$135

REF

2007

POLITICAL HANDBOOK
OF AFRICA
2007

REGIONAL POLITICAL HANDBOOKS OF THE WORLD

Political Handbook of Africa 2007

Editors: Arthur S. Banks, Thomas C. Muller, William R. Overstreet
Associate Editors: Judith Isacoff, John Riley Jr.
Assistant Editors: Tony Davies, Thomas Lansford
Contributing Editors: John Greenya, Brian Sulkis
Production Assistants: Nathaniel Bouman, Thomas Scalese, Erin Stanley, Kathleen Stanley

CQ Press

Sponsoring Editor: Doug Goldenberg-Hart
Chief, Editorial Acquisitions, Reference Publishing: Andrea Pedolsky
Managing Editor: Stephen D. Pazdan
Production Editor: Anna M. Schardt
Copy Editors: Sarah Bright, Mary Sebold, Anna Socrates, Anne Wendt
Production and Research: Timothy Arnquist, Kate Ostrander, Ilya Plotkin, Kate Stern
Manager, Electronic Production: Paul P. Pressau
Manager, Print and Art Production: Margot W. Ziperman

Senior Vice President and Publisher: John A. Jenkins
Director, Reference Publishing: Kathryn C. Suárez
Director, Editorial Operations: Ann Davies

President and Publisher, Congressional Quarterly Inc: Robert W. Merry

POLITICAL HANDBOOK OF AFRICA 2007

Introduction by Moses K. Tesi
Middle Tennessee State University

CQ PRESS

A DIVISION OF CONGRESSIONAL QUARTERLY INC.
WASHINGTON, D.C.

CQ Press
1255 22nd Street, NW, Suite 400
Washington, DC 20037

Phone: 202-729-1900; toll-free, 1-866-4CQ-PRESS (1-866-427-7737)

Web: www.cqpress.com

Cover design: TGD Communications
Composition: Pooja Naithani and the production staff at TechBooks-Delhi

Maps courtesy of International Mapping Associates

∞ The paper used in this publication exceeds the requirements of the American National Standard for Information Sciences–Permanence of Paper for Printed Library Materials, ANSI Z39.48-1992.

Printed and bound in the United States of America

10   09   08   07   06   1   2   3   4   5

Library of Congress Cataloging-in-Publication Data

Political handbook of Africa 2007.
   p. cm. – (Regional political handbooks of the world)
   Includes bibliographical references and index.
   ISBN-13: 978-0-87289-326-9 (alk. paper)
   ISBN-10: 0-87289-326-X (alk. paper)
   1. Africa–Politics and government–20th century–Handbooks, manuals, etc. 2. Africa–Politics and government–21st century–Handbooks, manuals, etc. 3. International agencies–21st century–Handbooks, manuals, etc. I. Title.

JQ1875.P63 2006
320.9603–dc22

                            2006037823

CONTENTS

INTERGOVERNMENTAL ORGANIZATION ABBREVIATIONS

Memberships in non-UN intergovernmental organizations are listed at the end of each country's section under Intergovernmental Representation. An asterisk in the list below indicates a nonofficial abbreviation. In the country profiles, associate memberships are in italics.

*AfDB	African Development Bank	*CWTH	Commonwealth
AMF	Arab Monetary Fund	EAC	East African Community
AMU	Arab Maghreb Union	EADB	East African Development Bank
AU	African Union	ECOWAS	Economic Community of West African States
BADEA	Arab Bank for Economic Development in Africa	IGAD	Inter-Governmental Authority on Development
BDEAC	Central African States Development Bank	IOC	Indian Ocean Commission
BOAD	West African Development Bank	IOR-ARC	Indian Ocean Rim Association for Regional Cooperation
*CAEU	Council of Arab Economic Unity	LAS	League of Arab States (Arab League)
CEEAC	Economic Community of Central African States	*MRU	Mano River Union
CEMAC	Central African Economic and Monetary Community	*NAM	Nonaligned Movement
*CENT	Council of the Entente	OAPEC	Organization of Arab Petroleum Exporting Countries
CEPGL	Economic Community of the Great Lakes Countries	*OIC	Organization of the Islamic Conference
CILSS	Permanent Inter-State Committee on Drought Control in the Sahel	OIF	International Organization of the Francophonie
Comesa	Common Market for Eastern and Southern Africa	SADC	Southern African Development Community
CPLP	Community of Portuguese Speaking Countries	UEMOA	West African Economic and Monetary Union

PART ONE

INTRODUCTION

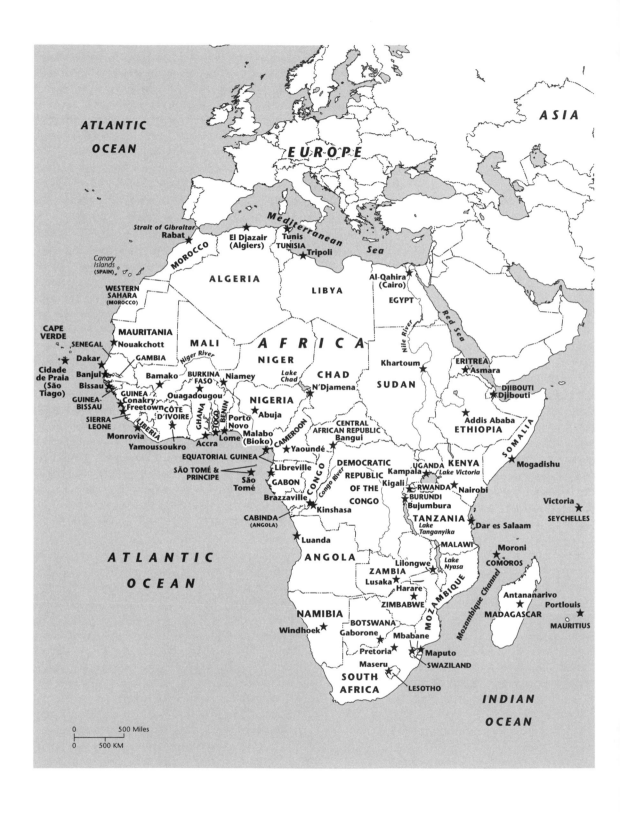

INTRODUCTION TO SUB-SAHARAN AFRICA*

Sub-Saharan Africa is the region of the African continent located immediately south of the Sahara that extends to the Cape of Good Hope in the southernmost part of Africa, where the Indian Ocean meets the Atlantic Ocean. Often referred to as black Africa, this region extends to the Red Sea in the northeast, the Indian Ocean (including the island countries of Mauritius, Seychelles, Comoro Islands, and Madagascar) in the east, and to the Atlantic Ocean in the west (also including the island nations of Cape Verde and Sao Tome and Principe).

Sub-Saharan Africa has a land mass of approximately 9.4 million square miles and a population of approximately 700 million, out of the continent's 11.6 million square miles and 900 million people. It is a region characterized by immense geographical, cultural, linguistic, historical, ethnic, and religious diversity on one hand, and vast similarities on the other. Politics in the region involves a complex and persistent pattern of interaction among these forces in varying configurations and with varying results.

For a region so massive, sub-Saharan Africa's geographic and demographic diversity ought to come as no surprise; yet the impressions of many outsiders are colored by myth and stereotypes. The image most people once had of sub-Saharan Africa came from tales about dense rain forests and wild animals in the jungle. Although the mass media has made significant progress during the past quarter century to provide a more accurate portrayal of the region's diversity, misconceptions still abound about the region's vegetation and hence its people. The reality is that less than 25 percent—a percentage that has been declining since the 1960s owing to deforestation by people in search of land and firewood—of sub-Saharan African vegetation is rain forest.

These forests and mangrove swamps are vegetation belts that are highly localized only in west-central Africa. Otherwise, tropical grasslands, mountain savanna, Sahel savanna, desert, and temperate forests—the principal vegetation belts of sub-Saharan Africa—are spread across the continent almost equally. Sub-Saharan Africa's main rivers, lakes, and mountain ranges also showcase both the uniformity and diversity of the area. Some of the world's major rivers flow through the region: the Nile in the northeast, the Zambezi in the southeast, the Niger in the west, and the Congo in the west-center. Sub-Saharan Africa's mountain ranges rise from the landscape, including the Drakensberg mountain ranges in South Africa, the Mount Kilimanjaro and Mount Kenya in east Africa, the Cameroon ranges in central Africa, and the Foutah Djallon mountains in west Africa.

For centuries before European imperialism these features combined to influence economic, political, and military activities in the region. Mountains and deserts provided groups of people natural protection from their enemies. The rivers and lakes served as means of transportation, their resources provided families with their livelihoods, and the fertile terrains along their banks were used for agriculture. They were also sub-Saharan Africa's main attractions as well as Africa's means of contact with the outside world. European explorers, merchants, missionaries, slave dealers, and empire builders made extensive use of Africa's rivers.

---

* North Africa is profiled in the introduction to *Political Handbook of the Middle East 2006* (CQ Press, 2006).

Economic activities in sub-Saharan Africa have always depended on the type of vegetation prevalent in the region. Although farming is the principal occupation of most people, many in the arid and semiarid regions—especially the region from Mauritania and northern Senegal across to the Ethiopian highlands and Somalia, and also in the southern savanna regions that run from northern Angola to Botswana and South Africa—also raise livestock. Crops in the tropical regions are a mix of perennial tree crops—palms, coffee, cocoa, and rubber—cultivated mainly for export, and food crops such as bananas, plantains, and cassava that are cultivated for local consumption. Farmers in the arid and semiarid regions of the savanna grow mainly cereals and legumes (corn, beans, and peanuts) or drought-resistant crops such as cotton.

Over the years, economic activities, while important in bringing about a measure of improvement in the traditional lifestyles once prevalent in the region, have also generated serious strains between people and their environment owing to the decreasing ability of the ecology to sustain the types of activities it once used to. This has had important economic consequences. These economic consequences have, in turn, fueled communal conflicts over resources in various countries in the region, including Kenya, Nigeria, Cameroon, Sudan, and Zimbabwe.

Sub-Saharan Africa is characterized by a cultural, linguistic, ethnic, and religious diversity unmatched in the world. It counts more than 2,000 ethnic groups and over 750 linguistic groups. With the exception of Lesotho, Comoro Islands, and to a lesser extent Somalia, which are ethnically homogenous, the countries of sub-Saharan Africa contain highly diverse ethnic, cultural, and linguistic populations. More than 250 language groups are found in Nigeria, more than 200 groups in the Democratic Republic of the Congo, over 120 in Tanzania, and more than 70 in Ethiopia. Ethnic fragmentation is as prevalent in countries with smaller populations as it is in larger ones: Ghana counts approximately 50 linguistic and ethnic groups, Côte d'Ivoire 60, Cameroon over 100, and the Republic of the Congo 70. Nigeria, South Africa, Kenya, Ethiopia, and Mozambique have ethnic populations that are larger than the populations of many countries. The Hausa, Yoruba, and Ibo, three of the largest groups in Nigeria, exceed 15 million people each. And in South Africa, the Zulu and Xhosa number around 10 million each; and the Oromo (Galla) in Ethiopia total more than 22 million. In these and other countries, many smaller groups numbering only a few thousand also dot the landscape.

Associated with ethnic diversity is cultural and linguistic fragmentation. While most sub-Saharan Africans speak the indigenous language of the ethnic groups they belong to, most also speak one or more European languages, mainly the language of the European country that colonized them. The addition of European languages to the highly fragmented cultural situation has deepened social fragmentation even more. But the language of the colonial power has also served to integrate all groups within a country around a common language that belongs to none of them and is therefore not considered threatening.

Religion as a source of identity in sub-Saharan Africa has been growing in importance during the past 20 years. With the exception of a few countries—Nigeria, Senegal, Somalia, and Sudan—religion has not been as galvanizing a force in most countries in the region as it has been in other parts of the world. Slightly more than half of the population of sub-Saharan Africa is Christian in religious belief while about one-third is Muslim; the remaining people follow various indigenous beliefs.

People in various parts of the region show varying degrees of identification with particular religious beliefs. Most of the states in west Africa (with the exception of Côte d'Ivoire, Ghana, Benin, and Sierra Leone) have populations that are predominantly Muslim. Nigeria, Africa's largest state, is split almost equally between Christians and Muslims. A similar split exists in Ethiopia. For the remaining countries in the region (with the exception of Sudan, Somalia, and Djibouti, which are predominantly Muslim), Christian majorities prevail. There once thrived in Ethiopia a Jewish community that, for various reasons—its marginalization by Ethiopia's government and its desire (supported by the Israeli state) to reunite with other Jews—evacuated to Israel. Only a few Jews remain in Ethiopia. A much larger Jewish community thrives in South Africa. South Africa and Tanzania also have a sizable number of Hindus.

European Colonialism

The modern states of sub-Saharan Africa are products of European imperialism that culminated with the partition of Africa at a conference of the major European powers held in Berlin in late 1884 and early 1885. Called by the German statesman Otto von Bismarck, the conference gathered to deal with the claims of European powers to various territories in Africa. The Berlin conference laid the ground rules for colonial acquisition, recognized colonies that had already been acquired, and agreed to the principles of freedom of navigation. Key to the ground rules was effective control of a colonial territory by the colonizer and notification of all participating states before a territory could be recognized as belonging to the claimant.

The result was the division of Africa into spheres of influence by the various European governments. Britain received much of east Africa, while France received much of west and central Africa. Britain also retained its Nigerian and Ghanaian territories, which proved to be prized possessions. King Leopold II of Belgium received the present-day Democratic Republic of the Congo, and Portugal retained Angola and Mozambique. Britain also retained its prized possessions in southern Africa—South Africa, Rhodesia (now Zimbabwe), Malawi, and Zambia. After 1885, European governments embarked on bringing their new African colonies under effective control in what they called pacification campaigns. The pacification of Africa was the name given to the wars that Europeans fought against African resistance as the Europeans advanced to bring territories under their effective control.

By 1900, European colonizers had succeeded in establishing control over most of the territories they claimed, although in some areas Africans continued to resist colonial rule. The Europeans' initial approach to governing the territories was to farm them out to European companies to rule and, in return, the companies kept part of the profits and returned the remainder to the home governments. In various parts of sub-Saharan Africa, European-chartered companies organized and eventually controlled much of the commerce, administration, and security. Along the Niger River, the Royal Niger Company wielded its authority; in Kenya and Uganda in east Africa it was the Imperial British East Africa Company; and in Rhodesia, the British South African Company prevailed. Company rule lasted into the 1920s for the French colonies and into the 1940s for the Portuguese colonies.

Company rule was practiced by all the colonial powers as a means of holding down costs while maximizing benefits for the colonial administration. It was usually brutal, exploitative, and dehumanizing. Many Africans were forced off their lands, while others were forced into day labor or into harvesting wild rubber or gathering ivory in return for a meager wage that they often were made to pay back in the form of taxes to the colonial administrations. Apart from its brutality, company rule was ineffective and did very little to cut costs. Consequently, it was later abandoned in favor of rule by governments.

The administration of the African colonies by the colonizing governments varied in many ways depending on the administrative models employed. In general, two broad approaches of colonial administration were used. The first—direct rule—was the approach that France, Belgium, Germany, and Portugal used. The second approach—indirect rule—was the policy that Great Britain adopted. The two approaches were based on the differing conceptions that the colonial powers held about the colonized people and their vision of colonialism in terms of where it would lead—that is, what the end game of colonialism would be.

The British, who adopted indirect rule, saw the colonized people and their cultures as much too different to be governed directly by European institutions and European personnel; they believed Europeans and Africans had very little in common. Indirect rule also envisioned a future in which the British would one day separate from the colonies. The point of such separation would come when the colonized people had developed to the level at which they could govern themselves. Accordingly, colonialism was viewed as a mission undertaken by the British to civilize the Africans; after they became civilized, they would be given their independence. At that point the British would feel they had accomplished their mission and would leave.

Indirect rule emphasized the use of indigenous African institutions and leaders—the chiefs, customary courts, and those customs the British agreed with—to govern the colonies. In African societies with social organizations that were more egalitarian, the colonial administrations created chiefs. In some societies where political authority was organized around a chief and a counsel of elders, the British dethroned the chief if the chief was considered not amenable to British purposes, was stubborn, or was seen as a threat to the stability of British rule. British indirect rule was developed in northern Nigeria and soon spread to the entire colony and to other British colonies.

Direct rule was based on a different philosophy and a distinct vision of imperial development. It stemmed from the vision that Africans could become like the French if they were given the opportunity to do so by acquiring French values and culture. Also known as "assimilation," the policy was built on the condescending premise that Africans were uncivilized and would want to be like French if only they were given the opportunity. Direct rule was also built on the ideals—*liberté, égalité, and fraternité*—of the French Revolution. The French believed that once Africans evolved through the acculturation process into civilized peoples, they would be given French citizenship with all the rights that went with it, without discrimination. This seemed contradictory because Africans were not treated as equals with the French unless they had become assimilated; neither could they determine their political destiny. Africans, in fact, did not have a choice; they were directed by the French. To become acculturated, Africans had to shed their African identity and replace their African cultures, values, spirituality, practices, and tastes with everything French. They had to denounce polygamy, convert to Christianity, adopt Christian names, and

acquire a European education. Assimilation into the French culture thus separated Africans from their own culture and their traditional social structures.

Direct rule as practiced by the Portuguese and Belgians was different from the French way mainly in terms of the outcome for assimilated Africans. Assimilated Africans fared far worse in the Portuguese and Belgian colonies than they did in French colonies: they had few of the same rights as their Belgian or Portuguese counterparts. Toward the end of colonial rule, however, France abandoned its policy of assimilation and adopted a policy of association. Association was based on the notion that Africans were much too different to be governed directly, so they should be allowed to develop within their own traditional institutions at their own pace.

Decolonization and the Colonial Legacy

Perhaps more than any other force, colonialism stands out as the most important in shaping contemporary sub-Saharan Africa, whether for good or for bad. No area of African society was left untouched by the forces of colonialism. Geopolitically, the European powers drew the map of the continent according to their own motives, creating what would eventually become the present-day states in the region. In the process, they did not appear to follow a particular formula based on the local facts on the ground. The outcome was a state system in the region, but it was plagued by problems. Boundaries were drawn artificially, sometimes cutting through a clan's territory and dividing families among different colonies (different independent states today). At other times when boundaries were drawn, little attention was paid to cultural differences, and different ethnic groups—some of which never got along—were gathered into a single state. Some states were so small that they were not viable economically, neither were they politically robust when it came to defending themselves. From the very beginning, many sub-Saharan African countries had little chance of competing in a world of major states.

Colonial economic activities also generated major disruptions in the region. Colonialism was motivated by three main goals: prestige (important for great-power status); captive markets for finished or manufactured European goods; and the need for raw materials for European factories, materials that could be extracted at artificially low costs. The mere existence of the territories satisfied the first objective whether the claimant was doing anything within it or not, just so long as the claimant was able to defend it from rivals. Securing colonies for markets and as sources of raw materials required the exploitation of those colonies. Exploitation required massive investment in infrastructure and investment in organizing the extraction of the raw materials and products from the region. Some of the main development-oriented activities of the colonial authorities—the building of roads, railways, and ports—were undertaken during this period. Typical roads and railways connected the sources of the various products in the hinterlands of the colonies with the coastal areas, for easy export of products to Europe.

The home governments considered colonialism a necessary undertaking, but they were unwilling to foot the bills. This limited the number of administrators who worked in the colonies. Most important, very little could be done in building colonial infrastructure such as roads, bridges, railways, and ports without a large infusion of money from the colonial budget. Colonial officials were thus left to devise strategies to raise the monies needed to put such infrastructure in place in order to exploit the resources of the colonies. The use of forced labor was one such strategy. Africans were often conscripted and forced to work on the various construction projects. At the same time, conscripts were often subjected to harsh and inhumane treatment that included constant whipping for what was called laziness and insubordination. Forced labor could succeed in the short run. The issue, however, was whether it could be sustained over a long period.

Investment in the acquisition of raw materials was also minimal. This was generally left to the domain of companies and enterprises. Some raw materials (minerals and wild rubber) were readily available in Africa's vast, marginally disturbed, terrain and required only labor and tools to extract. Forced labor was used in getting Africans to work in the mines for a bare minimum of compensation, especially in the Belgian Congo and in other colonies as well. For a pittance, Africans were also forced to tap wild rubber for the various concession companies; wild rubber was used in Angola and Mozambique by the Portuguese; in Cameroon by the Germans; in French Equatorial Africa by the French; and in Nigeria, Kenya, Uganda, and Rhodesia by the British—indeed, across the various colonies—in one form or another.

Cash crops (including tea, coffee, cocoa, cotton, peanuts, and bananas) were also introduced in the colonies. They were initially cultivated by European settlers whom the colonial administrators had lured into the colonies through offers of cheap land (acquired through the eviction of its African owners), low taxes, and cheap African labor. Africans who were evicted from their lands became landless and were thereafter compelled to work on the European farms for minimal wages. They then had to pay the taxes that were introduced in the colonies as a means of raising revenue because very little money was transferred from the home governments to the colonies. Over time, Africans were also brought into the cultivation of cash crops, in part to generate the cash needed to pay taxes. What was left after the payment of taxes was spent on European manufactured goods.

The imposition of taxes on the colonies significantly transformed African economic life. The traditional agricultural system that was based on subsistence farming was transformed into cash crop cultivation. People in areas where cash crops were not very productive sought work on European plantations or in mines so they were able to pay their taxes. African farmers sold their farm products only to European firms in the colonies organized purposely as middlemen between the African farmers and the overseas markets. The products were usually bought by the firms at below-market prices and then exported at higher prices, with the profits going to the middlemen. In addition, African farmers were forbidden to cultivate crops that might compete with European cultivators.

African businesses that emerged also found it difficult to compete with large European firms because they did not have access to capital (loans and other instruments for managing risk) from banks or insurers. Agricultural research and innovation were directed to the production of cash crops, while research and innovation on food crops lagged. Although many raw materials such as minerals and agricultural products were being produced in the region, they were not transformed into finished products there. Transformation and economies of scale (the jobs, other secondary industries, revenues, investments) all benefited the home country and not the colonies. Meanwhile, many of the finished products generated through such transformation were shipped back to Africa and sold there, creating more wealth for the home country.

The influx of European settlers under colonialism also contributed to the multicultural outlook of Africa. So did the arrival of Asians brought to work on plantations in South Africa and on railroads in Kenya and Uganda. Unfortunately, under the colonial administrations, the arrival of both European and Asian immigrants fueled the same process of subjugation of native Africans to the lowest ranks of the social and productive classes. In the postindependence period, these immigrant groups emerged to be the leading traders and owners of small businesses. Greek and Lebanese merchants dominated small businesses dealing in European products by interposing themselves between Africans and the European business and political classes.

Colonialism also affected education significantly, generating lasting changes. Much of the education was provided by missionaries, not by the colonial governments. Missionary education had a limited purpose in that it sought to enable Africans to read and write in order to read the Bible and undertake religious training. Only very few Africans received an education. Some sources place the ratio of those who had access to basic education (reading, writing, and history, mainly European history) to be one in ten in the most advanced of European colonies. In some of the worst, the figure was one in a hundred. Even so, some Africans advanced to pursue a university education, while still fewer continued to graduate school. Leading nationalist leaders in the region—Nnamdi Azikiwe (of Nigeria), Hastings Kamazu Banda (Malawi), Félix Houphouët-Boigny (Côte d'Ivoire), Jomo Kenyatta (Kenya), Nelson Rolihlahla Mandela (South Africa), Félix-Roland Moumié (Cameroon), Kwame N. Nkrumah (Ghana), Julius K. Nyerere (Tanzania), and Léopold Sédar Senghor (Senegal)—had university degrees; and Azikiwe, Banda, and Senghor earned doctorates. Whatever the level of education, exposure to education opportunities gave to the few fortunate Africans access to jobs at the lower echelon of the colonial administration, religious missions, and European firms.

After more than three quarters of a century of European colonial rule, the countries of sub-Saharan Africa gained independence in the 1950s and 1960s, beginning with Sudan in 1956 and Ghana in 1957. Guinea, a French colony in west Africa, gained its independence in 1958 when it alone opted for immediate independence in a referendum that the new French government of Charles de Gaulle conducted in all of France's African colonies that year.

In 1960, France hastily granted independence to 13 of its west and central African colonies (Cameroon, Central African Republic, Chad, Republic of the Congo, Benin, Gabon, Côte d'Ivoire, Mali, Mauritania, Niger, Senegal, Togo, and Burkina Faso) plus Madagascar in the Indian Ocean. The rest of the French colonies chose to continue within the French Union for two more years before eventual independence.

Britain's colonies in west Africa followed their French counterparts. Nigeria gained independence in 1960, Sierra Leone in 1961, and Gambia in 1965. Unlike the process in British west Africa (which had taken place peacefully), the decolonization process in the British colony of Kenya in east Africa was marred by much bloodshed. The Mau Mau insurrection, led by members of the Kikuyu tribe unhappy with the confiscation of indigenous lands and championing demands for independence since the 1920s, reached a climax in 1952. Britain's insistence on putting down the insurrection with military force only emboldened the group. The Mau Mau mounted a guerrilla campaign that preoccupied Britain for four years and accounted for the deaths of more than 10,000 Kenyans (contrasted with approximately 100 Europeans). Kenya eventually became independent in 1963 but only after neighboring Tanganyika (Tanzania) and Uganda had gained independence from Britain in 1961 and 1962, respectively.

The next phase of the collapse of the British African empire occurred in southern Africa. This took place uneventfully with the exception of the situation in the Rhodesian Federation that was composed of Nyasaland (now Malawi), Northern Rhodesia (Zambia), and Southern Rhodesia (Zimbabwe). The main sticking point in the decolonization process was the dissolution of the federation. Nationalists in Northern Rhodesia and Nyasaland opposed the federation and had been canvassing for its dissolution at the same time that they were mobilizing for an end to colonial rule. Because of the large European settler population in Southern Rhodesia, these nationalists feared domination by a minority settler population after independence. This fear eventually was given some support after Britain dissolved the federation. Following the dissolution of the federation, Northern Rhodesia and Nyasaland gained independence separately (and became known as Zambia and Malawi) in 1964. Southern Rhodesia (now Zimbabwe) was the exception in that it took a protracted civil war for it to gain independence. Other British colonies in southern Africa—Lesotho, Botswana, Swaziland, and Mauritius—became independent by 1968 without incident.

The situation in Rhodesia was a source of humiliation and embarrassment to the British government. The colonial government, dominated by white settlers, feared that Britain would abandon the colony and give independence to the territory on the basis of majority rule; thus the British would become a minority in the country of over 6 million black Africans. To prevent this, the administration, led by Ian D. Smith, a former military officer, uni-laterally declared independence from British rule. Unwilling to confront the white-dominated minority government, Britain was sidelined as black nationalists led by Robert Mugabe and Joshua Nkomo embarked on a guerrilla war against the minority government to establish black majority rule. With the support of South Africa, the Rhodesian government fought a long civil war that lasted until 1979. With very little support outside of South Africa and a global economic boycott against the country, the Smith government was forced to accept a return to British rule to oversee the transition of the territory through elections to independence and majority rule in 1980.

The two other colonial powers in sub-Saharan Africa, Belgium and Portugal, made the least sincere efforts in preparing a transition to the end of colonialism in Africa. Moreover, they were the poorest, and Portugal's colonies were the least developed of the European colonies. Belgium and Portugal were occupying large swaths of land that were much bigger and much richer than the home countries. The pearl of the Belgian colonies, the Belgian Congo, was 905,563 square miles in size and much larger than Western Europe. It also contained a diverse mix of valuable minerals, including tin, copper, diamonds, and cobalt. Portugal's main colonies, Angola and Mozambique, were each larger than Portugal and also provided a wide mix of mineral resources. On the basis of the rationale for colonialism—a source for raw materials, captive markets for finished European goods, and the prestige that went with colonial possession—both Belgium and Portugal could ill-afford to lose such benefits, and they had no intention of leaving. They had also done the least to foster indigenous socioeconomic and political development.

Following minor changes in colonial policy in the mid-1950s, blacks were allowed to participate in local government in the Belgian Congo. Not surprisingly, given what was happening in other African colonies, this gesture was considered insufficient by the various Congolese parties that emerged to advocate complete independence. These demands reached a climax in January 1959, when a riot in Kinshasa forced Belgium to reconsider its policy. Hastily, the Belgians called an all-party conference in Belgium in January 1960 to discuss the conditions for independence. The result of the conference was the drafting of a constitution, an agreement on elections to be held in May 1960, and independence on June 30. Within a matter of a few months, the Belgian Congo became independent. Independence was soon marred, however, by internal conflicts characterized by regional divisions, ideological differences, ethnic tensions, competing economic interests, and personality conflicts among the new political elite. These internal divisions were in turn manipulated and reinforced by Belgian business interests at home and in the country, as well as American cold war diplomacy. The result was a bitter civil war that broke out only a few months after independence.

In 1962, Rwanda and Burundi, which first had been colonized by Germany and later administered by Belgium, were also granted independence. In these two countries Belgium employed a colonial practice of manipulating ethnic divisions to suit its interests. Belgium favored the Tutsi ethnic group, whom it deployed as overlords to dominate the Hutu majority, a practice that exacerbated age-old antagonisms between the two groups. This ethnic animosity spilled over into a massacre of Tutsis by Hutus in 1959 in Rwanda. Animosity continued in both countries after they were granted independence in 1962. The worst acts of violence took place in the 1990s when the nations of the world stood by while in 1994 the Hutu majority massacred over 800,000 Tutsis. Unlike in Rwanda, where the majority Hutus had gained power after independence, in Burundi the minority Tutsis had by default gained control of the country at independence through their king, Mwambutsa IV. His failure to reconcile the two groups started the country on a course of ethnic massacres and countermassacres that continued into the early 21st century.

The Portuguese colonies of Angola, Mozambique, Cape Verde, Guinea-Bissau, and Sao Tome and Principe eventually gained independence in the mid-1970s, but the decolonization process in these countries was unplanned and bloodier than in other colonies. Decolonization was the result of both internal political dynamics in Portugal (including the overthrow of the dictatorial Salazar government in 1974 by junior military officers) and well-organized armed insurrections by African nationalists throughout the colonies. The new political leaders in Portugal moved to cut their losses by granting independence to the colonies, but this move came after a significant loss of life and destruction of property. Even so, just before independence in Angola in 1975, a civil war broke out between rival nationalist factions, the National Union for the Total Independence of Angola (UNITA), the National Front for the Liberation of Angola (FNLA), and the Popular Movement for the Liberation of Angola (MPLA). Mozambique, whose main nationalist party, the Marxist-leaning Mozambique Liberation Front (Frelimo), had led a guerrilla struggle against Portuguese colonialism, found itself fighting against reactionary, right-wing Mozambique National Resistance (Renamo) insurgents supported by some Portuguese settlers and South Africa.

In all, by the 1990s, only Namibia and South Africa remained under colonial control. South Africa, which administered Namibia under a League of Nations mandate, refused to grant independence to the territory and also refused to accept the transfer of the territory to the United Nations (UN) as a trust territory as had been the case with all other League of Nations mandates. South Africa's obstinacy fueled Namibian nationalism, which culminated in a military campaign begun by the South West Africa People's Organization of Namibia (SWAPO) in 1966. By the late 1980s, SWAPO's campaigns, pressure from the UN, and the changing international situation caused by the collapse of the Soviet Union created a climate that led to South Africa's agreement for a settlement. In 1990, Namibia became independent.

Meanwhile, although South Africa had itself gained independence from Britain in 1910, only its white population—approximately 12 percent of the total—enjoyed all the rights and privileges of independence and full citizenship. The white minority had designed and put in place a form of internal colonialism known as apartheid and used it politically, economically, and socially to subjugate, oppress, and exploit its nonwhite majority population. Under apartheid, nonwhites were divided into three categories: Coloureds, Asians, and blacks. A similar system was implemented in Namibia. International pressure, domestic mobilization, and costly guerrilla warfare by African nationalists (mainly the African National Congress [ANC]) forced the white minority government finally to end apartheid and negotiate a transfer of power to its majority black population in 1994. With South Africa's transfer to majority rule, colonialism in Africa, which had started a little over a century earlier, formally came to an end.

Politics in Postcolonial Africa

Experiments with Democracy, Nation Building, and One-Party Politics

Politics in sub-Saharan Africa's postcolonial era has been as intriguing as it has been challenging. For most Africans, independence was considered a means to an end rather than an end in itself. Most believed, naively perhaps, that independence would bring an end to the injustice, oppression, and exploitation that they suffered under colonial rule. They viewed colonialism as the source of their miseries and independence as their salvation: independence would lead to improvements in their social and economic situations through job creation; new roads, schools, and hospitals; the return of lands expropriated under colonialism; better prices for farm products; and greater openness and participation in determining their destiny. In short, independence was welcomed with high expectations and hope for a much better future in contrast with the dark memories of the colonial past. The challenge the postcolonial leaders faced was to devise strategies that would rally the people around a vision, a common agenda, and a strategy for governance that could confront the challenges of economic and political development and satisfy popular expectations.

The goals of nation building and socioeconomic development were adopted as the main objectives of postcolonial public policy, with each state de-

vising its own ideology and agenda on how to realize them. Thus, Africans and analysts alike measured politics in the postcolonial era by how well the new states fared in addressing their national goals. A gap began to develop between the citizens of the various countries and their political leaders regarding priorities and strategies. Political leaders sought to accomplish the nation-building goals before turning their attention to economic development, arguing that they needed national unity and political stability before they could deal with the daunting problems of economic development. Although ordinary Africans did not share this view, their political leaders proceeded to elaborate their visions.

The politics of African nation building was built on the widely held premise that the postcolonial countries were much too diverse ethnically and culturally and their political behavior and identities too narrowly focused on their ethnic or regional affinity groups to be guided by Western liberal democratic political philosophies or models. Drawing from the brief and limited experiences during the waning years of colonialism when limited home rule within a democratic framework was introduced in the colonies, and from their own experiences with democratic politics during the first few years of independence, political leaders in sub-Saharan Africa latched onto the single-party formula to serve as the basis for organizing politics.

During the final years of colonialism and the early years of independence, politics was more often dominated by ethnic or regional considerations than by considerations of the national interest. Political parties usually represented ethnic or regional constituencies rather than national mass movements, with voting during elections reflecting a similar ethnic or regional and parochial pattern. In a pluralist democratic political culture, this would be viewed as a healthy exercise in democratic rights and association. Political leaders in sub-Saharan Africa, however, saw the trend as undermining efforts at national unity. Emphasizing the need to forge a common national identity from the morass of ethnic and cultural pluralism, one country after another abolished multiparty democratic politics and replaced it with one-party politics. Despite differences in colonial experiences, levels of development, and history, by the mid-1970s most African nations—ranging from countries such as Senegal and Ghana (among the most assimilated into Western ways) to Tanzania, Zambia, Kenya, Cameroon, Côte d'Ivoire, and Gabon—had officially become one-party states.

The single-party systems established in sub-Saharan Africa differed from one country to another, but they also shared common traits. In most countries, the leaders employed tactics involving co-optation, intimidation, and coercion to do away with multiparty politics, while in other countries one-party rule emerged out of the dominant parties that controlled politics during colonialism, as was the case in Côte d'Ivoire and Tanzania. One-party systems also differed in terms of how the electoral process functioned. In most countries the party leadership merely prepared a list of candidates from different constituencies and submitted the list to the electorate, which was expected to legitimize the list through their votes for or against the entire list. Such systems made the party leadership very powerful, as they became brokers of party patronage and gatekeepers to public offices. Elections in some of the one-party systems such as in Kenya and Tanzania were slightly more competitive: the electorate chose from multiple names on the party lists for each electoral district.

Under one-party rule, other democratic institutions such as independent trade unions that were restructured and brought under the party's control were co-opted by the party, or they were allowed to operate as private entities under significant regulation and constraint. Moreover, the private press was usually subjected to censorship, and certain individual rights were significantly curtailed. The legal systems also suffered tremendously, with little or no independence from one-party rule. Political leaders appointed judges, which gave them considerable influence over the courts. In most instances, this lack of judicial independence resulted in a forfeiture of due process and the rule of law.

Military and Politics

Another key element in the political culture of postcolonial sub-Saharan Africa is the phenomenon of the military coup d'état and prolonged periods of military rule. Coup d'état, the military overthrow of a government, first took place in sub-Saharan Africa in Togo in 1963. President Slyvanus Olympio was ousted by military force and replaced by his political rival, Nicolas Grunitzky. In the same year, Benin experienced its own coup. A series of coups and a succession of military governments soon followed in some of the more prominent countries, including Nigeria in January 1966 and Ghana a month later. By the mid-1970s, it was easier to count the number of countries without military governments than those ruled by the military, as most countries had now succumbed to military rule.

Leaders of coups in sub-Saharan Africa explained their takeovers by citing features unique to their single country as well as common rationales. Coups often were staged during periods of great political turmoil, such as when sitting leaders made major, divisive decisions; when leaders seemed unwilling to take bold actions on matters judged to be of immense interest to the public; when the leaders did not invest in the military's welfare; and when the political leadership was viewed as too zealous. Coup leaders tended to justify their seizure of power in terms of saving the nation from civilian corruption, abuse of office by political leaders, and saving the country from ruinous factional politics that threaten to destroy national unity. Sometimes their rationalizations were focused on the poor performance of the economy, in which case coup leaders portrayed themselves being able to solve these difficult problems although their civilian or military predecessors had failed.

Ironically, the trend in the region has been for coup leaders or those they install in office to be changed mainly through later coups. Some countries—among them Nigeria, Ghana, Chad, Benin, and Burkina Faso—have experienced more than three coups. Most countries have experienced several forms of military rule, and only a few countries—Cameroon, Kenya, Tanzania, Namibia, Senegal, and Botswana—have either avoided coups entirely or prevented their success.

The record shows that military governments in sub-Saharan Africa have been just as corrupt, oppressive, divisive, and indecisive as their civilian counterparts. Moreover, the economies of certain countries (including Uganda, Central African Republic, Liberia, and Ghana) performed far better under civilian governments than under military rule. Ghana, for instance, while under successive military governments in the 1960s and 1970s, was without basic supplies even though it was among the richest of postindependent African countries. Successive military governments in Nigeria, culminating with that of Sani Abacha between 1993 and 1998, basically plundered the country and left it at the mercy of foreign creditors despite all its oil reserves and petrodollars. Liberia started experiencing its worst economic problems in the hands of Samuel Kanyon Doe, its military leader from 1980 to 1990.

Many military leaders have been just as ethnocentric as the civilian governments from which they seize power. Moreover, a disproportionate share of the notorious African dictators that the world has known, among them Idi Amin Dada of Uganda, Jean-Bédel Bokassa of the Central African Republic, Joseph D. Mobutu of Zaire (now the Democratic Republic of the Congo), and Sani Abacha of Nigeria, were military leaders. They were not only oppressive, they also bankrupted their public treasuries and pushed these countries countless years back as far as social relations and development are concerned.

The records of those military regimes that were average or moderate were not any better than their civilian counterparts on the index of governance. Most military governments banned political parties, and then their leaders took the civilian title of president. With some exceptions (as in Nigeria before Abacha's coup), press freedom was usually absent, as was due process and the rule of law. In Ghana under dictator Flt. Lt. Jerry John Rawlings,

judges were kidnapped and killed as a form of intimidation. The military government of Gen. Etienne Eyadéma of Togo used torture, press censorship, and control over the judiciary as a tool for sustaining power.

Military governments also had to take responsibility for creating some of the economic problems of their countries as well as failing to address them successfully. By the 1980s, most countries were under military rule and had been so for some time; therefore the military leaders could not blame their predecessors for their current problems in the economy.

Politics in the 1990s: A Return to Competitive Politics?

Politics in sub-Saharan Africa took a dramatic new turn in the 1990s after the 30 years of one-party dominance and military rule following independence. Almost without preparation, governments in the region were confronted with popular and sustained agitation for change to more democratic systems. These challenges were not necessarily new—many of these regimes had often faced such pressures in spite of immense restrictions placed on political activities. What was new in the renewed calls for democratization was the geopolitical context. The Berlin Wall had fallen only a year earlier, in 1989, and in the communist countries of Eastern Europe citizens had been organizing massive public demonstrations for democracy. Similar calls were being made in the Baltic states in the rapidly crumbling Soviet Union. In many Latin American countries like Chile, Argentina, and Nicaragua, military dictators and juntas were replaced with civilian governments via free and fair elections. Africans who had been used to organizing demonstrations and strikes for change felt even more energized by the demands for greater democracy around the world. More important, however, was the fact that the main external obstacles to their goals, the foreign supporters and benefactors of their autocratic governments, could now be on their side.

Foreign powers that had in the past often protected the authoritarian governments (or turned a deaf ear to the complaints of prodemocracy activists) for ideological and geopolitical reasons (that is, preventing international rivals from extending their sphere of influence) were now more willing to pressure African governments to open their political systems in a post–cold war international system. With agitation from below by students, intellectuals, and workers and pressure from foreign allies of the government that advocated democratic change (including the World Bank and the International Monetary Fund [IMF], which included political liberalization and an end to corruption among its conditions for loan financing of development projects), African governments were forced to take action.

Most regimes tried to resist at first, but they often found themselves at odds with those whose support they would need in order to fight a lengthy battle— the donor countries. In some cases, as happened in Cameroon, the initial reaction was to resist the pressure to reform, but many eventually relented (the Cameroon president, Paul Biya, initially refused to open up Cameroon's system, but upon his return from a trip to France, he agreed to do so). Even leaders known for their harsh rule relented: President Mobutu of Zaire (now Democratic Republic of the Congo) became an early adherent of democratization. Within a period of a year, when they realized that the wind of change was irreversible, much of the old guard jumped on the bandwagon and became adherents of democratization. As it turned out, most leaders simply wanted to work from within so as to control the process and its outcome, with an eye toward preserving their own political skins.

The process and pace of democratization varied significantly from country to country. Some governments, mainly governments in the French-speaking countries, pushed for the organization of a sovereign national conference that would be responsible for drafting a constitution, appointing a transitional government to run the country, and organizing elections. Benin, the first country to challenge its government to democratize, used this

formula. A second formula was that of amending the existing constitution and allowing for multiparty competitive politics. This formula was used by some French-speaking countries, among them Cameroon and Côte d'Ivoire. A third approach involved the drafting of a new constitution. Many English-speaking countries and countries making the transition from military rule employed this formula, among them Kenya, Nigeria, and Ghana. Not surprisingly, in some countries—Benin, Zambia, Republic of the Congo, Mali, and Malawi—the outcome of the elections that resulted was defeat for the incumbents. In many countries, including Togo, Cameroon, Kenya, Gabon, Ghana, and Burkina Faso, the incumbent leaders won under competitive elections. In many countries, the incumbent used various illicit tactics, ballot rigging, control of the media, finance, intimidation, and bribery to form parties in order to split the votes of the opposition to ensure victory. Nonetheless, by 2006, a number of countries had held three or more presidential elections and an equivalent number of legislative and local government elections under the new, more competitive political conditions.

Many countries in sub-Saharan Africa have taken major steps to open up their political systems. Across the region the media are much freer, there is greater individual freedom, and people are more able to organize and participate in politics than ever before. This is a far cry from the repressive political environment of the 1980s. However, these changes do not mean that sub-Saharan African countries are now full democracies. They can begin to approach that point only when elections can be conducted freely and fairly and then produce stable, peaceful leadership change. In contemporary sub-Saharan Africa, many of those who are leaders in 2006 were in power more than 20 years ago. Some countries have introduced term limits for political leaders, but such changes can be rolled back, as in Uganda and Chad, where the presidents later initiated constitutional changes so that they could run a third time (and in Nigeria as well, where a similar attempt by President Olusegun Obasanjo failed in 2006). These cases serve as a reminder that the leaders continue to contemplate manipulation of the countries' constitutions the way they used to routinely do under one-party or military rule.

Challenge of Development

Economic development preoccupied the newly independent states of sub-Saharan Africa almost to the same magnitude as the issue of nation building. Not least among the reasons was their view that economic development would enhance the efforts at nation building by deradicalizing the population and hence ensure stability. But besides the political need for development, the economic rationale was compelling: sub-Saharan Africa had emerged from colonialism without the capacity to sustain itself in a competitive global economy. While many of the countries had vast endowments of natural resources, the governments and productive sectors lacked the capacity to develop such resources. Worst of all, many had problems providing for some of the essential needs of their citizens—jobs, health care, education, and roads. The pursuit of economic development as a goal thus required fostering the productive capacity of societies, providing key goods and services for citizens, and finding ways to increase the size of national economies and raise living standards. These countries already had an economic base created during colonial rule. With few exceptions, and for better or worse, their leaders chose to build their economies upon the colonial framework, dominated by agriculture and mining. Efforts to build strong economies in the region have been undermined by a variety of factors, some of the leadership's making, others shaped by external forces.

Export-Oriented Agriculture, Import Substitution, Massive Industrialization, and Debt

Sub-Saharan Africa's leaders inherited economies that were based on commodities that in turn were dependent on exportation to the global market. In the years following independence, some countries chose to continue with an agriculture-oriented economic development policy. Countries that chose this strategy increased the cultivation of established agricultural commodities, and some diversified to other agricultural products as well. In Côte d'Ivoire, for example, the government embarked on a program of massive agricultural expansion, with much of that expansion based on large farms or plantations. Cultivators included many foreign planters, especially French nationals.

During the first decade and a half, this investment paid off, and many countries that had followed the model of development via agriculture were rewarded with high prices for their products in world markets, although world commodity prices fluctuated. Positive returns fueled even more investments in that sector. High prices for commodities continued in the 1970s, but then prices began to fall as production increased. This trend led to lower farm incomes as the global market reacted to the production increases with lower market prices. Consequently, farm incomes have fallen more than they have risen during the past 40 years. This situation adversely affected government revenues, leading to significant public deficits and a reduced capacity to provide services, maintain and develop infrastructure, and create an environment conducive to attracting investment capital. Faced with this state of affairs, African governments chose to borrow from international lenders to finance their budgets and continue national development plans.

While prices for Africa's main export commodities were falling, higher oil prices in the 1970s and 1980s not only reduced demands for Africa's agricultural products (as Western societies shifted their resources to pay for higher oil), but non-oil-producing sub-Saharan African countries also paid higher prices for the oil they were importing. With the exception of the oil-producing sub-Saharan African countries that saw increased revenues (at that time these comprised Nigeria, Gabon, Republic of the Congo, and Angola), African countries encountered only more deficits. In an effort to deal with the situation, these countries took on even greater debt to finance their budgets, provide services, and pay employees.

The persistence of the lower demand for agricultural products, and the high prices for oil that triggered a recession in the West hit sub-Saharan African economies hard. By the early 1980s, Africa's habit of borrowing to deal with the worsening economic conditions led to massive debt. Debt that in 1970 was $6 billion had increased by 1980 to $60.9 billion, by 1990 to $166 billion, and it continued upward to more than $200 billion in 2000. Interest on the debt also started to mount, so that Africa's export earnings were going mainly to service its debt without much left to reinvest in development projects or to finance annual budgets.

Efforts to deal with the regional economic crisis have centered on initiatives to reduce Africa's debt. Debt rescheduling, debt relief, debt forgiveness, and debt cancellation are some of the ideas that have been floated for addressing the problem. The fact that the bulk of the debt is owed to foreign governments, followed by international institutions, and then to private banks makes this even more complicated. Various enticements by the IMF and the World Bank have been put in place to help the countries; these include the Heavily Indebted Poor Countries initiative launched by the World Bank in 1996 to help cushion the burden that crushing external debt places on debtor countries and their economies. Countries that have completed the program have had their public debts and their debts to the IMF and World Bank cancelled or reduced.

Although sub-Saharan Africa's economic problems were partly the result of external factors, significant domestic factors were also involved. Apart from the continuation of the policy of dependence on agricultural commodities whose prices African countries had little direct influence on, African leaders made other costly mistakes by expanding other policies devised during colonial rule. They expanded some of the state-owned firms that they inherited from colonial governments, and they also created new ones. As part of the economic strategy of development, many countries in the region devised economic policies to promote industrialization. These policies, known as import substitution, called for the domestic manufacture of certain basic products so as to avoid importing them. The goal of import substitution was to generate economies of scale, create better-paying jobs, and generate new

sources of revenue. Import substitution was also meant to promote industrialization as an alternative to agriculture-led development.

To implement the policy of import substitution, African governments encouraged local firms to invest in the productive sectors identified for import substitution investments. Where local capital was unavailable or insufficient, the governments created parastatals (state-owned firms) to invest in and exploit the targeted sector. Products reserved for import substitution investments were shielded from competition with overseas products through the imposition of high tariffs on goods from foreign competitors. Some of the parastatals were monopolies, while others often had competitors in the domestic private sectors. Because the parastatals would still operate with subsidies from the state even if they did not make a profit, they tended to drive competitors out of the market. Moreover, some of the inputs that went into the products manufactured by import substitution firms were imported at high prices. The higher prices of these inputs were then passed on to consumers through higher prices for the finished products. Consequently parastatals developed into inefficient political tools used to reward supporters of the regimes. In some instances they became a place to banish politically ambitious individuals so as to take them out of the limelight. Accountability was often lacking, management laxity was rampant, and the government often subsidized their budgets. Rather than promote industrialization and diverse economic activities, the policy of import substitution ended up siphoning money from the state, driving away foreign investment and competition, and promoting corruption and rent seeking.

While import substitution focused on small and medium-size economic activities, another economic strategy that some countries used was the strategy of massive industrialization. This was based on investment in heavy industries so as to move the country overnight to the status of an industrialized economy. But this strategy required massive capitalization. In addition, it required the importation of inputs for production, massive energy supplies, the presence of a skilled labor force, and a large market for the finished goods. Ghana, for example, adopted this strategy and invested in the construction of a dam to supply the energy necessary for industrial production in addition to making investments in the industries themselves. However, with neither the monies for the inputs nor the markets for the finished goods, some of the industries in Ghana found they had to operate at less than full capacity. The strategy of massive industrialization was also plagued by the same problems as import substitution strategies, that is, dependence on public subsidies, inefficient parastatals, and the encouragement of rent seeking, which merely deepened the economic crisis.

Corruption

Corruption played a major role in both the unfolding economic crisis and the mounting debt burden in Africa. Initially this fact tended to be overlooked or was not always given serious attention by outside observers. The totality of corruption has now grown to encompass billions of dollars per year, and its persistence represents a serious threat to African economic and political development; yet no institutional mechanisms had been set up to deal with it until the late 1990s. Monetary corruption (graft, bribery, and fraud) is very expensive for an economy; thus, it tends to overshadow other, more subtle forms such as procedural corruption and nepotism. While monetary corruption siphons money directly from the system, procedural corruption siphons time. Nepotism deprives society of people's skills and the benefits of promotion through merit. All three forms are rampant in sub-Saharan Africa and are serious impediments to progress in contemporary African political systems.

Monetary corruption has a strong, negative impact on economic development. Money siphoned from the state deprives it of the ability to pay for vital services and products or pay down external debts, forcing governments to borrow at even higher prices. Moreover, the illicit money is redirected from public accounts for private gain, thus depriving the public as a whole of the benefits. The $5 billion that President Mobutu is said to have

stolen in Zaire could have paid for the building of several hospitals or other public infrastructure projects. Such is the cost of corruption, and all citizens pay for that individual transgression. In its annual corruption index, Transparency International, a Berlin-based organization that tracks corruption worldwide, lists most of the countries in sub-Saharan Africa among the most corrupt in the world. Critics call the worst African transgressor regimes "kleptocracies," implying that the regimes exist for no other purpose than to steal from public treasuries.

Structural Adjustment

As the economic crisis in the region deepened, the IMF and the World Bank stepped in to help with loans. Negotiations for these loans were often contentious because the loans came with strings attached. Both of these international financial institutions wanted guarantees that the loans would be repaid, and such guarantees required the African governments to agree to structural adjustment programs. Structural adjustments required the governments to restructure their economies to put them more in line with market economic principles. Structural adjustment programs generally included four main targets: revenue generation, reduction in the size of the government and public payrolls, market liberalization, and increasing productivity and demands. Specific steps ranged from reform of the country's tax system and tax collection, elimination of subsidies, removal of controls on agricultural prices, currency devaluation, tariff reduction, privatization of government-owned companies, and reducing and streamlining regulations.

Some African governments thought such structural adjustments would be political suicide; they believed such changes in policy would lead to political instability. This was particularly true about the elimination of many public subsidies, especially those on food. Moments after the implementation of structural adjustment programs in Zambia, which eliminated subsidies on grains, riots broke out in the country and a coup attempt was launched by disgruntled elements in the military.

Another contentious issue was that some of the measures hurt the most vulnerable because they involved cuts to basic services, social services, education, and health care. Also contributing to contentious relations between African governments and the two international lenders was the African governments' disapproval of the controls these institutions exercised over their economies. African leaders viewed such controls as infringements on their national sovereignty. In some countries, Nigeria for example, resentment and anger at the IMF's intrusion led to massive demonstrations that threatened the stability of the Nigerian government. After some countries signed agreements for structural adjustment loans, they found it difficult to stick with the program, although such structural adjustments would have helped in the long run. They eventually dropped out because of the sacrifices and hardships that the programs imposed, but dropping out only prolonged the economic crisis of sub-Saharan Africa.

HIV/AIDS

As sub-Saharan Africa sought solutions to its economic and political problems, another issue was brewing, an issue that would be as intractable as it was destructive. The HIV/AIDS epidemic will probably go down in history as Africa's worst public health epidemic, and it could not have come at a worse time, given the immense economic problems the region was already facing. Apart from not having adequate resources to mobilize against the epidemic, the stringent structural adjustment measures limited services—especially treatment—even more. As one tries to understand what the disease has done to the region, one cannot escape looking back to the early days to examine both actions and inactions. Although we need not dwell on hypotheticals, the debates and counterdebates about the African origin of the disease led to Africa's unwillingness to open its doors to experts working on it. To protect their national images, none of the African states wanted to be associated with a disease so terrible. For this and other reasons, sub-Saharan Africa's entry in the fight against AIDS came very late. By the time African governments confronted the epidemic, millions had been infected. Out of the more than 40 million people infected worldwide, 25 million—almost two-thirds of those infected—are in sub-Saharan Africa. In some countries, the percentage of the population affected is as large as 33 percent, although in others it is lower than 5 percent.

The AIDS epidemic is a health problem, but its impact extends deep into the very essence of African society, and it affects all aspects of African life. In economic terms, large public sums are required to deal with treatment, testing, and prevention. In addition, the most infected population cohort is the most productive in African societies, ranging in age from 20 to 49, which deprives the region of the backbone of its society and productive economy. Can countries in the region survive if they cannot produce for themselves?

Because AIDS is a disease transmitted through the most intimate aspects of human relationships, it is destroying the African family and is creating millions of orphans, many of whom are being cared for in orphanages or by community elders. Such care requires money, which is in short supply in the region. Will children who grow up in orphanages be able to acquire the values and traditions of their societies?

These are questions that have to be addressed by African governments. The more serious issue is finding ways of prolonging the lives of those infected with HIV but who have not yet developed AIDS. While scientific advances have led to the development of drugs that retard the mutation of the HIV virus into full blown AIDS, the cost of the drugs is much too high for the average African, whose annual income is less than $1,000. The challenge for African governments is to expand drug treatment by increasing the pool of recipients and to reduce the infection rate as they find ways of dealing with the social and economic problems the disease has generated.

The world has found various ways to support and help the effort to fight AIDS in Africa. After the United States increased its support to fight the epidemic during the final years of President Bill

Clinton's term of office, the George W. Bush administration increased the amount of aid to $15 billion. Also, various private initiatives—the Bill and Melinda Gates Foundation and the William J. Clinton Foundation's HIV/AIDS Initiative, for example—have focused attention on increasing access to drugs for a larger number of Africans infected with the virus.

Armed Conflict and Communal Violence

No single factor can explain the source of armed conflicts in sub-Saharan Africa. Conflicts in the region are the result of the multiple cleavages that cut across communities. These cleavages, including class, ethnicity, religion, geography, and ideology, are the breeding grounds for conflict. Their existence, however, does not necessarily mean that violence will occur and that if conflicts do take place they should succeed along preordained lines. Manipulation by the elites of Africa's various cleavages for their own purposes—turning various elements of the population or the government against each other—explains a great deal about the region's armed conflicts. Because the capacity of governments in sub-Saharan Africa is weak and the governments are often corrupt, their ability to respond is often inadequate or ineffective before the conflicts become lethal.

Armed conflicts are unfortunately major and regular occurrences in contemporary African politics. Very few countries have escaped armed conflicts of one form or another. Three broad types of armed conflicts have occurred in the region. The first is a conflict in which one group organizes a fighting force and militarily confronts the government or another group in the country over a particular grievance. This type of conflict has generated much instability, many casualties, and repercussions beyond the country through spillover into neighboring countries. This is also the type of armed conflict that often has invited foreign intervention. The second type of armed conflict is when one group in a country becomes involved in armed conflict with another group to settle a grievance. With few exceptions, this second form of communal conflict is often spontaneous. Effects of the second form could often be mitigated if the government would mediate impartially. A third common form of conflict is the coup d'état: one part of the government, usually the military, uses its guns to seize power. Sometimes this leads to tremendous bloodshed and extended conflict. At other times, the bloodshed is limited in time and scope.

Some of the continent's worst conflicts—among them the Nigerian civil war of 1967–1970; the conflicts in the southern African countries of Zimbabwe, Angola, Mozambique, Namibia, and South Africa during the 1970s, 1980s, and early 1990s; and the more recent civil war in Sudan—are cases of the first type of organized, armed conflict. During the 1970s and 1980s, armed conflicts in the Horn of Africa involving Eritreans, Somalis in the eastern region of Ogaden, Tigrayan people, and the Oromo (all groups in Ethiopia) fighting the government were also of the first type and had a similar effect. Other major conflicts that have taken place or are continuing in sub-Saharan Africa include the conflicts in the Great Lakes region involving Rwanda, Burundi, the Democratic Republic of the Congo, and Uganda. The civil wars in Sierra Leone and Liberia that ended in 2001 and 2003, respectively, and that in the western Darfur region of Sudan that began in 2003 are other examples.

Conflicts in the region during the cold war often led to foreign intervention because each of the superpowers, the United States and the Soviet Union, sought to expand its sphere of influence or to counter the influence of its adversary in the region. This intervention often prolonged and complicated the impacted conflict. Unilateral foreign intervention during the post–cold war era has been infrequent and, instead of helping one side fight and win, has tended to be multilateral and intended to either separate the fighting sides to broker a ceasefire or bring humanitarian supplies to victims of the fighting. Thus, UN and African Union peacekeepers and various international nongovernmental humanitarian organizations have deployed large contingents in various conflicts.

The specific context of armed conflict in sub-Saharan Africa is also very important, as most conflicts involve a cluster of factors rather than one specific factor that has caused a conflict. Most conflicts have either an ethnic, religious, or resource context to them, or they are based on a manipulation of ethnicity and religion by elites seeking political or economic power. No magic formula exists to predict whether a country that is ethnically and religiously fragmented will be involved in armed conflict, although ethnicity has played the principal role in conflicts in Nigeria, Sudan, Liberia, Rwanda, Ethiopia, and Burundi. In Sudan, ethnicity has been at the root of the civil war between the north and south, and ethnicity has continued to be the dominant factor in the conflict in the Darfur region in the early 21st century.

Religion as a source of conflict in sub-Saharan Africa has not been as widespread as it has been in other parts of the world, probably because family and ethnic ties are more important in sub-Saharan Africa than is religion. A family or a village may be split along religious lines, with half its members Muslims and the other half Christians. Religious conflicts that arise do not easily lead to violence when those involved are members of the same family, village, or ethnicity. And yet, even with the moderating social ties of ethnicity and family, religious violence in Africa has been growing.

Nigeria has been a hotbed for religious tensions that spill over on many occasions into armed conflicts. Two types of communal violence have been associated with the Muslim-Christian divide in Nigeria. The first is based on political competition between Christians and Muslims, which goes back to the early years of Nigeria's independence when Christians from the south dominated the country's public sector because of their educational attainments in comparison with the less-educated Muslims from the north. Even though the Muslim northerners resented this, they accepted it and worked to change the situation by using their political power derived from their larger numbers to reverse the situation. Muslim assertiveness met with resentment among southern Christians, and the result was the civil war of 1967–1970 that displayed elements of religious animosity. The second

form of religious conflict in Nigeria is associated with fundamentalist Islam's agenda of creating a theocracy. Since 2000, several Nigerian states in the predominantly Muslim north have instituted sharia, or Islamic law, and this has led to several confrontations with Christians. Violence between the two groups produced more than 3,000 deaths between late 1987 and 1993.

Sudan is another country in sub-Saharan Africa where religious conflicts have been profound. As in Nigeria, the conflict is between Muslims and Christians. Sudan adopted Islamic law in 1983, imposing it on the Christian south, at the same time that the south was at war with the mainly Arab north. Sudan also became a training ground for Osama bin Laden's al-Qaida followers in their fight against the United States and other Western targets. Although bin Laden was subsequently expelled from the country, the Islamist government has continued enforcing Islamic law.

Somalia is another country where Islamic law has only recently been introduced. The country has not had a viable central government since the overthrow of the government of Siad Barre in 1991. Years of civil war did not result in meaningful settlement, but peace talks between the warring factions finally generated a transitional government of national unity in 2004; however, the government has not been able to establish control of its entire territory. A group of Islamists sidestepped the new government (installed in the town of Baidoa and provided security by the African Union) to create a series of Islamic courts to rule territories under their control. The success of these courts so far has turned Somalia into another state in sub-Saharan Africa with Islamic law as its basic law. The Somali situation is much different from Nigeria or Sudan, given that Somalia does not have a viable central government but instead is controlled by warlords. The chaos and political turmoil make it easier for these factions to be infiltrated by or form alliances with groups with global terrorist missions rather than the local political goals that seem to concern the warlords today. Because more than 90 percent of Somalia's population is Muslim, the likelihood of the new laws remaining in place is unknown if political differences are settled. Ethiopia, an ally of the interim Somali government in Baidoa, is opposed to a theocratic government on its borders, a fact that could lead to problems with a Somali government that retains the Islamic courts and law.

Conflicts over resources—when groups and communities mobilize to demand what they consider to be their fair share of resources from the state—have been important components of conflicts in sub-Saharan Africa. This has been the case in the conflict in the Niger Delta region of Nigeria, for example, where armed regional groups have been battling oil companies and government troops.

Some conflicts are also motivated by the desire to control the government machinery to gain access to and control of the state's resources. Sometimes the resources might not have been the initial cause of the war, but once war begins, control over these resources becomes the basis for its continuation. Control over diamond fields in the war in Sierra Leone in the 1990s is one example. Charles Chankay Taylor's strategy in the Liberian war of the 1990s was to control the resource-rich region and the use it to finance his execution of the war. Laurent-Désiré Kabila in 1997 used a similar tactic. He went after mineral-rich Shaba against the government forces of Mobutu in the Democratic Republic of the Congo. And the discovery of oil in southern Sudan provided motivation for the intensification of the conflict by the country's government on one hand and by the Sudanese People's Liberation Army (SPLA) on the other.

The spillover of Africa's various communal armed conflicts is the consequent massive refugee population displaced by the ravages of the armed conflicts. Sub-Saharan Africa has one of the highest refugee populations in the world. UN figures put the number of refugees in the region at 4 million, second only to Asia with 9 million, out of a worldwide figure of 16 million refugees. The UN figure for sub-Saharan Africa does not include the millions of displaced people within their own countries. Often the countries that harbor the refugees, such as the Democratic Republic of the Congo, Chad, and Guinea, are themselves too poor and mired in their own armed conflicts to handle the influx.

Even more sobering are the many deaths that have resulted from armed conflicts. More than 800,000 people were killed in Rwanda alone in 1994, 4 million in the conflict in the Democratic Republic of the Congo that began in 1997, and 200,000 in Darfur in Sudan. A spillover is the instability that the conflicts often cause in neighboring countries. The conflict in Rwanda in 1994 ended up generating conflict in the Democratic Republic of the Congo through the large refugee population camped in eastern Congo. The civil war in Sierra Leone throughout the 1990s was the contagious effect of the Liberian war and the support Sierra Leone received from Liberia.

Subregional Issues

The preceding discussion provides the backdrop against which to view contemporary African politics, a backdrop that is constantly being reinforced by new issues. Upon closer examination, some of the issues that seem new are merely offshoots of older, still unresolved problems that feed off newer environments. That is the case with more recent challenges that have surfaced in specific subregions and countries. Whether these newer challenges are localized within a specific country or subregionally, they often have implications for regional and global security. Examples include the crisis in the Darfur region of Sudan, the instability in Somalia, the peace settlement in the Democratic Republic of the Congo, and the work of UN tribunals in Sierra Leone and in Arusha, Tanzania. In addition to these are the continental efforts within the framework of the African Union and its new vision, African Renaissance.

The Darfur Region of Sudan

The ongoing Darfur conflict represents, first, a major test of the international community's will to deal with the systematic massacre of a particular group of people for no other reason than that they are who they are. This is called genocide, but the Sudanese government and its supporters, including Russia and China, deny this. Second, the conflict exacerbates the poverty and misery in the region, a challenge that the government of Sudan or any government in Africa has failed to resolve for close to half a century. Apart from the 200,000 deaths from the conflict, it has created a refugee crisis. More than 2 million people have been displaced from their homes in Darfur, and over 200,000 have crossed into Chad. Third, the crisis is a test of the will to act on the part of the African Union and the United Nations before the numbers grow worse. In 1994, the UN failed to act decisively while similar ethnic massacres took place in Rwanda and Burundi. At that time the Organization of African Unity (now the African Union) was also ineffective. It appears that history is repeating itself only a little more than a decade later, and no clear end to the crisis is in sight. Fourth, the conflict has the potential of generating a regional war involving Chad, Sudan, and the Central African Republic. Chad already supports rebels in Darfur who are fighting against the Sudanese government, and Sudan supports Chadian rebels fighting to overthrow Chad's government. Rebels from Chad with bases in the Central African Republic have also been involved in operations to overthrow the Chadian government. The unpredictable nature of the situation came to the fore in April 2006 when Chadian rebels operating from bases in Darfur fought their way to Chad's capital, N'djamena, in April 2006 before being repelled. The rebels also initiated another offensive against the government in October 2006. Fifth, terrorist groups such as al-Qaida function best in chaotic situations where political order breaks down; thus, the possibility exists that al-Qaida could take advantage of the chaos in the region to build a base of operations there.

Somalia Again?

Somalia presents a dimension of chaos and insecurity rare even by African standards. For 15 years since the fall of the Siad Barre government in 1991,

Somalia has had no central government. It has been governed by warlords, each controlling a different part of the country. Attempts to get the different groups to negotiate the creation of a viable government (mediated by other African countries and the African Union) were unsuccessful until 2004, when an agreement was reached on a transition government. Even so, some warlords refused to give up their arms and support the transition government. Because Mogadishu, the capital, continued to be controlled by warlords, the government was forced to establish itself in the town of Baidoa. The division of the country among warlords has made it a constant battleground, resulting in continuing anarchy and easy accessibility to global terrorist groups, including al-Qaida, for recruitment and other operational needs. The bombing by al-Qaida cells of the U.S. embassies in Kenya and Tanzania in 1998 was traced to connections inside Somalia. Somali connections were also present in the attack on Israeli tourists in Kenya in 2002.

Efforts to set up a functioning central government have been complicated by the success of a new group known as the Islamic Courts Union (ICU) in seizing control of southern Somalia and Mogadishu, the capital, and uniting them under its control. The group stipulated its goal was to bring order and stability to the country through the institution of Islamic law, the sharia. However, Ethiopia views the ICU as a threat to its own interests, and some accounts say Ethiopia has deployed its forces in Somalia to protect the Baidoa government. Ethiopia fears that consolidation of an Islamic state on its border might embolden nationalist separatist groups within Ethiopia, especially in the Ogaden area occupied by ethnic Somali but also among the Oromo. The United States has also been concerned that the ICU could allow al-Qaida to build training camps in the country. The Bush administration even worked to preempt the success of the ICU by supporting an alliance of warlords to oppose it. Many fear that the situation could get out of hand and generate another subregional conflict in the Horn of Africa by bringing in Eritrea and other Islamic fighters on the side of the ICU.

Eritrea has already been supplying arms to the ICU, as has Ethiopia (to the Baidoa government), which has gone to war against Eritrea in the past.

International Terrorism

The United States has increasingly considered sub-Saharan Africa a crucial theater in the war on terrorism. Sub-Saharan Africa is a land of many porous borders, unstable governments, a large Muslim population, and a number of countries where no government exercises systematic authority throughout the territory. Some of the main terrorist groups, al-Qaida and *Hezbollah*, for example, have carried out operations in Africa against U.S. and Israeli targets, including the bombing of U.S. embassies in Tanzania and Kenya in 1998.

Some of those who carried out the bombing of the embassies were traced to Somalia. The Somali coast has also been a site used by pirates who have shot at cruise ships, probably in attempts to rob them. Somalia's attractiveness to terrorists and violent groups is due to the absence of any form of central authority with the power to govern throughout the territory. In 1995, Islamic terrorists used Sudan as a refuge as they planned and executed a plot to assassinate President Husni Mubarak of Egypt as his plane landed in Addis Ababa, Ethiopia, for an Organization of African Unity summit. Osama bin Laden, leader of al-Qaida, found safe harbor in Sudan before he was expelled to Afghanistan.

Al-Qaida and *Hezbollah* were also attracted to other trouble spots of Africa—Sierra Leone, Liberia, and the Democratic Republic of the Congo (DRC)—all of which waged long civil wars during the 1990s and, for the DRC and Sierra Leone, into the early 21st century. The warring groups in these countries financed their wars mainly through the sale of diamonds and, especially the DRC, other minerals. The UN ban on minerals from these countries gave al-Qaida, *Hezbollah*, and perhaps other terrorist groups an opportunity to play a crucial role in circumventing the UN ban. Diamonds from Sierra Leone were often taken to Liberia under the guard of Liberian security personnel. From Liberia,

the diamonds were then flown out of Africa. Al-Qaida and *Hezbollah* have also been linked to the diamond trade in the DRC. Other conflict areas in Africa, in Uganda, for example, where Lord's Resistance Army has been fighting the government for many years, provide territory conducive to international terrorist activities such as training and businesses used to raise funds.

Another attraction for global terrorist groups, especially jihadists, is the existence of sizable Muslim populations in many countries in the region (even though the Muslim population is smaller than the Christian population). But this advantage is stronger in eastern and southern Africa because many such terrorists, if they are of Arab or Asian descent, blend in more easily than they do in west and central Africa where Arab and Asian groups are much smaller and more easily segregated. Trouble spots in west and central Africa are better suited for raising funds through business activities than for establishing training camps. Thus, jihadist terrorists have been better established in Ethiopia, South Africa, Tanzania, and South Africa, countries where, although the Muslim population in relation to the entire population is small, the Arab and Asian segments of the population are much larger than in west and central African countries.

Fighting terrorists in Africa has been costly and complicated by economic factors and the nature of African borders. Africans have limited resources to put into intelligence gathering, communication, large counterterrorism units, and training programs. Various African countries have not been fully integrated by roads, railways, or by air. Roads are few and some are usable only during the dry season. Poverty and corruption fuel the instability in some of the countries of the region. Africa's large pool of unemployed people provides both breeding grounds for radical ideas and vulnerability to being recruited for a wage. Porous borders such as those shared by the DRC, Burundi, and Uganda provide ease of movement from one country to the other and allow terrorists to escape easily. Terrorists can also plan an operation in one country and execute it in another, as the Sudan-Chad border situation shows.

Fighting terrorism in Africa is also complicated by the fact that domestic groups seeking to overthrow their national governments could be viewed by those governments as al-Qaida-like organizations. If these dissident or illegal groups take refuge in a neighboring country, that neighbor might choose to deny requests for extradition to the home country. Such denials could unravel much of the cooperation that has been achieved in the global war on terrorism. War has brought African countries to cooperate with each other in ways they had not cooperated before. The war on terrorism has also led to new levels of cooperation between the United States and African governments in areas including information sharing, communication, interdiction, and the sharing of facilities. Djibouti and Kenya have allowed the United States to use their seaports and airports, and the United States has an intelligence-gathering post in Djibouti. Sudan, which once hosted Osama bin Laden, is reported to have allowed the United States to have access to files about certain suspects. Ethiopia and Kenya, both victims of terrorism associated with al-Qaida, have been working in collaboration with the United States to prevent al-Qaida from establishing a larger presence in Somalia. In addition, South Africa has an extradition agreement with the United States.

Niger Delta

Nigeria's Niger Delta presents one of the most enduring challenges that successive Nigerian governments have faced since the early 1990s. The estuary of the Niger River, the area where most of the country's crude oil is extracted, is covered by mangrove swamps that are difficult to access by people unfamiliar with them. Despite the oil produced in the area, poverty in the Niger Delta region is pervasive, and basic services are absent. In the delta, armed groups have been fighting the government, using tactics as varied as kidnapping, sabotage of infrastructure, and direct armed confrontation against government troops. Their grievance is

that the area produces the country's vast oil wealth but does not receive its fair share of development projects financed by the oil revenue. They also complain that the oil pollutes the delta's environment and damages their principal means of livelihood—fishing. The groups accuse the Nigerian government of a form of internal colonialism, wherein the oil revenue is used for projects in other parts of the country because they are the home areas of the powerful and influential politicians. The Nigerian government denies this accusation and has labeled the groups as bandits instead of people with genuine or legitimate grievances. Sometimes the actions of the protesting groups have gone beyond protests: group members have broken pipelines and siphoned oil that they sell later in the black market. They frequently kidnap employees of oil companies and hold them for ransom.

Recently their actions have become bolder, and they have actually engaged government troops and defeated them, suggesting they have sophisticated weapons, training, and discipline. The unusual boldness and persistence of the armed groups has led to the suspicion that they are acting with the complicity of government officials in either the delta region or in the national government. In any case, the groups are well coordinated as they siphon the oil into containers and then transport it to the point of sale, usually in neighboring countries.

The impact of the conflict in the delta region goes beyond Nigeria. Nigeria has been immensely affected because the conflict led to a 25 percent decrease in Nigeria's oil production in early 2006, affecting oil company earnings. In turn, global oil prices have also been affected, with prices rising or falling depending on rebel activity.

Efforts by the United States to diversify its energy sources have led the United States to develop stronger relations with the oil-producing countries of the Gulf of Guinea in west Africa (Nigeria, Angola, Equatorial Guinea, Gabon, Republic of the Congo, Cameroon, and inland Chad). Currently 15 percent of the U.S. oil supply comes from this region, and it has been projected that by 2015 the region will supply 25 percent of U.S. oil needs. The impact on the United States of disruptions to oil production in the Niger Delta and political instability in Nigeria could be great.

Special Court for Sierra Leone

Between 1996 and 2002, Sierra Leone went through one of the most brutal internal conflicts in the contemporary world. By the time the war ended, thousands of people had lost their lives and thousands more were maimed, not by land mines but by machetes. The magnitude of the brutality and the abuses that took place led to the creation of the Special Court for Sierra Leone in Freetown, Sierra Leone. The special court is administered jointly by the government of Sierra Leone and the UN and is charged with trying those with the highest responsibility for war crimes and crimes against humanity committed in Sierra Leone between 1996 and 2002. The court applies both Sierra Leone law and international law in its proceedings. The court differs from the International Criminal Tribunal for Rwanda (ICTR), located in Arusha, Tanzania, that hears cases about war crimes and crimes against humanity that took place during the Rwanda massacres because the ICTR was set up and funded by the UN Security Council. Charles Taylor, the former president of Liberia who was responsible for atrocities that took place during the Liberian civil war, was also indicted by the Special Court for Sierra Leone for his role in the brutal deaths or maiming of thousands of citizens of Sierra Leone during the war. Taylor's trial was later transferred to the Hague on grounds that he was a threat to peace.

Democratic Republic of the Congo

The Democratic Republic of the Congo (DRC), a former Belgian colony that gained independence in 1960, is one the most unstable countries in Africa. After many changes of government and one political crisis after another, army commander Joseph D. Mobutu seized power in 1965. He ruled the country, whose name he changed to Zaire in 1971, for 32 years (1965–1997) before he was ousted by Congolese rebels with the aid of troops from Rwanda. The Congolese leader of the rebel movement that ousted him, Laurent Désiré Kabila

became president. Within 15 months, the coalition of Rwandan soldiers and the new Congolese government had broken down and the groups were at war with each order. Rwanda had backed the Congolese Rally for Democracy (RCD) rebel group against Kabila's government, and Uganda had supported another Congolese group, the Movement for the Liberation of the Congo (MLC) in an effort to oust the Kabila government. Zimbabwe, Namibia, and Angola became alarmed and, in an effort to check any expansionist ambitions of Uganda and Rwanda, sent troops to back the DRC in what had now become a regional war. This nine-year conflict led to over 4 million deaths and created a massive refugee problem.

Following the peace accords that brought about a cease-fire, in 2002 South Africa hosted peace talks that ended with an agreement for bringing the rebel forces into the government and setting up a power-sharing arrangement in the DRC. The agreement also called for a new constitution and the establishment of a timetable for elections after the transitional period. The new constitution was approved in December 2005, it came into effect in February 2006, and the first round of the presidential elections was held in July of 2006 with no one getting a clear-cut majority. The second round of the presidential elections was held on October 29, 2006, between Joseph Kabila and Jean-Pierre Bemba, the opposition candidate. Voter turnout was 67 percent. With 65 percent of the votes counted, Kabila led Bemba, 61 percent to 39 percent. Thus, Kabila is expected to win the election considered the most important in the country's history.

A New Scramble for Africa

In the strategic thinking of the major global powers, Africa has become more important than ever before because of the changes that have taken place in the international system during the past decade. These changes include, in particular, the increasing insecurity associated with terrorism as well as the rise of India and China as global powers and their vast and expanding energy needs. For the

United States and Japan, which have been highly dependent on Middle Eastern oil, instability in that region has made that energy source too uncertain. The global war on terror has also influenced how the major powers, especially the United States, view the role Africa can play in global security. That role is one of partnership and cooperation.

The U.S. energy strategy is to diversify its oil suppliers as much as possible. Under that plan, sub-Saharan Africa is viewed as very important, despite the political risks. With 15 percent of current U.S. oil needs coming from Africa, the goal is that, by 2015, 25 percent of the U.S. oil supply will be from Africa. By 2020, that percentage is expected to rise further, and U.S. oil companies are investing billions of dollars—recently, $10 billion annually—in the oil sector in Africa. The United States will have to protect these sources of its energy; consequently it views Africa not just in terms of oil but also in terms of fighting terrorism. The United States has already been working with African countries on the fight against terrorism and other areas of mutual interest. India and China have placed Africa in their strategic thoughts about energy supplies as well. Thus, India and China have worked to increase investments and trade with Africa. Other countries, including Brazil and South Korea, have been working to increase their presence in Africa as well.

As 2006 comes to an end, the political situation in sub-Saharan Africa has been mixed. On the positive side, elections were held in the Democratic Republic of the Congo and we now await the results. In some of the trouble spots in the region, Sudan for example, the Darfur crisis remained unresolved, with no end in sight.

Select Bibliography

Bever, Edward. *Africa*. Phoenix, Ariz.: Oryx Press, 1996.

Bohannan, Paul, and Philip Curtin. *Africa and Africans*, 4th ed. Prospect Heights, Ill.: Waveland Press, 1995.

Cartey, Wilfred, and Martin Kilson, eds. *Independent Africa*. Vol. 2, The Africa Reader. New York: Random House, 1970.

Dagne, Ted. *Africa and the War on Terrorism*. Report no. RL31247. Washington, D.C.: Library of Congress, Congressional Research Service, 2002.

Edie, Carlene J. *Politics in Africa: A New Beginning?* Belmont, Calif.: Wadsworth/Thomson Learning, 2003.

Gordon, April A., and Donald L. Gordon, eds. *Understanding Contemporary Africa*, 3d ed. Boulder, Colo.: Lynne Rienner Publishers, 2001.

Liebenow, J. Gus. *African Politics, Crisis and Challenges*. Bloomington: Indiana University Press, 1986.

Shillington, Kevin. *History of Africa*, rev. 2d ed. New York: Palgrave Macmillan, 2005.

Tordoff, William. *Government and Politics in Africa*, 4th ed. Bloomington: Indiana University Press, 2002.

World Bank. *World Development Report 2000/2001: Attacking Poverty*. New York: Oxford University Press, 2000.

Wycoff, Karl. "Fighting Terrorism in Africa." Testimony before the House International Relations Committee, Subcommittee on Africa, Washington, D.C., April 1, 2004. http://www.state.gov/s/ct/rls/rm/2004/31077.htm.

Moses K. Tesi is professor of political science at Middle Tennessee State University and is the editor of The Journal of African Policy Studies.

PART TWO

GOVERNMENTS

ALGERIA

DEMOCRATIC AND POPULAR REPUBLIC OF ALGERIA

al-Jumhuriyah al-Jazairiyah
al-Dimuqratiyah al-Shabiyah

Note: Prime Minister Ouyahia resigned on May 24, 2006, and he was succeeded on the same day by Abdelaziz Belkhadem (National Liberation Front). Belkhadem announced a largely unchanged cabinet on May 25.

The Country

Located midway along the North African littoral and extending southward into the heart of the Sahara, Algeria is a Muslim country of Arab-Berber population, Islamic and French cultural traditions, and an economy in which the traditional importance of agriculture has been replaced by reliance on hydrocarbons, with petroleum and natural gas now accounting for more than 95 percent of exchange earnings. Women constitute only a small fraction of the paid labor force, concentrated in the service sector (particularly health care). The future role of women in government (and society as a whole) was one of the key issues separating the nation's Islamic fundamentalist movement from the dominant secularists in the 1990s.

For nearly two decades following independence Algeria was perceived by many as a model for Third World liberation movements: the socialist government attended to social welfare needs, while the economy grew rapidly as oil prices rose in the 1970s. Subsequently, declining oil revenues and poor economic management led to major setbacks. Once nearly self-sufficient in food, the country became highly dependent on foreign imports. Other problems included 25 percent unemployment, high population growth (more than one-half of the population is under 20 years old), an external debt estimated at more than $26 billion, a severe shortage of adequate housing, a widespread perception of corruption among government officials, and a spreading black market.

In the mid-1980s the government began to impose budget austerity while attempting to reduce state control of large industries and agricultural collectives, boost nonhydrocarbon production, and cultivate a free-market orientation. The pace of economic reform accelerated following an outbreak of domestic unrest in late 1988, which also

precipitated the launching of what was initially considered one of the continent's "boldest democratic experiments." Although political liberalization was seriously compromised during the 1990s by confrontation with the fundamentalists, the government persevered with its new economic policies, thereby gaining partial rescheduling of the external debt and additional credits from the International Monetary Fund (IMF) and the World Bank. Meanwhile, as mandated by the IMF, privatization accelerated, the collateral loss of some 400,000 jobs in the public sector contributing to growing popular discontent with fiscal policy. Burgeoning terrorist activity in the second half of the 1990s impaired foreign investment in a number of sectors, but it did not affect activity in the oil and gas fields in the southern desert, where oil reserves were estimated at about 16 billion barrels. Foreign investors were described in 2000 as exhibiting renewed interest in response to President Abdelaziz BOUTEFLIKA's free-market orientation and efforts to negotiate a settlement with antigovernment militants.

GDP growth of more than 5 percent was reported for 2004 and 2005, supported primarily by high oil and gas prices. As a result of significant budget surpluses, the government recently announced plans for large-scale spending increases designed to create jobs (official unemployment remained at more than 17 percent, with some observers suggesting the actual level could be twice that figure) and improve the housing and transportation sectors. Efforts were also launched to attract additional foreign investment to the non-hydrocarbon sector, although the IMF cautioned that substantial reform and modernization were still required in the banking system. International financial institutions also urged the government to accelerate its privatization program, described as having stalled recently in the wake of the budget surpluses and a lingering fondness among the population (as well as a number of government leaders) for public benefits associated with the socialist past. Meanwhile, Algeria signed an association agreement with the European Union in September 2005 and subsequently intensified its efforts to gain membership in the World Trade Organization.

Government and Politics

Political Background

Conquered by France in the 1830s and formally annexed by that country in 1842, Algeria achieved independence as the result of a nationalist guerrilla struggle that broke out in 1954 and yielded eventual French withdrawal on July 3, 1962. The eight-year war of liberation, led by the indigenous National Liberation Front (*Front de Libération Nationale*— FLN), caused the death of some 250,000 Algerians, the wounding of 500,000, and the uprooting of nearly 2 million others, as well as the emigration of some 1 million French settlers. The new Algerian regime was handicapped by deep divisions within the victorious FLN, particularly between commanders of the revolutionary army and a predominantly civilian political leadership headed by Ahmed BEN BELLA, who formed Algeria's first regular government and was elected to a five-year presidential term in September 1963. Despite his national popularity, Ben Bella exhibited an extravagant and flamboyant style that antagonized the army leadership, and he was deposed in June 1965 by a military coup under Col. Houari BOUMEDIENNE, who assumed power as president of the National Council of the Algerian Revolution.

During 1976 the Algerian people participated in three major referenda. The first, on June 27, yielded overwhelming approval of a National Charter that committed the nation to the building of a socialist society, designated Islam as the state religion, defined basic rights of citizenship, singled out the FLN as the "leading force in society," and stipulated that party and government cadres could not engage in "lucrative activities" other than those afforded by their primary employment. The second referendum, on November 17, approved a new constitution that, while recognizing the National Charter as "the fundamental source of the nation's policies and of its laws," assigned sweeping powers to

Political Status: Independent republic since July 3, 1962; one-party rule established by military coup July 5, 1965, and confirmed by constitution adopted November 19, 1976; multiparty system adopted through constitutional revision approved by national referendum on February 23, 1989; state of emergency declared for 12 months on February 9, 1992, by military-backed High Council of State and extended indefinitely on February 9, 1993; three-year transitional period declared by High Security Council effective January 31, 1994, as previously endorsed by National Dialogue Conference; constitutional amendments approved by national referendum on November 28, 1996, in advance of return to elected civilian government via multiparty local and national legislative elections in 1997.

Area: 919,590 sq. mi. (2,381,741 sq. km.).

Population: 29,100,867 (1998C); 32,023,000 (2005E), excluding non-resident nationals (estimated at upwards of 1 million in 1980).

Major Urban Centers (2005E): EL DJAZAIR (Algiers, 1,532,000), Wahran (Oran, 724,000), Qacentina (Constantine, 475,000). In May 1981 the government ordered the "Arabizing" of certain place names that did not conform to "Algerian translations."

Official Language: Arabic (French and Berber are also widely spoken. However, in December 1996 the National Transitional Council adopted legislation banning the use of French in the public sector as of July 5, 1998, with the exception that universities were given until July 5, 2000, to switch to the use of Arabic only. In the wake of unrest in Berber areas, the government announced in October 2001 that the Berber language—Tamazight—would be elevated to a "national" language.)

Monetary Unit: Dinar (official rate July 1, 2006: 73.09 dinars = $1US).

President: Abdelaziz BOUTEFLIKA (National Liberation Front—FLN); declared winner of controversial election of April 15, 1999, and sworn in for a five-year term on April 27 to succeed Maj. Gen. (Ret.) Liamine ZEROUAL (nonparty), who in September 1998 had announced his intention to resign prior to the scheduled completion of his term in November 2000; reelected (due to internal FLN disputes, as the candidate of the National Democratic Rally and the Movement for a Peaceful Society) on April 8, 2004, and sworn in for a second five-year term on April 19.

Prime Minister: (*See headnote.*) Ahmed OUYAHIA (National Democratic Rally); appointed by the president on May 5, 2003, to succeed Ali BENFLIS (National Liberation Front), who had been dismissed the same day; reappointed on May 1, 2005.

the presidency. The third referendum, on December 10, reconfirmed Colonel Boumedienne as the nation's president by an official majority of 99.38 percent. Two months later, in the first legislative election since 1964, a unicameral National People's Assembly was established on the basis of a candidate list presented by the FLN.

President Boumedienne died on December 27, 1978, and he was immediately succeeded by assembly president Rabah BITAT, who was legally ineligible to serve as chief executive for more than a 45-day period. Following a national election on February 7, 1979, Bitat yielded the office to Col. Chadli BENDJEDID, who had emerged in January as the FLN presidential designee during an un-

precedented six-day meeting of a sharply divided party congress.

At a June 1980 FLN congress, President Bendjedid was given authority to select members of the party's Political Bureau, and on July 15 he revived the military General Staff, which had been suppressed by his predecessor after a 1967 coup attempt by Col. Tahir ZBIRI. As a further indication that he had consolidated his control of state and party, Bendjedid on October 30 pardoned the exiled Zbiri and freed former president Ben Bella from house detention. (The latter had been released from 14 years' imprisonment in July 1979.)

Bendjedid was unopposed in his reelection bid of January 12, 1984, and on January 22 he appointed Abdelhamid BRAHIMI to succeed Col. Mohamed Ben Ahmed ABDELGHANI as prime minister. Thereafter, the regime was buffeted by deteriorating economic conditions, growing militancy among Islamic fundamentalists and students, and tension within the government, the FLN, and the army over proposed economic and political liberalization. The political infighting limited the effectiveness of reform efforts, critics charging that many of those entrenched in positions of power were reluctant to surrender economic and social privileges.

The pent-up discontent erupted into rioting in Algiers in early October 1988 and quickly spread to other cities, shattering Algeria's reputation as an "oasis of stability" in an otherwise turbulent region. Upwards of 500 persons died when the armed forces opened fire on demonstrators in the capital, while more than 3,000 were arrested. President Bendjedid thereupon adopted a conciliatory attitude, converting what could have been a challenge to his authority into a mandate for sweeping economic and political change. In a referendum on November 3, voters overwhelmingly approved a constitutional amendment reducing the FLN's political dominance by assigning greater responsibility to the prime minister and making him accountable to the assembly. Two days later, Bendjedid appointed Kasdi MERBAH, described as a "determined" proponent of economic liberalization, as the new ministerial leader, and on November 9 Merbah announced a new cabinet from which a majority of the previous incumbents were excluded. Collaterally, the president instituted leadership changes in the military and the FLN, the latter agreeing late in the month to open future legislative elections to non-FLN candidates. On December 22 Bendjedid was reelected to a third five-year term, securing a reported 81 percent endorsement as the sole presidential candidate.

The FLN's status was eroded further by additional constitutional changes in February 1989 that provided, among other things, for multiparty activity (see Constitution and government, below). Seven months later, arguing that economic reforms were not being implemented quickly enough,

Bendjedid named Mouloud HAMROUCHE, a longtime political ally, to succeed Merbah as prime minister.

A multiparty format was introduced for the first time in elections for municipal and provincial councils on June 12, 1990. Contrary to expectations, the Islamic Salvation Front (*Front Islamique du Salut*—FIS), the country's leading Islamic fundamentalist organization, obtained 53 percent of the popular vote and a majority of the 15,000 seats being contested. Responding to demands from the FIS and other opposition parties, President Bendjedid announced in April 1991 that two-stage national legislative elections, originally scheduled for 1992, would be advanced to June 27 and July 18. However, the FIS called a general strike on May 25 to demand additional electoral law changes, the immediate application of sharia (Islamic religious law), the resignation of Bendjedid, and scheduling of new presidential elections. Clashes in the capital between fundamentalists and police intensified in early June, leaving at least seven dead, and on June 5 Bendjedid declared a state of emergency, ordered the army to restore order, and postponed the legislative poll. He also called upon the foreign minister, Sid Ahmed GHOZALI, to form a new government.

On June 18, 1991, Ghozali, described as a "technocrat" committed to economic and political reform, announced his cabinet (the first since independence not to be dominated by FLN leaders) and pledged "free and clean" parliamentary elections by the end of the year. The schism between the government and the fundamentalists remained unbridged, however, and top FIS leaders and hundreds of their followers were arrested when new violence broke out in Algiers in early July.

Following a period of relative calm, the state of emergency was lifted on September 29, 1991, and two-round elections to a 430-seat assembly were scheduled for December 26, 1991, and January 16, 1992. Again testifying to the remarkable surge in fundamentalist influence, FIS candidates won 188 seats outright in the first round (compared to 25 for the Berber-based Socialist Forces Front [*Front des Forces Socialistes*—FFS] and only 15 for the FLN). With the FIS poised to achieve a substantial majority (possibly even the two-thirds majority needed for constitutional revision), Bendjedid initiated talks with the fundamentalists regarding a power-sharing arrangement.

On January 11, 1992, Bendjedid, apparently under pressure from military leaders upset with his accommodation of the FIS, submitted his resignation. The High Security Council (*Haute Conseil de Securité*—HCS), composed of Ghozali and other top officials, including three senior military leaders, announced that it had assumed control to preserve public order and protect national security. (According to the constitution, the assembly president was mandated to assume interim presidential duties, but the assembly had been dissolved by a secret presidential decree on January 4. Although the president of the Constitutional Council was next in the line of temporary succession, the council deferred to the HCS upon Bendjedid's resignation, reportedly ruling that "prevailing conditions" were not covered by the basic law.)

On January 12, 1992, the HCS canceled the second stage of the legislative election and nullified the results of the first. Two days later it announced that it had appointed a five-man High Council of State (*Haute Conseil d'État*—HCE) to serve as an interim collegial presidency. Mohamed BOUDIAF, vice president of the country's wartime provisional government, was invited to return from 28 years of exile in Morocco to assume the chair of the new body.

Following its "soft-gloved coup" in early 1992, the military launched what was described as an "all-out war" against the fundamentalist movement, arresting numerous FIS leaders (including moderates who had been counseling against violent confrontation) in addition to some 500 other FIS members. Bloody demonstrations throughout Algeria erupted shortly thereafter, and on February 9 the HCE declared a new 12-month state of emergency. With most constitutional rights effectively suspended by the declaration, the government intensified its anti-FIS campaign, while militant fundamentalists initiated guerrilla activity against police and security forces. The unrest continued following Ghozali's reappointment on February 23, even

relatively moderate fundamentalists being driven underground by a March decision of the Algerian courts, acting on an HCE petition, to ban the FIS as a legal party. Meanwhile, the nonfundamentalist population appeared to accept the military intervention with relief, since it feared political, legal, and social constraints should the FIS come to power.

HCE Chair Boudiaf was assassinated on June 29, 1992, while addressing a rally in the eastern city of Annaba. Official investigators subsequently concluded there was a broad conspiracy behind the attack without being able to identify those involved. Suspects ranged from militant fundamentalists to members of the "power elite" who may have felt threatened by Boudiaf's anticorruption efforts. (Only one person was arrested in connection with the incident—a member of the presidential guard who was convicted in June 1995 following a trial that shed little light on his motives or possible coconspirators.) On July 2 the HCS named Ali KAFI, the secretary general of the National Organization of Holy Warriors (a group of veterans from the war of independence) as Boudiaf's successor. Prime Minister Ghozali, blaming corrupt government officials and radical fundamentalists equally for the country's disorder, resigned on July 8. He was replaced on the same day by Belaid ABDESSELAM, longtime industry and energy minister under former president Boumedienne.

On February 9, 1993, the HCE extended the state of emergency indefinitely, declaring that steps toward restoration of an elected civilian government would be taken only after successful completion of the "antiterrorist" crackdown. Four months later it presented a blueprint for constitutional change, promising a democratic Muslim state and a free-market economy. In keeping with the new economic thrust, Prime Minister Abdesselam, viewed as strongly oriented towards state control of heavy industry, was replaced on August 21 by Redha MALEK, an advocate of privatization and other forms of liberalization geared to winning debt rescheduling from international creditors.

In October 1993 the HCE appointed an eight-member Committee for National Dialogue to negotiate an agreement among the legal political parties, labor organizations, and trade and professional groups on the nation's political future. However, talks were constrained by a mounting conviction among party leaders that full-scale civil war loomed unless the FIS was brought into the negotiations, a step the regime refused to accept. Consequently, the National Dialogue Conference held in Algiers in January 1994 was boycotted by nearly all the political parties, and its influence was extremely limited. The conference had been expected to name a president to succeed the HCE but failed to do so, reportedly because the military would not grant sufficient authority to a civilian leader. Therefore, on January 27 the HCS announced the appointment of Maj. Gen. (Ret.) Liamine ZEROUAL as president, his inauguration four days later coinciding with the dissolution of the HCE. Zeroual, who retained his former position as defense minister, was authorized to govern (in conjunction with the HCS) for a three-year transitional period, initial reports indicating he would seek a settlement with the FIS.

With debt rescheduling negotiations at a critical juncture, President Zeroual reappointed Prime Minister Malek on January 31, 1994, despite Malek's hard line regarding the FIS. Malek resigned on April 11, following the announcement of preliminary agreement with the IMF; he was replaced by Mokdad SIFI, who had held a number of ministerial posts recently. On April 15 Sifi announced the formation of a new government, described as largely comprising "technocrats" who would concentrate on economic recovery while leaving political and security issues to the president and the HCS. One month later the military-dominated regime set up an appointive National Transitional Council to act in a quasi-legislative capacity prior to elections tentatively scheduled for 1997. However, most of the leading parties boycotted the body, severely undercutting its claim to legitimacy.

A number of groups (including, most significantly, the FIS, FLN, and FFS) drafted a proposed national reconciliation pact in Rome in late 1994 and early 1995. The plan called for a cessation of antigovernment violence, the release of funda-

mentalist detainees, recognition of the FIS, and the convening of a national conference to establish a transitional government pending new national elections. Despite strong international endorsement of the proposal, the government quickly rejected it on the ground that no "credible" truce could be achieved. Further illustrating the sway held by the military's hard-liners, security forces subsequently launched a massive campaign against the Armed Islamic Group (*Groupe Islamique Armé*—GIA) and other militant factions that had claimed responsibility for a series of bombings and assassinations. At the same time, the Zeroual administration reportedly continued negotiations with the FIS in the hope that the Front's supporters could be reintegrated into normal political processes. However, the talks collapsed in mid-1995, and the regime subsequently began to implement its own schedule for a gradual return to civilian government.

The first stage of the transition was a presidential election conducted on November 16, 1995, in which Zeroual, running as an independent but with the support of the military, was elected to a five-year term with 61 percent of the vote. His closest competitor, Sheikh Mahfoud NAHNAH of the moderate fundamentalist *Hamas* Party, secured 25 percent of the vote, followed by Saïd SAADI of the Berber Rally for Culture and Democracy (*Rassemblement pour la Culture et la Démocratie*—RCD), with 9 percent, and Nourreddine BOUKROUH of the Algerian Renewal Party (*Parti pour le Renouveau de l'Algérie*—PRA), with 4 percent. President Zeroual's resounding first-round victory was initially seen as easing the "sense of crisis" somewhat, much of the electorate having apparently endorsed his continued hard line toward the militants. Zeroual, whose platform contained strong anticorruption language, was also reportedly perceived as a buffer, to a certain extent, against complete domination of political affairs by military leaders.

As anticipated, Prime Minister Sifi submitted his resignation following the successful completion of the election, and on December 31, 1995, President Zeroual appointed Ahmed OUYAHIA, former director of the president's office, to succeed Sifi. The government that was announced on

January 5, 1996, included several members from *Hamas* and the PRA, seemingly as a "reward" for their participation in the presidential poll, which had been boycotted by several major legal parties (including the FLN and the FFS) in protest over the lack of an agreement with the FIS.

In mid-1996 President Zeroual proposed a number of constitutional amendments granting sweeping new powers to the president and banning political parties based on religion (see Constitution and government, below). Some 38 parties and organizations endorsed the proposals, although the absence of several major legal groupings (including the FFS and RCD) and, of course, the FIS (which would have been precluded from any eventual legalization under the revisions) undercut the impact of the accord. The government subsequently reported that 85 percent of those voting in a national referendum on November 28 had supported the changes in the basic law. However, opposition leaders and some international observers questioned those results and described the government's claim of an 80 percent vote turnout as vastly inflated.

A new wave of antiregime attacks broke out shortly after the constitutional referendum of November 1996 and reached an unprecedented scale in July–August, despite (or perhaps because of) recent national legislative balloting and other progress toward full return to elected civilian government. Nevertheless, the administration proceeded with its timetable in 1997. Regulations for party registration were established in February, and new assembly elections were held on June 5, the balloting being dominated by the recently established progovernment National Democratic Rally (*Rassemblement National et Démocratique*—RND), with 156 seats, followed by the Movement for a Peaceful Society (*Mouvement pour une Société Paisible*—MSP, as *Hamas* had been renamed) with 69 seats, and the FLN with 62. After several weeks of reportedly intense negotiations, the MSP and the FLN agreed to join a new RND-led coalition government, which was announced on June 25 under the continued direction of Prime Minister Ouyahia. The RND also secured most of the seats in municipal elections conducted on October 23, although some were allocated to other parties after a judicial review of allegations of widespread fraud made by a number of groups, including the MSP and the FLN. The political transition was completed on December 25, 1997, with indirect elections to the Council of the Nation (the new upper house in the legislature), the RND winning 80 of the 96 contested seats. By that time, however, despite the progress on the institutional front, the wave of domestic violence had reached an unprecedented level.

As of early 1998 the government reported that about 26,000 people had died during the six-year insurgency, although other observers estimated the figure to be as high as 80,000. A special UN commission that visited Algeria at midyear placed the blame for the violence squarely on "Islamic terrorists" and argued that the Zeroual regime deserved international and domestic support. However, human rights organizations strongly criticized the UN report for inadequately addressing the harsh retaliatory measures on the part of government security forces. In that context, it appeared that differences of opinion had emerged within the military and political elite over how to proceed vis-à-vis the fundamentalists. Hard-liners subsequently appeared to continue to dominate that debate, possibly contributing to the surprise announcement in September by Zeroual (seen as having come to favor a dialogue with moderate Islamist leaders) that he would leave office prior to the completion of his term.

New presidential elections were initially set for February 1999 and then rescheduled for the following April. Meanwhile, Prime Minister Ouyahia resigned on December 14, 1998, and the following day the president appointed Ismail HAMDANI, a senator and former ambassador, to serve as head of a caretaker government pending completion of the presidential balloting. Hamdani's cabinet, installed December 19, differed only slightly from his predecessor's.

The April 15, 1999, presidential election proved to be highly controversial, as six of the seven candidates quit the race shortly before the balloting out of conviction that the poll had been rigged in favor of the military's preferred candidate, Abdelaziz BOUTEFLIKA, who had served as foreign minister in the 1960s and 1970s but had been on the political sidelines for 20 years. Despite the opposition's demand for a postponement, the election proceeded as scheduled, Bouteflika being credited with 74 percent of the vote. (The names of the other candidates had remained on the ballot despite the boycott. Official results declared former foreign affairs minister Ahmed IBRAHIMI, who ran as an independent but enjoyed the informal support of the FIS, to be the runner-up with 13 percent of the vote. None of the other candidates received more than a 4 percent vote share.)

Following surprisingly long negotiations, President Bouteflika named Ahmed BENBITOUR, a former foreign minister who was described as a "close friend" of the president's, as prime minister on December 23, 1999. On the following day, Benbitour formed a new government that included seven parties, all of whom remained in the cabinet named by Ali BENFLIS after he replaced Benbitour in late August 2000. However, the RCD left the coalition in May 2001 as the result of severe unrest within the Berber community (see Current issues, below).

The FLN dominated the May 30, 2002, legislative balloting, securing 199 seats, while the RND declined to 47. Prime Minister Benflis was reappointed on June 1, and on June 17 he formed a new government comprising FLN, RND, and MSP ministers.

Further successes by the FLN in the October 2002 elections appeared to kindle presidential aspirations in Benflis, who was dismissed by President Bouteflika on May 5, 2003; Ahmed Ouyahia returned to the prime ministerial post he had held from 1995 to 1998. In September 2003 Bouteflika also dismissed several pro-Benflis cabinet ministers, exacerbating tensions that subsequently split the FLN into two camps (see FLN, below, for details). The FLN dispute resulted in confusing circumstances under which Bouteflika was reelected (with 85 percent of the vote) on April 8, 2004, as the candidate of the RND and MSP, while Benflis

secured only 6.4 percent of the vote as the nominal FLN candidate.

Constitution and Government

The 1976 constitution established a single-party state with the FLN as its "vanguard force." Executive powers were concentrated in the president, who was designated president of the High Security Council and of the Supreme Court, as well as commander in chief of the armed forces. He was empowered to appoint one or more vice presidents and, under a 1979 constitutional amendment that reduced his term of office from six to five years, was obligated to name a prime minister. He also named an 11-member High Islamic Council selected from among the country's "religious personalities." The 1976 document also stipulated that members of the National People's Assembly would be nominated by the FLN and established a judicial system headed by a Supreme Court, to which all lower magistrates were answerable.

In late 1983, as part of a decentralization move, the number of administrative departments (*wilayaat*) was increased from 31 to 48, each continuing to be subdivided into districts (*dairaat*) and communes. At both the *wilaya* and communal (town) levels there were provisions for popular assemblies, with an appointed governor (*wali*) assigned to each *wilaya*. The various administrative units were linked vertically to the minister of the interior, with party organization paralleling the administrative hierarchy.

On January 16, 1986, a referendum approved a new National Charter that, while maintaining allegiance to socialism and Islam, accorded President Bendjedid greater leeway in his approach to social and economic problems, particularly in regard to partial privatization of the "inefficient" public sector. Additional constitutional changes were approved by referendum on November 3, 1988. The revisions upgraded the prime minister's position, declaring him to be the "head of government" and making him directly responsible to the assembly. In effect, the change transferred some of the power previously exercised by the FLN to the assembly, particularly in light of a decision later in the month to permit non-FLN candidates in future elections. The role of the FLN was further attenuated by reference to the president as the "embodiment of the unity of the nation" rather than "of the unity of the party and the state."

Another national referendum on February 23, 1989, provided for even more drastic reform. It eliminated all mention of socialism, guaranteed the fundamental rights "of man and of the citizen" as opposed to the rights of "the people," excised reference to the military's political role, and imposed stricter separation of executive, legislative, and judicial powers. In addition, the FLN lost its "vanguard" status with the authorization of additional "associations of a political nature." Continuing the transfer to a multiparty system, the assembly on July 2 established criteria for legal party status (see Political Parties and Groups, below), and on July 19 it adopted a new electoral law governing political campaigns. The new code established multimember districts for local and national elections, with any party receiving more than 50 percent of the votes to be awarded all the seats in each. However, reacting to complaints from newly formed opposition parties, the government in March 1990 approved a system of proportional representation for the June municipal elections. After intense debate, the electoral law was further changed in 1991 to provide for two-round balloting in single-member districts in future assembly elections.

In announcing a one-year state of emergency in February 1992, the newly formed High Council of State suspended a number of key constitutional provisions, and over the next ten months it ordered the dissolution of nearly 800 municipal assemblies controlled by the FIS since the 1990 elections. In furtherance of its antifundamentalist campaign, the High Council of State in October also created three secret courts in which persons over 16 years of age charged with "subversion" or "terrorism" could be sentenced without the right of appeal. The state of emergency was extended indefinitely in February 1993, a transitional government being named

a year later for a three-year period leading to proposed multiparty elections and a return to civilian leadership.

The electoral code was amended in 1995 to provide for multicandidate presidential elections, in two rounds if no candidate received a majority in the first round. Potential candidates were required to obtain the signatures of 75,000 voters to be placed on the ballot, and anyone married to a foreigner was precluded from running.

In connection with the planned transition to civilian government, the Zeroual administration in the spring of 1996 proposed a number of constitutional amendments, which were approved by national referendum on November 28. Among other things, the amendments banned political parties from referencing religious or ethnic "identities," while codifying Islam as the state religion and Arabic as the official national language. The president was given authority to govern by decree in certain circumstances and to appoint one-third of the members of a new upper house in the Parliament—the Council of Nations. That second provision was viewed as one of the most significant aspects of the new charter because it gave the president effective blocking power on legislation. (New laws require the approval of three-quarters of the Council of Nations.) A Constitutional Council was established in April 1998, while a juridical State Council was installed two months later.

Foreign Relations

Algerian foreign relations have gone through a series of changes that date back to the preindependence period, formal contacts with many countries having been initiated by the provisional government created in September 1958. Foreign policy in the immediate postindependence period was dominated by President Ben Bella's anti-imperialist ideology. The period immediately following the 1965 coup was essentially an interregnum, with President Boumedienne concentrating his efforts on internal affairs. Following the Arab-Israeli War of 1967, Boumedienne became much more active in foreign policy, with a shift in interest from Africa and the Third World to a more concentrated focus on Arab affairs. After the 1973 Arab-Israeli conflict, the theme of "Third World liberation" reemerged, reflecting a conviction that Algeria should be in the forefront of the Nonaligned Movement. Subsequently, Algeria joined with Libya, Syria, the People's Democratic Republic of Yemen, and the Palestine Liberation Organization to form the so-called "Steadfastness Front" in opposition to Egyptian-Israeli rapprochement. However, in conjunction with a softening Arab posture toward Egypt, Algiers resumed full diplomatic relations with Cairo in November 1988.

A major controversy erupted following division of the former Spanish Sahara between Morocco and Mauritania in early 1976. In February the Algerian-supported Polisario Front (see under Morocco: Disputed Territory) announced the formation of a Saharan Arab Democratic Republic (SADR) in the Western Sahara that was formally recognized by Algeria on March 6; subsequently, a majority of other nonaligned states accorded the SADR similar recognition. However, the issue split the Organization of African Unity (OAU), with Morocco withdrawing from the grouping in 1984 in protest over the seating of an SADR delegation. Concurrently, relations between Algeria and Morocco deteriorated further, with President Bendjedid pledging full support for Mauritania's "territorial integrity" and Morocco referring to the Polisarios as "Algerian mercenaries." Relations improved significantly in late 1987, however, and in May 1988 Rabat and Algiers announced the restoration of formal ties, jointly expressing support for settlement of the Western Saharan problem through a self-determination referendum. Subsequent progress in Morocco-Polisario negotiations permitted Algiers to concentrate on a long-standing foreign policy goal: the promotion of economic, social, and political unity among Maghrebian states (see separate section on Arab Maghreb Union).

Relations with Libya worsened in response to Tripoli's "unification" Treaty of Oujda with Rabat in August 1984 (see entries under Libya and Morocco) and continued to plummet as a result of Libya's expulsion of Tunisian workers in the summer of 1985. Algiers felt obliged, however, to defend the Qadhafi regime in the events leading up to the U.S. attacks on Tripoli and Benghazi in April 1986. Although Algeria resisted federation with its eastern neighbor (preferring to concentrate on more inclusive Maghrebian unity), agreement was reached in July 1988 for the free movement of people between the two countries and the launching of bilateral economic projects.

Ties with France, Algeria's leading trade partner, were temporarily strained by legislation in July 1986 making visas mandatory for all North Africans seeking entry into the former metropole; however, swift action by French authorities against Algerian opposition activists later in the year led to an improvement in relations. Earlier, in April 1985, President Bendjedid became the first Algerian head of state since independence to visit Washington, utilizing the occasion to secure Algeria's removal from a list of countries prohibited from purchasing U.S. weapons.

The victories of the Islamic fundamentalist movement in Algeria's 1990 and 1991 elections were characterized as generating "shock waves throughout northern Africa." The governments of Egypt, Libya, Morocco, and Tunisia (all struggling to contain fundamentalist influence) were reported to be greatly relieved by the military takeover in January 1992 and supportive of Algiers' anti-FIS campaign. The government/fundamentalist schism also led in March 1993 to the severing of ties with Iran, which the administration accused of supporting local terrorist activity. France, concerned over the possible influx of refugees should a fundamentalist government be established in Algiers, also supported the military regime.

President Bouteflika met with U.S. President George W. Bush in Washington in June 2001, their talks centering on "energy issues" rather than, as some reformists had hoped, democratization or good governance. Bouteflika returned to the United States late in the year to pledge Algeria's support for Washington's recently launched war on terrorism. Among other things, the aftermath of the September 11, 2001, attacks appeared to shine a more positive light, in the minds of many international observers, on the hard line adopted by the Algerian regime toward militant fundamentalism since 1992. In consonance with its renewed U.S. ties, the Algerian government refused in 2003 to permit domestic protests against U.S. actions in Iraq.

In March 2003 French President Jacques Chirac made the first formal state visit by a French leader to Algeria since the war of independence. The Algerian population warmly greeted Chirac, who pledged further "reconciliation" initiatives. (Relations with France deteriorated in early 2005 when the French parliament endorsed a bill that recognized the "positive role" that colonization had played in Algeria. President Bouteflika subsequently demanded that France formally apologize for its actions in Algeria, and a proposed French/Algerian "friendship treaty" remained unsigned as of April 2006.) Morocco also subsequently was reported to be seeking improved ties with Algeria, but the Algerian government remained committed to a self-determination referendum in the Western Sahara. Consequently, the border between Algeria and Morocco remained closed as of early 2006, although interest in negotiations on the issue appeared to have intensified.

Current Issues

Facing an extremely difficult task in convincing the Algerian populace and the international community of the legitimacy of the April 1999 presidential poll, President Bouteflika moved quickly to establish his leadership credentials by, among other things, announcing plans for a "civil concord," which proposed amnesty for most fundamentalist militants in return for their permanent renunciation of violence and surrender of arms. The pact easily secured legislative approval in the summer and was endorsed by 98 percent of those voting in a national referendum on September 16. By the end of the cut-off date for the amnesty in mid-January 2000, upwards of 6,000 guerrillas had reportedly accepted the government's offer. However, most of them came from the FIS-affiliated Islamic Salvation Army, which had already been

honoring a cease-fire since 1997. Significantly, the GIA rejected the peace plan, and deadly attacks and counterattacks continued on a nearly daily basis throughout the summer of 2000. By that time Bouteflika had achieved only mixed results on the political front as well, as evidenced by the eight-month wait for the formation of a new government following the presidential election. Some analysts attributed the delay to efforts by Bouteflika to consolidate his authority, even, in some cases, at the expense of the military leaders who had propelled him to power.

Despite the partial success of the civil concord, some 2,700 deaths were reported in 2000 from the ongoing conflict, and an upsurge of antigovernment violence was reported in December. In early 2001 President Bouteflika promised an "iron fist" in dealing with the remaining militants. However, the government faced a new crisis in April when riots broke out within the Berber population in the Kabylie region after a young man died under inadequately explained circumstances while in police custody. Government forces responded with a harsh crackdown, and some 1 million demonstrators reportedly participated in the antiregime protests that ensued in the Kabylie region and other areas, including Algiers. More than 60 people were killed and 2,000 injured in the clashes, which, fueled by economic malaise and long-standing concern over the authoritarian rule of what one journalist described as the "overwhelming power of an opaque military leadership," continued into 2002, prompting the leading Berber parties (the FFS and the RCD) to boycott the national legislative poll on May 30.

Deadly bomb attacks continued in 2003, mostly the work of the GIA offshoot called the Salafist Group for Preaching and Combat (*Groupe Salafiste pour la Prédication et le Combat*—GSPC). However, the level of violence was greatly reduced from its height earlier in the decade (as one reporter put it, dozens killed per month rather than dozens per day). Most observers credited President Bouteflika's resounding reelection in April 2004 to popular appreciation of the improved security situation, along with recent economic advances and Algeria's renewed international status in connection with the U.S.-led war on terrorism. For its part, the Algerian military appeared to step back from its previous level of background political involvement, possibly under the opinion that the "Islamist threat" had been for the most part overcome.

A January 2005 accord between the government and Berber representatives called for enhanced economic support for Berber areas and appeared to reduce unrest within the Berber community. Even more significant was a national referendum on September 29 that overwhelmingly endorsed the government's proposed national charter for peace and reconciliation. The charter called for amnesty for most of the Islamic militants involved in the civil war that had started in 1991, although leaders of the "insurrection" were barred from future political activity. Collaterally, the charter praised the role of the army in the conflict, effectively eliminating any possibility that excesses on the part of the security forces would be investigated. (It was estimated that 6,000–20,000 Algerians had "disappeared" as the result of the army's anti-insurgency measures.) Most major political parties supported the charter, and President Bouteflika staked his political future on its passage. The government reported a 97 percent yes vote and an 80 percent turnout, although the latter figure was broadly discounted by opponents of the initiative as well as some independent analysts. (It was noted that turnout in Berber regions appeared to be less than 20 percent.) Despite protests over the perceived heavy-handedness of the government in stifling effective opposition to the charter, the consensus appeared to be that the vote was a clear indication that the majority of Algerians were prepared to put the matter behind them. (It was estimated that the conflict had cost more than $30 billion and left 150,000–200,000 people dead.)

For its part, the U.S. government declared that Algeria was "moving in the right direction" and agreed to consider an Algerian request to purchase U.S. armaments, provided an understanding could be reached that the weapons would remain within the country. Algiers also announced increased cooperation with the North Atlantic Treaty Organization (NATO) regarding antiterrorism initiatives. Meanwhile, on the domestic front, the Bouteflika administration pledged to promote massive job creation through stimulus of the industrial and agricultural sectors throughout the country, assisted by development of new transportation networks. However, the state of emergency remained in effect "until terrorism is completely defeated," and security forces launched a campaign in March 2006 against militant holdouts (officially estimated as numbering less than 800 at that time) in remote mountainous regions.

Political Parties and Groups

From independence until 1989 the National Liberation Front was the only authorized political grouping, Algeria having been formally designated as a one-party state. Under constitutional changes approved in 1989, however, Algerians were permitted to form "associations of a political nature" as long as they did not "threaten the basic interests of the state" and were not "created exclusively on the basis of religion, language, region, sex, race, or profession." To operate legally, parties were also required to obtain government permits. The process of legalization began in August 1989, and multiparty activity was permitted for the first time at local elections in June 1990. By the end of 1991 there were nearly 60 legal parties. However, constitutional amendment of November 1996 and electoral law revision of February 1997 further restricted parties from referencing religion, ethnicity, or race. A number of existing groups were deregistered for failure to adapt to the changes by the deadline of April 1997. In addition, a number of other parties were told to disband in May 1998, either for failing to have the minimum of 2,500 members or for violating other new regulations. Twenty-three parties participated in the 2002 legislative balloting.

Government Parties

National Liberation Front (*Front de Libération Nationale*—FLN). Founded in November 1954 and dedicated to socialism, nonalignment, and pan-Arabism, the FLN led the eight-year war of independence against France. Although weakened by factionalism and disagreement over the role of the army in politics, the Front subsequently assumed complete control of Algerian political and governmental affairs.

By the late 1980s a cleavage was apparent within the FLN between an "old guard," dedicated to the maintenance of strict socialist policies, and a group, led by President Bendjedid, favoring political and economic liberalization. The reformers having manifestly gained the ascendancy, Mohamed Cherif MESSAADIA, the Front's leading socialist ideologue, was dismissed from the ruling Politburo in early November 1988. Subsequently, during the party congress in Algiers November 27–28, the Politburo itself was abolished, and the office of secretary general was dissociated from that of state president. (Bendjedid, however, was named to the newly created post of FLN president.) The delegates also voted to democratize the filling of FLN organs, approved the chief executive's proposals for economic reform, and nominated Bendjedid as sole candidate for a third presidential term. Although not specifically empowered by the congress to do so, the Central Committee in June 1989 endorsed the creation of a multiparty system, some continued opposition to Bendjedid's political and economic reforms notwithstanding.

Following the FLN's poor showing (about 34 percent of the popular vote) in the June 1990 municipal elections, a number of government officials were dismissed from the Politburo amid intense debate over how to check the rapid erosion of the Front's influence. In late June 1991 Bendjedid resigned as FLN president, and several other members of his administration relinquished their party posts as part of the government's effort to distance itself from FLN control. However, Abdelhamid MEHRI, Bendjedid's brother-in-law and close associate, was subsequently reelected FLN secretary-general.

Further illustrating the rapid decline in its electoral potency, the FLN won only 15 seats on the basis of a 24 percent vote share in the December 1991 first-round legislative poll. The party was subsequently reported to be divided over Bendjedid's resignation as president of the republic and the assumption of power by the High Security Council. Mehri initially charged the army with having conducted a coup d'état and suggested the FLN might join forces with other groups, including the FIS, to oppose the new regime. Subsequently, however, the FLN Central Committee announced it would support the High Council of State, assuming adherence to that council's pledge to return the nation to a democratic process. Meanwhile, despite widespread popular resentment over long-standing official corruption, FLN members reportedly remained entrenched in many formal and informal positions of local and national influence.

By late 1994 the FLN was firmly in the opposition camp, its leaders joining with those of the FIS, FFS, and other parties in negotiating a proposed plan for a return to civilian government. At the urging of Secretary General Mehri, the FLN formally endorsed a boycott of the 1995 presidential election, although it appeared that many party members voted anyway, a large percentage of their support reportedly going to President Zeroual. Mehri was subsequently dismissed as secretary general in January 1996 by the FLN Central Committee, and his successor, Boualem BENHAMOUDA, quickly distanced the FLN from the FIS and other antiregime groupings.

The 1995 electoral boycott having been widely acknowledged as a mistake, the FLN participated full force in the three 1997 elections and accepted junior partner status in the RND-led coalition government formed in June. However, despite the solidly proadministration stance of the FLN leaders, it was reported that a "reformist" faction, led by former prime minister Mouloud Hamrouche, continued to promote, among other things, a negotiated settlement with the FIS.

The FLN held its first congress in nine years in March 1998, electing a 210-member Central Committee and reelecting Secretary General Benhamouda, thereby underlining the party's return to a "conservative tendency." The FLN nominated military-backed Abdelaziz Bouteflika as its official candidate for the April 1999 presidential election, although a segment of the party supported Hamrouche, who ran as an independent and subsequently indicated his intention to form a new party. Benhamouda, viewed as a longstanding "rival" to Bouteflika, resigned as secretary general in September 2001; the post was later filled by Prime Minister Ali Benflis.

Following the resurgence of the FLN in the May 2002 assembly balloting (199 seats [to lead all parties] on a 35 percent vote share) and the October 2002 municipal elections, Benflis was reelected as FLN secretary general at a July 2003 congress, which also installed a pro-Benflis Central Committee. By that time it was clear that Benflis (who had been dismissed as prime minister in April 2003) planned to run for president in 2004, thereby causing a rupture in the FLN between his supporters and those of President Bouteflika. The FLN convention in December 2003 selected Benflis as the party's standard-bearer, but an Algerian court (apparently under pressure from the Bouteflika administration) "annulled" that nomination and ordered FLN funds frozen. After Benflis secured only 8 percent of the vote in the April 2004 balloting, he resigned as FLN secretary general. At a party congress in February 2005, Bouteflika was named "honorary president" of the party, his supporters having clearly regained party control.

In addition, Abdelaziz Belkhadem, described as close to Bouteflika and a potential link to the moderate Islamic movement, was reelected as secretary general.

Leaders: Abdelaziz BOUTEFLIKA (President of the Republic), Abdelaziz BELKHADEM (Secretary General).

National Democratic Rally (*Rassemblement National et Démocratique*—RND). Launched in February 1997 in support of the policies of President Zeroual, the RND dominated the subsequent assembly, municipal, and Council of the Nation balloting, in part due to substantial financing and other assistance from sitting government officials, many of whom ran for office under the RND banner. Formally committed to pluralism, a "modern" economy (including emphasis on privatization),

and "social justice," the RND was widely viewed primarily as a vehicle for entrenched authority to participate in an expanding democratic process without facing a genuine threat to its hold on power.

The first RND congress, held in April 1998, elected a National Committee and a 15-member National Bureau led by Secretary General Tahar BENBAIBECHE. However, a serious split subsequently developed in the party over whom to support in the April 1999 presidential balloting. Consequently, Benbaibeche, who had complained that military leaders had been inappropriately pressuring the RND to back Abdelaziz Bouteflika, was dismissed as secretary general in January 1999 and replaced by Ahmed Ouyahia, who had recently resigned as prime minister. Ouyahia quickly announced that Bouteflika, the official candidate of the FLN, enjoyed the support of most of the RND.

By early 2002 the RND was described as having failed to attract as much popular support as originally expected, apparently because of the party's ongoing ties to the military. The RND's representation in the National People's Assembly fell from 156 to 47 in the 2002 balloting. Ouyahia returned to the prime ministership in April 2003, and the RND supported Bouteflika in the 2004 presidential poll.

Leaders: Ahmed OUYAHIA (Prime Minister and Secretary General), Abdelkader BENSALAH (Speaker of the Council of the Nation).

Movement for a Peaceful Society (*Mouvement pour une Société Paisible/Harakat Mujitamas al-Silm*—MSP/*Hamas*). Formerly known as the Movement for an Islamic Society (*Mouvement pour une Société Islamique*—MSI) or *Hamas* (an acronym from that grouping's name in Arabic), the MSP adopted its current rubric in 1997 in light of new national restrictions on party references to religion. The MSP is a moderate Islamic fundamentalist organization distinct from the more militant Palestinian formation also known as *Hamas*. It advocates "coexistence" with groups of opposing views in a democratic political structure and the introduction "by stages" of an Islamic state that would maintain "respect for individual liberties."

Although it was reported in early 1992 that some *Hamas* members had been arrested in the sweeping antifundamentalist campaign, the government subsequently returned to its position that the grouping represented an acceptable moderate alternative to the FIS. Subsequently, Sheikh Mohamed BOUS-LIMANI, a founder of *Hamas*, was killed in late 1993, while another leader, Aly AYEB, was assassinated in September 1994, the attacks being attributed to radicals opposed to *Hamas*'s ongoing dialogue with the government.

Hamas leader Sheikh Mahfoud Nahnah, who had announced his support for the regime's "antiterrorist" campaign but had described the nation as stuck "in a political dead end" in view of the "lack of trust between people and authority," received 25 percent of the vote in the 1995 presidential election. Two members of the party were subsequently named to minor cabinet posts in the government formed in January 1996.

After finishing second in the June 1997 legislative balloting, the MSP joined the subsequent RND-led coalition government, a decision that was described as putting the party's "credibility on the line" vis-à-vis the more hard-line grouping, the MR (or *Nahda*), which was competing for Islamic support. The MSP subsequently continued to pursue a middle road; it strongly criticized perceived electoral fraud benefiting the RND in the October municipal elections but also demanded stricter security measures in early 1998 in the face of escalating terrorist attacks.

Nahnah attempted to run in the April 1999 presidential balloting, but his candidacy was disallowed, ostensibly on the ground that he had not provided proof he had participated in the country's "war of independence" as required of all presidential contenders under the 1996 constitutional revision. Nahnah died in July 2003 after a long illness.

The MSP, which had seen its assembly representation fall from 69 to 38 in the 2002 balloting, supported President Bouteflika in the 2004 presidential campaign. Not surprisingly, MSP leader Abou Djerra Soltani also strongly endorsed the 2005 national charter on peace and reconciliation.

Leader: Abou Djerra SOLTANI (President).

Other Legislative Parties

Movement for National Reform (*Mouvement pour la Réforme Nationale*—MRN). The MRN, also known as *Islah* (Arabic for "reform"), was launched in early 1999 to promote the presidential campaign of Sheikh Abdallah Djaballah, who had recently split from *Nahda*. The MRN, supportive of eventual establishment of an "Islamic State," won 43 seats in the 2002 assembly balloting, thereby becoming the largest opposition grouping. Djaballah won 4.9 percent of the vote in the 2004 presidential poll.

Leader: Sheikh Abdallah DJABALLAH (Party Leader and 2004 presidential candidate), Lakhdar Ben KHALIF.

Workers' Party (*Parti des Travailleurs*—PT). The Trotskyist PT was one of the groups that signed the proposed national reconciliation pact in early 1995. It secured four seats in the June 1997 assembly balloting and subsequently continued to urge the government to negotiate with the FIS. The PT improved dramatically to 21 seats in the 2002 assembly balloting on a vote share of 4.8 percent. PT leader and women's rights activist Louisa Hannoun, described as the first woman to run for president in the Arab world, won 1.2 percent in the vote in the 2004 poll.

Leader: Louisa HANNOUN.

Algerian National Front (*Front National Algérien*—FNA/*Jabhah al-Wataniyah al-Jazairiyah*). Organized in June 1999 in support of the "downtrodden," the FNA received official recognition the following November. It won eight seats in the 2002 legislative poll on a 3.2 percent vote share. However, the proposed presidential bid in 2004 of the FNA leader, Moussa Touati, was rejected by the Constitutional Council.

Leader: Moussa TOUATI.

Renaissance Movement (*Mouvement de la Renaissance/Harakat al-Nahda*—MR/*Nahda*). Previously called the Islamic Renaissance Movement (*Mouvement de la Renaissance Islamique/Harakat al-Nahda al-Islamiyya*—MRI/*Nahda*), the party dropped the "Islamic" portion of its rubric in early 1997 to conform to new national regulations. Initially a small, moderate fundamentalist grouping, *Nahda* was promoted in the mid-1990s by the government as a legal alternative to the banned FIS. The grouping performed "surprisingly well" in the June 1997 legislative balloting, finishing fourth with 34 seats. By that time *Nahda* had adopted a tougher stance than the other main legal Islamic party (the MSP), and its leaders ultimately declined to participate in the new RND-led coalition government.

A *Nahda* congress in early 1998 reportedly directed that some authority previously exercised by long-standing leader Sheikh Abdallah Djaballah be turned over to Secretary General Lahbib Adami. The apparent rivalry between the two came to a head late in the year when Adami announced that the party had agreed to support Abdelaziz Bouteflika, the military-backed FLN candidate, in the upcoming presidential balloting. Djaballah consequently left *Nahda* in January 1999 and formed the MRN (above), taking nearly half of the 34 *Nahda* assembly representatives with him. *Nahda* fell to only one seat in the 2002 assembly poll.

Leader: Lahbib ADAMI (Secretary General).

Algerian Renewal Party (*Parti pour le Renouveau de l'Algérie*—PRA). A moderate Islamic group that first surfaced during the October 1988 demonstrations, the PRA announced in 1989 that it would concentrate on economic issues, particularly a fight to end "state capitalism and interventionism." PRA leader Noureddine Boukrouh, described as a "liberal businessman," won 4 percent of the votes in the 1995 presidential election. Two PRA members were appointed to the January 1996 cabinet, but the party was not represented in the June 1997 government. The government disallowed Boukrouh's candidacy for the 1999 presidential election, citing insufficient signatures of support. However, Boukrouh joined the coalition government announced in December 1999. The PRA secured 2.2 percent of the vote in the 2002 assembly balloting.

Leaders: Noureddine BOUKROUH, Yacine TORKMANE.

Movement of National Harmony (*Mouvement de l'Entente Nationale*—MEN). The MEN secured 1.9 percent of the vote in the 2002 assembly balloting.

Leaders: Ali BOUKHAZNA, Amar LASSOUED.

Socialist Forces Front (*Front des Forces Socialistes*—FFS). Long a clandestine group, the predominantly Berber FFS was legalized in November 1989. Having earned the enmity of the government in 1985 when he briefly formed a "united front" with Ben Bella's MDS (below) to oppose the FLN, the FFS leader, revolutionary hero Hocine Aït-Ahmed, remained in Swiss exile until December 1989. The FFS boycotted the 1990 municipal elections but, after failing to create a multiparty coalition to "block" the FIS, presented over 300 candidates in the December 1991 legislative balloting on a platform that endorsed a "mixed economy," greater regional autonomy, and official recognition of the Berber language. The FFS won 25 seats (second to the FIS) on a 15 percent vote share in the first election round, Aït-Ahmed strongly criticizing cancellation of the second prior to returning to self-imposed exile in Switzerland. The FFS subsequently joined the FIS and the FLN as the leading proponents of the unsuccessful January 1995 peace plan and boycotted the 1995 presidential balloting. However, Aït-Ahmed then called for "conciliation" talks with the government in apparent recognition of the Zeroual regime's strengthened position following the election.

Aït-Ahmed, hitherto FFS general secretary, was elected to the newly created post of party president at the March 1996 FFS congress in Algiers. A 10-member secretariat and a 120-member national council were also installed. Dueling with the RCD for support within the Berber community, the FFS secured 20 seats in the June 1997 assembly balloting but was not invited to participate in the new RND-led government because of the Front's insistence that negotiations should proceed with the goal of incorporating the FIS into the legal political process. A special congress in February 1999 nominated Aït-Ahmed as the FFS candidate for the upcoming presidential balloting, despite the reported poor health of the aging leader, who had recently returned from his self-imposed exile. A May 2000 congress reelected Aït-Ahmed as FFS president amid reports of deepening divisions within the party. In the wake of severe unrest in Berber areas, the FFS boycotted the 2002 assembly balloting. The FFS also called for a boycott of the 2005 referendum on the national charter for peace and reconciliation, arguing that the charter would "consecrate impunity" for perpetrators of violent crimes on both sides of the recent conflict.

Leaders: Hocine AÏT-AHMED (President of the Party and 1999 presidential candidate), Samir BOUAKOUIR, Ahmed DJEDDAI (Secretary General).

Other Parties Competing in the 2002 Legislative Balloting

Ahd 54. A small, nationalist party, *Ahd 54* (*Ahd* is Arabic for "oath," reportedly a reference to principles espoused at the beginning of the war of independence) secured 0.9 percent of the vote in the 2002 assembly balloting. Its leader, human rights activist Ali Fawzi Rebaine, won 0.7 percent of the vote in the 2004 presidential poll.

Leader: Ali Fawzi REBAINE, Toufik CHELLAL.

Patriotic Republican Rally (*Rassemblement Patriotique Républicain*—RPR). The RPR is a successor to the Algerian Movement for Justice and Development (*Mouvement Algérien pour la Justice et le Développement*—MAJD), a reformist group launched in November 1990 by former prime minister Kasdi Merbah, who had resigned in October from the FLN Central Committee. In March 1992 Merbah described the recently installed High Council of State as "unconstitutional" and called for lifting the state of emergency and creation of a "government of national welfare." Merbah, a staunch antifundamentalist, was assassinated in August 1993, the government accusing Islamic militants of the act. However, no group claimed responsibility for the killing, and observers pointed out that Merbah had a broad spectrum of enemies.

In 1999 the government listed the RPR as the successor to the MAJD.

Leader: 'Abd al-Kader MERBAH (President).

National Party for Solidarity and Development (*Parti National pour la Solidarité et le Développement*—PNSD). The center-right PNSD won a reported 1.6 percent of the popular vote in the June 1990 municipal elections. It secured 1.8 percent of the vote in the 2002 assembly poll.

Leader: Mohamed Cherif TALEB (President).

Other parties that competed unsuccessfully in the 2002 assembly balloting included the **Front of Algerian Democrats** (*Front des Algériens Démocrates*—FAD), led by Tayeb KABRI; the **National Constitutional Rally** (*Rassemblement National Constitutionnel*—RNC), which in 2004 announced it had changed its name to the **Democratic National Front** (still under the leadership of Sassi MABROUK); the **National Movement of Algerian Youth** (*Mouvement National pour la Jeunesse Algérienne*—MNJA), led by Omar BOUACHA; the **National Movement of Hope** (*Mouvement National l'Espérance*— MNE), led by Mohamed HADEF; the **National Movement for Nature and Development** (*Mouvement National pour la Nature et le Développement*—MNND), led by Abderrahman AKIF; the **Progressive Republican Party** (*Parti Républicain et Progressiste*—PRP), which had won three seats in the 1997 assembly balloting under the leadership of Idriss KHADIR; the **Rally for Algeria** (*Rassemblement pour l'Algérie*—RPA), led by Mohamed HAMMOUMA; the **Rally for National Unity** (*Rassemblement pour l'Unité Nationale*—RUN), led by Yacine LEKHAL; and the **Union for Democracy and Liberties** (*Union pour la Démocratie et les Libertés*—UDL), which had won one seat in the 1997 assembly election.

Other Parties

Republican National Alliance (*Alliance Nationale Républicaine*—ANR). The ANR was formed in early 1995 by several former government officials, including Redha Malek, prime minister in 1993–1994, and Ali Haroun, a member of the 1992–1994 collective presidency. Formally opposed to any compromise with the Islamic fundamentalist movement, the ANR was considered a vehicle for a presidential bid by Malek. However, Malek was prevented from contesting the 1995 election because he failed to obtain the required 75,000 signatures of support. Malek was reelected chair of the party by the June 1996 ANR congress in Algiers, which also elected a new 145-member National Council.

Despite retaining a seat in the cabinet, the ANR in early 2002 was described as "steering clear" of the upcoming legislative poll.

Leaders: Redha MALEK (Chair), Ali HAROUN.

Rally for Culture and Democracy (*Rassemblement pour la Culture et la Démocratie*—RCD). Formed in February 1989 to represent Berber interests, the RCD proclaimed its commitment to "economic centralism," linguistic pluralism, and separation of the state and Islamic religion. It won 2 percent of the votes in the June 1990 municipal balloting.

In early 1994 Mohamed Ouramadane TIGZIRI, the RCD's national secretary, was assassinated, apparently as part of the militant fundamentalist campaign against groups such as the RCD that advocated a secular, Western-style political system. The RCD's strongly antifundamentalist leader, Saïd Saadi, is also prominent in the Berber Cultural Movement, described by the *New York Times* as having evolved into an influential political group in its campaign to have the Berber language sanctioned for use in schools and other public forums. Saadi captured 9 percent of the votes in the 1995 presidential poll, having been assured of the lion's share of Berber votes because of the boycott by the FFS, the RCD's primary competitor for support within that ethnic group. The RCD secured 19 seats in the June 1997 assembly elections but boycotted the December balloting for the new Council of the Nation. The RCD also announced in early 1999 that it was boycotting the upcoming presidential election. However, surprising many observers, the RCD subsequently joined the government coalition of December 1999, the party reportedly having become "increasingly closer" to President Bouteflika. The RCD left the coalition in May 2001 in the wake of severe government/Berber friction, and it boycotted the 2002 national and local elections. Saadi won 1.9 percent of the vote in the 2004 presidential poll.

The RCD strongly condemned the national charter for peace and reconciliation that was approved in 2005. The party also charged the government with fraud in regard to the official vote turnout for the related referendum. Meanwhile, another Berber grouping (the **Movement for the Autonomy of Kabylie,** led by singer Ferhat MLENNI) also rejected the charter as an exercise in "self-amnesty" by the Algerian authorities.

Leader: Saïd SAADI (President).

Democratic and Social Movement (*Mouvement Démocratique et Social*—MDS). The MDS rubric reportedly was recently adopted by the grouping formerly known as Challenge (*Ettahaddi*). Dedicated to "the revolutionary transition of Algeria to modernity and progress," *Ettahaddi* had been launched in January 1993 as successor to the Socialist Vanguard Party (*Parti de l'Avant-Garde Socialist*—PAGS). The PAGS had emerged in 1966 as an illegal, but generally tolerated, heir to the Algerian Communist Party (*Parti Communiste Algérien*—PCA), which had been proscribed shortly after independence. Supportive of the Boumedienne government but less so of the Bendjedid administration, the PAGS reportedly applauded the 1988 unrest as helpful in its effort to "reestablish itself," particularly among labor unionists. It offered a limited number of candidates in the 1990 municipal elections, without success, and boycotted the 1991, 1997, and 2002 legislative elections as well as the 1999 presidential poll.

Leader: Hachemi CHERIF (Secretary General).

Fidelity (*Wafa*). Organized by former foreign affairs minister Ahmed Taleb Ibrahimi following his 1999 presidential campaign in the hope of coordinating nationalist and Islamist opposition groups, *Wafa* was subsequently denied recognition by the government on the grounds that it was essentially an FIS "clone." Ibrahimi was rejected by the Constitutional Council as a presidential candidate in

2004 and subsequently threw his support behind Ali Benflis.

Leaders: Ahmed Taleb IBRAHIMI, Mohammed SAID, Rashid LERARRI.

Democratic Front (*Front Démocratique—* FD). An anti-Bouteflika grouping, the FD elected former prime minister Sid Ahmed Ghozali as its chair during the May 2000 inaugural congress. Ghozali was not permitted by the Constitutional Council to run in the 2004 presidential election, and he subsequently announced he was supporting Ali Benflis in that campaign.

Leader: Sid Ahmed GHOZALI (Chair).

Socialist Workers Party (*Parti Socialist des Travailleurs—*PST). Legalized in early 1990, the Trotskyite PST supports "radical socialism," nonpayment of Algeria's external debt, and secular government. The PST boycotted the 2002 assembly balloting.

Leader: Chawki SALHI.

Illegal Groups

Islamic Salvation Front (*Front Islamique du Salut—*FIS). The FIS was organized in early 1989 to represent the surging Islamic fundamentalist movement. Capitalizing upon strong antigovernment sentiment, it won control of a majority of town and departmental councils in the June 1990 municipal elections. Apparently to permit the broadest possible support for its effort to win national legislative control, the FIS leadership was subsequently reluctant to define its goals in specific terms. However, a significant proportion of the Front's supporters appeared committed to the adoption and enforcement of sharia throughout Algeria's theretofore relatively secular society and the imposition of measures such as the segregation of the sexes in schools and the workplace, a ban on alcohol consumption, and obligatory veils for women. FIS leaders also made it clear that a national fundamentalist government, even one that came to power through a multiparty election, would not feel bound to maintain a "Western-style" democracy.

In June 1991 FIS leader Dr. Abassi Madani, Ali Belhadj (his deputy), other members of the party's

Constitutional Council, and hundreds of FIS followers were arrested on charges of fomenting an "armed conspiracy against the security of the state" in connection with violent demonstrations in Algiers and other cities. Although hard-line FIS factions reportedly called for continued protest and an election boycott unless the detainees were released, the FIS ultimately participated in the December 26 legislative balloting under the leadership of the moderate Abdelkader HACHANI.

After winning 188 seats in the first round of the 1991 assembly poll, the FIS prepared to assume national political leadership, Hachani attempting to reassure the nonfundamentalist population that the FIS would "persuade, not oblige people into doing what we say." However, the party's plan to mount the world's first Islamic state via the ballot box was thwarted by the military takeover of the Algerian government in early January 1992. Nearly all of the remaining FIS national leaders, including Hachani, were subsequently arrested, as were hundreds of its local and provincial officials, with upwards of 30,000 FIS followers reportedly being placed in desert detention camps. In addition, Algerian courts in March formally banned the FIS as a political party upon petition of the High Council of State, which also ordered the dissolution of many municipal councils under FIS control and their replacement by appointed bodies. The Front was subsequently reported to be sharply divided between members remaining faithful to the group's official commitment to nonviolence and more radical adherents prepared to "move from words to rifles." It was generally believed that the latter were responsible for a number of attacks on Algerian security personnel during the rest of the year and for the subsequent emergence of armed groups such as the AIS and the GIA (below).

In July 1992 Madani and Belhadj were sentenced to 12 years in prison for conspiring against the authority of the state, five other leaders receiving shorter terms. However, the imprisoned FIS leaders reportedly met with Defense Minister Liamine Zeroual in December 1993 to discuss measures whereby the FIS could be reintegrated into the political mainstream. In the wake of Zeroual's appointment as president one month later, sporadic negotiations were reported between the government and the FIS, many reports suggesting that a breakthrough was imminent in mid-1995. However, the government finally declared the talks deadlocked, allegedly over the failure of the FIS leaders to renounce antiregime violence unequivocally. Consequently, no FIS participation was permitted in the 1995 presidential balloting, the Front calling upon supporters to boycott the election as a way of embarrassing the government. That strategy backfired, however, as heavy voter turnout and Zeroual's strong showing served to undercut the Front's insistence that it still held majority popular support. Postelection comments from some FIS leaders exhibited a conciliatory tone, observers suggesting that the Front would seek a compromise that would allow it to present candidates in the legislative elections planned for 1997. No such scenario developed in the first half of 1997, but, perhaps with the prospect of renewed negotiations in mind, the government released Madani on July 15, 1997, one week after Hachani had been freed when a court found him guilty of "inciting rebellion" in 1992 but sentenced him to time served. However, the nature of subsequent FIS/government talks was unclear, and Madani was placed under house arrest in September after he had called for UN mediation of the Algerian political impasse. Not surprisingly, the FIS urged its supporters to boycott the October local elections. It was reported in early 1999 that the FIS had encouraged its supporters to vote for former foreign affairs minister Ibrahimi in the April 1999 presidential balloting.

FIS leaders expressed the hope that President Bouteflika's civil concord of the second half of 1999 would lead to legalization of the party (perhaps under a different name), but prospects in that regard remained dim. Meanwhile, the circumstances surrounding the assassination of Hachani in Algiers in November 1999 were unclear, although the government attributed the murder to the GIA.

FIS leaders Madani and Belhadj were released from house arrest and prison, respectively, in July 2003, the former subsequently settling in Qatar. Both men were barred from political activity, although in 2005 Madani was reported to have contacted President Bouteflika regarding Madani's possible participation in discussion about the proposed general amnesty.

Bouteflika subsequently reportedly invited FIS leaders Rabeh Kebir and Anwar Haddam to return to Algeria, although Bouteflika indicated no inclination to permit the return of FIS leaders to political activity. In March 2006 the government announced that it would be up to the Algerian courts to determine Belhadj's fate in that regard.

Leaders: Dr. Abassi MADANI (in Qatar), Ali BELHADJ, Abdelkader BOUKHAMKHAM, Sheikh Abdelkader OMAR, Abdelkrim Ould ADDA (Foreign Spokesperson), Rabeh KEBIR (in Germany), and Anwar HADDAM (in the United States).

Islamic Salvation Army (*Armée Islamique du Salut*—AIS). The AIS, also previously referenced as the Armed Islamic Movement (*Mouvement Islamique Armée*—MIA), was an underground fundamentalist organization formed in response to the banning of the FIS in 1992. It was often described as the "military wing" of the FIS, although there were occasional reports of policy differences between the leaders of the two groups.

Initially, the AIS was formally committed to antiregime military activity, although, unlike the GIA (below), it attacked only "official" military and police targets. (Shortly after the formation of the AIS, its fighters, estimated at about 10,000 strong, were reported to be operating under a unified command with GIA guerrillas, but extensive fighting, apparently emanating from disputes over tactics, broke out between the two groups in early 1994.) In early 1995 AIS leaders called for dialogue with the government, indicating that they would accept any "peace settlement" negotiated by the FIS. The AIS declared a "cease-fire" in antigovernment attacks as of October 1, 1997, apparently to disassociate itself from the shocking (even by recent Algerian standards) wave of violence gripping the country.

In June 1999 the AIS agreed to a permanent cease-fire in connection with President Bouteflika's plans for a civil concord that included an amnesty for most AIS members and the restoration of their civil and political rights. In January 2000 AIS leader Madani MEZRAG signed documents formalizing the elements of the concord and announced the "dissolution" of the AIS, some 1,500 AIS members having reportedly been declared eligible for amnesty. Mezrag supported President Bouteflika's reelection bid in 2004 and endorsed the 2005 national charter for peace and reconciliation, indicating his desire to help form a new legal party among former FIS/AIS supporters.

Armed Islamic Group (*Groupe Islamique Armé*—GIA). The GIA is an outgrowth of antigovernment violence that first broke out in the mid-1980s around the city of Blida. In the 1990s the Group emerged as the most militant of the underground fundamentalist organizations, its targets including police, government officials, journalists, feminists, and foreigners. Vehemently anti-Western, the Group reportedly supported establishment of an Iranian-style "theocracy" in Algeria and firmly rejected dialogue with the military-backed Zeroual regime.

The GIA guerrilla force was once estimated at 2,500–10,000 fighters, some known as "Afghanis" in reference to their having fought with the *mujaheddin* in Afghanistan. In early 1994 the Group was reportedly in control of many rural areas and several urban districts. However, the government subsequently claimed that its intensive "antiterrorist" campaign had significantly weakened the GIA. Moreover, many GIA leaders were killed by security forces or rival Islamists. In addition, one leader, Sheikh Abdelhaq Layada, was arrested in Morocco in 1993 and extradited to Algeria, where he was sentenced to death following his conviction on terrorism charges (see below for information on his subsequent release).

In mid-1995 the GIA was placed on the U.S. State Department's list of "terrorist" organizations. Although deemed by mid-1996 to be stronger militarily than the AIS, the GIA was believed to have lost much of whatever popular support it might once have commanded as the result of its assassination campaign and sometimes indiscriminate bomb attacks.

Friction within the GIA was also apparent following the kidnapping and eventual murder of seven French Trappist monks in Algeria in the spring of 1996. After the GIA claimed responsibility for the deaths, GIA leader Dhamel ZITOUNI (a.k.a. Abu Abderrahmane Amin) was reportedly ousted from the Group. He was subsequently reportedly killed by Algerian security forces. The GIA leadership mantle subsequently reportedly fell to Antar ZOUABI, while reports surfaced in late 1997 of another GIA leader—Slimane MAHERZI (a.k.a. Abu Djamil), a young guerrilla who had reportedly served the militant fundamentalist cause in Afghanistan and Bosnia and Herzegovina.

The GIA was broadly accused of the bulk of the terrorist incidents of 1997–2000, most of which occurred in central Algeria, where the Group's influence was considered the strongest. As the attacks grew more random and increasingly targeted civilians, some observers suggested that discipline had broken down within the GIA, a correspondent for the *New York Times* describing the Group as a "loose organization of roving bandits, including outlaws with little or no ideological commitment to Islam."

Ahmed Zaoui, described as a prominent external leader of the GIA following his disassociation from the FIS in 1997, was reportedly in Burkina Faso in late 1998, having been expelled from Switzerland. The GIA's Zouabi strongly rejected the government's amnesty offer included in President Bouteflika's civil concord of the second half of 1999, and most GIA fighters reportedly followed his lead. Zouabi was reportedly killed by security forces in February 2002; Rachid Abou Tourab was subsequently reported to have been selected as the new GIA leader. Meanwhile, like the GSPC (below), the GIA was included on the list of "terrorist" organizations subject to asset seizure by the United States as part of the war on terrorism announced after the September 11, 2001, attack.

Noureddine Boudiafi reportedly assumed leadership of the GIA in 2004; however, he was subsequently arrested, and the GIA mantle reportedly fell to Younes CHAABANE, who was killed during a security sweep in early 2005. By that time, the government was describing the GIA as "nearly extinct."

Layada was released from prison in early 2006, apparently as part of the national peace and reconciliation process. However, some GIA fighters reportedly remained active at that point, having been blamed by the government for at least one attack in mid-2005.

Leaders: Sheikh Abdelhaq LAYADA, Noureddine BOUDIAFI (in prison), Mohammed SAID, Ahmed ZAOUI (in exile), Abdelmadjid DICHOU, Rachid Abou TOURAB, Ahmed BAICHE.

Salafist Group for Preaching and Combat (*Groupe Salafiste pour la Prédication et le Combat*—GSPC). Also referenced as Appeal and Struggle, the GSPC was established in 1999 by members of the GIA who were opposed to the parent group's targeting of civilians but remained committed to attacks on military sites and personnel. Although some reports suggested GSPC leaders had begun negotiations with the government in late 1999 regarding President Bouteflika's civil concord, that pact was ultimately rejected by the GSPC, which continued its guerrilla campaign. The GSPC was included on the list of proscribed organizations published by the United States following the September 11, 2001, terrorist attacks. Several reports suggested that some GSPC fighters might have independently established ties with Osama bin Laden's al-Qaida, although some observers doubted any formal connection between the two groups since the GSPC had never displayed any anti-U.S. sentiment.

By 2003 the GSPC was one of the few Islamist groups "still fighting," hard-liner Nabil SAHRAOUI having supplanted GSPC founder Hassan HATTAB as leader of the group. In October 2003 Sahraoui said that the GSPC supported bin Laden's *jihad* against "the American heretics," and the GSPC was held responsible for several attacks on Algerian forces in 2003–2004. However, Sahraoui was killed by the Algerian army in June 2004, analysts suggesting that GSPC forces had dwindled to 400–450 guerrillas by that time. Another GSPC leader, Amari SAIFI, was taken into custody in late 2004. (Saifi, also known as "El Para," was sentenced to life imprisonment in 2005, although in early 2006 his supporters were reportedly urging the government to consider an amnesty for him under the nation's new peace and reconciliation process.)

The government blamed the GSPC for several attacks in 2005, while the GSPC claimed responsibility for an attack on an army base in Mauritania in June 2005. (The GSPC said it was avenging the arrest by Mauritanian authorities of a group of alleged GSPC adherents, described by the Mauritania government as having ties to al-Qaida.) However, in late 2005, Hassan HATTAB, one of the founders of the GSPC, subsequently said he believed most GSPC supporters were now willing to consider an amnesty agreement.

Defenders of the Salafi Call (*Dhanat Houmet Daawa Salafia*). One of the few Islamist militant groups active in Algeria as of 2005, this "Taliban-trained" grouping, another offshoot of the GIA, was reported to comprise about 150–250 fighters in western Algeria. Like the GSPC, it has been declared a terrorist organization by the United States.

Leader: Mohammed BENSLIM.

Legislature

The 1996 constitution provided for a bicameral **Parliament** (*Barlaman*), consisting of a restructured National People's Assembly and a new upper house, the Council of the Nation. The former unicameral assembly, consisting of 295 members serving five-year terms, had been most recently elected on February 26, 1987, deputies being selected from a list of 885 candidates (three for every seat) that had been drawn up by the National Liberation Front (FLN). The first round of multiparty balloting for a new 430-member assembly was held December 26, 1991, with the Islamic Salvation Front (FIS) winning 188 seats, the Socialist Forces Front (FFS) 25, the FLN 15, and independents 3. A runoff round involving the top two vote-getters in the remaining districts was scheduled for January 16, 1992. However, the second poll was canceled on January 12

Cabinet

As of March 1, 2006 (*see headnote*)

Prime Minister	Ahmed Ouyahia (RND)

Ministers of State

Foreign Affairs	Mohamed Bedjaoui
Interior and Local Authorities	Noureddine Yazid Zerhouni (FLN)
Personal Representative of the Head of State	Abdelaziz Belkhadem (FLN)
Without Portfolio	Boudjerra Soltani

Ministers

Agriculture and Rural Development	Said Barkat
Commerce	El Hachemi Djaaboub (MSP)
Communication	Boujomah Hayshur
Culture	Khalida Toumi [f]
Employment and National Solidarity	Djamal Ould-Abbes
Energy and Mining	Chakib Khelil
Finance	Mourad Medelci
Fishing and Marine Resources	Smail Mimoune
Health, Population, and Hospital Reform	Amar Tou (FLN)
Higher Education and Scientific Research	Rachid Harraoubia (FLN)
Housing and Urban Affairs	Mohamed Nadir Hamimid
Industry	Mahmoud Khoudri
Justice, Keeper of the Seals	Tayeb Belaiz
Labor and Social Protection	Tayeb Louh (FLN)
National Education	Boubakeur Benbouzid (RND)
Posts and Information Technology	Boudjemaa Haichour (FLN)
Promotion of Investments	Abdelhamid Temmar
Public Works	Amar Ghoul (MSP)
Relations with Parliament	Abdelaziz Ziari (FLN)
Religious Affairs and Endowments	Bouabdallah Ghlamallah (RND)
Secretary General of the Government	Ahmed Noui
Small- and Medium-sized Enterprises and Crafts	Mustapha Benbada
Territorial Management and Environment	Cherif Rahmani
Tourism	Noureddine Moussa
Training and Professional Education	El Hadi Khaldi
Transportation	Mohamed Maghlaoui (RND)
War Veterans	Mohamed Cherif Abbas (RND)
Water Resources	Abdelmalek Sellal
Youth and Sports	Yahia Guiddoum

Ministers Delegate

Agriculture and Rural Development	Rachid Benaissa
Family and Women's Affairs	Nouara Saâdia Djaffar (RND) [f]
Finance	Karim Djoudi

Higher Education and Scientific Research	Souad Bendjaballah [f]
Interior and Local Communities	Daho Ould Kablia
Maghreb and African Affairs	Abdelkader Messahel
National Defense	Abdelmalek Guenaizia
Territorial Management and Environment	Abderrachid Boukerzaza
[f] = female	

by the High Security Council, which also declared the results of the first round invalid. Subsequently, it was revealed that the former assembly had been dissolved by a secret presidential decree on January 4.

In April 1992 the High Council of State announced the appointment of a 60-member National Consultative Council (*Majlis al-Shoura al-Watani*) to serve in an advisory capacity to the government pending new assembly elections. The National Dialogue Conference of early 1994, in turn, authorized the appointment of a three-year National Transitional Council (*Conseil National de Transition—* CNT), which at its initial sitting in May encompassed 63 seats filled by parties, 85 by professional associations and trade unions, and 30 by government nominees, with 22 reserved for nonparticipating secular parties. The CNT was dissolved on May 18, 1997, in preparation for the elections to the bodies authorized by the new constitution.

Council of the Nation (*Majlis al-Umma/ Conseil de la Nation*). The upper house has 144 members, 96 (2 from each *wilaya*) elected in secret ballot by an electoral college of the members of local councils and communal and *wilayaat* assemblies and 48 appointed by the president. The term of office is six years, although one-half of the initial members (elected on December 25, 1997) served only three years to permit 50 percent replenishment of the council every three years from that point. Following the balloting of December 30, 2003, the distribution of the elected seats was as follows: National Democratic Rally, 52; National Liberation Front, 31; Movement for a Peaceful Society, 10; Movement for National Reform, 2; Socialist Forces Front, 1.

Speaker: Abdelkader BENSALAH.

National People's Assembly (*Majlis Ech Chaabi al-Watani, Assemblée Popularie Nationale*). The lower house has 389 members, 381 representing the 48 *wilayaats* (each of which has at least 4 representatives) according to population, and 8 (4 in Europe and 4 in other Arab nations) elected by Algerians living abroad. Members are elected for a five-year term on a proportional basis from lists presented by parties or independents. Following the election of May 30, 2002, the distribution of seats was as follows: National Liberation Front, 199; National Democratic Rally, 47; Movement for National Reform, 43; Movement for a Peaceful Society, 38; Workers' Party, 21; Algerian National Front, 8; Movement of National Harmony, 1; Renaissance Movement (*Nahda*), 1; Algerian Renewal Party; and independents, 30.

Speaker: Amar SAADANI.

Communications

Press

After a long period of strict control of national and foreign press activities, the government introduced a new Information Code in mid-1989 that formally ended the state media monopoly and accorded journalists greater freedom of expression. It was succeeded in March 1990 by a more stringent code that mandated imprisonment for journalists who "offended" Islam or any other religion; the new regulations also stipulated that all new periodicals be printed in Arabic. However, the new strictures were not rigorously implemented, and an information "explosion" subsequently took place in the increasingly independent press. By mid-1991 there were reportedly more than 110 daily, weekly, and monthly periodicals, many of them fostered by a government program under which journalists in state-owned enterprises were offered a sum equal to two years' salary to help establish private publications. However, most of the new papers continued to be printed on government presses, which enabled the administration to suspend their issuance during the early phase of the 1991 state of emergency. Significant restrictions, largely directed at the Islamic fundamentalist press, were imposed following the declaration of a state of emergency in early 1992. A number of newspapers were also banned for a short time later in the year under a new decree permitting such action in cases of publications deemed to be operating "against public interest." In addition, journalists were permitted to report on "security matters" only with government authorization and only using information released by the state, stories on antigovernment activity consequently becoming quite limited. In part because they were often perceived as "apologists" for the government, journalists were subsequently targeted by fundamentalist radicals.

New restrictions, including harsh penalties in a revised penal code, have been imposed on the press in recent years, prompting protests from both domestic and international journalism organizations. Among other things, opposition candidates complained in 2002 about the high level of control exercised by the administration of President Boutcflika over all aspects of the media. Journalists have subsequently been jailed regularly for what the government calls "libel" but what free press advocates describe as legitimate criticism of officials. On the other hand, a reporter for *Middle East International* in 2005 opined that a degree of "genuine political debate" was apparent among some Algerian newspapers.

The following are dailies published in Algiers unless otherwise noted: *el-Moudjahid* (The Fighter, 440,000), former FLN organ in French; *Algérie Actualité* (255,000), government weekly in French; *Horizons* (200,000), in French; *al-Chaab* (The People, 150,000), former FLN information journal in Arabic; *al-Massa* (100,000), in Arabic. Other independent dailies include: *Le Soir de l'Algérie* (150,000), in French; *Al Khabar* (The News, 120,000), in Arabic; *El Watan* (The Nation, 80,000), in French; *Le Jeune Indépendant* (60,000), in French; *Al Djazair al-Joum* (54,000), in Arabic; *Le Matin*, in French; *La Tribune*, in French; *al-Jumhuriyah* (The Republic, Wahran, 20,000), former FLN organ in Arabic; *Liberté* (20,000), in French; *Le Monde Aujourd'hui*, in French; *Le Quotidien d'Oran* (Wahran), in French.

News Agencies

The domestic agency is the Algerian Press Service (*Wikalat al-Anba al-Jazairiyah/Algérie Presse Service*—APS). A number of foreign agencies maintain offices in Algiers.

Broadcasting and Computing

The government decreased its control over broadcasting services in 2000, although it retained a supervisory role. The former state-controlled *Télévision Algérienne* continues to service about a dozen stations. There were approximately 3.8 million television receivers and 250,000 personal computers serving 380,000 Internet users in 2003.

Intergovernmental Representation

Ambassador to the U.S.
Amine KHERBI

U.S. Ambassador to Algeria
Robert S. FORD

Permanent Representative to the UN
Youcef YOUSFI

IGO Memberships (Non-UN)
AfDB, AFESD, AMF, AMU, AU, BADEA, BIS, IDB, Interpol, IOM, LAS, NAM, OAPEC, OIC, OPEC, WCO

ANGOLA

REPUBLIC OF ANGOLA

República de Angola

The Country

The largest of Portugal's former African possessions, Angola is located on the Atlantic, south of the Congo River. The greater part of its territory is bounded on the north and east by the Democratic Republic of the Congo (DRC, formerly Zaire), on the southeast by Zambia, and on the south by Namibia. It also includes the small enclave of Cabinda in the northwest (bordered by the Republic of the Congo and the DRC), where important offshore oil deposits are being exploited. The overwhelming proportion of Angola's people are Bantus, who comprise four distinct tribal groups: the Bakongo in the northwest, the Kimbundu in the north-central region inland from Luanda, the Ovimbundu in the south-central region, and the Chokwe in eastern Angola. No native language is universally spoken, Portuguese being the only tongue not confined to a specific tribal area. Women have traditionally experienced equality with men in subsistence activities, and they were estimated to constitute 46 percent of the work force in 1996.

Because of its rail links with Zaire, Zambia, Zimbabwe, Mozambique, and South Africa, the port of Lobito served as a leading outlet for much of Central Africa's mineral wealth until independence was declared in 1975. Thereafter, civil war crippled the Benguela Railway and devastated much of the formerly prosperous economy, including the export of diamonds and coffee. Guerrilla activity resulted in massive migration of peasant farmers to cities or neighboring countries, and, despite its potential as a breadbasket for southern Africa,

Angola became dependent on food imports to stave off widespread famine. In addition, black market activity flourished, contributing to substantial degradation of the local currency. Although the government attempted to stimulate the economy by reducing state control over industry and agriculture, its efforts were hampered by corruption, bureaucratic inefficiency, and the allocation of more than half of its income to military expenditure. Only oil kept the economy afloat, generating more than 85 percent of revenue and attracting private foreign investment. Vowing to promote a "mixed economy" with additional free-market influence, Angola became a member of the International

Political Status: Formally independent upon departure of the Portuguese High Commissioner on November 10, 1975; government of the Popular Movement for the Liberation of Angola (MPLA) recognized by the Organization of African Unity on February 11, 1976; peace accord signed with rebel National Union for the Total Independence of Angola (UNITA) on June 1, 1991; multiparty democratic system approved by constitutional amendment on August 26, 1992.

Area: 481,351 sq. mi. (1,246,700 sq. km.).

Population: 5,646,166 (1970C); 13,912,000 (2005E). A census launched in 1982 was never completed; the 2005 figure is an extrapolation from recent UN estimates.

Major Urban Center (2005E): LUANDA (urban area, 2,825,000).

Official Language: Portuguese (although most Angolans speak tribal languages).

Monetary Unit: Kwanza (market rate July 1, 2006: 80.37 kwanzas = $1US).

President: José Eduardo DOS SANTOS (Popular Movement for the Liberation of Angola); designated by the Central Committee of the Popular Movement for the Liberation of Angola—Labor Party (MPLA-PT) and sworn in September 21, 1979, following the death of Dr. António Agostinho NETO on September 10; confirmed by an extraordinary congress of the MPLA-PT on December 17, 1980; reconfirmed in 1985 and 1990; mandate extended following popular election on September 29–30, 1992, and extended indefinitely by presidential order on January 29, 1999.

Prime Minister: Fernando ("Nando") Da Piedade Dias DOS SANTOS (Popular Movement for the Liberation of Angola); appointed by the president on December 6, 2002; formed new government on December 9, 2002. (The prime minister's post, previously held by Fernando José França Dias VAN-DÚNEM [Popular Movement for the Liberation of Angola], had been unfilled since a new government was installed on January 30, 1999, when President dos Santos assumed authority formerly exercised by the prime minister.)

Monetary Fund (IMF) and the World Bank in 1989, although assistance from those institutions was constrained prior to initial accommodation with leading rebel forces in June 1991.

The subsequent 18-month cease-fire, as well as military actions against other insurgents in the oil-rich Cabindan province, raised hopes for economic as well as political stability. However, such optimism was dashed in late 1992 by the outbreak of postelectoral violence, and in early 1993 coffee and cotton production were described as nonexistent while oil and diamond extraction had been severely constrained. Thereafter, in response to the 1994 peace accord and appeals from both government and rebel leaders, a conference sponsored by the European Union (EU) yielded pledges of nearly $1 billion to facilitate recovery from the country's 20 years of military devastation. During 1995–1997 Angola enjoyed average annual real GDP growth of approximately 10 percent; furthermore, inflation fell dramatically 1997–1998. However, with the return of civil war in late 1998 the government's economic energies again turned to fueling its war efforts.

In early 2000 the United Nations estimated that 4 million Angolans (approximately one-third of the population) had been directly affected by the conflict and that half of those individuals were "internally displaced." Furthermore, observers reported that approximately 200,000 Angolans had sought refuge in Zambia, while another 10,000 had recently fled to Namibia. On a more positive note, the dos Santos government reported that GDP had grown in real terms by 3.5 percent in 1999, largely due to oil-related production. However, inflation remained out of control at 3000 percent annually before declining to 305 percent in 2000 and 125 percent in 2001. New French investment pushed oil production to nearly 900,000 barrels per day in late 2001, underscoring the country's prominence in that sector. (Angola, already a major oil exporter to the United States and the second leading producer, next to Nigeria, in sub-Saharan Africa, is estimated to have reserves of more than 12.5 billion barrels.)

Despite its oil wealth, Angola remained in severe economic and social distress as of 2002 when the long-standing civil war finally concluded, leaving the nation's infrastructure in ruins and sapping government resources that might otherwise have gone to the health and education sectors. Life expectancy was estimated at less than 40 years, while 65 percent of the population lived below the poverty line and many people lacked basic medical care and educational opportunities. In addition, the IMF suspended its assistance after the war's end, citing, among other things, a lack of fiscal accountability on the part of the government. (Analysts suggested that billions of dollars in oil revenues had disappeared from government coffers and were hidden in secret offshore bank accounts.) In 2004 the government worked with the IMF on a plan to restore aid, but as of early 2006 no agreement had been reached. President dos Santos resisted renewed requests for fiscal transparency, a key obstacle to receiving IMF financial assistance. The IMF did, however, commend government officials for their commitment to lowering inflation, which was 10 percent at the end of 2005 and expected to be reduced to single digits in 2006. In addition, the IMF projected economic growth of 27.6 percent in 2006, boosted by the high price of oil. Meanwhile, the World Bank continued to give aid to the government to reduce the spread of AIDS, malaria, and tuberculosis.

GDP grew by nearly 15 percent in 2002 thanks to the robust energy sector and the return of international investment in the wake of the end of the civil war. Similar growth was achieved in 2004, which also saw inflation fall to more manageable levels. The government and transnational companies embarked on massive new initiatives to further exploit not only oil reserves but also Angola's significant deposits of diamonds, gold, uranium, iron ore, and other minerals and ores. However, as of early 2006, it was still not clear if economic expansion had extended substantial benefits to the general population, though the government had initiated an ambitious program of improving infrastructure (see Current issues, below).

Government and Politics

Political Background

Portuguese settlements were established in eastern Angola in the late 15th century by navigators seeking trade routes to India, but the territory's present boundaries were not formally established until the Berlin Conference of 1884–1885. In 1951 the colony of Angola became an Overseas Province of Portugal and was thus construed as being an integral part of the Portuguese state.

Guerrilla opposition to colonial rule broke out in 1961 and continued for 13 years, despite a sizable Portuguese military presence. At the time of the 1974 coup in Lisbon, there were three principal independence movements operating in different parts of Angola. The National Front for the Liberation of Angola (*Frente Nacional para a Libertação de Angola*—FNLA), which had established a government-in-exile in Zaire in 1963 under the leadership of Holden ROBERTO, controlled much of the north; the Soviet-backed Popular Movement for the Liberation of Angola (*Movimento Popular de Libertação de Angola*—MPLA), led by Dr. Agostinho NETO, controlled much of the central region plus Cabinda; the third group, the National Union for the Total Independence of Angola (*União Nacional para a Independência Total de Angola*—UNITA), operated in eastern and southern Angola under the leadership of Dr. Jonas SAVIMBI. On January 15, 1975, the three leaders signed an agreement with Portuguese representatives calling for the independence of Angola on November 11 (the 400th anniversary of the founding of Luanda). The pact provided for interim rule by a Portuguese high commissioner and a Presidential Collegiate consisting of one representative from each of the three liberation movements. During succeeding months, however, the FNLA and UNITA formed a tacit alliance against the MPLA, whose forces at the time of independence controlled the capital. On November 10 the Portuguese high commissioner departed after a brief ceremony at Luanda, and at midnight Neto proclaimed the establishment, under MPLA auspices, of the People's Republic of Angola. On November 23 the FNLA-UNITA announced the formation of a rival Democratic People's Republic of Angola, with the central highlands city of Huambo (formerly *Nova Lisboa*) as its capital.

Within a month of independence, some two dozen nations had recognized the MPLA government, although the Organization of African Unity (OAU) had urged all countries to withhold recognition until formation of a coalition government. Meanwhile, Cuba had dispatched upwards of 18,000 troops in support of the MPLA, while both Uganda and Zaire had threatened to break diplomatic relations with the Soviet Union because of its involvement in the Angolan war. The revelation that American money and equipment were being channeled to FNLA forces through Zaire posed the additional risk of a U.S.-Soviet confrontation. By late December the Cuban troops, equipped with Soviet armored vehicles and rocket launchers, had helped turn the tide in favor of the MPLA, and some 4,000–5,000 South African troops operating in support of the Huambo regime were substantially withdrawn a month later. In early February 1976 the MPLA launched a southern offensive that resulted in the capture of Huambo and other key cities, prompting declarations by the FNLA and UNITA that their forces would thenceforth resort to guerrilla warfare. On February 11 the OAU announced that the MPLA government had been admitted to membership, following formal recognition of the Neto regime by a majority of OAU member states.

The FNLA and UNITA continued to resist government and Cuban units from 1976 to 1978, and in early 1979 they announced formation of a joint military force. Nevertheless, it subsequently appeared that Roberto's FNLA had been virtually annihilated in the north and that only UNITA was offering organized opposition to the Luanda regime.

On September 10, 1979, President Neto died at Moscow, where he had been undergoing medical treatment. On September 21 he was succeeded by José Eduardo DOS SANTOS (the minister of planning) as chief of state, head of government, and chair of the ruling party, which had been renamed the MPLA–Labor Party (*MPLA–Partido Trabalhista*—MPLA-PT).

In September 1984 the remaining 1,500 guerrillas and 20,000 civilian members of COMIRA (*Conselho Militar para a Resistência de Angola*), which had been founded by former FNLA members, surrendered to the Luanda government under a 1979 amnesty provision, its military members being integrated into the MPLA-PT forces. However, the confrontation with UNITA settled into an intractable civil war: the U.S.-backed rebels, charged with brutal intimidation of the peasantry, continued to dominate much of the countryside, while the government, supported by 50,000 Cuban troops and extensive Soviet aid, remained in control of most urban areas.

With over 300,000 people dead, an estimated 1.5 million dislocated, and the country's economy and social infrastructure in shambles, attention in the latter part of the 1980s turned to negotiation of a political settlement to the military stalemate. One major breakthrough was achieved with an agreement in late 1988 for curtailment of foreign military involvement in Angola. Domestic reconciliation proved more difficult, however, as a much publicized cease-fire agreement brokered by Zairean President Mobutu at a meeting attended by the leaders of 16 African nations in mid-1989 lasted only a few weeks. Subsequently, despite further fighting, government-UNITA talks continued, yielding, with the involvement of both U.S. Secretary of State James Baker and Soviet Foreign Minister Aleksandr Bessmertnykh, a peace settlement signed at Washington on June 1, 1991, that provided for a multiparty election in late 1992. Responsibility for monitoring the accord and organizing elections was assigned to a Joint Political and Military Commission (*Comissão Comun Política e Militar*—CCPM), consisting of Portuguese, U.S., USSR, MPLA-PT, and UNITA representatives, which was bolstered in early June by the arrival of a 600-member United Nations Angola Verification Mission (UNAVEM).

In July 1992 dos Santos named former planning minister Fernando José França Dias VANDÚNEM to the recently restored prime ministerial post, without, however, relinquishing his powers of executive leadership. Thereafter, despite clashes between MPLA-PT and UNITA supporters, preelectoral activity continued, including the emergence of a number of opposition political parties and the return to Luanda of former MPLA-PT adversaries Holden Roberto and Jonas Savimbi, in August and September, respectively.

On August 26, 1992, the MPLA-PT endorsed constitutional revisions formalizing the government's dedication to a democratic system. Subsequently, the party also dropped "Labor Party" from its name. On September 8 dos Santos and Savimbi agreed to form a postelection unity government based on voting percentages derived from the balloting later that month. On September 28 the Angolan Armed Forces (FAA), drawn from the MPLA's Popular Armed Forces for the Liberation of Angola (FAPLA) and UNITA's Armed Forces for the Liberation of Angola (FALA), was inaugurated. However, at 8,000 troops, the FAA was far below its projected 50,000 strength, a shortfall attributed to UNITA's slow demobilization and consistent with reports that entire UNITA units remained intact outside the capital.

Although 11 presidential candidates and 18 political parties participated in balloting September 29–30, 1992, the polling was dominated by dos Santos, Savimbi, and their respective parties. On September 30 Savimbi, facing certain defeat, rejected the conclusions of international observers by declaring the balloting "rigged" and stated that he would "not accept defeat." By mid-October widespread violence was reported in the countryside, while for the first time UNITA and MPLA units clashed at the capital. Election results released on October 17 confirmed the MPLA's near two-to-one legislative victory, although dos Santos's 49.57 percent share of the presidential vote was constitutionally insufficient to avoid a second round against Savimbi, whose 40.07 percent vote share eclipsed nine other candidates by a wide margin. No presidential repolling subsequently occurred, as Savimbi's forces returned to military confrontation.

By October 1992 the MPLA-UNITA struggle had reached a previously unmatched intensity. On November 26 UNITA legislators boycotted the inaugural convention of the National Assembly, and, despite a new cease-fire agreement the following day, the fighting continued. On December 2 a transitional government was named, headed by Marcelino José Carlos MOCO, who had been appointed by dos Santos on November 27. Although dominated by MPLA members, the "unity" government provided for the participation of five opposition parties, featuring most prominently UNITA, which was assigned one full ministry and four deputy posts. Five days later UNITA agreed to join the government, and on December 20 the rebels reportedly accepted yet another peace plan, which was again ignored.

By mid-January 1993 tens of thousands of people had been reported killed, with Savimbi's forces on the defensive. On January 26 UN Secretary General Boutros Boutros-Ghali warned that if fighting continued, the remaining UN peacekeepers would be removed upon expiration of their mandate on April 30. The following day peace talks at Addis Ababa, Ethiopia, were abandoned. On March 6 UNITA recaptured its headquarters at Huambo after a pitched, 55-day battle that left over 12,000 dead, including 5,000 civilians. In addition to leaving the insurgents in control of over 70 percent of Angolan territory, the victory was described as pivotal to UNITA's transformation from a guerrilla force to a conventional army. Furthermore, UNITA's military advantage was evidenced by the government's subsequent willingness to make concessions at peace talks that opened on April 13 at Abidjan, Côte d'Ivoire. In mid-May the government agreed to a peace plan brokered by the UN, the United States, Russia, and Portugal that incorporated UNITA's demand for decentralized power sharing under a national unity government. However, days later UNITA rejected the agreement.

In response to UNITA's continued intransigence, the United States on May 18, 1993, announced its intention to recognize the dos Santos government, thus abandoning its attempt to use recognition to propel peace talks and formally signaling an end to its support for UNITA.

Subsequently, UNITA intensified its military activities, capturing oil-rich Soyo on May 26. On June 2 the UN Security Council unanimously declared UNITA responsible for the breakdown of peace negotiations and extended the UNAVEM mandate until July 15, albeit with a sharply reduced staff. In mid-July the UN continued the UNAVEM mandate until September 15 and threatened to impose an embargo on UNITA unless the rebels agreed to honor the 1991 accord, respect the 1992 elections, and enact a verifiable cease-fire. Heavy fighting nonetheless continued, and on August 20 the World Food Program agreed to a six-month emergency food operation to help alleviate the suffering from what one observer described as the "world's worst war." On September 20 UNITA announced a unilateral cease-fire; nevertheless, its military activities escalated, and on September 26 the UN imposed an embargo on oil and arms sales to the rebels. On October 30 and 31 UNITA agreed to withdraw from territory it had seized since the 1992 elections. However, the MPLA dismissed UNITA demands that "thousands of military prisoners" be released, UN forces be encamped in all towns it vacated, and UNITA fighters be integrated on an equal basis with government troops into an Angolan army.

In November 1993 a fresh round of peace talks opened at Lusaka, Zambia, and were reportedly going well until government negotiators insisted that UNITA civilian supporters be disarmed. Although the demand precipitated a temporary suspension of the talks, another cease-fire agreement was reported on December 10 to be near completion. However, three days later the negotiations were again suspended after UNITA accused the government of attempting to kill Savimbi in a bombing raid.

"Lusaka-2" negotiations were launched on January 5, 1994, with negotiators concluding an agreement on fundamental principles of national reconciliation on February 17. In March the government was reported to have offered four secondary ministerial posts to UNITA, which countered with a demand for the key portfolios of defense, interior, and finance. In late April agreement was reached on second-round conclusion of the presidential ballot-

ing that had been repudiated by UNITA in September 1992, although a deadlock ensued at midyear over UNITA's insistence that it be awarded the governorship of Huambo province. On September 5 the two sides agreed to a renewal of UNAVEM, whose existing mandate was scheduled to expire on September 30, and on October 31 they initialed a new peace agreement under which UNITA would be awarded eleven government portfolios and three provincial governorships. Nonetheless, heavy fighting continued, and on November 8 the rebel stronghold of Huambo again fell to government troops. Despite the absence of Savimbi, who was reported to have been wounded in an incident involving his own bodyguard, the latest peace accord was formally signed at Lusaka on November 20. On February 8, 1995, the UNAVEM mandate was extended for another six months amid evidence of tensions within UNITA because of hard-line opposition to Lusaka-2.

It was not until May 6, 1995, that a long-awaited meeting between dos Santos and Savimbi took place at Lusaka, at the conclusion of which the UNITA leader accepted his opponent as "president of my country." While there was no public mention at the meeting of demobilization of UNITA's guerrilla army, Savimbi later declared in talks with South African President Mandela that his group's revival of hostilities in late 1992 had been "stupid," and on May 31 the advance units of a projected 7,460-member UNAVEM peacekeeping force arrived in Angola.

On June 17, 1995, it was confirmed that Savimbi had been offered a vice presidency. While there was no immediate response from the UNITA leader, he was reported during a second meeting with dos Santos at Franceville, Gabon, on August 10 to have accepted, subject to a number of "understandings" that included a role in defining economic policy. On the other hand, Radio Angola announced prior to a joint appearance by the two rivals at the Brussels donor conference in September that Savimbi would not assume office until the demobilization or integration of UNITA military units had been completed in early 1996. The latter process was halted in December after government troops had launched a new offensive in northern Angola but

was resumed on the basis of a new timetable negotiated with Luanda on January 9, 1996.

The new timetable was immediately disregarded
by UNITA, only about 8,000 of whose 62,000-
strong army had reported to UN-supervised confinement camps by mid-February 1996. Direct talks
between dos Santos and Savimbi were held at Libreville, Gabon, on March 1, and the two leaders
agreed that a government of national unity would
be formed within four months and that a 90,000-
member national army would be created from existing guerrilla forces. A further agreement on May
24 specified an immediate start on the integration
of UNITA soldiers into a national force and the disarming of all civilians. Meanwhile, the UNAVEM
mandate had been renewed on May 8, this time for
only a two-month period, it being envisaged that
UN forces would extend their patrols to the whole
of the country.

The new agreements produced no greater urgency on UNITA's part, so that by the end of
May 1996 only some 23,000 UNITA forces had
been confined. Losing patience with the slow
rate of compliance, President dos Santos on June
8 appointed a new government in which Van-
Dúnem (then assembly speaker) returned to the
premiership. Charged in particular with launching an urgent assault on corruption and government inefficiency, the new ministerial list contained
no UNITA representatives, although government
spokesmen stressed that UNITA would be included
as soon as it had honored its undertakings under the
1994 Lusaka agreement. The UN Security Council
renewed the UNAVEM mandate in July and again
in October, the second extension including a warning to UNITA that sanctions would be imposed on
the group if it failed to comply with the Lusaka
agreement promptly. On November 13, 1996, the
National Assembly, citing a lack of electoral preparations, adopted a constitutional revision that extended its mandate for a period of two to four years.
On December 12 the UNAVEM mandate was extended to February 28, 1997, and the following day
UNAVEM officials declared that UNITA had fulfilled its obligations as delineated by the Lusaka
accord; however, the desertion of approximately

15,000 UNITA members from confinement centers
coupled with reports of UNITA's involvement in
the fighting at Zaire rekindled concerns regarding
Savimbi's dedication to the peace process. Subsequently, implementation of the peace accord stalled
in the first quarter of 1997, as Savimbi formally
rejected the offer of a vice presidential appointment and demanded instead a role as "principal
adviser" and the establishment of a "joint basic government." Both requests were promptly dismissed
by the dos Santos government, which further asserted that Savimbi remained unwilling to relinquish rebel-held territory and completely disarm
his forces.

On a more positive note, on April 9, 1997,
the National Assembly met for the first time with
its full complement of UNITA legislators and approved legislation naming Savimbi the "Leader of
the Largest Opposition Party." On the same day,
dos Santos took the first formal step toward the
establishment of a unity government, naming Van-
Dúnem as prime minister of a Unity and National
Reconciliation Government (*Governa da Unidade
e da Reconciliação Nacional*—GURN). Two days
later, more than a dozen foreign leaders attended
the inauguration of the GURN, which included
eleven UNITA members. Savimbi refused to attend, citing personal safety concerns.

On August 31, 1998, the dos Santos administration announced that UNITA's legislators and
cabinet members had been suspended because of
UNITA's failure to adhere to the dictates of the
Lusaka accord. However, most of the UNITA representatives were reported to have resumed their
duties in September, some now apparently operating under the rubric of the new UNITA-Renewal
faction (see UNITA under Political Parties). With
relations between the government and the Savimbi
faction of UNITA having deteriorated into full-
scale war, dos Santos formed a new government on
January 30, 1999, in which he left the prime minister's post unfilled and assumed the responsibilities of head of the government himself pending the
"return of constitutional normality." The new cabinet included several UNITA-Renewal representatives but no Savimbi supporters. Dos Santos also

announced he had taken over direct control of the armed forces as the government pursued what it hoped would be a final offensive against Savimbi's fighters.

In early 1999 the UN condemned the two combatants, asserting that their desire for a military conclusion to the strife had caused a humanitarian disaster; following the expiration of the mandate of the UN Observer Mission at Angola (UNOMA) on February 26, the peacekeepers were withdrawn. Meanwhile, heavy fighting continued, and by May approximately 10,000 people had been killed and 1 million dislocated.

By mid-1999 UNITA forces had reportedly closed to within 40 miles of Luanda; however, the government unleashed a fierce offensive highlighted by relentless air strikes. Reportedly aided by Western intelligence, government forces captured Bailundo in October, and in December UNITA forces fled from Jamba in the face of a government attack that originated, in part, from Namibia. For its open support of Luanda, Namibia suffered a wave of UNITA attacks. On the political front, President dos Santos continued to reach out to opposition party leaders at Luanda while at the same time remaining adamantly opposed to suggestions that he reopen negotiations with Savimbi.

In March 2000 the Angolan conflict once again captured international attention when the UN Sanctions Committee on Angola issued a report accusing individuals and institutions in nearly a dozen countries of ignoring sanctions against supplying or trading with the UNITA rebels. The document underscored the UN's efforts to tighten the application of sanctions, with the ultimate goal of derailing UNITA's war-making capabilities. (UNITA earlier had suffered another blow to its already severely tarnished image when the Southern African Development Community had formally branded Savimbi as a "war criminal.")

Significantly increased pressure on the government to resume peace negotiations was reported in 2001 from civic and religious groups as well as small opposition parties, a growing number of critics suggesting that the MPLA was using Savimbi and UNITA to distract attention from the administration's long-standing inability to confront the nation's social woes effectively. Savimbi declared himself available for new power-sharing talks, but dos Santos, apparently buoyed by recent military successes, adopted a hard line, demanding that UNITA forces lay down their arms as a precondition to negotiations. By the end of the year, government forces were reportedly in control of more than 90 percent of the country, UNITA having once again been reduced to waging a bush guerrilla campaign.

Savimbi was killed in a government ambush on February 22, 2002. On April 4, two days after the National Assembly had approved an amnesty for all participants in the long-standing civil war who now accepted a negotiated settlement, the government and UNITA signed a cease-fire that provided for disarmament of UNITA, integration of UNITA fighters into the Angolan military, and UNITA's return to normal political party activity.

In August 2002 the UN Security Council authorized the creation of the UN Mission in Angola (UNMA) to assist the government and UNITA in implementing the peace plan. (The UNMA was disbanded in February 2003.) An August 2 ceremony at Luanda formally marked the integration of 5,000 UNITA soldiers into the Angolan army.

Declaring an end to the "exceptional period" that had existed since 1999, President dos Santos on December 6 appointed Fernando Da Piedade Dias DOS SANTOS as prime minister. Collaterally, the administration, UNITA, and small opposition parties reportedly agreed on the delineation of authority between the president and the prime minister. However, the issue of upcoming elections remained unresolved as of early 2006 (see Current issues, below).

Constitution and Government

Under the 1975 constitution as amended, the government was headed by a president who also served as chair of the MPLA. In the event of presidential disability, the MPLA Central Committee was authorized to designate an interim successor, thus reinforcing the role of the party as the people's "legitimate representative." In December 1978 the positions of prime minister and deputy prime minister were abolished, while in November 1980 the legislative Council of the Revolution was replaced as the "supreme organ of state power" by a National People's Assembly, whose members were indirectly designated at meetings of locally elected provincial delegates. (The Council of the Revolution, subsequently renamed the Council of the Republic, continued to function as an advisory body.)

In late 1990 the government committed itself to a new constitution that would permit multiparty presidential and legislative elections. UNITA representatives were invited to help draft the document under the peace accord of June 1, 1991. Thus, on February 1, 1992, UNITA representatives (who boycotted a multiparty conference held January 14–26) agreed with the government that the September election should be held on the basis of proportional representation and that the post-electoral executive should be elected for a five-year term, while the assembly would serve for four years.

On August 26, 1992, the MPLA approved a revised constitution that, in addition to the February 1 stipulations, provided for a presidentially appointed prime minister to head a transitional government, the abolition of the death penalty, and, in keeping with the removal of "People's" from the Republic's formal name, the deletion of all constitutional references to "popular" and "people" as reflecting former Marxist tendencies. A new constitutional committee was established by the assembly in 1998 to address issues such as whether federal governors and the prime minister should be popularly elected and what authority should be invested in the latter. Negotiations between the government and the UNITA-led opposition on a new constitution began following the peace accord of 2002, but progress has continued at a slow pace. By the end of 2004, the National Assembly had abolished the Constitutional Commission (the object of a boycott by the opposition), announcing that constitutional revision would henceforth be handled by a government-dominated assembly committee. The constitution remained in the hands of the assembly in 2005 (see Current issues, below).

The country is divided into 18 provinces (*províncias*) administered by centrally appointed governors, with legislative authority vested in provincial assemblies. The provinces are further divided into councils (*concelhos*), communes (*comunas*), circles (*círculos*), neighborhoods (*bairros*), and villages (*povoações*).

Foreign Relations

On June 23, 1976, the United States exercised its right of veto in the Security Council to block Angolan admission to the United Nations. The stated reason for the action was the continued presence in Angola of a sizable Cuban military force. On November 19, however, the United States reversed itself, citing "the appeals of its African friends," and Angola was admitted on December 1. Senegal, the last black African state to withhold recognition of the MPLA-PT government, announced the establishment of diplomatic relations in February 1982, while the People's Republic of China, long an opponent of the Soviet-supportive regime, established relations in late 1983.

Relations with Portugal were suspended briefly in late 1976 and remained relatively cool prior to a June 1978 agreement providing for the mutual repatriation of Angolan and Portuguese nationals. Subsequently, relations were again strained by allegations of Portuguese-based exile support for UNITA rebels, although efforts were made to restore previously substantial trade links between the two countries.

Relations have fluctuated with neighboring Zaire (restyled the Democratic Republic of the Congo in 1997), which charged the Neto government with providing support for rebel incursions into Shaba (formerly Katanga) Province in March 1977 and May 1978. Shortly thereafter, President Mobutu agreed to end his support for anti-MPLA forces based in Zaire, in return for a similar pledge from President Neto regarding Zairean dissidents sited in Angola. In October 1979 the presidents of Angola, Zaire, and Zambia signed a more extensive trilateral nonaggression pact in Ndola, Zambia. Despite these agreements and a Kinshasa-Luanda security pact signed in early 1985, periodic accusations of Zairean support for Angolan insurgents continued to issue from Luanda.

In the south, Luanda's support for the South West African People's Organisation (SWAPO), which began operating from Angolan bases in the mid-1970s, resulted in numerous cross-border raids by South African defense forces deployed in Namibia. On the other hand, despite periodic encouragement of UNITA and an unwillingness to establish formal relations prior to the withdrawal of Cuban troops, both the Carter and Reagan administrations in the United States made overtures to Luanda, citing the need for Angolan involvement in the Namibian independence process. In early 1985 statements by dos Santos indicating a willingness to negotiate on Cuban troop withdrawal were offered by Washington as evidence of its "constructive engagement" policy in southern Africa; however, all contacts were suspended by Angola later in the year following U.S. congressional repeal of the "Clark Amendment" banning military aid to the insurgents, with repeated military activity by Pretoria having already reduced Luanda's willingness to negotiate. Relations with Washington deteriorated further in 1986, in the wake of a U.S. decision to give UNITA $15 million in military aid, including ground-to-air missiles.

By contrast, a series of meetings that commenced at London in May 1988 concluded at UN headquarters in New York on December 22 with the signing of two accords (one a tripartite agreement between Angola, Cuba, and South Africa, and the other a bilateral agreement among Angola and Cuba) for the phased withdrawal of Cuban forces, coupled with South African acceptance of the 1978 Security Council Resolution 435 that called for UN-supervised elections for an independent Namibia. Under the withdrawal provisions, to be monitored by UNAVEM, half of the Cubans were to leave by November 1989, with the remainder to depart by July 1991. For its part, Pretoria agreed to end military assistance to the UNITA rebels, while insisting that Luanda would be in violation of the accord if it permitted African National Congress (ANC) guerrillas to use its territory as a staging area for infiltration into Botswana, Namibia, or South Africa. (For the Namibia portion of the settlement, see articles on Namibia and South Africa.) In January 1989, three months ahead of schedule, Cuban troops began their withdrawal, although South Africa's apparent adherence to the accord was offset by a reported doubling of U.S. aid to the rebels.

In the wake of the June 1991 peace settlement, Washington pledged $30 million to assist UNITA in its transformation from a military organization into a political party, and, following a September summit meeting between presidents dos Santos and Bush, the United States reiterated its intent to restrict trade and investment until after multiparty elections. Nevertheless, dos Santos, citing a U.S. offer of humanitarian aid, electoral assistance, and the potential for postelection aid, stated that relations had reached a "turning point."

Resurgence of the Angolan civil war in late 1992 revived allegations by both combatants of military and financial intervention by neighboring states. Progovernment officials accused South Africa and Zaire of supporting UNITA efforts, while Namibia challenged UNITA to prove its allegation that Namibian forces were fighting alongside government troops.

Angola's foreign relations in 1993 were dominated by international efforts to thwart UNITA's widely condemned aggression and aid those adversely affected by the civil war. Most dramatically, on May 18 the United States announced its intention to recognize the Luanda government. The U.S. decision came after much exhortation by South Africa and Mozambique, both of whom feared that UNITA's refusal to accept the 1992 poll results might undermine their own election plans. Thereafter, France, Russia, and the United Kingdom announced that they were negotiating arms sales with the government.

Although both the MPLA and UNITA denied involvement in the fighting in Zaire in early 1997, observers there reported that MPLA units had provided at least rearguard and logistical assistance to Laurent Kabila's fighters, while UNITA forces had suffered heavy casualties fighting alongside the Mobutu regime's ultimately unsuccessful defenders. Meanwhile, at Luanda, government officials announced a reordering of their diplomatic priorities, with major emphasis being placed, in order of importance, on relations with the United States, France, and Angola's Asian economic partners. On June 30, 1997, the UNAVEM mandate expired, and its responsibilities were assumed by a new UN Observer Mission at Angola (UNOMA). In late October President dos Santos hosted a summit of the leaders of the Republic of the Congo, Democratic Republic of the Congo (DRC), and Gabon during which the four presidents agreed to isolate UNITA as well as the Cabindan guerrillas.

In 1998 Luanda alleged that Burkina Faso, Rwanda, Togo, Uganda, and Zambia were either supplying the UNITA rebels or offering them safe haven. Meanwhile, international attention focused on Angola's prominent role in the civil wars in the DRC and the Republic of the Congo. President dos Santos sought to justify Angola's involvement there as an attempt to help prevent a "bloodbath" and expansion of the fighting. In September, Angola, the DRC, and the Republic of the Congo signed a border security agreement. Meanwhile, Namibia's willingness to let anti-UNITA troops operate from within its borders proved pivotal to Luanda's military successes in late 1999 (see Current issues, below).

In December 1999 the Portuguese legislature approved a "vote of protest" against Angola's ongoing fighting, thus prompting Luanda to register its own complaint that Lisbon was attempting to interfere in its affairs. Thereafter, international attention turned to a UN investigation into alleged efforts by UNITA supporters to circumvent sanctions against supplying or trading with UNITA.

Following the mid-2002 peace accord in Angola, U.S. President George W. Bush welcomed President dos Santos at the White House, under-

scoring, among other things, the importance of Angolan oil to the United States. At the same time, however, ties between Angola and China intensified, resulting in major Chinese investment in Angolan oil production in 2004.

Current Issues

Almost immediately after the death of UNITA's Jonas Savimbi in February 2002 it became clear that most Angolans were more than ready for the nearly three-decade-long civil war to come to an end. The transformation of UNITA into a functioning political party and the reintegration of UNITA forces into the military and civil society occurred surprisingly swiftly and smoothly. (It was estimated that 500,000–1 million people had died in the conflict, with 4–5 million having been internally or externally dislocated.) Attention soon turned to plans for a return to a normal political process, including the writing of a new constitution scheduled to permit national elections, perhaps in 2007. In 2005 the MPLA remained strongly entrenched politically, despite regularly facing charges of corruption and economic mismanagement, particularly in regard to oil revenues. President dos Santos responded to severe criticism from the IMF and others by pledging greater transparency in governmental affairs and other reforms. The administration also embarked, with the assistance of eager foreign investors, on a series of massive projects designed to rebuild the nation's ravaged infrastructure. However, despite the appearance of an economic boom, observers cautioned that poverty and maldistribution of wealth were growing worse rather than better, leaving much of the population still without the basic services generally anticipated in resource-rich countries. In 2005 some 34,500 Angolans were repatriated from Zambia, where they had sought refuge during the civil war, putting a further strain on services.

The government was buffeted by allegations of corruption in 2005, one example being a line of credit from China meant for public works projects that some suggested was being used as a "political slush fund" for the upcoming elections.

Meanwhile, progress toward constitutional reform and elections slowed in 2005 as President dos Santos backed away from his initial affirmation that elections would be held in 2006. Sharp increases in oil revenues helped solidify the current administration's power, enabling it to rebuff opposition parties' attempts to impose political reforms. The constitution remained in the hands of the assembly in early 2006, and it was widely reported that elections would not be held until 2007, with *Africa Confidential* commenting that the government, by delaying elections a year, could then "steer a new constitution through parliament."

Political Parties

Angola was a one-party state for the first 16 years of its independence; however, in 1990 the government agreed to institute a multiparty electoral system, and, under legislation of March 26, 1991, more than 30 groups expressed interest in achieving formal party status. Thereafter, the imposition of strict registration guidelines limited participation in the September 1992 legislative balloting to 18 parties. (For information on several subsequent pro- and antigovernment coalitions, see the 2000–2002 *Handbook*.)

Government Parties

Popular Movement for the Liberation of Angola (*Movimento Popular de Libertação de Angola*—MPLA). Organized in 1956, the Soviet-backed MPLA provided the primary resistance to Portuguese colonial rule in central Angola prior to independence. During its first national congress, held at Luanda December 4–11, 1977, the party was formally restructured along Marxist-Leninist lines and redesignated as the MPLA–Labor Party (*MPLA–Partido Trabalhista*—MPLA-PT).

Reflecting the dos Santos administration's increasingly pragmatic approach to economic problems, the party's second congress in 1985 adopted a resolution promoting several "Western-style" reforms, without, however, altering its alliance with Cuba and the Soviet Union or its hostil-

ity to the United States and South Africa regarding the UNITA insurgency (below). At its third congress, held December 4–10, 1990, at Luanda, the MPLA-PT abandoned Marxism-Leninism in favor of "democratic socialism" and endorsed multiparty elections in the wake of a peace settlement with UNITA. In consonance with those decisions, the party decided to drop "Labor Party" from its name prior to the 1992 elections.

Dos Santos was reelected as MPLA president at the 1998 and 2003 congresses, apparently positioning himself at the latter for a run in the presidential elections tentatively scheduled for 2007.

Leaders: José Eduardo DOS SANTOS (President of the Republic and President of the Party), António Domingos Pitra da Costa NETO (Vice President of the Party), Gen. Juliao Mateus PAULO (Secretary General).

National Union for the Total Independence of Angola (*União Nacional para a Independência Total de Angola*—UNITA). Active primarily in southern Angola prior to the Portuguese withdrawal, UNITA, whose support is centered within the Ovimbundu ethnic group, joined with the FNLA (below) in establishing an abortive rival government at Huambo in November 1975 and subsequently engaged in guerrilla operations against Luanda. Although its ideology was of Maoist derivation, the party's image within black Africa suffered because of U.S. and South African military assistance. In late 1982 UNITA leader Jonas SAVIMBI asserted that no basic ideological differences separated UNITA and the MPLA-PT and that the removal of all Cuban troops would lead to negotiations with the government. Although his subsequent avowals of "anti-communism" and increased solicitation of aid from Pretoria and Washington reportedly generated internal dissent, Savimbi remained in control.

In the peace accord of June 1, 1991, UNITA agreed to recognize the legitimacy of the dos Santos government until the holding of multiparty elections in September 1992. In March 1992 two of UNITA's most senior officials, Secretary General Miguel N'ZAU PUNA and Gen. Tony da Costa

FERNANDES, left the party, ostensibly to focus on problems involving their native enclave of Cabinda. Late in the month, however, the two issued a statement at Paris charging UNITA with political killings and other human rights abuses. At midyear the party's election hopes were dealt another blow when Savimbi reportedly announced that a UNITA-led government would be composed of only black members, thus exacerbating the fear already existing in the mixed-race and Portuguese communities. Following the September election, Savimbi's rejection of the results and reports of UNITA military activities generated domestic and international condemnation. UNITA officials, however, blamed MPLA supporters for initiating the violence that broke out at Luanda in mid-October. In May 1993 UNITA's rejection of a peace plan that reportedly addressed most of Savimbi's demands appeared to reflect a split within the group between pro-negotiation moderates and fight-to-the-end hard-liners.

Meanwhile, on the diplomatic front, UNITA negotiators rejected demands in 1993 that its troops be withdrawn to their May 1991 positions, claiming that it feared MPLA reprisals against its supporters in the contested areas. In September the rebel leadership agreed to recognize the 1992 elections results. Thereafter, in late 1993 and into 1994 UNITA, propelled by Savimbi's apparently undiminished desire to rule Angola, continued its pattern of simultaneous diplomatic negotiations and military offensives.

On November 15, 1994, UNITA's Secretary General Eugénio Manuvakola signed a truce agreement on behalf of the rebels with the government. However, during a party congress in February 1995, UNITA hard-liners were reported to be dissatisfied with the peace agreement that was to have come into effect on November 22, and Manuvakola was replaced as secretary general by Gen. Paulo Lukamba Gato.

In addition to the four senior cabinet posts awarded the group in April 1997, UNITA representatives were also named to seven deputy ministerial positions. Amid speculation that UNITA was preparing to return to war, reports circulated at midyear that the group's military high command was planning on moving to the panhandle region along the Zambian border. Subsequently, General Manuvakola broke with the group, denouncing its hostile intentions.

Meanwhile, observers reported that a gap had developed between UNITA officials participating in the government at Luanda and those in Savimbi's inner circle, with the former attempting to distance themselves from the latter's confrontational stances. Evidence of the group's factionalization became apparent in February 1998 when the Luanda-based members ignored a Savimbi dictate to vote against a budget proposal. Thereafter, with the country once more poised for civil war, pro-Savimbi UNITA members fled Luanda in July, and, on August 31, the government announced the temporary suspension of UNITA representatives from the government and the assembly. In September Jorge Alicerces Valentim, a UNITA cabinet minister, announced that he and a number of other UNITA ministers and parliamentarians had aligned with General Manuvakola. Furthermore, the dissidents announced the suspension of Savimbi and, under the banner of UNITA-Renewal (UNITA-*Renavado*), appointed an interim group to lead the party until the convening of its next congress. Thereafter, a third UNITA strain emerged under the leadership of Abel Chivukuvuku, the party's parliamentary leader, and Armindo KASSESSA, both of whom had rejected UNITA-Renewal's entreaties. Chivukuvuku, reportedly popular with both UNITA military leaders and international mediators, in late October was reelected to his legislative post in what observers described as a direct "slap" at Valentim.

At what was labeled UNITA's ninth congress, delegates aligned with UNITA-Renewal convened at Luanda in mid-January 1999 and elected General Manuvakola president of the party. Meanwhile, Savimbi dismissed the Luanda-based factions as "irrelevant." Thereafter, the government intensified its efforts to persuade UNITA militants to disarm and play a role in the political process.

Following Savimbi's death in February 2002, UNITA quickly negotiated an accord with the government that ended the long civil war and provided for the integration of about 5,000 UNITA fighters into the Angolan armed forces. (Some 80,000 other fighters returned to civilian life.) The peace agreement also permitted reunification of the various UNITA factions, General Manuvakola suspending his UNITA-Renewal leadership to facilitate that initiative.

Again acting as a regular political party, UNITA elected its former representative at Paris, Isaias Samakuva, as its new president at a party congress in June 2003. (Samakuva defeated General Gato, who had served as interim leader since Savimbi's death.) In 2004 UNITA announced it was forming a Campaign for a Democratic Angola with some seven small parties in preparation for the next elections. In 2005 Samakuva announced his intention to run for the presidency. Meanwhile, a rift developed in the party after Valentim was removed from his ministry post in early 2005 and was then briefly suspended after publicly criticizing party leaders. He claimed party leaders were delaying his appointment to the assembly, though he was subsequently seated in April 2005.

Leaders: Isaias SAMAKUVA (President), Ernesto MULATO (Vice President), Abel CHIVUKUVUKU, Gen. Paulo Lukamba GATO, Gen. Eugénio MANUVAKOLA, Jorge VALENTIM, Mario VATUVA (Secretary General).

Angolan Democratic Forum (*Forum Democrático Angolano—FDA*). The FDA was organized by UNITA dissident and peace activist Jorge Chicoti to protest human rights abuses by the parent group and was registered in February 1992. Its ranks included a number of Angolan students overseas. The FDA secured one assembly seat in the September 1992 balloting.

The FDA's Paulo Tjipilica held the justice ministry in the MPLA-led cabinet until late 2004 and he was subsequently named the country's first "justice and ombudsman." Meanwhile, Chicoti continued to serve as deputy minister of foreign affairs.

Leaders: Jorge Rebelo Pinto CHICOTI (President), Paulo TJIPILICA, Manuel Adão DOMINGOS (Secretary General).

Other Parties

National Front for the Liberation of Angola (*Frente Nacional para a Libertação de Angola—FNLA*). Organized as a resistance group in 1962 in northern Angola, the FNLA was consistently the most anticommunist of the three major groups until the collapse of its forces in the late 1970s.

The FNLA was inactive throughout most of the 1980s; however, in 1991 longtime leader Holden Roberto announced his intention to seek the presidency and stated that the FNLA deserved to be accorded its earlier de facto parity with the MPLA-PT and UNITA. Nevertheless, at presidential and legislative balloting in September 1992 the FNLA fared poorly, with Roberto being held to 2.11 percent of the presidential vote and the party securing only five assembly seats.

At the FNLA's second congress in February 1999, delegates elected Lucas Ngonda party president. In addition, the party held balloting to fill its Central Committee and declared its willingness to participate in the government. The October 2004 congress reportedly agreed to have Roberto lead the party for the next ten months in an apparent effort to smooth over lingering friction between the FNLA's old guard and younger members. However, friction resumed in 2005 with division over Roberto's suspension of Secretary General Francisco MENDES in September, and the majority's discontent with Roberto's failure to hold another congress to elect new leadership. Roberto, however, maintained his leadership position.

Leaders: Holden ROBERTO (Party Leader), Lucas NGONDA and Ngola KABANGO (Deputy Leaders).

Social Renewal Party (*Partido Renovador Social—PRS*). The PRS finished third at the legislative balloting of September 1992 by winning six assembly seats.

At a congress in March 1999 Eduardo Kwangana was reportedly elected to lead the PRS; however, the incumbent party chief, António João Machicungo, rejected the polling, arguing that Kwangana's supporters had ignored party statutes in an effort to gain control of the grouping.

Leaders: António João MACHICUNGO, Eduardo KWANGANA, Lindo Bernardo TITO (Chair).

Democratic Renewal Party (*Partido Renovador Democrático*—PRD). The PRD was formed by survivors and sympathizers of the dissident Nito ALVES faction of the MPLA-PT, whose abortive 1977 coup attempt led to a violent purge of the parent party leadership. In September 1991 the PRD was the first party sanctioned by the Supreme Court to begin gathering the signatures necessary to secure legal status.

Leaders: Luís da Silva DOS PASSOS (President and 1992 presidential candidate), Noy da COSTA (Secretary General).

Liberal Democratic Party (*Partido Liberal Democrático*—PLD). The PLD won three legislative seats at the 1992 poll, party leader Anália de Victoria Pereira finishing tenth in the eleven-candidate presidential field. Pereira was renominated as party leader in July 2005 and was considered a possible candidate for the presidency in the next election.

Leaders: Anália de Victoria PEREIRA, Honorato LANDO.

Angolan National Democratic Party (*Partido Nacional Democrático de Angola*—PNDA). Originally styled the Angolan National Democratic Convention (*Convenção Nacional Democrática de Angola*—CNDA), the PNDA in September 1992 supported the presidential candidacy of Daniel Julio CHIPENDA, an independent who had reportedly left the MPLA in protest over the party's decision to present dos Santos as its standard-bearer. Chipenda captured only .52 percent of the presidential vote, with the PNDA winning one assembly seat.

At the party's national conference held May 23–24, 1997, delegates elected a new Central Committee and Political Bureau.

Leader: Geraldo Pereira João da SILVA (President).

Democratic Alliance of Angola (*Aliança Democrática de Angola*—ADA). Although garnering less than 1 percent of the vote, the ADA was able to win one assembly seat in September 1992.

Leader: Simba da COSTA.

Democratic Party for Progress–Angolan National Alliance (*Partido Democrático para Progresso–Aliança Nacional Angolano*—PDP-ANA). The PDP-ANA is a right-of-center humanist grouping previously led by a prominent university professor, Mfulumpinga Lando VICTOR, who was formerly affiliated with the FNLA. In mid-1992 Victor was named as a presidential candidate; however, there were no reports of his having received any votes in the September balloting, at which the party secured one assembly seat. Victor, a prominent opposition leader, was killed by unidentified gunmen in an attack at Luanda in July 2004. Sediangani Mbimbi, who had been acting president, was elected president of the party in April 2005, defeating Malungo Belo.

Leaders: Sediangani MBIMBI (Acting President), Malungo BELO.

Party of the Alliance of the Youth, Workers, and Farmers of Angola (*Partido da Aliança da Juventude, Operários e Camponeses de Angola*—PAJOCA). The PAJOCA won one seat at the legislative poll of September 1992.

Leader: Alexandre Sebastião ANDRE.

Social Democratic Party (*Partido Social Democrático*—PSD). The PSD secured one assembly seat in September 1992, while its presidential candidate, Bengue Pedro João, won less than 1 percent of the presidential vote.

Leaders: Bengue Pedro JOÃO, Dr. José Manuél MIGUEL.

Angolan Democratic Party (*Partido Democrático Angolano*—PDA). PDA leader António Alberto Neto finished third in the September 1992 presidential balloting, albeit with a vote share of 2.16 percent, far behind dos Santos and Savimbi.

Leader: António Alberto NETO.

Angolan Labor Party (*Partido Trabalhista Angolano*—PTA). The PTA was legalized in March 1995.

Leader: Angostinho PALDO.

Social Democratic Center (*Centro Democrático Social*—CDS). The CDS was legalized in November 1995.

Leaders: Mateus JOSE (President), Delfina Francisco CAPCIEL (Secretary General).

United Front for the Salvation of Angola (*Frente Unida para a Salvação de Angola*—FUSA). The FUSA was granted official registration by the Supreme Court in April 1996.

Leader: José Augusto da Silva COELHO (President).

Angola Democratic and Progress Support Party (*Partido de Apoio Democrático e Progresso de Angola*—PADPA). The PADPA's unsuccessful effort to organize a demonstration against a fuel-price hike in early 2000 was cited by observers as the impetus for a larger protest march soon thereafter. In August 2005 a senior party member was sentenced to 45 days in prison for an unauthorized protest outside parliament after his party was excluded from a panel set to supervise the next elections.

Leaders: Carlos LEITAO (President), Silva CARDOSA (Secretary General).

Minor parties also include the antiseparatist **Angolan Party of African Identity Conservative** (*Partido Angolano de Conservadora Identidade Africana*—PACIA); the **Angolan Democratic Party for Peace** (*Partido Democrático de Paz de Angola*—PDPA); the **Angolan Democratic Unity Movement for Reconstruction** (*Movimento Angolano de Unidade Democrática para a Reconstrução*—MAUDR); the **Angolan Liberal Party** (*Partido Angolano Liberal*—PAL); the **Angolan Independent Party** (*Partido Angolano Independente*—PAI); the **Angolan National Ecological Party** (*Partido Nacional Ecológico de Angola*—PNEA); the **Angolan Social Democratic Party** (*Partido Social Democrático de Angola*—PSDA); the **Front for Democracy** (*Frente para a Democracia*—FPD), led by Filomena Viera LOPES; and the **National Union for the Light of Democracy and Development in Angola** (*União Nacional para a Luz de Democracia e Desenvolvimento em Angola*—UNLDDA).

Separatist Groups

Since the early 1960s a number of groups have been active under the banner of the **Front for the Liberation of the Cabinda Enclave** (*Frente de Libertação do Enclave de Cabinda*—FLEC) in the oil-rich province of Cabinda, a sliver (7,300 sq. km.) of land between the Republic of the Congo and what is now the Democratic Republic of the Congo (formerly Zaire). The original FLEC was founded in August 1963 by Luis Ranque FRANQUE, who, encouraged by Portuguese authorities to continue separatist activities, refused to join other Angolan independence movements. In 1974 the Front's attempts to gain military control of the enclave were rebuffed by the MPLA and, in 1975, the movement broke into three factions: FLEC–Ranque Franque; FLEC-N'Zita, led by Henrique Tiaho N'ZITA; and FLEC-Lubota, led by Francisco Xavier LUBOTA. In November 1977 a splinter group styling itself the Military Command for the Liberation of Cabinda was organized, while in June 1979 the Armed Forces for the Liberation of Cabinda established another splinter, the Popular Movement for the Liberation of Cabinda (*Movimento Popular de Libertação de Cabinda*—MPLC). In the 1980s FLEC-UNITA, or UNIFLEC, was reported to be operating in Cabinda with South African assistance; however, the group's activities ceased following withdrawal of Pretoria's aid. In the early 1990s two other groups, the National Union for the Liberation of Cabinda (*União Nacional de Libertação de Cabinda*—UNLC), led by Lumingu Luís Caneiro GIMBY, and the Communist Committee of Cabinda (*Comité Comunista de Cabinda*—CCC), led by Kaya Mohamed YAY, were linked to separatist activities.

Anxious to create ties to the economically important region, both the government and UNITA named Cabindans to leadership positions in their parties. Nevertheless, in July 1991 a joint MPLA-PT/UNITA offensive was launched in Cabinda to eradicate the terrorists. Meanwhile, although past attempts to unify the numerous FLEC factions had proven short-lived, it was reported that four of the identifiable groups (FLEC-Lubota, the UNLC, CCC, and FLEC-R [*Renovada*]) were attempting to form a united front, FLEC N'Zita reportedly refusing to participate.

In mid-May 1993 FLEC responded to the U.S. recognition of Luanda by declaring that it did not extend to Cabinda and warning that "all those people with companies in Cabinda must choose between supporting the extermination of the Cabindan people or leaving the territory." Following UNITA's capture of Soyo in northwestern Angola in late May, the government, fearing a pact between the separatists and rebels, was reported to be attempting to form an alliance with a FLEC-R opponent, the **FLEC-Armed Forces of Cabinda** (*Forcas Armadas de Cabinda*—FLEC-FAC), which was reportedly being led by Henrique Tiaho N'Zita, his son, Emmanuel N'ZITA, and José Liberal NUNO. However, after a new guerrilla offensive in Cabinda from mid-1995, government and FLEC-R representatives meeting at Windhoek, Namibia, in April 1996 concluded a cease-fire agreement that was thought likely to be observed by the other FLEC factions. Such optimism proved ungrounded, however, as the government was subsequently unable to reach an agreement with the FLEC-FAC or Francisco Xavier Lubota's **Democratic Front of Cabinda** (*Frente Democrática de Cabinda*—FDC).

In September 1996 FLEC-R's Central Council advised its president, Jose Tiburcio LUEMBA, and a second party leader, Jorge Victor GOMES, not to attend a meeting at Brazzaville, Congo, with government officials. Their decision to ignore the committee led to their ouster at an extraordinary general assembly meeting on January 24, 1997. Subsequently, Antonio Bento BEMBE, theretofore party secretary general, and Arture TCHIBASSA, described by *Africa Confidential* as the group's "founder and most powerful leader," were named party president and secretary general, respectively.

Meanwhile, in early 1997 heightened military and political activity was reported in the enclave as the government launched an offensive reportedly aimed at dismantling the military capabilities of the separatists. Its cease-fire having formally lapsed in January, the FLEC-R's newly installed, more militant leadership also acknowledged having increased its military operations. In 1998

skirmishes between the militants and government forces reportedly intensified as the latter sought to neutralize its opponents (both FLEC and UNITA) in the region. Both FLEC-FAC and FLEC-R were reportedly involved in hostage-taking between 2000 and 2001, analysts suggesting that the proliferation of FLEC-related groupings had resulted in confusion among Cabinda's 400,000 inhabitants, most of whom apparently would opt for independence or at least autonomy if offered a choice.

The Angolan government launched what was reportedly considered a successful campaign against the Cabindan fighters in late 2002, following conclusion of the peace accord with the much larger UNITA forces. However, tension regarding "the forgotten war" continued into 2005. By that time FLEC-R and FLEC-FAC had reportedly agreed to operate together as FLEC, with Tiaho N'Zita as the group's leader and Bembe as secretary general. Although FLEC apparently indicated a willingness to negotiate with the government, no cease-fire had been achieved by February 2005, when a mass rally in Cabinda again underscored popular support for "self-rule." Meanwhile, an unprecedented strike by Catholic clergy fueled further unrest in 2005 after the Vatican sought to replace a retiring bishop with a non-Cabindan.

In a setback to FLEC, Bembe was arrested in mid-2005 in the Netherlands, where he had been invited by the Dutch foreign ministry to participate in peace negotiations regarding the situation in Cabinda. Bembe, who was arrested for his alleged role in the kidnapping of an American oil company employee several years earlier, was released on bail but subsequently disappeared near the end of 2005. Many observers suspected Bembe was taken to the United States, though the Dutch had denied a U.S. request for extradition. Meanwhile, Tchibassa was serving a 24-year sentence in the United States on the same charge.

Legislature

In accordance with the 1975 constitution, as amended, a 223-member National People's Assembly (*Assembleia Nacional Popular*) with a three-year term of office was elected in 1980 as

Cabinet

As of September 1, 2006

President	José Eduardo dos Santos (MPLA)
Prime Minister	Fernando Da Piedade Dias dos Santos (MPLA)
Deputy Prime Minister	Aguinaldo Jaime (MPLA)

Ministers

Agriculture and Rural Development	Gilberto Buta Lutukuta (MPLA)
Commerce	Joaquim Ekuma Muafumua (MPLA)
Culture	Boaventura Cardoso (MPLA)
Defense	Gen. Kundi Paihama (MPLA)
Education	António Burity da Silva (MPLA)
Energy and Water	José Maria Botelho de Vasconcelos (MPLA)
Family and the Promotion of Women	Candida Celeste da Silva (MPLA) [f]
Finance	José Pedro de Morais (MPLA)
Fisheries	Salomão Luheto Xirimbimbi (MPLA)
Foreign Affairs	João Bernardo de Miranda (MPLA)
Former Combatants and Veterans Affairs	Pedro José Van-Dúnem (MPLA)
Geology and Mines	Manuel Antonio Africano (UNITA)
Health	Sebastião Sapuile Veloso
Hotels and Tourism	Eduardo Jonatão Chingunji
Industry	Joaquim Duarte da Costa David (MPLA)
Interior	Gen. Roberto Leal Monteiro
Justice	Manualda Costa Aragao
Labor, Public Administration, and Social Security	António Domingos Pitra da Costa Neto (MPLA)
Minister in the Office of the Presidency, Diplomatic Affairs	Carlos Alberto Saraiva de Carvalho Fonseca
Minister in the Office of the Presidency, Economic Affairs	Augusto Archer de Sousa Mangueira
Minister in the Office of the Presidency, Legal Affairs	Carlos Manuel dos Santos Teixeira
Minister in the Office of the Presidency, Military Affairs	Manuel Hélder Dias
Minister in the Office of the Presidency, Civil Affairs and Regional Affairs	Américo Maria de Morais Garcia
Minister in the Office of the Presidency, Secretary of the Council of Ministers	Joaquim António Carlos dos Reis Júnior
Petroleum	Desidério da Graça Veríssimo da Costa (MPLA)
Planning	Ana Afonso Dias Lourenço (MPLA) [f]
Postal Services and Telecommunications	Licínio Tavares Ribeiro (MPLA)
Public Works	Francisco Higino Carneiro (MPLA)
Science and Technology	João Baptista Ngandagina (MPLA)
Social Assistance and Reintegration	João Baptista Kussumua (MPLA)
Social Communication (Information)	Manuel Rabelais
Territorial Administration	Virgílio Ferreira Fontes Pereira (MPLA)
Transport	André Luís Brandão (MPLA)
Urban Affairs and the Environment	Diekunpuna Sita José
Youth and Sports	José Marcos Barrica (MPLA)

[f] = female

successor to the Council of the Revolution, which had served as a legislature since formation of the republic. Subsequent balloting was deferred until late 1986, when the legislative term was extended to five years and the number of deputies increased to 289. The list of candidates, all members of the MPLA-PT, was drawn up by the assembly's Permanent Commission.

In late 1990 the MPLA-PT approved liberalization measures providing for election of a restyled **National Assembly** (*Assembleia Nacional*) on a multiparty basis. Following balloting held September 29–30, 1992, for 220 seats (three seats reserved for overseas Angolans not being filled by mutual agreement of the parties), the distribution was as follows: Popular Movement for the Liberation of Angola, 129; National Union for the Total Independence of Angola, 70; Social Renewal Party, 6; National Front for the Liberation of Angola, 5; Liberal Democratic Party, 3; and Angolan Democratic Forum, Angolan National Democratic Party, Democratic Alliance of Angola, Democratic Party for Progress–Angolan National Alliance, Democratic Renewal Party, Party of the Alliance of the Youth, Workers, and Farmers of Angola, and the Social Democratic Party, 1 each.

On November 13, 1996, the assembly overwhelmingly approved a constitutional revision extending the current legislature's mandate (due to expire on November 26) for a minimum of two and a maximum of four years. On April 9, 1997, the assembly met for the first time with the full complement of UNITA representatives in attendance. However, the status of the UNITA contingent became clouded in 1998 as relations between UNITA and the government deteriorated. The government announced on August 31, 1998, that the UNITA legislators had been suspended; however, many were subsequently permitted to reassume their seats under an agreement between the government and UNITA-Renewal, the new UNITA faction opposed to longtime UNITA leader Jonas Savimbi. At the same time, some of the UNITA legislators restated their allegiance to Savimbi. Following Savimbi's death in February 2002, the UNITA factions reunified as part of the broad peace accord with the government.

The government in 2004 announced plans to hold new assembly balloting in September 2006. (The assembly had again extended its own mandate for an indefinite period on October 17, 2000.) However, balloting was subsequently put off until 2007.

President: Roberto de ALMEIDA.

Communications

Press

Following nationalization of the press in 1976, the government required all news disseminated by the media to conform to official policy. The government announced that press liberalization would be addressed in the course of a constitutional review launched in late 1990. However, domestic and international watchdog groups strongly criticized the government between 2000 and 2001 for tightening controls on the media and otherwise pressuring journalists. The negotiation of a proposed new press law was one of the major areas of disagreement between the government and opposition parties in 2004 as plans were made for the next national elections. However, in February 2006 the National Assembly approved the new press law, granting freedom of the press by prohibiting censorship and revoking the state's monopoly over television and news agencies. It was not immediately clear who would operate these media outlets.

The following are Portuguese-language dailies published at Luanda: *O Jornal de Angola* (42,000); *Diário da República* (8,500), government news sheet. *Correio da Semana*, a weekly, is published at Luanda by the owners of *O Jornal*.

News Agencies

The domestic facility is the formerly government-operated Angolan News Agency (*Agência Noticiosa N'gola Press*—ANGOP). A limited number of foreign agencies maintain offices at Luanda.

Broadcasting and Computing

The principal broadcasting services are *Radio Nacional de Angola* and *Televisão Popular de Angola*, both formerly controlled by the government.

There were approximately 417,000 television receivers and 35,000 personal computers serving 49,000 Internet users in 2003.

Intergovernmental Representation

Ambassador to the U.S.
Josefina Pitra DIAKITÉ

U.S. Ambassador to Angola
Cynthia G. EFIRD

Permanent Representative to the UN
Ismael Abraão Gaspar MARTINS

IGO Memberships (Non-UN)
AfDB, AU, BADEA, CEEAC, Comesa, CPLP, Interpol, IOM, NAM, SADC, WCO, WTO

BENIN

REPUBLIC OF BENIN

République du Bénin

The Country

The elongated West African state of Benin (formerly Dahomey) lies between Togo and Nigeria, with a southern frontage on the South Atlantic and a northerly bulge contiguous with Burkina Faso and Niger. The country's population exhibits a highly complex ethnolinguistic structure, the majority falling within four major tribal divisions: Adja, Bariba, Fon, and Yoruba. The principal tribal languages are Fon and Yoruba in the south and Bariba and Fulani in the north. Approximately 70 percent of the people are animists, the remainder being almost equally divided between Christians (concentrated in the south) and Muslims (concentrated in the north). The labor force includes nearly three-quarters of the adult female population, concentrated primarily in the cultivation of subsistence crops. Female participation in government has traditionally been minimal; the first female cabinet member was named in 1989.

Benin is one of the world's poorest countries, with an average per capita income of only $3 per day. It has been reported recently that 60 percent of adults are illiterate, while only 50 percent of school-age children attend school. The country also ranks near the bottom in other "quality of life" measures. The economy is based primarily on agriculture, with cotton, cocoa, and various oilseeds serving as principal sources of foreign exchange. Most of its quite limited industrial development supports cotton and palm-oil production. Its major trading partner, France, subsidizes current expenses as well as basic development. Black-market activity is widespread, and contra-band trade, especially with Nigeria, is a significant source of income for many Beninois. Small deposits of oil and gas have been located, although exploitation has been minimal and significant impact from that sector on the economy is not currently anticipated.

The government adopted a strongly Marxist orientation in the mid-1970s but thereafter moved to privatize a number of state-run companies in an effort to counter high external debt, corruption, and severe economic stagnation. In addition, wide-ranging austerity measures were adopted, facilitating international aid agreements but also contributing to social unrest. In 1998 the International Monetary Fund (IMF) reported that Benin's

Political Status: Independent Republic of Dahomey established August 1, 1960; military regime established October 26, 1972, becoming Marxist one-party system 1972–1975; name changed to People's Republic of Benin on November 30, 1975; name changed further to Republic of Benin on February 28, 1990, by National Conference of Active Forces of the Nation, which also revoked constitution of August 1977; multiparty constitution approved by popular referendum on December 2, 1990.

Area: 43,483 sq. mi. (112,622 sq. km.).

Population: 6,752,569 (2002C); 7,107,000 (2005E).

Major Urban Centers (2005E): PORTO NOVO (240,000), Cotonou (789,000).

Official Language: French.

Monetary Unit: CFA Franc (market rate July 1, 2006: 513.01 francs = $1US). (The CFA franc, previously pegged to the French franc, is now permanently pegged to the euro at 655.957 francs = 1 euro.)

President: Boni YAYI (nonparty); elected in second-round balloting on March 19, 2006, and inaugurated on April 6 to succeed Brig. Gen. (Ret.) Mathieu KÉRÉKOU.

Prime Minister: (Vacant). (Adrien HOUNGBÉDJI [Party of Democratic Renewal] had been appointed prime minister by the president on April 8, 1996; however, following Houngbédji's resignation on May 8, 1998, President Kérékou did not name a successor, the post not being constitutionally required. President Yayi also did not include a prime minister in the cabinet he named in April 2006.)

GDP growth. Additional debt relief was announced in mid-2000, although concern was expressed in some quarters that the nation's poor were not benefiting from economic advancement. In that context, opposition surfaced to IMF/World Bank insistence on further privatization of state-controlled enterprises, particularly in the cotton and power sectors, out of fear for the loss of jobs and an increase in prices. GDP growth averaged more than 5 percent annually from 2000 through 2003, and in 2003 the World Bank approved $460 million in debt relief for Benin, in part due to economic reforms, including improved tax collection, instituted by the government. However, growth subsequently declined (to 2.7 percent in 2004) under the effect of rising oil and food prices and falling prices for cotton on the global market. In the opinion of many observers, potential economic development was the dominant concern among voters in the 2006 presidential elections (see Current issues, below).

Government and Politics

Political Background

Under French influence since the mid-19th century, the territory then known as Dahomey became self-governing within the French Community in December 1958. However, Dahomey permitted its Community status to lapse upon achieving full independence on August 1, 1960. During the next 12 years personal and regional animosities generated five military coups d'état, most of them interspersed with short-lived civilian regimes.

The country's first president, Hubert MAGA, was overthrown in October 1963 by Col. Christophe SOGLO, who served as interim head of state until the election in January 1964 of Sourou-Migan APITHY. In December 1965, after a series of political crises and a general disruption of civilian government, Soglo again assumed power as president of a military-backed regime. Another military coup, led by Maj. Maurice KOUANDÉTÉ on December 17, 1967, ousted Soglo and established an interim regime under Lt. Col. Alphonse ALLEY. Following an abortive attempt at a new

implementation of a structural adjustment program in the mid-1990s had resulted in "real income growth, a decline in inflation, and a reduction in internal and external imbalances." In August 1999 the IMF approved the release of further economic credits to Benin, citing the government's commitment to maintaining a "stable macroeconomic framework" as one of the reasons for "robust" election in May 1968, the former foreign minister, Dr. Émile-Derlin ZINSOU, was appointed president of a civilian administration. In December 1969 the Zinsou government was overthrown by Kouandété, and military rule was reinstituted. After another failed election in March 1970, the military established a civilian regime based on the collective leadership (Presidential Council) of the country's three leading politicians: Justin AHOMADEGBE, Apithy, and Maga. On October 26, 1972, following an unsuccessful coup attempt by Kouandété in February, the triumvirate was overthrown by (then) Maj. Mathieu KÉRÉKOU. The new president abolished the Presidential Council and Consultative Assembly and established a Military Council of the Revolution committed to a division of posts on the basis of regional equality.

On December 3, 1974, President Kérékou declared that Dahomey was to become a "Marxist-Leninist state," and two days later he announced that the nation's banks, insurance companies, and oil distribution facilities would be nationalized. Subsequently, he ordered the establishment of "Defense of the Revolution Committees" in all businesses to "protect the revolution from sabotage." On November 30, 1975, the country was styled a "people's republic" (to reflect the ideology officially embraced a year earlier) and was renamed Benin, after an African kingdom that had flourished in the Gulf of Guinea in the 17th century. The Benin People's Revolutionary Party (*Parti de la Révolution Populaire du Bénin*—PRPB) was established as the nucleus of a one-party system the following month. In August 1977 a new basic law was promulgated to reflect a commitment to three stages of development: a "revolutionary national liberation movement," a "democratic people's revolution," and a "socialist revolution."

In January 1977 a group of mercenaries had been repulsed by government forces in a brief but pitched battle in Cotonou. A UN mission of inquiry subsequently reported that the invaders had been flown in from Gabon under the command of an adviser to Gabonese President Bongo. The incident provoked an angry exchange between Presidents Kérékou and Bongo at a summit of the Organization for African Unity (OAU) in July 1978, after

which Bongo ordered the expulsion of some 6,000 Benin nationals from Gabon. Most of the mercenaries as well as 11 Benin "traitors" (including former president Zinsou in absentia) were condemned to death in May 1979.

President Kérékou was redesignated for a five-year term as head of state and government on July 31, 1984, having launched a government austerity program that included the proposed privatization of many parastatal enterprises that had not responded to a recent campaign to improve efficiency and curtail corruption. Economic difficulties continued, however, forcing further cutbacks in government spending, which in turn precipitated serious university disturbances in mid-1985.

Unrest intensified among students, teachers, and civil servants in early 1989 as the government, facing a severe cash shortage, withheld scholarship and salary checks. The PRPB nonetheless maintained complete control of legislative balloting on June 18, the single list that was advanced being credited with 89.6 percent voter approval. Subsequently, on August 2, Kérékou, the sole candidate, was reelected to another five-year presidential term by a reported 192–2 assembly vote.

In response to continued difficulties that included damaging charges of official corruption and widespread opposition to an IMF-mandated structural adjustment program, the government convened an unprecedented joint session of the PRPB Central Committee, the National Revolutionary Assembly Standing Committee, and the National Executive Council (cabinet) in late 1989. That meeting followed the lead of Eastern-bloc countries by abandoning formal adherence to Marxism-Leninism. It also called for a national conference in early 1990 to consider constitutional reforms. The resultant National Conference of Active Forces of the Nation (*Conférence Nationale des Forces Vivres du Pays*) met on February 19–28, 1990. Assuming the unexpected posture of a "sovereign" body, the conference revoked the 1977 basic law, dropped the word "People's" from the country's official name, dissolved the existing legislature, and named Nicéphore SOGLO, a former World Bank official, as interim prime minister pending the formation of a "transitional government." Kérékou, after initially terming the proceedings a "civilian coup d'état," endorsed the conference's decisions and was designated to remain head of state with the defense portfolio (but not command of the armed forces) removed from his jurisdiction.

A 50-member High Council of the Republic (*Haut Conseil de la République*—HCR) was installed on March 9, 1990, to replace the former National Revolutionary Assembly; three days later a new government, containing no carryovers from the previous administration, was announced. In April the preliminary text of a new constitution providing for a multiparty system was submitted to the HCR. After being presented for public comment and revision, it was approved by a reported 80 percent of those participating in a December 2 referendum.

At parliamentary balloting on February 17, 1991, none of two dozen competing parties secured a majority, the leading party winning only 11 of 64 seats. Subsequently, at a second-round presidential poll on March 24, Prime Minister Soglo was elected president, defeating Kérékou, who became the first incumbent chief executive in mainland Africa to fail in a reelection bid. General Kérékou's decision to run for reelection had been unexpected, having been announced less than a month before the presidential balloting. In an unusual appeal to the electorate, he had asked "forgiveness" from those who had suffered from "deplorable and regrettable incidents" during his 17 years of military-Marxist rule. The transitional government, in one of its concluding actions, responded to the *mea culpa* by granting immunity to Kérékou for any crimes committed while in office.

Hindered by the lack of an assembly majority, the Soglo administration's first year was marked by legislative inaction interspersed by confrontations with assembly president and former presidential candidate Adrien HOUNGBÉDJI. In June 1992 President Soglo secured his first assembly majority when the progovernment legislative bloc, styled Renewal, was expanded from 21 to 34 deputies from ten different parties. However, on October 11, 1993, the administration was dealt a setback when 15 members of Renewal quit the group to form a new coalition styled the Independents, thus

shattering the president's 16-month-old legislative majority.

First results of the legislative election of March 28, 1995, showed opponents of the president with a majority of seats. After repolling in 13 constituencies on May 28, the opposition held a 16-seat advantage in the assembly.

On January 17, 1996, the assembly rejected the administration's 1996 budget, and, in response, Soglo issued an edict enacting the budget, insisting that failure to implement his plan would imperil approximately $500 million of international assistance. Shortly thereafter, former president Kérékou announced his intention to contest the presidential elections scheduled for March, alleging that the incumbent's economic policies had devastated Benin's poor. Kérékou joined a field of seven other contenders, including Soglo; former assembly president Houngbédji of the Party of Democratic Renewal (*Parti du Renouveau Démocratique*— PRD); and Bruno AMOUSSOU, Houngbédji's assembly successor and leader of the Social Democratic Party (*Parti Social-Démocrate*—PSD).

President Soglo secured a slim lead over Kérékou (35.69 percent to 33.94) in the first round of presidential balloting on March 3, 1996. However, both Houngbédji and Amoussou, third and fourth place finishers, respectively, urged their parties to support Kérékou, and at second-round balloting on March 18 the former president was returned to power with a vote share of 52.49 percent. On April 1 the Constitutional Court rejected Soglo's claim that he had been the victim of polling fraud and a "vast international plot," and on April 6 Kérékou was officially inaugurated. (An inaugural ceremony on April 4 had been ruled inadmissible because Kérékou had failed to recite the entire vow.) On April 8 the new president named an 18-member government headed by Houngbédji in the reestablished post of prime minister. Houngbédji's PRD controlled the most cabinet portfolios, with four, while Amoussou's PSD was second, with three.

In early May 1998 Kérékou met with the leaders of a number of small opposition parties and reportedly pledged to increase their representation in his government. On May 8 Prime Minister Houngbédji and his PRD colleagues quit the government amid speculation that they were about to be demoted in a cabinet reshuffling. Six days later the president named a new government that did not include a prime minister.

At legislative balloting on March 30, 1999, opponents of the president, led by Soglo's Benin Renaissance Party (*Parti de la Renaissance du Bénin*—PRB) and the PRD, captured a one-seat majority (42 to 41) in the assembly. (The PRB, PRD, and their allies performed well in the pivotal capital region, while supporters of President Kérékou dominated balloting in the north.) Confronted with a choice between assuming their newly won legislative seats or remaining in the government, six legislators-elect subsequently quit their cabinet posts. On June 22 Kérékou named a new government that included representatives from ten presidential-supportive parties (up from seven). The PSD controlled the most posts (four), followed by the Action Front for Renewal and Development-Alafia (*Front Action pour la Renouvellement et le Développement-Alafia*—FARD-Alafia), which assumed two. No opposition members were included in the cabinet.

Seventeen candidates contested the first round of presidential balloting on March 4, 2001, with Kérékou finishing first with 45 percent of the vote, followed by Soglo (27 percent), Houngbédji (13 percent), and Amoussou (8 percent). However, Soglo challenged the results of the first round and refused to participate in the runoff, as did Houngbédji. Consequently, the balloting on March 22 pitted Kérékou against Amoussou, with the president easily winning another term by an 84–16 percent vote.

Significant economic growth and increased political stability appeared to solidify Kérékou's popularity prior to the March 30, 2003, National Assembly balloting, at which pro-presidential parties won 52 of 83 seats. Kérékou replaced about half the ministers in a June reshuffle, but he again declined to appoint a prime minister.

In the first round of presidential balloting on March 5, 2006, Boni YAYI, a prominent economist and regional banking executive, led 26 candidates

with 35.6 percent of the vote. He was followed by Houngbédji (24 percent), Amoussou (15.3 percent), and Léhady Soglo (the son of former president Soglo), who secured 8.5 percent of the vote. Yayi scored a landslide victory over Houngbédji in the runoff on March 19 with 75 percent of the vote. The new cabinet, appointed on April 8, comprised a number of technocrats, although the PSD and PRB also were reportedly represented.

Constitution and Government

The Marxist-inspired *Loi Fondamentale* of 1977 was rescinded in February 1990 by the National Conference, which authorized the formation of the High Council of the Republic (HCR) to exercise legislative power during the transition to a new regime. The constitution approved by referendum on December 2, 1990, instituted a multiparty presidential system headed by an executive elected for a five-year, once-renewable term, with National Assembly deputies serving four-year terms. (Presidential candidates must be between 40 and 70 years of age and have been a citizen for 10 years.) The new basic law also provided for a Constitutional Court, a Supreme Court, a High Court of Justice, an Economic and Social Council, and an Audiovisual Authority.

The country is divided into 12 provinces (6 prior to 1997), which are subdivided into 86 districts and 510 communes. Local administration is assigned to elected provincial, district, town, and village councils.

Foreign Relations

Throughout the Cold War era Benin adhered to a nonaligned posture, maintaining relations with a variety of both Communist and Western governments. Traditionally strong military and economic ties with France were reaffirmed during meetings in 1981 and 1983 between Presidents Kérékou and Mitterrand, following a revision of treaty relations in 1975.

Although its early regional links were primarily with other francophone states, Benin later sought to consolidate its interests with the broader African community. Relations with Lagos, initially strained by Nigeria's expulsion of foreign workers in the mid-1980s, subsequently improved to the point that Kérékou felt obliged in July 1990 to deny rumors that Benin was to become Nigeria's 22nd state.

Benin has been a strong supporter of multilateral development through the Economic Community of West African States, while bilateral ventures have been initiated with Ghana, Mauritania, and Togo. However, in early 1993 Benin's border with Togo was temporarily closed following an alleged attack on the private residence of Togo's President Eyadéma, although the rebels escaped into Ghana. By late March some 70–150 Togolese officers had reportedly arrived in Porto Novo claiming they were fleeing a purge of army personnel.

In March 1996 Nigeria closed its border with Benin, alleging that Porto Novo had failed to give notice prior to its own recent election-day closures and accusing Benin's security forces of illegal crossings. However, the border was reopened and relations smoothed when newly elected president Kérékou and his Nigerian counterpart, Gen. Sani Abacha, signed a cooperation agreement in April. Subsequent trade between the two countries allegedly occurred primarily in the "informal sector dominated by smuggling and unrecorded business," and in early 2000 Nigeria urged Benin to remove the remaining "obstacles to free trade."

A confrontation developed between Benin and Niger in mid-2000 over Lété and some 25 other islands in the Niger River, where sovereignty has been disputed for four decades. In April 2002 the two countries agreed to submit the case to the International Court of Justice, although the two countries in June had reached a tentative agreement to redraw the border to settle other disputes. Improved relations also were apparent in the initiation of joint border patrols and an agreement among Benin, Ghana, Nigeria, and Togo to build an oil pipeline through their countries. On a negative regional note, Chad severed economic ties with Benin in 2003 after Benin's government granted asylum to a group of exiled Chadian opposition figures.

Relations between Benin and the United States underwent a dramatic improvement in 2003 when the two countries agreed to cooperate on security and military issues. (The United States also announced more than $300 million in aid in early 2006 for port rehabilitation and the promotion of small businesses.) Benin also has recently become more involved in regional security, participating in several recent regional peacekeeping missions, including those in the Democratic Republic of the Congo, Liberia, and Côte d'Ivoire.

In July 2005 the ICJ allocated Lété (the most important of the disputed islands) to Niger, along with 15 of the other 25 islands. Also in 2005, Nigeria agreed to cede seven villages along its disputed border with Benin to Benin; collaterally, Benin ceded three villages to Nigeria. Meanwhile, a border dispute resurfaced between Benin and Burkina Faso, with Benin claiming sovereignty over territory beyond the Pendjari River. Burkina Faso contended the river constituted the border.

Current Issues

Supporters of the president appeared to win about 50 percent of the seats in the local elections of December 2002 and January 2003, the country's continuing north–south split remaining apparent in opposition mayoral victories in Cotonou (by former president Soglo of the PRB) and in Porto Nova (by former assembly president Houngbédji of the PRD). However, the Kérékou camp broke through the long-standing 50–50 electoral stalemate by winning 52 of 83 seats in the March 2003 assembly balloting, which marked the first time since 1990 that a president could count on a solid legislative majority.

Some observers worried that President Kérékou (constitutionally precluded from seeking a third term in 2006) might attempt to extend his tenure, particularly when he announced that the government did not have sufficient funds to conduct the March balloting. However, Kérékou ultimately accepted a peaceful democratic transition, resisting (apparently under heavy European pressure) the "temptation" to which a number of West

African leaders had recently succumbed to remain in power through heavy-handed measures. With both Kérékou (Benin's leader for 28 of the last 33 years) and Soglo (precluded from another presidential bid because of his age) out of the picture, the campaign drew 26 hopefuls, including a number of independents who apparently believed that the electorate was ready to move beyond oldtime politics and concentrate on the troubled economy. Among the independents was Boni YAYI, who recently had resigned after 12 years as head of the West African Development Bank. The political newcomer pledged to combat corruption, promote small- and medium-sized businesses (particularly in the food-processing sector), and increase budget allocations for education and youth employment programs. His landslide victory also was attributed in part to the fact that he was of mixed tribal descent, had been born in the country's "middle belt," and was a Christian from a predominantly Muslim family, which helped him bridge the ethnic, geographic, and religious divides so prevalent in previous elections. In addition, Yayi, an economic advisor in the Soglo administration in the early 1990s, was viewed as a "modernizer" whose regional contacts would prove useful in helping Benin to deal with its "economically aggressive" neighbors (most notably Nigeria).

Among other things, the 2006 presidential results were seen as a severe blow to the traditional political class. Perhaps as part of an effort by traditional power-brokers to recover some of their lost influence, the assembly in June 2006 extended its term from 2007 to 2008, ostensibly to permit joint national and municipal balloting and thereby save budget resources.

Political Parties

On April 30, 1990, at the conclusion of a closed-door congress at Cotonou, the ruling Benin People's Revolutionary Party (*Parti de la Révolution Populaire du Bénin*—PRPB) voted to dissolve itself. The PRPB had been the country's only authorized political formation from its December 1975 founding until installation of the Soglo government in March 1990. Delegates to the congress approved the launching of a new grouping, the Union of the Forces of Progress, to replace the PRPB.

By 2002 there were reportedly more than 160 registered parties, a total that, according to a number of Benin's political observers, presented a hindrance to political development. A number of parties and civic organizations that supported President Kérékou formed the Union for the Benin of the Future (*Union pour le Bénin du Futur*—UBF), which served as the core component of the Presidential Movement (*Mouvement Présidential*—MP) that dominated the 2003 legislative balloting. Included in the UBF were the PSD, RDL-Vivoten, FARD-Alafia, and NCC. It was reported that some 120 groups supported the MP. Subsequently, the UBF, under the leadership of Joseph GANAHO, reported in late 2004 that a number of small parties had disbanded and merged into the UBF. However, references to the UBF ceased in late 2005 as it became clear that the Kérékou government was coming to an end.

The formation of the Coordination of Political Forces for 2006 was announced in early 2005 by some ten "propresidential" parties and groups. The leader of the alliance, Idrissou IBRAHIMA, secured less than 1 percent of the vote in the first round of the 2006 presidential balloting.

Social Democratic Party (*Parti Social-Démocrate*—PSD). In June 1995 the PSD's leader and former presidential candidate, Bruno Amoussou, captured the assembly presidency. Thereafter, in March 1996 Amoussou failed to advance beyond the first round of presidential balloting; however, for rallying behind Mathieu Kérékou, the PSD was awarded cabinet posts in April.

At a party congress on January 29–31, 2000, PSD delegates elected Amoussou chair of a new 19-member National Executive Committee. Amoussou, described by *Africa Confidential* as a "kingmaker" for his role in the 1996 election and strongly positioned in the cabinet, enjoyed solid backing in portions of southern Benin.

Amoussou finished third in the first round of the 2006 presidential election with 15.3 percent of the vote as a candidate of an alliance of parties. The alliance supported Boni Yayi in the second round and reportedly secured four seats (two for the PSD) in Yayi's new cabinet.

Leaders: Bruno AMOUSSOU (Coordinator and 2006 presidential candidate), Felix ADIMI (First Vice Chair of the National Executive Committee), Emmanuel GOLOU (Parliamentary Leader).

Party of Democratic Renewal (*Parti du Renouveau Démocratique*—PRD). Led by (then) National Assembly president Adrien Houngbédji, the PRD won 9 legislative seats in 1991 and 19 in 1995, its support centering in the south around Porto Novo. Houngbédji finished third in the first round of presidential balloting in March 1996 with 18.72 percent of the vote. Subsequently, the PRD's support proved pivotal to Mathieu Kérékou in the second round of balloting, and the new president rewarded the party by appointing Houngbédji as prime minister and naming four other PRD members to his new cabinet.

In May 1998 Houngbédji and his PRD colleagues resigned from the government amid reports that the president was preparing to demote them in a cabinet reshuffling. The PRD was subsequently allied with a number of other parties in an anti-Kérékou coalition as of mid-2000. However, the groups were unable to agree on a joint presidential candidate for 2001. In February 2003 Houngbédji was elected mayor of Porto Nova, but he lost the assembly president's position in April 2003. He finished second to Boni Yayi in the 2006 presidential runoff with 25 percent of the vote.

Leader: Adrien HOUNGBÉDJI (Former President of the National Assembly, Former Prime Minister, and 2006 presidential candidate).

Benin Renaissance Party (*Parti de la Renaissance du Bénin*—PRB). The PRB was founded in March 1992 by Rosine Soglo, the wife of (then) President Nicéphore Soglo. In July 1993 President Soglo announced his intention to "come down into the arena" to help the PRB serve as a "catalyst" for Benin's democracy movement, and in July 1994 he assumed leadership of the party. On October 1, 1994, the PRB absorbed the small Pan-African Union of Democracy and Solidarity (*Union Panafricaine de la Démocratie et la Solidarité*—UPDS), but it managed to gain only 20 of 83 legislative seats in two rounds of balloting in March and May 1995.

Among the reasons cited for Soglo's electoral defeat in 1996 was his increasing reliance on a small circle of family members and the exclusion of the supporters who had helped him capture the presidency. Furthermore, his followers' strident attacks on Kérékou were described as having backfired on Soglo's campaign.

In August 1998 PRB dissidents led by Nicolas TCHOTCHONE left the party and formed the **African Movement for Development and Integration** (*Mouvement Africain pour le Développement et l'Intégration*—MADI), with Tchotchone calling for the establishment of a "new economic and political order."

In February 2003 Nicéphore Soglo was elected mayor of Cotonou. After the March 2003 elections, the PRB became the largest opposition party, with 15 seats.

With Nicéphore Soglo unable to run because of his age (over 70), the PRB presented his son, Léhady Soglo, as its 2006 presidential candidate. Léhady Soglo finished fourth in the first round of balloting with 8.5 percent of the vote. The PRB was reportedly given one seat in the new cabinet formed by President Boni Yayi following the election.

Leaders: Nicéphore SOGLO (President of the Party, Former President of the Republic, and 2001 presidential candidate), Léhady SOGLO (Deputy Major of Cotonou and 2006 presidential candidate), Rosine SOGLO (Chair).

Rally of Liberal Democrats for National Reconstruction (*Rassemblement des Démocrates Libéraux pour la Reconstruction Nationale*—RDL-Vivoten). Led by Séverin Adjovi, an advocate for the reelection of former president Kérékou, the RDL-Vivoten secured three seats at legislative balloting in 1995. Adjovi served as minister of defense from 1996 to May 1998, at which time he was named minister of communications, culture, and information.

At legislative balloting in 1999 the RDL-Vivoten reportedly campaigned along with four other groups under the banner of the **Movement for Citizens' Commitment and Awakening** (*Mouvement pour l'Engagement et le Réveil des Citoyens*—MERCI).

Adjovi secured 1.8 percent of the vote in the first round of presidential balloting in 2006.

Leader: Sévérin ADJOVI (2006 presidential candidate).

Action Front for Renewal and Development-Alafia (*Front Action pour la Renouvellement et le Développement-Alafia*—FARD-Alafia). At its launching in 1994 as a self-described "national unity party," FARD-Alafia claimed to control five National Assembly seats, which increased to ten in 1995.

In September 1995 FARD-Alafia's leader, Dr. Alafia Saka Saley, called for a grassroots campaign to persuade former president Kérékou to compete in the 1996 presidential elections. At a party congress in April 1997 Saka Kina captured the secretary general's post, succeeding Saley. In addition, a 25-member Bureau was created to handle administrative functions.

In June 1998 FARD-Alafia suffered the defection of parliamentarians who were subsequently reported to have formed a new grouping, the Car-DUNYA (below).

Leaders: Jerome Saka KINA (Secretary General), Dr. Alafia Saka SALEY.

Our Common Cause (*Notre Cause Commune*—NCC). The NCC was founded as a vehicle for the presidential ambitions of Albert Tévoédjré, a former deputy director of the International Labour Organisation. Formally registered as a separate party, the NCC won six assembly seats in February 1991, with its leader placing third in the March presidential contest.

In November 1995 the NCC announced its support of former president Kérékou in the upcoming presidential campaign, surprising some observers at the pairing of the northern military leader with Tévoédjre, a purportedly "radical" southerner. In

April 1996 Kérékou named Tévoédjre to his new government.

In late March 1997 a group of NCC dissidents, including Vice Chair Gratien Pognon, attempted to remove Tévoédjre from the party chairmanship. Accusing Tévoédjre of "single-handedly" controlling the party, the dissidents elected François Tankpinou as the new chair. However, the legality of their efforts was immediately challenged by Tévoédjre, who argued that the steering committee voting for his dismissal had lacked a quorum. Subsequent reports regularly referenced Tankpinou as the NCC chair, however.

Leader: François TANKPINOU (Chair).

African Movement for Democracy and Progress (*Mouvement Africain pour la Démocratie et le Progrès*—MADEP). Led by Séfou Fagbohoun, a wealthy businessman, the MADEP captured six seats in the 1999 legislative elections and in 2003 became the second-largest pro-presidential party, after the UBF. The MADEP's Antoine Idji Kolawolé finished fifth in the first round of the 2006 presidential poll with 3.25 percent of the vote.

Leaders: Séfou FAGBOHOUN (Chair), Antoine Idji KOLAWOLÉ (Speaker of the National Assembly).

Alliance (*Alliance*). The Alliance was a grouping of three propresidential parties formed prior to the 2003 legislative elections. The component parties were the **Congress of the People for Progress** (*Congrès du Peuple pour le Progrès*—CPP), led by Sédégnon ADANDE-KINTI; the **Movement for Development Through Culture** (*Mouvement pour le Développement par Culture*—MDC), led by Codjo ACHODE; and the **Party of the Beginning** (*Parti du Salut*—PS), led by Damien Alahassa.

Leader: Damien ALAHASSA.

Star Alliance (*Alliance Etoile*—AE). A platform for northern political figures, the AE includes the **Greens** (*Les Verts*); and the **Union for Democracy and National Solidarity** (*Union pour la Démocratie et la Solidarité Nationale*—UDSN), led by Adamou N'DIAYE. The AE secured four

Cabinet

As of September 1, 2006

President	Boni Yayi

Ministers

Administrative and Institutional Reform	Bio Gounou Idrissou Sina
Agriculture, Husbandry, and Fisheries	Cossi Gaston Dossouhoui
Development, Economy, and Finance	Pascal Irénée Koupaki
Culture, Sports, and Leisure	Théophile Montcho
Environment	Jean-Pierre Babatoundé
Family, Women's Affairs, and Children's Affairs	Guécadou Bawa Yorou Orou Guidou [f]
Foreign Affairs	Mariam Aladji Boni Diallo [f]
Health	Flore Gangbo [f]
Higher Education and Professional Formations	Mathurin Nago
Industry and Commerce	Moudjaïdou Issifou Soumanou
Justice (In Charge of Relations with Institutions)	Abraham Zinzindohoué
Labor and Public Affairs	Emmanuel Tiando
Mines, Energy, and Water Resources	Jocelyn Dégbè
National Defense	Issifou Kogui Nduro
Primary and Secondary Education	Colette Houeto [f]
Public Security and Local Collectives	Edgard Charlemagne Alia
Tourism and Handicrafts	Soumanou Toleba

Ministers Delegate

African Integration and Beninois Abroad	Albert Agossou
Budget	Albert Sègbégnon Houngbo
Communication and New Technologies	Venance Gnigla
Microfinance and Promotion of Small and Medium-Sized Enterprises	Sakinatou Abdou Alfa Orou Sidi [f]

[f] = female

seats in the March 1999 poll, and thereafter an AE representative was named to the cabinet. The AE backed an opponent of the PSD's Amoussou in a contest for the assembly presidency and was subsequently excluded from the government named in June 1999. In the 2003 elections, the AE won three seats.

Leader: Sacca LAFIA (Chair and Parliamentary Leader).

New Alliance (*Nouvelle Alliance*—NA). Led by Soulé Dankoro, the NA won two seats in the 2003 legislative elections. Dankoro won less than 1 percent of the vote in the first round of the 2006 presidential balloting.

Leader: Soulé DANKORO.

Car-DUNYA. The Car-DUNYA was formed in 1998 by eight assembly members who theretofore represented FARD-Alafia. At legislative balloting in 1999 three of the eight defectors retained their seats, and thereafter it was reported that efforts were being made to reconcile the two groups, with the goal of merging their memberships.

However, the Car-DUNYA was excluded from the government named in June 1999 after its legislators backed an opponent of the PSD's Amoussou in a contest for the assembly's top post.

Leader: Saka SALEY.

Communist Party of Benin (*Parti Communiste du Bénin*—PCB). Founded in 1977 as the Communist Party of Dahomey (*Parti Communiste du Dahomey*—PCD) and secretly functioning for the next 12 years as the sole opposition party, the PCB filed for legal recognition in early June 1993. In 1990 the party had boycotted the National Conference, labeling it a "plot between French imperialism and its Beninois lackeys."

Theretofore in opposition, the PCB allied itself with propresidential forces in May 1995, and at first-round presidential balloting in March 1996 PCB First Secretary Pascal Fatondji secured 1.3 percent of the vote. The PCB called for a boycott of the 2001 presidential balloting.

Leader: Pascal FATONDJI (First Secretary and 1996 presidential candidate).

Marxist-Leninist Communist Party of Benin (*Parti Communiste et Marxiste-Léniniste du Bénin*—PCMLB). The PCMLB was launched in early 1999 by dissident members of the PCB.

Leader: Magliore YANSUNNU.

Other groups allied with the President Kérékou prior to his retirement in 2006 included the **Alliance for Democracy and Progress** (*Alliance pour la Démocratie et le Progrès*—ADP), led by Sylvain Adekpedjou AKINDES; the **Alliance for Forces of Progress** (*Alliance des Forces du Progrès*—AFP), led by Valentin Aditi HOUDE; the **Chameleon Alliance** (*Alliance Caméléon*—AC); the **Key Force** (*Force Clé*—FC); the **Impulse for Progress and Democracy** (*Impulsion pour le Progrès et la Démocratie*—IPD), led by Théophile NATA; the **Movement for Development and Solidarity** (*Mouvement pour le Développement et la Solidarité*—MDS); the **Rally for Democracy and Progress** (*Rassemblement pour la Démocratie et le Progrès*—RDP); the **Rally for the Nation** (*Rassemblement pour la Nation*—RPN), led by De

Sodji Zanclan ABEO; and the **Together Party.** At legislative balloting in 2003, the AFP, FC, IPD, MDS, and RDP all captured seats.

The **African Congress for Democracy** (*Congrès Africain pour la Démocratie*—CAD) presented Lionel Jacques AGBO as its presidential candidate in 2006. The candidate of the **Rally of Liberal Democrats-Heviosso** (*Rassemblement des Démocrats Libéraux-Heviosso*) was Leandre DJAGOUE. Agbo and Djagoue each received less than 1 percent of the vote in the first round. Meanwhile, the candidate of the **Movement for an Alternative for the People**, Lazare SÉHOUÉTO, finished sixth in the first round with 2.1 percent of the vote.

Legislature

National Assembly (*Assemblée National*). Benin's unicameral legislature currently includes 83 deputies serving four-year terms and elected by party-list proportional representation in 24 constituencies. At the most recent election of March 30, 2003, the Presidential Movement coalition, which supported President Kérékou, won 52 seats (Union for the Benin of the Future, 31 seats; African Movement for Democracy and Progress, 9; Key Force, 5; Impulse for Progress and Democracy, 2; Alliance, 2; Alliance for Forces of Progress, 1; Movement for Development and Solidarity, 1; and Rally for Democracy and Progress, 1). Opposition parties gained 31 seats (Benin Renaissance Party, 15; Party of Democratic Renewal, 11; Star Alliance, 3; New Alliance, 2).

President: Antoine Idji KOLAWOLÉ.

Communications

Press

Press freedoms in Benin are considered among the most liberal in Africa. More than a dozen new press organs commenced publication in 1990, following abandonment of the prior censorship that had been imposed by the Kérékou regime. *Le Matin,* an independent daily, was launched in May

1994, and in August 1997 *Le Point Au Quotidien*, another independent daily, was founded. Other current publications include *La Nation* (4,000), government daily; *Le Matinal* (5,000), government daily; *L'Autre Quotidien; Les Echos du Jour* (3,000), independent daily; *Le Pointau Quotidien* (2,000), independent daily; *L'Aurore* (1,500); *Le Béninois; La Dépêche du Soir; Le Progrès; L'Oeil du Peuple; Fraternité; La Nouvelle Tribune; Le Soleil;* and *Le Nouvel Espoir.*

News Agency

The *Agence Bénin-Presse* operates as a section of the Ministry of Information.

Broadcasting and Computing

The government's *Office de Radio-diffusion et de Télévision du Bénin* broadcasts in French, English, and a number of indigenous languages throughout the country. There were approximately 301,000 television receivers and 26,000 personal computers, serving 70,000 Internet users in 2003.

Intergovernmental Representation

Ambassador to the U.S.
Segbe Cyrille OGUIN

U.S. Ambassador to Benin
Wayne E. NEILL

Permanent Representative to the UN
Simon Bodéhoussé IDOHOU

IGO Memberships (Non-UN)
AfDB, AU, BADEA, BOAD, CENT, ECOWAS, IDB, Interpol, IOM, NAM, OIC, OIF, PCA, UEMOA, WCO, WTO

BOTSWANA

REPUBLIC OF BOTSWANA

The Country

Landlocked Botswana, the former British protectorate of Bechuanaland, embraces a substantial area of desert, swamp, and scrubland situated on a high plateau in the heart of southern Africa. The country is bordered on the west by Namibia, on the south by South Africa, and on the northeast by Zimbabwe, with a narrow strip adjacent to Zambia in the north. The population is divided into eight main tribal groups, the largest of which is the Bamangwato (including an estimated 39,000 "San," or "bushmen," only 3,000 of whom continue to live in traditional nomadic fashion in the Kalahari desert). A majority of the people follow ancestral religious practices, but about 15 percent are Christian. Due in part to the large-scale employment of males in neighboring South African mines, 80 percent of households are headed by women who, however, cannot hold land title or control their crops, and therefore are denied access to funds and equipment under rural development programs. Female representation among senior officials has been limited.

At the time of independence Botswana was one of the world's poorest countries, dependent on stock-raising for much of its income because of an extremely dry climate that made large-scale farming difficult. Subsequent mineral discoveries initiated economic growth and raised per capita GNP to $2,980 in 2002. Botswana is one of the world's largest producers of diamonds, exports of which provide 75 percent of foreign exchange, 60 percent of government revenue, and 30 percent of gross domestic product. While extractive activity (also involving copper-nickel matte and coal) has yielded infrastructural gains, food production has

remained a problem. Although a large majority of the work force is involved in subsistence agriculture, the largely barren soil has led to a dependence on imported food that is only slowly being overcome. The government's free-enterprise orientation and conservative monetary policies have attracted substantial foreign aid. Meanwhile, the lucrative diamond industry has enabled the government to amass large financial reserves, although international advisers have called for diversification in order to insulate the economy from fluctuations in global demand for diamonds. In response, the government has created the International Financial Services Center (IFSC), which has launched a number of projects to attract foreign investment and companies.

Political Status: Independent republic within the Commonwealth since September 30, 1966.

Area: 231,804 sq. mi. (600,372 sq. km.).

Population: 1,680,863 (2001C); 1,815,000 (2005E).

Major Urban Centers (2005E): GABORONE (213,000), Francistown (91,000), Molepolole (64,000), Selebi-Pikwe (54,000).

Official Language: English (SeTswana is widely spoken).

Monetary Unit: Pula (official rate July 1, 2006: 6.02 pula = $1US).

President: Festus MOGAE (Botswana Democratic Party); sworn in on April 1, 1998, to succeed Sir Ketumile Joni MASIRE (Botswana Democratic Party), who had resigned the previous day; sworn in for a five-year term on October 20, 1999, following the legislative election of October 16; sworn in for another five-year term on November 1, 2004, following legislative election of October 30.

Vice President: Lt. Gen. (Ret.) Seretse Ian KHAMA (Botswana Democratic Party); appointed by the president on July 13, 1998, to succeed Festus MOGAE (Botswana Democratic Party), who had been elevated to the presidency on April 1; reappointed by the president on October 21, 1999; reappointed by the president on November 8, 2004.

Current government programs focus on agricultural improvements, educational expansion, the promotion of tourism, revitalization of the public sector, and efforts to promote investment in the private sector in the hope that diversification would counteract growing unemployment (20 percent in 1999) among unskilled workers. Real GDP growth averaged nearly 8.5 percent annually from 1980 through mid-1998, slowed (primarily due to decreased diamond exports) to 4 percent in the 1998–1999 fiscal year, and rebounded to 7.6 percent in 1999–2000. In 2002 the government launched a series of privatization programs in the telecommunications and public utilities sectors. In 2003 GDP growth was 5.4 percent, while inflation increased to 9.3 percent. Inflation has recently averaged about 8 percent annually, while unemployment has remained at 15 percent despite the government's stimulus initiatives. GDP growth in 2004 declined to 4.6 percent. According to the IMF, real GDP growth in 2005 was 3.8 percent and similar growth was expected in 2006.

Government and Politics

Political Background

A British protectorate from 1885, Botswana achieved independence within the Commonwealth on September 30, 1966, under the leadership of Sir Seretse KHAMA and has subsequently been regarded as a showplace of democracy in Africa. Following the National Assembly election of October 20, 1979, at which his Botswana Democratic Party (BDP) won 29 of 32 elective seats, President Khama was given a fourth five-year mandate. His death on July 13, 1980, led to the selection of Ketumile Joni MASIRE, vice president and minister of finance and development planning, to fill the remainder of the presidential term. Both Masire and Vice President Peter S. MMUSI were reappointed following the legislative election of September 8, 1984. However, the opposition Botswana National Front (BNF) showed surprising strength (20.2 percent) in that election and in simultaneous municipal balloting. At the election of October 7, 1989, the BNF vote share increased further to 26.9 percent (as contrasted with 64.8 percent for the BDP), although its representation fell from five (after a December by-election) to three. Presenting himself as the sole candidate, President Masire was reconfirmed by the Assembly and sworn in for a third term on October 10. On March 8, 1992, Mmusi, under pressure for alleged corruption, resigned the vice presidency in favor of Festus MOGAE, who retained his existing position as finance minister.

On May 12, 1993, representatives of the BDP, BNF, and four other parties met at Francistown to debate a recently released BNF proposal for electoral reform that included calls for the establishment of a multipartisan electoral commission to replace the existing presidentially appointed body and a lowering of the voting age from 21 to 18. Rebuffed by the government, the BNF declared six months later that it had tentatively decided to boycott the next election. Subsequently, however, it reversed itself, winning 13 legislative seats (to the BDP's 26) at the balloting of October 15, 1994. While the BDP's majority was sufficient to ensure the capture of all four nominated seats following President Masire's election to a third full term, the party's 53.1 vote share was the lowest in its 28 years of rule.

The unexpected gains of the BNF in 1994 were achieved despite rejection by the High Court at Lobatse of an opposition demand that the poll be canceled because of electoral roll deficiencies that allegedly favored the BDP. Contributing to the reduction in the BDF's majority were a series of corruption scandals, economic recession (triggered by declining diamond production and virtual collapse of the construction industry), and rising unemployment within a rapidly expanding urban population. Tensions generated by this combination erupted into serious antigovernment rioting at Gaborone in February 1995.

In late 1997 President Masire announced his intention to resign as head of state on March 31, 1998, and endorsed the succession of Vice President Mogae. Masire resigned as scheduled at an official ceremony that coincided with the conclusion of U.S. President Bill Clinton's visit to Botswana. On April 1 Mogae was inaugurated, and he announced the formation of a new cabinet on the same day. Two days later the new president nominated Lt. Gen. (Ret.) Seretse Ian KHAMA, son of Botswana's first president, to be his vice president. Khama, who had resigned from the military on March 31 to accept an appointment as minister of presidential affairs and public administration, captured a legislative by-election victory on July 6 (assembly membership being a prerequisite for the vice presidential slot) and, following assembly approval, assumed his new post on July 13. At new legislative balloting on October 16, 1999, the BDP secured 33 of 40 elective seats, and Mogae was consequently sworn in for a five-year presidential term. Mogae

announced a new cabinet on October 21, retaining Khama as vice president (and thereby the heir apparent as the next BDP presidential contender).

The BDP maintained its legislative dominance at the October 2004 assembly balloting, and President Mogae was sworn in for another five-year term on November 1.

Constitution and Government

The 1966 constitution provides for a president who serves as head of state and government, a Parliament consisting of a National Assembly and a consultative House of Chiefs, and a judicial structure embracing a High Court, a Court of Appeal, and a Magistrate's Court in each district. The National Assembly currently encompasses 57 directly elected members, who vote on four additional nominated members. Sitting as an electoral college, the assembly elects the president for a term coincident with its own. (In August 1997 the assembly approved by two-thirds majority a bill limiting the president to two five-year terms.) The House of Chiefs acts as a consultative body on matters of native law, customs, and land, and also deliberates on constitutional amendments. The president can delay for up to six months, but not veto, legislation.

In June 1996 the government accepted opposition demands for an independent electoral commission and agreed to consider lowering the voting age from 21 to 18 and granting proxy votes to Botswanans living abroad. The latter two measures, in addition to a bill designating the vice president as the president's successor, were approved by popular referendum in October 1997.

At the local level, Botswana is divided into nine districts and five towns, all governed by councils. Chiefs head five of the district councils, elected leaders the remaining four. The districts impose personal income taxes to generate revenue, the local funding being supplemented by central government grants.

Foreign Relations

Although generally pro-Western in outlook, Botswana belongs to the Nonaligned Movement and has consistently maintained diplomatic relations with members of the former Soviet bloc as well as with the People's Republic of China. Botswana's relations with South Africa, its major trading partner and the employer of over half its nonagricultural work force, have been problematic. While avoiding official contacts with Pretoria and participating as one of the six Front-Line States (also including Angola, Mozambique, Tanzania, Zambia, and Zimbabwe) opposing minority rule in southern Africa, it attempted to maintain peaceful coexistence with its neighbor prior to the abandonment of apartheid. Tensions heightened in 1985, however, when South African Defense Forces (SADF) mounted a cross-border attack on alleged havens for the African National Congress (ANC), killing 15 people. Botswana subsequently vowed not to condone any "terrorist activity" from its territory and forced numerous ANC adherents to leave the country. Nonetheless, the SADF conducted another raid near Gaborone in May 1986, prompting the Masire government to inform the other Front-Line States that it "would not stand in the way" of those who might wish to initiate economic sanctions against South Africa. Despite its denunciation of three more SADF raids, Gaborone announced a joint Botswanan/South African resource development project in 1988, further underlining what critics termed Botswana's contradictory position as a member of both the South African Customs Union (SACU) and the anti-apartheid South African Development Coordination Conference (SADCC, subsequently the Southern African Development Community—SADC), whose headquarters were in Gaborone.

In 1992 the Namibian government, under pressure from opposition politicians to clearly demarcate its borders, claimed a small island in the Chobe river that had previously been assumed to be part of Botswana. In late 1993, following a series of minor encounters in the area, a team of specialists was appointed to resolve the dispute. With no settlement ensuing, the two sides signed an agreement in February 1996 providing for the dispute to be submitted to the International Court of Justice (ICJ), whose ruling would be accepted as binding.

Meanwhile, tension had also been generated by work on a multimillion-dollar air base some 40 miles from Gaborone, and in April 1996 Botswana confirmed that it was purchasing substantial quantities of sophisticated weaponry from various countries. As the only neighbor with an unresolved territorial dispute with Botswana, Namibia voiced particular concern at the buildup. However, the Botswanan government contended that the purchases met legitimate defense requirements.

Under the aegis of the Namibian and Botswanan Joint Commission on Defense and Security, an accord was reached in May 1998 with both countries reportedly agreeing to resolve border disputes through diplomatic solutions. In late 1999 the territorial dispute was resolved when the ICJ ruled in favor of Botswana.

In 2002 Botswana and Namibia agreed to the repatriation of some 2,000 Namibian refugees in Botswana, while in 2003 the two countries established an eight-member commission to begin final demarcation of the border. The reported influx of some 100,000 refugees from Zimbabwe led the Botswanan government in 2004 to enact a number of measures, including the erection of an electric fence in some areas, designed to increase border security.

Current Issues

The run-up to the October 1999 elections proved embarrassing for the administration and electoral officials as a brief state of emergency was required to complete sufficient voter registration and chaos surrounded the validation of candidates. However, the recent splintering of the BNF (see Political Parties, below) precluded effective opposition to the BDP, especially when the rump BNF failed to reach an agreement with the new Botswana Alliance Movement (BAM). Following the election, President Mogae pledged that the government would continue the defense buildup of recent years while also addressing the problems of burgeoning unemployment among young people and the AIDS epidemic. (It was estimated that at least 30 percent of the nation's young adults were infected with the

AIDS virus, and life expectancy had fallen from 60 in 1990 to 47 in 1999 because of related deaths.)

Attention in 2001 was focused on the "land invasion" crisis in neighboring Zimbabwe (see article on Zimbabwe), negative publicity in the matter having adversely affected tourism in Botswana. President Mogae was among the leaders of several nations who pressured Zimbabwean President Mugabe to accede to the "rule of law" regarding land ownership in order to calm the turmoil. Mogae also attempted to facilitate a resolution to the civil war in the Democratic Republic of the Congo, which had contributed to an intensified campaign by nongovernmental organizations to convince potential diamond buyers to avoid gems emanating from areas of conflict. Among other things, the government feared that legitimate producers, such as those in Botswana, were being unfairly penalized by the antidiamond initiative. Meanwhile, on the domestic front, a degree of ethnic tension, previously not considered a problem, arose in 2001, particularly in regard to the Kalangas, who make up only 10 percent of the population but reportedly hold a majority of judicial posts. A national referendum in November endorsed revision of judiciary regulations; changes included an increase in the retirement age. Critics of the measures argued they were designed to fortify the Kalanga judicial influence.

Since 2001, the government has been challenged by domestic and international critics of its decision to forcibly resettle the last remaining bushmen out of the Central Kalahari Game Reserve. Some observers charged that the government's relocation initiative was designed to permit expanded mining on the tribal lands. By 2005 some 3,000 bushmen had been relocated, although others had resisted the government's financial inducements and pressure tactics. In 2006 several early court cases against the government on behalf of some of the bushmen were still unresolved. With tensions escalating over this matter, amid allegations of police brutality and arrests of some bushmen on charges of illegal hunting practices, the government denied mistreating the bushmen, stating that the bushmen could practice their culture outside the reserve and explaining that those arrested were "using horses,

donkey, spears, and dogs" to kill animals inside the reserve.

On the political front, although the BDP won 44 of the 57 elected seats in the October 2004 assembly balloting, the BDP totals for 11 of those 44 seats were outnumbered by the combined totals of the votes for the BNF and the Botswana Congress Party (BCP). The possibility of an eventual chink in the BDP's armor was also raised by internal disputes within the ruling party (see below). Meanwhile, President Mogae said in early 2006 he would not to seek a third term. At the same time, he said he would not leave office early (despite much speculation to that effect). Mogae's insistence on remaining in office and the bushmen cases were seen as stumbling blocks to a scenario in which some observers outlined Vice President Khama's early ascension to the presidency in 2008.

Political Parties

Government Party

Botswana Democratic Party (BDP). Founded in 1962 as the Bechuanaland Democratic Party, the BDP has been the majority party since independence. It advocates self-development on a Western-type democratic basis, cooperation with all states, and multiracialism. In June 1984 the BDP's president, Sir Ketumile Joni Masire, announced measures to "democratize" party nominations through a revamped primary system. However, all candidates remained subject to approval by a central committee dominated by government ministers.

During a BDP congress in July 1993 divisions within the party widened when Peter Mmusi and Daniel Kwelagobe, both of whom had been forced to resign from the government in 1992 for alleged involvement in a land transaction scandal, were elected chair and secretary general, respectively, while traditional southern leaders failed to secure leadership positions. Immediately thereafter, the Mmusi/Kwelagobe faction was reported to be in conflict with the party's "Big Five" cabinet members, led by Lt. Gen. Mompati S. Merafhe, who represented the BDP's propatronage, cattle-raising wing. Mmusi died in October 1994 and was eventually succeeded as BDP chair by Ponatshego KEDIKILWE, the minister of presidential affairs and public administration. The government reshuffling in late 1997 was reportedly hailed by party officials for balancing the number of northern and southern ministers.

On March 31, 1998, Masire resigned from both his national and party presidency posts, and on April 1 Festus Mogae assumed both positions. The BDP maintained its dominance in the 1999 assembly poll by securing 57 percent of the vote.

With Mogae's nomination of Lt. Gen. Seretse Ian Khama as the vice president of the republic, and thus the possible "heir," the factionalized structure of the BDP became more apparent. In June 2000 Kedikilwe resigned as minister of education, observers noting that Kedikilwe and BDP Secretary General Daniel K. Kwelagobe were uneasy with Khama, who had publicly called them the "old guard." However, at the party congress in July 2001 a compromise averted a possible crisis, and Khama was elected vice chair of the party, while Kedikilwe and Kwelagobe both kept their positions.

Kedikilwe was replaced by Khama as chair of the BDP at the 2003 congress, following which the party remained divided into two camps. One was led by Foreign Affairs Minister Mompati S. Merafhe and Education Minister Jacob NKATE, both of whom had supported Khama at the 2003 congress. The other faction was led by Kedikilwe and Kwelagobe. Discord between the factions was renewed at the July 2005 congress, but Kwelagobe managed to fend off a challenge for his post from Local Government Minister Margaret NASHA after Khama intervened on his behalf in an effort to keep peace in the party. All remaining top party positions went to the pro-Khama faction, with Nkate retained as deputy secretary general.

Strife continued to increase to the point that in early December 2005 the BDP High Command ordered the dissolution of party factions. The so-called K-K faction (Kedikilwe-Kwelagobe) refused to disband, upholding its battle over cabinet posts and insisting on a meeting with President Mogae to push for power sharing at all levels of government. Mogae finally agreed to a meeting in February 2006.

Leaders: Festus MOGAE (President of the Republic and of the Party), Sir Ketumile Joni MASIRE (Former President of the Republic and of the Party), Lt. Gen. (Ret.) Seretse Ian KHAMA (Vice President of the Republic and Chair of the Party), Lt. Gen. Mompati S. MERAFHE (Foreign Affairs Minister), Daniel K. KWELAGOBE (Secretary General).

Opposition Parties

Botswana National Front (BNF). The BNF is a leftist party organized after the 1965 election. Its principal leader, Dr. Kenneth Koma, was the only candidate to oppose Seretse Khama for the presidency in 1979, but he failed to retain his assembly seat. The party's share of the vote increased to 20 percent at the 1984 election, with its legislative representation growing from two to four; it also won control of the Gaborone city council.

In the late 1980s a number of right-wing members of the BNF defected to the BDP in response to the BNF's left-wing, procommunist orientation. In the wake of the October 1989 election, at which BNF assembly representation was reduced to three, Koma characterized its activists as "social democrats" who are "not Marxists." In the 1989 poll the BNF gained control of two local councils, including the capital, despite a loss of membership to two new splinter groups.

In August 1990 the BNF joined with the BPU and BPP (below) in forming a joint "Unity in Diversity" committee, which was formalized as a Botswana People's Progressive Front (BPPF) in October 1991. In 1993, however, Front members could not agree on whether they should boycott the next election if their demands for electoral reform were not met. As a result, the BNF contested the October 1994 poll in its own right, substantially increasing its vote share to 37.7 percent and winning 13 elective seats, including all 4 at Gaborone.

In mid-1998 the BNF was severely weakened by the withdrawal of a faction (reportedly including 11 legislators) led by Michael Kitso DINGAKE, who subsequently helped to form the Botswana Congress Party (BCP, below). The BNF was initially described in early 1999 as negotiating participation in the new Botswana Alliance Movement (BAM, below). However, delivering a blow to opposition legislative hopes of cutting into the BDP majority, the BNF ultimately decided to run its own candidates in all districts, securing 6 seats on 26 percent of the vote.

Although he did not take responsibility for the defeat, Koma announced in January 2000 that he would step down as the party's president. At a November 2001 congress, Otsweletse Moupo beat Peter WOKO, who was supported by Koma, and became the new BNF leader. Koma was expelled in 2002 for reportedly encouraging factionalism and moved on to help form the New Democratic Front (NDF) with other BNF dissidents in 2003 (see below).

In the 2004 elections, the BNF secured 12 seats. Following the election, a rift emerged within the party between supporters of Moupo and those of BNF Vice President Kopano Lekoma, who unsuccessfully challenged Moupo at the party conference in July 2005. In early 2006 the BNF appeared committed to cooperating with other opposition parties to wrest control from the BDP in the 2009 balloting.

Leaders: Otsweletse MOUPO (President), Nehemiah MODUBULE (National Chair), Akanyang MAGAMA (Secretary General), Kopano LEKOMA (Vice President of the Party).

Botswana Congress Party (BCP). The BCP was formally registered in June 1998 by a group of BNF legislators interested in pursuing more centrist policies than the left-leaning parent grouping (personal animosity between BNF leader Kenneth Koma and dissident leader Michael Dingake also reportedly contributed to the rupture.) The BCP secured 12 percent of the vote in the 1999 legislative poll but only 1 seat, Dingake theorizing the party had been punished by the voters by splitting the opposition ranks. In 2002 the BCP was reportedly engaged in unity talks with the BAM (below).

The party retained one seat in the 2004 election, and in 2005 it continued talks with the BAM and the BPP about a possible electoral coalition.

While the party suffered a number of defections (factionalism cited as the main reason) in early 2006, some 45 new members joined, including 3 from the BDP.

Leaders: Gilson SALESHANDO (Party President), Mokgweetsi KGOSIPULA (Secretary General), Gilson SALESHANDO (Publicity Secretary).

Other Parties Contesting the 2004 Legislative Elections

Botswana Alliance Movement (BAM). Formed by the three parties below and the BPP for the 1999 legislative balloting, the BAM secured only 5 percent of the votes (and no seats) in that poll after having failed to convince other anti-BDP parties, most notably the BNF, to join in a single opposition electoral coalition. Lepetu SETSHWAELO of the UAP served as the BAM's presidential candidate in 1999. The BAM was reportedly involved in unity talks with the BCP (above) during 2001. Although the parties did not merge before the 2004 elections (in which BAM received 2.84 percent of the vote and no seats in the assembly), talks continued about an electoral alliance between the BAM and other opposition groups for the 2009 elections. The BPP left the BAM prior to the 2004 election (see BPP, below), but in early 2006 met with the BCP, the BNF, and the BAM for unity talks.

Leaders: Lepetu SETSHWAELO, Lethogile SETHOKO (Chair), Matlhomola MODISE (Secretary General).

Botswana Progressive Union (BPU). Founded by a group of radicals in 1982, the BPU has never secured parliamentary representation.

Leaders: D. K. KWELE (President), R. K. MONYATSIWA (Secretary General).

Independent Freedom Party (IFP). The IFP was formed prior to the 1994 election by merger of the Botswana Independence Party (BIP), which had been launched in 1964 by a dissident

Cabinet

As of February 1, 2006

President	Festus Mogae
Vice President	Lt. Gen. (Ret.) Seretse Ian Khama

Ministers

Agriculture	Johnny Swartz
Communications, Science, and Technology	Pelonomi Venson [f]
Conservation, Wildlife, and Tourism	Kitso Mokaila
Education	Jacob Nkate
Finance and Development Planning	Baledzi Gaolathe
Foreign Affairs	Lt. Gen. (Ret.) Mompati Merafhe
Health	Sheila Tlou [f]
Labor and Home Affairs	Gen. Moeng Pheto
Lands and Housing	Ramadeluka Seretse
Local Government	Margaret Nasha [f]
Minerals, Energy, and Water Affairs	Charles Tibone
Presidential Affairs and Public Administration	Phandu Skelemani
Trade and Industry	Neo Moroka
Works and Transport	Lesego Mosomi [f]

Assistant Ministers

Agriculture	Peter Siele
Education	Moggie Mbaakanyi [f]
Finance	Duncan Mlazie
Labor and Home Affairs	Olifant Mfa
Local Government, Lands, and Housing	Ambrose Masalila
Works and Transport	Frank Ramsden

[f] = female

BPP faction, and the Botswana Freedom Party (BFP), which had been organized in 1989 by a former BNF member. The new formation won no legislative seats in 1994 on a vote share of 2.9 percent.

Leaders: Motsamai K. MPHO (BIP), Leach TLHOMELANG (BFP).

United Action Party (UAP). The UAP, also referenced as the Bosele Action Party (BAP), was launched in September 1997 by a group of BDP dissidents.

Leader: Lepetu SETSHWAELO.

Botswana People's Party (BPP). Founded in 1960 and for some years the principal minority party, the northern-based BPP advocates social democracy and takes a pan-Africanist line. It contested the 1994 election, winning no assembly seats on a vote share of 4.6 percent. The BPP was reportedly in disarray for most of 2000–2001. President Knight MARIPE resigned in July 2000, announcing that he had "nothing to offer" to the party. According to the *Africa News*, ten members of the party's National Executive Council, including the former chair Kenneth MKHWA and former secretary general Matlhomola MODISE, were expelled in November for "having failed to carry out a resolution which directed the party to withdraw from the BAM." The party left BAM prior to the 2004 legislative elections. The BPP gained only 1.91 percent of the vote and therefore no seats in the legislative balloting. After initially balking at unity terms, the BPP in October 2005 signed on to a memorandum of agreement with the BCP, BAM, and BNF to cooperate in ousting the BDP in 2009.

Leaders: Bernard BALIKANI, Cornelius GOPOLANG (Secretary General).

New Democratic Front (NDF). Formed in 2003 by dissidents from the BNF, including former BNF leader Kenneth Koma, the NDF is a center-left, social-democratic party. In the 2004 legislative elections, the NDF secured less than 1 percent of the vote. Koma stepped up in October 2005 to assist an NDF candidate in a by-election and was among those pushing for a unified opposition to unseat the BDP.

Leader: Dick BAYFORD.

Marx, Engels, Lenin, Stalin Movement of Botswana (MELS). Also reportedly referenced as the Mars Movement of Botswana, MELS presented two unsuccessful candidates in the 1999 legislative balloting, receiving only 0.1 percent of the vote. In the 2004 election, MELS again received 0.1 percent of the vote.

Leader: Themba JOINA.

Other Parties

Botswana Labour Party (BLP). Formed in September 1989 by former members of the BNF, the Labour Party espouses a program of neither "communism" nor "capitalism." The party did not offer candidates in 1989 or 1994. It was reportedly considering an alliance with the USP and SDP for the 1999 legislative balloting, but the initiative did not come to fruition.

Leader: Lenyeletse KOMA.

Other registered parties in 2004 included the **United Socialist Party** (USP), led by Nehemiah MODUBULE, now of the BNF; the **Social Democratic Party** (SDP), led by Rodgers SEABUENG; and the **Botswana Workers Front** (BWF), led by

Mothusi AKANYANG. The SDP fielded a single candidate in the 1999 local elections, but its candidate failed to win or to gather any significant support.

Legislature

The **Parliament** consists of an elective National Assembly with legislative powers and a consultative House of Chiefs.

House of Chiefs. The House of Chiefs is a largely advisory body of 15 members: the chiefs of the 8 principal tribes, 4 elected subchiefs, and 3 members selected by the other 12. Constitutional revision was being considered in early 2006 to increase the size of the upper house to 35.

Chair: Chief SEEPAPITSO IV.

National Assembly. The National Assembly, which sits for a five-year term, currently consists of 57 (raised from 40 in 2002) directly elected and 4 nominated members, in addition to the speaker and the (nonvoting) attorney general; the president serves ex officio. The most recent general election was held October 30, 2004, with the Botswana Democratic Party (BDP) winning 44 elective seats; the Botswana National Front, 12; and the Botswana Congress Party, 1.

Speaker: Patrick BALOPI.

Communications

In response to domestic and international criticism of proposed legislation on mass communications, Gaborone withdrew the bill from the legislature in early 1997 and announced that it would draft a new document after consulting with nongovernmental media groups. The original bill included provisions for strict governmental control of the fledgling industry. A new draft was presented in 2001, but it also faced criticism, especially from the International Federation of Journalists (IFJ), which claimed that the proposed Press Council would be given "extensive powers to impose fines and jail terms on journalists and publishers." In May the government allegedly decided to ban government advertising to the *Botswana Guardian* and the *Midweek Sun* after materials critical of the vice president had appeared in both papers. The papers sued the government in June, and in September the Botswana High Court ruled that the advertising ban was unconstitutional and violated the papers' freedom of expression. In an unprecedented move, the Botswana Media Workers Union was formed in 2005 to promote freedom of expression.

Press

All papers are published at Gaborone, except as noted: *Botswana Daily News/Dikgang Tsa Gompieno* (50,000), published by the Department of Information and Broadcasting in English and SeTswana; *Kutlwano* (23,000), published monthly by the Department of Information and Broadcasting in English and SeTswana; *The Reporter/Mmegi* (24,000), weekly; *Botswana Guardian* (17,000), weekly; *The Gazette* (16,000), weekly; *Midweek Sun* (13,800), weekly; *Northern Advertiser* (Francistown, 5,500), weekly; *Botswana Advertiser*, weekly; *Mmegi Monitor*, weekly; *The Voice*, bimonthly; *The Mirror*, bi-monthly.

News Agency

The Botswana Press Agency (BOPA) was established at Gaborone in 1981.

Broadcasting and Computing

The government-owned Radio Botswana operates six stations broadcasting in English and SeTswana to approximately 252,000 radio receivers. A number of private stations are expected to be launched in the wake of a recent government decision to terminate its monopoly. The TV Association of Botswana operates two low-power transmitters near Gaborone that relay programs from South Africa. In July 2000 the first state-owned television channel went on the air. In 2003 there were approximately 53,000 television receivers and 75,000 personal computers serving 70,000 Internet users.

Intergovernmental Representation

Ambassador to the U.S.
Lapologang Caesar LEKOA

U.S. Ambassador to Botswana
Katherine H. CANAVAN

Permanent Representative to the UN
Samuel Otsile OUTLULE

IGO Memberships (Non-UN)
ADB, AU, BADEA, CWTH, Interpol, NAM, SADC, WCO, WTO

BURKINA FASO

The Country

A land of arid savannas drained by the Mouhoun (Black), Nazinon (Red), and Nakambe (White) Volta rivers, Burkina Faso occupies a bufferlike position between the landlocked states of Mali and Niger on the west, north, and east, and the coastal lands of Côte d'Ivoire, Ghana, Togo, and Benin on the south. The most prominent of its numerous African population groups is the Mossi, which encompasses an estimated 50–70 percent of the population and has dominated much of the country for centuries. Other tribal groups include the Bobo, located near the western city of Bobo-Dioulasso, and the Samo. Mossi resistance to outside influence has contributed to the retention of tribal religion by a majority of the population, while 20 percent has embraced Islam and 10 percent Christianity. Women have traditionally constituted over half the labor force, producing most of the food crops, with men responsible for cash crops. Captain Compaoré's 1987 dismissal of a number of women appointed by his predecessor to politically influential posts was consistent with customary law that has been described as "unfavorable" to female property and political rights; however, subsequent cabinets have usually included several female ministers.

The former Upper Volta is one of the poorest countries in Africa, with GNP per capita estimated at $300. In addition, its illiteracy rate (more than 75 percent) is among the highest in the world. Over 80 percent of the population is engaged in subsistence agriculture; cotton, karité nuts, livestock, and peanuts are exported. (Cotton reportedly accounts for some 75 percent of exports and 30 percent of GDP, and Burkina Faso is one of Africa's largest cotton producers.) Mineral deposits, mainly manganese, remain largely unexploited due to a lack of transportation facilities. Industry, consisting primarily of the production of textiles and processed agricultural goods, makes only a small contribution to the GNP.

Since 1991 the government has adhered to a structural adjustment plan dictated by the International Monetary Fund (IMF) focusing on redirecting the economy from a "centralized to market-oriented one." In mid-2000 the IMF and the World Bank announced a $700 million debt relief package for Burkina Faso, contingent in part on further privatization and implementation of poverty-reduction policies. In November 2001 the IMF announced that the country's record on structural reforms was improving, although the fund called for refinements in the management of public finances. In the wake of additional reform by the government, the IMF endorsed debt relief of some $195 million for Burkina Faso in 2002. GDP grew by more than 6 percent annually in 1996–2005,

Government and Politics

Political Background

Under French control since 1896, what was then known as Upper Volta gained separate identity in March 1959 when it became an autonomous state of the French Community under Maurice YAMÉOGO, leader of the Voltaic Democratic Union (*Union Démocratique Voltaïque*— UDV) and a political disciple of President Félix Houphouët-Boigny of Côte d'Ivoire. Under Yaméogo's leadership, Upper Volta became fully independent on August 5, 1960. Though reelected for a second term by an overwhelming majority in 1965, Yaméogo was unable to cope with mounting student and labor dissatisfaction, and he resigned in January 1966. Lt. Col. Sangoulé LAMIZANA, the army chief of staff, immediately assumed the presidency and instituted a military regime.

Faithful to his promise to restore constitutional government within four years, Lamizana submitted a new constitution for popular approval in December 1970 and sponsored a legislative election in which the UDV regained its pre-1966 majority. Gérard Kango OUÉDRAOGO was invested as prime minister by the National Assembly in February 1971, while Lamizana was retained as chief executive for a four-year transitional period, after which the president was to be popularly elected. On February 8, 1974, however, the army, under General Lamizana, again seized control to prevent the political rehabilitation of ex-president Yaméogo. Declaring that the takeover was aimed at saving the country from the threat of squabbling politicians, Lamizana suspended the 1970 constitution, dissolved the National Assembly, and dismissed the cabinet. A new government was formed on February 11, with Lamizana continuing as president and assuming the office of prime minister.

In the wake of a ministerial reorganization in January 1977, the president announced that a constitutional referendum would take place by midyear, followed by legislative and presidential elections at which he would not stand as a candidate. The referendum was held November 27,

---

Political Status: Became independent as the Republic of Upper Volta on August 5, 1960; under largely military rule 1966–1978; constitution of November 27, 1977, suspended upon military coup of November 25, 1980; present name adopted August 4, 1984; multiparty constitution adopted by popular referendum on June 2, 1991.

Area: 105,869 sq. mi. (274,200 sq. km.).

Population: 10,312,609 (1996C); 13,391,000 (2005E).

Major Urban Center (2005E): OUAGADOUGOU (1,150,000).

Official Language: French.

Monetary Unit: CFA Franc (market rate July 1, 2006: 513.01 francs = $1US). (The CFA franc, previously pegged to the French franc, is now permanently pegged to the euro at 655.957 CFA francs = 1 euro.)

President: Capt. Blaise COMPAORÉ (Congress of Democracy and Progress); leader of military coup that overthrew Cdr. Thomas SANKARA, on October 15, 1987; popularly elected (as leader of the Popular Front) to a seven-year term on December 1, 1991; reelected to another seven-year term on November 15, 1998; reelected to a five-year term on November 13, 2005.

Prime Minister: Ernest Paramanga YONLI (Congress of Democracy and Progress); appointed by the president on November 7, 2000, to succeed Kadré Désiré OUÉDRAOGO (independent at time of appointment, subsequently a member of the Congress of Democracy and Progress), who had resigned the previous day; formed new government on November 12, 2000; reappointed by the president on June 6, 2002, and formed new government on June 11 following legislative balloting on May 5; reappointed by the president on January 6, 2006, and formed new government on January 7.

---

although growth has been dampened recently by low cotton prices and regional turmoil. Current development programs focus on the construction of rural roads and the expansion of irrigation systems.

with a reported 97.75 percent of the voters endorsing a return to democratic rule. Lamizana reversed himself, however, and announced his candidacy for the presidency in 1978. Rejecting an appeal by opponents that he abandon his military rank and campaign as a civilian, Lamizana retained his office in a runoff on May 29 after having obtained a plurality in first-round balloting on May 14. Earlier, on April 30, the regime-supportive Voltaic Democratic Union–African Democratic Assembly (*Union Démocratique Voltaïque–Rassemblement Démocratique African*—UDV–RDA) obtained a near-majority in a reconstituted National Assembly, which on July 7 designated Dr. Joseph Issoufou CONOMBO as prime minister.

Despite restrictions imposed on all but the leading political groups, Upper Volta remained only one of two multiparty democracies (the other being Senegal) in former French Africa until November 25, 1980, when the Lamizana regime was overthrown in a military coup led by former foreign minister Col. Sayé ZERBO. Officials of the ousted government, including the president and the prime minister, were placed under arrest, while a Military Committee of Recovery for National Progress (*Comité Militaire de Redressement pour le Progrès National*—CMRPN) suspended the constitution, dissolved the legislature, and banned political activity. A 17-member Council of Ministers headed by Colonel Zerbo as both president and prime minister was announced on December 7.

Accusing Zerbo of having "made the paramilitary forces an agent of terror," a group of noncommissioned officers mounted a coup on November 7, 1982, that installed Maj. Jean-Baptiste OUÉDRAOGO, a former army medical officer, as head of what was termed the People's Salvation Council (*Conseil de Salut du Peuple*—CSP). On August 4, 1983, Ouédraogo was in turn overthrown in a brief rebellion led by Capt. Thomas Sankara, who had been named prime minister in January, only to be arrested, along with other allegedly pro-Libyan members of the CSP, in late May. Immediately after the August coup, Sankara announced the formation of a National Revolutionary Council (*Conseil National de la Révolution*—

CNR) with himself as chair. A year later, following two failed counter-coup attempts, the name of the country was changed to Burkina Faso, a vernacular blend meaning "democratic and republican land of upright men."

In the wake of a state visit by Libya's Col. Muammar al-Qadhafi in December 1985, Cdr. Sankara declared that his country had "gone beyond the era of republics." He proclaimed the establishment of a Libyan-style "Jamahiriya" system aimed at linking national government policy to the wishes of the population as expressed through local people's committees.

Sankara was killed in a coup led by his second-in-command, Capt. Blaise COMPAORÉ, on October 15, 1987. Following the execution of a number of former government officials, Compaoré and his "brothers-in-arms," Maj. Jean-Baptiste LINGANI and Capt. Henri ZONGO, charged that Sankara had been a "madman" who had planned to consolidate power under a one-party system. Faced with substantial domestic hostility, Compaoré pledged to continue the "people's revolution," naming himself head of a Popular Front (*Front Populaire*—FP) administration. In March 1988 Compaoré announced a major government reorganization (see under Constitution and government, below), and, vowing to carry on the "rectification program" begun with the October coup, he appealed to elements that Sankara had labeled "entrenched interest groups"—labor unions, tribal chieftaincies, conservative civilians, and the military elite. However, Compaoré's efforts, hailed by some as welcome relief from Sankara's chaotic governing style, lacked his predecessor's wide popular appeal.

In September 1989 Lingani and Zongo, who had been named first and second deputy chair members, respectively, of the FP three months earlier, were arrested and summarily executed on charges of "betraying" the regime by attempting to blow up the plane on which Compaoré was returning from a state visit to the Far East. Three months later, another coup attempt was allegedly foiled by the president's personal guard, with the government subsequently denying press reports that several persons had been executed for involvement in the plot.

The first FP congress was held in Ouagadougou on March 1–4, 1990, with 3,000 delegates participating. The congress, which included representatives of a variety of unions and political groups, drafted a democratic constitution, which was approved by an assembly of 2,000 provincial delegates on December 15 and adopted by popular referendum on June 2, 1991.

On June 11, 1990, Compaoré dissolved the government and announced the opening of a 24-party consultative assembly to discuss implementation of a new constitution. The following day, however, 13 opposition parties walked out of the assembly when the government rejected their demands that the body be granted sovereign status and be expanded to include trade unionists, traditional leaders, and human rights organizations. On June 16 Compaoré named a 34-member transitional government consisting of 28 ministers and 6 secretaries of state, 21 of whom were members of the FP's core formation, the Organization for People's Democracy–Labor Movement (*Organisation pour la Démocratie Populaire–Mouvement Travailliste*—ODP-MT). However, three opposition members withdrew prior to the first cabinet meeting, and they were followed on August 17 by three more, including Herman YAMÉOGO (son of Upper Volta's first president), who had been assigned the agriculture portfolio only three weeks earlier.

In September 1990 Compaoré, who had resigned from the military as required by the new basic law, announced his presidential candidacy. Thereafter, in the run-up to presidential balloting, clashes intensified between the FP and opposition forces. On September 25 much of the opposition, loosely joined in a Coalition of Democratic Forces (*Coalition des Forces Démocratiques*—CFD), threatened to boycott elections if a national conference was not held. Compaoré responded by offering to hold a referendum on Burkina's transitional institutions. However, at the urging of government supporters, the proposal was quickly withdrawn. Thus, all four opposition presidential nominees (Pierre Claver DAMBA, UNDP Regional Director for Africa; the RDA's Gérard Kango Ouédraogo; Ram OUÉDRAOGO of the Union of Greens for the Development of Burkina [*Union des Verts pour le Développement du Burkina*—UVDB]; and Herman Yaméogo of the Alliance for Democracy and Federation [*Alliance pour la Démocratie et la Féderation*—ADF]) boycotted the December 1 balloting, in which Compaoré, running unopposed, won a renewed seven-year mandate.

Prospects for a representative legislature were dampened when only a quarter of the known parties indicated a willingness to participate in the projected January 1992 legislative poll. At the core of the complaint was the government's refusal to convene a national conference endowed with plenary powers to oversee the transition to a wholly democratic system. In mid-December 1991 opposition leaders had rejected an overture by President Compaoré to participate in a less authoritative National Reconciliation Forum, and the assemblage that was ultimately convened on February 11, 1992, was suspended nine days later because of a disagreement over live radio coverage of its deliberations. Nonetheless, 27 of 62 registered parties participated in the balloting that was eventually conducted on May 24, the ruling ODP-MT winning an overwhelming majority of seats.

On June 15, 1992, Compaoré dissolved the transitional government, and the following day he named economist Youssouf OUÉDRAOGO as prime minister. The cabinet named by Ouédraogo on June 20 included representatives from seven parties, although 13 of the 22 portfolios were awarded to the ODP-MT.

Prime Minister Ouédraogo resigned on March 17, 1994, after the mid-January devaluation of the CFA franc and subsequent collapse of a wage agreement with the trade unions. Three days later President Compaoré appointed Marc Christian Roch KABORÉ, theretofore minister of state in charge of relations with institutions, as Ouédraogo's successor.

On February 6, 1996, Prime Minister Kaboré resigned to assume the vice presidency of the Congress of Democracy and Progress (*Congress pour la Démocratie et le Progrès*—CDP), a newly formed government grouping created by the ODP-MT and a number of other groups. Kaboré, who was also named special advisor to the president, was replaced on the same day by Kadré Désiré OUÉDRAOGO, theretofore deputy governor of the Central Bank of West African States. The cabinet named on February 9 remained largely unchanged from its predecessor, and a reshuffle on September 3 was most noteworthy for Ouédraogo's assumption of the economy and finance portfolio.

In January 1997 the assembly approved constitutional amendments that abolished provisions limiting the number of presidential terms (previously two). The opposition strongly protested the change, arguing it was designed to insure Compaoré the presidency for as long as he desired.

Subsequently, in legislative balloting on May 11, 1997, the dominance of the pro-Compaoré groupings was underlined by the CDP's capture of 97 of 111 seats, a majority that swelled to 101 in June following elections in four constituencies where earlier results had been invalidated. In addition, the presidentially allied ADF secured 2 seats. The leading opposition party, the Party for Democracy and Progress (*Parti pour la Démocratie et le Progrés*—PDP), won 6 seats. On June 11 the president reappointed Ouédraogo prime minister and named a cabinet that was largely unchanged, with the notable exception that the ADF's Yaméogo was not returned to his post.

In April 1998 the Compaoré government announced the establishment of an independent electoral commission and charged it with organizing the presidential polling scheduled for late 1998. The government asserted that the creation of the commission was a sign of a willingness to install transparent electoral procedures. However, that assessment was rejected by many of the leading opposition groups, which, under the banner of the February 14 Group (*Groupe du 14 Février*—G14), a newly created coalition (see Political Parties, below), subsequently vowed to boycott the balloting unless further reforms were implemented. In September President Compaoré met with opposition leaders in an unsuccessful effort to break the impasse; consequently, in presidential polling on

November 15, the incumbent easily secured a second term, overwhelming several minor party candidates. Compaoré's 87.53 percent vote tally dwarfed the results of his nearest rival, the UVDB's Ram Ouédraogo, who secured just 6.61 percent; meanwhile, a number of observers described the relatively high voter turnout (58 percent) as a rebuke to the opposition.

Violent antigovernment protests broke out throughout the country in mid-December 1998 following the discovery of the bodies of Norbert ZONGO (a prominent independent journalist) and two colleagues in a burned vehicle outside of Ouagadougou. Zongo, a vocal critic of the administration, had reportedly been investigating the role the president's brother, François COMPAORÉ, had played in the death of one of Zongo's assistants. Subsequently, the president appointed an independent judicial commission to investigate the journalists' deaths; nevertheless, demonstrations continued through the first part of 1999.

On January 8, 1999, Prime Minister Ouédraogo and his government issued their pro forma resignations, as required by the constitution following presidential balloting. However, on January 11 Ouédraogo was reappointed by the president, and the government announced on January 15 was only slightly reshuffled.

In May 1999 the judicial commission issued a report that implicated the Presidential Guard in the Zongo killings. Subsequently, intensified antigovernment unrest erupted, and the leaders of a number of opposition groups were detained. The CDP dismissed the commission's findings as reflecting "partisan" concerns; nevertheless, President Compaoré created a 16-member Council of Elders on May 21 and asked its members (including three former heads of government) to help create an environment for "reconciliation and social peace." In August the council called for the establishment of a national unity government. Two months later, Prime Minister Ouédraogo reshuffled the cabinet, bringing into its ranks members of two theretofore opposition groups. However, members of the so-called "radical opposition" refused to participate, dismissing the government's entreaties as disingenuous and asserting that the political crisis would continue until those responsible for political killings were brought to justice.

In November 1999 Compaoré established two new bodies, the Consultative Commission on Political Reforms and the National Reconciliation Commission, which he charged with drafting "concrete proposals" for resolving the continuing imbroglio. However, opposition members refused to assume the seats set aside for them in the Consultative Commission, complaining that the president had reneged on an alleged pledge to make the commission's findings binding.

Antigovernment demonstrations continued through the end of 1999, and in the first days of 2000 the opposition criticized the administration's call for early legislative elections and condemned the "culture of impunity" engendered by the president. In late January CDP activists held a proreform rally, insisting that such efforts were the only way to derail the opposition's movement toward a "democratic coup d'état." The government subsequently announced plans for municipal elections to be held in late July, but the balloting was later delayed in view of opposition complaints about voter registration and electoral procedures.

In August 2000 three soldiers from the Presidential Guard were given prison sentences for having tortured to death one of Zongo's assistants in 1998. Subsequently, in October, the university in Ouagadougou was shut down by the government in response to several months of protests by students, teachers, and unions. After the government agreed to most of the protesters' demands, the university was reopened in December.

The municipal elections of September 2000 appeared to underscore the division between the moderate and radical opposition parties, as some of the latter refused to participate. On November 6, 2000, Prime Minister Ouédraogo resigned, and on November 7 the president appointed one of the ministers from the CDP, Ernest Paramanga YONLI, as the new prime minister. The CDP subsequently signed a "Protocol of Agreement" with a number of parties that consequently accepted posts in the new cabinet formed on November 12, their inclusion

being seen by some analysts as evidence of a new atmosphere of compromise and easing of tensions, as well as the split structure of the opposition.

In February 2001, in a further development on the prosecution of the political killings, a warrant officer was charged with the murder of Zongo. Implying that the investigations of the political killings had produced tangible results, the government organized a "National Day of Forgiveness" in March with the hopes of reconciling with the more radical opposition parties. However, the PDP, the Social Forces Front (*Front des Forces Sociales*—FFS), and some other parties refused to take part in the event.

Facing increased domestic and international criticism, the government authorized several significant electoral reforms prior to the 2002 assembly balloting, including a revision of the proportional voting system that had previously favored the CDP (it had won 69 percent of the vote in the 1997 balloting but had been awarded 97 of 111 seats). The measures appeared to produce the desired effect, as the CDP majority fell to 57 seats in the May 5 elections. The leading opposition parties were the ADF/African Democratic Rally with 17 seats and the PDP/Socialist Party with 10 seats. However, unlike the November 2000 cabinet, the new cabinet named by Prime Minister Yonli on June 11 did not include members of the opposition.

Following a controversial ruling by the Constitutional Court that permitted him to seek another term (see Current issues, below), President Compaoré was reelected with 80 percent of the vote against 12 other candidates in balloting on November 13, 2005. He subsequently reappointed Prime Minister Yonli to head a new government which, as formed on January 7, 2006, was again dominated by the CDP, although several small parties that had supported Compaoré in the presidential poll were also included.

Constitution and Government

The 1977 constitution called for a president and a National Assembly to be elected separately for five-year terms on the basis of a multiparty system.

After the constitution was suspended in November 1980, a period of uncertain military rule followed, yielding, in August 1985, a revised government structure intended to promote "the Burkinabè identity."

Under the new arrangement, President Sankara (as head of the National Revolutionary Council [CNR], the supreme political body) assumed responsibility for the proclamation of laws (*zatu*) in accordance with "the will of the people." The "revolutionary executive" was placed under the supervision of a People's Commission, acting in concert with a Ministerial Administrative Committee and a Ministerial Council. Within the villages, Revolutionary Defense Committees (*Comités pour la Défense Révolutionnaire*—CDR), which had taken over the function of tax collection from local chiefs in 1984, were designated as the ultimate repositories of "popular and insurrectional power." Earlier, a judicial reorganization had been announced, under which Popular Revolutionary Tribunals (*Tribunaux Populaires de la Révolution*—TPR) were established under the jurisdiction of Appeals Courts in Ouagadougou and Bobo-Dioulasso.

A new government was formed on October 31, 1987, two weeks after Sankara's overthrow. However, it was not until March 1988 that Captain Compaoré's Popular Front (FP) announced that the CDRs had been abolished and replaced by Revolutionary Committees. Described as "mass socio-professional organizations," the committees were mandated to meet every two years to modify FP programs, define the country's political orientation, and oversee admission into the FP. Although mimicking Sankara's call for extensive citizen involvement in government, the new regime ordered the banning of all political parties that did not align with the FP. Subsequently, the ban was relaxed for all but the most virulent opposition formations, and in August 1990 a commission was charged with drafting a new constitution. The multiparty document approved by popular referendum on June 2, 1991, provided for a separation of powers, a president and legislature elected by universal suffrage for seven- and five-year terms, respectively, and the establishment of an independent judiciary. The president has the right to name a prime minister, who must, however, be acceptable to the legislature. In April 2000 the Assembly of People's Deputies passed a law reducing the president's term from seven to five years, with a maximum of two terms. The new law did not affect the length of President Compaoré's current term. It also did not address the issue of "retroactivity," which led supporters of Compaoré to declare that he was eligible to run for a third term in 2005 (see Current issues, below). The country's Supreme Court is split into four separate courts, namely, the Constitutional Court, the Court of Appeals, the Council of State, and the government audit office.

Administratively, the country is divided into provinces, which are subdivided into departments, arrondissements, and villages. (In early 2006 the government announced that local elections would be held in April for 49 "urban communes" and 309 "rural communes.")

Foreign Relations

Upper Volta had consistently adhered to a moderately pro-French and pro-Western foreign policy, while stressing the importance of good relations with neighboring countries. However, after the 1983 coup, relations between Burkina Faso and France cooled, a result primarily of France's unease over Commander Sankara's vigorous attempts to rid the country of all vestiges of its colonial past (made manifest by the 1984 change in country name, the adoption of radical policies modeled on those of Ghana and Libya, and the widely publicized arrests of allegedly pro-French former government officials and trade unionists accused of plotting against the Sankara regime). Subsequent relations with francophone neighbors remained less than uniformly cordial, in part because of Sankara's blunt style in attacking perceived government corruption throughout the region and his strong ideological opinions.

In December 1985 a 20-year-long controversy involving the so-called Agacher Strip at Burkina's northern border with Mali yielded four days of fighting with approximately 300 dead on both sides. However, a ruling from the International Court of Justice on December 22, 1986, which awarded the two countries roughly equal portions of the disputed territory, largely terminated the unrest. Relations with another neighbor, Togo, were strained in 1987 over allegations of Burkinabè complicity (heatedly denied) in a September 1986 coup attempt against Togolese President Eyadema.

The October 1987 coup in Burkina Faso was manifestly welcomed by the region's most respected elder statesman, President Houphouët-Boigny of Côte d'Ivoire, with whom Captain Compaoré had long enjoyed close personal relations. Subsequently, in an attempt to gain recognition of his government and to repair strained ties with "Western-leaning" neighbors, Compaoré traveled to 13 countries during his first year in power. The long-standing border dispute with Mali was formally resolved in early 1988, followed by a resumption in relations with Togo and a border agreement with Ghana. Nevertheless, Compaoré also continued to maintain communist ties: in September 1988 he signed cooperation agreements with North Korea, and in September 1989 he was the first head of state to visit China following the crushing of that country's prodemocracy movement.

In September 1992 Malian president Alpha Oumar Konaré met in Ouagadougou with Compaoré to reactivate bilateral cooperation and to address Burkina's policy of allowing Tuaregs from Mali and Niger refuge in northern Burkina. On November 5 the United States recalled its ambassador to Burkina Faso, accusing the Compaoré government of continuing to supply arms to Charles Taylor's Liberian rebel forces despite Washington's earlier warnings about Ouagadougou's "destabilizing" involvement with Taylor.

On February 2, 1994, Ouagadougou reestablished relations with Taiwan after a 20-year lapse, thus precipitating China's suspension of relations one week later. Meanwhile, regional relations were dominated by the Tuareg dilemma, and in October Ouagadougou was the host site for successful negotiations between the Niger government and its Tuareg rebels. On a far less positive note, the refugee crisis along Burkina's border with Mali was exacerbated by intensified fighting between Tuaregs and Malian government forces. In January 1995 the United Nations reported that the number of Malian Tuareg refugees in Burkina Faso had risen to 50,000, up from 9,000 in 1993. In October Ouagadougou announced plans to send troops to join ECOMOG forces in Liberia, saying it had changed its policy because the peacemaking effort there appeared "more credible than previous ones."

Regional cooperation efforts topped Burkina's foreign policy agenda in 1996, Ouagadougou reaching agreement with Niger in March on the repatriation of that country's refugees. In March 1997 Burkina was the site for joint military exercises with Benin, Togo, and France, while in 1998 Compaoré hosted summits for representatives of combatants in the Eritrean and Ethiopian border conflict as well as participants in the civil war in the Democratic Republic of the Congo. Burkinabè troops also participated in the UN-sponsored peacekeeping mission in the Central African Republic from 1997 to 2000.

In November 1999 a violent land dispute erupted in Côte d'Ivoire between Ivorians and Burkinabè, and by the end of the year approximately 12,000 of the Burkinabè had crossed back into Burkina in search of refuge. Following a coup attempt in Côte d'Ivoire in January 2001, the two countries' relations were strained even further, as some Ivorian authorities unofficially implied that Burkina Faso may have been behind the overthrow effort. The Ivorian government subsequently began forced deportations of Burkinabè who lived or were working in Côte d'Ivoire. Estimates were that 20,000 Burkinabè expatriates were exported by 2002. Throughout 2002 and into 2003, the Ivorian government continued to blame its neighbor for promoting unrest, and there was another massive wave of Burkinabè refugees. The Compaoré government officially closed the border in September 2002 but reopened it a year later. By 2003, some 350,000 Burkinabè had fled Côte d'Ivoire. In 2003 Compaoré hosted a summit with his Ivorian counterpart and representatives of the main rebel groups in Côte d'Ivoire in an effort to improve bilateral relations.

The government also banned several Ivorian rebel groups from using Burkina Faso to undertake political activities in Côte d'Ivoire.

On another front, in March 2000 the United Nations accused the Compaoré administration of illegally circumventing international sanctions against financing or arming Angola's UNITA rebels. According to a UN report, Burkina Faso was a "de facto base of operations for UNITA's external activities in Africa." Ouagadougou denied the allegations, which linked Burkina Faso to UNITA during the year Compaoré chaired the Organization of African Unity (OAU, subsequently the African Union—AU). Similar allegations were made in July by American and British officials, and in December, mainly due to international accusations, Burkina Faso announced that it would set up a mechanism to control its weapons trade.

In mid-2003 President Compaoré was instrumental in launching a major effort among less-developed cotton-exporting nations to get industrialized nations to curb their domestic cotton subsidies. In that regard, Burkina Faso joined other West African countries and Brazil in filing a successful complaint with the World Trade Organization against U.S. cotton subsidies.

Current Issues

In October 2003 the government announced that it had foiled a coup plot by the arrest of some 15 senior military officials, including members of the presidential guard. It was subsequently reported that the alleged leader of the plot, Capt. Luther QUALI, had been in contact with officials in Togo and Côte d'Ivoire in September, further straining already tense relations between the Compaoré administration and those two nations. Regional issues subsequently remained in the forefront of Burkinabè politics, some opposition leaders calling in October 2004 for an investigation into the possibility that Compaoré had provided support for antigovernment activity in places such as Côte d'Ivoire and Mauritania. Critics also alleged that Compaoré had assisted former Liberian president

Charles Taylor in arming and training rebels from the Revolutionary United Front in Sierra Leone (see article on Sierra Leone for details).

In early 2005 Compaoré announced he would be a candidate for reelection despite the two-term limit implemented in 2000. (Compaoré's position was that the term limits could not be applied retroactively, meaning that, in theory, he was eligible for two more terms.) Not surprisingly, opposition leaders (already angered by the May 2004 reversal of election rules that had favored anti-CDP forces in the 2002 assembly poll [see Legislature, below, for details]) demanded that the Constitutional Court reject Compaoré's candidacy. However, the court quickly dismissed their demand, paving the way for Compaoré's landslide victory in November. Although his opponents cited numerous alleged irregularities, observers from the African Union and other organizations described the poll as generally fair. Compaoré clearly benefited from the failure of the opposition to coalesce behind a single candidate, while improved economic conditions also appeared to generate popular support for the incumbent. Attention subsequently turned to the local elections scheduled for late April 2006, which observers suggested might offer opposition parties a better chance for success. Meanwhile, another topic of discussion at that point was the possibility that Compaoré might be investigated by the UN court preparing to prosecute Taylor for his alleged war crimes in Sierra Leone.

Political Parties

Prior to the 1980 coup the governing party was the Voltaic Democratic Union–African Democratic Assembly (*Union Démocratique Voltaïque–Rassemblement Démocratique Africain*—UDV-RDA), an outgrowth of the Ivorian RDA. The UDV-RDA won 28 seats in the 1978 National Assembly election under the leadership of Malo TRAORÉ and Gérard Kango Ouédraogo. In opposition were the National Union for the Defense of Democracy (*Union Nationale pour la Défense de la Démocratie*—UNDD), organized by Herman

Yaméogo and the Voltaic Progressive Front (FPV), a socialist grouping led by Joseph KI-ZERBO that contained a number of UDV-RDA dissidents. Most such individuals subsequently left the country, Ki-Zerbo having been accused of planning a coup against Thomas Sankara in May 1984.

Political party activity was suspended in the immediate wake of Sankara's overthrow in 1987, although several groups maintained a highly visible identity, most importantly the Patriotic League for Development (*Ligue Patriotique pour le Développement*—Lipad), a Marxist organization that had been founded in 1973. In March 1988 Captain Compaoré declared that while his recently created Popular Front (FP) should not be construed as a political party, separate parties would be permitted to operate within it. A year later an apparent attempt was made to create a single government party (Organization for People's Democracy–Labor Movement —ODP-MT, below). In a return pendulum swing, the Popular Front was described on the eve of its first congress in March 1990 as consisting of "four national unions and seven political groups," although details regarding some of the components were sparse. In addition, it was reported that a number of nonlegalized (but otherwise unidentified) opposition groups had been invited to send representatives to the congress.

The multiparty constitution drafted by the 1990 congress was approved by popular referendum in June 1991. By November, 44 parties had been recognized. References to the Popular Front appeared to have been dropped following the formation of the Congress of Democracy and Progress (CDP) in February 1996.

In early 1998 ten opposition parties reportedly coalesced under the banner of the United Front for Democracy and the Republic (*Front Uni pour la Démocratie et la République*—FUDR), a grouping whose one identifiable demand—establishment of an independent electoral commission—was met in April (after which the coalition appeared to cease activities). Subsequently, the opposition mantle appeared to have been assumed by the **February 14 Group** (*Groupe du 14 Février*—G14), a nine-party

coalition that, under the leadership of the ADF, PAI, PDP, and FFS, attempted to organize a boycott of the November 1998 presidential elections after the Compaoré administration refused to make additional changes in the composition of the electoral commission.

In early 1999 yet another overlapping opposition coalition emerged—the **Collective of Mass Democratic Organizations and Political Parties** (*Collectif des Organisations Démocratiques de Masse et de Partis Politiques*—COD). Primarily comprised of union groups and political parties, the collective was led by a Sankarist, Thibaut Nan Halidou OUÉDRAOGO. Under the guidance of the leaders of the closely linked ADF and African Democratic Rally (RDA), the radical opposition refused to participate in any government-sponsored meeting or event. However, in late 1999 the Movement for Tolerance and Progress (MTP), which had theretofore been aligned with the G14, agreed to join the government. The COD and the G14 were further weakened when the ADF/RDA, CPS, MTP, PAI, and others signed a protocol with the CDP and were given cabinet posts in November 2000. There were additional significant shifts prior to the 2002 assembly balloting, the COD and G14 appearing to break apart and new coalitions, such as the Coalition of Democratic Forces, emerging as legislative opposition voices.

Some 15 opposition parties (including the UNIR/MS, UNDD, and PDS) launched an *Alternance 2005* coalition in a planned effort to present a single candidate in the 2005 presidential campaign. However, no such agreement was reached.

Primary Government Party

Congress of Democracy and Progress (*Congrès pour la Démocratie et le Progrès*—CDP). The CDP was formed on February 6, 1996, as a result of an agreement between the ODP-MT and a number of other parties, including the CNPP-PSD, the Rally of Independent Social Democrats (*Rassemblement des Social-Démocrates Indépendants*—RSI), the Group of Revolutionary

Democrats (*Groupement des Démocrates Révolutionnaires*—GDR), and the Movement for Socialist Democracy (*Mouvement pour la Démocratie Socialiste*—MDS). The Compaoré government's commitment to the new grouping was highlighted by the assignment of ODP-MT Executive Committee Chair Arsène Bongnessan Yè and Prime Minister Marc Christian Roch Kaboré to the CDP's presidency and vice presidency, respectively. (Some news reports described the CDP as a "merger" of the various parties, indicating that they might not retain autonomous identities within the Congress. Following is information on the OPD-MT and the CNPP-PSD as they existed immediately prior to the formation of the CDP. For information on the history of the RSI, GDR, MDS, and a number of other small parties reported to have joined the CDP, see the 2000–2002 *Handbook*.)

At a CDP congress on August 1, 1999, party delegates elected Kaboré to the newly created post of national executive secretary, a position that superseded both the party presidency and secretary generalship. Kaboré's ascendancy to the CDP's top post was described by some observers as evidence of a triumph for party moderates over hard-liners. Kaboré and the moderates appeared to extend their influence even further when he was elected as the new assembly president following the May 2002 legislative balloting. In June 2005 the CDP selected Compaoré as its candidate in the upcoming presidential balloting.

Leaders: Blaise COMPAORÉ (State President), Ernest Paramanga YONLI (Prime Minister), Marc Christian Roch KABORÉ (National Executive Secretary of the Party and President of the National Assembly), Pierre Joseph Emmanuel TAPSOBA, Salif DIALLO.

Organization for People's Democracy– Labor Movement (*Organisation pour la Démocratie Populaire–Mouvement Travailliste*—ODP-MT). The leftist ODP-MT was launched on April 15, 1989, as a means of unifying "all political tendencies in the country." Most prominently associated with the new

formation was the Union of Burkinabè Communists (*Union des Communistes Burkinabè*—UCB), the demise of which was announced by its leader, Clément Oumarou OUÉDRAOGO, on April 17, plus a number of dissidents from the former Union of Communist Struggles from which the UCB had earlier split.

During a congress in Ouagadougou in March 1991, the ODP-MT endorsed Compaoré's candidacy in the forthcoming presidential balloting and formally abandoned Marxism-Leninism in favor of free enterprise and a market economy. Meanwhile, in anticipation of multiparty elections, the ODP-MT moved to position itself as an independent grouping within the Popular Front, thus abandoning efforts to present the image of a nonhierarchical coalition. In July the party denounced opposition calls for a national conference, describing conference results elsewhere on the continent as equivalent to "civilian coup d'états."

In early 1996 the ODP-MT renounced its status as a "revolutionary party of the democratic masses" to become a "social democratic" party, shortly thereafter spearheading the formation of the CDP.

Leaders: Marc Christian Roch KABORÉ, Capt. Arsène Bongnessan YÈ, Naboho KANIDOUA (General Secretary).

National Convention of Progressive Patriots-Social Democratic Party (*Convention Nationale des Patriotes Progressistes–Parti Social-Démocrate*—CNPP-PSD). The CNPP-PSD was expelled from the Popular Front in March 1991 for criticizing ODP-MT policies and calling for a national conference. The party subsequently emerged as the opposition's most powerful force, winning 12 assembly seats as runner-up to the ODP-MT in May 1992.

Former party leader Pierre TAPSOBA's retirement from political life in May 1993 reportedly ignited a parliamentary power struggle that climaxed with the breakup of the CNPP-PSD's coalition with Joseph KI-ZERBO'S USDI (see under PDP, below).

The CNPP-PSD's decision to join its former Popular Front allies in the formation of the CDP in early 1996 was considered a major political victory for the Compaoré administration.

Leaders: Mamadou SIMPORÉ, Moussa BOLY.

Other Parliamentary Parties

Coalition of Democratic Forces (*Coalition des Forces Démocratiques*—CFD). Formed prior to the 2002 legislative election, the center-left CFD comprised the UVDB, the MTP, and a number of smaller parties. The CFD secured five seats in the assembly balloting. The new RDEB (see below), formed in October 2002, effectively became a member of the CFD in October 2002, when Ram Ouédraogo quit the UVDB but remained as the national coordinator of the CFD. The CFD secured five seats in the 2002 assembly balloting, and it was reported that the primary education and literacy cabinet post was awarded to a CFD member in June. However, the formal status of the CFD's relationship to the Compaoré administration remained unclear.

Leader: Ram OUÉDRAOGO (National Coordinator).

Greens of Burkina (*Les Verts du Burkina*). This party is a partial successor to the Union of Greens for the Development of Burkina (*Union des Verts pour le Développement du Burkina*—UVDB), launched in 1991. UVDB leader Ram Ouédraogo had the distinction of being the first opposition member to announce his presidential candidacy in 1991. However, prior to the December balloting, he withdrew in conjunction with the other opposition candidates.

In 1998 Ouédraogo campaigned for the presidency on a UVDB platform highlighted by a call for the elevation of water management issues to the forefront of national policymaking concerns. He finished second in the November presidential balloting, garnering just 6.61 percent of the vote. In October 1999 Ouédraogo was named a minister of state in the Kadré Ouédraogo government. He kept his position after the formation

of the new government in November 2000 but was not retained in June 2002.

Following the 2002 legislative balloting, disagreements broke out over the scope of cooperation between the UVDB and other opposition parties, and Ouédraogo left the UVDB to form the RDEB (below). The rump UVDB subsequently adopted the party's current rubric.

Leader: Ali Diaby KASSAMBA (President).

Rally of the Ecologists of Burkina (*Rassemblement des Ecologistes du Burkina*—RDEB). A moderate green party, the RDEB was formed by former UVDB leader Ram Ouédraogo in October 2002. He finished fifth in the 2005 presidential balloting with 2.03 percent of the vote.

Leader: Ram OUÉDRAOGO (President and 2005 presidential candidate).

Movement for Tolerance and Progress (*Mouvement pour la Tolérance et le Progrès*—MTP). The moderate Sankarist MTP was formed as an "anti-imperialist and national-progressive" grouping in late 1990. Its leader, Emmanuel Nayabtigungu Congo Kaboré, is a former CNR general secretary of government who has called for the maintenance of good relations with the Compaoré administration. To that end, in 1999 Kaboré accepted a post in the government. He kept his position after the formation of the new government in November 2000, but, as was the case with other "opposition" ministers, he was not retained in the June 2002 cabinet. Kaboré finished last in the 2005 presidential poll with 0.31 percent of the vote.

Leader: Emmanuel Nayabtigungu Congo KABORÉ (Secretary General and 2005 presidential candidate).

African Party for Independence (*Parti Africaine pour l'Indépendance*—PAI). Prior to Sankara's overthrow, the PAI's leader, Soumane Touré, was reportedly targeted for execution by the UCB. Despite Touré's reported allegiance to the Compaoré regime, the PAI joined the opposition February 14 Group in early 1998. However, in

August the PAI withdrew from the coalition, a schism having emerged in the party between factions led by Touré, who favored participating in the November presidential polling, and Philippe Ouédraogo, who agreed with boycott plans. At a September 13 meeting, Touré was ousted by Ouédraogo, and the group subsequently announced plans to observe the boycott. Rejecting this decision, Touré claimed that he and his followers represented the "true PAI" and continued to use the rubric. In November 2000 Touré's wing signed a protocol with the CDP and others and was given cabinet posts. Ouédraogo's wing stayed in opposition, however. The two factions subsequently fought over the right to use the PAI rubric.

The PAI won five seats in the 2002 assembly balloting, and it was reported that a PAI member was named to the June 2002 cabinet as minister of animal resources. However, apparently underscoring continued PAI disputes, Philippe Ouédraogo was subsequently described as the leader of a strongly anti-Compaoré faction in the assembly known as the Justice and Democracy Parliamentary Group.

Two PAI ministers were reportedly dismissed from the cabinet in September 2005 in an apparent response by Compaoré to Touré's announcement that he intended to oppose Compaoré in the upcoming presidential election. (Touré finished eighth in that poll with 1.12 percent, while Ouédraogo ran as the candidate of the PDS [below]).

Leaders: Soumane TOURÉ (2005 presidential candidate).

Alliance for Democracy and Federation/ African Democratic Rally (*Alliance pour la Démocratie et la Fédération/Rassemblement Démocratique Africaine*—ADF/RDA). The ADF/RDA, a merger between the ADF and RDA, was launched in May 1998. The ADF had been formed in December 1990 by Herman Yaméogo, founder of the UNDD, whose previous party had been expelled from the Popular Front in July 1990, largely because of criticism from intraparty critics of Yaméogo.

In February 1991 the ADF called for an immediate amnesty for all political prisoners, the appointment of a transitional government, and "democratization" of the press. By midyear Yaméogo had emerged as the opposition's most prominent government critic, denouncing Compaoré's unwillingness to hold a national conference and calling for the dissolution of the ODP-MT–dominated cabinet named on June 16. On July 26 Yaméogo was himself named agriculture minister, but on August 17 he and two other ADF members resigned from the government in a dispute over electoral procedure. Subsequently, Yaméogo announced his presidential candidacy; however, he and the other opposition candidates subsequently withdrew from the December 1 balloting. Somewhat inexplicably, Yaméogo again rejoined the cabinet as a minister of state in February 1992. The party participated in the May legislative poll, capturing four seats, and in June Yaméogo was redesignated minister of state. In legislative balloting in May 1997 the ADF fielded candidates in 33 of the 45 provinces but captured only two seats. Subsequently, Yaméogo was not included in the cabinet named in June. A leading component of the February 14 Group, the ADF boycotted the 1998 presidential elections. In December Yaméogo was detained by government security forces following the outbreak of anti-Compaoré unrest.

Formed in 1946 as an outgrowth of the Ivorian RDA, the RDA was a partner in the ruling UDV-RDA grouping that was unseated by the 1980 coup. At a party congress on October 13, 1991, former prime minister Gérard Kango Ouédraogo was selected as the party's presidential nominee, although he, like other opposition figures, subsequently withdrew his candidacy. The party captured six seats in the May 1992 balloting, and an RDA member, Clement SANOU, was included in the government named in June. Campaoré's appointment of Sanou was greeted with suspicion however, with *Africa Confidential* suggesting that the president was attempting to create friction within the RDA. The RDA presented candidates in slightly more than half of the polling districts in 1997, retaining only two seats.

The Party of the Convergence of Liberties and Integration (*Parti de la Convergence pour les Libertés et l'Integration*—PCLI) joined the ADF/RDA subsequent to the 1998 merger. The ADF/RDA signed a protocol with the CDP and others and was given cabinet posts in November 2000, although it returned to formal opposition status following the May 2002 legislative poll, in which it finished second to the CDP. Leadership disagreements within the ADF/RDA in 2003 led Yaméoga to quit the party and form the UNDD (below). Subsequently, the ADF/RDA supported President Compaoré in his reelection bid in 2005, and ADF/RDA leader Gilbert Ouédraogo was appointed to the new cabinet in January 2006.

Leaders: Gilbert Noël OUÉDRAOGO (President), Gérard Kango OUÉDRAOGO (Honorary President), Dabo HAMADOU (Vice President).

National Union for Democracy and Development (*Union Nationale pour la Démocratie et le Développement*—UNDD). The UNDD was launched in mid-2003 by Herman Yaméogo, one of the country's leading opposition figures, following a leadership squabble within the ADF/RDA. Among other things, Yaméogo had been accused by other ADF/RDA members of acting "too independently." The UNDD selected Yaméogo as its 2005 presidential candidate, but Yaméogo and the party formally withdrew the candidacy to protest the decision by the Constitutional Court to permit President Compaoré to run for another term. The UNDD called for "civil disobedience" in view of the court's ruling.

Leader: Herman YAMÉOGO (Chair), Mathieu N'DO.

Convention of Sankarist Parties (*Convention des Partis Sankaristes*—CPS). Also referenced as the Sankarist Panafrican Convention (*Convention Panafricaine Sankariste*), the CPS was formed in mid-1999 by the BSB, the United Social Democracy Party (*Parti de la Démocratie Sociale Unifié*—PDSU), a breakaway faction of the FFS and other

small groups. The CPS signed a protocol with the CDP and others and was given cabinet posts in November 2000, a decision that reportedly caused internal CPS tensions.

Leader: Ernest Nongoma OUÉDRAOGO (President).

Burkinabè Socialist Bloc (*Bloc Socialiste Burkinabè*—BSB). The BSB traces its lineage to the Democratic and Popular Rally–Thomas Sankara (*Rassemblement Démocratique et Populaire–Thomas Sankara*—RDP-TS), a clandestine resistance movement formed by supporters of the former president following the October 1987 coup. RDP-TS members were subsequently absorbed into the Sankarist Movement (*Mouvement Sankariste*—MS), an anti-Compaoré group, which was formed on August 4, 1988, the "revolution's" fifth anniversary. The MS, in turn, gave rise in November 1991 to the BSB (led by Ernest Nongoma Ouédraogo), which opposes Compaoré but is not part of the prodemocracy opposition.

The BSB boycotted the May 1992 assembly election, although one of its members, the **United Forces** (*Forces Unies*—FU), broke ranks to contest the poll. In August 1995 Ouédraogo was sentenced to six months imprisonment for allegedly accusing Compaoré of fraudulently amassing a personal fortune. Because of his conviction, Ouédraogo was forbidden from participating in the 1997 legislative elections; however, in March 1998 Compaoré pardoned him.

Leader: Ernest Nongoma OUÉDRAOGO.

Party for Democracy and Progress/Socialist Party (*Parti pour la Démocratie et le Progrès/Parti Socialiste*—PDP/PS). The PDP was launched in May 1993 by Joseph Ki-Zerbo in the aftermath of a struggle that erupted when a parliamentary coalition between Ki-Zerbo's Union of Independent Social Democrats (*Union des Sociaux-Démocrates Indépendants*—USDI) and the CNPP-PSD splintered following the retirement of the latter's leader.

Ki-Zerbo had previously been linked to the Voltaic Progressive Front (*Front Progressiste Voltaïque—* FPV), which he and a group of UDV-RDA dissidents had formed prior to the 1980 coup. The socialist-oriented FPV was proscribed until early 1991, when its longtime leader was amnestied; he returned from eight years in exile the following September.

The PDP, operating under the umbrella of the February 14 Group, boycotted the 1998 presidential elections. In May 2001 the PDP merged with the Burkinabè Socialist Party (*Parti Socialiste Burkinabè—*PSB), and the present name was adopted. Led by François Ouédraogo, the PSB was a breakaway formation from the PAI.

Under the leadership of Ki-Zerbo, described as one of the fiercest critics of the Compaoré administration, the PDP boycotted the 2000 municipal elections. However, the party presented candidates in the May 2002 assembly balloting, increasing its representation from six to ten. Disaffected PDP/PS members in 2002 formed a **People's Movement for Socialism/Federal Party** (*Mouvement du Peuple pour le Socialisme/Parti Féderal—*MPS/PF), which subsequently launched an electoral coalition with PAREN (below). Ali Lankoandé finished sixth (with 1.74 percent of the vote) as the candidate of the PDP/PS in the 2005 presidential election.

Leaders: Joseph KI-ZERBO (President), Sébastien ZABSONRE (General Secretary), François OUÉDRAOGO, Ali LANKOANDÉ (2005 presidential candidate).

Union for Rebirth/Sankarist Movement (*Union pour la Renaissance/Mouvement Sankariste—*UNIR/MS). Formed in 2000 under the leadership of Bénéwendé Sankara, the UNIR/MS won three seats in the 2002 assembly elections. In addition, Sankara, a lawyer and prominent human rights activist, finished second in the 2005 presidential poll with 4.95 percent of the vote.

Leader: Bénéwendé SANKARA (2005 presidential candidate).

Party for Democracy and Socialism (*Parti pour la Démocratie et la Socialisme—*PDS). After gaining representation in the 2002 assembly

balloting, the PDS reportedly presented Philippe Ouédraogo, formerly of the PAI (above), as its 2005 presidential candidate. He finished fourth with 2.28 percent of the vote.

Leader: Félix SOUBEIGA.

A number of minor parties gained representation in the assembly in the May 2002 elections including: the **Alliance for Progress and Freedom** (*Alliance pour le Progrès et la Liberté—*APL), led by Joséphine TAMBOURA-SAMA; the **National Convention of Progressive Democrats** (*Convention Nationale des Démocrates Progressistes—* CNDP), formed in 2000 and led by Alfred KABORÉ; the **Patriotic Front for Change** (*Front Patriotique pour le Changement—*FPC), a Sankarist party led by Tahirou Ibrahim ZON; and the **Union of Independent Progressive Democrats** (*Union des Démocrates et Progressistes Indépendants—*UDPI), which was formed in 2000 by dissidents from the G14 under the leadership of Longo DONGO.

Other Parties and Groups

Party for National Renaissance (*Parti pour la Renaissance Nationale—*PAREN). This party was launched in 1989 by Laurent Bado, who claimed that PAREN was neither socialist nor capitalist, but rather "Africanist." In August 2003 PAREN and the MPS/PF (above) formed an electoral coalition called the **United Opposition of Burkina** (*Opposition Burkinabè Uni—*OBU). As the PAREN/OBU candidate, Bado finished third in the 2005 presidential poll with 2.61 percent of the vote.

Leader: Laurent BADO (2005 presidential candidate).

African Convention for Democracy (*Convention Africain pour la Démocratie—*CAD). The CAD was reportedly admitted to the cabinet in November 2000.

Convention for Democracy and Federation (*Convention pour la Démocratie et la Fédération—* CDF). The CDF is a breakaway formation launched by, among others, a former ADF/RDA parliamentarian.

Cabinet

As of May 1, 2006

Prime Minister	Ernest Paramanga Yonli

Minister of State

Foreign Affairs and Regional Cooperation	Youssouf Ouédraogo

Ministers

Agriculture and Water Resources	Salif Diallo
Animal Resources	Tiémoko Konaté
Basic Education and Literacy	Marie Odile Bonkoungou [f]
Civil Service and Administrative Reform	Lassané Savadogo
Commerce and Promotion of Enterprise and Crafts	Bénoît Ouattara
Culture, Arts, and Tourism	Aline Koala [f]
Defense	Yéro Boly
Economy and Development	Seydou Bouda
Environment and Quality of Life	Laurent Sedego
Finance and Budget	Jean-Baptiste Marie Pascal Compaoré
Habitat and Urban Planning	Sékou Ba
Health	Bédouma Alain Yoda
Information	Joseph Kahoun
Infrastructure	Hyppolite Lingani
Justice and Keeper of the Seals	Boureima Badini
Labor and Social Security	Jerôme Bougouma
Mines, Quarries, and Energy	Abdoulaye Abdoulkader Cisse
Postal Service, Information Technology, and Communication	Joachim Tankoano
Promotion of Human Rights	Monique Ilboudo [f]
Relations with Parliament and Government Spokesman	Adama Fofana
Secondary and Higher Education and Scientific Research	Joseph Pare
Security	Djibril Yipéné Bassolet
Social Action and National Solidarity	Pascaline Tamini [f]
Sports and Leisure	Mori Ardouma Jean-Pierre Palm
Territorial Administration and Decentralization	Clément P. Sawadogo
Transportation	Gilbert Noël Ouédraogo
Women's Promotion	Gisèle Guigma [f]
Youth and Employment	Justin Koutaba
Secretary General of the Government and the Council of Ministers	Zakalia Kote

Ministers Delegate

Agriculture	Bonoudaba Dabire
Literacy and Nonformal Education	Amadou Diemdoba Dicko
Local Collectives	Soungalo Ouattara
Regional Cooperation	Jean de Dieu Somda
Technical and Professional Education	Hypolite Ouédraogo
Youth	Daniel Ouédraogo

[f] = female

Refuser's Front/African Democratic Rally (*Front de Refus/Rassemblement Démocratique Africain*—FR/RDA). The Refuser's Front is a breakaway faction of the RDA. Its leader, Frederic Fernand Guima, finished third in the 1998 presidential balloting.

Leader: Frederic Fernand GUIMA.

Social Forces Front (*Front des Forces Sociales*—FFS). A purported "Sankarist" group, the FFS was launched in October 1996. In 1998 the FFS gained national attention for its vocal role in the February 14 Group. The government accused FFS leader Norbert Tiendrébéogo of being involved in a coup plot in 2003, but Tiendrébéogo was subsequently exonerated. Tiendrébéogo finished seventh in the 2005 presidential poll with 1.6 percent of the vote.

Leader: Norbert Michel TIENDRÉBÉOGO (Chair and 2005 presidential candidate).

Other major parties that participated in the 2002 elections but failed to gain representation included the **National Democratic Party** (*Parti Démocratique National*—PDN), led by Karamoko KONÉ; the **Party for Progress and Social Development** (*Parti pour le Progrès et le Développement Social*—PPDS), led by Basile COMBARY; the **Unified Socialist Party** (*Parti Socialiste Unifié*—PSU), formed in 2001 by Benoît LOMPO; and the **Democrats and Patriots Group** (*Groupe des Démocrates et Patriotes*—GDP), led by Issa TIENDRÉBÉOGO.

Other new parties or groups created since the 2002 elections include the **Social and Democratic Convergence** (*Convergence Démocratique et Sociale*—CDS), formed in 2002 by a split in the UDPI and led by Valére SOMÉ; the **Ecological Party for the Development of Burkina** (*Parti Ecologique pour le Développement du Burkina*—PEDP), established in 2003; and the **Sankarist Democratic Front** (*Front Démocratique Sankariste*—FDS), which was created in 2004 by Fidéle KIENTÉGA and dissidents from the CPS.

Other small parties that participated in the 2005 presidential elections included the **Burkinabè Party for Refounding** (*Parti Burkinabè pour la Refondation*—PBR), whose candidate, Gilbert BOUDA, finished ninth with 1.04 percent of the vote; the **Socialist Alliance** (*Alliance Socialiste*—AS), whose candidate, Parqui Emile PARÉ, finished tenth with 0.87 percent of the vote; and the **Union for Democracy and Development** (*Union pour la Démocratie et le Developpement*—UDD), whose candidate, Toubé Clément DAKIO, secured 0.37 percent of the vote.

Legislature

The former National Assembly (*Assemblée Nationale*) was dissolved following the 1980 coup, and no successor body was established under the Sankara regime. The 1991 constitution provided for a 107-member Assembly of People's Deputies with a five-year mandate, balloting for which was initially scheduled for January 12, 1992, but subsequently postponed until May 24. The current basic law also provides for a second, consultative chamber (General Conference of the Nation [*Conférence Générale de la Nation*]), which had not been formally constituted as of early 2006.

Assembly of People's Deputies (*Assemblée des Députés Populaires*). In January 1997 the assembly approved a constitutional amendment increasing its seat total from 97 to 111. Election is conducted via a proportional system that was revised in advance of the 2002 balloting in order to promote greater opposition representation. Under the new changes, 90 deputies were elected in 2002 from 15 electoral districts (reduced from the previous 45 districts), and 21 deputies were elected from a national list. However, controversial legislation approved narrowly by the assembly in 2004 appeared to set the stage for a return to the old system for subsequent elections. Twenty-seven parties participated in the 1992 assembly balloting, 13 in 1997, and 30 in 2002.

The distribution of seats following the May 5, 2002, balloting was as follows: Congress of Democracy and Progress, 57; Alliance for Democracy and Federation/African Democratic Rally, 17;

Party for Democracy and Progress/Socialist Party, 10; African Party for Independence, 5; Coalition of Democratic Forces, 5; Party for National Renaissance, 4; Convention of Sankarist Parties, 3; Union for Renaissance/Sankarist Movement, 3; National Convention of Progressive Democrats, 2; Party for Democracy and Socialism, 2; Alliance for Progress and Freedom, 1; Patriotic Front for Change, 1; and Union of Independent Progressive Democrats, 1.

President: Marc Christian Roch KABORÉ.

Communications

Press

Under the present regime, there is a Written Press Board (*Direction de la Presse Ecrite*) charged with overseeing the media. The following are published in Ouagadougou (unless otherwise noted): *Observateur Paalga* (New Observer 8,000), independent daily; *Le Journal du Jeudi* (Thursday Journal, 8,000), independent weekly; *Le Matin* (The Morning, Bobo-Dioulasso), independent weekly; *Sidwaya* (Truth, 5,000), government daily; *Le Pays* (The Country, 4,000), independent daily; *Bulletin de l'Agence d'Information du Burkina* (200), twice-weekly government publication; *L'Indépendant* (The Independent), independent weekly; *Le Journal du Soir* (The Evening Journal); *Regard,* independent weekly; and *San Finna,* opposition weekly with connections to the National Union for Democracy and Development.

News Agencies

Agence d'Information du Burkina (AIB), a successor to *Agence Burkinabè de Presse* (ABP), is the domestic facility; *Agence France-Presse* and *Reuters* maintain offices in Ouagadougou.

Broadcasting and Computing

Radiodiffusion-Télévision du Burkina operates a number of radio and television stations, the latter concentrating on educational programming during the school year. There were approximately 196,000 television receivers and 26,000 personal computers serving 48,000 Internet users in 2003.

Intergovernmental Representation

Ambassador to the U.S.
Tertius ZONGO

U.S. Ambassador to Burkina Faso
Jeanine E. JACKSON

Permanent Representative to the UN
Michel KAFANDO

IGO Memberships (Non-UN)
AfDB, AU, BADEA, BOAD, CENT, CILSS, ECOWAS, IDB, Interpol, IOM, NAM, OIC, OIF, PCA, UEMOA, WCO, WTO

BURUNDI

REPUBLIC OF BURUNDI

Republika y'u Burundi (Kirundi)
République du Burundi (French)

The Country

Situated in east-central Africa, bordered by Rwanda, Tanzania, and the Democratic Republic of the Congo, Burundi is a country of grassy uplands and high plateaus. It is one of the most densely populated countries in Africa, with over 400 persons per square mile. There are three main ethnic groups: the Hutu (Bahutu), who constitute 84 percent of the population; the Tutsi (Batutsi, Watutsi), who are numerically a minority (15 percent) but have long dominated the country politically, socially, and economically; and the Twa, or pygmies (1 percent). A majority of the population is nominally Christian, primarily Roman Catholic. Women account for almost half of the labor force, although they are concentrated in subsistence activities, with men predominant in paid labor. Female representation in politics and government was traditionally minimal, although the prime minister from July 1993 to February 1994 was a woman. Under the new constitution adopted in 2005 significant female representation is guaranteed in the Parliament, and there are eight women in the current cabinet.

One of the world's least-developed countries (average per capita income is less than $1 per day), Burundi remains dependent on agriculture: more than 90 percent of its inhabitants are farmers, primarily at the subsistence level, while coffee typically accounts for about 80 percent of export earnings. The small industrial sector consists for the most part of agricultural processing. At present,

small quantities of cassiterite, gold, columbite-tantalite, and wolframite are extracted, while exploitation of a major deposit of nickel and potentially significant reserves of phosphate, petroleum, and uranium await construction of transport infrastructure.

Officials from the International Monetary Fund (IMF) in 1992 reported that the second phase of an economic reform program had produced "progress toward sustainable economic growth." However, the outbreak of civil conflict in 1993 and the subsequent withdrawal of international assistance yielded negative growth in 1993–1995. In

Political Status: Independent state since July 1, 1962; under military control from November 28, 1966; one-party constitution adopted by referendum of November 18, 1981; military control reimposed following coup of September 3, 1987; multiparty constitution adopted March 13, 1992, following referendum of March 9; military rule reimposed following coup of July 25, 1996; transitional constitution signed into law June 6, 1998; new transitional constitution providing for a three-year transitional period adopted October 27, 2001; new constitution approved by national referendum on February 28, 2005; transitional period concluded with local and national elections in June–September 2005.

Area: 10,747 sq. mi. (27,834 sq. km.).

Population: 5,139,073 (1990C); 7,056,000 (2005E).

Major Urban Center (2005E): BUJUMBURA (407,000).

Official Languages: Kirundi, French (Swahili is also spoken).

Monetary Unit: Burundi Franc (official rate July 1, 2006: 980.00 francs = $1US).

President: Pierre NKURUNZIZA (Hutu from the National Council for the Defense of Democracy–Forces for the Defense of Democracy); elected by the Parliament on August 19, 2005, and inaugurated for a five-year term on August 26 in succession to Domitien NDAYIZEYE (Front for Democracy in Burundi).

First Vice President (In Charge of Political and Administrative Affairs): Martin NDUWIMANA (Tutsi from the Union for National Progress); approved by the Parliament (upon nomination by the president) on August 29, 2005, and inaugurated the same day.

Second Vice President (In Charge of Social and Economic Affairs): Alice NZOMUKUNDA (Hutu from the National Council for the Defense of Democracy); approved by the Parliament (upon nomination by the president) on August 29, 2005, and inaugurated the same day.

mid-1996 it was estimated that fighting between Hutus and Tutsis had left over 150,000 dead in the previous three years, and, following the military coup in July, the nation's already extremely unstable security and economic conditions deteriorated even further.

The country's ongoing civil strife subsequently continued to constrain the government's ability to collect revenues, as did smuggling and a general economic downturn. GDP fell by an estimated 1 percent in 1999, partially as the result of the declining price for coffee (Burundi's main source of foreign exchange) and impaired transportation infrastructure, which significantly impeded the movement of goods. The transition government installed in late 2001 under a new power-sharing agreement (see Political background, below) immediately launched an appeal for international aid to assist reconstruction, combat what was described as an "alarming level of poverty," and facilitate the expected repatriation of hundreds of thousands of refugees from neighboring countries. Modest recovery, albeit from a very low base, subsequently

ensued, GDP growing by 2.1 percent in 2002 while inflation registered approximately 4 percent. The relative political stability also permitted the deployment of regional peacekeepers and the resumption of foreign aid by the IMF, the World Bank, and others.

Upon the installation of a new government of national unity in 2005, it was estimated that 300,000 people had lost their lives in the 12-year civil war. Collaterally, GDP had declined by more than a third. Among other distressing indicators, nearly 60 percent of the country's children suffered from stunted growth due to poor nutrition, according to one relief agency.

Government and Politics

Political Background

Established in the 16th century as a feudal monarchy ruled by the Tutsi, Burundi (formerly Urundi) was incorporated into German East Africa in 1895 and came under Belgian administration as a result of World War I. From 1919 to 1962 it formed the southern half of the Belgian-administered League of Nations mandate (later The United Nations Trust Territory) of Ruanda-Urundi. Retaining its monarchical form of government under indigenous Tutsi rulers (*mwami*), Urundi was granted limited self-government in 1961 and achieved full independence as the Kingdom of Burundi on July 1, 1962.

Rivalry between Tutsi factions and between Tutsis and Hutus resulted in the assassination of Prime Minister Pierre NGENDANDUMWE in January 1965 and an abortive Hutu coup the following October. The uprising led to repressive action by government troops under the command of Capt. Michel MICOMBERO. Named prime minister as the result of military intervention in July 1966, Micombero suspended the constitution, dissolved the National Assembly, and on November 28 deposed King NATARE V. In addition to naming himself president of the newly proclaimed Republic of Burundi, Micombero took over the presidency of the Union and National Progress (*Union et Progrés National*—Uprona), the Tutsi-dominated political party that was accorded monopoly status.

Despite antigovernment plots in 1969 and 1971, the Micombero regime was generally able to contain conflict in the immediate postcoup era. In 1972, however, the mysterious death of the former king and another attempted Hutu uprising provoked renewed reprisals by Micombero's Tutsi supporters. At least 100,000 deaths (largely of Hutus) ensued, with countless thousands fleeing to neighboring countries.

On November 1, 1976, Micombero was overthrown in a bloodless coup led by Lt. Col. Jean-Baptiste BAGAZA, who suspended the constitution and announced that formal power under the "Second Republic" would be assumed by a 30-member Supreme Council of the Revolution with himself as head of state. At an Uprona congress in December 1979 the council was abolished, effective January 1980, and its functions transferred to a party Central Committee headed by the president. On October 22, 1982, elections were held for a new National Assembly and for pro forma reconfirma-

tion of Bagaza as chief executive. Following his redesignation as party leader at the Uprona congress of July 25–27, 1984, Bagaza was nominated for a third presidential term (the first by direct election), obtaining a reported 99.6 percent of the vote in a referendum on August 31.

Bagaza's subsequent administration was marked by progressively more stringent measures against the Roman Catholic Church, which traditionally maintained strong links with the Hutu community. Many Tutsis eventually joined the condemnation of "dictatorial" anticlerical measures such as the expulsion and imprisonment of Church leaders and the proscription of weekday masses. Amid growing alienation, Bagaza was ousted in a bloodless revolt on September 3, 1987, while attending a francophone summit in Canada. The leader of the coup, Maj. Pierre BUYOYA, suspended the constitution, dissolved the National Assembly, and named a 31-member Military Committee for National Salvation (*Comité Militaire pour le Salut National*—CMSN) to exercise provisional authority. On September 9 the CMSN designated Buyoya as president of the "Third Republic," and on October 1 Buyoya announced the formation of a new government, pledging that the "military will not remain in power long."

On October 19, 1988, following a renewal of Tutsi-Hutu conflict, Buyoya named a 23-member cabinet that contained an unprecedented majority of Hutus, including Adrien SIBOMANA as occupant of the newly reestablished post of prime minister. However, the timetable for a return to constitutional rule remained unclear, and the CMSN, composed entirely of Tutsis, remained the dominant decision-making body until mid-1990, when it was replaced by the National Security Council (*Conseil National de Sécurité*—CSN), an 11-member civilian grouping of six Tutsis and five Hutus.

In furtherance of President Buyoya's campaign for ethnic reconciliation, a national charter calling for "unity, respect for human rights and freedom of expression" was endorsed by Uprona in December 1990 and adopted by popular referendum on February 5, 1991. In accordance with charter provisions calling for an end to military rule, Buyoya on March 22 empowered a 35-member constitutional commission to outline the framework of a multiparty system. The commission's report, released on September 10, served as the basis of a pluralist constitution that was approved by an overwhelming majority in a popular referendum on March 9, 1992, and promulgated four days later.

On November 17, 1992, President Buyoya appointed a national electoral commission charged with overseeing the legislative and presidential balloting scheduled for 1993. The 33-member body included two representatives from each of eight registered political parties, with the balance drawn from a broad spectrum of public and religious organizations.

At the presidential election of June 1, 1993, the Hutu opposition candidate, Melchior NDADAYE, was a better than three-to-one victor over Buyoya, and at legislative balloting on June 29 Ndadaye's Front for Democracy in Burundi (*Front pour la Démocratie au Burundi*—Frodebu) won 65 of 81 seats. Despite international praise for the electoral process, some 5,000 Tutsis took part in street demonstrations denouncing the "ethnic nature" of the Hutu victories, and on July 3 an abortive coup attempt by troops loyal to Buyoya was reported.

On July 10, 1993, Ndadaye reached out to the previously dominant ethnic group and included seven Uprona members in a new cabinet that was also headed by a Tutsi, Sylvie KINIGI, as prime minister. Pledging continuance of his predecessor's reconciliation program, Ndadaye in September amnestied 5,000 prisoners (earlier he had granted clemency to Bagaza, allowing the former president to return from six years in exile). In early October Ndadaye announced plans to begin the repatriation of the approximately 300,000 Burundians displaced by earlier conflicts.

Optimism engendered by the reconciliation effort was dashed on October 21, 1993, when Ndadaye, the National Assembly president, and a number of senior Hutu government officials were slain during an abortive military coup attempt spearheaded by Tutsi paratroopers. The rebellion ended within two days as senior military personnel, some

of whom had been implicated in the plot, sought to disassociate themselves from an ethnic frenzy unleashed by the president's assassination. In addition to a number of senior Tutsi officers from the Burore region, the coup plotters allegedly included Bagaza; the recently appointed army chief-of-staff, Col. Jean BIKOMAGU; and François NGEZE, a former interior minister and vocal critic of the new administration, who on October 21 was named president of the rebels' short-lived National Committee of Public Salvation (an appointment he later claimed was forced on him). Denying involvement in the uprising, Bikomagu on October 24 offered to aid in reestablishing the government in exchange for an amnesty; however, the offer was rejected by Prime Minister Kinigi, who said from refuge in the French embassy that she would remain underground until the military had returned to barracks and an international protective force had been established for the government.

By October 24, 1993, most of the rebel soldiers had fled Bujumbura in fear of a massing of progovernment troops and revenge-minded Ndadaye supporters. On November 2, following the arrest of at least ten of the plotters, including Ngeze, Kinigi emerged from her embassy sanctuary to retake control of the government. Six days later she met with 15 cabinet ministers under the protection of a French special forces unit to discuss ways of ending the tribal bloodbath that had left 10,000 dead and hundreds of thousands exiled in Rwanda, Tanzania, and Zaire.

On January 13, 1994, the National Assembly elected a Hutu moderate, Agriculture Minister Cyprien NTARYAMIRE, to the presidency. However, Ntaryamire and Rwandan President Habyarimana were killed in an airplane bombing over Kigali, Rwanda, on April 6, 1994. On April 8 Sylvestre NTIBANTUNGANYA, who had been elected assembly president on December 23, 1993, became Ntaryamire's acting successor.

Amid escalating violence, opposition leaders boycotted talks on the selection of a new president in June 1994. However, on July 13 a power-sharing agreement was concluded, under which Frodebu was to be awarded control of 9 provinces and 74 communes, with opposition groups being given 7 provinces and 48 communes. A follow-up "Convention on Government" was signed on September 10, under which 45 percent of cabinet posts, including the prime ministership and interior ministry, were to be allocated to the Uprona-led opposition, with the defense and justice portfolios reserved for "neutral persons." Subsequently, the convention's nomination of the acting president for a regular term was ratified by the National Assembly, with swearing-in ceremonies on October 1. Instability nonetheless continued, with the controversial election on December 3 of Frodebu's Jean MINANI as National Assembly speaker being defended by the Uprona prime minister, Anatole KANYENKIKO, who had succeeded Kinigi in February. Opposition to Minani led to his replacement by Léonce NGENDAKUMANA on January 12, 1995, while Kanyenkiko was, in turn, obliged to resign on February 15 after being expelled from Uprona for indiscipline in regard to the Minani affair. With the appointment of the Uprona-nominated Antoine NDUWAYO as Kanyenkiko's successor as prime minister on February 20, the political crisis appeared to ease, although Tanzania reported that some 25,000 refugees had crossed its border with Burundi since the first of the month.

A new cycle of fighting erupted following the murder on March 11, 1995, of a prominent Hutu leader, Ernest KABUSHEMEYE, prompting another wave of refugees into Zaire and Tanzania. Meanwhile, President Ntibantunganya rejected proposals (apparently advanced by U.S. officials) that the problems of Burundi and Rwanda be addressed by the creation of two ethnically based countries, in effect a "Hutuland" and a "Tutsiland." In July the UN announced the formation of a commission of inquiry into the October 1993 coup attempt and urged the feuding political groups to begin peace negotiations, warning that the UN could only play a minor role in ending the conflict.

Following the killing of at least 58 Tutsis at a displaced persons camp in early August 1995, Prime Minister Nduwayo claimed that former Rwandan soldiers and militiamen (both Hutu-dominated) were responsible for at least "two-thirds of the re-cent violence." Nduwayo's assertion worsened the already incendiary debate within the cabinet over which ethnic group was responsible for the latest round of violence, and on October 12 Ntibantunganya reshuffled the government, ousting the most vocal combatants and replacing them with less "partisan" ministers. The violence nonetheless continued, and in December three of the ten parties participating in the government withdrew.

With ethnic fighting intensifying, the United States and the European Union (EU) suspended aid payments to Burundi, citing the government's failure to end the violence. President Ntibantunganya and Prime Minister Nduwayo agreed in principle in early July 1996 to the deployment of foreign peacekeeping forces to quell ethnic violence and protect Burundi's infrastructure, borders, and political leaders. That plan was denounced by militants in both the Tutsi and Hutu camps, however, and, following the massacre by Hutu rebels of over 300 Tutsis in a camp on July 20, antigovernment demonstrations broke out in Bujumbura and other cities. After being stoned by Tutsi mourners at funeral services for the massacre victims, President Ntibantunganya sought refuge in the U.S. embassy on July 23. The next day Uprona announced it was withdrawing from the coalition government, and on July 25 the military declared that it had taken power, dismissed the government, suspended the constitution and the National Assembly, and appointed former president Buyoya head of state. (Prime Minister Nduwayo accepted his dismissal, but President Ntibantunganya subsequently insisted that he remained the nation's lawful head of state.) On July 31 Maj. Buyoya announced the appointment of Pascal Firmin NDIMIRA, a Hutu member of Uprona, as prime minister, and a new 25-member Uprona-based government was formed on August 2. Despite Maj. Buyoya's reputation as a "moderate" among Tutsi military leaders and the credit he had received for the orderly transfer of power three years earlier, the July 1996 coup was broadly denounced by the United Nations, Western capitals, and, most strongly, by neighboring states, who immediately imposed severe economic sanctions against Burundi. For his part, asserting that the military had taken over only to "stop the bloodshed," Maj. Buyoya called for a three-year transitional period prior to a return to civilian government and pledged to clamp down on military abuses.

On September 12, 1996, in the face of the strong international condemnation of the coup, Buyoya declared that the assembly suspension had been lifted and that political party activity could resume. However, only 37 of 81 legislators participated in the reopening of the assembly on October 7, contributing factors including the recent murder of a number of legislators, an opposition boycott, and apathy resulting from the fact that the suspension of the constitution had left the body virtually powerless. On October 11–12 regional leaders meeting in Arusha, Tanzania, decided to maintain the economic sanctions against Bujumbura despite the regime's announcement on October 11 that it intended to hold unconditional peace talks with the dominant rebel group—the National Council for the Defense of Democracy (*Conseil National pour la Défense de Démocratie*—CNDD). Moreover, in late 1996 both the UN and Amnesty International charged the regime with responsibility for the reoccurring massacres that had taken place since July.

In March 1997 the government announced that it had arrested eight people (five of whom belonged to former president Bagaza's Party for National Recovery [*Parti pour le Recouvrement National*—Parena]) for their alleged roles in a coup plot against the president as well as bomb attacks in Bujumbura. Despite continued violence, in mid-April regional leaders agreed to loosen sanctions on humanitarian supplies. On June 7 former president Ntibantunganya left the U.S. embassy, declaring his intention to resume his political life and calling for the opening of peace talks. One week later Buyoya asked for international assistance in establishing a genocide tribunal to punish those responsible for the recent ethnic violence. However, the UN Security Council rejected his request, citing continued high levels of instability.

Following intense negotiations on a power-sharing agreement between Buyoya and Hutu remnants in the assembly (led by Speaker Léonce

Ngendakumana), Buyoya signed a transitional constitution into law on June 6, 1998. Provisions included enlargement of the assembly, the formal recognition of established political parties, and formation of a transitional government. Consequently, Buyoya was officially sworn in as president on June 11, and the following day he appointed two vice presidents, including Frodebu leader Frederic BAMVUGINYUMVIRA, to assume responsibilities formerly held by the prime minister, whose post was abolished. On June 13 the president appointed a new cabinet, 13 of whose 22 members were Hutus, while the Transitional National Assembly was inaugurated on July 18, new members representing small parties as well as social and professional groups (see Legislature, below).

Regional leaders meeting in Tanzania in early September 1997 agreed to maintain economic sanctions against the Burundian regime, warning President Buyoya that "additional measures" would be considered unless progress was made toward restoration of civilian government. Buyoya had declined to participate in the summit's proposed peace talks, in part, reportedly, out of conviction that Tanzania was "pro-Hutu." (It was estimated that as many as 300,000 Hutu refugees were encamped inside the Tanzanian border.) In his defense, Buyoya appeared to be attempting to follow a difficult middle course between the militant Hutu guerrilla groups, who had been fighting since 1993 to take over the government, and predominately Tutsi hard-liners in the government and military, who opposed negotiations of any sort with the "rebels." At the same time, Western capitals remained concerned over the Buyoya regime's refusal to permit the resumption of normal political party activity as well as its highly controversial "resettlement" program in which perhaps as many as 600,000 people were confined to "refugee" camps. Although the government argued that the measures were designed to protect people displaced by guerrilla activity, critics argued that Hutus were being placed in the camps so that they could not offer support to the rebels.

Perhaps in part to improve his "battered image" in the West, President Buyoya in March 1998 agreed to participate in talks with representatives of Frodebu, the CNDD, and other factions. A series of peace talks began in June under the leadership of Julius Nyerere, the former Tanzanian president representing the regional nations who had imposed economic sanctions. During the fourth round of negotiations in January 1999, the sanctions were lifted, following earlier calls for their suspension or cessation by the EU and UN Security Council. The power-sharing agreement reached six months earlier between the government and the opposition appeared to have persuaded critics of the regime that it was making progress.

Peace negotiations in Tanzania dragged on through 1999, the slow pace of the discussions reflecting not only the complexity of the issues but also the reality that divisions had shifted in part from strictly along party lines to intraparty disagreements between peacemakers and hard-liners.

Following Nyerere's death in October 1999, former South African president Nelson Mandela assumed the task of facilitating the negotiations. He announced in May 2000 that an agreement in principle had been reached, and a partial, preliminary agreement was signed on August 28. However, details remained to be settled regarding highly sensitive issues such as the length and composition of a transitional government, the specifics of the new electoral system, and the integration of the nation's security forces. Highly contentious negotiations on these matters dragged on for months, as did efforts by the government to negotiate a cease-fire with the Hutu rebel groups that had rejected the accord— the Forces for the Defense of Democracy (*Forces pour la Défense de Démocratie*—FDD) and the National Forces of Liberation (*Forces Nationales de la Libération*—FNL). Finally, following mediation by the Organization of African Unity (OAU, subsequently the African Union—AU) and further efforts by Mandela, a power-sharing agreement was accepted on July 23, 2001, during a meeting in Arusha of 19 groups (representatives from the government, Transitional National Assembly, and all members of the pro-Hutu Group of Seven and pro-Tutsi Group of Ten—see listings in Political Parties and Groups, below).

On October 28, 2001, the assembly adopted a transitional constitution to implement the Arusha accords, and the following day the assembly confirmed Buyoya as president of the new transitional government and Domitien NDAYIZEYE, secretary general of Frodebu, as vice president. Buyoya was sworn in on November 1 for an 18-month term, after which he was to be replaced, according to the agreement, by Ndayizeye for the remaining 18 months of the transition period. (A Tutsi was scheduled to replace Ndayizeye as vice president following his elevation to president, although Buyoya announced he would not be a candidate for that post.) A new cabinet, comprising 15 political parties, was also installed on November 1, while on November 27 the assembly adopted legislation providing for a new transitional legislature (see Legislature, below, for details.)

In December 2002, through mediation by South Africa and Uganda, a broad cease-fire was reached with most of the remaining major rebel groups, including the FDD, thus paving the way for the deployment of a peace-monitoring force by the AU in February 2003. Under the terms of the transitional constitution, at the end of his 18-month term Buyoya turned the presidency over to Ndayizeye, who was inaugurated on April 30, 2003. That same day, Alphonse-Marie KADEGE of Uprona was appointed vice president.

Renewed fighting in July 2003 between the government and the FNL led the UN to withdraw its nonessential personnel from the country and had, by September, left 170 dead and created some 50,000 additional internal refugees. In October, in Pretoria, South Africa, peace negotiations under the leadership of South African President Thabo Mbeki led to an agreement that granted five cabinet posts to the primary CNDD faction, now known as the CNDD-FDD. Three provincial gubernatorial posts and the vice presidency of the assembly were also accorded to the CNDD-FDD. In return, the CNDD-FDD pledged to begin disarmament. To oversee that process, the AU peacekeeping force was increased to more than 3,000 troops. On November 16 the government and the CNDD-FDD signed a comprehensive peace agreement to implement the Arusha accords, and on November 23 Ndayizeye reshuffled the cabinet to form a government of national unity that included the CNDD-FDD. In December Pierre NKURUNZIZA, the leader of the CNDD-FDD, returned to Burundi for the first time since 1993, and 6,000 CNDD-FDD fighters began demobilization. However, at least one faction of the FNL continued its armed struggle.

On October 20, 2004, Ndayizeye signed a new draft constitution that had been approved by a special joint session of the legislature. The document called for permanent power sharing between the Tutsis and Hutus through a system of proportional representation (see Constitution and government, below). National legislative elections were subsequently scheduled for July 2005, and Ndayizeye's term was extended until the new elections, at which time a new president would be chosen by the legislature. (Subsequent presidents would be popularly elected.) Ndayizeye announced that he intended to retire from politics at the end of his current term. (The constitution was approved by voters in a national referendum on February 28, 2005, by a 92 percent margin.) On November 10, 2004, Vice President Kadege resigned following continued disagreements with the president over power-sharing arrangements and Kadege's opposition to the new constitution. Kadege was replaced the following day by Frederic NGENZEBUHORO of Uprona.

Communal elections were held on June 3, 2005, with the CNDD-FDD (now a legal party) securing more than 55 percent of votes and more than 1,780 of the 3,325 seats up for election. The CNDD-FDD also dominated the July 4 assembly balloting, and CNDD-FDD leader Nkurunziza was elected president (as the sole candidate) with 91 percent of the votes cast during a joint session of the assembly and the Senate on August 19. In keeping with constitutional requirements, Nkurunziza appointed a Tutsi from Uprona (Martin NDUWIMANA) as first vice president. Nkurunziza subsequently formed a new national unity government that included members from the CNDD-FDD, Uprona, Frodebu, Parena, and several small parties. However, Frodebu in March 2006 announced its withdrawal from the government (see Frodebu under Political Parties and Groups, below).

Constitution and Government

The constitution approved in March 1992 provided for a "semi-presidential, semi-parliamentary" government in which the president shared power with a prime minister, who appointed his ministerial colleagues. Both the president and legislature were popularly elected for five-year terms, with assignment to the latter by proportional representation. Political parties seeking legal status were required to pledge allegiance to the 1991 national unity charter and the "principles of respect for national sovereignty." Parties organized on an ethnic or regional basis were prohibited.

Following the abortive coup of October 1993, which claimed the lives of both the state and legislative presidents, the Constitutional Court declared the office of the former vacant and invoked a constitutional provision that, in such an eventuality, assigned interim power to the governmental collectivity headed by the prime minister.

The assembly's 1994 designation of Cyprien Ntaryamire as president was authorized by a constitutional amendment of January 9, while assumption of the office on an acting basis by assembly President Ntibantunganya in April was subject to a constitutional limit of three months, with a second such span subsequently authorized by the Constitutional Court. The constitution was suspended following the July 1996 coup, military leaders promising that a new institutional structure would be proposed within three years. The transitional constitution of June 6, 1998, restored a number of elements of the 1992 document, although the post of prime minister was abolished in favor of two new vice presidential positions and an expanded Transitional National Assembly was established.

Following the signing of the Arusha power-sharing accord in July 2001, the assembly adopted a "Constitution of Transition" on October 28 providing for a three-year transitional government. Power was concentrated in the presidency and vice presidency, with a Tutsi (President Buyoya) to serve as president for 18 months before being replaced for the next 18 months by a Hutu. Provision was also made for a new Transitional Parliament, to include a National Assembly and a Senate. Elections were scheduled to be held, under undetermined electoral arrangements, at the communal level by the end of the first 18 months of the transition and at the national level (for a new assembly and senate) by the end of the second 18-month period.

The new constitution approved via national referendum on February 28, 2005, was most noteworthy for its efforts to institutionalize Hutu/Tutsi power sharing. The new basic law provided for the new legislature to elect the next president, but subsequent chief executives will be popularly elected. The president is elected for a five-year term, renewable once. There are two vice presidents; if the president is a Hutu, then the first vice president must be a Tutsi, and vice versa. The first vice president must also be from a different party than the president. It was mandated that maximum cabinet membership be 60 percent for Hutus and 40 percent for Tutsis. The defense minister must be from a different ethnic group than the minister responsible for internal security, and no single ethnic group can make up more than 50 percent of military and security forces. (For details on the new Parliament, see Legislature, below).

For administrative purposes the country is divided into 17 provinces, each headed by an appointed governor. The provinces are subdivided into 129 communes as well as smaller districts, with elected communal and district councils directing local affairs.

Foreign Relations

Internal conflicts have significantly influenced Burundi's relations with its neighbors. During the turmoil of the Micombero era, relations with Rwanda (where the Hutu were dominant), as well as with Tanzania and Zaire, were strained. Under President Bagaza, however, a new spirit of regional cooperation led to the formation in 1977 of a joint Economic Community of the Great Lakes Countries (*Communauté Économique des Pays des Grande Lacs*—CEPGL), within which Burundi, Rwanda, and Zaire agreed to organize a development bank, exploit gas deposits under Lake Kivu, and establish a fishing industry on Lake Tanganyika.

Burundi is a member, along with Rwanda, Tanzania, and Uganda, of the Organization for the Management and Development of the Kagera River Basin. In February 1984 a revised plan for a 2,000-kilometer rail network linking the four countries was approved, thereby addressing Bujumbura's concern about Burundi's lack of access to reliable export routes; hydroelectric and communications projects by the organization also signaled greater economic cooperation, as did Burundi's entrance (along with the rest of CEPGL) into the Economic Community of Central African States.

Relations were poor between the first Buyoya government and Libya, where former president Bagaza was reported in early 1989 to have gained asylum. In April 1989 Bujumbura expelled Libyan diplomats and other Libyan nationals for alleged "destabilizing activities," reportedly in connection with a coup plot uncovered the previous month among Bagaza loyalists.

An August 1991 meeting of Burundian, Rwandan, and Ugandan representatives yielded agreement on efforts to contain ethnic destabilization movements operating near border areas; however, observers reported mounting grass-roots tensions stemming from persistent rumors of Tutsi "empire-building" ambitions. Although punctuated by crossborder rebel activities, negotiations continued in 1992 between Burundi and Rwanda on establishing cooperative security arrangements.

The October 1993 presidential assassination and coup attempt were immediately and unanimously condemned by international observers, with initial calls for economic and political isolation of the rebels giving way to plans to establish a regional peacekeeping force to bolster the government and stem the ethnic violence. However, with the Tutsi military and Uprona leadership openly hostile to intervention, UN and OAU officials resisted the Kinigi government's call for a large-scale intervention.

International efforts to contain ethnic violence were frustrated throughout 1995 by the intransigence of the combatants as well as by the Tutsi military leadership's adamant opposition to a foreign military presence. Burundi expressed wariness over Tanzanian and Ugandan mediation in the first half of 1996, suggesting that its east African neighbors were interested in expanding their territories. The July 1996 coup was broadly denounced by the UN, Western capitals, and, most strongly, by neighboring states, who immediately imposed severe economic sanctions against Burundi. Those sanctions were lifted on January 23, 1999, in conjunction with the initiation of peace talks in Arusha, Tanzania. During this period, Burundi's relations with its neighboring countries remained tense, and Burundian troops were sent into the Democratic Republic of the Congo (DRC, formerly Zaire) in an attempt to dislodge staging areas of the rebel FDD.

Burundi's troops reached 3,000 in the DRC prior to a withdrawal in January 2002. Meanwhile, continued fighting between the DRC government and its own rebels in the DRC prompted the flight of some 35,000 refugees to Burundi. In addition, some 324,000 refugees from fighting in Burundi reportedly continued to reside in Tanzania. Progress in the repatriation of refugees was reported in 2004–2005. Moreover, following the installation of a newly elected power-sharing government in Burundi in 2005, Burundi concluded an agreement with Uganda, Rwanda, and the DRC for establishment of a regional intelligence gathering unit.

Current Issues

The two main rebel groups (the FDD and FNL) remained adamantly opposed to the Arusha accord in late 2001 and, in fact, intensified their military activity. (Other rebel forces had accepted the Arusha provisions for their gradual integration into what would ultimately become ethnically balanced national defense and security forces.) Moreover, even within the political parties that had signed the power-sharing agreement, Tutsi and Hutu hardliners scoffed at the prospects for a permanent negotiated settlement and the potential for cohesiveness within the coalition government, which contained highly disparate elements. Nevertheless, President Buyoya and Vice President Ndayizeye pledged to "fight the ideology of genocide" and to promote national unity. Meanwhile, South Africa deployed peacekeeping troops in Burundi to protect the hundreds of thousands of Hutu refugees (including numerous prominent politicians) who had been invited to return to Burundi. The UN endorsed the South African initiative, which was soon augmented by forces from other neighboring countries; however, no official UN peacekeeping mission was authorized at that point in view of the lack of a cease-fire agreement from the rebels.

Fighting between government forces and both the FDD and FNL continued into the autumn of 2002, despite several attempts at negotiating peace settlements. However, the declaration of a cease-fire with the FDD in December and subsequent deployment of the AU peacekeeping force began to convince skeptics that a long-term settlement was possible. The UN in May 2004 authorized its own peacekeeping mission (the United Nations Operation in Burundi [*Opération des Nations Unies au Burundi*—ONUB]) to succeed the AU forces and supervise the disarmament of an estimated 40,000 "rebels." In December President Ndayizeye signed legislation creating a new national army and police force incorporating the former FDD fighters. At that point, sporadic, albeit intense, fighting between government forces and the FNL still presented a serious barrier to successful conclusion of the transitional government. However, in May 2005 most elements of the FNL finally agreed to a truce.

The CNDD-FDD completed a remarkable transition in 2005 from a former rebel group to the country's dominant political force. Observers attributed the CNDD-FDD's success to appreciation within the Hutu population for the past willingness of the CNDD-FDD to have "backed up" its political stance "with guns." In contrast, Hutu support for Frodebu had declined as the perception had apparently grown that its "engagement" with Uprona since the mid-1990s had been largely ineffective.

The three-month election cycle of mid-2005 was for the most part conducted peacefully, with only sporadic and isolated violence on the part of holdout FNL rebels being reported. EU and UN observers described the balloting as generally free and fair, prompting optimistic observers to suggest that the national unity government installed under the leadership of the CNDD-FDD had at least a modest chance of preserving the fledgling Hutu/Tutsi peace and addressing the nation's daunting economic and social needs. At the same time, cautious analysts cited several potential barriers to effective governmental action, including the inexperience of the new administration and concern (particularly within the Tutsi community) over the CNDD-FDD's militant background. (New president Pierre Nkurunziza had been sentenced, in absentia, to death by a court in Burundi in 1998 for his rebel activity before being covered by the amnesty provisions of the Arusha accord.) The international community broadly welcomed Burundi's first democratically elected government since 1993, which, among other things, was considered a significant triumph for South Africa's recent wide-ranging diplomatic efforts throughout Central Africa.

Despite the fact that some FNL rebel activity continued in mountainous areas near Bujumbura, the UN in April 2006 announced that ONUB peacekeepers would be withdrawn gradually throughout the rest of the year. (UN officials described the mission as "by and large a success story.") For its part, the new administration announced plans to raise the salaries of civil servants, provide greater aid to farmers (particularly in the famine-threatened north), expand health care (especially to pregnant women and mothers with young children), and modernize the coffee and sugar sectors. President Nkurunziza also pledged to implement anticorruption measures and to intensify the disarmament of former fighters and the civilian population as a whole. However, as of May, it remained unclear when (or if) a South African–style truth and recon-

ciliation commission would be established to deal with other lingering effects of the long civil conflict, which had cost the lives of more than 300,000 people.

In early September 2006 President Nkurunziza signed a cease-fire agreement with Agathon RWASA, the leader of the FNL rebel holdouts. Although the accord was heralded by some as the end of the country's 13-year civil war, negotiations were still required concerning the final disarmament of the FNL and its conversion into a political party.

Political Parties and Groups

Of the 24 political parties that contested Burundi's pre-independence elections in 1961, only Uprona survived, serving as the political base of the Micombero and Bagaza regimes. On April 16, 1992, a month after the constitutional revival of pluralism, President Buyoya signed a bill guaranteeing that the next election would be conducted on a multiparty basis.

On March 10, 1993, the government forwarded a "code of conduct" for signature by all active parties to promote "understanding and dialogue" during the "democratic process." By midyear 11 parties, including Uprona, had been legally registered. The government formed on March 1, 1995, encompassed Frodebu, Uprona, the RPB, PP, and six minor Tutsi-oriented nonparliamentarian groups that supported Uprona. In December three of the most vociferously anti-Hutu formations—Raddes, *Inkinzo*, and the PRP—withdrew from the government. Political party activity was suspended following the coup of July 1996 but was reactivated under the transitional constitution of June 1998. Many of the smaller parties were given seats in the 1998 Transitional National Assembly.

Two main groupings were involved in the negotiations from 1999–2001 of the Arusha accord providing for a new transitional government. Initially, Hutu-oriented parties coalesced in the Group of Six (G-6), which included Frodebu, CNDD, PP, PL, RPB, and Frolina. The G-6 subsequently became the G-7 with the addition of Palipehutu. Meanwhile, the pro-Tutsi Group of

Ten (G-10) included Uprona, Parena, *Inkinzo,* AV-*Intwari*, Abasa, Anadde, Raddes, PRP, PIT, and PSD. All of the G-7 and G-10 parties were offered seats in the new Transitional National Assembly, while 15 of the parties accepted seats in the new cabinet installed on November 1, 2001. However, strong dissident factions opposed to the Arusha accord were reported within many of the parties. The national unity government of November 2003 included Uprona, Frodebu, RPB, Raddes, *Inkinzo*, Anadde, Abasa, CNDD-FDD, PRP, Palipehutu, AV-*Intwari*, PSD, and PP.

Government Parties

National Council for the Defense of Democracy–Forces for the Defense of Democracy (*Conseil National pour la Défense de Démocratie–Forces pour la Défense de Démocratie—*CNDD-FDD). The CNDD-FDD is one of the successors to the CNDD that was formed in 1994 in Zaire following the assassination of President Ndadaye and the flight into exile of many Hutu political figures. The CNDD was led by Leonard Nyangoma, a former member of Frodebu and former cabinet minister who was branded a "warlord" by the Ntibantunganya government. From exile in Nairobi, Kenya, Nyangoma, who charged Frodebu with being terrorized by the "mono-ethnic Tutsi army," called in early 1995 for the deployment of a 5,000-man "international intervention force to protect the country's democratic institutions." If such intervention was not forthcoming, he asserted that the CNDD's armed wing—the Forces for the Defense of Democracy (*Forces pour la Défense de Démocratie—*FDD)—would have "no other choice but to step up popular resistance."

On March 25, 1996, the CNDD issued a list of conditions for a cease-fire, including the release of 5,000 Frodebu political prisoners; the return of government troops to their barracks; and the withdrawal of international arrest warrants for Nyangoma and his second-in-command, Christian SENDEGEYA. Although some observers cited the CNDD's willingness to negotiate as cause for optimism about scheduled peace talks, within weeks

the rebels had reversed their stance, vowing to keep fighting until the Tutsis gave "power back to the people." Rebel leader Nyangoma was excluded from peace talks in Arusha, Tanzania, in June, prompting a surge in FDD military activity.

In March 1997 the regime blamed CNDD operatives for deadly bomb attacks in Bujumbura, and the following month the government asserted that the rebels were being supported by former Rwandan "Interhamwe" fighters (see separate article on Rwanda) and Zairean Hutus. Meanwhile, observers reported that the CNDD's military efforts were focused in the south, central, and eastern regions.

In April 1997 the CNDD criticized regional leaders for easing sanctions on the regime in Burundi, and in June the rebels turned down an invitation to attend a peace conference in Geneva, Switzerland. However, the group subsequently agreed to participate in peace talks sponsored by regional leaders, earning the enmity of Palipehutu (below), with whose forces the FDD clashed repeatedly in late 1997 and early 1998. In March 1998 the CNDD began a purge that ousted at least seven leading figures, including Sendegeya. Relations between the CNDD, which attended the June 1998 peace talks, and the FDD, which was not invited (reportedly at the insistence of mediation leader Nyerere), came to a breaking point in May when CNDD leader Nyangoma sacked Jean-Bosco NDAYIKENGURUKIYE, head of the FDD, as well as Hussein Radjabu, a CNDD party official. However, CNDD spokesman Jerome Ndiho claimed that the party had, in fact, suspended Nyangoma and replaced him with Ndayikengurukiye. Nonetheless, Nyangoma attended the talks as CNDD president, and the CNDD joined the G-7. Observers in Bujumbura saw the split between the political and military wings of the rebel movement as the result of jockeying for positions of power in advance of a possible near-term settlement.

The Nyangoma faction subsequently became increasingly marginalized within the CNDD in favor of supporters of Ndayikengurukiye, who strongly criticized the finalization of the 2001 power-sharing accord with the government. Meanwhile, it was reported that Ndayikengurukiye had been ousted in September 2001 by a faction led by Pierre Nkurunziza and Radjabu. The anti-Ndayikengurukiye wing was described as "pro-Frodebu" and inclined to pursue further negotiations with the government, and it participated in a regional summit on Burundi's future in Pretoria in October. However, with both factions still claiming legitimacy, fierce fighting was reported in FDD strongholds in the east and south between the FDD and government troops in the last two months of the year following the installation of the new transitional government.

Elements of the FDD entered into negotiations with the government in 2002, with the Ndayikengurukiye faction signing a cease-fire in December and the Nkurunziza faction in October 2003. (By that time the Nkurunziza faction was referencing itself as the CNDD-FDD.) The CNDD-FDD was given four portfolios in the November 2003 cabinet, while one ministry was accorded to the Ndayikengurukiye faction of the CNDD.

In May 2004 Ndayikengurukiye announced that his group would thenceforth be known as *Kaza* (Welcome)-FDD. In early 2005 the interior ministry announced the formal registration of *Kaza*-FDD, the CNDD-FDD, and the CNDD (still under Nyangoma's leadership) as separate parties for the upcoming legislative elections. (See separate section on Nyangoma's CNDD, below).

The CNDD-FDD dominated the communal elections in June 2005 as well as the National Assembly and Senate balloting in July. Nkurunziza resigned as leader of the CNDD-FDD shortly before he was elected president of the republic in August. He was succeeded in the CNDD-FDD post by Radjabu, who was in turn succeeded at a February 2006 congress by Manassé Nzobonimpa. By that time, the CNDD-FDD had apparently made significant strides toward its goal of becoming a truly "national party" by having Tutsis fill a number of leadership posts.

Leaders: Pierre NKURUNZIZA (President of the Republic), Alice NZOMUKUNDA (Second Vice President of the Republic), Gervais RUFYIKIRI (Speaker of the Senate), Immaculée NAHAYO (Speaker of the National Assembly),

Hussein RADJABU, Manassé NZOBONIMPA (Secretary General).

Union for National Progress (*Union pour le Progrés National*—Uprona). Founded in 1958 as the *Union et Progrés National,* Uprona was dissolved after the 1976 coup but subsequently reemerged as the country's only authorized party. In December 1979, at its first national congress, the party elected a Central Committee of 48 members and pledged to return the country to civilian rule under President Bagaza's leadership. Following the 1987 coup and designation of Maj. Pierre Buyoya, previously a little-known Central Committee member, as president of the republic, all Uprona leaders were dismissed and formal party activity ceased. By early 1988 the party was again functioning, a Buyoya supporter having been selected as its new secretary general.

Thereafter, with Tutsis comprising 90 percent of Uprona's membership, party leaders attempted to recruit more Hutus and implement additional "democratization" measures. Thus, an extraordinary party congress in December 1990 for the first time named a Hutu as secretary general and approved the unity charter that was subsequently approved by popular vote in February 1991. In addition, the March 1992 Uprona congress approved a new Central Committee with a Hutu majority.

Uprona won only 16 of 81 legislative seats at the nationwide balloting of June 29, 1993. Subsequently, on July 2 party president Nicolas MAYUGI decried Frodebu's "antidemocratic" electoral victories, claiming they were based on "ethnic manipulation." Although observers described Mayugi's sentiments as pervasive in the Tutsi community, seven members of the government named on July 10, including the prime minister, were Uprona members. Similar concessions were made in the government arrangements of 1994–1995.

In 1995 and the first half of 1996, Uprona militants called for the ousting of President Ntibantunganya and repudiation of the power-sharing arrangements with Frodebu. Uprona also refused to negotiate with representatives from the CNDD, below, despite otherwise broad consensus that the latter's participation was imperative for any peace initiative. In addition, the party remained steadfastly opposed to foreign military intervention. Thus, in June 1996 Tanzanian President Nyerere labeled Uprona as one of the "main obstacles" to peace. It was therefore not surprising that Uprona was heavily represented in the new government formed following the July coup.

A split occurred in Uprona between those who supported Buyoya's efforts to reach a negotiated settlement with opposition groups in 1997–1998 and those opposed to any concessions to the "rebels." Uprona President Charles MUKASI, a member of the latter camp, was reportedly briefly detained in late 1997 for conducting a press conference in September 1997 in which he criticized the government for dealing with "genocidal" Hutu rebels. Ironically, Mukasi was one of the few high-ranking Hutus in the predominately Tutsi Uprona. The dispute over how to deal with the rebels came to a head in October 1998 when Mukasi expelled three members, including Luc Rukingama, a cabinet minister. Buyoya immediately reasserted his authority, and the Central Committee suspended Mukasi and replaced him with Rukingama as interim chairman. While divisions remained with the party, the Mukasi wing was subsequently largely marginalized.

Under the terms of the 2001 transitional constitution, Buyoya left his position as president of the republic in 2003 in favor of his Hutu vice president. New Uprona President Jean-Baptiste Manwangari opposed the constitution approved in February 2005 on the grounds that it provided insufficient guarantees for Tutsis.

Uprona won only 6.3 percent of the vote in local elections in June 2005 and 7.3 percent in assembly balloting in July, *Africa Confidential* subsequently describing the party as having "quietly accepted its defeat." Manwangari was defeated in his bid for reelection to the Uprona presidency at a congress in January 2006.

Leaders: Maj. Pierre BUYOYA (Former President of the Republic), Martin NDUWIMANA (First Vice President of the Republic), Aloys RUBUKA (President of the Party), Frederic NGENZEBUHORO (Former Vice President of the Republic), Jean-Baptist MANWANGARI (Former President of the Party).

Guarantor of Freedom of Speech in Burundi (*Inkinzo y Ijambo Ryabarundi*). Founded in 1993, *Inkinzo* (also referenced as the Shield of Freedom of Speech) joined the PRP and Raddes in their December 1995 withdrawal from the government. However, *Inkinzo* has participated in the two recent cabinets.

Leader: Dr. Alphonse RUGAMBARARA.

Movement for the Rehabilitation of the Citizen (*Movement pour la Réhabilitation du Citoyen*—MRC). After securing two seats in the 2005 assembly elections, the MRC (also referenced as the National Resistance Movement for the Rehabilitation of the Citizen) accepted the public service and social security portfolio in the new cabinet led by the CNDD-FDD.

Leaders: Laurent NZEYIMANA, Col. (Ret.) Epitace BAYAGANAKANDI.

Party for National Recovery (*Parti pour le Recouvrement National*—PRN or Parena). Launched in August 1994 by former head of state Col. Jean-Baptiste Bagaza, Parena was allegedly linked with a number of Tutsi militias. Bagaza, who had dismissed the 1993 elections as an "ethnic referendum," refused to sign the 1994 power-sharing agreement, saying there could be no solution that included Frodebu, and accused the president's party of planning a Tutsi genocide. In 1995 Bagaza reportedly concurred with calls for the establishment of a "Tutsiland" and a "Hutuland" as separate entities.

On January 18, 1997, the Buyoya regime's security forces placed Bagaza under house arrest, and on March 17 five senior party members were imprisoned for their alleged roles in a coup plot against the president. However, Bagaza was subsequently released and permitted to travel to neighboring countries to participate in discussions regarding a possible permanent solution to the instability in Burundi. The others were convicted in

January 2000 of plotting to kill Buyoya, but they were released in August 2000. Parena was frequently critical of the Arusha negotiations, accusing Buyoya of selling out Tutsi interests, but it eventually signed the accord. However, it subsequently declined to ratify various implementation measures. In November 2002 the government banned Parena and placed Bagaza under house arrest. However, the ban and arrest were suspended in May 2003. In February 2005 there were reports that a new rebel group, the **Justice and Liberty United Front,** had been formed to support Bagaza. However, Parena accepted a ministerial position in the new coalition government installed in September 2005.

Leaders: Col. Jean-Baptiste BAGAZA, Cyrille BARANCIRA (Secretary General).

Other Parliamentary Parties

Front for Democracy in Burundi (*Front pour la Démocratie au Burundi*—Frodebu). Frodebu was launched in support of a "no" vote at the referendum of March 1992, arguing that the government's failure to convene a national conference meant that there had been no opposition input to the constitutional draft. However, following the vote, the group's leadership announced, "We are ready to play the game."

Party leader Melchior Ndadaye won the presidency of the republic on June 1, 1993, with Frodebu securing 65 of 81 assembly seats on the basis of a 71.4 percent vote share. However, the October 21 assassination of President Ndadaye and a number of other prominent party members eviscerated Frodebu. Furthermore, a number of Frodebu leaders were tainted by their involvement in subsequent revenge attacks on Tutsis.

On December 23, 1993, Sylvestre Ntibantunganya, foreign minister and Ndadaye confidante, was elected party president and president of the National Assembly. Ntibantunganya became acting president of the republic on April 8, 1994, and president five months later.

Despite the emergence of militant anti-Tutsi emotions within Frodebu, a number of prominent leaders, including party president Jean Minani, called in 1995 for continued dialogue with their Tutsi counterparts. However, following the coup of July 1996, some Frodebu leaders urged supporters to join forces with the CNDD (below) in attempting to topple the Buyoya regime.

On February 6, 1997, Minani called on the international community to pressure the UN to send troops into Burundi and to observe the sanctions imposed on the regime in July 1996. In addition, he decried Bujumbura's "villagization" efforts for having created "concentration camps." The following week, party Secretary General Augustin NOJIBWAMI was jailed for "sabotaging the government's efforts to establish peace" after he echoed Minani's statements. In early 1998 Frodebu leaders reaffirmed their support for all-party talks toward a negotiated settlement of the conflict in Burundi, although the party was splitting into differing factions. For example, Minani remained in exile in Tanzania and attended the peace talks as the party's representative, while certain CNDD elements argued that they, not he, represented the genuine Frodebu leadership. In addition, in the wake of the power-sharing agreement of June 1998, Frodebu was authorized to keep the 65 legislative seats in the new Transitional National Assembly that it had obtained in 1993. However, the party had to appoint new legislators to more than 20 of the seats, the incumbents having either fled to exile or fallen victim to the recent violence. Concurrently, Nojibwami took over leadership of the Frodebu faction functioning in Burundi.

In July 1999 reports indicated that Minani had entered into an alliance with former president Bagaza and Parena (see above) in opposition to President Buyoya and Uprona, an initiative that was condemned by Nojibwami and others. This split was accommodated within the Arusha negotiations through the presence of the "internal" Nojibwani Frodebu wing in the National Assembly delegation to the talks. Minani led the main "external" Frodebu delegation. Following the installation of the new transitional government on November 1, 2001, Minani, who had recently returned to Burundi after more than five years in exile, was elected president of the new Transitional National Assembly.

After Frodebu's Domitien Ndayizeye became president of the republic in April 2003, Frodebu campaigned in support of the new constitution approved in February 2005. However, Frodebu secured only about 23 percent of the vote in the June 2005 local elections and July assembly poll. Many Frodebu supporters by that time had reprotedly defected to the CNDD-FDD.

Frodebu joined the national unity government installed in September 2005, but in March 2006 Frodebu announced it was withdrawing from the coalition. When the three Frodebu ministers opted to stay in the cabinet, they were expelled from the party.

Leaders: Domitien NDAYIZEYE (Former President of the Republic), Jean MINANI (President of the Party), Jean de Dieu MUTABAZI (Secretary General), Liboire NGENDAHAYO (National Executive Secretary).

National Council for the Defense of Democracy (*Conseil National pour la Défense de Démocratie*—CNDD). This grouping was reorganized under the CNDD rubric in early 2005 after sustained factionalization within the original CNDD (see CNDD-FDD, above, for details). The CNDD won four seats in the 2005 assembly poll and dominated balloting in local elections in Bururi Province, home of the CNDD leader.

Leader: Leonard NYANGOMA.

Other Parties

Burundi People's Rally (*Rassemblement du Peuple Burundien*—RPB). A Hutu party founded in 1992, the RPB finished third in the legislative balloting of June 1993, but with less than the minimum vote share needed to secure assembly representation. Its original leader, Ernest Kabushemeye, was assassinated on March 11, 1995.

Leaders: Balthazar BIGIRIMANA (President), Philippe NZOBONARIBA.

Rally for Democracy and Economic and Social Development (*Rassemblement pour la Démocratie et le Développement Economique et*

Social—Raddes). A virulently pro-Tutsi party, Raddes was allocated single cabinet posts in February 1994 and March 1995. However, in December 1995 Raddes joined the PRP and *Inkinzo* in withdrawing from the government and called for the president's ouster, charging him with responsibility for the ongoing civil strife. In January 1996 Raddes's president, Cyrille SIGEJEJE, was placed under arrest. Raddes was admitted into the Arusha peace talks in early 2000.

Leaders: Joseph NZEYIMANA (President), Astere NZISIBIRA.

National Alliance for Rights and Development (*Alliance Nationale pour les Droits et le Développement*—Anadde). The Tutsi-dominated Anadde was founded in 1992 and was given one ministry in March 1995. It was reportedly offered legislative representation in June 1998 but was unable to present a candidate due to party factionalization.

Leader: Patrice NSABABAWANGA.

African-Burundi Salvation Alliance (*Alliance Burundaise-Africaine pour le Salut*—Abasa). Abasa is a small Tutsi-dominated opposition group that in 1997 called for new national leadership, criticizing the Buyoya regime for lacking a "clear strategy."

Leaders: Terrence NSANZE (Former Permanent Representative to the UN), Serge MUKAMARAKIZA (in exile).

People's Reconciliation Party (*Parti de la Réconciliation du Peuple*—PRP). The promonarchist PRP was founded in September 1991 on a platform calling for a parliamentary monarchy with a prime minister and an ethnically mixed council of nobles. The group was officially recognized on July 1, 1992, and in November called it for the government to open negotiations with the opposition.

PRP candidate Pierre-Claver Sendegeya finished a distant third in the June 1, 1993, presidential balloting, and the party failed to secure representation at the subsequent legislative elections. Considered an extremist by the government, PRP leader Mathias Hitimana was arrested in August 1994, provoking a series of deadly street clashes by his followers that shut down the capital for three days.

The PRP was awarded a post in the government named in March 1995 but nine months later quit the cabinet, and in January 1996 Hitimana was again arrested. In July party militants took part in the anti-Ntibantunganya demonstrations that sought to vilify the president for agreeing to foreign intervention. Although the PRP was given a ministerial post in the transitional cabinet of November 2001, its minister left the government in July 2002. However, the party accepted a new post in 2003.

Leaders: Mathias HITIMANA (President), Pierre-Claver SENDE- GEYA (1993 presidential candidate), François MBESHERUBUSA, Jean Bosco YAMUREMYE.

Hutu People's Liberation Party (*Parti Libération du Peuple Hutu*—Palipehutu). Palipehutu was formed by Hutu exiles in Rwanda and Tanzania who opposed the long-standing political and economic dominance of Burundi's Tutsis. The government attributed the Hutu-Tutsi conflict of August 1988, as well as the attempted coup of November 1991, to Palipehutu activism, although there was no outside confirmation of either allegation. In 1990 Palipehutu founder Rémy GAHUTU died in a Tanzanian prison. (His successor, Etienne Karatasi, remained exiled in Denmark.)

In April 1992 Palipehutu forces, allegedly supported by Rwandan rebels, attacked military sites in northwest Burundi. In mid-July Palipehutu members were among 59 individuals convicted for their roles in the 1991 uprising; three weeks later 450 alleged Palipehutu members went on trial for their involvement in terrorist incidents.

In 1993 the party was split by the defection of its military leader, Cossan Kabura, who "declared war on the Ndadaye government." He subsequently founded the National Forces of Liberation (FNL, see below). In early 1997 *Africa Confidential* reported that Palipehutu and the FNL had agreed to form a military alliance with a group from the DRC styled the **National Council of Kivu Resistance** (*Conseil Nationale de Résistance du Kivu*— CNRK). Led by Arema Bin AMISI, the ethnic Bembe CNRK reportedly opposed the government of Laurent Kabila.

In the second half of 1997 Palipehutu leaders accused the CNDD of "collaborating" with the Buyoya regime by agreeing to join peace talks. Severe intra-Hutu fighting was subsequently reported between Palipehutu forces and the CNDD's armed wing, the FDD. In early 2000 it was reported that FNL fighters had clashed in Burundi with Rwandan Hutu guerrilla groups with which it had previously been allied. Palipehutu eventually joined the G-7 grouping at the Arusha talks and was a signatory to the August 28, 2000, accord, although the FNL did not accept the agreement. Palipehutu reportedly joined the national unity government installed in 2003. However, Palipehutu-FNL continued military action against the government (see FNL, below, for details).

Leaders: Etienne KARATASI, Antoine SEZOYA-NGABO.

National Liberation Front (*Front de Libération Nationale*—Frolina). A small movement composed primarily of militant Hutu refugees, Frolina (previously referenced as *Umbumwé* [Solidarity]) was organized in the mid-1980s. It reportedly conducted a guerrilla attack on a Burundi military installation in Mabandal on August 13, 1990. Four days later the group's leader, former Palipehutu member Joseph Karumba, was arrested in Tanzania.

In June 1992 Karumba was linked to militant refugees in Mpanda, Tanzania. In announcing their intent to arrest the group, Tanzanian officials reported that Karumba had recently sought their assistance in "liberating" Burundi. However, Karumba was subsequently granted asylum in Tanzania, from which he conducted Frolina's political affairs while Frolina fighters, referenced as the People's Armed Forces, engaged in sporadic guerrilla action in Burundi through 1998. In signing the Arusha accord of August 2000, Karumba agreed that Frolina forces would eventually be incorporated into the national forces of Burundi, although a militant Frolina wing reportedly remained opposed to that measure and other Arusha

Cabinet

As of May 1, 2006

President	Pierre Nkurunziza (CNDD-FDD)
First Vice President (In Charge of Political and Administrative Affairs)	Martin Nduwimana (Uprona)
Second Vice President (In Charge of Social And Economic Affairs)	Alice Nzomukunda (CNDD-FDD) [f]

Ministers

Agriculture and Livestock	Elie Buzoya (formerly Frodebu)
Commerce and Industry	Denise Sinankwa (CNDD-FDD) [f]
Communications, Information, Relations with Parliament, and Government Spokesman	Karenga Ramadhani (CNDD-FDD)
Defense and War Veterans	Maj. Gen. Germaine Niyoyankana (ind.)
Energy and Mines	Herman Tuyaga (CNDD-FDD)
External Relations and International Cooperation	Antoinette Batumubwira (CNDD-FDD) [f]
Finance	Dieudonne Ngowembusa (CNDD-FDD)
Good Governance	Venant Kamana (CNDD-FDD)
Interior and Public Security	Brig. Gen. Evariste Ndayishimiye (CNDD-FDD)
Justice and Keeper of the Seals	Clotilde Niragira (CNDD-FDD) [f]
National Education and Culture	Saidi Kiwea (CNDD-FDD)
National Solidarity, Human Rights, and Gender	Françoise Ngendahayo (*Inkinzo*) [f]
Office of the President (AIDS Control)	Dr. Triphonie Nkurunziza (Parena) [f]
Planning, Development, and Reconstruction	Marei-Goreth Nizigama (Uprona) [f]
Public Health	Dr. Barnabe Bonimpa (formerly Frodebu)
Public Service and Social Security	Juvenal Ngowenubusa (MRC)
Public Works and Equipment	Potame Nizigire (CNDD-FDD)
Territorial Development, Environment, and Tourism	Odette Kayitesi (formerly Fodebu) [f]
Transport, Posts, and Telecommunications	Jean Bigirimana (CNDD-FDD)
Youth and Sports	Jean-Jacques Nyenimigabo (CNDD-FDD)

[f] = female

"concessions." Frolina named four of its members to the new Transitional National Assembly in late 2001; however, no ministers in the new cabinet were identified as belonging to Frolina. Karumba was among the former rebels who were "demobilized" in mid-2005.

Leader: Joseph KARUMBA.

Other past government parties have included the **Alliance of the Brave** (AV-*Intwari*), a small grouping that joined the transitional legislature and participated in subsequent peace talks; the **Independent Workers' Party** (*Parti Indépendent de Travailleurs*—PIT), which is led by Nicéphore NDIMURUKUNDO and Etienne NTAHONZA and which held portfolios in the cabinets of 1994, 1995, 2001, and 2003; the **People's Party** (*Parti Populaire*—PP), a pro-Frodebu grouping that is led by Shadrack NIYONKURU and Appolinaire BUTOYI and which was allocated one cabinet ministry in 1995, 2001, and 2003; and the **Social Democratic Party** (*Parti Social-Démocrate*—PSD), a pro-Uprona Tutsi grouping (led by Vincent NDIKUMASABO and Godefroy HAKIZIMANA) that had been awarded the civil service ministry in March 1995.

Other political parties and groups include the **Democratic Forum** (*Forum Démocratique—* FODE), formed in 1999 and led by Deogratias BABURIFATO; the **Liberal Alliance for Development** (*Alliance Libérale Pour la Développement— Imboneza*), created in 2002 and led by Joseph NTIDENEREZA; the **New Alliance for Democracy and the Development of Burundi** (*Alliance Nouvelle Pour la Démocratie et le Développement au Burundi*), formed in 2002 by Jean-Paul BU-RAFUTA; the **Party for Democracy and Reconciliation** (*Parti pour la Démocratie et la Réconciliation—* PDR), formed in 2002 and led by Augustin NZOJIBWAMI; and the **Union for Peace and Development** (*Union pour la Paix et le Développement—* UPD), established in 2002 and led by Freddy FERUVI.

Active Rebel Group

National Forces of Liberation (*Forces Nationales de la Libération—* FNL). Founded in the mid-1990s by Palipehutu military leader Cossan KABURA (referenced in previous *Handbooks* as Kabora Kossani), the FNL (often referenced as the Palipehutu—FNL) subsequently conducted guerrilla actions against government forces, primarily in and around Bujumbura. The hard-line FNL separated from Palipehutu completely when the latter agreed in 1999 to participate in the Arusha peace talks.

In late February 2001 it was reported that Kabura had been "ejected" from the FNL by a faction led by Agathon Rwasa, said by that time to command some 90 percent of the FNL's fighters. Rwasa and his supporters criticized Kabura for failing to convene a national congress to discuss strategy. Apparently to underscore its militancy, the Rwasa faction invaded Bujumbura in early March in an apparent takeover attempt that was eventually repulsed by government forces. Both FNL factions condemned the July power-sharing accord, and intensified FNL attacks were reported late in the year.

In December 2002 dissident members of the FNL formed the **FNL-Icanzo** under the leadership of Alain MUGABARABONA. Following the cease-fire between the government and the FDD, the FNL subsequently remained the only major rebel group still fighting the transitional government. The group became increasingly marginalized and lost much of its foreign support following an attack in August of 2004 on a UN refugee camp in Gatumba, Burundi. The government and several neighboring states subsequently designated the FNL a terrorist organization. FNL forces were repulsed in a December 2004 attack but managed to assassinate the governor of Bubanza Province in January 2005.

In May 2005 the government and the FNL reportedly signed a peace deal whereby both sides agreed to cease fighting. Additional agreements to allow the FNL to participate in upcoming elections or future governments remained elusive, however.

In October 2005 reports surfaced that Rwasa had been ousted as chair of "Palipehutu-FNL" in favor of a "pronegotiation" leadership including Jean-Bosco Sinadayigaya as chair. However, Rwasa's faction continued antigovernment activity in the hills around Bujumbura into May 2006, having reportedly forged an alliance with rebels in the DRC. (See Current issues, above, for subsequent developments.)

Leaders: Agathon RWASA and Jean-Bosco SINDAYIGAYA (leaders of competing factions).

Legislature

The National Assembly (*Assemblée Nationale*), then a one-party, 65-member body, was suspended following the September 1987 coup. Although President Buyoya promised to revive the body within "one to two years," the suspension remained in effect until the multiparty election of June 29, 1993, at which the Front for Democracy in Burundi (Frodebu) won 65 seats in an enlarged body of 81 and the Union for National Progress (Uprona) won 16, no other formation meeting a threshold of 5 percent of the vote.

The assembly was once again suspended following the military coup of July 25, 1996. Although that decree was formally lifted in September, the assembly subsequently remained in disarray, many of its members having died in the recent violence or fled the country.

A Transitional National Assembly was inaugurated on July 18, 1998, under provisions of the June 6 transitional constitution. The assembly was expanded to 121 members; Frodebu and Uprona kept their 1993 allocations (65 and 16, respectively), although more than 20 vacant Frodebu seats had to be filled with new members. Of the 40 new seats, 27 were filled by government-appointed representatives of social and professional organizations. The remaining seats were reserved for small political parties. The following parties were subsequently reported to have appointed legislators: the Alliance of the Brave, the Burundi People's Rally, the Guarantor of Freedom of Speech in Burundi, the Independent Workers' Party, the People's Party, the People's Reconciliation Party, the Rally for Democracy and Economic and Social Development, and the Social Democratic Party. Several other parties were apparently invited to participate but were unable to appoint legislators due to internal wrangling. Consequently, four seats were not filled upon the inauguration of the new assembly.

In late October 2001 the Transitional National Assembly adopted a new "Constitution of Transition" providing for a new bicameral Parliament as envisioned by the recent Arusha peace accord. The new National Assembly was enlarged to 170 members, approximately 60 percent Hutu and 40 percent Tutsi; Frodebu and Uprona kept their previous allocation of seats, while the above eight small parties were allocated four seats, as were each of seven other groupings (the African-Burundi Salvation Alliance, the Hutu People's Liberation Party, the Liberal Party, the National Alliance for Rights and Development, the National Council for the Defense of Democracy, the National Liberation Front, and the Party for National Recovery [Parena]). New seats were also allocated to civic, professional, and social groups. The new assembly convened (minus designees from Parena) for the first time on

January 4, 2002, and elected Frodebu's Jean Minani as its president.

The new constitution approved in February 2005 codified the bicameral **Parliament** (*Parlement*) consisting of a Senate and a National Assembly elected for five-year terms.

Senate (*Sénat*). The upper house comprises 34 indirectly elected members (1 Hutu and 1 Tutsi from each province as selected by electoral colleges comprised of members of the local councils within each province), all former presidents (currently 4), 3 members of the Twa ethnic group, and enough women (currently 8) to make the number of female senators at least 30 percent of the total. (There are currently 49 members.) The first elections in the provincial electoral colleges took place on July 29, 2005. Of the 34 seats filled in that process, 30 were reportedly secured by the National Council for the Defense of Democracy–Forces for the Defense of Democracy, 3 by the Front for Democracy in Burundi, and 1 by the National Council for the Defense of Democracy.

Speaker: Gervais RUFYIKIRI.

National Assembly (*Assemblée Nationale*). The lower house comprises 100 members directly elected by party-list proportional representation, enough additional members (currently 15) to fulfill the constitutional mandates that 60 percent of the regular seats are filled by Hutus and 40 percent by Tutsis and that 30 percent of the regular seats are filled by women, and three members of the Twa ethnic group. At the first balloting of July 4, 2005, the National Council for the Defense of Democracy (CNDD-FDD) won 59 seats; the Front for Democracy in Burundi (Frodebu), 25; the Union for National Progress (Uprona), 10; the National Council for the Defense of Democracy, 4; and the Movement for the Rehabilitation of the Citizen, 2. Of the 15 additional seats subsequently allocated to meet the constitutional mandates, 5 each were given to the CNDD-FDD, Frodebu, and Uprona.

Speaker: Immaculée NAHAYO.

Communications

Press

A new media law in 2003 provided for broad journalistic freedom, and only one arrest of a journalist has subsequently been reported. The following are published in Bujumbura: *Le Renouveau du Burundi* (20,000), government daily, in French; *Umbumwé* (20,000), weekly, in Kirundi; *Burundi Chrétien,* weekly publication of the Gitega Archbishopric, in French; *Ndongozi Yaburundi,* Catholic fortnightly, in Kirundi. In June 2004 a new newspaper, *La Tribune du Burundi*, began publication as a monthly.

News Agency

Daily bulletins are issued by the official *Agence Burundaise de Presse.*

Broadcasting and Computing

The government facility, *La Voix de la Révolution/La Radiodiffusion et Télévision Nationale du Burundi* (RTNB), broadcasts in French, Kirundi, and Swahili. *Radio Publique Africaine* (a popular nationwide station) was temporarily shut down by the government in mid-2005 for alleged bias in its election coverage. Another popular raido station is the independent *Bonesha FM.* There were approximately 13,000 personal computers serving 14,000 Internet users in 2003.

Intergovernmental Representation

Ambassador to the U.S.
Antoine NTAMOBWA

U.S. Ambassador to Burundi
Patricia Newton MOLLER

Permanent Representative to the UN
Joseph NTAKIRUTIMANA

IGO Memberships (Non-UN)
AU, AfDB, BADEA, CEEAC, CEPGL, Comesa, Interpol, NAM, OIF, WCO, WTO

CAMEROON

REPUBLIC OF CAMEROON

République du Cameroun

The Country

Situated just north of the equator on the Gulf of Guinea and rising from a coastal plain to a high interior plateau, Cameroon is the product of a merger in 1961 between the former French and British Cameroon trust territories. Its more than 100 ethnic groups speak 24 major languages and represent a diversity of Christian (53 percent), traditional African (25 percent), and Muslim (22 percent) religious beliefs. Reflecting its dual colonial heritage (the source of lingering political cleavage), Cameroon is the only country in Africa in which both French and English are official languages. In 1996 women were reported to constitute 38 percent of the official labor force.

Cameroon's economy has long been primarily rural and, despite the discovery of major oil deposits in 1973, agriculture continues to provide a large share of the country's export earnings. Coffee, cocoa, and timber are among the most important agricultural products, but bananas, cotton, rubber, and palm oil also are produced commercially. Oil production declined from a high of 9.2 million metric tons in 1985 to 7.7 million tons in 1991. Apart from agricultural processing and oil-related activity, industrial development has focused on aluminum smelting from both domestic and imported bauxite. Current initiatives are aimed at hydroelectric expansion, the resolution of long-standing transportation problems, and the development of medium-sized farms to halt the exodus of rural youth to urban areas. The economy faltered during the mid-1980s and early 1990s under the influence of depressed oil and other commodity prices, sus-tained capital flight, rising external debt (approaching $6 billion in early 1992), and widespread corruption and inefficiency in state-run enterprises. Initially shunning involvement with the International Monetary Fund (IMF), the government since 1988 has negotiated agreements with it and other international lenders in a context of budget austerity and a commitment to privatization.

Following the devaluation of the CFA franc in 1994, Cameroon's inflation rate rose to 25.8 percent in 1995. However, from 1996 to 1998 the country enjoyed an average real GDP growth rate of approximately 5.0 percent annually, according to the IMF, as overall world economic activity increased and inflationary pressures eased. On the other hand,

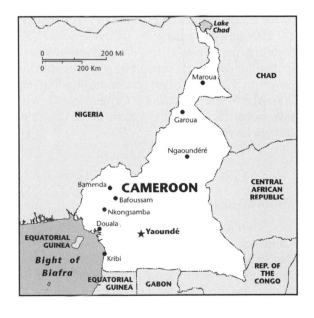

analysts urged the government to continue efforts to increase transparency in the public sector, warning that corrupt official practices were endangering economic progress. To that end, in late 1999 the IMF asked the government to set up a system whereby oil revenues would be directly deposited in a monitorable state budget. In addition, the IMF counseled Yaoundé to continue its efforts to raise the "non-oil revenue-to-GDP ratio." While the IMF and the World Bank subsequently praised the government's efforts regarding structural reforms and anticorruption measures, concerns were raised over the pace of privatization and poverty reduction. In 2000 the World Bank granted Cameroon $2 billion in a multi-year debt reduction program; however, the program was suspended in 2004 due to perceived financial mismanagement by the government and a slowdown in the pace of reforms.

Real GDP grew by 5.3 percent, and inflation was less than 3 percent, in fiscal year 2000–2001. While oil production decreased from 164,000 barrels per day in the 1990s to just 85,000 by 2002, GDP growth nonetheless averaged 4.3 percent annually from 2001 to 2004 as the non-oil sector expanded. Inflation remained low, although there was an increase to 4.8 percent in 2002–2003 as the result of higher food costs. The overall improvement in the economy was further supported by the opening of the Chad–Cameroon pipeline in 2003. In 2005 the IMF was encouraged by the government's efforts to generate non-oil revenue and approved several million dollars to support its poverty reduction programs. However, at the same time, heading into 2006 the World Bank cited Cameroon's "harsh" investment climate as the reason for its dearth of foreign investors.

Government and Politics

Political Background

A German protectorate before World War I, Cameroon was divided at the close of that conflict into French and British mandates, which became UN trust territories after World War II. French Cameroons, comprising the eastern four-fifths of the territory, achieved autonomous status within the French Community in 1957 and, under the leadership of Ahmadou Babatoura AHIDJO, became the independent Republic of Cameroon on January 1, 1960. The disposition of British Cameroons was settled in February 1961 by a UN-sponsored plebiscite in which the northern and southern sections voted to merge with Nigeria and the former French territory, respectively. On October 1, 1961, the Federal Republic of Cameroon was formed, with Ahidjo as president and John Ngu FONCHA, prime minister of the former British region, as vice president.

The federal structure was designed to meet the challenge posed by Cameroon's racial, tribal, religious, and political diversity. It provided for separate regional governments and political organizations, joined at the federal level. A transition to unitary government began with the 1965–1966 merger of the regional political parties to form the Cameroon National Union (UNC) under the leadership of President Ahidjo and was completed on June 2, 1972, following a referendum on May 20 that indicated overwhelming support for the adoption of a new constitution. Subsequently, President Ahidjo faced no organized opposition, and on April 5, 1980, he was reelected to a fifth successive term. However, in an unanticipated move on November 4, 1982, Ahidjo announced his retirement in favor of his longtime associate, Prime Minister Paul BIYA. Immediately following his installation as president, Biya, a southerner, named a northern Muslim, Maigari Bello BOUBA, to head a new government designed to retain the somewhat tenuous regional and cultural balance that had been established by the former head of state. Bouba was dismissed in August 1983, following a coup attempt that allegedly involved Ahidjo, then resident in France. (Ahidjo died at his longtime alternative home in Senegal on November 30, 1989.)

President Biya was unopposed for reelection on January 14, 1984, and immediately following his inauguration on January 21 the National Assembly voted to abolish the post of prime minister and to abandon "United Republic of Cameroon" as the country's official name in favor of the

Political Status: Independence proclaimed 1960; federation established 1961; one-party unitary republic declared June 2, 1972; multiparty system introduced under legislation approved December 6, 1990.

Area: 183,568 sq. mi. (475,442 sq. km.).

Population: 10,493,655 (1987C); 16,888,000 (2005E).

Major Urban Centers (2005E): YAOUNDÉ (1,525,000), Douala (875,000).

Official Languages: French, English.

Monetary Unit: CFA Franc (official rate July 1, 2006: 513.01 francs = $1US). (The CFA franc, previously pegged to the French franc, is now permanently pegged to the euro at 655.957 CFA francs = 1 euro.)

President: Paul BIYA (Democratic Rally of the Cameroon People—RDPC); served as prime minister 1975–1982; installed as president on November 6, 1982, to complete the term of Ahmadou Babatoura AHIDJO, who had resigned on November 4; reelected without opposition on January 14, 1984, and April 24, 1988; reelected for a five-year term in multicandidate balloting on October 11, 1992, for a seven-year term on October 12, 1997, and for another seven-year term on October 11, 2004.

Prime Minister: Ephraim INONI (RDPC); appointed by the president on December 8, 2004, to replace Peter Mafany MUSONGE (RDPC).

pre-merger "Republic of Cameroon." The following April Biya survived another coup attempt by elements of the presidential guard. While reportedly dealing harshly with the rebels, the administration nevertheless initiated steps toward democratization. Elections for local and regional bodies within the government party, which had been renamed the Democratic Rally of the Cameroon People (RDPC), also referenced in English as the Cameroon People's Democratic Movement (CPDM) in 1985, were held in 1986, followed by local government elections in 1987 that, for the first time, featured competitive balloting, albeit within

an RDPC/CPDM framework. Alternative candidates also were presented for National Assembly balloting on April 24, 1988; however, each of the two lists was restricted to ruling party nominees, with opponents attacking the "snail's pace" of liberalization, continued repression of dissent, and barriers to any genuine political challenge to Biya, who was unopposed in the presidential poll.

In emulation of trends elsewhere in Africa and beyond, democratization advocates intensified their pressure in late 1989 and early 1990. Initially, the government responded harshly: eleven opposition leaders were arrested in February 1990, and a massive prodemocracy demonstration in the western town of Bamenda was violently broken up by security forces, leaving at least six people dead. However, in the wake of growing domestic and international criticism, President Biya announced in June that a multiparty system would be introduced and other reforms implemented. Consequently, on December 6 the National Assembly enacted legislation restricting the government's authority to deny legal status to opposition groups, and the formal recognition of new parties began in early 1991. On the other hand, Biya's refusal to call a national conference (similar to those convened in other regional countries) to determine the nation's political future provoked continued antigovernment demonstrations.

In an effort to force the government's hand regarding a national conference, opposition parties in June 1991 launched a *villes mortes* ("dead cities") campaign during which shops were closed on weekdays to undercut tax revenue. In response, the government put seven provinces under military administration and temporarily banned several of the parties responsible for the general strike. However, faced with ongoing unrest, Biya announced in October that new legislative elections would be moved up by a year to early 1992. He also convened a meeting of government and opposition leaders that in November established a ten-member committee to oversee constitutional reform. In addition, the government promised to release detainees from earlier protests in return for discontinuation of the *villes mortes* campaign.

In the March 1, 1992, assembly balloting the RDPC/CPDM won 88 seats, enough to ensure its continued government control in coalition with the small Movement for the Defense of the Republic (MDR). However, the results were tainted somewhat by the refusal of some groups, most importantly the anglophone Social Democratic Front (SDF) and a faction of the Cameroonian People's Union (UPC), to participate in the election. Boycott leaders insisted that a ban on coalition or independent candidates favored the government formation and that the early balloting made it impossible for fledgling opposition parties to organize effectively. On April 9 President Biya announced the appointment of Simon ACHIDI ACHU, an Anglophone, as prime minister. However, Achidi Achu's designation failed to stem ongoing ethnic and political violence, while the regime's efforts to quell the unrest were described as "repressive."

In September 1992 Biya announced that presidential elections scheduled for March 1993 would be advanced to October 11 and, following a widely criticized run-up to the poll, Biya subsequently claimed a narrow victory over SDF leader John FRU NDI and four other candidates. On October 15 the Supreme Court rejected a petition by Fru Ndi and the third-placed Maigari Bello Bouba, now leader of the National Union for Democracy and Progress (UNDP), to annul the balloting on the basis of prepoll and election day irregularities. The polling process also was denounced by international observers, who charged that inspectors were denied access to some balloting sites. On October 23 the official election results were released, confirming Biya's victory, with 39.98 percent of the vote, over Fru Ndi (35.97 percent) and Bouba (19.22 percent). Subsequently, nationwide antigovernment rioting was reported, the most serious incidents occurring at Bamenda in Fru Ndi's home province. Six days later Fru Ndi was placed under house arrest as violent street protests continued despite the declaration of a state of emergency at Bamenda.

On November 25, 1992, Achidi Achu was reappointed by Biya, and two days later a new government, including a number of opposition members, was named. Further efforts by the regime to ease post-election tensions included the release of Fru Ndi in early December, termination of the state of emergency at Bamenda on December 29, and the freeing of some 175 political prisoners in January 1993. However, renewed violence was reported in March as the opposition increased pressure on Yaoundé to hold a national conference.

In November 1994 President Biya announced that a "debate" on the constitution, in addition to scheduling of municipal elections, would be forthcoming; however, he refused to agree to a sovereign conference and gave no date for the local balloting, which had already been postponed several times. In early April 1995 Biya pledged that elections would be held by the end of the year, and on April 24, 64 new local districts were created by presidential decree. In November, buoyed by the IMF's endorsement of his administration's 1995–1996 economic and financial reform plan, the president ordered that local elections be held in January 1996.

Propelled by a candidate list nearly twice the size of its closest competitor, the RDPC/CPDM captured 57 percent of the posts at municipal balloting on January 21, 1996. The SDF followed with 27 percent, while the UNDP and Cameroonian Democratic Union (UDC) garnered the remainder. The administration's decision to place presidential appointees in 20 municipalities that the opposition claimed to have captured at the local balloting drew immediate condemnation and calls for civil disobedience from opposition leaders. In March at least five people were killed when antigovernment demonstrators clashed with security forces. Subsequent antigovernment initiatives were undermined, however, by the opposition's intraparty factionalization and their mutual distrust. On September 19 the president announced that he had appointed businessman Peter Mafany MUSONGE to replace Achidi Achu as prime minister. The new government formed the following day was generally described as being of the "technocrat" variety.

Debate between legislative candidates over such "substantive" issues as Biya's economic and political reform programs was overshadowed during the run-up to the May 17, 1997, legislative elections by the opposition's outcry over the administration's allegedly fraudulent handling of electoral preparations. Subsequently, both domestic and international observers charged that the ruling party's capture of 109 seats had been severely tarnished by blatant irregularities and the violent intimidation of opposition candidates and supporters. At second-round polling in early August the RDPC/CPDM captured all of the undecided seats (raising its total to 116), and at mid-month the Supreme Court dismissed opposition appeals for fresh elections. Meanwhile, the administration rejected widespread calls for it to establish an independent electoral commission prior to presidential balloting (scheduled for October) and refused to meet with opposition leaders, whose preelection demands also included a shortening of the presidential term from seven to five years, equal distribution of state campaign funds, and access to the state-run media. In September the leading opposition legislative parties (the SDF, UNDP, and UDC) announced that they would not take part in the presidential elections and called on voters to observe another *villes mortes* boycott to undermine the polling.

At balloting on October 12, 1997, Biya easily recaptured the presidency, reportedly securing 92 percent of the vote; meanwhile the nearest of the six minor party candidates to compete garnered less than 3 percent. However, administration claims that 84 percent of eligible voters had participated in the polling were disputed by the opposition, which labeled the elections a "farce" and asserted that a boycott by over 80 percent of the electorate had made them the "victors." On December 7 Biya reappointed Musonge as prime minister; three UNDP representatives, including former prime minister Bouba, were included in the reshuffled government announced the same day. Reshuffles were announced on March 18, 2000, and April 27, 2001. The most recent cabinet included members from the RDPC/CPDM, the UNDP, the UPC, and independents.

Municipal elections originally scheduled for January 2001 were postponed first to January 2002 and then to June 30. Although the government gave technical reasons for the postponements, opposition parties claimed that the government was stalling the operation of the democratic process. In any event, the RDPC/CPDM dominated the local balloting as well as the National Assembly poll conducted the same day. President Biya also was easily reelected on October 11, 2004, securing a reported 70.8 percent of the vote against 15 rivals. On December 8 Biya appointed Ephraim INONI to head a new cabinet that included members of the RDPC, UNDP, UPC, and the MDR. (The SDF and UDC reportedly declined cabinet representation.)

Constitution and Government

The 1972 constitution provided for a unitary state headed by a strong executive directly elected by universal suffrage for a five-year term. In November 1983 independents were authorized to seek the presidency upon securing the endorsement of at least 50 prominent figures from each of the country's provinces, although the incumbent presented himself as the sole, party-backed candidate in both 1984 and 1988 (the 1988 poll being advanced by one year to coincide with legislative balloting). The president is assisted by a cabinet drawn from the civil service rather than the legislature. Members may return to their former positions upon termination of their ministerial duties. Under a constitutional revision of January 1984, the president of the assembly becomes, in the event of a vacancy, chief executive, pending the outcome, within 40 days, of a presidential election at which he cannot stand as a candidate. Legislative authority is vested in a National Assembly whose normal five-year term may be lengthened or shortened at the discretion of the president. The judicial system is headed by a Supreme Court and a High Court of Justice; there also are provincial magistrates and a court of appeal.

Under a constitutional amendment of December 23, 1995, the presidential term was extended to seven years and the maximum number of terms reduced to two. In addition, provision was made for the establishment of a bicameral legislature; however, details on the formation of the second chamber, a Senate, had not, as of early 2006, been further delineated.

Cameroon is administratively divided into 10 provinces, each headed by a provincial governor appointed by the president. The provinces are subdivided into regions and local districts, the latter totaling 340 (307 rural, 22 urban, and 11 special regime districts) following the creation of 64 new jurisdictions in April 1995.

Foreign Relations

Cameroon maintains relations with a wide variety of nations. Ties with France remain especially strong, with Yaoundé becoming a full participant in francophone affairs during the May 1989 summit at Dakar, Senegal.

Dominating foreign policy concerns for many years was the civil war in neighboring Chad, which resulted in an influx of some 100,000 refugees into the country's northern provinces. Thus the Ahidjo government took part in several regional efforts to mediate the dispute prior to the ouster of the Libyan-backed Queddei regime in Chad in mid-1982; later Cameroon served as a staging ground for France's support of the Habré government.

Relations with other neighboring states have been uneven. Border incidents with Nigeria, resulting in a seven-month suspension of diplomatic relations in May 1981, continued into early 1987, with Lagos threatening "to take military reprisals" against alleged incursions by Cameroonian *gendarmes* into Borno State. However, relations improved thereafter.

In October 1992 the Biya regime's alleged manipulation of presidential balloting drew widespread criticism from Western observers, including the European Community, Germany, and the United States, with the latter two announcing the suspension of aid payments in mid-November. On the other hand, Paris's continued support of the regime drew outcries from Cameroonian opposition leaders.

In late 1993 conflict again erupted with Nigeria in the form of an alleged Cameroonian troop raid into Nigeria's Cross River State and the re-ported dispatch of some 500 Nigerian soldiers to two islands off the Bakassi peninsula that were claimed by Cameroon. Underlying the dispute was the presence of substantial oil reserves along an ill-defined border between the two countries. In early 1994 Cameroon announced that it had filed a suit at the International Court of Justice (ICJ). Subsequently, during an Organization of African Unity (OAU) summit at Tunis in June, President Biya and the Nigerian head of state, Gen. Sani Abacha, agreed to set up a joint committee under the leadership of Togolese President Gnassingbé Eyadéma. However, the conflict reignited in early September with a Nigerian attack that left 10 Cameroonian soldiers dead. In mid-October Nigeria claimed to have indisputable proof of its claim to the Bakassi region in that a 1913 agreement transferring the area to German Kamerun had never been ratified because of the outbreak of World War I. Two months later the OAU formally agreed to mediate the dispute. Amid reports of low-level skirmishes between Cameroonian and Nigerian forces, the two countries traded charges throughout 1998 that the other was attempting to influence the ICJ's decision (originally due in July but subsequently delayed when the Court was forced to defend its jurisdiction). On a more positive note, tension in the region eased palpably when more than 200 prisoners were exchanged in November.

At a summit at Yaoundé in June 1999, Biya and his Nigerian counterpart, Gen. Abdulsalam Abubakar, reportedly held "breakthrough" talks regarding the Bakassi region. However, in early 2000 the Nigerian military was placed on "maximum alert" following Lagos's discovery that France was constructing a military base near the peninsula in Cameroon. Furthermore, Nigerian officials accused Cameroonian forces of regularly firing on its forces. The ICJ urged the two to maintain the "status quo" while waiting for a final ruling. Although minor skirmishes continued in 2000 and 2001, the Nigerian Cross River state opened its Cameroonian border in June 2000.

In 2002 the ICJ ruled in favor of Cameroon in its boundary dispute with Nigeria, but Lagos initially refused to accept the decision. However, after UN-brokered mediation talks in Geneva in August 2003, the two countries agreed to settle the dispute, and a three-year demarcation project was initiated. The development of the new border was overseen by the UN-sponsored Cameroon–Nigeria Mixed Commission. By December 2003 Nigeria had withdrawn from 32 villages and turned control of them over to Cameroon, while Cameroon had turned one village over to Nigeria. In January 2004 the two countries agreed to reopen diplomatic ties and to establish joint patrols in the disputed region until final demarcation was completed. In July 2004 a second round of territorial exchange occurred. However, Nigeria failed to meet the next round of transfer requirement on September 15, 2004, leading to renewed UN efforts to finalize a settlement. The UN reported success in partial demarcation by the end of 2005.

On November 1, 1995, Cameroon was officially granted membership in the Commonwealth. Although a full participant in francophone affairs, Yaoundé had campaigned for membership as part of an effort to appease secessionist leaders in the former British Cameroons region.

Current Issues

Attention in mid-2000 centered on continued secessionist unrest in the North-West and South-West provinces (see the Southern Cameroon National Council under Regional Groups in Political Parties, below) and the controversial pipeline proposed to carry oil from southern Chad to the Cameroonian port of Kribi. In June the World Bank endorsed the $3.7 billion project, despite criticism from environmentalists and human rights activists, the latter arguing that the expected windfall from the pipeline would likely be misused by what they considered to be already a highly corrupt and mismanaged government. The pipeline was completed in 2003, with Cameroon expecting to receive $500 million from Chad for leasing the pipeline over 25 years.

Opposition parties and secessionists were angered by the visit of a delegation from the Commonwealth Secretariat in August 2000 that ex-pressed "satisfaction" with the development of democracy in Cameroon. They also strongly criticized the creation of a National Electoral Observatory in October 2001 to oversee the upcoming municipal and national balloting, charging that the body was controlled by President Biya. Accusations of fraud and other irregularities surrounded the June 30, 2002, local and national elections in which the RDPC/CPDM was credited with resounding victories. (Reruns were ordered for some 17 assembly seats.) The SDF launched a two-month boycott of legislative activity to protest the perceived heavy-handedness of the administration, which in 2003 presented what it called reform of the electoral oversight body to meet opposition demands. However, even international observers criticized some aspects of the October 2004 presidential poll. Meanwhile, Biya's subsequent appointment of Ephraim Inoni as the new prime minister in December was seen as an attempt to "promote national unity." Inoni, a career civil servant who had represented Cameroon in its contentious negotiations with Nigeria (see Foreign relations, above), was expected to be popular among the English-speaking population. In addition, the expanded cabinet reportedly included some 17 Muslims.

In mid-2005 Biya loyalists were lobbying for an amendment to the constitution that would allow the president to serve a third seven-year term. Several opposition parties vehemently opposed such a move, with some suggesting it was a ploy by Biya meant only to test reaction to the idea.

Political Parties

Cameroon had only one legal party (the Cameroon National Union [UNC], later the Democratic Rally of the Cameroon People [RDPC]/Cameroon People's Democratic Movement [CPDM], below) from 1966 until early 1991 despite the fact that the 1972 constitution guaranteed the right of political parties to organize and to participate in elections. In June 1990 President Biya announced that the government, which had theretofore refused to legalize opposition parties, would no longer stand in the way of a multi-party system. In December the National Assembly passed new legislation covering the registration of parties, and as of November 2000, nearly 170 parties had been legalized.

Prior to the 2004 presidential balloting a group of nine opposition parties (including the SDF, UDC, UPC, MDP, and MLDC, below) formed a National Coalition for Reconciliation and Reconstruction (NCRR) with the goal of coalescing behind a single candidate. However, the SDF (the leading party in the coalition) subsequently withdrew following a dispute over the selection of the NCRR standard-bearer. The NCRR candidate, Adamon Ndam Njoua of the UDC, finished third in the balloting with 4.4 percent of the vote.

Government and Government-Supportive Parties

Democratic Rally of the Cameroon People (*Rassemblement Démocratique du Peuple Camerounais*—RDPC). Formerly the Cameroon National Union (*Union Nationale Camerounaise*—UNC), the RDPC was until early 1991 the only officially recognized party. The RDPC is also referenced in English as the Cameroon People's Democratic Movement (CPDM). The UNC was formed in 1966 by merger of the Cameroon Union (*Union Camerounaise*); the former majority party of East (French) Cameroons; and of several former West (British) Cameroons parties, including the governing Kamerun National Democratic Party (KNDP), the Kamerun United National Congress (KUNC), and the Kamerun People's Party (KPP). The present name was adopted, over significant anglophone resistance, at a 1985 congress that also established a National Council as the party's second-highest body. The latter, at its first meeting held November 24–26, 1988, urged that Cameroon maintain its nonaligned foreign policy, called for the imposition of stiff antiembezzlement measures, and asked citizens to accept the "necessary compromise between freedom and order."

At the party's fifth congress held June 28–30, 1990, President Biya called for a loosening of sub-version laws and told party members to expect political "competition," the way for which was cleared by the National Assembly's approval of a pluralism law in December. The RDPC/CPDM won 88 seats in the March 1992 legislative elections, subsequently forming a coalition with the MDR (below) to create a working majority in the assembly. At an extraordinary RDPC/CPDM congress on October 7, 1995, Biya secured a new five-year term as party president.

Beginning with the resignation of Ayissi NVODO in October 1996, the RDPC/CPDM and Biya were stung by the defection of three prominent party statesmen and their declarations of presidential candidacy. Following Nvodo in that regard were Albert NDZONGANG and the minister of health and Biya's personal physician, Titus EDZOA, who accused the administration of "permanent attempts to humiliate him." Edzoa was subsequently arrested on fraud charges, and in mid-1997 Nvodo, who had been ill, died. On the other hand, the party's success at legislative balloting in May was attributable, in part, to its recruitment of prominent UNDP and SDF leaders. In addition, observers credited the party's legislative gains to the adoption of a preelection primary process and the support of Prime Minister Musonge's ethnic Sawa constituency in the South-West and Littoral provinces.

The government named in December 1997 reflected, in part, a shift of power within the RDPC/CPDM from those sympathetic to Edzoa, who had been sentenced to 15 years in prison in October, and more senior members to a youthful cadre with "technocratic" tendencies in line with the prime minister's. In April 2001 Biya reshuffled the cabinet and replaced Edouard AKAME Mfoundou, minister of state in charge of economy and finance and an influential figure within the party. The reshuffle was reportedly part of Biya's attempt to increase control over his faction-ridden party.

Leaders: Paul BIYA (President of the Republic and of the Party), Ephraim INONI (Prime Minister), Joseph-Charles DOUMBA (Secretary General), Grégoire OWONA (Deputy Secretary General).

National Union for Democracy and Progress
(*Union Nationale pour la Démocratie et le Progrés*—UNDP). Seen primarily as a vehicle for supporters of former president Ahidjo, the UNDP was formed in 1991 under the leadership of Samuel Eboua. In early 1992, however, it was reported that Eboua had been "squeezed out" of his position by former prime minister Maigari Bello Bouba, who had recently returned from exile. After a last-minute reversal of a proposed electoral boycott, the UNDP won 68 seats in the March legislative balloting, running most strongly in the predominately Muslim northern provinces. Bouba was subsequently described as the "strongman of the opposition."

In the immediate aftermath of the October 1992 presidential election the UNDP leader, who had finished third, joined SDF leader Fru Ndi in petitioning the Supreme Court to annul the controversial poll. Nevertheless, in late November two party members, Hamadou MOUSTAPHA and Issa Tchiroma BAKARY, accepted cabinet ministries, and in early 1993 Fru Ndi denounced Bouba for negotiating with President Biya on the formation of a unity government.

On November 8, 1994, the UNDP announced a boycott of the National Assembly, pending the release of 30 party activists who had been arrested in July. While the walkout was abandoned four weeks later, the UNDP Central Committee confirmed in late December that Moustapha and Bakary had been expelled from the party (the latter proclaiming the formation of a rival UNDP). Although advancing the second-highest number of candidates (180) at the 1996 local elections, the UNDP finished third at the balloting. Highlighting the UNDP's electoral showing was the victory of former president Ahidjo's son, Mohamed AHIDJO, who had returned from exile two years earlier. Subsequently, the party was buffeted by a power struggle between Bouba and the virulently anti-Biya Mohamed Ahidjo.

Still reeling from the loss of Moustapha and Bakary in 1994, the UNDP fared poorly at legislative balloting in May 1997, its representation dropping to 13 seats. Having reached an impasse in its dialogue with the administration concerning a possible unity government, the UNDP helped spearhead a boycott of the October presidential elections, after which Bouba disputed the government's claims to a high voter turnout. Nevertheless, in December Bouba announced that he had accepted a cabinet post, asserting that Biya was seeking to incorporate opposition leaders in his government and admitting that his appointment was part of an apparent presidential effort to isolate Fru Ndi. Bouba remained in the cabinet following the March 2000 reshuffling, although substantial criticism was reported at the UNDP congress in June over his decision to stay in the government despite what delegates charged was a distinct lack of progress regarding the political liberalization promised by the Biya administration in the 1997 compact. (The dissent to Bouba became more apparent with the resignation of UNDP Vice President Nicole OKALA in July.) The congress formally criticized the government's human rights record and demanded broad changes in the electoral code and establishment of an independent election commission prior to the 2002 balloting.

Leader: Maigari Bello BOUBA (Party Leader), Pierre Flambeau NGAYAP (Secretary General).

Cameroon People's Union (*Union des Populations Camerounaises*—UPC). The Marxist–Leninist UPC was formed in 1948 and, although outlawed in 1955, continued to operate clandestinely in Cameroon, its membership fragmenting into pro-Soviet and Maoist factions in the 1960s. Sporadic UPC guerrilla activity presented no serious challenge to the Ahidjo regime, and by 1971 most UPC adherents had been forced into exile. Headquartered at Paris, the UPC subsequently served as the most prominent of the groups opposing Cameroon's one-party regime, claiming thousands of "militants" in both France and Cameroon.

In October 1990 UPC Secretary General Ngouo WOUNGLY-MASSAGA, having been accused by colleagues of "anti-social behavior and embezzlement," broke with the party and returned to Cameroon, where he eventually organized the People's Solidarity Party (*Parti de la Solidarité du*

Peuple—PSP). Upon legalization of the UPC in 1991 most former exiles returned, including Ndeh Ntumazah, the "last surviving founder of the UPC," who reportedly enjoyed a "larger-than-life" reputation in Cameroon despite his 20-year absence. The party subsequently split regarding the March 1992 legislative elections, Ntumazah leading a partial boycott of the balloting despite Secretary General Augustin Frederick Kodock's decision that the UPC should participate. Presenting candidates in about half of the 180 districts, the UPC won 18 seats, thereby becoming the third-leading parliamentary party.

In May 1992 the party was a founding member of the National Convention of the Cameroonian Opposition (see under PDC, below), and in September Henri Hogbe Nlend was described as a UPC presidential candidate. However, there were no reports of his having garnered any votes or of the UPC having taken part in the elections. In February 1995 Woungly-Massaga returned to the UPC, which absorbed his PSP.

Intraparty tension mounted following the UPC's poor showing at the January 1996 municipal elections, where it won only 3 of 336 contests, and in April the party announced a number of dismissals and reportedly sought closer ties with the RDPC/CPDM. In early May the UPC's parliamentary leader, Charles Oma BETOW, and three other senior leaders announced the removal of Secretary General Kodock, labeling his party management "disastrous." For his part, Kodock argued that his detractors had met illegally, thus invalidating their motion. Kodock was named minister of state for agriculture in the government announced on September 20, a UPC conference earlier in the month reportedly revealing at least four factions in the grouping.

At legislative balloting in May 1997 Kodock's "pro-Biya" wing forwarded 35 candidates while Ntumazah and his followers supported an additional 17; subsequently, the group's representation plummeted from 16 posts to 1 as Kodock alone secured a seat. At presidential polling in October the party once again forwarded Henri Hogbe Nlend, who secured only 2.8 percent of the vote.

In December Nlend was named minister of scientific and technical research in the new cabinet. As of mid-2001 the UPC was reportedly split into two competing factions, out of which Kodock's became increasingly "anti-Biya," while Nlend's wing was representing the "pro-Biya" orientation.

In the 2002 legislative elections the national election board treated the two factions as a single party, although candidates identified themselves as UPC (N) for the Nlend supporters and UPC (K) for the Kodock supporters. Kodock accepted a cabinet post after the balloting and continued to serve in the reshuffled cabinet after the presidential elections in 2004. The UPC (N) participated in the anti-Biya presidential electoral coalition in 2004.

Leaders: Henri Hogbe NLEND (1997 presidential candidate and UPC [N] Leader), Augustin Frederick KODOCK (UPC [K]) Leader).

Movement for the Defense of the Republic (*Mouvement pour la Défense de la République*—MDR). The northern-based MDR, supported primarily by the small Kirdi ethnic group, was organized shortly before the March 1992 legislative balloting in an apparent effort to dilute the electoral strength of the UNDP (above), the region's dominant party. Six of the MDR's 32 candidates won assembly seats, enough to make the party a crucial element in formation of the subsequent government. Five MDR members were appointed to the cabinet in April, including party leader Dakole Daissala, who had been placed in detention following the 1984 coup attempt. Although never formally charged or tried, Daissala had remained in jail until 1991, when he began what was viewed as an extraordinary ascent to governmental prominence.

At legislative balloting in May 1997 the MDR managed to recapture only one of its legislative posts. Subsequently, the party was not included in the government named in December. The MDR failed to gain any seats in the 2002 elections, but Daissala joined the government in 2004 as minister of transport.

Leader: Dakole DAISSALA (President).

Opposition Parties

Social Democratic Front (SDF). The SDF was launched in early 1990 in the English-speaking town of Bamenda in western Cameroon. Shortly thereafter a number of its leaders were arrested for belonging to an illegal organization, and an SDF rally in May was broken up by security forces, leaving several people dead. However, following the government's endorsement of political liberalization in June, the SDF detainees were released, and the party (legalized in 1991) became one of the most active opposition groups. Although it would probably have secured substantial representation, particularly in the anglophone western provinces, the SDF boycotted the March 1992 legislative election on grounds that there was insufficient time for opposition parties to organize effectively and that the electoral code favored the RDPC/CPDM.

Party president John Fru Ndi's strong showing in the October 1992 presidential balloting was heralded by the SDF as evidence that its appeal was not limited to the anglophone community. Hence, the party continued to distance itself from the Cameroon Anglophone Movement, the self-described "socio-cultural association" headquartered at Buea in the South-West province, which advocated a return to the 1972-style federal government system. In November the SDF rejected calls for a unity government headed by Biya, insisting that his handling of the presidential balloting and Fru Ndi's arrest proved that he could not be trusted. Instead it called for a two-year transitional program to be highlighted by the establishment of a new electoral code and the convening of a constitutional conference to draw up a new basic charter.

In May 1994 Secretary General Siga AS-SANGA was dismissed by the party's disciplinary council for making approaches to the government on possible SDF participation in a government of national unity. Five months later Fru Ndi spearheaded the launching of the Allies' Front for Change (FAC, below), prior to yielding the office under a revolving presidency system to Samuel Eboua (then of the UNDP) in January 1995.

In early 1995 the SDF experienced a deep crisis that resulted in the departure or exclusion from its executive committee of a dozen influential members. One of those excluded, party treasurer Jean DJOKOU, accused Fru Ndi of "secret management and swindling the party finances," while others complained of the lack of attention to francophones within the party, most of whom strongly supported a unitary state.

During the run-up to balloting in January 1996 the SDF suspended its membership in the FAC and issued a list of 105 candidates. At the January 21 polling the party secured victories primarily in large towns and "traditional fiefdoms." Subsequently, the party's performance at legislative balloting in May 1997 (43 seats captured) fell shy of analysts' predictions. Thereafter, SDF militants took to the streets to protest the government's alleged fraudulent administration of the polling, and on June 12 a number of party members were arrested. Nevertheless, on June 17 Fru Ndi called on the party's legislators to assume their seats. Fru Ndi's "statesman-like" decision to distance himself and the SDF from violent dissention had its roots, according to some analysts, in his ambitions for the presidential elections scheduled for October. Subsequently, Fru Ndi and other senior SDF members traveled to African and Western capitals to gain allies in their efforts to pressure the recalcitrant Biya administration into addressing the opposition's preelectoral demands. While such visits reportedly improved Fru Ndi's standing with the international community, Biya's stance remained unchanged. Consequently, on September 12 at Paris Fru Ndi announced the SDF's decision to boycott the presidential polling.

The SDF's (then) secretary general, Tazoacha Asonganyi, led the party's negotiating team at talks with the government, which opened in December 1997. For his part, Fru Ndi, who had earlier threatened to expel any member who joined the government, had reportedly adopted a "wait and see" position. The talks collapsed in early 1998, and in mid-February the SDF formed a "common front" with the UDC (below). In July the SDF suffered its most traumatic infighting since 1995, as 10 of the party's 43 legislators resigned from the party to protest Fru Ndi's leadership, which they reportedly characterized as "authoritarian." Subsequently, Fru Ndi ousted Souleimane MAHAMAD, theretofore SDF vice chair, in October after Mahamad convened an extraordinary party congress that served as an anti–Fru Ndi forum. In lopsided balloting at the SDF's annual congress in April 1999, Fru Ndi retained the party's top post.

The SDF protested that the 2002 legislative elections were flawed because of government interference, and Fru Ndi launched a boycott of the assembly and municipal councils. However, in July Fru Ndi announced an end to the boycott, prompting a group of SDF dissidents to form a new party (see AFP, below).

The SDF was instrumental in the formation of the anti-Biya electoral coalition, the NCRR, in April 2004. However, Fru Ndi withdrew the SDF from the NCRR in September after a dispute over the manner in which the coalition's presidential candidate would be chosen. Fru Ndi instead ran as the SDF's candidate and received 17.4 percent of the vote.

Rifts in the party developed in late 2005 after Asonganyi criticized party leadership for being ineffectual as a catalyst for change in Cameroon and said he would not run for party chair at the next congress in May 2006. Meanwhile, party members Paulinus Toh JUA and Ben MUNA vowed to challenge Fru Ndi at the next congress. Following Asonganyi's remarks, at a reportedly "stormy" session of party leaders, he was suspended, prompting protest by some members who walked out. Subsequently, he was replaced as secretary general by Dr. Michael NDOBEGANG. Asonganyi was dismissed from the party in early 2006 after the party found him guilty of six "charges," including questioning or criticizing party policies, ideals, and hierarchy. Shortly thereafter, Ndobegang resigned over Asonganyi's expulsion.

Leaders: John FRU NDI (President).

Cameroonian Democratic Union (*Union Démocratique du Cameroun*—UDC). The UDC was formed in 1991 under the leadership of Adamou Ndam Njoya, who held several senior posts in the Ahidjo administration. Although the party boycotted the March 1992 legislative election, Ndam Njoya subsequently competed in the October 1992 presidential elections, gaining 3.62 percent of the vote.

In 1997 Ndam Njoya was a leading advocate of the opposition's boycott of the October presidential polling, although the party had secured five seats in the May legislative balloting. Following the 2002 elections the UDC became the third-largest party in the assembly with five seats. Ndam Njoya helped form the anti-Biya coalition in the 2004 presidential election and was the coalition's candidate for the presidency. He placed third with 4.4 percent of the vote.

Leader: Adamou NDAM NJOYA.

Other Parties and Groups

Movement for the Liberation of Cameroonian Youth (*Mouvement pour la Libération de la Jeunesse Camerounaise*—MLJC). At legislative balloting in May 1997 the theretofore little-known MLJC secured one seat. It did not gain any seats in the 2002 balloting, and a subsequent leadership dispute led members of the MLJC to leave the party and establish a new political group (see MLDC below).

Leader: Dieudonné TINA.

Movement for the Liberation and Development of Cameroon (*Mouvement pour la Libération et le Développement du Cameroun*—MLDC). The MLDC, formed by dissident members of the MLJC, participated in the anti-Biya electoral coalition in 2004.

Leaders: Marcel YONDO, Jean PAHAI.

Alliance of Progressive Forces (*Alliance des Forces Progressistes*—AFP). Created in 2002, the AFP was formed by former members of the SDF who opposed Fru Ndi's leadership and willingness to compromise with President Biya.

Leader: Maidadi Saidou YAYA.

Social Movement for the New Democracy (*Mouvement Social pour la Nouvelle*

Démocratie—MSND). The MSND, said to have support among the urban middle class, was formed in 1991 by Yondo Black, a former president of the Cameroon Bar Association who had been active in the prodemocracy movement for several years, at times in conjunction with the organizers of the SDF. Black had been arrested in February 1990 for his activities and sentenced to three years' imprisonment for "subversion," but was released in August. Black ran for the presidency in 2004 but received only 0.36 percent of the vote.

Leader: Yondo Mandengue BLACK.

Allies' Front for Change (*Front des Alliés pour le Changement*—FAC). The FAC was launched in October 1994 under the guidance of SDF leader John Fru Ndi, although he and his party withdrew from the grouping to campaign independently for the 1996 municipal elections. The FAC was initially reportedly composed of 15 parties; however, only the 3 parties immediately below were subsequently identified as members.

The status of the Front was further clouded in October 1997 when the MDP's Samuel Eboua campaigned for the presidency under his party's banner (below).

Leaders: Njoh LITUMBE (President, PLD), Victorin Hameni BIELEU (UFDC), Samuel EBOUA (MDP).

Liberal Democratic Party (*Parti Libéral Démocrate* –PLD). The PLD was formed in 1991 under the leadership of Njoh Litumbe, who subsequently visited the United States as a spokesman for the opposition groups in Cameroon.

Leader: Njoh LITUMBE.

Union of Democratic Forces of Cameroon (*Union des Forces Démocratiques du Cameroun*—UFDC). The UFDC was considered one of the more important groups to boycott the March 1992 legislative election, its leader, Victorin Hameni Bieleu, having served as president of an opposition coordinating committee in 1991. On November 3, 1992, Bieleu was arrested for his involvement in antigovernment protests. Bieleu ran for the presidency in 2004 but received less than 1 percent of the vote. He was reported to be mobilizing support from his "militants" in the diaspora in early 2005 in preparation for the 2007 legislative elections.

Leader: Victorin Hameni BIELEU.

Movement for Democracy and Progress (*Mouvement pour la Démocratie et le Progrés*—MDP). The MDP is headed by former UNDP leader Samuel Eboua, who was elected to a FAC leadership post in February 1996. Eboua's 1997 presidential campaign yielded just 2.4 percent of the vote at October balloting.

Leader: Samuel EBOUA (1997 presidential candidate).

Cameroonian Party of Democrats (*Parti des Démocrates Cumerounais*—PDC). The PDC is Cameroon's member of the Christian Democratic International. One of its leaders, Louis-Tobie Mbida, was instrumental in launching an antigovernment coalition, the **National Convention of the Cameroonian Opposition** (*Convention Nationale de l'Opposition Camerounaise*—CNOC), in early 1992.

Leaders: Louis-Tobie MBIDA (President), Gaston BIKELE EKAMI (Secretary General).

Action for Meritocracy and Equal Opportunity Party (AMEOP). At presidential balloting in October 1997 the anglophone AMEOP's candidate, Joachim Tabi Owono, secured less than 1 percent of the vote.

Leader: Joachim Tabi OWONO (1997 presidential candidate).

Integral Democracy of Cameroon (*Démocratie Intégrale du Cameroun*—DIC). The DIC's presidential candidate in 1992 and 1997 was its leader, Blazius Isaka. He received less than 1 percent of the vote in October 1997. He also received less than 1 percent of the vote in the 2004 presidential balloting.

Leader: Blazius ISAKA (1992, 1997, and 2004 presidential candidate).

In January 1994 Jean-Michel TEKAM, leader of the **Social Democratic Party of Cameroon** (*Parti Social-Démocrate du Cameroun*—PSDC), announced the launching of an opposition united front that reportedly included the **Progressive Movement** (*Mouvement Progressif*—MP), led by Jean-Jacques EKINDI, as well as the MSND and a branch of the UPC (above). The new group declared itself open to all other opposition formations, including the SDF. Included in the government named in December 1997 was Antar GASSAGAYE, theretofore identified as leader of the **National Progress Party** (*Parti National du Progrès*—PNP). However, both Tekam and Ekindi ran in the 2004 presidential elections as candidates for their respective parties (the PSDC and the MP).

Other parties that contested the 2002 legislative or the 2004 presidential elections included the **Alliance for Development and Democracy** (*Alliance pour la Démocratie et le Développement*—ADD), led by 2004 presidential candidate Garga Haman ADJI; the **Justice and Development Party** (JDP), which promotes the rights of English-speaking Cameroonians under the leadership of publisher Boniface FOBBIN, who was the JDP's 2004 presidential candidate; and the **African Movement for New Independence and Democracy** (*Mouvement Africain pour la Nouvelle Indépendance et la Démocratie*—MANIDEM), led by Anicet EKANE and comprised of former members of the UPC.

(For a list of some 40 other small parties and groups, see the 1999 edition of the *Handbook*.)

Regional Groups

Southern Cameroon National Council (SCNC). The leading vehicle for expression of secessionist sentiment in the former British Cameroons region, the SCNC originally served as the elected executive organ of the Southern Cameroon People's Conference (SCPC), an umbrella organization for a number of professional and trade associations, political parties, youth groups, and other grassroots bodies opposed to the domination of francophone influence in the country. The SCPC was the successor to the All Anglophone Conference (AAC), which first met in 1993 in an effort to persuade the nation's francophone leadership to return to the federal structure of the 1960s in which the anglophone region enjoyed broad autonomy. The SCPC rubric was subsequently adopted in part because the term *anglophone* was deemed too "colonial" and "limiting" and in part to reflect the region's shift in favor of independence based on a perceived lack of interest in dialogue regarding autonomy on the part of the Biya administration. Most observers subsequently referred to the SCNC when discussing affairs in the Southern Cameroons, prompting the SCPC, for the sake of clarity, to formally adopt the SCNC name for itself.

In August 1995 an SCNC delegation petitioned the United Nations to mediate between the secessionists and Yaoundé, warning that lack of intervention would result in "another Somalia." Two months later the Council released a proposed timetable for independence, and the Cameroonians responded by arresting a number of SCNC adherents. SCNC founding chair Sam Ekontang ELAD resigned in late 1996, ostensibly due to illness, and he was succeeded by former Cameroonian diplomat Henry Fossung.

In late March 1997 more than 200 SCNC supporters were arrested, many in connection with what the government said was an attack on the headquarters of security forces at Bamenda in which several people were reportedly killed. The crackdown apparently suppressed SCNC activity for more than a year as Fossung reportedly returned to his outlying village to maintain a low profile. In April 1998 a group led by SCNC treasurer Arnold Yongbang attempted to revive the organization, electing Esoka NDOKI MUKETE, the "charismatic" provincial chair of the SDF, as the new SCNC chair. However, that decision was challenged as "undemocratic" by Fossung and others, including the influential SCNC–North America (SCNC-NA), and the Council remained factionalized and, consequently, ineffective.

In October 1999 a military tribunal at Yaoundé sentenced nine SCNC members to prison for their roles in the alleged 1997 attack, prompting renewed turmoil in the North-West and South-West provinces (which the SCNC prefers to reference as the Northern and Southern zones). Shortly thereafter, the SCNC again petitioned the UN for recognition, and in December it was reported that SCNC militants, under the leadership of Ndoki Mukete (who had been forced to resign his SDF post because that party does not endorse independence for the anglophone region), planned to declare independence by the end of the year. However, Fossung continued to oppose such a unilateral declaration, and the Cameroonian government indicated it would react harshly to any independence announcement. Consequently, Ndoki Mukete was reported to be "traveling abroad" on December 30 when SCNC militants took over the radio station at Buea to declare the establishment of the Federal Republic of the Southern Cameroons. Ndoki Mukete was subsequently described as having left the SCNC, the effective leadership mantle falling to Frederick Ebong Alobwede, who had read the independence declaration and been arrested with a number of supporters shortly thereafter following a series of pro-independence demonstrations.

An SCNC meeting in late January 2000 again attempted to resolve the leadership dispute, Fossung continuing to describe himself as chair and disavowing the recent declaration. In February the Northern and Southern zones each elected their own executive bodies, and those groups then elected a new SCNC executive body, with Ebong as chair, thereby "president" of the newly announced republic. The Council remained formally committed to nonviolence, although that philosophy was expected to be reconsidered at a "constituent assembly" scheduled for late September in which a constitution secretly adopted in 1996 also was scheduled for review. (The constitution reportedly calls for a federal structure for the Southern Cameroons based on 13 essentially tribal-based provinces.) Meanwhile, the Biya administration maintained its hard line toward the SCNC, and no dialogue was reported between the government and the secessionists as of midyear. In October 2001 violent clashes between police and SCNC demonstrators on the 40th anniversary of unification left three dead and dozens injured. In July 2001 Ebong announced the formation of his "cabinet," and the SCNC boycotted the 2002 legislative elections and the 2004 presidential polling.

In late 2005 several party members, including the chair of one of the factions, were arrested after illegal demonstrations. Party official Chief AYAMBA Ette Otun was released but soon rearrested for his role in launching Radio Free Southern Cameroons (see Broadcasting and computing, below), which aired programs highly critical of the administration. In early 2006 one of the detainees died, his supporters alleging his death was the result of torture.

Leaders: Henry FOSSUNG (head of faction opposed to independence declaration), Frederick EBONG Alobwede (Chair of the SCNC and President of the Federal Republic of the Southern Cameroons), Dr. Ngala NFOR (Vice Chair of the SCNC and Chair of the Northern Zone Executive Committee), Dr. Martin LUMA (Spokesman), Andrew AZONG-WARE (Secretary General).

South West Elite Association (SWELA). The reactivation of SWELA was announced in March 2000, apparently at the urging of Prime Minister Musonge in the hope of countering the secessionist movement in South-West province led by the SCNC. SWELA leaders subsequently voiced support for a "united Cameroon."

Leader: Lyonga Efase KANGE (Secretary General).

Guerrilla Group

National Liberation Front of Cameroon (*Fronte de la Libération Nationale du Cameroun—* FLNC). The anti-Biya FLNC is led by Mbara Guerandi, who reportedly fled from Cameroon in 1984 following his indictment for participating in an alleged coup attempt. In late 1997 it was reported that Guerandi, now based in Burkina Faso, had reached agreement with antigovernment rebels in Chad to coordinate guerrilla activities.

Leader: Mbara GUERANDI (in exile in Burkina Faso).

Cabinet

As of February 1, 2006

Prime Minister	Ephraim Inoni (RDPC/CPDM)
Deputy Prime Minister	Ali Amadou (RDPC/CPDM)

Ministers of State

Culture	Ferdinand Léopold Oyono (ind.)
Justice	Ali Amadou (RDPC/CPDM)
Planning, Development, and Land Management	Augustin Frederick Kodock (UPC)
Posts and Telecommunications	Maigari Bello Bouba (UNDP)
Secretary General of the Presidency	Jean-Marie Atangana Mebara (RDPC/CPDM)
Territorial Administration and Decentralization	Marafa Hamidou Yaya (RDPC/CPDM)
Town Planning and Housing	Etienne-Charles Lekene Donfack (RDPC/CPDM)

Ministers

Agriculture	Clobaire Tchatat (RDPC/CPDM)
Civil Service and Administrative Reform	Benjamin Amana Amana (RDPC/CPDM)
Communication	Pierre Moukoko Mbonjo (RDPC/CPDM)
Economy and Finance	Polycarpe Abah Abah (RDPC/CPDM)
Employment and Professional Training	Zacharie Perevet (RDPC/CPDM)
Environment	Pierre Hele (RDPC/CPDM)
Foreign Affairs	Laurent Esso (RDPC/CPDM)
Forests and Wild Animals	Hilman Egbe Achu (RDPC/CPDM) [f]
Higher Education	Jacques Fame Ndongo (RDPC/CPDM)
Labor and Social Insurance	Robert Nkili (RDPC/CPDM)
Lands	Louis Marie Abogo Nkono (RDPC/CPDM)
Livestock, Fisheries, and Animal Industries	Aboubakari Sarki (RDPC/CPDM)
Mines, Industry, and Technological Development	Charles Sale (RDPC/CPDM)
National Education	Haman Adama (RDPC/CPDM) [f]
Public Health	Urbain Olanguena Awono (RDPC/CPDM)
Public Works	Martin Aristide Okouda (RDPC/CPDM)
Scientific and Technical Research	Madeleine Tchuent (ind.) [f]
Secondary Education	Louis Bapes Bapes (RDPC/CPDM)
Small and Medium Enterprises and Social Economy	Bernard Messengue Avom (ind.)
Social Affairs	Cathérine Bakang Mbock (RDPC/CPDM) [f]
Sport	Philippe Mbarga Mboa (RDPC/CPDM)
Tourism	Baba Amadou (RDPC/CPDM)
Trade	Luc Magloire Mbarga Atangana (ind.)
Transport	Dakole Daissala (MDR)
Water and Power	Alphonse Siyam Siwe (RDPC/CPDM)
Women and the Family	Suzanne Mbomback (ind.) [f]
Youth	Adoum Garoua (RDPC/CPDM)

[f] = female

Legislature

The **National Assembly** (*Assemblée Nationale*) currently consists of 180 members elected for five-year terms. At the April 1988 election voters in most districts were permitted to choose between two lists (in the case of single-member constituencies, between two candidates) presented by the Cameroon People's Democratic Movement.

Multiparty balloting was introduced at the March 1, 1992, election, which was brought forward one year in response to pressure from the nation's burgeoning prodemocracy movement. However, no independent or coalition candidates were permitted, contributing to the decision by some opposition groups to boycott the poll. The number of parties participating in legislative balloting increased from 32 in 1992 to 40 in 1997, and the number of parties securing seats rose from four to seven, respectively. Following the most recent legislative elections on June 30, 2002 (with reruns on September 15), the seat distribution in the National Assembly was as follows: the Democratic Rally of the Cameroon People, 149; the Social Democratic Front, 22; the Cameroonian Democratic Union, 5; the Cameroon People's Union, 3; and the National Union for Democracy and Progress, 1.

President: Djibril Cayavé YEGUIE.

Communications

Press

Prior censorship has long been practiced in Cameroon, and journalists have occasionally been detained for publishing "sensationalist" or "tendentious" material. Although President Biya announced in June 1990 that restrictions on the press would be loosened in consonance with the government's political liberalization program, the censorship law was retained, and several newspapers were suspended in 1991 for publishing articles criticizing the administration. The principal newspapers are *Le Tribune du Cameroun/Cameroon Tribune* (Yaoundé), government daily in French (66,000) and English (20,000); *Cameroon Post* (50,000), weekly in English; *La Gazette* (Douala, 35,000), twice weekly in French; *Le Messager* (34,000), independent fortnightly in French; *Le Combattant* (21,000), independent weekly in French; *Cameroon Outlook* (Victoria, 20,000), thrice weekly in English; *Politiks* (10,000), independent daily in French; *Mutations*, biweekly independent; *La Révélation; L'Action.* In September 1992 *Le Messager* was one of several publications temporarily suspended by the government; the editor of *Le Messager* was imprisoned for nine months in 1998 for printing a "false story" about President Biya. In October 2001 the opposition publication *La Nouvelle Expression* reportedly came under scrutiny for stories on the secessionist movement. On the eve of the 2004 presidential elections, several media outlets, including *Mutations* and more than a dozen radio and television stations, were suspended. Speculation was that the action was taken to prevent criticism of President Biya prior to the election and suspensions were lifted after the election.

News Agencies

The former *Agence Camerounaise de Presse* (ACAP) was replaced in 1978 by the *Société de Presse et d'Edition du Cameroun* (Sopecam), which, under the Ministry of Information, is responsible for the dissemination of foreign news within Cameroon and also for publication of *Le Tribune du Cameroun.* The principal foreign agency is *Agence France-Presse.*

Broadcasting and Computing

The *Office de Radiodiffusion-Télévision Camerounaise* (CRTV) is a government facility operating under the control of the Ministry of Information and Culture. Programming is in French, English, and more than two dozen local languages, with 24-hour programming launched in 2005. There were approximately 580,000 television receivers and 100,000 personal computers serving 60,000 Internet users in 2003. An opposition radio station, Radio Free Southern Cameroons, began broadcasting in English an hour a week in late 2005 under the aegis of the SCNC (see Political Parties, above). Also in late 2005, a radio station operated by the Seventh-Day Adventist church began broadcasting.

Intergovernmental Representation

Ambassador to the U.S.
Jerome MENDOUGA

U.S. Ambassador to Cameroon
R. Niels MARQUARDT

Permanent Representative to the UN
Martin BELINGA EBOUTOU

IGO Memberships (Non-UN)
AfDB, AU, BADEA, BDEAC, CEEAC, CEMAC, CWTH, IDB, Interpol, IOM, NAM, OIC, OIF, PCA, WCO, WTO

CAPE VERDE

REPUBLIC OF CAPE VERDE

República de Cabo Verde

The Country

Cape Verde embraces ten islands and five islets situated in the Atlantic Ocean some 400 miles west of Senegal. The islands are divided into a northern windward group (Santo Antão, São Vicente, Santa Lúcia, São Nicolau, Sal, and Boa Vista) and a southern leeward group (Brava, Fogo, São Tiago, and Maio). About 60 percent of the population is composed of *mestiços* (of mixed Portuguese and African extraction), who predominate on all of the islands except São Tiago, where they are outnumbered by black Africans; Europeans constitute less than 2 percent of the total. Most Cape Verdeans are Roman Catholics and speak a Creole version of Portuguese that varies from one island to another. Partly because of religious influence, women have traditionally been counted as less than 25 percent of the labor force, despite evidence of greater participation as unpaid agricultural laborers; female representation in party and government affairs has been increasing slowly, and the current government contains six women.

The islands' economy has historically depended on São Vicente's importance as a refueling and resting stop for shipping between Europe and Latin America. The airfield on Sal has long served a similar function for aircraft, although substantial revenue losses were experienced in the late 1980s because of a denial of landing rights to South African planes as a matter of "morality and solidarity with the rest of Africa." Corn is the major subsistence crop, but persistent drought since the late 1960s has forced the importation of it and other foods. The Monteiro administration's World Bank–supported

efforts to both privatize state-run enterprises and attract foreign investment were underlined in 1995 by the sale of 40 percent of the telecommunications facility to Portuguese investors. In June 1997 efforts to rehabilitate the island's infrastructure were boosted by a loan from the African Development Fund of $4.9 million for road projects.

Cape Verde in 1998 adopted a structural reform program prescribed by the International Monetary Fund (IMF) with the aim of "restoring financial stability" in the wake of a dismal economic performance in the first half of the decade. Debt reduction and private sector growth topped the government's goals. GDP grew in real terms by 8.6 percent in 1999, and 6.8 percent in 2000, in part due to

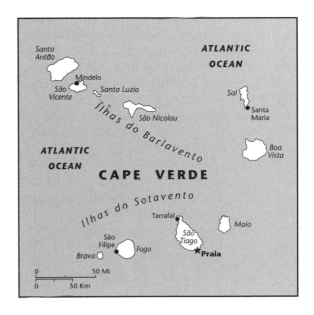

increased tourism and greater export of manufactured goods. On the negative side, unemployment grew during that time period, and by 2002 some 36 percent of the population was reportedly living in poverty. The IMF, World Bank, and African Development Bank subsequently provided significant additional assistance to support the government's economic restructuring. The country's GDP growth, which for the past several years had been described by the IMF as "robust," dipped to 4.5 percent in 2004, in part because of the drought's effect on agriculture (see Current issues, below). However, the IMF predicted 6 percent growth for 2005, bolstered by construction and continued low inflation.

Government and Politics

Political Background

Cape Verde was uninhabited when the Portuguese first occupied and began settling the islands in the mid-15th century; a Portuguese governor was appointed as early as 1462. During the 1970s several independence movements emerged, the most important being the mainland-based African Party for the Independence of Guinea-Bissau and Cape Verde (*Partido Africano da Independência do Guiné-Bissau e Cabo Verde*—PAIGC), which urged the union of Cape Verde and Guinea-Bissau, and the Democratic Union of Cape Verde (*União Democratica de Cabo Verde*—UDCV), which was led by João Baptista MONTEIRO and rejected the idea of a merger.

An agreement signed with Portuguese authorities on December 30, 1974, provided for a transitional government prior to independence on July 5, 1975. A 56-member National People's Assembly was elected on June 30, 1975, but only the PAIGC participated; the results indicated that about 92 percent of the voters favored the PAIGC proposal of ultimate union with Guinea-Bissau. Upon independence, the assembly elected Aristides PEREIRA, the secretary general of the PAIGC, as president of Cape Verde. On July 15 Maj. Pedro PIRES, who had negotiated the independence agreements for

both Cape Verde and Guinea-Bissau, was named prime minister of Cape Verde. However, the question of eventual unification with Guinea-Bissau remained unresolved, both governments promising to hold referendums on the issue. In January 1977 a Unity Council composed of six members from each of the national assemblies was formed, although in December the two governments asserted that it was necessary to move cautiously, with initial emphasis to be placed on establishing "a common strategy of development." Both countries continued to be ruled through the PAIGC, President Pereira serving as its secretary general and President Luis Cabral of Guinea-Bissau as his deputy.

On September 7, 1980, the assembly adopted Cape Verde's first constitution with the expectation that a collateral document under preparation in Guinea-Bissau would be virtually identical in all key aspects. On November 14, however, the mainland government was overthrown, and on February 12, 1981, the Cape Verdean assembly voted to expunge all references to unification from the country's basic law. Although formal reconciliation between the two governments was announced in mid-1982, the parties agreed that there would be no immediate resumption of unification efforts. Meanwhile, the offshore component of the ruling party had dropped the reference to Guinea in its title.

In keeping with currents elsewhere on the continent, the National Council of the African Party for the Independence of Cape Verde (PAICV, as the PAIGC had been restyled in 1981) announced in April 1990 that the president would henceforth be popularly elected and that other parties would be permitted to advance candidates for the assembly. On July 26 Pereira stepped down as PAICV party leader, declaring that the head of state should be "above party politics."

In the country's first multiparty balloting on January 13, 1991, the recently formed Movement for Democracy (*Movimento para Democracia*—MPD) won 56 legislative seats on the strength of a 68 percent vote share, compared to the PAICV's 23 seats. Prime Minister Pires announced his resignation on January 15, and on January 28 he was

Political Status: Former Portuguese
dependency; became independent July 5, 1975;
present constitution adopted September 25,
1992.

Area: 1,557 sq. mi. (4,033 sq. km.).

Population: 434,812 (2000C); 484,000 (2005E).

Major Urban Centers (2005E): CIDADE DE
PRAIA (São Tiago, 129,000), Mindelo
(67,000).

Official Language: Portuguese.

Monetary Unit: Cape Verde Escudo (official
rate July 1, 2006: 87.70 escudos = $1US).
(The escudo has been pegged to the Portuguese
escudo since 1998.)

President: Gen. (Ret.) Pedro Verona Rodrigues
PIRES (African Party for the Independence of
Cape Verde); elected by popular vote on
February 25, 2001, and inaugurated on March
22 for a five-year term, succeeding António
Mascarenhas MONTEIRO (nonparty, backed
by Movement for Democracy); reelected to
another five-year term on February 12, 2006,
and inaugurated on March 6.

Prime Minister: José Maria Pereira NEVES
(African Party for the Independence of Cape
Verde); appointed by the president on February
1, 2001, and sworn in (along with the new
cabinet) on the same day in succession to
António Gualberto DO ROSARIO (Movement
for Democracy) following legislative election
of January 14; reappointed by the president
and sworn in on March 8, 2006, following
legislative election of January 22.

succeeded by the MPD's Carlos Alberto Wahnon de
Carvalho VEIGA, who formed an MPD-dominated
interim government pending the upcoming presidential poll. Continuing the PAICV's decline, President Pereira was defeated in the February 17 balloting by António Mascarenhas MONTEIRO, who
had the support of the MPD, by a vote of 74 to
26 percent. Following Monteiro's inauguration on
March 22, a permanent Veiga government was installed on April 4.

In legislative balloting on December 17, 1995,
the MPD once again secured an absolute major-

ity, capturing a reported 60 percent of the vote, the
clear-cut legislative triumph being described by observers as validation of both the government's economic policies and Prime Minister Veiga, who had
vowed to resign if faced with the political "instability" of having to form a coalition government.
In addition, the PAICV's failure to increase its legislative representation reportedly convinced former
prime minister Pires to shelve plans for a presidential campaign. President Monteiro was reelected
unopposed in the presidential balloting of February 18, 1996.

On July 29, 2000, Prime Minister Veiga, who
had become increasingly at odds with President
Monteiro on several issues, including economic
policy, announced he would no longer serve as
prime minister in order to prepare for a campaign
to succeed Monteiro (limited to two terms by the
constitution) in the 2001 elections. Veiga argued
that his decision meant that Deputy Prime Minister António Gualberto DO ROSARIO should be
elevated to the premiership at least on an interim
basis. However, the PAICV labeled the maneuvering unconstitutional, and President Monteiro also
criticized the action as undermining his authority
to appoint the prime minister. (Among other things,
it was not clear if Veiga was officially resigning or
merely "suspending" his prime ministerial responsibilities.) An institutional crisis was finally averted
when Veiga subsequently submitted a formal resignation letter. On October 6 President Monteiro
invited do Rosario to form a new government that,
as constituted on October 9, comprised all but one
of the incumbent ministers.

In legislative balloting on January 14, 2001, the
PAICV won 47 percent of the vote and 40 seats.
On January 26 President Monteiro invited PAICV
leader José Maria Pereira NEVES to form a new
government, which was sworn in on February 1.
Subsequently, former prime minister Pires of the
PAICV was elected after two rounds of presidential balloting on February 11 and February 25, defeating Veiga and two independent candidates (see
Current issues, below). Pires again defeated Veiga
in the presidential balloting of February 12, 2006,
securing 50.92 percent of the vote versus Veiga's

49.02 percent, following the PAICV's winning 41 seats in legislative balloting on January 22. Neves was reappointed to head another PAICV government and was sworn in along with the new government on March 8.

Constitution and Government

The constitution of September 7, 1980, declared Cape Verde to be a "sovereign, democratic, unitary, anti-colonialist, and anti-imperialist republic" under single-party auspices. Legislative authority was vested in the National People's Assembly, which elected the president of the republic for a five-year term. The prime minister was nominated by the assembly and responsible to it. The basic law was amended in February 1981 to revoke provisions designed to facilitate union with Guinea-Bissau, thus overriding, inter alia, a 1976 judiciary protocol calling for the merger of legal procedures and personnel. The likelihood of a merger was virtually eliminated by adoption of the mainland constitution of May 1984, which emulated its Cape Verdean counterpart by lack of reference to the sister state.

On September 28, 1990, the National People's Assembly approved constitutional and electoral law revisions, forwarded in early 1990 by the PAICV National Council, which deleted references to the party as the "ruling force of society and of state," authorized balloting on the basis of direct universal suffrage, and sanctioned the participation of opposition candidates in multiparty elections that were subsequently held in January and February 1991.

A new constitution that came into force in September 1992 provided for direct presidential election to a five-year term, with provision for a run-off if no candidate secures a majority in the first round. Legislative authority is vested in a popularly elected national assembly of between 66 and 72 deputies. The assembly's normal term is also five years, although it may, in certain circumstances, be dissolved by the president. The prime minister continues to be nominated by and responsible to the assembly, though appointed by the president. On the prime minister's recommendation the president appoints the Council of Ministers, whose members must be assembly deputies. The court system features a Supreme Court of Justice, beneath which are courts of first and second resort. There also are administrative courts, courts of accounts, military courts, and tax and customs courts. In July 2004 the government announced plans to create a Constitutional Court in 2005.

At present there are 17 local government councils, which are popularly elected for five-year terms.

Foreign Relations

Cape Verde has established diplomatic relations with some 50 countries, including most members of the European Union (EU), with which it is associated under the Lomé Convention. Formally nonaligned, it rejected a 1980 Soviet overture for the use of naval facilities at the port of São Vicente as a replacement for facilities previously available at Conakry, Guinea. The Pereira government subsequently reaffirmed its opposition to any foreign military accommodation within its jurisdiction. In March 1984 Cape Verde became one of the few non-Communist countries to establish relations with the Heng Samrin government of Cambodia and, following a visit by Yasir Arafat in August 1986, it exchanged ambassadors with the Palestine Liberation Organization.

The country's closest regional links have been with Guinea-Bissau (despite a 20-month rupture following the ouster of the Cabral government in November 1980) and the other three Lusophone African states: Angola, Mozambique, and Sao Tome and Principe. Relations with Bissau were formally reestablished in July 1982 prior to a summit meeting of the five Portuguese-speaking heads of state in Praia held September 21–22, during which a joint committee was set up to promote economic and diplomatic cooperation.

Following the MPD legislative victory in January 1991, the new prime minister, Carlos Veiga, declared that no major foreign policy changes were contemplated, although he moved quickly to strengthen relations with anti-Marxist groups in Guinea-Bissau, Angola, and Mozambique.

In August 1998 international attention focused on Praia as the recently launched Community of Portuguese Speaking Countries (CPLP), under Monteiro's leadership, and the Economic Community of West African States (ECOWAS) forged a cease-fire agreement between the combatants in Guinea-Bissau.

The government established diplomatic and trade relations with China in 2001, while in 2002 it launched a broad initiative to gain preferential trade relations with the European Union. Subsequently, a sea-border agreement with Mauritania in December 2003 offered the hope for additional oil and mineral exploitation.

Current Issues

The MPD lost control over five key municipalities in local balloting in February 2000. In addition, a degree of discord developed within the MPD in midyear as President Monteiro described the recent privatization of the national fuel company as having lacked transparency, a charge that was sharply rejected by Prime Minister Veiga. The friction intensified later in the year as the result of the controversy surrounding Veiga's relinquishing of his prime ministerial duties (see Political background, above). Also contributing to declining MPD popularity was rising unemployment, linked, in the mind of some voters, to the government's recent structural adjustment efforts and additional promarket emphasis. Consequently, most observers were not surprised by the January 2001 legislative victory by the PAICV, led by José Neves, a symbol of the "new generation" in Cape Verdean political affairs. At the same time, the presidential campaign pitted the warhorses of the two dominant parties against one another in a poll whose closeness called to mind the 2000 balloting in the United States. The National Electoral Commission initially declared former prime minister Pires the victor in the second round by 17 votes, a margin that was reduced to

12 following Supreme Court rulings on challenges from both sides. Despite contending that the balloting had been marred by fraud, Veiga accepted the final verdict and successfully urged his supporters to remain calm in the face of the exasperating defeat. Among other things, Pires's victory precluded the need for a PAICV/MPD "cohabitation" government, which the PAICV argued would have been a severe hindrance to its economic plans. Despite its center-left orientation, the Neves government presented a development plan in early 2002 calling for intensified cooperation with the private sector, particularly in regard to promoting tourism and otherwise attracting foreign investment, goals that reportedly also influenced a March 1 cabinet expansion.

Drought contributed to famine conditions prior to heavy rains in 2003, while some 30 percent of the arable land was reportedly plagued by locusts. For its part, the government pledged to promote economic growth by constructing a new international airport, improving roads and other infrastructure, and supporting small businesses. However, it was not clear how much enthusiasm the population was retaining for the PAICV administration. In what some observers suggested could be a precursor to the national election scheduled for early 2006, the MPD won control of 9 of 17 municipal councils in the March 2004 local balloting. That proved to be of little help in maintaining any momentum for the MPD, however, as the party secured only 29 of 72 seats in the legislative election of January 22, 2006. Further, party leader Veiga again lost to rival Pires in the presidential balloting of February 2006, and though Veiga and his MPD supporters challenged the legislative results on the basis of fraud, the Supreme Court dismissed those claims. As of early 2006 the court had not ruled on similar allegations by Veiga regarding the presidential election results.

Political Parties

Although a number of parties existed prior to independence, the only party that was recognized for

15 years thereafter was the African Party for the Independence of Guinea-Bissau and Cape Verde (PAIGC). The reference to Guinea-Bissau was dropped and the party restyled the African Party for the Independence of Cape Verde (PAICV), insofar as the islands' branch was concerned, on January 20, 1981, in reaction to the mainland coup of the previous November.

Government Party

African Party for the Independence of Cape Verde (*Partido Africano da Independência de Cabo Verde*—PAICV). The PAICV's predecessor, the PAIGC, was formed in 1956 by Amílcar Cabral and others to resist Portuguese rule in both Cape Verde and Guinea-Bissau. Initially headquartered in Conakry, Guinea, the PAIGC began military operations in Guinea-Bissau in 1963 and was instrumental in negotiating independence for that country. Following the assassination of Cabral on January 20, 1973, his brother, Luís, and Aristides Maria Pereira assumed control of the movement, Luís Cabral serving as president of Guinea-Bissau until being overthrown in the 1980 coup.

At an extraordinary congress held February 13–17, 1990, the National Council endorsed constitutional changes that would permit the introduction of a multiparty system, and in April the council recommended that further reforms be adopted in preparation for legislative and presidential elections. In August Maj. Pedro Pires was elected PAICV secretary general, replacing Pereira, who was defeated for reelection as president of the republic on February 17, 1991, and promptly announced his retirement from politics.

At a party congress on August 29, 1993, Pires was appointed to the newly created post of party president to exercise "moral authority." Aristides Lima, the party's parliamentary leader, was subsequently elected to the vacated general secretary position. Pires won reelection to the PAICV's top post at a party congress in September 1997, staving off a challenge by newcomer José Neves.

Apparently bolstered by his party's success in local balloting in February 2000, Pires announced in

March that he was stepping down from his PAICV post to prepare for presidential balloting scheduled for 2001. A June PAICV congress elected Neves to succeed Pires in a reported 204–157 vote over PAICV Vice President Felisberto Viera. In the legislative elections in January 2001, the PAICV won 47 percent of the vote, and Pires secured 46 percent of the votes in the first round of presidential voting in February and was elected in a stunningly close race in the second round with 49.43 percent of the vote. In local elections in March 2004, the PAICV suffered a major defeat by losing control of the council on Sal Island, the country's major tourist destination. In response to the losses, Neves reshuffled the cabinet in April. Pires was reelected in 2006, and the PAICV won a majority of seats in the 2006 assembly elections.

Leaders: Pedro Verona Rodrigues PIRES (President of the Republic), José Maria Pereira NEVES (Prime Minister and President of the Party), Manuel Inocencio SOUSA (Vice President of the Party), Aristides Raimundo LIMA (Secretary General and the Speaker of the National Assembly), Rui SEMEDO (National Secretary).

Opposition Parties

Movement for Democracy (*Movimento para Democracia*—MPD). Then a Lisbon-based opposition grouping, the MPD issued a "manifesto" in early 1990 calling for dismantling of the PAICV regime, thereby prompting the ruling party to schedule multiparty elections. In June the MPD held its first official meeting in Praia, and in September it met with the PAICV to discuss a timetable for the balloting that culminated in MPD legislative and presidential victories of January and February 1991.

The MPD retained legislative control in 1995, although its seat total dropped from 56 to 50. In addition, President António Monteiro, an independent who enjoyed the support of the MPD, was reelected unopposed to a second term as president of the republic in February 1996. However, in the wake of estrangement between Monteiro and the MPD's Carlos Veiga, prime minister from March

1991 to October 2000 (see Political background and Current issues, above, for details), the party secured only 39 percent of the vote in the January 2001 legislative poll, losing control to the PAICV. Meanwhile, Veiga finished second in the first round of presidential balloting in February with 45 percent of the vote before losing an excruciatingly close race in the second round. (He finally was credited with only 17 fewer votes [on a 49.42 percent vote share] than his PAICV opponent. The MPD did very well in local elections in March 2004, gaining control of nine municipal councils, up from six). The elections confirmed the leadership of Agostinho Lopes, who had been subject to increasing dissatisfaction after the 2001 national elections. However, in 2006 the MPD's power showed signs of decline as Veiga again lost a presidential bid and the party won only 29 seats in the legislative election (see Political background, above).

Leaders: Agostinho LOPES (President of the Party), Carlos Alberto Wahnon de Carvalho VEIGA (Former Prime Minister, Former Chair of the Party, and 2001 and 2006 presidential candidate).

Cape Verdean Independent and Democratic Union (*União Caboverdeana Independente e Democrática*—UCID). The UCID is a right-wing group long active among the 500,000 Cape Verdean emigrants in Portugal and elsewhere. In mid-1990 the UCID, whose local influence appeared to be limited to one or two islands, signed a cooperation agreement with the MPD.

In legislative balloting in December 1995, the UCID received 5 percent of the vote, the third-largest tally, but failed to secure representation. The UCID was one of the components, with the Democratic Convergence Party (PCD) and the Labor and Solidarity Party (PTS), in the Democratic Alliance for Change (*Aliança Democrática para a Mudança*—ADM), which fielded candidates in the 2001 legislative election. (The ADM won 6 percent of the vote and two assembly seats [one each for the PCD and the PTS] in 2001.) There was no reference to the ADM in the 2006 elections. In the 2006 leg-

islative balloting, the UCID placed a distant third with 2.64 percent of the vote (two seats).

Leaders: Antonio MONTEIRO (President), Celso CELESTINO (Former President).

Other Parties

Democratic Socialist Party (*Partido Socialista Democrático*—PSD). Launched in 1992, the PSD was legalized on July 14, 1995. The party's platform calls for greater governmental support for development programs and the elimination of "injustices." The PSD secured less than 1 percent of the vote in the 1995, 2001, and 2006 legislative balloting.

Leader: João ALEM.

Democratic Renewal Party (*Partido da Renovação Democrática*—PRD). Established in July 2000, the PRD is an offshoot from the MPD. The party won 3.2 percent of the vote in the 2001 legislative balloting but failed to secure any seats. In 2003 the PRD joined with the PCD in discussions on a new coalition ahead of the 2006 legislative elections. The PRD won less than 1 percent of the vote in balloting on January 22, 2006.

Leader: Simao MONTEIRO.

Democratic Convergence Party (*Partido da Convergência Democrática*—PCD). The PCD was launched in 1994 by Dr. Enrico Correira Monteiro, a dissident MPD legislator, whose reelection to the assembly in 1995 was the group's sole electoral victory. In 2003 the PCD began efforts to create a new electoral coalition with the PRD to oppose the MPD and PAICV ahead of the 2006 legislative elections. There was no reference to the PCD in the 2006 elections, however.

Leader: Dr. Enrico Correira MONTEIRO (President).

Labor and Solidarity Party (*Partido de Trabalho e da Solidariedade*—PTS). This grouping is a "socialist-oriented" party that was launched by the mayor of São Vicente, Onesimo Silveira, in May 1998. In a confusing series of events following the formation of the ADM, Silveira announced his plans to run for president in 2001

Cabinet

As of March 1, 2006

Prime Minister	José Maria Pereira Neves

Ministers

Agriculture, Environment, and Fishing	Maria Madalena Brito Neves [f]
Culture	Manuel Monteiro da Veiga
Decentralization and Regional Development	Ramiro Azevedo
Defense and State Reform	Maria Cristina Lopes Almeida Fontes Lima [f]
Economy, Growth, and Competitiveness	João Pereira Silva
Education	Filomena Martins [f]
Finance and Public Administration	João Pinto Serra
Foreign Affairs, Cooperation, and Communities	Victor Borges
Internal Administration	Julio Correia
Justice	José Manuel Andrade
Labor and Solidarity	Sidónio Monteiro
Prime Minister's Adjunct Minister, Quality of Life	Sara Lopes [f]

Secretaries of State

Agriculture	Rosa Rocha [f]
Education	Octávio Ramos Tavares
Finance	Leonesa Fortes [f]
Foreign Affairs	Domingos Mascarenhas
Public Administration	Romeu Modesto
Youth and Sports	Américo Nascimento

Ministers of State

Health	Basilio Ramos
Infrastructure, Transport, and the Sea	Manuel Inocencio Sousa

[f] = female

as an independent before withdrawing from the race several days prior to the balloting. (He had previously been listed as the successful ADM/PTS candidate in the January 2001 assembly poll.)

Legislature

The unicameral **National People's Assembly** (*Assembleia Nacional Popular*) became a 79-member bipartisan body in the election of January 14, 1991. (The membership was reduced to 72 in 1995.) The normal term is five years, although the body is subject to presidential dissolution. Following the most recent balloting on January 22, 2006, the African Party for the Independence of Cape Verde won 41 seats; Movement for Democracy, 29; and Cape Verdean Independent and Democratic Union, 2.

Speaker: Aristides Raimundo LIMA.

Communications

Press

The Cape Verdean press, described by the *Financial Times* as "relatively free," includes the following, all published in Praia, unless otherwise noted: *Novo Jornal Cabo Verde* (5,000), government-supported biweekly; *A Semana* (5,000), PAICV weekly; *Boletim Informativo* (1,500), published weekly by the Ministry of Foreign Affairs; *Boletim Oficial*, government weekly; *Terra Nova*, published monthly by the Catholic Church; *Unidade e Luta*, PAICV organ.

News Agency

The domestic facility is Cabopress, headquartered in Praia; several foreign bureaus also maintain offices in the capital.

Broadcasting and Computing

The government-controlled *Radio Nacional de Cabo Verde* broadcasts over two stations located in Praia and Mindelo, and a number of private radio stations reportedly had started by early 2006; limited television service, launched in 1985 by *Televisão Nacional de Cabo Verde*, transmits from Praia to about 2,000 receivers. In 2003 approximately 3,600 personal computers served 20,000 Internet users.

Intergovernmental Representation

Ambassador to the U.S.
Jose BRITO

U.S. Ambassador to Cape Verde
Roger Dwayne PIERCE

Permanent Representative to the UN
Maria de Fatima LIMA DA VEIGA

IGO Memberships (Non-UN)
AfDB, AU, BADEA, CILSS, CPLP, ECOWAS, Interpol, IOM, NAM, OIF, WCO

CENTRAL AFRICAN REPUBLIC

CENTRAL AFRICAN REPUBLIC

République Centrafricaine

The Country

The Central African Republic (CAR) is a landlocked, well-watered plateau country in the heart of Africa. Its inhabitants are of varied ethnic, linguistic, and religious affiliations. In addition to French and many tribal dialects, Sango is used as a lingua franca. A majority of the population is Christian, and there also are sizable animist and Muslim sectors.

About four-fifths of the inhabitants are employed in farming and animal husbandry, primarily at a subsistence level. Leading exports include diamonds, coffee, timber, and cotton. Most of the small industrial sector is engaged in food processing, while uranium resources have been developed with French and Swiss partners. Economic diversification, long impeded by a lack of adequate transportation facilities, was further constrained by the personal aggrandizement during 1976–1979 of self-styled Emperor Bokassa, a virtually empty national treasury at the time of his ouster in September 1979 being only partially mitigated by marginal increases in commodity exports in ensuing years. France remains the country's main source of imports, chief market for exports, and principal aid donor.

Recent development programs have focused on trade promotion, privatization of state-run operations, encouragement of small- and medium-sized enterprises, civil service reductions, and efforts to combat widespread tax and customs fraud. Such measures have earned Bangui the tentative support of the International Monetary Fund (IMF) and the World Bank, although the implementation of many of the government's proposed administrative and structural changes has been criticized as slow and ineffective. In the mid-1990s political turmoil significantly diverted attention from economic development; however, following the restoration of stability in Bangui, the republic recorded real GDP growth of 5.1 percent in 1997 and 3.0 percent in 1998, with inflation of 1.8 percent being registered in 1998. In July 2000 the IMF noted that, despite ongoing social and political problems, the government had made progress in restructuring the

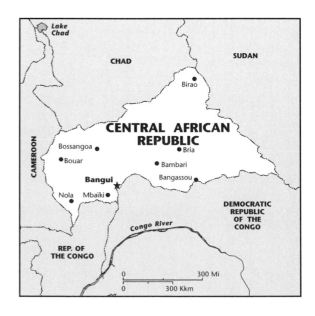

Political Status: Became independent August 13, 1960; one-party military regime established January 1, 1966; Central African Empire proclaimed December 4, 1976; republic reestablished September 21, 1979; military rule reimposed September 1, 1981; constitution of November 21, 1986, amended on August 30, 1992, to provide for multiparty system; present constitution adopted January 7, 1995, following acceptance in referendum of December 28, 1994; civilian government suspended following military coup on March 15, 2003; new constitution adopted by national referendum on December 5, 2004, providing for a return to civilian government via national elections that were held March–May 2005.

Area: 240,534 sq. mi. (622,984 sq. km.).

Population: 2,463,616 (1988C); 4,006,000 (2005E).

Major Urban Center (2005E): BANGUI (783,000).

Official Language: French. The national language is Sango.

Monetary Unit: CFA Franc (official rate July 1, 2006: 513.01 francs = $1US). (The CFA franc, previously pegged to the French franc, is now permanently pegged to the euro at 655.957 CFA francs = 1 euro.)

President: Gen. François BOZIZÉ Yangouvonda (nonparty); declared himself president on March 16, 2003, following the overthrow of Ange-Félix PATASSÉ (Central African People's Liberation Movement); popularly elected in two-round balloting on March 13 and May 8, 2005, and inaugurated for a five-year term on June 11.

Prime Minister: Elie DOTÉ (nonparty); appointed by the president on June 13, 2005, succeeding Célestin-Leroy GAOMBALET (nonparty).

health care or basic services such as electricity, running water, or sanitation systems. (The CAR ranked among the lowest ten countries in the Human Development Report prepared by the United National Development Program.) Financial affairs were further complicated by the arrest of more than 20 government officials in 2002 on charges of embezzling some $3 million in government funds, prompting the IMF and World Bank to suspend some aid programs temporarily. International financial institutions also reacted negatively at first to the coup of March 2003, although aid was resumed in 2004 after the new administration implemented initiatives designed to fight corruption and increase government revenue.

Real GDP grew by only 1 percent in 2004 and was expected to increase by about the same amount in 2005. In view of the country's continued economic difficulties (including increasing debt), the IMF called for "urgent fiscal consolidation" to contain spending and bolster revenue. While commending the country's peaceful transition to an elected government in 2005, the IMF was highly critical in its assessment of the management of public resources and security, citing widespread corruption. However, in early 2006 the IMF's confidence in the government following successful elections was evidenced by its approval of $10.2 million in emergency assistance to help stabilize the economy.

Government and Politics

Political Background

Formerly known as Ubangi-Shari in French Equatorial Africa, the Central African Republic achieved independence on August 13, 1960, after two years of self-government under Barthélemy BOGANDA, founder of the Social Evolution Movement of Black Africa (*Mouvement de l'Évolution Sociale de l'Afrique Noir*—MESAN), and his nephew David DACKO, the republic's first president. As leader of MESAN, President Dacko rapidly established a political monopoly, dissolving the principal opposition party in December 1960

banking system, although the proposed privatization of the petroleum sector was still lagging behind other reforms. Real GDP grew by 3.4 percent in 1999 and 4.1 percent in 2000, although aid agencies reported that two-thirds of the population continued to live in poverty and had little access to and banning all others in 1962. Dacko was ousted on January 1, 1966, in a military coup led by Col. Jean-Bédel BOKASSA, who declared himself president. Bokassa abrogated the constitution, dissolved the assembly, assumed power to rule by decree, took over the leadership of MESAN, and became chief of staff and commander in chief of the armed forces.

Following his assumption of power, Bokassa survived a number of coup attempts, often relying on French military intervention. Designated president for life by MESAN in 1972, he assumed the additional office of prime minister in April 1976 but relinquished it to Ange-Félix PATASSÉ the following September, when a new Council of the Central African Revolution (*Conseil de la Révolution Centrafricaine*—CRC) was established. In the context of widespread government and party changes, Bokassa further enhanced his image as one of Africa's most unpredictable leaders by appointing former president Dacko to be his personal adviser.

On October 18, during a state visit by Libyan leader Muammar al-Qadhafi, Bokassa revealed that he had been converted to Islam and would henceforth be known as Salah al-Din Ahmad Bokassa. On December 4 he announced that the republic had been replaced by a parliamentary monarchy and that he had assumed the title of Emperor Bokassa I. On December 7 the emperor abolished the CRC, and the next day he abandoned his Muslim name because of its incompatibility with the imperial designation.

In the wake of a lavish coronation ceremony in Bangui on December 4, 1977, the Bokassa regime became increasingly brutal and corrupt. In mid-1979 Amnesty International reported that scores of schoolchildren had been tortured and murdered after protesting against compulsory school uniforms manufactured by the Bokassa family. In August an African judicial commission confirmed the report, the emperor responding with a series of arrests and executions of those who had testified before the commission.

On the night of September 20–21, 1979, while on a visit to Libya, the emperor was deposed, with French military assistance, by former president Dacko. While several prominent members of the Bokassa regime were arrested, the "government of national safety" that was announced on September 24 drew widespread criticism for including a number of individuals who had held high-ranking posts in the previous administration. (Bokassa lived in exile until he returned in 1987 to face trial on charges of murder, torture, and cannibalism. Following conviction on the murder charge he was imprisoned until his sentence was commuted in 1993. Prolonged ill health having precluded any subsequent extensive political activity on his part, Bokassa died in November 1996.)

In a presidential election on March 15, 1981, Dacko was credited with 50.23 percent of the votes cast, as contrasted with 38.11 percent for his closest competitor, former prime minister Patassé. Alleged balloting irregularities triggered widespread violence in the capital prior to Dacko's inauguration and the naming of Simon Narcisse BOZANGA as prime minister on April 4. In mid-July opposition parties were temporarily banned after a bomb explosion at a Bangui theater, and on July 21 the army, led by Gen. André-Dieudonné KOLINGBA, was asked to restore order. Six weeks later, on September 1, it was announced that Dacko, known to be in failing health, had resigned in favor of a Military Committee for National Recovery (*Comité Militaire pour le Redressement National*—CMRN), headed by General Kolingba, which suspended the constitution, proscribed political party activity, and issued a stern injunction against public disorder.

Patassé and a number of senior army officers were charged with an attempted coup against the Kolingba regime on March 3, 1982, after which the former prime minister took refuge in the French Embassy in Bangui. He was flown out of the country a month later.

Internal security merged with regional concerns in late 1984 after an opposition group led by Alphonse M'BAIKOUA, who had reportedly been involved in the alleged 1982 coup attempt, joined with Chadian *codo* rebels in launching border insurgency operations. The following April Bangui and N'Djamena began a joint counterinsurgency campaign that failed to curb the rebels, most of whom sought temporary refuge in Cameroon.

In keeping with promises to launch a gradual return to civilian rule, Kolingba dissolved the CMRN in September 1985 and placed himself, in the dual role of president and prime minister, at the head of a cabinet numerically dominated by civilians, although military men remained in the most powerful positions. At a referendum on November 21, 1986, a reported 91 percent of the electorate approved a new constitution, under which General Kolingba continued in office for a six-year term. The constitution also designated a Central African Democratic Rally (*Rassemblement Démocratique Centrafricain*—RDC) as the nucleus of a one-party state, General Kolingba having asserted that a multiparty system would invite "division and hatred as well as tribalism and regionalism."

Balloting for a new National Assembly was held in July 1987, although voter turnout was less than 50 percent, apparently because of opposition appeals for a boycott. In May 1988, in what the government described as the final stage of its democratization program, more than 3,000 candidates, all nominated by the RDC, contested 1,085 local elective offices.

On March 15, 1991, General Kolingba divested himself of the prime ministerial office, transferring its functions to his presidential coordinator, Edouard FRANCK. In late April, pressured by international aid donors and encountering increased social unrest, Kolingba abandoned his opposition to pluralism. On May 18 the regime offered to accelerate political reform in exchange for an end to civil strife, and on June 7 a national commission was established to revise the constitution and prepare for the introduction of multipartyism. In July the government announced that political parties were free to apply for legal status. Subsequently, a broad-based committee was named to prepare for the convening of a national conference on February 19, 1992. However, during an early 1992 visit to the United States, President Kolingba referred to the projected talks as a "great national debate" that "cannot be a sovereign national conference."

Because of its lack of plenary power, the conference that convened on August 1, 1992, was boycotted by most opposition groups and was accompanied by street demonstrations and antigovernment strikes. On August 30 the National Assembly adopted a number of conference recommendations, including party registration guidelines, and on September 7 Kolingba announced plans for presidential and legislative elections on October 25. The ensuing campaign was described as "tense and disorganized" and polling (with Kolingba apparently running next-to-last behind Dr. Abel GOUMBA Guéne of the Concertation of Democratic Forces [*Concertation des Forces Démocratiques*—CFD], former prime minister Patassé, and former president Dacko) was suspended by the government, which charged that "premeditated acts of sabotage" had curtailed the distribution of voting materials. On November 28, the last day of his constitutional term, President Kolingba announced that new elections would be held on February 14 and 28, 1993, and on December 4 he appointed Timothée MALENDOMA of the Civic Forum (*Forum Civique*—FC) to succeed Franck as prime minister.

In a January 17, 1993, radio broadcast General Kolingba announced the formation of a National Provisional Political Council of the Republic (*Conseil National Politique Provisoire de la Républic*—CNPPR), headed by former president Dacko, to oversee public affairs until the installation of an elected government. However, doubts about the regime's commitment to a democratic transfer of power persisted as the president's mandate, which had officially ended on November 28, was extended, and the elections scheduled for February 14 and 28 were postponed until May.

On February 26, 1993, following what observers described as three months of political paralysis in Bangui, Kolingba dismissed Malendoma and his transitional government for "blocking the democratic process" and named Enoch Dérant LAKOUÉ, leader of the Social Democratic Party (*Parti Social-Démocrate*—PSD) as the new prime minister. In late April the president overrode an electoral commission recommendation and further postponed elections until October, prompting an outcry by the CFD's Goumba, who accused Kolingba and Lakoué of conspiring to use the delay to revive their flagging presidential campaigns.

On June 11, 1993, Prime Minister Lakoué announced that elections would be brought forward to August. The policy reversal came only six days after the French minister of cooperation, Michel Roussin, reportedly told Kolingba that continued aid was directly linked to the speed of reform. At the August 22 poll eight candidates, including Africa's first female contender, Ruth ROLLAND, vied for the presidency while 496 candidates contested 85 legislative seats. Although the election was conducted in the presence of international observers, Kolingba, faced with unofficial tallies showing that he had finished in fourth place, attempted to halt release of the official results; however, he was obliged to reverse himself upon domestic and international condemnation of what Goumba described as the "last convulsion of his regime."

In second-round presidential balloting on September 19, first-round plurality winner Patassé defeated Goumba 53.49 to 46.51 percent. In concurrent rounds of legislative balloting, Patassé's Central African People's Liberation Movement (*Mouvement de Libération du Peuple Centrafricaine*—MLPC) won 34 seats, followed by the CFD, whose members collectively won 17. Meanwhile, on September 1 Kolingba had released thousands of convicted criminals, the most prominent of whom was former Emperor Bokassa.

On October 25, 1993, Patassé named an MLPC colleague, Jean-Luc MANDABA, as prime minister. Five days later Mandaba announced the formation of a coalition government that drew from the MLPC, the Liberal Democratic Party (*Parti Liberal-Démocratic*—PLD), the CFD-affiliated Alliance for Democracy and Progress (*Alliance pour la Démocratic et le Progrés*—ADP), supporters of former president Dacko, and members of the outgoing Kolingba administration.

Prime Minister Mandaba was forced to resign on April 11, 1995, upon the filing of a nonconfidence motion signed by a majority of National Assembly members, who charged him with corruption, maladministration, and a lack of communica-

tion between the executive and legislative branches. President Patassé promptly named as his successor Gabriel KOYAMBOUNOU, a senior civil servant who announced that combating financial irregularities would be one of his principal objectives.

In early April 1996 a newly formed opposition umbrella group, the Democratic Council of the Opposition Parties (*Conseil Démocratique des Partis de l'Opposition*—CODEPO), organized an anti-Patassé rally in Bangui. An even more serious challenge developed on April 18 when several hundred soldiers, angered over payment arrears, left their barracks in the Kasai suburb of Bangui and took control of important locations in the capital. The rebels went back to their barracks several days later, after French troops were deployed in support of the government, but they returned to the streets on May 18. The rebellion finally ended on May 26 after French forces, supported by helicopter gunships, engaged the mutinous soldiers in fierce street battles. Patassé, describing the nation as "shattered" by the near civil war, replaced Koyambounu on June 6 with Jean-Paul NGOUPANDÉ, a former ambassador to France. Thereafter, in a further attempt to stabilize the political situation, Patassé's MLPC and the major opposition parties signed a pact under which, among other things, the authority of the prime minister was to be extended so as to dilute presidential control. Moreover, on June 19 Ngoupande announced the formation of what was optimistically described as a "government of national unity."

On November 16, 1996, another mutiny erupted in Kasai, and by early December the rebellious soldiers, who were demanding the president's resignation, were reportedly in control of several sections of the capital. In late December, amid reports that over a third of the city's population had fled as the fighting took on a "tribal character," the government and rebels appeared to agree to a ceasefire; however, it was subsequently reported that Capt. Anicet SAULET, the leader of the mutineers, had been detained by his own forces for having signed the accord. In early January 1997 French and government troops forced the rebels from a number of their strongholds in an offensive sparked by the assassination of two French troops on January 4.

On January 25, 1997, in Bangui, Patassé and Saulet signed a peace accord that had been brokered by an inter-African mediation group comprising representatives of Burkina Faso, Chad, Gabon, and Mali. The agreement included provisions for a general amnesty for the mutinous soldiers, the reintegration of the rebels into their old units, and the deployment of a regional peacekeeping force styled the Inter-African Mission to Monitor the Bangui Accords (*Mission Internationale du Suivi des Accords de Bangui*—MISAB). On January 30 Patassé appointed Foreign Minister Michel GBEZERA-BRIA to replace Prime Minister Ngoupandé, and on February 18 a new 28-member cabinet, the Government of Action for the Defense of Democracy (*Gouvernement pour l'Action et la Défense de la Démocratie*—GADD), was installed. Although the MLPC retained all the key posts, the GADD included representatives from ten parties, including nine members from four "opposition" groups. On March 15 the National Assembly voted to extend amnesty to those remaining rebels who agreed to be disarmed by the peacekeepers within 15 days; however, clashes broke out later in the month when a number of the rebels resisted the peacekeeping forces.

On May 5, 1997, the nine opposition cabinet ministers announced the "suspension" of their postings and called for nationwide strikes to protest the deaths two days earlier of three alleged mutinous soldiers being held in police custody. Amid mounting tension, on May 20 the rebels' two cabinet representatives (they had been appointed in April as part of the Bangui agreement) also quit the government. Subsequently, more than 100 people, primarily civilians, were killed in Bangui and the Kasai camp during clashes between rebel and government troops, the latter again supported by French troops, before another cease-fire was signed on July 2.

MISAB, which had the endorsement of the UN Security Council, began disarming the army mutineers in mid-July, and in late August the government released the last of more than 110 detainees connected to the "revolt." Consequently,

the nine cabinet members who had walked out in May formally rejoined the government of September 1. Tension continued at a somewhat reduced level into 1998, prompting the convening of a national conference in late February. On March 3 the conference's participants, including the opposition parties coalesced under the banner of the influential Group of 11 (G-11), signed a reconciliation pact aimed at improving interparty relations and reducing the lawlessness gripping the country.

A new UN peacekeeping force (*Mission des Nations Unies dans la République Centrafricaine*—MINURCA) took over MISAB and French responsibilities on April 15, 1998, with a mandate that included assisting in preparations for legislative elections. In early August the polling was postponed amid opposition criticism of the government's organization of the balloting, and in October MINURCA's mandate was extended as the peacekeepers began preparations for the elections that had been rescheduled for November/December.

Approximately 30 parties forwarded candidates for the 109 seats (enlarged from 85) available at first-round legislative balloting on November 22, 1998, the MLPC emerging with a small lead after that round. However, opposition groups signed an electoral pact under the banner of the Union of Forces Supporting Peace and Change (*Union des Forces Acquises à la Paix et au Changement*—UFAPC), whereby they agreed to back the leading opposition candidates in the undecided contests. As a result, following second-round balloting on December 13, the UFAPC-affiliated parties controlled 55 seats (led by the RDC with 20) and the MLPC 47. However, the small PLD (2 seats) and five independents subsequently confirmed their allegiance to the MLPC, and Patassé supporters were ultimately able to gain legislative control when, under highly controversial circumstances, a legislator-elect from the PSD defected to the MLPC. (The opposition charged the MLPC with "hijacking" the results of the election through bribery but lost its legal challenge when the Constitutional Court ruled that legislators represented their electorates and not their parties, thereby deeming the defection to have been legal.) Most opposition legislators boycotted the convening of the new assembly in early January 1999, and ten opposition cabinet members resigned from the government in protest against the MLPC's actions. On January 4 Patassé named Finance and Budget Minister Anicet Georges DOLOGUÉLÉ to replace Gbezera-Bria as prime minister. However, the UFAPC rejected Patassé's authority in the matter, arguing that it should have control over the appointment as holder of the true legislative majority.

On January 15, 1999, Prime Minister Dologuélé announced a new cabinet comprising eight ministers from the MLPC, four from the PLD, four from the opposition Movement for Democracy and Development (*Mouvement pour la Démocratic et la Développement*—MDD), one from the MLPC-allied National Convention (*Convention National*—CN), and eight independents. However, three of the MDD members resigned several days later, party leaders reiterating their support for the UFAPC.

The opposition ended its assembly boycott in early March 1999, apparently in part due to the government's agreement to let UFAPC members sit on a new election commission charged with overseeing the upcoming presidential poll. On September 19, Patassé secured another six-year term by winning 51.6 percent of the vote in the first-round balloting, defeating nine other candidates, including Kolingba, Dacko, and Goumba. Dologuélé was subsequently reappointed to head another MLPC-led government, the UFAPC having declined overtures to join the cabinet. In January 2000 the administration issued several decrees designed to restructure the armed forces so as to reduce the likelihood of a repeat of the 1996–1997 mutinies. Among other things, the size and authority of the powerful presidential guard were to be reduced. Subsequently, the MINURCA peacekeepers formally withdrew on February 15, while Paris announced an increase in aid to Bangui for military training. The Patassé/Dologuélé administration announced that its new top priority was to attract international economic assistance. However, the image-building campaign stalled in April when a series of scandals involving alleged money-laundering

and other corrupt practices precipitated a cabinet reshuffle amid opposition complaints that economic reforms contained in the 1997 peace accord were being ignored.

Because of increasing economic difficulties, the government was unable to pay the salaries of the state employees and military personnel for most of 2000. The worsening situation prompted the UN Security Council to urge the government in January 2001 to defuse tensions by paying off the arrears. Although trade unions were calmed by a partial payment (completed with the help of the World Bank, France, and Libya), the government's handling of the situation cost Dologuélé his post, as he was replaced by the president in April 2001 by the MLPC's Martin Ziguélé. On April 6 Ziguélé announced a new cabinet that included the MLPC, the PLD, the CN, the African Development Party (*Parti Africain du Développement*—PAD), the Democratic Union for Renewal/Fini Kodro (*Union Démocratique pour le Renouveau/Fini Kodro*—UDR/FK), one independent, and others.

In May 2001 the government managed to suppress a coup attempt reportedly masterminded by the former president and de facto leader of the RDC, André-Dieudonné Kolingba, who nevertheless remained at large. (It was subsequently reported that Kolingba had traveled to Uganda and then, in September 2002, to France. By that time he had been sentenced in absentia to death for his role in the coup attempt. Sentences in absentia also were handed down against more than 500 other participants.) Human rights activists voiced concern over the alleged acts of retaliation against Kolingba's Yakoma ethnic group. Reportedly, more than 200 people were killed and 50,000 displaced in the fighting following the coup attempt. Some cabinet members, as well as Gen. François BOZIZÉ, the chief of staff and close associate of Patassé, were also implicated in the conspiracy. Following a reshuffle in August that replaced those ministers allegedly supportive of the coup, Patassé dismissed Bozizé in late October. Government troops subsequently fought Bozizé loyalists who offered armed resistance to an effort to arrest the general. After Bozizé fled to Chad in November, the situation got increasingly "internationalized" (see Foreign relations, below), as many neighboring countries worked to arrange negotiations among Patassé, Kolingba, and Bozizé. In what some saw as a possible sign of compromise, the Central African Republic's courts dropped legal proceedings against Bozizé in December. However, sporadic skirmishes broke out along the Chadian border in the first half of 2002, the CAR government accusing Chad of supporting rebellious CAR soldiers. The Organization of African Unity called upon the UN to send peacekeepers to the CAR, but no such action ensued. Among other things, Western capitals objected to the continued presence in the CAR of Libyan troops and tanks, which had rushed to Patassé's aid in May 2001. For his part, Bozizé in September 2002 announced his intentions of ousting Patassé by force.

In October 2002 government forces supported by Libyan troops turned back pro-Bozizé rebels who were advancing on Bangui. However, after the Libyan troops withdrew in January 2003 in favor of a 350-member peacekeeping force from the Central African Economic and Monetary Community (*Communauté Économique et Monétaire de l'Afrique Centrale*—CEMAC), Bozizé's forces entered Bangui on March 15 while Patassé was out of the country on a diplomatic mission. (Patassé's plane reportedly tried to return to the CAR but was forced away by gunfire.) The following day Bozizé declared himself president, suspended the constitution, and disbanded the National Assembly. On March 23 Bozizé appointed what was termed a government of national unity (comprising five major parties) under the leadership of Abel Goumba of the Patriotic Front for Progress. At the end of May, Bozizé established a 98-member National Transitional Council (*Conseil National de Transition*—CNT) to oversee the planned return to civilian government under a revised constitution within 18–30 months. Goumba was dismissed in favor of Célestin-Leroy GAOMBALET on December 12.

The revised constitution was approved by a reported yes vote of 90.4 percent in a national referendum on December 5, 2004. In accordance with the provisions of the new constitution, the first parliamentary and presidential elections were held in two rounds of balloting on March 13 and May 8, 2005. Bozizé lacked a majority with 43 percent of the vote in the first round, with MLPC leader Ziguélé receiving 24 percent, and the RDC-backed Kolingba, 16 percent. In the two-way runoff, Bozizé, with the support of some of the other presidential candidates who had received only a small percentage of votes, defeated Ziguélé with 64.6 percent of the vote. For his part, Ziguélé called for the election to be invalidated, claiming soldiers intimidated voters, but the constitutional court dismissed the allegations as unfounded. Meanwhile, a coalition of business groups and small political parties that had formed under the name National Convergence (*Kwa na Kwa*—KNK) to support Bozizé won 42 legislative seats, while the former ruling party (the MLPC) won only 11 seats, and independents won 34.

A new government, composed largely of members of the KNK, was sworn in on June 19. The cabinet was reshuffled on January 31, 2006; it included members of seven parties in addition to the dominant KNK.

Constitution and Government

The imperial constitution of December 1976 was abrogated upon Bokassa's ouster, the country reverting to republican status. A successor constitution, approved by referendum on February 1, 1981, provided for a multiparty system and a directly elected president with authority to nominate the prime minister and cabinet. The new basic law was itself suspended on September 1, 1981, both executive and legislative functions being assumed by a Military Committee for National Recovery, which was dissolved on September 21, 1985. The constitution approved in November 1986 was a revised version of the 1981 document, one of the most important modifications being confirmation of the RDC as the country's sole political party. The 1986 basic law also provided for a Congress consisting of an elected National Assembly and a nominated Economic and Regional Council.

In June 1991 General Kolingba appointed a national commission to draft constitutional amendments providing for political pluralism, and in July the government announced that parties could apply for legal status. Other amendments approved at the "grand national debate" of August 1992 included creation of a semipresidential regime with executive authority vested in a prime minister and stricter separation of executive, legislative, and judicial powers. The basic law that was ratified in a referendum in December 1994 retained those provisions, while expanding the permissible mandate of the head of state to two six-year terms and specifying that the prime minister will implement policies proposed by the president, who is to "embody and symbolize national unity." In addition, the new charter (formally adopted on January 14, 1995) expanded the judicial system by adding a Constitutional Court to the existing Supreme Court and High Court of Justice and provided for an eventual substantial devolution of state power to directly elected regional assemblies.

The constitution was suspended following the coup of March 2003, although the 1995 basic law served as a model in many areas for the new constitution that was approved by national referendum on December 5, 2004, and entered into effect on December 27. The new constitution reduced the presidential term from six to five years (renewable once), while the prime minister (to be appointed by a majority within the new 105-member National Assembly) was given expanded powers.

Foreign Relations

As a member of the French Community, the country has retained close ties with France throughout its changes of name and regime. A defense pact between the two states permits French intervention in times of "invasion" or outbreaks of "anarchy," and French troops, in the context of what was termed "Operation Barracuda," were prominently involved in the ouster of Bokassa. By contrast, in what appeared to be a deliberate policy shift by the Mitterrand government, some 1,100

French troops remained in their barracks during General Kolingba's assumption of power and, despite debate over alleged French involvement in the Patassé coup attempt, the French head of state declared his support for the regime in October 1982. French troops remained permanently stationed at the Bouar Military base and were instrumental in propping up the Patassé administration during the army revolt of April–May 1996.

The civil war in neighboring Chad long preoccupied the CAR leadership, partly because of the influx of refugees in the country's northern region. In addition, trepidation about foreign intrusion not only from Chad but also from throughout Central Africa prompted Bangui in 1980 to sever diplomatic ties with Libya and the Soviet Union, both of which had been accused of fomenting internal unrest. Relations with the former, although subsequently restored, remained tenuous, with two Libyan diplomats declared *persona non grata* in April 1986. Formal ties were reestablished with the Soviet Union in 1988 and with Israel in January 1989, President Kolingba visiting Tel Aviv in July 1989 to ratify a development cooperation agreement. In July 1991 China severed diplomatic relations with Bangui after the Kolingba regime had reestablished links with Taiwan.

In the run-up to the August 1993 balloting, Abel Goumba emerged as France's "consensus candidate" while his primary competitor, Ange-Felix Patassé, was reportedly viewed with trepidation by Paris because of commercial links to Washington and other Western capitals. On August 28 Paris condemned Kolingba's efforts to stall the release of election results, suspended all aid payments, and stated that French troops and materials were no longer at the president's disposal.

Tension with the CAR's "new" neighbor, the Democratic Republic of the Congo (DRC), developed in 1997, and in February 1998 fighting was reported along their shared border. However, in May the two signed a defense pact, and thereafter CAR troops were reported to be assisting the forces of DRC President Kabila. The CAR was subsequently described as trying to maintain a neutral position in regard to the intertwined conflicts that produced what one reporter called a "ring of fire" in the region into mid-2000.

Relations between the CAR and the DRC soured, with the increasingly close ties between President Patassé and the DRC rebels, most prominently the forces loyal to Jean-Pierre Bemba (see article on the DRC). Patassé employed Bemba's troops and Libyan military detachments to suppress the coup attempt in May 2001. The CAR's relations with Chad also became strained in late 2001 after Gen. François Bozizé, who was accused by Patassé of having been involved with the coup attempt, fled to Chad in November. In December Patassé and Chadian President Idriss Déby met in Libreville, Gabon, for talks under the auspices of CEMAC, which deployed an ultimately ineffective peacekeeping force to the CAR after Bozizé's successful coup in 2003. In the years following the coup, the peacekeeping forces spread out beyond the capital to the troubled northern and eastern regions as violence increased. In early 2006, CAR leaders met with the leaders of six other African countries in their continuing efforts to defuse the escalating tensions at the border of Chad and Sudan. For its part, the CAR extended its relations with Sudan by signing an agreement with the latter and the United Nations High Commissioner for Refugees (UNHCR) providing for the return of the first group of 10,000 Sudanese refugees who had lived in the CAR for 16 years.

Current Issues

The March 2003 coup was initially condemned by regional powers and the broader international community. However, General Bozizé quickly muted much of the criticism by pledging a quick return to civilian government and initiating a campaign to combat the corruption that had been widely perceived as systemic in the Patassé administration. Moreover, mass demonstrations in Bangui appeared to support the coup leaders, and most political parties (including Patassé's MLPC) soon expressed a desire to look to the future rather than dwell on the events leading up to the takeover. Also well received were the appointments of leaders from a broad spectrum of political and civic groups to the transitional national government led by "opposition" leader Abel Goumba as well as to the CNT. Not surprisingly, the new government won additional domestic support when it paid public salaries for the first time in two years and launched a series of economic reforms. Those measures also prompted a quick resumption of aid from France and the EU, assisted by Bozizé's generally pro-Western policies and rhetoric.

In June 2003 the government launched a program to disarm and demobilize 5,700 fighters, including soldiers loyal to either Bozizé or Patassé. Meanwhile, in early 2004 the government reached a compromise with former rebels who had been blamed for numerous clashes with troops in the capital. The Chadian government provided mediators for the talks with the rebels, many of whom were former Chadians who helped bring Bozizé to power. Subsequently, heightened tension was reported in late 2004 in northern CAR, where unidentified armed fighters were said to have occupied a town close to the border with Chad.

The December 2004 constitutional referendum appeared to put a final plan in place for the return to civilian government. However, a sour note was struck, in the opinion of many observers, by Bozizé's subsequent announcement that he would be a candidate for president. (After seizing power in 2003 the general insisted he had no political ambitions and would not seek elected office.) Despite such concerns, national elections were held successfully in March and May 2005 with high voter turnout (72.7 percent and 67.3 percent, respectively).

Despite hopes for peace following the elections, violence escalated in the northern regions, forcing thousands to flee to Chad in early 2006. The government for years had dismissed the violence by attributing it to local bandits. However, in an unexpected announcement in March 2006, Bozizé's office for the first time blamed rebels linked to Patassé for the attacks.

In early 2006 the assembly granted Bozizé the authority to "rule by decree" for three months. The president reportedly planned to use the temporary power to deal with "contentious" economic matters, including government salary arrears. Foreign donors were described as hopeful that Bozizé would also eventually prove able to smooth over the country's longstanding ethnic tensions.

Political Parties and Groups

The 1980 constitution called for the establishment of a multiparty system, but General Kolingba banned political parties in the wake of the 1981 coup and did not include their legalization in his promise of future civilian rule since to do so would invite "weakening and paralysis of the state and make it prey to individualistic demands." In late 1983 the three main opposition parties (FPP, MLPC, and MCLN, below) formed a coalition styled the Central African Revolutionary Party (*Parti Révolutionnaire Centrafricain*— PRC), which the RPRC (see below, under Central African Movement for National Liberation) subsequently joined. In 1986 the FPP and MLPC also formed a United Front (*Front Uni*) that sought restoration of the 1981 constitution. No opposition grouping was accorded legal status upon formation of the regime-supportive RDC in 1986.

In September 1990 the government arrested 25 members of the opposition Coordination Committee for the Convocation of a National Conference (*Comité de Coordination pour la Convocation de la Conférence Nationale*—CCCCN), including its chair, Aristedes SOKAMBI. In late October, during an extraordinary congress in Berberati, the RDC voted against the introduction of a multiparty system. However, in April 1991 President Kolingba reversed the Berberati decision, declaring that "Henceforth, all kinds of thought . . . can be expressed freely within the framework of parties of their choice." Three months later the regime officially overturned its ban on political party formations. Subsequently a number of somewhat shifting opposition coalitions emerged.

Following the formation of an MLPC-led "unity" government in June 1996, 11 opposition parties, most of whom were theretofore aligned under the banner of the Democratic Council of the Op-

position Parties (*Conseil Démocratique des Partis de l'Opposition*—CODEPO), formed the **Group of Eleven** (G-11), under the leadership of former CODEPO president Dr. Abel GOUMBA Guéne. Four G-11 members (the ADP, FPP, PSD, and RDC) were awarded a total of nine cabinet posts in February 1997. On May 5, 1997, the G-11 cabinet members announced that they had "suspended" their participation in the government and called for national strikes to protest the death three days earlier of three alleged rebel soldiers. However, they returned to their portfolios in September.

Throughout most of 1998 the G-11 coordinated the activities of the main opposition groups; however, during the run-up to legislative balloting the G-11 appeared to have been superseded by the **Union of Forces Committed to Peace and Change** (*Union des Forces Acquises à la Paix et au Changement*—UFAPC), which comprised a number of parties (including the RDC, PSD, FPP, MDD, FODEM, and FC), labor unions, and human rights organizations. (See Political background, above, for details regarding the UFAPC and the legislative balloting and subsequent cabinet formation.) The UFAPC, also routinely referenced as the UFAP, proved unable to coalesce behind a single candidate for the first round of presidential balloting in September 1999, although an accord was reported if a second round had been required. Despite apparent objections from some components, the UFAPC rejected overtures from President Patassé to join the new cabinet in early November, and the grouping was subsequently described as in disarray following the withdrawal of the PSD and FPP and was reduced to limited membership as of late 1999.

Following the March 2003 coup, a government of national unity was formed with members from the FPP, RDC, FODEM, PSD, MDD, and the PUN. The MLPC and the MDI-PS were subsequently added to the cabinet.

After General Bozizé in 2004 announced his intention to seek the presidency in 2005, a coalition called the National Convergence (see below) was formed to support his candidacy, though Bozizé ran as an independent.

National Convergence (*Kwa na Kwa*—KNK). This coalition of business groups and small political parties was formed in 2004 to support Gen. François Bozizé's presidential bid in 2005. The KNK also entered candidates in the 2005 legislative balloting and secured by far the most seats (42).

Leader: Jean-Eudes TÉYA.

Central African Democratic Rally (*Rassemblement Démocratique Centrafricain*—RDC). The RDC was launched in May 1986 as the country's sole legal party, General Kolingba declaring that the formation would represent "all the various tendencies of the whole nation" but would deny representation to those who "seek to impose a totalitarian doctrine." At an extraordinary party congress on August 17, 1991, one month after the official endorsement of multipartyism, President Kolingba resigned as party president, saying he wanted to operate "above politics." Kolingba nonetheless ran as the RDC's 1993 presidential candidate, failing to make the second-round ballot because of a fourth-place finish on the first.

In mid-1995 party militants organized antigovernment demonstrations to protest the imprisonment of party leader and *Le Rassemblement* editor Mathias Gonevo Reapogo, who had been convicted of publishing an "insulting" article about President Patassé. Furthermore, the RDC leadership denounced the administration for its "policy of exclusion as well as arbitrary arrests." However, following the aborted army mutiny of April–May 1996, the RDC (unlike most other opposition groupings) signed the national unity agreement and was given four ministries in the government announced on June 19. The RDC cabinet members resigned in early 1999, the RDC, whose strongest support comes from the south, having finished second in the 1998 legislative poll with 20 seats. Kolingba also finished second in the 1999 presidential balloting with 19.4 percent of the vote. The party remained part of the UFAPC (above) as of late 1999. The RDC and Kolingba were reportedly involved with the failed coup attempt in May 2001. Subsequently, numerous party officials and members were arrested, although Kolingba remained at large. The RDC's activities were suspended for three months in June, with the government threatening to shut down the party permanently in late 2001. In late 2004, however, Kolingba announced his intention to return to the CAR and run for the presidency in 2005. He received 16.36 percent of the vote, while his party won 8 assembly seats. Days after the balloting, Kolingba's camp claimed that a shooting incident outside his residence between his guards and soldiers had been an assassination attempt, but the government dismissed the matter as "confusion" in communications between the two sides. Subsequently, one of Kolingba's sons was reportedly named to the new cabinet announced in early 2006.

Leaders: André-Dieudonné KOLINGBA (Former President of the Republic, de facto Leader of the Party, and 2005 presidential candidate), Louis-Pierre GAMBA (Deputy President), Honoré NZASSIWE, Mathias Gonevo REAPOGO (imprisoned), Daniel LAGANDI (Secretary General).

Movement for Democracy and Development (*Mouvement pour la Démocratie et le Développement*—MDD). The MDD was launched in January 1994 by former president David Dacko. MDD members were given four posts in the Dologuélé cabinet announced on January 15, 1999. However, party leaders, denying any interest in participating in an MLPC-led government, pressured three of the appointees to quit several days later. (The fourth member, who remained in government reportedly against the wishes of the grass roots, was not reappointed in the new cabinet formed in April 2001.) Dacko, who had won 20 percent of the presidential vote in 1993, finished third with 11.2 percent in 1999, his strength being the greatest in the capital region in the South. Dacko died in 2003.

There was no reference to the MDD in the 2005 election, although leader Auguste Boukanga reportedly ran as a presidential candidate under the banner of the Union for Renewal and Development. In 2006, one MDD member held a cabinet position.

Leaders: Auguste BOUKANGA.

Democratic Forum for Modernity (*Forum Démocratique pour la Modernité*—FODEM). FODEM was launched in the summer of 1997 by Agriculture Minister Charles Massi, who had recently been held hostage by rebellious soldiers and, reportedly, had been persuaded of the merits of their case. Massi was dismissed from the government in December, ostensibly because of his dealings in the diamond sector.

FODEM was officially recognized in May 1998, and in September Massi was cleared of the charges that had led to his removal from government in 1997. Massi won 1.3 percent of the vote in the 1999 presidential balloting and 3.2 percent in the 2005 presidential elections. He backed Bozizé in the 2005 runoff and was appointed a minister of state in 2006.

Leader: Charles MASSI (2005 presidential candidate).

National Unity Party (*Parti de l'Unité Nationale*—PUN). Led by former prime minister Jean-Paul Ngoupandé, the PUN won three seats in the late 1998 legislative balloting. Following the 1999 presidential balloting, in which Ngoupandé won 3.1 percent of the vote, a PUN member was named to the new cabinet albeit reportedly without the endorsement of the party leadership and was not reappointed in the new cabinet formed in April 2001. In the 2005 presidential balloting, Ngoupandé won 5.08 percent of the vote in the first round and backed Bozizé in the second round. Subsequently, he was appointed to the cabinet as one of the ministers of state.

Leader: Jean-Paul NGOUPANDÉ (Former Prime Minister and 2005 presidential candidate).

Central African People's Liberation Movement (*Mouvement de Libération du Peuple Centrafricaine*—MLPC). The MLPC was organized in Paris in mid-1979 by Ange-Félix Patassé, who had served as prime minister from September 1976 to July 1978 and was runner-up to Dacko in the presidential balloting of March 1981. At an extraordinary congress held September 14–18, 1983, Patassé was accorded a vote of no confidence and replaced with a nine-member directorate as part of

a move from "nationalism" to "democratic socialism." A communiqué released in Paris in July 1986 announced that the MLPC had joined forces with the FPP (below) to present a united front against the Kolingba government, with subsequent news stories again referring to Patassé, reportedly living in Togo, as the MLPC's leader. The party was granted legal status in September 1991.

In early 1993 Patassé, who had reportedly been running second when presidential balloting was suspended in October 1992, accepted an appointment to the CNPPR, despite allegations that Kolingba was using the Council to co-opt the most prominent opposition figures. In March, on the other hand, the party refused to enter the Lakoué government.

Patassé was elected president of the republic in 1993, while MLPC candidates secured a plurality of 34 legislative seats. The MLPC, whose strength is concentrated in the north, advanced to 47 legislative seats in 1998. Following his appointment as prime minister in January 1999, former MLPC stalwart Anicet Georges Dologuélé reportedly asserted that he wanted to be regarded as an independent. Patassé replaced him as the prime minister on April 1, 2001, with his close associate and leading party member, Martin Ziguélé, who then formed another MLPC-dominated cabinet on April 6. Following his ouster in March 2003, Patassé went into temporary exile in Togo. The MLPC subsequently endorsed General Bozizé's schedule for a return to civilian government. After Patassé's proposed candidacy was rejected by the transitional constitutional court, Ziguélé was named as the MLPC standard-bearer for the 2005 elections but he ultimately lost to Bozizé in the second round of presidential balloting.

At least one member of the MLPC was reportedly named to the cabinet in early 2006, although Patassé clearly remained at odds with the government. In April the Bozizé administration asked the new International Criminal Court to investigate alleged crimes on Patassé's part during the 2003 turmoil.

Leaders: Ange-Félix PATASSÉ (Former President of the Republic and of the Party), Martin

ZIGUÉLÉ (Former Prime Minister), Luc Apollinaire DONDON (Vice President of the Party), Francis Albert OUKANGA (Secretary General).

Alliance for Democracy and Progress (*Alliance pour la Démocratie et le Progrès*—ADP). A founding member of the CFD (see Political background, above), the ADP applied for legal status in late 1991. In October 1992 (then) party leader Jean-Claude CONJUGO was killed by government forces during a union-organized demonstration. However, the party was one of five groups represented in the government named on October 30, 1993, thereby breaking with the CFD. One of the party's leaders, Olivier Gabirault, ran for president in 2005, finishing last with less than 1 percent of the vote.

Leaders: Jacques MBOITEDAS, Olivier GABIRAULT, Tchapka BREDE (National Secretary).

Patriotic Front for Progress (*Front Patriotique pour le Progrès*—FPP). Launched initially by Abel Goumba Guéne as the Congo-based Ubangi Patriotic Front–Labor Party (*Front Patriotique Oubanguien–Parti Travailliste*—FPO-PT), the FPP repudiated the Dacko government in 1981, called for the withdrawal of French troops, and forged links with the French Socialist Party and other European socialist groups. Linkage with the MLPC was announced in 1986, the two groups calling for a boycott of the 1987 legislative balloting and the creation of a multiparty system as envisioned by the 1981 constitution. Between September 1990 and March 1991 Goumba was imprisoned for his involvement with the CCCCN. Leader of the core party of the opposition's Concertation of Democratic Forces (*Concertation des Forces Démocratiques*—CFD), Goumba was reported to be outpolling his four competitors at the abortive presidential balloting of October 1992 but fell to second place in 1993 and fourth place in 1999 (with 6.6 percent of the vote).

Goumba was appointed prime minister in the transitional government named following the March 2003 coup, but he was replaced in that post in December and named "honorary vice president." After receiving less than 3 percent of the vote in the first round of the 2005 presidential balloting, Goumba claimed widespread fraud. He was subsequently dismissed as honorary vice president on March 16. The official government explanation for his removal was that the new constitution did not provide for a vice president, but observers said his refusal to join those backing Bozizé cost him the post. However, in mid-2005, Goumba was appointed as "mediator of the republic" to improve relations between citizens and the government.

Leaders: Dr. Abel GOUMBA Guéne (President), Patrice ENDJIMOUNGOU (Secretary General).

Social Democratic Party (*Parti Social-Démocrate*—PSD). For the October 1992 balloting the PSD offered as a presidential candidate its leader, Enoch Dérant Lakoué, who was reportedly running in last place when the poll was aborted. In February 1993 Lakoué accepted appointment as Prime Minister Malendoma's successor.

During the first half of 1993 the PSD suffered numerous defections while Lakoué's own popularity continued to plummet. Thus, by the June 11 opening of a party congress, the PSD was, according to *Africa Confidential*, "run almost entirely by [Lakoué] family and friends."

At legislative balloting in 1998 the PSD captured six seats; however, one successful candidate, Dieudonné KOUDOUFARA, immediately defected to the MLPC, giving that party and its allies a disputed one-vote legislative majority. Two other PSD legislators reportedly followed Koudoufara's example in March 1999. Lakoué finished seventh in the 1999 presidential balloting with only 1.3 percent of the vote. The cabinet announced in November 1999 included a PSD member, but he was not reappointed in the new cabinet formed in April 2001. In 2005, the party won four seats in the assembly.

Leader: Enoch Dérant LAKOUÉ (Former Prime Minister).

Löndö Association. (*Levons-nous*). This human rights group won one assembly seat in 2005 balloting.

Movement for Democracy, Independence, and Social Progress (*Mouvement pour la Démocratie, l'Indépendance, et le Progrès Social*—MDI-PS). Formed in 1991 in an effort to develop a national party that would avoid the regional and ethnic group influences that were dominating other groupings, the MDI-PS was one of the few remaining members of the UFAPC as of late 1999.

Leader: Daniel NDITIFEI BOYSEMBE (Secretary General and Former Finance Minister).

Liberal Democratic Party (*Parti Liberal-Démocratic*—PLD). The PLD was launched prior to the 1993 legislative balloting, at which it won seven seats. The party was given four portfolios in the January 1999 cabinet, having won two seats in the late 1998 balloting as part of the "presidential majority" supportive of the MLPC. Former leader Nestor KOMBO-NAGUEMON reportedly committed suicide in 2004.

National Convention (*Convention National*—CN). Founded in October 1991 by David Galiambo, the CN won three seats in the 1993 National Assembly poll. It was represented in the cabinet from 1999 to 2003.

Leader: David GALIAMBO.

Civic Forum (*Forum Civique*—FC). Theretofore in opposition, the Civic Forum was suspended by the CFD in August 1992 for continuing its participation in the "grand national debate." On December 4 FC leader Gen. Timothée Malendoma was appointed prime minister by President Kolingba. However, scarcely more than two months later, on February 26, 1993, he was dismissed for "blocking the democratic process." As of late 1999 the FC was one of the few parties that remained part of the UFAPC (see above).

Leader: Gen. (Ret.) Timothée MALENDOMA (Former Prime Minister).

People's Union for the Republic (*Union du Peuple pour le République*—UPR). The recently formed UPR secured one seat in the 1998 legislative poll.

Democratic Movement for the Renaissance and Evolution of Central Africa (*Mouvement Démocratique pour la Renaissance et l'Evolution en Centrafrique*—MDREC). In mid-1992, MDREC party leader Joseph Bendounga, a pro-democracy advocate, was arrested and sentenced to six months' imprisonment for criticizing the president. The group secured one legislative seat in 1993. Bendounga, the mayor of Bangui, supported incumbent President Patassé in the 1999 presidential poll. Through 2001 the MDREC remained supportive of the MLPC and Patassé. The party named Bendounga as its candidate for the 2005 presidential election, but his name did not appear in the list of results.

Leaders: Joseph BENDOUNGA, Léon SEBOU (Secretary General).

Social Evolution Movement of Black Africa (*Mouvement de l'Évolution Sociale de l'Afrique Noire*—MESAN). The present MESAN is a faction-torn remnant of the group founded in 1949 and once headed by former president Dacko. The party won one assembly seat in 1993 balloting, and a MESAN member was appointed minister of communication in June 1996.

Leaders: Prosper LAVODRAMA and Joseph NGBANGADIBO (Faction Leaders).

Union of Democrats for Central African Renewal (*Union des Démocrates pour le Renouveau Centrafricain*—UDRC). The theretofore unknown UDRC was a founding member of CODEPO.

Central African Republican Party (*Parti Républicain Centrafricain*—PR). Also a former member of the CFD, the PR participated in the Malendoma government with its leader, Ruth Rolland, who had previously denounced the regime for tribalism and the misappropriation of public funds, accepting the Social and Women's Affairs portfolio. Subsequently, Rolland became the first African woman to present herself as a presidential candidate, although finishing last in 1993 with a mere 1 percent vote share. Rolland died in June 1995.

Central African Movement for National Liberation (*Mouvement Centrafricaine pour la Libération Nationale*—MCLN). The pro-Libyan MCLN, organized in Paris by Dr. Rodolphe Idi

Lala, a former member of the FPP, claimed responsibility for the July 1981 theater bombing in Bangui, in the wake of which it was outlawed. Idi Lala, who was condemned to death in absentia by a military court in May 1982, was challenged as leader in late 1983 by elements within the party that declared the bombing "off target"; at the time of its entry into the Central African Revolutionary Party (*Parti Revolutionnaire Centrafricain*—PRC), its leadership included former members of the Kolingba government who had been involved in the 1982 coup attempt. These individuals, especially Gen. Alphonse M'Baikoua, were subsequently involved in guerrilla action in the north, with the assistance of Chadian insurgents.

In late 1987 *Africa Confidential* reported that about 50 MCLN members were in prison in Bangui and described Gen. François Bozizé, then reportedly an MCLN leader operating from Libya, as a "constant headache" to Kolingba. In January 1988 Idi Lala was reported to have been arrested in Benin, and in October 1989 Bangui confirmed that Bozizé had been in detention in the Central African Republic since August, when Benin had agreed to "extradite" him, reportedly for a $3 million fee. In October 1991 Bozizé was acquitted of charges stemming from the 1982 coup attempt, and he was subsequently identified as leader of the Popular Rally for the Reconstruction of Central Africa (*Rassemblement Populaire pour la Reconstruction de la Centrafrique*—RPRC). Bozizé secured 1.5 percent of the presidential vote in 1993 as a technically independent candidate, having recently returned from nine years in exile. He was subsequently named chief of staff of the armed forces under President Patassé. Bozizé was dismissed in October 2001 by Patassé for allegedly having been involved in the attempted coup d'état in May. He left the country in November but returned to lead a successful overthrow of the Patassé government in March 2003.

The cabinet formed in April 2001 also included members from two small, previously unreferenced groups—the **African Development Party** (*Parti Africain du Développement*—PAD) and the **Democratic Union for Renewal/Fini Kodro** (*Union Démocratique pour le Renouveau/Fini Kodro*—UDR/FK).

Other Group

Patriotic Front for the Liberation of Central Africa (*Front Patriotique pour La Libération du Centrafrique*—FPLC). The formation of the FPLC was announced in Brazzaville, Congo, in June 1996 by exiled former CAR soldiers who had supported the army rebellion in April and May and opposed French intervention on behalf of the CAR government. The FPLC leaders promised "armed resistance" to both the Patassé administration and "French occupation."

Leaders: Lt. Jean Bertrand BIAMBA, Maj. Leopold ADETO, Dr. Jean Paul MANDAKOUZOU.

Legislature

The 1986 constitution provided for a bicameral Congress (*Congrès*) encompassing a largely advisory Economic and Regional Council composed of nominated members and an elective National Assembly with a five-year mandate.

The assembly was suspended following the March 2003 coup, and self-declared President Bozizé on March 30 established a 98-member National Transitional Council (*Conseil National de Transition*—CNT). The members were chosen by the president to represent the military, clergy, trade unions, political parties, human rights groups, and other sectors. The December 2004 constitutional revision provided for the creation of a new 105-member **National Assembly**. Following two rounds of balloting on March 13 and May 8, 2005, the distribution was as follows: the pro-Bozizé National Convergence coalition, 42 seats; the Central African People's Liberation Movement, 11; the Central African Democratic Rally, 8; the Social Democratic Party, 4; the Patriotic Front for Progress, 2; the Alliance for Democratic Progress, 2; the Löndö Association, 1; independents, 34; and undeclared, 1.

Speaker: Célestin-Leroy GAOMBALET.

Cabinet

As of March 1, 2006

Prime Minister	Elie Doté (ind.)

Ministers

Agriculture and Rural Development	Lt. Col. Parfait-Anicet Mbay (KNK)
Civil Service, Labor, and Social Security	Jacques Bothy
Energy, Mines, and Waterworks	Maj. Sylvain Ndoutingai (KNK)
Family and Social Affairs	Solange Pagonéndji Ndackala (ind.) [f]
Finance	Théodore Dabanga (KNK)
Interior	Lt. Col. Michel Sallé (KNK)
Justice	Paul Otto (ind.)
National Education	Charles Armel Doubane (ADP)
Posts and Telecommunications	Fidèle Ngouandjìka (KNK)
Public Health	Bernard Lala Bonamna (ind.)
Reconstruction of Public Buildings	Timoléon MbaiKoua (MLPC)
Secretary General of the Government and Relations with Parliament	Laurent Ngon Baba
Tourism	Col. Muhammad Mardi Marboua
Trade	Beatrice-Emilie Epaye (ind.) [f]
Water	Emanuel Bizo
Youth and Sports	Desiré Kolingba (RDC)

Ministers Delegate

Agriculture	Adamou Mahamat (ind.)
Equipment and Transport	Jean-Prosper Wodobodé (MDD)
Finance	Nicolas Nganzé (ind.)
National Education	Aurélien-Simplice Zingas (RDC)

Ministers of State

Communication	Jean-Études Téya (KNK)
Equipment and Transport	Charles Massi (FODEM)
Foreign Affairs, Regional Integration, and Francophone Affairs	Jean-Paul Ngoupandé (PUN)

[f] = female

Communications

Press

The following are published in Bangui: *E Le Songo* (2,000), daily tabloid in Sango; *Renouveau Centrafricaine* (1,000), weekly in French; *Journal Officiel de la République Centrafricaine,* fortnightly in French; *Terre Africaine*, weekly in French; *Le Rassemblement*, RDC organ; *Le Démocrate,* independent daily; *The Courier;* and *Le Citoyen*, independent. In May 2000 journalists in the CAR conducted a one-day strike to protest what they perceived as the government's efforts to "gag" the press, criticizing in particular the recent arrest of several editors and reporters for publishing anti-Patassé stories. In December 2004 the CNT decriminalized a range of press offenses including "defamation" and the publication of "false material," thereby overturning a restrictive 1998 press law that had been used in July 2004 to charge the editor of *Le Citoyen* with slander. In 2005 protests were voiced against a proposal by the acting communications minister to reinstitute censorship.

News Agency

The official facility is *Agence Centrafricaine de Presse* (ACAP).

Broadcasting and Computing

The government-controlled *Radio-diffusion-Télévision Centrafrique* broadcasts in French and Sango to some 24,000 television receivers. In 2003 approximately 8,000 personal computers serviced 5,000 Internet users.

Intergovernmental Representation

Ambassador to the U.S.
Emmanuel TOUABOY

U.S. Ambassador to the Central African Republic
(Vacant)

Permanent Representative to the UN
Fernand POUKRÉ-KONO

IGO Memberships (Non-UN)
AfDB, AU, BADEA, BDEAC, CEEAC, CEMAC, Interpol, NAM, OIF, WCO, WTO

CHAD

REPUBLIC OF CHAD

République du Tchad

The Country

Landlocked Chad, the largest in area and population among the countries of former French Equatorial Africa, extends from the borders of the equatorial forest in the south to the Sahara Desert in the north. Its unevenly distributed population is characterized by overlapping ethnic, religious, and regional cleavages; the more populous south is largely Negroid and animist, while the north is overwhelmingly Sudanic and Muslim. There is a Christian minority, estimates of which vary from 5 to 33 percent. Of the country's 12 major ethnic groups, the largest are the Saras in the south and Arabs in the center, north, and east. However, the Zakawa clan (an estimated 5 percent of the population) has dominated political affairs since the installation of the Déby regime in 1990. French is an official language, but Chadian Arabic has recognized status in the school system, and the major black tribes have their own languages. Women constitute roughly 21 percent of the official labor force and more than 65 percent of unpaid family workers. Female participation in government and politics, traditionally close to nonexistent, has increased slightly in recent years; the government has also recently introduced new legislation designed to protect certain rights of women, reportedly generating criticism form conservative elements of the population.

The economy is almost exclusively agricultural, nearly one-half of the gross national product being derived from subsistence farming, livestock-raising, and fishing. Cotton, grown primarily in the south, accounts for over 70 percent of export earnings, with cotton-ginning being the most important industry. Uranium and other mineral deposits are believed to be located in the northern Aozou Strip, long the source of a territorial dispute with Libya (see Foreign relations, below), while significant oil reserves have recently been discovered in the west and south (see below). Gold and diamonds also are mined.

Despite aid from such sources as the UN Development Programme, the World Bank, and the African Development Fund, widespread civil war through much of the 1970s, 1980s, and early 1990s precluded measurable economic development. In the mid-1990s the government began to privatize

Political Status: Independent since August 11, 1960; military regime instituted in 1975, giving way to widespread insurgency and ouster of Transitional Government of National Unity in 1982; one-party system established by presidential decree in 1984; constitution of December 10, 1989, suspended on December 3, 1990, following military coup; interim national charter announced February 28, 1991; transitional national charter adopted by Sovereign National Conference effective April 9, 1993; present constitution approved by national referendum on March 31, 1996, and revised by national referendum on June 6, 2005.

Area: 495,752 sq. mi. (1,284,000 sq. km.).

Population: 6,279,931 (1993C); 9,121,000 (2005E). The 1993 figure includes an adjustment of 1.4 percent for underenumeration.

Major Urban Center (2005E): N'DJAMENA (864,000).

Official Languages: French and Arabic. In addition, some 25 indigenous languages are spoken.

Monetary Unit: CFA Franc (official rate July 1, 2006: 513.01 francs = $1US). (The CFA franc, previously pegged to the French franc, is now permanently pegged to the euro at 655.957 CFA francs = 1 euro.)

President: Col. Idriss DÉBY (Patriotic Salvation Movement); self-appointed on December 4, 1990, following overthrow of the government of Hissène HABRÉ on December 2; confirmed by national charter adopted February 28, 1991; reconfirmed by the Sovereign National Conference on April 6, 1993; popularly elected to a five-year term in two-stage multiparty balloting on June 2 and July 3, 1996, and sworn in on August 8; reelected on May 20, 2001, and sworn in for another five-year term on August 8; reelected for another five-year term on May 3, 2006.

Prime Minister: Pascal YOADIMNADJI (Patriotic Salvation Movement); appointed by the president on February 3, 2005, to replace Moussa FAKI (Patriotic Salvation Movement).

many state-run enterprises and to adopt other measures designed to promote free-market activity, earning support from the International Monetary Fund (IMF) for its efforts. However, the IMF urged Chadian leaders to move beyond "crisis management" and "fiscal stabilization" to long-term policies designed to combat poverty.

Chad remains one of the poorest nations in the world, with a per capita annual income of less than $300. An estimated 80 percent of the population lives below the poverty level, nearly one-third of that number existing in near-starvation conditions. The illiteracy rate is estimated at 75 percent. Chad is also widely considered to be one of the world's most corrupt nations, with a "culture of clans and warlordism" dominating much of everyday existence and contributing to insurgencies that have compromised development efforts.

Prospects for economic advancement are focused almost exclusively on exploitation of the southern oil fields, which are estimated to contain at least 900 million barrels of oil. A pipeline to carry

the oil through Cameroon to the Atlantic Ocean was opened in October 2003, a consortium led by the Exxon Mobil Corporation having earmarked more than $4 billion for the extraction and piping processes. Significant financing was also provided by the World Bank, which was given control of an escrow fund containing Chad's portion of the oil revenue. As part of the arrangements with the World Bank, the Chadian government agreed to direct two-thirds of that revenue toward improving living standards and deposit 10 percent into a special fund to be reserved for use after the oil reserves were exhausted.

GDP grew by more than 30 percent in 2004 under the influence of the oil program and significantly increased foreign investment. However, growth declined to 13 percent in 2005 as the result of internal unrest and political discord that also prompted a serious dispute between the government and the World Bank (see Current issues, below). At that point Chad was exporting approximately 160,000 barrels of oil per day.

Government and Politics

Political Background

Brought under French control in 1900, Chad became part of French Equatorial Africa in 1910 and served as an important Allied base in World War II. It was designated an autonomous member state of the French Community in 1959, achieving full independence under the presidency of François (subsequently N'Garta) TOMBALBAYE one year later. Tombalbaye, a southerner and leader of the majority Chad Progressive Party (*Parti Progressiste Tchadien*—PPT), secured the elimination of other parties prior to the adoption of a new constitution in 1962.

The northern (Saharan) territories—historically focal points of resistance and virtually impossible to govern—remained under French military administration until 1965, when disagreements led Chad to request the withdrawal of French troops. Dissatisfaction with Tombalbaye's policies generated progressively more violent opposition and the formation in 1966 of the Chad National Liberation Front (*Front de Libération National Tchadien*—Frolinat), led by Aibrahim ABATCHA until his death in 1969, and then by Dr. Abba SIDDICK. French troops returned in 1968 at the president's request, but, despite their presence and reconciliation efforts by Tombalbaye, the disturbances continued, culminating in an attempted coup by Frolinat in 1971 (allegedly with Libyan backing). In a further effort to consolidate his regime, Tombalbaye created the National Movement for Cultural and Social Revolution (*Mouvement National pour la Révolution Culturelle et Sociale*—MNRCS) in 1973 to replace the PPT.

On April 13, 1975, Tombalbaye was fatally wounded in an uprising by army and police units. Two days later, Brig. Gen. Félix MALLOUM, who had been in detention since 1973 for plotting against the government, was designated chair of a ruling Supreme Military Council. The new regime, which banned the MNRCS, was immediately endorsed by a number of former opposition groups, although Frolinat remained aloof.

Following a major encounter between Libyan and Frolinat forces in the Tibesti Mountains in June 1976, Frolinat military leader Hissène HABRÉ attempted to negotiate a settlement with the Malloum regime but was rebuffed. In September Habré lost control of the main wing of Frolinat to Goukhouni OUEDDEI, who elected to cooperate with the Libyans, and in early 1978 Frolinat launched a major offensive against government forces in Faya-Largeau, about 500 miles northeast of the capital. Subsequently, on February 5, the government announced that it had concluded a cease-fire agreement with a rebel group, the Armed Forces of the North (*Forces Armées du Nord*—FAN), loyal to Habré, and a truce also was reached with Oueddei's People's Armed Forces (*Forces Armées du Peuple*—FAP), the largest Frolinat faction, in late March. However, the FAP resumed military operations in April, its advance being repulsed only with major French assistance. As of midyear the northern two-thirds of the country remained in the effective control of one or the other of the competing Frolinat factions.

On August 29, 1978, President Malloum announced the appointment of Habré as prime minister under a "basic charter of national reconciliation" pending the adoption of a permanent constitution. However, a serious rift developed between Malloum and Habré later in the year, and an abortive coup on February 12, 1979, by forces loyal to the prime minister was followed by a month of bloody, but inconclusive, confrontation between the rival factions. On March 16 a four-party agreement was concluded in Kano, Nigeria, involving Malloum, Habré, Oueddei, and Aboubakar Mahamat ABDERAMAN, leader of a "Third Army"—the Popular Movement of Chadian Liberation (*Mouvement Populaire de la Libération Tchadienne*—MPLT). Under the Kano accord, Oueddei on March 23 became president of an eight-member Provisional State Council, which was composed of two representatives from each of the factions and was to serve until a new government could be constituted. French troops were to be withdrawn under a truce guaranteed by Cameroon, the Central African Empire, Libya, Niger, Nigeria, and Sudan. At a second Kano conference held April 3–11, however, the pact broke down, primarily because agreement could not be reached with five other rebel groups, one of which, the "New Volcano," headed by the Revolutionary Democratic Council (*Conseil Démocratique Revolutionaire*—CDR) of Ahmat ACYL, had apparently become a leading beneficiary of Libyan support in the north. Meanwhile, former Malloum supporter Lt. Col. Wadal Abdelkader KAMOUGUÉ, commander of the Chadian Armed Forces (*Forces Armées Tchadiennes*—FAT), had launched a secessionist uprising in the south, also with Libyan backing.

On April 29, 1979, a second provisional government was announced under Lol Mahamat CHOUA of the MPLT, with Gen. Djibril Negue DJOGO, former army commander under President Malloum, as his deputy. However, the Choua government was repudiated by the six "guarantor" states during a third meeting in Lagos, Nigeria, held May 26–27, no Chadian representatives being present. In early June fighting erupted in N'Djamena between Frolinat and MPLT contingents, while other altercations occurred in the east, south, and north (where an invasion by a 2,500-man Libyan force, launched on June 26, met stiff resistance). In another effort to end the turmoil, a fourth conference convened August 20–21 in Lagos, attended by representatives of 11 Chadian groups and 9 external states (the original 6, plus Benin, Côte d'Ivoire, and Senegal). The August meeting resulted in the designation of Oueddei and Kamougué as president and vice president, respectively, of a Transitional Government of National Unity (*Gouvernement d'Union National de Transition*—GUNT), whose full membership, announced on November 10, included 12 northerners and 10 southerners.

Although the Lagos accord had called for demilitarization of N'Djamena by February 5, 1980, fighting resumed at the capital on March 21 between Defense Minister Habré's FAN and President Oueddei's FAP, the latter subsequently being reinforced by Kamougué's FAT and elements of the post-Lagos Front for Joint Action, of which Acyl was a leader. The coalescence of all other major forces against the FAN occurred primarily because of the perception that Habré, contrary to the intent of the Lagos agreement, had sought to expand his sphere of influence. While the FAN, clearly the best-organized of the military units, continued to maintain control of at least half the city, the Organization of African Unity (OAU, subsequently the African Union—AU) and such regional leaders as Togo's President Eyadéma arranged several short-lived cease-fires in late March and April.

Moving into a vacuum created by the removal of the last French military contingent on May 17, 1980, Libya on June 15 concluded a military defense treaty with the Oueddei government. By early November, 3,000–4,000 Libyan troops had moved into northern Chad and also had established a staging area within 40 miles of N'Djamena. Habré's position in the capital came under attack by Libyan aircraft, and fighting in the countryside spread as the government attempted to sever the FAN's link to its main base at Abéché, near the Sudanese border. An assault against FAN-controlled sectors of the capital was launched by government and Libyan forces on December 6, after Habré had rejected an OAU-sponsored cease-fire. Five days later the FAN withdrew from the city, some elements retreating toward Abéché and others crossing into Cameroon.

On January 6, 1981, the governments of Chad and Libya announced a decision to achieve "full unity" between their two countries. The action prompted OAU Chair Siaka Stevens of Sierra Leone to convene an extraordinary meeting of the OAU's Ad Hoc Committee on Chad in the Togolese capital of Lomé, where, on January 14, representatives of 12 governments repudiated the proposed merger, reaffirmed the validity of the 1979 Lagos accord, called on Libya to withdraw, and authorized the formation of an OAU peacekeeping force. Subsequently, it was reported that President Oueddei had been opposed to unification and had signed the agreement in Tripoli under duress, the Libyans expressing their disenchantment with his lack of "Islamic fervor" and calling for his replacement by Acyl. Both Vice President Kamougué and Frolinat's Dr. Siddick vehemently opposed the plan, the former terming it an "impossible marriage" and the latter fleeing to Sudan in April after resigning as health minister.

In late May 1981 the transitional government announced that several faction leaders had agreed to disarm and join in the formation of a "national integrated army" in anticipation of a Libyan withdrawal. Nonetheless, factional conflict continued, while at midyear a revitalized FAN mounted an offensive against Libyan and Libyan-backed government troops in the east. In mid-September, during a two-day meeting in Paris with Oueddei, French authorities agreed to provide logistical support to an OAU force to supplant the Libyans, and in November most of the latter were withdrawn after Benin, Gabon, Nigeria, Senegal, Togo, and Zaire had undertaken to form a 5,000-man contingent to maintain order, supervise elections, and assist in establishing a unified Chadian army.

During early 1982 FAN forces regained control of most of the eastern region and began advancing on N'Djamena, which fell on June 7, GUNT President Oueddei fleeing to Cameroon before establishing himself at the northern settlement of Bardai on the border of the Libyan-controlled Aozou Strip. Upon entering the capital, the Council of the Commander in Chief of the FAN (*Conseil du Commandement en Chef des FAN*—CCFAN) assumed political control, and on June 19 it named Habré to head a 30-member Council of State. Earlier, on June 11, OAU Chair Daniel arap Moi had ordered the withdrawal of the OAU force, which, at maximum strength, had scarcely exceeded 3,000 men, two-thirds from Nigeria. During the ensuing months, the FAN, with assistance from FAT units, succeeded in gaining control of the south. On September 29 the CCFAN promulgated a Fundamental Act (*Acte Fondamental*), based on the August 1978 charter (which had been effectively abrogated in 1979), to "govern Chad until the adoption of a new constitution." In accordance with the new act, Habré was sworn in as president of the republic on October 21. Following his investiture, the new chief executive dissolved the Council of State in favor of a 31-member government that included Dr. Siddick; DJIDINGAR Dono Ngardoum, who had served briefly as prime minister under Oued-

dei in May; and Capt. Routouane YOMA, a former aide of Colonel Kamougué. As stipulated in the Fundamental Act, Habré also announced the formation of a 30-member National Consultative Council (*Conseil National Consultatif*—CNC) to serve as the state's "highest advisory organ." Two months later N'Djamena announced that the FAN and FAT would be consolidated as the Chadian National Armed Forces (*Forces Armées Nationales Tchadiennes*—FANT).

After the declaration in Algiers in October 1982 of a "National Peace Government" by 8 of the 11 signatories of the 1979 Lagos accord, Oueddei forces regrouped in Bardai with renewed support from Tripoli. By May 1983 GUNT units were advancing south, and, with the aid of 2,000 troops and several MIG fighters supplied by Libya, they captured the "northern capital" of Faya-Largeau on June 24. Habré immediately called for international assistance and received aid from Egypt, Sudan, and the United States, with France avoiding direct involvement despite a 1976 defense agreement (see Foreign relations, below). FANT troops recaptured Faya-Largeau on June 30, only to lose it again on August 10, while France, under mounting pressure from the United States and a number of francophone African countries, began deploying troops along a defensive "red line" just north of Abéché on August 14. The French—who eventually numbered some 3,000, in addition to 2,000 Zairean troops—imposed a tenuous cease-fire for the remainder of the year, while calling for a negotiated solution between the two factions. In November the OAU announced that it would sponsor "reconciliation talks" in Addis Ababa and issued invitations to all participants in the Lagos conference, but protocol demands by Habré led to their eventual cancellation. While Habré continued to urge France to aid him in a full-scale offensive against Oueddei, the Mitterrand government refused, at one point urging "a federation of Chad" as a means of ending the conflict. Meanwhile, in the wake of renewed fighting, the "red line" was moved 60 miles north.

In April 1984 Libyan leader Muammar al-Qadhafi proposed a mutual withdrawal of "Libyan support elements" and French forces, with talks thereupon initiated between France and Libya that yielded an accord on September 17. The French pullout was completed by the end of the year; Libya, however, was reported to have withdrawn less than half of its forces from the north, and the political-military stalemate continued. Meanwhile, the Habré regime had attempted to consolidate its power with the June formation of the National Union for Independence and Revolution (*Union Nationale pour l'Indépendence et la Révolution*—UNIR), the first legally recognized political party in Chad since the 1975 banning of the MNRCS.

In a statement issued in Tripoli on October 15, 1985, Oueddei was declared dismissed as FAP leader. The GUNT president repudiated the action and on November 5 announced the release of Acheikh ibn OUMAR, leader of the GUNT-affiliated CDR, who reportedly had been arrested a year earlier. On November 11 the Habré administration responded by concluding a "reconciliation agreement" with a breakaway faction of the CDR, the Committee for Action and Concord (*Comité d'Action et de Concord*—CAC).

In February 1986 GUNT forces mounted an offensive against FANT troops at the center of the "red line," but by early March they had been repulsed, reportedly with heavy losses. On June 19 FAT leader Kamougué announced from Paris his resignation as the GUNT vice president, while in August Oumar declared that the CDR had "suspended collaboration" with the GUNT but would "maintain solidarity with all anti-Habré factions." Clashes between CDR and GUNT units followed, the latter offering to open peace talks with N'Djamena; however, the Habré government insisted that the GUNT would first have to repudiate the Libyan intervention. Subsequently, during a meeting of GUNT factions in Cotonou, Benin, in mid-November, Oueddei was "expelled" from the grouping, with Oumar being named its president. In late December, as FANT forces were reported to be moving north, fighting broke out between FAP units loyal to Oueddei and what Libyan sources characterized as Oumar's "legitimate" GUNT.

On March 22, 1987, in what was seen as a major turning point in the lengthy Chadian conflict, FANT troops captured the Libyan air facility in Ouadi Doum, 100 miles northeast of Faya-Largeau. Deprived of air cover, the Libyans withdrew from Faya-Largeau, their most important military base in northern Chad, abandoning an estimated $1 billion worth of sophisticated weaponry. On August 8 Chadian government troops captured the town of Aozou, administrative capital of the northern strip; however, it was retaken by Libyan forces three weeks later. Chad thereupon entered southern Libya in an unsuccessful effort to deprive it of air support in the continued struggle for the disputed territory. Subsequent international and regional criticism of the Chadian "invasion" led Habré to accept a September 11 cease-fire negotiated by OAU chair Kenneth Kaunda of Zambia; however, by late November the government reported FANT clashes with Libyan troops crossing into eastern Chad from Sudan.

In early 1988 Habré charged that Libya was still violating Chadian air space and backing antigovernment rebels despite Qadhafi's pledge of support for OAU peace-treaty negotiations. Nonetheless, Chad and Libya agreed in mid-October to restore diplomatic relations and "resolve peacefully their territorial dispute" by presenting their respective Aozou strip claims to a special OAU committee (see Foreign relations, below, for subsequent developments).

In April 1989 Habré survived a coup attempt that allegedly involved a number of senior government officials, including former FANT commander Idriss DÉBY, who subsequently mounted a series of cross-border attacks from sanctuary in Sudan. Eight months later, Chadian voters approved a constitution to replace the Fundamental Act. One of its provisions extended Habré's incumbency for another seven years; others formalized the UNIR's supremacy and authorized an elected National Assembly, balloting for which was conducted in June 1990.

In November 1990 a variety of antigovernmental forces, allied under Déby's leadership in the Patriotic Salvation Movement (*Mouvement Patriotique du Salut*—MPS), mounted a decisive offensive against FANT troops in eastern Chad. The rebels captured Abéché on November 30, reportedly prompting large-scale desertion by government troops. With France having announced that it would not intervene in what was characterized as an "internal Chadian power struggle," the MPS was left with a virtually unimpeded path to N'Djamena; consequently, Habré and other government leaders fled to Cameroon. (Habré was indicted in February 2000 in Senegal and charged with torture during his term in power. In June, however, the court ruled that Senegal did not have jurisdiction over the case, a decision that was heavily criticized as being politically motivated; human rights groups, which had filed the initial complaint against Habré, appealed to a higher Senegalese court. In March 2001 the appeals court upheld the lower court's ruling, President Wade of Senegal stating that he was prepared to send Habré to a third country to face trial. As of mid-2006 Habré remained in Senegal, although there had been attempts to extradite him to Belgium by victims of the regime who were Belgian citizens. In January 2006 the AU heads of state had voted not to order the extradition of Habré to Belgium [Senegal had asked for the vote].)

On December 3, 1990, one day after having occupied the capital, Déby suspended the constitution and dissolved the assembly; on December 4 he announced that a provisional Council of State had assumed power with himself as president and a fellow commander, Maldoum BADA ABBAS, as vice president. On February 28 an interim National Charter was adopted, and on March 5 the Council of State was dissolved in favor of a new Council of Ministers and an appointed Provisional Council of the Republic. The vice presidency was abandoned upon formation of the new government, Bada Abbas being named minister of state for the interior and former National Assembly president Jean ALINGUÉ BAWOYEU being appointed to the revived post of prime minister.

The overthrow of the Habré regime generated minimal international concern or domestic protest, in part because of reports that the deposed government had engaged in widespread human rights abuses. For his part, President Déby pledged to work toward implementation of a mul-

tiparty democracy in which "fundamental rights" would be guaranteed. However, the new regime also insisted that "security issues" took precedence over political liberalization.

In response to opposition demands for the convening of a Sovereign National Conference (*Conférence Nationale Souveraine*—CNS) to chart the nation's political future, Déby tentatively scheduled such a body for May 1992. Meanwhile, the Council of Ministers adopted guidelines for registering parties.

In mid-October 1991 fighting broke out in N'Djamena, the government subsequently announcing that it had thwarted an attempted coup. Among those arrested and charged with complicity in the overthrow effort was Bada Abbas, although the government later appeared to acknowledge that the allegations against him were unfounded.

The regime faced an even more serious challenge in late 1991 when Habré loyalists, organized as the Movement for Development and Democracy (*Mouvement pour le Développement et la Démocratie*—MDD), launched an invasion from the Lake Chad border region. The campaign enjoyed some initial success, and, as the rebels advanced on N'Djamena in early January 1992, French paratroopers reinforced the brigade of 1,110 French soldiers permanently stationed near the capital. In addition to its symbolic significance, the French reinforcement permitted the release of additional Chadian troops to confront the rebels, and within days the government reported that the MDD forces were in full retreat. In the wake of the insurgency, security forces arrested a number of prominent opposition leaders and launched what was perceived as a reprisal campaign against suspected MDD supporters, former officials in the Habré administration, and members of the fledgling Rally for Democracy and Progress (*Rassemblement pour la Démocratie et le Progrès*—RDP). Shortly thereafter, in response to pressure from Paris, the government announced an amnesty for those recently detained as well as those implicated in the October coup attempt, including Bada Abbas, who upon his release from prison was named to the Provisional Council of the Republic. Reaffirming its commitment to democratization, the regime began legalizing opposition parties, including the RDP, in March. However, the CNS opening scheduled for May was postponed indefinitely because of ongoing security concerns, the government having reported another coup attempt in April.

On May 19, 1992, the National Charter was modified to strengthen the authority of the prime minister, and the following day Alingué Bawoyeu was replaced by Joseph YODEYMAN. On May 22 a new Council of Ministers was announced that included representatives of newly organized parties, although a number of them subsequently resigned from the "coalition" government as the result of policy disputes. Following a minor reshuffle in October, the government announced that the CNS would convene on January 15, 1993, with a mandate to appoint a new prime minister, select a "transitional" legislature, and draw up constitutional revisions that would lead, following a national referendum on the proposals, to multiparty presidential and legislative balloting. Significantly, the CNS was not empowered to replace Déby, who was viewed as having the best chance to maintain a semblance of stability in an increasingly divided society. Thus, Déby remained as president and commander in chief of the armed forces under the transitional national charter adopted at the conclusion of the CNS on April 6, 1993. Quasi-legislative authority was extended to a Higher Transitional Council (*Conseil Supérieur de Transition*—CST), whose members were elected by the CNS. In addition, broad responsibility for economic and social policies was conferred on the prime minister, Dr. Fidèle MOUNGAR, a southerner named by the CNS to form the first transitional government. The CNS, supported by some 40 political parties (recognized and unrecognized), several rebel movements, and numerous trade and professional associations, approved a transitional period of up to 12 months pending the drafting of a permanent constitution and the holding of national elections. However, the CST was authorized to extend the charter's authority for an additional year, if necessary.

Despite the prime minister's expression of confidence that he and the president could work together, friction between the two leaders quickly surfaced, Déby being particularly critical of the new government's "amateurish" economic program. The dispute culminated with the CST forcing Dr. Moungar's resignation via a nonconfidence motion on October 28. After three rounds of voting, the CST on November 6 elected Delwa Kassiré KOUMAKOYÉ, the outgoing justice minister, to succeed Dr. Moungar. A new cabinet was named one week later, followed by a minor reshuffle in January 1994 in which MPS dominance was maintained despite the continued presence of ministers from anti-Déby parties. Subsequently, on April 4, the CST voted to extend the transitional period for 12 more months in view of the nation's seeming inability to reverse political fragmentation, with a major cabinet reshuffle following on May 17.

In November 1994 President Déby pledged that the constitutional referendum would be held in early 1995 and would be followed soon thereafter by presidential and legislative elections. In preparation for those events, he announced a general amnesty on December 1 for all political detainees and exiles (with the notable exception of former President Habré); he also reshuffled the cabinet on December 13.

The CST approved a new electoral code and a draft constitution in January 1995; however, the subsequent registration of voters was strongly criticized by opposition leaders, who claimed the process was skewed in favor of the MPS. Acknowledging that the validity of the new voter lists was questionable, the CST postponed the constitutional referendum indefinitely and in early April extended the transitional period for another 12 months. Collaterally, the CST dismissed Prime Minister Koumakoyé on April 8 for failing to "create the proper conditions" for elections, replacing him with Djimasta KOIBLA, who suspended his activity within the Union for Democracy and the Republic (*Union pour la Démocratie et la République*—UDR) upon assuming national office.

The extension of the nation's transitional political status was controversial, opponents noting that a National Reconciliation Committee appointed in 1994 had negotiated peace accords with several rebel groups and thereby reduced security concerns. Consequently, with the Déby regime reportedly facing international pressure to proceed with democratization, the constitutional referendum was finally conducted on March 31, 1996. The new basic law (see Constitution and government, below) was approved by 63.5 percent of the voters in what officials reported to be a 69 percent turnout. (Not surprisingly, the "no" vote was heaviest in the south, where sentiment had long preferred federal status that would accord substantial autonomy to the region.) As approved by the referendum, Déby remained in office pending new presidential balloting, while the CST continued to operate until the election of a new legislature. In addition, although the cabinet submitted an essentially pro forma resignation on April 18, Déby reappointed Koibla the next day to head an interim government that included all but one of the incumbent ministers.

Fifteen candidates contested the first round of presidential balloting on June 2, 1996, Déby being credited with 43.9 percent of the votes. His closest rival was former southern military leader and GUNT vice president Kamougué, running under the banner of the Union for Renewal and Democracy (*Union pour le Renouveau et la Démocratie*—UDR), who secured 12.4 percent of the votes. Other contenders included Saleh KEBZABO of the National Union for Development and Renewal (*Union National pour le Développement et le Renouvellement*—UNDR), 8.6 percent; former prime minister Alingué Bawoyeu of the UDR, 8.3 percent; and the RDP's Choua, 5.9 percent. Déby was subsequently elected to a five-year term on July 3 in the second-round balloting, defeating Kamougué 69.1 percent to 30.9 percent. Following his inauguration on August 8, Déby again named Prime Minister Koibla to head the significantly revamped government announced on August 12.

Although opposition parties charged that "massive fraud" had occurred in the first round of the presidential election in June 1996, international observers reportedly expressed satisfaction with the conduct of the balloting. The vote shares garnered by President Déby and Colonel Kamougué appeared to reflect the long-standing cultural, religious, and ethnic divide between southern Chad and the rest of the country. Meanwhile, Western capitals (most importantly Paris) signaled their support for President Déby as Chad's best hope for ongoing stability, despite concern over his administration's human rights record and its ties with Sudan and collateral support for the Islamic fundamentalist movement.

Elections to the new National Assembly were held on January 5 and February 23, 1997, with MPS candidates ultimately securing 65 of 125 seats following a redistribution ordered by the national electoral commission upon appeal by the governing party (which was initially credited with only 55 seats). Election monitors described the balloting as "relatively free and fair." On the other hand, there was widespread domestic and international condemnation of the allegedly progovernment bias of the national electoral commission, especially regarding alleged irregularities in the initial tallies. However, Western leaders appeared willing to overlook such heavy-handed tactics, perhaps out of appreciation for the relative stability of the Déby regime in a region of recent intense political and military turbulence. For its part, the government continued to pursue cease-fire agreements with various rebel groups, as observers warned that tribal influences remained the most serious threat to the regime and the fledgling democratic process.

On May 16, 1997, President Déby appointed Nassour OUAÏDOU Guelendouksia to succeed Koibla as prime minister, a number of incumbents retaining their posts in the new cabinet announced on May 21. Ouaidou also headed the reshuffled cabinet appointed on January 1, 1998. However, on December 13, 1999, in the wake of economic turbulence, President Déby appointed a "technocrat," Negoum YAMASSOUM, as prime minister. Yamassoum's new cabinet, announced December 14, included ministers from the MPS, UNDR, and URD. Déby was reelected to another term in controversial balloting (the opposition objected to de facto control by the MPS over the electoral commission) on May 20, 2001, and, following his inauguration on August 8, he reappointed Yamassoum as prime minister.

The MPS maintained its dominance in the April 21, 2002, National Assembly balloting (postponed from 2001 on the grounds that the government lacked sufficient funds to conduct the poll). On June 11 President Déby appointed Haroun KABADI as prime minister, but he was succeeded by Moussa FAKI on June 24, 2003, and Pascal YOADIM-NADJI on February 3, 2005.

A national referendum was held on June 6, 2005, on constitutional changes proposed by the assembly, the most contentious being elimination of the two-term presidential limit, which thereby permitted Déby to seek another term. Most opposition parties, many of which had served in Déby governments, strongly condemned the revisions and urged a boycott of the referendum. However, the government announced that 58 percent of voters participated in the referendum and that the changes were approved by a 66 percent yes vote. Subsequently, Déby reshuffled the cabinet on August 7; the most significant change involved his consolidation of control of the armed forces through the transfer of the defense ministry to the office of the president.

Following the outbreak of renewed rebel activity (some on the part of military deserters incensed over the constitutional changes) in late 2005, the assembly in January 2006 voted 129–0 (with opposition legislators boycotting the vote) to postpone the assembly elections scheduled for April 2006 until April 2007, citing security and budget concerns. In controversial balloting on May 3, Déby was reelected to another five-year presidential term, officially securing 77.5 percent of the votes against only four other candidates. Nearly all opposition parties called for a boycott of the election in view of the recent failed rebel takeover attempt (see Current issues, below, for additional information).

Constitution and Government

The 1962 constitution was abrogated in April 1975 by the Malloum government, which issued a provisional replacement in August 1978. A successor document, derived from the Malloum charter, was promulgated by the CCFAN in September 1982. A new constitution, commissioned by President Habré in 1988 and adopted by popular referendum in December 1989, provided for a strong presidency and a directly elected National Assembly, nonpartisan balloting for which was conducted on July 8, 1990. The 1989 basic law and its institutions were suspended indefinitely by the Déby regime on December 3, 1990.

Following approval by the Sovereign National Conference, a new transitional government structure, headed by President Déby and a Higher Transitional Council (CST), was formally launched on April 9, 1993. Initially scheduled to remain in place for 12 months, its mandate was twice extended for terms of like duration in April 1994 and April 1995.

A 17-member Constitutional Committee, established in December 1993, drafted a new basic law in 1994 calling for establishment of a bicameral legislature and a strong presidential system based on the French model. The changes were endorsed by the CST in January 1995, but the national referendum was postponed until March 31, 1996, when the proposed constitution was endorsed by 63.5 percent of the voters.

The new basic law provided for direct popular election (in two-round balloting, if necessary) of the president for a maximum of two five-year terms. The prime minister is appointed by the president, although he is also held "responsible" to the legislature. The members of the National Assembly serve four-year terms. The constitution also authorized the creation of a Constitutional Council and a Supreme Court, both of which were installed in April 1999.

Although the 1996 constitution provided for a new Senate, that body was never constituted, and a constitutional revision approved by national referendum on June 6, 2005, eliminated references to the Senate in favor of an advisory body called the Economic, Social, and Cultural Council, whose members were to be appointed by the president, subject to approval by the assembly. However, no appointments had been made as of May 2006. In a more controversial area (see Current issues, below), the amendments also permitted President Déby to seek a third term and removed an age restriction of 70 for the president.

In early 2000 the government doubled the number of prefectures (previously 14) and sub-prefectures, which are administered by government appointees. The cited reason was to promote de-centralization of government functions. However, critics claimed that the reforms also had the effect of further cementing the ruling party's hold on power.

Foreign Relations

Chad's internal unrest was exacerbated for a long time by conflict with Libya over delineation of their common border. The dispute was intensified in 1975 by Libya's annexation of an area of some 27,000 square miles in northern Chad (the Aozou Strip) that was said to contain substantial iron ore and uranium deposits. Beginning in 1977 Libyan representatives consistently identified the territory in question as part of "southern Libya," largely on the basis of a 1935 agreement between France and Italy that the latter had failed to ratify. In August 1989 Chad and Libya concluded a pact providing for mutual withdrawal from the disputed territory, an exchange of prisoners of war, agreement not to support one another's opponents, and the cessation of media "attacks" upon each other. However, subsequent negotiations failed to produce a permanent settlement to the dispute, with Chad accusing Libya of supporting rebels operating out of Sudan and Libya charging Chad with foot-dragging on the prisoner release. As a result of the impasse, the case was referred to the International Court of Justice (ICJ) in September 1990. Even though relations between the two countries improved significantly following the year-end victory by the MPS, whose fighters had reportedly been supplied with Libyan arms, the Aozou dispute remained in the hands of the ICJ, which in February 1994 ruled in favor of Chad by a vote of 16–1. After initially appearing to hesitate in the matter, Libya formally accepted the ICJ ruling in April, and the withdrawal of Libyan troops from the territory was completed by the end of May. Shortly thereafter President Déby met with Libya's Colonel Qadhafi in Tripoli to sign a treaty of friendship and co-operation. In February 2006 the two countries signed a declaration calling for full normalization of relations.

Relations with France have been complicated since the mid-1970s, when French involvement in the civil war was intensified by rebel kidnapping of a French national. In March 1976 a new co-operation pact was concluded, France agreeing to come to Chad's defense in the event of external, but not domestic, attack. Despite this assertion, French forces aided government troops throughout the late 1970s in stemming rebel, most notably Frolinat, offensives. By contrast, a French decision not to intervene in the fighting that broke out in November 1990 was considered critical to the success of the MPS campaign. Not surprisingly, the new Chadian president in early 1991 invited the approximately 1,100 French troops to remain in the country for security purposes, and their presence was considered a psychological factor in the Déby regime's ability to withstand several subsequent overthrow attempts.

Chadian affairs also were of particular interest to a number of other Western nations in the 1980s, especially in relation to the Habré government's dispute with Libya. Thus, U.S. surveillance photographs and anti-aircraft weapons were allegedly used by Habré forces during the 1987 struggle in southern Libya. However, concern over developments in Chad subsequently waned, the United States' protest over the events of late 1990 being relatively moderate, despite apparent Libyan support for the victorious rebel forces.

In September 1998 Chad sent more than 2,000 troops to support the Kabila regime in the civil war in the Democratic Republic of the Congo (DRC). In April 1999 the Déby administration announced that the force (some 200 of which had been killed) would be withdrawn soon, as regional mediators attempted to broker a settlement to that intractable dispute, which had drawn in some half-dozen of the DRC's neighbors (see article on the DRC for details). Meanwhile, troops from Nigeria and Niger continued to assist in flushing out Chadian rebels in the Lake Chad region. (Fighting had broken out between Nigerian and Chadian troops in April 1998 over possession of an island in the lake; however, the conflict had settled down quickly, the two countries agreeing to leave formal demarcation of the boundary to the Lake Chad Basin Commission.) Chad's relations with Sudan and Libya also continued to improve, some observers suggesting that the Déby regime was hoping to dilute the country's long-standing dependence on French support or at least increase its negotiating leverage with Paris.

In early 2000 the French ambassador was expelled by the government in a sign of further cooling of Franco–Chadian relations. However, diplomatic relations were subsequently restored, and in 2002 French President Chirac became the first French head of state to visit Chad.

Tension intensified with the Central African Republic (CAR) in 2001 when Chad provided refuge for Gen. François Bozizé, one of the main protagonists in the CAR's infighting (see article on the CAR for details). However, relations improved when Bozizé assumed control in the CAR, and Chad sent troops to help maintain order in the CAR following the takeover. (There are currently an estimated 15,000–20,000 refugees from the lawless northern provinces of the CAR in southern Chad.)

In 2002 Chad joined Algeria, Mauritania, and Niger in signing the "Pan Sahel Initiative" with the United States whereby U.S. forces were to be deployed to the region to help combat terrorism, drug trafficking, and arms smuggling. As part of that project, Chadian and U.S. troops reportedly broke up an Algerian rebel operation in Chad in 2004.

The intense fighting that broke out in the Darfur region of Sudan in early 2003 had major repercussions for Chad. Some 200,000 refugees from the non-Arab population of Darfur fled across the border into Chad, populated by many of the same ethnic groups as those in Darfur (including President Déby's Zakawa group). Sudan subsequently accused Chad of permitting Sudanese rebels to operate out of Chad, while Chad made similar accusations about Chadian rebels in Sudan. President Déby was prominent in efforts to mediate a settlement to the Darfur violence in 2005 (see Current issues, below, for subsequent developments).

Current Issues

In the presidential poll of May 20, 2001, President Déby faced six main challengers, all of whom protested alleged bias in the voter registration process and the administration of the election. Déby secured 68 percent of the vote in the first round, thereby avoiding a runoff. However, the opposition candidates declared the results fraudulent and launched a campaign of civil disobedience that resulted in their arrest and brief detention. The European Union "regretted" the many shortcomings in the organization of the poll and expressed concerns about the restriction of political liberties by the government. The opposition also charged that the 2002 assembly balloting was fraudulent.

Criticism of President Déby's "increasingly autocratic rule" intensified in May 2004 when the assembly proposed an amendment to the constitution to permit him to run for a third term. The opposition parties called for a boycott of the June constitutional referendum on the matter and described the government's official results of the voting as "imaginary." More threatening to the regime was the desertion of members of the presidential guard and other military forces in October and the collateral organization of well-armed rebel groups along both sides of the Sudanese border. In addition, the government reported that it had thwarted an attempted coup in November on the part of soldiers at two bases, which prompted a "sweeping purge" of the military by Déby, who formed a new security force under his direct command. In other manifestations of popular discontent, protest demonstrations broke out in the city of Pala in December and government workers went on strike in the capital, demanding payment of four months of salary arrears. All in all, the "increasingly isolated" Déby faced what one journalist characterized as "enormous dissent," not only because of the third-term issue but also because of the widespread perception that two years of windfall oil revenues had been mismanaged.

In late December 2005 the assembly approved new legislation permitting the administration to allocate additional oil revenue toward the general budget, which critics argued Déby would use almost exclusively to purchase armaments. The World Bank, which had been charged with allocating the oil revenues, decried the change as a violation of a prior agreement (see The Country, above, for details) and in January 2006 suspended the disbursement of $125 million in accumulated revenues. The Bank also halted its own lending program to Chad. The Déby administration responded with a threat to halt oil production altogether if the Bank did not reverse its course, sending a shiver through the world's oil markets.

Opposition parties strongly criticized the assembly's decision in January 2006 to postpone the upcoming April elections for a year, arguing that the government was simply trying to maintain its control of the legislature prior to the presidential balloting scheduled for May. Further mass military defections to the newly formed United Front for Change (*Front Uni pour le Changement*—FUC) were reported in February, and more than 100 soldiers were arrested in March in relation to an alleged attempt to shoot down Déby's plane. The unrest culminated in a rapid incursion by FUC forces from the Sudanese border that reached the outskirts of N'Djamena on April 13 before encountering significant resistance. The rebels were finally repulsed at the steps of the assembly building; more than 300 people were killed in the fighting, which also severely damaged eastern portions of N'Djamena. Déby accused the Sudanese government of backing the FUC, announcing that a "state of hostility" existed between Chad and Sudan. (Most analysts agreed with Déby's assertions, suggesting that Sudan, which had supported Deby's takeover in 1990, was now convinced that the Chadian government was providing assistance to the largely Zakawa rebel groups fighting the *Janjaweed* militias in Darfur [see article on Sudan for details].)

Significantly, France sent an additional 150 troops to its garrison in Chad during the April 2006 rebel incursion, and a French jet fired warning shots over the rebel forces in an apparent indication that France would not tolerate any attacks on French citizens. Although the French forces did not assist government troops in repulsing the rebels, their presence underscored the widespread perception that France preferred that Déby remain in power. Other Western countries also appeared to consider Déby the most likely leader to prevent Chad from descending further into ethnic/regional/political fragmentation that might threaten oil flows or lead to installation of a "pro-Sudan" administration. Consequently, western criticism was moderate concerning the May presidential election, which Chadian opposition parties characterized as Déby simply "installing himself for life." (Déby's only opponents were "three cronies" and one candidate from a minor opposition party.) Realpolitik also appeared to play a role in the World Bank's decision to resume lending to Chad in May and to agree to begin releasing oil revenue gradually upon the anticipated adoption of more transparent accounting practices by the Chadian administration. The accord also permitted the government to close the fund that had been established for the "post-oil" years and, apparently, to direct additional resources to security matters.

Political Parties and Groups

Prior to the collapse of the Habré regime and the suspension of the constitution on December 3, 1990, by Idriss Déby, single-party government control had been exercised by the National Union for Independence and Revolution (*Union Nationale pour l'Indépendence et la Révolution*—UNIR). President Déby, governing in the name of the Patriotic Salvation Movement (MPS, below), declared himself to be a supporter of multipartyism, and on October 1, 1991, the Council of Ministers authorized the legalization of parties provided they "shun intolerance, tribalism, regionalism, religious discrimination, and recourse to violence." The first parties were recognized in March 1992.

In 2004 some 20–30 opposition parties (including the URD, AND, RDP, and others formerly aligned with the MPS) formed the **Coordination of Parties for the Defense of the Constitution** (*Coordination des Parties pour la Défense de la Constitution*—CPDC) to protest, among other things, the MPS plan to revise the constitution to permit another presidential term for Déby. The CPDC also demanded revision of the electoral code, appointment of a truly independent election commission, and the use of international election observers at future balloting. Having failed to affect the plans of the MPS, the CPDC (whose components were considered to be in agreement on the constitutional issues "but little else") called for a boycott of the 2005 national referendum and the 2006 presidential election. Following the rebel attack on N'Djamena in April 2006, CPDC spokesman Ibni Oumar Mahamat Saleh said the CPDC was neither prorebel nor progovernment, although it opposed violent overthrow of the administration.

Legislative Parties

Patriotic Salvation Movement (*Mouvement Patriotique du Salut*—MPS). The MPS was formed in Libya in March 1990 by a number of groups opposed to the regime of President Hissne Habré. The movement was headed by Idriss Déby, a former Chadian military leader and presidential advisor, who had participated in an April 1989 coup attempt. In addition to Déby's **April 1 Action** (*Action du 1 Avril*), the MPS included the southern-based **Movement for Chadian National Salvation** (*Mouvement pour le Salut National du Tchad*—Mosanat), which was reported to have clashed with government troops in March 1989; and remnants of the **Chadian Armed Forces** (*Forces Armées Tchadiennes*—FAT), another southern grouping with extensive involvement in Chadian affairs (see Political background, above).

The MPS endorsed a prodemocracy platform, while "preaching neither capitalism nor socialism." After having ousted the Habré government in late 1990, it gained the allegiance of a number of other groups, including the **Chadian People's Revolution** (*Révolution du Peuple Tchadienne*—RPT), formed in Libya in January 1990 by several hundred Chadians of "various political tendencies" under the leadership of Adoum TOGOI.

After proclaiming himself president, Déby governed in the name of the MPS, remaining as president of the republic and commander-in-chief of the armed forces under the transitional charter approved by the Sovereign National Conference in April 1993. An extraordinary MPS congress held April 10–11, 1996, "unanimously" selected Déby as the party's presidential nominee, the MPS leader subsequently receiving the endorsement of a number of minor parties grouped as the Republican Front during his successful campaign. The MPS initially was credited with winning 55 seats in the assembly elections of early 1997 but was subsequently given additional seats following a controversial review by the national electoral commission. Its final total was placed at 65, which gave the MPS a working majority in the 125-member legislature.

In early 1999 the Liberal Party for Unity and Solidarity (*Parti Libéral pour l'Unité et la Solidarité*—PLUS), led by Braham AHMAT, merged with the MPS.

Leaders: Idriss DÉBY (President of the Republic and Chair of the Party), Mahamet HISSENE (Secretary General), Pascal YOADIM-NADJI (Prime Minister of the Republic).

Union for Renewal and Democracy (*Union pour le Renouveau et la Démocratie*—URD). The URD was legalized in May 1992 under the leadership of Lt. Col. Wadal Abdelkader Kamougué, a former commander of FAT forces in southern Chad who had served as a GUNT vice president (see Political background, above) and was subsequently a member of the Provisional Council of the Republic. In April 1993 Kamougué was named minister of civil service and labor in the Moungar government, retaining the post until May 1994.

Kamougué was the runner-up to President Déby in the first round of the June 1996 presidential election, earning a reported 12.4 percent of the votes. Although the URD leader alleged major irregularities had occurred in that balloting, he ultimately agreed to stand against Déby in the second round, in which he was credited with 30.9 percent of the votes. Kamougué's strong performance in the 1996 race established him and the URD as the nation's leading opposition force, particularly in view of its strong southern support. The URD finished second to the MPS in the 1997 legislative balloting with 29 seats. Kamougué was elected president of the new assembly, and the URD subsequently participated in MPS-led cabinets. In the 2001 presidential election Kamougué received 6 percent of the vote. The URD, which won 3 seats in the 2002 assembly poll, subsequently moved into the opposition camp to protest various constitutional changes engineered by the MPS.

Leaders: Lt. Col. Wadal Abdelkader KAMOUGUÉ (1996 and 2001 presidential candidate and Former President of the National Assembly), Sangde NGARNOUDJIBE (Secretary General).

National Union for Development and Renewal (*Union National pour le Développement et le Renouvellement*—UNDR). The UNDR is led by Saleh Kebzabo, who was a minister of public works and transportation in the Moungar government and ran third in the first round of the June 1996 presidential election with 8.6 percent of the vote. He subsequently announced the UNDR's alliance with the MPS and threw his support to President Déby for the second round, thereby earning appointment to the cabinet formed in August. The party won 15 seats in the 1997 legislative poll, reportedly participating in an electoral alliance with the MPS. News reports surrounding recent political activity described the UNDR as primarily representing the interests of Muslims in the southwest of Chad.

Kebzabo was named minister of mines, energy, and oil in January 1998, but he and two UNDR secretaries of state left the government four months later. However, Kebzabo and four UNDR colleagues were named ministers in the December 1999 cabinet reshuffle. Kebzabo ran for president

in 2001 but received only 7 percent of the vote. The UNDR won six seats in the 2000 assembly poll and was subsequently referenced as being firmly in the opposition camp.

Leader: Saleh KEBZABO (President and 2001 presidential candidate).

National Alliance for Development (*Alliance Nationale pour le Développement*—AND). Nabia NDALI, a member of the AND, was named minister of civil service and labor in the May 1992 cabinet. However, he resigned two months later following a dispute between AND leaders and Prime Minister Yodeyman, who was initially described as "close" to the AND but was subsequently reported to have been formally expelled from the group.

The AND was initially reported to have won no seats in the 1997 assembly balloting but, following a review by the national electoral commission, it was subsequently awarded two. AND President Salibou Garba was a member of the cabinet from May 1994 to April 2002, although he was subsequently referenced as a leader of the opposition's CPDC.

Leader: Salibou GARBA (President).

Rally for Democracy and Progress (*Rassemblement pour la Démocratie et le Progrès*—RDP). The RDP held its organizational congress in December 1991, its leadership including the mayor of N'Djamena, Lol Mahamat Choua, who had been proposed as president of an eventually aborted provisional national government in 1979. A number of RDP members were reportedly among those killed or arrested by Chadian security forces during the crackdown that followed the coup attempt of January 1992. (It was believed that the RDP was subjected to reprisal because of the support it enjoyed among the Kanem ethnic group, centered in the Lake Chad area, where the rebels had apparently received popular assistance.) Nevertheless, the RDP in early March was one of the first political parties to be legalized and was considered one of the leading components of the opposition coalition prior to the designation of Choua as chair of the Higher Transitional Council (CST) in April 1993.

In October 1994 Choua was replaced as CST chair, the RDP leader subsequently accusing the Déby regime of human rights violations, including the harassment of many RDP members. Choua was credited with 5.9 percent of the vote in the first round of the 1996 presidential election. In a surprise development, Choua supported President Déby in the 2001 presidential election.

The RDP secured 14 seats in the 2002 assembly balloting and subsequently supported the Déby administration and served in the cabinet until November 2003, when it withdrew from the government to protest Déby's announced plans to seek a third term. Choua subsequently served as a prominent figure in the anti-Déby CPDC.

Leaders: Lol Mahamat CHOUA (Former Chair of the Higher Transitional Council), Chetti Ali ABBAS.

Front of Action Forces for the Republic (*Front des Forces d'Action pour la République—* FFAR). Described as a "separatist" grouping, the FFAR won one seat in the 1997 legislative balloting. Its legislator, Ngarledjy Yorongar, subsequently became a prominent critic of government policy regarding the development of oil fields in southern Chad. He received a surprising 14 percent of the vote while finishing second in the 2001 presidential election. Although Yorongar called for a boycott of the 2005 constitutional referendum and the 2006 presidential poll, he and the FFAR did not participate in the CPDC.

Leaders: Yorongar LEMOHIBAN, Ngarledjy YORONGAR (2001 presidential candidate).

National Assembly for Democracy and Progress (*Rassemblement National pour la Démocratie et le Progrès—*RNDP). Formed in the spring of 1992, the RNDP (also regularly referenced as VIVA-RNDP) was subsequently described as a prominent exponent of the formation of opposition coalitions; its leader, Delwa Kassiré Koumakoyé, served as spokesman for a number of such groups. Koumakoyé was named justice minister in the reshuffled transitional government announced in June 1993 and was elected prime minister in

November. Following his dismissal in April 1995, Koumakoyé charged that he had been made a scapegoat by President Déby and the Higher Transitional Council, whom he described as bearing true responsibility for the delay in national elections.

In March 1996 Koumakoyé was sentenced to three months in prison for the illegal possession of weapons, the RNDP leader accusing the Déby regime of manufacturing the charge in order to thwart his presidential ambitions. The following September it was announced that Koumakoyé had been named spokesperson for a new opposition alliance called the Democratic Opposition Convention, which claimed the allegiance of more than 20 parties. The RNDP was initially credited with having secured four seats in the 1997 legislative poll, but all were given to other parties following the review by the national electoral commission. Koumakoyé won 2 percent of the votes in the 2001 presidential poll.

The RNDP has served in all cabinets since the 2002 assembly balloting, at which it won five seats. Koumakoyé, now considered to be aligned with Déby, was one of five candidates in the 2006 presidential election; he finished second with 8.8 percent of the vote.

Leader: Delwa Kassiré KOUMAKOYÉ (Former Prime Minister, President of the Party, and 2001 and 2006 presidential candidate).

National Union (*Union National—*UN). The UN was established in early 1992 by Abdoulaye Lamana, a former Chadian ambassador to Belgium. Its members reportedly included a number of former Frolinat adherents, notably Mahamat Djarma, former deputy to Frolinat leader Goukhouni Oueddei. An April 1996 party congress selected Lamana as its presidential nominee, the UN chair finishing well down the list among the 15 candidates in the first round of balloting. According to initial reports, the party won two seats in the 1997 legislative balloting, but they were taken away following the postelection review by the national electoral commission. Lamana was named minister of mines, energy, and oil in May 1998 but was not included in the reshuffled cabinet announced in December 1999. In 2005 Lamana was reportedly serving as chair of the government-appointed committee established to oversee the allocation of oil revenues.

Leaders: Abdoulaye LAMANA (Chair), Mahamat DJARMA.

Other minor parties that gained a single seat in the National Assembly in the 2002 election included **Action for the Renewal of Chad** (*Action pour le Renouvellement du Tchad*—ART), led by Oumar BOUCHAR; the **Chadian Social Democratic Party** (*Parti Social-Démocrate du Tchad*—PSDT), a southern grouping led by businessman Niabe ROMAIN; the **Convention for Democracy and Federalism** (*Convention pour la Démocratie et le Fédéralisme*—CDF), led by Ali GOLHOR; the **National Rally for Democracy in Chad–Le Réveil** (*Rassemblement National pour la Démocratie au Tchad–Le Réveil*—RNDT-Le Réveil), whose leader, Albert Pahimi PADACKET, was appointed agriculture minister in 2005 and was a presidential candidate in 2006; the **Party for Democracy and Integral Independence** (*Parti pour la Démocratie et l'Indépendance Intégrale*—PDI); the **People's Movement for Democracy in Chad** (*Mouvement Populaire pour la Démocratie au Tchad*—MPDT) whose leader, Mahamat ABDOULAYE, was appointed to the cabinet in 2005 and was a presidential candidate in 2006; and the **Rally for the Republic–LINGUA** (*Rassemblement pour la République*–LINGUA—RPR-LINGUA), led by Mersile Atti MAHAMAT.

Other Parties

Action for Unity and Socialism (*Action pour l'Unité et le Socialisme*—Actus). Actus is a former GUNT tendency that in March 1990 announced it was regrouping with the **Revolutionary Movement of the Chadian People** (*Mouvement Révolutionnaire du Peuple Tchadien*—MRPT), another GUNT faction led by Bire TITINAN, to form a joint **Rally for Democratic Action and Progress** (*Rassemblement pour l'Action Démocratique et le Progrès*—RADP). However, Actus leader Dr.

Fidèle Moungar was appointed to the May 1992 cabinet under his own formation's rubric, not that of the RADP. Dr. Moungar was subsequently named to form a transitional government in April 1993, although he was forced to resign as prime minister in October following passage of a nonconfidence motion by the Higher Transitional Council. The Actus leader was disqualified from running for president in 1996 by the Chadian Court of Appeal on the ground that he did not meet the nation's residency requirements. Actus was at first reported to have won four seats in the 1997 legislative poll, but that number was ultimately halved by the national electoral commission. There has subsequently been little reference to Actus in news reports.

Leader: Dr. Fidèle MOUNGAR (Former Prime Minister).

Union for Democracy and the Republic (*Union pour la Démocratie et la République*—UDR). The UDR was launched by Jean Alingué Bawoyeu in March 1992 and formally recognized a month later. Although Alingué Bawoyeu was replaced as prime minister in May, the new cabinet included Djimasta KOIBLA, another UDR member. However, after being named prime minister in April 1995, Koibla was subsequently described as having taken a leave of absence from the party. Meanwhile, the UDR moved into a position as one of the main opposition parties, Alingué Bawoyeu receiving 8.3 percent of the vote in the first round of the 1996 presidential election. He also was one of the main critics of the government's involvement in the Democratic Republic of the Congo in 1998 and 1999. Alingué Bawoyeu ran for president in 2001, receiving only 2 percent of the ballots cast. The UDR boycotted the 2002 legislative elections, and Alingué Bawoyeu subsequently remained a vocal critic of the government and proponent of formation of opposition coalitions.

Leader: Dr. Jean ALINGUÉ BAWOYEU (President of the Party and 2001 presidential candidate).

Party for Freedom and Development (*Parti pour la Liberté et le Développement*—PLD). Formed in late 1993 to promote the "rehabilitation" of Chad, the PLD captured three seats in the

1997 legislative elections. The PLD's candidate, Ibni Oumar Mahamat Saleh, secured 3 percent of the vote in the 2001 presidential election. The PLD boycotted the 2002 legislative elections. Saleh subsequently served as a spokesman for the CPDC.

Leaders: Ibni Oumar Mahamat SALEH (2001 presidential candidate), Paul SARADORI.

National Convention for Social Democracy (*Convention National pour la Démocratie Sociale—CNDS*). The leader of the CNDS, former Habré minister Adoum Moussa Seif, won 4.9 percent of the vote in the first round of the 1996 presidential election, and the party won one seat in the 1997 legislative balloting. In 1998, however, Seif was described in news reports as heading a rebel group in the Lake Chad region, the Armed Resistance Against Anti-Democratic Forces. The rump CNDS, under the leadership of Adoum Daye ZERE, supported President Déby in his 2001 re-election campaign and has not been regularly referenced in subsequent news reports.

National Salvation Council for Peace and Democracy (*Conseil de Salut National pour la Paix et la Démocratie—CSNPD*). The southern-based CSNPD was founded in mid-1992 by ex-soldiers who had recently defected from the nation's northern-dominated military. An estimated 200 CSNPD supporters were reportedly killed by government troops in early 1993, and sporadic fighting continued into 1994. In mid-1994 the CSNPD and the government concluded a peace agreement providing for a cease-fire and the integration of CSNPD officers into the national army. Collaterally, the CSNPD was declared to be a legal party. One member, Baihon Maloum ELOI, was minister of mines, energy, and petroleum from December 1994 to April 1995, while CSNPD leader Col. Moise Nodji KETTE also served in the cabinet from April 1995 to April 1996.

Union of Democratic Forces (*Union des Forces Démocratiques—UFD*). The UFD also was one of the minor parties represented in the May 1992 coalition government, although its subsequent relationship with the government was un-

clear. News reports suggested a connection between the UFD and the kidnapping of four French nationals in Chad in 1998.

Leader: Ngawara NAHOR.

National Alliance for Democracy and Renewal (*Alliance Nationale pour la Démocratie et le Renouveau—ANDR*). The ANDR was founded in early 1993 by Prime Minister Yodeyman in the wake of his estrangement from the AND.

Leader: Joseph YODEYMAN (Former Prime Minister).

Rally of the Chadian People (*Rassemblement du Peuple Tchadien—RPT*). The RPT was legalized in April 1992, and one of its members, Jeremie BEADE TOIRIA, was appointed minister of commerce and industry in the coalition cabinet announced in May. However, at the urging of his party, Beade Toiria resigned the post in October to protest the government's temporary ban on trade union activities.

Leader: Dangbe LAOBELE DAMAYE.

Convention of Chadian Social Democrats (*Convention des Social-Démocrates Tchadiens—CSDT*). The CSDT was established in April 1992 to promote establishment of a "new Chad" in which national unity would provide "peace and security in a country beset by internal wars for far too long." Several former Habré cabinet ministers were reportedly among its members. The CSDT supported President Déby in the 2001 election.

Leader: Younous IBEDOU.

Alliance for Chadian Democracy (*Alliance pour la Démocratie du Tchad—Adet*). Based in Paris, Adet was established in April 1992 by Tidjani Thiam, described as a petroleum trader with links to several regional states, including Libya. In late 1993 the organization, also referenced as the Democratic Alliance (*Alliance Démocratique—AD*), announced it had formed a coalition with two other expatriate groupings—the **Democratic National Union** (*Union National Démocratique—UND*), led by Facho BALAAM; and the **Democratic Revolutionary Council–Rejection Front** (*Conseil Démocratique Révolutionnaire–Front du*

Rejet—CDR-FR), led by Gaileth Bourkou MAN-DAH.

Leader: Tidjani THIAM.

Also active have been the **African Party for Progress and Social Justice** (*Parti Africain pour le Progrès et la Justice Sociale*—PAPJS), led by Neatobei Didier VALENTIN; the **Chadian Democratic Rally** (*Rassemblement Démocratique du Tchad*—RDT); the **Democratic Revolutionary Council** (*Conseil Démocratique Révolutionnaire*—CDR), led by Aboubakar Adzalo BARRAKA and former foreign minister Acheikh ibn OUMAR; the **Democratic Union for Chadian Progress** (*Union Démocratique pour le Progrès Tchadien*—UDPT), led by Elie ROMBA, who was among the also-rans in the 1996 presidential election; the **National Alliance for Progress and Development** (*Alliance Nationale pour le Progrés et le Développement*—ANPD); the **National Alliance for Solidarity and Democracy** (*Alliance Nationale pour la Solidarité et la Démocratie*—ANSD), formed in 1997 under the leadership of Mang Igri TAIDA; the **National Movement of Chadian Renovators** (*Mouvement National des Rénovateurs Tchadiens*—MNRT), led by Ali Muhammad DIALLO; the **New African Socialist** (*Socialiste Africain Rénové*—SAR), which fielded a candidate, Ibrahim KOULAMALLAH, in the 2006 presidential election; the **People's Action for Unity and Development** (*Action du Peuple pour l'Unité et le Développement*—APUD), which was registered in March 1996 under the leadership of Beshir Disco HAMAT; the **Rally for Development and Progress** (*Rassemblement pour le Développement et le Progrès*), led by Mamadou BISSO; the **Rally for Progress and Social Justice** (*Rassemblement pour le Progrès et la Justice Sociale*—RPJS), registered in January 1996 and the first Chadian party to be led by a woman (Leopoldine Adoun NDARADOUNRY); the **Rally of Chadian Nationalists** (*Rassemblement des Nationalistes Tchadiennes*—RNT); the **Revolutionary Council of the Chadian People** (*Conseil Révolutionnaire du Peuple Tchadien*—CRPT), led by Harmed JACOB; the **Socialist**

Movement for Democracy in Chad (*Mouvement Socialiste pour la Démocratie au Tchad*—MSDT), led by Albert Mbainaido DJOMIA; and the **Union of Democratic Forces–Republican Party** (*Union des Forces Démocratiques–Parti Républicain*—UFD-PR), led by Gali Gatta NGOTHE.

Other Groups

United Front for Change (*Front Uni pour le Changement*—FUC). The FUC was formed in December 2005 by the **Rally for Democracy and Liberties** (*Rassemblement pour la Démocratie et les Libertés*—RDL) and a number of other groups, some of which comprised deserters from the Chadian army as well as Chadian exiles in Sudan opposed to the recent constitutional changes and the "dictatorial rule" of President Déby. The RDL had been formed earlier in the year in the Darfur region of Sudan and had launched an unsuccessful attack on the Chadian city of Adré near the Sudanese border on December 18. RDL leader Mahamat Nour, who had branched out of the ANR (below), was instrumental in the organization of the FUC, which demanded the convening of a national forum to address the country's political future, the installation of a transitional government, and new elections. (Nour is a member of the Tama ethnic group, which reportedly led to leadership tension within the FUC, a predominantly Zakawa grouping.) The FUC, also referenced as the United Front for Democratic Change, attempted a military takeover of the government in April 2006, the Déby government alleging that the Sudanese government was supporting the FUC (see Current issues, above, for additional information).

Leaders: Mahamat NOUR, Col. Regis BECHIR.

Platform for Change, National Unity, and Democracy (*Socle pour le Changement, l'Unité, et la Démocratie*—SCUD). The SCUD was formed in October 2005 by a group of some 300 deserters from the Presidential Guard and other government forces. It reportedly attracted members of Déby's Zakawa clan, including members of his family such as Tom Erdimi (Déby's nephew and a former cabinet minister), who no longer supported the president. SCUD forces reportedly subsequently engaged government troops in eastern Chad, but the SCUD did not participate in the failed April 2006 attack on N'Djamena led by the FUC.

Leaders: Tom ERDIMI, Timan ERDIMI, Yaya Dilla DJEROU.

Movement for Democracy and Justice in Chad (*Mouvement pour la Démocratie et la Justice en Tchad*—MDJT). Led then by Youssef TOGOIMI, a former minister in the Déby administration, the MDJT launched guerrilla activity against government troops in late 1998 in northern Chad and by April 1999 was claiming control of substantial territory. It was still active in mid-2001, although there was little independently verifiable information on the breadth and scope of its activities. The government was sufficiently concerned about the MDJT to periodically issue communiqués minimizing the extent of the rebellion. The grouping reportedly draws its support from the Toubou ethnic group, described as a "traditional warrior community" in the Tibesti mountain region along the border with Niger. President Déby met with Togoimi in Libya in early 2001, but no agreement resulted. In 2002 Togoimi was killed by a land mine, and one faction of the MDJT left the group to participate in the formation of the FUDP (below). The government subsequently was reported to have negotiated a cease-fire with a number of local MDJT commanders, and a broader accord was brokered in January 2003, many MDJT elements reportedly accepting amnesty for an end to attacks. In August 2005 the government signed a final agreement with the MDJT that provided for the eventual integration of remaining MDJT fighters into the national army.

Leader: Col. Hassan Abdallah MARDIGUE.

United Front for Democracy and Peace (*Front Uni pour la Démocratie et la Paix*—FUDP). Formed in 2005 by dissidents from the MDJT as well as members of rebel groups based in Benin seeking a negotiated peace settlement, the FUDP subsequently was joined by a number of other parties and rebel groups, including the MDD.

Movement for Development and Democracy (*Mouvement pour le Développement et la Démocratie*—MDD). The MDD was formed in 1991 as the political arm of pro-Habré rebel forces, which in late December launched an attempted overthrow of the Déby regime from the western border, where they had been camped since Habré's ouster a year earlier. Although the government at first estimated the MDD strength at more than 3,000, it was subsequently reported that only about 500 had participated in the attempted coup. Following the rebel defeat in January 1992, MDD leaders alleged that some of its members had been "kidnapped" from Nigeria by Chadian troops and executed in N'Djamena. Although a spokesman initially claimed that MDD leader Goukhouni Guët had been among those killed, the Chadian government subsequently reported that he was alive but imprisoned.

Despite the highly publicized announcement of several peace agreements during the rest of 1992, fighting continued between government troops and MDD followers, who sometimes referred to themselves as the Western Armed Forces (*Forces Armées Occidentales*—FAO). In early 1993 the MDD was reportedly split into a pro-Habré faction known as the National Armed Forces of Chad (*Forces Armées Nationales Tchadiennes*—FANT), led by Mahamat Saleh FADIL, and an anti-Habré faction loyal to Guët, about whom no further information was forthcoming. Members of the latter faction were reportedly invited to the Sovereign National Conference that began in January, but the FANT, described by *Africa Confidential* as "much feared in N'Djamena by both government and opposition," remained outside the national reconciliation process.

In January 1994 the MDD announced an alliance with another guerrilla group, the **National Union for Democracy and Socialism** (*Union National pour la Démocratie et le Socialisme*—UNDS), and called upon other anti-Déby rebels to join them in united military activity. A year later, however, the MDD was described as still split into two factions "fighting each other, not Déby." Meanwhile, Habré remained in exile in Senegal, the general amnesty of December 1994 having specifically excluded him.

The apparent reunification of the MDD factions was reported in April 1995, and an extraordinary congress in August elected a new 16-member executive bureau headed by Mahamat Seïd Moussa Medella. Subsequently, in November, an agreement was announced between the government and the MDD calling for the cessation of hostilities, exchange of prisoners, and the integration of some MDD guerrillas into the national army. Some MDD fighters subsequently remained in conflict with government forces, however, and factionalization on that issue surfaced within the grouping again in 1998. The MDD joined the FUDP in 2003. By that time there were two main factions of the MDD: one led by Ibrahim Malla Mahamet, the other led by Issa Faki Mahamet.

Leaders: Goukhouni GUËT (in detention), Aboubarkaye HAROUN (Representative in Paris), Ibrahim Malla MAHAMET (Chair of the Executive Bureau).

Chad National Liberation Front (*Front de Libération National Tchadien*—Frolinat). Frolinat was established in 1966 by northerners opposed to the administration of President Tombalbaye, a southerner. The organization eventually suffered such severe factionalization that Frolinat became little more than a generic name for various groups originally based in the north, including splinters loyal to subsequent Chadian presidents Goukhouni Oueddei and Hissène Habré.

Following Habré's capture of N'Djamena in 1982, most of the factions opposed to his Frolinat/FAN coalesced under a reconstituted GUNT. During 1983 and 1984, dissent among GUNT factions over the extent of Libyan involvement led to reported dissolution of the coalition, although pronouncements continued to be issued in its name. During a meeting in Sebha, Libya, on August 7, 1984, most of the pro-Libyan military components of GUNT joined in forming the National Council

of Liberation (*Conseil National de la Libération*—CNL), which was succeeded by a more inclusive Supreme Revolutionary Council (*Conseil Supréme de la Révolution*—CSR) a year later. By 1986, however, anti-Libyan sentiment appeared to have gained the ascendancy, with Oueddei being removed as CSR chair (and president of GUNT) in November. Thereafter, the CSR declined in importance, many of its component groups having announced their dissolution and acceptance of integration into UNIR. Although Oueddei announced a cabinet reshuffle in May 1988 in an attempt to consolidate his position among remaining GUNT factions, he was described in mid-1990 as "essentially marginalized" as an antigovernment influence.

Continuing to position himself as the leader of Frolinat, Oueddei made a highly publicized return from exile to meet with President Déby in May 1991 and suggested that cooperation with the new regime was possible if opposition political parties were permitted. Subsequently, however, Oueddei returned to Algiers and, following the abortive October coup, was reportedly informed that he was again not welcome in his homeland. During an interview in mid-1992 Oueddei described Frolinat as "still an armed liberation movement" but one that was "currently not fighting" and dedicated, for the time being, to "resolving problems through dialogue." Oueddei, described as remaining widely respected by the public and considered a potential mediator among Chad's many ethnic and political adversaries, participated in the Sovereign National Conference in early 1993. Although he was reported in 1995 to be still harboring presidential ambitions, there was little evidence of his influence in the nation's 1996 democratization process. In December 1998 Oueddei issued a statement in Algiers calling for an "uprising" against the Déby government, and in early 1999 Frolinat announced its support for the Toubou rebels in northern Chad.

Leaders: Goukhouni OUEDDEI (Former President of the Republic), Mahmoud Ali MAHMOUD.

Armed Forces for a Federal Republic (*Forces Armées pour une République Fédérale*—FARF). A guerrilla movement based in oil-rich southern Chad, the FARF signed a peace accord with the government in April 1997, but fighting broke out again the following October, triggering what some observers described as a violent crackdown by the government against civilians in that region. A new peace agreement was reached in May 1998, under which FARF forces were to be integrated into the national army. In addition, the FARF was scheduled to transform itself into a political party called the Forum of Alliances for the Federal Republic (*Forum des Alliances pour le République Fédérale*—also FARF). However, it was announced in December that the FARF had in fact joined the MPS; that decision was reported by Dienambaye BARDÉ, brother of the popular FARF leader Lookein BARDÉ, who was believed to have died in the early 1998 fighting.

Chadian National Front (*Front National du Tchad*—FNT). A rebel force operating in central and eastern Chad, the FNT signed a peace agreement with the government in October 1992 under which its members were to be integrated into official civilian and military positions and the group was to be considered for formal party status. However, some of the rebels rejected the integration scheme, and renewed fighting was reported between them and government forces in late 1993 and much of 1994. Another peace accord was announced in late 1994, under which the FNT was to be integrated in the Chadian army. Once again, however, some FNT elements challenged the authority of those who had signed the agreement on behalf of the Front. In 2003 dissident members of the FNT joined the United Front for Democracy and Peace (see above).

Leader: Alarit BACHAR (Secretary General).

National Council for Chadian Recovery (*Conseil National de Redressement du Tchad*—CNRT). The CNRT was established under the leadership of Col. Abbas KOTY, a former member of the Déby cabinet who fled the country in mid-1992 after the regime charged him with plotting a government takeover. The CNRT subsequently initiated guerrilla operations in southern Chad, but Colonel Koty returned to the country in August

1993 for reconciliation talks. An agreement was announced in mid-October whereby the rebellion was to be terminated and the CNRT converted to a legal party. However, several days later Colonel Koty was killed by security forces trying to arrest him for allegedly planning a coup attempt. The CNRT subsequently strongly denied the charges, but his successors, including his brother Hisséne Koty, ordered the resumption of military activity in the wake of the government's "murder" of their leader.

Leaders: Hisséne KOTY (President), Idriss Agar BICHARA.

National Alliance of Resistance (*Alliance Nationale de la Résistance*—ANR). Formed in the mid-1990s by five rebel groups, the ANR grew to include eight antigovernment groups operating in the eastern part of the country. The ANR signed a peace agreement with the government in January 2003 with a long-term plan to transition to a formal political party, and Col. Mahamat GARFA (an ANR founder) joined the MPS-led cabinet later in the year. However, one faction of the ANR refused to accept the cease-fire and continued fighting under the leadership of Mahamat Nour (see FUC, above).

Legislature

As provided for in the constitution approved by national referendum in December 1989, a 123-member unicameral National Assembly (*Assemblée Nationale*) was elected by direct universal suffrage for a five-year term on July 8, 1990. However, the assembly was dissolved on December 3 upon the overthrow of the Habré regime. Subsequently, President Déby appointed a Provisional Council of the Republic (*Conseil Provisoire de la République*) to serve as an interim consultative body, which in turn was replaced by a 57-member Higher Transitional Council (*Conseil Supérieur de Transition*—CST) elected by the CNS in April 1993. The national constitutional referendum in March 1996 authorized the CST to continue to function pending the installation of the new

Cabinet

As of May 1, 2006

Prime Minister	Pascal Yoadimnadji

Minister of State

Infrastructure	Adam Younousmi

Ministers

Agriculture	Albert Pahimi Padacket
Assistant Secretary General to the Government	Mariam Ali Moussa [f]
Civil Service, Labor, and Job Promotion	Fatime Kimto [f]
Commerce, Industry and Handicrafts	Ngarmbatina Carmel Sou [f]
Communication and Government Spokesman	Hourmadj Moussa Doumngor
Decentralization (in the Prime Minister's Office)	Mahamat Abdoulaye
Environment and Water	Hissene Ahmat Senoussi
Finance and Economy	Abbas Mahamat Tolli
Foreign Affairs and African Integration	Ahmad Allammi
Justice and Guardian of the Seals	Edouard Ngarta Mbaihoroum
Livestock	Mahamat Allamine Bourma Tréyé
Mines and Energy	Yousouf Abassaiah
Oil	Mahamat Hassan Nasser
Planning, Economy, and Cooperation	Mahamat Ali Hassan
Posts and Telecommunications	Mahamat Garfa
Primary and Secondary Education	Mahamat Maouloud Izzadine
Public Health	Moussa Kadam
Regional Administration	Mahamat Ali Abdallah Nassour
Secretary General to the Government	Djividi Boukar
Security and Immigration	Brig.-Gen. Routouang Yoma Golom
Social Action and Family	Hassan Terab [f]
State Control and Morals	Mahamat Bechir Okormi
Territorial Development, Urban Planning, and Housing	Chene Adoum [f]
Tourist Development	Oumar Kadjallami Boukar
Youth and Sports	Oumar Boukar

Ministers Delegate

Delegate to the President for National Defense	Bichara Issa Djadallah
Economy and Finance	Nadjaita Marangaye
Foreign Affairs and African Integration	Dillah Lucien
Higher Education, Scientific Research, and Professional Training	Oumar Idriss al-Faroukh
Transport (in the Ministry of Infrastructure)	Emmanuel Nadinger

[f] = female

bicameral legislature. Elections (for a four-year term) to the new 125-member **National Assembly** were held on January 5 and February 23, 1997. In February 2001 the assembly extended its mandate until at least April 2002.

Following the election to an expanded 155-member assembly on April 21, 2002, and subsequent by-election for 3 seats, it was reported that the Patriotic Salvation Movement held 108 seats; the Rally for Democracy and Progress, 14; the Front of Action Forces for the Republic, 10; the National Union for Development and Renewal, 6; the National Assembly for Democracy and Progress, 5; the Union for Renewal and Democracy, 3; and Action for the Renewal of Chad, the Chadian Social Democratic Party, the Convention for Democracy and Federalism, the National Alliance for Development, the National Rally for Democracy in Chad–Le Réveil, the National Union, the Party for Democracy and Integral Independence, the People's Movement for Democracy in Chad, and the Rally for the Republic–LINGUA, 1 each. In January 2006 the assembly voted to postpone new elections (scheduled for April 2006) until at least April 2007.

President: Nassour Guelengdouksia OUAÏDOU.

Note: The constitutional revision approved bynational referendum on June 6, 2005, eliminated references to the Senate, which hadnever been filled since being provided for in the 1996 constitution. The legislaturethereby formally became a unicameral body.

Communications

The Ministry of Information controls most media.

Press

The following are published in N'Djamena: *Info-Tchad*, daily bulletin of the official news agency, ATP; *Al-Watan*, government weekly; *N'Djamena-Hebdo* (10,000), independent weekly; *L'Observateur* (10,000), independent weekly; *Le Temps*, independent weekly. Journalists from *L'Observateur* and *Le Temps* were arrested in the first half of 2005 for articles critical of the administration, prompting strong protest from domestic and international journalism organizations.

News Agencies

The domestic agency is *Agence Tchadienne de Presse* (ATP). *Agence France-Presse* and Reuters also maintain offices in N'Djamena.

Broadcasting and Computing

Radiodiffusion Nationale Tchadienne (RNT) broadcasts in French, Arabic, and local languages, while an independent radio station, *Radio Liberté*, began operations in June 2000. However, in October 2002 the station was suspended following critical reports about the president; it resumed broadcasting in December 2003. In April 2006, the government announced that private media companies could provide broadcasts of election coverage, subject to monitoring by the High Commission for Communication. *Télé-Chad* transmits from N'Djamena to some 12,850 TV sets. As of 2003, some 14,000 personal computers served 15,000 Internet users.

Intergovernmental Representation

Ambassador to the U.S.
Mahamoud Adam BECHIR

U.S. Ambassador to Chad
Marc McGowan WALL

Permanent Representative to the UN
Mahamat Ali ADOUM

IGO Memberships (Non-UN)
AfDB, AU, BADEA, BDEAC, CEEAC, CEMAC, CILSS, IDB, Interpol, NAM, OAU, OIC, OIF, WCO, WTO

COMORO ISLANDS

UNION OF THE COMOROS

Union des Comores (French)

The Country

Located in the Indian Ocean between Madagascar and the eastern coast of Africa, the Union of the Comoros consists of three main islands: Ngazidja (Grande Comore), site of the capital, Moroni; Nzwani (Anjouan); and Mwali (Mohéli). A fourth component of the archipelago, Mahoré (Mayotte), is claimed as national territory but remains under French administration. The indigenous inhabitants in the Comoros derive from a mixture of Arab, Malagasy, and African strains; Islam is the state religion.

Volcanic in origin, the islands are mountainous, with a climate that is tropical during the rainy season and more temperate during the dry season. There are no significant mineral resources, and soil conditions vary, being comparatively rich on Mayotte and substantially poorer on the more populous islands of Nzwani and Ngazidja. Economically, the islands have long suffered from an overemphasis on the production of export crops, such as vanilla, cloves, olives, and perfume essences—the latter shipped primarily to France—and an insufficient cultivation of foods, particularly rice, needed for local consumption. Only a small percentage of the population is engaged in salaried work, and the government remains highly dependent on foreign assistance to cover administrative and developmental expenses as well as trade deficits. Development has been severely hampered since independence in 1975 by some 20 coups or coup attempts, sustained interisland conflict, and widespread corruption.

Per-capita annual income (about $380) declined in the 1990s, while real GDP growth was marginal throughout most of the decade before falling by 1.1 percent in 2000 in the wake of severe political uncertainty following a bloodless military coup in April 1999. The turmoil also depressed tourism, impeded government economic plans, and precipitated a sharp decline in donor support. However, the international community pledged substantial aid in 2002 in response to negotiations that had led to the establishment of the Union of the Comoros (see Political background, below), which proponents hoped would, among other things, resolve separatist pressures on Nzwani. The World Bank and the European Union (EU) coordinated

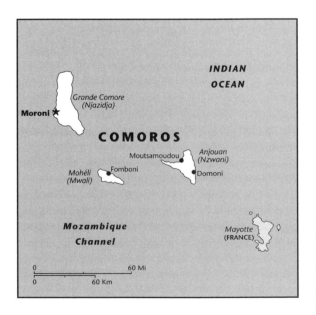

Political Status: Former French dependency; proclaimed independent July 6, 1975; Federal Islamic Republic of the Comoros proclaimed in constitution approved by national referendum on October 1, 1978; constitution of October 20, 1996, suspended following military coup of April 30, 1999; new constitution providing for the Union of the Comoros adopted by national referendum on December 23, 2001.

Area: 718 sq. mi. (1,860 sq. km.), excluding the island of Mahoré (Mayotte), which was retained as a "Territorial Collectivity" by France in 1976 and redesignated a French "Departmental Collectivity" in 2001.

Population: 446,817 (1991C), excluding an estimated 50,740 residents of Mahoré; 840,000 (2005E), excluding Mahoré.

Major Urban Centers (2005E): MORONI (Ngazidja [Grande Comore], 43,000), Mutsamudu (Nzwani [Anjouan], 24,000), Fomboni (Mwali [Mohéli], 13,000).

Official Languages: Arabic, French (a majority speaks Comorian, a mixture of Arabic and Swahili).

Monetary Unit: Comoros Franc (official rate July 1, 2006: 384.76 francs = $1US). (Previously pegged to the French franc, the Comoros franc is now permanently pegged to the euro at 491.968 francs = 1 euro.)

President of the Union: Ahmed Abdallah Mohamed SAMBI (National Front for Justice); elected in Union-wide runoff election on May 14, 2006, and inaugurated for a four-year term on May 26 in succession to Col. Assoumani AZALI.

Vice Presidents of the Union: Ikililou DHOININE (Mwali) and Idi NADHOIM (Ngazidja); elected on May 14, 2006, and inaugurated on May 26 for term concurrent with that of the president, succeeding Rachid Ben MASSOUNDI (Mwali) and Mohamed Caabi El YACHROUTU (Nzwani).

President of Mwali (Mohéli): Mohamed Saïd FAZUL; elected in runoff balloting on the island of Mwali on April 7, 2002, and inaugurated for a five-year term on May 19.

President of Ngazidja (Grande Comore): Abdou Soule ELBAK; elected in runoff balloting on the island of Ngazidja on May 19, 2002, and inaugurated for a five-year term on May 29.

President of Nzwani (Anjouan): Col. Mohamed BACAR; elected in first-round balloting on the island of Nzwani on March 31, 2002, and subsequently inaugurated for a five-year term.

the "Friends of Comoros" to support the transition. However, the International Monetary Fund (IMF) rejected a request from the Comoros for additional assistance, citing continued power-sharing contention between the island governments and the Union government. GDP grew by only 2.1 percent in 2003 and 1.9 percent in 2004, in part due to declining vanilla prices, while inflation rose to 4.5 percent in 2004.

In 2005 the IMF began a one-year monitoring program to see if the Union government could qualify for badly needed debt reduction through an announced plan of privatization, tax reform, and cessation of government control of commodity prices. The monitoring program was subsequently extended until June 2006, international donors (led by France) having pledged an additional $280 million in aid pending the IMF's review of a proposed Comoran poverty-reduction program.

Government and Politics

Political Background

Ruled for centuries by Arab sultans and first visited by Europeans in the 16th century, the Comoro archipelago came under French rule in the 19th century: Mayotte became a French protectorate in 1843; Anjouan, Grande Comore, and Mohéli were added in 1886. In 1912 the islands were joined administratively with Madagascar, from where they were governed until after World War II. Because of the lengthy period of indirect rule, the Comoros suffered comparative neglect, as contrasted with the nearby island of Réunion, which became an overseas French department in 1946.

In the wake of a 1968 student strike that was suppressed by French police and troops, France agreed to permit the formation of legal political parties in the archipelago. In December 1972, 34 of the 39 seats in the Comoran Chamber of Deputies were claimed by a coalition of proindependence parties: the Democratic Rally of the Comoran People, led by Prince Saïd Mohamed JAFFAR; the Party for the Evolution of the Comoros, which was linked to the Tanzania-based National Liberation Movement of the Comoros; and the Democratic Union of the Comoros, led by Ahmed AB-DALLAH Abderemane. The other five seats were won by the anti-independence Popular Movement of Mahoré, headed by Marcel HENRY. As a result of the election, the chamber named Abdallah president of the government, succeeding Prince Saïd IBRAHIM, co-leader, with Ali SOILIH, of the People's Party (*Umma-Mranda*), which had campaigned for a more gradual movement toward independence. The new government immediately began negotiations with Paris, and an agreement was reached in July 1973 providing for a five-year transition period during which France would retain responsibility for defense, foreign affairs, and currency. The only unresolved issue was the status of Mayotte, whose inhabitants remained strongly opposed to separation from France.

In a Comoran referendum held December 22, 1974, 95 percent of participating voters favored independence, despite a negative vote from Mayotte, where 25 percent of the registered electorate abstained. On July 6, 1975, a unilateral declaration of independence was voted by the territorial Chamber of Deputies, which designated Abdallah as head of state and prime minister. The action was timed to preempt the passage of legislation by the French National Assembly calling for an island-by-island referendum on a Comoran constitution—a procedure designed to allow Mayotte to remain under French jurisdiction. Having announced his intention to sever economic as well as political ties with France, the increasingly dictatorial Abdallah (who was visiting Anjouan at the time) was ousted on August 3 in a coup led by Ali Soilih and supported by a National United Front of several parties. On August 10 governmental power was vested in a 12-member National Executive Council headed by Prince Jaffar, who was appointed president and prime minister. In September, following an armed

invasion of Anjouan by forces under Soilih, Abdallah surrendered and was subsequently exiled. At a joint meeting of the National Executive Council and the National Council of the Revolution on January 2, 1976, Soilih was named to replace Jaffar as head of state, and the National Council of the Revolution was redesignated as the National Institutional Council. The presidency was also divorced from the premiership, and on January 6 Abdellahi MOHAMED was named to the latter post.

As president, Soilih encountered substantial resistance in attempting to mount a Chinese-style program designed to "abolish feudalism." During a month-long *"Période Noire"* in 1977, civil servants were dismissed, the regular governmental machinery temporarily dismantled, and the "people's power" vested in a 16-member National People's Committee of recent secondary-school graduates. The "revolution" also included establishment of people's committees at island, district, and local levels, despite numerous skirmishes between people's militia forces and Islamic traditionalists. Between April 1976 and January 1978, at least three unsuccessful countercoups against the regime were mounted.

During the night of May 12–13, 1978, President Soilih was ousted by a group of about 50 mercenaries under the command of Col. Bob DENARD (the alias of Gilbert BOURGEAUD), a Frenchman previously involved in rebellions elsewhere in Africa and southern Arabia. The successful coup resulted in the return of Ahmed Abdallah, who joined Mohamed AHMED as co-president of a Political-Military Directorate that also included Denard. It was subsequently reported that Soilih had been killed on May 29 in an attempt to escape from house arrest. An exclusively "political directorate" was announced on July 22 in view of the "calm" that had resulted from a decision to return to traditional Islamic principles.

Co-president Ahmed resigned on October 3, 1978, following the approval by referendum two days earlier of a new constitution that had proclaimed the establishment of the Federal Islamic Republic of the Comoros. Abdallah was thus enabled to stand as the sole candidate in balloting held October 22. Following a legislative election that concluded on December 15, Salim Ben ALI was designated prime minister, a post he continued to hold until he was dismissed by the president on January 25, 1982. His successor, Foreign Minister Ali MROUDJAE, was appointed on February 8, with the rest of the cabinet being named a week later. President Abdallah was unopposed in his bid for reelection to a second six-year term on September 30, 1984.

Amid evidence of serious dissent within the government, Abdallah, following his reelection, secured a number of constitutional amendments that abolished the position of prime minister and reduced the powers of the Federal Assembly. These actions precipitated a coup attempt by junior members of the presidential guard on March 8, 1985, while the chief executive was on a private visit to Paris. Subsequently, the Democratic Front, a Paris-based opposition group, was charged with complicity in the revolt, many of its domestic supporters being sentenced to life imprisonment in early November, although some were granted presidential amnesty at the end of the year.

At legislative balloting on March 22, 1987 (denounced as manifestly fraudulent by regime opponents), the entire slate of 42 candidates presented by President Abdallah was declared elected. Ostensibly open to any citizen wishing to compete as an independent, polls on two of the islands (Anjouan and Mohéli) involved only presidential nominees. By contrast, opposition candidates were advanced in 20 constituencies on Grande Comore.

In July 1987 the president announced that civil servants who had been dismissed for political reasons would be rehired; however, a "clarification" issued in August indicated that the policy would apply only to those suspected of complicity in the 1985 coup attempt—not to those supporting opposition candidates at the 1987 balloting. In November, the president survived another coup attempt with the assistance of Colonel Denard who, although officially retired, had remained in control of the country's small security force.

On November 4, 1989, an ostensible 92 percent of the participants in a national referendum approved a constitutional amendment permitting Abdallah to seek a third term. Little more than three weeks later, on November 27, he was assassinated in a reported clash between the Presidential Guard and forces loyal to a former army commander, Ahmed MOHAMED. Subsequent evidence suggested, however, that Abdallah had been killed by his own troops on order of Colonel Denard. Abdallah was succeeded, on an interim basis, by the president of the Supreme Court, Saïd Mohamed DJOHAR, who was elected to a regular six-year term on March 4 and 11, 1990, in the country's first contested presidential balloting since independence. Three months earlier, Denard, who denied complicity in the Abdallah assassination, was deported (in the company of some 30 other mercenaries) to South Africa, with the Presidential Guard being supplanted by a contingent of French paratroopers. The latter were credited with thwarting a coup attempt by four mercenaries allegedly linked to Mohamed TAKI Abdoulkarim, the runner-up at the March presidential poll, on the weekend of August 18–19.

On August 3, 1991, the new president of the Supreme Court, Ibrahim Ahmed HALIDI, failed in an attempt to oust Djohar by judicial impeachment and was arrested, along with a number of colleagues (they were ultimately released on December 2). Ten days later, amid mounting social unrest, public demonstrations were banned, and on August 27 a major cabinet shakeup was announced, from which the president's own party, the Comoran Union for Progress (*Union Comorienne pour le Progrès*—UCP/*Udzima*), dissociated itself.

In October 1991 five domestic participants in an Opposition Union accepted an invitation from the exiled Mohamed Taki to meet in Paris to discuss the formation of an interim government of national union and the scheduling of a National Conference. Subsequently, Taki and his associates met with Djohar in Paris, and on November 25 Taki and Djohar returned together to Moroni. On December 17 the president announced his willingness to enter into a pact of reconciliation with his opponents, on condition that they not challenge the legitimacy of his incumbency or attempt to destabilize the regime.

On December 31, upon endorsement of the pact by all of the then-recognized parties, Djohar dissolved the existing government, and on January 6, 1992, he appointed a broadly based nine-member successor, with Taki described somewhat vaguely as "coordinator of government action."

The long-sought National Conference, encompassing nearly two dozen parties, met from January 24 to April 8, 1992, and approved the draft of a new constitution, which was endorsed by a 74 percent majority in a referendum of June 7. Meanwhile, on May 8 President Djohar announced the formation of a new cabinet headed by Taki that was supposed to serve until the next election. However, following Taki's designation of a former mercenary as the country's international investment adviser, the president dismissed the government on July 4 and named a new transitional administration with no ministerial head.

On September 26, 1992, while President Djohar was visiting Paris, a group of some 30 Defense Forces officers mounted a coup attempt, which was put down the following day. Additional clashes occurred on October 13 and 21, with the president, at opposition insistence, announcing a third postponement of the legislative poll to November 8. At first-round balloting that was further deferred until November 22, only 4 of 42 seats were filled outright. A second round on November 29 was scarcely more conclusive, none of the 22 participating groups winning a majority of seats.

The vacant post of prime minister was filled on January 1, 1993, with the appointment of Ibrahim Abderemane HALIDI (not related to Ibrahim Ahmed Halidi), who announced the appointment of a 12-member cabinet five days later. A period of extreme instability ensued. On February 25 the president ordered an extensive cabinet reshuffle, and on May 19 Prime Minister Halidi was himself ousted by a parliamentary vote of no confidence for his "manifest inability to rally support" and the "inability of the government to cope with social problems." On May 25 the president called upon Saïd Ali MOHAMED to form a new government, which, however, drew support from only 13 of the 42 MPs; thus, to forestall another no-confidence

vote, the president on June 18 dissolved the assembly. Despite a declaration of support for Mohamed at the time of dissolution, Djohar dismissed him the following day, naming a former adviser, Ahmed Ben Cheikh ATTOUMANE, as his successor.

Although the constitution called for legislative balloting within 40 days of dissolution, a series of postponements delayed the poll until mid-December 1993. In the wake of the first cancellation, the president issued a decree ousting Electoral Commission members deemed hostile to the administration; a second decree established new constituency boundaries and revoked a requirement that ministers resign before standing for election. Both were branded as unconstitutional, and in early November, Djohar, in a concession to the opposition, removed the incumbent chair of the Electoral Commission.

Despite the blatant gerrymandering and other irregularities, all four individuals elected at first-round legislative balloting on December 12, 1993, were from the opposition, with the second round on December 20 characterized in one report as a "veritable masquerade." Thus, after the opposition had appeared to have swept the entire island of Anjouan, the voting was declared "null and void." The interior ministry then pronounced that government candidates had triumphed, while on Mohéli the secretary general of the presidency, whose candidacy had been formally invalidated in the first round, was permitted to contest the second. Understandably, the opposition called for cancellation of the second-round results, failing which it announced that it would participate in no further electoral activity and would take up no seats in the Federal Assembly.

On January 2, 1994, President Djohar named Mohamed Abdou MADI, secretary general of the recently launched Rally for Democracy and Renewal (*Rassemblement pour la Démocratie et le Renouveau*—RDR), to head a new government of regime supporters. In the wake of a scandal following attempted privatization of the national air carrier, *Air Comores*, coupled with a prolonged strike by schoolteachers and hospital workers, Prime Minister Madi was dismissed on October 13 and replaced by a relatively obscure education official, Halifa HOUMADI. In the ninth government change in 40 months, Houmadi was himself replaced on April 29, 1995, by former finance minister Mohamed Caabi El YACHROUTU.

The last four months of 1995 were marked by a degree of instability that was remarkable, even by Comoran standards. On the night of September 27–28 Colonel Denard reappeared as the leader of 30-odd mercenaries who, with local support, seized President Djohar and established a "military committee of transition" headed by a little-known army captain, Ayouba COMBO. Meanwhile, Prime Minister Yachroutu, who had sought refuge in the French embassy, called on France to intervene. On October 3 Combo announced that he was withdrawing in favor of Mohamed Taki Abdoulkarim and Prince Saïd Ali KEMAL as civilian joint presidents. The next day 900 French troops landed and quickly rounded up the mercenaries. They did not, however, reinstate the 80-year-old Djohar, who was flown to the nearby French island of Réunion, with Yachroutu proclaiming himself "interim president in accordance with the constitution." Yachroutu thereupon named a new Government of National Unity, which Djohar repudiated from Réunion by announcing a rival government headed by former prime minister Saïd Ali Mohamed.

On December 3, 1995, a somewhat diverse group of Comoran political leaders assembled in Paris in an effort to persuade Yachroutu to cancel a snap presidential election that he had scheduled for January 21. Yachroutu responded by calling for two-stage balloting on January 28 and February 7, arguing that although the dates fell within the month-long Muslim feast of Ramadan, postponement would mean loss of Comoran consideration in the current cycle of World Bank/IMF structural-adjustment programming. Subsequently, however, he relented and postponed the voting to March 6 and 16. He also agreed to send representatives to a conference, sponsored by the Organization of African Unity (OAU, subsequently the African Union—AU) in Antananarivo, Madagascar, concerning Djohar's possible return, although insisting that planning for the presidential poll would

make it impossible for him (Yachroutu) to attend in person.

The Madagascar gathering yielded agreement on January 23, 1996, that Djohar would return to Moroni as president but would cease to have any executive authority forthwith and would accept a new electoral code that effectively barred him from seeking reelection by specifying an obligatory 40–70 age range for a presidential candidate (he was over 80). With some 50 French troops remaining on station to guarantee order, presidential balloting accordingly went ahead on March 6 and 16, with 15 candidates contesting the first round. Of these, Mohamed Taki Abdulkarim of the National Union for Democracy in the Comoros (*Union National pour la Démocratie aux Comores*—UNDC) headed the poll with 21.3 percent and went on to secure a 64.3 percent second-round victory over Abbas DJOUSSOUF, leader of the Movement for Democracy and Progress, standing as candidate of the Forum for National Recovery (*Forum pour le Redressement National*—FRN).

Sworn in on March 25, 1996, President Taki assigned the premiership to Tadjidine Ben Saïd MASSONDE (*Udzima*), who named a government on March 28 that included several of the presidential candidates eliminated in the recent first round. On April 11 President Taki dissolved the assembly and announced that new balloting would take place on October 6 (notwithstanding a constitutional requirement of elections within 40 days of dissolution), adding that a referendum on a new constitution would be held before the end of June (later rescheduled to October). In August, Taki formally proposed the establishment of a single "presidential" party, with opposition forces grouped into two parties. Among the critics of the proposal were two government parties, both of whom subsequently lost their cabinet postings. On October 6 the pro-presidential National Rally for Development (*Rassemblement National pour le Développement*—RND) was formed, Taki confidante Ali Bazi SELIM being named to head the group.

On October 20, 1996, a new constitution that increased presidential powers and restricted political party formations was approved by 85 percent of those voting in a popular referendum. The new charter had been championed by Taki and the RND, but its controversial amendments had elicited opposition condemnation and calls for a boycott of the referendum. Thereafter, relations between the administration and opposition continued to deteriorate, and on November 10, 1996, the opposition announced that it would boycott the upcoming legislative elections after the government refused to establish an independent electoral commission. Consequently, at balloting on December 1 and 8, RND candidates faced little competition, capturing an overwhelming majority of the assembly seats contested, with the remaining seats being secured by the Islamic National Front for Justice (*Front National pour la Justice*—FNJ) and an independent candidate. On December 27 Ahmed ABDOU, a former assistant to ex-president Abdallah, was named prime minister, replacing Massonde, who had resigned on December 11.

Antigovernment strikes and violent demonstrations erupted in early 1997, sparked by the Taki administration's failure to fulfill an earlier pledge to pay civil-servant salary arrears. On Nzwani, where the government's increasing inability to provide basic services had already fueled simmering secessionist emotions, the unrest quickly gained intensity, and in mid-March deadly clashes erupted between strikers and government security forces following the arrest of Abdou ZAKARIA, the leader of the Democratic Front Party (*Parti du Front Démocratique*—PFD). Subsequently, amid reports that the demonstrators were in open rebellion, the government dismissed the Anjouan governor.

Following the arrest of secessionist leader Abdallah IBRAHIM and the banning of antigovernment parties in late July 1997, full-scale rioting broke out in the Anjouan capital of Mutsamudu. Thereafter, separatist militants affiliated with the Anjouan People's Movement (*Mouvement du Peuple d'Anjouan*—MPA) gained control over key island facilities, and on August 3 the MPA declared independence from the Comoros government and announced its intention to petition France for a return to overseas territory status. On August 5 the MPA named Ibrahim, who had been released from detention, president of the breakaway state and head of a 12-member cabinet. Meanwhile, separatists on Mwali also declared their independence. For its part, France rebuffed the entreaties from the secessionists and urged them to respect Comoros' "territorial integrity." Subsequently, under pressure from the OAU, which had also refused to recognize the declaration of independence, the MPA agreed to participate in reconciliation talks with the Taki administration in Ethiopia in September.

On September 3, 1997, seaborne government forces attempting to regain control of Anjouan suffered heavy casualties before being repelled by separatist fighters, who also took dozens of the "invaders" captive. The government's ill-fated offensive, which it had at first declared a success, drew sharp OAU criticism, and reconciliation talks were indefinitely postponed. On September 8 Ibrahim announced the creation of the "State of Anjouan" and declared that he would rule by decree. Meanwhile, amid rumors in Moroni of an impending military coup, President Taki dissolved the Abdou government and assumed absolute power on September 9. On September 13 Taki formed a State Transition Committee, an advisory body that included three representatives from Nzwani and two from Mwali.

On October 26, 1997, secessionist officials in Nzwani organized a referendum on independence that reportedly received a 99 percent affirmative vote. Two days later Ibrahim was formally appointed head of the provisional government of Nzwani (the island's traditional name having been readopted by the secessionists) and was charged with drafting a constitution and preparing for elections. Such efforts were delayed, however, when in mid-November Ibrahim's provisional government again succumbed to OAU pressure and agreed to attend talks with the Taki administration in Ethiopia in December. On December 7 Taki appointed Nourdine BOURHANE, a former cabinet official with ties to Nzwani, to head a government that included a number of members of the State Transition Committee.

From December 10 to 14, 1997, representatives of the Taki government and secessionist representatives from Nzwani and Mwali met in Addis Ababa, Ethiopia, for OAU-sponsored "reconciliation" talks, which failed to yield any major breakthroughs, although both sides agreed to reconvene in 1998. In mid-February 1998 fighting erupted in Nzwani between Ibrahim's forces and a dissident faction led by Mohamed Abdou MADI, who, Ibrahim claimed, had the backing of the OAU. Unable to dislodge Ibrahim, Madi was forced to flee, and a number of his fighters were arrested.

At a constitutional referendum on February 25, 1998, voters in Nzwani reportedly approved a basic document that called for the revocation of all Comoran laws. Thereafter, despite OAU calls for the secessionists to delay further provocations, Ibrahim named CHAMASSI Ben Saïd Omar as prime minister of Nzwani in March. However, Ibrahim and his new prime minister subsequently clashed, and in July Chamassi and his supporters reportedly attempted to oust Ibrahim. Fighting between the various factions on Nzwani, including Mahdi's reorganized militants, continued through the end of 1998.

Following violent antigovernment rioting by civil servants in Moroni in mid-May 1998, Taki dismissed the Bourhane government on May 29, and on May 30 he named a cabinet that did not include a prime minister. On November 5 Taki died of a heart attack. The following day former prime minister Tadjidine Ben Saïd Massonde assumed the presidency as constitutionally mandated because of his position as president of the High Council of the Republic (the country's Constitutional Court). On November 22 Massonde named the FRN's Abbas Djoussouf to head an interim government. Djoussouf's appointment and subsequent formation of an FRN-dominated (with six seats) cabinet was denounced by the RND, whose governmental representation had fallen to four seats. Meanwhile, Massonde called for a loosening of economic sanctions against the secessionists on Nzwani and appealed to their leaders to participate in an internationally sponsored, interisland conference. However, plans for the meeting were derailed by the outbreak of fierce fighting on Nzwani in December 1998. Sub-

sequently, Massonde announced that presidential elections would be postponed until the secessionist crisis was resolved, and in February 1999 the High Court approved the extension of his mandate.

At an OAU-mediated conference held in Antananarivo, Madagascar, April 19–25, 1999, representatives from Ngazidja, Nzwani, and Mwali reached agreement on a pact that granted the latter two increased autonomy within the republic (to be restyled the Union of Comoran Islands) and charged the Massonde administration with preparing for general elections in April 2000. The delegation from Nzwani departed, however, without signing the accord, and violent demonstrations subsequently erupted on Ngazidja, where protesters reportedly chanted anti-Nzwani slogans and attacked people who had been born on Nzwani. On April 30, Armed Forces Chief of Staff Col. Assoumani AZALI announced that, in an effort to stem the unrest, the military had assumed control of the country, ousted the president and government, and suspended the constitution, legislature, and judiciary.

Among Colonel Azali's first acts upon seizing power was to announce his intention to honor the Madagascar accord, including its provisions for presidential and legislative elections in 2000. Nevertheless, the coup was widely condemned by the international community, with the criticisms from the OAU and France being among the more strident.

Facing continued international isolation, on December 7, 1999, President Azali announced the formation of a new government headed by Bianrifi TARMIDI as prime minister, which he hoped would be viewed more positively because of the inclusion of several political parties. Meanwhile, events continued to percolate on Nzwani, where a referendum on January 23, 2000, endorsed independence by a reported vote of 95 percent. In response, the OAU on February 1 imposed economic sanctions on the separatists.

In April 2000 several demonstrations protested the passing without action of the one-year deadline for Azali's promised withdrawal from power. Among other things, Hachim Saïd HACHIM resigned his post as chair of the National Salvation

Coordination (*Coordination de Salut National—* CSN), a grouping of former party figures and civic leaders that had been formed to support Azali, to protest the delay. For his part, the president claimed he had been unable to act as expected due to the intransigence of the leaders of Nzwani. However, in August, Azali and Lt. Col. Saïd ABEID Abdéréman reached agreement on a preliminary plan for a new federal entity that would provide each island with substantially expanded autonomy. Although the OAU lambasted the accord as contrary to the guidelines established in Madagascar in April 1999, the agreement appeared to represent the best hope for a negotiated settlement to date, despite the at times violent opposition of hard-line separatists on Nzwani.

On May 6, 2000, Colonel Azali was sworn in as president, and he appointed a cabinet-like state council with six ministers from Ngazidja, four from Mwali, and two from Nzwani, promising to turn over the reigns of authority to a civilian government within one year. He also introduced a new "constitutional charter" authorizing himself, as president, prime minister, and minister of defense, to rule by decree (in conjunction with a "state committee") while negotiations continued toward the adoption of a new constitution. Meanwhile, Abeid, the former French officer who had "elbowed out" Ibrahim for dominance on Nzwani, announced the formation of a government on that island and indicated that Nzwani would not adhere to the Madagascar agreement, prompting the OAU to threaten sanctions and even military intervention.

On November 29, 2000, the president named Hamada Madi "BOLERO," one of his chief negotiators with Nzwani, to replace Prime Minister Tamadi. Bolero formed a new government on December 10, although he was unable to persuade opposition parties to join.

On February 17, 2001, a potentially landmark agreement was reached in Fomboni, the capital of Mwali, by members of the military junta, the former separatists on Nzwani led by Colonel Abeid, delegates from Mwali, and representatives from political parties and civic organizations. Based on that accord, a national referendum on a new constitution establishing a Union of the Comoros was held on

December 23, voters responding with a reported 76 percent "yes" vote. Meanwhile, on Nzwani, Colonel Abeid had been overthrown in a bloodless coup in August that had left control in the hands of Maj. Mohamed BACAR, who had quickly signaled his support for the proposed new federal system.

On January 17, 2002, President Azali nominated Prime Minister "Bolero" to head a new transitional government (installed on January 20) to prepare for presidential elections for the Union as well as for each island. For his part, Azali on January 21 resigned as president, as he was constitutionally required to do in order to compete in the upcoming balloting for the presidency of the Union. The primary was held March 17 on Ngazidja, with Azali finishing first with 39.8 percent of the vote, followed by Mahamoud MRADABI with 15.7 percent. Also on March 17, voters on Mwali and Nzwani approved the requisite new local constitutions. However, the constitutional referendum on Ngazidja failed, prompting a rerun (this time successful) on April 9.

Although the top three finishers in the March 17, 2002, primary on Ngazidja were authorized to compete in the Union-wide balloting for president of the Union on April 14, Azali ultimately ran unopposed because the other two candidates boycotted the poll to protest what they considered to be "anomalies" in the first round and ongoing questions about the integrity of electoral rolls. The national election commission ruled the results of April 14 to be void in view of the boycott, but the commission was dissolved for "incompetence" on April 23 by the follow-up committee charged with overseeing implementation of the 2001 Fomboni Agreement. A special commission was subsequently established to review the matter, and Azali's victory was confirmed on May 8. Azali was sworn in as president of the Union on May 26, and on June 5 he announced his Union cabinet, which comprised his two vice presidents and only three other members. Meanwhile, separate presidential balloting on each of the islands had resulted in Bacar's election as president of Nzwani, the selection of a then Azali supporter—Mohamed Saïd FAZUL— on Mwali, and a victory on Ngazidja for Abdou Soule ELBAK, an outspoken critic of Azali.

Elections for the proposed island and Union assemblies were postponed indefinitely in March 2003 in the wake of ongoing conflict over power-sharing issues and an apparent coup plot against Azali emanating from Ngazidja. However, at a meeting sponsored by the AU in Pretoria, South Africa, in August, representatives of the island and Union governments appeared to settle several contentious issues, including how tax revenues would be shared. The accord also provided for each island to have its own police force, while the army would remain under Union control. Azali and the three island presidents ratified the agreement on December 20 and established a national committee to oversee its implementation.

Balloting for the three island assemblies was held on March 14 and 21, 2004. The Azali, pro-Union camp fared poorly in the face of coordinated opposition efforts. (Pro-Bacar candidates won 20 of 25 seats on Nzwani, pro-Elbak candidates won 14 of 20 seats on Ngazidja, and pro-Fazul candidates won 9 of 10 seats on Mwali.) The opposition (now formally coalesced as the Camp of the Autonomous Islands [*Camp des Îles Autonomous*— CdIA] also dominated the April 18 and 25 balloting for the Assembly of the Union, securing 12 directly elected seats compared to 6 for the pro-Azali Convention for the Renewal of the Comoros (*Convention pour le Renouveau des Comores*—CRC). Because of its control of the island assemblies, the CdIA also gained all 15 of the indirectly elected seats in the Assembly of the Union.

On July 13, 2004, President Azali formed a new Union cabinet in which CRC members held a majority of the portfolios. However, the "opposition" was given three seats—one from Nzwani, one from Mwali, and one from the Islands Fraternity and Unity Party. Elbak declined an invitation to appoint a cabinet member from Ngazidja, citing Azali's perceived foot-dragging in devolving power to the islands. Azali announced another cabinet reshuffle in early July 2005.

In primary balloting on Nzwani for the president of the Union on April 16, 2006, moderate Islamist leader Ahmed Abdallah Mohamed SAMBI of the National Front for Justice (*Front National pour la Justice*—FNJ) led 13 candidates with 23.7 per-

cent of the vote, followed by two "secular" rivals— Mohamed DJAANFARI (a retired French air force officer) with 13.10 percent and former prime minister Ibrahim Halidi (who had Azali's endorsement) with 10.37 percent. In the nationwide runoff balloting among the three on May 14, Sambi was declared the winner with 58 percent of the vote. He formed a new cabinet on May 27.

Constitution and Government

The 1992 constitution provided for the popular election of a president, by runoff balloting if necessary to secure a majority, for a once-renewable five-year term. It also provided for a legislature consisting of a Senate of 15 members (5 per island, chosen by regional councillors for six-year terms) and a Federal Assembly, popularly elected (subject to dissolution) for four years by a single-vote, two-round ballot. Of the assembly's 42 members, 20 represented Ngazidja, 17 Nzwani, and 5 Mwali. A prime minister, named by the president, was drawn from the party holding or commanding a majority in the assembly.

The constitution approved by popular referendum on October 20, 1996, superseded the 1992 charter and included provisions for an enhanced presidency, wherein the chief executive was elected by popular mandate for a six-year term and given the exclusive rights to initiate any future constitutional changes and to appoint the prime minister and island governors. The 1996 constitution also abolished the Senate and enlarged the popularly elected Federal Assembly by 1 seat to a total of 43. Members of the assembly served four-year terms (subject to dissolution) and the seats were distributed geographically as follows: Ngazidja, 20; Nzwani, 17; and Mwali, 6. The document forbade independent candidates from vying for elected office and further stipulated that political parties needed to secure 2 assembly seats on each island to maintain legal status.

The 1996 constitution was suspended by the military junta that assumed power on April 30, 1999, and all state institutions were dissolved. On May 6, 1999, Col. Assoumani Azali, the leader of the junta, proclaimed a new "constitutional charter" with himself as president and head of a State Committee empowered to govern pending the return to civilian government. A progovernment "national congress" in Moroni on August 7, 2000, adopted a "national charter" that extended the authority of the president (as chosen by the military) even further. Among other things, the new document called for the president to appoint a prime minister and envisioned the eventual establishment of a vaguely defined "legislative council."

Following extensive and difficult negotiations among government officials, opposition parties, and representatives of Mwali and Nzwani, a national referendum on December 23, 2001, approved a new federal structure for the renamed Union of the Comoros. (The complete official name of the country had previously been the Federal Islamic Republic of the Comoros.) Autonomy was granted to the three island components of the Union to a much greater degree than in previous constitutions, especially in regard to finances. Meanwhile, the Union government was given responsibility for religion, currency, external relations, defense, nationality issues, and national symbols. New constitutions were also subsequently adopted by referenda on each island, although the division of authority between the island governments and the Union government was insufficiently delineated to prevent the immediate outbreak of confusion, especially on Ngazidja (see Current issues below).

The president of the Union serves a four-year term, with the office rotating among the islands each term. Two vice presidents, one from each of the islands not holding the presidency, also serve. The president and vice presidents constitute a Council of the Union. A primary election is held on the island scheduled to assume the presidency (Ngazidja was chosen as first in the rotation, to be followed in order by Nzwani and Mwali). The top three vote-getters in the primary earn a place on the ballot in subsequent Union-wide balloting. Each presidential candidate must select two vice-presidential running mates, one from each of the islands that the presidential candidate does not represent, prior to the Union-wide poll. The president

is authorized to appoint a prime minister and cabinet, although the new basic law requires that all the islands be represented in the federal government. Legislative power was vested in an elected Assembly of the Union (see Legislature, below, for details). The new constitutions for the islands also provided for direct election of their presidents and island assemblies.

The Union's other prominent institution is the High Council, which serves as a constitutional court and is responsible for validating election results as well as ruling on questions regarding the division of authority between the federal and island governments. Members of the High Council are appointed (for six-year terms) by the president and vice presidents of the Union, the president of the Assembly of the Union, and the presidents of the island governments. The judiciary is headed by a Supreme Court.

Foreign Relations

Comoran foreign relations have long been dominated by the Mayotte (Mahoré) issue. On November 21, 1975, French military personnel resisted an "invasion" by Ali Soilih and an unarmed contingent that attempted to counter the Mahori "secession." At the end of the year, France recognized the sovereignty of the other three islands, but referenda held on Mayotte in February and April 1976 demonstrated a clear preference for designation as a French department. On December 16 the French Senate ratified a measure according the island special standing as a *collectivité territoriale*, with that status being extended on December 6, 1979, for another five years. In October 1981 President Abdallah pressed for French withdrawal during a Paris meeting with President Mitterrand, who, he noted, had in 1975 opposed detachment of the island from the rest of the archipelago. He repeated the argument during a visit to France in June 1984, the French government responding that a further referendum on the issue would be deferred because the inhabitants of Mayotte were not sufficiently "well informed" on the options open to them. The decision was endorsed by the French National

Assembly in a bill approved on December 19, and no subsequent referendum has been held.

On January 20, 1995, a mass demonstration was mounted outside the French embassy in Moroni to protest a decision by French prime minister Edouard Balladur to reimpose a requirement that Comoros citizens obtain entry visas for travel to Mayotte. Thereafter, Mohamed Taki contested the March 1996 presidential election on a public platform of Islamic traditionalism and moderate nationalism, depicting his main rival as the candidate preferred by the French government. However, once in office Taki confirmed that the existing defense agreement with France would not only be maintained but also expanded to cover the external defense of the Comoros and to allow a French military presence on the islands.

In early 1997 French financial aid was suspended pending Moroni's restarting discussions with the IMF and World Bank on the establishment of a structural adjustment program. In 1998 international attention focused on the crisis on Nzwani. In March, France rejected the secessionists' call for the reestablishment of links as "unrealistic"; meanwhile, the OAU, whose mediation efforts were rebuffed by the separatists, adopted an increasingly hard-line stance against the breakaway movement. (In early December the OAU urged its members to comply with Moroni's call for military intervention to end the violence.)

The OAU and most of the rest of the international community strongly criticized the coup of April 1999, while the OAU continued to pressure the separatists on Nzwani into early 2001 (see Political background for further information). However, most capitals ultimately endorsed, as did the OAU, the political settlement subsequently reached regarding the new constitutional structure for the Comoros. France restored full ties with the Comoros in September 2002 and signed several economic agreements in 2005.

Current Issues

Not surprisingly, considering the chaos of recent years, the balloting for president of the Union of the Comoros in the spring of 2002 was highly controversial and, in the opinion of major opposition parties, a "fiasco" that undercut the legitimacy of President Azali's victory. Following Azali's appointment of his new cabinet in June, it also quickly became clear that the Union was facing a potentially fatal institutional crisis involving the failure of the union and island constitutions to fully delineate the separation of power between the federal and island authorities. (The *Indian Ocean Newsletter* described the problem as "Four presidents for three islands.") Conflict was most apparent on Ngazidja, where that island's president, Abdou Soule Elbak, attempted to make appointments and even occupy office space that Azali considered within the purview of the federal administration.

The contentious island and Union legislative elections in 2004 did little to settle the simmering power-sharing issues, particularly with the anti-Azali, "anti-Union" CdIA controlling all of the legislatures. Tension also intensified when the pro-Azali camp introduced legislation that would have permitted Azali to run for president of the Union again in 2006. (According to the rotating mechanism codified in the constitution, the next Union president was scheduled to be elected from Nzwani.) Although the proposed revision was withdrawn in the face of public protests, political uncertainty continued to pose a threat to the April 2006 primary election on Nzwani, prompting the AU to send a contingent of peacekeepers and police officers to help ensure peaceful balloting. (Local forces were confined to their barracks.) Surprising those analysts who predicted that the Comoros was not yet ready for a peaceful transfer of power, the April primary and May nationwide balloting proceeded in a generally orderly fashion, the AU characterizing the voting as "free, transparent, and credible." New president Sambi presented himself as a political newcomer devoted to combating corruption, by, among other things, developing an independent judiciary and investigating the perceived widespread "embezzlement" of government funds in recent years. Some observers suggested that Sambi, a Muslim theologian educated in Iran, might promote the installation of an Islamic regime, but he declared that Comorans were currently opposed to such a change and that he would accept public opinion on the matter. A successful businessman, Sambi pledged that his administration's activities would involve "more economics and less politics."

Political Parties

In 1979 the Federal Assembly effectively voided an endorsement of pluralism in the 1978 constitution by calling for the establishment of a single-party system, which prevailed until the resanctioning of multiparty activity in December 1989. Under the Djohar presidency, Comoran parties were mostly aligned into progovernment and opposition camps. The latter presented joint lists at the December 1993 election and in January 1994 launched the ten-party Forum for National Recovery.

The October 1996 constitution included a number of regulations for political party activity that the Taki administration had been advocating since assuming power the previous March, including requiring political parties to control two legislative seats on each of the islands in order to maintain legal status, allowing the formation of only two opposition parties, and forbidding independent candidates from vying for elected office. Thus, as of late 1998 the RND was the Comoro Islands' only legal party, although both the National Front for Justice and a successful independent candidate had reportedly assumed their legislative seats following the December 1996 balloting. The December 2001 constitution permitted parties to operate without hindrance, provided they respect "national sovereignty, democracy, and territorial integrity."

Presidential Party

National Front for Justice (*Front National pour la Justice*—FNJ). The FNJ is a moderate Islamic party led by Ahmed Abdallah Mohamed Sambi (nicknamed "Ayatollah" because of his theological training in Iran). At December 1996 legislative balloting the FNJ captured its first-ever seats, including one by Sambi.

FNJ members were not immediately linked to the unrest on Anjouan in 1997, and at midyear the group issued a statement saying that it was not a separatist body. However, the FNJ expressed sympathy for critics of government "negligence" and called for establishment of a "proper federal state."

The FNJ eventually joined the government following the coup of April 1999 but withdrew in October 2001 to protest the decision to remove "Islamic" from the name of the country in the constitution being readied for a national referendum in December.

Sambi, a prominent businessman in addition to being a popular cleric, was elected president of the Union in 2006.

Leaders: Ahmed Abdallah Mohamed SAMBI (President of the Union), Ahmed ABOUBACAR, Soidiki M'BAPANOZA, Ahmed RACHID.

Other Parties and Groups

Convention for the Renewal of the Comoros (*Convention pour le Renouveau des Comores*—CRC). The CRC was launched in September 2002 by members of the Movement for Socialism and Democracy (*Mouvement pour le Socialisme et la Démocratie*—MSD), which had been formed in July 2000 by Abdou Soefou after he and his supporters were expelled from the FDC (below) for supporting President Azali following the April 1999 coup. The CRC was described as an extension of the National Salvation Coordination that had been formed following the coup. The CRC was established to provide Azali with a party prior to the elections for island and Union assemblies.

Although Azali captured the Union presidency in 2002, the CRC was overshadowed by anti-Azali parties in the 2004 balloting for the Assembly of the Union. Subsequently, the CRC fractionalized in its efforts to present a candidate for the 2006 Union presidential elections. One group, led by former prime minister Mohamed Abdou Madi (who had sought the CRC nomination), reportedly backed Union Vice President Mohamed Caabi El Yachroutu, while Soefou and Azali supported Ibrahim Halidi of the MPC (below). El Yachroutu secured 9.56 percent of the vote in the presidential primary.

Leaders: Col. Assoumani AZALI (Former President of the Union of the Comoros), Abdou SOE-FOU (Secretary General).

Movement for the Comoros (*Movement pour les Comores*—MPC). Formed in 1997 by Saïd Hilali, an advisor to President Mohamed Taki Abdoulkarim, the MPC stressed "national unity" under a federal government. Ibrahim Halidi, the MPC's secretary general, finished third in the April 2006 primary, having secured the endorsement of President Azali's faction of the CRC as well as the Chuma and Djawabu parties (below). Among other things, Halidi, who had served briefly as prime minister in 1993, promised greater "friendship" with France if elected.

Leaders: Ibrahim Abderemane HALIDI (Secretary General and 2006 candidate for president of the Union), Saïd HILALI.

Rally for a Development Initiative with Enlightened Youth (*Rassemblement pour une Initiative de Développment avec une Jeunesse Avertie*—RIDJA). Launched in April 2005 by Saïd Larifou, a prominent lawyer who had led antigovernment protests in 2003, the RIDJA was a vocal opponent of efforts to rewrite the constitution to permit President Azali to run for another term. The RIDJA candidate for the presidency of the Union in 2006, Chadhouli Abdou, finished seventh with 3.12 percent of the vote in the primary.

Leaders: Saïd LARIFOU, Chadhouli ABDOU (2006 candidate for president of the Union).

Djawabu Party. This party's candidate, Youssouf Saïd SOILIHI, won 6.7 percent of the vote in the 2002 primary election for president of the Union. In 2006 the party supported Ibrahim Halidi of the MPC in his campaign for president of the Union.

Camp of the Autonomous Islands (*Camp des Îles Autonomous*—CdIA). Launched by the five parties below and other smaller groups, the CdIA campaigned for the island and assembly elections in 2004 on a platform calling for greater autonomy for the islands and support for the three island presidents. On the island of Ngazidja, the coalition is commonly referenced as Autonomy (*Mdjidjengo*).

The CdIA dominated the 2004 balloting for the Assembly of the Union, capturing 12 of the 18 directly elected seats and all of the 15 indirectly elected seats. However, references to the CdIA subsequently declined significantly, suggesting that its mission had been purely electoral. Components of the CdIA endorsed various candidates in the April 2006 primary election for president of the Union, although the three island presidents endorsed Ahmed Abdallah Mohamed Sambi in the May final balloting.

Leaders: Mohamed Saïd FAZUL (President of Mwali), Abdou Soule ELBAK (President of Ngazidja), and Col. Mohamed BACAR (President of Nzwani).

Movement for Democracy and Progress (*Mouvement pour la Démocratie et le Progrs*—MDP). The MDP, also styled the Popular Democratic Movement (*Mouvement Démocratique Populaire*), is a Moroni-based formation that was awarded the production and industry portfolio in the cabinet of May 1992 and campaigned in favor of the 1992 constitution. It later became the leading element of an anti-Djohar alliance called the Forum for National Recovery (*Forum pour le Redressement National*—FRN), of which MDP leader Abbas Djoussouf was the principal spokesman.

The FRN was originally launched in January 1994 by opposition parties that had presented joint lists at the December 1993 elections. President Djohar's eventual agreement to a transfer of power served to relax FRN discipline, in that a majority of its components put up candidates for the March 1996 presidential contest in their own right. Following the 1996 election, parties that had supported the failed candidacy of Djoussouf reorganized under the FRN rubric. In October the group was bolstered by the addition of the Chuma and the Forces for Republican Action (*Forces pour l'Action Républicaine*—FAR), which had rejected President Taki's call for the establishment of a single presidential party. Subsequently, the FRN organized boycotts of both the October 20 constitutional referendum and the December legislative balloting.

On January 18, 1997, Djoussouf and Mustapha Saïd CHEIKH were detained and questioned about their roles in the unrest that had erupted at the beginning of the year. On March 1 senior French government officials met with FRN leaders in an effort to persuade them to establish a dialogue with the Taki administration. However, the opposition's relations with the government subsequently worsened when security officials accused the FRN of financing student disturbances in Moroni. Ironically, observers cited the FRN's financial difficulties as the main reason the group failed to secure a more prominent negotiating role in the late 1997 reconciliation talks.

Djoussouf was appointed prime minister in November 1998, and he subsequently formed an FRN-dominated cabinet. Not surprisingly, he strongly protested the April 1999 coup, announcing the withdrawal of the MDP from the FRN when it appeared that some FRN components had acquiesced to the government of self-proclaimed President Azali. Djoussouf subsequently became the dominant figure in the opposition camp as it participated in negotiations on the creation of a new federal structure; he signed the Fomboni Agreement of February 2001 in that capacity and urged his supporters to vote "yes" in the December constitutional referendum. Djoussouf finished fourth in the primary election for president of the Union in 2002 by securing 7.9 percent of the vote, analysts suggesting he probably would have made the top three and thereby qualified for the runoff if the FRN had been preserved.

Leaders: Abbas DJOUSSOUF (1996 and 2002 presidential candidate), Fouad Mohamed AHMED.

Democratic Front of the Comoros (*Front Démocratique des Comores*—FDC). The FDC was formerly an exile group led, within the Comoros, by its secretary general, Mustapha Saïd Cheikh, who was imprisoned for complicity in the 1985 coup attempt until President Abdallah's assassination. It was one of the opposition groups invited to participate in the Djohar administration of August 1990. Subsequently, it campaigned in favor of the 1992 constitution and was a leading component of the FRN.

Some FDC members supported the government of President Azali following the April 1999 coup and were expelled from the party.

Cheikh won 3.4 percent of the vote in the primary election for president of the Union in 2002 and subsequently served as a major founding member of the CdIA.

Leaders: Mustapha Saïd CHEIKH, Ahmed Saïd ALI, Abdou MHOUMADI (2002 candidate for president of Grande Comore), Abdallah HALIFA (Secretary General).

Islands' Fraternity and Unity Party (*Chama cha Upvamodja na Mugnagna wa Massiwa*–Chuma). Chuma resulted from a "patriotic alliance to fight the antidemocratic regime of Ahmed Abdallah" that had been formed in the 1980s by the Paris-based National Committee for Public Salvation (*Comité National de Salut Public*—CNSP), an exile group led by Prince Saïd Ali Kemal, and two other exile groups, the Comoran National United Front (*Front National Uni des Komores*—FNUK) and the Union of Comorans (*Union des Komoriens*—Unikom). Kemal headed the economy and trade ministry in the first Djohar administration.

Chuma did not immediately adhere to the FRN, since Kemal was abroad at the time of the FRN's creation. Having stood unsuccessfully in the March 1996 presidential election, Kemal was appointed to the first post-Djohar government, but he was dismissed in August for opposing President Taki's proposal for a merger of government parties. Subsequently, Chuma announced that it was aligning with the FRN.

Kemal urged his supporters to vote "no" in the constitutional referendum of December 2001, arguing that the proposed federal structure would lead to the "Balkanization" of the Comoros. Kemal finished third in the primary election on Grande Comore for president of the Union in March 2002 with 10.8 percent of the vote; he called for a boycott of the runoff in April. Chuma supported Ibrahim Halidi of the MPC in the 2006 balloting for president of the Union, Kemal serving as one of Halidi's vice-presidential running mates.

Leaders: Prince Saïd Ali KEMAL (1996 and 2002 presidential candidate).

National Rally for Development (*Rassemblement National pour le Développement*—RND). The RND was officially launched on October 6, 1996, as a formal merger of the National Union for Democracy in the Comoros (*Union National pour la Démocratie aux Comores*—UNDC) and a number of former FRN parties under the leadership of a confidante of Mohamed Taki, Ali Bazi Selim. The formation of a single "presidential" party was first proposed by (then) newly elected President Taki in August 1996 on the grounds that almost all of the eliminated first-round candidates had supported his candidacy in the runoff balloting.

Subsequent intraparty competition for the RND's 26 elected Central Committee seats was described as "fierce," and the results—14 seats for Selim's supporters and 12 for a "youth wing" led by Abdoul Hamid Affretane—underlined reports of deep divisions in the fledgling grouping. Additional seats were set aside for the general secretaries of the parties joining the RND as well as for what was described as the Comoran "diaspora." Thereafter, despite the RND's electoral success at December 1996 legislative balloting, observers reported that its members' support for Taki remained their only commonality.

In November 1998 the RND denounced the appointment of the FRN's Djoussouf to the top government post. Subsequently, the RND's cabinet representation fell to four seats, and in early 1999 two former RND members were appointed to the government (see Maecha Bora Party, below).

One faction of the RND reportedly backed the new administration of President Azali after the coup of 1999, while another, led by Omar Tamou, lobbied for the reinstatement of former interim president Massonde. Mtara MAECHA, the former foreign minister who secured 7.86 percent of the vote in the primary election on Ngazidja for president of the Union, was identified as the candidate of the RND's "revival wing." Maecha reportedly supported Ahmed Abdallah Mohamed Sambi in the May 2006 balloting for president of the Union.

Leaders: Ali Bazi SELIM (President of the Party), Abdoul Hamid AFFRETANE (Secretary General, "Revival Wing"), Mouni MADI, Mouazoir ABDALLAH.

Comoran Party for Democracy and Progress (*Parti Comorien pour la Démocratie et le Progrès*—PCDP). The PCDP is led by Ali Mroudjae, who was an *Udzima* leader prior to President Abdallah's assassination and subsequently held the production and industry portfolio under Djohar. The party joined *Udzima* in moving into opposition in November 1991. Mroudjae secured 4.2 percent of the vote in the primary election of president of the Union in 2002. Abdou Soule Elbak, the President of Ngazidja, is a former deputy in the PCDP and is still referenced regularly as a member of the party. Meanwhile, several members of the PCDP serve in Elbak's cabinet on Ngazidja. Adinane was the candidate of the PCDP in the 2006 primary for Union president, but he received less than 3 percent of the vote and did not qualify for the general election.

Leaders: Loufti ADINANE (Chair), Ali MROUDJAE (Secretary General).

Maecha Bora Party. Maecha Bora is led by two RND dissidents, Issoufi Saïd Ali and 1996 presidential candidate Ali Ben Ali, who were named to the Djoussouf government in early 1999.

Leaders: Issoufi Saïd ALI, Ali Ben ALI (1996 presidential candidate).

Comoran Popular Front (*Front Populaire Comorien*—FPC). Also known as the *Front Populaire Mohélien* (FPM), the FPC was awarded the education portfolio in the government of May 1992 and campaigned for the new constitution; it later joined the FRN.

Mohamed Hassanali, leader of the FPC, was the leading vote-getter in the first round of balloting for president of Mwali in 2002 with 26.2 percent of the vote; however, he was defeated in the run-off.

Leaders: Mohamed HASSANALI, Abdou MOUSTAKIM (Secretary General).

Comoran Union for Progress (*Union Comorienne pour le Progrès*—UCP/*Udzima*). Launched as a regime-supportive group in 1982 by President Abdallah, *Udzima* was the sole legal party until 1989. *Udzima* presented Saïd Mohamed Djohar, interim president following Abdallah's assassination in November 1989, as its official candidate in the presidential balloting of March 1990. However, *Udzima* withdrew its support from Djohar in November 1991 and moved into opposition in protest over the formation of a coalition administration three months earlier. It did not participate in the 1992 balloting after its principal leaders had been either imprisoned or driven into hiding because of alleged complicity in the September coup attempt.

A member of the opposition FRN from January 1994, *Udzima* experienced internal divisions after President Djohar had agreed to a transfer of power, with the result that two candidates (Omar Tamou and Mtara Maecha) from *Udzima* stood in the March 1996 presidential election. Although both were eliminated in the first round, the *Udzima* leader, Tadjidine Ben Saïd Massonde, was appointed prime minister by the successful UNDC candidate. Massonde resigned as prime minister in December 1996, but he was named, due to his position as president of the High Council of the Repub-

lic, as interim president of the Republic following President Taki's death in November 1998. Confusion subsequently surrounded *Udzima*'s membership, as news reports referenced Massonde, Tamou, and Maecha as being members of the RND in 1999. In early 2002, Tamou, former *Udzima* secretary general, returned to the Comoros after two years in France.

Republican Party of the Comoros (*Parti Républicain des Comores*—PRC). The PRC was formed in the second half of the 1990s by Mohamed Saïd Abdallah Mchangama, then president of the Federal Assembly, and Hamada Madi "Bolero," who served as PRC secretary general until rallying to the cause of President Azali following the coup of April 1999. Mchangama, the son-in-law of former president Djohar, had been instrumental in the launching of the Rally for Democracy and Renewal (*Rassemblement pour la Démocratie et le Renouveau*—RDR) in December 1993 by merger of the Dialogue Proposition Action (*Mwangaza*), led by Mchangama, and dissidents from other parties. Personal rivalries had resulted in three prominent RDR members, including Mchangama, contesting the March 1996 presidential election, all being eliminated in the first round.

Mchangama called for dialogue with the Azali administration following the coup of April 1999, but the PRC was described as a member of the opposition in early 2001.

Leader: Mohamed Saïd Abdallah MCHANGAMA.

Other parties include the **Rally for Change** (*Rassemblement pour le Changement*), led by Mohamed ZEINA, described as being close to the center-right Rally for the Republic in France; **Shawiri,** based in Moroni and led by Col. Mahamoud MRADABI; and **Shawiri-Unafasiya** (SU), formed in 2003 by former members of *Shawiri* and led by Hadji Ben SAID.

Separatist and Other Groups

Anjouan People's Movement (*Mouvement du Peuple d'Anjouan*—MPA). The MPA emerged as

Cabinet

As of September 1, 2006

President	Ahmed Abdallah Mohamed Sambi (Nzwani)
Vice Presidents	Ikililou Dhoinine (Mwali)
	Idi Nadhoim (Ngazidja)

Ministers

Agriculture, Fishing, Industry, Handicrafts, and Environment	Siti Kassim [f]
Finance, Budget, and Economy	Hassani Hamadi
Foreign Affairs and Cooperation	Ahmed Ben Saïd Djaffar
Health, Solidarity, and Civil Service	Ikililou Dhoinine
Justice and Public Affairs and Keeper of the Seals	M'Madi Ali
National Education, Research, Arts, Culture, Youth, and Sports	Abdourahim Saïd Bacar
Territorial Development, Town Planning, Housing, and Energy	Naïlane Mhadji
Transportation, Posts and Telecommunications, Communication, and Tourism	Idi Nadhoim
Chief of Staff (Responsible for Defense)	Mohamd Abdul Wahab
Secretary General of the Government	Mohamed Bacar Dossar

[f] = female

the most prominent of the secessionist groups in Anjouan after the arrest of its leader, Abdallah IBRAHIM (a prominent businessman), on July 22, 1997, served as a rallying cry for antipresidential and separatist militants. Ibrahim was released days later, and on August 5 he was named president of the "State of Anjouan" (later changed to Nzwani). The MPA lobbied against the Union constitution of December 2001. In February 2002 it named Col. Mohamed Bacar, then the military ruler of Nzwani, as MPA honorary chair. Following Bacar's election to the presidency of Nzwani in March, some elements of the MPA joined the island government, and two MPA members were appointed to the nine-member Nzwani cabinet. Bacar emerged as the most vocal proponent of autonomy for the islands. However, other members of the MPA remained staunch secessionists and denounced Bacar for even his limited cooperation with the Union government. Abdullah Mohamed emerged as the leader of the hard-line secessionist wing of the party. In 2005 Mohamed and other members of the MPA were arrested for antigovernment activity.

Leaders: Abdullah MOHAMED (Leader of Separatist Faction).

Organization for the Independence of Anjouan (*Organization pour l'Indépendance d'Anjouan*—OPIA). Theretofore a propresidential grouping, the OPIA in late 1996 grew critical of the Taki administration and was subsequently linked to the growing number of antigovernment demonstrations in Anjouan. In mid-1997 leadership of the OPIA reportedly shifted from former armed forces chief of staff Col. Ahmed Mohamed HAZI to Mohamed Ahmed Abdou. Critics of Abdou, who has also been identified as a spokesman for the **Coordination Committee of Anjouan,** accused him of placing his personal ambitions ahead of the movement's. The OPIA steadfastly maintained its separatist stance into mid-2002, although subsequent references to OPIA activity have been very limited.

Leader: Mohamed Ahmed ABDOU.

Legislature

The 1992 constitution provided for a bicameral legislature. However, the Senate, which was to have 15 members (5 from each island) indirectly elected to six-year terms, was never named and was abolished by the 1996 basic charter. Prior to the April 1999 coup, legislative authority was vested in a Federal Assembly (*Assemblée Fédérale*), which comprised 43 members directly elected for four-year terms (subject to dissolution).

Under the December 2001 constitution, an Assembly of the Union was established as well as assemblies for each of the three islands that comprise the Union.

Assembly of the Union (*Assemblée de l'Union*). The assembly comprises 33 members—18 directly elected (9 from Ngazidja, 7 from Nzwani, and 2 from Mwali) and 15 indirectly elected by the 3 island assemblies (5 each). In the direct balloting on April 18 and 25, 2004, the Camp of the Autonomous Islands (CdIA) secured 12 seats, and the propresidential Convention for the Renewal of the Comoros, 6. All 15 indirectly elected seats were filled by the CdIA, anti-Azali coalitions having earlier won heavy majorities in all three island assemblies.

Speaker: Saïd Dhoifir BOUNOU.

Communications

Press

The nation's print media includes two weeklies, the state-owned *Al Watwan* (1,500) and the independent *L'Archipel*. A new daily, *Le Matin,* was introduced in March 2002. There is also a monthly, *La Tribune de Moroni.* The editor of *L'Archipel* was detained by the government for three days in March 2006 following the publication of an article critical of security officials. The arrest prompted an outcry from international media watchdogs.

News Agency

The domestic facility is the *Agence Comores-Presse* (ACP), located in Moroni.

Broadcasting and Computing

The government-operated *Radio-Comores* served some 96,000 receivers in 1999. The country's first independent radio station, *Radio Tropiques FM,* was closed down after one week of transmission in April 1991 and again in July 1993, at which time its director was arrested for "disturbing the peace." The one remaining independent outlet, *Udzima's Voix des Îles,* was silenced in February 1994, although news bulletins from *Radio France Internationale* began transmitting via satellite in March, and a number of new independent stations were subsequently launched. However, the Union and island governments continued to censor private stations, one station being suspended in 2005 after broadcasting programs critical of the government. In 1989 the French government provided 5 million francs for construction of the islands' first television station, which in 2003 served some 3,000 households. There were approximately 5,000 personal computers serving an equal number of Internet users in 2003.

Intergovernmental Representation

Ambassador to the U.S.
(Vacant)

U.S. Ambassador to the Comoros
James D. McGEE (resident in Madagascar)

Permanent Representative to the UN
(Vacant)

IGO Memberships (Non-UN)
AfDB, AMF, AU, BADEA, Comesa, IDB, Interpol, IOC, LAS, NAM, OIC, OIF, WCO

DEMOCRATIC REPUBLIC OF THE CONGO

République Démocratique du Congo

Note: In the first round of presidential balloting on July 30, 2006, President Joseph Kabila, running as an independent but supported by the People's Party for Reconstruction and Democracy and some 30 other parties in the Alliance for a Presidential Majority (*Alliance pour la Majorité Présidentielle*—AMP), was credited with 45 percent of the vote. Second place (20 percent of the vote) went to Vice President Jean-Pierre Bemba, the candidate of the Movement for the Liberation of the Congo and some 23 other parties aligned in the Rally of Congolese Nationalists (*Regroupement des Nationalists Congolais*—RENACO). The runoff was scheduled for October 29, although the announcement of the first-round results (characterized as fraudulent by Bemba and other candidates) triggered violent demonstrations in Kinshasa. Meanwhile, preliminary results from the July 30 voting for the 500-seat National Assembly indicated that the AMP had secured approximately 224 seats, followed by RENACO, approximately 100 seats; the Unified Lumumbist Party, approximately 34 seats; the Coalition of Congolese Democrats, approximately 30 seats; and the Congolese Rally for Democracy, approximately 15 seats.

The Country

Known prior to independence as the Belgian Congo and variously thereafter as the Federal Republic of the Congo, the Democratic Republic of the Congo (for the first time), Congo-Kinshasa, and Zaire, the Democratic Republic of the Congo (DRC) is situated largely within the hydrographic unit of the Congo River basin, in west-central Africa. The second-largest of the sub-Saharan states, the equatorial country is an ethnic mosaic of some 200 different groups. Bantu tribes (Bakongo, Baluba, and others) represent the largest element in the population, about half of which is Christian. Among the rural population, women are responsible for most subsistence agriculture, with men the primary cash-crop producers; in urban areas women constitute more than a third of wage earners, most of whom also engage in petty trade on the black market to supplement family income.

The DRC has major economic potential based on its great natural wealth in mineral resources, agricultural productivity sufficient for both local consumption and export, and a system of inland waterways that provides access to the interior and is the foundation for almost half of the total hydroelectric potential of Africa. Mineral extraction dominates the economy: cobalt and copper,

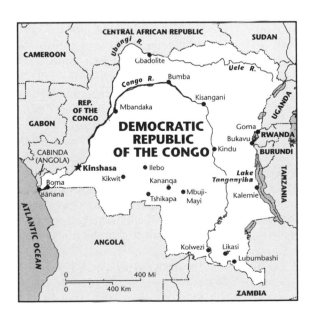

diamonds, tin, manganese, zinc, silver, cadmium, gold, and tungsten are among the commercially exploited reserves. Offshore oil began flowing in late 1975, while important agricultural products include coffee, rubber, palm oil, cocoa, and tea. Despite these assets, per capita income is one of the lowest in Africa, and the economy has for some years hovered on the brink of disaster. Consequently, infant mortality is high, and primary and secondary education is poor. In addition, universities, once among the continent's finest, are currently neglected, while the country (nearly the size of Western Europe) remains largely devoid of roads outside the major cities.

The International Monetary Fund (IMF) and World Bank provided assistance in the early 1990s in response to government austerity measures and liberalization of the investment code. However, in June 1994 the IMF suspended Zaire's voting rights and called on the Mobutu administration to take steps to eliminate its debt arrears. Corruption charges against regime members and a counterfeiting scandal overshadowed Zaire's economic adjustment efforts in the second half of 1994, and on December 31 the government announced that its foreign reserves had dwindled to two thousand dollars and "a few Swiss francs." At the time of the rebel takeover of Kinshasa in May 1997 the economy was in collapse, and the new government immediately announced its intention to focus on rebuilding and expanding the country's infrastructure. Despite barriers such as the DRC's $14 billion external debt, Western investors reportedly expressed eagerness to participate in development, the administration having proclaimed its intention to incorporate free-market practices in its economic system despite President Laurent Kabila's former Marxist orientation. However, in early 1998 the IMF suspended its loan program after Kabila reneged on a pledge to resume debt payments. Subsequently, economic issues were relegated to the background when civil war broke out in August (see Political background, below). Real GDP fell by 5.6 percent in 1997, 1.6 percent in 1998, 10.4 percent in 1999, and 4.3 percent in 2000. Real annual per capita GDP had declined to $85 by the end

of 2000 from $224 in 1990. The alarming situation was also marked by hyperinflation (107 percent in 1998, 70 percent in 1999, and 554 percent in 2000), an estimated 2 million internally displaced persons, and some 350,000 refugees from other countries.

Increased mineral (primarily diamonds) and oil exports helped foster GDP growth of 3 percent in 2002 and 5 percent in 2003. The IMF and World Bank approved a reduction of some 80 percent of the DRC's external debt in 2003, and continued economic improvement was expected in the wake of the partial conclusion of the five-year civil war in 2003 and the installation of a transitional national unity government. However, overall international economic and humanitarian aid remained minimal as the world diverted its attention from what the UN called one of the globe's "worst human crises." (An estimated 3–4 million people had died as the result of the recent civil war, mostly from conflict-related disease and starvation. In addition, one-fifth of the country's children were dying by the age of five, contributing to "1,200 unnecessary deaths per day," while 1.6 million people remained internally displaced, mostly in the "lawless" east.)

GDP grew by nearly 7 percent in 2004, and additional debt relief was subsequently promised by the government's commercial creditors. The IMF and World Bank also pledged an additional $2.4 billion in aid, provided the administration combats corruption in the state-owned oil company and systemic graft throughout other sectors. The IMF also chided the government for spending too much on "security concerns" and too little on poverty-reducing programs.

Government and Politics

Political Background

The priority given to economic rather than political development during Belgium's 75-year rule of the Congo contributed to an explosive power vacuum when independence was abruptly granted in June 1960. UN intervention, nominally at the request of the central government headed by President Joseph KASAVUBU, helped check the

Political Status: Independent republic established June 30, 1960; one-party constitution of February 1978 modified in June 1990 to accommodate multiparty system; all government institutions dissolved on May 17, 1997, following rebel takeover of the capital, and executive, legislative, and judicial authority assumed the same day by a self-appointed president backed by the military; interim constitution providing for a transitional national government approved April 2, 2003, by various groups participating in the Inter-Congolese National Dialogue; new constitution endorsed by national referendum on December 18, 2005, and promulgated on February 18, 2006, providing for new national elections later in the year.

Area: 905,562 sq. mi. (2,345,409 sq. km.).

Population: 29,916,800 (1984C); 56,057,000 (2005E).

Major Urban Centers (2005E): KINSHASA (7,000,000), Mbuji-Mayi (1,300,000), Lubumbashi (1,275,000).

Official Languages: French. Kikongo, Lingala, Swahili, and Tshiluba are classified as "national languages."

Monetary Unit: Congolese Franc (market rate July 1, 2006: 440.50 francs = $1US).

President: Joseph KABILA; appointed by the Legislative and Constituent Assembly–Transitional Parliament on January 24, 2001, and inaugurated on January 26 to succeed his father, Laurent Désiré KABILA (Alliance of Democratic Forces for the Liberation of Congo-Zaire), who had died on January 18 of injuries suffered in an assassination attempt two days earlier; inaugurated as interim president on April 7, 2003, in accordance with peace agreement signed on April 2. [**Note:** New presidential elections, postponed several times in 2005 and the first half of 2006, were held on July 30, 2006. *See headnote.*]

Vice Presidents: Jean-Pierre BEMBA (Movement for the Liberation of the Congo), Abdoulaye YERODIA Ndombasi (People's Party for Reconstruction and Democracy), Arthur Z'ahidi NGOMA (Forces of the Future), and Azarias RUBERWA Manywa (Congolese Rally for Democracy); inaugurated on July 17, 2003, in accordance with peace settlement signed in April.

centrifugal effects of factionalism and tribalism and preserve the territorial integrity of the country during the troubled early years, which witnessed the removal and death of its first prime minister, Patrice LUMUMBA, and the gradual collapse of separatist regimes established by Albert KALONJI in Kasai, Moïse TSHOMBE in Katanga (now Shaba Region), and Antoine GIZENGA in Stanleyville (now Kisangani). The withdrawal of UN peacekeeping forces in 1964 did not mark the end of political struggle, however, with Tshombe, who was appointed interim prime minister in July, and Kasavubu subsequently vying for power of what became (for the first time) the Democratic Republic of the Congo in August. On November 24, 1965, the commander of the army, Maj. Gen. Joseph D. MOBUTU, who had previously held control of the government from September 1960 to February 1961, dissolved the civilian regime and proclaimed himself president of the "Second Republic."

During 1966 and 1967 Mobutu put down two major challenges to his authority by white mercenaries and Katangan troops associated with the separatist activities of former prime minister Tshombe. Pierre MULÉLÉ and Gaston N'GALO, leaders of the rebellion against the central government in 1963 and 1964, were executed in 1968 and 1969, respectively; Tshombe died in captivity in Algeria in June 1969. Other plots were reported in 1971, one of them involving former associates of Mobutu, who in 1970 had been directly elected (albeit as sole candidate) to the presidency following establishment of the Popular Movement of the Revolution (*Mouvement Populaire de la Révolution*— MPR). Shortly thereafter, in an effort to reduce tension and solidify national unity, Mobutu embarked upon a policy of "authenticity," which included the general adoption of African names, and the country was officially redesignated the Republic of Zaire in October.

The country's Shaba Region was the scene of attempted invasions in March 1977 and May 1978 by rebel forces of the Congolese National Liberation Front (*Front de la Libération Nationale Congolaise*—FLNC) directed by a former Katangan police commander, Nathaniel MBUMBA. The first attack, repulsed with the aid of some 1,500 Moroccan troops airlifted to Zaire by France, was said to have failed because of Mbumba's inability to enlist the aid of other groups opposed to the Mobutu regime, particularly the Popular Revolutionary Party (*Parti de la Révolution Populaire*—PRP) of eastern Zaire, led by Laurent Désiré KABILA. In 1978, government forces were initially assisted by French and Belgian paratroopers, whose presence was defended as necessary to ensure the orderly evacuation of Europeans, and subsequently by a seven-nation African security force that was not withdrawn until July–August 1979.

The 1977 Shaba invasion was followed by a series of government reforms that included the naming in July of MPINGA Kasenda to the newly created post of first state commissioner (equivalent to prime minister) and the holding of direct elections in October to urban councils, to the National Legislative Council (*Conseil Législatif National*—CLN), and for 18 seats on the MPR Political Bureau. Having been reconfirmed by referendum as MPR president, Mobutu was invested for a second seven-year term as head of state on December 5.

In March 1979 the National Executive Council (cabinet) was reorganized, with André BOBOLIKO Lok'onga being named to replace Mpinga, who became permanent secretary of the MPR. Jean NGUZA Karl-I-Bond was designated first state commissioner on August 27, and Bo-Boliko assumed the new position of party executive secretary. In April 1981 Nguza resigned while on a trip to Belgium, declaring that he would have been imprisoned had the announcement been made prior to his scheduled departure; N'SINGA Udjuu Ongwakebi Untube was named as his successor. N'singa was in turn replaced by Joseph Léon KENGO wa Dondo in a major government reorganization on November 5, 1982, following a single-party (but multiple-candidate) election to the CLN September 18–19.

Again presenting himself as the sole candidate, President Mobutu was reelected for a third seven-year term on July 27, 1984. Fifteen months later, on October 31, 1986, he announced that the post of first state commissioner had been abolished, Kengo wa Dondo being redesignated as foreign minister; however, the office was restored in the course of a major ministerial reshuffling in January 1987, with former finance minister MABI Mulumba being designated its incumbent. Mabi was in turn succeeded on March 7, 1988, by SAMBWA Pida Nbagui. In the fourth cabinet reshuffling of the year, Sambwa was removed on November 26 and Kengo returned to the post he had held 1982–1986.

On April 24, 1990, bowing to rising demands for social and political change, Mobutu announced an end to Zaire's one-party system: during the ensuing year the constitution would be revised to permit the formation of trade unions and at least two additional parties. One day later he named the incumbent secretary general of the Economic Community of Central African States, Vincent de Paul LUNDA Bululu, to succeed Kengo wa Dondo as head of a substantially restructured "transitional" government that was installed on May 4.

The euphoria generated by the prospect of a liberalized "Third Republic" quickly dissipated with continued repression of opposition activity and a presidential declaration that the launching of a limited multiparty system would not take place for at least two years. The result was a bloody confrontation at the University of Lubumbashi on May 11, 1990, during which more than 50 student protesters were reported to have been killed. The legislature responded in late June by altering the constitution to accommodate the regime's April promises and reduce Mobutu's powers. Domestic and international impatience with the government's economic and human rights policies nonetheless continued, and in late November the basic law was further amended in favor of "full" multiparty democracy. On December 31 the president pledged that both presidential and legislative elections, in addition to a referendum on yet another new constitution, would be held in 1991.

On March 3, 1991, most of the more than five dozen political parties issued a demand that the government call a National Conference to consider more extensive constitutional revision. A month later, President Mobutu set April 29 as the date for such a meeting, although the three leading opposition groups indicated that they would not participate. On May 2 the National Conference was postponed following the massacre of 42 opposition supporters by security forces; it was subsequently rescheduled, initially for July 10 and then for July 30. Meanwhile, on July 22 the regime announced that Étienne TSHISEKEDI wa Malumba, leader of the opposition Sacred Union (*Union Sacrée*) coalition, had agreed to become prime minister, and on July 25 MULUMBA Lukoji, who had been named on March 15 to succeed Lunda, was dismissed. However, under pressure from Sacred Union members, Tshisekedi denied that he had accepted the government's offer, and on July 27 Mulumba was returned to office.

The National Conference finally convened on August 7, 1991, but was suspended a week later after opposition delegates had walked out, protesting that they had been harassed by the police and that the meeting had been illegally packed with regime supporters. The conference reconvened on September 16 after Mobutu had agreed to grant it sovereign powers but was again suspended after a near-riotous first day. On September 29 Mobutu agreed to a reduction of presidential powers and formation of a cabinet dominated by the opposition. The next day Tshisekedi was elected prime minister, triggering a power struggle between the heads of state and government that prevented a scheduled resumption of the National Conference on October 2. On October 14 Tshisekedi secured acceptance of his cabinet nominees, but seven days later he was dismissed by Mobutu. Tshisekedi immediately challenged the legality of the action, and the Sacred Union refused the president's invitation to nominate a successor. Mobutu responded on October 23 by naming Bernadin MUNGUL Diaka, the leader of a small Sacred Union affiliate, to head a new government. Encountering an increasingly violence-prone public, the president on November 22 agreed to a Senegalese-mediated accord with the Sacred Union that stipulated that the next prime minister would be a mutual choice

that would "of necessity, come from the ranks of the opposition." Thereupon, former prime minister Jean Nguza Karl-I-Bond, nominally an opposition leader but an opponent of Tshisekedi, presented himself as a candidate for the position and was immediately expelled from the Sacred Union. Apparently hoping to exploit the opposition's disarray, Mobutu disregarded the accord of three days before and designated Nguza as prime minister on November 25.

Mobutu's third seven-year term as president expired on December 4, 1991, but he refused to step down, insisting that he would remain in office until elections could be scheduled. On December 11 the National Conference reconvened, naming Laurent MONSENGWO Pasinya, the archbishop of Kisangani and an outspoken critic of Mobutu, as its president the following day.

On January 14, 1992, Prime Minister Nguza ordered suspension of the National Conference on the grounds that some of its decisions were "provoking a political crisis," and in early February he called for the convening of a smaller "national round table" to draft a new constitution and set a timetable for elections. On April 6 the conference resumed, and 11 days later it disregarded a government order by asserting its sovereign status. On June 21 President Mobutu again suspended the conference after it had begun debate on the choice of a new prime minister, insisting that such an appointment was a presidential prerogative. That objection notwithstanding, a "global comprehensive policy on transition" was reached on July 30, whereby Mobutu would remain in office for the duration of the interregnum, with former prime minister Tshisekedi being redesignated as head of government.

On August 29, 1992, Tshisekedi named a 21-member cabinet, which, unlike his previous short-lived administration, included no Mobutu associates or MPR members. On September 4 the ban on political demonstrations was lifted, and on September 19 the National Conference revealed details of a draft multiparty, parliamentary-style constitution that it promised to present for a referendum prior to general elections. Meanwhile, Mobutu announced that the MPR would "take no part in the government of national union" and that he too would be presenting a draft constitution. On October 5 Mobutu ignored the National Conference's August dissolution of the CLN, and, supported by the 20,000-strong Special Presidential Division (*Division Spéciale Présidentielle*—DSP), he reconvened the CLN for constitutional debate. However, with both Tshisekedi and National Conference president Monsengwo urging a boycott of the "rebellious" legislature, the proceedings were poorly attended and quickly halted.

On December 1, 1992, Mobutu ordered the dissolution of the Tshisekedi government and the National Conference. Thereafter, faced with the prime minister's refusal to step aside, the president ordered DSP troops deployed throughout the capital and released new 5-million zaïre notes, which he insisted were necessary to pay the army. Meanwhile, on December 6, the National Conference concluded its sitting, electing Monsengwo as head of a transitional legislature (the High Council of the Republic [*Haut Conseil de la République*—HCR]) and demanding that Mobutu abandon his efforts to dissolve the transitional government.

On January 7, 1993, Mobutu declared that he would ignore the HCR's "ultimatum" that he recognize the Tshisekedi government, describing the HCR as having been established "according to antidemocratic procedures." Consequently, the HCR authorized the government to seek foreign intervention to force Mobutu to comply with its dictates and, after accusing Mobutu of "high treason" for "blocking the functioning of the country's institutions at every level," declared its intent to begin impeachment proceedings. On January 20 Tshisekedi announced that he would include MPR members in a "reconciliation" cabinet, and the Sacred Union, announcing a unilateral truce, suspended its demonstrations in support of Mobutu's ouster. However, a new crisis erupted on January 28, when DSP troops attacked anti-Mobutu forces in the capital. On January 29 Belgium and France dispatched troops to protect their citizens, and within days more than 45 people were reported killed, including the French ambassador. On February 3 Belgium, France, and the United States issued a joint statement blaming Mobutu for the breakdown in public order and threatened to isolate the president unless he transferred his executive powers to the prime minister. Mobutu responded two days later by announcing the dismissal of Tshisekedi because of his "inability" to form a national unity government and initiated legal proceedings against him for offenses against state security. On February 9 the HCR, while reportedly chastising Tshisekedi for failing to form a government more acceptable to the president, rejected the dismissal order.

The HCR's efforts to initiate a dialogue between Mobutu and Tshisekedi collapsed on February 24, 1993, when soldiers surrounded the HCR building and demanded that the council recognize the new zaïre note. The siege ended on February 26 following Western diplomatic intervention, and on March 5 Mobutu met with Monsengwo. Although the two failed to reach agreement, Mobutu on March 9 inaugurated a "conclave of the last chance," which, he claimed, had HCR support. On March 17 the conclave, which was boycotted by the HCR, named former Sacred Union spokesman Faustin BIRINDWA as prime minister. Birindwa, who had been expelled from the Sacred Union on March 1 for "political truancy," was confirmed by Mobutu on March 29 at the opening of an extraordinary session of the CLN, which had been charged by the president to adopt a "Harmonized Constitutional Text" drafted by the mid-March conference.

On April 2, 1993, Mobutu, in an effort to bolster both his and the CLN's legitimacy, promulgated constitutional amendments establishing the CLN as a transitional institution equal in status to the HCR and confirming the president's right to appoint the prime minister. Concurrently, Birindwa announced a government highlighted by the appointment of Nguza as deputy prime minister for defense. On April 5 Sacred Union activists organized a general strike to protest Birindwa's action, and on April 9 Tshisekedi, who had rejected Birindwa's right to name a cabinet, presented his own reshuffled government, which was approved by the HCR on April 13. On May 7 the Birindwa government released an election timetable calling for a constitutional referendum on July 30 to be followed three months later by elections to choose among the competing governmental institutions. The HCR promptly disputed Birindwa's legal right to call a referendum and urged the opposition to boycott any such proceedings.

In mid-July 1993 the Mobutu regime announced that it had dispatched presidential guardsmen to Kasia, Kivu, and Shaba provinces to help quell ethnic violence that had reportedly claimed more than 3,000 lives. By August the number of casualties had reportedly doubled, eliciting charges by foreign observers that the president's forces were exacerbating the situation in an effort to slow the democratization process. Thereafter, negotiations in September between the regime-supportive Political Forces of the Conclave (*Forces Politiques du Conclave*—FPC) and the Sacred Union of Radical Opposition (*Union Sacrée de l'Opposition Radicale*—USOR), a successor to the Sacred Union, yielded a draft Constitutional Act of the Transition. However, efforts to finalize the accord remained stalled through the remainder of the year as the FPC continued to reject the USOR's demand that Tshisekedi's prime ministerial status be recognized, arguing that the National Conference's authority had been superseded by the HCR. Meanwhile, at a December 14 rally attended by former prime minister Nguza, Shaba governor Gabriel KUNGUA Kumwanza, in an action that evoked memories of the 1960 secession, declared the province's "total autonomy" from Zaire and reversion to its former name of Katanga.

On January 4, 1994, Mobutu issued an ultimatum to the deadlocked FPC and USOR leaderships, ordering them to implement the September 1993 agreement by January 12. Consequently, the two sides agreed on January 11 to the formation of a national unity government that included members from both Birindwa's and Tshisekedi's cabinets, thus precipitating Mobutu's January 14 dismissal of Birindwa and dissolution of the CLN and HCR. In addition, Mobutu directed the newly organized High Council of the Republic–Parliament of Transition (*Haut Conseil de la République– Parlement de Transition*—HCR-PT) to deliberate on the prime ministerial candidacies of Tshisekedi

and Mulumba Lukoji, who was backed by moderate opposition parties. However, on January 17 Tshisekedi rejected Mobutu's right to dissolve the original HCR and called for a "dead city" general strike on January 19 (the date the new legislature was scheduled to convene).

On January 23, 1994, the HCR-PT held its inaugural meeting, and two days later it appointed Monsengwo as its president. Thereafter, on April 8 the HCR-PT endorsed a second transitional constitution act, inaugurating a 15-month transitional period to culminate in general elections. Although the new document was immediately endorsed by USOR "moderates," Tshisekedi and his supporters denounced it, declaring that a provision calling for the declaration of prime ministerial candidacies implied that the post was vacant; nonetheless, on April 19 Tshisekedi reportedly accepted the accord's terms. Following the HCR-PT's acceptance of the credentials of seven prime ministerial candidates (including Tshisekedi) on May 2, Tshisekedi's followers announced their intention to boycott the proceedings and rebuked their USOR coalition partners for nominating candidates to compete against Tshisekedi. Two weeks later, the split within the USOR was formalized when the Tshisekedi faction ousted a number of parties aligned with former prime minister Kengo wa Dondo's Union for the Republic and Democracy (*Union pour la République et la Démocratie*—URD). On May 13 the HCR-PT appointed a commission to "quickly" define the criteria for choosing a prime minister, and on June 11 it ratified a list of seven individuals that did not include Tshisekedi because "he had not made a proper application to be a candidate." On June 14 the HCR-PT restored Kengo wa Dondo as prime minister, and on July 6 Kengo wa Dondo named a new government. For his part, Tshisekedi insisted that he remained Zaire's legitimate prime minister.

In August 1994 Kengo wa Dondo announced the formation of two electoral preparation commissions and pledged to adhere to a transitional schedule calling for prompt elections. Two months later the USOR rejoined the HCR-PT, and on November 16 Kengo wa Dondo reshuffled his cabinet to allow USOR members to assume posts that had been set aside for them in July. Subsequently, already strained relations between Kengo wa Dondo and Mobutu further deteriorated when Mobutu refused to endorse Kengo wa Dondo's nominee to head the Central Bank of Zaire. Meanwhile, Kengo wa Dondo announced in mid-December that long overdue presidential and parliamentary elections, as well as a constitutional referendum, would be held in July 1995; however, in May 1995 the balloting was again postponed.

Subsequently, FPC interim president Mandungu BULA Nyati orchestrated a legislative alliance between his party and the USOR that on June 30, 1995, provided overwhelming support for a two-year extension of the political transition period and, on July 2, successfully forwarded a motion calling for the resignation of HCR-PT president Monsengwo. Thereafter, amid reports that the alliance was planning to force his ouster, Prime Minister Kengo wa Dondo invited the "whole spectrum of the political class" to hold a dialogue and reportedly sought opposition participation in the reshuffled government he named on July 23. However, his entreaties were rebuffed by the USOR, which described the new cabinet as "illegal."

In February 1996 Kengo wa Dondo ousted 23 cabinet ministers, including all remaining opposition sympathizers, and filled their slots with his supporters, thereby rejecting the FPC's call for a new division of cabinet portfolios. Underscoring the level of factionalization in Kinshasa, the prime minister's allies boycotted the inauguration of the National Elections Commission (*Commission des Élections Nationales*—CEN) on April 3, claiming that they had been excluded from leadership positions. Meanwhile, the CEN was charged with preparing for a constitutional referendum in December 1996, presidential and legislative elections in May 1997, and local balloting in June and July 1997.

In May 1996 fighting broke out between Banyamulenge Tutsis and Rwandan Hutu refugees in the eastern region of South Kivu. Tension had been escalating there since an estimated 700,000–1,000,000 Hutus had fled Rwanda to Zaire in 1994 following the takeover of Kigali by Tutsi military forces. Among the refugees were members of *Interahamwe*, the Hutu militia that had been implicated in the massacre of hundreds of thousands of Tutsis and Hutu "collaborators" in Rwanda in April 1994 (see article on Rwanda). The Hutu militants subsequently gained control of the camps in Zaire, providing a degree of security for the Hutu refugees, who feared reprisals from Tutsis on both sides of the border for the recent "genocide" in Rwanda. Conflict quickly developed between the refugees and the Banyamulenge Tutsis who numbered an estimated 400,000 in eastern Zaire, where their ancestors had migrated 200 years earlier and where they had achieved a high level of unofficial governmental autonomy. For their parts, the Rwandan government accused the *Interahamwe* of cross-border attacks in western Rwanda while the Zairean government claimed that Banyamulenge militants were being armed and trained in Rwanda.

On October 8, 1996, amid escalating hostilities in the region, the deputy governor of Kivu, citing a 1981 law stripping the Tutsis of their Zairean citizenship, ordered them to leave the country within a week or risk annihilation. Although the governor was immediately suspended for his comments, thousands of Tutsis fled the area. At the same time, the Banyamulenge fighters, now reportedly numbering 3,000, launched an offensive that resulted in the quick rout of the Hutu fighters from the refugee camps and the retreat of the Zairean troops.

On October 29, 1996, Kinshasa declared a state of emergency in North and South Kivu as theretofore sporadic firefights between Rwandan and Zairean regular forces escalated into intense cross-border shelling. Collaterally, Kinshasa accused the Rwandan and Ugandan governments of attempting to take advantage of the absence of President Mobutu, who continued to convalesce in France from the effects of cancer surgery in August. Meanwhile, the Tutsi rebels, now widely identified as associated with the Alliance of Democratic Forces for the Liberation of Congo-Zaire (*Alliance des Forces Démocratiques pour la Libération du Congo-Zaire*—AFDL) and led by longtime anti-Mobutu guerrilla Laurent Kabila, continued to gain territory along Zaire's eastern border. Their numbers growing with the addition of militants from dissident ethnic groups, AFDL fighters reportedly faced little resistance from fleeing Hutus and Zairean troops (many of whom were accused of pillaging the towns they were assigned to protect).

Earlier, in Kinshasa on October 6, 1996, the HCR-PT had adopted a draft constitution that it pledged to present for a referendum in December. The proposed charter was immediately denounced by the USOR's Tshisekedi, who argued that the constitution produced by the 1991–1992 National Conference should be presented unaltered for referendum.

Thereafter, faced with continued AFDL advances, the HCR-PT on November 1 called for the expulsion of all Tutsis from Zaire. On November 2 the AFDL captured Goma, and on November 4 Kabila announced a unilateral cease-fire to allow international aid groups to facilitate the repatriation of the refugees, the bulk of whom (700,000) were reportedly massed near Mugunga. Amid international cries for the deployment of a military intervention force to stave off a humanitarian disaster, the AFDL on November 11 agreed to open a corridor for aid to reach the refugees and subsequently drove off the remaining Hutu militiamen in the area. Consequently, from November 15 to 19 more than 400,000 Hutu refugees, apparently convinced that it was now safer in Rwanda than in Zaire, flowed across the border, thus effectively dampening international support for the UN's military deployment plans (see Foreign relations, below).

On November 21, 1996, the AFDL declared an end to its cease-fire, and over the following several days it announced the appointment of its own officials to administrative positions in the Kivu regions. By early December the rebels had encircled Kisangani, Zaire's fifth-largest city, and reportedly controlled five large towns and a wide swath of territory. On December 17 a visibly ailing Mobutu returned to Kinshasa, and the following day he appointed a new chief of staff, Gen. Mahele Lioko BOKUNGU, and charged him with ending the rebellion. Mobutu met with a broad spectrum of political leaders on December 19 in an attempt to establish a government of national unity to confront the AFDL advance. However, Tshisekedi and his Union for Democracy and Social Progress (*Union pour la Démocratie et le Progrès Social—* UDPS) boycotted the meeting, effectively dooming its chances for success. Consequently, following a week of reportedly intense debate within the presidential circle, Mobutu on December 24 reappointed Kengo wa Dondo as prime minister.

The AFDL drive across Zaire proceeded quickly in early 1997, forcing a tide of Hutu refugees ahead of it, as demoralized Zairean troops offered little effective resistance to the rebels, who were substantially supported by Rwandan forces. (France, the last nation to drop a strong pro-Mobutu stance, described the AFDL as an "invading army.") On March 23 Prime Minister Kengo wa Dondo resigned, although he accepted caretaker status pending establishment of a new government. In what appeared to be a desperate final effort at a political settlement that would preclude a humiliating surrender, Mobutu on April 2 appointed longtime foe Tshisekedi as prime minister, and a new cabinet was announced the following day, which included six spots reserved for the AFDL. Conflict between security forces and UDPS supporters subsequently broke out in Kinshasa, and Mobutu abruptly dismissed Tshisekedi on April 9, replacing him with Gen. Likulia BOLONGO, former defense minister, who named a cabinet dominated by the military on April 11.

With the international community calling for a negotiated settlement and establishment of a transitional government to avoid widespread bloodletting as the AFDL neared Kinshasa, Mobutu agreed to meet with Kabila and South African president Nelson Mandela on a boat moored off the Zairean coast on May 4. However, although Mobutu reportedly expressed a willingness to relinquish power to a transitional government, final arrangements for his departure were never settled. Mobutu ultimately fled Kinshasa for Togo (and eventually Morocco, where he died on September 7) at the last moment on May 16. Following a brief but murderous rampage by Mobutu loyalists against "traitors" in Kinshasa, AFDL forces entered the capital on

May 17. Kabila, still located in the east, immediately declared himself president of the renamed Democratic Republic of the Congo (DRC) and ordered all governmental institutions dissolved.

Kabila arrived in Kinshasa on May 20, 1997, and, after conferring with leaders of various political groupings, made the first appointments to his new cabinet on May 22. However, to the great dismay of long-standing Mobutu opponents, the new regime announced there would be no role for Tshisekedi, whose supporters immediately organized a protest demonstration. In view of the unrest, Kabila on May 26 ordered the suspension of all political party activity and banned mass gatherings of any sort. Surrounded by the presidents of Angola, Burundi, Rwanda, Uganda, and Zambia, Kabila took the presidential oath of office on May 29, having promised a referendum on a new constitution by the end of 1998 and new legislative and presidential elections by April 1999.

After 32 years of Mobutu's dictatorial rule, the populace initially appeared, for the most part, to welcome the AFDL forces as "liberators" in May 1997. Regional leaders also strongly endorsed the regime of President Kabila, reflecting their long-standing complaint that Mobutu had permitted their opponents to conduct rebel activity against them from Zaire. The support from Western capitals was somewhat more cautious, particularly as reports surfaced of the alleged massacre of Hutus by the AFDL during its march across the country. Concern on that front deepened throughout the year and into early 1998 as the administration appeared to stonewall a UN investigation. In addition, widespread domestic disenchantment was reported by early 1998, particularly in regard to the stifling of political party activity and the dismissive treatment accorded to the UDPS and former prime minister Tshisekedi, described as the most popular political figure in the country. Ethnic tensions also continued to simmer, as evidenced by anti-AFDL rebel activity in several regions and reported growing concern over the heavy Tutsi influence at all levels of the AFDL administration. For his part, Kabila argued that "outsiders" did not appreciate the difficulties facing the DRC and that it was appropriate for his government to concentrate on reconstruction and the restoration of order while proceeding at a moderate pace toward general elections in 1999.

In April 1998 the UN withdrew its investigators, asserting that the Kabila government had purposely blocked their inquiry. Meanwhile, relations deteriorated between the president and the Rwandan-backed Banyamulenge Tutsis who had guided him to power; furthermore, increasing ethnic unrest was reported in the provinces bordering Rwanda and Uganda. In late July, Kabila demanded that Rwanda withdraw all of its remaining forces (he had reportedly become convinced that Kigali was preparing to overthrow his government). On August 2 government soldiers stationed in the east were attacked by Banyamulenge rebel forces supported by Rwandan troops. Within days the rebels had opened a second front within striking distance of Kinshasa, and, at a mid-August summit in Goma, the anti-Kabila forces—now bolstered by the addition of "Mobutists" and other former Kabila supporters—formed the Congolese Rally for Democracy (*Rassemblement Congolais pour la Démocratie*—RCD). Meanwhile, the rebel forces continued to capture large swaths of territory and appeared prepared to launch a full-scale attack on Kinshasa; however, in late August Zimbabwean and Angolan troops fighting on behalf of Kabila launched a counteroffensive against the RCD, and soon thereafter Kabila's defenders (now including Namibia and Chad) had fought the rebels to a standstill.

Fierce clashes were reported throughout the end of 1998 and in early 1999, and concern grew among regional and international observers that the fighting would spread beyond the DRC's borders. Peacemaking efforts were stymied, however, by Kabila's refusal to negotiate with the RCD, which he had described as a front for Rwandan and Ugandan invasion forces.

A cease-fire agreement was signed in July 1999 at a meeting in Lusaka, Zambia, of the six countries then involved in the fighting in the DRC (Angola, Namibia, and Zimbabwe on the government side; and Rwanda and Uganda in support of differing RCD factions and increasingly in conflict with one another) as well as Jean-Pierre BEMBA, the "Mobutist" leader of an increasingly important rebel force backed by Uganda, called the Movement for the Liberation of the Congo (*Mouvement pour la Libération du Congo*—MLC). The Lusaka accord envisioned the withdrawal of all foreign troops from the DRC, the disarming of local militias under the supervision of a Joint Military Commission, and the eventual deployment of UN peacekeepers. The ruptured RCD (see Political Parties and Groups, below) signed the agreement in August, but renewed fighting quickly broke out between the RCD factions, both of which had repudiated the agreement by the end of the year. (Among other things, the RCD infighting served as a surrogate for the conflict between the forces from Uganda and Rwanda, each of whom was viewed in many quarters as participating in the exploitation of the DRC's mineral wealth.) Nevertheless, in November the UN Security Council authorized the creation of the UN Organizational Mission in the Democratic Republic of the Congo (*Mission de l'Organisation des Nations Unies en République Démocratique du Congo*—MONUC) to assist in monitoring any eventual peace settlement. (In February 2001 the Security Council authorized up to 5,000 personnel for MONUC.)

President Kabila was shot by one of his bodyguards on January 16, 2001, and was declared dead from the wounds two days later. (The motive for the attack and any possible related conspiracy remained unclear, the assailant having been shot to death immediately after the attack.) On January 24 Kabila's son, Maj. Gen. Joseph KABILA, theretofore his father's chief of staff, was selected by the transitional legislature (installed by Laurent Kabila in August 2000 [see Legislature, below]) to succeed his father. Joseph Kabila immediately called for an intensification of talks toward national reconciliation, and in February another tentative UN-brokered accord was reached. The following month the first MONUC forces arrived in the DRC, but the proposed withdrawal of other foreign troops was delayed, in large part due to Rwanda's insistence that the Hutu militias be disarmed as a precondition to withdrawal. In April, Kabila appointed a new cabinet from which antinegotiation ministers were purged. Fighting, often intense, among RCD factions and between government forces and the rebels continued throughout 2001 and into early 2002 as peace talks inched toward a settlement.

In July 2002 the DRC and Rwanda finally reached a conclusive agreement providing for the withdrawal of the 20,000 Rwandan troops in the DRC starting in mid-September. Two months later a similar accord was struck with Uganda, setting the stage for intensification of talks (known as the Inter-Congolese National Dialogue) involving the government, domestic opposition parties, and rebel groups regarding a permanent resolution of the civil war. Under the weight of heavy international pressure, a potentially historic accord was signed in mid-December in Pretoria, South Africa, by Kabila, the RCD factions, the MLC, and representatives of opposition parties and civil society. The accord provided for a cease-fire and installation of a transitional government pending new national elections within 30 months. Power in the interim government was to be shared, with Kabila, as president, being assisted by four vice presidents and a transitional legislature, whose members would be selected, on a carefully allocated basis, by the signatories.

The warring factions approved a new interim constitution providing for the installation of Kabila's national unity government in April 2003. Integral to the composition of the cabinet was the inclusion of the four vice presidents (see Vice Presidents, above). More than half of the cabinet members represented either opposition or rebel groups. In late June most of the former combatants agreed in principle to their integration into a unified national army in which power sharing was to be carefully delineated. The integration began in August, with Kabila appointing several former rebel commanders to prominent positions. Rebel groups, civil organizations, and opposition parties were also represented prominently in Kabila's appointments in May 2004 to new provisional governments for the country's ten regions and capital district.

On May 5, 2005, the transitional legislature approved the draft of a new constitution (see below for details) for consideration via national referendum, which on December 18 endorsed the new basic law with an 84 percent yes vote. President Kabila signed the new constitution into effect on February 18, 2006, and new national elections were planned for later in the year.

Constitution and Government

A constitution drafted under President Mobutu's direction and approved by popular referendum in 1967 established a strong presidential system, certain features of which were drastically modified by amendments enacted in August 1974. Decisions of the MPR's Political Bureau were made binding upon both executive and legislative branches, thus making the Political Bureau the supreme state organ, while the MPR chair was designated president of the republic. The trend toward synthesis of government and party institutions was further exemplified by the creation of a National Executive Council (whose members were restyled state commissioners), in effect a fusion of the former cabinet with the Executive Council of the MPR. These changes were affirmed in a new constitution promulgated on February 15, 1978, in which the party was characterized as "the Zairean Nation organized politically" with an ideological commitment to "Mobutism." Beginning in 1977 members of the CLN were elected every five years from a list of candidates approved by the MPR.

In April 1990 the president ordered a transition to a tripartite polity, which he hoped could be introduced without a return to the "tribal factionalism" that had prevailed during the 1960s. In late June the CLN approved constitutional amendments that provided for separation of the responsibilities of the head of state and government (including removal from the former of foreign-policy powers), the formation of trade unions, and the organization of two additional political parties. However, the three-party system was condemned by the opposition, and on November 23, amid growing unrest, the basic law was further amended to allow for the unlimited organization of political parties.

On September 19, 1992, the National Conference adopted a draft multiparty constitution that included provisions for the creation of a bicameral parliamentary system, the replacement of the zaïre with the franc, the disenfranchisement of the military, and the designation of four indigenous languages (Kikongo, Lingala, Swahili, and Tshiluba) as official languages.

After President Mobutu's attempts in October to revive the CLN for debate on an alternative draft constitution had proved futile, a "political conclave" of pro-Mobutu parties met in Kinshasa March 9–19, 1993, to draft a so-called Harmonized Constitutional Text, which was approved by the reconvened CLN on March 31 and promulgated by the president on April 2. It purported to override the mid-1992 dissolution of the CLN, establishing it as a transitional body on par with the presidency and the HCR. Furthermore, the Mobutu charter reconfirmed the president's right to appoint the prime minister while redirecting the government's accountability from the HCR to the president and CLN.

On May 7, 1993, the Birindwa government introduced an electoral timetable that included plans for a constitutional referendum on July 30. One week later, in response to confusion over which constitution would be voted on—the Harmonized Constitutional Text or the National Conference charter—the government announced that a special commission would be convened to draft a single text. On May 25 HCR chair Monsengwo denounced the referendum plans as "irregular and illegal." Subsequently, the referendum was rescheduled for October.

Negotiations between presidential and opposition party leaders in September 1993 resulted in the adoption of a draft Constitutional Act of the Transition (*Acte Constitutionnel de la Transition*). The act delineated a transitional governance system that included a diminished presidency, the absorption of the current memberships of the HCR and CLN into a restyled, 500-member High Council of the Republic–Parliament of Transition (see HCR-PT, under Legislature, below), and a cabinet empowered with central bank and military oversight. However, the act remained unratified until January 14, 1994. Subsequently, it was superseded by a second transitional charter drafted by the HCR-PT and signed by President Mobutu on April 8, 1994. The new document called for a 15-month transitional period that was to include a referendum on the new constitution and conclude, prior to the May 1995 postponement, with general elections.

On October 6, 1996, the HCR-PT adopted yet another draft charter that it pledged to present for referendum. The document included provisions for a federal state (styled the Federal Republic of Zaire), a two-chamber parliament, a popularly elected president, and an expansion of the number of regions from 10 to 26. However, no action was taken regarding the proposed charter in view of the government takeover of May 1997. President Laurent Kabila appointed a constitutional commission in September 1997 to produce a new draft basic law by the end of March 1998. The commission was expected to endorse a strong presidential system based on the U.S. model. On March 30, 1998, the commission reportedly adopted a draft basic charter that included provisions for the creation of an elective vice-presidential post, the establishment of an enhanced judiciary system topped by a Supreme Court, and the dissolution of the prime minister's post. Subsequently, President Kabila issued a decree authorizing the formation of a 300-member Legislative and Constituent Assembly, which upon inauguration was to be charged with preparing for a constitutional referendum and legislative elections. Although the assembly was inaugurated in August 2000, no action was taken on the proposed constitution prior to Kabila's death in January 2001, after which the nature of the country's next constitutional arrangements were a primary focus of discussions between the government and rebel forces regarding a permanent peace settlement.

An interim constitution providing for a transitional government was adopted in April 2004 by most of the participants in the Inter-Congolese National Dialogue. The bicameral transitional legislature established by that accord (see Legislature, below, for details) subsequently (in May 2005) approved a draft of a new permanent constitution that was endorsed by national referendum in December. The new basic law provides for a "semipresidential" system in which the prime minister will have greater authority than in the past. The president's term was set at five years, renewable once. The minimum age for presidential candidates was reduced to 30, a measure clearly inserted to permit current President Joseph Kabila (34) to run for the office. Presidential balloting was to be conducted by direct vote under a two-round (if necessary) majoritarian system. The president was mandated to appoint the prime ministerial candidate selected by the majority party (or coalition of parties needed to make a majority) in the National Assembly, the lower house of the new Parliament (see Legislature, below, for details on the Parliament).

The new constitution permitted the current transitional government to remain in place until new national elections were held. Other important aspects included provisions to protect freedom of religion, expression, and political pluralism and to strengthen the judiciary. Citizenship was extended to members of all ethnic groups that were residing in the country at the time of independence.

The new constitution also called for significant devolution of governmental authority to the provinces, the number of which were to be extended from 10 to 26 (including the capital "province" of Kinshasa). Provincial authority was to be shared by presidentially appointed governors and directly elected provincial assemblies. Provinces will be further subdivided into communes and cities. Judicial authority at the national level was invested in a Constitutional Court, a Court of Cassation, and a High Military Court.

Foreign Relations

The DRC has generally pursued a moderate line in foreign policy while avoiding involvement in non-African issues. Relations with Belgium, its former colonial ruler, were periodically strained following independence, partly because vocal anti-Mobutu factions were based in Brussels. However,

Belgium remained a major aid donor. Development efforts following independence led to enhanced economic ties with Japan, the United States, and Western European countries, especially France, which Kinshasa in 1986 called its new European "fountainhead."

Relations with former French territories in central Africa have fluctuated. The Union of Central African States was formed with Chad in 1968, and more than 3,000 Zairean troops were sent to Chad in support of President Habré in 1983. In addition, Burundi and Rwanda joined Zaire in establishing the Economic Community of the Great Lakes Countries, the object being an eventual common market. Relations with Zambia have remained cordial despite a Zairean claim (resolved in 1987) to part of that country's northern Kaputa and Lake Mweru districts. In the west, border incidents involving the Republic of the Congo have periodically erupted, while in the east Zairean troops were given permission by Kampala in July 1987 to cross into Ugandan territory to engage rebels associated with the Congolese National Movement (see Political Parties, below).

A lengthy cold war between Zaire and Angola was formally terminated as the result of a visit by Angolan President Neto to Zaire in August 1978 and a reciprocal visit by President Mobutu to Angola the following October. The latter concluded with the signing of a cooperation agreement between the two governments and a mutual pledge to proceed with the establishment of a commission under the Organization of African Unity (OAU, subsequently the African Union—AU) to guard against rebel violations from either side of the 1,250-mile common border. By 1987, however, it had become apparent that the United States was deeply involved in covert activities in the vicinity of the Belgian-built air base at Kamina in southern Zaire, with plans to remodel the facility for delivery of supplies to the Angolan rebel forces led by Jonas Savimbi. Such collusion notwithstanding, President Mobutu joined in April with the heads of state of Angola, Mozambique, and Zambia in concluding, in Luanda, a declaration of intent to reopen the Benguela railroad, which had effectively

been closed by Angolan guerrilla operations since 1976.

In May 1982 Kinshasa announced that it was resuming diplomatic relations with Israel, reversing a rupture that had prevailed since the 1973 Arab–Israeli war. Earlier, President Mobutu had stated that the suspension was originally intended as a gesture of support for Egypt but was no longer justified in view of the return of the last of the occupied Egyptian territories in April, as provided by the 1979 peace treaty. In response, a number of Arab governments severed relations with Zaire, while regional leaders expressed concern at the Israeli "reentry" into Africa. In November, Israel's defense minister, Ariel Sharon, flew to Zaire to conclude arrangements for the supply of arms and the training of Zairean forces, particularly a "presidential battalion" under Mobutu's direct command. Further military-aid commitments were secured by Mobutu during a May 1985 visit to Israel, the regional backlash being tempered in 1986 by Zaire's resumption of participation in the OAU after a two-year hiatus occasioned by the OAU's admission of the Saharan Arab Democratic Republic.

In January 1989 President Mobutu, who had been strongly criticized in the Belgian press for financial aggrandizement, announced that he was abrogating agreements defining his country's postcolonial relations with Belgium; in addition, Zaire would halt payments on its more than $1 billion Belgian debt and explore alternatives to shipping its minerals to Belgium for refining. However, the dispute was settled and relations normalized at midyear.

In May 1990 Mobutu, labeling Brussels the "capital of subversion," rejected Belgian and European Community (EC, subsequently the European Union—EU) appeals for an international inquiry into the slayings at Lubumbashi University. Consequently, on May 24 Belgium halted aid payments, and, following Kinshasa's decision to sever diplomatic links on June 22, Belgium withdrew a debt-cancellation pledge. In August the U.S. Lawyers' Commission for Human Rights released a report describing Zaire's human rights record as a "systematic pattern of abuses." Subsequently, on

November 5 the U.S. Congress voted to suspend military aid and redirect humanitarian aid through nongovernmental agencies.

On September 24, 1991, France and Belgium ordered their troops to Zaire to protect foreign nationals threatened by widespread rioting and looting. One month later France and Belgium announced their disengagement from Kinshasa and called for regional intervention. Mobutu responded by vowing to stay in power and accusing international forces of "wanting my head at any price." In November, U.S. officials described Mobutu as having "lost the legitimacy to govern" and called for the regime to begin sharing power with the opposition.

In June 1992 the government announced that it was seizing the assets of all foreign oil companies as a means of alleviating chronic fuel shortages. While officials insisted that the measure was only temporary and promised reimbursement, the companies argued that the action was equivalent to confiscation, given Zaire's lack of currency reserves.

The appointment of the Tshisekedi government in August 1992 paved the way for an end in October to a ten-month-old aid embargo by the EC, although the EC stated its intention to continue to withhold funding until it received guarantees that it would be channeled to the appropriate recipients. Subsequently, in early December 1992 Prime Minister Tshisekedi's Western supporters criticized President Mobutu's attempts to dissolve the government, with Belgium reportedly preparing for a possible military role; the likelihood of such intervention increased dramatically in mid-January 1993 after the HCR had granted the government authorization to seek foreign assistance in ousting the president. Thereafter, following the outbreak of widespread military rioting in Kinshasa, Belgian and French troops were deployed at Kinshasa to protect their citizens.

On February 3, 1993, Belgium, France, and the United States issued a joint statement that described Mobutu as the architect of Zaire's ruin, called for the president's resignation, and threatened "total political and economic isolation" of his regime if he refused to capitulate. In late February,

Western diplomats continued to pressure Mobutu, warning him that he would be held personally responsible for the lives of the HCR members then being held captive in Kinshasa. The siege ended the following day.

Following the establishment of the Birindwa government in early April 1993, Mobutu's relations with Zaire's three largest donors deteriorated further. On April 7 the EC, which followed the lead of several of its members in repudiating the legal status of the new regime, reaffirmed its support for the Tshisekedi government, announced an embargo on arms sales to Zaire, and imposed visa restrictions on Mobutu and his allies. The Birindwa government responded by denouncing the "interference" in its internal affairs, expelling two Belgian diplomats, and, while rebuffing a CLN call to sever ties with the Europeans, warning against further Western action.

In September 1993 the Mobutu administration characterized as "tendentious" Amnesty International's release of a report critical of its human rights record. In February 1994 the international rights monitor accused the regime of continued complicity in human rights violations, charging the Mobutu-controlled military with responsibility for "indiscriminate executions." Moreover, international observers reporting on the plight of Rwandan refugees encamped along the Zairean border in mid-1994 accused Zairean troops of attacking refugees and confiscating their property. However, the Mobutu regime's support for French peacekeeping efforts in Rwanda was allegedly rewarded with an easing of international pressure on its domestic policies, and in mid-1994 France, Belgium, and the United States recognized the Kengo wa Dondo government.

On September 1, 1994, Zaire announced that the approximately 1.2 million Rwandan refugees in Zaire would have to leave by the end of the month. Although observers described the demand as unrealistic, it provoked renewed dialogue on the refugees' plight, and on October 24, Rwanda, Zaire, and the United Nations High Commission for Refugees (UNHCR) signed an agreement designed to facilitate their repatriation. However, during the first half of 1995 no further diplomatic progress was reported and conditions in the approximately 40 camps continued to deteriorate. On August 18, 1995, Zaire again ordered the expulsion of the refugees, citing rumors that both Rwanda and Burundi were preparing to attack the camps to suppress rebel groups. Within five days, 15,000 people were forcibly repatriated, while more than 100,000 others fled into the countryside. Pressured by the international community to end the expulsions, Kinshasa halted the program on September 7 and signed an accord with the UNHCR that, echoing the events of 1994, provided for the repatriation of the refugees by December.

Subsequently, in February 1996, Zairean troops, under UNHCR supervision, began sealing off the camps (in an effort to isolate them from the local communities) and urging the refugees to return home. The program was quickly abandoned, however, when the troops, demanding payment of salary arrears, left their posts.

Reportedly concerned about who would actually benefit from a militarily backed humanitarian aid program, as well as fearing involvement in a Somalia-like imbroglio, a number of regional and international capitals, including Washington, reacted warily toward a French- and Spanish-led call for foreign intervention in eastern Zaire in 1996. However, faced with the onset of what aid agencies predicted would ultimately be mass starvation, Canada, South Africa, and the United Kingdom had agreed to participate by November 11. Further bolstered by a U.S. commitment of 1,000 troops on November 13, the UN-sponsored, Canadian-led multinational force of 15,000 troops began deployment preparations on November 14. The efforts were suspended, however, following the subsequent mass repatriation of hundreds of thousands of refugees to Rwanda between November 15 and 19. Consequently, despite continued French lobbying for the dispatch of a military force, wide support for the plan dissipated, and at a meeting of the representatives of 29 countries and 6 aid agencies in Stuttgart, Germany, the operation was officially abandoned on November 22.

The DRC's foreign relations from 1998 to 2001 turned on the roles its neighbors played on both sides of the civil war that erupted in August 1998. Officially supporting the Kabila government with troops were Zimbabwe, Angola, Namibia, and Chad. In addition, Equatorial Guinea, Eritrea, Gabon, and Sudan expressed their sympathies with the DRC government but adopted far smaller roles in the dispute than did the aforementioned. On the side of the rebels, Rwanda and Uganda provided such a large amount of personnel and supplies that the Kabila administration accused them of invading DRC territory. To a lesser extent the insurgents were aided by Angolan rebels and supporters in Burundi. Noting the number of countries directly involved in the fighting, a Western official in late 1998 warned that the region was on the brink of the first "African world war."

Uganda had withdrawn its forces from the DRC by May 2003, and the two countries in 2004 agreed to cooperate in suppressing rebel groups on both sides of their border. However, relations with Rwanda remained strained, the DRC charging that Rwanda was still "stoking discontent" as of 2005.

In December 2005 the International Court of Justice (ICJ) ruled in favor of the DRC in regard to the case the DRC had filed charging Uganda with an "illegal incursion" into the DRC during the 1998–2003 conflict and the "plunder" of the DRC's natural resources. Uganda was ordered by the ICJ to pay reparations to the DRC, although a final amount was not determined. (The DRC was reportedly seeking $6–10 billion.) A similar DRC case against Rwanda remained under ICJ review as of early 2006.

Current Issues

An estimated 3–4 million people may have died in the 1998–2003 civil war, which had also destabilized the entire region. As of early 2005 the UN reported that sporadic but intense fighting in resource-rich areas of the country was still leading to the deaths of thousands of people per month. Although most major rebel groups had been integrated into the national army, small ethnic militias (often under the direction of local warlords) continued to terrorize the population. Meanwhile, the MONUC forces (whose mandate was extended to help train new police and security forces) suffered blistering criticism themselves for allegedly committing rapes while also failing to protect women from mass assaults by militiamen.

For his part, President Kabila was described in 2005 as "lurching from crisis to crisis," having reportedly survived several coup attempts in 2004. In January 2005 the government announced that the new national elections tentatively scheduled for June 2005 would not be held until June 2006, prompting massive public protests (led in large part by the UDPS). The government defended its decision on the grounds that all militias needed to be disarmed before voting could take place. Difficulties in registering some 26 million prospective voters and implementing electoral procedures were also cited in the delay.

Despite charges of widespread corruption, continued conflict in the east, and ongoing miserable conditions for the average citizen, the transitional government survived for the rest of 2005, buoyed in part by the constitutional referendum in December. Government officials reported a turnout of 60 percent for the referendum vote, which EU observers described as free and fair. Few analysts challenged the official tally of an 84 percent yes vote, most major parties and factions (with the notable exception of the UDPS) having supported the new basic law as representing at least a chance for the country to put its seemingly interminable chaos behind it. Thirty-three presidential candidates were registered for the first round of presidential elections (most recently rescheduled for July 30, 2006), despite a controversial $50,000 registration fee. In addition, candidates from more than 200 parties registered for the assembly balloting, whose first round was also scheduled for July 30. However, serious concerns remained over the boycott by the UDPS of the polls and the apparent intention of rebel militias in the resource-rich east to disrupt the balloting. The force strength of MONUC (already the largest and most expensive such UN deployment) was increased to more than 17,000 peacekeepers and military police to help try to preserve order during the elections. The EU also promised to send 1,500 troops of its own to assist in oversight. The West was generally perceived as supportive of a potential presidential victory by Kabila, who held massive leads in public opinion polls, particularly when it became clear that Étienne Tshisekedi of the UDPS would not be a candidate. However, underscoring the fragility of the situation, the government announced in May that it had uncovered another coup plot. Meanwhile, the UN appealed for massive additional aid to deal with a humanitarian crisis the UN characterized, in a reference to the Indian Ocean death toll in late 2004, as a "tsunami every six months."

Political Parties and Groups

All existing parties were outlawed in 1965. For the greater part of the next quarter century the only legal grouping was the Popular Movement of the Revolution (*Mouvement Populaire de la Révolution*—MPR). Established under General Mobutu's auspices in April 1967, the MPR progressively integrated itself with the governmental infrastructure. The formation in 1980 by a number of parliamentarians of the opposition Union for Democracy and Social Progress (UDPS) was countered by the MPR, which effectively co-opted most of the UDPS domestic leadership and severely repressed the remainder.

In April 1990 the president announced that the MPR, the UDPS, and one other party would be granted legal status during a "transitional period" culminating in a multiparty election in December 1991. Thereupon, more than 60 groups presented themselves for the remaining legal party position. However, in the face of manifest dissatisfaction with the pace and breadth of his reform program, Mobutu reversed himself in October and lifted the numeric restriction; as a result, 28 parties were registered by January 31, 1991, the applications of 94 others having been rejected as "incomplete."

An additional 38 parties were registered by mid-February, a majority of which were reportedly sympathetic to the MPR, and by March 30 a total of 58 parties had accepted the government's terms for the National Conference scheduled to convene on April 29. Meanwhile, however, leaders of the Sacred Union (*Union Sacrée*), an opposition coalition that included the influential UDPS, Union of Federalists and Independent Republicans (UFERI), and Democratic and Social Christian Party (PDSC), announced plans to boycott the conference, refused to recognize the recently named transitional government, and called for President Mobutu's resignation. Thereafter, while the 159 parties registered for the May 3–19 National Conference preparatory committee were described as largely proregime, Mobutu's continued reluctance to enact reforms had begun to alienate many groups, and by midyear the Sacred Union was credited with a membership of approximately 150 parties. The Sacred Union adopted the rubric of the Sacred Union of the Radical Opposition (*Union Sacrée de l'Opposition Radicale*—USOR) in 1993. (For an extensive history of the USOR, defunct as of 1998, see the 1999 *Handbook*.)

Governmental authority was taken over in May 1997 by Alliance of Democratic Forces for the Liberation of Congo-Zaire (*Alliance des Forces Démocratiques pour la Libération du Congo-Zaire*—AFDL), a predominantly Tutsi grouping of three rebel factions and the ADP (see RCD, below) that had been formed in November 1996 under the leadership of Laurent Kabila, a non-Tutsi "Lumumbist" who had been linked to anti-Mobutu militant groups since the 1960s. (For more information on the AFDL, which was dissolved by Kabila in 1999, see the 2005–2006 *Handbook*.) The AFDL immediately suspended all political party activity indefinitely, but President Kabila in late January 1999 lifted the ban on the formation of new political parties without, however, addressing the status of the previously existing parties. Moreover, the requirements for registering new parties demanded organizational and financial resources beyond most prospective groupings, while restrictions (such as a ban on any parties with connections to international organizations) also served to preclude participation.

Joseph Kabila ordered the barriers to party activity lifted in May 2001, and more than 150 parties had reportedly registered by the end of the year. However, in many cases, it was impossible to determine if the new parties were in fact positioned to genuinely affect domestic affairs.

In March 2004 Kabila signed a new law designed to grant parties access to media and provide them with state grants. The law also barred parties from involvement in fighting or military actions against the government. By 2005 more than 400 parties had reportedly registered with the Central Election Commission, with some 213 reportedly presenting candidates for the legislative balloting scheduled for 2006.

During the negotiations for the Pretoria Accord of 2002, 15 of the largest opposition political parties formed an alliance called the Opposition General Assembly (OGA) to coordinate strategy and priorities. As a result of the discussions, one of the four vice-presidential posts was designated for Arthur Z'ahidi NGOMA (Forces of the Future), the president of the OGA. Ngoma's appointment was opposed by some opposition parties, while other groups later became dissatisfied with his performance and called for his resignation. The result was a fracturing of the OGA.

Propresidential Party

People's Party for Reconstruction and Democracy (*Parti du Peuple pour la Reconstruction et la Démocratie*—PPRD). Formed in March 2002, the PPRD, composed mainly of former regime supporters and members of the government, was seen primarily as a political vehicle for President Joseph Kabila. Kabila initially asserted that he was not formally a member of the party, and, even though press reports routinely referenced him as the PPRD presidential candidate in 2006, Kabila announced that he would officially run as an independent in order to be the candidate of "all the Congolese people."

Leader: Vital KAMERHE (Secretary General).

Other Parties and Groups

Union for Democracy and Social Progress (*Union pour la Démocratie et le Progrès Social—* UDPS). The UDPS was the outgrowth of an effort in late 1980 to establish an opposition party within Zaire dedicated to the end of President Mobutu's "arbitrary rule." Subsequently, the government arrested, sentenced, and eventually amnestied a number of its members. The leadership was thrown into disarray in late 1987 when UDPS President Frédéric KIBASSA Maliba and several other prominent party members joined the Central Committee of the MPR (below) following a meeting with President Mobutu in which an agreement was reportedly reached to permit the UDPS to operate as a "tendency" within the governing formation. However, other leaders, including Secretary General Etienne Tshisekedi wa Malumba, vowed to remain in opposition and press for creation of a multiparty system, accusing government security forces of continuing to imprison and torture UDPS adherents.

During a visit to the United States in November 1990, Tshisekedi declared, "The people of Zaire are demanding that he [Mobutu] must go," and, following the party's official registration on January 16, 1991, he announced his presidential candidacy. Thereafter, the party stated that it would boycott any national conference not granted sovereign status and would refuse to join in a transitional government as long as Mobutu remained president.

On September 30, 1991, Tshisekedi agreed to be named prime minister, but two weeks later, following a struggle with Mobutu for executive authority, he was dismissed. Refusing to accept the validity of the president's action, Tshisekedi on November 1 chaired the first meeting of a parallel cabinet. On August 14, 1992, the National Conference voted to return Tshisekedi to the post of prime minister, which he retained until his controversial ouster on December 1.

Tshisekedi served as prime minister for one week in April 1997 as Mobutu desperately attempted to find a political solution to his impending ouster by the AFDL. The UDPS supporters were subsequently described as welcoming to the AFDL and new president Laurent Kabila; however, the relationship deteriorated quickly when Kabila declined to name Tshisekedi to his new government. The UDPS leader was detained in June 1997, and in February 1998 he was placed under house arrest for violating the ban on party activity and sent to his home village. In July, Tshisekedi was returned to Kinshasa and released. In early 1999 the UDPS leader and his opposition allies in Kinshasa reportedly refused the Kabila administration's invitation to participate in a national conference.

Following Kabila's death in early 2001, Tshisekedi proved to be one of the few old-time party leaders able to retain significant influence. Among other things, he participated in peace and reconciliation negotiations in conjunction with rebel groups and other opposition figures. Nonetheless, the UDPS refused to participate in the 2003 transitional government, and in 2005 it organized a series of demonstrations and rallies to protest the postponement of elections.

Under Tshisekedi's direction (called "dictatorial" by some party dissidents), the UDPS called for a boycott of the December 2005 constitutional referendum. Although Tshisekedi in early 2006 appeared ready to rejoin the political process in preparation for a presidential bid, he ultimately called for a boycott of the presidential and legislative balloting to protest the government's refusal to conduct new voter registration. (Some UDPS dissidents registered for the assembly poll, prompting their expulsion from the party.) Tshisekedi had been considered President Kabila's potentially most serious rival, while the UDPS, which claims support of some 30 percent of the electorate, had been expected to perform well (and perhaps lead) the legislative election.

Leaders: Etienne TSHISEKEDI wa Malumba (President of the Party), Rémy MASSAMBA Makiesse (Secretary General).

Congolese Rally for Democracy (*Rassemblement Congolais pour la Démocratie—*RCD). The RCD was formed in mid-August 1998 in Goma by the leaders of the predominantly Banyamulenge Tutsi rebels who had launched a military offensive against the government of Laurent Kabila on August 2. Ernest WAMBA dia Wamba, a theretofore largely unknown academic, emerged from the Goma meeting as the leader of the anti-Kabila forces. In addition, the RCD's leadership committee included Arthur Z'ahidi Ngoma, the prominent founder of the anti-Mobutu and subsequently anti-Kabila Forces of the Future, as well as two former Kabila government ministers, Bizima KARABA and Déogratias BUGERA. Bugera had been the leader and founder of the People's Democratic Alliance (*Alliance Démocratique des Peuples*—ADP), a military grouping of Tutsis that had been described as the dominant component of the AFDL as it marched across Zaire to seize the capital in May 1997 but had been ordered out of Kinshasa by the president in late July 1998.

In early 1999 RCD dissidents led by Bugera broke away from the group and formed the Reformers' Movement (*Mouvement des Réformateurs*—MR), and in February Ngoma formed the Union of Congolese for Peace, which he asserted would seek a peaceful solution to the country's crisis. Further intraparty friction was reported in March between Wamba dia Wamba, who allegedly sought a "political" end to the civil war, and a promilitary faction led by Alexis Tambwe and former prime minister Vincent de Paul Lunda Bululu. Meanwhile, a hard-liner, Emile ILUNGA, assumed command of the RCD's military operations amid reports that Wamba dia Wamba was losing control of the group. In May, Ilunga replaced Wamba dia Wamba as president of the RCD, and the group split into two warring factions, Ilunga's being backed by Rwanda, and Wamba dia Wamba's by Uganda. In October the latter faction adopted the rubric **RCD–Liberation Movement** (*RCD—Mouvement de la Libération*—RCD-LM). Ilunga was succeeded as president of the main RCD faction (now referenced as RCD-Goma) in October 2000 by Adolphe Onusumba Yemba. Meanwhile, yet another faction (**RCD–National** [RCD-N]) had broken off in June 2000 under the leadership of Roger Lumbala Tshitenge. In May 2001 Antipas NYAMWISI

Mbusa forcefully took control of the RCD-LM from Wamba dia Wamba.

The RCD groups participated in the Inter-Congolese National Dialogue and were signatories to the Pretoria Accord. Under the terms of the agreement, RCD-Goma secretary general Azarias Ruberwa Manywa was appointed one of four vice presidents of the republic in July 2003. The RCD factions agreed to disarm and a portion of their troops were integrated into the national security forces. In addition, the RCD factions received seats in both the Senate and National Assembly and posts in the transitional cabinet. The RCD-Goma briefly suspended participation in the transitional government in 2004 to protest the massacre of Tutsis in neighboring Burundi and what it viewed as the failure of the DRC government to take stronger action to protect refugees.

For the 2006 presidential election Ruberwa was listed as the official candidate of the RCD, although press reports continued to reference him as the candidate of RCD-Goma, while Lumbala ran as a candidate of the RCD-N and Nyamwisi as the candidate of the **Forces of Renewal** (*Forces du Renouveau*—FR).

Leaders: Antipas NYAMWISI Mbusa (RCD-LM), Adolphe ONUSUMBA Yemba (RCD-Goma), Roger LUMBALA Tshitenge (RCD-N), Azarias RUBERWA Manywa (Vice President of the Republic and Secretary General of RCD-Goma).

Movement for the Liberation of the Congo (*Mouvement pour la Libération du Congo*—MLC). The MLC was launched in Equateur Province in November 1998 by Jean-Pierre Bemba, a "Mobutist" who was allegedly funded by Ugandan sources. Subsequently, bolstered by a series of military successes against government forces, the MLC agreed to coordinate its actions with the RCD, which was backed by Rwanda. That alliance proved short-lived, however, in view of the conflict that soon developed between Uganda and Rwanda.

Like the other major rebel groups, the MLC participated in the Inter-Congolese National Dialogue and signed the Pretoria Accord. MLC fighters were subsequently integrated into the national security forces, and the party became a member of the transitional government. MLC leader Bemba was sworn in as one of four vice presidents for the DRC on July 17, 2003, and the MLC was given equal representation with the RCD-Goma and the opposition alliance in the cabinet and the transitional legislature.

Leaders: Jean-Pierre BEMBA (2006 presidential candidate).

Alliance for the Renaissance of Congo (*Alliance pour la Renaissance du Congo*—ARC). The ARC was formed in April 2006 by National Assembly President Olivier Kamitatu, who had recently left the MLC along with a number of others opposed to MLC leader Jean-Pierre Bemba. The ARC indicated it would present some 200 candidates in the upcoming assembly poll, while supporting Antipas Nyamwasi Mbusa for president.

Leader: Olivier KAMITATU (President of the National Assembly).

Federalist Christian Democracy. This party is led by Pierre Pay-Pay wa Syakassighe, a former central bank governor who, as the candidate of the 18-party **Coalition of Congolese Democrats** (*Coalition des Démocrates Congolais*—CODECO), was considered one of President Kabila's leading rivals in the 2006 presidential race.

Leader: Pierre Pay-Pay wa SYAKASSIGHE.

Unified Lumumbist Party (*Parti Lumumbiste Unifiée*—PALU). Another party claiming adherence to its namesake's teachings, the PALU is headed by Antoine Gizenga, the former leader of one of the three separatist regimes that emerged in Zaire following Belgium's withdrawal in 1960. On July 29, 1995, at least ten party members were killed during a clash with government security forces outside the parliamentary building.

Leader: Antoine GIZENGA (2006 presidential candidate).

Popular Movement for Renewal (*Mouvement Populaire Renouveau*—MPR). Founded in 1967 as the principal vehicle of the Mobutu regime and known until August 1990 as the Popular Movement of the Revolution (*Mouvement Populaire de la Révolution*), the MPR was long committed to a program of indigenous nationalism, or "authenticity." Prior to political liberalization in 1990 each Zairean was legally assumed to be a member of the party at birth.

The 1988 MPR Congress reaffirmed support for the country's single-party system. However, in May 1990 President Mobutu, after signaling the introduction of a multiparty system, stepped down as MPR chair, stating that he would henceforth serve "above parties"; he resumed the post in April 1991. During Mobutu's absence the party split into factions led by N'SINGA Udjuu Ongwakebei (the new chair) and Felix Vunduawe te Pemako, who termed the restructured entity "illegitimate" and presented himself as leader of a "group to renew the People's Revolution."

Faced with vigorous Western opposition to Mobutu's continuance in office, the party at an April 1993 general meeting called on the Birindwa government to sever diplomatic relations with Belgium, France, and the United States, all of which were accused of "stirring up hatred, division, and destruction" and engaging in "neo-colonialism, imperialism . . . and terrorism against Zaire."

Mobutu died of prostate cancer in September 1997, only months after his ouster from Kinshasa by the AFDL. Subsequently, the MPR (with the term "Revolution" once again being used routinely in its references, rather than "Renewal") split into two factions, one led by Vunduawe and a second led by Catherine Nzuzi wa Mbombo. Nzuzi was subsequently jailed for 20 months before being released by Joseph Kabila. She was appointed minister for solidarity and humanitarian affairs in the 2003 transitional government.

Leaders: Felix VUNDUAWE, Catherine NZUZI wa Mbombo (2006 presidential candidate).

Innovating Forces of the Sacred Union (*Forces Innovatrices de la Union Sacrée*—FONUS). FONUS is led by Joseph Olenghankoy, a hard-line USOR member who was arrested in 1994 for declaring the government guilty of "unconstitutional" behavior and in 1998 for engaging in illegal party activity. Olenghankoy was appointed minister of transport and communication in the 2003 transitional government.

Leader: Joseph OLENGHANKOY (2006 presidential candidate).

Democratic and Social Christian Party (*Parti Démocrate et Social Chrétien*—PDSC). A member of the Christian Democratic International, the PDSC applied for legal status in mid-1990 in a bid to secure what was then expected to be the third and final party slot. The party was ultimately recognized in early 1991, and by midyear it had emerged as one of the most influential groups in the Sacred Union.

The PDSC was one of the "moderate" USOR parties that, aligned under the banner of the Union for the Republic and Democracy (*Union pour la République et la Démocratie*—URD), had advocated better relations with the Mobutu regime and a more democratic process within the USOR. (Other groups in the URD included the UDI, below; the **Nationalist Common Front** [*Front Commun Nationaliste*—FCN], led by Gerard KAMANDA wa Kamanda [a former minister in the Mobutu and Tshisekedi governments and the FCN presidential candidate in 2006] and MANDUNGU-BULA Nyati; and the **Planters' Solidarity Party** [*Parti du Solidarité du Planteurs*—PSP], led by Pierre LUMBI Okongo, a former external relations minister.) The URD was expelled from the USOR in May 1994 after, in the climax of a long-running feud, it nominated three candidates for the prime minister's post despite the USOR's official designation of Etienne Tshisekedi as the sole USOR candidate. There has been little reference to PDSC activity since 2002.

Leaders: André BO-BOLIKO Lok'onga, Tuyaba LEWULA (Secretary General).

Union of Independent Democrats (*Union des Démocrates Indépendants*—UDI). Led initially by former planning minister Alexis TAMBWE, the UDI was a party of businessmen and technocrats. In June 1994 Prime Minister Kengo wa Dondo was described as the group's "spiritual father." Following his dismissal as prime minister in April 1997, Kengo wa Dondo fled the country in advance of the AFDL takeover of Kinshasa in May. In February 1998 he was named prime minister of a "government-in-exile" announced in Brussels, Belgium. He returned to the DRC in 2003 to resume political activity, although it was not clear if the UDI continued to function.

Leaders: Joseph Léon KENGO wa Dondo.

Union of Federalists and Independent Republicans (*Union des Fédéralistes et Républicains Indépendants*—UFERI). UFERI was created by the August 6, 1990, merger of the National Federation of Committed Democrats (*Fédération Nationale des Démocrates Commettres*–Fenadec) and the Independent Republicans' Party (*Parti des Républicains Indépendants*—PRI), which had been launched in April by state commissioner of foreign affairs Jean Nguza Karl-I-Bond. At the time of the merger, Nguza described the new grouping, which he was subsequently named to head, as a "serious adversary to the MPR." The party was officially registered on January 16, 1991, and soon thereafter was described as one of the most prominent groups in the Sacred Union coalition. In September UFERI asserted that it would only join in a government formed by a sovereign national conference, and in October UFERI agreed to support the Sacred Union's efforts to reinstate Etienne Tshisekedi as prime minister; nevertheless, on November 21 Nguza, dismissing coalition criticism, agreed to assume the prime minister's post, from which he was ultimately obliged to resign on August 17, 1992.

Subsequently, Nguza warned that UFERI's Katangan supporters would not accept Tshisekedi's appointment, and violent clashes between the two groups were reported. Furthermore, the "ethnic cleansing" of Kasais from Shaba (formerly Katanga) Province, which by mid-1993 had reportedly resulted in thousands of deaths and dislocations, was allegedly sanctioned by Mobutu and executed by Nguza's supporters. In April 1993 Nguza was named deputy prime minister for defense in the Birindwa government. In mid-1996 UFERI leaders denounced the Kengo wa Dondo government for its "anti-democratic behavior" after the party was banned from organizing political activities in Katanga. Nguza died of a heart attack in July 2003, and there has subsequently been little reference to UFERI activity.

Leader: Gabriel KYUNGU wa Kumwanza.

Congolese National Movement (*Mouvement National Congolais*—MNC). From the 1970s to the 1990s, the MNC was an exile group with at least two discernible current factions, the Congolese National Movement–Lumumba (*Mouvement National Congolais–Lumumba*—MNC-L), whose military wing operated as the Lumumba Patriotic Army (*Armíe Patriotique Lumumba*—APL), and the Reformed Congolese National Movement (*Mouvement National Congolais Rénové* – MNCR). The MNC became visible in 1978 when its president was detained by Belgian authorities and expelled to France, with similar action taken against its secretary general in 1984 after the group claimed responsibility for a series of March bombings in Kinshasa. In 1985 the MNC emerged as the most active of the external groups: in April it issued a statement calling Mobutu "an element of instability in central Africa" and listing those allegedly killed by government troops during disturbances in eastern provinces in late 1984. In September 1985 leaders of both the MNC-L and the MNCR joined with the Swiss-based Congolese Democratic and Socialist Party (*Parti Démocratique et Socialiste Congolaise*), led by Allah FIOR Muyinda, in inviting other opposition groups to participate in a joint working commission to oversee "activities [to be launched] over the whole country in coming days." MNCR leader Paul-Roger Mokede was named president of the exile provisional government at a meeting in Switzerland in September 1987 but rejected the designation on the grounds that Zaire could not "afford the luxury" of a parallel regime.

In September 1994 a group identifying itself as the MNC-L was reportedly "formed" in Kinshasa by "nationalists" and Lumumbists under the leadership of Pascal TABU, Mbalo MEKA, and Otoko OKITASOMBO. The older, or original, MNC faction became known as the MNC–*Lumumba Originel* or Original Lumumba (MNC-LO).

In early 1998 François Lumumba, eldest son of the former prime minister, charged that the regime of Laurent Kabila was denying freedom of expression to him and other family members. Lumumba emerged as leader of the MNC-L. He was briefly detained by the government in 2000.

Leaders: François Tolenga LUMUMBA (MNC-L).

Mai-Mai Ingilima. The Mai-Mai was an ethnic Bahunde militia whose members were described as "armed mystics" for their belief, among others, that the grass headgear they wear in battle possesses the power to turn their enemies' bullets into water (*mai-mai* is the Swahili word for water). Credited with disarming Hutu fighters and Zairean soldiers at the start of the 1996 rebellion, the Mai-Mai forces were expected to coordinate their actions with the AFDL as the fighting moved into northern Zaire; however, in December 1996 Mai-Mai militiamen were accused of attempting to assassinate AFDL commander Kissasse, who allegedly wanted them to disarm and report for training. In early 1997 further clashes between the rebel groups were reported, and later in the year the Mai-Mai grouping was described as fully confrontational with the national army of the new Kabila regime in pursuit of regional autonomy for South Kivu. Thereafter, beginning in August 1998, the Mai-Mai was described as alternately cooperating with and clashing with elements of the RCD, in addition to continuing its antigovernment military activities. However, by 2002 the Mai-Mai militias were widely considered to be supportive of the government of Joseph Kabila. The Mai-Mai became formally allied with the Kabila government during the Inter-Congolese National Dialogue that culminated in the Pretoria Accord, and Mai-Mai were subsequently given cabinet posts and seats in the transitional government. However, some Mai-Mai forces subsequently turned hostile to the government under the leadership of a warlord identified as GÉDÉON and assumed control of regions of Katanga. After his forces were accused of attacks on civilians, Gédéon surrendered to MONUC in April 2006.

Union of Congolese Patriots (*Union des Patriotes Congolais*—UPC). The UPC was formed as an antigovernment militia by members of the Hema ethnic group in the Ituri region. Although the UPC was reportedly subsequently registered as a political party, its leader, Thomas LUBANGA, was turned over to the new International Criminal Court (ICC) in March 2006 to face charges of war crimes and human rights abuses. By that time, some remnants of the UPC had reportedly helped launch the MRC (below).

Congolese Revolutionary Movement (*Mouvement Révolutionnaire Congolais*—MRC). The MRC was reportedly formed in Uganda in the second half of 2005 by Congolese rebels who had not accepted the peace process and integration into the proposed national army. MRC participants reportedly included remnants of the UPC (above), the Patriotic Resistance Front of Ituri (*Front de Résistance Patriotique en Ituri*—FRPI), the Front for National Integration, the People's Army of Congo, and the RCD. Government forces launched an offensive against the MRC in eastern DRC in March 2006.

Other parties presenting presidential candidates in 2006 included **Christian Democracy** (*Démocratie Chrétienne*—DC, Eugene Ndongala DIOMI); the **Socialist Liberal Union** (*Union Socialiste Libérale*—USL, Bernard Emmanuel SUILA); the **Rally of Social and Federalist Forces** (*Rassemblement des Forces Sociales et Féderalists*—RFSF, Vincent de Paul LUNDA Bululu [former prime minister]); the **Convention for the Republic and Democracy** (*Convention pour la République et la Démocratie*—CRD, Christophe N'KODIA Pwango Mboso); the **Rally for a New Society** (*Rassemblement pour une Nouvelle Société*—RNS, Alafuele KALALA Mbuyi); the **Union of Mobutist Democrats** (*Union des Démocrates Mobutistes*—UDEMO, François Joseph Nzanga Ngbangawe MOBUTU [a son of former president Mobutu who had

returned from exile in 2003]); the **Movement of Democrats** (*Mouvement des Démocrates*—MD, Justine Kasa-Vubu M'POYO); the **Alliance of Congolese Democrats** (*Alliance des Démocrates Congolais*—ADECO, Jonas Kadiata Nzemba MUKAMBA); **Renewal for Development and Democracy** (*Renouveau pour le Développement et la Démocratie*—RDD, Osee Ndjoko MUYIMA); the **Political Coalition of Christians** (*Coalition Politique des Chrétiens*—CPC, Jacob Souga NIEMBA); the **Party for Peace in the Congo** (*Parti pour la Paix au Congo*, Marie Thérèse Mpolo Nene NLANDU); the **Union for the Defense of the Republic** (*Union pour la Défence de la République*—UDR, Wivine Kavidí N'LANDU); and the **African Congress of Democrats** (*Congrès Africain des Démocrates*—CAD, Harsan Uba THASSINDA).

Other groups include the **Congolese People's Movement for the Republic** (*Mouvement Populaire Congolais pour le Républic*—MPCR), led by Jean-Claude VUEMBA; the **Congolese Socialist Party,** led by Christian BADIBANGI; the **Forces of the Future** (*Forces du Futur*—FDF), led by Arthur Z'ahidi NGOMA, who had been jailed from November 1997 to June 1998 and subsequently became an RCD leader before going into exile in France (see RCD, above) and then returning to serve as vice president of the republic from 2003 to 2006 (Ngoma ran for president in 2006 as the candidate of a party called **Camp of the Fatherland** [*Camp de la Patrie*]); the **Liberal Democratic Christian Party** (*Parti Libéral Démocrate Chrétien*—PLDC), led by Ramond TSHIBANDA; the **Movement for Solidarity, Democracy, and Development** (*Mouvement pour la Solidarité, la Démocratie, et le Développement*—MSDD), whose leader, Christophe LUTUNDULA Apala, chaired the legislative committee that recently investigated alleged corruption in the issuance of government contracts during the 1998–2003 civil war; the **National Alliance of Democrats for Reconstruction** (*Alliance Nationale des Démocrates pour la Reconstruction*–Anader), formed in 2001 under the leadership of Raphaël Kumba ki LUTETE; the **National Convention for Political**

Action; the **People's Party for Reconstruction and Development** (*Parti du Peuple pour la Reconstruction et la Démocratie*—PPRD), a social-democratic party formed in 2003 and led by Jean-Baptiste NKOY; and the **Union of the Congolese Left** (*Union de la Gauche Congolaise*—UGC), formed in 2000 and led by Delphin BANZA. In addition, a coalition of small left-wing parties, the **Coordination of Lumumbist Mulelist Kabilist Revolutionary Nationalist Forces** (*Coordination des Nationalistes Révolutionnaires Lumumbistes Mulelistes Kabilistes*—LMK), was formed in 2002. Another alliance, the **United Front of Congolese Nationalists** (*Front Uni des Nationalistes Congolais*—FUNC), was formed in 2004 as a coalition of left and center-left parties.

Other rebel groups include the **Nationalist and Integrationist Front** (*Front Nationaliste Integrationiste*—FNI), an ethnic Lendu separatist group active in Ituri and suspected of being responsible for attacks against MONUC forces and whose military leader, Etiene LONA, surrendered to the UN in March 2005; the **Congolese Patriots Union–Kisembo** (UPC-Kisembo), a breakaway faction of the UPC, led by Floribert Kisembo BAHEMUKA; the **Forces of Patriotic Resistance**, a group linked to the FNI; and the **Front for the Liberation of Eastern Congo**, a rebel group composed of former members of the RCD. In addition, the **Rwanda Democratic Liberation Front**, a Rwandan Hutu rebel group, remains active in South Kivu and has conducted raids into Rwanda and attacks on DRC government installations and security forces.

Legislature

In September 1992 the 210-member unicameral National Legislative Council (*Conseil Législatif National*— CLN), elected in 1987 from a list of MPR-approved candidates, was dissolved by the National Conference. On October 5 President Mobutu recalled the CLN; however, with both Prime Minister Tshisekedi and National Conference president Laurent Monsengwo Pasinya urging a boycott, the sessions were poorly attended and quickly abandoned. On December 6 the National Conference elected a 453-member High Council of the Republic (*Haut Conseil de la République*—HCR) to function as a transitional legislature.

On March 29, 1993, Mobutu, who refused to accept the legislative authority of the HCR, again reconvened the CLN, with members unable or unwilling to attend the session reportedly being replaced by pro-Mobutu soldiers. Two days later the CLN approved constitutional amendments, drafted by a "conclave" of pro-Mobutu parties March 9–19 that, following presidential promulgation on April 2, established the body as a transitional institution equal in status to the president and the HCR.

On January 14, 1994, Mobutu announced the dissolution of both the CLN and HCR, asserting that the two bodies would be reconstituted as a single body styled the High Council of the Republic–Parliament of Transition (*Haut Conseil de la République–Parlement de Transition*—HCR-PT). Despite opposition claims that the president had no right to dissolve the HCR, the new body, with more than 500 members, was inaugurated on January 23, and on January 25 it appointed former HCR president Monsengwo Pasinya as its leader.

On January 28, 1996, Monsengwo resigned as HCR-PT speaker—five months after an alliance of pro-Mobutu and opposition parliamentarians had passed a motion demanding his resignation. Subsequently, control of the HCR-PT passed to its two vice presidents, André Bo-Boliko Lok'onga and Anzuluni BEMBE Isinyonyi. The HCR-PT was ordered dissolved in May 1997 following the overthrow of the Mobutu regime.

On August 21, 2000, a new Legislative and Constituent Assembly–Transitional Parliament was inaugurated. President Laurent Kabila directly appointed 60 of the 300 members, while the remaining members were selected in consultation with a presidentially appointed commission.

The December 2002 Pretoria Accord provided for the establishment of a bicameral legislature through an interim constitution. The representatives from both chambers were appointed from the major political parties, civic groups, and rebel

Cabinet

As of May 1, 2006

President	Joseph Kabila (PPRD)
Vice Presidents	Jean-Pierre Bemba (MLC)
	Azarias Ruberwa Manywa (RCD-Goma)
	Abdoulaye Yerodia Ndombasi (PPRD)
	Arthur Z'ahidi Ngoma (FDF)

Ministers

Agriculture, Fisheries, and Livestock	Constant Ndom Ndam Ombel (MLC)
Budget	François Mwamba Tshishimbi (RCD)
Culture and Arts	Philémon Mukendi (PPRD)
Economy	Pierre Manoka (RCD)
Energy	Salomon Banamuhere (PPRD)
Environment and Conservation	Anselme Enerunga (Mai-Mai)
Finance	Marco Banguli (PPRD)
Foreign Affairs and International Cooperation	Raymond Ramazani Baya (MLC)
Foreign Trade	Chantal Ngalula Mulumba [f]
Health	Emile Bongeli Yekolo
Human Rights	Marie Madeleine Kalala [f]
Industry and Small and Medium Enterprises	Mukendi Tshambula (PPRD)
Interior, Decentralization, and Security	Théophile Mbemba Fundu (PPRD)
Justice and Keeper of the Seals	Honorius Kisimba Ngoy
Labor and Social Security	Balamage Nkolo
Land Affairs	Venant Tshipasa
Mines and Hydrocarbons	Ingele Ifoto
National Defense	Adolphe Onusumba Yemba
Planning	Denis Sesanga Ipungu
Post and Telecommunications	Gertrude Kitembo (RCD-Goma) [f]
Press and Information and Government Spokesman	Henri Moua Sakanyi (PPRD)
Primary and Secondary Education	Paul Musafiri (MLC)
Public Administration	Anasthase Matenda Kyelu
Public Works and Infrastructure	José Engwanda (MLC)
Regional Cooperation	Antipas Nyamwisi Mbusa (RCD-LM)
Rural Development	Pardonné Kaliba Munanga (Mai-Mai)
Scientific Research	Gérard Kamanda Wa Kamanda
Social Affairs	Laurent-Charles Otete Omanga
Solidarity and Humanitarian Affairs	Catherine Nzuzi wa Mbombo (MPR) [f]
State Properties	Célestin Vunabandi (RCD-Goma)
Tourism	José Engwanda (MLC)
Transport and Communication	Heva Muakasa [f]
Universities	Théo Baruti
Urban Development and Housing	John Tibasima Ateenyi
Women and Family	Faida Mwangila (RCD-Goma) [f]
Youth and Sports	Jacques Lungwana

[f] = female

factions. Both chambers of the **Parliament** were inaugurated on August 23, 2003.

The constitution promulgated in February 2006 provided for a new bicameral parliament comprising a Senate and a National Assembly. That new Senate was slated to include members indirectly elected for five-year terms by provincial councils as well as all former presidents of the republic. The National Assembly was slated to comprise members directly elected for five-year terms from 169 constituencies (some with only 1 seat). New assembly elections were most recently scheduled for July 30, 2006. Provincial elections (required for the indirect election of the Senate) were planned for later in the year.

Senate (*Sénat*). The interim Senate consists of 120 members appointed through negotiations following the Pretoria Accords. Each of the five major political groups received 22 positions, including propresidential parties (led by the People's Party for Reconstruction and Democracy); the opposition alliance; the Congolese Rally for Democracy (RCD-Goma); the Movement for the Liberation of Congo; and civic groups. In addition, the Mai-Mai received 4 seats; the RCD-Liberation Movement, 4; and the RCD-National, 2. (*See headnote.*)

President: Pierre Marini BODHO.

National Assembly (*Assemblée Nationale*). The interim National Assembly comprises 500 deputies appointed from the major political groups in the DRC. The five main groups each received 94 seats, including propresidential parties (led by the People's Party for Reconstruction and Democracy); the opposition alliance; the Congolese Rally for Democracy (RCD-Goma); the Movement for the Liberation of Congo; and civic groups. The RCD–Liberation Movement was given 15 seats; the Mai-Mai, 10; and the RCD–National, 5.

President: Olivier KAMITATU.

Communications

Newspapers were increasingly subject to government control under the Mobutu regime, and a "restructuring" of the press reduced the number of papers being issued. Strict control was also reported under the administration of Laurent Désiré Kabila. Opposition parties have accused state media of favoring the PPRD over other parties, and journalists have been arrested for reporting on demonstrations. In addition, the state media regulatory agency has suspended licenses of broadcast media for "biased reporting" of antigovernment activities. In late 2005 journalism watchdog organizations reported that press freedom was "deteriorating."

Press

The following are dailies published in Kinshasa, unless otherwise noted: *Mjumbe* (Lubumbashi); *Boyoma* (Kisangani); *Le Potentiel* (8,000); *L'Avenir; Le Phare* (4,000), close to the UDPS; *La Référence; Le Forum; Courier d'Afrique* (15,000); *La Depeche* (Lubumbashi, 20,000); *Salongo; Le Journal* (three times per week); *L'Alerte,* independent.

News Agencies

The domestic facility is the Congolese Press Agency (*Agence Congolaise de Presse*—ACP); *Agence France-Presse, Xinhua,* and Pan-African News Agency also maintain bureaus in Kinshasa.

Broadcasting and Computing

Radio broadcasting is provided by the government over the national station, *La Voix du Congo,* and regional stations. Commercial television is provided by the government-operated, commercial Television Congolaise. There are also several private radio and television stations broadcasting from Kinshasa. MONUC temporarily sponsors a radio station called *Radio Okapi.* However, television and radio broadcasts from Kinshasa do not reach some parts of the country, including the volatile eastern region. There were approximately 5.2 million radio and 208,000 television receivers in 1999, unsettled conditions precluding more recent assessments, save for a report of 50,000 Internet users in 2002.

Intergovernmental Representation

Ambassador to the U.S.
Faida MITIFU

U.S. Ambassador to the Democratic Republic of the Congo
Roger A. MEECE

Permanent Representative to the UN
Atoki ILEKA

IGO Memberships (Non-UN)
AfDB, AU, BADEA, CEEAC, CEPGL, Comesa, Interpol, IOM, NAM, OIF, PCA, SADC, WCO, WTO

REPUBLIC OF THE CONGO

République du Congo

The Country

The Republic of the Congo is a narrow 800-mile-long strip of heavily forested territory extending inland from the Atlantic along the Congo and Ubangi rivers. It is bordered on the west by Gabon, on the north by Cameroon and the Central African Republic, and on the east and south by the Democratic Republic of the Congo (formerly Zaire). The members of the country's multitribal society belong mainly to the Bakongo, Matéké, Mbochi, and Vili tribal groups and include numerous pygmies, who are thought to be among the first inhabitants of the area. Linguistically, the tribes speak related Bantu languages; French, although the official language, is not in widespread use. There is, however, a lingua franca, Mouman Koutouba, which is widely employed in commerce. In recent decades there has been substantial rural-to-urban migration, with close to 50 percent of the population now living in or near Brazzaville or Pointe Noir. Partly because of its level of urbanization, the Republic of the Congo has a literacy rate estimated at 70–85 percent, one of the highest in black Africa. About half of the population adheres to traditional religious beliefs, while Roman Catholics, Protestants, and Muslims comprise the remainder.

Although the country possesses exploitable deposits of manganese, copper, lead-zinc, and gold, its leading resources are oil and timber, with the first accounting for more than 88 percent of export earnings in 2003. The economy was severely compromised following the five-month civil war of mid-1997, which, among other things, heavily damaged the capital and reduced GDP growth from about 6.3 percent in 1996 to a negative rate in 1997.

The International Monetary Fund (IMF) and the World Bank suspended aid to the Republic of the Congo in 2000 because of the perceived failure of the government to enact economic reforms. Partial aid was restored in 2004, although the government by that time faced heavy international criticism on an important regional issue–diamond exporting (see Current issues, below). Meanwhile, the Republic of the Congo remained one of the poorest countries in the world (annual per capita income of approximately $700), although increased revenue from high oil prices had at least permitted the government to pay off arrears in civil-servant salaries.

High oil prices, along with increased stability since the end of the civil war, helped bolster the

economy in 2005, when real GDP growth of 6.5 percent was recorded. It was expected to be about the same in 2006. In another positive development, in early 2006 the World Bank and the IMF approved the Republic of the Congo for debt relief under the Heavily Indebted Poor Countries Initiative (HICP). The country was to receive some $5 billion in aid but was still required to address concerns over transparency in government and finances.

Government and Politics

Political Background

Occupied by France in the 1880s, the former colony of Middle Congo became the autonomous Republic of the Congo in 1958 and attained full independence within the French Community on August 15, 1960. The country's first president, Fulbert YOULOU, established a strong centralized administration but resigned in 1963 in the face of numerous strikes and labor demonstrations. His successor, Alphonse MASSAMBA-DÉBAT, was installed by the military and subsequently reelected for a five-year term. Under Massamba-Débat the regime embraced a Marxist-type doctrine of "scientific socialism," and the political system was reorganized on a one-party basis. In 1968, however, Massamba-Débat was stripped of authority as a result of differences with both left-wing and military elements. A military coup led by Capt. Marien NGOUABI on August 3 was followed by the establishment of a National Council of the Revolution to direct the government.

Formally designated as head of state in January 1969, Ngouabi proclaimed a "people's republic" the following December, while a constitution adopted in January 1970 legitimized a single political party, the Congolese Labor Party (*Parti Congolais du Travail*—PCT). Three years later, a new basic law established the post of prime minister and created a National Assembly to replace the one dissolved in 1968.

President Ngouabi was assassinated on March 18, 1977, and the PCT immediately transferred its powers to an 11-member Military Committee headed by Col. Jacques-Joachim YHOMBI-OPANGO, which reinstituted rule by decree. Former president Massamba-Débat, who was accused of having plotted the assassination, was executed on March 25. On April 3 it was announced that Maj. Denis SASSOU-NGUESSO had been named first vice president of the Military Committee and that Maj. Louis-Sylvain GOMA, who retained his post as prime minister, had been named second vice president.

Responding to pressure from the Central Committee of the PCT after having made disparaging remarks about the condition of the country's economy, General Yhombi-Opango, as well as the Military Committee, resigned on February 5, 1979. The Central Committee thereupon established a ruling Provisional Committee and named Sassou-Nguesso as interim president. At an extraordinary congress March 26–31, the party confirmed Sassou-Nguesso as president, while on July 8 the voters approved a new constitution and elected a People's National Assembly in addition to district, regional, and local councils. On July 30, 1984, the president was elected for a second term, and on August 11, as part of a reshuffling aimed at "strengthening the revolutionary process," he named Ange-Edouard POUNGUI to succeed Goma as prime minister.

In July 1987, 20 military officers linked to a group of Paris-based exiles were arrested on charges of plotting a coup. Thereafter, an alleged co-conspirator, Lt. Pierre ANGA, who charged that Sassou-Nguesso had participated in the murder of former president Ngouabi, led a rebellion in the north. Reports of attacks by rebel forces continued until July 4, 1988, when the killing of Anga by government troops ended the uprising.

On July 30, 1989, Sassou-Nguesso was reelected for a third term at the fourth PCT party congress. However, continued debate over the foundering economy led to an extraordinary congress on August 5 and 6 at which a moderate technocrat, Alphonse POATY-SOUCHLATY, was named to succeed Poungui as prime minister.

During the ensuing year, pressure mounted for abandonment of the PCT's claim to political

Political Status: Independent since August 15, 1960; one-party People's Republic proclaimed December 31, 1969; multiparty system authorized as of January 1, 1991; constitution approved in referendum of March 15, 1992, suspended in October 1997 following overthrow of the government; current constitution adopted by referendum of January 20, 2002.
Area: 132,046 sq. mi. (342,000 sq. km.).
Population: 2,591,271 (1996C); 3,913,000 (2005E).
Major Urban Center (2005E): BRAZZAVILLE (1,275,000).
Official Language: French.
Monetary Unit: CFA Franc (official rate July 1, 2006: 513.01 francs = $1US). (The CFA franc, previously pegged to the French franc, is now permanently pegged to the euro at 655.957 CFA francs = 1 euro.)
President: Gen. Denis SASSOU-NGUESSO (Congolese Labor Party); sworn in on October 25, 1997, following the military overthrow of the government of Pascal LISSOUBA (Pan-African Union for Social Democracy) on October 23; elected for a seven-year term on March 10, 2002, and inaugurated on August 10.
Prime Minister: Isidore MVOUBA (Congolese Labor Party); appointed by the president on January 7, 2005. (The position of prime minister is not mandated in the current constitution, and the last person to serve in the post was Bernard KOLELAS [Congolese Movement for Democracy and Integral Development], who lost the premiership when the position was "abolished" by President Sassou-Nguesso on November 3, 1997.)

exclusivity, and in October 1990, confronted with a general strike that had brought the country to a standstill, and acting on a party decision reached three months earlier, General Sassou-Nguesso announced that a multiparty system would be introduced on January 1, 1991, followed by the convening of an all-party National Conference to chart the nation's political future. On January 14 he

appointed a "transitional" government headed by former prime minister Goma, Poaty-Souchlaty having resigned on December 3 in protest over the president's call for the introduction of pluralism.

The National Conference, which encompassed representatives of 30 parties and 141 associations, convened for a three-month sitting on February 25, 1991, eventually approving the draft of a new democratic constitution, dropping "People's" from the country's name, transferring most presidential powers to the prime minister, scheduling a constitutional referendum for November, and calling for multiparty local, legislative, and presidential elections during the first half of 1992. On June 8, two days before its conclusion, the conference elected André MILONGO prime minister. Four days later, Milongo named a 25-member cabinet, which on September 15 was reduced to 15 ministers amid charges that members of the opposition coalition Forces of Change (*Forces de Changement*—FDC) were overrepresented.

After a series of postponements, the March 15, 1992, referendum on the new basic law was credited with securing 96 percent approval. Meanwhile, the Milongo government had barely survived a January 19 army mutiny triggered by allegations that transfers of senior officers had been politically motivated. Municipal elections, originally scheduled for March, were eventually held on May 3, while two-stage legislative balloting that was to have been held in April and May was also delayed, with numerous complaints of irregularities at the first stage on June 24.

At second-stage assembly balloting on July 24, 1992, the Pan-African Union for Social Democracy (*Union PanAfricaine pour la Démocratie Sociale*—UPADS) emerged as the clear winner, as it did in a Senate poll two days later, albeit without securing a majority in either body. At first-round presidential balloting on August 2, the UPADS nominee, Pascal LISSOUBA, led a field of 17 candidates but secured only 35.9 percent of the vote, thus necessitating a second round against Bernard KOLELAS of the Congolese Movement for Democracy and Integral Development (*Mouvement Congolais pour la Démocratie et le Développement Intégral*—MCDDI), who had garnered 22.9 percent. Among those eliminated in the first round were Sassou-Nguesso and Milongo, with vote shares of 16 and 10 percent, respectively. On August 11 the UPADS and PCT announced a coalition, with the outgoing president urging his followers to support the UPADS leader. Thus reinforced, Lissouba outdistanced Kolelas at the second round on August 16 by a margin of 61.3 to 38.7 percent. In the wake of his victory Lissouba promised a broadly representative government and indicated that he would petition the National Assembly to pardon Sassou-Nguesso and other top officials for crimes committed while in office. On September 1 Lissouba named Maurice-Stéphane BONGHO-NOUARRA of the National Alliance for Democracy (*Alliance Nationale pour la Démocratie*—AND) as prime minister. Six days later Bongho-Nouarra announced a cabinet that included a number of opposition leaders, although Kolelas declined to join them.

In late September 1992 the UPADS-PCT pact dissolved over the choice of a National Assembly president. Shortly thereafter, the PCT concluded an Opposition Coalition (*Coalition de l'Opposition*—CO) with Kolelas's recently formed Union for Democratic Renewal (*Union pour le Renouveau Démocratique*—URD), itself a seven-party antigovernment alliance that included the MCDDI. The CO moved quickly to assert itself and on October 31 successfully moved a no-confidence vote against the government. On November 11 the coalition called for a campaign of civil disobedience and strikes in an effort to force Lissouba to name a CO member as prime minister. On November 14 Bongho-Nouarra resigned, praising President Lissouba for attempting to "pull Congo out of the abyss." Subsequent negotiations between Lissouba and Kolelas led to an impasse, and on November 17 the president, accusing the coalition of "despicable and premeditated acts," dissolved the National Assembly and scheduled a new election for December 30. A wave of civil unrest promptly paralyzed the capital's commercial sector, and by the end of November opposition legislators and security forces were described as in "open con-

frontation." On December 2 the military occupied Brazzaville, dispersed demonstrators, ordered the government and opposition to form a unity government headed by a compromise prime minister, and suspended election preparations. Four days later, Lissouba appointed Claude-Antoine DACOSTA, an agronomist and former World Bank representative, as prime minister. The government named by Dacosta on December 25 included 12 members from the CO and 9 with links to the president.

At rescheduled assembly balloting on May 2 and June 6, 1993, President Lissouba's 60-party Presidential Tendency (*Tendance Présidentielle*) was credited with winning 69 of 125 seats. However, insisting that the first round had been "tarnished by monstrous irregularities," the opposition demanded a rerun in 12 constituencies and boycotted the second-round balloting. Furthermore, on June 8 Kolelas called for a campaign of civil disobedience to force new elections, thus igniting widespread violence. Subsequent negotiations to stem the unrest failed, as the Opposition Coalition rejected Lissouba's offer to rerun the second round. On June 22 the CO boycotted the National Assembly's inauguration, and the following day, concurrent with Lissouba's appointment of Yhombi-Opango as prime minister, it named Jean-Pierre THYSTERE-TCHICAYE of the Rally for Democracy and Social Progress (*Rassemblement pour la Démocratie et le Progrès Social*—RDPS) to head a parallel "national salvation" government.

On July 7, 1993, amid what Lissouba now labeled an "armed rebellion," a curfew was imposed in Brazzaville. Negotiations remained at an impasse until late July, when Gabonese and UN mediators brokered an unofficial disarmament pact, and on August 4 government and opposition negotiators in Libreville, Gabon, signed an agreement calling for an internationally supervised rerun of the second round of assembly elections and the establishment of a seven-member, international arbitration committee to rule on first-round disputes. On August 16, with the violence abating, a month-old state of emergency in Brazzaville was rescinded, and on September 17 the curfew was lifted. Meanwhile, the Senate agreed to a rerun of the June voting, although it rejected establishment of the arbitration committee on the grounds that the August accord had been a "private deal among political parties."

At the second-round rerun in October 1993 the Opposition Coalition won 7 of the 11 contests, increasing its representation to 56 seats, while the Presidential Tendency's majority fell to 65. However, in early November the cease-fire collapsed, with dozens of people reported killed in the capital when government forces responded to the kidnapping of two government officials and a sniper attack with a fierce assault on opposition strongholds. The coalition immediately cited artillery attacks on the Bacongo District of Brazzaville as a means of creating a violent "smoke screen" behind which the government was attempting to impose its will. Despite bilateral calls in late November for a cease-fire and disarmament, fighting continued into 1994, with a government blockade of Bacongo in January, renewed clashes in Brazzaville in July, and student demonstrations in the capital in November.

On January 23, 1995, CO unity was shattered by URD agreement to participate in a restructured Yhombi-Opango government, a move that was flatly rejected by the PCT. Another Coalition member, the National Union for Democracy and Progress (*Union Nationale pour la Démocratie et Progrés*—UNDP), echoed the PCT's sentiments, declaring that it would take no part in the government's "chaotic management of the country" and accusing President Lissouba of being "a past master in juggling and manipulation as a divide-and-rule strategy."

Regional divisions remained at the fore in 1995 as the Lissouba administration sought to end the northerners' dominance of the 25,000-member military as well as to disarm and integrate the numerous militias that were organized during the 1993 civil unrest and continued to cause widespread instability. In August, Lissouba declared that the military would be restructured to reflect a "tribal and regional equilibrium"; however, the military leadership and opposition strenuously objected to the plan, particularly efforts to integrate Lissouba loyalists. On September 1–6

government troops attempting to disarm militiamen loyal to Sassou-Nguesso met fierce resistance in Brazzaville. Consequently, on November 3 Lissouba proposed assimilating all militiamen into the armed forces. Nevertheless, two days later, National Defense Minister (and former prime minister) Maurice-Stéphane Bongho-Nouarra rejected an administration attempt to absorb 250 militiamen with alleged presidential loyalties, saying that he wanted to depoliticize the recruitment process.

On December 24, 1995, the leaders of the Congo's major propresidential and opposition tendencies signed a peace pact that included provisions for the disarmament and subsequent integration of the former combatants into the national army. However, efforts to implement the accord were dealt a setback on February 14, 1996, when more than 100 recently integrated former militiamen with ties to the UPADS led a violent mutiny in M'Pila that left 5 people dead and 40 others injured. The rebellion ended on February 19 after negotiations between the government and rebellious troops yielded another integration agreement favoring the latter. Consequently, the opposition United Democratic Forces (*Forces Démocratiques Unies*—FDU) boycotted the peace process for a month, denouncing the government's willingness to "reward" the mutineers and calling for equal representation in the armed forces.

On August 23, 1996, Prime Minister Yhombi-Opango resigned. His replacement, David Charles GANAO, leader of the Union of Democratic Forces (*Union des Forces Démocratiques*—UFD), on September 2 organized a new government that was nearly evenly split between old and new ministers. A partial Senate election in October did not change the balance of power.

Preparations for presidential elections (scheduled for July 27, 1997) had begun in earnest on May 4, 1996, when the National Census Commission (*Commission Nationale pour le Recensement*—CNR) was inaugurated. However, the CNR was immediately immersed in controversy when the opposition sharply criticized the appointment of President Lissouba as the commission's chair, arguing that it undermined the government's pledge to "ensure transparency" during the electoral run-up. Lissouba subsequently resigned from the CNR chairmanship; however, the appointment of Prime Minister Yhombi-Opango as his successor proved equally unsatisfying to the opposition, which called for establishment of an independent commission. Thereafter, in July, MCDDI leader Kolelas announced his presidential candidacy, joining a field that already included Lissouba and Gen. Jean-Marie Michel MOKOKO of the Movement for Congolese Reconciliation (*Mouvement pour la Réconciliation Congolaise*—MRC).

Tensions between supporters of Sassou-Nguesso and Lissouba, the two leading presidential candidates, increased as the election approached. In May 1997 Sassou-Nguesso survived an assassination attempt while campaigning, and on June 5 the army surrounded his home, claiming it was part of an effort to disarm private militias. The showdown quickly escalated into civil war, and by mid-July about 4,000 were dead. President Lissouba successfully petitioned the Constitutional Court to postpone the election and extend the expiration date of his mandate, as of July 22. The action only enraged Sassou-Nguesso's forces, and fighting spread north despite mediation efforts by the United Nations and the Organization of African Unity (OAU).

Lissouba appointed Kolelas, then mayor of Brazzaville, as prime minister on September 9, 1997, replacing Ganao, who had resigned on the same day. Kolelas formed a new unity government on September 13, but allies of Sassou-Nguesso declined the posts reserved for them. Kolelas was backed by a 40-party movement, the Republican Space for the Defense of Democracy and National Unity (*Espace Républicain pour la Défense de la Démocratie et Unité Nationale*—ERDDUN), though apparently it was identified too closely with Lissouba forces to have credibility with the rebels.

With the participation of a variety of mercenaries and regular troops from neighboring countries, the civil war continued into mid-October, with Sassou-Nguesso triumphantly entering the destroyed capital on October 23 and being sworn in as president two days later. On November 3 Sassou-Nguesso named a new, broadly representative transitional government but abolished the position of prime minister and initially reserved the defense portfolio for himself.

On January 5–14, 1998, the government hosted the National Forum for Reconciliation, Unity, Democracy, and the Reconstruction of the Congo that was attended by more than 1,400 participants, most of them, however, from within parties or other organizations identified with the FDU. The forum endorsed a "flexible" three-year transition to democracy during which a new constitution would be drafted and a national constitutional referendum held. New presidential and legislative elections would follow. The forum elected a 75-member National Transition Council to oversee the process, but it also accused the ousted president, Lissouba, and his allies of a planned "genocide" and urged that they be brought before the appropriate judicial venue. Meanwhile, Lissouba and Kolelas proclaimed a government in exile, with the former prime minister calling for a campaign of civil disobedience in opposition to the Sassou-Nguesso regime.

Throughout 1998, militias loyal to Lissouba and Kolelas—the so-called Cocoyes (in the south) and Ninjas (in the central Pool region), respectively—continued to battle the Cobra militias, which supported Sassou-Nguesso, forcing tens of thousands of civilians to flee and causing thousands of deaths. In December a major battle for control of Brazzaville erupted, and it wasn't until mid-1999 that victories by the army and Cobra forces made the eventual outcome a near-certainty. In August, Sassou-Nguesso offered amnesty to opposition militiamen who surrendered their arms, and on November 16 a peace plan, including the amnesty and a cessation of hostilities, was accepted by most of the opposition forces. Lissouba and Kolelas, still abroad, rejected the agreement. In late December, President Omar Bongo of Gabon, who had assumed the role of mediator between the interim government and the opposition militias, oversaw the signing of a second peace agreement, and by early 2000 the conflict appeared to have reached a conclusion. The 1990s had witnessed an estimated

20,000 deaths due to civil strife, with some 800,000 made homeless. On May 4, 2000, Kolelas and his nephew, former minister of the interior Col. Philippe BIKINKITA, having been tried in absentia, were sentenced to death for crimes committed against prisoners in 1997.

Although some areas of the country remained under militia control, in January 2001 the government announced that a "non-exclusive national dialogue" on a draft constitution, the peace plan, and national reconstruction would be held. Local sessions were conducted throughout the country in March and were followed by a convention in Brazzaville April 11–14. Although some representatives of former governments participated, Lissouba and Kolelas continued their opposition. The convention concluded by adopting the constitutional draft, which was approved in final form by the National Transition Council in September. The new basic law, which retained a strong presidency and a bicameral parliament, was endorsed by 84 percent of the voters at a public referendum on January 20, 2002, although much of the opposition leadership urged a boycott. A month earlier, Lissouba had been convicted in absentia of treason and misappropriation of funds and sentenced to 30 years in prison.

Sassou-Nguesso, facing no significant opponent following the withdrawal of former prime minister Milongo from the race, was elected to a seven-year term in presidential balloting on March 10, 2002. Having received 89.4 percent of the vote, Sassou-Nguesso was sworn in on August 14. In two-stage balloting for the new 137-seat National Assembly on May 26 and June 20, the president's PCT and the allied FDU won 83 seats, while indirect elections for the 66-seat Senate on July 11 produced an even greater majority for the government.

The PCT and FDU reportedly secured more than two-thirds of the seats in local balloting on June 30, 2002, a number of opposition parties having boycotted those elections to protest perceived mismanagement in the recent presidential poll. Consequently, the new Council of Ministers appointed on August 18 did not include any members of the opposition.

On January 7, 2005, President Sassou-Nguesso appointed Isidore MVOUBA of the PCT to what the president called the "honorary" post of prime minister and reshuffled the cabinet. In a partial Senate election on October 2, 2005, the PCT won 23 of 30 contested seats, with 6 of the remaining seats reportedly going to members of government coalition parties, and 1 to an independent.

Constitution and Government

The 1979 constitution established the Congolese Labor Party (PCT) as the sole legal party, with the chair of its Central Committee serving as president of the republic. Under a constitutional revision adopted at the third PCT congress in July 1984, the president was named chief of government as well as head of state, with authority to name the prime minister and members of the Council of Ministers.

The 1979 document was abrogated and a number of existing national institutions dissolved by the National Conference in May 1991. President Sassou-Nguesso remained in office pending the election of a successor, while a 153-member Higher Council of the Republic (*Conseil Supérieur de la République*—CSR) was appointed to oversee the implementation of conference decisions.

The constitution endorsed by the CSR on December 22, 1991, and approved by popular referendum on May 3, 1992, provided for a president elected for a once-renewable five-year term. The head of state, authorized to rule by decree in social and economic matters, appointed a prime minister capable of commanding a legislative majority. The bicameral parliament consisted of an indirectly elected Senate sitting for a six-year term and a directly elected National Assembly with a five-year mandate, subject to dissolution. A Supreme Court headed the judicial system, with a High Court of Justice empowered to rule on crimes and misdemeanors, with which the president, members of Parliament, and other government officials could be charged. A Constitutional Court interpreted the constitutionality of laws, treaties, and international agreements.

The 1992 constitution was suspended by the new Sassou-Nguesso regime following its military takeover in October 1997. During the subsequent transitional period, the republic was governed by Sassou-Nguesso as self-appointed president with the assistance of a National Transitional Council (see Legislature, below). In November 1998 the regime established a 26-member committee to rewrite the constitution, and in November 2000 the government approved a draft document that was then discussed in March and April 2001 as a key element in a "non-exclusive national dialogue." With the participation of many opposition groups (but not those closest to Bernard Kolelas and Pascal Lissouba), the draft was approved on April 14, and a final version was endorsed by referendum on January 20, 2002.

The current constitution retains a bicameral parliament and provides for a directly elected president, serving a once-renewable seven-year term, who functions as both head of state and head of government. The president has sole power to appoint and dismiss government ministers, but he does not have the power to dismiss parliament. Nor does the legislature have the power to remove the president. Members of parliament forfeit their seats if they switch parties during the legislative term.

The judicial branch is headed by a Supreme Court. There are also Courts of Appeal, a Court of Accounts and Budgetary Discipline, and a Constitutional Court. Local administration is based on ten regions (subdivided into 76 districts and 5 municipalities) and the capital district, each with an elected Regional Council.

Foreign Relations

The People's Republic of the Congo withdrew from the French Community in November 1973 but remained economically linked to Paris. In June 1977 it was announced that diplomatic ties with the United States would be resumed after a 12-year lapse, although the U.S. embassy was not reopened until November 1978, and ambassadors were not exchanged until May 1979.

For many years Brazzaville maintained close relations with Communist nations, including the People's Republic of China, Cuba, and the Soviet Union, signing a 20-year Treaty of Friendship with the USSR in May 1981. While the Congo remained on relatively good terms with its other neighbors, recurrent border incidents strained relations with Zaire (now the Democratic Republic of the Congo) despite the conclusion of a number of cooperation agreements, the most notable being the economic and social "twinning" of the countries' capital cities in February 1988. Subsequent reports of mutual deportations and a mass exodus of Zaireans from the Congo were downplayed by Brazzaville and Kinshasa as an exaggeration of the international press.

As an active member of the OAU, the Republic of the Congo hosted a number of meetings aimed at resolving the civil war in Chad, although it tacitly endorsed the claims of Chadian leader Hissein Habré by serving as a staging area in 1983 for Habré-supportive French troops. In 1986 President Sassou-Nguesso was selected the OAU's chief mediator in the Chadian negotiations. In early 1987 he embarked on a nine-nation European tour to emphasize the gravity of the economic situation facing sub-Saharan Africa and the need for effective sanctions against South Africa. Further enhancing the country's image as regional mediator was the choice of Brazzaville for international peace talks on the Angola-Namibia issue in 1988 and 1989. Because of his key role in the Namibian negotiations Sassou-Nguesso in mid-February 1990 was the first African leader to be welcomed to Washington, by U.S. president George H. W. Bush.

In early 1989 Brazzaville became the first francophone African capital to negotiate a debt swap, trading shares in agriculture, timber, and transport industries to a U.S.-based lender in return for debt reductions. Another financial "first" for the government was the signing of a comprehensive investment agreement with the United Kingdom in May 1989. Later Sassou-Nguesso met with Cameroon's Paul Biya and Gabon's Omar Bongo as part of an ongoing effort by the three to create a joint bargaining unit to negotiate with external creditors.

The 1997 overthrow of the Lissouba government reportedly involved a number of foreign powers. President Lissouba claimed that the Sassou-Nguesso forces included a coalition of Rwandan Hutu militiamen and elements of the defeated army of Zaire's Mobutu Sese Seko, though Lissouba's own fighters also were reported to include former Mobutu forces. The participation of the former Zairean elements on the rebel side was apparently enough to induce the new neighboring Kabila regime of the Democratic Republic of the Congo, whose capital of Kinshasa had been shelled from Brazzaville, to send troops in support of Lissouba, even though he had been one of Africa's last supporters of Mobutu. Meanwhile, the apparent entry into the fray by Angola on the side of the insurgents helped turn the tide with tanks and air power. Lissouba had reportedly hired mercenaries from the National Union for the Total Independence of Angola (UNITA), the rebel group whose participation gave Angola another reason to support Sassou-Nguesso. The Angolans were also keen to eliminate the separatist movement in Cabinda, an oil-rich Angolan province bordering the Republic of the Congo, where the separatists were suspected of having bases.

The insurrection of 1997, starting just three weeks after the Kabila victory in the neighboring Democratic Republic of the Congo, disturbed Western diplomats and African democrats, who suggested that both conflicts, ostensibly civil wars, were actually regional wars in which African armies crossed their borders to enforce political change in a neighboring country. In October the U.S. State Department protested Angola's involvement in the Republic of the Congo and threatened to cut off aid.

Following the outbreak of a rebellion in the Pool region of the Republic of the Congo in 2002 (see Current issues, below), Angola sent troops to assist the Congolese forces in dealing with the insurrection. (Angola, the Democratic Republic of the Congo, and the Republic of the Congo had signed an agreement in 1999 to cooperate regarding border and refugee issues.) Although observers noted problems regarding the fairness and transparency

of the 2002 elections under the new constitution, the balloting lent a degree of credibility to Sassou-Nguesso and his government, particularly within Africa.

In early 2006, the Republic of the Congo was chosen over Sudan to head the African Union (AU) as a result of opposition to the situation in Darfur, where the AU had peacekeepers.

Current Issues

As was expected, the exiled opposition questioned—with some justification–the legitimacy of Sassou-Nguesso's overwhelming election victory in March 2002. Nevertheless, even if the president could not fairly claim nearly 90 percent support nationwide, the Congolese voters were presented with no realistic alternative to his continued presidency. Since returning to power in 1997 Sassou-Nguesso had effectively marginalized his two principal opponents, Lissouba and Kolelas, whose refusals to participate in any of the recent government-sponsored reconciliation initiatives, had injured their standing among the internal opposition. Moreover, neither the former president nor the former prime minister, facing arrest if they returned from exile, could meet the constitutional requirement of a two-year residency before seeking the presidency. Prior to the May–June 2002 National Assembly election, the leaders of the principal domestic opposition parties formed the latest in a series of multiparty coalitions, the Convention for Democracy and Salvation (*Convention pour la Démocratie et le Salut*—Codesa), but their inability to present a unified electoral option left Sassou-Nguesso's political forces in full control of the national government.

The complexity of recent Congolese politics and attendant wide-spread unrest largely derive from historic tribal fault lines that tended to be obscured during the lengthy period of authoritarian rule. Thus, on the eve of the 1997 civil war, the three leading political groups represented quite different regional constituencies: Sassou-Nguesso's previously ruling PCT was strongest in the Cuvette region of the north; President Lissouba's UPADS was rooted in the largely rural Niari, Bouenza, and Lekoumo ("Nibolek") regions of the south; and Kolelas's URD dominated in the central Pool region, which includes the capital, and in the coastal oil city of Pointe-Noire.

Reconciling long-standing differences within the country's diverse population remained Sassou-Nguesso's principal challenge following his reelection in March 2002. Despite incentives for the country's many militia groups to surrender their weapons, some remained heavily armed and capable of offering resistance. The most serious violence occurred in the Pool region, where National Assembly elections in May and local balloting in June were postponed. Leading the rebellion was the National Resistance Council (*Conseil National de Résistance*—CNR), which called for greater autonomy for the region. (See CNR under Rebel Group, below, for additional information.) An estimated 10,000 people were displaced by the fighting. Following the signing of a cease-fire agreement in March 2003, the EU pledged financial aid in support of demobilization of the CNR's so-called Ninjas, and some 2,300 rebels subsequently were reported to have laid down their arms. However, the region had not been completely pacified as of late 2005. The government also reported in April 2005 that it had thwarted a coup plot among a group of soldiers.

In July 2004 the Republic of the Congo was excluded from the UN-sponsored Kimberley process, under which an international commission was authorized to certify that diamond sales in the region were not funding armed conflict. The oversight group alleged that the Republic of the Congo was being used to smuggle diamonds out of the Democratic Republic of the Congo. (It was estimated that diamond exports from the Republic of the Congo exceeded actual production in the country by as much as 100 times.)

In early October 2005, some opposition parties boycotted the partial senate elections (see Political background, above) based on what they claimed was the government's pretense of a democratic system. Later that month, Kolelas was allowed to return to Brazzaville to bury his wife, prompting

renewed clashes between Ninja rebels loyal to Kolelas and government troops in the city's southern districts. Subsequently, Sassou-Nguesso, backed by a unanimous vote in the National Assembly, granted Kolelas amnesty.

In December 2005, Kolelas apologized to the Congolese people for his role in the civil war and indicated his interest in reconciliation, leading some observers to speculate that his leaning toward supporting Sassou-Nguesso might cost him his party leadership. Problems plagued the country in late 2005, as floods displaced thousands in Brazzaville, and the head of the state oil company was implicated in corruption (despite government promises of reform). In addition, several generals, among others, were acquitted of killing hundreds of refugees who went missing in 1999, prompting outcry from human rights observers.

Political Parties

The Republic of the Congo became a one-party state in 1963 when the National Revolutionary Movement (*Mouvement National Révolutionnaire*—MNR) supplanted the two parties that had been politically dominant under the preceding administration: the Democratic Union for the Defense of African Interests (*Union Démocratique pour la Défense des Intérêts Africains*—UDDIA) and the African Socialist Movement (*Mouvement Socialiste Africain*—MSA). The MNR was in turn replaced by the Congolese Labor Party (PCT) in 1969, coincident with the declaration of the People's Republic. On July 4, 1990, the PCT agreed to abandon its monopoly of power, and nearly two dozen opposition groupings were formally legalized as of January 1, 1991. Thereafter, estimates of the number of parties ranged to upward of 100.

Following Denis Sassou-Nguesso's return to power in 1997, an already complex political party system, in which personal, tribal, and regional loyalties typically overpowered ideology, became further entangled. (See the 1999 *Political Handbook* for more detailed information about the period preceding the 1999 civil conflict.) In 2002 a reported 141 parties and alliances presented candidates for at least one of the 137 National Assembly seats. At that time the principal formations were Sassou-Nguesso's PCT and the allied United Democratic Forces; the opposition Convention for Democracy and Salvation (Codesa), a new multiparty alliance led by former prime minister André Milongo of the Union for Democracy and the Republic (UDR); the Pan-African Union for Social Democracy (UPADS), led from exile by former president Pascal Lissouba; and the Congolese Movement for Democracy and Integral Development (MCDDI), led from exile by former prime minister Bernard Kolelas.

Government Coalition

Congolese Labor Party (*Parti Congolais du Travail*—PCT). The PCT monopolized Congolese political life from its launching in 1969 until its agreement in 1990 to allow the formation of opposition groups. In mid-1992 the PCT finished third in the National Assembly election (19 seats) and fifth in the Senate poll (5 seats). On August 2 the party's fall from power was seemingly completed by Sassou-Nguesso's inability to proceed beyond the first round of presidential balloting; however, it allied itself with the UPADS for the second round and was included in the government named on September 1. The alliance broke down shortly thereafter, with the PCT entering into a new coalition with Bernard Kolelas's Union for Democratic Renewal (*Union pour la Renouveau Démocratique*—URD), a seven-party alliance that included the MCDDI and the RDPS (below).

Although generally listed as a member of the FDU, the PCT ran in its own right at the May–June 2002 National Assembly election, winning 53 seats. PCT candidates won 15 lower-house seats in 1993. In the October 2, 2005 partial Senate elections, the PCT won most of the 30 contested seats, with 21 going to the party's "new direction" wing and 2 to an unidentified dissident faction.

Leaders: Gen. Denis SASSOU-NGUESSO (President of the Republic), Ambroise NOU-MAZALAYE (President of the Senate and Secretary General of the Party).

United Democratic Forces (*Forces Démocratiques Unies*—FDU). The FDU was launched in September 1994 as a six-party coalition of the PCT; the **Convention for the Democratic Alternative** (*Convention pour l'Alternatif Démocratique*—CAD), led by Alfred OPIMBA; the **Liberal Republican Party** (*Parti Libéral et Républicain*—PLR), led by Nicéphore FYLA; the **National Union for Democracy and Progress** (*Union National pour la Démocratie et le Progrès*—UNDP), led by Pierre N'ZE; the **Patriotic Union for National Reconstruction** (*Union Patriotique pour la Réconstruction Nationale*—UPRN), led by Auguste-Célestin GONGARAD-NKOUA; and the **Union for National Renewal** (*Union pour le Renouveau National*—URN), led by Gabriel BOKILO.

The FDU's leaders came mainly from the northern Congo, in contrast to the central and southern linkages of the URD, the FDU's Opposition Coalition (*Coalition de l'Opposition*—CO) ally prior to the entry of the Kolelas grouping into the government in January 1995. In June 1997 the FDU assumed the name Democratic and Patriotic Forces (*Forces Démocratiques et Patriotiques*—FDP) and during the ensuing civil war was closely linked to the Cobra militias, which supported Sassou-Nguesso. The FDP then served as the backbone of the new Sassou-Nguesso government, before returning to the FDU designation in 1998.

By 2002 it was reported that the FDU comprised nearly 30 parties, including the recently formed **Club 2000,** led by Wilfrid NGUESSO. At the 2002 National Assembly election the FDU won 30 seats, thereby guaranteeing President Sassou-Nguesso a large majority in the lower house.

Leader: Lekoundzou Itihi OSSETOUMBA (President).

Principal Government-Supportive Parties

Rally for Democracy and Social Progress (*Rassemblement pour la Démocratie et le Progrs Social*—RDPS). Despite dissident withdrawals, the RDPS secured both upper- and lower-house representation in the 1992 legislative balloting.

The party's leader, Jean-Pierre Thystere-Tchicaye, a former PCT member, was eliminated from presidential contention by capturing only 5.8 percent of the first-round vote. At legislative balloting in 1993 the RDPS secured ten seats. Thystere-Tchicaye was named prime minister of a short-lived parallel government named by the Opposition Coalition, and then in mid-1994 was elected mayor of the country's second-largest city, Pointe-Noire.

In late 1996, in anticipation of the scheduled 1997 presidential election, the RDPS joined the Union for the Republic (*Union pour la République*—UR) of Benjamin BOUNKOULOU and the Movement for Democracy and Solidarity (*Mouvement pour la Démocratie et la Solidarité*—MDS) of Paul KAYA in forming a coalition called the Movement for Unity and Reconstruction (*Mouvement pour l'Unité et la Réconstruction*—MUR). After the civil war of 1997 the party was reportedly divided over the extent to which it should cooperate with the government. In 2002 the party's cofounder and former secretary general, Jean-Félix Demba TELO, ran for president as an independent, finishing fourth, with 1.7 percent of the vote.

In 2001 the RDPS had concluded a cooperation agreement with the PCT. In August 2002 Thystere-Tchicaye was selected to serve as speaker of the new lower house.

Leader: Jean-Pierre THYSTERE-TCHICAYE (President of the Party and Speaker of the National Assembly).

Union of Democratic Forces (*Union des Forces Démocratiques*—UFD). Although close to President Lissouba, the UFD's leader, David Charles Ganao, was reportedly backed by the opposition to succeed André Milongo as National Assembly president because of his reputation for nonpartisanship. Ganao was replaced as prime minister in September 1997 when President Lissouba appointed the MCDDI's Bernard Kolelas to succeed him in an effort to settle the civil war. In January 1998 the UFD broke with the opposition, urging its members to support the reconciliation and reconstruction efforts of the Sassou-Nguesso government, and in February Sebastien EBAO was

elected chair. At the time, Ganao was in exile, but by November 2001 he had resumed control of the party and, in a turnaround, concluded an electoral pact with Sassou-Nguesso's PCT.

Leader: David Charles GANAO (Chair).

Opposition Parties and Alliances

Congolese Movement for Democracy and Integral Development (*Mouvement Congolais pour la Démocratie et le Développement Intégral*—MCDDI). A right-of-center group and former member of the Forces of Change (*Forces de Changement*—FDC) coalition, the MCDDI was formed in 1989 by Bernard Kolelas, who had served as an adviser to former prime minister Milongo. In 1990 Kolelas was a leader of the opposition movement that successfully campaigned for multipartyism. In the first local and municipal elections in 1992 the party ran second, while Kolelas was runner-up in the subsequent presidential poll, with 38.7 percent of the vote. The MCDDI and the RDPS (above) were the principal members of the Union for Democratic Renewal (*Union pour la Renouveau Démocratique*—URD) alliance that was launched in mid-1992, and shortly thereafter formed the Opposition Coalition with the PCT.

At legislative balloting in 1993 the MCDDI secured 28 seats, half of the opposition's total. Meanwhile, Kolelas's leadership role in what the Lissouba administration labeled an "armed rebellion," made him a target for progovernment forces, and in October his residence in Brazzaville was hit by artillery fire. In a demonstration of antigovernment sentiment, Kolelas was elected mayor of Brazzaville in July 1994.

Kolelas maintained an opposition stance against the Lissouba government as well as a complex relationship with Sassou-Nguesso, ostensibly an ally but also a rival when the two were 1997 presidential candidates. However, during the four-month insurrection of 1997, Kolelas attempted to mediate between the Lissouba government and the Sassou-Nguesso rebels, before joining the government as prime minister in September. He fled the country when the government fell in October, and the party effectively split into two wings, one remaining loyal to Kolelas and the other, headed by Michel Mampouya, supporting the new interim regime. Mampouya himself accepted a cabinet post and assumed party leadership. In the 2002 legislative election, Kolelas called for a boycott, but Mampouya, despite contending that "there is only one MCDDI," headed a slate of unsuccessful candidates.

Kolelas was pardoned by the government in late 2005 following his return from exile to bury his wife in Brazzaville.

Leaders: Bernard KOLELAS (in exile), Michel MAMPOUYA, Jacques MAHOUKA.

Pan-African Union for Social Democracy (*Union PanAfricaine pour la Démocratie Sociale*—UPADS). Previously a member of the National Alliance for Democracy (*Alliance Nationale pour la Démocratie*—AND), a coalition of 40-plus parties that objected to the 1991 Milongo government, the UPADS ran alone in the 1992 municipal, legislative, and presidential elections. The party's pre-electoral prospects were bolstered by attracting numerous dissidents from the RDPS (above) and the UNDP, which had been a leading component of the prodemocracy movement (and which later helped form the FDU). In legislative polling at midyear the UPADS secured a plurality of seats in both houses. Following the first presidential round in August, the party concluded a pact with the PCT that ensured the second-round victory of the UPADS candidate, Pascal Lissouba. The alliance, upon which a legislative majority had been forged, was dissolved soon after Lissouba's inauguration.

The UPADS was the key player in the Presidential Tendency (*Tendance Présidentielle*), formed prior to the National Assembly balloting of June 1993 by a large number of pro-Lissouba parties (including many that would establish Codesa in 2002). The formation controlled a majority of seats following the second-round repolling in October. The UPADS retained its legislative plurality in 1993 but was weakened on January 27, 1995, by the withdrawal of 12 of its MPs, who complained of be-

ing marginalized and subsequently formed a new grouping, the Union for the Republic (UR).

At a UPADS congress on December 30, 1995, Lissouba was reelected to the party's top post. In addition, a 220-member National Council was formed in an apparent attempt by party leaders to appease its largest internal tendency, the "Reforming Democrats Group," which complained of the lack of party-wide deliberations. In the midst of the 1997 civil war the UPADS was a principal member of the 40-party self-described peace movement called the Republican Space for the Defense of Democracy and National Unity (*Espace Républicain pour la Défense de la Démocratie et de l'Unité Nationale*—ERDDUN).

Following the overthrow of President Lissouba, the UPADS split into two wings, one headed by Lissouba from abroad and the other led by Martin Mberi, a member of the National Council who became a minister in the new government of Sassou-Nguesso. In 2001 Mberi left and formed the CNRS (below), but the UPADS remained divided over strategy. It presented a slate of candidates for the 2002 National Assembly election and won three seats, although Lissouba had urged his supporters to boycott the balloting. In March the UPADS presidential candidate, Kignoumbi Kia MBOUNGOU, had finished second, with 2.8 percent of the vote.

Leaders: Pascal LISSOUBA (in exile), Alphonse Ongagou DATCHOU (Acting Leader).

Convention for Democracy and Salvation (*Convention pour la Démocratie et le Salut*—Codesa). Formation of Codesa was announced in late March 2002 by a dozen parties, including those discussed below. An anti-PCT/FDU coalition, Codesa is the latest in a series of unwieldy opposition formations in which individual parties have historically failed to coalesce, thereby diminishing their effectiveness as an electoral force. The UDR won six seats in the 2002 assembly balloting, while the rest of Codesa was credited with two seats. Codesa was factionalized over the question of whether to participate in subsequent local and regional elections. Most of the major Codesa components, including the UDR (below), ultimately boycotted that balloting.

The party's deputy president was initially an independent candidate for president in 2002 but withdrew from the race before the balloting. The party boycotted the partial Senate elections of 2005.

Leaders: André MILONGO (President); Anselme MACKOUMB-OU-NKOUKA and Saturnin OKABE (Vice Presidents); Hervé Ambroise MALONGA.

Union for Democracy and the Republic
(*Union pour la Démocratie et la République—* UDR). Launched following a split in the MCDDI (above) and subsequently characterized as "close to the Presidential Tendency," the UDR secured six assembly seats in the first two rounds of balloting in May and June 1993; however, as a result of the second-round rerun in October, its representation dropped to two seats. Its leader, André Milongo, had run for president in 1992 but was eliminated in the first round upon securing only 10.2 percent of the vote. In July 1993 Milongo's selection as assembly president drew sharp criticism from the Opposition Coalition.

In 2002 Milongo withdrew from the presidential election shortly before the March balloting, which he characterized as a "masquerade." At the subsequent National Assembly election the UDR won six seats to lead the opposition.

Leader: André MILONGO.

Union for Democracy and Social Progress
(*Union pour la Démocratie et le Progrs Social—* UDPS). The UDPS was formed in 1994 by merger of the Union for Development and Social Progress (*Union pour le Développement et le Progrs Social—*UDPS), led by Jean-Michel Boukamba-Yangouma, and the People's Party for Social Democracy and Defense of the Republic (*Parti Populaire pour la Démocratie Sociale et la Défense de la République—*PPDSDR), led by Stanislas BATHEAS-MOLLOMB. A breakaway faction of the Union for Social Progress and Democracy

(*Union pour le Progrs Social et la Démocratie-* UPSD) of former prime minister Ange-Edouard Poungui, the original UDPS had secured one assembly seat in 1993.

In December 2001 the UDPS leader headed formation of a "joint platform," encompassing some 40 parties and other groups, that had as its initial purpose ensuring a fair and open electoral process for the 2002 elections.

Leader: Jean-Michel BOUKAMBA-YANGOUMA.

Rally for Democracy and Development
(*Rassemblement pour la Démocratie et le Développement—*RDD). Founded in 1990, the RDD was subsequently a core component of the Forces for Change, the anti-PCT coalition. The RDD won six assembly seats in 1993, with its leader, former president Yhombi-Opango, being named prime minister on June 23. He resigned in August 1996 to run the presidential campaign of President Lissouba.

Leaders: Brig. Gen. Jacques-Joachim YHOMBI-OPANGO (Former President of the Republic), Saturnin OKABE (President).

National Convention for the Republic and Solidarity
(*Convention Nationale pour la République et la Solidarité—*CNRS). The CNRS was organized in late 2001 by Martin Mberi, who had served as leader of the UPADS following President Lissouba's flight into exile. An advocate of cooperation with the Sassou-Nguesso regime, he had served as minister of reconstruction and urban development until resigning in May 2001, at least in part because of objections to the extent of presidential powers in the proposed constitution. Initially a candidate for president in 2002, he pulled out of the race shortly before the balloting.

Leader: Martin MBERI.

Congolese Renewal Party
(*Parti Congolais du Renouveau—*PCR). The PCR was formed in late 1992 by a group of PCT dissidents who rejected the PCT's alliance with Bernard

Kolelas's URD in favor of continued contacts with the recently elected President Lissouba and his UPADS. During the 1997 civil war the party's president was frequently described as a spokesman for Lissouba. In October 2001 the party's secretary general, Wilson Abel Ndessabeka, resigned and went on to help organize the ADP coalition (below).

Leader: Gregoire LEFOUABA.

Republican Convention (*Convention pour la République*—CR). The CR is led by Hervé Ambroise Malonga, a lawyer and former member of the Constitutional Council who was detained by the government from November 1998 until October 1999. On various occasions he has served as an opposition spokesman.

Leader: Hervé Ambroise MALONGA.

Alliance for Democracy and Progress (*Alliance pour la Démocratie et le Progrès*—ADP). The ADP, which dates from 2001, reportedly included up to 14 opposition parties, although the establishment of Codesa in March 2002 apparently reduced its ranks to half a dozen parties. Following the May Assembly balloting, some reports indicated that the ADP had joined Codesa.

Leader: Wilson NDESSABEKA.

Patriotic Front for Dialogue and National Reconciliation (*Front Patriotique pour le Dialogue et la Réconciliation Nationale*—FPDRN). The Paris-based FPDRN is an umbrella grouping of various exiled political leaders close to former president Lissouba. Although it boycotted the initial round of the national dialogue on reconciliation in March 2001, a number of its leaders returned to the Congo for the concluding April session.

Leader: Augustin POIGNET (President); Jean-Michel BOUKA-MBA-YANGOUMA and André MILONGO (Deputy Presidents).

The leaders of four small parties ran for the presidency of the republic in 2002. Angéle BANDOU, a nun who first sought the presidency in 1992 and who ran as the nominee of the **Party of the Poor** (*Parti des Pauvres*—PAP), finished third,

with 2.3 percent of the vote. Luc Adamo MATELA, leader of the **Convention for Democracy and the Republic** (*Convention pour la Démocratie et la République*—CDR), garnered 1.6 percent of the vote. Côme MANCKASSA, a journalist by profession and leader of the **Congolese Union of Republicans** (*Union Congolaise des Républicains*—UCR), won 1.3 percent. Bonaventure MIZIDY, head of the **Republican Liberal Convention** (*Convention Républicaine des Libéraux*—CRL), finished last, with 1.0 percent of the vote.

There are more than 100 additional small parties, many of which have participated since the early 1990s in various alliances of shifting membership. Those parties and coalitions mentioned in the next paragraph are among the most recently reported organizations.

Formation of a **Party for the Reconstruction, Reconciliation, and Revival of the Congo** (*Parti pour la Reconstruction, la Reconciliation, et la Renaissance du Congo*—PRRRC), headed by Georges LOUMBABOU, was reported in April 2000. In August 2001 creation of an **Alliance for the Congo** (*Alliance pour le Congo*) was announced by Justine KOMBA. In December 2001 Ivan Norbert GAMBE announced formation of a **National Center** (*Centre National*) alliance consisting of the **National Party** (*Parti National*), the **National Convention for Democracy and Development** (*Convention Nationale pour la Démocratie et le Développement*—CNDD), the **Republican Convention for Democracy and Progress** (*Convention Républicaine pour la Démocratie et le Progrés*—CRDP), and the **Party for National Conscience** (*Parti pour la Conscience Nationale*—PCN). Gambe, who described the Center as devoted to pluralistic democracy and economic progress, stated that the new grouping neither supported the government nor belonged to the opposition. In January 2002 Michel Mboussi NGOUARI, who had been associated with the rebel National Resistance Council (see below), indicated that the **National Movement for the Liberation of the Congo** (*Mouvement Nationale pour la Libération du Congo*—MNLC) had been established as a political party; the MNLC had been one

Cabinet

As of March 1, 2006

President	Denis Sassou-Nguesso
Prime Minister	Isidore Mvouba

Ministers

Agriculture, Livestock, and Fisheries	Jeanne Dambendzet [f]
Commerce, Consumption, and Supplies	Adelaide Moundele-Ngollo [f]
Communications, in Charge of Relations with Parliament; Government Spokesman	Alain Akouala
Construction, Town Planning, Housing, and Land Reforms	Claude Alphonse Ntsilou
Coordinator for Government Action and Privatization	Isidore Mvouba
Culture, Arts, and Tourism	Jean-Claude Gakosso
Energy and Water	Bruno Jean-Richard Itoua
Equipment and Public Works	Brig. Gen. Florent Ntsiba
Finance, Economy, and Budget	Pacifique Issobeika
Forestry and Environment	Henri Djombo
Health and Population	Dr. Alphonse Gando
Higher Education and Scientific Research	Henri Ossebi
Industrial Development and Promotion of the Private Sector	Emile Mabondzot
Justice, Human Rights, and Keeper of the Seals	Gabriel Entsa-Ebia
Labor, Employment, and Social Security	Gilbert Ondongo
Land Reform and Preservation of Public Property	Lamyr Nguele
Maritime Economy and Merchant Marine	Louis-Marie Nombo Mavoungou
Mines, Mineral Industries, and Geology	Pierre Oba
Minister in the Presidency in Charge of Development Cooperation	Justin Ballay Megot
Minister in the Presidency, in Charge of National Defense and Veterans' Affairs	Jacques-Yvon Ndolou
Posts and Telecommunications, in Charge of New Technologies	Philippe Mvouo
Primary and Secondary Education, in Charge of Literacy	Rosalie Kama [f]
Promotion of Women and the Integration of Women in Development	Jeanne-Françoise Lekomba Loumeto [f]
Scientific Reform and Technological Innovation	Pierre-Ernest Abandzounou
Security and Public Order	Gen. Paul Mbot
Small and Medium Enterprises and Handicrafts	Parfait Aimé Coussoud-Mavoungou
Social Affairs, Solidarity, Humanitarian Action, Disabled War Veterans, and Family Affairs	Emilienne Raoul [f]
Sports and Youth	Marcel Mbani
Technical Education and Professional Training	Pierre Michel Nguimbi
Territorial Administration and Decentralization	François Ibovi
Transport and Civil Aviation	André Okombi-Salissa

Ministers of State

Civil Service and Administrative Reform	Jean-Martín Mbemba
Foreign Affairs and Francophone Affairs	Rodolphe Adada
Hydrocarbons	Jean-Baptiste Tati-Loutard
Planning, Territorial Management, and Economic Integration	Pierre Moussa

[f] = female

of the opposition military groups that agreed to the November 1999 cease-fire.

Rebel Group

National Resistance Council (*Conseil National de Résistance*—CNR). Having emerged from militia groups loyal to former president Lissouba, the CNR's "combat wing" (known as "Ninjas") was led by Frederic Bitsangou (alias Pastor Ntoumi). By 2002 the CNR had reportedly broken with Lissouba in pursuit of greater autonomy for the Pool region. Although some factions (including the MNLC, above) broke from the CNR to form legal parties, the Ninjas launched attacks on government and security sites that forced the postponement of Assembly balloting in Pool in 2002. The CNR and the government signed a cease-fire in March 2003 that called for the exchange of prisoners, demobilization of CNR fighters and their integration into national security forces, and a general amnesty. Nevertheless, some Ninja groups continued to conduct operations against government forces and international aid workers. Bitsangou subsequently called for CNR's inclusion in a proposed new government of national unity, but President Sassou-Nguesso refused that request. In mid-2005 the CNR announced that it hoped to participate as a political party in future elections in Pool.

Leaders: Frederic BITSANGOU, Ane Philippe BIBI.

Legislature

The former 133-member People's National Assembly (*Assemblée Nationale Populaire*) was dissolved by the 1991 National Conference, with assignment of its functions to an appointed but broadly representative Higher Council of the Republic (*Conseil Supérieur de la République*—CSR), a 153-member body charged with implementing National Conference decisions.

The constitution endorsed by the CSR in December 1991 and approved by popular referendum in May 1992 provided for a bicameral Parliament (*Parlement*) composed of a Senate and National Assembly. Following the civil war of mid-1997, the parliament was replaced by the National Transitional Council (*Conseil National de la Transition*—CNT), whose 75 members were elected in mid-January 1998 at a reconciliation forum attended by more than 1,400 delegates. The CNT candidate lists were put forward by political and legal commissions as well as the government. The forum recommended that the CNT exercise quasi-legislative authority pending the proposed election of a new bicameral assembly following a constitutional referendum. The constitution approved by referendum in January 2002 restored a bicameral system, with the **Parliament** comprising a Senate and a National Assembly.

Senate (*Sénat*). The upper house is a 66-member body–6 senators from each region and from the capital—indirectly elected by local and regional councils for a six-year term. Initial balloting was held on July 11, 2002, in all regions except Pool, where violence had forced postponement of voting. (Balloting in Pool had not been held as of October 2005.) In the future, one-third of the membership is to be renewed every two years. Of the 60 seats filled on July 11, 2002, the Congolese Labor Party reportedly won 44 seats; the United Democratic Forces, 12; the Convention for Democracy and Salvation, 1; others (civic organizations and independents), 3. In partial elections held on October 2, 2005, for 30 seats, the PCT won 23, with 6 going to government coalition parties and 1 independent.

President: Ambroise NOUMAZALAYE.

National Assembly (*Assemblée Nationale*). The lower house has 137 members, directly elected for five-year terms. Balloting is conducted in two rounds, with a majority needed for election. Of the 129 seats filled at the initial election of May 26 and June 23, 2002, the Congolese Labor Party reportedly won 53 seats, the United Democratic Forces, 30; the Union for Democratic Renewal, 6; the Pan-African Union for Social Democracy, 3; the Convention for Democracy and Salvation, 2; other parties, 16; independents, 19. Balloting for the eight seats in the Pool area was postponed because of militia activity and had not been held by mid-2005.

Speaker: Jean-Pierre THYSTERE-TCHI-CAYE.

Communications

Legislation passed in 2000 outlawed censorship and assured freedom of information, although libeling senior authorities or inciting ethnic conflict are among those offenses punishable by fines. In September 2005 *Radio Moka,* a community station based in Impfondo, was suspended indefinitely by the government on allegations of "lack of impartiality" in news coverage.

Press

Mweti (7,000) is a French-language daily published in Brazzaville. Other dailies include *Aujourd'hui; L'Eveil de Pointe-Noire;* and the *Journal de Brazzaville.*

News Agencies

The official news agency is *Agence Congolaise d'Information* (ACI); the *Agence d'Information d'Afrique Centrale* (ADIAC) is also located in the capital. Resident foreign bureaus include *Agence France-Presse,* the Pan-African News Agency, and Reuters.

Broadcasting and Computing

Broadcasting is dominated by the state-owned *Radiodiffusion-Télévision Nationale Congolaise* (RTNC), which offers programming in French, English, Portuguese, and a variety of indigenous languages. In April 1997 the government established a new official radio station, *Radio Brazzaville.* Television service is limited; approximately 62,000 television receivers were reportedly in use in 2003, while 15,000 personal computers served an equal number of Internet users.

Intergovernmental Representation

Ambassador to the U.S.
Serge MOMBOULI

U.S. Ambassador to the Republic of the Congo
Robert WEISBERG

Permanent Representative to the UN
Basile IKOUEBE

IGO Memberships (Non-UN)
AfDB, AU, BADEA, BDEAC, CEEAC, CEMAC, Interpol, IOM, NAM, OIF, WCO, WTO

CÔTE D'IVOIRE

République de Côte d'Ivoire

Note: In November 1985 the United Nations responded affirmatively to a request from the Ivorian government that *Côte d'Ivoire* be recognized as the sole official version of what had previously been rendered in English as Ivory Coast and in Spanish as *Costa de Marfil*.

The Country

A land of forests and savannas, with a hot, humid climate, Côte d'Ivoire is the richest and potentially the most nearly self-sufficient state of former French West Africa. Indigenous peoples fall into five principal ethnic groups: Ashanti-Agni-Baoule, Kru, Malinké, Mandé, and Lagoon dwellers. A substantial percentage of the population consists of migrant workers, mostly from Burkina Faso, Ghana, and Mali. There has traditionally also been a sizable non-African expatriate community consisting primarily of Lebanese and French. A majority of the population is either Muslim (40 percent) or Christian (30 percent), with the balance adhering to traditional religious practices. Women constitute approximately 33 percent of the adult labor force, primarily in agriculture; female representation in government is minimal, although there have been several women in recent cabinets.

The economy experienced rapid growth following completion in 1950 of the Vridi Canal, which transformed Abidjan into a deepwater port. An impressive average real growth rate of 7.5 percent was reported for 1960–1980, but a variety of factors led to a severe five-year recession thereafter. Although agriculture now accounts for only one-fourth of total GDP, Côte d'Ivoire is one of the world's leading producers of cocoa and Africa's primary exporter of coffee, bananas, and tropical woods.

The country's image as a model African economy was tarnished in the 1980s by debts attributed to extensive government borrowing in the 1970s. In the first half of the 1990s, sagging cocoa and coffee prices, the decimation of lumber-producing forests, and the government's inability to make debt payments prompted economic reform and diversification efforts. Such measures enabled Côte d'Ivoire to rebound quickly from the inflationary effects of the 1994 CFA franc devaluation, and between 1995 and 1998 the country experienced an average real GDP annual growth rate of more than 6 percent. However, Côte d'Ivoire's fiscal situation remained fragile. The International Monetary Fund (IMF)

and the World Bank cited poor economic management and a multitude of perceived governance problems as contributing to the country's difficulties. (The IMF temporarily suspended aid in 1999 because of perceived corruption within the administration.) In light of the political uncertainty that followed a military coup in December 1999, the economy shrunk by 2.5 percent in 2000 and 1.5 percent in 2001.

The resumption of civil war in 2002 (see Political background and Current issues, below) strained the economy even further, GDP declining by 3.8 percent in 2003. The IMF and World Bank suspended some aid and debt-reduction programs because of the strife, which also compromised major trade routes through the north of the country to neighboring states and prompted a sharp decline in foreign investment. GDP fell by 2.3 percent in 2004, but a UN-sponsored peace initiative in 2005 offered hope for economic recovery. Also encouraging was the opening of new oil fields in the Baobab region in 2005. The country's oil production reached 80,000 barrels per day, and the transitional government signed additional exploration agreements with several foreign companies. It was also announced in April 2006 that Cote d'Ivoire had qualified for IMF and World Bank debt relief.

Government and Politics

Political Background

Established as a French protectorate in 1842, Côte d'Ivoire became part of the Federation of French West Africa in 1904, an autonomous republic within the French Community in 1958, and a fully independent member of the Community in August 1960, although its membership was abandoned with the adoption of its present constitution two months later. Its dominant political figure since the 1940s was Félix HOUPHOUËT-BOIGNY, who in 1944 organized the *Syndicat Agricole Africain,* an African farmers union, and was one of the founders of the African Democratic Rally (*Rassemblement Démocratique Africain*—RDA), an international political party with branches in numerous French African territories. As leader of the RDA's Ivorian branch, the Democratic Party of the Ivory Coast (*Parti Démocratique de la Côte d'Ivoire*—PDCI), Houphouët-Boigny served in the French National Assembly from 1946 to 1959, became prime minister of the autonomous republic in 1959, and served as president from 1960 until his death in 1993.

The postcolonial era was relatively stable by African standards. Most vocal opposition to the regime came from students, and there were periodic demonstrations and university closings. Another source of tension was the presence of many foreign workers, with whom indigenous Ivorians sporadically clashed in competition for jobs. An alleged antigovernment conspiracy in 1963 resulted in the arrest and imprisonment of numerous party and government officials; however, subsequent evidence indicated that the plot was not a serious threat, and a majority of the prisoners were released. Additional attempts at subversion were suppressed in 1970 and 1973.

The election of an enlarged National Assembly on November 9 and 23, 1980, marked the first time since independence that nominees were not confined to a single PDCI list. Although all 649 office seekers were party members, incumbents captured only 26 of 147 seats, while a similar infusion of new representatives occurred at municipal balloting later in the month.

On May 30, 1990, the government was compelled by increasingly strident protests to authorize opposition party activity. On October 28 Houphouët-Boigny won a seventh term in office, capturing a reported 82 percent of the vote, while Laurent GBAGBO, leader of the opposition Ivorian Popular Front (*Front Populaire Ivoirien*—FPI), was credited with the remainder. On November 7, one day after the National Assembly approved creation of the post, the highly regarded governor of the Central Bank of West African States (*Banque Centrale des États de l'Afrique de l'Ouest*—BCEAO), Alassane OUATTARA, was appointed prime minister.

On December 7, 1993, Houphouët-Boigny died in his Yamoussoukro palace of complications

Political Status: Independent since August 7, 1960; present constitution adopted October 31, 1960; under de facto one-party regime prior to legalization of opposition parties on May 30, 1990; constitution suspended and governmental authority assumed by the military following a bloodless coup on December 24, 1999; new constitution providing for a return to civilian government approved by national referendum on June 23–24, 2000.

Area: 124,503 sq. mi. (322,463 sq. km.).

Population: 15,366,672 (1998C); 17,176,000 (2005E).

Major Urban Center (2005E): Abidjan (4,100,000). In March 1983 the interior city of YAMOUSSOUKRO (484,000, 2005E) was designated as the nation's capital. However, as of late 2005 many government offices remained in Abidjan (the former capital), and most foreign governments were also still maintaining their embassies there.

Official Language: French.

Monetary Unit: CFA Franc (official rate July 1, 2006: 513.01 francs = $1US). (The CFA franc, previously pegged to the French franc, is now permanently pegged to the euro at 655.957 CFA francs = 1 euro.)

President: Laurent GBAGBO (Ivorian Popular Front); elected on October 20, 2000, and inaugurated for a five-year term on October 27 to succeed Gen. Robert GUEÏ, who had come to power via a coup on December 24, 1999; term extended for one year following UN Resolution 1633, which endorsed the postponement of elections scheduled for October 2005.

Prime Minister: Charles Konan BANNY (nonparty); appointed by the president on December 5, 2005, and sworn in on December 7 to succeed Seydou DIARRA (nonparty); formed new multiparty government on December 28, 2005.

stemming from an operation earlier in the year. On the same day, Prime Minister Ouattara held a cabinet meeting in the presidential offices; however, that evening National Assembly president Henri Konan BÉDIÉ announced that he had assumed presidential power in accord with a 1990 constitutional amendment. Two days later Ouattara resigned, apparently unwilling to cooperate with Bédié, his (then) PDCI rival. On December 9 the Supreme Court confirmed Bédié's succession, and the following day the president appointed Daniel Kablan DUNCAN prime minister. On December 15 Duncan, a former economy minister described as a "technocrat," named a 24-member interim cabinet. Underscoring his professed dedication to economic reform, the prime minister retained the economy and finance ministry for himself.

In preparation for presidential and legislative elections scheduled for late 1995, the PDCI-dominated National Assembly voted overwhelmingly on December 8, 1994, to adopt a new electoral code that the opposition had strongly criticized as biased in favor of the government. The run-up to the 1995 poll was marked by violent protests against the code, its new provisions (requiring parents and grandparents of presidential candidates to have been of Ivorian birth) having thwarted the aspirations of Ouattara, Bédié's main challenger and the consensus leader of the opposition Republican Front (*Front Républicain*—FR). Moreover, the government refused to appoint an independent electoral commission, and in September it banned all demonstrations for three months. However, the FR continued its antigovernment marches, and on October 2 at least five people were killed when government forces attempted to disperse protestors. Meanwhile, the field of presidential contestants (which had numbered 11) continued to dwindle as candidates announced their intention to observe the FR's call for an electoral boycott. Consequently, at presidential balloting on October 22, President Bédié easily won reelection, capturing 96.25 percent of the tally while his sole adversary, Francis WODIÉ of the Ivorian Workers' Party (*Parti Ivoirien des Travailleurs*—PIT), secured a meager 3.75 percent. Although the government claimed a 62 percent voter participation rate, the opposition reported much lower figures.

Following a meeting with Bédié in early November 1995, the FR announced its intention to participate in legislative balloting. However, the FR proved unable to agree on a joint list of candidates; consequently, at assembly balloting on November 26 the PDCI retained all 148 of its seats while the FPI and the Rally of Republicans (*Rassemblement des Républicains*—RDR) managed only small gains.

Prime Minister Duncan submitted his pro forma resignation on January 24, 1996, although he was immediately reappointed by the president. The "continuity government" announced on January 26 largely mirrored the previous one, although a new ministry was created for Yamoussoukro, the titular national capital.

In May 1996 the government confirmed rumors that a coup attempt led by senior military officers had been thwarted prior to the 1995 assembly balloting. (The administration had previously maintained that the clashes were between government security forces and opposition militants.) On August 10 the administration removed Minister of Sports Gen. Robert GUEÏ, who was the army chief of staff in 1995 and had subsequently been linked by junior military officials to the "conception and preparation" of the coup plot (a charge he denied). Moreover, between November 1996 and January 1997 the government dismissed eight senior officers, including Gueï, from the armed forces and penalized at least four others for their alleged roles in the 1995 coup attempt.

On June 30, 1998, the PDCI-dominated assembly approved constitutional amendments that dramatically increased the scope of the chief executive's powers and, two years after it was first proposed, provided for the establishment of an upper legislative body, or Senate (see Constitution and government, below). Opposition legislators boycotted the assembly vote, asserting that the PDCI had ignored their legislative recommendations, including a call for the amendments to be submitted to a national referendum. Subsequently, antigovernment demonstrations erupted in Abidjan in September; however, the ruling party and the FPI began discussions that yielded a "good governance," prodemocracy pact on December 24. Four days later the National Assembly took action on a key element of the agreement, adopting a draft law that authorized the government to grant amnesty to opposition activists jailed during the 1995 unrest. Electoral reform was the focus of the accord's other major directives, most notably the financing of presidential election campaigns and the establishment of a national electoral commission. Meanwhile, although the agreement elicited nearly universal acclaim from Ivorian political leaders, the praise was tempered somewhat by opposition demands that the government begin negotiations with all of the major parties. Subsequently, in March 1999, the PDCI launched talks with the RDR on establishing the conditions necessary for elections in 2000 and the drafting of a "consensus constitution." However, the discussions quickly stalled, and attention in Abidjan turned toward the potential for an electoral confrontation between Bédié and Alassane Ouattara, the latter having reportedly announced his intention to relinquish his position as IMF deputy secretary general to mount a presidential campaign as the RDR's standard-bearer.

Growing dissatisfaction over Bédié's autocratic rule contributed to his overthrow in a bloodless military coup on December 24, 1999. General Gueï, the dominant figure in the junta, assumed the presidency of a transitional National Committee of Public Salvation (*Comité National de Salut Public*—CNSP), promising he would cede power within a year to a democratically elected president. In January 2000 membership on the CNSP was expanded to include the PDCI, FPI, and RDR, although ultimate control remained in the hands of the military. Gueï subsequently appeared to be maneuvering to consolidate his power in anticipation of a possible run for the presidency, despite his previous pledge that he would not be a candidate. The question of candidate eligibility was significant in the preparation of the new draft constitution, which originally required that a person needed only one parent of Ivorian nationality to be a legal candidate, a provision that would have permitted Ouattara to run. However, at Gueï's insistence, the draft basic law was redrawn to require that both parents of a presidential candidate had to be Ivorian citizens. In early October, the Supreme Court, headed by Gueï's former legal adviser, confirmed that Ouattara's candidacy was invalid, as was that of Emile Constant BOMBET, the potential candidate of the RDR.

The new constitution was approved in a national referendum July 23–24, 2000 (see Constitution and government, below, for details). Due to administrative and logistical problems, presidential balloting was subsequently postponed until October 22. Gueï and the FPI's Laurent Gbagbo were the primary contenders, a boycott by the PDCI and RDR having reduced the rest of the field to several candidates from minor parties. Voter turnout was low, only 35 percent, in large part due to the RDR boycott. When initial results suggested a Gbagbo victory, Gueï attempted to dismiss the Independent Electoral Commission and declare himself victor. However, massive street demonstrations erupted to protest Gueï's actions, and he was forced to abdicate power and accept the legitimacy of the victory by Gbagbo, who was sworn in as president on October 27. One day later Gbagbo named Pascal Affi N'GUESSAN of the FPI to head a new cabinet dominated by the FPI but also including members of the PDCI and PIT.

New assembly balloting was held on December 10, 2000, the RDR boycotting the poll because Ouattara was again declared ineligible to be a candidate. The FPI scored considerable gains, securing 96 seats to 77 for the PDCI. (Elections were not held for 28 northern seats due to violence related to the RDR boycott.)

The PDCI significantly improved its legislative standing in the January 14, 2001, balloting for 26 of the 28 seats that had not been filled the previous December, winning 17 of the contests. However, the FPI subsequently established a more comfortable plurality by negotiating a cooperation agreement with independent legislators who in February formed the new, pro-Gueï Union for Democracy and Peace in Côte d'Ivoire (*Union pour la Démocratie et la Paix de la Côte d'Ivoire*— UDPCI). On January 24 a new cabinet, again led by N'Guessan, was appointed, with the FPI, PDCI,

and PIT accepting portfolios. Municipal elections in March 2001 were most noteworthy for the success of the RDR, which, among other things, shed some of its reputation as a "one man" or "one region" party by gaining control of local councils throughout the country.

Under heavy international pressure, President Gbagbo convened a Forum for National Reconciliation in October 2001, which upon its conclusion in January 2002 had heard from Gbagbo, Bédié, Gueï, and Ouattara. The "big four" attended negotiations together in late January to review the forum's proposals, which, among other things, called for Ouattara to be issued a nationality certificate. Based on the success of those talks, the RDR joined the new government named on August 5.

In the wake of efforts to resolve a bitter civil war that broke out in September 2002, Gbagbo in January 2003 appointed Seydou DIARRA, a well-respected independent, to lead an ultimately star-crossed national unity cabinet. Following the postponement of national elections scheduled for October 2005, independent Charles Konan BANNY was named to head a new transitional government that was installed on December 28 (see Current issues, below, for information on the Diarra and Banny governments).

Constitution and Government

The 1960 constitution provided the framework for a one-party presidential system based on the preeminent position of President Houphouët-Boigny and the PDCI. Although other parties were not proscribed, no challenge to the PDCI was permitted until May 1990 when the government authorized the registration of opposition groups. The president, elected by universal suffrage for a seven-year term (extended from five in 1998), had wide authority, which was enhanced in November 1990 to include the designation of a prime minister. The cabinet (selected from outside the legislature) was responsible only to the chief executive. In September 1997 President Bédié established the National Strategy and Prospects Council, an advisory body whose members were to serve three-year terms. In 1998 the National Assembly approved constitutional amendments that, in addition to lengthening the president's mandate, removed presidential term limits and authorized the chief executive to postpone elections (and the release of polling results) and appoint some members of a proposed new Senate. Furthermore, the amendments delineated new eligibility requirements for the nation's top post, including ten years of residency immediately predating presidential polling and proof of Ivorian ancestry for both of the aspirant's parents.

The membership of the unicameral National Assembly was increased from 147 to 175 in 1985. By virtue of a 1990 change in the basic law, the president of the assembly, who was theretofore designated to head an interim government upon the death, resignation, or incapacity of the chief executive, was authorized to complete the remainder of the mandate. In October 1996, officials of the ruling PDCI proposed the establishment of a legislative upper house, or Senate. The new body was created by constitutional amendment in 1998; however, as of mid-1999 there had been no further reports of efforts to organize the Senate (one-third of whose members were to be presidential appointees).

The military junta that assumed power in a bloodless coup on December 24, 1999, immediately suspended the constitution. However, a new basic law was presented for a national referendum July 23–24, 2000, with 87 percent of the voters, according to official reports, approving the document. Much of the language in the 1960 constitution was retained in the 2000 version. A strong presidential system was confirmed; among other things the president retained the authority to appoint the prime minister and, in consultation with the prime minister, the Council of Ministers. The president's term was reduced to five years, renewable once. The post is selected through direct universal suffrage in two-round (if necessary) majoritarian balloting. Restrictions were also placed on presidential candidates regarding their parentage and formal nationality, again prompting substantial controversy (see Political background, above). (The National Assembly in December 2004 passed legislation to allow citizens with only one Ivorian parent to run for office, although President Gbagbo

insisted a national referendum would be required for the change to be implemented.) The National Assembly remained the sole legislative body, the Senate, which had never been established, being formally abolished. For the first time, the new constitution included detailed protection for human rights. Other noteworthy provisions included one granting civil and penal immunity for people involved in the 1999 coup.

The judiciary is headed by a Constitutional Council comprising three members appointed by the president and three appointed by the president of the assembly. There are also a High Court of Justice (whose members are elected by the assembly), a Court of Cassation, and local appeals courts. The new constitution also created the post of a presidentially appointed mediator of the republic to serve as a national ombudsman.

The country is divided for administrative purposes into 58 departments, each headed by a prefect appointed by the central government, but with an elected council. Municipalities (numbering nearly 200) have elected councillors and mayors.

Foreign Relations

In line with its generally pro-French orientation, Côte d'Ivoire has adhered to a moderate policy in African affairs and a broadly pro-Western posture. In the 1980s, relations with neighboring states were periodically strained, particularly in the wake of growing xenophobic sentiment in Côte d'Ivoire, especially among the mainly Christian population in the south. Although ties with neighboring Burkina Faso had previously been weakened because of its links with Libya and Ghana, Burkinabe leader Capt. Blaise Compaoré, who led the 1987 overthrow of Col. Thomas Sankara's government, long enjoyed close personal relations with Houphouët-Boigny. Relations with the Central African Republic, cool upon the provision of sanctuary to former emperor Bokassa, improved once the ex-sovereign departed for Paris in late 1983. Relations with Israel, which had been broken off in 1973, were reestablished in December 1985, an Arab League threat in late 1986 to break ties with Côte d'Ivoire resulting in transfer of the Ivorian embassy from Jerusalem to the less controversial location of Tel Aviv.

In the early 1990s, France, the country's leading financial donor and cultural influence, appeared to lose interest in maintaining a high profile in its former protectorate. In 1990 France stunned Côte d'Ivoire by refusing Houphouët-Boigny's request for troops to help quell an uprising of military conscripts, and in 1991 the number of French nationals employed in Côte d'Ivoire fell to its lowest level in several decades. In April 1992 Abidjan responded to French immigration restrictions with a requirement that French nationals apply for Ivorian visas; it reacted in a similar manner to the imposition of visa requirements for Ivorians by Denmark, Italy, Germany, Norway, and the United Kingdom in early 1995.

Burdened by the presence of 200,000 refugees along its western border, Côte d'Ivoire's diplomatic efforts to resolve the Liberian crisis continued through 1992. In September 1994, 15,000 refugees from renewed fighting in Liberia were reported to have crossed into Côte d'Ivoire in the largest such influx since 1992.

Cross-border violence continued to mar Côte d'Ivoire's relations with its neighbors in 1996. Consequently, in September, Abidjan, citing the need to stem attacks on its nationals as well as foreign refugees, established a military "operational zone" along its border with Liberia. Meanwhile, relations with Guinea were strained after its troops occupied an Ivorian border village in March. In April 1997 the Bédié government and the United Nations Office of the High Commissioner for Refugees (UNHCR) reached agreement on a plan to repatriate the approximately 200,000 Liberians still living in Côte d'Ivoire.

The Organization of African Unity (OAU, subsequently the African Union—AU) and the Economic Community of West African States (ECOWAS) did not agree with General Gueï's successful efforts to bar the presidential candidacy of Alassane Ouattara in the summer of 2000, and they subsequently exerted considerable diplomatic pressure to undermine Gueï's legitimacy. The international community, particularly the European Union (EU), also strongly urged all of the key political figures in Côte d'Ivoire to participate fully in the reconciliation process so as to permit resumption of aid.

Current Issues

More than 300 people died in violence that erupted following the October 2000 presidential election, much of it centered on conflict between the RDR and security forces as well as between the predominantly Muslim northern supporters of the RDR and the predominantly Christian southern supporters of the FPI. Continued political tension and unrest in the military were reflected in an unsuccessful military coup attempt in early January 2001. Fighting was also reported in the west between Ivorians and migrant workers from Burkina Faso who generally supported the RDR.

Hope was widespread in August 2002 that a return to stability was in the offing in view of the RDR's decision to join the cabinet. However, in mid-September a group of soldiers about to be demobilized launched antigovernment attacks that soon left more than half of the country in the hands of the new Patriotic Movement of Côte d'Ivoire (*Mouvement Patriotique de la Côte d'Ivoire*— MPCI). France sent additional troops to augment its 500-member permanent garrison in case a quick evacuation was required but declined to assist the government militarily, calling the conflict a domestic issue. For its part, the Gbagbo administration blamed the insurrection on supporters of General Gueï, who was killed under murky circumstances in a seemingly nonmilitary situation on the first day of fighting.

With the predominantly Muslim MPCI holding significant portions of the northern and central regions, the government in late September 2002 reportedly instituted harsh countermeasures that led the RDR to withdraw its support for the administration. Meanwhile, two new rebel groups (the Movement for Justice and Peace [*Mouvement pour la Justice et la Paix*—MJP] and the Ivorian Popular Movement for the Greater West [*Mouvement*

Populaire Ivoirien du Grand Ouest—MPIGO]) had emerged in the west. With the conflict having developed into a full-blown civil war, France deployed some 2,500 troops to try to maintain order in Côte d'Ivoire, while regional leaders initiated mediation efforts. In January 2003 an agreement was reached under the auspices of ECOWAS under which Gbagbo was to remain president while allowing security authority to be assumed by a new prime minister. For their part, the rebel groups agreed to end hostilities, with both sides being guaranteed amnesty for any human rights violations. ECOWAS peacekeepers joined French forces in an effort to patrol the cease-fire line.

The appointment of Seydou Diarra as prime minister in January 2003 appeared to be a promising development, since he was widely respected by opposition groups as well as the international community. (Diarra's subsequent willingness to negotiate with the rebels reportedly contributed to friction between him and President Gbagbo.) After intense negotiations, it was announced that a new cabinet would be formed comprising ten members from the FPI, eight from the PDCI, seven from the RDR, seven from the MPCI, one from the MJP, one from the MPIGO, and additional ministers from small established parties. However, the unity cabinet essentially collapsed before it began work when antigovernment protests (asserting that Gbagbo had reneged on his pledge regarding the prime minister's authority) were met with violent suppression. Fighting resumed in several areas, and even international observers were unable to pinpoint which side was to blame.

In June 2003 the UN Security Council authorized the creation of UN peacekeeping for Côte d'Ivoire, but fighting continued, the three rebel groups coalescing in August under the banner of the New Forces (*Forces Nouvelles*—FN). Meanwhile, progovernment demonstrations for the most part appeared to be conducted by the Coordination of Young Patriots (*Coordination des Jeunes Patriotes*—CJP), which was strongly criticized for alleged responsibility for a campaign of violence against opposition leaders and foreigners. The CJP was banned in September, but its hallmark at-

tacks continued. For his part, Guillaume SORO, the leader of the FN, announced his forces would not lay down their arms until Gbagbo surrendered his security power. In response, the UN imposed an arms embargo on the country in November 2004. However, subsequent reports indicated that the government and rebel groups were able to violate the embargo easily.

By the end of 2004 some 250,000 Ivorians had fled the civil war to neighboring countries, and 600,000 people had been displaced internally. In addition, tensions had grown between the government and French peacekeepers, French forces having "destroyed" the Ivorian air force after a government attack on a rebel base had accidentally left nine French soldiers dead.

President Gbagbo and FN leader Soro met at a summit in April 2005 sponsored by South African President Mbeki and reached yet another tentative peace agreement. As stipulated in the May accord, the rebels began to disarm in late June, while rebel and government forces started to withdraw from conflict zones. The cease-fire continued throughout the summer, despite ethnic clashes in cocoa-producing areas that left more than 100 dead in June. (Gbagbo deployed special police and security forces in Abidjan in the wake of that turmoil.)

In July 2005 the assembly endorsed legislation required by the recent peace agreement that provided for public financing of political campaigns, a new voter registration campaign, reform of citizenship laws, and establishment of a new election commission in preparation for the presidential and legislative elections scheduled for October. However, the FN temporarily withdrew from the peace process in September, claiming that South African officials were exhibiting a bias toward the Gbagbo administration. Consequently, upon the recommendation of UN Secretary General Kofi Annan that the elections be postponed, the UN Security Council on October 21 endorsed the extension of Gbagbo's presidential mandate for up to 12 months. The UN also called upon Gbagbo to appoint a new prime minister with enhanced powers to lead a new transitional government.

The AU and ECOWAS endorsed the UN's decision, but the FN rejected the action and demanded that Soro be named as the nation's new prime minister. Collaterally, FN forces "remobilized," and Gbagbo created new elite security forces to deal with the potential resumption of fighting. However, in November the FN returned to negotiations that, after 16 other candidates were rejected, led to the appointment of Charles Banny, a governor of the Bank of West African States, to the premiership. His government comprised representatives of the FPI, FN, PDCI, MPCI, PIT, RDR, and UDPCI and was seen as maintaining the necessary balance among the main factions.

Prime Minister Banny, an independent described as "pro-French," soon clashed with President Gbagbo over the extent of Banny's authority. Consequently, the UN established an International Working Group (IWG) to assist the new transitional government. In one of its first decisions, the IWG in January 2006 announced that it would not endorse the proposed extension of the mandate of the current assembly (a primary source of support for Gbagbo). The president's supporters (many of them youths commonly referred to as the "young patriots") subsequently launched a series of protests that included the occupation of UN headquarters in Abidjan and attacks on foreign businesses. In response, the UN threatened to impose travel restrictions and financial sanctions on any Ivorian leaders perceived as encouraging the unrest, and general calm returned. On January 27 Gbagbo announced that the mandate of the assembly had in fact been extended for up to one year; the IWG described the extension as a violation of the spirit of the peace agreements but took no formal action. A number of parties boycotted the subsequent assembly activity.

Another round of peace talks was held by the main factions in February 2006, with tentative agreement being reached for new national elections in October. Collaterally, the UN bolstered its peacekeeping mission by transferring troops to it from the successful UN initiative in Liberia. Voter registration began in May, along with an intensified campaign to disarm former rebel groups and pro-government militias. However, as of early September it appeared that the elections might be postponed once again.

Political Parties

On May 30, 1990, Côte d'Ivoire ceased to be a one-party state with the legalization of nine opposition groups; at first-round legislative balloting on November 25 their number exceeded two dozen, while in May 1991 the government recognized 14 more, some of which were alleged to be PDCI fronts created to dilute opposition cohesiveness. By July 1993 40 of the reported 82 active political parties had been recognized. The July 2002 constitution provided for unrestricted party activity "within the law."

In advance of presidential elections scheduled for October 2005, opposition groups formed a loose electoral coalition known (in homage to former president Houphouët-Boigny) as the **Rally of Houphouëtistas for Democracy and Peace** (*Rassemblement des Houphouëtistas pour la Démocratie et la Paix*—RHDP). The group subsequently became commonly known as the G7 after the FN agreed to work with the coalition. (G7 referred to the fact that it contained seven groups— the FN, PDCI, RDR, UDPCI, MFA, and two minor parties.) In July 2005 the RDR's Alassane Ouattara and the PDCI's Henri Bédié held discussions in Paris aimed at agreement on a single opposition candidate to challenge Gbagbo in the planned presidential elections. Alphonse Djedjé Mady (the secretary general of the PDCI) was appointed as the nominal leader and spokesperson for the G7. After the presidential elections were postponed, the G7 organized mass protests against Gbagbo in Abidjan in November 2005. The G7 supported the proposed appointment of the FN's Guillaume Soro as prime minister in December 2005 but endorsed Charles Banny after his appointment. The G7 also organized mass protests and a boycott of the assembly after it was announced that the mandate of the assembly would be extended. The parties and groups within the G7 continue to operate as independent entities and use the coalition only as a coordinating body.

Government Parties

Ivorian Popular Front (*Front Populaire Ivoirien*—FPI). The FPI was founded by history professor Laurent Gbagbo, who was granted a state pardon for dissident activity upon his return to Côte d'Ivoire in September 1988. At its founding congress on November 19–20, 1989, the FPI adopted a platform calling for a mixed economy with a private sector emphasis. Legalized on May 30, 1990, and becoming thereafter the unofficial leader of a coalition that included the PIT and USD, the party called for President Houphouët-Boigny's resignation, the appointment of a transitional government, and freedom of association. It endorsed Gbagbo's bid to succeed the incumbent chief executive at its first legal congress on September 16, 1990. Angered at apparent electoral irregularities and claiming fraudulent tallying, FPI supporters clashed with government forces during and after the October 28 presidential balloting, with 120 reportedly being arrested. Thereafter, in mid-1991 the FPI refused to join in an opposition call for a national conference, insisting instead that Houphouët-Boigny's government resign.

Reportedly believing that the FPI would be offered the premiership in a transitional government, Gbagbo publicly backed Henri Konan Bédié of the PDCI in the months prior to Houphouët-Boigny's death in December 1993. However, when it became apparent that Bédié would not extend such an offer, Gbagbo broke off negotiations with the ruling party.

In February 1994 Gbagbo called for repeal of the constitutional amendment detailing presidential succession procedures, the establishment of a transitional government, the creation of a West African currency, and the holding of "clean" elections. In July 1995 Gbagbo called the government's electoral code "legalized fraud," and he subsequently withdrew from the presidential campaign.

In July 1998 the FPI boycotted an assembly vote on constitutional amendments that increased the chief executive's powers. (An FPI call for the amendments to be subjected to a national referendum had been rejected by the PDCI.) Subsequently, the party reportedly played a leading role in organizing antigovernment demonstrations in Abidjan. On a more conciliatory note, the FPI and the government agreed in October to hold discussions on the country's "political future," and in December the two signed an accord that was described as starting them on the "road to achieving a new national consensus."

In the wake of the December 1999 coup, the FPI joined the cabinet in January 2000 after having successfully lobbied for greater representation than originally offered by General Gueï. Following Gbagbo's election as president of the republic in October 2000, he appointed the FPI's Pascal Affi N'Guessan to head a new FPI-dominated cabinet. N'Guessan, who had managed Gbagbo's presidential campaign, succeeded Gbagbo as FPI leader in mid-2001.

Following the renewed civil war in 2002, a number of propresidential groups affiliated with the FPI emerged. Foremost among them was the CJP (see Current issues), led by a close Gbagbo ally, Charles Blé GOUDE. The CJP organized a number of demonstrations in support of the president, but it was banned in September 2003 for the alleged use of violence and intimidation.

Following the extension of President Gbagbo's term in October 2005, the FPI filled seven seats (the most of any party) in the new transitional government installed in December. Subsequently, there were reports in early 2006 that Gbagbo was forming a new political organization to support his upcoming bid for reelection, apparently in an effort to broaden his base of appeal.

Leaders: Laurent GBAGBO (President of the Republic), Pascal Affi N'GUESSAN (Former Prime Minister and President of the Party), Sylvain Miaka OURETA (Secretary General).

Democratic Party of Côte d'Ivoire (*Parti Démocratique de la Côte d'Ivoire*—PDCI). Established in 1946 as a section of the African Democratic Rally (*Rassemblement Démocratique*

Africain—RDA), the PDCI (often referenced as the PDCI-RDA) was the country's only authorized party for the ensuing 44 years, although other parties were never formally banned. The PDCI held its ninth congress in October 1990, five months after the decision to allow political competition. Although reportedly divided into fractious "old and new guards" in response to the country's mounting socioeconomic problems, the congress endorsed President Houphouët-Boigny's bid for a seventh term, proposed the naming of a prime minister, and revived the office of party secretary general.

Divisions within the party were underscored in mid-1992 when Djény KOBINA, a spokesman for the party's so-called progressive wing, called for the release of opposition leaders detained in February. Thereafter, despite the PDCI's denial of intraparty conflict, Prime Minister Alassane Ouattara announced in early 1993 that he would seek the party's 1995 presidential nomination, thus highlighting the widening gulf between his northern, Muslim followers and the southern, predominantly Catholic supporters of the National Assembly president and presidential "heir apparent," Henri Konan Bédié. In the wake of Houphouët-Boigny's death and Bédié's subsequent succession, there were reports that Ouattara was planning to launch his own party and that the old-line "barons of *houphouëtisme*" had aligned with him and were demanding an extraordinary PDCI congress to reconsider succession policy. Nonetheless, Bédié was unanimously elected party chair in April 1994.

In June 1994 Kobina's wing, including a number of senior party officials, broke from the party to form the RDR (below), with a loss to the PDCI of nine assembly seats. Subsequently, Ouattara, who had accepted an IMF post in May, disavowed his PDCI membership. (He joined the RDR in 1995.)

Discouraged by the party's primary system, a number of PDCI legislative aspirants reportedly opted to compete as independents in the general elections in 1995; however, there was no indication of their having secured seats. Intraparty dissension continued to plague the PDCI through early 1996;

nevertheless, the group was victorious in 158 of the 196 municipal electoral contests held on February 11.

At the PDCI's tenth congress, held October 28–31, 1996, party delegates reportedly approved the establishment of a "high leadership," which included an executive branch and five commissions (political, economic, human resources, security, and environmental affairs). Furthermore, a 400-member deliberative body that had been created in 1990 was expanded into a 1,500-member parliament led by a "council of old ones" and charged with aiding the party president in charting "major political directions." In addition, Bédié and Laurent Dona-Fologo were reelected as party president and general secretary, respectively.

Following the overthrow of the PDCI government by the coup of December 1999, Bédié fled to Paris, from where he attempted to retain control of the party. Although disagreement existed regarding the extent to which the PDCI should cooperate with the coup leaders, several party members joined the transitional government of Gen. Robert Gueï, who subsequently tried to secure the PDCI nomination for president of the republic. However, the party rejected Gueï's plan, nominating instead former interior minister Emile Constant BOMBET, whose candidacy was ultimately ruled invalid by the Supreme Court. The PDCI accepted three posts in the new cabinet appointed in October 2000 and has participated in all subsequent cabinets.

Bédié returned from France in October 2001 and was reelected as PDCI president at the April 2002 party congress. In 2003 the PDCI temporarily suspended participation in the government along with other parties. However, its ministers rejoined the cabinet in August 2004.

Bédié returned in September 2005 from one year of self-imposed exile in order to participate in the presidential election then scheduled for October. After those elections were postponed, Bédié was active in negotiations regarding the installation of a new transitional cabinet in which the PDCI was accorded four seats. In March 2006 a PDCI congress selected Bédié as the party's candidate in the presidential poll scheduled for October.

Leaders: Henri Konan BÉDIÉ (President of the Party and Former President of the Republic), Laurent DONA-FOLOGO (Former Secretary General), Alphonse Djedjé MADY (Secretary General).

Ivorian Workers' Party (*Parti Ivoirien des Travailleurs*—PIT). The PIT was formally recognized in May 1990, although a PIT rally three months later was dispersed by government forces. The party captured one seat in the November legislative balloting. Three PIT leaders were among those given prison terms in March 1992 for involvement in the February rioting.

In view of President Houphouët-Boigny's manifestly poor health upon his return to Côte d'Ivoire on November 19, 1993, the PIT and other opposition parties called for the establishment of a transitional government, declaring that "there is a political vacancy in the presidency and a political, institutional, economic, and social stalemate."

At presidential balloting in 1995 PIT leader Francis Wodié captured less than 4 percent of the vote. Wodié's candidacy had been sharply criticized by his opposition colleagues, who cited the PIT leader's own advocacy of a boycott in 1990. In August 1998 Wodié was appointed to the Bédié government, while party members also held posts in 2000 in the transitional governments of Gen. Guéï. Wodié secured 5.7 percent of the vote in the October 2000 presidential balloting, and the PIT participated in all of the subsequent FPI-led cabinets, including the 2005 transitional government.

Leader: Francis WODIÉ (General Secretary and 2000 presidential candidate).

Rally of Republicans (*Rassemblement des Républicains*—RDR). The essentially centrist RDR was launched in June 1994 by ex-PDCI members, led by Djény Kobina and a number of ministers from the government of former prime minister Alassane Ouattara who had operated within the parent formation for the previous three years as a "reform" wing loyal to Ouattara. On October 5, at the RDR's first official press conference, Kobina announced that the new grouping controlled 30 National Assembly seats and had a membership of 1.5 million. Initially, the RDR could claim only to have "excellent relations" with Ouattara, whose willingness to campaign under the RDR's banner was considered necessary to the party's electoral viability. However, in January 1995 Kobina announced that Ouattara had joined the party.

In July 1995 the RDR officially endorsed Ouattara as its presidential candidate; however, the government refused to rescind the electoral code, and on August 2 Ouattara, who was ineligible under the new provisions, abandoned his campaign plans, citing his respect for Ivorian laws, even those he considered "aberrant." Thereafter, on November 22 the constitutional court rejected Kobina's appeal of the nullification of his legislative candidacy, both of his parents reportedly being Ghanaian.

Meanwhile, the RDR had earlier helped to launch the Republican Front (*Front Républicain*—FR), an electoral alliance that also included the FPI and the UFD (see ADS, below). In April 1995 the FR initiated a series of public meetings aimed at pressuring the government to withdraw the controversial electoral code. FR-organized protest rallies continued throughout 1995, and in October the front spearheaded an "active boycott" of the presidential elections. Subsequently, after a meeting with President Bédié in early November, the coalition agreed to participate in legislative elections. However, staggered by its leaders' legal problems and unable to agree on a joint candidate list, coalition members fared poorly at assembly balloting. Flagging coalition cohesiveness was underscored by the decision by the RDR and the FPI to forward competing candidates in more than 100 municipal electoral races in February 1996.

Djény Kobina died in October 1998, and he was succeeded as RDR secretary general by Henriette Dagbi Diabaté, who reportedly became the first woman to hold such a powerful post in an Ivorian political party. Thereafter, in the wake of the signing of the government-FPI accord, the RDR urged the Bédié administration to begin separate negotiations with each of the prominent opposition parties.

In early 1999 Ouattara confirmed that he would be the RDR's standard-bearer at the 2000 presidential elections. A number of party leaders were detained late in the year, prompting violent antigovernment demonstrations in RDR strongholds.

The RDR initially welcomed the December 1999 coup, since General Gueï was widely viewed as supportive of Ouattara, who returned from exile on December 29. A number of RDR members were appointed to Gueï's transitional cabinet, but relations between the RDR and military leaders subsequently deteriorated as Gueï began to retreat from his pledge not to run for president. Several RDR officials were detained in the wake of an aborted coup in early July 2000, while Ouattara's subsequent exclusion from the presidential campaign (see Political background, above) signalled a final rupture with Gueï. Following Gueï's failed attempt to manipulate the presidential balloting in October, RDR supporters fought with security forces as well as partisans of the FPI. The RDR's "outside" status continued into December, Ouattara being ruled ineligible to compete in the legislative balloting, which the RDR boycotted. However, some RDR members ignored the boycott and campaigned for assembly seats under the rubric of the **RDR–Movement of Moderate Activists and Candidates** (*RDR–Mouvement des Militants et Candidates Modérés—RDR-MMCM*).

Secretary General Diabaté was briefly detained by the government following the unsuccessful coup attempt in January 2001, and a number of RDR members remained imprisoned throughout the summer in connection with the violence that had erupted in late 2000. Despite the government pressure, the RDR performed very well in the March 2001 local elections, securing victories in the south, west, and center of the country as well as the traditional RDR strongholds among the northern Muslim population.

Following the outbreak of civil war in 2002, Ouattara went into exile, from where he reportedly became the opposition's leading presidential candidate. However, President Gbagbo continued to consider Ouattara ineligible to run due to his failure to meet residency and citizenship requirements, despite a National Assembly ruling to the contrary in December 2004. In December 2005 Gbagbo issued a decree allowing Ouattara to campaign in future presidential elections, and Ouattara returned from exile in January 2006. Meanwhile, the RDR had received five seats in the December 2005 transitional government.

Leaders: Alassane Dramane OUATTARA (Former Prime Minister), Amadou Gon COULIBALY (Deputy Secretary General), Henriette Dagbi DIABATÉ (Secretary General).

New Forces (*Forces Nouvelles—FN*). The FN was launched in August 2003 by the three main rebel groups opposing the Gbagbo government, including the **Patriotic Movement of the Côte d'Ivoire** (*Mouvement Patriotique de la Côte d'Ivoire—MPCI*), the predominately Muslim northern grouping that had initiated the 2002 civil war. The other FN components were the **Movement for Justice and Peace** (*Mouvement pour la Justice et la Paix—MJP*) and the **Ivorian Popular Movement for the Greater West** (*Mouvement Populaire Ivoirien du Grand Ouest—MPIGO*), both based in western regions of the country and formed after the 2002 strife had commenced. In April 2003 the leader of the MPIGO, Félix DOH, was killed by government forces.

Under the Marcoussis Accords of January 2003, the three FN components were allocated posts in the cabinet of March 2003. However, the FN representatives did not take their seats until August 2004.

In 2005 friction was reported within MPIGO over the apparent efforts by Roger BANCHI (one of MPIGO's leaders and a cabinet minister) to forge closer relations with President Gbagbo. (Banchi left the cabinet in July, officially for personal reasons.) After the FN's efforts to have Guillaume Soro (the FN secretary general) named prime minister failed in October, the FN was given six posts (including Soro as minister of state for reconstruction and reintegration) in the new transitional cabinet installed in December. However, the status of the MJP and MPIGO within the FN at that point was unclear, some reports indicating that the MJP and MPIGO had left the ranks of the umbrella organization.

Leader: Guillaume SORO (Secretary General).

Union for Democracy and Peace in Côte d'Ivoire (*Union pour la Démocratie et la Paix de la Côte d'Ivoire*—UDPCI). The UDPCI was launched in February 2001 by former members of the PDCI who had left that party to support Gen. Robert Gueï in the 2000 presidential campaign. (As many as 14 of the successful "independent" candidates in the December 2000 assembly balloting were subsequently identified as belonging to the PDCI dissident group; most were believed to have participated in the formation of the UDPCI.) General Gueï was elected president of the UDPCI in May 2002. On September 19, 2002, Gueï was killed when fighting erupted between government forces and rebels. The UDPCI joined the national unity government in 2002 and participated in the 2005 transitional government.

Leaders: Paul Akoto YAO, Alassane SALIF N'DIAYE (Secretary General).

Democratic Citizen's Union (*Union Démocratique Citoyenne*—UDCY). Launched in January 2000, the UDCY criticized the PDCI for failing to make the "necessary changes" to promote national "reconciliation and reconstruction." UDCY Chair Theodore Mel Eg, mayor of the Cocody District in Abidjan, was credited with 1.5 percent of the vote in the October 2000 presidential balloting, while the party secured one seat in the December legislative poll. The UDCY was given one cabinet post in 2003, and Eg was appointed minister of culture and Francophone affairs in the 2005 transitional government.

Leader: Theodore MEL EG (Chair).

Movement of Forces for the Future (*Mouvement des Forces pour l'Avenir*—MFA). The MFA, formed in 1995, was credited with one seat in the December 2000 legislative balloting, although little other information concerning the grouping was available. In 2003 the MFA joined the national unity government, and it remained in the 2005 transitional government.

Leader: Kobenan ANAKY (Secretary General).

Other Parties and Groups

Alliance for Democracy and Socialism (*Alliance pour la Démocratie et le Socialisme*—ADS). The launching of the left-wing ADS was announced in mid-2000 by the PPS, Renaissance, **Party for the Protection of the Environment** (*Parti pour la Protection de l'Environnement*—PPE), and the **Party for National Reconstruction and Democracy** (*Parti pour la Reconstruction Nationale et la Démocratie*—PRND). However, there were few subsequent reports of ADS activity.

Party for Social Progress (*Parti pour le Progrès Social*—PPS). The predominantly ethnic Djoula PPS is led by Bamba Morifére, reportedly one of the wealthiest opposition politicians. During the run-up to legislative balloting in November 1995 Morifére was jailed for alleged financial fraud and subsequently given a four-month suspended sentence, a verdict the FPI's Gbagbo decried as "shameful."

The PPS had been one of the members of the Union of Democratic Forces (*Union des Forces Démocratiques*—UFD), an opposition grouping launched in December 1992. Other UFD members had included the PIT, the UND, the **Social Democratic Movement** (*Mouvement Démocratique et Social*—MDS), and the **African Party for the Ivorian Renaissance** (*Parti Africain pour la Renaissance Ivoirienne*—PARI). PPS leader Morifére had served as president of the UFD. His proposed candidacy (presumably under the ADS rubric) for the 2000 presidential election was rejected by the Supreme Court.

Leader: Bamba MORIFÉRE.

Renaissance. Initially known as FPI-Renaissance, this grouping was formed on September 27, 1996, under the leadership of Don Mello Ahoua, who claimed that his faction would remain within the FPI but would work independently to promote "democracy" within the larger body. However, in July 1997, following an alleged shooting attack on Ahoua's car

Cabinet

As of May 1, 2006

Prime Minister	Charles Konan Banny (ind.)

Ministers of State

Development and Planning	Paul Bouabré (FPI)
Reconstruction and Reintegration	Guillaume Soro (FN)

Ministers

Administrative Reform	Hubert Oulaye (FPI)
Agriculture	Amadou Gon Coulibaly (RDR)
Communications	Charles Konan Banny (ind.)
Culture and Francophonie	Theodore Mel Eg (UDCY)
Defense	Rene Kouasi (ind.)
Domestic Commerce	Moussa Dosso (FN)
Economic Infrastructure	Patrick Achi (FN)
Family, Women, and Children	Jeanne Peuhmond (RDR) [f]
Fight Against AIDS	Christine Adjobi (FPI) [f]
Finance and Economy	Charles Konan Banny (ind.)
Fishery Resources and Livestock	Alphonse Douaty (FPI)
Foreign Affairs	Youssouf Bakayoko (PDCI)
Handicrafts and Tourism	Amadou Koné (FN)
Health and Public Hygiene	Remi Allah Kouadio (PDCI)
Higher Education and Scientific Research	Ibraham Cisse (RDR)
Industry and Promotion of the Private Sector	Marie Tehoua Amah (PDCI)
Interior	Joseph Dja Ble (ind.)
Justice and Guardian of the Seals	Mamadou Kone (FN)
Labor and Civil Service	Hubert Oulaye (FPI)
National Education	Michel N'Guessan Amani (FPI)
National Reconciliation	Sebastian Danon Djedje (FPI)
Mining and Energy	Leon Emmanuel Monnet (FPI)
Regional Integration and African Unity	Albert Mabri Toikeusse (UDPCI)
Relations with Parliament and Other Institutions	Sebastian Danon Djedje (FPI)
Solidarity and War Victims	Louis-Andre Dakoury Tabley (FN)
Technical Education and Professional Training	Youssouf Soumahoro (FN)
Telecommunications and New Information Technologies	Hamed Bakayoko (RDR)
Transport	Kobenan Anaky (MFA)
Urban Planning and Housing	Marcel Tanoh (RDR)
Water and Forests	Jacques Andoh (PIT)
Youth, Civil Education, and Sport	Dagobert Banzio (PDCI)

Ministers Delegate

Communications	Martine Studer Coffi (ind.) [f]
Finance and Economy	Charles Diby Koffi (ind.)

[f] = female

and threats to faction members, the group withdrew from the FPI.

Leader: Don Mello AHOUA (Coordinator).

Union of Social Democrats (*Union des Sociaux-Démocrates*—USD). The USD describes itself as a "compromise between capitalism and socialism." Longtime leader Bernard ZADI-ZAOUROU resigned as USD general secretary in July 2000. The presidential candidacy of his successor, Jerome Climanlo Coulibaly, was subsequently rejected by the Supreme Court. Following the outbreak of civil war in 2002, Coulibaly emerged as a major opposition figure to the Gbagbo regime.

Leader: Jerome Climanlo COULIBALY (General Secretary).

Republican Party of Côte d'Ivoire (*Parti Républicain de la Côte d'Ivoire*—PRCI). The PRCI is a right-wing grouping organized in 1987. In September 1995 party leader Robert Gbai-Tagro withdrew from the presidential race, citing electoral code shortcomings as his reason. In January 2000 Gbai-Tagro announced his support for General Gueï, leader of the recent coup.

Leader: Robert GBAI-TAGRO.

National Union for Democracy (*Union National pour la Démocratie*—UND). In December 1994 the UND was credited with one assembly seat.

Leader: Amadou KONE.

Other recently formed groups and parties include the **New Democratic Alliance of Côte d'Ivoire for Justice, Development, and Peace,** formed in October 2005 by Charles Ble Ble, who had been a ranking member of the FPI and the mayor of Saioua; and the **Coalition of Republican Forces of Côte d'Ivoire** (*Coalition des Forces Républicaines de Côte d'Ivoire*—COFREPCI), formed in 2005 by former Army chief of staff Mathias DOUÉ as an opposition group to Gbagbo's regime. (For a list of small parties from the 1990s, some of which may still be active, see the 1999 and 2000–2002 *Handbooks.*)

Legislature

The **National Assembly** (*Assemblée Nationale*) is a unicameral body with 225 members (raised in 2000 from 175) serving five-year terms. The assembly was suspended following the December 1999 coup, but balloting for a new legislature was held on December 10, 2000, with the Ivorian Popular Front winning 96 seats; the Democratic Party of Côte d'Ivoire (PDCI), 77; the Ivorian Workers' Party, 4; the Rally of Republicans/Movement of Moderate Activists and Candidates (RDR-MMCM), 1; the Democratic Union of Côte d'Ivoire, 1; the Movement of Forces of the Future, 1; and independents, 17. Balloting was not held at that time for 28 seats in northern constituencies because of unrest affiliated with an election boycott by the main faction of the RDR. Balloting for 26 of the outstanding seats was conducted on January 14, 2002, with the PDCI winning 17 to increase its total to 94, the RDR-MMCM winning 4 to increase its total to 5, and independents winning 5 to increase the total number of independents to 22. The mandate of the current assembly was extended for up to one year by a controversial presidential decree in late January 2006 (see Current issues).

President: Mamadou KOULIBALY.

Communications

Press

The following are published daily in Abidjan, unless otherwise noted: *Notre Voie,* FPI newspaper; *Fraternité-Matin* (80,000), official PDCI organ; *Ivoir Soir* (50,000), PDCI organ launched in 1987 to concentrate on social and cultural events as a complement to *Fraternité-Matin; Le Patriote,* RDR organ; *La Voix d'Afrique,* monthly regional magazine; *Le Populaire Nouvelle Formule*, independent daily; *Le Jour* (16,000), independent; *Le National,* "fiercely nationalist" daily supportive of former president Henri Konan Bédié; *Le Libéral;* and *Tassouma,* close to the RDR.

News Agencies

The domestic agency is *Agence Ivoirienne de Presse* (AIP). *Agence France-Presse,* the Associated Press, and Reuters maintain offices in Abidjan.

Broadcasting and Computing

The government-operated Ivorian Radio and Television (*Radiodiffusion-Télévision Ivoirienne*) transmitted to approximately 736,000 television receivers in 2003, while some 154,000 personal computers served 120,000 Internet users.

Intergovernmental Representation

Ambassador to the U.S.
Daouda DIABATÉ

U.S. Ambassador to Côte d'Ivoire
Aubrey HOOKS

Permanent Representative to the UN
Djessan Philippe DJANGONÉ-BI

IGO Memberships (Non-UN)
AfDB, AU, BADEA, BOAD, CENT, ECOWAS, IDB, Interpol, IOM, NAM, OIC, OIF, UEMOA, WCO, WTO

DJIBOUTI

REPUBLIC OF DJIBOUTI

République de Djibouti (French)
Jumhuriyah Djibouti (Arabic)

The Country

Formerly known as French Somaliland and subsequently as the French Territory of the Afars and the Issas, the Republic of Djibouti is strategically located in East Africa just south of the Bab el Mandeb, a narrow strait that links the Gulf of Aden to the Red Sea. Djibouti, the capital, was declared a free port by the French in 1949 and has long been an important communications link between Africa, the Arabian peninsula, and the Far East. The largest single population group (40 percent) is the ethnically Somalian Issa tribe, which is concentrated in the vicinity of the capital, while the Afar tribe (35 percent) is essentially nomadic and ethnically linked to the Ethiopians. The remaining 25 percent consists largely of Yemeni Arabs and Somalis.

Serviced by a number of international airlines and heavily dependent on commerce, Djibouti also provides Ethiopia with its only railroad link to the sea. The country is largely barren, with less than 1 percent of its land under cultivation, few known natural resources, and little industry; consequently, the government relies extensively on aid from France and other Western donors, several Arab countries, and various multilateral organizations. Real GDP declined by around 3 percent a year in the first half of the 1990s, before stabilizing in 1996, as structural adjustment measures negotiated with the International Monetary Fund (IMF) in April began to bring a measure of credibility to government finances. Meanwhile, it was estimated that about 40 percent of the potential work force was unemployed. In 1998 and early 1999

Djibouti's economic agenda was dominated by continued negotiations with the IMF and France, the latter's decision to reduce its military presence having sparked concern in Djibouti about potential financial repercussions. In October the IMF approved a new three-year loan to support the government's reform program, encouraging privatization of state-run enterprises, market liberalization, and change in labor regulations. The IMF, while urging the government to maintain fiscal austerity, also called for greater attention to poverty-reducing efforts and other social programs. IMF disbursements were suspended for six months in 2000–2001, the fund demanding that greater attention be

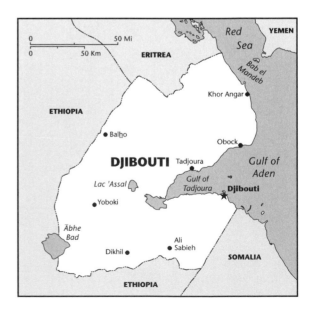

Political Status: Former French dependency; proclaimed independent June 27, 1977; new constitution with provisions for limited multiparty elections in effect as of September 1992; limit on the number of parties lifted in September 2002.

Area: 8,958 sq. mi. (23,200 sq. km.).

Population: 755,000 (2005E), including nonnationals. There has been no census since 1960–1961.

Major Urban Center (2005E): DJIBOUTI (599,000).

Official Languages: French and Arabic.

Monetary Unit: Djibouti Franc (official rate July 1, 2006: 174.70 francs = $1US).

President: Ismail Omar GUELLEH (Popular Rally for Progress); elected on April 9, 1999, and inaugurated for a six-year term on May 8 in succession to Hassan GOULED Aptidon (Popular Rally for Progress); reelected (as the sole candidate) to another six-year term on April 8, 2005.

Prime Minister: Dileita Mohamed DILEITA (Popular Rally for Progress); appointed by the president on March 4, 2001, and sworn in on March 7 to succeed Barkat GOURAD Hamadou (Popular Rally for Progress), who had announced his resignation on February 6; reappointed on May 21, 2005.

paid to the "inefficiency of public expenditures" and a lack of transparency in government finances. Real GDP growth of only 1 percent and inflation of 2.4 percent were reported for 2000. Subsequently, the administration was forced to grapple with social unrest triggered by two oil price increases, budgetary pressures associated with Djibouti's hosting of the Somalia National Peace Conference and the need to demobilize the bulk of the soldiers who had been recruited to deal with hostilities in northern Afar regions in the 1990s but were no longer needed in view of the recent formal peace accord.

Pervasive poverty and high unemployment remained priorities addressed by a 2004 review. The government pledged to improve revenue collection, adopt free-trade-zone legislation, and promote

development of the port of Doreleh. In late 2005 the economy was bolstered by a funding agreement with the World Bank for $17 million to support the education and energy sectors. In accordance with the country's first self-monitored program with the IMF, plans were under way for reforms in taxes, banking, and public administration. Real GDP growth for 2005 was projected to be about 4.5 percent, up from 3 percent the previous year, with inflation contained to about 3 percent.

Government and Politics

Political Background

The area known as French Somaliland was formally demarcated by agreement with Emperor Menelik II of Ethiopia in 1897 following a half-century of French penetration that included a series of treaties with indigenous chiefs between 1862 and 1885. Internal autonomy was granted in 1956, and in 1958 the voters of Somaliland elected to enter the French Community as an Overseas Territory. Pro-independence demonstrations during a visit by President de Gaulle in August 1966 led to a referendum on March 19, 1967, in which a majority of the predominantly Afar voters opted for continued association with France. Somali protest riots were severely repressed, and the name of the dependency was changed to Territory of the Afars and the Issas to eliminate exclusive identification with the Somali ethnic group.

On December 31, 1975, a UN General Assembly resolution called on France to withdraw from the territory, and during 1976 extensive discussions were held in Paris between leading tribal representatives and the French government. In the course of the talks, France tacitly agreed that the Afar president of the local Government Council, Ali AREF Bourhan of the National Union for Independence, no longer represented a majority of the population; consequently, Paris approved a new nationality law governing eligibility for a second referendum on independence. Aref subsequently resigned, and on July 29 a new ten-member council, composed of six Issas and four Afars, was formed.

On May 8, 1977, 98.8 percent of the electorate voted for independence, while simultaneously approving a single list of 65 candidates for a Chamber of Deputies. Following the passage of relevant legislation by the French Parliament, the territory became independent as the Republic of Djibouti on June 27. Three days earlier, Issa leader Hassan GOULED Aptidon of the African People's League for Independence had been unanimously elected president of the Republic by the chamber. On July 12 President Gouled named Afar leader Ahmed DINI Ahmed to head a 15-member Council of Ministers.

On December 17, 1977, Dini and four other Afar cabinet members resigned amid charges of "tribal repression," the duties of prime minister being assumed by the president until the designation of a new government headed by Abdallah MOHAMED Kamil on February 5, 1978. Mohamed Kamil was in turn succeeded by Barkat GOURAD Hamadou on September 30, 1978. Gourad, an Afar advocate of "detribalization," formed subsequent governments on July 7, 1981 (following the reelection of President Gouled on June 12), on June 5, 1982 (after a legislative election on May 21), and on November 23, 1987 (after balloting on April 24).

Although all of the cabinets formed since independence had ostensibly been designed to strike a careful balance in tribal representation and all three prime ministers named by President Gouled had been Afars, charges of Issa domination persisted, and most members of the opposition Djibouti People's Party (*Parti Populaire Djiboutien*— PPD) formed in August 1981 were from the ethnic minority. The regime's immediate response was to arrest PPD leader Moussa Ahmed IDRISS and the party's entire 12-member executive committee. However, all were released by early January 1982, after the enactment of legislation establishing Gouled's Popular Rally for Progress (*Rassemblement Populaire pour le Progrès*—RPP) as the sole authorized party.

Despite a constitutional limit of presidential tenure to two terms, Gouled was permitted to run again in 1987 on the ground that he had initially been appointed by the Chamber of Deputies rather than having been popularly elected. As sole candidate, the incumbent was reported to have secured 90 percent of the vote in the April 24 poll.

In 1990 the regime's reported backing of the rebels in Somalia sparked internal conflicts between the Issa majority and Afar/Gadabursi kinsmen of Somalian leader Siad Barre; as a consequence, the government on January 9, 1991, arrested 68 people for alleged involvement in a "vast plot" to incite "civil war" between the Afar and Issa communities. While most were soon released, the detention of seven "ringleaders," including former chief minister Ali Aref Bourhan, was confirmed by the interior ministry on January 17; three days later it was announced that "about 20" individuals had been formally charged with attempting to overthrow the government. At midyear, ethnic clashes were reported between Issas and Oromos, and in October Afar rebel forces, having coalesced as the Front for the Restoration of Unity and Democracy (*Front pour la Restauration de l'Unité et de la Démocratie*—FRUD), launched attacks on government installations.

In response to the fighting, France urged Djibouti to institute "rapid" liberalization of its political system, and on November 27, 1990, the government revealed plans for a referendum "to consult" the population "on changes to be made in the political domain." On December 19 it announced that the referendum would be held in May 1992, but only if rebel activity had ceased. Eleven days later an RPP spokesman reported that legislative elections to be held immediately after the referendum would be open to candidates from "several parties." Meanwhile, the slaying by government forces of 40 Afars and the wounding of 50 others in a Djibouti slum severely eroded what support remained for the regime. Thereafter, 14 parliamentarians led by Mohamed AHMED Issa ("Cheiko") formed a parliamentary opposition group, and in mid-January 1992 the health and public service ministers resigned, with the former decrying the regime's "war logic." Concurrently, a French spokesman insisted that the escalating civil war was an "internal matter" not covered by a defense agreement concluded between the two countries in 1977. Nonetheless, a French military contingent was deployed in late February to implement a cease-fire between government and FRUD units. Subsequently, a committee formed by President Gouled presented a preliminary draft of a new constitution, which was not, however, acceptable to the rebels, since it would retain a strong presidency.

On June 20–24, 1992, representatives of most of the leading opposition groups (under the banner of the United Opposition Front of Djibouti [*Front Uni de l'Opposition Djiboutienne*—FUOD] under Political Parties and Groups, below) met in Paris to forge a common front against the Gouled regime. The session concluded with a demand for a "transitional government led by a prime minister from the ranks of the opposition," who would be charged with initiating a democratic transitional process that would include the drafting of a multiparty constitution.

In a national referendum on September 4, 1992, a reported 97 percent of the voters approved the draft constitution presented by the administration, providing for, among other things, multiparty activity, although a separate vote also endorsed a proposal to limit the number of legal parties to four. Subsequently, FRUD and other opposition members of FUOD boycotted the legislative balloting of December 18 (at which the RPP was awarded all of the seats) as well as the presidential election of May 7, 1993, at which President Gouled defeated four other candidates by a wide margin in securing reelection to a fourth term.

In mid-1994 a split developed within FRUD between supporters of its newly designated president Ali MOHAMED Daoud, who favored peace talks with the government, and his recently ousted predecessor, former prime minister Dini, who, along with most of the FUOD leadership, supported continued resistance. The peace talks, which reportedly had commenced as secret negotiations between Prime Minister Gourad and the "New FRUD" secretary general, Ougoureh KIFLE Ahmed, continued intermittently for several months, eventually yielding a reconciliation agreement on December 26 that in a cabinet reshuf-

fle of June 8, 1995, provided the Kifle faction with two ministerial portfolios.

The December 1994 accord yielded greatly reduced hostilities in 1995, although by early 1996 dissension within the government had become intense, with the justice minister and RPP secretary general, Moumin BAHDON Farah, leading those who contended that the agreement had not brought real peace and stability to Djibouti. The dominance of the pro-accord camp was demonstrated on March 27 when Bahdon was dismissed from the government, together with Ahmed BOULALEH Barre, the defense minister. Bahdon and his allies subsequently launched a new opposition group, Group for the Democracy of the Republic. Collaterally, the episode showed that in the bitter contest between possible successors to an increasingly infirm Gouled, ascendancy had been gained by the president's nephew and *chef de cabinet*, Ismail Omar GUELLEH.

In assembly elections on December 19, 1997, the RPP—"New FRUD" electoral coalition captured all 65 seats (54 by the RPP and 11 by "New FRUD"), garnering a reported 78.55 percent of the vote tally compared to 19.19 percent for the Party of Democratic Renewal and 2.25 percent for the National Democratic Party. On December 28 President Aptidon reappointed Gourad as head of a reshuffled government.

In February 1999 President Gouled announced that he would not seek reelection at balloting scheduled for the following April, and the RPP promptly chose Guelleh as its presidential candidate. Guelleh captured 74.09 percent of the vote on April 9, 1999, easily outdistancing his sole competitor, Moussa Ahmed Idriss. Despite gaining the endorsement of the newly formed Unified Djiboutian Opposition (see Political Parties, below), Idriss garnered just 25.78 percent of the vote. Prime Minister Gourad was reappointed on May 10, and a reshuffled cabinet was formed two days later.

After 22 years in office, Prime Minister Gourad announced his resignation in February 2001; he was succeeded on May 7 by Dileita Mohamed DILEITA, a former chief of the presidential staff. In the wake of a comprehensive agreement between the administration and FRUD, several FRUD members were included in the new cabinet installed on July 4. In addition, in September 2002 President Guelleh announced the establishment of a full multiparty system. The ruling Union for a Presidential Majority still won all 65 seats in balloting for the Chamber of Deputies on January 10, 2003. Also undercutting the administration's stated goal of broader governmental participation, Guelleh was the only candidate in the April 8, 2005, presidential balloting. He appointed a new government on May 22.

In regional and communal elections on March 10 and 31, 2006, the RPP won overwhelming victories, further solidifying the president's power down to the local level.

Constitution and Government

The Chamber of Deputies established under the 1977 independence referendum was empowered to act as a constituent assembly pending adoption of a formal constitution. In that capacity it approved a number of measures in 1981 dealing with the presidency and the legislature. On February 10 it decreed that candidates for the former could be nominated only by parties holding at least 25 chamber seats, with balloting by universal suffrage and election for a six-year term that could be renewed only once. Following the presidential election of June 12 (at which the incumbent was the only candidate), the opposition PPD was organized, but it was denied legal status on the basis of a "National Mobilization" law approved on October 19 that established a one-party system. As a result, all of the candidates at the parliamentary elections of 1982 and 1987 were presented by the government-supportive RPP. A new constitution providing for a qualified multiparty system (with a maximum, for at least ten years, of four parties being permitted) became effective in September 1992. The president, who appoints the prime minister and otherwise exercises broad authority, is limited to two six-year terms. In September 2002 the government eliminated all restrictions on party registration.

The colonial judicial structure, based on both French and local law, was technically abolished at independence, although a successor system based on Muslim precepts remains imperfectly formulated. For administrative purposes the republic is divided into five districts, one of which encompasses the capital. Local elections to regional assemblies, envisioned under recent decentralization plans negotiated by the government with groups such as FRUD, were held in March 2006.

Foreign Relations

Djibouti's small size and its mixed population of Ethiopian-oriented Afars and Somali-oriented Issas make it highly vulnerable in a context of historic friction between its two neighbors. Despite bilateral accords in 1986 and 1987, Somalia has long regarded Djibouti as a "land to be redeemed," while the nearly 500-mile railroad between the port of Djibouti and Addis Ababa was viewed by Ethiopia as vital to its export-import trade during the lengthy revolt in its Red Sea province of Eritrea. The country's security depends in part on a French garrison, which was of crucial importance during the prolonged Soviet military presence in Ethiopia and South Yemen.

In January 1986 President Gouled hosted a six-nation conference to set up an Intergovernmental Authority on Drought and Development in East Africa (IGADD, subsequently the Intergovernmental Authority on Development—IGAD), which marked the first meeting between the Ethiopian head of state, Lt. Col. Haile-Mariam, and President Siad Barre of Somalia since the two countries went to war in 1977. The other states participating in the conference as IGADD members were Kenya, Sudan, and Uganda. Subsequently, peace talks between the 1977 combatants, mediated by Djibouti, were held in Addis Ababa in May, with Gouled reaffirming his country's role in the peace negotiations during a state visit to Ethiopia in September. A second IGADD summit was held in March 1988, with the Djibouti president being elected to a second term as the authority's chair.

The repatriation of some 50,000 Ethiopians who had fled to Djibouti during the Ogaden conflict began in 1983 but was subsequently halted because of the drought; it was resumed in December 1986 amid charges that the "voluntary" program would in fact expose the refugees to potential mistreatment. By 1987 it was estimated that fewer than 20,000 expatriates remained, with Djibouti insisting that they too would have to leave since resources were lacking for their assimilation.

The early 1990 intensification of the Somalian civil war, coupled with Djibouti's continued tacit support of the Somalian National Movement (SNM), an Issa rebel group, resulted in a deterioration of relations between Djibouti and Mogadishu and mutual border militarization. Midyear diplomatic efforts, including a heads of state meeting in May, were inconclusive, and in October Somalian claims of military intrusion yielded closure of the maritime border, while igniting ethnic hostilities in Djibouti. Meanwhile, observers described Djibouti's dependence on French security forces and aid (renewed for ten years in July) as motivation for publicly siding with allied forces in the Gulf crisis, despite a number of Djibouti-Baghdad military and economic agreements.

The outbreak of ethnic violence in 1991 severely strained Djiboutian-French relations. In October Paris, which had deployed troops in March to disarm Ethiopian soldiers fleeing into Djibouti, dismissed the government's claims that Ethiopian Afars were seeking to establish a "greater Afaria" and ordered its troops to remain in their barracks. Concurrently, France pressed the Gouled regime to accelerate political liberalization and enter into cease-fire negotiations with the rebels. In November France rejected Djibouti's request for supplies and labeled the regime's international efforts to solicit weapons as "intolerable." Following the government's violent suppression of Afar slum dwellers in Djibouti in December, Paris warned Djibouti that it would suspend economic aid unless there was immediate "democratization," and in February 1992 France intervened to enforce a standoff between government and rebel forces that continued for the remainder of the year. Relations with Paris improved in the wake of the December 1994 peace accord that the government signed with a FRUD faction, with French defense minister Charles Dillon confirming, during a visit to Djibouti in January 1996, that France would maintain its military presence in the republic. On the other hand, as French economic aid continued its precipitous decline (from $77 million in 1977 to $21 million in 1996) a number of Djiboutian economic planners rallied behind efforts to broaden ties with other countries in the region.

An unresolved territorial dispute flared in mid-April 1996 when Djiboutian and Eritrean forces clashed in a northern border area claimed by Eritrea on the strength of a 1935 colonial-era map. In June the Organization of African Unity (OAU, subsequently the African Union—AU) authorized Djibouti, Burkina Faso, and Zimbabwe to mediate the border dispute; however, in November Eritrea severed relations with Djibouti, accusing the Gouled administration of supporting Ethiopia's military campaign. (In early 1999 the OAU named a new negotiating team after the delegates from Burkina Faso and Zimbabwe refused to enter Eritrea without their banned Djiboutian colleagues [see separate articles on Eritrea and Ethiopia for more details].) Normal relations were reestablished with Eritrea following the conclusion of the conflict, in part assisted by the two countries' similar stances regarding events in Somalia.

In late 2001 and early 2002 Djibouti was frequently referenced as having achieved a higher international profile due to its potentially strategic geographic location in regard to the West's war on terrorism. Among other things, President Guelleh agreed to allow the United States to establish a military base in Djibouti, while also endorsing an ongoing French military presence. At the same time, the Guelleh regime, cognizant of the status of Islam as the nation's majority religion, evinced a strongly pro-Arab and pro-Palestinian posture in regard to the turmoil in the Middle East. In September 2003 Djibouti expelled some 80,000 illegal immigrants, mostly Ethiopians and Somalis. It was subsequently reported that U.S. concerns over possible attacks on Western interests had led the government of Djibouti to detain several hundred suspects.

Current Issues

The first months of President Guelleh's administration were marked by the same heavy-handed tactics for which its successor was noted. Domestic and international critics charged the new government with the illegal detention and abuse of "New-FRUD" sympathizers and other human rights abuses, while a crackdown on the opposition press (see News Media, below) and seemingly unnecessarily harsh treatment of Moussa Ahmed Idriss of the PPD (see introduction to Political Parties and Groups, below) were also condemned. However, the government's image shed some of its tarnish in February 2000 when a cease-fire was signed with FRUD militants on May 12 (see FRUD, below, for details).

In early December 2000 it was reported that a group of police officers had taken over several government buildings as part of a coup attempt after their commander had been demoted by the president. However, the mini-revolt was put down within eight hours and was not considered an influence in the subsequent resignation of longtime Prime Minister Gourad, whose health reportedly had recently declined significantly. New Prime Minister Dileita, an Afar (in the power-sharing tradition that has held since independence), did not name a new cabinet immediately as negotiations continued with FRUD on a permanent political settlement. Under the accord, the government pledged to help rebuild areas damaged by the earlier insurgency and agreed to intensify decentralization efforts. Although some FRUD demands (such as greater Afar representation in the civil service and establishment of an independent judiciary) were not fully addressed, the Front was sufficiently satisfied to agree to join the new "national unity" government and to start preparing for formal party status. Despite the lifting of the restrictions on the number of parties in 2002, the opposition alleged fraud and other irregularities in the January 2003 legislative elections. (Opposition leader Ahmed Dini Ahmed bitterly criticized the electoral structure, which denied antigovernment parties any seats though they had won 37 percent of the vote.) On a more positive note, new electoral rules not only permitted but required female candidates for the first time. In fact, ten seats in the Chamber of Deputies were set aside for women.

The opposition parties boycotted the April 2005 presidential balloting, citing what they perceived as a continued lack of transparency in the electoral process. President Guelleh nevertheless ran an "active campaign" in order to boost voter turnout.

In late 2005 clashes were reported between Afar rebels and government troops, precluding a full reconciliation in the wake of Guelleh's election. Following regional and communal balloting in March 2006, the FRUD's hopes for decentralization were shattered after the party's losses to Guelleh's RPP in every area.

Drought was a major concern in early 2006 in the Horn of Africa, prompting U.S. president George W. Bush to pledge some $92 million to the countries facing starvation, including Djibouti. The UN appealed for $426 million for the same relief effort.

Political Parties and Groups

Negotiations with the French that culminated in the referendum of May 8, 1977, were conducted by a United Patriotic Front representing five of the territory's major political groups. In preparing a list of candidates for the assembly election that accompanied the referendum, the Front acted under the name of the Popular Independence Rally (*Rassemblement Populaire pour l'Indépendance*—RPI). Its successor, the Popular Rally for Progress (RPP), was the only participant in the presidential election of June 1981 and continued as the country's only legal political party until the legislative balloting of December 1992.

In July 1997 former justice minister Moumin Bahdon Farah announced in Paris that the Group for the Democracy of the Republic (GDR) had formed a coalition with the United Opposition Front of Djibouti (FUOD) and a faction of the Party of Democratic Renewal (PRD) led by Kaireh ALLALEH Hared to campaign, according to the *Indian Ocean Newsletter*, for "the installation of a democratic legal framework" in anticipation of legislative elections in late 1997. However, a strong opposition challenge failed to materialize as, in addition to the PRD, both the Front for the Restoration of Unity and Democracy (FRUD) and the National Democratic Party (PND) suffered from factionalization.

In anticipation of upcoming presidential elections, by early 1999 a number of opposition leaders had declared their intention to campaign for the chief executive's post, including: Abbate Ebo Adou of the Action for Revision of Order in Djibouti (ARDD), the PND's Aden Robleh Awaleh, and the PRD's Abidillahi Hamareiteh. However, in February the aforementioned withdrew from the race as their parties, under the reported direction of the GDR's Bahdon, formed an electoral alliance, subsequently styled the **Unified Djiboutian Opposition** (*Opposition Djiboutienne Unifiée*—ODU), which then chose Moussa Ahmed IDRISS, a former independence fighter who had only recently resigned from the RPP, as its standard-bearer. Following his defeat in the 1999 presidential polling, Idriss was arrested in September for "attacking the morale of the armed forces" by publishing an article critical of the government in *Le Temps*. Idriss, along with 19 of his supporters, were found guilty and sentenced to four months imprisonment; however, Idriss was released in December after being given amnesty at the beginning of Ramadan, and he was subsequently invited to resume his role as a member of the Chamber of Deputies.

According to a separate measure approved in connection with the September 1992 constitutional referendum, a maximum of only four legal parties was established for a ten-year period. However, on September 4, 2002, President Guelleh announced the introduction of a full multiparty system. Some eight parties participated in the 2003 legislative elections, four each in progovernment and opposition electoral blocs.

Government-Supportive Parties

Union for a Presidential Majority (*Union pour la Majorité Présidentielle*—UMP). Formed as an electoral bloc prior to the 2003 legislative elections by the following four groups, the UMP secured all 65 seats in that balloting with a reported 62 percent of the vote. The four groups also backed Guelleh in the 2005 presidential election.

Leaders: Ismail Omar GUELLEH (RPP), Ali Mohamed DAOUD (FRUD), Aden ROBLEH Awaleh (PND), Moumin BAHDON Farah (PPSD).

Popular Rally for Progress (*Rassemblement Populaire pour le Progrès*—RPP). The RPP was launched on March 4, 1979, its leading component being the socialist African People's League for Independence (*Ligue Populaire Africaine pour l'Indépendance*—LPAI). Long the principal spokesman for the Issa majority, the LPAI was not represented in the Afar-dominated pre-independence Chamber of Deputies, although two of its members held ministerial posts.

The RPP was the first political group to be legalized under the "pluralist" constitution of 1992 and was credited with a clean sweep of chamber seats in December. In February 1994 it was reported that President Gouled would step down as RPP chair at a party congress scheduled for early March; however, in an apparent effort to avoid a conflict between potential successors, he accepted reelection at the congress that finally convened on May 26. Thereafter, in September 1996, Gouled announced his intention to serve out his presidential term (despite his failing health) and also to retain the party leadership until 1999.

In September 1996 the party announced the composition of its reshuffled Executive Committee, highlighted by the appointment as third deputy chair of Ismail Omar Guelleh, the apparent front-runner in the party's bitter contest to succeed the increasingly infirm Gouled. At a party congress on March 19–20, 1997, Gouled was reelected chair, while party delegates also elected a 125-member Central Committee and adopted a resolution confirming its alliance with the "New FRUD." Guelleh, who had succeeded Gouled as president of the republic in 1999, was also elected as the new RPP chair in March 2000, Gouled having retired from party activity.

The party won a majority in all five regional and three communal area elections in March 2006.

Leaders: Ismail Omar GUELLEH (President of the Republic and President of the Party), Hassan GOULED Aptidon (Former President of the Republic and Former Chair), Dileita Mohamed DILEITA (Prime Minister and Vice President of the Party), Idriss ARNAOUD Ali (Secretary General of the Party and Speaker of the Chamber of Deputies).

Front for the Restoration of Unity and Democracy (*Front pour la Restauration de l'Unité et de la Démocratie*—FRUD). The Afar-dominated FRUD was organized in Balho in northern Djibouti in August 1991 by nominal merger of the three groups below on a platform calling for the overthrow of President Gouled's "tribal dictatorship" and the installation of a democratic multiparty system. Responsibilities for political and military operations were assigned to a 17-member executive committee.

In September 1991 leaders of FRUD and the MNDID (see under PND, below) met in Ethiopia, and one month later their combined forces clashed with government troops in Djibouti's southern Yokobi region. Front officials denied government claims that their forces were Ethiopian Afars, although admitting that they had been trained across the border. Meanwhile, a second rebel summit, this time including the Democratic Union for Djiboutian Justice and Equality, was held in Somaliland.

The FRUD representative in the capital, Abbate Ebo Adou of the AROD, was arrested in December 1991, but he was released following French intervention in February 1992. Two months later a small armed Gadabursi movement, the **Front of Democratic Forces** (*Front des Forces Démocratiques*—FFD), led by Mahmoud ABAR Derane and Omar CHARDIE Bouni, was reported to have linked up with FRUD. The following August, during a congress in an area "liberated" by FRUD, the incumbent president, Mohamed ADOYTA Yusuf, was named first vice president, while former Prime Minister Ahmed DINI Ahmed, theretofore resident in Yemen, was named FRUD president.

Meanwhile, FRUD had been instrumental in the June 1992 formation in Paris of the United Opposition Front of Djibouti (*Front Uni de l'Opposition Djiboutienne*—FUOD), an alliance of Afar and antiregime Issa groups. (See 2000–2002 *Handbook* for additional information on FUOD.)

A rather confused FRUD leadership picture emerged during the first half of 1994. On February 22 it was reported that Dini had been ousted and a new executive committee appointed with Ougoureh Kifle Ahmed as its secretary general. Subsequently, Kifle was said to have been engaged in a series of peace talks with the government that were opposed by supporters of Dini. At a "reconciliation" meeting of FRUD factions on June 21–25, Ali Mohamed Daoud (a.k.a. Jean Marie) was formally designated as the successor to Dini, who, from residence in Addis Ababa, Ethiopia, continued to reject the posture of political conciliation displayed by the current leadership. By late July the latter itself appeared to back away from continued peace talks by issuing a series of demands calling for ethnic balance in the government and armed forces. Meanwhile, FUOD had refused to recognize the new FRUD leadership, continuing to support the FRUD-Dini group, which, during a September congress "in the northern part of the country," named a rival seven-member executive committee sworn "to pursue the armed struggle against the Gouled regime."

In December 1994 the "New FRUD" leadership concluded an agreement with the government (from which the group's deputy secretary general, Ibrahim Chehem Daoud, dissociated himself) that called for an end to armed resistance and integration of FRUD units into the regular military, an alliance with the RPP that would include cabinet portfolios for two FRUD faction members, and the reform of electoral lists prior to the next election. In accordance with the agreement, the legalization of FRUD as the fourth political party permitted under Djibouti's constitution was announced by the interior minister on March 9, 1996, although the split between the legalized "New FRUD" and the FRUD-Dini faction remained unresolved at that stage.

Ending over 19 years in exile, FRUD-Dini Vice President Adoyta Yusuf returned to Djibouti in November 1996, along with some 15 supporters. Their return was facilitated by high-level negotiations between the Djiboutian prime minister and his Ethiopian counterpart and sparked speculation that Adoyta would join the Gouled cabinet. In March 1997 the FRUD's longtime European representative, Ismael Ibrahim Houmed, also returned from exile.

The "New FRUD" held its first congress on April 15–16, 1997, officials revealing that they had signed a secret political platform with the ruling party in December 1994 that included provisions for both higher profile joint governmental activities and the preparation of a shared list of candidates for the legislative balloting scheduled for December 1997. Furthermore, party delegates elected a multiethnic, 21-member Executive Committee and a 153-member National Committee. The former's composition underlined the party's pledge to include non-Afars in leadership positions.

Meanwhile, the "New FRUD's" tightened alliance with the government widened the chasm between it and the FRUD-Dini faction, which, according to the *Indian Ocean Newsletter*, continued to enjoy support from the grassroots groups that viewed the "New FRUD" with "little esteem." Underscoring the reportedly widespread antipathy felt toward the "New FRUD," demonstrators on May 1, 1997, disrupted the group's attempt to open an office in a predominantly Afar neighborhood in the capital. Following the FRUD-Dini's alleged attack on government forces in September, the Gouled administration authorized a military offensive against the rebel militants and urged its allies abroad to deny asylum to the FRUD-Dini's exiled leadership. Consequently, a number of FRUD-Dini faction leaders were extradited to Djibouti, while others were reported to have been forced to leave their safe havens. On November 10–12 the FRUD-Dini organized a congress within Djibouti's borders where delegates reelected Dini chair and elected a 13-member political bureau. Furthermore, the faction asserted that, while it was committed to further warfare, it remained open to establishing a dialogue with the government.

On November 26, 1997, FUOD president Ahmed Issa died. He was succeeded by Mahdi Ibrahim Ahmed, who in November 1998 called for an interim government including the main opposition parties prior to the 1999 presidential balloting. However, there were few subsequent reports of FUOD activity, attention focusing on government negotiations with the remaining FRUD antigovernment forces.

In March 1998 FRUD-Dini and PRD delegates appealed to IGAD ministers meeting in Djibouti to intervene in the strife, claiming that foreign mercenaries were assisting government forces in the latest outbreak of fighting. The militants' entreaties were shelved by IGAD, and skirmishes were reported throughout the year and into 1999.

In November 1999 Dini suggested a Ramadan cease-fire and negotiations toward a peace settlement, and, following a series of secret meetings in France, an accord was signed on February 7, 2000, in Paris providing for an immediate cessation of hostilities, reciprocal prisoner releases, the eventual reintegration of the militants into their former jobs, and further discussions regarding the proposed devolution of political authority to the regions (primarily in the north of the country) involved in the rebel activity. Dini returned to Djibouti in late March from his long exile in France, and a FRUD-Dini congress on April 5–6 endorsed the Paris accord and reaffirmed its confidence in Dini's leadership, although the faction's fighters were to remain armed pending negotiation of a comprehensive peace settlement. Meanwhile, it was unclear how the recent agreement would ultimately affect the seven-year FRUD factionalization.

A final agreement was reached in May 2001 for, among other things, the demobilization of FRUD forces, which subsequently proceeded smoothly, facilitated by a September amnesty bill. FRUD also contributed several ministers to the July 2001 "postwar cabinet." However, friction continued within FRUD, particularly when Dini announced plans to launch a party called FRUD-National, which would seek countrywide membership that would include a significant non-Afar segment. Reports indicated that some FRUD continued to object to Dini's perceived efforts to place his personal imprint on the movement, while the so-called "Armed-FRUD" still remained skeptical of the peace process in general.

FRUD formalized its relationship with the RPP with the launching of the UMP prior to the 2003 legislative poll, while Dini established his own opposition party (see ARD, below). By that time there did not appear to be an armed FRUD rump of any consequence, though in late 2005 battles between Afar rebels and government troops were reported in the northern area of the country.

Leaders: Ali Mohamed DAOUD (President), Ougoureh KIFLE Ahmed (Secretary General).

Action for Revision of Order in Djibouti (*Action pour la Révision de l'Ordre à Djibouti*—AROD). The most prominent of the FRUD partners, AROD was launched on March 11, 1991, by Abbate Ebo Adou and Mohamed Adoyta Yusuf, theretofore leader of the Union of Democratic Movements (*Union des Mouvements Démocratiques*—UMD). The UMD had been organized in Belgium in February 1990 by the merger of the MNDID (see under PND, below) and Adoyta's Democratic Front for the Liberation of Djibouti (*Front Démocratique pour la Libération de Djibouti*—FDLD), itself a product of the June 1979 consolidation of two Afar groups—the National Union for Independence (*Union Nationale pour l'Indépendance*—UNI) and the Ethiopian-based Popular Movement for the Liberation of Djibouti (*Mouvement Populaire pour la Libération de Djibouti*—MPLD).

Relations with an intellectual faction, the **Alliance of Forces for Democracy** (*Alliance des Forces pour la Démocratie*—AFD), which joined AROD soon after the AFD's launching by Ali MOHAMED Ali ("Coubba") in Djibouti in 1989, were reportedly subsequently strained by AFD disagreements with the FRUD leadership.

In July 1998 Ebo Adou reportedly began efforts to position himself for a presidential campaign as a joint FRUD/PRD candidate. However, Ebo's alleged self-promotion reportedly angered a number of prominent FRUD leaders, and he was expelled from the coalition in December.

Leaders: Mohamed ADOYTA Yusuf (President), Abbate EBO Adou, Iwad HASSAN (Spokesman).

Front for the Restoration of Right and Equality (*Front pour la Réstauration du Droit et de l'Egalité*—FRDE). The FRDE was created on April 29, 1991, by Mohamed Aramisse Souleh and other former MPLD and FDLD members, on a platform urging the violent removal of the Issa regime.

Leader: Mohamed ARAMISSE Souleh.

Djibouti Patriotic Resistance Front (*Front de la Résistance Patriotique de Djibouti*—FRPD). The FRPD is a small group with links to Ali Aref Bourhan, the former chief minister who was arrested on January 17, 1991, for his alleged involvement in a "vast plot" to incite ethnic war.

Leader: Ali MAKI.

National Democratic Party (*Parti National Démocratique*—PND). The PND was reported to have been launched in Paris in late 1992 by Aden Robleh Awaleh, theretofore leader of the Djiboutian National Movement for the Installation of Democracy (*Mouvement National Djiboutien pour l'Instauration de la Démocratie*—MNDID). A former Gouled cabinet member and vice president of the RPP, Robleh had formed the MNDID in early 1986 after fleeing Djibouti in the face of government allegations that he had been a "silent partner" in a bombing. He accused the government of harassing him out of fear that he might become a presidential contender and called on other antigovernment exiles to join the MNDID and create unified opposition to the "tyranny" of President Gouled.

The party's initial communiqué called for promulgation of a constitution that would terminate the single-party system and usher in a "true liberal democracy." Robleh, who traveled widely during 1986–1987 in search of support for the MNDID, established his headquarters in Paris, with a reported branch in Addis Ababa. Some "personal rivalries" were reported within the MNDID in 1989, hindering efforts to form a common anti-Gouled front with other opposition groups. Subsequently, although the MNDID was not officially linked to FRUD, the two groups held a September summit in Ethiopia, and one month later MNDID forces were identified as part of the FRUD-led rebel unit that clashed with government troops.

In September 1993 Robleh met in Paris with the PRD's Djame, the two leaders subsequently reiterating the opposition's 1992 appeal for a transitional government of national unity. Nonetheless, Robleh joined his PRD counterpart in endorsing the December 1994 accord between "New FRUD" and the government.

In April 1996 a Paris judge issued an international arrest warrant against Robleh and his wife in connection with a French inquiry into a September 1990 grenade attack on a cafe in Djibouti in which a six-year-old French child had been killed and 15 people (mostly French nationals) injured. Suspected by French investigators of having been the brains behind the attack, the PND leader had reportedly fled Paris to seek refuge in Morocco.

In May 1997 Robleh's decision to suspend party spokesperson Farah ALI Wabert exacerbated an already growing chasm between the chair and his opponents on both the Political Bureau and National Council. Subsequently, all of the Political Bureau members, with the exception of Mahdi AHMED Abdillahi, who was also wanted for the 1990 attack, endorsed a letter urging Robleh to resign by August 31, 1997. According to the *Indian Ocean Newsletter*, Robleh's detractors were critical of his unwillingness to cooperate with other opposition groupings and claimed that the legal travails that have

dogged him since 1996 hampered his ability to run the party. A Paris court sentenced five defendants in absentia to life imprisonment for the 1990 attack. However, the case against Robleh was deferred, and he was briefly considered as the potential PND candidate for president in 1999 until the party joined the ODU. A number of PND were reportedly arrested in late 1999 for what the government termed an illegal street demonstration. In April 2001 Robleh was given a six-year suspended sentence after being convicted of complicity in the 1990 attack.

Leaders: Aden ROBLEH Awaleh (1993 presidential candidate), Moussa HUSSEIN, Abdallah DABALEH.

People's Social Democratic Party (*Parti Populaire Social Democrate*—PPSD). The PPSD was launched in 2002 under the leadership of Moumin Bahdon Farah, who had been dismissed as justice minister in March 1996 and had subsequently helped to establish the Group for the Democracy of the Republic (*Groupement pour la Démocratie de la République*—GDR) to oppose President Gouled. (For additional information on the GDR, see the 2000–2002 *Handbook*.)

Leader: Moumin BAHDON Farah.

Other Parties

Union for a Democratic Alternative (*Union pour l'Alternance Démocratique*—UAD). Formed prior to the 2003 legislative elections, the UAD won 37 percent of the vote, but no seats, prompting UAD leaders to appeal (unsuccessfully) for cancelation of the results based on allegations of fraud. The UAD boycotted the April 2005 presidential election, arguing that the electoral process lacked transparency and that the opposition was being denied fair access to the media.

Leaders: Ahmad Youssouf HAMED (ARD), Souleiman Farah LODON (MRDD), Mohamed Daoud CHEHEM (PDD), Ismael Guedi HARED (formerly head of UDJ).

Cabinet

As of March 1, 2006

Prime Minister	Dileita Mohamed Dileita

Ministers

Agriculture, Livestock, and Marine Affairs	Abdoulkader Kamil Mohamed
Commerce and Industry	Rifki Abdoulkader Bamakhrama
Communication, Culture, Posts and Telecommunications, Government Spokesman	Ali Abdi Farah
Employment and Solidarity	Houmed Mohamed Dini
Energy and Natural Resources	Mohamed Ali Mohamed
Equipment and Transportation	Ismaël Ibrahim Houmed
Finance, National Economy, and Privatization	Ali Farah Assoweh
Foreign Affairs and International Cooperation	Ali Abdi Farah
Housing, Urban Planning, Environment, and Relations with Parliament	Elmi Obsieh Waiss
Interior and Decentralization	Yacin Elmi Bouh
Justice, Muslim and Penal Affairs, and Human Rights	Mohamed Barkat Abdillahi
National Defense	Ougoureh Kifle Ahmed
National Education	Abdi Ibrahim Absieh
Presidential Affairs and Investment Promotion	Osman Ahmad Moussa
Public Health	Abdallah Abdillahi Miguil
Youth, Sports, Leisure, and Tourism	Hassan Farah Miguil

Delegate Ministers

Attached to the Minister of Foreign Affairs (International Cooperation)	Hawa Ahmed Youssouf [f]
Attached to the Minister of Justice (Religious and Muslim Affairs)	Cheikh Mogue Dirir Samatar
Attached to the Prime Minister (Women, Family, and Social Affairs)	Aïcha Mohamed Robleh [f]

[f] = female

Republican Alliance for Democracy (*Alliance Republicaine pour la Démocratie*—ARD). The ARD was registered in 2002 under the leadership of former FRUD leader Dini, who subsequently became the most prominent spokesman for the UAD. Dini's death in September 2004 reportedly left both the ARD and the URD at sea in regard to leadership.

Leader: Ahmad Youssouf HAMED.

Movement for Democratic Renewal and Development (*Mouvement pour le Renouveau Démocratique et le Développement*—MRDD). Legalized in 1992, the MRDD is an offshoot of the Party of Democratic Renewal (PRD), which had been formed in 1992 and served as a leading opposition grouping. (See 2000–2002 *Handbook* for additional information on the PRD.) MRDD leader Daher Ahmed FARAH is editor of the opposition weekly *Le Renouveau*, which has been the object of repeated closures by the government.

Leaders: Daher Ahmed FAHER, Souleiman Farah LODON.

Djibouti Development Party (*Parti Djiboutien pour le Développement*—PDD). The PDD served as a founding component of the UAD, but PDD leader Mohamed Daoud Chehem angered the other UAD parties in early 2005 by flirting with a possible presidential candidacy (subsequently abandoned).

Leaders: Mohamed Daoud CHEHEM, Bouha Daoud AHMED (Secretary General).

Union for Democracy and Justice (*Union pour la Démocratie et la Justice*—UDJ). The UDJ was established in 2002 under the leadership of Ismael Guedi Hared, a former cabinet director for President Gouled. UDJ Secretary General Farah Ali WABERI reportedly resigned from his post in March 2005 to protest the UAD's decision to boycott the upcoming presidential election.

Leader: Ismael Guedi HARED.

Union of Reformed Partisans (*Union des Partisans Reformés*—UPR). The launching of the UPR was announced in early 2005 under the leadership of Ibrahim Chehem Daoud, a former FRUD leader. The UPR endorsed President Guelleh in the 2005 presidential balloting.

Leaders: Ibrahim CHEHEM Daoud, Adou Ali ADOU (Secretary General).

Legislature

The **Chamber of Deputies** (*Chambre des Députés*) is a unicameral body of 65 members elected for five-year terms. Prior to 1992 there was no alternative to a single list presented by the Popular Rally for Progress (RPP). Under the system of limited pluralism approved in September 1992 a total of four parties was permitted to compete for chamber seats. However, the limit on the number of parties was eliminated in 2002. At the most recent balloting on January 10, 2003, the Union for a Presidential Majority captured all 65 seats.

President: Idriss ARNAOUD Ali.

Communications

Press

The pro-government *La Nation de Djibouti* (4,000) twice a month in Arabic and French, while *Carrefour Africain* (500), a Roman Catholic publication, is also issued twice monthly. *Le Temps*, an opposition monthly associated with 1999 UMO presidential candidate Moussa Ahmed Idriss, was banned in September 1999, and one of its editors was sentenced to six months in prison for "disseminating false news." Shortly thereafter two French journalists were expelled for articles deemed by the government to have "tarnished" the country's "image." Another opposition weekly, *Le Renouveau*, also closed down temporarily in October when its editor was jailed.

News Agencies

The domestic facility is *Agence Djiboutienne d'Information*. In addition, *Agence France-Presse* maintains an office in Djibouti.

Broadcasting and Computing

Radiodiffusion-Télévision de Djibouti transmitted in French, Afar, Somali, and Arabic to approximately 72,000 television receivers, while 15,000 personal computers served 6,500 Internet users in 2003.

Intergovernmental Representation

Ambassador to the U.S. and Permanent Representative to the UN
Roble OLHAYE

U.S. Ambassador to Djibouti
Marguerita Dianne RAGSDALE

IGO Memberships (Non-UN)
AfDB, AFESD, AMF, AU, Comesa, IGAD, IDB, Interpol, LAS, NAM, OIC, OIF, WTO

EGYPT

ARAB REPUBLIC OF EGYPT

Jumhuriyat Misr al-Arabiyah

The Country

Situated in the northeast corner of Africa at its juncture with Asia, Egypt occupies a quadrangle of desert made habitable only by the waters of the Nile, which bisects the country from south to north. Although the greater part of the national territory has traditionally been regarded as wasteland, Egypt is the most populous country in the Arab world: 90 percent of the people are concentrated in 4 percent of the land area, with population densities in parts of the Nile Valley reaching 6,000 per square mile. (An ambitious project was inaugurated in 1997 whereby the government plans to build a 150-mile canal northwest into the desert from Lake Nasser [formed by the Aswan High Dam] in the south. It is hoped that the $2 billion irrigation project will permit significant agricultural expansion and population relocation. Another massive irrigation canal is under construction eastward from the Nile along the northern coast into the Sinai Peninsula.) Arabic is universally spoken, and more than 80 percent of the ethnically homogeneous people adhere to the Sunni sect of Islam, much of the remainder being Coptic Christian. Women were listed as 29 percent of the paid labor force in 1996, with the majority of rural women engaged in unpaid agricultural labor; urban employed women tend to be concentrated in lower levels of health care and education.

Completion of the Aswan High Dam in 1971 permitted the expansion of tillable acreage and of multiple cropping, while the use of fertilizers and mechanization also increased production of such crops as cotton, wheat, rice, sugarcane, and corn, although Egypt still imports more than 50 percent of its food. Much of the population continues to live near the subsistence level, high rural-to-urban migration having increased the number of urban unemployed. A growing industrial sector, which employs 30 percent of the labor force, has been centered on textiles and agriprocessing, although the return by Israel of Sinai oil fields in 1975 permitted Egypt to become a net exporter of petroleum. Other natural resources include gas, iron ore, phosphates, manganese, zinc, gypsum, and talc.

The reopening of the Suez Canal (closed from the 1967 war until 1975) helped stimulate the gross domestic product, which displayed average annual real growth of 9 percent from mid-1979 to mid-1983. By 1985 economic conditions had sharply

Political Status: Nominally independent in 1922; republic established in 1953; joined with Syria as the United Arab Republic in 1958 and retained the name after Syria withdrew in 1961; present name adopted September 2, 1971; under limited multiparty system formally adopted by constitutional amendment approved in referendum of May 22, 1980.

Area: 386,659 sq. mi. (1,001,449 sq. km.).

Population: 61,452,382 (1996C); 73,855,000 (2005E), including Egyptian nationals living abroad.

Major Urban Centers (2005E): AL-QAHIRA (Cairo, 8,090,000), al-Giza (5,957,000), al-Iskandariyah (Alexandria, 3,990,000), Es-Suweis (Suez, 688,000), Bur Said (Port Said, 562,000).

Official Language: Arabic.

Monetary Unit: Egyptian Pound (market rate July 1, 2006: 5.76 pounds = $1US).

President: Muhammad Husni MUBARAK (National Democratic Party); appointed vice president on April 15, 1975; succeeded to the presidency upon the assassination of Muhammad Ahmad Anwar al-SADAT on October 6, 1981; confirmed by national referendum of October 13 and sworn in for a six-year term on October 14; served additionally as prime minister from October 14, 1981, to January 2, 1982; sworn in for a second presidential term on October 13, 1987, for a third term on October 13, 1993, and for a fourth term on October 5, 1999, following unanimous nomination by the People's Assembly on June 2 and confirmation in national referendum of September 26; elected to a fifth six-year term in limited multicandidate balloting on September 7, 2005, and inaugurated on September 27.

Prime Minister: Ahmed NAZIF; asked by the president on December 27, 2005, to form a new government, which was installed on December 31.

deteriorated as the decline in world oil prices not only depressed export income but severely curtailed remittances from Egyptians employed in other oil-producing states; in addition, tourism, another important source of revenue, declined because of regional terrorism and domestic insecurity. Currently compounding the difficulties are rapid population growth (an increase of approximately one million every nine months), an illiteracy rate estimated at nearly 50 percent, a high external debt, and an inefficient, bloated, and often corrupt bureaucracy of some six million civil servants.

In the early 1990s the government pledged to privatize state-run enterprises, reduce tariffs and price subsidies, devalue the Egyptian pound, and pursue further economic liberalization. Progress has been slow, despite the appointment of Prime Minister Ahmed NAZIF, a younger and more technologically savvy presence in the government. While the International Monetary Fund in 2005 noted Egypt's progress in structural reforms, it cited the need for privatization and debt reduction. Meanwhile, the populace has repeatedly demonstrated its frustration over the slow pace of significant change. Real GDP growth of 4.8 percent was reported in mid-2004–2005 and was projected to be 5 percent in 2006, with inflation hovering around 8 percent. Privatization, especially of banks, has been slow, but the government indicated it was responding to IMF recommendations to make monetary policies its highest priority. Tourism remained a top source of revenue, accounting for 12 percent of GDP in 2005.

Government and Politics

Political Background

The modern phase of Egypt's long history began in 1882 with the occupation of what was then an Ottoman province by a British military force, only token authority being retained by the local ruler (khedive). After establishing a protectorate in 1914, the United Kingdom granted formal independence to the government of King FUAD in 1922 but continued to exercise gradually dwindling control, which ended with its evacuation of the Suez Canal Zone in 1956. The rule of Fuad's successor,

King FAROUK (FARUK), was abruptly terminated as the result of a military coup on July 23, 1952. A group of young officers (the "Free Officers"), nominally headed by Maj. Gen. Muhammad NAGIB, secured Farouk's abdication on June 18, 1953, and went on to establish a republic under Nagib's presidency. Col. Gamal Abdel NASSER (Jamal Abd al-NASIR), who had largely guided these events, replaced Nagib as prime minister and head of state in 1954, becoming president on June 23, 1956.

The institution of military rule signaled the commencement of an internal social and economic revolution, growing pressure for the termination of British and other external influences, and a drive toward greater Arab unity against Israel under Egyptian leadership. Failing to secure Western arms on satisfactory terms, Egypt accepted Soviet military assistance in 1955. In July 1956, following the withdrawal of a Western offer to help finance the High Dam at Aswan, Egypt nationalized the Suez Canal Company and took possession of its properties. Foreign retaliation resulted in the "Suez War" of October–November 1956, in which Israeli, British, and French forces invaded Egyptian territory but subsequently withdrew under pressure from the United States, the Soviet Union, and the United Nations.

On February 1, 1958, Egypt joined with Syria to form the United Arab Republic under Nasser's presidency. Although Syria reasserted its independence in September 1961, Egypt retained the UAR designation until 1971, when it adopted the name Arab Republic of Egypt. (A less formal linkage with North Yemen, the United Arab States, was also established in 1958 but dissolved in 1961.)

Egypt incurred heavy losses in the six-day Arab-Israeli War of June 1967, which resulted in the closing of the Suez Canal, the occupation by Israel of the Sinai Peninsula, and an increase in Egypt's military and economic dependence on the USSR. Popular discontent resulting from the defeat was instrumental in bringing about a subsequent overhaul of the state machinery and a far-reaching reconstruction of the Arab Socialist Union (ASU), then the nation's only authorized political party.

A major turning point in Egypt's modern history occurred with the death of President Nasser on September 28, 1970, power subsequently being transferred to Vice President Anwar al-SADAT. The new president weathered a government crisis in 1971 that included the dismissal of Vice President Ali SABRI and other political figures accused of plotting his overthrow. A thorough shake-up of the party and government followed, with Sadat's control being affirmed at a July ASU congress and, two months later, by voter approval of a new national constitution as well as a constitution for a projected Federation of Arab Republics involving Egypt, Libya, and Syria. At the same time, the pro-Soviet leanings of some of those involved in the Sabri plot, combined with Moscow's increasing reluctance to comply with Egyptian demands for armaments, generated increasing tension in Soviet-Egyptian relations. These factors, coupled with Sadat's desire to acquire U.S. support in effecting a return of Israeli-held territory, culminated in the expulsion of some 17,000 Soviet personnel in mid-1972.

The apparent unwillingness of U.S. President Nixon in 1972 to engage in diplomatic initiatives during an election year forced Sadat to return to the Soviet fold to prepare for another war with Israel, which broke out in October 1973. After 18 days of fighting a cease-fire was concluded under UN auspices, with U.S. Secretary of State Henry Kissinger ultimately arranging for peace talks that resulted in the disengagement of Egyptian and Israeli forces east of the Suez Canal. Under an agreement signed on September 4, 1975, Israel withdrew to the Gidi and Mitla passes in the western Sinai and returned the Ras Sudar oil field to Egypt after securing political commitments from Egypt and a pledge of major economic and military support from the United States.

Although he had intimated earlier that he might step down from the presidency in 1976, Sadat accepted designation to a second six-year term on September 16. On October 26, in the first relatively free balloting since the early 1950s, the nation elected a new People's Assembly from candidates presented by three groups within the ASU. Two weeks later, the president declared that the new groups could be termed political parties but indicated that they would remain under the overall supervision of the ASU. The role of the ASU was further reduced in June 1977 by promulgation of a law that permitted the formation of additional parties under carefully circumscribed circumstances, while its vestigial status as an "umbrella" organization was terminated a year later.

On October 2, 1978, Sadat named Mustafa KHALIL to head a new "peace" cabinet that on March 15, 1979, unanimously approved a draft peace treaty with Israel. The People's Assembly ratified the document on April 10 by a 328–15 vote, while in a referendum held nine days later a reported 99.95 percent of those casting ballots voiced approval. At the same time, a series of political and constitutional reforms received overwhelming support from voters. As a result, President Sadat dissolved the assembly two years ahead of schedule and called for a two-stage legislative election on June 7 and 14. Sadat's National Democratic Party (NDP) easily won the multiparty contest—the first such election since the overthrow of the monarchy in 1953—and on June 21 Prime Minister Khalil and a substantially unchanged cabinet were sworn in. On May 12, 1980, however, Khalil resigned, with President Sadat assuming the prime ministership two days later.

By 1981 Egypt was increasingly dependent on the United States for military and foreign policy support, while growing domestic unrest threatened the fragile political liberalization initiated in 1980. In an unprecedented move in early September, the government imprisoned more than a thousand opposition leaders, ranging from Islamic fundamentalists to journalists and Nasserites.

On October 6, 1981, while attending a military review in Cairo, President Sadat was assassinated by a group of Muslim militants affiliated with *al-Jihad* ("Holy War"). The assembly's nomination of Vice President Muhammad Husni MUBARAK as his successor was confirmed by a national referendum on October 13, the new president naming a

cabinet headed by himself as prime minister two days later. On January 2, 1982, Mubarak yielded the latter office to First Deputy Prime Minister Ahmad Fuad MUHI al-DIN.

The NDP retained overwhelming control of the assembly at the March 1984 election, the right-wing New Wafd Party being the only other group to surpass the 8 percent vote share needed to gain direct representation. However, popular discontent erupted later in the year over measures to combat economic deterioration and numerous opposition leaders, accused of "fomenting unrest" were arrested. Meanwhile, Islamic fundamentalists continued a campaign for the institution of full *sharia* law that provoked a new wave of arrests in mid-1985.

At his death in June 1984 Muhi al-Din was succeeded as prime minister by Gen. Kamal Hasan ALI. Ali was replaced in September 1985 by Dr. Ali Mahmud LUTFI, who, in turn, yielded office on November 12, 1986, to Dr. Atif Muhammad SIDQI, a lawyer and economist whose appointment appeared to signal a willingness to institute drastic reform measures sought by the IMF and World Bank. Anticipating a resurgence of opposition and facing court challenges to the legality of an assembly that excluded independent members, the president confounded his critics by mounting a referendum in February 1987 on the question of legislative dissolution. The subsequent election of April 6 reconfirmed the NDP's control, and on October 5 Mubarak received public endorsement for a second term.

President Mubarak's swift response to the Iraqi invasion of Kuwait in August 1990 received widespread domestic support, and, at balloting on November 29 to replenish the assembly (whose 1987 election had been declared illegal in May 1990), the ruling NDP won an increased majority. The landslide victory was tarnished, however, by low voter turnout and an election boycott by three leading opposition parties and the proscribed, but prominent, Muslim Brotherhood. On December 13 Dr. Ahmad Fathi SURUR was elected assembly president, assuming the responsibilities left vacant by the assassination of the previous speaker, Dr. Rifaat al-MAHGOUB, on October 12.

Following a May 1991 cabinet reshuffle, Mubarak indicated that measures would be considered to reduce the NDP stranglehold on government activity. However, the state of emergency in effect since 1981 was extended for three more years, Mubarak citing ongoing "subversion" by fundamentalist militants as justification. Subsequently, international human rights organizations charged that the administration was continuing to torture and otherwise abuse its opponents, particularly the fundamentalists, with whom a state of "all-out war" was said to exist by 1992. For their part, the militants, vowing to topple the "corrupt" Mubarak government and establish an Islamic state, intensified their guerrilla campaign against police, soldiers, government officials, and tourists.

On July 21, 1993, the assembly nominated Mubarak for a third term by a vote of 439–7, and the president received a reported 95 percent "yes" vote in the national referendum of October 4, opposition leaders strongly questioning the accuracy of the tally. Although President Mubarak had promised an infusion of "new blood" into his administration, many of the previous cabinet members were reappointed in the reshuffle announced on October 14 by Prime Minister Sidqi.

On June 26, 1995, Mubarak narrowly escaped assassination when a group of alleged fundamentalists opened fire on his motorcade after his arrival in Addis Ababa, Ethiopia, for a summit of the Organization of African Unity (OAU). It was the third attempt on his life in 22 months. In September 1996, three defendants were sentenced to death by an Ethiopian court for their role in the 1995 attack, which President Mubarak blamed on the militant Islamic Group (see Illegal Groups under Political Parties, below).

Despite the regime's rhetorical commitment to broadening the governmental role of lesser parties, the NDP again completely dominated the legislative elections of late 1995, opposition leaders claiming they had been hamstrung by new press restrictions and the ongoing ban (under the long-standing state of emergency) on political demonstrations. On the other hand, the appointment of Dr. Kamal Ahmed al-GANZOURI as prime minister on January 3, 1996, launched what was widely perceived as significant economic liberalization.

The level of violence between the government and fundamentalist militants peaked in 1995 when more than 400 were killed from a combination of terrorist attacks and government reprisals against militant strongholds. International human rights organizations criticized the mass detention of political prisoners and "grossly unfair" trials leading, in many cases, to executions.

Sporadic incidents occurred throughout 1996 and into early 1997. In view of continued conflict with fundamentalist militants, the state of emergency in early 1997 was extended (and remained in effect as of mid-2006), permitting the government to continue to detain "terrorists" without formal charges for lengthy periods and to try defendants in special courts. Meanwhile, local elections in April again failed to reveal any hint of a political challenge to NDP control, nearly half of the ruling party's candidates running unopposed.

In mid-1997 imprisoned fundamentalist leaders reportedly called for a "cease-fire," and Egypt's vital tourist industry continued to revive. However, the government, apparently unconvinced that a truce had been achieved, proceeded with several mass trials and imposed harsh sentences on a number of defendants. Subsequently, militants massacred some 70 tourists at an ancient temple at Luxor in November, again bringing the conflict to the forefront of world attention. By that time, most observers agreed that a split had developed in the militant camp and that the faction committed to violence comprised possibly only several hundred guerrillas. It was also widely believed that there was little popular support for the militants, and only a few serious incidents were reported in 1998. By early 1999 the government had released an estimated 5,000 of the 20,000 people detained since the crackdown had begun, and in March the Islamic Group renounced violent methods.

All political parties having been distinctly "marginalized," President Mubarak faced no challenge to his nomination in June 1999 by the People's Assembly for a fourth term, duly confirmed by an official "yes" vote of 94 percent in a national referendum on September 26. Upon his inauguration, Mubarak announced the appointment of Atef Muhammad OBEID as the new prime minister. Subsequently, the NDP ultimately again won unchallenged control of the assembly in 2002. Some 70 percent of the NDP candidates also ran unopposed in the April 2002 municipal elections.

In June 2004, for the first time in Egypt's history, a member of the opposition leftist National Progressive Unionist Party—NPUP (al-Hizb al-Watani) won a seat in the Shura Council, and in October 2004, a third political party was allowed to form (see Constitution and government, below). Prime Minister Obeid resigned in 2004 and was succeeded by Ahmed Nazif, former minister of communications and information technology, who at age 52 was considerably younger than other government leaders.

President Mubarak was elected in controversial multicandidate balloting in September 2005 with 88 percent of the vote, most notably defeating Ayman NUR, formerly jailed leader of the leftist Tomorrow Party (al-Ghad), and then-leader of the New Wafd Party—NWP Hizb (al-Wafd al-Gadid), Numan GOMAA (see Political Parties and Groups, below). Seven other candidates each received less than 1 percent of the vote. Mubarak asked Prime Minister Nazif to form a new cabinet, which was sworn in at year's end.

Legislative elections in November and December 2005 resulted in the NDP retaining an overwhelming majority, but significant inroads were made by independents affiliated with the outlawed Muslim Brotherhood, whose representation increased more than five-fold to 88 seats. Runoffs for 12 undecided seats had not been held as of early 2006 (see Legislature, below).

Constitution and Government

Under the 1971 constitution, executive power is vested in the president, who is nominated by the People's Assembly and elected for a six-year term by popular referendum. The president may appoint vice presidents in addition to government ministers and may rule by decree when granted emergency powers by the 454-member assembly, which functions primarily as a policy-approving rather than a policy-initiating body. (Since assuming the presidency in 1981, Mubarak has chosen to rule without a vice president.) In May 1990 the Supreme Constitutional Court invalidated the 1987 assembly elections, claiming the electoral system discriminated against opposition and independent contenders. Consequently, the government abolished electoral laws limiting the number of independent candidates, rejected the "party list" balloting system, and enlarged the number of constituencies.

For only the third time since forming in 1977, Egypt's Political Parties Committee allowed the creation of a new political party, Tomorrow (al-Ghad), in February 2004. On June 9, 2005, the assembly approved a draft law to elect the president by direct, secret balloting, replacing the referendum system. This followed adoption of a constitutional amendment in May 2005 to allow Egypt's first multicandidate presidential election. The amendment was approved in a public referendum, albeit marked by huge public demonstrations over what is still perceived as too much government control over potential candidates.

A Consultative Council (Majlis al-Shura), formerly the Central Committee of the ASU, is composed of 140 elected and 70 appointed members. It serves in an advisory capacity as an "upper house" of the assembly. In addition to the Supreme Constitutional Court, the judicial system includes the Court of Cassation, geographically organized Courts of Appeal, Tribunals of First Instance, and District Tribunals. A Supreme Judicial Council is designed to guarantee the independence of the judiciary. Emergency laws, in effect since 1981, provide the government with broad arrest and detention powers. In addition, special military courts were established in late 1992 for the prosecution of those charged with "terrorist acts" in connection with the conflict between the government and militant Islamic fundamentalists.

For administrative purposes Egypt is divided into 26 governorates, each with a governor appointed by the president, while most functions are shared with regional, town, and village officials. In April 1994 the People's Assembly approved legislation whereby previously elected village mayors would thenceforth be appointed by the Interior Ministry.

Constitutional amendments passed by the assembly on April 30, 1980, and approved by referendum on May 22 included the following: designation of the country as "socialist democratic," rather than "democratic socialist," and designation of the Islamic legal code (*sharia*) as "the" rather than "a" principal source of law.

Foreign Relations

As the most populous and most highly industrialized of the Arab states, Egypt has consistently aspired to a leading role in Arab, Islamic, Middle Eastern, African, and world affairs and has been an active participant in the UN, the Arab League, and the Organization of African Unity. For a number of years, its claim to a position of primacy in the Arab world made for somewhat unstable relations with other Arab governments, particularly the conservative regimes of Jordan and Saudi Arabia, although relations with those governments improved as a result of the 1967 and 1973 wars with Israel. Relations with the more radical regimes of Libya and Syria subsequently became strained, largely because of their displeasure with the terms of the U.S.-brokered disengagement. Thus a January 1972 agreement by the three states to establish a loose Federation of Arab Republics was never implemented.

Formally nonaligned, Egypt has gone through a number of distinct phases, including the Western orientation of the colonial period and the monarchy, the anti-Western and increasingly pro-Soviet period initiated in 1955, a period of flexibility dating from the expulsion of Soviet personnel in 1972, and a renewed reliance on the West—particularly the United States—following widespread condemnation of Egyptian-Israeli rapprochement by most Communist and Arab governments.

On November 19, 1977, President Sadat began a precedent-shattering three-day trip to Jerusalem, the highlight of which was an address to the Israeli *Knesset*. While he offered no significant concessions in regard to the occupied territories, was unequivocal in his support of a Palestinian state, and declared that he did not intend to conclude a separate peace with Israel, the trip was hailed as a "historic breakthrough" in Arab-Israeli relations and was followed by an invitation to the principals in the Middle Eastern dispute and their great-power patrons to a December meeting in Egypt to prepare for a resumption of the Geneva peace conference. Israeli Prime Minister Begin responded affirmatively, but all of the Arab invitees declined. Consequently, on December 5 Egypt broke relations with five of its more radical neighbors (Algeria, Iraq, Libya, Syria, and South Yemen).

A dramatic ten-day "summit" convened by U.S. President Carter at Camp David, Maryland, in September 1978 yielded two documents—a "Framework for Peace in the Middle East" and a "Framework for a Peace Treaty between Israel and Egypt"—that were signed by President Sadat and Prime Minister Begin at the White House on September 17. By mid-November details of a peace treaty and three annexes had been agreed upon by Egyptian and Israeli representatives. Signing, however, was deferred beyond the target date of December 17 primarily because of Egyptian insistence on a specific timetable for Israeli withdrawal from the West Bank and Gaza, in addition to last-minute reservations regarding Article 6, which gave the document precedence over treaty commitments to other states. Thus, on March 8, President Carter flew to the Middle East for talks with leaders of both countries, and within six days compromise proposals had been accepted. The completed treaty was signed by Begin and Sadat in Washington on March 26, and on April 25 the 31-year state of war between Egypt and Israel officially came to an end. On May 25 the first Israeli troops withdrew from the Sinai under the terms of the treaty and negotiations on autonomy for the West Bank and Gaza opened in Beersheba, Israel.

The Arab League responded to the Egyptian-Israeli rapprochement by calling for the diplomatic and economic isolation of Egypt. By midyear all league members but Oman, Somalia, and Sudan had severed relations with the Sadat regime, and Cairo's membership had been suspended from a number of Arab groupings, including the league, the Arab Monetary Fund, and the Organization of Arab Petroleum Exporting Countries. Egypt succeeded in weathering the hard-line Arab reaction largely because of increased economic aid from Western countries, including France, West Germany, Japan, and the United States, which alone committed itself to more aid on a real per capita basis than had been extended to Europe under the post–World War II Marshall Plan.

Although Egypt and Israel formally exchanged ambassadors on February 26, 1980, a month after opening their border at El Arish in the Sinai to land traffic, negotiations on the question of Palestinian autonomy were subsequently impeded by continued Jewish settlement on the West Bank, the Israeli annexation of East Jerusalem in July 1980, and the invasion of Lebanon in June 1982. Following the massacre of Palestinian refugees at Sabra and Chatila in September 1982, Cairo recalled its ambassador from Tel Aviv. (Relations at the ambassadorial level were ultimately reestablished in September 1986, despite tension over Israel's bombing of the PLO headquarters in Tunis in October 1985.)

The Soviet intervention in Afghanistan in December 1979 generated concern in Egypt, with the government ordering Moscow in February 1980 to reduce its diplomatic staff in Cairo to seven, while offering military assistance to the Afghan rebels. In 1981, accusing the remaining Soviet embassy staff of aiding Islamic fundamentalist unrest, Cairo broke diplomatic relations and expelled the Soviet ambassador. Relations were resumed in September 1984, as the Mubarak government departed from the aggressively pro-U.S. policy of the later Sadat years, while a three-year trade accord was signed by the two governments in late 1987.

Relations with most of the Arab world also changed during President Mubarak's first term, Egypt's stature among moderate neighbors being enhanced by a virtual freeze in dealings with Israel after the 1982 Lebanon invasion. Although relations with radical Arab states, particularly Libya, remained strained, Egypt's reemergence from the status of Arab pariah allowed it to act as a "silent partner" in negotiations between Jordan and the PLO that generated a 1985 peace plan. However, the subsequent collapse of the plan left the Mubarak administration in an uncomfortable middle position between its "good friend" King Hussein and the PLO, whose Cairo offices were closed in May 1987 after the passage of an "anti-Egyptian" resolution by the Palestine National Council.

During an Arab League summit in Amman, Jordan, in November 1987, the prohibition against diplomatic ties with Egypt was officially lifted, although the suspension of league membership remained in effect. It was widely believed that the threat of Iranian hegemony in the Gulf was the principal factor in Cairo's rehabilitation. Egypt, which had severed relations with Iran in May 1987 upon discovery of a fundamentalist Muslim network allegedly financed by Tehran, possessed the largest and best-equipped armed force in the region. Following the Amman summit, Egypt authorized reopening of the PLO facility, instituted joint military maneuvers with Jordan, increased the number of military advisers sent to Iraq, and arranged for military cooperation with Kuwait, Saudi Arabia, and the United Arab Emirates.

By January 1989 only three Arab League countries—Libya, Lebanon, and Syria—had not renewed diplomatic relations with Cairo, and Egypt returned to full participation in the organization during its Casablanca, Morocco, summit in May. Meanwhile, a dispute that had marred relations with Israel since the latter's 1982 withdrawal from the bulk of the Sinai was resolved on February 26, when the two countries agreed to reaffirm Egyptian sovereignty over Taba, a beach resort on the northern tip of the Gulf of Aqaba.

Lebanon and Syria restored diplomatic relations with Cairo in 1989, and relations with Libya also improved as President Mubarak journeyed to Libya in October to meet with Col. Muammar al-Qadhafi, the first such visit by an Egyptian president since 1972. Meanwhile, Cairo increased pressure on Jerusalem to begin negotiations with the Palestinians in the West Bank and Gaza Strip, forwarding a ten-point plan to speed the onset of elections and lobbying the United States to exercise its diplomatic influence over Israel.

Egyptian-Iraqi relations were rocked in June 1989 by Baghdad's imposition of remittance restrictions on foreign workers, leading to the repatriation of 1 million Egyptians, many of whom complained about Iraqi mistreatment. In what was clearly his boldest foreign relations move, President Mubarak spearheaded the Arab response to Iraq's incursion into Kuwait in August 1990. At an Arab League summit in Cairo on August 10 the Egyptian leader successfully argued for a declaration condemning the invasion and approving Saudi Arabia's request for non-Arab troops to help it defend its borders. Subsequent Egyptian efforts to facilitate an Iraqi withdrawal were rebuffed by Baghdad. Overall, more than 45,000 Egyptian troops were deployed to Saudi Arabia, elements of which played a conspicuous role in the liberation of Kuwait.

In the wake of Iraq's defeat in 1991, policy differences arose between Egypt and its allies. Cairo had long urged that postwar regional security be entrusted to an all-Arab force. By contrast, Gulf Cooperation Council (GCC) members indicated that they looked with favor on a continued U.S. presence in the area. Particularly irksome was a Saudi statement that the monarchy did not welcome the permanent stationing of Egyptian forces on its soil, Cairo subsequently withdrawing all its troops by the end of August. A corollary to the dispute over military policy was increased uncertainty as to the level of economic aid that Egypt could expect from its oil-rich neighbors. For their part, Western creditors quickly rewarded Cairo for its support during the Desert Shield and Desert Storm campaigns. Shortly after the defeat of Iraqi forces, the United

States and Gulf Arab states forgave about $14 billion of Egypt's $50 billion external debt, and Paris Club members subsequently agreed to gradually write off another $11 billion. Globally, its prestige was enhanced by the selection of its leading diplomat, former deputy prime minister Boutros BOUTROS-GHALI, as the secretary general of the United Nations effective January 1, 1992.

Egyptian officials reportedly played an important advisory role in the secret talks that led up to the accord between Israel and the PLO in September 1993. In addition, Egypt won the backing of other North African governments for its hard-line antifundamentalist posture. Cairo's relations with Amman improved after a three-year rift caused by Jordan's pro-Iraqi stand during the Gulf crisis. In early February 1995 President Mubarak hosted Jordan's King Hussein, Israeli Prime Minister Yitzhak Rabin, and PLO Chair Yasir Arafat in a regional summit designed to revitalize prospects for implementation of the Israel/PLO peace accord. The summit also reportedly addressed growing tension between Egypt and Israel regarding nuclear weapons.

By mid-1995 tension with Egypt's southern neighbor, Sudan, had intensified because of an intimation by Mubarak that Sudanese officials had played a role in the June 26 assassination attempt in Ethiopia. In June Sudan accused Egypt of provoking a clash in the disputed border region of Halaib, with Mubarak declaring his support for exiled opponents of the fundamentalist Khartoum regime. In 2004, Egypt reluctantly agreed to send military officers as observers to Sudan, but stopped short of getting involved in attempting to resolve the Sudanese civil war.

On March 13, 1996, Egypt hosted the so-called "terrorism summit" of some 27 heads of state and government in the wake of suicide bomb attacks in Israel earlier in the month that appeared to threaten the Middle East peace process. Following the election of Benjamin Netanyahu as Israel's new prime minister in May, President Mubarak became more critical of him over the next six months in the face of what he described as Netanyahu's "lack of action" in implementing the Israeli/PLO peace accord. The Egyptian president intensified his attacks on Netanyahu's policies in 1997, particularly in regard to the expansion of Jewish settlements in the West Bank. In early 1998 Mubarak strongly objected to U.S. plans to take military action against Iraq after Baghdad blocked the activities of UN weapons inspectors. Meanwhile, by that time significant improvement had been registered in relations between Egypt and Sudan, the two countries having apparently agreed to address each other's "security" concerns, i.e., Sudanese support for fundamentalist militants in Egypt and Egyptian support for antiregime activity in Sudan, particularly on the part of southern rebels. Full diplomatic relations were restored between Sudan and Egypt in December 1999, following a visit by Sudan's President Bashir to Cairo. Relations with Iran were also reported to have improved later in 1998, but in 2005 they were again strained after a security court convicted an Egyptian of plotting to assassinate the president and of spying for Iran.

President Mubarak welcomed the election of Ehud Barak as prime minister of Israel in May 1999 as a "hopeful sign" regarding a peace settlement between Israel and the Palestinians, and Egypt was a prominent mediator in negotiations through mid-2000. However, Egypt recalled its ambassador to Israel in November 2000 in response to the Israeli bombing of the Gaza Strip. Egyptian/Israeli relations cooled even further following the election of hard-liner Ariel Sharon as prime minister of Israel in February 2001. By 2004, however, after Sharon had unveiled his unilateral disengagement plan for the Gaza Strip, in consultation with Egypt and the United States, relations between Egypt and Israel had begun to thaw. Egypt's role in security arrangements in Gaza were vital to the process and widely seen as enhancing Egypt's role as a power broker in the region. In December 2004, Egypt and Israel conducted their first prisoner exchange, marking a shift in relations and paving the way for a December 12 pact between the two countries on exports. In February 2005, Mubarak again helped mediate between Israel and the Palestinians, adopting a high-profile diplomatic role.

Current Issues

Under increasing pressure from prodemocracy activists, as well as from the United States, President Mubarak in February 2005 called for a constitutional amendment to allow multicandidate elections. Unprecedented public demonstrations and calls for Mubarak to step down preceded his historic announcement. The amendment was approved in a referendum in May 2005, but the government still faced vehement criticism for the restrictive conditions it placed on potential candidates; for example, leaders of the recognized parties can run, but independent candidates must get the backing of 250 members of the assembly and local councils. Four opposition parties immediately announced a boycott of the presidential elections scheduled for September 2005. Egyptian authorities had attempted to ban referendum-day protests, but large demonstrations took place nonetheless. The government also arrested members of the opposition Muslim Brotherhood. The ongoing crackdown against Islamists and other opposition groups sparked bold, massive protests, leading to further arrests. The leftist Tomorrow, the one new party granted a permit, saw its leader Ayman NUR jailed for six weeks on charges of forging signatures on his political party application. His June 2005 trial was postponed until after presidential elections, in which he ran a distant second to Mubarak. Subsequently, Nur was sentenced on December 24 to five years in prison. The European Union joined Washington in condemning Nur's conviction, which was reportedly jeopardizing a free trade agreement with the United States in early 2006.

Even with obvious moves toward reform, the emergency law decreed in 1981 remains in effect, and human rights organizations have continued to report ongoing abuse and torture by security services around the country. Amid growing opposition and calls for reform, Mubarak said in early 2006 he planned to replace the emergency law, set to expire in May 2006, with anti-terror legislation.

While the presidential election in 2005 was trumpeted as a move toward democratization, most observers considered the election to be a very limited step toward reform. Some 19 candidates were disqualified, the government refused to allow international monitors, turnout was extremely low, and laws severely restricting political activity remained in place. Assembly elections a few months later were marked by violence, with at least nine people allegedly killed by government security forces who reportedly blocked some polling stations in opposition strongholds. Hundreds of supporters of Muslim Brotherhood-backed candidates were arrested during the three-stage elections. While the NDP again dominated in the results, candidates allied with the Muslim Brotherhood increased their representation fivefold, thus consolidating the group's position as the strongest opposition force. In what was regarded as a move to preserve the NDP's power, the government postponed local elections (scheduled for April 2006) for two years. However, officials said the delay was to give the assembly more time to adopt laws that would increase the role of local governments.

Terrorist attacks plagued Egyptian tourist areas in 2005 and 2006. After three bomb explosions in the southern Sinai resort of Dahab on April 24, 2006, killed at least 24 people, Israel closed its border with Egypt for security reasons. Within days, Egyptian authorities arrested 10 people, linking some of them to previous attacks.

Political Parties and Groups

Egypt's old political parties were swept away with the destruction of the monarchy in 1953. Efforts by the Nasser regime centered on the creation of a single mass organization to support the government and its policies. Following unsuccessful experiments with two such organizations, the National Liberation Rally and the National Union, the Arab Socialist Union—ASU (al-Ittihad al-Ishtiraki al-Arabi) was established as the country's sole political party in December 1962.

Prior to the legislative election of October 1976 President Sadat authorized the establishment of three "groups" within the ASU—the leftist National Progressive Unionist Assembly (NPUA), the centrist Egyptian Arab Socialist Organiza-

tion (EASO), and the rightist Free Socialist Organization (FSO)—which presented separate lists of assembly candidates. Following the election, Sadat indicated that it would be appropriate to refer to the groups as distinct parties, though the ASU would "stand above" the new organizations. A law adopted on June 27, 1977, authorized the establishment of additional parties under three conditions: (1) that they be sanctioned by the ASU; (2) that, except for those established in 1976, they include at least 20 members of the People's Assembly; and (3) that they not have been in existence prior to 1953.

On February 4, 1978, the ASU Central Committee modified the impact of the 1977 legislation by permitting the *Wafd*, the majority party under the monarchy, to reenter politics as the New Wafd Party (NWP). Less than four months later, however, representatives of the NWP voted unanimously to disband the party to protest the passage of a sweeping internal security law on June 1. Subsequently, President Sadat announced the formal abolition of the ASU, the conversion of its Central Committee into a Consultative Council (*Majlis al-Shura*) to meet annually on the anniversary of the 1952 revolution, and the establishment of a new centrist group that, on August 15, was named the National Democratic Party (NDP). In an April 1979 political referendum, the voters overwhelmingly approved removal of the first two conditions of the 1977 law, thus clearing the way for the formation of additional parties. In May 1980 a constitutional amendment, also approved by referendum, removed reference to the defunct ASU as the sole source of political activity, thus formally legitimizing the limited multiparty system. In July 1983 the assembly approved a requirement that parties obtain 8 percent of the vote to gain parliamentary representation. One month later, the NWP announced that it was "resuming public activity," a government attempt to force the group to reregister as a new party being overturned by the State Administrative Court the following October.

At the 1984 election only the NDP and the NWP won elective seats, the former outdistancing the latter by a near 6–1 margin. In 1987 the

NDP obtained a slightly reduced majority of 77.2 percent, the remaining seats being captured by the NWP and a coalition composed of the Socialist Labor Party (SLP), the Liberal Socialist Party (LSP), and "Islamists" representing the Muslim Brotherhood (see below). Following a Supreme Court decision in May 1990 that overturned the results of the 1987 balloting, the government enacted a number of electoral changes, including reversal of the 8 percent requirement.

In 2002 the administration introduced controversial new regulations that precluded political activity on the part of any group receiving money from overseas that had not been approved by and channeled through the government. Opponents of the regime decried the measure as an attempt to throttle parties who might be funded by foreign prodemocracy organizations. In 2005, ten parties formed an alliance to promote reforms (see Other Legislative Parties, below). Still other parties are summarily banned.

Government Party

National Democratic Party—NDP (*al-Hizb al-Watani al-Dimuqrati*). The NDP was organized by President Sadat in July 1978 as the principal government party, its name being derived from that of the historic National Party formed at the turn of the century by Mustapha Kamel. In late August it was reported that 275 deputies in the People's Assembly had joined the new group, all but 11 having been members of the Egyptian Arab Socialist Party—EASP (*Hizb Misr al-Arabi al-Ishtiraki*), which, as an outgrowth of the EASO, had inherited many of the political functions earlier performed by the ASU. The EASP formally merged with the NDP in October 1978. President Mubarak, who had served as deputy chair under President Sadat, was named NDP chair at a party congress on January 26, 1982.

Two months after his pro forma reelection in October 1993, President Mubarak announced the composition of the new NDP political bureau, most leadership posts being retained by incumbents despite the president's campaign pledge to revitalize both the NDP and the national administration. In November 1998 the NDP nominated Mubarak as its candidate for the 1999 presidential election. Official NDP candidates reportedly won only 27 percent of the seats in the 2000 assembly balloting, although many successful independent candidates joined (or rejoined) the party to give it 388 out of 442 elected seats. Analysts attributed the poor performance of the official NDP candidates to public perception that the party lacked an ideological foundation and existed only to rubber-stamp the administration's agenda.

President Mubarak was reelected as chair of the NDP at the September 2002 congress, while his son, Gamal MUBARAK, who has been mentioned as a possible successor to his father, was elevated to a new post of head of the NDP's policy board.

In 2005, the NDP won the two-thirds majority (variously reported as 320 to 324 seats) needed to amend the constitution, which will determine how Mubarak's successor will be chosen.

Leaders: Muhammad Husni MUBARAK (President of the Republic and Chair of the Party), Muhammad Safwat al-SHERIF (General Secretary), Kamal al-SHAZLY (Assistant General Secretary).

Other Legislative Parties

Prior to the assembly elections of 2005, opposition leaders announced on October 8 they had formed a coalition of ten parties and movements seeking greater representation in the legislative body. Independent candidates allied themselves with movements or groups not officially recognized by the government. The **National Front for Political and Constitutional Change,** led by former prime minister Sidqi, was an apparent partial successor to the **Consensus of National Forces for Reform** (*Tawafuq al-Qiwa al-Wataniyah lil-Islah*), a group of eight opposition parties formed in 2004. Notably excluded from the 2005 coalition was the Tomorrow Party (*al-Ghad*), reportedly because of dissension within that party. Among those included were **Arab Dignity** (*Karama al-Araybia*), established by disenchanted Nasserists and led by Hamdin SABAHI; **Enough** (*Kifaya*), also referenced as the **Egyptian Movement for Change**, which includes leftists, liberals and Islamists, co-founded in 2004 by George ISHAQ and Amin ESKANDAR; the **Labor Party**; the **Center** (*Hizb al-Wasat*), an offshoot of the Muslim Brotherhood, led by Abdul-Ela MADI; and three parties already represented in the assembly.

New Wafd Party—NWP (*Hizb al-Wafd al-Gadid*). Formed in February 1978 as a revival of the most powerful party in Egypt prior to 1952, the NWP formally disbanded the following June but reformed in August. In 1980 a "new generation of *Wafd* activists" instigated demonstrations in several cities, prompting the detention of its leader, Fuad SERAGEDDIN, until November 1981. In alliance with a number of Islamic groups, most importantly the proscribed Muslim Brotherhood (below), the NWP won 15 percent of the vote in May 1984, thus becoming the only opposition party with parliamentary representation. In 1987 the NWP won 35 seats (23 less than in 1984), the Brotherhood having entered into a de facto coalition with the SLP and the LSP (below). The NWP boycotted the *Shura* poll in 1989, complaining that electoral procedures remained exclusionary; it also boycotted the 1990 assembly elections, although party members running as independents retained at least 14 seats.

Following the 1995 national balloting, NWP leaders charged that electoral fraud had been the "worst in history." The NWP also boycotted the April 1997 local elections. However, although the NWP had urged a boycott of the 1993 presidential poll, it urged a "yes" vote for President Mubarak in 1999. Serageddin died in August 2000 and was succeeded as party leader by Numan GOMAA, who was a distant third in 2005 presidential balloting. The party won six seats in the 2005 assembly elections.

Following internal strife in early 2006, Gomaa refused to give up control, and in April he was arrested after a highly publicized incident at party headquarters between rival factions that resulted in the death of one member. The assembly's Political Parties Committee subsequently ruled that

Mustapha Al Tawil was the legitimate leader of the party.

Leaders: Mustapha AL TAWIL, El Sayed BADAWI (Secretary General), Yaseen Tag al-DIN (Deputy Secretary General).

Liberal Socialist Party—LSP (*Hizb al-Ahrar al-Ishtiraki*). The Liberal Socialist Party, which was formed in 1976 from the right wing of the ASU, focuses on securing a greater role for private enterprise within the Egyptian economy while protecting the rights of workers and farmers. The party's assembly representation fell from 12 to 3 seats in June 1979 and was eliminated entirely at the 1984 balloting, on the basis of a vote share of less than 1 percent. It obtained three elective seats in 1987 as a member of a Socialist Labor Party–led coalition. It subsequently discontinued its alliance with the SLP and Muslim Brotherhood. It boycotted the November 1990 poll, although one of its members reportedly won a seat as an independent. The party won one seat in the 2000 and 2005 assembly elections and supported Mubarak in the 2005 presidential election.

Leader: Hilmi SALIM.

National Progressive Unionist Party—NPUP (*Hizb al-Tajammu al-Watani al-Taqaddumi al-Wahdawi*). Although it received formal endorsement as the party of the left in 1976, the NPUP temporarily ceased activity in 1978 following the enactment of restrictive internal security legislation. It contested the June 1979 assembly election on a platform that, alone among those of the four sanctioned parties, opposed the Egyptian-Israeli peace treaty, and it failed to retain its two parliamentary seats. In both 1979 and 1984 the party leadership charged the government with fraud and harassment, although on the latter occasion, President Mubarak included a NPUP member among his assembly nominees. In November 1990 the NPUP resisted opposition appeals for an electoral boycott and captured six assembly seats; meanwhile, the party led opposition criticism against U.S. military involvement in the Gulf. The NPUP urged a no vote against Mubarak in the 1993 presidential referendum and called for a boycott of the 1999 poll. The party won one seat in the 2005 assembly elections.

Leaders: Rifaat al-SAID, Abu al-Izz al-HARIRI (Deputy Chair).

Tomorrow Party (*al-Ghad*). Officially recognized by the government in October 2004, this leftist party became only the third new party allowed since 1977. Tomorrow seeks constitutional reform to reduce the power of the presidency and an end to the country's emergency law. Espousing a commitment to social justice, the party is made up largely of dissidents from the NWP. Former leader Ayman Nur, jailed for six weeks in 2005 (see Current issues, above), came in a distant second to Mubarak in the September 2005 presidential election. A rift over leadership occurred after the election between Nur's supporters and those led by Musa Mustafa Musa. His splinter group elected him the new party leader on October 1, 2005, though Nur insisted he was still party president. Nur was sentenced to five years in prison in December 2005 following his conviction on charges that he forged documents used to register his party. On December 30, however, the party's general assembly elected Naji al-Ghatrifi to be its new leader, named Nur its honorary leader, and sacked four dissident members. The party won one seat in the 2005 assembly elections.

Leader: Naji al-GHATRIFI (Chair).

Other Parties That Participated in Recent Elections

Nasserist Arab Democratic Party —NADP. Also referenced simply as the Nasserist Party, the NADP, formed in 1992, won one seat in the 1995 assembly balloting, three in the 2000 poll, and none in the 2005 elections. Its platform called for the government to retain a dominant role in directing the economy and to increase the provision of social services.

Leader: Diaeddin DAOUD.

National Party (*Hizb al-Umma*). A small Muslim organization, the National Party has ties to the supporters of Dr. Sadiq al-MAHDI, former prime minister of Sudan. It participated unsuccessfully in the 2000 assembly balloting on a platform that called for the strengthening of the "democratic process."

Leader: Ahmad al-SABAHI Awadallah (Chair and 2005 presidential candidate).

Green Party (*Hizb al-Khudr*). The Green Party, recognized by the Political Parties Tribunal in April 1990, was reported to have emerged in response to a 1986 newspaper column by (then) Vice President Abdel Salam DAOUD that criticized his countrymen's lack of interest in environmental issues. The formation claimed 3,000 members and, while professing no interest in gaining political power, participated unsuccessfully in the 1990 legislative campaign. The party supported President Mubarak in the 2005 presidential campaign.

Leader: Abdul Moneim al-AASAR (Chair).

Other parties that participated in the 2005 elections were the **Democratic Unionist Party**, led by Ibrahim TURK; the **Egyptian Arab Socialist Party**, led by Wahid al-UQSURI; the **Generation Party** (*al-Gayl*), led by Naji al-SHAHABI; the **National Accord Party**, led by Al-Sayyid Rifaat al-AGRUDI; **Solidarity** (*al-Takaful*), a socialist grouping led by Usama Mohammad SHALTOUT; the **Egypt 2000 Party** (*Misr*), led by Fawsi Khalil Mohammad GHAZAL; the **Social Constitutional Party**, led by Mamduh Mohammad QINAWI; and the **National Rally for Democratic Change**, whose leader, former Prime Minister Sidqi, was coordinator of the ten-party National Front coalition.

Other Parties and Groups

Muslim Brotherhood (*al-Ikhwan al-Muslimin*). Established in 1928 to promote creation of a pan-Arab Islamic state, the Brotherhood was declared an illegal organization in 1954 when the government accused its leaders, many of whom were executed or imprisoned, of plotting a coup attempt. However, for many years the Mubarak government tolerated some activity on the part of the Brotherhood since it claimed to eschew violence, as a means of undercutting the militant fundamentalist movement. With much of its support coming from the northern middle class, the Brotherhood retains the largest following and greatest financial resources among Egypt's Islamic organizations despite the emergence of more radical groups. It dominates many Egyptian professional associations, collaterally providing a wide range of charitable services in sharp contrast to inefficient government programs.

The Brotherhood secured indirect assembly representation in 1984 and 1987. Although the Brotherhood boycotted the 1990 assembly balloting, joint SLP/Brotherhood candidates contested a number of seats in November 1992 municipal elections. Many Brotherhood adherents were removed from local and national appointive positions in 1992–1993 as a side effect of the government's antifundamentalist campaign. Friction with the government intensified further in early 1995 when a group of Brotherhood members were charged with having links to the militant Islamic Group (below). The government arrested more than 50 members of the group in July on charges of belonging to an illegal organization. Sentences of up to five years in prison were handed down against most of the defendants in early November, essentially precluding effective Brotherhood participation in the legislative balloting later that month. (It was subsequently reported that only one successful assembly candidate could be identified as a Brotherhood adherent.) The Brotherhood urged a boycott of the April 1997 local elections, claiming that many of its supporters and preferred candidates had been subjected to government "intimidation."

In January 1996 a number of former Brotherhood members reportedly launched a **Center Party** (*Hizb al-Wasat*) along with representatives of the Coptic community in an avowed effort to "heal the breaches" within the Egyptian populace. However, the government denied the party's request for recognition and arrested some 13 of its founders with purported Brotherhood ties. In August seven of the defendants were convicted of antigovernment activity by a military court and sentenced to three years in prison. *Al-Wasat* was again denied legal status in May 1998, the government describing it as insufficiently different from other parties

to warrant recognition. (See Other Legislative Parties, above.)

A number of the officially independent candidates in the 2000 assembly balloting were clearly identifiable as belonging to the Brotherhood, and 17 of them were elected, permitting the return of the Brotherhood to the assembly after a ten-year absence. Though Brotherhood leaders subsequently again denied any connection to militant groups, a number of Brotherhood members were arrested in the government crackdown on Islamists in late 2001 and early 2002.

The death of 83-year-old leader Mamoun al-HODAIBI on January 9, 2004, was seen as an opportunity to attract the younger generation, but on January 14 the party selected an "old guard" successor: Muhammad Mahdi Akef, 74. He maintained that the Brotherhood would not change its approach. Akef had been convicted in 1954 of the attempted assassination of President Nasser and served 20 years in prison.

While Akef called for dialogue with the government, in May 2004 security forces arrested 54 members of the Brotherhood and for the first time targeted the organization's funding sources, closing various businesses and the group's website. In March 2005, some 84 members were arrested in police raids in the midst of massive demonstrations, said to be the largest in Cairo's history. The Brotherhood ran 120 candidates as independents in the November–December 2005 assembly elections, securing 88 seats in balloting marked by violence, including the death of one Brotherhood supporter. It was widely reported that government security forces blocked some polls and detained scores of group members. Brotherhood leaders said they would use the gains made in representation to push for the abolition of laws that restrict political activity.

Leaders: Muhammad Mahdi AKEF, Mohamed HABIB, Mahmoud EZZAT (Secretary General), Mohamed HILAL.

Another group, referenced as the **Social Justice Party**, was formed in 1993 and led by Mohammad Abdul AALA. It was suspended in 2003.

Illegal Groups

Holy War (*al-Jihad*). A secret organization of militant Muslims who had reportedly split from the Muslim Brotherhood in the second half of the 1970s because of the latter's objection to the use of violence, *al-Jihad* was blamed for attacks against Copts in 1979 and the assassination of President Sadat in 1981. In the first half of the 1980s it appeared to be linked to the Islamic Group (below), but the two organizations emerged with more distinct identities during the mid-1980s. Although some observers described *al-Jihad* as continuing to seek recruits, particularly in the military, its influence appeared to have diminished in the late 1980s as the result of government infiltration of its ranks and growing support for the Islamic Group. However, security officials charged that a revival of the group was attempted in the first half of the 1990s in conjunction with the increasingly violent fundamentalist/government conflict. A number of reported *al-Jihad* supporters were imprisoned in mid-1993 on charges of plotting the overthrow of the government, while, according to authorities, about 30 members were arrested in an April 1994 security sweep. Meanwhile, members of an apparent splinter, variously referenced as New *Jihad* or the Vanguards of Conquest (*Talai al-Fath*), were subsequently given death sentences for complicity in assassination plots against top government officials. Some reports linked that activity to Ayman al-ZAWAHIRI, a former Cairo surgeon who had been imprisoned (and reportedly subjected to extreme torture) for three years following the assassination of President Sadat. Zawahiri was also reportedly linked to the bombing of the Egyptian embassy in Pakistan in 1995.

In 1998, in the wake of the Luxor attack of 1997, Zawahiri and his brother, Mohammad al-ZAWAHIRI, were described as attempting to "reorganize" *al-Jihad* from Afghanistan, where they had reportedly established ties with the *al-Qaida* network of Osama bin Laden. (Ayman al-Zawahiri had not been seen in Egypt since 1986.) Among other things, Ayman al-Zawahiri endorsed bin Laden's 1998 call for attacks on "Jews and Crusaders" (the latter a reference to Americans and their allies). At that point it appeared that a portion of *al-Jihad*, having been effectively suppressed in Egypt, had shifted away from a goal of overthrowing the Egyptian government to a global anti-Western campaign in concert with al-Qaida. However, some members of *al-Jihad* reportedly objected to that new focus and split from Zawahiri.

A number of alleged *al-Jihad* adherents received long prison terms in early 1999, while nine were sentenced to death in absentia, including Ayman al-Zawahiri and Yasser al-SIRRI, a London-based leader. Zawahiri was also indicted in absentia in 1999 in the United States for his alleged role in the planning of the bombings of the U.S. embassies in Kenya and Pakistan in 1998. Following the attacks on the United States in September 2001 that were quickly attributed to al-Qaida, Zawahiri, noted for his organizational skills, was described as the number two leader, after bin Laden, in that network. Some reports linked Zawahiri to the July 2005 bombings in Sharm El-Sheikh, Egypt, that killed at least 64 people. As of mid-2006, he continued to elude U.S. authorities.

Islamic Group (*Gamaat i-Islami*). The Islamic Group surfaced in the late 1970s as the student wing of the Muslim Brotherhood, subsequently breaking from that organization and aligning (until the mid-1980s) with *al-Jihad* in seeking overthrow of the government. Having gained adherents among the poor in the Cairo slums and the villages in southern Egypt, it served as a loosely knit, but highly militant, umbrella organization for as many as three dozen smaller organizations. The government accused the Group of spearheading attacks on security forces, government officials, and tourists beginning in 1992, and hanged a number of its members who had been convicted of terrorist activity.

Egyptian authorities in the mid-1990s asked the United States to extradite Sheikh Omar ABDEL RAHMAN, the blind theologian who is reputed to be the spiritual leader of the Islamic Group and had been in self-imposed exile in the New York City area since 1990. In April 1994 Sheikh Abdel Rahman was sentenced in absentia by an Egyptian security court to seven years in prison for inciting his followers to violence in 1989. In addition, 25 codefendants received jail terms of various lengths. In January 1996 Sheikh Abdel Rahman was sentenced to life in prison in the United States following his conviction on charges of conspiring to commit a series of bombings in the New York City area. Eight codefendants were given prison terms of 25 years to life. Meanwhile, Safwat Abd al-Ghani, viewed as the political leader of the Group, was confined to prison in Egypt on a charge of illegal weapons possession. Ghani and other Islamic Group defendants had initially been charged with murder in the 1990 assassination of Assembly President Rifat al-Mahgoub; however, the charges were dismissed in 1993 following a court ruling that confessions had been extracted from them by torture.

Talaat Yassin HAMMAN, described by Egyptian authorities as the "military commander" of the Islamic Group, was killed by security forces in April 1994. His "intended successor," Ahmad Hassan Abd al-GALIL, also died in a shoot-out with police the following November. It was subsequently reported that Group military activities were being conducted under the leadership of Mustapha HAMZA and Rifai TAHA, apparently based in Afghanistan.

Two members of the Group were executed in February 1995 after being convicted of a bombing in which a German tourist was killed, while two others were executed in late March for the attempted killing of Nobel laureate Naguib MAHFOUZ in October 1994. The Egyptian government also accused the Group (and Hamza in particular) of being behind a June 1995 attempt on the life of President Mubarak in Ethiopia.

In mid-1996 reports surfaced that a faction of the Islamic Group had signaled an interest in negotiations with the government. However, that possibility was apparently rejected by the Mubarak administration. Factionalization within the Group was also apparent in 1997, particularly in regard to a "cease-fire" ordered by its imprisoned leaders at midyear. Although the militants responsible for the attack at Luxor in November appeared linked to the Group, long-standing Group leaders disavowed responsibility, suggesting they were no longer in control of at least some "rogue" guerrilla cells. Subsequently, spokesmen for the Group emphasized that it had reached "political maturity" and had renounced violence in favor of attempting to establish an Islamic state in Egypt through the political process. Sheikh Abdel Rahman appeared to endorse that shift in late 1998 when he called on his followers to pursue "peaceful means," and the Islamic Group announced in March 1999 that a unilateral cease-fire was in effect. That cease-fire remained in effect through mid-2005. Islamic Group members still committed to violence reportedly subsequently joined the al-Qaida network of Osama bin Laden. In April 2006, it was reported that Egyptian authorities had released 950 members of the organization, though officials denied having released that number and said those who were released posed no risk to national security.

Leaders: Safwat Abd al-GHANI, Salah HASHEM, Talaat Fuad QASIM (Spokesman in Europe).

Islamic Liberation Party (*Hizb al-Tahrir al-Islami*). This radical political movement wants to create an Islamic society in Egypt and is on the United States' list of foreign terrorist organizations.

In September 2002 some 51 defendants were given jail sentences in connection with the alleged activity of a clandestine organization known as *al-Waad* (The Pledge). First arrested on charges of belonging to an illegal organization, the defendants were also subsequently accused of planning violent acts in pursuit of the establishment of an Islamic state in Egypt. In early 2005 an Egyptian court upheld a five-year sentence for Mohammed Abdel Fattah, convicted along with 24 others the previous year, but Fattah managed to escape. He and the others were accused of trying to reorganize the party, which has been banned since 1974.

Also subject to government crackdowns have been the Islamic fundamentalist **Survivors from Hell** (*al-Najoun Min al-Nar*), charged in 1988 with

Cabinet

As of April 1, 2006

Prime Minister	Ahmed Mahmoud Muhammad Nazif
Deputy Prime Minister	Yussef Amin Wali

Ministers

Agriculture	Amin Ahmed Muhammad Othman Abaza
Civil Aviation	Lt. Gen. Ahmad Shafiq
Communications and Information Technology	Tariq Muhammad Kamal
Culture	Faruq Abd al-Aziz Husni
Defense and Military Production	Fld. Mar. Muhammad Hussein Tantawi Sulayman
Education	Youssri Saber Husayn al-Gamal
Electricity and Energy	Hassan Ahmed Younes
Finance	Yussef Boutros-Ghali
Foreign Affairs	Ahmed Ali Abu al-Ghayt
Foreign Trade and Industry	Rashid Muhammad Rashid
Health and Population	Hatem Moustafa Moustafa al-Gabaly
Higher Education	Hani Mafouz Helal
Housing, Utilities, and Urban Communities	Ahmed al-Maghrabi
Information	Anas Ahmed al-Fiqy
Interior	Gen. Habib al-Adli
International Cooperation	Fayza Abu-al-Naga [f]
Investment	Mahmoud Muhiy al-Din
Irrigation and Water Resources	Mahmoud Abd al-Halim Abu Zayd
Justice	Mahmoud Abu Lail Rashid
Legal Affairs and Parliamentary Councils	Mufid Mahmoud Mahmoud Shebab
Manpower and Immigration	Aisha Abdel Hady Abdel Ghany [f]
Petroleum	Amin Sameh Samir Fahmi
Planning and Local Development	Othman Muhammad Othman
Religious Trusts	Mahmoud Hamdi Zakzuk
Social Security	Ali Moselhi
Tourism	Ahmed al-Maghrabi
Transport	Isam Abd al-Aziz Sharaf

Ministers of State

Administrative Development	Ahmed Mahmoud Darwish
Environmental Affairs	Majid George Ghattas
Military Production	Sayed Abdou Moustafa Meshal

[f] = female

the attempted murder of two anti-Muslim former government ministers, and **Denouncement and Holy Flight** (*Takfir wa al-Hijra*). (Some 245 members of the latter were reportedly arrested in April 1996.) An obscure Islamic group, **Islamic Pride Brigades of the Land of the Nile**, claimed responsibility for a bombing in the heart of Cairo in April 2005.

Clandestine left-wing formations against which the government has moved energetically in the past included, most prominently, the **Egyptian Communist Party** (*al-Hizb al-Shuyui al-Misri*). Founded in 1921, the party subsequently experienced numerous cleavages that yielded, among others, the **Egyptian Communist Labor Party** and the Maoist **Revolutionary Current.** In 1990 another splinter, the **People's Socialist Party**, was launched under the leadership of veteran Communist Michel KAMEL, who later died in exile in France.

Two Islamist groupings—the **Reform (***Islah***) Party**, formed in 1997 under the leadership of Gamal SULTAN; and the **Islamic Law (***Sharia***) Party**—sought permission to participate in the 2000 assembly elections, but their applications were emphatically rejected by the government.

Legislature

The **People's Assembly** (*Majlis al-Shaab*) is a unicameral legislature elected in two-round balloting for a five-year term. As sanctioned by a popular referendum, President Sadat dissolved the existing assembly (which had two years remaining in its term) on April 21, 1979, and announced expansion of the body from 350 to 392 members, in part to accommodate representatives from the Sinai. Prior to the election of May 27, 1984, the assembly was further expanded to 458 members, including 10 appointed by the president.

On May 19, 1990, the Supreme Constitutional Court voided the results of an assembly poll of April 6, 1987, because of improper restrictions on opposition and independent candidates, and an October 11 referendum approved formal dissolution of the body. A new election, boycotted by most of the leading opposition formations, was held November 29 and December 6, 1990, the assembly having been reduced to 454 members, including the 10 presidential appointees.

Elections to the current assembly were held in November–December 2005. First-round balloting was conducted for three groups of districts on three days (November 9 and 20 and December 1); second-round balloting was held six days after each first round. The government reported that some 5,000 candidates competed for 444 seats. The results for 12 seats were annulled. The government reported the seat distribution for the remaining 432 seats as follows: the National Democratic Party (NDP), 265; the New Wafd Party (NWP), 6; the National Progressive Unionist Party (NPUP), 1; the Liberal Socialist Party, 1; the Tomorrow Party, 1; independents 157; and vacant, 1. However, it was widely agreed that 88 of the independent candidates were clearly identified as allied with the Muslim Brotherhood, while many of the remaining independents were considered allied with the NDP. (Most news reports credited the NDP with having secured 320–324 seats.) Ten parties and groups fielded candidates under a coalition referenced as the National Front for Change.

President: Dr. Ahmad Fathi SURUR.

Communications

The Supreme Press Council, established under a constitutional amendment in May 1980, oversees newspaper and magazine activity while government boards also direct the state information service, radio, and television. The government retains 51 percent ownership (exercised through the *Shura*) of many major newspapers and consequently exercises substantial editorial control. Although the development of an active and often highly critical opposition press was permitted in the 1980s, significant censorship has been imposed in recent years in conjunction with the conflict between the government and Islamic fundamentalist militants. A new press law was adopted in May 1995 providing for prison sentences and heavy fines for, among other things, "insulting" public officials or state institutions. However, in June 1996 some of the harshest elements of the new code were rescinded after the government was strongly criticized by domestic and international journalists for attempting to "muzzle" the press.

In February 2005, the president announced an end to imprisonment for various publication offenses, yet three months later, three journalists from an independent daily were found guilty of libeling the housing minister and sentenced to a year in jail. In July 2005 the government reshuffled the leadership of the press, appointing new heads to all the major government dailies.

Press

The following are Cairo dailies published in Arabic, unless otherwise noted: *al-Ahram* (1,000,000 daily, 1,200,000 Friday), semiofficial with *al-Ahram al-Massai* as an evening daily; *al-Akhbar* (800,000), Saturday edition published as *Akhbar al-Yawm* (1,100,000); *al-Jumhuriyah* (650,000), semi-official; *al-Misaa; Le Journal d'Egypte* (72,000), in French; *Egyptian Gazette* (36,000), in English; *Le Progrès Egyptien* (22,000), in French; *al-Hayat*. Among other newspapers are *al-Destour*, independent weekly; *al-Usbu*, independent "nationalist" weekly; and *al-Masr al-Yawm*. The party organs include the Socialist Labor Party's bi-weekly *al-Shaab* (50,000), which was closed in April 2005; the Socialist Liberal weekly *al-Ahrar;* the National Progressive Unionist weekly *al-Ahali;* The New Wafd's daily *al-Wafd;* the NDP's weekly *Shabab Beladi;* the Nasserist Arab Democratic Party's *al-Arabi;* the Tomorrow Party's *al-Ghad;* the National Party's weekly *al-Umma;* and the Green Party's weekly *al-Khudr.*

News Agencies

The domestic agency is the Middle East News Agency—MENA (*Wakalat al-Anba al-Sharq al-Awsat*). In addition, numerous foreign bureaus maintain offices in Cairo.

Broadcasting and Computing

The Egyptian Radio and Television Union (ERTU) operates numerous radio stations broadcasting in Arabic and other languages, and some three dozen television stations transmitting in two programs. Commercial radio service is offered by Middle East Radio (*Idhaat al-Sharq al-Awsat*). There were approximately 18.7 million television receivers and 1.5 million personal computers serving 2.7 million Internet users in 2003.

The first Egyptian communications satellite was launched by the European Space Agency in 1998; some 80 channels were expected to be broadcast regionally by the satellite, known as "Nilesat," under the control of the ERTU.

Intergovernmental Representation

Ambassador to the U.S.
Nabil FAHMY

U.S. Ambassador to Egypt
Francis Joseph RICCIARDONE Jr.

Permanent Representative to the UN
Maged Abdelfattah ABDELAZIZ

IGO Memberships (Non-UN)
AfDB, AFESD, AMF, AU, BADEA, CAEU, Comesa, IDB, Interpol, IOM, LAS, NAM, OAPEC, OIC, OIF, PCA, WCO, WTO

EQUATORIAL GUINEA

REPUBLIC OF EQUATORIAL GUINEA

República de Guinea Ecuatorial

Note: Prime Minister Borico and the entire cabinet resigned on August 10, 2006, after having been criticized for poor performance by President Obiang. The president subsequently appointed Ricardo Mangue Obama Nfube of the Democratic Party of Equatorial Guinea to head a new cabinet that was appointed on August 16.

The Country

The least populous and the only Spanish-speaking black African nation, Equatorial Guinea consists of two sharply differing regions: the mainland territory of Río Muni, including Corisco, Elobey Grande, and Elobey Chico islands as well as adjacent islets; and the island of Bioko (known prior to 1973 as Fernando Póo and from 1973 to 1979 as Macías Nguema Biyogo), including Pagalu (known prior to 1973 as Annobón) and adjacent islets in the Gulf of Guinea. Río Muni, whose area is 10,045 square miles (26,017 sq. km.), accounts for more than nine-tenths of the country's territory and about three-quarters of its total population; Bata is the principal urban center. Bioko's area covers 785 square miles (2,034 sq. km.); Malabo is the chief town and the capital of the republic.

The two basic ethnic groups, both Bantu sub-groupings, are the Fang, who reportedly account for the majority of the population, and the Bubi, primarily located in Bioko. (Bubi/Fang friction remains an important issue on Bioko, while resentment has also reportedly surfaced among the rest of Fang over the dominance within that group of President Obiang's Mongomo sub-clan.) Other elements include the Kombe and various coastal tribes in Río Muni, and Fernandinos (persons of mixed racial descent) in Bioko. Roman Catholicism is the religion of approximately 80 percent of the population.

Until the discovery of oil in the mid-1990s, the economy was dominated by agriculture, the principal exports being cocoa, coffee, and timber. Industry consisted primarily of small-scale agriprocessing operations, while a small fishing sector also operated. Following the August 1979 coup, substantial aid was tendered by Spain, France, and other international donors to help Equatorial Guinea recover from the economic devastation of the Macie era, during which most skilled workers were killed or fled the country, cocoa

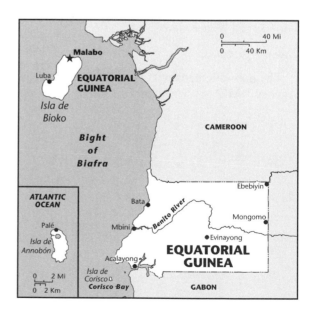

production and per capita GNP plummeted, and such essential urban services as power and water were disrupted. In contrast to the Eastern-bloc affiliation of its predecessor, the post-Macie government adopted generally pro-Western, free-market policies. However, economic recovery was initially slow, the adverse effects of high budget and trade deficits, inflation, and a burdensome external debt being only partially offset by improvements resulting from Equatorial Guinea's admission to the franc zone in 1985. Cocoa and timber prices also declined in the late 1980s, further complicating the situation.

Equatorial Guinea's economic prospects surged dramatically in the mid-1990s when significant oil and gas reserves were discovered off the north coast of Bioko. Pumping began in 1996 and had reached more than 100,000 barrels per day by early 1999; concurrently, GDP grew by nearly 100 percent in both 1997 and 1998. However, there was broad concern over the distribution of the oil wealth, reports indicating that it had been concentrated in the hands of only 5 percent of the population. Members of President Obiang's sub-clan were believed to have benefited most extensively, and international donors restricted aid over the lack of transparency in the oil sector and perceived widespread corruption in government and business. Meanwhile, it has been estimated that as much as 75 percent of the population remained impoverished, the World Bank and International Monetary Fund (IMF) insisting that income from oil exploitation be redirected toward social services and infrastructure development.

By the end of 2001, the country's long-term economic prospects had been buoyed by additional discoveries of oil and potentially lucrative gas deposits. After peaking at nearly 50 percent in 2001 (earning Equatorial Guinea the reputation of having the world's fastest-growing economy), GDP growth slowed to 10 percent in 2005. Naturally, the ongoing oil boom underpinned the expansion as production rose to 356,000 barrels per day; however, the non-oil sector also grew by an average of 5 13 percent in 2005. The increased revenue provided the government with regular budget surpluses, although critics continued to cite perceived corruption and inefficiency, and widespread poverty persisted. The IMF urged interim strategies in 2005 to help the country meet its poverty reduction objectives.

Government and Politics

Political Background

The former territory of Spanish Guinea, with Spanish sovereignty dating from 1778, was granted provincial status in 1959 and internal autonomy in 1964, achieving full independence under the name of Equatorial Guinea on October 12, 1968. The pre-independence negotiations with Spain had been complicated by differences between the mainland Fang, whose representatives sought the severance of all links with Spain, and the island Bubi, whose spokesmen advocated retention of some ties with Spain and semiautonomous status within a federal system. A compromise constitution and electoral law, submitted for popular approval in a UN supervised referendum on August 11, 1968, was accepted by 63 percent of the people, the substantial adverse vote reflecting Bubi fears of mainland domination as well as Fang objections to the degree of self-rule accorded the islanders. In presidential balloting a month later, MACÍAS Nguema Biyogo, a mainland Fang associated with the Popular Idea of Equatorial Guinea (*Idea Popular de Guinea Ecuatorial*—IPGE), defeated the head of the pre-independence autonomous government, Bonifacio ONDO Edu of the Movement for the National Unity of Equatorial Guinea (*Movimiento de Union Nacional de Guinea Ecuatorial*—MUNGE).

In 1969 President Macías seized emergency powers during a major international crisis involving tribal rivalries, personality conflicts, allegations of continued Spanish colonialism, and conflicting foreign economic interests. Following an unsuccessful coup d'état led by Foreign Minister Atanasio N'DONGO Miyone of the National Movement for the Liberation of Equatorial Guinea (*Movimiento Nacional de Liberación de la Guinea Ecuatorial*—Monalige), the president arrested some 200

Area: 10,830 sq. mi. (28,051 sq. km.).

Population: 300,000 (1983C); 519,000 (2005E).

Major Urban Centers (2005E): MALABO (Bioko, 90,000), Bata (Río Muni, 70,000).

Official Language: Spanish. (French was adopted as a "commercial" language in September 1997 during a period of friction between Malabo and Madrid. In addition various African dialects are spoken, and pidgin English serves as a commercial lingua franca.)

Monetary Unit: CFA franc (official rate July 1, 2006: 513.01 CFA francs = $1US). (The CFA franc, previously pegged to the French franc, is now permanently pegged to the euro at 655.957 CFA francs = 1 euro.)

President: Gen. Teodoro OBIANG Nguema Mbasogo (Democratic Party of Equatorial Guinea), assumed power as president of a Supreme Military Council following the ouster of MACIE (formerly Francisco Macías) Nguema Biyogo Ñegue Ndong on August 3, 1979; inaugurated October 12, 1982, following confirmation for a seven-year term by constitutional referendum on August 15; reelected for seven-year terms on June 25, 1989, February 25, 1996, and, in early elections, on December 15, 2002.

Prime Minister: (*See headnote.*) Miguel Abia Biteo BORICO (Democratic Party of Equatorial Guinea); named by the president on June 14, 2004, to replace Cándido Muatetema RIVAS, who had resigned on June 11; formed new government on June 16, 2004.

individuals, most of whom (including N'Dongo) were executed. An accompanying panic, aggravated by the extralegal activities of Macías's youth militia, provoked the flight of the country's Spanish population. Subsequently, a highly centralized, single-party state was instituted, Macías's control being formalized by his assuming the presidency for life in July 1972. Along with other Equatorial Guineans, Macías dropped his Christian name (Francisco) on September 26, 1975; in 1976 he also changed his surname from Macías to Macie.

The 11-year rule of Macías/Macie (during which the country became widely known as the "Auschwitz of Africa") was terminated on August 3, 1979, in a coup led by the president's nephew, Lt. Col. Teodoro OBIANG Nguema Mbasogo, who assumed the presidency of a Supreme Military Council that later in the month named Capt. Florencio MAYÉ Elá and Capt. Salvador ELÁ Nseng as first and second vice presidents, respectively. In February 1980 Elá Nseng was succeeded by Capt. Eulogio OYO Riquesa, presiding officer of the military tribunal that had ordered Macie's execution on September 29, 1979, for crimes that included genocide, treason, and embezzlement. The government was further reshuffled in early December 1981, the first vice presidency becoming vacant in the wake of Mayé Elá's assignment to the United Nations and Capt. Cristino SERICHE Bioko succeeding Oyo Riquesa as second vice president.

Concurrent with the adoption, by referendum, of a new constitution on August 15, 1982, Colonel Obiang was confirmed as president for a seven-year term. Subsequently, Captain Seriche was named prime minister, the two vice-presidential roles being eliminated. The first National Assembly election mandated by the new constitution was held on August 28, 1983.

An attempted coup of unclear origin (the third since 1981) failed to unseat Colonel Obiang in July 1986 while he was in France attending Bastille Day celebrations. At first, the government denied a revolt had occurred; a month later, however, Eugenio ABESO Mondu, a former diplomat and a member of the National Assembly, was executed for his alleged involvement, with 12 others, including prominent cabinet members and military officers, being sentenced to jail terms.

In late 1987 President Obiang launched a government formation, the Democratic Party of Equatorial Guinea (*Partido Democrático de Guinea Ecuatorial*—PDGE), as a precursor to political liberalization. However, there was little immediate movement in that direction: as in 1983 a July 1988 legislative poll was strictly pro forma, and Obiang was the only candidate at presidential balloting in June 1989. Although Obiang hailed his reelection as the launching of a democratization process and invited political exiles to return, he rejected suggestions that a multiparty system be introduced, arguing that "political pluralism would send convulsions through the population." However, in 1990 failure to implement political reforms severely constricted foreign aid and investment. As a result, an extraordinary PDGE congress in August endorsed the adoption of a democratic constitution, which was overwhelmingly approved in a referendum of November 17, 1991. On January 23, 1992, the president appointed a new administration, headed by Silvestre SIALE Bileka as prime minister, to serve "as a prelude to the introduction of multiparty politics," and in late May the government legalized the first two of six parties.

Meanwhile, tensions between Obiang and the opposition continued to mount, with the latter accusing the government of killing an opposition activist, Feliciano MOTO, and attempting to intimidate prodemocracy advocates. The regime denied involvement in Moto's death, but in September 1992 the president's brother, National Security Director Armando NGOR Nguema, was linked to the violent breakup of a meeting of the newly formed Joint Opposition Platform (*Plataforma de la Oposición Conjunta*—POC).

Political discord continued into 1993, with Washington in mid-January accusing the Obiang regime of engaging in torture, intimidation, and unlawful imprisonment of its opponents. On March 3 the U.S. ambassador was called home for "consultations" after allegedly being targeted by a government-inspired death threat. A week later the UN Commission for Human Rights (UNCHR) announced that it would appoint a special rapporteur to monitor conditions in Equatorial Guinea.

At poorly attended legislative balloting on November 21, 1993, the PDGE, aided by the POC's boycott, dominated the eight-party field, capturing 68 of the 80 seats. Both Spain and the United States denounced the proceedings, while the POC termed the low voter turnout a "slap in the face to the dictatorship" and insisted that absentee voters should be considered its supporters. Undeterred, the government on December 6 imposed a ban on unauthorized opposition demonstrations. Furthermore, the cabinet named two weeks later, again headed by Prime Minister Siale Bileka, included no opposition members.

International and domestic dissatisfaction with the Obiang regime continued to mount in 1994. In January Spain suspended aid payments to Malabo, protesting the president's apparent attempts to derail the democratization process, and in February Amnesty International condemned the government's human rights record. In April the administration urged opposition members to participate in a voter registration drive organized to prepare for municipal elections (then) scheduled for November. However, in August negotiations were suspended with a prominent opposition party, the Progress Party of Equatorial Guinea (*Partido del Progresso de Guinea Ecuatorial*—PPGE), after its leader, Severo MOTO Nsa, had criticized the government, and on October 5 two people were killed in a clash between government troops and demonstrators in Malabo. Subsequently, the government suffered a major setback when House speaker Felipe Ondo OBIANG Alogo and his deputy, Antonio Pascual Oko EBOBO, both prominent PDGE members, resigned on October 25, because of the "very poor management" that had led Equatorial Guinea into a "disastrous social and economic situation."

The nation's first multiparty municipal elections were held on September 17, 1995, the PDGE being credited with victories in 18 of the 27 localities. However, domestic and international observers challenged the government's voting tally, the POC arguing that the opposition had really garnered about 80 percent of the votes.

In yet another questionable tactic, Obiang decreed on January 12, 1996, that presidential elections would be held on February 25, three months before his term was set to expire. Opposition leaders immediately denounced the president's actions as unconstitutional and designed to preclude effective organization on their part. By late January a number of opposition candidates had emerged, including the PPGE's Moto and three from the POC. However, the subsequent run-up was reportedly marked by gross malfeasance, including harassment of opposition activists and replacement of a UN-compiled electoral list with a government list that excluded voters in regions that had supported the opposition in previous polling. Consequently, most opposition candidates ultimately withdrew and called on their supporters to boycott the election.

At the February 25, 1996, polling President Obiang was credited with 97.85 percent of the votes. However, citing the prepolling malpractice, apparent election day irregularities, and the dearth of impartial international election monitors, most observers dismissed the election as a sham. On March 29 Obiang appointed Angel Serafin Seriche DOUGAN to succeed Prime Minister Siale Bileka. Several parliamentary parties joined the expanded cabinet announced on April 9, although, not surprisingly, the major opposition groupings declined Obiang's invitation to join in a government of national unity. On January 15, 1998, Dougan and his cabinet resigned in accordance with a presidential mandate that required the prime minister to submit his government for review after two years in office. Two days later, Obiang reappointed Dougan head of a reshuffled government. In mid-January 1998 Prime Minister Dougan's claim to having preserved "national unity" during his first term was challenged in Bioko Island, where ethnic Bubi separatists reportedly attacked government offices. (The Bubi were the dominant group on the island until independence but since then have been surpassed in numbers by the Fang.) Denying a role in the violence, leaders of the Movement for the Self-Determination of the Island of Bioko—MAIB (see Political Parties, below) charged the government with a "veritable genocide" and reaffirmed their desire for self-rule. In March the Obiang administration denied charges by Amnesty International that it was torturing separatist prisoners. Thereafter, a military court sentenced 15 of the separatists to death in June for their alleged roles in the uprising, although the president commuted the death sentences in September following the prison death of a dissident who had reportedly been beaten by security forces. (The president's acts of clemency came amid speculation that his international economic sponsors were reconsidering their support.) Meanwhile, the government had reportedly arrested dozens of opposition activists in an apparent attempt to disrupt their preparations for legislative balloting (then scheduled for late 1998, but subsequently postponed until early 1999). At balloting on March 7, 1999, the PDGE increased its legislative dominance, capturing 75 of the 80 posts in polling that was reportedly again marked by widespread irregularities. On July 9 Obiang reappointed Dougan prime minister, and on July 22 Dougan announced a streamlined and reshuffled cabinet.

The PDGE reportedly won 230 of 244 seats and control of all 30 municipal councils in the local elections of May 28, 2000. Observers described the balloting as generally free and fair, although its significance was greatly undercut by the fact that three leading independent parties boycotted what they described as just the most recent "electoral farce." Some analysts suggested that Western capitals were ignoring the lack of democratic progress (to say nothing of continued human rights violations) in view of the dramatic surge of oil production.

In light of continued corruption allegations against various government officials, President Obiang reportedly asked Prime Minister Dougan to resign as early as October 2000, although it wasn't until February 23, 2001, that Dougan acquiesced to the pressure. Incoming prime minister Cándido Muatetema RIVAS, a former deputy secretary general of the PDGE, pledged the new government, which included members of several small parties in junior positions, would protect the "economic" and "social" rights of all citizens while maintaining the "stability" that the country has enjoyed for more than two decades. For its part, the "frail" opposition charged that oil proceeds were being diverted to promote a "clan dictatorship," a reference to reports of maneuvering within the president's ethnic group to ensure long-term retention of power.

Amid continuing political turmoil and continued government suppression of the opposition, President Obiang moved the next presidential balloting up from February 2003 to December 15, 2002. Most opposition parties ultimately boycotted the election, and Obiang was reelected with 97.1 percent of the vote. Although Obiang had promised to appoint a government of national unity, he reappointed Rivas to head a reshuffled cabinet that was again dominated by the PDGE and included two of Obiang's sons.

The PDGE and its allies (the newly formed Democratic Opposition Coalition) won 98 of 100 seats in the April 25, 2004, balloting for the House of People's Representatives. They also secured nearly all of the seats in concurrent municipal elections. Prime Minister Rivas resigned on June 11 and was succeeded three days later by Miguel Abia Biteo BORICO.

Constitution and Government

The 1982 constitution provided for an elected president serving a seven-year term and for a Council of State, one of whose functions was to screen candidates for presidential nomination. A National Council for Economic and Social Development was linked to the administration in a consultative capacity, while legislative functions were assigned to a unicameral National Assembly, whose members were elected for five-year terms.

The basic law of November 1991 called for a separation of functions between the president and prime minister, while authorizing competing parties. At the same time, it severely limited opposition activity by banning from presidential or parliamentary eligibility all individuals who had not been continuously resident in the country for the preceding two years. In addition, it stipulated that the head of state could "not be impeached, or called as a witness before, during and after his term of office." Subsequent legislation on the formation of political parties specified that no such group could be organized on a tribal, regional, or provincial basis.

In late 1980 the country was divided into 6 provinces (4 mainland and 2 insular) as part of a process of administrative reform, while there are currently 30 elected municipal governments.

Foreign Relations

While officially nonaligned, the Macie regime tended to follow the lead of the more radical African states. Diplomatic relations were established with—and aid received from—several Communist regimes, including the Soviet Union, the People's Republic of China, Cuba, and North Korea. Relations with Gabon and Cameroon were strained as a result of territorial disputes, while by 1976 the mistreatment of Nigerian contract workers had led Lagos to repatriate some 25,000 people, most of them cocoa plantation laborers. By contrast, the Obiang regime has striven for regional cooperation, with a Nigerian consulate opening in Bata in 1982 and a joint defense pact being concluded during a three-day official visit to Lagos by President Obiang in January 1987. Economic agreements were signed with Cameroon and the Central African Republic in 1983, and Obiang was active in the formation of the Central African Economic Community, announced in October 1983. Two months later, Equatorial Guinea became the first non-French-speaking member of the Central African Customs and Economic Union (UDEAC). As the only African country with Spanish as its official language, Equatorial Guinea was also anxious to develop links with Latin America and was accorded permanent observer status with the Organization of American States (OAS).

At the time of Macie's ouster, France was the only Western power maintaining an embassy in Malabo, although Spain had long been purchasing export commodities at above-market prices. Madrid made its first overture to the new regime in December 1979 with a state visit by King Juan Carlos, in the wake of which economic and military assistance was tendered; in 1983, it played a leading role in renegotiating the country's $45 million foreign debt. Nevertheless, following Equatorial Guinea's admission to the franc zone in 1985, Malabo emphasized rapidly expanding ties with France and francophone West African countries.

Frayed by Spain's criticism of Equatorial Guinea's political and human rights practices, ties between the two countries weakened steadily during 1993. In August the government of Equatorial Guinea charged Madrid with inciting antigovernment violence at Annobon Island. In late November Spain formally refused to underwrite the legislative balloting, saying it failed to meet "minimum requirements," and following the expulsion of its consul general in Bata, Madrid recalled its ambassador. Among other Western observers, only France openly supported the electoral process, with the United States and the United Nations refusing to provide poll watchers.

In September 1997 Equatorial Guinea temporarily suspended diplomatic relations with Spain after Madrid refused to repeal the refugee status of PPGE leader Severo Moto Nsa. (For further details about the Moto case, see the PPGE below and the 1998 edition of the *Handbook*.)

In mid-1999 Equatorial Guinea filed a complaint against Cameroon with the International Court of Justice (ICJ) after it was revealed that Yaoundé had made territorial claims to a section of the Gulf of Guinea that included Bioko Island. Fueling the Malabo-Yaoundé dispute, as well as an ongoing border disagreement between Equatorial Guinea and Nigeria, were the recent discoveries of offshore oil deposits. In an effort to reduce tensions and increase cooperation in the Gulf region, a Gulf of Guinea Commission was established in November by Equatorial Guinea, Angola, Congo, Gabon, Nigeria, and São Tome e Príncipe. Subsequently, in September 2000, Equatorial Guinea and Nigeria settled their border dispute, each country gaining sovereignty over one of the two major disputed oil fields.

Full economic ties with Spain were restored by 2001, and Madrid in 2003 forgave some $65 million of Equatorial Guinea's external debt. In addition, Spain offered diplomatic support to Equatorial Guinea when Gabonese troops occupied the disputed island of Mbagne. Gabon subsequently offered to withdraw its troops in exchange for an oil-sharing agreement that would cover the island and its surrounding waters, but President Obiang rejected that proposal. In January 2004 Gabon and Equatorial Guinea agreed to abide by the decision of a UN mediator appointed to investigate the dispute. However, by early 2006 the dispute had yet to be resolved.

The United States reopened its embassy in Equatorial Guinea in 2003 as U.S. companies continued to dominate oil exploration and production in Equatorial Guinea.

Current Issues

The already strained relations between the regime and the opposition deteriorated even further when the government in March 2002 initiated a major crackdown that included the arrest of numerous party leaders. The government claimed it was responding to an alleged coup conspiracy, although the opposition and some members of the international community accused Obiang of merely trying to clear the way for his reelection.

In the aftermath of Obiang's victory in the December 2002 presidential elections, a new cabinet was formed that included the president's son Teodoro Nguema OBIANG Mangue as minister of agriculture, fisheries and animal husbandry. Speculation continued that Obiang's son was being prepared as his successor. Meanwhile, international observers widely agreed with Obiang's domestic critics that the presidential poll and the legislative elections of April 2004 were deeply flawed—or even fraudulent and invalid.

In December 2003 a number of senior military officers were arrested on suspicion of plotting a coup, and most were given secret trials beginning in February 2004. Meanwhile, in March 2004, 19 others were arrested in a separate alleged coup plot. Finally, in a bizarre series of events that attracted substantial worldwide attention, Zimbabwe detained 70 suspected mercenaries en route to Equatorial Guinea. Simon MANN, a former British special forces officer, was charged with masterminding the plot. The group went on trial in Zimbabwe in July 2004, and many pleaded guilty to minor offenses, including illegal possession of weapons and immigration violations, and received minor sentences. On August 25, 2004, Mark THATCHER, son of former British prime minister Margaret THATCHER, was arrested in South Africa and charged with providing $275,000 to support the coup. On January 19, 2005, he pleaded guilty in exchange for a large fine ($506,000), a suspended jail sentence, and the opportunity to leave South Africa for the United States. A condition of his release was that Thatcher answer questions about his role for Equatorial Guinean prosecutors. Later that year Malabo lost its claim for civil damages in the case in a British court.

Obiang accused a variety of foreign governments, including Spain and the United Kingdom, of being involved in the coup attempt and ordered the forced deportation of several hundred foreign nationals. Obiang also ordered the arrest of a number of opposition figures, and accused exiled members of the opposition of involvement in the attempted overthrow. Most of the mercenaries were released from prison in Zimbabwe in May 2005.

Early in 2006, U.S. Secretary of State Condoleezza Rice drew criticism for meeting with President Obiang in Washington in the wake of State Department accusations of torture and other human rights violations, particularly regarding prisoners. One day earlier Obiang had signed a U.S. aid agreement.

Political Parties

Political parties were banned in the wake of the 1979 coup. In late 1987 President Obiang announced the formation of a government party (the Democratic Party of Equatorial Guinea—PDGE), as part of what he called a democratization process that might eventually lead to the legalization of other groups. In late 1991 and early 1992 the Obiang regime approved legislation that (albeit with restrictive provisions, including a requirement that applicant groups pay a deposit of approximately $110,000) provided a legal framework for the formation of political parties. In May 1992 two parties, the Liberal Democratic Convention (CLD) and the Popular Union (UP), were registered, and by the end of the year four more had been legalized.

During February 10–March 18, 1993, the government sponsored an assembly of the PDGE and the (then) ten legal opposition parties to discuss ways to improve the "democratization process," including lessened restrictions on party activities and increased access to state funds and media. Nevertheless, charging a lack of government action, most opposition parties declared that they would boycott elections then scheduled for August. Ultimately, eight parties, including the PDGE, took part in the November balloting; however, the three leading members of the Joint Opposition Platform (POC) refused to participate. After suffering from what they perceived as government electoral abuses in the September 1995 municipal elections, many opposition parties boycotted the February 1996 presidential poll.

For its part, the POC was unable to agree upon a single candidate in the chaotic run-up to the 1996 presidential election and was subsequently reported to have "collapsed in acrimony" over the issue. Two parties previously associated with the POC (the CLD and the Social Democratic Union [UDS, below]) accepted cabinet posts in April 1996.

In October 1997 the two most prominent former POC members, the Progress Party of Equatorial Guinea (PPGE) and the UP, joined with the Union for Democracy and Social Development (UDDS) and the Republican Democratic Force (FDR) to form a new coalition, the **National Liberation Council.** The Council's platform was highlighted by a pledge to "bring a change of government . . . at all costs." In December the legislature passed a law forbidding the formation of coalitions prior to legislative balloting (then scheduled for mid-1998, but subsequently postponed until March 1999).

In early 2000 Victorino BOLEKIA Bonay, the leader of the opposition **Democratic and Progressive Alliance** (*Alianza Demócratica y Progresiva*—ADP) and former mayor of Malabo, announced that the opposition, including the Convergence for Social Democracy (CPDS) and the UP, would boycott municipal balloting scheduled for May. According to Bolekia, the opposition would only participate if the government agreed to conduct a fair electoral census, invited international observers to oversee the polling, and, in addition to a number of other demands, allowed opposition activists freedom of expression and movement.

Various, and at times overlapping, opposition alliances were formed in 2000 and 2001, the most prominent of which was the **Democratic Opposition Front** (*Frente de la Oposicion Démocratica*—FOD) that included the UP, the Progressive Democratic Alliance (ADP), the CPDS, the PPGE, and the Social Democratic Party (PSD). The FOD was launched in November 2000. In December the **Equatorial Guinea National Resistance** (*Resistencia Nacional Guinea Ecuatorial*—RENAGE) was launched in Barcelona, Spain; it included the UP, the UDDS, the FDR, the MAIB, and the Union of Independent Socialists (UDI). In March 2001 a new opposition alliance was reportedly formed by the UP, the CPDS, the PPGE, the FDR, the UDI, the MAIB, the National Alliance for the Restoration of Democracy (ANRD), the UDDS, the Party of the Democratic Coalition, and the Forum for Democracy in Equatorial Guinea (see below). Although instrumental in the formation of all of the above opposition alliances, the Popular Union (UP) accepted a junior cabinet post in March 2001. However, the UP campaigned against the dominant PDGE in the 2004 elections.

Government and Government-Supportive Parties

Democratic Party of Equatorial Guinea (*Partido Democrático de Guinea Ecuatorial*—PDGE). The PDGE was launched in October 1987 by President Obiang, who said it would be used to address the country's development problems while promoting national unity and "respect for the constitution and freedoms." Shortly thereafter, the House of Representatives approved a law requiring all public officials and salaried employees to contribute 3 percent of their salaries to the new formation.

During an extraordinary party congress in Bata on August 4–6, 1991, party delegates urged the government to establish short-, medium-, and long-term plans to lead to the legalization of other political groups. The party also adopted resolutions calling for the adoption of a multicandidature presidential system and the drafting of a law on press rights.

At the PDGE's second national congress on March 20–26, 1995, President Obiang reaffirmed the party's preeminent role in the implementation of public policy and the PDGE has since remained the dominant government party. In legislative elections in 2004 the PDGE and its allies in the Democratic Opposition (see below) received 87.9 percent of the vote and 98 of the 100 seats in the legislature. In local elections, the PDGE and its allies won 237 of 244 posts.

Leaders: Brig. Gen. Teodoro OBIANG Nguema Mbasogo (President of the Republic), Miguel Abia Biteo BORICO (Prime Minister), Filiberto Ntutumu NGUEMA (Secretary General), Santiago NGUA Mfumu (Deputy Secretary General), Alberto Sima NGUEMA (Vice President), Cristina Djombe DJAGANI (Vice President).

Democratic Opposition (Electoral Coalition). Formed in 2004, this coalition of eight propresidential parties campaigned with the support of the PDGE in both legislative and local elections. The coalition gained 30 seats in the legislature, and legislators from two of the parties—the Liberal Democratic Convention and the Social Democratic Union—were appointed to posts in the government. The Democratic Opposition also campaigned with the PDGE in the concurrent municipal elections, winning, with the PDGE, 237 of 244 posts.

Leaders: Alfonse MOKUY (CLD), Carmelo MODU Akune (UDS).

Liberal Democratic Convention (*Convención Liberal Democrática*—CLD). Also identified as the Liberal Party (*Partido Liberal*—PL), the CLD was legally recognized in May 1992. In November Santos Pascual BIKOMO Nanguande, who had previously been linked to the **People's Alliance** (*Alianza del Pueblo*—AP), was named to serve as CLD chair until the party's first congress. An attempt to hold such a congress in January 1994 was blocked by the government after Bikomo had charged it with election irregularities.

The CLD was credited with winning one legislative seat in November 1993. Although an original member of the POC, the CLD supported President Obiang in the February 1996 presidential balloting, and Bikomo was named information minister in the new April government. Although Bikomo left his post in 1997, the CLD remained a government-supportive party and held junior ministries following the 1999 and 2004 elections.

Leader: Alfonse MOKUY (President).

Social Democratic Union (*Unión Demócrata Social*—UDS). Formerly a Gabon-based grouping affiliated with the ADP and the **Democratic Social Union** (*Unión Social Democrática*—USD), the UDS was officially recognized in October 1992 under the leadership of Carmelo Modu Akune. In November it was reported that the UDS leadership had expelled Akune for pursuing "ideals which ran counter to the principles" of the party, and had named Angel Miko Alo Nchama as interim chair. However, Modu was subsequently again described as the leader of the UDS, which won five legislative seats in November 1993. After supporting President Obiang for reelection, Modu was named minister of state for labor and social security in the April 1996 cabinet and has subsequently held several government posts.

Leaders: Carmelo MODU Akune, Angel Miko Alo NCHAMA.

Social Democratic and Popular Convention (*Convención Social Demócrata y Popular*—CSDP). The CSDP is reportedly split into two factions. The first, led by Rafael Obiang, apparently remains aligned with the POC, having boycotted the 1993 parliamentary elections and the 1996 presidential balloting. The second, led by Secundio Oyono Avong, participated in the 1993 legislative campaign, winning six seats. The latter also forwarded Oyono Avong as a presidential contender in 1996, several reports describing him as the only opposition candidate

not to withdraw from the campaign prior to balloting. On May 9, 2002, party Secretary General Placido Mico Abogo was arrested on charges of conspiracy to assassinate the president. He was pardoned in August 2003.

Leaders: Rafael OBIANG, Secundio OYONO AVONG (1996 presidential candidate), Placido Mico ABOGO (Secretary General).

Social Democratic Coalition Party (*Partido de Coalición Social Demócrata*—PCSD). The PCSD was officially registered in 1993. In early 1996 party leader Buenaventura Mezui Masumu announced his presidential candidacy; however, he withdrew from the campaign in February to protest the government's allegedly fraudulent preelection activities. In the 2004 legislative and municipal elections, the PCSD garnered less than 1 percent of the votes.

Leader: Buenaventura Mezui MASUMU.

Social Democratic Party (*Partido Social Demócrata*—PSD). Formed by Marcellino Mangue MBA and recognized as a party in 1992, the PSD was formerly affiliated with the anti-Obiang group, the Party of the Democratic Coalition (see below). However, it joined the pro-presidential coalition in 2004.

Leader: Benjamín BALINGA (President).

Other members of the Democratic Opposition include the **Progressive Democratic Alliance** (*Alianza Democrática Progresista*—ADP), led by Victorino BOLEKIA; the **Democratic National Union of Equatorial Guinea** (*Unión Democrática Nacional*—UDENA), led by José MECHEBA; and the **Liberal Party** (*Partido Liberal*—PL).

Other Parties and Groups

Popular Union (*Unión Popular*—UP). The UP was legally recognized in May 1992. However, in October party members were detained and beaten by government security forces, and in March 1993 the group reportedly concluded a merger agreement with the PPGE (although there was no confirmation of the accord).

In August 1993 the government announced that a UP activist, Pedro MOTU Mamiaka, had committed suicide while in detention. However, Amnesty International accused security forces of torturing him to death, and the UP described the killing as another demonstration of the government's persecution of dissenters.

The UP presented Andrés Moisés Mba Ada as a candidate in the 1996 presidential campaign, reportedly angering more senior politicians in the POC. In April 1998 the UP claimed that the government had detained 200 of its activists during a nationwide crackdown on opposition members. Furthermore, in August the group charged the government with expelling its members from electoral oversight committees.

The UP won four seats in the 1999 legislative balloting, but party leaders ordered the UP legislators to refuse to take their seats as a protest against perceived electoral fraud on the part of the government. However, two of the legislators reportedly disobeyed the orders of the UP leaders, producing a split in the party between those members who support a degree of cooperation with the PDGE and those who insist on substantial reform of the political process prior to such compromise. The former faction seemed to have captured the party's higher positions with the election of Jeremias ONDO Ngomo to replace Mba as the president in October 2000. The UP then reversed its previous decision to boycott the assembly, and Ondo accepted a junior post in the new government formed in March 2001. The UP Secretary General, Fabián Nsue Nguema, was subsequently arrested for treason but was pardoned in November 2002. The UP reportedly remained active in various opposition alliances, and it joined the boycott of the 2004 legislative election.

Leaders: Jeremias ONDO Ngomo (President), Andrés Moisés MBA Ada (Former President), Fabián Nsue NGUEMA (Secretary General).

Socialist Party of Equatorial Guinea (*Partido Socialista de Guinea Ecuatorial*—PSGE). Citing legislative constraints on party activity, the PSGE in January 1992 described President Obiang's multiparty advocacy as an attempt to "deceive" international observers. Subsequently, party leader Tomas Mecheba Fernández called for foreign intervention, "military if necessary," to force the regime to cease its human rights violations. The PSGE later supported cooperation with the PDGE, and Fernández accepted a junior post in the cabinet in 2001. However, the party did not gain seats in the 2004 legislative election and did not participate in the subsequent cabinet.

Leader: Tomas Mecheba FERNANDEZ (President).

Convergence for Social Democracy (*Convergencia para la Democracia Social*—CPDS). The CPDS was launched in Paris in May 1984 by the two groups below, which set as their goal talks with President Obiang designed "to democratically transform all the state institutions, to guarantee fundamental liberties, and to promote a policy of cooperation with neighboring countries and the Western world." The party was legally recognized in February 1993; however, on September 19, two days after he was convicted of murder in a summary military trial, CPDS activist Romualdo Rafael NSOGO was executed. Subsequently, CPDS leaders denounced the regime, accusing it of killing Nsogo in an attempt to intimidate the opposition.

In early 1996 the CPDS presented Anoncio NZE Angue as its presidential candidate, although he withdrew from the campaign to protest, along with the other POC candidates, the government's tactics prior to the balloting. Nze was reportedly arrested in March for possessing CPDS documents referring to the Obiang administration as "an unreconstructed family dictatorship." At that time *Africa Confidential* referred to the CPDS as the "most radical" opposition group and the least likely to participate in national unity talks with the government.

In early 1998 a CPDS spokesman reportedly accused the West of refusing to put pressure on the Obiang administration to enact political and social reforms because of Western "economic interests" in the country. In April the group claimed that nearly 50 of its members had been arrested by government security forces.

The CPDS won one seat at legislative polling in March 1999 but its representative subsequently refused to assume the post as a protest over the government's alleged electoral malfeasance. The CPDS won two seats in the 2004 legislative balloting, but denounced the results because of alleged voting problems. At a party congress in January 2005, Santiago Obama Ndong was elected party president.

In May 2005, the party's newspaper, *The Truth* (*La Verdad*), allegedly was shut down by the government, a month after several CPDS activists were arrested following clashes with security forces. The government denied any crackdown on the group.

Leaders: Santiago Obama NDONG (President), Celestino Bonifacio BACALE (2002 presidential candidate).

Democratic Movement for the Liberation of Equatorial Guinea (*Reunión Democrática para la Liberación de Guinea Ecuatorial—RDLGE*). Formed in 1981, the Paris-based RDLGE announced a provisional government-in-exile in March 1983 following the failure of reconciliation talks between its leader and Colonel Obiang in late 1982. The RDLGE is considered a relatively moderate opposition group, the formation of the CPDS apparently representing its response to the creation by more strident groups of the *Junta Coordinadora* (below).

Leader: Manuel Rubén NDONGO.

African Socialist Party of Equatorial Guinea (*Partido Socialista Africano de Guinea Ecuatorial—PSAGE*). Based in Oviedo, Spain, the PSAGE was little known prior to its CPDS alliance with the RDLGE.

Progress Party of Equatorial Guinea (*Partido del Progreso de Guinea Ecuatorial—PPGE*). Also referenced as the People's Party of Equatorial Guinea, the PPGE was formed in Madrid in early 1983 by Severo Moto Nsa, a former secretary of state for information and tourism. Moto and other PPGE leaders returned to Malabo in mid-1988, apparently believing that the government had adopted a conciliatory attitude toward its opponents.

However, a PPGE petition for recognition as a legal party was denied, and Moto returned to exile. In September several PPGE members, including Secretary General José Luis Jones, were jailed in connection with an alleged coup plot. Given a lengthy prison sentence shortly after his arrest, Jones received a presidential pardon in January 1989; also departing the country, he condemned the June presidential poll as "clearly not valid."

In August 1991 Moto planned a second termination of exile to campaign for a multiparty system and the holding of free elections, but the government refused to renew his passport until May 1992, when he returned to Malabo. In early September PPGE members were among those detained in another government crackdown on dissident activity. Nonetheless, the party was legalized in October.

In July 1994 the government severed relations with the PPGE after Moto allegedly "defamed" the Obiang regime, and in November the PPGE leader accused Obiang of involvement in the death of his brother, Vincente MOTO. Subsequently, in March 1995, Moto was sentenced to 18 months in prison for allegedly bribing a government official and defaming the head of state. A far more severe sentence of 28 years was imposed on Moto in April by a military tribunal investigating an alleged coup plot. The sentences were condemned by a number of Western governments, and, following the intercession of French President Jacques Chirac, President Obiang amnestied Moto on August 3.

Moto announced his candidacy for president in early 1996; however, like most other opposition candidates, he withdrew immediately prior to the balloting and urged PPGE supporters to boycott the election. Nevertheless, at midyear Moto was reported to have indicated the willingness of the PPGE and some of the other remaining POC component groups to reopen discussions with the Obiang government.

In June 1997 the government banned the PPGE after it was revealed that Moto had allegedly been planning to overthrow the Obiang government. The following month the party ousted Moto after he restated his willingness to use violence to topple the government. On August 18 Moto was convicted, in absentia, of high treason and sentenced to at least 30 years in jail. Concurrently, the government ordered the PPGE to dissolve.

In October 1997 Moto, who was still being identified by observers as the PPGE's leader, surfaced in Kinshasa, the Democratic Republic of the Congo, as the organizer of a new antigovernment coalition. Subsequently, the PPGE suffered another blow when its first and second deputy leaders reportedly defected to the PDGE in early 1998.

In early 1999 Moto filed suit in Spain against the Obiang government, charging it with engaging in "state terrorism and genocide." Furthermore, Moto announced that his party would boycott legislative polling in March. For its part, Malabo called on Madrid to expel Moto, who had reportedly been residing there for two years. The PPGE also boycotted the 2004 elections, joining with other exile groups to form a government-in-exile in Spain with Moto as its leader.

In late 2005, Spain revoked political asylum for Moto but refused to return him to Equatorial Guinea or any other country that would not guarantee his safety.

Leaders: Severo MOTO Nsa (President), Armengol ENGONGA (Vice President), José Luis JONES (Secretary General).

Republican Democratic Force (*Fuerza Demócrata Republicana*—FDR). In October 1997 this grouping was reported among the founders of the National Liberation Council. Subsequently, its cofounders, Felipe Ondo Obiang and Guillermo Nguema Ela, were described by party members as having been "abducted"; however, the government then admitted holding the two, and in mid-November they were released without explanation. In March 1998 the two were rearrested and charged with making defamatory comments about the president. They were released in March 2000, at which time they vowed to continue their campaign against the administration. In 2003, Amnesty International reported that Ondo was being held by the government and tortured. The government denied reports that security forces had killed Ondo, saying that he had been transferred from one prison to another.

Leaders: Felipe ONDO Obiang, Guillermo NGUEMA Ela, Bonifacio NGUEMA.

Union for Democracy and Social Development (*Unión para la Democracia y el Desarrollo Social*—UDDS). The UDDS was the core component of the Opposition Coordination of Equatorial Guinea (*Coordinación Oposición de Guinea Ecuatorial*—COGE), launched in March 1992 by several groups, including the PR, the Zaire-based **Movement for the National Unification of Equatorial Guinea** (*Movimiento para la Unificación Nacional de Guinea Ecuatorial*—MUNGE); the **Republican Party of Equatorial Guinea** (*Partido Republicano de Guinea Ecuatorial*—PRGE); the **National Movement for the Reliberation of Equatorial Guinea** (*Movimiento Nacional para la Reliberación de Guinea Ecuatorial*–Monarge); and the PSGE, which subsequently joined the POC.

Led by vociferous regime critic Antonio Sibacha Bueicheku, the UDDS in early 1993 called on the Guinean clergy to publicly denounce the Obiang administration's human rights record and urged the EC and France to impose sanctions to stem the "perpetual violations." On May 31 five UDDS members were detained when security forces raided a party meeting. Consequently, in early June the party exhorted opposition members to fight the "last dictatorship." In early 1994 the party applauded Spain's decision to suspend aid to Equatorial Guinea and urged other donors to follow suit. In 2004 the UDDS renewed its request for intervention by the UN, the United States, France, and Spain to help bring about political change.

It was unclear what effect the UDDS's membership in the National Liberation Council coalition in 1997 had on the COGE.

Leader: Antonio SIBACHA Bueicheku, Aquilino Nguema Ona NCHEMA (Secretary General).

National Alliance for the Restoration of Democracy (*Alianza Nacional de Restauración Democrática*—ANRD). Founded in 1974, the Swiss-based ANRD announced in August 1979 that it would regard the ouster of Macie as nothing more than a "palace revolution" unless a number of conditions were met, including the trial of all individuals for atrocities under the former dictator and the establishment of a firm date for termination of military rule.

In April 1983 the ANRD was instrumental in the launching of the Coordinating Board of Opposition Democratic Forces (*Junta Coordinadora da las Fuerzas de Oposición Democrática*), formed by a group of Spanish-based exile formations, then including the PPGE, to present a united front against President Obiang, whom it accused of failing to live up to the people's expectations and exhibiting a lack of respect for the law. The *Junta* denounced the August 1983 legislative balloting as a "sham" and called for an economic embargo of the Obiang regime by regional governments. Other participants in the *Junta* included the **Movement for the Liberation and Future of Equatorial Guinea** (*Movimiento de Liberación y Futuro de Guinea Ecuatorial*—Molifuge), the **Liberation Front of Equatorial Guinea** (*Frente de Liberación de Guinea Ecuatorial*—Frelige), and the **Democratic Reform** (*Reforma Democrática*). The ANRD boycotted the 2004 legislative elections.

Leader: Luis Ondo AYANG (Secretary General).

Union of Independent Democrats (*Unión Democrática Independiente*—UDI). Formation of the Revolutionary Command Council of Socialist Guinean Patriots was announced in September 1981 by Daniel Oyonoh, a former secretary of state for economy and finance, as a union of three internal groups-the Union of Independent Democrats (*Unión de Demócratas Independientes*—UDI), the Revolutionary Movement, and the Socialist Front. In addition to political liberalization, the new formation called for the withdrawal of foreign troops from Equatorial Guinea, a reference to the Moroccan and Spanish troops in the presidential guard. The extent of the council's subsequent activity has been unclear, although in mid-1999 it was reported that the council and Bubi nationalists had agreed to coordinate their activities. The UDI rubric was routinely referenced in news reports in the early 2000s.

Leader: Daniel OYONOH (UDI).

Four other anti-Obiang groups are the **Party of the Democratic Coalition,** led by Francisco JONES; the **People's Alliance of Equatorial Guinea,** led by Miguel ESONO; the **Forum for Democracy in Equatorial Guinea;** and the **National Movement for the Liberation of Equatorial Guinea** (*Movimiento Nacional de Liberación de la Guinea Ecuatorial*—Monalige), a continuation of an historic group (see Political background).

In April 2005 it was reported that former prime minister Christino Seriche Malabo BIOKO had joined exiled opposition activists in Spain and founded the **Vanguard for the Defense of Citizens' Rights** (VDDC) in December 2004 "to promote the establishment of a 'real' democratic state" in Equatorial Guinea.

Separatist Groups

April 1 Bubi Nationalist Group. The Bubi Nationalist coalition was launched in Madrid in April 1983 by a number of groups advocating independence for the island of Bioko (formerly Fernando Póo) where the Bubi people then constituted a majority. The Bubi organizations had been excluded from the *Junta Coordinadora* because of their opposition to its goal of promoting a "national identity." The new Bubi formation subsequently issued a number of manifestos calling for an end to alleged human rights abuses against the islanders.

Leader: Bwalalele BOKOKO Itogi (Secretary General).

Movement for the Self-Determination of the Island of Bioko (*Movimiento par la Autodeterminación de la Isla de Bioko*—MAIB). The Movement's role in the Bubi nationalist movement came under increased scrutiny following the arrest of a number of its members in July 1995. In late January 1998 the Movement denied government charges that it had organized deadly attacks on Bioko Island, countering that, following the incidents earlier in the month, the island's residents had been subjected to killing and torture by government forces and that 800 people had been arrested.

In June 1998, 15 Movement members were sentenced to death for their alleged roles in the January uprising. In addition, one of the group's leaders, Martin PUYE, was given a 20-year prison term; however, Puye, who, along with a number of the

Cabinet

As of May 1, 2006 (*see headnote*)

Prime Minister	Miguel Abia Biteo Borico (PDGE)
First Deputy Prime Minister	Marcelino Oyono Ntutumu (PDGE)
Second Deputy Prime Minister	Ricardo Mangue Obama Nfube (PDGE)

Ministers

Agriculture and Forests	Teodoro Nguema Obiang Mangue (PDGE)
Defense	Gen. Antonio Mba Nguema (ind.)
Economics, Trade, and Promotion of Entrepreneurship	Jaime Ela Ndong
Education, Science, and Sport	Cristbóal Mañana Ela (PDGE)
Finance and Budget	Marcelino Owono Edu (PDGE)
Fisheries and Environment	Fortunato Ofa Mbo Nchama
Foreign Affairs, International Cooperation, and Francophone Affairs	Pastor Micha Ondo Bile (PDGE)
Health and Social Welfare	Justino Obama Nve (PDGE)
Information, Tourism, and Culture	Alfonso Nsue Mokuy (CLD)
Infrastructure and Urbanism	Aniceto Ebiaca Mohete (PDGE)
Interior and Local Corporations	Clemente Engonga Nguema Onguene (PDGE)
Justice and Prisons	Angel Masie Mibuy (PDGE)
Labor and Social Security	Enrique Mercader Costa (PDGE)
Mines, Industry, and Energy	Atanasio Ela Ntugu Nsa (PDGE)
National Security	Col. Manuel Nguema Mba (ind.)
Planning, Economic Development, and Public Works	Carmelo Modu Akune (UDS)
Presidency, in charge of Special Duties	Alejandro Evuna Owono (PDGE)
Promotion of Women	Jesusa Obono Engono (PDGE) [f]
Regional Integration	Baltasar Engonga Edjo (PDGE)
Secretary General to the Government, in charge of Administrative Coordination and Parliamentary Relations	Antonio Martin Ndong Ntutumu (PDGE)
Transport, Technology, Posts, and Telecommunication	Demetrio Elo Ndong Nsefumu (PDGE)

Secretaries of State

Culture and Tourism	Prudencio Botey Sobole
Economy, Commerce, and Entrepreneurship	Jose-Angel Borico Moises
Energy	Francisco Mabale Nseng
Housing and Urbanism	Fidel Nsue Micha
Information, Radio, and Television	Purificación Opo Barila [f]
Interior and Local Affairs	Leocadio Ndong Moñung
International Cooperation	Victoriana Nchama Nsue Okomo [f]
Mines	Gabriel Mbega Obiang Lima
National Defense	Santiago Mauro Nguema
National Security	Francisco Edu Ngua
Planning, Economic Development, and Public Investment	Jose Ela Oyana
Post Office and Transport	Francisco Mba Olo Bahamonde
Public Works and Administrative Planning	Salvador Mangue Ayingono
Treasury and Budget	Melchor Esono Edjo
Women's Development	Purificación Buari Lasaquero [f]
Youth and Sports	Pedro Mabale Fuga

[f] = female

other Movement defendants, had showed signs of being tortured, died in jail in July. In August the president commuted the remaining death sentences to terms of life imprisonment.

Leaders: Anacieto BOKESSA, Weca CHICAMPO, Paco AUDIJE.

Legislature

The present constitution provides for a unicameral **House of People's Representatives** (*Cámara de Representantes del Pueblo*) to meet for a five-year term. The PDGE-dominated, 41-member legislature elected in July 1988 was dissolved by the president in early July 1993. At balloting on March 7, 1999, for the 80-member House (enlarged to its current size in 1993), the Democratic Party of Equatorial Guinea (PDGE) won 75 seats; the Popular Union (UP), 4; and the Convergence for Social Democracy (CPDS), 1. As of mid-2000 the legislators from the UP and the CPDS had refused to fill their seats as a protest against the government's conduct of the election. However, the UP later reversed its decision. In 2003, the legislature was enlarged to 100 seats in preparation for the 2004 elections. On April 25, 2004, the PDGE won 68 seats; the Democratic Opposition, 30; and the CPDS, 2.

President: Salomon NGUEMA Owono.

Communications

Press

The following are published irregularly in Malabo: *Ebano* (1,000), in Spanish; *Poto Poto* (Bata), in Spanish and Fang; *Unidad de la Guinea Ecuatorial*. In January 1994 the weekly *El Sol* became the first private newspaper to be recognized by the government. Two new independent papers, *Tiempo* and *La Nation*, were reportedly granted operating licenses in 2000. Other publications include *La Opinion* (an independent weekly) and an opposition magazine called *La Verdad*.

News Agency

The only facility currently operating in Malabo is Spain's *Agencia EFE*.

Broadcasting and Computing

Radio Nacional de Guinea Ecuatorial (RNGE) broadcasts over two stations in Malabo and one in Bata in Spanish and vernacular languages. There are also English-language stations, Radio Africa and Radio Earl Africa, which offer music and religious programming from Malabo. The government's *Television Nacional*, owned by President Obiang's son, transmits over one channel in Malabo. There were approximately 4,200 television receivers and 5,000 personal computers serving 2,000 Internet users in 2003.

Intergovernmental Representation

Ambassador to the U.S.
Purificacion Angue ONDO

U.S. Ambassador to Equatorial Guinea
R. Niels MARQUARDT (resident in Cameroon)

Permanent Representative to the UN
Lino Sima EKUA AVOMO

IGO Memberships (Non-UN)
AfDB, AU, BADEA, BDEAC, CEEAC, CEMAC, Interpol, NAM, OIF

ERITREA

STATE OF ERITREA

The Country

With a coastline stretching some 750 miles along the African border of the Red Sea, Eritrea is bordered on the northwest by Sudan, on the south by Ethiopia, and on the southeast by Djibouti. Home to many ethnic groups (including the Afar, Bilen, Hadareb, Kunama, Nara, Rashida, Saho, Tigray, and Tigrigna), its people are almost equally divided as Christians and Muslims.

The leading agricultural products are cereals, citrus fruits, cotton, and livestock (including camels and goats); fish are plentiful in the vicinity of islands off the Red Sea port of Massawa, while mineral resources include copper, gold, iron ore, and potash. The region's economic infrastructure was severely crippled by a long (1962–1991) war of independence from Ethiopia, the output of most industries being reduced during the conflict to a fraction of capacity. Conditions improved following the end of that war, and, although GNP per capita ($115) remained one of the world's lowest, agricultural production had increased four-fold by May 1993. With the installation of a famine early warning system and infrastructural improvements, a return to agricultural self-sufficiency was reported by late 1994. Subsequently, Eritrea's real GDP growth averaged 6.0 percent annually for 1994–1998, while annual inflation averaged 8.2 percent for the same period. However, that rapid progress came to a halt with the outbreak of a border war with Ethiopia (Eritrea's main export market) in May 1998. By the time hostilities ended (at least temporarily) in 2000, it was estimated that GDP had fallen by 9 percent.

The government launched a five-year, $249 million economic recovery program in 2000, concentrating on agriculture, infrastructure, and support for the private sector. However, the economy subsequently continued to languish, particularly as a final resolution of the conflict with Ethiopia proved elusive and the expense of an army of 350,000 soldiers siphoned resources away from development programs. GDP grew by only 1.8 percent in 2004, while remittances from abroad declined substantially. As of early 2006 it was estimated that two-thirds of the population remained dependent on food aid.

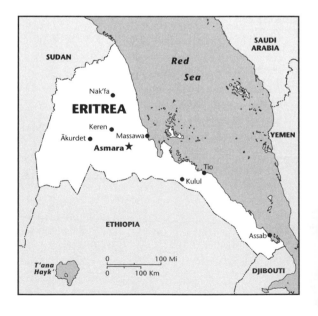

Political Status: Former Italian colony; became part of UN-sponsored Ethiopian–Eritrean Federation in September 1952; annexed as a province of Ethiopia in November 1962; declared independent on May 24, 1993, following secessionist referendum of April 23–25; new constitution approved by the Constitutional Assembly on May 23, 1997, but largely unimplemented as of mid-2006.

Area: 46,774 sq. mi. (121,144 sq. km.).

Population: 2,748,304 (1984C); 4,445,000 (2005E), including nonresidents.

Major Urban Centers (2005E): ASMARA (554,000), Keren (89,000).

Principal Languages: Tigrigna and Arabic.

Monetary Unit: A new currency—the nakfa—was introduced on July 15, 1997. For a transitional period the government agreed to exchange the nakfa on a one-to-one basis with the Ethiopian birr, previously the most commonly circulated currency. The introduction of the new currency was considered a factor in the outbreak of hostilities between Eritrea and Ethiopia in 1998 because it unsettled financial conditions at the border and complicated government-to-government transactions (see Political background, below). Consequently, the future of the nakfa appeared uncertain throughout the war, which concluded in late 2000. As of July 1, 2006, the government rate of exchange was 13.50 nakfa = $1US.

State President and Chair of the Executive Council of the People's Front for Democracy and Justice: ISAIAS Afwerki; named secretary general of the Eritrean People's Liberation Front in 1987; named head of Provisional Government of Eritrea following defeat of Ethiopia's Mengistu regime in May 1991; named state president on May 22, 1993; named chair of the People's Front for Democracy and Justice Executive Council on February 16, 1994.

Government and Politics

Political Background

After several centuries of intermittent Ethiopian and Ottoman control, the coastal area of what became known as Eritrea was occupied in the 1880s by Italy, which in 1890 proclaimed it a colony and in 1935–1936 used it as a staging area for its conquest of Ethiopia. Administered by Britain in the immediate post–World War II era, it was declared by the United Nations in 1952 to be an autonomous component of an Ethiopian federation. Ten years later it was annexed by Ethiopia, with Eritreans who opposed the action mounting a guerrilla campaign that lasted until the downfall of the Mengistu regime in May 1991 (see article on Ethiopia for additional information).

On June 15, 1992, the Eritrean People's Liberation Front (EPLF) announced the formation of a Provisional Government of Eritrea (PGE), headed by its secretary general, ISAIAS Afwerki. In a referendum on April 23–25, 1993, 99.8 of those participating voted for independence, which was accepted by Ethiopia on May 3 and became effective on May 24, with Isaias assuming the title of president. The EPLF was succeeded by the People's Front for Democracy and Justice (PFDJ) in February 1994.

At independence Eritrea's overriding concern was recovery from decades of economic neglect and military devastation. Although the country before World War II had, by African standards, been measurably industrialized, the subsequent damage to its infrastructure was estimated at more than $2 billion. In addition, the port of Massawa had been all but destroyed by enemy bombardment. The divorce from Ethiopia was nonetheless described by *Africa Confidential* as "pragmatic," with no reparations being sought from Addis Ababa and no indication that a return of Ethiopian assets was being considered. By 1994 a "Greening of Eritrea Campaign" that involved an emphasis on small-scale peasant agriculture, coupled with the assignment of army units to rural rehabilitation projects, had yielded surprising results, including praise from foreign aid donors.

The new Eritrean state subsequently exhibited a decided assertiveness on territorial issues, as evidenced by strained relations with Yemen, Djibouti, and Sudan (see Foreign relations, below). Nevertheless, many international observers expressed surprise in May 1998 when a crisis erupted between Eritrea and Ethiopia over a disputed territory within their ill-defined border region. On May 13 Ethiopia accused Eritrea of having forcibly occupied the Badme Triangle region in "northwest Ethiopia." On the following day, Eritrea claimed that Ethiopian troops had in fact initiated the skirmish on "sovereign Eritrean territory." Subsequently, with both sides claiming to possess colonial Italian maps as evidence of their sovereignty claims, open warfare erupted in the region in late May. Meanwhile, in an attempt to explain the outbreak of fighting, analysts suggested that relations between the two countries had been deteriorating since Eritrea introduced its own currency, the nakfa, in 1997. That decision had been followed by Ethiopia's insistence that all trade between the two must be in hard currency—a move that adversely affected the Eritrean economy and set off a series of tit-for-tat exchanges that increased tension between the two and, arguably, set the stage for the 1998 conflict.

Amid reports of continued fighting, the Organization of African Unity (OAU, subsequently the African Union—AU) and the United Nations spearheaded diplomatic attempts to settle the dispute in the second half of 1998; however, Eritrea rejected cease-fire proposals in both June and November, asserting that they favored Ethiopia. On November 18 Djibouti broke off relations with Eritrea after the latter accused Djibouti of backing Ethiopia throughout the mediation process. Meanwhile, independent sources confirmed reports that both Eritrea and Ethiopia were expelling each other's citizens in great numbers.

In late January 1999 Eritrea rejected a UN-backed OAU troop withdrawal plan, and within a week full-scale warfare had recommenced, with Ethiopia reported to have launched massive offensives on the Badme front and against the Eritrean port city of Assab. In late February Eritrea acknowledged having lost the Badme territory and agreed to abide by the OAU proposal. Nevertheless, fierce fighting continued through March.

The July 1999 Algiers Summit of the OAU formally endorsed a peace plan that would have returned both sides to their prewar positions and would have established a border demarcation mechanism. However, the proposed deal collapsed in September, in part due to Ethiopian concerns over technical aspects of the plan, particularly regarding the proposed Eritrean withdrawal. The subsequent months saw relatively little fighting, but Ethiopia launched a major offensive in May 2000 that concluded in a June truce after Ethiopian forces had reclaimed all the land previously lost and had advanced deep into Eritrea. In addition to a cease-fire, the combatants also agreed to eventual deployment of international peacekeepers. A final peace accord was signed by Isaias and President Meles of Ethiopia in Algiers, Algeria, on December 12. In April 2001 an independent boundary commission (the Eritrea-Ethiopia Boundary Commission—EEBC) established a 15-mile-wide buffer zone comprised exclusively of territory that belonged to Eritrea prior to the conflict. A UN Mission for Ethiopia and Eritrea (UNMEE)—comprised of some 4,200 peacekeepers from about 40 nations—was charged with monitoring the buffer zone. In March 2003, the border commission clarified its ruling, awarding the disputed town of Badme to Eritrea (see Current issues section for subsequent developments).

Constitution and Government

On May 22, 1992, the Provisional Government of Ethiopia issued a proclamation on Eritrea's transitional government structure. It stated that, prior to the adoption of a permanent constitution, the EPLF Central Committee would serve as the country's legislative body. Executive authority was invested in a 28-member Advisory Council (subsequently a 24-member State Council), chaired by the EPLF secretary general. In addition, a judiciary was authorized to function independently of the EPLF Central Committee, the Advisory/State

Council, and the secretary general. The new basic law provided for the country's ten provinces to be headed by governors, each of whom was also authorized to serve on the Advisory/State Council.

On May 22, 1993, Secretary General Isaias was proclaimed president of Eritrea. Concurrently, a transitional National Assembly was established. (By a resolution of the PFDJ congress a year later, the assembly became a 150-member body encompassing the 75 members of the PFDJ's Central Committee, plus a number of indirectly elected members.) In March 1994 the National Assembly approved a resolution to establish a 50-member Constitutional Commission to prepare a draft basic law for the country. The commission issued its recommendations in 1996, and a special 527-member Constitutional Assembly was subsequently elected in direct balloting and charged with preparing a final document. As unanimously approved by the Constitutional Assembly (which subsequently dissolved) on May 23, 1997, the new constitution provides for a directly elected National Assembly, which is authorized to select a president, who is granted strong executive authority. The president term was set at five years, renewable once. A multiparty system was envisioned, although its final structure was left to the current National Assembly as were details regarding other electoral matters. No precise timetable was established for the final implementation of the new constitution. Among other things, the 1998–2000 border war with Ethiopia served as an obstacle to implementation, while critics of President Isaias continued as of mid-2006 to accuse him of dragging his feet on the issue and lacking enthusiasm for establishment of genuine multiparty activity.

In May 1995 the National Assembly approved legislation dividing the country into six provinces, each of which would be further divided into regions, subregions, and villages. In early November the legislators decided that 30 percent of the provincial council seats would be reserved for women and gave the provinces nonethnic names (Southern Red Sea Region, Northern Red Sea Region, Anseba Region, Gash Barka Region, South Region, and Central Region).

Regional elections were held on May 20, 2004, but National Assembly elections were repeatedly postponed and remained unscheduled as of mid-2006.

Foreign Relations

A number of countries, including the United States, recognized Eritrea on April 27, 1993. All-important recognition by Ethiopia on May 3 paved the way for the proclamation of independence three weeks later. On October 10 Eritrea and Ethiopia concluded an agreement on freedom of cross-border transit for citizens of the two countries. By the end of the year Eritrea had been admitted to the United Nations and most of its affiliated bodies.

In late 1993 Eritrea complained of an attack by an armed Islamic group that had infiltrated from Sudan. A similar outbreak in November 1994 yielded a rupture in diplomatic relations with Khartoum, which the Asmara leadership had privately charged with "Islamic and imperialistic ambitions." Subsequent peace talks in Sana, Yemen, broke down in late December after Sudan had refused to condemn infiltrators that Eritrea had accused of destabilizing activities. Eight months earlier, at the conclusion of a defense treaty with Ethiopia, a foreign ministry spokesman had declared that "Eritrea, in collaboration with Ethiopia if necessary, will make a short shrift of militant Islam."

On November 11, 1995, a simmering dispute between Eritrea and Yemen over claims to three small islands in the Red Sea erupted into armed confrontation. The three islands, Greater Hanish (Hanish Al Kubra), Lesser Hanish (Hanish Al Suhrah), and Zukar (Jabel Zukar) had been retained by Britain when it withdrew from Aden in 1967 but were handed over to South Yemen three years later. Subsequently, the archipelago came under Yemeni development as a center for tourists, particularly French scuba enthusiasts. The November firefight, occasioned by the presence of Yemeni troops on Greater Hanish, was followed by a more bloody encounter on December 15–17. Thereafter, the two sides agreed to a cease-fire monitored by a four-member committee composed of one representative each from Eritrea and Yemen, plus diplomats from the U.S. embassies in Eritrea and Yemen.

Mediated by the UN and France, subsequent talks yielded signature of an accord in Paris on May 21, 1996, under which Eritrea and Yemen renounced the use of force and agreed to submit the dispute to binding arbitration by a panel of five judges, with Eritrea and Yemen appointing two each and these four naming the fifth. Nevertheless, the dispute flared up again in early August, when Eritrean troops occupied Lesser Hanish, withdrawing at the end of the month only on the express order of the UN Security Council. (In October 1998 the International Court of Justice [ICJ] ruled largely in Yemen's favor in the dispute, granting it sovereignty of the so-called Zukar-Hanish island groups while ceding Eritrea control over a smaller island grouping. Moreover, the ICJ asserted that traditional fishing patterns— both Eritrean and Yemeni—should be protected. Both countries promptly agreed to comply with the decision.)

The relationship between Eritrea and Sudan continued to deteriorate in 1996–1997 as the former joined forces with Ethiopia and Uganda to form a regional front to contain militant Islamic fundamentalism (see article on Ethiopia). In late July 1996 Khartoum claimed that its troops had repulsed an incursion by Eritrean forces as tensions mounted along their shared border. Subsequent UN-directed efforts to repatriate Eritrean refugees from Sudan ground to a halt in May 1997 after Eritrea expelled the UN workers for allegedly engaging "in activities incompatible with their mission"; however, some observers asserted that Eritrea was trying to slow the repatriation process because many of the refugees were Muslim and loyal to the opposition. Sudanese-Eritrean relations plummeted further in June when Eritrean officials announced that they had uncovered an alleged Sudanese-backed plot to assassinate President Isaias. Following the tentative conclusion of the Eritrean/Ethiopian war in late 2000, Eritrea concluded a border security agreement with Sudan in July 2001, though it was widely reported that Sudan subsequently continued

to support anti-government movements in Eritrea (see Political Groups section).

Relations with the United States, European Union, and the UN remained tenuous in mid-2006 due to what was perceived in the West as President Isaias's "confrontational approach" to UN-MEE (see Current issues). Meanwhile, Eritrea reportedly by that time had significantly increased its ties with Pakistan in regard to oil exploration and other "entrepreneurial" activity. Eritrea also continued to provide aid to numerous Ethiopian opposition groups as an expression of its anger over the impasse in final border demarcation.

Current Issues

The ferocity of the 1998–2000 border war with Ethiopia was very difficult for the international community to comprehend, since the narrow strip of land in question held few natural resources and was generally considered a poor candidate for development. The estimates of the number of Eritrean deaths in the conflict ranged from 20,000 to 50,000, while some 60,000 people were displaced. In addition, the government reportedly spent $1 billion on armaments to conduct the campaign against its former Ethiopian allies, thereby dealing a severe blow to an economy already in desperate need of investment. Some analysts attributed Eritrea's intensity in the dispute to a "sense of indomitability" arising from the long war of independence and to a degree of hubris on the part of President Isaias. Although Isaias and his administration continued to maintain that Eritrea had been waging a defensive war and declared "victory" in the final settlement, most observers concluded that Ethiopia had, in fact, achieved military superiority prior to the cease-fire.

President Isaias appeared to retain broad popular support throughout the war, although what one journalist called "quiet questions" were raised over the possibility that the president may have misjudged Eritrean capabilities. Following the war, criticism intensified noticeably, beginning with the issuance in late 2000 of the so-called "Berlin Manifesto" on the part of PFDJ supporters outside the country who argued that constitutional implementation was being unnecessarily delayed and that power remained inordinately concentrated in the president's hands. Subsequently, in May 2001, a number of influential government and party officials also broke ranks with Isaias (see PFDJ under Political Groups, below). Disconcerting many international donors, Isaias responded with a crackdown in September, arresting a number of government and party officials for "disloyalty." He also clamped down on the independent press.

Meanwhile, final border demarcation was left to the EEBC, whose ruling in April 2002 allocated sufficient territory to each side to permit each to claim satisfaction, although overall the decision appeared to favor Ethiopia. In March 2003, the border commission officially awarded the disputed town of Badme to Eritrea, but the Ethiopian government did not announce it accepted the ruling "in principle" until November 2004. Despite the demarcation, border skirmishes continued to flare up, land mines were periodically detonated, and the UN expressed concerns over Eritrea's lack of cooperation with the peacekeeping force patrolling the border. Although his external reputation continued to decline, Isaias still clung to his hard line, and opposition groups continued to coalesce and regroup (see Political Groups, below), some of them backed by the governments of Sudan, Yemen, and Ethiopia.

In October 2005 the Eritrean government banned UNMEE helicopter flights and other activity in the disputed border area to protest Ethiopia's unwillingness to accept the proposed final demarcation and to return Badme to Eritrean control. Although the Security Council threatened to impose sanctions on Eritrea for its unilateral action, Isaias continued to maintain that sanctions would be more appropriate if leveled at Ethiopia. (Isaias claimed that Eritrea was the "law-abiding party" in the dispute and that Ethiopia was receiving preferential treatment from the west because of President Meles's assistance in the U.S.-led "war on terror.") The two countries were described as once again "on the brink" in November in view of continued troop and tank buildups and an Eritrean demand (reluctantly accepted by the Security Council) that all western troops be withdrawn from UNMEE.

Complicating matters for Eritrea was a report in mid-December by an independent claims commission at the Permanent Court of Arbitration that adjudged that Eritrea had initiated the 1998 war by invading Badme. (The commission collaterally held both sides liable for property damage and abuse of civilians during the conflict.)

Clearly annoyed by Isaias's "belligerence" regarding UNMEE, UN Secretary General Kofi Annan in January 2006 argued that the peacekeeping mission be downgraded or even converted into a "defensive force" on the Ethiopian side of the temporary security zone. Subsequently, with tensions at the border having receded, the Security Council in late May decided to cut the UNMEE force by 1,000 soldiers and to extend the mission's mandate by only four months, instead of the normal six-month extension. The council also insisted that Ethiopia abide by the EEBC's border ruling and that Eritrea lift the ban on UNMEE flights. Meanwhile, as of midyear new assembly elections remained unscheduled and little other movement toward genuine democratic activity appeared in the offing. Among other things, Isaias's critics accused him of focusing on the "false issue" of sovereignty at the expense of attention to the nation's many economic and political problems.

Political Groups

In late 2000 the National Assembly approved statutes providing for eventual formation of political parties, although critics argued that accompanying restrictions might present an effective barrier to genuine multiparty activity. While describing party activity as "acceptable" in theory, the assembly in early 2002 upheld a ban on the legalization of parties, and the PFDJ remained the sole legal party as of mid-2006.

Opposition to the EPLF/PFDJ has primarily involved shifting, often overlapping, and mostly ineffective coalitions, usually led by the ELF (below). In November 1996 it was reported that the ELF had initiated formation of an Eritrean National Alliance (ENA), together with the ELF-NC and a faction of the EIJM. Reportedly established with the assistance of Sudan, the ENA, whose components were described as having "fundamentalist tendencies," called for the ousting of the Isaias government and the installation of a multiparty system. ENA Chair Abdella Idriss of the ELF also called for investigation of alleged human rights violations on the part of the administration. Significantly, the ELF-RC declined to join the ENA because of the inclusion of the EIJM faction in the alliance.

In March 1999 the ENA appeared to be superseded by a broader coalition of opposition groups styled the Alliance of Eritrean National Forces (AENF) that included the ELF, ELF-NC, ELF-RC, the EISM (see EIJM, below), and a number of small Marxist formations. Despite enjoying the support of Ethiopia, the AENF was described as maintaining a low profile during the Eritrean-Ethiopian war, supporting the 2000 truce while continuing to call for the ouster of the Isaias government.

In late 2002 reports once again began to reference the ENA, described now as comprising some 13 parties and groups under the leadership of the ELF's Idriss as president and HIRUY Tedla Bairu of the small, recently formed **Eritrean Cooperative Party** (ECP) as secretary general. Although the revitalized ENA reportedly initially indicated it would not use military force to try to overthrow the government, it was reported in May 2003 that an ENA military wing had been established. By that time, it appeared that the ENA was receiving financial aid from Ethiopia, Sudan, and Yemen. Once again undermining effective opposition cohesion, the ELF-RC refused to participate in the alliance, arguing that Hiruy was under "foreign influence."

In early 2004 four ENA members (the ELF-NC, the **People's Democratic Front for the Liberation of Eritrea** [PDFLE], RSADO, and the DMLEK) joined the EPM in forming an opposition alliance called the Four Plus One. In October, additional small parties joined the grouping, which described itself as a means of strengthening the ENA rather than replacing it.

New ENA leaders were reportedly elected in January 2005, Hiruy replacing Idriss as president and Husayn KHALIFA succeeding Hiruy as secretary general. However, the ENA was again apparently superseded in February by the formation of the **Eritrean Democratic Alliance** (EDA), which included the ELF, ELF-RC, EDP, EPM, the members of Four Plus One, the small **Eritrean Federal Democratic Movement,** the "newly emerging" **National Salvation Front,** and, apparently, the **Eritrean Islamic Islah Movement** (EIIM). The role of the EIIM was controversial, since it supported the use of violence against government forces (EIIM fighters killed a number of Eritrean soldiers in early 2005) while other EDA components (notably the EDP and EPM) opposed the use of such force. Meanwhile, Hiruy and his EPC remained outside the EDA, with Khalifa being referenced as the EDA leader and Abdallah Aden of the EPM as his deputy. Hiruy subsequently criticized the EDA for "monopolizing" financial aid from Ethiopia, Sudan, and Yemen designed to support opposition activity in Eritrea. The EDA was described in early 2006 as "virtually paralyzed" by a lack of effective coordination.

Government Party

People's Front for Democracy and Justice (PFDJ). The PFDJ's predecessor—the Eritrean People's Liberation Front (EPLF)—was launched in 1970 as a breakaway faction of the Marxist-oriented Eritrean Liberation Front (ELF, below). The EPLF was an avowedly nonsectarian, left-wing formation supported by both Christians and Muslims in its pursuit of Eritrean independence. With an estimated 100,000 men and women under arms, the EPLF for much of its preindependence existence controlled large areas of the Eritrean countryside, establishing schools, hospitals, a taxation system, and other government services.

After the EPLF revised its ideology to accommodate multipartyism and a "regulated" market economy, in May 1991 the United States for the first time supported the EPLF's call for a self-determination referendum. Immediately after the subsequent Ethiopian defeat, Isaias Afwerki, who had been named secretary general of the EPLF at its 1987 congress, announced that the group was establishing a provisional government in Eritrea until a UN-supervised independence vote could be conducted. At independence on May 24, 1993, Isaias was installed as Eritrean president. At its 1994 congress, the EPLF adopted its present name and elected a 75-member Central Council and a 19-member Executive Council chaired by Isaias.

In the wake of the disastrous 1998–2000 war with Ethiopia, which, among other things, directed attention away from proposed political reform, a group of 15 prominent PFDJ leaders (including members of the Executive Council) published a letter in May 2001 criticizing Isaias's "autocratic" rule and demanding a "legal and democratic transition to a truly constitutional government." Isaias reacted harshly to the challenge, and some of the so-called G-15 were among those arrested in a government crackdown in September 2001. Subsequently, PFDJ dissidents who had escaped arrest by fleeing the country announced the formation of an EPLF-Democratic Party in exile (see EDP, below).

Leaders: ISAIAS Afwerki (President of Eritrea and Chair of PFDJ Executive Council); Yemane GEBREAB, Hagos GEBHREHIWET, Yemane GEBREMESKAL, and Zemeheret YOHANNES (PFDJ Department Heads); Ahmad al-Amin Mohammed SAÏD (Secretary General).

Opposition Groups

Eritrean Liberation Front (ELF). The predominantly Muslim ELF initiated anti-Ethiopian guerrilla activity in 1961 in pursuit of Eritrean autonomy. Its influence plummeted following the formation of the EPLF, and numerous splinter groups subsequently surfaced. By 1992 the ELF was considered to have become virtually nonexistent within Eritrea. However, in November 1996 it helped to launch the first of several opposition alliances (see above for subsequent developments).

Leader: Abdella IDRISS.

Eritrean Liberation Front–Revolutionary Congress (ELF-RC). The ELF-RC is a predominantly Muslim but nonfundamentalist and nonmilitary group that also includes some Christians.

Leaders: Ahmed NASSER, Gebrezgabiker TEWELDE (in Canada).

Eritrean Liberation Front–National Congress (ELF–NC). This group formed when the ELF–RC split into two groups in 2004.

Leader: Dr. BEYENE (Kidane).

Eritrean Islamic–Jihad Movement (EIJM—*Jihad Islammiya*). An Islamic fundamentalist group, the EIJM is largely based in Sudan and is devoted to armed operations within Eritrea. The Eritrean government claims that the EIJM is financed by the Sudanese government.

In August 1993 the military wing of the EIJM announced from Saudi Arabia that it had dismissed its Political Bureau, headed by Sheikh Mohammed ARAFA, for having established contact with the Eritrean government. For his part, Arafa continued to claim leadership of the group. The factions each operated under the EIJM label until 1998 when it was reported that the military wing had restyled itself the **Eritrean People's Congress** (EPC), while Arafa's followers had reorganized under the banner of the **Eritrean Islamic Salvation Movement** (EISM—*Harahat al Khalas al Islamiya*). Despite their differences, both groups agreed to join the AENF in early 1999. In 2003 the U.S. State Department reportedly listed EIJM as an alleged member of al-Qaida.

Eritrean Democratic Party (EDP). The EDP is a successor to the EPLF-Democratic Party that was formed in exile by PFDJ dissidents after the government crackdown of 2001. The founding EDP congress was held in Germany in early 2004, the party committing itself to nonviolent opposition to the Isaias government.

Leaders: Mesfin HAGOS, Mohammad Nur AHMED.

Red Sea Afar Democratic Organization (RSADO). The RSADO joined the ENA in 2002 to advocate for the rights of the Afar, an ethnic group in the southern Red Sea region. In 2004 its chair, Ibrahim HAROUN, survived an assassination attempt, which some critics alleged may have been plotted by the ruling PFDJ.

Democratic Movement for the Liberation of Eritrean Kunama (DMLEK). This group was a

Cabinet

As of June 1, 2006

President	Isaias Afwerki

Councillors

Agriculture	Arefaine Berhe
Commissioner for Eritrean Relief and Refugee Commission	Dragon Hailemelekot
Defense	Gen. Sebhat Ephrem
Education	Osman Saleh Mohammed
Energy and Mines	Tesfai Gebreselassie
Finance and Development	Berhane Abrehe
Foreign Affairs	(Vacant)
Health	Saleh Meki
Information (Acting)	Ali Abdu Ahmad
Justice	Fozia Hashim [f]
Labor and Human Welfare	Askalu Menkerios [f]
Land, Water, and Environment	Weldenkiel Ghebremariam
Marine Resources	Ahmad Haji Ali
National Development	Dr. Woldai Futur
Public Works	Abraha Asfaha
Tourism	Amna Nur Husayn [f]
Trade and Industry	Giorgis Teklemikael
Transportation and Communications	Woldemikael Abraha

[f] = female

founding member of the ENA. It calls for more autonomy for the Kunama—an ethnic group indigenous to the Gash-Setit areas of western Eritrea.

Leader: Kerneleos UTHMAN.

Eritrean People's Movement (EPM). The EPM was founded in May 2004 to bypass the ELF/EPLF divide. It reportedly had the support of Sudan, Ethiopia, Australia, Europe, and the United States.

Leaders: Adhanom GEBREMARIAN (Former Ambassador to Nigeria), Abdallah ADEN (Former Ambassador to Sudan), and Mohammed IBRAHIM.

In 2003 the **Afar Revolutionary Democratic United Front** (ARDUF), led by Mohamouda Gaaz, allegedly formed with the goal of establishing an Afar state within Ethiopia. In December 2004,

Gaaz, the Ethiopian Secretary of State for Youth and Sport, started to support a new Eritrean opposition organization, the Afar Federal Alliance (AFA), started by his cousin, Ahmed Saled Gaaz, a veteran of the EFF. The AFA wants to set up a regional state for Afars in Eritrea, similar to the Afar state in Ethiopia. Another ELF veteran now living in Djibouti, Mohamed Moumin Gaaz, also was reportedly involved in the creation of AFA. Gaaz reportedly was planning to run in the next national legislative elections in the Afar Regional State of Ethiopia.

Legislature

The proclamation by the Provisional Government of Eritrea on May 22, 1992, called for legislative authority to be exercised by the Eritrean

People's Liberation Front's Central Committee, which was subsequently augmented by representatives of provincial assemblies to form a transitional **National Assembly** (*Hagerawi Baito*). A resolution by the People's Front for Democracy and Justice (PFDJ) on May 1994 provided for the establishment of a successor body encompassing the 75 members of the PFDJ Central Council, 3 members from each provincial council (currently a total of 18 members following the establishment of six provinces in 1995), and 45 representatives of professional groups, women's organizations, and other social bodies. (The latter were selected by the State Council from lists recommended by the organizations involved.) The 1997 constitution provided for a unicameral legislature of directly elected members. However, elections were subsequently delayed for several reasons, notably the 1998–2000 war with Ethiopia and ongoing failure to finalize border arrangements (see Current issues). In early 2000 the assembly endorsed a new electoral law, declaring, among other things, that 30 percent of the seats in the next assembly election would be reserved for women. As of September 2006, new assembly elections had not been scheduled.

Chair: ISAIAS Afwerki.

Communications

Press

The principal press organ is *Hadas Eritrea* (New Eritrea, 25,000), published five times a week in Tigrigna and Arabic. There is also an English-language government-owned weekly, *Eritrea Profile*. In September 2001 the government closed down all 12 of the nation's privately owned newspapers and arrested a number of journalists because of the Eritrean/Ethiopian war and growing dissent over the authoritarian rule of the Isaias administration. The crackdown elicited an international outcry, but the government has not eased its hard-line position as of mid-2005. Opposition groups and others have started several online newspapers.

News Agency

The Eritrean news agency is ERINA, which provides a daily news update.

Broadcasting and Computing

The Eritrean national radio service is Voice of the Masses (*Dimtsi Hafash*), broadcasting in Afar, Amharic, Arab, Kunama, Tigre, and Tigrigna. Eri-TV, broadcasting from Asmara and Assab, can be received in about 90 percent of the country. There were approximately 4,000 television receivers and 12,000 personal computers serving 9,500 Internet users in 2003. The EDA opposition alliance reportedly started broadcasting as the Voice of Democratic Alliance in April 2005.

Intergovernmental Representation

Ambassador to the U.S.
Girma ASMEROM

U.S. Ambassador to Eritrea
Scott H. DeLISI

Permanent Representative to the UN
Araya DESTA

IGO Memberships (Non-UN)
AfDB, AU, Comesa, IGAD, Interpol, NAM, PCA, WCO

ETHIOPIA

FEDERAL DEMOCRATIC REPUBLIC OF ETHIOPIA

The Country

One of the oldest countries in the world, Ethiopia exhibits an ethnic, linguistic, and cultural diversity that has impaired its political unity and stability in spite of the preponderant position long occupied by the Christian, Amharic- and Tigrinya-speaking inhabitants of the central highlands. Among the more than 70 different ethnic groups, the Amhara and the largely Muslim Oromo (Galla) account for approximately 40 percent of the population each. Amharic, the working language, is spoken by about 60 percent of the people; Galla, Tigrinya, Arabic, Somali, and Tigray are also prominent among the country's 70 languages and over 200 dialects, while English, Italian, and French have traditionally been employed within the educated elite. The Ethiopian Orthodox (Coptic) Church embraces about 40 percent of the population, as does Islam. In 1994 women accounted for 37 percent of the labor force, the vast majority as unpaid agricultural workers. Although females have traditionally influenced decision making among the Amhara and Tigrayan peoples, their representation in the Mengistu government was minimal. There are 116 women in the current House of Peoples' Representatives, up from 42 in the previous membership, while there are 2 women in the cabinet.

One of the world's poorest countries in terms of per capita GNP (estimated at $130 in 1994), Ethiopia remains dependent on agriculture, with over 85 percent of its rapidly expanding population (among the largest in Africa) engaged in farming and livestock-raising. (Despite free-market reforms initiated in the second half of the 1990s, most land remains owned by the government.) Coffee, the principal crop, accounts for more than 40 percent of export earnings; cotton and sugar are also widely harvested. Agricultural success waxes and wanes in response to variable rainfall, and drought and famine have routinely "stalked the land," often generating massive, albeit not always sufficient, international aid shipments. Industrial development, primarily concentrated in nondurable consumer goods, was severely hampered by the 1962–1991 civil war in Eritrea and guerrilla activity in other regions. In 1992 the government launched an ambitious "agricultural-led industrialization" program. Gold and marble are mined commercially, and deposits of copper, potash, and natural gas are awaiting exploitation. Oil exploration rights have been granted recently, although they reportedly remain highly speculative.

Political Status: Former monarchy; provisional military government formally established September 12, 1974; Marxist-Leninist one-party system instituted September 6, 1984; Communist constitution approved by referendum of February 1, 1987, resulting in redesignation of the country as the People's Democratic Republic of Ethiopia; "state responsibility" assumed by rebel coalition upon surrender of the former regime's military commander and acting president in Addis Ababa on May 27, 1991; national charter and transitional government approved by multiparty National Conference that met on July 1–5, 1991; present constitution promulgated December 8, 1994; Federal Democratic Republic proclaimed August 22, 1995.

Area: 436,349 sq. mi. (1,130,138 sq. km.).

Population: 53,477,265 (1994C); 73,090,000 (2005E).

Major Urban Centers (2005E): ADDIS ABABA (2,890,000), Dire Dawa (270,000), Nazret (218,000), Gondar (186,000), Dese (161,000), Jimma (151,000), Harer (117,000).

Working Language: Amharic (all Ethiopian languages enjoy equal state recognition).

Monetary Unit: Birr (official rate July 1, 2006: 8.74 birr = $1US).

President: GIRMA Wolde Giorgis (nonparty); nominated by the Ethiopian People's Revolutionary Democratic Front and elected by the Parliament on October 8, 2001, to a six-year term, succeeding NEGASO Gidada (Oromo Peoples' Democratic Organization).

Prime Minister: MELES Zenawi (Tigray People's Liberation Front); elected by the House of Peoples' Representatives on August 23, 1995, succeeding TAMIRAT Layne (Amhara National Democratic Movement); reelected to another five-year term on October 10, 2000; reelected to a third five-year term on October 10, 2005.

In January 1996 the World Bank announced that it had helped negotiate forgiveness of some $250 million of Ethiopia's commercial debt, although nearly $4 billion of additional external debt continued to constrain economic advancement. In October the International Monetary Fund (IMF) approved a three-year loan totalling $127 million to support the government's medium-term economic reform program for 1996–1999. However, the IMF suspended the aid in October 1997 and requested that additional reforms be implemented. Subsequently, Addis Ababa began to "pursue prudent macroeconomic policies and implement important structural reforms," according to the IMF, and in October 1998 the fund approved the release of the second of three scheduled annual payments. In 1995–1997 Ethiopia's GDP grew in real terms by an annual average of 8.0 percent. Although Ethiopia was considered as of early 1998 to be positioned for sustained economic improvement, the 1998–2000 border war with Ethiopia (see Political background and Current issues, below) severely eroded the confidence of investors and redirected national funds desperately needed for social services toward the military. The conflict also slowed down the government's privatization campaign and plans to strengthen the financial sector.

GDP grew by 7.7 percent in 2000–2001 and 1.6 percent in 2001–2002 but fell by 3.9 percent in 2002–2003, mostly due to collapsing coffee prices and drought. Agricultural recovery in 2003–2004 produced much better growth (11.6 percent), although Ethiopia continued to rank 170 out of 177 countries in the UN's Human Development Index and 45 percent of the population was considered to be living in poverty. The World Bank, the IMF, and Russia offered debt relief in 2004, Ethiopia remaining as one of the world's biggest per capita recipients of emergency assistance (it was estimated that 11 million people depended on humanitarian aid). The economy grew by 8.8 percent in 2004–2005, according to the IMF, with inflation for that fiscal year registering 6.8 percent, although a significant increase in inflation was subsequently reported. The IMF called upon the government to reinvigorate the privatization program, accelerate structural reform, strengthen the nation's legal and regulatory framework, and devote more if its budget toward poverty reduction. The IMF announced additional debt relief for Ethiopia in late 2005 and called for increased donor assistance. However, that question had become problematic by that time because of severe political discord in Ethiopia (see Current issues, below).

Government and Politics

Political Background

After centuries of medieval isolation, Ethiopia began its history as a modern state with the reign of Emperor MENELIK II (1889–1913), who established a strong central authority and successfully resisted attempts at colonization by Italy and other powers. Emperor HAILE SELASSIE I (Ras TAFARI Makonnen) succeeded to the throne in 1930 on the death of his cousin, the Empress ZAUDITU. Confronted with a full-scale invasion by Fascist Italy in 1935, Haile Selassie appealed in vain for assistance from the League of Nations and remained abroad until Ethiopia's liberation by the British and the liquidation of Italy's East African Empire in 1941. In accordance with a decision of the UN General Assembly, the former Italian colony of Eritrea was joined to Ethiopia in 1952 as an autonomous unit in an Ethiopian-Eritrean federation. Abandonment of the federal structure by formal incorporation of Eritrea into Ethiopia in 1962 fanned widespread separatist sentiment in Eritrea.

Although the post–World War II period witnessed a movement away from absolute monarchy, the pace of liberalization did not meet popular expectations, and in early 1974 an uprising among troops of Ethiopia's Second Army Division gradually escalated into a political revolt. As a result, Prime Minister Tshafe Tezaz AKLILU Habte-Wold resigned on February 28 and was replaced by ENDALKACHEW Makonnen, who also was unable to contain discontent among military, labor, and student groups. By late spring many aristocrats and former government officials had been imprisoned, and on July 22 Endalkachew was forced to resign in favor of Mikael IMRU.

On September 12, 1974, the military announced that the emperor had been deposed and that a Provisional Military Government (PMG) had been formed under Lt. Gen. AMAN Mikael Andom. Initially, the military presented a united front, but rival factions soon emerged. On November 24 approximately 60 officials, including two former prime ministers and Aman Andom, were executed, apparently on the initiative of (then) Maj. MENGISTU Haile-Mariam, strongman of the little-publicized Armed Forces Coordinating Committee, or *Dergue*, as it was popularly known. After November 28 the *Dergue* acted through a Provisional Military Administrative Council (PMAC), whose chair, Brig. Gen. TEFERI Banti, served concurrently as acting head of state and government.

Former emperor Haile Selassie, in detention since his deposition, died in August 1975. Earlier, on March 21, the PMAC had decreed formal abolition of the monarchy while declaring its intention to organize a new national political movement "guided by the aims of Ethiopian socialism."

On February 3, 1977, following reports of a power struggle within the *Dergue*, General Teferi and six associates were killed in an armed encounter in the Grand Palace in Addis Ababa. Eight days later, Mengistu and Lt. Col. ATNAFU Abate were named chair and vice chair, respectively, of the PMAC in a proclamation that also modified the *Dergue* structure. However, Colonel Atnafu was executed on November 11 for alleged "counter-revolutionary crimes." Collaterally, antigovernment violence, dubbed the "white terror," flared in Addis Ababa amid indications of growing coordination between several opposition groups, including the Marxist Ethiopian People's Revolutionary Party (EPRP) and the more conservative Ethiopian Democratic Union (EDU). The Mengistu regime responded by mounting an indiscriminate "red terror" in December 1977–February 1978 based in part on the arming of civilians in urban dweller associations (*kebeles*).

The struggle for control in Addis Ababa was accompanied by military challenges on three major fronts. By March 1977 virtually all of northern Eritrea was under rebel administration, while government forces were being subjected to increased pressure by EDU guerrillas in the northwest. Moreover, in late July the government conceded that the greater part of the eastern region of Ogaden had fallen to insurgents of the Western Somalia Liberation Front (WSLF), who were supported by Somali regular forces. On September 7 Addis Ababa severed relations with Mogadishu because of the "full-scale war" that existed between the two countries. By mid-December, however, a massive influx of Cuban personnel and Soviet equipment had shifted the military balance in Ethiopia's favor, and most of the region was recovered prior to formal Somali withdrawal in March 1978. A renewed offensive was then mounted in Eritrea, and in late November government forces recaptured the last two major cities held by the rebels, the strategically important Red Sea port of Massawa and Keren, some 70 miles northwest of the provincial capital, Asmara.

Despite the success of the 1978 anti-insurgent campaigns, a major offensive in mid-1979 to wipe out remaining resistance in Eritrea proved ineffectual, with government control remaining limited to the principal towns and connecting corridors. Similar conditions prevailed in the Ogaden, where the WSLF and its ally, the Somali Abo Liberation Front (SALF), persisted in launching guerrilla attacks. In response, Ethiopia was reported to have initiated a "scorched-earth" policy—poisoning water supplies, killing herds of livestock, strafing settled areas–that further aggravated what the UN Office of High Commissioner for Refugees had earlier described as the world's worst refugee problem.

Following a number of unsuccessful attempts to unite existing Marxist parties, a Commission for Organizing the Party of the Working People of Ethiopia (COPWE) was formed in December 1979 to pave the way for a Soviet-style system of government. On September 10, 1984, COPWE's work was declared to have been completed, with Colonel Mengistu being designated secretary general of a new Workers' Party of Ethiopia (WPE); however,

the PMAC remained in effective control, pending completion of a civilian governing structure.

A commission appointed and chaired by Colonel Mengistu presented the draft of a new constitution in early 1987. A reported 81 percent of voters approved the document at a referendum on February 1, the government announcing three weeks later that the country would thenceforth be styled the People's Democratic Republic of Ethiopia (PDRE).

A unicameral national legislature (*Shengo*), elected June 14, 1987, convened September 9, and on the following day it selected Colonel Mengistu as the country's first president. The *Shengo* also named Lt. Col. FISSEHA Desta, theretofore deputy secretary general of the PMAC Standing Committee, as PDRE vice president and elected a 24-member State Council, headed by Mengistu and Fisseha as president and vice president, respectively. The former deputy chair of the PMAC Council of Ministers, Capt. FIKRE-SELASSIE Wogderes, was designated prime minister of an administration whose composition, announced on September 20, was largely unchanged from that of its predecessor.

The new government was greeted by vigorous rebel offensives: the Eritrean People's Liberation Front (EPLF) claimed a succession of victories over government troops beginning in September 1987, while in March 1988 the Tigray People's Liberation Front (TPLF) took advantage of Addis Ababa's setbacks in Eritrea to launch a renewed offensive in their 13-year struggle for autonomy. In April Mengistu, buffeted by military reversals and deteriorating troop morale, signed a cease-fire accord with Somali President Siad Barre, thus freeing troops for redeployment to Eritrea, most of which, despite the recapture of some rebel-held villages, remained under EPLF control.

Conditions worsened substantially for the central government during 1989. A failed military coup in mid-May, during which the defense and industry ministers were killed, provoked a purge of senior officers that yielded the loss of most seasoned commanders. Three months earlier the Ethiopian People's Revolutionary Democratic

Front (EPRDF), a base-broadening coalition recently established by the TPLF, had launched another offensive that dealt the government a series of major setbacks. In August Colonel Mengistu felt obliged to augment his army (already black Africa's largest at more than 300,000 men) by mass mobilization and conscription. A month later Mengistu accepted an overture by former U.S. president Jimmy Carter to open peace talks with the EPLF, subsequently accepting Carter and former Tanzanian president Julius Nyerere as cochairmen of the discussions. Meanwhile, preliminary negotiations with the EPRDF were launched in Rome in October, although they were linked by the Tigrayans to "the irrevocable fall of the current regime." In November, with EPRDF forces moving toward the capital, Prime Minister Fikre-Selassie was dismissed for "health reasons" and replaced, on an acting basis, by Deputy Prime Minister HAILU Yimanu. Shortly thereafter, fighting also broke out in the east between government troops and rebel forces of the Oromo Liberation Front (OLF). Faced with continued military adversity, diminished Soviet support, and renewed projections of widespread famine, President Mengistu in March 1990 formally terminated his commitment to Marxism. However, the regime remained on the brink of collapse as EPRDF troops advanced to within 150 miles of Addis Ababa and EPLF forces gained control of all of Eritrea except for several major cities.

In January 1991 the EPRDF and the EPLF, which had been coordinating military operations for two years, devised a "final" battle plan after the TPLF reportedly agreed to a self-determination referendum in Eritrea following the anticipated rebel victory. With the OLF also a participant, the anti-Mengistu alliance launched a decisive offensive in February.

In what was seen as a last-ditch effort to salvage his regime, President Mengistu on April 26, 1991, announced the appointment of former Foreign Minister TESFAYE Dinka, a moderate with ties to the United States and Western Europe, to the vacant position of prime minister and named Lt. Gen. TESFAYE Gebre-Kidan as vice president.

However, on May 21, as EPRDF troops encircled Addis Ababa, Colonel Mengistu, under pressure from U.S. officials to prevent further bloodshed, resigned as head of state and fled to Zimbabwe, Vice President Tesfaye becoming acting president. Three days later the EPLF sealed its control of Eritrea by capturing the towns of Asmara and Keren, and, with EPRDF fighters poised to attack the capital, General Tesfaye "effectively surrendered" on May 27. Under an agreement reached at a U.S.-brokered conference in London, the EPRDF took control of Addis Ababa on May 28 with only minimal resistance from hold-out government troops. On the same day TPLF leader MELES Zenawi announced the impending formation of an interim government that would assume responsibility for "the whole country" until Ethiopia's political future could be further defined. Concurrently, however, EPLF leader Isaias Afwerki announced the establishment of a separate provisional government for Eritrea. Although some friction was subsequently reported between the two groups, a multiparty National Conference was launched on July 1 to chart the country's political future. On July 3 the EPRDF and the EPLF (technically attending as an observer) announced an agreement whereby the former would support a referendum in 1993 on Eritrean independence in return for access to the Red Sea port of Assab. At the conclusion of the Conference two days later, a National Charter was adopted that offered guarantees of basic human rights, freedom of association, access to mass media, judicial independence, and substantial autonomy for the country's numerous ethnic groups. In addition, an 87-member Council of Representatives was named that on July 21 formalized Meles Zenawi's status as head of state. Subsequently, on July 29, the acting chief of government, TAMIRAT Layne, was confirmed as prime minister, with a 16-member cabinet being announced on August 10.

At the long awaited referendum in Eritrea of April 23–25, 1993, 99.8 percent of those participating voted for independence, and on May 3 Addis Ababa endorsed the action, which was formalized on May 24. Subsequently, balloting for a 547-member Ethiopian Constituent Assembly was held on June 5, 1994, with the EPRDF winning an overwhelming majority in reporting districts (polling in Dire Dawa and elsewhere in the east and southeast being postponed until August 28 because of unsettled conditions in the largely Somali-dominated region).

While most of the major non-EPRDF groups participated in the Constituent Assembly poll, all but the largely progovernment Ethiopian National Democratic Party (ENDP) objected to the constitution adopted on December 8, 1994, and declared their intention to boycott the federal and state elections of May 7, 1995. Despite two bilateral negotiating sessions between government and opposition delegates in Washington in February and Addis Ababa in March, no resolution of the impasse was found. Representatives of the opposition Council of Alternative Forces for Peace and Democracy in Ethiopia (CAFPDE), led by BEYENE Petros, complained of a "stranglehold" by the EPRDF on the police and armed forces, the detention of numerous regime opponents, and a ban on many party activities. For its part, the government, through its chief negotiator, DAWIT Yohannes, called for acceptance of Ethiopia's existing state bodies and denied that it held political prisoners, insisting that those incarcerated encompassed only "warmongers." As a result of the stalemate, the EPRDF and its constituent groups swept the May balloting.

On August 21, 1995, the recently elected House of Peoples' Representatives convened to accept a transfer of power from its military-backed predecessor, and on August 22, after formal proclamation of the Federal Democratic Republic of Ethiopia, the House elected NEGASO Gidada to the essentially titular office of federal president. On August 23 the legislators elected former interim president Meles Zenawi to the far more powerful office of prime minister.

The cabinet named by Prime Minister Meles Zenawi in 1995 did not represent a cross-section of Ethiopian politics; it was, however, carefully balanced along ethnic lines, containing four Amharas, four Oromos, two Gurage, and one representative each from the Afar, Hadiya, Harari, Kembata,

Somali, Tigray, and Welayita communities. By mid-1996 the government was reported to be under heavy external pressure to bring nonsecessionist opposition groups into the federal administration. However, the EPRDF resisted the appeals, apparently concentrating instead on what the *Indian Ocean Newsletter* described as efforts "to prove that all its opponents are apprentice terrorists."

In October 1995, after four months of deliberation, the High Court in Addis Ababa ruled that, as a signatory of the international convention on genocide, Ethiopia was competent to try members of the former regime on charges of crimes against humanity. Accordingly, it was announced that a trial would proceed for more than 70 defendants, including, all in absentia, former president Mengistu Haile-Mariam, former prime minister Fikre-Selassie Wogderes, and former vice president Fisseha Desta. The trial, which the *New York Times* called possibly the most extensive of its kind since Nuremberg, proceeded slowly in 1996, however. In addition to the current defendants, more than 1700 former soldiers, police, and "mid-level" administrators were also awaiting trial. On February 13, 1997, special prosecutors in Addis Ababa brought additional charges against Mengistu and more than 5,000 officials of the *Dergue* regime (3,000 of them in absentia). The trials were expected to last at least three years.

During March 1997 social discontent surfaced in segments of the Amhara population, resulting from the government's "land reform" projects, which were seen by opponents as a policy to serve the peasants close to the ruling EPRDF. Attention throughout the rest of the year focused on efforts by the EPRDF to negotiate agreements with Oromo, Somali, and Afar groups that would permit implementation of the delayed regional autonomy plan (see various sections below for further information).

With a swiftness that stunned observers, a border dispute between Ethiopia and Eritrea escalated in mid-1998 from what was initially depicted as a minor skirmish in early May into full-scale fighting by June. Among the many casualties of the war was their joint effort, along with Uganda, to contain Sudan's regional influence, in particular Khartoum's effort to spread militant Islamic fundamentalism. Indeed, in its quest for regional allies, Addis Ababa reportedly toned down its anti-Sudanese rhetoric and opened a dialogue with Khartoum.

The war with Eritrea dominated Ethiopian affairs for the remainder of 1998 through 2000. (See Political background in article on Eritrea for an extensive history of the conflict.) Nearly every segment of Ethiopian society, including the opposition parties, appeared to support the military campaign, and the EPRDF dominated the balloting that began in May 2000 for the House of Peoples' Representatives (see Legislature, below, for details), while Meles was reelected to a second five-year term as prime minister on October 10, 2000, by acclamation in the House of Peoples' Representatives. On October 8, 2001, GIRMA Wolde Giorgis was selected to succeed President Negaso, who had become embroiled in a dispute with Meles and his supporters over the outcome of the war (see Current issues, below).

New balloting for the House of Peoples' Representatives was held on May 15, 2005, initial results indicating a strong challenge to the EPRDF from two new opposition alliances—the Coalition for Unity and Democracy (CUD) and the United Ethiopean Democratic Forces (UEDF). Both opposition groups charged the government with widespread fraud in the conduct of the poll and the tallying of the votes, and reballoting was ordered by the National Election Board in a number of constituencies. However, the EPRDF was credited with winning all of the seats subject to reballoting, and the final results (released in September) accorded the EPRDF and its allies an even greater majority than originally projected, prompting severe domestic turmoil (see Current issues, below). Meles was reelected by a show of hands in the legislature in a session on October 10 that was boycotted by more than 100 opposition members. The new cabinet that was appointed the following day was widely reshuffled, although portfolios remained primarily in the hands of EPRDF components.

Constitution and Government

An imperial constitution, adopted in 1955, was abrogated when the military assumed power in 1974. The 1987 constitution provided for a Communist system of government based on "democratic centralism." In July 1991, two months after the overthrow of the Mengistu regime, a National Conference was convened that approved a transitional government charter providing for an 87-member quasi-legislative body, the Council of Representatives, drawn from the various national freedom units. The council, intended to serve for a 24-month period, was empowered to designate a chair who would serve as head of a transitional government. Subject to council approval, the chair would appoint a prime minister and other cabinet members. The council was directed to oversee the drafting of a constitution that would ensure the realization of "a completely democratic system" and to prepare the country for elections to a National Assembly under the new basic law.

The document promulgated in December 1994 provided for a new House of Peoples' Representatives as "the highest organ of State authority." Its members are directly elected for five-year terms from single member districts, with special representation of at least 20 seats for minority nationalities. In addition, representatives of Ethiopia's "nations, nationalities, and peoples" constitute a senate-like House of the Federation, whose functions include that of constitutional interpretation. The president of the republic is nominated by the House of Peoples' Representatives and elected for a once-renewable six-year term by a two-thirds vote of the two houses in joint session. A prime minister, who serves as chair of the Council of Ministers and commander in chief of the armed forces, is elected by the House of Peoples' Representatives from among those sitting as members of the majority party or coalition for a term normally coincident with the legislative mandate. The judiciary includes both Federal and State Supreme Courts, appointed by their respective legislative councils; there is also a Court of Constitutional Inquiry, whose principal activity is to review disputes for submission to the House of the Federation.

Ethiopia was traditionally divided into 15 provinces, exclusive of the capital. However, in late 1987 legislation was enacted to redraw the internal boundaries in favor of 24 administrative regions, plus (in an apparent effort to placate separatists) five "autonomous regions," four of which (Assab, Dire Dawa, Tigray, and Ogaden) would be coterminous with administrative regions, while Eritrea would contain three. The present republic encompasses the following nine states: Afar; Amhara; Beneshangul-Gumuz; Gambela Peoples; Harari People; Oromia; Somalia; Southern Nations, Nationalities, and Peoples; and Tigray. The federal capital, Addis Ababa, is a separate entity, although it also serves as the capital of Oromia. In addition, there is a separate Dire Dawa Administrative Council. (Both cities enjoy the same autonomy as the states; for example, each elects its own representatives to the national legislature.) New states may be created following majority approval by a nationality group and endorsement by a two-thirds vote of the relevant state council. A somewhat unusual guarantee of self-determination includes a right of secession if requested by a two-thirds majority of the group's legislative body, endorsed by a similar state council majority, and approved by a majority vote in a referendum called by the federal government.

Foreign Relations

A founding member of both the United Nations and the Organization of African Unity (OAU, subsequently the African Union—AU), Ethiopia under Emperor Haile Selassie was long a leading advocate of regional cooperation and peaceful settlement in Africa. Addis Ababa was the site of the first African summit conference in 1963 and remains the seat of the OAU Secretariat and the UN Economic Commission for Africa.

As a result of the emperor's overthrow in 1974, Ethiopia shifted dramatically from a generally pro-Western posture to one of near-exclusive dependence on the Soviet bloc. Moscow guided Addis Ababa in the formation of a Soviet-style ruling party and provided weapons and other assistance to military units (including some 11,000 Cuban troops) during the Ogaden war in 1977–1978; while initially maintaining a low profile in regard to the Eritrean secessionist movements (the two most important of which were Marxist-inspired), it gradually increased its support of counterinsurgency efforts. In 1988 the Soviets provided the government with 250,000 tons of grain for relief purposes, thus avoiding repetition of criticism it had received for failing to provide assistance during the 1984 famine. Meanwhile, despite the continued presence of 1,400 Soviet military advisors, Moscow's interest in supporting the Mengistu government's war against the rebels appeared to be waning and, in September 1989, Cuba announced plans to withdraw all its troops.

Because of ethnic links to Somalia and the presence of virtually equal numbers of Muslims and Christians in Eritrea, most Arab governments (with the exception of Marxist South Yemen) remained neutral or provided material support to the guerrilla movements. Most black African governments, on the other hand, tended to support Addis Ababa, despite an OAU posture of formal neutrality.

During the 1980s relations with neighboring countries were strained by refugees fleeing Ethiopia because of famine or opposition to the Mengistu regime's resettlement policies. Tensions with Somalia, including sporadic border skirmishes in 1987, centered on the Ogaden region, with Addis Ababa accusing Mogadishu of backing the secession efforts of the Somalian-speaking population. However, in April 1988 Mengistu and Somalia President Siad Barre signed a treaty calling for mutual troop withdrawal, an exchange of POWs, and an end to Somalian funding of the rebels.

Relations with Sudan also fluctuated after the Sudanese coup of April 1985. In mid-1986 Khartoum announced that it had ordered the cessation of Eritrean rebel activity in eastern Sudan, apparently expecting that Addis Ababa would reciprocate by reducing its aid to the Sudanese People's Liberation Army (SPLA). Subsequently,

Khartoum denounced continued Ethiopian support of the SPLA as "aggression." In 1988 the continued SPLA insurgency forced more than 300,000 southern Sudanese refugees across Ethiopia's border, many starving to death en route.

Although Ethiopia remained strongly linked to the Soviet Union, anti-American rhetoric became manifestly subdued during an influx of U.S. food aid, valued at more than $430 million, from 1984 through 1986. Following the government's March 1988 expulsion of international aid donors from rebel-held areas, Washington reportedly began channeling food supplies to northern Ethiopian drought areas through Sudanese and rebel organizations. The U.S. policy of limiting its support to humanitarian aid continued into 1989, despite the decision of international creditors to fund Addis Ababa's agricultural reform program. In April 1989 the Mengistu regime indicated a desire to resume full diplomatic relations with Washington (reduced to the chargé level in 1980) but withdrew the overture in the face of a cool U.S. response. Washington reportedly exerted considerable pressure on Colonel Mengistu to resign in May 1991, named an ambassador to the new government in June, and was one of a dozen foreign governments to send a team of observers to the National Conference in July.

The attempted assassination of Egyptian President Mubarak on June 26, 1995 (see Egypt article), initially led to friction between Cairo and Addis Ababa because of intimations from Egyptian intelligence sources that the attack might have been aided by members of Ethiopia's security forces. After an Egyptian investigation team had complained of their treatment to U.S. embassy officials, they were ordered to leave the country. Subsequently, Ethiopian-Sudanese relations again plummeted in the wake of charges by Addis Ababa that Khartoum was sheltering several people implicated in the Mubarak affair. In September 1996 an Ethiopian court sentenced three men to death in connection with the assassination attempt, which by then was being attributed to the Islamic Group (see Illegal Groups under Political Parties in article on Egypt). Ethiopian prosecutors charged that the defendants had received military training in "terrorist" camps in Sudan. Egyptian officials praised the verdict and finally commended the Ethiopian authorities for their handling of the case.

According to many observers the Ethiopian, Eritrean, and Ugandan governments tried to coordinate efforts in 1996–1997 to control the spread of Islamic fundamentalism in the Horn of Africa, a policy that was also promoted by the United States. The campaign was mainly directed toward isolating Sudan's NIF government (see article on Sudan), the Ethiopian government providing support to the Sudanese opposition, mainly the SPLA. It also endorsed the Sodere agreement signed in January 1997 by 26 Somalian factions, which was intended to sideline Somalia's self-declared "president" and United Somali Congress—SNA leader, Hussein Mohamed FARAH AIDID (see article on Somalia). In addition, Ethiopia reportedly convinced those factions to assist in the fight with the Islamic Union guerrillas that operate along the border of Ethiopia and Somalia.

Diplomatic tension between Kenya and Ethiopia flared up in March 1997 when some 40 people were killed in Kenya by tribesmen reportedly infiltrating from the Ethiopian border. The two governments subsequently agreed to cooperate to control their borders. Meanwhile, Britain temporarily suspended its aid program to the country after ASSEFA Maru, a member of the Ethiopian Teachers Association, was killed by policemen in May 1997. On November 24, 1997, Italian President Oscar Luigi Scalfaro, during a trip to Addis Ababa, formally apologized for the Italian invasion and occupation of Ethiopia between 1936–1941.

Current Issues

In describing the 1998–2000 border war with Eritrea, the *New York Times* said it was "hard to think of a more pointless and wasteful international conflict." As many as 60,000 Ethiopians lost their lives in the fighting, which, while sporadic, was described at its most intense moments as the biggest war in the world, although international attention was minimal. Despite the costs, the

Ethiopian populace embraced the cause with enthusiasm and wildly celebrated the country's military success and the government's proclamation of "victory." However, the terms of the peace accord (see Current issues in article on Eritrea for details) subsequently proved highly controversial in Ethiopia. Critics both within and outside the EPRDF accused Prime Minister Meles of having "caved in" by accepting a settlement that did not appropriately reflect the Ethiopian military dominance. Among other things, Meles's opponents decried the failure of the government to gain guaranteed access in the agreement to the Eritrean ports of Assab and Massawa. (Ethiopia had become landlocked by Eritrea's independence, and its economy had been severely constrained by the lack of port access since the outbreak of hostilities.) Tension over the matter culminated in an attempt by TPLF hard-liners to remove Meles from his party post in early 2001. Although Meles survived, the rebellion had spread to other components of the EPRDF, and Meles's position remained fragile. Student protests in April contributed to the sense of instability, and the government subsequently launched an extensive crackdown on its opponents, against many of whom it leveled corruption charges. Meanwhile, President Negaso sided with the critics, sealing his political fate in view of Meles's successful counterattack. Girma Wolde Giorgis, Negaso's successor, was not widely known, even though he was a member of the House of Peoples' Representatives. Significantly, however, Girma was a member of the Oromo ethnic group (as was Negaso), his selection apparently reflecting the TPLF's intensifying concern over the growing unease in Oromia and other southern regions regarding TPLF dominance at the national level. Meanwhile, battles were reported in 2002 between Ethiopian forces and fighters from the Oromo Liberation Front, Ogaden National Liberation Front, and other smaller secessionist and/or anti-EPRDF groups.

Severe food shortages were reported in early 2003, while additional complications for the government arose from renewed tension along the border with Eritrea in late 2003 and widespread ethnic clashes in the state of Gambela in mid-2004. By November 2004 it was clear that final peace talks between Eritrea and Ethiopia had broken down, Meles, under heavy domestic pressure, having refused to accept the UN's proposed demarcation of the border, particularly the decision that the town of Badme would be Eritrean. Despite the presence of 4,200 UN peacekeepers, Ethiopia deployed its own troops to control Badme. At the same time, Meles continued to be perceived as an important ally of the West, particularly in regard to Washington's "war on terrorism."

All in all, the turmoil was expected to give the newly reorganized opposition parties an opportunity to present a genuine challenge to the EPRDF in the legislative balloting of May 15, 2005. For the first time, opposition candidates were allowed to "campaign openly" and were granted some access to state-run media. The election was also keenly observed by the west, which hoped the poll would represent an important step in the maturation of Ethiopia's fledgling democratic process and solidify Meles's credentials as one of the new breed of reformist African leaders. However, the election and its aftermath had just the opposite effect. The CUD and UEDF immediately challenged the preliminary results as fraudulent, claiming that they should have been credited with a majority of the seats and that the vote had been rigged. Although at least token reballoting was ordered in some constituencies, Meles quickly signaled a hard-line attitude toward protesters by banning all demonstrations in Addis Ababa and placing the capital police under his direct control. Student demonstrators clashed with police in several cities in June, leaving some 40 people dead, and the antigovernment outcry intensified in September when the government's official final results gave the EPRDF and its allies more than 68 percent of the seats. For their part, EU observers concluded that the election had failed to meet international standards.

Unrest culminated in another deadly conflict between protesters and government forces on November 1, 2005, during an AU summit in Addis Ababa. The government blamed "stone-throwers" for initiating the battle, while the opposition blamed unnecessarily harsh reactions by security forces to a peaceful demonstration. Nearly 50 people died in the clashes, to which the government responded by detaining thousands of protesters and arresting nearly all of the CUD leadership, prominent members of other opposition parties, and a number of journalists and human rights activists. Those arrested were charged with treason, promoting violence, and attempting to overthrow the government. (Meles indicated his belief that the opposition forces were attempting to topple his regime by emulating the mass demonstrations that had proven effective in countries such as Georgia, Kyrgyzstan, and Ukraine.)

Human rights groups expressed outrage over the crackdown, and the World Bank, EU, and UK suspended aid to Ethiopia in an effort to pressure Meles to adopt a more conciliatory stance. However, the trials of the detainees opened in May 2006 , with Meles dismissing accusations regarding his "dictatorial rule." By that time, the prime minister was also facing growing international pressure regarding Ethiopia's continued refusal to accept the final decisions of the commission established to demarcate the border with Eritrea (see Current issues in article on Eritrea for details.)

Political Parties and Groups

Political parties were not permitted under the monarchy, while legal party activity during the period of rule by the Provisional Military Administrative Council did not emerge until the formation of the regime-supportive Workers' Party of Ethiopia (WPE) in 1984. The 1987 constitution reaffirmed the WPE's position as the country's only authorized party, describing it as the "leading force of the state and society" and granting it wide authority, including the right to approve all candidates for the National Assembly. As the Mengistu regime faced accelerating rebel activity and declining Soviet support, the WPE in March 1990 abandoned its Marxist-Leninist ideology, changed its name to the Ethiopian Democratic Unity Party (EDUP), and opened its ranks to former members of opposition groups in an unsuccessful effort to broaden its base of public support. Following the overthrow of the Mengistu government in May 1991, leaders of the interim government announced that the EDUP had been dissolved. As of 2006 it was reported that some 78 parties had been recognized, although a majority of them were operating only at the regional level.

Government Parties

Ethiopian People's Revolutionary Democratic Front (EPRDF). The EPRDF was launched in May 1988 by the TPLF in an effort to expand its influence beyond Tigray Province, over which it had recently achieved military dominance. Although the TPLF had long subscribed to Marxist-Leninist ideology, an EPRDF congress in early 1991 called for development of a "small-scale" economy in which farmers would lease land from the government and control the sale of their products. While the new platform called for tight government control of foreign trade, it also endorsed an expanded role for private investment in the economy. In another significant policy shift, the congress, while displaying a clear preference for a united Ethiopia, accepted Eritrea's right to self-determination.

Joined in a loose military alliance with the Eritrean People's Liberation Front (see article on Eritrea) and the OLF (below), the EPRDF led the march on Addis Ababa that ousted the Mengistu regime in May 1991. Assuming power in the name of the EPRDF, Meles Zenawi was confirmed as head of state by the National Conference pending the outcome, under a new constitution, of multiparty elections originally scheduled for 1993, but not held until May 1995. The EPRDF won over 90 percent of the seats in that balloting, and Meles was elected prime minister by the House of Peoples' Representatives in August, the office of president (which he had previously held) having been reduced to figurehead status. The EPRDF dominated the 2000 legislative balloting and unanimously reelected Meles as EPRDF chair at a congress on September 1, 2001, the prime minister having survived serious dissension within the TPLF and other EPRDF component groups (see below). The congress also selected a new 140-member council, a 38-member Executive Committee, and an 8-member "Control Commission."

Leader: MELES Zenawi (Prime Minister of the Republic and Chair of the EPRDF), ADDISU Legesse (Deputy Chair).

Tigray People's Liberation Front (TPLF). Formed in 1975 by former students who had been strongly influenced by Marxism-Leninism, the TPLF initially pursued independence or at least substantial autonomy for Tigray Province. However, its subsequent goal became the overthrow of the Mengistu regime and establishment of a new central government involving all ethnic groups. Established in 1985, a pro-Albanian Marxist-Leninist League of Tigray (MLLT) gained ideological ascendancy within the TPLF, and MLLT leader Meles Zenawi was elected TPLF chair at a 1989 congress. By that time the TPLF had become one of the country's most active antigovernment groups, its fighters having gained control of Tigray and pushed south toward Addis Ababa. The TPLF subsequently began to shed its ideological rigidity, reflecting both the growing worldwide disillusionment with communism and a need to broaden the front's philosophical base in preparation for a possible government takeover. Consequently, by the time TPLF soldiers captured Addis Ababa in the name of the EPRDF in May 1991, the front's leaders were describing themselves as supporters of Western-style multiparty democracy and limited private enterprise. However, disagreement was subsequently reported within the TPLF regarding the proposed privatization of state-run enterprises.

Following the tentative conclusion of the border war with Eritrea in 2000, hard-liners in the TPLF reportedly came close to ousting Meles in March 2001. Among other things, the dissidents, who included TEWOLDE Wolde-Mariam, then vice chair of the TPLF, strongly objected to the perceived lack of results in the peace accord as well as the imposition of economic austerity measures requested by the IMF and World Bank. Meles and his "reformist" supporters subsequently launched a purge of many of the critics.

Leader: MELES Zenawi (Prime Minister of the Republic and Chair of the TPLF).

Amhara National Democratic Movement (ANDM). The ANDM was initially established in 1980 as the Ethiopian People's Democratic Movement (EPDM) by former members of the EPRP (below) under the guidance of the TPLF. In 1986 a number of pitched battles were reported in Wollo Province between EPDM forces and government troops. Subsequent ideological controversy generated the creation of an Ethiopian Marxist-Leninist Force (EMLF) to serve the same function in the EPDM as the MLLT was serving in the TPLF. The EPDM joined the TPLF in the 1988 formation of the EPRDF and adopted its present name at its third congress in January 1994.

In October 1996 it was reported that former prime minister Tamirat Layne had been dismissed as ANDM secretary general during an emergency meeting of the Central Committee for "acting contrary to the principles for which the ANDM has stood during the last 16 years." Tamirat was also subsequently fired from his posts of deputy prime minister and minister of national defense as part of what was widely viewed as an anticorruption campaign. He was sentenced in 1999 to 18 years in prison on corruption charges.

Divisions were reported within the ANDM in 2005–2006, as some members objected to what they perceived as growing anti-Amhara rhetoric on the part of members of the TPLF and OPDO.

Leader: ADDISU Legesse (Chair and Deputy Prime Minister of the Republic), TEFERA Walwa, BEREKET Simeon, HI-LAWE Yosef.

Oromo Peoples' Democratic Organization (OPDO). The OPDO was formed in April 1990 under the direction of the TPLF, its membership reportedly comprising Oromo prisoners of war captured by the TPLF in sporadic clashes with the OLF (below). The OLF immediately challenged the creation of the OPDO as an "unfriendly and hostile gesture," and the OPDO's existence remained a source of friction between the TPLF and the OLF. During 1992 the OPDO was reported to have been weakened by the desertion of a number of its followers to the OLF.

The OPDO, as expected, dominated the May 2000 elections in the state of Oromia, securing 173 of 178 seats in the House of Peoples' Representatives and 535 of 537 seats on the State Council. As with the TPLF and SEPDF, the OPDO was subsequently riven by dissension generated by hard-liners unhappy with Prime Minister Meles, particularly in regard to the conclusion of the border war with Eritrea. Among the consequences of the fractionalization was the dismissal of Negaso Gidada, then president of the republic, from the OPDO central committee and his eventual departure from the party. The OPDO declined to 110 seats in the 2005 balloting for the House of Peoples' Representatives.

Leader: Abdullah GEMEDA (President), Junedi SADO (President of the State of Oromia).

Southern Ethiopia Peoples' Democratic Front (SEPDF). The SEPDF comprises many small, mostly ethnically based parties. It secured 112 of 123 seats from the state of Southern Nations, Nationalities, and Peoples in the 2000 balloting for the House of Peoples' Representatives. (For a list of component parties that gained representation, see Legislature in article on Ethiopia in the 2005–2006 *Handbook*.) A number of members of the SEPDF's Central Committee were dismissed in 2002 in the wake of friction attributed to ethnic disputes as well as disagreement reflective of similar problems in the OPDO and TPLF over the policies of Prime Minister Meles.

Leaders: HAILEMARIAM Desalegn (Chair), KASSU Illala.

Somali Peoples' Democratic Party (SPDP). The SPDP was launched in Jijiga in Ethiopia's state of Somalia in June 1998 by the Ethiopian Somali Democratic League (ESDL) and a progovernment faction of the ONLF (below) that had split from its parent grouping regarding the question of independence. (The ESDL and the ONLF faction had formed a victorious coalition in the 1995 elections in the region.)

The ESDL had been formed in February 1994 by the following progovernment eastern region groups: the **Eastern Ethiopian Somali League** (EESL), the **Eastern Gabdoye Democratic Organization** (EGDO), the **Ethiopian Somali Democratic Movement** (ESDM), the **Gurgura Liberation Front** (GLF), the **Rer Barreh Party**, the **Horyal Democratic Front** (HDF), the **Isa and Gurgura Liberation Front** (IGLF), the **Shekicho Peoples' Democratic Movement** (SPDM), the **Social Alliance Democratic Organization** (SADO), the **Somali Abo Democratic Union** (SADU), and the **Somali Democratic Union Party** (SDUP).

ESDL leader Abdul Mejid Hussein, who had been the target in July 1996 of an assassination attempt that the government blamed on separatist rebels, was named leader of the SPDP at its formation. He was succeeded in 2000 by Mohammad Drir, who had already taken over Hussein's cabinet post.

A pro-EPRDF formation, the SPDP won 19 of the 23 seats from the state of Somalia in the House of Peoples' Representatives and 148 of the 168 Somali State Council seats. Severe fractionalization was reported within the party in 2002, although the SPDP won all 23 seats from the state of Somalia in the 2005 poll.

Leaders: Mohammad DRIR (Chair), Abdulrashid Dulene RAFLE (Vice Chair), Sultan Ibrahim (Secretary General).

Other Legislative Parties

Coalition for Unity and Democracy (CUD). Launched in 2004 as an electoral coalition in advance of the 2005 legislative balloting by the following four groups, the CUD called for constitutional changes to reduce the authority of the executive branch and to promote democratization and human rights. Other campaign promises included intensified land privatization and a switch to proportional legislative balloting. Supported primarily by urban Amaharas, the CUD also called for a more highly centralized government in which the ethnically based states would be replaced by a return to the former provincial structure. Under the CUD proposals, the constitution would also no longer include provisions for legal regional secession.

The CUD was the leading opposition force in the May 2005 national elections, dominating the balloting in Addis Ababa and other cities. The government ultimately credited the CUD with winning 109 seats, although the coalition strongly challenged the accuracy of the final results and a number of its successful candidates refused to take their seats in the House of Peoples' Representatives. The question of whether or not to boycott the legislature apparently caused significant dissension within the coalition, and undercut efforts by CUD Chair Hailu Shawel to merge the CUD components into a single party. In September the AEUP, RE:MDSJ, and EDL reportedly announced support for the merger and creation of the Coalition for Unity and Democracy Party (CDUP). However, the UEDP-Medhin resisted that initiative, prompting the national election board to refuse recognition of the CUDP on the grounds that the CUDP required full participation of all of its electoral components.

Many of the CUD leaders (including Hailu) were arrested in the government crackdown of November 2005.

Leaders: HAILU Shawel (Chair), BIRTUKAN Mideksa (First Vice Chair), Lidetu AYALEW (Vice Chair), Berhanu NEGA, MULENEH Eyuel (Secretary General).

All Ethiopian Unity Party (AEUP). This party is an outgrowth of factionalization within the All-Amhara People's Organization (AAPO), which initially supported the EPRDF but went into opposition over the issues of ethnic regionalization. The AAPO's president, Dr. ASRAT

Woldeyes, was one of several AAPO leaders sentenced to prison in June 1994 for inciting armed opposition to the government. Asrat remained incarcerated until late 1998. Upon his release the ailing former physician for Emperor Selassie left the country for medical treatment.

After winning only one seat in the 2000 balloting for the House of Peoples' Representatives, the AAPO suffered internal division. Hailu Shawel, the vice president of AAPO, lost a bid for the AAPO presidency, and he formed his own grouping under the AEUP rubric in consonance with its stated goal of downplaying its Amharic orientation in favor of outreach to "all Ethiopians." By that time a number of former AAPO members reportedly had joined the new EDP (see UEDP-Medhin, below). Hailu subsequently became prominent in the formation of the CDU in 2005.

Leaders: HAILU Shawel (President), Makonnen BISHAW (Secretary General).

United Ethiopian Democratic Party–Medhin (UEDP-Medhin). The formation of the UEDP was announced in 2003 by several groups, including the Ethiopian Democratic Party (EDP) and the Ethiopian Democratic Action Group. The EDP, a moderate grouping espousing "unity and peace," was launched in December 1999 and secured two seats from Addis Ababa in 2000 in the House of Peoples' Representatives. The EDP was subsequently reported to be opposed to the conditions of the peace accord accepted by the Meles government with Eritrea. Founding members of the EDP included Lidetu Ayelaw, a former head of the AAPO youth wing. The relationship of the UEDP with another group with a similar name—the Ethiopian Democratic Union Party (EDUP)—was unclear, although it was reported that the UEDP–Medhin rubric had been adopted prior to the 2005 national balloting as a result of several formal mergers of former single parties.

Lidetu (who had been serving as the group's acting leader) was reportedly elected chair of the UEDP–Medhin in late 2005 after he broke with

CUD components on the issue of participation in the legislature. (Lidetu supported the decision by most of the successful UEDP–Medhin candidates to take their seats.) Among other things, Lidetu accused CUD leader Hailu of trying to form a single party of the CUD components that would be dominated by the AEUP. There was also uncertainty within the UEDP–Medhin regarding accepting the seats it had won in the Addis Ababa Council and whether to fill the seats under the rubric of the CUD or UEDP–Medhin.

Leaders: LIDETU Ayelaw (Chair), Admasso GEBEYHU.

Rainbow Ethiopia: Movement for Democracy and Social Justice (RE:MDSJ). Launched by prominent human rights activists in November 2004, the RE:MDSJ called upon the country's myriad opposition parties to coalesce in advance of the May 2005 legislative elections.

Leaders: Berhanu NEGA, Mesfin Wolde MARIAM.

Ethiopian Democratic League (EDL). The EDL was launched in 2002 by opponents of the Meles administration. The new party described itself as open to all Ethiopians, regardless of ethnicity or regionality. Founding members reportedly included Berhanu Nega (a prominent economist) and Mesfin Wolde Mariam (a human rights activist). Both men were arrested in 2002 on charges of having incited disturbances at the University of Addis Ababa the previous year, but they were subsequently released, in part due to heavy international pressure. They were also arrested in the November 2005 government crackdown, Nega and Mariam then being referenced as the leaders of the newly formed RE:MDSJ.

Leaders: Chekol GETAHUN, MULENEH Eyuel.

United Ethiopian Democratic Forces (UEDF). Launched in mid–2003 by the following groups and other parties (both within Ethiopia and in the diaspora) opposed to the EPRDF government, the UEDF (comprising mostly southern parties and dominated by Oromos) called for peaceful regime change, land reform, privatization of state-run enterprises, greater press freedom, and greater free-market influence in the economy. With the primary goal of defeating the EPRDF, the UEDF cooperated informally with CUD for the May 2005 elections, the two groups pledging to forge a coalition government if successful in the balloting. However, opposition to the EPRDF regime appeared to be the only genuine shared position between the UEDF and the CUD, as UEDF officials made it clear they strongly opposed the CUD's plan to redraw regional boundaries and establish a more highly centralized government. Many UEDF supporters also criticized the CUD's proposed land privatization proposal as a pretext for "Amhara land grabs" in the south.

The UEDF was credited with winning 52 seats in the House of Peoples' Representatives in 2005, all but one of the successful candidates reportedly taking their seats despite a CUD call for a boycott of the legislature. UEDF President Beyene Petros and Vice President Merera Gudina supported the decision to participate in the legislature and called for a national dialogue with the EPRDF and other parties toward installation of a national unity government. As a result, hard-line UEDF dissidents meeting in October announced that Beyene and Merera had been relieved of their UEDF leadership posts in favor of the EPRP's Fasika BELETE and Ayalsew DERSIE and that "underground" antigovernment was being considered. However, Beyene rejected the validity of the dissident action and continued to serve as UEDF spokesman, initialling a memorandum of understanding with the EPRDF and the OFDM providing for ongoing negotiations to resolve the nation's political problems in a peaceful manner and with respect for constitutional structures.

Leaders: BEYENE Petros, MERERA Gudina, DEREJE Kebede (Secretary General).

Council of Alternative Forces for Peace and Democracy in Ethiopia (CAFPDE). An umbrella organization for a number of opposition groupings, the CAFPDE was formed under the leadership of Beyene Petros, also the leader of the SEPDC, the core component of the CAFPDE. In 1994 Beyene described the constitutional revision then underway as "undemocratic" and inappropriately dominated by the TPLF. The CAFPDE declined to participate fully in the 1995 elections on the grounds that insufficient arrangements had been made for foreign observation of the polls.

The CAFPDE participated with other leading groups to form the Coalition of Ethiopian Opposition Political Organizations (CEOPO) in Paris in September 1998. However, Beyene subsequently withdrew the CAFPDE from CEOPO and declared the CAFPDE's intention to contest the 2000 legislative elections on its own. As a result, hard-liners within the CAFPDE announced that Beyene had been replaced as chair by KIFLE Tigneh Abate. However, the National Electoral Board ordered Beyene reinstated in January 2000.

The CAFPDE was credited with winning four seats in the House of Peoples' Representatives in the 2000 balloting, while the SEPDC secured two and the **Hadiya National Democratic Organization** (HNDO), a small grouping also led by Beyene, won three. Following the balloting, Beyene strongly criticized the EPRDF for the perceived "intimidation" of members of the CAFPDE and other opposition parties.

In 2006 Beyene announced that the CAFPDE had been renamed the **Ethiopian Social Democratic Party** (ESDP) in an effort to merge the CAFPDE components into a single party. By that time, with the ONC having been factionalized (see below), Beyene and others also described the ESDP as the dominant component of the UEDF.

Leader: BEYENE Petros (Chair).

Southern Ethiopia Peoples' Democratic Coalition (SEPDC). The SEPDC was launched in 1992 by a number of small parties representing some 34 different tribal groups and holding 16 seats in the 87-member Council of Representatives. (Participating groups included the **Burji People's**

Democratic Organization [BPDO], the **Gedo People's Democratic Organization** [GPDO], the **Gedo People's Unity Democratic Movement** [GPUDM], the **Gurage People's Democratic Front** [GPDF], the HNDO [see above], the **Kefa People's Democratic Union** [KPDU], the **Kembata People's Congress** [KPC], the **Omo People's Democratic Front** [OPDF], the **Sidama Liberation Movement** [SLM], the **Walayta People's Democratic Front** [WPDF], and the **Yem People's Democratic Movement** [YPDM].)

In March 1993 the SEPDC organizations participated in a "Peace for Ethiopia" conference in Paris that included the OLF and CO-EDF. In a statement issued at the conclusion of the conference, participants strongly condemned the current regime in Addis Ababa for its alleged repressive tendencies, while calling on it to permit nonviolent opposition activity. The Council of Representatives reacted by calling on SEPDC members to repudiate the conference resolutions. Five (the BPDO, GPDF, KPDU, KPC, and WFDF) agreed to do so while five that refused (the GPDO, HNDO, OPDF, SLM, and YPDM) were suspended from council participation.

Beyene Petros, the leader of the SEPDC and HNDO, left his post as a vice minister in the transitional government as a result of the events of 1993. He subsequently became chair of the CAFPDE. After having agreed to participate in the 2000 legislative elections, the CAFPDE and the SEPDC boycotted local elections in December 2001 in the state of Southern Nations, Nationalities, and Peoples.

Oromo National Congress (ONC). Formed in 1998 by political science professor Mcrera Gudina, the ONC pledged to support the rights of the Oromo people, including preservation of the right to self-determination. Although the ONC won only 1 seat in the 2000 elections in the House of Peoples' Representatives, it reportedly secured some 39 of the UEDF's 52 seats in the 2005 poll, dominating balloting in several southern areas. Most of the successful ONC candidates, including Merera, subsequently took their legislative seats, although debate was reported within the ONC on the question. The party was subsequently severely split as dissidents announced in September that they had expelled Merera from the ONC and had withdrawn the ONC from the UEDF. However, Merera dismissed those measures as invalid actions on the part of only a few disgruntled ONC members. The status of the party remained unclear as of early 2006, although the national election board indicated that it believed the dissident faction had the strongest legal claim to the ONC rubric.

Leaders: MERERA Gudina; TOLOSSA Tesfaye, TEFERA Legesse, DEYASA Leta (Leaders of Dissident Faction).

Oromo Federalist Democratic Movement (OFDM). After winning 11 seats in the May 2005 balloting for the House of Peoples' Representatives, the recently organized OFDM, which had resisted preelection overtures from the CUD and UEDF, called for a "national dialogue" between the opposition parties and the EPRDF. Among other things, the OFDM urged that no changes be made in the powers or boundaries of the nation's states.

Leader: Balcha DEMESKA.

Beneshangul-Gumuz Peoples' Democratic Party (BGPDP). Described as a pro-EPRDF party, the BGPDP secured six of the nine seats from the state of Beneshangul-Gumuz in the 2000 balloting for the House of Representatives and 71 of 80 State Council seats.

Leader: Mulualem BESSE.

Afar National Democratic Party (ANDP). The ANDP was formed in August 1999 by the merger of five groups in the state of Afar: the Afar Peoples' Democratic Organization (APDO), the Afar Revolutionary Democratic Union Front (ARDUF), the Afar National Democratic Movement (ANDM), the Afar National Liberation Front (ANLF), and the Afar Liberation Front Party (ALFP).

The APDO, established originally as the Afar Democratic Union, had adopted the APDO rubric in 1992. Having benefited from dissension within the ALF (see below), the APDO was subsequently described as exercising dominant political authority, in alignment with the EPRDF, in the Afar region under the leadership of Ismail ALISERIO.

The ARDUF was formed in 1991 to "liberate Afar territories" of the former autonomous region of Assab from Eritrean domination. The ARDUF subsequently became an anti-EPRDF secessionist movement under the leadership of former WPE first secretary and Assab governor Mohamoda Ahmed GAAS. Sporadic fighting was reported in 1996 between the ARDUF's armed wing, *Ugugumo* (Revolution), and TPLF forces. During 1997, however, the government initiated a policy of dialogue with the ARDUF to reach a reconciliation over the future of the Afar National Regional State. The discussions brought about a division within the ranks of the ARDUF between pro- and anti-agreement factions. Meanwhile, hard-liners led by Gaas apparently reached an agreement with the ONLF to coordinate the opposition to the current regime.

The ANDM, a pro-EPRDF formation, was launched in February 1995 by Ahmed Mohamed AHAW, a son of the influential Sultan of Biru in the northwestern Danakil region.

The ANDP secured all of the eight seats from the state of Afar in the 2000 balloting for the House of Peoples' Representatives and all but three of the Afar State Council seats, the grouping being widely perceived as a pro-EPRDF, pro-Meles party.

Gambela Peoples' Democratic Movement (GPDM). The GPDM was formed in 2003 following the dissolution of the Gambela Peoples' Democratic Front (GPDF), which had secured all three of the seats from the state of Gambela in the House of Peoples' Representatives in the 2000 balloting and most of the Gambela State Council seats. Although the GDPF had presented its candidates in 2000 without declaring a cooperative stance with any other parties, it was later described as supportive of the pro-Meles faction of the TPLF and EPRDF.

The GPDF resulted from a merger of the Gambela People's Liberation Party (GPLP), a party representing the Anyuak ethnic group that, allied with the EPRDF, had won the 1995 elections in Gambela; and the Gambela People's Democratic Unity Party (GPDUP), a Nuer party. However, the GPDF was reportedly later dissolved following the collapse of power-sharing arrangements and the outbreak of sporadic deadly fighting between the Anyuak and the Nuer.

The GPDM secured 3 seats in the 2005 voting for the House of Peoples' Representatives and nearly all of the Gambela State Council seats. It subsequently concluded a cooperation agreement with the EPRDF.

Leader: Ket TUACH.

Other parties securing seats in the 2005 balloting for the House of Peoples' Representatives included: the **Argoba National Democratic Organization**; the **Harari National League** (HNL), a pro-EPRDF formation that also won a majority in the Harari State Council in 2005; and the **Shecko Mejenger People's Democratic Unity Organization**.

Other Parties and Groups

Afar Liberation Front (ALF). Long considered the most important of the Afar groups, the ALF was organized in 1975. Although its leadership was then based in Jeddah, Saudi Arabia, the ALF also operated in Ethiopia's Hararge and Wollo Provinces, where it was supported by followers of Ahmed ALI Mirah, the sultan of Awsa. In July 1991 the sultan returned from 17 years in exile and nominally endorsed Eritrea's right to self-determination, although his nomadic subjects occupy a lengthy portion of the Red Sea coast and had long had as their principal objective an Afar state within an Ethiopian federation. In April 1995 the sultan suspended his son, Hanfareh ALI Mirah, as ALF chair in response to preelectoral dissension within the Front; however, the AFL Executive Committee refused to endorse the action. The leadership of the ALF subsequently remained unclear as some reports suggested that the sultan

and at least one of his sons had expressed support for the new Afar party (see ANDP, above), while other sons (including Umar ALI Mirah, Habib ALI Mirah, and Ousman ALI Mirah) continued to oppose the EPRDF. Renewed fighting between ALF hard-liners and Ethiopian forces was reported in mid-2002.

Oromo Liberation Front (OLF). Initially centered in the eastern and mid-country regions, the OLF in the late 1980s expanded its activities to the west and south. Although it represented the largest ethnic group in Ethiopia, the OLF was the least powerful militarily of the rebel units that toppled the Mengistu government. Previously committed to the creation of a new country of "Oromia" in what is currently southern Ethiopia, OLF leaders said in June 1991 that they would consider remaining part of a Ethiopian federation that provided for substantial regional autonomy. In mid-July the OLF concluded a "unity" pact with four other Oromo groups: the **Islamic Front for the Liberation of Oromia** (IFLO), the **Oromo Aba Liberation Front** (OALF), the **United Oromo People's Liberation Front** (UOPLF), and the OPDO (above). Earlier the OLF had occasionally allied itself with the EPLF (see under Eritrea entry) in skirmishes with the EPRDF, and it withdrew from the EPRDF-led coalition in June 1992 because of alleged electoral fraud, harassment of its members, and inadequate tribal representation. Two of its leaders, IBSSA Gutema and LENCHO Leta, were among opposition figures arrested in December 1993, the OLF Central Committee subsequently announcing that Lencho had been dismissed as the front's deputy secretary general. Both men were released in January 1994. Three months later the OLF and IFLO were reported to have agreed to offer coordinated opposition to the forthcoming draft constitution. In early 1995 a number of skirmishes took place between government troops and OLF militants, and it was subsequently reported that several hundred OLF supporters had been imprisoned as a result of the front's low-level guerrilla campaign.

In mid-1996 the OLF announced that it had signed a cooperation pact with the hard-line faction of the ONLF (below). The two groups pledged, according to the *Indian Ocean Newsletter*, to coordinate their diplomatic, political, and military activity to secure self-determination referendums for their respective regions. Minor skirmishes between security forces and OLF militants continued throughout 1997 as the front reportedly remained divided between pro- and antidialogue factions. The party engaged in reportedly fruitless discussions with the government in 1997, and at an extraordinary OLF congress in early 1998 the antidialogue faction appeared to have won control of the group's policy-making Executive Committee. The OLF was subsequently described as "reinvigorated," partly as the result of aid from Eritrea, and OLF antigovernment military activity in pursuit of independence was reported in mid-2002, although severe fractionalization was reported between OLF militants, led by Daoud Ibsa, and moderates inclined to negotiate with the government. The OLF remained "at war with the regime" in early 2005, although Galasa Dilbo, the OLF chair who had been under house arrest, had been permitted to leave for Nairobi, Kenya, in late 2004.

Prime Minister Meles reportedly offered in late 2005 to negotiate with the OLF toward a possible peace settlement, but the OLF continued to support "mobilization" against the EPRDF regime. Meanwhile, the front reportedly remained split between supporters of Gelasa and supporters of Ibsa.

Leaders: GELASA Dilbo (Former Chair, in exile), Daoud IBSA, (Chair), Harsan HUSSEIN (resident in Washington, D.C.), Shigat GELETA (resident in Berlin, Germany).

Oromo People's Liberation Front (OPLF). Characterizing the EPRDF as an "occupying enemy," the OPLF was launched in London in 1992 with the issuance of a program calling for the formation of an independent state of Oromia. The position was reiterated in December 1994 at a meeting in Nairobi, Kenya, with representatives of the UOPLF (under OLF, above) and the **Oromo People's Liberation Organization** (OPLO). However, during a congress in Harar in May 1995 a new central committee was appointed that excluded exiled

members of its predecessor and adopted a conciliatory attitude toward the EPRDF in view of a "climate of peace and development" that had allegedly been attained in eastern Ethiopia. Cooperation with the OLF and other Oromo groups was launched in 2000.

Ogaden National Liberation Front (ONLF). The secessionist ONLF was organized in January 1986, reportedly by militant WSLF members opposed to Ethiopian-Somali talks on the future of the Ogaden that did not involve participation by regional representatives. In April 1988 the ONLF criticized Somalia's cessation of aid to the Ogaden rebels as little more than an endorsement of Ethiopian troop redeployment to the north. In September 1996 the Ethiopian army conducted cross-border operations inside Somaliland against ONLF guerrillas.

In June 1998 an ONLF faction that had reportedly been cooperating with the progovernment ESDL since 1995 formed a separate grouping–the SPDP. For their part, ONLF secessionists continued to clash with government troops.

In April 2006 the ONLF claimed responsibility for several attacks on government troops. Approximately 1,000 ONLF fighters were reportedly training in Eritrea at that point.

Leaders: Mohamed Omar OSMAN, Mohamed Ismaïl Omar, Shimber Abdel KADIR, Mohamed HUSSEIN.

Western Somalia Liberation Front (WSLF). The WSLF, established in 1975, long advocated the incorporation of the Somali-speaking Ogaden region into a "Greater Somalia." During late 1977 the WSLF gained control of the greater part of the area with support from Somalian regular forces, but following the latter's withdrawal in March 1978 was forced to operate primarily from bases inside Somalia. At a congress in February 1981 the Front elected a Central Committee that committed itself to the establishment of a "free state of Western Somalia" independent of both Ethiopia and Somalia. WSLF activity declined in 1986, some of its leaders apparently having shifted their allegiance to the newly formed ONLF (below). WSLF antigovernment activity was most recently reported in 1999.

Ethiopian Democratic Union Party (EDUP). The conservative Ethiopian Democratic Union (EDU) fought government troops in the northwest in the late 1970s before collapsing as the result of a leadership crisis. With the reported support of conservative Arab governments, the EDU later resurfaced, albeit with minimal impact. Although a participant in the 1991 National Conference, the EDU was also a member of COEDF (below). It adopted the EDUP rubric prior to the 1995 elections. An opponent of the recent peace accord with Eritrea, the EDUP has complained of government harassment of its members. Cooperation with the EDP was under consideration in mid-2002.

Leader: Mengesha SEYOUM.

Coalition of Ethiopian Democratic Forces (COEDF). The COEDF was launched in April 1991 in Washington, D.C., by a number of groups (including the EDU, above) whose "common denominator" appeared to be concern over the implications of a government takeover by the EPRDF. Continued friction between the EPRDF and the COEDF subsequently hindered the latter's efforts to play a substantial role in national negotiations on Ethiopia's political future.

The four COEDF leaders listed below were among those arrested upon their arrival in Addis Ababa for the dissident peace conference of December 1993. In July 1996 the COEDF initiated the formation of an opposition alliance, the **Ethiopian Unity Front** (EUF), which brought together the COEDF, the **Beneshangul Peoples' Democratic Movement** (BPDM), and a majority faction within the **Kefagn Patriotic Front** (KPF).

The COEDF was reported to be seriously fragmented as of mid-1999; some members were promoting the CEOPO (see CAFPDE, above), while others were in negotiations with the government. The disintegration of the coalition was further highlighted by a report that even its core component, the EPRP, was reluctant to describe itself as operating under the COEDF banner.

Leaders: ABERA Yemaneab (in prison), GENENEW Assefa, GUENET Giram, MESFIN Tefer, Merera GUDINA (ONC).

Ethiopian People's Revolutionary Party (EPRP). The EPRP initiated an unsuccessful antigovernment guerrilla campaign in north-central Ethiopia in 1977. Its forces also battled with the TPLF in Tigray Province, its defeat there in 1978 precipitating a sharp split within the party. One faction served as the formative core of the EPDM in alliance with the TPLF while a rump group was relatively quiescent until a series of kidnappings and other guerrilla acts in Gojam Province in early 1987. Although the EPRP was committed to the overthrow of the Mengistu regime, its relations with the EPRDF and the EPLF were strained. Following the rebel victory in May 1991, the EPRP, with an estimated 5,000 fighters controlling parts of Gojam and Gondar Provinces, was described as the "only really organized opposition" to the TPLF-dominated interim government. Like the country's other previously Marxist formations, the EPRP now supports multiparty democracy.

In 2001 the EPRP called for renewed action against the "racist" TPLF-led regime, and there were several reports in 2002 of fighting between the EPRP and government forces. Some reports described the EPRP as a participant in the UEDF in 2005, although the government continued to describe the EPRP as an illegal organization.

Leader: Col. TADERSE Muleneh, Iyassu ALEMAYEHU (in exile).

Ethiopian People's Democratic Alliance (EPDA). Founded in 1982, the EPDA was an attempt by right-wing opponents of the PMAC to regroup elements of the EDU. The EPDA subsequently comprised an "internal" wing, headquartered in Sudan, and an "external" wing operating in Britain and the United States. Its strongly anticommunist posture reportedly generated $500,000 in annual support from Washington in the late 1980s, but the financing

Cabinet

As of June 1, 2006

Prime Minister	Meles Zenawi
Deputy Prime Minister	Addisu Legesse

Ministers

Cabinet Office	Berhanu Adelo
Capacity Building	Tefera Walwa
Culture and Tourism	Mahmad Dirir
Defense	Kuma Demekesa
Economic Development and Finance	Sufian Ahmed
Education	Sintayehu Woldemikael
Federal Affairs	Siraj Fegeta
Foreign Affairs	Seyoum Mesfin
Health	Dr. Tewodros Adhanon
Information	Berhan Hailu
Justice	Assefa Keseto
Labor and Social Affairs	Hassen Abdella
Mines and Energy	Alemayehu Tegenu
Revenue	Melaku Fenta
Rural Development	Addisu Legesse
Trade and Industry	Girma Biru
Transport and Communications	Junedi Sado
Water Resources	Asefaw Dingam
Women's Affairs	Hirut Dilebo [f]
Works and Urban Development	Kasu Ilala
Youth, Sports, and Culture	Aster Mamo [f]

[f] = female

---

was cut off as the result of changing U.S. policy toward the nominally left-wing rebels.

Other groups reportedly participating in the COEDF included the **All-Ethiopian Socialist Movement** (*Meison*) and the **Tigray People's Democratic Movement** (TPDM). (TPDM fighters reportedly have conducted guerrilla activity recently in concert with other armed groups, including a faction of the EPRP.) The **Oromo National Congress** (ONC), which was formed in 1998 by political science professor Merera Gudina and won one seat in the 2000 legislative balloting, was subsequently refer-

enced as a member as the COEDF, with Gudina reportedly later becoming a prominent leader of the CUD.

Islamic Union (*al-Itahad al-Islami*). Operating along the southern part of the border between Ethiopia and Somalia, the Islamic Union conducted guerrilla activity in the early 1990s in support of the establishment of an "Ethiopian Ogaden State." The grouping was accused by the government of several bomb attacks, prompting military countermeasures in the second half of 1996. On July 8, 1996, minister of transport and communication and the chair of the ESDL, Abdulmejid HUSSEIN, was shot and wounded by *Al-Itahad* members. Government forces subsequently conducted territorial and extra-territorial military operations against *Al-Itahad*, the organization losing its last major bases to an Ethiopian assault in July 1997. (See article on Somalia for information on *al-Itahad* activity in that country.)

Tigrayan Alliance for National Democracy (TAND). TAND surfaced in Washington, D.C., in February 1995 as an exile grouping that reportedly included the **Multi-National Congress Party of Ethiopia** (MNCPE), and the TPDM, as well as former members of the TPLF and EDC.

Other parties winning single seats in the 2000 balloting for the House of Peoples' Representatives were the **Gambela Peoples' Democratic Congress** (GPDC), an anti-EPRDF formation with support within the Nuer ethnic group; the **Sidama Hadicko Peoples' Democratic Organization;** and the **Siltie Peoples' Democratic Party**.

Small formations include the **Tigray Democratic Union** (TDU), an anti-TPLF grouping that launched an armed struggle in 2000 under the leadership of AREGAWE Bereh, one of the founders of the TPLF; the **Sidama Liberation Movement** (SLM), led by Yilma CHAMOLA; the **Oromo National Liberation Party** (ONLP), launched in October 2000 under the leadership of ESAYAS Shegaw to "liberate Oromia from poverty and suffering."

Groups formed in advance of the 2005 legislative poll included the **Afar Liberation Party**; the **All Ethiopian Democratic Party**, launched by former members of the EDUP; the **Dal-Webi Democratic Movement**, which operates in the state of Somalia; and the **Ethiopian Pan-Africanist Party**, led by Abd al-Fatah HULDAR.

Legislature

The constitution of December 1994 provides for an Ethiopian **Parliament** encompassing a House of the Federation selected by the states and a popularly elected House of Peoples' Representatives. Both bodies have five-year mandates.

House of the Federation (*Yefedershein Mekir Bete*). The upper House currently consists of 108 members (serving five-year terms) who represent Ethiopia's "nations and nationalities," each of which is entitled to at least one member, with an additional representative for each one million of its population (The regional distribution of seats is as follows: Southern Nations, Nationalities, and Peoples, 54; Amhara, 17; Oromia, 16; Tigray, 6; Somalia, 4; Beneshangul-Gumuz, 4; Gambela Peoples, 4; Afar, 2; Harari People, 1.) Members are designated by state councils, which may elect them directly or provide for their popular election. The House of the Federation was most recently replenished in October 2005 following the State Council elections of May–August.

Speaker: DEGEFE Bula.

House of Peoples' Representatives (*Yehizb Tewokayoch Mekir Bete*). The House of Peoples' Representatives consists of no more than 550 members (minority nationalities being accorded at least 20 seats) directly elected for a five-year term from single-member districts by a plurality of votes cast. The most recent balloting in eight states and the administrative regions of Addis Ababa and Dire Dawa was held on May 15, 2005. (The balloting in the state of Somalia was deferred due to security concerns and administrative difficulties in providing electoral access to the nomadic population.) However, the preliminary election results were strongly challenged by opposition parties, and reballoting was held in 31 constituencies on August 21. The elections in Somalia were held the same day.

The government released final results in September 2005 for a total of 546 contested seats. However, some opposition legislators (mostly from the Coalition for Unity and Democracy) declined to take their seats when the house convened in October in a protest over what they perceived as government malfeasance during the balloting. Most opposition parties continued to argue that they had been defrauded out of a number of seats. Following is the distribution of 526 seats as reported by the government, which announced that those elected for the remaining 20 seats had declined to be seated: Ethiopian People's Revolutionary Democratic Front, 327 (Oromo Peoples' Democratic Organization, 110; Southern Ethiopian Peoples' Democratic Movement, 92; Amhara National Democratic Movement, 87; Tigray People's Liberation Front, 38); Coalition for Unity and Democracy, 89 (All Ethiopian Unity Party, 43; United Ethiopian Democratic Party–Medhin, 36; Rainbow Ethiopia: Movement for Democracy and Social Justice, 8; Ethiopian Democratic League, 2); United Ethiopian Democratic Forces, 52; Somali Peoples' Democratic Party, 24; Oromo Federalist Democratic Movement, 11; Benshangul-Gumuz Peoples' Democratic Unity Front, 8; Afar National Democratic Party, 8; Gambela Peoples' Democratic Movement, 3; Argoba National Democratic Organization, 1; Harari National League, 1; Shecko Mejenger Peoples' Democratic Unity Organization, 1; independent, 1.

Speaker: TESHOME Toga Chanaka.

Communications

Communications media were strictly controlled by the Mengistu government and presented the official version of international and domestic events to a small circle of governmental officials, teachers, army officers, and other members of the educated elite. Increased press freedom was promised in the wake of Mengistu's ouster, although the successor regime's actual policy subsequently remained less than tolerant, Ethiopian journalists accusing the EPRDF of a campaign of "harassment and intimidation" that included arrests of reporters and closure of a number of newspapers. The government proposed a controversial new press law in late 2003 that would have limited the number of newspapers, but protests prevented its official adoption. However, in April 2005 it was reported that many of the measures perceived to be repressive were "discreetly" introduced, apparently forcing some journalists into exile. In addition, more than 20 journalists were among those arrested in the government crackdown of late 2005.

Press

Except as noted, the following are dailies published in Addis Ababa: *Addis Zemen* (41,000), in Amharic; *Ethiopian Herald* (37,000), government-controlled, in English; the *Daily Monitor* (6,000), in English; *Yezareitu Itiopia* (30,000), government weekly in Amharic and English; *Mebrek*, independent weekly; the *Addis Tribune* (6,000), weekly in English; *Moged*, independent weekly; *Tomas*, weekly; *Fortune*, independent; *The Capital, Iftin,* biweekly in Amharic.

News Agencies

The domestic facility is the Ethiopian News Agency (*Itiopia Zena Agelgilot*—Izea); a number of foreign bureaus maintain offices in Addis Ababa.

Broadcasting and Computing

Radio Ethiopia broadcasts locally and internationally in Amharic, English, Arabic, and a number of other languages. There are also several; autonomous stations, two of which (including the Voice of the Revolution of Tigray) oppose the government. The EPRDF also controls its own station—*Radio Fana.* Licenses for two FM stations were recently issued by the Ethiopian Broadcasting Agency. Ethiopian Television (*Itiopia Television*) has been broadcasting under government auspices since 1964. There were approximately 421,000 television receivers and 150,000 personal computers serving 75,000 Internet users in 2003.

Intergovernmental Representation

Ambassador to the U.S.
Samuel ASSEFA

U.S. Ambassador to Ethiopia
(Vacant)

Permanent Representative to the UN
Dawit YOHANNES

IGO Memberships (Non-UN)
AfDB, AU, BADEA, Comesa, IGAD, Interpol, NAM, PCA, WCO

GABON

GABONESE REPUBLIC

République Gabonaise

The Country

A tropical, heavily forested country on the west coast of Central Africa, Gabon is inhabited by a sparse population whose largest components, among more than 40 distinct ethnic groups, are the Fang and Eshira tribes. A sizable European (predominantly French) community also is resident. Indigenous Gabonese speak a variety of Bantu languages, with Fang predominating in the north. About 60 percent of the population is Christian (largely Roman Catholic), with most of the rest adhering to traditional beliefs; there also is a small Muslim minority. Women constitute over half of salaried workers in the health and trading sectors, although female representation in party and government bodies is minimal.

Abundant natural resources that include oil, high-grade iron ore, manganese, uranium, and timber provided Gabon with a per capita GNP of over $4,200 in the early 1980s. Oil output accounted for about three-fourths of Gabon's export earnings until 1986. By 1988 the economic impact of recession in the oil industry was dramatically underscored by a drop in per capita GNP to $2,620 (still one of the highest among black African states), with subsequent recovery to about $4,950 in 1993.

Real GDP growth averaged 3.3 percent annually in 1996–1998 before a severe recession hit in 1999, triggered by an 11 percent decline in oil production, a trend analysts predicted would decline for the foreseeable future based on Gabon's known reserves. GDP fell 9.6 percent in 1999, and the government inaugurated a structural adjustment program sponsored by the International Monetary Fund (IMF) in an effort to reduce public spending, diversify the economy, promote good governance, and address the severe external debt problem.

Since 2003 the economy has rebounded, aided by higher oil prices and external debt rescheduling. This in turn has contributed to a sharp improvement in fiscal accounts, aided by better tax administration and expenditure discipline. GDP growth was 1.5 percent in 2004, while inflation declined to 0.5 percent, reflecting wage moderation and the monetary discipline imposed by the fixed exchange regime. The overall budget surplus was maintained at 7.5 percent. In 2004 the IMF approved $47 million in assistance to Gabon's economic program. Government corruption reportedly

continued to increase, however, and in 2004 Transparency International cited Gabon as among the most corrupt African nations.

Although GDP growth in 2005 was only 2 percent, the IMF noted fiscal progress over the past three years, including structural reforms in non-oil sectors. The IMF also cited the country's poverty reduction strategy initiative, adopted in early 2006. Declining oil reserves over the next decade continued to be the major economic challenge, according to the IMF and the World Bank.

Government and Politics

Political Background

Colonized by France in the latter half of the 19th century and subsequently administered as a part of French Equatorial Africa, Gabon achieved full independence within the French Community on August 17, 1960. Its longtime political leader, President Léon MBA, ruled in a conservative yet pragmatic style and supported close political and economic relations with France. However, Mba's attempts to establish a one-party state based on his Gabon Democratic Bloc (*Bloc Démocratique Gabonais*—BDG) were resisted for several years by the Gabonese Democratic and Social Union (*Union Démocratique et Sociale Gabonais*—UDSG), led by Jean-Hilaire AUBAME. Only after an attempted coup by Aubame's army supporters had been thwarted by French military intervention in February 1964 and Mba's party had gained a majority in legislative elections two months later was the UDSG formally outlawed.

Mba was reelected to a seven-year presidential term in March 1967, but he died the following November and was succeeded by Vice President Albert-Bernard (subsequently El Hadj Omar) BONGO Ondimba. Officially declaring Gabon a one-party state in March 1968, Bongo announced a "renovation" policy that included conversion of the former ruling party into a new, nationwide political grouping, the Gabonese Democratic Party (*Parti Démocratique Gabonais*—PDG). The incumbent was the sole candidate for reelection to a fourth

term on November 9, 1986, having survived a coup attempt by military officers in 1985.

Pressured by a deteriorating economy and mounting protests against his regime, President Bongo announced in early March 1990 that a national conference would be called to discuss the launching of an inclusive political organization that would pave the way for eventual adoption of a multiparty system. However, the conference ended its month-long deliberations on April 21 with a call for the immediate introduction of democratic pluralism. The president responded by granting legal status to all of the participating organizations. Moreover, on April 29 he announced that longtime Prime Minister Léon MEBIAME would be succeeded by Casimir OYE MBA as head of a government that would include a number of opposition leaders.

First-round legislative balloting was held on September 23, 1990, the results of which were annulled in 32 of 120 constituencies because of alleged improprieties. At the conclusion of second-round balloting on October 21 and 28, 62 seats were declared to have been won by the PDG (including 3 seats by pro-PDG independents). Subsequently, the PDG tally was augmented by 4 seats, with 7 opposition parties being credited with a total of 54.

In May 1991 six of the seven opposition parties with legislative representation announced a boycott of parliamentary proceedings, called for a dissolution of the government, and demanded that the Bongo regime comply with the dictates of the 1990 national conference and the constitution adopted on March 14 (see Constitution and government, below). Subsequently, on June 7, two days after an opposition-led general strike, President Bongo announced the resignation of Oye Mba's government and called on the opposition, now united in the Coordination of Democratic Opposition (*Coordination de l'Opposition Démocratique*—COD), to join a "government of national consensus." On June 15 the opposition rejected his offer; three days later Oye Mba was reappointed, and a new government was named that included a limited number of opposition figures.

In July 1992 the PDG-dominated National Assembly rejected an unprecedented no-confidence

Political Status: Independent since August 17, 1960; present constitution, providing for "semi-presidential" regime, adopted March 14, 1991.

Area: 103,346 sq. mi. (267,667 sq. km.).

Population: 1,014,976 (1993C). Despite the 1993 figure, recent estimates vary widely, the *Africa Research Bulletin* in early 1995 suggesting a total of 800,000, while the UN had previously assumed a figure of 1,237,000 for 1992. Based on recent UN estimates, the 2005 total should be approximately 1,376,000.

Major Urban Center (2005E): LIBREVILLE (metropolitan area, 659,000).

Official Language: French.

Monetary Unit: CFA Franc (official rate July 1, 2006: 513.01 francs = $1US). (The CFA franc, previously pegged to the French franc, is now permanently pegged to the euro at 655.957 CFA francs = 1 euro.)

President: El Hadj Omar (formerly Albert-Bernard) BONGO Ondimba; elected vice president on March 19, 1967; succeeded to the presidency on December 2, 1967, upon the death of Léon MBA; reelected in 1973, 1979, 1986, 1993, and for a seven-year term, on December 6, 1998, and on November 27, 2005.

Vice President: Didjob DIVUNGUI DI NDINGE (Democratic and Republican Alliance); reappointed by the president on January 19, 2006.

Prime Minister: Jean Eyéghe NDONG (Gabonese Democratic Party), appointed by the president on January 20, 2006, to succeed Jean-François NTOUTOUME EMANE. A new government was sworn in on January 21, 2006.

motion by a vote of 72 to 45. The motion, filed by the opposition to protest the government's rescheduling of local elections, closely followed assembly approval of a new electoral code, which opposition leaders described as "antidemocratic." Despite their drawing together in mid-1993 to form a Committee for Free and Democratic Elections, opposition groups failed to unite behind a single slate, and at balloting on December 5 Presi-

dent Bongo was credited with winning reelection over 13 competitors by a narrow 51.18 percent majority. The result was immediately challenged by runner-up Paul MBA-ABESSOLE of the National Rally of Woodcutters (*Rassemblement National des Bucherons*—RNB), who accused Bongo of "high treason against the nation by an electoral coup d'etat," declared himself president, and announced the formation of a parallel "government of combat" headed by his party's secretary general, Pierre-André KOMBILA Koumba. On December 12 Mba-Abessole announced the formation of the High Council of the Republic (*Haut Conseil de la République*—HCR), which included a majority of the opposition presidential candidates, to serve as an advisory body for his parallel government. On December 14 Bongo, promising a multiparty government of "broad consensus," termed the formation of the alternative body an "anticonstitutional act," and postelectoral unrest quickly subsided as the regime deployed heavily armed regular and paramilitary forces. Meanwhile, legislative balloting originally scheduled for December 26 was postponed until March 1994.

In late January 1994 consumer prices skyrocketed, and widespread disturbances were reported after France halved the value of the CFA franc. On February 15 Mba-Abessole urged his supporters to "disobey all government directives" and threatened to expel party members who took part in Bongo's proposed unity government. One week later, nine people were killed when government troops supported by tanks destroyed the RNB's radio station and attacked Mba-Abessole's residence as a "punitive measure" for having incited "hatred, violence, and intolerance." In addition, elections were rescheduled for August 1994.

On March 11, 1994, Prime Minister Oye Mba resigned, stating that the country had entered a "new political phase"; however, Bongo reappointed him two days later, and on March 25 Oye Mba named a new government, which included no opposition members. On April 8 Libreville lifted the state of alert and curfew that had been imposed almost without interruption since December 9, 1993.

On September 27, 1994, following three weeks of internationally supervised negotiations in Paris, government and opposition representatives signed an agreement calling for the establishment of a transitional coalition government and an independent electoral commission empowered to oversee an electoral timetable providing for local and legislative elections in 12 and 18 months, respectively. Consequently, on October 11 Oye Mba again resigned, and two days later the president named a PDG confidant, Paulin OBAME-NGUEMA, as interim prime minister. Although Obame-Nguema's appointment was generally well received, the RNB continued to urge its members to refuse to participate in a Bongo-affiliated government and denounced the 27-member cabinet named by Obame-Nguema, which included six opposition members, for failing to reflect the opposition's legislative strength.

On February 3, 1995, the Constitutional Court, acting at the opposition's urging, ruled that the mandate of the current assembly could continue for the duration of the transition period defined by the 1994 accord. Three days later, opposition deputies ended their legislative boycott, and on April 21 President Bongo agreed to submit a package of constitutional reforms to voters, who provided an overwhelmingly positive response at balloting on June 25. The Bongo administration, however, proved reluctant to implement the Paris Accord, and in February 1996 the opposition called on France to pressure the government to adhere to the transitional schedule. Thereafter, in May, Bongo agreed to organize an electoral commission to schedule and oversee local and, subsequently, national legislative elections.

Local polling, originally scheduled for July 1996, was delayed until October 20 by organizational problems that remained largely unresolved as of election day. Consequently, there were widespread reports of incomplete electoral lists and ballot box shortages, as well as a voter turnout rate as low as 10–15 percent in some areas. Such problems were so severe in Libreville that balloting there was suspended and completed in late November. Opposition leaders claimed that the disorganization was part of a "deliberate" government at-

tempt to undermine the electoral system. Meanwhile, opposition candidates, led by the RNB, captured a clear majority of the contests.

The opposition fared far less well at National Assembly elections conducted on December 15 and 29, 1996, and January 12, 1997, as the governing PDG scored a decisive victory, securing 82 of the 120 assembly seats. At subsequent balloting on January 26 and February 9, 1997, to fill the Senate for the first time, the governing party again secured a substantial majority. Meanwhile, on January 27 President Bongo reappointed Obame-Nguema, who announced a cabinet the following day.

On March 20, 1997, the National Assembly approved draft constitutional amendments, which included provisions for the creation of a vice presidential post and lengthening of the presidential term to seven years (following the next election). Following Senate approval of the amendments in April, the president named Didjob DIVUNGUI DI NDINGE, leader of the Democratic and Republican Alliance, as his vice president on May 28.

In mid-April 1998 the government announced the formation of the National Democracy Council (*Conseil pour la Démocratie Nationale*—CND), a consultative body comprising the former and current leaders of a broad spectrum of governmental and opposition groups, and charged it with assisting in the organization of presidential elections then tentatively scheduled for late 1998. In October the government announced that the first round of balloting would be held on December 6, with a second round, if necessary, on December 20. The Bongo administration rebuffed subsequent opposition requests for additional preparation time, and in early November the HCR and other leading opposition groups withdrew from the national electoral commission to protest what they described as a perfunctory revision of an already suspect voter registration list. Meanwhile, intraparty factionalization undermined the ability of prominent opposition groups to coalesce behind a competitive challenger to the incumbent.

On December 6, 1998, President Bongo won a seven-year term at polling that his opponents charged was tainted by "massive fraud." Bongo's 66.6 percent vote share dwarfed the returns of six other presidential aspirants, with his nearest competitors, the HCR's Pierre MAMBOUNDOU and the RNB's Paul Mba-Abessole, capturing 16.6 and 13.4 percent, respectively. On January 24, 1999, Bongo named Jean-François NTOUTOUME EMANE to succeed Obame-Nguema, who had resigned two days earlier, and on January 25 a new government was named.

The PDG retained its legislative stranglehold in assembly balloting in December 2001 (see Legislature, below). On January 27, 2002, President Bongo reappointed Prime Minister Ntoutoume Emane; notably, however, the new cabinet announced the same day included three members of the RNB (including Mba-Abessole) and the leader of another opposition grouping, the Social Democratic Party (*Parti Social-Démocratique*—PSD).

In local elections in 2002, the PDG achieved an overwhelming victory, albeit with voter participation estimated at less than 20 percent in some areas. In Senate elections held in 2003, the PDG won 60 of the chamber's 91 seats, followed by the RPG, which took 8 seats.

On November 27, 2005, President Bongo won another seven-year term at balloting that was again challenged as fraudulent by his opponents. Bongo garnered 79 percent of the vote, easily defeating four challengers, most notably Pierre Mamboundou, whose affiliation was listed as the Union of Gabonese People (*Union du Peuple Gabonais*—UPG), 13.6 percent; and Zacharie MYBOTO, an independent affiliated with the newly formed Gabonese Union for Democracy and Development (*Union Gabonaise de la Démocratie et du Développement*—UGDD), 6.6 percent. Two other candidates each received less than 1 percent of the vote: Augustin Moussavou KING of the Gabonese Socialist Party (*Parti Socialiste Gabonaise*—PSG) and Christian-Serge MAROGA of the Rally of the Democrats (RDD). Turnout was recorded at 63.6 percent, with security forces voting on November 25 in a move decreed by Bongo to maintain order at civilian polling on November 27. Bongo was sworn in on January 19, 2006, retaining Vice President Divungui Di Ndinge and appointing a new prime minister, Jean Eyéghe Ndong, on January 20. A new government was installed on January 21.

Constitution and Government

Until 1991, when a qualified multiparty system was introduced, popular election was pro forma because of a requirement that all candidates be approved by the PDG. Constitutional amendments approved by the legislature on April 18, 1997, provided for a lengthening of the presidential term from five to seven years; in addition, the amended basic charter empowered the president to name both a vice president (appointees to the newly created post are not eligible to succeed the chief executive) and a prime minister, who must enjoy the confidence of the legislature. The head of the government is the prime minister, who is appointed by the president. The prime minister, in consultation with the president, appoints the Council of Ministers. In 2003 the National Assembly voted to revoke the constitutional limit on the number of terms to which the president may be reelected. This effectively guaranteed Bongo the presidency for life.

Members of the bicameral legislature, which comprises a Senate (created in March 1994 and filled in April 1997) and a National Assembly, are directly elected for five-year terms. There is an appointed Economic and Social Council, whose advice on relevant policy issues must be given legislative consideration. The judiciary includes a Supreme Court (divided into judicial, administrative, and accounting chambers) and Courts of Appeal, as well as a Constitutional Court and an extraordinary High Court of Justice to hear impeachment cases.

For administrative purposes Gabon is divided into 9 provinces and subdivided into 37 departments, all headed by presidentially appointed executives. Libreville and Port-Gentil are governed by elected mayors and Municipal Councils, while 4 smaller municipalities have partly elected and partly appointed administrations.

Foreign Relations

Following his accession to power in 1967, President Bongo sought to lessen the country's traditional dependence on France by cultivating more diversified international support. Regionally, Gabon withdrew in 1976 from membership in the Common African and Mauritian Organization, while diplomatic relations with Benin, broken in 1978 after Gabon's alleged involvement in a mercenary attack in Cotonou in 1977 and the expulsion in 1978 of 6,000 Beninese workers, were restored in February 1989. Relations with neighboring Equatorial Guinea suffered until the overthrow of the Macie regime in August 1979, by which time as many as 80,000 Equatorial Guinean refugees had fled to Gabon. Relations with Cameroon deteriorated in May 1981 with the expulsion of nearly 10,000 Cameroonians in the wake of violent demonstrations in Libreville and Port-Gentil. Subsequently, an overt campaign against immigrant workers further strained ties between Gabon and its neighbors. Libreville nonetheless continued to participate in the Economic Community of Central African States, hosting its third summit meeting in August 1987. During the same month, a presidential visit to the United States served to strengthen relations between the two countries, with Bongo pledging to protect American investments of more than $200 million and Washington agreeing to debt restructuring of some $8 million owed by Gabon for military purchases. Earlier, following a meeting with the Palestine Liberation Organization's Yasir Arafat in Tunisia, the regime reiterated its opposition to "apartheid, Zionism, and neocolonialism."

In 1988, despite President Bongo's stated intent, Gabon continued to be heavily dependent on French support, with annual aid hovering at $360 million. In February the government granted the European Economic Community fishing rights to Gabonese territorial waters; thereafter, cooperation agreements were negotiated with the Congo in June and Morocco in October. Meanwhile, the regime's battle with Libreville's large illegal population continued: in July 3,500 foreigners were arrested following Bongo's warning that tougher measures would be used to stop "clandestine immigration."

In late 1992, following two years of negotiations, Gabon and South Africa, which had long been trading partners, established full diplomatic relations. Meanwhile, Libreville's crackdown on illegal immigrants was underscored by the deportation of 7,000 Nigerians.

Angered at Paris's "silence" over French press reports critical of President Bongo, Libreville recalled its ambassador on April 21, 1995. However, relations were quickly restored as Paris reasserted its support for Bongo who, in turn, called for an end to anti-French demonstrations in Libreville.

In the late 1990s President Bongo returned to the role of regional mediator, assuming a prominent position in efforts to reduce tensions in the Republic of the Congo and Côte d'Ivoire. In November 1999 Libreville hosted a summit of the heads of state and foreign ministers of seven Gulf of Guinea nations (Angola, Cameroon, Democratic Republic of the Congo, Republic of the Congo, Equatorial Guinea, Nigeria, and Sao Tome and Principe) that yielded agreement to form a cooperative commission.

In 2003 relations with Equatorial Guinea became tense following Gabon's occupation of the uninhabited islands of Mbagne, Cocotiers, and Congas in the potentially oil-rich Corisco Bay, north of Libreville. Both countries agreed to negotiations under the auspices of the UN, with the aim of resolving the dispute by the end of 2006.

French support declined in 2005 along with Gabon's oil supply, leaving Bongo to look increasingly to China, which previously had agreed to import large quantities of Gabonese oil and had funded and built Gabon's parliamentary complex.

Current Issues

Decrying President Bongo's reelection on December 6, 1998, as an "electoral coup," the HCR's leader and presidential candidate, Pierre Mamboundou, called for an annulment of the balloting. Furthermore, in an increasingly tense Libreville, Mamboundou declared that his organization of a "dead city" operation would be only the first in a series of antigovernment protests aimed at forcing new elections. Unrest was reported in the capital in early 1999; however, observers described PDG infighting as a more immediate problem for the Bongo administration.

A number of opposition parties boycotted the first-round of assembly elections on December 3, 2001, accusing the administration of having "inflated" electoral rolls in favor of the PDG and its allies. The voting also was marred by sporadic violence and a repeat of the widespread irregularities that had been routinely noted in previous elections. Consequently, other opposition parties urged a boycott of the second-round on December 23, which was conducted peacefully thanks to heavy security measures but suffered from low turnout (as little as 20 percent in urban areas). The subsequent inclusion of the RNB and PSD in the new cabinet was billed by President Bongo as the inaugural of an "open government," with observers noting that the PDG's hegemony had become a significant concern for international donors.

Bongo is Africa's longest-serving president. Although the Paris Accord of 1994 required him to share power with the opposition, he has managed to neutralize his opponents with cabinet positions and state largesse. Many nominal political opponents allegedly are financially supported by Bongo. While the president has a stronghold on the country, the people reportedly are happy not to have ethnic conflict. The 2005 presidential election, while free of violence, saw 9 of 13 candidates disqualified by the elections commission. Another candidate, Pastor Ernest TOMO, withdrew a month prior to balloting and threw his support to Bongo, to whom he is related through marriage. The only international monitors allowed during polling were "some avowedly pro-Bongo French senators," according to *Africa Confidential*. Opponents' claims of vote-rigging were dismissed by a constitutional court in January 2006. Large-scale looting was reported in Libreville in the months following the election, with the opposition claiming five people were killed. The government said one person had died.

In early 2006, Bongo's name arose during the scandal involving U.S. lobbyist Jack Abramoff. It was alleged that Bongo paid $9 million in 2003 to several people, including Abramoff, to secure a meeting with U.S. President George W. Bush. Both Bongo and Bush denied any financial arrangement prior to their May 2004 meeting.

Political Parties

Officially declared a one-party state in March 1968, Gabon in practice had been under one-party government since the banning of the former opposition group, the Gabonese Democratic and Social Union (*Union Démocratique et Sociale Gabonais*—UDSG), in 1964. Twenty-six years later, in February 1990, President Bongo announced that the ruling Gabonese Democratic Party (PDG) would be dissolved in favor of a Gabonese Social Democratic Rally (*Rassemblement Social-Démocrate Gabonais*—RSDG), which would pave the way for a multiparty system. In early March he retreated somewhat by announcing that the PDG would continue as a unit within the RSDG. However, delegates to a national political conference in late April rejected the RSDG as a vehicle for phasing in pluralism over a three- to five-year period; Bongo responded by granting legal status (initially for one year) to all of the 13 opposition groups participating in the conference, 7 of which obtained parliamentary representation late in the year. In May 1991, 6 of the 7 parties announced a boycott of parliamentary proceedings and called for dissolution of the coalition government. Meanwhile, an effectively short-lived Coordination of Democratic Opposition (*Coordination de l'Opposition Démocratique*—COD) had been launched by 9 opposition groups, 3 of which merged in early 1992 to form the African Forum for Reconstruction (FAR).

On June 30, 1993, members of Gabon's major opposition parties, meeting in the United States, agreed to form a Committee for Free and Democratic Elections dedicated to establishing a "democratic state." Following presidential balloting on December 5, the committee was supplanted by the

High Council of the Republic (*Haut Conseil du Republic*—HCR), which had been organized by Fr. Paul Mba-Abessole, leader of the National Rally of Woodcutters (RNB) and runner-up in the controversial elections, to function as an advisory body for his "administration." The HCR, which reportedly included a majority of the opposition presidential candidates and parties, named Mba-Abessole and PGP leader Pierre-Louis AGONDJO-OKAWE president and vice president, respectively. On January 27, 1994, the HCR was restyled the High Council of Resistance (*Haut Conseil de Résistance*—HCR) and announced that it would no longer refer to Mba-Abessole as the president of the republic, although vowing to continue to resist the Bongo regime.

At an HCR meeting in December 1997 party delegates elected a new executive bureau headed by Pierre Mamboundou of the Union of Gabonese People (UPG). Furthermore, four HCR members (the FAR, the Movement for People's Social Emancipation [MESP], the RNB, and the UPG) signed a new cooperation accord on which they reportedly expected to base their 1998 presidential campaign. In May 1998 the HCR chose Mamboundou as its standard-bearer for the presidential elections due in December; however, in subsequent months the viability of the movement was cast in doubt by reports that it had been reduced to only four or five parties, including the RNB, which had decided to field its own presidential candidate. In November the HCR withdrew from the national electoral commission, declaring that the commission's "hasty" revision of the electoral list had set the stage for "massive fraud" at the presidential balloting.

Of Gabon's 35 registered political parties, 29 belong to the presidential majority in what Bongo euphemistically calls "convivial democracy." Bongo and his family have a strong grip on the military, and he enjoys the support of the French.

Government and Government-Supportive Parties

Gabonese Democratic Party (*Parti Démocratique Gabonais*—PDG). Officially established by President Bongo in 1968, the PDG succeeded the earlier Gabon Democratic Bloc (*Bloc Démocratique Gabonais*—BDG) of President Mba. The PDG's most powerful body is its Political Bureau, although the party congress is technically the highest organ. There also is an advisory Central Committee, which oversees a variety of lesser bodies. In September 1986 the Third PDG Congress expanded the Central Committee from 253 to 297 members and the Political Bureau from 27 to 44 members to give "young militants" more access to leadership roles. In 1988 party membership was approximately 300,000. On May 17, 1990, amid increasing political turmoil and criticism of the regime's reform efforts, Bongo resigned as party chair, citing a desire to serve above "partisan preoccupations."

In early 1993 (then) National Assembly President Jules BOURDES-OGOULIGUENDE joined Alexandre Sambat in resigning from the PDG to run as an independent presidential candidate. On October 19 President Bongo officially declared his candidacy for reelection, and on November 4 the PDG organized a "New Alliance for Democracy and Change" electoral pact that included the **Association for Socialism in Gabon** (*Association pour le Socialisme au Gabon*—APSG) and the **People's Unity Party** (*Parti de l'Unité du Peuple*—PUP), led by Louis-Gaston MAYILA, both of which had gained legislative representation in 1990, as well as the previously FAR-affiliated **Gabonese Socialist Union** (*Union Socialiste Gabonais*—USG). The PUP won 1 seat in the assembly balloting of 2001.

Leaders: Jacques ADIAHENOT, Ali Ben BONGO, Simplice Guedet MANZELA (Secretary General).

Rally for Democracy and Progress (*Rassemblement pour la Démocratie et le Progrès*—RPG). The RPG controlled a single seat in the Senate as of mid-2001.

Leader: Pierre EMBONI.

Democratic and Republican Alliance (*Alliance Démocratique et Républicaine*—ADERE). At balloting in 1996 and early 1997 the ADERE won a number of town council and Senate seats after reportedly forming alliances with local PDG chapters. Furthermore, in May 1997 President Bongo named a senior ADERE leader, Didjob Divungui Di Ndinge, vice president of the republic.

Leader: Didjob DIVUNGUI DI NDINGE (Vice President of the Republic).

Movement of Friends of Bongo (*Mouvement des Amis de Bongo*—MAB). A self-described "apolitical grouping" founded by President Bongo's associates in November 1994, the MAB is not a "PDG offshoot" according to its leaders, who claimed that the group was launched to combat "tribalism, nepotism, disinformation, incrimination, and all forms of corruption." Party leader Georges RAWIRI, who was president of the Senate, died in 2006.

National Union of Blacksmiths. This group was formed in early 1999 by Thierry A'Agendieu KOMBILA, who had been vice president of the pro-Bongo Union for Development and Liberty (*Union pour le Développement et la Liberté*—UDL) until it disintegrated in December 1998.

National Rally of Woodcutters/Rally for Gabon (*Rassemblement National des Boucherons/Rassemblement pour le Gabon*—RNB/RPG). Formerly the National Rectification Movement–Woodcutters (*Mouvement de Redressement National–Bucherons*/Morena–*Bucherons*), the party adopted the RNB rubric in February 1991 in an effort to more clearly distinguish itself from its parent.

A southern grouping whose claimed membership of over 3,000 (mostly from the Fang ethnic group) supported nonviolent change, the Woodcutters on June 22–24, 1990, mounted the first opposition congress since the multiparty system was legalized. At the 1990–1991 legislative balloting the group became the leading opposition party, securing more than twice as many seats as Morena-*Originels*. Despite its success, the formation accused the government of electoral fraud and intimated that it would refuse to participate in assembly proceedings. In 1991 the Woodcutters joined an opposition call for dissolution of the National Assembly and the mounting of internationally supervised elections.

In mid-1992 *West Africa* reported that strained relations between the RNB and the Gabonese Progress Party (PGP, below) threatened the COD coalition. The enmity reportedly stemmed from the PGP's charge that the RNB's boycott of the later rounds of the 1990 election caused the opposition's defeat, as well as PGP bitterness at the RNB's failure to consult other parties prior to calling a general strike in February 1992. Meanwhile, Fr. Paul Mba-Abessole, the RNB's leader, labeled PGP President Pierre-Louis Agondjo-Okawe a "dangerous Marxist." (Mba-Abessole, who was dismissed by Morena in 1990, returned to Libreville that year at Bongo's invitation, after 13 years in exile.)

In June 1993 the party's secretary general, Pierre-André Kombila Koumba, was named chair of the opposition Committee for Free and Democratic Elections. Five months later, during the run-up to presidential balloting, the Woodcutters and the **National Convention for Change** (*Convention Nationale pour le Change*—CNC) issued a joint statement accusing the Bongo regime of electoral fraud.

In February 1994 RNB members and the party's radio station, *Radio Liberté*, were attacked by government forces deployed to quell antigovernment unrest in Libreville, with RNB leaders subsequently claiming that a number of its members had been detained. The attack on the RNB facilities coincided with the launching of a union-led general strike, which the RNB had publicly supported. Thereafter, the RNB was the most prominent of the opposition parties opposed to any cooperation with the Bongo regime.

At local balloting in October–November 1996, the RNB reportedly secured 62 of 98 contested posts; however, the party fared poorly at subsequent assembly balloting, falling 8 seats short of its 1990 totals. On January 19, 1997, the RNB-dominated Libreville municipal council elected Mba-Abessole as mayor.

In January 1998 the RNB newspaper, *Le Bucherons*, was suspended by the government for two separate three-month periods for publishing articles "insulting" to the president. In addition, Kombila Koumba, the paper's editor, was fined and given a suspended sentence. In June Mba-Abessole announced that Kombila Koumba had been removed from his party post because of alleged "indiscipline"; however, Kombila Koumba rejected Mba-Abessole's authority to oust him and, at a mid-July congress of his supporters, Kombila Koumba was pronounced RNB president. Subsequently, both Mba-Abessole and Kombila Koumba announced their intention to campaign for the presidency under the splintered RNB banner. Furthermore, in October the Constitutional Court approved the campaign application of another RNB stalwart, Alain ENGOUNG-NZE, thus leaving the party with three presidential contenders. At balloting in December Mba-Abessole finished a distant third with 13 percent of the vote while Kombila Koumba and Engoung-Nze finished near the bottom of the seven-candidate field.

In October 2000 the party reportedly adopted a new name (the Rally for Gabon [RPG]), but subsequent news stories referenced the grouping as the RNB/RPG. Several months earlier, the RNB also had reportedly announced the formation of a Front of Parties for Change (*Front des Parties pour le Changement*—FPC) with three smaller parties—the Congress for Democracy and Justice, the Rally of Republican Democrats, and the Republican Union for Democracy and Progress.

Following the December 2001 legislative balloting, Mba-Abessole, who had recently adopted a stance favoring "convivial democracy," accepted an invitation from President Bongo for the RNB/RPG to participate in an "opening up" of the government, although some party members remained hostile to the initiative. Mba-Abessole and two other RNB/RPG members were included in the new cabinet installed in January 2002. Mba-Abessole, a deputy prime minister, supported Bongo in the 2005 presidential election, although a year earlier he had accused the government of being the leading violator of human rights in the country.

Leaders: Fr. Paul MBA-ABESSOLE (1993 and 1998 presidential candidate and Mayor of Libre-ville), Pierre-André KOMBILA Koumba (leader of dissident faction and 1998 presidential candidate), Vincent Moulengui BOUKOSSO.

Social Democratic Party (*Parti Social-Démocrate*—PSD). The PSD became a member of the COD following its formation in 1991. During its first congress in Libreville, on April 21, 1992, party president Pierre Claver Maganga-Moussavou was chosen as its 1993 standard-bearer, but he secured a vote share of under 4 percent.

In October 1996 Maganga-Moussavou was ousted from the Obame-Nguema cabinet after he led a vociferous protest against the government's rescheduling of elections. Subsequently, the party reportedly dismissed another PSD leader, Senturel Ngoma MANDOUNGOU, when he assumed Maganga-Moussavou's vacant post.

In November 1998 the PSD withdrew from the national electoral commission to protest its administration of the voter registration lists. Subsequently, at polling in December, Maganga-Moussavou once again secured less than 4 percent of the vote. The PSD leader joined the PDG-led cabinet of January 2002 as the minister of state for agriculture, livestock, and rural development. In June 2004 the group joined the parties making up the ruling coalition, and Maganga-Moussavou was named to the cabinet in September 2004.

Leader: Pierre-Claver MAGANGA-MOUSSAVOU (President of the Party and 1993 and 1998 presidential candidate).

Gabonese Party of Independent Centrists (PGCI). The PGCI is led by Jean-Pierre Lemboumba, one of President Bongo's closest advisers.

Leader: Jean-Pierre LEMBOUMBA, Jerôme OKINDA.

Other Parties and Groups

Gabonese Union for Democracy and Development (*Union Gabonaise de la Démocratie et du Développement*—UGDD). Formed in France on April 30, 2005, by Zacharie Myboto, the party had not been legalized by the November presidential election, forcing Myboto to run as an independent. A defector from the PDG, he formerly was a minister of public works and an administrative secretary of the party. In September 2005 President Bongo said he would seize his opponents' passports to prevent them from "insulting" him abroad. However, observers commented that Bongo wouldn't arrest Myboto, who is popular in Gabon, for fear of "annoying" international donors.

Leader: Zacharie MYBOTO (2005 presidential candidate).

African Forum for Reconstruction (*Forum Africain pour la Réconstruction*—FAR). Also referenced as the Action Forum for Renewal (*Forum d'Action pour le Renouveau*), FAR was launched in early 1992 by merger of the National Rectification Movement–Originals (*Mouvement de Redressement National*–Morena-*Originels*), which had secured 7 legislative seats in 1990–1991, and two smaller formations, the Gabonese Socialist Union (*Union Socialiste Gabonais*—USG), which had secured 3 seats, and the extralegislative Gabonese Socialist Party (*Parti Socialiste Gabonais*—PSG). The party's platform advocates the establishment of a "state of law and social justice" and a market economy, tempered by the "interests of the State."

Organized in 1981, Morena operated clandestinely within Gabon for the ensuing nine years, during which time, with support from the French Socialist Party, it formed a self-proclaimed government-in-exile in Paris. In 1981–1982 its domestic leaders were repeatedly arrested for distributing leaflets calling for a multiparty system. Many were sentenced to long prison terms, but by 1986 all had been released under a general amnesty that had been urged by French President Mitterrand. By early 1990 the party had given rise to a number of dissident factions, the most important of which was Morena–*Bucherons*, above, as distinguished from the essentially northern, ethnic Fang parent group led by Noël Ngwa-Nguema. At a Morena party congress on August 30, 1991, Executive Secretary Jean-Pierre Zongue-Nguema called for a revival of the COD and denounced the "duplicity" of opposition colleagues who had joined the Bongo government.

At presidential balloting in December 1993, party leader León Mbou-Yembi captured a bare 1.83 percent of the vote while Adrien NGUEMA Ondo, running under the National Rectification Movement-Unionist (*Mouvement de Redressement National*–Morena-*Unioniste*) banner, secured less than 1 percent.

In August 1998 the Forum's Morena wing reportedly split into two camps, which subsequently held separate congresses in Libreville and Lambarene under the leadership of Jean Clement BOUTAMBA and Felix Martin Ze MEMINI, respectively.

In the 2005 presidential election, Augustin Moussavou King ran as a candidate affiliated with the PSG, coming in a distant fourth.

Leaders: León MBOU-YEMBIT, Pierre ZONGUE-NGUEMA (COD Chair and Former Morena-Originel Leader), Noël NGWA-NGUEMA (Former Morena-*Originel* Executive Secretary), Vincent ESSOLOMONGEU (Secretary General).

Gabonese Progress Party (*Parti Gabonais du Progrès*—PGP). The president of the recently organized PGP, Pierre-Louis Agondjo-Okawe, called in April 1990 for dissolution of the transitional government on the grounds that it was inadequately representative of the Gabonese people. In May the death of party secretary general Joseph Rendjambe was a catalyst for renewed unrest throughout the country. Second runner-up in the 1990 legislative poll, the PGP is composed primarily of members of the Myéné ethnic group.

In July 1998 the party announced that Benoit Mouity-Nzamba would be its standard-bearer at presidential balloting in December; however, there were no further reports regarding his candidacy.

In February 2000 the PGP reportedly accused the government of "organizing electoral fraud" and called on the president to convene talks on electoral and "institutional" reforms. The party won three seats in the 2001 assembly elections. Party leader Agondjo-Okawe died on August 27, 2005.

Leaders: Anselme NZOGHE (Secretary General), Benoit MOUITY-NZAMBA.

Union of the Gabonese People (*Union du Peuple Gabonais*—UPG). In July 1989 the UPG, which is supported largely by the southern Bapounou ethnic group, was reported to have circulated leaflets critical of President Bongo in Paris; the following October, three of its members were arrested in Gabon for alleged involvement in a coup plot. In February 1990 party founder Pierre Mamboundou was expelled from France to Senegal, despite his denial of complicity in the attempted coup.

On July 14, 1992, UPG activists demonstrated in Libreville, calling for Mamboundou's amnesty. On November 2, 1993, the UPG leader was allowed to return from Senegal; however, his bid to stand as a presidential candidate in the December elections was rejected. Subsequently, on November 8–9 UPG demonstrators rioted in Libreville in a futile attempt to force the government to overturn the ban.

Mamboundou's preeminent role within the UPG was diminished on September 25, 1995, when party members elected his former coleader and recent nemesis, Sebastien Mamboundou MOUYAMA, chair. In August 1996 it was reported that Mouyama had launched a new political party called the **Alternative Movement** (*Mouvement Alternatif*—MA). However, Mamboundou ran as the UPG and HCR's presidential candidate in 1998, and he was routinely referenced as the UPG leader in the 2001 legislative campaign, calling for a boycott of the second round of balloting in view of what he termed the "indescribable disorder" of the first round. The legal status of the new group and its relationship with the UPG was not immediately clear.

Leaders: Pierre MAMBOUNDOU (2005 presidential candidate), David BADINGA.

Rally of the Democrats (RDD). Founded in 1993 by Christian-Serge Maroga, who defected from UPG, the party was legalized in 1997.

Leader: Christian-Serge MAROGA (2005 presidential candidate).

Alliance of Republicans for Development. (*Alliance des Républicains pour le Développement*—ARD). The formation of the ARD was announced in January 2001 under the leadership of the former mayor of Port-Gentil, who had reportedly been recently expelled from the PGP.

Leader: Marie-Augustine Houangni AMBOUROUE.

Circle of Liberal Reformers (*Cercle des Libéraux Réformateurs*—CLR). The CLR was formed in late 1992 by former minister of security Jean-Boniface Assele, the brother of President Bongo's former wife, who was expelled from the PDG along with two other founders of the new group. The party won representation in the assembly in 2001.

Leader: Jean-Boniface ASSELE.

Rally of Gauls (*Rassemblement des Gaulois*—RG). The RG was founded in February 1994 by a former Morena leader, Max-Anicet Koumba-Mbadinga, who had returned from exile in France. The Gauls, whose name is traceable to its founder's belief that Gabon's "history does not begin with Gabon, but with our Gallic origins," forwarded a platform advocating a return to "pre-independence origins" with an emphasis on close ties to France. The RG also called for a renaming of the country, arguing that "Gabon" is derived from the name of a Portuguese wine.

In January 1998 the RG gained legal recognition (three years after it first applied).

Leader: Max-Anicet KOUMBA-MBADINGA.

Independent Republicans' Party (*Parti Des Républicains Indépendants*—PRI). The PRI was launched in early 1995 by Anaclet Bissielo, who castigated fellow opposition leaders for their "repeated failures" in opposing the Bongo regime.

Leader: Anaclet BISSIELO.

Democratic and Social Union (*Union Démocratique et Sociale*—UDS). In April 1996 the newly legalized UDS organized a debate that focused on the June 1995 referendum and the proposed upcoming elections. The UDS argued that, contrary to the dictates of the 1994 Paris Accords, "nothing had been done" to prepare for the balloting.

Leader: Herve ASSAMANET.

Cabinet

As of May 1, 2006

Prime Minister	Jean Eyéghe Ndong (PDG)
Deputy Prime Ministers	Emmanuel Ondo Metogho (PDG)
	Georgette Koko [f]
	Me Louis Gaston Mayila
	Paul Mba-Abessole (RNB/RPG)

Ministers of State

Culture and Arts	Pierre Marie Ndong
Defense	Ali Bongo Ondimba (PDG)
Development Planning	Casimir Oyé Mba (PDG)
Economy, Finance, Budget, and Privatization	Paul Toungui (PDG)
Foreign Affairs, Cooperation, and Francophone Affairs	Jean Ping (PDG)
Housing, Town Planning, and Surveying	Jacques Adiahénot (PDG)
Human Rights, Reform, and Fight Against Corruption	Pierre-Claver Maganga-Moussavou (PSD)
Interior, Security, and Immigration	André Mba Obame
Public Health	Paulette Missambo (PDG) [f]
Public Works	Gen. Idriss Ngari (PDG)
Professional Education and Social Rehabilitation	Pierre André Kombila Koumba (RNB/RPG)

Ministers

Agriculture, Livestock Farming, and Rural Development	Faustin Boukoubi (PDG)
Civil Service, Administrative Reform, and State Modernization	Gen. Jean Boniface Assele
Commerce and Industrial Development	Paul Biyoghe Mba (PDG)
Communications and Information Technology, Post and Telecommunications, and Government Spokesman	René Ndemezo Obiang (PDG)
Decentralization and Regional Planning	Dieudonne Pambo
Emergencies	Jean Massima (PDG)
Family, Protection of Children, and Promotion of Women	Angélique Ngoma (PDG) [f]
Fight Against AIDS and Protection of Orphans of AIDS	Alice Lamou (PDG) [f]
Justice and Keeper of the Seals	Honorine Dossou Naki (PDG) [f]
Labor and Employment	Christiane Bitoughat [f]
Merchant Navy and Ports	Martin Mabala (PDG)
Mining, Energy, Oil, and Water Resources	Richard Onouviet (PDG)
National and Higher Education	Albert Ondo Ossa
Promotion of the Private Sector; Social Economy and Handicrafts	Marie Missouloukagne [f]
Small and Medium-Sized Enterprises and Industries	Senturel Ngoma Madoungou
State Controls and Inspections	Me Francine Meviane [f]
Urban Affairs, Protection of Widows and Orphans	Pierre Amoughe Mba (RNB/RPG)
Water, Forests, Fishing, and Environment	Emile Doumba (PDG)
Youth, Sports, and Leisure	Egide Boundono-Simangove

[f] = female

Movement for Democracy, Development, and National Reconciliation (*Mouvement pour la Démocratie, le Développement, et la Réconciliation Nationale*—MODERN). The MODERN was launched in November 1996 by the (then) minister of higher education, Gaston Mozogo.

Leader: Gaston MOZOGO OVONO.

Minor parties include the **Circle for Renovation and Progress** (*Cercle pour le Renouveau et le Progrès*—CRP); the **Congress for Democracy and Justice** (*Congrès pour la Démocratie et la Justice*—CDJ), which won a seat in the 2001 assembly elections, led by Jules Bourdes-Ogouliguende and Marc Saturnin Nan NGUEMA, a Fang who was formerly a secretary-general of OPEC and arrested in December 2004 on trumped-up weapons charges; the **Federation of Gabonese Ecologists** (*Fédération des Ecologistes Gabonaises*—FEG), an environmental group led by Alain DICKSON that has been highly critical of the dearth of environmentalists in the government; **Gabon of the Future** (*Gabon Avenir*), which was launched in 1999 under the leadership of Sylvestre OYOUOMI; the **Mebiame Group** (*Groupe Mébiame*—GM); the **Movement for People's Social Emancipation** (*Mouvement pour l'Emancipation Sociale du Peuple*—MESP); the **National Front** (*Front National*—FN), led by Martin EFAYONG; **Renaissance of the Gabonese Democratic Bloc,** led by Antoine Meyo MENDOUTOUME; the **Union for Democracy and Social Integration,** led by Nzebi Herve Patrick OPIANGAH, who was jailed in early 2005 after participating in a demonstration demanding legalization of the party the African movement of Development (MAD) and the National Rally of Woodcutters–Kombila (RNB-kombila), both of which won 1 seat in the 2001 assembly balloting.

In early 2006 it was reported that a group calling itself Bongo Must Go (*Bongo Doit Partir*—BDP), based in the United States, had joined with a group called *Mamba*, which claimed to have carried out "sabotage" attacks in Libreville in December 2005. The leaders of the BDP were Daniel MENGARA, a Fang, and Serge BESAC.

Legislature

In March 1994 the (then) unicameral National Assembly adopted a draft constitutional reform bill that provided for a Senate, or upper legislative house. Elections to fill the body were held for the first time in January–February 1997 (see below).

Senate (*Sénat*). Created by a constitutional amendment in 1994, the Senate is a 91-member body elected for a six-year term by members of municipal councils and departmental assemblies. First-ever balloting to fill the body was held on January 26 and February 9, 1997. After the most recent elections on February 9, 2003, the seats were distributed as follows: the Gabonese Democratic Party, 60; the National Rally of Woodcutters, 8; the Gabonese Progress Party, 4; the Democratic and Republican Alliance, 3; the Rally for Democracy and Progress and the Circle of Liberal Reformers, 1 each; and independents and others, 14.

*President:*René RADEMBINO-CONIQUET.

National Assembly (*Assemblée Nationale*). The sole legislative organ prior to 1997, the National Assembly is a 120-seat body whose members are elected for five-year terms. Following the most recent balloting on December 9 and 23, 2001, the allocation of seats was as follows: the Gabonese Democratic Party, 88; the National Rally of Woodcutters/Rally for Gabon, 8; the Democratic and Republican Alliance, 3; the Gabonese Progress Party, 3; the Circle of Liberal Reformers, 2; the Congress for Democracy and Justice, 1; African Movement of Development, 1; the Social Democratic Party, 1; the People's Unity Party, 1; the National Rally of Woodcutters/Kombila, 1; independents, 12; and 1 vacant seat. The election in one department was postponed until May 26, 2002, but the results were unknown.

President: Guy NDZOUBA-NDAMA.

Communications

Most news media are owned and operated by the government. In late 1999 four private radio and television stations were suspended by the

National Council of Communication for broadcasting illegally.

Press

The following are published in Libreville: *L'Union* (35,000), government daily; *Gabon-Matin* (18,000), published daily by the *Agence Gabonaise de Presse; La Relance,* weekly PDG organ; *Gabon d'Aujourd'hui,* published weekly by the Ministry of Communications.

News Agency

The domestic facility is the *Agence Gabonaise de Presse* (AGP).

Broadcasting and Computing

The government-controlled *Radiodiffusion-Télévision Gabonaise* broadcasts national and regional radio programs in French and local languages, plus educational television programming from Libreville and Port-Gentil. There also are two private channels, *Télé-Africa,* which broadcasts in French, and *Telediffusion du Gabon.* There were approximately 70,000 television receivers and 30,000 personal computers serving 35,000 Internet users.

Intergovernmental Representation

Ambassador to the U.S.
Jules Marius OGOUEBANDJA

U.S. Ambassador to Gabon
Reuben Barrie WALKLEY

Permanent Representative to the UN
Denis DANGUE REWAKA

IGO Memberships (Non-UN)
AfDB, AU, BADEA, BDEAC, CEEAC, CEMAC, IDB, Interpol, IOM, NAM, OIC, OIF, WCO, WTO

GAMBIA

REPUBLIC OF THE GAMBIA

Note: In presidential balloting of September 22, 2006, President Yahya Jammeh (Alliance for Patriotic Reorientation and Construction) was reelected for another five-year term with 67.3 percent of the vote, defeating Ousainu Darboe (United Democratic Party), who received 26.7 percent, and Halifah Sallah (People's Democratic Organization for Independence and Socialism), who received nearly 6 percent.

The Country

Situated on the bulge of West Africa and surrounded on three sides by Senegal, Gambia is a narrow strip of territory (varying from 6 to 10 miles wide) that borders the Gambia River to a point about 200 miles from the Atlantic. The population is overwhelmingly African, the main ethnic groups being Mandingo (40 percent), Fula (13 percent), Wolof (12 percent), and Jola and Serahuli (7 percent each); in addition, there are small groups of Europeans, Lebanese, Syrians, and Mauritanians. Tribal languages are widely spoken, although English is the official and commercial language. Islam is the religion of 80 percent of the people.

The economy has traditionally been based on peanuts, which are cultivated on almost all suitable land and which, including derivatives, typically account for upward of 80 percent of export earnings. Industry is largely limited to peanut-oil refining and handicrafts; unofficially, smuggling into Senegal has long been important. In the early 1990s the government implemented an economic recovery program sponsored by the International Monetary Fund (IMF), which emphasized agricultural development, reductions in external borrowing, promotion of the private sector, and government austerity; those measures were credited with stimulating an improvement in GDP and a decline in inflation. Nonetheless, a slump in the agriculture sector yielded virtually no real economic growth in 1993–1994. Western aid was severely curtailed

following the military coup of 1994, the Jammeh regime turning to new donors such as Libya and Taiwan to finance an ambitious infrastructure program. Thereafter, the government adopted another IMF-prescribed structural adjustment program with an emphasis on economic and financial reform. Such efforts were rewarded in 1998 with a real GDP growth rate of over 5 percent and single-digit inflation (3.8 percent according to the IMF). Meanwhile, the fund urged the government to continue to increase its support for the private sector. In early 2000 Banjul called on the international

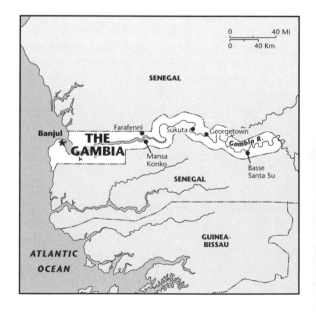

Political Status: Became independent member of the Commonwealth on February 18, 1965; republican regime instituted April 24, 1970; Gambian-Senegalese Confederation of Senegambia, formed with effect from February 1, 1982, dissolved as of September 30, 1989; most recent constitution approved by national referendum on August 8, 1996.

Area: 4,361 sq. mi. (11,295 sq. km.).

Population: 1,364,507 (2003C); 1,442,000 (2005E).

Major Urban Center (2005E): BANJUL (metropolitan area, 568,000).

Official Language: English.

Monetary Unit: Dalasi (market rate July 1, 2006: 28.00 dalasis = $1US).

President: (*See headnote.*) Yahya JAMMEH (Alliance for Patriotic Reorientation and Construction); installed as chair of the Armed Forces Provisional Ruling Council following military coup that overthrew the government of Alhaji Sir Dawda Kairaba JAWARA Sanyang (People's Progressive Party) on July 22, 1994; elected to a five-year presidential term on September 26, 1996; reelected on October 18, 2001, and sworn in for a second five-year term on December 21.

Vice President: Aisatou NJIE-SAIDY (Alliance for Patriotic Reorientation and Construction); appointed by the president on March 21, 1997, to fill previously vacant post; reappointed December 21, 2001.

investment community to assist African countries in their privatization efforts, asserting that state assets were being treated as "scrap" and sold off at extremely low prices.

Gambia experienced a severe economic downturn in 2002, partly due to a collapse in the peanut harvest. As a result, GDP declined by 3.2 percent, inflation rose to 13 percent, and the government's deficit ballooned to 8.1 percent of GDP. In addition, the currency lost 60 percent of its value against the euro and 45 percent of its value against the dollar. Meanwhile, unemployment approached 50 percent. Adding to the crisis was the rise in world oil prices and one of the world's fastest growing populations. In response to these economic shocks, the government created the National Emergency Fiscal Committee and implemented programs designed to spur growth. Real GDP growth declined to 5 percent in 2004 (from 7 percent the previous year), but on a more positive note, inflation plummeted 10 percent to single digits by early 2005, and fund managers were encouraged by the country's efforts to initiate reforms promoting transparency. However, economic recovery was jeopardized by the "near-disastrous effect" of a quasi-public entity charged with marketing and processing peanuts, according to the IMF. The company reportedly was unable to raise the money needed to buy what was to have been a bumper crop of nuts, which the IMF estimated would result in a substantial loss in exports.

Another setback to economic stability occurred in January 2006 when the president spontaneously announced a 10 percent salary increase for all government workers, an expenditure that was not accounted for in the recently approved budget.

Government and Politics

Political Background

Under British influence since 1588, Gambia was not definitively established as a separate colony until 1888. It acquired the typical features of British colonial rule, achieved internal self-government in 1963, and became fully independent within the Commonwealth on February 18, 1965. Initially a parliamentary regime (with the British monarch serving as head of state), Gambia changed to a republican form of government following a referendum in 1970.

For nearly three decades after independence leadership was exercised by the People's Progressive Party (PPP), headed by President Dawda K. JAWARA, although opposition candidates secured approximately 30 percent of the popular vote in the elections of 1972, 1977, and 1982. At the May 1979 PPP Congress—the first in 16 years—President Jawara rebuffed demands by some delegates that a one-party system be instituted, commenting that such a change could occur only through the ballot box. However, on November 1, 1980, amid allegations of a widespread antigovernment conspiracy, two opposition movements described by the president as "terrorist organizations" were banned, despite protests from the legal opposition parties.

A more serious threat to the Jawara regime developed in July 1981 when the capital was taken over by elements of Gambia's paramilitary Field Force and the Socialist and Revolutionary Labor Party, a Marxist-Leninist group led by Kukoi Samba SANYANG. The uprising was quelled with the aid of Senegalese troops dispatched under the terms of a 1965 mutual defense and security treaty. Subsequently, President Jawara and Senegalese President Diouf announced plans for a partial merger of their respective states in the form of a Senegambian Confederation, which came into effect on February 1, 1982.

The confederation, which critics branded as the equivalent of annexation by Senegal, was a major issue in the May 1982 presidential election, the first to be conducted by direct vote. However, with the government branding several members of the demonstrably divided opposition as participants in the 1981 coup attempt, Jawara secured a 73 percent majority. The president subsequently appeared to defuse the confederation issue by resisting immediate monetary union with Senegal, a proposal viewed with skepticism by many Gambians.

While President Jawara was returned to office at the general election of March 11, 1987, with a reduced majority of 59 percent, the PPP increased its representation in the 36-member House of Representatives from 28 to 31, most observers attributing the latter success to an economic upturn. Subsequently, amid widespread concern about Gambia becoming "Senegal's eleventh region," the administration evinced little interest in pursuing genuine Senegambian integration, and the confederation was dissolved with the consent of both countries as of September 30, 1989.

After declaring his intention to retire at a PPP congress in December 1991, Jawara reversed himself and stood for a fifth consecutive five-year term

in April 1992, reportedly to avoid further electoral slippage that might result in defeat for the ruling party. The outcome was a marginal decline of 5 elected House seats on a vote share virtually identical to that of 1985.

The Jawara government was overthrown on July 22, 1994, in a bloodless coup by junior army officers, who installed Lt. Yahya JAMMEH as chair of a five-member Armed Forces Provisional Ruling Council (AFPRC). Three days later the council named a 15-member government composed almost equally of military and civilian members. Antagonism toward the Jammeh government subsequently emerged from several quarters. In mid-August tension between the AFPRC and older military officials, who complained of being shunted aside, was underscored by the arrest of two high-ranking officers. Collaterally, friction continued between the AFPRC and members of Jawara's former government. Finally, on October 10, the European Union (EU) and the United Kingdom suspended economic and military assistance following Jammeh's dismissal of Finance Minister Bakary Bunja DARBO, the sole holdover from the previous administration.

In an attempt to mollify his critics, Jammeh in late 1994 announced a four-year transitional timetable that included plans for the drafting of a new constitution, an investigation into government corruption, a crackdown on crime, and a presidential election in November 1998. However, the four-year time frame drew widespread criticism, and in early February 1995 the AFPRC reduced it to two. Meanwhile, as the result of alleged participation in a coup attempt on January 27, two close associates of Jammeh on the AFPRC, Vice Chair Sana SABALLY and Interior Minister Sadibu HYDARA, were arrested and replaced by Capt. Edward SINGHATEY and Capt. Lamin BAJO, respectively. (In late December it was reported that Sabally had been given a nine-year sentence and that Hydara had died in prison.)

On April 10, 1995, the regime named a constitutional commission and charged it with drafting a document that would provide a legal framework for the holding of multiparty elections. However, in

October the defection of AFPRC spokesman Capt. Ebou JALLOW, amid charges that he had attempted to overthrow the regime, underscored the internal turmoil that had plagued the AFPRC and Jammeh's cabinet throughout 1995.

The draft constitution was released by the AFPRC in March 1996 and approved (according to government figures) by 70.4 percent of the voters in a national referendum on August 8, 1996, despite opposition charges that the new basic law had been carefully written to ensure that the Jammeh regime would continue in power. Jammeh subsequently announced that presidential elections would be held in September (months earlier than anticipated), with national legislative balloting to follow before the end of the year.

In voting on September 26, 1996, Jammeh was elected to a five-year presidential term as the candidate of the newly formed Alliance for Patriotic Reorientation and Construction (APRC). Official results credited him with 55.76 percent of the votes, his closest pursuer among the three other candidates being Ousainu DARBOE of the United Democratic Party (UDP) with 35.34 percent.

On November 8, 1996, the government announced that legislative elections, due on December 11, would be postponed until January 1997. The decision came after weeks of UDP-orchestrated antigovernment demonstrations. Subsequently, at balloting on January 2, 1997, President Jammeh's APRC captured 33 of the 45 contested seats (the president is empowered to name 4 additional legislators), giving the party the two-thirds majority necessary to pass legislation and make constitutional changes unimpeded. With 7 seats, Darboe's UDP finished a distant second.

Rebuffed in his attempt to name Edward Singhatey as vice president (the 27-year-old Singhatey failed a constitutional requirement that the deputy chief executive be at least 30 years old), Jammeh appointed a new 13-member cabinet on March 7, 1997, which did not include a vice president but placed Singhatey in the powerful post of minister to the president. However, following opposition criticism that the constitution mandated the appointment of a vice president, the president named Aisatou NJIE-SAIDY (his minister of health, social welfare, and women's affairs) to the post on March 21. Njie-Saidy thereby became the first female vice president in western Africa. The transformation from military to civilian rule was completed on April 17 when Jammeh replaced the last four military governors with civilians.

President Jammeh was reelected to a second term with 53 percent of the vote on October 18, 2001, the UDP's Darboe again proven to be his nearest competitor among four opposition candidates. The APRC dominated the January 2002 assembly balloting in light of a boycott by the major opposition grouping and subsequently dominated local and regional elections in April because of the continuing boycott (see Current issues, below).

In assembly by-elections on September 29, 2005, to replace 4 ousted members, 3 seats went to a newly formed opposition coalition, the National Alliance for Democracy and Development (NADD), and 1 seat was secured by the APRC (see Political Parties, below). A new assembly speaker, Belinda BIDWELL, was sworn in on April 19, 2006, to replace Sherif Mustapha DIBBA, who was arrested in connection with a March 21 coup attempt.

Constitution and Government

During the 12 years following adoption of a republican constitution in 1970, Gambia was led by a president who was indirectly elected by the legislature for a five-year term and was assisted by a vice president of his choice. The procedure was changed in 1982 to one involving direct election of the chief executive, who retained the authority to designate his deputy. Prior to the 1994 coup, the unicameral House of Representatives contained 50 members, of whom 36 were directly elected for five-year terms (save for presidential dissolution following a vote of nonconfidence); 5 seats were held by chiefs elected by the Assembly of Chiefs, while the remainder were held by 8 nonvoting nominated members and the attorney general. Subsequently, the 1996 constitution provided for a directly elected president with broad powers (including the authority to appoint the cabinet) and a National Assembly of elected legislators and presidential appointees. The assembly may order the resignation of the head of state or cabinet ministers by a two-thirds vote. The judicial system is headed by a Supreme Court and includes a Court of Appeal, magistrates' courts, customary tribunals, and Muslim courts.

At the local level the country is divided into districts administered by chiefs in association with village headmen and advisers. The districts are grouped into seven regions, which are governed by centrally appointed commissioners and area councils thus far containing a majority of elected members, with district chiefs serving ex officio. Banjul has heretofore been provided with an elected City Council.

Foreign Relations

While adhering to a formal policy of nonalignment, Gambia has long maintained close relations with the United Kingdom, its principal aid donor, and the African Commonwealth states. By far the most important foreign policy question, however, has turned on relations with Senegal. In 1967 the two countries signed a treaty of association providing for a joint ministerial committee and secretariat, while other agreements provided for cooperation in such areas as defense, foreign affairs, and development of the Gambia River basin. In early 1976 a number of new accords were concluded that, coupled with the need for Senegalese military assistance in 1980 and 1981, paved the way for establishment of the Confederation of Senegambia in February 1982. However, few of its goals had been seriously addressed at the time of the confederation's dissolution in 1989.

Relations deteriorated in the wake of the breakup with Senegal in 1989, with Banjul accusing Dakar of economic harassment (largely in connection with Senegalese attempts to limit the clandestine flow of reexport goods). However, a meeting between Presidents Jawara and Diouf in December 1989 proved beneficial, the Jawara administration reportedly attempting to stabilize relations so as not to jeopardize Gambia's recent economic improvement. Ties were further strengthened by the conclusion of a treaty of friendship and cooperation on January 8, 1991, that provided for annual political summits and the establishment of joint commissions to help implement summit agreements.

In September 1993 Senegal closed its borders with Gambia, voicing renewed frustration with illegal commerce. In November the two countries agreed to the establishment of a technical committee charged with creating a mechanism to alleviate the problem, which had plagued the former confederates since their 1989 split.

Regional relations were at the forefront of Gambia's foreign policy agenda in late 1999 and early 2000. In December 1999 President Jammeh played a leading role in facilitating the signing of a cease-fire pact by the Senegalese government and Casamance rebels, and in April 2000 Gambia and four other west African nations agreed to share a common currency by the end of 2002. However, the deadline was later advanced to the end of 2009. (The other prospective participants are Ghana, Guinea, Nigeria, and Sierre Leone.) Gambia also participated in the regional peacekeeping mission in Liberia by contributing 150 troops. These forces subsequently became part of the UN mission in Liberia.

In November 2000 a Commonwealth Ministerial Action Group visited Gambia, signaling a relative easing of relations that had reportedly been lukewarm since 1995, although Gambia continued to be criticized for its human rights record.

Relations between Gambia and Senegal remained tense in the early 2000s amid repeated claims that the Jammeh government provided aid to anti-government forces in Senegal. Subsequently, a 100 percent increase in duties on vehicles traveling through Gambia and a doubling of the cost of ferries between northern and southern Senegal temporarily led to the closing of the border between the two countries. Negotiations brokered by a Nigerian mediator in late 2005 led to "substantial progress" toward a resolution, with Senegal reportedly agreeing to remove its border blockade.

Current Issues

In September 1999 the Gambian *Daily Observer* reported that an assassination attempt had targeted President Jammeh, who had recently moved his government to his hometown (ostensibly because of renovation work being performed in Banjul). The government dismissed the story, and an *Observer* editor and reporter were arrested. However, following reports of violent clashes between rival groups of presidential guardsmen in Banjul in January 2000, Jammeh claimed that forces loyal to him had killed one guardsman and wounded a second who were facing arrest for allegedly plotting a coup. (Among the alleged targets of the dissidents were Jammeh and his government as well as all army officers above the rank of lieutenant.) In April the already tense capital was rocked by antigovernment demonstrations and rioting that erupted after security forces killed a student. At least 12 people died during the unrest. A commission of inquiry subsequently resulted in amnesties for both security forces involved in the shootings and the leaders of student groups.

The 2001 presidential campaign was marred by several violent incidents, but the balloting proceeded smoothly. Although international observers generally accepted the poll as free and fair, albeit with several significant criticisms, the UDP accused the government of electoral fraud. In late December the UDP and several of its coalition partners announced they would boycott the legislative election scheduled for January 17, 2002, on the grounds that the electoral commission was favoring the Jammeh administration by, among other things, permitting cross-district voting. The major opposition parties also boycotted the municipal and regional elections of April 2002, thereby again ensuring APRC dominance, as the APRC won 99 of 113 constituencies. Four assembly members were expelled in mid-2005 following their launch of the opposition coalition NADD. (The constitution states that elected representatives lose their seats if they change to a party other than the one they were affiliated with when elected.)

The administration continued to draw strong criticism for its repressive measures against the media, with one international group of journalists adding Jammeh to its list of "press freedom predators" in 2006. A former army chief was arrested after a coup attempt in March 2006, and one month later, thousands staged a pro-democracy, anti-coup demonstration. For his part, Jammeh warned the protesters against "external aggression" in matters of national concern.

On a brighter note, potentially significant oil deposits were reportedly discovered offshore, raising the possibility of dramatic revenue enhancement in five to ten years.

Political Parties

Prior to the 1994 coup, Gambia was one of the few African states to have consistently sanctioned a multiparty system, despite the predominant position held since independence by the ruling People's Progressive Party (PPP). Following the coup, all party activity was proscribed until August 14, 1996, when, in the wake of the recent approval of a new constitution, the government announced that the ban had been lifted. However, the regime's opponents described the new "preconditions" for party registration as "onerous" and accused President Jammeh of lacking commitment to genuine democratization. Such fears appeared justified when Jammeh announced shortly thereafter that the three main parties from the pre-coup era (the PPP, NCP, and GPP) had been banned. Under intense regional and other international pressure, Jammeh lifted the ban in July 2001 to permit full-party participation in the upcoming presidential election.

Five opposition parties formed a coalition on January 17, 2005, in Banjul to present a candidate to challenge Jammeh in the next presidential election at the end of 2006. The parties comprising the National Alliance for Democracy (NADD) were the National Democratic Action Movement (NDAM), the National Reconciliation Party (NRP), the People's Democratic Organization for Independence and Socialism (PDOIS), the PPP, and the UDP. The original coordinator of the NADD, which was officially registered a few months after its inception, was assembly minority leader Halifa SALLAH of the PDOIS. By March 2006, the UDP and the NRP had dropped out, and a new chair, Jallow SONKO, was elected. The group subsequently named Sallah its presidential candidate for the upcoming election.

Government and Government-Supportive Parties

Alliance for Patriotic Reorientation and Construction (APRC). Founded on August 26, 1996, as a vehicle for Col. Yahya Jammeh's presidential campaign, the APRC was a successor to the July 22 Movement (named in reference to the date of Jammeh's takeover in 1994), which had been launched in mid-1995. (Among other things, its leaders had committed the movement to "national unity," apparently in the hope of bridging the nation's ethnic divisions. The bulk of the support for the Jammeh regime at that point was described as emanating from the Jola ethnic group, which constitutes less than 10 percent of the population.) APRC founders announced they would pursue economic development based on free-market principles and cooperation with neighboring countries. Jammeh resigned his military position (as required by the constitution) shortly before the September 1996 presidential balloting.

In late 1999 Phoday MAKALO, theretofore the APRC's general secretary, reportedly fled the country amid allegations that he had embezzled party funds.

Leaders: Yahya JAMMEH (President of the Republic), Aisatou NJIE-SAIDY (Vice President of the Republic), Musa BITTAYE.

National Convention Party (NCP). The NCP was organized in late 1975 by Sherif Mustapha Dibba, former vice president of the Republic and cofounder of the PPP. Although jailed in August 1981 on charges of involvement in the July coup attempt, Dibba challenged Jawara for the presidency in 1982, securing 28 percent of the vote. The 5 leg-

islative seats won by the NCP in 1977 were reduced to 3 in 1982. A month after the election, Dibba was released from confinement, the charges against him having been vacated by a Banjul court. The party won 5 House seats in 1987 and 6 in 1992, Dibba running second to Jawara in the presidential balloting on both occasions. The NCP was banned from participating in 1996 elections but was reinstituted to legal status in July 2001. Dibba won 3.7 percent of the vote in the October presidential poll. Despite his previous criticism of President Jammeh and the APRC, Dibba announced an "alliance" between the NCP and the APRC prior to the legislative balloting of January 2002. Dibba was subsequently nominated by the president to the assembly, of which he was then elected speaker, thereby eliciting criticism from a number of other NCP stalwarts who wished to remain in strict opposition to the APRC.

Leader: Sherif Mustapha DIBBA (Former Speaker of the National Assembly).

Other Parties and Groups

United Democratic Party (UDP). Launched in August 1996 after the snap presidential election was announced, the UDP was described as having the support of the three parties (the PPP, NCP, and GPP) that had been banned by the Jammeh regime. UDP presidential candidate Ousainu Darbo, a prominent lawyer, ran second to Jammeh in the September 26 balloting, securing a reported 35.34 percent of the votes.

In May 1998 nine UDP members, including (then) party leader Lamin Waa JAWARA, were detained by government security forces. Another leader, Ousainu Darboe, and a group of UDP members were reportedly arrested in June 2000 in connection with an alleged confrontation with APRC militiamen. Darboe was subsequently released on bail and served as the presidential candidate of a UDP/PPP/GPP coalition, securing 32.7 percent of the vote in the October 2001 election. (The criminal case against Darboe and the other UDP members was in adjournment as of mid-2002 and later dismissed.)

The UDP/PPP/GPP coalition ultimately boycotted the January 2002 assembly elections. In November 2002 Jawara accused Darboe of misappropriating funds and was subsequently expelled from the UDP. Jawara then formed a new political party, the National Democratic Action Movement (below).

Leaders: Ousainu DARBOE (Secretary General, 1996 and 2001 presidential candidate), Yaya JALLOW (Deputy Secretary General), Momodou Shyngle NYASSI (Youth Wing Leader).

National Democratic Action Movement (NDAM). Formed by Lamin Waa JAWARA after he was expelled from the UDP in 2002, the NDAM has emerged as one of the leading opposition parties in spite of its short existence. Jawara was arrested in 2004 on charges of sedition and served six months in prison. The sentence reportedly increased his popularity among the opposition.

Leader: Lamin Waa JAWARA, Ousainou MBENGA (Deputy Secretary General).

People's Progressive Party (PPP). The moderately socialist PPP, which merged with the Congress Party (CP) in 1967, governed the country from independence until the 1994 coup. It sponsored adoption of the republican constitution in 1970 and long favored increased economic and cultural links with Senegal as well as maintenance of the Commonwealth association.

PPP Secretary General Dawda Jawara was reelected president of the republic in 1992, defeating four principal rivals with a 58.4 percent vote share. Following the July 1994 coup Jawara was granted political asylum by Senegal.

In November 1994 a number of PPP members were arrested for their alleged involvement in a failed coup plot, including a former cabinet minister, Mamadou Cadi CHAM, and the parliamentary vice president, Dembo JATTA. In June 1995 President Jammeh granted amnesty to the alleged conspirators; however, six months later at least 35 PPP activists were jailed and similarly charged. In addition, in January 1996 the AFPRC formally charged

Jawara with embezzlement, and in March his assets were seized.

In mid-1996 Jawara, in an announcement issued in London, strongly criticized the new constitution drafted by the Jammeh regime, describing the document as "tailor-made" to elect Jammah and designed to "confuse" matters in regard to basic individual rights. As with the NCP and the GPP, the PPP was banned from participating in the 1996 elections by the Jammeh government. After the ban was lifted in July 2001, the PPP teamed with the GPP and the UDP in launching an opposition coalition, which supported the UDP's Ousainu Darboe in the October 2001 presidential election. Jawara returned to Gambia in mid-2002 in response to the government's offer of amnesty. He resigned as leader of the PPP in December 2002 and was replaced by Omar Jallow. In 2006, the PPP reportedly was seeking an alliance with the UDP and the NRP.

Leaders: Yaya CEESAY (President), Omar JALLOW (Secretary General).

Gambia People's Party (GPP). The GPP was launched in early 1985 by former vice president Hassan Musa Camara and a number of other defectors from the PPP to oppose President Jawara at the 1987 general election. As the balloting approached, it was felt by many that the GPP had overtaken the NCP as the principal opposition grouping; however, Camara obtained only 13 percent of the presidential vote, with the GPP securing no legislative representation. Camara again finished third in 1992, while the GPP returned to the House of Representatives with 2 seats. Banned from participating in the 1996 elections (together with the PPP and the NCP), the GPP supported the UDP's candidate in the December 2001 presidential balloting.

Leaders: Hassan Musa CAMARA (Former Vice President of the Republic).

People's Democratic Organization for Independence and Socialism (PDOIS or DOY). The leftist PDOIS was formed at a congress that met from July 31 to August 19, 1986, to approve a lengthy manifesto that accused the PPP of compromising the country's sovereignty by agreeing to

Cabinet

As of May 1, 2006

President	Yahya Jammeh
Vice President	Aisatou Njie-Saidy [f]

Secretaries of State

Agriculture	Yankouba Touray
Communications, Information, and Technology	Neneh Macdouall-Gaye [f]
Education	Fatou Faye [f]
Finance and Economic Affairs	Musa Bala-Gaye
Fisheries and Water Resources	Bai Mass Taal
Foreign Affairs	Lamin Kaba Bajo
Forestry and the Environment	Edward Singhatey
Health and Social Welfare	Dr. Tamsir Mbowe
Interior	Col. Baboucarr Jatta
Justice, Attorney General	Sheikh Tijan Hydara
Local Government and Lands	Ismalia K. Sambou
Tourism and Culture	Susan Waffa-Ogoo [f]
Trade, Industry, and Employment	Alieu Ngum
Women and Social Affairs	Aisatou Njie-Saidy [f]
Works, Construction, and Infrastructure	Bala Garba Jahumpa
Youth and Sports, Religious Affairs	Samba Faal

[f] = female

the establishment of Senegambia on the basis of an "unequal relationship."

Party leader Sidia Jatta, who also had contested the 1992 election, secured a reported 2.87 percent of the vote in the 1996 presidential balloting and 3.2 percent in the 2001 presidential elections. The PDOIS was one of two opposition parties to participate in the 2002 legislative elections, winning two seats.

Leaders: Sidia JATTA (1992, 1996, and 2001 presidential candidate), Halifa SALLAH, Samuel SARR.

National Reconciliation Party (NRP). Formed quickly in August 1996, the NRP presented Hamat Bah as its candidate in the September 1996 presidential election, the well-known hotel owner garnering 5.52 percent of the votes according to official results. Bah ran again in 2001, securing 7.7 percent of the vote. The NRP won 1 seat in the 2002 assembly elections.

In March 2006, at least 2,500 NRP members reportedly defected to the APRC at a massive rally in Sankuba.

Leader: Hamat BAH (1996 and 2001 presidential candidate).

Gambia Party for Democracy and Progress (GPDP). The GPDP is a new opposition party formed by Henry GOMEZ. However, in April 2006 Gomez was quoted as endorsing Jammeh's plans for the country and praising his accomplishments.
Leader: Henry GOMEZ.

Legislature

Prior to its dissolution following the 1994 coup the unicameral House of Representatives contained

50 members, 36 of whom were directly elected by universal adult suffrage, plus 5 indirectly elected chiefs, 8 nominated members, and the attorney general (ex officio). The 1996 constitution provided for a 49-member **National Assembly,** 45 elected by popular vote in single-member constituencies and 4 appointed by the president. (The size of the assembly was increased to 53 [48 elected, 5 appointed] for the January 17, 2002, election in view of the recent population increase.) The term of the assembly is five years, unless it is dissolved earlier by the president.

All three parties represented in the legislature elected in 1992 (the People's Progressive Party, the National Convention Party, and the Gambia People's Party) were banned from participating in the January 2, 1997, balloting. Following the 1997 elections, the seat distribution was as follows: the Alliance for Patriotic Reorientation and Construction (APRC), 33; the United Democratic Party (UDP), 7; the National Reconciliation Party (NRP), 2; the People's Democratic Organization for Independence and Socialism (PDOIS), 1; and independents, 2.

New elections were held on January 17, 2002, although they were boycotted by the main opposition party—the UDP—and several smaller groupings. The governing APRC was declared the winner of 33 seats because no opposition candidates were presented for them. The APRC also won 12 of the 15 seats for which voting was held, giving it a total of 45 of the 48 elected seats. Of the remaining 3 elected seats, 2 were won by the PDOIS and 1 by the NRP. All of the 5 members subsequently appointed by the president were members of the APRC or APRC-supportive parties.

Speaker: Belinda BIDWELL.

Communications

The news media operated freely prior to the July 1994 coup, although the principal newspaper and national radio station were government owned. However, the Jammeh regime has applied constraints on the press in general and strongly attacked specific antigovernment reporting. Opponents of the administration also contend that the new Gambian constitution was written to permit "muzzling" of the media, and in November 1999 Reporters Without Frontiers described Gambia as one of a number of Commonwealth countries "flouting" press freedom.

In 2003 a state-run media agency, the National Media Commission, was created and given wide powers, including the power to arrest journalists and sentence them for up to six months. Additional press laws in 2004 and 2005 also were widely condemned as repressive.

Press

The following are English-language publications issued in Banjul: *The Gambia Daily,* state-owned; *The Gambia Weekly* (500), published by the Government Information Office; *The Gambia Times* (1,500), PPP fortnightly; *The Nation,* fortnightly; *The Daily Observer,* registered in 1992; *The Point* (4,000), twice-weekly; *The Worker,* thrice-weekly organ of the Gambia Labour Congress; *The Gambia Onward,* thrice-weekly; *Foroyaa* (Freedom), weekly; and the *Newswatch. Newsmonth,* an independent weekly, commenced publication in April 1993. A new daily introduced in 1999, *The Independent*, has accused the government of systematic harassment.

News Agency

The domestic facility is the Gambia News Agency (Gamna).

Broadcasting and Computing

Radio broadcasting is provided by the government-owned Radio Gambia, which relays BBC news and carries programs in English and local languages; Radio 1, a private FM outlet; and Radio Syd, a commercial station. The nation's first television station began broadcasting in January 1996, service having previously been available only via transmissions from Senegal. As of 2003 there were approximately 4,100 television receivers and 20,000 personal computers serving 30,000 Internet users.

Intergovernmental Representation

Ambassador to the U.S.
Dodou Bammy JAGNE

U.S. Ambassador to Gambia
Joseph D. STAFFORD III

Permanent Representative to the UN
Crispin GREY-JOHNSON

IGO Memberships (Non-UN)
AfDB, AU, BADEA, CILSS, CWTH, ECOWAS, IDB, Interpol, IOM, NAM, OIC, WCO, WTO

GHANA

REPUBLIC OF GHANA

The Country

Located on the west coast of Africa just north of the equator, Ghana's terrain includes a tropical rain forest running north about 170 miles from the Gulf of Guinea and a grassy savanna belt that is drained by the Volta River. While the official language of the country is English, the inhabitants are divided among more than 50 linguistic and ethnic groups, the most important being the Akans (including Fanti), Ashanti, Ga, Ewe, and Mossi-Dagomba. About 40 percent of the population is Christian, and 12 percent Muslim, with most of the rest following traditional religions. Over 40 percent of households are headed by women, who dominate the trading sector and comprise nearly 50 percent of agricultural labor; a smaller proportion of salaried women is concentrated in the service sector.

Agriculture employs nearly 60 percent of the population and accounts for about 20 percent of GDP, down from twice that level as late as the mid-1990s. Cocoa is responsible for 37 percent of exports; other important export commodities include gold, timber, and coffee. Manufacturing centers on food processing and the production of vehicles and textiles. Mining accounts for more than one-half of foreign exchange; in addition to gold, there are important deposits of diamonds, bauxite, and manganese.

According to the World Bank, per capita GNP declined by an average of 2 percent annually from 1980 to 1987. A subsequent return to modest economic growth largely resulted from the government's enactment of IMF-sponsored reform programs, including privatization of a number of government-controlled enterprises. However, the economy flagged in the mid-1990s, weighed down by rising debt payments. Although annual economic growth of over 4 percent was achieved from 1996 to 1999, per capita annual income remained at less than $500.

In early 2000 the World Bank refused to forward an anticipated loan, insisting that Accra's financial practices were not sufficiently transparent. The decision underscored widespread international and domestic concern over apparently pervasive corruption despite Ghana's image as a model for free-market orientation and democratization in Africa. Battered by tumbling cocoa and gold prices, the economy grew by only 1 percent in 2000, with inflation running at more than 30 percent annually.

By 2005 inflation had dropped to 6 percent, and GDP growth of 5.2 percent was recorded, while the IMF noted progress in structural reforms and

private-sector investment. However, poverty was unabated, particularly in the north. In early 2006 the IMF, the World Bank, and the African Development Bank canceled billions of dollars of debt owed by 13 of Africa's poorest countries, including Ghana, to allow resources to be funneled to poverty-reduction efforts. Also in 2006, the World Bank approved a $75 million loan for what was described as a model gold-producing project, predicted to generate between $300 million and $700 million for the country over the next 20 years.

Government and Politics

Political Background

The first West African territory to achieve independence in the postwar era, Ghana was established on March 6, 1957, through consolidation of the former British colony of the Gold Coast and the former UN Trust Territory of British Togoland. The drive to independence was associated primarily with the names of J. B. DANQUAH and Kwame N. NKRUMAH. The latter became prime minister of the Gold Coast in 1952, prime minister of independent Ghana in 1957, and the country's first elected president when republican status within the Commonwealth was proclaimed on July 1, 1960. Subsequently, Nkrumah consolidated his own power and that of his Convention People's Party (CPP), establishing a one-party dictatorship that neighboring states increasingly viewed with apprehension.

In 1966 the military ousted Nkrumah in response to increasing resentment of his repressive policies and financial mismanagement, which had decimated the country's reserves and generated an intolerably large national debt. An eight-man National Liberation Council (NLC) headed by Lt. Gen. Joseph A. ANKRAH ran the government. Promising an eventual return to civilian rule, the NLC carried out a far-reaching purge of Nkrumah adherents and sponsored the drafting of a new constitution. The NLC era was marked, however, by a series of alleged plots and corruption charges, with Ankrah resigning as head of state in April

1969 after admitting to solicitation of funds from foreign companies for campaign purposes. He was replaced by Brig. Akwasi Amankwa AFRIFA, who implemented plans for a return to civilian government.

Partial civilian control returned following a National Assembly election in August 1969 that designated Kofi A. BUSIA as prime minister. A three-man presidential commission, made up of members of the NLC, exercised presidential power until August 31, 1970, when Edward AKUFO-ADDO was inaugurated as head of state. The Busia administration was unable to deal with economic problems generated by a large external debt and a drastic currency devaluation, and in January 1972 the military, under (then) Col. Ignatius Kutu ACHEAMPONG, again seized control. The National Redemption Council (NRC), which was formed to head the government, immediately suspended the constitution, banned political parties, abolished the Supreme Court, and dissolved the National Assembly. In 1975 the NRC was superseded by the Supreme Military Council (SMC).

In the wake of accusations that "governmental activity had become a one-man show," General Acheampong was forced to resign as head of state on July 5, 1978, and he was immediately succeeded by his deputy, (then) Lt. Gen. Frederick W. K. AKUFFO. Promising a return to civilian rule by mid-1979, Akuffo quickly reconstituted a Constitution Drafting Commission, which subsequently presented its recommendations to an appointed, but broadly representative, Constituent Assembly that convened in mid-December.

In the wake of badly received efforts to secure constitutional immunity from future prosecution for existing government officials, Akuffo was ousted on June 4, 1979, by a group of junior military officers. The next day, an Armed Forces Revolutionary Council (AFRC) was established under Flt. Lt. Jerry John RAWLINGS, who had been undergoing court-martial for leading an unsuccessful coup on May 15. Having dissolved the SMC and the Constituent Assembly, the AFRC launched a "house cleaning" campaign, during which former presidents Acheampong, Afrifa, and Akuffo, in

Political Status: Independent member of the Commonwealth since March 6, 1957; under military control 1966–1969 and 1972–1979; Third Republic overthrown by military coup of December 31, 1981; constitution of Fourth Republic, approved in referendum of April 28, 1992, formally launched on January 7, 1993.

Area: 92,099 sq. mi. (238,537 sq. km.).

Population: 18,912,079 (2000C); 22,074,000 (2005E).

Major Urban Center (2005E): ACCRA (1,963,000).

Official Language: English.

Monetary Unit: New Cedi (market rate July 1, 2006: 9160 cedi = $1US).

President: John Agyekum KUFUOR (New Patriotic Party); elected on December 28, 2000, and sworn in for a four-year term on January 7, 2001, in succession to Flt. Lt. (Ret.) Jerry John RAWLINGS (National Democratic Congress); reelected on December 7, 2004, and sworn in for his second (and final) four-year term on January 7, 2005.

Vice President: Alhaji Aliu MAHAMA (New Patriotic Party); elected on December 7, 2004, and sworn in for a term concurrent with that of the president on January 7, 2005, in succession to Aliu MOHAMMED (New Patriotic Party).

addition to a number of other high-ranking military and civilian officials, were executed on grounds of corruption. Although the AFRC postponed promulgation of a new constitution until autumn, it did not interfere with scheduled presidential and legislative balloting on June 18. In a runoff presidential poll on July 9, Dr. Hilla LIMANN of the People's National Party, which had won a bare majority in the new National Assembly, defeated Victor OWUSU of the Popular Front Party; Limann was inaugurated on September 24.

The Limann government proved unable to halt further deterioration of the nation's economy and, in the wake of renewed allegations of widespread corruption, was overthrown on December 31, 1981, by army and air force supporters of Lieutenant

Rawlings, who was returned to power as head of a Provisional National Defense Council (PNDC). Three weeks later a 17-member cabinet was appointed that included a number of prominent individuals known for their "spotless integrity." Despite a number of subsequent coup attempts (two in 1985 alone), a combination of firmness toward opponents and radical state policy changes, including reorganization of the judicial and administrative structures, enabled the flight lieutenant to become Ghana's longest post–independence ruler, while district elections in late 1988 and early 1989 were viewed as heralding a return to civilian government.

In January 1991 President Rawlings instructed the National Commission for Democracy (NCD), which had recently sponsored a series of debates on the creation of regional and national assemblies, to draw on its findings, together with the content of past constitutions, in assembling a new national charter. Four months later the regime officially endorsed the NCD's plans for installation of a multiparty system and authorized a nine-member, ad hoc Committee of Experts to draft a constitution. On August 26 the document was submitted to a 258-member consultative assembly, Rawlings announcing that a referendum on the new basic law would be followed by presidential and legislative elections on November 3 and December 8, respectively.

On April 28, 1992, the new constitution was approved by 90 percent of the voters, and on May 17 the ban on political parties was lifted. Nevertheless, nine days later the High Court upheld the decision by the Interim National Electoral Commission (INEC) to continue a political parties law proscribing 21 parties outlawed in 1981 (see Political Parties, below). On September 14 Rawlings resigned from the air force to campaign for the presidency as a candidate for the National Democratic Congress (NDC), the political party successor to the PNDC.

At presidential balloting on November 3, 1992, Rawlings led the five-candidate field with 58.3 percent of the vote. Although international observers described the polling as "fair," attributing irregularities to deficient "organization and training," the four opposition contenders alleged widespread fraud, including NDC ballot stuffing. On November 13 the opposition announced it would boycott parliamentary balloting until a new electoral register was created (a demand rejected by the administration). Consequently, only 29 percent of eligible voters took part in the legislative poll of December 29, when pro-Rawlings candidates secured all but 2 of the 200 seats.

In February 1995 the government imposed a value-added tax that provoked widespread protests. Three months later the government offered to lower the tax rate, but the demonstrations continued, and in early June the measure was rescinded in favor of a reinstated sales tax. On July 21 Dr. Kwesi BOTCHWEY, who had championed Ghana's adoption of an IMF-prescribed economic reform program as well as the discarded tax, resigned as finance minister. Meanwhile, the withdrawal of Vice President Kow Nkensen ARKAAH's National Convention Party (NCP) from the presidential coalition in May reflected ruptured relations between Arkaah and Rawlings.

At presidential balloting on December 7, 1996, Rawlings and his vice presidential running mate, John Evans ATTA MILLS, defeated by a vote of 57.2–39.8 percent their main rivals, a Great Alliance ticket headed by the New Patriotic Party's (NPP) John KUFUOR, with Arkaah in the vice presidential slot. At concurrent legislative balloting the NDC retained a nearly 2 to 1 legislative majority, capturing 133 seats to the Great Alliance's 65. Subsequently, in January 1997 the Great Alliance disbanded acrimoniously.

President Rawlings's efforts to name a new government in early 1997 were complicated by difficulties in satisfying the various factions within the NDC as well as by the opposition's insistence that all prospective cabinet members, even incumbents, were subject to assembly approval. As a result, the full cabinet was not completed until midyear, after the opposition had apparently relented on the approval question.

Rawlings being constitutionally prevented from seeking a third term, the NPP's Kufuor led seven candidates in the first round of presidential balloting on December 7, 2000, with 48 percent of the vote and defeated the NDC's Atta Mills by 6 percent in the second round 3 weeks later. Meanwhile, the NPP had also secured a legislative majority in assembly balloting on December 7, setting the stage for installation of an NPP-led cabinet early in 2001.

In 2004 only four parties put forth presidential candidates. President Kufuor defeated NDC candidate Atta Mills 52.5 percent to 44.6 percent. (The NDC became the main opposition party.) The remaining two candidates had a combined vote of less than 3 percent. Edward MAHAMA of the Grand Coalition, which combined the People's National Convention (PNC), Every Ghanian Living Elsewhere (EGLE), and the Great Consolidated Popular Party (GCPP), received 1.9 percent. The final 1 percent went to George AGGUDEY of the CPP. The NPP also fared well in the 2005 assembly elections (see Legislature, below). A new government was sworn in on February 1, 2005; the cabinet was reshuffled on April 28, 2006.

Constitution and Government

On August 26, 1991, a consultative assembly of 258 members (117 drawn from district assemblies, 119 representing "identifiable" groups, and 22 governmentally appointed) began deliberations on a new constitution, a draft of which had been published by the government two weeks earlier. The document, which drew from Ghana's previous four constitutions as well as French basic law, was a multiparty instrument featuring a directly elected president; a presidentially appointed vice president; a military-civilian Security Council chaired by the president; a nonpartisan Council of State; a unicameral, directly elected legislative body; and a special committee on human rights and administrative justice.

The new constitution was approved by referendum on April 28, 1992, and on June 10 the PNDC was disbanded, although its ministerial personnel remained in office until March 22, 1993, despite the formal proclamation of Ghana's Fourth Republic on January 7.

Foreign Relations

External relations since independence have been pragmatic rather than ideological, the government unilaterally renouncing certain portions of the foreign debt and further disturbing creditor nations by taking partial control of selected foreign enterprises.

Relations with neighboring Togo have been strained since the incorporation of British Togoland into Ghana at the time of independence. In 1977 Ghana accused Togo of smuggling operations aimed at "sabotaging" the Ghanaian economy, while Togo vehemently denied accusations that it was training Ghanaian nationals to carry out acts of subversion in the former British territory. The border between the two countries was periodically closed, Accra repeatedly charging Togolese officials with spreading "vicious lies" about the Rawlings regime and "providing a sanctuary" for its opponents. In a February 1988 effort to interdict commodity smuggling (Togo, without mining, was being credited with multimillion-dollar gold export earnings), Rawlings declared a state of emergency in a number of Ghanaian towns along the Togolese border. The estrangement was substantially alleviated by an October 1991 treaty that resulted in the reopening of border crossings. However, in March 1993 Togolese President Eyadéma accused Ghana of involvement in an attack on his compound and in early January 1994 the two countries were reportedly "close to war" after Lomé charged Accra with supporting, at least tacitly, a second attack in Togo. On January 7 the Rawlings administration claimed it had no interest in "getting involved in Togo's internal affairs" and urged the Eyadéma government to stop blaming Ghana "whenever there is an armed attack or political crisis." The tension heightened on January 12 when Togolese troops killed 12 Ghanaians at a border post and Togolese naval officers imprisoned 7 Ghanaian fishermen.

In April 1994 Lomé blamed Accra for the "presence of bombs in Togo," thus igniting yet another round of acrimonious exchanges. On a more positive note, Accra appointed an ambassador to Togo in November, and on December 26 the border between the two countries was reopened. In July 1995 Rawlings and Eyadéma signed a cooperation agreement after which Togo appointed an ambassador to Ghana for the first time in over a decade.

Relations with other regional states have been mixed since the 1981 Ghanaian coup. The PNDC moved quickly to reestablish links with Libya (severed by President Limann in November 1980 because of the Qadhafi regime's presumed support of Rawlings), thereby clearing the way for shipments of badly needed Libyan oil. In April 1987 an agreement was signed with Iran for the delivery of 10,000 barrels of crude per day. Concurrently, a number of joint ventures were proposed in agriculture and shipping.

The 1987 overthrow of Burkina Faso's Thomas Sankara by Blaise Compaoré dealt a political and personal blow to Rawlings, who had hoped to form a political union with his northern neighbor by the end of the decade; instead, he encountered in the new Burkinabe president an ally of the Côte d'Ivoire's Houphouët-Boigny, with whom relations were strained. In April 1988, on the other hand, Rawlings and Nigeria's (then) president Gen. Ibrahim Babangida sought to ease tensions stemming from Nigeria's expulsion of Ghanaian workers in 1983 and 1985. In January 1989 the rapprochement yielded a trade agreement that removed all trade and travel barriers between the two countries.

Relations with Côte d'Ivoire worsened further in November 1993, when Ivorians seeking revenge for a murderous attack on supporters of their soccer team in Ghana killed 23 Ghanaian nationals and injured more than 100 others in Abidjan. Although Ivorian authorities established security areas for the Ghanaians, over 9,000 had reportedly fled the country by mid-month. In early 1997, on the other hand, Ivorian president Henri Konan Bédié made the first official visit to Ghana by an Ivorian head of state in nearly four decades. During his stay Bédié proposed broader economic and social ties between the two nations. Tensions heightened somewhat in 2005 after Ghanaian arms smugglers were arrested in the Ivorian town of Tantama, and President Kufuor attended the swearing in of Togo's illegal new leader, while other African countries denounced the coup. Meanwhile, Ghana indicated enhanced relations with Senegal by opening a new embassy in Dakar.

Current Issues

U.S. President Bill Clinton launched his tour of Africa from Ghana in March 1998, thus focusing international attention (generally favorable) on the democracy efforts of the Rawlings administration. However, Rawlings's subsequent announcement of his intention to support Vice President Atta Mills in the 2000 presidential race provoked sharp criticism from the NDC's reform faction, which, along with opposition observers, argued that the president was thereby seeking to retain unofficial political control following the end of his term. In early 1999 the reformers broke with the NDC, and in June launched the National Reform Party (NRP).

The administration's economic policies were also intensely scrutinized throughout 1999, with NDC opponents citing incidents of mismanagement and corruption as evidence of the ruling party's "inefficiency." In a rare display of unanimity, five of the most prominent opposition parties— the NPP, the People's Convention Party (PCP), the National Convention Party (NCP), the United Ghana Movement (UGM), and the new Reform Party—organized a nationwide demonstration in November against public sector layoffs and increased hospital and university fees. However, that protest was countered by the massive turnout at a pro-NDC rally in Accra in December.

The economy continued to decline in 2000, further eroding support for the NDC and contributing to what one observer described as classic "fin de régime" mismanagement on the part of the Rawlings administration. Most analysts attributed the presidential and legislative victories of the NPP in December largely to a general feeling among the population that it was simply "time for a change," since there were few significant policy differences between the two leading parties. In addition, it was widely acknowledged that candidate Atta Mills lacked the charisma that had carried the previ-

ous NDC standard-bearer to electoral success in the 1990s. For his part, Rawlings left office with relative equanimity, calming fears that a peaceful transfer of power from one party to another via free elections, a rare occurrence in the region, might be jeopardized. Meanwhile, John Kufuor's return to office in December 2004 marked the first time an erstwhile opposition party was reelected in the postcolonial period of almost 50 years. He pledged to intensify free-market economic policies while combating corruption. At the same time, he warned of the need for fiscal austerity, suggesting that various government subsidies, widely popular with the public, might need to be cut back. He also called for "unification," seemingly a reference to the country's potentially unstable ethnic, political, and religious mixes. In that regard, Kufuor established a truth and reconciliation commission to investigate, among other things, the bloodletting that followed the 1979 and 1981 coups. However, that initiative resulted not in harmony but rather severe NPP/NDC friction as the NDC refused to cooperate with the investigation, claiming it was being "demonized" by the NPP.

Human rights abuses and corruption were the focus of the newly launched African Peer Review Mechanism (APRM) in 2005, with Ghana among the first countries to be reviewed. The initial draft report was "unexpectedly critical," according to *Africa Confidential*, and proposed more funding for government oversight efforts. Accra reportedly planned a $2.8 billion program to address the concerns.

Tribal conflict flared up in 2005 between the Abudu and the Andani in the northern Dagbon Kingdom, despite a 1974 order that the rivals alternate control of the area. The feud reportedly remained unresolved. The greater cause for concern in 2006, however, was a new Representation of the People Amendment (ROPA), signed into law by President Kufuor on February 24. Five minority parties—the NDC, the NRP, the PNC, the GCPP, and the EGLE—unified in opposition, staging two demonstrations in which 9 members were arrested and 20 people injured. The law grants some 3 million Ghanaians living abroad the opportunity to vote, clearly benefiting the NPP, according to observers. Since those abroad account for the second-highest source of foreign revenue after cocoa, they should have a voice in how the country is run, supporters said. Opponents contended overseas voting without proper monitoring could easily be used to rig elections.

Political Parties

Political parties, traditionally based more on tribal affiliation than on ideology, were banned in 1972. The proscription was lifted in early 1979, with six groups formally contesting the June election. Following the coup of December 31, 1982, parties were again outlawed until May 17, 1992, when the ban was rescinded in accordance with the multiparty constitution approved on April 28. The new dispensation did not, however, reverse an earlier ruling banning 21 opposition parties, including the All People's Party (APP), Convention People's Party (CPP), National Alliance Party (NAP), Popular Front Party (PFP), Progress Party (PP), and Unity Party (UP). Future parties were also prohibited from using any of the symbols, names, or slogans of the proscribed parties. The Coordinating Committee of Democratic Forces of Ghana (CCDFG), an 11-party, mainly "Nkrumahist" coalition formed in August 1991, strongly objected to the new party provisions and asked the High Court to overturn them. However, the court sided with the ruling Provisional National Defense Council (PNDC).

Four new opposition parties (the New Patriotic Party [NPP], National Independence Party [NIP], People's Heritage Party [PHP], and People's National Convention [PNC]) presented candidates in the November 1992 presidential election. However, the opposition parties boycotted the December legislative elections, charging electoral fraud in presidential balloting on behalf of the National Democratic Congress (NDC), which had been formed to support the presidential campaign of PNDC Chair Jerry Rawlings.

In January 1993 the CCDFG was effectively superseded as the major opposition grouping by the new Inter-Party Coordinating Committee (ICC), which agreed to accept the "present institutional arrangements" but rejected the recent election results, calling for a new round of voting. However, the ICC was weakened somewhat the following August when the NPP (one of the strongest of the new groupings) decided to recognize the disputed election tallies.

Coordinated opposition activity next surfaced in early 1995, under the banner of the Alliance for Change. The NPP-dominated Alliance subsequently organized antigovernment demonstrations that forced the Rawlings administration to rescind the recently imposed value-added tax, the coalition's success encouraging it to announce its intention to present an electoral front in 1996. After drawn-out negotiations, which prompted the withdrawal of some components of the Alliance for Change, a new Great Alliance was announced in August 1996 by the NPP and the PCP. Despite being roiled by debate over the choice of legislative candidates until just prior to election day, Alliance-affiliated candidates captured over 60 legislative seats in December balloting. Nevertheless, the coalition subsequently collapsed as the NPP and PCP blamed each other for the opposition's failure to secure greater gains.

Government Parties

New Patriotic Party (NPP). The center-right NPP was launched in June 1992, its founders including former members of the old Progress Party, which had governed Ghana from 1969 to 1972 under Prime Minister Kofi Busia. The NPP's platform advocated the protection of human rights, the strengthening of democratic principles, and the holding of "free and fair elections." At the same time, the new grouping was widely viewed as devoted to the interests of the business class.

In 1994 the NPP sought to forge ties with other opposition groups, agreeing in November to back a single candidate in the next presidential election. Collaterally, it broke off negotiations with the NDC, stating that the government was uninterested in maintaining a dialogue. Meanwhile, the party experienced contentious internal debate over its own presidential candidates. At midyear the decision was postponed until 1995 as party leaders sought to placate its influential Young Executives Forum wing, which had funded Albert Abu BOAHEN's candidacy in 1992 but reportedly sought a new standard-bearer.

At the NPP congress on April 20, 1996, delegates chose John Kufuor as the party's presidential candidate. Kufuor declared his intent to forge a coalition with the PCP (see CPP, below), which was achieved in August with the establishment of the Great Alliance. As endorsed by an extraordinary NPP congress on August 31, the new Alliance selected Kufuor as its common presidential candidate and thereby the main threat to the Rawlings campaign.

After a number of postponements that NPP officials attributed to poor regional organization, the party convened its fourth congress in 1998. At balloting for leadership posts, Secretary General Agyenim BOATENG was ousted in favor of 39-year-old Dan BOTWE, whose victory highlighted what observers described as a youth movement within the party. At further intraparty balloting in October, Kufuor outpolled five other NPP would-be presidential candidates and secured the party's backing for another national campaign in 2000. In part, the NPP's success in the 2000 legislative balloting (100 seats versus 60 in 1996) was attributed to its "clean sweep" in areas dominated by the Ashanti ethnic group. Meanwhile, Kufuor secured 48.17 percent of the vote in the first round of the presidential election before winning the post with a 56.9 percent tally in the second round.

President Kufuor was reelected in 2004 with 52.6 percent of the vote in a race that saw a huge turnout and brought praise to Ghana as a stable if struggling democratic nation, especially in light of the civil unrest in neighboring Togo and Côte d'Ivoire.

In 2005 a rift developed over claims of financial irregularities by party chair Haruna ESSEKU, who withdrew just before the party's national congress in December. He was replaced by Peter Mac Manu,

with a new secretary general and first vice chair also elected.

Leaders: John Agyekum KUFUOR (President of the Republic), Alhaji Aliu MAHAMA (Vice President of the Republic), Peter Mac MANU (Chair), Hawa YAKUBU (First Vice Chair), Nana Ohene NTOW (Secretary General).

Convention People's Party   (CPP). The CPP considers itself the legitimate successor to the party of the same name formed by former president Nkrumah during the independence campaign. The revived grouping was launched in 1999 under the name Convention Party (due to a legal dispute over the use of the original rubric) as a result of a merger agreement between the People's Convention Party (PCP) and the National Convention Party (NCP).

The PCP had been formed in December 1993 as an apparent successor to the Nkrumahist ICC by the National Independence Party (NIP), the People's Heritage Party (PHP), and the People's Party for Democracy and Development (PPDD). (For further information on the NIP, PHP, and PPDD, see the 1999 *Handbook.*) A faction of the PNC also participated in the launching. (Organizers had reportedly rejected a demand from PNC leader Dr. Hilla Limann that he be named the new party's leader; consequently, only dissident PNC members joined the PCP.)

In early 1996 somewhat confusing reports indicated that the CPP rubric had been revived following a "merger" of the PCP and the NCP, the latter having split from the ruling Progressive Alliance the previous year. However, subsequent news stories routinely still referenced the PCP, and at least a portion of the NCP appeared to remain independent.

In the wake of its disappointing performance (five seats) at December 1996 balloting, the PCP blamed the NPP for the opposition's failure to secure greater representation; meanwhile, the PCP's claim to the Nkrumahist mantle in the Central, Western, and Brong Ahafo regions was undermined by its electoral defeats there.

The NCP had been the first group to be recognized following the lifting of the party ban in 1992.

However, it quickly was eclipsed in influence by the NDC, which had convinced PNDC Chair Rawlings to be its presidential candidate. Consequently, prior to the December 1992 legislative balloting, the NCP joined the NDC-dominated Progressive Alliance.

Although the NCP in November 1994 defended its ongoing alliance with the NDC as necessary for ensuring "national peace and stability," relations continued to deteriorate, particularly in regard to the relationship between the NCP's leader and vice president of the republic, Kow Nkensen Arkaah, and Rawlings. The vice president criticized governmental policy at a rally in May 1995, and shortly thereafter the NCP's executive board reportedly voted to withdraw from the Progressive Alliance.

In January 1996 Arkaah participated in the announcement of the "merger" of the NCP and the PCP in a revived CPP. However, other NCP leaders subsequently denounced that coalition, arguing that Arkaah was no longer the leader of their party nor its presidential candidate. Some influential party members later also criticized the Great Alliance formed in August by the NPP and the PCP.

Ending an eight-year legal battle on the issue, the CP was officially permitted to resume use of the CPP rubric in mid-2000. It campaigned for the December elections on a center-left platform that called for increased social spending and deceleration of the pace of economic reform. CPP candidate George HAGAN secured 1.78 percent of the vote in the first round of presidential balloting, the party throwing its support behind the NPP's John Kufuor in the second. The CPP accepted a cabinet post in January 2001, although the party subsequently emphasized that it disagreed with the NPP on many important issues.

In mid-2005 the party reportedly was engaged in unity discussions with the PNC in a move toward gaining political dominance, particularly as more youthful members defected to the CPP from the NPP and the NCD. Three CPP assembly members were dismissed by the party late in the year because they supported the ROPA (see Current issues, above), contrary to the party's position.

Leaders: Dr. Edmund DELLE (Chair), George AGGUDEY (2004 presidential candidate), Nii Noi DOWUONA (Secretary General).

Opposition Parties

Progressive Alliance (PA). The formation of the PA was announced in early December 1992 by the NDC (under whose banner PNDC Chair Jerry Rawlings had just been elected president of the republic), the NCP, and the EGLE Party. In part due to the fact that legislative elections were only weeks away, the three parties agreed that they would present competing candidates in some constituencies, with the PA components together winning 198 of the 200 seats.

In May 1995 the NCP, complaining of having been marginalized, withdrew from the PA while the small Democratic People's Party (DPP, below) joined the Alliance in September 1996. All three PA groups endorsed Rawlings as their 1996 presidential candidate and Atta Mills as their 2000 candidate. Although the PA appeared to remain technically in existence for the 2000 legislative balloting, only the NDC was credited with winning seats (as had been the case in 1996), and the role of the minor groupings remained negligible. In 2005 the PA was no longer listed as a political party.

National Democratic Congress (NDC). The NDC was formed on June 10, 1992, in Accra as a coalition of pro-Rawlings and pro-PNDC political and social clubs, including the New Nation Club and the Development Union. A number of factions emerged within the NDC from 1995 to 1996, including the December 31 Women's Movement (led by the president's wife, Nana Konadu RAWLINGS), which advocated sponsoring female candidates in 30 percent of the constituencies in the upcoming legislative elections. Despite concern over how the party would be able to accommodate its various strains, Jerry Rawlings was selected by acclamation as the NDC presidential nominee at the party's third annual national conference on September 6, 1996. Rawlings, who had been involved in a widely publicized conflict with Vice President Kow Nkensen Arkaah, subsequently selected little-known law professor John Evans Atta Mills as his 1996 running mate.

At the NDC's fourth congress in December 1998, party delegates approved reforms to the NDC charter, which included the designation of the Consultative Committee as the party's premier decision-making body. In addition, Rawlings was named NDC "Leader for Life" and, consequently, the Consultative Committee's president. Rawlings's ascension to the supreme party post was denounced by members of the NDC Reform Group, who had become increasingly combative following Rawlings's selection of Atta Mills as his would-be successor. In March 1999 the Reform Group announced it intended to form a separate party to compete in the 2000 elections (see National Reform Party, below).

A rift between those loyal to Rawlings and those who supported Chair Obed Yao ASAMOAH surfaced in late 2005, with the latter resigning in January 2006 as a consequence. In the fight for control of the party, Rawlings blamed Asamoah for the NDC losing in the 2004 election, and Asamoah's attempts at reconciliation were spurned. Subsequently, Asamoah declared he was forming a new party (see Democratic Freedom Party, below). The party elected pro-Rawlings candidate Kwabena Adjei to the chairmanship at its December 2005 congress.

Leaders: Kwabena ADJEI (Chair), John Evans ATTA MILLS (Former Vice President of the Republic and 2004 presidential candidate), Alhaji MUMUNI (2004 vice presidential candidate), Johnson Asiedu NKETIA (General Secretary).

Every Ghanaian Living Everywhere Party (EGLE). The (then) Eagle Club was formed in 1991, allegedly as a political affiliate of the PNDC. However, in mid-1992 the renamed EGLE Party declined to offer a blanket endorsement for all PNDC-NDC legislative candidates, positioning itself only as a pro-Rawlings grouping. EGLE did not put forth its own presidential candidate for the 2004 election, and instead joined in a Grand Coalition with the PNC and the GCPP to support Edward

Mahama. In 2006 the party reportedly had decided to rejoin the NDC to contest future elections.

Leaders: Nana Yaa OFORI-ATTA (Chair), Alhaji Rahman JAMATUTU (Vice Chair), Sam Pee YALLEY (General Secretary).

Democratic People's Party (DPP). The DPP joined the Progressive Alliance in September 1996 and quickly endorsed the presidential campaign of the NDC's Jerry Rawlings. However, in 2000 D. N. Ward-Brew, one of the DPP founders, accused the NDC of "marginalizing" the DPP and announced he was withdrawing the party from the PA. At the same time, Daniel Martin, claiming, with the apparent endorsement of the government, the chairmanship of the DPP, announced that the party would in fact remain in the PA and endorse the NDC presidential and vice presidential candidates. The DPP, by now considered a minor party, did not field a presidential candidate in 2004.

Leaders: D. N. WARD-BREW (Chair), Daniel D. K. MARTIN (General Secretary).

People's National Convention (PNC). The PNC was launched on May 30, 1992, by former president Dr. Hilla Limann, who finished third in the November presidential balloting. In late 1993 it was divided by Limann's initial antipathy toward opposition party unity talks and subsequently by his reported insistence that he be named the leader of any group that emerged therefrom. In October *West Africa* reported that among the PNC members opposing Limann was his close aide, Dr. Ivan ADDAE-MENSAH, who accused the former president of unconstitutional party activities, and by November a number of the PNC's constituent parties had reportedly broken off to join the PCP. In December Limann announced that despite the party schism he would continue to fend off merger efforts and "serve as a watchdog of the constitution."

Criticizing Rawlings's performance as leaving "much to be desired," Limann asserted in April 1994 that he "could prove equal to the task of leading Ghana again." However, at a party congress in Accra in early September 1996 Limann agreed to step aside to allow delegates "to inject fresh blood into the party." Subsequently, Dr. Edward Mahama was named the PNC's 1996 presidential candidate by acclamation, the PNC deciding to "go it alone" rather than participate in the Great Alliance formed by the NPP and the PCP. At balloting on December 7, Mahama secured just 3 percent of the presidential tally and the party won 1 legislative seat.

On January 23, 1998, former president Limann died. In September, at the PNC's third congress, Mahama was elected chair and chosen to represent the party at 2000 presidential polling, at which he secured 2.92 percent of the vote in the first round. (The PNC supported the NPP's John Kufuor in the second round.) During the 2000 presidential and legislative campaigns, the PNC claimed to be the legitimate successor to Kwame Nkrumah's original CPP, although it had lost a legal battle to use the CPP's rubric. The PNC's platform was described as "populist," albeit with a noticeable capitalistic bent. In 2004, Mahama again ran for the presidency as the PNC's candidate, but received only 1.9 percent of the vote. In mid-2005 the party reportedly was engaged in unity discussions with the CPP.

In 2006, First Vice Chair John NDEBUGRE was suspended because of his support for ROPA (see Current issues, above), in opposition to the party's position on the new law. Ndebugre subsequently resigned and was replaced by Alhaji Ahmed Ramadan.

Leaders: Dr. Edward MAHAMA (Chair and 1996, 2000, and 2004 presidential candidate), John EDWIN (President), Alhaji Ahmed RAMADAN (First Vice Chair), Gabriel PWAMANG (General Secretary).

Other Parties and Groups

United Ghana Movement (UGM). The UGM was launched in Accra in mid-1996 under the interim chairmanship of Dr. Charles Wereko-Brobby, a former Rawlings cabinet minister and prominent leader of the NPP who had expressed concern that an effective anti-Rawlings front would not be established by the NPP and CPP. After those two groups did in fact agree to a coalition in August, speculation arose that the UGM might be dismantled. However, it was subsequently reported that the

Movement had proceeded with its request for formal recognition. Earlier, Wereko-Brobby, a leader of the "professional, middle-class" component of the Alliance for Change, had announced his intention to support the proposed (eventually aborted) presidential candidacy of Kwiame PIANIM.

The UGM was granted formal recognition in January 1997, and Wereko-Brobby subsequently vowed to organize supporters in each of Ghana's voting districts to contest the presidential and legislative elections in 2000. However, Wereko-Brobby won only 0.34 percent of the vote in the first round of the presidential poll. In 2006 the party was listed as "in hibernation."

Leaders: Dr. Charles WEREKO-BROBBY (Chair and 2000 and 2004 presidential candidate), Eric K. DYTENYA (General Secretary).

National Reform Party (NRP). Originally organized to function as a reform-minded faction within the NDC, the NRP formally registered as an independent party in June 1999 with the intent of forwarding a candidate at the 2000 presidential elections. The Reform faction's decision to break with the NDC was reportedly precipitated by alleged attempts by the Rawlings camp to "undemocratically" control the party, in particular the president's pledge to back the presidential candidacy of Vice President Atta Mills.

Augustus Tanoh, a lawyer and businessman and former Rawlings ally, secured 1.21 percent of the vote in the first round of presidential balloting in December 2000. The NRP subsequently supported the NPP's John Kufuor in the second round, although party leaders resisted overtures to join the new cabinet, denying that Cecilia BANNERMAN, the new minister for manpower development and employment, was an official member of the NRP as claimed by the administration.

Leaders: Peter KPORDUGBE (Chair), Augustus Obuadum "Goosie" TANOH (2000 and 2004 presidential candidate), Kyeretwie OPOKU (General Secretary).

Great Consolidated Popular Party (GCPP). Formed in 1996, the GCPP, having lost its bid to be designated as the legitimate successor to the

Cabinet

As of May 1, 2006

President	John Agyekum Kufuor (NPP)
Vice President	Aliu Mahama (NPP)

Ministers

Civil Aviation	Gloria Akuffe [f]
Communications and Technology	Mike Oquaye (NPP)
Defense	Kwame Addo-Kufuor (NPP)
Education, Science, and Sports	Papa Owusu-Ankomah (NPP)
Energy	Joseph Kofi Adda (NPP)
Finance and Economic Planning	Kwadjo Baah Wiredu (NPP)
Fisheries	Gladys Asmah (NPP) [f]
Food and Agriculture	Ernest Debrah (NPP)
Foreign Affairs	Nana Akufo-Addo (NPP)
Health	Maj. (Ret.) Courage Qwashigah
Information and National Orientation	Kwamena Bartels
Interior	Albert Kan Dapaah
Justice and Attorney General	Joe Ghartey
Lands, Forestry, and Mines	Dominic Fobih (NPP)
Local Government, Rural Development, and Environment	Stephen Asamoah Boateng (NPP)
Manpower Development and Employment	Boniface Saddique
National Security	Francis Poku
Parliamentary Affairs	Felix Owusu Adjapong
Ports, Harbors, and Railways	Christopher Ameyaw Akumfi
Public Sector Reform	Paa Kwesi Nduom
Roads and Highways	Richard W. Anane (NPP)
Tourism and Diasporan Relations	Jake Okanka Obetsebi-Lamptey (NPP)
Trade, Industry, and Private Sector Development	Alan Kyeremateng (NPP)
Women's and Children's Affairs	Hajia Alima Mahama [f]
Works and Housing, Water Resources	Hackman Owusu Agyeman

Regional Ministers

Ashanti	Sampson Kwaku Boafo (NPP)
Brong Ahafo	Ignatius Baffour-Awuah
Central	Isaac Edumadze
Eastern	Yaw Barima
Greater Accra	Sheikh Ibrahim Codjoe Quaye (NPP)
Northern	Vacant
Upper East	Boniface Gambillah
Upper West	Ambrose Derry
Volta	Kofi Dzamesi
Western	Joseph Boahen Aidoo

[f] = female

original CPP, presented its chair, Daniel Lartey, as a presidential candidate in 2000. He won only 1.04 percent of the vote in the first round and endorsed the NPP's John Kufuor in the second round. The GCPP did not put forth a candidate for president in 2004.

Leaders: Daniel LARTEY (2000 presidential candidate).

Democratic Freedom Party (DFP). Founded in 2006 by former NDC chair Obed Yao Asamoah, the party was launched as an alternative opposition group after Asamoah lost his fight for control of the NDC to a pro-Rawlings faction. Asamoah said he hoped to attract those disillusioned with all of the main parties.

Leader: Obed Yao ASAMOAH.

Ghana Democratic Republican Party (GDRP). The GDRP was formed in the United States in 1992 by a group led by Dr. Kofi Amoah, who returned to Ghana that year. In 2005, however, Amoah's affiliation was unclear. In a published interview he was noncommittal on which party he would be affiliated with should he decide to enter politics.

Leaders: Nii ODARTY-LAWSON (General Secretary).

Legislature

The unicameral **National Assembly** elected in June 1979 was dissolved following the coup of December 31, 1981. In March 1992 Lieutenant Rawlings announced that balloting for a new assembly would be held on December 8. However, opposition candidates, angered by the administration's handling of the presidential elections ten days earlier, withdrew on November 13 from the campaign for the unicameral body's 200 seats, leaving 38 of the new constituencies with single candidates. Consequently, the government rescheduled the balloting twice as part of an only partially successful effort (23 candidates ran unopposed) to attract new candidates.

Following polling on September 18, 2005, the seats were distributed as follows: the New Patri-

otic Party (NPP), 128; the National Democratic Congress, 94; the People's National Convention, 4; the Convention People's Party, 3; and independents, 1.

Speaker: Ebenezer Begyina Sekhi HUGHES.

Communications

Under the 1979 constitution, state-owned media were required to "afford equal opportunities and facilities for the representation of opposing or differing views," and the Ghanaian press was one of the freest and most outspoken in Western Africa. However, since the 1981 coup, not only radio and television but also the leading newspapers have become little more than propaganda organs of the government.

Press

The following are published in English in Accra, unless otherwise indicated: *Ghanaian Voice* (100,000), bi-weekly; *The Pioneer* (Kumari, 100,000), daily; *The Mirror* (90,000), government-owned weekly; *Ghanaian Chronicle* (60,000), independent, three times a week; *Ghanaian Times* (50,000), government-owned daily; *Daily Graphic* (40,000), government-owned daily, *Echo* (40,000), weekly; *Weekly Spectator*, government-owned weekly.

News Agencies

The domestic facility is the official Ghana News Agency (GNA). AFP, AP, *Xinhua,* UPI, DPA, and ITAR-TASS maintain offices in Accra.

Broadcasting and Computing

In 1995 and 1996, the government ended the monopoly of the statutory Ghana Broadcasting Corporation by issuing radio and television licenses to more than three dozen private firms. There were some 2.8 million TV receivers and 90,000 personal computers serving 200,000 Internet users in 2003. The increase in the number of talk radio programs played a helpful role in disseminating information during the 2004 presidential elections.

Intergovernmental Representation

Ambassador to the U.S.
Fritz Kwabenam POKU

U.S. Ambassador to Ghana
Pamela E. BRIDGEWATER

Permanent Representative to the UN
Nana EFFAH-APENTANG

IGO Memberships (Non-UN)
AfDB, AU, BADEA, CWTH, ECOWAS, Interpol, IOM, NAM, WCO, WTO

GUINEA

REPUBLIC OF GUINEA

République de Guinée

The Country

Facing the Atlantic on the western bulge of Africa, Guinea presents a highly diversified terrain that ranges from coastal flatlands to the mountainous Foutah Djallon region where the Niger, Gambia, and Senegal rivers originate. The predominantly Muslim population includes over 2 million Fulani (Fulah); over 1.25 million Malinké (Mandingo, who have long been the dominant tribe); over 500,000 Soussou; 350,000 Kissi; and 250,000 Kpelle. While women are responsible for an estimated 48 percent of food production, female participation in government is minimal.

The majority of the population is dependent upon subsistence agriculture. Bananas, coffee, peanuts, palm kernels, and citrus fruits are important cash crops, although much foreign exchange is derived from mining. Guinea is one of the world's largest producers of bauxite, its reserves being exploited largely with the assistance of foreign companies. There are also valuable deposits of iron ore, gold, diamonds, uranium, and oil, in addition to substantial hydroelectric capability. Despite these resources, the GNP per capita was only $480 in 1990, reflecting an economy weakened by a quarter of a century of Marxist-inspired management. In the two years before his death, limited private enterprise was encouraged by Sékou Touré. Following its takeover, the CMRN announced a free-market economic policy and a series of economic liberalization measures involving banking and foreign investment. Development aid has since been obtained from a number of regional and European sources, notably France and Belgium. Structural adjustment efforts have focused on improving infrastructure as a necessary precondition to rejuvenating the agriculture sector, which in 1990 reportedly utilized less than 10 percent of available land.

By 1994 GNP per capita had risen marginally to $510, although real growth since 1985 had averaged only 1.3 percent. In late 1996 Guinea launched an economic reform program with the goals of restructuring the banking system, strengthening financial policies, and reducing corruption. In 1997 the International Monetary Fund (IMF) approved a three-year-loan package to support the country's efforts. Subsequently, the IMF reported that increased activity in the agriculture, construction, and trade sectors had spurred real GDP growth to

an annual average of 4.7 percent in 1997–1998; meanwhile, inflation was 1.9 percent in 1997 and 5.1 percent in 1998. In late 1999 Conakry asserted that it had made a "determined" effort to promote private sector development and had implemented strict expenditure controls and monitoring procedures as part of a "rigorous" financial management plan. Furthermore, the government projected a real GDP growth rate of over 5 percent in 2000 despite the continued effects of high petroleum prices. At the same time, the administration continued to call for international aid to help it cope with its large refugee population, made up of Sierra Leoneans and Liberians displaced by fighting in their respective countries. The United Nations High Commissioner for Refugees (UNHCR) reported that as of early 2001 Guinea was home to approximately 390,000 refugees and described the situation as "the most dramatic faced by the agency anywhere in the world."

In May 2001 the IMF approved a three-year arrangement for Guinea to "foster macroeconomic stability, promote growth, improve social services and reduce poverty." The country underwent a dramatic economic slowdown in 2003, with GDP growth declining to 1.2 percent. In addition, inflation rose to 14.8 percent. The economic contraction was the result of a range of factors, including poor harvests and a slump in manufacturing caused by significant problems with public utilities. The most significant negative consequence was a major rise in unemployment, with some estimates placing it as high as 70 percent. Meanwhile, food and fuel prices doubled.

Government reform of its tariff and auditing systems, along with other reforms, have led to promises of $800 million in debt relief and up to $82 million in economic aid as part of its arrangement with the IMF. However, delays in addressing structural problems, such as privatizing key industries, led some sources to withhold aid.

The economic forecast for 2005 was not much improved, with inflation expected to remain high and real GDP growth of only 3 percent. In an effort to improve structural reforms, reduce poverty, and bolster economic stability, the IMF approved a staff-monitored program for Guinea in 2005–2006, and noted that initial benchmarks had been met. Still, fund advisers cited the need for better monetary control, reform of public utilities, and a flexible exchange rate.

Government and Politics

Political Background

Historically part of the regional kingdom of Ghana, Songhai, and Mali, Guinea was incorporated into the French colonial empire in the late nineteenth century. Post–World War II colonial policy led to increasing political activity by indigenous groups, and in 1947 the Democratic Party of Guinea (PDG) was founded. Under the leadership of Ahmed Sékou TOURÉ, the PDG pushed for independence, and, following rejection of membership in the French Community in a referendum held September 28, 1958, Guinea became the first of France's African colonies to achieve complete independence. Since the PDG already held 58 of the 60 seats in the Territorial Assembly, Sékou Touré automatically became president upon establishment of the republic on October 2, 1958. Although the Soviet Union came to Guinea's aid following the abrupt withdrawal of French technical personnel and a collateral crippling of the new nation's fragile economy, Soviet nationals were expelled in 1961 after being charged with involvement in a teachers' strike.

Plots and alleged plots have dominated Guinea's history; at one time or another the United States, Britain, France, West Germany, the Soviet Union, and other countries have been accused of conspiring against the regime. The most dramatic incident occurred in November 1970 when Guinea was invaded by a force composed of Guinean dissidents and elements of the Portuguese army. The action was strongly condemned by the United Nations and resulted in a wave of arrests and executions. In July 1976 Diallo TELLI, the minister of justice and former secretary general of the Organization of African Unity (OAU, subsequently the African Union—AU), was arrested on charges of

Political Status: Independent republic since October 2, 1958; under one-party presidential regime until military coup of April 3, 1984; multiparty constitution approved by referendum of December 23, 1990, providing for five-year transition to civilian government.

Area: 94,925 sq. mi. (245,857 sq. km.).

Population: 7,156,406 (1996C); 8,603,000 (2005E). Both figures include refugees from Liberia and Sierra Leone, estimated at 640,000 in 1996.

Major Urban Center (2005E): CONAKRY (1,478,000).

Official Language: French, pending adoption of Soussou or Malinké. (Six other tribal languages are also spoken.)

Monetary Unit: Guinea Franc (market rate July 1, 2006: 5007 francs = $1US).

President of the Republic: Gen. Lansana CONTÉ (Party of Unity and Progress); named president by the Military Committee for National Recovery (CMRN) on April 5, 1984, following the deposition on April 3 of Lansana BEAVOGUI, who had been named acting president upon the death of Ahmed Sékou TOURÉ on March 26; popularly elected for a five-year term on December 19, 1993, and inaugurated on January 29, 1994; reelected to a second five-year term on December 14, 1998; reelected to a third term of seven years on December 21, 2003.

Prime Minister: Vacant, following the president's dismissal of Cellou Dalein DIALLO on April 5, 2006.

organizing an "anti-Guinean front" supported financially by France, the Côte d'Ivoire, Senegal, and the United States. Observers viewed Telli's possible complicity in a conspiracy, coupled with evidence of discontent within the people's militia, as indicative of a potentially serious threat to the Touré regime (the severity of which reportedly prompted the flight of nearly one-quarter of Guinea's population to neighboring countries). Subsequently, French sources reported that Telli had been assassinated in prison while awaiting trial.

President Touré was sworn in for the fifth time on May 14, 1982, after an election five days earlier in which he was credited with close to 100 percent of the votes cast. However, on March 26, 1984, Africa's longest-serving chief executive died while undergoing heart surgery in the United States. Prime Minister Lansana BEAVOGUI immediately assumed office as acting president, but on April 5 a group of junior military officers seized power in a bloodless coup and announced the appointments of Col. Lansana CONTÉ as president of the Republic and Col. Diarra TRAORÉ as prime minister. Despite Touré's legendary status, the military found themselves in control of what had been described as a police state, with widespread corruption permeating both governmental and party bureaucracies and an economy in shambles. While immediate action was taken by the postcoup administration to reduce political repression, the malfunctioning state-controlled economy presented a more intractable challenge.

Following the April 1984 takeover, power struggles were reported between President Conté and the internationally visible Traoré, the former consolidating his power by abolishing the prime minister's post and demoting Traoré to education minister in a December cabinet reshuffle. Subsequently, on July 4, 1985, while President Conté was out of the country, army elements led by Traoré declared the dissolution of the "corrupt" Conté administration and occupied sections of Conakry. The coup attempt was quelled by loyalist forces prior to the president's return on July 5, most of those involved being arrested, pending trial by military courts. Traoré and his co-conspirators were executed in jail shortly after their imprisonment, although there was no official confirmation of their deaths until 1987.

In late 1988 Conté himself criticized the corruption and "transitory" nature of the first four years of his regime. In an effort to counter domestic opposition to his stringent economic programs and inspire the return of Guinean expatriates, he called on men and women "without regard to their abode" to join in the drafting of a bipartisan constitution, which was approved by referendum on December 23, 1990.

On January 9, 1992, in keeping with the spirit of the new basic law, which called for a separation of powers between executive and legislative organs of government, General Conté relinquished the presidency of the quasi-legislative Transitional Committee for National Recovery (CTRN, under Constitution and government, below), while remaining president of the republic. Despite widespread popular protests during the remainder of 1992, the regime rejected appeals for a national conference and countered objections to the pace and breadth of reform by adopting draft laws increasing penalties for the organization of violent demonstrations and banning unauthorized public meetings.

In April 1993 the administration announced plans to hold presidential and legislative elections in the last quarter of the year; however, unrest continued as General Conté rebuffed the opposition's call for an independent electoral commission and all-party talks. In September the government, ignoring the opposition's demand for simultaneous polling, scheduled presidential elections for December 5, with legislative balloting to follow 60 days later. Furthermore, in the wake of violent clashes September 28 and 29 in Conakry, Conté banned all opposition demonstrations until after the elections.

On December 19, 1993, Lansana Conté retained the presidency, leading an 8-candidate field with 51 percent of the vote in polling marred by at least 12 deaths and charges of widespread irregularities. On December 23 the Supreme Court annulled voting results in two opposition districts where second-place finisher Alpha CONDÉ of the Rally of the Guinean People (RPG) had reportedly secured 90 percent of the vote, and on January 4, 1994, the court confirmed the incumbent's victory, ignoring opposition calls for a second round of balloting.

After three postponements, a National Assembly poll was held on June 11, 1995, with 21 of 46 legalized parties participating. Conté's Party of Unity and Progress (PUP) was credited with an absolute majority of 71 of 114 seats and the runner-up RPG with 19, the remainder being distributed across eight other contestants. Most opposition groups challenged the results, although foreign observers indicated that irregularities had been relatively isolated.

On July 5, 1995, the RPG, the Party for Renewal and Progress (PRP), and the Union for the New Republic (UNR), who among them controlled 37 seats, announced their intention to boycott the assembly and joined with nine other opposition parties to form the Coordination of Democratic Opposition (Codem). The new formation was denounced by the government, and Conté refused its entreaties to engage in extraparliamentary negotiations. Subsequently, Codem abandoned the boycott, and the inaugural session of the first democratically elected Guinean Assembly opened on October 5, 1995.

On February 2 and 3, 1996, 50 people were killed and more than 100 others wounded when approximately 2,000 soldiers demonstrating for higher wages and better working conditions rampaged through Conakry, ultimately attacking the presidential palace and taking the president hostage. During his brief captivity Conté reached agreement with the soldiers on amnesty for the mutineers, salary increases, and reform of the armed services; however, following the retreat of the rebellious troops, Conté dismissed reports that their attack on his government had occurred spontaneously and accused opposition activists of helping to organize the failed "coup" attempt. Thereafter, despite warnings from the insurgents that the "entire army" would retaliate if any of their comrades were arrested, by June at least 52 people had been detained for their roles in the incident, including Lt. Lamine DIARRA, one of the two alleged masterminds of the rebellion, his alleged co-conspirator, Cmdr. Gbago ZOUMANIGUI, having reportedly fled to Libya. (In August some 40 of the detainees were released after the state prosecutor ruled there was insufficient evidence against them.)

On July 9, 1996, Conté named an economist, Sidya TOURÉ, as Guinea's first prime minister since 1984. Touré's appointment was followed on July 17 by a major cabinet reshuffling that included the departure of interior minister Alseny René GOMEZ, theretofore considered the president's second-in-command. On November 3 Conté, in an apparent attempt to reestablish control of military and security forces, appointed himself to head a newly created national defense ministry. The decision came only one day after government forces allegedly orchestrated an attack against Alpha Condé and his RPG supporters that left over 50 people injured. In early 1997, the president proclaimed executive authority over the national bank.

In February 1998 the newly created State Security Council convened the trial of the military personnel allegedly responsible for the February 1996 uprising. However, in March the court proceedings were overshadowed by deadly clashes between opposition activists and government security forces in Conakry that left at least nine dead and a number of opposition figures imprisoned. In response to the government's subsequent refusal to release the jailed militants, opposition legislators affiliated with Codem boycotted the National Assembly. In September relations between the opposition and government deteriorated further when the government dismissed the opposition's call for the establishment of an independent electoral commission and created an electoral affairs committee, which it charged with preparing for presidential elections in December. In October tensions between the Conté administration and National Assembly President El Hadj Boubacar Biro DIALLO reached a nadir as the latter was suspended from the ruling party for criticizing the government's treatment of the alleged February 1996 insurgents (most of whom had been convicted and sentenced to prison in late September).

At presidential elections on December 14, 1998, President Conté won reelection, capturing 56.12 percent of the vote and easily outdistancing his four competitors. As anticipated, the polling results were immediately challenged by the opposition, whose top two contenders, Mamadou Boye BA of the Union for Progress and Renewal (UPR) and Alpha Condé, had officially secured 24.63 and 16.58 percent, respectively. On March 8, 1999, the president appointed Lamine SIDIMÉ (theretofore head of the Supreme Court) as prime minister, with no official explanation given for the change; on March

12 Conté named a moderately reshuffled government, which was sworn in on April 10.

Twice-postponed municipal elections were held on June 25, 2000, with the PUP winning more than three-quarters of the seats. Subsequently, on November 11, 2001, 98 percent of those voting in a national referendum endorsed a controversial constitutional amendment permitting President Conté to run for a third term in 2003, with the term of office being extended from five to seven years.

The PUP dominated the June 30, 2002, legislative balloting, securing 85 seats; the UPR finished second with 20 seats. Amid severe controversy over electoral procedures and government control of the media, the major opposition parties boycotted the presidential election of December 21, 2003, at which Conté was reelected with an official 95.6 percent of the vote.

In late February 2004, President Conté dismissed Prime Minister Sidimé without explanation, and François Lonseny FALL was appointed on March 1 to head a reshuffled cabinet with a broad mandate to improve economic conditions. However, following a severe breakdown in relations with Conté, Fall resigned on April 29 and went into exile in the United States. A new prime minister was not appointed until December 9, when Cellou Dalein DIALLO was named to the post.

The PUP swept the postponed municipal elections on December 18, 2005, securing more than three-quarters of the seats. On April 5, 2006, the president ordered a cabinet reshuffle that granted more control to Diallo, but hours later, after a surprise rescinding of the cabinet changes, the prime minister was dismissed for alleged gross misconduct.

Constitution and Government

The 1982 constitution was suspended and the Democratic Party of Guinea dissolved by the Military Committee for National Recovery (*Comité Militaire de Redressement National*—CMRN) in the wake of the April 1984 coup. Subsequently, Guinea was ruled by a president and Council of Ministers named by the CMRN, although the committee itself was dissolved on January 16, 1991, in favor of a Transitional Committee for National Recovery (*Comité Transitoire de Redressement National*—CTRN). The new body, which was to govern the country until the election of an all-civilian administration, included equal numbers of military and civilian personnel.

In a decree issued in May 1984, President Conté ordered that the name "People's Revolutionary Republic of Guinea," adopted in 1978, be dropped in favor of the country's original name, the Republic of Guinea. Subsequently, he announced the formation of a "truly independent judiciary" and revival of the theretofore outlawed legal profession. In August 1985 a Court of State Security was established, encompassing a supreme court judge, two military officers, and two attorneys, to try "crimes against the state."

A 50-member committee, led by Foreign Affairs Minister Maj. Jean TRAORÉ, was appointed in October 1988 to draft a new constitution, which was reportedly approved by 99 percent of the participants in a referendum on December 23, 1990. The new *loi fondamentale* validated replacement of the CMRN by the CTRN, which in turn yielded authority in 1995 to a civilian regime encompassing a president and unicameral legislature, both popularly elected under two-party (subsequently multiparty) auspices, and an independent judiciary. A presidential decree on June 19, 1997, established a consultative Economic and Social Council whose 45 members are appointed by the president upon the recommendation of various civic institutions.

The country is administratively organized into four main geographic divisions—Maritime, Middle, Upper, and Forest Guinea—which are subdivided into eight regions—Boké, Faranah, Kankan, Kindia, Labé, Mamou, N'Zérékoré, and Conakry. The Conakry region is subdivided into five "urban communes," while the remaining seven regions are subdivided into a total of 33 prefectures.

Foreign Relations

President Touré's brand of militant nationalism and his frequent allegations of externally provoked conspiracy led to strained international relations, including diplomatic ruptures with France (1965–1975), Britain (1967–1968), and Ghana (1966–1973). By January 1978, however, Conakry had moved to ease long-standing tensions with its immediate neighbors. Shortly thereafter, during a meeting in Monrovia, Liberia, attended by the presidents of Gambia, Guinea, the Côte d'Ivoire, Liberia, Senegal, and Togo, diplomatic relations with Senegal and the Côte d'Ivoire were restored, the participants pledging bilateral and multilateral cooperation in both political and economic spheres. In October 1980 Guinea acceded to the Mano River Union (MRU), formed seven years earlier to promote economic cooperation between Liberia and Sierra Leone, while in March 1982 Touré called for the unification of Guinea and Mali, arguing that economically the two countries were "two lungs in a single body." In subsequent years Conakry also increased its visibility in the Economic Community of West African States (ECOWAS).

In December 1978 French President Giscard d'Estaing visited Guinea, the first Western leader to do so in over two decades. The extremely warm reception he received was viewed as part of a broad effort to scale down assistance from Soviet and other Eastern Bloc countries in favor of Western aid and investment. In keeping with the policy shift, President Touré made a number of trips to the United States, Canada, and Western Europe from 1979 to 1983. However, distrust of the "father of African socialism" and an overvalued local currency discouraged large-scale Western involvement. By contrast, in the wake of the 1984 coup Prime Minister Traoré negotiated a broad aid package with France, while French and other foreign investment increased significantly upon the adoption of monetary and fiscal reforms recommended by the IMF.

Despite Guinean fears of a new "colonialism," raised by the influx of foreign merchants and military advisers into the capital, Conakry continued to pursue external assistance in developing its infrastructure and mineral resources, while concluding resource-development agreements with Morocco, Guinea-Bissau, and Liberia in 1989.

In early 1990 an influx of refugees fleeing the Liberian civil war quickly exhausted the reserves of Guinea's southern border region, and in May President Conté called for international aid to support refugees claimed to number 200,000. In August Conakry deployed troops to seal its southern border after a rebel incursion in alleged reprisal for Guinea's participation in ECOWAS activity in Liberia.

In September 1992, after a three-month cease-fire aimed at inducing Liberian and Sierra Leonean rebels to disarm and accept a full amnesty, Guinean and Sierra Leonean troops resumed their joint efforts to repel rebels in eastern and southern Sierra Leone. Meanwhile, the publication of a report claiming that Guinea had trained a Liberian paramilitary force assigned to interim Liberian president Amos Sawyer led to the detainment of its author. In August 1994, 35,000 Liberians were reported to have fled into Guinea, raising the five-year total to approximately 500,000.

In April 1996 Mali recalled its ambassador and criticized the Conté administration after Guinean troops stormed into the Malian embassy in Conakry in search of a leader of the February military uprising. Clashes between Malian and Guinean residents were subsequently reported in April and October near the border.

In April 1997 Belgium closed its consular offices after Conakry refused to release three Belgian nationals it had arrested in March for allegedly plotting to overthrow the government. Meanwhile, observers reported that Guinean security forces had arrested and then released 75 Liberian refugees on similar charges. Increasing incidents of "banditry" and violence along the Guinean-Liberian border were among the topics discussed by President Conté and Liberian President Charles Taylor during a summit in late 1997.

Amid reports that rebels from Sierra Leone had attacked a town in southern Guinea, in early December 1998 Conakry announced that it was closing its borders until after the presidential polling scheduled for December 14. Further Sierra Leonean cross-border activity was reported in early 1999, and in April Liberian troops threatened to en-

ter Guinean territory in pursuit of Liberian antigovernment rebels, whom Monrovia accused Conakry of at least tacitly supporting. In August at least two dozen people died when militants, allegedly operating from a base in Liberia, attacked a town in southern Guinea, and in mid-September Charles Taylor claimed that Guinean forces had killed several hundred Liberians during raids in April and August. Conté subsequently called his Liberian counterpart a "warmonger," although at the same time insisting that no problems existed between the two countries' peoples.

In March 2000 Guinea, Liberia, and Sierra Leone reportedly agreed to the immediate reactivation of the MRU secretariat. (Due to civil wars the body had been dormant since 1990.) However, Guinea and Liberia were subsequently described as still "trading destabilization accusations." (See Current issues, below, and article on Liberia for additional information.)

Economic relations between France and Guinea continued to remain strong through the early years of the 2000s, but Conakry also began to develop stronger security ties with the United States. The United States has provided military training and equipment for Guinea, including radio and vehicles, in a program to improve Conakry's military capabilities for regional peacekeeping missions. The appointment of Prime Minister Fall, an English-speaker and widely seen as pro-American, as opposed to pro-French, was perceived as a sign of Conté's desire to improve relations with the United States. One manifestation of the increased ties between the two countries was a decrease in Guinean support for Liberian rebel groups, as a result of diplomatic pressure from the United States, and broad support from Conakry for the United Nations peacekeeping mission in Liberia after the departure of Taylor from that country. By mid-2006, a marked decrease in violence at the border with Liberia was reported.

Current Issues

Legislative elections, originally due in June 2000, were initially rescheduled for the following

November. However, they were again delayed (with the approval of the opposition parties) in the wake of heavy fighting along the borders with Sierra Leone and Liberia. The conflict involved disputed control of diamond-producing areas in all three countries. President Conté charged that the Liberian government was supporting Guinean rebel groups (see Political Parties and Groups, below), much like Liberia was accused of supporting rebels in Sierra Leone to exercise de facto control of diamond mines. The conflict primarily pitted the Guinean and Sierra Leonean armies and Liberian rebels on one side and the Liberian military and Guinean and Sierra Leonean rebels on the other. Among other things, burgeoning regional war exacerbated the refugee crisis in Guinea, Conakry alleging that refugees in Guinea from Sierra Leone were harboring antigovernment rebels.

ECOWAS deployed troops in Guinean border areas in December 2000, and the completion of a peace accord in Sierra Leone in May 2001 (see article on Sierra Leone) appeared to offer the opportunity for resumption of normal political activity in Guinea. However, the opposition parties strongly objected to the November referendum that permitted a third, extended term for President Conté, calling the initiative a "constitutional coup d'état" designed to make Conté "president for life." (Although the government reported a turnout of 87 percent for the referendum, the opposition, which had called for a boycott, described that figure as outlandishly inflated.) When the opposition announced plans to boycott the new legislative elections scheduled for late December, the administration once again postponed the balloting indefinitely. The legislative poll finally took place on June 30, 2002, although most opposition parties boycotted the balloting.

Under heavy international pressure, the government established an interparty commission in 2003 in an effort to convince the opposition to return to full political participation. However, negotiations collapsed in September as the government reportedly refused to relinquish its tight control of the state media. Consequently, another opposition boycott was called for the December presidential election, at which Conté was challenged by only one

minor candidate after six others were rejected because of "technical errors" in their candidacy papers. Not surprisingly, international observers described the balloting as neither free nor fair.

The appointment of reformist Prime Minister Fall, described as "pro-American," in March 2004 was seen as part of ongoing efforts to improve relations with the United States. (Under U.S. pressure, Conakry had earlier decreased its support for Liberian rebel groups and endorsed the UN peacekeeping mission in Liberia.) However, Fall left office in less than two months to protest what he perceived as continued political repression and the unwillingness of Conté to pursue economic reform. From exile in the United States, Fall called upon the Guinean opposition parties to coalesce in order to challenge the Conté regime.

A number of public protests broke out in September 2004, and, following his appointment in December, reformist Prime Minister Diallo attempted to relaunch a dialogue with the opposition. In early 2005 he moved to lift a ban on private radio stations, but little progress ensued in his attempts to win over the opposition. Meanwhile, attention focused on the frail health of President Conté, for whom there appeared to be no obvious successor. The government reported an assassination attempt against Conté in January 2005, and reports surfaced about fears of a potential military coup if the president failed to live out his term. Despite calls late in the year by the Republican Front for Democratic Change (*Front de L'Alternance Démocratique—* FRAD) for the president to step down in favor of a government of national unity, observers pointed to ethnic and other differences among the opposition that could render such an alternative unlikely. The government was bolstered by an overwhelming PUP victory in December's municipal elections, postponed from 2004 because of allegations of widespread fraud, which were repeated after the 2005 balloting.

The president's deteriorating health (he was taken to Switzerland in March 2006, reportedly for emergency medical attention) prompted rising concern about the country's uncertain political future. In Conté's absence, a strike to protest low wages shut down the country for five days. As a result, the government reached an accord with unions that provided a 30 percent wage increase for civil service workers and a 10 percent tax cut on state employees' salaries. Further, an unprecedented National Consultation of opposition groups, unions, women's and youth groups, and civil societies resulted in unanimity on the need for a government of national unity to "rescue" the country. However, disarray followed a state radio broadcast on April 5, 2006, announcing extensive cabinet changes that bolstered the influence of Prime Minister Diallo. Within hours it was announced that the changes were rescinded and that Diallo had been dismissed because of alleged serious misconduct. Observers attributed the move to internal power struggles, raising questions about who was really in charge and who might assume control after Conté's death. For his part, Diallo denied claims that he was under house arrest and reiterated his support for Conté.

On a more positive note, the European Union in 2006 granted some $27 million in aid to help rebuild areas in Giunea's southeastern Forest Region, which was destroyed during conflicts in the late 1990s and early 2000s.

Political Parties and Groups

Prior to the 1984 coup, Guinea was a typical one-party state, according a monopoly position to the Democratic Party of Guinea (*Parti Démocratique de Guinée*—PDG) in all aspects of public life. The CMRN's initial promise of an introduction of "democracy" was reaffirmed in 1989 by President Conté, and the constitution approved in December 1990 included provisions for two parties, with numerous others being recognized in 1991 and 1992.

During 1993 a number of somewhat transitory opposition coalitions emerged, including Democratic Change (*Changement Démocratique*—CD), a 30-party grouping under whose banner activists clashed with police in Conakry in September. The principal opposition alliances in the run-up to the December presidential balloting were AGUNA (below) and the BPG, while nine of the nearly four dozen recognized parties were reportedly members of a "Presidential Tendency" headed by the PUP, below.

In August 1995 the "Presidential Tendency" splintered because of the failure of the PUP and a number of its erstwhile allies to reach agreement on a new assembly president; subsequently, the defecting parties formed the **Alliance of Democratic Forces** (*Alliance pour les Forces Démocratiques*—AFD), under the leadership of Oumar CAMARA. (Excluded from recent electoral preparations, the AFD has described the upcoming balloting as "useless" and asserted that the electorate felt "broad contempt" for both the Presidential Tendency and the Codem.)

Two somewhat overlapping opposition alliances were formed in 2001 to attempt to stop Conté from running for a third term. In July the UFR, the UFDG, and others formed the **Democratic Change in 2003** (*Alternance Démocratique en 2003*) to oppose the upcoming referendum on amending the constitution. Subsequently, opposition activity focused on the **Movement against the Referendum and for Democratic Change** (*Mouvement Contre le Referendum et pour l'Alternance Démocratique*—Morad), formed by the Codem, UFR, PGP, and four other parties.

Presidential Group

Party of Unity and Progress (*Parti de l'Unité et du Progrès*—PUP). The PUP nominated Gen. Lansana Conté as its presidential candidate in August 1993, subsequently becoming the core component of an informal regime-supportive coalition that included the **Democratic Rally for Development** (*Rassemblement Démocratique pour le Développement*—RDD), led by Georges Koly GUILAVOGUI.

At the PUP's first national congress held April 4–7, 1997, Conté was named as the party's candidate for upcoming presidential elections, and Aboubacar Somparé's theretofore interim appointment as PUP secretary general was made permanent.

In January 1998 members of the PUP's youth wing launched the **Movement for Lansana Conté's Reelection** (*Mouvement pour la Réélection de Lansana Conté*—MORELAC). In June the presidential supporters formed the **Association of Movements Affiliated to the Party of Unity and Progress**, a coalition of some 200 parties and groups chaired by Karim KANE. The groups were successful in the 2001 referendum to allow Conté to stand for a third term. In early 2005 feuding between Conté loyalists and those supporting the president's unofficial heir apparent, Youth Minister Fode Soumah, was reported. Late in the year, the party made a strong showing in both rural and urban areas in municipal elections.

Leaders: Gen. Lansana CONTÉ (President of the Republic), Sékou KONATE (Secretary General).

Democratic Party of Guinea–African Democratic Rally (*Parti Démocratique de Guinée–Rassemblement Démocratique Africain*—PDG-RDA). The leader of the PDG-RDA (a revival of former President Touré's party) secured less than 1 percent of the vote in the 1993 presidential balloting. In the wake of its poor showing the party splintered, with dissident members forming the **Democratic Party of Guinea–Renewed** (*Parti Démocratique de Guinée–Renouvellement*—PDG-R). In December 1994 the party suffered yet another mass defection when members claiming continued allegiance to former president Touré withdrew to launch the **Democratic Party of Guinea–Ahmed Sekou Touré** (*Parti Démocratique de Guineé–Ahmed Sekou Touré*—PDG-AST). In the 2002 legislative elections, the PDG-RDA won three seats.

Leader: Ismael Mohammed Gassim GUSHEIN.

Union for National Progress–Party of Unity and Development (*Union pour le Progrès National–Parti pour L'Unité et le Développement*—UPN-PUD). The PUD was one of seven parties that formed a coalition, **Guinean Alliance for National Unity** (*Alliance Guinéene pour L'Unité Nationale*—AGUNA), to support the presidential candidacy of Faciné TOURÉ. The PUD later merged with the pro-Conté UPN under the leadership of Mamadou Bhoye Barry. The UPN-PUD won one seat in the 2002 legislative

elections (the seat was won by Barry). Barry was the sole challenger to Conté in the 2003 presidential election.

Leader: Mamadou Bhoye BARRY.

Other Parties and Groups

Republican Front for Democratic Change (*Front de L'Alternance Démocratique*—FRAD). The FRAD was originally formed by a coalition of four parties in 2002 and then grew to include seven of the main opposition parties. FRAD emerged from previous anti-Conté groupings, principally the Coordination of the Democratic Opposition (*Coordination de l'Opposition Démocratique*—Codem). The Codem was formed by the RPG, PRP, UNR, and a number of other smaller parties to mount a legislative boycott in response to alleged ballot fraud at the June 1995 poll. In early February 1996 the group supported President Conté's handling of the military unrest in Conakry; however, after the president alleged that opposition activists had been involved in the uprising, Codem parliamentarians boycotted the assembly. Thereafter, intracoalition conflict was reported between the PRP's Siradiou Diallo, who advocated establishing a dialogue with the administration, and the RPG's Alpha Condé, who accused the regime of harassment and the illegal detention of opposition activists.

In late 1996 the Codem announced that it was forming a "resistance militia" in response to violent attacks against its members and to fend off security forces attempting to arrest its supporters. Thereafter, the coalition criticized the Conté administration for reducing the prime minister's powers. Underscoring its increasing hostility toward Conté's policies, the Codem in early 1998 established an Executive Secretariat to coordinate "acts of resistance" against the government. In March a number of opposition leaders, including the UNR's Mamadou Ba, were arrested after violent clashes erupted in Conakry between opposition protesters and government forces. Subsequently, the Codem boycotted legislative proceedings in an effort to persuade the government to release its imprisoned members. (In June Ba was given a "lenient verdict" and released.)

Codem boycotted the 2001 presidential referendum and announced that it would also boycott the upcoming legislative elections. In 2002 a split emerged in Codem over participation in the presidential elections, leading to the break-up of Codem and the creation of the FRAD by parties that planned to boycott the elections. The main difference between Codem and the FRAD was the absence of the Union for Progress and Renewal (see below). Nonetheless, many of the most prestigious and well-respected opposition figures, including Condé, Ba, Touré, and Boubacar Biro Diallo (then president of the assembly), joined the coalition. The FRAD led the opposition to the presidential election in 2003 and organized a succession of protests and demonstrations against the regime. In response, most of the FRAD's leadership figures, including Condé, Ba, and Touré, have been arrested for brief periods. In 2005 FRAD leaders called on the president to resign to allow for transition to a government of national unity.

Leaders: Mamadou BA (President), Alpha CONDÉ (RPG), Sidya TOURÉ (UFR), Jean-Marie DORÉ (UPG).

Rally of the Guinean People (*Rassemblement Populaire Guinéen*—RPG). In early 1991 Alpha Condé received an enthusiastic welcome from RPG members upon his return from exile. Subsequently, on May 19 government troops violently disrupted the party's attempt to hold an inaugural meeting.

In February 1993 the RPG and the UNR, below, were accused of inciting antigovernment violence in rural communities, and Condé subsequently appealed unsuccessfully for a joint opposition candidate in the December presidential poll, at which he was runner-up with a 19.55 vote share.

In 1994 the RPG adopted a new platform urging "peace, justice, and solidarity," and in April Condé reiterated the party's desire "to prepare for parliamentary elections in a transparent manner." Nonetheless, RPG activists subsequently accused the government of attempting to assassinate their leader, and in September 1995 at least one person was killed when RPG militants clashed with government security forces in Nzerekore.

On November 2, 1996, already-confrontational relations between the RPG and the government reached their nadir when government security forces allegedly organized an attack on a motorcade carrying Condé, and an RPG building was attacked by arsonists. Furthermore, on November 19 two prominent RPG leaders, Saliou CISSÉ and Keita BENTOUBA, were arrested. RPG leaders derided the arrests, reportedly describing them as a "dangerous, resounding slip-up," and in late December Codem officials cited the November incidents as catalysts for their decision to launch a militia.

The Codem's legislative boycott in early 1998 was prompted in part by the ransacking of the RPG's headquarters and the arrest of two RPG parliamentarians. Thereafter, in early December, Alpha Condé returned from self-imposed exile to campaign for the presidency. Despite the large turnouts that greeted his public appearances, the RPG candidate finished a distant third at the polling. Furthermore, on December 15 Condé was arrested as he prepared to enter Côte d'Ivoire, and a number of RPG activists were jailed for their alleged participation in the violent unrest that followed the release of the polling results. Having garnered substantial regional and global interest, the trial of Condé and more than 40 codefendants concluded in September 2000 with Condé being found guilty of sedition. His prison sentence was cut short by a presidential pardon in May 2001. Condé returned to Conakry in 2005 after two years of self-imposed exile in Paris to help organize the party ahead of the December municipal elections (in which the RPG won only a handful of seats.)

Leaders: Alpha CONDÉ (Secretary General and 1998 presidential candidate), Ahmed CISSÉ.

Union for the Progress of Guinea (*Union pour le Progrès de Guinée*—UPG). At the December 1993 balloting UPG secretary general Jean-Marie Doré secured less than 1 percent of the vote; nevertheless, Doré emerged as a prominent Codem spokesperson after the UPG secured 2 seats at the 1995 assembly balloting.

At presidential balloting in December 1998 Doré secured just 1.73 percent of the vote. The UPG left Codem in May 1996. Although the UPG took part in the 2002 legislative elections and won three seats, it boycotted the 2003 presidential elections. Doré is one of the main spokespersons for the FRAD.

Leader: Jean-Marie DORÉ (Secretary General and 1998 presidential candidate).

Union of Democratic Forces of Guinea (*Union des Forces Démocratiques de Guinée*—UFDG). The UFDG was one of the first parties applying for legal status in 1991. Its leader, Amadou Bâ Oury, was arrested on October 27, 1992, for alleged involvement in an attempted assassination of President Conté 11 days earlier, but he was released shortly thereafter in apparent acknowledgement by authorities that false testimony had been given against him.

In May 1996 the Union resurfaced as the leading opponent to the National Assembly's adoption of a law that rehabilitated former president Sékou Touré, calling it a "trivialization" of Touré's crimes. After he left the UPR, Mamadou Ba joined the UFDG and was elected president in October 2002. In 2005, Ba distanced himself from some FRAD members and expressed support for Prime Minister Diallo.

Leader: Mamadou BA.

Union of Republican Forces (*Union des Forces Republicains*—UFR). A small grouping formed in 1992, the UFR elected former prime minister Sidya Touré as its president in May 2000. The UFR subsequently was reported to have filed a suit against the government for having prevented its candidates from contesting the June municipal balloting. In 2004 Touré was

cleared of charges accusing him of plotting to overthrow the government.

Leader: Sidya TOURÉ (President), Bakary ZOUMANIGUI (Secretary General).

The FRAD also includes three minor parties: the **African Democratic Party** (*Parti Démocratique Africain*—PDA), led by Marcel CROS; the **Djama Party** (*Parti Djama*), a moderate Islamist party led by Mohamed Mansour KABA; and the **Union of Democratic Forces** (*Union des Forces Démocratiques*—UFD), led by Alpha Ibrahim SOW.

Union for Progress and Renewal (*Union pour le Progrès et le Renouvellement*—UPR). The UPR was launched in September 1998 as a merger of the Party of Renewal and Progress (*Parti pour le Renouveau et le Progrès*—PRP) and the Union for the New Republic (*Union pour la Nouvelle République*—UNR). While leadership of the new grouping was assumed by Siradiou Diallo, the PRP's secretary general and 1993 presidential candidate, the UNR's Mamadou Boye Ba was named the UPR's presidential candidate. Ba, who had been detained from March to June for his alleged role in the violent clashes in Conakry, finished second at the December balloting with 22 percent of the vote.

The UPR factionalized in 2002, with members who advocated dialogue with Conté and participation in elections remaining in the UPR under Diallo. Those UPR members who supported boycotting the upcoming legislative elections joined the Union of Democratic Forces of Guinea, of which Ba became president. Diallo died on March 14, 2004, of a heart attack, and the UPR elected Ousmane Bah as leader of the party. The UPR reportedly withdrew from the assembly in protest following municipal elections of December 2005, which the party claimed were "nothing short of electoral robbery."

Leader: Ousmane BAH (President).

National Alliance for Progress (*Alliance Nationale pour le Progrès*—ANP). The ANP formed prior to the 1995 legislative elections but remained a minor party for most of its history. However, it

Cabinet

As of May 1, 2006

President	Gen. Lansana Conté
Prime Minister	Vacant

Ministers

Agriculture and Animal Husbandry	Jean-Paul Sarr
Commerce, Industry, and Small and Medium-Scale Enterprise	Djénné Saran Camara [f]
Cooperation	Thierno Habib Diallo
Economy and Finance	Mady Kaba Kamara
Employment and Civil Service	Alpha Ibrahima Kéira
Environment	Sheikh Abdel Kader Sangare
Fisheries and Aquaculture	Ibrahima Sory Touré
Foreign Affairs	Sidibe Fatoumata Kaba [f]
Higher Education and Scientific Research	Sékou Décazy Camara
Information	Aissatou Bella Diallo [f]
Justice and Guardian of the Seals	Mamadou Sylla
Mines and Geology	Ahmed Tidiane Souare
Planning	Eugene Camara
Pre-University Education	Galema Guilavogui
Posts and Telecommunications	Jean-Claude Sultan
Public Health	Amara Cissé
Public Works and Transport	Bana Sidibe
Secretary General to the Government	Oury Bailo Bah
Secretary General to the Presidency	Fodé Bangoura
Security	Ousmane Camara
Social Affairs, Women's Promotion, and the Child	Mariama Aribot [f]
Technical Education and Training	Ibrahima Souma
Territorial Administration and Decentralization	Kiridi Bangoura
Tourism, Hotels, and Handicrafts	Sylla Koumba Diàkite [f]
Transport	Aliou Condé
Urban Affairs and Housing	Ouo-Ouo Blaise Foromo
Water Power and Energy	Dioubate Hadja Fatoumata Binta Diallo [f]
Youth, Sports, and Culture	Fode Soumah

[f] = female

was one of the few opposition parties not to boycott the 2002 legislative elections, and it won two seats in the assembly.

Leader: Sagno MOUSSA.

People's Party of Guinea (*Parti Guinéen du Peuple*—PGP). The PGP is an anti-Conté socialist party. At presidential balloting in December 1998 the PGP's candidate, Charles Pascal Tolno, received less than 1 percent of the vote. In 2003 Tolno was rejected as a presidential candidate by the Supreme Court. Jean-Marie Doré, now of the UPG, formerly was affiliated with the PGP.

Leader: Charles Pascal TOLNO (1998 presidential candidate).

Other registered parties include the **Democratic Union of Guinea** (*Union Démocratique* de Guinée—UDG), led by Sekou SYLLA; the **National Democratic Alliance** (*Alliance Démocratique Nationale*—ADN), led by Antoine SOROMO; the **Guinean Labor Party** (*Parti Guinéen du Travail*—PGT); the **Ecological Party of Guinea–the Greens** (*Parti Écologiste de Guinée–Les Verts*—PEG–Les Verts), led by Oumar SYLLA; and the **Rally for Peace and Development** (*Rassemblement pour la Paix et le Développement*—RPD).

Rebel Groups

In September 2000 the **Guinea Liberation Movement** (*Mouvement pour la Libération de Guinée*—MLG), suspected of working closely with Sierra Leone's **Revolutionary United Front** (RUF, see under Sierra Leone), reportedly infiltrated Guinean territory and engaged in fighting with the government forces. Another rebel group, the **Rally for Democratic Forces of Guinea** (*Rassemblement des Forces Démocratiques de Guinée*—RFDG), claimed responsibility for an attack on a town on the Liberian border.

In August 2001, Nfaly KABA, the leader of the **Union of the Forces for a New Guinea** (*Union des Forces pour une Nouvelle Guinée*—UFNG), vowed war on Guinea if President Conté did not step down. The UFNG's armed wing was reportedly led by former Major Gbago ZOUMANIGUI. In September a new exile opposition movement was formed in Bamako, Mali, under the leadership of Sheikh Mohamed KABA. The movement reportedly adopted the rubric of the **National Alliance of Democratic Patriots** (*Alliance Nationale des Patriotes Démocratiques*—ANPD).

Legislature

The 210-member People's National Assembly (*Assemblée Nationale Populaire*), elected from a single PDG list for a seven-year term on January 27, 1980, was dissolved in April 1984. Balloting for a successor body, originally scheduled for November 1992, was rescheduled in April 1993 for the last quarter of the year, but did not in fact occur until June 11, 1995.

National Assembly (*Assemblée Nationale*). The current assembly is a 114-member body with a five-year mandate. One-third of its deputies are elected by majority vote in single-member districts, two-thirds on a national list vote with proportional representation.

At legislative balloting on June 30, 2002, the Party of Unity and Progress won 85 seats; the Union for Progress and Renewal, 20; Union for the Progress of Guinea, 3; the Democratic Party of Guinea–African Democratic Rally, 3; the National Alliance for Progress, 2; and the Union for National Progress–Party of Unity and Development, 1. Most major opposition parties boycotted the elections.

President: Aboubacar SOMPARÉ.

Communications

All mass media are owned or controlled by the government. The government in 1992 introduced a National Communication Council (*Conseil Nationale de la Communication*—CNC) as a presidentially appointed regulatory body with the stated aim of "protecting the media from government and special interest encroachment and manipulation." However, the council was subsequently heavily criticized by human rights and media organizations for acting as a government tool to control and censor the media. Since the early 1990s numerous publications have been shut down permanently or temporarily, and journalists have been arrested and incarcerated.

Press

The press is subject to rigorous government censorship. The following have previously been published in Conakry: *Fonike,* government-owned daily; *Horoya* (Liberty, 20,000), weekly, in French and local languages; *Journal Officiel de Guinée,* fortnightly government organ; *Le Travailleur de Guinée,* monthly organ of the National Confederation of Guinean Workers. However, in late 1999 a Guinean media observer reported that of 40 independent newspapers once in publication only the following were still available: *L'Indépendant,* independent weekly; *L'Indépendant Plus,* weekly; *Le Lynx,* satirical weekly; *L'Oeil,* weekly; *La Lance; Le Globe*; and *Le Nouvel Observateur*.

News Agencies

The official news agency is *Agence Guinéenne de Presse* (AGP), which became operational in July 1986 as part of the UNESCO-supported West African News Agencies Development (WANAD) project. *Xinhua,* APN, and ITAR-TASS are represented in Conakry.

Broadcasting and Computing

The government-operated *Radiodiffusion Télévision Guinéenne* operates eight radio transmitting stations, with broadcasts in French, English, Portuguese, Arabic, and local languages. Television broadcasting, introduced in 1977, reaches some 376,000 TV sets, while 43,000 personal computers serviced 49,000 Internet users in 2003.

Intergovernmental Representation

Ambassador to the U.S.
Alpha Oumar Rafiou BARRY

U.S. Ambassador to Guinea
Jackson McDONALD

Permanent Representative to the UN
Alpha Ibrahim SOW

IGO Memberships (Non-UN)
AfDB, AU, BADEA, ECOWAS, IDB, Interpol, IOM, MRU, NAM, OIC, OIF, WCO, WTO

GUINEA-BISSAU

REPUBLIC OF GUINEA-BISSAU

República da Guiné-Bissau

The Country

Situated on the west coast of Africa between Senegal on the north and Guinea on the south, the Republic of Guinea-Bissau also includes the Bijagóz Archipelago and the island of Bolama. The population is primarily of African descent (principal tribes include the Balante, Fulani, Mandyako, and Malinké), but there are smaller groups of mulattoes, Portuguese, and Lebanese. The majority continues to follow traditional religious beliefs; however, there is a significant Muslim population and a small Christian minority.

Agriculture employs the vast majority of the population, with peanuts typically producing two-thirds of export earnings. Other important exports are palm products, fish, and cattle, while such crops as cotton, sugar, and tobacco have been introduced in an effort to diversify the country's output; industry is dominated by state enterprises and mixed ventures. The chief mineral resource may be petroleum (the extent of on- and offshore reserves is uncertain, although a number of Western oil companies have signed exploration contracts with the government). Economic development has been hindered by insufficient capital, skilled labor, and transport facilities. Consequently, the country remains one of the poorest in the world.

On May 2, 1997, Guinea-Bissau, citing its desire to "improve its regional trade position," joined the West African Monetary Union (*Union Monetaire Ouest-Africaine*—UMOA), thus abandoning the Guinea Peso in favor of the CFA franc. In addition, the government launched comprehensive tax and civil service reform programs. After three years

of steady annual increases (1995–1997), GDP declined in real terms by 21 percent in 1998 under the influence of civil war. Positive GDP growth (nearly 8 percent) returned in 1999 while annual inflation dropped to 2.1 compared to 8 percent in 1998. The International Monetary Fund (IMF) approved an emergency post-conflict assistance loan in January 2000 and a three-year debt reduction arrangement the following December. However, real GDP growth of only 0.2 percent was registered in 2001, and the IMF and other economic observers criticized the government for its handling of the economy.

In 2001 the IMF suspended debt relief to Guinea-Bissau because of the government's

Real GDP growth of about 2 percent was recorded for 2004 and 2005, though inflation remained at less than 1 percent. The country's economic situation remained "very difficult" following years of political instability and little new investment, according to the IMF, despite modest progress in tax reform and managing expenditures. The IMF in 2005 underscored the need to avoid domestic arrears as well as the need for more donor assistance.

Government and Politics

Political Background

First discovered by the Portuguese mariner Nuno Tristão in 1446, the territory long known as Portuguese Guinea did not receive a final delimitation of its borders until 1905. Initially, the country was plundered by slave traders, and consequent hostility among the indigenous peoples resulted in uprisings in the early twentieth century. The area was eventually pacified by military means, and in 1952 it was formally designated as an Overseas Province of Portugal.

In 1956 a group of dissatisfied Cape Verdeans under the joint leadership of Amílcar CABRAL, Luís de Almeida CABRAL, Aristides PEREIRA, and Rafael BARBOSA formed the African Party for the Independence of Guinea and Cape Verde (*Partido Africano da Independência da Guiné e Cabo Verde*—PAIGC). Failing to win concessions from the Portuguese, the PAIGC, with assistance from Warsaw Pact nations, initiated an armed struggle in 1963, and by the early 1970s the PAIGC claimed to control two-thirds of the mainland territory. On January 20, 1973, Amílcar Cabral was assassinated in Conakry, Guinea, allegedly by PAIGC dissidents but with the apparent complicity of the Portuguese military. Six months later, Aristides Pereira and Cabral's brother, Luís, were confirmed as party leaders by a PAIGC congress.

A government was formally organized and independence declared on September 23 and 24, 1973. The Portuguese authorities claimed the move was a "propaganda stunt," but the coup in Portugal in

Political Status: Achieved independence from Portugal on September 10, 1974; under rule of Revolutionary Council following coup of November 14, 1980; new constitution of May 16, 1984, amended on May 4, 1991; military control imposed following coup of May 8, 1999; present constitution promulgated July 7, 1999, under direction of military junta.
Area: 13,948 sq. mi. (36,125 sq. km.).
Population: 983,367 (1991C); 1,583,000 (2005E).
Major Urban Center (2005E): BISSAU (247,000).
Official Language: Portuguese (several local languages are also spoken).
Monetary Unit: CFA Franc (official rate July 1, 2006: 513.01 francs = $1US). (The CFA franc, previously pegged to the French franc, is now permanently pegged to the euro at 655.957 CFA francs = 1 euro.)
President: João Bernardo VIEIRA (independent); elected to a five-year term after second-round balloting on July 24, 2005, and sworn in on October 1, succeeding Henrique ROSA (nonparty), who had been installed as interim president following the military overthrow of Kumba YALA (Social Renewal Party) in 2003.
Prime Minister: Aristides GOMES (Pro-Vieira faction of the African Party for the Independence of Guinea and Cape Verde); appointed by the president and sworn in on November 2, 2005, to succeed Carlos GOMES (African Party for the Independence of Guinea and Cape Verde).

unwillingness to enact agreed-upon reforms. Conflict within the country led to a GDP decline of 7 percent in 2002; there was no measurable GDP growth in 2003. That year, donor states suspended aid after the government failed to demobilize ex-soldiers and continue economic restructuring. Following the coup of September 2003 and subsequent legislative elections, donors announced a limited resumption of aid in 2004, including $13 million from the World Bank.

April 1974 led to an informal cease-fire and negotiations with the rebel leaders. Although the talks failed to resolve the status of the Cape Verde Islands, an agreement signed August 26, 1974, provided for the independence of Guinea-Bissau as of September 10, 1974, and the removal of all Portuguese troops by October 31.

In the first balloting since independence, 15 regional councils were elected during December 1976 and January 1977, the councils in turn selecting delegates to a second National People's Assembly, which convened in March 1977; Cabral was reelected president of the republic and of the 15-member Council of State, while (then) Maj. João Bernardo VIEIRA was designated vice president of the republic and reconfirmed as president of the assembly. Vieira became principal commissioner (prime minister) on September 28, 1978, succeeding Maj. Francisco MENDES, who died on July 7.

The principal political issue of the late 1970s was a projected unification of Cape Verde with Guinea-Bissau, many mainland leaders—including President Cabral and other high officials of the binational PAIGC—being Cape Verdean *mestiços.* On November 10, 1980, an extraordinary session of the National People's Assembly adopted a new constitution that many black Guineans construed as institutionalizing domination by islanders; four days later a coup led by Vieira, a native Guinean, deposed the president. On November 19 the Council of State and the assembly were formally dissolved by a Revolutionary Council that designated Vieira as head of state, and, on the following day, the council announced a provisional cabinet, all but one of whose members had served in the previous administration. Shortly thereafter, President Vieira identified the basic reasons for Cabral's ouster as the country's social and economic difficulties, including severe food shortages; "progressive abandonment of the principle of democratic centralism"; and "corruption of the meaning of unity between Guinea-Bissau and Cape Verde."

At a PAIGC conference in November 1981 it was announced that presidential and legislative elections under a new constitution would be held in early 1982 and that the party would retain its existing name, despite the fact that in the wake of the coup its Cape Verdean wing had formally repudiated the goal of unification with the mainland. In May 1982 President Vieira instituted a purge of reputed left-wingers within the government and the PAIGC. Furthermore, he named Vítor SAÚDE Maria as prime minister, a post that had been vacant since the 1980 takeover. Continued instability persisted for the next two years, culminating in the ouster of Saúde Maria on March 8, 1984, for alleged antistate activity. The return to constitutional rule followed on March 31 with the election of eight regional councils, which, in turn, chose 150 deputies to a new National People's Assembly. The assembly convened on May 14 and two days later approved a new basic law that combined the offices of head of state and chief of government into the presidency of a revived Council of State, to which Vieira was unanimously elected.

A further attempt to overthrow the Vieira regime was reported on November 7, 1985, when security forces arrested some 50 individuals, including the first vice president, Col. Paulo CORREIA, and a number of other prominent military and civilian officials, who were apparently opposed to economic austerity moves and upset by a military anticorruption drive. Despite international appeals for clemency, Correia and five of his associates were executed in July 1986.

A new National Assembly was designated on June 15, 1989, by and from the regional councils, for which direct single-party balloting had been conducted on June 1. On June 19 General Vieira was reelected to a second term as president of the Council of State, which two days later named its former vice president, Col. Iafai CAMARA, as first vice president and its former secretary, Dr. Vasco CABRAL, as second vice president. Both of the vice presidencies were abandoned in a government restructuring of December 27, 1991, that marked another restoration of the post of prime minister, to which former agriculture minister Carlos CORREIA was appointed.

In July 1992 the PAIGC agreed to the formation of a national commission with responsibility for facilitating the country's first multiparty balloting. However, the elections, originally scheduled for November and December, were rescheduled in October for March 1993, at which time they were again postponed. In July the Council of State set March 27, 1994, as the new date for simultaneous presidential and legislative balloting, with a further postponement in February 1994 to late May. At the poll that was finally held on July 3, Vieira, who had resigned his commission to qualify as a candidate under a 1991 constitutional revision, was credited with winning 46 percent of valid presidential votes, as contrasted with 21.9 percent for runner-up Kumba YALA of the opposition Social Renewal Party (*Partido para a Renovação Social*—PRS); concurrently, the ruling PAIGC was awarded 64 of 100 parliamentary seats. Vieira went on to secure reelection by defeating Yala, who had been accorded unanimous opposition endorsement, in a runoff on August 7.

On October 25, 1994, Vieira named a senior PAIGC official, Manuel Saturnino da COSTA, to succeed Correia as prime minister. Observers attributed the delay between the election and Costa's appointment to a deep division in the ruling party between its founding members, including Costa, and their younger colleagues, who desired more "pragmatic" economic policy-making. On November 11 Costa named a new government, which included members of both PAIGC tendencies.

On May 27, 1997, President Vieira dismissed Costa in the midst of what the president described as a "serious political crisis." Costa's ouster came as government troops were deployed to quell riots sparked by state workers who were angered at poor working conditions and the government's failure to pay salary arrears. On June 5 Vieira reappointed Carlos Correia as prime minister, and Correia formed a new government the following day. However, Correia's appointment was immediately contested by opposition legislators, who asserted that the president was constitutionally required to consult with the assembly prior to naming a prime minister. Subsequently, a virtual legislative dead-lock ensued as opposition legislators refused to consider the government's initiatives while their legal challenge was being considered by the courts. On October 7 the Supreme Court ruled that the administration had erred, and on October 11 the president dismissed Correia; however, following negotiations with legislative leaders, on October 13 Vieira reappointed Correia.

In January 1998 President Vieira dismissed his military chief of staff, Gen. Ansumane MANE, charging him with "dereliction of duty" for allegedly failing to stem the illegal transfer of arms from Guinea-Bissau to Senegalese rebels. Subsequently, in early June, troops directed by General Mane overran the national airport and an army base in Bra as part of a declared effort to remove Vieira from power. Facing minimal resistance from a small contingent of pro-presidential forces, the rebels quickly secured control of a majority of the country. However, bolstered by Senegalese and Guinean troops, Vieira's loyalists fought the rebels to a standstill in Bissau. On August 26 regional mediators in Cape Verde brokered a cease-fire agreement that held until October, when fierce fighting was once again reported. In November the two sides signed a second cease-fire accord in Abuja, Nigeria. The accord included provisions for presidential and legislative balloting in March 1999, as well as the formation of a unity government comprising representatives selected by the president as well as the rebels. In addition, the agreement called for the replacement of the Senegalese and Guinean troops with a regional peacekeeping force supplied by the Economic Community of West African States (ECOWAS). On December 3 Vieira, under strong pressure from the military rebels, named Francisco FADUL, General Mane's aide-de-camp, to replace Correia as prime minister.

In early January 1999 the national balloting envisioned for March was indefinitely postponed as contentious debate continued in Bissau over implementation of the Abuja accord. Fierce fighting was reported in the capital in early February; however, a new cease-fire agreement (based on the Abuja document) was reached on February 4, and ECOWAS troops began arriving en masse soon thereafter. On

February 20 Fadul and his nine-member cabinet were sworn in.

Amid reports that troops loyal to the president were seeking to rearm, fresh fighting erupted on May 6, 1999, and the following day General Mane claimed that his forces had overthrown Vieira, who agreed to the unconditional surrender of the government on May 10. (Vieira left the country in June.) On May 14 Mane named the president of the assembly, Malam Bacai SANHA, interim president; furthermore, Mane announced that election preparations could continue as scheduled and that he would not be a presidential candidate. In early July the military junta promulgated a new constitution (see Constitution and government, below).

In the first round of presidential balloting on November 28–29, 1999, the PRS's Kumba Yala led a field of 11 presidential aspirants with 34.81 percent of the vote, while interim president Sanha finished second with 23.34 percent. Meanwhile, at concurrent legislative polling the PRS led a crowded field with 38 seats while the PAIGC's representation fell to 24, which was 4 less than the second-place Guinea-Bissau Resistance–Bah Fatah Movement (*Resistência da Guiné-Bissau–Movimento Bah-Fatah*—RGB-MB).

Having failed to garner the vote share necessary to stave off a second round of balloting, Yala faced off against Sanha on January 16, 2000. Yala won easily, capturing 72 percent of the vote, and on January 24 he named a PRS leader, Caetano NTCHAMA, prime minister. On February 19 Ntchama was sworn in as the head of a government that included representatives from four political parties and a number of independents, but no members of the PAIGC. However, Ntchama was buffeted by tensions between the PRS and the RGB-MB; in September the RGB-MB ministers were dismissed but they were reinstated shortly thereafter. In the meantime, conflict between President Yala and the former head of the junta, Ansumane Mane, resurfaced. In November, uneasy with some recent military appointments, Mane announced that he had "reinstated" himself as the chief of staff, and clashes were reported between

a few troops following Mane and the majority of the army, which remained loyal to the Yala. Some opposition figures, most prominently from the PAIGC, the Union for Change (*União para a Mudança*—UM), and the Democratic Alliance (*Aliança Democrática*—AD), were arrested for allegedly supporting Mane. On November 30, Mane was killed by government troops surrounding his enclave in Quinhamel, north of Bissau.

In January 2001 the RGB-MB left the governing coalition in reaction to an earlier reshuffle the party claimed unfairly favored the PRS. In March Yala dismissed Ntchama, who was reportedly having medical problems, and named an independent, Faustino Fadut IMBALI, as the new prime minister. Imbali had run in the 1999 presidential elections and had supported Yala in the second round in January 2000. He had also served in Ntchama's government as the deputy prime minister. Imbali formed a government including the PRS, the RGB-MB, the PAIGC, the Guinean Civic Forum (*Foro Civico da Guiné*—FCG), the Social Democratic Party (*Partido Social Democrata*—PSD), the Democratic Convergence Party (*Partido da Convergência Democrática*—PCD), and independents. The PAIGC and the RGB-MB, however, reportedly continued their critical stance toward Yala's presidency and some of Imbali's policies. Yala dismissed Imbali on December 7, 2001, and appointed Alamara NHASSE of the PRS as the new prime minister the following day. Nhasse's new government, formed on December 12, included members from the PRS and the PCD as well as independents.

In the wake of increasing tension between President Yala and Prime Minister Nhasse concerning ministerial and judicial appointments, Yala dismissed Nhasse on November 15, 2002. On November 16 Yala appointed Mario PIRES of the RPS to head a temporary caretaker government. Yala also dissolved the assembly and announced that new legislative elections would be held in early 2003. However, that balloting was postponed several times as the government was perceived as becoming increasingly authoritarian (see Current issues, below).

The military deposed President Yala on September 14, 2003, in a takeover that appeared to have broad domestic support. The army's chief of staff, Gen. Verissimo Correia SEABRA, proclaimed himself interim president and named a military council to conduct governmental affairs pending the appointment of a new civilian government. (Yala was permitted to "resign" as of September 17.) On September 28, Henrique ROSA, a prominent businessman with no formal political ties, was appointed interim president, while Antonio Artur SANHA of the PRS was designated head of a caretaker cabinet.

Negotiations between the major political groups and the military subsequently yielded an agreement providing for legislative elections within six months and presidential balloting within 18 months. Concurrently, a 56-member civilian Transitional National Council was appointed to advise the government pending the new elections. The PAIGC secured a plurality of 45 seats in the March 28 and 30, 2004, assembly poll, followed by the PRS with 35 seats. Carlos GOMES, the president of the PAIGC, was appointed prime minister on May 12 to head a cabinet comprising the PAIGC and independents.

In the first round of presidential balloting on June 19, 2005, the PAIGC's Sanha received 35.45 percent of the vote, followed by Vieira (running as an independent) with 28.87 percent, and Yala of the PRS with 25 percent. Ten other candidates, representing 6 other parties and independents, each won less than 3 percent of the vote. Since Sanha failed to gain a clear majority, he faced Vieira in a runoff on July 24. Several weeks later, Vieira was declared the winner with 52.35 percent of the vote. In August, the Supreme Court rejected Sanha's request to annul the election, and the PAIGC government finally conceded defeat on September 27. Amid continuing friction with Prime Minister Carlos Gomes, Vieira was sworn in on October 1, and on October 30 he dismissed the prime minister in favor of PAIGC dissident Aristides GOMES (see PAIGC under Political Parties, below). On November 9 Vieira appointed a five-party coalition government comprising the PAIGC (split into pro-Vieira and pro–Carlos Gomes factions), the PRS, the PCD, the United Social Democratic Party (*Partido Unido Social Democrata*—PUSD), and the Electoral Union (*União Eleitoral*—UE). In early 2006, court rulings upheld the appointment of Aristides Gomes, striking down the PAIGC's argument that it was unconstitutional since Gomes had been suspended from the party (for his support of Vieira) and that the president was obligated to appoint a majority-party member to head the government.

Constitution and Government

The constitution of May 1984 gave the PAIGC the right to define "the bases of state policy in all fields"; for legislative purposes it reestablished the National People's Assembly, members of which were to be designated by eight regional councils. The assembly was, in turn, empowered to elect a 15-member Council of State, whose president was to serve as head of state and commander in chief of the armed forces.

In early 1989 a six-member National Commission, headed by Fidélis Cabral D'ALMADA, was established by the PAIGC Central Committee to revise the constitution in accordance with recent economic reform and structural adjustment policies. Thereafter, in April 1990, President Vieira promised "freer and more democratic elections," and in August he characterized the democracy movement as "irreversible." On January 9, 1991, he formally committed himself to political pluralism in a speech that was promptly endorsed by the PAIGC. On May 4 the assembly approved a constitutional amendment voiding the republic's "revolutionary" character and stripping the PAIGC of its status as the "leading force in society." Both president and legislators were henceforth to be popularly elected for five-year terms. Four days later a framework law on political parties won legislative approval, with numerous opposition groups subsequently being recognized in preparation for the country's first contested elections (originally scheduled for late 1992, but not held until mid-1994).

In July 1999 the military junta led by Gen. Ansumane Mane discarded the 1991 basic law in favor of a new constitution that included provisions for presidential term limits (two five-year terms), the abolition of the death penalty, and the establishment of strict residency requirements for government officeholders. In November the junta drafted a new document, a so-called *Magna Carta*, reportedly styled after the basic law imposed in Portugal following its 1974 military coup; however, General Mane withdrew the controversial draft law (which provided for ten years of military rule) following an outcry from Bissau's political leaders. Furthermore, the junta amended the article of the July document that excluded would-be presidential candidates whose parents were foreign-born. In October 2000 President Yala named a State Council to "advise him on decisions such as declaration of war and state of emergency." Some observers suggested that the establishment of the council substantively finalized the transition to civilian rule. (For details of governmental arrangements following the September 2003 coup, see Political background, above.)

Foreign Relations

During the struggle for independence, Guinea-Bissau received economic and military assistance from many Communist countries, including the Soviet Union, Cuba, and China. A subsequent deterioration in relations with the USSR because of alleged encroachment upon the country's fishing grounds appeared to have been reversed in early 1978 with a promise of Soviet assistance in modernizing the country's fishing industry. In May 1982, on the other hand, President Vieira replaced two strongly pro-Soviet cabinet ministers with Western-trained "technocrats" and appealed for development aid from non-Communist sources.

In November 1980 Guinea was the first country to recognize Guinea-Bissau's Revolutionary Council; earlier disputes over offshore oil exploration rights had been defused by former Guinean President Sékou Touré's announcement that Guinea would cooperate with other African states in developing on- and offshore resources. Similar controversy with Senegal erupted in early 1984, involving questions about the legality of offshore borders drawn by the French and Portuguese governments before independence. In February 1985 the International Court of Justice (ICJ) offered a settlement of the Bissau-Conakry border question that was accepted by both governments, while in March a meeting between Vieira and Senegalese President Diouf resulted in assignment of the latter dispute to an ad hoc international tribunal. A decision by the tribunal on July 31, 1989, in favor of Senegal, was immediately rejected by Bissau in an appeal to the ICJ.

A further border clash with Senegal occurred in April and May 1990, leaving 17 dead and drawing charges by Dakar that Bissau was harboring Casamance separatist guerrillas (see article on Senegal). Tensions eased however in the wake of a meeting in the border town of São Domingos on May 29 at which the two countries agreed to a mutual troop withdrawal and termination of aid to each other's insurgent movements. In April 1991 Vieira called for the Casamance rebels to lay down their arms and take advantage of Senegal's multiparty system. Subsequently, in May Guinea-Bissau was the site of cease-fire talks between Dakar and Casamance representatives. However, in early February 1995 relations between Bissau and Dakar were again strained when Senegal bombed a Guinea-Bissau border village in retaliation for Bissau's alleged support of two recent Casamance rebel attacks against Senegalese military sites. Relations again eased on June 12, when a visit by Senegalese President Abdou Diouf produced a declaration to abandon border hostility and an agreement to share equally in offshore mineral and energy resources.

A meeting with President Pereira of Cape Verde in Mozambique on June 17–18, 1982, yielded an announcement that diplomatic relations would be restored. Despite "reconciliation," the unification sought by Cabral became more and more distant as island influence was purged from the mainland party, with no reference to eventual merger being mentioned in the 1984 Guinea-Bissau constitution.

The last vestige of the PAIGC alliances, a joint shipping line, was liquidated on February 29, 1988; both countries cited the nonviolent action as a sign of their "political maturation."

In early 1996 the Vieira administration agreed to ratify a 1993 maritime joint exploration pact with Senegal, ignoring its domestic critics' charges that the agreement unfairly favored the neighboring state, and in June Bissau and Dakar signed a security collaboration accord. (On the basis of such accords Senegal and Guinea dispatched troops to Guinea-Bissau in 1998 in an effort to quell the military uprising.)

In February 1999 the leaders of rebel forces in Guinea-Bissau claimed that French battleships had fired on their positions. Paris denied the charges. Following the military coup in May, ECOWAS peacekeeping forces departed, with both the junta and its regional sponsors agreeing that they were "redundant." On the other hand, a UN contingent arrived in Bissau in June in accordance with provisions in the February cease-fire. The UN officials were charged with organizing elections, and in March 2000 their mandate was extended. Among the myriad problems confronting international mediators was the need to smooth relations between Bissau and the Senegalese and Guinean governments, both of whom had sent troops in an ultimately futile attempt to reinforce the Vieira administration. Guinea-Bissau's relations with Senegal were further strained in April following an attack by Casamance rebels, who had (according to Senegal) infiltrated from Guinea-Bissau's territory. In March 2002, the leader of one of the main rebel factions was arrested and deported to Senegal. The situation subsequently improved and in September the border was reopened and a joint security commission was formed.

Although the international community initially condemned the overthrow of Yala, Guinea-Bissau's external relations were quickly repaired. Once Rosa assumed office, he made diplomatic visits to a number of neighboring states, and Portugal as well. International aid was resumed soon after the March 2004 elections and included pledges to provide the funds needed to pay the military and civil

service until after the June 2005 presidential elections. In addition, the small UN mission charged with monitoring the border between Senegal and Guinea-Bissau had its mandate extended for one year. Conflict at the border reignited in early 2006 (see Current issues, below), with the Casamance rebel leader reportedly refusing to participate in peace talks.

Current Issues

Conflict broke out between President Yala and the judiciary in late 2001 when Yala appointed three supreme court judges who had been dismissed in 1993. After criticism by coalition members RGB-MB and the PAIGC, the assembly in October approved a motion of no confidence against the president, who then threatened to suspend the legislature. A large demonstration in the capital in late November demanded that Yala resign. The appointment of Alamara Nhasse, theretofore minister of the interior and a "PRS strongman," as new prime minister did little to calm the waters, opposition parties denouncing the dismissal of Prime Minister Imbali despite Yala's assertion that Imbali's government should have been held accountable for the country's economic problems.

Political instability continued into mid-2002, Yala claiming he had survived a coup attempt in May that he attributed to "Gambian influence." President Yala's dismissal of Nhasse and dissolution of the assembly in November initiated a period of intensified repression of dissent that included the arrest of a number of prominent opposition figures and the closure of private radio stations that had criticized the administration. Tensions intensified in 2003 when soldiers threatened to mutiny over payment arrears and schools were closed because teachers had not been paid. Consequently, the September 2003 coup elicited little criticism within the populace, particularly after it had become clear that the military intended a quick return to civilian government through new elections.

The Rosa administration reopened schools after the World Bank loaned money for teacher salaries, and most international aid was restored after the May 2004 legislative elections were deemed free and fair by international observers. However, the new Gomes government faced severe problems, including rivalry among heavily armed ethnic groups, reported continued discontent within some sections of the military, and depressed economic conditions. Complicating matters in March 2005 was Yala's announcement that he planned to run as the PRS candidate in the June presidential balloting, despite the fact that he had been "banned" from politics for five years after the 2003 coup. (In May 2005 Yala and Vieira were declared eligible to run after both had initially been barred.) Subsequently, "serious tension" was reported after Yala insisted on May 15 he was still president, based on a court ruling that his forced resignation after the coup was invalid. A few days later, Yala briefly occupied presidential headquarters before being removed by government troops. A huge demonstration in support of Yala took place before the June first-round balloting, followed by violent protests in the capital days after his defeat in which three people were killed and five injured in clashes with police. Hundreds of Yala's backers accused the government of vote-rigging and reportedly tried to overrun the National Electoral Commission. Ultimately, Yala supported Vieira in the two-way runoff in July, which was conducted fairly, according to international observers.

Vieira dismissed Carlos Gomes as prime minister on October 30, replacing him with PAIGC dissident Aristides Gomes. The new coalition government was sworn in on November 10, though controversy continued to surround Vieira's choice of a prime minister (see PAIGC under Political Parties, below). In April 2006, the PUSD, one of ten parties that backed Vieira in his presidential bid, reportedly withdrew from the government, though it was unclear whether a formal action was taken.

Also in 2006, the army resumed its offensive against the Casamance rebels, resulting in some 12,000 civilians fleeing the border region and prompting calls for a cease-fire by the UN. By mid-May, the UN appealed for $3.6 million to help those most vulnerable in northern Guinea-Bissau who were cut off from the rest of the country by landmines, leaving farmers unable to get to the cashew fields in time for the harvest.

Political Parties

On May 8, 1991, the National People's Assembly approved the formation of opposition parties, thereby formalizing events set in motion in April 1990. The principal requirements for registration are that each group present to the Supreme Tribunal of Justice a petition signed by 1,000 eligible voters, at least 50 of whom must reside in each of the country's regions and the district of Bissau. By early 1993 more than two dozen parties had been formed, most of which had been legalized.

Government and Government-Supportive Parties

African Party for the Independence of Guinea and Cape Verde (*Partido Africano da Independência da Guiné e Cabo Verde*—PAIGC). Formed in 1956 by Amílcar Cabral and others, the PAIGC established external offices in Conakry, Guinea, in 1960 and began armed struggle against the Portuguese authorities in 1963. During its 28 years as the country's only lawful party, the PAIGC was formally committed to the principle of "democratic centralism." Its policy-making and administrative organs include a Central Committee (the Supreme Council of the Struggle), a National Council, a Permanent Committee, and a Secretariat.

Until the coup of November 1980 the party leadership was binational, with Aristides Pereira, president of Cape Verde, serving as secretary general and President Luis Cabral of Guinea-Bissau as deputy secretary. On January 19, 1981, the Cape Verdean branch decided to break with the mainland organization, proclaiming, on the following day, an autonomous African Party for the Independence of Cape Verde (PAICV).

In May 1990 General Vieira instructed the party to begin preparations for the introduction of political pluralism. Accordingly, the Central

Committee in July proposed the adoption of "integral multipartyism," and in September it announced a schedule for implementation of the new system, which was formally approved at an extraordinary party congress held January 21–25, 1991. At its fifth ordinary congress in November 1991 the PAIGC voted to widen intraparty democracy and restructure its executive apparatus by dropping the post of secretary general in favor of a party president and national secretary.

At the party's sixth ordinary congress in May 1998 delegates reelected Vieira to the PAIGC presidency and approved the appointment of Paulo Medina to the newly created post of permanent secretary. Despite Vieira's positive account of the meeting, observers asserted that the PAIGC emerged from the congress further factionalized. Thereafter, it was unclear what effect the military uprising of June 1998 would have on the PAIGC, although the vehemently anti-Vieira stance of Francisco Fadul, a longtime party member who was sworn in as prime minister in February 1999, appeared to portend further cleavage.

In the wake of Vieira's removal from office, Manuel Saturnino da Costa was chosen on May 12, 1999, to assume the PAIGC party presidency, and Flavio Provenca was named interim secretary. The party held an extraordinary congress in Bissau September 3–9, with the stated goal of preparing for presidential and legislative polling. Delegates voted to expel Vieira, Carlos CORREIA, and a number of former ministers affiliated with Vieira, and the (then) defense minister and ally of the Mane junta, Francis Benante, was elected as the new PAIGC president.

The PAIGC won 24 seats in the 1999 legislative elections, and its candidate, interim president of the republic Malam Bacai SANHA, won 23.34 percent of the votes in the first round in November 1999 presidential elections. He lost in the second round in January 2000 with 28 percent of the vote.

The PAIGC assumed an opposition stance to the PRS-led government formed in February 2000. The party reportedly came under intense scrutiny after allegedly supporting Ansumane Mane's failed bid to reinstate himself as the chief of staff in November. Benante was subsequently arrested and then released for alleged possession of arms, as were other opposition figures. The PAIGC accepted a post in the cabinet announced in March 2001 but remained highly critical of some of the administration's policies. In May the PAIGC voted in the legislature to approve the government's program, but only after amnesty was granted to prisoners from the events of the previous November. The new government appointed in December reportedly did not include any PAIGC members. In 2004 the PAIGC became the largest party in the assembly, receiving 33.88 percent of the vote and 45 seats. Party leader Carlos Gomes became prime minister on May 12, 2004, and subsequently formed a government of PAIGC members and independents. Gomes declared that he would not seek the presidency in 2005 and would instead concentrate on his role as prime minister. Following the election of Vieira in July, friction intensified within the party between those who supported Vieira, including party vice president Aristides Gomes, and those who remained loyal to Carlos Gomes. In September, Aristides Gomes and several other dissident members were suspended, and a month later 14 of the party's 45 legislators resigned, declaring themselves independents. Aristides Gomes joined with some of those dissidents and others from various opposition groups to form the **Forum for the Convergence of Development** (FCD), reportedly in an attempt to create a new majority in the assembly. The continued dissension between Vieira and the Carlos Gomes supporters in the PAIGC resulted in a delay in Vieira's inauguration until October because the pro-Gomes faction refused to recognize his authority. The rift culminated in Vieira's dismissal of the prime minister on October 30, and his appointment on November 2 of Aristides Gomes as the new prime minister. For its part, the PAIGC postponed indefinitely its extraordinary congress scheduled for October and in November named a new chair, Martin Ndafa Kabi. Meanwhile, Carlos Gomes' faction of the party continued to contest the appointment of Aristides Gomes, claiming it was unconstitutional, but court rulings in 2006 upheld Vieira's action. The final status of Aristides

Gomes and his supporters in the PAIGC remained unclear as of April 2006.

Leaders: Martin Ndafa KABI (Chair), Carlos GOMES, Malam Bacai SANHA (2005 presidential candidate), Manuel Saturnino da COSTA, Paulo MEDINA.

Social Renewal Party (*Partido para a Renovação Social*—PRS). The PRS was formed in January 1992 by seven defectors from the FDS (below) led by Kumba Yala, who accused the parent group of secretly collaborating with the PAIGC. Yala was runner-up to Vieira in the 1994 presidential balloting, with the party winning 12 of 100 assembly seats. In November Yala rejected an offer to join the Costa government. Meanwhile, the PRS reportedly teamed with the Union for Change (UM, below) and the Front of Struggle for the Liberation of Guinea (FLING, below) to form a voting bloc in the assembly.

On November 10, 1995, Yala told a Portuguese daily, *Jornal de Notícias*, that the PAIGC was bereft of both "international credibility" and the "confidence of the people." Calling for early elections, Yala warned that while the PRS was opposed to a civil war, its wide support within the military would allow it to take power in "five or ten minutes."

In January 1998 Yala announced that he would form a parallel government if elections (then scheduled for midyear) were postponed. Thereafter, the PRS joined with other opposition groups demanding Vieira's resignation in early 1999. The PRS won 38 seats in the 1999 legislative elections, and Yala won the presidency in January 2000 with 72 percent of the vote in the second round. In 2003 the party was rife with conflict between those who supported Yala and those who did not. This divide led party president Alamara Nhasse to resign his post and lead a group of defectors to form a new group, the National Reconciliation Party (see below).

In the March 2004 elections, the PRS came in second with 24.76 percent of the vote and 35 seats. After Yala's defeat in the June 2005 presidential election, at least three people were killed during a protest by his supporters and Sanha was briefly detained by police.

Leaders: Alberto NAMBEIA (Interim Chair), Kumba YALA (Former President of the Republic and 2005 presidential candidate), Ibrahima Sori DJALO, Caetano NTCHAMA (Former Prime Minister), Antonio Artur SANHA (Former Prime Minister and Secretary General).

United Social Democratic Party (*Partido Unido Social Democrata*—PUSD). The PUSD was led by former prime minister Vítor Saúde Maria, who left the PAIGC in 1984 and was a member of the FDS before launching the present formation in June 1991.

In March 1993 Saúde Maria denounced PRD leader da Costa's detainment for alleged involvement in a coup attempt, accusing the government of launching an unprovoked opposition crackdown. Saúde Maria died in October 1999. His replacement as party president, Francisco José Fadul, was chosen at a party congress in late 2000. In the 2004 elections, the PUSD became the third-largest parliamentary party with 16.1 percent of the vote and 17 seats. (On April 5, 2006, it was reported that the PUSD had withdrawn from the government in a dispute regarding the justice minister, although it was unclear what the status of the party was thereafter.)

Leader: Francisco José FADUL (Party President, Former Prime Minister, and 2005 presidential candidate).

United Platform (*Plataforma Unida*—PLATAF). This electoral coalition, led by Helder VAZ and Victor MANDINGA, was formed to contest the 2004 legislative elections. Two members of the coalition, the Democratic Front and the Democratic Convergence Party, were also linked in a separate coalition as the Democratic Alliance (see Democratic Convergence Party, below). In 2004, the former leader of the PLATAF, Francisca VAZ Turpin, filed papers to form a new party, the Union of Guinea-Bissau Patriots (UPG).

Democratic Convergence Party (*Partido da Convergência Democrática*—PCD). The PCD first surfaced in the early 1990s under the leadership of a former PAIGC member, Victor

Mandinga. The PCD apparently served as the core component of the **Democratic Alliance** (*Aliança Democrática*—AD) coalition that was credited with winning four seats (including one by Mandinga) in the 1999 legislative balloting. Mandinga supported Ansumane Mane in the events of late 2000, and he was briefly detained by security forces. Mandinga, routinely referenced as leader of the AD, subsequently remained a highly vocal and visible critic of President Yala. Meanwhile, several cabinet ministers installed in March 2001 and December 2001 were referenced as PCD members. In 2005, Mandinga was named minister of finance.

Leader: Victor MANDINGA.

Democratic and Social Front (*Frente Democrática e Social*—FDS). The FDS was launched in early 1990 by former PAIGC president Rafael Barbosa to fight against the "dictatorship" of the existing system. A cofounder of the PAIGC, Barbosa had been accused of collaboration with the Portuguese during the liberation struggle, convicted of treason in 1974, and imprisoned. He was released briefly upon Vieira's seizure of power in 1980, but was again imprisoned after calling for the expulsion of Cape Verdeans from Guinea-Bissau. He was formally amnestied in 1987.

Following a contentious FDS leadership meeting on January 15, 1992, the two-year-old group suffered its third split as seven members left to form the PRS. The FDS won a single seat in the legislature in 1999. In advance of the 2004 assembly election, the FDS formed a coalition with the PUSD, the PRD, and the LGBPE.

Leader: Rafael BARBOSA.

Front of Struggle for the Liberation of Guinea (*Frente da Luta para a Liberação da Guiné*—FLING). Formerly known as the Front for the Liberation and Independence of Guinea-Bissau (*Frente para a Libertação e Independência da Guiné-Bissau*, FLING claimed to have been organized in 1954 and, as a group opposed to the unification of Cape Verde and the mainland, to have initiated the armed struggle against Portugal. In March 1981 it was announced that it had been dissolved, with its militants accepted into the PAIGC, although remnants of the organization continued to be active, primarily as exiles. It assumed its present name, while retaining the original acronym, in 1991. Its leader, François Mendy Kankoila, returned in 1992 after 40 years in exile. The group applied for legalization in 1992 and won a single seat in 1994.

In June 1996 President Vieira sued Kankoila and suspended him from the National Assembly after Kankoila accused Vieira of orchestrating the disappearance of a FLING member.

Leaders: François Mendy KANKOILA, Catengul MENDES (1999 presidential candidate).

Other minor parties in the PLATAF include the **Group of Independent Democrats** (*Grupo de Democratas Independentes*—GDI), which was formed by Helder Vaz and dissidents from the RGB-MB; and the **Democratic Front** (*Frente Democrática*—FD), led by Canjura INJAI.

Electoral Union (*União Eleitoral*—UE). The UE was formed in 2002 to contest legislative elections by a group of small leftist and center-left parties. In the 2004 elections, the UE gained two seats in the assembly.

Leader: Joaquim BALDE.

Guinea-Bissau League for the Protection of the Ecology (*Liga da Guiné-Bissau para a Protecção da Ecologia*—LGBPE). The LGBPE applied for legalization in July 1993. The league's president, Bubacar Rachid Djalo, ran in the first round of the presidential elections in November 1999 and backed the PRS's Kumba Yala in the second round in January 2000. Djalo was given a junior cabinet post in the PRS-led government in February but was not reappointed in the new government formed in March 2001.

Leader: Bubacar Rachid DJALO (President and 1999 presidential candidate).

Social Democratic Party (*Partido Social Democrata*—PSD). Founded by dissident Guinea-Bissau Resistance–Bah Fatah Movement (RGB-MB) members, the PSD was legalized on August 21, 1995. It won three seats in the legislative elections in 1999 and backed the PRS's Kumba Yala in the second round of the presidential elections in January 2000. Although some PSD members had previously taken part in PRS-led coalition governments, the cabinet installed in December 2001 reportedly did not include any PSD members. Party leader Joaquim Balde was the spokesman for the National Transition Council following the coup in 2003.

Leaders: Joaquim BALDE (1999 presidential candidate), Gaspar FERNANDES (Secretary General), João Seco MANE.

Other minor parties in the UE include the **Guinean Socialist Party** (*Partido Socialista Guineense*—PSG), led by Cirilo VIEIRA; and the **Party of Renovation and Progress** (*Partido da Renovação e Progresso*—PRP), led by Mamadu DJALO.

Other Legislative Parties

United Popular Alliance (*Aliança Popular Unida*—APU). The APU was formed prior to the 2004 legislative elections as an electoral coalition between the ASG and the small **Guinean Popular Party** (*Partido Popular Guineense*—PPG), led by Joao Tatis SA. It won one seat in the 2004 assembly election. In May 2004 the APU signed an agreement with the PAIGC and the UE to "ensure stability." Sa ran last in the field of 13 first-round presidential candidates in 2005.

Socialist Alliance of Guinea-Bissau (*Aliança Socialista da Guiné-Bissau*—ASG). The ASG was launched in May 2000 under the leadership of Fernando Gomes, a human rights advocate. Gomes had run as an independent candidate in the first round of presidential elections in November 1999, receiving 7 percent of the vote. He backed Kumba Yala in the second round. Gomes and the ASG, however, were subsequently among the fiercest critics of the government, especially on the issues of human rights and freedom of the press. Gomes was briefly detained in late May 1999 for having released a communiqué strongly critical of the government.

Leader: Fernando GOMES.

Other Parties and Groups

Guinea-Bissau Resistance–Bah Fatah Movement (*Resistência da Guiné-Bissau–Movimento Bah-Fatah*—RGB-MB). Launched in Lisbon, Portugal, in 1986, the RGB-MB was technically precluded from using Bafata in its official title because of a legal prohibition of the use of an ethnic, regional, or (in this case) town name for political parties. As a result it substituted "Bah-Fatah" for "Bafata" prior to registration in December 1991. RGB-MB founder Domingos Fernandes Gomes returned after six years in exile on May 18, 1992. The party was runner-up to the PAIGC in the 1994 legislative poll, winning 19 seats. In November Fernandes refused an invitation to join the Costa government.

In late 1998 the RGB-MB announced that it would not participate in reconciliation talks with President Vieira and called for his resignation. The party had been a vocal critic of Vieira throughout the military uprising, which it had allegedly described as an internecine struggle within the PAIGC.

In the 1999 legislative elections, the RGB-MB won 28 seats and became the second-largest party in the legislature. In the first round of presidential balloting in November 1999 the RGB-MB's candidate was Helder VAZ Lopes, who had become the party chair in September. In the second round in January 2000 Vaz Lopes told his supporters to vote for a candidate of their choice.

The RGB-MB was included in the PRS-led government formed in February 2000. In September all the ministers from the party were dismissed, but they were reinstated shortly thereafter. In January 2001, however, the RGB-MB left the government in reaction to an earlier reshuffle the party claimed unfairly favored their senior partner, the PRS. In March the party was given representation in Faustino Imbali's new government, although it reportedly remained highly critical of Kumba Yala's presidency and of some of Imbali's policies. The government appointed in December reportedly did not include any RGB-MB members. In the 2004 legislative elections, the RGB-MB only received 1.85 percent of the vote and consequently no seats in the assembly. Party leader Domingos Fernandes Gomes announced he would run in the 2005 presidential election, but his name did not appear on the list of candidates. Party leader Salvador Tchongo dropped out the 2005 presidential race, citing financial difficulties and a lack of confidence in the process.

Leaders: Domingos FERNANDES Gomes (1994 presidential candidate), Salvador TCHONGO (President), Mario Ujssumane BALDE (Secretary General).

Union for Change (*União para a Mudança*—UM). The UM was originally organized prior to the 1994 election as a six-party electoral coalition that included the left-of-center Democratic Front (*Frente Democrática*—FD), led by Marcelino BAPTISTA; the United Democratic Movement (*Movimento para a Unidade e a Democracia*—Mude), led by Felintro Vaz MARTINS; the Democratic Party of Progress (*Partido Democrático do Progresso*—PDP); and the Party of Renovation and Development (*Partido da Renovação e Desenvolvimento*—PRD), a grouping of PAIGC dissidents led by João da Costa; as well as the FDS and LGBPE (above), which did not join their partners in a formal merger in November 1995. The Union secured six seats in 1994 and three in 1999. The party reportedly came under scrutiny after Ansumane Mane's failed bid to reinstate himself as the chief of staff in November 2000. The group's secretary general, Agnello Regala, was arrested for allegedly supporting Mane. He was released in December. In the 2004 election, the UM received only 2 percent of the vote and therefore no seats in the assembly.

Leaders: Manuel Rambout BARCELOS, Amine Michel SAAD (PDP), Agnello REGALA (Secretary General).

Guinean Civic Forum (*Foro Civico da Guiné*—FCG). The FCG's Antonieta Rosa Gomes competed in the 1999 presidential election, and in 2000 she was appointed to the Ntchama government. However, she was dismissed in November 2001. The new government appointed in December 2001 reportedly did not include any FCG members. The FCG received less than 1 percent of the vote in the 2004 elections. Gomes ran for president in 2005 on the FCG ticket in affiliation with the Social Democracy (SD) group.

Leader: Antonieta Rosa GOMES (1999 and 2005 presidential candidate).

National Union for Democracy and Progress (*União Nacional para a Democracia e o Progresso*—UNDP). The UNDP was formed in December 1997 by Aboubacar Balde, a former PAIGC official, who was reportedly angered at the ruling party's failure to organize a congress in mid-1997. The party was officially recognized in April 1998, and won one legislative seat in 1999. The UNDP reportedly came under scrutiny after Ansumane Mane's failed bid to reinstall himself as the chief of staff in November 2000. In the 2004 elections, the UNDP received 1.1 percent of the vote. Balde dropped out as a 2005 presidential candidate for financial reasons.

Leader: Aboubacar BALDE (1999 presidential candidate).

National Reconciliation Party (*Partido Nacional do Reconciliation*—PRN). Formed in October 2004 by former PRS leader Alamara Nhasse, the PRN drew a large number of senior PRS figures away from the PRS, including a former defense minister and the former mayor of Bissau.

Leader: Alamara NHASSE (Former Prime Minister).

Other minor parties that contested the 2004 legislative elections include the **Guinean Democratic Party** (*Partido Democrático Guineense*—PDG), led by Manuel CA; the **Manifest Party**

Cabinet

As of April 1, 2006

Prime Minister; Acting Interior Minister	Aristides Gomes (PAIGC)

Ministers

Agriculture and Rural Development	Sola Nquilin Na Bitchita (PRS)
Civil Service and Labor	Carlos Costa (PRS)
Defense	Helder Proenca (PAIGC)
Economy	Issufo Sanha (PAIGC)
Finance	Victor Mandinga (PCD)
Fisheries and Marine Economy	Abdu Mane (PAIGC)
Foreign Affairs and International Cooperation	Antonio Isaac Monteiro (PAIGC)
Health	Antonia Mendes Teixeira (PAIGC) [f]
Industry, Commerce, and Handicrafts	Pascoal Domingos Batica (PUSD)
Justice	Namuano Dias Gomes (PUSD)
Natural Resources	Aristides Ocante da Silva (PAIGC)
National and Higher Education	Tcherno Djalo (ind.)
Presidency of the Council of Ministers and Relations with Parliament	Rui Dia de Sousa (PAIGC)
Public Works and Urban Affairs	Carlitos Barai (PRS)
Regional Administration and Tourism	Francisco Conduto de Pina (PAIGC)
Social Solidarity, Family Affairs, and the Fight Against Poverty	Adelina Na Tamba (PRS) [f]
Transport and Communications	Admiro Nelson Belo (PRS)
Territorial Administration	Braima Embalo (UE)

Secretaries of State

Administrative Reform	Jose Braima Dafe (PUSD)
Budget, Treasury, and Fiscal Affairs	Jose Djo (PAIGC)
Energy	Augusto Poquena (PRS)
International Cooperation	Tibna Samba Nawana (PRS)
Planning and Regional Development	Purna Bia (PRS)
Public Order	Baciro Dabo (ind.)
Social Solidarity	Joao de Barros (ind.)
War Veterans	Nhasse Na Man (PAIGC)
Youth Culture and Sports	Mario Martins (PAIGC)

[f] = female

of the People (PMP); the **Movement for Democracy in Guinea-Bissau** (*Movimento Democrático Guiné-Bissau*—MDG), led by Silvestre ALVES; the **Party of National Unity** (*Partido da Unidade Nacional*—PUN), led by Idrissa DJALO; and the **Socialist Party of Guinea-Bissau** (PS-GB). A group listed as the **Labor Party** (PT) ran a candidate in the 2005 presidential election.

Legislature

The current **National People's Assembly** (*Assembleia Nacional Popular*) is a directly elected body of 102 members elected for five-year terms. At the most recent balloting of March 28 and 30, 2004, the African Party for the Independence of Guinea and Cape Verde secured 45 seats; the Social Renewal Party, 35; the United Social Democratic Party, 17; the Electoral Union, 2; the United Popular Alliance, 1.

President: Francisco BENANTE.

Communications

In October 1991 the National People's Assembly adopted a 55-article law providing for substantially greater freedom of the press than in a previous measure of December 1989. However, in 2002 and 2003 the government closed several private radio stations and fired reporters from the Guinea News Agency because of critical reports on the government. Following the 2003 coup, press restrictions were lifted.

Press

The following are published in Bissau: *Nô Pintcha* (6,000), official government daily; *Diario de Bissau*, independent daily; *Banobero*, independent weekly; *Expresso-Bissau*, independent weekly; *Baguerra*, PCD organ; *Voz da Guine* (6,000).

News Agency

The domestic facility is the Guinea News Agency (*Agência Noticiosa da Guinea*—ANG).

Broadcasting and Computing

Radio programming is offered by the government's *Radiodifusão Nacional da República da Guiné-Bissau* and *Rádio Liberdade*, which after a 16-year silence returned to the airwaves in 1990 to "renew and deepen" democracy; broadcasts are in Portuguese and Creole. Two independent stations were launched in 1995 and 1996. Television commenced on an experimental basis in 1989, but it still reaches a quite limited number of receivers. There were 19,000 Internet users in 2003.

Intergovernmental Representation

Ambassador to the U.S.
(Vacant)

U.S. Ambassador to Guinea-Bissau
Janice L. JACOBS (resident in Senegal)

Permanent Representative to the UN
Alfredo Lopes CABRAL

IGO Memberships (Non-UN)
AfDB, AU, BADEA, BOAD, CILSS, CPLP, ECOWAS, IDB, Interpol, IOM, NAM, OIC, OIF, UEMOA, WTO

KENYA

REPUBLIC OF KENYA

Jamhuri ya Kenya

The Country

An equatorial country on the African east coast, Kenya has long been celebrated for its wildlife and such scenic attractions as the Rift Valley. The northern part of the country is virtually waterless, and 85 percent of the population and most economic enterprises are concentrated in the southern highlands bordering on Tanzania and Lake Victoria. The African population, mainly engaged in agriculture and stock-raising, embraces four main ethnic groups: Bantu (Kikuyu, Kamba, Luhya), Nilotic (Luo), Nilo-Hamitic (Masai), and Hamitic (Somali). Non-African minorities include Europeans, Asians (mainly Indians and Pakistanis), and Arabs. In addition to Kiswahili and English, the most important languages are Kikuyu, Luo, and Luhya. A majority of the population is nominally Christian (approximately 38 percent is Protestant, and 28 percent is Catholic), but approximately 35 percent adheres to traditional religious beliefs; there is also a growing Muslim minority currently comprising 10 to 20 percent of the population.

Although the services sector now accounts for approximately 65 percent of Kenya's Gross Domestic Product (GDP), Kenya's economy continues to depend heavily on agriculture. Agricultural production continues to decline and accounts for less than 16 percent of the GDP (compared to 33.9 percent in 1984). This trend is particularly troubling because the vast majority of Kenyans rely upon subsistence farming. (Women produce more than men in the sector.) The main cash crops are coffee, tea, sisal, pyrethrum, and sugar. The coffee and tea sectors, once export leaders, are in steady decline; coffee has gone from being the first to the fourth major source of foreign exchange earnings since the late 1980s. Coffee production has fallen steadily due to high production costs, inefficient methods of cultivation, and corruption in the government-controlled cooperatives. In 2005 an acute drought struck much of the northern and eastern parts of Kenya and deviated agricultural production in these areas. Approximately, 2.5 million people (10 percent of the population) faced the risk of starvation, and the crisis required an international relief effort to contain.

The manufacturing sector has been growing, and now represents about 19 percent of GDP; important industries include food processing, the production

Political Status: Independent member of the Commonwealth since December 12, 1963; republic established in 1964; de facto one-party system, established in 1969, recognized as de jure by constitutional amendment on June 9, 1982; multiparty system approved by constitutional amendment on December 20, 1991.

Area: 224,960 sq. mi. (582,646 sq. km.).

Population: 28,686,607 (1999C); 34,467,000 (2005E).

Major Urban Centers (2005E): NAIROBI (urban area, 2,725,000); Mombasa (798,000).

Official Language: English (Kiswahili is the national language).

Monetary Unit: Kenya Shilling (principal rate July 1, 2006: 73.85 shillings = $1US).

President: Emilio Mwai KIBAKI (National Rainbow Coalition—NARC; National Rainbow Coalition of Kenya—NARC-Kenya) elected by popular vote on December 27, 2002, and inaugurated on December 30, 2002, for a five-year term, succeeding Daniel Teroitich arap MOI (Kenya African National Union—KANU), who had served as president since 1978.

Vice President: Arthur Moody AWORI (National Rainbow Coalition of Kenya—NARC-Kenya) appointed by the President on September 25, 2003, to succeed Michael Kijana WAMALWA (National Rainbow Coalition—NARC; Forum for Restoration of Democracy–Kenya—FORD-K), who died August 23, 2003.

the GDP has steadily expanded from 1.3 percent in 2003 to approximately 4 percent in 2005.

Although Kenya's economy was long considered one of the continent's healthiest, it has been subject since the mid-1980s to numerous pressures, including fluctuating fuel and commodity prices, an external debt of about $5 billion, high rates of natural population increase (currently estimated at 2.56 percent annually), escalating inflation (11 percent in 2005), and large foreign exchange losses (the current account deficit as a percentage of GDP rose to almost 27 percent in 2005) attributed to irregular banking activity. Kenya is still considered the banking and business center of East Africa, but the banking sector and the country's infrastructure suffered greatly from the corruption and neglect under the Moi regime. Health and educational services also deteriorated significantly, while unemployment rose steadily. (The government's official estimate places unemployment at 15 percent, while others estimate the rate at close to 40 percent.) Kenya has one of the highest infant mortality rates in the world, and more than half the population lives on less than $1 a day.

Kenya's relations with foreign donors have been strained since the early 1990s. Unsatisfied with the Moi regime's response to their economic conditions (austerity) and political prescriptions (instituting party pluralism and eradicating corruption), donors suspended aid payments in November 1991. The World Bank released some $350 million in frozen aid funds in April 1993, but only after a tumultuous period when President Moi agreed to a strict economic liberalization program and then reneged before finally acquiescing. Relations with both the IMF and the World Bank remained uncertain during the remainder of the decade (for more details, see *Political Handbook of the World 2000–2002*).

The IMF greeted the December 2002 election of President Kibaki with the hope that it might lift a 2001 loan freeze if the new government made progress in addressing the deficit, corruption, and privatization of state enterprises. But, the government's elimination of fees for public schools, its increase in salaries and perks for senior civil servants,

of textiles and clothing, and oil refining (almost entirely of imported crude). Tourism represents about 13 percent of GDP and is the second largest source of foreign exchange. In 2005, the Kenyan government reported that tourism rose nearly 16 percent above 2004 levels, an indication that the industry might have recovered from the adverse effects of the 2003 terrorist attacks in Mombassa, which led to a 1.5 percent decline in the country's GDP. These gains, coupled with general improvements in the tertiary sector have fueled relatively steady growth;

and the pay raises the National Assembly gave its members increased the public deficit. (The overall balance of tax revenue and public spending fell from 0.1 percent in 1995 to −2.9 percent in 2006.) By November 2003 the IMF approved a $253 million loan despite the government's difficulty in controlling the budget deficit and its delays in privatizing state-run enterprises. In November 2004 the World Bank agreed to assist the government in an audit of bank projects (most of which were administered during the Moi regime) in which corruption was suspected. The "Goldenberg" and "Anglo Leasing" scandals and the government's heavy-handed treatment of the press (see Current issues and Communications below) in 2006 caused the IMF and the World Bank to delay indefinitely the disbursement of a three-year, $327-million loan.

Government and Politics

Political Background

Kenya came under British control in the late nineteenth century and was organized in 1920 as a colony (inland) and a protectorate (along the coast). Political development after World War II was impeded by the Mau Mau uprising of 1952–1956, which was inspired primarily by Kikuyu resentment of the fact that much of the country's best land was controlled by Europeans. Further difficulties arose in the early 1960s because of tribal and political rivalries, which delayed agreement on a constitution and postponed the date of formal independence within the Commonwealth until December 12, 1963. An election held in May 1963 had already established the predominant position of the Kenya African National Union (KANU), led by Jomo KENYATTA of the Kikuyu tribe, who had previously been imprisoned and exiled on suspicion of leading the Mau Mau insurgency. Kenyatta accordingly became the country's first prime minister and subsequently, upon the adoption of a republican form of government on December 12, 1964, its first president. The principal opposition party, the Kenya African Democratic Union (KADU), dissolved itself and merged with KANU in 1964.

However, a new opposition party, the Kenya People's Union (KPU), emerged in 1966 under the leadership of the leftist Jaramogi Oginga Ajuma ODINGA, whose forced resignation as vice president in April 1966 caused a minor split in the ruling party and led to a special election in which the new group won limited parliamentary representation.

Both President Kenyatta and Vice President Daniel Teroitich arap MOI, a member of the small Kalenjin ethnic group, were unopposed for reelection in September 1974. Kenyatta died on August 22, 1978, and was immediately succeeded, on an interim basis, by Moi, who, as the sole KANU candidate, was declared president on October 10 to fill the remainder of Kenyatta's five-year term.

A veneer of apparent stability was shattered by an attempted coup by members of the Kenyan Air Force on August 1, 1982. The rebellion was quickly crushed by loyal military and paramilitary units, and the government announced the disbanding of the existing air force. President Moi dissolved the National Assembly on July 22, 1983, and called for a premature general election. The balloting was conducted on September 26, although Moi on August 29 was guaranteed a return to the assembly as an unopposed candidate and reelected to another presidential term as KANU's sole candidate for the office. Thereafter, he dealt harshly with rebel leaders, twelve of whom were executed in 1985.

In early 1986 the government launched a crackdown on dissidents, especially pamphleteering supporters of the Mwakenya movement, and dealt forcefully with unrest within the university community in late 1987. Internal and external critics continued to charge the government with human rights abuses. Some anti-Moi foment was attributed to resentment by Kikuyu tribesmen of the political ascendancy of Moi's numerically inferior Kalenjin group, amid evidence that members of the political elite had amassed large fortunes despite deepening national poverty.

Notwithstanding such controversies, the government experienced little real electoral challenge in early 1988. As the only candidate presented by KANU on February 27, Moi was declared reelected, again without the formality of a public vote, while party preselection eliminated most dissenters from assembly balloting on March 21. Several days later, Moi replaced his longtime vice president, Mwai KIBAKI, with the relatively unknown Dr. Josephat KARANJA. However, in April 1989 the assembly, apparently with the tacit support of the president, declared its nonconfidence in Karanja, who resigned on May 1. Moi immediately appointed George SAITOTI to the position, noting that his new deputy, who had earned praise for his handling of economic affairs, would retain the finance portfolio.

In February 1990 Foreign Minister Robert OUKO, whose popularity was viewed by many as having eclipsed that of the president, was assassinated before he could complete a highly publicized investigation of government and KANU corruption. Although domestic unrest intensified following the incident, in May Moi once again rejected calls for introduction of a multiparty system, insisting that such a change would exacerbate tribal cleavage. A KANU conference in December 1990 reendorsed the one-party system, while in February 1991 the government refused to recognize a National Democratic Party (NDP) organized by former vice president Odinga. However, multiparty advocates regrouped in midyear as the Forum for the Restoration of Democracy (FORD, under Political Parties, below), which, with widening popular support, continued the struggle for liberalization despite harassment by the authorities.

The administration's image was further tarnished on November 19, 1991, when Nicholas Kiprono BIWOTT, one of the president's closest political allies, was dismissed from the cabinet after an outside investigator had described him as a "prime suspect" in the Ouko murder. Shortly thereafter, international lenders and Western capitals informed Nairobi that economic assistance would be frozen until political and economic reforms were implemented. In response, Moi reluctantly reversed his position on multiparty pluralism, and following constitutional revision effective December 20, several new parties were legalized, prompting a number of cabinet and KANU officials to resign and join the opposition.

On October 28, 1992, Moi dissolved the National Assembly in preparation for the as yet unscheduled elections. Describing the action as his "secret weapon," Moi apparently sought to capitalize on the recent splintering of FORD into two factions, FORD-Kenya (FORD-K) and FORD-Asili (FORD-A), over the choice of a presidential candidate. At presidential balloting on December 29 Moi was challenged by two former vice presidents, Kibaki, founder of the Democratic Party (DP), and Odinga, leader of FORD-K, as well as FORD-A leader Kenneth MATIBA and four other candidates. Although winning only 36 percent of the vote, Moi easily outpolled his three top challengers. Meanwhile, at simultaneous legislative balloting KANU secured 100 assembly seats, well ahead of FORD-K and FORD-A, which won 31 seats each. Domestic and international observers criticized the polling as tainted by KANU intimidation tactics, electoral fraud, and vote rigging. Subsequently, on January 4, 1993, the two FORD groups and the DP, the latter controlling 23 assembly seats, announced the formation of an opposition coalition to "nonviolently" force the holding of new elections. However, only the DP honored a pledge not to sponsor candidates against other opposition parties. As a result, the coalition was in disarray at a by-election on June 27, 1994, that gave KANU three of seven seats. More importantly, an increasing number of disillusioned opposition MPs were crossing over to KANU, with the latter edging toward the two-thirds majority needed for constitutional revision.

The government's violent crackdown on dissidents in late 1996 signaled both an intensification of Moi's desire to suppress the proreform movement as well as the apparent ascendancy of hardliners within KANU. In early February 1997 the administration, citing "emergency" drought conditions, imposed the Preservation of National Security Act, which granted the government broad emergency powers, including the right to curtail political party activity. Thereafter, widespread antigovernment demonstrations were reported in late February 1997, and in April the ambassadors of 14 countries issued a joint statement condemning the government for using excessive force to suppress the continuing unrest and calling on the administration to remove restrictions on the opposition's freedoms of speech and assembly.

In mid-April 1997 the constitutional reform movement appeared to gain new focus when a number of prominent opposition leaders took part in a meeting of the National Convention Assembly (NCA), a proreform movement theretofore led by activist religious groups. For their part, KANU leaders rejected an invitation to attend the conclave and dismissed the NCA as a grouping of "tribalists"; moreover, the NCA's attempt to convene a meeting of its executive wing was banned in late May.

Under pressure from both domestic and international observers, President Moi on June 1, 1997, pledged to review the colonial-era laws that allowed security personnel to use force against illegal demonstrations; nevertheless, reports of government-initiated violence continued. Consequently, on July 17 the opposition announced its intention to launch a campaign of protest demonstrations culminating in a general strike in August. In response, the administration announced that it would establish a bipartisan parliamentary commission to review the constitution and expunge those laws designed to suppress the opposition. Real progress remained elusive, however, as the government rejected demands that NCA representatives be included on the commission.

On August 28, 1997, President Moi organized a meeting of over 120 KANU and opposition parliamentarians at which the two sides launched the Inter-Party Parliamentary Group (IPPG) to serve as a vehicle for drafting electoral reform measures. Subsequently, IPPG negotiators forged a series of draft constitutional amendments, which were approved by the legislature in late October and early November and signed into law by Moi on November 7. Meanwhile, the government approved the registration of twelve new parties, including, after some delay, Safina, a grouping launched in early 1995 by Paul MUITE (an opposition MP) and the noted paleontologist Dr. Richard LEAKEY (see Political Parties, below). On November 10 Moi dissolved the assembly, and the following day the government announced that presidential and legislative elections would be held in late December.

At the presidential balloting held December 29–30, 1997, President Moi won another five-year term by outdistancing a field of 14 candidates. The incumbent secured approximately 40 percent of the vote, while his nearest competitor, the DP's Kibaki, captured 31.1 percent. Meanwhile, at simultaneous legislative elections, KANU narrowly retained its majority, securing 113 seats. The DP finished second, with 41 seats overall, while a total of ten parties gained representation. Deriding the polling as fraudulent, a number of opposition officials immediately called for new elections, and Kibaki filed suit to have the results overturned. Dismissing criticism of the electoral process, on January 8, 1998, Moi named a new government, which did not, however, include a vice president.

The terrorist bombing of the U.S. embassy in Nairobi on August 7, 1998, and the resulting death of 247 Kenyans and 11 U.S. citizens caught the Moi government off guard. Security concerns surfaced again in early 1999 when it was revealed that a Kurdish militant, Abdullah Öcalan, had entered Kenya without going through proper immigration procedures, only to be captured and transported out of the country by Turkish security agents acting without Nairobi's consent. On February 18 Moi dismissed three top security officials and reshuffled his government in an apparent response to the incident.

Among those affected by the cabinet changes was finance minister Simeon NYACHAE, the government's most prominent anticorruption campaigner, who resigned from the government rather than accept a lesser post. Nyachae's demotion reportedly surprised observers, as it appeared to undermine the government's claims of greater economic accountability on the eve of fresh negotiations with the IMF. On April 3 Moi reappointed George Saitoti as vice president. (Saitoti had held the post until December 1997, after which Moi had left the post vacant, prompting speculation that his next deputy would be his hand-chosen successor.)

President Moi pulled a political rabbit out of his hat in June 1999 when he enticed Dr. Richard

LEAKEY (a prominent member of the Safina opposition party) to join the administration as cabinet secretary and head of the civil service. Leakey and his economic reform team were subsequently given high marks for probity and enthusiasm, although it remained unclear whether progress would be sufficient for the IMF and World Bank (who were demanding improved fiscal discipline, privatization, and anticorruption measures) to resume aid. That question became moot in April 2001 when Leakey resigned; allegedly powerful groups within the government had blocked his anticorruption efforts.

On June 12, 2001, Moi appointed Raila ODINGA and other members of the National Democratic Party (NDP) to his cabinet, thereby forming a "coalition" government. (In March 2002 KANU and the NDP formally merged.)

Moi in July 2002 selected Uhuru KENYATTA, the son of independence leader Jomo Kenyatta, as his preferred successor. However, public sentiment subsequently appeared to be turning solidly against KANU, which was expected to face a serious electoral challenge in December from a united opposition. On August 30, 2002, Moi dismissed Saitoti, who had earlier opposed Moi's selection of Kenyatta as his presidential successor. (The post remained vacant until November 4, when Moi appointed Wycliffe Musalia MUDAVADI from KANU as the new vice president.) In the meantime four cabinet ministers, including Odinga, resigned from the cabinet over Moi's selection of Kenyatta, and, with Saitoti, joined the opposition (see Political Parties, below). Moi dissolved the assembly on October 26, 2002, prior to the elections and before it had an opportunity to review proposed changes to the constitution drafted by the constitutional review commission. Moi dissolved the constitutional commission the following day, and on October 28 barred delegates from convening.

The results of the presidential and legislative balloting on December 27, 2002, swept KANU out of power in a decisive victory for the "Super Alliance" of the National Rainbow Coalition (NARC). The NARC presidential candidate, Mwai Kibaki, secured 62.3 percent of the vote, while Moi's hand-picked successor, Uhuru Kenyatta, captured only 31.2 percent. The remaining three presidential candidates won less than 6.4 percent of the vote. In the legislative elections, the constituent parties of NARC captured a majority of 125 of the 210 elected seats. KANU finished second with 64 seats. Five other parties secured seats in the National Assembly (see Legislature, below).

President Kibaki was inaugurated on December 30, 2002, and had a cabinet in place by January 6, 2003. His labor minister, Ahmed KHALIF, was killed in an airplane crash before the end of January (three other members of the cabinet were also seriously injured in the crash). Vice President Michael Kijana WAMALWA died of a serious illness on August 23, 2003. Kibaki named Arthur Moody AWORI the new vice president on September 25, 2003.

In a bid to shore up support for his government in the face of bitter factional infighting among the major parties within NARC, President Kibaki reshuffled the cabinet on June 30, 2004, and formed a "government of national unity" by including key opposition party leaders, including members of KANU and FORD-People (see Political Parties, below). Kibaki reshuffled the cabinet again on February 14, 2005, transferring some cabinet ministers and announcing a number of changes in the civil service, in reaction to charges of corruption against members of the government (see Current issues, below).

On November 23, 2005, Kibaki dismissed his entire cabinet in the wake of the no-vote for the constitutional referendum; seven of the 28 cabinet ministers campaigned against the proposed constitution (see Constitution and government, below). Political turmoil ensued as Kibaki announced the names of his new cabinet on national television only to have many of the newly appointed officials refuse to serve. Additionally, Kibaki refused to recall the National Assembly until March 22, 2006, out of fear that the parliament would pass a vote of no confidence. Lastly, Kibaki indicated that he would run for reelection in 2007, possibly under the banner of a new party, NARC-Kenya (see Political Parties, below). The formation of a new splinter party calls into question the viability of President Kibaki's NARC coalitional government.

In response to additional corruption charges stemming from two separate scandals, three additional members of the cabinet were dismissed in February and March 2006 (see Current issues, below). Five members of parliament died in an airplane crash in April 2006.

Constitution and Government

The 1963 constitution has been amended several times, mainly in the direction of increased centralization and the abrogation of checks and balances that were originally introduced at the insistence of the tribal and party opposition. Originally designated by the assembly, the chief executive is now popularly elected for a five-year term. In case of a presidential vacancy, the vice president (a presidential appointee) serves pending a new election, which must be held within 90 days. The National Assembly, initially bicameral in form, was reduced to a single chamber in 1967 by merger of the earlier Senate and House of Representatives. The president can dissolve the body and call a new election; a nonconfidence vote also results in dissolution, with both presidential and legislative balloting mandated within 90 days. All candidates for election to the assembly were required to be members of KANU prior to the December 1991 amendment, which authorized multiparty balloting. The judicial system is headed by the Kenya Court of Appeal and includes the High Court of Kenya, provincial and district magistrates' courts, and Muslim courts at the district level. Under controversial amendments approved in 1988 the president, who had been accorded the right in 1986 to replace the auditor and attorney generals, was further empowered to dismiss court of appeal and high court judges; concurrently, police were authorized to hold uncharged detainees for up to 14 days. An amendment passed in August 1992 required that successful presidential candidates secure 25 percent of the vote in at least five of the eight provinces. Defended by the government as a means to avoid election of a solely regional candidate, the law was criticized by

the opposition for unduly favoring the incumbent, whose support was drawn from a number of small, geographically widespread tribes. Amendments in 1997 permitted the formation of a coalition government, mandated a broad review of the constitution, and expanded the number of directly elected seats in the assembly from 188 to 210.

A constitutional review commission continued work in 2002 on a new draft constitution, projected to propose the establishment of a bicameral legislature and creation of the post of prime minister. President Moi dissolved parliament for the 2002 elections before any action was taken.

A popular plank of the NARC government electoral platform promised to deliver a new constitution that would reduce the powers of the president within six months, with a deadline of June 2003. The mistrust between the NAK and LDP party factions of NARC (see Political Parties, below), however, led to a stalemate over the formula for the diminution of executive power. Raila Odinga of the LDP rallied support for the creation of a robust prime minister in a constitutional arrangement similar to that of France. President Kibaki and his closest advisors in the NAK wing of NARC lost their enthusiasm for specific arrangements that would force the executive to substantively share power with another single figure, and for other reforms that might weaken NARC's ability to maintain its electoral advantage. A constitutional review conference opened on April 30, 2003, in the Bomas of Kenya, comprised of all the members of the National Assembly plus 406 delegates, but the divisions over a new power-sharing formula only sharpened during the proceedings. The promised deadline passed without approval of a new constitution, and popular agitation over the stalemate presented the NARC with a serious crisis, as a majority of Kenyans expected concrete reforms to prevent future abuses of executive power associated with the graft, corruption, and oppression of the previous regime. The situation became more polarized with the suspicious murder in September 2003 of Crispin MBAI, a key figure in the negotiations over executive power-sharing at the Bomas conference and a close associate of Odinga.

The stalemate continued into 2004 as the "Mt. Kenya" faction of the NAK wing of NARC sought assembly review and amendment of the Bomas draft, which supported the Odinga/LDP view of executive power-sharing and was approved in March by most of the 629 delegates to the review conference. The LDP wing countered that the draft could only be passed or defeated in toto, a position also favored by a majority of the delegates who attended the review conference. The government withdrew from the conference and sought passage of legislation that would permit the assembly to amend the Bomas draft. On June 28, 2004, President Kibaki announced that the 2004 revised date for a new constitution would also be missed. Riots broke out at pro-Bomas constitutional rallies in Nairobi and Kisumu as riot police moved to enforce a ban on antigovernment protests.

In 2005 the debate continued to rage in the assembly where a Parliamentary Select Committee on Constitutional Review (PSC) was formed to consider the status of changes to the Bomas draft. The LDP pulled out of the PSC after six of its party members were removed from the committee. Eventually, the NAK wing of NARC prevailed as the assembly amended the Bomas draft to weaken the prime minister, retain a powerful presidency, and maintain a unicameral legislature. The changes also altered the basis for the administration of Kenya's provinces; previous arrangements would be changed to create elective district administration with accountability to the central government. On July 22, 2005, the National Assembly approved the key terms of the revised constitution bill. A national referendum on the new constitution, required by a ruling of the High Court before a new constitution could have effect, was held on November 21, 2005.

The proposed constitution's key elements included provisions for land reform, women's rights, and the further establishment of regional religious courts. (Christian and other religious courts would be created to work in tandem with the Kadhi, or Muslim, courts, which apply religious law to issues such as personal status, marriage, and divorce.) Absent from the proposed constitution, generally

referred to as the Wako Draft, were provisions to establish a prime minister and to return to a bicameral legislature.

The referendum, which became known as the Banana and Orange Referendum (because the many illiterate voters were asked to choose from a symbol of a banana if they approved of the new constitution and an orange if they opposed it), was hotly contested. Both sides held a series of political rallies that were marred by violence; at least eight people were killed. The referendum ballot on November 21, 2005, drew a 53 percent voter turnout. The Wako draft constitution was soundly defeated, with approximately 58 percent voting against and only 42 percent favoring its passage. The failure dealt a blow to Kibaki's leadership and threatened the viability of his government (see Current issues, below).

Administratively, Kenya is divided into 40 rural districts grouped into seven provinces, exclusive of the Nairobi Extra Provincial District, which comprises the Nairobi urban area.

Foreign Relations

Generally avoiding involvement in "big power" politics, Kenya devoted its primary attention following independence to regional and continental affairs, supporting African unity and liberation movements in southern Africa. Regionally, it signed the Treaty for East African Cooperation at Kampala, Uganda, on June 6, 1967, providing for the formal launching of the East African Community (EAC) on December 1. The grouping (initially perceived as a model for multinational economic integration) was designed to preserve and expand arrangements established under British colonial rule in areas such as transportation and communications. Supporters also envisioned eventual creation of a common market, and the East African Development Bank (EADB) was established as a related institution (see article on EADB under Regional Development Banks). However, the EAC achieved little success, in part due to ideological differences between Kenya and socialist Tanzania and a variety of disputes between Kenya and

Uganda. The EAC was terminated in mid-1977 amid significant acrimony over distribution of its assets and collateral developments, including Tanzania's decision to close its border with Kenya. In November 1983 final agreement was reached regarding the EAC assets, and the Kenyan-Tanzanian border was reopened; relations with Dar es Salaam were further stabilized by the reestablishment of diplomatic relations in December. Relations with Uganda also improved in the immediate wake of the November agreement, although new tensions subsequently arose, with each country accusing the other of harboring insurgents and Nairobi exhibiting what some observers described as an "obsession" with perceived Ugandan hostility.

In 1994 the three former EAC members established a Tripartite Commission for East African Cooperation with the hope of reviving integrationist sentiment, and in 1996 Francis MUTHAURA, Kenya's former ambassador to the United Nations, was named executive secretary of the commission's new secretariat, headquartered in Arusha, Tanzania. Kenya was subsequently viewed as the leading proponent of cooperation, and a treaty for the formal reactivation of the EAC had been drafted by the spring of 1999. The proposed accord called for the gradual reduction of tariffs between members and establishment of a common external tariff as initial steps toward a possible monetary union and even, in the minds of the most ardent integrationists, eventual political federation. The presidents of the three countries involved were scheduled to meet to approve the new treaty by the end of 1999. However, considerable negotiation reportedly was necessary on details of the plan; Tanzania expressed concern that it would be overwhelmed by Kenya's much larger economy and continental leaders wondered how a revived EAC would interact with other groupings, such as the Common Market for Eastern and Southern Africa (Comesa) and the Southern African Development Community (SADC), which were promoting larger free-trade blocs. Meanwhile, Rwanda and Burundi were said to be eager for membership should the EAC be relaunched successfully. (For details on the subsequent formal reestablishment of the EAC, see separate article on the EAC in the Intergovernmental Organization section.)

Kenyan-Somali relations have been frequently strained by the activities of nomadic Somali tribesmen (*shiftas*) in Kenya's northeastern provinces and by long-standing Somalian irredentist claims. They reached a nadir in mid-1977 with the outbreak of hostilities between Somalia and Ethiopia in the latter's Ogaden region, when a Kenyan spokesman declared that an Ethiopian victory would be "a victory for Kenya." It was not until July 1984 that President Moi paid his first state visit to Mogadishu, in the course of which an agreement was concluded on border claims and trade cooperation, with Moi offering to help Somalian President Siad Barre "find a peaceful solution" to the dispute with Addis Ababa. The following September, several hundred ethnic Somali members of an exile group, the Northern Frontier District Liberation Front (NFDLF), responded to a government amnesty and returned to Kenya, declaring that the organization's headquarters in Mogadishu, Somalia, had been closed. Subsequently, in early December, Kenyan and Somalian representatives concluded a border security agreement, while other top *shifta* leaders responded to a second general amnesty in July 1985, declaring an end to the years of "banditry." Border incidents nonetheless continued, including the killing of four Kenyan policemen in September 1989 by Somali forces claiming to be in pursuit of antigovernment rebels.

In early 1992 Nairobi, seeking to repair strained regional relations, signed cooperation agreements with Ethiopia and Sudan. Furthermore, on May 8 Nairobi established formal relations with Pretoria, and in June Moi became the first African head of state to visit South Africa in 21 years. Meanwhile, the encampment of approximately 300,000 Somalian, 70,000 Ethiopian, and 30,000 Sudanese refugees along Kenya's borders was described by the regime as an economic burden and source of insecurity. In August the United Nations High Commission for Refugees (UNHCR) criticized Kenya for detaining thousands of refugees in squalid conditions in Nairobi and Mombasa. Thereafter, in January 1993, amid rumors that it was considering an involuntary repatriation and describing the refugee situation as increasingly untenable, Kenya urged the UNHCR to hasten their departure.

In October 1998 approximately 200 people were killed when Ethiopian forces crossed into Kenyan territory in pursuit of antigovernment rebels and their alleged Kenyan supporters. In late November regional peace talks opened; however, the security situation in northwestern Kenya remained extremely volatile. On the other hand, in April 2000 President Moi ordered the reopening of the border with Somalia, which had been closed since the previous August.

On November 28, 2002, terrorists bombed an Israeli-owned hotel in Mombasa, killing 11 Kenyans and three Israeli tourists. On the same day a shoulder-launched missile was fired at an Israeli airliner but missed its target. In December al-Qaida claimed responsibility for the attacks as it had for the 1998 bombing of the U.S. Embassy in Nairobi.

President Kibaki's new government faced renewed pressure from the United States and the United Kingdom in 2003 to crack down on terrorist activity in Kenya with new internal security measures and reforms in the Kenyan security services. The United States threatened cuts in foreign aid to Kenya to encourage the new government, which reorganized the key security units responsible for antiterrorist intelligence. Both the United States and the United Kingdom announced in late May 2003 heightened security alerts for travel to Kenya, and British Airways suspended flights. (The Israeli airline El Al suspended flights as well; the UK ban was lifted in late June for Nairobi, but not for Mombasa.) The travel alerts, warning of increased risk of a terrorist attack, were a blow to the Kenyan tourist industry already reeling from the November 2002 bombing and missile attacks. The alerts and threats of aid reduction may have prompted the government to submit a controversial Suppression of Terrorism Act in July 2003, which when introduced in the assembly was greeted with alarm by many government and opposition members and prompted hundreds of protesters in Nairobi. The bill, which proposed to strengthen the government's powers of detention of persons and permit searches without court authorization, was of particular concern to Muslim community leaders from the Coast and Mombasa and to human rights organizations. Due to widespread opposition from government and opposition MPs, the bill was blocked by an assembly committee. By January 2004 President Kibaki attempted to revive the bill with assurances to Muslim leaders that any measures that might lead to the targeting of Kenyan Muslims would be removed from the bill.

Nairobi advanced its regional security objectives in East Africa in 2003 by signing in March a Strategy and Plan of Action for implementing a security agreement reached with Tanzania and Uganda in 2001. In May 2003 two Kenyan army battalions were deployed on the border with Somalia to guard against infiltration by potential terrorists, and in June the government responded to the heightened terror alerts by suspending flights to Somalia. Police also arrested 36 suspects from a neighborhood of Somali refugees in Nairobi. In September Nairobi agreed to meet with Sudan to address cattle rustling and the illegal weapons trade. The Kenyan security forces continue to maintain a heightened presence on the Somali border. As the violence escalated in Mogadishu and southern Somalia in early 2006, these forces increasingly faced large numbers of refugees attempting to enter Kenya.

In March 2006, Kenyan police arrested two suspected terrorists in Nairobi with 55 pounds of ammonium nitrate and bomb-making material. The capital was placed on red alert; there was concern that the suspects were cooperating with terrorists from other countries.

Current Issues

The NARC government's first major policy initiative in January 2003 was to deliver on its campaign promise to eliminate the fees for the country's public primary schools and make school compulsory. The response to the new policy overwhelmed a school system unprepared for the return of so many children to classrooms. The cost of the program ballooned the public deficit at a time when

Nairobi was anxious to resume the flow of IMF and World Bank loans (see The Country, above) and forced the government to seek financial support for the program from foreign donors.

NARC's campaign pledges for economic revival proved more difficult to realize. The Moi regime had left the Kenyan economy in bad shape, by some estimates at least 20 years behind in overall economic development progress. The economic infrastructure, once one of the best in all of Africa, was in disrepair, especially the transportation infrastructure and the once-strong banking and financial services sector. State-owned enterprises were notoriously corrupt and mismanaged. International pressure to eliminate corruption in the public and private sectors and to privatize state enterprises (especially in energy, telecommunications, transportation, and ports), resisted by Moi for years, now gained significant traction as the new government needed foreign aid and loans to deliver on its promises to revive the economy. President Kibaki had promised to create 500,000 new jobs every year, a pledge that was impossible to achieve even with external assistance and proved even more challenging given the blows to the tourism (terrorism) and agriculture (severe drought) sectors. Moreover, the Kibaki government made slow progress in the privatization of government-controlled enterprises, given the entrenched interests within some of the governing coalition's factions attempting to keep control of these sectors as sources of patronage and graft.

NARC also pledged to crack down on corruption with a zero-tolerance platform. In 2003 President Kibaki was under popular and international pressure to put an end to public sector corruption and prosecute some of the worst abusers of the Moi regime. Kibaki moved quickly to dismantle entrenched political patronage networks as he purged some tainted members of the senior civil service and security forces in early February 2003, while others were reassigned or were left untouched. (Critics within the NARC government had hoped for a more comprehensive purge.) Soon thereafter, he dismissed the chief executives of three state enterprises. Kibaki opened the new session of the National Assembly on February 18, 2003, with the remarkably frank admission that "[c]orruption has undermined our economy, our politics, and our national psyche" and pledged to address the issue by introducing legislation. (A new law and code of ethics were later adopted requiring senior government officials to declare their assets upon entering and exiting office.) Within days of the speech before the assembly Kibaki suspended the chief justice of the High Court pending an investigation into allegations of corruption and torture of prisoners. Kibaki also named a high-profile antigraft crusader, John GITHONGO (former head of Transparency International in Kenya), as his anti-corruption chief.

In March 2003 the government opened a public inquiry, closely followed by the news media and the Kenyan people, into the infamous Goldenberg International corruption scandal that first surfaced in the 1990s. The inquiry addressed a scheme whereby nearly $600 million (the equivalent of approximately 10 percent of the country's annual GDP) was siphoned from the public coffers of the central bank to the Goldenberg firm (and, by implication, to a string of former and present government officials) in the form of export credits and state subsidies for gold and jewelry exports, exports that most likely never existed.

In October 2003 the government, in the wake of a report issued by a special commission investigating the conduct of the Kenyan judiciary, suspended 6 of the 9 judges in the court of appeals, 17 out of the 36 high court judges, and 82 of the 254 magistrates on grounds of "corruption, unethical conduct, and other forms of misbehavior."

By December 2003, however, problems with the government's anticorruption record emerged in new press accounts of irregularities in government procurement. By May 2004 new allegations surfaced over irregularities surrounding procurement contracts for police telecommunications equipment, forensic laboratories, and a new passport system (dubbed the Anglo-Leasing scandal). In July, British High Commissioner Sir Edward Clay publicly criticized the Kibaki government about a renewed tolerance within the NARC coalition for the corrupt practices of the past and an appetite among senior government officials for the trappings of office. The British, United States, and European Union governments immediately stepped up diplomatic pressure on Nairobi to investigate and prosecute any wrongdoing; the IMF and World Bank joined the chorus of donors calling for action, a renewed commitment to zero tolerance, and an end to the excessive salary increases and vehicle allowances for senior government officials.

On February 7, 2005, John Githongo resigned from his post as anticorruption chief, citing pressure from within the NARC cabinet to close his investigations of the procurement irregularities. The United States immediately suspended $2.5 million in anticorruption aid to Kenya. President Kibaki reshuffled the cabinet on February 14, 2005, in response to the mounting pressure from foreign governments, and on February 16, 2005, government prosecutors filed charges against six former government officials implicated in the procurement scandals.

Another matter of concern to the government was the escalation of long-standing tensions between the Masai and Kikuyu tribal communities over land, cattle, and water. Masai protests over the right to reclaim land leased for long periods under colonial era treaties, and access to water on these lands for Masai cattle herds, turned violent in August 2004 and January 2005. The government has linked the land reform issue to progress in constitutional reform, and President Kibaki pledged to establish order in the affected provinces. The land reform initiatives were defeated, however, in the no-vote on constitutional reform in November 2005.

In 2006 more details of the Goldenberg and Anglo-Leasing corruption scandals surfaced and threatened to bring down Kibaki's government, after John Githongo, now living in exile in the United Kingdom, alleged in a public letter to President Kibaki that the Kenyan government had issued phony contracts in 2002 to a nonexistent British firm to upgrade its passport system and forensic science laboratories. The Githongo Report alleged

that up to 30 members of the government had participated in the scheme, including Vice President Moody Awori, who denied any wrongdoing. George Saitoti (education minister), Kiraitu MURUNGI (energy minister), and David MWIRARIA (finance minister) resigned their cabinet positions in the wake of the allegations. Githongo also claimed that the money raised by graft was intended to fund the government's forthcoming election campaign.

Kenya is suffering one of the worst droughts in decades. The seasonal rains failed to appear in late 2005 or in early 2006; in the eastern and northern regions of the country up to 80 percent of the livestock have died, and approximately 3 million people face starvation. International organizations, such as the World Food Program, have issued urgent appeals for international assistance.

Political Parties

Before its unprecedented defeat in the face of a united opposition in the 2002 national elections, the ruling **Kenya African National Union** (KANU) had dominated the government structure and political life of Kenya since independence. KANU's one-time principal rival, the **Kenya People's Union** (KPU), was proscribed in 1969, although a one-party system was not formally mandated until June 1982. Under mounting domestic and external pressure, KANU endorsed pluralism in December 1991, and a number of other parties were legalized in the ensuing months.

On August 5, 1992, prospects for an opposition upset of the incumbents in presidential and legislative elections later that year were severely undermined when Masinde MULIRO, a prominent **Forum for the Restoration of Democracy** (FORD) leader who advocated opposition unity, died. One month later, torn by debate over the nomination of a presidential candidate, FORD broke into two competing factions (see below).

On November 30, 1995, members of FORD-K, FORD-A, the DP, and Safina launched an Opposition Alliance with its stated objectives being the political defeat of KANU, an end to tribalism and corruption, and the formation of a government of national reconciliation and reconstruction. Intraparty disputes plagued the opposition in 1996 and 1997. In March 1997 an Opposition Solidarity was formed by former FORD-K leader Raila Odinga in concert with the FORD-A's Kenneth MATIBA and Ngengi MUIGAI, a DP faction leader. Meanwhile, the Opposition Alliance claimed to have drafted FORD-K and DP faction leaders Michael Kijana Wamalwa and Mwai Kibaki, respectively, as well as FORD-A's Joseph Martin SHIKUKU. However, the fledgling Alliance–Solidarity rivalry was almost immediately overshadowed by the emergence of the National Convention Assembly (NCA), a proreform grouping. At the NCA's inaugural national convention in April Kivutha KIBWANA was appointed chair, and the group's executive committee drafted a number of well-known opposition figures, including Kibaki, Richard Leakey, Koigi Wa WAMWERE, and Islamic Party of Kenya (IPK) leader Sheikh Khalid Salim Ahmed BALALA.

In late August 1997 President Moi denounced the NCA as the instigator of the violent unrest gripping the country. Moreover, despite the NCA's subsequent decision to suspend protest activities to allow the government to fulfill its pledge to introduce reforms, the group was banned from holding meetings. In the face of violent dispersal of its meetings by government security forces, the NCA announced its intention to boycott presidential and legislative balloting. On the other hand, the Opposition Alliance had reportedly "folded up its umbrella," to distance itself from the ongoing violence and in response to the government's reform promises. The NCA subsequently continued to be an important stakeholder and government critic in the reform process by articulating alternate plans to those proposed by KANU.

A number of opposition alliances were formed in 2002 in preparation for the December presidential and legislative balloting. In February several groups (including the DP, FORD-K, NCA [also now referenced as the National Convention Executive Council—NCEC], UDM, and a faction of FORD-A) launched a **National Alliance for Change** (NAC), which was later restyled as the **National Alliance of Kenya** (NAK) under the party registration for the **National Party of Kenya** (NPK). Concurrently, FORD-People, Safina, KENDA, the NLP, and others established the People's Coalition of Kenya (PCK), also sometimes referenced as the "Third Force for Change." In mid-October the NAK and PCK joined the newly-formed LDP and its so-called "Rainbow Alliance" of former KANU and NDP faction leaders in an even larger opposition alliance called the **National Rainbow Coalition** (NARC), also referred to as the "Super Alliance." However, the selection of Kibaki as the NARC's presidential candidate caused problems with FORD-People leader Simeon Nyachae, who withdrew his party from the alliance and launched his own presidential campaign.

These 15 opposition parties in the "Super Alliance" were held together by a Memorandum of Understanding (MoU) signed before the December 2002 elections by the leadership of the constituent parties of the NAK and the LDP. In the MoU NAK and LDP agreed, if victorious, to divide cabinet positions equally in consultation among the party leaders and to name Raila Odinga prime minister once a new constitution was adopted.

After the election, President Kibaki unilaterally named NAK and LDP ministers to his NARC cabinet in early 2003 without regard to the equal division formula specified in the MoU. Moreover, the NARC eight-member Summit of NAK and LDP politicians did not convene, and within the first three months some members of the new government were questioning the Summit's utility. By late spring of 2003 heated disputes erupted between Kikuyu "Mt. Kenya" elements of NAK and Luo LDP leader Odinga, in league with the Luhya NARC politicians (who together constituted a "Western Alliance"), over the diminution of executive power in the new draft constitution, which the Mt. Kenya faction sought to derail. By August Kibaki publicly opposed the creation of a premiership, stating before a NARC parliamentary meeting, "there can never be two governments." The bitter ethnic and factional infighting jeopardized the long-anticipated constitutional reform process and threatened to bring down the government due to the size of the LDP voting bloc in the assembly (59 elected seats).

President Kibaki attempted to quell the party in-fighting by decreeing in December 2003 that all the parties in the coalition were "dissolved" and called for new party elections to transform NARC into a single party. The LDP and FORD-K ignored the demand and boycotted a February 2004 meeting convened to reach a new consensus on power shar-ing and to plan the dissolution of the constituent parties (see below). By March, FORD-K leader Musikari KOMBO asked Kibaki to halt the recruit-ment drive begun by Charity NGILU to avoid ir-reparable harm and avoid violent clashes between party activists. Subsequently, none of the NARC member parties unilaterally disbanded their orga-nizations, although Kibaki distanced himself from official status as leader of the DP.

The opposition KANU and FORD-People in the meantime allied in a Coalition for National Unity (CNU), which presented the factions within the NARC with opportunities to selectively seek the opposition's support on issues that divided the gov-ernment. Odinga and the LDP exploited this oppor-tunity by garnering KANU's support for the Bomas conference constitutional draft that endorsed curb-ing the power of the presidency, devolving power to district authorities, and creating a prime minis-ter. President Kibaki also exploited this opportunity on June 30, 2004, when he announced a cabinet reshuffle that produced a "government of national unity" by bringing in ministers from the opposition parties and demoting or removing key LDP cabinet members. By the end of 2004 many LDP MPs had crossed over to sit with the opposition parties in the assembly.

By mid-2005 the parliamentary groups of NARC were in disarray as members of the govern-ment and opposition camps crossed party lines to forge temporary and unstable alliances, and groups of MPs openly contemplated the formation of new political parties and party alliances in anticipation of the 2007 elections. The run-up to the constitu-tional referendum in November intensified this in-stability and maneuvering for political advantage.

Opposition to the November 2005 constitutional referendum united under the banner of the "Orange Team"; the "no vote" was symbolized by an orange. Building upon the defeat of the proposed constitu-tion, the LDP and KANU leadership, the power brokers behind the "Orange Team," took steps to form a coalition, the Orange Democratic Move-ment (ODM). Although ODM is still in its infancy and is subject to factional infighting, supporters are positioning the ODM to unite the disparate oppo-sitional parties in a bid to win control of the gov-ernment in the 2007 elections. Neither the institu-tional structure nor the party leadership has been finalized, but it appears ODM hopes to model itself after the successful NARC coalition—new mem-bers would maintain their original party member-ships.

In response to members of his own cabinet de-fecting to ODM, President Kibaki announced in March 2006 that he no longer considered NARC a viable party and that he identified with the newly formed NARC-Kenya party. Kibaki's announce-ment is widely seen as an indication that he plans to seek reelection in 2007, even though the 2002 MoU stipulated that he would step down after com-pleting his first term. ODM, KANU, and other op-position parties have responded to the president's statement, and his subsequent support for a NARC-Kenya candidate in the July 2006 by-election by challenging the legitimacy of his government and calling for a vote of no confidence in parliament. The coalition that elected the president has since unraveled.

The July 24, 2006, by-elections for five as-sembly seats (to replace the five MPs who died in the April airplane crash) were hotly contested by the new NARC-Kenya party and the KANU and LDP wings of ODM given the close margins on votes of no confidence in parliament. NARC-Kenya candidates prevailed in three of the five constituencies; KANU candidates won the other two. The balloting was marred by charges of vote buying (with money and food stores), violence, and allegations that government aircraft were used to transport NARC-Kenya politicians while cam-paigning and that government vehicles were used to ferry voters to the polls. LDP and KANU party leaders called on the Electoral Commission of Kenya (ECK) to nullify the results, and ECK officals complained of "the wanton violation of electoral rules by the Government."

Government Party

National Rainbow Coalition (NARC). The NARC was fashioned out of the October 2002 "Super Alliance" between the 14-party National Alliance for Kenya (NAK)—a restyled version of the National Alliance for Change—and the newly formed **Liberal Democratic Party** (LDP) and its "Rainbow Alliance" of KANU/NDP dissidents. From the beginning this grouping of politicians, ethnic interests, and wide-ranging political ideologies was one of political expedience more than enduring ties or shared policy goals. *Africa Confidential* framed NARC's inherent challenge: "[I]t isn't a party, it's a loose alliance of individuals and 15 parties. Its members range from leftists and trade unionists to 'tribal rights' ethnic chauvinists who have found common political cause."

Uniting the opposition to defeat the ruling KANU necessitated constructing a "big tent." NAK and LDP achieved this with the 2002 pre-election MoU that equally divided job responsibilities and cabinet positions should NARC prevail. The NARC platform promised to revive the economy and create hundreds of thousands of jobs, crack down on official corruption (and get foreign aid flowing again), ratify a new constitution that limited presidential power within six months, and institute free universal primary education.

After the NARC electoral victory the underlying tensions within the coalition began to appear almost immediately. President Kibaki never convened the NARC Summit, the top party organ made up of the constituent major party leaders, after the election, and the LDP neglected to designate one of its leaders as its summit representative, perhaps due to the difficulty of choosing faction leaders. From the very beginning the ethnic rivalries, dissension over broken MoU promises, and the division of power undermined the cohesion of NARC in government.

President Kibaki's efforts throughout 2004 and 2005 to fashion a more cohesive NARC by dissolving the constituent parties and opening NARC to an individual rather than a corporate basis for membership had the opposite effect. His move to invite opposition members into the government and demote several LDP cabinet members exacerbated the tensions and drove some LDP assembly members to sit with the opposition parties. The February 5, 2004, NARC party meeting in Nanyuki, convened to plan the dissolution of the constituent parties and broker a new consensus on power sharing, failed when only a fraction of the invited delegates attended. At a second Nanyuki meeting in April, members of the NARC committee for corporate membership voted down the plan to dissolve the member parties in favor of individual membership. The LDP, FORD-K, UDM, and IPK representatives voted in favor of retaining corporate membership, the FORD-A and SPARK delegates took a middle position, the DP representative remained neutral, and only the SDP and PPF leaders supported dissolution of parties and individual membership.

Calls for NARC party elections slated to begin February 26–27, 2005, at local levels, March 1 at the constituency level, and ending on March 11 were eventually scuttled. Opposition from three NARC factional leaders—Charity Ngilu (NPK), Raila Odinga (LDP), and Musikari Kombo (FORD-K)—led to a court battle over the NARC constitution.

In January 2005, 73 members of the assembly from the NAK wing of NARC formed a new lobby called National Reform Initiative (NARI) in response to their dissatisfaction with the pace and tenor of the government's economic, land, constitutional, and social service reforms. With the LDP wing of the coalition already in open rebellion, this left the future parliamentary cohesion of NARC in jeopardy. By mid-2005 assembly members from the Coast Province were openly meeting to discuss the formation of a regional party, further undermining NARC's cohesion.

The major party organs of NARC are the Summit, created by the MoU, the Party Council, and the Parliamentary Group. In theory the NARC Summit achieved some measure of party and ethnic balance among the coalition partners. The Summit consisted of the DP's Kibaki (Kikuyu), LDP's Odinga (Luo), Moody Awori (Luhya), and Najib Balala (Coast and Muslims), UDM's Kipruto KIRWA (Kalenjin), and the NPK's Charity Ngilu (Kamba). All of these organs have fallen away due to factional tensions. In practice NARC had two de facto secretariats, one unofficial group loyal to Kibaki and another official group under the leadership of Ngilu.

The movement of the LDP into opposition and the formation of NARC-Kenya in 2006 further divided NARC and undermined its viability. President Kibaki has declared NARC "dead," and Ngilu has retorted that the newly formed NARC-Kenya is little more than the DP with a different name and should not be confused with the NARC, which is still the ruling government party. At least 80 MPs have left the coalition, including Mutua Katuku and Alex KIBAKI (President Kibaki's son), as well as many cabinet ministers.

Leaders of the NPK, DP, and FORD-K met in June 2006, after the formal launch of NARC-Kenya, to discuss reinvigorating the NARC party organs now that Kibaki had distanced himself politically from the coalition. They also opened a dialogue with ODM leaders, fearing that no party or coalition would win enough seats in 2007 to control the government.

Leaders: Charity NGILU (Chair), Fidelis NGULI (Secretary-General), Bartha MBUVI (Vice Chair), Noah WEKESA (Council and Coordinating Committee Chair), Mutua KATUKU (National Recruitment Executive Committee Chair), Alex MUREITHI, Wanjala WELIME (Elections Board Chairs).

National Alliance Party of Kenya (NAK)/ **National Party of Kenya** (NPK). The NPK was launched in June 2001 under the leadership of Charity K. Ngilu, who had been the SDP presidential candidate in 1997. The NPK announced that it would work toward "gender equality" and "good governance" while "fighting poverty, ignorance and disease."

By 2002 Ngilu had moved the NPK into the NAC grouping to help launch the restyled NAK, turning over to the opposition alliance the party registration for the NPK to avoid delays or obstruction in party certification from the Moi government.

The NAK brought together 14 parties under one tent (with the NAK as one of the two pillars of NARC, the other being the LDP). Before the LDP joined forces with the NAK to form NARC, Ngilu was in line to receive the prime minister's post under the anticipated new constitution. Once LDP's "Rainbow Alliance" entered the scene, the premiership was promised to Raila Odinga of the LDP. Ngilu was named a cabinet minister by President Kibaki, however, was made chair of NARC, and was selected to sit on the NARC Summit.

In the party dissolution crisis that followed in 2004 (see above), Ngilu initially supported Kibaki on the question of individual or corporate membership in NARC, but by early 2005 she and other NPK party leaders had reversed course and registered the NPK independently again. The NPK joined the LDP and FORD-K in asking the courts to block the March 2005 NARC effort to dissolve the constituent parties and hold direct NARC party elections. The High Court, however, ruled against the injunction and cleared the way for NARC to hold grassroots elections. The ruling is widely seen as damaging to NPK's ability to organize and register voters for the 2007 elections. It is possible that the move toward grassroots elections might lead to the decertification of NPK.

NPK was not consulted during the creation of the NARC-Kenya party, and Ngilu has challenged the legitimacy of the new party by suggesting that NARC-Kenya is little more than the DP in a different form. Although she has not clearly defined NPK's relationship with ODM,

Ngilu does appear to be positioning herself to run for the 2007 presidency.

Leaders: Titus MBATHI (Chair), Fidelis NGULI (Secretary General), Charity K. NGILU (1997 presidential candidate), Cecily MBARIRE.

Democratic Party (DP). The DP, which draws support largely from the sizeable Kikuyu ethnic group, was formed in January 1992 by a number of former government officials, including Mwai Kibaki, a long-standing ally of President Moi who had recently resigned from the government and KANU to protest the administration's failure to address widespread official corruption. Kibaki challenged the Moi government on a number of economic issues, especially its continued allocation of funds to inefficient government-owned operations.

At the DP's annual meeting in November 1992 Kibaki's presidential candidacy was unanimously supported; at balloting in late December the DP standard-bearer finished third while party legislative candidates won 23 seats. In early January 1993 the DP agreed to form an electoral coalition with FORD-A and FORD-K, which displayed little effective cohesion at a by-election five months later.

Confronted with the DP's dire financial condition, its main factions agreed to shelve their differences and reelected Kibaki chair at a congress in March 1997. However, a number of party members subsequently signaled their interest in campaigning as the group's standard-bearer in the forthcoming presidential elections. The most noteworthy bid came from Charity K. Ngilu, a prominent assemblywoman, who joined the SDP (and later formed the NPK) after Kibaki received the group's nomination.

In early 1998 the DP accused propresidential militants of orchestrating the outbreak of ethnic violence in the Rift Valley, alleging that supporters of Kibaki's presidential bid were being targeted. (On January 23 the party had filed suit to have the balloting nullified.) Thereafter, the DP sought to form a multiparty, opposition government-in-waiting; however, subsequent negotiations among opposition leaders quickly fell apart, and in April the DP named a shadow cabinet composed of its own members. In October the DP overwhelmingly supported a nonconfidence motion against the government; however, as many as three of its legislators were alleged to have broken with the party on the issue. Kibaki subsequently continued to reject the assembly's constitutional review process, believing that it unfairly represented the interests of KANU and President Moi.

By 2002, the DP, under Kibaki's direction, played a key role in stitching together the NAC, NAK, and subsequently victorious NARC opposition party alliances to defeat KANU. Kibaki's election as president left him in the dual position of DP chair and NARC party boss. By December 2003 President Kibaki chose to distance himself publicly from any official role in the DP as he battled to dissolve the various parties within NARC in favor of direct NARC membership (see above). The DP, however, did not disband and continues to maintain a formal organization chaired by Kibaki, despite his public statements that the party ceased to exist after the formation of the NAK and despite his calls for DP members to support NARC.

At a June 2005 DP meeting in Nairobi, which was called to revitalize the party, 40 party leaders, who were members of the assembly, failed to attend, including President Kibaki, David Mwiraria, Chris MURUNGARU, Martha KARUA, Peter NDWIGA, and Kiraitu MURUNGI. The delegates who attended pledged to strengthen the party and avoid its personalization; however, by March 2006 it appeared that their efforts had failed. After announcing the formation of NARC-Kenya, President Kibaki declared that DP "had ceased to exist." The DP's national governing council unanimously voted to remove President Kibaki as its leader and endorsed Rose Waruhiu to act as chair until the National Delegates Council in July 2006. Waruhiu maintains that the party will not be dissolved and that it will field candidates in the 2007 general election either independently or with other political parties. Meanwhile, the party will support Kibaki, NARC, and the Government of National Unity.

Leaders: Rose WARUHIU (Acting Chair), David MWIRARIA (Vice Chair), Tabitha SEII (Vice Chair), Joseph MUNYAO (Secretary General), George NYAMWEYA (Deputy Secretary General), Karisa MAITHA (Treasurer), David MWENJE (Deputy Treasurer).

Forum for Restoration of Democracy–Kenya (FORD-K). The Luo-dominated FORD-K is the most direct outgrowth of the Forum for Restoration of Democracy (FORD), which was characterized by its multiparty founders in August 1991 as a "discussion group" in deference to the ban on political parties other than KANU. Despite seeming widespread support, FORD experienced problems in formulating a comprehensive platform and establishing a permanent party structure, following its legalization in December 1992. Leadership disputes contributed to the difficulties, one faction supported the presidential ambitions of Martin Shikuku while another aligned itself with Jaramogi Oginga Ajuma Odinga, the aging former vice president of the republic, who succeeded in being named interim chair, with Shikuku as interim secretary general. However, the picture clouded further in May 1992 when Kenneth Matiba, a Kenyan businessman recently returned from London, announced his presidential candidacy.

At FORD's inaugural congress on September 4, 1992, Odinga was selected as the party's presidential candidate. However, Shikuku and Matiba supporters boycotted the congress and subsequently broke off to form FORD-Asili (FORD-A, below). In early April 1993, despite a declaration of support by 51 opposition legislators for Odinga's assumption of the opposition leadership, the assembly speaker recognized FORD-A's Matiba. At the same time, intraparty opposition to Odinga's continued stewardship surfaced, with Kikuyu followers of (then) Deputy Chair Paul MUITE, an Odinga critic and

de facto leader of the FORD-K's "young turks," reportedly defecting to the FORD-A and DP, below. (Muite subsequently became a founder of Safina, below.)

In late June 1993 Odinga became leader of the opposition after a FORD-A legislator defected to KANU, and on July 15 he named a shadow cabinet. However, his subsequent efforts to improve relations with the Moi administration split the party, as supporters, led by his son, Raila Odinga, accused the anti-Moi faction aligned with Muite and (then) Secretary General Gitobu IMANYARA of seeking to gain control of the party. On September 18 the FORD-K national executive council stripped Imanyara of his post and named Munyua WAIYAKI as his replacement. The following day Muite resigned as deputy chair, and on September 21 Imanyara quit the party, announcing plans to launch a "new democratic opposition movement."

Following Odinga's death on January 20, 1994, (then) Deputy Chair Michael Kijana Wamalwa, a favorite of the late leader's sons, Raila and Oburu ODINGA, was named party chair. In June 1995 Secretary General Waiyaki resigned to help form the United Patriotic Party (UPP, below). Subsequently, a schism developed because of a leadership contest between Wamalwa and Raila Odinga. In December Odinga disregarded a court ruling banning internal party elections by having himself proclaimed chair at meetings in Kisumu and Nairobi (but not in Mombasa, where the police intervened). Wamalwa reacted by announcing that his faction would sponsor grassroots balloting in May and June. Relations between Wamalwa and Odinga sunk to a new low in early April 1996 when an extraordinary party congress, convened specifically to settle their leadership dispute, disintegrated into a riot after a party mediator, citing Wamalwa and Odinga's intransigence on procedural disagreements, declared their intraparty electoral contest "null and void" and resigned. Subsequently, on April 15 Wamalwa's supporters dismissed Odinga's claim that he had captured the party leadership. Friction continued throughout the year, culminating in Odinga's announcement in December that he was resigning from the party and joining the NDP. (On March 12 FORD-K officials openly supported a KANU candidate in a by-election contest with Odinga for the seat the latter had vacated when he left the party.)

At a FORD-K national delegates' conference on January 26, 1997, Wamalwa, James ORENGO, and Rachid MZEE were reelected chair, first vice chair, and second vice chair, respectively. Wamalwa was one of four prominent opposition leaders put under house arrest in May for their alleged roles in organizing antigovernment demonstrations. Subsequently, however, Wamalwa's opposition colleagues sharply criticized him after he met with President Moi to declare his intention to establish a dialogue with KANU.

Wamalwa's relations with KANU improved dramatically in 1998, and in October FORD-K legislators helped vote down a nonconfidence motion against the government. On the other hand, the October vote highlighted a split in the party between Wamalwa and a faction led by Orengo, who had tabled the motion. Wamalwa's ambivalent attitude toward KANU and what was considered by many his lackluster leadership style continued to cause dissension within the party, and Orengo attracted considerable publicity. Meanwhile, another anti-Wamalwa figure in the party, George KAPTEN, died under mysterious circumstances in 1999.

FORD-K was heavily involved in 2002 in the formation of a large anti-KANU opposition front, first NAK then the NARC "Super Alliance," but Orengo launched his own presidential bid through the SDP (below). Wamalwa was named vice president by President Kibaki in January 2003 but died in August. Musikari Kombo, a Luhya like Wamalwa, became acting chair of the party until he was elected at a subsequent party conference.

After forestalling a challenge to his leadership of the party from Mukhisa Kituyi in December 2005, Kombo took steps in 2006 to broaden the national appeal of the FORD-K party. In

March he opened a party office in the Thika district to build support in the central province. More significantly, Kombo has initiated talks with party members to "synergize the FORD family" for the purpose of campaigns and electoral support. Talks with Simeon Nyachae and the FORD-People yielded encouraging results while negotiations with FORD-A were stymied by FORD-A's own internal divisions (see below). Kombo has also entered a dialogue with DP and NPK leaders to reinvigorate the NARC party organs in the wake of the formal launch of NARC-Kenya and the exodus of cabinet ministers and MPs from NARC. The struggle with Kituyi for the FORD-K party leadership remains, however, and is likely to be settled later in 2006 either by Kombo conceding to holding party elections to generate a fresh mandate or, absent polls, by a court judgment expected in September.

Leaders: Musikari N. KOMBO (Chair), John MUNYES (Secretary General), Otieno K'OPIYO (Deputy Secretary General) Noah WEKESA (Director of Elections), Jael MBOGO (Organizing Secretary), Mukhisa KITUYI, Peter SHITANDA.

United Democratic Movement (UDM). The UDM was formed in 1998 under the leadership of Kipruto arap Kirwa, whose organization of an anti-Moi faction within KANU had cost him his post of assistant minister of agriculture in May. In early 1999 the group released a leadership roster, which reportedly included legislators thought to be KANU supporters. (Consequently, President Moi presented a motion that would forbid sitting assembly members to launching new groups.) The Moi administration suppressed UDM's formal registration.

UDM leaders took part in the 2002 negotiations to create the NAK and NARC (see above), and in return Kirwa was named agriculture minister in the NARC administration following the 2002 election. Kirwa formally registered UDM in March 2003. The current impetus for the UDM is to provide a party to champion the interests of the Kalenjin ethnic group, according to party Secretary General Stephen Tanis.

In the 2004–2005 NARC party dissolution battles, UDM leaders supported maintaining corporate membership for the parties within NARC. By 2006 the future of UDM was unclear. Kipruto Rono arap Kirwa (party leader and minister of agriculture) is embroiled in an alledged corruption scandal, and the party's influence at the national level appears diminished. Moreover, Kirwa and Stephen Tanis allied themselves with NARC-Kenya, calling into question the continued organizational independence of the UDM heading into the 2007 elections.

Leaders: Kipruto Rono arap KIRWA (Chair), Stephen TANIS (Secretary General).

Forum for Restoration of Democracy–Asili (FORD-A). The Kikuyu-dominated FORD-Asili (Kiswahili for "Original") was formally launched on October 13, 1992, by Kenneth Matiba and Martin Shikuku, a popular Luhya politician and former FORD interim secretary general. Matiba, who had suffered a stroke while under detention in 1990, returned from recuperation in London in May 1992 to a "hero's welcome." Immediately thereafter he announced his interest in becoming FORD's presidential candidate, thus aggravating an already contentious leadership struggle. In early September Matiba and Shikuku boycotted FORD's inaugural congress, at which Jaramogi Odinga, as expected, was selected the party's presidential candidate, and one month later FORD-A was founded.

On November 17, 1992, Matiba outpolled Shikuku for the group's nomination, and at nationwide presidential balloting in December he finished second with 26 percent of the vote. At simultaneous legislative balloting the party won 31 seats, tying FORD-K. On January 4, 1993, the party joined in a coalition with FORD-K and the DP to contest KANU's electoral victories and "coordinate activities." On April 8 the party was declared the official opposition party by the assembly speaker, and in early May

Matiba, as minority leader, named a shadow government with Shikuku in the vice presidential slot. However, in June FORD-A lost the assembly leadership when a party legislator defected to KANU. During 1994 the party leadership fell into disarray, with the still ailing Matiba openly sparring with Shikuku (whom some accused of being a KANU "mole") and with several MPs deserting to the government formation.

In March 1996 it was reported that Shikuku had lost his position as FORD-A secretary general to Kimani WANYOIKE while George NTHENGE had also been defeated (by Stephen Musila) in his bid to retain the party chairmanship.

Amid reports that Matiba and Shikuku had established separate headquarters, Matiba's faction held its own intraparty elections in May 1997. Subsequently, however, the polling was challenged in court by Shikuku and nullified. In June Matiba announced that he no longer recognized the legitimacy of the Moi government and resigned from the parliament. Thereafter, Matiba's alliance with the Opposition Solidarity and Shikuku's ties with the Opposition Alliance appeared to have superceded their allegiance to what *Africa Confidential* described as the "catastrophically split" FORD-A. In October Matiba formed the FORD-People (below). Shikuku announced his desire to run for the presidency in 2002 but was not one of the candidates on the December ballot.

In the 2002 elections some FORD-A leaders joined the NARC coalition under the NAK wing (John Michuki was subsequently appointed to the cabinet). The party also ran candidates for the National Assembly under the FORD-A party banner, independent of NARC, and secured two seats.

In 2005 party officials publicly asked Martin Shikuku to revamp the party as divisions both within the party and with FORD-People threatened to make FORD-A irrelevant in the upcoming 2007 elections. Julius Masiva (a Uasin Gishu branch official) charged that "Shikuku risks losing political credibility if he is going to leave the party to die. He should implement the views of the members." There is concern that the party will loose its official status as a registered party for failing to give returns as required by the Ministry of Justice and Constitutional Affairs.

Leaders: Martin SHIKUKU (Chair, 1997 presidential candidate), John MICHUKI, Ivuti MWANGU, Francis KAGWIMA, Wanguhu NGANGA.

Social Democratic Party (SDP). Subsequently registered as a legal party, the SDP was formed in early 1992 by National Assembly member Johnstone Makau, who called for the release of all political prisoners and the elimination of other human rights abuses.

In March 1997 the SDP added two former FORD-K leaders, Peter Anyang' Nyong'o and Joe Ager. Thereafter, in July, the party was thrust into the national spotlight when Charity K. Ngilu, an outspoken assembly member, launched her presidential campaign under the SDP banner. As was the case with a number of parties, the SDP was subsequently riven by factionalism, Ngilu's high profile reportedly rankling other SDP leaders. Indeed, she left the party in June 2001 to form her own grouping, the NPK (see above).

Although FORD-K's James Orengo in September 2002 declared his presidency under the SDP rubric, Nyong'o and others challenged that announcement. Orengo subsequently failed to win half of 1 percent of the national vote as an SDP candidate.

Peter Anyang' Nyong'o steered SDP into the NAK and NARC fold and joined the Kibaki cabinet. SDP was one of the few constituent parties to support individual membership as the basis for NARC during the 2004–2005 party dissolution dispute. In 2005 the party became embroiled in a leadership dispute that ended in litigation with the High Court elevating Peter Anyang' Nyong'o to the position of party chair.

Leaders: Peter ANYANG' NYONG'O (Chair), Mboro GATHUU (Secretary General), James Aggrey ORENGO (2002 presidential candidate), Johnstone MAKAU, Joe AGER.

Social Party for the Advancement of Reforms Kenya (SPARK). SPARK joined the NAK and then NARC groupings before the 2002 election. In the NARC dissolution disputes SPARK's representative on the April 2004 Nanyuki committee, William OKOTH, took a middle position by asserting that NAK partners had discussed merging into one party under the right circumstances.

Leaders: Joseph Owuor NYONG'O (Chair), Jackson MASIKA (Secretary), Benson WAIGURU (Treasurer), William OKOTH.

Progressive People's Forum (PPF). The little-known PPF is part of the NAK grouping under NARC. PPF's Mboya voted in support of individual membership (as opposed to corporate membership) in the NARC disputes over the basis for party membership at the April 2004 Nanyuki committee meeting.

Leaders: Lucas MBOYA

Party of Independent Candidates of Kenya (PICK). One of the earliest fringe parties after the advent of party pluralism, PICK was founded by a Nairobi businessman, John Harun MWAU, who styled himself as PICK party boss.

Leaders: G. N. MUSIMI (Chair), F. OLIEWO (Vice Chair), F. NGUGI (Secretary).

United Agricultural Party of Kenya (UAPK). The UAPK was established to "fight for rural development" and led by George KINYUA and Simon KITOBIO.

Liberal Party of Kenya. This party's 1997 presidential candidate was Wangari MAATHAI. Maathai formed a new environmental party in 2003 (see below).

Government-Supportive Parties

National Rainbow Coalition of Kenya (NARC-Kenya or NARC-K). NARC-K claims to be a "political vehicle" that will enable the current Kenyan leadership a "fresh start" to achieve "true Kenyan independence." Composed primarily of former members of NARC and DP who remain loyal to President Kibaki, NARC-Kenya seeks to free itself from the political corruption that plagued the country under President Moi and the scandals and factional infighting that have marred the Kibaki presidency. Although billed as a multiethnic party, the leadership derives most of its support from the Kikuyu ethnic group, and skeptics have charged that the formation of NARC-Kenya is little more than a political maneuver designed to bring the DP into power under a different name. (Kibaki is the founder of DP, see above.) At very least, the formation of NARC-Kenya appears to be an attempt to reconstitute the DP with the objective of attracting wider support within the Mt. Kenya region. Complicating matters further is Kibaki's relationship with NARC-Kenya. Kibaki has stated that he identifies with NARC-Kenya, and Vice President Awori (a Kibaki ally) has declared that President Kibaki was "behind the inspiration of leaders knitting together the values, policies and vision of the party." However, Kibaki was noticeably absent from NARC-Kenya's first public meeting, and he has yet to register as a member of the party.

Leaders: Kivutha KIBWANA (Chair), Stephen TARUS, Arthur Moody AWORI (Vice President of the Republic), Mutua KATUKU, Gideon KONCHELLAH, Raphael TUJU, Alex Muriithi KIBAKI, Njeru NDWIGA.

Forum for the Restoration of Democracy for the People (FORD-People). FORD-People was launched by Kenneth Matiba in October 1997, thus ending his battle with Martin Shikuku for control of FORD-A. Reportedly the most "distinguishing salient feature" of the FORD-People's charter (in comparison to the FORD-A's) is an intraparty electoral system wherein its candidates' nominations "will be under direct primary elections."

Upon Matiba's retirement in December 1998, his son Raymond MATIBA allegedly assumed control over the party; however, it was not immediately clear in what capacity the younger Matiba would function.

In December 2001 FORD-People invited former KANU minister Simeon Nyachae to join the party and serve as its presidential candidate. FORD-

People subsequently participated in the formation of the PICK and NARC. Nyachae pulled out of NARC almost immediately, however, after NARC refused to institute a primary to nominate a single candidate for the presidency. Nyachae ultimately ended up pursuing his own candidacy in the December 2002 election, a decision that reportedly caused serious rifts within FORD-People.

Nyachae and the other elected FORD-People ministers sat in opposition within the National Assembly, pledging to vote with NARC when it made good decisions. Nyachae was eventually brought into the cabinet by President Kibaki when he formed the government of national unification in June 2004.

At a December 2004 party conference Kipkalya Kones, Reuben Oyondi, and Farah Maalim were elected chair, vice chair, and secretary general, respectively.

In preparation for the 2007 presidential elections, FORD-People has met with FORD-Kenya with the aim of reviving the original FORD party. The talks were aimed at reaching an agreement on the process of determining a joint presidential nominee. Farah Maalim proclaimed that the "differences between party members have been ironed out and all were now united." The parties intend to play down the importance of reaching an agreement on a new constitution and instead have made economic development, energy resources, and drought recovery the primary issues for FORD-People. Simeon Nyachae announced in June 2006 that he plans to leave politics and not stand for election in 2007.

Leaders: Kipkalya KONES (Chair), Reuben OYONDI (Vice Chair), Farah MAALIM (Secretary General), Simeon NYACHAE (2002 presidential candidate), Henry OBWOCHA (Deputy Secretary General, Party Whip), Francis Munyialo OPAR (Party Organizing Secretary), D. S. MUTHUURI (Treasurer), Kimani WANYOIKE (Former Secretary General and 1997 presidential candidate).

Safina. Safina was launched in May 1995 by an opposition group that included Dr. Richard Leakey, a former director of the Kenya Wildlife Service. The group, which applied for registration on June 20, said that it would work with others to establish a viable alternative to KANU. However, a ruling party MP filed a suit in late July to block legalization of the formation on the grounds that its name (translated as "Noah's Arc") was "repugnant to good religious values." The emergence of Leakey (a second-generation White Kenyan) as head of an opposition group reportedly appeared to "unnerve both President Moi and KANU leaders." Among other things, Leakey had been successful in attracting foreign backing for his scientific activities and had served to heighten international awareness of Kenya's domestic turmoil. For its part, the government declared it had no intention of conferring legitimacy on a party "backed by foreigners."

Following his release from prison in December 1996, opposition activist Koigi Wa Wamwere joined Safina and called on the government to recognize the grouping. Official opposition to Safina remained strong, however, and in February 1997 security forces violently thwarted an attempt by party members to convene a meeting. Thereafter, Safina militants were reportedly deeply involved in the organization of antigovernment demonstrations, and at midyear Leakey, Paul Muite, and other party officials joined the NCA's executive wing.

In October 1997 Safina's bid for legalization was again rejected by the government; however, under pressure from moderate opposition leaders, the Moi administration reversed itself, and in November Safina was registered. Although legalized too late to forward a presidential candidate, Safina participated in the December 1997 legislative balloting, capturing three seats.

At Safina's first national convention on September 5, 1998, party delegates elected Farah Maalim interim chair and Mwandawiro MGHANGA secretary general. In addition, the party subsequently chose Josephine Odira SINYO to assume the parliamentary post vacated by Leakey, who had been restored to directorship of the wildlife service. Safina's cohesion subsequently suffered from Leakey's decision to join the KANU administration (see Current issues, above) and from a scandal involving alleged corruption on the part of key leaders.

Safina took part in the PCK negotiations to join forces with the NAK and LDP to form the NARC "Super Alliance," but Paul Muite, like Simeon Nyachae of FORD-People (see above), pulled out of NARC almost immediately after NARC refused to institute an electoral college to nominate a single candidate for the presidency. However, Muite has positioned Safina in support of President Kibaki's government by denouncing cabinet members who campaigned against the November 2005 constitutional referendum and by taking the unusually aggressive stance of publicly defending the Kibaki government's raid on *The Standard* newspaper (see Communications, below). Muite described the IMF and World Bank threats to withhold funds as "senseless and uncalled for fodder for the donors to fight the government."

Leaders: Paul MUITE (Chair), Peter MUNYA (Secretary General).

Sisi Kwa Sisi (SKS). Sisi Kwa Sisi purports to transcend religious barriers by uniting supporters of Islamic Party-Kenya and the Mungiki sect. The party won two seats in the 2002 legislative balloting and pledged to work with the NARC coalition to secure political and economic reforms.

Leaders: John Rukenya KABUGUA (Chair), Moffat Muia MAITHA, William Gitau KAABOGO.

Shirikisho Party of Kenya (SPK). Shirikisho was a little-known regional group that claimed one seat in the 1997 legislative balloting and retained the one seat in the 2002 election. The party draws it support from the Coast Province.

In 2005 allegations of misappropriation of funds granted from the Center for Multiparty Democracy surfaced from former party treasurer Mwakio NDAU. SPK party leader Harry Kombe met in Nairobi with a small number of LDP and KANU assembly members who expressed interest in joining SPK. At the same time, party leaders spurned a plan by the Third Progressive Force to form a new Coast Province party, and entertained talks of forming a coalition before the 2007 elections with the LDP and FORD-K representatives.

Leaders: Mashengu wa MWACHOFI (Chair), Abubakar YUSUF (Secretary General), Harry KOMBE.

Opposition Parties

The Orange Democratic Movement (ODM). Originally known as the Orange Team, ODM began as a coalition of disparate actors unified in their opposition to the November 2005 constitutional referendum (see above). ODM is an unsteady partnership between KANU and the LDP, allied by their common desire to defeat President Kibaki in the 2007 election. As a consequence, the party lacks a common ideology or political philosophy and is best understood as a pure opposition coalition. The party has no institutional structure and suffers from infighting among the leaders, which suggests that this is no more than a temporary coalition. Thus far, there are several prominent members seeking the ODM nomination for president, including William Ruto, Najib BALALA, Raila Odinga, Uhuru Kenyatta, Kalonzo MUSYOKA, and Musalia Mudavadi.

Leaders: William RUTO (Secretary-General), Joseph KAMOTHO, Uhuru KENYATTA, Raila ODINGA, Omingo MAGARA, Peter ODOYO.

Kenya African National Union (KANU). Originally drawing most of its support from Kenya's large Kikuyu and Luo tribes, KANU was formed in 1960, established its leading position at the election of May 1963, and subsequently broadened its constituency through absorption of the Kenya African Democratic Union (KADU) and the African People's Party (APP), both supported by smaller tribes. KANU principles include "African Socialism," centralized government, racial harmony, and "positive nonalignment."

Following President Moi's lead, KANU in December 1990 voted to retain the one-party system; however, on December 3, 1991, a special congress endorsed the president's about-face on the issue. A number of KANU adherents, including eleven National Assembly members, subsequently switched allegiance to new opposition parties, primarily FORD (below).

During the run-up to presidential and legislative balloting in late 1992 the party attempted to portray itself as a "stable alternative" to what it described as an internally divided, tribal opposition. On the other hand, it continued to suffer from a steady flow of defections as well as accusations that it was supporting Kalenjin tribesmen who were considered responsible for initiating ethnic clashes in the Rift Valley. Faring poorly in Nairobi, Nyanza, and Central Province, the party lost over half of its seats at assembly elections on December 29. Nevertheless, KANU retained an assembly majority, securing 100 seats, not including the 12 seats designated for presidential appointment.

In 1996 KANU was bolstered by the addition of a number of former opposition members as well as three legislative by-election victories. However, several factions subsequently emerged, notably KANU-A, ostensibly more open to political reform and internal party democracy; and KANU-B, which tended to reflect more centralized and traditionalist perspectives. With Moi's renomination for another (and possibly final) presidential term a foregone conclusion, the main issue within KANU in late 1996 was the selection of his vice presidential running mate for the 1997 campaign. Although George Saitoti retained a degree of support for continuing in office, it was reported that he and his supporters in the KANU-B faction (including Nicholas BIWOTT and party secretary general Joseph KAMOTHO) were being challenged by Simeon Nyachae, a cabinet minister, and his KANU-A colleagues.

At an October 1996 meeting the internecine competition reached a head as the two camps clashed over internal election policies, with the KANU-A wing seeking the introduction of a nationwide internal balloting system (apparently with the anticipation of snaring the secretary generalship) while KANU-B demanded continuation of the local branch elections (from which victors are chosen for top posts). For his part, President Moi came down firmly behind the KANU-B faction, either demoting or ousting

KANU-A ministers in a sweeping government reshuffling in January 1997.

In early 1998 Moi called on the party to rally behind constitutional reform efforts and pledged to expand KANU's dialogue with FORD-K and the National Development Party (NDP), a previously minor grouping that had been pushed into the limelight when former FORD-K leader Raila Odinga had joined it in December 1996. Meanwhile, a third faction (KANU-C) emerged within the party under the leadership of Kipruto arap Kirwa and other "youth-oriented" activists. Angered at the organizational efforts of the Kirwa faction, Moi called on KANU dissidents to quit the party in June; subsequently, Kirwa and his associates withdrew from the constitutional review process. (In January 1999 they formally broke with the party and formed the UDM [see above]).

The supremacy of the KANU-B faction within the party and government was reinforced by the February 1999 cabinet reshuffling, which included the demotion of Nyachae (who then left the government and, ultimately, the party [see FORD-People, above]). However, a number of prominent KANU-B leaders were subsequently accused of corruption in a report published by the assembly in May 2000.

Growing cooperation between KANU and the NDP led to the inclusion of several NDP members (including Odinga) in the cabinet in June 2001. Subsequently, in March 2002, the NDP decided to merge into KANU, with Odinga becoming KANU's secretary general. However, severe internal problems arose in July when President Moi selected Uhuru Kenyatta as his preferred successor. Odinga subsequently helped form the so-called "Rainbow Alliance" within KANU in conjunction with several other disaffected former leaders, including Saitoti, who had been ousted as vice president of the republic in August.

President Moi's selection of Uhuru Kenyatta (Kenyatta was formally nominated at a party congress in October) was designed to put a Kikuyu candidate on the party ballot, and maintain Moi's control over the party after he exited the presidency. The ploy split KANU and drove out the Rainbow dissidents. The Alliance formally left KANU in October to form the LDP (see above). NARC's nomination of Mwai Kibaki in October pitted two Kikuyu candidates as the presidential frontrunners, a fact that magnified the importance of the votes brokered by the other ethnic leaders in the LDP.

More KANU old guard resigned after the party's defeat in the December 2002 elections, throwing the party into turmoil. By April 2003, Moi announced that he would step down as party chair later in the year. Stepping into the role of official opposition party leader in the assembly, Kenyatta named a shadow KANU cabinet in June. At the September KANU executive meeting, Moi kept his pledge and resigned as chair without naming a successor. Kenyatta was subsequently named acting chair in April 2004.

KANU's party elections were held at a party congress in early 2005. Kenyatta took the chair in a landslide victory over rival faction leader Nicholas Biwott; Biwott disputed the outcome and moved to set up a rival KANU faction dubbed the New KANU Alliance Party.

As the principal opposition party uniting the Orange Team against the November 2005 constitutional referendum, KANU played a dominant role in shaping the ODM. Although KANU has not fully settled internal struggles over its level of commitment to the long-term development of ODM the party has signaled its willingness to work with their ODM partners to nominate a single opposition candidate and to work with ODM partners in the July 2006 by-elections. (In mid 2006 Kenyatta and Moi claimed KANU would go it alone while William Ruto, the party secretary general, pledged to continue to support ODM.)

In parliament KANU MPs aggressively challenged President Kibaki's paper-thin majority. For instance, in March 2006 six KANU members resigned their seats in the powerful House Business Committee after complaining that the government was underrepresenting KANU in committee assignments.

Who will emerge as the leading KANU presidential candidate for the 2007 election is unclear. Uhuru Kenyatta and William Ruto are considered the favorites. Kenyatta, backed by former President Moi, tried to disentangle KANU from the ODM before the July 2006 by-elections and has stepped up the verbal attacks on Odinga and other prominent LDP political rivals. Ruto openly supports the ODM alliance and leads a faction of KANU parliamentarians who actively cooperate and coordinate with ODM partners. Although Kenyatta will benefit from greater KANU institutional support, Ruto has won the endorsement of Kipkalya Kones (FORD-People Chair) and has openly courted the approval of Kalenjin elders, Moi being the exception. Former president Moi has signaled an intent to play a significant role in the final candidate selection.

Leaders: Uhuru KENYATTA (Chair and 2002 presidential candidate), Henry KOSGEY (Vice Chair), Chris Okemo (Vice Chair), William RUTO (Secretary General), Joseph NKAISERRY (Deputy Secretary General), Gideon NDAMBUKI (National Organizing Secretary), Billow KERROW (Treasurer), Wycliffe Musalia MUDAVADI (Vice President of the Republic and Vice Chair of the Party), Julius ole SUNKULI (Secretary General), Noah Katala NGALA (Assistant Secretary General), Justin MUTURI (Chief Whip), Kipyator Nicholas BIWOTT, Daniel T. arap MOI (Former president of the Republic and of the Party).

[Note: Although a constituent party of NARC in 2002–2003, the LDP was in virtual opposition during 2004–2005, and moved to the opposition side in 2006.]

Liberal Democratic Party (LDP). The LDP was launched in October 2002 by politicians who had formed the "Rainbow Alliance" faction within KANU and had left the party mainly in protest over President Moi's selection of Uhuru Kenyatta as his preferred successor for the presidency. The disaffected included former vice president George Saitoti, and former cabinet ministers Raila Odinga, Kalonzo Musyoka, William ole NTIMAMA, and Awiti ADHU. Nearly simultaneously the LDP leaders opened negotiations with the leadership of the NAK to form the "Super Alliance" National Rainbow Coalition (NARC) to defeat the ruling KANU party in the presidential and legislative elections. The LDP's base of support came from the western provinces, which when combined with the NAK's base in central Kenya and the Rift Valley gave the NARC a chance to win pluralities in enough provinces to secure the success of a NARC presidential candidate. The LDP and NAK signed the MoU in late October 2002 to cement the alliance before the December balloting. In the MoU they reached agreement on a broad platform of issues, including having a new constitution in place by June 2003 and a post-election formula for the division of jobs and power sharing.

President Kibaki, however, ignored the MoU's equality formula when he appointed the new cabinet, and with all the jockeying for power by the notables in the LDP, the LDP did not select one among equals to spearhead the NARC Summit, the supreme NARC party organ. Disputes within the NARC over the division of executive power between the president and a premier in the draft constitution further convinced Odinga and other LDP leaders that the LDP was being systematically undercut by a "Mt. Kenya" faction of Kikuyu and NAK power brokers close to Kibaki.

The LDP openly defied President Kibaki's attempts in 2004 and 2005 to dissolve the constituent parties of NARC in favor of creating a single party with individual membership. When Kibaki brought members of the opposition KANU and FORD-People into the cabinet (at the expense of LDP leaders, some of whom were demoted), in June 2003, LDP MPs crossed over to sit with the opposition in the National Assembly, declaring that the LDP was leaving the government. None of the LDP cabinet ministers, however, resigned from the government at that time.

In early 2005 the LDP actively sought alliances with other parties and groups in anticipation of the 2007 elections. The rivalries and presidential aspirations among LDP notables, however, made it difficult to schedule party elections. By June the party's National Executive Council postponed scheduled party elections indefinitely pending a revision of nomination and elections rules.

Also in June 2005, LDP MPs announced that they would once again sit with the other NARC MPs in the National Assembly. In March 2006, LDP officially broke from NARC when LDP MPs crossed over to the opposition's benches and signaled their support for ODM. (Only Mutinda Mutiso and former Education Minister George Saitoti remained on the Government side.)

LDP named Paddy Ahenda as party nominee for the 2007 presidential elections. The nomination elections were marked by corruption and apathy. By mid-2006, other LDP notables (e.g., Odinga, Balala, Musyoka, Mudavadi) were actively preparing bids for the ODM nomination for president, undercutting the importance of the LDP nomination process.

Leaders: David MUSILA (Chair), Joseph KAMOTHO (Secretary General), Joseph KHAMISI (Vice Chair), Andrew LIGALE (Deputy Secretary General), Paddy AHENDA (the party's 2007 presidential nominee), Raila ODINGA, Stephen Kalonzo MUSYOKA, Wycliffe Musalia MUDAVADI (Former Vice President), Najib BALALA, William ole NTIMAMA, Ochilo Mbogo AYACKO, Otieno KAJWANG'.

Labour Party of Kenya (LPK). The LPK joined the Orange Team in opposing the constitutional referendum and has allied itself with the LDP/KANU elements in the Orange Democratic Movement in anticipation of the 2007 national elections. Although a founding member of NARC, the LPK controls no seats in the assembly.

Leaders: Julia OJIAMBO (Chair).

Other Parties and Groups

Kenya National Congress (KNC). The KNC was launched on September 30, 1992, by Charles RUBIA, a former FORD-K member who claimed that he was seeking to reconcile the two FORD factions. The party captured one parliamentary seat in December 1992. In February 1994 Rubia, along with Chair Titus MBAATHI, Secretary General Kimani WANYOIKE, and five other leaders left the party to join FORD-A.

George Katana MKANGI, a long-time KNC politician, advocate of federalism, and 1997 presidential candidate, died in March 2004.

Leaders: S. Kathini Maloba CAINES (Vice Chair), Onesmus Musyoka MBALI (Secretary General), Chibule wa TSUMA (1992 presidential candidate).

Kenya Social Congress (KSC). Launched in June 1992, the KSC was led by George ANYONA, a former member of the National Assembly who was jailed from 1990 to 1992 on a sedition charge, and Onesmus Musyoka Mbali, a prominent businessman. The party was legally registered on October 27, 1992.

Anyona died in a car accident in November 2003. KSC held a national executive council meeting to elect new party leaders in Nairobi during July 2004.

Leaders: Mathius Ondeyo NYARIBARI (Chair), Andrew NYANGARESI (Vice Chair), Japheth OTUKE (Secretary General), Josiah NYAWACHI (Assistant Secretary General).

Kenya National Democratic Alliance (KENDA). Like the SDP, KENDA's initial policy statements concerned human rights issues, the party calling for, among other things, an end to detention without trial and political imprisonment. Legalized in early 1992, KENDA secured no assembly representation in December 1992, and its presidential candidate, Mukara NG'AND'A, captured only .11 percent of the vote.

In 1997 Koigi wa Wamwere campaigned for the presidency under the KENDA banner when his party, Safina, was unable to forward a candidate.

Leader: Joram Gaine KARIUKI (Chair), Patrick Ouma ONYANGO (Secretary), Winston Kimathi KANG'ETHE (Treasurer), Koigi wa WAMWERE (1997 presidential candidate).

National Labor Party (NLP), led by Joseph Kennedy KILIKU and Daniel Mogaka RAGUSU. In 2005 Kiliku had open discussion with the LDP's Kalonzo Musyoka about the latter using the party as a vehicle for Musyoka's run for the presidency in 2007. Kiliku also sought to broker his party, without success, as a platform for a revitalized Third Progressive Force (TPF).

United Patriotic Party (UPP). Included among the UPP's founders in June 1995 was Dr. Munyua Waiyaki, theretofore secretary general of FORD-Kenya, who indicated dissatisfaction with the administration of his former party.

Leader: Njuguna KUNGU (Chair), Dr. Munyua WAIYAKI (1997 presidential candidate).

Islamic Party of Kenya (IPK). Formed in January 1992 but denied legal status by the Moi government, the IPK announced in June that it would urge Muslims to boycott any future elections unless recognition was forthcoming. The administration responded on July 20 by formally banning the group, which had declared "total war" on the government, from participation in the forthcoming elections. One day later, party leader Khalid Salim Ahmed Balala was detained for the second time in as many months for allegedly urging Moi's assassination. In April and May 1993 Balala was alternately detained, released, and detained again as relations between the Muslims and KANU deteriorated.

On July 2, 1993, amid clashes in Mombasa between the IPK and the UMA (below), Balala accused the government of bombing his residence; subsequently, however, the IPK leader refused a Nairobi offer to investigate the incident. Thereafter, violent skirmishes between the IPK and UMA continued through the end of the year, with the latter claiming to be fighting on behalf of African Muslims against the IPK's "Arab" Muslims. Meanwhile, on October 9 Balala resigned from the IPK because of differences with Omar MWINGI, the group's interim chair.

In March 1995, John Garang, leader of the rebel Sudanese People's Liberation Army (SPLA), claimed that the IPK was engaged in subversive activities against the Kenyan government from a Khartoum-controlled region within Sudan.

As part of its effort to quell opposition unrest, the Moi government authorized Balala's return from a two-year forced exile in Germany in early July 1997. (In 1995 Balala's visa had been revoked while he was abroad, the government charging him with provoking unrest in Mombasa.) Upon his return in mid-July Balala announced that he had joined the NCA. On July 21 he dismissed the government's entreaties to the opposition as thinly veiled attempts to "emasculate" the proreform movement.

In 2004 Sheikh Mohammed Khalifa, the IPK party chair, announced that the party would seek formal registration with the government in order to protect the rights of Muslims and put forward a presidential candidate in 2007. Although the party remained unregistered in February 2006, IPK has endorsed the nomination of Najib Balala for president.

IPK also played an instrumental role in rallying coastal Muslims against the November 2005 constitutional referendum and to reject President Kibaki's newly created constitutional "review team."

Leaders: Mohammed KHALIFA (Chair), Ahmed AWADH (Secretary General), Khalid Salim Ahmed BALALA.

United Muslims of Africa (UMA). Described as a pro-KANU "rampart" against the IPK, with whom it engaged in street fighting in 1993 in Mombasa, the UMA is allegedly directed by a KANU parliamentarian, Rashid SAJJAD.

Leaders: Emmanuel MAITHA, Omar MASUMBUKO.

Mazingira Green Party of Kenya. In April of 2003 the noted environmental and human rights activist and assistant cabinet minister for environment Wangari MAATHAI formed the Green Party in the mold of Green parties in Europe. In 2004 Dr. Maathai was awarded the 2004 Nobel Peace Prize.

Leader: Wangari MAATHAI.

The following parties took part in the 1997 and 2002 presidential and legislative balloting: the **Umma Patriotic Party of Kenya**, led by Mbuthia THAIRU; the **Democratic Assistance Party,** led by Nyerere MANONDA; the **Green Africa Party,** led by Geoffrey Kibiria M'MWIRERIA.

Minor groups who put forward candidates or who were referenced in the 2002 election campaign included **Chama Cha Uma Party** (CCU), led by David Ngethe WAWERU (2002 presidential candidate); **Chama Cha Majimbo Na Mwangaza** (CCM), led by Leslie MWACHIRO; the **Mass Party of Kenya** (MPK), led by Georgr MWAURA; the **Economic Independence Party** (EIP), led by Stephen Wilfred Omondi OLUDHE; the **Federal Party of Kenya** (FPK), led by Winston Ogola ADHIAMBO; the **Kenya Patriotic Trust Party** (KPTP), led by Joseph KARANI; the **Kenya Republican Reformation Party** (KRRP), led by Lihanda SAVAI; **The People's Solidarity Union of Kenya** (PSUK), led by Fanuel LIYAI; the **Mau Mau War Veterans' Association,** led by King'ori MBOGO; the **National Progress Party** (NPP), led by Hussein ISMAEL; the **People's Party of Kenya** (PPK), launched to pursue "radical social democracy" and led by Harun WAWERU; the **United Democrats of Peace and Integrity in Kenya** (UDPIK), led by Ken NJIRU; the **Republican Party of Kenya** (RPK); **Kenyan African Democratic Development Union** (KADDU), led by Aluda ESSENDI; the **National Progressive Party** (NPP); and the **Kenya Citizens Congress** (KCC).

Other recently emerging groups include the **Alliance for Democracy** (*Muungano wa Ukombozi*); the **Kenya National Patriotic Party** (KNPP), led by Salim MWIROTHO; **Kenya Voice of Young People** (KVYP), a pro-Moi party; **Labour Party Democracy,** led by Mohamed Ibrahim NOOR; the **Patriotic Pastoralist Alliance of Kenya** (PPAK), founded in mid-1997 by Khalif ABDULLAHI, Ibrahim WOCHE, and Jackson LAISAGER; the **People's Union of Justice and Order** (PUJO), founded by former KANU member Wilson OWILI; the **Rural National Democratic Party** (RNDP), organized by Sebastian MUNENE to protect the rights of peasants and fishermen; the **Wakulima Party**, registered in October 2004; **Youth Associated with the Restoration of Democracy** (YARD), which under the leadership of Eliud Ambani MULAMA urges that the voting age be reduced to 18; and the **United Party** (UP), which was officially registered in early 1999.

(For information on pre-2002 Clandestine and Exile Groups, see the 2000–2002 *Handbook*.)

Legislature

The unicameral **National Assembly** currently consists of 210 members elected by universal suffrage in single-seat constituencies for five-year terms, plus 12 members appointed by the president and two ex officio members (the speaker of the National Assembly and the attorney-general), for a total of 224 members of parliament. Prior to the expansion of the assembly in 1997, there were 188 elected members and 12 appointed. From 1966 to the relegalization of political pluralism in December 1991, only KANU had been permitted to offer legislative candidates. Despite the 1991 law, the assembly in March 1992 vacated the seats of 11 parliamentarians who had defected from KANU.

On December 29, 1992, in the first multiparty balloting since 1969, the ruling Kenya African National Union secured 100 assembly seats, while six opposition parties shared the remaining 88 seats. The new assembly convened for the first time on January 26, 1993, but was suspended by President Moi the following day after clashes in and outside of the assembly building. The legislature reconvened on March 23, 1993, with 84 of the opposition legislators boycotting the session.

Following balloting for the expanded assembly held December 29–30, 1997, the ruling Kenya

Cabinet

As of July 1, 2006

President	Mwai Kibaki (NARC-K)
Vice President	Moody Awori (NARC-K)

Ministers of State in the President's Office

Provincial Administration and Internal Security	John Njoroge Michuki (NARC-K)
Public Service	Moses Akaranga (NARC)
Defense	Njenga Karume (NARC-K)
Immigration and Registration of Persons	Gideon Konchelah (NARC-K)
National Heritage	Suleiman Shakombo (NARC)

Ministers of State in the Vice President's Office

Youth Affairs	Mohammed Kuti (NARC-K)

Ministers

Agriculture	Kipruto Rono arap Kirwa (NARC-K)
Cooperative Development and Marketing	Peter Njeru Ndwiga (NARC-K)
East African and Regional Cooperation	John Koech (KANU)
Education, Science, and Technology	Noah Wekesa (NARC; FORD-K)
Energy	Henry Onyancha Obwocha (acting) (FORD-People)
Environment and Natural Resources	Kivutha Kibwana (NARC-K)
Finance	Amos Kimunya (NARC-K)
Foreign Affairs	Raphael Tuju (NARC-K)
Gender, Sports, Culture, and Social Services	Maina Kamanda (NARC-K)
Health	Charity Kaluki Ngilu (NARC; NPK) [f]
Housing	Peter Shitanda (NARC; FORD-K)
Information and Communications	Mutahi Kagwe (NARC)
Justice and Constitutional Affairs	Martha Karua (NARC-K) [f]
Labor and Human Resources Development	Newton Kulundu (NARC)
Lands	Kivutha Kibwana (NARC-K)
Livestock and Fisheries Development	Joseph Konzolo Munyao (NARC; DP)
Local Government	Musikari N. Kombo (NARC; FORD-K)
Planning and National Development	Henry Onyancha Obwocha (FORD-People)
Regional Development Authorities	Mohamed Abdi Mahamoud (NARC-K)
Roads and Public Works	Simeon Nyachae (FORD-People)
Tourism and Wildlife	Morris M. Dzoro (NARC-K)
Trade and Industry	Mukhisa Kituyi (NARC; FORD-K)
Transport	Chirau Ali Mwakwere (NARC-K)
Water and Irrigation	Mutua Katuku (NARC-K)

[f] = female

Note: Two parties are listed for ministers whose parties remain part of NARC.

African National Union secured 113 seats (107 elected, 6 appointed) while nine opposition parties shared the remaining 109 seats.

The December 27, 2002, election witnessed the end of KANU control of the assembly. Following the balloting the 210 elected seats were distributed as follows (appointed seats appear in parentheses): National Rainbow Coalition, 125 (7)*; Kenya African National Union, 64 (4), the Forum for the Restoration of Democracy–People, 14 (1); the Forum for the Restoration of Democracy–Asili, 2; Safina, 2; Sisi Kwa Sisi, 2; Shirikisho Party of Kenya, 1. [*Within the ruling National Rainbow Coalition, the elected assembly seats were divided as follows: Liberal Democratic Party, 59; Democratic Party, 39; the Forum for the Restoration of Democracy–Kenya, 21; National Party of Kenya, 6.] The next election is scheduled for December 2007.

Speaker: Francis Xavier ole KAPARO (ex officio).

Communications

Following the 2002 election, Kenya made significant strides in advancing free speech and developing a free press. The press grew noticeably bolder, publishing news articles and analysis critical of the government as a matter of routine and without the fear of intimidation or reprisals that were ever present under the Moi regime. Broadcasting was also a government monopoly until recently (see below).

The government introduced a bill in July 2004 that would have prevented ownership by the same media company of electronic and print versions of the same publications under the banner of avoiding media monopolies. Kenya's two largest news dailies also have electronic versions and are parts of larger media companies with television and/or radio divisions. In the face of opposition from the trade association for the media companies, the bill was dropped. In January 2004 the government arrested 15 news vendors on charges of selling publications that did not print the name and address of the publisher on the first or last pages—a violation of laws governing the publication of newspapers.

A government raid of *The Standard* newspaper and its sister television station KTN in March 2006, however, led many observers to question President Kibaki's commitment to free speech. The raids appeared to have been prompted by an article in *The Standard* claiming that a senior opposition figure had secret talks with President Kibaki. John Michuki, the minister for internal security, defended the attack by warning journalists working in Kenya that "if you rattle a snake, you must be prepared to be bit by it!" Rumors persist that the raid was led by government hired mercenaries.

Press

Newspapers are privately owned. Although newspapers evince a range of opinions, many are financially controlled by Europeans or by individuals who are close to political elites. The National Rainbow Coalition (NARC) attempted to launch a daily newspaper in 2004, but the venture, which would have been titled *The Dawn*, failed to raise the necessary funds to finance the start-up costs.

The following are English-language dailies published in Nairobi, unless otherwise noted: *Nation* (170,000 daily, 170,000 Sunday), independent; *Taifa Weekly* (70,000), weekly, in Kiswahili; *The Standard* (70,000 daily, 90,000 Sunday), moderate; *The People* (40,000); *Taifa Leo* (57,000), in Kiswahili; *Taifa Jumapili* (56,000), weekly, in Kiswahili; *Kenya Times* (52,000), KANU organ; *Kenya Leo* (6,000), KANU organ in Kiswahili.

News Agencies

The domestic facility is the Kenya News Agency (KNA); a number of foreign agencies also maintain bureaus in Nairobi.

Broadcasting and Computing

The Kenya Broadcasting Corporation (KBC) was formed in 1989 as a state agency to succeed the Voice of Kenya and the Voice of Kenya Television; it operates over an area extending from Nairobi to Kisumu, as well as from the coastal city of Mombasa. Kenya Times Media Trust (KTMT), a joint venture of KANU, U.S.-based CNN, and Australian

Rupert Murdoch, set up channel 62, a 24-hour commercial subscription service in 1989. Citizen TV, a commercial station, operates in Nairobi and surrounding areas. Nation TV was founded in 1999; it is a commercial station owned by Nation Media Group. Stellagraphics TV (STV) was formed in 1998 as a commercial station operating in Nairobi. Kenya Television Network (KTN-TV), formed in 1990, is a commercial station operating in Nairobi and Mombasa. A number of FM commercial radio stations broadcast from Nairobi. There were 794,000 television receivers in 1999 and 500,000 Internet users in 2005.

Intergovernmental Representation

Ambassador to the U.S.
Leonard NGAITHE

U.S. Ambassador to Kenya
William M. BELLAMY

Permanent Representative to the UN
Judith Mbula BAHEMUKA

IGO Memberships (Non-UN)
AfDB, AU, BADEA, Comesa, CWTH, EAC, EADB, IGAD, Interpol, IOM, IOR-ARC, NAM, PCA, WCO, WTO

LESOTHO

KINGDOM OF LESOTHO

The Country

Lesotho, the former British High Commission territory of Basutoland, is a hilly, landlocked enclave within the territory of South Africa. The Basotho people, whose vernacular language is Sesotho, constitute more than 99 percent of the population, which includes small European and Asian minorities. About 80 percent of the population is nominally Christian. The economy is largely based on agriculture and stock raising; diamond mining, which in the late 1970s accounted for more than half of export earnings, was discontinued in 1982. Lesotho is highly dependent on South Africa, its main trading partner, which employs 80 percent of the country's wage earners and is the principal supplier of energy. Because of the unusual employment pattern, women are primarily responsible for subsistence activities, although they are unable by custom to control household wealth.

Economic growth was stagnant in the early and mid-1980s, partly because of prolonged droughts that depressed agricultural output and compounded problems of unemployment, landlessness, and inflation. However, real GDP growth averaged 6 percent annually from 1987 to 1997, under the influence of the expansion of the manufacturing sector (and a collateral growth in exports) as well as the economic effect of investment in the massive Lesotho Highlands Water Project (LHWP, see Foreign relations, below). Severe political disruption in 1997 and 1998 (see Political background, below) contributed to a 3.6 percent decline in real GDP in fiscal year April 1998–March 1999. In December 1999 the government, in conjunction with the International Monetary Fund (IMF), announced a new economic-recovery program designed to attract foreign investment, diversify the manufacturing base, enhance tourism, privatize state-run enterprises and otherwise promote the private sector, reform tax policy, and overhaul the financial sector. In early 2001 the IMF described the program as off to a "good start" and approved a new three-year assistance package. However, the fund warned that the country continued to face a serious HIV/AIDS problem as well as widespread unemployment and poverty, while other observers cited rampant corruption in the government and civil service as a barrier to effective economic and political reform.

The economy was severely compromised in 2001 and 2002 as the result of massive food shortages resulting from drought and soil degradation. Agricultural production subsequently increased,

Political Status: Traditional monarchy, independent within the Commonwealth since October 4, 1966.

Area: 11,720 sq. mi. (30,355 sq. km.).

Population: 1,862,275 (1996C); 2,473,000 (2005E), excluding expatriate workers in South Africa (approximately 150,000 in 1999).

Major Urban Center (2005E): MASERU (185,000).

Official Languages: English, Sesotho.

Monetary Unit: Loti (principal rate July 1, 2006: 7.13 maloti = $1US). The loti is at par with the South African rand, although under a Tripartite Monetary Area agreement concluded between Lesotho, Swaziland, and South Africa on July 1, 1986, the rand has ceased to be legal tender in Lesotho.

Sovereign: King LETSIE III; became king upon the dethronement of his father, King MOSHOESHOE II on November 6, 1990; voluntarily abdicated upon his father's return to the throne on January 25, 1995; became king again on February 7, 1996, following the death of his father on January 15; took coronation oath on October 31, 1997.

Prime Minister: Bethuel Pakalitha MOSISILI (Lesotho Congress for Democracy); sworn in on May 29, 1998, following intraparty caucus election, replacing Ntsu MOKHEHLE (Lesotho Congress for Democracy); formed new government on June 3, 1998; formed new government on June 11, 2002, following legislative balloting of May 25.

although food shortfalls continued into 2005 and rising food prices contributed to high inflation and burgeoning governmental budget deficits. On the other hand, the growth of the textile industry was the country's main bright spot, with several large Taiwanese firms relocating to Lesotho (and generating an estimated 40,000 new jobs within a population suffering more than 30 percent unemployment) to take advantage of new U.S. laws eliminating or reducing quotas and tariffs on developing African states. (As of 2004 some 60 percent

of Lesotho's exports were going to the United States.) Real GDP growth declined slightly to 2 percent in 2005 (down from 3 percent the previous two years), attributed mainly to a continuing drought that affected agriculture and a manufacturing slowdown. Though inflation dropped to 3.7 percent (from 7.7 percent in 2003), the unemployment rate was estimated at 30 percent, according to the IMF. Fund managers urged authorities to expand the tax base, keep better track of public expenditures, and increase spending to reduce widespread poverty. On a more positive note, the fund commended Lesotho for continuing to pursue and strengthen regional trade and investment, particularly with South Africa.

Government and Politics

Political Background

United under MOSHOESHOE I in the mid-19th century, Basutoland came under British protection in 1868 and was governed from 1884 by a British high commissioner. A local consultative body, the Basutoland Council, was established as early as 1903, but the decisive move toward nationhood began in the mid-1950s and culminated in the attainment of full independence within the Commonwealth as the Kingdom of Lesotho in 1966. MOSHOESHOE II, the country's paramount chief, became king of the new state, and Chief Leabua JONATHAN, whose Basutoland National Party (BNP) had won a legislative majority in the preindependence election, became prime minister.

A trial of strength between the king and prime minister erupted in 1966 when the former's attempt to gain personal control over both foreign and domestic policy led to rioting by opposition parties; after being briefly confined to his palace, the king agreed to abide by the constitution. Further internal conflict followed the 1970 election, at which the opposition Basotho Congress Party (BCP) appeared to have outpolled the BNP. Voting irregularities were cited to justify the declaration of a state of emergency, a consequent suspension of the constitution, and the jailing of opposition leaders. Subsequently, the detainees were released, and the king, who had gone into exile, returned. The state of emergency was ultimately lifted in July 1973, but, in the wake of a coup attempt in January 1974 against his increasingly unpopular regime, the prime minister introduced new internal security measures (patterned after similar measures in South Africa) that proscribed the transmittal of outside funds to political groups within the country and authorized the jailing of individuals for 60 days without legal assistance. Between 1979 and 1982 numerous armed clashes were reported with the Lesotho Liberation Army (LLA), a guerrilla group affiliated with the outlawed "external" wing of the BCP under Ntsu MOKHEHLE, who claimed from exile that he was Lesotho's true leader on the basis of the election results invalidated in 1970.

In late 1984 the prime minister was mandated by an extraordinary general meeting of the BNP to call for a legislative election, and, with effect from December 31, the king dissolved an interim assembly that had been appointed after the abortive 1970 balloting. Following refusal by the five leading opposition parties to participate in the voting scheduled for September 17 and 18, 1985, Chief Jonathan announced that a formal poll would be unnecessary and declared all the BNP nominees elected unopposed.

On January 20, 1986, the Jonathan regime was toppled in a relatively bloodless coup led by Maj. Gen. Justin M. LEKHANYA, commander in chief of the Lesotho Paramilitary Force (LPF). Among the factors reportedly contributing to the coup were an economic blockade by South Africa (see Foreign relations, below) and power struggles within the BNP and the LPF. A decree issued on the day of the coup conferred executive and legislative powers on the king, who was to act in conjunction with a six-member Military Council and the Council of Ministers. On January 24 the king swore in Lekhanya as chair of the Military Council, with a largely civilian Council of Ministers being installed three days later. In February the king declared an amnesty for political offenders, and in March he banned all political activity pending the establishment of a new constitution. The new government quickly concluded a security pact with Pretoria and began to retreat from the Communist-bloc relations established by Chief Jonathan in the last years of his rule.

A new crisis erupted in early 1990 following the dismissal and arrest on February 19 of three Military Council members, two of whom were cousins of the king. Moshoeshoe refused to approve the appointment of replacement members and in a publicized letter to Lekhanya demanded an explanation for the arrests. The general responded two days later by declaring that supreme authority would "for the time being" be vested in himself and other members of the council, though the king would remain head of state. On February 22 he announced a major cabinet reshuffle that involved the dismissal of 9 of 18 ministers, including the king's brother, Chief Mathealira SEEISO, from his post as interior minister. On March 5 the council formally validated the action against the monarch, who left the country on March 10 for a "brief sabbatical" in the United Kingdom. The king was dethroned on November 6, and his son, Letsie David SEEISO, was sworn in as King Letsie III on November 12 after his accession had been approved by an assembly of 22 traditional chiefs.

On April 30, 1991, General Lekhanya was overthrown in a bloodless coup and replaced as chair of the Military Council by Col. Elias Phisoana RAMAEMA. Thereafter, an unsuccessful attempt to depose Ramaema on June 17 led to the arrest of 18 senior military officers, and, in an unrelated action, Lekhanya was placed under house arrest from August 2 to September 17 for allegedly plotting a return to power.

In April 1992 the former king announced that he would be returning to Lesotho in late May, apparently against the wishes of the Military Council. Complicating the situation was a report that King Letsie III was prepared to abdicate in favor of his father. During talks brokered by the Commonwealth secretariat in London in June, it was agreed that Moshoeshoe could return as head of the royal family, but not as monarch, and on July 20 he was accorded a warm reception in Maseru after a two-year absence.

After several postponements, a general election was held on March 27, 1993, at which the previously outlawed BCP swept all the 65 National Assembly contests, both General Lekhanya and BNP leader Evaristus SEKHONYANA being among the defeated. Although the results were disputed by the BNP, which subsequently rejected an offer of two nominated Senate seats, Ntsu Mokhehle was installed as head of a BCP government on April 2.

In mid-November 1993 coup rumors were sparked when the government's attempts to fulfill its promise to integrate former LLA soldiers into the Royal Lesotho Defense Force (RLDF) resulted in a confrontation between the latter's senior and junior officers. Furthermore, the RLDF's unwillingness to acquiesce to the new administration was, at least nominally, the catalyst for clashes between rival factions of the RLDF in January 1994. On April 14 dissident soldiers assassinated Deputy Prime Minister Selometsi BAHOLO and seized four other cabinet ministers for four hours in apparent response to government plans to investigate the January violence.

On August 17, 1994, King Letsie announced that he had removed the government of Prime Minister Mokhehle and that the country would be run by an appointed provisional council prior to the scheduling of new elections. The action was immediately challenged by thousands of rock-throwing protesters in a march on the royal palace, while a four-nation summit involving the leaders of Botswana, Zimbabwe, and South Africa was convened in Pretoria late in the month in an effort to resolve the crisis. On September 14 a meeting between the king and Mokhehle yielded an agreement that reinstated the latter and called for the abdication of the former in favor of his deposed father. A bill that provided for the monarchial transfer was approved on November 17, with Moshoeshoe II returning to the throne on January 25, 1995.

While the reaccession of King Moshoeshoe came about as a result of the tripartite intervention of late August 1994, the more important outcome was his son's agreement to restore democracy, lacking which South Africa had threatened an economic blockade of the landlocked enclave.

Subsequently, South Africa's deputy foreign secretary termed the Lesotho settlement "the first success of the Organization of African Unity's regional approach to conflict resolution."

On January 15, 1996, King Moshoeshoe was killed in an automobile accident while returning from a late-night visit to his cattle herds in the royal village of Matsieng, and on February 7 Crown Prince Letsic David ascended the throne for the second time as King Letsie III. The 32-year-old Letsie promised to "abstain from involving the monarchy in any way in politics or with any political parties or groups."

In late 1996 and early 1997 Lesotho's political landscape was dominated by a highly publicized struggle between Prime Minister Mokhehle and Molapo QHOBELA, the leader of the BCP's "modernizing" wing and deputy chief of the party's National Executive Commission (NEC). At a meeting held February 28–March 2, 1997, the NEC denounced Mokhehle's governance and voted to strip Mokhehle of his party leadership posts as the first step in an apparent effort to gain control of the government; however, in mid-April the High Court reinstated Mokhehle on an interim basis and ordered him to hold intraparty elections by the end of July. On June 7 Mokhehle and 37 BCP legislators defected from the BCP and announced the formation of the Lesotho Congress for Democracy (LCD). Furthermore, Mokhehle asserted that he would continue as prime minister, citing the LCD's control of a majority of the assembly seats. Consequently, on June 11 the BCP suspended its participation in the assembly, asserting that Mokhehle's "coup" was a blatant attempt to avoid the proposed intraparty balloting. In October Mokhehle's deputy, Bethuel Pakalitha MOSISILI, met with Botswanan, South African, and Zimbabwean leaders who had been charged by the Southern African Development Community (SADC) with mediating in the political stalemate. Thereafter, dismissing the BCP's continued attacks on its legitimacy, the LCD hosted the official coronation of King Letsie III on October 31.

In early 1998 Prime Minister Mokhehle announced that he would not run for reelection in balloting scheduled for May, citing declining health, and on February 27 the legislature was dissolved in anticipation of the polling. In elections on May 23 approximately 400 candidates from 12 parties vied for posts in the enlarged 80-seat assembly. Although the polling was initially described as "free and fair" by the SADC and Lesotho's Independent Electoral Commission (IEC), the LCD's capture of 78 seats (the BNP being credited with 1, and 1 remaining vacant) was immediately denounced as fraudulent by the opposition, whose subsequent demand for a recount was rejected by the IEC. On May 28 Mosisili was elected prime minister by an LCD intraparty caucus, and on June 4 a new government was sworn in. Nevertheless, opposition calls for an annulment of the elections continued. In late July the Court of Appeals ruled that only the king could annul elections.

On August 4, 1998, opposition demonstrators occupied the grounds outside the royal palace. On August 11 the SADC named a South African judge, Pius LANGA, to head an international team (referred to thereafter as the Langa Commission) charged with investigating the charges of electoral fraud. Meanwhile, tensions continued to mount at the royal palace, where several people were killed during clashes between the opposition and security forces and progovernment activists. On August 26 the Langa Commission released an interim report in which it accused the IEC of mishandling the vote tallying, and, under pressure from South Africa, the government agreed to a vote recount. However, on September 11, mutinous soldiers arrested more than 20 senior military officials after the dismissal of a military leader with alleged sympathies for the antigovernment demonstrators. Furthermore, the commander of the military, Lt. Gen. Makhula MOSAKENG, was forced to resign at gunpoint. On September 22, South Africa and Botswana, acting under the auspices of the SADC, deployed approximately 800 troops to Maseru at the request of Prime Minister Mosisili, who reportedly feared a coup attempt by the rampaging soldiers. The SADC forces were greeted by stiff resistance from the mutinous soldiers as well as opposition militants and were

unable to gain control of Maseru until September 29, by which time dozens of people had been killed and the city severely damaged by looting and burning.

By early October 1998 a majority of the RDLF had returned to the barracks, and between October 2 and 14 the SADC organized government and opposition negotiations that yielded an agreement to create a transitional executive committee that would operate parallel to the government and assist in organizing new elections in 15 to 18 months. The negotiators also agreed to restructure the IEC, draft a new code of conduct for political parties, and create guidelines for equitable access to media outlets for all political groups. Furthermore, it was concluded that Prime Minister Mosisili would remain in office during the transitional phase and that SADC forces would remain for an indefinite period. On December 9 a 24-member Interim Political Authority (IPA) was sworn in, and the following day two opposition party members were elected cochairs of the new body.

SADC peacekeeping forces completed their withdrawal in mid-May 1999, supporters describing the military intervention of the previous year as an "outstanding success." At the same time, the IPA expressed confidence that it would meet its deadline of organizing national elections by mid-2000, when the original IPA mandate was due to expire. Under pressure from international mediators concerned over potential delays, the IPA and the government in December 1999 reached an agreement to hold elections sometime in 2000, with the IPA mandate to be extended indefinitely until balloting was conducted. However, a planned election date in May 2000 was quickly scrapped as the IPA and the government argued over proposed restructuring of the parliament. The IPA and the government subsequently charged each other with attempting to delay the elections, although neutral observers suggested that it was the government that appeared to have the most to gain from such tactics. Plans to conduct the balloting in early 2001 also proved unrealistic in view of disagreement over voter registration and the addition of legislators selected via proportional representation to the assembly.

In legislative balloting on May 25, 2002, the LCD won a new term in office, and on June 11 Mosisili formed an all-LCD cabinet. Four more ministers were announced on July 11.

On April 30, 2005, the nation's first local elections were held, with a government stipulation that one-third of the elected seats be filled by women. Seven opposition parties tried to have the elections postponed, claiming irregularities, which some observers said may have affected voter turnout (reported to be about 30 percent). Though an official breakdown of results was not released, electoral officials announced May 9 that the LCD won "by a large margin," followed by independents, the opposition Basotho National Party (BNP) and the Lesotho People's Congress (LPC), and unspecified smaller parties. Failed elections were reported in 15 districts, attributed to the death of candidates, and new elections were to be scheduled to replace them.

Constitution and Government

Under the 1966 constitution, which was suspended in January 1970, Lesotho was declared to be an independent monarchy with the king functioning as head of state and executive authority being vested in a prime minister and cabinet responsible to the lower house of a bicameral parliament. In April 1973 an interim unicameral body was established, encompassing 22 chiefs and 71 nominated members. A return to bicameralism was voted in 1983, but the bill was never implemented and was voided after the 1986 coup by the Military Council, which announced the vesting of "all executive and legislative powers in HM the King"; the latter action was reversed by the council prior to the exile of Moshoeshoe in March 1990, the new monarch appearing to possess only ceremonial authority.

On July 4, 1991, a National Constituent Assembly approved the draft of a new constitution, which was promulgated following the legislative election of March 1993. The revised basic law restored the bicameral system and returned executive authority to a cabinet headed by a prime minister, without conclusively resolving the issue of the monarch's

role. The judicial system consists of a High Court, a Court of Appeal, and subordinate courts (district, judicial commissioners, central, and local). Judges of the High Court and the Court of Appeal are appointed on the advice of the government and its Judicial Service Commission. Local government is based on nine districts, each of which is administered by a commissioner appointed by the central government. In April 1997 the assembly approved a constitutional amendment that established an Independent Electoral Commission (IEC).

Foreign Relations

Lesotho's foreign policy was long determined less by its membership in the United Nations, the Commonwealth, and the Organization of African Unity (OAU, subsequently the African Union—AU) than by its position as a black enclave within the white-ruled Republic of South Africa. While rejecting the South African doctrine of apartheid and insisting on the maintenance of national sovereignty, the Jonathan government for some years cultivated good relations with Pretoria. Subsequent events, however, led to a noticeable stiffening in Maseru's posture. Following South Africa's establishment of the adjacent Republic of Transkei in October 1976, Lesotho requested a special UN Security Council meeting on the matter, complaining that its border had been effectively closed in an "act of aggression" designed to force recognition of Transkei. Subsequently, South African prime minister Pieter Botha accused Maseru of harboring militants from the African National Congress (ANC) among the approximately 11,000 South African refugees living in Lesotho. Friction over Chief Jonathan's refusal to expel the ANC supporters culminated in South Africa's institution of a crippling economic blockade, ostensibly to block cross-border rebel activity, on January 1, 1986. Pretoria denied charges of complicity in the subsequent overthrow of Chief Jonathan but lifted the border controls one week later when the new military regime flew 60 ANC members to Zimbabwe. The new relationship with South Africa was further demonstrated by the signature in October of a treaty authorizing commencement of the $2 billion Lesotho Highlands Water Project (LHWP), which had been under consideration for more than two decades. The three-phase project, expected to take 25 to 30 years to complete, will divert vast quantities of water to South Africa's arid Transvaal region in return for the payment of substantial royalties. (The project has been the attention of intense scrutiny recently in light of bribery charges against foreign contractors. In May 2002 a former chief executive of the LHWP was sentenced to a lengthy prison term for fraud and accepting bribes, while Canadian, French, and German companies were fined for paying bribes.)

In an attempt to broaden its international support both regionally and abroad, Lesotho has been an active member of the Southern African Development Coordination Conference (SADCC, subsequently the SADC), a body created in 1980 to lessen members' economic dependence on the then white-ruled regime. However, in view of its vulnerability to South African influence, Maseru, unlike other SADCC governments, did not seek sanctions against Pretoria for its apartheid policies. Rather, on May 21, 1992, the two governments formally established diplomatic relations.

In January 1994 the interwoven nature of relations between Lesotho and South Africa was evidenced by Pretoria's immediate and forceful response to the unrest in Maseru. Although the Commonwealth was subsequently credited with brokering an accord between the combatants, observers cited pressure from a task force created by South African president F. W. de Klerk and other southern African leaders as the reason for the speedy resolution of the dispute. Thereafter, speculation about the possible merger of the two countries continued, with the *Christian Science Monitor* quoting local observers as saying that, if not for the monarchy, Lesotho would be "swallowed up" by South Africa. In early 2001 it was reported that relations between the South African government and Lesotho's royal family were strained because of the former's failure to "come clean" on a "massacre" allegedly committed by its paratroopers during the SADC's intervention in 1998. However, relations subsequently

improved (apparently influenced by the successful 2002 legislative elections in Lesotho), culminating in a new cooperation protocol through which South Africa agreed to provide economic aid and technical assistance. In 2005 troops from Lesotho were being trained for use in future UN and SADC missions. Late that year, Prime Minister Mosisili visited China amid pledges by both countries for political and economic cooperation.

Current Issues

Although tension between the government and the opposition was reported in advance of the May 2002 legislative poll, the balloting was deemed generally free and fair by international observers, the new mixed system (which included 40 members elected on a proportional basis) having succeeded in providing minority parties with a significant legislative voice. Nevertheless, the government continued to face severe pressures from food shortages (accompanied by high prices that triggered street protests in November 2003) and the HIV/AIDS crisis (an estimated 31 percent of the population was infected). In November 2005 the government announced a plan to offer free HIV/AIDS testing to the entire population.

Meanwhile, the issue of accession continued to gain attention after the birth of a second daughter to the royal family in November 2005. While only male heirs to the throne are allowed, a government secretary in 2006 raised the issue of female inheritance as part of the ongoing speculation. In January, Foreign Affairs Minister Monyane Moleleki was wounded by gunfire near his home shortly after he had attended a national conference of the LCD, during which tensions reportedly heated up over the accession issue and hints that Moleleki might seek an unprecedented third term in the 2007 elections.

Political Parties

Political party activity was banned in March 1986 following the January coup that ended nearly 20 years of dominance by the Basotho National Party (BNP). Subsequently, the BNP joined four former opponents (the BCP, UDP, BDA, and CPL) in an informal "Big Five" alliance to demand that the ban be lifted in preparation for a return to civilian government. Ten days after the coup of April 30, 1991, the Military Council announced that party activity could resume as long as it did not degenerate into "divisive politics." However, it was not until nearly two years thereafter that a general election was authorized.

The 11 parties that had competed individually in the 1998 legislative balloting (the LCD, BCP, BNP, MFP, SDU, NPP, NIP, KBP, LEP, PFD, and CDP) were accorded two seats each on the Interim Political Authority (IPA) that was established in late 1998. The UDP and the LLP, which had contested the 1998 election as an alliance, each received one seat on the 24-member IPA.

In May 1999 a number of small parties (the PFD, NPP, NIP, KBP, CDP, CPL, and SDP) announced formation of an anti-LCD grouping called the Khokanyana-Phiri Democratic Alliance. In August another antigovernment grouping, the Setlamo Democratic Alliance, was formalized by the BNP, BCP, MFP, UDP, LLP, and LEP, which had been operating together informally since the beginning of the year.

Government Party

Lesotho Congress for Democracy (LCD). The LCD was launched by Prime Minister Ntsu MOKHEHLE, the (then) BCP interim president, on June 7, 1997, one month before the BCP was scheduled to hold intraparty elections for his post and just two days after a BCP spokesman had labeled him "permanently incapacitated." Subsequently, Mokhehle cited the LCD's control of a majority of the legislative posts (38 seats) as the basis for his continued control of the government. In early 1998 Bethuel Pakalitha Mosisili, theretofore deputy party leader, was elected to succeed Mokhehle as party leader, the latter declining to run for reelection due to poor health. (Mokhehle died in January 1999.)

Party infighting was reported in 2000, culminating in violence between rival factions in October

that precipitated police intervention. Some observers suggested the friction underscored a split between the youthful, possibly more progressive, supporters of Mosisili and a conservative faction led by Shakhane MOKHEHLE, brother of the LCD founder and current chair of the LCD. Subsequently, Mosisili was elected for another five-year term as party leader but Mokhehle was defeated 717–710 in his reelection bid by Sephiri Motanyane, described as a close associate of Mosisili's. Prominent LCD leaders, including Deputy Prime Minister Kelebone Maope and several other cabinet members, charged that the elections had been "rigged" and vowed to take the matter to court. Maope's faction left the party in September 2001 to form the Lesotho People's Congress (below). In April 2005 it was reported that the LCD had won the country's first locally-held elections.

Leaders: Bethuel Pakalitha MOSISILI (Prime Minister and Party Leader), Enoch Sephiri MOTANYANE (Secretary General), Motlohi MOENO (Deputy Secretary General).

Opposition Parties

Basotho Congress Party (BCP). Strongly antiapartheid and pan-Africanist in outlook, the BCP (formerly the Basutoland Congress Party) was split, following the abortive 1970 election, by the defection of (then) deputy leader Gerard P. Ramoreboli and several other members, who defied party policy and accepted nominated opposition seats in the interim National Assembly.

Banned in 1970, the main branch of the BCP continued to oppose the Jonathan government, claiming responsibility in the late 1970s for numerous armed attacks on police and BNP-supportive politicians. Concurrently, a Lesotho Liberation Army (LLA) of 500–1,000 operated, under external BCP direction and allegedly with South African support, in the country's northern mountains and from across the border. Despite overtures from the new regime in early 1986, the LLA called for revival of the 1966 constitution as a condition of abandoning antigovernment activity. However, in early 1989 external leader Ntsu Mokhehle returned to Lesotho, along with about 200 BCP supporters, presumably because of Pretoria's satisfaction with the current military government. Meanwhile, although the BCP remained committed to the establishment of a constitutional democracy, the LLA, apparently of no further use to South Africa, was reported to have been reduced to a few "rag-tag" dissidents.

Mokhehle and other party members attended the opening of the constituent assembly in June 1990, despite their earlier support of a boycott. Subsequently, the party was rumored to be interested in Lesotho's incorporation into South Africa. Formerly a socialist party, the BCP in its 1993 election manifesto declared its commitment to a mixed economy.

Controversy rocked the BCP in 1996 as the rift between the party's conservative elders, or *majela-thoki* ("those who want to be isolated"), and the younger, so-called modernizers widened. At a party congress March 9–10, delegates elected a new 12-member National Executive Commission (NEC). In addition, "conservative" Deputy Prime Minister Bethuel Pakalitha Mosisili, a potential Mokhehle successor, secured the party vice presidency, outpolling the incumbent, modernizer Molapo Qhobela. However, Qhobela and his supporters promptly filed suit to have the balloting overturned, alleging that the *majela-thoki* had rigged the elections. Subsequently, in May four prominent modernizer cabinet ministers, including Qhobela and Tseliso Makhakhe, were ousted from the government. One week later two other ministers aligned with them quit the cabinet.

In November 1996 the High Court ruled in favor of the Qhobela faction, annulling the March NEC polling and charging the members of the previous NEC with preparing new elections. At fresh balloting for the NEC on January 24, 1997, the modernizers retained their seats, reflecting their reportedly overwhelming numerical dominance within the party. On February 16 the remaining links between the two factions were fractured when the Mokhehle government ignored Qhobela's attempts to mediate an end to a police mutiny and violently squashed the rebellion. The progressives' dismay with Mokhehle was further compounded by testimony being made at South Africa's Truth and Reconciliation Commission (see separate article on South Africa) that, according to *Africa Confidential,* appeared to substantiate long-held rumors that Mokhehle and his LLA forces had cooperated with the apartheid-era regime's "death squads." At a BPC meeting on February 28 party delegates voted to remove Mokhehle from the party presidency; however, on April 18 the High Court reversed Mokhehle's ouster, declaring that it violated the BCP's charter and directing Mokhehle to serve as interim president (his term having expired in January) until new partywide elections could be held.

On June 7, 1997, Mokhehle announced that he and 37 other BCP legislators were leaving the party to form the LCD. On July 27 party delegates elected Qhobela as the BCP's new leader. Subsequently, on December 1 the Khauta KHASU-led Democratic Movement for Reconstruction (DMR) announced that it was disbanding so that its members could rejoin the BCP (Khasu, former BCP deputy leader G. P. RAMOREBOLI, and Phoka CHAOLANE had been expelled from the BCP in 1992).

In December 1998 Khauhelo RALITOPOLE, leader of the BCP's Women's League, was named cochair of the IPA. It was reported in early 2001 that two different executive committees—one led by Molapo Qhobela, former minister of foreign affairs and heretofore president of the BCP, and the other by Tseliso Makhakhe, former minister of education—were claiming legitimate control of the party. Following a court's decision to accord the pro-Makhakhe faction the legitimate use of the BCP rubric, the pro-Qhobela faction broke away in early 2002 to form the Basutoland African Congress (below).

Leader: Tseliso MAKHAKHE.

Basutoland African Congress (BAC). The BAC was launched in early 2002 by a breakaway faction of the BCP.

Leaders: Molapo QHOBELA, Maholela MANDORO (Secretary General).

Basotho National Party   (BNP). Organized in 1959 as the Basutoland National Party, the BNP has counted many Christians and chiefs among its members. It traditionally favored free enterprise and cooperation with South Africa while opposing apartheid. In the mid-1970s, however, it began co-opting policies originally advanced by the BCP, including the establishment of relations with Communist states and support for the ANC campaign against Pretoria. Growing internal division was reported in 1985 over who would succeed the aging chief Jonathan as prime minister. One faction was dominated by the paramilitary Youth League, armed and trained by North Korea, which reportedly planned a government takeover. The Youth League was disarmed and officially disbanded in a confrontation with the Lesotho Paramilitary Force on January 15, 1986, prior to the LPF-led coup of January 20. Although the BNP's national chair was named finance minister in the post-Jonathan administration, supporters of Chief Jonathan were barred from political activity. Chief Jonathan was detained briefly after the coup, released, and then placed under house arrest in August along with six BNP supporters for activities allegedly threatening national stability. They were released in September by order of the High Court with an admonition to refrain from political activity. The former prime minister died in April 1987.

On October 18, 1995, BNP leader Evaristus Retselisitsoe SEKHONYANA was sentenced to two years' imprisonment or a heavy fine after being convicted of sedition for having urged armed resistance to military units during the August unrest. Sekhonyana assumed a leading role in the interparty negotiations that were held in the aftermath of the September 1998 uprising; however, he died on November 18. At a BNP congress in March 1999, former military leader Justin Metsing Lekhanya was elected as the new party leader. At the 2002 legislative elections the BNP became the second-largest party in the assembly (21 seats) and the main opposition grouping. In 2005 the government rejected a proposal from the BNP to form a government of national unity.

Leaders: Justin Metsing LEKHANYA (Party Leader), Leseteli MALEFANE (Secretary General).

Lesotho People's Congress   (LPC). The LPC was established in October 2001 by an LCD breakaway group led by former deputy prime minister Kelebone Maope.

Leaders: Kelebone MAOPE (Party Leader), Shakhane MOKHEHLE (Secretary General).

Marematlou Freedom Party   (MFP). A royalist party, the MFP has long been committed to enlarging the king's authority. In other respects, its position has been somewhere between the BCP and the BNP. An offshoot Marematlou Party (MP), formed in 1965 and led by S. S. Matete, reemerged with the MFP in 1969. One of its members, Patrick Lehloenya, accepted a cabinet post as minister to the prime minister in late 1975, subsequently becoming minister of health and social welfare. The party's (then) president, Bennett Makalo KHAKETLA, was appointed minister of justice and prisons in the cabinet formed after the 1986 coup.

Leaders: Vincent Moeketse MALEBO, Tsitso LEANYA.

Sefate Democratic Union   (SDU). Founded by BCP dissidents, the SDU controlled the sole non-BCP legislative seat prior to the formation of the LCD in 1997.

Leader: Bofihla NKUEBE.

National Progressive Party   (NPP). The NPP was launched on October 22, 1995, by Chief Peete Nkoebe Peete, who had previously been a deputy leader of the BNP but had had a falling-out with Chief Sekhonyana. Peete declared that the new group would function in the tradition of the BNP's founder, Chief Leabua Jonathan.

Leader: Chief Peete Nkoebe PEETE.

United Democratic Party   (UDP). The UDP was formed in 1967 by two progovernment members of the BCP. However, in a 1982 manifesto the party called for the establishment of full diplomatic relations with Pretoria, the expulsion from Lesotho of all South African political refugees,

Cabinet

As of May 1, 2006

Prime Minister	Bethuel Pakalitha Mosisili
Deputy Prime Minister	Archibald Lesao Lehohla

Ministers

Agriculture and Food Security	Daniel Rakoro Phororo
Communications, Science, and Technology	Motsoahae Thomas Thabane
Defense and National Security	Bethuel Pakalitha Mosisili
Education and Training	Mohlabi Kenneth Tsekoa
Employment and Labour	Mpeo Mahase [f]
Finance and Development Planning	Timothy Thahane
Foreign Affairs	Monyane Moleleki
Forestry and Land Reclamation	Lincoln Ralechate Mokose
Gender, Youth, and Sports	Mathabiso Lepono [f]
Health and Social Welfare	Motloheloa Phooko
Home Affairs and Public Safety	Archibald Lesao Lehohla
Industry, Trade, and Marketing	Mpho Malie
Justice, Human Rights and Rehabilitation, Law and Constitutional Affairs	Refiloe M. Masemene
Local Government	Pontso Suzan Matumelo Sekatle [f]
Natural Resources	Mamphono Khatletla [f]
Parliamentary Affairs	Bethuel Pakalitha Mosisili
Prime Minister's Office	Mokone Lehata
Public Service	Bethuel Pakalitha Mosisili
Public Works and Transport	Popane Lebesa
Tourism, Culture, and Environment	Lebohang Ntsinyi [f]

[f] = female

and opposition to trade sanctions against the Botha regime. In early 1985 UDP leader Charles Mofeli branded the projected legislative balloting as a "farce" and accused Prime Minister Jonathan of attempting to create a one-party state. Mofeli was also one of the most vocal critics of the successor military regime, being detained briefly in 1987 for condemning its "abuse of power." The UDP contested the 1998 legislative balloting in an alliance with the LLP (below).

Leaders: Charles D. MOFELI (President), Molomo NKUEBE (Secretary General), Mthuthuzeli PATRICK.

National Independence Party (NIP). The NIP was formed in late 1984 by a former cabinet member who resigned from the Jonathan government in 1972. In an election manifesto issued in March 1985, the NIP called for the establishment of diplomatic relations with South Africa and the severance of links with Communist countries. In mid-1992 it criticized the government for scheduling elections "prematurely" and announced that it would boycott the balloting then scheduled for November. The party failed to win seats in the 2002 assembly elections.

Leader: Anthony C. MANYELI.

Communist Party of Lesotho (CPL). The small Communist Party, founded in the early 1960s and declared illegal in 1970, long drew its major support from Basotho workers employed in South Africa. The ban on its activities within Lesotho was reported to have been "partially lifted" by the Jonathan government in 1984. Since 1986, muted activity by CPL leaders has reportedly been tolerated, despite the party ban, although the CPL congress in early 1987 was held "in utmost secrecy." The congress called for the revitalization of trade union activities, particularly in the mineworkers' union, which is led by the CPL secretary general.

In mid-1992 the party announced that it would boycott the forthcoming legislative elections, criticizing their hasty scheduling. There were no recent references to the CPL.

Leaders: R. MATAJI (Chair), Nimrod SIJAKE, Jacob Mokhafisi KENA (Secretary General).

Kopanang Basotho Party (KBP). Lesotho's first feminist party, *Kopanang Basotho* (Basotho Unite) was launched in mid-1992 to protest what it termed "repressive and discriminatory" laws against women. By the end of the year it was reported to have a membership of some 30,000.

Leader: Limakatso NTAKATSANE.

United Party (UP). In late February 1996 United Party leader Makara Azael Sekautu and two soldiers were arrested for their roles in a botched coup attempt that government officials alleged had been planned since September 1995. Sekautu was released in 1998 and reportedly ran for a legislative seat as part of a UDP/LLP/UP electoral alliance. However, official government election results referenced the coalition as including only the UDP and LLP, and the UP did not secure representation on the IPA. The UP contested the 2002 assembly balloting without success.

Leader: Makara Azael SEKAUTU.

Lesotho Workers' Party (LWP). The LWP was formed in August 2001 by left-wing trade unionists and other labor leaders.

Leader: Billy MACAEFA.

Other parties participating in the IPA were the **Christian Democratic Party** (CDP), led by Thuso LITSOANE and Ntja THOOLA; the **Lesotho Educational Party** (LEP), led by Thabo S. PITSO; the **Lesotho Labour Party** (LLP), led by Patrick SALIE and Charles MOFELI; and the **Popular Front for Democracy** (PFD), led by Rakali KHITSAM and Lekhetho RAKUNE. Other parties include the **Social Democratic Party** (SDP), described upon its formation in 1998 as a "youth" party under the leadership of Masitise SELESO; and the **New Lesotho Freedom Party,** led by Manapo Majara P. KHOABANE.

Legislature

The bicameral parliament established under the 1966 constitution was dissolved in the wake of alleged irregularities at the election of January 27, 1970. An interim assembly of 22 chiefs and 71 nominated members, named on April 27, 1973, was dissolved as of December 31, 1984. Subsequent arrangements called for a Senate of 22 chiefs and an assembly of 60 elected and up to 20 nominated members. Since none of the opposition parties nominated candidates for balloting to have been conducted on September 17–18, 1985, Chief Jonathan canceled the poll and declared the BNP candidates elected unopposed. The 1983 Parliament Act, on which the action was based, was voided following the 1986 coup.

At present the **Parliament** is a bicameral body consisting of a nonelective Senate and an elective National Assembly.

Senate. The Senate contains 22 chiefs and 11 nominated members. A restructuring of the Senate (to make the body more "democratic" and "representative") was proposed for consideration by the Interim Political Authority (IPA), established in late 1998. However, little further information on proposed changes had surfaced as of 2005.

President: Chief Sempe LEJAHA.

National Assembly. At the election of May 23, 1998, approximately 400 candidates competed for 80 lower-house seats (an increase of 15 since the

1993 polling). The Lesotho Congress for Democracy (LCD) won 78 seats, the Basotho National Party (BNP) secured a sole position, and 1 seat was left vacant. The next election initially was not scheduled until 2003; however, early elections were envisioned as part of the late-1998 agreement negotiated between the government and the opposition following the military intervention of the SADC. After several postponements, it was announced in March 2001 that balloting would be conducted in 2002 for a new assembly, whose 80 members elected on a "first-post-the-post" system would be complemented by 40 members selected by proportional vote. In balloting on May 25, 2002, the LCD won 77 seats, followed by the BNP, with 21 seats; the Lesotho People's Congress, 5; the National Independence Party, 5; the Basotho Congress Party, 3; the Basutoland African Congress, 3; the Popular Front for Democracy, 1; the National Progressive Party, 1; the Marematlou Freedom Party, 1; and the Lesotho Workers' Party, 1. Two seats were left vacant.

Speaker: Nthohi MOTSAMAI.

Communications

Press

The following are published in Sesotho in Maseru, unless otherwise noted: *Moeletsi oa Basotho* (Mazenod, 20,000), Catholic weekly; *Leselinyana la Lesotho* ("Light of Lesotho," 15,000), published fortnightly in Morija by the Lesotho Evangelical Church; *Lentsoe la Basotho* (14,000), weekly government organ; *Lesotho Today* (7,000), government organ in English; *The Mirror* (4,000), independent weekly in English; *Lesotho Weekly; Makatolle,* weekly; *Mphatlatsane* (4,000), daily; *Mopheme* (The Survivor).

News Agency

The Lesotho News Agency (LENA), originally established in 1983, was relaunched in August 1990.

Broadcasting and Computing

The Lesotho National Broadcasting Service (LNBS) operates the government-owned, commercial Radio Lesotho, which transmits in Sesotho and English, while television from Maseru services approximately 43,000 receivers. There were some 21,000 Internet users in 2003.

Intergovernmental Representation

Ambassador to the U.S.
Molelekeng E. RAPOLAKI

U.S. Ambassador to Lesotho
June Carter PERRY

Permanent Representative to the UN
Lebohang Fine MAEMA

IGO Memberships (Non-UN)
AfDB, AU, BADEA, CWTH, Interpol, NAM, SADC, WCO, WTO

LIBERIA

REPUBLIC OF LIBERIA

The Country

Facing the Atlantic along the western bulge of Africa, Liberia is a country of tropical rain forests and broken plateaus. Established as a haven for freed American slaves, it became an independent republic more than a century before its neighbors. Prior to the escalation of domestic violence in 1990, a small "Americo-Liberian" elite (between 3 and 5 percent of the population), which traced its descent to the settlers of 1820–1840, was gradually being assimilated, with most of the other inhabitants, divided into 16 principal tribes and speaking 28 native languages and dialects, adhering to traditional customs and practicing indigenous religions. About 10 percent is Christian and 10–20 percent Muslim. Women comprise approximately 40 percent of the labor force, mainly in agriculture; female participation in government, traditionally minimal, increased marginally during the 1980s.

The Liberian economy is dependent on exports of iron ore, rubber, and timber, plus smaller quantities of diamonds and coffee. In 1989 iron ore accounted for more than half of export revenue, although the industry employed only 2 percent of the labor force. Industrial development also included diverse smaller enterprises centering on commodities such as processed agricultural goods, cement, plastic explosives, beverages, and refined petroleum. In addition, Liberia provided a "flag of convenience" for about 2,450 ships, or approximately one-fifth of the world's maritime tonnage.

During the decade preceding the collapse of the Doe regime in 1990, a decline in world commodity prices, combined with mismanagement of state enterprises, produced a severe fiscal crisis. In response, the government attempted to privatize national industries, mounted an anticorruption campaign, and promoted an agriculture-based "green revolution." Aggravating the situation was the suspension of aid in 1986 by the International Monetary Fund (IMF) because of Monrovia's failure to make scheduled payments on its external debt, which exceeded $1.7 billion by mid-1990. Of far greater consequence was the subsequent carnage caused by civil war and the interim government's lack of fiscal resources because of rebel activity. The government installed in mid-1997 pledged to focus its economic rehabilitation efforts on advancement of the private sector and reduction of the high unemployment rate. Real GDP grew by 20 percent in 1999, although per capita income reportedly remained at only one-third of prewar levels and unemployment was widespread.

Subsequently, the Liberian economy suffered from the country's increasing international isolation resulting from the government's perceived role in the burgeoning subregional conflict (see Foreign relations and Current issues, below). Among other things, the unrest led to a UN embargo on diamond sales (integrally related to arms traffic), a halt to many donor-financed development projects, and delays in the government's proposed fiscal reforms.

Intensified fighting in 2002 led to a dramatic decline in GDP in 2003 and created severe food and energy shortages and substantial internal and external displacement of large segments of the population. In March 2003 the IMF suspended Liberia because of the Taylor administration's failure to pay its dues and repay loans. The negotiation of a cease-fire and installation of a national transitional government in the second half of 2003 prompted international donors in February 2004 to pledge $520 million in humanitarian and economic assistance. Growth of 2.4 percent and 5.3 percent was achieved in 2004 and 2005, respectively.

In August 2005, Mittal Steel, the largest steel corporation in the world, announced that it would invest $900 million over a 25-year period in iron mines in northeastern Nimba County. The company would retain 70 percent of the revenues of the mines, with the government getting the rest. However, sanctions continued to constrain economic growth. In December 2005, the UN extended sanctions on timber and diamonds for an additional six months. (The timber sanctions were lifted in June 2006, although the UN left the diamond sanctions in place for at least six more months pending adoption of a program that would verify the origins of the diamonds.)

Following the 2005 elections, the IMF estimated that the country's fragile economic recovery would continue. GDP growth for 2006 was expected to rise to 7.7 percent, most of the expansion being tied to additional foreign aid, including resumed assistance from the IMF. The World Bank announced $55 million in aid for road repairs, improvements in the delivery of water, and other reconstruction. Meanwhile, China and other creditor nations wrote off some of Liberia's external debt.

In order to repair the country's reputation for financial mismanagement, the new administration launched a series of reforms in early 2006 designed, among other things, to increase the collection of unpaid taxes, improve auditing processes, and computerize the banking system. In exchange for the renewal of foreign aid, donor organizations and states, led by the United States, the European Union (EU), the United Nations (UN), the African Union (AU), and the Economic Community of West African States (ECOWAS), created the Governance and Economic Management Assistance Program (GEMAP), a three-year initiative under which international experts will assist members of the new Liberian government. (GEMAP officials are required to countersign all major government expenditures, a condition that has created significant resentment among Liberians.)

In April 2006 the IMF announced that Liberia was one of 11 countries that had qualified for debt relief under the Heavily Indebted Poor Countries (HIPC) initiative. (Liberia's foreign debt stood at about $3.2 billion.) As evidence of the daunting task facing the new government, it was estimated that 50 percent of the population survived on less than $1 per day. In addition, some estimates placed unemployment as high as 80 percent.

Government and Politics

Political Background

Liberia's political origins stem from a charter granted by the U.S. Congress to the American Colonization Society in 1816 to establish a settlement for freed slaves on the west coast of Africa. The first settlers arrived in 1822 with the financial assistance of U.S. President James Monroe, and in 1847 Liberia declared itself an independent republic under an American-style constitution. During the late 19th and early 20th centuries, such European powers as Britain, France, and Germany became involved in the country's domestic affairs and laid claim to portions of Liberian territory. After World War I, however, American political and economic influence was reestablished, with Firestone

Political Status: Independent republic established in 1847; under de facto one-party system from 1878; martial law imposed on April 25, 1980, following coup of April 12; new constitution approved by national referendum on July 3, 1984 (with full effect from January 6, 1986 [the date of the inauguration of the new president]); constitution effectively voided by rebel action in mid-1990; Interim Government of National Unity (supported militarily by the Economic Community of West African States Monitoring Group [Ecomog]) sworn in November 22, 1990; State Council of Liberian Transitional National Government sworn in March 7, 1994; new six-member State Council sworn in September 1, 1995, following cease-fire agreement of August 19; amended version of 1995 cease-fire agreement signed by faction leaders on August 16, 1996, after 1995 accord was rendered moot by an outbreak of violence in April; constitution of 1986 reaffirmed by the National Assembly on August 6, 1997, following presidential and legislative balloting on July 19; transitional government established October 14, 2003, following settlement of a civil war; new elected government installed January 16, 2006.

Area: 43,000 sq. mi. (111,369 sq. km.).

Population: 2,101,628 (1984C); 3,638,000 (2005E).

Major Urban Center (2005E): MONROVIA (571,000).

Official Language: English.

Monetary Unit: Liberian Dollar (market rate July 1, 2006: 54.00 dollars = $1US). The U.S. dollar also circulates.

President: Ellen JOHNSON-SIRLEAF (Unity Party); elected in second-round balloting on November 8, 2005, and inaugurated on January 16, 2006, for a six-year term to succeed the Chair of the National Transitional Government, Charles Gyude BRYANT (Liberia Action Party).

Vice President: Joseph N. BOAKAI (Unity Party); elected in second-round balloting on November 8, 2005, and inaugurated on January 16, 2006, for a term concurrent with that of the president, succeeding the Vice Chair of the National Transitional Government, Wesley Momo JOHNSON (United People's Party).

assuming operation in 1926 of the world's largest rubber plantation in Harbel.

Relative stability characterized internal politics under the guidance of the True Whig Party (TWP), which ruled continuously for more than a century after coming to power in 1878. Political authority was strongly centralized under the successive administrations of President William V. S. TUBMAN, who served as chief executive from 1944 until his death in 1971. Tubman was elected on a platform calling for unification of the country by integrating the Americo-Liberian and tribal groups and the promotion of foreign economic investment. Although these policies were maintained by Tubman's successor, William Richard TOLBERT Jr., limited economic imagination, insensitivity to popular feeling among indigenous Liberians, and allegations of maladministration and corruption contributed, in the late 1970s, to growing domestic opposition, including a wave of illegal strikes and widespread rioting in Monrovia in April 1979 over a proposed increase in the price of rice. Emergency powers were quickly granted to President Tolbert by the Congress, while later in the year municipal elections were postponed and tough labor laws enacted to end the stoppages.

Despite legalization in January 1980 of the People's Progressive Party (PPP), the country's first formal opposition in more than two decades, President Tolbert responded to a call for a general strike by PPP leader Gabriel Baccus MATTHEWS in March by asserting that the party had planned "an armed insurrection." Matthews and other PPP leaders were arrested, but on April 12, two days before their trial was to begin, a coup led by junior officers overthrew the government, President Tolbert and more than two dozen others being killed. A People's Redemption Council (PRC), chaired by Master Sgt. Samuel Kanyon DOE, was established, and on April 13 the PRC announced a civilian-military cabinet that included Matthews as foreign minister. On April 22, following a series of military trials,

13 former government and TWP officials—including the Tolbert administration's ministers of foreign affairs, justice, finance, economic planning, agriculture, and trade; the chief justice of the Supreme Court; and the presiding officers of the Congress—were publicly executed by firing squad. Three days later, the PRC suspended the constitution and instituted martial law.

In April 1981 the PRC appointed a 25-member commission to draft a new constitution, in keeping with Doe's promise of a return to civilian rule by April 1985. After a number of postponements for the avowed purpose of registering and educating voters, a constitutional referendum was held on July 3, 1984. On July 20 Doe announced that the document had been accepted, and on the following day he abolished the PRC and merged its membership with 57 hand-picked civilians to form an Interim National Assembly. Although the new assembly immediately elected him as its president, Doe characterized the status as temporary and announced that he would present himself as a candidate at a national election to be held in October 1985.

Because of restrictions imposed by the government-appointed electoral commission, neither Matthews nor the chair of the constitutional commission, Dr. Amos SAWYER, was allowed to campaign for the presidency, with their parties also being disqualified from presenting legislative candidates. As a result, three substantially weaker groups challenged Doe's recently launched National Democratic Party of Liberia (NDPL). Amid widespread allegations of electoral fraud and military intimidation, Doe claimed victory at the October 15, 1985, balloting on the basis of a 50.9 percent presidential vote share, while the NDPL was awarded 73 of the 90 assembly seats.

In June 1987, as part of an apparent effort to consolidate his power, President Doe dismissed four Supreme Court justices, thereby drawing criticism that he had exceeded his constitutional authority. Three months later the government reported that it had thwarted a coup attempt masterminded by former foreign minister Matthews.

During 1988 the regime continued to crack down on real or imagined opponents. In March, William Gabriel KPOLLEH, president of the Liberian Unification Party (LUP), was charged with leading a coup attempt, and in July, Doe's former PRC deputy, J. Nicholas PODIER, was slain in the wake of another alleged overthrow effort (reportedly the ninth since 1980).

In early 1990 what began as a seemingly minor insurrection in the northeastern border region of Nimba County gradually expanded to pose a major threat to the Doe regime. In late 1989 a number of villages had been overrun by a group of about 150 rebels led by Charles Chankay TAYLOR, who five years earlier had escaped from custody in the United States after being charged with the theft of Liberian government funds. In January 1990 the fighting assumed a tribal character, with the rebels (styling themselves the National Patriotic Front of Liberia [NPFL]) attacking members of the president's Krahn ethnic group, and government forces retaliating against Nimba's principal tribe, the Gio. By early June, after steady progress in a series of engagements with Liberian army units, rebel troops were advancing on Monrovia, and by mid-July a "reign of terror" was reported in the capital, with both sides engaging in atrocities against ethnic opponents and unarmed civilians. Meanwhile, an Independent NPFL (INPFL), which had broken with the Taylor group in February under the leadership of Prince Yormic Johnson, emerged as a major "third force" that succeeded in gaining control of central Monrovia on July 23.

With neither the United Nations nor the Organization of African Unity (OAU, subsequently the AU) taking action to ameliorate the conflict, ECOWAS organized a 4,000-man peacekeeping force styled the ECOWAS Monitoring Group (Ecomog), which arrived in Monrovia on August 25, 1990. The intervention was welcomed by Johnson but was bitterly denounced by Taylor, who insisted that the force had been assembled to avert defeat of the Doe regime by the NPFL.

On September 11, 1990, President Doe was killed by members of the Johnson group as the apparent result of an argument that had broken out during a meeting arranged by Ecomog. Government forces nonetheless continued their defense of the heavily fortified executive mansion under the presidential guard commander, Brig. Gen. David NIMLEY. During the next several days four individuals (Johnson, Taylor, Nimley, and the former constitutional commission chair, Amos Sawyer, who headed an Interim Government of National Unity [IGNU] from exile in Banjul, Gambia) proclaimed themselves president, with the last being recognized, on an interim basis, by ECOWAS on November 22. Six days later the three warring factions within Liberia concluded a cease-fire agreement in Bamako, Mali, and declared their intention to participate in a national conference to establish an interim government. Although Taylor was reported to have signed the accord only because of pressure from his two principal backers, Libya and Burkina Faso, the suspension of hostilities generally held into 1991, with the three faction leaders (including Gen. Hezekiah BOWEN, who had succeeded Nimley as head of the Armed Forces of Liberia [AFL]), agreeing to meet in Lomé, Togo, on March 15 to pave the way for a transitional regime. At the last moment, however, Taylor refused to attend without the participation of elected representatives from Liberia's 13 counties, all but one of which his forces claimed to control. A compromise structure was eventually agreed upon, providing for a president and two vice presidents (representing the IGNU, NPFL, and INPFL, respectively). However, there was little immediate progress toward implementation of the plan, and Ecomog experienced mounting pressure to move militarily against the obdurate Taylor. On June 30 the stalemate appeared to have been broken in the course of a meeting attended by Taylor, Sawyer, and five West African heads of government in Yamoussoukro, Côte d'Ivoire, that yielded agreement on the establishment of a commission to organize a national election.

Although the fighting subsided in July–August 1991, Taylor took no action to disarm his forces as mandated by the Yamoussoukro accord, while Johnson on August 6 announced that the INPFL was withdrawing from the tripartite regime. Faced with Taylor's hostility toward the composition of the Ecomog force, Côte d'Ivoire offered to seek Ecomog's replacement by a UN contingent, but the idea was rejected by Sawyer on August 19. Renewed hostilities thereupon broke out in the form of clashes between NPFL units, which had entered Sierra Leone in support of local dissidents, and Sierra Leonean troops, accompanied by a group from former president Doe's Krahn tribe that had styled itself the United Liberation Movement of Liberia for Democracy (Ulimo). Nonetheless, peace talks resumed in Yamoussoukro on September 16 and 17, yielding a new stand-down commitment by the Liberian factions in return for an Ecomog restructuring (primarily in response to NPFL charges that it was Nigerian-dominated).

A fourth summit in Yamoussoukro on October 29–31, 1991, drew a pledge by the NPFL to withdraw from Sierra Leone, disarm its forces, and relinquish Liberian territory under its control to Ecomog. It was also agreed that a buffer zone would be established between Liberia and Sierra Leone and that the Liberian election would be held within six months. On November 8 Johnson's INPFL announced that it would rejoin the interim government, although Ulimo leader Raleigh SEEKIE repudiated the peace agreement. While additional disagreements surfaced by early 1992, including a refusal by both the NPFL and INPFL to honor new banknotes issued by the Sawyer administration, a 13-member interim election commission was sworn in on January 13 with instructions to prepare for legislative and presidential balloting in August. A week later, in his annual message to Monrovia's Interim Assembly, President Sawyer offered NPLF leader Taylor the vacant post of vice president in the interim government on the condition that Taylor join in effective implementation of the most recent Yamoussoukro accord. However, no response was reported.

On April 7 and 8, 1992, ECOWAS representatives met in Geneva, Switzerland, with Sawyer, Taylor, the presidents of Burkina Faso, Côte d'Ivoire, and Senegal, and the vice president of Nigeria. The group reaffirmed its support of Yamoussoukro IV, including establishment of the

Ecomog buffer zone. On April 14 Taylor renounced the agreement, calling it "unbalanced and unsatisfactory," but on April 29 he again reversed himself. On April 30 Ecomog began deployment in border areas theretofore controlled by the NPFL.

In August 1992 heavy fighting broke out between NPFL and Ulimo forces, and in September the NPFL accused Ecomog of supporting the NPFL's ostensibly Sierra Leone-based opponents. Fighting also erupted in October in Monrovia between NPFL and Ecomog units and persisted for the remainder of the year. By early 1993 the ECOWAS contingent appeared to have gained the upper hand, and in March the NPFL was driven (briefly as it turned out) from its stronghold of Gbanga, with its control of the hinterland having been reduced from more than 90 to less than 40 percent. In early April Ecomog troops drove Taylor's forces from the strategic port city of Buchanan, and in May the southeastern port of Greenville also fell, confining the NPFL's maritime access to the small town of Harper near the Côte d'Ivoire border.

On July 25, 1993, in Cotonou, Benin, Liberia's leading combatants (the NPFL, Ulimo, and Ecomog) signed an OAU/UN-brokered peace accord, and on August 1 the lengthy conflict appeared to end, Taylor advising his followers (somewhat prematurely) "to return to your towns and village and begin to rebuild your lives. The war is over." On August 16 the three factions reached agreement on a transitional Council of State to consist of Bismark KUYON and David KPOMAKPOR (IGNU), Dorothy MUSULENG-COOPER (NPFL), and Dr. Mohamed SHERIFF and Thomas ZIAH (Ulimo). The new council proceeded to elect Kuyon, Musuleng-Cooper, and Sheriff as chair and first and second deputy chairs, respectively. However, a scheduled takeover from the Sawyer government on August 24 was postponed by Kuyon, pending the deployment of a peacekeeping force from throughout Africa to oversee disarmament. One week later Nigeria withdrew its personnel from Ecomog (approximately three-quarters of the force total), and on September 22 the UN Security Council voted to establish the UN Observer Mission in Liberia (UNOMIL) to ensure implementation of the Cotonou accord. Subsequently, the IGNU designated Philip A. Z. BANKS to succeed Kuyon, while the NPFL named Gen. Isaac MUSA to replace Musuleng-Cooper.

By late 1993 agreement had been reached on the structure of a unified interim assembly and on the allocation of most portfolios in a transitional government. However, it was not until March 7, 1994, that a restructured Council of State with Kpomakpor as chair was formally installed. Following intense bargaining over the distribution of portfolios, the formation was announced of a full Liberian National Transitional Government (LNTG), which first met on May 16. The transitional period was officially dated from the launching of the Council of State, with a six-month mandate to expire on September 7.

On August 4, 1994, NPFL leader Taylor declared that the transitional administration would have no "legal tenure" after September 7, when multiparty elections had been scheduled to take place. He also demanded a cabinet reshuffle, claiming that several key ministers no longer represented the NPFL, having recently been expelled from the organization for criticizing his leadership.

On September 7, 1994, Taylor joined AFL leader Bowen and Lt. Gen. Alhaji G. V. KROMAH, the leader of Ulimo's Mandingo-based Muslim faction (Ulimo-M), in a meeting on Lake Volta near Akosombo with Ghana president Jerry Rawlings and representatives of Ecomog, the OAU, and the UN secretary general. Five days later, an agreement was signed calling for an immediate end to hostilities; continuance until October 10, 1995, of the transitional government, headed by a new five-member Council of State; and the holding of presidential and legislative elections within a year. During the Akosombo meeting, however, the NPFL dissenters, led by Woewiyu, overran the NPFL headquarters in Gbarnga, forcing Taylor to seek refuge in Côte d'Ivoire.

On September 15, 1994, a rogue AFL group led by Charles JULUE, a former army general under President Doe, launched a predawn raid on the executive mansion in Monrovia. However, the attempted coup was of short duration, Ecomog forces recovering the complex within 24 hours and rescuing Julue from a pummeling by enraged civilians as he attempted to flee the capital.

In October 1994 both UNOMIL and Ecomog forces were substantially reduced as prospects for an end to the lengthy Liberian conflict receded, and on November 6 the Ghanaian and Nigerian governments (the largest contributors to Ecomog) convened a "last ditch" meeting in Accra that included, in addition to the signatories of the Akosombo accord, Gen. Roosevelt JOHNSON, leader of Ulimo's Christian-oriented Krahn faction (Ulimo-K); Dr. George E. S. BOLEY, head of the Krahn-based Liberian Peace Council (LPC); François MAS-SAQUOI, commander of the Lofa Defense Force (LDF); and Woewiyu, representing the NPFL dissidents. However, the meeting adjourned on November 29 with no agreement on the membership of a reconstituted Council of State.

Despite the failure of the November 1994 talks, follow-up discussions were launched in Accra in December, with the major warring groups (the NPFL, Ulimo-K, Ulimo-M, AFL, LNC, LDF, and the Woewiyu dissidents [now styled the Central Revolutionary Council–NPFL]) participating. On December 22 agreement was reached on a cessation of hostilities as of December 28 and on a Council of State to include one representative each from the NPFL, Ulimo, the AFL, and the LNC, with a fifth member to be selected by the NPFL and Ulimo from traditional chiefs. It was further agreed that the Council of State would give way to an elected government on January 1, 1996, after multiparty elections on November 1, 1995.

On January 25, 1995, the warring groups agreed to expand the Council of State from five to six members, but they continued to disagree as to its composition and adjourned the talks indefinitely on January 31. Subsequently, on February 6, Ghanaian mediators rejected a Taylor proposal for another five-man council to be chaired by an elderly traditional chief, Tamba TAYLOR (no relation to the NPFL leader), with Charles Taylor as first vice chair, Ulimo-M's Kromah as second vice chair, and the AFL's Bowen as third vice chair. It was not until August 19 that agreement on the makeup of the

new council was reached and a seemingly conclusive cease-fire declared. The six members inaugurated in Monrovia on September 1 included Charles Taylor, G. V. Kromah, and Dr. George E. S. Boley, in addition to three civilians: Chief Tamba Taylor, Oscar QUIAH, and Wilton S. SANKAWULO, a former university professor and newspaper columnist, who was named council chair.

On September 3, 1995, the Council of State announced the formation of a new Transitional Government. Twelve days later the UN Security Council voted unanimously to extend UNOMIL's mandate to January 31, 1996, and in October Ecomog responded positively to an appeal from its chair, President Rawlings of Ghana, for a fourfold increase in its troop level to oversee disarmament and demobilization of the various warring factions.

On April 6, 1996, renewed fighting broke out throughout Monrovia, sparked by the attempted arrest of Ulimo-K leader Johnson by NPFL and Ulimo-M fighters. Although Johnson's headquarters were easily taken, he escaped capture, and his forces and Krahn defectors from other factions took up arms throughout the city. By April 9 Johnson and his fighters, with several hundred hostages in tow, had been forced to retreat to their Monrovia barracks; however, "systematic" looting continued amid anarchic conditions in the capital.

On April 10, 1996, with extremely intense fighting reported around the U.S. embassy (where thousands of Liberian civilians and foreigners were reported to have sought refuge), the United States ordered the deployment of a warship to the Liberian coast to support an evacuation effort begun the previous day. On the same day the warring faction leaders agreed to a cease-fire; however, it was immediately abandoned after Johnson refused to surrender to Ecomog forces. On April 16, 1996, anti-Johnson militiamen laid siege to his base. Three days later a second cease-fire was announced, and on April 21 the Ulimo-K released the majority of its hostages. Furthermore, Ecomog commanders reported that they had secured the perimeter of Monrovia in an effort to stanch the flow of arms and fighters. Nevertheless, intense fighting reportedly continued.

An ECOWAS summit scheduled for May 8, 1996, in Ghana was canceled after a number of member states and faction leaders refused to attend; for his part, Charles Taylor claimed he and his "government" troops were needed in Monrovia to maintain order. Citing frustration with the "intransigence" of the warring faction leaders, Ghanaian President Rawlings threatened to withdraw Ecomog troops if peace negotiations were not promptly launched.

At ECOWAS's annual summit on July 27–28, 1996, its members pledged to organize Liberian elections within nine months. With fighting reported to have subsided, ECOWAS representatives and all of the faction leaders met in mid-August in Abuja, Nigeria, where they agreed to a revised version of the 1995 Abuja accord. The faction leaders also unanimously elected Ruth PERRY, a senator during the Doe era, to replace Sankawulo as Council of State chair. The cease-fire agreement was highlighted by a schedule for disarmament and demobilization (from November 22, 1996, to January 31, 1997), dissolution of the factions (January 31, 1997), presidential and legislative elections (May 31, 1997), and the inauguration of a new government (on June 15). On August 31 the UNOMIL mandate was extended, and on September 3 Perry was inaugurated, thus becoming the first-ever female African head of state.

Adding muscle to the August 1996 accord, ECOWAS threatened to impose sanctions on "any person or group obstructing the implementation" of the cease-fire agreement. Meanwhile, the United States pledged to finance the anticipated expansion of Ecomog troop strength. Subsequently, amid reports of mass starvation in those areas already cleared of fighters, Ecomog troops began deploying weeks ahead of the scheduled November start of the disarmament process. An assassination attempt against Charles Taylor at the presidential palace on October 31 resulted in suspension of Council of State activities and underscored the fragility of the cease-fire. Nevertheless, registration of political parties continued through the end of the year in preparation for the general elections scheduled for May 1997.

In mid-January 1997 the Council of State reconvened for the first time since the attempt on Taylor's life. Meanwhile, Ecomog's Nigerian leadership increased pressure on the former combatants to turn in their arms. Consequently, the disarmament campaign, which had theretofore elicited only a trickle of returns, accelerated to near conclusion by the end of the month, and, in accordance with the peace accord, on February 1 all the armed factions were declared officially dissolved. In mid-February presidential and legislative balloting was scheduled for May 30, and a seven-member electoral commission was established. Two weeks later, Taylor, Kromah, and Boley resigned from the Council of State to begin preparations for the presidential election. In early March, Perry appointed former information minister Henry ANDREWS as president of the electoral commission, and on April 2 the commission was officially sworn in. Meanwhile, former UN official and international banker Ellen JOHNSON-SIRLEAF emerged as Taylor's primary competition for the presidency in the wake of the splintering of an anti-Taylor coalition, the Alliance of Seven Parties (see Political Parties and Groups, below). In addition, 11 others registered as presidential candidates, and at least 13 parties announced their intention to compete for legislative posts. In mid-May the balloting was postponed to July.

In presidential and legislative balloting on July 19, 1997, Taylor and the restyled National Patriotic Party (NPP) overwhelmed their opponents, with Taylor and his vice presidential running mate, Enoch DOGOLEA, capturing approximately 70 percent of the votes and the NPP securing majorities in both the House of Representatives and the Senate. Although some analysts had forecast a tight race between Taylor and Johnson-Sirleaf, Taylor's well-financed campaign, his veiled threats to recommence fighting if he were to lose the elections, and his election-eve apology for his role in the civil war proved too much for Johnson-Sirleaf. She received just 9 percent of the vote, and the UP was also a distant second at legislative polling. International observers described the balloting as generally fair. However, a number of domestic critics characterized the balloting as irreparably tainted by irregularities. On August 2 Taylor and Dogolea were inaugurated, and by mid-month Taylor had finished appointing a predominantly NPP cabinet.

Fighting intensified in 2002 between government forces and the Liberians United for Reconciliation and Democracy (LURD) and the Movement for Democracy in Liberia (MODEL). As the rebels reached Monrovia in June 2003, peace negotiations between the warring factions were launched in Accra, Ghana. On June 17 the Accra Accord was signed, calling for withdrawal of the rebels to the north of Monrovia, deployment of an international peacekeeping force, and the resignation of Taylor in favor of a transitional government. Within days, however, Taylor reneged on his pledge to resign, and the rebels again advanced on Monrovia.

Near the end of July 2003 ECOWAS authorized the deployment of peacekeeping forces under the banner of the ECOWAS Mission in Liberia (ECOMIL). Some 3,250 ECOMIL troops (mainly from Nigeria) were dispatched to Monrovia in early August. Under intense international pressure, Taylor finally resigned on August 11 and left Liberia for Nigeria. Vice President Moses Zeh BLAH assumed presidential authority on an acting basis, and he quickly negotiated (on August 18) a new cease-fire and a so-called Comprehensive Peace Agreement with the rebels. In accordance with the peace plan, a national transitional government was installed on October 14, with Charles Gyude BRYANT of the Liberia Action Party (LAP) as chair. His cabinet comprised members of the pro-Taylor Government of Liberia (GOL), the LURD, the MODEL, and representatives of civic organizations. At the same time, a 76-member National Transitional Legislative Assembly (NTLA) was installed for a two-year period pending new legislative and presidential elections.

In the first round of presidential balloting on October 11, 2005, George WEAH (a former soccer star) of the Congress for Democratic Change (CDC) led 22 candidates with 28.3 percent of the vote. Ellen Johnson-Sirleaf of the Unity Party (UP) finished second with 19.8 percent. However,

Johnson-Sirleaf handily won the runoff balloting on November 8 with 59.4 percent of the vote. Meanwhile, in the October 11 balloting for the House of Representatives, the CDC led all parties with 15 seats. Since her party did not command a legislative majority, Johnson-Sirleaf (the first democratically elected female leader of a national government in Africa) formed a cabinet that included independents and members of several small parties.

Constitution and Government

The former Liberian constitution, adopted July 26, 1847, was modeled, save in the matter of federalism, after that of the United States. Executive authority was vested in the president, who was limited by a 1975 amendment to a single eight-year term, excluding time spent completing the unexpired term of a predecessor. The bicameral Congress consisted of an 18-member Senate and a 65-member House of Representatives.

The constitution approved in July 1984, with effect from President Doe's inaugural in January 1986, did not differ significantly from its predecessor. Rather than being elected for eight years, the president was restricted to a maximum of two six-year terms, while the legislature was styled the National Assembly. The Senate was increased to 26 members and the house reduced to 64. Suffrage was extended to all adults. The 1984 law also provided for relatively simple registration of political parties, with prohibitions against those considered dangerous to "the free and democratic society of Liberia." Administratively, the country was divided into 9 counties and 5 territories, with lesser units encompassing 30 cities and 145 townships. The number of counties has subsequently increased to 15.

Some of the provisions of the 1984 constitution were superseded by the Comprehensive Peace Agreement of 2003 and the Electoral Reform Act of 2004, which, among other things, established guidelines for elections to a new Senate and House of Representatives (see Legislature, below) and for new presidential/vice presidential balloting.

Foreign Relations

Many of the guiding principles of the OAU originated with President Tubman, who held a prominent position among moderate African leaders dedicated to peaceful change and non-interference in the internal affairs of other countries. President Tolbert was similarly respected in international forums, with the result that the April 1980 coup and his assassination were widely condemned.

Liberia's traditional friendship with the United States was reflected both in the extent of U.S. private investment and in the existence of a bilateral defense agreement. Despite initial U.S. criticism of the PRC takeover in 1980, neither proved to be seriously threatened. The Doe government's essentially pro-Western posture was reflected in its cool treatment of the Libyan and Soviet ambassadors (the latter being expelled in October 1983 for alleged involvement in an antigovernment conspiracy), while in July 1985 relations with Moscow were severed for "gross interference" stemming from links between student activists and the Soviet embassy in Monrovia. In May 1987, on the other hand, the embassy was permitted to reopen in the context of an overture to the eastern bloc, while in mid-1989 Doe renewed ties with former close confidant Muammar Qadhafi of Libya.

The core group of rebels led by Charles Taylor in early 1990 was reported to have been given commando training in Burkina Faso and Libya, while the initial point of entry into Nimba appeared to have been from neighboring Côte d'Ivoire. Although the United States maintained formal neutrality in the conflict, it appeared somewhat embarrassed by its support of the Doe regime and suspended trade concessions to Liberia in early May. Concurrently, the United States dispatched a naval flotilla to the region to evacuate American citizens wishing to leave. In March 1991, despite a continued display of reluctance to become involved in Liberian internal affairs, the United States was reported to have worked behind the scenes to persuade the NPFL's Taylor to participate in the roundtable discussions that yielded the abortive cease-fire of May 1991 and the equally abortive peace agreement of the following October.

In mid-1998 Liberia accused Guinea of attempting to destabilize Liberia through its role in Ecomog. Monrovia's diplomatic offensive against Guinean officials (who denied the charges) coincided with a heightening of tension between the Taylor administration and the Ghanaian and Nigerian governments over Monrovia's alleged support of rebels who were fighting the ECOWAS-backed government of Sierra Leone. In early 1999 the United States declared that it had uncovered evidence of Liberia's support for the rebels, and shortly thereafter Nigeria withdrew its remaining troops from Liberia, asserting that it could no longer maintain a mission there while Monrovia supported attacks against Nigerian troops in Freetown.

An armed incursion from Guinea into northwestern Liberia was reported in April 1999, prompting a state of emergency in Lofa County. Under ECOWAS mediation, a tripartite commission was formed to attempt to reduce friction in the diamond-rich areas at the conjunction of the borders of Liberia, Guinea, and Sierra Leone. Consequently, a degree of stability ensued, permitting the final Ecomog contingents to leave Liberia in October and the borders to be reopened with Sierra Leone (in October) and Guinea (in February 2000). However, major fighting erupted in mid-2000 along the border with Guinea, the Liberian government accusing the Guinean government of supporting anti-Taylor elements that had loosely coalesced as the LURD. Skirmishes continued into 2001, exacerbating already extensive refugee problems. Among other things, Liberian refugees in Guinea claimed they were being mistreated by the Guinean military, which in turn argued that the refugees were helping Guinean rebels (see article on Guinea for additional information). Meanwhile, President Taylor faced growing international pressure for his apparent continued support of the Revolutionary United Front (RUF) in Sierra Leone. The complicated subregional conflict pitted the militaries of Guinea and Sierra Leone, Liberian rebels, and certain tribal groups (notably the Kamajors) from

Sierra Leone on one side against the Liberian army and rebel groups from Guinea and Sierra Leone on the other. Much of the fighting involved control of rich mining areas, diamond production permitting various factions to buy armaments for their military campaigns.

In May 2001 the United Nations imposed an embargo on Liberian trade in diamonds and arms and barred senior Liberian officials from international travel as a means of encouraging Taylor's disengagement from the civil war in Sierra Leone. Combined with other pressure (including the suspension of EU development aid), the UN initiative appeared to have the desired effect in contributing to a tentative resolution of the situation in Sierra Leone (see article on Sierra Leone for details). However, fighting between the LURD and Liberian government continued into 2002, relations between Guinea and Liberia remaining tense until a somewhat surprising meeting in late February of the presidents of Liberia, Guinea, and Sierra Leone at which agreement was reached on enhanced border security, repatriation of refugees, and reactivation of the Mano River Union.

The intensification of the civil war in Liberia in late 2002 and early 2003 exacerbated tensions with regional powers as well as with the broader international community. Ghana, Nigeria, and Sierra Leone attempted to mediate a cease-fire as rebel forces moved on Monrovia. For their part many Western capitals urged President Taylor to resign. (Relations with the United States had deteriorated in late 2002 when evidence allegedly emerged that al-Qaida financiers may have been profiting from the Liberian diamond-smuggling trade.)

The UN endorsed the ECOWAS peacekeeping force in early August 2003, but by September ECOMIL had been superseded by a new UN force of 11,500 called the UN Mission in Liberia (UNMIL). Meanwhile, the United States pressed Nigeria to turn Taylor over to the UN for possible prosecution on charges related to his alleged activities in Sierra Leone.

In September 2005 Charles Bryant, the chair of Liberia's transitional government, attended a UN summit in New York where he deposited some

103 international treaties and agreements, part of a "backlog" that had accumulated over the past decade while Liberia had been a dysfunctional state.

The United States supported the continuing efforts to demobilize the militia groups in Liberia in 2005–2006, pledging some $200 million for the effort and providing American military advisors to help train a new security force. President Johnson-Sirleaf continued to press for expanded U.S. aid in 2006, meeting with President George W. Bush in March.

In November 2005, the UN expanded the mandate of UNMIL to include the capture of Charles Taylor and his transfer to the UN Special Court for Sierra Leone. In December 2005 the UN renewed sanctions that prohibited travel for some 60 Liberians who were suspected of involvement in the conflict in Sierra Leone.

After a lengthy campaign by a range of international bodies, on March 25, 2006, the Nigerian government announced that it would honor a request to extradite Taylor to stand trial before the UN Special Court for Sierra Leone. Taylor briefly escaped on March 28, but he was recaptured the following day. He was transferred to Monrovia, and then to the Special Court in Freetown, Sierra Leone. Johnson-Sirleaf subsequently requested that Taylor be transferred to The Hague to stand trial so that his presence in Sierra Leone did not destabilize the region.

Current Issues

In 1998 President Taylor wielded an increasingly heavy hand in response to domestic criticism, shutting down opposition media outlets, purging dissenters from the government, and, according to critics, covertly supporting violent attacks on opposition foes. In mid-September dozens of people were reportedly killed in Monrovia when presidential forces attempted to arrest Gen. Roosevelt Johnson, who had refused to release his grip on a section of the capital and was suspected of plotting to overthrow the government. During the fighting, Johnson and his entourage fled to the U.S. embassy, where they were allowed to enter only after Taylor's forces attacked and killed two of Johnson's associates and wounded two U.S. personnel. The following day, Johnson, Lt. Gen. Alhaji KROMAH of the All-Liberia Coalition Party (ALCOP), and approximately 20 others were charged with treason. Subsequently, Johnson and Kromah escaped from the country (the former by U.S. helicopter), and neither of the two men, nor half of their codefendants, appeared at the opening of their trial in November. (In April 1999, 13 of the "coup plotters" were sentenced to ten years in prison.)

At a July 1999 weapons-destruction ceremony, President Taylor declared the end of a "dark chapter" in Liberian history. (More than 200,000 people had died in the civil war.) It soon became clear, however, that many of Taylor's opponents had not given up their fight, as evidenced by LURD guerrilla activity in the northwest (see Foreign relations, above, and Political Parties and Groups, below). In August 2000 the administration charged a number of opposition figures (many in exile) with treason in connection with ongoing "dissident" activities. However, facing heavy international pressure for both his domestic policies and his involvement in regional conflicts, Taylor amnestied many of his opponents and urged them to return to Liberia to assume a role in the political process. Although the fragile peace in Sierra Leone offered some respite for Taylor and other participants in the interlocking regional disputes, the LURD offensive continued into early 2002. Opposition leaders also accused the administration in the first half of 2002 of increasingly repressive (and sometimes violent) measures against dissident voices in the media and elsewhere. In addition, international human rights activists charged Liberian security forces with numerous violations that were seen as contributing to a deteriorating political climate. Meanwhile, in May the UN extended its embargo on the purchase of diamonds from Liberia for 12 months in light of the intensified LURD/government fighting.

In January 2003 the government announced that new presidential and legislative elections would be held in October. However, rebel fighters launched an offensive in February that neared Monrovia in April, causing a mass exodus from the capital and making it clear that normal political activity was an impossibility without a cease-fire. Complicating matters for President Taylor was an indictment from the UN-sponsored court in Sierra Leone charging him with 17 counts of crimes against humanity in connection with his alleged role in that nation's recently resolved conflict. A warrant for Taylor's arrest on those charges remained outstanding even after he resigned the presidency in August and went into exile in Nigeria as part of the comprehensive cease-fire and agreement for installation of a new transitional government. For his part, Charles Gyude Bryant, the chair of the transitional government, dedicated his administration to the task of bringing Liberia "back from the brink of self-destruction." Priorities included the disarmament (with help from the UNMIL) of the former warring factions and assistance for some 300,000 internal or external refugees (as of November 2004). Sporadic clashes between Muslims and Christians in several areas of the country also contributed to the government's difficulties.

In April 2005 the transitional government signed a secretive deal with the West African Mining Corporation (Wamco). The agreement granted Wamco an exclusive contract to purchase all minerals in the western regions of Liberia, except in cases where prior contracts existed. In exchange, Wamco pledged to provide $2 million over two years to create local cooperatives and to pay the government $1 million directly. The agreement was heavily criticized by the UN and international financial organizations. For many in Liberia, the emergence of the details of the deal, combined with revelations of other alleged financial improprieties, tainted the tenure of the transitional government.

More than 20 candidates contested the first round of presidential balloting in October 2005. The subsequent runoff pitted George Weah, a former soccer star who ran a populist campaign and enjoyed the support of some elements of the former Taylor regime, against Ellen Johnson-Sirleaf, a long-standing member of the anti-Taylor opposition and a former World Bank official who was championed as the candidate who could best restore Liberia's international ties and garner much-needed foreign reconstruction aid. Weah initially alleged fraud surrounding his loss in the second round, although EU and ECOWAS observers described the balloting as generally free and fair and the national election commission dismissed Weah's complaints. Liberian security forces and UN peacekeepers used tear gas and riot batons to disperse protest demonstrations by Weah's supporters shortly after the balloting. Even more violent demonstrations broke out in December after Weah delivered a speech that was highly critical of the elections and Johnson-Sirleaf. However, in order to defuse the situation, Weah later in the month announced he had accepted his defeat and urged his supporters to do likewise.

On January 16, 2006, Edwin Melvin SNOWE was elected speaker of the house, defeating UP candidate Dusty WOLOKOLLIE on a vote of 48 to 13. Snowe, a son-in-law of former president Taylor, was under a UN travel ban and was widely associated with the previous regime.

Despite ongoing political tension throughout the country and the diversity of the new legislature, lawmakers in early 2006 appeared ready to work with the Johnson-Sirleaf administration. All of the new president's cabinet appointments were approved by March, as were most of her initial legislative proposals. The international community also responded positively to the completion of the elections (see The Country, above). Meanwhile, in late June former president Taylor was transferred to The Hague, Netherlands, to face trial by a temporarily moved session of the UN Special Court for Sierre Leone on charges of war crimes and crimes against humanity.

Political Parties and Groups

For more than a century prior to the 1980 coup, an Americo-Liberian elite had dominated Liberia's politics through the True Whig Party (TWP), most of whose leaders were subsequently assassinated or executed.

Upon the PRC's assumption of power in 1980, political party activity was suspended, a ban that was extended in December 1982 to any individual or group "caught making unfavorable speeches and pronouncements against the government."

The ban was repealed in July 1984, although only the National Democratic Party of Liberia (NDPL), Liberia Liberal Party (LLP), Liberia Action Party (LAP), and Liberia Unification Party (LUP) were permitted to contest the election of October 15, 1985.

In anticipation of presidential and legislative elections, the Alliance of Seven Parties was formed in February 1997 by the LAP, LUP, NDPL, TWP, the Liberian People's Party (LPP), the Unity Party (UP), and the United People's Party (UPP). On March 24 the alliance held intraparty primary elections to choose a presidential candidate for the upcoming elections; however, the victory of the LAP's Cletus Wotorson was immediately challenged, and both the UPP and LPP withdrew from the coalition, claiming that the LAP had engaged in fraud and "vote buying." With the alliance in disarray, the LPP, LUP, and TWP announced in June that they had switched their allegiance to UP presidential candidate Ellen Johnson-Sirleaf (although the LPP ultimately fielded its own candidate). Likewise, a coalition of the three most prominent Krahn parties—the Liberia Peace Council (LPC), the NDPL, and the Krahn faction of the United Liberation Movement of Liberia for Democracy (Ulimo)—proved unable to reach agreement on campaign tactics and splintered.

One manifestation of efforts to forge an anti-Taylor alliance was the Collaborating Political Parties (CPP), whose members included the All-Liberian Coalition Party, the Free Democratic Party, the LAP, the Liberian National Union, the LPP, the NDPL, the People's Democratic Party of Liberia, the Progressive People's Party, the Reformation Alliance Party, the TWP, UP, and UPP.

Prior to the October 2005 elections, 22 parties and groupings registered to contest the legislative and presidential elections.

Legislative Parties

Congress for Democratic Change (CDC). Formed in 2005 and led by former soccer star George Weah, the CDC is a populist party with broad appeal among Liberia's poor. Following the 2005 legislative balloting, the CDC became the largest party in the house with 15 seats. It gained 3 seats in the Senate. The party splintered in March 2006 when Samuel TWEAH Jr., the chair of the American branch of the party, resigned along with other leading CDC figures, citing financial irregularities and a dispute over whom the party should have supported for speaker of the house.

Leaders: George WEAH (Party President and 2005 presidential candidate), Lenn Eugene NAGBE (Secretary General), Acarous GRAY (Assistant Secretary General).

Liberty Party (LP). Formed in 2005, the LP is led by Charles Brumskine, who placed third in the October presidential polling with 13.9 percent of the vote. The LP secured 9 seats in the 2005 house elections, making it the second largest party in the chamber. It gained 3 seats in the Senate. At a party congress in February 2006, Brumskine announced that he would not stand as the party's presidential candidate in the 2011 elections, and a new slate of party leaders was elected, including a new national chair, Israel Akinsanya.

Leaders: Charles BRUMSKINE (Party President and 2005 presidential candidate), Israel AKINSANYA (Chair).

Coalition for the Transformation of Liberia (COTOL). Formed in July 2005 as an electoral coalition by the four parties below in preparation for the October presidential and legislative balloting, the COTOL chose the LAP's Varney G. Sherman as its presidential candidate. The COTOL became the largest Senate grouping with 7 seats and also won 8 seats in the house. Sherman placed fifth in the presidential election with 7.8 percent of the vote. Most of the COTOL components supported George Weah in the presidential runoff.

Leaders: Isaac F. MANNEH (Chair), Napoleon TOQUE (Vice Chair), Varney G. SHERMAN (2005 presidential candidate).

Liberia Action Party (LAP). The LAP was organized by Tuan WREH, a former supporter and political confidant of General Doe, who was subsequently joined by a number of Tolbert-era officials, including ex-finance minister Ellen Johnson-Sirleaf. In 1985 the LAP emerged as the NDPL's primary challenger following disqualification of the UPP (below), winning two Senate and eight house seats. It decided, however, to boycott legislative proceedings because of the detention of Johnson-Sirleaf and other party leaders for their alleged role in the 1985 coup attempt. In early 1986 Wreh and another LAP member were expelled from the party for agreeing to take their seats in defiance of the boycott. Johnson-Sirleaf, though pardoned in May 1986, fled to the United States claiming her life was in danger after her rearrest in July.

The subsequent naming of an LAP member, David FARHAT, to Doe's cabinet failed to abate the party's antigovernment criticism. The group derided the arrival of U.S. financial experts in early 1988 as a "disgrace to Africa, and Liberia in particular" and in September joined with the Unity Party (UP, above) in condemning the government's banning of student politics. In mid-1989 the leaders of the LAP, UP, and United People's Party (UPP, below) issued a joint communiqué calling on Doe to enact economic and political reforms and return to the tenets of the 1984 constitution. The government responded by dismissing Farhat from his position as finance minister, despite his being credited with increasing budgetary restraint and the repayment of U.S. loans. The LAP's Jackson F. DOE (no relation to the former chief executive) was widely believed to have been the actual winner of the 1985 presidential contest; he was reported in 1990 to have been executed by order of rebel leader Charles Taylor.

At a meeting of the Alliance of Seven Parties in March 1997, the LAP's presidential candidate, Cletus Wotorson, was chosen as the coalition's standard-bearer. However, charges that the primary had been rigged in his favor led to the splintering of the Alliance and prompted the LAP's most prominent member, Ellen Johnson-Sirleaf, to defect to the UP.

In 2003 LAP Chair Charles Gyude BRYANT was chosen as chair of the new transitional government, although he subsequently suspended his party activity to avoid the appearance of favoritism.

Leaders: Varney G. SHERMAN (Chair), Cletus WOTORSON (1997 presidential candidate).

Liberia Unification Party (LUP). Organized in 1984 by William Gabriel KPOLLEH, former president of the Monrovia Public School Teachers' Association, the LUP was initially viewed as a potential "Trojan horse" by the NDPL. Kpolleh surprised many observers by backing the LAP-led legislative boycott, with all four of the party's assembly members refusing to take their seats. In March 1988 the party's leader and deputy leader were arrested on charges of plotting to overthrow the government and were given ten-year prison sentences the following October. Kpolleh was released in 1991 and was later assassinated, although the LUP remained active.

Leaders: Isaac F. MANNEH (Chair).

True Whig Party (TWP). Founded in 1868 and Liberia's ruling party until banned in the wake of the 1980 coup, the TWP was revived in 1991. Many members of the TWP defected to either the CDC or the UP prior to the 2005 elections.

Leaders: Peter VUKU (Chair), Othello R. MASON (Secretary General).

People's Democratic Party of Liberia (PDPL). The PDPL was represented by George Toe WASHINGTON in the 1997 presidential balloting. The PDPL broke with the other parties in COTOL and supported Ellen Johnson-Sirleaf in the 2005 presidential runoff.

Leaders: Napoleon TOQUE (Chair), G. Narrison TOULEE (Secretary General).

Unity Party (UP). The UP was formed by Dr. Edward B. Kesselly, who had served as local government minister in the Tolbert administration and subsequently chaired the PRC's Constituent Advisory Assembly. The party elected one senator and two representatives in the 1985 balloting. In November 1988 Kesselly claimed that the government was attempting to "frame" him in an effort to squelch his anticorruption protests. (Kesselly died in 1993.)

In April 1997 former finance minister and UN official Ellen Johnson-Sirleaf defected from the LAP, below, and joined the UP to campaign for the presidency. The addition of Johnson-Sirleaf gave the UP newfound prominence and, subsequently, the backing of the TWP, LUP, and a number of LPP members. Despite early polling showing her with a higher popularity rating than Taylor, Johnson-Sirleaf and the UP's poorly financed efforts were ultimately no match for the NPP.

In late 1998 the UP pledged to continue participating in the electoral process if the government would guarantee the security of its candidates. In August 2000 the government issued an arrest warrant for Johnson-Sirleaf for her alleged role in the dissident activities in Lofa County. However, she was granted amnesty in July 2001 and returned to Monrovia in September.

Johnson-Sirleaf was one of the candidates to lead the NTLA in 2003 but failed to gain sufficient support. After she was chosen as the UP's 2005 presidential candidate, a number of prominent members of other parties reportedly defected to the UP in solidarity with her. In July, the newly-formed Liberia First Group signed an accord with the UP to support the UP and Johnson-Sirleaf in the elections. Johnson-Sirleaf won the presidency in the second round of balloting in November 2005, while the UP gained eight seats in the house and four in the Senate in the legislative elections.

Leaders: Charles CLARKE (Chair), Ellen JOHNSON-SIRLEAF (President of the Republic), Joseph BOAKAI (Vice President of the Republic), Walter WISNER (Secretary General).

Alliance for Peace and Democracy (APD). Formed as a coalition in advance of the October 2005 elections by the two parties below, the APD chose the LPP's Togba-Nah Tipoteh as its presidential candidate. He placed ninth in the first round of balloting with 2.3 percent of the vote. The APD secured five seats in the house and three seats in the Senate.

Leader: Marcus DAHN (Chair).

Liberian People's Party (LPP). The LPP was organized by former members of the Movement for Justice in Africa (Moja), whose leader, Togba-Nah Tipoteh, had been dismissed from the cabinet for alleged complicity in a countercoup attempt in August 1981. Moja was a Left-nationalist, Pan-Africanist formation organized in 1973 and banned in 1981, at which time Tipoteh went into exile. LPP leader Amos SAWYER, former chair of the PRC's national constitutional commission, was also charged with plotting against the regime in August 1984, although the allegation was widely interpreted as an attempt by General Doe to discredit a leading rival for the presidency in 1985. Reportedly in retaliation for his subsequent unwillingness to accept an offer to campaign as General Doe's running mate, an audit was initiated in early 1985 of Sawyer's finances as constitutional commission chair, thus permitting the electoral commission to deny registration to the LPP. In 1988 Sawyer testified against the Doe regime before a U.S. congressional committee considering revocation of Liberia's preferential trade status. In November 1990 he was named to head the ECOWAS-supported caretaker government, thereby reportedly earning the disapproval of some LPP stalwarts. Meanwhile, Tipoteh, an avowed supporter of Prince Johnson, returned to Monrovia in mid-1991 to preside over Moja's relaunching as a paramilitary formation styled the Black Berets/Moja, which was later disbanded.

The LPP was significantly fractionalized in regard to the 1997 presidential elections, partly due to the competing presidential ambitions of Sawyer, Tipoteh, and George Klay KIEH, Jr., another LPP founder. The party initially intended to back a joint opposition candidate forwarded by the Alliance of Seven Parties (see above). However, following the Alliance's nomination of Cletus Wotorson, Tipoteh declared that the Alliance's primary had been fraudulent and announced the withdrawal of the LPP from the grouping. Tipoteh then served as the LPP standard-bearer in the presidential balloting, although Sawyer, former LPP chair Dusty

Wolokollie, and other prominent LPP members supported various other candidates. Sawyer, Wolokollie, and others were subsequently expelled from the LPP. Meanwhile, Edwin Dennis-Weah, a prominent attorney, was selected by the LPP's national committee to succeed James Logan as secretary general, Logan reportedly having become disillusioned with the political infighting. For his part, Kieh resigned from the LPP and subsequently formed a New Deal Movement (below) that included a number of other disgruntled former LPP members.

Tipoteh has served as the primary spokesman within Liberia since 1997 for the LPP (which also has an active branch in the United States), and as of mid-2002 was the only announced candidate for the LPP presidential nomination for 2003. Among other things, he objected to the government's imposition of a state of emergency in February 2002 and subsequent ban on certain public gatherings, arguing that the measures could mask inappropriate harassment by the administration of legitimate opposition voices. Tipoteh also denounced the national electoral commission as partisan in favor of the NPP, earning a growing reputation as one of the nation's leading anti-Taylor voices. Meanwhile, some LPP leaders (including Dennis-Weah and Chair John Karweaye) remained outside Liberia as of mid-2002, as did numerous leaders from other opposition parties concerned over what they perceived as a deteriorating security situation in Liberia and increasingly heavy-handed behavior by the administration and security forces.

Leaders: Togba-Nah TIPOTEH (1997 and 2005 presidential candidate), Richard S. PANTON.

United People's Party (UPP). A centrist outgrowth of the pre-coup People's Progressive Party and viewed as the most serious threat to the NDPL, the UPP was organized by former PPP leader Gabriel Baccus Matthews, who had been dismissed as foreign minister in November 1981 because of opposition to a pro-U.S. posture by the Doe regime and had left the government again in April 1983 after serving for a year as secretary general of the cabinet. Although meeting legal requirements for registration, the UPP was not permitted to participate in the 1985 balloting because of its leader's "socialist leanings" and unofficially supported Jackson Doe of the LAP in the presidential race. A number of leading officials quit the party because of the exiled Matthews's unwillingness to join an opposition coalition in March 1986, which induced the government to permit his return from the United States and rescind its proscription of the formation in late September. Although labeled a "loyal opposition," in May 1989 the party was accused of printing "propagandist statements" in its newsletter, *UPP Times*. As of September 2001 the UPP was active in efforts to form a loose anti-Taylor opposition alliance.

The UPP's Wesley Johnson was chosen as vice chair of the transitional government in 2003.

Leaders: Marcus DAHN (Chair), Wesley JOHNSON.

National Patriotic Party (NPP). Restyled the National Patriotic Party in 1997, the small rebel group launched by Charles Taylor in Liberia's northeastern region in 1989 was originally called the National Patriotic Front of Liberia (NPFL). The NPFL dissidents reportedly included a number of former Liberian soldiers who had fled abroad after the 1985 coup attempt. By April 1990 the rebels were posing a serious threat to the Doe regime and three months later were in control of much of Liberia's hinterland as well as of large sections of Monrovia. The NPFL was precluded from consolidating its control of the country by opposition from Prince Yormic Johnson's breakaway INPFL and the intervention of an ECOWAS force (Ecomog) in August. The NPFL succeeded in gaining control of most of Liberia, except for the capital, by mid-1992, although experiencing reverses thereafter.

Charles Taylor received an enthusiastic reception upon his arrival in Monrovia to take a seat on the Council of State in September 1995. However, it was Taylor's attempt to arrest Ulimo-K leader Roosevelt Johnson on murder charges that ignited the violence that exploded in the capital on April 6, 1996, and in May, Taylor's announced plans to boycott an ECOWAS peace summit led, in part, to its cancellation. On the other hand, in July, Taylor publicly apologized for his role in the outbreak of fighting, asserting that he had underestimated the risk of his actions. Furthermore, on September 30 Taylor pledged to comply with the disarmament provisions of the August peace accord and cooperate with international peacekeepers. Subsequently, on October 7 the NPFL leader announced the establishment of a presidential campaign vehicle, the National Committee for the Promotion of Charles Ghankay Taylor.

On October 31, 1996, Taylor reportedly narrowly escaped an assassination attempt at the presidential mansion that claimed the lives of three of his bodyguards. Taylor accused the leaders of the LPC and Ulimo-K of planning the attack, but both denied involvement.

In accordance with the 1996 peace pact, on January 31, 1997, the NPFL's military wing was officially dissolved. On February 1 the interim National Patriotic Association of Liberia (NAPAL) was formed and charged with overseeing the transformation of the NPFL's political wing, the National Patriotic Party, into a legal political party, and in April the NPP was officially registered. Charles Taylor and the NPP scored easy electoral victories in July 1997, and, following his inauguration in August, the new president named a government dominated by NPP stalwarts.

The NPP provided the main base of support for Taylor in the subsequent civil war, and Taylor's actions appeared to undercut popular support for the NPP. Following Taylor's departure from Liberia in August 2003, many NPP members reportedly continued to support him, and he reportedly remained in contact with them as of mid-2005. However, other NPP stalwarts disassociated themselves from Taylor and joined other parties. In the first round of the 2005 presidential balloting, the NPP's Roland Massaquoi placed sixth with 4.1 percent of the vote.

In the legislative elections, the NPP won four seats in the house and three seats in the Senate. Taylor's wife, Jewel HOWARD-TAYLOR, was elected to the Senate.

Taylor was extradited from Nigeria in March 2006 and placed in the custody of the UN's Special Court for Sierra Leone.

Leaders: Charles Chankay (Ghankay/Gankay) TAYLOR (Former President of the Republic, under UN arrest), Lawrence GEORGE (Acting Chair), Roland MASSAQUOI (2005 presidential candidate), John WHITFIELD (Secretary General).

New Deal Movement (NDM). The NDM was launched in 1999 by a number of former LPP members, including George Klay Kieh Jr., a professor who had found his goal of running for president of the republic blocked by senior LPP leaders. The NDM achieved formal party status in mid-2002. Kieh received 0.5 percent of the vote in the first round of presidential balloting in 2005. The NDM gained three seats in the 2005 house elections, but did not secure any Senate seats.

Leaders: George Klay KIEH Jr. (2005 presidential candidate).

All-Liberia Coalition Party (ALCOP). The ALCOP was formed in November 1996 by Ulimo-M leader Lt. Gen. Alhaji G. V. Kromah, who said that the new party would serve as a vehicle for ethnic Krahns and Mandingos. Although Kromah claimed to have completely disarmed his militants by the end of January 1997, a raid on his headquarters in February unearthed an arms cache, and he was briefly detained. Underlining reports that his coalition-building efforts had failed, Kromah and ALCOP legislative candidates fared poorly at balloting in July. Subsequently, Kromah called for new elections, claiming that the July polling had been severely marred by irregularities.

In September 1998 Kromah was indicted for allegedly plotting a coup against Charles Taylor. Subsequently, Kromah fled the country and ignored a summons to appear in court in November. In April 1999 former Ulimo-M members clashed with government forces in northern Liberia; however, the government's allegations that Kromah was behind the incursion from Guinea remained unconfirmed.

In August members of the hitherto unknown **Joint Forces for the Liberation of Liberia** (JFLL), a group reportedly formed by former Ulimo-M members, clashed with security forces and briefly kidnapped foreign aid workers. Kromah received 7.8 percent of the vote in the first round of the 2005 presidential polling. In the legislative elections, Alcop secured two seats in the house and one in the Senate.

Leaders: David KORTIE (Chair), Lt. Gen. Alhaji G. V. KROMAH (1997 and 2005 presidential candidate).

National Democratic Party of Liberia (NDPL). Essentially a Krahn-based party, the NDPL was formed in August 1984 to support the policies and projected presidential candidacy of General Doe. Amid widespread opposition charges of fraud at the 1985 election, the NDPL, in addition to electing Doe, was awarded an overwhelming majority of seats in both houses of the National Assembly. President Doe was killed on September 11, 1990.

In early 1997 the NDPL, LPC, and Ulimo-K participated in the Alliance of Seven Parties under the NDPL's banner; however, following the Alliance's splintering, the Krahn ties also unraveled. Subsequently, former vice president Harry Moniba was the party's standard-bearer at presidential polling in July. Meanwhile, Moniba was also linked to a theretofore unknown formation, the **Liberian National Union** (LINU).

NDPL candidate Winston Tubman came in fourth in the first round of the 2005 presidential balloting with 9.2 percent of the vote. The NDPL secured one seat in the house and two seats in the Senate. Two posts in the subsequent Johnson-Sirleaf administration were given to members of the NDPL.

Leaders: Nyandeh SIGH (Chair), Harry MONIBA (1997 presidential candidate), Winston TUBMAN (2005 presidential candidate).

National Reformation Party (NRP). The NRP was formed by Martin Sheriff in 1996. In the 2005 presidential balloting, Bishop Alfred Reeves was the party's candidate and Sheriff was the vice presidential candidate. Reeves, a Christian prelate, and Sheriff, a leading Muslim, campaigned on a platform of religious harmony and a return to morality. Reeves received 0.3 percent of the vote in the first round of balloting, last among the 22 candidates. In the legislative elections, the NRP secured one seat in the house and one in the Senate. The NRP supported George Weah in the presidential runoff.

Leaders: Bishop Alfred REEVES (2005 presidential candidate), Martin SHERIFF (2005 vice presidential candidate and 1997 presidential candidate).

United Democratic Alliance (UDA). Formed prior to the 2005 elections as a coalition of the three small parties below, the UDA put forth John Morlu as its presidential candidate. Morlu ran a populist campaign that emphasized nonviolence and pledged to end corruption and improve social services. Morlu received 1.2 percent of the vote in the first round. The UDA won one seat in the 2005 legislative elections. The LINU and LEDP supported George Weah in the second round of the presidential poll.

Leaders: Aaron WESSEH (Chair), John MORLU (2005 presidential candidate).

Liberia National Union (LINU). The LINU was formed by former vice president of the republic and NDPL executive, Harry MONIBA, in 1996 as a party for the Lofan and Gbandi peoples. Moniba unsuccessfully contested the 1997 presidential elections as the LINU candidate. Moniba died in 2004. In May 2005, at a party congress, John Morlu was elected as the party's leader and candidate for the 2005 presidential elections. Morlu subsequently endeavored to broaden the appeal of the party outside of its traditional base.

Leader: John MORLU (Party Leader and 2005 presidential candidate), Aaron WESSEH (Chair), and Jerome GEORGE (Secretary General).

Liberia Education and Development Party (LEDP). The LEDP was formed in 2004 under the leadership of Rev. Hananiah Zoe. It is a Christian party that was initially created as a

vehicle for Zoe's presidential bid in 2005. However, Zoe subsequently agreed to join the UDA and support John Morlu for the 2005 presidential election.

Leaders: Rev. Hananiah ZOE (2005 presidential candidate), and Benedict MATADI (Chair).

Reformation Alliance Party (RAP). Formed in 1996, the RAP unsuccessfully contested the 1997 presidential elections. In July 2005 Dr. H. Boima Fahnbulleh Jr., the RAP 1997 presidential candidate (and a former foreign minister) resigned from the party. The RAP split with the other UDA parties and endorsed Ellen Johnson-Sirleaf in the 2005 presidential runoff.

Leader: Losine N. SARYON.

Other Parties That Participated in the 2005 Elections

Liberia Equal Rights Party (LERP). At a party convention in August 2005, delegates elected Joseph Korto as the LERP candidate for the 2005 presidential election. Korto won 3.3 percent of the vote (seventh place) in the first round of balloting. The LERP supported Ellen Johnson-Sirleaf in the November presidential runoff.

Leader: Joseph KORTO (2005 presidential candidate).

Reformed United Liberia Party (RULP). The RULP was formed in 2005 by William "Shad" Tubman, the son of former president William Tubman. The younger Tubman received 1.6 percent of the vote in the first round of the subsequent presidential poll; the RULP failed to secure any seats in the legislative elections. The RULP supported Ellen Johnson-Sirleaf in the 2005 runoff election but subsequently charged that the UP failed to honor a pre-runoff agreement that would have provided a cabinet position for the RULP.

Leaders: William "Shad" TUBMAN (2005 presidential candidate), Peter S. MENYOU.

Progressive Democratic Party (Prodem). Formed in 2004, Prodem was initially composed mainly of former LURD members, including former LURD leader Sekou Conneh, who was chosen as the party's presidential candidate. Conneh received only 0.6 percent of the vote in the first round of the presidential election, and the party did not gain any seats in the legislative elections. Following the November presidential runoff, Conneh was prominent in efforts to convince George Weah's supporters to accept the decision of the election commission to declare Ellen Johnson-Sirleaf the victor.

Leaders: Sekou CONNEH (2005 presidential candidate), Amara KROMAK (Chair), Jackie C. DEVINE (Secretary General).

National Party of Liberia (NPL). Formed in 2005 by former senator Armah Jallah, the NPL appealed mainly to Liberians from the Lofa region. Jallah claimed that God had asked him to seek the presidency; he received 0.4 percent of the vote. Richard SAMKA (an NPL executive) and other members of the party defected to the UP just prior to the October 2005 elections. The NPL endorsed George Weah in the 2005 presidential runoff.

Leader: Armah JALLAH (Party Founder and 2005 presidential candidate).

Union of Liberian Democrats (ULD). Formed in 2005 by Dr. Robert Kpoto, the ULD is a mainly Lofan grouping. In September 2005 senior members of the ULD broke away to form a new party—the **Progressive Independent Movement of the ULD** (PIMULD). The PIMULD supported the COTOL and Varney Sherman in the October 2005 elections, and both the ULD and the PIMULD endorsed George Weah in the November runoff. (Kpoto had received just 0.4 percent of the vote in the first round of the presidential poll.)

Leaders: Dr. Robert KPOTO (Party Founder and 2005 presidential candidate), George J. TARN (Chair).

Other parties and groups that participated in the 2005 elections include the **Free Democratic Party** (FDP), formed in 1996 and led by Ciapha GBOLLIE, George BORWAH, and David FARHAT (2005 presidential candidate); the **Freedom Alliance Party of Liberia** (FAPL), led by Margaret THOMPSON (2005 presidential candidate); the **Labor Party of Liberia** (LPL) led by Joseph WOAH-TEE (2005 presidential candidate); the **Liberia Destiny Party** (LDP), led by Nathaniel BARNES (2005 presidential candidate); the **Liberia First Group** (LFG), formed in 2005 and led by former LPP chair Dusty WOLOKOLLIE and LPP figure Commany WESSEH (the LFG supported the UP and Ellen Johnson-Sirleaf in the 2005 elections); and the **National Vision Party** (NATVIPOL), led by George M. KAIDII, who was also the party's 2005 presidential candidate.

The **Liberia National Alliance** (LNA) consists of the **Progressive People's Party** (PPP) and the **Independent Democratic Party** (IDP). The LNA chose PPP leader Chea CHEAPOO as its 2005 presidential candidate.

Other Parties and Groupings

Liberians United for Reconciliation and Democracy (LURD). The LURD claimed responsibility for antigovernment guerrilla activity launched in northwestern Liberia in mid-1999. A number of former Ulimo fighters reportedly participated in the organization of the LURD, and, as had been the case with Ulimo, Krahn-Mandingo infighting was subsequently reported within the new grouping. The Liberian government accused the Guinean government of supplying arms to the LURD, which appeared to include several anti-Taylor factions left over from the Liberian civil war as well as anti-Taylor elements from the complicated conflict in Sierra Leone. The LURD subsequently became the largest anti-Taylor group in Liberia, its fighters ultimately pressuring Taylor to leave the country in August 2003 (see Political background, above, for details).

In January 2004, Aisha CONNEH (the daughter of the president of Guinea and the wife of Sekou Damate Conneh, who had been named chair of the LURD in 1999) reportedly attempted unsuccessfully to gain control of the LURD in cooperation with Chayee DOE (the younger brother of former

Liberian president Samuel Doe). Chayee Doe was subsequently killed, while Sekou Conneh was reportedly suspended from the party. The LURD disbanded in late 2004, and many of its members reportedly joined the new **Progressive Democratic Party**, which chose Sekou Conneh as its 2005 presidential candidate.

Leaders: Lt. Gen. Charles JULU, Prince SEO, Sekou CONNEH, Gen. Joe WYLIE.

Liberia Peace Council (LPC). Organized in 1993, the LPC is a largely Krahn group that has engaged in numerous clashes with the NPFL in southeastern Liberia. In January 1996 the LPC was cited by observers as the only faction to have complied with the disarmament provisions of the August 1995 peace accord. However, such claims were subsequently undermined by reports of LPC–NPFL clashes, and in October LPC militants were accused of attempting to assassinate Charles Taylor.

In early 1997 the LPC participated in the Alliance of Seven Parties under the NDPL's banner. However, following the factionalization of the Alliance and breakup of the informal Krahn coalition, the LPC forwarded its chair, Dr. George BOLEY, as its presidential candidate. In early 1999 it was reported that Boley had fled the country in fear of attack by Taylor's security forces. The LPC subsequently disbanded, and many of its members, including Boley, reportedly joined the NDPL.

Movement for Democracy in Liberia (MODEL). Supported primarily by members of the Krahn ethnic group who had previously been core constituents of former president Samuel Doe, the MODEL was launched in 2001 and quickly emerged as a major anti-Taylor rebel force during the 2002–2003 civil war. MODEL leader Thomas Yaya NIMELY was named foreign minister under the peace agreement of August 2003. The MODEL disbanded in late 2004 under an agreement that also involved the LURD and pro-Taylor groups. Nimely chose not to form a political party, urging his supporters to join existing parties.

United Liberation Movement of Liberia for Democracy (Ulimo). Ulimo was initially a formation drawn primarily from the Krahn tribe of former president Doe. As such, it opposed the granting of concessions to the rebels by ECOWAS and Sawyer's interim government. By 1994 it had split into two factions: a Krahn-based Christian group, Ulimo-K, led by Gen. Roosevelt Johnson, and a Mandingo-based Muslim group, Ulimo-M, led by Lt. Gen. Alhaji G. V. Kromah. (The former is sometimes referenced as Ulimo-J and the latter confusingly [and incorrectly] as Ulimo-K.)

In early 1996 forces aligned with Johnson fought with Ecomog troops in Tubmanburg after the former refused to comply with the disarmament provisions of the 1995 peace accord. Subsequently, on March 11, 1996, the Ulimo-K's Executive Council and military commanders issued a joint statement announcing the dismissal of Johnson as party chair in favor of Brigadier Gen. William Karyee, citing Johnson's inability to forward the peace process as the reason for his ouster.

Krahn fighters from the AFL and LPC reportedly defected to the Ulimo-K during the fighting that ensued after militiamen loyal to the NPFL and Ulimo-M attempted to arrest Johnson on April 6, 1996. Thereafter, amid intense fighting in the capital, Johnson, who continued to be recognized as the faction's de facto leader, was flown to Ghana on May 3 by U.S. helicopters to attend an ECOWAS peace summit then scheduled for May 8.

Under pressure from international observers, on June 11, 1996, the Ulimo-K agreed to disarm, and in August a faction spokesman claimed that the group's militiamen had turned over their weapons to Ecomog troops. Moreover, in late September the two Ulimo factions reportedly agreed to a cessation of their mutual hostilities. However, in early October Ulimo-K fighters agreed to end their armed blockade of the highways leading to Tubmanburg and Cape Mount (where thousands of starving citizens were subsequently discovered) only under pressure from the Council of State and ECOWAS. Meanwhile, Ulimo-M leader Kromah announced his intention to compete in the May 1997

Cabinet

As of July 1, 2006

President	Ellen Johnson-Sirleaf (UP) [f]
Vice President	Joseph N. Boakai (UP)

Ministers

Agriculture	Christopher Toe
Commerce and Industry	Bankie King Akerele [f]
Education	Joseph Kortoe (LAP) [f]
Finance	Antoinette M. Sayeh [f]
Foreign Affairs	George Wallace
Gender Development	Vabah Gayflor [f]
Health and Social Welfare	Walter Gwenigale
Information, Culture, and Tourism	Johnny McCLain
Internal Affairs	Ambullai Johnson
Justice	Francis Johnson Morris [f]
Labor	Samuel Kofi Woods
Lands, Mines, and Energy	Eugene Shannon
National Defense	Brownie J. Samukai (ind.)
Planning and Economic Affairs	Toga McIntosh
Posts and Telecommunications	Jackson G. Doe (NDPL)
Public Works	Willis Knuckles
Transportation	Jeremiah Sulunteh (NDPL)
Youth and Sports	Jamesetta Howard-Wollokollie [f]
Chief of Staff	Morris Dukuly

[f] = female

presidential elections as the candidate of the new ALCOP (below).

Johnson's efforts to form an electoral coalition with the LPC and NDPL failed in early 1997; subsequently, Ulimo-K candidates performed poorly at balloting in July. In August, Johnson was appointed minister of rural development; however, Johnson continued to criticize the Taylor administration, accusing the president in early 1998 of filling the military with former NPFL militiamen. In March, Johnson was the target of what he described as the third recent attempt on his life; concurrently, it was reported that Taylor had removed Johnson from the cabinet with the goal of naming him to an overseas post (ambassador to India). Thereafter, clashes between Ulimo-K militants and

presidential forces were reported in neighborhoods controlled by Johnson, and in September an all-out attack by Taylor's troops forced Johnson and his family and close associates to seek refuge in the U.S. embassy, from where they were subsequently airlifted out of the country.

Many members of Ulimo were reportedly involved in the formation of the LURD in 1999. Subsequently, in 2004, Johnson died in exile in Nigeria. Most reports suggested that both Ulimo factions were defunct as of 2005.

Legislature

The National Assembly established by the 1984 constitution was a bicameral body consisting of a Senate and a House of Representatives, both elected by universal adult suffrage. Following the collapse of the Doe administration, the assembly was nominally superseded by interim bodies established by the Sawyer and Taylor regimes. Subsequently, in accordance with the 1993 Cotonou agreement, a 35-member Transitional Legislative Assembly (TLA) composed of representatives of the principal warring factions was inaugurated on March 7, 1994. On July 17, 1997, the TLA approved legislation that limited legislative terms to four years.

Balloting for the Senate and the House of Representatives was held on July 19, 1997, although those bodies ceased to function as a result of the civil war in the early 2000s. Under the terms of a recently completed peace agreement, an appointed 76-member National Transitional Legislative Assembly was established on October 14, 2003. Twelve seats were accorded to the pro-Taylor Government of Liberia (GOL), 12 to the Liberians United for Reconciliation and Democracy, 12 to the Movement for Democracy in Liberia, 18 to established political parties, 7 to representatives of civic organizations, and 15 to the nation's counties (1 for each of the 15 counties).

Under the terms of the 2003 peace agreement and the Electoral Reform Law of 2004, new elections were held for the House of Representatives and the Senate on October 11, 2005.

Senate: The Senate comprises 30 members (2 from each of the 15 countries) directly elected in a single round of voting. (The top two vote-getters in each county are declared the victors.) According to the guidelines adopted for the 2005 balloting, the first-place finishers in each county were elected for nine-year terms, the second-place finishers for six-year terms. All subsequent elections will be for nine-year terms. Following the initial election on October 11, 2005, the Coalition for the Transformation of Liberia won 7 seats; the Unity Party, 4; the National Patriotic Party, 3; the Congress for Democratic Change, 3; the Alliance for Peace and Democracy, 3; the Liberty Party, 3; the National Democratic Party of Liberia, 2; the All

Liberia Coalition Party, 1; the National Reformation Party, 1; and independents, 3.

President (pro tempore): Isaac W. NYENABO.

House of Representatives: The lower house comprises 64 members directly elected from single-member constituencies in single-round plurality voting for six-year terms. In the balloting on October 11, 2005, the Congress for Democratic Change secured 15 seats; the Liberty Party, 9; the Unity Party, 8; the Coalition for the Transformation of Liberia, 8; the Alliance for Peace and Democracy, 5; the National Patriotic Party, 4; the New Deal Movement, 3; the All Liberia Coalition Party, 2; the National Democratic Party of Liberia, 1; the National Reformation Party, 1; the United Democratic Alliance, 1; and independents, 7.

Speaker: Edwin Melvin SNOWE.

Communications

Press

The Doe regime did not impose formal press censorship, although the *Daily Observer* was repeatedly closed subsequent to its founding in February 1981 and was the object of an arson attack in March 1986, whereas *Footprints Today* and the *Sun Times* were shut down from April 1988 to March 1990. The following are issued in Monrovia: *Daily Observer* (30,000), independent; *The Herald* (3,000), Catholic weekly; *The New Liberian* (2,000), published daily by the Ministry of Information; *Footprints Today,* founded 1984; *Sun Times,* founded 1985. By early 1991 a number of new papers had been launched, including *The Inquirer* (independent), the *New Times, The Torchlight,* and *The Patriot,* a pro-Taylor organ. In addition the INPFL had commenced publication of *Scorpion.* Among other newspapers are the *Monrovia News,* the *New Democrat* (independent), the *Analyst* (independent), and the *Daily News.* Reporters of the latter newspaper were arrested and charged with "espionage" in February 2001 after an article critical of some government expenditures were published. In August 2000 the government had ordered formal censorship of news reporting on the fighting in Lofa County. Human rights and media organizations reported heavy pressure on the press that was critical of the government from 1999 to mid-2002.

News Agency

The official facility is the Liberian News Agency (Lina); *Agence France-Presse, Deutsche Presse Agentur,* Reuters, and UPI are represented in Monrovia.

Broadcasting

The government-controlled Liberian Broadcasting Corporation (LBS) operates one commercial radio station (ELBC) and one commercial television station (ELTV), while the government-operated Liberia Rural Communications Network (LRCN) transmits from three radio outlets (ELRG, ELRV, and ELRZ). Additional radio programming is offered by the Liberian-American-Swedish Minerals Company (Lamco) station ELNR, the Sudan Interior Mission's religious station ELWA, the ECOWAS Monitoring Group's Radio Liberty Monrovia (RLM), and a Voice of America transmitter in Monrovia. The government's heavy hand on the print media was extended to radio and television in 2000 when the private *Star* radio station and the Catholic-oriented *Radio Veritas* were shut down in March for broadcasts critical of the regime. Also, in August a British *Channel Four* TV crew was charged with "spying" while preparing a documentary linking the president to diamond smuggling and gunrunning in Sierra Leone. Following an international outcry, the crew was freed. There were approximately 964,000 radio and 95,000 television receivers in 1999.

Intergovernmental Representation

Ambassador to the U.S.
Charles A. MINOR

U.S. Ambassador to Liberia
Donald E. BOOTH

Permanent Representative to the UN
Lami KAWAH

IGO Memberships (Non-UN)
AfDB, AU, BADEA, ECOWAS, Interpol, IOM, MRU, NAM, WCO

LIBYA

Great Socialist People's Libyan Arab Jamahiriya

*al-Jamahiriyah al-Arabiyah al-Libiyah al-Shabiyah
al-Ishtirakiyah al-Uzma*

The Country

Extending for 910 miles along Africa's northern coast, Libya embraces the former Turkish and Italian provinces of Tripolitania, Cyrenaica, and Fezzan. Some 95 percent of its territory is desert and barren rockland, and cultivation and settlement are largely confined to a narrow coastal strip. Tribal influences remain strong within a population that is predominantly Arab (with a Berber minority) and almost wholly Sunni Muslim in religion. Arabic is the official language, but Italian, English, and French are also spoken. The government has made efforts in recent years to increase the education of females (about 50 percent of whom are reportedly illiterate), and women comprised 21 percent of the official labor force in 1996, up from less than 9 percent in the 1980s. Female representation in government continues to be minimal.

Libya's reputation as a country largely devoid of natural resources was rendered obsolete by the discovery of oil in the late 1950s; the ensuing development of export capacity resulted in its achieving the highest per capita GNP in Africa (more than $8,600 in 1980). However, world market conditions subsequently reduced the country's oil revenue from a high of $22 billion in 1980 to $5 billion in 1988, with per capita GNP declining to less than $5,500 through the same period. Oil production (about 1.6 million barrels per day) accounts for more than 95 percent of export income, the primary market being Western Europe. Other industry has been limited by the weakness of the domestic market, uneven distribution of the population, and a shortage of skilled manpower. Recent large-scale development has focused on building chemical and steel complexes, in addition to the controversial Great Man-Made River Project, a $30 billion plan to pipe water from aquifers deep below the Sahara Desert to coastal areas. The government hopes that the project, the first phase of which was inaugurated in mid-1991 and the second in 1996, will eventually permit dramatic agricultural expansion as well as provide bountiful drinking water to major cities.

Due to limited rainfall and an insufficient labor pool resulting from migration to the cities, agriculture currently contributes only minimally to domestic output. Barley, wheat, tomatoes, olives, citrus, and dates are the primary crops.

After decades of rigid state control of the economy, liberalization measures, including the promotion of limited private enterprise, were introduced in 1988. Results were initially viewed as encouraging, but domestic opposition was kindled by concurrent government efforts to eliminate food subsidies, reduce state employment, and trim financing for medical, educational, and other social programs. Consequently, about 70 percent of the economy remains under government control, and much of the populace still relies heavily on various subsidies. Falling oil prices in 1998 contributed to a devaluation of the dinar in November and cutbacks in the proposed 1999 budget before economic pressures were eased by the return of high oil prices in the second half of 1999 and 2000. Early in the 21st century, leader Muammar al-Qadhafi's perceived resistance to even modest free-market reforms constrained foreign investment, despite significant interest on the part of Western companies in tapping into the Libyan consumer market as well as participating in the potentially lucrative upgrading of the oil field infrastructure.

Economic affairs, particularly in regard to the West, changed dramatically in September 2004 when the United States lifted most of its long-standing unilateral sanctions against Libya. (UN sanctions, imposed in 1992, had been suspended in 2000 and formally lifted in September 2003.) Western companies immediately began to negotiate substantial oil contracts with Tripoli in conjunction with pledges from the Qadhafi regime to enact broad economic policy changes (see Foreign relations and Current issues, below). Real GDP dipped to 3.5 percent in 2005 (from 4.5 percent in 2004), with economic growth mainly in the non-oil sector, particularly construction, transportation, hotels, and trade. The International Monetary Fund (IMF) in 2005 urged Libya to ease trade restrictions and move toward a market economy, among other economic reforms.

Government and Politics

Political Background

Successively ruled by the Phoenicians, Greeks, Romans, Arabs, Spaniards, and others, Libya was under Ottoman Turkish control from the middle of the 16th century to the beginning of the 20th century. It was conquered by Italy in 1911 and 1912 and was ruled as an Italian colony until its occupation by British and French military forces during World War II. In conformity with British wartime pledges and a 1949 decision of the UN General Assembly, Libya became an independent monarchy under Emir Muhammad IDRIS al-Sanussi (King IDRIS I) on December 24, 1951. A constitution promulgated two months earlier prescribed a federal form of government with autonomous rule in the three historic provinces, but provincial autonomy was wiped out and a centralized regime instituted under a constitutional amendment adopted in 1963.

The 1960s witnessed a growing independence in foreign affairs resulting from the financial autonomy generated by rapidly increasing petroleum revenues. This period marked the beginnings of Libyan radicalism in Third World politics and in its posture regarding Arab–Israeli relations. Increasingly, anti-Western sentiments were voiced, especially in regard to externally controlled petroleum companies and the presence of foreign military bases on Libyan soil. The period following the June 1967 Arab–Israeli conflict saw a succession of prime ministers, including the progressive Abd al-Hamid al-BAKKUSH, who took office in October 1967. His reforms alienated conservative leaders, however, and he was replaced in September 1968 by Wanis al-QADHAFI. The following September, while the king was in Turkey for medical treatment, a group of military officers led by Col. Muammar al-QADHAFI seized control of the government and established a revolutionary regime under a military-controlled Revolutionary Command Council (RCC).

After consolidating his control of the RCC, Colonel Qadhafi moved to implement the goals of

Political Status: Independent state since December 24, 1951; revolutionary republic declared September 1, 1969; name changed from Libyan Arab Republic to Libyan Arab People's Republic in 1976; present name adopted March 2, 1977.

Area: 679,358 sq. mi. (1,759,540 sq. km.).

Population: 5,678,484 (2003C, provisional); 5,769,000 (2005E). Both figures include nonnationals.

Major Urban Centers (2003C): TARABULUS (TRIPOLI, 1,197,000), Banghazi (Benghazi, 680,000), Misratah (Misurata, 351,000), Surt (Sirte, 162,000). (Many secretariats have reportedly been relocated recently to Sirte—about 400 miles east of Tarabulus—and other cities.)

Official Language: Arabic.

Monetary Unit: Dinar (official rate July 1, 2006: 1.30 dinar = $1US).

Revolutionary Leader (De Facto Head of State): Col. Muammar Abu Minyar al-QADHAFI (Col. Moammar GADDAFY); assumed power as Chair of Revolutionary Command Council (RCC) following coup d'état of September 1, 1969; became prime minister in January 1970, relinquishing the office in July 1972; designated General Secretary of General People's Congress concurrent with abolition of the RCC on March 2, 1977, relinquishing the position March 1–2, 1979.

Secretary General of General People's Congress: Zanati Muhammad al-ZANATI; appointed by the General People's Congress on November 18, 1992, to succeed Abd al-Raziq al-SAWSA; most recently reappointed on March 1, 2000.

Secretary General of General People's Committee (Prime Minister): Al-Baghdadi Ali al-MAHMUDI; appointed by the General People's Congress on March 5, 2006, to succeed Shukri Muhammad GHANIM.

his regime, which reflected a blend of Islamic behavioral codes, socialism, and radical Arab nationalism. By June 1970 both the British and U.S. military installations had been evacuated, and in July the Italian and Jewish communities were dispossessed and their members forced from the country. In June 1971 an official party, the Arab Socialist Union (ASU), was organized, and in September the Federation of Arab Republics (a union of Egypt, Libya, and Syria) was approved by separate referenda in each country. The federation, while formally constituted at the legislative level in March 1972, became moribund shortly thereafter. Meanwhile, the regime had begun acquiring shares in the country's petroleum industry, resorting to outright nationalization of foreign interests in numerous cases; by March 1976 the government controlled about two-thirds of oil production.

Periodically threatening to resign because of conflicts within the RCC, Colonel Qadhafi turned over his prime-ministerial duties to Maj. Abd al-Salam JALLUD in July 1972 and was in seclusion during the greater part of 1974. In August 1975 Qadhafi's rule was seriously threatened by a coup attempt involving army officers—some two dozen of whom were ultimately executed; a number of drastic antisubversion laws were promptly enacted. In November a quasi-legislative General National Congress (renamed the General People's Congress a year later) was created, while in March 1977 the RCC and the cabinet were abolished in accordance with "the installation of the people's power" under a new structure of government headed by Colonel Qadhafi and the four remaining members of the RCC. The political changes were accompanied by a series of sweeping economic measures, including limitations on savings and consolidation of private shops ("nests of exploitation") into large state supermarkets, which generated middle-class discontent and fueled exile-based opposition activity. The government was further reorganized at a meeting of the General People's Congress in March 1979, Colonel Qadhafi resigning as secretary general (but retaining his designation as revolutionary leader and supreme commander of the armed forces) in favor of Abd al-Ati UBAYDI, who was in turn replaced as secretary general of the General People's Committee (prime minister) by Jadallah Azzuz al-TALHI.

At a congress session in January 1981, Secretary General Ubaydi was succeeded by Muhammad al-Zarruq RAJAB, who, in February 1984, was replaced by Miftah al-Usta UMAR and named to succeed Talhi as secretary general of the General People's Committee. Talhi was returned to the position of nominal head of government in a major ministerial reshuffle announced on March 3, 1986; in a further reshuffle on March 1, 1987, Talhi was replaced by Umar Mustafa al-MUNTASIR.

In October 1990 a government shakeup was undertaken that included the appointment of Abd al-Raziq al-SAWSA to succeed Umar as secretary general of the General People's Congress and Abu Zaid Umar DURDA to succeed Muntasir as head of the General People's Committee. Durda was reappointed in November 1992 while Sawsa was replaced by Zanati Muhammad al-ZANATI. The 1992 reorganization was otherwise most noteworthy for the designation of Muntasir, a moderate who had earlier cultivated a good working relationship with the West, as the equivalent of foreign secretary.

The sanctions imposed by the United Nations in 1992 (see Foreign relations, below) subsequently contributed to what was widely believed to be growing domestic discontent with the regime. Internal difficulties were most sharply illustrated by an apparent coup attempt in early October 1993, reportedly involving thousands of troops at several military locations. Although loyalist forces quashed the revolt in about three days, the government was described as "severely shaken" by the events.

In a cabinet reshuffle on January 29, 1994, Abd al-Majid al-QAUD was named to succeed Durda as secretary general of the General People's Committee. Qaud was succeeded on December 29, 1997, by Muhammad Ahmad al-MANQUSH, who was reappointed, along with most other senior ministers, in a cabinet reshuffle on December 15, 1998. On March 1, 2000, Manqush was succeeded by Mubarak Abdullah al-SHAMIKH, Colonel Qadhafi concurrently ordering a sharp reduction in the number of ministries in the name of further devolution of power to local "people's" bodies. SHAMIKH remained in his post during a reshuffle on October 1, 2000, but was replaced in a subsequent reorganization on June 13, 2003, by Shukri Muhammad GHANIM, theretofore the secretary for economy and trade. The secretary for public security, Nasr al-Mabruk ABDALLAH, was suspended on February 18, 2006, after a violent protest a day earlier at the Italian embassy in Benghazi. Six new secretaries were added to the cabinet in a reorganization on March 5, 2006, when the former assistant secretary general of the General People's Committee, Al-Baghdadi Ali al-MAHMUDI, was appointed to succeed Ghanim.

Constitution and Government

Guided by the ideology of Colonel Qadhafi's *Green Book,* which combines elements of nationalism, Islamic theology, socialism, and populism, Libya was restyled the Socialist People's Libyan Arab Jamahiriya in March 1977. The *Jamahiriyah* is conceived as a system of direct government through popular organs interspersed throughout Libyan society. A General People's Congress is assisted by a General Secretariat, whose secretary general serves as titular head of state, although effective power has remained in Colonel Qadhafi's hands since the 1969 coup. Executive functions are assigned to a cabinet-like General People's Committee, whose secretary general serves as the equivalent of prime minister. The judicial system includes a Supreme Court, courts of appeal, courts of the first instance, and summary courts. In 1988 the government also established a People's Court and a People's Prosecution Bureau to replace the unofficial but powerful "revolutionary courts" that had reportedly assumed responsibility for nearly 90 percent of prosecutions. In what was seen as an effort to placate the expanding Islamic fundamentalist movement, Colonel Qadhafi in April 1993 called for more widespread implementation of *sharia* (Islamic religious law), and in February 1994 the General People's Congress granted new powers to the country's religious leaders, including (for the first time under Colonel Qadhafi) the right to issue religious decrees (*fatwas*).

Libya's three provinces are subdivided into ten governorates, with administration based on "Direct People's Authority" as represented in local People's Congresses, People's Committees, Trade Unions, and Vocational Syndicates.

Foreign Relations

Under the monarchy, Libya tended to adhere to a generally pro-Western posture. Since the 1969 coup its foreign policy has been characterized by the advocacy of total war against Israel, a willingness to use petroleum as a political weapon, and (until 1998—see Current issues, below) a strong commitment to Arab unity that has given rise to numerous failed merger attempts with sister states (Libya, Egypt, Sudan, and Syria in 1969; Libya, Egypt, and Syria in 1971; Libya and Egypt in 1972; Libya and Tunisia in 1974; Libya and Syria in 1980; Libya and Chad in 1981; Libya and Morocco in 1984).

Libya's position within the Arab world has been marked by an improbable combination of ideological extremism and pragmatic compromise. Following the 1978 Camp David accords, relations were severed with Egypt, both sides fortifying their common border. Thereafter, Tripoli strove to block Cairo's reentry into the Arab fold (extending its condemnation to Jordan following the warming of ties between Jordan and Egypt) and provided support to Syrian-based elements of the Palestinian Liberation Organization (PLO) opposed to Yasir Arafat. Relations with the Mubarak government began to warm, however, during an Arab League meeting in Casablanca, Morocco, in May 1989 and, stimulated by a "reconciliation" summit in Mersa Metruh, Egypt, in October, continued to improve with a series of cooperation agreements in 1990 and the opening of the border between the two countries in 1991. By mid-decade, Egypt had become what one correspondent described as Libya's most important potential "bridge to the West," Cairo's supportive stance reflecting the importance of Libya

as a provider of jobs for Egyptian workers and the value attached by the Mubarak regime to Colonel Qadhafi's pronounced antifundamentalist posture.

Relations with conservative Morocco, broken following Tripoli's 1980 recognition of the Polisario-backed government-in-exile of the Western Sahara, resumed in 1981. Ties with neighboring Tunisia, severely strained during much of the 1980s, advanced dramatically in 1988, the opening of the border between the two countries precipitating a flood of option-starved Libyan consumers to Tunis. Regional relations stabilized even further with the February 1989 formation of the Arab Maghreb Union (AMU), although Colonel Qadhafi remained a source of controversy within the ineffective and largely inactive grouping.

A widespread expression of international concern in the 1980s and 1990s centered on Libyan involvement in Chad. Libya's annexation of the Aozou Strip in the mid-1970s was followed by active participation in the Chadian civil war, largely in opposition to the forces of Hissein Habré, who in 1982 emerged as president of the strife-torn country. By 1983 Libya's active support of the "National Peace Government" loyal to former Chadian president Goukhouni Oueddei (based in the northern Tibesti region) included the deployment of between 3,000 and 5,000 Libyan troops and the provision of air support for Oueddei's attacks on the northern capital of Faya-Largeau. Although consistently denying direct involvement and condemning the use of French troops in 1983 and 1984 as "unjustified intervention," Qadhafi agreed in September 1984 to recall "Libyan support elements" in exchange for a French troop withdrawal. The agreement was hailed as a diplomatic breakthrough for Paris but was greeted with dismay by Habré and ultimately proved to be an embarrassment to the Mitterrand government because of the limited number of Libyan troops actually withdrawn. Two and a half years later, in March 1987, the militarily superior Qadhafi regime suffered the unexpected humiliation of being decisively defeated by Chadian government forces, which, after capturing the air facility at Quadi Doum, 100 miles northeast of Faya-Largeau, forced the Libyans to withdraw from all but the Aozou Strip, leaving behind an estimated $1 billion worth of sophisticated weaponry.

In early August 1987, Chadian forces, in a surprise move, captured Aozou, administrative capital of the contested border area, although the town was subsequently retaken by Libya. Despite a September cease-fire, skirmishes continued as the Islamic Legion, comprised largely of Lebanese mercenaries, attacked Chadian posts from bases inside Sudan, with Libyan jets supporting counteroffensives in the Aozou Strip. A year later, the warring neighbors had resumed intermittent peace negotiations, Libya having reportedly lost 10 percent of its military capability, although retaining most of the disputed territory.

In July 1989 the Organization of African Unity (OAU, subsequently the African Union—AU) sponsored negotiations between President Habré and Colonel Qadhafi, which set the stage for the signing of a peace treaty by the countries' foreign ministers on August 31. The treaty called for immediate troop withdrawal from the disputed territory, exchange of prisoners of war, mutual "noninterference," and continued efforts to reach a permanent settlement. Relations subsequently deteriorated, however, with Habré accusing Libya of supporting Chadian rebels operating from Sudan. A year of talks having achieved little progress, the dispute was referred to the International Court of Justice (ICJ) several months before the ouster of the Habré regime in December 1990.

New Chadian president Idriss Déby announced in early 1991 that a "new era" had begun in relations between Chad and Libya, the belief being widespread that Libya had supplied arms and logistical support (but not personnel) to the victorious Chadian rebels. However, Déby subsequently described the Aozou issue as still a "bone of contention" requiring resolution by the ICJ. Consequently, hearings in the case began in June 1993 at The Hague, Netherlands, and in February 1994 the ICJ ruled by a vote of 16–1 that Libya had no rightful claim to the Aozou Strip or any other territory beyond the boundary established in a 1955 treaty between Libya and France. On May 30 the lengthy dispute ended with Libya's withdrawal and a sym-

bolic raising of the Chadian flag. Shortly thereafter, Colonel Qadhafi received President Déby in Tripoli for the signing of a friendship and cooperation treaty, which, among other things, provided for a Libyan–Chadian Higher Joint Committee to discuss mutual concerns. Following the inaugural meeting of the Committee in July, (then) Chadian prime minister Kassiré Koumakoyé reportedly described the Aozou issue as "settled for good," while announcing his country's support for Libyan efforts to have UN economic sanctions lifted.

Relations with the West have been problematic since the 1969 coup and the expulsion, a year later, of British and U.S. military forces. Libya's subsequent involvement in negotiations between Malta and the United Kingdom over British naval facilities on the Mediterranean island contributed to a further strain in relations with London. In December 1979 the United States closed its embassy in Tripoli after portions of the building were stormed and set afire by pro-Iranian demonstrators, while in May 1981 the Reagan administration ordered Tripoli to shut down its Washington "people's bureau" in response to what it considered escalating international terrorism sponsored by Colonel Qadhafi. Subsequent U.S.–Libyan relations were characterized as "mutual paranoia," with each side accusing the other of assassination plots amid hostility generated by U.S. naval maneuvers in the Gulf of Sirte, which Libya has claimed as an internal sea since 1973.

Simultaneous attacks by Palestinian gunmen on the Rome and Vienna airports on December 27, 1985, brought U.S. accusations of Libyan involvement, which Colonel Qadhafi vehemently denied. In January 1986 President Reagan announced the freezing of all Libyan government assets in U.S. banks, urged Americans working in Libya to depart, banned all U.S. trade with Libya, and ordered a new series of air and sea maneuvers in the Gulf of Sirte. (U.S. officials charged that Libya was harboring members of the Revolutionary Council of Fatah, the radical Palestinian grouping led by Abu Nidal and allegedly behind the 1985 attacks.) Three months later, during the night of April 14, eighteen F-111 bombers based in Britain, assisted by carrier-based attack fighters, struck Libyan military targets in Tripoli and Benghazi. The action was prompted by what Washington termed "conclusive evidence," in the form of intercepted cables, that Libya had ordered the bombing of a Berlin discotheque nine days before, in the course of which an off-duty U.S. soldier had been killed. The U.S. administration also claimed to have aborted a planned grenade and machine-gun attack on the American visa office in Paris, for which French authorities ordered the expulsion of two Libyan diplomats.

Tripoli's adoption of a more conciliatory posture during 1988 did not yield relaxation of tension with Washington, which mounted a diplomatic campaign against European chemical companies that were reported to be supplying materials for a chemical weapons plant in Libya. Despite Libyan denial of the charges, reports of U.S. readiness to attack the site were believed to be the catalyst for a military encounter between two U.S. F-14s and two Libyan MiG-23 jets over the Mediterranean Sea on January 4, 1989, which resulted in downing of the Libyan planes. Concern subsequently continued in some Western capitals over the alleged chemical plant (the site of a much-publicized fire in March 1990), as well as Libya's ongoing efforts to develop nuclear weapons. Suspicion also arose over possible Libyan involvement in the bombing of Pan Am Flight 103, which blew up over Lockerbie, Scotland, in December 1988, and the crash of a French DC-10 in Niger near the Chad border in September 1989.

Colonel Qadhafi was described as maintaining an "uncharacteristically low profile" following the August 1990 Iraqi invasion of Kuwait (which he publicly criticized) and the U.S.-led Desert Storm campaign against Iraqi forces in early 1991. However, the respite from the international spotlight proved short-lived as the investigations into the Lockerbie and Niger plane explosions once again focused Western condemnation on Libya.

In October 1991 the French government issued warrants for six Libyans (one of them a brother-in-law of Colonel Qadhafi) in connection with the Niger crash, while American and British authorities announced in mid-November that they had filed charges against two Libyan nationals in connection with the Pan Am bombing. In early December the Arab League Council expressed its "solidarity" with Libya in the Lockerbie matter and called for an inquiry by a joint Arab League–UN committee. Two days later a Libyan judge declared that the two suspects were under house arrest and that Tripoli would be willing to send judicial representatives to Washington, London, and Paris to discuss the alleged acts of terrorism.

On January 21, 1992, the UN Security Council unanimously demanded extradition of the Lockerbie detainees to either Britain or the United States and insisted that Libya aid the French investigation into the Niger crash. Although Libya announced its willingness to cooperate with the latter demand, which involved no extradition request, it refused to turn over the Lockerbie suspects, declaring it would try the men itself. Consequently, the Security Council ordered the imposition of selective sanctions, including restrictions on air traffic and an embargo of shipments of military equipment as of April 15.

On May 14, 1992, in partial compliance with the Security Council, Libya announced that it would sever all links with organizations involved in "international terrorism," admit UN representatives to verify that there were no terrorist training facilities on its soil, and take action to preclude the use of its territory or citizens for terrorist acts. In addition, a special session of the General People's Congress in June agreed that the Lockerbie suspects could be tried in a "fair and just" court in a neutral country as suggested by the Arab League. However, the Security Council reiterated its demand for extradition to the United States or United Kingdom, ordered that the sanctions be continued, and warned that stiffer measures were being considered. After mediation efforts by UN Secretary General Boutros Boutros-Ghali failed to resolve the impasse, the Security Council voted on November 11, 1993, to expand the sanctions by freezing Libya's overseas assets and banning the sales to Libya of certain oil-refining and pipeline equipment. The sanctions were subsequently regularly extended, although the

Security Council rejected a U.S. proposal for a total oil embargo.

Libya continued to face heavy pressure from the United States in 1996. In April, U.S. defense secretary William Perry warned that force would be used if necessary to prevent Libya from completing an alleged underground chemical weapons plant.

Attention in 1998 and 1999 remained focused on efforts to negotiate a resolution of the Lockerbie impasse, the Libyan government having previously argued (with the support of the OAU and the Arab League) that the suspects should be tried in a neutral country. Finally, Libya agreed in late March 1999 to send the two men (Abd al-Basset al-MEGRAHI and Lamin Khalifah FHIMAH) to the Netherlands in early April to face a trial under Scottish law before three Scottish judges. Colonel Qadhafi's acceptance of the plan apparently was predicated on assurances that the trial would not be used to attempt to "undermine" his regime. For their part, Washington and London appeared to compromise on the issue of the trial's location, in part at least, out of recognition that international support for continued sanctions was diminishing. The Security Council announced that the UN sanctions had been suspended as soon as the suspects arrived in the Netherlands on April 5. However, unilateral U.S. sanctions remained in place as long as Libya stayed on Washington's official list of countries perceived to be "state sponsors of terrorism."

An antiterrorism court in Paris convicted, in absentia, six suspects in the Niger plane crash case, including Abdallah SENOUSSI, Qadhafi's brother-in-law, in March 1999 and issued warrants for their arrest, which could be enforced only if they left Libya. Meanwhile, Colonel Qadhafi had also permitted German investigators to question Libyan intelligence officers concerning the 1986 Berlin disco bombing, although prosecution of the case had been thrown into disarray in 1997 when the main witness apparently recanted his previously incriminating testimony against alleged Libyan operatives. (Four defendants were convicted of the Berlin bombing in October 2001, the court also accepting the prosecution's argument that the Libyan secret service had been involved in planning the attack.)

In July 1999 full diplomatic relations were reestablished with the United Kingdom, which had severed ties after a British policewoman was killed during an anti-Qadhafi demonstration outside the Libyan mission in London. (It had been argued that the policewoman was killed by gunfire directed from the mission at the demonstrators.) Resolution of the dispute included Libya's agreement to cooperate in the investigation and to pay compensation to the victim's family.

The Lockerbie trial opened in May 2000, and on January 31, 2001, Megrahi was convicted of murder in connection with the bombing, the judges having accepted the admittedly circumstantial evidence that he had been at the airport when the bomb was allegedly planted and was working for Libyan intelligence at the time. Megrahi was sentenced to life in prison, but Fhimah returned to Libya after the judges did not convict him of any charges. (For subsequent developments see Current issues, below.)

Current Issues

Colonel Qadhafi announced in the late 1990s that he was turning his focus away from pan-Arabism and toward pan-Africanism, having described most other Arab states as "defeatist" in dealing with the West and Israel. The quixotic Libyan leader attended his first OAU summit in 20 years in July 1999 to promote his new vision and hosted a special summit in September to address proposed changes in the charter that would permit creation of OAU peacekeeping forces. Subsequently, Qadhafi participated prominently in efforts to resolve the conflicts in Sudan and Democratic Republic of the Congo and served as a mediator in the war between Eritrea and Ethiopia. However, Libya's image as a potential continental unifier suffered a severe blow in late September 2000 when scores of black African workers died in a series of attacks by Libyans on nonnational workers in a suburb of Tripoli. (Underscoring the continued deterioration of the African initiative, in 2003 Libya recalled its troops from the Central African Republic, a trade agreement with Zimbabwe collapsed, and Qadhafi abolished the ministry for African unity.)

In early 2001 Colonel Qadhafi criticized the conviction of one of the defendants in the Lockerbie trial (see Foreign relations, above) as politically motivated. However, by that time it was widely accepted that the Libyan government had not supported any terrorist activities or groups in several years and was genuinely interested in reintegration into the global community. Qadhafi had also improved his international image by cooperating extensively with the U.S.-led "war on terrorism," by freeing a number of political prisoners and by indicating a willingness to discuss the proposed payment of compensation to the families of the victims of the Lockerbie bombing.

Qadhafi subsequently continued his drive to improve Libya's international standing, and the initiative appeared to reach critical mass with an August 2003 announcement of final resolution of the Lockerbie affair. Under the carefully crafted language of the settlement, Libya accepted "responsibility for the actions of its officials" and agreed to pay an estimated $10 million (in three installments) to each of the families of the 270 killed in the attack. The UN Security Council formally lifted UN sanctions against Libya in September, permitting payment of the Lockerbie settlements to begin. In January 2004 Libya also agreed to pay a total of $170 million to the families of those killed in the 1989 Niger plane crash. The final piece of the puzzle appeared to be put in place in September 2004 when Libya agreed to pay $35 million to the non-U.S. victims of the 1986 bombing in Berlin.

Meanwhile, dramatic progress was also achieved regarding the other long-standing area of intense Western concern, that is, Libya's perceived pursuit of weapons of mass destruction (WMD). In December 2003 the United States and UK announced that after nine months of secret negotiations Qadhafi had agreed to abandon all WMD programs and to permit international inspectors to verify compliance. (Some analysts suggested that the process had been accelerated by the aggressive stance taken by the U.S. Bush administration against Iraq.) Washington announced in February 2004 that it would permit flights to Libya and allow U.S. oil companies to launch talks with Tripoli aimed at further exploitation of oil fields. Many U.S. commercial sanctions were lifted the following April, and in October the EU removed its embargo on arms sales to Libya, and other economic sanctions. Underscoring the dramatic transformation of the West's perception of Qadhafi, he was visited in 2004 by the British, French, and German heads of state, and a number of U.S. companies were awarded permits in 2005 for oil exploration. Collaterally, the Libyan regime, which celebrated its 35th year in power in 2004, pledged sweeping economic reforms to broaden trade and expand investment opportunities. Libya officially remained on the U.S. list of terrorist-sponsoring states, possibly in part to permit investigation of charges by Saudi Arabia that then-Crown Prince Abdallah (now king) had been the target of an assassination plot, but Libya and Saudi Arabia reestablished diplomatic relations in late 2005.

In a diplomatic move that observers said was also meant to send a message to Iran and North Korea (both developing nuclear capabilities), the United States restored full relations with Libya on May 15, 2006. The United States also removed Libya from its list of state sponsors of terrorism (the latter requiring congressional approval within 45 days). Some of the families of Lockerbie bombing victims were angered, however, that they had not been notified first and demanded that the U.S. Congress ensure Libya fulfilled its financial commitment to them. (Libya halted its final payment to the families until it was removed from the list of states sponsoring terrorism.) With diplomatic ties restored, further restrictions on American oil companies were lifted, allowing for increased exploration. For its part, Libya opened bidding on its oil reserves to international companies in an effort to boost production over the next ten years and bring in a projected $7 billion.

Political Parties

Under the monarchy, all political parties were banned. In 1971 an official government party, the Arab Socialist Union (ASU), was founded with the Egyptian ASU as its model. The formation was designed primarily to serve as a "transmission belt," helping implement government decisions at local levels and serving to channel local concerns upward to the central government; however, there was no public reference to it after 1975. At present all parties are proscribed, Colonel Qadhafi arguing that their legalization would only lead to disorder.

Opposition Groups

National Front for the Salvation of Libya (NFSL). Formation of the NFSL was announced in Khartoum, Sudan, on October 7, 1981, under the banner "Finding the democratic alternative." In September 1986 the Front published a list of 76 regime opponents that it claimed had been assassinated in exile, and in January 1987 it joined with a number of other exile formations in establishing a joint working group during a meeting in Cairo, Egypt. The NFSL also participated in the formation of the LNLA (below), which, however, announced its independent status in early 1994.

Operating out of Egypt and the United States, the NFSL was in the forefront of efforts to coordinate anti-Qadhafi activity in the first half of the 1990s, including a conference in Washington in late 1993 attended by most of the regime's leading opponents. However, a "statement of principles" of a proposed front was not negotiated.

In early 1994 it was reported that the NFSL had begun to transmit its antiregime radio program, the *Voice of the Libyan People,* via European Satellite. The program had previously been intermittently broadcast by shortwave radio from neighboring countries. In 1997 the NFSL issued a report alleging that more than 300 Qadhafi opponents had been killed by government operatives abroad or by domestic security forces between 1977 and 1994. In mid-2004 NFSL leaders warned Western leaders that the Qadhafi regime continued to hold political prisoners despite the country's improved international reputation.

Leaders: Ibrahim SAHAD, Mahmud DAKHIL, Muhammad Fayiz JIBRIL, Muhammad MAGARIAF (Secretary General). (Jabal MATAR, described as leader of the NFSL's "military wing," has been missing since 1990.)

Libyan National Liberation Army (LNLA). The LNLA, a paramilitary unit organized with covert U.S. backing to destabilize the Libyan government, was formed in Chad in 1988. The existence of the army, comprising an estimated 600–700 Libyan soldiers taken prisoner by Chadian forces and subsequently molded into an anti-Qadhafi force, became known following the overthrow of the Habré regime in late 1990. Washington quickly airlifted the Libyan *"contras"* out of Chad after the fall of Ndjamena, U.S. embarrassment over the affair increasing as the LNLA participants entered a "floating exile." About 250 eventually returned to Libya, the rest reportedly finding temporary asylum in Zaire and, subsequently, Kenya. In late 1991 some of the guerrillas were reported to have been moved to a Central Intelligence Agency (CIA) training base in the United States, and in April 1992 LNLA members participated in an NFSL congress in Dallas, Texas. Two years later, as the apparent result of a policy dispute, the LNLA severed its links to the NFSL. There has been little subsequent information regarding any LNLA activity.

Leaders: Col. Khalifa HIFTER, Braek SWESSI.

The **Libyan Alliance,** an anti-Qadhafi front, was announced in the late 1980s. Although *Middle East International* reported in late 1993 that most of its constituent groups had "drifted away," Mansur KIKHIA, a former Libyan foreign minister and UN representative, remained the group's titular secretary general. Kikhia, a human rights activist and one of Libya's most prominent dissidents, disappeared during a visit to Cairo in December 1993, his supporters subsequently charging he had been kidnapped by Qadhafi agents. In June 1994 the Libyan leader announced that Kikhia was alive, but he insisted that Tripoli had nothing to do with his disappearance and had no knowledge as to his whereabouts. In 1997 U.S. intelligence reports indicated that Kikhia had apparently been executed in Libya in early 1994. In 1998 an Egyptian court ordered the Egyptian government to pay Kikhia's wife $30,000 as the result of the apparent involvement of its security agents in turning Kikhia over to Libya.

Another anti-Qadhafi umbrella organization, the **Cooperation Bureau for Democratic and National Forces,** has been chaired by former foreign minister Abd al-Munim al-HUNI, who has been an exile in Egypt since breaking with the regime in the mid-1980s. (Other prominent members of the Bureau have included Izzidin GHADANSI, Bashir RABTI, and Abdullah SHARAFFEDIN.) Huni, who reportedly declined an invitation from Colonel Qadhafi in mid-1992 to return to Libya, subsequently participated in meetings with the NFSL and Libyan Alliance representatives to develop a common program. Like-minded overtures were reportedly made to former Libyan prime minister Abd al-Hamid al-BAKKUSH, who founded the Cairo-based **Libyan Liberation Organization** in 1982. (As of early 1999 there was little evidence that the alliance, the bureau, or the organization remained active.)

In May 1996 a number of opposition groups reportedly issued a statement condemning the "despotic practices" of the Qadhafi regime, according to the *Africa Research Bulletin,* which said signatories included the **Libyan Constitutional Union,** the **Libyan Nationalist Organization,** and the **Libyan Democratic Nationalist Grouping.** Also listed were a **Movement for Change and Reform** (a nationalist grouping) and the **Libyan Islamic Group,** an underground but nonviolent organization that has been compared to groups such as the Muslim Brotherhood in Egypt. A number of supporters of the Libyan Islamic Group (including professors and other professionals) were reportedly arrested in Benghazi and other northeast-

ern cities in mid-1998. Libyan security forces also reportedly clashed at that time with members of the **Libyan Islamic Fighting Group** (LIFG, also referenced as the Libyan Militant Islamic Group— LMIG), an Islamic fundamentalist grouping that had earlier been linked to the antigovernment disturbances in northeastern Libya in March 1996 and had claimed that it had planned an assassination of Colonel Qadhafi. The Libyan leader subsequently criticized the United Kingdom for permitting the group to maintain operations in London in view of its avowed goal of overthrowing the Libyan government. In 1998 leaders of the LIFG denied that UK intelligence forces had been involved in the earlier assassination plot, which was aborted when Qadhafi changed travel plans suddenly. (A "rogue" UK agent had reportedly alleged that the LIFG had been given money to assist in the plot, a charge that London vehemently denied.) The LIFG has been accused of having connections to the al-Qaida terrorist network, and in 2001 it was included on the U.S. list of terrorist organizations whose assets were to be frozen. Meanwhile, a number of LIFG members remained in prison in Libya in 2002. The United States and the UK reportedly helped Libya in 2006 in a crackdown on group members to prevent militants from plotting attacks against Qadhafi and against U.S. forces in Iraq.

Another group reportedly involved in recent clashes with security forces is the **Islamic Martyrs Movement,** whose reputed leader Muhammad al-HAMI, was believed to have been killed by government security forces in July 1996. (Abdullah AHMAD has subsequently been identified as a spokesman for the movement.) The grouping, described as operating out of the mountains near Benghazi, claimed that it had wounded Qadhafi in an attack on his motorcade on the night of May 31– June 1, 1998. (The government denied that such an attack had taken place.) Meanwhile, the formation of the **Libyan Patriots Movement** had been announced in London in January 1997, founders calling for the ouster of Colonel Qadhafi and creation of a "free Libya" based on free-market economic principles. In April 1998 the movement reportedly staged an attack on security forces in Benghazi.

Cabinet

As of June 1, 2006

Secretary General, General People's Committee	Al-Baghdadi Ali al-Mahmudi
Assistant Secretary General	Muhammad Ali al Houeiz

Secretaries

Agriculture, Livestock, and Water Resources	Abu-Bakr Mabruk al-Mansuri
Culture and Information	Nuri Dhaw al-Humaydi
Economy and Trade	Al-Tayyib al-Safi al-Tayyib
Finance	Ahmad Munaysi Abd-al-Hamid
Foreign Liaison and International Cooperation	Abdurrahman Muhammad Shalgam
General Education	Abd-al-Qadir Muhammad al-Baghdadi
Health and Environment	Muhammad Abu-Ujaylah Rashid
Higher Education	Ibrahim al-Zarruq Sharif
Industry, Electricity, and Mines	Fathi Hamad Bin Shitwan
Inspection and People's Control	Ibrahim Ali Ibrahim
Justice	Ali Umar al-Husnawi abu-Bakr
Planning	Ali Tahir al-Juhaimi
Public Security	Brig. Salih Rajab al-Mismari
Social Affairs	Bakhitah Abd-al-Alim al-Shalwi
Telecommunications and Transport	Ali Yusuf Zikri
Tourism	Ammar Mabruk al-Lutayyif
Workforce, Training, and Employment	Matuq Muhammad Matuq
Youth and Sports	Mustafa Miftah Belid al-Dersi

In August 2000 the formation of a new external opposition grouping—the **National Reform Congress**—was reported as a vehicle for promoting a multiparty system in Libya.

Legislature

The Senate and House of Representatives were dissolved as a result of the 1969 coup, Colonel Qadhafi asserting that all such institutions are basically undemocratic, "as democracy means the authority of the people and not the authority of a body acting on the people's behalf."

A government decree of November 13, 1975, provided for the establishment of a 618-member General National Congress of the ASU to consist of the members of the Revolutionary Command Council and leaders of existing "people's congresses," trade unions, and professional groups. Subsequent to its first session held January 5–18, 1976, the body was identified as the **General People's Congress** (GPC).

Secretary General: Zanati Muhammad al-ZANATI.

Communications

Press

In October 1973 all private newspapers were nationalized, and censorship remains heavy. The country's major daily, *al-Fajr al-Jadid* (The New Dawn, 40,000), is published in Tripoli in Arabic, by JANA. Also published daily in Arabic in Tripoli is the "ideological journal" *Al-Zahf al-Akhdar* (The Green March).

News Agencies

The official facility is the Jamahiriya News Agency (JANA). Italy's ANSA and Russia's ITAR-TASS maintain offices in Tripoli.

Broadcasting and Computing

Radio and television transmission in both Arabic and English is under the administration of the Great Socialist People's Libyan Arab Jamahiriya Broadcasting Corporation. There were approximately 988,000 television receivers and 140,000 personal computers serving 160,000 Internet users in 2003.

Intergovernmental Representation

There were no diplomatic relations between Libya and the United States until June 2004, when, in the wake of perceived progress toward the resolution of several long-standing areas of severe contention (see Foreign relations and Current issues, above), Washington announced it would open a liaison office in Tripoli.

Permanent Representative to the UN
(Vacant)

IGO Memberships (Non-UN)
AfDB, AU, AFESD, AMF, AMU, BADEA, CAEU, Comesa, IDB, Interpol, IOM, LAS, NAM, OAPEC, OIC, OPEC, PCA, WCO

MADAGASCAR

REPUBLIC OF MADAGASCAR

Repoblikan'i Madagasikara (Malagasy)
République de Madagascar (French)

The Country

The Republic of Madagascar, consisting of the large island of Madagascar and five small island dependencies, is situated in the Indian Ocean off the southeast coast of Africa. Although the population includes some 18 distinct ethnic groups, the main division is between the light-skinned Mérina people of the central plateau and the more Negroid peoples of the coastal regions (*côtiers*). The Malagasy language is of Malayo-Polynesian origin, yet reflects African, Arabic, and European influences. The population is about 36 percent Christian (predominantly Roman Catholic in the coastal regions, Protestant on the plateau) and about 9 percent Muslim, while the remaining 55 percent adhere to traditional beliefs. The nonindigenous population includes some 30,000 Comorans and smaller groups of French, Indians, Pakistanis, and Chinese. Women constitute more than 45 percent of the labor force, performing the bulk of subsistence activity. However, due largely to matriarchal elements in pre-colonial Malagasy culture, females are significantly better represented in government and urban managerial occupations than their mainland counterparts.

Agriculture, forestry, and fishing account for about two-fifths of Madagascar's gross domestic product but employ over four-fifths of the labor force, the majority at a subsistence level. Leading export crops are coffee, cloves, and vanilla, while industry is concentrated in food processing (notably seafood) and textiles. Mineral resources include deposits of graphite, chromium, and gemstones (particularly sapphires), in addition to undeveloped reserves of oil, bauxite, iron, nickel, and titanium.

Beginning in the early 1970s a large portion of the country's economic base, formerly dominated by foreign businesses, was nationalized by a strongly socialist regime. However, in the face of mounting difficulties with the external debt and worsening trade deficits, the administration in 1980 started to reverse its policies, introducing budget austerity, currency devaluations, and measures to reduce food imports by boosting agricultural production. Although such actions were applauded

Political Status: Established as the Malagasy Republic within the French Community in 1958; became independent with present system June 30, 1960; military regime established May 18, 1972; name of Democratic Republic of Madagascar and single-party system adopted in new constitution and Socialist Revolutionary Charter approved by national referendum on December 21, 1975; present name adopted in the new constitution of the Third Republic (codifying multiparty activity first authorized by presidential decree of March 1990) that was approved by national referendum on August 19, 1992, but was subsequently the subject of extensive political conflict (see Political background and Constitution and government, below); federal system established by constitutional amendments approved by national referendum on March 15, 1998, and promulgated on April 8.

Area: 226,657 sq. mi. (587,041 sq. km.).

Population: 12,092,157 (1993C); 16,908,000 (2005E).

Major Urban Center (2005E): ANTANANARIVO (1,581,000).

Official Languages: Malagasy, French.

Monetary Unit: New currency "ariary" introduced in July 2003 (official rate July 1, 2006: 2,165 ariarys = $1US).

President: Marc RAVALOMANANA (I Love Madagascar); proclaimed himself president on February 22, 2002, following a disputed first-round presidential election on December 16, 2001; inaugurated for a five-year term on May 6, 2002, to succeed Adm. Didier RATSIRAKA (Vanguard of the Malagasy Revolution), following a ruling by the High Constitutional Court confirming Ravalomanana's victory in the December 2001 election.

Prime Minister: Jacques SYLLA (I Love Madagascar); appointed by self-proclaimed President Ravalomanana on February 26, 2002; reappointed by the president on May 9, 2002, following the president's inauguration, to succeed Tantely René Gabrio ANDRIANARIVO (Vanguard of the Malagasy Revolution); reappointed by the president on June 16, 2002, following cabinet dissolution earlier that day; formed "government of national reconciliation" on June 18, 2002; reappointed on January 12, 2003, following legislative elections of December 15, 2002; formed new government on January 16, 2003.

by foreign creditors, no measurable economic progress was subsequently achieved.

In 1992 the International Monetary Fund (IMF) and the World Bank temporarily suspended their aid to Madagascar, calling for implementation of austerity measures and widespread economic reform. The government adopted (nominally at least) an adjustment strategy in 1994 focusing on the privatization of state-run enterprises, deregulation of various sectors, and liberalization of restrictions on foreign investment, although there was significant discord within the Zafy administration over implementation (see Political background, below). The IMF criticized the deceleration of the pace of reform following the installation of another Ratsiraka administration in early 1997. Following a period of sustained growth in the late 1990s, the country suffered a series of economic shocks. By the start of the new millennium it was reported that an esti-

mated 75 percent of the population lived in poverty and that the health and education infrastructures were dilapidated. The lingering effects of three cyclones in early 2000 as well as of weak export prices propelled the economy as a key issue in the controversial 2001 presidential campaign (see Political background, below). In 2002, the GDP declined by 12.7 percent as a result of violence and uncertainty associated with the contested presidential election. There was also a spike in inflation, which rose to 15.4 percent. By 2003, the economy began to recover, with GDP growing by 9.6 percent and inflation declining to 2.7 percent with the introduction of a new currency, the ariary. The IMF dispersed a $100 million credit for economic restructuring and arranged several multimillion dollar grants for economic reforms in 2002. Arrangements for substantial debt relief were concluded with the IMF and World Bank in 2004.

In part because of the effects of a devastating cyclone in 2004, GDP growth fell from 9.8 percent in 2003 to 5.3 percent in 2004. However, as of 2006 analysts were predicting significantly positive economic developments for Madagascar, based on expanded foreign investment (notably in pursuit of the exploitation of chromium, titanium, and offshore oil) and the country's accession in May to the Southern African Development Community (SADC), which was expected to expand regional trade opportunities. Meanwhile, aid from the World Bank and the European Union (EU) was earmarked for infrastructure projects (mostly the construction of roads) and programs designed to reduce poverty.

Government and Politics

Political Background

During the 18th century and most of the 19th century, Madagascar was dominated by the Mérina people of the plateau. However, after a brief period of British influence, the French gained control and by 1896 had destroyed the Mérina monarchy. Renamed the Malagasy Republic, it became an autonomous state within the French Community in 1958 and gained full independence on June 26, 1960, under the presidency of Philibert TSIRANANA, who governed with the support of the Social Democratic Party (*Parti Social Démocrate*— PSD).

Tsiranana's coastal-dominated government ultimately proved unable to deal with a variety of problems, including ethnic conflict stemming from Mérina opposition to the government's pro-French policies. In addition, economic reverses led to a revolt in 1971 by peasants in Tulear Province, while students, dissatisfied with their job prospects in a stagnating economy, mounted a rebellion in early 1972. In May having acknowledged his growing inability to rule, Tsiranana turned over his duties as head of state and chief of government to Maj. Gen. Gabriel RAMANANTSOA, who was confirmed for a five-year term by a referendum held October 8.

An attempted coup by dissident *côtier* officers led to Ramanantsoa's resignation on February 5, 1975; his successor, Col. Richard RATSIMANDRAVA, was assassinated six days later, with Brig. Gen. Gilles ANDRIAMAHAZO assuming the leadership of a Military Directorate. Andriamahazo was in turn succeeded on June 15 by Cdr. Didier RATSIRAKA, who as foreign minister since May 1972 had been instrumental in reversing Tsiranana's pro-Western policies in favor of a more Soviet-oriented and vigorously pro-Arab agenda. Subsequently, on December 21, 1975, voters approved a Socialist Revolutionary Charter and a new constitution that called for the establishment of a National Front for the Defense of the Malagasy Socialist Revolution (*Front National pour la Défense de la Révolution Socialiste Malgache*— FNDR) as an overarching political formation. The voters also designated Ratsiraka for a seven-year term as president of the newly styled Democratic Republic of Madagascar; thereby he continued his role as chair of a Supreme Revolutionary Council (*Conseil Suprême de la Revolution*—CSR) that had been established in 1972.

The new Ratsiraka government formed on January 11, 1976, was designed to reflect a regional balance of both military and civilian elements. It was reconstituted on August 20 following the accidental death of Prime Minister Joël RAKOTOMALALA on July 30 and his replacement by Justin RAKOTONIAINA on August 12. Local elections, the first since the constitutional revision, began in March 1977 and were dominated by the Vanguard of the Malagasy Revolution (*Antoky'ny Revolosiona Malagasy*—Arema), established by Ratsiraka a year earlier as the main FNDR component. Arema members also filled 112 of the 137 positions on the FNDR's single list of National Assembly candidates, which was approved by a reported 90 percent of voters on June 30. Ratsiraka subsequently appointed a new cabinet, headed by Prime Minister Lt. Col. Désiré RAKOTOARIJAONA.

President Ratsiraka was popularly reelected to a seven-year term on November 7, 1982, by a four-to-one margin over Monja JAONA of the National Movement for the Independence of Madagascar

(*Mouvement National pour l'Indépendence de Madagascar*—Monima), who had campaigned on a platform attempting to capitalize on growing domestic insecurity. Assembly elections scheduled for 1982 were postponed until August 23, 1983, at which time over 500 candidates from FNDR-affiliated groups were allowed on the ballot. Arema secured 117 seats on the basis of a 65 percent vote share.

In August 1985 an army raid in Antananarivo killed 19 leaders of the country's 10,000-member *kung fu* sect, which was reported to be plotting a revolution. However, this hard-line approach failed to deter burgeoning opposition to administration policies among students, civil servants, and some FNDR members.

On February 12, 1988, Lt. Col. Victor RAMA-HATRA (theretofore minister of public works) was named to succeed Colonel Rakotoarijaona as prime minister. While the latter's resignation was officially attributed to "health reasons," observers noted he had recently given the impression of distancing himself from the president.

With the FNDR increasingly unable to maintain control of its constituent groups, the scheduled 1988 assembly elections were postponed, ostensibly to permit their being held simultaneously with presidential balloting in November 1989. However, under powers granted by a constitutional amendment approved by the assembly in December 1988, Ratsiraka moved the presidential election up to March 12, 1989. Aided by disunity within the opposition, which fielded three candidates, Ratsiraka was reelected to another term, albeit with a reduced majority (63 percent) and with waning support in Antananarivo and other urban areas. The opposition remained in disarray after it announced a boycott of the election but then decided at the last minute to participate without having reached agreement on common candidates. Arema had little trouble maintaining its large majority in assembly balloting on May 28.

After the government thwarted a coup attempt in Antananarivo in July 1989, party leaders became increasingly critical of the administration's policies, and in early 1990 President Ratsiraka is-

sued a decree that abolished mandatory participation in the FNDR as of March 1. A number of new parties immediately emerged, six of which joined with the Christian Council of Churches of Madagascar (*Fikambanan'ny Fiangonana Kristiana Malagasy*—FFKM) in sponsoring a National Meeting for a New Constitution on May 23. Ten days earlier, three people had been killed and some two dozen injured in a coup attempt by the Republican Committee for Public Safety (*Comité Républican pour le Salut Publique*), whose 15 members reportedly included individuals involved in the 1989 coup attempt. Thereafter, highly publicized FFKM-opposition party conferences held August 16–19 and December 5–9 demanded abolition of the CSR, the formation of an all-party transitional government, and the convening of a constituent assembly to define the institutions of a Third Republic. Ratsiraka responded in January 1991 by announcing that he had asked the government to present a series of proposals to the assembly to bring the constitution into closer conformity with the "national and international context."

On July 28, 1991, following seven weeks of strikes and demonstrations by an opposition Active Forces (*Forces Vives/Hery Velona*) group, which in late June had announced the formation of an alternative "provisional" administration, Ratsiraka dissolved the government and announced that he would call for constitutional reform by the end of the year. On August 8 he appointed as prime minister the mayor of Antananarivo, Guy Willy RAZANAMASY, who, after being granted widespread executive powers, proclaimed a desire to lead his country "down the tortuous and difficult road to democracy." However, an interim government announced by Razanamasy on August 26 included no representatives of *Hery Velona,* the sizeable but moderate Movement for Proletarian Power (*Mpitolona ho'amin'ny Fanjakan'ny Madinika*—MFM), or the FFKM. As a result, the opposition launched a general strike and organized a protest rally in the capital of some 300,000 persons.

In the wake of continued unrest, Ratsiraka and Razanamasy agreed on October 29, 1991, to the formation of a new unity government that would include representatives of opposition formations, religious groups, and the armed forces. In addition, both the CSR and the assembly would be dissolved, with their functions transferred to a transitional High State Authority (*Haute Autorité d'État*—HAE) and a Committee for Economic and Social Recovery (*Comité pour le Redressement Économique et Social*—CRES). Finally, a new constitution would be drafted for submission to a popular referendum by the end of the year. *Hery Velona* leader Dr. Albert ZAFY was named HAE president on November 23. The result was a quadripartite distribution of power involving the prime minister, the HAE president, the CRES chair, and the increasingly marginalized president of the republic. On December 19 the cabinet was again reorganized to accommodate a more equitable distribution of opposition representatives. Thereafter, a 1,400-member National Forum met March 22–29, 1992, to draw up the new constitution, which was approved by referendum on August 19.

Zafy received 45.2 percent of the vote against seven other candidates in first-round presidential balloting on November 25, 1992. In a runoff against Ratsiraka on February 10, 1993, Zafy defeated the incumbent president by a two-to-one margin. Subsequent legislative balloting on June 16, 1993, gave Zafy supporters a majority of 75 of 138 seats on a 55 percent vote share, with the new assembly approving Francisque RAVONY as prime minister on August 9.

By mid-1995 the president and prime minister were at loggerheads, with Zafy accusing Ravony of a variety of shortcomings, including having impoverished the country through maladministration of its structural adjustment program. However, Zafy was unable to mount sufficient legislative support to secure Ravony's removal from office. As a result of the impasse, the two leaders arrived at an unusual compromise whereby Ravony would receive long-sought authorization to name a new cabinet (implemented on August 18, with the exclusion of Zafy supporters), while a constitutional referendum would be held to give the president opportunity to appoint the new prime minister.

Despite complaints of a return to authoritarianism, Zafy won a 63 percent "yes" vote at the referendum of September 17, 1995, and on October 30 he appointed Emmanuel RAKOTOVAHINY to succeed Ravony, who had resigned on October 13. Rakotovahiny's cabinet, appointed on November 10, was dominated by members of Zafy's National Union for Development and Democracy (*Union Nationale pour le Développement et la Démocratie*—UNDD), although the ongoing dispute regarding economic policy was underscored by the fact that the sentiments of the new finance minister, Jean-Claude RAHERIMANJATO, echoed those of former prime minister Ravony, not Zafy. That controversy came to a head in early May 1996 when IMF Director Michel Camdessus, during a visit to Antananarivo, announced that the government as constituted was not suitable to negotiate new agreements with the IMF and World Bank. Consequently, on May 17, the assembly passed a motion of nonconfidence in the government by a vote of 109–15. Although Rakotovahiny challenged the constitutionality of the vote, he submitted his resignation on May 20, and on May 28 Zafy appointed Norbert RATSIRAHONANA, chief judge of the High Constitutional Court, as the new prime minister. The cabinet announced by Ratsirahonana on June 5 was again comprised primarily of UNDD members, and many legislators boycotted Ratsirahonana's subsequent policy address to the assembly to protest the government's failure to alter its economic approach.

The executive/legislative conflict culminated on July 26, 1996, in a 99–39 assembly vote to remove Zafy from office on grounds that he had violated his oath of office by taking numerous actions contrary to the constitution and the "interests of the entire Malagasy people." Zafy challenged the legality of the decision, charging that the assembly was attempting a "constitutional coup." However, on September 5 the High Constitutional Court upheld the assembly's action and appointed Prime Minister Ratsirahonana to serve as interim president until new elections were held (within 90 days at the most). (Zafy, arguing he had "done nothing wrong to my country," nevertheless announced his resignation upon the issuance of the court's decision, in part, apparently, to become a candidate in the new presidential poll.) Ratsirahonana appointed an interim government (including representatives from a number of factions and parties) on September 13. Later in the month he presented the government's revised framework for economic policy to IMF officials, who indicated that at least theoretical progress was being made.

Fifteen candidates contested the first round of the special presidential balloting on November 3, 1996. The front-runner was former president Ratsiraka (who had returned in late September from 18 months of self-imposed exile in Paris), with 36.6 percent of the vote. He was followed by Zafy, 23.4 percent; Herizo RAZAFIMAHALEO (head of the "non–politician" Leader–*Fanilo* party), 15 percent; Ratsirahonana, 10 percent; and National Assembly Speaker Rev. Richard ANDRIAMANJATO, 5 percent. Runoff balloting between Ratsiraka and Zafy took place on December 29, Razafinahaleo having thrown his support to the former while Ratsirahonana endorsed the latter. Preliminary results showed Ratsiraka ahead by about 30,000 votes. However, final publication of the official results was suspended in early January after Zafy alleged that fraud had occurred within the interior ministry during vote tabulation.

On January 30, 1997, Ratsiraka was proclaimed president by virtue of a 51 percent share of the second-round polling. On February 21 Ratsiraka named Pascal RAKOTOMAVO, a business executive and Arema official, as prime minister. One week later Rakotomavo formed a new multiparty government.

On July 15, 1997, the High Constitutional Court approved the government's proposal to push back the next legislative elections (originally scheduled for mid-1997) to May 1998. Consequently, the term of the National Assembly (then set to expire in August) was extended to mid-1998. For its part, the opposition rejected the government's claim that the additional time was necessary to properly prepare for the balloting, calling the delays "illegal." Relations between the president and his opponents

plummeted when he announced plans to organize a constitutional referendum based on his proposal to return Madagascar to its pre-1995 provincial system. On February 4, 1998, opposition legislators failed in their effort to impeach Ratsiraka over the matter, and on March 15 the referendum was approved by a narrow margin (50.96 percent). The constitution of the Third Republic entered into force on April 8, providing for a federal system comprising six provincial governments. At the same time, changes in the structure of the central government led opponents of Ratsiraka to accuse him of attempting to consolidate power in a "presidential regime."

In legislative balloting on May 17, 1998, Arema captured 63 seats. The next largest bloc of seats, 32, went to a group of independent, but predominantly propresidential, candidates. The propresidential Leader–*Fanilo* party followed with 16. In the end, after further defections to Arema by a number of former moderate opposition groups, propresidential legislators reportedly controlled at least 90 percent of the assembly posts (albeit, in a body whose powers had been diminished by the March constitutional amendments). On July 6 a power struggle between Prime Minister Rakotomavo and Deputy Prime Minister Rajaonarivelo culminated in the resignation from the government of the latter along with 17 other ministers. Unable to govern and constitutionally obligated to resign following assembly elections, Rakotomavo left office on July 22. The following day the president appointed Tantely René Gabrio ANDRIANARIVO, an Arema stalwart and former deputy prime minister, to replace Rakotomavo, and on July 31 a new government was named in which Arema controlled all the key portfolios. The virtually unchallenged appointment of Arema members to all critical cabinet posts in July 1998 underscored the extent to which President Ratsiraka and Arema had secured control of Malagasy political affairs by way of constitutional referendum and legislative elections. On the other hand, the administration's economic recovery program continued to falter, with its halting privatization efforts and apparent unwillingness to adhere to international reform prescriptions undermining its chances of securing much needed financial aid. In late 1998 new economic initiatives were announced, with a focus on customs and revenue collection reforms accompanying further privatization pledges.

In March 1999 opposition activists ignored the government's refusal to grant them permission to organize a protest march and demonstrated in Antananarivo. It was widely believed that the unrest in the capital was the start of an intensive campaign to unseat the president, although the opposition remained essentially disorganized into early 2001, as evidenced by the weak performance of anti-Ratsiraka groupings in the March Senate election. (Arema dominated the first Senate elections on March 18, 2001, securing 49 of the 60 elected seats.) However, a number of smaller parties subsequently endorsed the presidential candidacy of Marc RAVALOMANANA, the supermarket magnate and mayor of Antananarivo who had gained strong support among the middle class with his promises to spur economic growth.

There were six candidates in the December 16, 2001, presidential balloting, which produced highly controversial and destabilizing results. The government reported that no candidate had secured 50 percent of the votes and that a runoff was required between President Ratsiraka (officially credited with 41 percent of the first-round votes) and Ravalomanana, who had been credited with a front-running 46 percent. However, Ravalomanana, supported by the I Love Madagascar (*Tiako I Madagasikara*—TIM) political association, argued that he had in fact won nearly 52 percent of the first-round votes, setting the stage for massive political turmoil in early 2002. Ravalomanana's supporters poured into the streets of the capital in late January to protest the government's ruling that a second round of presidential balloting was required. This argument was bolstered by international observers who concluded that massive tampering had occurred in the initial official tabulations.

As demonstrations continued, Ravalomanana declared himself president on February 22, 2002, and began installation of his own cabinet under the leadership of Jacques SYLLA. Ratsiraka responded by declaring a state of martial law. Conditions deteriorated in March as supporters of the two parallel governments clashed violently in Antananarivo, control of which was ultimately gained by Ravalomanana's forces while Ratsiraka's forces established a rival capital in the eastern city of Toamasina. Negotiations in Senegal in April pointed toward a compromise settlement. However, on April 17 the supreme court of Madagascar declared the initial published results of the December 16 voting void and ordered a recount, which, as reported by the High Constitutional Court, showed that Ravalomanana had indeed won a first-round majority of 51.5 percent. Ravalomanana was formally inaugurated on May 6, although Ratsiraka refused to accept the legitimacy of that situation and continued to fight it. However, the United States officially recognized Ravalomanana as president of Madagascar on June 26, and similar action by France on July 3 sealed the fate of Ratsiraka, who left the country on July 5 for eventual exile in France. (In August 2003, Ratsiraka and two former officials of the Central Bank were tried and sentenced in absentia to ten years hard labor for allegedly embezzling $8.25 million from the bank during the crisis.)

Once in office, Ravalomanana dramatically reduced the size of the cabinet from 30 to 20 posts. However, in the interest of national conciliation, he included a number of members of former Ratsiraka cabinets in the new government.

Early legislative elections were held on December 15, 2002, with Ravalomanana's TIM party winning a majority in the assembly of 103 seats. Their allies, the Patriot Front, an electoral alliance that supported Ravalomanana, gained an additional 22 seats. Arema's representation declined to 3 seats. Significantly, 23 deputies were elected as independents. The elections were remarkable in that they were the first in which foreign monitors were allowed to observe the polling. Following the balloting, Sylla was reappointed prime minister on January 12, 2003.

In local elections (boycotted by Arema) held on November 9 and 23, 2003, the TIM continued its electoral dominance and won the mayoral races in 27 of the country's 45 major cities.

Constitution and Government

Under the 1992 constitution a president is directly elected for a four-year term, by runoff between the two leading contenders if such is needed to secure a majority. Cabinet leadership is assigned to a prime minister, who was initially responsible to the legislature but whose appointment (from a legislative list) and dismissal are now presidential prerogatives. The bicameral Parliament consists of a Senate of both indirectly elected and nominated members and a National Assembly of deputies directly elected by proportional representation.

In 1995 Madagascar's former six provinces were replaced by 28 regions. The former 111 prefectures (*fivondronana*) were replaced by 148 departments and the former 1,252 subprefectures (*firaisana*) by 1,400 communes, of which 45 were urban.

The constitutional amendments of 1998 effectively reversed the changes incorporated in 1995, so as to establish, under the guiding principles of "humanism and ecology," a federal system wherein each of six semi-autonomous provinces would have its own governor, legislature, and economic and social councils. The central government retains control of diplomatic, defense, and budgetary efforts. The amended document also included provisions for the establishment of regional and communal districts; however, as of mid-2006 no further progress toward their creation had been reported.

Foreign Relations

During the Tsiranana administration, Madagascar retained close economic, defense, and cultural ties with France. In 1973, however, the Ramanantsoa government renegotiated all cooperation agreements with the former colonial power, withdrew from the Franc Zone, and terminated its membership in the francophone Common African and Malagasy Organization. Over the next several years a number of agreements with the Republic of South Africa were repudiated, diplomatic relations with Communist nations were established, and pro-Arab policies were announced. In 1979 the government offered the former Israeli embassy in Antananarivo to the Palestine Liberation Organization as a base for local activity, while support was consistently offered to African liberation movements.

Subsequently, there was a drift towards the West; ambassadorial links with Washington were restored in November 1980 after a lapse of more than four years, and aid agreements were negotiated with the United States, France, Japan, and a number of Scandinavian countries. On the other hand, talks were initiated in Moscow in 1984 on improving trade with the Soviet Union, and agreements to strengthen bilateral relations with China were announced in 1986. (Although the country let Taiwan open a special delegation in Antananarivo during President Zafy's term, President Ratsiraka overturned that decision in December 2000, announcing that Madagascar recognized "only one China, represented by the People's Republic.")

In a dramatic policy reversal in mid-1990, economic and air links were established with South Africa as President Ratsiraka, heralding President De Klerk's "courageous" efforts to reverse apartheid laws, sought Pretoria's aid in developing Madagascar's mineral and tourism industries. In September 1998 Ratsiraka attended an international conference in Durban, thus becoming the first-ever Malagasy head of state to visit South Africa. Subsequent regional negotiations focused on the prospect of Madagascar joining the SADC (achieved in 2006).

Following the disputed presidential election of 2001, several countries terminated diplomatic relations with Madagascar and the country was suspended from meetings of the African Union (AU). In June 2002 the Ravalomanana government was recognized by the United States; France and Senegal recognized the government in July of the same year. The AU suspension was lifted in July 2003 after the legislative elections.

In April 2006 German President Horst Köhler visited Madagascar to promote trade relations, and on a state visit to Madagascar in July French President Jacques Chirac apologized for the actions of French troops during a 1947 revolt against French rule. Meanwhile, President Ravalomanana visited China to bolster Sino-Malagasy economic relations.

Current Issues

In June 2004 a grenade attack at an Independence Day ceremony injured 30 people and led to speculation about renewed political violence. The following month there were separate grenade attacks on the homes of politicians associated with President Ravalomanana. These attacks coincided with a rise in street protests over poverty, the slow pace of economic reforms, and worsening inflation. In addition, reservists in the armed services who participated in the 2001–2002 political crisis held a number of protests in which they demanded more compensation for their service.

Tensions continued into 2005, security forces using tear gas and grenades to disperse an opposition rally in October led by former president Zafy in pursuit of an amnesty for those arrested for their roles in the 2001–2002 conflict. Further protests planned for March 2006 were cancelled after armed riot police were deployed in the capital. Meanwhile, President Ravalomanana announced that new presidential balloting would be held on December 3. He called for a conference of propresidential and opposition parties to try to negotiate terms that would preclude a repeat of the instability that had followed the last presidential poll. For its part, the opposition as of mid-year was reportedly making little progress in regard to coalescing behind a single candidate to challenge Ravalomanana.

Political Parties and Groups

While Madagascar has long featured multiple parties, they were required under the 1975 constitution to function as components of a national front (see Arema, below). The requirement was rescinded under a decree that became effective on March 1, 1990. A number of new groups promptly emerged, several of which participated in the launching of a somewhat loosely structured anti-Ratsiraka coalition that resulted from church-sponsored conferences later in the year. By early 1992 two opposition tendencies were evident: a relatively moderate grouping centered on the MFM (see PMDM/MFM, below) that evidenced a gradualist approach to constitutional change, and a more intransigent Living Forces group, led by the UNDD's Albert Zafy, that only grudgingly agreed to participate in the transitional regime but went on to capture the presidency in late February 1993 and a majority of legislative seats in mid-June.

By March 1998 two large opposition coalitions claimed the services of the leading anti-Ratsiraka politicians. The Panorama Group was organized in September 1997 under the leadership of former prime minister Ravony and was described as a counterbalance to the more radical Union of Democratic Active Forces (*Union des Forces Vives Démocratique*—UFVD), which was formed in early 1998 by Zafy. However, they were superseded in 2001 when most anti-Ratsiraka elements informally coalesced behind the presidential candidacy of Marc Ravalomanana.

In December 2004, several opposition parties agreed to form a parliamentary coalition to promote a "third way" between the progovernment TIM and the antigovernment Arema. The resultant grouping was named the **Parliamentary Solidarity for Democracy and National Union** (*Solidarité des Parlementaires pour la Défense de la Démocratie et de l'Unité National*—SPDUN). The SPDUN, which included several parties who had supported Ravalomanana in the 2002 presidential election, announced its intention to serve as the "loyal opposition" to the Sylla government. Included in the SPDUN were the AKFM-*Fanavaozana*, the RPSD-Nouveau, the PMDM/MFM, and the AVI. Rev. Richard Andriamanjato of the AKFM-*Fanavaozana* and Jean Eugené Voninahitsy of the RPSD-Nouveau were chosen as coleaders of the SPDUN.

In advance of the 2006 presidential elections, three opposition groupings formed another loose coalition called the **3 National Forces**

(*3 Forces Nationale*—3FN), led by former president Zafy. The 3FN consisted of Zafy's CRN (below), the SPDUN, and the **Rally of National Forces** (*Rassemblement des Forces Nationales*—RFN), led by Rev. Rafimanaheja EDMOND. The 3FN led a series of protests against the government in 2005 and sought a transitional government prior to the presidential polling.

Propresidential Parties

I Love Madagascar (*Tiaho I Madagasikara*—TIM). A "political association," the TIM was formed to support the presidential campaign of Marc Ravalomanana, the businessman who had been elected mayor of Antananarivo in 1999 as an independent. Ravalomanana's candidacy was also endorsed by numerous other parties, including the AVI, RPSD, PMDM/MFM, and *Grad-Iloafo*. The TIM became a formal party in mid-2002 and became the majority party in the assembly following the 2002 legislative elections, when it received 34.3 percent of the vote and 104 seats. The TIM also did well in local elections in November 2003, winning 27 of 45 major mayoral races.

In 2005, an internal power struggle emerged within the TIM, and Prime Minister Jacques Sylla failed to be reelected as the party's secretary general at a congress in January 2005. Reports suggested that Ravalomanana feared Sylla would challenge him in the next presidential election and therefore wanted to dismiss the prime minister in the summer of 2005. Nevertheless, the two continued to work together, as a rift between Ravalomanana and (then) assembly speaker Jean LAHINIRIAKO in 2006 moved to the forefront of party friction. Lahiniriako was ejected from the TIM and subsequently announced his intention to run for president in December.

Leaders: Marc RAVALOMANANA (President of the Republic), Jacques SYLLA (Prime Minister), Solofonantenaina RAZOARIMIHAJA (Chair).

Rally for Socialism and Democracy (*Rassemblement pour le Socialisme et la Démocratie*—RPSD). The RPSD is the current incarnation of the Social Democratic Party (*Parti Social Démocrate*—PSD) that was legalized in March 1990 as a revival of the party originally formed in 1957 by Philibert Tsiranana. (The group is still frequently referenced under the PSD rubric.) Although initially viewed as sympathetic to the Ratsiraka government, the party became increasingly critical of the rapid pace of its economic liberalization efforts and in the second half of 1990 moved into opposition. The party's prestige was bolstered by the addition of former MFM leaders Franck Ramarosaona and Evariste Marson in 1990 and 1992, respectively. The RPSD supported Albert Zafy in the second presidential round (after a bid by Marson had failed in the first) and went into opposition after the June 1993 poll. Jean-Eugène Voninahitsy, RPSD secretary general and vice president of the National Assembly, received just less than 3 percent of the vote in the first round of the 1996 presidential election.

The RPSD won 11 seats in legislative balloting in May 1998, and thereafter the group was reported to have joined Arema's legislative alliance. In late 2000, however, relations between Arema and the RPSD were strained when Voninahitsy was arrested on charges of insulting the head of state and "putting out false information." Earlier, he had criticized Ratsiraka for purchases made by the state. The RPSD subsequently left Arema's legislative faction by late 2000 and supported opposition candidate Marc Ravalomanana in the 2001 presidential campaign. Disaffected members of the RPSD left the party to join the Patriotic Front (FP) prior to the 2002 elections (two former RPSD members were elected as FP candidates in the balloting). The RPSD allied itself with the TIM in the election and secured 5 seats in the polling.

In 2003 dissidents led by former secretary general Jean Eugéne VONINAHITSY left the party to form a new group, the New RPSD or **RPSD-Nouveau**, which was subsequently active in the anti-Ravalomanana protests of October 2005.

Leaders: Pierre TSIRANANA (son of the former president), Evariste MARSON, André RESAMPA.

Opposition Parties

Patriot Front (*Firaisankinam-Pirenenai*— FP). The FP was an electoral alliance formed by the AVI and former members of the RPSD in 2002 to support the presidency of Marc Ravalomanana. The FP allied itself with the TIM in order to help to secure a propresidential majority in the 2002 legislative elections, at which the FP won 22 seats. However, the AVI had moved into the opposition camp by 2006, and the FP appeared defunct.

One Should Be Judged By One's Works (*Asa Vita Ifampitsanara*—AVI). In May 1998 the AVI won 14 assembly seats under the leadership of former prime minister and interim president Norbert Ratsirahonana, who had theretofore positioned the grouping as a moderate opposition party aligned with the Panorama Group. Subsequently, however, the AVI joined the Arema-led propresidential legislative alliance.

In what was considered an important development in the 2001 presidential campaign, Ratsirahonana withdrew his candidacy in late October and endorsed Marc Ravalomanana. The AVI joined the pro-Ravalomanana FP in 2002, and AVI members secured 20 of the coalition's 22 seats in the legislative elections. However, the AVI joined the SPDUN in 2006, thereby distancing itself from the president.

Leader: Norbert RATSIRAHONANA.

Militant Party for the Development of Madagascar (*Parti Militant pour le Développement de Madagascar*—PMDM/MFM). The PMDM/MFM is a successor name for the Movement for Proletarian Power (*Mouvement pour le Pouvoir Prolétarien/Mpitolona ho'amin'ny Fanjakan'ny Madinika*—MFM) formed in 1972 by student radicals who helped to overthrow President Tsiranana. The MFM initially opposed the Ratsiraka government and was not an FNDR component in the 1977 balloting. In what was called a "fitful collaboration" with the FNDR that led to internal divisiveness and "confusion," the group won three assembly seats in 1983. Although its leaders sub-

sequently cultivated an increasingly moderate outlook, a drive to reestablish support among student militants was reported in 1987, followed by a pronounced shift into opposition. The party obtained seven assembly seats in May 1989 after its leader, Manandafy Rakotonirina, placed second in the presidential balloting with 19 percent of the vote. After completing a "conversion to liberalism," the MFM pressed for the establishment of a market economy and a Western-style multiparty system.

Although it continues to be referenced by its earlier Malagasy initials, the party adopted its current name at a 1990 party congress during which the National Council elected a three-member National Bureau composed of the party's president, secretary general, and treasurer.

MFM leader Rakotonirina, who stood as a first-round presidential contender in 1992, supported Albert Zafy in the second round. Following the legislative poll of June 1993, the MFM went into opposition. It supported prime minister and interim president Norbert Ratsirahonana in the 1996 presidential balloting.

Like its former Cartel HVR partner, the AVI, the PMDM/MFM reportedly swung back over to the government camp following the May 1998 legislative elections but then supported opposition candidate Marc Ravalomanana in the 2001 presidential campaign. In the 2002 elections, the MFM won two seats in National Assembly.

Leaders: Manandafy RAKOTONIRINA (President), Germain RAKOTONIRAINY (Secretary General).

Vanguard of the Malagasy Revolution (*Avant-Garde de la Révolution Malgache/Antoky'ny Revolosiona Malagasy*—Arema). Arema was organized by Didier Ratsiraka in 1976 and subsequently served as the nucleus of the National Front for the Defense of the Malagasy Socialist Revolution (*Front National pour la Défense de la Révolution Socialiste Malgache*—FNDR), which was renamed the Militant Movement for Malagasy Socialism (*Mouvement Militant pour le Socialisme Malgache*—MMSM) in mid-1990. The 1975 constitution provided for organization of the FNDR as the country's overarching political entity, with a variety of "revolutionary associations" participating in the presidential balloting of November 1982 and the legislative election of August 1983 as FNDR components. However, beginning in early 1987 three FNDR members (the MFM, Vonjy, and Monima) initiated joint antigovernment activity and, in what constituted the demise of the FNDR's political monopoly, contested the 1989 presidential and legislative elections as the equivalent of opposition formations.

After losing the 1992 presidential election, Ratsiraka eventually moved to Paris, France, from where he regularly criticized the Zafy administration and what he described as the "chaos" of political affairs in Madagascar. In 1993 he formed the Vanguard for Economic and Social Recovery (*Avant-Garde pour le Redressement Economique et Social*—ARES) as a successor to Arema; however, the Arema acronym and earlier title continued to be used by his supporters and media groups.

On November 29, 1997, at Arema's first party congress since taking power the previous January, Deputy Prime Minister Pierrot Rajaonarivelo was elected to the secretary general's post vacated by Ratsiraka when he assumed the national presidency. In addition, the party established another governing body, styled the "national college." The party also reportedly adopted the Malagasy title, *Andry sy Riana Enti-Manavotra an'i Madagasikara,* or Supporting Pillar and Structure for the Salvation of Madagascar; however, it was not clear if the new label was an official name, and the Arema acronym once again remained in common use.

In legislative balloting in May 1998 Arema and its allies secured an overwhelming mandate (its forces reportedly controlled approximately 90 percent of the assembly seats). Meanwhile, intraparty relations between Rajaonarivelo and Prime Minister Rakotomavo reached a nadir on July 6 when Rajaonarivelo and 17 of his ministerial allies withdrew from the cabinet, thereby paralyzing the government and effectively destroying Rakotomavo's chances for reappointment.

In 2000–2001 disagreements were reported between Arema's liberal wing, headed by Rajaonarivelo, and the "orthodox" wing represented by ministers Nivoson Jacquit Rosat SIMON and Boniface LEVELO.

After failing to receive the party's endorsement for the 2001 Senate balloting, Arema member Jean André Soja presented an "Independent List of Jean André Soja" for the election in Toliara Province, securing three "independent" seats.

Following the violence surrounding the 2001 presidential election, Arema experienced a wide-scale loss of public support. Ratsiraka and other senior Arema figures, including Secretary General Pierrot Rajaonarivelo, went into exile in France. In the legislative balloting in 2002, Arema secured only three seats, and it boycotted local elections in 2003. In 2003 Rajaonarivelo was sentenced in absentia to five years in prison on several charges involving his alleged abuse of office while deputy prime minister. Reports subsequently indicated a growing split in the party, with one faction loyal to the exiled leadership and a second group (led by Assistant Secretary General Pierre RAHARI-JOANA) eager to distance itself from the exiles. In 2006 Rajaonarivelo called upon the government to issue an amnesty to potential candidates, such as himself, for the upcoming presidential poll whose sentences would otherwise preclude them from participating. Arema was also pressuring President Ravalomanana to hold meetings with Ratsiraka prior to the elections to negotiate the return of the Arema exiles.

Leaders: Adm. Didier RATSIRAKA (Former President of the Republic, in exile), Herivelsona RAMANANTSOA, Tantely René Gabrio ANDRIANARIVO (Former Prime Minister), José ANDRIANOELISON, Pierrot Jocelyn RAJAONARIVELO (Secretary General, in exile).

Leader-Fanilo. Launched in 1993 by a group of self-styled "nonpoliticians," Leader-Fanilo opposed President Zafy in the September 1995 referendum and expelled Trade and Tourism Minister Henri RAKOTONIRAINY for accepting cabinet reappointment two months later.

Party leader Herizo Razafimahaleo finished third in the first round of the 1996 presidential balloting with 15 percent of the vote and fourth in 2001 with 4.2 percent. (Three Leader-*Fanilo* cabinet members resigned from the government in early October 2001 after Razafimahaleo announced his intention to campaign for the presidency.) In balloting for the National Assembly in 2002, Leader-*Fanilo* gained two seats.

Leader: Herizo RAZAFIMAHALEO.

Other Parties and Groups

Congress Party for Madagascar Independence–Renewal (*Parti du Congrès de l'Indépendence de Madagascar–Renouveau*—AKFM-*Fanavaozana*). The AKFM-*Fanavaozana* was launched in 1989 by Rev. Richard Andriamanjato, the longtime leader of the AKFM-KDRSM (below), in opposition to the government's acceptance of IMF-mandated economic reforms. Although it only won three assembly seats in 1989, the new formation received substantial urban support in subsequent local elections.

Andriamanjato supported Albert Zafy in his presidential campaign of 1993; however, the two became estranged by early 1996. Andriamanjato, who was speaker of the assembly, led the subsequent legislative campaign against Zafy and ran as a candidate himself in the 1996 presidential election, securing 6 percent of the vote in the first round of balloting.

AKFM-*Fanavaozana* remained neutral in the 2001 presidential campaign, despite the fact that two party members were then holding cabinet posts. It did not gain any seats in the 2002 legislative elections.

Leader: Rev. Richard ANDRIAMANJATO.

Action and Reflection Group for the Development of Madagascar (*Groupe d'Action et Réflexion pour le Développement de Madagascar*—Grad-*Iloafo*). Grad-*Iloafo* was formed in mid-1991 by a former member of Monima (below), who left the latter in 1983 because of an "absence of democracy" within its ranks. Grad-*Iloafo* won a single seat in the legislative elections in 1998. It supported Marc Ravalomanana in the 2001 presidential campaign but failed to gain representation in the 2002 legislative balloting.

Leader: Tovonanahary RABETSITONTA.

Support Group for Democracy and Development in Madagascar (*Comité de Soutien à la Démocratie et au Développement de Madagascar*—CSDDM). The CSDDM was organized in December 1992 by Deputy Prime Minister Francisque Ravony in support of Albert Zafy's presidential bid. Ravony was named prime minister in August 1993, but he resigned in October 1995 because of the outcome of the September 17 constitutional referendum. Ravony was a prominent member of the coalition that supported Marc Ravalomanana in the 2001 presidential campaign.

Leaders: Francisque RAVONY (Former Prime Minister), José Yvon RASERIJAONA (Former Finance Minister and Secretary General of the Party).

National Reconciliation Committee (*Comité pour la Réconciliation Nationale*—CRN). The CRN was launched in 2002 by former president Albert Zafy and other prominent former officials in an attempt to foster a solution to the "post-election crisis" pitting the supporters of former president Ratsiraka against the supporters of President Ravalomanana. Zafy had previously served as the leader of the National Union for Development and Democracy (*Union Nationale pour le Développement et la Démocratie*—UNDD), a revival of a party originally organized in 1955. The UNDD was particularly strident in its denunciation of "corruption" under the Ratsiraka regime. Zafy, its founder, was foreign minister under President Ramanantsoa. In 1991 Zafy was named to head the High State Authority under the Provisional Government. In May 1993, following his election as president of the republic, he resigned as UNDD president, being accorded the title of honorary party president. Though it participated in the 1993 legislative poll as a *Forces Vives* member, the UNDD won seven seats in its own right. UNDD members dominated the November 1995 and May 1996 cabinets, but that was not the case in the September 1996 interim government. Zafy won 5.35 percent in the first round of presidential balloting in December 2001.

Zafy had also recently been affiliated with the Living Forces Rasalama Coalition (*Cartel Hery Velona Rasalama*—Cartel HVR), which had been launched in 1990 as the Committee of Living Forces (*Comité des Forces Vives*), an alliance of some 16 anti-Ratsiraka opposition parties, trade unions, and religious groups. The Cartel HVR rubric was assumed in 1993, although the grouping was also often subsequently referenced as *Forces Vives Rasalama* (Rasalama being the name of a 19th-century Christian martyr).

The only solid common bond among the components of the Living Forces appeared to be their opposition to the Ratsiraka regime, and cohesiveness subsequently deteriorated. Prior to presidential balloting in 1996 a number of parties disavowed their alliance membership.

In legislative balloting in May 1998 what remained of the pro-Zafy grouping competed under the banner of the recently established **Action, Truth, Development, and Harmony** (*Asa Fahamarianana Fumpandrosoana Arinda*—AFFA). Six AFFA candidates, including Zafy, were elected. The AFFA supported Zafy in the 2001 presidential election, but failed to gain any seats for itself in the 2002 legislative balloting.

The CRN never formally recognized the legitimacy of the presidency of Marc Ravalomanana and continued in 2005 and the first half of 2006 to call for a "transitional regime" to govern before new elections are held, lest the problems of 2001–2002 be repeated.

Leaders: Dr. Albert ZAFY (Former President of the Republic), Emmanuel RAKOTOVAHINY (Former Prime Minister).

Popular Impulse for National Unity (*Elan Populaire pour l'Unité Nationale/Vonjy Iray Tsy Mivaky*—VITM or Vonjy). A centrist, Catholic-oriented group formed in 1973 by followers of former president Tsiranana, Vonjy lost one of its seven seats at the 1983 election despite speculation that it might be runner-up to Arema. Subsequently, it split into pro- and anti-Arema factions, a division

that was seemingly resolved at an extraordinary congress held in February 1987 that adopted a solid posture of opposition. The party elected four members of the assembly in May 1989 after its leader placed third in the March presidential poll with a 15 percent vote share. Subsequently, the party was depleted by defections, primarily to the PSD, amid claims that its leadership was politically and financially corrupt. In December 1990 two Vonjy members, Joma ERNEST and Jean-Jacques RAFALIMANANA, were given prison sentences for their alleged involvement in the May coup attempt. The party captured one assembly seat in 1993. Vonjy supported President Ratsiraka in his 2001 reelection bid. The VITM won only .12 percent of the vote in the 2002 legislative elections.

Leader: Dr. Jérôme Marojàma RAZANABAHINY.

Congress Party for Madagascar Independence (*Parti du Congrès de l'Indépendance de Madagascar/Antokon'ny Kongresy Ho An'ny Fahaleovantenan'i Madagasikara-Komity Demokratika Manohana ny Republika Socialista Malagasy*—AKFM-KDRSM). The AKFM-KDRSM was founded as a left-wing alliance of radical and middle- and upper-class nationalist movements in which communist influence, largely of a pro-Soviet orientation, played a significant role. The party won 16 seats in the 1977 legislative election, 7 of which were lost in 1983. The Central Committee endorsed President Ratsiraka for reelection in early 1989, overruling party cofounder Richard Andriamanjato. Andriamanjato responded by forming the splinter AKFM-Renewal party. The AKFM rump won 2 seats in the 1989 election, but none in 1993 or 1998. In 2002, the AKFM-KDRSM received only .42 percent of the vote in the legislative elections.

Leaders: Rakotovao ANDRIANTIANA (Chair), Giselle RABESAHALA.

National Movement for the Independence of Madagascar/Madagascar for the Malagasy Party (*Mouvement National pour l'Indépendance de Madagascar/Madagasikara Otronin'ny Malagasy*—Monima). A left-wing nationalist party based in the south, Monima (also called *Monima Ka Miviombio*—Monima K) withdrew from the National Front after the local elections of March 1977, charging it had been the victim of electoral fraud. As a result, it was awarded no places on the National Front's list for the June legislative election. Its longtime leader, Monja JAONA, was under house arrest from November 1980 to March 1982, at which time he agreed to bring the group back into the FNDR and was appointed a member of the Supreme Revolutionary Council (SCR). He subsequently joined the 1982 presidential election as Commander Ratsiraka's only competitor, winning 20 percent of the vote. In December it was reported that he had been stripped of his membership on the SCR and again placed under house arrest for activities "likely to bring about the fall of the country." He was released in mid-August 1983, after undertaking a hunger strike, and returned to the legislature following the August 28 election as one of Monima's two representatives. The party's poor showing (less than 4 percent of valid votes cast) in 1983 was partly attributed to uncertainty, prior to Jaona's release, as to whether it would participate. Jaona secured only a 3 percent vote share in the 1989 presidential balloting and was the only assemblyman elected by the party in May. The aging leader was subsequently named chair of the SCR, having rejected calls from other opposition figures to join them in maintaining a solid anti-government front. Monima's deputy general secretary, René RANAIVOSOA resigned from the party in June 1990 following a dispute with Jaona, and established the **Democratic Party for Madagascar Development** (*Parti Démocratique pour le Développement de Madagascar*—PDDM/ADFM).

In early 1992 Joana was named a special advisor to the president, and on March 31 he was seriously wounded during a pro-Ratsiraka demonstration that included a clash with soldiers guarding the concluding session of the National Forum. Monima's influence has declined since Jaona's death, although the party pledged in 2000 to be more visible and reportedly endorsed President Ratsiraka in his subsequent reelection bid. In the 2002 legisla-

tive balloting, Monima won less than 1 percent of the vote.

Leader: Monja ROIDERO (Chair).

Socialist Monima (*Parti Socialiste Monima/ Vondrona Sosialista Monima*—VSM). The VSM was organized in late 1977 by a pro-Beijing group that had withdrawn from Monima. Subsequently unrepresented in the assembly, it supported MFM candidate Manandafy Rakotonirina for the presidency in 1989. The VSM did not participate in the 2002 legislative balloting.

Leaders: Tsihozony MAHARANGA (President), Romance RABETSITONTA, André RAZAFINDRABE (National Secretary).

Malagasy Christian Democratic Union (*Union Démocratique Chrétien Malgache*—Udecma). The tiny Udecma is a progressive Christian Democratic group formerly known as the *Rassemblement National Malgache* (RNM). It won two legislative seats in 1977, both of which were lost in 1983 and not recovered in 1989. The party took no official position in the 1989 presidential campaign.

Leader: Solo Norbert ANDRIAMORASATA.

Militant Malagasy Movement (*Mouvement Militant Malgache/ Malagasy Mivondrona Mitolona*—MMM). The MMM is led by a Udecma dissident, who had earlier been a pro-Ratsiraka activist within Arema.

Leader: Zaka Soa Max Halvanie RANDRIAMBAOMAHOVA.

Christian Democratic Movement of Madagascar (*Mouvement des Démocrates Chrétiens de Malgaches*—MDCM). Formed in 1990, the MDCM is a right-wing group whose platform calls for reentry into the Franc Zone and the establishment of relations with Israel and South Africa. Its leader was once a former minister under Tsiranana.

Leader: Jean-Jacques RAKOTONIAINA.

Christian Democratic Party of Madagascar (*Parti Démocrate Chrétien de Madagascar*—PDCM). One of the parties formed in the wake of the March 1990 decree, the PDCM has vied with Udecma and the MDCM for acceptance as

Cabinet

As of June 1, 2006

Prime Minister	Jacques Sylla

Ministers

Agriculture, Livestock, and Fisheries	Harison Edmond Randriarimanana
Civil Service, Labor, and Social Laws	Jean Theodore Ranjivason
Culture and Tourism	Jean Jacques Rabenirina
Decentralization and Development of Autonomous Provinces	Angelin Randrianarison
Economy, Finance, and Budget	Andriamparany Radavidson
Education and Scientific Research	Haja Nirina Razafinjatovo
Energy and Mines	Jaquis H. Rabarison
Environment, Water, and Forests	Gen. Charles Sylvain Rabotoarison
Foreign Affairs	Gen. Marcel Ranjeva
Health and Family Planning	Jean-Louis Robinson Richard
Industrialization, Commerce, and Development of the Private Sector	Roger-Marie Rafanomezantsoa
Interior and Administrative Reform	Lt. Gen. Charles Rabemananjara
Justice and Keeper of the Seals	Lala Henriette Ratsiharovala [f]
National Defense	Maj.-Gen. Petera Behajaina
Population, Social Protection, and Leisure	Andriamatoa Zafilaza
Posts, Telecommunications, and Communication	Clermont Gervais Mahazaka
Transport, Public Works, and Local Government	Roland Randriamampionona
Youth and Sports	Tombo Ramandimbisoa

Secretaries of State

Decentralization and Development of Autonomous Provinces	Eniavisoa
Public Security	Gen. Lucien Victor Razakanirina

[f] = female

Madagascar's internationally recognized Christian Democratic formation.

Leader: Alexis BEZAKA.

Rally for Madagascar's Muslim Democrats (*Rassemblement pour les Démocrates des Musulmans de Madagascar*—RDMM). The RDMM was officially recognized on September 30, 1997.

Leader: Jean-Louis RAZANABOHITRA.

Other parties include the **Malagasy Federalist Party,** a formerly pro-Ratsiraka grouping led by Henri LECACHEUR that reportedly endorsed Marc Ravalomanana in the 2001 presidential campaign, and the pro-Arema party, the **Toamasina**

Tonga Saina (TTS). Roland RATSIRAKA (the nephew of the former president, the mayor of Toamasina, and a member of the TTS) in 2006 announced his candidacy for the upcoming presidential election.

Legislature

The 1992 constitution provides for a bicameral **Parliament** (*Parlement*) consisting of a Senate and a National Assembly.

Senate (*Sénat*). The upper house has 90 members, 60 of which (10 from each province) are indirectly elected by electoral colleges comprised of the provincial councillors and mayors. The remaining 30 senators are appointed by the president in consultation with legal, economic, social, and cultural groups. The term of office is six years.

The first electoral college elections at the provincial level were held on March 18, 2001, resulting in the following seat distribution: Vanguard of the Malagasy Revolution, 49; Leader-*Fanilo*, 5; One Should Be Judged By One's Works, 2; Action, Truth, Development, and Harmony, 1; and independents (from the "Independent List of Jean André Soja" in Toliara Province), 3. The presidential appointments followed on April 17. President Ravalomanana appointed 30 members in July 2002, most of whom were reportedly members of his new I Love Madagascar party.

Speaker: Guy Rajemison RAKOTOMANORO.

National Assembly (*Assemblée Nationale*). The lower house encompasses 160 (formerly 138) members directly elected by proportional representation for five-year terms. At the most recent election of December 15, 2002, the I Love Madagascar party won 103 seats; the Patriotic Front, 22; the Rally for Socialism and Democracy, 5; the Vanguard of the Malagasy Revolution, 3; Leader-*Fanilo*, 2; the Militant Party for the Development of Madagascar, 2; and independents, 23. (The next election is due in December 2007.)

Speaker: Mahafaritsy Samuel RAZAKANIRINA.

Communications

Press

Media censorship in Madagascar was formally lifted in March 1989. A communication bill approved in December 1990 provided further liberalization, including the limitation of a requirement that journalists reveal their sources to state security personnel. The following are dailies published in Antananarivo in Malagasy, unless otherwise noted: *Midi-Madagasikara* (25,500), in French; *Madagascar Tribune* (formerly *Madagascar-Matin,* 12,000), government organ in French and Malagasy; *Imongo Vaovao* (10,000), AKFM organ; *Maresaka* (5,000), independent; *Sahy* (9,000), weekly; and *Maresaka* (5,000). In early 1995 two new papers were launched: *L'Express de Madagascar,* a bilingual independent daily, and the pro-Ravony *Valeurs-L'Hebdomadaire de Madagascar.*

News Agencies

In June 1977 the government replaced the existing *Agence Madagascar-Presse* with the *Agence Nationale d'Information "Taratra"* (Anta), which is responsible to the Ministry of Information and Ideological Orientation. A number of foreign bureaus maintain offices in the capital.

Broadcasting and Computing

In 1999 *Radio Nationale Malagasy,* a government-owned, commercial network, in addition to a number of private facilities, serviced some 3.3 million receivers, while *Télévision Nationaly Malagasy* offered programming for approximately 424,000 receivers in 2003. There were some 80,000 personal computers serving 70,500 Internet users in 2003.

Intergovernmental Representation

Ambassador to the U.S.
Narisoa RAJAONARIVONY

U.S. Ambassador to Madagascar
James D. McGEE

Permanent Representative to the UN
Zina ANDRIANARIVELO-RAZAFY

IGO Memberships (Non-UN)
AfDB, AU, BADEA, Comesa, Interpol, IOC, IOM, IOR-ARC, NAM, OIF, SADC, WCO, WTO

MALAWI

REPUBLIC OF MALAWI

The Country

Malawi, the former British protectorate of Nyasaland, is a landlocked southeastern African nation bordering the western side of 360-mile-long Lake Malawi (formerly Lake Nyasa). The country's name is a contemporary spelling of "Maravi," which historically referenced the interrelated Bantu peoples who inhabit the area. The main tribal groups are the Chewas, the Nyanja, and the Tumbuka. It is estimated that 75 percent of the population is Christian and 13 percent Muslim, with the remainder, except for a very small Hindu population, adhering to traditional African beliefs. A small non-African component includes Europeans and Asians. Three-quarters of adult females are subsistence agricultural workers, while the number of households headed by women has increased in recent years as men have relocated to pursue cash-crop labor.

About 85 percent of the population is engaged in agriculture, the most important cash crops being tobacco, tea, peanuts, sugar, and cotton. Development efforts have focused on integrated rural production, diversification in light industry (particularly agriprocessing and import substitution), and improved transportation facilities.

Although credited by the mid-1980s with being one of the few African states with a grain surplus, Malawi continued to suffer high rates of malnutrition, infant mortality, and poverty—a paradox widely attributed to an agricultural system favoring large estate owners. The economy was further stressed by chronic unemployment, trade imbalances, persistent inflation, and external debt pressures, prompting the government in the early 1990s to adopt adjustment measures sponsored by the International Monetary Fund (IMF), including the privatization of state enterprises. The reforms contributed to an economic resurgence in the mid-1990s. However, a downturn subsequently ensued, in part, according to the IMF, due to a slackening in the pace of reform as well as a slowdown in agricultural demand. Real GDP growth fell to 1.7 percent in 2000, with inflation steadying at 45 percent. In 2001 GDP declined by 4.1 percent, before posting a small recovery in 2002 and growing by 4.4 percent in 2003. In addition, inflation was brought down to 10 percent in 2003.

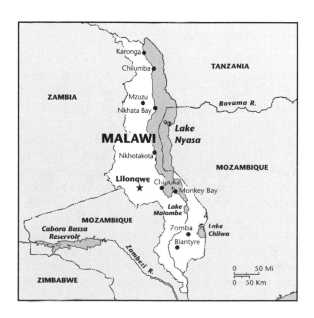

In 2000 Malawi was approved for $1 billion in debt reduction under the World Bank's Heavily Indebted Poor Countries (HIPC) initiative, and the IMF provided a $65 million loan for poverty reduction. However, excessive government spending, corruption, and the slow pace of economic reforms led international donors, including the World Bank, IMF, United States, and European Union (EU), to suspend some economic aid during 2001–2002, although humanitarian assistance continued in light of Malawi's worsening food crisis (caused by drought in some areas and severe flooding in others). Poor harvests in 2004 left some 5 million Malawians dependent on food aid, although agricultural production improved significantly in 2005. Meanwhile, the EU resumed full economic and development aid, including support for ports, hydroelectric facilities, and direct financial contributions to limit the government's deficit. In April 2006 the IMF reported that the new government had made progress in regard to economic reforms and approved a three-year aid program (contingent on continued reform and the meeting of certain economic benchmarks). The World Bank also approved aid to develop rural infrastructure.

Government and Politics

Political Background

Under British rule since 1891, the Nyasaland protectorate was joined with Northern and Southern Rhodesia in 1953 to form the Federation of Rhodesia and Nyasaland. Internal opposition to the federation proved so vigorous that a state of emergency was declared, with nationalist leaders H. B. M. CHIPEMBERE, Kanyama CHIUME, and Hastings Kamuzu BANDA being imprisoned. They were released upon the attainment of internal self-government on February 1, 1963, and dissolution of the federation at the end of that year. Nyasaland became a fully independent member of the Commonwealth under the name of Malawi on July 6, 1964, and a republic two years later, with Prime Minister Banda being installed as the country's president.

The early years of the Banda presidency were marked by conservative policies, including the retention of white civil service personnel and the maintenance of good relations with South Africa. Younger, more radical leaders soon became disenchanted, and in 1965 a minor insurrection was led by Chipembere, while a second, led by Yatuta CHISIZA, took place in 1967. Both were easily contained, however, and Banda became entrenched as the nation's political leader.

In March 1983, Dr. Attati MPAKATI of the Socialist League of Malawi (one of the two principal exile groups) was assassinated in Zimbabwe. In May, Orton CHIRWA, the former leader of the other main exile organization (the Malawi Freedom Movement—Mafremo) was found guilty of treason and was sentenced to death. (Chirwa had been jailed, along with his wife and son, since December 1981.) Subsequent appeals in December 1983 and February 1984 were denied, and Chirwa, who claimed that he and his family had been abducted from Zambia to permit their arrest, became an object of international human rights attention. Bowing to the pressure, Banda commuted the sentences to life imprisonment in June 1984. (Chirwa died in 1992 under unclear circumstances.)

In an apparent response to pressure from international aid donors, President Banda instructed the National Assembly in December 1991 to "make a final decision" on unipartyism, albeit prefacing his call for debate by commending the "successes" of his Malawi Congress Party (MCP), which had voted for a continuation of the existing system only three months before. Thus, despite the country's first mass protests against MCP rule in May 1992, no opposition groups were permitted to present candidates in legislative balloting on June 26–27. Somewhat unexpectedly, given another MCP vote against pluralism on October 2, President Banda on October 18 announced plans for a national referendum to decide Malawi's future political structure. On June 15, 1993, 63.5 percent of those participating voted in favor of a multiparty system.

On October 13, 1993, 11 days after Banda underwent emergency brain surgery, the office of the president announced the formation of a

Political Status: Independent member of the Commonwealth since 1964; republic under one-party presidential rule established July 6, 1966; constitution amended on June 22, 1993, to provide for multiparty activity following national referendum of June 15; new constitution enacted provisionally as of May 16, 1994, and adopted permanently (as amended) on May 18, 1995.

Area: 45,747 sq. mi. (118,484 sq. km.).

Population: 9,933,868 (1998C); 12,587,000 (2005E).

Major Urban Centers (2005E): LILONGWE (676,000), Blantyre (715,000), Mzuzu (107,000).

Official Language: English. (Chichewa is classified as a national language.)

Monetary Unit: Kwacha (official rate July 1, 2006: 138.99 kwacha = $1US).

President: Bingu wa MUTHARIKA (Democratic Progressive Party); popularly elected (as a member of the United Democratic Front) on May 20, 2004, and inaugurated for a five-year term on May 24, succeeding Bakili MULUZI (United Democratic Front).

First Vice President: Cassim CHILUMPHA (United Democratic Front); popularly elected on May 20, 2004, and inaugurated for a five-year term on May 24, succeeding Justin C. MALEWEZI (United Democratic Front).

Second Vice President: Vacant following the resignation of Chakufwa CHIHANA (Alliance for Democracy) on February 24, 2004.

---

the National Consultative Council (NCC) and the National Executive Council (NEC), charged with electoral preparation and oversight.

In early December 1993 the Presidential Council ordered the disarmament of the Malawi Young Pioneers (MYP), an MCP-affiliated paramilitary group whose recent killing of two regular army soldiers had exacerbated tensions between the two armed forces. The ensuing crackdown, resulting in 32 deaths and the reported flight of 1,000 pioneers to Mozambique, was denounced by the NCC, which accused the Presidential Council of having "lost control." Consequently, on December 7 a still visibly ailing Banda dissolved the Presidential Council and reassumed presidential powers. Shortly thereafter, Banda appointed a new defense minister, Maj. Gen. Wilfred John MPONERA, who, on January 7, 1994, announced the completion of MYP disarmament.

In the country's first multiparty election on May 17, 1994, voters decisively rejected bids by Banda and two other presidential candidates in favor of Bakili MULUZI of the United Democratic Front (UDF). In simultaneous legislative balloting, the UDF also led the field, although it fell short of a majority by five seats. Four days after his inauguration on May 21, President Muluzi announced a coalition government in which two minor parties— the Malawi National Democratic Party (MNDP) and the United Front for Multiparty Democracy (UFMD)—were allocated one portfolio each.

On July 21, 1994, the MCP and the Alliance for Democracy (Aford) announced the formation of a shadow government that included Banda's former second in command, John Tembo, as finance minister. However, the MCP-Aford pact was effectively terminated when Aford president Chakufwa CHIHANA accepted an appointment by Muluzi as second vice president designate and three other Aford members joined an expanded cabinet on September 24. Constitutional revision was required to accommodate Chihana's appointment (see Constitution and government, below).

In response to domestic and international criticism of the size of his cabinet, Muluzi reshuffled it and reduced its size from 35 to 32 members on

---

three-member Presidential Council, thus rejecting the opposition's call for a "neutral" president to rule in Banda's absence. The council was comprised of the MCP's recently appointed secretary general, Stephen Gwandanguluwe CHAKUAMBA Phiri, as well as MCP stalwarts John TEMBO and Robson CHIRWA. Nevertheless, preparations for the May 1994 multiparty balloting continued, with the assembly approving constitutional amendments reforming the electoral process and presidency (see Constitution and government, below) and authorizing the formation of two transitional bodies:

July 16, 1995. A more significant change occurred on July 27, when the UDF and Aford announced that they had signed an agreement to form a coalition government. However, in December relations between the two groups cooled when Aford leader Chihana accused the government of "lacking transparency" and failing to combat corruption.

On December 23, 1995, former president Banda and his five codefendants were acquitted of all charges relating to the murder of "reformist" politicians in 1983 (see MCP in Political Parties and Groups, below). Shortly thereafter, Banda apologized for the "pain and suffering" that had occurred while he was in office. However, he continued to deny personal responsibility, instead blaming "selfish individuals" in his government. Meanwhile, the new UDF-led government continued to press inquiries into a wide range of abuses that were alleged to have taken place under Banda's rule. Ultimately, although official scrutiny remained leveled at some of Banda's former confidants, investigative fervor in general dissipated substantially upon Banda's death on November 25.

On May 2, 1996, Chihana resigned from the government, saying that he wanted to concentrate on his party responsibilities. Six Aford cabinet ministers refused to comply with Chihana's demand that they resign from the government as well, and they declared themselves "independents." In response, Aford and the MCP suspended their participation in the assembly, accusing the UDF of attempting to secure a legislative majority by "poaching" their representatives as cabinet ministers. Assembly activity subsequently remained blocked (the UDF proving unable to muster a quorum) until April 1997, when Aford and the MCP ended their boycott after President Muluzi agreed to pursue constitutional amendments that would "prevent political horsetrading and chicanery." However, the matter was not resolved on July 24, when Muluzi appointed a new cabinet that still included Aford representatives against the wishes of Aford leaders.

On June 15, 1999, President Muluzi was reelected to a second five-year term with 51.37 percent of the vote, compared to 44.3 percent for runner-up Chakuamba, the joint MCP/Aford candidate. (Aford's Chihana had served as Chakuamba's vice presidential running mate.) In concurrent legislative polling the UDF secured a plurality of 93 of 193 seats. The opposition accused the government of numerous irregularities, including manipulation of the media and the voter registration process as well as vote rigging. The losing candidates also argued that a runoff should have been held because Muluzi's vote total had not surpassed the level of 50 percent of the registered voters. Although the international community generally accepted the balloting as free and fair and the courts in Malawi upheld the results, Chakufwa Chihana of Aford, the MCP/Aford vice presidential candidate, called for a campaign of civil disobedience to protest the government's actions. Muluzi's critics also challenged the cabinet he appointed on July 1 for containing too many ministers (21 of 36) from the southern part of the country, the UDF stronghold.

Corruption charges prompted the appointment of new cabinets in March and November 2000, although many incumbents were simply given new portfolios. Meanwhile, severe intraparty infighting continued to hamper both the MCP and Aford, as evidenced by their poor showing in the November 2000 local elections, which were dominated by the UDF, albeit in the context of a low voter turnout. Muluzi's second term was marked by a bitter dispute over proposed constitutional changes to allow a president to seek a third term. The initial proposal failed to gain the needed two-thirds majority in the assembly in 2002, and a second effort in the legislature was rebuffed in 2003. The UDF attempted to have the measure brought to the public in a national referendum. However, it became clear that the constitutional amendment would fail because of widespread opposition, and the referendum request was withdrawn. Muluzi subsequently announced that he would not seek a third term. Instead he handpicked his successor, economist Bingu wa MUTHARIKA, who had run as a presidential candidate in 1999 for the defunct United Party (UP).

Presidential polling in 2004 was delayed by two days as a result of complaints by opposition parties that some 1 million voters, including many of their supporters, had been purged from the list of eligible voters. However, the High Court accepted the government's explanation that only double registrations and ineligible voters had been eliminated from the rolls.

In January 2004 a coalition of seven small parties, calling itself *Mgwirizano* (Unity), was launched to present Chakuamba as a joint presidential candidate. However, President Mutharika was reelected in balloting on May 20 with 35.9 percent of the vote, compared to 27.1 percent for Tembo (the MCP candidate) and 25.7 percent for Chakuamba. In concurrent legislative balloting, the MCP secured 60 seats, followed by the UDF with 60. Opposition parties and candidates challenged the legitimacy of the polling. However, Chakuamba withdrew his objections and accepted the post of minister of agriculture in the new Mutharika government, which also included the UDF, the National Democratic Alliance, the *Mgwirizano* coalition, and independents. Many independent legislators agreed to support the UDF in the assembly, some 23 of them subsequently joining the UDF. Additional realignments occurred after a dispute within the UDF prompted Mutharika to form a new party (see Current issues, below).

Constitution and Government

The republican constitution of July 6, 1966, established a one-party system under which the MCP was accorded a political monopoly and its leader extensive powers as head of state, head of government, and commander in chief. Originally elected to a five-year presidential term by the National Assembly in 1966, Hastings Banda was designated president for life in 1971.

Following approval of a multiparty system in a national referendum on June 15, 1993, the assembly on June 22 amended the basic law to permit the registration of parties beyond the MCP. In November further revision abolished the life presidency and repealed the requirement that presidential candidates be MCP members. Following the return of ailing President Banda to active status in early December, an additional amendment was enacted to provide for an acting president in case of the president's incapacitation.

A new constitution (proposed by a National Constitutional Conference) was approved by the assembly on May 16, 1994, and entered into effect provisionally for one year on May 18. The new basic law incorporated the 1993 amendments while also providing for a new Constitutional Committee and a Human Rights Commission. It also authorized the eventual creation of a second legislative body (the Senate) no sooner than 1999. However, in January 2001, much to the consternation of opposition parties and some civic organizations, the assembly revised the basic law to eliminate reference to the proposed Senate. The government argued that the creation of the Senate would have burdened the country's fragile economy, but opponents claimed that the administration was in reality primarily concerned that the new body would have had the power to impeach the president. Following review and refinement by the Constitutional Conference, the new constitution was once again approved by the assembly and promulgated as a permanent document on May 18, 1995. One of the amendments approved by the assembly in November 1994 provided for a presidentially appointed second vice president. The first vice president is elected as a running mate to the president and assumes the presidency if that office becomes vacant. The president is not required to designate a second vice president, but any such appointment must be made outside the president's political party.

The 1995 constitution provided for a Western-style judicial system, including a Supreme Court of Appeal, a High Court, and Magistrates' courts. No mention is made of the so-called traditional courts (headed by local chiefs), which had been restored in 1970. For administrative purposes Malawi is divided into 3 regions, 24 districts, and 3 sub-districts, which are headed by regional ministers, district commissioners, and assistant district commissioners, respectively.

Foreign Relations

Malawi under President Banda's leadership sought to combine African nationalism with multiracialism at home and a strongly pro-Western and anti-Communist position in world affairs. Citing economic necessity, Malawi was one of the few black African states to maintain uninterrupted relations with white-ruled South Africa. A consequence of the linkage was a September 1986 meeting in Blantyre, during which the leaders of Mozambique, Zambia, and Zimbabwe reportedly warned Banda to change his policies, particularly concerning alleged Malawian support for Renamo rebels in Mozambique. Banda, while denying the allegations, nevertheless quickly concluded a joint defense and security pact with Mozambique. The government also reaffirmed its commitment to an effort by the Southern African Development Coordination Conference (SADCC, subsequently the Southern African Development Community—SADC) to reduce dependence on South African trade routes. To that end, Malawi in 1987 agreed to increase shipments through Tanzania, with which it had established diplomatic ties in 1985 despite long-standing complaints of Tanzanian aid to Banda's opponents. Relations with Zambia had also been strained by Malawi's claim to Zambian territory in the vicinity of their common border.

In 1994 the new Muluzi administration moved quickly to strengthen regional ties, the president traveling to Zimbabwe, Zambia, and Botswana. In addition, Malawi and Mozambique created a joint commission to locate and repatriate former rebels located in the opposite state. Malawi also endeavored to improve relations and security ties with the United States. In June 2003 five suspected al-Qaida terrorists were turned over to U.S. custody.

President Mutharika's anticorruption campaign won international praise from European states, the United States, and international organizations such as the IMF and the World Bank. As a result, donors increased aid and assistance to the government in 2004 and 2005.

Current Issues

Political affairs were chaotic in 2001 and 2002, with UDF hard-liners working to prevent defections to the new National Democratic Alliance (NDA, see Political Parties and Groups, below). Many of the administration's initiatives in that regard were overturned by the courts, leading to marked friction between the executive and legislative branches. Following the 2004 presidential and legislative elections, a leadership struggle within the UDF led to defections from the party.

Following the 2004 elections, new president Mutharika launched a broad anticorruption campaign that earned praise (and additional aid) from donors such as the EU and the United States. However, the initiative generated a rift between Mutharika and former president Muluzi, some of whose close allies (including several UDF leaders) were arrested on corruption charges. (Critics of Mutharika accused him of using the new anticorruption bureau as a personal political tool.) Consequently, supporters in the assembly of Muluzi (who remained leader of the UDF after leaving the presidency) began to block legislation presented by the Mutharika administration. The conflict culminated in the president's decision in February 2005 to quit the UDF and form a new Democratic Progressive Party (DPP), which attracted a number of Mutharika's supporters within the UDF and other parties and prompted significant legislative realignment.

In March 2005 the UDF and MCP attempted without success to impeach Mutharika for inappropriate use of government funds. At the same time, it was reported that the government was contemplating an investigation of former president Muluzi's alleged acquisition of millions of dollars during his presidential tenure. Relations between the executive and legislative branches deteriorated further when Mutharika moved his offices into the new assembly building, forcing the assembly to return to its old headquarters. Opposition parties (led by the UDF) again attempted to start impeachment proceedings against the president in June, and, in apparent retaliation, Mutharika removed the UDF's Cassim Chilumpha from his cabinet post, although Chilumpha remained vice president. Collaterally, Mutharika announced a cabinet reshuffle that raised the number of ministers from 27 to 33 so that he could include some of his independent supporters.

The assembly formally approved the start of impeachment proceedings in mid-October 2005, but the High Court ordered them stopped after pro-Mutharika demonstrations had deteriorated into "riots" in which opposition legislators were reportedly attacked. In any event, it had been widely expected that the impeachment motion would not have garnered the two-thirds assembly vote required for success. In addition, analysts suggested that much of the population considered the impeachment initiative a waste of time and resources, particularly in view of the nation's severe food crisis. Among other things, the assembly's blockage of the administration's proposed budget compromised the distribution of emergency food supplies. (The budget had also called for a pay raise of more than 350 percent for the president.)

The government conducted another string of arrests in November 2005 as part of its anticorruption campaign. Among those charged were two legislators who had led the recent impeachment drive and Vice President Chilumpha. However, the High Court ruled that Chilumpha could not be brought up on criminal charges while serving as vice president. In February 2006 Mutharika attempted to dismiss Chilumpha for "undermining the government," but the High Court declared the president lacked the constitutional authority for such a move. At the end of April Chilumpha and some 12 others (including senior members of the UDF) were arrested on treason charges, the administration accusing them of having plotted the assassination of Mutharika. The charges against most of those arrested were quickly dropped, but Chilumpha remained under house arrest as of July awaiting trial with two codefendants.

Political Parties and Groups

For nearly three decades prior to the 1993 national referendum, the Malawi Congress Party (MCP) was the only authorized political group, and it exercised complete control of the government. On June 29, 1993, the constitution was amended to allow for multiparty activity, and on August 17 the government announced that the first groups had been authorized to function as legal parties.

The **Mgwirizano** (Unity) coalition was formed in January 2004 by seven small parties opposed to the UDF and the rule of President Muluzi. The coalition included the Republican Party, the People's Progressive Movement, the Movement for Democratic Change, the People's Transformation Party, the Malawi Democratic Party, the National Unity Party, and the Malawi Forum for Unity and Development. It fielded a slate of candidates for the legislative election and chose Gwanda Chakuamba as the coalition leader and main presidential candidate. (John Malewezi also ran as a candidate for the People's Progressive Movement.) Following the legislative elections, some member parties decided to support newly elected President Mutharika after he reached out and incorporated party members in a coalition government. However, the coalition dissolved in February 2005 with the resignation of Chakuamba and the formation of the Democratic Progressive Party (see below).

In February 2006 it was reported that the MCP, Aford, and the NRP had agreed to form a "grand coalition" for subsequent elections.

Legislative Parties

Democratic Progressive Party (DPP). The DPP was launched in February 2005 by President Bingu wa Mutharika and other UDF dissidents who opposed UDF president Muluzi. Disaffected members of other parties and a number of independents also joined the UDF, which as of mid-2006 was credited with controlling some 74 assembly seats. DPP Vice President Gwanda Chakuamba was dismissed from the cabinet and expelled from the DPP in September 2005 after he strongly criticized President Mutharika.

Leaders: Bingu wa MUTHARIKA (President of the Republic and Party President), Uladi MUSSA (Party Vice President).

United Democratic Front (UDF). The UDF was founded in April 1992 by former MCP officials who operated clandestinely until October, when they announced their intention to campaign for a multiparty democracy. A party congress on December 30, 1993, chose UDF chair Bakili Muluzi to be the UDF's presidential candidate. Meanwhile, the UDF leaders were embarrassed by allegations, attributed to the MCP, that they had engaged in anti-opposition activities while MCP members.

Muluzi defeated incumbent president Banda and two other candidates in March 1994 with a 47.3 percent plurality of the vote. In the legislative balloting the UDF won a plurality of 84 of 177 seats. Muluzi was reelected with 51.37 percent of the vote in 1999, while the UDF increased its legislative plurality to 93 out of 193 seats in 1999.

Beginning in 2000, the party suffered serious internal divisions, leading to the formation of the anti-Muluzi NDA (above). In 2003, dissident members of the UDF left the party to form a new entity, the People's Progressive Movement (PPM), led by former UDF party vice president Aleke Banda. In the 2004 legislative elections the UDF lost its plurality and became the second-largest party (49 seats) in the assembly behind the MCP.

Following the 2004 presidential election, a leadership struggle emerged between Muluzi, who remained party president, and his hand-picked successor as Malawi's president, Bingu wa Mutharika. Among other things, Muluzi's supporters objected to elements of the broad anticorruption efforts by Mutharika, who in February 2005 left the UDF to form the DPP (above).

The UDF lead the subsequent effort to impeach President Mutharika, although its legislative representation had reportedly fallen to 30 by mid-2006 due to defections to the DPP. In addition, many UDF leaders faced corruption charges pressed by the Mutharika administration (see Current issues, above).

Leaders: Bakili MULUZI (President of the Party and Former President of the Republic), Kennedy MAKWANGWALA (Secretary General).

Malawi Congress Party (MCP). The MCP is a continuation of the Nyasaland African Congress (NAC), which was formed in 1959 under the leadership of President H. Kamuzu Banda. Overtly pro-Western and dedicated to multiracialism and internal development, the party was frequently criticized for being excessively conservative. It held all legislative seats prior to the multiparty poll of May 1994, when it ran second in both the presidential and legislative races.

On August 25, 1994, Banda retired from politics although he retained the title of MCP president for life. The 1994 vice presidential candidate, Stephen Chakuamba, assumed leadership of the party. Thereafter, in early 1995, the party was shaken by the arrests of Banda, John Tembo (longtime Banda associate and MCP leader), and others for alleged involvement in the killing 12 years earlier of Dick MATENJE and several other MCP cabinet ministers. At the time of his death, Matenje had headed an increasingly popular reform wing within the party that had clashed with Tembo and his supporters. Banda, Tembo, and their codefendants in the murder trial were acquitted on all charges in December. Related charges against Cecilia KADZAMIRA, Banda's longtime companion who had been the country's "official hostess" during the latter part of the Banda regime, had been dismissed prior to trial on technical grounds. However, the government continued to press the case by appealing the verdict to the High Court, which ultimately upheld the acquittal. Meanwhile, Tembo and Kadzamira were arrested in September 1996 on charges of conspiracy to commit murder in connection with an alleged plot to assassinate cabinet members in 1995. They were quickly released on bail, and it was subsequently unclear if the case would be pursued. Similar ambiguity existed regarding fraud charges against Tembo and Kadzamira stemming from alleged malfeasance during the accumulation of the vast Banda "economic empire." Banda himself had been the focus of a corruption investigation in early 1997, but the case was dropped later in the year when it became apparent that the former president had little time to live.

Conflict between Banda's supporters and MCP "reformists" continued through 1997, with the latter clearly gaining the ascendancy at the party convention in July. In a surprisingly decisive vote of 406–109, Tembo was defeated in the race for MCP president by Chakuamba, who immediately declared his intention to run for president of the republic in 1999, insisting that the MCP should merge with Aford (below) to present the strongest possible challenge to the UDF. However, the proposed merger was shelved in the wake of objections from MCP veterans, including Tembo, who had been elected unopposed as MCP vice president.

In intraparty polling in January 1999, Chakuamba defeated Tembo in a contest to decide who would be the MCP's standard-bearer in midyear presidential balloting. Subsequently, Chakuamba rejected suggestions that he choose Tembo as his running mate and named Aford's Chakufwa Chihana to his campaign ticket. On February 8 an electoral alliance for the presidential race between the two parties was officially inaugurated. Meanwhile, pro-Tembo activists staged demonstrations to protest what they (and reportedly Tembo) considered an affront. The MCP/Aford ticket finished second (with 44.3 percent of the vote) in the June presidential ballot, while the MCP secured 66 seats (on 33.82 percent of the vote) in the legislative poll. Meanwhile, tension between Chakuamba and Tembo continued, and in late May Tembo called upon Chakuamba to step down as party leader. In early June, Chakuamba called for an MCP boycott of the opening session of parliament, but his request was ignored and he was given a one-year suspension from the house (later voided by the High Court). On June 24 Speaker Sam Mpasu endorsed Tembo as new leader of the opposition in parliament, a decision that was subsequently challenged by Chakuamba.

The MCP infighting continued unabated into 2000, and the rival factions held separate conventions in August at which Chakuamba and Tembo were each declared party chair. However, the following summer the High Court nullified the parallel conventions. Meanwhile, the Chakuamba faction, which announced it had expelled Tembo and his supporters from the party, pursued ties with the NDA, the newly formed antigovernment group-

ing, while the Tembo faction was perceived as cooperating more and more with the administration. Chakuamba subsequently joined the Republican Party (below) in December 2003. The MCP became the largest party in the assembly after the 2004 elections, but Tembo lost his presidential bid. MCP Secretary General Kate KAINGA-KALULUMA joined the new Mutharika government and subsequently left the MCP to join the DPP. Subsequently, the MCP cooperated with the UDF's attempt to impeach President Mutharika, although internal MCP dissension was reported regarding that and other issues. (A dissident faction led by Respicious DZANJALIMODZI was reportedly challenging Tembo's supporters for party supremacy.)

Leaders: John TEMBO (Party Leader and 2004 presidential candidate), Louis CHIMANGO (Speaker of the National Assembly), Nicolas DOSUI.

Alliance for Democracy (Aford). Aford was launched in Lilongwe on September 21, 1992, by trade union leader and prodemocracy advocate Chakufwa Chihana, who at the time of the group's founding was awaiting trial on sedition charges. The grouping was led by a 13-member interim committee that included civil servants, academics, and businesspeople. Although Aford described itself as "not a party but a pressure group," the government on November 7 declared membership in the group illegal. In late December many of its members were arrested during demonstrations ignited by the sentencing of Chihana to three years imprisonment.

In March 1993 a spokesperson for the Zimbabwean-based Malawi Freedom Movement (Mafremo) announced that the group had dissolved and had merged with Aford. (Mafremo, in the wake of the 1981 arrest and imprisonment of its leader, Orton CHIRWA, had been relatively inactive until an early 1987 attack on a police station near the Tanzanian border that was attributed to the group's military wing, the Malawi National Liberation Army. Although initially based in Dar es Salaam, Mafremo had subsequently been reported to have secured Zimbabwean support through the efforts of a new leader, Dr. Edward YAPWANTHA, who was expelled from Zimbabwe in mid-1990, apparently as a result of improved Malawian-Zimbabwean relations.)

In mid-1994, Chihana, who had been granted a sentence reduction and released two days before the multiparty referendum, pressed President Banda to resign in favor of an MCP-UDF-Aford transitional government. In August Aford turned back a merger bid from another opposition party—the Congress for the Second Republic (CSR)—asserting an interest in the CSR's (then) exiled leader, Kanyama CHUIME, but not the party.

Following its third-place showing in the 1994 assembly balloting, Aford declined an invitation to participate in a government coalition with the UDF, which was five seats short of a legislative majority. On June 20 Aford signed a memorandum of understanding with the MCP, in which the two groups committed themselves to preservation of "the endangered national unity and security of the country." However, in September Chihana joined the Muluzi government as second vice president designate, while three other Aford members accepted cabinet posts. Although Chihana rejected reports that the party was defecting to the UDF, in January 1995 Aford announced the dissolution of its alliance with the MCP.

Relations between the UDF and Aford deteriorated over the next year, and on May 2, 1996, Chihana, who had criticized the UDF on several points in December 1995, resigned from the second vice presidency, ostensibly to devote more time to party affairs. In June it was reported that an Aford national congress had voted to withdraw from the government coalition and had ordered its members in the cabinet to resign their posts. However, most of the ministers refused to leave the government, and it was reported that at least six members of the Aford executive council rejected the decision to separate from the coalition with the UDF. In response, Chihana called for the ouster of the "renegade" members, who, according to some reports, were by then referring to themselves as "independents." The issue remained clouded throughout 1997 as the new cabinet announced in July included not only the previous Aford ministers but also several other Aford members. Meanwhile, at the party's annual congress in December, Aford delegates voted against a merger with the MCP that had been advocated by many within the Chihana camp.

In June 1998 two Aford legislators, Joseph MSEKAWANTHU and Edward MUSYANI, declared their independence from the party, charging that the party's "dictatorial" leadership policies had marginalized them. In October Aford officially acknowledged having decided to compete for the presidency on a joint ticket with the MCP, and in February 1999 Chihana agreed to campaign for the vice presidency on a ticket led by MCP leader Chakuamba. Aford was credited with 10.52 percent of the vote and 29 seats in the June 1999 assembly balloting.

Intraparty fighting continued in 2000–2001 in regard to issues such as the future of the alliance with the MCP and whether the party should cooperate with the government. While the faction around Chihana was reportedly in favor of continuing an antigovernment stance, another wing pressed to discontinue the alliance with the MCP and form a national unity government with the UDF. Aford won only 6 seats in the 2004 elections and supported the subsequent Mutharika government after Chihana was appointed minister of agriculture and food security, a post he left in February 2005. Four of Aford's legislators reportedly defected to the DPP in 2005.

Leaders: Chakufwa CHIHANA (President of the Party and Former Second Vice President of the Republic), Chipimpha MUGHOGHO (Chair).

Congress for National Unity (CONU). The CONU is led by a cleric who received .51 percent of the vote in the 1999 presidential poll. The CONU also participated unsuccessfully in the 1999 legislative balloting. In the 2004 elections CONU gained one seat in the assembly.

Leaders: Bishop Daniel NKHUMBWE (1999 presidential candidate), Silvester White CHABUKA (1999 vice presidential candidate).

Republican Party (RP). The RP was formed in 2004 by Gwanda Chakuamba and Stanley Masauli and other opponents of John Tembo from the MCP. Using the RP as the nucleus of the anti-Muluzi coalition *Mgwirizano*, Chakuamba placed third in the 2004 presidential balloting with 25.7 percent of the vote. He subsequently joined the government as minister of agriculture and food security. In the legislative elections, the RP became the third largest party with 15 seats.

In March 2005 Chakuamba resigned from the RP, along with a number of RP members, to join the new DPP. Chakuamba initially announced the dissolution of the RP, but the RP's executive council rejected the proposed "merger" with the DPP. The executive committee agreed that the RP would remain in the government.

Following his dismissal from the government and the DPP in September 2005, Chakuamba attempted to reassert control over the RP. However, he was formally expelled from the RP in October, and he subsequently announced the formation of the **New Republican Party** (NRP).

Leader: Stanley MASAULI (Interim Leader).

People's Progressive Movement (PPM). Formed in 2003 by former UDF vice president Aleke Banda and other members of the UDF opposed to the Muluzi faction of the UDF, the PPM joined the *Mgwirizano* coalition for the 2004 elections, gaining six seats in the assembly. Party member and former vice president of the republic John MALEWEZI ran as a presidential candidate for the PPM in 2004, placing fifth with just 2.5 percent of the vote. In 2005 a number of PPM members joined the DPP, although the PPM retained its status as an independent party.

Leader: Aleke BANDA (Party Leader), Mark KATSONGA.

Movement for Genuine Democratic Change (MGODE). The MGODE, created in 2003 by former members of Aford, joined the *Mgwirizano* coalition prior to the 2004 presidential and legislative elections, gaining three seats in the assembly balloting. In 2005 it was reported that the MGODE had been absorbed into the DPP.

Leaders: Sam Kandodo BANDA (Party President), Greene MWAMONDWE (Chair), Rodger NKWAZI (Secretary General).

National Democratic Alliance (NDA). The NDA was originally launched in early 2001 as a "pressure group" designed to promote "good governance" and to combat potential revision of the constitution that would permit President Muluzi to run for a third term. The new grouping also criticized the government's economic policies and urged installation of a "unity government" that would include the MCP. The NDA was founded by several dissident UDF members, the most prominent being Brown Mpinganjira, a longtime Muluzi loyalist who had been dismissed from the cabinet in November and had been arrested on corruption charges in late December. Mpinganjira, who had once been considered a possible successor to Muluzi, accused the government of trumping up the charges against him because of his outspoken opposition to a third term for Muluzi. The charges were subsequently dropped for lack of evidence.

At the inception of the NDA, Mpinganjira and the other UDF "rebels" insisted that they were still UDF members and that they were not trying to establish a new party. However, the UDF quickly expelled Mpinganjira and three other UDF legislators from the party for their NDA association. In late February 2001 another prominent UDF member, James Makhumula, also left the party in favor of association with the NDA, of which he eventually was named national chair. (Makhumula, a prominent and wealthy businessman, had been regarded as the "chief financier" of the UDF.)

Apparently in response to growing support for the NDA, the assembly in June 2001 passed an "antidefection law" that stated that legislators leaving the party under whose banner they were elected thereby forfeited their seats. In November the assembly voted to expel Mpinganjira and six others for violation of the new law. However, the High Court ordered the legislators reinstalled. Subsequently, the NDA was granted legal party status in preparation for the 2004 elections. Mpinganjira placed fourth in the 2004 presidential election with

Cabinet

As of September 1, 2006

President	Bingu wa Mutharika (DPP)
Vice President	Cassim Chilumpha (UDF)
Second Vice President	(Vacant)

Ministers

Agriculture and Food Security	Uladi Mussa (DPP)
Defense	Davis Katsonga (DPP)
Economic Planning and Development	David Faiti (RP)
Education and Vocational Training	Anna Kackiko [f]
Finance and Economic Planning	Goodall Gondwe (DPP)
Foreign Affairs and International Cooperation	Joyce Banda (DPP) [f]
Health	Marjorie Ngaunje [f]
Home Affairs and Internal Security	Bob Khamisa (UDF)
Industry, Trade, and Private Sector Development	Ken Lipenga (DPP)
Information and Tourism	Patricia Kaliati [f]
Justice and Constitutional Affairs	Bazuka Mhango (RP)
Labor and Social Development	Khumbo Chirwa (RP)
Lands, Housing, and Surveys	Henry Phoya (UDF)
Local Government and Rural Development	George Chaponda (UDF)
Natural Resources, Mines, and Energy	Henry Chimunthu Banda (DPP)
Public Services	Bingu wa Mutharika (DPP)
Social Development and Persons with Disabilities	Clement Khembo
Transport and Public Works	Henry Mussa (DPP)
Water Development and Irrigation	Sidik Mia
Women and Child Development	Kate Kainja Kaluluma (DPP) [f]
Youth, Sports, and Culture	Jaffalie Mussa (UDF)

[f] = female

8.7 percent of the vote, while the NDA gained eight seats in the assembly balloting.

Leaders: Brown MPINGANJIRA (President and 2004 presidential candidate), James MAKHU-MULA (Chair).

Other Parties That Contested the 2004 Legislative Election

Malawi Democratic Party (MDP). The MDP was legalized shortly after its formation in mid-1993, its leader running a distant fourth in the presidential balloting of May 17, 1994. Although having won no legislative seats, the MDP held the economic planning portfolio during the first four months of the Muluzi government and was given the housing portfolio in August 1995.

The MDP leadership reportedly called for the government's resignation in July 1995 after the party lost its sole post in a cabinet reshuffling. Two months later, the MDP's president and vice president, Kampelo Kalua and Unandi Banda, were arrested on intimidation charges; however, the two were subsequently acquitted.

Kalua received only 1.43 percent of the vote in the 1999 presidential vote, while no MDP legislative candidates were successful in either the 1999 or 2004 election.

Leaders: Kampelo KALUA (President and 1994 and 1999 presidential candidate), Unandi BANDA (Vice President), Lyson MILANZI (1999 vice presidential candidate).

Other parties that contested the May 2004 legislative elections included the **People's Transformation Party** (Petra), which gained one seat in the balloting; the **Malawi Forum for Unity and Development** (MAFUNDE), formed in 2002 under the leadership of George MNESA to fight corruption and end food shortages; the **National Unity Party** (NUP); the **New Congress for Democracy** (NCD), launched in 2004 by former MCP members and led by Hetherwick NTABA, who joined the Mutharika government as minister of health after the election (it was subsequently reported that Ntaba had joined the DPP and that the NCD had been dissolved); and the **Pamodzi Freedom Party** (PFP), established in 2002 and led by Rainsford NDIWO.

Legislature

Members of the unicameral **National Assembly** normally sit for five-year terms. From 1978 through 1992 candidates had to be approved by the MCP. The first multiparty balloting was held on May 17, 1994, for an enlarged body of 177 members. The number of legislators was increased to 193 for the balloting of July 15, 1999. In legislative balloting on May 20, 2004, the Malawi Congress Party secured 60 seats; the United Democratic Front, 49; the *Mgwirizano* coalition, 25 (the Republican Party, 15; the People's Progressive Movement, 6; the Movement for Genuine Democratic Change, 3; and the People's Transformation Party, 1); the National Democratic Alliance, 8; the Alliance for Democracy, 6; the Congress for National Unity, 1; and independents, 38. The six other seats were filled in subsequent by-elections. All were won by the newly formed, propresidential Democratic Progressive Party, which as of mid-2006 was reported to control more than 70 assembly seats in the wake

of substantial party defections and the inclusion in its ranks of many former independents.

Speaker: Louis CHIMANGO.

Communications

Press

Most newspapers are privately owned and operated. There is no formal censorship, but the government's refusal to tolerate any form of criticism was reflected in a 1973 decree that journalists who printed material "damaging to the nation's reputation" were liable to life imprisonment. In 1992 the press law was amended, reducing sentences for such crimes to five years; in addition, previously stringent restrictions on foreign journalists appeared to have been relaxed. In March 1993, on the other hand, opposition newspapers launched by Aford and the UDF were reported to have been banned. However, subsequent constitutional amendments eased press restrictions, and by November 1993 there were reportedly 12 newly licensed opposition newspapers. Censorship remains a problem; two journalists were arrested after publishing a story in which they suggested that the president was afraid of ghosts and had moved out of the presidential mansion because he believed it to be haunted. On March 15, 2005, the journalists were charged with publishing false stories and "causing ridicule" to the president.

The following are published in Blantyre, unless otherwise noted: *Boma Lathu* (100,000), Department of Information monthly in Chichewa; *Moni* (39,000), monthly in English and Chichewa; *Malawi News* (30,000), opposition weekly in English and Chichewa; *The Daily Times* (22,000), opposition daily in English; *Odini* (Lilongwe, 12,000), Catholic fortnightly in English and Chichewa; *The Independent* (10,000), independent weekly; *Malawi Democrat,* Aford publication; *Michiru Sun,* independent daily; *The New Express,* independent weekly; *Nation,* progovernment daily; *Mirror,* weekly; *Chronicle,* independent weekly; and *The Dispatch,* independent daily.

News Agency

The domestic facility is the Malawi News Agency (Mana).

Broadcasting and Computing

Radio service in English and Chichewa is provided by the statutory and semicommercial Malawi Broadcasting Corporation (MBC) and the privately owned Capital Radio Company. In July 1995 the government signed an agreement with TV3 of Malaysia to establish a television service by March 1996; however, Lilongwe canceled the deal in May 1996, citing the slow pace of implementation and poor equipment quality. Subsequent efforts to begin broadcasting were slowed by financial problems, although Television Malawi formally came into existence in 1999. There were some 35,000 television receivers and 14,000 personal computers serving 30,000 Internet users in 2003.

Intergovernmental Representation

Ambassador to the U.S.
Bernardo SANDE

U.S. Ambassador to Malawi
Alan W. EASTHAM Jr.

Permanent Representative to the UN
Brown Beswick CHIMPHAMBA

IGO Memberships (Non-UN)
AfDB, AU, BADEA, Comesa, CWTH, Interpol, NAM, SADC, WCO, WTO

MALI

REPUBLIC OF MALI

République du Mali

The Country

Of predominantly desert and semidesert terrain, landlocked Mali stretches northward into the Sahara from the upper basin of the Niger and Senegal rivers. The country's lifeline is the Niger River, which flows northeastward past Bamako, Ségou, and Timbuktu in Mali and then southeastward through Niger and Nigeria to the Gulf of Guinea. Mali's overwhelmingly Muslim population falls into several distinct ethnic groups, including the Bambara and other southern peoples, who are mostly sedentary farmers, while the Peul, or Fulani, as well as the warlike Tuareg pursue a nomadic and pastoral existence on the fringes of the Sahara. Women constitute 46 percent of the work force; female involvement in politics has traditionally been minimal.

Nearly 90 percent of the economically active population is dependent on agriculture, with cotton, peanuts, and livestock being the leading sources of foreign exchange. Although the country was once dubbed the potential "breadbasket of Africa," Mali's food output in recent decades has been severely depressed by periodic droughts, locust infestations, and land mismanagement. However, a return to agricultural self-sufficiency became a top priority for the Traoré government, which in its later years tried to boost production by loosening price and marketing controls. Industrial activity is concentrated in agriprocessing, some enterprises having recently been privatized as part of an overall retreat from state dominance of the economy. Extraction of minerals such as uranium, bauxite, ferronickel, phosphates, and gold, while drawing the interest of international investors, has been hindered by inadequate transport and power facilities. Some progress toward economic reconstruction has been registered with assistance from a variety of foreign sources, although Mali remains one of the world's dozen poorest countries.

In September 1993 the International Monetary Fund (IMF) and World Bank agreed to provide Mali with a four-year aid plan, but within two months the IMF had suspended the program, blaming continued budget overruns on fraud, extrabudgetary spending, and wage increases. In March 1994 the IMF reversed itself and approved an immediate disbursement of funds to help dampen economic and social turmoil generated by devaluation of the CFA

franc two months earlier. Annual GDP growth averaged about 5.7 percent from 1995 to 2000, with inflation falling into negative figures in 1999–2000. Among other things, the IMF urged an increased pace of privatization, harmonization of investment regulations and business laws, and greater efficiency in collection of tax revenues, which could permit increased social spending. In August 1999 the IMF approved a three-year loan to assist the government in its economic reform program, and additional aid was approved in 2000 and 2001.

In 2003 Mali completed a series of economic reforms and restructuring under the IMF's Heavily Indebted Poor Countries (HIPC) initiative, and, as a result, the country was granted $417 million in debt relief. In 2004 Mali received an IMF grant of $6.3 million to support continuing economic reforms through 2007.

Record gold and agricultural production in the early 2000s helped maintain strong economic growth, which averaged 5 percent annually in 2000–2004. Inflation remained low, at less than 1 percent in 2003, but the government's deficit rose as spending on infrastructure, including roads, increased significantly. Rising fuel prices and falling cotton prices constrained growth in 2005. However, gold production continued to increase. In 2006 the World Bank approved additional debt relief for Mali and provided other credits to support agriculture as well as poverty-reduction efforts.

Government and Politics

Political Background

Mali, the former French colony of Soudan, takes its name from a medieval African kingdom whose capital was located near the present capital city of Bamako. As a part of French West Africa, Soudan took part in the general process of post–World War II decolonization and became a self-governing member state of the French Community in 1958. Full independence within the community was achieved on June 20, 1960, in association with Senegal, with which Soudan had joined in January 1959 to form a union known as the Federation of Mali. However, Senegal seceded from the federation on August 20, 1960, and on September 22 Mali proclaimed itself an independent republic and withdrew from the French Community.

Mali's government, led by President Modibo KEITA of the Soudanese Union/African Democratic Rally (*Union Soudanaise/ Rassemblement Démocratique Africain*—US/RDA), gradually developed into a leftist, one-party dictatorship with a strongly collectivist policy at home and close ties to the Soviet bloc and the People's Republic of China. In late 1968 the Keita regime was ousted in a bloodless coup d'état led by Lt. Moussa TRAORÉ and Capt. Yoro DIAKITÉ under the auspices of a Military Committee of National Liberation (*Comité Militaire de Libération Nationale*—CMLN).

Reversing the economic policies of the Keita government, the military regime pledged that civil and political rights would soon be restored. However, further centralization of the military command took place in 1972 following the trial and imprisonment of Captain Diakité and two associates for allegedly plotting another coup. Subsequent coup attempts were reported in 1976 and 1978, the latter involving a reputed pro-Soviet faction of the CMLN that opposed a projected return to civilian rule under a constitution approved in 1974.

After a five-year period of transitional rule by the CMLN, civilian government was formally restored on June 19, 1979, when General Traoré was elected, unopposed, to a five-year term as president and prime minister. Earlier, in March, the Malian People's Democratic Union (*Union Démocratique du Peuple Malien*—UDPM) had been formally constituted as the country's sole political party. In 1982 the presidential term was increased to six years, resulting in the reelection of Traoré coincident with pro forma legislative balloting on June 9, 1985. Three days earlier the president had carried out a cabinet reshuffle that included the designation of Dr. Mamadou DEMBELE as prime minister. The latter office was abolished in the course of a further cabinet shakeup, on June 6, 1988, that preceded assembly renewal on June 26.

Widespread opposition to harsh conditions under the Traoré regime erupted into rioting in

Political Status: Independent republic
proclaimed September 22, 1960; military
regime established November 19, 1968;
civilian rule reestablished under constitution
approved in 1974 and promulgated June 19,
1979; 1974 constitution suspended on March
26, 1991, and replaced by interim Fundamental
Act on March 31; multiparty constitution
drafted by National Conference in July–August
1991, approved by popular referendum on
January 12, and formally proclaimed on
February 14, 1992.

Area: 478,764 sq. mi. (1,240,000 sq. km.).

Population: 9,790,492 (1998C); 13,810,000
(2005E).

Major Urban Center (2005E): BAMAKO
(1,995,000).

Official Language: French. Bambara is spoken
by the majority of the population.

Monetary Unit: CFA Franc (market rate July 1,
2006: 513.01 francs = $1US). (The CFA franc,
previously pegged to the French franc, is now
permanently pegged to the euro at 655.957
CFA francs = 1 euro.)

President: Amadou Toumani TOURÉ
(nonparty); popularly elected in second-round
balloting on May 12, 2002, and inaugurated for
a five-year term on June 8 to succeed Alpha
Oumar KONARÉ (Alliance for Democracy in
Mali).

Prime Minister: Ousmane Issoufi MAIGA
(nonparty); appointed by the president on April
29, 2004, to succeed Mohamed Ag AMANI
(nonparty), who had announced his resignation
on April 28.

Bamako and other towns during January 1991
and continued into February and March amid
mounting demands for the introduction of a multiparty system. On March 26 Traoré was ousted
by an army group under the leadership of Lt.
Col. Amadou Toumani TOURÉ, who formed a 17-
member Council of National Reconciliation (*Conseil de la Réconciliation Nationale*—CRN). On
March 30 the CRN joined with anti-Traoré political
leaders in establishing a Transitional Committee

for the Salvation of the People (*Comité de Transition pour le Salut du Peuple*—CTSP), comprised
of 10 military and 15 civilian members. On April 2
the CTSP announced the appointment of Soumana
SACKO, a highly respected senior official of the
UN Development Program, as prime minister. The
cabinet that was announced two days later consisted
largely of "unknown" technocrats, with military officers being awarded a number of key portfolios.

On April 5, 1991, the CTSP authorized the formation of political parties and declared its intention to rule for a nine-month period ending with
a constitutional referendum and multiparty elections. Traoré supporters were subsequently purged
from the government and military, and, following
a failed attempt to liberate the imprisoned former
president in June, a coup attempt by the (then) territorial administration minister, Maj. Lamine DIA-
BIRA, failed in mid-July.

At a National Conference on July 29–August
14, 1991, charged by the CTSP with the founding of a "third republic" based on "legality and
freedom," 1,000 delegates from 42 parties and 100
associations drafted a new constitution, which the
government pledged to put to a referendum on December 1 in anticipation of multiparty elections in
early 1992. However, in November the government
extended the transition period to March 26, 1992,
citing difficulties in establishing an electoral system and its inability to guarantee safe polling sites
for voters in the north, where Tuareg insurgents had
long been active.

On January 12, 1992, the new basic law was
approved by 98.35 percent of referendum participants. One week later the Alliance for Democracy in Mali (*Alliance pour la Démocratie au
Mali*—Adema) won a majority of seats in municipal balloting. Both polls, as well as legislative balloting in February–March, were marred
by low voter turnout, coupled with allegations
of electoral fraud and inappropriate CTSP support for Adema. In addition, a number of parties
protested a reported CTSP decision to assign Tuareg groups uncontested legislative seats as an outgrowth of a National Peace Pact concluded with the
rebels on March 25. Nonetheless, after a one-month

postponement, Adema leader Alpha Oumar KONARÉ led eight competitors in first-round presidential balloting on April 12 and went on to defeat Tréoulé Mamadou KONATÉ by a 40 percent margin two weeks later. On June 8 Younoussi TOURÉ, a former Central Bank president, was named to succeed Sacko as prime minister.

On May 18, 1993, the Supreme Court upheld death sentences that had been passed on former president Traoré and three associates for causing the "premeditated murder" of 106 persons during prodemocracy riots in the capital in March 1991. Meanwhile, an escalation of student riots, which had commenced seven months earlier, yielded arson attacks on a number of public installations, including the National Assembly building. On April 9, in response to the unrest, President Konaré announced the resignation of the Touré government and the appointment of its defense minister, Abdoulaye Sekou SOW, to head a new administration.

On November 7, 1993, citing austerity concerns, Prime Minister Sow downsized his fledgling cabinet; however, Adema membership in the reshuffled, technocratic government grew as its members replaced three nonparty ministers. On December 9 the government confirmed reports that an imprisoned former Traoré aide, Lt. Col. Oumar DIALLO, and five others had been charged with plotting to "topple democratic institutions" and "dispose" of anyone opposed to Diallo's release.

On February 2, 1994, Sow became the second consecutive prime minister to resign amid student protests over government spending decisions. Collaterally, Sow echoed his predecessor's complaint that Adema members had worked to undermine his premiership. Two days later President Konaré named an Adema member, Ibrahim Boubacar KEITA, as the new prime minister. On February 6 the cabinet was thrown into disarray when ministers from the National Congress for Democratic Initiative (*Congrés National d'Initiative Démocratique*—CNID) and the Rally for Democracy and Progress (*Rassemblement pour la Démocratie et le Progrès*—RDP) resigned, with CNID leader Mountaga TALL accusing the administration of having "marginalized"

non-Adema ministers. Subsequently, the government named by Keita on February 7 included only 16 members, 11 from Adema and 5 from minor parties.

The military conflict between the government and Tuaregs unofficially ended in June 1995 when the last active rebel group, the Arab Islamic Front of the Azawad, "unilaterally" halted its guerrilla campaign and announced its interest in peace negotiations. In November the government announced that approximately 20,000 Tuareg refugees had returned from exile in Mauritania. By February 1996 over 3,000 former rebels had reportedly been integrated into the armed forces.

On March 4, 1997, President Konaré dissolved the assembly in anticipation of assembly elections in April. The first of two rounds of balloting was held on April 13; however, the polling was marred by reported gross irregularities, including a shortage of balloting papers. Consequently, on April 25 the Constitutional Court annulled the first-round results and indefinitely postponed the second round. At the same time, the court ordered that preparations for presidential polling continue, thus ignoring opposition threats to boycott such balloting if it preceded the assembly balloting.

In presidential elections on May 11, 1997, Konaré garnered 95.9 percent of the vote, overwhelming his sole opponent, Mamadou Maribatourou DIABY of the small Unity, Development, and Progress Party (*Parti pour l'Unité, le Développement, et le Progrès*—PUDP). (Eight other opposition candidates boycotted the polling, which was marked by a low voter turnout and antigovernment demonstrations.) Subsequently, in two rounds of legislative balloting on July 20 and August 3, Adema candidates also easily dominated an electoral field depleted by an opposition boycott. On September 13 Konaré reappointed Prime Minister Keita, who rejected opposition calls for a "unity" government and named a cabinet on September 16 that was dominated by propresidential parties and moderate opposition groups.

President Konaré made a number of conciliatory gestures to his opponents in the second half of 1997, including releasing opposition members arrested during the violent unrest that surrounded the May–August polling and reducing the death sentences of former President Traoré and his associates to life imprisonment. The president's pledge to convene an all-inclusive national forum gained momentum in mid-April 1998, when a broad range of opposition groups responded positively to a conciliatory proposal brokered by former U.S. president Jimmy Carter. However, on April 20 hard-line opposition groups in the Collective of Opposition Political Parties (*Coordination des Partis Politiques de l'Opposition*—COPPO) refused to attend a government-sponsored summit, asserting that the government representatives lacked legitimacy and vowing to boycott the upcoming local elections and launch a civil disobedience campaign.

In balloting on June 21, 1998, Adema candidates captured an overwhelming number of mayoral and local council posts. In August the government announced that further local polling, then tentatively scheduled for November, would be postponed in the hopes of avoiding an opposition boycott. The Konaré administration reportedly remained intent on convincing opposition hard-liners to participate in future polling, since their previous boycotts had undermined the credibility of Mali's democratization and decentralization efforts. In January 1999 the government convened an internationally monitored national forum with the stated aim of allowing Malian political leaders input into the electoral process. However, only four of the parties aligned with the so-called radical opposition attended, and COPPO again urged its supporters not to vote in the May 2 and June 5, 1999, balloting, in which Adema secured about 60 percent of the seats on local councils.

Prime Minister Keita resigned on February 14, 2000, and was succeeded the following day by Mandé SIDIBE, one of President Konaré's economic advisors. The cabinet announced on February 21 included 15 new ministers.

Prime Minister Sidibe resigned on March 18, 2002, to contest the upcoming presidential election. He was succeeded by former president Modibo Keita. In the first round of presidential balloting on April 28, former military leader Amadou Toumani Touré, backed by a number of parties, finished first among over 20 candidates. He was elected president on May 12 by securing about 64 percent of the vote in a runoff against Soumaïla CISSÉ of Adema. Touré appointed Mohamed Ag AMANI (nonparty) as the new prime minister on June 9; on June 15 a new "national unity" cabinet was named that included members of a number of parties as well as independents.

In controversial assembly balloting on July 14 and 28, 2002, Hope 2002 (an alliance of parties upset over the conduct of the first round of the presidential poll) won 66 seats, followed by the Alliance for the Republic and Democracy (a coalition that included Adema and others) with 51 seats and Alternation and Change (a coalition of parties that had supported Touré in the presidential balloting) with 10.

In by-elections on October 20, 2002, Adema won all eight seats being contested and became the largest single party in the assembly with 53 seats. Hope 2002, with 66 seats, combined with 19 presidential-supportive deputies, including independents, to create a stable presidential majority within the legislature.

Local elections on May 30, 2003, were relatively free of the problems that had surrounded the 2002 presidential and assembly elections. Turnout was high (prompted by the government's campaign to encourage voting), and more than 20 parties won seats. Hope 2002 reportedly secured a majority of the mayoral posts.

Prime Minister Ag Amani resigned on April 28, 2004, and was replaced by former transport minister Ousmane Issoufi MAIGA (nonparty). Maiga formed a new cabinet on May 2.

Constitution and Government

The constitution adopted at independence was abrogated by the military in November 1968. A new constitution was approved by referendum on June 2, 1974, but did not enter into force until June 19, 1979. The constitution drafted by the National Conference of July 29–August 14, 1991, and approved by referendum on January 12, 1992, replaced the interim *Acte Fondamental* that the CTSP had promulgated in April 1991 following abrogation of the 1974 document. The current basic law includes an extensive bill of individual rights, a charter for political parties, guarantees of trade union and press freedoms, and separation of executive, legislative, and judicial powers. A directly elected president, who may serve no more than two five-year terms, appoints a prime minister and other cabinet members, who are, however, responsible to a popularly elected unicameral National Assembly. The judicial system is headed by a Supreme Court, which is divided into judicial, administrative, and fiscal sections. There is also a nine-member Constitutional Court, while a High Court of Justice is empowered to hear cases of treason.

Mali is administratively divided into eight regions, the eighth being created in May 1991 by the halving of a northern region as a concession to Tuareg separatists. The regions, headed by appointed governors, are subdivided into 46 districts (*cercles*) and 282 counties (*arrondissements*), also administered by appointed officials. Most municipalities have elected councils, which have been given increased authority in connection with the government's recent decentralization program.

Foreign Relations

Reflecting a commitment to "dynamic nonalignment," Mali improved its relations with France, Britain, the United States, and other Western nations under General Traoré. It also cultivated links to China and the former Soviet Union.

For two decades Mali was locked in a dispute with Burkina Faso (formerly Upper Volta) over ownership of the 100-mile long, 12-mile wide Agacher strip between the two countries. The controversy, which triggered a number of military encounters (including a four-day battle in December 1985), was finally settled by a ruling in late 1986 from the International Court of Justice that divided the disputed territory into roughly equal parts, with the border being defined in accordance with traditional patterns of nomadic passage. Similar clashes involving Mauritania were followed by a border demarcation agreement in May 1988.

Relations with Libya cooled perceptibly as a result of the latter's involvement in the Chadian civil war. In early 1981 a number of Libyan embassy personnel in Bamako were expelled in response to an effort to convert the mission into a "people's bureau"; relations were further exacerbated by the expulsion of some 2,500 Malian workers from Libya in 1985 as part of a drive by the Qadhafi regime to reduce its dependence on foreign labor. Subsequently, Mali charged Libya with supporting Tuareg insurgents in northern Mali.

In January 1991 the Algerian government mediated a truce between the Malian government and moderate Tuareg party leaders, which was hailed as paving the way toward more definitive resolution of the conflict 14 months later. In September 1992 President Konaré met with Burkinabé President Blaise Compaoré in Ouagadougou to discuss efforts to reactivate bilateral cooperation and resolve the status of Tuareg refugees in northern Burkina Faso. In October Mali announced that France had pledged to finance the integration of Tuareg forces into the Malian army and to equip "mixed" Tuareg-regular army patrols (provided for in the National Pact) to contain unassimilated rebel groups. Subsequently, international diplomatic efforts were credited with generating tripartite agreements among Algeria, Mali, and Niger, which resulted in the repatriation of thousands of Tuaregs from Algeria in August 1993 and the creation in January 1994 of accommodation centers in Algeria for exiles fleeing the adjacent two countries' drought and civil unrest. Negotiations between Mali and Algeria in February 1995 yielded an accord on border security issues.

Relations with France were strained in the late 1990s following France's expulsions of thousands of Malian illegal immigrants. In 1998, the two countries created a joint commission to repatriate Malians living illegally in France, and the French government agreed to fund programs to help the returning Malians reintegrate into society.

Mali, Mauritania, and Senegal agreed in 1999 to conduct joint patrols to combat "banditry" in border areas, which had also experienced sporadic conflict among ethnic groups. Meanwhile, reports surfaced of tension in the north between Tuaregs and the national army. Relations with Côte d'Ivoire were strained following a coup attempt in that country in January 2001, Ivorian authorities reportedly unofficially implying that Mali and Burkina Faso had backed the overthrow effort.

In July 2003 reports emerged that a group of European tourists who had been taken hostage by Islamic militants in Algeria were being held in a remote region of Mali. They were released on August 8 following negotiations led by former Tuareg rebels. Mali subsequently agreed to increase border security with Algeria and to increase antiterrorism cooperation with Algeria, Chad, and Niger.

The growing presence of foreign Islamic extremists, mainly from Pakistan and Afghanistan, prompted the government in 2004 to seek international counterterrorism aid. U.S. military advisors subsequently arrived in Mali to initiate an antiterrorism training program for the Malian armed forces. This followed several U.S.-sponsored military training exercises in Mali and several years of U.S. security assistance in the form of equipment and financial aid. The government also gave permission for U.S. special operations units to undertake antiterrorism missions in the north of the country, where Algerian militants had reportedly established a presence. The United States subsequently announced it would use its Malian base as a headquarters for regional antiterrorism efforts.

Mali signed a broad economic agreement with China in early 2006. In return for increased exports of cotton from Mali to China, China agreed to expand investment in Mali's agriculture, tourism, and telecommunications sectors.

Current Issues

In January 1999 former president Traoré again faced a death sentence, this time following conviction on embezzlement charges. Traoré's wife, Mariam CISSOKO, was also similarly sentenced. However, in September President Konaré commuted the sentences to life imprisonment with hard labor. Subsequently, in January 2000, Konaré granted a full pardon to former army chief of staff Col. Ousman COULIBALY, who was facing a death sentence for his role in the suppression of the demonstrations in 1991. The resignation of Prime Minister Keita in February 2000 was seen in some quarters as designed to permit him to concentrate on what was expected to be a campaign to succeed Konaré in the 2002 presidential balloting (the president having previously announced he would not attempt to circumvent the two-term limit despite being encouraged in that regard by his supporters). However, analysts also pointed out that Keita had faced increasing criticism over economic policy, the area of expertise for new Prime Minister Sidibe. It was also reported that former president Amadou Touré was gearing up for a presidential run, while at midyear COPPO leaders announced plans to present a coalition opposition candidate in the campaign. Indeed, Touré resigned from his army post in September 2001 as required by law to be able to run for the presidency in 2002.

Some 40 parties signed a "pact of good conduct" in January 2001 in preparation for the 2002 presidential and legislative balloting, domestic and international consensus having been reached that a repeat of the 1997 electoral dysfunction would seriously tarnish the image of one of the continent's most prominent democratic experiments. However, late in the year President Konaré suspended plans for a referendum on new electoral laws approved by the assembly in mid-2000 based on recommendations from the 1999 national forum. Konaré argued that public support for the referendum was minimal and that certain provisions of the new legislation could be constitutionally challenged. Among other things, the proposed changes called for adoption of proportional balloting for some assembly seats, a longtime objective of the opposition.

In February 2002 the assembly adopted new electoral legislation that did not require a referendum, thereby paving the way for first-round presidential balloting in late April and legislative elections in July. Most parties agreed to participate in the polls, although observers noted that the successful presidential candidate and legislative parties would face daunting challenges, including economic malaise resulting from depressed export prices and ongoing inadequacies in the health and education sectors. Among other things, such problems had contributed to the increased societal influence of "hard-line" Islamic activists, who accused the government and Malian "elites" of having siphoned off most Western aid for their personal benefit.

Following his victory in 2002, one of President Touré's first acts was to pardon former president Traoré in an attempt to promote national unity and reconciliation. However, sectional violence continued in the east, and violent crime also subsequently increased dramatically.

In September 2004 renewed fighting between Islamic groups in eastern Mali left 13 people dead. The fighting followed another incident of violence in western Mali in which 10 people were killed. Analysts suggested that a rise in Islamic "extremism" was creating a serious challenge to government efforts to maintain stability.

Attention in 2005–2006 turned to preparations for the presidential and assembly elections scheduled for 2007. Among other things, opposition parties hoped to capitalize on the apparent public perception that economic and political reforms were progressing more slowly than anticipated. Meanwhile, the "Tuareg issue" heated up again, as Tuareg fighters launched attacks on several cities and military bases in the north in May 2006. In July an accord was announced under which the rebels agreed to stop their militancy in return for intensified government investment in the region.

Political Parties

The only authorized party prior to the March 1991 coup was the **Malian People's Democratic Union** (*Union Démocratique du Peuple Malien*—UDPM), which had been launched by General Traoré in 1979. The UDPM was dissolved in the wake of Traoré's ouster.

The public demonstrations that preceded the 1991 coup were orchestrated by a number of groups (including Adema), which were linked by a Coordi-

nation Committee of Democratic Associations and Organizations, which joined the CRN in forming the CTSP on March 30, after which both it and the CRN were dissolved. On April 5 the CTSP authorized the formation of political parties, and by late 1991 approximately 50 formations, many with links to pre-1968 political personalities or groups, had applied for legal status. However, only 27 parties presented legislative candidates in 1992.

On May 11, 1992, representatives of 13 parties, including the US/RDA–Tréoule Konaté Tendency, Union for Democracy and Development (*Union pour la Démocratie et le Développement*—UDD), Soudanese Progress Party (*Parti Soudanais du Progrés*—PSP), RDP, and Union of Democratic Forces for Progress (*Union des Forces Démocratiques pour le Progrés*—UFDP), announced the formation of a **Front to Safeguard Democracy** (*Front Sauvegarde de la Démocratie*—FSD) under the reported leadership of Konaté and the RDP's Almamy SYLLA to conduct "a resolute and determined, but still democratic and constructive, opposition" to Adema. In August 1995 a number of senior leaders left the group following a dispute with Konaté. In October 1996 Adema initiated the formation of a progovernment alliance, the **National Convention for Democracy and Progress** (*Convention Nationale pour la Démocratie et le Progrés*—CNDP), which also included the Democratic and Social Convention (*Convention Démocratique Sociale*—CDS), the Party for National Renaissance (*Parti pour la Renaissance Nationale*—Parena), the **Malian Rally for Labor** (*Rassemblement Malien pour le Travail*—RAMAT), and others. The formation of another opposition alliance, the **Rally for Patriotic Forces** (*Rassemblement pour les Forces Patriotiques*—RFP), was reported by *Africa Confidential* in November. In July 1997 the following opposition parties boycotted legislative balloting after the president refused to reschedule presidential elections (held on May 11) until after assembly polling: the CNID, Popular Movement for Development (*Mouvement Populaire pour le Développement*—MPD), RDP, Rally for Democracy and Labor (*Rassemblement pour la*

Démocratie et le Travail—RDT), UFDP, and the US/RDA.

In 1998 observers reported a widening of the differences between the aforementioned parties (the so-called radical or hard-line opposition) and those opposition groups (moderates) pursuing a dialogue with the Konaré administration. Loosely coalesced under the banner of the **Collective of Opposition Political Parties** (*Coordination des Partis Politiques de l'Opposition*—COPPO), the former rejected the administration's plans for an all-inclusive national forum and demanded both a reform of the electoral system and direct talks with the president. On April 16 a number of opposition parties, including COPPO members, tentatively agreed to a proposal brokered by former U.S. president Jimmy Carter that called on the Konaré government to reformulate the electoral commission, reschedule municipal elections to June, and revise the electoral list in exchange for the opposition's agreement to recognize the results of the 1997 elections. However, on April 20 the radical groups refused to attend a government-sponsored meeting on the accord, and thereafter they boycotted the June polling. In January 1999 representatives from the Soudanese Progress Party (PSP) and three other COPPO-affiliated groups attended the national forum in defiance of the Collective's leadership. Subsequently, COPPO suspended the PSP, whose leader, Oumar Hammadoun DICKO, then announced his party's plans to participate in midyear polling.

Meanwhile, in late January 1999 three centrist groups, the COPP, PDP, and UDD, formed a **Convention for the Republic and Democracy** (*Convention pour la République et la Démocratie*—CRD), under the leadership of Mamadou GAKOU. In 2000 and 2001 a significant thaw was noted between the government and most opposition parties. As of June 2000 almost all of the parties that had boycotted the 1997 polling had decided to contest the presidential and legislative elections scheduled for 2002. Prior to the 2002 presidential and legislative elections, three main electoral coalitions emerged—the ACC, ARD, and Hope 2002 (below).

Legislative Parties

Alliance for Alternation and Change (*Alliance pour L'Alternance et le Changement*—ACC). Formed prior to the 2002 legislative elections with the goal of providing President Touré with a political base in the assembly, the ACC consisted of some 28 parties, including those listed below.

Leader: Ibrahim Boubacar BAH (President).

Party for National Renaissance (*Parti pour la Renaissance Nationale*—Parena). Active since March 1995, Parena was officially launched on September 18 after its founders, CNID dissidents Capt. Yoro Diakité and Tiéblé Dramé, lost their five-month legal battle for control of that party. A number of Parena leaders were former or current Konaré government ministers, a status reflected in the signing of the Parena-Adema cooperation pact in February 1996. Parena participated in the cabinet announced in 1997 but declined to accept any posts in the February 2000 government. Meanwhile, Diakité was reported to have formed a new party (see BARA, below).

In 2001 Parena distanced itself from Adema, and Dramé became the party's presidential candidate in 2002, finishing fourth in the first round of balloting with 3.99 percent of the vote. Parena reportedly won one of the ACC seats in the 2002 legislative poll.

Leaders: Tiéblé DRAMÉ (President), Amidou DIABATÉ (Secretary General).

Soudanese Union/African Democratic Rally (*Union Soudanaise/Rassemblement Démocratique Africain*—US/RDA). The Malian wing of the RDA was formed in the aftermath of an RDA convention in Bamako in 1946. Supported by a rural constituency, the group came to power with the formation of Modibo Keita's postindependence government in 1960 but went underground following his ouster in 1968.

At a special congress in January 1992, the US/RDA split over the selection of a presidential candidate. Tréoulé Mamadou KONATÉ, the son of an RDA founder and an advocate of purging "Stalinism" from the party, was selected initially, but the party leadership ultimately repudiated the action, nominating instead former UN official Baba Hakib HAIDARA. Subsequently, both stood as candidates, with Konaté outpolling his rival in the first round but securing only 30 percent of the second-round vote in a contest with Alpha Oumar Konaré. In October 1995 Konaté was killed in a car crash, and in January 1996 the party ousted Secretary General Mamadou Bachir Gologo in favor of Mamadou Bamou TOURÉ.

In mid-May 1998, 29 senior US/RDA members led by political secretary Daba DIAWARA issued a statement allying themselves with party leader Seydou Badian KOUATÉ, who, in defiance of the US/RDA's official stance, had declared that the group should recognize the government and participate in the local elections scheduled for June. Subsequently, Touré attempted to suspend the 29 members, who, in turn, rejected the legitimacy of his leadership, asserting that his earlier unwillingness to implement reconciliation initiatives approved by the party's governing organs had undermined his authority. The moderate tendency of the US/RDA participated in the 1999 local elections.

The US/RDA supported former Amadou Touré's presidential campaign in 2002. It reportedly won three seats as part of the ACC in the 2002 legislative balloting. In August 2003, Mamadou Bamou Touré resigned as secretary general of the party.

Leader: Mamadou Bachir GOLOGO (President).

Union of Democratic Forces for Progress (*Union des Forces Démocratiques pour le Progrés*—UFDP). The UFDP was launched in 1991 under the leadership of Demqo DIALLO, a prominent human rights advocate and champion of efforts to oust Moussa Traoré. A pro-Konaré grouping, the UFDP joined the CNDP in 1997 and criticized antigovernment protesters. Diallo

died in June 2001, and a July national congress of the party (now also sometimes referred to as the Union of Forces of Progress) elected Shaka Diarra as the new chair.

Leaders: Shaka DIARRA (Chair), Youssouf TRAORE (Secretary General).

Other minor parties in the ACC include: the **Democratic Bloc for African Integration** (*Bloc Démocratique pour l'Intégration Africaine*—BDIA), a liberal party formed in 1993 under the leadership of Youssouf TRAORÉ that won three seats in the 2002 assembly elections; the **Movement for African Independence, Renewal, and Integration** (*Mouvement pour l'Indépendence, la Renaissance, et l'Intégration Africaine*—MIRIA), established by dissident members of Adema, including Mohamed Lamine TRAORÉ; the **Malian Rally for Labor** (*Rassemblement Malien pour le Travail*—RAMAT), which won two seats in the 2002 legislative elections under the leadership of Abdoulaye MAKO; and the **Party for Democracy and Renewal** (*Parti pour la Démocratie et le Renouveau*—PDR), which won one seat in the 2002 assembly balloting under the leadership of Adama KONE.

Alliance for the Republic and Democracy (*Alliance pour la République et la Démocratie*—ARD). The ARD was formed by several groups, including those below, in advance of the 2002 elections. Adema and the UDD each presented their own candidates in the first round of the presidential poll but then cooperated in the presidential runoff and the legislative balloting.

Leader: Moussa Balla COULIBALY.

Alliance for Democracy in Mali/Pan African Party for Liberty, Solidarity, and Justice (*Alliance pour la Démocratie au Mali/ Parti Pan-Africain pour la Solidarité et la Justice*—Adema/PASJ). A principal organizer of anti-Traoré demonstrations and subsequently among those groups represented in the CTSP, Adema registered for legal status in April 1991. Adema candidates won substantial majorities in all three 1992 elections, securing 214 municipal council seats and 76 National Assembly seats. Adema also captured the presidency on April 26 with a 70 percent second-round vote share.

At the party's first congress on July 8–14, 1993, dissident members released a manifesto calling for the "appointment to positions of responsibility [within the party] . . . of competent men and women of integrity" and the "destruction of the old state apparatus." Moreover, former prime ministers Touré and Sow both cited subversive activities by "radical" elements within Adema as among their reasons for resigning from the party. Observers attributed the intraparty friction to a conflict between members identifying with the former prime ministers and favoring integration of non-Adema political groups into the government and a smaller faction advocating Adema's unilateral rule.

At a party congress on September 25–27, 1994, founding member and Chair Mohamed Lamine Traoré lost his post in an action spearheaded by Prime Minister Ibrahim Boubacar Keita, who had hinted at dramatic party changes at his investiture. Subsequently, Traoré, Secretary General Mohamedoun DICKO, and a number of other senior members resigned from the party; two months later the dissidents launched MIRIA (above).

In February 1996 Adema signed a cooperation agreement with Parena, a newly founded group led by former Konaré ministers and dissidents from the CNID, which called for the establishment of a committee to implement a joint government program and electoral alliance pact.

At an Adema congress on December 5–6, 1997, the agenda was dominated by debate on how to reintegrate disenfranchised opposition groups into the political process. In 1998 relations between Adema and the majority of its hard-line opponents grew more distant. On the other hand, at a much heralded summit in May, Adema and representatives of the MPR (below) discussed adopting cooperative tactics to avert further violence.

In February 1999 Adema held its fifth national congress amid reports that it was riven by intraparty squabbling. Although Konaré reportedly emerged from the congress heralding the health of his party, continued factionalization was subsequently reported between Keita's supporters and his critics, led by Secretary General Ali Nouhoun DIALLO. Despite such opposition, Keita was reelected as party chair in October. He resigned from all his party duties, however, in October 2000 in reaction to the advances registered by the "reformist" wing. Keita then launched his own formation, the RPM (below). Observers noted that Keita's exit did not calm the tensions in the party, especially with regard to the 2002 presidential nomination. In March 2002, in a bitterly contested party election, Adema chose Soumaïla Cissé over former prime minister Mandé Sidibe to be the party's presidential candidate. However, Cissé was defeated in the second round of the presidential poll. Subsequently, Adema's parliamentary majority was reduced from 128 seats to 53 in legislative balloting, although the party remained the largest single group in the assembly.

The electoral decline led to infighting within the party, and Cissé led a group of dissident Adema members in the formation of a new rival party, the URD (below).

In 2006 former defense minister Soumaylou Boubèye MAIGA announced he intended to seek Adema's nomination for the 2007 presidential election.

Leaders: Alpha Oumar KONARÉ (Former President of the Republic), Dioncounda TRAORÉ (Party President), Marimata DIARRA, Mandé SIDIBE (Former Prime Minister).

Union for Democracy and Development (*Union pour la Démocratie et le Développement*—UDD). Running on a platform calling for "security, good citizenship, and clean streets," the UDD, whose founder, Moussa Balla Coulibaly, was an official in the Traoré government, won 62 seats in the 1992 municipal elections.

In 1999 it was reported that the Socialist Party for Progress and Development had merged into the UDD. In late 2001 Coulibaly was nominated as the UDD's presidential candidate in the 2002 polling. Coulibaly was eliminated in the first round, and the UDD supported Soumaïla Cissé of Adema in the second round.

Leader: Moussa Balla COULIBALY (Chair and 2002 presidential candidate).

Hope 2002 (*Espoir 2002*). Hope 2002 was formed by some 15 parties, including those below, following the first round of the 2002 presidential balloting, which Hope 2002 described as "rigged" in favor of Adema. Hope 2002 supported Amadou Touré in the second round. In the legislative elections, Hope 2002 gained 66 seats and became the largest single group within the assembly.

Leader: Mountaga TALL (Spokesperson).

National Congress for Democratic Initiative (*Congrés National d'Initiative Démocratique*—CNID). Launched in 1990 as the National Committee for Democratic Initiative (*Comité National d'Initiative Démocratique*), the CNID was included in the April 1991 formation of the CTSP in recognition of its role in the overthrow of the Traoré regime. In 1992 the party, supported by a predominantly youthful constituency, secured 96 municipal and 9 National Assembly seats. On April 12 Mountaga Tall, the party's 35-year-old presidential candidate, finished third in the first presidential round, with 11.41 percent of the vote.

On March 26, 1995, on the eve of the party's first conference, a group of dissidents reacted to the expulsion of ten governing committee members by holding a rival conference of the "true" CNID (see Parena, above).

In 1998 the CNID emerged as one of the most prominent of the radical opposition groups, organizing boycotts of the June polling and allegedly attempting to interfere with polling. The group's stance toward the government reportedly softened in 2000 and 2001, and the CNID announced that it would participate in presidential and legislative polling in 2002.

Tall finished fifth as the CNID's candidate in the first round of presidential balloting in 2002 with 3.75 percent of the vote. The CNID subsequently joined Hope 2002 for the legislative poll, reportedly securing 13 of Hope 2002's seats.

Leader: Mountaga TALL (Chair).

Rally for Mali (*Rassemblement pour le Mali*—RPM). Launched initially in February 2001 as "Alternative 2000," the RPM was a breakaway faction from Adema supportive of former prime minister Ibrahim Kéita, who had left Adema in October 2000. Kéita placed third in the first round with 21.03 percent of the vote. The RPM gained 46 seats in the 2002 legislative balloting as part of Hope 2002. In September Keita was elected speaker of the assembly. In 2006 Keita announced plans to run for president again in 2007.

Leaders: Ibrahim Boubacar KEITA (2002 presidential candidate and Speaker of the Assembly), Bocary TRETA (Secretary General).

Patriotic Movement for Renewal (*Mouvement Patriotique pour le Renouveau*—MPR). The MPR, which describes itself as a descendant of the UDPM, was legalized in January 1995. Because of its ties to former President Traoré, the party was reportedly widely denigrated until 1997, when it assumed a prominent role in the opposition camp. In May 1998 at a highly publicized meeting with Adema, MPR representatives reportedly agreed to cooperate in efforts to control political violence. Collaterally, the MPR pressed the government to expedite the trials of the former president and his associates. Subsequently, following the splintering of the US/RDA in mid-1998, one observer described the MPR as the most "stable" of the moderate opposition groups. Nevertheless, in January 1999 MPR activists clashed with security forces when the former attempted to march from their own meeting to the site of the national forum.

The MPR was described by *Africa Confidential* in 1999 as being "openly aligned" with the imprisoned Traoré but committed to the pursuit of "national reconciliation." Indeed, in 2000 the group decided to participate in presidential and legislative elections in 2002, nominating Choguel MAIGA for president. Maiga received 2.71 percent of the vote, and the MPR joined Hope 2002 for the subsequent legislative balloting.

Leader: Choguel MAIGA (President and 2002 presidential candidate).

Rally for Democracy and Progress (*Rassemblement pour la Démocratie et le Progrès*—RDP). The RDP was one of the first groups reported to have formed in April 1991. It won 64 seats in the February 1992 municipal balloting. The RDP's Almamy Sylla gained less than 1 percent of the vote in the first round of presidential balloting in 2002.

Leaders: Almamy SYLLA, Abdul Wahab BERTHE.

Other minor parties in Hope 2002 include **the Party for Independence, Democracy, and Solidarity** (*Parti pour l'Indépendance, la Démocratie, et la Solidarité*—PIDS), formed by dissenters from the US/RDA in September 2001 and led by Daba DIAWARA; and the **Rally for Democracy and Labor** (*Rassemblement pour la Démocratie et le Travail*—RDT), formed in 1991 and led by Amadou Ali NIANGADOU.

African Solidarity for Democracy and Independence (*Solidarité Africaine pour la Démocratie et l'Indépendance*—SADI). Established in 2002 prior to the presidential elections, the SADI presented Oumar MARIKO as its presidential candidate. He received less than 1 percent of the vote in the first-round balloting. In the subsequent legislative elections, the SADI won six seats.

Leader: Cheick Oumar SISSOKO.

Union for the Republic and Democracy (*Union pour la République et la Démocratie*—URD). Launched in 2003 by former members of Adema who supported former presidential candidate Soumaïla Cissé, the URD is a centrist party that supports secularism and economic reforms.

Leaders: Soumaïla CISSÉ (former presidential candidate), Younoussi TOURÉ (Interim Party President).

Other Groups

Democratic and Social Convention (*Convention Démocratique Sociale*—CDS). The self-styled "centrist" CDS was launched by Mamadou Bakary Sangaré Kabakoro in 1996. Unlike its moderate opposition party peers, the CDS chose not to participate in the government named in September 1997, although it participated in the 1999 local elections. Sangaré received 2.21 percent of the vote in the first round of presidential balloting in 2002.

Leader: Mamadou Bakary SANGARÉ.

Party for Democracy and Progress (*Parti pour la Démocratie et le Progrès*—PDP). On February 8, 1994, the PDP leadership agreed to abandon its cabinet posting, reversing an earlier decision to ignore CNID and RDP calls for an opposition boycott. However, Boubacar Karamoko COULIBALY, the youth and sports minister, refused to resign, saying he would remain as an independent. In April 1994 dissidents led by Karim TRAORÉ broke from the PDP to form the **Malian Alliance for Democracy and Progress-Dambe** (*Alliance Malienne pour la Démocratie et le Progrès-Dambe*—AMDP-Dambe).

Leader: Mady KONATÉ.

Block of Alternatives for African Renewal (*Bloc des Alternatives pour le Renouveau Africain*—BARA). Formed in 1999 under the direction of Capt. Yoro Diakité, a former leader of Parena, the BARA pledged to pursue "unity" and "African integration." In 2001 BARA was reportedly working together with the UDD and the CND to support the presidential bid of UDD chair Moussa Balla Coulibaly. In 2005 BARA rejected proposed cooperation with the Touré administration.

Leaders: Capt. Yoro DIAKITÉ (Chair), Inza COULIBALY (Secretary General).

Cabinet

As of June 1, 2006

Prime Minister	Ousmane Issoufi Maiga

Ministers

African Integration and Malians Abroad	Oumar Hamadoun Dicko
Agriculture	Seydou Traoré
Armed Forces and Veterans	Mamadou Clapie Cissouma
Communications and Information Technology	Gaoussou Drabo
Culture	Sheik Oumar Sissoko
Economy and Finance	Abou-Bacar Traoré
Education	Mamadou Lamine Traoré
Employment and Professional Training	Diallo M'Bodjisene
Environment and Sanitation	Nancouma Keita
Equipment and Transport	Abdoulaye Koita
Foreign Affairs and International Cooperation	Bien Moctar Ouane
Health	Maiga Zeinab Mint Youba [f]
Industry and Commerce	Choguel Kokala Maiga
Investment, Small and Medium-Sized Business	Ousmane Thiam
Justice and Keeper of the Seals	Me Fanta Sylla [f]
Livestock and Fishing	Oumar Ibrahima Touré
Mines, Energy, and Hydraulics	Hamed Diane Semega
Promotion of Women, Children, and the Family	Berthe Aissata Bengaly [f]
Rural Development and Planning	Marimatia Diarra
Security and Civil Protection	Col. Sadie Gassama
Social Development, Solidarity	Djibril Tangara
State Properties, Land, and Housing	Soumare Aminata Sidibe [f]
Territorial Administration and Local Communities	Gen. Kafougouna Kone
Tourism and Cottage Industry	Bah N'diaye
Urban Development and Housing	Modibo Sylla
Youth and Sports	Moussa Balla Diakite

[f] = female

Mamadou Maribatourou Diaby, the incumbent's sole challenger in the 1997 presidential balloting, is a member of the **Unity, Development, and Progress Party** (*Parti pour l'Unité, le Développement, et le Progrés*—PUDP). Diaby also ran unsuccessfully for the presidency in 2002. Other minor parties include the **Civic Society** (*Société Civique*—SC); the **Movement for Democracy and Development** (*Mouvement pour la Démocratie et le Développement*—MPDD); the **Party for Unity and Progress** (*Parti pour l'Unité et le Progrés*—PUP), led by former UDPM official Nock Ag ATTIA; the **Popular Movement for Development** (*Mouvement Populaire pour le Développement*—MPD); the **Soudanese Progress Party** (*Parti Soudanais du Progrès*—PSP), which is led by African Development Bank consultant Oumar Hammadoun Dicko and which was awarded two assembly seats in 1992 by the Supreme Court after successfully suing Adema for electoral fraud.

On March 20, 1996, the rebel Azwad Liberation Front (*Front pour la Libération de l'Azaouad*—FLA), originally launched in Algeria in December 1991 as the Unified Movements and Fronts of Azawad (*Mouvements et Fronts Unifiés de l'Azaouad*—MFUA), was formally dissolved after its component groups (see 1995–1996 *Handbook,* p. 598) had announced their "unflinching attachment to the constitution of the Republic of Mali, to national unity, and to the territorial integrity of the country."

In August 1998 members of the **Barefooted Ones** (*Pied Nus*), a Muslim sect led by Cheikh Ibrahim Khalil KANOUTE, reportedly killed a judge in Dioila for imprisoning one of their colleagues and then clashed with local security officials. The group reportedly rejects all forms of Western and modern influences and has protested against the government's adherence to internationally prescribed economic structural adjustment programs.

In November 2001 the former leader of the PDP, Idrissa TRAORE, formed the **Party for Democracy and Self-Sufficiency** (*Parti pour la Démocratie et l'Autosuffisance*—PDA). Other active parties include the **National Democratic Convention** (*Convention Nationale Démocrate*—CND); the **Convention for Progress and the People** (*Convention pour le Progrès et le Peuple*—COPP), led by Mamadou Gakou; and the **Citizens' Party for Renewal** (*Parti Citoyen pour le Renouveau*—PCR), formed in July 2005, reportedly to provide President Touré with a political base for the 2007 elections.

Legislature

Following the March 1991 coup, the UDPM-dominated legislature was dissolved, with its powers assigned to the CTSP. The current **National Assembly** (*Assemblée Nationale*) contains 147 members serving (subject to dissolution) five-year terms. (In addition, Malians living abroad are represented by 13 legislators whom they select in separate polling.) In balloting on July 14 and 28, 2002, and after by-elections on October 20, Hope 2002

held 66 seats; the Alliance for the Republic and Democracy, 59 seats; the Alliance for Alternation and Change, 10; African Solidarity for Democracy and Independence, 6; and independents, 6.

President: Ibrahim Boubakar KEITA.

Communications

Press

The impact of the press has long been limited because of widespread illiteracy (80–90 percent) and, until the 1990s, little opportunity to publish dissenting or adversarial material. The following are published in Bamako: *L'Essor-La Voix du Peuple* (3,500), government daily; *Le Républicain,* independent daily; *Le Soudanais; Nouvel Horizon* and *Le Soir de Bamako,* independent dailies; *Liberté,* weekly; *L'observateur; L'Aurore,* biweekly; *Info-Matin,* pro-opposition daily; and *Le Continent,* weekly. *Les Echos* (25,000), initially a pro-government bimonthly, subsequently a daily, was launched in March 1989.

News Agencies

The National Information Agency of Mali (ANIM) and the Malian Publicity Agency (AMP) were merged in 1977 to form the official *Agence Malienne de Presse* (Amap); *Agence France-Presse* and a number of other foreign agencies maintain bureaus in Bamako.

Broadcasting and Computing

Radiodiffusion-Télévision Malienne (RTM) broadcasts news bulletins and programs in French, English, and the principal local languages; there are also more than a dozen private radio outlets. RTM transmissions were received by more than 160,000 television sets in 2003, while some 16,000 personal computers served approximately 32,000 Internet users. The staff of a private radio station were arrested in October 2003 and charged with "slander and incitement to violence" by the government. The arrests were criticized by press groups and opposition parties.

Intergovernmental Representation

Ambassador to the U.S.
Abdoulaye DIOP

U.S. Ambassador to Mali
Terrence P. McCULLEY

Permanent Representative to the UN
Sheikh Sidi DIARRA

IGO Memberships (Non-UN)
AfDB, AU, BADEA, BOAD, CILSS, ECOWAS, IDB, Interpol, IOM, NAM, OIC, OIF, UEMOA, WCO, WTO

MAURITANIA

ISLAMIC REPUBLIC OF MAURITANIA

al-Jumhuriyah al-Islamiyah al-Muritaniyah

The Country

Situated on the western bulge of Africa, Mauritania is a sparsely populated, predominantly desert country, overwhelmingly Islamic and, except in the south, Arabic in language. The dominant Beydane (Arabic for "white") Moors, descendants of northern Arabs and Berbers, have been estimated as constituting one-third of the population, with an equal number of Haratines (mixed-race descendants of black slaves) having adopted Berber customs. Black Africans, the most important tribal groups of which are the Toucouleur, the Fulani, the Sarakole, and the Wolof, are concentrated in the rich alluvial farming lands of the Senegal River valley. They have recently claimed to account for a much larger population share than is officially acknowledged, their case being supported by the government's refusal to release pertinent portions of the last two censuses. Racial tension, exacerbated by government "arabization" efforts, has contributed to internal unrest and conflict with several neighboring nations. Further complicating matters has been the de facto continuation of slavery, officially banned in 1980 but still reportedly encompassing an estimated 100,000–400,000 Haratines and blacks in servitude to Arab masters.

Before 1970 nearly all of the northern population was engaged in nomadic cattle raising, but the proportion had shrunk to less than one-quarter by 1986. Prolonged droughts, desertification, the loss of herds, and more recently, a devastating locust attack in 2004, which wiped out about half of the country's crops, have driven more Mauritanians to urban areas, where many depend on foreign relief aid. Many Mauritanians seek their livelihood in other countries.

The country's first deep water port, financed by China, opened near Nouakchott in 1986. Mauritania's coastal waters are among the richest fishing grounds in the world and generate more than half of foreign income, although the region is also routinely fished by foreign trawlers. In 2003 exploratory tests indicated the presence of offshore oil fields, prompting investments from international oil companies. The country's first offshore oil field, Chinguetti, went into production in February 2006. A second, larger field, Tiof, may go into production in 2009. The two fields are projected to

produce as much as 165,000 barrels per day, netting approximately $300 million a year.

To secure aid from international donors, the government initiated numerous economic reforms, the latter including privatization of state-owned enterprises, promotion of free market activity, and currency devaluation. The government also endorsed political liberalization, although genuine progress in that regard has been minimal, while international lenders called for measures to address the unequal distribution of wealth. (More than 50 percent of the population lives in poverty, and the social services sector is considered grossly inadequate.)

In 2002 the International Monetary Fund (IMF) and the World Bank announced that Mauritania had fulfilled its requirements for the Heavily Indebted Poor Countries (HIPC) initiative, resulting in debt relief of $1.1 billion. Real GDP growth of 3.3 percent and 5.4 percent was reported in 2002 and 2003, respectively, and inflation was relatively low. By 2004 real GDP grew about 7 percent, though inflation had soared to double digits, and GDP growth of 5 percent was projected for 2005. The IMF commended authorities for their plans to curtail government spending and to budget anticipated oil revenue for antipoverty programs. In May 2006 the IMF mission to Nouakchott noted that the transitional government was making progress on transparency and restoring economic stability since the coup in August 2005.

Government and Politics

Political Background

Under nominal French administration from the turn of the century, Mauritania became a French colony in 1920, but de facto control was not established until 1934. It became an autonomous republic within the French Community in 1958 and an independent "Islamic Republic" on November 28, 1960. President Moktar OULD DADDAH (died October 14, 2003), who led the country to independence, established a one-party regime with predominantly Moorish backing and endorsed a policy of moderate socialism at home combined with nonalignment abroad. Opposition to his 18-year presidency was periodically voiced by northern groups seeking union with Morocco, by inhabitants of the predominantly black south who feared Arab domination, and by leftist elements in both student and trade union organizations.

Under an agreement concluded in November 1975 by Mauritania, Morocco, and Spain, the Ould Daddah regime assumed control of the southern third of Western (Spanish) Sahara on February 28, 1976, coincident with the withdrawal of Spanish forces and Morocco's occupation of the northern two-thirds (see discussion under entry for Morocco). However, an inability to contain Algerian-supported insurgents in the annexed territory contributed to the president's ouster in a bloodless coup on July 10, 1978, and the installation of Lt. Col. Mustapha OULD SALEK as head of state by a newly formed Military Committee for National Recovery (*Comité Militaire de Recouvrement National*—CMRN). Ould Salek, arguing that the struggle against the insurgents had "nearly destroyed" the Mauritanian economy, indicated that his government would be willing to withdraw from Tiris El-Gharbia (the Mauritanian sector of Western Sahara) if a settlement acceptable to Morocco, Algeria, Mauritania, and the insurgents could be found. However, the overture was rejected by Morocco, and in October the Algerian-backed Popular Front for the Liberation of Saguia el Hamra and Rio de Oro (Polisario) announced that the insurgency would cease only if Mauritania were to withdraw from the sector and recognize Polisario's government in exile, the Saharan Arab Democratic Republic (SADR).

In March 1979 Salek reiterated his government's desire to extricate itself from the conflict but dismissed several CMRN members known to favor direct talks with Polisario. Subsequently, on April 6, he dissolved the CMRN itself in favor of a new Military Committee for National Salvation (*Comité Militaire de Salut National*—CMSN) and relinquished the office of prime minister to Lt. Col. Ahmed OULD BOUCEIF, who was immediately hailed as effective leader of the Nouakchott regime. On May 27, however, Ould Bouceif was killed in

Political Status: Independent republic since November 28, 1960; 1961 constitution suspended by the Military Committee for National Recovery on July 20, 1978; present constitution, providing for multiparty civilian government, approved by referendum July 12, 1991.

Area: 397,953 sq. mi. (1,030,700 sq. km.).

Population: 2,548,157 (2000C); 3,166,859 (2005E), excluding an estimated 170,000–240,000 former residents of Senegal who fled or were expelled to Mauritania following a 1989 border dispute.

Major Urban Center (2005E): NOUAKCHOTT (644,000). In recent years the population of Nouakchott has grown rapidly, many former nomads having taken up permanent residence in the capital since the 1970s.

Official Language: Arabic. (Three languages of the Black African community—Poular, Soninke, and Wolof—are constitutionally designated as national languages. French, an official language until 1991, is still widely spoken, particularly in the commercial sector. In addition, in 1999 the government designated French as the "language for science and technical subjects" in Mauritanian schools.)

Monetary Unit: Ouguiya (official rate July 1, 2006: 271.30 ouguiyas = $1US).

Head of State: Col. Ely Ould Mohamed VALL; assumed office as president of the Military Council for Justice and Democracy following coup of August 3, 2005, that ousted President Maaouya Ould Sidahmed TAYA (Democratic and Social Republican Party).

Prime Minister: Sidi Mohamed Ould BOUBACAR; appointed by the head of state on August 7, 2005, to succeed Sghair Ould MBARECK (Democratic and Social Republican Party).

an airplane crash and was succeeded (following the interim incumbency of Lt. Col. Ahmed Salem OULD SIDI) by Lt. Col. Mohamed Khouna OULD HAIDALLA on May 31.

President Ould Salek was forced to resign on June 3, the CMSN naming Lt. Col. Mohamed Mahmoud Ould Ahmed LOULY as his replacement. Colonel Louly immediately declared his commitment to a cessation of hostilities and on August 5, after three days of talks in Algiers, concluded a peace agreement with Polisario representatives. While the pact did not entail recognition of the SADR, Mauritania formally renounced all claims to Tiris El-Gharbia and subsequently withdrew its troops from the territory, which was thereupon occupied by Moroccan forces and renamed Oued Eddahab (the Arabic form of the province's original name, Rio de Oro).

On January 4, 1980, President Louly was replaced by Col. Ould Haidalla, who also continued to serve as chief of government. The following December Ould Haidalla announced that, as a first step toward restoration of democratic institutions, his largely military administration would be replaced by a civilian government headed by Sid Ahmad OULD BNEIJARA. Only one army officer was named to the cabinet announced on December 15, while the CMSN published a draft constitution four days later that proposed establishment of a multiparty system.

The move toward civilianization was abruptly halted on March 16, 1981, as the result of an attempted coup by a group of officers (who were allegedly backed by Morocco), Prime Minister Ould Bneijara being replaced on April 26 by the army chief of staff, Col. Maaouya Ould Sidahmed TAYA. A further coup attempt, involving an effort to abduct President Ould Haidalla at Nouakchott airport on February 6, 1982, resulted in the arrest of Ould Bneijara and former president Ould Salek, both of whom were sentenced to ten-year prison terms by a special tribunal on March 5.

On March 8, 1984, in a major leadership reshuffle, Taya returned to his former military post, and the president reclaimed the prime ministry, to which was added the defense portfolio. The following December Ould Haidalla was ousted in a bloodless coup led by Colonel Taya, who assumed the titles of president, prime minister, and chair of the CMSN.

Amid increasingly vocal black opposition to Moorish domination, Colonel Taya announced plans in mid-1986 for a gradual return to democratic rule (see Constitution and government, below), and local councils were elected in the country's regional capitals in December. However, north-south friction persisted, with three Toucouleur officers being executed and some 40 others imprisoned for involvement in an alleged coup attempt in October 1987.

Although the Taya regime was subsequently charged with systematic repression of opponents, particularly southerners, elections were held for councils in the principal townships and rural districts in January 1988 and 1989, respectively. New elections to all the municipal councils, originally planned for late 1989 but postponed because of a violent dispute with Senegal (see Foreign relations, below), were held in December 1990. Meanwhile, racial tension remained high because of reports that security forces had imprisoned thousands of black army officers and government officials, several hundred of whom had allegedly been executed or tortured to death. Although the government claimed that the arrests had been made in connection with a coup plot, opponents charged that the regime was merely intensifying an already virulent anti-black campaign.

On April 15, 1991, Colonel Taya surprised observers by announcing that a referendum would be held soon on a new constitution, followed by multiparty presidential and legislative elections. The draft constitution was released on June 10 by the CMSN, approved with a reported "yes" vote of nearly 98 percent in a national referendum on July 12, and formally entered into effect on July 21. Four days later, the CMSN adopted legislation on the legalization of political parties, six of which (including the regime-supportive Democratic and Social Republican Party [*Parti Républicain Démocratique et Social*—PRDS]) were quickly recognized. On June 29 Colonel Taya, expanding a partial program announced in March and April, declared a general amnesty for detainees held on state security charges, thereby somewhat mollifying black hostility.

In presidential balloting on January 24, 1992, Colonel Taya, as the PRDS nominee, was credited with winning 63 percent of the vote; his principal challenger, Ahmed OULD DADDAH, received 33 percent. Ould Daddah, the previously exiled brother of former president Moktar Ould Daddah, was supported by a number of the new political parties, including the influential Union of Democratic Forces (*Union des Forces Démocratiques*—UFD), which challenged the accuracy of the official election results.

On February 10, 1992, five opposition parties requested postponement of National Assembly elections scheduled for March 6 and 13 to avoid a repetition of what they claimed had been massive fraud at the presidential poll. Their appeal rejected, 6 of the 14 opposition groups, including the UFD, boycotted the balloting, in which the PRDS won an overwhelming majority of seats on a turnout of little more than a third of the electorate.

In indirect senatorial balloting on April 3 and 10, 1992, the participants were further reduced to the PRDS and the small Avante-Guard Party (*Parti Avant-Garde*—PAG), which received none of the available seats, as contrasted with 36 for the PRDS and 17 for independents. On April 18, following Colonel Taya's inauguration as president, Taya yielded the office of prime minister to a young "technocrat," Sidi Mohamed OULD BOUBACAR, who announced the formation of a new government on April 20.

Only the UFD and the recently formed Union for Democracy and Progress (*Union pour la Démocratie et le Progrès*—UDP) challenged the PRDS in municipal balloting on January 28 and February 4, 1994. The government party won control of 172 of the 208 municipal councils (as compared to 19 for independents and 17 for the UFD), prompting opposition charges of extensive electoral fraud. The opposition also questioned the results of the April Senate replenishment, in which the PRDS won 16 of 17 seats. In September it was reported that President Taya had dropped his military title in pursuit of a more civilian image. At the same time, the government launched a crackdown on Islamic "agitators," fundamentalists having reportedly gained converts by providing much-needed social services in urban areas.

Taya dismissed Ould Boubacar on January 2, 1996, replacing him with Cheikh el Avia Ould Mohamed KHOUNA. The December 12, 1997, elections won President Taya another six-year term, with an official 90 percent of the vote. The UFD and several other opposition parties boycotted the balloting in objection to the regime's failure to establish an independent electoral commission, among other things.

Despite growing opposition, President Taya's PRDS party maintained a firm grip on power, winning a majority of seats in the 1996 and 2001 National Assembly elections.

The Mauritanian cabinet underwent more than a dozen reshufflings between June 1997 and May 2003, prompting concerns about the stability of the government. On June 7, 2003, those concerns were validated when rebels stormed the presidential palace in a coup attempt that led to two days of fighting in the capital. After regaining power on June 9, President Taya began a crackdown on the Muslim extremists he blamed for the uprising. On July 7, 2003, Taya appointed Sighair Ould Mbareck as prime minister, replacing Khouna. Ould Mbareck is the first former slave to hold the position.

Four months later Taya was elected to his third term. His principal challenger, former president Ould Haidalla, who had assembled a coalition of prominent Islamists, Arab nationals, and reformers, won 18.7 percent of the vote. Ould Haidalla and several of his supporters were arrested and detained on the day before the election, then released, only to be arrested and released again the next day. International observers were not permitted to observe the elections, which were labeled fraudulent by Taya's opponents. In February 2005 Ould Haidalla was acquitted on charges relating to the 2003 and 2004 attempted coups. Four soldiers were found guilty and sentenced to life in prison.

In August and September 2004 government officials announced discovery of two more coup attempts, allegedly organized by former army officers Saleh Ould Hanenna and Mohamed Cheikhna.

Officials accused Libya and Burkina Faso of arming and financing the coup, charges the two countries denied.

However, the insurgency seemed to be on the rise. On June 16, 2005, gunmen ambushed a remote military outpost in northern Mauritania, killing 15 soldiers. An Algerian group called the Salafist Group for Call and Combat, which is affiliated with al-Qaida, claimed responsibility for the attack. The group said that the ambush was meant to avenge the imprisonment of Islamists in Mauritania.

A bloodless coup was staged on August 3, 2005, when Taya was in Saudi Arabia attending the funeral of King Fahd. A group of 16 security and army officers led by Col. Ely Ould Mohamed VALL established themselves as the ruling Military Council for Justice and Democracy (MCJD) with Vall as head of state. On August 5, the parliament was dissolved. Mbareck resigned as prime minister on August 7 and was immediately replaced by Ould Boubacar, ambassador to France, who resigned from the former ruling PRDS party on August 9. A new cabinet, described as consisting primarily of technocrats, was announced on August 10. The transitional government pledged to hold elections within two years (see Current issues, below). Most political parties, including the PRDS, ultimately gave their approval to the junta.

Constitution and Government

The constitution of May 23, 1961, which had replaced Mauritania's former parliamentary-type government with a one-party presidential system, was formally suspended by the CMRN on July 20, 1978. A Constitutional Charter issued by the Military Committee confirmed the dissolution of the National Assembly and the Mauritanian People's Party (*Parti du Peuple Mauritanien*—PPM) and authorized the installation of the committee's chair as head of state until such time as "new democratic institutions are established."

In December 1980 the CMSN published a constitutional proposal that was to have been submitted to a referendum in 1981. However, no balloting was held prior to the coup of December

1984. Subsequently, Colonel Taya indicated that the military would prepare for a return to democracy through a program called the Structure for the Education of the Masses that would involve the election of councilors at the local level to advise the government on measures to improve literacy, social integration, and labor productivity. In the series of municipal elections conducted in 1986–1990, voters chose from multiple lists of candidates approved by the government, although no formal political party activity was permitted.

The 1991 constitution declared Mauritania to be an "Islamic Arab and African republic," guaranteed "freedom of association, thought, and expression," and conferred strong executive powers on the president, including the authority to appoint the prime minister. Directly elected by universal suffrage in two-round voting, the president may serve an unlimited number of six-year terms. The new basic law also established a bicameral legislature (comprising a directly elected National Assembly and an indirectly elected Senate), as well as constitutional, economic and social, and Islamic councils.

The legal system traditionally reflected a combination of French and Islamic codes, with the judiciary encompassing a Supreme Court; a High Court of Justice; courts of first instance; and civil, labor, and military courts. In June 1978 a commission was appointed to revise the system according to Islamic precepts, and in March 1980, a month after the replacement of "modern" codes by Islamic law (*sharia*), the CMSN established an Islamic Court consisting of a Muslim magistrate, two councilors, and two *ulemas* (interpreters of the Koran). Earlier, in October 1978, a special Court of State Security had been created. The 1991 constitution provided for an independent judiciary with Islam serving as the "single source of law."

For administrative purposes the country is divided into 12 regions, plus the capital district of Nouakchott, and 32 departments; in addition, 208 urban and rural districts (areas populated by at least 500 inhabitants) were created in October 1988.

The Military Council for Justice and Democracy (MCJD) formed by the leaders of the August 2005 coup, maintained the 1991 constitution, supplementing it with a military council "charter" that stipulated the MCJD held power over the executive and legislative branches, dissolved the parliament, and gave the MCJD advisory power over the Constitutional Council. Constitutional amendments proposed by the transitional government were overwhelmingly approved by voters (97 percent) in a June 25, 2006, referendum to limit a president to two terms of five years each and set a maximum age limit of 75 for a president.

Foreign Relations

Mauritania has combined nonalignment in world affairs with membership in such groupings as the Arab League (since 1973) and, as of 1989, the Arab Maghreb Union (AMU). Following independence, economic and cultural cooperation with France continued on the basis of agreements first negotiated in 1961 and renegotiated in 1973 to exclude special arrangements in monetary and military affairs. As a consequence, French military advisers were recalled and Mauritania withdrew from the Franc Zone, establishing its own currency. In late 1979 a limited number of French troops and military instructors returned to ensure Mauritania's territorial integrity following Nouakchott's withdrawal from Western Sahara and the annexation of its sector by Morocco.

Mauritania's settlement with the Polisario Front was followed by restoration of diplomatic relations with Algeria, which had been severed upon Algiers' recognition of the Saharan Arab Democratic Republic (SADR) in 1976. During 1980–1982 Nouakchott maintained formal neutrality in Polisario's continuing confrontation with Morocco, withholding formal recognition of the SADR but criticizing Rabat's military efforts to retain control of the entire Western Sahara. In 1983 Colonel Ould Haidalla concluded a Maghreb Fraternity and Cooperation Treaty with Algeria and Tunisia that was implicitly directed against Rabat and Tripoli. On the other hand, declaring that the conflict in the Western Sahara had "poisoned the atmosphere," Colonel Taya subsequently attempted to return

Mauritania to its traditional posture of regional neutralism. While still maintaining its "moral support" for the SADR, which it officially recognized in 1984, the Taya regime normalized relations with Morocco and Libya, thereby balancing growing ties with Algeria that included the signing of a border demarcation agreement in April 1986.

Relations with Senegal have been tense since an April 1989 incident when violence erupted between villagers along the border with Senegal, provoking race riots in both nations' capitals that reportedly caused the death of nearly 500 people and injury to more than 1,000. During the ensuing months an estimated 170,000–240,000 Mauritanian expatriates fled Senegal, while Mauritania reportedly expelled 70,000 Senegalese and 40,000 of its own black residents. Mauritania and Senegal severed diplomatic relations in August, with each country accusing the other of instigating further violence. Although the countries restored ties in April 1992 and the border was partially reopened the following November, tension continued as black Mauritanians charged they were being prevented from returning to Mauritania and Senegal attributed widespread "banditry" along the border to the refugee situation. Despite several flare-ups, relations between the two countries improved after Senegal's President Wade expressed his support for the Taya regime, following the 2003 coup attempt in Mauritania, and extradited a suspected coup plotter to Mauritania.

Mauritania has also had strained relations with Mali, whose black-dominated Traoré regime accused Nouakchott in the late 1980s of supporting antigovernment activity among its ethnically Berber Tuareg population. Following the resolution of the Tuareg situation in the mid-1990s, relations with Mali have warmed.

Mauritania attracted an unusual amount of international attention for its support for Iraq in the 1990–1991 Gulf crisis, causing Western aid donors to sharply curtail their aid to Nouakchott. However, assistance was subsequently restored, apparently reflecting Western support for the Taya regime's strong antifundamentalist posture. The government has distanced itself from Iraq recently, expelling

Baghdad's ambassador in October 1995 amid reports of a coup plot among "pro-Baathist" elements. Among other things, the policy shift has contributed to improved relations with Gulf Arab states.

In November 1995 Nouakchott announced plans to open an "interest" office in Tel Aviv as part of what was expected to be eventual restoration of full relations with Israel. The action was condemned by some hard-line Arab states, including Libya, which recalled its ambassador and discontinued all aid to Mauritania. However, Tunisian mediation in early 1997 helped restore relations between Mauritania and Tripoli.

In late 1999 the Taya government completed the foreign policy reversal started in mid-decade by severing relations with Iraq and becoming only the third Arab state (after Egypt and Jordan) to establish full diplomatic relations with Israel.

French officials have been critical of Mauritania's human rights record, but relations between the two countries improved after France offered support to the Taya regime following the 2003 coup attempt.

The government has cooperated with the United States in several counterterrorism training programs beginning in 2003. Such programs target al-Qaida–affiliated groups operating in Mauritania and several neighboring countries. In a major decision, Mauritania announced in December that it was withdrawing from the Economic Community of West African States (ECOWAS); analysts suggested that Nouakchott had grown increasingly concerned over the possibility that the non-Francophone countries in ECOWAS would adopt a common currency to the detriment of the ouguiya. Subsequently, the Taya administration declared that it would focus on affairs in northern Africa, particularly through the proposed rejuvenation of the Arab Maghreb Union, rather than on its relations with its southern neighbors. (As an outgrowth of that orientation, Nouakchott was described in 2000 as having informally accepted the premise that the Western Sahara would remain a province of Morocco.)

Regional tensions increased in August and September 2004 after President Taya accused

Libya and Burkina Faso of arming renegade soldiers allegedly preparing to topple the Taya regime in two separate coup attempts. Both countries denied the accusations.

Following the August 2005 coup, Colonel Vall pledged to maintain Mauritania's relations with Israel. The African Union (AU) suspended Mauritania's membership a day after the coup but subsequently indicated the country would regain its seat after elections if a democracy were established.

Current Issues

Several human rights activists were arrested in 1998 after they participated in a French television documentary on slavery. Antislavery demonstrations ensued in Nouakchott, prompting further arrests and leaving some 20 people injured. Although President Taya pardoned the activists in March, his regime subsequently faced domestic and international criticism for its failure to enforce antislavery statutes. (The president's power base includes wealthy and extremely influential clan leaders, who are generally reported to be slave "owners.")

The municipal elections of early 1999 did little to enhance the country's democratic credentials as the PRDS and its allies won control of every council in the wake of a boycott by the UFD-led opposition, which also refused to participate in the Senate replenishment of April 2000. The government subsequently announced that the next local elections would be moved up to October 2001 to coincide with the scheduled National Assembly poll, with a degree of proportional representation to be introduced into both as a means of promoting inclusion of non-PRDS parties in the legislative process.

A series of large pro-Palestinian street demonstrations occurred in late 2000 following the breakdown of Israeli-Palestinian negotiations. However, the government quashed the protests and, despite heavy pressure from many Arab states, refused in early 2001 to revoke its recently established diplomatic ties with Israel. President Taya maintained his new strongly pro-United States stance which, among other things, had underpinned substantial Western aid. In 2002 the government continued its

crackdown on Islamists, Baathists, and suspected insurgents, arresting and detaining, among others, three "prisoners of conscience" from the opposition group Popular Front, according to Amnesty International. Following the June 2003 coup, almost 200 suspected insurgents were arrested and charged. None was sentenced to death; however, according to the defense, many were tortured in detainment.

President Taya's 2003 victory came amid widespread allegations of fraud, but his critics declined to pursue the matter through legal channels. French observers were not invited to monitor the elections, as they had done in 2001, and several opposition members, including Taya's main opponent, were arrested in the days leading up to the vote, prompting a warning form Human Rights Watch of a climate of "harassment of opposition members."

The crackdown on Islamists and other Taya opponents subsequently intensified; in the spring of 2005, the government arrested 30 alleged terrorists accused of attempting to destabilize the country. The government claimed to have linked many of the prisoners to a group affiliated with al-Qaida; however, opponents and some human rights groups charged that Taya was using Western fears of terrorism as an opportunity to silence his opponents. Training and financing for the crackdown came partly from the United States as part of its own counterterrorism efforts. Human rights groups cautioned that increasing tensions between Taya and Islamic groups, fueled by the impending infusion of oil money, could further destabilize the country.

Taya had become "despotic" since taking power and was "deeply unpopular," according to *Middle East International*, not only for his imprisonment of dissidents (Islamists, in particular), but also because of his perceived discrimination against Mauritania's poorer Arab population. Thus, the coup staged by a group of military officials on August 3, 2005, when Taya was out of the country, had domestic support—marked by exuberant street celebrations—and, ultimately, international acceptance, including financial support for promised elections. Col. Ely Ould Mohamed Vall, who, as president of the Military Council for Justice and

Democracy became head of state after the MCJD's takeover, immediately announced broad-ranging plans for democratic reform. He offered assurances that the transitional government would be in place for no longer than two years, and that neither he nor anyone in the MCJD would participate in elections scheduled in 2006 (local and parliamentary) and 2007 (presidential). In addition, he announced a general amnesty for political prisoners; implemented a constitutional referendum (see Constitution and government, above); and allowed Taya—in exile in Qatar—to return to Mauritania if he chose, though barring him from the 2007 presidential elections. While the coup initially met with international condemnation, attitudes soon softened, and in early 2006 the European Union offered some $7 million to support the transition, with other contributions reportedly coming from France, Spain, and Egypt. The United States was also reported to be working with the junta to organize multiparty elections as soon as possible. As of April, according to a Mauritanian census, nearly 1 million voters had been registered. Perhaps the most significant change under Colonel Vall's initial tenure was the amending of the constitution to set term limits for a president, eliminating the power of a "president-for-life," and possibly bringing the country closer to civilian rule with the introduction of multiparty elections.

Meanwhile in early 2006, Mauitania was reportedly becoming the latest point of departure for Africans trying to enter Europe illegally. Prime Minister Boubacar called for Western assistance after hundreds of migrants died, including 18 in the ocean off Mauritania, as thousands of others came through the country on their way to Europe.

Political Parties

Mauritania became a one-party state in 1964, when the Mauritanian People's Party (*Parti du Peuple Mauritanien*—PPM/*Hizb al-Shah al-Muritani*) was assigned legal supremacy over all governmental organs. The PPM was dissolved following the coup of July 1978. Although partisan activity was not permitted, some candidates in municipal elections in 1986–1990 were linked to informal groups such as the National Democratic Union (*Union National Démocratique*—UND) and the Union for Progress and Fraternity (*Union des Progrès et Fraternité*—UPF). In addition, unofficial opposition activity was conducted by several formations, including the National Democratic Movement (*Mouvement National Démocratique*—MND) and the United Democratic Front of Forces for Change (*Front Démocratique Uni des Forces du Changement*—FDUFC).

The constitution approved in July 1991 guaranteed "freedom of association," and subsequent legislation established regulations for the legalization of political parties. Groups based on race or region were proscribed, while Islamic organizations were declared ineligible for registration on the ground that Islam belonged to "all the people" and could not be "claimed" by electoral bodies.

In view of the near-total dominance of the Democratic and Social Republican Party (PRDS) in recent national and municipal elections, legislation was adopted in late 2000 providing for a degree of proportional representation in the 2001 assembly balloting and concurrent local polls. It was also announced that all parties securing at least 1 percent of the votes in the municipal elections would receive government financing (based on their total vote) and that "equal access" to the state-controlled media would be provided to opposition parties.

Following the coup of August 3, 2005, most political parties and groups backed the transitional junta. Though the PRDS initially denounced the coup, within little more than a month it appeared willing to support the junta, and in September abolished the post of party chair that had been held for 15 years by former president Taya. Various other parties began forming alliances in advance of scheduled parliamentary and presidential elections in 2006 and 2007, respectively.

Parties

Democratic and Social Republican Party (*Parti Républicain Démocratique et Social*—PRDS). The PRDS was launched in support of

President Taya by a longtime associate, Cheikh Sid Ahmed Ould Baba, who resigned from the cabinet and military in mid-1991 to concentrate on party politics. As the PRDS nominee, Taya won the January 1992 presidential poll by a substantial margin, and the PRDS assumed essentially unchallenged political control by winning large majorities in the subsequent National Assembly and Senate elections, which were boycotted by most opposition groups. The party also dominated the municipal and Senate balloting of early 1994.

In March 1995 the PRDS absorbed the Movement of Independent Democrats (*Mouvement des Démocrates Indépendants*—MDI), led by Bechir el-HASSEN, which had left the UFD (below) in June 1994.

The party won 70 of 79 seats in the 1996 legislative balloting on its own right and was also considered to enjoy the support of the seven independent legislators (some of whom were former PRDS members) and the RDU representative in the assembly. Taya was reelected as party leader at the second national congress held in November 1999. The PRDS won 64 of 81 seats in the assembly in the 2001 balloting and 15 out of 18 open seats in the April 2004 partial Senate elections. In 2003 President Taya won his third term in office.

Following the August 3, 2005, coup, Colonel Vall named PRDS member Sidi Mohamed Ould Boubacar as prime minister, and Boubacar quit the party on August 9. The PRDS initially objected to the junta, calling on its members to support the former regime. A few days later, however, it reportedly reversed itself and gave approval to the ruling MCJD (which reportedly did detain or interrogate members of Taya's government after the coup). Support for Taya, widely reported to be a repressive leader who imprisoned dissidents, particularly Islamists, had waned over the years, and his policy of engagement with Israel angered Arab nationalists, observers said. On September 19 the party took the further step of abolishing the chairmanship that Taya had held for 15 years. In October the party held an extraordinary congress

and reportedly changed its name to the Republican Democratic Party for Renovation (PRDR). However, the actions of the congress were canceled in November by a Mauritanian court, which also ordered the party's assets seized pending the outcome of a dispute within the party over whether an audit should have been conducted during the congress. Further turmoil was evidenced when the party's Islamist wing, led by Abdou MAHAM, severed its ties the same month, reportedly to join the Rally for Democracy and Unity (*Rassemblement pour la Démocratie et l'Unité*—RDU). On November 25 the PRDS elected Ethmane Ould Cheikh Abou Ali Maali, Mauritania's ambassador to Kuwait, as president.

Leaders: Ethmane Ould Cheikh Abou Ali MAALI (President), Cheikh El Avia Ould Mohamed KHOUNA (Former Prime Minister), Rachid Ould SALEH (Speaker of the National Assembly), Bela Ould MAKIYA (Secretary General).

Rally for Democracy and Unity (*Rassemblement pour la Démocratie et l'Unité*—RDU). Led by the mayor of Atar, who had served as a cabinet minister under Mauritania's first president, the center-right RDU was the first party (in August 1991) to be recognized by the present regime. It supported President Taya in the January 1992 presidential campaign but, after winning one seat in the first round of the March National Assembly election, broke with the government and boycotted the second round, as well as the subsequent Senate race. However, as of the 1996 legislative elections, in which it retained its seat, the RDU was once again described as allied with the PRDS, and the RDU leader was named an adviser to the president in the government announced in December 1998. In the 2004 Senate elections, the RDU won one seat.

Leader: Ahmed Moktar Sidi BABA.

Union for Democracy and Progress (*Union pour la Démocratie et le Progrès*—UDP). The UDP was legalized in June 1993, its ranks including prominent ex-UFD members, some of whom had also served in the administration of Mauritania's first president, Moktar Ould Daddah. UDP leaders pledged to work toward "restoration of national unity," which, in contrast to government policy, appeared to be aimed at conciliation with black Mauritanians. However, despite its professed multiracial stance, the UDP has recently been described as continuing, for the most part, to represent conservative Moorish interests.

The UDP participated in the 1994 municipal balloting, although it did not gain control of any of the 19 local boards for which it offered candidates, party leaders reportedly having encouraged supporters to vote for whichever opposition candidate had the best chance of defeating the PRDS candidate. Reportedly suffering from internal dissension, the UDP won no seats in the 1996 legislative poll. When UDP leader Hamdi OULD MOUK-NASS was appointed as a presidential adviser in December 1997, the UDP moved into a position as a government-supportive party. At the same time, some party members had reportedly aligned with the FPO (see AC, below), the recently organized leading opposition coalition.

Hamdi Ould Mouknass died in September 1999 and was succeeded as UDP president in May 2000 by his daughter, Naha Mint Mouknass, who thereby became one of the few female party leaders in the Arab world. She was also named a presidential adviser, reaffirming the rump UDP's ties to the government. The party made five nominations to the 2004 Senate elections but won none.

Leaders: Naha Mint MOUKNASS (President), Sheikh Saad Bouh CAMARA, Ahmed OULD MENAYA (Secretary General).

Action for Change (*Action pour le Changement*—AC). The AC by default became the "leading" opposition party when it won the only legislative seat in 1996 that did not go to the PRDS or PRDS supporters. Formed as the result of a split within the UFD (below), the AC was described as comprising the "most militant elements" of Haratine and black groupings. It appeared to be an outgrowth of *El-Hor,* formed in 1974 to promote Haratine interests and a component of the UFD until mid-1994. The group is led by Massoud Ould Boulkheir, a minister of rural development under former president Ould Haidalla. *African Confidential* several years ago described *El-Hor* as the "most likely effective opposition" to President Ould Taya and the PRDS because of the country's large Haratine population.

Before the 1996 balloting the AC called for a national census to be conducted to create complete and accurate voting lists. The AC legislator, Kebe Abdoulaye, was elected secretary of the National Assembly as part of what some observers described as a public relations exercise designed to illustrate the Taya regime's "inclusiveness." However, three members of the AC were among those arrested during the antislavery demonstration at the capital in February 1998.

In February 1997 the AC was a founding member (along with the Popular Progressive Alliance [APP], the UFD, PAG, and dissidents from the UDP [who referenced themselves as the UDP-2]) of the Front of Opposition Parties (*Front des Partis d'Opposition*—FPO), which described itself as committed to pluralism, a mixed economy, and the eradication of slavery. Although organized, among other things, to present joint opposition candidates, the Front boycotted the December 1997 presidential balloting because the regime denied its demand for creation of an independent electoral commission. The FPO components also boycotted the January 1999 municipal elections, while little reference to the FPO was made during the run-up to the 2001 balloting.

In late 2000 it was reported that Boulkheir and Abdoulaye were among the founding members of a new group, the **Alliance for Justice and Democracy** (*Alliance pour la Justice et la Démocratie*—AJD), which was officially recognized in 2001. (Subsequent leaders were Cisse Amadou CHEIKHOU and Alpha DIALLO [Secretary General].)

The AC became the leading opposition party when it won four seats in the 2001 legislative balloting. However, the government announced that it was withdrawing the AC's legal status, a decision that Boulkheir attributed to the administration's opposition to the AC's insistence on discussing the slavery issue.

The AC was permitted to keep its assembly seats despite a February 2002 Supreme Court decision upholding the group's dissolution. In August Boulkheir's application to register a new party, Convention for Change, was denied on the grounds that it was simply a new guise for the AC.

In October the AC was one of three groups to form the United Opposition Framework. The following March 2003 officials again denied the application for a new party, the Alliance for Democracy in Mauritania, citing its association with the AC, which the new group denied. In August 2004 Boulkheir was elected president of the APP (see below).

Leaders: Massoud Ould BOULKHEIR, Kebe ABDOULAYE, Mohamed Hafed Ould ISMAEL (Secretary General).

Rally of Democratic Forces (*Rassemblement des Forces Démocratiques*—RFD). The RFD was formed in 2001 by former members of the Union of Democratic Forces (*Union des Forces Démocratiques*—UFD), which had been legalized in October 1991 under the leadership of Hadrami Ould Khattry (former president of the FDUFC) and had originally encompassed a number of diverse opposition groups whose desire to oust the Taya regime appeared to be their only common bond. Widely viewed as the strongest opposition formation, the UFD supported Ahmed Ould Daddah, half-brother of former Mauritanian president Moktar Ould Daddah, in the January 1992 presidential election, while spearheading the subsequent legislative boycotts. In May 1992 it was announced that the supporters of Ahmed Ould Daddah had been incorporated into the union, which was reported thereupon to have adopted the name of Union of Democratic Forces–New Era (*Union des Forces Démocratiques–Ere Nouvelle*—UFD-EN). However, news reports often continued to use the original name when referencing the group.

The party remained highly critical of the government; Ahmed Ould Daddah, who was elected UFD president in June 1992, charged that official harassment was impeding "normal" party activity. After Ould Daddah was reconfirmed as leader in early 1993, several prominent members left the party and formed the UDP (see above). More serious were the announced defections in June 1994 of two of the union's most important components, *El-Hor,* which formed the AC (above) and the MDI, which joined the PRDS.

The UFD was one of only two opposition parties (the UDP being the other) to contest the municipal elections in early 1994, gaining a majority in 17 of the country's 208 local councils. It boycotted the 1992 legislative poll but obtained one Senate seat in 1994. The UFD competed unsuccessfully in the first round of 1996 legislative balloting but boycotted the second round, charging that the government had "tampered" with voting lists to excise supporters of the opposition. Although the UFD-EN boycotted the January 1999 municipal balloting, a "Bedredine" tendency of the UFD was reported to have participated in the poll.

In October 2000 the government banned the UFD-EN, accusing the party of inciting violence in connection with pro-Palestinian street demonstrations. Supporters subsequently launched the RFD, which won three assembly seats in the 2001 legislative balloting as well as control of four districts in municipal polls. Ahmed Ould Daddah was unanimously elected as president of the RFD in January 2002.

In April 2002 RFD won one seat in partial Senate elections, the first of Taya's radical opposition ever to do so. A year later, in May 2003, a senior RDF member was arrested in the wake of the U.S.-led attack on Iraq and subsequent crackdown on Mauritanian Islamic groups. That same month the government appointed a close associate of Ahmed Ould Daddah, Abdellahi Ould Souleimana Ould Cheikh Sidya, to a cabinet position in an apparent attempt to gain some RFD support.

In 2004, Ahmed Ould Daddah was charged with helping to finance the opposition Knights of Change (see below), a movement in exile that reportedly advocated the armed overthrow of the Taya government. Daddah was later acquitted.

Leader: Ahmed Ould DADDAH (President and 1992 and 2003 presidential candidate).

Union of Progressive Forces (*Union des Forces Progressives*—UFP). Formed by former members of the UFD, the UFP, whose leadership includes former Marxists, called for dialogue with the PRDS in order to "improve the political atmosphere." The new party won three seats in the 2001 assembly balloting. In 2003 the UFP supported Haidalla for president and joined other opposition groups in complaining of fraud following the Taya victory. The party considered boycotting the 2004 Senate elections but ultimately participated with two nominees. Both lost, one by a narrow margin, to PRDS candidates. In 2005 the party demanded the return of Mauritanian exiles and an end to slavery in the country, precepts it pushed for in the transitional program following the August coup.

Leader: Mohammed Ould MAALOUD.

Popular and Democratic Front (*Front Populaire et Démocratique*—FPD). The FPD, also recently referenced simply as the Popular Front, is led by former minister Mohamed Lemine Chbih Ould Cheikh Malainine, who finished second (with 7 percent of the vote) as an independent candidate in the December 1997 presidential polling. Malainine, a Muslim spiritual leader, was elected chair of the Front at its first congress in April 1998.

The formal relationship between the FPD and the FPO was unclear, but in early 2001 Malainine announced that the FPD would participate in the October legislative balloting, eliciting criticism from the UFD-EN. Despite Malainine's apparently conciliatory gesture toward the government, he was arrested in April on charges of conspiring with Libya to commit acts of terrorism and sentenced to five years in prison. Amnesty International described Malainine as a "prisoner of conscience" and charged that his arrest was merely an attempt to "stifle" the opposition. The sentence was also strongly condemned by other opposition parties. In October 2002 the FPD formed, with the Cavaliers for Change and RFD, the United Opposition Framework (UOF), which sought dialogue on democratic reform between the government and opposition groups.

Leaders: Mohamed Lemine Chbih Ould Cheikh MALAININE (President), Mohamed Fadel SIDIYA (Political Secretary).

El Sawab ("The Correct," "The Right Track"). El Sawab, formed in May 2004 by politicians close to former head of state Mohamed Khouna Ould Haidalla, says it has an "original" society program.

Leader: Cheikh Sidi Ould HANENNA, Mohamed Ould GUELMA.

Popular Progressive Alliance (*Alliance Populaire et Progressive*—APP). A number of APP members were arrested in early 1997 on "conspiracy" charges emanating from the group's allegedly "pro-Libyan" tendencies. The APP boycotted the 2001 elections. On August 1, 2004, Massaoud Ould Boulkheir, the former leader of the dissolved Action for Change, was elected president of the APP, replacing Mohamed El-Hafedh Ould Ismail. That same month the party won two seats in Nouakchott in the partial Senate elections.

Leader: Massaoud Ould BOULKHEIR (2003 presidential candidate).

Party for Democratic Convergence (PCD). Many Mauritanians refer to the PCD as "Haidalla's friends," but the Arabic initials of Ould Haidalla's party, formed in May 2004, reveal another allegiance: they spell El Hamd, literally, "praise to God." The PCD is composed of a wide range of groups who have been persecuted under the Taya regime, including many Black Mauritanians, Islamic radicals, and those who supported the 2003 coup attempt. The vice president of the group is former Nouakchott mayor Mohamed Jemil Ould Mansour, an accused Islamic radical who was arrested in 2003 but escaped from prison during the coup attempt and fled to Belgium. There Mansour helped found the **Mauritanian Forum for Reform and Democracy**, along with other political exiles from the 2003 coup. Upon returning to Mauritania, Mansour was arrested again and then released. In 2005 the ruling junta refused to recognize the party because it contended the party advocated the monopoly of Islam in politics.

Leader: Mohamed Khouna Ould HAIDALLA.

Avant-Garde Party (*Parti Avant-Garde—* PAG). The Baathist PAG was one of the minor parties legalized prior to the 1992 elections; however, it won no seats in the National Assembly poll and was equally unsuccessful in the Senate balloting, for which it was the only party other than the PRDS to present candidates. Apparently as a "reward" for participating, PAG leader Kattry Ould Taleb Jiddou was named secretary of state for literacy and traditional education in the cabinet announced in April; however, he was dismissed from the position in a January 1994 reshuffle. Jiddou and former PAG secretary general Abdoulaye Ould HAMED were among those arrested in November 1995 for allegedly forming a "secret organization" in support of Iraqi interests; all were acquitted in January 1996.

The PAG, also referenced as the National Vanguard Party (*al-Talia al-Watania*), was banned in late 1999 after Mauritania severed ties with Iraq. The Mauritanian government alleged that Iraq had "infiltrated" the party with plans to foment unrest within Mauritania.

Leaders: Kattry Ould Taleb JIDDOU, Mohamed ENAHOUI (Secretary General).

National Union for Democracy and Development (*Union Nationale pour la Démocratie et le Développement—*UNDD). Formed by Senator Tidjane Koita after he left the AC in 1997, the UNDD has been described as the "moderate opposition" and a proponent of dialogue between the PRDS and the more strident antiregime groups. None of the UNDD's candidates were successful in the 2001 assembly balloting.

Leader: Tidjane KOITA.

Mauritanian Renewal Party (*Parti Mauritanien pour le Renouvellement—*PMR). Shortly after legalization of the PMR, also referenced as the Party for Renewal and Concord, in mid-September 1991, its leaders charged that inappropriate links had been formed between the PRDS and long-standing national and municipal leaders, placing other groups at a disadvantage in forthcoming elections. The PMR leader finished third in the 1997 presidential balloting with less than 1 percent of the vote. (In April 2001 the government announced the recognition of a new party also known as the Mauritanian Renewal Party, led by Atiq OULD ATTIA.)

Leader: Moulaye al-Hassan OULD JEYDID (1997 and 2003 presidential candidate).

Socialist and Democratic Popular Union (*Union Populaire Socialiste et Démocratique—* UPSD). A conservative Moorish group recognized in late September 1991, the UPSD is also identified as the Social and Popular Democratic Union (*Union Démocratique Sociale et Populaire—* UDSP). It is led by Mohamed Mahmoud Ould Mah, a former mayor of Nouakchott, who at the time of his election to that post in 1986 was a member of the UND. Ould Mah was accorded a presidential vote share of 1.36 percent in January 1992 and 0.7 percent in December 1997.

Leader: Mohamed Mahmoud OULD MAH (1992 and 1997 presidential candidate).

National Pact (*Pacte National—*PN). Organized in mid-1992, the PN is led by a former PRDS member.

Leader: Mohamed Abdallah OULD KHARCY.

Democratic Center Party (*Parti du Centre Démocratique—*PCD). The PCD, also referenced as the Mauritanian Party of the Democratic Center (PCDM), supported Ahmed Ould Daddah in the January 1992 presidential balloting after its own leader withdrew from the race.

Leader: Benba Ould Sidi BADI.

Democratic Justice Party (*Parti pour la Justice Démocratique—*PJD). Legalized in late September 1991, the PJD supported Ahmed Ould Daddah in the 1992 presidential election.

Leader: Mohamed Abdallahi Ould El BANE.

Additional minor parties include the **Democratic and Social Union** (*Union Démocratique et Sociale—*UDS); the **National Party for Unity and Democracy** (*Parti National pour l'Unité et la Démocratie—*PNUD); and the **Party for Liberty, Equality, and Justice** (*Parti pour la Liberté, l'Egalité, et la Justice*). Several new parties were recognized in April 2001, including the **Mauritanian Liberal Democrats,** led by Mustapha

OULD LEMBRABET; the **Third Generation,** led by Lebat OULD JEH; the **Mauritanian Labor Party,** led by Mohamed Hafid OULD DENNA; and the **Democratic Alliance,** led by Mohamed Ould Taleb OTHMAN. The **National Renaissance Party** (*Parti de la Renaissance Nationale*— PRN) was established in mid-2001 under the leadership of Mohamed Ould Abdellaki Ould EYYE.

Other Groups

Patriotic Alliance (aka Democratic Alliance). Several Mauritanian political groups created the Patriotic Alliance on July 10, 2004. It is allegedly affiliated with Haidalla and those responsible for the failed 2003 coup.

The Salafi Group for Call and Combat (GSPC). This group, also referenced as the Salafist Group for Preaching and Combat, has Algerian roots but has been active in Mauritania, most notably in the attacks on a military outpost in June 2005. The GPSC is linked to al-Qaida according to the U.S. State Department.
Leader: Mokhtar BELMOKHTAR.

Umma. An Islamic fundamentalist organization, *Umma* (Nation) was formed in 1991 but was denied legal party status because of the constitutional prohibition against parties based on religion. However, it remained an important political grouping, particularly in light of its reported ties to the Islamic Salvation Front of neighboring Algeria, which achieved startling electoral success in late 1991. *Umma's* leader Cheikh Ould Sidi Yayia was among some 60 people detained briefly by security forces in September 1994 during a crackdown on "clandestine" Islamic organizations.
Leader: Cheikh Ould Sidi YAYIA.

Rally for the Rebirth of Black Africans (*Rassemblement pour la Renaissance des Négres-Africans de la Mauritanie*—RENAM). RENAM was established in 1989 in response to the ethnic violence along the border with Senegal, which the Mauritanian government was accused of using as an excuse to oppress black inhabitants. The mem-

bership of RENAM reportedly included exiles in Europe as well as secession-minded guerrillas in southern Mauritania.
Leader: Abdoulaye SOUMARE.

United Front for Armed Resistance in Mauritania (*Front Uni pour la Résistance Armée en Mauritanie*—FURAM). Also a black resistance group, FURAM was launched in Dakar in May 1990. In April 1991 its leaders described the political liberalization measures proposed by President Taya as a last-ditch effort by a "racist" regime to save itself and called for a transitional government pending "true national renewal."

African Liberation Forces of Mauritania (*Forces de Libération Africaine de Mauritanie*—FLAM). Organized in 1983 in opposition to what were perceived as repressive policies toward blacks, FLAM was believed responsible for an "Oppressed Black" manifesto that in 1986 was widely distributed within Mauritania and at the nonaligned summit in Zimbabwe. Based partly in Dakar, Senegal, the group also condemned reprisals against blacks by the Taya regime following an alleged coup attempt in 1987. Many FLAM supporters were reported to be among those who fled or were expelled to Senegal in 1989. Subsequently engaged in guerrilla activity, FLAM leaders announced in July 1991 that they were suspending "armed struggle" in response to the government's general amnesty and promulgation of a new Mauritanian constitution. FLAM endorsed Ahmed Ould Daddah in the January 1992 presidential election, after which it renewed its antigovernment military campaign near the Senegalese border. Leaders of the group stated in early 1995 that they were neither secessionists nor terrorists, reiterating their support for the establishment of a federal system that would ensure an appropriate level of black representation in government while protecting the rights of blacks throughout Mauritanian society. In a statement issued from Senegal, the FLAM in 1997 criticized a visit by French president Chirac to Mauritania on the ground that the trip was showing support for a "racist regime." In early 2001 the FLAM called upon the international community to exert pressure on the Mauritanian government to address the issue of black refugees remaining in Senegal and Mali as the result of the 1989 exodus. The group called for the boycott of elections scheduled by the transitional government for 2006 and 2007.

Leader: Saba THIAM (President).

Rally of Democratic Patriots (*Rassemblement des Patriotes Démocratiques*—RPD). Launched in Dakar, Senegal, in August 2000 by former members of the FLAM and the UFD, the RPD called for the return of black Mauritanians from Senegal to an "equal, united Mauritania."

Knights of Change. In 2006 the military organization known as the Knights of Change became a political party, referenced as the Mauritanian Party for Unity and Change (*Umat*). The Knights had staged several failed coup attempts against President Taya, and one of the leaders of the military wing, Maj. Saleh Ould Hanena, received a life sentence in February 2005 but was released by the new junta in September 2005.

Leader: Maj. Saleh Ould HANENA.

In May 1984 an **Organization of Mauritanian Nationalists** (*Organisation des Nationalistes Mauritaniens*—ONM) was formed in Dakar, Senegal, by Khadri OULD DIE, a former military officer, while another antiregime formation, the multiracial **Resistance Front for Unity, Independence, and Democracy in Mauritania** (*Front Résistance de l'Unité, Indépendance et Démocratie en Mauritanie*—Fruidem), was proclaimed in Paris in September 1989.

In 1994 security forces accused a number of previously unknown fundamentalist organizations, including **Call to Islam** and the **Mauritanian Islamic Movement** (*Hasim*) of conspiring to overthrow the government. The regime's crackdown on Islamic militants also included the dissolution of the **Cultural and Islamic Association of Mauritania,** which had wielded significant influence in government circles since its establishment in 1980. The government alleged that the association had been involved in the formation of *Hasim*.

In 2005, legal status was denied the **Democratic Forum Party**, led by Cheikh Ould Horma Ould BEBANA, after the party reportedly claimed to be the country's Islamic authority. Also in 2005, Mohamed Salek Ould DIDAH announced the formation of a new party referenced as the **Social Democratic Party** (SDP), and El Moustapha Ould OBEIDRAHMANE, who held several ministerial posts in the Taya regime, announced a new, as yet unnamed, party in August.

Legislature

The 1991 constitution provides for a bicameral legislature consisting of an indirectly chosen Senate and a popularly elected National Assembly. The parliament was dissolved by the Military Council for Justice and Democracy following the August 3, 2005, coup.

Senate (*Majlis al-Shuyukh*). The Senate is renewed by thirds every two years for six-year terms, with 53 of its 56 members selected by the country's mayors and municipal councilors and three by Mauritanians abroad. In the inaugural domestic balloting of April 3 and 10, 1992, the Democratic and Social Republican Party (PRDS) reportedly obtained 36 seats, whereas 17 were won by independents. The PRDS has maintained its large Senate majority, with a small handful of seats going to other groups. In the balloting of April 11, 2002, the PRDS won 16 of the 18 seats up for election, and the Rally of Democratic Forces won 1; the final seat required a runoff. After contesting the results of the 2003 elections, some opposition groups were wary of participating in the partial Senate elections of April 9 and 16, 2004, and considered a boycott. However, ultimately nine parties decided to participate. The PRDS won 15 seats, with 2 going to the Progressive Alliance (APP) and 1 to the Rally for Democracy and Unity (RDU).

President: Dieng Boubou FARBA.

National Assembly (*Majlis al-Watani*). The 81 deputies to the lower house are elected by direct universal suffrage, nominally for five-year terms. Theretofore, all deputies were elected on a

Cabinet

As of June 1, 2006

Prime Minister	Sidi Mohamed Ould Boubacar

Ministers

Civil Service and Labor	Mohamed Ould Ahmed Ould Jakkou
Communication	Cheikh Ould Ebbe
Culture, Youth, and Sport	Mehla Mint Ahmed [f]
Economic Affairs and Development	Hammada Ould Abed
Equipment and Transportation	Ba Ibrahima Demba
Finance	Abdellahi Ould Cheikh Sidiya
Fisheries and Maritime Affairs	Sidi Mohamed Ould Sidina
Foreign Affairs and Cooperation	Ahmed Ould Sid Ahmed
Health and Social Affairs	Qsaadna Ould Bahaida
Higher Education and Scientific Research	Naji Ould Mohamed Mahmoud
Interior, Post, and Telecommunications	Mohamed Ahmed Ould Mohamed Lemine
Justice	Maafoudh Ould Bettah
Literacy, Islamic Orientation, and Original Education	Yahya Ould Sid El Moustaph
Mines and Industry	Mohamed Ould Ismail Ould Abidna
Petroleum and Energy	Mohamed Ali Ould Sidi Mohamed
Primary and Secondary Education	Cheikh Ould Sid Ahmed
Rural Development and Environment	Gandega Silly
Trade, Handicrafts, and Tourism	Ba Abderrahmane
Water	Ali Ould Ahmadou

Secretaries of State

Civil Registry	Abdi Ould Horma
Maghreb Arab Union	Bissimillah Elih Ould Ahmed
New Technologies (Prime Minister's Office)	Manyana Sow Deina [f]
Secretary General of the Government	Ba Saidou Moussa
Women's Affairs	Nebghouha Mint Tlamid [f]

[f] = female

majoritarian basis. However, some proportional voting was introduced for the 2001 elections. In the most recent balloting of October 19 and 26, 2001, the Democratic and Social Republican Party won 64 seats; Action for Change, 4; the Rally for Democracy and Unity, 3; the Union for Democracy and Progress, 3; the Rally of Democratic Forces, 3; the Union of the Progressive Forces, 3; and the Popular and Democratic Front, 1.

Speaker: Rachid Ould SALEH.

Communications

All news media were owned and operated by the government until mid-1991 when legislation recognizing the principle of freedom of the press was passed in conjunction with the country's new constitution. However, the new law precluded the news media from "encouraging intolerance between tribes or races," and the government reportedly banned the September 1991 issue of the

Mauritanie Demain because the monthly magazine had reported on the alleged torture of black political detainees. In the weeks leading up to the 2003 presidential elections, authorities shut down four weekly newspapers. In March 2005 a freelance journalist was charged with "damaging the public image" of Mauritania and imprisoned after he interviewed a woman said to be a runaway slave, prompting protests from international organizations devoted to protecting the rights of journalists.

Press

The following are published in Nouakchott: *Ach Chaab,* government daily in Arabic and French; *Mauritanie Nouvelle,* independent in French; *La Calame,* independent weekly in French; *La Tribune,* independent weekly in French; *Eveil-Hebdo,* independent weekly in French; and *Journal Officiel,* government semimonthly in French.

News Agencies

The government facility is *Agence Mauritanienne de l'Information* (AMI); *Agence France-Presse* also maintains an office in Nouakchott.

Broadcasting and Computing

The state-owned *Office de Radiodiffusion et Télévision de Mauritanie* (ORTM) broadcasts to radio receivers in Arabic, French, and indigenous tribal languages, as well as to about 323,000 television sets in Arabic and French. There were some 30,000 personal computers serving 120,000 Internet users in 2003.

Intergovernmental Representation

Ambassador to the U.S.
Tijani Ould KERIM

U.S. Ambassador to Mauritania
Joseph LeBARON

Permanent Representative to the UN
Mohamed Ould TOLBA

IGO Memberships (Non–United Nations)
AfDB, AU, AFESD, AMF, AMU, BADEA, CAEU, CILSS, IDB, Interpol, IOM, LAS, NAM, OIC, OIF, WCO, WTO

MAURITIUS

REPUBLIC OF MAURITIUS

The Country

The island of Mauritius, once known as Ile de France, is situated 500 miles east of Madagascar, in the southwestern Indian Ocean; Rodrigues Island, the Agalega Islands, and the Cardagos Carajos Shoals (St. Brandon Islands) also are national territory. (Mauritius also claims Diego Garcia and other islands in the Chagos Archipelago, currently controlled by the United Kingdom as part of the British Indian Ocean Territory (see Foreign relations, below, for details). The diversity of contemporary Mauritian society is a reflection of its history as a colonial sugar plantation. African slave laborers were imported initially, and they were followed by the migration of Indians (who now constitute two-thirds of the population), Chinese, French, and English. Religious affiliations include Hinduism, to which 52 percent of the population adheres; Christianity (predominantly Roman Catholicism), 28 percent; and Islam, 17 percent. Women are significantly engaged in subsistence agriculture, although they comprise only 32 percent of the paid labor force. Four women served in the National Assembly and two in the cabinet as of early 2005.

Sugar production, to which over 90 percent of the arable land was devoted in the 1960s, traditionally accounted for an overwhelming proportion of the country's export earnings. However, rapidly falling prices after 1975 created severe economic difficulties that were partly overcome by expanded activity in the country's export processing zone (EPZ), by means of which investors were given tax and other incentives to set up ventures aimed at production for export. Excellent sugar harvests in the 1980s, expanded tourist activity, and increased exports of manufactured goods, coupled in 1989 with the opening of a local stock exchange and the authorization of offshore banking activity, subsequently yielded substantial economic growth. Most sales in sugar and other commodities are to the European Union (EU) under trade provisions of the Lomé Convention. However, South Africa has recently begun to vie with France as the leading supplier of goods to Mauritius, and economic ties have been expanded with a number of other southern African nations.

The overall strong economic performance in the 1990s led some experts to reference a "Mauritian miracle" and to describe the country as a "case study" in the successful management of a

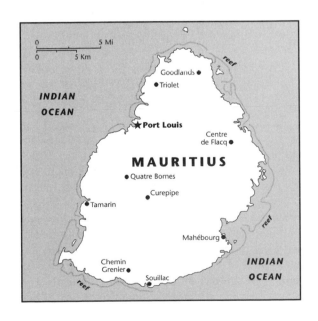

developing country that pursued "investor-friendly" policies. GDP growth averaged 5.7 annually from 1996–1999, although it measured only about 3 percent in 1999 because of the effects of a severe drought on agricultural production. Government initiatives focused on promoting offshore banking, information technology, garment manufacturing, and tourism (about 500,000 visitors annually). Job creation programs received top priority because unemployment grew from a negligible 1.5 percent in 1995 to a disturbing 8 percent in early 2001. The job situation may have contributed to the unrest at Port Louis in February 1999 (see Current issues, below); skeptics claimed that the wealthiest segment of the population had benefited disproportionately from recent growth and that significant tension continued to exist between the underprivileged Creole population and the Hindu majority.

Success in the sugar and tourism industries led to economic growth of 4.5 percent in 2003–2004. In its 2004 report the International Monetary Fund (IMF) described the country's social and economic achievements since independence as "impressive." However, unemployment reached 10.2 percent, and ongoing budget deficits contributed to debt. Moreover, threats to the sugar and textile industries (see Current issues, below) reportedly troubled voters at the July 2005 legislative balloting.

Government and Politics

Political Background

Because of its location, Mauritius had strategic importance during the age of European exploration and expansion, and the Dutch, French, and English successively occupied the island. France ruled Mauritius from 1710 to 1810, when Britain assumed control to protect its shipping during the Napoleonic wars. Political evolution began as early as 1831 under a constitution that provided for a Council of Government, but the franchise was largely restricted until after World War II. The postwar era also witnessed the introduction of po-litical parties and increased participation in local government.

An election under a system of internal parliamentary democracy initiated in 1967 revealed a majority preference for full independence, which was granted by Britain on March 12, 1968, with Sir Seewoosagur RAMGOOLAM of the Independence Party (IP) as prime minister. A state of emergency, occasioned by an outbreak of severe communal strife between Muslims and Creoles, was lifted in 1970, although new disorder brought its reimposition from December 1971 to March 1978.

Under constitutional arrangements agreed upon in 1969, the mandate of the existing Legislative Assembly was extended by four years. At the election of December 20, 1976, the radical Mauritian Militant Movement (*Mouvement Militant Mauricien*—MMM), led by Anerood JUGNAUTH and Paul BÉRENGER, won a plurality of legislative seats, but the IP and the Mauritian Social Democratic Party (*Parti Mauricien Social-Démocrate*—PMSD) formed a coalition that retained Prime Minister Ramgoolam in office with a slim majority. At the country's second postindependence balloting on June 11, 1982, the incumbent parties lost all of their directly elective seats, Jugnauth proceeding to form an MMM-dominated government on June 15.

In the wake of a government crisis in March 1983, which yielded the resignation of 12 ministers, including Bérenger, and the repudiation of the prime minister by his own party, Jugnauth and his supporters regrouped as the Mauritian Socialist Movement (*Mouvement Socialiste Mauricien*—MSM) and, in alliance with Ramgoolam's Mauritius Labour Party (MLP) wing of the IP and the PMSD, won a decisive legislative majority in a new election held August 21.

In February 1984 Ramgoolam's successor as MLP leader, Sir Satcam BOOLELL, was relieved of his post as minister of economic planning, whereupon the MLP voted to terminate its support of the MSM. However, 11 Labour deputies, under the leadership of Beergoonath GHURBURRUN,

Political Status: Constitutional monarchy under multiparty parliamentary system established upon independence within the Commonwealth on March 12, 1968; became a republic on March 12, 1992.

Area: 790 sq. mi. (2,045 sq. km.).

Population: 1,179,137 (2000C); 1,241,000 (2005E).

Major Urban Centers (2005E): PORT LOUIS (151,000), Beau Bassin/Rose Hill (109,000), Vacoas-Phoenix (107,000), Curepipe (84,000), Quatre Bornes (81,000).

Official Language: English (French is also used, while Creole is the lingua franca, and Hindi the most widely spoken).

Monetary Unit: Mauritian Rupee (official rate July 1, 2006: 30.81 rupees = $1US).

President: Sir Anerood JUGNAUTH (Mauritian Socialist Movement—MSM); elected by the National Assembly on October 7, 2003, to complete the five-year term (which began on February 25, 2002) of Karl Auguste OFFMANN (Mauritian Socialist Movement), who had resigned on September 30, 2003, apparently as part of the power-sharing agreement negotiated in 2002 by the MSM and the Mauritian Militant Movement (MMM). (Vice President Raouf Bundhun served as acting president between Offmann's resignation and Jugnauth's inauguration.)

Vice President: Raouf BUNDHUN (nonparty); elected by the National Assembly on February 25, 2002, for a term concurrent with that of the president.

Prime Minister: Navin RAMGOOLAM (Mauritian Labor Party); named prime minister on July 5, 2005, in succession to Paul Raymond BÉRENGER (Mauritian Militant Movement) following legislative election of July 3.

refused to follow Boolell into opposition and remained in the government alliance (initially as the Mauritian Workers' Movement—MWM and later as the Mauritian Labour Rally—RTM).

At municipal council balloting on December 8, 1985, the opposition MMM won 57.2 percent of the vote, decisively defeating the coalition parties, who captured only 36.8 percent, while the MLP was a distant third with 5.4 percent. Although insisting that the MMM victory represented a rejection of Jugnauth's policies, Bérenger did not immediately call for the government to resign. However, such an appeal was made in the wake of a major scandal at the end of the month, which stemmed from the arrest on drug charges of four coalition members at Amsterdam's Schipol Airport. Subsequently, the MLP agreed to reconcile with the MSM, and Boolell was awarded three portfolios and the post of second deputy prime minister in a cabinet reorganization August 8, 1986.

At an early election on August 30, 1987, called largely because of favorable economic conditions, a reconstituted Jugnauth coalition consisting of the MSM, the MLP, the RTM (subsequently absorbed by the MSM), the PMSD, and the Rodriguan People's Organization (*Organisation du Peuple Rodriguais*—OPR) retained power by capturing 41 of 62 elective legislative seats. In August 1988, however, the PMSD, whose leader, Sir Gaëtan DUVAL, had frequently been at odds with the coalition mainstream in domestic and foreign policy, withdrew from the government, forcing Jugnauth to form a new cabinet whose Assembly support had fallen to a majority of 10. Two months later the largely urban-based coalition suspended participation in municipal balloting to avoid the embarrassment of a major defeat, with the MMM (allied with several small parties) winning all of the seats in a two-way contest with the PMSD.

In an effort to strengthen his parliamentary position, Jugnauth in July 1990 concluded an electoral pact with the opposition MMM. However, the move angered a number of his fellow MSM ministers, as well as MLP leader Boolell. In August, after the government narrowly failed to secure the 75 percent approval necessary to make the country a republic within the Commonwealth, Jugnauth dismissed the dissident ministers and announced that he would continue as head of a minority administration with the parliamentary support of the MMM. A month later the MMM formally joined the government, with its president, Dr. Prem NABABSINGH, named deputy prime minister.

At an early election on September 15, 1991, the governing alliance won 59 of 62 legislative seats, far in excess of the 75 percent required to implement a change to republican status, which was approved by the Legislative Assembly on December 10, with effect from March 12, 1992. By agreement between the coalition's leading parties, Sir Veerasamy RINGADOO, who had been appointed governor general in January 1986, was designated nonexecutive president of the new republic for three months; he was succeeded on June 30 by the MMM's Cassam UTEEM.

In a cabinet reshuffle on August 18, 1993, Bérenger, who had been openly critical of government policies, was ousted as foreign minister. Two months later he was removed as MMM secretary general by the party's Political Bureau, which named Jean-Claude DE L'ESTRAC as his successor. However, the action was reversed on October 23 by the MMM Central Committee, which proceeded to name a new, pro-Bérenger party leadership. On November 16 Bérenger crossed the aisle to sit with the opposition, although he formally rejected the opposition leadership on the ground that he had no electoral mandate for such a role. A year later Bérenger and De L'Estrac resigned as MPs; only the former regained his seat at by-elections in January 1995.

After the MLP had in January 1995 rebuffed Prime Minister Jugnauth's offer of power sharing, the PMSD agreed in early February to join the coalition, which then encompassed the MSM, MTD, OPR, and the Mauritian Militant Renaissance, despite opposition from a number of leading PMSD members, with a cabinet realignment following on February 13. An early election was then called after Jugnauth had failed to secure passage of a constitutional amendment to introduce Asian languages (Hindi, Urdu, Tamil, Marathi, Telegu, Chinese, and Arabic) into the educational curriculum. The Creole opposition strongly opposed the amendment, which also provoked the withdrawal not only of the recently appointed PMSD members but also of the OPR representative, thus effectively shrinking the government coalition.

In an outcome not dissimilar to Prime Minister Jugnauth's 1982 electoral victory, an opposition MLP-MMM alliance swept the legislative balloting of December 20, 1995, with the MLP's Dr. Navin RAMGOOLAM, son of former prime minister Sir Seewoosagur Ramgoolam, forming a new government on December 31. It consisted of 13 MLP ministers, 9 MMM ministers (including Bérenger as deputy prime minister and foreign minister), and 1 OPR representative at the junior ministerial level. However, Bérenger was dismissed from the cabinet on June 20, 1997, and most of the other MMM ministers resigned their posts in protest. After reportedly failing to convince the PMSD to participate in the government, Ramgoolam on July 2 formed a new cabinet, which included only MLP ministers except for 1 OPR member and 1 independent (Dr. Ahmed Rashid BEEBEEJAUN, who had recently left the MMM rather than give up his portfolio for land transport, shipping, and public safety). Meanwhile, President Uteem was reappointed to another term, although his relationship with the MMM (which had promoted his initial appointment) remained unclear. Ramgoolam reshuffled his cabinet on October 25, 1998, reportedly to enhance the role of young MLP legislators in the government after an alliance formed between Bérenger's MMM and Jugnauth's MSM. The prime minister also attempted to shore up his control by including the recently formed Xavier Duval Mauritian Party (PMXD) in a cabinet reshuffle on September 26, 1999. However, in the legislative balloting on September 11, 2000, the MSM-MMM electoral coalition soundly trounced the MLP-PMXD alliance, securing 54 of the 62 elected seats. Consequently, Jugnauth returned as prime minister on September 17 to lead with Bérenger a MSM-MMM coalition government which required Jugnauth to resign after three years and Bérenger to assume the premiership.

On February 15, 2002, President Uteem resigned after he refused to approve an antiterrorism law recently passed by the National Assembly.

(Uteem argued that the new legislation could undermine national sovereignty in the name of US security concerns.) He was replaced by Vice President Andigi Verriah Chettiar, who resigned on February 18 after he also refused to sign the bill into law. In accordance with the constitution, Chief Justice Arriranga PILLAY replaced Chettiar as the interim president on February 18. (Pillay subsequently signed the controversial legislation.) On February 25 the National Assembly elected Karl Auguste OFFMANN and Raouf BUNDHUN as the president and vice president, respectively.

On September 29, 2002, the OPR won 10 of 18 seats in the new Rodrigues Regional Assembly, while the Rodrigues Movement won the remaining 8 seats.

Although many observers doubted the MSM-MMM "marriage" of 2000 would survive, Bérenger assumed the premiership on October 1, 2003, and Jugnauth took the largely ceremonial presidency on October 7. The most noteworthy of Bérenger's subsequent cabinet changes was the appointment of Pravind Kumar JUGNAUTH (the son of Anerood Jugnauth) as deputy prime minister and finance minister.

At balloting for 62 elected members of the National Assembly on July 3, 2005, the Social Alliance (led by the MLP) won 38 seats, while the alliance of the MSM and the MMM won 22 and the OPR won 2. Prime Minister Bérenger resigned on July 5 and was succeeded the same day by MLP leader Navin Ramgoolam, who formed a new cabinet comprising (for the most part) the parties that had formed the Social Alliance.

Constitution and Government

The Mauritius Independence Order of 1968, as amended the following year by the Constitution of Mauritius (Amendment) Act, provided for a unicameral system of parliamentary government with executive authority exercised by a prime minister appointed by the governor general (as the representative of the Crown) from among the majority members of the Legislative Assembly. In December 1991 the assembly approved a change to republican status as of March 12, 1992, with an essentially titular president, appointed by the assembly to a five-year term, replacing the Queen as head of state. The change also included creation of an indirectly elective vice presidency. The legislature (known under the present basic law as the National Assembly) includes a speaker, 60 representatives directly elected from 3-member districts on the main island, plus 2 from Rodrigues, and the attorney general, if not an elected member. In addition, up to 8 "best loser" seats may be awarded on the basis of party or ethnic underrepresentation as indicated by shares of total vote and total population, respectively. Judicial authority, based on both French and British precedents, is exercised by a Supreme Court, 4 of whose 5 judges (excluding the chief justice) preside additionally in Appeal, Intermediate, District, and Industrial court proceedings. There are also inferior courts and a Court of Assizes. In conformity with the practice of a number of other small republican members of the Commonwealth, final appeal continues to be to the Judicial Committee of the Privy Council at London.

Nine districts constitute the principal administrative divisions, with separate administrative structures governing the Mauritian dependencies: The Agalega and Cargados Carajos islands are ruled directly from Port Louis, while Rodrigues Island has a central government under a resident commissioner. On the main island, municipal and town councils are elected in urban areas and district and village councils in rural areas.

In 1991 a Rodrigues Local Council, comprising 21 members appointed by the Minister for Rodriguan Affairs, was established to exercise a degree of autonomy on Rodrigues. However, its mandate expired in 1996 amid political infighting concerning the issue. Subsequently, in November 2001, the National Assembly authorized creation of an elected Rodrigues Regional Assembly (see Legislature, below). In addition to enjoying the same authority as that of local bodies on the main island, the new Regional Assembly was empowered to propose bills to the National Assembly and to oversee development projects and otherwise administer internal initiatives.

Foreign Relations

Mauritius maintains diplomatic relations with most major foreign governments. One principal external issue has been the status of Diego Garcia Island, which was considered a Mauritian dependency until 1965, when London transferred administration of the Chagos Archipelago to the British Indian Ocean Territory (BIOT). The following year, Britain concluded an agreement with the United States whereby the latter obtained use of the island for 50 years. Following independence in 1968 Mauritius pressed its claim to Diego Garcia, while international attention was drawn to the issue in 1980 when Washington announced that it intended to make the island the chief U.S. naval and air base in the Indian Ocean. In July the Organization of African Unity unanimously backed Port Louis's claim, but efforts by Prime Minister Ramgoolam to garner support from the UK government were rebuffed.

In July 1982 Britain agreed to pay $4 million in compensation for its 1965–1973 relocation of families from the Chagos islands to Mauritius. In accepting the payment, Port Louis reversed its position in regard to Diego Garcia and insisted that existence of the U.S. base violated a 1967 commitment by the United Kingdom (denied by London) that the island would not be used for military purposes. The Diego Garcia issue resurfaced in 1989 when U.S.-Soviet détente seemed to reduce the strategic significance of the base and encourage those who supported regional demilitarization. In September a British Foreign and Commonwealth Office official stated that London did not "look unfavorably" on the Mauritian claim. In October Mauritius charged that the accidental bombing of the island by a U.S. fighter plane had endangered nearby civilian aircraft. The installation proved to be of major value to U.S. forces during the Gulf war of early 1991, and the British position thereafter appeared to harden, London's high commissioner to Port Louis declaring in mid-November that the question of British sovereignty over the Chagos archipelago was "not negotiable." The issue surfaced again in 1996 when the Ramgoolam government demanded a share of

the proceeds from fishing permits issued by the BIOT, while stressing that any such income should not be defined as rent for, and thus acceptance of, the U.S. naval base on the BIOT island of Diego Garcia. In October 2000 the British High Court ruled that some 2,000 inhabitants of Diego Garcia and other islands of the Chagos Archipelago had been "unlawfully removed" to Mauritius prior to independence, possibly opening the way for the return of Chagossians to all of the islands in question except, notably, Diego Garcia. (The Creole-speaking Chagossians have not assimilated well into mainstream Mauritian society; many of them live in poverty.) Suits have been filed for substantial UK and U.S. financial support for the proposed return, while Mauritius has continued to press its claim to sovereignty over the islands. In 2004 lawyers representing the Chagossians petitioned Queen Elizabeth to permit the Chagossians to return to the Chagos Archipelago and to compensate the Chagossians further for the UK's previous "unlawful actions." The petition also requested that the UK rebuild the infrastructure on the islands to permit the resumption of fishing and agriculture. Meanwhile, analysts suggested that Mauritius might pursue its claim over the islands through the International Court of Justice.

Many years earlier, in June 1980, the Ramgoolam government had announced that it was amending the country's constitution to encompass the French-held island of Tromelin, located some 350 miles to the north of Mauritius, thus reaffirming a claim that Paris had formally rejected in 1976. In December 1989 the Jugnauth administration announced that it would seek a ruling on Tromelin from the General Assembly's Committee on Decolonization. Six months later French President Mitterrand, during a tour of the Indian Ocean region, agreed to Franco-Mauritian discussions on the future of the island, although its status remained unchanged as of early 2005.

Mauritius is a member of the Indian Ocean Commission (IOC). In February 1995 it hosted a ministerial meeting to form a regional economic bloc, the Indian Ocean Rim Association for Regional Cooperation (IOR-ARC), which first met in Mauritius in March 1997. In August 1995 Mauritius became a member of the Southern African Development Community (SADC). It is also a member of the Common Market for Eastern and Southern Africa (Comesa). Mauritius is pushing for trade expansion through the IOR-ARC because it finds the IOC and Comesa ineffective.

Current Issues

The long-disenfranchised Creole population rioted in February 1999 after a popular singer died in police custody. Underlying the violence was friction between Creoles, the mixed-blood descendants of African slaves who constitute about 30 percent of the population, and Hindus, the dominant force in government and the extended public sector. The Ramgoolam administration was also buffeted by the resignation of several top officials, who were tainted by scandal, as well as by drought-induced economic decline. Consequently, in August the prime minister felt compelled to dissolve the National Assembly and call for new elections in September, four months early. The MSM and MMM quickly concluded an unbeatable electoral alliance, based on an agreement that former prime minister Jugnauth would reassume the reins of government for three years, with Bérenger serving as prime minister the following two years. The new administration appeared to have the support of the private sector, notably the sugar companies and the Catholic Church. Jugnauth declared the economy and internal security to be his top priorities.

In October 2003 Bérenger, a Creole, became the nation's first non-Hindu prime minister. He pledged to make economic progress the top priority of his administration, but rising unemployment and inflation subsequently appeared to erode support for the MSM-MMM alliance. Further complicating matters for the government were setbacks in the sugar industry (the EU announced sharp cutbacks in the prices it would pay for foreign sugar) and the textile sector (Chinese factories had become intense competitors). As a result, the MLP-led Social Alliance of former prime minister Navin Ramgoolam re-

gained the confidence of its old constituencies with its populist platform and won the July 2005 legislative poll. However, Ramgoolam's new government quickly faced daunting challenges, as a steep rise in oil prices combined with ongoing problems in the sugar and textile industries to buffet the country in 2006 with what commentators regularly referred to as an "economic triple shock."

Political Parties

A large number of political parties have contested recent Mauritian elections (more than 40, presenting 535 office seekers in 2000); few, however, have run candidates in most constituencies, and only a very limited number have secured parliamentary representation. Because most of the groups are leftist in orientation, ideological differences tend to be blurred, with recurrent cleavages based largely on pragmatic considerations.

Government and Government-Supportive Parties

Mauritius Labour Party (MLP). A Hindu-based party, the MLP (also referenced as the Workers' Party [*Parti des Travailleurs*—PTr]), under the leadership of Seewoosagur Ramgoolam, joined the country's other leading Indian group, the Muslim Action Committee (CAM), in forming the Independence Party (IP) prior to the 1976 election. Collectively, the MLP and the CAM won an overwhelming majority of 47 legislative seats at the 1967 preindependence balloting, whereas the IP retained only 28 in 1976 and lost all but 2 in 1982 (both awarded to the MLP on a "best loser" basis). A condition of the MLP joining the 1983 government alliance was said to be the designation of Ramgoolam as president upon the country's becoming a republic; following failure of a republic bill in December 1983, the longtime MLP leader was named governor general.

In February 1984, after MLP leader Sir Satcam Boolell was relieved of his post as minister of planning and economic development, the party went into opposition. It reentered the government in August 1986, with Boolell as second deputy prime minister. In September 1990 the MLP again moved into opposition, Seewoosagur Ramgoolam's son, Navin, succeeding Boolell as party leader and assuming the post of leader of the opposition. On the basis of a preelectoral accord with the MMM's Paul Bérenger, the younger Ramgoolam became prime minister following the MLP-MMM victory in December 1995. The MLP-MMM coalition dissolved in mid-1997 with Ramgoolam subsequently remaining the head of an all-MLP (with the exception of one OPR minister) cabinet. At that point the MLP was described as holding a majority of 35–37 seats in the assembly. With the MMM aligning with the MSM for the September 2000 assembly balloting, the MLP was left with only the PMXD and several small parties as electoral partners, their coalition securing 36.6 percent of the vote but only 6 of the 62 elected seats.

For the 2005 assembly elections, the MLP led a Social Alliance (Alliance Social) that included the new MSD, the PMXD, the MR, and the MMSN.

Leaders: Dr. Navin RAMGOOLAM (Prime Minister and Leader of the Party), Jean François CHAUMIERE (President), Sir Satcam BOOLELL (Honorary President), Dharam GHOKOOL (Secretary General).

Xavier Duval Mauritian Party (*Parti Mauricien Xavier Duval*—PMXD). A byproduct of interfamily conflict within the PMSD (below), the PMXD is led by Xavier Luc Duval, the son of the late PMSD leader, Sir Gaëtan Duval. Following his split with his uncle, Hervé Duval (the current PMSD leader), and the formation of the PMXD, Xavier Luc Duval was elected to the National Assembly in a by-election on September 19, 1999, on a MLP-PMXD ticket. He was subsequently named minister of industry, commerce, corporate affairs, and financial services in the new MLP-led cabinet announced on September 26, and the party ran in alliance with the MLP in the September 2000 legislative poll, Duval securing 1 of the "best loser" seats in the assembly following that poll. When the MLP's Navin Ramgoolam became

prime minister in 2005, he named Xavier Luc Duval one of his three deputy prime ministers.

Leaders: Xavier Luc DUVAL, Jacques PANGLOSE (Secretary General).

Republican Movement (*Mouvement Républicain*—MR). The MR was founded on the eve of the October 1996 municipal balloting, in which its leader, Rama Valayden, won a local council seat. Valayden had presented himself as an heir to the policies pursued by the late Sir Gaëtan Duval of the PMSD. The MR aligned with the MSM-MMM coalition in the September 2000 balloting, one MR member reportedly securing a seat as an alliance candidate. In May 2001 the MR decided to end its support for the government, and subsequent press reports referred to the MR as an "opposition party." The MR participated in the MLP-led Social Alliance in 2005, and Rama Valayden was named attorney general and minister of justice and human rights in the new Ramgoolam government.

Leaders: Rama VALAYDEN, Sada ETWAROO.

Mauritian Militant Socialist Movement (MMSM). The MMSM is a radical Hindu group led by former agriculture minister Madun Dullo. It participated in the MLP-PMXD electoral alliance in the September 2000 assembly poll and the MLP-led Social Alliance in 2005.

Leader: Madun DULLO.

Social Democratic Movement (*Movement Social-Démocrate*—MSD). The MSD was formed in March 2005 by four MSM legislators (including two who had recently resigned from the cabinet) to protest the proposed continuation of the MSM-MMM electoral alliance. The new party joined the Social Alliance for the July legislative balloting.

Leaders: Anil BAICHOO, Mukeshawr CHOONEE.

Opposition and Other Parties

Mauritian Socialist Movement (*Mouvement Socialiste Mauricien*—MSM). The MSM was organized initially on April 8, 1983, as the Militant Socialist Movement (*Mouvement Socialiste*

Militant) by Prime Minister Jugnauth following his expulsion, in late March, from the MMM. Prior to the 1983 election, the MSM, with the MLP, the PMSD, and the OPR, formed a coalition that secured a clear majority of legislative seats. In February 1984 the MLP withdrew from the alliance, although a number of its deputies remained loyal to the government.

The MSM secured 26 of the 41 elective seats won in August 1987 by the reconstituted five-party alliance, from which the PMSD withdrew a year later. The MLP again moved into opposition following an electoral agreement between the MSM and MMM in July 1990, with the new MSM-led alliance winning 59 of 62 elective seats in September 1991. In a disastrous loss in December 1995 all of the MSM deputies, including Jugnauth, lost their seats. However, the MSM formed a coalition with the MMM for the snap legislative elections in September 2000 and secured 54 of the elected seats with 51.7 percent of the vote.

Pravind Jugnauth succeeded his father as leader of the MSM in April 2003. In 2004 he called for retention of the MSM-MMM electoral alliance in the 2005 assembly balloting, prompting several prominent MSM members to quit the party to form the new MSD (above).

Leaders: Sir Anerood JUGNAUTH (President of the Republic), Pravind Kumar JUGNAUTH (Deputy Prime Minister and Chair of the Party), Dr. Beergoonath GHURBURRUN, Emmanuel Jean Leung SHING (Secretary General).

Mauritian Militant Movement (*Mouvement Militant Mauricien*—MMM). The leadership of the MMM was detained during the 1971 disturbances because of its "confrontational politics," which, unlike that of other Mauritian parties, was intended to cut across ethnic-communal lines. Following the 1976 election, the party's leadership strength was only 2 seats short of a majority; in 1982, campaigning in alliance with the Mauritian Socialist Party, it obtained an absolute majority of 42 seats.

In March 1983, 12 members of the MMM government of Anerood Jugnauth, led by Finance Minister Paul Bérenger, resigned in disagreement over economic policy and because they and their supporters believed that Creole should be designated the national language. Immediately thereafter, Jugnauth was expelled and proceeded to form the MSM (above), which, with its allies, achieved a decisive victory at the August 21 election.

Prior to the 1987 balloting, Bérenger, long viewed as a Marxist, characterized himself as a "democratic socialist." However, he was unsuccessful in securing an assembly seat on either a direct or "best loser" basis. The party itself campaigned as the leading component of a Union for the Future alliance, which included two minor groups, the **Democratic Workers' Movement** (*Mouvement des Travaillistes Démocrates*—MTD), then led by Anil Kumar BAICHOO and later by Sanjeet TEELOCK, and the **Socialist Workers' Front** (*Front des Travailleurs Socialistes*—FTS). On July 17, 1990, the MMM concluded an electoral accord with the MSM and MTD and formally entered the Jugnauth government on September 26.

In October 1993 Bérenger was briefly ousted as MMM secretary general, but he was returned to office by the party's Central Committee, which proceeded to expel the anti-Bérenger majority of Political Bureau members, including Prem Nababsingh and Dharmanand Goopt FOKEER, theretofore MMM president and chair, respectively, who remained members of the Jugnauth administration. In April 1994 Bérenger concluded an electoral pact with Navin Ramgoolam of the MLP under which, in the event of a coalition victory, Ramgoolam was to become prime minister and Bérenger his deputy. Two months later Nababsing and his supporters formally left the MMM to organize the Mauritian Militant Renaissance.

Bérenger resigned his parliamentary seat on November 29, 1994, after having charged the MSM of manipulating the 1991 election, despite having been a government minister at the time. He regained his MP status at a by-election in January 1995 and became deputy prime minister and foreign minister as a result of the MLP-MMM victory in December 1995. However, Bérenger was relieved of his cabinet posts in June 1997, and the MMM moved into opposition when all but one of the party's nine other ministers resigned from the government.

In August 1997 Bérenger spearheaded the organization of a National Alliance (*Alliance Nationale*—AN) in an apparent attempt to improve his chances of securing the top governmental post in the next election. In addition to the MMM, the AN comprised the PMSD, the RPR, and the MMSM. However, the grouping did poorly in an April 1998 by-election (the AN candidate finished third with 16 percent of the vote), and a correspondent for the *Indian Ocean Newsletter* described the AN as "having been shot at dawn." Bérenger subsequently joined with Jugnauth in late 1998 to announce a MMM-MSM "federation" that would present joint candidates in the next general election and share governmental responsibility in the event of success. The federation was formally established in January 1999, and, as expected, Bérenger assumed a deputy post in the coalition with the understanding that he would be named to a similar rank in a Jugnauth-headed government. Following the landslide victory of the MSM-MMM coalition in the September 2000 balloting, Bérenger was named deputy prime minister, with the understanding that he would succeed Jugnauth as prime minister in three years. Bérenger also negotiated a similar proposed arrangement with Pravind Jugnauth of the MSM prior to the 2005 balloting.

On April 8, 2006, Bérenger resigned his position as leader of the opposition in the assembly because relations between the MMM and the MSM deteriorated following the MMM-MSM coalition's defeat in the 2005 elections.

Leader: Paul BÉRENGER (Former Prime Minister), Premnath RAMNAH (Former Speaker of the National Assembly), Ivan COLLENDAVELLOO (General Secretary).

Rodriguan People's Organization (*Organisation du Peuple Rodriguais*—OPR). The OPR captured the two Rodrigues Island seats at the 1982 and 1983 balloting and, having earlier indicated that it would support the MSM-Labour alliance,

was assigned one cabinet post in the Jugnauth government of August 1983; it retained the post after the ensuing two elections. The OPR again won Rodrigues's two elective parliamentary seats in 1995, despite its affiliation with the Jugnauth administration. It joined the resultant MLP-led government, although its customary full ministerial responsibility for Rodrigues affairs was downgraded to junior level under the prime minister. The OPR regained the full cabinet authority for Rodrigues affairs in the new government announced in July 1997. The party again secured the two elective seats from Rodrigues in the 2000 and 2005 legislative polls.

Leaders: Louis Serge CLAIR (Former Rodrigues Island Minister and Leader of the Party), J. Benoit JOLICOEUR.

Mauritian Social Democratic Party (*Parti Mauricien Social-Démocrate*—PMSD). Composed chiefly of Franco-Mauritian landowners and middle-class Creoles, the PMSD initially opposed independence but subsequently accepted it as a fait accompli. Antisocialist at home and anticommunist in foreign affairs, it has long been distinguished for its francophile stance. The party was part of the Ramgoolam government coalition until 1973, when it went into opposition. It won 23 legislative seats at the 1967 election but retained only 8 in 1976, when it reentered the government. Reduced to 2 "best loser" seats in 1982, it won 4 on an elective basis in 1983 and 1987. The party withdrew from the alliance in August 1988 following a dispute over fiscal policy.

The party was awarded one "best loser" seat following the 1991 election. In January 1994 Sir Gaëtan Duval, the leader of the PMSD, failed in an attempt to persuade Prime Minister Jugnauth to form a common front to block the threatened electoral alliance between the MLP and the MMM. At a party congress on May 22 he turned the leadership over to his son, Xavier Luc Duval, under whom the PMSD retreated visibly from its theretofore rightist posture. The party joined the MSM-led coalition in February 1995, with the younger Duval being given the industry and tourism portfolios; however, the move was opposed by the PMSD Central Committee, which in April called on Duval to resign from the government (a move which he undertook only in October for a quite different reason—his opposition to the proposed Asian language amendment). The episode reflected a growing rift between the two Duvals, with Sir Gaëtan subsequently withdrawing from the PMSD to form the Gaëtan Duval Party (*Parti Gaëtan Duval*—PGD). As PGD candidate he reentered the assembly on a "best loser" basis after the December elections. Because the PMSD had failed to gain representation, the elder Duval effectively resumed its leadership until his death in May 1996, when his seat in the legislature passed to his brother, Hervé Duval. It was reported that Prime Minister Ramgoolam had approached Hervé Duval with a proposal to join the government in late June 1997 following the split in the MLP-MMM coalition. However, the PMSD leader decided to align instead with the MMM in the short-lived National Alliance opposition grouping, a decision that apparently exacerbated Duval's differences with Xavier Luc Duval, who subsequently formed his own grouping, the PMXD (above). At balloting in 2000 the PMSD was described as associated with the coalition led by the MSM and MMM. (Hervé Duval's supporters have also been referenced as the *Vrais Bleus* [True Blues].)

Leaders: Alan DRIVER (President), Hervé DUVAL, Clifford EMPEIGNE.

Green Party (*Les Verts*). The Green Party was reportedly aligned with the MSM-MMM electoral coalition in the September 2000 legislative balloting, and party leader Sylvio Louis MICHEL was named minister of fisheries in the new cabinet.

Leader: Sylvio Louis MICHEL.

Rodriguan Movement (*Mouvement Rodriguais*—MR). A regional rival of the OPR favoring U.S.-style federalism rather than separation, the MR was awarded two "best loser" seats following both the 1995 and 2000 legislative polls.

Leaders: Nicolas VON MALLY (Leader of the Opposition and Party Leader), Alex NANCY.

Resistance and Alternative. A center-left grouping launched in March 2005, Resistance and Alternative argued that the "big parties" had failed to solve the nation's problems.

Leader: Ashok SUBRON (Secretary General).

Party of God (*Hizbullah*). The Islamic fundamentalist *Hizbullah* obtained one assembly seat as a "best loser" in the December 1995 election. (Some subsequent reports referenced the seat as belonging to the **Mauritian Liberal Movement** [*Mouvement Libéral Mauricien*—MLM], described as *Hizbullah*'s "ally.") Reportedly draining Muslim support from the MMM, *Hizbullah* was credited with 5 percent of the vote in the September 2000 poll but did not receive a "best loser" seat.

Leader: Ceeal MEEAH.

Mauritian Socialist Party (*Parti Socialiste Mauricien*—PSM). The original PSM was formed in 1979 by the withdrawal from the MLP of a group of dissidents led by Harish Boodhoo. It was dissolved in May 1983 by absorption into the MSM, and Boodhoo was named deputy prime minister. In January 1986 Boodhoo resigned his government post in the wake of a disagreement with Prime Minister Jugnauth over drug policy, and he withdrew from the assembly the following November. Subsequently, he mounted an opposition campaign in his newspaper, *Le Socialiste*, and in June 1988 announced the PSM's revival. Boodhoo was aligned with the MSM-MMM alliance for the September 2000 balloting. However, the PSM apparently withdrew its support for the government in early 2002, and Boodhoo subsequently attempted to forge an opposition coalition.

Leader: Harish BOODHOO.

Rally for Reform (*Rassemblement pour la Réforme*—RPR). The RPR was launched in August 1996 by a dissident faction of the MSM led by Rama Sithanen (a former finance minister) and Sheila Bappoo (who had briefly been MSM secretary general). It formed an alliance with the PMSD for the October 1996 municipal elections, the combined list polling some 25 percent of the vote. In

Cabinet

As of July 1, 2006

Prime Minister	Navinchandra Ramgoolam (MLP)
Deputy Prime Ministers	Ahmed Rashid Beebeejaun
	Charles Gaëtan Xavier Luc Duval (PMXD)
	Rama Krishna Sithanen

Ministers

Agriculture, Food Technology, and Natural Resources	Arvin Boolell (MLP)
Arts and Culture	Mahendra Gowressoo (MLP) [f]
Civil Service Affairs and Administrative Reforms	Navinchandra Ramgoolam (MLP)
Commerce and Consumer Protection	Rajeshwar Jeetah (MLP)
Defense, Interior, and External Communications	Navinchandra Ramgoolam (MLP)
Education and Scientific Research	Dharambeer Gokhool (MLP)
Environment and National Development	Anil Kumar (MLP)
External Communications	Charles Gaëtan Xavier Luc Duval (PMXD)
Finance and Economic Development	Rama Krishna Sithanen (MLP)
Foreign Affairs, International Trade, and Regional Cooperation	Madan Murlidhar Dulloo (MLP)
Health and Quality of Life	Satya Veyash Faugoo (MLP)
Housing, Lands, and Fisheries	Mohammed Asraf Ally Dulull (MLP)
Industry, Medium Enterprises, Financial Services, and Corporate Affairs	Rajeshwar Jeetah (MLP)
Information Technology and Telecommunications	Marie Joseph Noël-Etienne
	Ghislain Sinatambou (MLP) [f]
Justice and Human Rights	Jaya Rama Valayden (MR)
Labor, Industrial Relations, and Employment	Vasant Kumar Bunwaree (MLP)
Local Government and Solid Waste Management	James Burty David (MLP)
Public Infrastructure and Land Transport	Ahmed Rashid Beebeejaun (MLP)
Public Utilities	Abu Twalib Kasenally (MLP)
Rodrigues and Outer Islands	Navinchandra Ramgoolam (MLP)
Social Security, National Solidarity, Senior Citizen Welfare, and Reform Institutions	Sheilabai Bappoo (MLP) [f]
Tourism and Leisure	Charles Gaëtan Xavier Luc Duval (PMXD)
Training, Skills Development, Productivity, and External Communications	Charles Gaëtan Xavier Luc Duval (PMXD)
Women's Rights, Child Development, and Family Welfare	Indranee Seebun (MLP) [f]
Youth and Sports	Sylvio Hock Sheen Tang Wah Hing (MLP) [f]

[f] = female

the September 2000 assembly balloting, the RPR was aligned with the MLP-PMXD coalition.

Leaders: Rama SITHANEN, Sheila BAPPOO.

Muslim Action Committee (*Comité d'Action Musulman*—CAM). The CAM has long represented the interests of the Indian Muslim community. Reports on the September 2000 legislative poll referenced a **Mauritian Action Committee** (*Comité d'Action Mauricien*—also CAM). It was not clear if any relationship existed between the two groups. In 2003 members of the Muslim Action Committee reportedly launched a new party called the **Muslim League** under the leadership of Farook Mohammed BACCUS.

Leader: Youssuf MOHAMMED (President).

National Mauritian Movement (*Mouvement National Mauricien*—MNM). Led by an ex-police chief who had criticized Prime Minister Ramgoolam's handling of the riots at Port Louis in early 1999, the right-wing MNM campaigned for the 2000 legislative balloting on a platform urging voters to renounce the country's "old parties." (Some confusion may exist over the name of this grouping, some electoral reports also referencing a **National Democratic Movement** [Raj Dayal].)

Leader: Col. Raj DAYAL.

In addition, there are two far-left organizations that remain active: **The Struggle** (*Lalit*), led by Lindsey COLLEN, and the **Socialist Workers' Party** (*Parti Socialiste Ouvriére*—PSO), whose secretary general is Didier EDMOND. (In 2005 *Lalit* called for the United States to close its military base on Diego Garcia and for all of the Chagos Archipelago to be returned to Mauritian sovereignty.)

Other parties participating in the September 2000 assembly elections were **Agricultural Planting Movement** (*Mouvement Planteur Agricole*—MPA); **Authentic Mauritian Movement** (*Mouvement Authentique Mauricien*—MAM); **Liberal Action Party** (*Parti Action Libéral*—PAL); **Mauritian Democracy** (*Démocratie Mauricienne*—DM); **Mauritian Democratic Movement** (*Mouvement Démocratique Mauricien*—MDM); **Mauritius Party Rights** (MPR); **National Democratic Movement** (*Mouvement Démocratique National*—MDN); **NouvoLizur,** a grouping led by former cabinet minister Joceline MINERVE which, among other things, supports "Chagossian rights"; **Party of the Mauritian People** (*Parti du Peuple Mauricien*—PPM); **Socialist Workers Movement** (*Mouvement Travailliste Socialiste*—MTS); **Tamil Council** (TC); and the **Mauritian Union** (*Union Mauricienne*—UM).

Legislature

The Mauritian **National Assembly** is a unicameral body containing 62 elected deputies (3 from each of the 20 constituencies on the main island and 2 from Rodrigues Island), plus up to 8 appointed from the list of unsuccessful candidates under a "best loser" system designed to provide "balanced" ethnic and political representation. The legislative term is five years, subject to dissolution. In the National Assembly elections held on July 3, 2005, the Social Alliance (led by the Mauritius Labor Party) won 38 of the 60 elected seats from the main island, the other 22 going to the coalition of the Mauritian Socialist Movement (MSM) and the Mauritian Militant Movement (MMM). The Rodriguan People's Organization (OPR) won the 2 elected seats on Rodrigues Island. In the subsequent best loser distribution of appointed seats, the Social Alliance was accorded 4 additional seats; the MSM-MMM coalition, 2; and the OPR, 2.

Speaker: Rajikeswur PURRYAG.

Rodrigues Regional Assembly. As authorized by a constitutional amendment approved by the National Assembly in November 2001, the Rodrigues Regional Assembly comprises 18 members, 12 elected from six constituencies on a first-past-the-post system and 6 elected on a proportional basis. In the first balloting for the assembly on September 25, 2002, the Rodriguan People's Organization secured 10 seats and the Rodriguan Movement, 8 seats. The assembly was inaugurated on October 15.

Communications

The traditionally free Mauritian press was subject to censorship under the state of emergency imposed in 1971, but restrictions were lifted on May 1, 1976. Radio and television are under semipublic control.

Press

The following are published daily at Port Louis in English and French, unless otherwise noted: *Weekend* (85,000), weekly; *Le Mauricien* (35,000);

Cinq Plus (30,000), weekly; *L'Express* (30,000); *Le Quotidien* (30,000); *Le Dimanche* (25,000), weekly; *Mauritius Times* (13,500), weekly; *Le Nouveau Militant* (6,000), MMM weekly; *Chinese Daily News* (5,000), in Chinese; *China Times* (3,000), in Chinese; *Maurice Soir* (2,000), in French; *The Sun,* MMM organ; *Vani,* PSM weekly.

Broadcasting and Computing

The Mauritian Broadcasting Corporation operates two national radio networks and two television channels. There were approximately 299,000 television receivers and 180,000 personal computers serving 150,000 Internet users in 2003.

Intergovernmental Representation

Ambassador to the U.S.
(Vacant)

U.S. Ambassador to Mauritius
(Vacant)

Permanent Representative to the UN
Somduth SOBORUN

IGO Memberships (Non-UN)
AfDB, AU, BADEA, Comesa, CWTH, Interpol, IOC, IOM, IOR-ARC, NAM, OIF, PCA, SADC, WCO, WTO

MOROCCO

KINGDOM OF MOROCCO

al-Mamlakat al-Maghribiyah

The Country

Located at the northwest corner of Africa, Morocco combines a long Atlantic coastline and Mediterranean frontage facing Gibraltar and southern Spain. Bounded by Algeria on the northeast and (following annexation of the former Spanish Sahara) by Mauritania on the south, the country is topographically divided into a rich agricultural plain in the northwest and an infertile mountain and plateau region in the east that gradually falls into the Sahara Desert in the south and southwest. The population is approximately two-thirds Arab and one-third Berber, with small French and Spanish minorities. Islam is the state religion, most of the population adhering to the Sunni sect. Arabic is the language of the majority, most others speaking one or more dialects of Berber; Spanish is common in the northern regions and French among the educated elite. Women comprise 35 percent of the paid labor force, concentrated mainly in textile manufacture and domestic service; overall, one-third of the female population is engaged in unpaid family labor on agricultural estates. While an increasing number of women from upper-income brackets have participated in local and national elections, they have thus far obtained only minimal representation.

The agricultural sector employs approximately 40 percent of the population; important crops include cereals and grains, oilseeds, nuts, and citrus fruits. One of the world's leading exporters of phosphates, Morocco also has important deposits of lead, iron, cobalt, zinc, manganese, and silver; overall, mining accounts for about 45 percent of export receipts. The industrial sector emphasizes import substitution (textiles, chemicals, cement, plastics, machinery), while tourism and fishing are also major sources of income. Trade is strongly oriented toward France, whose economic influence has remained substantial. Since the early 1980s the economy has suffered from periodic droughts, declining world demand for phosphate, rapid urbanization, and high population growth. Unemployment remains a problem, with youth and talent seeking opportunity in Europe. Economic growth has been disappointing according to a report by the country's Higher Planning Authority: Morocco has failed to meet targets in growth, investment, and exports during the past five years. One piece of

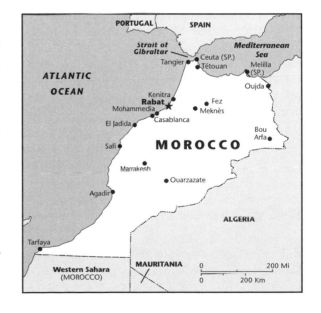

good news has been the improved performance of agriculture, which has benefited because of better rainfall, but it also points to Morocco's continued dependence on that sector of the economy. Remittances from workers abroad and steady tourist receipts have also helped the economic picture. Trade liberalization continues with the European Union, and in 2004 Morocco and the United States signed a free trade agreement. While these measures were expected to strengthen foreign business and investment, they also represented competition to Moroccan farmers and textile industries.

Living conditions remain low by regional standards, and wealth is poorly distributed. However, with its low inflation rate, cheap labor pool, and reputation as an "oasis of stability" in an otherwise turbulent region, Morocco is considered by some as a potential target for substantial Western (particularly European) investment. To encourage such interest, the government continues to privatize many state-run enterprises, address the high (52 percent) illiteracy rate, and reform the stock market, tax system, and banking sector. Recent political liberalization has also reportedly been aimed, at least in part, at securing additional Western support.

A more costly wage structure and higher oil subsidies contributed to a rapidly rising budget deficit and a concomitant drop in the GDP growth rate to 1.2 percent in 2005. On a more positive note, the 2004 free trade agreement with the United States took effect in January 2006, improving prospects for increased direct foreign investment. Concurrently, Morocco's decision to allow private purchase of shares in the largest state-owned bank and the state telecommunications company further enhanced the climate for foreign capital.

Government and Politics

Political Background

Originally inhabited by Berbers, Morocco was successively conquered by the Phoenicians, Carthaginians, Romans, Byzantines, and Arabs. From 1912 to 1956 the country was subjected to de facto French and Spanish control, but the internal authority of the sultan was nominally respected. Under pressure by Moroccan nationalists, the French and Spanish relinquished their protectorates, and the country was reunified under Sultan MOHAMED V in 1956. Tangier, which had been under international administration since 1923, was ceded by Spain in 1969.

King Mohamed V tried to convert the hereditary sultanate into a modern constitutional monarchy but died before the process was complete. It remained for his son, King HASSAN II, to implement his father's goal in a constitution adopted in December 1962. However, dissatisfaction with economic conditions and the social policy of the regime led to rioting at Casablanca in March 1965, and three months later the king assumed legislative and executive powers.

In June 1967 the king relinquished the post of prime minister, but the continued hostility of student and other elements led to frequent governmental changes. A new constitution, approved in July 1970, provided for a partial resumption of parliamentary government, a strengthening of royal powers, and a limited role for political parties. Despite the opposition of major political groups, trade unions, and student organizations, an election for a new unicameral House of Representatives was held in August 1970, yielding a pro-government majority. However, the king's failure to unify the country behind his programs was dramatically illustrated by abortive military revolts in 1971 and 1972.

A new constitution was overwhelmingly approved by popular referendum in March 1972, but the parties refused to enter the government because of the monarch's reluctance to schedule legislative elections. After numerous delays, elections to communal and municipal councils were finally held in November 1976, to provincial and prefectural assemblies in January 1977, and to a reconstituted national House of Representatives in June 1977. On October 10 the leading parties agreed to participate in a "National Unity" cabinet headed by Ahmed OSMAN as prime minister.

Osman resigned on March 21, 1979, ostensibly to oversee reorganization of the proroyalist

Political Status: Independent since March 2, 1956; constitutional monarchy established in 1962; present constitution approved March 1, 1972.

Area: 274,461 sq. mi. (710,850 sq. km.), including approximately 97,343 sq. mi. (252,120 sq. km.) of Western Sahara, two-thirds of which was annexed in February 1976 and the remaining one-third claimed upon Mauritanian withdrawal in August 1979.

Population: 29,891,708 (2004C); 30,310,000 (2005E), including Western Saharans (273,000 in 2005E).

Major Urban Centers (2005E): RABAT (1,654,000), Casablanca (2,957,000), Fez (967,000), Marrakesh (840,000), Oujda (406,000).

Official Language: Arabic.

Monetary Unit: Dirham (official rate July 1, 2006: 8.68 dirhams = $1US).

Sovereign: King MOHAMED VI, became king on July 23, 1999, following the death of his father, HASSAN II.

Heir to the Throne: Crown Prince HASSAN.

Prime Minister: Driss JETTOU (nonparty), appointed by King Mohamed in October 2002, replacing Abderrahmane YOUSSOUFI (Socialist Union of Popular Forces); reappointed on June 8, 2004.

National Assembly of Independents (RNI), although the move was reported to have been precipitated by his handling of the lengthy dispute over the Western Sahara (see Disputed Territory, below). He was succeeded on March 22 by Maati BOUABID, a respected Casablanca attorney.

On May 30, 1980, a constitutional amendment extending the term of the House of Representatives from four to six years was approved by referendum, thus postponing new elections until 1983. The king indicated in June 1983 that the legislative poll, scheduled for early September, would be further postponed pending the results of a referendum in the Western Sahara to be sponsored by the Organization of African Unity (OAU, subsequently the African Union—AU). On November 30 a new "unity" cabinet headed by Mohamed Karim LAMRANI was announced, with Bouabid, who had organized a new moderate party eight months earlier, joining other party leaders in accepting appointment as ministers of state without portfolio.

The long-awaited legislative poll was finally held on September 14 and October 2, 1984, with Bouabid's Constitutional Union (UC) winning a plurality of both direct and indirectly elected seats, while four centrist parties collectively obtained a better than two-to-one majority. Following lengthy negotiations, a new coalition government, headed by Lamrani, was formed on April 11, 1985.

Although King Hassan appeared to remain popular with most of his subjects, domestic opposition leaders and Amnesty International continued to charge the government with human rights abuses and repression of dissent, including the alleged illegal detention and mistreatment of numerous leftists and Islamic fundamentalists arrested in 1985 and 1986. On September 30, 1986, the king appointed Dr. Azzedine LARAKI, former national education minister, as prime minister, following Lamrani's resignation for health reasons.

Attributed in large measure to improvements in the economy, calm subsequently ensued, with domestic and international attention focusing primarily on the Western Sahara. Thus, a national referendum on December 1, 1989, overwhelmingly approved the king's proposal to postpone legislative elections due in 1990, ostensibly to permit participation by Western Saharans following a self-determination vote in the disputed territory.

In mid-1992, amid indications that the referendum might be delayed indefinitely or even abandoned, the government announced that forthcoming local and national elections would include the residents of Western Sahara as participants. On August 11 King Hassan reappointed Lamrani as prime minister and announced a "transitional cabinet" to serve until a postelection cabinet could be established under new constitutional provisions (see Constitution and government, below).

The basic law revisions were approved on September 4, 1992, by a national referendum, which the government hailed as a significant step in its ongoing democratization program. Widespread disbelief greeted the government's claim that 97.5 percent of the electorate had participated and that a 99.9 percent "yes" vote had been registered.

In balloting for directly elective house seats, delayed until June 25, 1993, the newly established Democratic Bloc (*Koutla*), a coalition of center-left opposition groups led by the old-guard *Istiqlal* party and the Socialist Union of Popular Forces (USFP), secured 99 seats. They won only 15 more in the September 17 voting in electoral colleges made up of local officials, trade unionists, and representatives of professional associations. Meanwhile, the National Entente (*Wifaq*), a group of center-right royalist parties, increased its representation from 116 at the first round of balloting to 195 after the second. The Democratic Bloc subsequently charged that the indirect election encompassed widespread fraud, an allegation that received some support from international observers.

Although King Hassan rejected the Democratic Bloc's demand that the results of the indirect poll be overturned, he did propose that the bloc participate in the formation of a new cabinet, the first of what the king envisioned as a series of alternating left-right governments. The offer was declined because of the monarch's insistence that he retain the right to appoint the prime minister and maintain de facto control of the foreign, justice, and interior portfolios. Consequently, Lamrani formed a new nonparty government on November 11.

With his poor health again cited as the official reason for the change, Lamrani was succeeded on May 25, 1994, by former foreign minister Abdellatif FILALI, a longtime close advisor to the king. On June 7 Filali presented the monarch with a ministerial list unchanged from that of his predecessor, while King Hassan continued to seek Democratic Bloc leadership of a new coalition government. The negotiations eventually collapsed in early 1995, in part because of the king's wish that Driss BASRI, long-term minister of state for interior and information, remain in the cabinet. The opposition parties had objected to Basri's influ-

ence for many years, charging that he had sanctioned human rights abuses and tolerated electoral fraud. Nonetheless, Basri retained the interior post on February 28 when Filali's new government, including 20 members of the National Entente, was announced.

Despite his failure to draw the leftist parties into the government, the king continued to pursue additional democratization, particularly regarding the proposed creation of an upper house of the legislature that, theoretically, would redistribute authority away from the monarchy to a certain degree. The king's proposal was affirmed by a reported 99.56 percent "yes" vote in a national referendum on September 13, 1996, most opposition parties having endorsed the amendment (see Constitution and government, below, for details).

Local elections were held on June 13, 1997, with seats being distributed along a wide spectrum of parties and no particular political dominance being apparent. Such was also the case with the November 14 balloting for a new House of Representatives as the *Koutla, Wifaq,* and a bloc of centrist parties each won about one-third of the seats. On the other hand, the indirect elections to the new House of Councilors revealed a decided tilt toward the *Wifaq,* not a surprising result considering its long-standing pro-government stance.

Continuing to pursue an alternating left-right series of governments, King Hassan was subsequently able to finally persuade the Democratic Bloc to assume cabinet control, and on February 4, 1998, he appointed Abderrahmane YOUSSOUFI of the USFP (which had won the most seats in the House of Representatives) as the next prime minister. As formed on March 14, the new cabinet included representatives from seven parties, although the King's supporters (most notably Basri) remained in several key posts.

King Hassan, whose health had been a concern since 1995, died of a heart attack on July 23, 1999; Crown Prince SIDI MOHAMED succeeded his father immediately, the official ceremony marking his enthronement as King MOHAMED VI being held on July 30. Shortly thereafter, the long-suspect Driss Basri was dismissed as minister of the interior and moved to Paris. The new king confirmed his support for Prime Minister Youssoufi and his government. The cabinet was reshuffled on September 6, 2000, with Youssoufi retaining the top post, but the new king replaced him with an independent, Driss JETTOU, in 2002. In 2004 the cabinet was again reshuffled, with many new cabinet appointments being made and Jettou remaining as prime minister.

Constitution and Government

Morocco is a constitutional monarchy, the Crown being hereditary and normally transmitted to the king's eldest son, who acts on the advice of a Regency Council if he accedes before age 20. Political power is highly centralized in the hands of the king, who serves as commander in chief and appoints the prime minister; in addition, he can declare a state of emergency, dissolve the legislature, veto legislation, and initiate constitutional amendments. Constitutional revisions approved in 1992 empowered the prime minister, instead of the king, to appoint and preside over the cabinet (albeit still subject to the king's approval); broadened the authority of the House of Representatives to include, inter alia, the initiation of confidence motions and the launching of investigations; and established new Constitutional and Economic/Social Councils. The preamble of the basic law was also altered to declare "the kingdom's attachment to human rights as they are universally recognized."

Until recently, legislative power had been nominally vested in a unicameral House of Representatives, one-third of whose members were indirectly designated by an electoral college. The new upper house (House of Councilors), provided for in the 1996 referendum, is elected indirectly from various local government bodies, professional associations, and employer and worker organizations. All members of the House of Representatives are now elected directly. Included in the new legislature's expanded authority is the power to censure the government and to dismiss cabinet members, although such decisions can still be overridden by the king.

The judicial system is headed by a Supreme Court (*Majlis al-Alaa*) and includes courts of appeal, regional tribunals, magistrates' courts, labor tribunals, and a special court to deal with corruption. All judges are appointed by the king on the advice of the Supreme Council of the Judiciary.

The country is currently divided into 49 provinces and prefectures (including four provinces in Western Sahara), with further division into municipalities, autonomous centers, and rural communes. The king appoints all provincial governors, who are responsible to him. In addition, the basic law changes of September 1996 provided for 16 regional councils, with some members elected directly and others representing various professional organizations.

Foreign Relations

A member of the UN and the Arab League, Morocco has been chosen on many occasions as a site for Arab and African Islamic conferences at all levels. It has generally adhered to a nonaligned policy, combining good relations with the West with support for African and especially Arab nationalism. Morocco has long courted economic ties with the European Community (EC, now the European Union—EU), although its request for EC membership was politely rebuffed in 1987 on geographic grounds. An association agreement was negotiated in 1995 with the EU, which reportedly had begun to perceive the kingdom as the linchpin of a European campaign to expand trade with North Africa.

Relations with the United States have been friendly, U.S. administrations viewing Morocco as a conservative counter to northern Africa's more radical regimes. An agreement was signed in mid-1982 that sanctioned, subject to veto, the use of Moroccan air bases by U.S. forces in emergency situations. Periodic joint military exercises have since been conducted, with Washington serving as a prime supplier of equipment for Rabat's campaign in the Western Sahara.

During early 1991 Rabat faced a delicate situation in regard to the Iraqi invasion of Kuwait the previous August. Many Arab capitals were critical of King Hassan for contributing 1,700 Moroccan troops to the U.S.-led Desert Shield deployment in Saudi Arabia and other Gulf states; domestic sentiment also appeared to be strongly tilted against Washington. However, the king defused the issue by permitting a huge pro-Iraq demonstration in the capital in early February and by expressing his personal sympathy for the Iraqi people during the Gulf war. His middle-of-the-road approach was widely applauded both at home and abroad.

Morocco's role in regional affairs has been complicated by a variety of issues. Relations with Algeria and Mauritania have been marred by territorial disputes (until 1970, Morocco claimed all of Mauritania's territory). The early 1970s brought cooperation with the two neighboring states in an effort to present a unified front against the retention by Spain of phosphate-rich Spanish Sahara, but by 1975 Morocco and Mauritania were ranged against Algeria on the issue. In an agreement reached in Madrid on November 14, 1975, Spain agreed to withdraw in favor of Morocco and Mauritania, who proceeded to occupy their assigned sectors on February 28, 1976, despite resistance from the Polisario Front, an Algerian-backed group that had proclaimed the establishment of an independent Saharan Arab Democratic Republic (SADR). Following Mauritanian renunciation of all claims to the territory in a peace accord with Polisario on August 5, 1979, Moroccan forces entered the southern sector, claiming it, too, as a Moroccan province.

Relations with Algeria were formally resumed in May 1988 prior to an Arab summit at Algiers on the uprising in the Israeli-occupied territories. The stage was thus set for diplomatic activity that in the wake of first-ever talks between King Hassan and Polisario representatives in early 1989 appeared to offer the strongest possibility in more than a decade for settlement of the Western Sahara problem. Although little progress was achieved over the next seven years on a proposed UN-sponsored self-determination vote, a new UN mediation effort in 1997 rekindled hopes for a settlement (see Disputed Territory, below). Relations with Algeria improved further following the 1999 election of

the new Algerian President, Abdelaziz Bouteflika, who suggested that bilateral affairs be handled independently of the conflict in the Western Sahara.

Long strained ties with Libya (which had been accused of complicity in several plots to overthrow the monarchy) began to improve with a state visit by Muammar Qadhafi to Rabat in mid-1983. The process of rapprochement culminated in a treaty of projected union signed by the two leaders at Oujda on August 13, 1984. An inaugural meeting of a joint parliamentary assembly was held in Rabat in July 1985, and commissions were set up to discuss political, military, economic, cultural, and technical cooperation. By February 1989, cordial relations paved the way for a summit in Marrakesh, during which Qadhafi joined other North African leaders in proclaiming the Arab Maghreb Union.

Morocco's attitude toward Israel has been markedly more moderate than that of many Arab states, in part because more than 500,000 Jews of Moroccan ancestry live in Israel. King Hassan was known to relish his conciliatory potential in the Middle East peace process and was believed to have assisted in the negotiations leading up to the Israeli/PLO agreement of September 1993. Israeli Prime Minister Yitzhak Rabin made a surprise visit to Rabat on his return from the historic signing in Washington, his talks with King Hassan being heralded as an important step toward the establishment of formal diplomatic relations between the two countries.

In late 2001 relations between Morocco and Spain were strained by disagreements over illegal immigration, fishing rights, and smuggling. In July 2002, the countries were involved in a brief military standoff over an uninhabited islet (called Perejil by Spain, Leila by Morocco, and claimed by both) off the coast of Ceuta. With U.S., EU, and Egyptian mediation, the two sides agreed to withdraw their troops from the islet and to begin cooperating on various issues. Tensions eased dramatically when Spain's conservative government was replaced by the Spanish Socialist Workers Party in March 2004. In January 2005, Spain's King Juan Carlos paid an official visit to Morocco, a further sign of improved relations.

U.S. Secretary of Defense Donald Rumsfeld visited Morocco in February 2006 and praised the king for his cooperation with U.S. counterterrorism efforts. (Morocco is a signatory to the U.S.-led Trans-Sahara Counterterrorism Initiative, a $500 million, seven-year program.) Anti-U.S. protesters, in particular the Moroccan Association for Human Rights, expressed displeasure that the state of domestic political freedoms and human rights in Morocco was apparently not among topics on the agenda.

Relations with Spain improved after the election success of the Spanish Socialist Workers Party in 2004, but stresses were evident surrounding the issue of illegal migration of Africans through Morocco into Spain. In September 2005 five migrants were killed and approximately 100 injured as they attempted to scale the security fences that divide Moroccan territory from the North African Spanish enclave of Ceuta; another six were killed during a similar incident in early October. Following a tightening of security in that location, Italy protested to Morocco that it was seeing an increase in illegal immigrants trying to cross the Mediterranean from Morocco to Italy in small boats.

Current Issues

Western capitals appeared to be generally satisfied with King Mohamed's efforts at democratization. His coalition government works efficiently, and the approval of young ministers indicates his commitment to moving Morocco forward. Past abuses of human rights, including the disappearance of dissenters, seem to have diminished. The status of women in Moroccan society has been officially reformed, with the legal age for marriage raised from 15 to 18 and polygamy virtually outlawed.

The rise of radical Islamists—spurred on by the suicide attacks and the war in Iraq—has been of concern to the palace. Several blasts on one day in early 2003 in Casablanca killed more than 40 people. Some 2,000 Moroccans were convicted for the bombings, with several given death sentences and others long prison terms. A new anti-terrorism law was swiftly passed amid concerns in the media that increased powers of detention and surveillance would erode the gains in human rights. Although a survey by the U.S.-based Pew Research Center indicated that 45 percent of Moroccans had a favorable view of Osama Bin Laden (compared with 65 percent in Pakistan and 55 percent in Jordan), Moroccans seemed to support the government's efforts to crack down on perpetrators of political violence. Also encouraging was the government's initiation of a new housing program and renewed efforts to industrialize the northern coast in recognition that poverty and joblessness in the slums had created potential breeding grounds for radicalism.

The rate of unemployment continued to be a thorny issue, as unemployed graduates frequently protested outside parliament, demanding government jobs. In December 2005, several students set themselves on fire during such a protest, reportedly yelling "a civil service job or death." While none died, a number were badly burned.

As 2005 came to a close, a Moroccan truth commission—formally called the Equity and Reconciliation Commission (IER)—released its final report on alleged human rights abuses during the reign of King Hassan. The commission, described as the first of its kind in the Arab world, had been set up in January 2004. The commission reported that between independence in 1956 and the end of Hassan's rule in 1999, nearly 600 people were killed, and opposition activists were systematically suppressed, with numerous instances of torture and disappearances. The commission heard from more than 16,000 people and recommended that more than 9,000 victims receive compensatory payments. Many prodemocracy activists, including the Moroccan Association for Human Rights, criticized the panel for its policy of withholding the names of those found responsible for the abuses and for not recommending prosecution of the perpetrators. They also disputed the IER's numbers, maintaining that at least 1,500 people had been killed during protests on March 21, 1965, alone, and another 500 to 1,000 in protests during 1981. The hearings were televised throughout the country, an event unprecedented in the region.

Political Parties

Government Parties

Democratic Bloc (*Bloc Démocratique*). Launched in May 1992 to promote the establishment of a "healthy democracy within the framework of a constitutional monarchy," the Democratic Bloc or *Koutla* ("coalition"), currently includes the following three groups. (The UNFP was reportedly an initial member of the bloc, but recent references have not listed it as a component.) All of the bloc's founding members except the PPS (under PRP, below) urged voters to abstain from the September 1992 constitutional referendum, while in February 1993 all except the UNFP withdrew from participation in the national commission created to supervise upcoming legislative elections. The protesters charged that the commission was failing to pursue electoral law revision necessary to ensure "free and fair elections." However, all of the bloc's components participated in the 1993 balloting, securing 114 seats overall, with affiliated labor organizations winning six more. Most of the bloc's success (99 seats) came in the direct election, leading to its contention that the results of the indirect election had been "falsified." After protracted debate, the bloc in November rejected King Hassan's invitation to name most of the ministers in a new government, insisting that it should be given a right of veto over all appointments. However, after its components secured 102 seats in the 1997 balloting for the House of Representatives, the *Koutla* agreed to lead a new coalition government, which was appointed in March 1998 under the leadership of the USFP's Abderrahmane Youssoufi. In October 2002, Youssoufi was replaced by the independent Driss Jettou, who was renominated in 2004.

Independence Party (*Parti de l'Istiqlal, or Istiqlal*—PI). Founded in 1943, *Istiqlal* provided most of the nation's leadership before independence. It split in 1959, and its members were relieved of governmental responsibilities in 1963. Once a firm supporter of the throne, the party now displays a reformist attitude and supports the king only on selected issues. Stressing the need for better standards of living and equal rights for all Moroccans, it has challenged the government regarding alleged human rights abuses. In July 1970 *Istiqlal* formed a National Front with the UNFP (below) but ran alone in the election of June 1977, when it emerged as the (then) leading party. It suffered heavy losses in both the 1983 municipal elections and the 1984 legislative balloting.

In May 1990 *Istiqlal* joined the USFP (below), the PPS (under PRP, below), and the OADP (below) in supporting an unsuccessful censure motion that charged the government with "economic incompetence" and the pursuit of "antipopular" and "antisocial" policies. In November 1991 *Istiqlal* announced the formation of a "common front" with the USFP to work toward "establishment of true democracy," and the two parties presented a joint list in 1993, *Istiqlal*'s 118 candidates securing 43 seats in the direct *Majlis* poll. As with many other long-standing Moroccan parties, *Istiqlal*'s older and younger members have been at odds recently. *Istiqlal* was the leading party in the June 1997 local elections but fell to fifth place in the November house balloting. In the 2002 direct elections, the party won 48 seats, and its secretary general, Abbas El Fassi, was named minister of state.

Leaders: Mohamed DOURI, Abbas EL FASSI (Secretary General).

Socialist Union of Popular Forces (*Union Socialiste des Forces Populaire*—USFP). The USFP was organized in September 1974 by the UNFP-Rabat Section (see UNFP, below), which had disassociated itself from the Casablanca Section in July 1972 and was accused by the government of involvement in a Libyan-aided plot to overthrow King Hassan in March 1973. The USFP subsequently called for political democratization, nationalization of major industries, thorough reform of the nation's social and administrative structures, and the cessation of what it believed to be human rights abuses by the government. It secured the third-largest number of legislative seats in the election of June 1977 but withdrew from the House in October 1981 in protest at the extension of the parliamentary term. A year later it announced that it would return for the duration of the session ending in May 1983 so that it could participate in the forthcoming electoral campaigns. The majority of nearly 100 political prisoners released during July–August 1980 were USFP members, most of whom had been incarcerated for alleged antigovernment activities in 1973–1977.

After 52 of its 104 candidates (the USFP also supported 118 *Istiqlal* candidates) won seats in the June 1993 *Majlis* balloting, the union was reportedly divided on whether to accept King Hassan's offer to participate in a coalition government, the dispute ultimately being resolved in favor of the rejectionists. Subsequently, the USFP was awarded only four additional house seats in the September indirect elections. First Secretary Abderrahmane Youssoufi resigned his post and departed for France in protest over "irregularities" surrounding the process. The party also continued to denounce the "harassment" of prominent USFP member Noubir EL-AMAOUI, secretary general of the Democratic Confederation of Labor (*Confédération Démocratique du Travail*), who had recently served 14 months in prison for "insulting and slandering" the government in a magazine interview.

Youssoufi returned from his self-imposed exile in April 1995, apparently in response to overtures from King Hassan, who was again attempting to persuade leftist parties to join a coalition government. Although observers suggested that the USFP would soon "redefine" the party platform and possibly select new leaders, a July 1996 congress simply reconfirmed the current political bureau. Meanwhile, one USFP faction was reportedly attempting to "re-radicalize" the party under the direction of Mohamed BASRI, a longtime influential opposition leader. In June 1995 Basri returned from 28 years in exile, during which he had been sentenced (in absentia) to death three times.

The USFP was the leading party in the November 1997 house balloting, securing 57 seats and distancing itself somewhat from its *Koutla* partner *Istiqlal* (32), with which it had been considered of comparable strength. Subsequently, the 74-year-old Youssoufi (once again being referenced as the USFP first secretary) was named by King Hassan to lead a new coalition government, although many younger USFP members reportedly opposed the party's participation. Internal dissent continued, as some radical members charged Youssoufi and the party administration with acting timidly in government and failing to push for further reforms in state institutions. Demands for a leadership change were reportedly voiced in the party congress in March 2001, especially by younger members and those associated with labor unions. However, Youssoufi managed to retain his post, prompting some members to leave the party to form the National Ittihadi Congress (CNI, below). USFP was the leading party in the 2002 elections, winning 50 seats.

Leaders: Mohammed El YAZGHI (First Secretary), Abdelwahed RADI, Fathallah OUALALOU.

Party of Renewal and Progress (*Parti du Renouveau et du Progrès*—PRP). The PRP is the successor to the Moroccan Communist Party (*Parti Communiste Marocain*), which was banned in 1952; the Party of Liberation and Socialism (*Parti de la Libération et du Socialisme*), which was banned in 1969; and the Party of Progress and Socialism (*Parti du Progrès et du Socialisme*—PPS), which obtained legal status in 1974. The single PPS representative in the 1977 chamber, Ali YATA, was the first Communist to win election to a Moroccan legislature. The fourth national congress, held in July 1987 at Casablanca, although strongly supportive of the government's position on the Western Sahara, criticized the administration's recent decisions to privatize some state enterprises and implement other economic liberalization measures required by the International Monetary Fund (IMF). However, by mid-1991 the PPS was reported to be fully converted to *perestroika,* a stance that had apparently earned the party additional support within the Moroccan middle class. In late 1993 Yata unsuccessfully urged his Democratic Bloc partners to compromise with King Hassan in formation of a new government.

The party's current name was adopted in 1994 in conjunction with its "repositioning" as a social democratic grouping under the growing influence of Ali Yata's son, Nadir. However, subsequent news reports have often still referenced the group under the PPS rubric. Ali Yata, who had been reelected to his post of PRP secretary general in mid-1995, died in August 1997 after being struck by a car. In March 2002 the PRP and the PSD (below) announced that they had launched the Socialist Alliance (*Alliance Socialiste*) and that they were planning to cooperate in the legislative poll in September. In that election the PRP collected only 11 seats.

Leaders: Nadir YATA, Khalid NACIRI, Ismail ALAOUI (Secretary General).

National Assembly of Independents (*Rassemblement National des Indépendant*—RNI). The RNI was launched at a Constitutive Congress held October 6–9, 1978. Although branded by left-wing spokesmen as a "king's party," it claimed to hold the allegiance of 141 of 264 deputies in the 1977 Chamber. Subsequent defections and other disagreements, both internal and with the king, resulted in the party's designation as the "official" opposition in late 1981. It won 61 house seats in 1984, thereafter returning to a posture of solid support for the king and the government. RNI leader Ahmed Osman, a former prime minister and former president of the House of Representatives, is one of the country's best-known politicians. Previously affiliated with the National Entente, the RNI participated (as did the MNP) in the November 1997 elections as an unaligned "centrist" party (winning 46 seats) and subsequently agreed to join the Koutla-led coalition government named in early 1998. In 2002 RNI won 41 seats.

Leaders: Ahmed OSMAN (President), Moulay Mustafa Ben Larbi ALAIOU.

Popular National Movement (*Mouvement National Populaire*—MNP). The MNP was organized in October 1991 by longtime Berber leader Mahjoubi Aherdane, who was ousted as secretary general of the MP in 1986. The new party won 25 house seats in 1993. A number of MNP members left the party in mid-1996 to form the MDS (below). The MNP won 19 seats in the 1997 balloting for House of Representatives, having shed its National Entente orientation. Ahmed MOUSSAOUI, the minister of youth and sports, was expelled from the MNP in April 2001 and was subsequently reported to have joined the new Democratic Union. The MNP won 18 seats in 2002.

Leaders: Mahjoubi AHERDANE (Secretary General), Hassan MAAOUNI.

Other Parties

Socialist Democratic Party (*Parti Socialiste et Démocratique*—PSD). The PSD was established in October 1996 by OADP members who disagreed with that group's rejection of King Hassan's proposed constitutional changes. The party won six seats in 2002 balloting.

Leaders: Abdessamad BELKEBIR, Mohamed Habib TALEB, Aissa QUARDIGHI (Secretary General).

Democratic Forces Front (*Front des Forces Démocratiques*—FFD). Launched in 1997 by PRP dissidents, the FFD won 9 seats in the November house balloting, and its leader was named to the March 1998 cabinet. In 2002 the party won 12 seats.

Leader: Thami KHYARI (National Secretary).

National Entente (*Entente Nationale*). The National Entente, also known as the *Wifaq* (Agreement) Bloc, initially comprised five center-right parties, the three listed below and the MNP and RNI (above). The UC, MP, PND, and RNI had served as leading government parties from April 1985 to

August 1992. In November 1993 King Hassan announced that the Entente, whose members held 195 of 333 seats in the recently elected House of Representatives, had decided not to enter the new government in order to permit component parties to concentrate on internal matters. However, after the failure of a protracted effort to persuade leftist parties to participate, 20 Entente members (9 from the UC, 8 from the MP, and 3 from the PND) were named to the cabinet formed in February 1995. Although the MNP and the RNI declined cabinet representation, they announced they would provide the government with legislative support. Those two parties were subsequently listed as operating outside the *Wifaq* umbrella for the 1997 elections, at which the UC, MP, and PND secured 100 house seats. In 2002 the three parties dropped to 55 seats.

Constitutional Union (*Union Constitutionelle*—UC). Founded in 1983 by Maati Bouabid, the UC is a moderate party that emphasizes economic self-sufficiency. Said to have royal support, the party won 83 house seats in 1984. The UC's representation fell to 54 seats in 1993, although it retained a slim plurality and one of its members was elected president of the new house. Bouabid died in November 1996, exacerbating problems within a party described as already in disarray. The UC was the second leading party in the November 1997 house balloting, winning 50 seats, but dropped to 16 in 2002.

Leader: Mohamed ABIED.

Popular Movement (*Mouvement Populaire*—MP). Organized in 1958 as a monarchist party of Berber mountaineers, the MP was a major participant in government coalitions of the early 1960s. It secured the second-largest number of legislative seats at the election of June 1977 and was third-ranked after the 1984 and 1993 elections.

In October 1986 an extraordinary party congress voted to remove the MP's founder, Mahjoubi Aherdane, from the post of secretary general, replacing him the Mohand Laenser. Aherdane subsequently formed a new Berber party (see MNP, above). In the 2002 elections the MP won 27 seats and Laenser was named minister of agriculture.

Leader: Mohand LAENSER (Secretary General).

National Democratic Party (*Parti National Démocrate*—PND). The PND was founded as the Democratic Independents (*Indépendants Démocrates*—ID) in April 1981 by 59 former RNI deputies in the House of Representatives. At the party's first congress on June 11–13, 1982, its secretary general, Mohamed Arsalane al-JADIDI, affirmed the PND's loyalty to the monarchy while castigating the RNI for not providing an effective counterweight to the "old" parties.

Leader: Abdallah KADIRI.

Justice and Development Party (*Parti de la Justice et du Développement*—PJD). The PJD was formerly known as the Popular Constitutional and Democratic Movement (*Mouvement Populaire Constitutionnel et Démocratique*—MPCD). The MPCD was a splinter from the Popular Movement. It won three legislative seats in 1977 and none in 1984 or 1993.

In June 1996 the moribund MPCD was rejuvenated by its merger with an unrecognized Islamist grouping known as Reform and Renewal (*Islah wa al-tajdid*), led by Abdelillah BENKIRANE. The Islamists were allocated three of the MPCD's secretariat seats, and Benkirane was generally acknowledged as the party's primary leader. He announced that his supporters had relinquished their "revolutionary ideas" and were now committed to "Islam, the constitutional monarchy, and nonviolence." The party won 9 seats in the House of Representatives in 1997, while Benkirane was successful in a by-election on April 30, 1999. The PJD has gained popularity, taking 42 seats in the House of Representatives in 2002, having won in most districts where it was permitted to run a candidate. In local elections in 2003, it scaled back the candidates it presented, with leader Saad Eddine OTHMANI explaining that the party did not want to scare off foreign investors with high-profile wins.

The PJD is widely expected to have significant success in the parliamentary elections in 2007, and observers anticipate that the party will become a partner in a government coalition.

Leader: Saad Eddine OTHMANI (Secretary General).

Action Party (*Parti de l'Action*—PA). The PA was organized in December 1974 by a group of Berber intellectuals dedicated to the "construction of a new society through a new elite." It won two legislative seats in 1977, none in 1984, and two in 1993 and 1997.

Leader: Mohammed EL IDRISSI.

Democratic Party for Independence (*Parti Démocratique pour l'Indépendance*—PDI). The PDI, a small but long-standing grouping (also referenced as the *Parti de la Choura et de l'Istiqlal,* or *Choura*), won three seats in the 1993 direct house election and a surprising six seats in the indirect election.

Leaders: Abdelwahed MAACH.

Democratic and Social Movement (*Mouvement Démocratique et Social*—MDS). Launched in June 1996 (as the National Democratic and Social Movement) by MNP dissidents, the Berber MDS is led by a former official of the interior ministry.

Leader: Mahmoud ARCHANE (Secretary General).

United Socialist Left (*Gauche Socialiste Unifiée*—GSU). The GSU is a left-wing formation that was launched at a constitutive congress in July 2002 when the OADP merged with three minor radical groupings, namely the Movement of Independent Democrats, the Movement for Democracy, and the Independent Left Potentials.

Leader: Mohamed Ben Said AIT IDDER (Secretary General).

Organization of Democratic and Popular Action (*Organisation de l'Action Démocratique et Populaire*—OADP). Claiming a following of former members of the USFP and PPS, the OADP was organized in May 1983. It obtained one seat in 1984 balloting and two

seats in 1993. A new 74-member Central Committee was elected at the third OADP congress, held November 5–6, 1994, in Casablanca.

The OADP was one of the few major parties to oppose the king's constitutional initiatives of 1996, some of its members subsequently splitting off to form the PSD (above) because of the issue. The OADP won four seats in the November 1997 *Majlis* elections. Although the OADP was a member of the ruling Democratic Bloc, it was not listed as having any members in the March 1998 cabinet. The OADP sources defined the group's stance as one of "critical" support of the coalition government.

Leader: Mohamed BENSAID (Secretary General).

National Union of Popular Forces (*Union Nationale des Forces Populaires*—UNFP). Formed in 1959 by former *Istiqlal* adherents, the UNFP subsequently became a coalition of left-wing nationalists, trade unionists, resistance fighters, and dissident members of minor parties. Weakened by internal factionalism, government repression, the disappearance of its leader Mehdi BEN BARKA (while visiting France in 1965), and the neutrality of the Moroccan Labor Union (UMT), the party subsequently split into personal factions. In 1972 the National Administrative Committee replaced the ten-person Secretariat General and three-person Political Bureau with a group of five permanent committees. The Political Bureau thereupon formed its own organization, UNFP–Rabat Section, which was banned for several months in 1973 for activities against the state and subsequently reorganized as the USFP (above). The UNFP formally boycotted the legislative elections of 1977 and 1984, as well as the municipal balloting of June 1983; it won no seats in 1993. Recent references to the Democratic Bloc have not listed the UNFP among its components, despite its previous inclusion in that umbrella group.

Leader: Moulay Abdallah IBRAHIM (Secretary General).

Party of the Democratic and Social Vanguard (*Parti de l'Avant-Garde Démocratique et*

Socia—PAGDS). Formed by USFD dissidents in 1991, the PAGDS boycotted the 1997 elections on the ground that its members had been harassed by the government.

Leader: Ahmed BENJELLAIME.

Other parties, a number of which won seats in 2002, include the **Alliance of Freedoms** (*Alliance des Liberté*—ADL), led by Ali BEL HAJ; the **Citizens' Initiatives for Development** (*Initiatives Citoyennes pour le Développement*—ICD), led by Mohammed BENHAMOU; the **Democratic Union** (*Union Démocratique*—UD), led by Bouazza IKKEN; the **Moroccan Liberal Party** (*Parti Marocain Libéral*—PML), led by Mohammed ZIANE; the **National Ittihadi Congress** (*Congrès National Ittihadi*—CNI), a breakaway group from the USFP led by Abdelmajid BOUZOUBAA; the **National Party for Unity and Solidarity** (*Parti National pour l'Unité et la Solidarité*—PNUS), led by Muhammad ASMAR; the **Party of Citizens' Forces** (*Parti des Forces Citoyennes*—PFC), led by Abderrahim LAHJOUJI; the **Party of Environment and Development** (*Parti de l'Environnement et du Développement*—PED), led by Ahmed AL ALAMI; the **Party of Promise** (*Parti al-Ahd*), led by Najib EL OUAZZANI; the **Party of Reform and Development** (*Parti de la Réforme et du Développement*—PRD), led by former RNI member Abderrahmane EL KOHEN; the **Party of Renewal and Equity** (*Parti du Renouveau et de l'Equité*—PRE), led by Chakir ACHEHBAR; and the **Social Center Party** (*Parti du Centre Social*—PCS), led by Lachen MADIH.

Clandestine Groups

Justice and Welfare (*Adl wa-al-Ihsan*). The country's leading radical Islamist organization, *Adl wa-al-Ihsan* was formed in 1980. Although denied legal party status in 1981, it was informally tolerated until a mid-1989 crackdown, during which its founder, Sheikh Abd Assalam Yassine, was placed under house arrest and other members were imprisoned. The government formally outlawed the group in January 1990; two months later, five of its most prominent members were given two-year prison terms, and Yassine's house detention was extended, touching off large-scale street disturbances in Rabat. Although the other detainees were released in early 1992, Yassine remained under house arrest, King Hassan describing fundamentalism as a threat to Moroccan stability. An estimated 100 members of *Adl wa-al-Ihsan* were reportedly among the prisoners pardoned in mid-1994, Yassine pointedly not among them. He was finally released from house arrest in December 1995 but was soon thereafter placed under "police protection" for apparently having criticized the government too strenuously. (Among Yassine's transgressions, in the eyes of the government, was his failure to acknowledge King Hassan as the nation's supreme religious leader.) His house arrest prompted protest demonstrations in 1998 by his supporters, whom the government also charged with responsibility for recent protests among university students and a mass demonstration in late December 1998 protesting U.S.–UK air strikes against Iraq. Although the group remained proscribed, Yassine was released from house arrest in May 2000. He reportedly continued to be critical of the royal family and the government, but based on Yassine's rejection of violence, the government tolerated the group's activities. However, in May 2006 the government arrested hundreds of *Adl wa-al-Ihsan* members across the country, apparently in reaction to rumors that the party had planned an uprising. Those rounded up were later freed, but party members claimed that materials such as computers and books had been seized from party offices.

In a separate matter, Yassine's daughter, Nadia YASSINE, head of the organization's feminist branch, was charged with insulting the monarchy after she gave an interview to a Moroccan newspaper in which she asserted that the monarchy "was not suitable for Morocco," that a republic would be preferable, and that the king's regime was likely to collapse soon. She faced up to five years in prison. After the United States expressed opposition to her prosecution, her trial was postponed indefinitely.

Leader: Sheikh Abd Assalam YASSINE.

Cabinet

As of June 1, 2006

Prime Minister	Driss Jettou (ind.)
Minister of State	Abbas El Fassi (*Istiqlal*)

Ministers

Agricultural, Rural Development, and Marine Fisheries	Mohand Laenser (MNP)
Communication, Spokesman of the Government	Mohamed Nabil Benabdallah (ind.)
Culture	Mohamed Achaari (USFP)
Energy and Mining	Mohammed Boutaleb (ind.)
Employment and Vocational Training	Mustapha Mansouri (*Istiqlal*)
Environment, Territory Development	Mohamed El-Yazghi (USFP)
Equipment and Transport	Karim Gellab (ind.)
Finance and Privatization	Fathallah Oualaou (USFP)
Foreign Affairs and Cooperation	Mohamed Benaissa (RNI)
Foreign Trade	Mustapha Mechahouri (ind.)
General Secretary of the Government	Abdessadek Rabiaa (ind.)
Habous (Religious Endowments) and Islamic Affairs	Ahmed Toufig (ind.)
Health	Mohammed Chaik Biadillah (ind.)
Industry, Trade, and Upgrading the Economy	Salaheddine Mezouar (ind.)
Interior	Chakib ben Moussa (ind.)
Justice	Mohamed Bouzoubaa (ind.)
Modernization of the Public Sector	Mohamed Boussaid (ind.)
National Education, Higher Education, Staff Training, and Scientific Research	Habib El Malki (ind.)
Relations with Parliament	Mohammed Saad El Alami (*Istiqlal*)
Social Development, the Family, and Solidarity	Abderrahman Harouchi (ind.)
Tourism, Handicraft, and Social Economy	Adil Douiri (*Istiqlal*)

Ministers Delegate (Ministries)

Foreign Affairs and Cooperation	Tayeb Fassi Fihri
Foreign Affairs, Moroccans Living Abroad	Nouzha Chekrouni [f]
Interior	Fouad Ali El-Himma

Secretaries of State

Agriculture, Rural Development, and Sea Fisheries	Mohamed Mohattane
Employment and Vocational Training	Said Oulbacha
National Education, Higher Education, Staff Training, and Scientific Research	Anis Birou
Social Development, Family, and Solidarity	Yasmina Baddou [f]
Youth	Mohammed El Gahs

[f] = female

In 1985 and 1986 there were a number of arrests of people appearing to be members of two left-wing groups: *Ila al-amaam* (To the Future), formed in the 1960s by a number of PPS Maoist dissidents, and *Qaidiyyun* (The Base), an outgrowth of a *23 Mars* group of the 1970s, most of whose supporters entered the OADP. Many of the detainees were released in mid-1989 under a royal amnesty. *Ila al-Amaam*'s former leader, Abraham SERFATY, was allowed to return to Morocco in late 1999. Members of another banned organization, *Shabiba al-islamiya* (Islamic Youth), have also been sentenced to prison terms, often in absentia, for antiregime activity. The group was founded by Abdelkarim MOUTIA, a former nationalist.

Legislature

The constitutional amendments of September 1996 provided for a bicameral **Parliament** (*Barlaman*) comprising an indirectly elected House of Councilors and a directly elected House of Representatives. Previously, the legislature had consisted of a unicameral House of Representatives, two-thirds of whose members were directly elected with the remainder being selected by an electoral college of government, professional, and labor representatives.

House of Councilors (*Majlis al-Mustasharin*). The upper house consists of 270 members indirectly elected for nine-year terms (one-third of the house is renewed every three years) by local councils, regional councils, and professional organizations. At the first election on December 5, 1997, the National Assembly of Independents won 42 seats; the Democratic and Social Movement, 33; the Constitutional Union, 28, the Popular Movement, 27; the National Democratic Party, 21; the Independence Party, 21; the Socialist Union of Popular Forces, 16; the Popular National Movement, 15; the Action Party, 13; the Democratic Forces Front, 12; the Party of Renewal and Progress, 7; the Socialist Democratic Party, 4; the Democratic Party for Independence, 4; and various labor organizations, 27. In the election to renew one-third

of the house on September 15, 2000, the National Assembly of Independents won 14 seats; the Popular National Movement, 12; the National Democratic Party, 10; the Popular Movement, 9; the Constitutional Union, 8; the Independence Party, 7; the Democratic and Social Movement, 6; the Democratic Forces Front, 5; the Socialist Union of Popular Forces, 3; the Party of Renewal and Progress, 2; the Action Party, 2; the Socialist Democratic Party, 2; the Democratic Party for Independence, 1; and various labor organizations, 3.

Speaker: Mustapha OUKACHA.

House of Representatives (*Majlis al-Nawwab*). The lower house has 325 members directly elected on a proportional basis for five-year terms. (Under electoral law revision of May 2002, 30 seats were set aside for women; those seats were to be contested on a proportional basis from national lists for the September 2002 balloting, while the other 295 seats were to be elected on a proportional basis from 92 multi-member constituencies.) Following the election of September 27, 2002, the distribution of seats was as follows: Socialist Union of Popular Forces, 50; Independence Party (*Istiqlal*), 48; Justice and Development, 42; National Assembly of Independents, 41; Popular Movement, 18; Constitutional Union, 16; National Democratic Party, 12; Democratic Forces Front, 12; Party of Renewal and Progress, 11; Democratic Union, 10; Democratic and Social Movement, 7; Socialist Democratic Party, 6; Party of Promise, 5; Alliance of Freedom, 4; Party of Reform and Development, 3; United Socialist Left, 3; Moroccan Liberal Party, 3; Party of Citizens' Forces, 3; Party of Environment and Development, 2; National Ittihadi Congress, 1.

Speaker: Abdelwahed RADI.

Communications

Press

Moroccan newspapers have a reputation for being highly partisan and outspoken, although those incurring the displeasure of the state face reprisal, such as forced suspension, and government control has at times been highly restrictive. The following are published daily in Casablanca in French, unless otherwise noted: *Le Matin du Sahara* (100,000), replaced *Le Petit Marocain* following government shutdown in 1971; *al-Alam* (Rabat, 100,000), Istiqlal organ, in Arabic; *L'Opinion* (Rabat, 60,000), Istiqlal organ; *Maroc Soir* (50,000), replaced *La Vigie Marocaine* in 1971; *al-Maghrib* (Rabat, 15,000), RNI organ; *al-Mithaq al-Watani* (Rabat, 25,000), RNI organ, in Arabic; *al-Anbaa* (Rabat, 15,000), Ministry of Information, in Arabic; *al-Bayane* (5,000), PRP organ, in French and Arabic; *Libération,* USFP organ; *al-Ittihad al-Ishtiraki,* USFP organ, in Arabic; *Risalat al-Umma,* UC organ, in Arabic; *Anoual* (Rabat), OADP weekly, in Arabic; *al-Mounaddama*, in Arabic. a*l-Mouharir,* a USFP organ, and *al-Bayane* were suspended in the wake of the June 1981 riots at Casablanca. The latter was permitted to resume publication in mid-July but, having had a number of its issues confiscated in early 1984 because of its reporting of further Casablanca disturbances, it was suspended again from October 1986 until January 1987. Two months later, the government seized an issue of *Anoual,* apparently in response to its coverage of prison conditions, and took similar action against *al-Bayane* in January 1988 because of its stories on problems in the educational system and recent demonstrations at Fez University. The USFP's *al-Ittihad al-Ishtiraki* was also informed that it would be censored because of its coverage of the student disturbances. In mid-1991 the government banned distribution of the first issue of *Le Citoyen,* a weekly established by political dissidents to promote government reform. Following the enthronement of the reform-minded King Mohamed VI in 1999, the government somewhat relaxed its grip on the print media. However, from 2000 through mid-2002 various issues of *Le Journal,* the independent weekly *L'Economiste, Maroc-Hebdo,* the Islamist weekly *Risalat al-Foutawah, Le Reporter al-Moustaquil, Le Quoditien du Maroc, Chamal, Demain,* and *Al-Sahifa* were banned. Domestic and international journalists' organizations criticized a libel law adopted in April 2002, accusing the government of eroding civil and press liberties by making it easier to file li-

bel suits. In May 2006, Human Rights Watch issued a report critical of tightening controls on the press, citing recent harassment of independent news weeklies that had questioned government policies.

News Agencies

The Moroccan Arab News Agency (*Wikalat al-Maghrib al-Arabi*—WMA), successor to the former *Maghreb Arabe Presse,* is an official, government-owned agency. Most major foreign agencies maintain offices in Rabat.

Broadcasting and Computing

Broadcasting is under the supervision of the Broadcasting Service of the Kingdom of Morocco (*Idhaat al-Mamlakat al-Maghribiyah*). The government-controlled *Radiodiffusion-Télévision Marocaine* provides radio service over three networks (national, international, and Berber) as well as commercial television service; transmission by a private television company was launched in 1989. In addition, the Voice of America operates a radio station in Tangier. There were approximately 7.1 million television receivers and 600,000 personal computers serving 800,000 Internet users in 2003.

Intergovernmental Representation

Ambassador to the U.S.
Aziz MEKOUAR

U.S. Ambassador to Morocco
Thomas RILEY

Permanent Representative to the UN
Mustapha SAHEL

IGO Memberships (Non-UN)
AfDB, AFESD, AMF, AMU, BADEA, EBRD, IDB, Interpol, IOM, LAS, NAM, OIC, OIF, PCA, WCO, WTO

Disputed Territory

Western Sahara

The region known since 1976 as Western Sahara was annexed by Spain in two stages: the coastal area in 1884 and the interior in 1934. In 1957, the year after Morocco attained full independence, Rabat renewed a claim to the territory, sending irregulars to attack inland positions. In 1958, however, French and Spanish troops succeeded in quelling the attacks, with Madrid formally uniting Saguia el Hamra and Rio de Oro, the two historical components of the territory, as the province of Spanish Sahara. Mauritanian independence in 1960 led to territorial claims by Nouakchott, with the situation being further complicated in 1963 by the discovery of one of the world's richest phosphate deposits at Bu Craa. During the next dozen years, Morocco attempted to pressure Spain into relinquishing its claim through a combination of diplomatic initiatives (the UN first called for a referendum on self-determination for the Sahrawi people in 1966), direct support for guerrilla groups, and a legal challenge in the International Court of Justice (ICJ).

Increasing insurgency led Spain in May 1975 to announce that it intended to withdraw from Spanish Sahara, while an ICJ ruling the following October stated that Moroccan and Mauritanian legal claims to the region were limited and had little bearing on the question of self-determination. Nevertheless, in November King Hassan ordered some 300,000 unarmed Moroccans, in what became known as the Green March, to enter the territory. Although Spain strongly objected to the action, a tripartite agreement with Morocco and Mauritania was concluded at Madrid on November 14. As a result, Spanish Sahara ceased to be a province of Spain at the end of the year; Spanish troops withdrew shortly thereafter, and Morocco and Mauritania assumed responsibility for Western Sahara on February 28, 1976. On April 14 Rabat and Nouakchott reached an agreement under which Morocco claimed the northern two-thirds of the region and Mauritania claimed the southern one-third.

The strongest opposition to the partition was voiced by the Popular Front for the Liberation of Saguia el Hamra and Rio de Oro (Polisario, see below), which in February 1976 formally proclaimed a government-in-exile of the Sahrawi Arab Democratic Republic (SADR), headed by Mohamed Lamine OULD AHMED as prime minister. Whereas Polisario had originally been based

in Mauritania, its political leadership was subsequently relocated to Algeria, with its guerrilla units, recruited largely from nomadic tribes indigenous to the region, establishing secure bases there. Neither Rabat nor Nouakchott wished to precipitate a wider conflict by operating on Algerian soil, which permitted Polisario to concentrate militarily against the weaker of the two occupying regimes and thus to aid in the overthrow of Mauritania's Moktar Ould Daddah in July 1978. On August 5, 1979, Mauritania concluded a peace agreement with Polisario at Algiers, but Morocco responded by annexing the southern third of Western Sahara. Meanwhile, Polisario launched its first raids into Morocco while continuing a diplomatic offensive that by the end of 1980 had resulted in some 45 countries according recognition to the SADR.

During a summit meeting of the Organization of African Unity (OAU) in Nairobi, Kenya, in June 1981, King Hassan called for a referendum on the future of the disputed territory, but an OAU special implementation committee was unable to move on the proposal because of Rabat's refusal to engage in direct negotiations or to meet a variety of other conditions advanced by Polisario as necessary to effect a cease-fire. As a result, conflict in the region intensified in the second half of the year.

At an OAU Council of Ministers meeting in Addis Ababa, Ethiopia, on February 22, 1982, a SADR delegation was, for the first time, seated, following a controversial ruling by the organization's secretary general that provoked a walkout by 18 member states, including Morocco. For the same reason, a quorum could not be declared for the next scheduled Council of Ministers meeting in Tripoli, Libya, on July 26, or for the 19th OAU summit, which was to have convened in Tripoli on August 5. An attempt to reconvene both meetings in November, following the "voluntary and temporary" withdrawal of the SADR, also failed because of the Western Sahara impasse, coupled with disagreement over the composition of a delegation from Chad. Another "temporary" withdrawal of the SADR allowed the OAU to convene the long-delayed summit in Addis Ababa in May 1983 at which it was decided to oversee a referendum in the region by the end of the year. Morocco's refusal to meet directly with Polisario representatives forced postponement of the poll, while the 1984 Treaty of Oujda with Libya effectively reduced support for the front's military forces. Subsequently, Moroccan soldiers crossed briefly into Algerian soil in "pursuit" of guerrillas, while extending the area under Moroccan control by 4,000 square miles. The seating of an SADR delegation at the 20th OAU summit in November 1985 and the election of Polisario Secretary General Mohamed Abd al-AZZIZ as an OAU vice president prompted Morocco's withdrawal from the organization.

At the sixth triennial Polisario congress, held in "liberated territory" in December 1985, Abd al-Azziz was reelected secretary general; he subsequently appointed a new 13-member SADR government that included himself as president, with Ould Ahmed continuing as prime minister. The following May a series of "proximity talks" involving Moroccan and Polisario representatives concluded at UN headquarters in New York with no discernible change in the territorial impasse. Subsequently, Rabat began construction of more than 1,200 miles of fortified sand walls that forced the rebels back toward the Algerian and Mauritanian borders. Polisario, while conceding little likelihood of victory by its 30,000 fighters over an estimated 120,000 to 140,000 Moroccan soldiers, nonetheless continued its attacks, hoping that the economic strain of a "war of attrition" would induce King Hassan to enter into direct negotiations—a position endorsed by a 98–0 vote of the 41st UN General Assembly. The UN also offered to administer the Western Sahara on an interim basis pending a popular referendum, but Rabat insisted that its forces remain in place. In 1987 the SADR reported an assassination attempt against Abd al-Azziz, alleging Moroccan complicity. Rabat denied the allegation and suggested that SADR dissidents may have been responsible.

Following the resumption of relations between Rabat and Algiers in May 1988, which some observers attributed in part to diminishing Algerian support for Polisario, progress appeared to be developing toward a negotiated settlement of the militarily stalemated conflict. On August 30, shortly after a new SADR government had been announced with Mahfoud Ali BEIBA taking over as prime minister, both sides announced their "conditional" endorsement of a UN-sponsored peace plan that called for a cease-fire and introduction of a UN peacekeeping force to oversee the long-discussed self-determination referendum. However, agreement was lacking on the qualifications of those who would be permitted to participate in the referendum and whether Moroccan troops would remain in the area prior to the vote. Underlining the fragility of the negotiations, Polisario launched one of its largest attacks in September before calling a cease-fire on December 30, pending face-to-face talks with King Hassan in January 1989. Although the talks eventually broke down, the cease-fire continued throughout most of the year as UN Secretary General Javier Pérez de Cuéllar attempted to mediate an agreement on referendum details. However, Polisario, accusing Rabat of delaying tactics, initiated a series of attacks in October, subsequent fighting being described as some of the most intense to date in the conflict. Another temporary truce was implemented in March 1990, and in June the UN Security Council formally authorized creation of a Western Saharan mission to supervise the proposed referendum. However, it was not until April 29, 1991, that the Security Council endorsed direct UN sponsorship of the poll, with the General Assembly approving a budget of $180 million, plus $34 million in voluntary contributions, for a UN Mission for the Referendum in Western Sahara (referenced by its French acronym, MINURSO). The mission's charge included the identification of bona fide inhabitants of the territory, the assembly of a voting list, the establishment of polling stations, and supervision of the balloting itself. The plan appeared to be in jeopardy when fierce fighting broke out in August between Moroccan and Polisario forces prior to the proposed deployment of MINURSO peacekeeping troops; however, both sides honored the UN's formal cease-fire date of September 6.

By early 1992 the broader dimensions of the Western Sahara conflict had significantly changed. The collapse of the Soviet Union and heightened internal problems for Polisario's principal backers, Algeria and Libya, created financial and supply problems for the rebels. At midyear it was estimated that more than 1,000 rank and file had joined a number of dissident leaders in defecting to Morocco. Meanwhile, Morocco had moved tens of thousands of settlers into the disputed territory, thereby diluting potential electoral support for Polisario. In addition, the proposed self-determination referendum, which the UN had planned to conduct in February, had been postponed indefinitely over the issue of voter eligibility, Polisario leaders charging that UN representatives had compromised their impartiality through secret dealings with Rabat. An unprecedented meeting, brokered by the UN at El Aaiún between Moroccan and Polisario representatives, ended on July 19, 1993, without substantial progress. The main difficulty lay in a dispute about voting lists, Polisario insisting they should be based on a census taken in 1974 and Morocco arguing that they should be enlarged to include the names of some 100,000 individuals subsequently settling in the territory.

A second round of face-to-face talks, scheduled for October 1993, was cancelled at the last moment when Polisario objected to the presence of recent defectors from the front on the Moroccan negotiating team. Although the prospects for agreement on electoral eligibility were regarded as slight, MINURSO began identifying voters in June 1994 with the hope that balloting could be conducted in October 1995. Registration proceeded slowly, however, and UN officials in early 1995 protested that the Moroccan government was interfering in their operations. In April, UN Secretary General Boutros Boutros-Ghali reluctantly postponed the referendum again, sentiment reportedly growing within the UN Security Council to withdraw MINURSO if genuine progress was not achieved shortly.

In May 1996 the Security Council ordered a reduction in MINURSO personnel, UN officials declaring an impasse in the voter identification dispute and observers suggesting that hostilities could easily break out once again. However, face-to-face contacts between Polisario and Moroccan officials resumed in September, but no genuine progress ensued. It was reported that only 60,000 potential

voters had been approved, with the cases of some 150,000 other "applicants" remaining unresolved at the end of the year.

New UN Secretary General Kofi Annan made the relaunching of the UN initiative in Morocco one of his priorities in early 1997 and in the spring appointed former U.S. Secretary of State James Baker as his personal envoy on the matter. Baker's mediation led to face-to-face talks between Polisario and representatives of the Moroccan government in the summer, culminating in the announcement of a "breakthrough" in September. Essentially, the two sides agreed to revive the 1991 plan with the goal of conducting the self-determination referendum in December 1998. They also accepted UN "supervision" in the region pending the referendum and agreed to the repatriation of refugees under the auspices of the UN High Commissioner for Refugees. MINURSO resumed the identification of voters in December 1997; however, the process subsequently again bogged down, with most observers concluding that the Moroccan government bore primary responsibility for the foot-dragging. Annan launched what he said would be his final push for a resolution in early 1999, calling for the resumption of voter registration at midyear leading up to a referendum by the end of July 2000.

In September 1999 several pro-independence riots in Western Sahara were suppressed by what some saw as an over-reaction by the police, who beat and arrested scores of demonstrators. The heavy-handedness of the security forces reportedly strengthened the resolve of King Mohamed VI to oust the "old guard" of the Moroccan regime, especially Interior Minister Driss Basri. Although the new king later espoused a more flexible stance toward the Western Sahara issue, UN special envoy Baker noted in April 2000 that he remained pessimistic about the prospects of a resolution of the conflict, citing Morocco's insistence that Moroccan settlers in Western Sahara be eligible in the proposed referendum. In September 2001 Polisario rejected Baker's proposal to grant the Western Sahara political autonomy rather than hold an independence referendum. Recent interest in oil drilling in the region reportedly further complicated the matter. In November 2002 King Mohamed described the notion of a self-determination referendum as "obsolete." In mid-2004 the UN Security Council adopted a resolution urging Morocco and Polisario to accept the UN plan to grant Western Sahara self-government. Morocco rejected the proposal and continued to insist that the area be granted autonomy within the framework of Moroccan sovereignty. In August 2005 Polisario released 404 Moroccan prisoners, the last of the soldiers it had captured in fighting. The front said it hoped that the gesture would lead to Moroccan reciprocity and then a peace settlement. In November 2005, the king renewed his call for autonomy for the region within "the framework of Moroccan sovereignty," but the Polisario Front quickly rebuffed what it referred to as the king's "intransigence."

The stalemate lasted into 2006. Morocco continued to administer the annexed territory as four provinces: three established in 1976 (Boujdour, Es-Smara, El-Aaiún) and one in 1979 (Oued ed-Dahab). The SADR administers four Algerian camps, which house an estimated 190,000 Sahrawis, and claims to represent some 83,000 others who remain in the Western Sahara.

Sahrawi Front

Popular Front for the Liberation of Saguia el Hamra and Rio de Oro (*Frente Popular para la Liberación de Saguia el Hamra y Rio de Oro*—Polisario). Established in 1973 to win independence for Spanish (subsequently Western) Sahara, the Polisario Front was initially based in Mauritania, but since the mid-1970s its political leadership has operated from Algeria. In consonance with recent developments throughout the world, the once strongly socialist Polisario currently promises to institute a market economy in "the future Sahrawi state," except in regard to mineral reserves (which would remain state property). The front also supports "eventual" multipartyism, its 1991 Congress, held in Tindouf, Algeria, pledging to draft a "democratic and pluralistic"

constitution to present for a national referendum should the proposed self-determination vote in the Western Sahara go in Polisario's favor. In other activity, the Congress reelected longtime leader Mohamed Abd al-Azziz as secretary general of the front and thereby president of the SADR. However, in August 1992 the defection to Morocco of the SADR foreign minister, Brahim HAKIM, served to point up the increasingly tenuous position of the rebel movement. Subsequently, a new SADR government-in-exile announced in September 1993 was most noteworthy for the appointment of hard-liner Brahim GHALI as defense minister.

In 1995 Polisario reportedly was still threatening to resume hostilities if the UN plan collapsed. However, it was widely believed that the front's military capacity had by then diminished to about 6,000 soldiers.

The Ninth Polisario Congress, held August 20–27, 1995, reelected Abd al-Azziz as secretary general and urged the international community to pressure the Moroccan government regarding its perceived stonewalling. In September a new SADR government was announced under the leadership of Mahfoud Ali Larous Beiba, a former SADR health minister. On October 12 the first session of an SADR National Assembly was convened in Tindouf, its 101 members having been elected via secret ballot at local and regional "conferences." A new SADR government was named on January 21, 1998, although Beiba remained as prime minister and a number of incumbents were reappointed. Beiba was succeeded on February 10, 1999, by Bouchraya Hamoudi Bayoun.

In the summer and fall of 2005, many Sahrawis had began referring to their campaign against Morocco as an "*intifada*," and Abd al-Azziz called for assistance from South Africa's Nelson Mandela and U.S. President George W. Bush in resolving the Western Sahara standoff.

Secretary General: Mohamed Abd al-AZZIZ (President of the SADR).

Prime Minister of the SADR: Bouchraya Hamoudi BAYOUN.

MOZAMBIQUE

REPUBLIC OF MOZAMBIQUE

República de Moçambique

The Country

Mozambique lies on the southeast coast of Africa, its contiguous neighbors being Tanzania on the north; Malawi and Zambia on the northwest; and Zimbabwe, South Africa, and Swaziland on the west and south. Mozambique's varied terrain comprises coastal lowlands, central plateaus, and mountains along the western frontier. The country is bisected by the Zambezi River, which flows southeastward from the Zambia-Zimbabwe border. The population, while primarily of Bantu stock, is divided into several dozen tribal groups, most speaking distinct local languages or dialects. A majority of the population is Christian (according to the 1997 census); about one-quarter of the population practices traditional religions, and there is a Muslim minority of about 18 percent. Catholic and Anglican churches, many of which were closed following independence, have regained influence as a result of the government's retreat from a rigidly Marxist-Leninist orientation. Women constitute 48 percent of the labor force, primarily in the agricultural sector; there are a number of female ministers, including the prime minister, in the current cabinet.

Agriculture remains the mainstay of the economy, employing two-thirds of the work force and providing the principal cultivated exports: cashew nuts, cotton, sugar, and tea. Seafood is also an important export. Following independence, agricultural output declined—particularly in production of sugar and cotton as well as of such minerals as coal and copper—as the government introduced pervasive state control and the Portuguese community, which possessed most of the country's tech-

nical and managerial expertise, left the country. In the early 1980s, however, the government began to encourage limited private ownership, foreign investment, and the development of family-owned and operated farms. For the most part, industry has been limited to processing agricultural commodities, although significant deposits of natural gas, as well as bauxite, iron, manganese, tantalite, uranium, and other ores await exploitation.

The economy contracted sharply from 1982 to 1986, as insurgency and drought inflicted widespread death and deprivation that necessitated massive emergency food imports and other aid. Subsequently, a recovery program sponsored by the International Monetary Fund (IMF) contributed to

moderate economic growth, although social conditions, particularly in rural areas, remained dismal as the result of rebel activity.

In June 1993 international donors pledged some $70 million to aid the estimated 4 million internally displaced Mozambicans and to launch a massive repatriation program in light of progress toward resolution of the longstanding civil war. However, returning refugees faced grim economic conditions, as reflected by an average annual per capita income of less than $80 (the world's lowest, according to the World Bank). The imposition by the government of fiscal austerity and other reforms subsequently sparked an impressive recovery, GDP growing by more than 10 percent annually from 1996–1999 and Mozambique becoming the "darling" of the IMF and World Bank, which had helped to negotiate substantial debt relief packages. However, despite having returned to food self-sufficiency, Mozambique remained among the lowest-ranked nations regarding development, and poverty was widespread, much of the population living in small villages lacking electricity or running water.

It was widely expected that GDP growth would again approach double digits in 2000 based on the continued inflow of substantial foreign investment. However, severe flooding early in the year significantly damaged those prospects. Indeed, the government announced that GDP growth for 2000 was only 2.1 percent, while inflation registered 12.7 percent for the year. The economy recovered in 2001, however, with real GDP rising by 13.9 percent. Through mid-2002, the World Bank, the IMF, and the World Trade Organization continued to praise the country's economic performance and the government's policies.

Growth continued through 2003, propelled by expansion in manufacturing, construction, and service industries. In 2004 the World Bank provided $790 million in grants for debt relief. In addition, the IMF pledged $7.7 million in assistance over a three-year period to support government efforts to reform and restructure the economy. (Banking reform and intensified privatization efforts were requested.) The IMF also approved $110 million to fund construction of a major railway in Zambezi Province as a conduit for manufactured goods and passengers to the interior of the country.

In 2005 it was reported that GDP had increased annually by an average of 8 percent over the past ten years, one of the highest long-term growth rates in Africa. Collaterally, the poverty rate had declined from 69 percent of the population in 1997 to 54 percent. Inflation had dropped to 8 percent in 2005.

Government and Politics

Political Background

Portuguese hegemony was established early in the 16th century, when Mozambican coastal settlements became ports of call for traders from the Far East. However, it was not until the Berlin Congress of 1884–1885 that Portuguese supremacy was formally acknowledged by the European powers. In 1952 the colony of Mozambique became an Overseas Province and, as such, was constitutionally incorporated into Portugal. In 1964 armed resistance to Portuguese rule was initiated by the Mozambique Liberation Front (*Frente de Libertação de Moçambique*—Frelimo), led by Dr. Eduardo MONDLANE until his assassination by Portuguese agents in 1969. Following Mondlane's death, Samora MACHEL and Marcelino DOS SANTOS overcame a bid for control by Frelimo Vice President Uriah SIMANGO and were installed as the movement's president and vice president, respectively. After the 1974 coup in Lisbon, negotiations in Lusaka, Zambia, called for the formation of a new government composed of Frelimo and Portuguese elements and for the attainment of complete independence in mid-1975. The agreement was challenged by leaders of the white minority, who attempted to establish a white provisional government under right-wing leadership. After the collapse of this rebellion on September 10, 1974, most of the territory's 250,000 whites migrated to Portugal or South Africa.

On June 25, 1975, Mozambique became an independent "people's republic," with Machel assuming the presidency. Elections of Frelimo-sponsored candidates to local, district, provincial, and national assemblies were held during

Political Status: Former Portuguese dependency; became independent as the People's Republic of Mozambique on June 25, 1975; present name adopted in constitution that came into effect on November 30, 1990.

Area: 309,494 sq. mi. (801,590 sq. km.).

Population: 16,542,740 (1997C); 19,434,000 (2005E). The 1997 figure includes an adjustment of 5.1 percent for underenumeration.

Major Urban Center (2005E): MAPUTO (1,122,000).

Official Language: Portuguese (a number of African languages are also spoken).

Monetary Unit: Metical (market rate July 1, 2006: 25,860 meticals = $1US). (In November 2005 the Assembly of the Republic approved legislation providing for the introduction of a "new metical" [worth 1,000 old meticals] as of July 1, 2006. Both old and new meticals were to be considered legal tender at least until the end of the year.)

President: Armando Emilio GUEBUZA (Mozambique Liberation Front); elected on December 1–2, 2004, and inaugurated on February 2, 2005, to succeed Joaquim Alberto CHISSANO (Mozambique Liberation Front).

Prime Minister: Luisa Dias DIOGO (Mozambique Liberation Front); appointed by the president on February 17, 2004, to succeed Dr. Pascoal Manuel MOCUMBI (Mozambique Liberation Front), who earlier had announced his intention to resign; reappointed by the president on February 3, 2005, following presidential and legislative elections on December 1–2, 2004.

September–December 1977. In an apparent easing of its commitment to Marxist centralism, the government took steps in the early 1980s to separate government and party cadres. However, a government reorganization in March 1986 reestablished party domination, with the Council of Ministers being divided into three sections, each directed by a senior member of the Frelimo Political Bureau.

On July 26, 1986, Mário Fernandes da Graça MACHUNGO, an economist who had overseen re-cent liberalization of the economy, was sworn in as prime minister, a newly created post designed to permit President Machel to concentrate on defense of the regime against the Mozambique National Resistance (*Resistência Nacional Moçambicana*—Renamo), which had grown from a relatively isolated opponent to an insurgent force operating in all ten provinces. Machel, who had remained a widely respected leader despite the country's myriad problems, died in a plane crash on October 19 and was succeeded on November 6 by his longtime associate, Foreign Affairs Minister Joaquim Alberto CHISSANO. Chissano extended the economic liberalization policies initiated by his predecessor, overtures to the West for emergency and development aid generally being well-received. However, domestic progress remained severely constrained by Renamo attacks on civilians and the concurrent destruction of farms, schools, and health facilities.

In part to seek accommodation with the rebels, Frelimo abandoned its commitment to Marxism-Leninism in July 1989. A year later, direct talks with Renamo representatives were launched in Rome, Italy, and in August 1990 Frelimo's Central Committee endorsed the holding of multiparty elections in 1991.

On November 2, 1990, following extensive National Assembly debate, a new, pluralistic constitution was adopted. Subsequently, a tenuous ceasefire negotiated with Renamo on December 1 broke down, the rebels withdrawing from the Rome talks. The talks resumed in May 1991, and five months later the rebels agreed to halt armed activity, to drop demands for a UN transitional government, and to recognize the government's authority. For its part, the government agreed to procedures by which Renamo could function as a political party following a formal cease-fire.

After several weeks of deadlock in the ninth round of the Rome talks, the parties finally agreed on a protocol, which was signed March 12, 1992. It provided for election to the Assembly of the Republic by proportional representation; the holding of simultaneous legislative and presidential balloting; the formation of a National Electoral Commission, one-third of whose members would be named by

Renamo; and government assistance to Renamo in establishing itself as a political grouping in every provincial capital. After another delay, the round continued with a June 10 agreement on the formation of a unified, nonpartisan army; the specifics of a cease-fire; and transitory arrangements before the general election. On August 5 Chissano and Renamo leader Gen. Afonso DHLAKAMA held their first ever face-to-face meeting, and on August 7 they reached an accord on a cease-fire and electoral preparations. Subsequently, despite reports of Renamo intransigence and an increasingly restive national army, Chissano and the rebel leader signed a peace treaty in Rome on October 4, ending the 16-year-old conflict. Included in the treaty were provisions for a cease-fire, multiparty elections within a year, the establishment of a 30,000-member army drawn equally from the existing forces, a political amnesty, and Western-financed repatriation of refugees. Five days later the assembly approved the treaty and the launching of the UNs' Operation in Mozambique (*Operação des Naões Unidas em Moçambique*—ONUMOZ), a peacekeeping force with responsibility for disarming both combatants, integrating troops into the new armed forces, organizing elections, and securing trade routes.

In April 1993 the UN Security Council voiced "serious concern" over implementation of the October 1992 accord because of a shortfall in funds for deployment of peacekeeping troops and the withdrawal of Renamo members from the cease-fire and control commissions established under the treaty. Renamo subsequently indicated that it would not return to the commissions until a number of logistical problems had been resolved and some $15 million to support its political activities had been received.

On June 3, 1993, the commissions resumed meeting, and on June 21 the disarmament program was launched. Two months later the Joint Commission for the Formation of the Mozambique Defense Armed Forces announced that it had reached agreement on creation of the inclusive Mozambique Defense Armed Forces. In addition, an August 27–September 3 meeting between Chissano and Dhlakama, their first since 1992, yielded an accord on territorial administration, following Renamo's retreat from insistence that it be given jurisdiction over the provinces it controlled. At a further meeting on October 16–20 the two agreed on the establishment of a 20-member electoral commission (to be composed of ten government appointees, seven Renamo officials, and three from other opposition parties). Thereafter, the peace process continued to advance as the government and Renamo settled electoral law differences and formally agreed to a demobilization plan that would commence on November 30 and continue for six months.

By mid-January 1994 over 50 percent of the rebels were reported to have arrived at demobilization sites. By contrast, the government was widely criticized for a compliance level of only 19 percent. Nonetheless, President Chissano, responding to a Security Council call for a transfer of power to democratically elected officials by the end of November, announced that the country's first multiparty balloting would take place on October 27–28.

At the long-deferred balloting (extended by one day to October 29), President Chissano was a clear victor, polling 53.7 percent of the vote, compared to 33.7 percent for his principal opponent, Renamo's Dhlakama. While the legislative outcome was much closer (129–112), no opposition members were named to the government subsequently formed under former foreign minister Pascoal Manuel MOCUMBI.

Under pressure from the opposition and international donors to broaden its definition of what constituted a viable polling district, the assembly, with Renamo support, approved a constitutional amendment in November 1996 that provided for the establishment of a local government electoral system wherein communities with a functioning administration and a "reasonable" local tax base would participate in polling. In early 1997 Renamo reversed itself, threatening to stalemate the assembly and boycott elections if the scope of the polling was not expanded. Nevertheless, in March 1997 the assembly approved the creation of a nine-member, bipartisan national elections commission, which it charged with preparing for balloting. In June it was announced that elections would be held in 23 cities and 10 towns (1 in each of the provinces) in December, one year after originally scheduled. Balloting was subsequently postponed until May 1998 and, once again, in March 1998 to June 30.

Thereafter, after months of threats, in April 1998 the partners in the Coordinating Council of the Opposition formally announced their intention to boycott the local polling, citing the government's unwillingness to allow their representatives to participate in the commission that was investigating alleged electoral roll fraud. The opposition's subsequent efforts to garner support for their boycott plans appeared to have succeeded dramatically, as on June 30 less than 20 percent of the electorate was reported to have participated in the balloting. In the immediate aftermath of the elections, during which Frelimo candidates easily overwhelmed a field of independent competitors, the opposition declared the polling "null and void" and threatened to launch a civil disobedience campaign if the results were upheld. Subsequently, however, the Renamo-led opposition announced that it would not hinder the efforts of the newly elected officials, asserting that it was turning its attention to preparing for general elections in 1999.

Chissano once again defeated Dhlakama (52.3–47.7 percent) in the presidential poll conducted on December 3–5, 1999, while Frelimo won 133 seats in the concurrent assembly balloting, compared to 117 seats for Renamo and its recently formed opposition alliance called the Renamo/Electoral Union (Renamo/*União Electoral*—Renamo/UE). After the Supreme Court rejected a Renamo/UE call for nullification of the results, Chissano was sworn in for another five-year term on January 15, 2000. Two days later he reappointed Mocumbi to head a new all-Frelimo cabinet, which was described as bringing "fresh blood" into the government while retaining the "tested core" of the previous administration.

In February 2003, Renamo announced that it would run alone in upcoming municipal elections,

thereby leading ten other opposition parties to form a new electoral coalition—the Movement for Change and Good Governance (*Movimento para a Mudança e Boa Governação*—MGB)—to oppose Frelimo and Renamo. In the municipal elections held on November 19, 2003, Frelimo won 28 mayoral posts and a majority of council posts in 29 municipalities, while Renamo won 5 mayor's races and council majorities in 4 municipalities (its best showing in municipal elections since multiparty elections were implemented). Although there was low voter turnout (estimated at 24.2 percent) and Renamo complained of irregularities, monitors from the European Union (EU) judged the elections free and fair, and the Constitutional Council confirmed the results in January 2004.

On February 19, 2004, former World Bank economist and Finance Minister Luisa Dias DIOGO was appointed prime minister. (Mocumbi had earlier announced his plans to retire from the premiership in order to take a UN job.) Diogo became the country's first female prime minister. Analysts suggested that she was appointed ahead of presidential and legislative elections in an effort to reinvigorate Frelimo and demonstrate a commitment by the party to economic reform.

Chissano having announced in 2001 that he would not seek reelection in 2004, Frelimo chose Armando GUEBUZA as its presidential candidate. In balloting on December 1–2, Guebuza won 63.74 percent of the vote. His closest rival was Dhlakama, who received 31.72 percent of the vote. In concurrent legislative balloting, Frelimo won 62.03 percent of the vote and 160 seats, while Renamo won 29.73 percent, and 90 seats. None of the other 23 parties received more than 2 percent of the vote. Both the presidential and legislative elections were heavily criticized by the opposition and international observers. Renamo protested to the Constitutional Council, and its deputies initially refused to take their seats in the assembly. Nonetheless, on January 20, 2005, the council certified the results. Diogo was reappointed as prime minister on February 3, and she subsequently formed a new cabinet of Frelimo appointees.

Constitution and Government

The 1975 constitution characterized the People's Republic of Mozambique as a "popular democratic state" while reserving for Frelimo "the directing power of the state and society," with decisions taken by party organs to be regarded as binding on all government officials. A subsequent constitution, adopted in August 1978, set as a national objective "the construction of the material and ideological bases for a socialist society." The president of Frelimo served as president of the republic and chief of the armed forces, while an indirectly elected People's Assembly was designated as the "supreme organ of state power."

The basic law approved by the assembly in November 1990 contained no reference to Frelimo or leadership of the working class, while "People's" was dropped from the state name. It provided for a popularly elected president serving a maximum of two five-year terms. The Council of Ministers continued to be headed by a presidentially appointed prime minister, with national legislators selected on a proportional basis in multiparty balloting. In addition to freedom of association and of the press, the new document guaranteed various human and civil rights, including the right to private property and the right to strike. A Supreme Court heads an independent judiciary.

A number of constitutional amendments were approved by the Assembly of the Republic in November 2004, although most of the basic elements of the 1990 text remained intact. (The president continued to hold the power to appoint the prime minister, cabinet ministers, and provincial governors.) The amendments reaffirmed the authority of the Constitutional Council (established in 2003) to rule on the constitutionality of legislation and to validate election results. Other changes provided for an Ombudsman (appointed by a two-third's majority in the assembly) to investigate allegations of misconduct by state officials, for the election of provincial assemblies (beginning in 2008), and for the establishment of an advisory Council of State (comprised of automatic members [such as former presidents, former assembly presidents, and the runner-up in the most recent presidential election], as well as members appointed by the president and the assembly). Although the new council was given no formal decision-making authority, the president was required to consult with the council on a broad range of matters, including the conduct of elections. The basic law revisions also removed the president's immunity from prosecution by authorizing impeachment by a vote of two-thirds of the assembly.

The governors of the country's ten provinces are appointed by the president, who may annul the decisions of provincial, district, and local assemblies. The city of Maputo (which has provincial status) is under the administrative direction of a City Council chair.

Foreign Relations

Avowedly Marxist in orientation until mid-1989, the Frelimo government was for many years the beneficiary of substantial economic, technical, and security support from the Soviet Union, Cuba, East Germany, and other Moscow-line states. However, links with the West began to increase in 1979. The UK and Brazil extended credit, and in 1982 Portugal resumed relations that had ceased in 1977 as a result of the nationalization of Portuguese holdings. Relations with the United States, troubled since 1977 by charges of human rights abuses, reached a nadir in 1981 with the expulsion of all U.S. embassy personnel for alleged espionage. Relations were reestablished in July 1983, and President Machel made a state visit to Washington in September 1985, securing economic aid and exploring the possibility of military assistance. President Chissano was similarly received in March 1990 by President George H. W. Bush, who promised an unspecified amount of U.S. aid for reconstruction and development. Meanwhile, in 1984 Mozambique had been admitted to the IMF and World Bank, signifying a desire on Maputo's part to become a more active participant in the world economy.

Despite its prominence as one of the Front-Line States committed to majority rule in southern

Africa, Mozambique maintained economic links to white-dominated South Africa as a matter of "realistic policy," with some 40,000 Mozambicans employed in South African mines and considerable revenue derived from cooperation in transport and hydroelectric power. However, relations were severely strained by South African support for the Renamo insurgents in the 1980s. In a 1984 nonaggression pact, the "Nkomati Accord," South Africa agreed to stop aiding Renamo in return for Mozambique's pledge not to support the African National Congress (ANC) in its guerrilla campaign against the South African minority government. The accord proved ineffective, however, as growing rebel activity fostered Mozambican suspicion of continued destabilization attempts by its white-ruled neighbor. In August 1987 the two countries agreed that the pact should be reactivated, prompting an unprecedented meeting between President Chissano and South African President Botha in September 1988, at which Botha again promised not to support the insurgents. In 1990 President Chissano announced that he was convinced that the new government in Pretoria had indeed halted its support of Renamo and that the two countries could now concentrate on economic cooperation.

The civil war also dominated Maputo's relations elsewhere in the region. The Zimbabwean government, declaring "If Mozambique falls, we fall," sent an estimated 10,000 troops to combat the Renamo rebels, particularly in the transport corridor to Beira, which played a central role in the Front-Line States' effort to reduce dependence on South African trade routes. In December 1986 Tanzanian President Mwinyi also agreed to make troops available to Mozambique, as did Malawi following a dispute over alleged Renamo bases within its borders (see Malawi article). In 1992 Zimbabwean president Robert Mugabe, along with Italian officials, played a major role in brokering the peace accord that was signed in Rome in October.

By early 1993 approximately 1.7 million Mozambicans had taken refuge in neighboring countries, Malawi housing 1.1 million. On June 12 Mozambique and the UN High Commission for Refugees (UNHCR) formally inaugurated a repatriation operation (beginning with exiles in Zimbabwe), which observers described as the largest ever in Africa, and by August 19 Mozambique had signed repatriation agreements with Malawi, Swaziland, and Zambia. The repatriation program was formally terminated on November 21, 1995, at which time the UNHCR announced that more than 1 million refugees had returned home.

The most surprising foreign policy development of 1995 was Mozambique's admission to the Commonwealth as the group's 53rd member. Its entry on a "unique and special case" basis had been urged by its anglophone neighbors as a means of enhancing regional trade, most importantly in cashew nuts, which critics insisted was effectively controlled by Indian and Pakistani interests.

In 1996 Mozambique negotiated security agreements with Malawi, Swaziland, and Zimbabwe in an effort to squelch the border violence attributed to *Chimwenje,* a shadowy grouping of Zimbabwean dissidents who were allegedly led and trained by former Renamo militiamen from bases along their shared borders (for more information on *Chimwenje* see article on Zimbabwe). Meanwhile, following approximately a year of negotiations, Mozambique signed an agreement with South Africa in May that provided South African farmers with access to Mozambican agricultural land. The deal was opposed by both Renamo leaders and Frelimo activists, who charged that "exporting white farmers to Mozambique" was favored by South Africa's ANC as a means of freeing up land for black settlement. At the same time, South Africa and Mozambique inaugurated the Maputo Corridor Development Project with the aim of redeveloping the trade route between Johannesburg and Maputo and refurbishing the latter's harbor. In 2002 the government initiated a program to resettle white farmers from Zimbabwe whose land had been expropriated.

Relations between Mozambique and the United States have improved in recent years. In 2002, Chissano, along with the leaders of Botswana and Angola, met with U.S. President George W. Bush in Washington, D.C., in a summit on development of the region. Mozambique is part of the U.S.

Africa Growth and Opportunity Act (AGOA) that offers preferential trade opportunities to African states. Relations with European states also remained strong, with both France and Russia agreeing in 2002 to cancel portions of Mozambique's debt. Meanwhile the EU increased direct annual aid to Mozambique to $131 million per year through 2007.

In 2002 and 2003 Mozambique conducted a series of cooperative military exercises with Portugal. (The two countries also have an agreement whereby soldiers from Mozambique are trained in Portugal.) Although the relationship between the two countries subsequently remained essentially strong, friction developed in 2005 over the proposed takeover by Mozambique of a hydroelectric plant on the Zambesi River for which the Portuguese government held 85 percent financial responsibility. New President Guebuza refused to accept the amount of back debt that Portugal demanded be paid by Mozambique prior to the transfer of ownership, and, although a tentative agreement was announced in late 2005, its implementation remained unfinalized as of mid-2006. Meanwhile, the Guebuza administration reached out to a broad range of other potential donors for assistance, achieving success most notably with China, Germany, and India.

Current Issues

International observers concluded that the December 1999 elections were generally free and fair, but the Renamo/UE alleged fraud on the part of the government. The significant support for the Renamo/UE in legislative balloting and Dhlakama's surprisingly strong challenge to President Chissano was attributed in large part to the ongoing political cleavage between southern Mozambique (Frelimo's stronghold) and the rest of the country. Among other things, voters in the northern and central areas were reportedly upset that the recent influx of foreign capital was concentrated in Maputo, while poverty remained widespread in rural areas. In addition, Renamo's charges of corruption in government circles appeared to have resonated with some segments of the population. Nevertheless, for

his part, Chissano described the election results as a vindication of Frelimo policies and called the balloting a "fundamental step" in the consolidation of democracy, which would earn the country further foreign assistance.

Tension between the government and the opposition rose significantly in November 2000, when more than 40 people were killed during countrywide protest demonstrations called by Renamo. Dhlakama had earlier announced that "all doors of dialogue were shut" following Chissano's unilateral appointment of governors in the provinces "won" by Renamo. Interestingly, the violent events were followed by a significant thaw in Frelimo/Renamo relations as Chissano and Dhlakama agreed to form "working committees" to discuss "their disagreements." Although it was announced that the government would take Renamo's "input into consideration" in appointing governors in the disputed provinces, the exact form of this accommodation remained unclear. Dhlakama also shied away from formally recognizing the president, acknowledging only that Chissano "was *de facto* governing the country." Analysts noted that the perceived toning down of Dhlakama's previously fiery rhetoric could be attributed in part to problems he was facing within his own party (see Renamo under Political Parties, below).

During the 2004 presidential campaign, divisions within Frelimo emerged between the supporters of Armando Guebuza (the Frelimo candidate) and Chissano. The new cabinet appointed following Guebuza's victory contained many new members and appeared to represent an attempt by the new president to break with Frelimo's "old guard." In addition to purging many "*Chissanoistas*" from their former posts throughout government ranks, Guebuza also launched a broad anticorruption initiative that often focused on members of the former administration. (Guebuza described the "remoralization" of government as his top priority.) Tensions between Frelimo and Renamo also remained high, although Dhlakama (who continued to refuse to accept the validity of the 2004 election results) agreed to take his seat on the new Council of State in December 2005 on the grounds that too many critical governmental decisions were being made without appropriate opposition influence. Underscoring the ongoing friction, a bipartisan assembly commission, established in 2005 to propose electoral law reforms, disbanded in April 2006 without reaching agreement.

Political Parties

For its first 15 years of independence Mozambique was a one-party state in which the Mozambique Liberation Front (Frelimo) was constitutionally empowered to guide the operations of government at all levels. However, after extensive national debate, the government concluded in 1990 that a "significant minority" of the population desired a multiparty system. Consequently, constitutional revision in October guaranteed freedom of association, with subsequent legislation establishing the criteria for party legalization. Following President Chissano's February 6, 1991, announcement that legislation sanctioning political party formations (approved in January) was now in effect, a number of groups announced their intention to hold inaugural congresses, and by January 1994, 13 political parties had been legally recognized. Some 25 parties contested the 2004 legislative elections.

Government Party

Mozambique Liberation Front (*Frente de Libertação de Moçambique*—Frelimo). Founded in 1962 by the union of three nationalist parties and led by Dr. Eduardo Mondlane until his death in 1969, Frelimo engaged in armed resistance to Portuguese rule from 1964 to 1974, when agreement on independence was reached. At its third national congress in 1977, the front was designated a Marxist-Leninist party (directed by a Central Committee, a Political Bureau, and a Secretariat), but at the fourth party congress in 1983 economic philosophy began to shift toward the encouragement of free-market activity. Following the death of Samora Machel in October 1986, the Central Committee designated his longtime associate, Joaquim Alberto Chissano, as its political leader.

Frelimo retreated even further from Marxist doctrine at the group's fifth congress in 1989.

Terming itself the vanguard of "the Mozambican people" rather than a "worker-peasant alliance," the party opened its membership to many formerly excluded groups, such as private property owners, the business community, Christians, Muslims, and traditionalists. The congress also called for a negotiated settlement with Renamo, bureaucratic reform, and emphasis on family farming rather than state agriculture.

Although President Chissano easily defeated Renamo's Afonso Dhlakama at the 1994 election, Frelimo as a party performed much more poorly, barely securing a majority of legislative seats. On a regional basis the results were quite mixed, the party substantially outpolling Renamo in the south, while being decisively defeated in the center and trailing marginally in the north.

In what was described as a break with "old guard" leadership, five of the Frelimo Central Committee's six members were replaced on July 24, 1995, and Manuel Tome was appointed as the party's new secretary general. In spite of these changes, corruption charges continued to dog the party. Observers attributed Frelimo's subsequent endorsement of a proposal to limit the geographic scope of municipal elections to weak support beyond its southern base. Challenged only by small opposition groups and independent candidates, Frelimo dominated balloting for local posts in June 1998. It secured 48.5 percent of the vote and 133 seats in the December 1999 legislative balloting.

During a party congress in June 2002, Chissano was reelected as Frelimo chair. However, former parliamentary leader Armando Guebuza was elected as the new secretary general and the party's 2004 presidential candidate despite the fact that Chissano had supported Herder MUTEIA for the post. Guebuza was elected president in the 2004 balloting, and Frelimo increased its seats in the assembly to 160. Significant friction was subsequently reported between President Guebuza and former members of the Chissano administration (see Current issues, above).

Leaders: Armando GUEBUZA (President of the Republic and Secretary General), Luisa Dias DIOGO (Prime Minister), Joaquim Alberto CHISSANO (Former President of the Republic and

Chair of the Party), Manuel TOME (Parliamentary Leader).

Opposition Group

Mozambique National Resistance/Electoral Union (*Resistência Nacional Moçambicana/ União Electoral*—Renamo/UE). Formed in mid-1999, the Renamo/UE electoral alliance secured 38.8 percent of the vote and 117 seats in the December legislative balloting, a surprisingly good result in the opinion of most analysts after what was generally viewed as a "threadbare" campaign and the grouping's ongoing lack of "coherent strategies." (Distribution according to component parties, which included those indented below as well as Unamo, was unavailable, although the influence of the non-Renamo parties was considered minimal, and most seats certainly went to Renamo members.) Collaterally, Renamo/UE presidential candidate Afonso Dhlakama won 47.7 percent of the votes in the presidential balloting in 1999.

Renamo contested municipal elections independently in 2003, but Renamo/UE ran in the presidential and legislative elections in 2004. The alliance was hurt by the defection of Renamo members to form the Party for Peace, Development, and Democracy (see below) and the loss of Unamo (see below).

Leaders: Afonso DHLAKAMA (Chair), Manecas DANIEL (Vice Chair), Maximo DIAS (Chair of the Renamo/UE General Assembly), João ALEXANDRE (Secretary General).

Mozambique National Resistance—MNR (*Resistência Nacional Moçambicana*—Renamo). Also known as the *Movimento Nacional da Resistência de Moçambique* (MNRM) and as the André Group, after its late founder, André Matade MATSANGAI, Renamo was formed in the early 1970s primarily as an intelligence network within Mozambique for the white Rhodesian government of Ian Smith. Following Rhodesia's transition to majority rule as "Zimbabwe" in 1980, Renamo developed into a widespread anti-Frelimo insurgency, relying on financial support from Portuguese expatriates and, until the early 1990s, substantial military aid from South Africa. The 20,000-member Renamo army, comprising Portuguese and other mercenaries, Frelimo defectors, and numerous recruits from the Shona-speaking Ndau ethnic group, operated mainly in rural areas, where it interdicted transport corridors and sabotaged food production. Widely condemned for terrorist tactics, including indiscriminate killing and mutilation of civilians, Renamo, although largely stalemating the government militarily, generally failed to gain external recognition. In an apparent attempt to foster its nationalist image, Renamo launched an "Africanization" program in 1987 that included replacements for white Portuguese at its Lisbon-based headquarters. Further image-building took place at the 1989 Renamo congress, which revamped the movement's internal bodies. The congress also declared that Renamo was no longer intent on overthrowing the government but was seeking instead a peace settlement under which it could participate as a recognized "political force" in free elections resulting from constitutional revision. However, the Renamo leadership appeared disconcerted when, in 1990, the government agreed to hold such elections. Thereafter, despite a December 1, 1990, cease-fire, Renamo's military activities continued, thus supporting a widely held view that apart from its advocacy of a multiparty system the group lacked a political agenda.

When rebel strikes coincided with the reopening of peace talks in March and May 1991, there was speculation that party president Gen. Afonso Dhlakama had lost control over some of his forces. Thereafter, in negotiations with the government in Rome, Renamo, weakened by dwindling finances and pressed by South Africa, the UK, and the United States to negotiate seriously, signed the first of a series of concessionary protocols By mid-1992 it was apparent that the lengthy rebellion was drawing to a close.

While Dhlakama failed in his bid to win the presidency from Chissano in December 1994, the results of the legislative poll left Renamo only marginally second to Frelimo. In May 1995 President Chissano stated that, while Dhlakama could not be styled leader of the opposition (because he was not an elected member of the People's Assembly), he would be accorded "dignified status."

Although Renamo's legislative initiatives were blocked in the Frelimo-controlled assembly in 1995–1996, observers credited Dhlakama with continuing to enhance both the group's and his own political viability. In November 1996 Renamo legislators reportedly gave unanimous support to a constitutional amendment altering local election laws. In early 1997, however, the party reversed itself, threatening to boycott upcoming balloting unless the 1996 bill was repealed. Amid escalating tensions, the party organized nationwide antigovernment demonstrations in May 1997.

Although Renamo officials publicly insisted that they had no interest in returning to an armed struggle, arson attacks and disruption of the water supply were reported in July 1997. Subsequently, Dhlakama denounced the government's use of force to suppress the unrest, reportedly warning that Renamo would not rule out using force to defend itself against government "aggression."

Citing the need for the party to be "more flexible," Dhlakama forced the ouster of Secretary General Jose de CASTRO and Assistant Secretary General Albino FAIFE in January 1998. João Alexandre was subsequently named to Castro's former post. A split was reported in 2000 between those Renamo members, including a number of legislators, who appeared to be interested in negotiating a settlement with Frelimo and those, led by Dhlakama, who at midyear were still refusing to accept the results of the December 1999 legislative and presidential elections. In September 2000 the party's former legislative leader, Raul DOMINGOS, was expelled for "having collaborated with Frelimo" and for "corruption" during secret talks he allegedly held with the government. (Some analysts noted

that Domingos had previously been seen as a possible successor to Dhlakama.)

Allegedly facing increasing dissent within the party, Dhlakama nevertheless was reelected as Renamo's president in November 2001.

At a subsequent party congress, a ten-member political committee was created as a means to decentralize party leadership and broaden the party's appeal. In the 2004 presidential elections, Dhlakama again ran as the party's candidate, receiving 31.74 percent of the vote. The Renamo-led electoral alliance won 29.73 percent of the vote in the concurrent legislative elections, its representation declining from 117 to 90 seats in the assembly. Renamo deputies initially boycotted the assembly to protest perceived irregularities in the polling, but, after the Constitutional Council upheld the results, the deputies were seated in January 2005.

A number of regional and local Renamo leaders reportedly defected to Frelimo in 2006, apparently in the hope of improving their chances in the upcoming provincial and municipal elections.

Leaders: Gen. Afonso Macacho Marceta DHLAKAMA (President), Ossufo QUITINE (Legislative Leader), Jafar Gulamo JAFAR (Spokesman), João ALEXANDRE (former Secretary General), Ossufo MOMAD (Secretary General).

Mozambican Social Democratic Party (*Partido Moçambicano da Social Democracia*—PMSD). The PMSD was launched as political heir to the Mozambican Nationalist Movement (*Movimento Nacionalista Moçambicana*—Monamo) at the conclusion of Monamo's first congress in May 1992. Monamo had been founded in 1979 by exiled former Frelimo members led by Máximo Dias, who in 1973–1974 had attempted to persuade the Lisbon government to negotiate with the insurgents. In the late 1980s Monamo merged with the West German–based Mozambique National Independent Committee (*Comité Nacional Independente de Moçambique*—Conimo) to form the Mozambican Political Union (*União Política Moçambicana*—Upomo). In 1989 the group called for an immediate cease-fire under UN auspices, the departure of foreign troops, and the holding of national elections. Upomo operated until adoption of the 1990 constitution, after which Dias returned to Mozambique and Monamo reportedly decided to seek legal party status on its own. (Despite the formal change of name in 1992, the Monamo acronym continues in use.)

The Monamo/PMSP participated in the 1994 balloting in a Patriotic Alliance (*Aliança Patriótica*—AP) with the FAP (immediately below) that won 1.95 percent of the vote.

In 2006 Dias reportedly threatened to leave the Renamo/UE coalition because of the dominance of Renamo. (He contended that Renamo consistently appointed its own members to any vacant party or government posts.)

Leader: Dr. Máximo Diogo José DIAS (Secretary General).

Patriotic Action Front (*Frente de Acção Patriótica*—FAP). Founded in 1991, the FAP was a proponent in 1992 of delaying multiparty elections and naming a two-year transitional government.

Leaders: José Carlos PALAÇO (President), Raulda CONCEIÇÃO (Secretary General).

National Convention Party (*Partido de Convenção Nacional*—PCN). In October 1992 the *Indian Ocean Newsletter* described the PCN as a possible "third force" between Frelimo and Renamo. Amid nationwide debate in late 1992–early 1993 on the implementation of the October peace treaty provisions, the party urged the government to adhere to the timetable that called for elections in late 1993. The PCN, led by Lutero Simango, son of former national vice president Uriah Simango, was also linked to controversial former chief of staff Col. Gen. Sebastião MABOTE, who became a vocal critic of the regime after his ouster from the government in 1991 for alleged participation in a coup plot.

Leaders: Lutero SIMANGO (Chair), Inácio CHIRE, Luís GUIMARÃES, Abel Gabriel MABUNDA (Secretary General).

Mozambique People's Progress Party (*Partido de Progresso do Povo Moçambicano*—PPPM). The PPPM held its inaugural congress in July 1992 and was legalized in December. In 1993 supporters of its (then) vice president, Miguel Mabote, withdrew to form the PT (below). The PPPM won 1.06 percent of the vote in the 1994 legislative poll.

Leader: Dr. Padimbe KAMATI (President), Che ABDALA (Secretary General).

Democratic Renewal Party (*Partido Renovador Democrático*—PRD). Denied legal status in September 1993, the (then) Mozambique Federal Party (*Partido Federal de Moçambique*—Pafemo) subsequently abandoned its original name and amended its constitution, deleting statutes that had been described as critical of the federal government. Consequently, in January 1994 the PRD became the 13th legally registered party. It secured 1.01 percent of the vote in the 1994 legislative poll.

Leaders: Maneca DANIEL (President), Mariano Janeiro BORDINA.

United Democratic Front (*Frente Democrática Unida*—FDU). The FDU was formed in late 1994 by Mariano Janeiro Turbina, former head of the defunct Pafemo (see PRD, above) and theretofore commander of an anti-Frelimo guerrilla force in central Mozambique.

Leader: Mariano Janeiro TURBINA.

United Front of Mozambique–Democratic Convergence Party (*Frente Unida de Moçambique–Partido de Convergência Democrática*—Fumo-PCD).

Linked to Germany's Christian Democrats, Fumo-PCD held its inaugural congress in Maputo in January 1993. The party secured 1.39 percent of the legislative votes in 1994. It joined the Renamo/UE in 1999 despite the objection of Fumo-PCD founder Domingos Arouca, who resigned from the party's presidency in protest. A

June 2000 Fumo-PCD congress offered Arouca the position of "honorary president," but he angrily refused the post.

Leaders: Jose Samo GUDO (President), Dr. Domingos António Mascarenhas AROUCA (Former President), Pedro LOFORTE (Secretary General).

The other minor parties participating in the Renamo/UE were the **Mozambique Independents Alliance**, led by Ernesto SERGIO and Khalid Hussein MAHOMED; the **National Unity Party**, led by Hipóloto de JESUS; and the **Ecological Party of Mozambique** (*Partido Ecologista de Moçambique*—Pemo).

Other Groups Contesting the 2004 Legislative Elections

Party for Peace, Democracy, and Development (*Partido para a Paz, Democracia, e Desenvolvimento*—PPDD). Formed in 2003 by disaffected members of Renamo, including Raul Domingos, the PPDD is a liberal party that promotes nonpartisanship in public administration. At the first party congress on October 4, 2003, Domingos was nominated to run for the presidency in 2004. He placed third in the balloting with 2.73 percent of the vote. The PPDD also came in third in the concurrent legislative elections with 2 percent of the vote. Most analysts believe that the PPDD pulled votes away from Renamo.

Leader: Raul DOMINGOS.

Movement for Change and Good Governance (*Movimento para a Mudança e Boa Governação*—MGB). The MGB was an electoral alliance formed prior to the 2004 elections to rally behind a single candidate for the presidency and to pool resources for the legislative elections. The MGB consisted of Unamo and the small **Party of All Mozambican Nationalists** (*Partido de Todos os Nativos Moçambicanos*—Partonamo). In the legislative elections, the MGB received .36 percent of the vote.

Leader: Carlos Alexandre REIS (Chair and 2004 presidential candidate).

Mozambican National Union (*União Nacional Moçambicana*—Unamo). Reportedly then in control of three battalions of rebel fighters in Zambezia province, Unamo was formed in 1987 by a Renamo breakaway faction. Subsequently, some of its leaders appeared to be operating from Malawi while others established an office in Lisbon. However, by late 1990, Unamo forces, stationed along the Malawian border, were reported to be "on good terms" with the government. Meanwhile, political leaders had returned from exile in anticipation of Unamo being recognized as a legal party, spokesmen indicating it would participate in upcoming legislative contests but would endorse President Chissano in his reelection bid.

In March 1991 the party formally characterized itself as a social-democratic "peaceful organization" with 20,000 members and offices in nine provinces. One year later it was the first opposition party granted legal status. However, in August 1992 party president Carlos Alexandre Reis was imprisoned for financial crimes for which he had been convicted and sentenced in absentia seven years earlier.

In April 1994 Unamo was alleged to be financing *Rombezia,* an armed group in northern Mozambique led by Manuel ROCHA and Octavio CUSTODIO, which was descended from the African National Union of Rombezia (*União Nacional Africana da Rombezia*—UNAR). The UNAR was believed to have been formed by the Portuguese secret police in the 1960s to promote an independent state in the Rovuma and Zambezia provinces (which gave the grouping its name).

Unamo secured only .73 percent of the vote in the 1994 legislative balloting and subsequently announced it was forming the extraparliamentary United Salvation Front (*Frente Unida de Salvação*—FUS) with the PSLD, PPPM, PT, PRD, Pacode, and Pimo. However, in 1999 Unamo chose, as did the PPPM and the PRD, to participate in the Renamo/UE, while the other FUS members either ran alone or in different coalitions. In 2004, however, Unamo joined the

MGB, while Reis ran as the Unamo candidate for the presidency. He received .9 percent of the vote.

Leaders: Carlos Alexandre REIS (President), Florencia João Da SILVA (Secretary General).

Democratic Union (*União Democrática*—UD). The UD was formed in 1994 as a coalition of Panade, Palmo, and the **National Party of Mozambique** (*Partido Nacional de Moçambique*—Panamo), led by Marcos JUMA and Chabane ASSANE. It secured 5.15 percent of the vote in the December legislative poll, thereby gaining nine seats and becoming only the third party, behind Frelimo and Renamo, to gain representation. (Earlier editions of the *Handbook* incorrectly assigned those seats to the Democratic Union of Mozambique [*União Democrática de Moçambique*—Udemo], a former separatist group in northern Mozambique.) However, Palmo left the UD in mid-1999, and the rump coalition of Panade and Panamo managed only 1.48 percent of the vote (and consequently no seats) in the December balloting. The UD only received .34 percent of the vote in the 2004 legislative elections. Juma reportedly led Panamo to join the Constructive Opposition Bloc in 2006.

Leaders: José Chicuarra MASSINGA, Marcos JUMA.

National Democratic Party (*Partido Nacional Democrático*—Panade). Panade was launched in late 1992 by José Massinga, a former foreign ministry official who was discharged in 1979 for alleged links to the U.S. intelligence network. The party's platform, based on "Christian values and human dignity," reportedly mirrored the teachings of activist Catholic bishops in central Mozambique. The group was legalized in 1993.

Leader: José Chicuarra MASSINGA.

Liberal Democratic Party of Mozambique (*Partido Liberal Democrático de Moçambique*—Palmo). Reportedly seeking legal recognition in late 1990, Palmo criticized the nonindigenous population for "controlling" the economy to the detriment of "original" (black) Mozambicans. At the

party's first congress on May 6–11, 1991, Martins Bilal won a hotly contested presidential contest over Dr. António Palange. Consequently, another prominent leader, Casimiro Miguel Nhamithambo, resigned from the party, criticizing it for "lacking democracy" and launching a breakaway group (PSLD, below).

In July 1998 a dispute between Bilal and Palange split Palmo, with Bilal claiming that the party's National Committee had suspended Palange, whose recent assumption of the UD leadership mantle had given him increased national prominence. For his part, Palange asserted that the committee had lacked a quorum and that it was Bilal who had in fact been dismissed from the party for financial malpractice. In November Palange was formally expelled from Palmo. He subsequently launched his own formation (CDU, below).

Palmo had filled 5 of the 9 legislative seats won by the UD in 1994. However, it split from the UD in August 1999, securing 2.47 percent of the vote and no seats in the December poll. In balloting in 2004, Palmo received 0.30 percent of the vote.

Leader: Martins Luis BILAL (Chair), Antonio MUEDO (Secretary General).

Labor Party (*Partido Trabalhista*—PT). The PT was formed in 1993 by a breakaway faction of the PPPM. In early 1997 the party's vice president and secretary general were expelled for allegedly embezzling PT funds. The PT contested several municipal races but failed to win any seats in 2003. The PT won .56 percent of the legislative vote in 1994, 2.69 percent in 1999, and .47 percent in 2004. In 2006 the PT was reported to have joined the Constructive Opposition Bloc led by Pimo.

Leaders: Miguel MABOTE (President), Luis MUCHANGA (Secretary General).

Social, Liberal, and Democratic Party (*Partido Social, Liberal e Democrático*—PSLD). The PSLD was formed by former Palmo leader Casimiro Nhamithambo, who complained of the parent group "lacking democracy." The PSLD, also referenced by the initials SOL, was a founding member in early 1999 of the Mozambican Opposition Union (*União Moçambicana da Oposição*—UMO), which its supporters hoped would serve as an electoral front for as many as a dozen parties. Nhamithambo initially served as the UMO secretary general, but he resigned from that post later in the year as the result of friction with Wehia RIPUA, the leader of anothr UMO component—the **Mozambique Democratic Party** (*Partido Democrático de Mocambique*—Pademo). Although Nhamithambo announced at that time that the PSLD would remain in the UMO despite the dispute, the PSLD ultimately contested the December 2000 legislative poll on its own, winning 2.02 percent of the vote. (Only three groups finally ran under the UMO banner: Pademo, the **Democratic Congress Party** [*Partido do Congresso Democrático*—Pacode], and the **Democratic Party for the Reconciliation of Mozambique**. Meanwhile, the UMO supported Renamo's Afonso Dhlakama in the presidential race after Ripua's candidacy was disallowed due to faulty nomination papers.) In 2004, the PSLD won .46 percent of the legislative vote.

Leader: Casimiro Miguel NHAMITHAMBO.

Independent Party of Mozambique (*Partido Independente de Moçambique*—Pimo). Described as a "thinly disguised Islamic party," Pimo won 1.23 percent of the legislative vote in 1994 and .71 percent in 1999. Pimo leader Yaqub Sibinde attempted to run for president in 1999, but his nomination was declared invalid by the Supreme Court. In 2003, Pimo won 3 posts in municipal elections in predominately Islamic areas. In 2004 Sibinde ran for the presidency and received .91 percent of the vote. In the concurrent legislative elections, Pimo received .59 percent of the vote. In 2006 Sibinde was reported to have formed an opposition alliance of 18 minor parties called the **Constructive Opposition Bloc**. Besides Pimo, other members of the Bloc included the PT and Panamo.

Leader: Yaqub Neves Salomão SIBINDE.

Democratic Liberal Party of Mozambique (*Partido Democrático Liberal de Moçambique*—Padelimo). Formed in 1998, Padelimo won .80 percent of the vote in the 1999 legislative balloting and .12 percent in 2004.

Leader: Joaquim José NYOTA.

Social Broadening Party of Mozambique (*Partido de Ampliação Social de Moçambique*—Pasomo). Pasomo won .05 percent of the legislative vote in 1999 and .52 percent in 2004.

Leader: Helder Francisco CAMPIRA.

Green Party of Mozambique (PVM). Formed in 1997, the PVM (also known as *Os Verdes* [The Greens]) split into two factions prior to the 1999 elections, one supportive of membership in Renamo/UE and the other committed to an independent campaign. In 2004, the independent faction gained .33 percent in legislative elections.

Leader: Armando Bruno João SAPEMBE.

Other parties or groups that contested the 2004 legislative elections included the **Broad Opposition Front** (*Frente Alargada da Oposição*—FAO), a coalition of conservative parties that included the small **Liberal Front** (*Frente Liberal*—LF) and received .25 percent of the vote; the **Party of Freedom and Solidarity,** which received .88 percent of the vote; the **National Reconciliation Party,** which received .6 percent of the vote; the **Ecological Party-Land Movement,** which received .4 percent of the vote; and the **Congress of United Democrats** (*Congresso dos Democratas Unios*—CDU), formed in January 2002 by António PALANGE following his expulsion from Palmo. A number of other minor parties also received less than 1 percent of the vote.

Other Parties and Groups

Mozambique Democratic Internationalist Party (*Partido Internationalista Democrático de Moçambique*—Pidemo). Pidemo was launched in early 1994 by João Kamacho on a platform advocating a federalist system of government.

Leader: João KAMACHO.

Mozambique Communist Party (*Partido Comunista de Moçambique*—Pacomo). The formation of Pacomo was announced on April 12, 1995.

Leader: Almeida TESOURA.

Other minor parties include the **Democratic Alliance of Mozambique** (*Aliança Democrática de Moçambique*—ADM), led by José Pereira BRANQUINHO; the **Democratic Confederation**

Cabinet

As of June 1, 2006

Prime Minister	Luisa Dias Diogo [f]

Ministers

Agriculture and Rural Development	Tomas Mandlate
Development and Planning	Aiuba Cuereneia
Education	Aires Bonifacio Aly
Energy	Salvador Namburete
Environmental Action Coordination	Luciano Andre de Castro
Finance and Planning	Manuel Chang
Fisheries	Cadmiel Muthemba
Foreign Affairs and Cooperation	Alcinda Abreu [f]
Health	Paulo Ivo Garrido
Industry and Commerce	Antonio Fernando
Interior	José Pacheco
Justice	Esperanca Alfredo Machavela [f]
Labor	Helena Taipo [f]
Mineral Resources	Esperanca Bias [f]
National Defense	Gen. (Ret.) Tobias Dai
President's Office with Responsibility for Parliamentary Affairs	Isabel Manuel Nkavandeka [f]
President's Office with Responsibility for Diplomatic Affairs	Francisco Caetano J. Madeira
Public Works and Housing	Felicio Zacarias
Science and Technology	Venancio Simao Massingue
State Administration	Lucas Chomera
Tourism	Fernando Sumbana Júnior
Transport and Communications	Antonio Francisco Mungwambe
War Veterans' Affairs	Feliciano Salomao Gundana
Women and Social Action Coordination	Virgília B. N. Santos Matabele [f]
Youth and Sports	David Simango

[f] = female

Note: All of the above are members of the Mozambique Liberation Front.

of **Mozambique** (*Confederação Democrática de Moçambique*—CDM), led by Domingos CARDOSO; the **Mozambique Agrarian Party** (*Partido Agrário de Moçambique*—PAM); the **Revolutionary Party of the United Socialist People of Mozambique** (*Partido Revolucionário do Povo Socialista Unido de Moçambique*—Prepsumo); the **Social Democratic Party** (*Partido Social Democrático*—PSD), led by Cárlos MACHEL; and the **Waterworkers and Farmers of Mozambique** (*Regedores e Camponeses de Moçambique*—Recamo), led by Arone SIJAMO.

Legislature

A People's Assembly (*Assembleia Popular*), consisting of Frelimo's (then) 57-member Central Committee, was accorded legislative status at an uncontested election in December 1977. The body was increased to 210 members in April 1983 by the addition of government ministers and vice ministers, provincial governors, representatives of the military and of each province, and ten other citizens. While its term was not constitutionally specified, the original mandate was set by law at five years. The lengthy poll eventually conducted in August–December 1986 was for 250 deputies, indirectly elected by provincial assemblies from a list of 299 candidates presented by Frelimo. The name of the body was changed to the Assembly of the Republic in the 1990 constitution, which also provided for future elections to be conducted by direct universal suffrage on a multiparty basis.

Assembly of the Republic (*Assembleia da República*). The current legislature is a unicameral body of 250 members elected on a proportional basis for five-year terms. Parties must secure 5 percent of the votes on a nationwide basis to gain representation. At the balloting of December 1–2, 2004, the Mozambique Liberation Front won 160 seats and the Mozambique National Resistance/Electoral Union, 90.

President: Eduardo MULEMBWE.

Communications

Press

After having maintained strict control of the media since independence, the government in 1990 permitted substantial press liberalization. In late 1991 a press law was ratified, giving existing publications six months to reregister in accordance with new provisions, including revised ownership rules. In July 2001 the New York–based Committee to Protect Journalists reported that Mozambican journalists were exhibiting a degree of self-censorship in regard to investigations into corruption because of intimidation emanating from the November 2000 murder of a reporter from the independent daily, *Metical,* which subsequently went out of business. Among other things, journalists complained that the government's investigation of the murder lacked intensity. The following are published in Maputo and Beira, respectively: *Notícias* (33,000), government controlled, and *Diário de Moçambique* (16,000). In 1993 *Mediacoop,* a cooperative publishing venture founded by a group of independent journalists, launched *Mediafax,* a daily, and in early 1994, *Savana,* a weekly. Other publications include the progovernment weekly *Domingos* (25,000) and the pro-Renamo *Imparcial.*

News Agencies

The official facility is the Mozambique Information Agency (*Agência de Informação de Moçambique*—AIM); a number of international agencies are represented in Maputo.

Broadcasting and Computing

Government broadcast facilities include *Rádio Moçambique* and *Televisão de Moçambique.* There were approximately 122,000 television receivers and 90,000 personal computers serving 60,000 Internet users in 2003.

Intergovernmental Representation

Ambassador to the U.S.
Armando Alexandre PANGUENE

U.S. Ambassador to Mozambique
Helen R. MEAGHER LA LIME

Permanent Representative to the UN
Filipe CHIDUMO

IGO Memberships (Non-UN)
AfDB, AU, BADEA, CPLP, CWTH, IDB, Interpol, IOR-ARC, NAM, OIC, SADC, WCO, WTO

NAMIBIA

REPUBLIC OF NAMIBIA

The Country

Bordered on the north by Angola and Zambia, on the east by Botswana, on the southeast and south by South Africa, and on the west by the Atlantic Ocean, Namibia consists of a high plateau bounded by the uninhabited Namib Desert along the Atlantic coast, with more desert land in the interior. The inhabitants are of diversified origins, although the Ovambo constitute by far the largest ethnic group (a majority of 51 percent in the 1981 census, slightly less than 50 percent on the basis of a 1986 estimate). A substantial exodus has reduced the white population, traditionally engaged in commercial farming and ranching, fish processing, and mineral exploitation, from approximately 12 percent to 6.6 percent. Other groups include the Kavango, the Herero, the Damara, the Nama, and those classified as "coloured." The country is one of the world's largest producers of diamonds, which yield about half of export earnings, and uranium; copper, lead, zinc, tin, and other minerals are also available in extractable quantities. These resources yielded substantial economic growth during the 1970s; subsequently, falling mineral prices, extended periods of drought, and internal insecurity caused severe recession, marked by 40–50 percent unemployment, 13–16 percent inflation, and severe budgetary problems. In July 1990 international donors committed $200 million to help offset a $270 million fiscal shortfall caused by South Africa's withdrawal from the economy. GDP growth averaged 5 percent annually in 1990–1993 and 3 percent annually in 1994–1999; inflation measured 8.8 percent in 1997. Current economic policies focus on further exploitation of the country's rich fisheries, export manufacturing, promotion of private investment, and programs designed to ameliorate the severe maldistribution of wealth and an unemployment rate estimated to be as high as 35 percent.

Steady economic growth continued in the early 2000s, with GDP increasing by an average of 3–4 percent annually. Significantly, inflation fell to 5 percent by 2004 after the Bank of Namibia cut interest rates from 12.75 percent to 5 percent over a four-year period. One of the main growth sectors of the Namibian economy was commercial fishing, which accounted for one-third of total exports in the early 2000s. A 2002 agreement to allow Namibian craft to fish in South African territorial waters further expanded the sector.

In addition to continued mineral exploitation and fishing, international firms have invested $800 million in the development of natural gas fields,

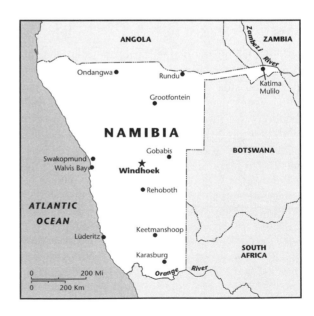

scheduled to begin production in 2006. Long-term plans are to use the fields to produce electricity for export to surrounding states, including South Africa. In an effort to ameliorate unemployment and poverty, the government launched a controversial land redistribution program in 2004 (see Current issues, below) in order to increase farm ownership among black Namibians. The program continued to be of regional interest in 2006, with Namibia and four other nations meeting in Pretoria in March for a five-day conference on the subject. Despite the economic challenges of an unemployment rate exceeding 20 percent and widespread poverty, real GDP growth was projected to be 3.5 percent in 2005, according to the International Monetary Fund (IMF), owing mainly to "surging" diamond production. The prevalence of HIV/AIDS in the country (an estimated 20 percent of the population) continued to be a major concern.

Government and Politics

Political Background

South West Africa came under German control in the 1880s, except for a small enclave at Walvis Bay, which had been annexed by the United Kingdom in 1878 and subsequently became a part of South Africa. Having occupied the whole of South West Africa during World War I, South Africa was granted a mandate in 1920 to govern the area under authority of the League of Nations. Declining to place the territory under the UN trusteeship system after World War II, South Africa asked the UN General Assembly in 1946 for permission to annex it; following denial of the request, Pretoria continued its rule on the strength of the original mandate.

Although the international status of the territory and the supervisory authority of the United Nations were repeatedly affirmed in advisory opinions of the International Court of Justice (ICJ), the court in 1966 declined on technical grounds to rule upon a formal complaint by Ethiopia and Liberia against South Africa's conduct in the territory. The UN General Assembly then terminated the mandate in a resolution of October 27, 1966, declaring

that South Africa had failed to fulfill its obligations. A further resolution on May 19, 1967, established an 11-member UN Council for South West Africa, assisted by a UN commissioner, to administer the territory until independence (originally set for June 1968) and to prepare for the drafting of a constitution, the holding of an election, and the establishment of responsible government. The council was, however, refused entry by the South African government, which contended that termination of the mandate was invalid. South Africa subsequently disregarded a number of Security Council resolutions to relinquish the territory, including a unanimous resolution of December 1974 that gave it five months to initiate withdrawal from Namibia (the official name adopted on December 16, 1968, by the General Assembly).

Beginning in the mid-1960s, South Africa attempted to group the black population into a number of self-administering tribal homelands ("Bantustans"), in accordance with the so-called Odendaal Report of 1964. Ovamboland, the first functioning Bantustan, was established in October 1968, but its legitimacy was rejected by the UN Security Council. Fully implemented, the partition plan would have left approximately 88,000 whites as the largest ethnic group in two-thirds of the territory, with some 675,000 black inhabitants confined to the remaining third.

Both the Organization of African Unity (OAU, subsequently the African Union—AU) and the South West Africa People's Organization (SWAPO) consistently pressed for full and unconditional self-determination for Namibia. In May 1975, however, Prime Minister Vorster of South Africa stated that while his government was prepared to "exchange ideas" with UN and OAU representatives, it was not willing to accede to the demand that it "acknowledge SWAPO as the sole representative of the Namibian people and enter into independence negotiations with the organization."

On September 1, 1975, the South African government convened a constitutional conference in Turnhalle, Windhoek, on the future of the territory. SWAPO and other independence groups boycotted

Political Status: Former German territory assigned to South Africa under League of Nations mandate in 1920; declared to be a United Nations responsibility by General Assembly resolution adopted October 27, 1966 (resolution not recognized by South Africa); subject to tripartite (Angolan-Cuban-South African) agreement concluded on December 22, 1988, providing for implementation from April 1, 1989, of Security Council Resolution 435 of 1978 (leading to UN-supervised elections on November 1 and independence thereafter); independence declared on March 21, 1990.

Area: 318,259 sq. mi. (824,292 sq. km.).

Population: 1,826,854 (2001C); 2,161,000 (2005E). Both area and population figures include data for Walvis Bay (see Political background and Foreign relations, below).

Major Urban Center (2005E): WINDHOEK (282,000).

Official Language: English.

Monetary Unit: Namibian Dollar (market rate July 1, 2006: 7.13 dollars = $1US). Introduced on September 13, 1993, the Namibian dollar is at par with the South African rand, which is also legal tender in Namibia.

President: Hifikepunye POHAMBA (South West Africa People's Organization of Namibia); popularly elected on November 15–16, 2004, and inaugurated on March 21, 2005, to succeed Samuel (Sam) Daniel Shafilshuna NUJOMA (South West Africa People's Organization of Namibia).

Prime Minister: Nahas ANGULA (South West Africa People's Organization of Namibia); appointed by the president following parliamentary elections on November 15–16, 2004, and sworn in on March 21, 2005, to succeed Theo-Ben GURIRAB (South West Africa People's Organization of Namibia).

the conference and organized demonstrations against it. As a result, the Ovambos, with approximately half of the territory's population, were represented by only 15 of 135 delegates. At the second session of the conference, held March 2–19, 1976, Chief Clemens KAPUUO, then leader of the Herero-based National United Democratic Organization, presented a draft constitution that called for a bicameral legislature encompassing a northern chamber of representatives from Bantu areas and a southern chamber that would include representatives from the coloured and white groups. On August 18, during the third session of the conference, a plan was advanced for the creation of a multiracial interim government to prepare Namibia for independence by December 31, 1978. Despite continued opposition from SWAPO, the conference's constitution committee unanimously approved a resolution on December 3 that called for establishment of the interim government within the next six months.

Although a draft constitution calling for representation of the territory's 11 major racial and ethnic groups was approved by the Turnhalle delegates on March 9, 1977, and was subsequently endorsed by 95 percent of the white voters in a referendum on May 17, it continued to be opposed by SWAPO as well as by a "contact group" of diplomats representing the five Western members of the UN Security Council (Canada, France, the Federal Republic of Germany, the United Kingdom, and the United States). The Western delegation visited Windhoek on May 7–10 and subsequently engaged in talks with South African Prime Minister Vorster in Cape Town, in the course of which it indicated that the Turnhalle formula was unacceptable because it was "predominantly ethnic, lacked neutrality, and appeared to prejudice the outcome of free elections." The group added, however, that the appointment of an administrator general by the South African government would not be opposed insofar as it gave promise of contributing to "an internationally acceptable solution to the Namibia question." For his part, Vorster, prior to the appointment of Marthinus T. STEYN as administrator general on July 6, agreed to abandon the Turnhalle proposal for an interim government, to accept the appointment of a UN representative to ensure the impartiality of the constituent election in 1978, and to initiate a withdrawal of South African troops to be completed by the time of independence. He insisted, however, that the South African government had no intention of abandoning its jurisdiction over Walvis Bay and certain islands off the South West African coast. (Governed as part of South Africa until 1922, when it was assigned to South West Africa for administrative purposes, Walvis Bay was reincorporated into South Africa's Cape Province in August 1977.)

During November and December 1977 representatives of the "contact group" engaged in inconclusive discussions with leaders of SWAPO and of the black African "Front-Line States" (Angola, Botswana, Mozambique, Tanzania, and Zambia). The main problem concerned South African security forces within Namibia, SWAPO asserting that their continued presence would influence the outcome of the projected election despite a UN presence. Nonetheless, Administrator General Steyn moved energetically to dismantle the territory's apartheid system, including abolition of the pass laws and the Mixed Marriages Act, in preparation for the 1978 balloting.

On March 27, 1978, Chief Kapuuo, who had assumed the presidency of the Democratic Turnhalle Alliance (DTA, see Political Parties, below), was shot and killed by unknown assailants on the outskirts of Windhoek. The assassination removed from the scene the best-known tribal figure apart from SWAPO leader Sam NUJOMA, who denied that his group had been involved. Three days later the Western nations presented Prime Minister Vorster with revised proposals calling for a cease-fire between SWAPO guerrillas and the 18,000 South African troops in the territory. The latter force would be expected to withdraw from the border areas and gradually decrease to 1,500, with UN troops being positioned to maintain order in preparation for Constituent Assembly balloting. South Africa accepted the plan on April 25 after receiving assurances that the status of Walvis Bay would not be addressed until after the election, that the reduction of its military presence would be linked to "a complete cessation of hostilities," and that some of its troops might be permitted to remain after the election if the assembly so requested. On July 12 SWAPO agreed to the Western plan, which had also been endorsed by the Front-Line States. The UN

Security Council approved the plan on July 27, but Pretoria reacted bitterly to an accompanying resolution calling for the early "reintegration" of Walvis Bay into South West Africa and subsequently announced that its own final approval would be deferred. In early September South African Foreign Minister Botha denounced the size of the proposed UN military force for the territory, and two weeks later he indicated that his government had reversed itself and would proceed with an election of its own before the end of the year. Undaunted, the Security Council on September 29 approved Resolution 435, which called for the formation of a 7,500-member UN Transitional Assistance Group (UNTAG) to oversee free and fair elections, while declaring "null and void" any unilateral action by "the illegal administration in Namibia in relation to the electoral process." Administrator General Steyn nonetheless proceeded to schedule balloting for a Constituent Assembly, which on December 4–8, without SWAPO participation, gave the DTA 41 of 50 seats.

In May 1979 the South African government agreed to the Constituent Assembly's request that the body be reconstituted as a National Assembly, although without authority to alter the status of the territory. Collaterally, conflict between SWAPO guerrilla forces and South African troops intensified, the latter carrying out a number of preemptive raids on SWAPO bases in Angola and Zambia. By midyear negotiations between UN and South African representatives had not resumed, Pretoria having rejected a contact group proposal to establish bases for SWAPO forces in Namibia as a counter to South African installations. In an effort to break the deadlock, Angolan President Agostinho Neto, a few weeks before his death in September, proposed the creation of a 60-mile-wide demilitarized zone along the Angolan-Namibian border to prevent incursions from either side. He also pledged that Angola would welcome a UN civilian presence to ensure that any guerrillas not wishing to return to Namibia to participate in an all-party election would be confined to their bases.

Although Pretoria agreed to "the concept" of a demilitarized zone, discussions during 1980 failed to yield agreement, and on November 24 UN Secretary General Kurt Waldheim called for a meeting in Geneva in January 1981 to discuss all "practical proposals" that might break the lengthy impasse. Earlier, DTA spokesmen had urged repeal of the General Assembly's 1973 recognition of SWAPO, arguing that the root of the problem lay in the fact that "the UN is required to play a neutral role in respect of implementation but at the same time is the most ardent protagonist of SWAPO."

During 1981–1982 units of both the South West Africa Territorial Force (SWATF) and the South African Defence Force (SADF) conducted numerous "search and destroy" raids into Angola, Pretoria insisting that the withdrawal of Cuban troops from the latter country was a necessary precondition of its own withdrawal from Namibia and the implementation of a UN-supervised election. Thus, Prime Minister Botha declared at a Transvaal National Party congress in September 1982 that his government would never accede to Namibian independence unless "unequivocal agreement [could] first be reached" on the linkage issue. Subsequently, an Angolan spokesman indicated that a partial withdrawal of Cuban forces was possible if Pretoria would agree to reduce the size of its military presence to 1,500 troops and discontinue incursions into his country. The overture prompted a secret but inconclusive series of talks between Angolan and South African ministerial delegations on the island of Sal in Cape Verde in early December, the South African foreign minister subsequently asserting that responsibility for a Cuban withdrawal was "the task of the Americans."

In November 1983 a Multi-Party Conference (MPC) of seven internal groups, including the DTA, was launched in Windhoek in an effort to overcome the standoff. Although the "Windhoek Declaration of Basic Principles" that was issued on February 24, 1984, did little more than reaffirm the essentials of the earlier UN plan, South African Prime Minister Botha announced in March that his government would be willing to enter into negotiations with all relevant parties to the dispute, including the Angolan government and UNITA, the Angolan rebel movement that enjoyed de facto

SADF support. However, the overture was rejected by SWAPO on the ground that only Namibian factions should be involved in independence discussions. Collaterally, Angola offered to participate as an observer at direct negotiations between SWAPO and Pretoria. Two months later Zambian President Kenneth Kaunda and South West African Administrator General Willem VAN NIEKERK jointly chaired a meeting in Lusaka that was attended by representatives of South Africa, SWAPO, and the MPC, while a meeting between van Niekerk and SWAPO president Nujoma was held in Cape Verde on July 25. Although unprecedented, the bilateral discussions also proved abortive, as did subsequent talks involving Washington, Luanda, SWAPO and/or Pretoria; progress on the issue was further inhibited in mid-1985 by evidence of continued U.S. and South African support for UNITA.

After lengthy discussion with the MPC, on June 17, 1985, Pretoria installed a Transitional Government of National Unity (TGNU), with a cabinet, 62-member legislature, and Constitutional Council of representatives from the MPC parties. Having largely excluded Ovambos, the new administration was estimated to command the support of perhaps 16 percent of the population and was further limited by Pretoria's retention of veto power over its decisions; not surprisingly, international support for the action was virtually nonexistent. While the TGNU's "interim" nature was stressed by Pretoria, which mandated a formal constitution within 18 months, stalled negotiations with Angola and continued SWAPO activity provoked South African intimations that the arrangement could lead to a permanent "regional alternative to independence."

In early 1986 Pretoria proposed that independence commence August 1, again contingent upon withdrawal of the Cubans from Angola. The renewed linkage stipulation, termed by the United Nations as "extraneous," prompted both Angola and SWAPO to reject the plan as nothing more than a "public relations exercise." In September a UN General Assembly Special Session on Namibia strongly condemned South Africa for effectively blocking implementation of the UN plan for Namibian independence and called for the imposition of mandatory sanctions against Pretoria; however, U.S. and UK vetoes precluded the passage of resolutions to such effect by the Security Council.

During 1987 South Africa continued to seek Western recognition of the TGNU as a means of resolving the Namibian question. However, even within the TGNU, differences emerged regarding a draft constitution and the related question of new elections to second-tier legislative bodies.

In 1988 the long drawn-out dispute moved toward resolution. A series of U.S.-mediated negotiations among Angolan, Cuban, and South African representatives that commenced in London in May and continued in Cairo, New York, Geneva, and Brazzaville (Republic of the Congo), concluded at UN headquarters on December 22 with the signing of an accord that linked South African acceptance of Resolution 435/78 to the phased withdrawal, over a 30-month period, of Cuban troops from Angola. The agreement provided that the resolution would go into effect on April 1, 1989, with deployment of UNTAG (approximately 7,100 individuals from 22 countries.) As ratified by the Security Council on February 16, the timetable further provided that South African troop strength would be reduced to 1,500 by July 1, followed by the election of a constituent assembly on November 1 and formal independence for the territory by April 1990.

Ten groups were registered to contest the slightly deferred Constituent Assembly election of November 7–11, 1989, with SWAPO winning 41 of 72 seats and the DTA winning 21. On February 16, 1990, the assembly elected Nujoma to the presidency of the new republic. He was sworn in by UN Secretary General Pérez de Cuéllar during independence ceremonies on March 21, with Hage GEINGOB being installed as prime minister of a 20-member cabinet.

In July 1993 Namibia and South Africa agreed to joint administration of Rooikop Airport at Walvis Bay, and on August 18 South African President de Klerk announced that his government had agreed to relinquish its claim to the port. The actual withdrawal on March 1, 1994, was hailed as completing the process of Namibian independence.

On July 18, 1994, Windhoek's already battered economic record was dealt a further blow when the auditor general released a report criticizing the Nujoma government for widespread financial mismanagement and accusing three ministries of criminal fraud. However, on December 6, one day before Namibia's first presidential and legislative elections since independence, South African President Nelson Mandela announced his country's plans to forgive Namibia's $190 million debt. Thereafter, propelled by Mandela's timely largess and SWAPO's enduring image as the party of independence, President Nujoma and SWAPO legislative candidates easily outpaced the opposition at balloting on December 7–8, capturing approximately 76 percent of the presidential vote and 53 assembly seats. Nujoma's sole competitor, Mishake MUYONGO of the renamed DTA of Namibia (who received 23 percent of the vote), cited SWAPO's dominance in the north and declared that the elections left Namibia divided along ethnic lines. Although SWAPO captured the two-thirds assembly majority necessary to amend the constitution, Nujoma had announced earlier that any proposed changes would be submitted to popular referendum. SWAPO reportedly gained control of 27 of 45 local councils at the February 1998 balloting, followed by the DTA of Namibia with nine.

On October 16, 1998, the SWAPO-dominated National Assembly approved a constitutional amendment that granted President Nujoma the opportunity to compete for a third presidential term and increased the powers of the office. On October 30 the assembly voted against a DTA of Namibia proposal to hold a popular referendum on the bill, despite its earlier pledges to the contrary, and on November 19 the National Council also passed the third-term amendment, leaving final approval to Nujoma, who signed the bill into law in 1999. Despite continued opposition objections to the constitutional revamping, Nujoma was easily reelected for a third term in balloting on November 30–December 1, 1999, securing 76.8 percent of the vote, while SWAPO maintained its assembly dominance in concurrent legislative balloting. On August 27, 2002, Nujoma appointed cabinet minister Theo-Ben GURIRAB as the new prime minister.

In late March 1999 Nujoma slightly reshuffled his government, appointing several prolabor deputy ministers in what observers described as an apparent attempt to counter the formation of a new party, the Congress of Democrats (CoD), by Ben ULENGA, a former independence fighter and trade unionist who had recently left SWAPO as the result of his opposition to the third term for Nujoma. The CoD, which called for an anticorruption drive among public officials and for the withdrawal of Namibian troops from the Democratic Republic of the Congo (DRC), was expected by some observers to offer SWAPO its first genuine electoral challenge, perhaps enough to cost the ruling party its comfortable legislative majority. However, SWAPO easily maintained more than enough seats to permit constitutional revision at will.

Although President Nujoma volunteered in April 2001 to seek a fourth term if he believed that popular will favored such a decision, late in the year he announced that he had ruled out another term. Meanwhile, tension was reported between Nujoma and Prime Minister Geingob, resulting in the appointment of Theo-Ben Gurirab to the premiership in August 2002. (Geingob declined Nujoma's offer of another cabinet post.)

In May 2004 a SWAPO party convention nominated Hifikepunye POHAMBA (the minister of lands, resettlement, and rehabilitation) as the party's presidential candidate in the November elections. Pohamba was challenged by six other candidates: Ben ULENGA (CoD), Katuutire KAURA (DTA of Namibia); Kuaima RIRUAKO (National Unity Democratic Organization—NUDO); Justus GAROËB (United Democratic Front—UDF); Henk MUDGE (Republican Party—RP); and Jacobus PRETORIUS (Monitor Action Group—MAG). Pohamba received 76.3 percent of the vote in the November 15–16, 2004, elections, with his closest rivals being Ulenga with 7.34 percent and Kaura with 5.2 percent (all of the other candidates received less than 5 percent). In the concurrent legislative elections,

SWAPO maintained its dominance in the legislature, winning 55 of the 72 seats (the CoD won 5; the DTA, 4; NUDO, 3; UDF, 3; the RP, 1; and the MAG, 1). Following the elections, a new cabinet composed of SWAPO members was chosen, with Nahas ANGULA, the former minister of higher education, training, and employment creation, as prime minister.

Constitution and Government

On February 9, 1990, the Constituent Assembly approved a liberal democratic constitution that became effective at independence on March 21. The document provides for a multiparty republic with an executive president, selected initially by majority vote of the legislature (but by direct election thereafter) for a maximum of two five-year terms. (An amendment was approved in 1998 to permit incumbent President Nujoma to serve a third term, although the two-term limit will still exist for future presidents.) The bicameral legislature encompasses a National Assembly elected by proportional representation for a five-year term and a largely advisory National Council consisting of two members from each geographic region who are elected by regional councils for six-year terms. A Council of Traditional Leaders advises the president on the utilization and control of communal land. Provision is made for an independent judiciary, empowered to enforce a comprehensive and unamendable bill of rights, considered to be the centerpiece of the document. Capital punishment and detention without trial are outlawed. The basic law also calls for a strong affirmative action program.

Regional and local units of elective government, delineated on a purely geographical basis, are to function "without any reference to the race, colour or ethnic origin" of their inhabitants.

Foreign Relations

At independence Namibia became the 50th member of the commonwealth and shortly thereafter the 160th member of the United Nations. For economic reasons, it was deemed necessary to continue trading with South Africa; at the same time it viewed continuance of Pretoria's apartheid policies as precluding the establishment of normal diplomatic relations. Thus South Africa was permitted to maintain a mission in Windhoek that did not have the status of a full-fledged embassy.

In September 1990 it was reported that discussions (South Africa rejected the term "negotiations") had begun on the future status of South African-controlled Walvis Bay, title to which was claimed in both countries' constitutions. The talks continued in March 1991 without yielding agreement, Pretoria indicating that the only concession it would consider would be some form of joint administration of the enclave, but in November the two governments agreed to establish an interim joint administration committee. On August 21, 1992, the Walvis Bay Joint Administrative Body was formally launched. Meanwhile, neither government retreated from its territorial claim, with South Africa insisting that it would withhold a final decision until after it had formed a post-apartheid government. However, on August 16, 1993, in a major decision of the multiparty forum convened to decide on the future of South Africa, the South African government delegation agreed under pressure from the African National Congress and other participants to transfer the Walvis Bay enclave to Namibia. South Africa, however, refused in November 2000 to continue negotiations with Namibia on the precise position of the Orange River border between the two countries. The disagreement over the border issue continued through late 2002.

A seemingly less consequential dispute with a neighboring country has turned on the status of Sedudu, a small island in the middle of the Chobe River along the southern border of Namibia's Caprivi Strip. The island had been assumed to be part of Botswana until 1992, when Namibia advanced a claim that yielded a number of armed skirmishes in the area. Following an unsuccessful mediation attempt by President Mugabe of Zimbabwe, the two nations agreed in early 1995 to forward the dispute to the ICJ. On December 15, 1999, the ICJ ruled in favor of Botswana regarding Sedudu, and Namibia announced that it would accept the decision.

In an effort to end illegal trading across its border with Angola (which had been closed since September 1994), Windhoek ordered troops to fire at vehicles attempting to cross the frontier in 1995. Encountering continued insecurity along the border, Namibian authorities decided in September to create a "control unit" in support of defense and police efforts to monitor contraband traffic. On the other hand, a meeting between Namibian and Angolan officials in March 1996 was described as "positive," and in April Namibia welcomed the arrival of UN troops in southeastern Angola, suggesting that, when the peacekeepers had established themselves, the border might be reopened. In July 1997 an international human rights group accused the Nujoma administration of being responsible for the disappearance of over 1,700 Angolans since the 1994 crackdown.

In late August 1998 President Nujoma confirmed speculation that Namibian forces had been sent to the Democratic Republic of the Congo at the request of the DRC's president, Laurent Kabila, to help Kabila's army fight Rwandan-backed rebels. While effectively acknowledging domestic critics' assertions that his office had acted unilaterally, Nujoma attributed his decision to join Angola and Zimbabwe in aiding the DRC to the "spirit of Pan-Africanism, brotherhood and international solidarity." Thereafter, in late October the DRC rebellion topped the agenda of Nujoma's summit with South African President Mandela. The latter had been a critic of involving the forces of the members of the Southern African Development Community (SADC) in the violence. The country's involvement with the conflict in DRC was widely criticized by the Namibian opposition during 1999 and 2000. Following the assassination of Kabila in 2001, Namibian troops were withdrawn under the auspices of a UN agreement.

In February 2001 Namibia joined Angola and Zambia in the establishment of a tripartite mechanism aimed at improving security along their mutual borders, Windhoek having continued to provide the Angolan government with military support in the campaign against UNITA.

After the cease-fire agreement between the Angolan government and UNITA (see article on Angola), the Namibian government began repatriating Angolan refugees, with 20,000 having been returned by the end of 2003.

In 2001 descendants of Hereros killed by the Germans during their occupation of the country filed a suit in the United States against the German government, seeking $2 billion in reparations. Although the suit was dismissed in 2004, Germany formally apologized for the role played by its colonial officials in the 1904–1907 Herero uprising against German rule. Nonetheless, relations between Germany and Namibia remain close, and Germany continues to be a leading Namibian donor.

Relations between Namibia and Brazil increased significantly during Nujoma's tenure as president. Brazilian companies were contracted to explore the edges of Namibia's continental shelf in order to determine the country's formal oceanic boundaries. In addition, under the terms of the 2002 Naval Cooperation Agreement, Brazil provided assistance to construct a naval port at Walvis Bay and to train Namibian naval officers in return for the purchase of Brazilian-built vessels for the Namibian navy. Namibia has also developed closer military ties with Russia. A 2001 bilateral military accord called for Russian technical and military assistance and the eventual purchase of Russian-built MiG fighters.

In late 2005, following President Pohamba's visit to Beijing, relations with China were enhanced as the two countries signed extradition and trade agreements, and China pledged continued economic and social assistance to Namibia.

Current Issues

Following approval of the constitutional amendment granting President Sam Nujoma the opportunity to compete for a third presidential term,

Windhoek's attention in late 1998 turned to the intertwined issues of regional council elections (November 30) and secessionist activity in the Caprivi Strip region. Observers ascribed low voter participation in regional polling to both apathy and the adherence of DTA of Namibia supporters to a boycott called by the party in protest of the government's refusal to postpone balloting in those regions affected by the alleged uprising. (See Caprivi Liberation Front under Illegal Groups in Political Parties and Groups, below, for additional information.)

Following the 2004 elections, which were initially described as free and fair by foreign observers, opposition groups took the electoral commission of Namibia to court over alleged irregularities. The charges were prompted by the discovery of uncounted ballots that had been removed from polling places. A recount in March 2005 confirmed the SWAPO victory, although opposition parties gained a small number of additional votes. Otherwise, the electoral developments were most noteworthy for the smooth presidential transition after 15 years of rule by the "father of the nation," Sam Nujoma.

Following several stalled initiatives to redistribute land from white-owned farms to landless blacks, the government intensified its program to expropriate the farms in 2004. Previous efforts had been based on the voluntary sale of land and had resulted in the transfer of approximately 10 percent of the country's 7,000 white-owned farms to members of the majority population (and the resettlement of some 25,000 people). The government's new plan called for the expropriation of about one-third of the remaining white-owned farms, although the government pledged that owners would be compensated. In 2005 the budget for land purchases was doubled to $8 million, and Namibia received $10.4 million from Germany for training and technical assistance for the new farmers (although not for land costs). The government announced it hoped to maintain the vitality of the agricultural sector in order to avoid the problems that resulted from expropriations in countries such as Zimbabwe. In 2006 the government was still grappling with ways to improve the program and speed its implementation. Another issue still unresolved in 2006 pertained to the discovery of eight mass graves in late 2005, reported to be the remains of SWAPO liberation fighters killed the day the UN resolution on Namibian independence was signed. Government officials called for a "truth commission" but as of June 2006 had not come up with a plan on whether to exhume the bodies or how to deal with the graves.

Political Parties and Groups

Government Party

South West Africa People's Organization of Namibia (SWAPO). Consisting mainly of Ovambos and formerly known as the Ovambo People's Organization, SWAPO was the largest and most active South West African nationalist group and was recognized prior to independence by the United Nations as the "authentic representative of the Namibian people." Founded in 1958, it issued a call for independence in 1966 and subsequently initiated guerrilla activity in the north with the support of the OAU Liberation Committee. Further operations were conducted by the party's military wing, the People's Liberation Army of Namibia (PLAN), from bases in southern Angola. A legal "internal wing" engaged in political activity within Namibia, although it was the target of arrests and other forms of intimidation by police and South African military forces. SWAPO's cofounder, Andimba TOIVO JA TOIVO, was released from 16 years' imprisonment on March 1, 1984, and was immediately elected to the organization's newly created post of secretary general. In February 1988, at what was described as the largest such meeting in the movement's history, 130 delegates representing about 30 branches of SWAPO's internal wing reaffirmed their "unwavering confidence" in the exiled leadership of Sam Nujoma and their willingness to conclude a cease-fire in accordance with implementation of the UN independence plan. Nujoma returned to Namibia for the first time since 1960 on September 14, 1989, and was elected president of the new republic by the Constituent Assembly on February 16, 1990.

At a party congress in December 1991, the first since the group's inception, delegates reelected Nujoma and Rev. Hendrik Witbooi, party president and vice president, respectively, while Moses GAROËB captured the secretary generalship from Toivo ja Toivo. The congress also elected a new Central Committee (enlarged from 38 to 67 members) and adopted a revised constitution, expunging references to the PLAN and changing descriptions of the group from a "liberation movement" to a "mass political party."

At presidential and legislative balloting in December 1994 President Nujoma and SWAPO legislative candidates captured approximately 70 percent of the vote. However, some internal friction was subsequently reported between Nujoma loyalists and the party's "pragmatists" over Nujoma's allegedly heavy-handed direction of party affairs. Thereafter, in what observers described as a possible shift of power to the group's younger leaders, in April 1996 Deputy Minister of Foreign Affairs Netumbo Ndaitwah was named party secretary general. He replaced Garoëb, who had resigned days earlier.

In May 1997, at SWAPO's second congress since independence, party delegates adopted a resolution supporting amendment of the constitution to allow Nujoma a third presidential term. In addition, SWAPO Vice President Witbooi retained his post, staving off a challenge by Prime Minister Hage Gottfried Geingob, while cabinet member and Nujoma confidante Hifikepunye Pohamba was elected secretary general.

On the eve of the extraordinary party congress of August 29–30, 1998, Ben Ulenga, Namibia's high commissioner to Britain and a SWAPO central committeeman, resigned from his overseas post to protest the plans to allow Nujoma a third term as well as the deployment of Namibian troops in the DRC. Ulenga's public denouncement of the Nujoma amendment, the first by a ranking SWAPO member, colored the late August proceedings, at which the congress rebuffed calls from party dissidents for a debate on the issue and formally approved the proposed bill. In November the party voted to suspend Ulenga, who had recently led "like-minded" colleagues in the formation of a self-described bipartisan grouping. (In early 1999 Ulenga launched the Congress of Democrats, below.)

Meanwhile, at regional council balloting in December 1998 SWAPO easily won the majority of the posts at polling marked by low voter turnout. In the legislative election in November–December 1999 the party got 76.1 percent of the vote and won 55 seats in the National Assembly. Nujoma easily was reelected president with 76.8 percent of the vote. At the August 2002 congress, the party's politburo underwent a significant change, with new officers being elected. Some analysts noted that new prime minister Theo-Ben Gurirab, new SWAPO vice president Hifikepunye Pohamba, and new secretary general Ngarikutuke Tjiriange were among the possible successors to Nujoma, who had announced in late 2001 that he would not seek a fourth presidential term.

In May 2004 Pohamba was chosen as Nujoma's successor at a party conference. Nujoma was reelected as party president with his term set until 2007. In November 2004 Pohamba was elected president of Namibia with 76.3 percent of the vote. In the concurrent legislative elections, SWAPO won 55 seats. Gurirab was subsequently elected speaker of the assembly, and Nahas Angula was appointed prime minister.

Party infighting erupted in 2005 after SWAPO secretary and deputy works minister Paulas KAPIA was accused in a scandal involving state funds (the opposition claimed Nujoma was involved as well; he refuted the allegations.) Kapia resigned his government post and his assembly seat, and was suspended from the party. Some observers suggested that it was President Pohamba who forced the resignation of Kapia, a Nujoma protégé; subsequently, Nujoma returned Kapia to the party payroll. The rift between "Nujomaists" and backers of former foreign minister Hidipo HAMUTENYA, who took over Kapia's assembly seat, deepened after Jesaya NYAMU, a leading party member for some 40

years (and loyal to Hamutenya), was dismissed from the party in late 2005 for alleged "serious misconduct." The vote to oust him reportedly divided the party between backers of Nujoma and Hamutenya, with some observers speculating that Hamutenya might throw his support to Pohamba in an effort to remove Nujoma from the party presidency.

Leaders: Samuel (Sam) Daniel NUJOMA (Former President of the Republic and President of the Party), Theo-Ben GURIRAB (Speaker of the National Assembly), Rev. Hendrik WITBOOI, Hifikepunye POHAMBA (President of the Republic and Vice President of the Party), Ngarikutuke TJIRIANGE (Secretary General).

Other Parties Participating in the 2004 Legislative Elections

DTA of Namibia. The grouping known as the Democratic Turnhalle Alliance (DTA) until adoption of the abbreviated form in November 1991 was launched in the wake of the Turnhalle Conference as a multiracial coalition of European, coloured, and African groups. Advocating a constitutional arrangement that would provide for equal ethnic representation, the DTA obtained an overwhelming majority (41 of 50 seats) at the Constituent Assembly balloting of December 4–8, 1978, and was instrumental in organizing the Multi-Party Conference in 1983. Its core formations were the white-based Republican Party (RP), organized in October 1977 by dissident members of the then-dominant South West Africa National Party (SWANP), and the Herero-based National United Democratic Organization (NUDO), which had long advocated a federal solution as a means of opposing SWAPO domination. (For a list of other groups participating in the formation of the DTA, see the 1999 *Handbook*.)

At a Central Committee meeting on November 30, 1991, DTA officials announced the transformation of the coalition into an integrated political party. The committee also reelected the party leaders to permanent positions, adopted a new constitution, and announced that the group would thenceforth be known as the DTA of Namibia.

An intraparty chasm between former RP leader Dirk MUDGE and a faction led by party president Mishake MUYONGO and information secretary Andrew Matjila widened in the wake of the DTA of Namibia's poor showing at regional and local council elections in November–December 1992. At a central committee meeting in February 1993, the Muyongo faction pressed Mudge to resign, arguing that his former ties to South Africa had contributed to the party's loss of electoral support from all but small-town whites and the Herero and Caprivi communities. In April Mudge announced that he would be vacating his parliamentary seat, insisting that he had made the decision for purely personal reasons and would retain the DTA of Namibia chairmanship. In mid-1994 Matjila broke with the party, and less than a year later Mudge resigned his party post and bowed out of politics. Thereafter, at balloting in December, Muyongo secured only 23 percent of the presidential vote, while the party's parliamentary representation fell to 15 seats, the DTA of Namibia claiming that there had been widespread voting irregularities.

On August 25, 1998, the DTA of Namibia's Executive Committee suspended Muyongo from the party presidency and named Vice President Katuutire Kaura interim party leader after Muyongo called for the secession of the Caprivi Strip region from Namibia. Muyongo subsequently assumed control of the militant Caprivi Liberation Movement (see CLF, under Illegal Groups, below).

The legislative elections on November 30– December 1, 1999, proved nearly disastrous for the DTA of Namibia as the party secured less than half of what it did in 1994, winning only 9.5 percent of the vote and 7 seats in the National Assembly. In the presidential election, Kaura received 9.6 percent of the vote. In early April 2000 the DTA of Namibia and the UDF formed an opposition coalition when the negotiations with the CoD broke down.

The DTA of Namibia won four seats in the 2004 legislative elections while its presidential candidate, again Kaura, placed third with 5.2 percent of the vote. The defections of DTA of Namibia members to the RP and NUDO hurt the party most in the December Regional Council elections, where voters split among the three parties, giving SWAPO its greatest success ever in such balloting. The DTA of Namibia had 16 candidates elected to the councils in the 1998 elections but only 2 in the 2004 balloting.

Leaders: Johan DE WAAL (Chair), Katuutire KAURA (President and 2004 presidential candidate), Nico SMIT (Secretary General).

United Democratic Front (UDF). The UDF is led by Justus Garoëb, longtime head of the **Damara Council,** which withdrew from the MPC in March 1984; chair of the group is Reggie Diergaardt, leader of the **Labour Party,** a largely coloured group that was expelled from the DTA in 1982 but participated in the MPC subsequent to its November 1983 meeting. Two small leftist groups were also Front members: the **Communist Party of Namibia** (CPN) and the Trotskyist **Workers' Revolutionary Party** (WRP). The UDF ran a distant third in the November 1989 election, winning four assembly seats. At balloting in November– December 1992 the party was unable to lessen the gap between itself and the two major parties, capturing only 1 of 13 regional council seats.

In a November 1993 action opposed by other clan chiefs, UDF president Garoëb was enthroned as the king of Damara. Thereafter, observers attributed Garoëb's failure to participate in the December 1994 presidential balloting, despite a pledge to the contrary, to the UDF's poor financial condition. Meanwhile, the party, securing only 2 percent of the vote, lost two of its four assembly seats.

In late 1998 a UDF spokesman denounced SWAPO's legislative efforts to grant Nujoma a third term. The UDF received 2.9 percent of the vote in the legislative elections on November 30– December 1, 1999, and won two seats in the National Assembly while Garoëb secured 3 percent of the vote in the presidential poll.

In the 2004 presidential balloting Garoëb gained 3.8 percent of the vote, while the UDF gained an additional seat in the assembly.

Leaders: Justus GAROËB (King of Damara, President of the Party, and 2004 presidential candidate), Eric BIWA (Chair).

Congress of Democrats (CoD). The CoD was launched in March 1999 by former SWAPO stalwart Ben Ulenga, who had been suspended by SWAPO in 1998 after he criticized efforts to permit President Nujoma to run for a third term and had formed a grouping styled Forum for the Future. Included in the CoD's platform were calls for a smaller cabinet and the withdrawal of Namibian troops from the DRC. The CoD won 9.9 percent of the votes in the legislative elections held on November 30–December 1, 1999. It won 7 seats in the National Assembly and became the official parliamentary opposition, supplanting the DTA of Namibia. Ulenga received 10.5 percent of the vote in the presidential election.

The CoD lost support in the 2004 elections; Ulenga only received 7.34 percent of the presidential vote while the party fell to five seats.

Leaders: Ben ULENGA (President and 2004 presidential candidate), Nora SCHIMMING-CHASE (Vice President), Kalia GERTZE (Secretary General).

South West Africa National Union (SWANU). Formerly coordinating many of its activities with SWAPO's internal wing, the Herero-supported SWANU joined with the Damara Council and a number of smaller groups to form a multiracial coalition in support of the Western "contact group" solution to the Namibian problem. SWANU's president, Moses Katjioungua, participated in the 1983 MPC meeting and in September 1984 was reported to have been replaced as party leader by Kuzeeko Kangueehi, who indicated that the group would leave the MPC, with a view to possible merger with SWAPO. In October, on the other hand, Katjioungua was again identified as holding the presidency, with Kangueehi described as the leader of a dissident faction (subsequently styled SWANU-Left).

The incumbent's anti-SWAPO orientation was reflected by his inclusion in the "national unity" cabinet of 1985. A founding member of the Democratic Coalition of Namibia (DCN), SWANU abruptly dropped out of the grouping in November 1994 while Katjioungua stayed within the DCN. SWANU formed an electoral alliance with the **Workers' Revolutionary Party** (below), which received less than 0.5 percent of the vote in the legislative election on November 30–December 1, 1999. SWANU secured less than 1 percent of the vote in the 2004 legislative elections.

Leaders: Dr. Rihupisa KANDANDO (President), Kuzeeko KANGUEEHI (Vice President), Hitjevi Gerson VEII.

Monitor Action Group (MAG). A conservative, predominantly white grouping, the MAG won one assembly seat in December 1994. The MAG received 0.7 percent of the vote in the legislative election on November 30–December 1, 1999, and won one seat in the National Assembly.

In the 2004 polls Jacobus Pretorius received 1.2 percent of the presidential vote, while the party retained its single seat in the assembly.

Leader: Jacobus W. F. ("Kosie") PRETORIUS (2004 presidential candidate).

Republican Party (RP). Originally part of the DTA, the RP was reestablished as an independent party in 2003 under the leadership of Henk Mudge, the son of Dirk Mudge, the leader of the former Republican Party within the DTA. The conservative RP won 1.9 percent of the vote in the 2004 elections and gained a seat in the assembly for the first time. In addition, the younger Mudge ran as a presidential candidate; he came in fifth with 1.95 percent of the vote.

Leaders: Henk MUDGE (2004 presidential candidate), Carola ENGELBRECHT (Secretary General).

National Unity Democratic Organization (NUDO). Led by the Herero High Chief, Kuaima Riruako, former members of NUDO left the DTA of Namibia in 2003 to reestablish their Herero-based party. In the 2004 elections NUDO secured

4.79 percent of the vote and three seats in the assembly. Riruako came in third with 5.2 percent of the vote in the presidential poll.

Leader: Kuaima RIRUAKO (2004 presidential candidate).

Namibia Democratic Movement of Change (DMC). Established by former DTA of Namibia member Frans Goagoseb, the DMC received 0.53 percent of the vote in the 2004 legislative poll.

Leaders: Frans GOAGOSEB (President), Claudia NAMISES (Secretary General).

Other Parties and Groups

Workers' Revolutionary Party (WRP). The Trotskyite WRP was formed in 1989 and was part of the UDF. The WRP contested the 1994 legislative election and received 0.19 percent of the vote. For the 1999 balloting, the WRP formed an electoral alliance with SWANU (above).

Leaders: Werner MAMUGWE, Hewat BEUKES.

Christian Democratic Action for Social Justice (CDA). Supported principally by Ovambos, the CDA was formed in January 1982 by members of the National Democratic Party who withdrew from the DTA because of the latter's failure to organize as a unified grouping. The CDA contested the 1989 independence vote, and the party's leader subsequently announced it was withdrawing from politics.

Leader: Rev. Peter KALANGULA (President).

Federal Convention of Namibia (FCN). Strongly opposed to the UN independence plan, the FCN was organized by J. G. A. Diergaardt, a former minister of local government and leader of the **Rehoboth Free Democratic Party** (*Rehoboth Bevryder Demokratiese Party*—RBDP). The RBDP was an outgrowth of the former Rehoboth Liberation Front (RLF), which endorsed the partition of Namibia along ethnic lines and obtained one assembly seat in 1978 as representative of part of the Baster community, composed of Afrikaans-speaking people with European customs. The RFDP was an original member of the

MPC but in 1987 joined the SWANP in opposing the draft constitution endorsed by other TGNU members.

In 1994 the FCN chose former Women's Party (WP) leader Hileni LATVIO as its presidential candidate; however, Latvio failed to register her candidacy by the appropriate date and was denied an extension. The FCN won less than 0.5 percent of the vote in the 1999 legislative elections and won no seats.

Leader: Kaptein J. G. A. (Hans) DIERGAARDT (Chair).

National Democratic Party for Justice (NDPFJ). The launching of the NDPFJ was announced in November 1996 by SWAPO dissidents who in May 1995 had coalesced as SWAPO-Justice. The latter dissolved in 1997, and its leader, Nghiwete NDJOBA, subsequently joined the CoD. Ndjoba died in February 2004.

Namibia Movement for Independent Candidates (NMIC). The NMIC was launched in July 1997 on a platform stressing the need to incorporate Namibian youths into the political process. In September 1998 NMIC became affiliated with the DTA of Namibia (above).

Leader: Joseph KAUANDENGE.

Illegal Groups

Caprivi Liberation Front (CLF). Formed in 1994, the CLF has sought autonomy or independence for the Caprivi Strip, a narrow portion of northern Namibia that juts about 250 miles into central Africa, touching the borders of Angola, Botswana, Zambia, and Zimbabwe. The strip, theretofore part of the British protectorate of Bechuanaland (subsequently Botswana), was ceded to Germany, colonial ruler of South West Africa, in 1890 as part of a land swap that included Britain's assumption of control in Zanzibar. The region is part of the former ancestral kingdom of Barotseland, which also included portions of Zambia, Botswana, and Zimbabwe. In the 1970s and 1980s the strip was used by South African forces as a base for military activities against independence

Cabinet

As of June 1, 2006

Prime Minister	Nahas Angula
Deputy Prime Minister	Dr. Libertina Amathila [f]

Ministers

Agriculture, Water, and Rural Development	Nick Iyambo
Defense	Maj. Gen. Charles Namoloh
Education	Nangolo Mbumba
Environment and Tourism	Willem Konjore
Finance	Saara Kuugongelwa-Amathilia [f]
Fisheries and Marine Resources	Abraham Iyambo
Foreign Affairs	Marco Hausiku
Health and Social Services	Richard Kamwi
Home Affairs and Immigration	Rosalia Nghidinwa [f]
Information and Broadcasting	Netumbo Nandi-Ndaitwah [f]
Justice and Attorney General	Pendukeni Iivula-Ithana [f]
Labor	Alpheus Naruseb
Lands, Resettlement, and Rehabilitation	Jerry Ekandjo
Mines and Energy	Errki Nghimtina
Presidential Affairs	Albert Kawana
Regional and Local Government and Housing	John Pandeni
Safety and Security	Peter Tsheehama
Trade and Industry	Immanuel Ngatjizeko
Without Portfolio	Ngarikutuke Tjiriange
Women's Affairs and Child Welfare	Marlene Mungunda [f]
Works, Transport, and Communications	Joel Kaapanda
Youth, Sport, and Culture	John Mutorwa

[f] = female

fighters in Namibia as well as against the Angolan government.

In 1998 the Namibian government reported that a security sweep had uncovered training bases in Caprivi for the CLF-affiliated Caprivi Liberation Army. Several thousand Caprivians subsequently fled to Botswana, including Mishake Muyongo, the CLF/CLA leader who been dismissed from both SWAPO and the DTA of Namibia for his secessionist sentiments. In early August 1999 a small group of alleged CLA members attacked security locations in the town of Katima Mulilo, the fighting leaving at least 16 dead. The insurgents were quickly routed, but the Namibian government declared a state of emergency in the region for three weeks and implemented what critics described as a heavy-handed crackdown that allegedly included the abuse of detainees. Among the factors reportedly fueling antigovernment sentiment among Caprivians (primarily from the Lozi ethnic group) is the political and economic dominance of Ovambos in Namibia.

Leader: Mishake MUYONGO (under asylum in Denmark).

Legislature

The Namibian **Parliament** consists of an indirectly elected National Council and a National Assembly whose voting members are directly elected.

National Council. The largely advisory upper house is a 26-member body containing two members from each of 13 regional councils; the term of office is six years. The national body launched its first session on May 11, 1993, following regional and local elections on November 29–December 4, 1992, at which the South West Africa People's Organization of Namibia (SWAPO) won control in 9 regions and the Democratic Turnhalle Alliance of Namibia (DTA of Namibia) in 3, with the United Democratic Front (UDF) holding the balance of power in 1. After SWAPO gained control of 12 of the 13 regional councils in balloting on November 30–December 1, 2004, the distribution of seats in the National Council was SWAPO, 24; the DTA of Namibia, 1; and the UDF, 1.

President: Asser Kuveri KAPERE.

National Assembly. The 72 members of the current lower house were initially elected on November 7–11, 1989, to the Namibian Constituent Assembly, which at independence assumed the functions of an ordinary legislature with a five-year mandate. The lower house balloting of November 15–16, 2004, resulted in the distribution of seats as follows: the South West Africa People's Organization of Namibia, 55; the Congress of Democrats, 5; the DTA of Namibia, 4; the National Unity Democratic Organization, 3; the United Democratic Front, 3; the Republican Party, 1; and the Monitor Action Group, 1. In addition to the elected members, up to six nonvoting members may be named by the president.

Speaker: Dr. Theo-Ben GURIRAB.

Communications

Press

Although there are generally few restrictions on the press, in 2001 the government forbade state agencies and institutions from advertising or purchasing *The Namibian* in response to articles that were critical of the government. The following newspapers are English dailies published in Windhoek, unless otherwise noted: *New Era* (25,000), weekly; *Die Republikein* (12,000), DTA organ in Afrikaans, English, and German; *The Namibian* (11,000); *Windhoek Observer* (10,000), weekly; *Allgemeine Zeitung* (5,000), in German; *Windhoek Advertiser,* daily (5,000); *Namibia Economist; Namibia News; Namibia Today,* pro-SWAPO; *Tempo,* weekly; *Namib Times,* biweekly, published in Walvis Bay; *The New Era,* government biweekly; and the regional *Caprivi Vision.*

News Agencies

A Namibian Press Agency (Nampa) was launched by SWAPO in November 1987; the Italian-based Inter Press Service (IPS) and the South African Press Association maintain offices in Windhoek.

Broadcasting and Computing

The Namibian Broadcasting Company (NBC), formerly the South West Africa Broadcasting Company (SWABC), is accountable to the Ministry of Information and Broadcasting, although with a mandate to operate as an independent service. However, in October 2002 President Nujoma ordered the NBC to stop broadcasting foreign programs. In addition, during the 2004 elections opposition parties charged that NBC provided the government party, SWAPO, with a disproportionate share of airtime and refused some requests to broadcast opposition advertisements. Radio broadcasts, which commenced in 1979, are transmitted over eight channels in 11 regional languages; television service, initiated in 1981, broadcasts in English, with a commitment to add ethnic languages when feasible. The country's first private commercial radio station commenced operation in April 1994. There were approximately 73,000 television receivers and 191,000 personal computers serving 65,000 Internet users in 2003.

Intergovernmental Representation

Ambassador to the U.S.
Hopelong Uushona IPINGE

U.S. Ambassador to Namibia
Joyce A. BARR

Permanent Representative to the UN
Martin ANDJABA

IGO Memberships (Non-UN) AfDB, AU, Comesa, CWTH, Interpol, NAM, SADC, WCO, WTO

NIGER

REPUBLIC OF NIGER

République du Niger

The Country

A vast landlocked country on the southern border of the Sahara, Niger is largely desert in the north and arable savanna in the more populous southland, which extends from the Niger River to Lake Chad. The population includes numerous tribes of two main ethnic groups: Sudanese Negroes and Hamites. About 75 percent of the population is classified as Sudanese Negro, with Hausa being the predominant subgroup (56 percent); Hamites, found in the north, include the nomadic Tuareg, Toubou, and Peulh subgroups. The population is largely (85 percent) Muslim, with smaller groups of animists and Christians. While French is the official language, Hausa is the language of trade and commerce and is constitutionally classified, along with Arabic and five other tribal languages, as a "national" language. Women constitute a minority of the labor force, excluding unpaid family workers.

Agriculture and stock raising occupy 90 percent of the work force, the chief products being millet and sorghum for domestic consumption and peanuts, vegetables, and live cattle for export. The country's major exports are cotton and uranium, of which Niger is one of the world's top five producers. Coal, phosphates, iron ore, gold, and petroleum have also been discovered, but their exploitation awaits development of a more adequate transportation and communication infrastructure. Niger's economy declined in the 1980s, with agriculture suffering from both floods and drought. Also, a decrease in uranium demand contributed to a severe trade imbalance and mounting foreign debt. The introduction of austerity measures, while generating substantial social unrest, yielded assistance from the International Monetary Fund (IMF) and debt rescheduling from the Paris Club. In June 1996 the IMF approved a new three-year loan to facilitate further structural adjustments.

The government's economic policies in 1996–1998, which focused on privatization of state-run enterprises, were described as "broadly satisfactory," with GDP growth rising from 2.8 percent in 1997 to 10.4 percent in 1998. However, political turmoil and an eight-month imposition of military rule following the assassination of President Maïnassara halted economic progress, as some external financing was frozen and domestic arrears (including the payment of civil service salaries)

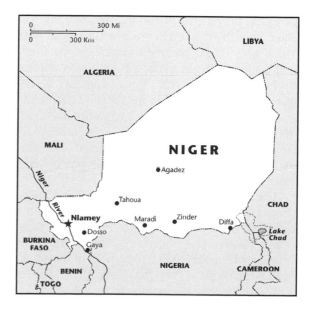

accumulated. GDP consequently contracted by 0.6 percent in 1999, although a degree of fiscal stability returned after a democratically elected civilian government was installed late in the year. GDP grew by an average of about 1.5 percent per year between 2001 and 2003 in view of returned support from the IMF and World Bank, which have endorsed the new government's commitment to structural reform and financial transparency. Drought and widespread devastation by locusts in 2004 weakened the economy and resulted in a lack of trade and subsequent GDP growth of less than 1 percent. Because of progress the country made in economic reforms, however, the IMF provided substantial debt relief at the end of 2005. The fund projected GDP growth of about 4 percent for Niger in 2006, though analysts suggested that long-term prospects for Niger (one of the poorest and least developed countries in the world) largely would depend on enhanced regional economic cooperation.

Government and Politics

Political Background

An object of centuries-old contention among different African peoples, Niger was first exposed to French contact in the late 19th century. Military conquest of the area began prior to 1900 but, because of stiff resistance, was not completed until 1922, when Niger became a French colony. Political evolution began under a constitution granted by France in 1946, with Niger becoming a self-governing republic within the French Community in 1958 and attaining full independence in August 1960. Although its membership in the community subsequently lapsed, Niger has retained close economic and political ties with its former colonial ruler.

The banning of the Marxist-oriented *Sawaba* (Freedom) Party in 1959 converted Niger into a one-party state under the Niger Progressive Party (*Parti Progressiste Nigérien*—PPN), headed by President Hamani DIORI, a member of the southern Djerma tribe. Thereafter, Djibo BAKARY led *Sawaba* elements to continue their opposition ac-

tivity from abroad, with terrorist incursions in 1964 and 1965 that included an attempt on the president's life. The Diori government, carefully balanced to represent ethnic and regional groupings, was reelected in 1965 and 1970 by overwhelming majorities but proved incapable of coping with the effects of the prolonged Sahelian drought of 1968–1974. As a result, Diori was overthrown on April 15, 1974, by a military coup led by Gen. Seyni KOUNTCHÉ and Maj. Sani Souna SIDO, who then established themselves as president and vice president, respectively, of a Supreme Military Council (*Conseil Militaire Suprême*—CMS). On August 2, 1975, Kountché announced that Sido and a number of others, including Bakary, had been arrested for attempting to organize a second coup.

A National Development Council (*Conseil National pour le Développement*—CND), initially established in July 1974 with an appointive membership, was assigned quasi-leadership status in August 1983, following indirect election of 150 delegates. Earlier, on January 24, Oumarou MAMANE had been appointed to the newly created post of prime minister; on August 3 he was named president of the reconstituted CND. Hamid AL-GABID replaced him as prime minister on November 14.

President Kountché died in a Paris hospital on November 10, 1987, after what was apparently a lengthy illness. He was immediately succeeded by the army chief of staff, (then) Col. Ali SAIBOU. After being formally invested by the CMS on November 14, the new president named Algabid to head an otherwise substantially new government.

On August 2, 1988, following a July 15 cabinet reorganization that included the return of Mamane as prime minister, Saibou announced the formation of a National Movement for a Developing Society (*Mouvement National pour une Société de Développement*—MNSD) as the "final step in normalization of Niger's politics." The CND, whose constituent functions had been reaffirmed by Saibou in December 1987, was given the task of further defining the role of the MNSD.

Adding to the complexity of the restructuring process was General Saibou's declaration on

Political Status: Former French dependency; independence declared August 3, 1960; military regime established April 15, 1974; constitution of September 1989, providing for single-party military/civilian government, suspended on August 4, 1991, by a National Consultative Conference that had declared itself a sovereign body on July 30; multiparty constitution of December 27, 1992, suspended by military coup on January 27, 1996; new constitution adopted on May 22, 1996, following approval by national referendum on May 12; constitution suspended by the military-based National Reconciliation Council on April 11, 1999; new multiparty constitution providing for return of civilian government approved by national referendum on July 18, 1999, and promulgated on August 9.

Area: 489,189 sq. mi. (1,267,000 sq. km.).

Population: 10,790,352 (2001C); 12,283,000 (2005E).

Major Urban Center (2005E): NIAMEY (including suburbs, 991,000).

Official Language: French.

Monetary Unit: CFA Franc (official rate July 1, 2006: 513.01 CFA francs = $1US). (The CFA franc, formerly pegged to the French franc, is now permanently pegged to the euro at 655.975 CFA francs = 1 euro.)

President: Mamadou TANDJA (National Movement for a Developing Society—Victory); elected in second-round balloting on November 24, 1999, and sworn in for a five-year term on December 22; reelected in second-round balloting on December 4, 2004, and sworn in for a record five-year term on December 21. (Prior to Tandja's first term Maj. Daouda Malam WANKÉ had served as head of state and chair of the newly formed National Reconstruction Council; he was appointed on April 11, 1999, following the assumption of power by a military junta in the wake of the assassination of President Ibrahim Baré MAÏNASSARA on April 9.)

Prime Minister: Hama AMADOU (National Movement for a Developing Society—Victory); appointed by the president on December 31, 1999, and sworn in on January 3, 2000, to succeed Ibrahim Assane MAYAKI; formed new government on January 5, 2000; reappointed by the president on December 24, 2004, and formed new government on December 30, 2004.

January 1, 1989, that the initial congress of the MNSD would elect the membership of a Supreme Council of National Orientation (*Conseil Suprême de la Orientation Nationale*—CSON) to replace the CMS, while the CND would become an advisory Economic and Social Council (*Conseil Economique et Social*—CES). On May 17 Saibou was elected president of the CSON, thereby becoming, under a new constitution approved in September, the sole candidate for election as head of state on December 10. Saibou was credited with more than 99 percent of the votes, as was the single list of 93 MNSD candidates concurrently elected to the new National Assembly.

The post of prime minister was eliminated upon the formation of a new government on December 20, 1989. However, it was reestablished in a March 2, 1990, reshuffle precipitated by student-government confrontations in Niamey; Aliou MA-HAMIDOU, a government industrial executive, was named to the position. Three months later, the CSON committed itself to "political pluralism," and in mid-November, after encountering further dissatisfaction with his policies, Saibou announced that a National Consultative Conference would convene to consider constitutional reform.

The conference opened on July 29, 1991, with 1,204 delegates from 24 political groups and 69 mass organizations in attendance. After declaring its sovereignty and electing André SALIFOU as chair, the conference suspended the constitution on August 9 and transferred all but ceremonial presidential powers from Saibou to Salifou. It was decided at the time that Prime Minister Mahamidou would remain in office. However, on November 1, in the wake of an inquiry into the May 1990 massacre of Tuareg nomads by government troops, Amadou CHEIFFOU was named to succeed Mahamidou for a 15-month transition to multiparty balloting scheduled for January 31,

1993. On November 2 the conference appointed a 15-member High Council of the Republic (*Haut Conseil de la République*—HCR), chaired by Salifou, to serve as a constituent assembly and provisional legislature for the duration of the transitional period. The following day the conference voted to disband the HCR in favor of another form of transitional government.

Cheiffou announced the creation of a transitional government on November 4, 1991, which was then dissolved on March 23, 1992, in the wake of a failed military coup on February 28; a new cabinet was named on March 27. In early July Cheiffou survived a nonconfidence motion triggered by a mid-June decision to recognize Taiwan in exchange for an economic aid package, an arrangement that the HCR branded as contravening National Conference resolutions. The split between Cheiffou and the HCR proved short-lived, as the two agreed at an August 7 meeting to reconcile their differences. Meanwhile, preparations for a constitutional referendum and multiparty election proceeded haltingly. The new constitution was finally approved on December 26 by 89 percent of referendum voters, despite observations that the polling was marred by irregularities.

In late December 1992 the government admitted it had lost control over troops assigned to the northeastern Tuareg region where the insurgent Front for the Liberation of Air and Azaouad (FLAA) had resumed activity, further complicating the transitional process. Seven months earlier, the government had responded to the FLAA capture of some 28 military personnel and two officials of the recently restyled MNSD-*Nassara* by giving the army control of security in the region, a decision criticized by local Tuareg officials as equivalent to imposing a state of emergency. Frustrated by the rebels' unwillingness to release their prisoners, the army, apparently without government approval, arrested 186 alleged FLAA rebels and supporters, including a number of prominent Tuareg members of the transitional administration. Tuareg officials denounced a subsequent soldiers-for-civilians exchange offer and appealed to the UN for assistance. A Niamey offer to create a "forum for national reconciliation" in November was rebuffed by the Tuaregs, who questioned the government's ability to provide for their safety.

Following a National Assembly election on February 14, 1993, the MNSD-*Nassara,* with a plurality of 29 seats, appeared likely to form a coalition with one or more of its competitors, as a means of retaining control of the government. However, two days later, nine opposition parties, decrying the possibility of MNSD-*Nassara* controlling 50 assembly seats and continuing its rule, formed a majoritarian Alliance of Forces of Change (AFC). At the first round of presidential balloting on February 27 MNSD-*Nassara* candidate Mamadou TANDJA led the eight-candidate field with 34.22 percent of the vote, followed by Mahamane OUSMANE of the Democratic and Social Convention-*Rahama* (CDS-*Rahama*), with 26.59 percent. However, at the second round on March 27, Ousmane was able to surpass Tandja with 54.42 percent of the vote, thanks to solid AFC backing; he was sworn in for a five-year term on April 16. The next day Mahamadou ISSOUFOU, leader of the Nigerien Party for Democracy and Socialism-*Tarayya* (PNDS-*Tarayya*), was appointed prime minister. Issoufou named a cabinet on May 23.

In early 1994 opposition legislators launched a boycott against the Assembly, but all 33 were arrested for advocating civil disobedience following violent antigovernment demonstrations on April 16–17. Among those incarcerated for their roles in the unrest were Tandja and the leaders of two theretofore AFC parties, André Salifou of the Union of Democratic Patriots and Progressives–*Chamoua* (UPDP-*Chamoua*) and Issoufou ASSOUMANE of the Democratic Union of Progressive Forces–*Sawaba* (UDFP-*Sawaba*). Their defection lent credence to reports of discord within the AFC, apparently stemming from the president's poorly received efforts to seize Mahamadou Issoufou's prime ministerial powers.

The AFC lost its assembly majority on September 25, 1994, when the PNDS-*Tarayya* broke with the coalition, complaining it had been marginalized by the CDS-*Rahama.* Prime Minister Issoufou resigned on September 28, and Ousmane named CDS-*Rahama* cabinet minister Abdoulaye SOULEY as the new head of government the same day. However, on October 16, two days after the MNDS-*Nassara* and PNDS-*Tarayya* had successfully orchestrated an assembly nonconfidence vote, the 11-day-old Souley government was forced to dissolve. The following day Ousmane reappointed Souley, who proffered the same cabinet. A second nonconfidence vote ensued and, faced with the choice of appointing a prime minister from the new parliamentary majority or dissolving the National Assembly and holding a new legislative election, Ousmane chose the latter.

On January 9, 1995, three days before the election, the MNSD-*Nassara* coalition threatened a boycott due to alleged voter registration fraud and the assassination of an opposition candidate, Seydou Dan DJOUMA. Nevertheless, the coalition participated in the poll and captured 43 legislative seats; AFC-affiliated groups secured the remaining 40. Ousmane ignored MNSD-*Nassara's* request that he name Hama AMADOU as prime minister, despite the party's assembly majority, and instead appointed another MNSD-*Nassara* member, Amadou Boubacar CISSÉ, on February 8. Two days later the MNSD-*Nassara* expelled Cissé, and on February 20 the assembly voted to censure the new prime minister. The following day Ousmane dismissed Cissé and appointed Amadou, who subsequently formed a cabinet drawn from supporters of the new governing coalition.

Despite differences within the Tuareg leadership, a final peace accord was signed on April 25, 1995. On June 12, the National Assembly unanimously decided to grant full amnesty to all participants of the civil war. Meanwhile, political turmoil continued in Niamey as the AFC, which had earlier accused the MNSD-*Nassara* and its partners of "monstrous irregularities" during the January polling, criticized Prime Minister Amadou's new government for failing to represent "half of the population." Ousmane refused Amadou's call for a cabinet meeting on July 6, in an apparent attempt to avert a vote on his own non-cabinet appointments. Amadou contended that Ousmane lacked the authority to name government officials

and responded by ordering riot police to prevent Ousmane-appointed administrators from entering their offices. Despite subsequent negotiations, Amadou dismissed the officials in question on August 1; however, a Niamey court immediately reinstated them. On August 4 the prime minister held a cabinet meeting without Ousmane, who promptly declared all cabinet decisions "null and void."

In early October 1995 opposition parliamentarians aligned with Ousmane declared that the prime minister had deliberately violated the constitution by convening the cabinet without presidential approval and called for his censure. However, their attempt to pass a nonconfidence motion on October 8 failed (in part because some members boycotted the vote to protest the absence of the assembly speaker). In November international mediators met with the president and prime minister in what was described as a successful attempt to end the constitutional impasse, although the question of who controlled government appointments remained unresolved.

On January 27, 1996, at least ten people were killed in a military coup directed by Army Chief of Staff Col. Ibrahim Baré MAÏNASSARA, who claimed that he had acted to end the "absurd, irrational, and personalized crisis" gripping the Nigerien government. Following seizure of the presidential palace and assembly building, Maïnassara announced the "dismissal" of the president and prime minister (both of whom had been arrested), the dissolution of the assembly, suspension of political party activity, and his own installation as chair of the National Salvation Council (*Conseil pour le Salut National*—CSN), an 11-member military body organized to govern until a civilian government could be reestablished. On January 30 the CSN designated Boukari ADJI, vice governor of the Central Bank of West African States (BCEAO), as prime minister.

In February 1996 Maïnassara appointed a 100-member Committee of Wisemen to act as an advisory council and a 32-member Coordinating Committee for the Democratic Renewal to supervise the restoration of a democratic government and draft a new constitution. At a meeting chaired by

Maïnassara on February 12, Ousmane and Amadou publicly acknowledged the "constitutional problems" that had prompted the coup and endorsed the CSN's early governing efforts.

On February 17, 1996, the CSN announced a timetable for the return to a democratically elected government, which called for a constitutional referendum in September and presidential and legislative elections by the end of the year. However, under pressure from France, which on March 6 became the first international donor to renew ties with the junta, the CSN released a revised timetable that moved the schedule up by three months. On March 27 the regime established a transitional legislature, the National Forum for Democratic Renewal, consisting of members from the Committee of Wisemen and the Coordinating Committee, as well as former National Assemblymen. The National Forum met for the first time on April 1 and six days later it approved a draft constitution that included provisions for a second legislative body (a Senate), as well as a government wherein the prime minister would be accountable to the president. On April 19 the National Forum released yet another transitional timetable, rescheduling the constitutional referendum to May 12, presidential balloting to July 7, and legislative elections to September 22.

The constitutional referendum was approved on May 12, 1996, by 92 percent of the voters—though the election was poorly attended. Maïnassara revoked the ban on political parties May 19, and lifted the state of emergency four days later. Meanwhile, a clash between government forces and rebels near Lake Chad was reportedly the first such incident since early March, when Tuareg and Toubou leaders had agreed to implement a unilateral cease-fire as a sign of support for the military regime.

In balloting July 7–8, 1996, Brig. Gen. Maïnassara (who was promoted on May 14) captured the presidency, securing 52 percent of the vote, according to government figures. However, the election was marred by the junta's termination of the Independent National Electoral Commission (CENI) on the second day of voting and installation of a National Electoral Commission (CNE) filled with Maïnassara's supporters. Dismissing the regime's claim that it had dissolved the CENI to end the "corruption" of ballots by opposition activists, Maïnassara's top three challengers (former president Ousmane, MNSD-*Nassara* chair Mamadou Tandja, and former National Assembly president Mahamadou Issoufou) filed a petition to have the results overturned. (Ousmane had been credited with 19.75 percent of the vote, Tandja 15.65 percent, and Issoufou 7.6 percent. The fifth candidate, Moumouni DJERMAKOYE of the ANDP-*Zaman Lahiya,* secured 4.77 of the vote; he did not formally contest the results.) The Supreme Court officially validated Maïnassara's electoral victory July 21, and on August 23 the new president named a cabinet, again led by Prime Minister Adji, which included no military officials.

Following his inauguration on August 7, 1996, President Maïnassara attempted to negotiate an agreement that would prompt angry opposition groups to participate in upcoming legislative elections. Among other things, he dissolved the CNE on August 30 and announced the formation of a new electoral commission. However, the opposition, most of which coalesced in September as the Front for the Restoration and Defense of Democracy (FRDD), demanded that the members of the CENI be reappointed and that other measures be taken to ensure fair elections. Unconvinced of the regime's democratic intentions, the FRDD ultimately boycotted the balloting for a new National Assembly held on November 23, paving the way for the National Union of Independents for Democratic Renewal (UNIRD), which had recently been established by supporters of resident Maïnassara, to win 59 of the 83 seats. Declaring the transition to civilian government complete, Maïnassara dissolved the CSN on December 12. On December 21 he appointed a new government, headed, ironically, by Amadou Cissé, whose attempted appointment to the premiership in February 1995 had triggered the constitutional crisis leading up to the January 1996 coup.

Antigovernment sentiment culminated in large-scale demonstrations in the capital in early January 1997. Maïnassara responded with a crackdown that resulted in the arrest of the FRDD leaders; however, the detainees were released after ten days, regional leaders having apparently persuaded the president to adopt a less harsh approach.

On March 31, 1997, Maïnassara dissolved the Cissé government in response to the opposition's agreement to set aside its preconditions for entering into negotiations (i.e., dissolution of the assembly and organization of fresh elections) and accept cabinet postings. However, talks between the two sides quickly broke down, and no opposition members were included in the government named on June 13. The opposition rejected subsequent government entreaties, and unrest was reported throughout the country. Consequently, on November 24 Maïnassara again dismissed the Cissé government, accusing it of "incompetency" and failing to ease political tensions.

On November 27, 1997, Ibrahim Assane MAYAKI was named to replace Cissé, and on December 1 a new government was appointed. Despite Maïnassara's pledge to include opposition figures in the new cabinet, only one minister, Tuareg leader Rhissa ag BOULA, came from outside the pro-presidential coalition of parties. Moreover, a number of Cissé ministers were reappointed.

Opposition candidates captured a majority of the contested seats at local, municipal, and regional balloting on February 7, 1999. Heightened government-opposition tension was consequently reported in Niamey after the Supreme Court (acting, according to the opposition, under pressure from the administration) ordered extensive repolling in early April.

On April 9 President Maïnassara was assassinated at the Niamey airport upon returning from a trip to Mecca, reportedly by members of the presidential guard. Troops immediately took control of the capital, and Prime Minister Mayaki dissolved the assembly, suspended political party activities, and asserted that he and his cabinet would continue governing until a "unity" government was formed. After two days of uncertainty, however, junior army officers announced on April 11 that they had assumed power and formed a National Reconciliation Council (*Conseil de Réconciliation Nationale*— CRN), whose chair, Maj. Daouda Malam WANKÉ

(theretofore commander of the presidential guard), was also named head of state. The junta suspended the constitution and formally dissolved the government and Supreme Court. In addition, the results of the February elections were annulled. At the same time, the military announced a nine-month transitional plan that would culminate in the inauguration of an elected president. On April 16, 1999, the CRN named an interim government that included Wanké as the head of government, Mayaki in a diminished prime ministerial role, and a number of FRDD ministers.

A new constitution, designed, among other things, to resolve the presidential/prime-ministerial power-sharing confusion of the early to mid-1990s, was approved by 90 percent of the vote in a national referendum on July 18, 1999, although turnout was estimated at only 32 percent. Seven candidates ran in the presidential election on October 17, and in runoff balloting on November 24 Mamadou Tandja of MNSD-*Nassara* defeated Mahamdou Issoufou of PNDS-*Tarayya*, 60 percent to 40 percent. The MNSD-*Nassara* also secured a plurality in new assembly balloting on November 24, and in coalition with the CDS-*Rahama* controlled a comfortable majority of 55 legislative seats. Tandja was inaugurated on December 22 and, upon the recommendation of the assembly, named fellow party member Hama AMADOU as prime minister on December 31. In addition to the MNSD-*Nassara* and CDS-*Rahama*, the new cabinet announced on January 5, 2000, also included representatives of two small, nonlegislative parties–the UFPDP-*Sawaba* and PUND-*Salama*– as well as two leaders of former Tuareg rebel organizations. However, in a reshuffle on September 17, 2001, the ministers from the UFPDP-*Sawaba* and PUND-*Salama* were dropped from the cabinet.

The country's first municipal elections, postponed from May 4, 2004, were successfully held on July 24, 2004, with councilors elected to represent 206 communities.

Tandja was reelected in 2004, after winning the first round of balloting on November 16 and easily defeating Issoufou in second-round balloting on December 4 with 65.5 percent of the vote. He named a new cabinet on December 30, which included five women and retained Amadou as prime minister. The assembly, also elected on December 4, seated seven members from a new party formed earlier in the year by former transitional leader Cheiffou: the Rally for Social Democracy (RSD).

Constitution and Government

In January 1984 President Kountché created a National Charter Commission, largely comprised of CND members, to develop a constitutional framework that was ultimately endorsed in a national referendum on June 14, 1987. On December 17 of the same year, General Saibou announced the formation of a national "reflection committee" to finalize guidelines for the new basic law, which was approved by popular referendum on September 24, 1989. Capping the government structure was the CSON, whose 67 civilian and military members (14 serving as a National Executive Bureau) were elected by the MNSD and whose president became sole candidate for election to the presidency of the republic. The 1989 document, which also provided for a National Assembly of 93 MNSD-approved members and for a judiciary headed by a presidentially appointed Supreme Court, was suspended by the National Conference on August 9, 1991.

By mid-1992 the presidency had been reduced to an essentially symbolic institution, as true executive power was exercised by the prime minister who until early 1993 answered to a quasi-legislative High Council of the Republic (HCR). One of the functions of the HCR was to oversee the drafting of the new basic law, which was approved by national referendum on December 27, 1993. The document provided for a directly elected president to serve a once-renewable five-year term. A presidentially nominated prime minister was responsible to a unicameral National Assembly whose 83 members were also elected for five-year terms.

Upon its ascension to power in early 1996 the CSN military regime suspended the 1993 document and appointed a commission to draft a new charter. The new constitution, which was approved by national referendum on May 12, 1996, featured an executive branch headed by a powerful president, thus clearly distinguishing itself from its predecessors. Meanwhile, in early June the regime created a ten-member High Court of Justice and granted it sole authority to prosecute the president and government members.

The 1996 basic law was suspended by the CRN on April 11, 1999, and an interim Consultative Council (*Conseil Consultative*—CC) was appointed in May by the new military head of state, Maj. Daouda Malam Wanké, to draft yet another constitution. As approved in a national referendum on July 18, the new basic law accorded strong power to the president to prevent a reoccurrence of the difficulties experienced in interpreting the 1993 document with regard to the authority of the prime minister versus the president.

Foreign Relations

Prior to the 1974 coup Niger pursued a moderate line in foreign affairs, avoiding involvement in East-West issues and maintaining friendly relations with neighboring states, except for a brief period of territorial friction with Dahomey (subsequently Benin) in 1963–1964. The Kountché government established diplomatic links with a number of communist states, including China and the Soviet Union, and adopted a conservative posture in regional affairs, including a diplomatic rupture with Libya from January 1981 to March 1982. Tripoli was periodically charged thereafter with backing anti-Niamey forces, including those involved in a late 1983 coup attempt and northern Tuareg rebel activity in 1985 and 1990. However, a bilateral security agreement in December 1990 eased tensions between Niger and Libya.

Niamey's relations with neighboring Algeria and Mali have been complicated since October 1991 by the resurgence of militant Tuareg activities across their shared borders. In March 1992 a meeting between Prime Minister Cheiffou and Tuareg officials in Algeria yielded a two-week truce. However, the truce was allowed to lapse, and in February 1993 Nigerien and Malian troops clashed, after reportedly mistaking each other for Tuareg units. The January 1996 military coup in Niger drew condemnation from both regional and international observers, with France, the European Union, and the United States suspending aid payments. Although Paris resumed cooperation in March 1996, Washington reiterated its stance following the controversial July presidential elections.

A number of regional and other international capitals condemned the military takeover in April 1999; France, for example, promptly broke off its relations with Niger and suspended all aid. Such pressure was considered influential in the subsequent quick return to civilian rule, after which normal international relations were reestablished and external financial assistance was resumed.

In May 2000 a long-standing dispute between Niger and Benin over ownership of Lete Island and a number of smaller islands in the Niger River resurfaced. After mediation by the Organization of African Unity (OAU, subsequently the African Union—AU) failed to produce successful border delineation, the case was submitted to the International Court of Justice (ICJ) in mid-2001. In 2005 the ICJ ruled that 16 of the 25 disputed islands, including Lete, belonged to Niger.

Current Issues

Although the events of April 1999 had, in the opinion of many observers, all the earmarks of a military coup d'état, CRN Chair Wanké did not acknowledge any involvement in the killing of President Maïnassara. Instead, he argued that the junta had assumed power only as a result of the chaos that ensued following the "tragic accident." In any event, it did not appear that an intense investigation into the death of the manifestly unpopular Maïnassara would be conducted, as the general populace and political party leaders seemed primarily concerned with the junta's plans for return to civilian government—which, to the surprise of some analysts, was accomplished rather smoothly by the end of the year. (Wanké died on September 15, 2004, at age 58.) Both the presidential and legislative polls were described as fairly conducted

by international observers, and the results were accepted in most domestic quarters. The administration of President Tandja, who had campaigned on a platform calling for national unity, was widely credited by the international financial community for having stabilized the economy. However, the newly formed opposition group known as the Coordination of Democratic Forces (*Coordination des Forces Démocratiques*—CFD) criticized the government for "ruling by edict" in order to accommodate the IMF and other lenders. The CFD organized street protests and presented several censure motions in the assembly, which were ultimately unsuccessful. Eyebrows were also raised by the decision to grant amnesty to everyone involved in the 1996 coup and the events of April 1999. Also, the government faced pressure from student protesters and Islamic organizations, some of whom had been banned in November 2000 for "disturbing the peace." On a positive note, however, most former rebel groups were officially disarmed as of mid-2000; a weapons-burning ceremony in September symbolized the end of large-scale rebellion.

Tension between the government and the opposition continued into 2002, with the opposition criticizing the government's heavy-handed response to a midyear mutiny by soldiers in the southeastern town of Diffa over payment arrears and working conditions. Although the revolt was quickly squashed, the government limited civil liberties and press freedoms. In April 2003 a pilot project was launched to rid the southeast Nigerien region near Chad of weapons. Under the auspices of the UN, communities that handed in small arms were to receive public works and health and education assistance.

Slavery continues to be a major part of the culture and in March 2005 some 3,000 people in the capital protested the detention of anti-slavery activists. The government, for its part, denies that slavery exists. Niger faced a food crisis in 2005, which government authorities refused to label a "famine" despite the dire needs of a third of the population. UN and other aid was lagging, which analysts said was due to similar suffering by some 4 million people in other poor regions. By 2006, the IMF joined the now urgent appeal for donor assistance. Violent protests and kidnappings of petroleum industry workers occurred at midyear, reportedly by militant groups angered over what they said was the lack of oil profits being used to aid impoverished communities.

Political Parties

Political parties were not permitted in Niger during the more than 13 years of the Kountché regime. The National Movement for a Developing Society (MNSD, below) was established as a government formation in 1988, and some 15 parties received provisional recognition in the five months following President Saibou's November 1990 acceptance of a multiparty system. All party activity was suspended in the wake of the January 1996 coup, but the ban was soon lifted on May 19. However, the new standards guiding party formations and activities were described as restrictive. Nevertheless, numerous coalitions were formed in 1996–1998, though alliances continued changing. Most notably, the once powerful Alliance of Forces of Change (*Alliance des Forces de Changement*—AFC) appeared to have collapsed by the late 1990s. (For further information on the AFC, see p. 680 of the 1998 *Handbook*.)

Political party activity was suspended immediately following the April 1999 military takeover; however, within days of President Maïnassara's death the leading opposition groups announced their intention to cooperate with the military junta, and the suspension was lifted.

In March 2000 the PNDS-*Tarayya,* RDP-*Jamaa,* ANDP-*Zaman Lahiya,* and a number of smaller parties formed a loose antigovernment coalition called the Coordination of Democratic Forces (*Coordination des Forces Démocratiques*—CFD). In response the MNDS-*Nassara* and several allies, including the CDS-*Rahama,* announced the creation of an Alliance of Democratic Forces (*Alliance des Forces Démocratiques*—AFD) in July. The ANDP-*Zaman Lahia* joined the AFD coalition on July 8, 2002.

The following year the CFD protested President Tandja's coalition approval of a new law eliminating the requirement that ministers seeking elected office must first resign from their government position. The CFD members were angry that they had not been consulted, as electoral changes were usually made by consensus in the past.

Government Parties

National Movement for a Developing Society–Victory (*Mouvement National pour une Societé de Développement Nassara—MNSD-Nassara*). General Saibou announced the formation of the MNSD on August 2, 1988. Rejecting calls for a multiparty system, he claimed that the new group would allow for the "plural expression of opinions and ideological sensibilities," while paving the way for a normalization of politics in Niger.

General Saibou was reelected MNSD chair at a party congress on March 12–18, 1991, during which a transition to multipartism was formally endorsed. The military also announced its withdrawal from politics, and the MNSD added the Hausa word *Nassara* (Victory) to its name. On July 12, just as the party prepared to enter the competitive arena, Saibou resigned his chairmanship, citing a need to serve in a nonpartisan capacity.

At legislative balloting on February 14, 1993, the MNSD-*Nassara* secured 29 seats, 7 more than its nearest competitor; however, the subsequent formation of the AFC coalition relegated the then-ruling party to minority status. Accusing the new group of procedural irregularities, the MNSD-*Nassara* refused to promote a candidate for the National Assembly presidency in April; thereafter, it spearheaded numerous protests against the government's alleged "constitutional violations." In October ten party members were sentenced to prison for engaging in violent clashes with security forces, and in March 1994 Mamadou Tandja, the MNSD-*Nassara*'s leader and former 1993 presidential candidate, was arrested for his alleged role in an antigovernment demonstration in Niamey.

The MNSD-*Nassara* again captured 29 seats in legislative balloting in January 1995, thus retaining its position as the dominant partner in the parliamentary coalition it had led since late 1994. Tandja secured 15.65 percent of the vote during presidential balloting in July 1996. Tandja and his fellow PNDS-*Tarayya* and CDS-*Rahama* presidential competitors (below) subsequently sought to have the elections nullified, claiming "massive fraud," but the Supreme Court promptly dismissed their petitions.

In September 1996 the MNSD-*Nassara* joined the PNDS-*Tarayya*, CDS-*Rahama,* and several other small groups in launching the Front for the Restoration and Defense of Democracy (*Front pour la Restauration et la Défense de la Démocratie—* FRDD), which immediately became the primary opposition to the Maïnassara regime. The leaders of the front demanded the restoration of the "original" Independent National Commission (CENI), equal access to the media, and supervision of the balloting by the Organization of African Unity and/or the United Nations as preconditions for FRDD participation in the upcoming national elections. Despite some apparent compromise on the part of the government, the FRDD ultimately called for a boycott of the legislative balloting.

Following prodemocracy demonstrations in Niamey in early January 1997, the leaders of the three main FRDD components were arrested and reportedly threatened with prosecution by a tribunal especially created for that purpose by President Maïnassara. However, the party leaders and 60 other detainees were released ten days later and immediately urged the resumption of antigovernment demonstrations.

Each of three main FRDD components presented its own presidential candidate in the first round of balloting in 1999, and Mamadou Tandja led with 32.3 percent. Thanks in part to the support of former president Mahamane Ousmane of the CDS-*Rahama,* Tandja was elected with 59.9 percent of the vote in the second round. For the November 1999 legislative balloting the MNSD-*Nassara* was portrayed as still aligned with the

CDS-*Rahama,* but no longer with the PNDS-*Tarayya.*

Tandja again took the lead in the presidential elections of 2004, taking 40.7 percent of the vote in the first round of balloting on November 16. He retained his post in the second round of balloting on December 4 with a resounding victory (65.5 percent of the vote) by striking alliances with ANDP-*Zaman Lahiya* candidate Moumouni Djermakoye (who was fifth in first-round balloting) and Amadou Cheiffou of the Rally for Social Democracy-*Gaskiya* who ran as an independent (fourth in the first round), and gaining the support of the CDS's Ousmane, who garnered just 24.6 percent of votes in the first round, and Hamid ALGABID of the Democratic Rally of the People-*Jamaa* (sixth place in the first round). MNSD captured 47 legislative seats, a gain of 9 from the previous elections, though it failed to gain an absolute majority of the expanded 113-member assembly (see Legislature, below). The legislative election coincided with the second round of the presidential elections on December 4.

Leaders: Col. (Ret.) Mamadou TANDJA (President of the Republic), Hama AMADOU (Prime Minister of the Republic and Secretary General of the Party).

Democratic and Social Convention–Rahama (*Convention Démocrate et Sociale–Rahama—* CDS-*Rahama*). In the legislative balloting of February 1993 CDS-*Rahama* captured 22 seats, the most of any opposition party. Its candidate Mahamane Ousmane, who had finished second in the first round of balloting, captured the presidency with 54.42 percent of the vote in the second round of presidential balloting on March 27. In January 1995 the party increased its assembly representation to 24 seats. Ousmane was ousted from office in the January 1996 coup; his bid to regain the presidency in the July balloting fell short as he came in second (at least according to government tallies) with 19.75 percent of the vote. He finished a close third in the first round of presidential balloting in 1999 with 22.5 percent of the vote. The

CDS-*Rahama* subsequently threw its support behind Mamadou Tandja of the MNSD-*Nassara* for the second round. In the 2004 presidential balloting, Ousmane was again third in the first round of voting, and again threw his support behind Tandja in the second round. CDS-*Rahama* won 22 seats in the assembly balloting of 2004.

Leaders: Mahamane OUSMANE (Speaker of the National Assembly and Former President of the Republic), Nabram ISSOUFOU.

Nigerien Alliance for Democracy and Progress–Zaman Lahiya (*Alliance Nigérienne pour la Démocratie et le Progrès–Zaman Lahiya—ANDP-Zaman Lahiya*). On August 28, 1992, ANDP-*Zaman Lahiya* vice president Birgi Raffini, a former Saibou government official, was arrested during an army crackdown on suspected FLAA rebels and sympathizers. He was released in early 1993, and his party won 11 seats in legislative balloting that February. ANDP-*Zaman Lahiya's* candidate, Moumouni Adamou Djermakoye, secured only 15 percent of the vote in the first round of presidential balloting, but his support for the CDS-*Rahama's* Ousmane was described as pivotal to Ousmane's presidential victory. In April Djermakoye was named National Assembly president. The party's legislative representation fell to 9 seats in January 1995.

At presidential balloting in July 1996 Djermakoye received only 4.77 percent of the vote, finishing last in the five-candidate field. The ANDP-*Zaman Lahiya* was the only major party not to boycott the November 1996 elections, at which it secured eight seats.

In 1998 the ANDP-*Zaman Lahiya* joined the PUND-*Salama* and the PNA (see below) to form a pro-Maïnassara group called the Alliance of Democratic Social Forces (*Alliance des Forces Démocratiques et Sociales—AFDS*). Djermakoye won 7.7 percent of the votes in the first round of presidential balloting in 1999 and endorsed Mahamadou Issoufou of the PNDS-*Tarayya* in the second round. The ANDP-*Zaman Lahiya* agreed to join the progovernment Alliance of Democratic Forces in 2002.

In 2004, presidential candidate Djermakoye received only 6.1 percent of the vote in the first round of balloting, the fifth of six candidates. Since his party belongs to the ruling coalition, his support in the second round likely went to Tandje. ANDP-*Zaman Lahiya* won five seats in the assembly election of 2004.

Leaders: Moumouni Adamou DJERMAKOYE (Party President, 1999 and 2004 presidential candidate, and Former National Assembly President), Birgi RAFFINI (Vice President).

Rally for Social Democracy–Gaskiya (*Rassemblement pour Sociale Democrate—RSD-Gaskiya*). The RSD-Gaskiya split off from CDS in January 2004. Amadou Cheiffou, a former transitional prime minister from 1991 to 1993 and party leader, ran as an independent presidential candidate in 2004, receiving only 6.3 percent of the vote in the first round of balloting. However, the new party did win seven seats in the assembly and subsequent representation in the cabinet of President Tandje.

Leader and founder: Amadou CHEIFFOU (Former Prime Minister and 2004 presidential candidate).

Democratic Rally of the People–Jamaa (*Rassemblement Démocratique du Peuple–Jamaa—RDP-Jamaa*). The RDP-*Jamaa* held its inaugural congress on August 14–19, 1997, and was the party of then-President Maïnassara. Thereafter the party emerged as the leader of a loose coalition of parties that supported the president. At local and municipal polling in early 1999, the RDP-*Jamaa* reportedly captured the largest number of seats; however, the military junta that came to power in April nullified the balloting.

Intraparty fighting erupted over the choice of a 1999 presidential nominee, leading former Prime Minister Amadou Boubacar Cissé and his supporters to leave the party (see UDR, below). Meanwhile, Hamid Algabid of the RDP-*Jamaa* won 10.9 percent of the vote in the first round of presidential balloting and supported Mahamadou Issoufou of the PNDS-*Tarayya* in the second round. In the first round of presidential elections in 2004, Algabid won only 4.9 percent of the vote, finishing in last place. He supported Tandja in the second round. The party won only six seats in the Assembly elections of 2004.

Leaders: Hamid ALGABID (Chair and 1999 and 2004 presidential candidate), Abdourahamane SEYDOU (Secretary General).

Other Legislative Parties

Nigerien Party for Democracy and Socialism–Tarayya (*Parti Nigerien pour la Démocratie et le Socialism–Tarayya—PNDS-Tarayya*). In the legislative election of February 1993 the PNDS-*Tarayya*, then affiliated with the AFC, won 13 seats. Having gained only a 16 percent vote share in the first round of 1993 presidential balloting, party leader and presidential candidate Mahamadou Issoufou was eliminated from the runoff election; he was subsequently named prime minister.

On September 25, 1994, the PNDS-*Tarayya* withdrew from the AFC, claiming that it had been "betrayed" by its coalition partners, and three days later Issoufou resigned his prime ministerial post. In mid-October the PNDS-*Tarayya* joined with the MNSD-*Nassara* in a successful nonconfidence motion against the Souley government. In the January 1995 legislative poll the party won 12 seats; Issoufou was then elected National Assembly president. He captured 7.6 percent of the vote as the party's standard-bearer in the July 1996 presidential elections. He fared significantly better in 1999, finishing second in the first round with 22.8 percent of the vote before losing the runoff with 40.1 percent. Once aligned with the MNSD-*Nassara* and the CDR-*Rahama* in the FRDD, the PNDS-*Tarayya* competed against those parties in the 1999 legislative balloting in alliance with the RDP-*Jamaa* and ANDR-*Zaman Lahiya*.

Issoufou faced a runoff with incumbent President Tandja in 2004, after winning 24.6 percent of the votes in first-round balloting. In the second round, Tandja handily defeated his rival with 65.5 percent of the vote. However, the PNDS-*Tarayya*

ran in coalition with a number of small parties and won 17 seats in the 2004 legislative election (see Legislature, below).

Leaders: Mahamadou ISSOUFOU (Former National Assembly President and 1999 and 2004 presidential candidate), Mohammed BAZOUM.

Nigerien Democratic Front–Mutunci (*Front Démocratique Nigerien–Mutunci—FDN-Mutunci*). The launching of the FDN-*Mutunci* in late January 1995 represented a redefinition of the Nigerien Progressive Party (*Parti Progressiste Nigerien—PPN*), which had previously operated as the local section of the African Democratic Rally (*Rassemblement Démocratique Africaine—RDA*) under the PPN/RDA rubric. The new name was adopted shortly after the group withdrew from the AFC, as it was being increasingly dominated by CDS-*Rahama*. The platform advanced by the FDN-*Mutunci* calls for the "preservation" of Niger's sovereignty and the "strengthening of national cohesion." The party won one seat at the January 1995 balloting and none in November 1996.

Ide Oumarou was elected chair of FDN-*Mutunci* at a party congress in October 1998. Thereafter, he announced that the group (still widely referred to as the PPN/RDA) would align itself with parties supporting President Maïnassara. It ran in coalition with smaller parties for the 2004 assembly elections (see Legislature, below).

Former party chair Ide Oumarou died in February 2002. At the time of his death he had been vying with RDA leader Abdoulaye Diori Hamani, son of the country's first president, for chairmanship of the party.

Leaders: Dan Dicko DANKOLODO (Former Chair), Oumarou Garba YOUSSOUFOU (1993 presidential candidate), Léopold KAZIENDE.

Niger Party for Self-Management (*Parti Nigérien pour l'Autogestion—PNA*). Former CDS vice chair Sanoussi Jackou formed the

PNA in early 1997. It supported Mamadou Tandja in the 1999 presidential balloting despite its previous affiliation with the AFDS. Chair Jackou received a four-month suspended prison sentence in May 2002 after he was accused of slander and inciting racial hatred. In January 2005 he was released after serving a one-month prison sentence for insulting an ethnic group during a radio broadcast.

In the 2004 legislative elections the PNA allied in various coalitions along with PNDS-*Tarayya* (see Legislature, below).

Leader: Sanoussi JACKOU.

Nigerien Social Democratic Party–Alheri (*Parti Social Démocrate du Niger–Alheri—PSDN-Alheri*). At legislative balloting in January 1995 the PSDN-*Alheri* increased its representation from one seat to two. The group did not appear to participate in the November 1996 balloting, but it returned in 2004 to regain one seat.

Leaders: Gagara GREIMA, Malam Adji WAZIRI, Katzelma Omar Mahaman TAYA (1993 presidential candidate).

Other Parties

Union of Popular Forces for Democracy and Progress–Sawaba (*Union des Forces Populaires pour la Démocratie et le Progrès–Sawaba—UFPDP-Sawaba*). The UFPDP-*Sawaba* is an offshoot of the UDN-*Sawaba* (below). It was led by Djibo Bakary, a 74-year-old former prime minister and former opponent of President Diori, from May 1957 to December 1958. He was unanimously elected party president in February 1992. Running on a platform calling for national unity and increased dialogue with the Tuareg rebels, Bakary captured 1.68 percent of the presidential vote in February 1993. The party lost both of its former legislative seats in January 1995 and was equally unsuccessful in the November 1996 balloting. Bakary died in 1998.

The UFPDP-*Sawaba* supported Mamadou Tandja in the 1999 presidential poll and was rewarded with a cabinet seat in the January 2000 government. However, the UFPDP-*Sawaba* minis-ter, Issoufou Assoumane, was not reappointed in the September 2001 reshuffle; he formed a new political party (USN, below) in October.

Party for National Unity and Development–Salama (*Parti pour l'Unité Nationale et la Développement–Salama—PUND-Salama*). Previously unknown, the pro-Tuareg PUND-*Salama* won three assembly seats in January 1995, including two seats in non-Tuareg districts, but was unsuccessful in the November 1996 balloting.

Although aligned with the ANDP-*Zaman Lahiya* in the pro-Maïnassara AFDS (launched in 1998), the PUND-*Salama* supported Mamadou Tandja of the MNSD-*Nassara* in the 1999 presidential campaign. The PUND-*Salama* was accorded a seat in the January 2000 cabinet but lost the post in the September 2001 reshuffle.

Leader: Pascal MAMADOU.

National Union of Independents for Democratic Renewal (*Union National des Indépendants pour le Renouveau Démocratique—UNIRD*). The UNIRD was launched in 1996 as an electoral vehicle for supporters of President Maïnassara. It won 56 seats in the November assembly balloting and 3 more at subsequent by-elections, its political dominance enhanced even further by pledges of support from several smaller legislative parties and independents. However, its presidential candidate, Amadou Djibo, won only 1.7 percent of the vote in the first round of presidential balloting, so the party endorsed Mahamadou Issoufou in the second round. The UNIRD secured no seats in the 1999 legislative poll.

Leaders: Moutari MOUSSA (Former Speaker of the National Assembly), Amadou DJIBO (1999 presidential candidate).

Union of Democratic Patriots and Progressives–Chamoua (*Union des Patriotes Démocratiques et Progressistes–Chamoua—UPDP-Chamoua*). The UPDP-*Chamoua* is led by André Salifou, who was named National Conference chair in August 1991. Salifou's position in the transitional government disqualified him from running for the presidency, and the party advanced Illa Kane, who captured only 2.55 percent of the vote.

In April 1994 Salifou and a number of UPDP-*Chamoua* activists were arrested for alleged involvement in an antigovernment demonstration reportedly triggered by President Ousmane's attempts to marginalize his AFC partners. Subsequently, the UPDP-*Chamoua* broke from the AFC, and in January 1995 the party lost one of its two assembly seats. The party won four seats in the November 1996 legislative balloting, at which time it was described as aligned with the UNIRD in support of the Maïnassara regime. Salifou won 2.1 percent of the vote in the first round of the 1999 presidential balloting.

Leader: André SALIFOU (Chair and 1999 presidential candidate).

Party for People's Dignity (*Parti pour la Dignité du Peuple-Daraja*—PDP-*Daraja*). The PDP-*Daraja* was launched in October 1995 and secured three assembly seats in November 1996. It supported Mamadou Tandja in the second round of the 1999 presidential poll.

Leader: Ali TALBA.

Workers' Movement Party–Albarka (*Parti du Mouvement des Travailleurs–Albarka*—PMT-*Albarka*). The PMT-*Albarka* was formed in the early 1990s by the merger of the People's Union for Democratic Action (*Union Monde pour l'Action Démocratique*—UMAD) and the Workers' Liberation Party. The group won two seats in the 1996 legislative balloting. It supported Mamadou Tandja in the 1999 presidential balloting.

Leader: Omar Idi ANGO.

Movement for Democracy and Progress–Alkawali (*Mouvement pour la Démocratie et le Progrés–Alkawali*—MDP-*Alkawali*). The MDP-*Alkawali,* also called the Movement for Democracy and Panafricanism, secured one seat in the 1996 assembly balloting. It supported Mamadou Tandja in the 1999 presidential campaign.

Leader: Dr. Mai Manga BOUKAR.

Union for Democracy and Progress (*Union pour la Démocratie et le Progrés*—UDP). The UDP was one of several small parties to participate in the launching of the FRDD. However, at intraparty balloting in 1998 Abdoulaye Tondi defeated the incumbent UDP president, Bello Tiousso GARBA, and the party subsequently moved into the propresidential camp. In 1999 the UDP supported Mamadou Tandja for president.

Leader: Abdoulaye TONDI (President).

Union for Democracy and Social Progress–Amana *(Union pour la Démocratie et le Progrès Social–Amana*—UDPS-*Amana*). On August 28, 1992, (then) UDPS-*Amana* leader Akoli Daouel was imprisoned during the army's crackdown on suspected Tuareg dissidents.

A deadly grenade attack on a UDPS-*Amana* meeting at Agades in October 1994 was blamed on Tuaregs angered by ongoing negotiations with the government. Thereafter, in the legislative balloting of January 1995, the party doubled its parliamentary representation to two seats.

Although technically an opposition grouping, the UDPS-*Amana* was awarded a cabinet portfolio by Prime Minister Amadou in February 1995. However, under pressure from opposition allies, who termed the appointment "regrettable," the minister was expelled from the party. The UDPS-*Amana* won three seats in the November 1996 assembly elections.

Leaders: Mohamed ABDULLAHI (Chair), Mohamed MOUSSA, Akoli DAOUEL.

Nigerien Democratic Union–Sawaba (*Union Démocratique Nigerien–Sawaba*—UDN-*Sawaba*). The UDN-*Sawaba* failed to win any seats in the legislative balloting of February 1993 or January 1995.

Leader: Karimou MAMAN.

Niger National Front (*Front National du Niger*—FNN). The FNN was launched in early 1993 on a platform calling for "greater justice" for Peulh nomads through reversal of "persecution and arbitrary actions" against the group.

Leader: Salifou SADIKOU (Secretary General).

Other parties and groups active in 2001 included the **Union of Independent Nigeriens** (UNI), led by Djibo Tinder; the **Union for Democracy and the Republic–Tabbat** (UDR-Tabbat); the radical Islamist **Alliance for Democracy and Progress** (*Alliance pour la Démocratie et le Progrès–Zumunci*—ADP-*Zumunci*), led by Issoufou BACHAR; the **Democratic and Socialist Renewal Union** (*Union Démocratique et Socialiste du Renouveau*—UDSR), led by Ibrahim Abdou GAUGE; the left-wing **Revolutionary and Democratic Organization of Niger** (*Organisation Révolutionnaire et Démocratique du Niger*—ORDN); the **Nigerien Party for Socialism** (*Parti Nigérien pour le Socialisme–Imani*—PNS-*Imani*), led by Boukari Maman SANI; the **Party for Democracy and Renewal** (*Parti pour la Démocratie et le Redressement*—PRD), led by Moumouni YACOUBA; the **Party of Consultation and Peace** (*Parti de la Concertation et de la Paix–Chawara*—PCP-*Chawara*), led by Katzelma Omar TAYA; the **Patriotic Movement for Solidarity and Progress** (*Mouvement Patriotique pour la Solidarité et le Progrès–Anoura*—MPSP-*Anoura*), led by Moussa OUMAROU; the **Popular Front of National Liberation** (*Front Populaire de Libération Nationale–Chamsya*—FPLN-*Chamsya*), led by Jamboy Sabo DIALLO; the **Rally for a Green Sahel** (*Rassemblement pour un Sahel Vert–Niima*—RSV-*Niima*), led by Adamou GARBA; the **Republican Party for Liberties and the Progress of Niger** (*Parti Républicain pour les Libertés et le Progrès de Niger–Nakowa*—PRLPN-*Nakowa*), led by Alka ALMOU; the **Revolutionary Organization for the Defense of Democracy** (*Organisation Révolutionnaire pour la Défense de la Démocratie*—ORDD), led by Mama SUNI; the **Revolutionary Organization for the New Democracy** (*Organisation Révolutionnaire pour la Démocratie Nouvelle–Tarmamoua*—ORDN-*Tarmamoua*), led by Maman Sadi ADAMOU; the **Union for Democracy and Republic** (*Union pour la Démocratie et la République*—UDR), a splinter from the RDP-*Jama'a* formed in September 1999 by former prime minister Amadou Boubacar

CISSÉ; the **Union for the Republic** (*Union pour la République*—UPR), led by Karimou MAMAN; the **Union of Independent Democrats** (*Union des Démocrates Indépendants*—UDI) led by Ali Sirfi MAIGA; the **Union of Nigerien Socialists** (*Union des Socialistes Nigérien*—USN), a splinter from the UFDPD-*Sawaba* formed in October 2001 by Issoufou ASSOUMANE, who was the minister of environment and desertification in Hama Amadou's cabinet until September 17, 2001.

Former Rebel Groups

Organization of the Armed Resistance (*Organisation de la Résistance Armée*—ORA). ORA emerged in March 1995 upon the temporary demise of the CRA when the FLAA withdrew from the coalition (see below). Successful implementation of a final peace agreement, signed by Rhissa ag Boula on behalf of the ORA on April 25, 1995, was viewed as depending on the resolution of differences between the FLAA and CRA chair Mano Dayak. In June the ORA denounced the inclusion of the so-called "self-defense" groups in the proposed amnesty, arguing that the groups were responsible for attacks on Tuareg civilians.

At the end of 1996 the FPLS and the ARLN reportedly left ORA to join the new UFRA (below) in an attempt to "rationalize" the Tuareg leadership situation. At that point it was not clear if Boula's FLAA would maintain the ORA structure, as FLAA appeared to be the dominant, and perhaps only, component in the ORA. Furthermore, the FLAA also appeared to have distanced itself from the 1995 accord. Such concerns were at least temporarily eased in September 1996 when the ORA reportedly integrated a number of its fighters into the government's newly formed "peacekeeping detachment." (In 1998 the ORA and the CRA turned in their weapons when parliament granted amnesty to the rebel groups in March.) In 1997 Boula was named to the Mayaki government. He remained in the new governments announced in January 2000 and September 2001, but was dismissed from his post as tourism minister in the Tandja government on February 13, 2004. Boula was then arrested and jailed for his alleged involvement in the assassination of a militant member of the ruling party, MNSD-*Nassara,* in January (see FLAA, below). He was released in March 2005, allegedly after his brother, rebel leader Mohamed ag Boula (see below), claimed he would not release four kidnapped soldiers until his brother was freed. (The hostages returned home in February 2005 after Libya helped secure their release.)

Leaders: Rhissa ag BOULA (Chair), Attaher ABDOULMOUMINE (Vice Chair).

Front for the Liberation of Air and Azaouad (*Front de Libération de l'Aïr et l'Azaouad*—FLAA). The Nigerien FLAA is a 400–1,000 member military wing of the greater Tuareg nomadic movement also active in Algeria and Mali. The FLAA "blue people," so-called because of the staining of their skin by their traditional blue cloth robes, are based in the Aïr mountains approximately 600 miles northeast of Niamey. The FLAA insurgency began in 1990 in response to the "exploitation and persecution" of the Tuareg nomads and sought the withdrawal of government forces and a broader distribution of the region's uranium ore wealth—although the Nigerien government denied the existence of any armed Tuareg group until early 1992.

FLAA activity increased dramatically in October 1991, as Tuareg officials criticized the recently concluded National Conference for failing to respect their "needs." Niamey responded to Tuareg demands for a troop withdrawal and greater autonomy in early 1992 by declaring its readiness to enter into formal negotiations with the insurgents. In mid-March the government reported that it had met with FLAA leaders, and on May 12 Niamey announced a truce, which Algeria and France would help mediate. Two weeks later, however, it accused the FLAA of violating the accord and authorized the army to take responsibility for security in the north. On August 27 Nigerien troops, later described as renegades by Niamey, launched a crackdown on alleged FLAA dissidents and sympathizers and arrested 186 people, including prominent Tuareg officials in the transitional government. The FLAA declared war and launched a series of offensives in early September. On September 14 FLAA representatives in Paris called on the United Nations to help end the "arbitrary treatment and terror imposed on the Tuareg civilian community."

Although the government claimed to have released 57 of the Tuareg detainees by late December 1992, the FLAA issued an ultimatum on December 31, threatening an even deeper crisis if all Tuareg prisoners were not immediately released. On January 9, 1993, nine MNSD-*Nassara* negotiators were killed and 20 FLAA fighters were killed or wounded when the FLAA launched an attack on the venue of negotiations with traditional Tuareg chiefs. In mid-March the FLAA, responding to MNSD-*Nassara* electoral losses, announced a truce as a peace offering to the new government; in April it released 26 prisoners of war and agreed to extend the truce as a goodwill gesture to President Ousmane. However, by midyear the party was buffeted by the defection of a number of top officials, led by Mano Dayak.

After the arrest of Rhissa ag Boula (see ORA, above), a leftist publication reported that resistance fighters had met in April 2004 and agreed to reestablish FLAA. In October 2004, combatants claiming to be members of FLAA clashed with government troops in the Aïr Mountains. Mohamed ag BOULA, brother of FLAA founder Rhissa ag Boula, claimed responsibility for the attack. In 2005 it was reported that several hundred former FLAA members had joined the Libyan army (some analysts said Tripoli was suspected of financing the Tuareg rebellion in 1991).

Leaders: Mohamed ag BOULA, Mohammed EWANGAI.

Union of Forces of the Armed Resistance (*Union des Forces de la Résistance Armée*— UFRA). The UFRA was formed in November 1996 by the FPLS and the ARLN (theretofore members of the ORA), the FFL, and three other groups: the **People's Army for the Liberation of the North** (*Armée du Peuple pour la Libération du Nord*—APLN), the **Popular Front for the Liberation of Northern Niger** (*Front Populaire pour la Libération du Niger Nord*—FPLNN), and the **United Revolutionary Movement** (*Mouvement Révolutionnaire Uni*—MRU). It was reported that a ten-member executive committee had been established under the chairmanship of the FPLS's Mohamed Anako, who endorsed the April 1995 accord with the government and called upon other Tuareg groups to join UFRA to complete its implementation. Although one stated goal of the UFRA was to reduce confusion concerning the Tuareg leadership, its immediate effect was just the opposite.

In September 1996 the UFRA was among the rebel groups reported to have been integrated into the national "peacekeeping detachment." However, amid reports that its leadership was unhappy with government "mop up" offensives in early September 1997, the UFRA rejected the government's call for all rebel groups to complete disarmament procedures by September 30 and formed an alliance with the FARS, the **Coalition of Toubou and Tuareg Armed Resistance**. Clashes between the new alliance and government forces left at least 50 people dead before a cease-fire was announced in November. In June 1998 it was reported that the UFRA had completely disarmed.

Leader: Mohamed ANAKO (Chair).

Popular Front for the Liberation of the Sahara (*Front Populaire pour la Libération de la Sahara*—FPLS). The FPLS was launched on January 28, 1994, by Mohamed Anako and Issad Kato, who pledged to cooperate with existing Tuareg groups. In April 1999, Anako was reportedly appointed minister without portfolio and special adviser to head of state Maj. Daouda Wanké, a move some observers said was meant to avert further violence following Wanké's ascension after the assassination of President Maïnassara.

Leaders: Mohamed ANAKO, Issad KATO.

Revolutionary Army for the Liberation of Northern Niger (*Armée Révolutionnaire pour la Libération du Niger Nord*—ARLN). The ARLN refused to participate in negotiations with the government in October 1993, but reversed that position in 1994. Emerging from splits within the ARLN in October 1994 and March 1995 were the **Liberation Forces Front** (*Front des Forces pour la Libération*—FFL) and the **Revolutionary Liberation Movement of the North** (*Mouvement Révolutionnaire pour la Libération du Niger Nord*—MRLN), led by Ibrahim ROUMAR.

Leader: Mohammed ABDOULMOUMINE.

Coordination of Armed Resistance (*Coordination de la Résistance Armée*—CRA). Originally formed in January 1994 by the FLAA, FPLS, ARLN, and FLT (below), the CRA met in Tenere in early February to elect an executive bureau and draft a platform calling for the creation of an autonomous Tuareg territory and Tuareg representation in the armed forces, government, and National Assembly. The coalition participated in talks with the government in Ouagadougou, Burkina Faso, in late February and in Paris in June, which ultimately resulted in a preliminary peace accord on October 9.

The CRA splintered in March 1995 following a disagreement between FLAA leader Boula and CRA chair Mano Dayak over the latter's approach to renewed peace negotiations. Immediately thereafter, Boula reorganized the CRA members, including the Dayak-led FLT, under the ORA banner; however, in June the FLT withdrew from the coalition. In July Dayak announced that he had revived the CRA; he would no longer respect the peace agreement and further negotiations would have to include his new Toubou and Arab allies (below).

In October 1995 FLT militants were accused of violating the peace accord; however, Dayak continued to negotiate with the government, and CRA officials pledged to proceed with peace talks following his death in a plane crash in December. Thereafter, at a summit of the leaders of the

Cabinet

As of June 1, 2006

Prime Minister	Hama Amadou

Ministers

Agricultural Development	Labo Moussa
Animal Resources	Abdoulaye Djina
Basic Education and Literacy	Hamani Harouna
Civil Service and Labor	Kanda Siptey [f]
Commerce and Promotion of the Private Sector	Habi Mahamadou Salissou
Culture, Arts, and Communication	Oumarou Hadary
Equipment	Seini Oumarou
Finance and Economy	Ali Lamine Zeine
Foreign Affairs, Cooperation, and African Integration	Aïchatou Mindaoudou [f]
Government Spokesman	Mohamed Ben Omar
Handicrafts and Tourism	Amadou Nouhou
Interior and Decentralization	Mounkaila Modi
Justice and Keeper of the Seals	Mati Moussa
Mines and Energy	Mohamed Abdoulahi
National Defense	Hassane "Bonto" Souley
Population and Social Development	Boukari Zila Mahamadou [f]
Privatization and Restructuring of Enterprises	Gazobi Laouali Rahamou [f]
Promotion of Women and Protection of Children	Ousmane Zeinabou Moulaye
Public Health and the Fight Against Endemic Diseases	Ary Ibrahim
Relations with Institutions	Mohamed Ben Omar
Secondary and Higher Education, Research, and Technology	Ousmane Galadima
Territorial and Community Development	Mahaman Moussa
Transport	Souleymane Kane
Urban Affairs, Housing, and Census	Diallo Aïssa Abdoulaye
Vocational Education, in Charge of Youth Employment	Abdou Daouda
Water Resources, Environment, and the Fight Against Desert Encroachment	Abdou Labo
Youth and Sport	Abdourahamane Seydou

Secretaries of State

Economic Reform	Hamida Arzake
Endemic Diseases	Abdoulwahid Halimatou Ousseini [f]

[f] = female

Tuareg and Toubou fronts in Kawar on March 8, 1996, the CRA agreed to recognize the 1995 peace accord and joined the others in declaring a unilateral ceasefire as a sign of support for the military regime. Consequently, the junta offered to include the CRA in its "application" of the treaty, and the group signed the accord on April 2.

A split between the CRA and the ORA was reported in November 1996, with the emergence of the new UFRA (see above). Included in the "new" CRA were a number of Toubou and Arab autonomous movements based in the southeast who had complained of being ignored by the peace process.

Leaders: Mohamed AOUTCHEKI Kriska (FLT), Mohammed AKOTE.

Front for the Liberation of Tamoust

(*Front pour la Libération de Tamoust*—FLT). The FLT was launched in July 1993 by Mano Dayak, previously one of the FLAA's chief negotiators, and a number of other former FLAA officials who sought continuation of the truce agreement reached with Niamey in March. The FLT was the only Tuareg group to renew the accord in September; a month later its status was bolstered by the addition of another FLAA defector, Mohamed Aoutcheki Kriska.

FLT officials reportedly welcomed the 1996 coup, asserting that the military could "settle certain questions which could not be settled during the period of democracy," and on February 22 Aoutcheki was named as a special adviser to CSN Chair Maïnassara.

Leaders: Mohamed AOUTCHEKI Kriska, Mohammed EKIJI (Secretary General).

Democratic Renewal Front

(*Front Démocratique pour le Renouvellement*—FDR). The FDR surfaced in May 1994 in the Lake Chad region under the leadership of Cpl. Ahmed Mohammed, a Nigerien who had served in the Libyan army. A militant group of members from the Arab Choa, Toubou, and Kanouri ethnic groups (who Mohammed claimed had been excluded from the greater Tuareg movement), the FDR professed dedication to "conducting the political and military battle" necessary to bring about the "annihilation" of the present governing system. The FDR's platform also advocated the division of Niger into federal states with boundaries conforming to "geographical and social reality."

In the first half of 1995 the FDR's clashes with government and Tuareg forces reportedly left over 40 people dead. At the same time, the group called attempts to implement the April 1995

peace accord the "facade of democracy" and urged Niamey to recognize their demands for autonomy. FDR/government clashes continued throughout 1996 and 1997.

In August 1998 the FDR signed a peace accord with the government, and party spokesperson Issa Lamine was named to the cabinet in January 2000.

Leaders: Cpl. Ahmed MOHAMMED, Mamane KODELAMI Ali, Goukouni ZENE, Issa LAMINE (Spokesperson).

Rebel Group

Armed Revolutionary Forces of the Sahara (*Forces Armées Révolutionnaires de la Sahara*—FARS). The primarily Toubou and Arab FARS gained international attention in February 1997 for kidnapping a Canadian aid worker and three Nigerien security officials in an effort to dramatize demands for an inquiry into the death of 14 FARS fighters in a clash with government forces the month before. Following peaceful resolution of that crisis, the FARS signed a cease-fire agreement with the government in June; however, that accord proved short-lived, and the FARS was subsequently reported to have formed an alliance with the UFRA before the latter grouping disarmed in 1998. In September 2001 the government launched a major crackdown that, among other things, resulted in the death of a FARS leader, Chahayi BARKAYE. In an effort to establish peace, France agreed to help finance the reintegration of some 250 FARS rebels into the northern region of Bilma.

Leader: Barka OUARDOUGOU.

Legislature

The unicameral **National Assembly** (*Assemblée Nationale*) was enlarged to 113 members in 2003, based on an increase of nearly 3 million in the country's population between 1988 and 2001 (the assembly had previously consisted of 83 members). Members are elected for five-year terms. The assembly elected in January 1995 was dissolved by the National Salvation Council on January 27,

1996, and replaced on March 27 by a 600-member transitional body known as the National Forum for Democratic Renewal, which included former assemblymen as well as members of various advisory groups supportive of the new military regime. Balloting for a new assembly was held on November 23–though it was boycotted by most major opposition groups.

On April 10, 1999, Prime Minister Mayaki suspended the assembly in the wake of the assassination of President Maïnassara. Balloting to refill the body was held on November 24, 1999, with the National Movement for a Developing Society–Victory securing 38 seats; the Democratic and Social Convention–*Rahama,* 17; the Nigerien Party for Democracy and Socialism–*Tarayya,* 16; the Democratic Rally of the People–*Jamaa,* 8; and the Nigerien Alliance for Democracy and Progress–*Zaman Lahiya,* 4.

The most recent rounds of balloting were held on November 16, 2004, and December 4, 2004. The National Movement for a Developing Society–Victory won 47 seats; the Democratic and Social Convention–*Rahama*, 22; the Nigerien Party for Democracy and Socialism–*Tarayya* (PNDS-*Tarayya*), 17; the coalition of the PNDS-Tarayya, the Niger Progressive Party–African Democratic Rally/Niger Party for Self-Management (PPN-RDA/PNA), 4; the coalition of PNDS-Tarayya, the Union of Independent Nigeriens/Union for Democracy and the Republic-Tabbat, 2; the coalition of the PNDS-*Tarayya*, the PPN-RDA, 2; and the Nigerien Social Democratic Party–*Alheri*, 1.

Speaker: Mahamane OUSMANE.

Communications

Press

The following are published in French in Niamey: *Le Sahel* (5,000), daily news bulletin of the government Information Service; *Le Sahel Dimanche* (4,000), weekly publication of the government Information Service. An independent monthly, *La Marche,* was introduced in August 1989, while an independent weekly, *La Républicain* (3,000), commenced publication in 1991. Other publications include *Le Tribune du Peuple* (3,000), daily in French, and the weekly, *Le Démocrate.* There are a number of other small newspapers, some of which were subjected in 2000 to government crackdowns, which, in turn, led journalists to charge that the administration was intent on "silencing" the independent press. Journalists in Niger have been periodically arrested and detained on charges of defamation and "inciting ethnic hatred."

News Agency

The government launched *Agence Nigérienne de Press* (ANP) in late 1986.

Broadcasting and Computing

The *Office de Radiodiffusion-Télévision du Niger* (ORTN) operates *La Voix du Sahel,* a government radio service broadcasting in French, English, and indigenous languages, and also services nine television stations. There were approximately 576,000 television receivers and 8,000 personal computers serving 17,500 Internet users in 2003.

Intergovernmental Representation

Ambassador to the U.S.
Aminata Maiga DJIBRILLA

U.S. Ambassador to Niger
Bernadette Mary ALLEN

Permanent Representative to the UN
Aboubacar Ibrahim ABANI

IGO Memberships (Non-UN)
AfDB, AU, BADEA, BOAD, CENT, CILSS, ECOWAS, IDB, Interpol, IOM, NAM, OIC, OIF, UEMOA, WCO, WTO

NIGERIA

FEDERAL REPUBLIC OF NIGERIA

The Country

The most populous country in Africa and one of the most richly endowed in natural resources, Nigeria extends from the inner corner of the Gulf of Guinea to the border of Niger in the north and to Lake Chad in the northeast. Included within its boundaries is the northern section of the former United Nations Trust Territory of British Cameroons, whose inhabitants voted to join Nigeria in a United Nations–sponsored plebiscite in 1961. Nigeria's topography ranges from swampy lowland along the coast, through tropical rain forest and open plateau country, to semidesert conditions in the far north. The ethnic pattern is similarly varied, with tribal groups speaking more than 250 languages. The Hausa, Fulani, and other Islamic peoples in the north, the mixed Christian and Islamic Yoruba in the west, and the predominantly Christian Ibo in the east are the most populous groups. In the absence of reliable information (ethnic identification being excluded from the 1991 census), it has been estimated that nearly half the population is Muslim, with 35 percent Christian and the remainder adhering to traditional religious practices. Numerous traditional rulers retain considerable influence, particularly in rural areas. Women are responsible for the bulk of subsistence farming, and their participation in the paid work force (about 36 percent) is concentrated in sales and crafts.

Nigeria's natural resources include petroleum and natural gas, hydroelectric power, and commercially exploitable deposits of tin, coal, and columbite. Oil production of 2.2 million barrels per day accounts for an estimated 90 percent of exports and provides 80 percent of the government's revenue; some 60–90 percent of Nigerian crude, con-

sidered ideal for gasoline production, is exported to the United States. The leading cash crops are cocoa, peanuts, palm products, and cotton, with timber and fish also of importance. The oil boom of the 1970s produced rapid industrial expansion led by consumer nondurables, vehicle assembly, aluminum smelting, and steel production. However, a world glut reduced oil revenue from $26 billion in 1980 to $5.6 billion in 1986, precipitating industrial contraction and cutbacks in government and personal spending, with per capita income dipping by more than half (from $670 to $300) during 1979–1988. Thus, a structural adjustment program launched in 1986 was actually more stringent than a number of International Monetary Fund (IMF) austerity plans that Lagos had previously been unwilling to adopt. It focused on reviving non-oil exports, achieving a

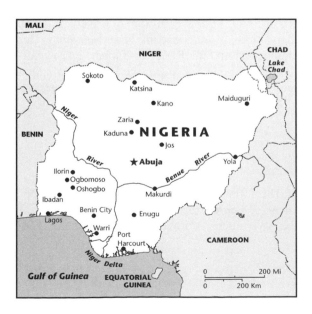

Political Status: Independent member of the Commonwealth since 1960; republic established in 1963; civilian government suspended as the result of military coups in January and July 1966; executive presidential system established under constitution effective October 1, 1979; under military rule following successive coups of December 31, 1983, and August 27, 1985; constitution of Third Republic promulgated May 3, 1989; existing state organs dissolved following military takeover of November 17, 1993; 1979 constitution restored and Provisional Ruling Council established on November 21, 1993; current constitution entered into effect May 29, 1999, with installation of new civilian government.

Area: 356,667 sq. mi. (923,768 sq. km.).

Population: 88,992,220 (1991C), 130,445,000 (2005E). The 1991 census was undertaken with far greater care than a 1973 predecessor, the results of which were officially repudiated as being grossly inflated insofar as the northern count was concerned. On the other hand, estimates in 1988 ranged as high as 105 million, raising the possibility that the 1991 figure might be unrealistically low. The suspicion was enhanced in November 1994 by the Constitutional Convention's "rejection" of the 1991 results.

Major Urban Centers (1991C): ABUJA (107,069), Lagos (5,195,247), Kano (2,166,554), Ibadan (1,835,300), Kaduna (933,642), Benin City (762,719), Port Harcourt (703,421), Maiduguri (618,278), Zaria (612,257), Ilorin (532,089), Jos (512,300). The 1991 figure for Lagos was unquestionably conservative, a UN estimate for mid-2000 being 10,103,000. Other 2000 estimates: Kano (2,763,000), Ibadan (2,284,000), Kaduna (1,273,000).

The transfer of government offices from the longtime capital of Lagos to the new capital of Abuja was officially described as completed on December 12, 1991.

Official Language: English (the leading indigenous languages are Hausa, Igbo, and Yoruba).

Monetary Unit: Naira (official rate July 1, 2006: 128.40 naira = $1 US).

President: Gen. (Ret.) Olusegun OBASANJO (People's Democratic Party); directly elected on February 27, 1999, and inaugurated for a four-year term on May 29; reelected on April 19, 2003, and sworn in for a second four-year term on May 29.

Vice President: Abubakar ATIKU (People's Democratic Party); elected on February 27, 1999, and inaugurated on May 29, for a term concurrent with the president; reelected on April 19, 2003, and sworn in for a second four-year term on May 29.

realistic naira exchange rate, and discouraging the purchase of luxury goods. Not surprisingly, nationwide protests against the program were reported in 1987 and 1988, with particularly violent confrontations erupting in May–June 1989.

In January 1994 the Abacha government presented a budget that abandoned virtually all of the 1986 reforms. Subsequently, in the wake of sharp criticism from international lenders, the January 1995 budget revived free-market policies. The economy nonetheless remained severely distressed under the influence of rampant official corruption, external debt of more than $33 billion, and ongoing concern over the nation's political future. Abacha's successor, Gen. Abdulsalam Abubakar, moved quickly in 1998 to mend relations with the World Bank and the IMF, pledging to speed up the privatization of state-run industries and combat corruption. Moreover, in January 1999 the government abolished the heavily criticized dual-rate system of foreign exchange (which had allowed officials and favored segments of the business community to purchase U.S. dollars at one-fourth the market rate), and Lagos announced the end of its ten-year rift with the IMF, with which it had begun new negotiations on easing its huge debt burden. Nigeria's GDP grew in real terms by 6.4 percent in 1996, 3.9 percent in 1997, 2.3 percent in 1998, 2.5 percent in 1999, 3.2 percent in 2000, and 4 percent in 2001. Annual inflation was estimated at 20 percent in 2001. Although the IMF approved new lending in August 2001, it subsequently continued to criticize the government's economic management.

Increased federal and state spending subsequently undermined the government's efforts to secure foreign assistance for debt relief. In 2002 the IMF suspended Nigeria's participation in its debt reduction program because of excessive government spending. The World Bank also reduced its lending program to Nigeria by half in 2003. Rising oil and gas revenues offset higher federal and state spending in 2004. In addition, the government implemented a new long-range program to repair decaying infrastructure such as roads and pipelines. The National Economic Empowerment and Development Strategy (NEEDS) program was also launched in an effort to restore international confidence in the Nigerian economy. Meanwhile the government initiated a broad effort to recover part of the estimated $2.2 billion that was reportedly funneled out of the country during the tenure of President Abacha (see Current issues, below).

High oil prices provided significant additional resources in 2004–2005 for the government, which, among other things, established a $6 billion "emergency fund." GDP growth remained at about 3.5 percent annually for 2004–2005, although inflation jumped to 20 percent in the latter year. Satisfied with the government's recent reform efforts, the IMF in 2005 announced new aid and support for additional debt relief. Late in the year, the Paris Club of creditor nations accepted an agreement under which Nigeria could fulfill its obligation to them by paying only $12 billion of the $30 billion owed. In April 2006 the government announced that it had made its final payment to the Paris Club members.

Government and Politics

Political Background

Brought under British control during the 19th century, Nigeria was organized as a British colony and protectorate in 1914, became a self-governing federation in 1954, and achieved independence within the Commonwealth on October 1, 1960. Under the guidance of its first prime minister, Sir Abubaker Tafawa BALEWA, Nigeria became a republic three years later, with the former governor general, Dr. Nnamdi AZIKIWE of the Ibo tribe,

as president. The original federation consisted of three regions (northern, western, and eastern); a fourth region (the midwestern) was created in 1963.

Though initially regarded as one of the most potentially viable of the new African states, independent Nigeria was beset by underlying tensions resulting from ethnic, religious, and regional cleavages. Weakened by strife and tainted by corruption, the federal government was overthrown on January 15, 1966, in a coup that cost the lives of Prime Minister Balewa and other northern political leaders and resulted in the establishment of a Supreme Military Council (SMC) headed by Maj. Gen. Johnson T. U. AGUIYI-IRONSI, the Ibo commander of the army. Resentment by northern Muslims of the predominantly Ibo leadership and its subsequent attempt to establish a unitary state resulted on July 29 in a second coup, led by a northerner, Col. (later Gen.) Yakubu GOWON. Events surrounding the first coup had already raised ethnic hostility to the boiling point. Thousands of Ibo who had settled in the north were massacred before and after the second, while hundreds of thousands began a mass flight back to their homeland at the urging of eastern leaders.

Plans for a constitutional revision that would calm Ibo apprehensions while preserving the unity of the country were blocked by the refusal of the Eastern Region's military governor, Lt. Col. Odumegwu OJUKWU, to accept anything less than complete regional autonomy. Attempts at conciliation having failed, Colonel Gowon, as head of the federal military government, announced the assumption of emergency powers and the reorganization of Nigeria's 4 regions into 12 states on May 28, 1967. Intended to equalize treatment of various areas and ethnic groups throughout the country, the move was also designed to increase the influence of the eastern region's non-Ibo inhabitants. The eastern region responded on May 30 by declaring independence as the Republic of Biafra, with Ojukwu as head of state. Refusing to recognize the secession, the federal government initiated hostilities against Biafra on July 6. Peace plans were subsequently proposed by London, the Commonwealth, and the Organization of African Unity (OAU, subsequently the African Union—AU). However, Ojukwu rejected them repeatedly on the ground that they failed to guarantee Biafra's future as a "sovereign and independent state." Limited external support, mainly from France, began to arrive in late 1968 and enabled Biafra to continue fighting despite the loss of most non-Ibo territory, massive casualties, and a growing threat of mass starvation. A series of military defeats in late 1969 and early 1970 finally resulted in surrender of the rebel forces on January 15, 1970.

The immediate postwar period was one of remarkable reconciliation, as General Gowon moved to reintegrate Ibo elements into Nigerian life. Not only were Ibo brought back into the civil service and the military, but the federal government also launched a major reconstruction of the devastated eastern area. Normal political life remained suspended, however, and on July 29, 1975, while Gowon was attending an OAU meeting in Kampala, Uganda, his government was overthrown in a bloodless coup led by Brig. (later Gen.) Murtala Ramat MUHAMMAD. In October the SMC charged a 50-member committee with drafting a new constitution that would embrace an "executive presidential system."

Muhammad was assassinated on February 13, 1976, during an abortive coup apparently provoked by a campaign to wipe out widespread government corruption. He was succeeded as head of state and chair of the SMC by Lt. Gen. (later Gen.) Olusegun OBASANJO, who had been chief of staff of the armed forces since the 1975 coup.

A National Constituent Assembly met in 1977 to consider the constitution proposed by the committee established two years earlier. The assembly endorsed a draft on June 5, 1978, although the SMC made a number of changes before the new basic law was promulgated on September 21, at which time Nigeria's 12-year-old state of emergency was terminated and the ban on political parties was lifted.

Elections were contested in mid-1979 by five parties that had been approved by the Federal Electoral Commission (Fedeco) as being sufficiently national in representation. Balloting commenced on July 7 for the election of federal senators and continued, on successive weekends, with the election of federal representatives, state legislators, and

state governors, culminating on August 11 with the election of Alhaji Shehu SHAGARI and Dr. Alex EKWUEME of the National Party of Nigeria (NPN) as federal president and vice president, respectively. Following judicial resolution of a complaint that the NPN candidates had not obtained a required 25 percent of the vote in 13 of the 19 states, the two leaders were inaugurated on October 1.

By 1983 public confidence in the civilian regime had waned in the face of sharply diminished oil income, massive government overspending, and widespread evidence of official corruption. Nonetheless, the personally popular Shagari easily won reelection in the presidential balloting of August 4. Subsequent rounds of the five-week election process, marred by evidence of electoral fraud and by rioting in Oyo and Ondo states, left the ruling NPN in control of 13 state houses, 13 governorships, and both houses of the National Constituent Assembly. After the balloting, the economy continued to decline, with an austerity budget adopted in November further deepening public discontent. On December 31 a group of senior military officers (most of whom had served under Obasanjo) seized power. On January 3, 1984, Maj. Gen. Muhammadu BUHARI, formerly Obasanjo's oil minister, was sworn in as chair of a new SMC, which launched a "war against indiscipline," reintroduced the death penalty, and established several special tribunals that moved vigorously in convicting numerous individuals, including leading politicians, of embezzlement and other offenses.

In the wake of increasing political repression and a steadily worsening economy, Buhari and his armed forces chief of staff, Maj. Gen. Tunde IDIAGBON, were deposed by senior members of the SMC on August 27, 1985. The ensuing administration, headed by Maj. Gen. (later Gen.) Ibrahim BABANGIDA as chair of a new Armed Forces Ruling Council (AFRC), abolished a number of decrees limiting press freedom, released numerous political detainees, and initially adopted a more open style of government that included the solicitation of public opinion on future political development. However, there was a countercoup attempt late in the year by a group of disgruntled officers, several of whom were executed in March 1986.

In September 1987, the Babangida regime announced a five-year agenda for return to civilian government. The schedule called for promulgation of a new constitution and lifting of the ban on political parties in 1989, gubernatorial and state legislative elections in 1990, and federal legislative and presidential elections in 1992. To guard against tribal and religious fractionalization, the AFRC adopted the recommendation of a university-dominated "Political Bureau" that only two political parties be sanctioned. Late in 1987 Babangida announced that most former and current leaders, including himself and the rest of the AFRC, would be barred from running in forthcoming elections. Local nonparty elections were held on December 12, 1987; however, many of the results from that poll were invalidated, and further balloting was conducted on March 26, 1988.

In May 1989 General Babangida lifted the ban on party politics, calling on parties to register with the National Electoral Commission (NEC) and announcing details of a draft constitution that had been presented to him in April by the National Constituent Assembly. Although more than 50 parties were reportedly interested in securing recognition, a short enrollment period and a complex application process limited the number of actual petitioners to 13, 6 of which were subsequently recommended to the AFRC for further reduction to 2. However, on October 7, amid reports of the arrest of "illegal" party members, Babangida cited "factionalism" and "failing marks" on preregistration examinations as reasons for dissolving all 13 parties and substituting in their place the regime-sponsored Social Democratic Party (SDP) and National Republican Convention (NRC).

In January 1990 General Babangida cancelled state visits to Italy and the United States in the wake of widespread unrest provoked by a December 29 reshuffle of senior military and civilian officials. The tension culminated in a coup attempt on April 22 in Lagos by middle-ranked army officers, with at least 30 persons being killed in heavy fighting.

On August 30, 1990, General Babangida announced another extensive cabinet reshuffle and the appointment of Vice Admiral Augustus AIKHOMU to the newly created position of vice president of the republic. Shortly thereafter, in furtherance of General Babangida's plan to "demilitarize" politics, Aikhomu and a number of other senior government leaders retired from military service, while ten military state governors were replaced by civilian deputies pending the upcoming gubernatorial elections. Meanwhile, organization of the SDP and NRC continued under stringent government supervision, with two-party local elections being held on December 8.

Neither of the parties secured a clear advantage in the 1990 local poll or in gubernatorial and State Assembly elections in December 1991, although the SDP won control of both the Senate and House of Representatives in National Constituent Assembly balloting on July 4, 1992. Party presidential primaries (on August 7 and again on September 12, 19, and 26) were invalidated on grounds of widespread irregularities, with presidential balloting originally slated for December 5 being rescheduled to June 1993. Concurrently, General Babangida announced that the AFRC would be replaced by a National Defense and Security Council (NDSC) and that the existing Council of Ministers would be abolished in favor of a civilian Transitional Council to pave the way for the planned installation of a new government on August 27, 1993. On December 15, 1992, Chief Ernest Adegunle SHONEKAN was named to chair the Transitional Council, which, along with the NDSC, was formally installed on January 4, 1993.

The long-delayed presidential balloting went ahead on June 12, 1993, with the SDP candidate, reputed billionaire Moshood Kashimawo Olawale ("MKO") ABIOLA, the apparent winner over the NRC's Bashir Othma TOFA. However, on June 16 the NEC bowed to a court injunction restraining it from announcing the outcome. The two parties thereupon agreed to form an interim coalition government if General Babangida would authorize a return to civilian rule by the previously agreed upon date of August 27. The general's response being negative, serious rioting erupted in Lagos on July 5, followed by the announcement that a new election, from which the earlier candidates would be excluded, would take place on July 31. Not surprisingly, this plan was scuttled, with Babangida naming Shonekan as head of an Interim National Government (ING) before stepping down as president on August 26.

On September 19, 1993, the NEC announced that new presidential and local elections would be held on February 19, 1994. However, on November 10 the Federal High Court unexpectedly pronounced the ING unconstitutional, and on November 17 Shonekan resigned in favor of a new military administration headed by Defense Minister Sani ABACHA, who had long been viewed as the "power behind the throne" of both the Babangida and Shonekan governments. Subsequently, Abacha formally dissolved both the ING and the National Constituent Assembly, banned the SDP and NRC, and, on November 24, announced the formation of a Provisional Ruling Council (PRC) comprised of senior military figures and several members of a new cabinet-level Federal Executive Council (FEC).

On April 22, 1994, the regime outlined the first phase of a political transition program that called for the convening of a constitutional conference to prepare a draft basic law for approval by the PRC. Elections were held nationwide in May to select the conference participants, although the balloting was boycotted by a number of prodemocracy groups as well as organizations representing southern interests.

On June 22, 1994, Moshood Abiola, who, based on the 1993 poll, had declared himself president 11 days earlier, emerged from hiding to address a rally in Lagos; he was arrested the following day for treason. On June 27 General Abacha opened a National Constitutional Conference (NCC), which was promptly adjourned for two weeks because of "logistical problems." Subsequently a large number of strikes erupted to protest Abiola's arrest and resumption of the NCC. The most serious of the stoppages was by the oil unions, whose resistance crumbled in late August after the PRC had replaced their leaders with military-appointed administrators.

On September 6, 1994, the PRC issued several new decrees that restricted the media and precluded legal challenges to action taken by the regime in regard to "the maintenance of law and order." Further underscoring the regime's hard-line approach, the new 25-member PRC formed on September 27 contained only military officers, even though 4 of the 11 members on the previous council had been civilians. Meanwhile, NCC sessions continued, and in October the conference gave its preliminary endorsement to a draft constitution (see Constitution and government, below). In addition, the NCC in December formally notified the military that the transition to a civilian government was expected to be accomplished by January 1, 1996. Initially appearing to support that schedule, the PRC dissolved the FEC on February 8, 1995, so that members of the council could "prepare for their upcoming political careers." However, the new FEC, which was appointed on March 20, reportedly favored an extension of military control, the apparent policy change being attributed to turbulence surrounding the recent arrest of a group of military officers and civilians in connection with an alleged coup plot. Consequently, on April 25 the NCC reversed its earlier decision regarding the deadline for a return to civilian government and approved a new resolution granting the Abacha regime what amounted to an "open-ended tenure." As a result, the final NCC report, submitted to Abacha on June 27, contained the draft of a new basic law but no proposed timetable for its implementation.

The international criticism prompted by the apparent retrenchment on democratization intensified sharply when minority rights activist Kenule SARO-WIWA and other members of the Movement for the Survival of the Ogoni People (MOSOP) were hung on November 10, 1995, soon after their conviction on what were perceived outside the government to be highly dubious murder charges. However, the regime angrily rejected what it termed external meddling in its domestic affairs and refused to reevaluate its proposed timetable, which called for the government to turn authority over to an elected civilian government on October 1, 1998.

Local elections were held on March 16, 1996, although political parties remained proscribed. The campaign period was limited to only five days, and balloting was conducted by having voters line up behind their preferred candidate, a practice long criticized by prodemocracy activists. Facing ongoing internal and external pressure, the government

in June issued regulations for the proposed legalization of a limited number of political parties, five
of which were recognized in September. Six new
states were established on October 1, and the government announced that 183 additional municipalities would be created for the next local elections,
with balloting to be conducted on a limited multiparty basis.

The local elections were held on March 15,
1997, followed by balloting for state assemblies on
December 6. Meanwhile, on November 17 President Abacha announced that the cabinet had been
dissolved, a number of incumbent senior ministers
being left out of the government appointed on December 18.

At national legislative elections on April 25,
1998, the United Nigeria Congress Party (UNCP)
reportedly captured the majority of the seats. Voter
turnout was described as scant (as little as 10 percent in some areas), with many Nigerians apparently heeding the opposition's call for a boycott
of the contest. Subsequently, at least seven people
were killed and dozens arrested when government
forces clashed with prodemocracy demonstrators
in Ibadan in early May. Meanwhile, Abacha was
reportedly named as the candidate of all the legal
parties for the upcoming presidential election.

On June 8, 1998, Abacha died of an apparent
heart attack, and the following day Gen. Abdulsalam ABUBAKAR was sworn in as his replacement. Opposition militants derided Abubakar's
inaugural pledge to adhere to his predecessor's
transitional program, and in mid-June government
troops forcibly broke up an opposition demonstration. Thereafter, Abubakar approved the release of
dozens of political prisoners, and in early July UN
Secretary General Kofi Annan announced that the
regime was preparing to release all political prisoners, including Abiola, who had reportedly agreed to
relinquish his claim to the presidency. However, on
July 7 (the eve of his release) Abiola fell ill during
a meeting with a high-level U.S. mission and died.

On July 8, 1998, Abubakar dissolved the five
legal parties as well as the government named by
Abacha. Two weeks later he called for the creation
of an "unfettered" democracy and announced that

he would soon release all political prisoners and
allow the free formation of political parties. To
that end, in early August the regime appointed a
14-member electoral commission, the Independent
National Electoral Commission (INEC), which it
charged with overseeing a transitional schedule expected to culminate in the return to civilian rule
in May 1999. On August 21 Abubakar named a
new cabinet, which included only five holdovers
from the Abacha government. Four days later, the
INEC released an electoral timetable calling for
local elections in December, gubernatorial polling
in January 1999, and legislative and presidential balloting on February 20 and 27, respectively.
Twenty-five political groups applied for provisional
legal status between August 27 and September
5, and nine were subsequently registered. However, at local elections in December only three
of those parties—the People's Democratic Party
(PDP), the All People's Party (APP), and the Alliance for Democracy (AD)—secured the minimum vote tally (at least 5 percent in 24 of the 36
states) required to maintain their legal status and
continue on to the next electoral stages. (The PDP,
under the leadership of Gen. Obasanjo, led all parties in the local balloting with approximately 60
percent of the vote.)

At gubernatorial elections held January 9–30,
1999, the PDP once again overwhelmed its competitors, capturing 21 of the 36 state houses (unrest in the state of Bayelsa had forced officials to
postpone balloting there from January 9 to January
30). Seeking to prevent further PDP domination,
the APP and AD subsequently announced their intention to form an electoral alliance and forward
a joint candidate for president. On February 5 the
INEC ruled that such an alliance would be illegal;
however, faced with an APP/AD threat to boycott
further elections, the commission subsequently reversed itself, although it precluded the two groups
from using a single symbol on ballot papers.

The PDP won approximately two-thirds of the
seats in both the Senate and House of Representatives at poorly attended legislative polling
on February 20, 1999. In presidential balloting
on February 27 General Obasanjo completed the

sweep for the PDP, capturing 62.8 percent of the vote and easily defeating Samuel Oluyemisi ("Olu") FALAE, the APP/AD candidate. International observers asserted that the elections "generally" reflected "the will of the people" but refused to describe them as "free and fair" because both sides appeared to have tried to rig the balloting. Obasanjo was sworn in on May 29, and on the same day the new constitution (signed by Abubakar on May 5) also came into effect. On June 28 Obasanjo swore in a new 47-member cabinet, claiming the large size was necessary to represent Nigeria's ethnic and regional diversity. The government included representatives from all 36 states as well as ministers from all three registered parties. Obasanjo dismissed ten members of the cabinet on January 30, 2001, in the wake of intensifying criticism over the government's economic policies. A reshuffled cabinet was announced on February 8.

Political discord increased significantly in June 2001 when religious and ethnic conflict between Christians and Muslims in the northern state of Bauchi left 1,000 dead. Another 1,000 were killed in continuing violence in the region before the end of the year. One area of dispute was Muslim efforts to implement sharia, or Islamic religious law. In addition, a series of general strikes by oil workers threatened to disrupt production.

The registration of political parties having begun in 2002, multiparty legislative and presidential elections were held on April 12, 2003. The PDP again won a commanding majority in both the House of Representatives and the Senate, its strongest opposition coming from the All Nigeria People's Party (ANPP), the successor to the APP. Gubernatorial races were also held on April 19, and the PDP secured 29 of the 36 governorships. The PDP also won about two-thirds of the total seats in the state assemblies in elections held May 3.

The presidential elections held on April 19, 2003, were contested by 20 candidates. Obasanjo was reelected with 62 percent of the vote. His closest rival was former SMC chair Buhari, with 32 percent. No other candidate received more than 3.5 percent of the vote. Buhari challenged the results, but the federal Court of Appeal ruled in favor of

Obasanjo, who was inaugurated on May 29. However, it was not until July 17 that Obasanjo was able to form a new federal government. Obasanjo's second term was initially marked by efforts at economic reform, including the development and implementation of the National Economic Empowerment and Development Strategy (NEEDS), and a broad range of anticorruption campaigns, but strikes and other problems in the petroleum sector continued to constrain the government's efforts. On May 18, 2004, because of the escalating violence in the region, Obasanjo declared a state of emergency for Plateau State and ordered the federal government to take control from the state governor and assembly. This marked the first time that the federal government had taken over a state since 1962 (see Current issues, below).

Constitution and Government

Before General Muhammad's assassination in February 1976, he had announced that the 12 states created in 1967 would be expanded to 19 to alleviate the domination of subunits by traditional ethnic and religious groups, thus helping "to erase memories of past political ties and emotional attachments." A decree establishing the new states was subsequently promulgated by General Obasanjo. A centrally located area of some 3,000 square miles was also designated as a federal capital territory, with the federal administration to be transferred (a process declared completed in late 1991) from Lagos to the new capital of Abuja.

In September 1987 two new states, Katsina and Akwa Ibom, were created out of territory formerly in Kaduna and Cross River, respectively. President Babangida subsequently announced that his administration would not consider further changes. However, in August 1991 he reversed himself with a decision to further increase the number of states to 30 based on "social justice, the principle of development, and the principle of a balanced federation." On October 1, 1996, President Abacha announced the creation of six more states, one in each region, arguing that the expansion would serve the "decentralization" process. It was also announced that 183 new municipalities would be established, bringing the total to 776.

Region (Pre-1967)	State (1967)	State (1987)	State and Capital (1996)
Northern	Benue Plateau	Benue	Benue (Makurdi) †Kogi (Lokoja)*
		Plateau	Plateau (Jos) ‡Nassatawa (Lafia)
	Kano	Kano	Kano (Kano) †Jigawa (Dutse)
	Kwara	Kwara	Kwara (Ilorin)
	North-Central	Kaduna	Kaduna (Kaduna)
		Katsina	Katsina (Katsina)
	North-Eastern	Bauchi	Bauchi (Bauchi) ‡Gombe (Gombe)
		Borno	Borno (Maiduguri) †Yobe (Damaturu)
		Gongola	†Adamawa (Yola) †Taraba (Jalingo)
	North-Western	Niger	Niger (Minna)
		Sokoto	Sokoto (Sokoto) †Kebbi (Birnin Kebbi) ‡Zamfara (Gusau)
Eastern	East-Central	Anambra	Anambra (Akwa) †Enugu (Enugu)
		Imo	Imo (Owerri) †Abia (Umuahia) ‡Eboniyi (Abakaliki)**
	Rivers	Rivers	Rivers (Port Harcourt) ‡Bayelsa (Yenagoa)
	South-Eastern	Cross River	Cross River (Calabar)
		Akwa Ibom	Akwa Ibom (Uyo)
Mid-Western	Mid-Western	Bendel	†Delta (Asaba)
			†Edo (Benin)
Western	Lagos	Lagos	Lagos (Ikeja)
	Western	Ogun	Ogun (Abeokuta)
		Ondo	Ondo (Akure) ‡Ekiti (Ado-Ekiti)
		Oyo	Oyo (Ibadan) †Osun (Oshogbo)

†created in 1991
‡created in 1996
*also includes territory from Kwara
**also includes territory from Enugu

The 1979 constitution established a U.S.-style federal system with powers divided among three federal branches (executive, legislative, and judicial) and between federal and state governments. Executive authority at the national level was vested in a president and vice president who ran on a joint ticket and served four-year terms. To be declared the victor on a first ballot, a presidential candidate was required to win a plurality of the national popular vote and at least one-quarter of the vote in two-thirds of the (then) 19 states. Legislative power was invested in a bicameral National Assembly comprising a 95-member Senate and a 449-member House of Representatives.

Upon assuming power on December 31, 1983, the Supreme Military Council (SMC) suspended those portions of the constitution "relating to all elective and appointive offices and representative institutions." A constitutional modification decree issued in January 1984 established a Federal Military Government encompassing the SMC; a National Council of States, headed by the chair of the SMC and including the military governors of the 19 states, the chief of staff of the armed forces, the inspector-general of police, and the attorney general; and a cabinet-level Federal Executive Council (FEC). The decree also provided for state executive councils headed by the military governors. Following the coup of August 1985, the SMC was renamed the Armed Forces Ruling Council (AFRC), and the FEC was renamed the National Council of Ministers. The chair of the AFRC was empowered to serve as both the head of state and chief executive. However, responsibility for civilian "political affairs" was delegated to a chief of general staff. Following the AFRC's announcement in September 1987 of a five-year schedule for return to civilian government, a 46-member Constitution Review Committee was created to prepare a revision of the 1979 basic law.

In May 1988 a 567-member Constituent Assembly was established to complete the work of the Constitution Review Committee. The most controversial issue faced by the assembly was the proposed institution of sharia (Islamic religious law), which was not favored by Muslim president

Babangida or the Christian population. Unable to reach agreement, the assembly provided two separate and divergent submissions on the matter, which the president stated the AFRC would review in the context of "the national interest."

The draft constitution of the "Third Republic," presented to the AFRC by the Constituent Assembly in April 1989, mirrored the 1979 basic law with the notable addition of anticorruption measures and extension of the presidential term to six years. The document took no position on sharia, as Babangida claimed the issue would constrain debate on other provisions and should be addressed separately at a future time. The existing judiciary was left largely intact, although it was enjoined from challenging or interpreting "this or any other decree" of the AFRC.

A new National Assembly was elected on July 4, 1992, and convened on December 5. Presidential balloting was, however, deferred until June 12, 1993, with a return to constitutional government scheduled for the following August 27. In the meantime, a Transitional Council, with a chair as nominal head of government, was designated to serve in a quasi-executive capacity. The system nonetheless remained tutelary, since both legislative and executive actions were subject to review by the president and the military-civilian National Defense and Security Council (NDSC). Coincident with President Babangida's resignation in 1993, the Transitional Council was abolished, not in favor of a constitutional government but of an Interim National Government (ING), which was in turn superseded by the Provisional Ruling Council (PRC)/Federal Executive Council (FEC) in November.

The 369 participants in the constitutional conference that convened on June 27, 1994, had been selected in widely boycotted balloting on May 23 and 28 from a list of PRC-approved candidates. The conference's recommendations were formally submitted to the PRC on June 27, 1995, and the provisions in the new proposed basic law called for a presidency that would rotate between the north and the south, the election of three vice presidents, the creation of several new states, and the installation of a transition civilian government pend-

ing new national elections. However, many of the 1995 document's provisions were not included in the draft charter released by the Abubakar regime for comments in September 1998. The new draft more resembled the 1979 constitution, providing for a strong, executive president who is responsible for nominating a cabinet that is subject to senate approval. At the state level, power is vested in a popularly elected governor and the state legislature. In early 1999 the regime announced that it had agreed on details of the new constitution, which was promulgated into law in May. The 1999 document specifies a federal system with the 36 states and federal capital territory. The states are divided into 776 local government districts and municipalities. Both the executive president and the two-house legislature serve four-year terms. The upper house, the Senate, has 109 members, whereas the lower House of Representatives has 360 members. The legislature and the president are elected by universal suffrage.

Foreign Relations

As a member of the United Nations (UN), the Commonwealth, and the OAU, Nigeria adhered (following independence) to a policy of nonalignment, opposition to colonialism, and support for liberation movements in all white-dominated African territories. It actively participated in OAU committees and negotiations directed toward settling the Chadian civil war, the Western Saharan conflict, and disputes in the Horn of Africa. At the regional level, Nigeria was the prime mover in negotiations leading to the establishment in 1975 of the Economic Community of West African States (ECOWAS) and spearheaded the ECOWAS military and political involvement in Liberia in 1990 and Sierra Leone in 1998.

Benin and Cameroon have challenged Nigerian territorial claims along the Benin-Nigeria border and in offshore waters, respectively. In 1989 President Babangida sought to repair relations that had been strained by expulsion of illegal aliens by the Shagira regime, primarily by providing Benin with financial assistance. Cameroon and Nigeria continued to assert rival claims to the Bakassi Peninsula, several deaths having been reported during military clashes in 1994 in that oil-rich region. Briefs in the case were submitted to the International Court of Justice (ICJ) during the first half of 1995, but tension stemming from the dispute subsequently remained high. Seeking to repair relations even as legal wrangling over the region continued, president-elect Obasanjo visited Cameroon in early 1999.

In 2002 the ICJ ruled in favor of Cameroon in the border dispute. The governments of both Cameroon and Nigeria subsequently entered into the UN-brokered talks to implement the decision. By 2003 Nigeria had turned over more than 30 small villages to Cameroon in exchange for control of a small area. A second round of territorial exchange occurred in July 2004, and diplomatic relations were also restored between the two countries. However, in September the Obasanjo administration refused to participate in a third round of land exchange. That led to a new UN effort (see article on Cameroon).

Relations with Benin were also strengthened in the early 2000s. Joint border patrols were initiated in 2002 between the two states, who subsequently agreed to redraw their borders. Three areas claimed by Nigeria were turned over to the government in Lagos in return for its release of seven areas claimed by Benin. In addition, in May 2003 Nigeria and Benin agreed, along with Ghana and Togo, to the construction of a 1,000-kilometer pipeline to transship oil.

Following independence Nigeria maintained relations with both eastern and western governments, establishing strong economic ties with Britain, Canada, the Soviet Union, and the People's Republic of China. Nigeria's current leading export partner is the United States, although relations with the U.S. government were somewhat strained when the Nigerian government, after having criticized Iraq's invasion of Kuwait in August 1990, remained neutral during the armed confrontation of early 1991.

Relations between Lagos and London, weakened by the flight to Britain of a number of political associates of former president Shagari, were for-

mally suspended in mid-1984, when British police arrested a Nigerian diplomat and expelled two others for the attempted kidnapping of former transport minister Umaru DIKKO, who was under indictment in Nigeria for diversion of public funds. Full relations with the United Kingdom resumed in February 1986, with Dikko being denied asylum in early 1989.

Despite Nigeria's reported admission to full membership in the Organization of the Islamic Conference (OIC) in 1986, intense Christian opposition yielded the appointment of a commission to evaluate the implications of the move. As a result, the country formally repudiated its links to the conference in 1991, although the OIC continues to list Nigeria as one of its members. Muslims objected strenuously to the 1991 reversal of an 18-year lapse in relations with Israel, although the Babangida regime two years earlier had recognized the Palestinian claim to statehood.

In April 1994 the U.S. State Department accused Nigerian government officials of complicity in a global drug trafficking network that supplied upwards of 40 percent of the heroin entering the United States. However, the United States stopped short of imposing economic sanctions because of "vital national interests."

In February 1998 Nigerian troops were at the vanguard of the ECOWAS Monitoring Group (Ecomog) that invaded Freetown, Sierra Leone, in an effort to restore to power the democratically elected government of Ahmed Tejan Kabbah. (Kabbah had been forced into exile in the aftermath of the military coup [see separate article on Sierra Leone for further details].) In March 1999 Nigerian president-elect Obasanjo reiterated his country's commitment to restoring peace in Sierra Leone and pledged to keep Nigerian troops there as long as necessary. In 2004 Nigeria still had 2,400 troops in Sierra Leone.

The Obasanjo administration was also active in international efforts to resolve the Liberian civil war. In 2003 Liberian leader Charles Taylor accepted a Nigerian proposal whereby he would receive asylum in Nigeria in exchange for surrendering power. Taylor left Liberia for Nigeria in

August 2003 and settled in Calabar. Nigeria then contributed 1,500 troops to the UN-sponsored peacekeeping mission to Liberia in October 2003.

The new civilian regime installed in 1999 received much international praise for its attempt to eliminate widespread corruption and its commitment to democratic practices. Among other things, the United States restored military ties and announced that Nigeria would receive $10 million in military aid. In addition, a U.S.-Nigerian committee was established in 2005 to address regional security issues as well as to combat violence in Nigeria's oil-producing areas.

Reports surfaced in 2006 that Nigeria was pursuing negotiations with China toward an agreement whereby Chinese companies would be granted oil licenses in return for as much as $4 billion in infrastructure grants. Nigeria also reportedly agreed to purchase military aircraft from China.

In March 2006 former Liberian leader Taylor tried to flee from Nigeria when it became apparent that President Obasanjo planned to extradite him. However, Taylor was captured and turned over to a special UN court for trial on charges of having committed war crimes.

Current Issues

Widespread disbelief greeted the government's announcement in March 1995 that it had uncovered a coup plot involving some 150 military officers and prominent civilians, including former head of state Olusegun Obasanjo. Prodemocracy groups argued that the Abacha regime, already considered one of the most repressive in Nigeria's history, had concocted the charges as part of an effort to "clear the political landscape of opposition" (a claim that was lent further credence in June when several other dissidents were arrested). The international community also expressed concern over the regime's hard-line tactics, particularly after a report was issued in July that a secret military tribunal had given a life sentence to Obasanjo, one of the continent's most respected "elder statesmen" and the only Nigerian military leader ever to have turned control over to an elected civilian government.

U.S. president Bill Clinton was among the world leaders calling for clemency for Obasanjo and the other prisoners, and his administration imposed aid and diplomatic sanctions to pressure Abuja on the matter. Meanwhile South African president Nelson Mandela urged an embargo on arms sales to Nigeria until Moshood Abiola was released from prison, where he was awaiting trial on charges of treason for having declared himself president after the 1993 balloting. In addition, in September a special Commonwealth committee suggested that economic sanctions (including a possible embargo on Nigerian oil exports) be applied unless democratization measures were adopted quickly.

President Abacha reacted angrily to the criticism, promising "retaliatory measures" against western nations attempting to "destabilize Nigeria." However, in what was seen as an attempt to ward off further sanctions, Abacha on October 1, 1996, proposed a three-year transition to civilian government (see Political background, above) and commuted the sentences of the March 1995 "coup plotters." (All death sentences were reportedly changed to life imprisonment, whereas Obasanjo's term was reduced to 15 years.) External reaction to the transition proposal was tepid at best, and, in any event, prospects for improvement in the regime's image were obliterated upon the hanging of activist Kenule Saro-Wiwa and eight others in early November. International concern having turned to outrage, the Commonwealth heads of government suspended Nigeria's membership, the European Union (EU) discontinued all development cooperation, and many nations withdrew their diplomatic representatives from Nigeria.

Consequently, Nigeria entered 1996 in the role of a "pariah state," and developments over the next year did little to alter that situation. The government refused to permit Commonwealth representatives into the country until November and, even then, blocked access to prisoners such as Obasanjo and Mobiola. (The Commonwealth subsequently appeared split between hard-liners such as Canada and the United Kingdom, who were willing to consider an oil embargo, and others, most notably African states, who appeared content to maintain the current level of pressure on the Abacha regime.) In addition, following a fact-finding mission to Nigeria in March, the UN Human Rights Committee accused the government of a wide range of abuses.

President Abacha also faced internal challenges in 1996, as evidenced by several "purges" of the military leadership (including a revamping of the PRC membership) and the reported outbreak of fighting between Sunni and Shiite Muslims in Kaduna in September. In addition, local elections in March and recognition of five political parties in September elicited only scorn from prodemocracy groups. Furthermore, economic conditions remained dismal for ordinary Nigerians, faced with rapidly rising prices as well as corruption within the government and the business sectors that had been described as among the most pervasive in the world.

Two bomb attacks in Lagos killed several soldiers and wounded more than 30 other people in January and February 1997, no groups claiming responsibility. The government subsequently intensified its crackdown on opposition groups, among other things charging Nobel Prize winner Wole SOYINKA (in self-imposed exile) and 14 other dissidents with treason in March. Spokesmen for the regime linked several subsequent attacks to the National Democratic Coalition (NADECO), although impartial observers strongly questioned any such link and suggested the government was merely attempting to silence some of its most effective critics. Harassment was also reported of journalists who questioned the regime. On another and perhaps more genuinely threatening front, the regime reported that a coup attempt had been uncovered in late December. Meanwhile, in October the Commonwealth heads of government had decided to continue Nigeria's suspension for another year, and expulsion was threatened in case General Abacha failed to carry through with the proposed return to civilian government by October 1, 1998. Consequently, attention in early 1998 focused on plans for legislative elections in April and presidential balloting in August. Initial analysis of the latter was less than encouraging, however, as Abacha at-

tempted to secure the nomination of all the legal parties before his death in June.

Upon assuming office in June 1998, General Abubakar initially signaled his intent to follow Abacha's electoral schedule. However, he soon abandoned his deceased predecessor's plan, annulled the recent legislative results, dissolved the five legal parties, appointed a new government, and pledged to hand over power to a popularly elected civilian government in 1999. Those efforts were met with praise (albeit guarded) from most international observers, and in October 1998 the EU announced a partial lifting of sanctions against Nigeria. Moreover, in March 1999 the United States ended its sanctions, thereby paving the way for new IMF and World Bank loans. Meanwhile, Britain dispatched a high-level mission to Lagos to discuss Nigeria's readmission to "the world economic and political community," and in April the Commonwealth's foreign ministers recommended that Nigeria's suspension be lifted. At the same time, the incoming Obasanjo administration and PDP-dominated legislature confronted economic, political, and social problems of immense proportions. Among the most pressing issues awaiting the new government were violent political and social unrest in the economically critical oil-producing regions, a decayed infrastructure, and a treasury depleted by corruption. As a first step in Obasanjo's anticorruption program, in June he expelled 60 senior military officers and suspended all contracts negotiated by the Abacha government.

Ethnic tensions in the oil-producing Niger Delta escalated throughout the fall of 1999, resulting in the deployment of 2,000 government troops to the state of Bayelsa.

Religious violence claimed hundreds of lives and dominated Nigerian affairs in 2000–2002 as a dozen northern states instituted sharia despite opposition from the federal government. (Some analysts suggested that the northern states were employing sharia as another "weapon" in their long-standing effort to wrest authority from the federal government.) The issue received extensive international attention in November 2002 when the Miss World contest in the northern city of Kaduna had to be cancelled in light of deadly rioting sparked by a newspaper article that had inflamed portions of the Muslim population.

Strikes and violence continued during the 2003 presidential poll, although foreign observers described the election as generally free and fair, with some irregularities, including voter intimidation and ballot tampering in 13 states. The main opposition candidate, former SMC chair Buhari, contested the results, but his challenge was dismissed by an appeals court. Meanwhile, following the elections, striking oil employees took 97 foreign workers hostage on offshore petroleum rigs. The hostages were released after negotiations among the striking workers, the government, and the main union. In June a nationwide strike began over the rising price of fuel, and security forces killed several protestors. The strike ended in July after the government agreed to implement price controls on fuel and investigate the actions of security forces. A second major nationwide strike was called in October because of perceived government inaction; however, the government preempted the strike with the arrest of several union leaders. In October 2004 unions launched another general strike after the government announced a 25 percent increase in fuel prices. Clashes between police and demonstrators during the strike again left several dead and dozens wounded.

Tensions between Christians and Muslims escalated into renewed violence in May 2004 when some 600 people were killed and more than 30,000 fled their homes in the northern city of Kano. Religious fighting in Plateau State led Obasanjo to declare a state of emergency on May 18, 2004. The president suspended the authority of the governor and state assembly and appointed a federal official to oversee the state for six months.

Ethnic groups in the Niger Delta threatened to force foreign oil companies out of the area in October 2004 amid violence and interethnic strife. The uncertainty created during the crisis led the price of oil on the international market to increase significantly.

As part of President Obasanjo's economic reform efforts, he continued to seek a reduction of Nigeria's foreign debt burden in 2004. He received a pledge from the United Kingdom to partially reduce its total debt, and in addition, the United Kingdom pledged to trace the $2.1 billion that reportedly had been funneled through British banks during the Abacha regime. This followed a March 2005 decision by the Swiss government to return $458 million inappropriately banked by Abacha. Obasanjo also launched a major anticorruption initiative in 2004, and investigations were initiated against several officials, including the state governor of Plateau, who was arrested in London by Nigerian and British police for money laundering. In addition, the education minister was fired and charged with bribing federal officials in March 2005, and the national police chief resigned in January 2005 amid allegations that he embezzled $7 million.

The government convened a National Political Reforms Conference (NPRC) in February 2005 in an effort to ease tensions among the regions. After contentious debate, the conference in April issued a report that called for increased oil revenues to be allocated to southern and eastern regions and rejected the proposed revision of the constitution to permit Obasanjo to run for a third term. The latter issue was permanently put to rest in May 2006 when the Senate blocked an amendment presented by supporters of a third term. (Obasanjo agreed to abide by that ruling.) Attention thenceforth turned to what observers agreed would be a turbulent campaign leading up to the 2007 presidential and legislative elections. In June Obasanjo signed a new electoral law designed to reduce fraud in the elections by, among other things, limiting donations to campaigns and strengthening the authority of the election commission.

The other dominant issue in late 2005 and early 2006 was sustained severe discord in the oil-rich Niger Delta region. Two groups—the Niger Delta's People's Volunteer Force (NDPVF) and the Movement for the Emancipation of the Niger Delta (MEND)—claimed responsibility for a number of attacks on pipelines and kidnappings designed to disrupt production in pursuit of greater autonomy for the region and compensation for environmental damage done by oil companies in the state of Bayelsa. In June 2006 MEND declared a "cease-fire" after a Nigerian court ordered Shell (the country's largest oil-producer) to pay $1.5 billion for environmental "reparations."

Political Parties and Groups

Upon assuming power in December 1983, the Supreme Military Council (SMC) banned all political parties, arrested many of their leaders, and confiscated their assets. The ban was lifted on May 3, 1989, and 13 parties were legalized, 2 of which were to be selected to contest upcoming elections. However, the government, having become dissatisfied with that process, subsequently dissolved the existing parties and, on October 7, 1989, two new parties—the Social Democratic Party (SDP) and the National Republican Convention (NRC)—were created by presidential decree. The political platforms of the new groups were dictated by the regime, which also provided financial support until January 1991 when it declared the parties to be "on their own." Subsequently, the SDP and the NRC were dismantled when all party activity was banned by the Abacha regime on November 18, 1993.

On June 27, 1995, General Abacha announced that the ban on "political activity" had been lifted, although "rallies and campaigns" remained restricted and other constraints continued as a consequence of the country's severe political turmoil. On June 17, 1996, the National Electoral Commission of Nigeria (NECON) announced the regulations for registration of parties, which were required, among other things, to secure the signature of 40,000 voters from each region and to forswear accepting money from external sources. The regulations promised public financing for the recognized groups. Some 23 political associations reportedly purchased the registration forms, but only 15 completed them within the 30-day limit imposed by the NECON. On September 30 NECON announced that five parties had been recognized; the other aspirants were ordered to dissolve immediately. Although the NECON argued that the selections had

been based on an unbiased "point system," opposition leaders called the process a "sham," observers generally supporting their assessment that the newly recognized parties all shared a "conservative" point of view, which meant tacit support of the current military regime and its proposed transition schedule. Meanwhile, no opponents of the Abacha government appeared to have gained a legal foothold.

In April 1998 all five legal parties nominated Abacha to be their presidential candidate at balloting then scheduled for August. However, following Abacha's death in June, his successor, General Abubakar, dissolved the five parties and called on political associations to register with the newly created Independent National Electoral Commission (INEC). Between August 27 and September 9, 25 political groups applied to the INEC for provisional legal status. Only nine of the applicants met the baseline qualifications—including maintaining functional offices in 24 states—and at local elections in December only three of those groups, the People's Democratic Party (PDP), the All People's Party (APP), and the Alliance for Democracy (AD), secured the voting tally necessary to maintain their legal status and move onto legislative and presidential elections. The other six were reportedly deregistered. Three new parties (the NDP, UNPP, and APGA) were registered in June 2002, and by 2006 some 35 parties had been legalized.

Parties That Participated in the 2003 Elections

People's Democratic Party (PDP). The PDP was formed in Lagos in August 1998 as an umbrella for more than 60 organizations, including many from the so-called Group of 34, which registered among its leaders traditional chiefs, businesspeople, academicians, and a strong contingent of retired generals. Alex EKWUEME, a former national vice president, and Jerry GANA emerged from the PDP's inaugural meetings as the group's chair and second in command, respectively. The party presented a platform that reflected its broad political base—advocating the "guided" deregulation of the economy, respect for human rights, and improved funding for health care and education.

In late October 1998 Gen. Olusegun Obasanjo, the military head of state between 1976 and 1979, joined the PDP, and, with Obasanjo at the helm, the party subsequently swept local and gubernatorial elections, won a majority in the assembly, and in February 1999 captured the national presidency.

In January 2003 the PDP elected Obasanjo as its presidential candidate for the upcoming elections, which he won with 62 percent of the vote. The PDP also retained its majorities in the federal Senate and House of Representatives and among state governors and state assemblies.

Feuding developed in 2005 between President Obasanjo and Vice President Abubakar Atiku over the proposed constitutional amendment to permit Obasanjo to seek a third term (see Current issues, above). The split also appeared to reflect the schism between the party's founding members ("concerned elders") led by Atiku and the "progressive faction" led by Obasanjo. A party congress elected Ahmadu Ali as the PDP chair, and Obasanjo's supporters blamed Ali for the defeat of the constitutional amendment. Subsequently, a PDP faction led by Solomon Lar declared itself the real leadership of the party and sued for access to the PDP assets.

Leaders: Gen. Olesegun OBASANJO (President of the Republic), Ahmadu ALI (Chair), Abubakar ATIKU (Vice President of the Republic), Solomon LAR (Leader of dissident faction), Chief Ojo MADUEKWE (National Secretary).

All Nigeria People's Party (ANPP). The ANPP is a successor to the All People's Party (APP), a center-right grouping established in September 1998 by some 14 Ibo and Hausa-Fulani political associations, including the People's Congress (PC), the New Era Alliance (NEA), the National Unity Forum (NUF), and the Democratic Vanguard (DV). Within the APP's ranks were some former members of the five parties dissolved in July 1998, as well as so many associates of for-

mer president Abacha that APP detractors derisively labeled the group the "Abacha's People's Party." The APP forwarded its own candidates for local, gubernatorial, and national legislative balloting in late 1998 and early 1999, capturing one-quarter of the governorships and representation in both assembly bodies. On the other hand, prior to the 1999 presidential balloting, the APP formed an electoral alliance with the AD (below). After the AD's standard-bearer, Samuel Oluyemisi Falae, outpolled the APP's proposed candidate, Oghonnaya ONU, in intra-alliance balloting, the APP backed Falae's presidential bid.

Membership in the APP largely came from the northern region. In July 2000 the party claimed to have reorganized in an attempt to widen membership to the southeast, with particular focus on the Igbo tribe. As part of the APP's reorganization, the party set up a monitoring mechanism to ensure that the party's elected officials lived up to the party platform. (The APP tended to support the implementation of sharia in northern states.)

In May 2002 the APP announced its intention to change its name to the ANPP in anticipation of a planned merger with the then-unrecognized UNPP (below). However, both parties subsequently suffered internal factionalization over the proposed merger, with one APP faction demanding retention of the party's original rubric. In November a special APP national convention ratified the name change, although only a portion of the UNPP membership joined the group.

In the 2003 elections Muhammadu Buhari ran as the ANPP's presidential candidate and received 32 percent of the vote. In the legislative elections, the ANPP secured 96 seats in the house and 27 in the senate, making it the largest opposition party.

Leaders: Modu SHERIFF (National Chair), Etubon ASUQUO (National Secretary).

Alliance for Democracy (AD). The Yoruba-dominated AD draws on a long tradition of leftist, nationalist politics that originated before independence under the guidance of Chief Obafemi AWOLOWO and continued more recently in the

National Democratic Coalition (NADECO, below). The AD called for greater regional autonomy and constitutional reform, and AD candidates sought office in late 1998 and 1999 on a platform promising privatization of state-run enterprises, reduction of Nigeria's debt burden, and free education and health care. In early 1999 the AD formed an electoral alliance with the APP in preparation for presidential balloting, and an AD moderate, Samuel Oluyemisi ("Olu") Falae, subsequently captured the right to head the alliance ticket.

Falae finished a distant second at the February 1999 elections, which he decried as rigged in favor of the PDP. Subsequently, he petitioned the Court of Appeals to overturn the election results; however, when the court rejected his bid in early April, he reportedly abandoned his legal challenge.

In late 1999 the party factionalized over a leadership dispute. Yusuf MAMMAN, who became chair in December, was accused of misconduct for neglecting to call a party convention. The northern faction then suspended his position on December 20 and elected Adamu SONG as pro tem chair. Both men claimed the leadership post in the spring of 2000. Because of the split, the AD did not field a candidate in the 2003 presidential election. In the legislative elections, the AD won 34 seats in the house and 6 in the senate.

Leader: Ahmed ABDULKADZR (Chair).

National Democratic Party (NDP). Described as a "pan-Yoruba" party, the NDP was launched in 2001 as a merger of several groups in pursuit of "true federalism." Ike NWACHUKWU, the NDP candidate in the 2003 presidential election, received less than 1 percent of the vote. In legislative balloting, the NDP secured 2 percent of the vote in the house and gained one seat. It received less than 2 percent of the vote in senate elections and no seats.

In April 2006, the NDP announced that former president Ibrahim Babangida would be the party's candidate in the 2007 presidential election.

Leaders: Aliyu Habu FARU (Chair), Kenny MARTINS, Idongesit NKANG (National Secretary).

United Nigeria People's Party (UNPP). The UNPP is a successor to the United Nigeria Democratic Party (UNDP), which was launched in August 2001 by, among others, former members of the PDP and supporters of former president Babangida. The UNDP changed its name to the UNPP in May 2002 to avoid confusion with the UN Development Program (also UNDP). The UNPP subsequently was splintered by a proposed merger with the APP; although some UNPP members joined the new ANPP, a rump UNPP continued to operate. Jim NWOBODO, the UNPP candidate in the 2003 presidential poll, secured 0.43 percent of the vote. In the concurrent legislative balloting, the UNPP secured 2.72 percent of the vote in the senate (but no seats) and 2.8 percent of the vote and two seats in the house.

In 2006, it was reported that many members of the UNPP had defected to the newly-formed Movement for Restoration and Defense of Democracy (MRDD, below).

Leaders: Mallem Salek JAMBO (Chair), Ukeje NWOKEFORO (National Secretary).

All Progressive Grand Alliance (APGA). Launched in April 2002, the APGA is led by a prominent chief of the Southern Igbo ethnic group, Chekwas Okorie. However, its founders criticized those who branded the APGA as an "Igbo party," arguing instead that it intended to represent "all the marginalized people of Nigeria." Okorie came in third in presidential balloting in 2003 with 3.29 percent of the vote. The party also gained two seats in the house but none in the senate in 2003.

A faction of the party led by Chief Victor UMEH claimed to be the legitimate leadership of the APGA in 2005–2006, and the party was reported to be on the verge of a split.

Leaders: Chief Chekwas OKORIE (Chair), Said Baba ABDULLANI (National Secretary).

People's Redemption Party (PRP). The PRP was formed in 2002 under the leadership of Balarabe Musa, who was also the party's unsuccessful presidential candidate in 2003. The PRP won one seat in the house in 2003.

Leader: Balarabe MUSA.

Other parties participating in the 2003 elections included (all received less than 1 percent of the vote and no representation in the legislature): the **People's Salvation Party** (PSP), which was created in 2002 and is led by Alhaji WADA NAS; the **National Conscience Party** (NCP), formed in October 1994 by Gani FAWEHINMI, an attorney and political activist who was arrested in mid-1995; the **Justice Party** (JP), led by former NADECO member Ralph OBIOHA and former NDP member Chris OKOTIE (2003 presidential candidate); the **Movement for Democracy and Justice** (MDJ), led by Kalli Al-Gazali ALH and Mohammed Dikko YUSUF (2003 presidential candidate); the **Progressive Action Party** (PAC), led by A. C. NWODO; the **People's Mandate Party** (PMP), led by Arthur NWANKWO (who was also the party's 2003 presidential candidate); the **All Peoples' Liberation Party** (APLP), led by Alhaji Umar Mohammed; the **New Nigeria Peoples' Party** (NNPP), chaired by B. O. ANIEBONAM; and the **United Democratic Party** (UDP), formed in 1998.

Other Groups

Campaign for Democracy (CD). Formed in late 1991 by some 40 human rights, labor, and social organizations, the Lagos-based CD was subsequently at the forefront of efforts to force the military to turn authority over to a civilian government. Having released, against court orders, what it described as reliable figures concerning the June 1993 presidential balloting, the CD organized a general strike in response to the government's refusal to permit the installation of Moshood Abiola as president. A number of CD leaders and members were detained in the subsequent standoff with the Abacha regime, with the coalition calling for a sovereign national conference to establish a transitional government pending new elections. In 1996 CD leader Dr. Beko Ransome-Kuti was sentenced to prison on charges (dismissed as spurious by many observers) related to the alleged coup plot in March.

Leader: Dr. Beko RANSOME-KUTI.

National Democratic Coalition (NADECO). Organized in May 1994 by a group of former politicians, retired military officers, and human rights activists, NADECO demanded that the Abacha regime yield to an interim government led by Moshood Abiola, the apparent winner in the aborted 1993 presidential election. As in the case of other prominent antigovernment figures, several NADECO leaders were temporarily detained, including the revered 87-year-old ex-governor of Ondo, Michael AJASIN. NADECO unsuccessfully supported a People's Progressive Party for recognition in 1996, and Ajasin angrily denounced the failure of the regime to legalize opposition groupings.

Wole Soyinka, the prominent exiled critic of the government who was involved in the reported formation of several external groups (see Nalicon, immediately below), was identified as a NADECO leader in 1997. Soyinka (in absentia) and other NADECO supporters were charged with treason in March 1997 for their antiregime activities. In early May 1998 NADECO's secretary general, Ayo Opadokum, was among 20 opposition activists arrested when a rally at Ibadan turned violent.

Beginning in mid-1998 the Abubakar regime released a number of opposition figures and was reportedly preparing to release Moshood Abiola when Abiola died. In October Soyinka, who had been a leading advocate for Abiola's release, returned from exile, where most recently he had been calling for the formation of a South African-style human rights tribunal to investigate the alleged abuses of Nigeria's military regimes. Subsequently, NADECO Chair Ndubuisi Kanu stated that the organization would resume its role as unofficial opposition, although it would not assume the status of political party.

Leaders: Commodore Ndubuisi KANU (Chair), Bolaji AKINYEMI, Wole SOYINKA, Ayo OPADOKUM (Secretary General).

National Liberation Council of Nigeria (Nalicon). Formed in exile in June 1995 by Wole Soyinka (winner of the 1986 Nobel Prize for Literature, who had fled Nigeria in November 1994) and other government critics, Nalicon advocated a "boycott" of the Abacha regime, which it accused of, among other things, massive human rights abuses. In April 1996 Soyinka announced that several exiled opposition groups had formed a United Democratic Front of Nigeria (UDFN), which called for an international embargo on Nigerian oil sales as part of the effort to topple the government.

Leader: Wole SOYINKA.

Movement for the Survival of the Ogoni People (MOSOP). MOSOP pressed the government for years on the rights of the indigenous Ogoni ethnic group in oil-rich southwestern Nigeria. Having previously suggested that a self-determination referendum would be appropriate, MOSOP has more recently concentrated on forcing the government to share the oil wealth more equitably with the local population.

Kenule SARO-WIWA (a well-known author, minority rights activist, and longtime MOSOP leader) was arrested in 1994 on murder charges involving the death of four progovernment Ogoni leaders. Saro-Wiwa vehemently denied the charges, calling them a blatant attempt by the Abacha regime to silence his criticism. Most internal and external observers remained extremely skeptical of Saro-Wiwa's guilt, and western and African capitals urged his release. However, Saro-Wiwa and eight others were found guilty by a special military tribunal in late October 1996 and, following ratification of the sentences by the PRC, were hanged on November 10. The executions prompted an international outcry that contributed significantly to the government's sustained isolation in 1996–1998.

MOSOP subsequently attempted to change the constitution so that the presidency would rotate on a regional basis.

Leader: Ledum MITEE.

Arewa People's Congress (APC). The APC is a northern nationalist group that formed as a counter to the militant nationalist Yoruba OPC (see below). It has pledged to protect "northerners" in the southwest region.

Movement for the Actualization of the Sovereign State of Biafra (MASSOB). An Ibo group formed by lawyer and activist Ralph Uwazurike in 1999, MASSOB advocates the secession of Biafra and is opposed to the introduction of sharia in northern states. In October 2005 Uwazurike and six members of MASSOB were arrested on charges of treason and organizing an illegal organization.

Leader: Ralph UWAZURIKE.

O'odua People's Congress (OPC). The OPC is a militant organization that advocates secession of the Yoruba. It was allegedly behind a November 1999 dispute between Yoruba and Hausa merchants in the Lagos market that killed dozens. In addition, the OPC was blamed for several attacks in early 2000, including the murder of a Banga police officer. Some members of the OPC support the spread of sharia in northern states in the hope that the issue will further divide the country and thereby make Yoruba secession easier to obtain.

United Democratic Forum (UDF). The UDF was launched by a group of moderate northerners and so-called "Middle-Belters" who oppose the implementation of sharia as well as the northern nationalist APC. The UDF was formed by Suleman TAKUMA, a Nuper from the Niger state.

Advanced Congress of Democrats (ACD). The ACD was formed in April 2005 to oppose President Obasanjo's bid for a third presidential term. The party attracted a number of elected officials at the state and national level, including members of the house and senate, as well as senior PDP figures, including former chair of the PDP, Audu OGBEH. The party is mainly comprised of Northerners and is essentially an anti-PDP formation. After Obasanjo announced that he would not stand for a third term, the party announced a progressive platform that emphasized honesty in politics and government campaign. The ACD attracted members from other parties, principally the Alliance for Democracy.

Leaders: Lawal KAITA (Former Governor of Kaduna), Ghali Umar NA'ABA (Former President of the House of Representatives), Abubakar RIMI (Former Governor of Kano).

Movement for Restoration and Defense of Democracy (MRDD). The MRDD was formed in February 2006 by disaffected members of the UNPP and the PRP. The MRDD opposed President Obasanjo's bid for a third term.

Leader: Alh JIMETA (National Chair).

Other groups mentioned in news reports in the past decade include the **Democratic Alternative,** led by Alao AKA-BASHORUM, the attorney for detained 1993 presidential candidate Moshood Abiola; the **Eastern Mandate Union,** formed by tribal leaders and politicians from southeastern Nigeria under the leadership of Patrick Dele COLE and Chuba OKADIGBO; the **Liberal Democrats** (LD), formed in August 1998 in Abuja and led by Baghir TOFA; the **Movement for National Reconciliation,** led by Anthony ENAHARO; the **National Conscience Party,** formed in October 1994 by Gani FAWEHINMI, an attorney and political activist who was arrested in mid-1995; the **National Democratic Movement** (NDM), led by Emmanuel OSAMOR; the **New Democratic Party** (NDP); the **Nigerian People's Movement,** which represents the interests of the Igbo ethnic group in eastern Nigeria; the **Northern Elders' Forum,** a conservative group; the **People's Democratic Congress** (PDC), which was launched in August 1998 in Enugu by Chief Emeka OJUKWU, who had been active in the Biafra independence movement; the **People's Liberation Party** (PLP), a coalition of youth organizations formed at Abuja in September 1998 under the leadership of Goodnews Guben ABBE; the **United Action for Democracy** (UAD), which organized anti-Abacha rallies in early May 1998; the **United Democratic Congress,** led by Alhaji Usman ABATEMI; and "**Vision '99.**"

Groups formed after 2000 include the Fourth Dimension, formed in 2001 by former military officers and led by Adm. (Ret.) Augustus AIKHOMU; **National Frontier,** created in 2001 by several former governors and senior military officers and led by Edwin Ume EZEOKE; **IBB Vision 2003,** established in 2002 as a political front for former president Ibrahim Babangida; and the **National Solidarity Party** (NSP), formed in 2001 by ex-military officers.

The **African Democratic Congress** (ADC) was formed in 2006 by Chief Okewo OSUI, and the **Fresh Democrats** were established in 2006 under the leadership of Chris OKOTIE.

In addition, the following groups have been linked to unrest in the Niger Delta area: the **Ijaw Youth Organization,** which is composed of radical elements of the ethnic Ijaw tribe who have asserted their desire for a role in Nigerian political life and greater benefits from the oil removed from their territory; the **Federated Niger Delta Izon Communities** (FNDIC), who warned foreign oil workers to leave the region in late 1998 because their safety could "no longer be guaranteed"; and the Ijaw-dominated **Rivers' States Coalition.** In January 1999 Ijaw-related unrest caused the postponement of a gubernatorial election, and further violence was reported throughout the beginning of the year.

In 2005 a new insurgent group—the **South-South Liberation Movement**—was launched with the goal of creation of a Niger Delta Republic. The movement was reportedly led by a former Nigerian Army warrant officer, John ADIE. Meanwhile, the **Niger Delta's People's Volunteer Force** (NDPVF), led by Mujahid DOKUBO-ASARI, was reported to have undertaken a number of attacks on oil production facilities. Dokubo-Asari was arrested for treason in September 2005, an appeals court rejecting bail for the jailed leader in June 2006. NDPVF members repeatedly warned of new attacks if Dokubo-Asari was not released. Although jailed, Dokubo-Asari reportedly negotiated the release of foreign hostages on several occasions.

The most active and militant of the Niger Delta groups has been the **Movement for the Emancipation of the Niger Delta** (MEND), which emerged in early 2006 when it conducted a series of attacks on oil production facilities. MEND was

Cabinet

As of September 6, 2006

President	Gen. (Ret.) Olusegun Obasanjo
Vice President	Atiku Abubakar

Federal Executive Councilors

Agriculture and Rural Development	Adamu Bello
Aviation	Babaloa Borishade
Commerce	Aliyu Modibbo Umar [f]
Communications	Obafemi Anibaba
Cooperation and Integration in Africa	Lawan Guba
Culture and Tourism	Chief Fani Kayode
Defense	Rabiu Kwankaso
Education	Obiageli Ezekwesili [f]
Environment	Helen Esuene [f]
Federal Capital Territory	Mallam Nasir el-Rufai
Finance	Nenadi Esther Usman [f]
Foreign Affairs	Joy Ogwu [f]
Health	Eyitayo Lambo
Housing and Urban Development	Rahman Olusegun Mimiko
Industry	Fidelis Naanmiap Tapgun
Information and National Orientation	Frank Nweke Jr.
Intergovernmental Affairs, Youth Development, and Special Duties	Grace Ogwuche [f]
Internal Affairs	Oluyemi Adenijl
Justice and Attorney General	Chief Bayo Ojo
Labor, Employment, and Productivity	Hassan Muhammed Lawal
Police Affairs	Broderick Bozimo
Power and Steel	Liyel Imoke
Science and Technology	Isoun Turner
Solid Minerals Development	Leslye Obiora [f]
Sports and Social Development	Bala Bawa Ka'oje
Transport	Precious Sekibo
Water Resources	Muktari Shagari
Women Affairs	Maryam Ciroma [f]
Works	Chief Cornelius Adebago

Ministers of State

Agriculture and Rural Development	Bamidele F. Dada
Education	Sayyad Abba Ruma
Finance	Elias N. Mbam
Foreign Affairs	Abubakar Tanko
Health	Halima Tayo Alao [f]
Internal Affairs	Joseph O. Itotoh
Petroleum Resources	Edmund Dakoro
Power and Steel	Ahmed Abdulhamid
Transport	Habibu Aliyu Mohammed
Water Resources	Salome Audu Jankada
Works	Malam Yahaya Abdulkarim

[f] = female

subsequently believed responsible for the kidnapping of foreign oil workers. It repeatedly demanded compensation from foreign oil companies for environmental damage done in the Niger Delta and demanded the release of NDPVF's Dokubo-Asari. MEND reportedly finances its operations through large-scale bunkering of oil.

Legislature

The former **National Assembly,** encompassing a Senate and a House of Representatives, was dissolved in December 1983. It was revived under the 1989 constitution, with an election of members to four-year terms in both houses on July 4, 1992. However, the new body did not convene until December 5 and was again dissolved in the wake of the November 1993 coup.

Five parties approved by the Abacha regime were permitted to contest the balloting for a new assembly on April 25, 1998. According to preliminary results, the United Nigeria Congress Party captured a comfortable majority of the seats; however, the election results were annulled, and the five parties were dissolved following Abacha's death in June. New elections were held on February 20, 1999, among the three parties that had achieved the required electoral threshold in the December 1998 local elections (see Political background, above).

Senate. The upper chamber consists of 109 seats: 3 from each state and 1 from the Federal Capital Territory of Abuja. Following the balloting of April 12, 2003, the seats were distributed as follows: the People's Democratic Party, 76; the All Nigeria People's Party, 27; and the Alliance for Democracy, 66.

President: Kenechukwu NNAMANI.

House of Representatives. The lower house consists of 360 seats, with the actual number of seats per state being apportioned on the basis of population. Following the balloting of April 12, 2003, the seats were distributed as follows: the People's Democratic Party, 223; the All Nigeria People's Party, 96; the Alliance for Democracy, 34; United Nigeria People's Party, 2; All Progressive

Grand Alliance, 2; National Democratic Party, 1; and the People's Redemption Party, 1; vacant, 1.

President: Aminu MASARI.

Communications

The Nigerian media returned to their position among the freest and most active in Africa following repeal, after the coup of August 1985, of the previous regime's Decree No. 4, which had authorized numerous media suspensions and the imprisonment of journalists for "inaccurate reporting." On the other hand, the popular and outspoken weekly *Newswatch,* whose founding editor-in-chief Dele Giwa was killed by a letter bomb in 1986, was banned for several months in 1987 for publishing details of the government's political transition plan, while a British freelance journalist was expelled in July 1991 because of reports on the country's fiscal problems that the regime found unacceptable. On August 15, 1994, the Abacha regime closed down the country's most respected newspaper, the *Guardian,* after it had published a report that government officials were at odds over the release of Moshood Abiola. Subsequently, two other prominent dailies—the *National Concord* and the *Punch* (both owned by Abiola)—were temporarily banned in 1995, and stringent restrictions were placed on the rest of the media.

Press

The following are published daily in Lagos, unless otherwise noted: *Times* (420,000 daily, including evening edition, 100,000 Sunday), government owned; *Nigerian Tribune* (Ibadan, 109,000), independent; *Nigerian Observer* (Benin City, 150,000, 60,000 Sunday), state owned; *Nigerian Standard* (Jos, 100,000 daily, 130,000 Sunday), state owned; *New Nigerian* (Kaduna, 80,000), federal-state owned; *Nigerian Chronicle* (Calibar, 50,000 daily, 163,000 Sunday), state owned; *New Democrat* (Kaduna South, 100,000); *Sketch* (Ibadan, 64,000 daily, 125,000 Sunday), government owned; *The Renaissance* (Enugu, 50,000).

News Agencies

The official News Agency of Nigeria (NAN) was established in 1978. A number of foreign agencies maintain offices in Lagos.

Broadcasting and Computing

In November 1975 the government assumed control of all radio and television broadcasting facilities, placing them under a newly created National Broadcasting Corporation that was itself superseded in 1978 by the nominally independent Federal Radio Corporation of Nigeria (FRCN) and Nigerian Television Authority (NTV). Subsequently, numerous regional and state broadcast facilities were launched. There were approximately 8.6 million television receivers and 900,000 personal computers serving 750,000 Internet users in 2003.

Intergovernmental Representation

Ambassador to the U.S.
George Achulike OBIOZOR

U.S. Ambassador to Nigeria
John CAMPBELL

Permanent Representative to the UN
Aminu Bashir WALI

IGO Memberships (Non-UN)
AfDB, AU, BADEA, CWTH, ECOWAS, Interpol, IOC, IOM, NAM, OPEC, PCA, WCO, WTO

RWANDA

REPUBLIC OF RWANDA

République Rwandaise (French)
Republika y'u Rwanda (Kinyarwanda)

The Country

Situated in the heart of Africa (adjacent to Burundi, Tanzania, Uganda, and the Democratic Republic of the Congo), Rwanda consists mainly of grassy uplands and hills endowed with a temperate climate. The population comprises three main ethnic groups: the Hutu, or Bahutu (85 percent); the Tutsi, or Batutsi (14 percent); and the Twa, or pygmies (1 percent). There are about equal numbers of Roman Catholics and animists, with small Protestant (9 percent) and Muslim (1 percent) minorities. In addition to English, French, and Kinyarwanda (the three official languages), Kiswahili is widely spoken. Women account for about half of the labor force, primarily as unpaid agricultural workers on family plots; female representation in government and party posts is minimal, though the 2003 constitution called for increased participation by women in all levels of government, civil service, and policymaking.

Economically poor, Rwanda has been hindered by high population growth (it is one of the most densely populated states in Africa), inadequate transportation facilities, distance from accessible ports, and the ravages of civil war. Over 90 percent of the people depend on agriculture for their livelihood, and goods are produced largely for local consumption. Coffee is the leading cash crop and principal source of foreign exchange, although tea cultivation is expanding. Industry is concentrated in food processing and nondurable consumer goods, but the mining of cassiterite and wolframite ore is also important. International assistance has focused on economic diversification, while recent state budgets have concentrated on agricultural and infrastructural development. Rwanda's GNP per capita rose to $270 in 1991 but then plunged because of economic and social carnage in 1994 (see Political background, below).

Despite the subsequent problems associated with civil war and the massive displacement and return of perhaps 2 million Rwandans, as of mid-2002 Rwanda was continuing to make considerable progress in rebuilding its economy. Due to the improved security situation, favorable weather conditions, additional foreign aid, increased food production, and the partial revival of exports, real GDP

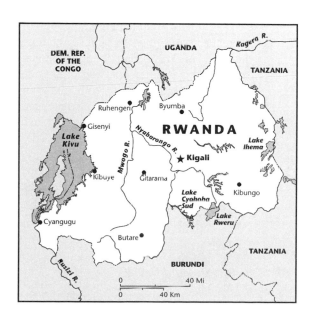

had grown by 13.8 percent in 1997, 8.9 percent in 1998, 7.6 percent in 1999, 6.0 percent in 2000, and 6.7 percent in 2001 (according to the International Monetary Fund [IMF]), while annual inflation had fallen into negative figures by the end of 2001. Reinforcing the country's economic infrastructure subsequently became the primary focus of governmental policy, which attracted substantial donor assistance. The IMF and World Bank, noting the progress in structural reform, offered debt relief, while at the same time encouraging the government to improve its revenue-collection system and intensify the privatization of state-run enterprises. A drought in 2003 cut agricultural production and caused growth to slow, while inflation rose to 9.4 percent. In addition, proposed economic reforms and privatization initiatives remained uncompleted. By 2004, only 30 of 74 state-owned enterprises scheduled for privatization had made the transition to private ownership. The international community also closely monitored the termination of the current transitional government and the return to a fully-elected civilian administration as well as resolution of the huge backlog of criminal cases arising from the conflict of 1994 (see Political background and Current issues, below).

Rwanda achieved GDP growth of 3.7 percent in 2004 and 6 percent in 2005, and the government was credited with continued liberalization of the economy and retrenchment in public spending. In 2005 the IMF and World Bank announced that Rwanda had met the requirements for large-scale debt reduction through the Heavily Indebted Poor Countries (HIPC) initiative. The IMF also pledged additional lending for poverty reduction programs. For its part, the government launched programs designed to attract foreign investment, particularly in regard to an ambitious plan to make Rwanda a "high-tech hub" for central Africa by extending phone and Internet service into rural areas.

Government and Politics

Political Background

Like Burundi, Rwanda was long a feudal monarchy ruled by nobles of the Tutsi tribe. A German protectorate from 1899 to 1916, it constituted the northern half of the Belgian mandate of Ruanda-Urundi after World War I and of the Belgian-administered trust territory of the same name after World War II. Resistance to the Tutsi monarchy by the more numerous Hutus intensified in the 1950s and culminated in November 1959 in a bloody revolt that overthrew the monarchy and led to the emigration of thousands of Tutsis. The Party of the Movement for Hutu Emancipation (*Parti du Mouvement de l'Émancipation Hutu*— Parmehutu), founded by Grégoire KAYIBANDA, won an overwhelming electoral victory in 1960, and Rwanda proclaimed itself a republic on January 28, 1961, under the leadership of Dominique MBONYUMUTWA. Since the United Nations did not recognize the action, new elections were held under UN auspices in September 1961, with the Hutu party repeating its victory. Kayibanda was accordingly designated president on October 26, 1961, and trusteeship status was formally terminated on July 1, 1962. Subsequently, Tutsi émigrés invaded the country in an attempt to restore the monarchy; their defeat in December 1963 set off mass reprisals against the remaining Tutsis, resulting in 10,000–15,000 deaths and the flight of 150,000–200,000 Tutsis to neighboring countries.

The Hutu-dominated government consolidated its position in the elections of 1965 and 1969. Moreover, with President Kayibanda legally barred from seeking another term in the approaching 1973 election, the constitution was altered to assure continuance of the existing regime. The change fanned hostility between political elements from the northern region and those from the southern and central regions, the latter having dominated the government since independence. Beginning in February 1973 at the National University in Butare, renewed Hutu moves against the Tutsis spread quickly to other areas. The government did not attempt to quell the actions of the extremists, and continued instability raised the prospect of another tribal bloodbath or even war with Tutsi-ruled Burundi. In this context, a bloodless coup took place on July 5, 1973.

The new government, under Maj. Gen. Juvénal HABYARIMANA, moved quickly to dissolve the

Political Status: Republic proclaimed January 28, 1961; independent since July 1, 1962; multiparty constitution adopted June 10, 1991, but full implementation blocked by ethnic-based fighting; peace agreement signed August 4, 1993, in Arusha, Tanzania, providing for transitional government and multiparty elections by 1995; twenty-two month transitional period announced January 5, 1994; new transitional government installed on July 19, 1994, by the Rwandan Patriotic Front (FPR) after taking military control in the wake of "genocide" of April 1994; new constitution (providing for a four-year, FPR-led transitional government but including provisions of the 1991 basic law and the 1993 Arusha peace agreement) adopted by the Transitional National Assembly on May 5, 1995; transitional period extended by the FPR for four years on June 8, 1999; new constitution providing for full transition to civilian rule adopted on June 4, 2003, following a national referendum on May 26.

Area: 10,169 sq. mi. (26,338 sq. km.).

Population: 8,128,553 (2002C); 8,928,000 (2005E).

Major Urban Center (1993E): KIGALI (276,000).

Official Languages: English, French, Kinyarwanda. (English was designated as an official language by the National Assembly in January 1996.)

Monetary Unit: Rwanda Franc (official rate July 1, 2006: 552 francs = $1US).

President: Maj. Gen. Paul KAGAME (Rwandan Patriotic Front); named interim president by the Supreme Court on March 24, 2000, following the resignation the previous day of Pasteur BIZIMUNGU (Rwandan Patriotic Front); elected in a permanent position by the combined Transitional National Assembly and cabinet on April 17, 2000, and inaugurated on April 22; reelected by popular vote on August 25, 2003, and inaugurated for a seven-year term on September 12.

Prime Minister: Bernard MAKUSA; appointed by the president on March 8, 2000, to succeed Pierre-Célestin RWIGEMA (Republican Democratic Movement), who had resigned on February 28; formed new government on March 20, 2000; reappointed by the president on October 11, 2003, and formed new government on October 19, following legislative elections on September 30.

---

legislature, ban political organizations, and suspend portions of the constitution. A civilian-military government, composed largely of young technocrats, was subsequently installed, and it established a more centralized administrative system. A regime-supportive National Revolutionary Movement for Development (*Mouvement Républicain National pour le Développement*—MRND) was organized in mid-1976 and was accorded formal status as the sole legal party under a new constitution adopted by referendum on December 17, 1978. Subsequently, it was announced that the same poll had confirmed Habyarimana for an additional five-year term as president.

In 1980 the administration declared that it had foiled a coup attempt allegedly involving current and former government officials, including Maj. Théonaste LIZINDE, who had recently been removed as security chief after being charged with corruption. Lizinde received a death sentence, which was subsequently commuted to life imprisonment.

Single-party legislative balloting was conducted in 1981, 1983, and on December 26, 1988. Habyarimana, the sole candidate, was accorded additional five-year terms as president by means of referendums in 1983 and on December 19, 1988. In July 1990 Habyarimana called for the drafting by 1992 of a new national charter, which would separate governmental and MRND powers, reduce the size of the bureaucracy, and establish guidelines for the creation of a multiparty system. However, political reform was delayed by an October 1990 invasion from bases in Uganda of the Tutsi-dominated Rwandan Patriotic Front (*Front Patriotique Rwandais*—FPR), obliging the government to call in French, Belgian, and Zairean troops to help repel an FPR advance on Kigali. In March 1991 a cease-fire was negotiated, although fighting continued intermittently thereafter.

On April 6, 1991, a National Synthesis Commission was charged with revising the constitution, and a draft charter was completed on April 30. On June 2 the president announced the legalization of multiparty politics, and the revised constitution was adopted on June 10, one year ahead of schedule. (Earlier, plans for a national referendum were reportedly abandoned for economic reasons.) On October 12 Justice Minister Sylvestre NSANZIMANA was named to the newly created post of prime minister, and on December 30 he announced the installation of a bipartisan administration drawn from what was now termed the National Republican Movement for Democracy and Development (*Mouvement Républicain National pour la Démocratie et le Développement*—MRNDD) and the Christian Democratic Party (*Parti Démocratique Chrétien*—PDC), one of a number of newly registered formations.

In April 1992 the Social Democratic Party (*Parti Social-Démocrate*—PSD), Liberal Party (*Parti Liberal*—PL), and Republican Democratic Party (*Parti Démocratique Républicain*—MDR), which had refused to enter the government unless an opposition leader was named prime minister, agreed to join an expanded five-party administration headed by the MDR's Dismas NSENGIYAREMYE pending legislative balloting within a year. In early June the new administration's plan to expedite a debate on a national conference and then hold general elections was foiled when the FPR ejected government forces from a large area of northern Rwanda and threatened to continue its advance unless granted a role in the administration. During preliminary talks held June 5–7 in Paris, the FPR and the government agreed to revive the March 1991 cease-fire and hold a full-scale peace conference.

The first round of talks held July 10–14, 1992, in Arusha, Tanzania, with Western and regional observers in attendance, yielded a truce and a new cease-fire to take effect July 19 and 31, respectively. Thereafter, despite reports of continued fighting, negotiations continued, and on October 31 a power-sharing protocol was announced. On January 10, 1993, following two months of debate on the composition of a transitional government, a formal peace agreement was signed that would give the FPR, MDR, PDC, PL, and PSD a majority of seats in the cabinet and National Assembly. The

MRNDD, which was assigned six cabinet seats, and a weakened presidency, denounced the agreement, saying that it categorically refused to participate in the future broad-based transitional government. By early February more than 300 people, predominantly Tutsis, had reportedly been killed in violent anti-accord demonstrations allegedly orchestrated by the MRNDD and the Coalition for the Defense of the Republic (*Coalition pour la Défense de la République*—CDR), an openly anti-Tutsi group, which had been excluded from the government. In response to continuing violence, the FPR announced that it was withdrawing from peace negotiations, and on February 8 it launched an attack on government forces in northern Rwanda near the site of a recent Tutsi massacre. However, the deployment of additional French troops (bringing their number to 600), officially to protect foreign nationals, enabled the regime to survive.

Following further negotiations with the FPR in Arusha in March 1993, Habyarimana was able in July to appoint a new coalition government of the same five "internal" parties, although this time with a more accommodating faction of the MDR, headed by Agathe UWILINGIYIMANA as prime minister. Renewed Arusha talks subsequently yielded a new 300-page treaty that was signed by President Habyarimana and FPR chair Alexis KANYERENGWE on August 4. Under the new accord, a Hutu prime minister acceptable to both sides would be named and the FPR would be allocated 5 of 21 cabinet posts in a government to be installed by September 10, with multiparty presidential and legislative elections to be held by mid-1995. In addition, a united military force would be formed, 40 percent of which would be Tutsi and 60 percent Hutu. Earlier, on June 22, the UN Security Council had voted to establish a UN Observer Mission Uganda–Rwanda (UNOMUR) to verify that no external military assistance was reaching the FPR. In accordance with the August agreement, the Security Council voted on October 4 to establish a UN Assistance Mission in Rwanda (UNAMIR), which was mandated to monitor the cease-fire and to contribute to security and national rehabilitation in the run-up to the planned elections.

Bickering among the Rwandan parties and delays in UNAMIR deployment made it impossible to meet a September 1993 deadline for the start of the transitional period or a revised target date of December 31. Thus, a new timetable was announced by Habyarimana when, on January 5, 1994, he assumed the presidency for a 22-month transitional period preparatory to multiparty elections in October 1995. However intense criticism from both the FPR and the "internal" prodemocracy parties forced the president to postpone the designation of a transitional government and interim legislature. The assassination by unknown assailants on February 21 of PSD leader and government minister Félicien GATABAZI, a Hutu who had promoted rapprochement with the FPR, provoked a new crisis. On February 22 Habyarimana declared an indefinite extension of the transitional phase amid street clashes in which the chair of the Hutu CDR, Martin BUCYANA, was slain by a mob of PSD supporters.

Previous violence in Rwanda paled in significance compared with the wholesale slaughter that followed the death of Habyarimana on April 6, 1994. Both he and President Ntaryamira of Burundi died when their plane was shot down on approach to Kigali airport. (No official determination has been made regarding responsibility for the downing of the plane.) The reaction of Hutu militants in Rwanda, led by the Presidential Guard and CDR militia, was to embark on an orgy of killing, not only of Tutsis but also of Hutus believed to favor accommodation with the FPR. Among those murdered within hours of the president's death were Prime Minister Uwilingiyimana and members of her family, at least one minister, Constitutional Court Chair Joseph KAVAUNGANDA, and ten Belgian soldiers of the UNAMIR force.

As prescribed by the constitution, the president of the National Development Council, Theodore SINDIKUBWABO, assumed the presidency on April 9, 1994, appointing an interim government headed by Jean KAMBANDA as prime minister and including the five parties represented in the previous coalition. Although a broader-based transitional administration was promised within

six weeks, the FPR rejected the legitimacy of the new government (claiming that the presidency should have passed to the president of the yet-to-be-inaugurated transitional legislature) and declared a new military offensive. On April 12, as FPR forces closed in on Kigali, the new government fled to Gitarama, some 30 miles to the south. Meanwhile, French, Belgian, and U.S. troops had been deployed in Rwanda to evacuate foreign nationals. On April 14, upon completion of the transfer of the foreign nationals, Belgium withdrew its 420-strong contingent from UNAMIR. That action, coupled with the failure of UN mediators to arrange a lasting cease-fire, prompted the UN Security Council, in a controversial decision on April 22, to vote unanimously for a reduction of UNAMIR from 2,500 to 270 personnel.

The FPR offensive and the effective absence of an international military presence served to incite the Hutu militants in Rwanda to even greater savagery against the Tutsi minority and presumed Hutu opponents. Gangs of machete-wielding soldiers and militia members reportedly roamed the countryside, engaging in systematic and indiscriminate slaughter of men, women, and children. Although numbers were impossible to verify, the death toll was estimated to be at least 200,000 by late April and perhaps as high as 800,000—a scale of killing officially described by the UN as "genocidal." The carnage caused a mass exodus from the country, both of surviving Tutsis and of Hutus fearing FPR vengeance. By early May some 1.5 million refugees had crossed into neighboring countries, creating one of the most severe humanitarian crises ever to afflict independent Africa.

Following widespread criticism of its April 22 decision, the UN Security Council on May 17, 1994, reversed itself by approving the creation of a UNAMIR II force of 5,500 troops, while embargoing arms supplies to the Rwandan combatants. Mainly at U.S. insistence, however, only 150 unarmed observers were initially dispatched, followed by an 800-strong Ghanaian contingent charged with securing Kigali airport. Deployment of the bulk of the force was contingent on a further report from the UN secretary general on its duration, mandate, and composition, and on the attitude of the warring factions to a heightened UN presence. The immediate reaction of the FPR to the UN decision was one of suspicion that UNAMIR II would forestall its imminent military victory. On May 30, with FPR forces controlling portions of Kigali, UN mediators succeeded in bringing about talks between government and rebel representatives. However, little of substance resulted from these and subsequent meetings, while a cease-fire agreement signed under the auspices of the Organization of African Unity (OAU, subsequently the African Union—AU) in Tunisia on June 14 was equally ineffectual. Accounts continued to emerge from Rwanda of atrocities, some allegedly committed by advancing FPR forces. Especially deplored in the West was the murder on June 9 by FPR soldiers (later described as "renegades" by the FPR leadership) of the (Hutu) archbishop of Kigali, two Hutu bishops, and ten Catholic priests.

The UN Security Council on June 9, 1994, unanimously extended the UNAMIR mandate for a six-month period and approved the speedy deployment of two further battalions, which were to protect civilians in Rwanda and facilitate the international relief effort. However, difficulties and delays in assembling and equipping the UNAMIR force (most of which was to be provided by African states) led France to propose on June 15 that it should dispatch 2,500 troops pending the arrival of the enlarged UNAMIR contingent. The Security Council endorsed the French proposal on June 22 (albeit with five members abstaining), and French troops (supported by a small Senegalese contingent) arrived in Rwanda the next day. The result was the establishment of a large "safe area" southeast of Lake Kivu for surviving Tutsis as well as for Hutus fleeing the advancing FPR forces.

The FPR leadership expressed strong opposition to the French deployment, disputing the French claim to nonpartisanship in the conflict in light of the French record of support for the Hutu-based Habyarimana regime. Moving quickly to consolidate its position, the FPR completed its capture of Kigali on July 4, 1994, and two weeks later declared itself the victor in the civil war. On July 19

the Front installed a new transitional government, with a moderate Hutu, Pasteur BIZIMUNGU, as president, and another Hutu, Faustin TWAGIRA-MUNGU (the opposition's nominee for the post following the August 1993 agreement) as prime minister. The FPR military commander, Maj. Gen. Paul KAGAME, became vice president and defense minister, while Tutsis took most of the remaining portfolios. In addition to the FPR and MDR, the PDC, PL, and PSD were represented in the new administration, while the MRNDD and CDR were excluded.

Because of widespread reports of mass killings, the Office of the UN High Commissioner for Refugees (UNHCR) in September 1994 suspended its policy of encouraging Rwandan refugees in Zaire to return home, and on November 8 the Security Council established an International Criminal Tribunal for Rwanda (ICTR) to prosecute those responsible for genocide "and other serious violations of international humanitarian law." Subsequently, the 70-member Transitional National Assembly provided for under the 1993 Arusha agreement convened in Kigali on December 12 (see Legislature, below).

On April 22, 1995, the image of the FPR-controlled government was severely tarnished by the Tutsi-dominated army's massacre of some 2,000 Hutus in the Kibeho refugee camp near Gikongoro. The universally condemned action slowed the voluntary return of Rwandans from Zaire, in addition to setting back efforts to secure badly needed international aid. This and other atrocities by the victorious Tutsis were reportedly the reason for the resignation of Prime Minister Twagiramungu on August 28, with Pierre-Célestin RWIGEMA, the relatively obscure primary and secondary education minister, being named three days later as Twagiramungu's successor and the head of a government which included a number of new Tutsi members in posts formerly assigned to Hutus. By all accounts, however, Major General Kagame remained the most powerful figure in the administration, and on March 24, 2000, he moved into the presidency following the resignation of President Bizimungu. Earlier, on March 8, Bernard

MAKUSA, a relatively unknown former ambassador to Burundi and Germany, was appointed to succeed Rwigema as prime minister.

Prime Minister Rwigema's resignation in late February 2000 was attributed to his deteriorating relationship with the Transitional National Assembly (which was investigating alleged financial improprieties on the part of government officials) as well as conflict with other MDR leaders. Likewise, an intraparty power struggle in the FPR apparently contributed to the resignation of President Bizimungu in March. The installation of Major General Kagame as president merely formalized his already de facto authority. Kagame called upon all Rwandan refugees to return home and pledged to pursue national reconciliation, although his status as the nation's first Tutsi president since independence created additional unease for those already concerned over the lack of Hutu representation in government. That worry was not alleviated by the March 2001 district elections, in which party activity was again barred and most of the successful candidates appeared to be aligned with the FPR.

In April 2003 the Transitional National Assembly approved a new draft constitution that was put before voters in a national referendum on May 26, 2003. The new basic law was approved by a 93.4 percent vote and became effective June 4. Among other provisions, the constitution created a bicameral legislature and provided for direct elections of the president. In an effort to prevent further ethnic conflict, the constitution also prohibited any parties based solely on race, gender, or religion. However, some opposition parties and international human rights groups charged that this provision was enacted to reinforce the political domination of the FPR.

Prior to the presidential elections, the constitutional court ruled that the MDR and the PDC were illegal parties because of their role in the events of 1994. Consequently, the MDR candidate—former prime minister Twagiramungu—and the PDC candidate—Jean-Népomuscéne NAYINZIRA—were forced to run as independents. At the balloting on August 25, 2003, Kagame was elected with 95.1 percent of the vote, followed by Twagiramungu with 3.6 percent and Nayinzira with 1.3 percent.

Legislative balloting took place September 29–30 and October 2, 2003. Of the 53 directly contested seats, a coalition led by the FPR secured 40 seats; the PSD, 7; and the PL, 6. Makusa was reappointed prime minister and formed a new government on October 19.

Constitution and Government

Under the 1978 constitution, executive power was vested in a president elected by universal suffrage for a five-year term, the president of the MRND being the only candidate. He presided over a Council of Ministers, which he appointed, with the secretary general of the MRND being empowered to serve as interim president should the incumbent be incapacitated. A unicameral National Development Council, also elected for a five-year term, was to share legislative authority with the president and, by four-fifths vote, could censure (but not dismiss) him.

On June 10, 1991, President Habyarimana signed into law a new charter distinguished by the introduction of a multiparty system and the separation of executive, legislative, and judiciary powers. Under the 1991 constitution, executive powers were shared by the president and a presidentially appointed prime minister, who named his own cabinet. In addition, the legislature's presiding officer was empowered to serve as interim president if the incumbent left the country or became incapacitated. The constitution also stated that while political party formations could organize along ethnic and tribal lines, they had to be open to all.

On May 5, 1995, the Transitional National Assembly that had convened five months earlier adopted a new constitution incorporating the essentials of the 1991 document as well as elements of the 1993 power-sharing peace agreement. On June 8, 1999, the FPR secretary general announced that the transition period, initially scheduled to expire in 1999, would be extended to 2003.

The new constitution adopted on June 4, 2003, created a bicameral legislature and provided for a directly elected president, limited to two seven-year terms. Amendments to the constitution in October 2005 reduced the number of provinces from 12 to 5, the number of districts from 106 to 30, and the number of "sectors" (local administrative units) from 1,545 to 416. The consolidation was seen as a way to save money and streamline government. In February 2006 the language in the constitution regarding property rights was strengthened to assist returning refugees in recovering their property.

The judiciary, headed by a Supreme Court, includes magistrates', prefectural, and appeals courts; a Court of Accounts; a Court of Cassation; and a Constitutional Court composed of the Court of Cassation and a Council of State. The president and vice president of the Supreme Court are elected by the Senate. (See Current issues, below, for information on the recent creation of local village courts outside the regular system.)

Foreign Relations

Under President Kayibanda, Rwandan foreign policy exhibited a generally pro-Western bias but did not exclude relations with a number of Communist countries, including the Soviet Union and the People's Republic of China. Following the 1973 coup, however, the country took a pronounced "anti-imperialist" turn; Rwanda became the first African nation to break relations with Israel as a result of the October 1973 Arab-Israeli war, and it also contributed to the support of liberation movements in southern Africa. At the same time, President Habyarimana initiated a policy of "opening" (*l'ouverture*) with adjacent countries. Despite a tradition of ethnic conflict between Burundi's ruling Tutsis and Rwanda's ruling Hutus, a number of commercial, cultural, and economic agreements were concluded during a visit by Burundian President Micombero in June 1976, while similar agreements were subsequently negotiated with Tanzania and Côte d'Ivoire. Burundi, Rwanda, and Zaire established the Economic Community of the Great Lakes Countries in 1976; two years later, Burundi, Rwanda, and Tanzania formed the Organization for the Management and Development of the Kagera River Basin.

Relations with Uganda were strained for several decades following independence by large numbers of refugees crossing the border in both directions to escape tribal-based hostilities. Following the overthrow of Ugandan President Apollo Milton Obote in 1985, some 30,000 Ugandan refugees returned from Rwanda. However, more than 200,000 Rwandan Tutsis remained in Uganda. Rwanda in 1986 urged that all the refugees be given Ugandan citizenship, but Uganda granted the status only to those with ten years of official residency. Despite continued concern over the refugee issue, agreements on trade, security, and communications strengthened relations between the countries in 1986 and 1987. On the other hand, a Ugandan plan to restrict property rights of foreigners was one of the reported impulses for the invasion of northern Rwanda by Ugandan-based rebels of the FPR in October 1990. Ugandan President Museveni denied any prior knowledge of the attack and criticized the rebels, many of whom were recent deserters of the Ugandan military; nonetheless, relations between Uganda and Rwanda deteriorated as the FPR made military inroads in the early 1990s.

In 1995 and 1996 Rwanda's foreign relations continued to be defined by the encampment of an estimated 2 million Rwandans outside its borders. In August 1995 the UN lifted its embargo on the sale of weapons to Rwanda after months of lobbying by Rwanda, which claimed that members of the former Hutu government now exiled in Zaire were engaging in cross-border guerrilla attacks. In response to the end of the embargo, Kinshasa launched a violent and unsuccessful repatriation program, claiming that Kigali was preparing to attack the refugee camps. A subsequent repatriation attempt in February 1996 strained relations even further, and throughout the first half of 1996 the two capitals accused each other of employing "destabilization" tactics. Meanwhile, in mid-April the FPR cheered the withdrawal of the last UN peacekeepers from Rwanda. (The Tutsi regime held the UN forces responsible for both allegedly collaborating in the 1994 genocide and undermining the regime's attempts to govern.) During the second half of 1996 a stunning sequence of events in Burundi, Zaire, and Tanzania, respectively, resulted in the repatriation of approximately 650,000 refugees to Rwanda. In Burundi the military coup by Tutsi officers in late July reportedly sparked fear of reprisal attacks among the refugees, and, following the departure of 130,000 people, Bujumbura on August 27 announced the closing of the last of its camps. Thereafter, in mid-November, several hundred thousand refugees were reported to have fled back across the border from their encampments in eastern Zaire after an allegedly Kigali-funded rebellion on behalf of Zairean Tutsis, the Banyamulenge, resulted in the rout of Zairean troops and Rwandan Hutu militiamen who had been seeking to establish a "Hutuland" in the region. In December Tanzanian government forces, with the tacit and unprecedented approval of the UN Office of High Commissioner for Refugees (UNHCR), forcibly repatriated over 200,000 refugees to Rwanda.

In 1997 Rwanda, along with five other nations, supported the forces of Laurent Kabila in Zaire, hoping a rebel victory there would enable Rwanda to close the rear bases of the Hutu guerrillas as well as the camps where they sought refuge. After the Kabila victory, the refugee camps along the border were closed, but guerrillas drifted across into Rwanda with returning refugees and regrouped in Rwanda. Meanwhile, Rwandan government forces who had crossed the border into the former Zaire remained in two provinces, North and South Kivu, in a de facto occupation apparently with Kabila's tacit approval. Relations between Kinshasa and Kigali subsequently deteriorated, as Kabila distanced himself from Tutsi influence, prompting hostility among the Banyamulenge Tutsis in the eastern portion of the Democratic Republic of the Congo (DRC), as Zaire had been renamed. In July 1998 Kabila announced an end to military cooperation with Rwanda, and in August a full-fledged rebellion broke out against his administration (see article on the DRC). By November Rwanda acknowledged that its troops were allied with the anti-Kabila rebels, claiming that the DRC government was rearming the Hutus responsible for the 1994 genocide.

In an unexpected turn of events, forces from Rwanda and Uganda, previously allied in support of anti-Kabila rebels in the DRC, clashed in northeast DRC in August 1999, with underlying factors apparently including support for different anti-Kabila factions in the DRC and perhaps most importantly, rivalry regarding eventual preeminence in the region. Fighting between the Rwandan and Ugandan troops erupted again in the spring of 2000.

In November 2001, Kagame began a series of meetings with the leader of Uganda, Lt.-Gen. Yoweri Museveni. Following mediation efforts by South Africa and the United Kingdom, in 2003, the two governments agreed to take stronger action to prevent rebels and dissident groups from crossing each other's borders and initiating conflicts. In addition, the two heads of state agreed on the voluntary repatriation of 26,000 Rwandans remaining in refugee camps in Uganda. In July 2002 a peace accord was signed in Pretoria, South Africa, between Rwanda and the DRC. By October, all 23,400 Rwandan troops had withdrawn from the DRC, and in September 2003 the two countries reestablished diplomatic relations.

In March 2005, the government offered to contribute troops to the proposed UN peacekeeping mission in Darfur, Sudan. Rwanda eventually lent 2,000 soldiers to that effort.

In May 2006 President Kagame met with U.S. President George W. Bush in Washington. The United States announced at the meeting that it was increasing its bilateral aid to Rwanda.

Current Issues

By the end of 1997 an estimated 1.5 million refugees had returned, but the FPR regime still fell short of fulfilling what it had delineated as one of the top prerequisites for national reconciliation—resolution of the judicial process for the tens of thousands of predominantly Hutu prisoners imprisoned (in reportedly subhuman conditions) for their alleged roles in the 1994 genocide. In fact, the FPR continued to be plagued by charges, largely unsubstantiated, that the Tutsi-controlled military was engaging in its own campaign of revenge killings. Meanwhile, the ICTR—26 justices assigned to more than 100,000 cases—proceeded at a glacial pace, hampered, according to a January 1998 UN internal investigation, by a mismanaged judicial system. By the end of 1997, three years after the massacres, the ICTR had not convicted a single defendant. Kigali's judicial efforts, which disposed of less than 300 cases in 1997, also foundered when a plea-bargaining program failed to break the logjam, causing observers to note that, barring new developments, most prisoners would die in prison long before their cases could come to trial.

Meanwhile, the toll from ethnic conflict increased in the second half of 1997 (with at least 6,000 more murders during the year, according to UN monitors) as Hutu guerrillas grew in strength and began making daylight raids, particularly in the northwest, where they had wide popular support. Although the guerrillas appeared to have no hope of a military victory, their attacks seemed aimed at making Rwanda ungovernable.

During ICTR testimony in February 1998 the former UNAMIR commander in Rwanda said he had advised the UN leadership of the impending genocide and asked for authorization (never granted) to prevent it. Similarly, a report by the Belgian parliament released in February 1998 claimed the Belgian, French, and U.S. governments also had credible advance warning of the genocide. U.S. President Bill Clinton visited Rwanda in March as part of an African tour, and he acknowledged that the United States and other Western nations had been slow to react to the developments of 1994. (In July 2000 an OAU panel strongly criticized the United States, France, Belgium, the UN, and others—including church groups—for failing to prevent or stop the genocide and called for a "significant level of reparations.")

In April 1998 Rwanda publicly executed 22 persons convicted of murders committed during 1994, and by June thousands of other prisoners had pleaded guilty, apparently to avoid death sentences.

In early September the ICTR (recently expanded by the UN in response to widespread criticism) issued its first guilty verdict. Shortly thereafter, the tribunal sentenced former interim prime minister Jean Kambanda to life in prison following his conviction on genocide charges. (Kambanda had admitted his guilt earlier and had reportedly provided evidence against other officials.)

Despite the ongoing judicial quagmire, a degree of normalcy had returned to Rwanda by early 1999, as evidenced by the successful completion of nonparty local elections in March, the first balloting since 1988. At the same time, however, instability persisted near the DRC border, hundreds of thousands of civilians having moved into camps protected by government troops. International attention also remained focused on the Rwandan government's significant role in the DRC civil war (see article on the DRC). Under those circumstances, it was not surprising that the transitional government in July extended its mandate for four more years, with FPR leaders concluding that security conditions did not permit the organization of multiparty elections.

The return to normality continued with the government in December 2001 adopting a new flag, national anthem, and national seal. However, Hutu groups continued to assert periodic discrimination and retaliation by the FPR-dominated government. Domestically, hopes for Tutsi-Hutu reconciliation rested, in part, on the reestablishment in early 2002 of the traditional *gacaca* system, in which elected village judges were to adjudicate the cases of some 90,000 detainees still facing charges relating to the events of 1994. (Most of the other cases, involving those accused of ordering mass killings or participating in rapes, were to be handled by the normal court system. Meanwhile, the "masterminds" of the genocide still faced trial at the ICTR, which as of April 2002 had arrested 60 of the 75 people who had been indicted so far. Only eight convictions had been achieved by that time, although a number of high-profile cases were on the docket for the remainder of the year.)

In January 2003, the government ordered the release of 40,000 detainees, but reserved the right to arrest the released people if new evidence emerged. By the end of the year, some 25,000 had been released. Survivor groups severely criticized the measure, claiming that many involved in the genocide were being released. Meanwhile, the *gacaca* courts began to adjudicate an increasing number of cases. In August 2003, one *gacaca* court convicted 105 people in a mass two-day trial.

The passage of the new constitution and subsequent presidential and legislative elections in 2003 finalized the transition to civilian government. Defeated presidential candidate Faustin Twagiramungu protested the official results, claiming that widespread irregularities had occurred. However, the Supreme Court ruled against him, and international observers characterized the balloting as generally free and fair, despite certain significant problems.

By March 2005 the ICTR had convicted 22 defendants and acquitted 3. In addition to complaints about the continued slow pace of case resolution, criticism emanated from Rwandan Hutus over the fact that no Tutsis had been indicted by the ICTR, despite Hutu assertions that revenge killings and other atrocities had been committed by Tutsis from the FPR in 1994. Meanwhile, the *gacaca* courts faced a backlog of some 95,000 cases by the end of the year. Tension also arose from the release of documents from the Kambanda trial that appeared to support Tutsi arguments that the Hutu attacks in 1994 had been well coordinated and discussed in advance at high levels of government.

Reports surfaced in mid-2006 of a possible power struggle within the Kagame administration. For his part, the president pointed to the nation's recent economic progress (see The Country, above) as evidence of effective governance. He also emphasized that a former Rwandan finance minister had recently been named president of the African Development Bank, while another Rwandan had been named one of the four deputy directors of the World Trade Organization. Kagame described those events as indications of success in his efforts to elevate the status and visibility of Rwanda in the international community.

Political Parties

A one-party state after the 1973 coup, Rwanda adopted a multiparty constitution on June 10, 1991. By mid-1993 it was reported that 17 parties, including the preexisting National Republican Movement for Democracy and Development (MRNDD), had been recognized. However, the MRNDD was not included in the government installed in July 1994 after the military victory of the FPR over the forces of the previous regime. Party candidates were not permitted at the March 1999 village elections or the March 2001 communal balloting, the government concluding that party activity might exacerbate ethnic tensions.

Under the terms of the 2003 constitution, the government has the power to ban political parties that might advocate civic unrest or exacerbate ethnic differences. Using this provision, the government banned the MDR, PDC, and several smaller parties prior to the 2003 elections (see below).

Government and Progovernment Parties

Rwandan Patriotic Front (*Front Patriotique Rwandais*—FPR). Currently the dominant political force in Rwanda, the FPR is a largely Tutsi formation that invaded Rwanda in October 1990 from Uganda under the command of Rwandan refugees who were formerly officers in the Ugandan armed forces. However, most of the original leadership, including FPR founder Fred RWIGYEMA, were killed in fighting with government troops in late 1990 and early 1991.

Buoyed by a series of stunning victories in early June 1992, which yielded control of much of northern Rwanda, the FPR called on the Rwandan government to integrate FPR members into both the military and the government, reduce the president's power, allow all refugees to return, and hold multiparty elections. The FPR signed the Arusha peace agreement on August 4, 1993, but implementation was subject to repeated delays. The massacres of Tutsis and moderate Hutus, which followed the death of President Habyarimana in April 1994, impelled the FPR to launch a new offensive, which brought it to power three months later. The victory was attributed largely to the military leadership of Maj. Gen. Paul Kagame, who, although designated as vice president in the new regime, was widely regarded as its preeminent figure. Kagame consolidated his power when he was elected FPR president in February 1998 and president of the republic in March 2000. Kagame was subsequently reelected president for a seven-year term in 2003. During legislative elections, the FPR led an electoral coalition that received 73.78 percent of the vote and 40 seats. (The FPR gained 33 seats alone.)

Leaders: Maj. Gen. Paul KAGAME (President of the Republic and President of the Front), Col. Alexis KANYARENGWE (Former President of the Front), Charles MURIGANDE (Secretary General).

Christian Democratic Party/Centrist Democratic Party (*Parti Démocratique Chrétien*—PDC). The PDC accepted one cabinet post in the governments of December 1991 and April 1992. A PDC member also served in the Makusa government until March 2001. Prior to the 2003 presidential elections, the PDC was banned. It reconstituted itself as the **Centrist Democratic Party** (*Parti Démocrate Centriste*—PDC) before legislative elections, and the reconstituted PDC joined the FPR-led coalition. It won three seats. Former PDC President Jean-Népomuscéne Nayinzira placed third in the national presidential polling in 2003.

Leader: Alfred MUKEZAMFURA.

Social Democratic Party (*Parti Social-Démocrate*—PSD). One of the first three opposition parties to be recognized under the 1991 constitution, the PSD was one of several prodemocracy parties that accepted cabinet posts from April 1992, and in August 1993 it was a signatory of the Arusha peace agreement. The assassination of its leader, Félicien GATABAZI, in February 1994 sparked the violence in Rwanda, which escalated to genocidal proportions from April onward. Following the death of President Habyarimana two months later, PSD president Frederic NZAMURAMBAHO and vice president Felicien NGANGO also died. The PSD's Juvénal Nksui, then speaker of the assembly, was sacked by the legislature in March 1997 and

accused of incompetence after failing to sign into law a bill passed by the assembly that would make the president accountable to it. The PSD won six seats in the 2003 legislative elections. Party leader Vincent Biruta was elected to the Senate and was subsequently elected speaker of that body. The PSD participated in the subsequent Kagame unity government.

Leader: Vincent BIRUTA (Speaker of the Senate), Juvénal NKSUI (Former Speaker of the Assembly), Jacqueline MUHONGAYRIE.

Liberal Party (*Parti Liberal*—PL). Joining the MDR and PSD in refusing to enter the Nsanzimana government of December 1991, the PL accepted three cabinet posts under the MDR's Dismas Nsengiyaremye in April 1992 and also participated in subsequent coalitions, becoming as a consequence split into progovernment and antigovernment factions. The latter joined the government installed by the FPR following its military victory in July 1994. The PL's Joseph SEBARENZI became speaker of the assembly when that body sacked Juvénal Nksui (see PSD, above); however, Sebarenzi resigned his speaker's position in January 2000 amid a power struggle within the party and in the face of parliamentary criticism. He was subsequently reported to have assumed self-imposed exile in the United States. Prosper Higiro became party chair in 2001. In the 2003 elections, the PL secured seven seats. The PL was given a cabinet post in the subsequent Kagame unity government.

Leaders: Prosper HIGIRO (Chair), Esdra KAYIRANGA, Joseph MUSENGIMANA, Odette NYIRAMIRIMO.

Other progovernment parties that contested the 2003 legislative elections included the **Islamic Democratic Party** (*Parti Démocratique Islamique*—PDI), formed in 1992 and led by André Bumaya HABIB; the **Rwandan People's Democratic Union** (*Union Démocratique du Peuple Rwandais*—UDPR), formed in 1992 and led by Adrien RANGIRA; and the **Rwandan Socialist Party** (*Parti Socialiste Rwandais*—PSR), a workers' rights party launched in 1991 and led by Medard RUTIJANWA.

Other Parties and Groups

Party for Progress and Concord (*Parti pour le Progrès et la Concorde*—PPC). The PPC was formed in 2003 after the MDR was outlawed. It is comprised mainly of Hutus. In the 2003 legislative elections, the PPC received 2.2 percent of the vote, below the 5 percent threshold needed for representation.

Leader: Christian MARARA.

Republican Democratic Movement (*Mouvement Démocratique Républicain*—MDR). A predominantly Hutu party, which draws its support from the central Rwandan capital region, the MDR is a direct descendant of Grégoire Kayibanda's Parmehutu—MDR, which was banned in 1973. The current party was legally registered on July 31, 1991, and in November it led, along with the recently recognized PL and PSR (above), a march in Kigali in support of a national conference. From April 1992 the MDR headed successive coalition governments that included other prodemocracy parties, although the appointment of the MRD's Agathe Uwilingiyimana as prime minister in July 1993 was strongly opposed by an antiregime MDR faction. Meanwhile one of the MDR's leaders, Emmanuel GAPYISI, who had also served as president of the Forum for Peace and Democracy (a group opposed to both President Habyarimana and the FPR), had been assassinated on May 19, 1993.

The MDR was a signatory of the August 1993 Arusha peace agreement with the rebel FPR, and Faustin Twagiramungu (of the MDR antiregime wing) became the agreed nominee of the prodemocracy parties for the premiership in the envisaged transitional government. Many MDR members, including Uwilingiyimana, were killed by Hutu extremists in the bloodletting that followed President Habyarimana's death in April 1994. Early in May the antigovernment MDR faction formed an alliance called the Democratic Forces for Change (*Forces Démocratiques pour le Changement*—FDC) with the opposition faction of the PL, the PDC, and the PSD (above). The eventual military victory of the FPR resulted in Twagiramungu being appointed prime minister of a transitional government in July; he resigned in late August 1995.

The appointment of Pierre-Célestin Rwigema as Twagiramungu's prime ministerial successor exacerbated the intraparty rift between Twagiramungu's antiregime followers and the so-called "liberal" wing of the party, led by Rwigema and Anastase GASANA, the foreign affairs minister whom Twagiramungu's allies had labeled an FPR "straw man." For his part, Gasana was a vocal critic of the former prime minister, describing his government as guilty of "inaction and inefficiency." In December 1995 Twagiramungu rejected as "null and void" a motion forwarded by Gasana, Jean-Pierre BIZIMANA, and Laurien NGIRABANZI to force him from his party post. Subsequently, in March 1996 Twagiramungu split from the MDR to create a new anti-FPR grouping (see FRD, below).

In August 1998 the MDR's executive committee was dissolved, and party president Bonaventure UBALIJORO, who had been arrested in July, was dismissed and succeeded by Prime Minister Rwigema. In March 1999 four members of the party were expelled from the legislature, three for alleged involvement with the *Interahamwe*, the extremist Hutu militias. The fourth, Jacques M*aniraguha*, had repeated allegations made by a local official on trial for genocide that Prime Minister Rwigema had armed the *Interahamwe* just before the genocide of 1994. In April the prime minister, on behalf of the party, asked the Rwandan people to forgive the MDR for its role in 1994. Rwigema was subsequently reported to have feuded with other MDR leaders, and the party's political bureau approved changes in MDR governing bodies (although keeping Rwigema as party president) prior to Rwigema's resignation from his prime minister's post in February 2000. Rwigema subsequently moved to the United States, Rwanda issuing an international warrant for his arrest in connection with the events of 1994. Meanwhile, the MDR, which had expelled Rwigema in August 2000, reaffirmed its support in 2001 for the "collegial" power-sharing agreement with the FPR.

Prior to the 2003 legislative elections, the National Assembly voted to dissolve the MDR under the terms of the 2003 constitution. Former MDR member Twagiramungu ran for the presidency in 2003 and placed third. Many members of the MDR joined the new Hutu-based party, the Party for Progress and Concord (*Parti pour le Progrés et la Concorde*—PPC).

Party for Democracy and Renewal (*Parti pour la Démocratie et le Renouveau*—PDR). Formed in mid-2001 by former president Pasteur Bizimungu after he had resigned his government post following an apparent disagreement with Maj. Gen. Kagame of the FPR, the PDR (also known as *ubuyanja*, Renewal) was subsequently banned by the government on the grounds that the new grouping promoted ethnic hostility. Bizimungu, a Hutu who had served as an "icon of reconciliation" during his presidency, was arrested in mid-2002. He was convicted in 2004 on charges of embezzlement and incitement to civil disobedience and sentenced to 15 years in prison.

Leader: Pasteur BIZIMUNGU (Former President of the Republic).

Rally for Return and Democracy (*Rassemblement pour la Démocratie et le Retour*—RDR). Based in the refugee camps of eastern DRC, the RDR is the most prominent of the exile political groupings. The RDR has been critical of the UNHCR's compliance with FPR demands, claiming that a forced repatriation of the Hutu refugees "would mean handing over the refugees to their torturers." In January 1997 the RDR denounced the genocide trials of Hutus as a "mockery of justice," claiming, for example, that alleged murderers were falsely accused by those who wanted their property. In June the RDR reportedly decided to become a political party, while in April 2000 the grouping reacted in a conciliatory manner to President Kagame's inaugural speech in which he urged exiles to return home.

Leaders: Charles NDEREYENE, François NZABAHIMANA.

Resistance Forces for Democracy (*Forces de Résistance pour la Démocratie*—FRD). The FRD, listed in a previous edition of the *Handbook* under its provisional name, United Political Forces, was launched by former Hutu prime minister Faustin Twagiramungu and former interior minister Seth SENDASHONGHA in Brussels on March 26, 1996, following their breaks from the MDR and FPR, respectively. Both had been sacked by the government in August 1995 after objecting to an expansion of army power, which the military claimed was necessary to hunt down perpetrators of genocide. Highlighting the new party's platform were calls for the ouster of the Tutsi regime (which the FRD cited as an unbreachable impediment to the return of Rwanda's primarily Hutu refugees) and the drafting of a new power-sharing constitution based on the 1993 Arusha peace agreement. Furthermore, the FRD accused the FPR regime of engaging in "genocide" against the Hutu population. Two of the party's key leaders were in exile, Twagiramungu in Brussels and Sendashongha in Nairobi, when the latter was assassinated in May 1998. Moderates had wanted Sendashongha to return to Kigali to lead reconciliation efforts. Twagiramungu strongly criticized President Kagame's call in April 2000 for exiles to return to Rwanda, charging that Kagame was attempting to cover up his "crimes against humanity." Nonetheless, Twagiramungu returned to Rwanda in June 2003 and launched a bid for the presidency as an independent. He placed second in the balloting, but challenged the results. His challenge was overturned by the Supreme Court.

Leader: Faustin TWAGIRAMUNGU (Former Prime Minister).

Democratic Forces for the Liberation of Rwanda (*Forces Démocratiques pour la Libération du Rwanda*—FDLR). Described in 2004 and early 2005 as one of the last major organized resistance groups outside Rwanda, the Hutu FDLP was accused by some Western leaders of involvement in the killing of civilians in the DRC. In March 2005 the FDLR formally apologized for its role in the 1994 killings in Rwanda. In April 2005 the FDLR declared it was disarming, and the leadership announced the group's intention

Cabinet

As of June 1, 2006

Prime Minister	Bernard Makusa (ind.)

Ministers

Agriculture and Animal Resources	Anastase Murekezi
Commerce, Industry, and Tourism	Protais Mitali
Defense	Maj. Gen. Marcel Gatsinzi (ind.)
Education	Jean d'Arc Mujawamariya
Finance and Economic Planning	James Musoni
Foreign Affairs	Charles Murigande (FPR)
Health	Jean-Damascène Ntawukuliryayo (PSD)
Infastructure	Stanislas Kamanzi
Internal Security	Sheikh Fazil Musa Harerimana
Justice	Edda Mukabagwiza [f]
Labor and Civil Service	Paul-Manasseh Nshuti
Lands, Environment, Forestry, Water, and Mines	Christophe Bazivamo (FPR)
Local Government and Social Affairs	Protais Musoni
President's Office	Solina Nyirahabimana [f]
President's Office in charge of Science, Technology, and Research	Romain Murenzi (PL)
Prime Minister's Office in charge of Gender and Women in Development	Valérie Nyirahabineza (ind.) [f]
Prime Minister's Office in charge of Information	Laurent Nkusi (PL)
Youth, Culture, and Sports	Joseph Habineza

Ministers of State

Agriculture	Daphrose Gahakwa
Energy and Communication	Albert Butare
Environmental Protection	Patricia Hajabakiga [f]
Finance and Economic Planning	Monique Nsanzabaganwa [f]
Foreign Cooperation	Rosemary Museminari [f]
HIV/AIDS and other Infectious Diseases	Innocent Nyaruhirira
Industry and Investment Promotion	Vincent Karega
Primary and Secondary Education	Joseph Murekeraho
Rural Development and Social Affairs	Christine Nyatanyi [f]
Skills Development and Labor	Angelina Muganza [f]
Water and Natural Resources	Bikoro Munyanganizi

[f] = female

to return to Rwanda from the DRC and to try to establish a legal political movement.

FDLP leader Ignace MURWANASHYAKA was arrested in Germany in April 2006 on alleged immigration violations. The Rwandan government asked for his extradition, but the German government refused the request.

It was reported in early 2002 that two exile groups in Belgium—the **African Democratic Congress** and the **Movement for Peace,**

Democracy, and Development—had launched a new anti-Kagame coalition called the **Rwandan Democratic Alliance**. Another opposition coalition—the **Alliance for Democracy and National Recovery**—was reportedly launched in Brussels in April under the leadership of Valens KAJEGUHAKWA.

Legislature

Prior to the resumption of hostilities between the Rwandan armed forces and the Rwandan Patriotic Front in April 1994, the legislature consisted of a unicameral National Development Council (*Conseil pour le Développement National*) of 70 members elected on December 26, 1988, from 140 candidates nominated by the MRND. Under the terms of the power-sharing agreement reached by the government and FPR on January 10, 1993, and confirmed by the Arusha peace agreement of August 4, 1993, a transitional legislative body was formally launched on December 12, 1994.

Under the terms of the 2003 constitution, a bicameral **Parliament** was created.

Senate. The Senate consists of 26 indirectly elected members who serve eight-year terms. Twelve senators are elected by regional councils; eight are appointed by the president; four are elected by a regulatory forum of the country's political parties; and the remaining two are elected by university staffs and faculty. In addition, former presidents of the republic can request to be members of the Senate. The first senators were sworn in on October 10, 2003.

Speaker: Vincent BIRUTA.

Chamber of Deputies. The lower house consists of 80 members who serve five-year terms. Fifty-three are directly elected by a system of proportional representation in which parties must achieve a 5 percent threshold to gain representation. Two deputies are elected by the National Youth Council and one by the Federation of the Associations of the Disabled. The remaining 24 deputies are elected by a joint council, which includes representatives from provincial, district, and city governments, as well as members of the executive committees of women's groups at various regional levels. Following the balloting of September 29–30 and October 2, 2003, the 53 popularly elected seats were divided as follows: Rwandan Patriotic Front, 33; Liberal Party, 7; Social Democratic Party, 6; Centrist Democratic Party, 3; Islamic Democratic Party, 2; Rwandan People's Democratic Union, 1; and the Rwandan Socialist Party, 1.

Speaker: Alfred MUKEZAMFURA.

Communications

Press

On August 14, 1991, the legislature adopted a press law guaranteeing, with certain restrictions, a free press. Most papers stopped publishing as the result of the 1994 genocide, although the situation has since returned to normal. The press is generally considered to be supportive of the government and exercises a degree of self-censorship in that regard. There are no daily papers; the government information office in Kigali publishes *Imvaho* (The Truth, 51,000), a weekly in Kinyarwanda, and *La Relève* (Relief, 1,700), a monthly in French. The weekly *Umuseso* is generally perceived as the most independent publication; progovernment (according to the journalism watchdog organization Reporters Without Frontiers) publications include *The New Times, L'Enjeu, Grand Lacs Lebdo,* and *L'Horizon.*

News Agency

The official facility is *Agence Rwandaise de Presse* (ARP).

Broadcasting and Computing

The government-controlled Radio Rwanda broadcasts daily in Kinyarwanda, Kiswahili, and French. Deutsche Welle Relay Kigali broadcasts in German, French, English, Hausa, Kiswahili, Portuguese, and Amharic. The government's Television Rwanda is the only TV facility. There were approximately 718,000 radio and 864,000 television receivers in 1999, with some 30,000 Internet users reported in 2003.

Intergovernmental Representation

Ambassador to the U.S.
Zac NSENGA

U.S. Ambassador to Rwanda
Michael R. ARIETTI

Permanent Representative to the UN
Joseph NSENGIMANA

IGO Memberships (Non-UN):
AfDB, AU, BADEA, CEEAC, CEPGL, Comesa, Interpol, IOM, NAM, OIF, WCO, WTO

SAO TOME AND PRINCIPE

DEMOCRATIC REPUBLIC OF SAO TOME AND PRINCIPE

República Democrática de São Tomé e Príncipe

The Country

Located in the Gulf of Guinea some 125 miles off the coast of Gabon, Sao Tome and Principe embraces a small archipelago of two main islands (after which the country is named) and four islets: Cabras, Gago Coutinho, Pedras Tinhosas, and Rolas. Volcanic in origin, the islands exhibit numerous craters and lava flows; the climate is warm and humid most of the year. Of mixed ancestry, the indigenous inhabitants are mainly descended from plantation laborers imported from the African mainland. The Portuguese population, estimated at more than 3,000 before independence, has reportedly declined to less than 100. Roman Catholicism is the principal religion. Women constitute about one-third of the economically active population and hold a limited number of leadership positions in politics and government.

Sao Tome and Principe was once the world's leading producer of cocoa, although production has declined in recent years. Tourism and construction now contribute more to economic growth, and oil revenues from the Gulf are expected to dominate the economy in coming years. Most food is imported, often in the form of donations, with copra, coffee, palm kernels, sugar, and bananas produced domestically. Consumables dominate the small industrial sector. The country relies heavily on foreign aid because cyclical droughts, low world cocoa prices since 1980, and the flight of Portuguese managers and skilled labor at independence haven taken a toll on the economy. The government began moving away from a Marxist orientation in the mid-1980s; recent emphasis has been on denationalization (most importantly in the cocoa industry), encouragement of foreign investment, reduction of subsidies, currency devaluation, and other "pragmatic" liberalization measures that have won the support of the International Monetary Fund (IMF) and World Bank. In addition, the government has tried to diversify the economy by developing fishing and tourism.

In 1998 the World Bank ranked Sao Tome and Principe third on its list of the world's 40 most heavily indebted poor countries. Consequently, the government adopted a structural adjustment program proposed by the IMF, which was designed to reduce the budget deficit, address the high external debt, intensify privatization, promote foreign

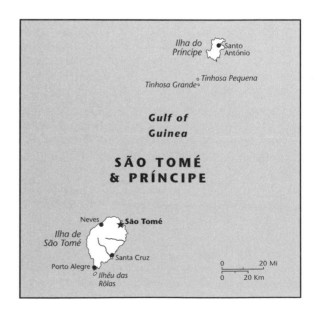

Political Status: Achieved independence from Portugal on July 12, 1975; constitution of November 5, 1975, revised in December 1982, October 1987, August 1990, and March 2003.

Area: 387 sq. mi. (1,001 sq. km.).

Population: 137,599 (2001C); 188,000 (2005E).

Major Urban Center (2005E): SAO TOME (53,600).

Official Language: Portuguese.

Monetary Unit: Dobra (market rate July 1, 2006: 6,825 dobras = $1US).

President: Fradique de MENEZES; popularly elected (as a member of Independent Democratic Action) on July 29, 2001, and sworn in for a five-year term on September 3 to succeed Miguel Anjos da Cunha Lisboa TROVOADA (Independent Democratic Action); reelected (as the candidate of the alliance of the Democratic Movement of Forces for Change and the Party of Democratic Convergence) on July 30, 2006, and inaugurated for a second five-year term on September 3.

Prime Minister: Tomé Soares da VERA CRUZ (Democratic Movement of Forces for Change); appointed by the president following the legislative elections on March 26, 2006, and inaugurated on April 21 as head of a minority government in succession to Maria do Carmo SILVEIRA (Movement for the Liberation of Sao Tome and Principe–Social Democratic Party).

investment, and reduce unemployment. GDP grew by 2.5 percent in 1999 and 2.9 percent in 2000, while inflation continued its downward trend to 13 percent in 1999 and 9.6 percent in 2000. In early 2000 the IMF congratulated the government for having achieved "a good measure of stability" in the economy, and the IMF subsequently agreed to a three-year support program designed to solidify the recent structural reforms, combat widespread poverty, and alleviate the "unsustainable" external debt burdens. In the latter regard, the Paris Club of creditor nations approved a three-year debt reduction plan. The country expected to receive the benefit of another $200 million in debt relief in 2006, in accordance with terms of an IMF-sponsored Highly Indebted Poor Countries (HIPC) program. Meanwhile, offshore oil surveys have brought rough estimates of large deposits of oil in the Gulf. No reserves have yet been proven, but Sao Tome and Principe shares an economic development zone with Nigeria that is believed to hold more than 10 billion barrels of crude. The petroleum resources are scheduled to be developed in accordance with an arrangement that will give Nigeria 60 percent of the revenue and Sao Tome and Principe 40 percent.

Government and Politics

Political Background

Discovered by Portuguese explorers in 1471, Sao Tome and Principe became Portuguese territories between 1522 and 1523 and, collectively, an Overseas Province of Portugal in 1951. Nationalistic sentiments became apparent in 1960 with the formation of the Committee for the Liberation of Sao Tome and Principe (CLSTP). In 1972 the CLSTP became the Movement for the Liberation of Sao Tome and Principe (MLSTP), which quickly became the leading advocate of independence from Portugal. Based in Gabon under the leadership of Dr. Manuel Pinto da COSTA, the group carried out a variety of underground activities, particularly in support of protests by African workers against low wages.

In 1973 the Organization of African Unity (OAU, subsequently the African Union—AU) recognized the MLSTP, and in the same year Portugal granted the country local autonomy. After the 1974 military coup in Lisbon, the Portuguese government began negotiations with the MLSTP, which it recognized as sole official spokesperson for the islands. The two agreed in November 1974 that independence would be proclaimed on July 12, 1975, and that a transitional government would be formed under MLSTP leadership until that time. Installed on December 21, 1974, the transitional government council encompassed four members appointed by the MLSTP and one by Portugal. Upon independence, da Costa assumed the presidency and promptly designated his MLSTP associate, Miguel Anjos da Cunha Lisboa TROVOADA, as prime minister. In December 1978, however, Trovoada was relieved of his duties, and in October 1979 he was arrested on charges that he had been involved in a projected coup, one of a series that da Costa claimed to have foiled with the aid of Angolan troops. The president subsequently served as both head of state and chief executive without serious domestic challenge, despite Trovoada's release in 1981. In late 1987 the government, which had already introduced many economic liberalization measures, launched a political liberalization campaign as well (see Constitution and government, below). One of the first official changes was the revival of the office of prime minister; Celestino Rocha da COSTA was appointed to the post in January 1988.

The reform process culminated in an August 1990 referendum that endorsed abandonment of the country's single-party system, and on January 20, 1991, the recently legalized Party of Democratic Convergence (PCD) out-distanced the now restyled MLSTP-Social Democratic Party (MLSTP-PSD) by winning 33 of 55 National Assembly seats. On February 8 the PCD General Secretary, Daniel Lima dos Santos DAIO, was named to head a new government, and on March 3 former prime minister Trovoada secured election as head of state. President da Costa had earlier announced his retirement from public life.

Prime Minister Daio, who was viewed as being responsible for economic hardship generated by an IMF-mandated austerity program, was dismissed on April 22, 1992, in favor of his finance minister, Norberto José d'Alva COSTA ALEGRE. Despite an MLSTP-PSD call for a unity government, the cabinet announced by Costa Alegre on May 16 was composed solely of PCD members.

On July 2, 1994, Trovoada sacked Costa Alegre in favor of Evaristo de CARVALHO, who, although a PCD member, had long been close to the president. Four days later Carvalho was expelled from the PCD, which called for a new presidential election. Trovoada responded on the nights of July 7 and 8 by appointing a Carvalho-recommended government of "presidential friends." On July 10, after the PCD had announced that it intended to introduce a motion declaring the new administration unconstitutional, Trovoada dissolved the National Assembly and called for the election of a successor.

At legislative balloting on October 2, 1994, the MLSTP-PSD returned to power with the capture of a near-majoritarian 27 seats, while the PCD and President Trovoada's recently legalized Independent Democratic Action (ADI) party each secured 14. On October 25 Trovoada appointed MLSTP-PSD secretary general Carlos Alberto Dias Monteiro da GRAÇA prime minister. Although da Graça had pledged to form a government of "national union," he named a cabinet dominated by MLSTP-PSD members on October 28.

On August 16, 1995, a group of Cuban-trained rebel soldiers led by Lt. Orlando das NEVES stormed the presidential palace, taking President Trovoada prisoner; however, Trovoada resumed his duties a week later after issuing a pardon to the officers who had seized him. Among the concessions reportedly made to secure Trovoada's release were pledges to name the long-anticipated unity government and restructure the military.

In anticipation of the formation of a multiparty government on December 29, 1995, the MLSTP-PSD, the ADI, and the Opposition Democratic Coalition (Codo) signed a cooperation pact. Two days later, MLSTP-PSD deputy secretary general Armindo Vaz de ALMEIDA was named to replace da Graça as prime minister, and on January 5, 1996, he named a cabinet that included seven members from the MLSTP-PSD, four from the ADI, and one from Codo, despite Codo's lack of legislative representation.

At delayed presidential balloting on June 30, 1996, Trovoada led a five-man field with 40.85 percent of the vote, followed by former president da Costa (39.14 percent), the PCD's Alda BANDEIRA (14.63 percent), former prime minister da

Graça, and Armindo TOMBA, an anticorruption journalist. In a second-round runoff on July 21, Trovoada defeated da Costa on a 52–48 percent split.

On September 20, 1996, an assembly non-confidence motion reportedly orchestrated by the assembly president, Fortunato PIRES, forced the resignation of the Almeida government. Later MLSTP-PSD efforts to have Pires appointed to the vacant post were blocked, however, by Trovoada and the ADI, and on November 13 Trovoada appointed the MLSTP-PSD's deputy secretary general, Raúl Bragança NETO, prime minister. On November 28 Neto named a government that included six MLSTP-PSD ministers, three from the PCD, and one independent.

Shrugging off responsibility for Sao Tome and Principe's economic plight, the MLSTP-PSD captured a majority of the legislative seats (31) at polling on November 8, 1998, with the ADI improving to 16 seats and the PCD falling to 8. The MLSTP-PSD subsequently nominated Guilherme Posser da COSTA, a former foreign minister and ambassador, to be the next prime minister, and Costa and his government (comprising MLSTP-PSD members only) were sworn in on January 5, 1999.

In first-round presidential balloting on July 29, 2001, businessman Fradique de MENEZES (56.3 percent of the vote) defeated former president Manuel Pinto da Costa (38.4 percent) and three minor candidates. Several attempts to form a "cohabitation" government failed, in part because President Menezes rejected cabinet recommendations from the MLSTP-PSD. Menezes, who had been inaugurated in September, consequently dismissed Prime Minister Costa and his cabinet and then named former prime minister Carvalho to head a "presidential initiative" government including members from the ADI and the PCD. Calling the minority government "unconstitutional," the MLSTP-PSD walked out of the assembly, precipitating a political crisis that prompted President Menezes to dissolve the assembly on December 7 and call for early elections. Concurrently, news sources reported that the leading political parties had agreed to allocate cabinet posts according to the seats won by each party in the new legislative balloting.

In the assembly poll on March 3, 2002, the MLSTP-PSD secured a one-seat plurality of 24 seats over the new electoral coalition formed by the PCD and the recently launched, pro-Menezes Democratic Movement of Forces for Change (MDFM). On March 26 the president appointed Gabriel COSTA (a former leader of the MLSTP-PSD but now an independent described as "close" to the MDFM) as the new prime minister. The cabinet that took office in April contained, according to the previously determined proportion, members of the MLSTP-PSD, the MDFM-PCD coalition, and the new Uê Kédadji alliance that had been formed by the ADI, Codo, and others prior to the assembly poll, in which Codo captured third place with 8 seats.

Following a dispute between Prime Minister Costa and Defense Minister Victor MONTEIRO, President Menezes dismissed Costa and the rest of the cabinet on September 27, 2002. On October 3 the president appointed Maria das NEVES de Souza (MLSTP-PSD) as the new prime minister. On October 6 das Neves announced her new cabinet, which again included members of her own party, the coalition of the MFDM and PCD, and the Uê Kédadji alliance.

In November 2002 the National Assembly approved a resolution for constitutional reform altering the semipresidential system to reduce presidential power. Despite President Menezes's objections, the new constitution took effect in March 2003, reducing presidential power but maintaining a semipresidential system.

A bloodless military coup in June 2003 briefly deposed Menezes while the president was in Nigeria, but negotiations led to his return to office July 23. He appointed Damiao ALMEIDA prime minister on September 17, and a reshuffled cabinet made up of MLSTP-PSD and ADI was sworn in the next day. The minister of natural resources and environment, Arlindo CARVALHO, resigned May 16,

2005, over delays in the allocation of oil exploration licenses, and on June 3 the prime minister and entire cabinet also resigned. Maria do Carmo SILVEIRA was named prime minister June 7 and her new cabinet, with MLSTP-PSD members holding 8 of the top 12 positions, was appointed the next day. In legislative elections on March 26, 2006, Menezes's MDFM won 23 seats, surprising many by finishing ahead of the MLSTP-PSD, which fell to 20 seats. The ADI took 11 seats. Menezes subsequently named Tomé Soares da VERA CRUZ—an engineer who had previously held the position of minister of natural resources—as head of a new minority MDFM-PCD government.

On July 30, 2006, with the backing of the MDFM-PCD, Menezes was reelected president, winning 60.6 percent of the vote. Menezes's main opponent, former foreign minister Patrice TROVOADA, backed by the ADI and the MLSTP-PSD, received 38.8 percent of the vote. A third candidate, independent Nilo GUIMARÃES, got 0.6 percent of the vote.

Constitution and Government

The 1975 constitution, as revised in 1982, identified the MLSTP as the "directing political force" for the country, provided for an indirectly elected National Popular Assembly as the supreme organ of state, and conferred broad powers on a president, who was named by the assembly for a five-year term.

In October 1987 the MLSTP Central Committee proposed a number of constitutional changes as part of a broad democratization program. Theretofore elected by the People's District Assemblies from candidates nominated by an MLSTP-dominated Candidature Commission, legislators would now be chosen by direct and universal suffrage. Independent candidates would be permitted in addition to candidates presented by the party and "recognized organizations," such as trade unions or youth groups. The president would be elected by popular vote rather than being designated by the assembly; however, only the MLSTP president (elected by secret ballot at a party congress) could stand as a candidate. In the course of approving the reform program, the assembly provided for the restoration of a presidentially appointed prime minister.

As a consequence of the August 1990 referendum, a multiparty system was introduced, together with multicandidature presidential balloting. The National Assembly conferred local autonomy upon Principe in 1994, and elections were held there in March 1995 for a seven-member regional assembly and a five-member regional government (headed by a president). The new bodies were installed April 29, 1995.

The judiciary is headed by a Supreme Court, whose members are designated by and responsible to the assembly. Administratively, the country is divided into two provinces (coterminous with each of the main islands) and 12 counties (11 of which are located on Sao Tome).

Foreign Relations

Despite the exodus of much of the country's Portuguese population from 1974 to 1975, Sao Tome and Principe continued to maintain an active commercial trade with the former colonial power, although the generally cordial relations were strained in mid-1983 over a projected aid package and the activities of Lisbon-based groups opposed to the da Costa regime. Following independence, diplomatic relations were established with the Soviet Union and the Eastern-bloc countries as well as the major western states. Relations with other former Portuguese dependencies in Africa, particularly Angola, have been close; in 1978 some 1,000 troops from Angola, augmented by a small contingent from Guinea-Bissau, were dispatched to Sao Tome to guard against what President da Costa claimed to be a series of coup plots by expatriates in Angola, Gabon, and Portugal. However, most of the troops were withdrawn by the mid-1980s as part of a rapprochement with the West that included a bilateral military cooperation agreement with Lisbon and the signing of a three-year fishing pact with the European Community in 1987.

Regional relations have also improved, and growing ties with nearby francophone nations underscore the fact that France is now the country's leading trade partner. In November 1999 Sao Tome and Principe joined six of its Gulf of Guinea neighbors (Angola, Cameroon, Republic of the Congo, Equatorial Guinea, Gabon, and Nigeria) in agreeing to establish the Gulf of Guinea Joint Commission (GGJC) to coordinate "cooperation and development" in the oil- and fish-rich region. In early 2001 Sao Tome and Principe reached an accord with Nigeria to establish a Joint Development Zone (JDZ) in disputed waters in the Gulf of Guinea, thereby ending years of dispute over economic exploitation of the oil- and fish-rich waters. It was agreed that Nigeria would receive 60 percent and Sao Tome and Principe 40 percent of the revenue from joint oil-licensing revenues.

Tensions arose between Sao Tome and Principe and Nigeria over the awarding of operating rights in the JDZ in May 2005, but cooperation between the two countries over oil development appears to be on track.

Recently, Sao Tome and Principe's relationship with the United States has drawn closer. In February 2005, the U.S. Navy sent the submarine tender USS Emory S. Land to the Gulf of Guinea area. Sao Tome and Principe was one of several nations in the Gulf of Guinea region that received training for local security forces, as well as assistance with numerous other infrastructure projects.

Current Issues

The probability of petroleum wealth remains uppermost in the minds of residents of Sao Tome and Principe and has had a dramatic effect on its politics. The stakes are enormous. With no oil yet pumped, the little country of some 150,000 citizens should receive millions of dollars in signature bonuses for the awarding of geographic blocs to giant oil companies that want to explore for oil, plus a share of the oil eventually produced. The signature bonuses alone could amount to $412 million, with Nigeria receiving 60 percent and Sao Tome and Principe receiving 40 percent, a bonanza for a country whose total tax revenues for 2004 were less than $15 million. The front-end signature bonus designated in the treaty with the consortium exploring the first bloc should provide Sao Tome and Principe with $49 million, approximately 10 times the country's annual revenue from its largest export crop, cocoa.

The potential windfall also raises fears of corruption by government officials handling the oil accounts. In an early sampling of trouble, a bloodless coup in 2003 that temporarily deposed President Menezes was undertaken by a military group proclaiming their concerns about how the oil wealth would be managed. Menezes had admitted receiving a $100,000 payment from the Environmental Remediation Holding Corporation (ERHC), a Nigerian company that made lucrative deals in the JDZ that most observers believe were not favorable to Sao Tome. Following the coup in 2003 the president was reinstated after negotiations with the rebels, but more oil-related trouble loomed. Amid charges and counter-charges of corruption, by September 2004 the government had changed six times in three years. Questions and angry debate continue concerning terms of the contract with ERHC, with accusations being leveled that the company has neither sufficient resources nor adequate experience to have been entrusted with the area's drilling rights, but instead received the contract due to "sweetheart" arrangements among various Nigerian investors and certain politicians from Sao Tome and Principe. There is also some outrage over the fact that ERHC is exempt from paying any signing bonuses, unlike the other signatories. However, news reports allege that many officials involved felt somewhat boxed in by the fact that opening an investigation into terms of the treaty could work to the country's disadvantage—if the probe delayed signings with consortiums interested in drilling in other blocs past the time of the first explorations. Officials fear that initial drilling could reveal "dry holes"—news that could dampen enthusiasm on the part of other consortiums to sign further agreements, or at least affect the terms they would be willing to extend.

The awarding of five blocs of the JDZ on May 31, 2005, brought further disagreement. Patrice Trovoada, oil adviser to President Menezes and an oil broker himself, protested the awarding of the best blocs to a consortium of U.S. companies, claiming irregularities and influence peddling. Others countered that his protests merely reflected his relationship with an independent U.S. company, Anadarko, which he championed to receive operating rights in one of the blocs. Trovoada was fired as oil adviser, and Menezes had to dismiss his own chief of staff, Mateus RITA, from the bilateral Joint Ministerial Council after disclosures that Rita owned 500,000 shares in the ERHC. Menezes then flew to Abuja, Nigeria, and signed off on the bloc awards, which provoked further crises. Prime Minister Damiao Vaz de Almeida resigned and Maria do Carmo Silveira of the MLSTP-PSD was named prime minister. A new cabinet heavily loaded with MLSTP-PSD members was named the next day. In June 2005, blocs 2 through 6 were allocated, and production-sharing contracts were signed with the highest bidders the following November. In January 2006, Chevron became the first oil company to begin exploratory drilling within the blocks.

The smooth transfer of millions of dollars in signature bonuses for oil development rights depends on how well the new government operates. Despite the accusations and frequent shifts in power, outsiders believe Sao Tome and Principe stands a better chance than most new petro-states of straightening out its priorities. Few ethnic tensions exist because the population shares a history as former plantation slaves to the Portuguese, who operated the country as an overseas province until independence in 1973. The Sao Tome government has begun developing rules and institutions for the oil sector that were not present in other new oil states. Late in 2004 a revenue management law was co-drafted by a team from New York's Columbia University and signed into law. The new law sets up an oversight committee and requires the government to give priority to poverty reduction and social spending in health, education, and infrastructure. It remains to be seen whether these priorities actually prevail.

Some citizens, apparently angered at the perceived failure of the government to improve basic services in recent years, barricaded the roads leading to some polling places during the March 26, 2006, legislative elections. (Repolling was held in a number of districts a week later.) Not surprisingly, economic issues, particularly involving oil, appeared to dominate public concerns in the elections. Observers suggested that Prime Minister Vera Cruz and his new minority government faced a difficult task in placating a restive population until the oil spigot is turned on, as currently anticipated, in 2010.

Political Parties

Government Parties

Democratic Movement of Forces for Change (*Movimiento Democrático das Forças para da Mudança*—MDFM). The MDFM was formed in late 2001 by former members of the ADI (below) close to President Menezes. The MDFM later established an electoral alliance with the PCD (below) for legislative balloting in 2002. That alliance won the largest number of seats, 23, in the March 2006 voting.

Leader: Tome Soares da VERA CRUZ (Prime Minister and Secretary General).

Party of Democratic Convergence (*Partido da Convergência Democrática*—PCD). The PCD was launched in 1987, initially as an underground movement styled the Reflection Group (*Grupo de Reflexão*—GR), which surfaced as an open opposition formation following the introduction of multipartyism in August 1990.

In January 1996 the PCD named party president Alda Bandeira de CONÇEICÃO as its presidential candidate. At the same time, despite Miguel Trovoada's entreaties, the party refused to participate in the government formed in early 1996. Following Bandeira's third-place finish in the first round of presidential polling in June, the PCD switched its support to Trovoada. Subsequently, although it was at first reported to have backed the choice of Assembly President Pires as the successor to outgoing prime minister Almeida, the PCD, in accord with the MLSTP-PSD, supported the appointment of Raúl Bragança Neto in November and became the junior partner (with three portfolios) of the subsequent coalition government.

At legislative polling in November 1998 the PCD's representation fell from 14 to 8 seats. The party was not included in the new government installed in January 1999, its votes no longer being required for the MLSTP-PSD to command a legislative majority. Since 2000 the PCD has been part of the Democratic Platform, and it supported the ADI's candidate in the 2001 presidential election. The PCD was given cabinet posts in the new cabinet in September 2001. The PCD entered into an electoral alliance with the MDFM (above) for the legislative balloting in 2002 and 2006, winning 23 seats in each poll.

Leader: Leonel Mario D'ALVA.

Opposition Parties

Movement for the Liberation of Sao Tome and Principe–Social Democratic Party (*Movimento de Libertaçã de São Tomé e Príncipe-Partido Social Democrata*—MLSTP-PSD). The outcome of an earlier Committee for the Liberation of Sao Tome and Principe (*Comité de Libertação de São Tomé e Príncipe*—CLSTP), the MLSTP was founded in 1972 and gradually became the leading force in the campaign for independence from Portugal. At its first congress in 1978, the movement defined itself as a "revolutionary front of democratic, anti-neocolonialist, and anti-imperialist forces"; however, it did not formally adopt Marxism-Leninism despite the ideology's influence on its leaders and their economic policies. MLSTP-PSD served as the country's only authorized political group until the adoption of a multiparty system in August 1990. Two months later, (then) President da Costa retired from leadership of what had been redesignated the MLSTP-PSD.

Da Costa returned to party activity from retirement in 1998 in preparation to run for the presidency in July 2001. He was defeated by Fradique de Menezes of the ADI, and the MLSTP-PSD was excluded from the new government. De Menezes dissolved the National Assembly in December and announced new legislative elections in March 2002, after which a new, more broadly based government would be formed. In that election no party obtained an overwhelming majority, with the MLSTP-PSD winning 24 of the 55 seats, the MDFM-PCD securing 23, and the UK, a coalition of five other parties, winning the other 8. The new coalition government, although headed by an independent, Gabriel da Costa, included representatives of the MLSTP-PSD, the MDFM-PCD, and the UK, as well as a number of independents. De Menezes dismissed da Costa in September 2002 and appointed Maria das Neves de Souza of the MLSTP-PSD as his successor. She remained in office for two years until Menezes dismissed her in September 2004 amid accusations of her involvement in financial scandals. Appointed in her place was Damiao Vaz d'Almeida, also of the MLSTP-PSD. In February 2005, former prime minister and vice president of the party Guilherme Posser da Costa replaced Manuel Pinto da Costa as the party's president. In June 2005 the MLSTP-PSD threatened to resign from the government and force new parliamentary elections. After negotiations de Menezes and the MLSTP-PSD agreed to form a new government and avoid early elections. Maria do Carmo Silveira, a respected head of the Central Bank and a member of the MLSTP-PSD, became the new prime minister and finance minister.

In the March 2006 legislative elections, the party finished second behind thd MDFM-PCD, winning 20 seats.

Leader: Guilherme Posser da COSTA (President).

Independent Democratic Action (*Acção Democrática Independente*—ADI). The ADI was formed in 1992 under the leadership of President Trovoada's political advisor, Gabriel Costa, and participated in municipal elections of that year as an "independent group." It was legally registered in early 1994, at which time Trovoada was identified as a member. The ADI won 14 seats in the 1994 assembly balloting and 16 in 1998, claiming

Cabinet

As of July 1, 2006

Prime Minister	Tomé Soares da Vera Cruz (MDFM)
Deputy Prime Minister	Maria dos Santos Tebus Torres (PCD) [f]

Ministers

Defense and Internal Affairs	Lt. Col. Oscar Aguiar Sacramento Sousa (MDFM)
Economy	Cristina Maria Fernandes Dias (MDFM) [f]
Education, Culture, Youth, and Sport	Maria de Fatima Leite de Sousa Almeida (MDFM0 [f]
Finance and Planning	Maria dos Santos Tebus Torres (PCD) [f]
Foreign Affairs	Carlos Gustavo dos Anjos (PCD)
Health	Arlindo Vicente de Assunçao Carvalho (PCD)
Justice and Parliamentary Affairs	Justino Tavares Veiga
Labor, Solidarity, Women, and the Family	Maria de Cristo dos Santos Raposo de Carvalho (MDFM) [f]
Natural Resources and the Environment	Maule de Deus Lima (MDFM)
Public Administration, State Reform, and Territorial Administration	Armindo Vaz Rodrigues Aguiar (PCD)
Public Works and Infrastructure	Delfim Santiago das Neves (MDFM)
Social Communication and Regional Integration	Tomé Soares da Vera Cruz (MDFM)

[f] = female

irregularities in the latter poll. In 2000 the ADI began to collaborate with the PCD, Codo, UNDP, and PPP in an alliance called the "Democratic Platform." In the presidential election in July 2001, the ADI candidate, Fradique de Menezes, captured the presidency with the support of the Democratic Platform parties. In September the ADI formed a coalition government with the PCD. In November the ADI formed an alliance with the Democratic Platform parties and the PRD to counter the MLSTP-PSD in legislative elections in 2002. Menezes fell into disagreement with pro-Trovoada factions within the party. Those close to Menezes launched the MDFM (above) in late 2001. The ADI participated in the UK (see below) from late 2001 until seceding from the coalition, in which it had been the principal entity, in early 2006. The ADI won 11 seats on its own in the March 2006 elections.

Leader: Patrice TROVOADA (Secretary General).

New Wave Movement *(Movimento Novo Rumo–NR)*. This newly formed party won one seat in the March 2006 legislative elections.

Leader: Joao GOMES.

Other Parties and Groups

Uê Kédadji (UK). The UK was established in late 2001 as an alliance of the ADI (above) and Codo (see below) and the **National Union for Democracy and Progress** *(União Nacional para a Democracia o Progresso—*UNDP), the **People's Progress Party** *(Partida Progresso do Povo—*PPP), and the **Democratic Renovation Party** (PRD), led by Armindo GRAÇA. The UNDP and the PPP had been recognized in September 1998 and were part of the Democratic Platform, formed in 2000, that supported the ADI candidate in the 2001 presidential balloting. After the 2002 balloting, the UK held eight seats in the legislature. The

ADI left the alliance in early 2006, and the UK failed to win any seats in the legislative elections in March.

Opposition Democratic Coalition (*Coligação Democrática da Oposição*—Codo). Codo was launched in March 1986 as an alliance of two Lisbon-based opposition groups, the **Independent Democratic Union of Sao Tome and Principe** (*União Democrática Independente de São Tomé e Príncipe*—UDISTP) and the **Sao Tome and Principe National Resistance Front** (*Frente da Resistência Nacional de São Tomé e Príncipe*—FRNSTP), to combat what they called the "totalitarianism" of the da Costa government. Although the UDISTP previously had taken the position that its goals were to be reached through "peaceful means," its association with the FRNSTP, generally considered a more radical group, led to a Codo posture that did not rule out "recourse to armed struggle."
Leader: Manuel Neves e SILVA.

Among the other groups active as of 2002 were the **Sao Tome Workers' Party** (*Partido Trabalhista São Tomense*—PTS), led by Anacleto ROLIM; the **Democratic Renovation Party of Progress** (*Partido da Renovação Democrática*—PRD), led by Armindo GRAÇA; the **Popular Party of Progress** (*Partido Popular do Progresso*—PPP), led by Francisco SILVA; and the **National Union for Democracy and Progress** (*Uniao Nacional para Democracia e Progresso*—UNDP), led by Manuel Paixao LIMA.

Legislature

Formerly an indirectly elected National Popular Assembly (*Assembleia Popular Nacional*) of 40 members, the current **National Assembly** (*Assembleia Nacional*) is a unicameral body of 55 members directly elected for five-year terms. In the most recent balloting of March 26, 2006 (and reruns in 18 districts on April 2), the electoral alliance of the Democratic Movement of Forces for Change and the Party of Democratic Convergence won 23 seats; the Movement for the Liberation of Sao Tome and Principe–Social Democratic Party, 20; Independent Democratic Action, 11; and the New Way Movement, 1.
President: Francisco DA SILVA.

Communications

Press

The following are published in Sao Tome: *Diário da República*, government weekly; *Notícias*; *Nova República*; *O País Hoje* (Country Today); *O Parvo; Tribuna.*

News Agency

In mid-1985 the Angolan News Agency, ANGOP, joined with Sao Tome's national radio station in establishing STP-Press.

Broadcasting and Computing

Radio programming is transmitted by the official *Rádio Nacional de São Tomé e Príncipe* (RNSTP). *Televisão de São Tomé e Príncipe,* which began broadcasting on a limited basis in 1992, today services some 68,000 sets. There were approximately 15,000 Internet users in 2003.

Intergovernmental Representation

Ambassador to the U.S. and Permanent Representative to the UN
Ovidio Manuel Barbosa PEQUENO

U.S. Ambassador to Sao Tome and Principe
R. Barrie WALKLEY (resident in Gabon)

IGO Memberships (Non-UN)
AfDB, AU, BADEA, CEEAC, CPLP, Interpol, NAM, OIF

SENEGAL

REPUBLIC OF SENEGAL

République du Sénégal

The Country

Senegal is situated on the bulge of West Africa between Mauritania on the north, Mali on the east, and Guinea and Guinea-Bissau on the south. Gambia forms an enclave extending into its territory for 200 miles along one of the area's four major rivers. The predominantly flat or rolling savanna country has a population of varied ethnic backgrounds, with the Wolof, whose language is widely used commercially, being the largest group. French, the official language, is spoken only by a literate minority. In the 1988 census 94 percent of the population was identified as Muslim, the remainder being animist or Christian. Islamic "brotherhoods" exercise significant economic and political influence throughout the country, most of them espousing what Western observers would describe as a moderate version of Islam. One such group is the Mouride brotherhood, said to represent as many as two million Sufi Muslims around the city of Touba. The illiteracy rate, while declining in recent years, remains at 62 percent, somewhat higher than for the continent as a whole.

About 70 percent of the population is employed in agriculture; peanuts, the principal crop, once accounted for one-third of export earnings, but production has declined. Cotton, sugar, and rice (most supplies of which have traditionally been imported) have become the focus of agricultural diversification efforts, while fishing, phosphate mining, oil refining, and tourism have grown in importance. Economic difficulties, as exemplified by rising prices and high urban unemployment, have been addressed since 1977 by a series of adjustment programs that have reduced the role of the state in most sectors, liberalized trade measures, and limited government spending, These programs earned Senegal a high level of foreign aid, generous terms in rescheduling its more than $4.2 billion external debt, and support from the International Monetary Fund (IMF). Overall economic improvement was minimal in the early 1990s, and in 1994 the IMF extended additional credit to Dakar to support programs it had adopted to offset the devaluation of the CFA franc, including a reduction of custom tariffs and a "moderate wage policy." GDP grew by an average of more than 5 percent annually from 1996 to 2000, earning praise from the IMF and World Bank. At the same time, Senegal

Political Status: Former French dependency, independent since August 20, 1960; presidential system established under constitution promulgated March 7, 1963; Senegalese-Gambian Confederation of Senegambia, formed with effect from February 1, 1982, dissolved as of September 30, 1989.

Area: 75,750 sq. mi. (196,192 sq. km.).

Population: 6,896,808 (1988C); 10,591,000 (2005E).

Major Urban Center (2005E): DAKAR (2,167,000).

Official Language: French.

Monetary Unit: CFA Franc (official rate July 1, 2006: 513.01 francs = $1US). (The CFA franc, previously pegged to the French franc, is now permanently pegged to the euro at 655.957 francs = 1 euro.)

President: Abdoulaye WADE (Senegalese Democratic Party); elected in second-round balloting on March 19, 2000, and inaugurated for a seven-year term on April 1 in succession to Abdou DIOUF (Socialist Party).

Prime Minister: Macky SALL (Senegalese Democratic Party); appointed by the president on April 22, 2004, to succeed Idrissa SECK (Senegalese Democratic Party), who resigned on April 21.

entered the new millennium with an economy that remained peasant-based and stressed by unequal distribution of wealth, high unemployment, an external debt of $3.5 billion, and deteriorating social services. Nonetheless, Senegal subsequently experienced steady, if modest, economic growth, which was accompanied by low inflation. As the result of sound fiscal policy, the government was also able to lower deficits and increase tax revenue.

In April 2003 Senegal was granted $33 million from the IMF for economic restructuring from 2003 to 2005. A year later, the IMF declared that Senegal had completed the necessary steps under the Heavily Indebted Poor Countries (HIPC) initiative. As a result, Senegal was accorded nearly $500 million in debt relief, thereby reducing its debt to $1.9 billion. Meanwhile, GDP growth of 6 percent

was reported for 2004, with inflation of only 1.4 percent.

In 2006, the World Bank announced that Senegal was one of 17 countries that qualified for additional debt relief under the Multilateral Debt Relief Initiative.

Government and Politics

Political Background

Under French influence since the 17th century, Senegal became a French colony in 1920 and a self-governing member of the French Community in November 1958. In January 1959 it joined with the adjacent French Soudan (now Mali) to form the Federation of Mali, which became fully independent within the Community on June 20, 1960. Two months later Senegal seceded from the federation, and the separate Republic of Senegal was proclaimed on September 5. President Léopold Sédar SENGHOR, a well-known poet and the leader of Senegal's strongest political party, the Senegalese Progressive Union (*Union Progressiste Sénégalaise*—UPS), governed initially under a parliamentary system in which political rival Mamadou DIA was prime minister. An unsuccessful coup in December 1962 resulted in Dia's arrest and imprisonment (until his release in 1974) and the establishment by Senghor of a presidential form of government under his exclusive direction. In an election held under violent conditions on December 1, 1963, Senghor retained the presidency, and his party won all of the seats in the National Assembly, as it also did in the elections of 1968 and 1973.

In response to demands for political and constitutional reform, Senghor in early 1970 reinstituted the post of prime minister, while a constitutional amendment adopted in 1976 sanctioned three political parties, the ideology of each being prescribed by law. In early 1979 a fourth, essentially conservative, party was also accorded recognition. Additional parties were legalized under legislation enacted in April 1981.

Although he had been overwhelmingly reelected to a fourth five-year term on February 26, 1978,

President Senghor resigned on December 31, 1980, and, as prescribed by the constitution, was succeeded by Prime Minister Abdou DIOUF. The new administration extended the process of political liberalization, most restrictions on political party activity being lifted in April 1981. Coalitions were proscribed, however; thus the opposition did not present a serious threat to the ruling Socialist Party (*Parti Socialiste*—PS) in the presidential and legislative balloting of February 27, 1983, Diouf winning reelection with 83 percent of the vote, and the PS capturing 111 of 120 assembly seats. At the subsequent poll of February 28, 1988, Diouf was reported to have been reelected by 73 percent of the vote, with the PS being awarded 103 assembly seats. Controversy surrounding this election and its aftermath tarnished Senegal's long-standing democratic reputation. While the major opposition parties boycotted local elections in November 1990, a number of their leaders, including Abdoulaye WADE, Diouf's principal opponent in the 1982 and 1988 presidential campaigns, were named to a government headed by Habib THIAM on April 7, 1991. However, in October 1992 Wade and three other cabinet members from Wade's Senegalese Democratic Party (*Parti Démocratique Sénégalais*—PDS) resigned from the government, claiming they had been marginalized by their PS colleagues and included in only "trivial" decision making.

At first-round balloting on February 21, 1993, President Diouf was credited with winning 58 percent of the valid vote, thus eliminating the need for a second round. Wade was runner-up with a vote share of 32 percent. In the legislative poll of May 9, the PS won a reduced majority of 84 assembly seats, with the PDS securing 27 seats.

On May 15, 1993, the Constitutional Council's vice president, Babacar SEYE, was assassinated by a group identifying themselves as the People's Army. On May 16 Wade and a number of his PDS colleagues were detained after one of the alleged conspirators, Cledor SENE, claimed to be acting on their orders. On June 7 Sene recanted his story, publicly apologized to Wade for attempting to "decapitate" the PDS. Thereafter, relations

between government and opposition grew increasingly acrimonious, as two PDS deputies, Mody SY and Samuel SARR, remained imprisoned for alleged involvement in the assassination, and the PDS mounted a demonstration in late July on behalf of their release. On August 24 the National Assembly further aggravated the situation by approving an emergency economic austerity plan that called for cuts in civil service salaries. Implementation of the measure was temporarily suspended following a general strike on September 2. In early October Wade and his wife, Viviane WADE, who had previously been released, were rearrested for their alleged involvement in Seye's assassination, and on November 5 over 130 opposition activists were arrested for participating in an antigovernment rally organized by the PDS and the African Party for Democracy and Socialism/And Jëf (*Parti Africain pour la Démocratie et le Socialisme/And Jëf*—PADS/AJ). (*And Jëf* is a Wolof expression meaning "to unite for a purpose.") Violent clashes erupted during a demonstration against the effects of the mid-January 1994 CFA devaluation, and the government moved quickly to indict Abdoulaye Wade and Landing SAVANE, leader of the PADS/AJ, for "breach against the state security," a charge for which 73 others were also being detained. However, on May 26 the Wades and their fellow PDS members were cleared of involvement in the Seye assassination, and at midyear Sy and Sarr were released after launching hunger strikes. In August Wade and Savane were acquitted of the February charges. In October three people were sentenced for their roles in Seye's assassination, although no motive was revealed.

In March 1995 the Diouf administration scored what appeared to be a major political victory when Wade accepted a cabinet-level post. As a result, the government contained three of the four leading groups previously aligned as regime opponents. In addition, although Wade had previously refused to enter the government unless the PDS was given half the posts in a 20-member cabinet, he now agreed to accept only 5 portfolios in a 33-member cabinet.

Amid reports of increasing violations of a two-year-old cease-fire between the government and secessionist Casamance rebels in southern Senegal, security forces in May 1995 arrested Fr. Augustin DIAMACOUNE Senghor, leader of the Movement of Democratic Forces of Casamance (*Mouvement des Forces Démocratiques de la Casamance*—MFDC). Full-scale fighting erupted following Diamacoune's detention, and in mid-June the cease-fire was formally abandoned. In September the government attempted to start peace talks in Ziguinchor, but fighting continued as MFDC militants refused to negotiate until Diamacoune, who had been placed under house arrest, was freed. In response to the release of a number of his associates in early December, Diamacoune called for an end to the uprising, and on December 30 charges against him were dropped. The following day Diouf announced the creation of a parliamentary upper house, a Senate, which he described as the first step in an effort to decentralize power through a process of "regionalization."

In early 1996 the Diouf administration announced that independent candidates would be prohibited from participating in the rural, regional, and municipal elections scheduled for November. Grassroots groupings and small opposition parties then accused Diouf of retreating from his pledge to decentralize power. Electoral preparations were threatened by the renewal of Casamance rebel activity, and in May the president's party rebuffed proposals to form an independent electoral commission. At balloting on November 24 the PS won what was described as a landslide victory, although voter turnout was reported at only about 50 percent, and opposition parties criticized some aspects of the way the elections were conducted.

In March 1997 President Diouf convened a conference to review the 1996 elections with the purported aim of improving polling procedures. However, 19 opposition parties accused the PS of attempting to dominate the proceedings and withdrew from the conference in May. In August the Diouf administration, in an abrupt about-face, announced that it would establish an independent electoral commission, the National Elections Observatory (*Observatoire National des Elections*—ONEL), and published a draft electoral reform document that opposition leaders described as meeting "80 percent" of their demands.

At legislative balloting on May 25, 1998, PS candidates dominated an 18-party field, winning 93 seats in the expanded 140-member assembly; the PS's nearest two competitors, the PDS and the newly formed Union for Democratic Renewal (*Union pour le Renouveau Démocratique*—URD), secured 23 and 11 seats, respectively. Although the PDS, URD, and four other parties petitioned to have the polling results overturned because of alleged fraudulent tallying, the ONEL and international observers described the elections as generally free and fair. On July 3 Diouf named Mamadou Lamine LOUM to replace Thiam as prime minister, and the following day a new cabinet that included only one non-PS member was announced. Elections to fill the legislature's newly formed upper house, or Senate, were held on January 24, 1999, candidates affiliated with the PS winning all 45 elective seats. In August 1998 the PS-dominated assembly had voted 93–1 to abolish the limit on presidential terms, thereby permitting the Diouf presidency to continue past 2000. All but two opposition legislators boycotted the session, and the following day all of the leading opposition politicians condemned the assembly vote at an unprecedented joint news conference.

Eight candidates contested the first round of presidential balloting on February 27, 2000, with Diouf securing 43 percent of the vote and Wade 30 percent. Most of the other candidates threw their support to Wade in the second round, which he won, 58.7 to 41.3 percent. Following his inauguration on April 1, Wade appointed Moustapha NIASSE of the Alliance of Forces for Progress (*Alliance des Forces pour le Progrès*—AFP) as prime minister to head a coalition cabinet that also included the PADS/AJ, the Independence and Labor Party (*Parti de l'Indépendance et du Travail*—PIT), and the Democratic League–Labor Party Movement (*Ligue Démocratique–Mouvement pour le Parti du Travail*—LD-MPT).

As promised during the 2000 presidential campaign the PDS and its allies presented a number of constitutional amendments for a national referendum on January 7, 2001. The measures, which abolished the presidentially appointed Senate and otherwise reduced the president's authority, were approved by 94 percent of the voters in a reported 66 percent turnout.

Invoking a provision in the new basic law that authorized the president to call for new legislative elections after the most recently elected assembly had served for at least two years, Wade dissolved the assembly on February 15, 2001, and ordered new elections for April 29. Meanwhile, friction between Wade and Niasse intensified, and the prime minister left his post (having either resigned or been dismissed, depending on whose account was accurate) on March 3. He was succeeded by Mame Madiou BOYE, an independent who had been serving as justice minister; Boye thereby became Senegal's first female prime minister.

The PDS-led "Sopi" (Wolof for "Change") coalition (see Political Parties, below) dominated the April 29, 2001, assembly balloting, despite the defection of the AFP and the PIT from the government. The new government named by Boye on May 12 was again led by the PDS and several of its smaller electoral partners.

On November 4, 2002, President Wade dismissed Prime Minister Boye in the wake of a ferry disaster that claimed 1,200 lives and attracted intense international scrutiny. Wade appointed Idrissa SECK, his chief of cabinet, to form a new government. The ferry disaster continued to dominate Senegalese politics for the next several years, and the chief of staff of the armed forces and the chief of staff of the air force were both removed because of the military's slow response to the disaster.

In August 2003 the Seck government resigned in response to growing public discontent with the inquiry into the ferry's sinking and negative reaction to the government's response to severe flooding that year. Seck was reappointed prime minister and asked to develop a government of national unity, but most opposition parties declined to join the government, which remained largely dominated by propresidential parties. Tensions between Wade and Seck resulted in the latter's dismissal as prime minister on April 21, 2004; former interior minis-

ter Macky SALL was named the next day to lead a reshuffled cabinet. Seck was subsequently charged with subversion and embezzlement and kicked out of the PDS (see Current issues, below). Wade conducted several cabinet reshuffles in 2005–2006 in an apparent effort to increase his control over the government and party ahead of the 2007 presidential elections.

Constitution and Government

Senegal is administratively divided into eleven regions, each headed by a presidentially appointed governor who is assisted by an elected Regional Assembly; the regions are divided into departments. The constitution provides for a president elected by direct universal suffrage, with runoff balloting for the two top contenders if none secures an absolute majority. Under amendments approved in 1991, presidents were limited to two terms, although the incumbent (Abdou Diouf), already elected twice, was permitted to stand one more time. An amendment in 1993 extended presidential terms to seven years. The two-term restriction was formally abandoned in 1998, thereby permitting Diouf to contest the 2000 balloting as well. Amendments in 2001 reimposed the two-term limit and returned the length of the term to five years. The president appoints the prime minister (the office having been abolished in 1983 and revived in 1991), who in turn appoints the Council of Ministers in consultation with the president. Legislative power was vested in a unicameral National Assembly until December 31, 1995, when President Diouf announced the creation of a Senate to act as an upper house. The first Senate was elected in January 1999, but that body was abolished in the 2001 constitutional amendments. Under initial procedures, half of the assembly members were elected from Senegal's departments, on a "first past the post" basis, the other half by proportional representation from a national list. However, electoral changes adopted in 1989 provided that national lists would be dropped from future elections, with all members being chosen on a departmental basis. Only parties registered at least four months before an election were allowed to participate; neither independent candidacies nor opposition coalitions were permitted. However, the combination of departmental and national lists was reestablished for the April 2001 assembly election in accordance with the January constitutional revisions. Party restrictions were also lifted as were barriers to electoral coalitions. The principal judicial organs, under a system revised in 1992, include a Constitutional Council, one of whose functions is to rule on electoral issues; a Council of State; a Court of Cassation; and a Court of Appeal; with magistrate courts at the local level. In addition, a High Court of Justice, chosen by the assembly from among its own membership, is responsible for impeachment proceedings. Elections for municipal and rural community councilors were held in May 2002.

Foreign Relations

Formally nonaligned, Senegal has retained especially close political, cultural, and economic ties with France. An active advocate of West African cooperation, it has participated in such regional groupings as the Economic Community of West African States, the Permanent Inter-State Committee on Drought Control in the Sahel, and the Organization for the Development of the Senegal River. (The members of the latter are Mali and Mauritania.) Regional relations improved substantially as the result of a "reconciliation" pact signed in Monrovia, Liberia, in March 1978, ending five years of friction with Guinea and Côte d'Ivoire.

Under President Senghor, Senegal maintained a generally conservative posture in African affairs, refusing to recognize Angola because of the presence of Cuban troops there, supporting Morocco against the claims of the insurgent Polisario Front in the Western Sahara, and breaking relations with Libya in mid-1980 because of that country's alleged efforts to destabilize the governments of Chad, Mali, and Niger as well as Senegal. Reflecting the "spirit of our new diplomacy"—essentially an effort to introduce greater flexibility in its relations with other African governments—Dakar announced in February 1982 that it would reverse its long-standing support of the Angolan resistance movement and recognize the MPLA government in Luanda. Ties with Algeria were strengthened in the course of reciprocal visits by the respective heads of state in 1984 and 1985; relations with Libya eased as the result of a visit by Colonel Qadhafi in December 1985 and were formally restored in November 1988.

In light of the unusual geographic relationship between the two countries, one of Senegal's most prominent regional concerns has been its association with Gambia. A 1967 treaty provided for cooperation in foreign affairs, development of the Gambia River basin, and, most important, defense. Consequently, Senegalese troops were dispatched to Banjul, Gambia, in October 1980 amid rumors of Libyan involvement in a projected coup and again in July 1981 when an uprising threatened to topple the Jawara administration (see article on Gambia). The latter incident was followed by an agreement to establish a Confederation of Senegambia, completed on February 1, 1982. Although the component states remained politically independent entities, the Confederation agreement called for the integration of security forces, the establishment of an economic and monetary union, and the coordination of policies in foreign affairs, internal communications, and other areas. A joint Council of Ministers and an appointed Confederal Assembly were established, and it was agreed that the presidents of Senegal and Gambia would serve as president and vice president, respectively, of the confederation. In practical terms, however, little progress was made in actualizing the confederation, Gambia in particular appearing to procrastinate in the endeavor. Many Gambians criticized what was perceived as an unequal relationship, while Gambian government and business leaders questioned the wisdom of their country's proposed entrance into the franc zone. Economic union was also hindered by the fact that Gambia had long favored liberal trade policies in contrast to Senegal's imposition of high protective tariffs. In August 1989 Senegal unilaterally withdrew some of its troops from Gambia, and President Diouf declared that the confederation, having "failed in its purpose," should be "frozen." Gambian President Jawara responded by suggesting it be terminated completely, and a protocol was quickly negotiated formally dissolving the grouping as of September 30. Despite a presidential summit in December 1989, relations remained cool through 1990 as Senegal enacted trade sanctions aimed at stemming the importation of foreign goods via its relatively duty-free neighbor. In January 1991 the two countries moved to reestablish bilateral links by the conclusion of a treaty of friendship and cooperation. As finalized in June, the treaty provided for annual summits and the establishment of joint commissions to ensure implementation of summit agreements.

In May 1989 the third conference of francophone heads of state met in Dakar amid deepening hostility between Senegal and Mauritania that had been triggered by a dispute on April 9 over farming rights along their border. Rioting in both Dakar and Nouakchott had ensued, causing death or injury to several hundred people and the cross-repatriation of an estimated 150,000–300,000, including a substantial number of Moors, who had dominated the crucial small-business retail sector in the Senegalese capital. The situation continued in crisis for the balance of the year. Relations remained broken, with a continuing exodus (forced, according to Senegalese charges) of blacks from Mauritania to Senegal; Nouakchott announced preparations for a possible war. In January 1990 border forces exchanged artillery fire across the Senegal River, but diplomatic efforts, led by Organization of African Unity (OAU, subsequently the African Union—AU) president Hosni Mubarak, helped avert additional violence. By early 1991 relations had again deteriorated, as Nouackchott accused Senegal of aiding antigovernment rebels and Dakar charged Mauritania with arming Casamance separatists with Iraqi weapons. Meanwhile, relations with Guinea-Bissau, already strained by Bissau's refusal to recognize a July 1989 international court decision favoring Senegal in their maritime border dispute, were exacerbated by a clash in May 1991 that left 17 dead and by reports that Bissau was also supporting the Casamance rebels.

A May 1991 rapprochement between Dakar and the Casamance insurgents had a positive effect on relations with both Guinea-Bissau and Mauritania.

The choice of the former as the site for the signing of a cease-fire agreement signaled a further lessening of tensions, and on July 18 an agreement to reopen the Senegalese-Mauritanian border paved the way for restoration of diplomatic relations on April 23, 1992. However, on December 12 tension again flared with the bombing by Senegalese forces of alleged Casamance bases in northern Guinea-Bissau. Four days later the Senegalese government offered its apologies after Bissau had protested the violation of its border, and on December 22 it was reported that Casamance leader Diamacoune had been expelled from Guinea-Bissau.

In May 1994 Dakar demanded the withdrawal of Iran's ambassador, accusing Teheran of supporting the activities of the Islamic fundamentalist movement in Senegal. Fear of the spread of Islamic fundamentalism also dominated a meeting among Senegal, Mali, and Mauritania in January 1995, with the three agreeing to "combat fanaticism in all its forms." On February 10 Senegalese aircraft bombed a suspected Casamance rebel base in Guinea-Bissau, Dakar ignoring Bissau's subsequent demand for an explanation of the attack. However, in September Dakar and Bissau signed a security cooperation pact, and in December the prospect of closer relations improved markedly when Bissau agreed to withdraw its earlier objections to the 1989 court ruling on their shared maritime border. In 1996 Senegal continued to enjoy improved relations with its neighbors, signing cooperation agreements with Guinea, Guinea-Bissau, Mali, and Mauritania. On a less positive note, efforts to repatriate the Mauritanian refugees residing in Senegal since 1989 were only haltingly successful.

In June 1998 President Diouf deployed troops to Guinea-Bissau to shore up the embattled government there, underlining Dakar's concern that the Casamance region in Senegal would erupt in violence if the pro-Casamance Bissaun rebels secured power in Guinea-Bissau (see article on Guinea-Bissau). The administration's military strategy initially drew widespread support; however, by August opposition leaders had begun to question the effort. In March 1999 the last of the Senegalese troops were withdrawn. In 2001 armed forces from Guinea-Bissau destroyed the main Casamance rebel bases in that country. In 2002 separatist groups launched a new round of negotiations with the Senegalese government following the appointment of a new government peace commission. The government committed to a number of infrastructure programs in the province and released some government-held rebels on bail. In response the rebels adopted a cease-fire, although rebels opposed to the negotiations continued to launch minor attacks.

Wade enhanced the international status and influence of Senegal during the early 2000s by, among other things, condemning antidemocratic tendencies among African leaders. Senegal also served as an active force for regional peace by contributing peacekeeping troops to operations in the Democratic Republic of the Congo, Côte d'Ivoire, and Liberia.

Wade has maintained close ties with France but has also reached out to other major powers. In February 2002 he hosted Tony Blair, the first British prime minister to visit Senegal. During the meeting Blair pledged support for the New Partnership for Africa's Development (NEPAD), an organization launched through the OAU in October 2001 to promote socioeconomic recovery in Africa. In April 2002 Wade hosted the first major NEPAD conference. Wade also worked to improve relations with the United States and met with U.S. President George W. Bush in Senegal in July 2003. In addition, Senegal pledged to cooperate with the United States in the global war on terrorism. In 2003 Wade angered France by his refusal to condemn the U.S.-led war in Iraq.

On December 30, 2004, the government and the main rebel group in Casamance, the MFDC, signed a comprehensive peace settlement, although some minor rebel factions continued to fight the central government. (In March 2006, fighting between competing factions of the MFDC displaced 5,000 civilians along the border between Senegal and Guinea-Bissau.)

Tensions emerged in 2005 over a Gambian decision to double the tariff on ferry traffic on the Gambia River, which prompted Wade to close border crossings. The dispute was later resolved with a 15 percent reduction in the tariffs.

In October 2005, Senegal reestablished diplomatic relations with the People's Republic of China, ending Senegal's long-standing recognition of Taiwan. Economic relations between Dakar and Beijing were the main reason for the action, as trade between the two countries had increased by 25 percent per year since 2003. In April 2006, the prime minister led a trade delegation to China in an effort to further enhance trade and investment in Senegal.

Current Issues

The peaceful transfer of presidential power from the PS to the PDS in 2000 was widely hailed as a triumph for the constitutional process in a continent more often known for violent changeovers. Despite having served as chief executive since 1981, President Diouf conceded gracefully. For 75-year-old Abdoulaye Wade the victory was a testament to perseverance (the campaign was his fifth) and to growing support for his long-time populist message. The new president quickly launched a number of ambitious projects designed to promote agro-industry, with particular emphasis on private-sector development. At the April 2001 legislative balloting, the public appeared still to be in the mood for a change, giving Wade a nearly two-thirds majority to work with in the assembly. By mid-2002, however, some analysts suggested that economic realities were beginning to impinge on the new administration's honeymoon, while the PS and other opposition parties were reportedly achieving more effective coordination.

In 2004 the government announced plans to build a new capital city some 150 kilometers from Dakar. The new capital would allow for a centralized and modern government center and would facilitate economic development through new construction and the renovation of existing government facilities for private development. In July 2005, parliament passed a measure that changed the location of the proposed capital to a new site near Kebemer.

Public opposition was provoked in January 2005 by a law designed to pardon those responsible for political crimes or acts committed since 1983 and to help promote the peace settlement in Casamance. Opposition groups asserted that the law was an attempt to cover up past crimes by former government officials and asked the Constitutional Council to examine the measure.

On July 15, former prime minister Seck was arrested on charges of embezzlement and later with endangering national security. On August 3 parliament voted to strip Seck of immunity and forced him to appear before a special anticorruption court. The court dismissed the embezzlement and subversion charges, and the former prime minister was released from prison in February 2006. Seck continued to face a minor charge of overspending government funds; however, his release allowed him to launch his 2007 presidential campaign, reports indicating that he hoped to draw support from the PDS and other progovernment parties.

In late 2005 legislative elections scheduled for May 2006 were postponed until February 2007, ostensibly to save money by combining the polling with presidential elections. Wade redirected the $13 million allocated for the 2006 balloting to help relocate Senegalese displaced by flooding. Opposition leaders met in Dakar in December 2005 and issued a joint statement condemning the postponement. Several opposition parties also launched discussions about the formation of electoral alliances prior to the 2007 balloting. Meanwhile, in spite of his age, Wade announced his intention to campaign for reelection.

Poverty remains Senegal's main social and economic problem. Estimates are that some 57 percent of the population lives in poverty. In response, the government has expanded spending on social programs so that education and health care now account for more than half the national budget. Wade has set a goal of reducing poverty in Senegal by half by 2015. The government has also launched an ambitious bid to make Senegal a leading tourist destination among Muslims. In March 2005 Wade conducted a tourism conference for Muslim foreign ministers. The country hopes to increase the number of wealthy tourists from Muslim states such as Morocco and Tunisia.

Political Parties

In March 1976 the National Assembly approved a constitutional amendment authorizing three political parties, each reflecting a specific ideological "current" that President Senghor had declared to exist in Senegalese society. Senghor's own Socialist Party (PS) adopted the centrist position of "democratic socialism," while the two other legal parties, the Senegalese Democratic Party (PDS) and the African Independence Party, were assigned "liberal democratic" and "Marxist-Leninist" postures, respectively. In early 1979 the amendment was altered to permit the legal establishment of a fourth, essentially right-wing, party—the Senegalese Republican Movement. The process of liberalization reached a conclusion in April 1981, when the assembly removed most remaining restrictions on party activity. More than 60 groups currently enjoy legal status.

A number of opposition parties including the PDS, the PADS/AJ, and the MSU operated in a loose coalition called Uniting to Change Senegal until that grouping's demise following the PDS's decision to join the government in 1995. After the PDS withdrew from the government in March 1998, it spearheaded the formation of an Alliance of Forces for Change (*Alliance des Forces pour le Changement*—AFC), which also included the PADS/AJ, the CDP, and the PIT. The AFC was superseded in late 1999 by the formation of an opposition coalition known as Alternance 2000 to challenge the PS in the 2000 presidential balloting. The new coalition, which endorsed Abdoulaye Wade of the PDS in the first round of the presidential election, was dominated by the PDS but also included the LD-MPT, PADS/AJ, MSU, PIT, UDF, ADN, and FAR/Yoon Wi. In early 2000 Alternance 2000 joined with a number of other opposition groupings, including the AFP, CDP, and URD, to form the Front for Fair and Transparent Elections (*Front pour la Régularité et la Transparence des Elections*—FRTE) to combat what the members perceived to be efforts by the PS to sabotage the election. The FRTE was not an electoral coalition; several members, including Alternance 2000, the AFP, CDP, and URD, presented their own presidential candidates in the first round.

Following the first round of presidential balloting on February 27, 2000, a number of groups previously aligned in the FRTE (including Alternance 2000, the AFP, CDP, and FSD) formed the Front for Change (*Front pour l'Alternance*—FAL) to support Wade in the second round after the PDS/Alternance 2000 leader promised that his victory would be followed by installation of a coalition government. Meanwhile President Diouf of the PS was also endorsed in his reelection bid by a coalition called the Patriotic Convergence (*Convergence Patriotique*—CP), which included the PDS-R, BGC, and others.

The FAL essentially collapsed when Moustapha Niasse of the AFP resigned as prime minister in early March 2001 and the AFP cabinet members also left the government. Consequently, the PDS organized the *Sopi* Coalition, which ultimately included upwards of 40 smaller groups (including the LD-MPT, CDP, UDF, ADN, and PSR), to contest the April 29 assembly balloting. Meanwhile, the AFP, PIT, PPS, and a number of other opposition parties formed a loose preelection coalition called the Front for Defense of Democracy (*Front pour la Défence de la Démocratie*—FDD), under the leadership of the PIT's Amath DANSOKHO. The *Sopi* Coalition was credited with winning 89 of the legislative seats. Subsequently, opposition parties (including the PS, AFP, URD, and PIT) organized a Permanent Framework for Consultation (*Cadre Permanent de Concertation*—CPC) to work against the policies of the PDS-led government. In response, the PDS organized a grouping known as the Convergence of Actions around the President for the 21st Century (*Convergence des Actions autour du Président en Perspective du 21ème Siècle*—CAP-21). The CAP-21, which included the PADS/AJ, the LD-MPT, and some 20 other smaller groups, contested the May 2002 municipal balloting as an electoral coalition, as did the CPC.

Government and Government-Supportive Parties

Senegalese Democratic Party (*Parti Démocratique Sénégalais*—PDS). The PDS was launched in October 1974 as a youth-oriented opposition group to implement the pluralistic democracy guaranteed by the Senegalese constitution. Although standing to the left of President Senghor on certain issues, it was required by the constitutional amendment of March 1976 to adopt a formal position to the right of the government party. Having charged fraud in both the 1980 and 1983 legislative elections (although the PDS was one of two opposition parties to gain representation on the latter occasion), PDS leaders participated in the 1984 municipal boycott and asserted their regret at having campaigned in 1983. Following the return from abroad of party leader Abdoulaye Wade in early 1985, the PDS led a number of mass prayer demonstrations for radical change, with Wade calling for "a transitional government of national unity."

As the major force in Senegal's growing opposition movement, the PDS appeared to pose a genuine threat to the PS in the 1988 legislative and presidential campaigns, partly as a result of its alliance with the LD-MPT and the PIT (below). Although presidential candidate Wade was officially credited with 26 percent of the vote, widespread indications of electoral abuse suggested that his actual total may have been higher.

In 1991 Wade attributed his acceptance of a cabinet post to fears that continued opposition activity would destabilize the country. However, Wade resigned from the government in October 1992 in what was viewed as an attempt to recapture the allegiance of PDS members estranged by his alliance with Diouf. Shortly thereafter Wade announced that the party would present candidates at the forthcoming legislative poll and entered the presidential contest in which he ran second to the incumbent, with a 32.03 percent share of the vote.

In July 1993 the PDS, ignoring a government ban, organized a demonstration for the release of jailed party deputies Mody Sy and Samuel Sarr, both of whom had been held since mid-May for their alleged involvement in the assassination of the Constitutional Council's vice president. On October 1 Wade, who had himself been detained for two days after the assassination, was arrested along with his wife for their alleged roles in the killing. Within days a number of other prominent PDS leaders, including Abdoulaye FAYE and Ousmane NGOM, were also implicated in the assassination.

On November 5, 1993, a number of party members were arrested for leading antigovernment demonstrations, and on February 18, 1994, Wade was reimprisoned for his participation in rioting, which erupted following the devaluation of the CFA franc. At a perfunctory military trial on February 24 Wade was convicted of a "breach against state security." However, on May 26 charges against him and his associates in connection with the 1993 assassination were dropped. Wade was one of five PDS leaders to accept cabinet portfolios in August 1995.

In March 1998 the PDS withdrew from the government and legislature after the PS legislators increased the size of the latter. At the same time Wade reportedly predicted that the PDS would win as many as 80 seats at polling in May. However, the party fell far short of such expectations, securing just 23 seats, and in June Ousmane Ngom and a number of other party leaders left the grouping to form the Senegalese Liberal Party (below). In July Wade resigned his assembly post, saying that he would focus his efforts on resolving the PDS's intraparty disputes.

Wade finished second with 30.97 percent of the vote in the first round of presidential balloting in February 2000. However, after securing the support of most of the other first-round runners-up, Wade went on to defeat President Diouf in the second round in March with 58.7 percent of the vote, setting the stage, in conjunction with the PDS legislative victory in April 2001, for one of the continent's most remarkably peaceful shifts in political power.

In April 2002 it was reported that the **Party for Progress and Citizenship** (*Parti pour le Progrès et la Citoyenneté*—PPC) had agreed to merge with the PDS. The PPC, formed in 2001 by Mbaye Jacques DIOP after he quit the PS, had secured one seat in the 2001 legislative balloting. A similar decision to merge with the PDS was also reported on the part of the **Senegalese Democratic Party–Renewal** (*Parti Démocratique Sénégalais–Rénovation*—PDS-R), which had been organized in June 1987 by an anti-Wade faction within the PDS that announced as its goal the establishment of a "truly secular and pluralist democracy." PDS-R candidates secured minuscule legislative vote shares in the 1988 and 1993 elections, while supporting Diouf for president on both occasions. Serigne Lamine DIOP, the PDS-R secretary general, was named minister of justice and keeper of the seals in the Loum government formed in July 1998, the party having secured one seat in the May legislative balloting.

In April 2005, 14 PDS members of parliament announced their intention to leave the party and form a new group, the **Forces of Change.** After it was ruled that the 14 would have to resign their seats and campaign in special elections, they returned to the PDS.

Wade's main political rival within the PDS, Idrissa Seck, was dismissed as prime minister in April 2004. In August Seck was also dismissed from his post as PDS executive secretary, and he and several of his supporters were expelled from the party. Seck later announced he would contest the 2007 presidential elections.

Leaders: Abdoulaye WADE (President of the Republic and Secretary General), Macky SALL (Prime Minister).

Democratic League–Labor Party Movement (*Ligue Démocratique–Mouvement pour le Parti du Travail*—LD-MPT). A self-proclaimed independent Marxist group with links to Senegal's leading teachers' union, the LD-MPT contested both the 1983 and 1984 elections. At its second congress in December 1986, the League's secretary general, Abdoulaye Bathily, called for "disorganized alliances" between opposition parties and advanced an economic "alternative to the recipes of the International Monetary Fund and the World Bank" as a means of establishing a socialist society. The party supported PDS candidate Abdoulaye Wade in the 1988 presidential poll but presented its own legislative candidates, securing no seats on a 1.4 percent vote share.

In April 1988 LD-MPT Secretary General Bathily was given a suspended sentence for having organized an illegal antigovernment demonstration, while five other party activists were indicted on similar charges late in the year. In 1990 Bathily intensified his criticism of the Diouf administration's policies and called for a non-Diouf "unity" government. Thereafter, despite the co-option of a number of opposition colleagues, Bathily initially refused Diouf's offer of a cabinet portfolio, citing Dakar's repressive policies in Casamance. However, Bathily ultimately agreed to become environment minister in June 1993, with the party being awarded a second portfolio in August 1995. Following the May 1998 legislative poll (at which it won three seats), the LD-MPT declined to participate in the next government. Instead it proposed the formation of a unified opposition front against the PS and President Diouf. Six of the 89 successful candidates from the *Sopi* Coalition in the 2001 legislative balloting were identified as LD-MPT members. Two LD-MPT deputies briefly served in the government in 2005, before disputes with Wade led to their dismissal during a cabinet reshuffle.

Leader: Dr. Abdoulaye BATHILY (1993 presidential candidate and Secretary General).

African Party for Democracy and Socialism/And Jëf (*Parti Africain pour la Démocratie et le Socialisme/And Jëf*—PADS/AJ). The PADS/AJ was formed in 1991 by merger of the Revolutionary Movement for the New Democracy (*Mouvement Révolutionnaire pour la Démocratie Nouvelle*—MRDN) and two other left wing groups, the People's Democratic Union (*Union pour la Démocratie Populaire*—UDP) and the Socialist Workers' Organization (*Organisation Socialist des Travailleurs*—OST).

Also known as *And Jëf*, a Wolof expression meaning "to unite for a purpose," the MRDN was a populist southern party of the extreme left that included former socialists and Maoists. It was

permitted to register in June 1981 but joined the 1983 and 1984 election boycotts. In 1988 one of its leaders, Landing Savane, won 0.25 percent of the vote as a presidential candidate. The UDP was organized in 1981 by a pro-Albanian MRDN splinter group, while the OST was a small Marxist-Leninist formation launched in 1982.

Landing Savane ran a distant third as the 1993 presidential nominee of the PADS/AJ. For the May legislative balloting the party participated with the RND (below) in a **Let Us Unite** (*Jappoo Liggeeyal*) **Senegal** coalition that won three assembly seats. In November Savane was arrested for organizing a demonstration against the Diouf administration's economic austerity program. Given a suspended sentence for the incident, the PADS leader was rearrested in February 1994 and, along with Wade, he was subsequently convicted of provoking antigovernment riots.

The PADS/AJ captured four seats in the 1998 legislative balloting; subsequently it cooperated with the PIT and PLS to run a joint slate of candidates at the January 1999 Senate elections under the banner of "*And Fippu*." After supporting Abdoulaye Wade of the PDS in the 2000 presidential campaign, the PADS/AJ secured two seats in the 2001 legislative poll (on 4.1 percent of the vote) and subsequently joined the PDS-led parliamentary faction. Savane and Mamadou Diop were given posts in subsequent PDS-led governments.

Leaders: Landing SAVANE (Secretary General), Mamadou DIOP.

Convention of Democrats and Patriots (*Convention des Démocrates et des Patriotes*—CDP). Also known as *Garab-Gi* ("The Cure"), the CDP was founded in May 1992 by Iba Der Thiam, a former education minister and UNESCO Executive Council member, who promptly announced his presidential candidacy. Thiam also proposed the signing of a nonaggression pact by opposition parties to encourage election monitoring as well as joint endorsement of the leading opposition candidate at the first round of presidential balloting.

In December 1994 the CDP and the RND (below) issued a joint statement rejecting the

Uniting to Change coalition's call for the drafting of a national consensus program, describing it as a self-serving PDS maneuver. However, after Thiam secured 1.2 percent of the vote in the first round of the 2000 presidential poll, he threw his support behind Wade in the second round, becoming the coordinator of the FAL. The CDP, noted for its antipoverty platform and, more recently, an increasingly Islamic orientation, secured one seat as a member of the *Sopi* Coalition in the 2001 legislative balloting. In May 2005, it was reported that the CDP had agreed to merge with the PDS.

Leader: Iba Der THIAM (1993 and 2000 presidential candidate and Secretary General of the Party).

Movement for Socialism and Unity (*Mouvement pour le Socialisme et l'Unité*—MSU). The MSU was registered in 1981 as the People's Democratic Movement (*Mouvement Démocratique Populaire*—MDP), which, led by longtime Senghor opponent Mamadou Dia, called for a program of socialist self-management of the economy. Dia was one of the few prominent Senegalese political figures to oppose establishment of the Senegambian Confederation. The MDP contested the 1983 general election but boycotted subsequent balloting.

The MSU was listed as a member of Alternance 2000, and official government sources indicated that one MSU member was elected in the 2001 legislative balloting as a member of the *Sopi* Coalition. However, perhaps indicating a split within the party, news reports described the MSU, under the leadership of Sheikh Tidiane BA, as aligning with the PIT for the assembly elections. As of 2002 Ba was still being described as an opponent of the Wade government.

Leaders: Mamadou DIA (Former Prime Minister), Mouhamadou N'DIAYE (National Coordinator).

Action for National Development (*Action pour le Développement National*—ADN). Organized in mid-1996 under the leadership of Mamadou Moustapha Diop, the ADN participated in the *Sopi* Coalition in the 2001 legislative balloting.

Leader: Mamadou Moustapha DIOP.

Senegalese Republican Party (*Parti Sénégalais Républicain*—PSR). In the first round of the 2000 presidential election the PSR's Ousseymou Fall secured 1.12 percent of the vote. Subsequently, the party joined the *Sopi* Coalition for the 2001 legislative poll.

Leaders: Ousseymou FALL (2000 presidential candidate), Ely Madiodo FALL (Secretary General).

Front for Socialism and Democracy (*Front pour le Socialisme et la Démocratie*—FSD). Launched under the direction of a prominent Muslim leader, Cheikh Abdoulaye Dieye, the FSD captured one seat in the 1998 legislative balloting on a platform emphasizing care for the elderly and women. Dieye captured 0.97 percent of the first-round vote in the 2000 presidential election, and the FSD subsequently joined the FAL.

Leader: Cheikh Adoulaye DIEYE.

Other pro-Wade formations include the **Senegalese Democratic Rally** (*Rassemblement Démocratique Sénégalais*—RDS), led by Abdou Latif GUEYE; the **Union of Senegalese Patriots;** the **Popular Democratic Rally** (*Rassemblement Démocratique Populaire*—RDP), formed by Ibrahim Masseck DIOP; the **Democratic Union for Federalism/Mboloomi** (*Union Démocratique pour le Fédéralisme/Mboloomi*—UDF/Mboloomi); and the **Union for Democratic Renewal/Front for Change** (*Union for Democratic Renewal/Front pour l'Alternance*—URD/FAL), a breakaway faction from the URD (below) that joined the *Sopi* Coalition for the 2001 legislative balloting under the leadership of Mahmout SALEH.

Opposition Parties

Socialist Party (*Parti Socialiste*—PS). Known until December 1976 as the Senegalese Progressive Union (*Union Progressiste Sénégalaise*—UPS), the PS consistently held a preponderance of seats in the National Assembly until 2001. A moderate Francophile party long identified with the cause of Senegalese independence, the UPS was founded by Léopold Senghor in 1949 in a secession from the dominant local branch of the French Socialist Party. From 1963 to 1974 it was the only legal party in Senegal; it absorbed the only significant opposition grouping, the leftist *Parti de Regroupement Africain-Sénégal* (PRA) in 1966 in furtherance of Senghor's "national reconciliation" policy. In early 1981, following his resignation of the presidency, Senghor withdrew as party secretary general. During an extraordinary conference in March 1989, the PS voted to assign internal authority to a ten-member Executive Committee that was directed to recruit new members and assist in "rejuvenation" of the party. At the PS congress in 1990, Abdou Diouf was reappointed secretary general and given unchecked control of a restructured, "non-hierarchical," 30-member Politburo.

The PS experienced unprecedented levels of intraparty violence prior to its 1996 congress, spurring a call from Diouf for "reconciliation." Meanwhile Diouf and Ousmane Tanor Dieng were elected to the newly created party presidency and executive secretaryship, respectively, with the latter assuming administrative responsibilities previously assigned to the secretary general.

In March 1998 a PS faction, led by Djibo KA, broke off from the party and formed the URD (below). Among the reasons cited for Ka's decision was Diouf's reported elevation of Dieng to the status of heir apparent.

Another prominent PS member, Moustapha Niasse, left the PS after 40 years to form the AFP (below), the recent departures contributing to Diouf's failure in his 2000 reelection bid. Although Diouf was reconfirmed as the PS leader at an October 2000 congress, he subsequently announced plans to retire from politics.

The PS led the opposition to the 2006 postponement of legislative elections and tried to rally opposition parties. The PS was also reported to be active in efforts to form an electoral coalition ahead of the 2007 balloting.

Leaders: Abdou DIOUF (Former President of the Republic), Mamadou Lamine LOUM (Former Prime Minister), Cheikh Abdoul Khadre CISSOKHO (Former National Assembly President), Ousmane Tanor DIENG (Secretary General).

Alliance of Forces for Progress (*Alliance des Forces pour le Progrès*—AFP). Formed by Moustapha Niasse in the fall of 1999 after he had left the PS, the AFP supported Abdoulaye Wade in the second round of the 2000 presidential election after Niasse had finished third in the first round with 16.76 percent. Under an apparent electoral agreement with Wade, Niasse was named prime minister in Wade's first cabinet, but he subsequently quit that post in early 2001. The AFP, some of whose support comes from the Tidjane Islamic Brotherhood, competed alone in the 2001 legislative elections, finishing second to the *Sopi* Coalition.

Leader: Moustapha NIASSE.

Union for Democratic Renewal (*Union pour le Renouveau Démocratique*—URD). The URD, originally styled the Democratic Renewal (*Renouveau Démocratique*—RD), was formed by former interior minister Djibo Ka in November 1997 to act as a reform group within the PS; however, in December Ka and ten of his dissident colleagues were suspended from the PS for three months. Subsequently, Ka declared his intention to forward an independent list of candidates at legislative balloting in May 1998. In March 1998 the PS rejected Ka's list, and on April 1 he resigned from the group and formally launched the URD. Having emerged from the 1998 legislative polling with 11 seats, the URD presented Ka as its candidate in the first round of the 2000 presidential election. He finished fourth with 7.08 percent of the vote and somewhat surprisingly threw his support to Abdou Diouf in the second round. A split in the URD regarding that decision (one faction joined the *Sopi* Coalition) apparently contributed to the URD's decline to three seats following the 2001 legislative poll.

Leader: Djibo KA (Secretary General and 2000 presidential candidate).

Independence and Labor Party (*Parti de l'Indépendance et du Travail*—PIT). Organized by a group of PAI dissidents and permitted to register in 1981, the PIT was recognized by Moscow as Senegal's "official" Communist Party. It contested both the 1983 and 1984 elections but won no assembly or town council seats. The party joined the LD-MPT in supporting PDS presidential candidate Wade in 1988, while its legislative candidates won only 0.8 percent of the vote and no seats. The PIT secretary general was among those arrested after the elections, but the charges were later dismissed. In mid-1989 the PIT entered into negotiations with the ruling Socialist Party, and the party was awarded two portfolios in the cabinet reshuffle of August 1995. However, both ministers were ousted a month later in the wake of a PIT Central Committee statement critical of the Diouf administration.

The PIT was a member of Alternance 2000 in support of the 2000 presidential bid of Abdoulaye Wade, and the party's secretary general, Amath Dansokho, served in the first Wade cabinet. However, the two leaders subsequently quarreled and Dansokho resigned from the government in early 2001. Dansokho was briefly arrested in July 2005 for making antigovernment statements.

Leader: Amath DANSOKHO (Secretary General).

Alliance Jëf Jël. Formerly known as the Alliance for Progress and Justice/Jëf Jël, this grouping adopted its current name at a party congress in June 2000.

Leaders: Talla SYLLA (President), Moussa TINE.

National Democratic Rally (*Rassemblement National Démocratique*—RND). Established in February 1976, the RND described itself as a "party of the masses." It applied, without success, for recognition in September 1977, and two years later its founder, Cheikh Anta DIOP (who died in 1986), was ordered to stand trial for engaging in unauthorized party activity. The RND was legalized in June 1981; it subsequently repeatedly criticized the government for its position on Chad and for its "systematic alignment with the positions of France and the United States." Evincing an anti-Wade orientation, the RND retained its single legislative seat in 2001, although it garnered only 0.7 percent of the vote.

Leader: Madior DIOUF (Secretary General).

Senegalese Liberal Party (*Parti Libéral Sénégalais*—PLS). The PLS was formed in June 1998 by Ousmane Ngom and a number of other PDS defectors after they failed to gain central committee posts in their former party. At the group's founding meeting, Ngom described the PLS as a vehicle of "liberalism" and denounced Wade's rule of the PDS as monarchical. The PLS participated in the 1999 Senate election in an And Fippu Coalition, which also included the PIT and PADS/AJ.

Leader: Ousmane NGOM.

Other Parties Contesting the 2001 Legislative Elections

African Independence Party (*Parti Africain de l'Indépendance*—PAI). Founded in 1957 and composed mainly of intellectuals in southern Senegal, the PAI was legally dissolved in 1960 but was subsequently recognized as the "Marxist-Leninist" party called for by the 1976 constitutional amendment. Claiming to be the "real PAI," a clandestine wing of the party denounced recognition as a self-serving maneuver by the Senghor government. In March 1980 two leaders of the splinter faction, Amath Dansokho and Maguette THIAM, were charged with inciting workers to strike, but in 1981 they were permitted to register the group as a distinct party (see PIT, above). Having unsuccessfully contested the 1983 election, the PAI joined the November 1984 boycott. In early 1987 the formation of a front uniting the PAI with the MDP (see under MSU, above) and the former Communist Workers' League (*Ligue Communiste des Travailleurs*—LCT) was announced, although no legislative candidates were presented by any of the three in 1988.

The PAI supported Abdou Diouf in the 2000 presidential campaign and presented its own candidates (unsuccessfully) in the 2001 legislative poll.

Leaders: Majhemouth DIOP (President), Balla N'DIAYE (Vice President), Bara GOUDIABY (Secretary General).

Senegalese Republican Movement (*Mouvement Républicain Sénégalais*—MRS). The MRS is a self-styled "right-wing" party organized by former National Assembly vice president Boubacar GUÈYE. In August 1977 the party applied for legal recognition, which was not granted until February 1979. It supports human rights, free enterprise, and private property. At the domestic political level, it has urged parliamentary election of the president; regionally, it has proposed the introduction of a common currency for OAU member countries.

Leader: Demba BA (Secretary General).

Party for the African Renaissance (*Parti pour la Renaissance Africaine*—PARENA). Devoted primarily to the issues of women's rights and the "lack of transparency" in governmental affairs, PARENA attempted to present its leader, Mariame Ly Wane, as a presidential candidate in 2000 but she was disqualified on technical grounds.

Leader: Mariame Ly WANE.

Senegalese People's Party (*Parti Populaire Sénégalais*—PPS). Legalized in December 1981, the PPS was also organized by a number of PAI adherents, who did not immediately delineate its program, indicating only that they supported the "restructuring of Senegalese society on new and scientific bases." Some of its members have been involved in demonstrations led by Casamance separatists (see MFDC, below). The party received only 0.2 percent of the vote in the 1983 legislative and presidential elections and did not participate in 1988 or 1993.

Leaders: Semou Pathe GUEYE, Magatte LOUM, Dr. Oumar WANE (Secretary General).

Other parties that competed unsuccessfully in the 2001 legislative balloting were the **Rally of Ecologists of Senegal** (*Rassemblement des Écologists du Sénégal*—RES); **Party of Renewal and Citizenship** (*Parti de la Renaissance et de la Citoyenneté*—PRC); the **Assembly of African Workers–Senegal** (*Rassemblement des Travailleurs Africains–Sénégal*—RTA-S), a social-democratic party recognized in March 1997; the **Reform Movement for Social Development** (*Mouvement de la Réforme pour le Développement Social*—MRDS); the **Movement for Democracy and Socialism/Naxx

Jarinu** (*Mouvement pour la Démocratie et le Socialisme/Naxx Jarinu*—MDS/NJ); the **Union for the Republic** (*Union pour la République*—UPR); the **Social Democratic Party/Jant-Bi;** the **Democratic Union of Progressive Patriotic Forces** (*Union Démocratique des Forces Progressistes Patriotiques*—UDFP); and the **Citizens' Movement for a Democracy of Development** (*Mouvement des Citoyens pour une Démocratie de Développement*).

Other Parties and Groups

Senegalese Democratic Union–Renewal (*Union Démocratique Sénégalais–Rénovation*—UDS-R). Organized in February 1985 and legally recognized in July, the UDS-R is led by Mamadou Fall, a well-known trade-union leader and former deputy, who was expelled from the PDS while in the assembly for "divisive activities." Fall describes himself as a "progressive nationalist" seeking to promote the "unification of healthy forces." The party presented no candidates in 1988. It secured one legislative seat in May 1993, which it retained in 1998.

Leader: Mamadou Puritain FALL (Secretary General).

Other parties include the **Action Front for Renewal/"The Way"** (*Front d'Action pour le Renouveav/Yoon Wi*—FAR/Yoon Wi), led by Bathie SECK; the **Gainde Centrist Bloc** (*Bloc des Gainde Centristes*—BGC), which captured a single seat in the May 1998 legislative balloting under the leadership of PDS dissident Jean-Paul DIAS, who was arrested in April 2006 for antigovernment remarks; the **Reform Party** (*Parti de la Réforme*—PR), whose leader, Abdourahim AGNE, was arrested in May 2005 for sedition; and the **Rally for Unity and Peace** (*Rassemblement pour l'Unité et la Paix*—RUP), a Louga-based grouping headed by Moctar N'DIAYE.

Illegal Groups

Movement of Democratic Forces of Casamance (*Mouvement des Forces Démocratiques de la Casamance*—MFDC). The MFDC was launched as a clandestine grouping advocating the secession of the Casamance region of southern Senegal. Many supporters, including MFDC leader Fr. Augustin Diamacoune Senghor, were jailed following demonstrations in the provincial capital of Ziguinchor in the early 1980s, and another 152 people were arrested in 1986 for allegedly attending a secret MFDC meeting. Diamacoune and most of the other detainees were subsequently released, the government being perceived as having adopted a more conciliatory approach in dealing with the separatist issue. However, new MFDC-army clashes were reported in late 1988.

In a series of actions that commenced in mid-1990, Diamacoune and most other MFDC civilian leaders were arrested or forced into exile following a resurgence of separatist violence spearheaded by *Attika* ("Fighter"), the MFDC's military wing. The uprising, which the separatists claimed was the result of their being economically and socially marginalized, continued through late 1990. However, in May 1991, following a series of secret meetings with ethnic Diola parliamentarians negotiating on Diouf's behalf, MFDC leaders agreed to a cease-fire and disarmament. Reports of the negotiations supported observers' suspicions that the separatists encompassed a limited number (300–500) of ethnic Diolas.

In April and May 1992 renewed separatist activity was attributed to a militant MFDC splinter and despite an escalating verbal confrontation between Dakar and the MFDC leadership over the military's allegedly heavy-handed response to the violence, the Diouf administration, as late as September, absolved the MFDC leadership of blame for the cease-fire breakdown.

On July 8, 1993, the MFDC signed a cease-fire agreement with the government that included provisions for further negotiations, a bilateral prisoner release, the deployment of French military observers, and the establishment of a refugee repatriation program. However, renewed clashes were reported three days later, and open fighting resumed following the government's killing of an MFDC activist in September. Thereafter, no serious cease-fire violations were reported until January 1995,

when a pro-independence faction led by Léopold SANIA rejected the peace accord and resumed guerrilla activities. Following a government air attack on an alleged MFDC base in Guinea-Bissau in February, the rebels denied having personnel there.

In April 1995 the government deployed an additional 1,000 troops in the Casamance region in response to persistent breaches of the cease-fire, including the disappearance of four French tourists who were assumed to have been kidnapped by the MFDC. In late April the government announced the arrest of some 50 suspected activists, including Father Diamacoune, and in mid-July the separatists formally abandoned the cease-fire. While Diamacoune's imprisonment served as a rallying point for MFDC faithful during the 1995 crisis, his influence with party militants reportedly had already begun to wane. Subsequently, despite his declaration of a unilateral cease-fire in January 1996, rebel attacks continued throughout the first half of the year.

After a year of relative calm in the region, fierce fighting broke out in August 1997 as the government responded to renewed rebel activity with a massive offensive, and by late September over 100 people were reported dead. Meanwhile, the fighting widened the split in the MFDC between the hardline northern wing, led by Mamadou Sane, and Diamacoune's predominantly southern followers, who were described as prepared to abandon their demand for independence in return for a government promise to speed development of the region. In early 1998 the two factions were reported to be in open conflict. Furthermore, troops from Guinea-Bissau were reportedly laying siege to Sane's long-time safe havens within Bissau's border.

In March 1998 the government claimed to have killed 50 MFDC fighters preparing to attack a village near Ziguinchor. Thereafter, fighting was reported throughout the region during the run-up to legislative polling; however, the government deployed a large number of forces to the area for the balloting period, and few incidents were reported.

Amid reports that the MFDC was preparing to enter into negotiations with the Diouf administration, the group's military and political leaders met in Banjul, Gambia, in April 1999. However, on

April 30, 17 people were reported killed in a clash between the rebels and government forces, thus underscoring continued reports that the movement was splintered.

Some MFDC fighters were reported to have disarmed in mid-1999, and another questionable cease-fire was announced late in the year. However, the leadership dispute within the MFDC continued, as did the low-level war between rebels and government troops. Additional negotiations were launched in December 2000, new Senegalese President Abdoulaye Wade having declared resolution of the conflict a top priority for his government. A peace pact was again announced in March 2001, ostensibly providing for a cease-fire, release of prisoners, return of refugees and displaced persons, and infrastructure rehabilitation, particularly road repairs. It also appeared that Diamacoune and his supporters had renounced their secessionist stance and instead had agreed to pursue greater autonomy for the region while remaining a part of Senegal. The accord was greeted hopefully by many observers, especially following a face-to-face meeting between Wade and Diamacoune and the MFDC's call for fighters to lay down their guns for the April national legislative balloting. Banditry and sporadic killings continued, however, precluding finalization of a permanent settlement.

At a mid-2001 MFDC Congress, Diamacoune was moved to the group's presidency, a role considered more ceremonial in nature than his previous post. Meanwhile, Sidi Badji, a hard-liner perceived as a rival to Diamacoune, was reportedly named head of military affairs. Badji subsequently claimed the secretary general's position, and the power struggle between his "radical" faction (which also included military commander Salif SADIO) and Diamacoune's "peacemaking" faction continued into mid-2002. On September 19, 2004, Diamacoune became honorary president, while Biagui became the effective leader of the MFDC. Meanwhile, continuing violence barred much rehabilitation of the poverty-stricken region. The MFDC signed a peace agreement with the government on December 30, 2004. The MFDC plans to reestablish itself as a legitimate political party and contest legislative elections in 2007. In March 2006, the Sadio-led faction of the MFDC launched attacks against other MFDC groupings. In response, security forces from Guinea-Bissau launched an offensive against MFDC positions in an attempt to end the factional fighting.

Leaders: Fr. Augustin DIAMACOUNE Senghor (Honorary President), Mamadou SANE, Sidi BADJI, Jean-Marie BIAGUI (Secretary General).

Men and Women Fighting for Truth (*Dahira Moustarchidine wal Moustarchidate*). A radical Islamic youth movement, the group, also known as "Guides," was banned on February 17, 1994, two days after a violent protest in Dakar calling for President Diouf's ouster. A month earlier the group's leader, Mostapha Sy, had been sentenced to a one-year prison term for an antigovernment speech at a PDS rally in October 1993.

Leader: Mostapha SY.

Legislature

The **National Assembly** currently consists (as authorized by constitutional revision in January 2001) of 120 members, 65 elected on a majoritarian basis at the department level and 55 elected on a proportional basis from national party lists. Members serve five-year terms, although the assembly is subject to presidential dissolution after two years. The 2001 constitutional revision also eliminated the Senate, a 45-member body (elected by the assembly and local, municipal, and regional officials) that had first been elected in January 1999.

At the most recent assembly balloting of April 29, 2001, the *Sopi* Coalition (led by the Senegalese Democratic Party) won 89 seats; the Alliance of Forces for Progress, 11; the Socialist Party, 10; the Union for Democratic Renewal, 3; the African Party for Democracy and Socialism/And Jëf, 2; and the Senegalese Liberal Party, the Party for Progress and Citizenship, the Alliance Jëf Jël, the National Democratic Rally, and the Independence and Labor Party, 1 each. (The elections due in May 2006 were postponed to 2007).

President: Pape DIOP.

Cabinet

As of July 1, 2006

Prime Minister	Macky Sall (PDS)

Ministers of State

Economy and Finance	Abdoulaye Diop (ind.)
Fisheries	Djibo Leyti Ka
Foreign Affairs	Cheikh Tidiane Gadio (ind.)
Infrastructure, Equipment, and Transport	Habib Sy
Justice; Keeper of the Seals	Cheikh Tidiane Sy

Ministers

Agriculture and Water	Farba Senghor
Armed Forces	Bécaye Diop (PDS)
Civil Service, Labor and Professional Organizations	Adama Sall
Commerce	Mamadou Diop (PDS/AJ)
Culture and Communication	Mame Birame Diouf
Decentralization and Regional Planning	Ousmane Ngom
Education	Moustapha Sourang (ind.)
Environment and Conservation	Thierno Lo
Expatriates	Abdoul Diop
Family and Social Development	Aida Mbodj [f]
Health, Hygiene, and Medical Prevention	Issa Mbaye Samb [f]
Housing and Construction	Oumar Sarr
Industry and Handicrafts	Bineta Samb Ba [f]
Information and Government Spokesman	Bacar Dia
International Cooperation and Regional Cooperation	Lamine Ba
Livestock	Oumou Khairy Gueye Seck [f]
Mining and Energy	Madicke Niang
NEPAD and Good Governance	Abdoul Aziz Sow
Parliamentary and African Union Relations	Awa Fall Diop [f]
Planning and Sustainable Development	Mamadou Sidibe
Posts, Telecommunications, and Information and	Joseph Ndong (PDS)
New Communication Technologies	Joseph Ndong (PDS)
Prevention, Public Hygiene, and Sanitation	Abdou Fall
Scientific Research and Technology	Yaye Kene Gassama Dia
Small- and Medium-Sized Enterprises and	Marie-Pierre Sarr Traore [f]
Women's Entrepreneurship and Micro-Finance	Marie-Pierre Sarr Traore [f]
Sport	Daouda Faye
Technical and Professional Education	Georges Tendeng
Tourism and Air Transport	Ousmane Masseck Ndiaye
Urban and Regional Planning	Assane Diagne
Youth	Aliou Sow

Ministers Delegate	
Budget	Adjibou Soumare
Literacy, National Languages, and Francophonie	Diegane Sene
Local Development	Sokhna Toure Fall [f]
Preschool Education	Ibrahima Fall [f]
[f] = female	

Communications

Press

Newspapers are subject to government censorship and regulation, although a number of opposition papers have recently appeared in the 1990s, some evading official registration by means of irregular publication, and restrictions have eased significantly in recent years. The following, unless otherwise noted, are published daily in French in Dakar: *Le Soleil* (45,000), government-owned; *Sud Quotidien* (30,000), independent; *Wal Fadjiri* (The Dawn, 15,000), independent Islamic daily; *Le Matin,* independent; *Le Populaire,* independent; *L'Actuel; Tract; La Pointe; Afrique Nouvelle* (15,000), Catholic weekly; *Sénégal d'Aujourd'hui* (5,000), published monthly by the Ministry of Communications; *Nouvel Horizon,* independent weekly; *Eco Hebdo,* weekly.

News Agencies

Agence de Presse Sénégalaise (APS) is the official facility; the Pan-African News Agency (PANA), as well as a number of foreign agencies, also maintain offices in Dakar.

Broadcasting and Computing

Broadcasting is controlled by the *Radiodiffusion-Télévision du Sénégal* (RTS). In July 1994 *SUD FM,* Senegal's first private radio station, joined two radio networks, *Radio Sénégal-Inter* and *Radio Sénégal II.* On November 14, 2005, West African Democracy Radio (WADR) began broadcasting from Dakar throughout West Africa. The station was created with support from the Open Society Initiative for West Africa. A number of new independent radio stations have started broadcasting recently, their aggressive reporting having reportedly contributed to the opposition's electoral victories in 2000 and 2001. In addition to the state television channel, there are several semi-private stations. There were approximately 395,000 television sets and 220,000 personal computers serving 225,000 Internet users in 2003.

Intergovernmental Representation

Ambassador to the U.S.
Amadou Lamine BA

U.S. Ambassador to Senegal
Janice L. JACOBS

Permanent Representative to the UN
Paul BADJI

IGO Memberships (Non-UN)
AfDB, AU, BADEA, BOAD, CILSS, ECOWAS, IDB, Interpol, IOM, NAM, OIC, OIF, PCA, UEMOA, WCO, WTO

SEYCHELLES

REPUBLIC OF SEYCHELLES

Repiblik Sesel
République des Seychelles

The Country

The Seychelles archipelago consists of some 115 islands in the Indian Ocean about 600 miles northeast of Madagascar. Over 85 percent of the population is concentrated on the largest island, Mahé, which has an area of approximately 55 square miles (142 sq. km.); most of the remainder is distributed between the two northern islands of Praslin and La Digue. Most Seychellois are of mixed French-African descent and adhere to Roman Catholicism. There are small minority groups of Indians and Chinese. Nearly 98 percent of adult women are classified as "economically active," largely in subsistence agriculture; women are, however, more likely than men to be literate.

Tourism is a significant source of national income and employs about 30 percent of the labor force. Small-scale industries provide about one-quarter of GDP, while the fishing sector produces about 30 percent of export earnings. The export of copra has declined sharply in recent years, and other cash crops are limited in scope. The economy is also underpinned by a growing offshore banking sector. (Hopes that oil would deliver economic salvation receded in October 1995 when a British company abandoned exploratory drilling south of the islands, though renewed optimism was evidenced when a U.S. firm was awarded a similar bid in 2005.) After recording moderate increases during the previous several years, GDP contracted by 3 percent in 1999, with consumer prices rising by 6.2 percent. The slump was attributed by the International Monetary Fund (IMF) and other observers to

a recent fall in tourism revenues, the government's continued heavy involvement in the economy, and a dramatic shortage of foreign currency reserves. Modest improvement was achieved in 2000, with GDP growing by 1.2 percent, but the economy subsequently dropped again, with real GDP declining significantly in 2002–2005. (In early 2005 the Paris Club canceled Seychelles' debt following the December 2004 Indian Ocean tsunami.) Though real GDP growth was projected to improve somewhat in 2006, it was still expected to remain in negative numbers (−1.4 percent, compared to −2.3 percent in 2005.) The government has recently solicited foreign investment for the tourism sector and

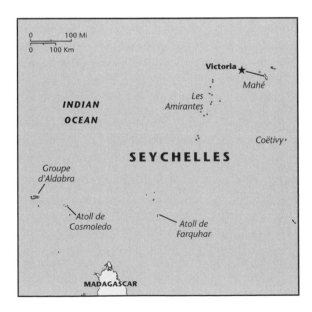

Political Status: Independent member of the Commonwealth since June 29, 1976; present constitution approved by referendum of June 18, 1993.

Area: 171 sq. mi. (429 sq. km.).

Resident Population: 75,876 (1997C); 83,500 (2005E); some 30,000 Seychellois live abroad, mainly in Australia and the United Kingdom.

Major Urban Center (2005E): VICTORIA (25,100).

National Languages: Creole, English, French. (Creole had replaced English and French as the official language in 1981, but all three languages were codified as "national languages" in the 1993 constitution.)

Monetary Unit: Seychelles Rupee (official rate July 1, 2006: 5.52 rupees = $1US).

President: James Alix MICHEL (Seychelles People's Progressive Front); installed as president on April 14, 2004, following the retirement of France Albert RENÉ (Seychelles People's Progressive Front); elected to a five-year term in presidential balloting of July 28–30, 2006, and inaugurated on August 1.

Vice President: Joseph BELMONT (Seychelles People's Progressive Front); nominated by the president on April 15, 2004, and confirmed by the National Assembly on April 16; elected with running mate President Michel in balloting of July 28–30, 2006, and inaugurated on August 1.

promoted Seychelles as a provider of offshore financial services. However, the IMF noted there is little such activity in the latter area because of the lack of financial supervision in Seychelles. The IMF cited an "urgent" need for banking reforms and legislation that would criminalize the financing of terrorism.

Government and Politics

Political Background

Following a half-century of French rule, Seychelles became a British possession under the Treaty of Paris in 1814. Originally administered from Mauritius, it became a Crown Colony in 1903. A partially elected governing council was established in 1967, and limited self-government under a chief minister was introduced in 1970. Following a constitutional conference in London in March 1975, the legislative assembly established in 1970 was increased from 15 to 25 members, the 10 new members being nominated by the two parties in the government coalition. Concurrent with the achievement of independence on June 29, 1976, the former chief minister, James R. MANCHAM, was designated president, and the former leader of the opposition, France Albert RENÉ, became prime minister.

On June 5, 1977, while the president was attending a Commonwealth conference in London, the government was overthrown in a near-bloodless coup that installed René as the new head of state. In balloting on June 23–26, 1979, conducted under a single-party socialist constitution adopted on March 26, René was confirmed in office for a five-year term.

After assuming power, President René encountered a series of external and internal challenges to his authority. In November 1979 he announced the discovery of an antigovernment plot "sponsored from abroad" that allegedly involved ousted president Mancham and a force of mercenaries based in Durban, South Africa. Among the 85–100 people arrested in the wake of the allegations were the head of the country's immigration service, a former minister of finance, and a French citizen who had been advising the Seychelles police force. A potentially more serious threat was averted in November 1981 with the detection at Mahé's Pointe Larue airport of a group of mercenaries led by the celebrated Col. Michael ("Mad Mike") Hoare, an Irishman who had been involved in a number of African destabilization efforts during the previous two decades. In the course of a pitched battle with units of the Seychelles People's Defence Force (SPDF), some 45 of the invaders commandeered an Air India Boeing 707 and ordered the pilot to fly them to Durban, where they eventually surrendered to South African police. Released on bail in early December, the mercenaries were rearrested on January 5, 1982, in the wake of mounting international criticism. Most were given modest jail sentences under the South African Civil Aviation Offenses Act, Colonel Hoare ultimately being released in May 1985.

In August 1982 some 150 lower-ranked members of the SPDF seized key installations on Mahé in an abortive protest against alleged ill-treatment by senior military officials, while in September 1986 a number of army officers loyal to the minister of defense, Col. Ogilvy BERLOUIS, were charged with plotting to assassinate the president. In London, the exile Seychelles National Movement (*Mouvement National Seychellois*—MNS) claimed knowledge of the 1986 plot, saying that the principals had been divided as to its implementation; subsequently, Colonel Berlouis resigned his post and left the country for Britain.

Despite exile opposition calls for a boycott, President René was reelected by a reported 92.6 percent of the vote on June 17, 1984, after having announced that those failing to participate would lose their right to public assistance. The National Assembly was subsequently replenished at single-party balloting on December 5, 1987, while the president was accorded a third term on June 9–11, 1989. In early 1990 President René declared that recent developments in Eastern Europe were of no concern to his administration, and at midyear he insisted that the Seychelles would "continue on the same path" with no acceptance of political change. However, in November he adopted a somewhat different posture by commenting favorably on the possibility of a reform referendum, albeit with reference only to the conduct of intraparty affairs. In March 1991 he was further reported to favor limited administrative decentralization through the reestablishment of district councils, whose members would, however, have to be supporters of the ruling Seychelles People's Progressive Front (SPPF).

On September 12, 1991, the assembly approved a Local Government Bill that provided for the multiple candidature, one-party election of local councils, whose heads were to meet with the Central Committee of the SPPF to rule on the desirability of a referendum on constitutional revision. However, in a remarkable turnabout on December 3, an extraordinary SPPF congress (meeting with the council heads elected two days earlier and identified as constituting a new assembly) voted unanimously to endorse an unexpected proposal by René to introduce a pluralist system. Under the plan (formally approved by the assembly on December 27), opposition parties would be permitted to register by January 1992 and a Constituent Committee would be elected by proportional representation in July to draft a new constitution. Earlier, the president had called on all political exiles, including his predecessor, to return to the Seychelles, provided that they retract their "accusations" against his regime.

At the Constituent Committee balloting on July 26, 1992, the SPPF won 14 seats on the basis of a 58.4 percent vote share, while the Democratic Party (DP) of former president Mancham was awarded 8 seats on the basis of a 33.7 percent share; no other groups secured representation. On September 18 the DP delegation withdrew from the constitutional talks, charging the SPPF with "bulldozer tactics" in attempting to meet a presidential deadline for a referendum on the document in November and a general election in December. Six days later Mancham announced a DP boycott of the proceedings, with the SPPF delegation (which constituted a quorum) indicating that it would continue alone. On October 6 opposition objectives became more specific: (1) separation of the overlapping roles of district councilors and local party officials; (2) termination of links between the SPPF and the armed forces; (3) a halt to state funding for the SPPF; (4) unhindered access to the media, including autonomy for the Seychelles Broadcasting Company; and (5) deletion of an electoral provision that would allocate nondirectly elective legislative seats in accordance with the distribution of the presidential vote.

In the face of opposition criticism, the draft constitution secured the approval of only 53.7 percent of the votes cast (60 percent being needed for acceptance) at the referendum of November 15, 1992. The DP thereupon returned to the Constituent Committee and participated in the approval on May 7, 1993, of a revised draft that received popular endorsement by 73.6 percent of participating voters on June 18. At a general election under the new basic law on July 23, President René retained his office on the basis of a 60 percent vote share, while the SPPF was victorious in all but one of the directly elective constituencies.

New presidential and assembly elections were held on March 20–22, 1998, with President René and the SPPF again winning by convincing margins. René was reelected with 67 percent of the vote, 7 points higher than he had scored in the 1993 election; in addition, James MICHEL, whom René had appointed as vice president the previous year, was elected as René's running mate. (Michel had taken on a number of René's former duties as a consequence of the president's ill health and was widely considered to be the likely presidential successor.) René's nearest competitor was Rev. Wavel RAMKALAWAN, leader of the United Opposition (UO), who secured 20 percent of the vote, while former president Mancham of the DP finished with 14 percent. The DP also fared poorly in the assembly balloting, winning only one seat (down from the five they had held previously). Meanwhile, the SPPF, with 30 legislative seats, improved its total by 3 from 1993; the UO became the main opposition party, such as it was, with 3 assembly seats.

Following the approval by the National Assembly in 2000 of a constitutional amendment allowing the president to call presidential elections separately from legislative elections, René called for an early presidential poll on August 31–September 2, 2001. Once again facing Ramkalawan (representing the Seychelles National Party [SNP] as the UO had been renamed), René was reelected with 54.19 percent of the vote. Ramkalawan, however, significantly improved his vote share to 44.95 percent, partly because of Mancham's decision not to run. The cabinet announced by René on September 5 included reshuffled assignments but no new members.

In October 2002 the assembly voted to dissolve itself and hold new legislative balloting on December 4–6. Although the SPPF retained its plurality (23 of 34 seats on a 54 percent vote share), the SNP improved from 3 to 11 seats (on a 40 percent vote share).

President René, citing the fact that he was "getting older," resigned the presidency on March 31, 2004, and Michel was inaugurated as his successor on April 14. Joseph BELMONT, a cabinet member since 1982, was confirmed as vice president by the assembly on April 16. An opposition (SNP) motion to dissolve the assembly to allow for parliamentary elections at the same time as presidential balloting in 2006—a year ahead of schedule—was rejected by the full body in May 2006. Presidential elections subsequently were held July 28–30, 2006, in which the incumbent Michel and running mate Vice President Belmont garnered 53.73 percent of the votes. Michel, elected for a five-year term, defeated the SNP's Ramkalawan and running mate Annette GEORGES (45.71 percent of the vote), and independent Philippe BOULLÉ (0.56 percent). A reshuffled cabinet was sworn in on August 9, 2006.

Constitution and Government

The 1993 constitution provides for a multiparty presidential system, under which the chief executive is elected for a thrice-renewable five-year term. Legislative authority is vested in a unicameral National Assembly. Constitutional amendments introduced in July 1996, following their adoption by an SPPF congress in late May, created the post of vice president and also increased the number of directly elective seats in the assembly from 22 to 25, while reducing the proportional seats to a maximum of 10 subject to a threshold of 10 percent of the vote.

The judiciary encompasses a Court of Appeal, a Supreme Court (part of which sits as a Constitutional Court), an Industrial Court, and magistrates' courts. Local government, seemingly necessary for geographic reasons, was abolished in 1971 following problems growing out of a district council system that had been introduced in 1948. However, the councils were revived in 1991.

Foreign Relations

The main objectives of Seychelles' foreign policy following independence were the "return" of a number of small islands and island groups administered since 1965 as part of the British

Indian Ocean Territory and designation of the Indian Ocean as a "zone of peace." In March 1976, prior to debate on the Seychelles independence bill in the House of Commons, the British government indicated that arrangements had been made for the return to Seychelles of the islands of Aldabra, Desroches, and Farquhar; however, the Chagos Archipelago would remain as the sole component of the British Indian Ocean Territory. Included in the archipelago is Diego Garcia, where the United States, under an agreement concluded with Britain in 1972, maintained military and communications facilities. There was also a U.S. space-tracking station on the island of Mahé, where, despite the Diego Garcia issue, relations between American personnel and the Seychellois were relatively cordial. In July 1989, while visiting Washington, President René agreed to a five-year extension of the station's lease, which in 1984 provided 5 percent of the state's revenue. In 1995 Washington announced it was closing the station in a cost-cutting move and transferring its activity to a new facility on Diego Garcia.

Relations between Seychelles and South Africa were by no means enhanced as a result of the 1981 coup attempt on Mahé. The South African proceedings against Colonel Hoare and his associates were confined entirely to air piracy charges on the ground that judicial notice could not be taken of activities beyond Pretoria's jurisdiction. The defendants nonetheless argued that the coup had been undertaken with arms supplied by the South African Defence Force and with the full knowledge of the National Intelligence Service (NIS). The trial judge agreed that it would be "naive" to assume that the NIS was unaware of the plot, since one of the mercenaries was a former NIS agent. This finding was not disputed by Prime Minister P. W. Botha, who nevertheless argued that "neither the South African Government, the Cabinet nor the State Security Council" had been informed and that "no authorization was therefore given for any action." Significantly, 34 of the mercenaries convicted on the air piracy charges were given time off for good behavior and released on November 27, 1982, after spending only four months in prison. By early 1992 relations between the two countries had noticeably warmed, permitting the establishment of consular and trade (though not ambassadorial) relations.

In mid-1988 Seychelles established formal diplomatic relations with the neighboring island states of Mauritius and the Comoros. The three, along with Madagascar and France (representing Réunion), are members of the Indian Ocean Commission (IOC) set up in 1982 to promote regional cooperation and economic development.

Relations with the United States were also damaged in 1996 by the withdrawal of the U.S. satellite-tracking operations on Mahé (which yielded $4.5 million a year to the Seychelles treasury) and by the closure of the U.S. embassy in Victoria (responsibility for Seychelles transferring to the U.S. ambassador to Mauritius). In addition, a U.S. State Department report in March criticized Seychelles' human rights record, referring to the ruling party's "pervasive system of political patronage and control over government jobs, contracts, and resources." (Similar criticisms were included also in the department's 2001 report.) In the wake of increasing global terrorist attacks, the United States in 2005 pledged continued support to the Seychelles military (see Current issues, below).

Current Issues

There was little effective challenge to President René and the SPPF at the 1998 general elections. UO President Ramkalawan subsequently emerged as the primary government critic, his uncompromising stance reportedly garnering a degree of additional public support in view of growing economic difficulties, which included a large trade imbalance, debt payment arrears, and slumping tourism. The IMF urged a reduction in spending on state-run enterprises and other structural reforms, and the administration imposed modest austerity measures in late 1998. However, the private sector subsequently continued to press for trade liberalization measures, particularly the elimination of the government's monopoly on the sale of certain products. The administration remained opposed to the reforms as of mid-2000, earning further reproach from the IMF, World Bank, and the African Development Bank. The government also continued to promote the offshore banking sector, despite the fact that Seychelles had already been placed on the list of questionable "tax havens" by the Organization for Economic Cooperation and Development (OECD).

René's call for early presidential elections in 2001 was viewed by some observers as an attempt to show the world, particularly foreign investors, that his government had not lost popular support. It was also noted that a convincing victory might have permitted René to implement the austerity measures being demanded by the international financial community. However, the president's 54 percent vote share in the balloting was widely perceived as surprisingly narrow and unlikely to empower the government to launch any bold economic initiatives. In addition, runner-up Wavel Ramkalawan accused the government of voter intimidation and other electoral abuses, and he and his SNP boycotted René's inaugural. (International observers were divided on whether the elections were completely free and fair, although it was generally conceded that the alleged violations, even if true, would not have been sufficient to have altered the final outcome of the race.)

René in March 2002 rejected the reforms outlined by the IMF on the grounds that they would "cripple the economy." However, following the SPPF's decline in the early assembly elections in December, dialogue was reopened with the IMF and several requested reforms were enacted. Subsequently, the European Parliament in 2003 questioned the status of human rights in Seychelles following a crackdown on SNP supporters. In addition, in early 2004 opposition leaders argued that the René administration was attempting to limit their voice in the assembly and decrease the authority of the assembly overall. Consequently, René's decision to relinquish the rest of his presidential term to his longtime ally James Michel in April 2004 was not a complete surprise. René, 68, said he was retiring because he wanted to turn power over to a "younger person" who would nevertheless continue the policies pursued by René since the 1977 coup. (René's 27-year tenure was one of the longest ever for an African head of state.)

The Indian Ocean tsunami of December 2004 produced few casualties in Seychelles but caused some $30 million in damage. Significantly, considering earlier tension (see Foreign relations, above) the United States promised reconstruction aid. Among other things, U.S. officials said that the United States and Seychelles had developed a good "military-to-military relationship." Washington reportedly viewed Seychelles as important geographically as a transit area for visiting U.S. ships. There were also concerns that Seychelles could be used as a transfer point by terrorists seeking access to Africa.

The SNP initially demanded early presidential elections upon René's resignation, claiming the SPPF was simply attempting to provide Michel with a "training ground" for the 2006 election. (Michel's elevation to the presidency was constitutionally authorized.) However, SNP leader Ramkalawan subsequently accepted Michel's presidency, Michel reportedly having made reconciliation overtures to long-standing René opponents. For his part, Michel pledged to concentrate on improving the economy, with emphasis on dialogue with the private sector (a potentially significant policy shift). Meanwhile, René continued to serve as the leader of the SPPF and retained significant political influence in general. In mid-2006, Ramkalawan was unsuccessful in his bid to dissolve the assembly so that concurrent elections could be held with presidential balloting (see Political background, above). While all 11 legislators of the SNP voted in favor of the motion, all 22 members of the SPPF voted against, the majority party contending that the minority party lacked the authority to call for dissolution of the assembly.

Political Parties

Prior to the 1977 coup, government was shared by the centrist Seychelles Democratic Party (SDP), led by President James R. Mancham, and the left-of-center Seychelles People's United Party (SPUP), headed by Prime Minister France René. Following the coup, René stated that the SDP "has not been banned, it has simply disappeared." The government-supportive Seychelles People's Progressive Front (SPPF) was the sole legal party from June 1978 until January 1991, following which other parties, including Mancham's Democratic Party were recognized. Provision was also made for the financial support of parties from public funds.

Government Party

Seychelles People's Progressive Front —SPPF (*Front Populaire Progressiste des Seychelles*—FPPS). The SPPF was organized in early 1978 as successor to the SPUP. Like its predecessor, it advocated a broad spectrum of "progressive" policies while attempting to cultivate relations with Catholic clergy sympathetic to its approach to social issues. Upon the retirement of Secretary General Guy SINON in May 1984, President René was named to succeed him as head of an expanded secretariat of 13 members, René's former position as party president being abolished.

In an address before the SPPF annual congress in 1985, René called for improvements in agriculture, employment, and housing, while emphasizing that "the rights of the majority come before the rights of the individual." Delegates to the party's fifth congress in 1991 approved a Central Committee declaration that "the SPPF believes in the one-party system and in the socialist option" but left open the possibility of a future referendum on multipartyism. It also endorsed revival of an earlier system of party-controlled elective district councils, prior to approving a return to political pluralism at an extraordinary congress in December (see Political background, above). Most of the previous members were retained in the Central Committee elected at the May 1998 SPPF congress. René was reelected as party chair during the annual SPPF conference on April 3, 2005, even though many observers had expected him to vacate the post following his resignation as president of the Republic in 2004.

Leaders: James Alix MICHEL (President of the Republic and Secretary General of the Party),

Joseph BELMONT (Vice President of the Republic), France Albert RENÉ (Former President of the Republic and Chair of the Party), Daniel FAURE, Francis MACGREGOR (Speaker of the National Assembly).

Opposition Party

Seychelles National Party (SNP). The SNP is the successor to the United Opposition (UO), which changed its name at a July 1998 congress. The UO had been formed by the three parties immediately below to oppose the 1993 constitution in both its original and final forms. Its candidate, Philippe Boulle, ran a distant third in the presidential balloting of July 23, while its legislative success was limited to a single proportionally allocated seat. Boulle announced his retirement from politics in September 1995 (see National Alliance Party, below) during the party's first convention, at which its member of parliament, Rev. Wavel Ramkalawan, defeated Gabriel Hoareau of the MNS for the party presidency. Ramkalawan finished second in the 1998 presidential election with 20 percent of the vote. The UO won three seats in parliament to become the leading opposition group, and Ramkalawan (who was reelected as party leader during the July 1998 congress at which the SNP rubric was adopted) subsequently attracted substantial press coverage for his "fierce" criticism of the René administration. While relations between Ramkalawan and René appeared to improve during the 2002 elections, government forces launched a crackdown on an SNP demonstration in July 2003. The SNP subsequently won 11 seats in the December 2002 legislative elections. During the party's annual convention in August 2005, Ramkalawan appealed to Nichol Gabriel, former interim leader of the Democratic Party (DP), to form an alliance with the SNP prior to the upcoming elections (see DP, below).

Leaders: Rev. Wavel RAMKALAWAN (President of the Party and 1998, 2001, and 2006 presidential candidate), Annette GEORGES (Treasurer and Ramkalawan's 2006 running mate), Roger MANCIENNE (Secretary).

Seychelles Party (*Parti Seselwa*—PS). Led by Jean-François Ferrari, son of Maxime Ferrari (former foreign minister and leader of the RPSD, see below), and formerly referenced most frequently by its French rubric, *Parti Seychellois,* the free enterprise-oriented PS was, prior to its legalization, the domestic clandestine affiliate of the RPSD/UDM (see below). The younger Ferrari remained party leader upon the return of his father, who occupied himself primarily with the launching of a new *Institut Seychellois pour la Démocratie.* Jean-François Ferrari, publisher of the opposition weekly *Regar*, was among those arrested in the July 2003 crackdown.

Leaders: Rev. Wavel RAMKALAWAN, Jean-François FERRARI (Secretary).

Seychelles National Movement (*Mouvement National Seychellois*—MNS). The MNS was originally formed in Brussels in 1984 as an affiliate of the MPR (below).

Leaders: Gabriel (Gaby) HOAREAU (President), Robert FRICHOT (Vice President), Terry SANDAPIN (Secretary).

National Alliance Party (NAP). The NAP was organized in early 1992 by Philippe Boullé and Kathleen Pillay, a former UDM (see below) leader. (Boulle later ran as the UO's presidential candidate in balloting in 1993 and announced his retirement in 1995 from active politics. However, he ran as an independent candidate in presidential balloting in 2001, securing only 0.86 percent of the vote, and again in 2006, winning a mere 0.56 percent.)

Leader: Kathleen PILLAY (Secretary).

Other Parties and Groups

Democratic Party (DP). The DP was legalized in March 1992 as a revival of the former SDP. Its leader, Sir James Mancham, returned from exile on April 12, 1992. Subsequently, the DP and the SPPF were viewed as the country's two principal political "currents."

Mancham was reelected party leader at an extraordinary party congress on March 18, 1995, from which his intraparty opponents were excluded. (DP dissident Christopher GILL, one of those expelled from the congress for complaining about Mancham's "tightfisted" control, subsequently announced the formation of a New Democratic Party. Gill, the only DP member to gain a directly elected legislative seat in 1993, was reported in late 1997 to have crossed over to the SPPF, despite his previous extremely negative analysis of the René government.) The DP was beaten badly in the 1998 elections, securing only one parliamentary seat, while Mancham won only 14 percent of the vote in the presidential balloting. Mancham declined to run in the 2001 presidential election. The DP polled only 3.1 percent in the 2002 elections, thereby losing its seat in the assembly. Mancham retired as party leader in January 2005, although he subsequently was reportedly involved in planning a conference of opposition leaders designed to promote "reconciliation."

In 2006 party leaders formed an alliance with the SNP to counter the SPPF in upcoming elections. The DP supported the SNP's Ramkalawan in the presidential election (DP members being assured of several ministerial posts if Ramkalawan were elected). In a related move in March 2006, the DP replaced interim leader Nichol Gabriel—who observers said was reluctant to consider the alliance—with Paul Chow, reportedly of the party's "old guard" who gave his full backing to the SNP alliance. Gabriel assumed the post of party secretary.

Leaders: Paul CHOW (Leader), Bernard ELIZABETH, Sir James R. MANCHAM (Former President of the Republic), Paul CHOW (Former Secretary), Nichol GABRIEL (Secretary).

The only other party to present candidates in the 2002 assembly balloting was the **Social Democratic Alliance**, which fielded one candidate. However, several independent candidates contested the elections.

A British-based organization known simply as the Resistance Movement (*Mouvement pour la Résistance*—MPR) appeared to have been implicated in the November 1981 coup attempt, while a South African-based Seychelles Popular

Cabinet

As of August 9, 2006

President	James Alix Michel
Vice President	Joseph Belmont

Ministers

Arts, Culture, and Sports	Sylvette Pool [f]
Community Development and Youth	Vincent Meriton
Education	Bernard Shamlaye
Environment and Natural Resources	Ronald Jumeau
Finance	Daniel Faure
Foreign Affairs and International Cooperation	Patrick Pillay
Health	MacSuzy Mondon [f]
Investment, Industry, and Technology	Jacquelin Dugasse
Land Use and Habitat	Joel Morgan
Social Affairs and Employment	Marie-Pierre Lloyd [f]

[f] = female

Anti-Marxist Front (SPAMF) announced late in the year that it had known of the mercenary effort but had declined to participate on the ground that it was unworkable. A third group, the Seychelles Liberation Committee (*Comité de la Libération Seychelles*—CLS) was launched in Paris in 1979.

In November 1985 MPR leader Gérard HOAREAU was assassinated outside his London residence by an unknown assailant. Former president Mancham charged the René government with the killing, which was vehemently denied by a spokesman for the Seychelles embassy. A month earlier David JOUBERT, a former Mancham cabinet official, had announced the revival of the SDP as a London-based exile formation, although Mancham, who had become a British citizen, dissociated himself from the action.

During a speech before a House of Commons committee in February 1990 Mancham invited all of the exile groups to join him in a Crusade for Democracy in Seychelles (CDS) and subsequently called for the formation of an opposition United Democratic Front (UDF). A less conservative London exile, former foreign minister

Dr. Maxime FERRARI, displayed ambivalence toward the Mancham overture and in December 1990 launched a Rally of the Seychelles People for Democracy (*Rassemblement du Peuple Seychellois pour la Démocratie*—RPSD) that, somewhat unrealistically, appeared to seek common ground between Mancham and René.

A meeting of Seychelles opposition groups in Brussels, Belgium, on March 15–17, 1991, included representatives of the MNS, the SDP, and the RPSD, as well as of the Alliance for the Restoration of Democracy and Pluralism (*Alliance pour la Restauration de la Démocratie et du Pluralisme*—ARDP), led by Christophe SAVY, and the Seychelles Organization for Liberty (*Organisation Seychelloise pour la Liberté*—OSL), led by Desiré André UZICE. Those in attendance (Mancham being conspicuous by his absence) denounced "the obstinacy" of President René "in maintaining his single, totalitarian, party in power." Another non-Mancham conference organized by RPSD leader Ferrari in Munich, Germany, on July 21–24 concluded with the formation of an exile United Democratic Movement (UDM).

Legislature

The unicameral **National Assembly** (*Assemblée Nationale*) has 25 directly contested seats from 25 single-member constituencies, plus up to 10 seats allocated on a proportional basis to parties winning at least 10 percent of the vote. (A party gets one proportional seat for each 10 percent of the vote it receives in the balloting for the directly contested seats.) The term of office is five years. The results of the most recent elections on December 4–6, 2002, were as follows: Seychelles People's Progressive Front, 23 (18 directly contested, 5 proportional); and the Seychelles National Party, 12 (7 directly contested and 5 proportional).

Speaker: Francis MACGREGOR.

Communications

Press

The following are published in Victoria in Creole, English, and French: *The Seychelles Nation* (3,500), daily government organ; *Seychelles Today,* monthly published by the Ministry of Finance; *L'Echo des Îles* (2,900), pro-SPPF Catholic weekly; *The People* (1,000), SPPF monthly; *Seychelles Review,* DP monthly; and *Nouvo Vizyon,* the SNP's Creole-language newsletter. *Regar,* a nongovernment weekly, was forced to suspend publication temporarily in December 1994 after losing a libel case to the head of presidential security. Another nongovernmental organ, the *Independent,* was advised by the state-owned printing facility in mid-1995 that its stories would thenceforth be vetted before publication because of complaints by opposition leader Mancham of "irresponsible and provocative" reporting of the DP's internal problems.

The U.S. State Department's 2001 report on human rights in Seychelles expressed concern over the potential effects on press freedom of a new Broadcasting and Telecommunications bill, which had been approved in early 2000. In early 2002 the Paris-based journalists' rights association, Reporters Without Frontiers, protested what it described as the government's "harassment" of *Regar* through heavy financial penalties resulting from libel lawsuits filed by some top government officials. Government opponents also criticized the high registration fees that are required to launch private radio and television stations.

News Agency

The official facility is the *Seychelles Agence de Presse* (SAP).

Broadcasting and Computing

In early 1992 President René announced that the government-controlled Radio-Television Seychelles (RTS) would be granted autonomous status equivalent to that of the British Broadcasting Corporation (BBC), and in early May its name was changed to the Seychelles Broadcasting Corporation (SBC). The system broadcasts locally from Victoria in English, French, and Creole. A missionary facility, the Far East Broadcasting Association (FEBA), services several domestic radio stations and transmits in a wide variety of languages to other Indian Ocean islands, South Asia, the Middle East, and Eastern and Southern Africa; in September 1995, however, FEBA announced that it was cutting back some of its operations because of "high operating costs." There were approximately 22,400 television receivers and 14,000 personal computers serving an equal number of Internet users in 2003.

Intergovernmental Representation

Ambassador to the U.S. and Permanent Representative to the UN
Emile Patrick Jérémie BONNELAME

U.S. Ambassador to the Seychelles
(Vacant)

IGO Memberships (Non-UN)
AfDB, AU, BADEA, Comesa, CWTH, Interpol, IOC, NAM, OIF, WCO, WTO

SIERRA LEONE

REPUBLIC OF SIERRA LEONE

The Country

Facing the South Atlantic and nearly surrounded by the Republic of Guinea on the northwest, north, and east, Sierra Leone ("lion mountain") encompasses three geographic regions: a peninsula in the west; a western coastal region, which consists of mangrove swamps and a coastal plain; and a plateau in the east and northeast. The indigenous inhabitants range over 12 principal tribal groups, the most important being the Mende in the south and the Temne in the north. There are also numerous Creole descendants of freed slaves. A variety of tribal languages are spoken, with Krio, a form of pidgin English, serving as a lingua franca. Traditional religions predominate, but there are many Muslims in the north and Christians in the west.

The agricultural sector of the economy employs about two-thirds of the work force. Rice is the main subsistence crop, while cocoa, coffee, and palm kernels are the leading agricultural exports. Gold, bauxite, and rutile are among the minerals extracted, with a rapidly dwindling diamond reserve providing approximately 20 percent of export earnings in 1992 (down from 60 percent in 1980). The International Monetary Fund (IMF), the World Bank group, and the European Community/ Union (EC/EU) have been among the international agencies extending recent aid in support of efforts to revive an economy that has deteriorated markedly since the mid-1970s. Until quite recently, the assistance proved largely ineffectual, inflation rising to nearly 110 percent in 1990, with the balance of payments severely weakened by declining rice production and commodity smuggling. Upon assuming power in April 1992 the STRASSER regime stressed its intent to honor Sierra Leone's international obligations. Subsequently, the regime's first budget, released in July, was highlighted by a three-year public investment plan formulated with World Bank assistance, and inflation for the year declined sharply to 36 percent. In March 1994 the IMF rewarded Freetown's restructuring efforts by reopening credit lines that had been frozen since 1988. Economic activity reportedly ground to a virtual standstill during the military's control of power from May 1997 to February 1998. A blockade of the Freetown harbor was lifted in late February 1998, thus allowing commercial activity to resume.

In late 1998 observers reported that mining and agriculture sectors in the north and east had been decimated by fighting. Furthermore, the subsequent return to full-scale civil war effectively

Political Status: Independent member of the Commonwealth since April 27, 1961; republic proclaimed April 19, 1971; one-party constitution adopted June 1978; multiparty constitution approved by popular referendum on August 23–30, 1991, with effect from September 24; government overthrown in military coup of April 29, 1992; ruling military council overthrown and replaced by "reconstituted" military council on January 16, 1996; democratically elected president inaugurated on March 29, 1996; government overthrown in military coup of May 25, 1997; ruling military council forcibly removed by regional forces on February 13, 1998; previously elected government reinstalled on March 10, 1998; July 1999 Lomé peace accord and UN peacekeepers unable to halt ongoing violence; cease-fire agreed between government and insurgents on May 16, 2001; previously elected president and majority party won elections of May 14, 2002.

Area: 27,699 sq. mi. (71,740 sq. km.).

Population: 3,700,000 (1985C), including a 5.2 percent adjustment for underenumeration; 5,412,000 (2005E).

Major Urban Center (2005E): FREETOWN (824,000, including suburbs).

Official Language: English.

Monetary Unit: Leone (market rate July 1, 2006: 2,976 leones = $1US).

President: Ahmad Tejan KABBAH (Sierra Leone People's Party); elected on March 16, 1996, to succeed Brig. Gen. Julius Maada BIO (Chair, Supreme Council of State); sworn in on March 29; ousted in military coup led by Major Johnny Paul KOROMA (Armed Forces Revolutionary Council) on May 25, 1997; returned to office on March 10, 1998, following Koroma's removal by the Economic Community of West African States Monitoring Group on February 12; reelected on May 14, 2002, and sworn in for another four-year term on May 19.

Vice President: Solomon BEREWA (Sierra Leone People's Party); elected on May 14, 2002, and sworn in on May 19 for a term concurrent with the president's in succession to Albert Joe DEMBY (Sierra Leone People's Party).

dashed hopes for economic growth in 1998 and 1999. In December 1999 the IMF approved emergency assistance for the country to ease the government's efforts to reconstruct the economy, and a cease-fire in 2001 fostered the resumption of normal activity.

Diamond mining, the country's third largest employer, has been a prime beneficiary of the cessation of hostilities. The smuggling of "blood diamonds," a key feature of the civil war, was curbed by a United Nations diamond embargo on Sierra Leone in 2000 and a subsequent diamond-certification scheme known as the Kimberley process. Since then, the government has regained partial control over the diamond trade, enabling it to raise $126 million in tax revenues on the industry in 2004 alone.

Economic growth improved in 2005–2006, with a further decline in inflation (to 9.5 percent) and increased foreign investment in oil and mining. The IMF approved a new three-year poverty reduction program for Sierra Leone, citing the government's "considerable progress" toward economic stability and addressing widespread poverty. (The IMF noted that 80 percent of the population lives on less than $1US per day.) The fund urged the government to enforce tax regulations, accelerate privatization efforts, and diversify and expand exports to bolster revenue. Real GDP growth in 2006 was expected to be about 6 percent. According to a 2006 UN report, corruption and mismanagement of public revenue continued to be of great concern.

Government and Politics

Political Background

Growing out of a coastal settlement established by English interests in the 18th century as a haven for freed slaves, Sierra Leone became independent within the Commonwealth in 1961. Political leadership from 1961 to 1967 was exercised exclusively through the Sierra Leone People's Party (SLPP), a predominantly Mende grouping led successively by Sir Milton MARGAI and his half-brother, Sir Albert M. MARGAI. Attempts to establish a one-party system under the SLPP were successfully resisted by the opposition All People's Congress (APC), a predominantly Temne formation headed by Dr. Siaka P. STEVENS, a militant trade-union leader belonging to the smaller Limba tribe.

Following an unexpectedly strong showing by the APC in the election of 1967, Stevens was appointed prime minister, but he was prevented from taking office by Brig. David LANSANA's declaration of martial law on March 21. Two days later, Lt. Col. Andrew JUXON-SMITH assumed the leadership of a National Reformation Council (NRC) that suspended the constitution, dissolved the parties, and ruled for the ensuing 13 months. The NRC was itself overthrown in April 1968 by a group of noncommissioned officers, the Anti-Corruption Revolutionary Movement, which restored civilian government with Stevens as prime minister.

The ensuing decade was marked by a series of coup attempts and government harassment of political opponents. In 1973 official intimidation contributed to an SLPP boycott of the general election, with the APC winning all but one of the seats in the House of Representatives. In 1975 six civilians and two soldiers were executed in Freetown after being convicted of an attempt to assassinate (then) Finance Minister Christian KAMARA-TAYLOR and take over the government. Under a new constitution adopted by referendum in early June 1978, Sierra Leone became a one-party state; President Stevens was reinvested for a seven-year term on June 14.

In early 1985 the president announced his intention to retire, naming army commander Maj. Gen. Joseph Saidu MOMOH as his successor. The new president was confirmed in single-party balloting on October 1; Stevens transferred power to him on November 28, although formal swearing-in ceremonies were not held until January 26, 1986. The House of Representatives was renewed in a multicandidate, one-party poll held on May 29–30, a year prior to expiry of its normal term.

Momoh's accession was greeted with enthusiasm that subsided when a campaign to "instill military discipline" in fighting corruption and managing the economy failed to yield tangible results. By mid-1990 the Momoh regime's inability to check inflation, generate the funds for civil service salary payments, or maintain basic services had provoked widespread civil unrest and calls for the adoption of a new, multiparty constitution. Consequently, at an extraordinary APC meeting in August, President Momoh named economist Peter TUCKER to head a National Constitution Review Commission to explore government reorganization along "democratic lines." (At the same time, Momoh described multiparty activity as incompatible with Sierra Leone's tribal structures and widespread illiteracy.)

In late March 1991, less than a week after having reiterated his opposition to the idea, Momoh announced that he welcomed the introduction of a multiparty system. Two months later, the Tucker Commission submitted its report, and in early June the life of the existing House of Representatives was extended to enable it to approve a pluralistic basic law. On July 2, following intense debate both within and outside the government, the House of Representatives ratified the new constitution, and on August 23–30 the document was approved by popular referendum; over 60 percent of the 2.5 million participants reportedly favored its enactment. On September 23 President Momoh named a transitional government to rule until multiparty elections that were tentatively scheduled for late 1992. One day later the constitution was promulgated, and on September 30 the ban on political parties was officially lifted.

On April 29, 1992, army units, angered at a lack of pay and the failure of the government to provide them equipment to end a 13-week rebellion in eastern Sierra Leone, ousted President Momoh, who flew to exile in Guinea. On May 1 Capt. Valentine Strasser and (then) Lt. Solomon Anthony James MUSA were named chair and vice chair, respectively, of a National Provisional Ruling Council (NPRC). On May 2 the NPRC appointed a 19-member government, which included several members of the NPRC and six civilians. Two days later the NPRC dissolved the legislature and suspended political activity. On July 14 Captain Strasser announced that the NPRC would thenceforth be known as the Supreme Council of State (SCS) and would no longer be involved in day-to-day administration. Concurrently, ministers were redesignated as secretaries of state, with Musa serving in the quasi-prime ministerial post of chief secretary. In October a 15-member advisory council was established with a mandate to work out the "modalities" of a return to multipartyism, with an emphasis on involving citizens in the democratization process.

In mid-December 1992 the regime established a special military tribunal "in the interest of maintaining peace, security, and public order" and to assure that criminals were "rapidly punished." On December 28 government troops violently repulsed an alleged coup attempt by the so-called Anti-Corruption Revolutionary Movement (ACRM), a grouping of pro-Momoh civilians and military personnel (some of whom were already incarcerated). On December 30, following a summary military trial, 26 people (9 ACRM members and 17 others who had been convicted of high treason for their involvement in an earlier incident) were executed. The executions drew international condemnation; several Western donors announced suspension of aid payments.

On April 29, 1993, amid reports of widespread disillusionment with the one-year-old "revolution," Strasser announced the commencement of a three-year transition period to culminate in multiparty elections. In addition, the chair promised to launch an inquiry into the special military tribunal's activities and to ease some security measures.

In a government reshuffle on July 5, 1993, Capt. Julius Maada BIO replaced Musa as SCS vice chair and chief secretary. Musa's dismissal came amid reports that he had clashed with Strasser about the return to multipartyism and that he harbored his own presidential ambitions. In December Dr. James JONAH was appointed chair of the newly established Interim National Electoral Commission (INEC), which had been charged with preparing for presidential and legislative elections tentatively scheduled for 1995.

In 1994 the Strasser regime's credibility was impaired by the alleged complicity of government troops in widespread banditry and its inability to suppress the military activities of the Revolutionary United Front (RUF, below), a Sierra Leonean offshoot of Charles Taylor's National Patriotic Front of Liberia (NPFL, see Liberia article) led by Foday Savannah SANKOH; the Strasser regime claimed the RUF had been organized to punish Sierra Leone for its peacekeeping role in Liberia. By midyear RUF-related violence was reportedly responsible for the deaths of hundreds of individuals and the dislocation of thousands. Consequently, in July the State Advisory Council, noting that "local people must be collaborating" with the insurgents, announced the creation of a National Security Council charged with ending the hostilities. Thereafter, despite reports that most of the country was "lawless," the government released a draft constitution in October, which included provisions for a return to civilian rule by 1996.

On November 12, 1994, the junta executed 12 soldiers in an apparent attempt to intimidate the so-called "sobels" (soldiers during the day, rebels at night) whom observers described as increasingly beyond Freetown's control. On November 25, bolstered by reports that an offensive had severely weakened the rebels, the Strasser government called on the RUF to begin negotiations on a peace accord and cease-fire, pledging that they would be allowed to form a political party in preparation for multiparty elections. The RUF, which had gained international attention two weeks earlier when it had kidnapped two British citizens, initially rejected the offer but on December 4 met with government negotiators for discussions, which were described as "frank." However, the rebels' kidnapping campaign continued into 1995; they reportedly seized an additional 15 foreigners by February. (All of the hostages were eventually handed over to International Red Cross representatives on April 20.)

On March 31, 1995, Captain Strasser announced a major government restructuring, under which

Health and Social Services Secretary Lt. Col. Akim GIBRIL would become chief secretary in place of Bio, who remained SCS vice chair while assuming the position of chief of the defense staff "to provide additional mettle" to the armed forces in its campaign against the RUF. On April 27 Strasser promised to lift the ban on political parties and relinquish power to a democratically elected president in January 1996. He also offered the RUF a truce to negotiate an end to the conflict that had claimed some 5,000 lives since 1991. On May 18 he asked the Economic Community of West African States (ECOWAS) to broker negotiations with the rebels; however, the RUF rejected the initiative, calling instead for Strasser to convene a sovereign national conference to decide the future of the country.

On June 21, 1995, the regime lifted the ban on political parties, but two days later it issued a list of 57 people, headed by former president Momoh, who were ineligible to compete in the upcoming balloting. On August 18 the government convened a National Consultative Conference; however, despite its earlier entreaties, the RUF refused to attend. Among the rulings adopted by the conference were the postponement of balloting until February 1996 and the organization of simultaneous presidential and legislative polling.

On October 3, 1995, a coup attempt led by at least eight senior military officers was quashed by troops loyal to Strasser, who was out of the country. The failed uprising highlighted the growing chasm in the SCS between those who opposed the return to a civilian government and its advocates, purportedly led by Strasser.

On January 16, 1996, Strasser was overthrown by his second-in-command, Brig. Gen. Julius Bio, who claimed that Strasser had been scheming to retain the presidency; Bio announced that he would lead a "Reconstituted" Supreme Council of the State (RSCS). At his inauguration the following day, Bio promised to continue preparations for "transparent, free, and fair" elections and urged the RUF to begin peace talks. In response, the RUF announced a one-week, unconditional cease-fire and called for postponement of the elections, saying

it would not negotiate with a civilian government. Subsequently, Bio expressed interest in rescheduling the balloting; however, following a meeting with the leaders from a number of the newly recognized political groups on January 24, he reiterated his intent to adhere to the pre-coup electoral schedule.

At the first round of legislative and presidential balloting on February 26–27, 1996, the SLPP captured 36.1 percent of the vote, easily outpacing the United People's Party (UNPP, below), which finished second with 21.6 percent, and 11 other parties. Meanwhile, SLPP presidential candidate Ahmad Tejan KABBAH and UNPP leader John KARIFA-SMART finished first and second, respectively, in their 12-candidate race. However, because neither captured a majority, a second round of balloting was held on March 15, with Kabbah winning with a 59.49 percent of the vote tally.

The Kabbah administration moved quickly to build on the peace initiative its predecessor had begun with the RUF, and on April 23, 1996, agreement was reached between Kabbah and Sankoh on a "definitive" cease-fire and the establishment of committees to draft disarmament and peace accords. On May 30 Freetown announced that it had reached agreement with the RUF on 26 of 28 articles in a proposed peace plan, leaving unresolved only the timetable for the withdrawal of foreign troops and the establishment of a national debt commission. However, the rebels continued to refuse to recognize the Kabbah government publicly and insisted that the cease-fire was only provisional. At the same time, the administration's announced intention to reduce the military ranks from 18,000 to approximately 4,000 added the threat of yet another military coup to a domestic security landscape already populated by RUF dissidents, "sobels," and escaped prisoners.

On September 8, 1996, at least six soldiers were arrested after senior military officials were alerted to their alleged plans to overthrow the government, and within a week 150 more soldiers were purged in response to an executive order demanding the dismissal of suspected dissidents. Meanwhile, a series of clashes between government forces and rebels in the east threatened the six-month-old cease-fire. However, when government troops reportedly gained the upper hand on the battlefield, President Kabbah and RUF leader Sankoh signed a peace treaty at Abidjan, Côte d'Ivoire on November 30. Highlighting the accord were provisions for the immediate end to hostilities, the demobilization and disarmament of the RUF, and the integration of rebel soldiers into the national army. Furthermore, the agreement entitled the RUF to transform itself into a legal political party.

Sporadic fighting was reported throughout late 1996 and early 1997; the RUF and government accused each other of violating the peace accord. In addition, clashes were reported between alleged "sobels" and ethnic Kamajor militiamen allied with the president. On March 12 the RUF's Sankoh was detained in Nigeria, and on March 15 he was dismissed from the RUF by senior party officials who accused him of blocking implementation of the peace accord. Subsequently, Sankoh's supporters threatened to attack Freetown unless he was returned from Lagos.

On May 25, 1997, junior army officers fighting alongside RUF militants overran the prison where the defendants in the September 1996 coup plot were being held. Subsequently, under the leadership of one of the freed prisoners, Maj. Johnny Paul KOROMA, the combined forces took control of Freetown and overthrew the government (with Kabbah fleeing to Guinea). On May 28 the military junta abolished the constitution and banned political parties. Meanwhile, 300,000 people reportedly fled the country amid heavy fighting between the junta's forces and Nigerian-led ECOWAS troops, who had launched a countercoup offensive. On June 1 the junta established a 20-member Armed Forces Revolutionary Council (AFRC) and named Koroma its chair. Unable to dislodge the rebel soldiers, the Economic Community of West African States Monitoring Group (Ecomog) announced a cease-fire on June 2. Nevertheless, regional and international observers vowed not to let the coup stand and refused to recognize the Koroma regime.

On June 17, 1997, Major Koroma was sworn in as the leader of the AFRC, and he subsequently agreed to participate in internationally mediated negotiations. However, the talks were promptly abandoned after the junta leader demanded a four-year term. Frustrated with Koroma's intransigence, ECOWAS officials tightened sanctions against the AFRC in late August, and on September 2 Ecomog forces bombed Freetown in an effort to enforce an embargo on imported goods. Furthermore, on October 8 the UN Security Council adopted a resolution empowering Ecomog forces to enforce oil and arms sanctions against the regime. On October 24, under pressure of heavy shelling, AFRC negotiators agreed to a peace plan that included provisions for a disarmament process (beginning December 1), Kabbah's reinstallment on April 22, 1998, immunity for the junta's forces, and a future government role for RUF leader Sankoh. Despite the accord, clashes continued between the AFRC and Ecomog forces, and in mid-December 1997 Koroma asserted that the timetable for implementing the pact would be delayed.

Following a week of particularly intense fighting, Ecomog forces captured Freetown on February 13, 1998. On February 17 ECOWAS announced the formation of an interim "special supervision committee," headed by Vice President Albert DEMBY and the Nigerian leader of the Ecomog forces, Col. Maxwell Khobe. On February 20, 25 of the AFRC leaders were captured as they attempted to escape into Liberia (Koroma is widely believed to be dead or in hiding somewhere in West Africa). President Kabbah was officially reinstated on March 10 and promptly named a 15-member cabinet.

As of March 1998 Ecomog-directed, pro-presidential forces reportedly controlled 90 percent of Sierra Leone. In addition to attempting to wrest control of the remainder of the country from the remnants of the combined AFRC-RUF forces, the reinstalled Kabbah government faced a myriad of other challenges, including resurrecting a devastated economy; reintegrating tens of thousands of dislocated and homeless citizens; and reestablishing relations with Sankoh and the RUF, many of whose fighters reportedly had hidden their weapons when confronted by the Ecomog offensive. Meanwhile, the Kabbah administration pressed ahead with legal actions against former Koroma coup members and their alleged collaborators. In October Freetown ignored observers' calls for leniency and executed 24 people for treasonous acts, including Koroma's brother, Brig. Gen. Samuel KOROMA. On October 23 Sankoh, who had been returned for trial from Nigeria in July, was sentenced to death for similar offenses. (Collaterally, on November 5 former president Momoh received a ten-year jail term for his ties to Koroma, who remained a fugitive.) Following Sankoh's sentencing, a dramatic upsurge in rebel attacks against civilians was reported; thousands subsequently fled to the capital to escape a campaign marked by atrocities. Despite initial depictions of the violence as being the rebels' last gasp, the RUF and its AFRC military allies advanced to within striking distance of Freetown by December.

In late December 1998 RUF commander Sam BOCKARIE rejected calls for a cease-fire, and on January 6, 1999, the rebels invaded the capital. Approximately 5,000 people were killed before Ecomog troops regained control of the city in midmonth. Thereafter, President Kabbah agreed to let Sankoh participate in cease-fire negotiations; however, apparently emboldened by reports of Ecomog gains elsewhere in the country, Kabbah insisted that the rebels respect the dictates of the 1996 peace accord. Consequently, negotiations proceeded fitfully through February and early March. On March 16 Bockarie broke off talks, reportedly suspecting the government of employing delaying tactics while it won back territory. Subsequently, the Kabbah administration came under pressure from its two largest military backers, the United Kingdom and Nigeria, to seek a negotiated end to its "unwinnable" war.

On May 18, 1999, President Kabbah and rebel leader Sankoh signed an agreement in Togo calling for a cease-fire effective May 25, and a formal peace accord was signed in July. The agreement promised to give the RUF and the AFRC four key government posts and extended total amnesty to RUF and AFRC leaders, including Sankoh, as well as former head of state Momoh, who had been charged with collaborating with the AFRC junta. Amid reports of internal divisions, the RUF and the AFRC agreed to demobilize and disarm and also dropped their demands for an immediate withdrawal of Ecomog troops. The AFRC wing that accepted Koroma's call to stop violence immediately was then reincorporated into the political arena. In October the UN Security Council authorized the United Nations Mission in Sierra Leone (UNAMSIL) to replace the Ecomog troops gradually. In November Sankoh was given powers equivalent to those of vice president, and the RUF and the AFRC were allocated non-senior cabinet posts. Concurrently, the RUF decided to transform itself into a registered political party, adopting the rubric Revolutionary United Front Party (RUFP). However, the issues of demobilization and disarmament created problems during much of early 2000, and in May the peace agreement broke down as UNAMSIL was moving to replace the Ecomog troops. RUF fighters and some renegade AFRC militia (linked with Eddie KANNEH's wing, which was uneasy with Koroma's call to stop the violence) attacked UNAMSIL detachments, and 19 civilians were killed by Sankoh's bodyguards during a demonstration in front of his residence. Although Sankoh fled the country following the incident, he was apprehended in Nigeria on May 17. Due to advances by UNAMSIL, the pro-government Kamajor militia (styled as the Civil Defense Force [CDF]), Guinean forces opposed to the RUF, and renegade AFRC forces, the rebels were on the defensive for much of the year. In November the RUF agreed once again to commit itself to the peace process and to disarm its troops and relinquish most of its territory to government and UNAMSIL control. In February 2001 Kabbah asked the National Assembly to postpone the presidential and legislative elections due to be held in February and March because of the "uncertain security situation." He also reshuffled his cabinet to include some opposition figures.

As Liberian President Charles Taylor tried to distance himself from the RUF in an effort to clean up his country's image as a protector of the rebels, the RUF signed a peace agreement in May 2001, and another cease-fire was implemented. In August it was announced that elections were expected to be held in June 2002 under a "constituency electoral system," although in September the National Electoral Commission advised the assembly to adopt a proportional representation system instead. Despite criticism from the opposition that Kabbah was trying to eliminate his potential rivals in the coming elections, as well as fears that some RUF forces might resume fighting, the country appeared to be moving toward some form of normalization.

At a dramatic weapons-burning ceremony on January 18, 2002, which marked the completion of the disarmament process, President Kabbah declared the "war is over," and the four-year state of emergency was formally lifted on March 1. (An estimated 50,000 people died as a result of the conflict.) Attention subsequently focused on the campaign for the presidential and assembly balloting.

In presidential balloting on May 14, 2002, President Kabbah was elected to another four-year term by securing more than 70 percent of the vote against eight opponents. (Kabbah's running-mate, Solomon BEREWA, the sitting minister of justice and attorney general and also from the SLPP, was elected to the vice presidency in succession to Albert Joe Demby, who had been dropped from the ticket at the SLPP congress in March.) In concurrent voting for the National Assembly, which had been expanded to comprise 112 members elected on a proportional basis, the SLPP secured 83 seats, followed by the All People's Congress (APC) with 27 seats, and the Peace and Liberation Party PLP) with 2 seats. A new cabinet of the SLPP and several independents was sworn in on July 9.

After the elections, international troops who had overseen the cease-fire ending Sierra Leone's civil war began to withdraw. On July 28, 2002, 400 British troops withdrew, leaving a contingent of military advisers to train the Sierra Leonean army. In November UNAMSIL began the gradual withdrawal of its 17,500-man force, culminating in the removal of all troops by the end of 2005. UNAMSIL was replaced by a small contingent of military advisers—the United Nations Integrated Office in Sierra Leone (UNIOSL)—charged with monitoring the security situation and guarding the war crimes tribunal (see Current issues, below).

The cabinet was reshuffled on September 6, 2005.

Constitution and Government

The 1991 constitution provided for a popularly elected executive president, who could serve for no more than two five-year terms; a parliament, whose members could not serve simultaneously as ministers; and a State Advisory Council composed of 12 paramount chiefs (one from each local district) and ten "emergent citizens" nominated by the president. There was no limit on the number of political parties, provided they met basic requirements. The judicial system included a Supreme Court and a Court of Appeal, as well as a lower tier of high, magistrates', and native courts.

The somewhat complex executive structure proclaimed by the newly styled Supreme Council of State on July 14, 1992, called for the designation of three SCS members as "principal liaison officers," each of whom would oversee a number of government departments (successors to the former ministries). The department heads were to be styled secretaries of state under a chief who would report to the SCS. Meanwhile, the SCS had assumed a quasi-legislative function by the issuance of decrees. In October 1994 the SCS released a draft basic charter, which included stipulations that future presidents must be at least 39 years old and native-born Sierra Leoneans.

Sierra Leone is administratively divided into three provinces (Northern, Eastern, Southern), in addition to a Western Region that includes Freetown. The provinces are subdivided into 12 districts and 147 chiefdoms.

Foreign Relations

Sierra Leone has long subscribed to a generally pro-Western foreign policy, while maintaining diplomatic relations with the former USSR, several

East European countries, the People's Republic of China, and North Korea. Regionally, it has been an active participant in the Organization of African Unity (OAU, subsequently the African Union— AU) and a long-standing member of OAU committees established to resolve the disputes in Chad and the Western Sahara. Traditionally cordial relations with bordering states were strained by the overthrow of civilian governments in Liberia and Guinea; however, the three countries signed a security agreement in September 1986 and revived the Mano River Union plan for economic cooperation. Tension with Liberia flared again in July 1988 with the expulsion of 63 Sierra Leonean nationals in the wake of a coup attempt against the Doe regime; however, the dispute was seemingly resolved during a two-day "reconciliation summit" in Lomé, Togo, in mid-September. In early 1989 continuing efforts by Freetown to "intensify existing friendly relations" with regional neighbors led to the establishment of joint economic and social commissions with Nigeria and Togo.

Civil war in neighboring Liberia topped Freetown's foreign policy agenda in 1990 as ECOWAS's peacekeeping forces, including Sierra Leonean troops, were dispatched from Freetown. In November Momoh described the influx of Liberian refugees as "stretching thin" his government's resources and characterized Liberian rebel leader Charles Taylor, who had threatened retaliation for Sierra Leone's involvement, as "ungrateful." In March 1991 Taylor, angered by Freetown's participation in the ECOWAS operation, began launching raids into Sierra Leone, and Nigeria and Guinea were reported in mid-April to have dispatched troops to aid in repulsing the intruders. Meanwhile, Freetown also accused Libya, Burkina Faso, and Côte d'Ivoire of aiding the rebels.

By early November 1991 the government and its allies claimed to have routed the guerrillas, and Guinean forces began their withdrawal. However, a cease-fire signed earlier in Yamassoukro, Côte d'Ivoire, proved short-lived; in December Taylor charged Freetown with backing incursions by the Liberian United Movement for Freedom and Democracy (ULIMO), a group linked to the de-posed Doe regime. ULIMO admitted to having engaged Taylor's forces but denied being based in Sierra Leone.

During the second half of 1992 Captain Strasser reportedly developed close ties with Nigerian military leader Gen. Babangida, who in early 1993 agreed to provide Sierra Leone with military advisers. Subsequently, Sierra Leone and ULIMO forces were reported to have participated in joint operations against RUF rebels.

In March 1994 the Strasser government pressed Ecomog commanders to establish a buffer zone along its shared border with Liberia, citing increased rebel activity as well as the volatility of Liberia's disarmament process. One month later, the Strasser government expelled Germany's ambassador to Freetown, claiming that his "undiplomatic" behavior, including meetings with Liberia's Taylor, were undermining Sierra Leone interests and threatening relations between the two countries. However, other reports linked the German's ouster to his defense of a Sierra Leonean journalist who had been arrested for criticizing Strasser. In September 1995 seven Guinean soldiers, stationed at Sierra Leone in fulfillment of a defense pact between the two nations, were killed during a clash with the RUF.

In July 1998 the UN Security Council announced the establishment of a United Nations Mission in Sierra Leone (UNAMSIL), which it charged with overseeing peacekeeping efforts. In February 1999 UNAMSIL personnel accused Nigerian members of Ecomog of executing civilians suspected of aiding the antigovernment insurgents. Subsequently, observers in Lagos reported that support for continued involvement in Sierra Leone had reached a new low. Meanwhile, Liberia, Libya, and Burkina Faso were alleged to be supplying the rebels with armaments and refuge. Following the agreement reached between the Sierra Leonean government and the RUF in May 1999 (see Current issues, below), there were signs of a thaw in relations with Liberia and Libya. In October the Liberian border was reopened, and in December Sierra Leone and Liberia established a joint security committee.

However, with the breakdown of the agreement and the resumption of violence in May 2000, Sierra Leone's relations with all three countries suspected of helping the RUF deteriorated once again. Although the Mano River Union summit held in May and attended by Sierra Leone, Liberia, Guinea, and Mali "deplored the attacks by the RUF," Kabbah's government and much of the international community continued to charge Liberia with assisting the rebels. With the RUF rebels crossing into the Guinean territory, and the Guinean President Lasana Conté accusing Sierra Leonean and Liberian refugees in his country of assisting the rebels, the Mano River region became a crisis zone and the scene of a severe refugee tragedy.

After the fighting in Liberia's Lofa county intensified in early 2001, Liberian President Charles Taylor renewed his claim that the Sierra Leonean and Guinean authorities were assisting the Liberian rebels. In March the ambassadors of Sierra Leone and Guinea were expelled from Liberia.

There were some signs of thaw, however, after the Sierra Leonean government and the RUF signed a new peace agreement in May 2001. In early October UN Secretary General Kofi Annan announced that he was pleased with the progress made by the Mano River Union members toward restoring peace in West Africa. In January 2006 representatives from Sierra Leone, Liberia, and Guinea met to discuss ways to restore peace in the Mano River basin. Also in 2006, Sierra Leone became a full member of the Community of Sahel and Saharan States (CEN-SAD).

Current Issues

In accordance with the Lomé Accord, a Truth and Reconciliation Commission (TRC), based on the South African model, was established in 2002 as a forum to enable Sierra Leoneans on both sides of the conflict to relate their wartime experiences. Amputations, rape, and mass killings were common human rights violations during the decade-long conflict. The same year, at the government's request, the United Nations helped establish a special court in Freetown to try the most serious cases of war crimes. In March 2003 the court issued indictments against Foday Sankoh, Sam Bockarie, Johnny Paul Koroma, and former internal affairs minister Sam HINGA NORMAN. Bockarie, a notoriously brutal RUF field commander, and Koroma, then minister of the interior and former head of the Civil Defense Force (CDF), fled to neighboring Liberia. On May 5 Bockarie was killed, allegedly on orders of Liberian President Charles Taylor, who also was indicted in connection with his role in the war but continued to live in exile in Nigeria. On June 29, 2003, the chronically ill Sankoh—the Revolutionary United Front's former leader—died, reportedly of a heart attack, in a Freetown prison. By mid-2005, the court had indicted 13 people, of whom two had died, two had eluded arrest, and nine were in custody. Taylor was captured in March 2006 (reportedly "on the run" with bags of cash) and jailed in Sierra Leone on eleven charges related to war crimes. In June he was transferred to The Hague to stand trial after Swedish lawmakers approved a law allowing a Scandinavian country to imprison Taylor if he is convicted. (The UN had asked the International Criminal Court in the Netherlands to hold the trial to avoid potential problems in the region if the trial were held in Africa; the court agreed on condition that Taylor be jailed in another country if convicted.)

Meanwhile, the government faced increasing criticism by war victims and human rights organizations for delays in implementing the TRC's recommendations, although some groups described the recommendations as "vague and noncommittal."

In anticipation of presidential and legislative elections scheduled for 2007, Sierra Leone's numerous political parties and groups began forming new alliances in an effort to counter the overwhelming political power of the SLPP and the APC and to mount a challenge to Vice President Solomon Berewa, who was expected to be the aging President Kabbah's successor as the SLPP's presidential candidate. The main coalition as of mid-2005 was the Third Force, which included the UNPP, the People's Democratic Party (PDP), and several other parties. Meanwhile, the head of the National

Electoral Commission drew criticism for reportedly drawing new election boundaries in 2006, which apparently favored the SLPP.

Political Parties

During Sierra Leone's first 17 years of independence, the principal political groupings were the Sierra Leone People's Party (SLPP), strongest in the Mende area of the south, and the All People's Congress (APC), based in the Temne region of the north. The SLPP dominated from 1961 to 1967 and the APC from 1967 to 1978, when it was accorded monopoly status. Following adoption of the 1991 constitution, a number of new parties emerged, most of which were accorded legal recognition prior to the suspension of political activity in May 1992.

By late 1992 the regime had released the majority of the political figures detained in the aftermath of the coup, the most prominent of whom included SLPP leader Salia JUSU-SHERRIFF and National Action Party (NAP) co-founder Dr. Sheka KANU.

The ban on political party activity was rescinded on June 21, 1995, in preparation for elections promised by early 1996. In August the Interim National Electoral Commission granted provisional registration certificates to approximately 15 groups, 11 of which were granted permission in November to participate in the upcoming elections.

Political parties were banned by the Koroma military junta upon its seizure of power in May 1997. Following his reinstallation in March 1998, President Kabbah authorized parties to resume their activities. His decision to include representatives from only four groups in his reshuffled government was criticized by his opponents, who had expected a more inclusive cabinet.

Following the July 1999 peace and power-sharing agreement, Kabbah reshuffled his cabinet in November, and the rebels (the RUF and AFRC) were given four non-senior posts. After the resumption of fighting in May 2000, however, the three rebel ministers were jailed. In March 2001 Kabbah reshuffled his cabinet to replace retiring and jailed rebel ministers. In an effort described as "forming a more inclusive national unity government" but criticized by opponents as "trying to silence and co-opt" his rivals, Kabbah appointed four new ministers. Three came from the opposition National Unity Party (NUP), People's Democratic Party (PDP), and UNPP to supplement Kabbah's SLPP-dominated government (which had also included civilians); one minister came from the Democratic Center Party (DCP). The latter party, chaired by Aiah Abu KOROMA, reportedly dissolved in 2002 after pledging its support to Kabbah. However, the UNPP, NUP, and PDP announced they were not supporting Kabbah's rule by joining the government but were merely trying to help the country in difficult times. (In 2003, however, NUP leader John BENJAMIN joined the SLPP, following the party's former chair, Dr. John KARIMU, who defected in 2001.) Indeed, the APC, People's Democratic Alliance (PDA), People's National Convention (PNC), People's Progressive Party (PPP), PDP, and UNPP had formed an opposition alliance styled as the Grand Alliance (GA) in August 2000 (see below). A number of smaller parties reportedly joined the GA later. Although the GA members had announced their attempt to "unite under a single political party in due course," by mid-2001 various internal rifts seemed to have rendered that aim difficult to achieve. The APC and UNPP subsequently left the alliance.

In the May 14, 2002, balloting, 11 parties presented candidates for the presidency, and 12 parties were represented in the legislative contest.

Sierra Leone People's Party (SLPP). Led by former second vice president Salia Jusu-Sheriff, whose identification with the Momoh regime was viewed as a political liability, the SLPP was launched as a revival of the party outlawed in 1978.

Ahmad Tejan Kabbah, a 64-year-old veteran politician and former UN development worker, emerged as the SLPP's presidential candidate after an intraparty contest with Charles MARGAI in early 1996. Subsequently, at parliamentary balloting in February 1996, the SLPP secured ten more seats than its nearest competitor while its allies (the

PDP, APC, NUP, and DCP) gained an additional 24 seats.

In mid-1998 Kabbah reportedly signaled that he would not seek another term in office. Among those cited by observers as potential successors were Margai, cabinet member Harry WILL, and Sam Hinga Norman, whose command of Kamajor militias had won him wide acclaim. Kabbah reversed his previous announcement, however, during a period of peace, which was followed by a resumption of violence and another time of peace from 1999 to 2001, when he won enough support to ensure another election victory for himself and his party in 2002. Former military leader Julius Bio returned to Sierra Leone in 2004 after ten years in exile and reportedly stated his interest in party leadership while condemning the current regime for its alleged corruption and incompetence. Margai left the party in 2005 after losing the leadership post—and, thus, the opportunity to be the party's presidential candidate—to Solomon Berewa, whom *Africa Confidential* said was "generally referred to as President Number Two" because Kabbah delegated many official duties to him. Margai started the **People's Movement for Democratic Change** (PMDC, below) with other SLPP defectors. Bio announced he would not leave to follow Margai and reiterated his support for the SLPP.

Leaders: Solomon BEREWA (Vice President of the Republic and Party Leader), S. U. M. JAH (Chair), Ahmad Tejan KABBAH (President of the Republic), Prince HARDING (Secretary General).

All People's Congress (APC). Leftist and republican in outlook, the APC was formed in 1960 by Dr. Siaka Probyn Stevens in a split with a dissident group headed at that time by Albert M. Margai. Although strongest in Temne territory, the party was not exclusively tribal in character, drawing its support from wage-earning and lower-middle-class elements in both Temne and non-Temne areas. The APC won all but one of the legislative seats in the 1973 election, which was boycotted by the opposition SLPP; it won all but 15 seats in 1977 and was constitutionally unopposed in 1982

and 1986. At the conclusion of an APC conference in August 1985, despite strong support for (then) first vice president Sorie KOROMA, Maj. Gen. Joseph Momoh was nominated as the sole candidate to succeed Stevens as president of the republic. While yielding the post of secretary general to Momoh, Stevens retained the title of chair, as well as the primary loyalty of much of the party's membership, until his death in June 1988. Momoh was reelected unopposed to the party's top post at the tenth APC conference in January 1989, which also yielded abandonment of the positions of chair and vice chair and adoption of a demanding "Code of Conduct" for political leaders and public servants.

At an APC Central Committee and Governing Council joint session on August 17–20, 1990, President Momoh, pressured by calls for political reform, proposed an "overhauling" of Sierra Leone's political system. However, his support in March 1991 for the adoption of a multiparty constitution generated deep fissures within the party. In mid-July two of its leaders resigned their posts, and ten others were suspended for criticizing the document that was approved in late August. In early 1992 the party further redefined its policies and principles, and, by providing for rank-and-file balloting, underwent sweeping personnel changes.

APC presidential candidate Edward Mohammed Turay captured just 5.1 percent of the vote at 1996 balloting, while the party finished fourth in the legislative contest. At the 2002 elections, APC presidential candidate Ernest Bai Koroma won 22.3 percent of the vote, and the party finished second in the legislative election, winning 27 seats.

Koroma ran unopposed for the party leadership in September 2005 and was tapped to represent the APC in the next presidential election. Meanwhile, party member Amara Alkalie KAMARA announced that he would also be a presidential candidate in 2007.

Leaders: Ernest Bai KOROMA (Minority Leader in Parliament and 2002 presidential candidate), Edward Mohammed TURAY (1996 presidential candidate), Mohamed Aka KOROMA (Acting Secretary General).

Peace and Liberation Party (PLP). Established in 2001, the PLP is led by the former AFRC leader Johnny Paul Koroma. It was linked with the Grassroots Awareness movement, one of many peace promotion organizations. At the May 2002 elections, Koroma came in third in the presidential race, while the party won 3.6 percent of the vote—and two seats—in the legislative contest.

Leaders: Johnny Paul KOROMA (whereabouts unknown; 2002 presidential candidate), Darlington MORRISON (Chair), Bai MORROW, Amadu BAH (Spokesperson).

Revolutionary United Front Party (RUFP). The Revolutionary United Front (RUF) surfaced in early 1991 as a group of Sierra Leone dissidents who had joined forces with Liberian guerrillas loyal to Charles Taylor along the Sierra Leone–Liberia border, where diamond smuggling had been estimated to yield some $100 million annually. In July 1992 the rebels rejected an appeal by the Strasser regime to surrender and negotiate a resolution of their estrangement from Freetown, demanding instead a national interim government and free democratic elections.

In August 1993 the RUF was described as "unorganized" amid indications that attempts had been made to oust its leader, Foday Sankannah Sankoh (who earlier had been rumored to have died). On December 30 Sankoh's personal bodyguards surrendered when government troops overran Pujehin, and in early 1994 the RUF leader was reported to have barely escaped arrest during fighting at Kailahun, which resulted in the further capture of elite rebel troops.

Thereafter, although estimates of the actual number of RUF members fluctuated between 100 and 1,000, the group, which had reportedly broken into four units, was credited with orchestrating military activities in over two-thirds of the country. At the same time, its casualty rate climbed precipitously, and by October 1994 some observers suggested that the government's war with the rebels was nearly concluded. However, in early November the RUF appeared to be invigorated when its seizure of two British nationals drew international attention, and on November 28 the rebels rejected Freetown's cease-fire entreaties, saying it would only negotiate with the British government.

On January 18–20, 1995, the RUF captured two of the country's most important mines; however, the rebels suffered numerous casualties in a government counter-offensive that dislodged the insurgents. Subsequently, the RUF requested that the International Committee of the Red Cross act as a mediator in the conflict.

Confronted with a reorganized Sierra Leonean Army and near starvation conditions in areas under their control, RUF political leaders in September 1995 reportedly sought a dialogue with Freetown. However, rebel military activities continued unabated, underscoring the reported split between RUF moderates and militants.

Following the overthrow of the Strasser regime in mid-January 1996, the RUF announced a one-week unconditional cease-fire, and on February 25 the rebels held their first direct talks with the new government in Côte d'Ivoire, where they unsuccessfully sought a delay in nationwide elections. Subsequently, the rebels were blamed for disrupting polling in a number of regions. At a meeting with Brigadier General Bio on March 24, Sankoh agreed to a cease-fire but refused to recognize the civilian government-elect. Thereafter, the Kabbah government expressed "cautious optimism" following a meeting between Sankoh and the new president on April 22–23, which yielded a "definitive" cease-fire. The final accord signed on November 30 permitted the RUF to begin functioning as a political movement immediately, with the understanding that it would apply for formal party recognition within 30 days.

Subsequently, implementation of the peace pact stalled because Sankoh refused to meet with officials seeking to finalize the scheduling of the RUF's disarmament and reintegration, and in early 1997 the government accused Sankoh of failing to meet his responsibilities as dictated by the accord. Following a meeting with Nigerian officials, Sankoh was arrested in Lagos on March 12. Three days later, a senior RUF official, Philip Sylvester PALMER, announced that Sankoh had been dismissed from the RUF for "thwarting the peace process." The arrest and ouster of Sankoh (an "international conspiracy" according to his followers) sparked fierce internecine fighting between his loyalists and opponents.

RUF militants played a major role in the fighting, which led to President Kabbah's overthrow in May 1997, and in June at least three RUF representatives were included in the AFRC. Moreover, the AFRC's exhaustive diplomatic efforts to win Sankoh's freedom from detention in Nigeria fueled reports that the RUF was steering the junta's activities. During negotiations with the AFRC in late 1997, representatives of the Kabbah administration agreed to find a role for Sankoh upon their proposed reinstallation in Freetown. Meanwhile, RUF fighters who had aligned with rebel soldiers were being targeted by Ecomog troops.

Following the peace agreement with the government in July 1999, the RUF was promised cabinet posts, and Sankoh was given powers equivalent to those of vice president. In the meantime, the RUF decided to transform itself into a registered political party (the RUFP). However, after the breakdown of the agreement and the resumption of fighting in May 2000, Sankoh was jailed, and Issa Sesay replaced him as the interim leader. In June the government asked the UN to set up a special court to try Sankoh and other RUF officials for "war crimes."

Before and after the RUF's announcement of commitment to the peace process once again in May 2001, there were signs of a split within the organization. Reportedly, the faction for continuing the war, represented by an uneasy coalition of Sam Bockarie and Dennis Superman Mingo, was in conflict with the official leadership of Sesay and the faction committed to the peace process.

The RUFP's presidential candidate, Alimamy Pallo BANGURA, came in fourth, with 1.7 percent of the vote, in May 2002, while the party won 2.2 percent of the vote—and no seats—in the legislative contest.

Sesay, who had been indicted by the special court on war crimes charges, was replaced as interim leader in January 2005 by Peter VANDY. The following month, however, Vandy resigned from the party and joined the SLPP, declaring his belief in the SLPP as the party of reconciliation and multiparty democracy. In early 2006 Sesay remained in detention on war crimes charges. Meanwhile, party official Omrie Golley was charged in 2006 with plotting to overthrow the government.

Leaders: Samuel Gbessay KAMU (Acting Leader), Issa SESAY (in detention), Gibril MASSAQUOI (Spokesperson), Dennis Superman MINGO, Omrie GOLLEY (Peace and Political Council Chair; in detention), Jonathan KPOSOVA (Secretary General).

United National People's Party (UNPP). The UNPP secured 17 seats behind a 21 percent vote tally at balloting in February 1996. Meanwhile, its leader, banker John Karifa-Smart, placed second in concurrent presidential balloting. In March 1997 Karifa-Smart was charged with contempt and suspended from the assembly. He also unsuccessfully attempted in April 2001 to expel some legislators from the party due to differences on certain policies. Karifa-Smart came in last, with 1 percent of the vote, in the May 2002 presidential election, and the UNPP failed to win any seats in the legislative contest, with 1.3 percent of the vote. In May 2005 the UNPP joined in coalition with the National Unity Movement (below) in advance of the next presidential elections. It backed out of a so-called merger with the RUFD after some of the latter's leaders were charged with war crimes.

Karifa-Smart reportedly left politics in 2006, and Abdul Kadi Karim was elected as party leader and 2007 presidential candidate.

Leaders: Abdul Kadi KARIM (Party Leader), Soufian KARGBO (Secretary General), John KARIFA-SMART (1996 and 2002 presidential candidate).

Grand Alliance Party (GAP). Initially formed in August 2000 as a broad coalition in opposition to the SLPP, the GAP splintered in 2001. A number of small parties kept the alliance alive, but it won only 2.4 percent of the vote in the May 2002 legislative election, not enough to secure a seat. Its candidate in the 2002 presidential election, Raymond KAMARA, won 0.6 percent of the vote.

Cabinet

As of June 1, 2006

President	Ahmad Tejan Kabbah (SLPP)
Vice President	Solomon Berewa (SLPP)

Ministers

Agriculture and Food Security	Sama Sahr Mondeh
Community Development and Local Government	Sidikie Brima
Defense	Ahmad Tejan Kabbah (SLPP)
Development and Economic Planning	Mohamed B. Daramy
Education, Science, and Technology	Alpha T. Wurie (SLPP)
Energy and Power	Lloyd During
Finance	John O. Benjamin (SLPP)
Foreign Affairs and International Cooperation	Momodu Koroma
Health and Sanitation	Abbator Thomas [f]
Information and Broadcasting	Septimus Kaikai
Internal Affairs	Pascal Egbenda
Justice and Attorney General	Frederick M. Carew (SLPP)
Labor, Industrial Relations, and Social Security	Alpha O. Timbo
Lands, Country Planning, Forestry, and Environment	Alfred Bobson Sesay
Local Government	Sidique Brima
Marine Resources	Chernor Jalloh (UNPP)
Mineral Resources	Alhaji Mohamed Swarry Deen (SLPP)
Political and Parliamentary Affairs	Eya Mbayo
Social Welfare, Gender, and Children's Affairs	Shirley Y. Gbujama (SLPP) [f]
Tourism and Culture	Okere Adams (SLPP)
Trade and Industry	Kadi Sesay (PDP) [f]
Transport and Communications	Prince A. Harding
Works, Housing, and Technical Maintenance	Caiser J. Boima
Youth and Sports	Dennis Bright

Ministers of State

Presidential Affairs	Sheku Sesay
Eastern Region	Sahr Randolph Fillie-Faboe
Southern Region	S. U. M. Jah (SLPP)
Northern Region	Alex Alie Kargbo

[f] = female

People's Democratic Party (PDP). The PDP was characterized by *West Africa* as the "loudest" of the new parties, whose "main handicap is the uncharismatic quality" of its leader, former information minister Thaimu BANGURA. In September 1991 Bangura had been named chair of a United Front of Political Movements (UNIFORM), a six-party opposition formation that was subsequently dissolved.

At balloting in February 1996, Bangura placed third in the presidential contest, with 16.1 percent of the vote, and the party won 12 seats.

Subsequently, as an apparent reward for supporting Kabbah in the second round of presidential balloting, the PDP secured three cabinet portfolios.

Bangura died in March 1999. Following infighting between Osman Kamara and former NPRC member Abdul Rahman KAMARA to replace Bangura, Osman Kamara was elected chair. Abdul Rahman Kamara quit the party to form his own organization, the **People's Democratic Alliance** (PDA) in November. In a cabinet reshuffle in March 2001, Osman Kamara was given the post of the trade and industry minister, although he claimed that the PDP was still an opposition party. He was subsequently replaced. The PDP, with 1 percent of the vote, failed to win a seat in the legislative election of May 2002. The party did not present a presidential candidate but came out in support of Kabbah.

Leader: Osman KAMARA (Secretary General).

Young People's Party (YPP). Described as "one of the most promising new parties" by *Africa News,* the YPP was formed in April 2001 mainly by university students. Andrew Duramani TURAY placed last in the 2002 presidential election with 0.2 percent of the vote.

Leader: Sylvia BLYDEN (Executive Leader).

National Democratic Alliance (NDA). The NDA fielded candidates for the legislature but not the presidency in 2002. The party reconvened in 2005 after having been inactive for several years.

Leaders: Ansu MASSAQUOI (Acting Chair), Amadu JALLOH, Francis BAWOH (Secretary General), Abdul BAH.

Movement for Progress (MOP). Formed in 2002 to promote "good governance and positive change," the MOP supported the creation of the special war crimes court and presented the only female candidate in 2002, longtime political activist Zainab Bangura. She garnered less than 1 percent of the vote.

Leader: Zainab BANGURA (Chair and Leader and 2002 presidential candidate).

Citizens United for Peace and Progress (CUPP). Founded in 2001 (and registered on September 28) by Sierra Leoneans in the United States, the CUPP advocates "justice for victims" of the decade-long civil war. The party presented a presidential candidate in 2002, Washington lawyer Raymond Bamidele THOMPSON (who received 0.4 percent of the vote), but no legislative candidate.

People's Movement for Democratic Change (PMDC). Registered by the government in April 2006, the PMDC was founded by Charles Margai, who left the SLPP after he lost his bid for the chairmanship, to promote a civilian, democratic government. Margai was arrested in 2006 on a variety of charges related to disorderly behavior against the government.

Leaders: Charles MARGAI, Ansu LANSANA (Secretary General).

In addition to the 11 parties that competed in the May 2002 presidential and legislative balloting, other groups include the **People's Progressive Party** (PPP), led by former ECOWAS executive secretary Dr. Abass BUNDU; the **People's National Convention** (PNC), led by 1996 presidential candidate Edward KARGBO; the **National Unity Movement** (NUM), led by Reginald SCHLENKER-WILLIAMS; the **National Alliance Democratic Party** (NADP), led by Mohamed Yahya SILLAH; the **National People's Party** (NPP); and the **Sierra Leoneans Advocate for Progress** (SLAP), led by Christian JOHNSON.

In February 2000 two new parties were formed, the **Liberal Democratic Party** (LDP) and the **Sierra Leone Socialist Party** (SLSP).

Legislature

The Sierra Leone **National Assembly** is a 124-member unicameral body. At the general elections of May 14, 2002 (the first since February 1996), the Sierra Leone People's Party captured 83 seats; the All People's Congress, 27; and the Peace and Liberation Party, 2. In addition to these 112 members, elected directly to five-year terms, 12 seats were filled by paramount chiefs, representing the 12 provincial districts.

Speaker: Edmond K. COWAN.

Communications

Press

A variety of media rights conferred by the 1991 constitution were effectively abrogated by the post-coup military government, which issued a series of decrees limiting freedom of the press, introducing prior censorship, and severely curtailing private speech. One such enactment outlawed reports "likely to cause alarm, despondency or be prejudicial to the public safety, public tranquility and the maintenance of public order," while another declared illegal any attempt to influence public opinion "orally or otherwise." On March 30, 1994, new press guidelines set minimum financial and educational standards for publishers and journalists, respectively. Among the nation's daily newspapers are the government-controlled *Daily Mail* (Freetown, 10,000) and the independent *Standard Times;* weekly organs include *The Weekend Spark* (20,000), *Progress* (7,000), *The New Globe, The New Breed,* the independent *Weekly Democrat,* and the pro-APC *We Yone.* The independent *Concord Times* is published three times a week; *The New Shaft* (10,000), twice weekly.

News Agencies

The domestic facility is the Sierre Leone News Agency (Slena), established in 1980 after President Stevens complained about "the image given to Third World countries by the press in developed countries." Reuters, TASS, *Xinhua,* and *Agence France-Presse* are among the foreign agencies that maintain bureaus in Freetown.

Broadcasting and Computing

The government-owned Sierra Leone Broadcasting Service (SLBS) operates a number of radio stations broadcasting in English, Krio, Limba, Mende, and Temne; it also provides limited commercial television service. ABC TV is a private television network. Radio stations include Radio Democracy, a pro-government station originally set up as the voice of the Kabbah government in exile; Radio UNAMSIL, the UN network; Believers Broadcasting Network, a Freetown Christian station; Voice of the Handicapped, founded to serve Sierra Leone's victims of mass amputations carried out during the civil war; and private stations KISS FM (Bo) and SKYY FM (Freetown). There were approximately 70,000 television receivers and 9,000 Internet users in 2003.

Intergovernmental Representation

Ambassador to the U.S.
Ibrahim M. KAMARA

U.S. Ambassador to Sierra Leone
Thomas N. HULL III

Permanent Representative to the UN
Joe Robert PEMAGBI

IGO Memberships (Non-UN)
AfDB, AU, BADEA, CEN-SAD, CWTH, ECOWAS, IDB, Interpol, IOM, MRU, NAM, OIC, WCO, WTO

SOMALIA

SOMALI REPUBLIC

Jamhuuriyada Soomaaliyeed

Note: On May 18, 1991, the (then) president of the Somali National Movement (SNM), Abdurahman Ahmed Ali ("Taur"), announced that northwestern Somalia (British Somaliland prior to its incorporation into Somalia in July 1960) had seceded to form an independent Republic of Somaliland. Although the self-proclaimed entity had received no international recognition as of 2006, it is accorded a separate write-up following the present article. An "autonomous region" was declared in the northeastern area of Puntland in 1998; information on that region is contained in this article.

Note: Following numerous cabinet dismissals and resignations from May to early August 2006, President Yusuf Ahmed announced on August 7 that the entire cabinet had been dismissed, although Prime Minister Ghedi remained in office. A new cabinet was announced on August 21.

The Country

The easternmost country in Africa, Somalia (including Somaliland) encompasses a broad band of desert and semidesert territory extending eastward along the Gulf of Aden and continuing southwestward to a point just south of the equator. The Somalis, a people of nomadic and pastoral traditions, share a common religion (Islam) and a common language (Somali). However, interclan rivalry has generated numerous economic and political cleavages, particularly between northern and southern groups. Nonindigenous inhabitants include Arabs, Ethiopians, Italians, Indians, and Pakistanis.

The economy is largely undeveloped, virtually no growth having been achieved in the last three decades and the country remaining one of the world's poorest with annual per capita GNP falling below $110 in the early 2000s. Agriculture accounts for two-thirds of economic activity, although it is compromised by irregular rainfall. The country possesses some mineral deposits that thus far have not been commercially exploited. Although fishing, textile, and food processing industries have been established, much of the country's foreign exchange is derived from livestock

and livestock-related products. In addition, Somalia has long been the world's largest producer of myrrh, an incense that is widely used in the Gulf region, China, and France. Development projects, including the construction of a dam for hydroelectric and irrigation purposes across the Juba River

in the south, came to a virtual halt following the collapse of the central government in 1991. Meanwhile, inflation, drought, inefficiency in state enterprises, bureaucratic corruption, the presence of refugees from neighboring Ethiopia, and disruptions occasioned by civil war and interclan hostilities subsequently contributed to an overall state of destitution so severe that three-quarters of the population was estimated in mid-1992 to be at risk of starvation. The situation was only partially alleviated by the United Nations and other relief suppliers in 1993–1994. As of 1999 Somalia remained at the bottom of the UN development index, ongoing interclan violence in the south constraining the ability of the international community to deliver aid. The interim national government (unrecognized in several key regions) that was installed in 2000 declared infrastructure development to be second only to security among its priorities. However, Somalia subsequently remained what one UN official described as a "black hole of anarchy" that lacked sufficient institutional structure to process foreign aid that could assist in addressing the dearth of health, educational, and security services. As momentum developed toward the resolution of the long-standing hostilities, the World Bank relaunched some of its aid programs to Somalia in 2003. Optimists also predicted that the installation of a new transitional government in late 2004 to early 2005 would finally permit a semblance of normal attention to the country's dire economic and social conditions. The European Union (EU) subsequently pledged humanitarian and reconstruction aid, while UN agencies and other aid organizations launched food-distribution initiatives in the drought-affected south. However, the resumption of conflict in the spring of 2006 (see Current issues, below) prompted many aid groups to withdraw personnel and suspend assistance.

Government and Politics

Political Background

Divided into British, French, and Italian sectors at the end of the 19th century, Somalia was partially reunited in 1960 when British Somaliland in the north and the Italian-administered Trust Territory in the south achieved their independence and promptly merged to form the United Republic of Somalia. Large numbers of Somalis remained in Ethiopia, Kenya, and the French Territory of the Afars and the Issas (subsequently Djibouti), and the new Somali regime announced that their inclusion in a "Greater Somalia" was a leading political objective.

The Somali Youth league (SYL) was the country's principal political party at independence and formed the republic's initial governments. During the late 1950s and early 1960s Somalia pursued a strongly irredentist policy toward Ethiopia and Kenya, relying increasingly on aid from the Soviet Union and other communist states. A change of policy occurred in 1967 with the presidential election of Abdirashid Ali SHERMARKE and his appointment of Mohamed Haji Ibrahim EGAL as prime minister. Under Egal's leadership, Somalia maintained its demand for self-determination for all Somalis but emphasized reduced dependence on the communist world, conciliation with neighboring states, and the cultivation of friendly relations with Western countries.

The Egal regime was ousted by military units under the command of Maj. Gen. Mohamed SIAD BARRE on October 21, 1969, in an action that included the assassination of President Shermarke. Pledging to reduce tribalism and corruption, the new military government launched a restructuring along socialist lines of what was now termed the Somali Democratic Republic. Although briefly interrupted by antigovernment plots in 1970 and 1971, the program moved forward at a deliberate pace. In 1970 foreign banks and other foreign-controlled enterprises were nationalized, and in October 1972 local government reorganization was begun. On July 1, 1976, the Supreme Revolutionary Council (SRC) that had been established in the wake of the 1969 coup was abolished, and its powers were transferred to a newly created Somali Revolutionary Socialist Party (SRSP) of which Siad Barre was named secretary general. Civilian government was nominally reinstituted following

Political Status: Independent republic established July 1, 1960; revolutionary military regime installed October 21, 1969; one-party state proclaimed July 1, 1976; multiparty system authorized on December 25, 1990, but unimplemented prior to the assumption of power by rebel forces on January 27, 1991; national charter providing for three-year transitional national government adopted by Somali National Peace Conference July 16, 2000, in Arta, Djibouti; Transitional Federal Charter approved January 29, 2004, providing for a four-year transitional government.
Area: 246,199 sq. mi. (637,657 sq. km.), including Somaliland (68,000 sq. mi.; 176,120 sq. km.).
Population: 7,114,431 (1987C); 10,764,000 (2005E). Both figures include Somaliland, estimated at 4,997,000 in 2005.
Major Urban Center (2005E): MOGADISHU (1,257,000, preliminary, including suburbs).
Principal Language: Somali.
Monetary Unit: Somali Shilling (official rate July 1, 2006: 1,340 shillings = $1US). (The United Nations reported an operational rate as of August 1, 2006, of 14,406 shillings = $1US. Earlier, as many as four versions of the shilling reportedly remained in circulation, including some apparently printed by local businessmen, thereby rendering attempts to determine a genuine national currency rate essentially futile. A degree of stability was anticipated following the 2004 comprehensive peace settlement, although it was clear that the UN rate was more "real" than the official rate.)
President: Col. Abdullahi YUSUF AHMED; elected by the Transitional Federal Parliament on October 10, 2004, and inaugurated the same day to succeed nominal Interim President Abdiqassim SALAD HASSAN.
Prime Minister: Ali Mohammed GHEDI; appointed by the president on November 3, 2004; lost confidence motion in the Transitional Federal Parliament (TFP) on December 11, 2004; reappointed by the president on December 13, 2004, and confirmed by the TFP on December 23.

popular approval of a new constitution on August 25, 1979, the one-party election of a People's Assembly on December 30, and the assembly's election of General Siad Barre as president on January 26, 1980.

A state of emergency was declared on October 21, 1980, following a resurgence of conflict with Ethiopia (for a discussion of earlier hostilities, see Foreign relations, below). Radio Mogadishu announced two days later that the SRC had been reconstituted. The emergency decree was rescinded on March 1, 1982, despite reports of a northern army mutiny in mid-February and sporadic border incidents that persisted thereafter. At the legislative election of December 31, 1984, 99.8 percent of the voters were reported to have cast ballots, with less than 1 percent opposing the SRSP's nominees.

In May 1986 Siad Barre suffered severe injuries in an automobile accident, and First Vice President Lt. Gen. Mohamed Ali SAMATAR served as de facto chief executive for several months. Although Siad Barre recovered sufficiently to be the sole candidate for reelection to a seven-year presidential term on December 23, 1986 (in the country's first direct balloting for the position), his poor health and advanced age generated intense speculation as to a successor. Samatar appeared to be a leading candidate, particularly after being additionally named to the new post of prime minister in January 1987. However, in the wake of a government reshuffle in December, all references to his vice presidential role ceased. Given the constitutional significance of the office in regard to succession, the change was interpreted as reflecting Siad Barre's desire to be succeeded either by a family member or an individual from his Marehan clan, to which Samatar did not belong.

During 1988 the Somali National Movement (SNM), a northwestern rebel group that had joined Ethiopian units in a cross-border assault the year before, mounted a broad offensive that eventually succeeded in driving government forces from most of the region's rural areas by mid-1989. President Siad Barre thereupon announced the appointment of a constitutional review committee charged with laying the groundwork for a multiparty system that would permit the SNM to engage in electoral activity, provided it did "not solely seek to satisfy tribal interests." Meanwhile, other clan-based groups had taken up arms, including the United Somali Congress (USC) in the center and the Somali Patriotic Movement (SPM) in the south.

On September 3, 1990, in the wake of heightened rebel activity, Prime Minister Samatar was dismissed in favor of Mohamed HAWADIE MADAR. On January 20, 1991, as USC forces converged on the capital, Umar ARTEH GHALIB, a former foreign minister who had only recently been released from house arrest, was asked to form an essentially transitional government, and six days later Siad Barre departed for exile in Kenya. (He died in Nigeria on January 2, 1995.) On January 28, one day after assuming control in Mogadishu, the USC appointed its principal financial backer, Ali MAHDI MOHAMED, to the post of interim president. Mahdi, in turn, named Arteh Ghalib to head a reconstituted administration on January 29. However, neither appointment proved acceptable to the SNM, which, after rejecting two invitations to attend "national reconciliation" meetings with its erstwhile allies, announced the secession of the former British Somaliland on May 18 (see article on Somaliland). Subsequently, Gen. Mohamed Farah AIDID was elected USC chair at the party's third congress held July 4–5, provoking a bitter dispute with President Mahdi because the two came from different Hawiye subclans. In early September at least 300 people were killed in a clash between the two factions in Mogadishu, while more intense fighting, which erupted in mid-November, resulted in the slaughter of at least 4,000 civilians by the end of the year, with some 100,000 having fled the city.

In early February 1992 General Aidid was dismissed as USC chair, formalizing the cleavage between the group's pro- and anti-Mahdi factions. The action came after the announcement by UN Secretary General Boutros Boutros-Ghali of the first of a number of cease-fires, none of which proved effective despite the arrival in Mogadishu in late March of a UN technical team to monitor the conflict and develop a mechanism for delivering relief supplies. On April 24, in response to the team's recommendations, the Security Council authorized the creation of a United Nations Operation in Somalia (UNOSOM) to "facilitate an immediate and effective cessation of hostilities . . . and provide urgent humanitarian assistance." Meanwhile, General Aidid launched a new opposition grouping called the Somali National Alliance (SNA).

On June 6, 1992, representatives of 11 Somali factions, meeting in Bahr Dar in northwest Ethiopia, agreed to support a UN-implemented cease-fire and convene a "comprehensive and joint conference" to "smooth the way" for the establishment of a provisional government in Somalia within three months. However, by late August, with reports that some 2,000 people were perishing daily from starvation, arrangements were made for the deployment of a 500-member UN peacekeeping force to guard relief supplies. In mid-September, responding to heightened evidence of famine, U.S. President George H. W. Bush ordered four warships with 2,400 marines to the Somali coast. On October 1 the United Nations announced that it was increasing its peacekeeping body to 1,200, despite protests from General Aidid, whose forces claimed control of two-thirds of the capital and most of southern Somalia. On November 27 Washington offered to provide 30,000 troops as part of a UN military intervention effort to thwart the theft of food aid. General Aidid thereupon reversed himself and hailed the U.S. overture as a way to "solve our political, economic, and social problems." On December 4 President Bush ordered the U.S. forces to Somalia as part of a projected multinational United Task Force (UNITAF) of some 35,000 soldiers.

Despite the breakdown of peace talks among 14 warring Somali factions in early January 1993, agreement was subsequently reached on a cease-fire and the appointment of a seven-member committee to lay the groundwork for a national reconciliation conference in mid-March. Meanwhile, the U.S. forces committed to "Operation Restore Hope" commenced a withdrawal, preparatory to handing peacekeeping operations over to a new 28,000-member UN Operation in Somalia (UNOSOM II) in early May.

Intense fighting erupted in the southern port city of Kismayu in mid-March 1993 between forces commanded by Siad Barre's son-in-law, Gen. Mohamed SAID HERSI, and Col. Ahmed UMAR JESS, an ally of General Aidid. However, at the conclusion of the conference in Addis Ababa, Ethiopia, on March 27, 1993, it was announced that agreement had been reached on a Transitional National Council for Somalia, which was given a mandate to lead the country to elections within two years.

On May 4, 1993, the UN formally assumed control of the multinational relief effort led since December by a U.S. commander. Unlike previous peacekeeping missions, however, the UN troops were provided with rules of engagement that permitted them to use offensive force to disarm Somali clans. This mandate was invoked on June 11 in retaliation against General Aidid, whose faction was accused of ambushing and killing 23 Pakistani peacekeepers on June 5. The action, which commenced with an attack by U.S. helicopter gunships on Aidid's Mogadishu compound, concluded on June 17 with a ground assault that failed to curb the general's military capability, Aidid himself evading capture. On November 16 the UN Security Council revoked its warrant for the arrest of Aidid, who nonetheless boycotted a further UN-sponsored peace conference in Addis Ababa in November.

A more positive note was sounded at a January 1994 meeting in Mogadishu of elders of Mahdi's Abgal and Aidid's Habr Gedir subclans. Two months later, the two leaders met for the first time in over a year in Nairobi, and on March 24 they signed a somewhat vaguely worded peace accord that called for the formation of a coalition government during a "national reconciliation" meeting on May 15. However, no action was taken on the date specified, and in late June heavy factional fighting again broke out in Mogadishu.

Frustrated in its efforts to reconcile Somalia's rival factions, the UN Security Council voted on November 4, 1994, to withdraw the UNOSOM II force by March 31, 1995. In fact, the UN completed its withdrawal on March 1. Eleven days later Aidid and Mahdi concluded an agreement for joint control of the port and airport, both of which reopened on March 14. However, by mid-May the agreement appeared to be fading, each side charging the other with violating its terms, and on May 25 Aidid's sector of Mogadishu came under shelling from the north. On June 12 Aidid was formally ousted as SNA leader by a joint SNA-USC conference called by his longtime ally and fellow Habr Gedir subclansman, Osman HASAN ALI ("Osman Ato"), who was named the general's successor. Aidid, who refused to accept the conference action, responded by convening a meeting of representatives from a number of groups of supporters who unanimously elected him Somali "president" for a three-year term. On June 16 Interim President Mahdi joined Osman Ato in condemning Aidid's "self-appointment."

In late August 1995 fighting broke out along a Green Line demarcating sectors of Mogadishu controlled by Aidid and Mahdi. The clash was apparently triggered by Aidid's efforts to confiscate weapons from civilians as part of a "rehabilitation and disarmament" drive, which followed the failure of a "reconciliation" conference launched by Osman Ato in Nairobi with the support of the Organization of the Islamic Conference (OIC). In September Aidid's forces captured the important town of Baidoa, some 90 miles northwest of the capital.

Aidid and his militiamen continued their offensive through early 1996, scoring a number of victories outside of the capital, including the capture of at least two more towns, before being slowed by the Mahdi-allied Rahanweyn Resistance Army (RRA). Subsequently, theretofore low-level hostilities erupted into widespread fighting following the collapse of peace talks in April. Particularly intense clashes were reported in Mogadishu, where, in July, the warring factions were reported to be preparing for an all-out battle for control of the capital. However, on August 1, 1996, General Aidid died from wounds reportedly suffered one week earlier in a battle against Ato's forces in the Medina neighborhood of Mogadishu. Calling Aidid's death an opportunity to launch fresh peace negotiations, Mahdi and Ato immediately announced a cease-fire.

Optimism was quickly dampened, however, by the SNA's election of Aidid's son, Hussein Mohamed Farah AIDID, as "interim president of Somalia." At his "inauguration" on August 4, 1996, Aidid, a U.S.-educated former Marine who had returned to Somalia a year earlier, pledged to gain revenge on his father's killers, and renewed fighting was subsequently reported in Mogadishu. Meanwhile, international observers had persuaded Aidid, Mahdi, and Ato to accept the establishment of a commission to prepare for reconciliation negotiations, and in Nairobi on October 15 the three agreed to begin a cease-fire, remove roadblocks between the areas under their control, and facilitate the distribution of humanitarian aid. The cease-fire proved short-lived, however, with fighting beginning anew in late October.

In mid-November 1996 representatives of 26 groups, including nearly all of the major factions (with the notable exception of Aidid's), convened in Sodere, Ethiopia, for peace talks sponsored by the Organization of African Unity (OAU, subsequently the African Union—AU). On January 3, 1997, the participants announced the creation of a 41-member National Salvation Council (NSC) under the leadership of five faction leaders (including Mahdi and Ato), as well as an 11-member National Executive Committee (NEC). The NSC was charged with organizing a national reconciliation conference (then scheduled for June 1997) at which a transitional government would be formed. For his part, Aidid rejected the NSC's entreaties to participate, reasserting that he was already the "legitimate leader of all Somalia."

Despite the efforts of the NSC's preparatory committee in the first half of 1997, prospects for an all-inclusive agreement remained slim as Aidid continued to refuse to participate and actively sought to resuscitate the October 1996 accord, meeting and signing new pacts with Ato and Mahdi in Cairo, Egypt, in early and late May, respectively. In June the NSC rescheduled the proposed reconciliation conference to November; however, in October the conference was postponed indefinitely, ostensibly because of a lack of international funding. On the other hand, Egypt continued its efforts

to provide an alternative to the now-stalemated Sodere plan, and in early December Aidid and leaders of other factions signed an accord in Cairo that included provisions for a "government of national union." The NSC ratified the accord in early January 1998 and scheduled a national reconciliation conference for February 15 to select a transitional president, a prime minister, a 13-member Presidential Council, and a 189-member Council of Deputies. However, the conference was postponed, and, despite subsequent efforts to resuscitate the pact, Somalia remained without a national governing authority. (On March 20 Aidid had reportedly renounced his claim to the presidency and, restyling himself "co-president," had pledged to cooperate with nominal president Mahdi.)

On July 23, 1998, a conference of some 300 leaders from the northeast region of Puntland declared the establishment of an autonomous government under the presidency of Col. Abdullahi YUSUF AHMED, a longtime military and political leader (see Somali Salvation Democratic Front under Political Parties and Groups, below). Although the conference also established a 66-member House of Representatives (appointed by local leaders, essentially on a subclan basis), a charter endorsed by the house (as well as an informal council of traditional leaders) in September rejected secession for the region, calling instead for eventual establishment of a federal system in which regional governments would enjoy extensive autonomy. A transitional government of three years' duration was initially envisioned for Puntland.

On May 2, 2000, in Arta, Djibouti, Ismail Omar Guelleh, the new president of Djibouti, convened a Somali National Peace Conference (SNPC) of prominent Somali figures representing a wide range of constituencies, including religious groups, the business community, traditional elders, intellectuals, women's organizations, and clans. (The conference was endorsed by the UN, OAU, and the Inter-Governmental Authority on Development [IGAD].) On July 16 the SNPC approved a national charter providing for a three-year Transitional National Government (TNG) to be led by a

Transitional National Assembly (TNA, appointed on a clan basis) and a president (elected by the TNA). The TNA convened for the first time in Arta on August 13, and on August 27 it elected Abdiqassim SALAD HASSAN, a former deputy prime minister and interior minister in the Siad Barre regime, as president. On October 2 Salad Hassan appointed Ali Khalif GALAYDH, a professor and prominent businessman, as prime minister. Galaydh announced his first ministerial appointments, carefully balanced among clans, on October 20. Although the fledgling interim central government subsequently moved to Mogadishu, its potential effectiveness remained in serious question because it had not received the endorsement of Somaliland, the regional administration established in Puntland, or most factional militia leaders. Of the prominent Somali "warlords," only Mahdi had attended the SNPC. He was subsequently appointed to the new assembly and pledged his support to the TNG.

In February 2001 Prime Minister Galaydh announced a cabinet reshuffle, with the pro-Mahdi faction of the USC formally joining the government. However, Galaydh's government, apparently being blamed by the public for the lack of progress in negotiations with the recalcitrant warlords, lost a confidence motion in the assembly by a reported vote of 141–29 on October 28. President Salad Hassan on November 12 named Hasan Abshir FARAH, a former cabinet member, to replace Galaydh. Following the successful negotiation of a power-sharing agreement with several minor warlords in late December, Farah announced a new cabinet on February 16, 2002.

Meanwhile, political affairs in Puntland also remained complicated. As the conclusion neared of the three-year mandate accorded the transitional government of Yusuf Ahmed in 1998, it was announced in late June 2001 that the Puntland House of Representatives and clan elders had extended the government's authority for another three years, the Puntland administration continuing to reject the legitimacy of the TNG. However, Puntland Chief Justice Yusuf Haji NUR in early July declared the extension "unconstitutional" and announced he

had assumed authority as "acting president" pending new regional elections. Yusuf Ahmed rejected Nur's dictate, and fighting was reported in August between Yusuf Ahmed's forces (reportedly supported by Ethiopia) and those of Nur's (believed to have the support of the TNG and, according to charges from Yusuf Ahmed, the Islamic Union [see Political Parties and Groups, below].) With Yusuf Ahmed now "ruling" from the city of Galkacyo and Nur controlling the regional capital of Garowe, a controversial congress of clan elders opened in Garowe in late August. On November 14 the congress, deemed "illegal and destabilizing" by Yusuf Ahmed, elected Jama Ali JAMA, a former army colonel who had been imprisoned for part of the Siad Barre regime, as the new president of Puntland from among 12 candidates. Although Jama was inaugurated on November 19, Yusuf Ahmed's forces by May 2002 had effectively regained control of the region. The TNG subsequently continued to reference Jama as the "legitimate" president, but Yusuf Ahmed was still exercising full authority as the year ended.

Further complicating the situation in Somalia was the announcement of the formation on April 1, 2002, of an autonomous government in the self-described State of Southwestern Somalia, the third such breakaway administration (the others being Somaliland and Puntland) to be formed. Although internal dissension was reported on the matter, the new regional government was launched under the umbrella of the Somali Reconciliation and Reconstruction Council (SRRC), a loose coalition of southern factions that had been launched in 2001 in opposition to the TNG (see Somali National Alliance under Political Parties and Groups, below, for additional information on the SRRC). Col. Hassan Mohammed NUR ("Shatigadud") of the RRA was named president of the new administration, also slated to include a cabinet and 145-member legislature.

Most of the major factions in the Somalian conflict resumed negotiations in October 2002 in Kenya, although Somaliland declined to attend. On July 5, 2003, the parties appeared to agree on a transitional peace plan, but Salad Hassan rejected the proposal, claiming that Prime Minister Farah had exceeded his authority by agreeing to allow too much power to remain at the regional level under the tentative agreement. On August 9 Salad Hassan dismissed Farah as prime minister, naming Osman JAMA ALI (former deputy prime minister) to the post. However, Jama Ali resigned on November 28, reportedly due to conflict with the president. He was succeeded on December 8 by Mohamed Abdi YUSUF, the deputy speaker of the TNA, which subsequently endorsed a new 37-member cabinet. Meanwhile, in Puntland, Yusuf Ahmed had initiated peace talks with rival groups in May 2003 that had yielded an agreement under which he was fully recognized as president while former opponents were named to the new Puntland cabinet.

In January 2004 several hitherto reluctant rebel and opposition groups (including the RRA) joined the peace negotiations in Kenya, and on January 29 some 42 factions and warlords signed a potentially historic comprehensive accord based on a Transitional Federal Charter (TFC) that provided for a transitional legislature that would elect a president and confirm a new transitional government. The TNA approved the settlement on February 9, and the new legislature (the Transitional Federal Parliament—TFP) was filled by clan and subclan appointees by early August.

In the third round of balloting for a national president in the TFP on October 10, 2004, Yusuf Ahmed was elected by a vote of 189–79. (Eleven candidates had contended the first round.) On November 3 the new president appointed Ali Mohammed GHEDI as prime minister, but the TFP on December 11 voted down his first proposed cabinet, apparently because a number of clans were not happy with their representation. However, an expanded and revised Transitional Federal Government (TFG) won TFP approval on January 7, 2005, all activity occurring in Kenya due to continued unsettled conditions in Somalia. Somaliland remained divorced from the new institutions, although the breakaway status of the State of Southwestern Somalia appeared resolved by Colonel Shatigadud's inclusion in the new national government.

Constitution and Government

For the decade after the October 1969 coup, supreme power was vested in the Central Committee of the SRSP, whose secretary general served as head of state and chief executive. For all practical purposes these arrangements were continued under a constitution approved in 1979, which provided additionally for a People's Assembly of 177 members, 171 of whom were nominated by the party and 6 by the president. The president was popularly elected for a seven-year term after having been nominated by the SRSP as the sole candidate. These and other provisions of the 1979 basic law were effectively suspended with the collapse of the Siad Barre regime in January 1991, following which the independent republic of Somaliland was declared in May in the northwest (see separate article for details on the administration in Somaliland).

In part with the goal of encouraging eventual participation by the administrations already established in Somaliland and Puntland, the national charter adopted by the SNPC in July 2000 called for a federal system with strong regional governments. Pending formal establishment of such a system under a new constitution, the SNPC authorized a three-year TNG, with legislative responsibility delegated to an appointed House of Representatives. The charter also promised an independent judiciary, protection of the freedom of expression and other human rights, and support for multiparty activity. (For details of new transitional institutions established through the Transitional Federal Charter of January 2004, see Political background, above.)

Administratively, the country is divided into 15 regions, which are subdivided into 70 districts, plus the city of Mogadishu.

Foreign Relations

Although a member of the United Nations, the AU, and the Arab League, Somalia has been chiefly concerned with the problems of its own immediate area, where seasonal migrations by Somali herdsmen have long strained relations with neighboring states. The most serious disputes have been with Ethiopia. Somali claims to the Ogaden desert region precipitated conflicts beginning in 1963 that escalated into a full-scale war in 1977–1978 when government troops entered the region, eventually to be driven back by an Ethiopian counteroffensive. The war had international implications, producing a reversal of roles for the Soviet Union and the United States in the Horn of Africa. Ethiopia, previously dependent on the United States for military support, was the recipient of a massive influx of arms and advisers from the Soviet Union and Cuba. Collaterally, Somalia, which had developed an extensive network of relations with communist countries, broke with Moscow and Havana in favor of reliance on the West, eventually agreeing in 1980 to make port facilities available to the U.S. Rapid Deployment Force for the Middle East in return for American arms. Somalia normalized relations with the USSR in 1986 and Cuba in 1989 but continued to receive substantial military aid from the United States.

Although the 1979 constitution called for "the liberation of Somali territories under colonial occupation"—implicitly referencing Somali-populated areas of Kenya as well as of Ethiopia—the Somalis promised that they would not intervene militarily in support of external dissidents. Tense relations and occasional border hostilities continued, however, with Ethiopia supporting the major Somali opposition groups in guerrilla operations. In January 1986 President Siad Barre and Ethiopian leader Mengistu Haile-Mariam established a joint ministerial commission to resolve the Ogaden question, but no results were achieved during the ensuing year, with Somalia condemning Ethiopia for a cross-border attack in February 1987. Following major Ethiopian reverses at the hands of Eritrean secessionists in the north, Siad Barre and Mengistu conferred during a drought conference in Djibouti in March 1988 and agreed to peace talks in Mogadishu in early April. The discussions yielded a communiqué that pledged a military "disengagement and separation," an exchange of prisoners, the reestablishment of diplomatic relations, and the joint cessation of support for opposition groups.

In early August 1996 Ethiopian forces attacked three towns in Somalia's Gedo region in an apparent attempt to squash the activities of the Islamic Union (see Political Parties and Groups, below), which had claimed credit for bombings and assassination attempts in Ethiopia as part of its campaign for the Ogaden region's independence. The offensive continued into 1997, and by early February Ethiopian troops had reportedly overrun the Islamic fighters' last base in the region. Ethiopia's military advances proved costly on the diplomatic front, however, as a number of Somalian faction leaders, most important the SNA's Aidid, condemned the "occupation" and refused to participate in the peace process launched in November 1996 in Sodere, Ethiopia. Thereafter, Aidid's efforts to revive the short-lived Nairobi accord of October 1996 were actively supported by Kenya and Egypt. The latter championed the establishment of a unified and centrally governed Somalia as opposed to an Ethiopian diplomatic advance, which one analyst labeled "divisive." Much of southern Somalia subsequently came under Ethiopian influence as the result of Ethiopian initiatives relating to its war with Eritrea in 1998–2000. The TNG in Somalia subsequently accused Ethiopia of supplying weapons to anti-TNG warlords in Somalia. Meanwhile, the activities of the Islamic Union also attracted the interest of the United States because of the latter's "war on terrorism" following the terrorist attacks in September 2001.

Many African states recognized the TFG established in late 2004 and early 2005 to govern Somalia, and the AU authorized a contingency peacekeeping force for possible deployment in Somalia. Meanwhile, the European Union pledged financial and technical aid for the new administration, but the United States as of mid-2005 had developed only "informal ties" with the TFG. Negotiations over the size and makeup of the proposed AU peacekeeping force continued through 2005, and the outbreak of hostilities in Mogadishu in early 2006 appeared to jeopardize the plan.

In April 2006 Prime Minister Ghedi gave the United States permission to patrol the waters off the coast of Somalia to suppress piracy. (Some 35 pirate attacks had been reported in 2005.) Reports had also previously surfaced that U.S. marines and special forces had undertaken several covert antiterrorist operations in Somalia, prompting minor rioting and protests in some cities.

Current Issues

The establishment of regional administrations in Banaadir (encompassing Mogadishu) and Puntland in mid-1998 exemplified what observers described as a potential "bottom up" approach to ending Somalia's civil strife. However, the country's political, economic, and social quagmire subsequently remained intractable, despite the efforts of regional and international mediators. Significantly, unofficial Islamic courts began operating throughout much of the country in the late 1990s, reportedly backed by the business community in the hope of combating rampant banditry and other criminal activity. Islamic militias also apparently challenged the control of long-entrenched warlords in some areas.

The establishment of the Transitional National Government (TNG) in mid-2000 evoked "high emotion" in many domestic sectors as hope spread that nearly a decade of fighting, which had left hundreds of thousands of people dead and millions displaced, was coming to an end. However, despite the fact that mass demonstrations greeted President Salad Hassan in Mogadishu following his inauguration in August, it quickly became clear that the new administration remained tenuous because of the absence of support from numerous warlords, including General Aidid. Salad Hassan and new prime minister Galaydh declared "law and order," national reconciliation, and infrastructure rehabilitation to be their top priorities. Intense negotiations were subsequently reported between the TNG and recalcitrant warlords, but security issues remained unresolved, costing Galaydh the premiership in late 2001.

The peace talks launched in Kenya in October 2002 were attended by a number of regional leaders as well as representatives of Somalia's civil society. Although some of the warlords at the negotiations endorsed an immediate cease-fire, sporadic fighting continued in several parts of Somalia. The addition of holdout rebel groups to the negotiations in January 2004 appeared to break the long-standing impasse and offer the best chance to date to end the national nightmare. However, underscoring the continued fragility of the security situation, the Transitional Federal Government (TFG) established in late 2004 and early 2005 remained in Kenya until April 2005. Fighting was reported when Prime Minister Ghedi finally attempted to settle his government in Mogadishu, and most government operations were shifted to more stable cities in the south. Meanwhile, it was unclear how the new national government would ultimately affect the autonomous government in Puntland (where Mohamed Muse HERSI had been elected president in January), and there was no indication of possible reconciliation from Somaliland.

Tensions over where the government should locate subsequently continued to constrain the TFG's effectiveness, as did reported clan rivalries within the cabinet. Consequently, plans for the demobilization of clan militias in favor of a unified national army failed to produce significant results. Underscoring the fragility of the situation, a bomb exploded following an address by Prime Minister Ghedi in May 2005 in Mogadishu, killing more than 15 people. Ghedi, the cabinet, and some legislators subsequently settled in Jowhar, while other legislators attempted to operate out of Mogadishu. Ghedi survived another assassination attempt during a trip to Mogadishu in November, an event that triggered a new round of fighting in the capital. At the same time it was reported that Islamic fighters were filtering into Mogadishu to support the Islamic Courts Union (ICU, see Political Parties and Groups, below).

The full TNA met for the first time in Baidoa in February 2006. However, it remained clear that the TFG lacked the military means to confront the warlords who had controlled Mogadishu for the past 15 years. Following severe rioting in February, prompted by the publication of cartoons in Denmark deemed offensive to Muslims, fighting intensified in Mogadishu between the ICU militias and the warlords, who had formed the Alliance for the Restoration of Peace and Counter-Terrorism (ARPCT). (It was widely reported that the ARPCT received financial and intelligence support from the United States, which apparently had earlier recruited the warlords to assist in capturing suspected al-Qaida members in Somalia.) Street conflict quickly grew into major battles that culminated in the Islamists routing the warlords and taking control of Mogadishu and surrounding areas in June. The ICU subsequently established a Council of the Islamic Courts to govern the capital.

Much of the population in Mogadishu reportedly welcomed the ICU victory as representing relief from the violence, "arbitrary rule," and "exploitation" that had marked the reign of the warlords. At the same time, concern was voiced over the potential for the imposition of extreme religious strictures. It was also unclear whether the ICU would decide to try to extend its control throughout the rest of the country. (Hard-liners in the group reportedly called for an Islamic state that would also include parts of Ethiopia, Kenya, and Djibouti.) The international community urged negotiations between the TFG (located in Baidoa) and the Islamists toward creation of a government of national unity. However, talks remained stalled as of mid-August. The Inter-Governmental Authority on Development agreed to send 6,800 peacekeepers to Somalia in case of a comprehensive agreement, but the Islamists, already reportedly infuriated by Ethiopian support for the TFG, rejected the proposal outright.

Political Parties and Groups

From the time of its inaugural congress in June 1976 to the nominal authorization of a multiparty system in December 1990, the Somali Revolutionary Socialist Party (SRSP) was the country's only authorized political formation. The SRSP virtually ceased to exist with the collapse of the Siad Barre regime in January 1991, at which time a large number of additional groups, almost all of them clan-based, emerged from clandestine or insurrectionary activity. The most important of the

new formations was the United Somali Congress (USC), organized in January 1989. Subsequently, in November 1993, several components of the USC helped to launch the **Somali Salvation Alliance** (SSA), a loose coalition that also included components of the SDM, SAMO, SPM, SSDF, NSA, and SSNM, as well as the **Somali Democratic Front,** led by Ali MOHAMED HAMED; the **Somali National Democratic Union** (SNDU); and the **Somali National Union** (SNU), led by Mohamed RAJIS MOHAMED. The SSA was supportive of Ali MAHDI MOHAMED (who had become the nominal president of Somalia in 1991 following the ouster of Gen. Siad Barre) in his leadership fight with Gen. Mohamed Farah Aidid and, after 1996, General Aidid's son, Hussein Mohamed Farah Aidid. Both Aidids were supported by the Somali National Alliance (SNA, see below); consequently, other groups routinely added SSA or SNA to their names to indicate their positions regarding the leadership fights.

Severe splintering continued in the SSA in the second half of the 1990s, some factions accusing Mahdi of pursuing a self-serving agenda. Mahdi attended the Somali National Peace Conference (SNPC) in Djibouti in 2000, was chosen as a member of the new Transitional National Assembly, and subsequently fully supported the interim central government led by President Salad Hassan. Although references continued in early 2001 to Mahdi's leadership of the SSA, he by that time faced a challenge from antigovernment dissidents for use of the SSA rubric (see USC-SSA, below). Mahdi's supporters reportedly considered a "revival" of the SSA in mid-2002, but the initiative did not subsequently appear to maintain momentum.

Islamic Courts Union   (ICU). A fundamentalist movement devoted to the creation of an Islamic state in Somalia governed by sharia (Islamic religious law), the ICU was formed in 2004 by some five of the Islamic courts that had arisen in and around Mogadishu since the mid-1990s and had become the capital's de facto judiciary. Dominated by the Hawiye clan, the ICU created its own militia to protect the courts and help to enforce the courts' decisions. Following the example of successful fundamentalist movements elsewhere in the world, the Union also set up schools and hospitals in Mogadishu, reportedly gaining popular support for these and other services.

By late 2005 the ICU had grown to include 11 courts, bolstered by a militia force of at least 1,500 Somalis as well as, reportedly, a number of militant Islamists from other countries. In early 2006, the Ifka Halam court led by Sheikh Hassan Dahir Aweys (a hard-line former leader of the Islamic Union currently on the U.S. list of terrorism suspects) launched a campaign to drive the warlord militias out of Mogadishu. The ICU victory was secured in June, and the ICU subsequently announced the establishment of an 88-member Council of the Islamic Courts to govern Mogadishu. Aweys was selected as leader of the new council, while Sheikh Sharif Ahmed, the moderate chair of the ICU, was named head of the council's executive committee.

Leaders: Sheikh Hassan Dahir AWEYS (Leader of the Council of the Islamic Courts); Sheikh Sharif AHMED (Chair of the ICU).

United Somali Congress (USC). Organized in January 1989 by members of the Hawiye clan of central Somalia, the USC was instrumental in the ouster of President Siad Barre in 1991, and the grouping's principal financial backer, Ali Mahdi Mohamed, was shortly thereafter named interim president of the republic. However, at the party's third congress held July 4–5, Gen. Mohamed Farah Aidid was elected USC chair, provoking a bitter dispute with Mahdi and clashes between their respective factions in the autumn that produced widespread death and dislocation in Mogadishu. The USC subsequently remained split between pro-Mahdi and pro-Aidid factions referenced as the USC-SSA and USC-SNA, respectively. Further splintering occurred in June 1995 when Osman Hasan Ali ("Osman Ato"), a longtime ally of Aidid's, turned against the general and was named chair of a dissident USC-SNA.

In February 2001 Muhammad Qanyarsh AFRAH, a USC leader, was named to the cabi-

net. However, a major USC-SSA faction, under the leadership of Musa Sudi YALLAHOW (who had challenged Mahdi for the SSA leadership in 1999) and Umar Muhammad MAHMUD ("Umar Finish"), continued to reject participation in the government. Further splintering occurred in December when Umar Finish and his supporters signed the proposed expanded power-sharing agreement, while Yallahow opposed the pact. Fighters loyal to Yallahow engaged TNG troops routinely throughout 2002, and his faction remained an integral part of the Somali Reconciliation and Reconstruction Council (SRRC) and joined in the launching of the breakaway autonomous administration in the southwest (see Political background, above). Some factions joined in the negotiations, which resulted in the 2004 TFC, and Osman Ato and Yallahow joined the 2004 transitional government.

Somali National Alliance (SNA). The SNA was launched by Gen. Mohamed Farah Aidid following the leadership conflict in 1992 in the USC (see above). The SNA claimed the support of some two dozen affiliates, including factions of the USC, SDM, SPM, SSDF, and SSNM.

In October 1994 General Aidid, responding to the announcement by his adversary, Ali Mahdi Mohamed, of a Group of Twelve alliance, announced a G-12 of his own that encompassed Aidid supporters from the previous five formations; a number of SSA dissidents; the **National Democratic Union** (NDU); an SNU faction led by Umar MUNGANI AWEYS; an SAMO faction led by Sheikh JAMA HUSSEIN; a faction of the **Somali National Democratic Union** (SNDU) led by Ali ISMAIL ABDI and Ahmad MAHMUD ATO; and a United Somalia Party (USP) faction led by Hasan Haji UMAR AMI. The other two places on Aidid's G-12 list were assigned to a northwestern clan grouping, the Somali Democratic Alliance (SDA), and Somaliland's Somali National Movement (SNM), which Abdurahmane Ahmed Ali insisted that he still led (see the Somaliland article for both groups).

In May 1995, Osman Hasan Ali ("Osman Ato"), a longtime adviser to General Aidid, broke with

Aidid and announced he had assumed the leadership of the SNA. Osman Ato and his supporters were subsequently referenced as representing a dissident branch of the USC-SNA.

Several additional groups reportedly supported General Aidid at the time of his presidential self-proclamation in June 1995, including the **Somali Democratic Movement–Original** (SDM–*Asalow*), led by Dr. Yusuf ALI YUSUF, and an SPM faction led by Barreh UGAS GEDI.

Following the death of General Aidid in August 1996, his son, Hussein Mohamed Farah Aidid, an American-educated former U.S. Marine, was elected "president" and SNA leader, respectively, in a three-day, two-part electoral process that reportedly split the clan along generational lines. Older members criticized his lack of experience and his links to the United States, while younger members heralded his military background and "charisma." Subsequently, although there was widespread speculation that the younger Aidid would only serve as a figurehead for the SNA's militia, he immediately pursued reconciliation pacts with a number of SNA clan leaders whom his father had alienated.

In April 1997 approximately 800 SNA militants broke off from the grouping, accusing the Farah Aidid "government" of corruption and complaining that they had not been given the respect due a national army. SNA militiamen subsequently battled with forces from the RRA (below) for control of Baidoa.

Aidid, whose militia continued to control portions of Mogadishu and surrounding areas, declined to participate in the SNPC, held in Arta, Djibouti, in 2000, and rejected the resultant transitional government. In early 2001 Aidid, still referring to himself as chair of the SNA, was announced as chair of the Somali Reconciliation and Reconstruction Council (SRRC), a new grouping of some 21 southern faction leaders committed to establishing their own interim central government as an alternative to the "Arta" plan.

Other prominent SRRC members included the RRA, SSNM, and a main faction of the SPM. Aidid was elected as the first SRRC chair, while Mawlid

MA'ANE MAGMUD was named as the group's general secretary. However, Ma'ane Magmud, described as the leader of the Bantu community in Somalia, broke from the SRRC and endorsed the December 2001 power-sharing agreement between the TNG and several warlords and faction leaders. The SRRC subsequently continued to serve as the primary challenge to the TNG's authority, and in April 2002 it announced the formation of a breakaway state in southern Somalia. Farah Aidid supported the 2004 TFC and was appointed a deputy prime minister and the internal affairs minister in the December transitional government.

Leader: Hussein Mohamed FARAH AIDID (Chair).

Rahanweyn Resistance Army (RRA). Assisted by troops from Ethiopia, the RRA in 1999 seized control of much of south-central Somalia (home to the Digil and Mirifle clans) and expelled Ethiopian rebel groups from the region. The RRA was a core component of the Somali Peace Alliance (SPA), established in August 1999 to promote the "rebuilding" of a central government through the initial establishment of a number of autonomous regional governments. (The SPA was led by Col. Abdullahi Yusuf Ahmed of Puntland and also included the pro-Ethiopian wing of the SNF.) In December 2000 the leader of the RRA, Col. Hassan Mohammed Nur ("Shatigadud"), rejected the authority of the TNG, and the RRA subsequently indicated plans to set up its own regional administration. In January 2001 the SPA appeared to have been superseded by a National Restoration Council (NRC), itself a precursor, in part at least, to the SRRC (see SNA, above). Colonel Shatigadud was elected president of the Southwestern Regional Government announced in April 2002, although some RRA members, led by Muhammad Ibrahim HABSADE and Sheikh Adan MADOBE, opposed that initiative. Fierce fighting was subsequently reported between the two RRA factions. Shatigadud was appointed agriculture minister in December 2004. However, in June 2005, there were reports that Shatigadud's militia forces were regrouping and preparing for renewed attacks. Madobe was appointed minister of justice in the subsequent transitional government.

Leaders: Col. Hassan Mohammed NUR ("Shatigadud"), Mohamed Ali Adeh QALINLEH.

Somali National Front (SNF). The SNF was launched in 1991 by Darod clan interests in southern Somalia as a guerrilla force seeking the return to power of Siad Barre. Led by the former dictator's son-in-law, Gen. Mohamed Said Hersi ("Morgan"), the group was described as a "fair-weather-ally of Mahdi Mohamed."

In 1997 SNF militants clashed with Islamic Union fighters fleeing invading Ethiopian troops. Clashes between the SNF and Islamic militants continued into 1998, with the SNF allegedly receiving funding from Ethiopia. In addition, fighting between the SNF and SSDF was reported in the south. Moreover, beginning in April, the SNF suffered from intraparty battles in Kismayu, where General Morgan attempted to fend off attacks by fighters loyal to Omar HAJI MASALEH. (Haji Masaleh and his militiamen were reportedly supported by Mogadishu warlords Farah Aidid and Ali Mahdi.) Severe splintering continued into 2002; by that time General Morgan was no longer referenced as an SNF leader, the progovernment, anti-Ethiopian SNF faction reportedly led by Col. Abdouzarak Issak BINI and the main pro-Ethiopian faction, which joined the NRC and SRRC, led by Mohamad Sayyid ADEN.

Somali Patriotic Movement (SPM). The SPM surfaced in 1989 on behalf of Ogadeni soldiers of the southern Darod clan who formerly supported Siad Barre but had initiated antigovernment attacks in the area between the Juba River and the Kenyan border in an effort to gain autonomy for the region.

The SPM's leader, Gen. Adan Abdullahi Noor ("Gabio"), was one of five NSC cochairs appointed in early 1997. By that time the SPM was split into at least two main factions—one led by Noor and General Morgan (formerly of the SNF, above) and one led by Col. Umar Jess, who had once partnered with the SNM in Somaliland before joining the SPM in alliance with General Aidid in 1992. Fighting between the two factions for control of the rich agricultural region of the Juba Valley was subsequently reported, as were skirmishes between SPM fighters and those from the rival Juba Valley Alliance (see below). Neither faction reached an agreement with the TNG, Noor and his supporters participating in the launch of the SRRC. Morgan was one of the few major warlords who did not participate in the negotiations over the TFC. He later agreed to support the TFP but opposed the election of Yusuf Ahmed as President.

Leaders: Gen. Adan Abdullahi NOOR ("Gabio"), Gen. Mohamed Said HERSI ("Morgan"), Col. Ahmed Umar JESS.

Islamic Union (*A-Itihad al-Islami*). The Islamic Union was initially described by the *New York Times* as a "faction made up of fervently religious people, mostly from the Ogadeni clan of Somalia," dedicated to gaining independence for the Ogaden region. Throughout the first half of 1996 the Union claimed responsibility for a number of terrorist attacks in Addis Ababa, Ethiopia, including the attempted assassination of a cabinet member. In August Ethiopian forces attacked three Union-controlled towns in the Gedo region of Somalia and claimed to have killed over 200 Islamic fighters before withdrawing. Consequently, Union leader Sheik Hassan Dahir Aweys declared a "holy war" against Ethiopia and accused Ethiopia of harboring plans to occupy Somalian territory.

In late 1996 Hussein Farah Aidid reportedly sought to establish a dialogue with the Union, and in early 1997 the latter announced its interest in attaining legal party status. However, such concerns were subsequently overshadowed when an Ethiopian offensive into Somalia drove Union fighters from their last remaining military base in the Gedo region. Compounding the Union's military woes, SNF forces were reported to be attacking Union fighters retreating from the border region. In 1998 the Union accused Ethiopia of orchestrating assassination attempts against its leaders.

The United States expressed concern in the early 2000s about possible links between the Islamic Union and al-Qaida, although Union leaders have steadfastly denied any connection to terrorist activities or proclivities. However, the Union has supported the growing influence of Islamic courts in Somalia. Meanwhile, Col. Yusuf Ahmed, the leader of Puntland, accused the Islamic Union of being behind efforts by Jama Ali Jama to secure power in that autonomous region (see Political background, above, for details). However, some analysts have described reports of Union influence in Somalia as "overblown." In 2005 Yusuf Ahmed reported that the Union had ceased any major operations in Somalia. Many of the fighters of the Islamic Union were subsequently reported to have joined the Islamic Courts Union (above).

Somali Salvation Democratic Front (SSDF). The SSDF was initially organized in 1982 as the Democratic Front for the Salvation of Somalia (DFSS) by merger of three dissident groups: the Somali Salvation Front (SSF), the Democratic Front for the Liberation of Somalia (DFLS), and the Somali Workers' Party (SWP). The SSF (also known as Sosaf) had been formed in 1976 as the Somali Democratic Action Front (Sodaf), with headquarters in Rome, Italy, the change of name and relocation to Addis Ababa occurring in early 1979. Its leader at the launching of the DFSS was Col. Abdullahi Yusuf Ahmed, who had defected from Somalia with a group of army officers in 1978 following an abortive coup attempt. Most SSF members were drawn from the secessionist-oriented Mijarteyn tribe of northeastern Somalia, some of whom were executed after the coup had failed.

The DFLS, another Ethiopian-backed group, was led at the time of the merger by Abderahman AIDID AHMED, reportedly a former chair of the SRSP Ideological Bureau. The SWP, a Soviet-supported movement headquartered in South Yemen, was led by Hussein SAID JAMA, a former member of the SRSP's Central Committee.

At the inauguration of the DFSS, Yusuf Ahmed was named chair, Said Jama vice president, and Aidid Ahmed secretary general. A party congress in March 1983 elected a 21-member central committee and a nine-member executive committee and adopted a constitution and a political program

that called for the overthrow of the Siad Barre regime, the removal of U.S. bases from Somalia, and the establishment of "genuine peace and cooperation based on the brotherhood of the Horn of Africa." However, some DFLS and SWP members reportedly were excluded from the new formation at the 1983 congress, and Said Jama and Aidid Ahmed were removed from their leadership positions the following November. In January 1984 it was reported that a number of DFSS members opposed to Yusuf Ahmed's leadership had accepted government amnesty, as had about 200 guerrillas in May. In July 1985 Said Jama was reported to have founded a splinter group, the **Somali Patriotic Liberation Front** (SPLF), based, like its SWP predecessor, in Aden, South Yemen. In October 1985 Yusuf Ahmed, who had been criticized for his attempts to lessen Ethiopian influence over the DFSS and for his unwillingness to facilitate further merger of Somali opposition movements, was arrested in Ethiopia and replaced as chair by Gen. Mohamed ABSHIR MUSSE.

In 1989 the DFSS leadership announced that the organization was no longer pursuing military confrontation with the government but was hoping for legal recognition as a political party should proposed political liberalization measures be implemented. What had been restyled as the SSDF split in May 1993, with Yusuf Ahmed concluding an accord with General Aidid, while the rump group under Abshir Musse became a member of the G-12 grouping led by Ali Mahdi. In 2000 the SSDF was referenced as supporting the TNG, an initiative opposed by Yusuf Ahmed, then the leader of the autonomous administration in Puntland. There subsequently was little reference to the SSDF.

Northern Somalia Alliance (NSA). The NSA was formed in 1997 by the merger of the United Somalia Front (USF) and the United Somalia Party (USP). The USF was launched in 1989 to represent the Issa community in the northwest (Somaliland). Subsequently, Somaliland's President Ahmed Ali pledged that the party would participate in future multiparty elections. Prior to its alliance with the USF, little was known about the northwest-based

Cabinet

As of June 1, 2006 (*see headnote*)

Prime Minister	Ali Mohammed Ghedi
Deputy Prime Ministers	Hussein Mohamed Farah Aidid
	Salim Haji Aliyow Ibrow
	Mohamoud Mohamed

Ministers

Agriculture	Hassan Mohammed Nur ("Shatigadad")
Air and Land Transport	Adan Hasan
Animal Husbandry and Forestry	Ibrahim Muhammad Isaq
Cooperative Development	Muhammad Abdulbhi Kamil
Commerce	Musa Sudi Yallahow
Constitution and Federation	Abdallah Derow Isaq
Culture and Social Services	Abdi Hashi Abdullahi
Defense	Abdirahman Mahmud Ali
Education	Ali Abdullahi Osoble
Energy	Muhammed Nurani Bakar
Finance	Salim Haji Aliyow Ibrow
Fishing and Marine Resources	Hasan Abshir Farah
Foreign Affairs	Abdullah Sheikh Ismail
Health	Abdiaziz Sheikh Yusuf
Higher Education	Hasayn Muhammed Sheikh Husayn
Industry	Abdi Muhammed Tarah
Information	(Vacant)
Internal Affairs	Hussein Mohamed Farah Aidid
Justice	Sheikh Adan Madobe
Labor	Salah Ali Farah
Lands and Settlement	Mowlid Ma'ane Mahmud
Monetary Affairs	Abdikarim Ahmad Ali
National Assets	Mahmud Sayid Adan
National Security	Muhammed Qanyare Afrah
Planning and International Cooperation	Abdirizaq Usman Hasan
Petroleum	Yusuf Ahmad Muhammad
Ports and Marine Transport	Ali Isma'il Abdi
Posts and Communications	Ali Ahmad ("Jengali")
Public Works and Housing	Uthman Hasan Ali Ato
Reconciliation and Somali Communities Abroad	Sheikh Adan Sheikh Muhammad
Reconstruction and Resettlement	Col. Barre Aden Shire
Regional Cooperation	Isma'il Mahmud Hurre ("Buba")
Religious Affairs	Omar Mohamed Mohamud
Rehabilitation and Training of Militia	Botan Ise Alin
Rural Development	Muhammad Mahmud Guled
Science and Technology	Isma'il Hasan Jama
Settlement and Disaster Management	Muhammad Usman Maye
Sports and Youth Affairs	Ahmad Abdullahi Dakir

Tourism and Wildlife	Muhammad Mahmud Hayd
Water and Mineral Resources	Mahmud Salad Nur
Welfare of Disabled and Orphans	(Vacant)
Women's and Family Affairs	Fowzia Muhammad Sheikh [f]
Ministers of State	
Defense	Ali Muhammad Hared
Foreign Affairs	Ibrahim Sheikh Ali Hafun
Parliament and Government Relations	Abdrahman Adan Ibdi
Presidency	Khalid Umar Hashi
Prime Minister's Office	Abdulqadin Mahmud Dakane
[f] = female	

USP except for its opposition to Somaliland's independence. News reports have made few references to the NSA in recent years.

Leaders: Abdurahman DUALEH ALI (USF Chair); Ali Sheikh IBRAHIM ARAYE (USF); Gen. Mohamed OSMAN ALI (USF Secretary General); Mohamed ABDI HASHI (USP).

Southern Somali National Movement (SSNM). A south coastal formation, the SSNM is led by Abdi Warsame ISSAQ, who withdrew from the SNA in August 1993 to enter the pro-Mahdi G-12. In August 1997 one faction of the SSNM rejoined the pro-Aidid wing of the SNA. The SSNM-SNA, now under the leadership of Abdullahi Sheikh ISMAIL, participated in the formation of the SRRC in 2001 and the subsequent negotiations over the TFC. Ismail was appointed foreign minister in the transitional government installed in late 2004.

Somali Democratic Movement (SDM). The SDM is a Rahanweyn clan grouping that in early 1992 split into pro- and anti-Mahdi factions. Following Aidid's capture of Baidoa in August 1995, pro-Mahdi militants within the SDM formed the Rahanweyn Resistance Army (RRA, see above). As have most Somali parties and groups, the SDM has remained severely factionalized since the mid-1990s.

Leader: Abdulkabir Mohamed ADAN.

Other groups include the **Juba Valley Alliance** (JVA), which, under the leadership of Col. Barre Aden SHIRE ("Hirale"), has confronted the RRA and "Ethiopian influence" in the Juba Valley (Shire was appointed minister for reconstruction and resettlement in the December 2004 transitional government); the **Muslim Youth Party,** formed in late 2002 under the leadership of Ibrahim Muhammad HASSAN; the **Peace and Development Party,** organized in 2002 under the leadership of Gedi Shadron ABDULLAHI and Abdullahi Hassan AFRAH; the **Somali African Muki Organization** (SAMO), an ally of the RRA; the **Somali Democratic Party,** originally formed in 1993 in the Gedo region and reportedly relaunched in 2002 under the leadership of Abdi Barre ABDI and Omar Ibrahim MOHAMOUD; the **Somali Islamic Party** (SIP), which in 2002 called for a foreign peacekeeping force to be deployed in Somalia; the **Somali Peace Loving Party,** whose chair, Khalid Umar ALI, was reportedly involved in efforts to mediate between the TNG and opposition factions; the **Somali Solidarity Party** (SSP), formed in Mogadishu under the leadership of Abdulrahman Musa MUHAMMED and Muhammad UTHMAN; the **Somali Unification Party,** a small grouping led by warlord Hussein Haji BOD, who ultimately endorsed the 2000 reconciliation initiative with the TNG; the **Unity for the Somali Republic Party** (USRP), launched in 1999 under the leadership of Abdi Nur

DARMAN; and the **National Democratic League**, formed in 2003 and led by Abdiwahid Abdulle ABDI.

Legislature

The former People's Assembly was dissolved after the overthrow of the SRSP government in January 1991. On August 13, 2000, a Transitional National Assembly (TNA) was inaugurated in accordance with the national charter adopted by the Somali National Peace Conference meeting in Arta, Djibouti. The TNA comprised 245 members appointed for a three-year term pending national elections. Each of four major clan groupings (Darod, Hawiye, Dir, and Digil-Mirifleh) was allowed to appoint 44 members, while 24 seats went to smaller clans and subclans. In addition, 25 seats (also reportedly allocated on a clan basis) were designated specifically for women, while Djibouti's President Ismail Omar Guelleh was given 20 appointments. (The charter had initially envisioned a 225-member TNA, but the 20 appointments were extended to President Guelleh, who had hosted the peace conference, to accommodate groupings [mostly small clans and subclans] who objected to their perceived marginalization in the first distribution of seats.) The TNA began formal legislative sessions in October in Mogadishu, although many members reportedly stayed away due to security concerns. Meanwhile, the government of Somaliland, the administration of the self-declared autonomous region of Puntland, and a number of major faction leaders in and around Mogadishu did not accept the authority of the TNA.

In January 2004 most of the parties involved in the political and military conflict in Somalia agreed to a comprehensive agreement that included provision for the creation of an appointed **Transitional Federal Parliament** (TFP) to serve for four years, following which direct elections were to be held for a permanent legislature. The TFP, sworn in on August 29, comprised 275 deputies; each of the four major clans appointed 61 members, while 31 seats were allocated to smaller clans and subclans.

Speaker: Sharif Hasan Sheikh ADAN.

Communications

Press

The press is undeveloped and circulation is low. During the Siad Barre era, the only daily was the government's *Xiddigta Oktobar* (October Star), which ceased publication after the former president's overthrow. Current periodicals published in Mogadishu include *Ayaamaha,* described as supportive of Hussein Farah Aidid; *Qaran* (Nation, 2,000), daily; *Xog-Ogaal,* daily; the *Mogadishu Times;* and *Sooyal.* The newspaper *Sahan* is published in the Puntland region.

News agencies

The domestic agency is the Somali National News Agency (Sonna).

Broadcasting

The previously government-owned Somali Broadcasting Service, now controlled by General Aidid's faction, operates Radio Mogadishu. Intermittent television service transmits to some 160,000 receivers in the vicinity of Mogadishu.

Intergovernmental Representation

Ambassador to the U.S.
The Washington embassy closed on May 8, 1991.

U.S. Ambassador to Somalia
(Vacant)

Permanent Representative to the UN
Elmi Ahmed DUALE

IGO Memberships (Non-UN)
AfDB, AFESD, AMF, AU, CAEU, IDB, IGAD, Interpol, LAS, NAM, OIC

SOMALILAND

REPUBLIC OF SOMALILAND

The Country

The northwest portion of the Somali Republic as constituted in 1960, Somaliland extends some 400 miles eastward from Djibouti along the Gulf of Aden. Most of the terrain is desert or semidesert, and it is estimated that nomadic animal-herders still constitute about one-half of the population. While sharing, as throughout Somalia, a common religion (Islam) and a common language (Somali), the people are divided into numerous clans and subclans, which contributed to the 1991 break with the south as well as subsequent difficulty in forging a wholly unified regime in the north.

Largely stable and peaceful since 1997, Somaliland has nevertheless failed to achieve international recognition for its independence as the result of concern, particularly among African leaders, that the "Balkanization" of Somalia would embolden secessionists throughout the continent. Consequently, international aid has been constrained, and the economy has depended primarily on remittances from workers abroad (an estimated $300 million in 2005). About 60 percent of the population reportedly relies on agriculture, including livestock, for a living, and annual GDP per capita is currently estimated at only $200. To attract the interest of the international private sector, the government has adopted a free-market orientation, including liberal investment policies. Development plans focus on expanding the production of frankincense and myrrh, exploiting rich coastal fishing grounds, and exploring the potentially lucrative gem sector. It has been estimated that up to two-thirds of the budget goes to military spending, much of it in the form of what are essentially "bribes" to former clan militiamen who have agreed to stop fighting each other in return for employment in the police force. Few resources are therefore available for educational, health, or infrastructure purposes. However, a degree of economic progress (particularly around Hargeisa and the port of Berbera) has been reported in recent years, lending support, in the opinion of some analysts, to the contention of the government that Somaliland would best be served by remaining outside the political and economic "maelstrom" of Somalia proper. Perhaps significantly, the European Union (EU) pledged in 2006 to increase its aid to Somaliland. Meanwhile, oil companies from South Africa, Malaysia, and India were authorized by the Somaliland administration to pursue offshore oil exploration.

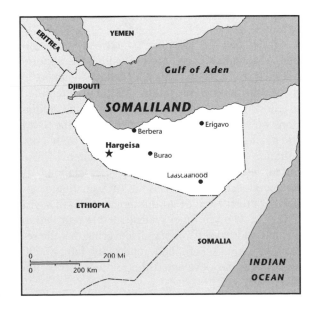

Government and Politics

Political Background

A British protectorate since 1887, Somaliland was overrun by Italian forces at the outbreak of World War II but was recaptured by Britain in 1941. The protectorate was terminated on June 26, 1960, and on July 1 Somaliland joined its theretofore Italian-administered counterpart in the south to form what was styled the United Republic of Somalia, prior to its redesignation as the Somali Democratic Republic in 1969.

In 1988 the Somali National Movement (SNM), a rebel group that had joined with Ethiopian units in a cross-border assault the year before, mounted a broad-gauged offensive that succeeded in driving government forces from most of the northern region's rural areas by mid-1989. However, the government continued its heavy bombing campaign against Hargeisa and other towns, much of the northern population reportedly fleeing to Ethiopia to escape the "genocidal campaign" of the Siad Barre regime. Meanwhile, elsewhere in Somalia, other clan-based groups had taken up arms, most important among them the United Somali Congress (USC) in central regions and the Somali Patriotic Movement (SPM) in the south (see Political Parties and Groups in article on Somalia for details).

On January 27, 1991, USC forces assumed control in Mogadishu, the Somalia capital, and appointed their principal backer, Ali Mahdi Mohamed, to the post of interim president. Ali Mahdi attempted to convene a "conference of national reconciliation" on February 28 but was rebuked by the SNM for having taken the initiative without prior consultation. A second such effort on March 14 also failed, and on May 18 the north proclaimed its independence as the Republic of Somaliland under the presidency of Abdurahman AHMED ALI ("Taur"). Many refugees subsequently returned to Somaliland from Ethiopia, discovering that the recent fighting, which had reportedly left 40,000 dead, had also devastated the region's infrastructure.

Ahmed Ali's control proved to be somewhat tenuous, and he did not attend a grand *shir* (gathering) of leading tribal, political, and military figures in Somaliland that met for most of February 1993 to discuss clan relations and the formalization of independence. Subsequently, a "parliamentary" meeting of the SNM Central Committee was convened to implement the *shir*'s conclusions. On May 5 the same body named Mohamed Ibrahim EGAL, a former prime minister of Somalia who had been imprisoned by the Siad Barre regime for many years, to succeed Ahmed Ali as president, with Col. Abdurahman ALI, who had been sacked as education minister in February, as vice president.

During a meeting with Gen. Mohamed Farah Aidid of the Somali National Alliance (SNA) in Ethiopia in April 1994, Ahmed Ali unexpectedly called for Somaliland to rejoin Somalia. The appeal was immediately rejected by President Egal, who branded his predecessor as a traitor and termed Somaliland's independence as "irrevocable." Egal reiterated the position in late May by rejecting inclusion in a federal state and indicating that Somaliland would shortly be issuing its own currency and passports.

On October 15, 1994, fighting erupted in Hargeisa airport between government forces and defecting militiamen of the Issaq subclan of Eidegalla. By late November the rebels appeared to control most of the capital, despite claims by President Egal to the contrary, and by early December about three-quarters of the city's population had reportedly fled.

In January 1995, having embarked on a build-up of arms (reportedly supplied by Albania) and with an army increased to more than 3,000 men, Egal mounted an offensive that succeeded in driving the rebels from Hargeisa. On May 9 a spokesman in Nairobi announced the government's appointment of a Peace Committee, although the Mogadishu-based Ahmed Ali continued to support anti-Egal forces. Further clashes occurred in Hargeisa airport in August 1995 and along the frontier with Djibouti three months later. On the latter occasion the government blamed the Djibouti regime for providing support to dissident Issa militiamen belonging

Political Status: Former British Somaliland Protectorate; joined with (Italian) Trust Territory of Somalia on July 1, 1960, to form Somali Republic; announced secession as independent state on May 18, 1991; constitution endorsing independence and providing for multiparty activity approved by national referendum on May 31, 2001.

Area: 68,000 sq. mi. (176,120 sq. km.).

Population: 4,997,000 (2005E).

Major Urban Centers (1984E): HARGEISA (90,000), Berbera (83,000).

Principal Language: Somali.

Monetary Unit: Somaliland Shilling, which became Somaliland's sole legal tender on January 31, 1995, with an initial value of 100 Somali shillings = $1US. Due to the lack of international recognition of Somaliland's self-declared independent status, the exchange value of the shilling is not reported in regular currency listings. However, in July 2006 a market rate was reported of approximately 6,500 shillings = $1US.

President: Dahir Riyale KAHIN (United and Democratic People's Alliance); sworn in (based on his position as vice president and thereby the constitutionally authorized presidential successor) on May 3, 2002, following the death of Mohamed Haji Ibrahim EGAL (initially Somali National Movement, subsequently United and Democratic People's Alliance) the same day; popularly elected on April 14, 2003, and sworn in for a five-year term on May 16.

Vice President: Ahmad Yusuf YASIN (United and Democratic People's Alliance); named by the president on May 16, 2002, and approved by the legislature on May 21; popularly elected on April 14, 2003, and sworn in on May 16 for a five-year term.

to the United Somali Front (see Political Parties, below).

On the political front, meanwhile, in May 1995 the SNM Central Committee, acting as an interim parliament, reelected Egal president. In July Egal appointed a ten-member constitutional draft-

ing committee that he charged with writing a new basic charter within 12 months. However, immediately thereafter, the president employed a Sudanese constitutional consultant who, along with the president and a reportedly shrinking circle of presidential advisors, drew up a draft document that included provisions for a U.S.-style presidency. In response to Egal's proposed constitution, the Central Committee, many of whose members were described as "infuriated" by the president's actions, presented a rival draft highlighted by a parliamentary democracy. The constitutional deadlock continued through mid-1996, thus "forcing" Egal to continue governing by decree.

Concurrent with the expiration of its own charter, the advisory Council of Elders in October 1996 convened a 315-member National Communities Conference to which President Egal presented the two draft documents. In early 1997 the conference provisionally approved a new constitution (see Constitution and government, below), and on February 23 the delegates reelected Egal to a five-year term (the incumbent secured 223 votes in what observers described as remarkably "amicable" polling). In May Egal appointed a new government.

In December 1997 President Egal submitted his resignation to the legislature, complaining of a "lack of collaboration" from his government and other senior officials. Citing the need for stability, the legislators voted overwhelmingly to reject his request, thus compelling the incumbent to continue at his post. Meanwhile, a number of analysts attributed Egal's actions to his desire to fortify his position amid accusations of rampant corruption as well as to underline Somaliland's independence claims at the same time that Somalian faction leaders held unity talks in Cairo, Egypt.

Constitutional amendments were proposed by the government in mid-1999 with the goals of strengthening the role of the president and responding to opposition demands for greater judicial independence. Following a number of further revisions, the new constitution received a reported 97 percent endorsement from those voting in a national referendum on May 31, 2001. Among other things, the new basic law contained an article affirming Somaliland's status as an independent republic. (The Somaliland government had declined to participate in reconciliation talks launched in 2000 in Somalia proper. See article on Somalia for details.) The first multiparty elections under the new constitution were initially scheduled at the local level for December 2001. However, they were subsequently postponed, and in early 2002 the legislature reportedly extended Egal's term of office (as well as that of Vice President Dahir Riyale KAHIN) until February 2003, although opponents of the administration criticized that decision and demanded that another all-inclusive conference of clan elders be held to determine the presidential status.

President Egal died on May 3, 2002, and he was succeeded on the same day by Kahin, following endorsement by an emergency meeting of legislative and ministerial representatives. Kahin's administration subsequently underscored its commitment to independence by declining to participate in the conference launched in Kenya in late 2002 regarding potential power-sharing in Somalia. Local elections were conducted in December 2002, with Kahin's United and Democratic People's Alliance (*Ururka Dimuqraadiga Ummadda Bahawday*—UDUB) securing a reported 41 percent of the vote, followed by the Solidarity Party (*Hisbiga Kulmiye*) with 19 percent and the Justice and Welfare Party (*Uruka Caddaalada Iyo Daryeelka*—UCID) with 11.2 percent. Those three parties consequently qualified for legal status under new constitutional provisions (see Political Parties and Groups, below, for details).

In presidential balloting on April 14, 2003, Kahin was reelected by a razor-thin margin (42.08 percent to 42.06 percent) over Ahmed Mohamed MOHAMOUD ("Silanyo") of *Kulmiye*. A new "propresidential" government was announced on July 3.

In Somaliland's first national legislative balloting since its declaration of independence, the UDUB secured a plurality of 33 seats in the elections to the House of Representatives on September 25, 2005. However, following the elections,

the UCID and *Kulmiye* announced a cooperation agreement that produced immediate results—the election of a member of the UCID as speaker.

Constitution and Government

The government established in the wake of the May 1991 independence proclamation encompassed a president and vice president, appointed by the SNM, initially for a two-year transitional period during which a constitution was to be drafted that would permit the holding of open, multiparty elections. On May 28 *Radio Hargeisa* announced that the SNM leadership had also approved the formation of a high court and a civil service, in addition to the appointment of an attorney general, an auditor general, and a Central Bank governor.

In early July 1995 President Egal announced that a ten-member constitutional drafting committee had been appointed and that a basic law for Somaliland would be forthcoming within the ensuing 12 months. Meanwhile, the SNM Central Committee continued to serve as an interim legislature and electoral body for the presidency. In early 1997 the National Communities Conference provisionally approved a constitution that provided for a bicameral legislature (see Legislature, below), an electoral system of direct universal suffrage, and the organization of political parties (although groups with "tribal" or religious affiliations were proscribed). Among the details to surface subsequently about the document were stipulations that future presidents and their spouses be both native Somalians and Muslims. In late 1998 the legislature reportedly approved the implementation of measures based on Islamic religious law.

The 1997 constitution was approved with the provision that it be presented to a national referendum within three years. A one-year extension was granted in February 2000 and a three-month extension in February 2001, with the referendum finally being held on May 31, 2001. The new basic law confirmed Somaliland's independence, strengthened the executive branch, confirmed Islam as the "national faith," provided for a free press, and endorsed multiparty elections at all levels of government through universal suffrage. Somaliland is divided into 6 regions and 30 districts.

Foreign Relations

Refusals to attend "reconciliation" conferences in Djibouti in 1991 were defended by SNM leaders on the ground that the meetings were called to address matters of domestic concern to "Southern Somalia." However, relations between Djibouti and Somaliland had been less than cordial because of conflict between the Issa community common to both countries and the Issaq grouping in Somaliland.

Despite what was described as a "flurry of meetings" designed to promote international recognition, by mid-1995 no foreign government had complied, partly because of long-standing opposition by the Organization of African Unity (OAU, subsequently the African Union—AU) to secessionist regimes and partly because of uncertainties surrounding continued anarchic conditions in the south. Significantly, while Somaliland had agreed in 1993 to the introduction of 500 UN peacekeepers to supervise the distribution of relief supplies, it rejected any deployment of U.S. troops on the ground that its claim to autonomy would thereby be jeopardized. In May 1994 President Egal threatened to expel any UN personnel advocating reintegration into Somalia.

In mid-1995 President Egal was reported to have sent a fax message to the (then) Israeli prime minister, Yitzhak Rabin, proposing the establishment of "strategic links" between their two countries. Egal spoke of the need to counter Islamic fundamentalism in the Horn of Africa, attributed with some degree of imprecision to "the growing influence of Saudi Arabia and the pro-Islamic Yemen."

Egal's efforts to gain international support bore fruit in late 1997 as Djibouti announced that it would exchange diplomatic credentials with Hargeisa. Furthermore, in early 1998 Italy told Egal that it would support an EU proposal to grant Somaliland "semi-diplomatic" recognition. For his part,

Egal agreed to accept the offer of limited recognition for an interim period. Such concerns dominated Somaliland's foreign policy agenda through early 1999, with reports of Hargeisa's enhanced international standing being balanced by continued calls from regional leaders for Somaliland to be included in a unified Somalia.

Relations with Djibouti deteriorated in 2000 when that country's leadership played a major role in the establishment of the transitional government in Somalia. However, Somaliland and Djibouti agreed to "normalize" their ties again in 2001. By that time it was clear that, in addition to opposing the notion of reunification with Somalia, Somaliland was in the midst of an ongoing territorial dispute with the Puntland autonomous region in Somalia.

Intense lobbying efforts were reported in 2004 by officials from Somaliland to convince the UK government to recognize Somaliland's status as a fully independent nation. UK lawmakers visited Somaliland, and London agreed to help pay costs involved in the 2003 presidential poll. In addition, British companies reportedly began negotiations with Somaliland regarding offshore oil exploration. However, no official recognition was forthcoming, as most of the international community pressed (unsuccessfully) the Kahin administration to participate in the comprehensive Somalia peace talks. The AU and the Arab League in 2005 declined requests for membership from Somaliland. Kahin traveled to six African states in 2006 to lobby for recognition, and an AU fact-finding mission concluded that Somaliland's status was "unique" and that recognition of its independence would not open a "Pandora's box" of new secessionist movements across the continent as African leaders had been fearing.

Current Issues

In early 1999 President Egal reportedly indicated that Somaliland would be willing to consider reunification talks with Somalia, should warlords there negotiate a cease-fire and establish a permanent central government. However, until such progress was achieved by its "brothers in the south," Somaliland would continue to strengthen its own governmental institutions. At the same time, Egal pushed for international development aid, reportedly receiving a degree of "empathy" but little actual support from countries reluctant to appear at odds with OAU and UN hopes that all of Somalia, including Somaliland, be reunified under a single federal system. For most observers, the May 2001 constitutional referendum appeared to settle the independence question.

President Egal's death in May 2002 was widely viewed as creating conditions that could lead to instability, since his hand had been firmly placed on the governmental tiller for so many years. However, new President Kahin managed the transition smoothly, and the first multiparty municipal elections were conducted without incident in December.

President Kahin's reelection in April 2003 was noteworthy for his amazingly small margin of victory (80 votes out of nearly 490,000 cast). His Solidarity Party challenger initially protested the results, but, following a ruling from the Constitutional Court that validated the outcome, he urged his supporters to accept the verdict.

In October 2003 the government initiated a series of "antiterrorism" measures following an attack on westerners that Kahin blamed on illegal immigrants with connections to militant Islamic organizations. Among other things, foreigners without legal permits were expelled from the country.

After numerous postponements, balloting for the first elected House of Representatives was held in September 2005, as Somaliland remained divorced from the nascent reconciliation in Somalia (see article on Somalia for details). Severe tension was reported over Somaliland's plan to include the disputed territory of Sool along the border with Puntland in the poll. (Fighting had broken out in that area between forces from Somaliland and Puntland in 2004.) However, the balloting was completed in Sool without violence.

Foreign observers described the 2005 elections as generally fair and free, further bolstering Somaliland's argument that it represented an oasis of developing democracy in an otherwise turbulent region and should be rewarded with international recognition. On a more negative note, however, conflict over the election of the speaker of the House of Representatives prompted a walkout by UDUB legislators and riots outside the parliament buildings. After securing the speaker's post, the UCID/*Kulmiye* coalition presented a legislative agenda calling, among other things, for sweeping anticorruption measures and a reduction in the president's national security powers. Meanwhile, the government announced that security forces had arrested a group of heavily-armed men accused of plotting the assassination of public officials and other terrorist acts. (The government characterized the detainees as members of al-Qaida who had been trained in Afghanistan.)

In May 2006 the House of Elders (currently appointed) announced that it had extended its term of office until October 2010 even though elections had been scheduled for October 2006. President Kahin supported the extension, and he and the House of Elders were strongly criticized by UCID and *Kulmiye* leaders for seemingly trying to hold on to a degree of legislative authority through extraconstitutional means.

Political Parties and Groups

The constitution endorsed by national referendum in May 2001 provided for multiparty activity, with the restriction that parties could not be based on tribal/clan or religious affiliations. It was determined that groups would be provisionally recognized prior to proposed local elections (originally scheduled for December 2001), with those gaining at least 20 percent of the vote in four of Somaliland's six regions to be granted permanent registration prior to subsequent presidential and national legislative balloting. The first parties were registered in October 2001, but the municipal elections were postponed until December 2002, at which time the first three groups below gained legal status by meeting the constitutional requirement regarding vote totals.

Official Parties

United and Democratic People's Alliance (*Ururka Dimuqraadiga Ummadda Bahawday*—UDUB). Launched in June 2001 by President Egal, the UDUB was subsequently routinely referenced as the "ruling" party in Somaliland. Although some observers viewed the UDUB as primarily a personal vehicle for Egal, the party was reportedly "resuscitated" by President Kahin following Egal's death in May 2002. The party went on to dominate the December 2002 municipal elections and to achieve a plurality in the 2005 legislative balloting on a vote share of 40.7 percent.

Leaders: Dahir Riyale KAHIN (President of the Republic), Ahmad Yusuf YASIN (Vice President of the Republic), Usman GARAD (Secretary).

Solidarity Party (*Hisbiga Kulmiye*). Established in early 2002, *Kulmiye* is led by Ahmed Mohamed Mohamoud ("Silanyo"), who was chair of the SNM from 1984–1990. Silanyo had resigned from the Egal government in 2001, indicating his desire to campaign for the presidency. *Kulmiye* finished second to the UDUB in the December 2002 municipal balloting, securing, according to the government, about 83,000 votes to UDUB's 198,000. Silanyo finished second in the very close vote for president in April 2003. Subsequently, when the Kahin government was criticized by world leaders for refusing to participate in the Somalian peace negotiations, Silanyo announced that he supported Kahin in the matter.

Kulmiye finished second in the 2005 legislative balloting with 30.3 percent of the vote. Following the election, *Kulmiye* announced a cooperative agreement with the other "opposition" party—the UCID (below).

Leader: Ahmed Mohamed MOHAMOUD ("Silanyo").

Justice and Welfare Party (*Ururka Caddaalada Iyo Daryeelka*—UCID). Established as a "modern" party devoted to "good governance," the staunchly nationalist UCID was described as an outgrowth of a Social Democratic Party that had been previously organized within the diaspora.

UCID leader Farah Ali ("Warabe") was one of the founders of the SNM and currently owns a private construction company. The UCID secured an estimated 50,000 votes in the December 2002 municipal elections, good for third place among the six contesting parties. Warabe placed third in the 2003 presidential election with 16 percent of the vote. The UCID secured 29 percent of the vote in the 2005 legislative elections, and, after announcement of a UCID/*Kulmiye* cooperation agreement, the UCID's Abdirahman Muhammad Irro was elected speaker of the House of Representatives.

Leader: Farah ALI ("Warabe"), Abdirahman Muhammad IRRO (Speaker of the House of Representatives).

Other Parties and Groups

Somali National Movement (SNM). The SNM was organized in London, United Kingdom, in April 1981 by an exile group that declared its commitment to the overthrow of the existing Mogadishu regime but did not wish to ally itself with either the United States or the Soviet Union. Deriving most of its support from Somaliland's Issaq clan, the SNM long supported greater autonomy for the area, a "more equitable" distribution of resources, and political democratization. Ideologically, however, the movement suffered from a lack of cohesion, apparently counting Marxist, pro-Western, and Islamic fundamentalist groups within its ranks.

Following the Ethiopian-Somali agreement in April 1988, the SNM was left with no external source of support as its fighters were forced to leave Ethiopia. Subsequently, the SNM initiated wide-scale military activity against the government in the north and announced the capture of Hargeisa, the country's second city, in December 1989. The SNM formed an operational alliance with Somalia's other leading rebel groups in mid-1990. Reportedly, the SNM leadership was initially willing to participate in a federal system after the fall of the Siad Barre regime in January 1991, but it bowed to rank-and-file sentiment in opting for independence in May.

Cabinet

As of August 1, 2006

President	Dahir Riyale Kahin
Vice President	Ahmad Yusuf Yasin

Ministers

Agriculture	(Vacant)
Civil Aviation	Aw Nuur Amin
Commerce (Interim)	Hasan Wadaad
Culture and Heritage	Usman Ali Bile
Defense	Ismail Aden Boss
Development of Rural Areas	Fuad Adan Cade
Education	Hasan Haji Mahmud Warsame
Family Planning	Fadhuma Sudi Hasan [f]
Finance	Hussein Ali Dualeh
Fisheries and Coastlines	Mohammed Oday
Foreign Affairs	Edna Adan Ismail [f]
Health and Labor	Usman Qasim Qodah
Information and National Guidance	Abdullahi Muhammad Duale
Interior	Ismail Aden Osman
Justice	Ahmad Hasan Ali Libah
Livestock	Idris Ibrahim Abdi
Mineral and Water Resources	Qasim Sheikh Yunis Ibrahim
Parliament	Abdi Hassan Buuni
Planning	Ahmed Haji Dahir
Post and Transport	Hasan Abdi Khayr
Presidency	Nuh Ahmad Usman
Public Works	Said Sulub
Rehabilitation, Reconstruction, and Resettlement	Abdillahi Hussein Iman
Religion	Sheikh Mohamed
Sports	Mahmud Said Muhammad

Ministers of State

Foreign Affairs	Said Muhammad Nuur
Interior	Adan Mire Muhammad
Public Works	Adan Ahmed Muhammad
Rehabilitation, Reconstruction, and Resettlement	Yasin Fardoon

[f] = female

After being ousted from the Somaliland presidency in favor of Ibrahim Egal in May 1993, Abdurahman Ahmed Ali took up residence in London before surfacing in Mogadishu in August 1994 as a pro-Aidid opponent of secession. In September President Egal denounced a claim from Ahmed Ali that Ahmed Ali remained SNM chair. Thereafter, in early 1996 it was reported that Ahmed Ali was advising an anti-Egal rebel group in the Burao region.

Anti-Egal forces within the SNM accused the president of corruption in 1997 and threatened to launch a legal challenge against the composition of the National Communities Conference. However, such opposition reportedly failed to materialize. The SNM subsequently remained fractionalized concerning Egal's role and other issues, the president's critics also questioning his commitment to independence. Egal in 2001 formed his own political party (see the UDUB, above), with several other former SNM leaders following suit. The SNM ceased to function as a political entity after the 2001 referendum.

United Somali Front (USF). Emphasizing the deep cleavage between Somaliland's Issaq and Issa communities, the latter (reportedly with encouragement from Djibouti) organized the USF in early 1991. Subsequently, President Ahmed Ali approved the action and pledged that USF supporters could participate in future multiparty elections. While claiming to be neutral in the dispute over Somaliland's future, the front's leadership joined Ahmed Ali in calling for federalism rather than independence. The USF participated in peace talks in 2000. The USF subsequently became increasingly marginalized, and it did not participate in the 2002 local elections.

Leader: Abdurahman DUALEH ALI (Chair).

The three other parties reported by the government to have participated (in addition to the UDUB, UCID, and *Kulmiye*) in the December 2002 municipal elections were the **Asad Party,** which won 9 percent of the vote and was led by Suleiman Mohamed ADEN, a longtime rival of President Egal's who returned to Hargeisa in 2001; the **Sahan Party,** a moderate grouping led by Musa BIHE that secured 10.8 percent of the vote; and the **Hormood Party**, which gained 9.2 percent of the vote. The three parties ceased to be active after the 2002 local elections.

Legislature

Following Somaliland's declaration of independence in 1991, the Central Committee of the So-

mali National Movement (SNM) served as a nominal "provisional" legislature for several years, although its actual authority was limited due to the subclan conflict that left substantial territory outside SNM control. In May 1993 the SNM "parliament" endorsed the recommendation of a recently concluded grand *shir* (gathering) for the formal establishment of a two-chamber legislature, comprising a House of Elders and a House of Representatives (initially to be appointed on a clan basis but ultimately to be filled by elections). The two chambers began to operate shortly thereafter, although some clan seats in the House of Representatives remained vacant until August 1994. The new constitution approved by national referendum in 2001 provided for a bicameral **Parliament**.

House of Elders (*Golaha Guurtida*). The upper house is authorized to review legislation passed by the House of Representatives and to approve legislation on its own in regard to religion, culture, and security. It comprises 82 members and a number of nonvoting honorary members. The first elections to the House of Elders were scheduled for October 2006, but in a controversial decision the current appointed membership decided in May 2006 to extend its mandate until October 2010.

Speaker: Saleban Muhammad ADAN.

House of Representatives (*Golaha Wakiilada*). The lower house comprises 82 members directly elected via proportional representation (in six regions) for five-year terms. At the first elections for the house on September 29, 2005, the United and Democratic People's Alliance reportedly secured 33 seats; the Solidarity Party, 28; and the Justice and Welfare Party, 21.

Speaker: Abdirahman Muhammad IRRO.

Communications

Press

Freedom of the press was codified in the constitution approved by national referendum in 2001, although some observers have suggested that government control is still exercised over journalists. Newspapers published in Hargeisa include *Jamhuuriya* (The Republic, 2,500), an independent daily that was closed by the government in 1997–1998 for printing articles critical of the government; *Huuriya* (Liberty), daily; *Mandeeq*, progovernment daily; *al-Moujahid* (The Fighter), a weekly launched in 1985 by the SNM; and *The Republican*, an English-language weekly. In October 2003 the editor of *Jamhuuriya* was briefly detained for publishing "antigovernment" stories.

Broadcasting

In May 1991 the former *Radio Hargeisa* was renamed *Radio Somaliland Republic*. Private radio stations are banned. There is no television service.

Intergovernmental Representation

As of September 2006 Somaliland was not a member of the United Nations.

IGO Memberships (Non-UN)
None

SOUTH AFRICA

REPUBLIC OF SOUTH AFRICA

Republiek van Suid-Afrika
Unofficial African Name: Azania

The Country

Industrially the most developed country in Africa, the Republic of South Africa is a land of rolling plateaus within a mountainous escarpment that rims its territory on the seaward side and separates the coastal cities of Cape Town and Durban from the inland centers of Johannesburg and Pretoria. The country is peopled by four separate ethnic elements as unequal in numbers as they used to be in political status. The largest but historically least-favored group, comprising approximately 78 percent of the population, consists of the Xhosa, Zulu, and Sotho, who are collectively known as the Bantu; next in order of size is the white community, 10 percent; "Coloureds," or persons of mixed blood, 9 percent; and Asians, mainly Indians living in KwaZulu-Natal Province, 3 percent.

Some three-fifths of the whites are "Afrikaners," who trace their descent from the Dutch, German, and French Huguenot settlers who colonized the country from the 17th century onward. Traditionally agrarian in their social traditions and outlook, they speak Afrikaans, a language closely related to Dutch; are predominantly affiliated with the Dutch Reformed Church; and were the most resolute supporters of the policy of separation of the races (apartheid). The remainder of the whites are largely English-speaking, identify with the British tradition, and have been more involved in business and industry.

South Africa has become a highly urbanized country, with half of the white population, a third of the blacks, and most Coloureds and Asians residing in and around the dozen large cities and towns. The social and economic differences between the white and non-white groups are reflected in the country's literacy rates, estimated at 98 percent for whites but only 85 percent for the country as a whole.

In 1998 women constituted 38 percent of the paid labor force. White women are concentrated in the clerical and service sectors; in predominantly white areas, black women work mainly as domestic servants and casual agricultural laborers. Elsewhere, traditional law restricts female land ownership, although male migration to white-controlled employment sites has left women largely in control of subsistence agriculture. Female participation

in government was long limited to minor representation by white women in both national and provincial legislatures; however, women of all races were prominent in the anti-apartheid movement. The awarding of cabinet portfolios to women in the current administration has fulfilled a pledge by former president Mandela that they would be given one-third of all posts at all levels.

The first African country to experience the full force of the industrial revolution, South Africa now has an advanced economy that plays an important role in world economic affairs. It is the world's leading gold producer, supplying nearly one-third of global output; other important mineral products include diamonds, copper, asbestos, chrome, platinum, and vanadium. The principal resource deficiency is oil, although recently discovered ocean reserves are now being tapped. There are, however, abundant coal reserves, which provide a large share of primary energy. Agriculturally, the country is self-sufficient in most foods (except coffee, rice, and tea) and exports wool, maize, sugar, and fruits. Although agriculture now contributes only about 3 percent of GDP, it continues to employ about 10 percent of the labor force. The manufacturing sector, spurred by governmental efforts during the apartheid era to promote industrial self-sufficiency, presently accounts for approximately 25 percent of GDP, with mining adding another 6 percent. Industry as a whole employs about 25 percent of workers. South Africa's leading trade partner is the European Union, with which it concluded in 2000 a free-trade agreement that is planned to cover some 90 percent of transactions by 2012.

Gross domestic product (GDP) growth has averaged only 1.5 percent annually since 1974, contrasted with an average yearly population increase of 2.5 percent. This creeping poverty was exacerbated in the late 1990s by the Russian and Asian economic crises, which contributed to a trade decline and the collateral dampening of GDP growth to only .7 percent in 1998. Meanwhile, unemployment, heavily concentrated in the black population, remained at 35 to 40 percent, with inflation at about 9 percent in 1998. Growth recovered to 2.1 percent in 1999 and then advanced to 3.4 percent in 2000. In the latter year the government introduced an inflation-targeting strategy with a goal of containing consumer price inflation at 3 to 6 percent by 2002.

Mbeki's economic ministers are reportedly among the developing world's best and have restored sound fiscal management and modest growth in gross domestic product. Their Black Economic Empowerment program has begun to redress apartheid's untenably skewed economic legacy. The foreign exchange market is one of the developing world's most liquid, and the corporate sector is solid. The strength of the rand has contributed to a dissipation of inflationary pressures and enabled the Reserve Bank to reconstitute its net international reserve position. The GDP growth was running at an annualized 4.8% in the second quarter of 2005 (compared to 3.7% in 2004 and 2.8% in 2003). However, unemployment continued to remain very high, fluctuating between 30 percent and 40 percent. Some of the joblessness is due to South Africa's belated entry into the global economy and some to administrative inefficiencies. Violent crime is still a scourge. The African National Congress (ANC) has put job creation at the top of its agenda, promising to halve unemployment by 2014. An expanded public works program aims to prime the pump by creating one million jobs within five years. South African labor, while abundant, is expensive. The national trade union federation, COSATU, is a partner in government and is therefore in a position to obtain high wage settlements. AIDS also tends to push labor costs up and will continue to drag the economy down over the next decade. The disease hits working-age adults disproportionately and pushes up absenteeism and insurance costs. It is said to reduce the GDP by at least two percentage points each year.

There has been a subtle shift in the direction of economic policy from market-led to state-led growth. While large-scale privatization remains in disfavor, the focus is on public-private partnerships and public works programs to create jobs. All economic sectors are required to draw up charters committing themselves to black economic empowerment.

Political Status: Fully independent state since 1934; republican regime established May 31, 1961; Interim Constitution ratified on December 22, 1993, with effect from April 27, 1994, for a five-year term; new text signed into law on December 10, 1996, effective February 4, 1997, with certain provisions implemented gradually through 1999.

Area: 470,882 sq. mi. (1,221,037 sq. km.).

Population: 44,819,770 (2001C); 46,745,000 (2005E).

Major Urban Centers (urban areas, 2005E): PRETORIA (administrative capital, 2,534,000), Cape Town (legislative capital, 3,143,000), Bloemfontein (judicial capital, 793,000), Durban (4,610,000), Johannesburg (3,974,000). In 2005–2006 a move was underway to change the name of the administrative capital from Pretoria to TSHWANE. As of August 2006 the change was meeting strong resistance in some quarters.

Official Languages: There are eleven official languages, of which English and Afrikaans are the languages of record.

Monetary Unit: Rand (principal rate July 1, 2006: 7.13 rand = $1US).

President: Thabo Mvuyelwa MBEKI (African National Congress); inaugurated June 16, 1999, for a five-year term, in succession to Nelson Rolihlahla MANDELA (African National Congress), following unopposed election by the National Assembly on June 14; reelected April 23, 2004, to a second five-year term.

Deputy President: Phumzile Gloria MLAMBO-NGCUKA (African National Congress), appointed by the President and sworn in on June 27, 2005, succeeding Jacob Gedleyihlekisa ZUMA (African National Congress).

Government and Politics

Political Background

The Republic of South Africa as it exists today is the result of a long and complicated process of interaction between indigenous peoples and the Dutch and British colonists who came to exploit the territory. The original Cape Colony was settled by the Dutch in the 17th century but fell into British hands as a result of the Napoleonic wars. Discontented Boers, or Afrikaners (largely, but not exclusively, farmers of Dutch or French Huguenot descent) trekked northward in 1835–1837, commencing a half-century subjugation of the Zulu and other native peoples and establishing the independent republics of Transvaal and Orange Free State. Following the discovery of diamonds and gold in the late 19th century, the two Boer republics were conquered by Britain in the Anglo-Boer War of 1899–1902. In 1910 they were joined with the British colonies of the Cape and Natal (annexed in 1843) to form the Union of South Africa, which obtained full independence within the Commonwealth in 1931.

Although South Africa joined with Britain in both world wars, its British and Commonwealth attachments progressively weakened as the result of widespread anti-British sentiment and racial preoccupations. The National Party (*Nasionale Party*—NP), led by Daniel F. MALAN, came to power in 1948 with a program strongly reinforcing racial separation under white "guardianship." It proceeded to enact a body of openly discriminatory legislation that was further amplified under Hendrik F. VERWOERD (1958–1966). Segregation was strictly enforced, the already token political representation of non-whites was progressively reduced, and overt opposition was severely repressed. Similar policies were applied in South West Africa, a former German territory occupied by South Africa in World War I and subsequently administered under a mandate from the League of Nations (see entry under Namibia).

Increasing institutionalization of segregation under the Verwoerd regime led to international condemnation. External opposition was intensified by the "Sharpeville incident" of March 21, 1960, during which South African police fired on African demonstrators, killing 69 of them. In view of the increasingly critical stand of other Commonwealth members, South Africa formally withdrew from the grouping and declared itself a republic on May 31, 1961.

Prime Minister Verwoerd was assassinated by a deranged white man in September 1966, but his successor, Balthazar J. VORSTER, continued Verwoerd's policies, bringing to fruition the idea of separating the blacks into separate tribal homelands, or "Bantustans." These areas, encompassing approximately 13 percent of the country's land, were ultimately intended to house upwards of three-quarters of the population. However, a series of minor concessions to the blacks brought about a challenge from the right-wing, or *verkrampte* ("unenlightened" or "ultra-Conservative"), faction of the National Party under the leadership of Dr. Albert HERTZOG, who formed the Refounded National Party (*Herstigte Nasionale Party*—HNP) to compete in the 1970 election. The NP easily survived his challenge, the HNP winning no legislative seats on a 3.6 percent vote share, although the longtime opposition United Party (UP) made some gains. At the next parliamentary balloting in April 1974 the NP increased its majority, with the UP losing five seats to the other opposition group, the Progressive Party (PP), which had for some years held only a single seat.

The 1974 Portuguese revolution and subsequent changes in Angola and Mozambique further isolated the South African regime. Early in 1975 the government announced a policy of "ending discrimination" within South Africa and of working for détente in external affairs. The new policy was accompanied by a partial relaxation in apartheid regulations, including a repeal of "Masters and Servants" legislation, portions of which had been in existence for over a century. During the following year, however, the country experienced its worst outbreak of racial violence since the Sharpeville episode in 1960. The rioting, which began in Soweto, near Johannesburg, in mid-June, grew out of black student protests against the compulsory use of Afrikaans as a medium of instruction. Although the government announced in early July that it would begin phasing out Afrikaans at

the primary and secondary school levels, the disturbances spread to townships around Pretoria and, in late August and early September, to the heart of Cape Town. Despite the unrest, the Vorster government gave no indication of abandoning its commitment to "separate development" of the races, with the official position being that the policy was not based on race but on the conviction that, within South Africa, blacks made up distinct "nations" to which special political and constitutional arrangements should apply. It was in accordance with this philosophy that nominal independence was granted to the territory that would become known as the black homelands: Transkei in October 1976, Bophuthatswana in December 1977, Venda in September 1979, and Ciskei in December 1981.

Rioting intensified during 1977 amid growing signs that the Vorster government had succumbed to a siege mentality, although its white support increased substantially. Drastic new security legislation was approved, including a Criminal Procedure Bill that substantially augmented the powers of the police while severely limiting the rights of individuals in judicial proceedings. On September 12 Steven BIKO, one of the country's most influential black leaders, died in suspicious circumstances while in police detention. On October 19 the government instituted its most drastic crackdown in two decades, closing the leading black newspaper, arresting its editor, and banning a number of protest groups, including the Black Consciousness movement founded by Biko in 1969. Apparent white endorsement of these moves was revealed in a parliamentary election on November 30, at which the NP captured 134 of 165 lower-house seats.

On September 20, 1978, Prime Minister Vorster announced his intention to resign for reasons of health. Nine days later he was elected by a joint session of Parliament to the essentially titular post of president, succeeding Nicolaas J. DIEDERICHS, who had died on August 21. One day earlier the NP elected Defense Minister Pieter W. BOTHA as its new leader (hence prime minister) over Foreign Minister Roelof F. ("Pik") BOTHA and Plural Relations and Development Minister Cornelius P. MULDER. In November a long-simmering scandal involving alleged corruption and mismanagement of public funds in the Department of Information implicated a number of individuals, including Mulder, who was forced to resign from the government prior to his formal expulsion from the NP in May 1979. On June 4 President Vorster also resigned after being charged with participation in a variety of clandestine propaganda activities and of giving false evidence in an effort to conceal gross irregularities in the affair. He was immediately succeeded, on an interim basis, by Senate president Marais VILJOEN, who was elected to a full term as head of state by Parliament on June 19. Despite the scandal and increasingly vocal opposition from both the HNP and remaining *verkrampte* elements within the NP, the Botha government remained in power with a marginally reduced parliamentary majority after the election of April 29, 1981, having campaigned on a twelve-point platform, first advanced in 1979, that called for constitutional power-sharing among whites, Coloureds, and Asians, with "full independence" for the black homelands.

In a referendum conducted November 2, 1982, a Constitution Bill, providing for an executive state president and a tricameral parliament excluding blacks, was endorsed by 66 percent of white voters, and was approved by the House of Assembly on September 9, 1983. After balloting for delegates to the Coloured and Indian chambers in August 1984, Prime Minister Botha was unanimously elected president by an electoral college of the majority parties in each House on September 5, and he was inaugurated at Cape Town on September 14.

Faced with mounting internal unrest and near-universal foreign condemnation, the government in April 1985 abandoned two bastions of segregationist legislation: the Mixed Marriages Act and a portion of the Immorality Act that outlawed sex across the color line, while the prohibition of multiracial political movements was lifted in June. These moves, while provoking an immediate backlash by right-wing extremists, were received by black and moderate white leaders as "too little, too late." Clashes between police and demonstrators increased, yielding nearly 300 deaths (mainly of

blacks) by midyear. On July 21, in the first such action in a quarter-century, a state of emergency was declared in 36 riot-stricken black districts and townships in the Johannesburg and eastern Cape regions. On August 15, in a speech at Durban, President Botha rejected demands for further racial concessions, insisting that they would constitute "a road to abdication and suicide" by white South Africans. In mid-September, however, he indicated that Parliament would be asked in early 1986 to consider modification of a leading bulwark of residential segregation, the Group Areas Act, with possible revocation of the country's pass laws. The laws required adult black South Africans, on pain of imprisonment, to carry a pass at all times. This hated document showed what, if any, white areas the holder was allowed to enter, and at what times of day.

In an address at the opening of Parliament on January 31, 1986, President Botha shocked the extreme right by declaring that "We have outgrown the outdated colonial system of paternalism, as well as the outdated concept of apartheid." In late April he announced that a bill would be introduced terminating the pass laws, though the legislation would not affect segregation in schools, hospitals, and residential areas. Earlier, on March 7, the partial state of emergency imposed eight months before was rescinded; however, a nationwide state of emergency was declared on June 12 to quell anticipated violence on June 16, the anniversary of the Soweto uprising.

Although the term of the House of Assembly had been extended from 1986 to 1989 to coincide with the five-year mandates of the Coloured and Indian chambers, President Botha announced in January 1987 that an early election for a new white chamber would be held on May 6. The results of the poll reflected a distinctly rightward swing by the white voters: the NP won 123 of the 166 directly elective seats, while the far-right Conservative Party of South Africa (CPSA), with 22 seats, displaced the liberal Progressive Federal Party (PFP, a direct descendant of the PP) as runner-up.

During the ensuing months the government increased the practice of grudgingly yielding on the substance of apartheid while severely limiting the freedom of its opponents. A variety of new press restrictions were announced in August, while the government banned the activities of numerous groups. Banned groups included labor unions; civic, educational, and youth associations; the umbrella United Democratic Front (UDF), which linked some 650 anti-apartheid organizations; and a new Committee for the Defence of Democracy (CDD), organized at Cape Town in March 1988. In September a major constitutional crisis was averted by the government's withdrawal of five bills, designed to tighten residential segregation laws, upon which the two non-white parliamentary chambers had refused to act. Throughout the period numerous long-incarcerated regime opponents were released, while others, primarily from the "new generation" of UDF and other leaders, were arrested and convicted of treason.

On January 18, 1989, President Botha suffered a stroke, and Constitutional Development Minister J. Christiaan HEUNIS was sworn in as acting chief executive the following day. On February 2 Botha resigned as NP leader, with Education Minister Frederik W. DE KLERK being named his successor. On March 13 the party's parliamentary caucus voted unanimously that de Klerk should also become state president; Botha, however, refused to step down and on March 15 resumed the presidency, vowing to stay in office for the remainder of his term. Less than five months later a dispute erupted over Botha's not being advised of a meeting that de Klerk and Foreign Minister "Pik" Botha had scheduled with Zambian President Kenneth Kaunda. Terming the proposed meeting "inopportune" and complaining of having been ignored in the matter, President Botha resigned on August 14, with de Klerk succeeding him on an acting basis the following day.

At balloting for all three legislative chambers on September 6, 1989, the NP retained its overall majority in the House of Assembly, although its share of the vote fell to less than half (48.6 percent). On September 14 de Klerk was named by the parliamentary electoral college to a regular five-year term as president.

On February 2, 1990, de Klerk announced the lifting of bans against the ANC, the Pan-Africanist Congress (PAC), and the South African Communist Party (SACP), and on February 11 he freed the long-incarcerated ANC leader, Nelson Rolihlahla MANDELA. However, on April 17, two weeks before the start of talks with ANC leaders, the president flatly rejected majority rule on the ground that it would "lead to the domination and even the suppression of minorities." He also rejected a demand by right-wing whites for racially-based partition of the country and proposed a system under which power would be shared by all groups and minority rights would be constitutionally guaranteed. For its part, the ANC indicated that it would not engage in full negotiations until the nearly four-year state of emergency had been rescinded (effected in three of the four provinces on June 8) and all political prisoners and exiles had been amnestied.

On June 1, 1990, the government introduced legislation to rescind the Reservation of Separate Amenities Act that had sanctioned "petty apartheid" at public locations, such as beaches, libraries, and places of entertainment. Left in place were the Group Areas Act, which provided for racially segregated residential areas; the Lands Acts of 1913 and 1936, which reserved 87 percent of the country's land for the white minority; and the Population Registration Act, which mandated the classification of South Africans by race from birth.

On June 27, 1990, de Klerk stated that he was prepared to negotiate a new constitution that would eliminate all aspects of apartheid, and on August 7, one day after his second meeting with the president, Mandela announced that the ANC was suspending its 30-year armed struggle. In early October de Klerk and the leaders of the six "self-governing" homelands agreed to scrap the Lands Acts, and on October 15 the Separate Amenities Act was formally repealed; four days later emergency rule was lifted in Natal. Subsequently, in a historic move, de Klerk asked the National Party to open its rolls to all races.

In a "Manifesto for the New South Africa," proclaimed in a speech opening the 1991 Parliament session on February 1, President de Klerk indicated that not only would the Lands and Group Areas acts soon be repealed, but the Population Registration Act would be eliminated prior to constitutional revision. Two weeks earlier the government and the ANC had agreed to convene an all-party conference on the constitutional drafting process, although Chief Mangosuthu BUTHELEZI, leader of the Zulu-based *Inkatha* Freedom Party (IFP), responded coolly, while the CPSA, the PAC, and the Azanian People's Organization (Azapo) indicated that they would not participate. Meanwhile, on January 29, the ANC's Mandela and *Inkatha's* Buthelezi met for the first time in 30 years to defuse the bitter rivalry that had caused the death of more than 4,000 persons and had split the anti-apartheid movement. However, within two days of the leaders' reconciliation renewed fighting had broken out between their followers.

The Lands and Group Areas acts were abolished on June 5, 1991, as was the Population Registration Act five days later. Revocation of the Population Act left the capacity to vote (promised by the government under the new constitution) as the major remaining obstacle to black emancipation.

The first session of the Convention for a Democratic South Africa (Codesa), held December 20–21, 1991, featured a "declaration of intent" whereby constitutional proposals would require the approval of both the ANC and the government, with the latter pledging to employ its parliamentary majority to translate Codesa's decisions into law. Meanwhile, the de Klerk administration had become embroiled in an "Inkathagate" scandal stemming from evidence that the South Africa Defence Force (SADF) had been engaged over a three-year period in providing IFP members with anti-ANC military training.

On February 20, 1992, President de Klerk announced that a "whites-only" referendum would be held March 17 to renew his mandate for negotiating with anti-apartheid organizations. The projected poll was immediately denounced by white extremist groups as well as by the leftist PAC and Azapo, which had long demanded that a new basic law be approved by a broadly based constituent assembly rather than by the existing non-black Parliament. The result of the referendum was a triumph for the president, with 68.7 percent of the participants endorsing continuation of the reform process.

The Codesa II session held May 15–16, 1992, proved unproductive, largely because the parties were unable to resolve an impasse over the size of the majority required for interim legislative approval of key constitutional provisions. It was followed on May 27 by the issuance of a six-month study on the sources of internal violence by a commission headed by Richard GOLDSTONE, a respected South African jurist. While not completely exonerating the government, the commission found no evidence of "a sinister and secret organization orchestrating political violence on a wide front." Rather, it attributed the disturbances in the townships to "the political battle between supporters of the African National Congress and the *Inkatha* Freedom Party." The conclusions of the commission were sorely tested on June 17, when South African police were accused of transporting a group of Zulu-speakers to Boipatong township, south of Johannesburg, where a bloody massacre ensued that claimed 45 lives. After touring Boipatong, ANC Secretary General Cyril RAMAPHOSA insisted that the slaughter was a government response to the launching of an ANC mass action campaign designed to force majority rule. While the government vehemently denied the charge, Nelson Mandela declared on June 21 that negotiations were "in tatters," and the ANC Executive Committee voted two days later to withdraw from Codesa.

ANC suspicions that the Goldstone Commission had not uncovered the whole truth about township violence were confirmed when a raid on a covert operations center of Military Intelligence in Pretoria yielded information that impelled President de Klerk to announce on December 19, 1992, that illegal activities by senior SADF officers were under investigation. In further reports, the commission in October 1993 found strong circumstantial evidence of security force involvement in the violence. In March 1994 it cited allegations of a conspiracy among senior police officers involving a "third force" of *agents provocateurs* tasked with anti-ANC destabilization in collaboration with the IFP.

Meanwhile, a "record of understanding" drawn up in September 1992 between the ANC and the NP had given renewed impetus to constitutional talks, which were resumed in March 1993 within what was later designated the Multi-Party Negotiating Process (MPNP). The 26 parties involved included several that had boycotted Codesa, notably the PAC and the SACP, the latter being a leading component of the Concerned South Africans Group (COSAG) of apartheid-era formations, including the IFP. The MPNP came under immediate strain as a result of the assassination on April 10 of Chris HANI, SACP general secretary and an ANC executive member. However, counsels of restraint from Mandela and others prevented the violent reaction in the black townships from getting out of control.

Negotiating breakthroughs came in May and June 1993, when most of the MPNP parties agreed that nonracial elections for a five-year transitional government of national unity would take place on April 27, 1994. Also crucial was the ANC's shift from insistence on a centralized state to acceptance of a federal structure with entrenched powers for provincial governments. The concession did not prevent the IFP and the CPSA from withdrawing from the MPNP shortly before the publication on July 26 of a draft interim constitution providing for equal citizenship rights for all races and a nine-province federal structure integrating the black homelands into the new South Africa. In September the remaining MPNP parties also reached agreement on the creation of a multiracial Transitional Executive Council (TEC), which as approved by Parliament on September 23 was to operate alongside the government in the election run-up to ensure fair play and to monitor the operations of the security forces. After the package of texts had been formally adopted by the MPNP on November 18, the TEC was installed on December 7. Finally, on December 22 Parliament ratified the Constitution of the Republic of South Africa Bill by 237 votes to 45, most of those against being CPSA members.

The problem of reconciling opponents, both white and black, to the settlement remained. In May 1993 the CPSA had joined with various right-wing Afrikaner groups to form the Afrikaner People's Front (*Afrikaner Volksfront*—AVF) under the leadership of Gen. (Ret.) Constand VILJOEN, a former head of the SADF, with the central aim of achieving self-determination for Afrikaners in a separate homeland. In June tensions mounted when armed members of the Afrikaner Resistance Movement (*Afrikaner Weerstandbeweging*—AWB), a highly visible paramilitary group led by Eugene TERRE'BLANCHE, forcibly occupied the building in Johannesburg where MPNP talks were in progress, with no resistance from police. In October the AVF, together with the IFP and other conservative black elements, launched the Freedom Alliance as successor to COSAG. Its constituent elements at first presented a united front against the constitutional settlement, although a January 1994 decision in favor of electoral participation by the Ciskei government (originally a Freedom Alliance member) was a serious setback.

The situation was transformed in March 1994 when the AWB and other Afrikaner paramilitaries, apparently sanctioned by the AVF, tried to protect the Bophuthatswana government of Chief Lucas MANGOPE (a Freedom Alliance member) from ANC-led protests against his decision to boycott the elections. Order was restored by speedy deployment of SADF troops, the Afrikaners being routed with 3 fatalities among at least 60 deaths overall and Mangope being removed from office by decision of the TEC on March 12. In light of this debacle and earlier divisions in the Freedom Alliance, Viljoen broke ranks with the AVF by forming the Freedom Front (*Vryheidsfront*—VF), which registered for the elections, whereas the CPSA and the other AVF formations maintained their nonparticipatory stance. The split marked the effective collapse of the Freedom Alliance, as confirmed by the eleventh-hour decision of the IFP on April 19 that it too would contest the forthcoming elections, despite a last-minute bout of bloodletting in Johannesburg on March 28 in which over 50 IFP demonstrators had been killed.

The IFP's participation ensured that South Africa's first multiracial balloting, to be held April 26–29, 1994, would be relatively free of violence. According to the Independent Electoral Commission and numerous foreign observers, it was in the main conducted fairly. As expected, the ANC registered an overwhelming victory in the national contest, winning 252 of 400 seats in the new National Assembly, against 82 for the NP, 43 for the IFP, 9 for the VF, and 14 for three smaller parties. In simultaneous polls for new provincial assemblies, the ANC won majorities in seven provinces, losing only Western Cape (to the NP) and KwaZulu-Natal (to the IFP).

Elected president by unanimous vote of the new Assembly on May 9, 1994, Nelson Mandela was sworn in the following day. Under the terms of the constitutional settlement, the ANC's Thabo MBEKI became first deputy president and de Klerk second deputy president. The new cabinet installed on May 11 contained 19 ANC representatives, 5 from the NP, and 3 from the IFP (including Chief Buthelezi as home affairs minister). The new Senate, its members designated by the newly elected provincial assemblies, convened on May 20, with the ANC holding 60 of 90 seats.

The widespread jubilation accompanying the installation of Nelson Mandela as South African president on May 10, 1994, tended to obscure a variety of problems confronting the new administration. Far-right Afrikaners continued to press for political autonomy, although talks between Mandela and CPSA leader Ferdi HARTZENBERG in Pretoria on August 12 suggested that the AVF did not intend to resort to force. As for the IFP, while Chief Buthelezi had accepted cabinet membership, relations between his Zulu-based formation and Mandela's ANC remained tense. Intensifying post-election controversy was the disclosure on May 19 that on the eve of the election some 7.4 million acres of state land in KwaZulu, about a third of the ex-homeland's area, had been transferred to the control of the Zulu King Goodwill ZWELITHINI under legislation adopted by the outgoing KwaZulu Assembly and approved by President de Klerk, without the knowledge of the ANC. Although the new

minister of land affairs, Derek HANEKOM (ANC), announced on June 15 that the transfer would stand, the affair angered many ANC members, who suspected that its purpose had been to entice the IFP into the electoral process.

A year after the advent of majority rule, the most serious political problem facing the government was the disaffection of the IFP and its Zulu supporters, centering on their demand for a degree of autonomy for KwaZulu-Natal that fell little short of independence, including a constitutionally recognized role for the Zulu monarchy. Accompanied by periodic clashes between ANC and IFP supporters, the confrontation worsened in April 1995 when IFP members withdrew from the Constituent Assembly charged with drafting a permanent constitution. Although Chief Buthelezi remained a member of the government, he asserted that his party would not accept any constitution drawn up in its absence and repeated his demand for international mediation of KwaZulu-Natal's dispute with the central authorities. ANC ministers and officials responded that a formal international role in the dispute would imply acceptance of KwaZulu-Natal's claim to separate status; they also insisted that drafting of the new constitution would proceed according to schedule, if necessary without IFP participation.

ANC-IFP relations were further aggravated by President Mandela's admission on June 1, 1995, that he had personally authorized ANC officials "to shoot to kill if necessary" in the March 1994 clashes near the party's Shell House headquarters at Johannesburg, in which over 50 IFP demonstrators had died. Amid IFP calls for his impeachment over this admission, the president sought to regain the initiative by proposing on June 14 that responsibility for the pay and perquisites of tribal chiefs should be transferred from the provincial authorities to the central government. Such a change would pose a special threat to Chief Buthelezi's power base in the KwaZulu-Natal countryside, where control of the purse strings sustained the IFP's network of support among tribal chiefs. Serious IFP-ANC clashes in August 1995 were followed on December 25 by an attack by IFP supporters on the village of Shobashobane (an ANC enclave in

KwaZulu-Natal) in which at least 19 people were killed, with the security forces failing to intervene.

In sharp contrast, relations between the ANC and the white minority continued to be accommodating, with occasional rifts within the transitional government being quickly resolved. The discovery by the ANC justice minister in January 1995 that the outgoing NP government had secretly granted indemnities from prosecution to over 3,500 policemen and security officials provoked a cabinet crisis in which de Klerk claimed that he and the NP had been subjected to "insulting attack." However, the possibility of an NP withdrawal receded when de Klerk and Mandela agreed in a face-to-face meeting on January 20 that a "fresh start" should be made. More surprisingly, the president also established working relations with several Afrikaner groups that had vigorously opposed black majority rule, with a disavowal of violence by General Viljoen and the VF seen as particularly helpful. Most Afrikaner leaders welcomed an offer by Mandela on June 27 that a nonbinding referendum be held to ascertain the views of Afrikaners on the proposal for a separate Afrikaner state (*volkstaat*), the president accepting that it was the government's duty "to consider their concerns and fears in a responsible, sensitive and constructive manner."

Two days after the endorsement of the new constitution in Parliament, F. W. de Klerk announced on May 10, 1996, that the NP was withdrawing from the government of national unity with effect from June 30. He cited the diminishing influence of the NP on government policy, the refusal of the ANC to include power-sharing arrangements in the new constitution, and the need for an effective opposition. Commentators considered that the decision was motivated by a desire to assert the NP's independence well in advance of legislative elections in 1999. The party subsequently also withdrew from all provincial governments except that of Western Cape, where it was in the majority. President Mandela appointed ANC members to replace the outgoing NP ministers and abolished the post of second deputy president vacated by de Klerk.

Much domestic attention subsequently focused on the initial proceedings of the Truth and Rec-onciliation Commission (TRC), which had been created in July 1995 to investigate human rights abuses and political crimes of the apartheid era with the aim of consigning their legacy to history. Chaired by Archbishop Desmond TUTU (head of the Anglican Church in South Africa until his retirement in June 1996), the TRC was empowered to grant judicial amnesties to people confessing to apartheid-era crimes (depending on their gravity) if it was satisfied that full disclosure had been made and that the crime in question had been politically motivated. The TRC began a scheduled two years of hearings in April 1996, its authority to grant amnesties being upheld by the Constitutional Court in July after the families of several murdered political activists had argued that the commission's power to protect human rights violators from prosecution and civil damages denied them the opportunity to obtain justice through the courts.

Former state president de Klerk gave evidence to the TRC on August 21, 1996, stating that the security forces had not, to his knowledge, been authorized during the period of NP government to commit human rights abuses, although he apologized for suffering caused by the apartheid system. However, Eugene DE KOCH, a former colonel in the South African police who was convicted in the same month for murder and other crimes during the apartheid era, subsequently claimed in court that members of the former NP government had had full knowledge of a systematic campaign by the police, armed forces, and covert security units against apartheid opponents. Furthermore, in testimony to the TRC in October, several former members of the police claimed that former president P. W. Botha and two former ministers, Louis LE GRANGE and Adriaan VLOK, had ordered state violence against anti-apartheid organizations in the 1980s. (Botha was convicted in August 1998 for refusing to appear before the TRC, although in June 1999 his appeal was upheld on technical grounds.) In May 1997 de Klerk, in a second appearance, again denied knowledge of human rights violations. He retired from politics in August, and the NP inaugurated a new leadership under Marthinus van SCHALKWYK, by which time the party had ended its cooperation with the TRC on the grounds of political bias.

In September 1997 the deadline for submitting petitions to the TRC passed. Among those who did not file and attempted to stave off the TRC's calls to testify were former president Botha and a number of apartheid-era judicial officials. The ANC was the most prominent of the organizations to apply and in its petition admitted to torture, abuse, and even executions; however, the party attempted to justify such actions as being in the name of the "dirty war" fought against apartheid.

The dominant event of 1998 was the October release of a comprehensive report from the TRC. Having reviewed evidence from some 20,000 people, the TRC described apartheid as a "crime against humanity." It also declared the government responsible for a large majority of the abuses committed between 1960 and 1994, condemning the NP regime for a broad range of atrocities that included kidnappings, torture, killings, and bombings. However, the ANC and other liberation groups as well as extreme right organizations were also held accountable for violent acts. Not surprisingly, the report sparked controversy, and every major party rejected its conclusions to some degree. The report cited prominent individuals from across the entire political spectrum for human rights abuses. They included P. W. Botha, Chief Buthelezi, General Viljoen, Eugene Terre'Blanche, and President Mandela's ex-wife, Winnie MADIKIZELA-MANDELA, one of the country's most popular female politicians and an ANC leader, who was implicated in a dozen violent acts, including murder. Although the activities of two of the TRC's three committees—the Reparation and Rehabilitation Committee and the Human Rights Violations Committee—drew to a close with the release of the report, the mandate of the Amnesty Committee, with over 1,000 cases yet to review, was extended by act of Parliament "until a date determined by the President."

In December 1997 President Mandela had resigned as ANC president and was succeeded, as expected, by Thabo Mbeki, who led the ANC into the June 2, 1999, national elections. The ANC emerged from the balloting with 266 National Assembly seats, 1 short of the two-thirds majority needed to amend the constitution, prompting party leaders to quickly negotiate a coalition with the Minority Front (MF), an ethnic Indian party that had won a single seat. On June 14 the National Assembly elected Mbeki, without opposition, as president, and he took the oath of office two days later. On June 17 the new president named ANC deputy leader Jacob ZUMA as deputy president and appointed a cabinet in which Chief Buthelezi retained his position as home affairs minister.

Simultaneous elections to the National Assembly and the provincial assemblies took place on April 14, 2004. A total of 21 parties presented candidates in the national ballot while 37 parties contested the provincial elections. The ANC emerged as the dominant party at both national and provincial levels. It gained 279 of the 400 National Assembly seats with 69.7 percent of the votes while the DA took 50 seats with 12.4 percent of the votes cast and the IFP 28 seats with 7.0 percent. The ANC took control of seven of the nine provincial assemblies. Although it failed to win outright majorities in KwaZulu-Natal and Western Cape, the ANC nominated premiers to head all nine provincial governments. The Democratic Alliance, led by Tony LEON, remained the official opposition.

Members of a reconstituted version of the old apartheid-era ruling party known as the New National Party (NNP), and the Azanian People's Organization were included in the cabinet, which contained 12 women, including the foreign minister. Several members of the South African Communist Party (SACP), which held no parliamentary seats, were included by virtue of their dual membership in the ANC. The NNP had an electoral pact with the ANC but received only 1.65 percent of the vote, down from 6.87 percent in 1999. The United Democratic Movement made a better showing with 2.2 percent of the vote (compared with 3.42 percent in 1999), and the newly-formed Independent Democrats, led by Patricia de LILLE, received 1.73 percent. In August Marthinus van Schalkwyk announced the dissolution of the NNP and with some of his colleagues joined the ANC.

However former president F. W. de Klerk refused to follow Schalkwyk into the ANC. In September, when elected officials at the local level were permitted to change parties during a "floor-crossing window," two-thirds of NNP councilors joined the ANC. In June former president Nelson Mandela officially retired from public life.

On April 23 the Assembly re-elected Mbeki to serve a second term, but Buthelezi, who had held the post of minister of home affairs since 1994, was not reappointed.

Constitution and Government

Under the Interim Constitution adopted by the outgoing Parliament on December 22, 1993, executive power was exercised by a president named for a five-year term by the National Assembly. Legislative authority was vested in a bicameral Parliament consisting of a Senate, 10 of whose 90 members were elected from each of nine regional legislatures, and a National Assembly, half of whose 400 members were elected from national and half from regional party lists. The two houses sat jointly as a Constituent Assembly, which debated and approved a permanent constitution (see below). The Interim Constitution detailed rights of citizenship, which for the first time constituted a universal bill of rights applying equally to all races, to be safeguarded by a Constitutional Court as the supreme judicial authority. In its first major ruling on June 6, 1995, the Court decided unanimously to abolish the death penalty in South Africa.

The four historic provinces (Cape, Natal, Orange Free State, and Transvaal) were replaced by nine new provinces: Eastern Cape, Eastern Transvaal (now Mpumalanga), KwaZulu-Natal, Northern Cape, Northern Transvaal (now Limpopo), North-West, Orange Free State (now Free State), Pretoria-Witwatersrand-Vereeniging (PWV, now Gauteng), and Western Cape, each with an elected legislature. Under the new provincial structure, the four "independent" and six "self-governing" black homelands created by the previous regime were effectively abolished. (For details regarding the "independent" homelands, see

the 1993 edition of the *Handbook,* pp. 762–772.) Town and city councils were established as multiracial, with white and black voters each electing 30 percent of the councilors and the remainder being selected on a nonracial basis.

In November 1995, following 18 months of work by the Constituent Assembly, the first draft of the new permanent constitution was published, with the main political parties reaching agreement on a final version on May 7, 1996, shortly before the expiry of the deadline set during the transitional period. The following day the text was approved overwhelmingly by Parliament. The NP voted in favor, despite its reservations over provisions relating to labor relations, property rights, language, and education, in order to safeguard concessions already secured from the ANC. The IFP was absent for the vote, maintaining its boycott of the Constituent Assembly, from which it had withdrawn in April 1995. Ratified in its final version on December 4 by the Constitutional Court, which had previously rejected certain draft clauses, particularly in relation to the reduction of provincial powers, the new constitution was finally signed into law on December 10 by President Mandela in a ceremony at Sharpeville. The IFP, which had briefly returned to the Constituent Assembly on October 1 before withdrawing again on October 7, accepted the legitimacy of the new document.

The new constitution took effect February 4, 1997, although some provisions (such as those concerning budget responsibilities) were not to be implemented until later in the year and the power-sharing provisions of the 1993 interim constitution were to remain in force until the 1999 general elections. The new basic law incorporated many essentials of the 1993 text, although it abandoned the principle that all parties with 5 percent of the vote should be represented in the cabinet. It also provided for a National Council of Provinces to replace the existing Senate, with the aim of enhancing the influence of the provinces on the policy of the central government—although it fell short of guaranteeing the provincial powers that the IFP had demanded. In addition, it enshrined an extensive bill of rights, one of the most liberal in the world. In the future, changes to the constitution would require the approval of at least two-thirds of the members of the National Assembly and at least six of the nine provinces represented in the National Council.

With regard to ordinary legislation, the powers exercised by the two houses vary. Bills affecting the republic as a whole are introduced in the National Assembly and, if passed, proceed to the National Council, where the members, voting individually, may concur or may propose changes for consideration by the Assembly. Bills affecting the provinces may be introduced in either house, but in the Council each of the nine provincial delegations has one vote. If the two chambers disagree on a provincial bill, an 18-member mediation committee (9 members from each chamber) attempts to reconcile the differences and return compromise legislation for a new vote in both houses. Failing that, the National Assembly may pass the bill with a two-thirds vote and send it on for presidential signature.

In early 1997 the legislature approved the creation of a National House of Traditional Leaders, aiming to provide a forum for the leaders of tribal groups and increasing communication between the legislature and the provinces. The new body was inaugurated on April 17. Members are named by provincial-level Houses of Traditional Leaders. In 2001 the Department of Justice and Constitutional Development, responding largely to requests from rural areas, announced that traditional leaders would be permitted to function as Commissioners of Oaths. At the same time, the Department of Provincial and Local Government has begun the process of more clearly delineating the powers and functions of the traditional leadership.

Provincial governments are led by elected legislatures of 30 to 80 members. Each legislature elects a provincial premier, who heads an Executive Council. Beneath the provincial level are six recently established metropolitan municipalities ("megacities," incorporating surrounding townships)—Cape Town, Durban Unicity, Ekurhuleni (East Rand), Johannesburg, Nelson Mandela (Port Elizabeth), and Tshwane (Pretoria). There are also 47 district municipalities and 231 local munic-

ipalities. Legislatures are elected at each municipal level. In 2000 the proportion of traditional representatives on councils was raised from 10 percent to 20 percent. The smaller jurisdictions are represented throughout the governmental system by the South African Local Government Association (SALGA).

Foreign Relations

Although South Africa was a founding member of the United Nations, its international standing was greatly impaired as a result of the racial restrictions maintained in its own territory and, until late 1988, that of Namibia (South West Africa). In the post–World War II period its rejection of external advice and pressure resulted in an atrophy of international contacts, notably through its departure from the Commonwealth in 1961, its suspension from membership in the Economic Commission for Africa in 1963, and its withdrawal or expulsion from a number of UN Specialized Agencies. It was also denied participation in the UN General Assembly, which repeatedly condemned the policy and practice of apartheid and advocated "universally applied economic sanctions" as the only means of achieving a peaceful solution to the problem. The UN Security Council, while stopping short of economic measures, called as early as 1963 for an embargo on the sale and shipment to South Africa of military equipment and materials.

Relations with the United Nations were further aggravated by South Africa's refusal to apply economic sanctions against Rhodesia, as ordered by the Security Council in 1966, and its long-standing refusal to relinquish control over Namibia, as ordered by both the General Assembly and the Security Council. Despite its political isolation on these key issues, Pretoria refrained from quitting the world body and attempted to maintain friendly political relations and close economic ties with most Western countries. Regionally, it belonged to the Southern African Customs Union (SACU), along with Botswana, Lesotho, Swaziland, and, later, Namibia. It also cooperated closely with the Ian Smith regime in Rhodesia over economic and defense matters, assisting its neighbor in circumventing UN sanctions. However, in accordance with its policy of seeking détente with neighboring black regimes, it publicly called for a resolution of the "Rhodesian question," endorsing in 1976 the principle of black majority rule if appropriate guarantees were extended to the white minority of what became in 1980 the Republic of Zimbabwe.

For more than a decade the government mounted repeated forays into Angola in its protracted conflict with Namibian insurgents, while relations with Swaziland and Mozambique were aggravated by the presence of ANC guerrilla bases in both countries, despite the conclusion of a non-aggression pact with the former in 1982 and a similar agreement with the latter (the "Nkomati accord") in May 1984.

During 1985 Western states came under increased pressure to impose sanctions on the Botha government. U.S. President Reagan had long opposed any action that would disrupt the South African economy, but, faced in mid-September with a congressional threat to act on its own, he ordered a number of distinctly modest punitive actions, with the countries of the European Community (EC, subsequently the EU) following in an equally restrained manner. The principal American prohibitions focused on bank loans and the export of nuclear technology and computers, while the Europeans imposed an oil embargo, halted most arms sales, and withdrew their military attachés. In addition, substantial corporate divestment occurred, particularly by U.S. firms. None of these sanctions presented a serious challenge to South Africa, which was, however, sufficiently aggrieved to threaten an embargo on the export of strategic metals to the United States.

Pretoria's capacity to act with impunity in regard to neighboring states was amply demonstrated during 1986. On January 1 Lesotho was effectively blockaded, and three weeks later its government was overthrown by forces more supportive of South African efforts to contain cross-border attacks by ANC guerrillas. Subsequently, on May 19, ANC targets in Botswana, Zambia, and Zimbabwe were

subjected to bombing attacks by the South African Air Force, in addition to ground raids by units of the SADF. Additional forays were conducted against alleged ANC bases in Swaziland late in the year and in Zambia in early 1987.

During 1988 South Africa's regional posture softened dramatically. In September President Botha traveled to Mozambique for his first state visit to a black African country. "Fruitful and cordial" discussions were held with President Chissano on a variety of topics, including the supply of power from Mozambique's Cahora Bassa hydroelectric facility, the status of Mozambican workers in South Africa, and "reactivation and reinforcement" of the Nkomati agreement of March 1984, which promised mutual non-aggression between South Africa and Mozambique. Subsequently, Botha visited Zaire and Côte d'Ivoire for talks with presidents Mobuto and Houphouët-Boigny, respectively. The most important development, however, concerned the Angola-Namibia conflict. During a November meeting at Geneva, Switzerland, Pretoria accepted a U.S.-mediated agreement, previously endorsed by Angola and Cuba, for the phased withdrawal of Cuban troops from Angola, accompanied by a withdrawal of all but 1,000 South African troops from Namibia and a UN-supervised election seven months thereafter in implementation of UN Security Council Resolution 435 of 1978. A protocol finalizing the agreement was signed at Brazzaville, Congo, on December 13, followed by the formal conclusion of a tripartite peace accord at UN headquarters in New York on December 22 (for details, see articles on Angola and Namibia). Not addressed by the Namibia settlement was the status of the port enclave of Walvis Bay, which, although historically South African territory, had been administered since 1977 as part of South West Africa. Preliminary discussions on the issue were launched in March 1991, but it was not until August 16, 1993, in a major decision of the multiparty forum convened to decide the future of South Africa, that the South African government delegation agreed under pressure from the ANC and other participants to transfer the Walvis Bay enclave to Namibia.

Formal conveyance occurred at midnight on February 28, 1994.

In a setback for ANC efforts to increase Pretoria's diplomatic isolation, in September 1990 President de Klerk was received at the white House by U.S. President George H. W. Bush. A few days earlier Foreign Minister Botha had announced that South Africa was prepared to accede to the UN Nuclear Non-Proliferation Treaty (see International Atomic Energy Agency, under UN: Related Organizations) in furtherance of an effort to make the African continent a nuclear weapons–free zone.

The progress made in dismantling apartheid during 1991 yielded significant diplomatic gains for Pretoria on both a global and an African continental basis. Most economic embargo measures imposed by Western nations (save in regard to military items) were relaxed, and in April 1992, after a number of political exchanges with neighboring regimes, President de Klerk made a highly symbolic state visit to Nigeria for talks with the incumbent chair of the Organization of African Unity (OAU, subsequently the African Union —AU), Ibrahim Babangida. No less symbolic was South Africa's reacceptance into international sports activity.

On July 1, 1993, President de Klerk and ANC President Mandela held separate meetings at Washington with U.S. President Clinton and three days later were joint recipients of Liberty Medals at Philadelphia, with President Clinton in attendance. The end of apartheid was further celebrated on October 15, when de Klerk and Mandela were jointly awarded the 1993 Nobel Peace Prize. Concurrently, most UN economic sanctions against South Africa were terminated.

During 1994 South Africa gradually reentered the international community. On June 1 it rejoined the Commonwealth after a break of 33 years; two weeks later it became the 53rd member of the OAU. On June 23, following the Security Council's lifting of its long-standing arms embargo on South Africa, the suspension of Pretoria's participation in the UN General Assembly was rescinded, thus facilitating the reactivation of South African membership in UN specialized agencies. Two months later, South

Africa joined the Southern African Development Community (SADC), and in October it signed a cooperation agreement with the EU.

President Mandela's independent line in foreign policy included the cultivation of relations with anti-Western regimes, such as those of Cuba and Libya, which had supported the ANC during the apartheid era. Nevertheless, relations with the United States were also strengthened, and in 1996 Mandela made successful visits to Germany, the United Kingdom, and France.

In November 1996 the South African government announced that it was canceling its diplomatic relations with Taiwan, one of its foremost trading partners, and establishing formal relations with the People's Republic of China with effect from the end of 1997. Although President Mandela said that South Africa wanted to maintain its links with Taiwan on the highest level short of diplomatic ties, in mid-December Taiwan recalled its ambassador for an indefinite period in protest over the South African decision.

South Africa remained a dominant force in regional affairs in 1998, one of its most striking decisions involving the deployment of troops to help restore order in Lesotho in the fall (see article on Lesotho for details). President Mandela also continued to pursue a role as Africa's most prominent peacemaker, becoming heavily involved, for example, in efforts to resolve the conflict in the Democratic Republic of the Congo. In addition, the government further exhibited the independent nature of its foreign policy by extending ties with Iraq and North Korea, despite strong objections from Washington and several EU capitals.

South Africa has emerged in recent years as the continent's most vigorous and ambitious diplomatic power. Mbeki was the leading figure behind the newly created African Union and New Partnership for Africa's Development (NEPAD) and was instrumental in brokering peace in Burundi and the Democratic Republic of the Congo. South Africa provided 3,000 troops in the Democratic Republic of the Congo and Burundi as part of UN peacekeeping operations, and Pretoria also has shouldered most of the financial burden. South African companies have struck out north with strong investment strategies. With 40 percent of sub-Saharan Africa's GDP, South Africa is the only country capable of projecting both military power and economic clout. However, South Africa has been criticized for its relations with Zimbabwe, as being insufficiently distanced from the Mugabe government. As one of the richest and most stable countries in Africa, South Africa attracts more refugees, both political and economic, than it can well accommodate. Some critics have described policies and procedures for granting refugees permanent resident status as arbitrary and inconsistent, as they seem to vary throughout the country.

South Africa has consistently opposed the U.S.-led war in Iraq and has promoted relations with many countries with whom the United States is at odds. Nevertheless, the United States considers South Africa as an ally in its efforts to promote democracy in the continent. President George W. Bush pointedly included South Africa in the itinerary during his tour of Africa in 2003.

In June 2006, Chinese premier Wen Jiabao visited South Africa and, addressing a crowd of more than 800 Chinese and South African business people at a forum in Cape Town, declared, "South Africa is China's key partner of strategic cooperation in Africa."

Current Issues

At the June 1999 balloting the dominance of the ANC was evident not only at the national level, but also in the provinces, where it retained outright majorities in seven, formed a coalition government with the IFP in KwaZulu-Natal, and won a plurality in Western Cape. In the national balloting, the Democratic Party, led by Tony LEON, displaced the NNP as the leading opposition formation, winning 38 seats (up from 7 in 1994), while the NNP managed only 28, a net loss of 54. Facing diminished prospects, in June 2000 the NNP joined the DP in forming a Democratic Alliance (DA), the expectation being that a full merger of the parties would eventually occur. The DA surprised many

observers by winning 23 percent of the national vote at the December municipal elections, but policy and leadership clashes ultimately led the NNP to part ways with the DP in October 2001. In abandoning the DA for a closer relationship with the ANC, the NNP's van Schalkwyk noted that the two erstwhile antagonists no longer had significant ideological differences. Thus, at the end of 2001 the only opposition formations with more than a handful of National Assembly members were the rump DA (the DP plus the small Federal Alliance) and the United Democratic Movement.

Despite its predominance, in 2000–2002 the ANC often found no clear direction toward resolving fundamental national issues. Criticism of its Growth, Employment, and Redistribution (GEAR) program was voiced not only by the opposition, but also by the closely allied Congress of South African Trade Unions (COSATU) and the South African Communist Party (SACP). Both faulted the ANC's turn toward market-oriented economics, including its privatization plans for such industries as energy, transportation, and telecommunications. They objected partly on ideological grounds and partly from concern over potential job losses, the rate of unemployment having failed to move significantly lower than the 37 percent average of 1997–1999, and economic growth having remained well below the level needed for achieving real reductions in poverty. At the same time the pace of land redistribution was slow, with the Land Claims Commission and white landowners often in dispute over fair market value. By July 2000 only 3 percent of farmland had been redistributed, far from the 30 percent called for by Parliament in 1994. As a consequence, landless blacks became increasingly impatient as the government attempted to avoid the domestic turmoil and international condemnation associated with the more radical expropriation policy in neighboring Zimbabwe.

In 2000–2002 the Mbeki administration drew withering criticism for its failure to present a cohesive plan for fighting the HIV/AIDS crisis. In April 2000 President Mbeki lent support to a scientifically discredited argument attributing AIDS to causes other than HIV infection, but by

October the resultant uproar had led him to temper his comments. Although the government and AIDS activists joined forces to win a patent fight against international pharmaceutical companies, more often than not they were at odds over treatment, costs, and drug distribution, particularly with regard to preventing mother-to-child transmission. Meanwhile, an estimated 11 percent of the South African population has been infected with HIV (at least one estimate places the number at 25 percent), and in 2000 AIDS accounted for 40 percent of all deaths in the 15–49 age group. Such daunting statistics prompted the International Monetary Fund to warn in 2001 of likely "significant demographic changes" in South Africa and of "far-reaching economic and social consequences, including lower economic growth and exacerbation of poverty." In October 2002 the government reversed itself and announced that it would look into making crucial antiretroviral drugs available through the public health system. Criticism of the government's response to the problem has continued, however.

The Mbeki administration also struggled to maintain an anticorruption campaign. In June 2001 public hearings opened into a December 1999 arms deal involving the purchase of surface ships, submarines, helicopters, and jet aircraft from a number of EU countries, at a cost of $5.4 billion. Despite accusations that officials had received kickbacks and engaged in other illegalities, in November the resultant report concluded that the procurement procedure had been flawed but not corrupt, although individuals who had derived "some form of benefit from the acquisition process" could be held criminally liable. The National Assembly opposition condemned the report as a whitewash.

The Truth and Reconciliation Commission intended to release the final volumes of its report in 2002, but publication was delayed when the IFP went to court in opposition to conclusions that it had been responsible for major violations of human rights. At the same time, the government, apparently fearing a loss of foreign investment, offered no support for various class action lawsuits, filed in the United States and elsewhere, against banks and multinational corporations that allegedly extended material support to the apartheid-era regime.

Meanwhile, even as South Africa's official examination of its apartheid-era abuses neared a conclusion, a more recent wave of violence frequently commanded the headlines. An Islamic group, the People Against Gangsterism and Drugs (PAGAD), drew considerable attention. Some members admitted involvement in vigilante attacks against drug traffickers, but PAGAD also allegedly conducted unrelated pipe bombings in the Cape Town vicinity. Among the dozens of targets were a police station and a U.S.-owned restaurant, raising the possibility of political motivation by at least some PAGAD elements. Since 2002 PAGAD activities have diminished considerably.

The extreme right-wing Warriors of the Boer Nation claimed responsibility for a wave of bomb blasts in Soweto on October 30, 2002. The attacks came in the context of a crackdown by authorities against extremist white elements. In November the National Intelligence Agency reported that it had broken up a plot by another group, the Boer Freedom Action (*Boere Vryheids Aksie*—BVA), to poison township water supplies and attack power and other infrastructure facilities.

In 2004 the ANC consolidated its hegemonic position in South African politics. In 2002 the Constitutional Court had allowed deputies to change parties without losing their seats. Following this ruling, members of the UDM and NNP defected to the ruling party, giving it a two-thirds majority, while the FA and the *Afrikaner Eenheidsbeweging* lost all their seats. South Africa was becoming more and more a one-party state like many of the African states to the north. At the provincial level members of the IFP defected to the ANC in KwaZulu-Natal.

The Truth and Reconciliation Commission's final report was presented to the president in 2003. The Commission had granted amnesty to 1,200 people but had rejected more than 5,000 applications. After rejecting a suggestion that a special tax be imposed on companies that had gained from apartheid, Mbeki announced that those designated victims by the TRC would receive a single payment of $3,800 each.

Land redistribution has dominated the public policy agenda along with HIV/AIDS during Mbeki's second term. Fifty thousand white farmers own 87 percent of the country's agricultural land. In 2004 Mbeki signed into law the controversial Restitution of Land Rights Amendment Act, which gives the state the right to expropriate land for restitution purposes without a court order or the seller's agreement. The act applies only to land from which blacks were forcibly removed under the colonial and apartheid regimes. The expropriated farmer will reportedly receive just and equitable compensation. The government's goal is to transfer 30 percent of all agricultural land from white to black farmers by 2014. By mid-2006 there were indications that land redistribution was not going fast enough to meet that goal, and that the government might move away from its stated "willing buyer, willing seller" policy in the direction of forced expropriation.

In June 2005 Schabir SHAIK, financial adviser to deputy president Jacob ZUMA, was found guilty of two counts of corruption and one of fraud in one of the most closely watched criminal trials since the end of apartheid. On June 15, Zuma, whom the judge had called "compliant," was dismissed from the office of deputy president, and two weeks later he was charged with two counts of bribery. In the months that followed, a groundswell of popular support developed for Zuma, a key figure in the fight against apartheid; the powerful trade union COSATU described the pending legal action as a "political trial," and called on President Mbeki to reinstate Zuma. At year's end, however, matters became further complicated when Zuma was charged with raping the 31-year-old daughter of a friend. In May 2006, a judge found Zuma not guilty of rape, and within days he was reinstated as ANC deputy president. Analysts said Zuma emerged "battered but not destroyed." His trial on the bribery charges began at the end of July, but has been postponed until early September so that the judge could consider a motion to dismiss the charges. The outcome of the trial will be a major factor in Zuma's quest to succeed Mbeki as president of South Africa.

Political Parties

During most of the apartheid era South Africa's leading party was the predominantly Afrikaner National Party, which came to power in 1948 and steadily increased its parliamentary strength to a high of 134 (81 percent) of lower house seats at the November 1977 election, before falling to 98 seats (57 percent) in 1989. While not as extremist as the Reconstituted National Party, the Conservative Party of South Africa, or a variety of smaller formations, the National Party was long committed to the general principle of white supremacy. Parties advocating more liberal racial policies fared poorly, with only the Progressive Party winning representation in the House of Assembly at the 1974 election; in 1977, however, a successor organization, the Progressive Federal Party (PFP), became the leading opposition party, with 17 seats, which were increased to 26 in 1981. In 1989 the PFP joined with two other moderate groups to form the Democratic Party, which won 33 directly elective seats in the September balloting.

At the post-apartheid election of April 26–29, 1994, the African National Congress secured an overwhelming majority of National Assembly seats on a vote share of 62.6 percent, followed by the National Party with 20.4 percent and the *Inkatha Freedom Party* with 10.5 percent.

Some 40 parties, including a number of new groupings, appeared in the run-up to the balloting of June 2, 1999; the government announced that some 16 had been authorized to contest the election to the National Assembly, while 10 more planned to offer candidates at the provincial level only. As of late 2001 over 100 parties were officially registered with the Independent Electoral Commission.

Government Parties

African National Congress (ANC). Organized in 1912 and long recognized as South Africa's leading black formation, the ANC was banned from 1960 to 1990. In October 1989 Walter SISULU, who had been imprisoned for 26 years, was one of seven prominent ANC leaders released from custody by the de Klerk administration; release of the organization's most charismatic figure, Nelson

Mandela, occurred on February 11, 1990, while its president, Oliver TAMBO, was permitted to return from more than three decades' exile on December 13. (Tambo died in 1993.) On May 28–31, 1992, the ANC held a policy conference at Johannesburg, during which it celebrated its evolution from a liberation movement to a political party and replaced a 1955 commitment to comprehensive nationalization with an emphasis on a mixed economy. In January 1994, prior to its assumption of power, it did, however, announce an ambitious program to end economic apartheid by redistributing land, building more than a million low-income dwellings, assuming state control of the mining industry, and breaking up white-owned conglomerates. The draft plan, known as the Reconstruction and Development Program, drew immediate criticism from the country's business leaders and yielded a caveat from Mandela that it required "a substantial amount of additional work to be anywhere near what we want it to be."

Among those elected on the ANC ticket in the party's landslide election victory in April 1994 was Winnie Mandela, the controversial estranged wife of the new president, whose 1991 conviction for kidnapping and being an accessory to assault did not deter her appointment as a deputy minister in the new government. Also elected was the ANC secretary general, Cyril RAMAPHOSA, who on May 22 was named by the ANC parliamentary caucus to chair the joint Assembly-Senate sittings that would draft the definitive version of the post-apartheid constitution. In a strengthening of radical elements in the party leadership, Winnie Mandela regained her position on the ANC executive at the 49th congress in December, when First Deputy President Thabo Mbeki succeeded the ailing Sisulu as ANC vice president, thus becoming President Mandela's heir apparent. Mrs. Mandela's dismissal from the government in March 1995, following her public assertions that it lacked radicalism, drew official endorsement from ANC bodies, although she retained strong rank-and-file support. The Mandelas' 38-year marriage ended in divorce in March 1996.

In November 1995 the ANC won 66.4 percent of the votes cast in South Africa's first democratic local elections. In August 1996 President Mandela formally notified the ANC executive committee that he would not seek a second presidential term in the elections due in 1999 and that he would relinquish the ANC presidency at the party's next national conference in 1997.

In April 1997 Winnie Mandela retained her position as president of the ANC's Women's League, despite the party's apparent backing of her challengers, and in September she announced her intention to campaign for the ANC's deputy presidential post. Once again the party backed her opponent, Jacob Zuma, but what ultimately derailed her aspirations was her alleged role in apartheid-era violence, and she withdrew from the deputy leadership race.

As expected, at the ANC's congress held December 16–20, 1997, Nelson Mandela announced his retirement from the party's top post and his chosen successor, Thabo Mbeki, was unopposed in the subsequent election for party president. Also unopposed in their runs for party posts were Zuma, Kgalema Motlanthe (secretary general), and Mendi MSIMANG (treasurer general). For her part, Winnie Mandela secured a seat on the National Executive Committee.

The ANC unsuccessfully tried to block release of the comprehensive TRC report in the fall of 1998, objecting to conclusions that the ANC had been responsible for human rights abuses and acts of terrorism against its opponents during the anti-apartheid campaign and prior to the 1994 balloting. Party officials, led by Mbeki, condemned the report as "scurrilous," but President Mandela, in a pointed departure from the views of his successor, acknowledged that some of the abuses reported by the TRC had occurred and chastised the other ANC leaders for their angry response. Winnie Mandela was singled out in the TRC report for her alleged role in violent acts committed by the Mandela United Football Club, described as her "private army." Nevertheless, she remained popular in the ANC and was placed high on its candidate list for the June 1999 balloting, thereby assuring her election to the Assembly.

At the June 1999 elections the ANC widened its parliamentary majority to 266 seats (with a 66.4

percent vote share) and retained control of seven provincial legislatures. It joined the IFP in a coalition government in KwaZulu-Natal and then in November 2001, having negotiated a cooperation agreement with the NNP, joined in forming a new administration in the ninth province, Western Cape, where it held a plurality of Council seats.

Considerable controversy greeted an April 24, 2001, televised accusation by Minister of Safety and Security Steve TSHWETE that three prominent party members—Cyril Ramaphosa, former Mpumalanga premier Mathews PHOSA, and former Gauteng premier Tokyo SEXWALE—had conspired against President Mbeki's leadership. All three were regarded in some quarters as potential challengers to Mbeki. On December 4 Tshwete publicly apologized.

On October 18, 2001, Winnie Madikizela-Mandela was arrested and charged with fraud and theft involving some $108,000 in dozens of bank loans to fictitious members of the ANC Women's League. Earlier in the month ANC Whip Tony YENGENI had resigned following his arrest for alleged illegal acquisition of an automobile in connection with the controversial 1999 $5.4 billion arms deal with EU countries.

The ANC remains closely tied, through a Tripartite Alliance, to the COSATU and to the South African Communist Party (SACP), despite the latter's recent objections to ANC labor and privatization policies. The three organizations have a considerable overlap in membership, and in recent elections COSATU and SACP candidates have been included on the ANC candidate list.

The ANC's entrenchment as the dominant party in South African politics has been helped by the splintering of opposition parties and the iconic status of ANC leaders such as Mandela and Mbeki. Although voter turnout in South Africa is historically low, the ANC has made heavy inroads among Zulus, working-class people, Indians, and Coloureds. It still has not won over many white voters, who generally vote for the DA or other white liberal or right-wing parties. Most South Africans believe that only the ANC has the interests of blacks at heart and are therefore prepared to overlook its deficiencies. While South Africans are keenly aware of the dangers of a one-party state, they also realize that the ANC's strength has helped to create one of the most stable countries in Africa. The ANC has also vigorously pursued the attrition of its opponents by wooing legislators and career politicians with jobs and favors. The ANC has made floor-crossing respectable and has helped to create a big tent in which even rival political ideologies can flourish. In a survey conducted by Harvard University two out of three South Africans believe the ANC wields too much power, and that the boundary between party and state is becoming blurred. The same survey reveals that eight out of ten South Africans believe that this poses no threat to democracy.

The outcome of Jacob Zuma's legal problems is likely to have a profound effect on the ANC's future. He is estranged from president Mbeki, but remains popular with many ANC members. Some observers have suggested that controversy over Zuma could go as far as to break up the ANC, with unpredictable consequences for South Africa's future. If Zuma is not convicted he is likely to be a candidate for president in the elections of 2009, the crucial first transfer of power in which Nelson Mandela is neither the incoming nor the outgoing president.

Leaders: Thabo MBEKI (President of the Republic and of the Party), Phumzile MLAMBO-NGCUKA (Deputy President of the Republic), Jacob ZUMA (Deputy President), Patrick LEKOTA (National Chairperson), Kgalema MOTLANTHE (Secretary General).

South African Communist Party (SACP). The SACP was formed in 1953, following dissolution, a year earlier, of the original Communist Party of South Africa (CPSA), which had been organized in 1921. The SACP has long cooperated closely with the ANC, to a number of whose senior organs SACP members have been appointed. The party's former chair, Dr. Yusef DADOO, died in 1983, while its former general secretary, Moses MABHIDA, died at Maputo, Mozambique, in March 1986. A year later, following his appointment as Mabhida's successor, Joe SLOVO resigned as chief of staff of the ANC's military wing, *Umkhonto we Sizwe*. He returned to South Africa in April 1990. The party gathered for a "relaunching"—its first public rally within South Africa in 40 years—on July 29, 1990.

In a stinging opening address to the SACP's first legal congress on December 8, 1991, Slovo insisted that former Soviet President Gorbachev had "completely lost his way" and that what was being buried in Eastern Europe was not true socialism. Subsequently, Slovo was elected party chair, with the longtime chief of *Umkhonto we Sizwe,* Chris HANI, being named his successor as general secretary. Hani was assassinated on April 10, 1993.

The SACP, as such, did not contest the 1994 election, its candidates being included on the ANC list. Subsequently, Slovo was awarded the housing portfolio in the Mandela administration, but he died in January 1995. The party candidates were again merged with those of the ANC for the 1999 balloting. About 80 of the ANC's 266 National Assembly representatives have SACP membership, as do a number of cabinet ministers.

The SACP is one of only a few Communist parties in Africa today. But its ideology has been diluted since 1994 when it moved in as a coalition partner with the ANC in a national government. Many of its leaders, such as Chair Charles Nqakula, Jeff RADEBE, and Essop PAHAD, are now cabinet ministers. Since the SACP is now in the position of having to defend ANC policies and programs, hardliners in the party feel that the party's own principles have suffered.

Leaders: Charles NQAKULA (National Chair), Geraldine FRASER-MOLEKETI (Minister of Public Service and Administration), Blade NZIMANDE (General Secretary), Jeremy CRONIN (Deputy General Secretary).

Azanian People's Organization (Azapo). Azapo was launched as a black consciousness movement in early 1978; however, its founders, Ishmael MKHABELA and Lybon Mabasa, were immediately detained, and it did not hold its first congress until September 1979. (Mabasa was subsequently described as the leader of the **Social-ist Party of Azania**.) Although never a mass party, it enjoyed the support of black intellectuals. Avowedly nonviolent, it adopted a hard line on the possibility of negotiating with the white government and was strongly anti-Codesa. In early 1994 Azapo declared its opposition to the forthcoming all-party election and announced that it would intensify its struggle until land had been returned to the country's blacks. Although Azapo had boycotted the 1994 balloting, it was registered for the 1999 elections, at which it won .2 percent of the vote and one National Assembly seat. In January 2001 the Azapo leader, Mosibudi Mangena, was named deputy minister of education. After its poor performance in the 2004 elections it held unity talks with the Pan Africanist Congress and the Socialist Party of Azania.

Leaders: Mosibudi MANGENA (President), Pandelani NEFOLOVHODWE (Deputy President), Zithulele N. A. CINDI (National Chair).

United Democratic Movement (UDM). The UDM was launched on September 27, 1997, by former NP secretary general Roelf MEYER and former ANC deputy minister Bantu Holomisa on a self-described moderate and nonracial platform. The new grouping was reportedly immediately bolstered by the enrollment of a number of young, liberal NP defectors. Its first secretary general, Sifiso NKABINDE, was murdered in January 1999.

The UDM subsequently was reported to be gaining popular support, and it competed in the 1999 Assembly campaign on a pledge to narrow the gap between rich and poor without imperiling the wealth of the financial elite. The party won 14 seats on a 3.4 percent vote share. In January 2000 Meyer announced his retirement from politics, and the Second National Congress in December 2001 confirmed Holomisa as president.

The UDM is identified with Xhosa interests in Eastern Cape province. It supported the ANC during the latter's bitter struggle with the IFP for control of the KwaZulu-Natal legislature. Floor crossing has cost the UDM heavily. Nine members defected to the ANC, and Mogoboya Ramodike left to form his own party. However the party retains one deputy ministerial post, Ntopile KGANYAGO, Public Works, and for this reason is included among government parties here.

Leaders: Bantu HOLOMISA (President), Gerhard KOORNHOF (Deputy President/Finance Spokesperson), Malizole DIKO (Secretary General).

Other Parliamentary Parties

Democratic Alliance (DA). The DA was established in late June 2000 by the Democratic Party (DP); the New National Party (NNP); and the small Federal Alliance (FA), which earlier in the month had agreed to present its candidates for upcoming local elections on the DP list. Formal merger of the three was delayed, however, pending passage of legislation permitting party consolidations. Initially seen as an attempt by the principal white formations to form a united front, the DA registered considerable success at the December municipal elections, taking 23 percent of the national vote and capturing Cape Town from the ANC. However, differences within the leadership resulted in the departure of the NNP from the DA in November 2001, and local defections in October 2002 delivered control of Cape Town to an ANC-NNP coalition. In 2004 the Democratic Alliance emerged as the principal opposition party in the national parliament with 50 seats.

Leaders: Tony LEON (President and Leader of the Opposition), Joe SEREMANE (Chairperson), Donald LEE (Deputy Chairperson).

***Inkatha* Freedom Party** (IFP). Although predominantly a Zulu organization, the *Inkatha,* in response to charges of tribalism, voted at a general conference in July 1990 to transform itself "from a liberation movement into a political party" that would be open to all races; however, most observers felt that the organization remained primarily a vehicle for the expression of Zulu interests in KwaZulu.

Bitterly opposed to the ANC and frequently engaged in violence with its larger rival, *Inkatha* declared in mid-1993 that it would not participate in the 1994 election and joined in an improbable alliance with the leading right-extremist parties and representatives of nominally independent Bophuthatswana and Ciskei in a Concerned South Africans Group (COSAG) that was subsequently styled the Freedom Alliance. Following the ouster of Bophuthatswana's Lucas Mangope in March 1994, however, the Alliance disintegrated, and *Inkatha* agreed on April 19 to abandon its boycott of the election. It placed third. The group was awarded three portfolios in the ensuing Mandela administration, including the designation of *Inkatha* leader Buthelezi as home affairs minister. It nevertheless continued its deep disagreement with the ANC over constitutional and other issues, boycotting the Constituent Assembly charged with drafting a new constitution.

The intraparty schism between those members favoring continued participation in the national government (so-called moderates) and the Buthelezi-led, anti-ANC faction widened in early 1997. At a meeting of the National Council in January, the IFP's national chair, Frank MDLALOSE, and Secretary General Jiba JIYANE resigned and were replaced by Buthelezi supporters Ben NGUBANE and Zakhele KHUMALO, respectively. Subsequently, in March, 13 IFP activists were convicted for their roles in the slaying of 19 ANC members in 1995.

The TRC accused the IFP of having caused the death of nearly 4,000 opponents in KwaZulu in 1982–1994, attributing ultimate responsibility for the violence in large part to Chief Buthelezi, who did not testify before the commission or request amnesty. Subsequently, the IFP election campaign in 1999 focused on economic issues. At the June balloting the party won 34 seats in the National Assembly on an 8.6 percent vote share. It continued as national government partner of the ANC, with which it also formed a coalition in KwaZulu-Natal.

The IFP has suffered considerable erosion of support as a result of perceived ANC bulldozer strategies. Relations between the IFP and ANC are now at their lowest ebb since 1994, when the IFP joined the government of national unity. The main arena of the quarrel between the two parties is KwaZulu-Natal, where, in late 2002, the ruling IFP ejected two ANC ministers from the provincial government and formed a partnership with the opposition Democratic Alliance. While Buthelezi and chair Lionel MTSHALI were renominated at the 2004 national congress in Ulundi, Musa ZONDI was nominated for the revived position of secretary general that had been abolished in 1998. The IFP also launched a campaign to shed its image as an exclusively Zulu party and appeal to the broader multiracial community. The IFP no longer has any representation in the government.

Leaders: Chief Mangosuthu (Gatsha) BUTHELEZI (President of the Party).

African Christian Democratic Party (ACDP). The ACDP, a conservative Christian group, was organized prior to the 1994 balloting, at which it won two seats on a 0.5 percent vote share; it also secured representation in three provincial assemblies. In 1997 the ACDP expressed outrage at the government's decision to legalize abortion. The party also contested the 2004 elections, at which it won 1.4 percent of the vote and six assembly seats.

Leaders: Kenneth MESHOE (President), Jo-Ann DOWNS (Deputy President).

Independent Democrats (ID). The ID is South Africa's newest political party, formed in March 2003 under the leadership of Patricia de LILLE. De Lille is a former trade unionist and a long-time member of and MP for the Pan Africanist Congress, which she left to form the ID. With the motto "Back to Basics," the ID's policies are fairly centrist. The party agrees with the ANC on the economy, health, and jobs, although de Lille outspokenly differs on HIV/AIDS.

Freedom Front Plus. This group was founded in 2004 as successor to **Freedom Front** (*Vryheidsfront*—VF). The VF was launched by Gen. (Rct.) Constand VILJOEN in March 1994 following a split in the Afrikaner People's Front (AVF; see discussion under CPSA, below) over the issue of participation in the April election, with the VF opting to register to present the case for a "white homeland." Several prominent members of the Conservative Party also defected to the new

grouping. In late March the VF stated that its objective was a confederal South Africa based on the "inalienable and non-negotiable" right of self-determination for Afrikaners and all other groups. Subsequent to the April poll, at which it placed fourth with 2.2 percent of the vote, the Front insisted that blatant irregularities had occurred at 80 percent of the voting stations. Having achieved a measure of accommodation with the government under black majority rule, the VF welcomed President Mandela's proposal of June 1995 that a consultative referendum should be held to ascertain Afrikaners' views on the concept of a separate Afrikaner state.

In the TRC report issued in October 1998, General Viljoen was held accountable for certain acts of violence committed by right-wingers during the run-up to the 1994 balloting. Meanwhile, the VF was described as hoping to cooperate with the DP for the 1999 election, at which it won only 0.8 percent of the vote and three National Assembly seats (a loss of six). In August Viljoen was reelected party leader by one vote over Pieter Mulder, but in March 2001 he announced his retirement from active politics. On March 31 Mulder was unanimously elected as his successor. The Freedom Front Plus manifesto calls for self-determination for local communities.

Leaders: Pieter MULDER (Party Leader), Abrie OOSTHUIZEN (Chair).

Pan Africanist Congress of Azania (PAC). A militant ANC offshoot that was also banned in 1960, the PAC long sought to unite all black South Africans in a single national front. Based at Lusaka, Zambia, the Congress announced in May 1979 the establishment in the Sudan of a "June 16 Azania Institute" (named after the June 1976 Soweto uprising) to instruct displaced South African students in a variety of academic and artisan skills. Its underground affiliate, the Azanian People's Liberation Army (APLA), was relatively small, compared to the military wing of the rival ANC. The PAC's longtime leader, John Nyati POKELA, died in June 1985; its president, Zephania MOTHOPENG, was released from nine years' imprisonment in November 1988, while another leader, Jafta MASEMOLA, was released in October 1989. In September 1990 the PAC rejected a government invitation to participate in constitutional talks, branding the overture as "not serious or honest." In October the PAC joined the ANC and some 60 other groups (*Inkatha* being the most notable exception) in the attempted formation of a united Patriotic Front. However, the PAC subsequently broke with the Mandela-led formation in opposing Codesa, insisting that it would settle for nothing less than "a democratically elected constituent assembly." The PAC has abandoned its more radical programs, and it concentrates on the plight of the poor and related issues.

The PAC announced in early 1994 that it was abandoning armed struggle, thus permitting it to register for the April election. The party won 1.2 percent of the vote and five Assembly seats. Following a protracted leadership struggle, Clarence MAKWETU stepped down as PAC president in December 1996 and was replaced by Mmutlanyane Mogoba.

Under Mogoba's leadership the PAC in 1997 evinced a conciliatory attitude toward whites, while party leaders also expressed an interest in opening a dialogue with the ANC, the PAC's longtime rival. Subsequently, in January 1999, it was announced that the APLA had been officially disbanded, and the PAC was registered to contest the June national elections, at which it won three seats on a 0.7 percent vote share. In July 2001 the PAC, responding to delays in land distribution and government housing construction, began helping thousands of homeless people occupy a wasteland near Johannesburg. The government quickly evicted them.

Leaders: Mmutlanyane MOGOBA (President), Michael Ngila MUENDANE, Thami ka PLAATJIE (Secretary General).

United Christian Democratic Party (UCDP). The UCDP was founded by Chief Lucas Mangope, former president of the Bophuthatswana homeland. The conservative formation includes in its platform support for the authority of traditional leaders. Despite reports that Mangope considered

merging the UCDP with the newly formed UDM in 1997, it contested the 1999 elections independently, winning three seats in the National Assembly on a .8 percent vote share. In 2004 it retained its three seats.

Leaders: Lucas MANGOPE, Paul DIT-SHETELO (Parliamentary Leader).

Minority Front (MF). The MF represents the rights of Indians in South Africa; it participated without success in the 1994 balloting but won one National Assembly seat in 1999 on a vote share of 0.3 percent. It then formed an alliance with the ANC, giving the latter the 267 votes needed to amend the constitution.

Leaders: Amichand RAJBANSI, Sunklavathy RAJBALLY (Member of the National Assembly).

Other Parties and Groups

New National Party (NNP). The NNP is the name adopted by the National Party (*Nasionale Party*—NP) at a December 1998 congress in an effort to reshape its image from that of the party that had promoted apartheid. A product of a number of splits and mergers extending back to the period before World War II, the NP had come to power under the leadership of Daniel F. MALAN in 1948, and in 1951 it absorbed the Afrikaner Party. Supported by the great majority of Afrikaners and by a growing number of English-speaking South Africans, it became the majority party in 1953. For many years the party's official doctrine stressed rigorous anticommunism and separate development of the nonwhite races, with the Bantu homelands developing into independent states. The so-called *verligte* ("enlightened") faction under former prime minister Balthazar VORSTER sought to reconcile these policies with the promotion of white immigration, solidarity among all white South Africans, and the pursuit of friendly relations with the outside world, including black African states. These ideas were rejected by the opposing *verkrampte* ("unenlightened") faction, which tended to regard the party as a vehicle of specifically Afrikaner nationalism and opposed the inclusion of English-speaking elements in the membership. The dismissal of *verkrampte* leader Dr. Albert Hertzog in the course of a cabinet reorganization in 1968 was generally interpreted as establishing the predominance of the Vorster faction. Hertzog and other conservative elements withdrew in 1969 to form the Refounded National Party (below). Vorster's influence within the party eroded sharply following the eruption of a Watergate-type scandal (see Political background, above) that forced his resignation as state president in mid-1979.

President Pieter BOTHA resigned as party leader at the party's annual caucus on February 2, 1989, with F. W. de KLERK being elected his successor in a contested vote. At the general election of September 6, the NP retained control of the House of Assembly by a substantially reduced majority. Four months earlier, in a parliamentary speech, de Klerk had asserted that although South Africans should anticipate "drastic changes," the NP was committed to "a constitutional dispensation which will not be conducive to majority rule," since such a condition would be "unjust to minorities." On August 31, however, he announced that the party would thenceforth be open to members of all races.

Following the March 1992 referendum on constitutional revision, de Klerk announced that South Africa's whites had "closed the book on apartheid" and reiterated an earlier pledge that the NP would utilize its parliamentary majority to implement decisions that called for admission of all South Africans to the political process. The NP emerged from the election of April 1994 as the second-ranked party, with de Klerk being named second deputy president in the Mandela administration. A feature of the party scene thereafter was an increasing number of defections from the NP to the ANC, including those of some senior figures.

In February 1996 the NP minister of provincial affairs and constitutional development, Roelf Meyer, announced his resignation from the government to assume the new post of NP secretary general. While remaining a member of the National Assembly and taking over the party's parliamentary leadership, Meyer was charged with charting a new future and image for the NP in the post-apartheid era. To that end, de Klerk announced in May 1996 that the NP was withdrawing from the government of national unity in order to form the parliamentary opposition and to redefine itself as a distinctive political force.

Subsequently, the NP was stunned when Meyer resigned from the party in May 1997 and announced the formation of a new grouping (see UDM, above). In June de Klerk reportedly reached agreement with Freedom Front leader Constand Viljoen to increase the level of cooperation between their two groups. However, de Klerk announced his intention to resign from politics in August. The former national president had been the target of withering criticism from the TRC after he had testified in May that he knew nothing about human rights abuses during his years in leadership positions. Following a reportedly bruising intraparty battle between the party's conservative and moderate wings, Marthinus van SCHALKWYK, a relative unknown, was elected party president.

The TRC strongly condemned former president Botha for the violence, including murder and torture, committed by government security forces during his tenure as prime minister (1978–1984) and president (1984–1989). For his part the unrepentant Botha accused the TRC of "witchhunts" and refused to testify, earning a conviction for contempt that was later overturned on technical grounds.

For the June 1999 balloting the NNP reportedly sought an electoral alliance with the IFP or the Democratic Party (DP), but neither overture succeeded. In the national election the party saw its vote share drop to 6.9 percent; as a consequence its National Assembly representation fell to 28 seats, down from 82 in 1994. In the provinces it won enough West Cape Council seats to form a coalition government with the DP.

On June 25, 2000, the DP and NNP announced that they would merge as the Democratic Alliance (DA), with van Schalkwyk becoming the new formation's deputy chair under the DP's Tony Leon. Policy and personal disputes between the two leaders subsequently surfaced, however, and on October 21, 2001, the NNP withdrew from the DA and announced that it was prepared to seek closer ties to the ANC, with which it no longer had prohibitive policy differences. On November 27 the ANC and NNP announced a cooperative pact, the most immediate consequence being formation of a new ANC-NNP administration in Western Cape. Looking further ahead, the NNP leadership anticipated greater participation throughout government, including at the cabinet level.

On August 7, 2004, the NNP asked its members to join the ANC and agreed to fight all future elections under the ANC banner. The decision sounded the death knell for South Africa's second-oldest party, founded in 1914, two years after the formation of the ANC. While the party was not formally disbanding until September 2005, Marthinus van Schalkwyk said that he was applying for ANC membership and advised his colleagues to do likewise. Support for the NNP in 2004 was only 1.7 percent, compared to 20 percent in 1994 and 7 percent in 1999. Most of the hard-core NNP voters have shifted their allegiance to the DA. By mid-2006 defections of its National Assembly members had reduced its parliamentary representation to zero. The party appeared to have some vestigial existence on the national level, but the scope of its activity was unclear.

Alliance for Democracy and Prosperity (ADP). The ADP is a new political party launched by Nelson RAMODIKE, formerly of the United Democratic Movement.

Conservative Party of South Africa (*Konserwatiewe Party van Suid-Afrika*—CPSA). The CPSA was formally launched in March 1982 by a group of right-wing MPs who had been expelled from the NP for opposing the government's proposals for constitutional reform, which, it was argued, would eventually lead to power-sharing with blacks. During its inaugural rally at Pretoria, it was announced that three formations had agreed to merge with the CPSA: the National Conservative Party—NCP (*Nasionale Konserwatiewe Party*); the "Action for Our Future" (*Aksie Eie Toekoms*—AET); and the South Africa First Campaign (SAFC), a relatively obscure English-speaking group.

The NCP had been organized in November 1979 (initially as the Action Group for National Priorities) by Dr. Connie Mulder, who had been ousted as a government minister for his role in the Information Department scandal. The AET had been formed in February 1981 by a number of Afrikaner intellectuals who favored rejection of the constitutional proposals and the establishment of separate homelands for all racial groups. Both the NCP and AET had participated in the 1981 election without securing parliamentary representation and were reported in October to have concluded a separate alliance with the *Kappie Kommando,* an Afrikaner women's group, and the extremist Afrikaner Resistance Movement (AWB, below). Dr. Mulder died in 1988.

The CPSA was runner-up to the NP at the elections of 1987 and 1989. It rejected the Codesa commitment to an "undivided" South Africa, insisting on the right of self-determination, including the possibility of a white homeland. In May 1993 it participated in the formation of the Afrikaner People's Front (*Afrikaner Volksfront*—AVF), founded to oppose majority rule, partly on the initiative of a "Committee of Generals" headed by Gen. (Ret.) Constand Viljoen, who became the AVF convener. The AVF linked over 20 rightist Afrikaner groups, including the AWB as well as the Afrikaner People's Union (*Afrikaner Volksunie*—AVU), chaired by G. KRUGER. The Reconstituted National Party (HNP, below) was originally a member but withdrew after finding the grouping unwieldy. Seeking a commitment to the creation of a white homeland, the AVF in October entered into the Freedom Alliance with conservative black elements, but the somewhat implausible coalition collapsed in March 1994 when Viljoen opted to register his new Freedom Front for the April elections. (In late 1996 the AVF reportedly disbanded with the intention of allowing its constituent organizations to develop individual roles.)

Despite the collapse of the Freedom Alliance, the CPSA boycotted the election of April 1994 and thereafter mounted a campaign for the UN to classify Afrikaners as an oppressed indigenous people. The CPSA did not contest the 1999 election independently but offered support to the AWB. Thereafter the CPSA continued to seek amnesties from the TRC for two members who had been convicted of murdering Communist leader Chris Hani in 1993. In 2003 the party amalgamated with the Freedom Front to form the Freedom Front Plus, but it is still registered with the South African Independent Electoral Commission as a national-level party.

Afrikaner Resistance Movement (*Afrikaanse Weerstands- beweging*—AWB). Founded in 1973, the extreme right-wing AWB became the most visible of the Afrikaner paramilitary formations opposed to majority rule. In June 1993 armed AWB members invaded the Johannesburg building where constitutional talks were in progress, meeting no resistance from the police on duty. Having been convicted and fined in October for electoral violence in 1991, controversial AWB leader Eugene Terre'Blanche in November urged whites to arm themselves for "inevitable" civil war. In March 1994, however, the failure of AWB and other Afrikaner paramilitaries to preserve the Bophuthatswana regime contributed to the collapse of the broad Freedom Alliance of conservative forces. In April 1996 ten AWB members were imprisoned for their part in a bombing campaign aimed at disrupting the 1994 election.

Further arrests of AWB activists were reported in early 1997. Moreover, in June Terre'Blanche was sentenced to prison for six years for allegedly attempting to murder a black laborer. (In March 2001 he lost his most recent appeal and began serving his sentence.) He was released in 2004. He was also condemned by the TRC for his role in the 1993–1994 violence.

Leaders: Eugene TERRE'BLANCHE, Piet "Skiet" RUDOLPH.

New Labour Party (NLP). Peter Maraais quit the NNP in 2003 to create the New Labour Party. Marais was Mayor of Cape Town and premier of the Western Cape.

Leaders: Peter MARAIS, Colin Francois DU SART (Contact).

Refounded National Party (*Herstigte Nasionale Party*—HNP). The HNP is a right-wing Calvinist party organized by Dr. Albert HERTZOG following his dismissal from the government in 1968. The party, which adopted the racist doctrine that blacks are genetically inferior to whites, competed in four subsequent elections without securing parliamentary representation. Dr. Hertzog (son of original National Party founder J. B. M. Hertzog) relinquished the HNP leadership in May 1977. In March 1979 the NP-dominated Parliament, by amendment to a 1978 electoral act, refused to register the HNP as a political party, although it was permitted to contest most constituencies (none successfully) in 1981 by producing 300 signatures in support of each nomination. It secured its first parliamentary seat, previously held by the NP, at a by-election in October 1985 but was unable to retain it in 1987. Although the HNP withdrew from the AVF shortly after its formation in May 1993, it nevertheless joined the AVF in boycotting the April 1994 election.

The HNP's attempts to reach a broader constituency were reportedly hindered in 1997 by its well-publicized conflicts with other Afrikaner groups, most notably the VF. It was reported in 1998 that the HNP was hoping to contest the 1999 balloting, but it did not appear on the final list of approved parties. Longtime leader Jaap MARAIS died in August 2000 and was officially succeeded by Willem Marais at a March 2001 party congress.

Leaders: Willem MARAIS (Chair), L. J. van der SCHYFF (Chief Secretary).

Legislature

Prior to 1981 the South African **Parliament** was a bicameral body consisting of a Senate and a House of Assembly, from which blacks lost their previous limited representation in 1959, with Coloureds also being excluded in 1968. The Senate (consisting largely of members designated by the provincial assemblies) was abolished, effective January 1, 1981, some of its duties being assumed by a newly created President's Council of nominated members. A separate South African Indian

Cabinet

As of July 1, 2006

President	Thabo Mvuyelwa Mbeki
Deputy President	Phumzile Gloria Mlambo-Ngcuka [f]

Ministers

Agriculture and Land Affairs	Lulu Xingwana [f]
Arts and Culture	Pallo Jordan
Communications	Ivy Matsepe-Casaburri [f]
Correctional Services	Ngconde Balfour
Defense	Mosiuoa Lekota
Education	Naledi Pandor [f]
Environment and Tourism	Marthinus van Schalkwyk
Finance	Trevor Manuel
Foreign Affairs	Nkosazana Dlamini Zuma [f]
Health	Mantombazana Tshabalala-Msimang [f]
Home Affairs	Nosiviwe Mapisa-Nqakula
Housing	Lindiwe Nonceba Sisulu [f]
Intelligence	Ronnie Kasrils (SACP)
Justice and Constitutional Affairs	Bridgitte Mabandla [f]
Labor	Membathisi Mdladlana
Minerals and Energy	Buyelwa Patience Sonjica [f]
Presidency	Essop Pahad
Provincial and Local Government	Sydney Mufamadi (SACP)
Public Enterprises	Alec Erwin
Public Service and Administration	Geraldine Fraser-Moleketi [f] (SACP)
Public Works	Angela Thoko Didiza [f]
Safety and Security	Charles Nqakula (SACP)
Science and Technology	Mosibudi Mangena (Azapo)
Social Development	Zola Skweyiya
Sport and Recreation	Makenkesi Stofile
Trade and Industry	Mandisi Mpahlwa
Transport	Jeff Radebe
Water Affairs and Forestry	Benedicta Lindiwe Hendricks [f]

Governor, Reserve Bank	Tito Mboweni

[f] = female

Note: Except as otherwise stated, all ministers are members of the African National Congress. People designated SACP are also members of the ANC.

Council of 15 elected and 15 appointed members was abolished upon adoption of the 1983 constitution.

The 1983 document provided for a tricameral body encompassing a House of Assembly, a continuation of the former lower house; a House of Representatives, representing Coloured voters; and a House of Delegates, representing Indian voters. Each was empowered to legislate in regard to its "own" affairs, while the assent of all was required in regard to "general" affairs.

The interim constitution, which was in effect from April 27, 1994, to February 4, 1997, was the first to be based on the one-man, one-vote principle. It provided for a Senate of indirectly elected members and a directly elected National Assembly, both with five-year mandates. The two bodies sat jointly as the Constituent Assembly that drafted the permanent basic law, which entered into effect on February 4, 1997, and, among other things, replaced the Senate with a National Council of Provinces.

National Council of Provinces. The National Council replaced the Senate on February 6, 1997, at which time 54 permanent members (6 from each of the nine provinces) and 36 special delegates (4 from each province) were inaugurated. Members are elected by each provincial legislature from among its own ranks. Each delegation is headed by the provincial premier.

Delegations are required to reflect the party makeup of the provincial legislatures. As of mid-2006, the breakdown of the 54 permanent representatives was as follows: African National Congress, 38; Democratic Alliance, 10; *Inkatha* Freedom Party, 2; United Christian Democratic Party, 1; Freedom Front Plus, 1; Independent Democrats, 1; United Democratic Movement, 1.

Chair: Mosiuoa LEKOTA.

National Assembly. The lower house contains 400 members, 200 of whom are elected by proportional representation from national party lists and 200 from regional lists. All serve a five-year term. At the election of April 15, 2004, the African National Congress won 279 seats; the Democratic Alliance, 50; the *Inkatha* Freedom Party, 23; the New National Party, 9; the United Democratic Movement, 9; the African Christian Democratic Party, 6; the Freedom Front Plus, 4; the United Christian Democratic Party, 3; the Pan Africanist Congress, 3; the Azanian People's Organization and the Minority Front, 1 each. Since the election many members of the National Assembly have changed party, usually moving to the ANC. As of August 2006 the South African government website shows the African National Congress with 293 seats; the Democratic Alliance, 47; the *Inkatha* Freedom Party, 23; the United Democratic Movement, 6; the Independent Democrats, 5; the African Christian Democratic Party, 4; the Freedom Front Plus, 4; the National Democratic Convention, 4; the United Christian Democratic Party, 3; the Pan Africanist Congress, 3; the Minority Front, 2; the Azanian People's Organization, 1.

Speaker: Baleka MBETE [f].

Communications

Press

Newspapers are published in both Afrikaans and English, the English-language press having by far the larger circulation because its readership among non-whites outweighs the numerical preponderance of Afrikaners in the white population. After years of restrictions and censorship under the white minority government, the 1993 majority-rule constitution guaranteed freedom of expression in the media. All newspapers are owned by conglomerates. One of the more prominent companies is New Africa Media, a black-owned consortium that controls the newspaper with the largest circulation, *The Sowetan*, as well as the large publishing business, Times Media Limited. Print media reaches only 20 percent of the population because of the high rates of illiteracy. The majority of the population receives news through radio and television. The following are English dailies, published at Johannesburg unless otherwise noted: *Sunday Times* (458,000); *Rapport* (350,000, Sunday), in Afrikaans; *The Sowetan*

(225,000), leading African-oriented daily; *The Star* (162,000 weekdays, 130,000 Saturday); *The Citizen* (140,000 weekdays, 110,000 Saturday), tabloid; *City Press* (130,000), African-oriented weekly; *Sunday Tribune* (Greyville, 113,000); *Ilanga* (Durban, 120,000), twice weekly, in Zulu; *Beeld* (110,000), in Afrikaans; *Argus* (Cape Town, 110,000); *Die Burger* (Cape Town, 105,000), in Afrikaans; *Daily News* (Greyville, 80,000); *UmAfrica* (Mariannhill, Natal, 60,000), independent weekly in Zulu and English; *Natal Mercury* (Durban, 40,000); *Die Transvaaler* (40,000), in Afrikaans; *Business Day* (40,000); *Financial Mail* (30,000), weekly; *Mail and Guardian* (30,000), leading independent; *Pretoria News* (Pretoria, 25,000).

News Agencies

Domestic service is provided by the South African Press Association (SAPA), an independent agency cooperatively owned by the country's major newspapers; a number of foreign bureaus maintain offices at Johannesburg or elsewhere.

Broadcasting and Computing

The government-owned South African Broadcasting Corporation (SABC) owns and controls the majority of radio and television outlets. It is managed by black executives and broadcasts news in all the main languages of South Africa. SABC-TV commands 85 percent of the market, and SABC dominates radio with 11 stations. The only commercial station is e.tv, which is received by 75 percent of the population. It is owned by a black-owned consortium. There is some self-censorship as a result of official sensitivity to criticism. Black journalists who criticize the government can be accused of disloyalty, and white journalists of racism. There were approximately 8.0 million television receivers and 3.6 million personal computers serving 3.2 million Internet users in 2003.

Intergovernmental Representation

Ambassador to the US
Barbara MASEKELA

US Ambassador to South Africa
(Vacant)

Permanent Representative to the UN
Dumisani Shadrack KUMALO

IGO Memberships (non-UN)
AfDB, AU, BIS-BIZ, CWTH, Interpol, IOM, IOR-ARC, NAM, PCA, SADC, WCO, WTO

SUDAN

REPUBLIC OF THE SUDAN

Jumhuriyat al-Sudan

The Country

The largest country in Africa, Sudan borders on nine neighboring states as well as the Red Sea and forms part of the transitional zone between the continent's largely desert north and its densely forested, subtropical south. The White Nile flows north for almost 2,500 miles, from the Ugandan border, past the river's union with the Blue Nile near Khartoum, to Egypt above Aswan. Approximately 70 percent of the population is Arab and/or Muslim and occupies the northern two-thirds of the country, while the largely black south is a mix of Christian and animist. The geographic, ethnic, and religious cleavages have yielded political discord marked by prolonged periods of southern rebellion.

The economy is predominantly agricultural, although only a small part of the arable land is actually cultivated. Cotton is the most important cash crop, followed by gum arabic, of which Sudan produces four-fifths of the world supply. Other crops include sesame seeds, peanuts, castor beans, sorghum, wheat, and sugarcane. The country has major livestock-producing potential, and large numbers of camels and sheep are raised for export. At present, industry is largely limited to the processing of agricultural products and the manufacture of light consumer goods.

Sudan was plagued in the 1980s and 1990s by persistent drought, which led to the death by starvation of more than 200,000 people in 1985 and 1988, as well as by fighting in the south, which impeded relief efforts and dislocated large segments of the population. In 1999 it was estimated that as many as 1.5 million Sudanese had died in the previous 16 years as the result of famine and war, while more than 2 million were in danger of starving as a result of the most recent drought. The situation was further exacerbated by a twofold refugee crisis: An estimated 1 million people, fleeing both the southern insurgency and drought conditions, sought refuge in Khartoum or in neighboring countries while, ironically, large numbers of civilians poured into Sudan to escape fighting in adjacent lands.

One result of the economic distress was an external debt of more than $15 billion and excessive reliance on foreign aid, for many years provided largely by the United States, West Germany, Britain, and Saudi Arabia. However, Western

Political Status: Independent republic established
in 1956; revolutionary military regime instituted in
1969; one-party system established in 1971;
constitution of May 8, 1973, suspended following
military coup of April 6, 1985; military regime
reinstituted on June 30, 1989; ruling military
council dissolved and nominal civilian government
reinstated on October 16, 1993; nonparty
presidential and legislative elections held on March
6–17, 1996; new constitution providing for limited
multiparty system signed into law on June 30,
1998; peace agreement signed between the
government of Sudan and the Sudanese People's
Liberation Movement on January 9, 2005,
effectively ending a civil war between the north
and the south; six-year power-sharing period
initiated on July 9, 2005, with the signing of an
interim constitution.

Area: 967,494 sq. mi. (2,505,813 sq. km.).

Population: 24,940,683 (1993C); 35,123,000
(2005E). The 1993 figure does not include an
adjustment for undercounting, while a government
estimate of 40,200,000 for 2005 appears to be too
high.

Major Urban Centers (1993C): KHARTOUM
(947,483), Omdurman (1,271,403), Port Sudan
(308,195), Kassala (234,622).

Official Language: Arabic (English has been
designated the "principal" language in the southern
region).

Monetary Unit: Dinar (market rate July 1, 2006:
217.55 dinars = $1US).

President and Prime Minister: Umar Hassan
Ahmad al-BASHIR (National Islamic Front
[subsequently National Congress]); installed as
chair of the Revolutionary Command Council for
National Salvation (RCC) following overthrow of
the government of Prime Minister Sadiq
al-MAHDI (Umma Party) on June 30, 1989,
succeeding the former chair of the Supreme
Council, Ahmad al-MIRGHANI (Democratic
Unionist Party); assumed title of prime minister
upon formation of government of July 9, 1989;
named president by the RCC on October 16, 1993;
elected to a five-year term as president in nonparty
multicandidate balloting on March 6–17, 1996, and
inaugurated on April 1; formed new government
on April 21, 1996; reelected on December 13–20,
2000, and inaugurated for a second five-year
presidential term on February 13, 2001; formed
new government on February 23, 2001.

First Vice President: Salva KIIR Mayardit (Sudan
People's Liberation Movement); appointed on
August 11, 2005, to succeed John GARANG
(Sudan People's Liberation Movement), who died
in a helicopter crash on July 30.

Second Vice President: Ali Uthman Muhammad
TAHA (National Islamic Front [subsequently
National Congress]); appointed on February 17,
1998, to succeed Maj. Gen. al-Zubayr Muhammad
SALIH, who had died in a plane crash on February
12.

assistance, save for contributions to UN food relief
operations, was cut back sharply in the 1990s amid
concern over Khartoum's alleged human rights
abuses and its failure to pursue democratization.
In addition, responding to what it perceived to be
long-standing government mismanagement of the
economy, the International Monetary Fund (IMF)
in 1990 declared Sudan to be a "noncooperating"
state. Negotiations were resumed in early 1992 after Khartoum agreed to reduce agricultural subsidies, privatize financially untenable government
enterprises (including large cooperative farms),
and institute a series of austerity measures. However, Sudan's voting rights in the IMF were for-

mally suspended in August 1993 because of an accumulation of arrears, and in early 1994 the country
reportedly faced the prospect of becoming the first
member ever to be expelled from the Fund. However, in 1998 the IMF described Sudan as having
made "substantial progress" regarding economic
reform, which had included austerity measures that
had earlier prompted antiregime protests while failing to curb the estimated 100 percent annual rate of
inflation. Moreover, in August 1999 the IMF lifted
its Declaration of Noncooperation from Sudan because of its progress in implementing macroeconomic policies. Economic gains were reflected in
the reported real GDP growth of 6 percent and

inflation of 16 percent for 1999. Government expectations remained high for further economic recovery due to new oil revenue that was expected to reduce the need to borrow. Nevertheless, the civil war continued to drain resources in all regions and to force substantial internal and external dislocations. The situation was made worse by fighting in Darfur in the west, starting in early 2003, with an estimated 113,000 villagers fleeing to Chad by January 2004 and a death toll leading U.S. officials to declare the killing a genocide (see Current issues, below).

By 2005 the economic outlook for Sudan had become more positive, according to the IMF, which projected real GDP growth to be 8 percent that year, owing primarily to higher revenues from oil and other sectors. The IMF cautioned, however, that progress in resolving Sudan's $15 billion debt hinged on resolution of the Darfur crisis and successful implementation of the peace agreement with the Sudanese People's Liberation Movement (SPLM). Encouragingly, in 2006 it was reported that oil production had doubled since 2004 due to new investments by energy firms from India and China.

Government and Politics

Political Background

Historically known as the land of Kush, Sudan was conquered and unified by Egypt in 1820–1821. Under the leadership of Muhammad Ahmad, the MAHDI ("awaited religious leader"), opposition to Egyptian administration broke into open revolt in 1881; the insurrection had succeeded by 1885, and the Mahdist state controlled the region until its reconquest by an Anglo-Egyptian force in 1896–1898. Thereafter, Sudan was governed as an Anglo-Egyptian condominium, becoming self-governing in 1954 and fully independent on January 1, 1956, under a transitional constitution that provided for a democratic parliamentary regime. A civilian government, led successively by Ismail al-AZHARI and Abdallah KHALIL, was overthrown in November 1958 by Lt. Gen. Ibrahim ABBUD, whose mil-

itary regime was itself dislodged following protest demonstrations in October and November 1964. The restored constitutional regime, headed in turn by Sir al-Khatim KHALIFA, Muhammad Ahmad MAHGUB, and Dr. Sadiq al-MAHDI (a descendant of the 19th-century religious leader), was weakened both by political party instability and by revolt in the southern provinces.

Beginning in 1955 as a protest against Arab-Muslim domination, the southern insurgency rapidly assumed the proportions of a civil war. Led by the *Anyanya* (scorpion) movement under the command of Joseph LAGU, the revolt prompted military reprisals and the flight of thousands of refugees to neighboring countries. While moderate southern parties continued to seek regional autonomy within the framework of a united Sudan, exile groups worked for complete independence, and a so-called Provisional Government of Southern Sudan was established in January 1967 under the leadership of Agrev JADEN, a prominent exile leader.

An apparent return to normalcy under a new Mahgub government was interrupted in May 1969 by a military coup organized by a group of nationalist, left-wing officers led by Col. Jafar Muhammad NUMAYRI. With Numayri assuming the leadership of a ten-man Revolutionary Council, a new civilian administration, which included a number of communists and extreme leftists, was formed by former chief justice Abubakr AWADALLA. Revolutionary activity continued, however, including successive communist attempts in 1969 and 1971 to overthrow the Numayri regime. The latter effort succeeded for three days, after which Numayri regained power with Egyptian and Libyan help and instituted reprisals that included the execution of Abd al-Khaliq MAHGUB, the Communist Party's secretary general.

Reorganization of the government continued with the issuance of a temporary constitution in August 1971, followed by Numayri's election to the presidency in September. A month later, in an effort to consolidate his position, Numayri dissolved the Revolutionary Council and established the Sudanese Socialist Union (SSU) as the only recognized political party. Of equal significance was the ratification in April 1973 of a negotiated settlement that temporarily brought the southern rebellion to an end. The terms of the agreement, which provided for an autonomous Southern Sudan, were included in a new national constitution that became effective May 8, 1973. In November the Southern Region voted for a Regional People's Assembly, while the first national election under the new basic law took place in May 1974 for a 250-member National People's Assembly.

In September 1975 rebel army personnel led by a paratroop officer, Lt. Col. Hassan Husayn USMAN, seized the government radio station in Omdurman in an attempted coup. President Numayri subsequently blamed Libya for instigating the uprising, which was quickly suppressed. The attack had been preceded by an army mutiny in Akobo on the Ethiopian border in March and was followed by an uprising in Khartoum in July 1976 that reportedly claimed 300 lives. At a news conference in London on August 4, former prime minister Mahdi, on behalf of the outlawed Sudanese National Front (SNF), a coalition of former centrist and rightist parties that had been organized in late 1969, accepted responsibility for having organized the July rebellion but denied that it had involved foreign mercenaries.

In the months that followed President Numayri undertook a broad-ranged effort to reach accommodation with the dissidents. In July 1977 a number of SNF leaders, including Dr. Mahdi, returned from abroad and were immediately appointed to the Central Committee of the SSU. A year later the Rev. Philip Abbas GHABUSH, titular president of the SNF, expressed his conviction that the government was committed to the building of "a genuine democracy in Sudan" and ordered the dissolution of both the internal and external wings of the Front.

In early 1980 the north was divided into five new regions to provide for more effective local self-government, and in October 1981 the president dissolved both the National Assembly in Khartoum and the Southern Regional Assembly to facilitate decentralization on the basis of new regional bodies to which certain legislative powers would be devolved. Concurrently, he appointed Gen. Gasmallah Abdallah RASSA, a southern Muslim, as interim president of the Southern Region's High Executive Council (HEC) in place of Abel ALIER, who nonetheless continued as second vice president of the Republic. Immediately thereafter a plan was advanced to divide the south into three regions based on the historic provinces of Bahr al-Ghazal, Equatoria, and Upper Nile.

The projected redivision of the south yielded three regional blocs: a "unity" group led by Vice President Alier of the numerically dominant Dinka tribe, who branded the scheme a repudiation of the 1973 agreement; a "divisionist" group led by former rebel commander Joseph Lagu of the Wahdi tribe of eastern Equatoria; and a "compromise" group, led by Clement MBORO and Samuel ARU Bol, which styled itself "Change Two" (C2) after an earlier "Wind for Change Alliance" that had opposed Alier's election to the HEC presidency. None of the three obtained a majority at an April 1982 election to the Southern Regional Assembly, and on June 23 a divisionist, Joseph James TOMBURA, was designated by the assembly as regional president with C2 backing (the alliance being styled "C3"). Six days later President Numayri named General Lagu to succeed Alier as second vice president of the Republic. Earlier, on April 11, Maj. Gen. Umar Muhammad al-TAYYIB (who had been designated third vice president in October 1981) was named to the first vice presidency in succession to Lt. Gen. Abd al-Majid Hamid KHALIL, who had been dismissed on January 25.

As expected, President Numayri was nominated for a third term by an SSU congress in February 1983 and reelected by a national plebiscite held April 15–26. In June the tripartite division of the south was formally implemented, with both the HEC and the southern assembly being abolished.

In the face of renewed rebellion in the south and rapidly deteriorating economic conditions, which prompted food riots and the launching of a general strike in Khartoum, a group of army officers, led by Gen. Abd al-Rahman SIWAR al-DAHAB, seized power on April 6, 1985, while the president was returning from a trip to the United States.

Numayri's ouster was attributed in part to opposition by southerners and some urban northerners to the adoption in September 1983 of Islamic religious law (sharia).

On April 9, 1985, after discussions between the officers and representatives of a civilian National Alliance for the Salvation of the Country (NASC) had proved inconclusive, General Siwar al-Dahab announced the formation of a 14-member Transitional Military Council (TMC), with himself as chair and Gen. Taq al-Din Abdallah FADUL as his deputy. After further consultation with NASC leaders, Dr. al-Gizouli DAFALLAH, who had played a prominent role in organizing the pre-coup demonstrations, was named on April 22 to head an interim Council of Ministers. On May 25 a seven-member southern cabinet was appointed that included representatives of the three historic areas (henceforth to be known as "administrative regions"). Concurrently, the Sudanese People's Liberation Army (SPLA), which had become the primary rebel force in the south under the leadership of Col. John GARANG, resumed antigovernment military activity.

Adhering to its promise to hold a national election within a year, the TMC sponsored legislative balloting on April 1–12, 1986, despite continued insurgency that precluded returns in 41 southern districts. The new body, serving as both a Constituent and Legislative Assembly, convened on April 26 but was unable to agree on the composition of a Supreme (Presidential) Council and the designation of a prime minister until May 6, with a coalition government being formed under former prime minister Mahdi of the Umma Party (UP) on May 15. The UP's principal partner was the Democratic Unionist Party (DUP), which had finished second in the assembly balloting. Although several southern parties were awarded cabinet posts, most "African bloc" deputies subsequently boycotted assembly activity because of alleged underrepresentation and a lack of progress toward sharia repeal.

The Council of Ministers was dissolved on May 13, 1987, primarily because of a split within the DUP that had weakened the government's capacity to implement policy decisions. A new government was nonetheless formed on June 3 with little change in personnel. On August 22 the DUP formally withdrew from the coalition because of a dispute over an appointment to the Supreme Council, although it indicated that it would continue to cooperate with the UP. Eight months later the DUP rejected a proposal by Mahdi for formation of a more broadly based administration that would include the opposition National Islamic Front (NIF). Undaunted, the prime minister resigned on April 16, 1988, to make way for a government of "national reconciliation." Reappointed on April 27, he issued an appeal for all of the parties to join in a proposed national constitutional conference to decide the role of Islam in a future state structure. He formed a new administration that included the DUP and NIF on May 14.

In July 1988 the DUP, reversing an earlier position, joined the fundamentalists in calling for a legislative vote on the introduction of sharia prior to the constitutional conference. On September 19, following the government's introduction of a sharia-based penal code, the southern deputies withdrew from the assembly, and in mid-November, purportedly with the prime minister's approval, DUP representatives met with SPLA leader Garang in the Ethiopian capital of Addis Ababa to negotiate a peace treaty that would entail abandonment of the sharia legislation, the lifting of the state of emergency, and the eventual convening of a national constitutional conference. However, rioting subsequently broke out in Khartoum, and on December 20, in the wake of a reported coup attempt and suspension of parliamentary debate on policy toward the south, Prime Minister Mahdi declared another state of emergency. On December 28 the DUP withdrew from the government in response to Mahdi's failure to recognize the agreement with the SPLA, the DUP ministerial posts being refilled by NIF representatives. On February 27, 1989, after another cabinet reshuffle in which the DUP did not participate, Mahdi threatened to resign if the army did not give him a free hand in working for peace with the rebels. On March 5 some 48 parties and trade unions indicated their general acceptance of the November peace accord, and on March 22 a new governing coalition was announced composed of the UP, the DUP, and representatives of the unions and southern parties, with the NIF in opposition.

In May 1989, while complaining that Khartoum had "done absolutely nothing" to advance the cause of peace, Colonel Garang announced a cease-fire in the south, and a month later he met with northern representatives in Addis Ababa for peace talks mediated by former U.S. president Jimmy Carter. Shortly thereafter, Khartoum agreed to implement the November 1988 accords and schedule a September constitutional conference. However, the plan was nullified on June 30, when the Madhi regime was overthrown in a military coup led by Brig. Gen. Umar Hassan Ahmad al-BASHIR, who assumed the chairship of a Revolution Command Council for National Salvation (RCC). The RCC immediately suspended the constitution, dissolved the Constituent Assembly, imposed emergency rule, and freed military leaders arrested on June 18 for allegedly plotting an earlier coup. Claiming that factionalism and corruption had led to economic malaise and an ineffective war effort, the military regime banned all political parties and arrested senior government and party leaders. On July 9 Bashir assumed the additional office of prime minister, heading a 21-member cabinet composed primarily of career bureaucrats drawn from the NIF and supporters of former president Numayri.

Despite claims that "peace through negotiation" was its first priority, the new government rejected the November 1988 treaty, suggesting instead that the sharia issue be decided by national referendum. However, the SPLA, which sought suspension of sharia while negotiations continued, resumed military activities in October.

A major cabinet reshuffle on April 10, 1990, was construed as a consolidation of Islamic fundamentalist influence, and on April 24 a total of 31 army and police officers were executed in the wake of an alleged coup attempt the day before. Another reshuffle in January 1991 was followed by the introduction of a nine-state federal system (see Constitution and government, below), and on

March 22 a new sharia-based penal code was instituted in the six northern states, prompting a strong protest from the SPLA.

In the wake of heavy fighting between his supporters and several SPLA breakaway factions in the south, Garang announced a unilateral cease-fire in late March 1993 as far as the conflict with government troops was concerned. Khartoum endorsed the cease-fire several days later, and a new round of peace talks with Garang representatives resumed in Abuja in late April. The government also initiated parallel negotiations in Nairobi, Kenya, with the SPLA dissidents, who had recently coalesced as the SPLA-United. However, both sets of talks were subsequently suspended, with fighting between government forces and Garang's SPLA faction having resumed near the Ugandan border by midyear.

On July 8, 1993, Prime Minister Bashir announced a cabinet reshuffle that was most noteworthy for what was described as an "overt increase in NIF involvement." Subsequently, in a surprise, albeit essentially cosmetic, return to civilian control, the RCC dissolved itself on October 16 after declaring Bashir president and granting him wide authority to direct a transitional government. Shortly thereafter, Bashir announced his administration's commitment to a largely undefined democratization program that would lead to national elections by the end of 1995. Nevertheless, the new cabinet announced on October 30 appeared to solidify NIF control even further, lending support to opposition charges that the military-fundamentalist alliance had no true intention of loosening its stranglehold on political power.

Following a September 1993 summit of the regional Inter-Governmental Authority on Drought and Development (IGADD, later the Inter-Governmental Authority on Development—IGAD), a quadripartite committee of representatives from Ethiopia, Eritrea, Kenya, and Uganda was established to mediate the Sudanese conflict. However, the talks ended in deadlock in late 1994 after the two sides had "adopted irreconcilable positions on southern self-determination and the relationship between state and religion."

On March 27, 1995, Bashir announced a unilateral two-month cease-fire to facilitate another peace initiative launched by former U.S. president Jimmy Carter. While the truce was cautiously supported by the leading southern factions, no progress was reported in resolving the conflict, despite a two-month extension of the cease-fire on May 25.

Indicative of what some construed as a weakening northern regime, widespread rioting broke out in several locations, including Khartoum and Port Sudan, in September 1995. The outbreaks, which appeared to be spontaneous, involved both student protesters and conservative elements angered by low salaries and food shortages. Further violence erupted in Khartoum in early January 1996 between police and Muslim fundamentalists calling for conversion of the country's Christians and animists to Islam.

In January 1996 the regime announced that elections would be conducted in March for president and a new National Assembly. However, that balloting (conducted March 6–17) was boycotted by nearly all the major opposition groups, most of whom had coalesced under the banner of the National Democratic Alliance (NDA). Some 40 independent candidates contested the presidential balloting, with Bashir being elected to a five-year term on the strength of a reported 75.7 percent share of the vote. Bashir was sworn in on April 1, and on the same day the new assembly convened and unanimously elected the NIF's Hassan Abdallah al-TURABI (long considered the dominant political leader in the country) as its president. On April 21 Bashir appointed a new cabinet, which did not include (despite previous speculation to the contrary) any members of the SPLA-United or the Southern Sudan Independence Movement (SSIM), the two southern groups with which the government had recently signed a peace accord.

In January 1997 a major rebel offensive was reportedly launched under the leadership of a more cohesive and potent NDA. In April the regime reached another agreement with the SSIM, the SPLA-United, and four other SPLA breakaway groups, calling for suspension of sharia in the south and further discussions regarding autonomy there.

Subsequently, with both the government and the SPLA having claimed military success, a preliminary agreement was reached in July on the resumption of peace talks under a "framework of principles" proposed by IGAD, which envisioned an eventual self-determination plebiscite in the south. However, negotiations, formally opened in October, were quickly suspended until April 1998, and fighting continued.

Elections were held for ten southern gubernatorial posts in November 1997, and on December 1 the SSIM's Riak MACHAR was named head of a new Southern States' Coordination Council (SSCC) and given a four-year mandate to govern the south pending a decision on its permanent political status. However, the exercise was widely viewed as futile, if not surreal, considering Colonel Garang's depiction of the SSCC as a "sham."

A plane crash on February 12, 1998, killed First Vice President Maj. Gen. al-Zubayr Muhammad SALIH (one of the president's oldest and most trusted associates) and a number of other government officials. On March 8 Bashir finally settled on Ali Uthman Muhammad TAHA, considered second in authority in the NIF, to succeed Salih. In addition, the NIF had an enhanced presence in the extensively reshuffled cabinet, which also included dissident Umma members and representatives of the southern rebels who had aligned with Khartoum.

In the face of heavy international pressure for political reform, the assembly, on March 28, 1998, approved the government's proposed new constitution, which, among other things, authorized the legalization of "political associations." The new basic law was endorsed by a reported 96.7 percent "yes" vote in a national referendum in late May and signed into law by President Bashir on June 30, the ninth anniversary of the coup that had brought him to power. On November 23 the assembly approved the Political Association Act, which established the laws governing party activity, and registration of parties began in January 1999.

In the wake of rapidly escalating conflict between Bashir and Turabi, Turabi proposed a series of constitutional amendments in November 1999 to curb Bashir's power. Bashir responded by announcing a three-month state of emergency and dissolving the National Assembly on December 12, 1999 (effective December 13). Bashir's declaration occurred a mere 48 hours prior to the scheduled National Assembly vote regarding Turabi's proposed amendments. On the heels of these events, the cabinet formally issued its resignation on January 1, 2000. Bashir appointed a new cabinet on January 25, retaining his backers in some ministry posts. The power struggle continued, however, because Turabi, although he held no official position, remained secretary general of the National Congress (NC), the successor to the NIF. Meanwhile, the government also was buffeted in February by the departure of Machar and a number of his supporters from the government because of the perceived failure of Bashir to implement the 1997 accord.

On March 12, 2000, the cabinet extended the state of emergency until the end of the year. Bashir further consolidated power by removing Turabi as secretary general of the NC and replacing him with Ibrahim Ahmed OMAR.

Despite seemingly positive negotiations between the government and the UP (see UP under Political Parties and Groups, below), the UP led an opposition boycott of assembly and presidential elections on December 13–23, 2000. Consequently, the NC secured 355 of the 360 contested assembly seats, while Bashir was elected to a second five-year term with a reported 86.5 percent of the vote. (After returning from 14 years in exile in May 1999, former president Numayri, as the candidate of the Popular Working Forces Alliance, finished second with 9.6 percent of the vote in the presidential poll.) DUP dissidents were included in the new cabinet named on February 23, 2001, as were UP dissidents in the reshuffle of August 19, 2002. Two DUP dissidents were also among those named to the cabinet in a reshuffle on November 30, 2002.

Following the signing of the peace agreement in January 2005 between the government and the SPLM (see Current issues, below), a new 30-member power-sharing cabinet was announced on September 22, 2005. Fifteen posts went to the NC, 9 to the SPLM, and 6 to northern and southern opposition groups. On October 21, the first cabinet of the Government of South Sudan was appointed. The 22-member southern unity cabinet included 16 seats designated for the SPLM, 3 for the NC, and 3 for other south Sudan opposition groups.

Constitution and Government

The 1973 constitution provided for a strong presidential form of government. Nominated by the Sudanese Socialist Union for a six-year term, the president appointed all other executive officials and served as supreme commander of the People's Armed Forces. Legislative authority was vested in the National People's Assembly, a unicameral body that was partially elected and partially appointed.

The Southern Sudan Regional Constitution, abrogated by the June 1983 redivision, provided for a single autonomous region governed, in nonreserved areas, by the president of a High Executive Council (cabinet) responsible to a Regional People's Assembly. Each of the three subsequent regions in the south, like the five in the north, was administered by a centrally appointed governor, acting on the advice of a local People's Assembly. In a move that intensified southern dissent, President Numayri announced in June 1984 the incorporation into the north of a new province (*Wahdah*), encompassing territory theretofore part of the Upper Nile region, where oil reserves had been discovered.

Upon assuming power in 1985, the Transitional Military Committee (TMC) suspended the 1973 basic law, dissolved the central and regional assemblies, appointed a cabinet composed largely of civilians, and assigned military personnel to replace regional governors and their ministers. An interim constitution was approved by the TMC in October 1985 to provide a framework for assembly elections. The assembly members chosen in April 1986 were mandated to draft a new basic law, although many southern districts were unrepresented because of rebel activity. The assembly's charge to act as a constituent body appeared to have ceased with Prime Minister Mahdi's call in April 1988 for the convening of a national constitutional conference.

In January 1987 the government announced the formation of a new Administrative Council for the South, comprising representatives of six southern political parties and the governors of each of the three previously established regions. The Council, although formally empowered with only "transitional" authority, was repudiated by both the "unity" and "divisionist" groups. Subsequently, following the signing of a pro-pluralism "Transitional Charter" on January 10, 1988, to serve as an interim basic law, the Council was suspended, and the administration of the southern provinces was assigned to the regional governors.

During negotiations between the Mahdi regime and southern rebels in early June 1989, an agreement was reached to open a constitutional conference in September. However, the Bashir junta rejected the June agreement and suspended the Transitional Charter. Subsequently, a national "political orientation" conference, held April 29–May 2, 1991, in Khartoum, endorsed the establishment of a pyramidal governmental structure involving the direct popular election of local councils followed by the successive indirect election of provincial, state, and national lawmaking bodies. On February 13, 1992, Prime Minister Bashir appointed a 300-member Transitional National Assembly, and he was named president on October 16, 1993, by the RCC, which then dissolved itself. Elections were held on March 6–17, 1996, to a new National Assembly, with concurrent nonparty balloting for president.

On February 5, 1991, the RCC announced the establishment of a new federal system comprising nine states—six (Central, Darfur, Eastern, Khartoum, Kordofan, and Northern) in the north and three (Bahr al-Ghazal, Equatoria, and Upper Nile) in the south that were subdivided into 66 provinces and 281 local government districts. The states, each administered by a federally appointed governor, deputy governor, and cabinet of ministers, were given responsibility for local administration and some tax collection, although control over most major sectors remained with the central govern-

ment. In early February 1994 President Bashir announced that the number of states had been increased from 9 to 26, new governors being appointed later in the month. A Southern States Coordination Council was named in December 1997 to govern the south pending final determination of the region's status, but the authority of the new body remained severely compromised by the opposition of the main rebel group, the SPLA.

On March 22, 1991, a new penal code based on sharia went into effect in the north, the government announcing that the issue would be "open" in regard to the south, pending the outcome of peace negotiations.

The new constitution, which went into effect on June 30, 1998, annulled most previous decrees by the Bashir regime, thereby permitting the reintroduction of a multiparty system. The new basic law described Islam as "the religion of the majority," although it notes the "considerable number of Christians and animists" in the country and guarantees freedom of religion. The controversial issue of sharia, particularly as it might apply to the south, was skirted, the constitution stating only that the "religion, customs, and consensus of the Nation shall be the sources of legislation."

Following the peace agreement reached on January 9, 2005, between the government and the SPLM, an interim constitution was signed on July 9, 2005, allowing for power sharing during a six-year transitional period. Whether the south would continue under Khartoum's rule was to be determined by a referendum in 2011. The south was given a large degree of autonomy, with Garang being named president of the south, as well as first vice president of Sudan. (Salva KIIR Mayardit replaced Garang as president of the south and first vice president of Sudan on August 11, 2005, following the latter's death on July 30.)

Foreign Relations

During much of the Cold War Sudan pursued a policy of nonalignment, modified in practice by changing international circumstances, while focusing its attention on regional matters. Prior to the

1974 coup in Ethiopia relations with that country were especially cordial because of the prominent role Haile Selassie had played in bringing about a settlement of the initial southern rebellion. Subsequently, Addis Ababa accused Khartoum of providing covert support to Eritrean rebels, while Sudanese leaders charged that SPLA camps were flourishing in Ethiopia with the approval of the Mengistu regime. Not surprisingly, relations between the two countries improved dramatically following the May 1991 rebel victory in Ethiopia; the presumed SPLA contingents subsequently were forced back into Sudan by Ethiopian troops and the Bashir regime became a vocal supporter of the new leadership in Addis Ababa. By contrast, the secular administration in Asmara charged in early 1994 that Sudan was fomenting fundamentalist antigovernment activity in the new nation of Eritrea, and in December it severed relations with Khartoum.

Soon after taking power in 1969 Prime Minister Numayri forged close ties with Egyptian President Nasser within a federation scheme encompassing Sudan, Egypt, and the newly established Libyan regime of Colonel Qadhafi. Although failing to promote integration, the federation yielded joint Egyptian-Libyan military support for Numayri in defeating the communist insurgency of June 1971. However, Numayri was reluctant to join a second unity scheme—the abortive 1972 Federation of Arab Republics—because of Libyan-inspired conspiracies and opposition from the non-Arab peoples of southern Sudan. President Sadat's own estrangement from Qadhafi during 1973 led to the signing of a Sudanese-Egyptian agreement on political and economic coordination in February 1974. In subsequent years Sadat pledged to support Numayri against continued Libyan attempts at subversion, and Sudan followed Egypt into close alignment with the United States. While rejecting the Egyptian-Israeli peace treaty of 1979, Sudan was one of the few Arab states that did not break diplomatically with Cairo.

Libya, which announced that it would terminate its support of the SPLA rebels, was the first country to recognize the post-Numayri regime, urging the TMC to sever Sudanese links with Egypt. Close military and economic ties were thereupon reestablished with Tripoli, relations with Cairo remaining cool, in part, because of Egyptian President Mubarak's refusal to extradite Numayri for trial by the new Khartoum government.

In October 1988 Prime Minister Mahdi, reportedly desperate for arms, signed a unity proposal with Colonel Qadhafi, which was immediately denounced by the DUP and in January 1989 labeled "inappropriate" by the United States following reports that Libyan forces had used chemical weapons in attacks on SPLA forces. Concurrently, Washington, whose nonintervention policy had drawn increasing criticism from international aid groups, announced its intention to supply aid directly to drought victims in areas under SPLA control rather than through allegedly corrupt government channels. Four months later Washington cut off all nonfamine relief support because of Khartoum's failure to service its foreign debt. The ban was reaffirmed (with specific reference to economic and military aid) in March 1990 because of Khartoum's human rights record and lack of democratic commitment. Later in the year relations with the United States deteriorated even further when Sudan refused to join the UN anti-Iraq coalition, a decision that also cost the Bashir government financial support from Saudi Arabia and Egypt. In addition, many Arab states subsequently expressed concern over the growing influence of Islamic fundamentalism within the Bashir regime. On the other hand, Iran, anxious to support the fundamentalist cause, became a major source of Sudanese economic and, according to some reports, military aid.

In August 1994 authorities in Khartoum seized the long-sought international terrorist Ilich Ramírez Sanchez (a.k.a. "Carlos"), who was flown to Paris for trial on charges stemming from a 1983 attack in the French capital. In return, France was reported to have exercised its influence with the Central African Republic (CAR) to provide Sudanese military transit through CAR territory to the south Sudanese combat zone. In addition, Khartoum appeared to seek French assistance in restoring its relations with the United States in the wake of disappointment with the level of aid forthcoming from its alliance with Iran.

Meanwhile, relations with other neighboring states had deteriorated sharply. In September 1994 Egypt was accused of moving troops into Sudan's northern Halaib region, which was believed to contain substantial oil deposits, and relations plummeted further in mid-1995 after President Mubarak had intimated that the NIF might have been involved in the failed attempt on his life in Addis Ababa on June 26. In the south, Uganda canceled a 1990 agreement providing for a military monitoring team on its side of their border, and in April 1995 it broke relations because of the alleged bombing of a Ugandan village by Sudanese government forces; however, relations were restored in mid-June as the result of talks between presidents Bashir and Museveni that were brokered by Malawian president Bakili Muluzi.

By late 1995 Sudan had come under widespread criticism for its alleged sponsorship of international terrorism, including possible involvement in the Mubarak assassination attempt. On December 19 a group of Organization of African Unity (OAU, subsequently the African Union—AU) foreign ministers, meeting in Addis Ababa, called on Khartoum to extradite three Egyptians wanted for questioning in the Mubarak affair, and on January 31, 1996, the UN Security Council adopted a unanimous resolution to the same effect. Earlier, as an expression of its displeasure, Ethiopia had ordered a reduction in Sudan's embassy staff to four, the closure of a Sudanese consulate, and the banning of all nongovernmental organizations linked to the Sudanese regime.

In 1997 and early 1998, Eritrea, Ethiopia, and Uganda cooperated to constrain the spread of militant fundamentalism in the Horn of Africa, further straining relations with Sudan, which accused the other governments of supporting the SPLM and NDA. (Relations with Ethiopia subsequently improved, however, in conjunction with the outbreak of hostilities between that nation and Eritrea, which Khartoum charged was still backing Sudanese rebels.) Meanwhile, South African President Nelson Mandela played a prominent role in efforts to bring the Bashir regime and its opponents together for peace talks under the aegis of IGAD.

An improvement in regional and international relations was noted in 1999 and 2000 due, in large part, to a "charm offensive" on Bashir's part. Sudan reestablished diplomatic relations with the United Kingdom, Kuwait, Ethiopia, Eritrea, Egypt, and Tunisia. In addition, in December 1999 Sudan and Uganda signed an accord agreeing not to support rebel forces working to overthrow each other's respective governments. Sudan later requested that the UN Security Council lift sanctions imposed in 1996 following accusation of its involvement in the attempted assassination of Mubarak. The Security Council unanimously approved the request in September 2001.

Throughout 2004 and early 2005, the international response to the staggering human rights abuses in Darfur was slow to materialize (see Current issues, below). In April 2005 the UN Security Council voted to refer 51 Sudanese—many of them said to be high-ranking NIF officials—for prosecution in connection with crimes against humanity in Darfur. That same month, Western countries pledged $4.5 billion in urgent food aid for southerners displaced by the civil war.

In response to continuing attacks on Uganda by the Lords Resistance Army (LRA) from bases in Sudan, the newly installed Government of South Sudan signed a security protocol with Uganda in October 2005 calling for joint efforts to suppress the LRA. Reports indicated that the increased security collaboration led many members of the LRA to flee to the Democratic Republic of the Congo. Meanwhile, relations with Chad worsened in 2005 as Chadian rebels launched a series of attacks from bases in Sudan. By December 2005 Chadian President Idriss Déby described the two countries as being in a state of "belligerency" (see entry on Chad).

Current Issues

Running counter to the liberalization taking place throughout much of Africa, the Bashir regime and its fundamentalist supporters were charged with widespread abuse (including torture and execution) of political opponents in the 1990s, in addition to mistreatment of non-Muslim ethnic groups. The resultant curtailment of Western support exacerbated the country's long-standing economic crisis, and observers periodically questioned the government's capacity to survive. However, due in part to the weakness of opposition political forces, the administration proved more resilient than anticipated.

In November 1997 Washington denounced the Bashir government's poor human rights record and alleged support for international terrorism and imposed economic sanctions against Sudan that included a ban on Sudanese exports and seizure of Sudanese assets in the United States. In addition, U.S. Secretary of State Madeleine Albright met with Colonel Garang and other NDA leaders in Uganda. The friction between the United States and Sudan subsequently intensified, and on August 20, 1998, U.S. missiles destroyed a pharmaceutical plant in Khartoum, in response to the bomb attacks on the U.S. embassies in Kenya and Tanzania on August 7. Washington claimed the Sudanese facility was producing chemicals used to make nerve gas and that it was connected to the "terrorist network" of militant Islamic fundamentalist Osama bin Laden. However, no evidence supporting the U.S. charges was forthcoming, and many observers ultimately concluded that Washington had erred regarding the possible connection of the plant to nerve gas production. For its part, the government in Khartoum, which had expelled bin Laden from the country in 1996 under U.S. pressure, strongly denied the U.S. accusations and branded U.S. President Clinton a "war criminal." Ironically, the episode generated a degree of sympathy on the international stage for Sudan, whose image also was improved by its new constitution and the return (notionally at least) of multipartyism in early 1999. At the same time, however, the conflict in the south remained generally as intractable as ever; of particular interest to both sides were the oil-rich regions of the Upper Nile and the Nuba mountains.

Apparently as part of an overall effort to enhance his regime's image, President Bashir announced an amnesty for his opponents in June 2000. The SPLM, NDA, and most other opposition groups remained skeptical of the offer, however, and the political climate deteriorated when the state of emergency was again extended in January 2001 and former NIF strongman Turabi and several of his associates were arrested in February after Turabi's Popular National Congress (PNC) had signed an accord with the SPLA to "resist" the government. (Most of the PNC members were released by presidential order in October, but Turabi remained under house arrest until October 2003. He was rearrested on March 31, 2004, along with ten military officers and seven PNC members for what government officials said was a plot to stage a coup. Some reports claimed that those arrested had links to rebels in the western province of Darfur [see below]. Turabi was released on June 30, 2005, when Bashir announced the release of all political detainees.)

Following the al-Qaida attacks in the United States in September 2001, the Sudanese government came under additional international scrutiny. One apparent outgrowth of that increased attention was significant progress toward resolution of the southern conflict, which had led to the death of more than 1 million people (as casualties of either the fighting or related food shortages) and the dislocation of 4 million more. A tentative cease-fire was negotiated under U.S. mediation in January 2002, and although there was sporadic fighting in the first half of the year, with the NIF reportedly bombing civilians, a potentially historic accord was signed in Kenya on July 20 by representatives of the government and the SPLM. The agreement, mediated by the IGAD, envisioned the establishment of a joint, six-year transitional administration for the south to be followed by a self-determination referendum in the region. The government also reportedly agreed that sharia would not be imposed in the south. The two sides signed a Comprehensive Peace Agreement on January 9, 2005, in Nairobi, bringing to an end the 21-year war in the south and, ironically, making former enemies Garang and Bashir partners in a new government.

The agreement called for national elections within four years and a referendum on independence for the south to be held in six years. It also stipulated the sharing of power and a 50–50 split of oil profits between the north and the south. In addition, it called for a six-month "pre-interim" period to draft a new constitution; a transitional government in Khartoum under Bashir; a separate administration in the south headed by a first vice president; a national assembly to be appointed within two weeks of the drafting of the interim constitution, with members divided roughly 70–30 north-south, with full legislative authority by 2011; and shared governance by the NC and SPLM of Kordofan and Blue Nile. The SPLM was authorized to keep its army in the south but agreed to withdraw from the east, while the regime agreed to withdraw its troops from the south in two and a half years.

Meanwhile, despite the far-reaching agreement between north and south, another huge and bloody struggle in the western region of Darfur continued unabated. The war, which erupted in February 2003, had been preceded by tribal clashes for years. Escalation occurred when the Darfur Liberation Front claimed in February 2003 to have seized control of Gulu, and government forces were sent to retake the village in early March. The conflict, fueled by the scarcity of water and grazing land, became an increasingly fierce rivalry between Arab tribesmen who raised cattle and needed the land and black African farmers who relied on the water. The fighting intensified in 2004, as black Africans accused the government in Khartoum of using the mounted, Arab *Janjaweed* militias, sometimes accompanied by fighters in Sudanese military uniforms, to force people from their land.

The government in Khartoum steadfastly refused to apply self-rule to the west, as it had in its agreement with the south. While some 113,000 refugees fled across the border into Chad, fighting continued to intensify, and the U.S. administration of George W. Bush called on the parties to negotiate. The insurgent groups—the Sudan Liberation Movement/Army (SLM/A) and the Justice and Equality Movement (JEM)—claimed that the government had neglected the impoverished areas for years. The UN High Commissioner for Refugees decried the "scorched-earth" tactics used by the

government and militias in response to the rebellion in Darfur and appealed for serious efforts to resolve the conflict.

In May 2004 the *New York Times* reported that an estimated 1 million people had been uprooted by the conflict in Darfur. That same month, human rights workers charged that the government had used the *Janjaweed* to implement a policy resembling ethnic cleansing. Peace talks began in mid-July, as demanded by U.S. Secretary of State Colin Powell, but soon dissolved when Khartoum rejected the rebels' conditions, including a time frame for disarming the militias. After the threat of punitive measures in short of sanctions by the UN Security Council on July 29, 2004, and a reported protest by 100,000 people in Khartoum against a Security Council resolution, the rebel groups and the government agreed to meet in Nigeria for peace talks in late August. As talks broke down days later and the UN pressed for more monitoring, Powell declared, on September 10, that the United States considered the killing, rape, and destruction in Darfur to be genocide. On behalf of the United States, the secretary asked for urgent action by the Security Council.

On November 9, 2004, the government agreed to ban military flights over Darfur and signed two deals with the rebels after two weeks of talks in Nigeria. However, no agreement was reached on a long-term resolution to the fighting, and violence resumed within weeks. With Washington still pressing the UN for action, on March 23, 2005, the Security Council unanimously approved a resolution calling for 10,000 peacekeepers for Darfur and southern Sudan. However, resistance from the Sudanese government to a UN mission led to the repeated continuation of the AU Mission in Sudan. Another round of peace talks between the two rebel groups and the government was scheduled for later in the year. Rwanda and Nigeria were among the countries that began to send peacekeeping forces into Darfur in July 2005. In May 2005, NATO agreed to assist the AU-led mission in Darfur with transport and other logistical aid. The AU force eventually numbered some 7,000. By September 2005, estimates of those killed in the conflict ranged from 70,000 to 300,000, and 2–3 million people were believed to have been displaced.

On another unsettling front, a tense military situation in eastern Sudan in the states of Kassala and the Red Sea Hills began to escalate in 2005. The Beja people of the east had also long complained about the government ignoring them. Fighting continued through mid-2005 between government and rebel groups, which combined in February as the Eastern Sudan Front (see Political Parties and Groups, below).

On July 10, 2005, Bashir ended the national state of emergency in all but three of Sudan's provinces: Darfur, Kasala, and Red Sea Hills. Bashir also ordered the release of hundreds of political prisoners, including Turabi. The SLM/A subsequently launched a new offensive in Darfur, and the AU initiated a new round of peace talks between the government and the SLM/A and the JEM in Abuja, Nigeria. The AU developed a comprehensive peace plan, which the Sudanese government accepted on April 30, 2006. The plan called for the disarmament of the *Janjaweed* militias, elections within three years, and the provision of $500 million for the establishment and operation of an autonomous regional authority. One faction of the SLM/A signed the agreement, but another major SLM/A faction and the JEM refused to sign. Meanwhile, Sudan rejected a proposal from UN Secretary General Kofi Annan in April 2006 to replace the AU mission with a more expansive UN-led operation that would have included European and, possibly, U.S. forces.

Political Parties and Groups

Following the 1969 coup, all political parties, except the Sudanese Communist Party (SCP), were outlawed. After the failure of the SCP coup in July 1971, it also was driven underground, and many of its leaders were arrested. The following October President Numayri attempted to supplant the existing parties by launching the Sudanese Socialist Union, modeled after the Arab Socialist Union of Egypt, which remained the country's only recognized political group until its suspension by the

TMC in April 1985. More than 40 parties were reported to have participated in the post-Numayri balloting of April 1986, although only the Umma Party (UP), Democratic Unionist Party (DUP), and National Islamic Front (NIF) obtained substantial legislative representation.

In July 1989 the newly installed military regime imposed a new ban on political groups and arrested numerous party leaders. Although most of the detainees were eventually released, the ban continued, with Bashir announcing in late 1990 that the regime had no intention of reestablishing a multiparty system.

In response to the NIF's assumption of substantial, albeit unofficial, political power, a number of the other parties (including the DUP, UP, and SCP), the SPLM, trade union and university organizations, and some disaffected military leaders) formed a loose antigovernment coalition known as the **National Democratic Alliance** (NDA). An NDA Summit, held in London, England, on January 26–February 3, 1992, called for the establishment of a transitional government in Sudan pending the formulation of a new constitution that would create a multiparty democracy, ensure human rights, and preserve the nation's religious and ethnic "diversity." A second NDA summit in London in February 1994 demonstrated, according to *Middle East International,* that the Alliance "exists only on paper," as no consensus was reached on the pivotal questions of proposed self-determination for the south and the role of sharia in the state envisioned by the NDA. By contrast, a third summit in Asmara, Eritrea, on June 15–23, 1995, yielded agreement that, if and when the opposition gained power, "religion should be separate from politics," and that a referendum should be held in the south on its secession from the republic. The NDA called for a boycott of the March 1996 presidential and general elections, describing them as a "farce." In June the Alliance charged the Bashir regime with having imposed "religious fanaticism" on Sudan and having established a "politically backward" system of government. A joint NDA military command was established in October under the direction of the SPLM's Col. John Garang.

The NDA suffered a blow in March 2000 when the UP withdrew from the Alliance in the wake of a preliminary agreement between Bashir and UP leader Sadiq al-Mahdi (see UP, below, for additional information). It also was suggested that Mahdi may have been distressed by the authority being exercised by DUP leader and NDA Chair Usman al-Mirghani as well as the military dominance of the SPLM within the Alliance. For its part, the NDA subsequently continued to insist that Bashir step down in favor of a government of national reconciliation. In May 2001 the UP declined an invitation to rejoin the NDA, although Mahdi and Mirghani subsequently met in an effort to assist in devising a comprehensive peace plan. Although both the UP and DUP tentatively endorsed the proposed accords between Khartoum and the SPLM in 2002, the NDA was not officially included in those negotiations. In January 2005, the government reached an agreement in Cairo with the NDA that would reintegrate it into politics.

The new constitution signed into law in June 1998 authorized the formation of political "associations," and the government began to register parties in January 1999 under guidelines provided by the Political Association Act approved by the assembly in November 1998. Wide latitude was given to a government-appointed registrar of political associations to rule on applications; among other things, groups could be denied legal status if their activity was deemed incompatible with the country's "cultural course," an apparent reference to the government's Islamization campaign. The March 2000 Political Organizations Act for the Year 2000 amended the 1998 act to allow the formation of parties opposed to the government; however, it maintained government power to close down any party. In addition, parties not registered, while permitted to operate freely, were precluded from participating in elections until registered. Subsequently, in August 2002, President Bashir called for a lifting of the ban on parties that had been represented in the legislature at the time of his assumption of power.

National Congress   (NC). The NC is a partial successor to the National Islamic Front (*al-Jabhah*

al-Watani al-Islami—NIF), which was organized prior to the April 1986 balloting by the leader of the fundamentalist Muslim Brotherhood, Dr. Hassan Abdallah al-Turabi, who as attorney general had been largely responsible for the harsh enforcement of sharia law under the Numayri government. The NIF displayed unexpected strength by winning 51 legislative seats but refused to enter the government until May 1988 because of the UP commitment to revise the sharia system, which the NIF had long wished to strengthen rather than weaken. The NIF gained a number of ministerial seats vacated by the DUP in December 1988 but withdrew from the coalition upon the latter's return in March 1989. Although Turabi was arrested in July 1989, along with the leaders of many other parties, he was released in December and soon became one of the new regime's most influential supporters. As it became more and more identified with fundamentalism, the Bashir government appointed numerous NIF adherents to key government posts, most observers agreeing that the Front had become a de facto government party. NIF/Muslim Brotherhood supporters also were reported to be directing the Islamic "security groups," which had assumed growing authority since 1990, particularly in dealing with government opponents.

Turabi, one of the world's leading Islamic fundamentalist theoreticians, was subsequently routinely described as the country's most powerful political figure. A follower of Iran's late Ayatollah Khomeini, he called for the creation of Islamic regimes in all Arab nations, a position that caused concern in several nearby states (particularly Egypt) as well as in major Western capitals. The NIF's "number two," Ali Uthman Muhammad Taha, was named foreign minister in February 1995 and first vice president in early 1998.

It was reported in 1996 that Turabi had directed that the NIF be renamed the National Congress (NC), apparently to reflect a proposed broadening of its scope to serve as an umbrella political organization open to all citizens and to act as a quasi-institutional governing body. Subsequent news reports appeared to use the two names interchangeably, with the NIF rubric predominating. In January

1999 it was announced that a National Congress had been officially registered as a political party, while reports in March indicated similar status had been accorded to a National Islamic Front Party. It was not immediately clear what relationship, if any, the two groupings had to each other or the traditional NIF. Meanwhile, reports (officially denied) surfaced of friction between Turabi and party reformists as well between Turabi and Sudanese President Bashir, who was named chair of the recently established NIF advisory council. Tensions between Turabi and Bashir resulted in the removal of Turabi as general secretary in May. Turabi subsequently formed a new party, the Popular National Congress (PNC, below), and Bashir's supporters formally used the NC rubric in the December 2000 elections.

Leaders: Umar Hassan Ahmad al-BASHIR (President of the Republic and Chair of the Party's *Shura* Council), Ibrahim Ahmed OMAR (Secretary General), Ahmad Abder RAHMAN, Ali Uthman Muhammad TAHA (First Vice President of the Republic), Ali al-Haj MUHAMMAD, Muhammad Ahmad SALIM (Registrar of Political Associations).

Popular (People's) National Congress (PNC). The PNC is an Islamic fundamentalist organization that was formed by the Turabi faction of the NIF/NC. Turabi had earlier accused President Bashir of betraying the NC's Islamist tenets. Thus, Turabi claimed he was merely adding "Popular" to the original party's name and expelling members who had produced the crisis. Nevertheless, the PNC officially registered as a district party in July 2000. Turabi described the PNC as a "comprehensive *shura* organization," which indicated it would be outside the government. The PNC has few policy differences with the NC.

Turabi and several of his PNC supporters were arrested in February 2001 (see Current issues, above). Turabi was released in October 2003 and rearrested on March 31, 2004. The registrar of political parties issued a decree on April 1, 2004, to suspend the PNC's activities, following Turabi's arrest. Turabi was released as part of the general amnesty issued by Bashir in July 2005.

Leaders: Hassan Abdallah al-TURABI, Ali al-Hajj MUHAMMAD (Secretary General).

Umma (People's) Party (*Hizb al-Umma*— UP). A moderate right-of-center formation, the UP has long been led by former prime minister Mahdi. Strongest among the Ansar Muslims of the White Nile and western Darfur and Kordofan provinces, it obtained a plurality of 100 seats at the 1986 assembly balloting. Most of its members traditionally advocated the repeal of sharia law and were wary of sharing power with the fundamentalist NIF. Despite an historic pro-Libyan, anti-Egyptian posture, the party cultivated good relations with Western countries based, in part, on Mahdi's personal ties to Britain.

Prime Minister Mahdi and Idriss al-Banna were arrested shortly after the military coup in June 1989 (the latter being sentenced to 40 years in jail for corruption); Mahdi was released from prison and placed under house arrest in January 1990, amid rumors that the UP was considering some form of cooperation with the new regime. Subsequently, in light of growing fundamentalist influence within the Bashir government, the UP announced an alliance with the SPLM (see Other Groups, below) dedicated to overthrowing the government; ending the civil war; and reintroducing multiparty, secular democracy. The southern liaison notwithstanding, the UP membership was reported to be deeply divided following Mahdi's release from house arrest in May 1991. One faction apparently considered negotiations with the current regime to be pointless, while another supported the convening of a national conference (with full NIF participation), which would organize a national referendum on the nation's political future. With southern groups tending more and more to support independence for their region, the UP in early 1994 was described as "open" on the question. Mahdi was rearrested in June 1994 on charges of plotting against the government and again in May 1995 for a three-month period. He was reportedly invited by the Bashir regime to join the new government formed in April

1996 but declined and eventually fled to Asmara, Eritrea, in December.

The UP was one of the first groups to seek recognition in early 1999, the pronegotiation faction having apparently gained ascendancy. For his part, Mahdi in November concluded an agreement with Bashir known as the "Call of the Homeland Accord," which proposed a new, pluralistic constitution for Sudan and a four-year transitional period that would conclude with a self-determination referendum for the south. Consequently, in March 2000 Mahdi announced that the UP had withdrawn from the NDA, which he criticized for refusing to negotiate with the government, and directed the *Umma* militia to honor a cease-fire. Mahdi returned to Sudan in November after four years of exile in Egypt, but the UP nonetheless boycotted the December legislative and presidential elections, arguing that the balloting should be postponed pending comprehensive "national reconciliation." The UP also declined Bashir's invitation to join the cabinet in February 2001, again on the premise that a "bilateral" agreement was not appropriate while other opposition groups remained in conflict with the government. However, a UP splinter faction, led by Mubarak al-Fadil al-Mahdi, accepted ministerial posts in August 2002 and in the 2005 unity government.

Leaders: Dr. Sadiq al-MAHDI (Former Prime Minister), Idris al-BANNA, Mubarak Abdullah al-MAHDI, Mubarak al-Fadil al-MAHDI (Assistant to the President of the Republic and dissident faction leader), Sarrah NAGDALLA, Umar Nur al-DAIM (Secretary General).

Democratic Unionist Party (*al-Hizb al-Ittihadi al-Dimuqrati*—DUP). Also right of center, the DUP draws its principal strength from the Khatmiya Muslims of northern and eastern Sudan. Based on its second-place showing at the 1986 poll, the DUP was the UP's "junior partner" in subsequent government coalitions, although internal divisions prevented the formulation of a clearly defined outlook. The faction led by party chair Usman al-Mirghani included pro-Egyptian traditionalists once linked to the Numayri regime, who were re-

luctant to repeal sharia until an alternative code was formulated. Younger members, on the other hand, urged that the party abandon its "semi-feudal" orientation and become a secular, centrist formation capable of attracting nationwide support. In early 1986 the DUP reunited with an offshoot group, the Democratic People's Party (DPP), and subsequently appeared to have absorbed the small National Unionist Party (NUP), which had drawn most of its support from the Khartoum business community.

The party withdrew from government participation in late December 1988 because of failure to implement a southern peace accord that it had negotiated, with the prime minister's approval, a month earlier; it rejoined the coalition on March 22, 1989. Party leaders Usman and Ahmad al-Mirghani were arrested following the June 1989 coup, but they were released at the end of the year and subsequently went into exile in Egypt.

Although significant divisions apparently remained on both questions, the DUP was described by *Middle East International* in early 1994 as still officially opposed to independence for the south and "not adverse to some form of Islamic state" for Sudan. The latter issue apparently had contributed to the defection in 1993 of the DUP faction led by former deputy prime minister Sharif Zayn al-Abidin al-HINDI, who advocated the separation of church and state despite his position as a religious leader. A possible change in the DUP's stance toward fundamentalism and southern secession may have been signaled by the party's participation in subsequent NDA summits.

DUP Chair Mirghani described the guidelines adopted in late 1998 for legalization of parties as too restrictive, and his supporters did not submit a request for registration, although a splinter group reportedly sought recognition under the DUP rubric. Ahmad al-Mirghani returned from exile in November 2001, but Usman al-Mirghani, who had been elected chair of the NDA in September 2000, remained outside the country despite requests from the Sudanese government for his return. Meanwhile, a DUP splinter faction, calling itself the DUP–General Secretariat, had accepted cabinet posts in the government in February 2001 and in the 2005 unity government.

Leaders: Usman al-MIRGHANI (Chair), Ahmad al-MIRGHANI, Dr. Ahmad al-Sayid HAMAD (Former DDP Leader), Ali Ahmed al-SAYYED, Mohammed al-AZHARI, Ali Mahmoud HASSANEIN.

United Democratic Salvation Front (UDSF). The USDF was formed in 1999 by southern Sudanese political figures and dissidents from the SPLA under the leadership of Riak Machar. The UDSF included representatives of rebels groups who had signed the 1997 peace accord with the government in Khartoum and was seen as a progovernment grouping that advocated a peaceful resolution of the north-south conflict. In January 2000, Machar resigned as chair, and he rejoined the SPLA in 2002. He was replaced by Elijah HON at a party congress. In September 2001, the party's general secretary, Ibrahim al-TAWIL, led a large group of UDSF members in a defection to the NC. In October 2001, in an effort to unify the party, new leadership elections were conducted, and Eng Joseph Malwal was chosen chair. In March 2003 the USDF signed a cooperation agreement with the NC and was subsequently included in successive cabinets, including the 2005 unity government.

Leaders: Eng Joseph MALWAL (Chair), Faruq GATKOUTH (General Secretary).

Sudanese Communist Party (*al-Hizb al-Shuyui al-Sudani*—SCP). Founded in 1946 and a leading force in the struggle for independence, the SCP was banned under the Abbud regime and supported the 1969 Numayri coup, becoming thereafter the sole legal party until the abortive 1971 uprising, when it was again outlawed. The SCP campaigned as a recognized party in 1986, calling for opposition to Islamic fundamentalism; repeal of sharia; and the adoption of a secular, democratic constitution. It displayed no interest in joining the government coalition in 1988 but accepted one cabinet portfolio in March 1989. Secretary General Muhammad Ibrahim Nugud Mansur was arrested following the June 1989 coup, and in September four more party members were detained for alleged involvement in an antigovernment protest. Nugud

was released from prison in February 1990 but was placed under house arrest until May 1991, at which time he was freed under what the government described as a blanket amnesty for all remaining political detainees. The SCP, operating primarily from exile, subsequently remained active in the anti-NIF opposition, some members of the NDA complaining in late 1992 that the SCP's influence continued at a higher level than was warranted in view of communism's worldwide decline. SCP reformers have recently urged the party to shed its communist orientation in favor of a more moderate left-of-center posture that would attract wider popular participation, but the group's "older generation of leaders" has thus far resisted such a move. The party leadership was reportedly critical in late 1998 and early 1999 of the closer ties apparently being established by UP leader Sadiq al-Mahdi with the NIF government.

Leaders: Muhammad Ibrahim NUGUD Mansur (Secretary General), Ali al-Tijani al-TAYYIB Babikar (Deputy Secretary General).

Progressive People's Party (PPP). The PPP is one of the two major "Equatorial" parties (see SAPC, below) representing Sudanese living near the Zairian and Ugandan borders. Both the PPP and SAPC, unlike the SSPA, are "pro-divisionist," calling for strong provincial governments within a weak regional administration for the south.

Leader: Elioba SURUR.

Sudanese African People's Congress (SAPC). Sudan's other "Equatorial" party, the SAPC was initially represented by Pacifico LOLIK on the Supreme Council named in 1986. However, Lolik was reportedly expelled from the party in 1987 for supporting government plans for a unified southern administration.

Leader: Morris LUWIYA.

Sudanese People's Federal Party (SPFP). As in the case with several other southern parties, the SPFP was awarded a ministry in the coalition government of May 1986.

Leader: Joshua Dei WAL.

Islamic Socialist Party (ISP). A little-known nonregional party, the ISP received attention in

1987 when its leader was named to the Supreme Council as a neutral candidate after a dispute between the UP and the DUP over the filling of a vacancy.

Leader: Mirghani al-NASRI.

Sudanese National Party   (*al-Hizb al-Watani al-Sudani*—SNP). The SNP is a Khartoum-based party that draws most of its support from the Nuba tribes of southern Kordofan. The SNP deputies joined the southerners in boycotting the assembly in 1986 on the grounds that "African bloc" interests were underrepresented in the cabinet. In November 1987 the party's leader, Rev. Philip Ghabush, was branded a "dictator" by dissidents.

The SNP was officially registered in April 1999, Ghabush having announced his support for the new constitution and laws regarding party formation.

Leader: Rev. Philip Abbas GHABUSH.

Sudanese African Congress   (SAC). A southern party based in Juba, the SAC was awarded the ministry of labor in the first post-Numayri cabinet but has since been unrepresented in the government. The SAC represents a more radical viewpoint than the SSPA, calling for a shift in the Sudanese power structure to give the south more voice in national administration. At present the SAC appears strongly oriented toward the SPLM (below), several of its leaders having reportedly joined the movement by 1987.

Leader: Walter Kunijwok Gwado AYOKER.

Sudan African National Union   (SANU). A small southern party based in Malakal, SANU (adopting the same name as a pre-Numayri party) supports the division of the south into separate regions for administration.

Leader: Andrew Wieu RIAK.

National Alliance for the Salvation of the Country   (NASC). A loose coalition of professional groups, trade unions, interdenominational church groups, and political parties, the NASC was formed in 1985 as an extension of the National Salvation Front (NSF) established the year before. The NASC was instrumental in organizing strikes and other demonstrations that preceded the ouster of President Numayri, but its subsequent efforts to negotiate a north–south reconciliation through a proposed constitutional conference have been largely unproductive.

Leader: Awad al-KARIM Muhammad.

Sudanese Movement of Revolutionary Committees   (SMRC). Established in May 1985 as an outgrowth of the Libyan-backed Sudanese People's Socialist Front (SPSF) formed the previous year, the SMRC adopted an ideology based on the "Green Book" of Colonel Qadhafi. By late 1987, however, it was reported that most "revolutionary committee" activity had ceased in the face of popular disinterest.

Nile Valley Conference   (NVC). In seeking official recognition in early 1999, the NVC announced it would pursue "unity" between Sudan and Egypt and otherwise promote regional action.

Leader: Lt. Gen. Umar ZARUG.

Islamic Umma Party   (*Hizb al-Umma al-Islamiya*—IUP). In applying for recognition in early 1999, the IUP announced it would advocate sharia as the sole source of law while promoting "Mahdist" ideology and a nonaligned foreign policy. The IUP was officially registered in April 1999 and convened its first general congress with delegates from all parts of Sudan the same month.

Leader: Wali al-Din al-Hadi al-MAHDI.

Alliance for People's Working Forces.   The Alliance was organized in early 1999 in support of the proposed return of former president Numayri to Sudan. Numayri returned to Sudan after 14 years in exile and officially registered the party in May 1999. He then announced that he would contest the presidential elections scheduled to take place mid-October 2000.

Leader: Kamal al-Din Muhammad ABDUL-LAH.

Party of God   (*Hizb Allah* or *Hezbollah*). In submitting their application for legal status in early 1999, *Hezbollah* leaders called for national unity based on Islamic rule and sharia and praised the NIF-led government for having promoted national dialogue and democratization.

Leader: Sulayman Hasan KHALIL.

Other groups that have applied for recognition include the **Future Party** (*Hizb al-Mustaqbal*), led by Abd al-Mutal Abd al-RAHMAN; **Islamic–Christian Solidarity,** launched under the leadership of Hatim Abdullah al-Zaki HUSAYN on a platform of religious harmony and increased attention to social problems; the **Islamic Path Party,** led by Hasab al-RASUL; the **Islamic Revival Movement,** led by Siddiq al-Haj al-SIDDIQ; the **Islamic Socialist Party,** led by Sabah al-MUSBAN; the **Liberalization Party; the Moderate Trend Party,** led by Mahmud JINA; the **Muslim Brothers,** led by Sheikh Sadiq Abdallah Abd al-MAJID; the **National Popular Front,** led by Umar Hasan SHALABI and devoted to pan-Arab and pan-Islamic unity; the **National Salvation Party;** the **New Forces Association,** led by Abd al-Rahman Ismail KIBAYDAH; the **Popular Masses' Alliance,** founded by Faysal Muhammad HUSAYN in support of policies designed to assist the poor; the **Socialist Popular Party,** led by Sayyid Khalifah Idris HABANI; the **Sudanese Central Movement,** led by Muhammad Abu al-Qasim Haji HAMAD; the **Sudan Federal Party,** launched by Ahmed DIRAIGE (a leader of the Fur ethnic group) in support of a federal system; the **Sudan Green Party,** led by Zakaraia Bashir IMAN; and the **Sudanese Initiative Party,** led by Jafar KARAR.

The formation of a **National Democratic Party** (NDP) was reported in February as a merger of several small groupings with leftist or nationalist orientations.

Other Groups

Sudanese People's Liberation Movement (SPLM). The SPLM and its military wing, the Sudanese People's Liberation Army (SPLA), were formed in 1983 by Col. John Garang, until then an officer in the Sudanese army. Sent by the Numayri administration to negotiate with mutinous soldiers in southern garrisons, Colonel Garang joined the mutineers and, under his leadership, the SPLA became the dominant southern rebel force. The SPLM and SPLA were supported by Libya prior to Numayri's ouster, when Tripoli endorsed the new regime in Khartoum. The SPLA called a cease-fire immediately following the coup but thereafter initiated military action against the Khartoum government after failing to win concessions on the southern question. Relying on an estimated 20,000 to 25,000 troops the SPLA subsequently gained control of most of the nonurban south; sporadic negotiations with various northern representatives yielded several temporary cease-fires but no permanent solution to the conflict.

The SPLM, which in 1987 began to downplay its initial self-description as "Marxist-Leninist," did not propose secession for the south. Instead, it supported a unified Sudan in which the south would be granted a larger voice in national affairs and a greater share of the nation's economic development programs. However, under pressure from secession-oriented splinters, the SPLM's leaders in 1992 reportedly endorsed the proposed division of Sudan into two highly autonomous, albeit still confederated, states, with the south operating under secular law and the north under sharia.

Prior to mid-1991 the SPLA maintained large training camps in southern Ethiopia with the apparent blessing of the Mengistu regime. Following the change of government in Addis Ababa, however, its units were forced back across the border. In August the Movement was severely splintered when a group of second-tier leaders headquartered in the eastern town of Nasir announced their intention to wrest SPLA control from Garang, whom they accused of perpetrating a "dictatorial reign of terror." Long-standing tribal animosity also appeared to contribute to the split, support for the Nasir faction coming primarily from the Nuer ethnic group, which has had a stormy relationship with Garang's Dinka supporters since the creation of the SPLA (see Anyanya II Movement, below). Several months of fighting between the two factions left thousands dead, Garang's supporters charging the dissidents with the "massacre" of Dinka civilians in January 1992. Although a temporary reconciliation between the SPLA factions was achieved at the Abuja peace talks with the government in June, sporadic fighting resumed later in the summer.

In September 1992 William Nyuon BANY, who had been conducting negotiations with the splinter group on behalf of Garang, defected from the main SPLA branch to form his own faction, which in April 1993 coalesced with other anti-Garang groups as the SPLA-United (below). In early 1994 negotiations between the SPLA and the SPLA-United yielded a tentative cease-fire agreement in which Garang reportedly agreed to support a proposed self-determination vote for the south, which most observers believed would endorse secession. Although discussion also focused on possible reunification of the southern forces, there appeared to be ongoing friction between Garang and the SPLA-United's Riak Machar concerning their prospective leadership roles.

In April 1994 some 500 delegates attended the first SPLA-SPLM conference since 1983. The conference was reportedly called to shore up Garang's authority in the face of competition from the SPLA-United. The SPLM leader was put in charge of the joint military command announced by the NDA in October 1996 after the SPLA-United and Machar's SSIM signed a peace accord with the Bashir government. (See Current issues, above, for information on negotiations between the SPLM and the government.)

In late 2004 rumors surfaced of a "revolt" against Garang by some SPLA officers who favored the independence of the south and wanted Salva Kiir Mayardit to replace Garang as head of the SPLA. However, Kiir reminded the rebel officers of the uprising against Garang in 1991. The rebel officers were impatient with Garang's seeming ineffectiveness in negotiations with Khartoum.

On July 30, 2005, Garang died in a helicopter crash, an event that ignited rioting leading to the death of more than 100 people. He was succeeded as SPLM leader by his deputy, Kiir. Kiir appointed Machar as vice president of the Government of Southern Sudan in August 2005.

Leader: Salva KIIR Mayardit (First Vice President of the Republic, President of South Sudan, and Party Chair), Riak MACHAR (Vice President of South Sudan).

Sudanese People's Liberation Army–United (SPLA-United). The formation of the SPLA-United was announced in early April 1993 in Nairobi, Kenya, by SPLA dissidents who opposed the "one-man rule" of longtime SPLA leader John Garang. Included in the grouping was the Nasir faction (which had been fighting with Garang's forces since August 1991 [see SPLM, above]); William Nyuon Bany's self-styled **Forces of Unity;** and the so-called Kerubino Group, formed in February by Kerubino Kwanyin Bol and several other dissidents who had escaped from a Garang prison in the fall of 1992.

As of early 1994 the SPLA-United was facing heavy domestic and international pressure to reconcile with the SPLA, internecine fighting having yielded numerous civilian casualties and exacerbated famine conditions in the south. At the same time, the SPLA-United's advocacy of independence for southern Sudan appeared to be gaining widespread support.

A number of splits in the SPLA-United occurred in early 1995, the most important of which was the withdrawal of Nasir faction leader Riak Machar to form a Southern Sudan Independence Movement (SSIM). Concurrently, Nyuon Bany was expelled from the SPLA-United on the ground that he was collaborating with Khartoum, although by early 1996 the rump group was itself reportedly an ally of the north, with Nyuon Bany resuming a pro-Garang posture within the SSIM. In April the SPLA-United and the SSIM signed an agreement with the government in which they endorsed the preservation of Sudan's "known boundaries," apparently thereby relinquishing their drive for independence. Several factions of the SPLA-United were among the groups that reached a peace accord with the government in April 1997.

The SPLA-United, under Lam Akol, subsequently gained strength through a merger with the Southern Sudan Defense Forces (SSDF) led by Machar. As an outgrowth of that agreement, Machar was named head of the new Southern States Coordination Council (SSCC, see Political background, above). However, Machar later pulled out of the government, accusing President Bashir of failing to consult with him regarding governmental appointments. Machar subsequently became the leader of the UDSF (above). Meanwhile, Akol continued to serve in Bashir's cabinet until August

2002, when he was dismissed after he and several supporters had announced they were leaving the NC to form a new party. By that time, Machar and his supporters had reintegrated into the SPLA as southern groups in general attempted to present as unified a front as possible in the increasingly promising peace negotiations. SPLA leader Akol was subsequently appointed foreign minister in the 2005 government of national unity.

Leader: Lam AKOL.

Sudan Liberation Movement/Army (SLM/A). This group is a successor of sorts to the Darfur Liberation Front, a rebel group organized to combat the perceived repression in Darfur. The rebels split into two groups in 2004, as the SLM/A vehemently opposed Khalil Ibrahim, a radical opponent of Khartoum (see JEM, below). The SLM/A claimed to represent the region's black African farmers, who were angry over perceived government support for Arab militias. One faction of the SLM/A, known as the *Mani Arkoi* and led by Minni Minawi, signed the AU-backed 2006 Darfur peace accord, but the main SLM/A body, led by party chair Abdallah Wahid Mohamed Ahmad Nur, rejected the agreement.

Leader: Adballah Wahid Mohamed Ahmad NUR (Chair), Mustafa TIRAB (General Secretary), Minni MINAWAI (Leader of the *Mani Arkoi* faction).

Justice and Equality Movement (JEM). The JEM split from the SLM in mid-2004, further complicating peace negotiations with Khartoum, with each of the groups at odds with the others based on tribal rivalries. It reportedly is supported by Islamists close to Hassan Abdallah al-Turabi. In May 2006 the JEM refused to sign the AU-supported Darfur peace plan.

Leader: Khalil IBRAHIM Mohamed.

National Movement for Reform and Development in Dafur. This rebel group, which operates in the north and west, split from the JEM in August 2004 after its leader accused the JEM's Ibrahim of trying to have him assassinated. This group officially announced its formation on October 26, 2004.

Leader: Jibril Abdel KARIM, Nourene Manawi BARTCHAM.

Eastern Sudan Front. Formed on February 1, 2005, this group, which operates in the east, is composed of two rebel groups: the Free Lions Association, whose members are Rashaida tribesmen, and the Beja Congress, which represents the non-Arab, nomadic Beja tribes. Unrest in the impoverished area of eastern Sudan, long ignored by the government, began as a grassroots movement in the 1990s and gained strength with the return of Umar Muhammad TAHIR, the exiled Beja Congress leader, in November 2003. The Congress was banned by the government in October 2003 for its use of violence.

Anyanya II Movement. *Anyanya II,* so-named in emulation of the *Anyanya* (scorpion) southern insurgency of earlier decades (see Political background, above), was formed in late 1983, when the Nuer faction broke from the recently formed SPLA. Although the Movement continued its antigovernment activity until the ouster of President Numayri, it subsequently became a progovernment guerrilla group, regularly engaging SPLA troops around the Upper Nile city of Malakal. Despite reports in 1987 of an agreement between *Anyanya II* and the SPLA to curtail hostilities arising from their longstanding ethnic rivalry, *Africa Report* stated in late 1990 that the Movement was once again engaging in anti-SPLA activity, reportedly with the support of Khartoum. In the second half of 1991 *Anyanya II* aligned itself with the Nasir faction of the SPLA but by early 1996 had once again adopted a pro-Khartoum posture.

Leader: David Dogok PUOCH (Secretary General).

Patriotic Resistance Movement of South Sudan (PRMSS). The PRMSS was established in Nairobi, Kenya, in late 1993 by southern Sudanese critical of both SPLA factions. The new grouping, believed to derive its support primarily from

Cabinet

[as of July 1, 2006]

President and Prime Minister	Umar Hassan Ahmad al-Bashir (NC)
First Vice President	Salva Kiir Mayardit (SPLM)
Second Vice President	Ali Uthman Muhammad Taha (NC)

Ministers

Agriculture and Forestry	Mohammed al-Amin Essa Kabashi (NC)
Animal Resources	Qalwak Danek (NC)
Cabinet Affairs	Denik Alor Cole (SPLM)
Culture and Youth	Mohammed Youssef Abdullah (NC)
Defense	Lt. Gen. Abdel-Rahim Hussein (NC)
Education	(Vacant)
Energy and Mining	Awad Ahmed al-Jaz (NC)
Environment and Urban Planning	Ahmed Babakr (NC)
External Trade	George Bornik Neyami (SPLM)
Federal Governance	Abdel-Basit Sabdarat (NC)
Finance	Al-Zubair Hassan Ahmed (NC)
Foreign Affairs	Lam Akol (SPLM)
Health	Tabita Shwkaya (SPLM) [f]
Higher Education and Scientific Research	Peter Cock (SPLM)
Humanitarian Affairs	Kosti Manibi (SPLM)
Industry	Jalal Yusuf Mohammed Digair (DUP)
Information and Communications	El-Zahawi Ibrahim Malik (UP)
Interior	Zubair Bashir Taha (NC)
International Cooperation	Al-Tijani Saleh Fadel (NC)
Investment	Malik Akar Ayar (SPLM)
Irrigation and Water Resources	Kamal Ali Mohammed (NC)
Justice	Mohammed Ali al-Mardi (NC)
Labor, Public Service, and Human Resources	Alson Manani Makaya (NC)
Parliamentary Affairs	Joseph Okilo (SPLM)
Religious Guidance and Endowments	Azhari al-Taji Awad al-Sayyed (NC)
Republic Affairs	Maj. Gen. Bakri Hassan Salih (NC)
Science	(Vacant)
Tourism	Joseph Malwal (UDSF)
Transport and Roads	Kol Manyak Gok (SPLM)
Welfare and Social Development	Samia Ahmed Mohammed (NC)

[f] = female

the Equatoria region of Sudan, reportedly favors a self-determination vote for the south.

Leaders: Alfred Lado GORE, Philip TONGUN, Barri WANJI.

Sudan Invincible Forces of Democracy (SIFD). Formation of the SIFD was announced in Nairobi in late 1993 by southerners seeking a peaceful settlement to the fighting between SPLA factions as well as between the government and the SPLA.

Leader: David Idilla LOBUIN.

Legitimate Command. The Command is a Cairo-based group of former Sudanese officers opposed to the Bashir regime that claims the support of "democratic" officers in the Sudanese army. The Command has participated in NDA summits in recent years, some observers going so far as to describe it as the NDA's "military wing."

Leader: Fathi Ahmad ALI.

Sudan Federal Democratic Alliance (SFDA). The SFDA was launched in London in February 1994 under the chairship of Ahmed Dreige, a former Numayri cabinet member. The group has deemed "all means to be legitimate" in securing an end to the Bashir regime and has proposed a substantially decentralized federal structure for Sudan in which the traditional parties would play no role.

Leaders: Ahmed DREIGE (Chair), Sherif HARIR, Suleiman RAHAL.

Sudan Alliances Forces (SAF). The SAF is a rebel group operating in eastern Sudan, reportedly from bases in Ethiopia and Eritrea. In late 1996 it was described as a participant in the NDA, although its fighters were not believed to be under the direct command of the SPLA's Colonel Garang.

Leader: Brig. Gen. Abd al-Aziz Khalid OSMAN.

Nobility Movement (*al-Shahamah*). This is a rebel group reportedly formed in October 2004 in West Kordofan state by a former leader of the progovernment paramilitary Popular Defense Forces. The leader, Musa Ali Muhammadayn (also a former governor of al-Rashad province), was dismissed from that post when he decided to remain loyal to Turabi in the latter's confrontations with Bashir.

Leader: Musa Ali MUHAMMADAYN.

Sudanese National Movement for the Eradication of Marginalization. This rebel group, about which little is known, reportedly operates in Darfur. It claimed responsibility for an attack on an oil field in Darfur on December 20, 2004.

Legislature

Under the Numayri regime, the size and composition of the unicameral National People's Assembly changed several times, the assembly elected in 1974 being the only one to complete its full constitutional term of four years. All existing legislative bodies were dissolved by the TNC in April 1985.

On April 1–12, 1986, balloting was held for 260 members of a 301-member Constituent Assembly, voting being postponed in many southern districts because of rebel activity. The assembly was dissolved by the Bashir regime in July 1989.

On February 13, 1992, Prime Minister Bashir announced the appointment of a 300-member Transitional National Assembly, which met for the first time on February 24. Included in the new assembly were all members of the Revolutionary Command Council (RCC); a number of RCC advisors; all cabinet ministers and state governors; and representatives of the army, trade unions, and former political parties. The prime minister decreed that the assembly would sit for an indeterminate period, pending the selection of a permanent body as the final step of the new pyramidal legislative structure envisioned by the government.

Elections to a new 400-member **National Assembly** were conducted on March 6–17, 1996, all candidates running as independents because political parties remained banned. Most of the 275 elected members of the assembly were selected during that balloting, although in October President Bashir appointed eight legislators from constituencies in the south, where voting had been deemed impossible due to the civil war. When the assembly convened on April 1, the elected legislators were joined by 125 legislators who had been selected in January by representatives of local and state councils and numerous professional associations.

At the most recent balloting, held December 13–23, 2000, the National Congress won 355 of 360 contested seats, the remaining 5 being secured by independents. (Most major opposition groups boycotted the balloting, and elections were not held in three southern provinces due to the civil war.) On December 20, 2004, the National Assembly amended the constitution to extend the term of the sitting legislature for one year. Legislators serve four-year terms.

In accordance with the Comprehensive Peace Agreement signed January 9, 2005, seats in the legislature were divided based on a power-sharing quota, with the NC holding 52 percent of the seats; the SPLM, 28 percent; northern opposition parties, 14 percent; and southern opposition parties, 6 percent. The new 450-member "national unity" assembly—appointed by decree by Bashir—convened for the first time on August 31, 2005. Also under the agreement, the south established its own assembly, the South Sudan Transitional Legislative Assembly, which convened for the first time on September 29, 2005.

President: Ahmed Ibrahim al-TAHIR.

Communications

Press

The Bashir government banned all newspapers and magazines with the exception of the weekly military paper, *al-Guwat al-Musallaha* (Armed Forces), upon its assumption of power in June 1989. The following September two new dailies were issued under government auspices, *al-Engaz al-Watani* and *al-Sudan al-Hadith.* In May 1990 a new English-language weekly, *New Horizon,* was launched. In April 1993 it was reported that *al-Khartoum,* one of the dailies banned in 1989, had resumed publication from exile in Cairo, Egypt. Two months later the government announced a relaxation of its press monopoly; however, in April 1994 the country's sole privately owned paper, *al-Sudan al-Dawli,* was shut down for criticizing the NIF's continued support of the regime.

On May 10, 2003, the *Khartoum Monitor,* Sudan's only English-language daily, was banned. On August 12, 2003, reportedly to bolster support for his regime, President Bashir issued a decree supposedly to end press censorship.

News Agencies

The domestic facility is the Sudan News Agency (SUNA) (*Wakalat al-Anba al-Sudan*). A number of foreign agencies maintain bureaus in Khartoum.

Broadcasting and Computing

Republic of Sudan Broadcasting (*Idhaat al-Jumhuriyah al-Sudan*) is a government facility transmitting in Arabic, Amharic, Somali, and Tigrinya as well as in English and French. Television service is provided by the commercial, government-controlled Sudan Television Service. There were approximately 9 million television receivers and 290,000 personal computers serving 300,000 Internet users in 2003.

Intergovernmental Representation

Ambassador to the U.S.
(Vacant)

U.S. Ambassador to Sudan
(Vacant)

Permanent Representative to the UN
(Vacant)

IGO Memberships (Non-UN)
AfDB, AFESD, AMF, AU, BADEA, CAEU, Comesa, IDB, IGAD, Interpol, IOM, LAS, NAM, OIC, PCA, WCO

SWAZILAND

KINGDOM OF SWAZILAND

The Country

Bordered on the north, west, and south by South Africa and on the east by Mozambique, Swaziland is the smallest of the three former British High Commission territories in southern Africa. The country comprises a mountainous western region (Highveld), a middle region of moderate altitude (Middleveld), an eastern lowland area (Lowveld), and the so-called Lubombo plateau on the eastern border. About 97 percent of the population is Swazi African, the remainder being of European and Eurafrican (mixed) stock. English is an official language, but siSwati (akin to Zulu) prevails among the indigenous population; Afrikaans is common among the Europeans, many of whom are of South African origin. Christianity is the religion of approximately half the people; there are a few Muslims, the remainder adhering to traditional beliefs. Women constitute about 37 percent of the work force; female participation in government, with the exception of the former queens regent, has been minimal.

The economy is quite diversified, given the country's small land area and population, although its composition, particularly in the mining sector, is changing. Production of iron ore, which accounted for 25 percent of export earnings in 1967, had virtually ceased by the end of the 1970s, while asbestos reserves, after 40 years of extraction, were also approaching depletion. Coal mining, on the other hand, underwent rapid development, while other minerals, such as tin, barites, and silica, were found in commercially exploitable quantities. Under normal conditions, water supplies are sufficient not only to support agriculture, which yields sugar, forest products, and livestock, but also to provide

a potential hydroelectric power base. Swaziland experienced real GDP growth of 3.6 percent in 1996 and 3.7 percent in 1997, partially as the result of the government's implementation of economic reforms suggested by the International Monetary Fund (IMF) and the World Bank. Growth declined to about 2 percent in 1998 due to deteriorating economic conditions in South Africa and the effects of the Asian financial crisis.

Growth of 3.5 percent was achieved in 2002, mainly due to expansion of the textile industry, which took advantage of reduced U.S. tariffs and quotas designed to assist developing African nations. However, the economy subsequently continued to suffer from high unemployment, persistent poverty, localized food shortages and, according to some international donors, irresponsible spending

Political Status: Independent monarchy within the Commonwealth since September 6, 1968.

Area: 6,703 sq. mi. (17,363 sq. km.).

Population: 929,718 (1997C); 1,101,000 (2005E).

Major Urban Centers (2005E): MBABANE (administrative capital, 78,000), Lobamba (royal and legislative capital, 11,000), Manzini (33,000).

Official Languages: English, siSwati.

Monetary Unit: Lilangeni (official rate July 1, 2006: 7.13 emalangeni = $1US). The lilangeni is at par with the South African rand, although under a Tripartite Monetary Area agreement concluded among Swaziland, Lesotho, and South Africa on July 1, 1986, the rand ceased to be legal tender in Swaziland.

Sovereign: King MSWATI III; installed on April 25, 1986, succeeding (as Head of State) Queen Regent Ntombi THWALA.

Prime Minister: Absalom Themba DLAMINI; appointed by the king on November 14, 2003, to succeed Paul SHABANGU, who had been serving in an acting capacity since the dismissal of Sibusiso Barnabas DLAMINI by the king on September 30, 2003, following the legislative election of September 20–October 18.

on the part of the royal family. In addition, Swaziland faced one of the highest rates of HIV/AIDS infection in the world; UN officials estimated in 2004 that 39 percent of adults were infected. After many years of seeming failure to implement a plan to combat the pandemic, the government in 2004 declared a national emergency regarding the issue and solicited international assistance in trying to halt the spread of the disease. (In 2005 the infection rate among one age group of teens declined for the first time.) The economy continued its downward trend, with real GDP growth of 1.8 percent in 2005, compared to 2.1 percent in 2004. Little progress was made in reducing poverty, according to the IMF, which cited, among other reasons, the high rate of HIV/AIDS infection, a prolonged drought, and the removal of textile quotas in other countries, resulting in factory closings that contributed to Swaziland's 30 percent unemployment rate. The IMF urged the government to reduce its budget deficit and increase privatization in order to attract investors.

Government and Politics

Political Background

Swaziland came under British control in the mid-19th century when a Swazi ruler requested protection against his people's traditional enemies, the Zulu. Kept intact when the Union of South Africa was formed in 1910, the territory was subsequently administered under native rulers by the British high commissioner for South Africa. Preparations for independence began after World War II and culminated in the promulgation of internal self-government in 1967 and the achievement of full independence within the Commonwealth in 1968 under King SOBHUZA II, who subsequently exercised firm control of the country's political institutions. Following small gains by the semiradical Ngwane National Liberation Congress (NNLC) in a 1972 parliamentary election and frustration of his attempts to have an opposition MP deported, the king in April 1973 repealed the constitution, abolished the legislature, introduced a detention act, and banned all opposition political activity. On August 21, 1982, King Sobhuza died, having technically reigned from the age of one in 1899, although he had not been formally enthroned until 1921 and had not been recognized as paramount ruler by the British until 1966. He was succeeded as head of state by Queen Mother Dzeliwe SHONGWE, authorized to act as regent until a successor king was designated and reached maturity.

The naming of Prince Bhekimpi DLAMINI to succeed Prince Mabandla Fred DLAMINI as prime minister in March 1983 seemed to mark the ascendancy of conservative elements within the royal house. In August Queen Regent Dzeliwe also was ousted from power, reportedly because she differed over the interpretation of her role with traditionalists within the *Liqoqo,* historically an advisory council of royal family members that had been elevated to the status of Supreme Council of State shortly before Sobhuza's death. Queen Regent Dzeliwe was replaced by Ntombi THWALA, the mother of Prince Makhosetive, who was named successor to the former sovereign on August 10. Two months later, however, Prince Mfanasibili DLAMINI and Dr. George MSIBI, who were prominently involved in the palace coup that installed Queen Regent Ntombi, were dismissed from the *Liqoqo*.

On April 25, 1986, two years earlier than originally planned, Prince Makhosetive assumed the title of King MSWATI III in an apparent effort to halt the power struggle that had followed his father's death. The 19-year-old king, the world's youngest monarch, moved quickly to consolidate his control, formally disbanding the *Liqoqo* in June and appointing Prince Sotsha DLAMINI, a relatively obscure former police official, as prime minister on October 6.

After authorizing the arrest in May 1987 of 12 people allegedly involved in the palace intrigue of recent years, the king dissolved parliament in September, one year early. Assembly elections were held in November, and the government was extensively reorganized at the end of the month. Although the king's bold action at the outset of his reign surprised some observers, most Swazis appeared to support his exercise of monarchical prerogative as a means of preserving stability.

The king formally assumed full executive authority at age 21 on April 19, 1989. Three months later he dismissed Prince Sotsha as prime minister, replacing him with Obed Mfanyana DLAMINI. The new prime minister was the founder and former secretary general of the Swaziland Federation of Trade Unions (SFTU), a background that appeared to strengthen the government's capacity to deal with a growing number of labor disputes.

On October 9, 1992, one month before the expiration of its term, the king dissolved Parliament and declared that, with the assistance of his cabinet (which would be restyled a Council of Ministers and act as a caretaker government), he would rule by decree until the adoption of a new constitution and the holding of elections. Balloting scheduled for November was postponed until 1993 to allow for the redefinition of constituencies and compilation of a voters' register. The monarch's action followed his approval of a draft charter that called for retention of the monarchy and the revival of multipartyism (banned in 1973 by King Sobhuza II).

Fearing a conservative backlash if the reform movement outpaced the prerogatives of the royal court and powerful traditional chiefs, the constitutional commission recommended that decisions regarding political parties be deferred. Consequently, candidates at the House of Assembly elections on September 18 and October 11, 1993, competed on a nonparty basis; nonetheless, the polling marked the first time that legislators had been popularly elected and royal family members had been prohibited from participating. Underscoring the change, Prime Minister Obed Dlamini and all but three cabinet ministers lost their seats. As a result, on October 25 King Mswati named Andreas FAKUDZE as interim prime minister with responsibility for all 16 ministries. Ten days later the king appointed Prince Jameson Mblini DLAMINI, a conservative, to succeed Fakudze. Traditionalists hailed the monarch's choice, although the government named by Dlamini on November 10 included several reformists.

A follow-up round to the 1993 balloting was held on October 2, 1994, with voters selecting secretaries for the country's 55 regions (*Inkundla*). The new officials were described as links between legislators and their constituents, as well as coordinators of development activities in their areas.

The SFTU called a general strike (the most comprehensive in recent years) on March 13–14, 1995, to secure acceptance of a variety of demands, including the reinstatement of summarily dismissed state employees. The action was called off after the government appointed a select committee to consider the grievances. Subsequently, the SFTU called for another strike on July 17, which was called off after the House of Assembly had imposed severe penalties for work stoppages. In mid-August the Senate endorsed a statement by King

Mswati that Swazis did not want multiparty politics. Three months later, a well-attended opposition conference rejected the royal assessment.

On January 22–29, 1996, the SFTU organized a widely observed general strike, which was abandoned only after the king ordered the strikers back to work, threatening "to go to war" if necessary to end the action. Although some observers described the SFTU as "tarnished" by its capitulation to the monarch's threat, on February 16, three days before a scheduled resumption of the strike, King Mswati promised to reform the constitution and consider lifting the political party ban. Subsequently, the union suspended plans for a renewed action; however, prodemocracy rallies continued.

On May 8, 1996, the king dismissed Prime Minister Dlamini, promising "concrete democratic changes." Subsequently, the king named Deputy Prime Minister Sishayi NXUMALO as acting prime minister, but Nxumalo immediately asserted that the Swazi people were not ready for political parties, which he described as ill-suited for the "close-knit, non-ethnic, traditional society." Nevertheless, on July 26 the king announced the creation of a 29-member Constitutional Reform Commission (CRC) with responsibility for drafting a new constitution and named former finance minister and IMF executive director, Dr. Sibusiso Barnabas DLAMINI, as the new prime minister. The cabinet was reshuffled on November 13, the king pledging emphasis on economic development and the pursuit of foreign investment and trade.

In April 1998 the king once again reshuffled the government, most notably replacing Deputy Prime Minister Nxumalo with Arthur KHOZA and naming the former to head the Swaziland Investment Promotion Authority (SIPA). Thereafter, in an apparent effort to quell increasingly vocal calls for reform from prodemocracy activists, the king abruptly dissolved the House of Assembly in August in anticipation of balloting in October.

As in 1993, at elections on October 16 and 24, 1998, candidates for the House of Assembly competed on a nonparty basis. Observers attributed the low voter turnout to voter apathy and the prodemoc-

racy forces' call for an electoral boycott; in addition, union activists reportedly threatened would-be voters. On November 13 the king reappointed Dlamini as prime minister, and on November 20 a new government was sworn in.

On May 31, 2003, the king dissolved the assembly and appointed a special council to act as a caretaker government until elections were held. Paul SHABANGU was appointed as the interim prime minister, although no other cabinet posts were filled. The nonparty elections, which were boycotted by most of the major opposition groups, were conducted on September 20 and October 18. The king appointed five women to the assembly (there had been no women in the previous assembly). Following the elections, the king dismissed Shabangu and appointed Absalom Themba DLAMINI as prime minister on November 14. The cabinet was reshuffled on February 23, 2006, and one minister was replaced on May 24, 2006.

Constitution and Government

For some years after independence, King Sobhuza was reported to have been working on a revised Western-style constitution. However, in March 1977 he announced that he had abandoned the effort in favor of a form of traditional government based on tribal councils (*Tinkhundla*), which was formally introduced in October 1978. Under the *Tinkhundla* electoral system, which was voided by decree on October 9, 1992, polling was held without political campaigns or electoral rolls for an 80-member electoral college charged with naming four-fifths of a 50-member House of Assembly, which in turn named half of a 20-member Senate. Ten members of each were designated by the monarch, who also named the prime minister and other cabinet officials.

On February 14, 1992, a royal constitutional commission appointed by the king in late 1991 presented a draft charter for a multiparty electoral system, which was given preliminary approval by the monarch in October. The proposal called for a two-stage balloting process beginning with polling in the 210 *Tinkhundla* for local representatives from among candidates chosen by the chiefs. At the second round of the secret balloting, first round victors from four to six *Tinkhundla* were to compete against one another in *Inkhundla* elections for berths in an expanded House of Assembly and Senate of 55 and 20 members, respectively (the monarch having the right to appoint 10 additional members to each.) The plan, while serving as a partial blueprint for the 1993 and 1998 polls, lacked formal approval, and its status remained distinctly uncertain. A Constitutional Reform Committee (CRC) formed in 1996 proceeded haltingly. In January 2001 a draft constitution report from the CRC was criticized by the opposition and human rights groups as a "doctored document" and "not a truly representative report because group submissions were denied." The long-awaited new draft constitution was presented to the king in November 2003 but he did not sign it into law until July 26, 2005, after ordering the legislature to amend sections regarding religion and taxing the royal family. The new constitution promulgated on February 8, 2006, has no specific language to legalize political parties (and stipulates that candidates for election must run as individuals.) Though the constitution contains a bill of rights guaranteeing limited freedoms, the king retains ultimate authority (see Current issues, below).

The judiciary, whose members are appointed by the king, encompasses a High Court, a Court of Appeal, and district courts. There are also 17 Swazi courts for tribal and customary issues. Swaziland is divided for administrative purposes into four districts, each headed by a commissioner appointed by the central government.

Foreign Relations

Swaziland is a member of the UN, the Commonwealth, and the African Union (AU, formerly the Organization of African Unity—OAU). It maintains close relations with South Africa as a result of geographic proximity, administrative tradition, and economic dependency (more than 80 percent of the Kingdom's imports are from South Africa, and a substantial portion of its national income consists of remittances from Swazis employed in the neighboring state). Despite OAU strictures, Swaziland concluded a secret nonaggression pact with Pretoria in 1982 and subsequently strove to contain African National Congress (ANC) activity within its territory.

A series of major raids on purported ANC strongholds by South African security forces in 1986 led to vehement protests by the Swazi government and a December visit by South African Foreign Minister Roelof "Pik" Botha, who reaffirmed his government's commitment to the 1982 pact and pledged that the incursions would cease. However, in July 1987 two top ANC officials and a Mozambican woman companion were killed in Mbabane. Two additional killings by alleged South African agents in August brought the total number of ANC deaths in 1987 to 11.

Despite its ties to South Africa, Swaziland established diplomatic relations with Mozambique during 1976. The action was prompted by a need to facilitate the movement of goods through the Mozambique port of Maputo. The Mozambique Embassy in Mbabane was Swaziland's first resident mission from independent Africa, and a security accord was concluded between the two countries in mid-1984.

In September 1989 it was reported that Swaziland and South Africa had agreed on a border adjustment that would bring the largely Swazi-populated South African homeland of KaNgwane within the kingdom. However, no date was given for the formal transfer, which remained unimplemented in mid-1999. In 2001 the king launched a new initiative to discuss border issues with South Africa; however, no progress was subsequently reported toward a settlement.

In March 2005 the king and South African president Thebo Mbeki were scheduled to hold a summit, which activists had hoped Mbeki would use to push for reforms, but the meeting was postponed indefinitely. South African activists continued their efforts in support of democratization in Swaziland by staging a border blockade in 2006. Eight people were shot and wounded on the South African side of the border.

In late 1997 relations between Swaziland and Mozambique were strained after it was reported that a Swazi prince leading a committee studying their shared border had asserted that Swazi territory legally encompassed all of Mozambique's Maputo Province. (The claim was dismissed by Maputo, which declared that it had never been formally contacted by Swaziland.) In 1998–1999 relations between the two turned on repatriation issues. In 1999 Swaziland relocated 500 Mozambicans and began a program to force Mozambicans living in Swaziland to register for military service.

Current Issues

In 2000 opposition pressure for political reforms continued, but the government exhibited little concession. In November a general strike called by the SFTU led to the arrests of a number of prominent trade union and opposition leaders. The king's perceived heavy-handed approach to the prodemocracy movement was criticized by the opposition through 2001 and into 2002. Several neighboring countries (notably South Africa) and other international observers also questioned the regime's policies, particularly following a royal decree in June 2002 permitting the king to overturn court rulings, ban newspapers, and impose penalties on those charged with "ridiculing" royal authority or the government. Events surrounding the drafting of a new constitution also appeared to dampen prospects for liberalization. In August 2001 the CRC had in fact proposed enlarging the king's authority and maintaining the ban on political parties.

The draft constitution was formally presented to the king in November 2003. As expected, the document did not call for the legalization of parties and appeared to many observers to strengthen, rather than weaken, the monarch's authority. Among other things, the proposed new basic law reaffirmed the king's power to appoint the prime minister, cabinet, judges, and other government officials. It also

authorized the king to dissolve the assembly and veto any legislation. Although reference was made to rights for women, freedom of expression, and other issues generally addressed by modern constitutions, the opposition immediately dismissed the draft as unacceptable. Leading the campaign against approval was the Coalition of Concerned Civil Organizations (CCCO), launched by business, professional, and legal organizations. Unions, religious groups, and the banned political parties subsequently joined the CCCO in trying to force revision of the draft. However, their efforts were fruitless, as the king signed the new constitution into law in July 2005. The constitution maintains the power of the monarchy and includes a provision that a ruler who does not perform can be removed, his authority then being assumed by the Queen Mother. A bill of rights within the constitution guarantees equality under the law and freedom of religion, speech, and assembly, though the king may suspend certain rights if he finds them to be in conflict with the (undefined) public interest. Observers questioned the commitment to women's rights, citing the fact that women historically have been grouped with minors under the law, and given that the king still has the authority to "claim" and marry underage girls. The CCCO noted that under the constitution the king enjoys legal immunity and protection against investigation by the Swaziland Human Rights Commission.

Perhaps a positive note for prodemocracy activist was that the government issued guidelines for the creation and registration of nongovernmental organizations—a move some said could be a precursor to legal political activity. Opposition leader Obed Dlamini of the NNLC vowed to challenge the constitution by attempting to register his party. The king, for his part, said in 2006 that the country was not ready for political parties and criticized foreign countries that pushed for reforms in Swaziland. Meanwhile, the government blocked a protest rally organized by the People's United Democratic Movement (Pudemo) and banned a women's group from registering as an organization. Tensions in the country were heightened by reports that the king built several lavish palaces for his wives, bought them luxury cars, and otherwise continued to spend large amounts of money, while two-thirds of the population lived on less than $1US per day. On a more positive note, after tough new anticorruption laws were approved in 2006, the king held the country's first summit to address the major problem of graft.

Political Parties

During 1994 a number of parties, including Pudemo (below), joined with human rights and other groups to form a Confederation for Full Democracy in Swaziland (CFDS). During a visit to Johannesburg in September, CFDS representative Sabelo DLAMINI termed the 1993 nonpartisan poll a "pseudo election" and warned of civil war that might spill over into South Africa if Swaziland's "undemocratic government" did not agree to free elections. On November 13, 1995, the CFDS sponsored a conference of political and labor groups that called on King Mswati to go into voluntary exile "until we have sorted our political problems out."

In early 1996 the CFDS appeared to have been superseded by the **Swaziland Democratic Alliance** (SDA), a coalition that included Pudemo; the Swaziland Federation of Trade Unions (SFTU), an 80,000 member grouping led by Jan SITHOLE; and representatives of the Institute for Democracy and Leadership (Ideal), led by Dr. Jerry GULE. Organized to "try to force change," the alliance led a march on the prime minister's office and parliamentary building, which was noteworthy mainly for the paltry number of activists who participated. In early 1999 the SDA was bolstered by the addition of the NNLC (below) to its ranks, and in April the NNLC's Obed Mfanyan Dlamini was elected, along with Pudemo's Jerry NXUMALO and Sithole, to lead the reorganized alliance. In 2003 Obed Dlamini was elected to parliament, and a year later the NNLC reportedly had decided to participate in national elections, which, observers said, would most likely mean the end of the SDA, as other alliance members opposed such participation.

Former Government Party

Imbokodvo National Movement (INM). The *Imbokodvo* ("Grindstone") Movement dominated the political scene during the late 1960s and was the only political group permitted to function openly after 1973. The leadership of the party has been vacant since the dismissal of Prince Mabandla Dlamini as prime minister in March 1983. The royalist *Sive Siyingaba* cultural-political group, an offshoot of the INM, called on the king in January 2000 to lift the ban on political parties.

Illegal Opposition and External Groups

People's United Democratic Movement (PUDM or Pudemo). Initial reports about Pudemo surfaced in 1989 when the government accused the group of illegally circulating political pamphlets. In mid-1990 it was reported that, after a period of inactivity, the group had resumed actively campaigning for electoral reform, multiparty democracy, and an end to corruption. The party unilaterally proclaimed its "legality" in February 1992.

In August 1993 party president Kislon SHONGWE reportedly requested refuge at the UK's high commission in Mbabane after he was listed among opposition figures being sought for distributing "seditious pamphlets." A month later Pudemo officials countered international praise for the government's electoral preparations, contending that the balloting could not be considered democratic if the 20-year-old state of emergency remained in place and political parties were not able to participate.

On January 1, 1996, Pudemo threatened to make the country "ungovernable" if the monarch failed to adopt a multiparty democratic system of government. Subsequently, it called for the establishment of an interim government to oversee a transition to democratic rule. Underscoring its more militant stance, Pudemo subsequently replaced Shongwe, who was described as "uncombative," and Secretary General Dominic MNGOMEZULU with Mario Masuku and Bonginkhosi Dlamini, respectively. Masuku was named to the constitutional

Cabinet

As of June 1, 2006

Prime Minister	Absalom Themba Dlamini
Deputy Prime Minister	Albert Shabangu

Ministers

Agriculture and Cooperatives	Mtiti Fakudze
Economic Planning and Development	Rev. Absalom Dlamini
Education	Constance Simelane [f]
Enterprise and Employment	Lufto E. Dlamini
Finance	Majozi Sithole
Foreign Affairs and Trade	Mathendele Moses Dlamini
Health and Social Welfare	Njabulo Mabuza
Home Affairs	Prince Gabheni Dlamini
Housing and Urban Development	Mabili Dlamini
Justice and Constitutional Affairs	Prince David Dlamini
Natural Resources and Energy	Dumsile Sukati [f]
Public Service and Information	Themba Msibi
Public Works and Transport	Elijah Shongwe
Regional Development and Youth Affairs	Chief Sipho Shongue
Tourism and Environment	Thandi Shongwe [f]

[f] = female

review commission established in May but subsequently resigned on the ground that it had become apparent that the King had no intention of lifting the political party ban. In November 2000, Pudemo was among the forces of opposition to join the general strike called by the SFTU during which Masuku was arrested, together with other opposition leaders. Masuku was acquitted of sedition charges in August 2002.

In 2005 the king accused 13 Pudemo members of firebombing homes and offices of government officials; all were released, but one member was fined $800 after pleading guilty to treason and testifying that Pudemo was behind the attacks. The government cracked down on a Pudemo rally in March 2006, arresting several party members, including Masuku (who was released the same day). Party leaders said they staged the protest to test the constitution's provision regarding political freedom.

Leaders: Mario MASUKU (President), Jerry NXUMALO, Bonginkhosi DLAMINI (Secretary General).

Ngwane National Liberation Congress (NNLC). The NNLC was at the forefront of opposition activities in the 1970s but thereafter was reported to have become defunct. At a meeting of the resuscitated body in December 1998, former prime minister Obed Mfanyana Dlamini was elected president of the congress, and in April 1999 he reportedly agreed to enter into the SDA. In the 2003 legislative elections, Dlamini was elected to the assembly after campaigning as a nonpartisan. In 2005 party member Jimmy HLOPHE, running as an unaffiliated individual, won an assembly seat in a special election following the death of a member of parliament.

Leader: Obed Mfanyana DLAMINI (President of the Party and Former Prime Minister).

Swazi Liberation Movement (Swalimo). The avowedly revolutionary Swalimo was launched in 1978 by Dr. Ambrose Zwane, formerly leader of the NNLC.

Leaders: Dr. Ambrose Phesheya ZWANE, Dumisa DLAMINI (Secretary General).

Swaziland Progressive Party (SPP). The SPP is an outgrowth of the former Swazi Progressive Association, founded in 1929.

Leader: J. J. NQUKU (President).

Swaziland United Front (SUF). The SUF was organized in 1962 as an offshoot of the SPP.

Leader: Matsapa SHONGWE.

Swaziland National Front (Swanafro). Swanafro is a small Manzini-based formation.

Leaders: Elmond SHONGWE (President), Glenrose DLAMINI (Secretary General).

Swaziland Solidarity Network (SSN). Based in South Africa and led by a South African, Solly Mapaila, the SSN is a "pressure group" that has been critical of the Swaziland regime's alleged efforts to squelch prodemocracy activity. In October 1997 Mapaila, who was himself banned from the kingdom for allegedly fomenting unrest, accused the monarch of maintaining a list of ANC officials it sought to ban from entering the country. The SSN launched a campaign in 2000 calling for the international community to "isolate" Swaziland until political reforms are enacted. It renewed its calls for international action in 2005, citing the king's reported extravagant spending while most of the population lives in extreme poverty.

Leader: Solly MAPAILA (Chair), Lucky Lukhele (Spokesperson).

Bombings in Mbabane in October and November 1998 were blamed on a militant group styled the "Black Tigers." An underground grouping called the Makhundu Congress claimed responsibility for a December 2000 bombing of a police and army camp.

Legislature

On October 9, 1992, King Mswati dissolved the bicameral **Parliament** (*Libandla*) in preparation for new elections scheduled to follow the adoption of a new multiparty constitution in 1993. However, further deliberation on the draft charter was suspended, and the 1993 and 1998 elections were held on a nonparty basis.

Senate. The Senate is composed of 30 members, 20 chosen by the monarch plus 10 elected by the House of Assembly from within its own ranks. The current upper house was appointed in late October 2003.

President: Chief Gelani ZWANE.

House of Assembly. Enlarged by 15 seats since the 1992 elections, the assembly consists of 65 members, 55 popularly elected (1 for each district) in addition to 10 monarchial appointees. Approximately 250 candidates participated in the most recent lower house balloting, which commenced on September 20 and concluded on October 18, 2003.

Speaker: Charles Sgayoyo MAGONGO.

Communications

In October 1997 the government established the Swaziland Media Council, a seven-member regulatory body.

Press

The following are published in Mbabane in English: *Times of Swaziland* (18,000), independent daily; *Swaziland Observer* (11,000), independent daily; *The Swazi News* (7,000), independent weekly. Publication of the *Swaziland Observer* was suspended from February 2000–January 2001 due to pressure from the government. In May 2001 the government banned two independent publications (*The Guardian of Swaziland* newspaper, and a weekly magazine, *The Nation*) for "operating illegally."

Broadcasting and Computing

The nation's radio sets receive commercial programs from the government-controlled Swaziland Broadcasting and Information Service and the privately owned Swaziland Commercial Radio, in addition to religious programs from Trans World Radio. The state-owned Swaziland Television Broadcasting Corporation (STBC) transmits to about 130,000 receivers. There were 30,000 personal computers serving 27,000 Internet users in 2003.

Intergovernmental Representation

Ambassador to the U.S.
Ephraim Mandlenkosi HLOPHE

U.S. Ambassador to Swaziland
Lewis W. LUCKE

Permanent Representative to the UN
Phesheya Mbongeni DLAMINI

IGO Memberships (Non-UN)
AfDB, AU, BADEA, Comesa, CWTH, Interpol, NAM, PCA, SADC, WCO, WTO

TANZANIA

UNITED REPUBLIC OF TANZANIA

Jamhuri ya Muungano wa Tanzania

The Country

The United Republic of Tanzania combines the large territory of Tanganyika on the East African mainland and the two islands of Zanzibar and Pemba off the East African coast. Tanzania's people are overwhelmingly of African (primarily Bantu) stock, but there are significant Asian (largely Indian and Pakistani), European, and Arab minorities. In addition to the indigenous tribal languages, Swahili (Kiunguja is the Zanzibari form) serves as a lingua franca, while English and Arabic are also spoken. A majority of the population (over 60 percent on the mainland and over 90 percent on Zanzibar) is Muslim, the remainder adhering to Christianity or traditional religious beliefs. Women are estimated to comprise nearly 50 percent of the labor force, with responsibility for over 70 percent of subsistence activities; Tanzanian women have a relatively high level of literacy and are represented in most levels of government and party affairs.

The economy is primarily agricultural, benefiting from few extractive resources except diamonds. The most important crops on the mainland are coffee, cotton, and sisal, which collectively account for approximately two-fifths of the country's exports. The economies of Zanzibar and Pemba are based on cloves and coconut products. Industry, which accounts for about 15 percent of the gross domestic product, is primarily limited to the processing of agricultural products and the production of nondurable consumer goods, although there is an oil refinery that is dependent on imported crude. Modernization plans were enhanced by the completion in mid-1976, with Chinese financial and technical assistance, of the Tanzania-Zambia Railway (Tazara), which links Dar es Salaam and the Zambian copper belt; however, chronic maintenance and management problems have limited Tazara's effectiveness in resolving bottlenecks in the transport sector.

Since 1979 the country has encountered serious economic difficulty, exacerbated by a decline in cash-crop output and rapid population growth. Assistance from the International Monetary Fund (IMF) was suspended in 1982, necessitating severe budget cutbacks. Four years later, faced with an external debt crisis, the government acceded to IMF demands for devaluation of the Tanzanian shilling, price increases for food producers, and

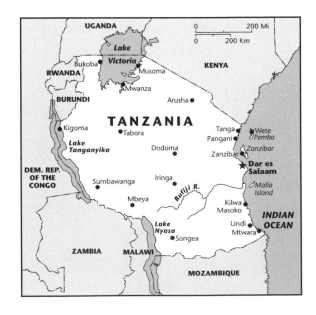

Political Status: Independent member of the Commonwealth; established in its present form April 26, 1964, through union of the Republic of Tanganyika (independent 1961) and the People's Republic of Zanzibar (independent 1963); one-party constitution adopted April 25, 1977; multiparty system legalized June 17, 1992.

Area: 364,898 sq. mi. (945,087 sq. km.), encompassing Tanganyika, 363,948 sq. mi. (942,626 sq. km.) and Zanzibar 950 sq. mi. (2,461 sq. mi., the latter including Pemba (350 sq. mi., 906 sq. km.).

Population: 34,569,232 (2002C); 35,426,000 (2005E).

Major Urban Centers (2005E): DAR ES SALAAM (2,692,000), Mwanza (219,000), Zanzibar (town, 217,000), Tanga (190,000), Dodoma (169,000). The deadline for the transfer of government operations to a new capital in Dodoma has been extended numerous times. Although the National Assembly now sits in Dodoma, it remains uncertain when, or even if, full governmental relocation will occur.

Official Languages: English, Swahili.

Monetary Unit: Shilling (official rate July 1, 2006: 1,255 shillings = $1US).

President: Jakaya KIKWETE (Revolutionary Party of Tanzania); elected on December 14, 2005, and sworn in for a five-year term on December 21 to succeed Benjamin William MKAPA (Revolutionary Party of Tanzania).

Vice President: Ali Mohamed SHEIN (Revolutionary Party of Tanzania); nominated by the president on July 13, 2001, and sworn in on the same day following confirmation by the National Assembly to succeed Omar Ali JUMA (Revolutionary Party of Tanzania), who had died on July 4; reelected concurrently with the president on December 14, 2005, and sworn in on December 21.

Prime Minister: Edward LOWASSA (Revolutionary Party of Tanzania); appointed by the president on December 29, 2005, following the general elections of December 14, and confirmed by the National Assembly and sworn in on December 30, 2005, in succession to Frederick Tluway SUMAYE (Revolutionary Party of Tanzania).

President of Zanzibar: Amani Abeid KARUME (Revolutionary Party of Tanzania); elected October 29, 2000 (with a partial rerun on November 5), and sworn in for a five-year term on November 8 to succeed Dr. Salmin AMOUR Jima (Revolutionary Party of Tanzania); reelected on October 30, 2005, and sworn in for a second five-year term on November 2.

liberalization of export-import regulations. Additional economic reforms were pledged during 1991 negotiations with the IMF, which had expressed concern over the slow pace of privatization of state-run enterprises and apparent widespread corruption in the government bureaucracy.

In early 1993 the IMF released an analysis of Tanzanian economic reform efforts during 1986–1992, which noted progress in the previous two years but urged the government to increase its efforts in four areas: liberalizing agricultural markets and prices, privatizing parastatals and state-run industries, controlling inflation, and reducing the money supply. More overt criticism resulted from a December 1994 informal meeting of Tanzanian fund donors in Paris that focused on financial mismanagement, including the government's poor record in customs collection and its frequent issuance of tax exemptions. However, in November 1996 the IMF approved a $234 million three-year credit to assist the economic reforms endorsed by the new Mkapa administration. Thereafter, gains were reported in the mining, agriculture, and tourism sectors. On the other hand, observers described the overall standard of living as dismal, citing drought-induced famine and an economy burdened by large debt-service payments. In April 2000 the IMF and World Bank agreed to support a comprehensive debt relief package for Tanzania, encouraged by reduction in the size of the public sector and greater influence of the free market.

GDP growth averaged about 6 percent annually in the early 2000s, based on expansion in the manufacturing, mining, and construction sectors. GDP growth was 6.3 percent in 2004 and 6.8 percent in 2005, while inflation was 4 percent in 2004 but rose to 6.9 percent in 2005. Poverty levels consequently declined, although drought in 2004 caused severe food shortages that required substantial international assistance. The IMF provided grants and loans under the Fund's Poverty Reduction and Growth Facility (PRGF) initiative. In 2006, Tanzania was one of 17 countries approved for additional debt relief through the World Bank's Heavily Indebted Poor Country (HIPC) initiative.

Government and Politics

Political Background

The former British-ruled territories of Tanganyika and Zanzibar developed along separate lines until their union in 1964. Tanganyika, occupied by Germany in 1884, became a British-administered mandate under the League of Nations and continued under British administration as a United Nations trust territory after World War II. Led by Julius K. NYERERE of the Tanganyika African National Union (TANU), it became independent within the Commonwealth in 1961 and adopted a republican form of government with Nyerere as president in 1962.

Zanzibar and Pemba, British protectorates since 1890, became independent in 1963 as a constitutional monarchy within the Commonwealth. However, little more than a month after independence, the Arab-dominated government of Sultan Seyyid Jamshid bin Abdullah bin KHALIFA was overthrown by African nationalists, who established a People's Republic with Sheikh Abeid Amani KARUME of the Afro-Shirazi Party (ASP) as president.

Following overtures by Nyerere, the two countries combined on April 26, 1964, to form the United Republic of Tanganyika and Zanzibar, renamed the United Republic of Tanzania later in the same year. Nyerere became president of the unified state, and in September 1965 he was overwhelmingly confirmed in that position by popular vote in both sections of the country. Karume, in addition to becoming first vice president of Tanzania, continued to head the quasi-independent Zanzibar administration until April 1972, when he was assassinated. Nyerere thereupon appointed Aboud JUMBE to succeed Karume as first vice president and as leader of the ASP.

On February 5, 1977, TANU and the ASP merged to form the Revolutionary Party of Tanzania (CCM); subsequently, a new constitution was adopted on April 25, according the CCM a "dominant" role in the Tanzanian governmental system. On November 5, 1980, Prime Minister Edward SOKOINE announced his retirement for reasons of health, and two days later the president named Cleopa David MSUYA as Sokoine's successor. Sokoine returned as prime minister on February 24, 1983, but was killed in an automobile accident on April 12, 1984; he was succeeded 12 days later by Salim Ahmed SALIM. Earlier, on January 27, Vice President Jumbe had submitted his resignation in the wake of mounting secessionist agitation on Zanzibar, Ali Hassan MWINYI having been named his replacement on January 30.

Carrying out a pledge made in early 1984 to step down as head of state upon the expiration of his existing term, Nyerere withdrew from contention at the 1985 CCM congress in favor of Vice President Mwinyi, who was overwhelmingly nominated as the sole candidate for the October presidential balloting. Because of a constitutional prohibition against Zanzibaris occupying both presidential and prime ministerial offices, Prime Minister Salim was replaced following the October 27 poll by Justice Minister Joseph S. WARIOBA, who also assumed the post of first vice president; concurrently, Idris Abdul WAKIL, who had been elected president of Zanzibar on October 13, became second vice president, while Salim was named deputy prime minister and minister of defense.

Mwinyi's elevation to the presidency and his encouragement of private enterprise appeared to stem secessionist sentiment on Zanzibar. However, discord attributed to a variety of economic, religious, and political motives broke out again in late 1987. An apparent power struggle developed between Wakil and supporters of Chief Minister Seif Sharif HAMAD, a leader from the northern island of Pemba (where 90 percent of the islands' cloves are produced), after Hamad was dropped from the CCM Central Committee. On January 23, 1988, Wakil, claiming that dissidents were plotting a coup, suspended the Zanzibari government; three days later he announced a new administration in which Hamad was replaced by Omar Ali JUMA. In May Hamad and six of his supporters were expelled from the CCM for alleged "antiparty" activity. Observers reported a continued "undercurrent of rebellion" on the islands, however, and Hamad was arrested in May 1989 on charges of organizing illegal meetings, the government also accusing his supporters of forming a political group, *Bismallah* ("In the name of God"), dedicated to "breaking the union."

Mwinyi continued to consolidate his authority during 1990; in March he ousted hard-line socialist cabinet members who opposed his economic policies, and, following Nyerere's retirement on August 17, he was elected CCM chair. On October 28 the president won reelection for a second five-year term, and on November 8 he named John S. MALECELA first vice president and prime minister, replacing Warioba. Meanwhile, on October 21 Salmin AMOUR had been elected president of Zanzibar and second vice president of the republic after Wakil had declined to seek reelection to the posts.

On June 17, 1992, President Mwinyi signed a bill legalizing opposition parties. The legislation had been approved by the National Assembly on May 7 and by the Zanzibar House of Representatives on May 14, following endorsement by the CCM in February. On July 1 the CCM became the first group to be officially registered under the new law, and by the end of August, 12 of the reportedly 35 parties that had requested application forms had been granted provisional registration.

In late 1992 the government released a tentative multiparty electoral schedule, beginning with municipal and local balloting in 1993 and concluding with national elections in 1994–1995. Subsequently, the Civic United Front (CUF), a promi-

nent opposition grouping, and four smaller parties threatened to boycott the polling, saying that the delays favored the CCM and calling instead for the convening of a constitutional conference before any elections were held.

In February 1993, Zanzibari membership in the Organization of the Islamic Conference (OIC) was categorized as "unconstitutional" and "separatist" by a Tanzanian parliamentary commission. (The membership was reportedly withdrawn in August 1993, although uncertainty on the question continued into 2000 [see Membership in OIC article].) The affair highlighted continued debate within the government over the two regions' respective roles, as well as a growing schism between Christians and Muslims, which was further evidenced by the anti-Muslim rhetoric of the increasingly popular Democratic Party leader, Rev. Christopher MTIKILA, and the militant activities of the Council for the Dissemination of the Koran in Tanzania (*Balukta*) (see under Political Parties, below).

In April 1993, at the first balloting since the introduction of multipartyism, the CCM, aided by a CUF boycott, easily won two Zanzibari municipal by-elections. However, fiscal problems, coupled with the Muslim fundamentalist issue, continued to bedevil the ruling party. By late 1994, with less than a year remaining before the next presidential poll, its leadership had fallen into disarray, with former president Nyerere criticizing President Mwinyi as a political weakling and attacking Prime Minister Malecela and CCM Secretary General Horace KOLIMBA as "hooligans" who should resign their positions. The immediate upshot was an extraordinary event: a total ministerial boycott of a cabinet meeting called by the president. Mwinyi responded on December 4 by dissolving the National Assembly, and on December 5 he named a new government headed by former prime minister Cleopa Msuya. Meanwhile, the assembly, two days before the dissolution, had approved a constitutional amendment that created a furor on Zanzibar by specifying that henceforth the island president would no longer become a union vice president unless specifically elected as the president's running mate.

In preparation for the first nationwide multiparty elections, the CCM in July 1995 elected Minister of Science Benjamin William MKAPA as its presidential nominee, President Mwinyi being ineligible for a third term. The balloting of October 29 featured more than 1,300 legislative candidates, with nine opposition parties announcing that they would form a postelectoral coalition if it would give them a parliamentary majority. However, in results that were hotly disputed, Mkapa was credited with winning 61.8 percent of the valid presidential votes, while the CCM garnered 186 of 232 elective assembly seats. Earlier, in even more contentious Zanzibari balloting on October 22, the National Electoral Commission (NEC) had announced that President Amour had been reelected on a 52 percent vote share, with the CCM having been awarded 26 of 50 elective seats in the Zanzibar House of Representatives. Mkapa subsequently named former agriculture minister Frederick Tulway SUMAYE to head a new cabinet, which contained a majority of relatively young newcomers and excluded nearly all former ministers who had been tinged by charges of corruption.

Of 13 opposition parties that contested the 1995 election, only 4 obtained legislative representation. Their disappointing capture of only 24 percent of the seats on a near 40 percent share of the vote was attributed by many to the majority electoral system and by some to widespread electoral fraud, particularly in the Zanzibari balloting, in which the opposition's Seif Hamad was widely believed to have attracted more than the 48 percent vote share officially credited to him in the presidential poll.

Mkapa's economic and political reform efforts in 1996 drew broad praise. Such advances were overshadowed, however, by the political stalemate in Zanzibar where the CUF continued to boycott the legislature in protest over the CCM's alleged rigging of the 1995 elections. In addition, the government's anticorruption campaign was tarnished by the resignation of several ministers in late 1996 and early 1997 following bribery and abuse of power investigations, which also prompted a cabinet reshuffle in February 1997.

In January 1998 Commonwealth mediators introduced a seven-point plan to ease the tension in Zanzibar. However, both sides rejected the accord, with President Amour of Zanzibar asserting that there was no crisis. In March the Commonwealth released another proposal that was subsequently reported to have been positively received by the CCM and CUF negotiators. The government continued its crackdown on alleged CUF militants in early 1999, but an agreement was finally signed by the CCM and the CUF providing for the return of the CUF to the National Assembly, the award of two additional assembly seats to the CUF, and the creation of an independent electoral commission to oversee the elections scheduled for October 2000. Each side subsequently charged the other with foot-dragging in implementing some provisions of the accord, and tension remained substantial on the island, exacerbated by the death in October 1999 of former president Nyerere, whose considerable domestic and international prestige and influence had been credited with holding the shaky union together despite significant opposition on both the mainland and the islands. Attention in early 2000 focused on the attempt by Zanzibari President Amour to have the constitution amended to permit him to run for a third term. After reportedly "tumultuous" debate, the CCM rejected the appeal from Amour, who had been widely criticized on Zanzibar for hardline tactics including the arrest of prominent CUF members on treason charges (see CUF under Political Parties, below).

Balloting for the National Assembly and Zanzibar's House of Representatives as well as for the presidencies of Tanzania and Zanzibar was held on October 29, 2000. However, reruns were required in 16 island constituencies on November 5 because of ballot problems in the initial poll. (The CUF and many other opposition parties boycotted the reruns, arguing that new voting should have been ordered in all island constituencies.) Final results showed President Mkapa easily securing a second five-year term with 71.7 percent of the vote against three rivals. In addition, the CCM maintained its stranglehold on the assembly and a comfortable majority in the House of Representatives.

Meanwhile, the CCM's Amani Abeid Karume, the son of the first president of independent Zanzibar, was declared winner of the Zanzibari presidential poll with 67 percent of the vote. On November 23, President Mkapa reappointed Prime Minister Sumaye to head a significantly reshuffled CCM cabinet.

On October 27, the vice presidential candidate of the Party for Democracy and Progress (Chadema) party unexpectedly died and consequently, the NEC postponed presidential and legislative balloting on the mainland until December 14 but allowed balloting for offices in Zanzibar to go forward. The Zanzibari elections were marked by flaws and violence, which required a new round of voting in approximately one-third of the districts (see Current issues). Incumbent President Karume was reelected, and the CCM retained its majority in the Zanzibari legislature. Opposition parties decried the balloting and challenged the results.

The CCM candidate, Foreign Minister Jakaya MIKWETE, easily won the 2005 presidential election in Tanzania with more than 80 percent of the vote. In addition, the CCM increased its majority in the National Assembly. Edward LOWASSA was appointed prime minister on December 29, and a CCM cabinet was approved by the assembly on January 6, 2006.

Constitution and Government

An "interim" document of 1965 was replaced on April 25, 1977, by a "permanent" constitution, although the system of government was essentially unaltered. A number of amendments were adopted prior to the 1985 election; significantly, however, Tanzania remained a one-party state, with controlling influence exercised by the CCM at both national and regional levels. Legislation authorizing multiparty activity was approved in 1992 (see Political background, above).

The president is elected by universal suffrage for no more than two five-year terms. Since 1995 the vice president has also been elected as part of a national president/vice president ticket. (Previously, Tanzania had two vice presidents: the president of Zanzibar [who served as first vice president if the president was from the mainland] and a presidentially appointed prime minister. The December 1994 constitutional amendment ending the automatic designation of the Zanzibar president as one of the two vice presidents left the insular region without mandated representation at the national executive level.) The prime minister is currently appointed by the president subject to confirmation by the National Assembly. Cabinet ministers are also appointed by the president.

The National Assembly, more than four-fifths of whose members are at present directly elected, sits for a five-year term, subject to presidential dissolution (in which case the president himself must stand for reelection). The judicial system on the mainland is headed by a High Court and includes local and district courts. In August 1979 a Tanzanian Court of Appeal was established to assume, inter alia, the functions of the East African Court of Appeal, which had ceased to exist with the collapse of the East African Community in 1977. All judges are appointed by the president.

Tanzania's 25 administrative regions (20 on the mainland, 5 on Zanzibar) are each headed by a regional commissioner appointed by the central government. Below the regional level there are municipalities, town councils, and, in rural locations, area or district councils.

On October 13, 1979, a new constitution for Zanzibar was promulgated by its Revolutionary Council after having been approved by the CCM. Under the new system, designed to provide for "more democracy" without contravening the union constitution of Tanzania, the president of Zanzibar is directly elected for a five-year term and held to a maximum of two successive terms. There is also a largely elected House of Representatives endowed with the legislative authority previously exercised by the Revolutionary Council. The latter, however, has been retained as a "high executive council" of cabinet status, with members appointed by the president.

In 2000 the Thirteenth Amendment was ratified by a two-thirds majority in the National Assembly. The measure expanded presidential prerogatives to include the appointment of ten members to the National Assembly and permited election of the president by a plurality instead of a majority of voters. The amendment also increased the percentage of seats reserved for women from 15 percent to 20 percent. In February 2005 the Fourteenth Amendment was ratified by the assembly. The measure had a number of provisions, including a section that allowed the prime minister to act as president in the absence of the president and vice president. It also loosened the rules surrounding electoral campaigning.

Foreign Relations

Tanzania belongs to the United Nations and most of its Specialized Agencies, the Commonwealth, and the African Union. In addition, it participated with Kenya and Uganda in the East African Community (EAC) until the organization was dissolved in mid-1977. Under President Nyerere's leadership, Tanzania pursued a policy of international nonalignment and of vigorous opposition to colonialism and racial discrimination, particularly in southern Africa, maintaining no relations with Pretoria and strongly supporting the effort of the Front-Line States to avoid South African trade routes. In addition, declaring South African destabilization efforts in nearby states to be a direct threat to Tanzania, the government in 1987 sent troops to Mozambique to assist Maputo in the fight against Renamo rebels. (The troops were withdrawn in December 1988, in part, reportedly, because of the cost of their maintenance.) Tanzania also gave asylum to political refugees from African countries, and various liberation groups were headquartered in Dar es Salaam.

Relations with Britain were severed from 1965 to 1968 to protest London's Rhodesian policy. Relations with the United States have been strained at times by Tanzanian disagreement with U.S. policies on Africa and, until Washington's rapprochement with Peking, by U.S. uneasiness over Tanzanian acceptance of military and economic aid from China.

Long-standing friction with Uganda escalated into overt military conflict in late 1978 (see article on Uganda). After a six-month campaign that involved the deployment of some 40,000 Tanzanian troops, the forces of Ugandan president Idi Amin were decisively defeated, Amin fleeing to Libya. Subsequently, under an agreement signed with the government of Godfrey Binaisa, approximately 20,000 Tanzanians remained in the country to man security points pending the training of a new Ugandan army. During 1980 Kenya and Sudan were among the regional states expressing concern over the continuing presence in Uganda of the Tanzanian troops, the last of which were finally withdrawn in May–June 1981.

Relations with Kenya improved measurably upon the conclusion of a November 1983 accord among the two and Uganda on the distribution of EAC assets and liabilities. The border between Tanzania and Kenya, originally closed in 1977 to "punish" Kenya for allegedly dominating Tanzania's economy, was reopened, and the two countries reached agreement on a series of technical cooperation issues. Rapprochement was further enhanced in December, when the three former EAC members exchanged high commissioners in an effort "to facilitate expansion and consolidation in economic matters." (See Foreign relations in article on Kenya for information regarding the recent reactivation of the EAC.)

In September 1995 Prime Minister Msuya appealed to the UN High Commissioner for Refugees (UNHCR) to aid in the repatriation of more than 800,000 Burundian and Rwandan refugees living in border area camps. In January 1996 the Tanzanian Army turned back an estimated 17,000 Rwandan Hutu refugees fleeing violence in Burundi; however, three days later the government reversed itself and reopened its border. In February relations between Tanzania and Burundi were enhanced by an agreement on border security and refugee repatriation; however, in March, as fighting in Burundi spilled over Tanzania's border, Dar es Salaam rejected the appointment of a Burundian ambassador for the second time, asserting that it was "not siding with either" of the combatants in its neighbor's burgeoning civil war.

Conditions deteriorated significantly toward the end of 1996 when large numbers of Hutu refugees crossed Burundi from Zaire (where Tutsis had destroyed Hutu camps and assumed control of the eastern part of the country) into Tanzania. Burundi's President Buyoya accused Tanzania of supporting Hutu "rebels" and criticized former Tanzanian president Nyerere for spearheading the regional economic sanctions against Burundi. A number of cross-border skirmishes, substantial troop build-up on both sides, and diplomatic posturing were reported throughout 1997, and in February 1998 regional leaders, including President Mpaka, agreed to maintain the sanctions they had first imposed on Burundi in 1996. However, in early 1999 Dar es Salaam lifted its sanctions and announced that it was reestablishing diplomatic relations with Bujumbura. Subsequently, in March, Tanzania ordered the 20,000 Rwandan refugees remaining within its borders to return home, describing security conditions there as safe. However, tension continued into 2000 because of the presence in Tanzania of Rwandan and (especially) Burundian refugees and guerrillas. For example, Tanzanian security forces "arrested" over 160 Burundian Hutu "militiamen" in early 2000.

By the end of 2002, the UN estimated that there were 540,000 Burundian refugees in Tanzania. However, in light of the normalization of relations between the two countries, the governments subsequently launched a broad effort to repatriate the refugees. Additional border crossings were opened, and by the end of 2003 there were 324,000 refugees left. Meanwhile, by February 2004 Tanzania had returned all identifiable Rwandan refugees; according to UN estimates, 20,000 remained in Tanzania illegally.

Earlier, on August 7, 1998, 11 Tanzanians had been killed in Dar es Salaam when alleged militant Islamic fundamentalists set off simultaneous bomb blasts at U.S. embassies in Tanzania and Kenya. (For further details see article on Kenya.)

The European Union (EU) provided $1.9 million in aid to support the 2001 peace accord between the government and the CUF and $14.82 million to assist Burundian refugees. Collaterally, relations between Tanzania and the United Kingdom have remained strong. The UK agreed in 2003 to provide assistance for Tanzania's refugee repatriation efforts, and in 2005 the UK announced that Tanzania would be the first African country to benefit from an initiative to write off the debt of poorer countries. Later in 2005, however, a diplomatic row occurred between the two countries when Tanzania unilaterally ended a $143.5 million water privatization project funded jointly by Britain and the World Bank. The Tanzanian government charged that the foreign companies involved in the project were not fulfilling their obligations. In 2006, the United States granted Tanzania $11 million for an anti-corruption campaign and included the country among six other African states to receive funding from a $1.2 billion initiative to suppress malaria. The United States recently increased its security assistance to Tanzania for counterterrorism efforts.

Current Issues

A key factor in President Mkapa's successful reelection bid in late 2000 was the fractured nature of the opposition, which was unable to agree on a single candidate to challenge him. International observers were generally satisfied with the conduct of the presidential and legislative balloting on the mainland but strongly criticized the situation on the islands. Commonwealth officials described the Zanzibar polls as a "shambles" resulting from "either massive incompetence or a deliberate attempt to wreck at least part of this election." Despite appeals to rerun the voting throughout the islands, the government agreed to new voting in only 16 of 50 constituencies there, leading the CUF and many of the other opposition parties to boycott that round and refuse to accept the final official results of the national and Zanzibari elections as legitimate.

Reflecting widespread anger over the perceived biased nature of the election administration, the CUF in late January 2001 organized demonstrations in Zanzibar and mainland Tanzania, demanding new elections. The government banned the demonstrations and proceeded to disperse the protesters. At least 40 people were killed by police on Pemba under highly questionable circumstances, while some detainees were allegedly subjected to torture and other ill-treatment.

After protracted negotiations, on October 10, 2001, the CCM signed an agreement with the CUF to end the political impasse that had followed the January violence. The accord addressed a number of human rights issues and called for establishment of an independent commission of inquiry into the unrest and provision of compensation to those affected. A Zanzibar court subsequently freed two senior opposition party officials after the state dropped murder charges against them.

In April 2002 the Zanzibari House of Representatives approved constitutional amendments designed to codify several of the changes approved in October 2001. Among other things, the reforms called for restructuring of the electoral commission to include opposition representation. Also envisioned were the establishment of permanent voter lists and reform of the judiciary. In 2004 the Revolutionary Council on Zanzibar announced plans for a new flag, national anthem, and identity cards for the island.

Politics on Zanzibar were subsequently reported to be increasingly influenced by Islamic activism, in part by supporters of the Union for Awakening and Islamic Forums (*Uamsho*), which organized several antigovernment demonstrations that led to the arrest of some top opposition leaders. There was widespread violence prior to the October 2005 elections; government and opposition groups were accused of attacks. The government reportedly launched a series of raids on the headquarters of opposition parties and arrested a number of opposition leaders. Subsequent rioting left some 14 people dead, and the administration suspended registration of new parties. Meanwhile, in April 2005, CCM offices were bombed on Zanzibar, and a party official was murdered in a separate incident. Police subsequently arrested four activists in connection with the bombing. After the polling in Zanzibar, CUF members and supporters rioted to protest the results, and security forces used tear gas and force to disperse the protesters. Opposition groups complained that the CCM sponsored groups

of youths (dubbed *Janjaweed* after the Sudanese militias) who intimidated voters, and that voters in some districts were either turned away from polling stations or had their ballots destroyed. International observers noted some irregularities but described the voting as generally free and fair. Polling on the mainland was not marred by violence, according to international monitors.

A long-term drought continued to affect Tanzania in 2006. In April the government ordered farmers and ranchers to stop encroaching on game preserves and national parks by June. The drought reduced the country's hydroelectric output and caused mandatory blackouts in some areas of the country.

Political Parties

Constitutional amendments in 1992 allowed the formation of political parties other than the CCM. The first multiparty elections were held in 1995. Nonetheless, the CCM has continued to dominate the legislature and the presidency. In February 2003 opposition parties formed an electoral coalition to oppose the CCM in presidential and legislative balloting in October 2005. The coalition chose Bob Nyanga MAKANI of the Party for Democracy and Progress (*Chama Cha Demokrasia na Maendeleo*–Chadema) as its chair. Besides Chadema, the coalition included the Civic United Front (CUF), the United Democratic Party (UDP), the National Convention for Constitution and Reform-Maguezi (NCCR-Maguezi), the Tanzania Democratic Alliance Party (Tadea), the National Reconstruction Alliance (NRA), the Democratic Party (*Chama Cha Demokrasi*–CCD), the National League for Democracy (NLD), the United People's Democratic Party (UPDP), and the Forum for Restoration of Democracy (FORD). The only major opposition parties that did not join the alliance were the Tanzania Labor Party (TLP) and the Justice and Development Party (*Chama cha Haki na Usitawi Chausta*). The alliance failed to present a unified candidate list for the 2005 legislative balloting and could not unite behind a single candidate in the mainland presidential polling.

Some parties supported the CUF candidate, while a group of four parties rallied behind the NCCR-Maguezi candidate.

Government Party

Revolutionary Party of Tanzania (*Chama Cha Mapinduzi*—CCM). The CCM was formally launched on February 5, 1977, two weeks after a merger was authorized by a joint conference of the Tanganyika African National Union (TANU) and the Afro-Shirazi Party (ASP) of Zanzibar. During the January conference, President Nyerere had asserted that the new organization would be "supreme" over the governments of both mainland Tanzania and Zanzibar. Subsequently, a National Executive Committee (NEC) was named by a process of hierarchical (indirect) election, with the NEC, in turn, appointing a smaller Central Committee, headed by President Nyerere.

Founded in 1954, TANU had been instrumental in winning Tanganyika's independence from Britain in 1961. It served after independence as the nation's leading policymaking forum, nominating the president and candidates for election to the National Assembly. Its program, as set forth in the 1967 Arusha Declaration and other pronouncements, called for the development of a democratic, socialist, one-party state.

The ASP, organized in 1956–1957 by Sheikh Abeid Amani Karume, had played a minor role in Zanzibari politics until the coup of 1964. Subsequently, it became the dominant party in Zanzibar and the leading force in the Zanzibar Revolutionary Council. Communist and Cuban models influenced its explicitly socialist program.

During the CCM's national conference in 1982, delegates approved a series of proposals advanced by the NEC to reestablish a separation of powers between party and state, particularly at the regional and local levels. Delegates to an extraordinary national party conference in February 1992 unanimously endorsed the introduction of a multiparty system. At the party's fourth national conference, held in Dodoma on December 17–20, Ali Hassan Mwinyi, who had succeeded Nyerere as state president and party chair in 1985 and 1990, respectively, was reelected chair. In addition, delegates elected (then) Prime Minister Malecela and Dr. Salmin Amour, a Zanzibari, as vice chairmen.

During the first half of 1993 acrimonious debate between the party's mainland and island factions over the selection process for the vice presidency and military leadership led to the cancellation of two CCM meetings. Furthermore, the party experienced rifts over how to respond to Christopher MTIKILA, the (then) prominent leader of the CCD (below).

In July 1995 Benjamin William Mkapa, then minister of science, education, and technology, defeated two opponents in intraparty balloting for designation as the CCM presidential nominee, and he was subsequently credited with a 61.8 percent vote share in the October–November general election. Underlining his commitment to a reform-minded agenda, Mpaka named only one senior CCM party official to his technocrat-dominated cabinet. Although observers praised the new president's early initiatives, a split emerged within the party between Mpaka's supporters and old guard members aligned with former first vice president and prime minister Malecela and former party secretary general Horace Kolimba.

At party balloting on June 22, 1996, Mpaka easily captured the party chairship and, bringing his reform efforts to bear on the CCM, began to replace "old guard" members with his supporters. In February 1997 Horace Kolimba publicly denounced the new team of CCM leaders for their lack of "vision" (a charge that was promptly seconded by the CCM's Pius MSEKWA, speaker of the assembly). Furthermore, Kolimba accused the party of abandoning its "socialist" origins. The intraparty flap and public relations imbroglio arising from Kolimba's statements quickly dissipated in March after Kolimba died of a heart attack while defending his position to party officials. At a party congress in 1997, Mkapa was reelected to the party's top post by acclamation; meanwhile, Mkapa's continued efforts to infuse fresh blood into the CCM resulted in the election of a number of new faces to top posts. On the other hand, John Malecela's retention of the vice chairship was described by observers as a reminder of the continued influence (albeit waning), of the party's old guard.

In 1998 the CCM experienced further intraparty tension when, after minimal consultation, Mkapa appointed a three-member CCM team to meet with Commonwealth officials in charge of the negotiations to end the Zanzibar stalemate. Several powerful CCM leaders were subsequently reported to be considering forming a breakaway group in reaction to the CCM-CUF agreement of early 1999. However, as the October 2000 national elections approached, the CCM exhibited greater unity and discipline. A March 2000 special congress rejected an intense effort by controversial Zanzibar President Amour to have the constitution amended to permit him to run for a third term. The CCM also subsequently agreed to delay further consideration of proposed constitutional amendments that had been condemned by opposition groups on both the mainland and Zanzibar.

At a June 2000 CCM congress, President Mkapa was selected without opposition to run for a second term in the October poll. Concurrently, Amani Abeid Karume, a longtime member of the Zanzibari cabinet, was chosen as the CCM candidate for president of Zanzibar from among four candidates, including one supported by Amour. Karume was widely viewed as a strong candidate for the post based on his anticorruption image and the fact that he was the son of Abeid Amani Karume, the first president of independent Zanzibar.

Mkapa was reelected party chair at the 2002 CCM party convention. By April 2005, 11 CCM members had declared their intention to run to succeed Mkapa as president. At a party congress in May, Foreign Minister Jakaya Kikwete was chosen as the party's candidate for the mainland presidency. Kikwete subsequently won the national balloting and was sworn in as president in December 2005. Edward Lowassa, former water minister, was appointed prime minister and formed a CCM government. At a party congress in June 2006, Kikwete was elected party chair.

Leaders: Jakaya KIKWETE (President of the Republic and Chair of the Party), Benjamin William MKAPA (Former President of the Repub-

lic), John MALECELA (Vice Chair, Mainland), Ali Hassan MWINYI (Former President of the Republic), Ali Mohamed SHEIN (Vice President of the Republic), Edward LOWASSA (Prime Minister), Amani Abeid KARUME (President of Zanzibar and Vice Chair, Zanzibar), Samwel SITTA (Speaker of the National Assembly), Salim Ahmed SALIM (Member of the Executive Committee and Former Secretary General of the Organization of African Unity), Philip MANGULA (Secretary General).

Opposition Parties

Civic United Front (CUF). Also referenced as the People's Party (*Chama Cha Wananchi—CCW*), the CUF was founded in late 1991 by former NCCR-Maguezi leader James MAPALALA, a lawyer who had also been instrumental in the February 1990 establishment of the Civil and Legal Rights Movement. Mapalala was reportedly arrested following the creation of the CUF, which was then deemed to be an illegal formation.

As in the case of other opposition groups, the CUF has been wracked by internal dissent; party chair Mapalala went so far in 1994 as to institute court action against his deputy, Seif Sharif Hamad, and Secretary General Shaaban MLOO. Although Hamad was officially declared runner-up to Salmin Amour in Zanzibar's 1995 presidential race, many observers felt he was the actual victor. Labeling the Amour government "illegal," the CUF refused to assume its Zanzibar parliamentary seats and accused the government of falsely arresting its members. Thereafter, despite a ban on its activities, CUF-directed unrest spread, with observers attributing incidents of arson and harassment to the group.

The split between the CUF's mainland and island wings widened dramatically in early 1997 when the former passed a resolution recognizing Amour's Zanzibar government. Intraparty dissension continued to plague the CUF throughout the year, and, in December, 14 members were arrested for their alleged roles in a coup plot in Zanzibar. In early 1998 further arrests of CUF dissidents were reported.

In May 1998 Mapalala broke with the CUF, announcing that he had formed a new group, the Justice and Democracy Party (below). Meanwhile, at Commonwealth-brokered negotiations with the Amour administration, CUF islanders agreed to participate in legislative proceedings, abandoning the position that Amour had to be removed prior to the representatives being seated.

The trial of the 18 CUF members (including four members of the House of Representatives) arrested in 1997–1998 formally opened in February 1999, the charge against them having been upgraded to treason, which carried a mandatory death sentence upon conviction. Proceedings were subsequently postponed until January 2000, when another short session resulted in further delay until at least August. Meanwhile, domestic and international human rights groups criticized the prolonged imprisonment of the defendants, whom Amnesty International described as "prisoners of conscience," and the apparent political nature of the charges.

At a general congress in early June 2000, Hamad was once again selected as the CUF candidate for president of Zanzibar in the balloting scheduled for October. The CUF candidate for president of Tanzania, Ibrahim Lipumba, finished second in the 2000 poll with 16.3 percent of the vote, while Hamad was credited with 33 percent of the vote in the controversial balloting for president of Zanzibar (see Current issues, above). Meanwhile, all of the 16 seats the CUF secured in the 2000 balloting for the Zanzibar House of Representatives came from CUF strongholds on Pemba. In the 2005 elections, Hamad was again the CUF's candidate for the presidency of Zanzibar. Hamad was defeated in controversial balloting in which he received 46.07 percent of the vote. (Only 32,000 votes separated Hamad from the winning candidate.) In the legislative balloting in Zanzibar, the CUF increased its seats in the house to 19. Lipumba was also the CUF candidate for president of Tanzania in 2005, but he was again defeated, securing only 11.68 percent of the vote. The CUF remained the largest opposition party with 30 seats in the Tanzanian assembly.

Leaders: Seif Sharif HAMAD (1995, 2000, and 2005 candidate for President of Zanzibar, Secretary General), Ibrahim LIPUMBA (1995, 2000, and 2005 candidate for President of Tanzania and Chair of the Party).

Party for Democracy and Progress (*Chama Cha Demokrasia na Maendeleo*—Chadema). Chadema was launched in 1993 by former finance minister Edwin I. M. Mtei. It was awarded three elected assembly seats in 1995.

In 1997 Chadema stunned observers when it forwarded the controversial Rev. Christopher Mtikila as a candidate at a legislative by-election contest. (Described by *Africa Confidential* as a "fiery xenophobic evangelist," Mtikila, theretofore leader of the CCD, below, has been a staunch critic of the mainland's union with Zanzibar.)

Chadema supported the CUF candidate in the 2000 presidential poll; in concurrent legislative balloting the party improved its representation to four of the elected seats. The Chadema vice presidential candidate in the 2005 mainland elections died on October 27, 2005, causing a postponement of the balloting until December 14. The party's presidential candidate, Freeman Mbowe, placed third with 5.9 percent of the vote. Chadema secured five of the elected seats in the legislative polls.

Leaders: Freeman MBOWE (2005 presidential candidate and Chair), Edwin I. M. MTEI (2000 presidential candidate), Willbroad SLAA (Secretary General).

Tanzania Labor Party (TLP). This small party's profile grew significantly in 1999 when leading opposition figure Augustine Mrema and over 1000 of his followers joined after leaving the NCCR-Maguezi. Mrema won 7 percent of the vote in the 2000 presidential poll, while the TLP secured three of the elected seats in concurrent assembly elections. In mid-2001 the TLP was reportedly riven by factions devoted to Mrema and party founder Leo LWEKAMWA.

The TLP opposed the opposition coalition formed for the October 2005 election and decided to contest the balloting independently. Its candidate, Mrema, placed fourth with less than one percent of the vote. The TLP secured one seat in the assembly.

Leaders: Augustine MREMA (2000 and 2005 presidential candidate and Chair), Rajabu TAO.

United Democratic Party (UDP). The UDP's John Cheyo ran fourth in the 1995 presidential race, with a 3.94 percent vote share; in the assembly balloting the party ran fifth, winning three elective seats. In 1997 the UDP added a fifth seat when Cheyo scored an upset victory in a by-election contest expected to be won by a NCCR-Maguezi candidate. Cheyo secured 4.2 percent of the vote in the 2000 presidential poll. The UDP was a member of the opposition electoral coalition in the 2005 balloting and supported the CUF candidate in the presidential election. The party secured one seat in the assembly.

Leaders: John CHEYO (1995 and 2000 presidential candidate and Chair), Teddy Kassela BANTU (Secretary General).

National Convention for Constitution and Reform–Maguezi (NCCR-Maguezi). The NCCR-Maguezi was formed in the first half of 1991 as an outgrowth of the Steering Committee for a Transition Towards a Multiparty System, a broad-based organization comprising leading businessmen and lawyers as well as political dissidents and student activists. Its initial chair, Abdallah Said FUNDIKIRA, and vice-chair, James K. Mapalala, subsequently formed splinter organizations (below), although their successors vowed to keep the committee at the forefront of the "multiparty debate" and to push for its legalization. The party was again split in 1994 when Secretary General Prince Mahinja BAGENDA and several of his supporters withdrew to form the **National Convention for Constitution and Reform–***Asili* (the Swahili word for "original").

In April 1995 Augustine Lyatonga MREMA, who had been dismissed as minister of Labor and Youth Development in February for "indiscipline" and who withdrew from the CCM a month later, was selected as the NCCR-Maguezi's standard-bearer for the presidential election in October. Mrema was credited with only 27.8 percent of the vote, while his party captured only 16 of 232 elective assembly seats.

Asserting that the current constitution unfairly hampered the opposition's electoral ambitions, the NCCR-Maguezi announced in early 1997 that its

top priority for the year would be to pressure the government into organizing a constitutional conference. However, in May the party's stated agenda was overshadowed when Mabere MARANDO, the NCCR-Maguezi's secretary general, and Masumbuko LAMWAI, a NCCR-Maguezi parliamentarian and former CCM member, attempted to oust Mrema, who had accused Marando of acting in complicity with the CCM. During the subsequent legal and political infighting, the Central Committee reportedly aligned behind Marando and his supporters and the National Executive Committee with Mrema. The reportedly irreconcilable nature of the split was underscored by the unwillingness of the two factions (styled the NCCR-Mrema and NCCR-Marando) to cooperate on by-election campaigns, thus, according to observers, costing the group winnable legislative seats. Furthermore, in October both factions sent representatives to an opposition summit.

After sustained legal and political infighting between the two camps, in April 1999 Mrema announced that he was leaving the NCCR-Maguezi to join the TLP (see below). Lamwai subsequently rejoined the CCM. The NCCR-Maguezi won only one elected seat in the 2000 legislative poll, while its proposed presidential candidate, Edith LUSINA, was precluded from running for failure to secure sufficient advance signatures of support.

In the 2005 presidential election, four parties, including the FORD, NRA, UMD, and the UPDP, agreed to support the NCCR-Maguezi candidate, Sengondo Mvungi. The NCCR-Maguezi failed to gain any seats in the assembly.

Leaders: James MBATIA (Chair), Sengondo MVUNGI (2005 presidential candidate), Hussein Mwaiseje POLISYA (Secretary General).

Other Parties Competing in the 2005 Election

Tanzania Democratic Alliance Party (Tadea). The previously London-based Tadea was founded by Oscar Salathiel KAMBONA, a former TANU secretary general and Nyerere cabinet member who went into voluntary exile in 1967 after government authorities alleged he had been involved in a coup plot. Kambona was also one of the founders of the Tanzania Democratic Front (TDF), formed in London by a number of exile opposition groups to promote the introduction of a multiparty system. Tadea was registered in Tanzania in 1993.

In 1996 the Tadea was buffeted by allegations that its officials had misused publicly funded campaign finances.

The party joined the opposition alliance to contest the 2005 elections and supported the CUF mainland presidential candidate.

Leaders: John D. LIFE-CIIIPAKA (Chair), Charles Dotto LUBALA (Secretary General).

Union for Multiparty Democracy (UMD). The UMD was organized in late 1991 by Abdallah Said Fundikira, a well-known Tanzanian businessman, and others who had previously been involved in the NCCR. They proposed that a national conference be held to draft a new Tanzanian constitution that would permit multiparty activity. In addition, the UMD suggested that the union between the mainland and the islands of Zanzibar and Pemba be reevaluated. Following the formation of the UMD, Fundikira was arrested and released on bail after being charged with establishing an illegal organization. The UMD was nonetheless registered in 1993. The UMD supported the NCCR-Maguezi candidate in the 2005 presidential elections and failed to gain any seats in the assembly.

Leaders: Chief Abdallah Said FUNDIKIRA (President of the Party and 1995 candidate for President of the Republic), Stephen M. KIBUGA (Vice President), Hussein Hassan YAHAYA (Secretary General).

National Reconstruction Alliance (NRA). Former industries and trade minister Kigoma Ali MALIMA resigned from the CCM on July 16 to become the NRA's 1995 presidential candidate; however, he died unexpectedly on August 5. Following the elections, the party reportedly faced an audit of its campaign financing practices amid allegations that it had misused public funds.

The NRA joined the electoral coalition that supported the NCCR-Maguezi candidate in the 2005 elections.

Leaders: Rashid MTUTA (Chair), Maoud RATUU (Secretary General).

Forum for Restoration of Democracy (FORD). FORD was formed in April 2001 by CUF dissidents, led by Ramadhani MZEE, to oppose the CUF's bellicose stance versus the CCM. The FORD supported the NCCR-Maguezi candidate in the 2005 presidential balloting.

Leaders: Ramadhani MZEE (Chair), Natanga NYAGAWA (Secretary General).

Justice and Development Party (*Chama cha Haki na Usitawi Chausta*—Chausta). The Justice and Development Party was launched in Zanzibar in May 1998 by former CUF leader James Mapalala. According to Mapalala, the new party was founded on the principle of development of the "individual." The party was officially recognized in late 2001.

Leaders: James MAPALALA (Chair), Joseph MKOMAGU (Secretary General).

Democratic Party (*Chama Cha Demokrasi*—CCD). The CCD was formed in late 1991 in anticipation of the introduction of a multiparty system. The CCD is sometimes referred to as the DP. Soon thereafter, the party was thrust into the national limelight by the August 1992 conviction of its leader, Christopher Mtikila, on charges of illegal assembly. The High Court subsequently dismissed the charges against Mtikila, whose nationalistic rhetoric had made him increasingly popular. However, in January 1993, Mtikila was arrested on charges of having fomented sedition and rioting by a speech in which he had accused the government of having "sold [Tanzania] to Arabs and Gabacholics [Asians]," urged Indo-Pakistanis, Arabs, Somalians, and Zanzibaris to emigrate, and warned that blood would flow if the alleged favoritism to foreigners continued. He was rearrested a number of times thereafter on a variety of charges, including the leadership of illegal demonstrations.

In 1997 Mtikila ran as a Chadema candidate in a legislative by-election, thus casting uncertainty on the future of the CCD, which had been unable to secure official recognition because of its unwillingness to accept Zanzibar as a legitimate part of the country.

The CCD's candidate in the 2005 presidential election was Mtikila who placed sixth in the balloting.

Leaders: Christopher MTIKILA (2005 presidential candidate and Chair), Natanga NYAGAWA (Secretary General).

The other small parties that competed unsuccessfully in the 2005 assembly balloting were the **National League for Democracy** (NLD), led by Emmanuel J. E. MAKAIDI (Chair) and Michael E. A. MHINA (Secretary General); the **Progressive Party of Tanzania** (PPT-*Maendeleo*), formed in 2003 and led by 2005 presidential candidate Anna SENKORO and Peter Kuga MZIRAY (Chair); **Jahazi Asilia**, which received less than 1 percent of the vote in the 2005 balloting and is led by Abuu Juma AMOUR (Chair); and the **Sauti Ya Umma** (SAU), formed in 2005 and led by Paulo KYARA (2005 presidential candidate and Chair).

Other Parties and Groups

Zanzibar Organization.   An offshoot of the former Zanzibar Nationalist Party, a predominantly Arab group that was influential prior to the 1964 union, the Zanzibar Organization reportedly supports full independence for Zanzibar, having recently been active within the growing Islamic fundamentalist movement on the island. Members of its leadership reportedly reside in several Gulf states.

Leader: Ali MOSHEN.

Other parties that were registered prior to the 2005 elections but did not participate in the balloting include the **National Democratic Union** (*Nduta*), the **Tanzania Organization for Democracy and Development** (*Topodd*), **Solidarity of United Party** (*Supa*), the **Party for Liberation of Poor People** (*Chudewama*), and the **National Democratic Party for Rehabilitation** (NDPR-*Marejesho*). The **Tanzanian People's Congress** (TPC) was registered in November 2004, but its status was revoked on May 7, 2005, after the National Electoral Commission ruled that the grouping had failed to complete required paperwork.

Banned Grouping

Council for the Dissemination of the Koran in Tanzania   (*Balukta*). *Balukta* is a militant Islamic group that was proscribed by the government in early 1993 amid rumors that it was considering reorganization as a political party. In April approximately 40 members, including leaders Yahya Hussein and Kassim bin Jumma, were arrested on charges stemming from their involvement in a campaign to forcibly close butcher shops selling pork in Muslim districts. The action was depicted by the government as part of a larger destabilization campaign, which included attacks on alcohol distributors and the recruitment of approximately 500 youths for the group's military wing, the Islamic Army, in preparation for a *Jihad* (Holy War). In June 1993 charges against many of the *Balukta* members, including Sheikh Hussein, were dropped. Financial and military support for *Balukta* reportedly originates in Iran and is funneled through the Islamic Party of Kenya.

Leaders: Sheikh Yahya HUSSEIN, Sheikh Kassim bin JUMMA.

Legislature

The Tanzania **National Assembly** (*Bunge*), also referenced as the Union Parliament, has a five-year mandate, barring dissolution. The current assembly includes 232 members directly elected in single member constituencies (182 on the mainland and 50 on the islands). The constitution requires that women hold 20 percent of the assembly seats, an increase of 5 percent with the elections in 2000. Following every general election, parties in the assembly must nominate (according to the seats they hold) a number of women to fill any remaining seats of the 20 percent allotted them. The Zanzibar House of Representatives elects 5 of its members to the assembly, and the Tanzanian attorney general

Cabinet

As of July 1, 2006

President	Jakaya Kikwete
Vice President	Ali Mohamed Shein
President of Zanzibar	Amani Abeid Karume
Prime Minister	Edward Lowassa

Ministers of State in the President's Office

Good Governance	Philip Sang'ka Marmo
Political Affairs and Civil Societies	Kingunge Ngombale Mwiru
Public Service Management	Hawa Abdulrahman Ghasia

Ministers of State in the Vice President's Office

Environment	Mark James Mwandosya
Union Affairs	Dr. Hussein Ali Mwinyi

Ministers of State in the Prime Minister's Office

Parliamentary Affairs	Juma Jamaldin Akukweti
Regional Administration and Local Government	Mizengo Kayanza Peter Pinda

Ministers

Agriculture and Food Security	Joseph Mungai
Community Development, Women's Affairs, and Children	Sofia Simba [f]
Defense and National Service	Juma Kapuya
East African Cooperation	Andrew Chenge
Education and Vocational Training	Margareth Sitta [f]
Energy and Mineral Resources	Ibrahim Msabaha
Finance	Zakia Meghji [f]
Foreign Affairs and International Cooperation	Asha Rose Migiro [f]
Health and Welfare Development	David Mwakyusa
Home Affairs	John Zefania Chiligati
Industries and Trade	Nazir Karamagi
Information, Culture, and Sport	Mohammed Seif Khatibu
Infrastructure Development	Basil Mramba
Justice and Constitutional Affairs	Mary Nagu [f]
Labor, Youth Development, and Sports	Jumanne Maghembe
Lands, Housing, and Human Settlement	John Magufuli
Livestock Development	Shukuru Kawambwa
Natural Resources and Tourism	Anthony Diallo
Planning, Economy, and Empowerment	Juma Ngasongwa
Public Safety and Security	Harith Bakari Mwapachu
Science, Technology, and Higher Education	Peter Msola
Water	Stephen Masatu Wassira

[f] = female

is entitled to a legislative seat. Another revision made in 2000 allows the president to appoint 10 members. At the most recent balloting of December 14, 2005, the Revolutionary Party of Tanzania (CCM) secured 206 of the directly elected seats; the Civic United Front (CUF), 19; the Party for Democracy and Progress (Chadema), 5; the United Democratic Party (UDP), 1; and the Tanzania Labor Party (TLP), 1. Following the election, the CCM was authorized to nominate an additional 58 women legislators; the CUF, 11; and Chadema, 6.

Speaker: Samwel SITTA.

The Zanzibar **House of Representatives** is a 75-member body encompassing 50 elected members, 5 regional commissioners, 10 presidential nominees, and 10 members representing women and selected organizations. At the balloting of October 30, 2005, the Revolutionary Party of Tanzania won 30 of the elected seats, and the Civic United Front won 19. (One election had to be rerun.)

Speaker: Pandu Amir KIFICHO.

Communications

Press

The Newspaper Ordinance of 1968 empowered the president to ban any newspaper if he considered such action to be in the "national interest," while the Newspaper Act of 1976 declared that government approval was required for the creation of any new publications. Additionally, the Zanzibar House of Representatives in September 1988 approved the imprisonment of authors of articles deemed critical of the government. Although press restrictions were eased somewhat as the country implemented its multiparty system, four newspapers, according to 1996 reports, had been temporarily suspended by the government since 1993, with a number of others having been "warned." The following papers are published in Dar es Salaam: *Uhuru* (100,000), CCM daily, published Sunday as *Mzalendo* (116,000), in Swahili; *Mfanyakazi* (70,000 Wednesday, 120,000 Saturday), in Swahili;

Daily News (50,000), formerly the *East African Standard,* government-owned daily, in English; *The Guardian,* independent, in English.

News Agencies

The principal domestic facility has been the government-operated Tanzanian News Agency (*Shihata*), established in 1976. However, according to reports in April 2000, the National Assembly had voted to abolish *Shihata* and transfer its responsibilities to the government's information department (*Maelezo*). There is also a privately owned Press Service of Tanzania.

Broadcasting and Computing

The two government-owned radio stations are Radio Tanzania, which broadcasts in Swahili and English, and Radio Tanzania Zanzibar, which broadcasts in Swahili. The two stations operate transmitters on approximately 20 different frequencies. In November 1993 the archdiocese of Dar es Salaam launched Radio Tumaini (Hope) "to educate society on several social problems"; the privately owned Radio One also broadcasts from Dar es Salaam. There is a government-run, noncommercial television station on Zanzibar and a government-run and an independent station on the mainland. There were approximately 742,000 television receivers and 200,000 personal computers serving 250,000 Internet users in 2003.

Intergovernmental Representation

Ambassador to the U.S.
Andrew Mhando DARAJA

U.S. Ambassador to Tanzania
Michael RETZER

Permanent Representative to the UN
A. Augustine MAHIGA

IGO Memberships (Non-UN)
AfDB, AU, BADEA, Comesa, CWTH, EAC, EADB, Interpol, IOM, IOR-ARC, NAM, SADC, WCO, WTO

TOGO

REPUBLIC OF TOGO

République Togolaise

Note: President Faure Gnassingbé appointed a new prime minister, Yawovi Madji Agboyibo of the Action Committee for Renewal party (CAR), to form a new government in September 2006, in a first step toward forming a government of "national unity" as provided for in the "universal political agreement" that had emerged from negotiations among Togolese government and opposition political leaders in August. Prime Minister Agboyibo, who replaced Edem Kodjo of the Panafrican Patriotic Convergence party, appointed a new coalition cabinet on September 20, and announced that new legislative elections would be held in June 2007.

The Country

Wedged between Ghana and Benin on Africa's Guinea Coast, the small Republic of Togo extends inland from a 31-mile coastline for a distance of 360 miles. Eighteen major tribal groups are located in its hilly, hot, and humid territory, the best known being the culturally dominant Ewe in the south, whose traditional homeland extends into Ghana; the Mina, another southern people; and the Kabiyé in the north, who staff most of the country's small army. Although French has been accorded official status, most people use indigenous languages, with Ewe being predominant in the south and Twi in the north. About 75 percent of the population adheres to traditional religious beliefs; the remainder embrace Christianity (20 percent, mainly Roman Catholics) and Islam (5 percent). Somewhat more than half of adult women are in the work force, predominantly in the agricultural and trading sectors; however, there are few women in the government.

The economy depends primarily on subsistence agriculture, the three most important crops being cocoa, coffee, and cotton. Phosphate is the leading export, and oil refining, steel fabrication, and cement production are assuming increasing indus-

trial importance. Smuggling has long been a source of contention with Ghana; as much as a third of Togo's cocoa exports originates in the neighboring state and is smuggled into Togo in exchange for luxury items that are much cheaper than in other parts of Africa. Development in the 1980s focused largely on tourism, agriculture, and a new

free port in Lomé. The World Bank and other international institutions, encouraged by the government's commitment to budget austerity and the privatization of some state-run enterprises, supported these and other efforts to recover from the fall of commodity prices on the world market. However, the economy came to a virtual standstill in 1991, declining sharply thereafter by 8.8 percent in 1992 and by an even more calamitous 13.5 percent in 1993. In addition, foreign aid donors, most notably France and the United States, halted aid payments to protest military and presidential obstruction of democratization efforts. In September 1994 France announced its intention to renew civil and military cooperation agreements, in addition to writing off part of Togo's debt, and in early 1995 the European Union (EU) activated its aid program after a three-year suspension; however, the United States was unwilling to follow suit, reportedly citing the "lack of guarantees for the ongoing democratic process." Togo adopted structural reforms proposed by the International Monetary Fund (IMF) in the mid-1990s, and GDP grew by an annual average of 6.9 percent in 1995–1997. However, GDP declined by about 1 percent in 1998, due to a bad crop harvest and a sharp increase in government spending prior to the disputed June presidential election. (The EU, which had financed much of that electoral process, subsequently suspended its aid payments after announcing it would not recognize President Eyadéma's reelection.) Meanwhile, the IMF urged the government to intensify its privatization efforts, adopt stricter banking regulations, and improve tax collection. GDP rose by 2.7 percent in 1999 but declined by 0.5 percent in 2000, the IMF attributing the economic deterioration, in part, to policy weaknesses, including the slow pace of reform in the public sector. GDP growth returned to 2.7 percent in 2001, with an inflation rate of 3.9 percent for the year.

GDP grew by 4.2 percent in 2002, 2.7 percent in 2003, and 3.0 percent in 2004, fueled by increased agricultural output and expanded phosphate production. Inflation was 3.4 percent in 2004. The government's fiscal status was also improved by better tax collection procedures. However, most international donors continued to withhold assistance due to the Eyadéma regime's poor human rights record and failure to implement democratic reform. In 2004, the EU resumed aid after Togo met 22 preconditions, and in September 2005, the IMF resumed aid to the country. In April 2006 the World Bank included Togo among 11 countries that qualified for debt relief under the Heavily Indebted Poor Countries (HIPC) initiative.

Government and Politics

Political Background

The present Republic of Togo is the eastern section of the former German Protectorate of Togoland, which became a League of Nations mandate after World War I and was divided into separate zones of British and French administration. After World War II France and Britain continued to administer the eastern and western sections, respectively, as United Nations trust territories. Following a UN-supervised plebiscite, Western (British) Togoland became part of the new state of Ghana on the latter's accession to independence in 1957. Eastern (French) Togoland, which became a French-sponsored autonomous republic in 1956, achieved complete independence in agreement with France and the United Nations on April 27, 1960.

Sylvanus OLYMPIO, leader of the predominantly Ewe party then known as the Togolese Unity Committee (CUT), became the country's first chief executive. Olympio's somewhat dictatorial rule, coupled with his alienation of the army by the imposition of an austerity program, contributed to his assassination in 1963. Nicolas GRUNITZKY, Olympio's chief political rival, succeeded him as president and attempted to govern on a multiparty basis with northern support. Grunitzky failed, however, to establish firm control and was deposed in 1967 by (then) Maj. Etienne EYADÉMA, a northerner who was chief of staff of the armed forces. Acting in the name of a National Reconciliation Committee (NRC), Eyadéma suspended the constitution, outlawed political activity, and instituted

Political Status: Independent republic since 1960; personal military rule imposed in 1967; one-party state established November 29, 1969; Third Republic proclaimed on January 13, 1980, under constitution adopted in referendum of December 30, 1979; constitution suspended by a National Conference on July 16, 1991; multiparty constitution adopted by popular referendum on September 27, 1992.

Area: 21,622 sq. mi. (56,000 sq. km.).

Population: 2,703,250 (1981C); 5,132,000 (2005E).

Major Urban Center (2005E): LOMÉ (835,000).

Official Language: French.

Monetary Unit: CFA Franc (official rate July 1, 2006: 513.01 francs = $1US). (The CFA franc, previously pegged to the French franc, is now permanently pegged to the euro at 655.957 CFA francs = 1 euro.)

President: Faure Essozimma GNASSINGBÉ (Rally of the Togolese People); elected on April 24, 2005, and inaugurated on May 4 following an extended constitutional crisis triggered by the death on February 5 of his father, Gen. Gnassingbé EYADÉMA (Rally of the Togolese People), who had been president since 1967.

Prime Minister: Edem KODJO (Panafrican Patriotic Convergence); appointed by the president on June 9, 2005, to succeed Koffi SAMA (Rally of the Togolese People).

direct military rule. Later the same year, he dissolved the NRC and declared himself president. The Rally of the Togolese People (RPT), a regime-supportive party, was established in 1969 and, in that year and in 1971, made pro forma attempts (which were described as overruled by the "popular will") to return the nation to civilian rule.

A constitution drafted in 1969 was accepted by a reported 98 percent of the registered electorate on December 30, 1979, in balloting at which General Eyadéma (whose first name had been "Africanized" to Gnassingbé in 1974) stood as the sole candidate for a seven-year term as president. Concurrently, a unicameral General Assembly was constituted on the basis of a single list of candidates presented by the RPT.

In September 1986 the government reported that it had rebuffed a coup attempt allegedly fomented in Ghana and Burkina Faso by supporters of the exiled sons of former president Olympio. However, some external critics suggested that the seriousness of the coup attempt may have been overstated by the Eyadéma regime to shift attention away from earlier reports of torture and illegal detention of political prisoners. On December 21 President Eyadéma was unopposed in election to a further seven-year term.

In early October 1990 the imposition of lengthy jail terms on two opposition figures for alleged antigovernment activity ignited a series of protests and strikes. On October 10 President Eyadéma responded by telling a RPT Central Committee meeting that the country's "apprenticeship in democracy" was complete and preparations should be made for a multiparty system. However, the establishment of a constitutional commission and scheduling of a referendum for late 1991 failed to appease government critics, with violent protests continuing into 1991.

In March 1991 ten opposition groups formed a Front of Associations for Renewal (FAR) under the leadership of Yawovi AGBOYIBO, and four days later, after a meeting with FAR representatives, the president agreed to accelerate reforms. In mid-April he authorized the legalization of opposition parties and pledged to hold multiparty elections within a year. Nevertheless, violent demonstrations continued, fueled by the discovery of the bodies of 30 slain protestors in a Lomé lagoon. Subsequently, in the course of negotiations with opposition leaders, Eyadéma agreed to transfer power to a prime minister to be elected by a National Conference on Togo's Future, which convened in Lomé on July 8. On July 16 the opposition-dominated conference declared its sovereignty, dissolved the National Assembly, abrogated the 1980 constitution, and stripped Eyadéma of all but ceremonial powers, thus prompting a government and army withdrawal from the proceedings. On July 23 the government rejoined the conference, and, at its close on August

28, the president publicly accepted most of its findings, including a diminished presidency, the election of Joseph Kokou KOFFIGOH as prime minister, and the replacement of the RPT-dominated National Assembly with an interim High Council of the Republic (HCR). However, Eyadéma's military supporters continued to reject both the conference's sovereignty claims and the new government, in particular Koffigoh's assumption of the defense ministry. Subsequently, military coup attempts on October 1 and 8 ended only after public appeals from Eyadéma that the troops return to their barracks.

In mid-October 1991 the HCR, under pressure from newly enfranchised party leaders to establish control of the government, formally ousted Eyadéma, and on November 26 the council banned the RPT on the eve of a party congress. The following day rebel troops surrounded Koffigoh's residence, and on December 2 the troops announced that they had "reclaimed" strategic points throughout Togo and had called on Eyadéma to name a new prime minister and dissolve the HCR. On December 3 Koffigoh was seized by the rebel soldiers and brought to Eyadéma, whereupon the prime minister announced his "surrender" and agreed to Eyadéma's request that he form a national unity government, assignments to which were announced on December 30.

On January 29, 1992, the government issued a revised electoral calendar that called for a constitutional referendum and municipal balloting in early April, a legislative poll in late May, and a presidential election in June. The schedule was subsequently abandoned because of widespread violence, including the May 5 wounding of opposition leader Gilchrist OLYMPIO, son of the former president, in an attack for which Capt. Ernest GNASSINGBÉ, the president's son, was implicated two months later. On August 13 negotiations between a presidential delegation and representatives of eight opposition parties on resumption of the transitional process were suspended, and on August 23 the government, citing ongoing unrest, cancelled a constitutional referendum. Meanwhile, following extensive talks between the president and prime minister, at which the latter reportedly agreed to a number of concessions reversing earlier limitations on the president's power, the transition period, scheduled to expire on August 28, was extended to December 31.

On September 27, 1992, a new constitution was endorsed in a referendum by 99.09 percent of the voters. Concurrently, a new electoral calendar was released, which called for balloting to take place between October and December. However, the democratization process was halted on October 22 with seizure of the National Assembly building by pro-Eyadéma troops, who demanded the release of frozen RPT funds in return for the release of 40 legislative hostages. The crisis was resolved the following day when the HCR agreed to release the funds; however, Koffigoh declared the HCR's action invalid because it was performed under duress, while Eyadéma, who had supported earlier efforts to free the funds, called for sanctions against the intruders. Unappeased by the government's response, the opposition organized a general strike on October 26 to protest the military's action.

On November 11, 1992, Eyadéma, in a direct affront to the prime minister and HCR, rejected as "unconstitutional" Koffigoh's dismissal of two propresidential cabinet ministers, one of whom had reportedly threatened to have the prime minister arrested. The United States responded on November 13 with suspension of $19 million in aid payments. Three days later Togolese unions, acting in concert with the Democratic Opposition Collective (COD-2), launched a general strike, which they warned would continue until the government agreed to the formation of a politically neutral security force, a new government, free and fair elections, prosecution of the troops implicated in the October National Assembly incident, and international monitoring of the transitional period. Meanwhile, Koffigoh's repeated compromises with Eyadéma appeared to have cost him the support of the COD-2, whose leaders, in early January 1993, refused to meet with him.

On January 13, 1993, Eyadéma dismissed Koffigoh, claiming that the transitional government's mandate had ended on December 31, 1992.

However, five days later, in an action that the HCR described as "unconstitutional," he reappointed Koffigoh to his post. Tensions were further heightened on January 25 when security forces killed at least 20 people demonstrating in support of the arrival of French and German mediators. Nationwide clashes between prodemocracy and government forces were subsequently reported, and at the end of the month, amid reports of rampaging soldiers and an imminent civil war, 300,000 Togolese fled to Benin and Ghana.

Negotiations to break the downward political and social spiral opened on February 11, 1993, in Colmar, France, with representatives of the president, the government, the HCR, and the opposition in attendance; however, Eyadéma's delegation soon withdrew because of the opposition's demand for political neutralization of the armed forces. Three days later, following negotiations between the president and prime minister, during which the former reportedly pledged to keep troops loyal to him in their barracks, Koffigoh was named to head a "crisis government" dominated by presidential loyalists. The HCR rejected the legality of the new administration, calling it the product of a "constitutional coup d'état," and in early March COD-2 leader Olympio reportedly declared that a "short, foreign military intervention" might be necessary to break the stranglehold on the democratization process.

On March 25, 1993, Eyadéma's top military aide was among a number of military personnel reportedly killed when the president's residence came under attack from raiders who fled into Ghana. Olympio, who was accused of planning the attack, countered by charging that the incident was part of a purge of army dissidents. Lending credence to his argument, over 140 former Eyadéma troops were reported to have fled Togo by early April, claiming that a presidentially sanctioned ethnic cleansing campaign was indeed under way. Despite the unrest, an election timetable was subsequently released, which called for new presidential and legislative balloting. However, most of the opposition boycotted the long-deferred presidential poll of August 25 at which Eyadéma was credited with

reelection amid increasing evidence that he had regained most of his pre-1991 powers.

In late September 1993 the COD-2 threatened to boycott legislative elections then scheduled for December unless the government agreed to provide access to state-controlled media, redefine voting constituencies, and increase the number of poll watchers. The balloting was further postponed until February following renewed fighting near Eyadéma's residence on January 5, 1994, which left more than 60 dead.

The multiparty poll, which was finally mounted on February 6 and 20, 1994, was marred by violence, with RPT militants accused of attacking opposition candidates. International observers nonetheless endorsed the results, which included a majority of 43 seats for the opposition Patriotic Front (FP) and 35 for the RPT. Subsequently, however, the Supreme Court, responding to petitions filed by the RPT, vacated three seats won by the opposition. Therefore, the FP's overall lead was imperiled, pending by-elections, which, having initially been scheduled for May, were deferred. Criticizing the Court's action, the FP's leading components (the Action Committee for Renewal—CAR and the Togolese Union for Democracy—UTD) threatened to boycott the National Assembly; however, the coalition's unanimity was sorely tested on April 22, when the president, in apparent violation of an earlier agreement, rejected CAR leader Yawovi Agboyibo as the FP's prime minister designate in favor of the UTD's Edem KODJO.

In mid-1994 a RPT characterization of the FP as a "facade of a coalition" seemed increasingly apt, as the CAR resisted UTD entreaties to join Kodjo's government. Earlier, on May 20, the CAR, which unlike the UTD had carried through on a legislative boycott, announced that it was abandoning the action, explaining that the regime's failure to mount by-elections by the legally mandated date of May 15 was tantamount to a confession that "conditions for legality, transparency, and security" had not been met. In December the CAR once again withdrew from the assembly, but in April 1995 President Eyadéma and Agboyibo reached an agreement on electoral reform, which called for equal representation for government and opposition parliamentary groups on all electoral commissions. As a result, the CAR rejoined the assembly in August; however, an alliance of RPT and UTD parliamentarians defeated the reform bill in February 1996.

Already strained relations between President Eyadéma and Prime Minister Kodjo deteriorated sharply in May 1996 when the Supreme Court supported Eyadéma's assertion that he alone controlled the appointment of senior administrative officials. For his part, Kodjo reportedly accused the president of establishing a "parallel government." Subsequently, following the RPT's capture of three assembly seats (and consequently a narrow legislative majority) at early August by-election balloting, Kodjo resigned on August 19, citing his desire to avoid the "legal war," which he described as likely to arise from the lack of an "obvious majority." The following day Eyadéma appointed Planning and Territorial Development Minister Kwassi KLUTSE as Kodjo's successor, and on August 27 the new prime minister announced the formation of a new government.

On December 3, 1996, the National Assembly voted to adopt a RPT-drafted document delineating the responsibilities of a new Constitutional Court. The poll was boycotted by the CAR, which had unsuccessfully sought to broaden the court's powers to include mediation of electoral disputes. (The new body was inaugurated in March 1997.) Thereafter, in September, the opposition boycotted an assembly vote on a new electoral code after attempts to persuade the legislature to include provisions for an independent electoral body were rebuffed. The code, approved unanimously by the propresidential legislators, provided for a nine-member commission (four from the propresidential forces and four from the opposition, in addition to an appointed chair).

Following presidential balloting on June 21, 1998, President Eyadéma was credited with a vote share of 52 percent and Gilchrist Olympio of the Union of Forces of Change (UFC) with 34 percent. The remainder of the tally was shared by four other candidates, led by Yawovi Agboyibo with 9.6

percent. However, the polling process was widely criticized by both domestic and international observers. Furthermore, two days after the polling, the chairperson of the electoral commission, Awa NANA, resigned, claiming that her efforts to prepare provisional electoral results had been blocked by "unidentified" individuals widely believed to be presidential supporters. Subsequently, the opposition, led by Olympio, who claimed that he had actually won the election with a 59 percent vote share, refused the president's offer to join a unity government and organized a number of demonstrations and work stoppages. Amid reports of mounting violence, on August 19 Prime Minister Klutse resigned; however, the president reappointed Klutse the following day, and on September 1 Klutse named a government that included a number of new members but no prominent opposition leaders.

In December 1998 government and opposition leaders announced that they had made progress in their efforts to organize a dialogue. Thereafter, however, the preparations ground to a halt as the two sides proved unable to agree on a venue for the proposed talks. Subsequently, in early 1999, the opposition announced its intention to boycott legislative polling then scheduled for early March. The Eyadéma administration rejected calls to delay the balloting until after interparty talks and proceeded with electoral preparations, albeit delaying the start of polling for two weeks.

Following legislative balloting on March 21, 1999, and two subsequent by-elections, the RPT, facing only limited competition from independent candidates and two minor parties, was credited with having won 79 of the 81 seats. On April 17 Klutse dissolved his government and offered his resignation, although he agreed to continue thereafter on a caretaker basis. On May 22 the president appointed Eugene Koffi ADOBOLI, a former official of the United Nations Conference on Trade and Development, as Klutse's successor. Facing continuing criticism for his inability to improve the economic condition, however, Adoboli resigned on August 25, 2000, one day after a vote of no-confidence against his government in the legislature. The president named Agbéyomé Messan KODJO of the RPT as Adoboli's successor on August 29.

On June 27, 2002, President Eyadéma appointed Koffi SAMA of the RPT to replace Prime Minister Kodjo. (Kodjo was subsequently expelled from the RPT for criticizing the president; he later went into exile.) Sama was sworn in on June 30, and he announced his cabinet on July 5.

The RPT dominated the October 27, 2002, assembly balloting (72 of 81 seats), in part, due to a boycott by most opposition parties. Sama was reappointed as prime minister on November 13. In December the RPT-controlled assembly approved a constitutional revision that removed the limit on the number of presidential terms for one person, thereby permitting Eyadéma to seek another term in the election scheduled for 2003. The assembly also lowered the eligibility age for presidential candidates from 45 to 35, a measure apparently designed to permit the eventual succession of Eyadéma's son, Faure Essozimma GNASSINGBÉ, who was only 37 years old at the time. Moreover, the basic law was changed to require presidential candidates to have resided in Togo for one year prior to the election. That provision prevented Gilchrist Olympio, who had been in exile in France, from contesting the election; he urged supporters to vote for Emmanuel BOB-AKITANI, the vice president of the UFC.

In the presidential poll of June 1, 2003, Eyadéma was credited with 58 percent of the vote, followed by Bob-Akitani (34 percent), and four minor candidates. Prime Minister Sama and his cabinet resigned on June 23, but the president reappointed Sama on July 1. On July 29 Sama formed a new cabinet that included a few members of minor opposition parties and, notably, Faure Gnassingbé.

President Eyadéma died of a heart attack on February 5, 2005. His son, Faure Gnassingbé, backed by the military and Sama, was immediately named interim president, although the constitution required the speaker of the assembly to fill a presidential vacancy. Because the current speaker, Fambaré NATCHABA, was out of the country at the time, the assembly, on February 6, elected Gnassingbé to replace Natchaba as speaker, and Gnass-

ingbé was sworn in as president the following day to serve until the end of his father's term in 2008. The assembly also rescinded the constitutional provision that new presidential elections be held within 60 days in case of a vacancy. However, in the wake of intense domestic and international criticism, the assembly, on February 21, voted to reverse its decisions (see Foreign relations, below). Gnassingbé resigned as speaker and interim president on February 25 and was succeeded in both positions by Abbas BONFOH (hitherto the deputy speaker) pending new elections. In highly controversial balloting on April 24, Gnassingbé was credited with 60 percent of the vote and runner-up Bob-Akitani with 38.25 percent. After the Constitutional Court validated the results on May 3, Gnassingbé was sworn in on May 4. On June 9, the president appointed Edem Kodjo of the Panafrican Patriotic Convergence (*Convergence Patriotique Panafricaine—* CPP) as prime minister in an attempt to reach out to opposition groups. Kodjo's new cabinet, formed on June 20, comprised mostly members of the RPT, although several small opposition parties agreed to join. Efforts to form a broader unity government were rebuffed by the major opposition parties.

Constitution and Government

The 1979 constitution provided for a highly centralized system of government headed by a strong executive presiding over a cabinet of his own selection and empowered to dissolve a single-chambered National Assembly after consulting the Political Bureau of the RPT. It detailed a judicial system headed by a Supreme Court that included a Court of Appeal and courts of the first and second instance, with special courts for administrative, labor, and internal security matters.

On July 16, 1991, the National Conference on Togo's Future abrogated the 1979 basic law, transferred all but ceremonial presidential powers to a prime minister, and dissolved the legislature, with assignment of its powers to a High Council of the Republic (HCR), pending the promulgation of a new constitution and the holding of multiparty elections.

A draft constitution accepted by the HCR on July 2, 1992, called for a semi-presidential system with the head of state elected to a once-renewable five-year term and a prime minister chosen by the president from a parliamentary majority and responsible to the legislature, which would also have a five-year mandate. Other projected institutions included a High Court of Justice and a Supreme Court, in addition to a Constitutional Court, an Accounts Court, and an Economic and Social Council. On September 27 the new basic charter was approved by 99.08 percent of the participants in a nationwide referendum. In March 1997 a seven-member Constitutional Court was appointed to serve a seven-year term.

The country is divided for administrative purposes into five provinces, which are subdivided into prefectures that were formerly administered by presidentially appointed chiefs and "special delegations" (councils) but are now subject to prefectural and municipal elections on the basis of direct universal suffrage.

Foreign Relations

Togo's foreign policy has long been based on nonalignment, although historical links have provided a foundation for continued financial and political support from the West. Bowing to pressure from the Arab bloc, diplomatic relations with Israel were severed from 1973 to 1987.

Although one of the smallest and poorest of the African states, Togo has played a leading role in efforts to promote regional cooperation and served as the host nation for negotiation of the Lomé conventions between the European Community (EC) and developing African, Caribbean, and Pacific (ACP) countries. It worked closely with Nigeria in organizing the Economic Community of West African States (ECOWAS) in May 1975 and, having assumed observer status earlier with the francophone West African Economic Community (CEAO), joined the CEAO states in a Non-Aggression and Defense Aid Agreement (ANAD) in 1979. Its major regional dispute concerns the status of Western Togoland, which was incorpo-

rated into Ghana in 1957. A clandestine "National Liberation Movement of Western Togoland" has been active in supporting Togo's claim to the 75-mile-wide strip of territory and has called for a new UN plebiscite on the issue. There have been numerous incidents along the Ghanaian border, and the Eyadéma and Rawlings regimes regularly accused each other of destabilization efforts, including the "harboring" of political opponents. Heated exchanges occurred with Ghana and, to a lesser degree, Burkina Faso, following the reported coup attempt in Togo in September 1986. However, Eyadéma avoided charging Accra and Ouagadougou with direct involvement in the plot, and relations were largely normalized by mid-1987, Lomé calling for help from regional organizations to keep further enmity from developing. In December 1991 the Koffigoh administration announced that a comprehensive cooperation agreement had been reached with Ghana.

Togo's foreign affairs in 1992 and early 1993 were determined in great part by its domestic political turmoil. In early November 1992 both Benin and Ghana reported deaths of their nationals in border incidents involving Togolese security forces, although their complaints were relatively low-keyed in apparent support of the transitional government. On November 13 a deteriorating political situation led the United States to suspend all but humanitarian aid payments. Thereafter, in late January 1993, a French and German mediation effort was cut short when 20 prodemocracy demonstrators were killed by government forces outside the negotiation site. In mid-February, France, citing the death of the demonstrators and lack of progress towards democracy, announced restrictions on aid payments. France's decision came only weeks after its former president, Valéry Giscard D'Estaing, had written a controversial letter in support of Eyadéma.

Meanwhile, relations between Togo and Ghana continued to worsen. In March 1993 rebels, who had attacked the Eyadéma compound, retreated into Ghana, setting off an exchange of accusations between the two capitals. In early January 1994 Togo and Ghana were described as "close to war" after Lóme once again accused Accra of aiding alleged anti-Eyadéma insurgents in an attack on the president's residence. For its part, Ghana described the unrest in Togo as "the consequence of the government's refusal to establish a credible democratic process" and called on Lomé to resist always accusing Ghana "whenever there is an armed attack or political crisis." Such charges notwithstanding, relations between the two improved dramatically by midyear; on November 16 diplomatic ties were formally restored, and in December Eyadéma ordered the reopening of their shared border. Lomé's relations with Paris improved when France agreed to reschedule and forgive Togolese debt in May 1995.

In August 1998 the Togolese government reported that troops based near Lomé had been attacked by opposition-affiliated "terrorists" based in Ghana; however, the opposition countered that the fighters were actually government provocateurs who had attacked the headquarters and homes of UFC members. Collaterally, the incident proved to be a showcase for improved relations between Accra and Lomé (the two nations' presidents having signed cooperation agreements in Accra earlier in the year) because Ghana deployed forces to carry out a joint operation with Togolese troops pursuing the alleged "aggressors." However, conflicts over property rights were reported in 1999 along the border between Togo and Ghana, and in March 2001 Togo closed the border without explanation. The border was reopened and relations between the two sides improved dramatically with the election of John Kufuor as president of Ghana.

In 1998 Eyadéma helped mediate the conflict in Guinea-Bissau. Togolese troops also joined the international peacekeeping mission in Guinea-Bissau, and Eyadéma played a role in efforts to end the conflicts in Liberia and Sierra Leone. In addition, Togolese troops participated in the ECOWAS mission in Liberia and the UN mission in Sierra Leone. In light of Togo's importance to regional peacekeeping operations, the United States initiated joint training exercises with the Togolese military in April 2002.

France was the first country to accept Gnassingbé's victory in the 2005 presidential election; Chirac sent formal congratulations to the new president on May 5, 2005.

In February 2006 Gnassingbé traveled to China to promote increased economic interaction between the two countries. (In 2005 trade between Togo and China was worth more than $500 million).

Current Issues

Togolese officials came under intense scrutiny in May 1999 when Amnesty International (AI) released a report titled "Togo: Reign of Terror," which cited numerous human rights violations and claimed that hundreds of government opponents had been executed during the 1998 election campaign. Defiantly, the government arrested several opposition leaders for having "provided erroneous information" to the AI investigators.

In July 1999 representatives of the government and opposition met in Lomé with international mediators and, under heavy pressure from, among others, French President Jacques Chirac, reached an agreement, which included Eyadéma's pledge that he would not seek reelection in 2003 and that new legislative elections would be conducted. An independent electoral commission was established in December, a new election code was adopted in March 2000, and, following heated debates and several setbacks, the electoral commission announced in January 2001 that the new legislative balloting would be conducted in October.

Relations between the government and the opposition remained severely strained in late 2001 and the first half of 2002. Particularly galling to the opposition was an amendment to the electoral code approved by the assembly in February 2002 that required future presidential candidates to have resided in Togo for 12 consecutive months. Critics described the new law as designed to prevent another presidential run by the UFC's Gilchrist Olympio, who remained outside the country. The opposition parties also strongly objected to the government's offer of only 5 seats on the proposed

20-member electoral commission. In view of the impasse on that membership, the government in May appointed a committee of judges to oversee the new legislative elections, which, having already been postponed from October 2001 and March 2002, were finally held in October 2002 without the participation of most opposition parties.

Critics strongly challenged the assembly's decision to permit Eyadéma to run for a third term in 2003 and described the election results as fraudulent. Although international observers accepted the poll as generally free and open, it was noted that the administration had limited the number of opposition rallies and had constrained access to the government-controlled media. Subsequently, the government appeared to soften its stance by releasing some 500 political prisoners, overturning repressive press restrictions, and promising genuine negotiations designed to bring the opposition into the political process. As part of the reform effort, Prime Minister Sama attempted to create an independent electoral commission, but the UFC, CAR, and other opposition parties refused to participate, citing what they perceived to be a continued lack of transparency in the entire election process. As a result, municipal and regional elections scheduled for December 2004 were postponed indefinitely.

President Eyadéma's death in February 2005 ended Africa's longest presidential reign (38 years) and plunged Togo into a complicated constitutional crisis (see Political background, above, for details). Faure Gnassingbé's takeover prompted numerous demonstrations that led to the death of protesters who clashed with police. In addition, regional organizations such as ECOWAS and the African Union condemned the Togolese military for attempting what was perceived as essentially a coup d'état. On February 9, the International Organization of the Francophonie suspended Togo's membership. On February 20, ECOWAS imposed a range of sanctions on Togo, including suspension of the country's membership, a travel ban on Togolese officials, and an arms embargo. Five days later, the AU endorsed sanctions by individual member states. The United States and the EU offered support for the ECOWAS and AU sanctions. These actions

apparently triggered Gnassingbé's decision to relinquish the presidency and campaign in new elections scheduled for April 24, 2005. Opposition parties sought a postponement to give them more time to campaign. However, the government rejected any delay and even dismissed the interior minister on April 22 when he publicly called for additional time to prepare better for the balloting.

Gnassingbé's election in April (which the opposition and international observers again described as fraudulent) triggered a new wave of violence and the flight of more than 30,000 people to neighboring countries. The UN reported that more than 500 people were killed in post–election violence. (There was approximately $7 million in property damage.) Turmoil continued throughout the summer, despite Gnassingbé's pledge to support new legislative elections if reconciliation could be achieved with the opposition. Gnassingbé undertook a range of actions to mollify the opposition, including the November 2005 release of 460 political prisoners.

Political Parties

Political parties were banned after the 1967 coup. Two years later, the official Rally of the Togolese People (RTP) was organized as the sole legitimate political party. However, on April 12, 1991, the Eyadéma regime, besieged by antigovernment strikes and protests, reversed the RPT's 24-year-old monopoly. Opposition activities were coordinated by a Front of Associations for Renewal (*Front des Associations pour le Renouvellement—* FAR), a coalition of human rights, prodemocracy, and student groups, which, three days after its launching on March 15, had been promised a national conference by the president if it would halt its demonstrations. In May the FAR was superseded by a Democratic Opposition Collective (*Collectif de l'Opposition Démocratique—*COD), which in turn gave way to the National Council for the Safeguard of Democracy (*Conseil National pour la Sauvegarde de la Démocratie—*CNSD) in late December. In July 1992 the CNSD was succeeded by a revived Democratic Opposition Collective (COD-2).

In early 1993 the COD-2 appeared to split into two wings: a "moderate" faction aligned under the banner of the Patriotic Front (FP, below) and a "radical" component, the Union of Forces of Change (UFC, below). Although the FP joined the UFC in boycotting the 1993 presidential election, the linkage was abandoned in early 1994 as the FP ignored the UFC's call for a boycott of legislative balloting. (In July 1997 ties between the two groups were reestablished; however, a proposed electoral coalition, which would have also included the Party for Democracy and Renewal [PDR, below], collapsed following the UFC's withdrawal late in the year.)

In early 2002 a group of opposition parties formed The Front (see below), which subsequently participated in the October launching of the Coalition of Democratic Forces (*Coalition des Forces Démocrates*—CFD) with other groups, including the Panafrican Patriotic Convergence and the UFC. The CFD sought to present a single candidate for the June 2003 election but ultimately boycotted that balloting due to perceived unwillingness on the part of the administration to permit full electoral participation by the opposition. Prior to the 2005 presidential election, six opposition parties agreed to support the candidacy of Bob- Akitani, including the UFC, the PDR, the **Action Committee for Renewal** (*Comité d'Action pour le Renouveau*—CAR), the **Democratic Convention of African People** (*Convention Démocratique des Peuples Africains*—CDPA), **Alliance of Democrats for Integrated Development** (*Alliance des Démocrates pour le Développement Intégré*—ADDI), and the **Union for Democracy and Solidarity–Togo** (*Union pour la Démocratie et la Solidarité–Togo*—UDS–Togo).

Rally of the Togolese People (*Rassemblement du Peuple Togolais* –RPT). Formed in 1969 under the sponsorship of President Eyadéma, the RPT was Togo's sole legal party until its constitutional mandate was abrogated by the National Conference in July 1991. In February 1994 the RPT captured 33 of the 57 seats decided in the first round of assembly balloting; however, the party subsequently fell short of an overall majority by winning only

two second-round seats. The RPT's three victories at legislative by-election balloting in August 1996 left the party in control of 38 of 57 seats. It also claimed the vote of former interim prime minister Koffigoh and two former opposition legislators who held seats as independents. In November the RPT absorbed the Union for Justice and Democracy (*Union pour la Justice et la Démocratie*—UJD), a small grouping that controlled two assembly seats. At the RPT's congress on January 9–11, 1997, the party continued its recent swing back towards a hard-line posture and away from the proreform, youth movement that had characterized a 1994 congress. Evidencing the sea change were the appointments to the Central Committee of a number of old guard stalwarts. In November the party was bolstered by the addition of another minor party, the **Movement for Social Democracy and Tolerance.** The RPT captured 79 seats in the 1999 assembly balloting and 72 in 2002.

Following the death of President Eyadéma in February 2005, his son, Faure Gnassingbé, was elected RPT president.

Leaders: Faure Essozimma GNASSINGBÉ (President of the Republic and the Party), Koffi SAMA (Former Prime Minister), Dama DRAMANI (Secretary General).

Coordination of New Forces (*Coordination des Forces Nouvelles*—CFN). Formed in June 1993 by several parties, including the Union of Democrats for the Republic (*Union des Démocrates pour la République*—UDR), the Togolese Social Liberal Party (*Parti Social-Liberal Togolais*—Solito), and several professional associations, the CFN is led by former prime minister Joseph Kokou Koffigoh under a banner describing the party as "resolutely committed to an irreversible democratic process." At legislative balloting in February 1994 the CFN won one seat. In November 1995 a CFN member, Euphrem Seth DORKENOU, was named to the Kodjo government. The CFN participated (unsuccessfully) in the March 1999 legislative elections, although the party was considered pro-Eyadéma and Koffigoh was named to the cabinet formed in August 2000.

The CFN also failed to win seats in the 2002 elections.

Leaders: Joseph Kokou KOFFIGOH (Former Prime Minister), Nicolas NOMEDJI (Executive Secretary).

Coordination of Political Parties of the Constructive Opposition (*Coordination des Partis de L'Opposition Constructive*—CPOC). Formed in 2002, the CPOC emerged as a formation of opposition parties, which agreed to participate in elections and in the government. The CPOC originally included the Rally for Support for Democracy and Development (RSDD); the **Believers' Movement for Equality and Peace** (*Mouvement des Croyants pour L'Egalité et la Paix*—MOCEP), which won one seat in the 2002 elections and is led by Comlangan Mawutoé D'ALMEIDA; the **Togolese Youth Movement—Juvento** (*Mouvement de la Jeunesse Togolaise*—Juvento), a nationalist youth movement that won two seats in the 2002 assembly elections and is led by Monsilla DJATO and Abalo FIRMIN; and the **Union for Democracy and Social Progress** (*Union pour la Démocratie et le Progrès Social*—UDPS), which won two seats in the 2002 elections and is led by Sekodona SEGO.

Following the 2002 legislative elections, one seat in the government was given to CPOC member Henry OLYMPIO of the RSDD. After the 2003 presidential elections, the government was reshuffled, and a second seat was given to the CPOC. However, Olympio resigned in August 2003 and was replaced by D'Almeida. The RSDD was subsequently expelled from the CPOC.

Rally for Support for Democracy and Development (*Rassemblement pour le Soutien pour la Democratie et le Developpement*—RSDD). The RSDD is led by Henry Octavianus Olympio, a cousin of the opposition leader Gilchrist Olympio of the UFC. Henry Olympio served in the cabinet of Kwassi Klutse and was appointed minister of democracy and promotion of the rule of law in the government formed by Prime Minister Adoboli in June 1999. However, he was dismissed from the latter post in June 2000.

Olympio was appointed minister for relations with the assembly in 2002, but he resigned in August 2003 over a dispute with the prime minister in which the RSDD leader sought a different cabinet post. Olympio secured less than 1 percent of the vote in the 2005 presidential poll.

Leader: Henry Octavianus OLYMPIO (2005 presidential candidate and Chair).

Panafrican Ecologist Party (*Parti Écologiste Panafricain*—PEP). Another RPT-supportive grouping, the PEP also participated unsuccessfully in the 1999 legislative election.

Leader: Essohanam LAWANI.

Panafrican Patriotic Convergence (*Convergence Patriotique Panafricaine*—CPP). The CPP was formed in August 1999 with the formal merger of the UTD (below); the **Party of Democrats for Unity** (*Parti des Démocrates pour l'Unité*—PDU); the **Democratic Union for Solidarity** (*Union Démocratique pour la Solidarité*—UDS); and the **African Party for Democracy** (*Parti Africain pour la Démocratie*—PAD). The CPP was among the main opposition groups that continued talks with the government in 2000 and 2001 and was subsequently active in the formation of the independent electoral commission and the CFD. CPP leader Edem Kodjo was named prime minister in June 2005.

Leaders: Edem KODJO (Prime Minister), Jean-Lucien Savide TOVE.

Togolese Union for Democracy (*Union Togolaise pour la Démocratie*—UTD). Aligned with the CAR, the UTD secured seven seats (one subsequently vacated) at legislative balloting in February 1994, and on April 22 its leader and former secretary general of the Organization of African Unity, Edem Kodjo, was chosen by the president to head a new government. In March 1995 the UTD temporarily withdrew from the National Assembly following a dispute with the RPT over the assignment of responsibility for two government bodies. Improved UTD-RPT relations were highlighted in November when Kodjo included a number of new RPT representatives in his enlarged cabinet. Furthermore, in February 1996 the UTD's votes were pivotal to an RPT-led assembly rejection of an opposition bid for an independent electoral commission. Thereafter, however, relations between the two deteriorated, and in August 1997 Kodjo claimed to have been attacked by government security forces. Subsequently, the UTD leader reportedly announced his intention to boycott forthcoming presidential elections, asserting that the polling would be rigged in favor of the incumbent. Nonetheless, Kodjo ran as the candidate for the CPP in the 2003 presidential election, placing fifth with just 1 percent of the vote.

The Front (*Front Uni de l'Opposition—Le Front*). The Front was formed by the four opposition parties below in 2002 in order to coordinate anti-regime efforts, including negotiations over elections and government policy.

Leader: Yawovi AGBOYIBO (National Coordinator).

Action Committee for Renewal (*Comité d'Action pour le Renouveau—CAR*). The CAR was one of the leaders, along with the UTD, below, in the formation in October 1992 by "moderate" COD-2 parties of the Patriotic Front (*Front Patriotique—FP*), which sought to maintain links with the government despite the objection of other coalition partners. The FP boycotted presidential balloting in August 1993. However, dismissing calls from the more militant UFC for a second boycott, the FP split from its ally and participated in the February 1994 legislative balloting. The CAR captured 36 seats (2 of which were subsequently vacated); however, despite an earlier pledge, President Eyadéma refused to appoint Yawovi Agboyibo, the CAR's leader and presidential candidate, prime minister.

At a mid-March 1994 meeting, the FP, attempting to dispel rumors that dissension would render the coalition unable to assume a governing role, issued a communiqué demanding the

right to form a cabinet. On March 26 the group agreed that the next prime minister would be a CAR member, and two days later it nominated Agboyibo as its choice for the post. Consequently, on April 22 the CAR denounced the appointment of the UTD's Edem Kodjo as prime minister as a "blatant and inadmissible violation" of the March agreement, called on Kodjo to "reconsider" his position, and declared that it would not participate in a UTD-led government, thereby effectively ending the Front's existence. Nevertheless, the following day Kodjo insisted that the FP was still viable and that he controlled a parliamentary majority (albeit a tenuous one in light of a Supreme Court ruling that had invalidated three FP electoral victories).

The CAR boycotted assembly by-election balloting in August 1996, thus conceding the loss of two more seats. Meanwhile, party officials complained that they had been the victim of a RPT-orchestrated "smear campaign." In October the party's legislative seat total dropped to 32 after a deputy defected to the RPT. (Earlier, two other CAR legislators had quit the party, switching their allegiances to the Eyadéma camp.)

The CAR reportedly organized a number of antigovernment demonstrations beginning in late 1996 and continuing through 1997. Furthermore, the group spearheaded concurrent legislative boycotts. In November 1997 Agboyibo, whom *Africa Confidential* described as seeming to "seek outright confrontation with the government," was attacked after attending a function at the U.S. embassy.

Following presidential elections in June 1998, Agboyibo reportedly asserted that the UFC's Olympio was the true top vote-getter. For his part, Agboyibo finished third in the balloting with 9 percent of the tally. The CAR joined the opposition boycott of the 1999 balloting. Agboyibo was found guilty of defamation charges in August 2001. Although a court of appeal nullified a six-month sentence against him in January 2002, he was held on additional conspiracy charges. In mid-March the president ordered his release for the "sake of national reconciliation."

Agboyibo ran for the presidency in 2003 and placed third with 5.2 percent of the vote. In the 2005 presidential election, CAR supported the candidacy of Bob-Akitani.

Leaders: Yawovi AGBOYIBO (1993, 1998, and 2003 presidential candidate), Dodji APEVON (Secretary General).

Democratic Convention of African People (*Convention Démocratique des Peuples Africains*—CDPA). In December 1989 CDPA members Godwin TETE and Kuevi AKUE were arrested for distributing antigovernment leaflets. Their sentencing in October 1990 led to violent protests, which in turn were followed by the government's decision to move towards a multiparty system. The CDPA was legalized in 1991.

In September 1992 the house of CDPA leader Nguessan Ouattara was bombed during a wave of political assassination attempts allegedly orchestrated by Eyadéma supporters. In 1993 the CDPA initiated the formation of the **Panafrican Social Democrats' Group** (*Groupe des Démocrates Sociaux Panafricains*—GDSP), an opposition coalition that also included the PDR and PSPA (below). (After boycotting the 1994 legislative elections, the GDSP was subsequently dissolved.)

In August 1997 the CDPA's founder and secretary general, Léopold Gnininvi, returned from a four-year, self-imposed exile, and at presidential elections in June 1998 he captured less than 1 percent of the vote.

The CDPA joined the boycott of the 2002 legislative elections and was one of the founding parties of both the CFD and The Front. In 2003, CDPA General Secretary Léopold Gnininvi registered to run in the presidential election, but he subsequently withdrew from the race. The CDPA joined the coalition that supported Bob-Akitani's candidacy in the 2005 presidential elections.

Leaders: Nguessan OUATTARA, Léopold GNININVI (Secretary General and 1998 and 2003 presidential candidate), Emmanuel GUKONU (First Secretary).

The other parties in the Front included the **Alliance of Democrats for Integrated Development** (*Alliance des Démocrates pour le Développement Intégré*—ADDI), led by Nagbandja KAMPATIBE, and the **Union for Democracy and Solidarity–Togo** (*Union pour la Démocratie et la Solidarité–Togo*—UDS–Togo), led by Antoine FOLLY. Both the ADDI and the UDS–Togo were part of the coalition that supported the candidacy of Bob-Akitani in the 2005 presidential balloting.

Union of Forces of Change (*Union des Forces du Changement*—UFC). The UFC coalition is led by Gilchrist Olympio, who has long been linked to the MTD (below). In July 1993 the Eyadéma government issued an arrest warrant that linked Olympio to an attack on the president's residence in March, and in early August the UFC leader, who had been calling for a new electoral register, was disqualified from presidential polling for refusing to return to Togo for a medical checkup. Subsequently, the UFC spearheaded a successful boycott of the balloting by its (then) COD-2 partners; however, its calls for a boycott of assembly balloting in February 1994 were ignored. In December 1997 UFC Secretary General Jean-Pierre Fabre was arrested and briefly detained after he sought to investigate the alleged murder of opposition activists by government security forces.

Although officially declared the runner-up at June 1998 presidential balloting, Olympio, who had been blocked from entering Togo from his base in Ghana during the closing days of the campaign, claimed that he had received 59 percent of the vote, not the 34 percent with which he had been credited. Subsequently, the UFC was at the forefront of the antigovernment actions that followed the polling, and in August UFC headquarters were attacked by unknown assailants. Although remaining critical of the French government's previous support of the Eyadéma regime, the UFC followed President Jacques Chirac's call for reconciliation and joined talks with the government in July 1999 along with the CAR and UTD.

The UFC helped form the antiregime CFD in 2002 but withdrew from the group in 2003. Olympio returned to contest the presidential election in 2003 but failed to meet the residency requirements. Bob-Akitani ran as his proxy and placed second in the balloting. Akitani also finished second in the disputed April 2005 presidential poll. In September 2005, UFC member Gabriel Sassouvi DOSSEH-ANYROH was dismissed from the party after he accepted a cabinet post in the Gnassingbé government.

Leaders: Gilchrist OLYMPIO (1998 presidential candidate), Jean-Pierre FABRE (Secretary General), Emmanuel BOB-AKITANI (2005 presidential candidate and Vice President of the Party).

Togolese Movement for Democracy (*Mouvement Togolais pour la Démocratie* — MTD). Prior to the legalization of political parties in April 1991 the MTD was a Paris-based organization, which claimed in 1980 that 34 people released from confinement on January 13 were "not real political prisoners" and that hundreds of others remained incarcerated. It disclaimed any responsibility for a series of bomb attacks in 1985, while charging that the Eyadéma regime had "unleashed a wave of repression" in their wake. In mid-1986 MTD Assistant Secretary General Paulin LOSSOU fled France in the face of a decision by authorities to expel him to Argentina for his "partisan struggle" against the Eyadéma regime. Several reported MTD members were imprisoned in 1986 for distributing anti-Eyadéma pamphlets, but all of their sentences were commuted by 1987.

The government accused the MTD of complicity in the September 1986 coup attempt, insisting that they planned to install Gilchrist Olympio, exiled son of the former chief executive, as president. Olympio, who was sentenced to death in absentia for his alleged role in the plot, described the charges as "preposterous," suggesting that internal dissent had generated the unrest. Olympio returned to Lomé on July 6, 1991, under an April 12 general amnesty, to participate in the National Conference. Although claiming no interest in avenging his father's death, Olympio described the existing regime as lacking "legitimacy." Subsequently, *Africa Confidential* cited his influence in Joseph Kokou Koffigoh's capture of the prime ministerial post.

In May 1992 Olympio was critically wounded in an assassination attempt which took the lives of four others, including MTD leader Eliot OHN. Following his return from rehabilitation in Europe, Olympio emerged as the opposition's most prominent spokesman, and in early 1993 he reportedly suggested that ECOWAS establish a presence in Togo to counter the reemergence of pro-Eyadéma military factions as well as help facilitate the transitional process.

Leader: Gilchrist OLYMPIO (Party Leader).

Socialist Renewal Pact (*Pacte Socialiste pour le Renouveau* — PSR). The PSR's 2003 presidential candidate placed fourth with 2.3 percent of the vote. The PSR was part of the six-party coalition that endorsed Bob-Akitani in the 2005 presidential polling. PSR leader Tchessa Abi broke with other opposition parties and joined the cabinet in June 2005.

Leaders: TCHESSA ABI (Party Leader), Maurice Datuku PERE (2003 presidential candidate).

Union of Independent Liberals (*Union des Libéraux Indépendants* — ULI). The ULI was launched on August 25, 1993, by Jacques Amouzou, an independent presidential candidate, who pledged to "bridge" the gap between the president and the opposition.

Leader: Jacques AMOUZOU (1993 and 1998 presidential candidate).

Unity Party for Economic and Social Development (*Parti Unité pour le Développement Économique et Social* — PUDES). The PUDES was formed on November 14, 1993, according to its founder Essogo Juwe Binizi, to combat "tribalism" and fight for "reconciliation, . . . enhancing job creation, and ensuring a fairer distribution of the nation's wealth."

Leader: Essogo Juwe BINIZI (Chair).

Also legalized in 1991 were the **People's Movement for Democracy and Development** (*Mouvement du Peuple pour la Démocratie et le Développement*—MPDD); the **Togolese Alliance for Democracy** (*Alliance Togolaise pour la Démocratie*—ATD), led by Adani Ifé ATAK-PAMEVI, who was an independent presidential candidate in 1993; the **Togolese Communist Party** (*Parti Communiste Togolais*—PCT); the **Togolese Progress Party** (*Parti du Progrès Togolais*—PPT); and the **Togolese Social Democratic Party** (*Parti Social-Démocrat Togolais*—PSDT). (There have been few references to the above groups since the mid-1990s.)

In addition to the CAR, UTD, and PDU, a number of other parties were assigned posts in the September 1992 government, including the centrist **Alliance of Democrats for the Republic** (*Alliance des Démocrates pour la République*—ADR), which contested the early legislative elections in August 1996; the **Party of Action for Democracy** (*Parti d'Action pour la Démocratie*—PAD), led by Francis EKOH; the **Togolese Union for Reconciliation** (*Union Togolaise pour la Réconciliation*—UTR), led by Bawa MANK-OUBU; and the **Union for Labor and Justice** (*Union pour le Travail et la Justice*—UTJ), which also contested the legislative elections in 1994.

Other parties that emerged in 1992 and 1993 included the **Nationalist Movement for Unity** (*Mouvement Nationaliste de l'Unité*—MNU), led by Koffitse ADZRAKO; the **Togolese Democratic Party** (*Parti Démocratique Togolais*—PDT), led by Mba KABASSEMA; and the **Movement of October 5th** (*Mouvement du 5 Octobre*—MO5), a militant group led by Bassirou AYEWA and whose name was derived from the date of the first anti-Eyadéma demonstration. In February 1993, MO5 members were reported to have built barricades throughout Lomé to protest the late January killing of opposition demonstrators by government security forces.

In October 1994 five terrorists, who were linked to a group of Togolese exiles led by Logo DOS-SOUVI, were arrested as they prepared to launch a strike in southern Togo from their camp in Ghana's Volta region. In early 1997 former interior minister Kokou MASSEME was arrested in Ghana, where he had reportedly formed a "national liberation army."

Among other formations are the **Party for Democracy and Renewal** (*Parti pour la Démocratie et le Renouvellement*—PDR), led by Zarifou AYEWA (who joined the cabinet in June 2005); the hard-line Marxist-Leninist **Pan-African Socialist Party** (*Parti Socialiste PanAfricain*—PSPA), led by Francis AGBOBLI; the **Workers' Party** (*Parti des Travailleurs*—PT), led by Claude AMENGAVI; the **National Front** (*Front National*—FN), led by Amela AMELA VI; the **Movement of Republican Centrists** (*Mouvement des Républicains Centristes*—MRC), led by Kabou Gssokoyo ABASS; the **Party for Renewal and Redemption**, whose leader, Nicholas LAWSON, won 1 percent of the vote in the 2005 presidential poll; and the **Party for Renewal and Social Progress** (*Parti pour le Renouveau et le Progrès Social*—PRPS), led by Agbessi MAWOU. In 2005, the **Initiative and Development Party** was formed by Adanu Kokou KPOTUI as the country's 63rd registered party. It was followed in September by the formation of the **Democratic Alliance for the Motherland** by former prime minister Agbéyomé Messan KODJO and former speaker of the assembly Maurice Dahuku PERE.

Legislature

On July 16, 1991, the National Conference dissolved the existing National Assembly and subsequently transferred its powers to a High Council of the Republic (*Haut Conseil de la République*—HCR) for a transition period leading to multiparty elections. In early 1993 the HCR, already involved in a constitutional debate with the president over his efforts to reverse the prime minister's dismissal of two cabinet members, once again found itself in conflict with Eyadéma, who, in response to criticism of his dismissal and then reconfirmation of the prime minister, argued that the HCR's mandate had expired along with the transition period. Subsequently, after numerous postponements,

Cabinet

As of September 20, 2006

Prime Minister	Yawovi Madji Agboyibo (CAR)

Ministers of State

Agriculture, Livestock, and Fishing	Yves Mado Nagou
Foreign Affairs and African Integration	Zarifou Ayéva (PDR)
Mines and Energy	Léopold Messan Gnininvi (CDPA)

Ministers

Civil Service, Labor, and Employment	Katari Foli-Bazi
Commerce, Industry, and Handicrafts	Jean-Lucien Savi de Tové
Communication and Civic Formation	Gahoun Egbor
Cooperation and NEPAD	Gilbert Bawara
Culture, Tourism, and Leisure	Gabriel Sassouvi Dosseh-Anyroh
Decentralization and Regional Planning	Yendja Yentchabré
Defense and Veterans Affairs	Kpatcha Gnassingbé
Economy and Development	Daniel Kloutsé
Environment and Forest Resources	Issifou Okoulou-Kantchati
Equipment, Transport, Posts, and Telecommunications	Kokouvi Dogbé
Finance and Privatization	Payadowa Boukpessi
Health	Charles Kondi Agba
Higher Education and Research	Messan Adimado Aduayom
Human Rights, Democracy, and Reconciliation	Célestine Akouavi Aïdam [f]
Justice and Keeper of the Seals	Sela Polo
Population, Social Affairs, and Promotion of Women	Maïmounatou Ibrahima [f]
Primary and Secondary Education	Komi Klassou
Relations with the Institutions of the Republic	Tchessa Abi (PSR)
Security	Col. Atcha Titikpina
Small and Medium Size enterprises and Free Zone Promotion	Bernard Edjaidé Walla
Technical Education and Professional Training	Antoine Agbéwanou Edoh
Territorial Administration and Decentralization	Kwesi Séléagodji Ahumey-Zunu
Urban Affairs	Comlan Mally
Water and Water Resources	Yao Florent Maganawé
Youth and Sports	Richard Tipoé

[f] = female

Togo's first multiparty balloting took place over two rounds on February 6 and 20, 1994.

National Assembly (*Assemblée Nationale*). The National Assembly is composed of 81 members directly elected for five-year terms. At the most recent balloting on October 27, 2002, the Rally of the Togolese People won 72 seats; the Rally for Support for Democracy and Development 3; the Union for Democracy and Social Progress, 2; the Togolese Youth Movement, 2; the Believers' Movement for Equality and Peace, 1; and independents, 1.

President: Abbas BONFOH.

Communications

For many years the media were almost exclusively government controlled. A highly restrictive press code adopted in October 1990 was significantly relaxed in early 1991; however, in June 1998 yet another more stringent code was adopted. In early 2000 a new press bill further limited press freedom and made "defamation of the government" an offense subject to a prison sentence. In 2000 and 2001 numerous independent and pro-opposition publications came under government scrutiny. In April 2000 the director of the independent weekly *L'Exilé* was arrested, and his newspaper was suspended for six months.

A second repressive law was passed in 2002 and allowed fines of up to $7,500 and sentences of five years in prison for defaming the president. The law also imposed lesser penalties for defamation of members of the government and the assembly. However, many of the new measures were repealed in August 2004 as part of Togo's effort to restart international aid. Suppression and intimidation of opposition media continued, and in October 2005 there were widespread protests to denounce attacks on opposition journalists.

Press

The following are published in French in Lomé: *Togo Presse* (15,000), government-owned daily; *Le Combat du Peuple,* pro-opposition weekly; *L'Exilé, Abito, Le Regard, L'Aurore, Le Nouvel Echo,* and *Le Nouveau Journal,* all independent weeklies; *Le Nouvel Éclat,* pro-government weekly; *Le Courrier du Golfe* and *Forum-Hebdo,* independent bimonthly; *La Dépêche,* bimonthly; and *L'Echos d'Afrique,* a pro-CDPA publication.

News Agencies

Agence Togolaise de Presse (ATOP) is the official facility; *Agence France-Presse* and *Deutsche Presse-Agentur* maintain bureaus in Lomé.

Broadcasting and Computing

The government-operated *Radiodiffusion du Togo* broadcasts from Lomé in French, English, and indigenous languages. *Télévision Togolaise* began programming in Lomé in 1973; other transmitters are located in Alédjo-Kadara and Mont Agon. By the end of 2000, three private channels, *Radio Télévision Delta Santé, Radio Télévision Zion-To* (with a Christian orientation), and *Djabal Nour* (with a Muslim orientation) were still operating, while a fourth, *TV2,* was on the air in 2002. There were approximately 156,000 television receivers and 160,000 personal computers serving 210,000 Internet users in 2003.

Intergovernmental Representation

Ambassador to the U.S.
(Vacant)

U.S. Ambassador to Togo
David B. DUNN

Permanent Representative to the UN
(Vacant)

IGO Memberships (Non-UN)
ADF, AfDB, AU, BADEA, BOAD, CENT, ECOWAS, Interpol, IOM, NAM, OIC, OIF, PCA, UEMOA, WCO, WTO

TUNISIA

REPUBLIC OF TUNISIA

al-Jumhuriyah al-Tunisiyah

The Country

Situated midway along the North African littoral between Algeria and Libya, Tunisia looks north and eastward into the Mediterranean and southward toward the Sahara Desert. Along with Algeria and Morocco, it forms the Berber-influenced part of North Africa known as the "Maghreb" (West) to distinguish it from other Middle Eastern countries, which are sometimes referred to as the "Mashreq" (East). Tunisia's terrain, well wooded and fertile in the north, gradually flattens into a coastal plain adapted to stock-raising and olive culture, and becomes semidesert in the south. The population is almost exclusively of Arab and Berber stock, Arabic in speech (save for a small Berber-speaking minority), and Sunni Muslim in religion. Although most members of the former French community departed after Tunisia gained independence in 1956, French continues as a second language, and small French, Italian, Jewish, and Maltese minorities remain. Women, who constitute approximately 31 percent of the paid labor force, are the focus of relatively progressive national policies on equal rights, educational access for girls, and family planning. In addition, by presidential decree 20 women were elected to the national legislature in 1999 and 43 in 2004. Moreover, the current government includes female ministers and secretaries of state.

About one quarter of the working population is engaged in agriculture, which is responsible for about 13 percent of GNP; the main products are wheat, barley, olive oil, wine, and fruits. Petroleum has been a leading export, although there is also some mining of phosphates, iron ore, lead, and zinc. Industry has expanded to more than 30 percent of GDP, with steel, textiles, and chemicals firmly established. Most development is concentrated in coastal areas, where tourism is the largest source of income; however, poverty is widespread in the subsistence farming and mining towns of the south. Rising oil exports underpinned rapid economic growth in the 1970s, but declining prices and reserves precipitated a tailspin in the early 1980s. Consequently, high unemployment, a large external debt, and growing budget and trade deficits led the government, with encouragement by the International Monetary Fund (IMF) and World Bank, to abandon much of its former socialist orientation in favor of economic liberalization in the second half

of the decade. Led by growth in the agriculture and food processing sectors, the economy rebounded strongly in the 1990s as the government endorsed further privatization and measures designed to attract foreign investment. As a result, the IMF has touted Tunisia as an example of how effective adjustment programs can be in developing nations if pursued faithfully. At the same time economic advances have not been accompanied by significant democratization measures, and government at all levels remains totally dominated by the ruling party.

GDP grew at an annual average of 5.7 percent from 1996–2000, with inflation running at 3 percent in 2000. The most worrisome economic indicator involved unemployment, estimated at 15 percent (higher among young workers). Although the IMF in early 2001 continued to praise the government for "prudent" economic policies, the fund called for intensification of the privatization program (the government still controls 40 percent of economic production). Real GDP growth was 6.2 percent for 2005, though unemployment remained high. The IMF in 2006, while again commending the government's fiscal policies that continued to help strengthen the economy, urged reduction of the country's external debt and reform of the banking sector. GDP growth was projected to be 8.4 percent for 2006, according to the IMF, partly due to the country's opening up "substantially" to foreign trade.

Government and Politics

Political Background

Seat of the Carthaginian empire destroyed by Rome in 146 BC, Tunisia was successively conquered by Romans, Arabs, and Turks before being occupied by France in 1881 and becoming a French protectorate under a line of native rulers (beys) in 1883. Pressure for political reforms began after World War I and in 1934 resulted in establishment of the nationalist Neo-Destour (New Constitution) Party, which spearheaded the drive for independence under the leadership of Habib BOURGUIBA. Nationalist aspirations were further stimulated by World War II, and an initial breakdown in independence negotiations led to the outbreak of guerrilla warfare against the French in 1952. Internal autonomy was conceded by France on June 3, 1955, and on March 20, 1956, the protectorate was terminated, with the country gaining full independence.

A national constituent assembly controlled by the Neo-Destour Party voted on July 25, 1957, to abolish the monarchy and establish a republic with Bourguiba as president. A new constitution was adopted on June 1, 1959, while Bourguiba's leadership and that of the party were overwhelmingly confirmed in presidential and legislative elections in 1959 and 1964.

Bourguiba was reelected in 1969, but his failing health precipitated a struggle for succession to the presidency. One-time front-runner Bahi LADGHAM, prime minister and secretary general of the party, was apparently too successful: the attention he received as chair of the Arab Superior Commission on Jordan and as effective executive during the president's absences led to a falling-out with an eventually rejuvenated Bourguiba; he was dismissed in 1970 and replaced by Hedi NOUIRA. President Bourguiba encountered an additional challenge from Ahmed MESTIRI, interior minister and leader of the liberal wing of the party. The liberals succeeded in forcing democratization of the party structure during the Eighth Party Congress in October 1971, but Bourguiba subsequently reasserted his control over the party apparatus. Mestiri was expelled from the party in January 1972 and from his seat in the National Assembly in May 1973, while Bourguiba was named president for life on November 2, 1974.

In February 1980 Prime Minister Nouira suffered a stroke, and on April 24 Mohamed MZALI, the acting prime minister, was asked to form a new government. Mzali was reappointed following a general election on November 1, 1981, in which three additional parties were allowed to participate, although none secured legislative representation.

Political Status: Independent state since 1956; republic proclaimed July 25, 1957; under one-party dominant, presidential regime.

Area: 63,170 sq. mi. (163,610 sq. km.).

Population: 9,910,872 (2004C); 10,031,000 (2005E).

Major Urban Centers (2005E): TUNIS (734,000), Sfax (Safaqis, 269,000), Ariana (252,000), Ettadhamen (116,000).

Official Language: Arabic; French is widely spoken as a second language.

Monetary Unit: Dinar (market rate July 1, 2006: 1.32 dinars = $1US).

President: Gen. Zine El-Abidine BEN ALI (Democratic Constitutional Assembly); appointed prime minister on October 2, 1987; acceded to the presidency upon the deposition of Habib BOURGUIBA on November 7; returned to office, unopposed, at elections of April 2, 1989, and March 20, 1994; reelected in multicandidate balloting on October 24, 1999, and on October 24, 2004.

Prime Minister: Mohamed GHANNOUCHI (Democratic Constitutional Assembly); appointed by the president on November 17, 1999, to succeed Hamed KAROUI (Democratic Constitutional Assembly), who had resigned the same day.

Bourguiba dismissed Mzali on July 8, 1986, replacing him with Rachid SFAR, theretofore finance minister.

Gen. Zine El-Abidine BEN ALI was named to succeed Sfar on October 2, 1987, reportedly because of presidential displeasure at recent personnel decisions. Five weeks later, after a panel of doctors had declared the aged president medically unfit, Bourguiba was forced to step down in favor of Ben Ali, who designated Hedi BACCOUCHE as his prime ministerial successor.

Although widely termed a "bloodless coup," the ouster of Bourguiba and succession of Ben Ali were in accord with relevant provisions of the Tunisian constitution. Moreover, the takeover was generally welcomed by Tunisians, who had become increasingly disturbed by Bourguiba's erratic behavior and mounting government repression of the press, trade unions, legal opposition parties, and other sources of dissent, including the growing Islamic fundamentalist movement. (Following his deposition, Bourguiba retired from public view. He died in April 2000.)

Upon assuming office the Ben Ali government announced its commitment to domestic pluralism and launched a series of wide-ranging political and economic liberalization measures, which included the legalization of some political parties, the loosening of media restrictions, and the pardoning of more than 8,000 detainees, many of them fundamentalists. Additionally, in late 1988, the new regime negotiated a "national pact" regarding the country's political, economic, and social future with a number of political and labor groups. However, the Islamic Tendency Movement (*Mouvement de la Tendance Islamique*—MTI) refused to sign the accord, foreshadowing a steady deterioration in relations between the fundamentalists and the government.

Presidential and legislative elections, originally scheduled for 1991, were moved up to April 2, 1989, Ben Ali declaring they would serve as an indication of the public's satisfaction with the recent changes. No one challenged the popular Ben Ali in the presidential poll, but the legal opposition parties and fundamentalist independent candidates contested the House of Representatives balloting, albeit without success.

On September 27, 1989, Ben Ali dismissed Baccouche and named former Justice Minister Hamed KAROUI as prime minister. The change was reportedly precipitated by disagreement over economic policy, Baccouche having voiced concern over the "social effects" of the government's austerity program. Shortly thereafter, the government announced the formation of a "higher council" to oversee implementation of the national pact, although several opposition parties and MTI followers, now operating as the Renaissance Party (*Hizb al-Nahda*—generally referenced as *Nahda*) boycotted the council's meetings. Charging that the democratic process was in reality being "blocked" by the government, the opposition also refused to contest municipal elections in June 1990 or national by-elections in October 1991. Apparently in response to criticism that the government's enthusiasm for democratization had waned as its antifundamentalist fervor had surged, electoral law changes were adopted in late 1993 to assure opposition parties of some legislative representation in the upcoming general election (see Legislature, below). Nevertheless, the RCD, officially credited with nearly 98 percent of the vote, won all 144 seats for which it was eligible in the balloting for a 163-member House on March 20, 1994. On the same date, Ben Ali was reelected without challenge, two potential independent candidates being stricken from the ballot by their failure to receive the required endorsement of at least 30 national legislators or municipal council presidents.

The RCD won control of all 257 municipal councils in local elections on May 21, 1995. While opposition candidates (standing in 47 municipalities) won only 6 of 4,090 seats, it was the first time since independence that the opposition had gained any such representation at all.

Ben Ali was reelected to a third full presidential term (then the constitutional limit) in balloting on October 24, 1999, securing more than 99 percent of the vote against two candidates presented by small opposition parties. Meanwhile, the RCD again secured all the seats for which it was eligible (148) in the concurrent legislative poll. Two days after being sworn in for his new term, President Ben Ali appointed Mohamed GHANNOUCHI, theretofore the minister for international cooperation and foreign investment, as the new prime minister.

Constitutional revision in 2002 removed the limit on the number of presidential terms, thereby permitting Ben Ali on October 24, 2004, to seek a fourth term, which he won with 95 percent of the vote against three other minor candidates. On the same date the RCD won all 152 seats contested on a district basis for an expanded assembly.

In the municipal election of May 8, 2005, to renew 264 councils comprising 4,366 seats, the RDC garnered 93.9 percent of the vote, while 4 oppo-

sition parties and 1 independent won representation with 6.1 percent of the vote. Three opposition groups whose candidates were barred from running boycotted the election.

Constitution and Government

The constitution of June 1, 1959, endowed the Tunisian Republic with a presidential system backed by the dominant position of the (then) Neo-Destour Party. The president was given exceptionally broad powers, including the right to designate the prime minister and to rule by decree during legislative adjournments. In addition, the incumbent was granted life tenure under a 1975 amendment to the basic law. In the wake of President Bourguiba's ouster in 1987, the life presidency was abolished, the chief executive being limited to no more than three five-year terms. (See Current issues, below, for details of constitutional revision in 2002 affecting the presidency.) The succession procedure was also altered, the president of the House of Representatives being designated to serve as head of state for 45–60 days, pending a new election, at which he could not present himself as a candidate. Other changes included reduction of the role of prime minister from leader of the government to "coordinator" of ministerial activities.

The legislature was a unicameral body until 2005, with only a House of Representatives.

The House of Representatives (styled the National Assembly until 1981 and also referenced as the Chamber of Deputies) is elected by universal suffrage for a five-year term. Under Bourguiba it had limited authority and in practice was wholly dominated by the ruling party, whose highly developed, all-pervasive organization served to buttress presidential policies both nationally and locally. Constitutional changes approved in July 1988 contained measures designed to expand the House's control and influence, although their impact has been minimal. Consultative bodies at the national level include a Social and Economic Council and a Higher Islamic Council. The judicial system is headed by a Court of Cassation and includes three courts of appeal, 13 courts of first instance, and

51 cantonal courts. Judges are appointed by the president. A new constitution approved in a referendum on May 26, 2002, and signed into law by the president on June 2, 2002, introduced a second legislative body, provisions for an upper house (House of Advisers, see below, under Legislature), removed presidential term limits, and raised the age limit for a presidential candidate to 75 (from 70), among other things.

Tunisia is administratively divided into 23 provinces, each headed by a governor appointed by the president. The governors are assisted by appointed government councils and 264 elected municipal councils.

Foreign Relations

Tunisia assumed a nonaligned posture at independence, establishing relations with both Eastern and Western countries, although placing particular emphasis on its relations with the West and with Arab governments. It became a member of the United Nations in 1956 and is active in all the UN-related agencies. It joined the Arab League in 1958 but boycotted its meetings from 1958 to 1961 and again in 1966 as a result of disagreements with the more "revolutionary" Arab states. As a signal of its support for peace negotiations (particularly the 1993 accord between Israel and the Palestine Liberation Organization), Tunisia exchanged low-level economic representatives with Israel in October 1994 in what was considered a possible precursor to eventual establishment of full diplomatic relations. However, Tunisia recalled those representatives from Israel in 1997 as part of the broad Arab protest over a perceived intransigence on the part of the Netanyahu administration in Israel.

Beginning in 1979 a series of agreements were signed with Algeria, culminating in a March 1983 "Maghreb Fraternity and Co-Operation Treaty," to which Mauritania acceded the following December. Relations with Libya, though reestablished in 1982 after a 1980 rupture over seizure of a southern town by alleged Libyan-trained insurgents, continued to be difficult. President Bourguiba's visit to Washington in June 1985 led to a mass expulsion of Tunisian workers from Libya, as well as reported Libyan incursions into Tunisia and efforts to destabilize its government. After suspending relations with Tripoli in September 1986, Tunis resumed relations a year later following a pledge by Libya to reimburse the expelled workers. Further economic and social agreements, including provisions for the free movement of people and goods between the two countries, were announced in 1988 as Tunisia stepped up its call for regional cooperation and unity, the latter bearing fruit with the formation of the Arab Maghreb Union in February 1989 (see article under Intergovernmental Organizations). Also in 1988, relations were reestablished with Egypt after an eight-year lapse.

The Iraqi invasion of Kuwait in August 1990 appeared to precipitate a change in Tunisia's theretofore unwavering pro-Western orientation. Although critical of the Iraqi occupation, Tunis strongly condemned the subsequent deployment of U.S. troops in Saudi Arabia and the allied bombing of Iraq in early 1991. However, security forces clamped down on large-scale pro-Iraqi demonstrations during the Gulf war, apparently out of concern that the situation might be exploited by Islamic fundamentalists.

President Ben Ali welcomed the antifundamentalist stance adopted by the Algerian military in early 1992, and Tunis was subsequently in the forefront of efforts among North African capitals to coordinate an "antiterrorist" campaign against Muslim militants. In October 1991 Tunisia recalled its ambassador from Sudan, charging Khartoum with fomenting fundamentalist unrest and providing sanctuary and financial support for groups intent on overthrowing the Tunisian government.

Tunisia is prominent among those nations hoping to develop economic cooperation, and possibly a free trade area, in the Mediterranean region. "Partnership" discussions have been emphasized with the European Union (EU), the focus of an estimated 80 percent of Tunisia's trade, and Tunis signed an association agreement with the EU in 1995 that provided for the progressive reduction of tariffs (and elimination of many by 2008).

Current Issues

Government/fundamentalist conflict dominated domestic affairs in the early and mid-1990s, the Ben Ali regime denouncing *Nahda* adherents as "terrorists" intent on seizing power. However, the government's own hard-line tactics were the subject of increasing domestic and international condemnation, human rights organizations accusing security forces of arbitrary detention and widespread mistreatment of prisoners. Government critics also alleged that the antifundamentalist campaign was being used to deflect attention from the RCD's continuing status as "virtually a state party" and the retention of as many as 2,000 political prisoners. The situation was seen as creating a problem for Western capitals: on the one hand, the administration's economic policies had generated widespread success while, on the other, its human rights record was difficult to condone. In 1998 the U.S. State Department described the Ben Ali administration as "intolerant of dissent," and Amnesty International charged that human rights activists in Tunisia had themselves become the targets of intimidation and imprisonment.

Once again adopting a seemingly unnecessarily restrictive stance, the administration announced that candidates in the 1999 presidential election would be allowed to run only if they had served five years as the leader of a party currently represented in the legislature. Only two challengers qualified and, although the administration heralded the multicandidate nature of the balloting as an important democratization step, critics dismissed the poll as a "parody," citing the fact that each opposition candidate won less than 0.5 percent of the vote. The RCD's total domination of the concurrent legislative poll and the municipal elections in May 2000 further supported the argument that the legal opposition parties remained "subservient or marginalized."

Perhaps in response to growing criticism in the West over human rights issues and the lack of genuine political liberalization, the government released some political prisoners in late 1999 and appeared to accept a more vocal dissent in 2000. How-

ever, this modest "Tunisian spring" was the focus of a crackdown in early 2001 as the administration faced intensifying attacks from domestic human rights organizations and challenges in the form of several high-profile petitions and manifestos.

In November 2001 the government introduced controversial proposed constitutional amendments that, among other things, called for the revocation of presidential term limits and the raising of the maximum age of presidential candidates from 70 to 75. Critics described the changes as being designed to permit Ben Ali, currently 65, to govern for many more years. A national referendum on May 26, 2002, approved the basic law revisions by more than 99 percent, according to official reports.

Another focus of attention in 2002 was a reported increase in activity on the part of radical Islamic militants. In April an Islamic Army for the Liberation of Holy Places claimed responsibility for a bomb attack on a synagogue on the island of Djerba that killed more than 20 people. Several months later it was reported that a senior al-Qaida leader had suggested that al-Qaida had also been involved in the bombing.

Despite continued criticism from human rights groups, there appeared to be little subsequent improvement in the treatment of political prisoners. Collaterally, in the wake of the September 11, 2001, terrorist attacks in the United States, Washington concentrated less on the issue of human rights and more on Tunisia's antiterror efforts. (In December 2003 the Ben Ali administration adopted broad new antiterrorism legislation that critics claimed could be used to apply harsh penalties to nearly any crime.) Prior to the October 2004 presidential and legislative balloting, Ben Ali pledged to "deepen the democratic exercise," but opposition parties characterized those elections as a "charade" that was simply propelling Ben Ali toward a "life presidency." Among other things, the opposition candidates claimed they were victims of intense harassment by the government prior to the balloting.

In apparent response to ongoing criticism from human rights groups, the government agreed in early 2005 to change its detention policy, promising to hold prisoners in solitary confinement for no more than 10 days. (Human Rights Watch claimed Tunisia resorted to lengthy isolation terms for leaders of outlawed Islamist parties as a way of eradicating the Islamist movement.) Subsequently, in September 2005, the Tunisian Human Rights League (*Ligue Tunisienne des Droits de l'Homme*—LTDH [see Other Groups under Political Parties, below]) was banned from holding its conference.

Syria extradited 21 suspected Tunisian Islamists in 2005, raising concerns in Tunis and Washington. Tunisia, according to observers, has been intent on reassuring its Western allies that it will not allow extremists to stir trouble abroad, concurrently intensifying the government's resolve to exclude such groups from the country's political process.

Political Parties

Although not constitutionally mandated, Tunisia was effectively a one-party state from the time the Communist Party (PCT) was banned in January 1963 until its return to legal status in July 1981. In June 1981 the government had announced that recognition would be extended to all parties obtaining at least 5 percent of the valid votes in legislative balloting on November 1. On September 9 the PCT indicated that it would participate in the election after receiving official assurances that the 5 percent requirement would not be imposed in its case, and in 1983 recognition was extended to two additional opposition parties, the Popular Union Party (*Parti de l'Unité Populaire*—PUP) and the Democratic Socialist Movement (*Mouvement des Démocrates Socialistes*—MDS [below]). All three boycotted the 1986 election because of the rejection of many of their candidate lists and administrative suspension of their publications. In November 1987 the Ben Ali government endorsed the legalization of any party that would consent to certain conditions, one (advanced by the House of Representatives in April 1988) being that "no party has the right to refer, in its principles, its objectives, its activities or its programs, to religion, language, race or a regime," a stipulation that served as a

barrier to the legalization of militant Islamic groups. Prior to the 1989 balloting, the government party (RCD, below) offered to head an electoral front that would have guaranteed at least minimal opposition representation in the house. However, the proposal was rejected, ultimately to the dismay of the legal opposition parties, none of which succeeded in winning more than 3 percent of the popular vote. In April 1991 the Ben Ali government agreed to provide the six legal opposition parties with moderate state financial support and limited access to government-controlled television and radio broadcasting facilities. Subsequently, in what the administration described as a further effort to strengthen the role of the opposition parties, the RCD also offered not to present candidates for the House by-elections in October. However, the opposition boycotted the balloting as a protest against the government's unwillingness to revise the electoral law or reduce the RCD's "stranglehold" on the civil service. Electoral law changes guaranteed the opposition a minimal number of seats in the March 1994 national elections, but non-RCD candidates still secured less than 3 percent of the votes even though all the legal parties participated. The government announced in 1997 that the House would be expanded for the 1999 balloting and that electoral revision would attempt to promote opposition representation of up to 20 percent. The House was expanded to 182 members for the 1999 balloting, electoral revision in 1998 having guaranteed opposition representation of at least 34 members.

Government Party

Democratic Constitutional Assembly (*Rassemblement Constitutionnel Démocratique*—RCD). Founded in 1934 as the Neo-Destour Party, a splinter from the old Destour (Constitution) Party, and known from October 1964 as the Destourian Socialist Party (*Parti Socialiste Destourien*—PSD), Tunisia's ruling party was given its present name in February 1988 to provide new impetus to "the practice of democracy" within its ranks. Its moderately left-wing tendency was of less political significance than its organizational strength, derived in large part from affiliated syndicates representing labor, agriculture, artisans and merchants, students, women, and youth. Party members have filled most major government positions since independence.

At the 12th party congress in June 1986 President Bourguiba personally selected a new 90-member Central Committee and 20-member Political Bureau, ignoring party statutes calling for election by delegates. By the end of the year the PSD had ended a 1985 rift in returning to close alignment with the General Union of Tunisian Workers (*Union Générale des Traivailleurs Tunisiens*—UGTT). A special "Congress of Salvation," held in Tunis July 29–31, 1988, endorsed the political liberalization policies of new President Ben Ali (who was reelected party chair), included a number of young party members in a new 150-member Central Committee, and named a new 12-member Political Bureau.

At a congress held July 29–31, 1993, Ben Ali was unanimously reelected party chair and designated as the RCD presidential candidate in the elections scheduled for March 1994. A new Central Committee was selected, more than half of its 200 members serving for the first time in a reflection of the RCD's "revitalization" campaign that also included enlargement of the Political Bureau to include several young cabinet ministers and the first female member. In addition, the congress reconfirmed its commitment to free-market economic policies and stated its strong opposition to Islamic fundamentalist "militancy."

The third RCD congress, held July 30–August 22, 1998, reelected Ben Ali as chair and nominated him as the party's candidate for the 1999 presidential election, which he won with more than 99 percent of the vote. In the 1999 legislative balloting, the RCD secured 92 percent of the vote; municipal elections in May 2000 and May 2005 produced similar support for the RCD.

On October 24, 2004, Ben Ali won a fourth term with 95 percent of the vote against three other minor candidates.

Political Bureau: Gen. Zine El-Abidine BEN ALI (President of the Republic and President of the Party), Mohamed GHANNOUCHI (Prime Minister and Second Vice President of the Party), Hamed KAROUI (First Vice President of the Party and Former Prime Minister), Hédi MHENNI (Secretary General), Abdelaziz BEN DHIA, Abderrahim ZOUARI, Chedli NEFFATI, Dali JAZI, Fouad MBAZAA (President of the House of Representatives), Habib BEN YAHIA, Abdallah KALLEL, Neziha ZARROUK, Ali CHAOUCH.

Other Legal Parties

Democratic Socialist Movement (*Mouvement des Démocrates Socialistes*—MDS). Organized as the Democratic Socialist Group in October 1977 by a number of former PSD cabinet ministers who sought liberalization of the nation's political life, the MDS was refused formal recognition in 1978, although its leader, Ahmed Mestiri, had served as an intermediary between the government and the trade union leadership in attempting to resolve labor unrest. The new grouping was runner-up at the 1981 election but obtained only 3.28 percent of the vote, thus failing to secure either legislative representation or legal status. However, recognition was granted by President Bourguiba in November 1983.

Mestiri was arrested in April 1986 and sentenced to four months in prison for leading demonstrations against the U.S. bombing of Libya. The conviction automatically disqualified him from running for legislative office, the MDS thereupon becoming an early advocate of the November electoral boycott. (Under the amnesty program initiated by the Ben Ali government in late 1987, Mestiri was pardoned for the conviction.) The MDS fared poorly in the 1989 balloting, and Mestiri was criticized for rejecting the RCD's preelection offer of an electoral front with the MDS and other parties. Subsequently, Mestiri resigned as MDS secretary general, assistant secretary general Dali Jazi having earlier quit the party to join the government. Mestiri was reported to have left the party altogether in early 1992, as criticism grew of the "authoritarian" approach of its new leader, Mohamed Mouada. Factionalization also contributed to the "suspension" by the MDS of another of its prominent leaders, Mustafa BEN Jaafar.

The MDS supported President Ben Ali for reelection in 1994 but challenged the RCD in the national legislative balloting. Although no MDS candidates were successful on their own, ten were subsequently seated in the house under the proportional arrangement enacted to guarantee a multiparty legislature.

In early October 1995 Mouada published a letter criticizing the "lack of political freedom" in Tunisia. Within days he was arrested on charges of having had illegal contacts with representatives of the Libyan government, and in February 1996 he was sentenced to 11 years in prison. Mouada dismissed the charges as "obviously politically motivated," and his conviction was widely condemned by international observers. Khemais CHAMMARI, a member of the MDS as well as the House of Representatives, was also given a five-year sentence in July for "attacking state security." Both men were released in December, although Mouada was briefly detained again one year later. Meanwhile, an MDS congress in May 1997 had elected Ismaïl Boulahia to the new leadership post of secretary general, his discussion of the future of the "new MDS" apparently reflecting a diminution of Mouada's authority. However, Boulahia was not eligible to contest the 1999 presidential election, since he had not held his MDS post the requisite five years, and he subsequently announced the MDS was supporting President Ben Ali for reelection. Meanwhile, the party secured 13 seats in the legislative balloting of 1999, again thanks solely to electoral law guarantees regarding opposition representation.

Mouada was held under house arrest for one month in late 1999 on a charge of defaming the government, and in early 2001 he issued a joint declaration with *Nahda* leader Rachid Ghanouchi calling for creation of a joint antigovernment front. However, apparently underscoring continued disagreement within the MDS regarding the extent of cooperation with the regime, Boulahia met with President Ben Ali in early 2001 and praised his commitment to "democratic values." The party

supported Ben Ali in the 2004 presidential election and won representation in municipal elections of 2005. Meanwhile, Ben Jafaar continued his heavy criticism of the administration through an unrecognized grouping called the Democratic Forum for Labor and Liberties (*Forum Démocratique pour le Travail et les Libertés*—FDTL), of which he was described as the secretary general, and the National Council for Tunisian Freedoms (*Conseil National pour les Libertés*—CNLT [below]), of which he was a founding member.

Leaders: Mohamed MOUADA, Ismaïl BOULAHIA (Secretary General).

Renewal Movement (*Harakat Ettajdid/ Mouvement de la Rénovation*—MR). The Renewal Movement is heir to the Tunisian Communist Party (*Parti Communiste Tunisien*—PCT), which was founded in 1934 as an entity distinct from the French Communist Party. The PCT was outlawed in 1963 and regained legality in July 1981. Historically of quite limited membership, the party secured only 0.78 percent of the vote at the 1981 legislative balloting. Prior to the opposition boycott, the PCT had intended to participate in the 1986 election in alliance with the RSP (below). Delegates to the party's 1987 congress denounced IMF-supported changes in the government's economic policies, particularly the emphasis on the private sector and free-market activity. Subsequently, the PCT supported the political reforms instituted by the Ben Ali government, before joining the MDS and MUP in boycotting the municipal elections in 1990 to protest the "failure" of democratization efforts.

The party's new name was adopted at an April 1993 congress, leaders announcing that Marxism had been dropped as official doctrine in favor of a "progressive" platform favoring "democratic pluralism." None of the MR's 93 candidates was successful in the 1994 national legislative balloting, although four MR members were subsequently seated in the House under the proportional arrangement established for opposition parties. Party leaders complained of widespread fraud in the legislative balloting and described Tunisia's slow pace of political liberalization as a national "scandal."

The MR secretary general, Mohamed Harmel, was constitutionally prohibited from contesting the 1999 presidential election due to his age (70). The MR was accorded five seats in the legislature elected in 1999.

MR Chair Mohamed Ali el-Halouani was one of three candidates to oppose President Ben Ali in the 2004 elections. In a rare occurrence, MR supporters demonstrated in Tunis after el-Halouani complained that the party had been blocked from distributing its manifesto. El-Halouani received about 1 percent of the vote and denounced the poll as a "sham."

Leaders: Mohamed Ali el-HALOUANI (Chair and 2004 presidential candidate), Boujamma RMILI, Mohamed HARMEL (Secretary General).

Unionist Democratic Union (*Union Démocratique Unioniste*—UDU). Legalized in November 1988, the UDU was led by Abderrahmane TLILI, a former member of the RCD who had resigned from the ruling party to devote himself to the unification of various Arab nationalist tendencies in Tunisia. Tlili garnered 0.23 percent of the vote in the 1999 presidential balloting, the UDU securing seven of the seats distributed to the opposition following the concurrent legislative poll.

Tlili was sentenced to nine years in prison in 2004 on embezzlement charges relating to his former government tenure. The UDU supported President Ben Ali in the 2004 presidential election and won representation in municipal elections in 2005.

Popular Union Party (*Parti de l'Unité Populaire*—PUP). The PUP is an outgrowth of an "internal faction" that developed within the Popular Unity Movement (MUP, below) over the issue of participation in the 1981 legislative election. Although garnering only 0.81 percent of the vote in 1981, it was officially recognized in 1983 as a legal party, subsequently operating under its current name. The PUP attempted to offer candidates for the 1986 balloting, but most were declared ineligible by the government. The party therefore

withdrew three days before the election, citing the same harassment that had led to the boycott by other opposition groups. It participated in "national pact" discussions with the government in 1988, thus asserting an identity separate from that of its parent. PUP Secretary General Mohamed Belhadj Amor won 0.31 percent of the vote in the 1999 presidential campaign, during which he expressed deep dismay over the failure of the so-called "opposition parties" to mount any effective challenge to the RCD. He subsequently resigned the PUP leadership post. His successor, Mohamed Bouchiha, received 3.8 percent of the vote in the 2004 election.

The party won representation in the 2005 municipal elections.

Leaders: Jalloud AZZOUNA, Mohamed Belhadj AMOR (1999 presidential candidate), Mohamed BOUCHIHA (Secretary General and 2004 presidential candidate).

Progressive Democratic Assembly (*Rassemblement Démocratique Progressiste*—RDP). The RDP had been established as the Progressive Socialist Assembly (*Rassemblement Socialiste Progressiste*—RSP) by a number of Marxist groups in 1983. The pan-Arabist RSP was tolerated by the Bourguiba government until mid-1986. It formed a "Democratic Alliance" with the PCT and planned to field candidates for the 1986 balloting. However, the coalition boycotted the election after the government disqualified some of its candidates and sentenced 14 of its members to six-month jail terms for belonging to an illegal organization. The party was officially recognized in September 1988. The RSP did not secure any of the legislative seats reserved for opposition parties in 1994 or 1999, and it called for a boycott of the municipal elections of May 2000. The RSP changed its name to the RDP in July 2001 in an effort to "broaden its ideological base." The RDP reportedly included many Marxists as well as moderate Islamists and liberals.

RDP Secretary General Ahmed Chebbi was blocked from contesting the 2004 presidential election because of a recent decree by President Ben Ali that candidates could be presented only by parties with legislative representation. The RDP consequently called for a boycott of the presidential balloting and withdrew its candidates from the legislative poll.

Leader: Ahmed Néjib CHEBBI (Secretary General).

Liberal Social Party (*Parti Social Liberal—* PSL). Formed to advocate liberal social and political policies and economic reforms, including the privatization of state-run enterprises, the PSL was officially recognized in September 1988 under the name of the Social Party for Progress (*Parti Social pour le Progrès* —PSP). The current name was adopted at the first party congress, held in Tunis on October 29–30, 1994. The PSL secured 2 of the 34 seats reserved for opposition parties in the 1999 legislative balloting. PSL Secretary General Mounir Beji won less than 1 percent of the vote in the 2004 presidential poll.

At the party congress in April 2005, Beji was reelected president, and the party changed its name to the Liberal Social Democratic Party (PSDL). The party won representation in the May 2005 municipal elections.

Leaders: Hosni HAMMANI, Mounir BEJI (President of the Party and 2004 presidential candidate).

Democratic Forum for Labor and Liberties (*Le Forum Démocratique pour le Travail et les Libertés*—FDTL). Legalized in 2002, the FDTL called for a boycott of the 2004 elections and urged opposition parties to work toward cohesion.

Leader: Mustafa BEN JAFAAR.

Other Groups

Popular Unity Movement (*Mouvement de l'Unité Populaire*—MUP). The MUP was formed in 1973 by Ahmed Ben Salah, a former "super-minister" who directed the economic policies of the Bourguiba cabinet from 1962 to 1969. Ben Salah was sentenced to ten years' imprisonment in 1969 for "high treason," although the action was generally attributed to his having fallen out of favor with Bourguiba. After his escape from prison in 1973, Ben Salah directed the MUP from exile, urging the

government to return to the socialist policies of the 1960s. The movement reorganized itself as a political party in June 1978 but was unable to gain legal recognition. In early 1981 friction developed within the MUP leadership after the government granted amnesty to all members theretofore subject to legal restriction, the sole exception being Ben Salah. Ben Salah subsequently declared his opposition to the group's participation in the November 1 balloting, causing a split between his supporters and an "internal" faction (see PUP, above). After maintaining a high international profile throughout his exile, Ben Salah returned to Tunisia in 1988 in the wake of Bourguiba's ouster. However, the MUP did not sign the "national pact" of late 1988, primarily to protest the government's refusal to restore Ben Salah's civil rights, a requirement for his participation in national elections. The MUP joined two legal parties (the MDS and the PCT, above) in an antigovernment coalition in 1990.

Ben Salah was one of several opposition leaders who issued a joint communiqué in London in November 1995 attacking the Tunisian government as repressive. In 1996 the MUP leader was described by *Africa Confidential* as no longer commanding a significant popular base, and he returned to Tunisia from ten years of voluntary exile in Europe in September 2000.

Leader: Ahmed BEN SALAH (General Secretary).

Renaissance Party (*Hizb al-Nahda/Parti de la Renaissance*—PR). Also known as the Renaissance Movement (*Harakat al-Nahda/Mouvement de la Renaissance*), *Nahda* was formed as the Islamic Tendency Movement (*Mouvement de la Tendance Islamique*—MTI) in early 1981 by a group of Islamic fundamentalists inspired by the 1979 Iranian revolution. Charged with fomenting disturbances, many MTI adherents were jailed during a series of subsequent crackdowns by the Bourguiba government. However, the MTI insisted that it opposed violence or other "revolutionary activity," and the Ben Ali government pardoned most of those incarcerated, including the movement's leader, Rachid Ghanouchi, shortly after assuming power. The new regime also initiated talks that it said were designed to provide moderate MTI forces with a legitimate means of political expression in order to undercut support for the movement's radical elements. As an outgrowth of that process, the MTI adopted its new name in early 1989; however, the government subsequently denied legal status to *Nahda,* ostensibly on the grounds that it remained religion-based. Undaunted, the group quickly established itself as the government's primary opposition, its "independent" candidates collecting about 13 percent of the total popular vote (including as much as 30 percent of the vote in some urban areas) in 1989 legislative balloting.

Nahda boycotted "higher council" negotiations and municipal elections in 1990, Ghanouchi remaining in exile to protest the lack of legal recognition for the formation and the continued "harassment" of its sympathizers. Friction intensified late in the year following the arrest of three groups of what security forces described as armed extremists plotting to overthrow the government. Although the government alleged that some of those arrested had *Nahda* links, the party leadership strongly denied the charge, accusing the regime of conducting a propaganda campaign aimed at discrediting the fundamentalist movement in order to prevent it from assuming its rightful political role.

On October 15, 1991, the government announced that it had uncovered a fundamentalist plot to assassinate President Ben Ali and other government officials in order to "create a constitutional vacuum." However, *Nahda* leaders again denied any connection to violent antigovernment activity, reiterating their commitment to "peaceful methods" of protest and stressing that their vision for the "Islamization" of Tunisia was "compatible" with democracy and a pluralistic society. The disclaimers notwithstanding, the government flatly labeled *Nahda* "a terrorist organization" and intensified the campaign to "silence" it. Thousands of suspected *Nahda* sympathizers were detained, many later claiming that they had been tortured or otherwise abused in prison (a charge supported by Amnesty International). At a widely publicized trial in mid-1992 about 170 *Nahda* adherents were

convicted of sedition. A number were sentenced to life imprisonment, including Ghanouchi and several other leaders who were tried *in absentia*. The government subsequently issued an international arrest warrant for Ghanouchi, who was living in London, but in mid-1993 the United Kingdom granted him political asylum. In 1994 Ghanouchi dismissed the recent Tunisian presidential and legislative elections as "a joke." Despite the "banned and fragmented" status of *Nahda,* Ghanouchi was described in 1996 as still the only possible "serious challenger" to Ben Ali. A number of *Nahda* adherents were released in November 1999 from long prison terms. In March 2001 Ghanouchi, in conjunction with MDS leader Mohamed Mouada, proposed establishment by *Nahda* and the legal opposition parties of a National Democratic Front to challenge the RCD, suggesting to some observers that *Nahda* hoped to return to mainstream political activity. However, *Nahda* remained relatively quiescent during the 2004 election campaign.

Leaders: Rachid GHANOUCHI (President, in exile), Habib ELLOUZE, Sahah KARKAR (in exile), Sheikh Abdelfatah MOURROU (Secretary General).

Commandos of Sacrifice (*Commandos du Sacrifice*—CS). Although the government insisted that the CS was the "military wing" of *Nahda,* the group's leader, Habib Laasoued, described it as independent and, in fact, a rival to *Nahda* for support among fundamentalists. About 100 members of the commandos were convicted in mid-1992 of planning terrorist acts, although the trials were surrounded by allegations of human rights abuses and other governmental misconduct. Laasoued, who was sentenced to life imprisonment, reportedly acknowledged that the commandos had engaged in theoretical discussions of *jihad* (Islamic holy war) but denied that any antigovernment military action had actually been endorsed.

Leader: Habib LAASOUED (imprisoned).

Party of Tunisian Communist Workers (*Parti des Ouvriers Communistes Tunisiens*—POCT). An unrecognized splinter of the former PCT, the POCT is led by Hamma Hammani, who had been the director of the banned newspaper *El Badil* (The Alternative). Hammani was sentenced to eight years in prison in early 1994 on several charges, including membership in an illegal organization, his case being prominently cited in criticism leveled at the government by human rights organizations. Hammani and another POCT member who had been imprisoned with him were pardoned by President Ben Ali in November 1995. A number of POCT members were convicted in July 1999 of belonging to an illegal association, but most were released later in the year. Hammani and several associates were charged again in absentia in 1999 for having been members of an unrecognized group. In February 2002 they were retried and committed to various prison sentences. In September, however, Hammani and some of the others were released following a hunger strike that had attracted increasing international scrutiny to their case. Hammani called for a boycott of the 2004 elections.

Leader: Hamma HAMMANI.

Several human rights groups have been prominent in the increasingly vocal opposition movement in recent years. They include the unrecognized National Council for Tunisian Freedoms (*Conseil National pour les Libertés Tunisiennes*—CNLT), founded in 1998 by, among others, Moncef MARZOUKI, who had unsuccessfully attempted to run for president in 1994. In a case that attracted wide international attention, Marzouki was sentenced in December 2000 to one year in prison for belonging to an illegal organization. Meanwhile, as of early 2001 the status of the officially sanctioned Tunisian Human Rights League (*Ligue Tunisienne des Droits de l'Homme*—LTDH) remained unclear, a Tunisian court having ordered new elections for LTDH leadership posts. The leaders elected in October 2000, including LTDH President Mokhtar TRIFI, had sharply condemned the Ben Ali government after wresting control of the organization from RCD adherents. Trifi was arrested in March 2001.

In mid-1994 it was reported that a militant Islamic group had been organized among Tunisian exiles under the leadership of Mohamed Ali el-HORANI to support armed struggle against the Ben Ali government. The group, which reportedly adopted the name of Algeria's outlawed **Islamic Salvation Front** (*Front Islamique du Salut*—FIS), was described as critical of *Nahda's* official rejection of violence. References have also been made to a **Tunisian Islamic Front** (*Front Islamique Tunisien*—FIT), which reportedly has committed itself to armed struggle against the Ben Ali regime. In addition, some 14 members of a fundamentalist group called *Ansar* were sentenced to jail terms in December 2000 for belonging to an illegal organization, which the government described as having Iranian ties.

Legislature

House of Representatives (*Majlis al-Nuwab/Chambre des Députés*). The lower house consists of 189 members serving five-year terms. Under a new system adopted for the 1994 election, most representatives (148 in 1999 and 152 in 2004) are elected on a "winner-takes-all" basis in which the party whose list gains the most votes in a district secures all the seats for that district. (There are 25 districts comprising 2 to 10 seats each.) The remaining seats (19 in 1994, 34 in 1999, and 37 in 2004) are allocated to parties that failed to win in any districts, in proportion to the parties' national vote totals.

From the establishment of the house in 1959 until 1994, members of the ruling party (RCD) occupied all seats. Although six opposition parties were permitted to offer candidates at the 1989 balloting and a number of independent candidates sponsored by the unsanctioned Renaissance Party also ran, the RCD won all seats with a reported 80 percent of the vote. RCD candidates also won all 9 seats contested in October 1991 by-elections, which were boycotted by the opposition parties. The house was enlarged from 141 members to 163 for the 1994 election and to 182 for the 1999 balloting. The membership was expanded to 189 seats for the most recent election on October 24, 2004, President Ben Ali decreeing that 43 seats be filled by women. The RCD won all 152 seats that were

Cabinet

As of July 1, 2006

Prime Minister	Mohamed Ghannouchi
Secretary General of the Government in Charge of Relations with the House of Representatives and the House of Advisors	Mounir Jaidane

Ministers

Agriculture and Water Resources	Mohamed Habib Haddad
Communication Technologies	Montassar Ouaïli
Culture and Heritage Preservation	Mohamed El Aziz Ben Achour
Development and International Cooperation	Mohamed Nouri Jouini
Director of Presidential Cabinet	Tadh Ouderni
Education and Training	Sadok Korbi
Employment and Professional Integration of Youth	Chadli Laroussi
Equipment, Housing, and Territorial Management	Samira Khayach Belhadj [f]
Finance	Mohamed Rachid Kechiche
Foreign Affairs	Abdelawahab Abdallah
Higher Education	Lazhar Bou Ouni
Industry, Energy, and Small and Medium Enterprises	Afif Chelbi
Interior and Local Development	Rafik Belhaj Kacem
Justice and Human Rights	Béchir Tekkari
Minister of State (Special Advisor to the President)	Abdelaziz Ben Dhia
National Defense	Kamel Morjane
Prime Minister's Office	Zouhair Mdhaffer
Public Health	Ridha Kechrid
Religious Affairs	Boubaker El Akhzouri
Scientific Research, Technology, and Development of Training	Taieb Hadri
Social Affairs, Solidarity, and Tunisians Abroad	Ali Chaouch
State Property and Land Affairs	Ridha Grira
Tourism	Tijani Haddad
Trade and Handicrafts	Mondher Zenaïdi
Transport	Abderrahim Zouari
Women, Family, Children, and Elderly Affairs	Salova Ayachi Labben [f]
Youth, Sports, and Physical Education	Abdallah Kaâbi

[f] = female

---

contested on a district basis. However, under the proportional system for distributing 37 additional seats, five other parties were allocated seats as follows: The Democratic Socialist Movement, 14; the Popular Union Party, 11; the Unionist Democratic Union, 7; the Renewal Movement, 3; and the Liberal Social Party, 2.

President: Fouad MBAZAA.

House of Advisers. (*Majlis al-Mustasharin*). The upper body was seated after balloting on July 3, 2005, following a national referendum on May 26, 2002, that provided for several constitutional changes, the creation of the upper House among them. The upper chamber comprises 126 members, 85 of whom are directly elected and 41 appointed by the president, all serving six-year terms.

The members include 14 from each of the 3 main professional unions and federations (the employers' federation, the trade unions, and the farmers' union), and 43 representatives from various regions of the country. Half of the members are renewed every three years.

President: Abdallah KALLEL.

Communications

The media during most of the Bourguiba era were subject to pervasive party influence and increasingly repressive government interference. The Ben Ali government initially relaxed some of the restrictions, although the fundamentalist press remained heavily censored and mainstream publications continued to practice what was widely viewed as self-censorship, bordering on what one foreign correspondent described as "regime worship." In addition, several foreign journalists were subsequently expelled and some international publications were prevented from entering the country for printing articles critical of the government. (The French dailies *Le Monde* and *Libération* were banned from March 1994 until March 1995 because of their coverage of events prior to the national elections.) In recent years international journalists' groups have called for Western nations to apply pressure upon the Tunisian government to reduce what has been widely perceived as pervasive restraints on freedom of the press, including the arrests of journalists.

Press

The following, unless otherwise noted, are published daily in Tunis: *As-Sabah* (The Morning, 50,000), government-influenced, in Arabic; *al-Amal* (Action, 50,000), RCD organ, in Arabic; *L'Action* (50,000), RCD organ, in French; *Le Temps* (42,000), weekly in French; *La Presse de Tunisie* (40,000), government organ, in French; *Le Quotidien* (The Daily, 30,000), independent, in French; *Le Renouveau* (23,000), RCD organ, in French; *La Presse-Soir,* evening; *as-Sahafa,* in Arabic; *al-Huriyya,* in Arabic; *as-Shourouq* (Sunrise), independent, in Arabic.

News Agencies

The domestic facility is *Tunis Afrique Presse*—TAP (*Wakalah Tunis Afriqiyah al-Anba*); in addition, a number of foreign bureaus maintain offices in Tunis.

Broadcasting and Computing

The *Etablissement de la Radio-diffusion-Télévision Tunisienne* (ERTT) operates a radio network broadcasting in Arabic, French, and Italian. It also operates three television channels, one of which links the country with European transmissions. The first privately owned radio station was launched in 2003, and the first private television station began broadcasting in early 2005. (Although President Ben Ali portrayed these developments as expansion of freedom of the press, thus far programming on the new stations has lacked political commentary.) There were approximately 3.9 million television receivers and 400,000 personal computers serving 630,000 Internet users in 2003.

Intergovernmental Representation

Ambassador to the U.S.
Mohamed Nejib HACHANA

U.S. Ambassador to Tunisia
William J. HUDSON

Permanent Representative to the UN
Ali HACHANI

IGO Memberships (Non-UN)
AfDB, AFESD, AMF, AMU, AU, BADEA, IDB, Interpol, IOM, LAS, NAM, OIC, OIF, WCO, WTO

UGANDA

REPUBLIC OF UGANDA

The Country

Landlocked Uganda, located in east-central Africa, is bounded on the east by Kenya, on the south by Tanzania and Rwanda, on the west by the Democratic Republic of the Congo (DRC), and on the north by Sudan. The country is known for its lakes (among them Lake Victoria, the source of the White Nile) and its mountains, the most celebrated of which are the Mountains of the Moon (the Ruwenzori), lying on the border with the DRC. The population embraces a number of African tribal groups, including the Baganda, Banyankore, Basoga, and Iteso. For many decades a substantial Asian (primarily Indian) minority engaged in shopkeeping, industry, and the professions. In 1972, however, the Amin government decreed the expulsion of all noncitizen Asians as part of a plan to put Uganda's economy in the hands of nationals, and at present only a scattering of Asians still reside in the country. Approximately 60 percent of the population is Christian and another 15 percent is Muslim, with the remainder adhering to traditional African beliefs. Women are primarily responsible for subsistence agriculture, with most male rural labor being directed toward cash crops; women also dominate trade in rural areas, although not in the cities. The government is considered progressive regarding women's rights, with a number of seats in the current parliament being reserved for women. One-third of the seats in local councils must, by law, also go to women.

Agriculture, forestry, and fishing contribute about one-third of Uganda's gross domestic product (GDP); industry, which is growing in importance, accounts for about 21 percent of GDP. Services account for the remainder. Coffee is the principal crop (Uganda is one of Africa's leading producers), followed by cotton, tea, peanuts, and tobacco.

Beginning in the late 1960s Uganda experienced two decades of violence arising from tribal warfare, strongman governments, rebel activity, and coups that left more than 800,000 dead, many of them reportedly victims of military atrocities. The resultant drop in agricultural and industrial output combined with heavy capital flight to produce severe economic distress. The regime installed in 1986 attempted to kindle recovery through enhanced exploitation of resources and renegotiation of the external debt in light of improved internal security. In the process, Uganda became a "major hope" of the International Monetary Fund (IMF)/World Bank approach to economic reform in sub-Saharan

Political Status: Independent member of the Commonwealth since October 9, 1962; republican constitution adopted on September 8, 1967; personal military rule (instituted on January 25, 1971) overthrown with establishment of provisional government on April 11, 1979; military regime installed on January 29, 1986; present constitution adopted on September 22, 1995, with effect from October 8.

Area: 93,104 sq. mi. (241,139 sq. km.).

Population: 24,748,977 (2002C); 27,282,000 (2005E).

Major Urban Center (2005E): KAMPALA (metropolitan area, 1,337,000).

Official Language: English (Swahili and Luganda are widely used).

Monetary Unit: New Shilling (principal rate July 1, 2006: 1,865 new shillings = $1US).

President: Lt. Gen. Yoweri Kaguta MUSEVENI; sworn in on January 29, 1986, following the overthrow of Lt. Gen. Tito OKELLO Lutwa on January 27; popularly elected on May 9, 1996, and inaugurated for a five-year term on May 12; reelected for another five-year term on March 12, 2001; reelected in multiparty balloting on February 23, 2006, and inaugurated for another five-year term on May 12.

Vice President: Gilbert Balibaseka BUKENYA, appointed by the president on June 6, 2003, succeeding Dr. Speciosa Wandira KAZIBWE, who resigned; reappointed by the president on May 23, 2006.

Prime Minister: Apolo NSIBAMBI; appointed by the president on April 6, 1999, succeeding Kintu MUSOKE; reappointed on July 13, 2001; reappointed by the president following elections on February 23, 2006, and sworn in with the new cabinet on June 2, 2006.

Africa. The success of economic reform was minimal through 1993; annual per capita gross national product (GNP) remained less than $200, while schools and health facilities continued to be severely underfinanced.

In mid-1995 planning for privatization reforms was under way, calling for the abolition of government subsidies to state-owned companies, except for public utilities, where the support was to be phased out over a four-year period.

In May 2000 the IMF and World Bank announced that Uganda had qualified for $2 billion in debt service relief over the next 20 years based on the government's adherence to its comprehensive reform program and continued economic progress. By mid-2005 real economic growth was offset by one of the highest population growth rates in the world and widespread poverty. Subsequently, the IMF in 2006 cited poverty reduction as the foremost economic issue for Uganda and urged reforms to curb corruption. Unhappy with the country's slow progress toward democratization and alleged corruption in government spending, the UK, traditionally Uganda's biggest donor, and three other donor countries canceled millions of dollars in aid to Kampala. On a more positive note, the IMF projected GDP growth of 6.6 percent for 2006.

Government and Politics

Political Background

Uganda became a British protectorate in 1894–1896 and began its progress toward statehood after World War II, achieving internal self-government on March 1, 1962, and full independence within the Commonwealth on October 9, 1962. A problem involving Buganda and three other traditional kingdoms was temporarily resolved by granting the kingdoms semiautonomous rule within a federal system. The arrangement enabled Buganda's representatives to participate in the national government, and the king (*kabaka*) of Buganda, Sir Edward Frederick MUTESA II, was elected president of Uganda on October 9, 1963. The issue of national unity versus Bugandan particularism led Prime Minister Apollo Milton OBOTE, leader of the Uganda People's Congress (UPC) and an advocate of centralism, to depose the president and vice president in February 1966. A constitution eliminating Buganda's autonomous status was ratified in

April 1966 by the National Assembly, which consisted mainly of UPC members. Failing in an effort to mobilize effective resistance to the new government, the *kabaka* fled the country in May, and a new republican constitution, adopted in September 1967, eliminated the special status of Buganda and the other kingdoms. Earlier, on April 15, 1966, Obote had been designated president by the National Assembly for a five-year term. In December 1969 he banned all opposition parties and established a one-party state with a socialist program known as the Common Man's Charter.

On January 25, 1971, Maj. Gen. Idi AMIN Dada, commander in chief of the army and air force, mounted a successful coup that deposed Obote while the president was abroad at a Commonwealth meeting. In addition to continuing the ban on opposition political activity, Amin suspended parts of the constitution, dissolved the National Assembly, and secured his own installation as president of the Republic.

Following an invasion by Tanzanian troops and exile forces organized as the Uganda National Liberation Army (UNLA), the Amin regime, which had drawn worldwide condemnation for atrocities against perceived opponents, was effectively overthrown with the fall of Kampala April 10–11, 1979, with Amin fleeing to Libya. Concurrently, the National Consultative Council (NCC) of the Uganda National Liberation Front (UNLF) designated Professor Yusuf K. LULE, former vice chancellor of Makerere University, as president of the republic and head of a provisional government. On June 20 the NCC announced that Godfrey Lukongwa BINAISA, a former attorney general under President Obote, had been named to succeed Lule in both capacities.

After a series of disagreements with both the NCC and the UNLF's Military Commission, Binaisa was relieved of his authority on May 12, 1980. On May 18 the chair of the Military Commission, Paulo MUWANGA, announced that a three-member Presidential Commission had been established to exercise executive power through a cabinet of ministers on advice of its military counterpart, pending a national election later in the year.

Former president Obote returned from Tanzania on May 27, 1980, and in mid-June agreement was reached between party and UNLF representatives on four groups that would be permitted to participate in the presidential/legislative campaign. Following balloting December 10–11, the UPC declared that it had secured a majority in the National Assembly, thus assuring Obote's reinvestiture as chief executive. Although the runner-up Democratic Party (DP) denounced the results as fraudulent, most victorious DP candidates took their legislative seats. The Uganda Patriotic Movement (UPM), led by former president Lule and his former defense minister, Yoweri MUSEVENI, refused to accept the one seat it had won. After shedding the party apparatus, Lule and Museveni formed a National Resistance Movement (NRM) and initiated a guerrilla campaign against Obote through the affiliated National Resistance Army (NRA).

During the next five years, while the UNLA achieved some success in repulsing the rebels, the NRA continued to hold the agriculturally important "Luwero triangle" north of Kampala, as well as its traditional strongholds in the Banyankore-dominated southwest. During the same period, many army actions against civilians were reported, including the harassment, wounding, or killing of DP members; by mid-1985, more than 200,000 were estimated to have died, either from army "excesses" or official counterinsurgency efforts.

On July 27, 1985, in a self-proclaimed attempt to "stop the killing," Brig. Basilio Olara OKELLO led a senior officers' coup against Obote, who had lost much international support and was again forced into exile. Two days later the constitution was suspended, and Obote's army chief of staff, Lt. Gen. Tito OKELLO Lutwa, was sworn in as chair of a ruling Military Council. On August 6 General Okello called for all guerrilla groups, including former Amin soldiers, to join his army, while naming Paulo Muwanga, who had served as Obote's vice president, as prime minister and DP leader Paul SSEMOGERERE as minister of the interior. Unlike most other resistance leaders, Museveni, the dominant NRM figure following Lule's death in January 1985, did not accede to Okello's call for "unity," citing continued abuses by army personnel who routinely failed to defer to Okello. In contrast, the NRA had a reputation for being well disciplined, relatively free of tribal rivalries, and far less brutal toward civilians.

By September 1985, when the first of a series of Kenyan- and Tanzanian-mediated peace talks began in Dar es Salaam, NRA forces had taken control of a number of strategic towns and supply routes, while another Obote associate, Abraham WALIGO, replaced Muwanga as prime minister. In November Museveni announced that "in order to provide services pending an agreement with the regime in Kampala," an "interim administration" was being established in rebel-held areas. A peace pact signed in Nairobi on December 17 gave Museveni the vice-chairmanship of the Military Council while providing for the dissolution of all existing armed units and the recruitment, under external supervision, of a new, fully representative force. However, the accord did not take effect: After failing to attend "celebrations" scheduled for January 4, 1986, Museveni, citing continuing human-rights abuses, launched a drive on Kampala, which culminated in the overthrow of the six-month-old Okello regime on January 27. Two days later, while NRA forces consolidated their control, Museveni was sworn in as president, thereafter appointing a cabinet that included as prime minister Dr. Samson KISEKKA, formerly the NRM's external spokesman. In an attempt to prevent further civil war, Museveni also named representatives of other major political groups to his government. However, some UNLA units that had not disbanded fled to the north and the east, where they and other rebel groups continued to resist the NRA.

In mid-1986 Museveni absolved his immediate predecessor, General Okello, of atrocities committed by troops under his command. No such tender was made to former presidents Amin and Obote, with Museveni calling for their repatriation from exile in Saudi Arabia and Zambia, respectively, to face charges by a special commission of inquiry established to review the "slaughter" of Bantu southerners by their Nilotic followers. (Obote died in Zambia in October 2005.)

In February 1988 Museveni named three deputy prime ministers, including DP leader Ssemogerere, to assist the ailing Kisekka. In addition, the cabinet was reshuffled to include more representatives from the north and east, where rebel activity continued to impede national reconciliation. An even more drastic reshuffle was ordered in April 1989 coincident with conversion of the theretofore appointive National Resistance Council (see under Constitution and government, below) into a largely elective body. Six months later the council voted to extend the government's interim mandate (originally limited by President Museveni to four years) to January 1995. The action was justified by the minister of justice on the grounds that the country lacked the "essential political machinery and the logistics for the evolution of a democratic and a permanent stable government."

On January 22, 1991, Museveni appointed Kisekka to the new, largely ceremonial position of vice president, with George Cosmas ADYEBO, a 43-year-old economist, named prime minister. The government subsequently conducted a "final sweep" against rebel forces in the north and east, and in July Kampala reported that its troops had decimated the rebel forces, killing 1,500 insurgents between March and July (many, Amnesty International charged, after perfunctory military trials) and absorbing many others into the NRA. In August the government described the remaining rebels, predominantly from Joseph KONY's Uganda Democratic Christian Army, as "thugs" who had been reduced to raiding villages for food and whose earlier atrocities prevented their reintegration.

In January 1993 Museveni, who continued to reject domestic and international calls for the immediate introduction of multipartyism on the grounds that it would exacerbate religious and ethnic cleavages, announced plans for nonparty elections by the end of 1994. In February the NRC passed a constituent assembly bill that called for the delay of multiparty politics until at least the year 2000 (see Constitution and government, below).

Earlier, in what was described by critics as political repayment to the Baganda people for supporting the NRA struggle in the early 1980s, Museveni had begun negotiating with Baganda to restore its monarch. Consequently, on July 31, 1993, the son of Mutesa II, Ronald Muwenda MUTEBI, was crowned *kabaka,* an event described as a purely "ceremonial" action. Collaterally, pro forma recognition was granted to the coronation of Patrick David Matthew Olimi KABOYO II as monarch of the smaller Toro kingdom. (Kaboyo died on September 13, 1995, and was succeeded by his three-year-old son, Oyo Nyimba Kabamba IGURU IV.) On June 11, 1994, the oldest of Uganda's historic kingdoms was restored, with the crowning of Solon Iguri GAFABUSA I as king of the Bunyoro tribe. (The crowning of John BARIGYE as monarch of Uganda's Ankore kingdom was indefinitely delayed because of disputes within the clan leadership.) Meanwhile, on February 11, 1996, Henry Wako MULOKI, the Basoga's traditional leader, was reinstalled as *kyabazinga* (king) at a ceremony attended by Museveni.

On March 28, 1994, nonparty balloting was held to fill the 214-seat Constituent Assembly. As anticipated, NRM-affiliated candidates captured the majority of the seats (114), although the president's actual assembly supporters were reported as numbering only 93.

In December 1994 the government announced that nonparty general elections would be held by late 1995; however, they were deferred until April–May 1996. Meanwhile, the Constituent Assembly on September 22 approved a new basic law that continued the ban on political campaigning and provided that the NRC would remain in existence for another five years. Upon promulgation of the document on October 8, the constituent body was dissolved.

At Uganda's first presidential balloting on May 9, 1996, President Museveni captured 74.2 percent of the vote, easily outpolling his two competitors, the DP's Ssemogerere (23.7 percent) and an Islamic candidate, Mohamed MAYANJA Kibirige (2.1 percent). Although Museveni controlled the media and local councils administering the polling, international observers described the polling as "fair."

Thereafter, at "no-party" legislative polling staged between June 6–27, 1996, NRM candidates

secured or were appointed to 271 of the 276 available posts. On July 6 Museveni named an enlarged cabinet that included only NRM members.

In early 1998 Museveni named his half-brother, Gen. Salim SALEH, as defense minister, a post held theretofore by the president himself. The appointment of Saleh, who had been credited with coordinating the government's highly successful offensives against its various rebel opponents in mid-1997, underscored Museveni's apparent dedication to a total rout of the Lord's Resistance Army (LRA—see Political Parties and Groups, below), whose call for a cease-fire in July had been rejected. (Saleh resigned in December after allegations of corrupt financial dealings were made against him.)

In May 1998 Museveni reshuffled the government and, following the retirement of Prime Minister Musoke, on April 6, 1999, the president named Apolo NSIBAMBI to head a substantially altered cabinet. In a referendum on June 29, 2000, 90 percent of the voters endorsed continuance of the "no-party" system.

On March 12, 2001, President Museveni was reelected to another five-year term, securing 69 percent of the vote compared to 28 percent for his nearest rival, Kizza BESIGYE, Museveni's former doctor and former military ally. Subsequently, the NRM retained its stronghold on the parliament in elections held on June 26, 2001. Although a dozen sitting cabinet members lost their legislative seats, most of them were beaten by other Museveni supporters. Following the elections, Museveni reappointed Prime Minister Nsibambi to head a significantly altered cabinet, which was sworn in on July 24. A constitutional referendum on July 28, 2005 (see Constitution and government, below), allowed for the registration of political parties, among other things, in advance of presidential and parliamentary elections on February 23, 2006. In the multiparty presidential election, Museveni defeated four challengers by garnering 59.26 percent of the vote. His nearest rival, Kizza Besigye, running as the Forum for Democratic Change (FDC) candidate, received 37.39 percent of the vote. The Democratic Party's John SSEBAANA Kizito won 1.58 percent, and an independent candidate and Miria OBOTE, widow of the former president and candidate of the Uganda People's Congress (UPC), each won less than 1 percent.

In parliamentary elections the same day, the NRM retained power, winning 187 seats, while five opposition parties also won representation (see Legislature, below). A reshuffled and enlarged cabinet, again led by Prime Minister Apolo Nsibambi, was sworn in on June 2, 2006.

Constitution and Government

The 1962 constitution was suspended by Prime Minister Obote in February 1966. A successor instrument adopted in April 1966 terminated the federal system but was itself replaced in September 1967 by a republican constitution that established a president as head of state, chief executive, and commander in chief of the armed forces. While he did not formally revoke the 1967 constitution when he came to power, President Amin in February 1971 assumed judicial as well as executive and legislative powers. Subsequently, though martial law was never declared, military tribunals tried both civil and criminal cases and authorized numerous public executions. With but minor modification, the 1967 constitution was reinstated by the UNLF as the basis of postmilitary government in 1980; it was suspended by the Military Council in mid-1985 and remained inoperative thereafter.

On February 1, 1986, while in the process of organizing an interim government dominated by members of his National Resistance Movement (NRM), President Museveni announced the formation of a National Resistance Council (NRC) to serve as an appointive surrogate for the former National Assembly. The NRC was converted into a largely elective body of 278 members in February 1989.

In early 1993 a 15-member commission, appointed by President Museveni in February 1989, released a report proposing the delay of multipartyism for seven years, during which time a largely elected Constituent Assembly would draft a new constitution. (Representatives of special interest groups, including the NRA, NRC, women, youths, and unions, were subsequently added to the 214-member parliament elected in March 1994.) However, the charter that emerged in September 1995 was promulgated without submission to a promised referendum. More importantly, it continued the ban on partisan activity (save behind closed party doors). In the wake of intense criticism from U.S. and British authorities, regime opponents sought to have the ban rescinded but were told that such action could be initiated only by the legislature elected under the constitution as adopted. The "no-party" system was subsequently endorsed by national referendum in June 2000.

Local government has assumed a variety of forms since 1971, the Amin and Lule governments both having reorganized the provincial and district systems. Currently, under initiatives adopted by the Museveni administration, local affairs are handled by several tiers of elected "resistance councils" ranging from village to regional levels.

President Museveni established a Constitutional Review Commission in 2001 to examine possible adaptations to the constitution regarding political parties, federalism, the size of parliament, and voter and candidate eligibility. Opponents criticized the commission as having a pro-NRM bias, having little genuine authority, and failing to reflect the broad spectrum of Ugandan public opinion.

In January 2004 the government initiated negotiations with opposition parties on the transition to multiparty politics and the future system of government. Six months later a court ruling invalidated (on a technicality) the 2000 referendum. Subsequently, as pressure for a multiparty system continued, the parliament voted in May 2005 in favor of a national referendum on a multiparty political system, abolishing the two-term limit on the presidency, and granting the president the authority to dissolve parliament in case of a constitutional crisis. In balloting of July 28, 2005, the amendments were approved by 92.44 percent of voters.

Foreign Relations

From independence, Uganda based its foreign policy on anticolonialism, retaining moderate

Western support from its consistently nonaligned posture. However, reacting to criticism by the Amin regime of U.S. policies in Vietnam, Cambodia, and the Middle East, Washington terminated its economic assistance program in mid-1973 and subsequently closed its embassy because of public threats against officials and other Americans residing in the country. Three years later, in an event of major international import, Israeli commandos raided Entebbe airport during the night of July 3–4, 1976, to secure the release of passengers of an Air France airliner that had been hijacked over Greece by Palestinian Arab guerrillas and flown to Uganda via Libya. Denying allegations that he had cooperated with the hijackers, Amin protested Israel's action and accused Kenya of aiding in its implementation.

Tensions with both Kenya and Tanzania resulted not only in the collapse of the tripartite East African Community (EAC) in June 1977 but ultimately in the Tanzanian military intervention of early 1979 (see Political background, above). The latter action came in the wake of an ill-conceived incursion into northern Tanzania in October 1978 by Ugandan troops, with effective Tanzanian withdrawal from Uganda not occurring until mid-1981 due to retraining requirements of the post-Amin Ugandan army. The two neighbors were critically involved in discussions between the short-lived Okello regime and the NRA, Kenyan president Moi being credited with brokering the December peace agreement between Okello and Museveni. Following Museveni's takeover in January 1986, both governments were quick to recognize the new regime, as was the United States. Nevertheless, relations with Kenya were subsequently strained by a series of border incidents, mutual accusations over the harboring of political dissidents, and Nairobi's displeasure at Ugandan links with Libya, particularly as manifested in an April 1989 trade accord. During a summit of the Ugandan, Kenyan, and Tanzanian presidents in Nairobi on November 22, 1991, the three declared an interest in reactivating cooperation efforts and appointed a three-member commission to draft an agreement.

Kampala concluded a security accord with Sudan in mid-1987 but subsequently charged that Khartoum was still aiding anti-Museveni rebel forces. Border tension intensified following the June 1989 coup in Sudan, precipitating the signing of another mutual nonaggression pact in April 1990, which provided for a Sudanese monitoring team on the Ugandan side of their border after Khartoum had accused Kampala of aiding the southern Sudanese rebels. Meanwhile, the Museveni administration accused former president Obote of training soldiers in Zambia, intimating that Lusaka was turning a blind eye to the activity.

Unrest in the Sudan and Zaire/Democratic Republic of the Congo has dominated Uganda's regional relations since the early 1990s. In October 1992 Kampala warned its northern neighbor that it would mount an "appropriate response" against Sudanese troops crossing the border in pursuit of rebels, and in January 1993 it expressed its concern that a Sudanese plot to launch an Islamic fundamentalist movement in Uganda was under way. Meanwhile, the approximately 20,000 Sudanese refugees within Uganda's borders were joined by thousands of Zairians fleeing unrest in their country.

In October 1994 Uganda canceled the 1990 agreement with its northern neighbor and ordered Sudan to withdraw its monitoring group, accusing it of activity incompatible with its mandate. In April 1995 Kampala severed relations with Khartoum, alleging improper activity by Sudanese diplomatic personnel and the sponsorship of a cross-border rebel attack on April 20. A subsequent agreement to adhere to "the principle of good neighborliness" and to work toward "the gradual and eventual restoration of full diplomatic relations" failed to bring an end to the border hostilities, with at least a limited number of Ugandan units operating in support of Sudanese rebels and the NRA conducting raids on Ugandan rebel bases inside Sudan.

Relations were restored with Kenya in January 1996 following a border summit between the two countries' leaders. The discussions also yielded mutual pledges to revive the dormant

EAC. However, the continuing fragile nature of Ugandan-Kenyan ties was subsequently underlined by Nairobi's charge that the Museveni regime was supporting Kenyan rebels.

Meanwhile, rebel-related activities along their shared border continued to buffet Ugandan-Sudanese relations in 1996, with President Museveni reportedly stating at midyear that the situation "could not get much worse unless the two countries went to war." Nevertheless, on September 9 diplomatic representatives from the two countries signed an agreement in Khartoum that reestablished ties. Highlights of the Iranian-brokered accord included provisions for the cessation of "hostile propaganda" and the removal of rebel groups from within approximately 60 miles of the border. In December 1999 President Museveni signed an agreement with Sudanese authorities calling for mutual elimination of support for rebel movements, but in mid-2000 Museveni complained that Sudan was not living up to its end of the bargain. Relations between Sudan and Uganda appeared to improve in 2001, as Sudan reportedly permitted Ugandan forces to conduct military action in Sudan against rebels in the Lord's Resistance Army (LRA). However, Uganda continued to accuse Sudan of helping the LRA, and rebel attacks—some targeting aid workers—continued.

Regional observers described Uganda as playing a crucial role in Laurent Kabila's ouster of the Mobutu government in Zaire (subsequently the Democratic Republic of the Congo—DRC) in 1997. Kampala denied actively supporting Kabila, although admitting that its troops had crossed the border in pursuit of Ugandan rebels. Clashes occurred in August 1999 and the spring of 2000 between previously allied Ugandan and Rwandan troops in Kisangani in north-central DRC. A UN-sponsored disengagement agreement in June 2000 brought relative peace to the area, although tensions between Ugandan and Rwandan military forces remained high. Negotiations between senior levels of the two governments under British auspices in November 2001 failed to resolve the underlying strains between the two countries.

On a positive note, in July 2003 a tripartite agreement was signed among Uganda, Rwanda, and the office of the UN High Commissioner on Refugees, providing for the voluntary repatriation of some 26,000 Rwandans in refugee camps in western Uganda. In February 2004 the two countries signed a bilateral agreement to strengthen cooperation in several fields. Yet Uganda still accuses Rwanda of aiding the rebel People's Redemption Army (PRA), said to operate in eastern Congo and West Nile. Uganda claims the PRA is the armed wing of the new opposition group Forum for Democratic Change (FDC) and its exiled leader, retired colonel Kizza Besigye. The FDC claimed to know nothing of the PRA and accused the government of inventing the connection to discredit the FDC. Both Uganda and Rwanda are accused of meddling in the Ituri Province of the DRC, arming rebels there in exchange for minerals. Museveni and Rwandan President Paul Kagame tried to defuse the situation. In May 2005, three Ugandan soldiers were tried for spying against Rwanda, and months later, as tensions eased, Uganda and Rwanda signed an extradition treaty to crack down on criminals crossing the borders. Meanwhile, Uganda denied UN claims that it was trading weapons for minerals with the DRC.

Current Issues

Uganda, for many years, was the African darling in the eyes of Western nations, which donated millions to back President Museveni's efforts toward democratization and economic reform. Bolstered by an IMF program, the economy recorded average growth of 6 percent in the late 1990s, and inflation plummeted from 240 percent in the late 1980s to 3 percent in the 1990s. However, corruption continued to be of concern, as well as rampant poverty among Uganda's rapidly growing population.

The 20-year war with rebels in the north continued to drain the economy well into the 2000s. According to the U.S. aid agency World Vision, the conflict cost Uganda more than $1.6 billion in lost economic development and left 1.5 million people displaced in refugee camps. The LRA's recruitment methods reportedly included abduction of children and cutting off the lips and noses of those who refused to cooperate. Peace talks collapsed in 2004, and hostilities continued, although Ugandan forces captured or killed several rebel leaders. In 2005 the International Criminal Court (ICC) took the unprecedented step of issuing arrest warrants for five LRA leaders, Joseph Kony among them, for alleged war crimes.

Key domestic issues were addressed in July 2005 with the launch of a multiparty system and extension of the president's time in office beyond the two-term limit as stated in the amended constitution. The national referendum on constitutional amendments did away with the "no-party" system in effect since Museveni took over in 1986, leaving the president's NRM to dominate government. Six opposition groups boycotted the referendum, claiming it was too costly and unnecessary as the groups' fundamental right to political association should not be subject to a vote. Observers said the national referendum was meant to placate donor nations that had been pressing for political reforms. The referendum also strengthened the NRM, which advocated the multiparty system prior to balloting (ostensibly to rid the party of dissenters), and allowed Museveni to take credit for progress toward democratization. The president's power was further increased by his securing a third elected term in multiparty balloting. Museveni's key challenger, Kizza Besigye, was arrested on rape and treason charges in Kampala shortly after he returned to Uganda in 2005 and declared he would be the FDC presidential candidate. His arrest sparked rioting in the capital city; ultimately, he was released on bail and cleared of the rape charge. While Besigye finished a distant second to Museveni, his FDC party secured 39 seats in parliamentary elections. The NRM, however, retained its dominance in the legislature. Given a new mandate, Museveni vowed his government would begin resettling villagers displaced by LRA rebels.

President Museveni attempted to conduct peace talks with Kony in July 2006, ultimately offering the rebel leader amnesty if Kony would agree to give up fighting. Following negotiations in August and a unilateral cease-fire called by Kony, the LRA and Museveni signed a peace treaty to be finalized on September 12. Under provisions of the agreement, the rebels were to leave Uganda and their bases in Sudan and the Democratic Republic of the Congo for areas designated and protected by the government of southern Sudan. Meanwhile, the Ugandan government acceded to the ICC order that it compensate families of those killed by LRA rebels.

Political Parties and Groups

In 1986 President Museveni ordered the suspension of political party activity pending the adoption of a new constitution, although several parties were allowed to maintain offices and small staffs. The 1989 elections were conducted on a "nonparty" basis, even though members of at least four parties (the Conservative Party [CP], the DP, UPC, and UPM) ran for office with their affiliations obvious to voters. Several others, principally political wings of military groups that had been absorbed by the NRA, had by then been effectively dissolved.

In March 1990 the government extended the formal party ban until 1995, President Museveni continuing to question the advisability of restoring a full-fledged multiparty system. Museveni's official explanation for banning political party activity was that it would cause ethnic divisions within the country. NRM officials claimed the country operated under a no-party system, although the opposition charged that the NRM operated as a party even though it claimed not to be one. Originally the ban on all party activity was to last until 2000, when the question of a multiparty system would be addressed in a referendum. The announced result of that referendum was that voters had said yes to a continued "no-party" system with the NRM in control, although the legality of the election was questioned by the opposition. Ultimately, a court invalidated the referendum on a technicality, but the issue of multiparty activity persisted and was addressed in a referendum on June 28, 2005, and a number of political groups emerged in Uganda to address the reforms and to contest the 2006 elections.

Originally the referendum questions of a multiparty versus a no-party system and the extension of presidential term limits were to appear on the same ballot. A "yes" vote for multiparty activity would have also meant a "yes" for term-limit extensions. In a remarkable show of independence in June 2005, Parliament voted to allow citizens to vote on each issue separately. Both amendments were approved by voters, though opposition groups styled the G6 (the FDC, UPC, DP, CP, the Justice Forum [JEEMA], and the Free Movement) boycotted the referendum, and turnout was low (officially 47 percent, though reports from exit polls put turnout at about 20 percent). Multiparty presidential and parliamentary elections were held for the first time in 20 years in February 2006.

Dominant Government Party

National Resistance Movement (NRM). The NRM was formed following the controversial 1980 election by former president Yusuf K. Lule and Yoweri Museveni, the former directing the political wing from exile in London and the latter leading internal guerrilla activity through the National Resistance Army (NRA). Upon his assumption of the presidency in January 1986, Museveni declared that the NRM was a "clear-headed movement" dedicated to the restoration of democracy in Uganda. Despite the ineffectiveness of subsequent membership drives, Museveni on several occasions suggested that the NRM could become the centerpiece of a one-party or limited-party state in which wide-ranging political expression would be permitted but ethnic and religious sectarianism avoided.

In a dramatic turnaround, however, Museveni sponsored the motion in parliament in 2005 for a national referendum on a multiparty system versus a "no-party" system. Museveni championed multiparty political activity, observers said, to appease western donors by assuring them of his intention to move toward a more democratic society. In addi-

tion, the multiparty ballot question was paired with a provision that would eliminate the two-term limit on the presidency, thus virtually assuring Museveni of a third five-year term. In the 2006 parliamentary elections, the NRM won 187 seats.

Leaders: Lt. Gen. Yoweri MUSEVENI (President of the Republic and Chair of the NRM), Moses KIGONGO (Vice Chair), Crispus KIYUNGA (National Political Commissar), Ofwono OPONDO (Spokesperson).

Other Legislative Parties

Uganda People's Congress (UPC). The largely Protestant UPC was formed in 1960 with a stated commitment to "African socialism." It served as the ruling party under former president Apollo Milton Obote from independence until 1971 and again from late 1980 to 1985. Despite the inclusion of several UPC adherents in the initial Museveni administration, friction persisted between the government and Obote loyalists, particularly hardliners who launched splinters such as the UPF in response to the pro-Museveni posture of their former colleagues.

In February 1991 the **October 9 Movement,** an Obote-led UPC faction named after the date of Ugandan independence, was reportedly operating from a Nairobi-subsidized "training camp" along the Ugandan border in Kenya. Obote's chief of staff was identified as Lt. Col. John OGORE; also listed as movement leaders were Peter OTAI, former commander of the **Uganda People's Army** (UPA), and Peter OWILI, known as "the butcher of Nile Mansions" for the brutal interrogation methods he employed during Obote's presidency.

Despite living in exile in Zambia, Obote continued to control the UPC, and in June 1996 he ordered Assistant Secretary General Cecilia OGWAL not to participate in parliamentary elections. However, Ogwal, who had been credited with maintaining party unity after Obote's departure, defied his edict and captured a seat. Consequently, Obote dismissed her and named James RWANYARARE party spokesman and chair of the UPC's Presidential Policy Commission (i.e., de facto party leader).

For her part, Ogwal rejected Obote's authority to intervene and announced the formation of her own "task force," an act one observer described as an intraparty "coup" attempt. Her underfinanced splinter was subsequently described as unlikely to challenge Rwanyarare, although she remained a controversial figure in the party. In 2005 Obote dismissed Rwanyarare and dissolved the Presidential Policy Commission, replacing it with a Constitutional Steering Committee. Ultimately, a court ordered the party to sort out its differences following the death of Obote in October 2005. The former president's widow, Miria Kalule Obote, was elected party leader in November 2005. She placed last in 2006 presidential balloting with less than 1 percent of the vote. (She was the first woman presidential candidate in Uganda and the first woman to lead a major political party.) In concurrent parliamentary elections, the UPC won eight seats.

Leaders: Miria Kalule OBOTE (Party Leader and 2006 presidential candidate), Peter WALU-BIRI (Secretary General), Akhbar Adoko NEKYON, Livingstone Okello OKELLO.

Democratic Party (DP). An advocate of centralization and a mixed economy that draws on a solid Roman Catholic base, the DP enjoys widespread support in southern Uganda. Officially, it ran second to the UPC in the post-Amin balloting of December 1980, winning 51 of 126 legislative seats, although the results were strongly challenged. The DP subsequently was weakened by defections to the UPC and sporadic harassment, killing, or detention of its leadership by the Obote government. While DP president Paul Ssemogerere joined the Okello cabinet, most DP leaders supported Museveni's NRA in continued guerrilla fighting. Several members of the DP executive committee were included in Museveni's first cabinet, and, despite reports of some deterioration in DP–NRM relations, Ssemogerere was named second deputy prime minister and foreign minister in February 1988; he retained both posts in the cabinet reorganization of July 1991.

In mid-1992 Ssemogerere was the reported leader of a cabinet revolt against Museveni's re-quest for extension of the ban on political party activities; however, in May 1993 he advised party activists to curtail operations in the face of a presidential decree banning theretofore implicitly acceptable activities. In June 1995 the DP leader resigned as second deputy prime minister and minister of public service to position himself for the forthcoming presidential campaign.

In early 1996 the DP and the UPC forged an unofficial alliance, the Inter-Party Coalition (IPC), on the premise that in return for its support of DP candidates at the 1996 elections the UPC would be the opposition's standard-bearer at the next national elections. Subsequently, a number of UPC leaders made campaign appearances with Ssemogerere; however, following the DP leader's overwhelming electoral defeat, the UPC's Obote reportedly denied the coalition's existence. Collaterally, observers speculated that the alliance had cost Ssemogerere the votes of the Baganda people, who had been oppressed by Obote's regime and continued to resent him. Although Ssemogerere described the presidential polling as "rigged" in favor of the incumbent and subsequently boycotted the June legislative balloting, suggestions that the party would go into opposition were greeted with skepticism by observers, who cited the DP's history of participation in NRM governments. Subsequent to the June 2000 referendum (which the DP boycotted) on political party activity, Ssemogerere announced his intention to resign the party presidency, but he stayed on until his retirement in 2005. Factions within the party clashed in advance of the 2005 constitutional referendum but reportedly reunited a month later. John Ssebaana Kizito was elected party leader in November 2005, ending Ssemogerere's 25-year reign, and faction leader Hajji Ali Sserunjogi was elected vice president. Ssebaana finished third behind Museveni in the 2006 presidential election with 1.58 percent of the vote. In concurrent parliamentary elections, the DP won 11 seats.

Leaders: John SSEBAANA Kizito (President and 2006 presidential candidate), Hajji Ali SSERUNJOGI (Vice President), Joseph MUKIIBI (Chair), Ebil OTTOO (Secretary General).

Forum for Democratic Change (FDC). This opposition group was formed in July 2004 by a merger of the Reform Agenda, the Parliamentary Advocacy Forum, and the National Democratic Forum. The FDC's leader in exile, retired colonel Kizza Besigye, had challenged Museveni in the 2001 presidential election. Several opposition members of parliament previously affiliated with the UPC and DP reportedly joined the new group, which declared its intentions of becoming "a strong, democratic, mass organization."

Besigye returned from the United States in 2005 in order to participate in 2006 elections and drew large crowds at a number of rallies in areas that traditionally had supported Museveni. In what observers said was an attempt to prevent Besigye from challenging Museveni in the 2006 elections, Besigye was arrested in Kampala for allegedly supporting the rebel PRA based in the DRC and charged with treason. He was also charged with rape in connection with a 1997 case but was cleared of that charge in March 2006. Earlier, the FDC nominated him as the group's presidential candidate, and Besigye was freed on bail a month ahead of the 2006 presidential election. He came in a distant second to Museveni. The party won 39 seats in the concurrent parliamentary elections.

Leaders: Dr. Kizza BESIGYE (Party Leader and 2001 and 2006 presidential candidate), Sulaiman KIGGUNDU (Chair), Alice ALASO (Secretary General), Sam AKAKI (Spokesperson), Salaami MUSUMBA, Geoffrey EKANYA.

Conservative Party (CP). The CP is a small formation whose leader, prime minister of Baganda in 1964–1966, participated in the Okello and Museveni governments. CP has adopted to some extent the positions of the **Baganda Royalist Movement,** which has long sought restoration of the traditional Kingdom of Baganda.

In early 2005, rival factions divided the group, and a lengthy dispute over leadership ensued until May, when Mayanja Nkangi, on one side, reconciled with Yusufu Nsubuga Nsombu and John Ken Lukyamuzi on the other. Lukyamuzi, who supported the DP's Ssemogerere in the 1996 presidential election over Museveni, initially supported the FDC's Besigye in 2006, then said he would run for president but did not appear on the ballot. He was forced to leave Parliament in 2006 for allegedly breaking the law by failing to disclose his wealth. Subsequently, a dispute over his leadership of the party remained unresolved as of midyear. The party won 1 seat in the 2006 parliamentary elections.

Leaders: John Ken LUKYAMUZI (Secretary General), Ashe James SEKAGGYA (Vice Chair), Mayanja NKANGI, Yusufu NSUBUGA NSOMBU.

Justice Forum (Justice, Education, Economy, Morality, African unity—JEEMA). The Justice Forum was formed in October 1996 by Mohamed Mayanja Kibirige, who secured only 2.1 percent of the vote in the 1996 presidential election, to rally support for his candidacy in the 2001 presidential election. (Kibirige received just 1 percent of the vote in 2001.) In 2004 the group, which reportedly seeks a democratic, federal system of government, rejected a merger with the FDC.

Kibirige initially announced he would seek the presidency in 2006 but later withdrew.

Leaders: Mohamed MAYANJA Kibirige (President and 1996 and 2001 presidential candidate), Alex OJOK (Vice President), Hussein KYANJO (Secretary General).

Other Groups

Progressive Alliance Party (PAP). Established in April 2005 by Bernard Kibirige, a former aide to Brig. Henry TUMUKUNDE, who was dismissed from his post as Uganda's military intelligence chief, the PAP has had a divisive history.

Its leaders deny that they are front men for Tumukunde, who was arrested in May 2005. (Tumukunde played a key role in Museveni's 1996 and 2001 elections, allegedly using "strong-arm" tactics and military intelligence to help the president.) Meanwhile, a rival intelligence chief and former supporter of Museveni, David Pulkol, left the FDC to join the PAP in September 2005, prompting accusations from Kibirige and other party members that Pulkol was sent by the NRM to spy on and "destroy" the party. Subsequently, however, Pulkol, who also had ties to Tumukunde, was elected party president and nominated as the party's presidential candidate for the 2006 election. Infighting in the party was blamed for his failing to meet the registration deadline, and in 2006 the group supported Kizza Besigye's FDC candidacy. A month before the election, about 100 PAP members linked to Tumukunde defected to the NRM and demanded Tumukunde's release. Reportedly, many of the defectors had been part of a "task force" organized by Tumukunde to support Museveni's 2001 bid, and they left the PAP in part because the party had no presidential candidate for 2006.

Leaders: David PULKOL (President), Bernard KIBIRIGE (Secretary General), Dr. Kaddu MULINDWA (Interim Chair).

Other groups include The **Freedom Movement,** part of the so-called G6 group of opposition parties that opposed the 2005 constitutional referendum; **Forces for Change,** a splinter opposition group formed in March 2005 by Nasser Ntege SSEBA-GALA and David Pulkol (who later joined the PAP); the **Reform Party,** a breakaway group from the FDC, led by Robert NDYOMUGYENYI; the **National Peasants Party,** led by Erias WAMALA; the **Republican Women and Youth Party,** led by Stella NAMBUYA; the **People's Independent Party,** led by Yahaya KAMULEGEYA; **Movement for Democratic Change,** led by Paulsen KITIMBO; the **Action Party,** led by Nelson OCHEGER; the **National People's Organization,** led by Abdu JAGWE; the **National Convention for Democracy,** led by Haji Jingo KAAYA; the **Farmers Party of Uganda,** led by Mudde Bombakka NSKIO; and the **National Unity, Reconciliation, and Development Party,** led by Sam SSEKAGYA.

Guerrilla Groups

Lord's Resistance Army (LRA). The LRA first emerged in the late 1980s as Lakwena Part Two, a small, predominantly Acholi successor group to the Holy Spirit Movement that had been led by "voodoo priestess" Alice LAKWENA from 1986 until her flight to Kenya in 1987. Under the leadership of Joseph Kony, the anti-NRA rebels remained active in northern Uganda, and in early 1991 the militants reportedly began referring to themselves as the Uganda Democratic Christian Army. Following inconclusive negotiations with government representatives in early 1994, Kony and his supporters launched a new offensive under their current name, claiming they were fighting "a holy war against foreign occupation" and seeking to install a government guided by the biblical Ten Commandments.

Casualties linked to the insurgency reached a one-month high of approximately 200 in March 1996. Observers attributed the violent upsurge to the recent arrival from Sudan of freshly armed and trained LRA fighters, many of whom were believed to have been Ugandan youths kidnapped by Kony in 1995. Kidnappings and disfigurements of uncooperative villagers have caused an international condemnation of the LRA. Several attempts at peace talks have failed. In June 1996 Museveni offered amnesty to the "ordinary fighters" affiliated with the LRA and a second group, the West Bank Nile Front (WBNF, see below), but pledged to prosecute the groups' leaders.

LRA bases in Sudan came under sustained attack by Sudanese rebel forces and the Ugandan Army beginning in April 1997, and in July LRA commanders reportedly called for a cease-fire. Subsequently, in the second half of 1997 Kony led his fighters in a series of cross-border raids, although the LRA had been forced to break into much smaller fighting cells than its usual 150–200 member units. Despite heavy casualties, according to government officials, the LRA continued to replenish its ranks by abducting teenage Ugandans and forcing them to march to Sudan for training and indoctrination.

In late 1998 a group of LRA dissidents led by Ronald Otim KOMAKECH reportedly split from the group following a dispute over the LRA's alleged targeting of civilians; subsequently, Komakech formed the **LRA–Democratic** and allied the splinter with the **Uganda National Front** (UNRF, below). The level of LRA activities actually increased after a December 1999 treaty between Sudan and Uganda ostensibly designed to end support for guerrilla groups. LRA activity subsided in 2000–2001, largely due to behind-the-scenes negotiations mediated by the U.S.-based Carter Center in Atlanta, which tried to initiate talks with LRA leader Kony and his backers, the Sudanese government. In February 2001, however, LRA rebels attacked a northern Ugandan town and abducted 40 people. In March Ugandan wildlife authorities suspended game-viewing activities in parts of the northwestern Murchison Falls National Park following an alleged LRA ambush in which at least 10 people were killed. In 2004 gains made by the Ugandan People's Defense Force (UPDF) against the rebels seemed to compel the LRA to seek a cease-fire. By mid-2005, however, talks had not made significant progress. Meanwhile, evidence of cooperation between Sudanese and Ugandan troops against the LRA raised hopes that combined pressure might force Kony's group into meaningful negotiations. In 2005 the ICC issued arrest warrants for Kony and other LRA leaders.

Leaders: Joseph KONY, Vincent OTTI, Oti LAGONY (Military Commander).

Allied Democratic Forces (ADF). The ADF is reportedly composed of remnants of the late Amon BAZIRA's National Movement for the Liberation of Uganda, and Islamic militant fighters, styled the *Salaaf Tabliqs,* allegedly funded by the Sudanese government. ADF activity was first reported in 1995, but the group did not achieve prominence until 1997 when its numbers were reportedly swollen by the addition of former Zairean government forces and Rwandan Hutu *Interhamwé* fighters.

A government offensive in mid-1997 decimated the ADF's fighting strength and drove a majority of its fighters deep into the mountains of the Democratic Republic of the Congo. However, ADF militants were allegedly responsible for grenade attacks in Kampala in early 1998, and thereafter the ADF launched a series of attacks that claimed dozens of civilian lives. In February 1999 the ADF was accused of orchestrating a deadly bomb attack in Kampala. A number of ADF militants were killed

in subsequent government raids, while the ADF was accused of killing both civilians and soldiers in several incidents throughout the rest of the year. In April 2000 the Ugandan government pulled out 2,000 soldiers from eastern DRC, claiming that the threat of cross-border ADF incursions was greatly reduced. Ugandan authorities in July arrested 28 ADF recruits accused of undertaking bomb attacks that have killed 67 people and injured 262 others since 1997. The ADF had resorted to urban terrorism after its ground insurgency was defeated in the mountains straddling Uganda's western border with the Democratic Republic of the Congo. Some ADF rebel leaders and fighters allegedly were trained in terrorist Osama bin Laden's Afghan camps, and in December 2001 the United States listed the ADF as a terrorist organization. Clashes between Ugandan forces and ADF rebels continued into 2006, with security forces arresting and killing many suspected ADF members in the western forests of Uganda. The militants reportedly were fleeing the DRC following fighting between the Congolese army and UN peacekeeping forces.

Leaders: Jamir MUKULU, Yusuf KABANDA.

West Bank Nile Front (WBNF). The WBNF was formed during the Obote era by West Nile people who had reportedly been forced to flee to Sudan and Zaire to escape government persecution. Although President Museveni successfully integrated most of the dissident West Nile leaders into his NRM regime and facilitated the repatriation of the majority of the remaining refugees, the WBNF, allegedly funded by Sudan and Zaire, remained active through the 1990s under the leadership of Maj. Juma ORIS. Prior to the 1996 presidential elections the WBNF was reported to have penetrated close to the provincial capital of Arua before being driven back by government forces.

In early 1997 WBNF bases in Zaire were overrun by Ugandan forces, and the rebels fled into Sudan where they suffered further heavy losses at the hands of Sudanese rebels. Oris was reportedly killed in February, and in March the group's deputy commander, Abdulatif Toya, was captured in Sudan. In August another WBNF leader, Hajji

Cabinet

As of August 1, 2006

Prime Minister	Apolo Nsibambi
First Deputy Prime Minister	Eriya Kategaya
Second Deputy Prime Minister	Henry Kajura
Third Deputy Prime Minister	Ali Kirunda Kivejinja
Office of the President	Beatrice Wabudeya [f]
Prime Minister's Office	Adolf Mwesige

Ministers

Agriculture, Animal Husbandry, and Fisheries	Hillary Onek
Defense	Dr. Crispus Kiyunga
East African Affairs	Eriya Kategaya
Education and Sports	Namirembe Bitamazire
Energy and Mineral Development	Daudi Migereko [f]
Finance	Dr. Ezra Suruma
Foreign Affairs	Sam Kutesa
Gender, Labor, and Social Development	Syda Bumba [f]
Health	Dr. Steven Mallinga
Information Communications Technology	Hamu Mullira
Information and National Guidance	Ali Kirunda Kivejinja
Internal Affairs	Ruhakana Rugunda
Justice and Constitutional Affairs and Attorney General	Kiddu Makubuya
Lands, Housing, and Urban Development	Omara Atubo
Local Government	Maj. Gen. Kahinda Otafiire
Public Service	Henry Kajura
Public Works	John Nasasira
Relief and Disaster Preparedness	Tarsis Kabwegyere
Security	Amama Mbabazi
Trade and Industry	Janat Mukwaya [f]
Water and Environment	Maria Mutagamba [f]
Without Portfolio	Dorothy Hyuha [f]

[f] = female

Kabeba, was arrested by government forces. In recent years WBNF activities have been extremely limited.

Leaders: Abdulatif TOYA (under arrest), Hajji KABEBA (Zairean-based Commander, under arrest), Zubair ATAMVAKU.

United Freedom Front/Army (UFF/A). The UFF/A was founded in London, United Kingdom, in February 1999 by Herman Ssemuju, former leader of the **National Freedom Party,** who had fled Uganda in 1998. (Ssemuju had run for president in 1996.) Among those in attendance at the UFF/A's launching were representatives of the LRA and ADF.

Leader: Herman SSEMUJU.

Other rebel groups have been formed in opposition to the government since Museveni's takeover in 1986, but their activities have mostly subsided or their members have been absorbed by government amnesties. The **Uganda National Front** (UNRF) led by Ali BAMUZE, for example, began softening its stance toward the regime in 1998, and in June 2002 the government announced that a cease-fire with the UNRF had been reached. In 1994 most of the *Ruwenzuru,* a 30-year-old Bakonjo autonomist group from the west, surrendered to the government, and responses to presidential amnesty continued after that.

However, it was reported that NRM supporters secured more than 200 of the elected seats.

Following the most recent balloting on February 23, 2006 (the first held on a multiparty basis following the 2005 constitutional revision), the seat distribution was as follows: National Resistance Movement, 187; Forum for Democratic Change, 39; Democratic Party, 11; Uganda People's Congress, 8; Justice Forum, 1; Conservative Party, 1; independents, 29.

Speaker: Edward SSEKANDI Kiwanika.

Legislature

The former National Assembly was dissolved following the July 1985 coup. On February 1, 1986, an appointed National Resistance Council (NRC) of 23 members was sworn in to serve as an interim legislature, its enactments being subject to presidential approval. Additional members were named in subsequent months, and in mid-1987 the NRC was expanded to include the cabinet as well as deputy and assistant ministers. In early 1989 the council was further enlarged to 278 members, of whom 210 were indirectly elected (168 on a district constituency basis, 34 as regional women's representatives, 5 representing youth organizations, and 3 representing trade unions), with the remaining 68 appointed by the president.

Balloting for a new, formally recognized **Parliament** was held on a "no-party" basis in June 1996. Government-supportive candidates captured or were appointed to 271 of the 276 available seats, while unrecognized opposition candidates reportedly secured the remaining 5 posts. Balloting was again held on a nonparty basis on June 26, 2001, for 214 chamber seats. (There are also 81 indirectly elected legislators who are selected by various interest groups, predominately the National Resistance Movement—NRM). In addition, members of the cabinet who are not already sitting legislators serve as ex-officio members of Parliament.) Supporters of opposition parties were allowed to run on an individual basis, and several were elected.

Communications

Press

The press under the Amin regime was subject to very strict censorship and saw an extremely high rate of attrition. Substantial relaxation occurred after the installation of President Binaisa in June 1979. In March 1981 the Obote government banned a number of papers that had been critical of the UPC and subsequently took additional measures against both foreign and domestic journalists who had commented unfavorably on the security situation within Uganda. The press has enjoyed relative freedom under the current regime. Several private radio stations and private television stations report on local political developments. The largest newspapers and broadcasting facilities that reach rural areas remain state-owned. Governmental corruption is reported. Opposition positions are also presented, but the coverage is often not balanced. Journalists have asked Parliament to enact a freedom of information act so that the public is not denied information. Intermittently journalists are arrested, but generally their cases have been handled fairly in the country's judicial system. The following, unless otherwise noted, are English-language dailies published in Kampala: *New Vision* (40,000), NRM organ launched in March 1986 as successor to the *Uganda Times,* which had ceased publication in early 1985; *The Monitor* (34,000), weekly; *Taifa Uganda Empya* (24,000), in Luganda; *Topic* (13,000), radical weekly; *Focus*

(13,000), weekly; *Ngabo* (7,000), independent, in Luganda; *Munno* (15,000), Catholic daily, in Luganda; *The Star* (5,500), independent; *The Citizen,* DP organ; *The Financial Times; Munnansi News Bulletin,* DP weekly in Luganda.

News Agencies

The domestic facility is the Uganda News Agency (UNA); a number of foreign agencies maintain bureaus in Kampala.

Broadcasting and Computing

The Ministry of Information and Broadcasting controls Radio Uganda, which broadcasts in 24 languages over two networks, and Uganda Television, which broadcasts primarily in English. There is also an independent television outlet broadcast-

ing in the Kampala area. There were approximately 650,000 television receivers and 103,000 personal computers serving 125,000 Internet users in 2003.

Intergovernmental Representation

Ambassador to the U.S.
Perezi Karukubiro KAMUNANWIRE

U.S. Ambassador to Uganda
Steven Alan BROWNING

Permanent Representative to the UN
Francis K. BUTAGIRA

IGO Memberships (Non-UN)
AfDB, AU, BADEA, Comesa, CWTH, EAC, EADB, IDB, IGAD, Interpol, IOM, NAM, OIC, PCA, WCO, WTO

ZAMBIA

REPUBLIC OF ZAMBIA

Note: In preliminary results from the presidential balloting on September 28, 2006, the Movement for Multiparty Democracy (MMD) candidate and incumbent president Levy Patrick Mwanawasa won reelection with a plurality of 43 percent of the vote; Michael Sata of the Patriot Front (PF) placed second with 29 percent; Hakainde Hichilema of the United Democratic Alliance (UDA) placed third with 25 percent. In legislative balloting on the same day, the MMD won 73 seats; PF, 43 seats; UDA, 26 seats; the United Liberal Party, 2 seats; and the National Democratic Front, 1 seat. Independent candidates won 3 seats and results for 2 seats were not yet available.

The Country

Landlocked Zambia, the former British protectorate of Northern Rhodesia, is bordered by the Democratic Republic of the Congo, Tanzania, and Malawi on the north and east, and by Angola, Namibia, Zimbabwe, and Mozambique on the west and south. Its terrain consists primarily of a high plateau with abundant forests and grasslands. The watershed between the Congo and Zambezi river systems crosses the northern part of the country. The bulk of the population belongs to various Bantu tribes, the most influential being the Bemba in the north and the Lozi, an offshoot of the Zulu, in the southwest. (Tribal influences remain highly influential in political affairs.) Nonindigenous groups include a small number of whites (mainly British and South African), Asians, and persons of mixed descent concentrated in the "copper belt" in the north. Nearly three-quarters of native Zambians are nominally Christian, almost equally divided between Catholics and Protestants; the remainder adhere to traditional African beliefs. The official language is English, but Afrikaans and more than 70 local languages and dialects are spoken. Women comprise approximately one-third of the labor force, not including unpaid agricultural workers. Although a number of women involved in the independence struggle achieved positions of influ-

ence in the former ruling party, female representation is minimal at local levels.

Zambia is one of the world's largest producers of copper and cobalt. The former accounts for 75 percent of export earnings, but Zambia's share of the world copper market has declined significantly in the wake of a nearly 80 percent decline in production, attributed in large part to mismanagement of state-owned mines. Zinc, coal, cement, lime,

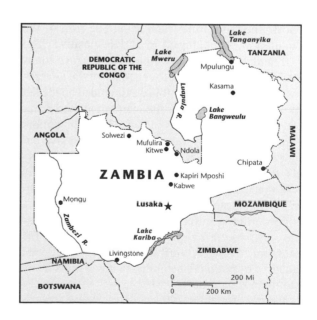

sulphur, and magnetite are among other minerals being extracted. Agriculture employs two-thirds of the labor force, with maize, peanuts, tobacco, and cotton constituting the chief commercial crops. Because of a booming copper industry, Zambia, until the early 1970s, enjoyed one of Africa's highest standards of living, with rapid development of schools, hospitals, and highways. However, a subsequent decline in copper prices yielded infrastructural decay, rising unemployment within the rapidly growing and highly urbanized population, a foreign exchange shortage, an external debt of more than $6 billion, and the erosion of social services. Although the government had exercised budgetary restraint and relaxed its control of the economy in accordance with International Monetary Fund (IMF) strictures dating to the mid-1970s, rioting over price increases in late 1986 prompted Lusaka to abandon austerity measures and break with the IMF. However, economic reform measures were reinstated in 1998, paving the way for renewal of relations with international lenders and donors. In 1992 the Chiluba government launched a privatization program; however, market reform was subsequently seen as having failed to help the nation's poor (an estimated 83 percent of the population). Funds for education and health remained severely constrained at a time when about one-fifth of the population was believed to be HIV-positive. The IMF and World Bank continued to approve loans (Western aid accounted for one-half of the government's budget), and Zambia was included on the list of countries eligible for the international community's new debt-relief program. However, donors expressed concern over the apparent pervasive nature of corruption in government affairs at all levels. Particularly disappointing to foreign observers was the decision in 2002 of South African mining giant Anglo-American to abandon the massive copper mining initiative it had launched in Zambia only two years earlier. Among other things, the economic distress contributed to the emergence of a degree of political instability that was unusual by Zambian standards.

Severe drought in 2002 caused a decline in agricultural production that left 25 percent of the population temporarily dependent on food aid. Collaterally, the pace of economic reform slowed, prompting the temporary suspension of IMF and World Bank assistance. However, real GDP growth averaged 4.8 percent a year in 2004 and 2005, in part due to soaring copper prices and the investment of $1 billion by mining companies. In addition, the Group of Eight in 2005 canceled Zambia's $2.5 billion debt. Real GDP growth of nearly 6 percent was forecast for 2006, with inflation projected to decline from 15.9 percent to about 10 percent. Meanwhile, the Zambian administration earlier declared a national emergency in regard to HIV/AIDS and began providing free drugs to those infected.

Government and Politics

Political Background

Declared a British sphere of influence in 1888, Northern Rhodesia was administered jointly with Southern Rhodesia until 1923–1924, when it became a separate British protectorate. From 1953 to 1963, it was linked with Southern Rhodesia and Nyasaland (now Malawi) in the Federation of Rhodesia and Nyasaland, which was dissolved at the end of 1963 in recognition of the unwillingness of the black majority populations in Northern Rhodesia and Nyasaland to continue under the political and economic domination of white-ruled Southern Rhodesia. A drive for Northern Rhodesia's complete independence, led by Harry NKUMBULA and Kenneth D. KAUNDA, concluded on October 24, 1964, when the territory became an independent republic within the Commonwealth under the name of Zambia (after the Zambezi River). Kaunda, as leader of the majority United National Independence Party (UNIP), became head of the new state; Nkumbula, whose African National Congress (ANC) had trailed in the preindependence election of January 1964, became leader of the opposition. The political predominance of Kaunda and his party was strengthened at the general election of December 1968, Kaunda winning a second five-year term as president and the UNIP again capturing an overwhelming

Political Status: Independent republic within the Commonwealth since October 24, 1964; under one-party, presidential-parliamentary system from 1972 to adoption of multiparty constitution on August 29, 1991.

Area: 290,584 sq. mi. (752,614 sq. km.).

Population: 10,285,631 (2000C); 11,044,000 (2005E).

Major Urban Center (2005E): LUSAKA (metropolitan area, 1,647,000).

Official Language: English.

Monetary Unit: Kwacha (official rate July 1, 2006: 3,505 kwachas = $1US).

President: (*See headnote.*) Levy Patrick MWANAWASA (Movement for Multiparty Democracy); popularly elected (in disputed balloting) on December 27, 2001, and inaugurated on January 2, 2002, for a five-year term in succession to Frederick Jacob Titus CHILUBA (Movement for Multiparty Democracy).

Vice President: Lupando MWAPE (Movement for Multiparty Democracy); appointed by the president on October 4, 2004, to replace Nevers MUMBA (National Citizens' Coalition) following Mumba's dismissal on the same day.

legislative majority. In December 1972 Kaunda promulgated a law banning all parties except the UNIP and introduced what was termed "one-party participatory democracy." In December 1978 he was reelected for a fourth term following disqualification of Nkumbula and former vice president Simon M. KAPWEPWE.

On August 27, 1983, the president dissolved the National Assembly to pave the way for an October 27 election, in which, as sole presidential candidate, he garnered 93 percent of the vote and was returned to office for a fifth five-year term. Two years later Kaunda transferred both the prime minister and the UNIP secretary general to diplomatic posts; Defense Minister Alexander Grey ZULU was chosen to head the party, while Prime Minister Nalumino MUNDIA was replaced by Minister of Education and Culture Kebby MUSOKOTWANE.

Following a UNIP restructuring that was generally interpreted as enhancing his personal control of both party and government, Kaunda, again the sole candidate, was elected for a sixth presidential term on October 26, 1988, with a reported 96 percent "yes" vote. On the other hand, eight cabinet members were defeated in assembly elections held the same day, apparently reflecting increased opposition to government policy. Shortly after the election, Kaunda reshuffled the cabinet, and on March 15, 1989, he named Gen. Malimba MASHEKE to replace the young and popular Musokotwane as prime minister; the subsequent posting of Musokotwane to a diplomatic mission lent credence to the view that he had become a political threat to Kaunda.

In early 1990 the regime rejected a number of proposals for liberalization of the Zambian political system. However, by midyear the government had grudgingly agreed to implement reforms in an attempt to appease increasingly vociferous critics, particularly among the trade and business communities. In the wake of a coup attempt in June and price riots in July, Kaunda agreed to a voter registration drive and the freeing of a number of political prisoners. In September, following a series of major prodemocracy rallies, the president announced plans for multiparty elections by October 1991. On December 4 the National Assembly legalized the formation of political parties, and on December 30 the Zambian Congress of Trade Unions (ZCTU) aligned itself with the leading opposition group, the Movement for Multiparty Democracy (MMD).

In 1991 the regime's practices, including strict control of the media, drew MMD condemnation and led to violent clashes between MMD and UNIP supporters. Nevertheless, on August 2 the National Assembly approved a new multiparty constitution, and, following its formal signing on August 29, the president dissolved the legislature and allowed the state of emergency decree to lapse for the first time since independence. On October 31, in balloting supervised by former U.S. president Jimmy Carter and representatives of the Commonwealth and the Organization of African Unity (OAU, subsequently the African Union—AU), the MMD's Frederick

CHILUBA won 74 percent of the presidential vote and the movement's candidates captured 125 of 150 assembly seats.

The MMD secured a vast majority of the 1,190 local council seats contested on November 30, 1992; however, the ruling party's victories were tainted by a lack of competition in approximately 400 councils, coupled with voter apathy (less than 10 percent of eligible voters reportedly having participated). Observers attributed the apparent growing disenchantment among voters to the effects of a severe economic austerity program compounded by the perception of unmitigated governmental corruption.

On March 4, 1993, the administration's prestige was further damaged when Chiluba declared an indefinite state of emergency and 25 UNIP members, including three of former president Kaunda's sons, were arrested on charges relating to an alleged coup plot. On March 9 the president shortened the detention without trial period from 28 to 7 days, apparently seeking to combat domestic and international charges that his administration had overreacted to reports about the alleged plot, and on May 25 the state of emergency was lifted.

In August 1993 15 prominent MMD officials resigned from the government and National Assembly because of the Chiluba administration's alleged unwillingness to investigate corruption and drug trafficking charges against powerful cabinet ministers; the MMD defectors, citing a "critical national crisis of leadership and governance," launched the National Party (NP). Chiluba dismissed the resignations as the "teething problems" of democratic reform; however, in December international aid donors meeting in Paris voted to withhold aid payments until Lusaka investigated the allegations, and on January 6, 1994, the ZCTU called on the Chiluba administration to dissolve the government. Consequently, on January 11, 1994, Chiluba reshuffled his cabinet, claiming to have ousted tainted ministers, and in March the World Bank agreed to release suspended aid payments despite opposition protestations that the president had shielded corrupt ministers while dismissing two who had sought to expose malfeasance.

On July 3, 1994, Vice President Levy MWANAWASA resigned, citing alleged irresponsibility and greed among his colleagues. On the following day Chiluba named Brig. Gen. Godfrey MIYANDA, theretofore a minister without portfolio, to replace Mwanawasa.

In October 1994 former president Kaunda officially announced that he would end his retirement to campaign for early presidential elections, saying "there is a crisis in Zambia. . . . I have accepted the call to come back." Thereafter, in February 1995, Kaunda, who had been under surveillance since August 1994 because of allegations that his return was being financed by foreign backers, was charged with attempting to hold an illegal political party meeting. Meanwhile, the MMD sought to block his presidential eligibility by pressing for a constitutional amendment that would disqualify anyone not born in Zambia of Zambian-born parents (Kaunda's parents having been born in Malawi). Such an amendment, as well as a second amendment disqualifying any person who had already been twice-elected president, were included in a draft document issued on June 16. The proposed charter was released despite the objections of an independent constitutional review commission, which had declared the amendments "rubbish" and accused the MMD of having bribed its authors.

On May 16, 1996, the National Assembly approved the Constitution of Zambia Amendment Act 1996, and 12 days later the president sanctioned the measure, thus officially banning Kaunda from future elections. Subsequent opposition efforts to have the constitutional changes suspended and the upcoming balloting held in accordance with the 1991 document were dismissed in September by the president and High Court, respectively. On the other hand, in an effort to dampen mounting opposition charges that electoral preparations were being "rigged," Chiluba agreed to provide opposition representatives with equal access to the media and oversight of vote tabulation. On October 19 Chiluba dissolved the assembly and announced that presidential and legislative elections would be held on November 18. (The opposition's subsequent charge that the government's mandate would expire on October 31 and that any of its actions thereafter would be illegal were dismissed by the regime as "immature.") On October 23 Kaunda announced that the UNIP would boycott the November elections to protest the constitutional changes and the government's alleged manipulation of the voter registration drive.

As anticipated, President Chiluba and the MMD secured landslide victories at polling on November 18, 1996, with the former capturing 69.5 percent of the vote and his party 131 of the 150 seats contested. Their victories were marred, however, by alleged electoral irregularities and by what one observer described as a "revolt of MMD voters" in high-profile contests won by independents and opposition candidates. Thereafter, amid widespread opposition calls for a campaign of civil disobedience to force the government to hold fresh elections, Chiluba put the military on alert on November 28. On December 2 Chiluba named a new cabinet that was described as "tribalist" because of the preponderance of members from the Northern and Luapula regions (Chiluba is from the latter).

Tensions remained high in Lusaka throughout the first half of 1997 as the Chiluba administration, now reportedly under the direction of MMD hardliners, was sharply denounced by both domestic and international observers for introducing legislation that would strictly regulate both the media and nongovernmental organizations. (In March the latter law went into effect, but in April the government suspended the controversial Press Council Bill.) In early August antigovernment demonstrations in Lusaka turned into rioting, and, at an illegal opposition rally on August 23, Kaunda and Roger CHONGWE, leader of the Liberal Progressive Front, were shot and wounded in what Kaunda described as an assassination attempt.

On October 28, 1997, a group of junior military officers led by Capt. Steven LUNGU (aka "Captain Solo") took over a government radio station and declared that they had established a "National Redemption Council" and were prepared to overthrow the government. Within hours the reportedly drunken rebels were overpowered by forces loyal

to the president; nevertheless, the government declared a state of emergency, and in the following weeks more than 80 mid-level officers and dozens of opposition members were detained, with a number of others reportedly fleeing the country amid reports that those arrested were being tortured.

On December 2, 1997, Chiluba demoted his vice president, Brig. Gen. Godfrey Miyanda, to the education ministry and named as his replacement Lt. Gen. Christon TEMBO. Furthermore, Chiluba drastically reshuffled both the government and the military leadership.

In late April 2001 a fractured MMD congress agreed to seek constitutional revision to permit President Chiluba to run for a third term, prompting massive protest demonstrations and significant external condemnation. Under heavy pressure, Chiluba finally declared he would not seek reelection. However, on May 4 he dissolved the cabinet, permitting him to appoint a new government on May 6 that pointedly did not include theretofore Vice President Tembo and some 11 other MMD members who had opposed the third-term initiative.

Former vice president Mwanawasa became the surprise MMD candidate in the December 27, 2001, presidential balloting, securing, according to official results, a narrow victory (28.69 percent to 26.76 percent) over the second-place finisher, Anderson K. MAZOKA of the United Party for National Development (UPND). However, opposition parties charged that the balloting had been rigged and demanded a court review. (The Supreme Court launched a review of the charges but closed the case in November 2004.) Meanwhile, the MMD was also credited with pluralities in the concurrent assembly and municipal elections, the UPND easily outdistancing the other contenders to secure its position as the dominant opposition grouping. Not surprisingly, considering the electoral challenge, no opposition parties were represented in the cabinet appointed by Mwanawasa on January 7, 2002. However, Mwanawasa appointed members of the UNIP and the Forum for Democracy and Development (FDD) to junior cabinet positions in a May 28, 2003, reshuffle. He also named Nevers MUMBA, a prominent pastor and leader of the National Citizens' Coalition (NCC), as vice president. Mumba was in turn succeeded by Lupando MWAPE of the MDD on October 4, 2004, and by 2005 it was reported that the non-MDD cabinet members had been replaced by MDD stalwarts.

On April 5, 2006, the assembly adopted a controversial electoral reform bill establishing the president's authority to set election dates and requiring only a plurality in a single-round election to decide presidential balloting, among other provisions (see Current issues, below). The bill was promulgated on May 19, and in July President Mwanawasa called for tripartite elections to be held on September 28, 2006. (*See headnote.*)

Constitution and government

Zambia's 1964 constitution was superseded by the adoption at a UNIP conference in August 1973 of a constitution of the "second republic" that reaffirmed the introduction in 1972 of a one-party system and further provided for the sharing of authority between the party and traditional organs of government. To further emphasize the role of the UNIP, its secretary general (rather than the prime minister) was designated the nation's second-ranking official.

On August 2, 1991, the National Assembly adopted a new constitution that provided for multiparty elections, a two-tiered parliament, abandonment of the post of prime minister in favor of a revived vice presidency, and a presidentially appointed cabinet. In 1993 President Chiluba named a 22-member commission to revise the 1991 document. Draft amendments, released in June 1995 in expectation of a constituent assembly and national referendum, were approved by the National Assembly on May 16, 1996, and by President Chiluba on May 28. The Constitution of Zambia Amendment Act 1996 limits participation in presidential polling to Zambian-born citizens whose parents were also born in Zambia and disqualifies traditional chiefs and anyone who has lived abroad during the previous 20 years. The chief executive is limited to two five-year terms.

The judiciary embraces a Supreme Court, a High Court, and various local courts. Administratively, the country is divided into nine provinces, including the city of Lusaka and its environs, which are subdivided into 55 districts.

Foreign Relations

While pursuing a generally nonaligned foreign policy (an 18-year coolness with Britain having been ended by a Kaunda state visit to London in 1983), Zambia consistently opposed racial discrimination in southern Africa and provided sanctuary for numerous exile groups engaged in guerrilla operations against white-controlled territories. Prior to the constitutional changes in South Africa, Zambia's prestige among Front-Line States was pronounced. In the wake of treaties concluded by Angola and Mozambique with South Africa, Lusaka became the headquarters of the African National Congress (ANC), making it a target for bomb attacks in May 1986 by South Africa forces, who also crossed the border on a "reconnaissance mission" in April 1987 that left several persons dead. Kaunda assumed the chairmanship of the Front-Line grouping in early 1985, vowing to promote increased mutual support among member governments. In 1986 he denounced the United States and the United Kingdom for "conspiring" to support the South African government, warning they would share responsibility for the impending anti-apartheid "explosion." Zambia was also in the forefront of a regional plan to lessen reliance on South African trade routes that included rehabilitation of the Benguela Railway in Angola and the Tanzania-Zambia (Tanzam) link to Dar es Salaam. In other regional affairs, troops were at times deployed in border clashes with Malawi and Zaire, the latter agreeing in 1986 to a joint review and demarcation of disputed territory that yielded a settlement in 1989. (Disputes continued to erupt in 2005 at the border, reportedly notorious for illegal crossings and smuggling.) In November 1989 a joint security commission was established with Mozambique in an attempt to thwart cross-border guerrilla activity.

Since its ascension to power in October 1991, the Chiluba government's foreign policy agenda was topped by relations with international creditors. In late 1991 the government negotiated a release of the aid allocations suspended in September when the Kaunda regime had allowed debt repayment and austerity programs to lapse. The government's decision to sever diplomatic ties with Iran and Iraq for their alleged financing of coup plotters against Chiluba was described in *Africa Confidential* as owing more to "fundamentalist Christian and anti-Muslim" tendencies within the administration than to substantive evidence of foreign involvement. Furthermore, the Chiluba government experienced slow progress in establishing relations with regional neighbors, many of whom were Kaunda supporters and had expressed distrust of the new administration's criticism of the ANC as well as of its links to South African commercial interests.

The Zambian assembly's approval of a controversial constitutional amendment bill in May 1996 provoked widespread disapproval from Zambia's Western donors, and in June a number of them suspended aid payments. Regionally, however, the Southern African Development Community (SADC) was described by observers as having adopted a "passive" position after the Chiluba government rebuffed its initial intervention efforts, and South Africa, the only SADC member considered powerful enough to influence Lusaka, refused to assume a leadership role.

Aid donors remained unwilling to restart payments through the first half of 1997; however, in July the suspension was partially lifted. Negotiations on further relaxation of payment restrictions were postponed after Lusaka imposed a state of emergency from October until March 1998. In May 1998 the World Bank agreed to a new aid package contingent on Lusaka enacting economic and political reforms; in particular, the bank pressed the government to speed privatization efforts and improve its human rights record.

Zambian-Angolan relations deteriorated in early 1999 as Luanda threatened military action against Zambia if Lusaka continued its alleged support for Angolan rebels. Thereafter, in a thinly veiled reference to Luanda, the Chiluba administration blamed "external forces" for a series of bombings in Lusaka. Later agreements between Luanda and Lusaka appeared to ease the tension, however, although a large Angolan refugee population subsequently continued to create difficulties for the Zambian government, as did an influx of refugees from fighting in the Democratic Republic of the Congo. A joint UN-Zambian program to repatriate Angolan refugees subsequently had substantial success, although there continued to be sporadic raids by Congolese rebels into Zambia. In response, the government increased border patrols. The final repatriation of some 34,500 Angola refugees was reported to be under way in 2005, though many were still living in camps in remote areas of Zambia in 2006.

In November 2004 the Zambian military launched a series of training exercises overseen by French military experts. The operations were part of a larger regional initiative through which France hoped to promote military cooperation among Tanzania, Zambia, and Zimbabwe that could lead, among other things, to joint regional humanitarian operations.

Current Issues

Political affairs in the early 2000s were dominated by the question of whether the constitution would be revised by national referendum to permit President Chiluba to seek a third term. Civic groups strongly objected to the initiative, and public anti-Chiluba demonstrations in March 2001 prompted mass arrests and a crackdown on meetings devoted to discussion of the question. Although nearly one-third of the delegates walked out of the MMD congress in late April, Chiluba's bid received official party endorsement, prompting another wave of street protests before the campaign was abandoned. By that time, many analysts had concluded that the party wrangling, resentment over Chiluba's autocratic style, and the perception of substantial corruption in government circles had made the MMD vulnerable in advance of the December elections.

However, although they had proven successful in a number of recent by-elections, some of the opposition parties appeared to be regionally or tribally based and therefore of limited national scope, while the UNIP remained in disarray. In addition, despite much negotiation on the matter, the opposition failed to coalesce behind a single presidential candidate, permitting the MMD's Levy Mwanawasa to eke out a victory in the first-past-the-post contest among 11 candidates. Second-place finisher Anderson Mazoka of the UPND and a number of the other losing candidates immediately charged that the presidential balloting had been severely tainted by, among other things, the intimidation of voters and ballot-box stuffing. International observers agreed that electoral preparations had been seriously flawed, while EU monitors concluded it would be "unsafe" to accept the official results as accurately reflecting the will of the voters. Meanwhile, the president dedicated his new government to combating corruption, a campaign that quickly appeared to place him at odds with many MMD stalwarts, including his predecessor. In July 2002 the National Assembly lifted the immunity from prosecution previously enjoyed by former president Chiluba. As a result, Chiluba was arrested on a wide range of corruption charges. Some 150 other senior figures from the Chiluba government, including the chief of the army and the country's intelligence head, were also arrested. Initial reports estimated that tens of millions of dollars may have been embezzled during the ten years of the Chiluba administration.

The appointment of opposition legislators to the cabinet in May 2003 was seen as an effort by President Mwanawasa to deal with plummeting popular support for the MMD in the wake of the Chiluba scandals. The administration had also been recently confronted by public protests over the effects of austerity measures. Further complicating matters for the government was the decision in August 2004 to postpone the local elections scheduled for November for two years because of financial constraints. Finally, Chiluba was rearrested in September 2004 (the initial charges had been botched by the prosecution), and supporters of the former

president split from the MDD to form the Party for Unity, Democracy, and Development (PUDD). (The trial for Chiluba and the others from his administration got under way in 2006.)

As attention in 2005 turned to the 2006 presidential and legislative polls, opposition leaders called for drafting of a new constitution that would, among other things, establish at least a degree of proportional representation in the assembly. The government's critics also demanded revision in the makeup and authority of the electoral commission to help avoid the problems experienced in 2001. However, the electoral reform law adopted by the assembly and endorsed by President Mwanawasa in 2006 rejected the electoral commission's recommendations, including the stipulation that presidential balloting be decided by majority vote. The new law gives the president the authority to set the date of elections (President Mwanawasa set the date for September), which opposition groups claimed would not give them enough time to prepare. Meanwhile, several opposition groups formed alliances in advance of the elections (see Political parties, below), but observers said the opposition was in "disarray," as it had been assumed elections would not be held until closer to the end of the year.

Political Parties

In December 1972, the United National Independence Party (UNIP) became the country's only legal political party. During the late 1980s reformists called for a multiparty system, with President Kaunda repeatedly dismissing the idea as unworkable because of "too many tribal conflicts." However, in September 1990 he bowed to mounting pressure and agreed to termination of the UNIP monopoly. Three months later, the president signed a National Assembly bill legalizing the formation of political parties, and in August 1991 a multiparty constitution was adopted. Thereafter, on October 31 the UNIP, the Movement for Multiparty Democracy (MMD), and 12 smaller parties participated in the first multiparty balloting since 1968.

Dominant Government Party

Movement for Multiparty Democracy (MMD). Formed in mid-1990 as a loose alliance of anti-UNIP groups in support of a voter registration drive, the MMD applied for legal party status immediately following legislative approval of a multiparty system in December. Among other things, the group issued a manifesto declaring its commitment to a free-market economy.

In June 1991 the MMD denounced a proposed draft constitution on the grounds that it would advance an excessively powerful presidency; the party threatened to boycott upcoming elections if it were adopted. Consequently, President Kaunda met in July with MMD leaders to forge a compromise document. Meanwhile, violent clashes between MMD and UNIP supporters continued, and in September the MMD complained that limiting the campaign period to two months favored the incumbents. Nevertheless, at the October 31 balloting Frederick Chiluba of the MMD defeated Kaunda's bid for reelection, with the MMD also winning an overwhelming majority of National Assembly seats. Subsequently, at sparsely attended balloting in late November 1992, the party captured nearly 75 percent of 1,190 local council seats.

In early 1993 a growing interparty chasm was reported between those members urging faster governmental reform and a second, reportedly more influential faction, which was concerned less with reform and more with "strengthening the political and financial interests of the . . . commercial class." Founding member and party chair Arthur Wina was one of 14 prominent MMD officials who withdrew from the grouping in August to protest the dismissal of cabinet ministers identified as having exposed corruption and drug trafficking by their colleagues. Thereafter, more members left the party as its popularity plummeted amid allegations that top officials were sheltered from the effects of the government's economic austerity program. On the other hand, in November 1993 Enoch Kavindele, leader of the United Democratic Party, dissolved his party and joined the MMD, claiming that he and Chiluba shared similar development strategies.

Internal friction, based in part on tribal differences as well as the personal ambition of various MMD leaders, was reported throughout the rest of the 1990s, although the party retained solid political control at both the national and local levels. Fractionalization reached its apex in early 2000 when it became apparent that President Chiluba's supporters were intent on constitutional revision that would permit him a third term. Some 400 delegates walked out of the MMD congress in Lusaka at the end of April to protest the initiative; however, the remaining delegates dutifully endorsed Chiluba as the MMD candidate in the upcoming presidential race, calling for a national referendum on the proposed constitutional change. In the wake of massive protest demonstrations, Chiluba several days later announced he had decided not to seek a third term, but at the same time more than 20 senior members of the MMD (including some 11 cabinet members) were expelled from the party, some of them subsequently helping to form new opposition parties.

In August 2001 Levy Mwanawasa, a prominent attorney and former vice president of the republic, was selected as the new MMD standard-bearer. Critics initially described Mwanawasa as Chiluba's hand-picked successor, but tension was apparent between the two MMD leaders following Mwanawasa's controversial victory in the national balloting, the new president, among other things, reportedly rejecting Chiluba's suggestions for cabinet appointments. Following Chiluba's arrest on corruption charges in 2004, the former president's supporters defected from the MMD and formed the PUDD (below).

The National Citizens' Coalition (NCC), sometimes referred to as the National Christian Coalition, merged with the MDD after the MDD's leader, prominent pastor Nevers Mumba, was appointed vice president in 2003. (Mumba had run for the presidency in 2001 but had received only 2.2 percent of the vote.) In October 2004 Mumba was dismissed as vice president following his comments accusing opposition parties of taking funds from foreign sources. He was forced to leave the party in 2005 after he reportedly accused

President Mwanawasa and his wife of using government money to buy party convention votes.

Although Mwanawasa won the party leadership by a landslide in 2005, providing him a mandate to seek a second term as president of the republic in 2006, rifts in the party were reported among rivals who campaigned against him.

Leaders: Levy Patrick MWANAWASA (President of the Republic), Lupando MWAPE (Vice President of the Republic), Samuel MIYANDA (Secretary General).

Other Legislative Parties

In advance of the September 2006 presidential election, three legislative parties—the UPND, UNIP, and FDD—formed the **United Democratic Alliance** (UDA), with the leader of each party serving as co-president.

United Party for National Development (UPND). Described as representing the interests of urbanized Zambians, the UPND was launched on December 1998 under the leadership of business leader Anderson Mazoka, who had recently left the MMD. The party quickly became a major opposition grouping, winning four of the six legislative by-elections it had contested as of mid-2000. Mazoka, running with the support of the NP (below), secured an official 26.76 percent of the vote in the 2001 presidential balloting, although his supporters charged he had actually won the election and challenged the results in court. Meanwhile, the UPND easily became the leading opposition party by securing 49 seats in the concurrent legislative balloting.

Following Mazoka's death in 2006, a rift developed in the party, with members from the Southern Province backing Mazoka's widow as successor while party officials approached ZCTU president Leonard HIKAUMBA over the party's acting president, Sakwiba SIKOTA. After the party's divisive and chaotic convention in July, in which Lusaka businessman Hakainde Hichilema was elected president, Sikota resigned (along with party vice president Robert SICHINGA and secretary general Logan SHEMENA), and he subsequently formed the United Liberal Party (below). Sikota blamed "tribalism and violence" for the party's election upheaval, though the election was declared fair by the Foundation for Democratic Process (FODEP). Sikota's departure reportedly left the party in disarray, with party vice president for economic and political affairs Patrick Chisanga trying to mend fences.

Leaders: Hakainde HICHILEMA (President), Patrick CHISANGA (Spokesperson).

United National Independence Party (UNIP). The UNIP was formed as a result of the 1958 withdrawal of Kenneth D. Kaunda, Simon M. Kapwepwe, and others from the preindependence African National Congress (ANC), led by Harry Nkumbula. The UNIP was banned by the British in March 1959, reconstituted the following October, and ruled Zambia from independence until October 1991.

On May 29, 1990, in announcing that the National Council had approved the holding of a referendum on multipartyism, President Kaunda stated that it would be "stupid" for the party not to explain to the public that approval of such a system would be equivalent to "courting national disaster." Nevertheless, at the 25th meeting of the UNIP National Council on September 24, 1990, Kaunda announced that referendum plans would be canceled and a multiparty constitution adopted prior to the 1991 poll.

At an extraordinary party congress held August 6–7, 1991, Kaunda faced a leadership challenge from businessman Enoch Kavindele; however, under pressure from party stalwarts, Kavindele withdrew his bid, and Kaunda won unanimous reelection as party president. Thereafter, at nationwide balloting on October 31, both Kaunda and the UNIP suffered resounding defeats, the former capturing only 24 percent of the presidential vote and the latter being limited to 26 assembly seats. In the wake of his electoral defeat, Kaunda resigned as party leader on January 6, 1992, but reversed himself four months later.

Fueled by the defection of a number of party members to Kavindele's newly formed United

Democratic Party (UDP) and the UNIP's poor showing at local elections in November 1992, speculation mounted in early 1993 that Kebby Musoktwane, who had been elected party president at an extraordinary congress on October 1, would be supplanted by Maj. Wezi Kaunda, head of the UNIP's military wing and son of the former president. However, Wezi Kaunda, along with his two brothers, Tilyenji Kaunda and Panji KAUNDA, were among approximately 25 people, including 7 UNIP central committee members, arrested in March 1993 on charges stemming from an alleged coup plot. For its part, the party denied charges that it had planned to overthrow the Chiluba administration, with Musoktwane insisting that he had aided the government in exposing the plot.

In June 1993 former president Kaunda resigned from the party, citing a desire to become "father" to all Zambians and complaining that he had been denied a pension by the Chiluba government. In March 1994 approximately 85 members of the now defunct UDP rejoined the UNIP. (Prior to its dissolution in late 1993 UDP membership had been dominated by UNIP defectors.) In June 1994 the UNIP was instrumental in the formation of the Zambia Opposition Front (Zofro), an opposition umbrella organization that included the **Independent Democratic Front** (IDF), led by Mike KAIRA; the **Labour Party** (LP), led by Chipeza MUFUNE; the **National Democratic Alliance** (NDA), led by Yonam PHIRI (the NDA was reportedly deregistered in 1998); the **National Party for Democracy** (NPD), led by Tenthani MWANZA; and the **Zambia Progressive Party** (ZPP).

Although Kaunda's decision in May 1995 to return to political life was coolly received by Musoktwane and his youthful supporters, the former president encountered little difficulty in being reelected to the UNIP presidency on June 28. Kaunda continued to enjoy broad party support throughout 1995 and the first half of 1996 despite intensive government efforts to discredit him. However, in June 1996 former party secretary general Benjamin Mibenge called for an extraordinary UNIP congress to elect a new leader, asserting, according

to *Africa Confidential,* that it was time to break "the myth that Dr. Kaunda can forever lead the party." Meanwhile, the government arrested seven people (including Kaunda) with ties to the UNIP, charging them with complicity in a wave of bombings and bomb threats allegedly masterminded by a terrorist group called *Black Mamba,* Kaunda's nickname during Zambia's independence drive.

In early October 1996 Zofro announced it would back single candidates in the upcoming legislative balloting. Meanwhile, Kaunda declared his intention of running for president again despite the recent controversial amendment that appeared to have disqualified him. However, later in the month the UNIP announced plans to boycott the legislative balloting, citing what it described as the "mismanagement" of the voter registration drive and charging the government with manipulating the constitution. Furthermore, Kaunda asserted that the continued imprisonment of six prominent party members on treason charges had undermined the UNIP's electoral preparations. The charges were dropped on November 1. (Charges against Kaunda had been dismissed earlier.)

In April 1997 a simmering intraparty rivalry between Kaunda's supporters and members opposed to his continued domination exploded into public view as the two groups clashed at a UNIP function. Internecine concerns were subsequently overshadowed, however, by violent encounters between the UNIP and supporters of the Chiluba government. In June the UNIP and its opposition allies called for foreign intervention to ease the political and social "crisis" gripping Lusaka. Two months later Kaunda accused the government of attempting to assassinate him and Roger Chongwe, leader of the **Liberal Progressive Front** (LPF), a small party allied with the UNIP.

In January 1998 Kaunda was indicted by the government for his alleged role in the October 1997 coup attempt. The UNIP president was held under house arrest until June 1, when the government, under intense international pressure, dropped the charges. In June Kaunda said he would retire from the UNIP, although he agreed to serve as party president on an acting basis until his successor was elected. Subsequently, members of the UNIP's youth wing were reported to have rallied behind the succession ambitions of Wezi Kaunda. However, Wezi died in November 1999 after being attacked by gunmen in his driveway.

Kenneth Kaunda officially retired from the UNIP presidency at the beginning of an extraordinary congress in Ndola in May 2000. He was succeeded by Francis NKHOMA, a former central bank governor, although severe factionalization was subsequently still reported in the party, particularly in regard to the new president's positive comments about potential cooperation with the MMD, of which he had been a member from 1990 to 1994. Tilyenji Kaunda was elected to the UNIP presidency in April 2001 and won 9.96 percent of the votes in the December presidential election. In 2003 the UNIP announced it would cooperate with the ruling MMD, and UNIP legislators were appointed to junior cabinet posts.

Leaders: Tilyenji KAUNDA (President and 2001 presidential candidate), Njekwa ANAMELA (Vice President), Richard BANDA (Chair).

Forum for Democracy and Development (FDD). Reportedly enjoying support among students and other urban dwellers, the FDD was launched in 2001 by former MMD members opposed to efforts by President Chiluba to run for a third term. Party founders included Lt. Gen. Christon Tembo, who had been dismissed as vice president of the republic by Chiluba in May. Tembo finished third in the 2001 presidential balloting, securing 12.96 percent of the vote according to the official results. The FDD expelled four members in 2003 after they accepted cabinet posts in the MMD-led government. Several other FDD members subsequently left the party and joined the MMD. Former finance minister Edith Nawakwi was elected party president in 2005.

Leaders: Edith NAWAKWI (President), Lt. Gen. Christon S. TEMBO (2001 presidential candidate).

Heritage Party (HP). The HP was formed in 2001 by Brig. Gen. Godfrey Miyanda, a former MMD stalwart and former vice president of the republic, who had left the ruling party in the dispute over a proposed third term for President Chiluba. He rejected pressure to join with the FDD; subsequently, some FDD and MDD members reportedly defected to the party in 2001. Miyanda secured 7.96 percent of the vote in the 2001 presidential balloting, according to official results, and the party gained 4 seats in the legislative balloting.

Leader: Brig. Gen. Godfrey MIYANDA (2001 presidential candidate).

Zambia Republican Party (ZRP). The formation of the ZRP was announced in February 2001 as a merger of the Zambia Alliance for Progress (ZAP, see below), the Republican Party (RP), and the small National Republican Party.

The RP, with support centered in the copper belt, had been founded in mid-2000 by wealthy businessman Ben Mwila and a number of his supporters following their expulsion from the MMD. (Mwila had incurred the wrath of other MMD leaders by indicating a desire to run for president of the republic while a possible third term for President Chiluba was still under consideration.)

Both Mwila and Dean Mungomba of the ZAP announced their presidential ambitions prior to the creation of the ZRP, and friction quickly materialized between the two. Consequently, Mungomba announced that he and his supporters were withdrawing from the ZRP to resume ZAP activity, although a number of former ZAP members remained in the new grouping.

Mwila was officially credited with 4.84 percent of the vote as the ZRP candidate in the 2001 presidential poll. Among other things, the ZRP platform called for increased privatization of state-run enterprises and the extension of agricultural subsidies.

Leaders: Benjamin Yorum MWILA (President and 2001 presidential candidate), Ben KAPITA (Chair), Sylvia MACEBO (Secretary General).

Patriotic Front (PF). The PF was formed in 2001 by disgruntled former MMD members, including Michael Sata, who resigned as MMD secretary general in September to protest what he described as the irregular method of selection of Levy Mwanawasa as the MMD's standard-bearer. Sata was credited with 3.35 percent of the vote in the 2001 presidential poll.

In 2005 Sata was tried for alleged espionage (unresolved as of mid-2006), and in 2006 Sata and party secretary general Guy Scott were charged with defaming the president after Sata allegedly leaked a letter written by President Mwanawasa. Sata claimed the letter was a forgery and a "trap."

Leader: Michael SATA (President and 2001 presidential candidate), Guy SCOTT (Secretary General).

Other Parties Participating in the 2001 Elections

Agenda for Zambia (AZ). The agenda was launched in October 1996 by Akashambatwa Mbikusita Lewanika and his sister, Inonge, the NP's former secretary general and interim chair, respectively. Although the group reportedly fielded fewer than six candidates at legislative polling in November, it captured two formerly MMD-held seats. For his part, Lewanika finished fourth in presidential balloting.

In late 1998 the agenda asserted its support for separatists operating in the Caprivi Strip region of Namibia. In a related matter, the AZ also supports self-rule for "Barotseland" in southwestern Zambia (see BPF, below).

After receiving only 0.56 percent of the vote in the 2001 presidential balloting, Inonge Mbikusita Lewanika disbanded the party and joined the MMD. In 2003 she was appointed Zambia's ambassador to the United States after having served as special envoy to the AU.

Leaders: Akashambatwa   Mbikusita LEWANIKA (1996 presidential candidate), Inonge Mbikusita LEWANIKA (2001 presidential candidate).

Social Democratic Party (SDP). The SDP was formed in mid-2000 under the leadership of former diplomat Gwendoline Konie with the goal of addressing issues of special importance to women and young people. Konie, one of the first women to lead a Zambian party, won 0.58 percent of the vote in the 2001 presidential poll. She retired from pol-

itics in 2005 after establishing a nongovernment organization to help women in the prevention of HIV/AIDS.

Leader: Gwendoline KONIE (President and 2001 presidential candidate).

National Leadership for Development (NLD). The NLD was launched in mid-2001 by Yobert Shamapande, a former UN official and relative newcomer to domestic politics. Running on a platform that emphasized education, poverty reduction, gender balance in government, and better health services, Shamapande won 0.54 percent of the vote in the 2001 presidential balloting. Thereafter, Shamapande pledged his support to President Mwanawasa's policies.

Leader: Yobert SHAMAPANDE (President and 2001 presidential candidate).

Zambia Alliance for Progress (ZAP). The ZAP was formally launched in June 1999 by the Zambia Democratic Congress (Zadeco), the National Lima Party (NLP), and a nonparty organization called the National Pressure Group, although it had initially been perceived as a much larger opposition grouping. However, parties such as the AZ, NP, LP, and NCC ultimately declined to join the ZAP, which would have required dissolution of those parties as distinct entities, and, for the AZ and NP, loss of their parliamentary seats.

Zadeco was formed in mid-1995 by several former MMD members of parliament and more than 80 cadres from Kabwata and Kanyama constituencies, who expressed their disillusionment with the parent party. In early 1996 Zadeco leaders reportedly alienated a number of supporters when they issued a handpicked candidate list, thus dashing expectations of intraparty polling. Thereafter, Zadeco president Dean Mungomba was described as at the "forefront" of opposition activists threatening unrest if the Chiluba government remained in office after its mandate expired on October 31, 1996. Mungomba won 12 percent of the votes in the 1996 presidential poll, while Zadeco secured two seats in the concurrent legislative balloting.

Suspected of having played a role in the abortive October 1997 coup, Mungomba was imprisoned and reportedly beaten by government security forces; meanwhile, Zadeco's secretary general, Azwell Banda, fled to Zimbabwe. Thereafter, Zadeco called for international intervention to ease the tensions gripping Lusaka.

In April 1998 a Zadeco faction led by Eden JERRY and Don CHISANDO broke from the group and formed the **Zambia Democratic Congress–Popular Front** (Zadeco-PF), which its founders asserted was based on the same principles as Zadeco, but without the "undemocratic" leadership. Meanwhile, Mungomba remained imprisoned until December 1998, when the charges against him were dropped.

The NLP had been launched on August 11, 1996 by Guy Scott, a former agriculture minister and MMD parliamentarian (later of the PF), and Ben Kapita, the president of the Zambian National Union of Farmers. At legislative balloting in November, NLP candidates, campaigning on a platform calling for protection of Zambian farmers from foreign competitors, secured 6.6 percent of the vote but no seats.

The first ZAP general congress in July 2000 selected Mungomba as the party's candidate for the 2001 presidential contest. However, Mungomba subsequently participated in the creation of the ZRP in February 2001, apparently with the hope of securing the new grouping's nomination. After withdrawing from the ZRP several months later, Mungomba continued to present himself as the ZAP presidential candidate before leaving the race in October. By that time critics described the rump ZAP as a "one-man show," and the party secured less than 0.2 percent of the votes in the legislative balloting.

After Mungomba's death in 2005, Zadeco secretary general Langton SICHONE said the party would disband. In 2006, however, Zadeco was still active, though divided by a rift between Sichone (who was reportedly expelled) and leader Dan Pule.

Leader: Dan PULE (President).

National Party (NP). The NP was launched on August 16, 1993, by MMD defectors, including prominent party officials and legislators, who had become disenchanted with the Chiluba administration's apparent unwillingness to combat cabinet-level corruption and drug trafficking. Soon thereafter, former UNIP deputy secretary general Kennedy Shepande joined the new grouping, raising NP hopes of a possible alliance with other UNIP elements.

Pledging to be a "receptive and listening party," the NP appointed Inonge Mbikusita Lewanika interim chair, making her Zambia's first female political party leader. However, in October 1996 the party announced that Lewanika and her brother, Akashambatwa Mbikusita Lewanika, theretofore NP secretary general, had left the party to form the Agenda for Zambia (above). Meanwhile, party leader Humphrey MULEMBA called on President Chiluba to develop a "dialogue" with opposition parties to address electoral grievances. In early 1997 the NP called for an independent inquiry into what it asserted were the suspicious circumstances surrounding the recent deaths of three party leaders.

In October 1998 the NP suspended three of its assemblymen after they voiced support for the presidential candidacy of Anderson Mazoka, a party member and business leader who had continued to seek backing for his electoral ambitions despite the party's decision to forward its secretary general, Ludwig SONDASHI. Subsequently, Mazoka broke from the NP and formed the UPND (above), although the NP and UPND announced an electoral pact in 2000.

NP President Daniel LISULO, a former prime minister and UNIP stalwart under President Kaunda, died in August 2000. (Lisulo had briefly organized a United Democratic Congress Party [UDCP] in the early 1990s before joining the MMD and then joining other MMD defectors to the NP. He had succeeded Mulemba as NP leader upon Mulemba's death in February 1998.)

Zambia United Development Party (ZUDP). The ZUDP was launched in 2001 by businessman Wilson Mukupa as a grouping dedicated to antipoverty efforts. The ZUDP presented candidates, without success, in the 2001 local elections.

Leader: Wilson MUKUPA.

Other Parties and Groups

An alliance of smaller parties, styled as the **National Democratic Front** (NDF), formed prior to the 2006 presidential election. The NDF included the **All People's Congress** (APC); the Party for Unity, Democracy, and Development (PUDD); the Zambia Democratic Congress (Zadeco); the Reform Party (RP); and the ZRP. The APC, led by Kenny NGONDO, later withdrew over a dispute with alliance leader, former vice president of the republic Nevers Mumba. The **Zambia Direct Democracy Movement** (ZDDM), led by Edwin SAKALA, later was reported to have joined the alliance.

Party for Unity, Democracy, and Development (PUDD). The PUDD was formed in September 2004 by former members of the MMD who supported former President Frederick Chiluba. It also attracted dissident members of the PF who opposed the party's leader, Michael Sata. Former party leader Dan PULE led a cadre of defectors to Zadeco in 2005. Subsequently, former MMD national chair Chitalu Sampa became interim leader of PUDD. The party sought to draw disaffected political figures into a new coalition ahead of the 2006 legislative elections, and though there was speculation that Chiluba might use the new party to challenge President Mwanawasa in the 2006 presidential election, Chiluba's health and legal problems (see Current issues, above) cast doubt on his candidacy.

Leaders: Chitalu SAMPA (President), Josiah CHISHALA (National Chair).

Reform Party (RP). The Reform Party was founded in 2005 by supporters of former vice president of the republic Nevers Mumba after he was expelled from the MDD. (He reportedly had planned to challenge President Mwanawasa for the party presidency.) Mumba said he would be the Reform Party candidate in the 2006 presidential election.

Leader: Nevers MUMBA.

United Liberal Party. Former UPND acting president Sakwiba Sikota formed the United Liberal Party in July 2006 after his failed bid to become UPND president. He broke away with several other senior officials of UPND, accusing the latter party of corruption and tribalism. Many of his supporters were reported to be from his home Western Province.

Leader: Sakwiba SIKOTA.

Barotse Patriotic Front (BPF). References to the BPF first appeared in 1998 in regard to calls for independence or autonomy for a portion of western Zambia that had, along with regions in what are now Namibia and Botswana, been known as Barotseland. That kingdom of Lozi-speakers had enjoyed what one journalist called "half-independence" under British colonial rule. The area in Zambia became part of that country at independence in 1964 under an autonomy agreement with the UNIP under which the tribal chieftain was to retain significant powers, particularly in regard to control of land and resources. Lozi leaders subsequently claimed that UNIP had abrogated the agreement by stripping the chief of many of his powers.

The BPF in 1999 supported the secessionist activities of the Caprivi Liberation Front, which represents Lozi-speakers in Namibia (see Illegal Groups in article on Namibia for details). The BPF also called for a self-determination vote in western Zambia, prompting the detention of BPF leader Imasiku Mutangelwa on sedition charges. The BPF has acted in concert with a Barotse Cultural Association, while a Forum for the Restoration of Barotseland in July 2001 petitioned the OAU and the UN to conduct a self-determination referendum. In 2004 the BPF renewed its call to restore the name Barotseland to the Western Province and for the constitution of Zambia to uphold the 1964 agreement.

Leaders: Imasiku MUTANGELWA (President), Pumulo YUSIKU (Executive Secretary).

Minor parties include the **Democratic Party** (DP), led by businessman Emmanuel MWAMBA; the **Progressive Parties Alliance**, led by Paul BANDA; the **Unity Party for Democrats** (UPD), led by Matthew PIKITI; the **Zambia Democratic Party** (ZDP), led by Susan JERE; the **Zambia Progressive Party** (ZPP), led by Ambran ZAPU; and the **Zambia United Development Party,** led by Wilson MUKUPA.

Cabinet

As of August 1, 2006

President	Levy Patrick Mwanawasa
Vice President	Lupando Mwape

Ministers

Agriculture and Cooperatives	Mundia Sikatana
Commerce, Trade, and Industry	Dipak Patel
Communications and Transport	Abel Chambeshi
Community Development and Social Services	Steven Manjata
Defense	Wamundila Muliyokela
Education	Brian Chituwo
Energy and Water Development	Felix Mutati
Finance and National Planning	Ngandu Magande
Foreign Affairs	Lt. Gen. Ronnie Shikapwasha
Health	Sylvia Masebo [f]
Home Affairs	Bates Namuyamba
Information and Broadcasting	Vernon Mwaanga
Labor and Social Security	Mutale Nalumango [f]
Lands	Rev. Gladys Nyirongo [f]
Legal Affairs	George Kunda
Local Government and Housing	Andrew Mulenga
Mines and Mineral Development	Kalombo Mwansa
Science, Technology, and Vocational Training	Judith Kapijimpanga [f]
Sport, Youth, and Child Development	George Chulumanda
Tourism, Environment, and Natural Resources	Kabinga Pande
Works and Supply	Marina Nsingo [f]

[f] = female

Legislature

The current **National Assembly** is a unicameral body consisting of 150 elected members, 8 presidentially appointed members, and the speaker, who is elected by the members of the assembly from outside their membership. The term of office is five years. Prior to the 1991 election candidates were required to be members of the United National Independence Party (UNIP) and endorsed by that party's Central Committee. The most recent elections were held on December 27, 2001, with the Zambia Electoral Commission reporting the following distribution of elected seats: the Movement for Multiparty Democracy, 69; the United Party for National Development, 49; UNIP, 13; the Forum for Democracy and Development, 12; the Heritage Party, 4; the Zambia Republican Party and the Patriotic Front, 1 each; and independents, 1. (*See headnote.*)

Speaker: Amusaa K. MWANAMWAMBWA.

Communications

Prior to its electoral defeat in October 1991, the UNIP exercised rigid control over the news media. Since then, a flourishing, essentially free press has emerged.

Press

In April 1980, following publication in the *Times of Zambia* of an article critical of the government, President Kaunda warned that press freedoms might be curtailed. Subsequently, on October 1, 1982, the *Times,* which had long been dominated by the UNIP, was acquired outright from the British conglomerate Lonrho. The following are English-language newspapers published in Lusaka: *National Mirror* (40,000), Catholic weekly; *Zambia Daily Mail* (40,000), government owned; *Weekly Post* (40,000), influential independent, launched in July 1991; *Times of Zambia* (32,000 daily, 44,200 Sunday), government owned; *The People,* independent weekly.

In 1998 a number of *Weekly Post* staff members were arrested after their paper reported that the Zambian military would be incapable of fending off an Angolan invasion.

News Agencies

The Zambia News Agency (Zana) is the domestic facility; *Agence France-Presse, Deutsche Presse-Agentur,* and Reuters are among the foreign agencies maintaining bureaus in Lusaka.

Broadcasting and Computing

The government-supervised Zambia National Broadcasting Corporation (ZNBC) controls both radio and television. Radio Zambia transmits in English and seven Zambian languages, while Television-Zambia provides programming for approximately 323,000 television receivers. There were some 95,000 personal computers serving 68,200 Internet users in 2003.

Intergovernmental Representation

Ambassador to the U.S.
Inonge Mbikusita LEWANIKA

U.S. Ambassador to Zambia
Carmen Maria MARTINEZ

Permanent Representative to the UN
Tens C. KAPOMA

IGO Memberships (Non-UN)
AfDB, AU, BADEA, Comesa, CWTH, Interpol, IOM, NAM, PCA, SADC, WCO, WTO

ZIMBABWE

REPUBLIC OF ZIMBABWE

The Country

Bordered by Botswana, Zambia, Mozambique, and South Africa, Zimbabwe occupies the fertile plateaus and mountain ranges between southeastern Africa's Zambezi and Limpopo rivers. The population includes approximately 12 million Africans, mainly Bantu in origin; some 200,000 Europeans; and smaller groups of Asians and people of mixed race. The Africans may be classified into two multitribal groupings, the Shona (about 75 percent) in the north and the Ndebele, concentrated in the southern area of Matabeleland. Shona-Ndebele rivalry dates to the 19th century and has contributed to a pronounced north-south cleavage. The majority of the European population is Protestant, although there is a substantial Catholic minority; the Africans include both Christians and followers of traditional religions; the Asians are a mixture of Hindus and Muslims.

In 1982 a Legal Age of Majority Act significantly enhanced the legal status of women (including the right of personal choice in selecting a marital partner, the right to own property outright, and the ability to enter into business contracts); it has, however, been unevenly utilized because of its conflict with traditional law. In 1996 about 44 percent of the paid labor force was estimated to be female; black women are responsible for most subsistence agriculture (cash-crop production had been undertaken mainly by some 4,500 white farmers who at one time owned more than 70 percent of the arable land); white and Asian women are concentrated in the clerical and service sectors.

Zimbabwe is well endowed with natural resources that have yielded a relatively advanced economy oriented toward foreign trade (to which tobacco is a large contributor). The country exports asbestos, chrome, copper, and other mineral products to a wide variety of foreign markets, while agricultural self-sufficiency, until recently, has permitted export of maize and other food crops to shortage-plagued neighbors. Although international trade sanctions were imposed on Zimbabwe (then Rhodesia) from 1965 to 1979, its economy prospered for much of the period because of continued access to trade routes through Mozambique (until 1976) and South Africa, which became the conduit for up to 90 percent of Rhodesian imports and exports. The lifting of sanctions at the end of 1979 further stimulated the economy, although drought and falling commodity prices subsequently contributed to fiscal difficulties, including budget deficits and persistent inflation. In

Political Status: Became self-governing British Colony of Southern Rhodesia in October 1923; unilaterally declared independence November 11, 1965; white-dominated republican regime proclaimed March 2, 1970; biracial executive established on basis of transitional government agreement of March 3, 1978; returned to interim British rule on basis of cease-fire agreement signed December 21, 1979; achieved de jure independence as Republic of Zimbabwe on April 18, 1980.

Area: 150,803 sq. mi. (390,580 sq. km.).

Population: 11,631,657 (2002C); 13,004,000 (2005E). The 2002 figure appears to involve substantial underenumeration.

Major Urban Center (including suburbs, 2005E): HARARE (formerly Salisbury, 1,527,000).

Official Language: English (Shona and Sindebele are the principal African languages).

Monetary Unit: Zimbabwe dollar (official rate, July 1, 2006: 101,196 dollars = $1US).

President: Robert Gabriel MUGABE (Zimbabwe African National Union–Patriotic Front); sworn in as prime minister on April 18, 1980, following legislative election of February 14 and 27–29; reconfirmed following election of June 30 and July 1–2, 1985; elected president by parliament on December 30, 1987, and inaugurated for an anticipated six-year term on December 31, succeeding the former head of state, Rev. Canaan Sodindo BANANA; reelected for a six-year term, following constitutional revision, by popular vote March 28–30, 1990; reelected for another six-year term March 16–17, 1996; reelected for another six-year term March 9–11, 2002.

Vice President: Joseph MSIKA (Zimbabwe African National Union–Patriotic Front); appointed by the president on December 21, 1999, in succession to Joshua Mqabuko NKOMO (Zimbabwe African National Union–Patriotic Front), who died on July 1; reappointed following election of March 2002.

Vice President: Joyce MUJURU (Zimbabwe National Union–Patriotic Front); appointed by the president on December 6, 2004, to succeed Simon MUZENDA, who died in 2003.

addition, unemployment was aggravated by a growing pool of workers seeking better jobs as the result of rapid educational advances for blacks. The government consequently relaxed its control of the economy in favor of private business, industry, and agriculture, while an accelerated rate of disinvestment by foreign companies prompted revision of the country's investment guidelines.

In September 1995 the International Monetary Fund (IMF) announced the nonrenewal of loans for balance-of-payments support for six months in the wake of what were viewed as unacceptable projections of deficit reduction in the 1995–1996 budget. Following President Robert MUGABE's reelection in March 1996 the Zimbabwean business community lobbied the administration to enact the reforms sought by international lenders, including military and civil service budget cuts.

Zimbabwe continues to suffer gravely from severe deterioration of economic, social, and political conditions, in part due to controversy surrounding the government's land redistribution program (see Political background and also Current issues, below). The government has also been buffeted by allegations of corruption and broad mismanagement of the economy, marked by a bloated and inefficient civil service, massive budget deficits, and a soaring inflation rate. Poverty was widespread, and the rate of adults with HIV was 25 percent (though that figure was reported to have declined by 2006).

Real GDP declined by 8.2 percent in 2004 and by 7.2 percent in 2005, while inflation ballooned to a record 620 percent in 2004, then dropped to around 400 percent by the end of 2005. Further exacerbating the faltering economic situation, Zimbabwe was nearly forced to withdraw from the IMF in 2005 because it owed $175 million in arrears. In early 2006, however, following a payment of $9 million, Zimbabwe avoided expulsion but lost its IMF voting rights and access to general resources of the fund. Despite calls for reforms by the IMF and the UN, the government refused help or intervention. By April 2006 conditions grew more dire as the country's inflation rate hit 1,042.9 percent, among the highest in the world; millions of people were said to be suffering from food shortages;

and the infant mortality rate was also reported as likely the highest in the world. The government devalued the currency and subsequently introduced emergency reforms, issuing new currency in August and seizing cash from citizens and businesses in an effort to curtail black market trade.

Government and Politics

Political Background

Originally developed and administered by the British South Africa Company, Southern Rhodesia became an internally self-governing British colony in 1923 under a system that concentrated political power in the hands of its white minority. In 1953 it joined with Northern Rhodesia (now Zambia) and Nyasaland (now Malawi) in the so-called Federation of Rhodesia and Nyasaland. However, Southern Rhodesia reverted to separate status in 1963 when the federation was dissolved and Northern Rhodesia and Nyasaland prepared to claim their independence. A new constitution granted to Southern Rhodesia by Britain in December 1961 conferred increased powers of self-government and contained various provisions for the benefit of the African population, including a right of limited representation in the Legislative Assembly. However, the measure failed to resolve a sharpening conflict between African demands for full political equality based on the principle of "one-person, one-vote" and white Rhodesian demands for permanent white control.

In view of the refusal of Britain to agree to independence on terms that would exclude majority rule, the colonial government under Prime Minister Ian D. SMITH on November 11, 1965, issued a Unilateral Declaration of Independence purporting to make Rhodesia an independent state within the Commonwealth, loyal to the queen but free of external constraints. Britain repudiated the action, declared the colony to be in a state of rebellion, and invoked financial and economic sanctions; however, it refused to use force against the Smith regime. British Prime Minister Harold Wilson met personally with Smith in December 1966, after which

UN sanctions were imposed, and again in October 1968, but no agreement was reached.

Rhodesia approved a new constitution on June 20, 1969, declaring itself a republic; subsequently, Britain suspended formal ties with the separatist regime. However, further British initiatives under Conservative leadership resulted in a set of proposals for settlement of the dispute in November 1971. These proposals were declared unacceptable by independent African leaders at the United Nations, and they were dropped in May 1972 after a 15-member British commission under Lord PEARCE found them equally unacceptable to the majority of Rhodesia's African population.

On December 8, 1974, an agreement was concluded in Lusaka, Zambia, by Bishop Abel MUZOREWA of the African National Council (ANC), Joshua NKOMO of the Zimbabwe African People's Union (ZAPU), Ndabaningi SITHOLE of the Zimbabwe African National Union (ZANU), and James CHIKEREMA of the Front for the Liberation of Zimbabwe (Frolizi), whereby the latter three, representing groups that had been declared illegal within Rhodesia, would join an enlarged ANC executive under Bishop Muzorewa's presidency for a period of four months to prepare for negotiations with the Smith regime aimed at transferring power to the majority. Three days later Prime Minister Smith announced that, upon the receipt of assurances that insurgents within Rhodesia would observe a cease-fire, all black political prisoners would be released and a constitutional conference would be held without preconditions. On December 15, however, Smith again reiterated his government's opposition to the principle of majority rule.

In March 1975 Sithole, who had returned to Salisbury in December, was arrested by Rhodesian authorities on charges of plotting to assassinate his rivals in order to assume the ANC leadership. He was released a month later, following the intervention of Prime Minister Vorster of South Africa. A few days earlier the Zambian government had announced that the Lusaka offices of ZANU, ZAPU, and Frolizi would be closed in accordance with its interpretation of the December 1974 agreement and the subsequent recognition of the ANC by the Organization of African Unity (OAU, subsequently the African Union—AU). ZANU spokesmen responded by charging that the presidents of Botswana, Tanzania, and Zambia had secretly agreed at the December talks to reconstitute the ANC leadership under the presidency of Nkomo without consulting Rhodesian African leaders.

During an ANC executive committee meeting in Salisbury on June 1, 1975, fighting broke out between ZANU and ZAPU representatives, and ZANU announced that it would not send delegates to an ANC congress scheduled for June 21–22. Frolizi also indicated that it would be unrepresented because the government had refused to grant its delegates an amnesty to return to Rhodesia. On June 16 Bishop Muzorewa announced that the proposed congress would not take place "due to serious administrative and other extreme difficulties."

Following an inconclusive meeting in Victoria Falls held August 25–26, 1975, by the leaders of Rhodesia, South Africa, Zambia, and the ANC, the Nkomo faction, meeting in Salisbury on September 27–28, elected Nkomo president of the ANC within Rhodesia. On December 1 Nkomo and Prime Minister Smith concluded a series of meetings by signing a Declaration of Intention to Negotiate a Settlement of the Rhodesian issue. Under the agreement, which was repudiated by external ANC leader Bishop Muzorewa (then resident in Zambia) and by ZANU leader Sithole, all members of the ANC negotiating team were guaranteed freedom to enter Rhodesia to attend the projected talks.

Early 1976 witnessed an intensification of guerrilla activity by Mozambique-based insurgents under the leadership of former ZANU secretary general Robert MUGABE, the closing of the Mozambique border on March 3, and a breakdown in the talks between Nkomo and Smith on March 19. In early September it was reported that South African Prime Minister Vorster had agreed to a U.S.-British offer to provide upwards of $2 billion in financial guarantees to Rhodesia's white settlers, contingent upon Salisbury's acceptance of majority rule. Prime Minister Smith subsequently announced that he had accepted a comprehensive package tendered by U.S. Secretary of State Henry Kissinger in a meeting on September 19 in Pretoria, South Africa, that called for a biracial interim government and the establishment of majority rule within two years. Britain responded to the Kissinger-Smith accord by convening a conference in Geneva between a white delegation led by Smith and a black delegation that included Nkomo, Mugabe, Muzorewa, and Sithole. However, the conference, which ran from October 28 to December 14, failed to yield a settlement, with the black leaders rejecting the essentials of the Kissinger plan by calling for an immediate transfer to majority rule and the replacement of the all-white Rhodesian army by contingents of the nationalist guerrilla forces. Alternative proposals advanced by the black leadership pointed up major differences among the various factions. Mugabe and Nkomo demanded a British presence in Rhodesia (rejected by Sithole) while refusing to accept Sithole's and Muzorewa's proposals for an election prior to the transfer of power. Earlier, on September 9, Sithole had announced the withdrawal of ZANU from the ANC, which since its formation in December 1974 had been split into two wings led by Bishop Muzorewa and ZAPU leader Nkomo. Collaterally, Mugabe claimed the leadership of ZANU, while the Sithole group within Rhodesia became known as ANC-Sithole and the Muzorewa group as the United African National Council (UANC).

In September 1976 Mugabe called for a unified military command of all guerrilla forces, and on October 9 he announced the formation of a Patriotic Front (PF) linking ZANU and ZAPU units. Although subsequently endorsed by the OAU and the front-line states—Angola, Botswana, Mozambique, Tanzania, and Zambia—the PF failed to achieve full integration because of the Soviet orientation of ZAPU, many of whose recruits had been trained by Cubans in Angola, and the Chinese orientation of ZANU, most of whose recruits had been trained in Tanzania. To complicate matters further, a dissident ZANU group withdrew its cadres from Mugabe's leadership on October 11 and formally redesignated Sithole as party president;

however, Sithole and Muzorewa continued to assume a relatively moderate posture during 1977, engaging in sporadic negotiations with the Smith regime, while Nkomo and Mugabe constituted the core of a more radical external leadership.

In January 1977 three moderate white groups—the Rhodesian Party, the Centre Party, and the National Pledge Association—created the National Unifying Force to campaign for the effective removal of discriminatory legislation and a meaningful accord with the black majority. However, more crucial pressure was exerted by rightist elements within the ruling Rhodesian Front (RF) following the front's decision in March to liberalize constitutional provisions regarding land tenure. The dissidents were expelled from the RF on April 29 and organized themselves as the Rhodesian Action Party (RAP) on July 4. Since the RF thus lost the majority required for constitutional amendment, a new election was called for August 31, at which the front regained all 50 seats on the European roll.

During 1977 a number of British proposals were advanced in hopes of resolving the impasse on interim rule. In January, concurrent with an announcement that resumption of the Geneva discussions would be indefinitely postponed, Ivor RICHARD, British representative to the UN and chair of the Geneva Conference, called for the appointment of a British resident commissioner in Salisbury who would play a balancing role in the negotiations with "a great deal of constitutional power." He further proposed an interim Rhodesian Council embracing 20 blacks (5 from each of the leading nationalist factions) and 10 whites (5 British and 5 Rhodesian). The proposal was immediately rejected by Prime Minister Smith, who conveyed his government's opposition to any form of British presence. In September, however, a revised version of the proposal was endorsed by the UN Security Council. Under the new plan, a British resident commissioner (Field Marshal Lord CARVER) would be appointed for a period of six months, during which arrangements would be made for a new constitution and a one-person, one-vote general election. The plan also called for the creation of a new Rhodesian army containing mixed black-white

units and the appointment of a UN special representative (Indian Lt. Gen. Prem CHAND, former commander of the UN Force in Cyprus, who was named to the new post on October 4). While the initial reaction by all parties was encouraging, both Nkomo and Mugabe subsequently insisted that transitional control be exercised by the PF rather than by the British commissioner. The change in attitude was occasioned largely by a dispute regarding the timing of a general election, PF leaders insisting, because of Bishop Muzorewa's apparent widespread popularity, that the election be deferred for as long as three years after independence. Subsequently, Prime Minister Smith declared that the British settlement plan had failed and resumed discussions, based on a revision of the earlier Kissinger package, with Muzorewa and Sithole. In December Nkomo declared that front leaders would not join the "fake so-called internal settlement talks by Smith and his puppets."

Despite the intransigence of the PF, an agreement was reached on March 3, 1978, by Smith, Muzorewa, Sithole, and Mashona Chief Jeremiah S. CHIRAU of the Zimbabwe United People's Organization (ZUPO) to form a transitional government that would lead to black rule by the end of the year. Accordingly, an Executive Council comprising the four was established on March 21, while a multiracial Ministerial Council to replace the existing cabinet was designated on April 12. On May 16 the Executive Council released preliminary details of a new constitution that would feature a titular president elected by parliament sitting as an electoral college. In the face of escalating guerrilla activity, however, the existing House of Assembly voted on June 26—despite the unanimous objection of its black members—to renew the state of emergency that had been in effect since 1965 for another year. More importantly, although all racial discrimination was formally abolished on October 10, the projected national election was postponed in early November, following the failure of a renewed effort to convene an all-party conference, until April 1979.

A new constitution was approved by the assembly on January 20, 1979, and endorsed by 84 percent of the white voters in a referendum on January 30. Although condemned by the UN Security Council by a 12–0 vote (with 3 abstentions) on March 8, a lower-house election was held on April 10 and 17–20 for 20 white and 72 black members, respectively, at which the UANC won 51 seats in the face of a boycott by the PF parties. Following a Senate election on May 23, Josiah GUMEDE of the UANC was elected president of Zimbabwe/Rhodesia, and on May 29 he requested Bishop Muzorewa to accept appointment as prime minister.

On June 7, 1979, U.S. President Carter rejected an appeal for recognition of the new government, expressing doubt that the election had been either free or fair since "the black citizens . . . never had a chance to consider or to vote against the Constitution," while the white minority retained control of the police, the army, the justice system, and the civil service. Earlier, the newly appointed British prime minister, Margaret Thatcher, had stated that responsibility for deciding on the legality of the Muzorewa government lay with the UK parliament, although Foreign and Commonwealth Secretary Lord Carrington argued in the House of Lords that it would be "morally wrong to brush aside an election in which 64 percent of the people of Rhodesia cast their vote."

Following renewed guerrilla activity by PF forces in mid-1979, British and other Commonwealth leaders issued a call for talks between representatives of the Muzorewa government and the Patriotic Front. The discussions, which commenced on September 10 and ran for 14 weeks, yielded a cease-fire agreement on December 5 that called for Britain to reassume full administrative authority for an interim period, during which a new and carefully monitored election would be held as a prelude to the granting of legal independence. On December 7 the terms of the agreement (which was not formally signed by the principals until December 21) were approved by parliament, and Lord SOAMES was appointed colonial governor, with Sir Anthony DUFF as his deputy. On December 12 Lord Soames arrived in Salisbury, where he was welcomed by members of the former government of Zimbabwe/Rhodesia, who, one day earlier, had approved a parliamentary bill terminating the Unilateral Declaration of Independence and transferring authority to the British administration.

White and common roll elections were held in February 1980, the Rhodesian Front winning all 20 white seats and Mugabe's ZANU-PF winning a substantial overall majority in the House of Assembly. Accordingly, Mugabe was asked by Lord Soames on March 4 to form a cabinet that included 16 members of ZANU-PF, 4 members of Nkomo's Patriotic Front–ZAPU, and 2 members of the RF. The new government was installed during independence day ceremonies on April 18 following the inauguration of Rev. Canaan Sodindo BANANA, a Mugabe supporter, as president of the republic.

The period immediately after independence was characterized by persistent conflict between armed forces of ZANU-PF and PF-ZAPU (units of Mugabe's Zimbabwe African National Liberation Army [ZANLA] and Nkomo's Zimbabwe People's Revolutionary Army [ZIPRA], respectively). To some extent the difficulties were rooted in tribal loyalties, with most ZANLA personnel having been recruited from the northern Shona group, while ZIPRA had recruited primarily from the Ndebele people of Matabeleland. During 1981 the level of overt violence subsided, the government announcing in November that merger of the two guerrilla organizations and the former Rhodesian security force into a 50,000-man Zimbabwean national army had been completed. However, personal animosity between Mugabe and Nkomo continued, threatening the viability of the coalition regime. On February 17, 1982, Nkomo and three other ZAPU government members were dismissed in a major cabinet reorganization, Nkomo declaring that his group should thenceforth be construed as an opposition party. By 1984 violence on the part of dissident Nkomo supporters had produced major confrontations with government forces in Matabeleland, while defections from Ian Smith's party, renamed the Conservative Alliance of Zimbabwe (CAZ), had reduced its strength in the assembly to seven.

After a series of postponements attributed to a need to redraw electoral districts and prepare new voter lists, the first postindependence legislative elections were held in mid-1985. Smith's CAZ rallied to regain 15 of the 20 white seats on June 27, while in common roll balloting held July 1–4, Mugabe's ZANU-PF won all but 1 of the non-Matabeleland constituencies, raising its assembly strength to 64 as contrasted with ZAPU's 15. Although the results fell short of the mandate desired by Mugabe for introduction of a one-party state, ZAPU members, including Nkomo, responded to overtures for merger talks, which eventually yielded an agreement on December 22, 1987, whereby the two parties would merge, with Nkomo becoming one of two ZANU-PF vice presidents. Three months earlier, following expiration of a constitutionally mandated seven-year entrenchment, the white seats in both houses of parliament had been vacated and refilled on a "non-constituency" basis by the assembly. On December 31 Mugabe, having secured unanimous assembly endorsement the day before, was sworn in as executive president; concurrently, Simon MUZENDA was inaugurated as vice president, with the post of prime minister being eliminated.

The Senate was abolished as of the balloting of March 28–30, 1990, at which Mugabe won 78 percent of the presidential vote and ZANU-PF swept all but four seats in the House of Assembly. Following the election, a second vice presidency was established by constitutional amendment, with Nkomo being named to the post.

On May 1, 1993, the government released a list of 70 farms, encompassing approximately 470,000 acres, which it planned to purchase for redistribution under authority of the 1992 Land Acquisition Act. Subsequently, the powerful Commercial Farmers' Union (CFU), representing approximately 4,000 white farmers, denounced the government for violating its pledge to buy only "derelict and underutilized" properties. Furthermore, Western donors reportedly warned the Mugabe administration that it risked suspension of aid payments if it followed through with its proposed acquisitions. In August the president responded that his government would seize the properties without compensation and expel "resistant" whites if domestic and "racist" foreign interference continued, and in September he dismissed a legal challenge to the Land Act as futile. However, following the revelation in early 1994 that a majority of the 98 parcels appropriated under the act had been granted to senior government officials and civil servants, Mugabe suspended the program in April.

At presidential balloting held March 16–17, 1996, President Mugabe captured a third term. The president's victory was tarnished, however, by the withdrawal of his only two competitors, Sithole and Muzorewa, during the week prior to balloting. Both men complained of being harassed by government security forces, and they charged that the electoral system unfairly favored the incumbent. Furthermore, voter turnout was reported to have been only 32 percent, the first polling since independence to attract less than 50 percent of the electorate. Thus, even with an official 92 percent vote share (Sithole's and Muzorewa's names remained on the ballot, and both garnered votes), Mugabe reportedly secured only 28.5 percent of the potential vote, far from the mandate for which he had campaigned.

ZANU-PF reportedly won most of the seats in local elections in August 1999, although low turnout again tarnished the results. Shortly thereafter, opposition forces coalesced as the Movement for Democratic Change (MDC), which lobbied strongly against the constitutional revision proposed by the government that, among other things, would have made Mugabe president for life, given him the power to dissolve parliament, and endorsed the administration's land redistribution program. Underscoring growing internal discontent, 55 percent of those voting in a national referendum held on February 12–13, 2000, rejected the proposed changes in the basic law.

ZANU-PF barely withstood an electoral challenge from the MDC in new assembly balloting held June 24–25, 2000, securing 62 of the 120 elective seats. Subsequently, in presidential balloting on March 9–11, 2002, Mugabe won another term, defeating Morgan TSVANGIRAI of the MDC 56 to 42 percent, although the MDC, as it had with the legislative balloting, rejected the results as fraudulent. (A court ruling in 2006 rejected Tsvangirai's charge of voter fraud in the 2002 election.)

In the legislative elections of March 31, 2005, ZANU-PF made a strong recovery, winning 78 seats, which, coupled with its 30 appointive seats, gave the president's party a two-thirds majority. The MDC won 41 seats, and 1 seat went to an independent candidate. The president reshuffled the cabinet on April 15, 2005, moving house speaker Emmerson MNANGAGWA to a ministry post, among other changes. On August 30, 2005, the House of Assembly voted 103–29 to establish a new 66-member Senate (see Constitution and government, below), in addition to other constitutional amendments. In the first polling for 50 Senate seats on November 26, 2005, the ZANU-PF won 43 and the MDC won 7. Several other parties and independent candidates failed to win representation.

Constitution and Government

The constitution that issued from the 1979 London talks provided for a president designated for a six-year term by the (then) two houses of parliament sitting as an electoral college. Executive authority was vested in a cabinet headed, by a prime minister, with the appointment going to the person best able to command a legislative majority. However, in late 1987 the post of prime minister was abolished in favor of an executive presidency. The (then) unicameral legislature consisted of a 150-member House of Assembly, 120 of whom are popularly elected (see Legislature, below) for five-year terms. There is also an Advisory Council of Chiefs and an ombudsman, appointed by the president, to investigate complaints against actions by political authorities. The judicial system is headed by a High Court (with both general and appellate divisions) and includes magistrate courts at the local level. A national referendum in 2000 defeated proposed changes to enhance presidential authority (see Political background, above, for details).

Since 1980, the assembly has amended the constitution numerous times, most recently in August 2005, when it approved the establishment of an upper house, the Senate (see Legislature, below). Other constitutional amendments approved by the assembly in 2005 denied owners the right to appeal government expropriation of their land and empowered the government to confiscate passports, in the interest of national security, with no right to appeal.

The country is currently divided into ten provinces: West, Central, and East in Mashonaland; North and South in Matabeleland; Midlands; Manicaland; Masvingo; Harare; and Bulawayo (though the latter two are cities, they have provincial status). Each is headed by a centrally appointed provincial governor and serves, additionally, as an electoral district. Local government is conducted through town, district, and rural councils.

Foreign Relations

Zimbabwe became a member of the Commonwealth upon achieving de jure independence in April 1980; it was admitted to the OAU (subsequently the African Union—AU) the following July and to the United Nations in August. In January 1983 it was elected to a seat on the UN Security Council, where its representatives assumed a distinctly anti-American posture. The strain in relations with the United States culminated in 1986 with Washington's withdrawal of all aid in response to strongly worded attacks from Harare on U.S. policy regarding South Africa. Despite (then) Prime Minister Mugabe's refusal to apologize for the verbal onslaughts, the aid was resumed in August 1988.

In regional affairs, Harare occupied a leading position among the front-line states bordering South Africa, concluding a mutual security pact with Mozambique in late 1980 and hosting several meetings of the Southern African Development Coordination Conference (now the SADC). It also provided active support for the Maputo government's anti-insurgency campaign, with approximately 10,000 troops being stationed in Mozambique in 1986, primarily to defend the transport corridor to Beira on the Indian Ocean, which the front-line states viewed as crucial to diminish reliance on South African trade routes. In June 1988 Zimbabwe and Mozambique signed a military cooperation agreement aimed at containing the border activities of the rebel Mozambique National Resistance (Renamo). Nonetheless, news reports in January 1990 that some 60 Zimbabwean civilians had been killed by Renamo insurgents during the preceding six months, prompted Mugabe to extend state of emergency measures. In July Harare closed the border in an attempt to contain the unrest, while the Chissano government engaged in peace talks with Renamo. Thereafter, in compliance with a Chissano-Renamo accord, Zimbabwe on December 28 completed the withdrawal of its troops to defensive positions along Mozambique's trade routes, ceding control of previously held territory to Mozambique government forces. In April 1993, Harare withdrew its remaining troops.

The Zimbabwean government initially declined, for the sake of its own domestic "reconciliation," to provide bases for black nationalist attacks on South Africa. However, the antiapartheid African National Congress (ANC) continued to operate from Zimbabwean territory, its cross-border attacks yielding retaliatory incursions by South African troops into Zimbabwe.

In February 1997 Zimbabwe and South Africa signed a defense agreement; however, their ties were subsequently strained by what Harare asserted were unfair South African trade practices and Pretoria's crackdown on illegal Zimbabwean immigrants. In February 1998 Zimbabwe, South Africa, and Namibia signed an extradition treaty.

In mid-1998 President Mugabe dispatched troops to the Democratic Republic of the Congo (DRC) to shore up the presidency of Laurent Kabila, from whose administration Harare reportedly sought mining concessions. At the peak of the conflict, an estimated 12,000 Zimbabwean troops were in the DRC, President Mugabe also strongly endorsing the succession of Joseph Kabila to the DRC presidency after the death of Laurent Kabila in early 2001. The support from Zimbabwe was considered crucial to the lasting power of the DRC administration, although the economic drain on scarce Zimbabwean resources contributed to growing anti-Mugabe sentiment. The last contingent of Zimbabwean troops left the DRC in November 2002.

In 2005 Zimbabwe was reelected to the UN Human Rights Commission, drawing sharp criticism from Western countries, among others, citing Zimbabwe's appalling human rights record.

Zimbabwe increasingly turned to South Africa and to China for financial aid as economic conditions worsened (most Western donors had frozen aid after Mugabe enacted the controversial land redistribution program). South Africa loaned $470 million to bail Zimbabwe out of IMF and humanitarian crises in 2005, and China signed a $1.3 billion energy deal with the Mugabe government in 2006.

Current Issues

A possible settlement appeared in the making in early 1999 concerning the incendiary question of land redistribution. According to the plan, the Zimbabwean government was to buy land from the dominant white farmers for use by black farmers, while the international community was to provide substantial aid for the development of infrastructure related to agriculture. However, the government's true intentions remained obscure as President Mugabe continued to threaten to expropriate the white farms and donor countries demanded significant economic reform on the part of the administration before releasing the promised financial assistance. Consequently, Mugabe attempted to secure authority to seize white farms through proposed constitutional revision. When the national referendum in February 2000 rejected the measure, the so-called invasion of some 1,600 farms by blacks (many from influential war veterans' groups) began. Collaterally, the administration, according to a rising chorus of domestic and international critics, launched a campaign of intimidation against opposition parties, particularly the surging MDC, in advance of the assembly balloting scheduled for June. Attendant disorder left more than 30 people dead as Mugabe promised additional resettlement in language described by one critic as "radical, racist rhetoric." The president issued a special decree in May empowering himself to pursue his land redistribution initiative; the courts ruled that measure unconstitutional, but Mugabe refused to enforce a court order to evict the black "settlers" from the disputed farms.

Conditions continued to deteriorate following the June 2000 legislative balloting, with the MDC claiming it had been fraudulently deprived of many seats. International observers were reluctant to characterize the balloting as fair, and observers subsequently warned that Zimbabwe could implode, especially when rioting broke out in October. Despite such warnings, Mugabe appeared to harden his stance, pardoning thousands of ZANU-PF adherents who had been implicated in the pre-election violence. Throughout the first half of 2001, the administration also stepped up its attacks on journalists and reform-minded judges, while white-owned businesses in the cities also became the target of "invasions." (Whites, less than 2 percent of the population, still controlled more than 50 percent of industry and commercial agriculture.) The United Kingdom at midyear withdrew its financial support to protest the takeovers, and unrest increased in August following the "evacuation" of some white farmers. Little progress in settling the dispute ensued during the remainder of the year. The assembly in January 2002 approved legislation banning public gatherings without police approval as an apparent means of undercutting the MDC challenge to Mugabe in the March presidential poll. The Commonwealth suspended Zimbabwe and imposed sanctions, including travel bans and aid restrictions, to protest the heavy-handedness of the administration, with the United States weighing in that Mugabe's governance was "illegitimate and irrational." For his part, Mugabe called his reelection a "stunning blow to imperialism" and condemned the "blatant racism of the West." The farm crisis continued unabated throughout the rest of the year as the country appeared to be approaching financial collapse.

By the end of 2002 more than 28 million acres had been transferred to black Zimbabweans from white commercial farmers, but observers said the majority was redistributed, not to poor farmers, but to high-ranking government officials, army officers, and judges with ties to the ZANU-PF. In 2005 the governor of the central bank called on the government to allow some of the white farmers whose land had been seized to resume growing crops to bolster output. Reportedly, lack of expertise among black farmers who had received land, as well as drought conditions early in the year, resulted in what was described as an "economic catastrophe." Urgent requests by UNICEF to bring in food aid were rejected by government officials, who insisted the country had enough food. Ultimately, however, the government agreed to allow UN assistance, but only under strict conditions.

With no abatement of the crisis, the government allegedly used food to buy votes in the March 31, 2005, assembly elections (the vote-buying was cited by a Zimbabwe judge in October), increasing its ZANU-PF representation by 16 seats, mainly with support from poor rural areas. The MDC again alleged massive fraud, although AU observers endorsed the elections, albeit citing some concerns, and the South African Development Community (SADC) observer mission found the election to be credible. The ZANU-PF returned with a landslide victory in balloting for a newly established Senate in November 2005, though critics pointed to the very low turnout of 19.5 percent as evidence of voter apathy coupled with a boycott by some members of the opposition MDC. The government party also benefited from a major rift in the MDC, which subsequently split into two factions (see Political Parties, below).

Further exacerbating the declining economic and social conditions, the government in 2005 launched Operation Marambatsvina ("drive out rubbish") purportedly to rid urban areas of black market traders. Shantytowns were burned and bulldozed, initially displacing some 200,000 people. The MDC charged that the program was meant to punish urban dwellers who voted against the ZANU-PF. While the government said the operation was designed to "restore social order," critics claimed that by dispersing urban dwellers, the government reduced the possibility of an uprising and drove people back to rural areas in the aftermath of the economic collapse due to the land redistribution program. After a visit by a UN official to assess the situation, President Mugabe pledged to spend hundreds of thousands of dollars over three years to rebuild homes and businesses. However, the slum clearing continued into 2006 under another program called Operation Roundup. By May 2006, both operations had cleared an estimated 700,000 people from Harare.

Also in 2006, white farmers were invited to lease back their land from the government under a 99-year agreement, but the few white farmers still in Zimbabwe were reported to be largely uninterested in the offer.

Political Parties

Prior to the "internal settlement" agreement of March 1978, Rhodesian parties could be broadly grouped into (1) the all-white Rhodesian Front (RF), which maintained overwhelming predominance in the elections of 1965, 1970, 1974, and 1977; (2) a number of small white opposition groups on the right and left of the ruling front; and (3) a variety of black opposition parties ranging from relatively moderate formations under such leaders as Bishop Abel Muzorewa, Reverend Ndabaningi Sithole, and Chief Jeremiah Chirau, to the more radical and overtly insurgent groups led by Robert Mugabe and Joshua Nkomo. The principal African leaders agreed during a summit conference at Lusaka, Zambia, in December 1974 to work together under Bishop Muzorewa of the African National Council (ANC) to achieve majority rule in Rhodesia, but disagreements precluded the creation of a unified black movement. The moderate leaders thereupon joined the RF's Ian Smith in establishing a transitional government to prepare for a one-person, one-vote election originally scheduled for December 1978 but subsequently postponed to April 1979, while Mugabe and Nkomo entered into a somewhat tenuous Patriotic Front (PF) committed to the military overthrow of the biracial regime.

Although Nkomo expressed a desire to continue the alliance, Mugabe's Zimbabwe African National Union–Patriotic Front (ZANU-PF) and Nkomo's Patriotic Front–Zimbabwe African People's Union (PF-ZAPU) contested the common roll election of February 27–29, 1980, as separate entities, ZANU-PF winning 57 of 80 assembly seats and PF-ZAPU winning 20.

Nkomo's PF revived its earlier ZAPU designation following the government rupture of February 1982, while ZANU-PF moved toward the establishment of a one-party state that was consummated, on a de facto basis, with the signature of a merger agreement by Mugabe and Nkomo on December 22, 1987. However, on August 2, 1990, 21 of 26 ZANU-PF Politburo members voted against Mugabe's appeal for a constitutional amendment to institutionalize the one-party system.

At a convention of the Zimbabwe Congress of Trade Unions (ZCTU) in Harare in late February 1999, the ZCTU announced that it had coalesced with the **National Constitutional Assembly (NCA),** 30 civic groups, and a number of human rights, trade, and student organizations to form a political movement dedicated to pressuring the Mugabe government to enact economic, electoral, and constitutional reforms. Morgan Tsvangirai and Gibson Sibanda, leaders of both the ZCTU and the new coalition, had emerged in 1998 as point men for the anti-Mugabe forces. The NCA subsequently served as a major force in the creation of the nation's first effective opposition party, the Movement for Democratic Change (below).

By 2005 the MDC had emerged as the chief opposition party and the only one of consequence. None of the numerous smaller parties had been able to elect any of their members to the parliament. In August 2006, opposition leaders, including those from the two MDC factions (below), announced they would form an alliance in an effort to unseat the ZANU-PF.

Government Party

Zimbabwe African National Union–Patriotic Front (ZANU-PF). ZANU was formed in 1963 as a result of a split in the Zimbabwe African People's Union (ZAPU), an African nationalist group formed in 1961 under the leadership of Joshua Nkomo. Nkomo had in 1957 revived the dormant ANC, which was banned in 1959. He then was elected from exile as the president of a new National Democratic Party, which was declared illegal in 1961, leading to the formation and quick banning of ZAPU. ZANU, led by Ndabaningi Sithole and Robert Mugabe, was also declared illegal in 1964, and both ZANU and ZAPU initiated guerrilla activity against the Rhodesian government announced in November 1965.

In December 1974 ZANU President Sithole agreed to participate (along with ZAPU) in the enlargement of the African National Council to serve as the primary organization for negotiating with the Smith government (see Political background, above, for further information). However, Mugabe opposed such discussions and went into exile in Mozambique, from where he contested Sithole's dominance in ZANU. By late 1976 Mugabe was widely recognized as ZANU's leader, and he concluded a tactical (Patriotic Front—PF) agreement with Joshua Nkomo of ZAPU, although a minority of the ZANU membership apparently remained loyal to Sithole. The PF alliance broke down prior to the 1980 assembly election, Nkomo's group campaigning as PF-ZAPU and Mugabe's as ZANU-PF. Both parties participated in the government formed at independence, although ZANU-PF predominated with 16 of 22 ministerial appointments.

At ZANU-PF's third ordinary congress held December 19–21, 1989, the Politburo was enlarged from 15 to 26 members, the Central Committee was expanded from 90 to 150 members, a national chairmanship was created, and ZAPU was formally incorporated into the party (despite rejection of its demands for a sole vice presidency filled by Nkomo and an expunging of the group's Marxist-Leninist tenets). Furthermore, in an apparent expression of dissatisfaction with reform-minded East European regimes, the party's socialist orientation was redefined to emphasize the Zimbabwean historical, cultural, and social experience. Ultimately, on June 22, 1991, the party agreed to delete all references to Marxism, Leninism, and Scientific Socialism from the party's constitution.

While Mugabe's party leadership subsequently remained unchallenged, the increasing independence of ZANU-PF legislators and local leaders was highlighted in August 1992 by the assembly's rejection of an administration request for a new cabinet post, as well as by reports of regional leaders ignoring candidates forwarded by the national party in favor of their own local choices.

At a party congress in December 1995 Mugabe loyalists blocked efforts to open a party-wide dialogue on the question of presidential succession. At the same time, analysts predicted that party power would soon devolve to a younger generation of financially oriented technocrats and grassroots activists.

The revelation in April 1997 that senior party officials close to Mugabe had allegedly plundered the pension fund of war veterans created a rift in the party between its military and political wings. Meanwhile, analysts, and Mugabe himself, were reportedly critical of the party's senior leadership for having become preoccupied with positioning themselves for possible presidential succession. Reports that the popularity of the president as well as that of the party was waning were underlined in 1998 by the paltry turnout at Mugabe's public appearances and party rallies. Defying both international donors and ZANU-PF moderates, the Central Committee in December urged the president to forge ahead with plans to seize white-owned properties.

Despite the schisms within ZANU-PF, Mugabe was reelected without opposition as party president in 1999. Subsequently, in controversial balloting, ZANU-PF retained a narrow majority in the assembly in June 2000 and Mugabe was reelected to another term as president of the Republic in 2002.

Party solidarity began to disintegrate in 2004 after five party officials were arrested on espionage charges (three of whom were later convicted of spying for South Africa), and a purge of the party targeted members who opposed Mugabe's choice of Joyce Mujuru as vice president of the republic. Mujuru was appointed over house speaker Emmerson Mnangagwa, regarded by many as the president's likely successor. In 2005 Mnangagwa was moved to a low-profile ministry post when the president reshuffled the cabinet following the ZANU-PF's substantial victory in the March assembly election. The president also dismissed from the party information minister Jonathan MOYO after Moyo chose to run as an independent in the assembly balloting. (Moyo won a seat.) At midyear, Mugabe confirmed his plan to retire when his term expires in 2008, but he said he intended to remain active in the party until the 2009 national congress.

Leaders: Robert Gabriel MUGABE (President of the Republic and of the Party), Joseph MSIKA and Joyce MUJURU (Vice Presidents of the Republic and of the Party), Simba MAKONI, Emmerson MNANGAGWA, Didymus MUTASA, John NKOMO (National Chair).

Other Parliamentary Party

Movement for Democratic Change (MDC). Launched in September 1999, the MDC was an outgrowth of the ZCTU/NCA (see above), its core components including workers, students, middle-class intellectuals, civil rights activists, and white corporate executives opposed to the perceived corruption of the ZANU-PF government as well as its management of the economy. Many of the MDC adherents had been members of the Forum Party of Zimbabwe, which had been established in 1993 under the leadership of Enoch DUMBUT-SHENA (a retired chief justice) and David Coltart (see 1999 *Handbook* for details on the Forum Party).

In a rapid rise, the MDC secured 57 seats in the 2000 assembly balloting. MDC leaders claimed fraud on the part of the government in some 37 of the 62 seats secured by the ZANU-PF. Following party leader Morgan Tsvangirai's loss in the 2002 presidential election, he was charged with treason. That charge was later dropped, and in 2004 he was acquitted of a separate treason charge involving a plot to assassinate Mugabe.

Prior to the November 2005 Senate election the party was deeply divided between Tsvangirai's faction, which opposed participation in the balloting, and a faction led by party secretary general Welshman Ncube that planned to field candidates. Sub-

sequently, 26 members who had been expelled by Tsvangirai stood for election, with only 7 winning Senate seats. A month later the MDC split, leaving the lawful leadership of the party in question. Tsvangirai maintained he was still in charge of the party, despite dissidents claiming he had been expelled. At the party congress in March 2006, Tsvangirai was reelected president and Isaac Matongo was reelected chair.

Several members of an alleged terrorist cell reported to have MDC connections were arrested in 2006 and charged with plotting to overthrow President Mugabe. The **Zimbabwe Freedom Movement** reportedly had ties to former Rhodesian security forces and was supposedly coordinated by two members of the MDC.

Leaders: Morgan TSVANGIRAI (President of the Party and 2002 presidential candidate), Thokozani KHUPE (Vice President of the Party), Isaac MATONGO (Chair).

Pro Democracy MDC. In early 2006, this dissident faction of the MDC was formed by party secretary general Welshman Ncube after a dispute with the MDC president over participation in the 2005 Senate election. Ncube's faction, styled the Pro Democracy MDC, named former MDC vice president Gibson Sibanda as acting president. The pro democracy group held a congress in February 2006 and elected former student activist Arthur Mutambara, 39, as party president, and Sibanda as vice president. Ncube retained the post of secretary general. The following month, however, Mutambara said it was wrong for MDC members to have contested the Senate elections and he urged those who were elected to resign. Further, he proposed reconciling with Tsvangirai's faction, and as of July, the leaders of both factions vowed to work together to unseat the ZANU-PF.

Leaders: Arthur MUTAMBARA (President), Gibson SIBANDA (Vice President), Welshman NCUBE (Secretary General).

Other Parties

Zimbabwe African National Union–Ndonga (ZANU-Ndonga). ZANU-Ndonga was formerly led by Ndabaningi Sithole, a vocal supporter of Mozambique's Renamo grouping, who announced from exile in the United States that, despite government threats to arrest and prosecute him on treason charges, he would return to Zimbabwe during an October 1991 meeting of the Commonwealth leaders in Harare; in actuality his return was postponed until early 1992. The party, which had controlled the sole opposition parliamentary seat in the late 1980s and retained it in 1990, suffered thereafter from criticism that Sithole's reform proposals were unrealistic and out of touch. By mid-1993, the grouping was described as "disorganized," although at least 18 of its members were reported as being arrested in mid-1994 after engaging in a clash with ZANU-PF supporters near the capital. Its parliamentary representative was killed in an automobile accident in October 1994, but the seat was recaptured by Sithole at a by-election held December 19–20.

In October 1995 Sithole was charged with participation in a plot to assassinate President Mugabe. Shortly thereafter William NAMAKONYA, a Sithole bodyguard who allegedly confessed to being a member of the Mozambique-based Chimwenje rebel group, was found guilty of possessing illegal arms, while on December 1 Simon MHLANGA, a Sithole supporter, was found guilty of having been illegally engaged in guerrilla training.

In March 1996 Sithole, who remained free on bail, announced his withdrawal from the presidential campaign, charging that security forces were harassing his supporters. In late 1997 Sithole was found guilty of treason and sentenced to two years in prison. In January 1998 Sithole, who remained free while preparing an appeal, called for the drafting of a new constitution, asserting that amending the current document, as suggested by other political leaders, would fail to bring down the Mugabe administration.

ZANU-Ndonga supported the MDC in the 2000 legislative campaign, although the party was credited with gaining one seat from the rural district of Chipinge on its own. Sithole died in December 2000, his appeal of his 1997 sentence having never been heard. With Zimbabwe's politics now only a two-party affair, ZANU-Ndonga became increasingly irrelevant. In 2005 it lost a seat in rural Chipwge South that it had held since 1980.

Leaders: Wilson KHUMBULA (President), Gideon CHINOGUREI (Secretary General).

United Party (UP). The UP was launched in October 1994 by former UANC leader Bishop Muzorewa and his supporters, following their withdrawal from the Zimbabwe Unity Movement (ZUM). In December it merged with the small Forum Party for Democracy (FPD) in what was briefly styled the United Parties before reverting to the singular form. The UP joined ZUM in boycotting the 1995 balloting. Following the Supreme Court's rejection of his bid to postpone presidential balloting, on March 15, 1996, Bishop Muzorewa announced his withdrawal from the contest, charging that the electoral laws unfairly favored the ZANU-PF.

In the run-up to the June 2000 assembly balloting, the UP announced it was participating in an electoral coalition with ZANU-Ndonga, the ZUD, and the LPZ called the Foundation for Democracy in Zimbabwe (FODEZI). However, complete cohesion in that regard was not achieved, and FODEZI components presented competing candidates in some districts. By 2005 UP had all but disappeared as a political party.

Leaders: Bishop Abel MUZOREWA (President of the Party and 1996 presidential candidate).

Zimbabwe Union of Democrats (ZUD). Officially launched in December 1998, the ZUD is a vehicle for independent legislator Margaret Dongo, who had been credited with revealing the ZANU-PF's role in the veterans' pension fund scandal. (In February 1998 Dongo was reportedly the target of an unsuccessful bomb attack.) Dongo failed in her reelection bid in 2000. There is general agreement that ZUD has, as one observer put it, "sunk into political oblivion." Dongo surfaced to contest the 2005 assembly election as an independent.

Leaders: Margaret DONGO (President), Isaac MANYEMBA (Secretary General).

Popular Democratic Front (PDF). The PDF was originally founded in 1994 as the **Front for**

Popular Democracy (FPD) by Austin Chakawodza, who in 1996 emerged as a prominent opposition spokesman and is based in London. In 1999 Chakawodza announced that the group had adopted the PDF rubric, denouncing some of his internal critics for "masquerading" as the FPD. As a very small opposition party, the PDF has little or no influence on the ruling powers.

Leader: Austin CHAKAWODZA (Chair).

National Democratic Union (NDU). Founded in 1979, the NDU is a very small, conservative Mashonaland grouping that participated in the 1990 legislative poll. In early 1998 the NDU reportedly petitioned the Supreme Court to overturn the Mugabe administration's land reform proposals.

Leader: Mark MUCHABAIWA.

Zimbabwe Integrated Party (ZIP). Originally launched as the Zimbabwe Integrated Program, a nongovernmental organization devoted to promoting development projects, the ZIP secured 0.02 percent of the legislative vote in 2000 under the leadership of Heneri Dzinotyiwei, a mathematics professor and businessman. In June 2006 it was reported that Dzinotyiwei had joined Morgan Tsvangirai's faction in the MDC.

Leader: Heneri DZINOTYIWEI.

Liberty Party of Zimbabwe (LPZ). Described as having a base among migrant workers in South Africa, the anti-Mugabe LPZ secured 0.06 percent of the vote in the 2000 legislative balloting. In 2002 a split in the party reportedly occurred over whether to support Mugabe and his controversial land reforms. LPZ was not a factor in the elections of 2002 and 2005.

Leaders: Canaan MOYO, George MOYO, Jabulani NDLOVU (Secretary General).

Federal Party of Zimbabwe (FPZ). The FPZ, also referenced as the FP, was formed in Bulawayo in December 1994 by a group of dissidents from the Forum Party of Zimbabwe to contest the "tribal domination" imposed on Matebeleland by ZANU-PF. It advocates a Zimbabwe of five provinces, each headed by its own prime minister. It also calls for limiting the term of the country's president. In 1999 the party reportedly was dissolved as members joined the MDC in an effort to unseat the ZANU-PF.

Leaders: Twoboy JUBANE.

Zimbabwe Unity Movement (ZUM). The ZUM was launched in April 1989 by the so-called bad boy of Zimbabwe politics, Edgar Tekere, in opposition to President Mugabe's efforts to establish a one-party state. It won two House of Assembly seats in March 1990, with Tekere securing a 16 percent vote-share as Mugabe's only competitor in the presidential race. The party subsequently splintered when Tekere rejected a new ZUM constitution and proposal to restructure the party hierarchy.

Professing a desire to topple the Mugabe government, the ZUM in early 1994 announced a merger with the United African National Congress (UANC) of preindependence government leader Bishop Abel Muzorewa. The unification under the ZUM rubric failed, however, to attract new members, and by mid-1994 the group was suffering from internal tensions. Three months later Bishop Muzorewa and his supporters withdrew to form the United Party, (above). ZUM boycotted the 1995 election and was described as a "spent force" by 1999.

Leader: Edgar TEKERE.

Zimbabwe People's Convention (ZPC). The ZPC was formed by former student leaders in mid-1998 on a prodemocracy and anti-Mugabe platform. Subsequently, the ZPC incorporated the members of the Zimbabwe National Liberation War Collaborators' Association. In 2000, party secretary general Obey Mudzingwa and another high-ranking party official were reported to have joined the MDC.

Leader: Obey MUDZINGWA.

Democratic Party (DP). Launched by ZUM expellees (including Emmanuel MAGOCHE) in 1991, the DP held its inaugural congress in September 1992. In early 1996 the DP was identified as

Cabinet

As of July 1, 2006

President	Robert Gabriel Mugabe
Vice Presidents	Joseph Msika
	Joyce Mujuru [f]

Ministers

Agriculture	Joseph Made
Defense	Sidney Tigere Sekeramayi
Economic Development	Rugare Gumbo
Education, Sports, and Culture	Aeneas S. Chigwedere
Energy and Power Development	Gen. Mike Nyambuya
Environment and Tourism	Francis Nhema
Finance	Herbert Murerwa
Foreign Affairs	Simbarashe Mumbengegwi
Health and Child Welfare	David P. Parirenyatwa
Higher and Tertiary Education	Stanislaus Mudenge
Home Affairs	Kembo C. D. Mohadi
Industry and International Trade	Obert Mpofu
Information and Publicity	Paul M. Mangwana (Acting)
Justice, Legal, and Parliamentary Affairs	Patrick Chinamasa
Local Government, Public Works, and National Housing	Ignatius Chombo
Mines	Amos Midzi
National Security	Didymus Mutasa
Policy Implementation	Webster Shamu
Public Services, Labor, and Social Welfare	Nicholas Goche
Rural Housing and Social Amenities	Emmerson Mnangagwa
Science and Technology	Olivia Muchena [f]
Small and Medium Enterprise Development	Sithembiso G. Nyoni [f]
State Enterprises, Anti-Monopolies, and Anti-Corruption	Paul M. Mangwana
Transport and Communications	Chris Mushowe
Water Resources and Infrastructural Development	Munacho Mutezo
Women's Affairs, Gender, and Community Development	Oppah Muchinguri [f]
Without Portfolio	Elliott T. Manyika

Ministers of State

Indigenization and Empowerment	Josiah Tungamirai
Land and Resettlement Programs	Flora Buka [f]

[f] = female

an organizer of the reform-minded MPC grouping. Constitutional reform has been one of the DP's priorities, and in 2004 the party urged the government to present a democratic constitution before the 2005 legislative elections, calling the constitution at the time "colonial and illegitimate."

Leader: Wurayayi ZEMBE (President of the Party).

Other parties participating in the 2000 balloting (all of which received less than 0.1 percent of the vote) included the **Zimbabwe Progressive Party** (ZPP), led by Justine CHIOTA; the **African National Party** (ANP); the **National People's Alliance** (NPA); and the **Zimbabwe Congress Party** (ZCP).

Other parties participating in the 2005 Senate election included the ANP, the **Multiracial Open Party–Christian Democrats** (MOP-CD); **Peace Action is Freedom for All** (PAFA); the **Zimbabwe African People's Union-Federal Party** (ZAPU-FP), led by Paul SIWELA; and the **Zimbabwe Youth in Alliance** (ZIYA), led by Daniel MBANJE and Bernard NYIKADZINO. All of the parties received less than 2 percent of the vote.

Other parties and groups include the **Committee for a Democratic Society** (Codesa), a Matebeleland-based party launched in 1993 under the leadership of Soul NDLOVU; the **Conservative Alliance of Zimbabwe** (CAZ), an offshoot of the former Rhodesia Front now led by Gerard SMITH and Mike MORONEY; the **Multi-Racial Open Party** (MOP); the **Transparency Front;** the **United People's Movement** (UPM), led by former ZANU-PF minister Jonathan MOYO; the **United People's Party** (UPP), led by former ZANU-PF official Daniel SHUMBA; the **Zimbabwe Independence Party** (ZIP); and the **Zimbabwe People's Democratic Party** (ZPDP), led by Isabel MADANGURE. In addition, there reportedly are two groups claiming the name of the **Zimbabwe Labor Party,** one led by Alois MACHOKOTO and the other by David MATANGANYIDE, and the **Zimbabwe National Congress** (ZINC), led by Godwin MUTAMBIRWA.

Legislature

Zimbabwe has had four legislatures since 1978, the first three bicameral (for details see the 1989 edition of the *Handbook*). As of March 1990 the upper house (Senate) was abolished, the legislature thereupon becoming a unicameral body, the House of Assembly, The bicameral legislature was reinstituted in 2005, following a constitutional amendment approved by the house on August 30 to establish an upper chamber Senate.

Senate. The upper body was seated following single-round, plurality system balloting of November 26, 2005. The Zimbabwe African National Union–Patriotic Front won 43 seats and the Movement for Democratic Change won 7. The Senate comprises 66 members, 50 of whom are directly elected (5 from each of the 10 provinces). The nonelective seats comprise 8 held by traditional chiefs, 6 members appointed by the president, and 1 each for the president and deputy president of the Council of Chiefs. All serve five-year terms.

President: Edna MADZONGWE.

House of Assembly. In the most recent balloting of March 31, 2005, the seat distribution was as follows: the Zimbabwe African National Union-Patriotic Front, 78; the Movement for Democratic Change, 41; and independents, 1. The elective seats are determined via direct universal suffrage in a single-round plurality system in 120 single-member constituencies. The assembly also contains 30 nonelective seats: 8 traditional chiefs selected by their peers, 10 provincial governors appointed ex officio by the president, and 12 members appointed by the president. All serve five-year terms.

Speaker: John NKOMO.

Communications

Press

In early 1981 the government purchased 42 percent of the shares of the (South African) Argus group, thereby acquiring control of the largest newspapers in Zimbabwe, which it subsequently published through Zimbabwe Newspapers Ltd. Current government-controlled dailies include *The Herald* (122,000), published in Harare, and *The Chronicle* (45,000), published in Bulawayo. Weeklies produced by Zimbabwe Newspapers Ltd. include *Sunday Mail* (159,000), published in Harare, and *Sunday News* (50,000), published in Bulawayo.

A number of privately owned papers now exist, the best-selling of which is the *Daily News,* published in Harare. Independent weeklies published in Harare include the *Financial Gazette* (35,000), *The Standard,* the *Zimbabwe Independent,* and the *Zimbabwe Mirror.*

In mid-1998 the government passed a bill forbidding foreign ownership of media outlets. Relations between the Mugabe administration and the independent press subsequently deteriorated sharply, and journalists charged the government with widespread harassment and intimidation during and after the 2000 legislative campaign. Meanwhile, independent observers strongly criticized the government-controlled media for exhibiting a strongly pro–ZANU-PF bias in covering the election.

News Agencies

In October 1980 the South African Press Association relinquished its interest in the Salisbury-based Inter-African News Agency, the latter being reorganized as the Zimbabwe Inter-African News Agency (ZIANA). *Agence France-Presse,* AP, Reuters, and UPI are among the foreign agencies that maintain bureaus in Harare.

Broadcasting and Computing

The Zimbabwe Broadcasting Corporation (ZBC) regulates radio and television stations; service is in English and a variety of African languages. Although ZBC is formally an independent statutory body, it is dependent on public funds and has been broadly criticized in recent years for a progovernment orientation in presenting the news. There were approximately 454,000 television receivers and 620,000 personal computers serving 600,000 Internet users in 2003.

Intergovernmental Representation

Ambassador to the U.S.
Machivenyika Tobias MAPURANGA

U.S. Ambassador to Zimbabwe
Christopher William DELL

Permanent Representative to the UN
Boniface G. CHIDYAUSIKU

IGO Memberships (Non-UN)
ADF, AfDB, AU, BADEA, Comesa, Interpol, IOM, NAM, PCA, SADC, WCO, WTO

PART THREE

INTERGOVERNMENTAL ORGANIZATIONS

AFRICAN UNION (AU)

Established: Charter of the predecessor Organization of African Unity (OAU) adopted May 25, 1963, in Addis Ababa, Ethiopia; Treaty Establishing the African Economic Community (AEC)—the Abuja Treaty—adopted June 3, 1991, by the OAU heads of state and government in Abuja, Nigeria, and entered into force May 12, 1994; Constitutive Act of the African Union (AU) adopted July 11, 2001, by the OAU heads of state and government in Lomé, Togo, and entered into force May 26, 2001. (The OAU remained in existence during a one-year transitional period ending July 8, 2002; the Abuja Treaty remains a cornerstone of the AU.)

Purpose: To "achieve greater unity and solidarity" among African states; to "accelerate the political and socio-economic integration of the continent"; to "promote and defend African common positions"; to "promote peace, security and stability"; to "promote democratic principles and institutions, popular participation and good governance"; to assist in Africa's effort "to play its rightful role in the global economy and in international negotiations"; and to "promote sustainable development at the economic, social and cultural levels."

Headquarters: Addis Ababa, Ethiopia.

Principal Organs: Assembly of Heads of State and Government; Executive Council; Peace and Security Council (15 members); Permanent Representatives Committee; Pan-African Parliament; Economic, Social, and Cultural Council; Commission.

Chair of the Commission: Denis Sassou-Nguesso (Republic of the Congo).

Membership (53): Algeria, Angola, Benin, Botswana, Burkina Faso, Burundi, Cameroon, Cape Verde, Central African Republic, Chad, Comoro Islands, Democratic Republic of the Congo, Republic of the Congo, Côte d'Ivoire, Djibouti, Egypt, Equatorial Guinea, Eritrea, Ethiopia, Gabon, Gambia, Ghana, Guinea, Guinea-Bissau, Kenya, Lesotho, Liberia, Libya, Madagascar, Malawi, Mali, Mauritania, Mauritius, Mozambique, Namibia, Niger, Nigeria, Rwanda, Sahrawi Arab Democratic Republic, Sao Tome and Principe, Senegal, Seychelles, Sierra Leone, Somalia, South Africa, Sudan, Swaziland, Tanzania, Togo, Tunisia, Uganda, Zambia, Zimbabwe. Madagascar, which was suspended by the OAU in June 2002 as a consequence of a disputed change of government, remained under suspension by the AU until reinstated in July 2003.

Working Languages: Arabic, English, French, Kiswahili, Portuguese, Spanish, and "if possible," other African languages.

Origin and development. The OAU was the most conspicuous result of the search for unity among the emerging states of Africa, a number of whose representatives participated in the first Conference of Independent African States in April 1958 in Accra, Ghana. However, common action was seriously impaired by the division of the newly independent states into rival blocs, notably the "Casablanca group" led by Ghana and Guinea, which stressed left-wing socialism, radical anticolonialism, and pan-Africanism, and the more moderate "Monrovia group," which favored a cautiously evolutionary and more subregional approach to African problems. In an attempt to heal this split, a 20-state summit conference of African leaders met May 22–25, 1963, in Addis Ababa at the invitation of Emperor Haile Selassie of Ethiopia, and agreed to form the OAU.

Intense controversy erupted in February 1982 over the seating of a delegation from the Sahrawi Arab Democratic Republic (SADR)—the national name adopted by the Polisario Front guerrillas in the Western Sahara. The 19th Assembly of Heads of State was unable to convene in August in Tripoli, Libya, because of Moroccan-led opposition to SADR attendance. An effort was made to reconvene the meeting in November, after the SADR was induced to "voluntarily and temporarily" withdraw from participation; however, a new boycott resulted from Libya's refusal to admit Chadians representing the Hissein Habré government. The summit was finally convened in June 1983 in Addis Ababa with Libya's boycott still in effect and the SADR seat remaining vacant. Morocco withdrew from the organization following the return of the SADR in October 1984; in support of Morocco, Zaire suspended its membership, but returned as a participant at the 1986 summit.

The OAU long functioned as a sounding board for African opinion on such problems as colonialism and racial discrimination. Thus, the Liberation Committee assisted the South West African People's Organization in the fight for Namibian independence and supported the African National Congress and the Pan-Africanist Congress in their struggle for majority rule in South Africa. At the same time, attention also focused on refugee problems, human rights issues, and the continent's deteriorating economic condition, including what the OAU called its "excruciating debt burden."

In June 1991, meeting in Abuja, Nigeria, the assembly passed the Treaty Establishing the African Economic Community (AEC), which reflected both the OAU's mounting concern that world events were "marginalizing" Africa and the members' desire to reverse the continent's declining economic prospects. To be implemented in six phases over a 30-year period, the Abuja Treaty (as the AEC founding document is commonly called) sought to remove trade and travel barriers and spur development through economic integration, with the ultimate goal of creating an economic union controlled by a Pan-African Parliament and marked by a single African currency. A Court of Justice would also be established. The treaty's first phase called for the strengthening of existing regional economic bodies in anticipation of their eventual merger.

With South Africa registering progress toward a political settlement, the 1993 OAU summit in Cairo, Egypt, focused on the broader question of conflict resolution throughout the continent. In its Cairo Declaration the summit endorsed the proposed creation of an OAU "mechanism" to help prevent or resolve conflicts both between and within states, although the heads of state declined to authorize establishment of an OAU peacekeeping force, as requested by Secretary General Salim Ahmed Salim of Tanzania.

Final arrangements on the Mechanism for Conflict Prevention, Management, and Resolution were completed at a November 1993 foreign ministers meeting, and an OAU Peace Fund was established to help finance endeavors under the new interventionist mandate. However, concern was expressed during the 1994 summit at Tunis, Tunisia, that OAU efforts in this area were doomed to ineffectiveness unless the organization's financial status was strengthened. With many members in arrears and additional resources appearing scarce, critics suggested the OAU would be unable to sustain the expensive peacekeeping missions probably needed to resolve the numerous "internal wars" raging on the continent. Such concerns appeared validated when proposed OAU intervention in Rwanda, widely discussed at the summit, was quickly abandoned in favor of French and UN action. The Tunis summit also marked the admission of postapartheid South Africa as the OAU's 53rd member.

The July 1996 summit in Yaoundé, Cameroon, considered the possibility of sending a peacekeeping mission to Burundi. Regarding such operations, much of the international community, led by the United States, continued to call for the implementation of an OAU intervention mechanism using "all-African" forces. Although the concept had significant support within the OAU as well, the logistical problems and political ramifications associated with intervention in domestic conflicts remained a barrier to effective action.

Civil strife and its aftermath were also among the dominant themes of the OAU's annual summit in June 1997 in Harare, Zimbabwe. On one hand, the body applauded the ouster of Zairean President Mobutu Sese Seko by Laurent Kabila's rebel forces (while urging the latter to fulfill his pledge to hold elections within two years in the newly proclaimed Democratic Republic of the Congo); on the other hand, the OAU gave its approval to the use of force to remove the military junta that seized control of Sierra Leone in late May.

In the second half of 1997, OAU energies were directed at attempting to settle the growing separatist crisis in the Comoro Islands. In August the OAU reported it had convinced the leaders of the independence movements on Anjouan and Moheli Islands to participate in reconciliation talks, and in November the OAU dispatched an eight-member military observation force to the region.

The June 1998 summit in Ouagadougou, Burkina Faso, opened with calls for an end to the fighting between Eritrea and Ethiopia. To help mediate the conflict, summit participants agreed to send a mission to the region from the Mechanism for Conflict Prevention, Management, and Resolution. However, the mission came under criticism from South African President Nelson Mandela, who said it was ineffective. He called instead for the development of alternative means to resolve conflicts on the African continent. Mandela also recommended that the OAU abandon one of its core principles, that of nonintervention, arguing that African nations had a responsibility to protect other Africans living under oppressive regimes.

The 35th OAU summit met July 12–14, 1999, in Algiers, Algeria. Among the notable achievements were passage of a Convention on the Combating and Elimination of Terrorism, which entered into force in December 2002, and an agreement that the OAU would no longer recognize any government that came to power by unconstitutional means. Considerable attention was again devoted to the ongoing conflicts in the continent, particularly

involving Ethiopia and Eritrea, the Democratic Republic of the Congo (DRC), and the Comoros.

The Algiers summit also marked the return of Libya's Mu'ammar al-Qadhafi, who had not attended OAU heads of state meetings in more than 20 years and who now proposed that an extraordinary summit be held to consider establishing a "United States of Africa." As a result, on September 8–9, 1999, the heads of state and government reconvened in Sirte, Libya, and agreed to formation of the African Union as successor to the OAU. Following subsequent negotiations, African leaders signed the Constitutive Act of the AU at the OAU summit July 10–12, 2000, in Lomé, Togo.

At the OAU's fifth extraordinary summit, held March 1–2, 2001, in Sirte, the OAU declared the AU to be established, although the Constitutive Act did not technically enter into force until May 26, 30 days after ratification by the 36th OAU state. The OAU remained in existence for a one-year transition period, during which technical arrangements, such as for financial transfers, were worked out and remaining protocols for various AU organs drafted. On July 9–10, 2002, the heads of state and government, meeting in Durban, South Africa, inaugurated the AU.

Structure. The Assembly of Heads of State and Government, the supreme decision-making organ of the AU (as it was of the OAU), now meets twice annually in ordinary session to define overall AU policy and to supervise the activities of the other AU organs. Substantive decisions are made by consensus or, failing that, a two-thirds majority. A simply majority suffices on procedural questions.

The Executive Council, comprising the foreign ministers or other designated representatives of all member states, meets at least twice a year to confer on preparation for meetings of the assembly, the implementation of assembly decisions, the AU budget, and matters of intra-African cooperation and general international policy. Assisting the Executive Council is the Permanent Representatives Committee, made up of ambassadors accredited to the AU. An advisory Economic, Social, and

Cultural Council (ECOSOCC) was launched in March 2005.

Among the actions taken by the July 2002 inaugural summit in Durban was adoption of a Protocol Relating to the Establishment of the Peace and Security Council (PSC) of the African Union. On December 26, 2003, Nigeria became the 27th AU state to deposit its instrument of ratification, thereby bringing the protocol into force. Consisting of 15 members elected with due regard for "equitable regional representation and rotation," the PSC includes in its mandate supervision of a planned African Standby Force equipped to intervene in crisis situations (see Activities, below). Pending constitution of the PSC, the Central Organ of the OAU's Mechanism for Conflict Prevention, Management, and Resolution continued to meet.

The Pan-African Parliament, established under a protocol to the AEC treaty, is envisaged as evolving into a directly elected organ with full legislative powers. Initially, however, it comprises five representatives chosen by and from within the member states' legislatures and reflecting "the diversity of political opinion in each." The inaugural parliamentary session was held March 18–20, 2004, in Addis Ababa.

The AU Commission replaced the OAU's Secretariat. The Commission chair, who is elected by the assembly for a four-year term, is assisted by a deputy and eight elected commissioners. The commissioners separately oversee the Peace and Security Directorate, the Political Affairs Department, the Directorate of Infrastructure and Energy, the Social Affairs Directorate, the Department of Trade and Industry, the Rural Economy and Agriculture Directorate, the Department of Economic Affairs, and the Human Resources, Science and Technology Department. Also coming under the purview of the Commission are the Women, Gender, and Development Directorate; the Afro-Arab Cooperation Department; the Pan African Tsetse and Trypanosomiasis Eradication Campaign (PATTEC); the Programming, Budget, Finance, and Accounting Directorate; the Administration Department; the Office of Legal Counsel; the Policy Analysis Support Unit (PASU); and the Protocol Services Unit. In addition, the Commission services the Conference on Security, Stability, Development, and Cooperation in Africa (CSSDCA), which was established by the 2000 OAU summit in Lomé and has a primary role in monitoring and evaluation.

The Constitutive Act additionally called for the formation of seven "specialized technical committees": Rural Economy and Agricultural Matters; Monetary and Financial Affairs; Trade, Customs, and Immigration Matters; Industry, Science, and Technology; Energy, Natural Resources, and the Environment; Transportation, Communication, and Tourism; Health, Labor, and Social Affairs; and Education, Culture, and Human Rights. The assembly may create additional specialized technical committees.

An organ yet to be established is the Court of Justice, which was provided for in the Abuja Treaty. Three new financial institutions are also mentioned in the founding act: an African Central Bank, an African Monetary Fund, and an African Investment Bank. At the eighth Ordinary Session of the Executive Council, held January 16–17, 2006, in Addis Ababa, the first members of the African Court on Human and People's Rights were elected. Creation of this body was proposed in a protocol to the 1981 African Charter on Human and People's Rights.

Related specialized agencies, all previously associated with the OAU, include the African Accounting Council, the African Civil Aviation Commission (AFCAC), the African Telecommunications Union (ATU), the Pan-African Institute of Education for Development, the Pan-African News Agency (PANA), and the Pan-African Postal Union (PAPU).

Activities. Based loosely on the model of the European Union (EU), the AU was envisaged as building on existing elements of the OAU—for example, the AEC and the Mechanism for Conflict Prevention, Management, and Resolution—but with a stronger institutional structure. It was also expected to serve as a means of achieving faster sustainable economic development and integration and as a better vehicle for representing unified African positions in international forums and organizations.

During the 2001–2002 transition year, with many AU procedures yet to be codified and key organs yet to be established, conflicts continued to occupy much of the OAU's attention. In May 2001, for example, the Mechanism for Conflict Prevention, Management, and Resolution participated in a meeting in Togo that addressed ongoing problems in Burundi, Comoros, the DRC, Republic of Congo, and the Mano River region of Guinea, Liberia, and Sierra Leone.

The OAU's 37th and final full summit convened July 9–11, 2001, at Lusaka, Zambia, at which time Amara Essy of Côte d'Ivoire was elected OAU/AU secretary general. On the economic front, the summit launched a New Africa Initiative (NAI) with the goal of ending poverty, war, and disease in Africa by 2015 through, among other things, better governance, foreign investment in a more open marketplace, and sustainable development. The NAI represented a consolidation of the Millennium Partnership for the African Recovery Program (MAP), which was proposed in 2000 by the presidents of Algeria, Nigeria, and South Africa, and Senegal's Omega Plan. Having attracted wide support from the developed world and from the UN Economic Commission for Africa, the plan was renamed the New Partnership for Africa's Development (NEPAD) at an October 23 OAU meeting in Abuja, where, in the wake of the September 11 attacks against the United States, terrorism was also a principal discussion topic.

In addition to adopting the PSC's founding protocol, the inaugural AU Assembly of Heads of State and Government in Durban stressed the parallel need for a unified defense and security policy. Although the Constitutive Act continued to uphold the OAU-era principle of noninterference in members' internal affairs, it also set forth "the right of the Union to intervene in a Member State pursuant to a decision of the Assembly, in respect of grave circumstances, namely: war crimes, genocide and crimes against humanity." It also stated, in accordance with a declaration adopted July 2000 in Lomé, that any regime coming to power through unconstitutional means could be suspended from the organization and have sanctions imposed. (As

a consequence of the declaration, Madagascar was suspended from the OAU/AU from June 2002 until July 2003, although international calls for action against the Mugabe regime in Zimbabwe went unheeded.)

The first extraordinary AU summit, meeting February 3, 2003, in Addis Ababa, approved several amendments to the Constitutive Act, making explicit, for example, that the "African Diaspora" should participate in building the organization and that the AU will ensure women's "full and effective participation" in decision making ("particularly in the political, economic and socio-cultural areas"). In a significant expansion of the AU's military authority, the extraordinary assembly session also approved extending the grounds for intervention in a member state to include "a serious threat to legitimate order."

On the same day, summit attendees reconvened as the Seventh Ordinary Session of the Central Organ of the Mechanism for Conflict Prevention, Management, and Resolution at the Heads of State and Government Level. The session examined a half dozen "conflict situations" in the continent and expressed its "deep concern" regarding the worsening tensions over Iraq. With regard to Burundi, the Central Organ approved the deployment of troops, as agreed to by the disputants in their December 2002 cease-fire agreement. The first military contingent arrived in late April 2003. As of June 1, 2004, the African Mission in Burundi (AMIB) gave way to a UN-sponsored peacekeeping mission, which was approved unanimously by the Security Council in May. At that time, there were about 2400 AU personnel, including troops from Ethiopia, Mozambique, and South Africa, and military observers, the latter from Burkina Faso, Gabon, Mali, Togo, and Tunisia. The AMIB was generally regarded as a significant contribution to a peace process that concluded with parliamentary and presidential elections in July–August 2005.

The second ordinary session of the assembly met July 10–12, 2003, in Maputo, Mozambique, where a primary focus continued to be organizational matters. In addition to authorizing the Commission and the Executive Council to continue their preparations for getting the PSC operational as soon as possible after completion of the protocol ratification process, the assembly asked the EU to consider funding PSC missions through a Peace Support Operation Facility. The assembly also advanced toward establishment of another major AU organ by approving the Protocol of the Court of Justice of the African Union and sending it on to the individual states for ratification. The assembly did likewise with a Convention on the Prevention and Combating of Corruption and also supported efforts to draft an international code of conduct for counterterrorism. Among other decisions, the assembly decided to hold a 2004 Extraordinary Summit on Employment and Poverty Alleviation in Africa.

The second extraordinary session of the assembly met February 27–28, 2004, in Sirte, at which time it adopted the Common African Defense and Security Policy (CDSP), as called for in the Constitutive Act and the PSC protocol. Asserting that the causes of intrastate conflict, in particular, necessitate a new, multidimensional emphasis on "human security," the CDSP defines defense as encompassing "both the traditional, military, and state-centric notion of the use of the armed forces of the state to protect its national sovereignty and territorial integrity, as well as the less traditional, non-military aspects which relate to the protection of the people's political, cultural, social and economic values and ways of life." Identified among the CDSP's "building blocks" are various regional groups and mechanisms: the Convention for the Elimination of Mercenaries in Africa (adopted by the OAU in 1977); the African Charter on Human and People's Rights (1981); the African Charter on the Rights and Welfare of the Child (1990); the Declaration and Plan of Action on Drug Use and Illicit Trafficking Control in Africa (1996); the Kempton Park Plan of Action on a Landmine-Free Africa (1997); the African Nuclear-Weapon-Free Zone Treaty (Treaty of Pelindaba, 1998); the Algiers Convention on the Prevention and Combating of Terrorism (1999); the Bamako Declaration on an African Common Position on the Illicit Prolifera-

tion, Circulation, and Trafficking of Small Arms and Light Weapons (2000); and the Declaration on the Framework for an OAU Response to Unconstitutional Changes of Government (2000).

The assembly also requested the commission to convene a panel of experts for advice on revising a draft Non-Aggression and Common Defense Pact in the light of two related proposals: a draft Pact against Aggression and on Mutual Assistance, which had been offered by the Republic of the Congo, and a draft Treaty for a Common Defense and the Establishment of a United Army for the African Union, which Libya had advanced. Among other actions, the extraordinary session adopted the Sirte Declaration on the Challenge of Implementing Integrated and Sustainable Development on Agriculture and Water in Africa.

By the end of 2003 the PSC protocol entered into force, and on March 15, 2004, the Executive Council elected the following as initial PSC members: Algeria, Ethiopia, Gabon, Nigeria, and South Africa, all serving three-year terms; and Cameroon, Republic of the Congo, Ghana, Kenya, Lesotho, Libya, Mozambique, Senegal, Sudan, and Togo, all serving two-year terms. One of the first tasks of the PSC is to organize the African Standby Force (ASF), now planned to be fully operational by 2010. This force is to incorporate police and civilian components as well as military personnel, in keeping with the broad mission of the ASF, which includes possible preventive deployment, peacekeeping, and postconflict disarmament and demobilization.

With regard to regional economic development, NEPAD has begun moving forward with support not only from the African Regional Economic Communities (RECs), but from the UN, the Group of Eight (G-8), the EU, and other international organizations. In 2002 it adopted a Declaration on Democracy, Political, Economic, and Corporate Governance and developed an African Peer Review Mechanism (APRM), which the AU's 2003 Maputo summit described as intended to "foster the adoption of policies, standards and practices leading to political stability, high economic growth, sustainable development and accelerated regional and continental economic integration." The Maputo summit, in its Declaration on the Implementation of NEPAD, acknowledged the importance of integrating NEPAD and its organs (Heads of State and Government Implementation Committee, Steering Committee, and Secretariat) into the AU structures and processes. It also called on member states and the RECs to assist NEPAD in implementing programs in such priority areas as agriculture and infrastructure and in developing detailed sectoral action plans in culture, education, environment, health, science and technology, and tourism.

Collaterally, the AU has indicated its intention to accelerate the AEC schedule, for which it will rely heavily on the RECs. Five of the RECs, collectively providing continent-wide coverage, have been described as "pillars" of the AEC process: the Arab Maghreb Union (AMU), the Common Market for Eastern and Southern Africa (Comesa), the Economic Community of Central African States (CEEAC), the Economic Community of West African States (ECOWAS), and the Southern African Development Community (SADC).

In its July 6–8, 2004, summit held in Addis Ababa, the AU endorsed an estimated $1.7 billion for three years to fund a strategic development plan. It also discussed Darfur and adopted a declaration on gender equality. On September 8–9, 2004, an extraordinary summit was held in Ouagadougou to discuss poverty alleviation and employment. This meeting gave particular attention given to the role of agriculture, education, infrastructure, small- and medium-sized enterprises, and the integration of women into formal employment. The session coincided with issuance of a World Bank report criticizing excessive bureaucratic regulation in Africa, which it said discouraged business enterprise.

At the January 30–31, 2005, summit in Abuja, the assembly decided to meet twice annually. The African Union Non-Aggression and Common Defense Pact was adopted, but by early 2006 only 15 countries had signed and none had ratified it.

The summit participants also agreed to disperse organs geographically: the African Central Bank to a country in West Africa, the Court of Justice to East Africa, the African Monetary Fund to Central Africa, and the Pan-African Parliament to Southern Africa.

The fifth regular summit, held July 4–5, 2005, in Sirte, focused on economic matters. The meeting called for a full cancellation of all African countries' debts and for "the abolition of subsidies that stand as an obstacle to trade"—an issue slated for discussion at the forthcoming G-8 summit in Scotland. The final declaration also called for two permanent African seats at the UN Security Council, as well as five nonpermanent seats. The AU was only able to offer small contingents for peacekeeping missions to Somalia and the Darfur region of Sudan in 2005, contingents generally considered too small to be fully effective. As of April 2006 the Somalia contingent had not actually deployed, the latest proposal suggesting that AU force should take over from a proposed mission by the Inter-Governmental Authority on Development (IGAD), which played a major role in the Somali peace process. (IGAD consists of Eritrea, Ethiopia, Djibouti, Kenya, Uganda, Sudan, and Somalia.) Meanwhile, AU leaders continued to discuss the proposal that the AU assume full responsibility for NEPAD, including NEPAD's well-scrutinized "peer-review" process through which nations agreed to be assessed regarding good governance, democratic reforms, human rights, and development progress.

A complication to the AU's peacekeeping efforts in Darfur was Sudan's bid at the sixth AU summit (held January 23–24, 2006, in Khartoum, Sudan) to assume the organization's presidency for the year. Amid accusations of genocide over the Sudanese government's role in the Darfur conflict, it withdrew its bid in favor of the Republic of the Congo (Congo-Brazzaville), but with suggestions that it might renew its bid in 2007. The AU's peacekeeping force in Darfur, funded by the United States and the EU but at odds with the Sudan government, appeared to be making little progress in stopping the violence. On March 10, 2006, the AU announced it would turn over peacekeeping to the UN on September 30, 2006. In the meantime, it urged bringing its African Mission In Sudan (AMIS) up to full strength of approximately 6200 military personnel, including more than 1500 police. (See the article on Sudan.)

Also in March 2006, the AU decided, on the PSC's recommendation, to send more than 400 personnel (mostly troops and some police) to the Comoros between April and June to help ensure tranquility during presidential elections and the installation of the new president.

ARAB LEAGUE

al-Jami'a al-'Arabiyah

Official Name: League of Arab States.

Established: By treaty signed March 22, 1945, in Cairo, Egypt.

Purpose: To strengthen relations among member states by coordinating policies in political, cultural, economic, social, and related affairs; to mediate disputes between members or between members and third parties.

Headquarters: Cairo, Egypt. (In 1979 the league transferred its headquarters from Cairo to Tunis, Tunisia, because of Egypt's peace treaty with Israel. In early 1990 members agreed unanimously to return the headquarters to Cairo, although some offices were scheduled to remain in Tunis. Extensive debate on the issue was reported later in the year as an outgrowth of the schism arising from the Iraqi invasion of Kuwait, but the relocation was formally completed January 1, 1991.)

Principal Organs: Council of the League of Arab States (all members), Economic and Social Council (all adherents to the 1950 Collective Security Treaty), Joint Defense Council (all adherents to the 1950 Collective Security Treaty), Permanent Committees (all members), Arab Summit Conferences, General Secretariat.

Secretary General: Amr Mahmoud Moussa (Egypt).

Membership (22): Algeria, Bahrain, Comoro Islands, Djibouti, Egypt, Iraq, Jordan, Kuwait, Lebanon, Libya, Mauritania, Morocco, Oman, Palestine, Qatar, Saudi Arabia, Somalia, Sudan, Syria, Tunisia, United Arab Emirates, Yemen.

Official Language: Arabic.

Origin and development. A long-standing project that reached fruition late in World War II, the league was founded primarily on Egyptian initiative following a promise of British support for any Arab organization that commanded general endorsement. In its earlier years the organization focused mainly on economic, cultural, and social cooperation, but in 1950 a Convention on Joint Defense and Economic Cooperation was concluded that obligated the members in case of attack "immediately to take, individually and collectively, all steps available, including the use of armed force, to repel the aggression and restore security and peace." In 1976 the Palestine Liberation Organization (PLO), which had participated as an observer at all league conferences since September 1964, was admitted to full membership. Egypt's participation was suspended from April 1979 to May 1989 because of its peace agreement with Israel.

Structure. The principal political organ of the league is the Council of the League of Arab States, which meets in regular session twice a year, normally at the foreign ministers level. Each member has one vote in the council; decisions usually bind only those states that accept them, although a two-thirds majority vote on financial and administrative matters binds all members. The council's main functions are to supervise the execution of agreements between members, to mediate disputes, and to coordinate defense in the event of attack. There are numerous committees and other bodies attached to the council, including permanent committees dealing with finance and administration, legal affairs, and information.

The council has also established an Administrative Court, an Investment Arbitration Board, and a Higher Auditing Board. Additional ministerial councils, attended by relevant ministers or their representatives, are held in a dozen areas including transport, justice, health, telecommunications, and environmental affairs.

Three additional bodies were established by the 1950 convention: a Joint Defense Council to function in matters of collective security and to coordinate military resources; a Permanent Military Commission, comprised of representatives of the general staffs, to draw up plans for joint defense; and an Economic Council, comprised of the ministers of economic affairs, to coordinate Arab economic development. The last was restructured as an Economic and Social Council in 1977. An Arab Unified Military Command, charged with the integration of strategy for the liberation of Palestine, was formed in 1964.

The General Secretariat is responsible for internal administration and the execution of council decisions. It also administers several agencies, including the Bureau for Boycotting Israel (headquartered in Damascus, Syria).

Membership in the league generally carries with it membership in an array of specialized agencies, including the Arab Bank for Economic Development in Africa (BADEA) and the Arab Monetary Fund (AMF), as well as a variety of other bodies dealing with economic, social, and technical matters.

Nearly three dozen ordinary and extraordinary Arab Summit Conferences have been held since the first one met in 1964. Summit resolutions give direction to the work of the council and other league organs, although the organization's charter did not provide a framework for convening summits.

Activities. After many years of preoccupation with Arab-Israeli issues, the league's attention in 1987 turned to the Iraq-Iran conflict as Arab moderates sought a united front against Iran and the potential spread of militant Islamic fundamentalism. An extraordinary summit conference held November 8–11 in Amman, Jordan, condemned "the Iranian regime's intransigence, provocations,

and threats to the Arab Gulf States" and called for international "pressure" to encourage Iran to accept a UN-sponsored cease-fire. Although Syrian and Libyan opposition blocked a proposed restoration of membership privileges to Egypt, the summit declared that members could establish relations with Cairo individually. A number of countries, including the Persian Gulf states, quickly did so.

Palestinian issues quickly returned to the forefront of the league's agenda in early 1988 because of the uprising (*intifada*) in the Gaza Strip and West Bank. A June summit affirmed "moral, political, and diplomatic" support for the *intifada* while most of the members made individual financial pledges to the PLO. The major development at the May summit in Casablanca, Morocco, was the readmission of Egypt, whose president Husni Mubarak urged the other attendees to stop "wasting time and opportunities" for formulating a "vision" for peace in the Middle East.

A special summit in late May 1990 in Baghdad, Iraq, although convened at the PLO's urging to discuss the mass immigration of Soviet Jews to Israel, focused primarily on U.S. policy. In condemning Washington as bearing a "fundamental responsibility" for Israel's "aggression, terrorism, and expansionism," the league reflected growing frustration among Arabs over the lack of progress in peace negotiations as well as an increased militancy, most forcefully expressed by Iraqi President Saddam Hussein. In an apparent effort to reinforce Arab political unity, the leaders agreed to hold regular annual summits in Cairo, beginning in November.

The prospect for effective cooperation was severely compromised by Iraq's takeover of Kuwait on August 2, 1990, which split the league into two deeply divided blocs. On August 10, the majority (comprising Bahrain, Djibouti, Egypt, Kuwait, Lebanon, Morocco, Oman, Qatar, Somalia, Syria, Saudi Arabia, and the United Arab Emirates) voted to send a pan-Arab force to guard Saudi Arabia against possible Iraqi attack; several members (most notably Egypt and Syria) ultimately contributed troops to the U.S.-led liberation of Kuwait in early 1991. The minority included members overtly sympathetic to Baghdad (such as Jordan, the PLO, and Sudan) and those that, while critical of the Iraqi invasion, were adamantly opposed to U.S. military involvement.

Although both sides continued to promote an "Arab solution" throughout the Persian Gulf crisis, the schism precluded the league from playing any meaningful negotiating role. Symptomatic of the disarray in the Arab world, long-time league secretary general Chedli Klibi of Tunisia resigned in September 1990 after a blistering personal attack by Saudi Arabian officials. The league observer at the United Nations also resigned soon after, citing his inability to cope with Arab fragmentation.

Following the coalition victory over Iraqi forces and the restoration of the Kuwaiti government in early 1991, it appeared that Egypt, the leading Arab coalition member, had regained league dominance, although "intense animosities" reportedly remained from the Persian Gulf crisis. Evidence of Cairo's standing included the May appointment by the Arab League Council of Egypt's retiring foreign minister, Ahmad Ismat Abd al-Magid, as the next secretary general.

In September 1993 the Arab League's foreign ministers gave quick approval to the recently negotiated peace accord between Israel and the PLO. However, the league subsequently announced it would not lift the Arab economic boycott against Israel until Israeli troops withdrew from all the occupied territories. The ban, adopted at the creation of the Jewish state in 1948, precluded any direct commercial contact between Arab countries and Israel. In 1951 a secondary boycott was declared against any companies in the world that conducted business with Israel, followed by a tertiary boycott against any companies dealing with those companies already blacklisted. However, the secondary and tertiary boycotts have been widely ignored recently, and in September 1994 the members of the Gulf Cooperation Council (Bahrain, Kuwait, Oman, Qatar, Saudi Arabia, and United Arab Emirates) announced their formal abandonment. Nevertheless, for the Arab League as a whole the boycotts remained formally in place. In addition, league officials remained skeptical of the proposed formation of a regional economic cooperation union that would include Israel, as had been proposed by the Middle East and North Africa Summit, held October 30–November 1, 1994, in Casablanca, Morocco. The league argued that its members should establish an Arab Free Trade Association that would exclude Israel.

In the wake of the victory of the right-wing Likud party of Benjamin Netanyahu in the May 1996 Israeli elections, the league held its first full summit since 1990 on June 21–23 in Cairo to address, among other things, Netanyahu's perceived retreat from previous Israeli positions regarding the Palestinian self-rule process. The summit reaffirmed its positions supporting full Israeli withdrawal from the occupied territories, Palestinian self-determination, and an end to settlement building in the West Bank. However, divisions among members on the issue were readily apparent, with moderate states such as Jordan and Egypt leading successful efforts to dilute stronger language proposed by Syria. In other activity, the summit again criticized Iraq, which was not invited to the session, for its lack of cooperation with the United Nations and issued a statement of support for Bahrain and the United Arab Emirates in their disputes with Iran.

The summit's final communiqué also called for greater Arab solidarity and a strengthening of the organization's institutions, although skeptics noted a "hollow ring" to the language. The prospects for institutional reform were also constrained by financial difficulties: only four members (Egypt, Jordan, Saudi Arabia, and Syria) had paid their full dues, while the remaining members were a combined $80 million in arrears. As a consequence, the league was forced to close several foreign offices and reportedly had difficulty meeting its payroll at times.

In November 1997, despite the league's financial troubles, 17 members agreed to proceed with the establishment of the Arab Free Trade Zone in 1998, with the goal of cutting customs duties by 10 percent a year until their elimination at the end of 2007. In other activity during the year, the Arab League foreign ministers, meeting in March in Cairo, recommended that members reactivate the economic boycott against Israel and cease all activity geared toward normalizing relations with that country, given the stalled peace process. For the same reason, the league also urged a boycott of the fourth Middle East and North Africa economic conference held in November in Qatar.

In late 1997 and early 1998 the league expressed concern over rising tension between Iraq and Western capitals. It reportedly encouraged Baghdad to adopt a more conciliatory posture while at the same time warning against "unilateral" U.S. action. An emergency summit convened in early January 1999 to address Iraq's request that the league condemn the recent U.S.-UK air assaults. However, the final statement from the summit was mild in tone, expressing "uneasiness and concern" over the attacks while at the same time criticizing Baghdad for its "provocative" rhetoric. Similarly, an Arab League Council session in March declined to label (as Baghdad had demanded) the "no-fly zones" in Iraq as illegal.

Another recent focus of attention is antiterrorism. An accord was signed in April 1998 by the interior and justice ministers of the league's members, who pledged to exchange evidence in terrorist investigations and extradite suspects. The Arab states also agreed not to harbor or assist groups responsible for terrorist acts against Arab nations, although an exemption was granted regarding "national liberation" groups.

In March 2000 the council addressed Israel's announcement of a pending pullout from its "security zone" in southern Lebanon by warning that renewed Palestinian attacks could result unless Israel provided for the repatriation of Palestinians from refugee camps in the region. The league basically adopted what had been the Syrian position on the matter, rejecting the pullout in the absence of a comprehensive peace agreement—clearly, an effort by Syria to interweave the issue of an Israeli pullout from the occupied Golan Heights.

Although the league subsequently cosponsored peace talks in Djibouti on the Somali conflict, from late September 2000 league concerns were largely dominated by the renewal of the Palestinian *intifada,* which quickly led to the first emergency

summit in four years on October 20–21 in Cairo. As in the past, however, league reaction was far from unified. Libya's Colonel Qadhafi pointedly avoided the session altogether, anticipating, from his hard-line perspective, an inadequate response to the renewed hostilities. Iraq's representative called for holy war (*jihad*), while the majority endorsed a halt to further diplomatic normalization with Israel. (At the time, Mauritania, Morocco, Oman, Qatar, and Tunisia had representative offices in Israel.) The summit communiqué continued to call for a renewal of the peace process, while the participants agreed to set up a $1 billion fund to aid Palestinians affected by the uprising and Israeli counteractions.

The Amman summit of March 27–28, 2001, marked the first regular summit since 1990, with Iraq in attendance as a full participant. The *intifada* remained a principal subject, although no significant new initiatives resulted. Presummit speculation centered largely on efforts to repair the rift between Iraq and Kuwait, but only marginal progress toward that end occurred. The league ended up calling once again for an end to the sanctions against Iraq but also for Baghdad to work out its differences with the United Nations over inspections and related issues. In other matters, the summit advocated accelerating the movement toward free trade as well as forming a customs union and promoting cooperative development in areas such as transport, telecommunications, and information technology. Two months later on May 16, Amr Mahmoud Moussa, theretofore Egypt's foreign minister, began his tenure as the league's new secretary general.

At the 14th Arab League summit, held March 27–28, 2002, in Beirut, Lebanon, attention focused on Iraqi-Kuwaiti relations and on a "land-for-peace" plan offered by Saudi Arabia's Crown Prince Abdullah to settle the Arab-Israeli conflict. Although Iraq and Kuwait appeared ready to resolve their differences, with Baghdad saying it would henceforth respect Kuwait's territorial integrity and sovereignty, positive international expectations for the Saudi plan were undercut even before the summit got under way. In the context of continuing Israeli-Palestinian violence,

PLO leader Yasir Arafat initially rejected Israeli conditions for his departure from Ramallah and ultimately decided not to attend the summit for fear the government of Israeli Prime Minister Sharon would not permit his return. Egypt's President Mubarak and Jordan's King Abdullah also chose not to attend, while several of the smaller Persian Gulf states sent less senior delegations. In addition, on the summit's opening day the Palestinian delegation withdrew over Lebanon's refusal to permit a satellite address by Arafat. As a consequence of these developments, Crown Prince Abdullah's plan failed to register as great an impact as had been anticipated, although it was endorsed by the attendees.

The Saudi plan called for normalization of relations with Israel and affirmed that state's right to security. In return, Israel was expected to withdraw from all occupied territories and recognize a Palestinian state with East Jerusalem as its capital. The summit's concluding Beirut Declaration both called for a "just solution" to the Palestinian refugee problem and rejected "all forms of Palestinian repatriation which conflict with the special circumstances of the Arab host countries."

In October 2002, Libya's Qadhafi announced he would pull his country from the organization because of its demonstrated inability to deal effectively not only with the Palestinian situation, but also the looming crisis involving Iraq and the United States. A March 1, 2003, summit in Sharm el Sheikh, Egypt, to discuss the Iraq crisis left the league divided after a heated exchange between Qadhafi, who attacked Saudi Arabia for permitting U.S. forces on its soil, and Crown Prince Abdullah. The summit concluded with condemnation of any "aggression" against Iraq but also called for Baghdad's compliance with UN weapons inspections. As late as April 2003, Libya maintained its intention to withdraw from the league, but in May, apparently at the urging of the Egyptian president, Qadhafi reversed himself.

With regard to the "road map" for peace in the Middle East that was formally introduced April 30, 2003, by the "quartet" of the European Union, the United Nations, Russia, and the United States,

the Arab League expressed its cautious support. The league welcomed the June decision of militant Palestinian groups to introduce a three-month cease-fire, but a league spokesman cautioned that Israel had yet to "implement its obligations" and cease assassinations, incursions, demolitions, and seizures. He further urged the United States in particular to ensure Israeli compliance with the terms of the peace initiative. On February 25, 2004, in the course of oral presentations before the International Court of Justice in The Hague, the league argued that the separation barrier being erected on Palestinian land by Israel was illegal and "an affront to international law."

In December 2003, the league sent its first official delegation to Iraq, signaling a change in attitude from its earlier criticism of the U.S. invasion in March.

A league summit scheduled for March 29, 2004, in Tunis was abruptly called off two days in advance of the opening because of divisions over peace overtures to Israel, with tensions heightened following Israel's assassination of the leader of the radical Palestinian group *Hamas* just days prior to the summit. The resulting outrage in the Arab world inflamed league ministers and complicated plans to relaunch the Saudi-backed peace initiative adopted at the 2002 Beirut summit. The collapse of the Tunis summit was widely reported as reflective of the turmoil in Arab ranks.

The rescheduled Tunis summit of May 22, 2004, was marred the first day by the walkout of Libya's Qadhafi, who again threatened to withdraw from the league. Qadhafi said he was "disgusted" by the treatment of Saddam Hussein and Yasir Arafat and wholly dissatisfied with the summit agenda. Furthermore, 10 of the 22 league members did not attend the two-day summit, which ultimately issued a strongly worded denunciation of abuse inflicted on Iraqi prisoners by U.S. forces, pledged further reforms to be launched in league countries, and called for an international security force for the Palestinians. The league also called for an extensive UN role in rebuilding Iraq.

An emergency session of the league was called August 8, 2004, to address ways to help Sudan resolve the humanitarian crisis in Darfur, but little was reported from that event. The issue was again addressed at a meeting specific to that purpose on May 16, 2005, producing a resolution promoting resumption of negotiations between the Sudan government in Khartoum and the Darfur rebels.

On March 22–23, 2005, only 13 of 22 leaders attended the league summit in Algiers, and the resolutions adopted "were of comparatively little significance," according to the *New York Times*. However, plans were unveiled for an Arab common market by 2015 and a regional security system. The participants also approved establishment of an interim Arab Parliament, which met for the first time on December 27, 2005, in Cairo. The parliament has 88 representatives, 4 from each Arab League member, but has no legislative authority, leaving its responsibilities and importance unclear, apart from serving as a forum on Arab issues. It was decided that this interim legislature would move to Syria, meeting twice a year with the aim of creating a permanent Arab legislature by 2011. Mohammad Jassim al-Saqr, a Kuwaiti described as a liberal, was elected its speaker.

The Arab League's response to the landslide victory of the militant group *Hamas* in the January 2006 Palestinian Authority elections has been mixed. Secretary General Moussa said *Hamas* should renounce violence against Israel and recognize its right to exist, if it expects to function as a legitimate government. On the other hand, at its March 28–29, 2006, summit in Khartoum, the league pledged to contribute $55 million a month toward the operation of the Palestinian Authority, at a time when some foreign funding appeared likely to be withdrawn because of *Hamas*'s intransigence.

The 2006 summit, like its predecessor, was not attended by the heads of several member states, for reasons including poor security and Sudan's position on the Darfur crisis. In addition to its commitment to the Palestinian Authority, the league pledged $150 million to support the mission of African Union peacekeepers in Darfur. This aid, however, was scheduled to begin in October 2006, the month after the AU was expected to hand over its responsibilities to a UN force. At the meeting's conclusion the Saudi Arabian representative withdrew his country's offer to host the 2007 meeting, leaving it instead to be held in Egypt.

ARAB MAGHREB UNION (AMU)

Established: By the Arab Maghreb Treaty, signed by the heads of state of the member countries on February 17, 1989, in Marrakesh, Morocco, effective July 1, 1989.

Purpose: "To strengthen the bonds of brotherhood which bind the member states and their peoples to each other . . . to work gradually towards the realization of the freedom of movement of [the member states'] people, goods, services, and capital . . . to safeguard the independence of every member state . . . to realize the industrial, agricultural, commercial, and social development of the member states . . . by setting up joint ventures and preparing general and specialized programs . . . to initiate cooperation with a view to developing education at various levels, to preserving the spiritual and moral values derived from the tolerant teachings of Islam, to safeguarding the Arab national identity."

Headquarters: Casablanca, Morocco.

Principal Organs: Presidential Council (heads of member states), Council of Prime Ministers, Council of Foreign Ministers, Consultative Council, Judicial Body, Follow-up Committee, Specialized Ministerial Commissions, General Secretariat.

Secretary General: Mohamed Habib Benyahya (Tunisia).

Membership (5): Algeria, Libya, Mauritania, Morocco, Tunisia.

Official Language: Arabic.

Origin and development. The idea of a unified northern Africa was first voiced by Arab nationalists in the 1920s and subsequently received widespread support throughout the turbulence of World War II and the independence movements of the 1950s and early 1960s. By contrast, the postindependence era yielded a variety of territorial disputes, political rivalries, and ideological differences that blunted meaningful integration efforts. However, the Maghrebian movement regained momentum following the 1987 rapprochement between Algeria and Morocco (see articles on those countries). Meeting together for the first time in June 1988 in Algiers, Algeria, the leaders of the five Maghrebian countries appointed a commission and five subcommittees to draft a treaty that would encompass the "Greater Arab Maghreb." After intensive negotiations, the treaty was signed February 17, 1989, following a two-day summit in Marrakesh, Morocco, with formal ratification following shortly thereafter.

Although the five heads of state appeared arm-in-arm after the summit, reports indicated that volatile Libyan leader Mu'ammar al-Qadhafi, upset at the rejection of his proposal that Chad, Mali, Niger, and Sudan be brought into the union, had attended only at the last minute. After the summit Qadhafi continued to push for "one invincible Arab nation" from the Atlantic to the Persian Gulf, and, apparently at his insistence, the Arab Maghreb Treaty left AMU membership open to other countries "belonging to the Arab nation or the African group."

Structure. The supreme political organ of the AMU is the Presidential Council, comprising the heads of state of the member nations; the chair of the council rotates among the heads of state, who are assisted by a Council of Prime Ministers. The Council of Foreign Ministers is empowered to attend sessions of the Presidential Council and is responsible for preparing summit agendas. Reporting to the Council of Foreign Ministers is a Follow-up Committee, comprising the members' secretaries of state for Maghreb affairs, who are mandated to oversee the implementation of integrationist measures. In addition, Specialized Ministerial Commissions have been established in five areas (with each commission empowered to create subsidiary committees): interior, human resources (judicial affairs, youth and sports, culture and information, labor and social affairs, higher education and scientific research, health), infrastructure (transport, public works, housing and urban development, posts and communications), economy and finance (financial and monetary affairs, commerce, energy and mines, industry, tourism and crafts), and food security.

The original treaty provided for a Consultative Council of ten representatives from each member state; in 1994 the size of each delegation was increased to 30. The Consultative Council meets in ordinary session once a year and in emergency session at the request of the Presidential Council, to which it submits recommendations and draft resolutions. The treaty also calls for a "judicial body," consisting of two judges appointed by each member state, to "deal with disputes concerning the implementation of the treaty and the accords concluded within the framework of the Union." A small General Secretariat operates from Morocco, the participants having pledged to keep the union's bureaucracy to a bare minimum.

Activities. Despite economic and political differences among its members, the AMU was perceived at its formation as having the capacity to provide a significant regional response to the single internal market being planned then by the European Community (EC, later the European Union—EU). In subsequent months preliminary agreement was reported on the establishment of a regional airline and unification of postal and telecommunications services. In addition, several joint industrial projects were approved, and a campaign was launched to vaccinate children against an array of diseases. However, by early 1990, AMU proponents acknowledged that progress had been slower than anticipated in reducing trade barriers, facilitating the movement of people across national borders, and otherwise moving toward economic integration. Consequently, the AMU heads of state, during a January summit in Tunis, Tunisia, agreed to appoint a secretary general, establish a permanent headquarters, and implement other changes to strengthen AMU authority and effectiveness. It was also announced that the AMU defense and foreign ministers were asked to study ways of achieving "cooperation and coordination" in security matters. Nevertheless, several difficult political issues continued to work against regional unity, including Mauritania's displeasure over lack of support from Morocco in its border dispute with Senegal (see articles on Mauritania and Senegal), irritation among several members over positions taken by Libya's Colonel Qadhafi, and failure to resolve the Western Sahara dispute (see Morocco article).

A lack of cohesion was also evident during a July 1990 summit in Algiers, as the heads of state were unable to agree on a location for the permanent AMU headquarters or to select a secretary general. Moreover, as was the case in many Arab organizations, activity within the AMU was subsequently constrained by events associated with Iraq's invasion of Kuwait in August. Although Morocco adopted a solidly anti-Iraq stance and contributed troops to the U.S.-led Desert Shield operation, the other AMU members opposed the presence of U.S. troops in the Persian Gulf. In addition, strong pro-Iraq sentiment surfaced within all of the AMU states, creating concern among some officials over a possible backlash against those North African countries perceived by the EC and other Western nations to have been on the "wrong side" of the Persian Gulf crisis. As a result, the AMU summit in Ras Lanuf, Libya, in March 1991 called on the Arab League to work quickly to heal divisions created by the war so a pan-Arab consensus could be reached on economic, political, and security issues.

During the 1991 summit the AMU heads of state (with the exception of Libya's Colonel Qadhafi, whose absence was unexplained) agreed to establish the organization's General Secretariat in Casablanca, the Maghreb Consultative Council in Algeria, the Maghreb University and Science Academy in Libya, the Maghreb Court in Mauritania, and a Maghreb Bank for Investment and External Trade (*Banque Maghrébine d'Investissement et de Commerce Extérieur*—BMICE) in Tunisia. In October, Mohammed Amamou of Tunisia was selected as the AMU's first secretary general. However, most of the AMU's planned initiatives subsequently remained unimplemented as conflict among the members left the impression, in the words of the *Middle East International*, that the union was "dead, if not quite buried."

One major stumbling block to effective regional action was the imposition of limited sanctions by the United Nations against Libya in the spring of 1992 because of Tripoli's refusal to turn over two suspects in the bombing of an airliner over Lockerbie, Scotland, in the late 1980s. Despite strong protests from Colonel Qadhafi, Libya's AMU partners honored the sanctions, although the AMU summit held November 10–11 in Nouakchott, Mauritania, urged the UN to reconsider its position. The summit also issued a declaration condemning the "terrorism" stemming from militant Islamic fundamentalism in the region and called for "concerted effort" to keep it in check.

Some rhetorical commitment to union aims returned at the sixth AMU summit, held after several postponements April 2–3, 1994, in Tunis. In addition to urging faster implementation of previous agreements, the AMU leaders called for intensified trade and security negotiations with the EU. However, the Libyan regime, which, prior to the summit, had bluntly labeled the AMU a "failure," reportedly remained "bitter" that the AMU members were still upholding the UN sanctions. For their part, the AMU leaders expressed "concern" over the effects of the sanctions on the Libyan people and called for a "just, honorable, and swift settlement" based on "international laws, resolutions, and charters."

The next AMU summit was postponed indefinitely after Libya announced it would not assume its scheduled chair tenure because of the Lockerbie impasse. Following the apparent resolution of the sanctions issue in early 1999, observers suggested that a revival of AMU progress was at hand, but the AMU remained essentially moribund because of differences between Morocco and Algeria over the latter's support for the Polisario insurgents in the Western Sahara. The 35th session of the Follow-up Committee convened in Algiers in mid-May, ostensibly to relaunch the union, but little came of the meeting. In August, newly crowned King Mohamed of Morocco proposed to Algerian President Bouteflika that the AMU be reinvigorated, and a month later a Moroccan spokesman described the union as "still a fundamental project in our view." Nevertheless, a summit anticipated for November never occurred, and in February 2000, Tunisian President Ben Ali, marking the union's 11th anniversary, once again urged that the AMU be revived, calling it "a strategic choice and an historical aspiration."

A March 2001 meeting of the Council of Foreign Ministers in Algiers was partly undercut by Morocco's unenthusiastic participation. Later in the year, however, it appeared that the Moroccan and Algerian leaders attempted to work around the Western Sahara issue. The fourth session of the Consultative Council met in September in Rabat, Morocco, after a lapse of nine years. In October 2001 the AMU trade ministers announced agreement on a draft free trade area and customs union, while a foreign ministers meeting in January 2002 was viewed as a prelude to a seventh summit in mid-2002, eight years after the sixth. At the January session the ministers appointed Habib Boularès of Tunisia as successor to Secretary General Amamou.

The anticipated June 2002 summit ultimately fell victim to continuing differences over the Western Sahara. Earlier, Colonel Qadhafi offered to mediate the dispute between Algiers and Rabat, with the Polisario Front expressing conditional support for the proposal. Morocco, however, termed the offer unrealistic, and in early June, King Mohamed indicated he would not attend the summit. As a consequence, the meeting was postponed indefinitely.

The Council of Foreign Ministers convened January 3–4, 2003, in Algiers, where one of the concerns was the need for the AMU to adapt to the challenges posed by increasing globalization. The concluding communiqué again denounced Israeli aggression against Palestinians, called for the lifting of sanctions against Iraq as well as remaining sanctions against Libya, and condemned terrorism (while noting the right of resistance against foreign occupation). The foreign ministers also supported continuation of the "5 + 5 dialog" on Mediterranean issues, begun in 1991 with France, Italy, Spain, Portugal, and Malta.

On December 22, 2003, a day before the much-discussed AMU summit was to have been held, the AMU foreign ministers, meeting in Algiers, indefinitely postponed the meeting. The cancellation followed announcements that the king of Morocco, the president of Mauritania, and the Libyan leader had all declined to attend. Shortly before, Mauritania accused Libya of financing a plot to overthrow Mauritania's government. After the cancellation Colonel Qadhafi indicated the summit might be rescheduled following Algeria's 2004 presidential election. A subsequent attempt to hold a summit in Tripoli in May 2005 was canceled at the last minute as the king of Morocco declined to attend because of the dispute with Algeria over Western Sahara. Algeria had reiterated its support for the Polisario insurgents in that territory.

The Council of Foreign Ministers continues to meet, exploring ways to revitalize the union and to address such pressing local issues as drought and agriculture, the latter with particular reference to genetically modified crops. In February 2006 the secretary general said the union would be active in monitoring elections over the next year to facilitate Mauritania's return to democracy, following the August 3, 2005, coup there.

ARAB MONETARY FUND (AMF)

Established: By Articles of Agreement signed April 27, 1976, in Rabat, Morocco, with effect from February 2, 1977.

Purpose: To correct disequilibria in the balance of payments of member states; to promote the stability of exchange rates among Arab currencies, rendering them mutually convertible; to promote Arab economic integration and development; to encourage the creation of a unified Arab currency; and to coordinate policies in other international monetary and economic forums.

Headquarters: Abu Dhabi, United Arab Emirates.

Principal Organs: Board of Governors (all members), Board of Executive Directors (9 members), Loan and Investments Committees.

Director General: Jassim al-Mannai (Bahrain).

Membership (22): Algeria, Bahrain, Comoros, Djibouti, Egypt, Iraq, Jordan, Kuwait, Lebanon, Libya, Mauritania, Morocco, Oman, Palestine, Qatar, Saudi Arabia, Somalia, Sudan, Syria, Tunisia, United Arab Emirates, Yemen. (The memberships of Iraq, Somalia, and Sudan were suspended in February 1993 because of payments arrears. Sudan reached a repayment agreement, and its membership was reactivated in April 2000.)

Official Language: Arabic.

Origin and development. Although a proposal to form an Arab Payments Union was made by the Arab Economic Council in the 1960s and a meeting was subsequently held for that purpose, the idea was discarded as attention was drawn to more pressing political issues. With the quadrupling of oil prices in 1974, however, concern once again focused on the issue of monetary problems. The objective was now more ambitious: an organization to deal with recycling, or investing, Arab "petrodollars" to decrease dependence on foreign handling of surplus funds. This goal is clearly implicit in the Articles of Agreement signed in April 1976. Since then, the AMF has gradually expanded its mission to promote economic integration and development, to aid Arab financial institutions, to encourage intra-Arab trade, and to assist member countries in structural financial reforms.

Structure. The Board of Governors, comprising one governor and one alternate governor from each member state, serves as the fund's general assembly and holds all administrative powers. Meeting at least once a year, it is responsible for capitalization, income distribution, the admission and suspension of members, and the appointment of the fund's director general. The Board of Executive Directors, consisting of the director general and eight experts elected for three-year terms from the member states, performs tasks assigned it by the Board of Governors. Subsidiary departments include the Economic and Technical Department, the Economic Policy Institute, and the Treasury and Investments Department.

One of the AMF's principal aims is to foster the economic integration of member states. Thus the fund has guaranteed loans to Arab countries to correct payment imbalances resulting from unilateral or pan-Arab development projects. It has also used its capital as a catalyst to advance Arab financial instruments and has promoted creation of a unified Arab currency. It provides technical assistance to the monetary and banking agencies of member countries, largely through training seminars in such areas as branch banking and accounting, bank supervision and internal auditing, and documentary credit. It also cooperates with other Arab and international organizations to discuss and promote areas of common interest.

In late 1987 the AMF launched a restructuring program apparently with widespread support from Arab bankers; its "fresh priorities" included the creation of a regional securities market and the strengthening of securities markets in member states to provide long-term financing for development. In September 1988 the fund endorsed further changes, such as an emphasis on "productive projects" leading directly to economic growth, rather than on the infrastructural programs of earlier years. Although not yet willing to say it would attach conditions to AMF loans, the Board of Executive Directors announced its intention to take a more active interest in how loans were used. The board also approved the creation of an Economic Policy Institute to assist member states in formulating national policies as well as to promote the development of financial strategies for the Arab countries as a group.

Attention subsequently shifted to the Arab Trade Financing Program (ATFP), established by the AMF and other pan-Arab financial institutions to promote trade among Arab countries. The AMF agreed to provide $250 million of the initial $500 million of authorized capital and was accorded control of five of the nine seats on the program's board of directors. Approved in 1989, the ATFP was scheduled to become operational in 1990 but its launching was delayed by the Persian Gulf crisis. The first ATFP loan agreement (with Morocco) was signed in January 1992.

As was the case with most Arab financial institutions, AMF activity was severely curtailed by the 1990–1991 Gulf War, although it began to rebound in the mid-1990s. Cumulative approvals reached 718.8 million Arab Accounting Dinars (AAD) ($2.9 billion) for 103 projects as of January 1, 1998. Since then, most loans have involved a new Structural Adjustment Facility (SAF), which was set up to support reforms in the financial sector.

In March 2003 the AMF changed its general lending policy, replacing its traditional fixed-interest loans with two types of market-related variable rates on new loans, and allowing member countries to choose between the two. Following the U.S.-led invasion of Iraq in the spring of 2003, the AMF played a role in attempts to rebuild Iraqi national life. In March 2004 the fund organized, in conjunction with the International Monetary Fund (IMF), a course on "Macroeconomic Management and Policies" for Iraqi officials from the Central Bank of Iraq and the Iraqi ministries of finance and planning. This course was held at the AMF's headquarters in Abu Dhabi. The fund declined, however, to write off Iraq's debts, with Egypt's the largest in its portfolio, but declared it would seek repayment when the country's situation improved. At this time the fund approved the reinstatement of Sudan, having approved an agreement to settle its arrears, estimated at nearly $93 million.

The year 2005 was characterized by the beginning of a run-up in oil prices, combined with the sinking value of the U.S. dollar against other major currencies. As a result, the fund's conservative management made adequate progress, and its educational arm held several conferences and seminars for its member banks on national and international money management.

By early 2006, the AMF warned that the oil boom was discouraging Arab governments from making public sector investments in national infrastructure. Instead, the money flow was forcing more such investment into the private sector, where it would be less centrally managed. The year 2006 also saw the unexpected victory of Hamas in Palestinian Authority elections. The fund announced that it would allocate 10 percent of 2005's net profits, approximately $50 million, to aid Palestinians, but none of it would go to the Hamas-led government.

CENTRAL AFRICAN ECONOMIC AND MONETARY COMMUNITY (CEMAC)

Communauté Economique et Monétaire de l'Afrique Centrale

Established: By the Central African Customs and Economic Union (UDEAC) under a treaty signed March 15–16, 1994, in N'Djamena, Chad; formally succeeded the UDEAC in June 1999, following ratification of the treaty by the member states.

Purpose: To promote socioeconomic integration and sustainable development in Central Africa in the context of monetary and economic unions.

Headquarters: Bangui, Central African Republic.

Principal Organs: Conference of Heads of State, Council of Ministers of the Central African Economic Union, Ministerial Council of the Central African Monetary Union, Executive Secretariat.

Executive Secretary: Jean Nkuete (Cameroon).

Membership (6): Cameroon, Central African Republic, Chad, Republic of the Congo, Equatorial Guinea, Gabon.

Official Language: French.

Origin and development. Prior to attaining independence, the Central African Republic, Chad, the Congo, and Gabon were joined in the Equatorial Customs Union (*Union Douanière Equatoriales*—UDE), which sought to harmonize the fiscal treatment of industrial investments. In June 1961 Cameroon joined the UDE, and by mid-1962 an external common tariff had been established. In 1964 the members began more comprehensive economic cooperation, including coordination of development policies, especially in the fields of infrastructure and industrialization, and on December 8 they signed in Brazzaville, Congo, a treaty establishing the Central African Customs and Economic Union (*Union Douanière et Economique de l'Afrique Centrale*—UDEAC), effective January 1, 1966.

In early 1968 Chad and the Central African Republic announced their intention to withdraw from the UDEAC, but the latter reversed itself later in the year. Chad's withdrawal became effective January 1, 1969, although N'Djamena continued to participate in some activities. In December 1975 it was granted observer status in the Council of Heads of State and ultimately rejoined the group in December 1984. Equatorial Guinea joined the UDEAC in December 1983.

The November 1992 UDEAC summit endorsed the creation of a Central African Economic and Monetary Community (*Communauté Economique et Monétaire de l'Afrique Centrale*—CEMAC). Prompted in part by repercussions from the 50 percent devaluation of the CFA franc in January 1994, a UDEAC summit on March 15–16 in N'Djamena signed a treaty creating CEMAC. Although another summit on December 21–22 in Yaoundé, Cameroon, reaffirmed the integrationist commitment, decisions were again delayed on a timetable for the implementation of CEMAC provisions.

At the February 5, 1998, summit, Gabonese President Omar Bongo urged members to ratify the CEMAC treaty, stating that the establishment of the Central African Monetary Union would "mark the end of recovery and the beginning of a new dynamism." The only country to have ratified the treaty by that time was the Central African Republic, but the ratification process accelerated thereafter, and the inaugural CEMAC summit was held in June 1999, in Malabo, Equatorial Guinea.

Structure. The Conference of Heads of State meets at least once a year to coordinate the general monetary and economic policies of the participating states. The CEMAC treaty created a Monetary Union (*Union Monétaire de l'Afrique Centrale—*UMAC), which is under the direction of a Ministerial Council, and an Economic Union (*Union Economique de l'Afrique Centrale*—UEAC), directed by a Council of Ministers. Specialized institutions integrated into the UEAC are the Interstate Customs School, the Subregional Multisectoral Institute for Applied Technology, the Subregional Institute for Statistics and Applied Economics, and the Development Bank of the Central African States (*Banque de Développement des Etats de l'Afrique Centrale*—BDEAC). The UMAC incorporates the Bank of the Central African States (*Banque des Etats de l'Afrique Centrale—*BEAC) and the Banking Commission of Central Africa. The treaty also called for formation of a Community Parliament and a Community Court of Justice.

The chief administrative officer of the CEMAC is an executive secretary, who heads an Executive Secretariat with various divisions and offices responsible for administrative and financial affairs; agriculture, food security, and the environment; the common market; economic analysis; education and culture; industrial commerce and tourism; juridical and institutional affairs; and transport and telecommunications.

Activities. As forerunner of the CEMAC, the UDEAC adjusted common external customs tariffs; coordinated legislation, regulations, and investment codes; harmonized internal taxes; and developed common industrialization projects, development plans, and transport policies. In 1973 the BEAC was established as a central bank for all UDEAC members and Chad, and it continues in that capacity for the CEMAC.

In January 1978 the UDEAC heads of state adopted additional measures designed to facilitate economic unity. These included a projected common income tax, community administration of waterways between Bangui and Brazzaville, and harmonization of legislation dealing with migration and industrialization. In addition, members agreed to increase cooperation in business and civil service administration, to standardize customs procedures, and to establish common structures for scientific and technical research, transportation, communications, and tourism. Subsequently, the UDEAC played a major role in formation of the Economic Community of Central African States (*Communauté Economique des Etats de l'Afrique Centrale*—CEEAC), an association of 11 French- and Portuguese-speaking states, established in October 1983 (see separate article).

The late 1980s saw the UDEAC make little specific headway on regional economic integration, although a declaration issued at the conclusion of the organization's 1988 summit reaffirmed the members' commitment to that goal. The declaration also noted the willingness of members to accept "reasonable social costs" affiliated with structural adjustment policies, provided industrialized nations would accept the "realities" of Africa's economic problems and increase their development assistance.

A lack of meaningful action also characterized the 1989 summit, the heads of state deciding that the economic crises affecting member states would preclude significant UDEAC financing. In light of continuing financial constraints, the December 1990 summit ordered sharp cutbacks in the UDEAC secretariat staff while deferring consideration of a regional value-added tax and/or a community integration tax. A new secretary general, Thomas Dakayi Kamga of Cameroon, was named at the December 1991 summit, with several modifications regarding customs collections being approved in the hope of alleviating the UDEAC's financial difficulties. A plan was also adopted to abolish import restrictions in mid-1992, although implementation was delayed in the wake of concerted opposition from business interests in member states.

Activity over the next several years focused on establishment of the CEMAC, which was expected to be a more effective vehicle for regional integration. CEMAC was formally inaugurated at a summit on June 25–26, 1999, in Malabo, collateral with the summit of the CEEAC. The two organizations again held parallel summits in June 2000 in Libreville, Gabon, where the CEMAC attendees remarked positively on the ongoing development of institutional arrangements, including formation of an interparliamentary commission; announced their intention to revitalize the BDEAC; and called attention to the challenges presented by economic globalization and the concomitant need for stronger regional and subregional integration. In May–June 2001 the CEMAC/CEEAC trade ministers met in Yaoundé to prepare for ACP (African, Caribbean, and Pacific) trade negotiations with the European Union. At the second regular CEMAC summit, held in mid-December 2000 in N'Djamena, the national leaders agreed to accelerate introduction of a common passport and to establish a regional stock exchange in Libreville.

The focus of attention at an extraordinary summit held in early December 2001 in Libreville was the volatile political situation in the Central African Republic (CAR), where the armed forces chief, General François Bozize, was dismissed because of his alleged involvement in a failed May 2001 coup against President Ange-Félix Patassé. The CEMAC leaders established an ad hoc commission of Presidents Bongo of Gabon, Déby of Chad, and Sassou-Nguesso of the Republic of Congo to encourage the disputants to negotiate. Shortly after the December 5 conclusion of the Libreville session, the CEMAC leaders convened for a previ-ously scheduled annual summit in Yaoundé, where plans for a joint air transport company, introduction of the common passport, and medium-term customs and tax reforms were discussed. The summit also addressed the need to combat money laundering and to restructure the BDEAC. Another topic considered by the attendees was the possible inclusion of Angola, the Democratic Republic of Congo, and Sao Tome and Principe in subregional discussions with the European Union (EU).

Beginning in early 2002 the CEMAC's attention became increasingly diverted by the deteriorating situation in the CAR. An extraordinary summit on August 15 in Brazzaville authorized dispatch of an observer team to the CAR as a consequence of escalating tensions with Chad, which gave refuge to General Bozize. Meanwhile, Bozize loyalists continued to threaten the CAR's internal security. A CEMAC crisis summit in early October 2002 was followed in late January 2003 by the fourth ordinary Conference of Heads of State, which urged the CAR government to open talks with the rebels and called on the two neighboring states to resolve their differences. By that time a CEMAC peacekeeping force was already being deployed to the CAR, replacing a contingent that Libya sent in May 2001 to protect President Patassé's government. On March 15, 2003, however, General Bozize mounted a successful coup, which led the CEMAC Conference of Heads of State, meeting June 2–3 in Libreville, to officially recognize the successor regime. The decision came following General Bozize's presentation of a plan for the rapid restoration of democracy. The conference then called for international humanitarian assistance for the CAR as well as other measures to restore the country's peace and security. Several hundred CEMAC troops from Gabon, Chad, and the Republic of the Congo remained deployed in the CAR with a mandate that included protecting the capital and provincial towns, securing transportation routes, disarming combatants, and restructuring the CAR armed forces.

Meanwhile, the CEMAC moved forward on various initiatives, including improvements in cross-border land transport and initiation of the public/private Air CEMAC. This airline, which was initially expected to begin operations by the end of 2003, encountered difficulties in starting up, and its first flight was last heard of as projected for the end of 2005. Its future seems unclear. In addition to their involvement in negotiating partnership agreements with the EU, the CEMAC trade ministers continued to formulate a common position for international trade forums. Other CEMAC concerns included food security and self-sufficiency and sustainable use of the region's forests.

The fifth Heads of State Conference, held January 28, 2004, in Brazzaville, Republic of the Congo, produced a nonaggression pact, an agreement on judicial cooperation between the member states, and an agreement on extradition. The sixth conference was held February 11, 2005, in Libreville. It encouraged peace and civic responsibility in the troubled states of the Central African Republic, Côte d'Ivoire, and Togo, and expressed concern about the deteriorating situation in Darfur.

The seventh conference, held on March 14–15, 2006, in Bata, Equatorial Guinea, was marked by the early return home of the president of Chad, Idriss Deby, in face of an attempted coup against him; the coup failed. The conference, noting the slow progress of subregional integration, set up a task force, due to report in 2008, to see what could be done.

COMMON MARKET FOR EASTERN AND SOUTHERN AFRICA (COMESA)

Established: By treaty signed November 5, 1993, in Kampala, Uganda, and effective December 8, 1994.

Purpose: To promote wide-ranging regional economic cooperation, particularly in the areas of agriculture, industry, transportation, and communications; to facilitate intraregional trade through the reduction or elimination of trade barriers and the establishment of regional financial institutions; to establish a common external tariff and internal free trade zone; and to pursue "economic prosperity through regional integration."

Headquarters: Lusaka, Zambia.

Principal Organs: Authority of Heads of State and Government, Council of Ministers, Committee of Governors, Intergovernmental Committee, Court of Justice, Secretariat.

Secretary General: Erastus J. O. Mwencha (Kenya).

Membership (21): Angola, Burundi, Comoros, Democratic Republic of the Congo, Djibouti, Egypt, Eritrea, Ethiopia, Kenya, Libya, Madagascar, Malawi, Mauritius, Rwanda, Seychelles, Sudan, Swaziland, Tanzania, Uganda, Zambia, and Zimbabwe. (In 1996 signatories Lesotho and Mozambique announced they would not ratify the Comesa treaty but were instead "withdrawing" from Comesa. However, in 1997 Mozambique announced it was only "suspending" its affiliation.)

Origin and development. The creation of a permanent organization to coordinate economic cooperation among eastern and southern African states was first proposed in the mid-1970s by the United Nations' Economic Commission for Africa and subsequently endorsed by the Organization of African Unity (OAU) in its 1980 Lagos Plan of Action for the continent's overall economic development. After what were described as "tough negotiations" arising from the seeming incompatibility of some of the national economies in the region and given that many potential members relied on the production of the same commodities, the Preferential Trade Area for Eastern and Southern African States (PTA) was launched on December 21, 1981, by nine nations—the Comoro Islands, Djibouti, Ethiopia, Kenya, Malawi, Mauritius, Somalia, Uganda, and Zambia. Lesotho, Swaziland, and Zimbabwe joined in 1982, followed by Burundi and Rwanda in 1984, Tanzania in 1985, Mozambique and Sudan in 1988, Angola in 1990, and Eritrea, Madagascar, Namibia, and Seychelles in 1993. Zaire also applied for admission in the early 1990s, but consideration of its request was postponed because of its domestic turmoil.

The operational phase of the PTA began in 1984 when tariffs on some goods traded between members were reduced, and a PTA financial clearinghouse, run by the Reserve Bank of Zimbabwe, was established to permit trade based on members' national currencies. In addition, a PTA Trade and Development Bank was opened in 1986 in Bujumbura, Burundi, although it moved to Nairobi, Kenya, in 1994.

At the January 1992 PTA heads of state meeting, delegates conceded that the organization had little to show for its first ten years of existence. Many tariffs on trade between members remained high, most of the region's communications and transportation facilities were still subpar, and members' arrears continued to undercut the potential effectiveness of the PTA Secretariat. In addition, most members were preoccupied with turbulent domestic affairs to the apparent exclusion of regional concerns. Nevertheless, supporters of integration expressed the hope that spreading democratization and free market emphasis in the region would soon translate into greater economic cooperation. Toward that end, PTA officials proposed a merger with the Southern African Development Community (SADC), whose overlapping membership and objectives were producing a "parallel existence" between the two groups that was seen as counterproductive. However, the SADC, historically much more successful in attracting international financial support because of its highly visible face-off with apartheid-era South Africa, rejected the proposed union, at least for the time being.

Many of the PTA's original tasks were expanded in the treaty establishing the Common Market of Eastern and Southern Africa (Comesa), which was signed during the PTA's 12th summit on November 5, 1993, in Kampala, Uganda. Following ratification of the Comesa treaty by enough signatories for the accord to enter into force on December 8, 1994, officials and journalists routinely began to refer to Comesa as the "successor" to the PTA, even though several PTA members—Lesotho, Mozambique, and Somalia—ultimately opted not to join Comesa, and two nonmembers of the PTA—Democratic Republic of Congo and Egypt (1998)—did join. Tanzania withdrew in September 2000. The renamed Eastern and Southern Africa Trade and Development Bank continues to be known less formally as the PTA Bank, and the autonomous *Compagnie de Réassurance de la Zone d'Echanges Préférentiels* (ZEP-RE) is similarly styled the PTA Reinsurance Company in English.

Structure. At the apex of Comesa is the Authority of Heads of State and Government, which establishes by consensus fundamental policy and directs subsidiary organs in pursuit of the Common Market's objectives. The Council of Ministers monitors and reviews the performance of administrators and financial managers in addition to overseeing the organization's programs and projects. An Intergovernmental Committee, comprising permanent secretaries from the member countries, develops and manages cooperative programs and action plans in all sectors except finance and monetary policy, which is the domain of a separate Committee of Governors of the members' central banks. There are also a number of technical committees and a Secretariat, the latter, following a recent reorganization, including five divisions: Administration; Trade, Customs, and Monetary Harmonization; Investment and Private Sector Development; Infrastructure Development; and Information and Networking. The secretary general serves a once-renewable, five-year term. A Court of Justice is responsible for interpreting the Comesa treaty and for adjudicating related disputes between members.

The PTA Bank is the most prominent of various Comesa-established autonomous institutions, which also include the Comesa Bankers' Association (BAPTA), the Comesa Metallurgical Industries Association (Comesamia), the Comesa Telecommunications Company (Comtel), the Eastern and Southern Africa Business Association (ESABO), the Federation of National Associations of Women in Business (Femcom), the Leather and Leather Products Institute (LLPI), and the Pharmaceutical Manufacturers of Eastern and Southern Africa (Pharmesa).

Activities. The initial Comesa summit was held December 7–9, 1994, in Lilongwe, Malawi; however, whereas the treaty had 22 signatories at that point (all the PTA members except Djibouti, Seychelles, and Somalia, plus Zaire), it had only been ratified by 12 (Burundi, Comoro Islands, Eritrea, Ethiopia, Kenya, Madagascar, Malawi, Mauritius, Sudan, Tanzania, Uganda, and Zambia). Thus, although plans were discussed for eventual cooperation in the areas of customs, transportation, communications, agriculture, and industry, formal arrangements remained incomplete, partly because of uncertainties over the relationship between the PTA/Comesa and the SADC.

The outlook for Comesa was further clouded in late 1995 when South Africa announced it did not intend to join. At the end of 1996 Mozambique and Lesotho announced their "withdrawal" from Comesa, and speculation arose that Namibia might follow suit; most SADC members seemed to prefer distinguishable north and south zones of economic cooperation (see SADC article). In 1996 the SADC countries once again vetoed Comesa's offer to merge as a single trade zone. Kenya, Tanzania, and Uganda considered turning away from Comesa activity in favor of the proposed reactivation of their old East African Community (EAC).

In late January 1997, Secretary General Bingu Mutharika was suspended during an investigation into the recent management of funds within the Secretariat. Mutharika resigned in April (although he continued to deny any wrongdoing), and Erastus Mwencha of Kenya succeeded him in an acting capacity.

Mwencha officially replaced Mutharika at the third Comesa summit, held in mid-1998 in Kinshasa, Democratic Republic of Congo (formerly Zaire). Summit participants agreed to eliminate tariffs and the need for visas within the Common Market by 2000 and to admit Egypt as the first North African member. Egypt officially became a member after ratifying the Comesa treaty later that year, but progress toward the removal of tariffs was slower than hoped. Comesa members were urged to reduce the tariffs by 90 percent by October 1998, but as of early December only Madagascar had done so. Despite this, Comesa still hoped for their total removal in 2000. In other activities, the Comesa Court of Justice, established under the Comesa treaty, held its first session in September 1998, and the PTA Development Bank decided to invite countries from outside the region to become members in an effort to increase the bank's capital.

Speaking at the fourth Comesa summit May 24–25, 1999, Kenyan President Daniel arap Moi called for greater subregional cooperation, which he described as crucial for achieving high economic growth rates and attracting investment capital. Otherwise, he warned, the Comesa countries would face being marginalized by ongoing economic globalization and competition from other trading blocs. As a key step toward further integration, the summit established a committee charged with preparations for introducing a Free Trade Area (FTA). (Many Comesa members had already reduced tariffs by 60–90 percent on goods produced within the grouping.) The summit participants, acknowledging the collateral importance of regional stability, also agreed to study setting up a mechanism for maintaining peace and security.

Arguably the most significant event in the organization's history occurred at an extraordinary summit in Lusaka, Zambia, on October 31, 2000, when nine Comesa members—Djibouti, Egypt, Kenya, Madagascar, Malawi, Mauritius, Sudan, Zambia, and Zimbabwe—inaugurated Africa's first FTA, enabling duty-free trade in goods, services, and capital and eliminating for the participants other nontariff barriers to trade. Political concerns in several states, including Burundi, Rwanda, and Eritrea, delayed their participation, and for Namibia and Swaziland membership in the Southern African Customs Union (SACU) made their entry into Comesa's FTA problematic. Moreover, in what was generally acknowledged to be a major setback, Tanzania withdrew from Comesa in September 2000, citing the need to streamline its international memberships and preferring to remain in the SADC because of the latter's emphasis on capacity building for goods production.

Although no additional members joined the FTA by late 2003, others were expected to do so before attainment of Comesa's next major goal: introducing in 2004 a customs union and tiered Common External Tariff (CET) for capital, raw materials, intermediate goods, and finished goods. Another target date, 2025, has been set for formation of a full-fledged economic community that would feature a monetary union and the free movement of goods, services, capital, and people.

The sixth Comesa summit, held May 22–23, 2001, in Cairo formally endorsed moving ahead with the CET despite problems in administering the FTA, including disputes between Zambia and Zimbabwe, Egypt and Sudan, and Egypt and Kenya. One of the major difficulties was determining how to compensate local industries damaged by the expansion of competition. At the same time, a May 22 meeting of Comesa and the SADC leaders suggested the rivalry between the two organizations had abated somewhat. In fact, they decided to form a Secretariat-level task force charged with coordinating programs and activities.

The 2001 summit's final communiqué directed Comesa to move forward in such areas as gender policy, e-commerce, and food security. Later in the year Comesa launched in Nairobi an African Trade Insurance Agency (ATIA), with funding from the World Bank group, the European Union (EU), and Japan, to protect investors against political risks. In addition, on October 29 Comesa and the United States signed a significant Trade and Investment Framework Agreement.

The May 23–24, 2002, summit in Addis Ababa, Ethiopia, saw the reappointment of Secretary General Mwencha. The attendees also authorized the return of the Comesa Trade and Development Bank to Bujumbura and signed a protocol for establishing a Fund for Cooperation, Compensation, and Development.

The organization's eighth summit, held March 17, 2003, in Khartoum, Sudan, focused on the anticipated introduction of the Customs Union and accompanying CET in December. Meanwhile, Secretary General Mwencha reported, intra-Comesa trade had expanded at a rate of 30 percent per year since the 2000 launch of the FTA. At the end of 2003 the FTA still had only nine members, although Rwanda was expected to join early in 2004. Rwanda and Burundi had announced in March 2003 they were preparing to join, as were Namibia and Swaziland, assuming that remaining issues involving their SACU memberships were resolved. Namibia actually left in July 2003, intending to concentrate on its relationship with SACU. The summit also called for further development of basic infrastructure; discussed food security, particularly in light of recurrent crises in the Horn of Africa; and emphasized the need to strengthen regional peace and security. With regard to trade, Comesa agreed to adopt a regional approach in pursuit of an Economic Partnership Agreement with the EU. In addition, while noting that the textile sector was particularly benefiting from improved access to U.S. markets under the U.S. Africa Growth and Opportunity Act (AGOA), the summit participants called for closer cooperation in other sectors, especially agriculture. In other business, the summit received a request for membership from Libya.

The ninth summit was held on June 7–8, 2004 in Kampala, Uganda. Trade and investments within the community were discussed, as was the plan to move to a customs union by the end of the year. For the first time a business summit ran concurrently with the Heads of State and Government meeting, attracting more than 600 delegates. At the tenth summit on June 2–3, 2005, in Kigali, Rwanda, Comesa admitted Libya. Twenty-one countries now belong to Comesa.

THE COMMONWEALTH

Established: By evolutionary process and formalized December 31, 1931, in the Statute of Westminster.

Purpose: To give expression to a continuing sense of affinity and to foster cooperation among states presently or formerly owing allegiance to the British Crown.

Commonwealth Center: The Secretariat is located in Marlborough House, London, which also serves as the site of Commonwealth meetings in the United Kingdom.

Principal Organs: Meeting of Heads of Government, Secretariat.

Head of the Commonwealth: Queen Elizabeth II.

Secretary General: Donald McKinnon (New Zealand).

Membership (53, with years of entry): Antigua and Barbuda (1981), Australia (1931), Bahamas (1973), Bangladesh (1972), Barbados (1966), Belize (1981), Botswana (1966), Brunei (1984), Cameroon (1995), Canada (1931), Cyprus (1961), Dominica (1978), Fiji (reentered 1997), Gambia (1965), Ghana (1957), Grenada (1974), Guyana (1966), India (1947), Jamaica (1962), Kenya (1963), Kiribati (1979), Lesotho (1966), Malawi (1964), Malaysia (1957), Maldives (1982), Malta (1964), Mauritius (1968), Mozambique (1995), Namibia (1990), Nauru (1999), New Zealand (1931), Nigeria (1960), Pakistan (reentered 1989, but suspended following military coup of October 1999; readmitted on May 22, 2004), Papua New Guinea (1975), St. Kitts-Nevis (1983), St. Lucia (1979), St. Vincent and the Grenadines (1979), Samoa (1970), Seychelles (1976), Sierra Leone (1961), Singapore (1965), Solomon Islands (1978), South Africa (reentered 1994), Sri Lanka (1948), Swaziland (1968), Tanzania (1961), Tonga (1970), Trinidad and Tobago (1962), Tuvalu (2000), Uganda (1962), United Kingdom (1931), Vanuatu (1980), Zambia (1964). (Zimbabwe, a member since 1980, withdrew in 2003.)

Working Language: English.

Origin and development. A voluntary association that gradually superseded the British Empire, the Commonwealth traces its origins to the mid-1800s, when internal self-government was first introduced in the colonies of Australia, British North America (Canada), New Zealand, and part of what was to become the Union of South Africa. The increasing maturity and independence of these overseas communities, particularly after World War I, eventually created a need to redefine the mutual relationships between the United Kingdom and the self-governing "dominions" that were collectively coming to be known as the "British Commonwealth of Nations." The Statute of Westminster, enacted by the British Parliament in 1931, established the principle that all members of the association were equal in status, in no way subordinate to each other, and united by allegiance to the Crown.

The original members of the Commonwealth, in addition to the United Kingdom, were Australia, Canada, the Irish Free State, Newfoundland, New Zealand, and the Union of South Africa. In 1949 Newfoundland became a province of Canada, and the Irish Republic became an independent state outside the Commonwealth. South Africa ceased to be a member upon becoming a republic in 1961 because of the opposition of the other Commonwealth countries to Pretoria's apartheid policies; however, it was readmitted June 1, 1994, following the installation of a multiracial government. Pakistan withdrew in 1972 but rejoined in 1989, although its membership was suspended in response to the coup of October 1999.

The ethnic, geographic, and economic composition of the Commonwealth has been modified fundamentally by the accession of former colonial territories in Asia, Africa, and the Western Hemisphere. This infusion of racially non-white and economically less developed states had significant political implications, including modification of the Commonwealth's unwritten constitution to accommodate the desire of many new members to renounce allegiance to the British Crown and adopt a republican form of government. In 1949 the pattern was set when Commonwealth prime ministers accepted India's formal declaration that, on becoming a republic, it would accept the Crown as a symbol of the Commonwealth association and recognize the British sovereign as head of the Commonwealth. The movement toward a multicultural identity was solidified by the Declaration of Commonwealth Principles adopted by the heads of government at their 1971 Singapore summit. In addition to acknowledging the organization's diversity, the Singapore Declaration enumerated a set of common principles, including the primacy of international peace and order; individual liberty regardless of racial, ethnic, or religious background; people's "inalienable right to participate by means of free and democratic processes in framing the society in which they live"; opposition to "colonial domination and racial oppression"; and the "progressive removal" of wide disparities in wealth and living standards.

The new thrust was further evidenced by a North-South summit in October 1981, which reflected that most Commonwealth members were developing countries. Subsequently, a 1982 report, *The North-South Dialogue: Making It Work*, proposed many institutional and procedural reforms to facilitate global negotiations on development and related issues, and a 1983 document, *Towards a New Bretton Woods*, proposed short-, medium-, and long-range changes to enhance the efficiency and equity of the international trading and financial system.

A declaration in October 1987 that Fiji's Commonwealth status had lapsed followed two successive coups, abrogation of the country's constitution, and proclamation of a republic. Readmission required the unanimous consent of the Commonwealth members, and Fiji's application remained blocked until mid-1997 by India on the grounds that appropriate constitutional recognition had yet to be given to the island's Indian population. Fiji was finally readmitted effective October 1, 1997, following the adoption of a new constitution in July, but its membership was suspended in May 2000 following displacement of the elected government. Full participation was restored in late 2001, following democratic elections in August through September.

The October 1991 summit in Harare, Zimbabwe, was noteworthy for the adoption of a declaration redefining the Commonwealth's agenda. The Harare Declaration, drafted under the guidance of a ten-member High Level Appraisal Group, committed all Commonwealth countries, regardless of their political or economic conditions, to promote democracy, human rights, judicial independence, equality for women, educational opportunities, and the principles of "sound economic management."

In a departure from precedent, membership was granted on November 13, 1995, to Mozambique, even though it had never been a British colony and was not at least partly English speaking. A "unique and special" case regarding Mozambique had been presented by its Anglophone neighbors because of regional trade concerns. In 1999 Nauru became the 53rd full member of the Commonwealth after 31 years as a special member, and Tuvalu, also a special member (from 1978), became the 54th full member in 2000. In 2005 Nauru resumed its status as a special member, a category of membership available to very small countries.

In March 2002 Zimbabwe's participation in Commonwealth meetings was suspended as a consequence of a widely condemned presidential election earlier in the month. In response to its continued suspension, Zimbabwe withdrew effective December 7, 2003.

Structure. One of the least institutionalized intergovernmental organizations, the Commonwealth was virtually without permanent machinery until the establishment of its Secretariat in 1965. The symbolic head of the organization is the reigning British monarch, who serves concurrently as constitutional sovereign in those member states that still maintain their traditional allegiance. Since World War II, the heads of government have held biennial meetings, and specialized consultations occur periodically among national ministers responsible for such fields as foreign affairs, defense, finance, education, agriculture, health, trade, legal affairs, science and the environment, and women's and youth affairs. National finance ministers normally convene in the nearest convenient Commonwealth site on the eve of the annual fall meetings of the International Monetary Fund and World Bank to discuss monetary and economic issues.

The Secretariat organizes meetings and conferences, collects and disseminates information on behalf of the membership, and is responsible for implementing collective decisions. The secretary general, who currently serves a four-year term, is assisted by three deputies with responsibilities for political affairs, economic and social development, and development cooperation. Since its reorganization in 2002, the Secretariat has encompassed nine divisions: Communications and Public Affairs, Corporate Services, Economic Affairs, Gender and Human Resources Development, Governance and Institutional Development, Legal and Constitutional Affairs, Political Affairs, Science and Technology, and Special Advisory Services. The organization's technical assistance program is financed primarily through the Commonwealth Fund for Technical Cooperation (CFTC).

The fund is supported by all Commonwealth countries on a voluntary basis, and its governing body includes representatives of all contributors. In addition, a Commonwealth Equity Fund, designed to encourage private sector investment in the emerging stock markets of developing countries,

was launched in 1990 and was followed in 1995 by formation of a Commonwealth Private Investment Initiative (CPII). The latter was established to help geographic regions attract capital for small- and medium-sized ventures and for former state enterprises that were being privatized. The first CPII investment fund, for Sub-Saharan Africa, was established in 1996, and others followed. On the political front, a Commonwealth Ministerial Action Group (CMAG) was created in November 1995 to provide guidance toward "good governance" in countries undergoing transition to democracy.

The autonomous Commonwealth Foundation, the formation of which was authorized by the Commonwealth heads of government in 1965, supports nongovernmental organizations, professional associations, and other such bodies. Known informally as the "unofficial Commonwealth," the foundation directs its attention to "inter-country networking, training, capacity-building, and information exchange." The Commonwealth of Learning, likewise authorized by the heads of government and located in Vancouver, Canada, was established in 1987 to promote distance learning and thereby improve access to education and training. Some three dozen additional Commonwealth associations, institutes, councils, and other groups were also established over the years, largely to promote development or disseminate information in such fields as forestry, health, telecommunications, education, journalism, law, and sports. Most are based in London.

Activities. The Secretariat's divisions oversee Commonwealth activities. Among the most prominent, the Political Affairs Division participates in organizing Commonwealth Heads of Government Meetings (CHOGMs), conducts research, aids various committees in their tasks, and monitors political issues and developments of importance to Commonwealth members. Since 1990 its observer missions have also monitored election campaigns, preparations for balloting, and elections in some two dozen Commonwealth countries around the globe, and in 1999 it drafted a "Framework for Principles for Promoting Good Governance and

Combating Corruption." The Economic Affairs Division conducts research and analysis and supports expert groups in such areas as North–South economic relations, protectionist tariffs, reform of the international financial system, debt management, and youth unemployment. Its purview also includes environmental concerns and sustainable development. In the area of technical assistance and development, CFTC provides training, expertise, and advice in the promotion of economic growth, public sector reform, poverty alleviation, infrastructural and institutional development, and capacity building. A Commonwealth Youth Program likewise funded through voluntary contributions, is an effort to encourage youth participation in economic and social development. Among more recent innovations, in 1995 the heads of government endorsed a Commonwealth Plan of Action on Gender and Development.

During the 1980s and early 1990s, the Commonwealth was most prominently identified with its efforts to end apartheid in South Africa, although debate frequently raged within the organization over tactics, especially the imposition of sanctions. Accordingly, the formal readmission of South Africa at midyear was the highlight of 1994, newly elected South African President Nelson Mandela hailing the "sterling contribution" of the grouping to the installation of a nonracial government in Pretoria.

The heads of government meeting held November 8–13, 1995, in Auckland, New Zealand, was dominated by discussion of recent events in Nigeria, which resulted in the suspension of Nigeria's membership and the launching of efforts (ultimately largely unsuccessful) by the Commonwealth to influence the actions of the military regime in Abuja. The governments of Gambia and Sierra Leone were also criticized for their perceived failure to support genuine democratization; the summit established CMAG in part to "guide" developing Commonwealth countries toward abiding by the principles enunciated in the 1991 Harare Declaration.

Nigeria, Gambia, and Sierra Leone were also major topics at the 1997 Commonwealth heads of government meeting held in Edinburgh, Scotland.

While praising the role Nigeria played in the Liberia conflict, the summit decided to continue the former's suspension because of ongoing human rights abuses and the suppression of democracy by the government. The summit also indicated it might impose sanctions if they would help move Nigeria toward democracy. Sierra Leone was also suspended (until the restoration of President Tejan Kabbah's government in March 1998), and the summit called on Commonwealth members to support the UN and ECOWAS sanctions imposed on that country. In contrast, the government in Gambia was praised for having made progress toward genuine democratization.

Another focus of attention at the summit was the promotion of economic prosperity. The heads of government adopted the Edinburgh Commonwealth Economic Declaration, which called for continued global economic integration with greater attention to the smaller, less developed countries that believed they were being "left behind." To assist the smaller countries, the Commonwealth leaders agreed to support efforts to develop a successor to the Lomé Convention, to offer duty-free access to certain markets, and to establish a Trade and Investment Access Facility (TIAF) with initial funding from Australia, Canada, New Zealand, and the United Kingdom. The Commonwealth leaders also endorsed establishing a Commonwealth Business Council, which would meet every two years to ensure that the voice of the "business community" was heard.

In October 1998 CMAG concluded that the Nigerian government had taken enough steps toward democracy to warrant a lifting of sanctions and a resumption of Nigerian participation in some Commonwealth activities. Full participation was restored May 29, 1999, following presidential elections the previous February. In other activities during the year, a Commonwealth ministerial mission lobbied leading providers of aid and loans to developing countries on behalf of small island states, arguing they deserved special consideration because of their extreme exposure to outside political, economic, and environmental forces.

At the November 12–15, 1999, Commonwealth summit in Durban, South Africa, the organization established a ten-member High-Level Review Group (HLRG) comprising the heads of government of Australia, India, Malta, Papua New Guinea, Singapore, South Africa, Tanzania, Trinidad and Tobago, United Kingdom, and Zimbabwe. The HLRG was assigned the task of recommending how the Commonwealth could best meet 21st century challenges. Issues facing the organization included what measures to take in response to corrupt governments and how to reconcile promotion of good governance with the principle of national sovereignty and noninterference in internal affairs. In this context, a number of Commonwealth countries called for expanding CMAG's mandate to allow firmer action where democratic practices were perceived as under threat—for example, in cases of arbitrarily postponed elections, restrictions on freedom of speech and the press, and evidence of persistent human rights violations. To date, such proposals have been met with less than unanimity, however, given that many Commonwealth countries have questionable records with regard to political pluralism and press independence.

Also at the Durban heads of government session, Donald McKinnon, former deputy prime minister and foreign minister of New Zealand, was elected to succeed Chief Eleazar Chukwuemea (Emeka) Anyaoku of Nigeria as secretary general, effective April 2000. McKinnon, who received wise praise for his role in resolving the Bougainville crisis in Papua New Guinea, subsequently indicated that his priorities would include obtaining debt relief for developing countries, promoting democracy, and facilitating technology transfers. The heads of government also confirmed Pakistan's suspension from Commonwealth activities in the wake of the previous month's coup in Islamabad.

Pakistan (like Fiji, Gambia, Sierra Leone, and the Solomon Islands) continued to be one of the countries on the CMAG agenda for 2001. Recent threatening events in Zimbabwe were also discussed at CMAG's March 19–20 session. Collaterally, HLRG established three working groups to consider the Commonwealth's political role,

including conflict prevention and the mandate of CMAG; its developmental role, including how to reduce the "digital divide"; and Commonwealth governance and structures.

The CHOGM scheduled for October 2001 was postponed in the wake of the September 11 terrorist attacks in the United States and then rescheduled for March 2–5, 2002, in Coolum, Australia. The meeting's concluding declaration called for a rationalized and streamlined organizational structure, as HLRG's report recommended. Emphasis was also given to "people-centered economic development," good governance and human rights, efforts to bridge the widening gap between rich and poor, and the elimination of terrorism. (Some African participants, however, although condemning the September 11 al-Qaida attacks, expressed concern that the definition of terrorism was too closely tied to U.S. and Western concerns and ignored, for example, that a number of present-day African leaders had themselves been branded as terrorists during the colonial and apartheid eras.) In addition, the assembled heads of government voiced support for the New Partnership for Africa's Development (Nepad), which was launched in 2001 under the auspices of the Organization of African Unity (OAU), and endorsed a new assistance effort for small states. Countries continuing under CMAG scrutiny included Fiji, Pakistan, the Solomon Islands, and Zimbabwe.

In keeping with a summit recommendation that they pursue more active consultations, the Commonwealth foreign ministers convened for the first time in September 2002, during the opening days of the annual UN General Assembly session in New York. At that time the ministers agreed to hold annual meetings.

The next CHOGM, which was held December 5–8, 2003, in Abuja, Nigeria, was dominated by the Zimbabwe issue. Although many African states argued that the Mugabe government could best be engaged by lifting the suspension, opponents prevailed. The Commonwealth proceeded to form a balanced committee of leaders from Australia, Canada, India, Jamaica, Mozambique, and South Africa to pursue "national reconciliation" in

Zimbabwe and a rapid return of that country to full participation, but Zimbabwe's governing party quickly voted to terminate membership in the Commonwealth. In acknowledging the withdrawal, Secretary General McKinnon, who was elected to a second term at the CHOGM, expressed his hope that Zimbabwe would rejoin "in due course, as have other members in the past." Also at the CHOGM, membership applications from the Palestinian Authority, Rwanda, and Yemen were rejected.

Four and a half years after the military coup that brought Gen. Pervez Musharraf to power, Commonwealth ministers decided to restore full membership to Pakistan at a May 2004 meeting in London. Ministers insisted that General Musharraf uphold his pledge to step down as chief of the army by the end of the year and expected the country to move forward with democratic reforms. Some African nations, including Nigeria and Tanzania, objected to the readmission of Pakistan because they feared that military rulers, who thought that international sanctions could be reversed, might take power in other countries.

The marriage of Prince Charles, Queen Elizabeth's son and heir to the throne, to Camilla Parker Bowles in April 2005 had implications for the Commonwealth. The British Department of Constitutional Affairs stated on March 21 that Parker Bowles would automatically become queen when Charles became king, despite Charles's declarations to the contrary, unless parliaments of the UK and the Commonwealth countries of which the UK monarch was head of state all agreed to a change in the law. On March 23 the Commonwealth Secretariat announced that Charles would not automatically succeed Queen Elizabeth as head of the Commonwealth when he became king. Instead, the various Commonwealth heads of government would elect the next head of the Commonwealth. Appointing anyone other than the British monarch to this symbolic position would mark a substantial shift away from the organization's British and imperial roots.

The next CHOGM, which was held November 25–27, 2005, in Valletta, Malta, declared that Pakistan could remain a member in full standing as long as General Musharraf resigned from the military within two years. Ugandan President Yoweri Museveni was much criticized for the arrest on treason charges of Uganda's main opposition leader, Col. Kiza Besigye. The European Union received criticism for maintaining agricultural subsidies and for a 36 percent cut in the guaranteed price of sugar—a matter of great concern to Commonwealth Caribbean countries. The summit issued a Statement on Multilateral Trade, calling for agreement on trade subsidies at forthcoming World Trade Organization talks. The 2007 CHOGM meeting will take place in Uganda, unless Commonwealth members continue to question Museveni's policies.

COMMUNITY OF PORTUGUESE SPEAKING COUNTRIES (CPLP)

Comunidade dos Países de Lingua Portuguesa

Established: By statutes signed July 17, 1996, in Lisbon, Portugal, with immediate interim effect pending completion of ratification procedures by member states.

Purpose: To promote "concerted political and diplomatic action" between sovereign and equal member states in the international arena; to assist cooperation, "particularly in the economic, social, cultural, juridical, technical, and scientific fields"; to implement projects "for the promotion and diffusion of the Portuguese language."

Headquarters: Lisbon, Portugal.

Principal Organs: Conference of Heads of State and Government, Council of Ministers, Standing Committee of Ambassadors, Executive Secretariat.

Executive Secretary: Luis de Matos Monteiro da Fonseca (Cape Verde).

Membership (8): Angola, Brazil, Cape Verde, Guinea-Bissau, Mozambique, Portugal, Sao Tome and Principe, Timor-Leste.

Official Language: Portuguese.

Origin and development. The idea of creating a grouping of Portuguese-speaking countries, in emulation of the (mainly) English-speaking Commonwealth and the Francophonie network, was proposed following the accession to independence of Portugal's colonies in the mid-1970s. Protracted civil war in Angola and Mozambique contributed to the delay in implementation, as did a lack of enthusiasm on the part of Brazil, in which nearly 80 percent of the world's 200 million Portuguese speakers live. Eventually, however, the regular ministerial conferences of the seven Lusophone countries yielded a decision by their foreign ministers, meeting in February 1994 in Brasília, that an institutional community should be established. Further instability in Angola and disagreements on funding contributed to the postponement of an intended mid-1995 launch, and it was not until July 1996 that the founding summit convened at the Portuguese capital.

The heads of state of Angola, Brazil, Cape Verde, Guinea-Bissau, Mozambique, Portugal, and Sao Tome and Principe duly signed the statutes of the new community, enunciating eight principles that would govern it: sovereign equality of the member states; no interference in internal matters; respect for national identity; reciprocal treatment; upholding of peace, democracy, the rule of law, human rights, and social justice; respect for territorial integrity; promotion of development; and promotion of mutually advantageous cooperation. The community would be open to any other state with Portuguese as its official language, subject to unanimous decision of the existing members. It was agreed that the statutes would come into effect immediately on a "temporary" basis and would "become definite after conclusion of constitutional formalities by all of the member states."

Timor-Leste, the former Portuguese Asian colony of East Timor, was admitted as the eighth CPLP member at the organization's fourth summit, on July 31–August 1, 2002.

Structure. The CPLP's statutes prescribe that political decisions be achieved by consensus. The highest organ is the Conference of Heads of State and Government, which meets every two years (unless two-thirds of the members request an extraordinary meeting) and is headed by a president serving a two-year term. Responsibility for the coordination and definition of CPLP activities and approval of its budget is vested in the Council of (Foreign) Ministers, which convenes at least annually and is headed by a president serving a one-year term. The Standing Committee of Ambassadors, currently those in Lisbon, meets at least once a month, charged in particular with supervising the implementation of conference and council decisions by the Executive Secretariat, which is the main executive organ of the CPLP. The secretariat is headed by an executive secretary elected by the Conference of Heads of State and Government for a two-year term, renewable once.

Activities. The intention of the CPLP to adopt the Commonwealth model of an outward-oriented organization, rather than the metropolitan focus characteristic of Francophonie, was highlighted by the appointment of the former Angolan prime minister, Dr. Marcolino José Carlos Moco, as the organization's first executive secretary. This orientation was also apparent in the initial diplomatic tasks that the new community set for itself, namely support for Brazil's quest to become a permanent member of the UN Security Council, and advocacy of self-determination for the inhabitants of East Timor (a Portuguese colony annexed by Indonesia exactly 20 years before the launching of the CPLP). In 1997 the CPLP foreign ministers met for two days to discuss cooperation in the areas of security, services, and immigration.

The second Conference of Heads of State and Government was held in July 1998 in Praia, Cape Verde. The CPLP leaders called on Indonesia to conduct a self-determination referendum in East Timor, which sent an observer delegation to the summit. The summit also condemned renewed rebel activity in Angola, formed a contact group to help negotiate a settlement to the fighting in Guinea-Bissau, and reelected Secretary General Carlos Moco to a second two-year term.

In May 2000 the CPLP defense ministers met in Luanda, Angola, and agreed to establish a joint military force that would cooperate with UN missions in addition to undertaking peacekeeping and humanitarian assignments within the CPLP member countries. As a follow-up to the decision, the community conducted its first joint military maneuvers in October 2000 in Portugal.

On July 17–18, 2000, six of the seven CPLP heads of state (excluding Angola's José Eduardo dos Santos) convened at Maputo, Mozambique, for the third CPLP summit. In addition to electing Brazil's Dulce Maria Pereira as successor to Executive Secretary Carlos Moco, the participants issued a concluding declaration that acknowledged the prevention and treatment of AIDS and other diseases as a prerequisite for sustained development and security, supported the ongoing reconciliation process in Guinea-Bissau, reinforced the importance of international compliance with UN sanctions against the rebel National Union for the Total Independence of Angola (UNITA), and asserted that peace, democracy, and human rights would be accorded maximum priority. Also at the summit, Portugal indicated it would finance an International Institute for the Portuguese Language (*Instituto Internacional da Língua Portuguesa*), to be sited in Cape Verde, as well as a long-distance learning network.

Coincident with independence festivities in May 2002 in Dili, Timor-Leste, the CPLP Council of Ministers held an extraordinary meeting, at which time the newly formed government of the world's newest state requested admission to the CPLP. As expected, the CPLP states granted formal membership at the fourth CPLP summit, held July 31–August 1 in Brasília. Timor-Leste thus became the first Asian member of the community

The group has focused in recent years on shared security concerns, the spread of HIV/AIDS, and promotion of shared culture. Cultural exchange has include the establishment of a Lusophone Culture Day (*Dia da Cultura Lusófona*), the CPLP Games (last held in 2005 in Angola), and the attempt to create a FIFA-sanctioned CPLP soccer event. Additionally, the increased ease of movement of CPLP citizens was furthered by changes in visa rules and the installation of a special entry port for CPLP citizens at the Lisbon airport. The organization has also worked to aid in member state crises such as the coup in Sao Tome and Principe and the election controversy in Guinea-Bissau.

A goal of the organization has been to create a CPLP parliamentary assembly. General Secretary Luis Fonseca accepted a proposal to create a working group to that end at the 5th Portuguese Speaking Forum held in April 2006 in Luanda, Angola.

COUNCIL OF ARAB ECONOMIC UNITY (CAEU)

Established: By resolution of the Arab Economic Council of the League of Arab States on June 3, 1957, in Cairo, Egypt, effective at its first meeting May 30, 1964.

Purpose: To provide a flexible framework for achieving economic integration of Arab states.

Headquarters: Cairo, Egypt.

Principal Organs: Council, General Secretariat.

Secretary General: Ahmed Guweili (Egypt).

Membership (11): Egypt, Iraq, Jordan, Kuwait, Libya, Mauritania, Palestine, Somalia, Sudan, Syria, Yemen. (Egypt's membership was suspended from 1979 to 1988. Although not a de jure state, Palestine succeeded the Palestine Liberation Organization as a member following formation of the Palestinian Authority in 1994.)

Official Language: Arabic.

Origin and development. In January 1956 the Arab League agreed on the necessity for an organization that would deal specifically with the economic problems of Arab countries. As a result, on June 3, 1957, a resolution was passed creating the Council of Arab Economic Unity. The organization officially came into existence May 30, 1964.

In December 1988 the CAEU announced it was lifting a nine-year suspension of Egypt's membership that had been occasioned by Cairo's conclusion of a peace agreement with Israel.

In March 1990, Kuwait announced its intention to withdraw over the council's "poor performance" and that CAEU objectives overlapped those of other Arab organizations. Continuing disputes over budget assessments and shortfalls, including Kuwait's back dues, also played a part in the decision. The CAEU lost its only other Gulf member when the United Arab Emirates withdrew in late November 1999, immediately after a summit of the Gulf Cooperation Council.

Structure. The Council, consisting of the economic, finance, and trade ministers of member states, meets twice a year to discuss and vote on the organization's agenda. The General Secretariat oversees implementation; it also has responsibility for drawing up work plans, which are presented to the council.

Activities. Since its inception, activities have focused on furthering economic development and encouraging economic cooperation among Arab countries. To promote these ends, the Council established an Arab Common Market in 1964. Seven years later the market achieved its initial aim of abolishing all taxes and other duties levied on items of trade between Arab countries. The second part of the plan, a customs union of all members, has not yet been fully implemented. Emphasis has also been given to forming joint Arab companies and federations, to coordinating agricultural and industrial programs, and to improving road and railway networks. Industries in which joint ventures and federations or unions have been formed include textiles, processed foods, pharmaceuticals, fertilizers, building materials, iron and steel, shipping, petrochemicals, and information technology. The CAEU has also promoted harmonization of statistics and data collection.

The CAEU was thrown into disarray by the Persian Gulf crisis in August 1990. Several prominent CAEU members participated in the U.S.-led coalition that succeeded in driving Iraqi forces from Kuwait in early 1991. Subsequently, in part to restore a sense of normalcy to Arab affairs, as well as for humanitarian reasons, the CAEU repeatedly called on the UN Security Council to discontinue its sanctions against Iraq.

The CAEU continues to encounter considerable difficulty in achieving its economic goals. The planned introduction in 1998 of an Arab Free Trade Zone, which had the support of most Arab League members as well as the overlapping CAEU membership, was undermined by requests for exceptions involving nearly 3,000 commodities.

The CAEU Council session held June 6–7, 2001, was notable primarily because it constituted the first such meeting in Baghdad, Iraq, since the 1991 Gulf war. At the session Egypt, Iraq, Libya, and Syria announced they were establishing their own free trade zone, which once again called into question the CAEU's long-term prospects.

The December 2002 CAEU Council session heard Arab League Secretary General Amr Mussa warn of the political, economic, and social consequences posed by threats to the Arab world, principally U.S. antagonism toward the Iraqi government as well as the ongoing Israeli confrontation with Palestinian militants. Also in 2002 the CAEU established a committee to encourage inter-Arab investment by redirecting some of the estimated $1 trillion in Arab funds that are invested elsewhere. More recently, a CAEU-sponsored economic conference in Cairo also called for the repatriation of investment capital, particularly in view of rapid Arab population growth and an unemployment rate that was already approaching 20 percent.

In 2004 the CAEU acceded to the 2001 Agadir (Morocco) Declaration, which was seen as a step toward creating a pan-Arab free trade zone. Initial signatories were Morocco, Jordan, Tunisia, and Egypt. The declaration also proposed launching a Mediterranean Arab Free Trade Association, bringing together various Arab countries with bilateral partnerships with the EU and other foreign entities. Its Council session that year produced a strongly negative report concerning unemployment in Arab countries. It stated it was finalizing details of an Arab Investment Map (AIM), a means of connecting Arab investors with Arab prospective investment recipients. The intent was to make it as easy for Arabs to invest inside the Arab world as it is elsewhere. The CAEU is now concentrating on the AIM. It continues to push for Arab economic self-sufficiency and to warn against domination of key economic sectors by outside entities.

COUNCIL OF THE ENTENTE

Conseil de l'Entente

Established: May 29, 1959, in Abidjan, Côte d'Ivoire, by a convention signed by representatives from countries that were once part of French West Africa.

Purpose: To promote political, economic, and social coordination among the member states.

Headquarters: Abidjan, Côte d'Ivoire.

Principal Organs: Council, Ministerial Council, Mutual Aid and Loan Guarantee Fund, Secretariat.

Administrative Secretary: Paul Kouamé (Côte d'Ivoire).

Membership (5): Benin, Burkina Faso, Côte d'Ivoire, Niger, Togo.

Official Language: French.

Origin and development. The Council of the Entente was formed in 1959 by Benin (then Dahomey), Burkina Faso (then Upper Volta), Côte d'Ivoire, and Niger; Togo joined in 1966. In its early years the Entente was seen as a vehicle for Côte d'Ivoire, by far the most economically and politically powerful member, to promote its preeminence in west Africa.

In 1966 the Entente adopted a convention that established the Mutual Aid and Loan Guarantee Fund to promote economic development and regional integration; to assist in preparing specific economic projects; to obtain assistance from donor organizations; and to promote increased trade, commerce, and investment among Entente members and their neighbors. In 1970 an associated Economic Community of Livestock and Meat (*Communauté Economique du Bétail et de la Viande*—CEBV) was established to provide technical and financial support for the region's cattle industry.

Structure. The organization's principal organ, the Council, encompasses the members' heads of state; the location of meetings rotates among the capitals of the members. Council sessions are preceded by meetings of the Ministerial Council, which is comprised of representatives of the five governments.

In accordance with a modified structure adopted in December 1973, a board of directors (the five heads of state) governs the Mutual Aid and Loan Guarantee Fund. Its management committee handles administrative and financial matters, such as the approval of guarantees. The Entente's Secretariat considers applications for guarantees, the reduction of interest rates, and the extension of loan repayment periods. It also provides regional centers with support for technical assistance, development, and cooperation.

Activities. The member states established a port and harbor administration, a railway and road traffic administration, and a unified quarantine organization. Development programs have concentrated on food production, village water projects, expansion of tourism, and energy.

In the 1990s, institutional effectiveness remained marginal at best because member states, several of them beset by sustained political turmoil, failed to make their allotted financial contributions. Consequently, the members' heads of state convened for the first time in 11 years on October 31, 1994, in Kara, Togo, in an effort to "relaunch" the organization, which the participants characterized as "an irreplaceable framework for debate and solidarity." Nevertheless, Benin boycotted the Council summit held in Kara in February 1996 to protest the presence of Col. Ibrahim Baré Maïnassara, who had led a coup in Niger. Other Council leaders exhorted Colonel Maïnassara to return Niger to civilian government. During the February 20, 1997, summit, the heads of state expressed their concerns about regional security; they feared that the turmoil in the Great Lakes countries would spread to neighboring states. The summit called for the removal of all outside forces from Burundi, Rwanda, and Zaire to promote stability.

At the August 1998 Council meeting, the heads of state denounced illegal arms trade in the region and the associated rise in crime. They also discussed ongoing conflicts in Africa and expressed concern about renewed fighting in Angola. The Council gave its support to the Economic Community of West African States (ECOWAS) and the Community of Portuguese-Speaking Countries (CPLP), which were mediating the crisis in Guinea-Bissau. Entente leaders also signed agreements to establish a regional tourist visa and enhance cooperation among the members' national lotteries.

At the Entente summit of March 2000, the leaders of the five member states were joined by President Obasanjo of Nigeria for discussions on regional security. This was the first time the head of a nonmember state attended a Council summit. Meeting again in mid-February 2001 in Kara, the Entente executives conducted wide-ranging discussions on political, economic, social, peace, security, and regional stability matters.

The summit's final communiqué voiced support for the free movement of goods and people in the region, closer integration through ECOWAS and the West African Economic and Monetary Union (*Union Economique et Monétaire Ouest-Africaine*—UEMOA), and rapid adoption of the founding statute for the OAU-sponsored African Union. Five months later, in late July, the five Entente countries initiated their regional tourist visa.

In March 2002 the five members' security ministers and their counter-part from Mali met in Niamey, Niger, to discuss regional security issues, including illegal arms sales, banditry, and child trafficking. Shortly thereafter, the Entente Council's tourism ministers met to review implementation of the regional visa and to identify possible improvements. The prospects for including Ghana and Mali in the regime were also discussed.

In early July 2002 the Entente leaders met in Lomé, Togo, but two months later attention turned from regional cooperation to instability in Côte d'Ivoire. In September a failed coup, continuing conflict, and a resultant flow of refugees complicated the already strained relations between Côte d'Ivoire and Burkina Faso, and their border was closed as a consequence. Although France helped broker a peace agreement between the Ivorian government and rebel forces in March 2003, the border remained closed until September 2003. Burkina Faso's president did not attend an extraordinary "mini-summit," which was held in May in Lomé to promote reconciliation in Côte d'Ivoire. Since that time, regional conflicts have severely limited the organization's ability to function.

EAST AFRICAN COMMUNITY (EAC)

Established: By Treaty for the Establishment of the East African Community, which was signed November 30, 1999, in Arusha, Tanzania, and entered into force July 7, 2000; community formally launched January 15, 2001.

Purpose: To coordinate trade, monetary, defense, and sectoral policies with a view toward establishment of a customs union, a common market, a monetary union, and, eventually, a political federation of the partner states.

Headquarters: Arusha, Tanzania.

Principal Organs: Summit, Council of Ministers, Coordination Committee, Sectoral Councils, Sectoral Committees, East African Court of Justice, East African Legislative Assembly.

Secretary General: Juma Volter Mwapachu (Tanzania).

Membership (3): Kenya, Tanzania, Uganda.

Official Language: English. Kiswahili is to be developed as a lingua franca.

Origin and development. The original East African Community (EAC) of Kenya, Tanzania, and Uganda was established in 1967 but collapsed in July 1977, although its affiliated East African Development Bank (EADB), which had been established under an annex to the original treaty, was reorganized by the founding states in 1980 and continues to function. (For background on the original EAC and its collapse, see the section on foreign relations in the Kenya article.) In 1984 the former EAC members signed a Mediation Agreement to explore ways of resuming cooperation, which led in 1993 to an Agreement for the Establishment of the Permanent Tripartite Commission for East African Cooperation. A corresponding Secretariat began operations in Arusha, Tanzania, in March 1996 under Executive Director Francis Muthaura of Kenya.

The main task of the Tripartite Commission soon became negotiation of a new EAC treaty, the three neighboring states having confirmed in 1997 their intention to reestablish the EAC. On November 30, 1999, Presidents Daniel arap Moi of Kenya, Benjamin Mkapa of Tanzania, and Yoweri Musaveni of Uganda signed in Arusha the new Treaty for the Establishment of the East African Community. The requisite ratifications having been completed, the treaty entered into force on July 7, 2000, with the EAC being formally launched at a meeting of the three leaders on January 15, 2001.

Structure. The Summit, consisting of the heads of state or government of the three members, provides "general direction and impetus" to the EAC. It meets annually or in extraordinary session at the request of one member state. The summit chairmanship rotates annually; decisions are reached by consensus. The Council of Ministers, which meets at least twice a year, comprises the members' ministers for regional cooperation plus any other ministers designated by the individual states. As the principal EAC policymaking organ, the council reviews and oversees the EAC's programs, establishes oversight Sectoral Councils from among its own members, and appoints working Sectoral Committees.

A Coordination Committee, which also convenes at least twice a year, includes the member states' permanent secretaries responsible for regional cooperation; other permanent secretaries may also be named to it by each state. Its responsibilities include implementing council decisions and coordinating the work of the Sectoral Committees. The latter have responsibilities for such concerns as agriculture and food security; energy; education, culture, and sports; fiscal affairs; gender and community development; labor/employment, refugee management, and movement of persons; and transport, commerce, and meteorology.

The Secretariat is headed by a secretary general, who is selected by the summit for a five-year term on a rotational basis. The secretary general is assisted by two deputies, one for Projects and Programs and the other for Finance and Administration.

The treaty also provided for an East African Court of Justice to interpret and apply the treaty, although the Council of Ministers may extend the court's jurisdiction to other areas, subject to protocol approval. The East African Legislative Assembly comprises 5 ex officio and 27 elected members; the latter are selected by the three national assemblies, but sitting deputies and government ministers are excluded.

Activities. Even before conclusion of the new EAC treaty in 1999, the three prospective member states had concluded a 1997–2000 East African Cooperative Development Plan in which they agreed to work toward harmonizing policies in key sectors, making their currencies convertible, easing border crossings, reducing bilateral tariffs, identifying needed infrastructural projects, and bringing investment incentives and codes in line with each other. The first session of the EAC Council convened January 13, 2001, immediately before the first summit, which officially launched the organization. At the second EAC summit, held two months later, the heads of state agreed to move ahead with the Second Cooperative Development Strategy (2001–2005).

Looking ahead, the EAC anticipated quick completion of a Protocol on the Customs Union as well as closer coordination of monetary and fiscal policies, banking regulations, and value added tax (VAT) rates. The EAC also requested the participation of agencies and offices involved in such areas as tourism, posts and telecommunications, investment promotion, and scientific research, plus the participation of civil groups representing, for example, women, youth, professionals, and workers.

The heads of state met for a third time on November 30, 2001, to launch the Court of Justice and the Legislative Assembly and to sign a revised Memorandum of Understanding on Cooperation in Defense, updating a document that they had completed in April 1998. The possible future membership of Rwanda and Burundi was also discussed, but at an April 11, 2002, summit any such expansion was indefinitely postponed. Observers attributed the decision primarily to internal strife in Burundi and Rwanda's involvement in the war in the Democratic Republic of the Congo. Moreover, the EAC leaders saw as their principal short-term goal not expansion, but completion of a Protocol on the Establishment of the East African Customs Union. The Parliamentary Assembly, meeting in early June, renewed a quarter-century-old debate on forming an East African political federation, but the discussion was regarded as largely symbolic at the time.

The heads of state convened again on November 30, 2002, in Arusha, Tanzania, where the topics under discussion included a common external tariff (CET), the community's road network, and development of the Lake Victoria area. In an extraordinary summit on June 20, 2003, in Nairobi, the leaders reached tentative agreement on the CET, including a maximum rate of 25 percent (to be lowered to 20 percent five years after introduction of the customs union). The EAC also reaffirmed its commitment to antiterrorism but cautioned that travel bans imposed on the region by other countries were hampering the tourism industry. The customs union protocol was ultimately approved by the

EAC Council of Ministers on November 30, 2003, with the document then being signed by the heads of state in a summit on March 2, 2004 in Arusha. It came into force January 1, 2005, and apart from some complaints by Kenya that Uganda was cheating, it was generally considered a success.

At the seventh summit of heads of state, held on April 5, 2006, in Arusha, an application from Rwanda and Burundi to join the community was passed forward for detailed negotiation, with the expectation that final action would be taken at the next ordinary summit meeting in November 2006.

ECONOMIC COMMUNITY OF CENTRAL AFRICAN STATES (CEEAC)

Communauté Economique des Etats de l'Afrique Centrale

Established: By treaty signed by the heads of state of the member countries on October 18, 1983, in Libreville, Gabon.

Purpose: Initially, to end customs duties and other restrictions on trade between the member countries and establish a common market; more recently, to also promote regional integration, security, and stability.

Headquarters: Libreville, Gabon.

Principal Organs: Conference of the Heads of State and Government, Council of Ministers, Secretariat.

Secretary General: Louis-Sylvain Goma (Republic of the Congo).

Membership (11): Angola, Burundi, Cameroon, Central African Republic, Chad, Democratic Republic of the Congo, Republic of the Congo, Equatorial Guinea, Gabon, Rwanda, Sao Tome and Principe.

Official Languages: French, Portuguese.

Origin and development. In 1977 President Mobutu Sese Seko of Zaire proposed a merger of the three-member Economic Community of the Great Lakes Countries (CEPGL, below) with the four-member Central African Customs and Economic Union (*Union Douanière et Economique de l'Afrique Centrale*—UDEAC) to form a francophone Central African grouping. The proposal resurfaced in 1981, yielding the UDEAC Libreville Declaration in December, which called for the establishment of a group comprising the members of the CEPGL and the UDEAC plus Angola, Chad, Equatorial Guinea, and Sao Tome and Principe. The resulting ten-member CEEAC (plus Angola as an observer) was formally inaugurated December 21, 1985, in Libreville, Gabon, in accordance with a treaty concluded October 18, 1983, in Libreville. Angola became a full member in 1999.

Structure. The principal government body of the CEEAC is the Conference of Heads of States and Government, which meets annually. There is also a Council of Ministers, a Court of Justice, a Consultative Commission, and a Secretariat.

Activities. At the formal launching of the CEEAC, Secretary General Lunda Bululu declared that the aim of the organization was to "promote and reinforce cooperation and a sustained and balanced development in all areas of both economic and social activity between member states." The 1986 summit charged the secretary general with the drafting of a program of action aimed at increasing intracommunity trade, and also requested that he prepare a study on community transport and communications infrastructure. In July the central bank governors of the member states met in Libreville to consider the establishment of a clearinghouse for the diverse national currencies in use in the area.

At the 1988 summit, support was again voiced for customs, financial, transportation, and communications integration within the community, although there appeared to be little hope for implementation of such plans in the near future given mounting arrears in members' budget contributions—a problem that has perpetually plagued the CEEAC. The 1989 summit underscored the lack of CEEAC consensus on how to reduce trade barriers, the summit leaders deciding to extend debate on the question until at least 1991. However, a "greater sense of urgency" was reported at the 1990 summit, partly in response to challenges posed by the European Community's impending single market and the attention being given to developments in Eastern Europe, possibly to the detriment of African interests. The CEEAC leaders authorized the free circulation within the region of several categories of individuals, such as students and researchers, starting in 1991; agreed to establish a CEEAC bank in Kigali to finance intraregional trade; called for additional airline cooperation among members; and gave priority to road and bridge projects that would facilitate trade within the community. However, the group still appeared "timid" in the opinion of some observers.

Addressing their critics at the 1991 summit, CEEAC leaders expressed the opinion that small regional groupings such as their own should work toward the creation of an economic community covering all of Africa to achieve international negotiating leverage. Underscoring the difficulties facing the smaller organizations, the CEEAC summit on May 17–18, 1992, in Bujumbura, Burundi, achieved little discernible progress because most member states were preoccupied throughout the year by wide-ranging political changes precipitated by the rapid spread of prodemocracy movements in the region.

The community remained in financial crisis in early 1993, and in March staff members went on strike to protest salary arrears. The CEEAC staff went on strike again in May 1994, reportedly criticizing Secretary General Kasasa Mutati Chinyata for not addressing employee concerns. Subsequently, CEEAC activity was severely constrained by ongoing political turmoil within several key member states. Nonetheless, in response to the region's rapidly changing political and governmental landscape, the CEEAC members, under the auspices of the United Nations, drafted a proposed mutual nonaggression pact: defense ministers and/or military leaders from five members (Central African Republic, Congo, Equatorial Guinea, Gabon, and Sao Tome and Principe) initialed the accord in October 1994. Discussion also took place on the creation of a regional conflict prevention body and the designation of special "peacekeeping" forces within members' armed forces. The organization nevertheless remained hamstrung by continuing financial difficulties as well as by regional and intrastate political disturbances.

Meeting in extraordinary session in February 1998 in Libreville, the community heads of state agreed on the necessity of reinvigorating the organization. Accordingly, the summit requested assistance from the UN Economic Commission for Africa in evaluating the CEEAC budget and financial structure, operations, and salaries. The following July, Louis-Sylvain Goma, a former prime minister of the Republic of the Congo, was appointed CEEAC secretary general.

The inauguration of recently reelected Gabonese President Bongo in January 1999 provided an opportunity for "mini-summit" consultations that for the first time included Angola as a full CEEAC member. A month later the member states, convening in Yaoundé, Cameroon, as the UN Standing Advisory Committee on Security Questions in Central Africa, reached agreement on establishing a Council for Peace and Security in Central Africa (COPAX), which was envisaged as a political forum for consultation in the event of threats to peace and security in the region. Also included under COPAX would be a nonstanding multinational force for peacekeeping, security, and humanitarian relief efforts.

In late June 1999 in Malabo, Equatorial Guinea, the CEEAC and the Central African Economic and Monetary Community (*Communauté Economique et Monétaire de l'Afrique Centrale*—CEMAC, successor to the UDEAC) met in parallel sessions to discuss regional security and economic concerns. At the summit the CEEAC leaders stated their intention to make the organization "a model of regional and subregional integration" as well as a "lynch-pin within the African economic community." They also agreed to form a CEEAC Parliament, a center for human rights, and a peace and security council. A third extraordinary CEEAC summit in February 2000 in Malabo ratified the COPAX agreement and a mutual assistance pact. A month earlier, eight CEEAC member states (excepting Angola, the Democratic Republic of the Congo, and Rwanda) joined eight Western countries (Belgium, France, Italy, Netherlands, Portugal, Spain, United States, United Kingdom) in military exercises designed to improve regional peacekeeping and crisis intervention capabilities. Both the UN and the Organization of African Unity (OAU, subsequently the African Union—AU) had endorsed the training activities.

Opening speakers at the tenth ordinary summit, held June 13–17, 2002, in Malabo, once again called attention to the organization's precarious financial status. Although the CEEAC was designated as one of the five regional "pillars" of the AU's African Economic Community (along with ECOWAS, Comesa, the SADC, and the AMU), its financial difficulties and relative lack of integration have diminished its role. Specific measures adopted by the summit called for creation of an "autonomous financing mechanism," liberalized freedom of movement for nationals of the member states, supported ongoing efforts with the UN Food and Agriculture Organization (FAO) to establish a regional food security program, and directed the Secretariat to negotiate financial assistance from the African Development Bank. In addition, with regard to peace and security issues, the attendees approved declarations supporting peace efforts in Angola, Equatorial Guinea, and the Republic of the Congo and also adopted standing orders for three COPAX organs: the Defense and Security Committee, the Early Warning Mechanism of Central Africa, and the nonpermanent Multinational Force of Central Africa. A number of CEEAC states have yet to ratify the COPAX agreement.

In July 2003 the CEEAC condemned a coup in Sao Tome and Principe and then participated in a successful mediation effort led by the Community of Portuguese-Speaking Countries (CPLP). On August 19, 2003, the CEEAC heads of state and government met in Brazzaville and established an International Monitoring Committee for Sao Tome and Principe.

A UN report released in November 2003 attributed regional instability to widespread poverty and a "crisis of governance," including a lack of transparency and insufficient respect for human rights. These difficulties were exacerbated by such factors as conflicts over the region's abundant natural resources, smuggling and drug trafficking, and the movement of mercenaries and militias across borders. The report called on the Security Council to assist in the economic stabilization of CEEAC countries that are "emerging from conflict" and those that are undertaking democratic reforms.

Despite the troubled political climate in the region, CEEAC leaders have called for the establishment of a free trade area by 2007 and a customs union by 2008. Some beginnings of this union may have been seen in August 2004, when Cameroon, the Central African Republic, and the Republic of the Congo abolished visas for certain categories of skilled workers and academics.

CEEAC has also made some effort to address the region's instability. The military chiefs of the CEEAC countries declared, at their annual meeting held April 24–26, 2006, in Brazzaville, that they would work together to promote regional peace. In April 2006 the secretary general declared that CEEAC was ready to send observers to the Democratic Republic of the Congo to help ensure a fair outcome in the June 2006 elections in that country.

ECONOMIC COMMUNITY OF THE GREAT LAKES COUNTRIES (CEPGL)

Communauté Economique des Pays des Grands Lacs

Established: By convention signed by the heads of state of the member countries on September 26, 1976, in Gisenyi, Rwanda.

Purpose: To promote regional economic integration; to increase security and welfare for the region; to facilitate political, cultural, technical, and scientific cooperation among the members; and to contribute to the strengthening of national sovereignty and African unity.

Headquarters: Gisenyi, Rwanda.

Principal Organs: Conference of Heads of States, Council of Ministers and State Commissioners, Consultative Commission, Specialized Technical Commissions, Permanent Executive Secretariat.

Membership (3): Burundi, Democratic Republic of the Congo, Rwanda.

Official Language: French.

Origin and development. The first proposal for the creation of an organization concerned with the social, cultural, economic, and political problems of the Central African subregion emerged from discussions held during a 1966 summit of the heads of state of Burundi, Rwanda, and the Democratic Republic of the Congo (DRC). On August 29, at the conclusion of their four-day meeting in Kinshasa, the three leaders signed a mutual security pact, while Burundi and the DRC signed trade and cultural agreements that contained provisions for closer policy coordination and cooperation. The Kinshasa agreement was reaffirmed during a tripartite summit in 1974 and was strengthened with the addition of clauses on refugees, undesirable aliens, and joint promotion of tourism, communication, and social security measures. In May 1975 the three states' foreign ministers met to discuss a drafted general convention on economic, technical, scientific, and cultural cooperation, the final version of which, establishing the Economic Community of the Great Lakes Countries, was signed by the heads of state of Burundi, Rwanda, and Zaire on September 20, 1976. In 1980 the Development Bank of the Great Lakes States (*Banque de Développement des Etats des Grands Lacs*—BDEGL) was inaugurated in Goma, Zaire, to finance community projects. The subsequent Economic Community of Central African States (*Communauté Economique des Etats de l'Afrique Centrale*—CEEAC, above) was formally launched in October 1983 by a treaty signed in Libreville, Gabon, to which all three CEPGL states were signatories. Although left open to "any country in the region which wished to join it in order to contribute to the strengthening of African unity," CEPGL's own membership has remained at three.

Structure. The legal authority of CEPGL is vested in the Conference of the Heads of State, which normally meets once a year to approve the community's budget and action program. Preparation for annual summits and the implementation of CEPGL resolutions are responsibilities of the Council of Ministers and State Commissioners. Technical and administrative assistance for both groups is provided by the Permanent Executive Secretariat. The organization's five Specialized Technical Commissions address political and juridical affairs; society and culture; planning, agriculture, industry, and natural resources; commerce, finance, immigration, and tourism; and public works, energy, and transport.

Activities. Although emerging from a mutual security pact during South Africa's apartheid era, CEPGL in its first two decades focused much of its activities on economic issues. To promote economic development and integration, the community proposed a number of projects, including development of the Ruzizi River Valley for hydroelectric power, methane gas extraction from Lake Kivu, coordination of members' transportation and communications networks, and joint cement, bottling, and agricultural materials production. The CEPGL also acted to harmonize regulation in car insurance and investment, to increase freedom of movement of goods and people, and to coordinate health, agricultural, and other basic research.

The 14th summit was delayed twice because of the civil war in Rwanda before finally being held in the nation's northeastern city of Gisenyi on August 2, 1992. The CEPGL heads of state agreed to seek resolution of border security problems through "regular official contacts." However, a resumption of full CEPGL activity was subsequently precluded by extremely unsettled conditions in the region, including the political stalemate in Zaire, the deaths of the presidents of Burundi and Rwanda in April 1994, and subsequent Hutu-Tutsi conflict in those two countries.

Following the installation of a government led by the Tutsi-dominated Rwandan Patriotic Front in Rwanda in 1994, the defense ministers of the CEPGL countries met June 10, 1995, in Bujumbura, Burundi, to "reactivate" the community's security arrangements. It was concluded that joint forces would patrol the community's common borders, under the direction of a tripartite CEPGL subcommission. Specifically, the patrols were mandated to combat "armed, destabilizing elements" near the borders, a reference to antigovernment activity emanating from among the estimated 2 million (mainly Rwandan) Hutu refugees in Zaire. However, CEPGL intentions were subsequently overwhelmed by the massive dislocations and fighting that developed in the region in 1996 as Hutu-Tutsi conflict crossed the borders of the three member states and precipitated extreme turmoil, including the rebel victory in Zaire in 1997 and its return to the name of the Democratic Republic of the Congo (see articles on Burundi, Democratic Republic of the Congo, and Rwanda). Through 2004 continuing conflict and a lack of cordial bilateral relations among the members kept the CEPGL in limbo. A meeting in April 2005 in Lubumbashi, Democratic Republic of the Congo, with the EU commissioner of development and humanitarian aid, Louis Michel, was said at the time to mark a new beginning for unity in the Great Lakes region. The sum of 50 million euros was promised for this purpose.

ECONOMIC COMMUNITY OF WEST AFRICAN STATES (ECOWAS/CEDEAO)

Communauté Economique des Etats de l'Afrique de l'Ouest
Comunidade Economica dos Estados da Africa do Oeste

Established: By Treaty of Lagos (Nigeria), signed May 28, 1975; amended by Treaty of Cotonou (Benin), signed July 24, 1993; entry into force of the latter announced July 30, 1995.

Purpose: "To promote cooperation and integration leading to the establishment of an economic union in West Africa in order to raise the living standards of its peoples, and to maintain and enhance economic stability, foster relations among member states and contribute to the progress and development of the African Continent."

Headquarters: Abuja, Nigeria.

Principal Organs: Authority of Heads of State and Government; Council of Ministers; Community Parliament; Economic and Social Council; Specialized Technical Commissions; Community Court of Justice; ECOWAS Bank for Investment and Development; Executive Secretariat.

Executive Secretary: Mohamed Ibn Chambas (Ghana).

Membership (15): Benin, Burkina Faso, Cape Verde, Côte d'Ivoire, Gambia, Ghana, Guinea, Guinea-Bissau, Liberia, Mali, Niger, Nigeria, Senegal, Sierra Leone, Togo.

Official Languages: English, French, Portuguese, and "all West African languages so designated by the Authority."

Origin and development. The Economic Community of West African States received its greatest impetus from discussions in October 1974 between Gen. Yakubu Gowon of Nigeria and President Gnassingbé Eyadéma of Togo. The two leaders advanced plans for a more comprehensive economic grouping than the purely francophone West African Economic Community (*Communauté Economique de l'Afrique de l'Ouest—*CEAO; see the article on the UEMOA), which had been recently launched by Côte d'Ivoire, Dahomey (later Benin), Mali, Mauritania, Niger, Senegal, and Upper Volta (later Burkina Faso). The treaty establishing ECOWAS was signed by representatives of 15 West African states on May 28, 1975, in Lagos, Nigeria, and by the end of June had been formally ratified by enough signatories (seven) to become operative. However, it took until November 1976 for an agreement to be worked out on protocols to the treaty. The delay resulted in part from Senegal's effort to make its ratification dependent upon a broadening of the Community to include Zaire and several other francophone states of Central Africa. Ultimately, it was decided that any such expansion would be unrealistic. Portuguese-speaking Cape Verde joined in 1977.

At their 1981 summit ECOWAS leaders agreed in principle to a mutual defense pact under which military units would carry out joint maneuvers and would be mobilized to defend a member under external attack or to act as a peacekeeping force in the event of intra-Community conflict.

In 1991 a special committee was established to propose revisions to the ECOWAS treaty. After extensive negotiation the committee's proposals were adopted in the Treaty of Cotonou, approved at the July 1993 ECOWAS summit. The treaty was designed to make summit decisions binding on all members and also expanded ECOWAS's political mandate. Members agreed, for example, to the peaceful settlement of interstate disputes, the protection of human rights, and the promotion of democratic systems of governance. In addition, a number of new bodies, such as a Community Parliament and an Economic and Social Council, were authorized.

At the conclusion of a summit on July 28–29, 1995, ECOWAS announced that sufficient ratifications had been received for the treaty to enter into effect, although the Parliament and a Community Court of Justice were not inaugurated until 2000 and 2001, respectively. Meanwhile, Mauritania, apparently objecting to moves toward greater military and monetary integration, had announced in December 1999 its intention to withdraw from the organization, effective December 2000.

Structure. The basic structure of ECOWAS consists of an Authority of Heads of State and Government; a Council of Ministers with two representatives from each member; an Executive Secretariat headed by a secretary who is appointed for a four-year period; a Community Court of Justice to settle disputes arising under the treaty; an Economic and Social Council; and eight Specialized Technical Commissions: Administration and Finance; Food and Agriculture; Environment and Natural Resources; Human Resources, Information, and Social and Cultural Affairs; Industry, Science and Technology, and Energy; Political, Judicial, and Legal Affairs and Regional Security and Integration; Trade, Customs, Taxation, Statistics, Money, and Payments; and Transport, Communications, and Tourism. The ECOWAS Community Parliament of 120 national representatives began its inaugural session in November 2000 in Abuja. The Community Court of Justice was inaugurated in January 2001. A Council of Elders has also been formed recently.

The Treaty of Lagos authorized creation of a Fund for Cooperation, Compensation, and Development (FCCD), supported by members' contributions, the revenues of Community enterprises, and grants from non-ECOWAS countries. In addition to financing mutually approved projects, the fund, headquartered in Lomé, Togo, was established to compensate members who suffered losses due to the establishment of Community enterprises or to the liberalization of trade. Upon ratification of treaty changes approved by the Authority in December 2001, the FCCD was reconfigured as the ECOWAS Bank for Investment and Development (EBID), which has the broader mission of financing private investment in infrastructure as well as such public sector activities as poverty reduction.

Activities. Although the May 1990 summit marked the 15th anniversary of the signing of the ECOWAS treaty, the mood was described as "far from celebratory" in light of the domestic problems facing several key members, ongoing disputes between others, and a persistent fiscal shortfall. Despite the absence of half of the heads of state and past ECOWAS difficulty in translating plans into action, several major resolutions were approved. They included the creation of a Standing Mediation Committee to intervene in regional disputes, the approval of a common residency card for the Community, and support for reliance on ECOWAS as the "single economic community in West Africa," an oblique reference to "competing" organizations, such as the CEAO, the Mano River Union, and the Council of the Entente.

Purely economic concerns were pushed into the background by ECOWAS's controversial involvement in the civil war that broke out in Liberia in August 1990. An ECOWAS Monitoring Group (Ecomog) was formed and sent to Liberia to facilitate a cease-fire, organize an interim government, and oversee the holding of new national elections. However, only Gambia, Ghana, Guinea, Nigeria, and Sierra Leone supplied soldiers for the group, and a proposed special ECOWAS summit was canceled because of differences among the members. A tenuous cease-fire was finally negotiated at an extraordinary summit in late November, but the political situation in Liberia remained chaotic.

During the second half of 1991 ECOWAS endorsed the peacemaking efforts of a committee involving the heads of state of Burkina Faso, Côte d'Ivoire, Gambia, Nigeria, and Togo, which in late October yielded the so-called Yamassoukro IV peace accord. The agreement, signed by interim Liberian President Amos Sawyer and Charles Taylor, head of the National Patriotic Forces of Liberia (NPFL), directed Ecomog troops to supervise the disarmament and encampment of rebel forces throughout Liberia, establish a "buffer zone" along the Liberia-Sierra Leone border, and facilitate the holding of elections. However, the NPFL subsequently refused to permit implementation of the agreement. Consequently, the ECOWAS summit on July 27–29, 1992, in Dakar, Senegal, displaying rare unanimity, agreed to impose economic sanctions against NPFL-held Liberian territory if Taylor's forces continued to undermine Ecomog efforts.

To the surprise of some observers, Ecomog began to gain the upper hand in early 1993. Subsequently, in what was seen as a remarkably successful response to the ECOWAS intervention, a peace accord (negotiated with UN assistance) was signed by Liberia's warring factions in July. The appearance of success produced an atmosphere of enthusiasm during the ECOWAS summit in Cotonou, Benin, on July 22–24, *West Africa* voicing the opinion that the Community had become "planted much more firmly on the international map as a serious and credible organization." Hoping to capitalize

on the newfound cohesion, the summit signed the Treaty of Cotonou, a revision of the original Lagos Treaty. The new accord was designed to speed up implementation of a regional common market, which would include, progressively, a monetary union, an internal free trade zone (providing for the free movement of people, goods, services, and capital), and a common external tariff and trade policy. The signatories also committed themselves to "solidarity and collective self-reliance" and pledged to refrain from any aggressive action against another ECOWAS member. In general, ECOWAS was seen as trying to secure its position as the West African "pillar" of the African Economic Community fashioned by the Organization of African States (OAU, subsequently the African Union—AU).

Despite continued concern over the failure of some members to make their allotted financial contributions to the Community, at the August 1994 summit the heads of state and government once again affirmed their confidence in the organization's future. The 18th ECOWAS summit, held July 28–29, 1995, in Accra, Ghana, was described as a "lackluster" event, with only six heads of state among the attendees. Contributing to the Community's malaise were ongoing difficulties in implementing the Liberian peace accord and the sustained political crisis in Nigeria. Despite reports that members' arrears had climbed to over $100 million, the summit leaders reaffirmed their commitment to regional economic cooperation and authorized the use of a "West African traveler's check" as a possible precursor to a common currency. (The check was officially introduced in 1998.)

Throughout 1996 the ECOWAS agenda remained dominated by the problems associated with the Liberian peace process. However, the situation brightened in August with the signing of the Abuja Accord, which directed Ecomog to disarm and demobilize the warring factions by January 31, 1997.

In a change from past summits, an "optimistic" attitude was reported at the meetings held in Abuja, Nigeria, on July 27–28, 1996, only four heads of state failing to attend. Nevertheless, it was clear that problems, such as high arrears, were continuing to impede ECOWAS operations. In order to provide operating funds it was agreed that a small levy on imports from nonmembers would be imposed. (Introduced in July 2003, the Community levy amounted to 0.5 percent of customs duties.)

The major topics of discussion at the summit of August 28–29, 1997, in Abuja were the July election of Charles Taylor as president of Liberia and the May coup in Sierra Leone. In recognition of the apparent resolution of the long-standing Liberian conflict, ECOWAS lifted its sanctions. However, Ecomog troops were directed to remain in the country to help "in the restructuring of Liberia's national army and police force." Meanwhile, ECOWAS responded to the overthrow of the Kabbah government in Sierra Leone by recommending a boycott and blockade of the country and the deployment of Ecomog contingents to enforce them. (See article on Sierra Leone for subsequent developments.)

At the October 1998 ECOWAS summit most of the discussions were devoted to promoting peace and stability in the region. Toward this end, the summit participants agreed to ban the trade in and manufacture of small arms throughout ECOWAS and called on other parts of Africa to do the same. The summit also approved a peace accord that ECOWAS representatives had helped to negotiate in Guinea-Bissau (see Guinea-Bissau article for more information) and that committed the Community to providing peacekeeping forces in that country as of early 1999. In what was perhaps the boldest move at the summit, ECOWAS also endorsed a conflict resolution mechanism authorizing ECOWAS to intervene in the internal affairs of its member states if the security of the region were threatened.

The December 9–10, 1999, summit in Lomé, Togo, was highlighted by approval of a draft protocol for the Permanent Mechanism for the Prevention, Management, and Settlement of Conflicts and the Maintenance of Peace in the Region. The Authority also approved creation of a Mediation and Security Council; endorsed conversion of Ecomog into a permanent standby force capable of enforcement, peacekeeping, and humanitarian missions; and voiced continuing support for the Community-

wide moratorium on the manufacture, export, and import of light\break weapons.

Although ECOWAS failed to achieve a common external tariff by its target of January 2000, in April the anglophone Gambia, Ghana, Guinea, Liberia, Nigeria, and Sierra Leone, plus Portuguese-speaking Cape Verde, reached agreement on establishing by 2003 a new West African monetary union in parallel to the francophone West African Economic and Monetary Union (*Union Economique et Monétaire Ouest-Africaine*—UEMOA). In February 2000, apparently setting aside what the ECOWAS chair and president of Mali, Alpha Oumar Konare, termed the anglophone/francophone "distractions" that had long impeded economic integration, ECOWAS and the UEMOA had agreed to a joint action plan that envisaged, in part, a merger of the UEMOA and the proposed second monetary union into a single zone by 2004. On November 17, 2000, the ECOWAS Convergence Council, consisting of the member states' finance ministers and central bank governors, approved establishment of a transitional West African Monetary Institute (WAMI) in Accra, Ghana, in preparation for the inauguration of a West African Central Bank (WACB). The initial time frame for these developments ultimately proved to be too optimistic, however, because of "macroeconomic and political instability," and thus the introduction of the second monetary zone was later delayed until 2005, with the date for the merger of the two zones to be decided by the Authority in 2005.

Throughout 2000, developments in Guinea, Liberia, and Sierra Leone continued to generate international concern. The December 2000 summit authorized positioning Ecomog monitors along the three countries' borders, as had been previously proposed in 1999, shortly before Ecomog's Liberian mission had effectively ended. Nevertheless, neither Guinea nor Liberia signed a requisite Status of Forces Agreement. The 25th annual ECOWAS summit, which convened in Dakar, Senegal, on December 20–21, called attention to positive developments in the troubled Mano River region but also approved sanctions against recalcitrant rebel groups in Liberia and asked the

Liberian government to undertake a "national reconciliation policy." In addition, the summit took a major step toward creation of the second regional monetary zone, encompassing Gambia, Ghana, Guinea, Nigeria, and Sierra Leone. (The general view was that conditions in Liberia and Cape Verde would prevent their immediate participation.) Among other actions, the summit adopted a special regional food security program, voiced support for the recently established Intergovernmental Action Group against Money Laundering (GIABA) in Dakar, and approved protocols on fighting corruption and human trafficking and on promoting democracy and good governance.

The 26th session of the Authority of Heads of State and Government, held in Dakar on January 26–31, 2003, focused its attention on economic and security issues. Having been designated as the West African coordinator and monitor for the AU-sponsored New Partnership for Africa's Development (Nepad), ECOWAS reaffirmed its support for the initiative. The summit participants also praised steps taken with the UEMOA toward harmonizing trade liberalization measures, the eventual goal being a regional common market. In addition, progress was noted in the areas of Community water resource management; energy coordination and development, particularly with regard to a planned West Africa Gas Pipeline project involving Benin, Ghana, Nigeria, and Togo; preparations for negotiating an Economic Partnership Agreement (EPA) with the EU; and funding of the EBID. (Member states may use the new Community levy to pay their shares of called up capital.) However, economic and political difficulties had pushed back until 2005 the introduction of the second regional monetary zone and a single currency.

With regard to security, the session heard extensive reports on developments in Côte d'Ivoire and Liberia. In addition to expressing its support for the French-sponsored Marcoussis Accord earlier in the month, ECOWAS remained committed to deployment of a peacekeeping ECOWAS Mission in Côte d'Ivoire (ECOMICI), formation of which had been approved in December 2002. A

September 2002 emergency meeting on the crisis in Côte d'Ivoire had established a contact group of Ghana, Guinea-Bissau, Mali, Niger, Nigeria, and Togo. Shortly after the summit, on February 4, 2003, the UN Security Council authorized deployment of the ECOMICI, which numbered over 1,800 troops by the end of the year. With respect to the troubled Mano River area, the January summit called upon the international community to provide additional development assistance to Sierra Leone, where peace had taken hold, but it expressed regret over renewed hostilities in Liberia between the government and rebel forces.

Issues of peace and security continued to dominate the region throughout 2003. Events in Côte d'Ivoire, Liberia, and also Guinea-Bissau prompted a number of emergency summits and other meetings. In early July, following the failure of yet another negotiated cease-fire in Liberia, ECOWAS agreed to dispatch several thousand troops to Monrovia, and the resultant ECOWAS Mission in Liberia (ECOMIL) was deployed in August.

The ECOWAS summit on December 19, 2003, in Accra saw Executive Secretary Mohamed Ibn Chambas and other speakers lament that the repeated political and military crises in the region had diverted ECOWAS from its goal of furthering economic integration and regional development. Chambas also asserted that a lack of political will in some member countries had delayed integration. Nevertheless, those attending the brief summit reiterated a commitment to establishing a West African free trade area by the end of 2005 and introducing a customs union by 2008.

The ECOWAS summit on January 19, 2005, in Accra was marked by dissension over Côte d'Ivoire, whose president, Laurent Gbagbo, was forced to hear declarations that he and his country's various faction leaders must "search their hearts." ECOWAS peacekeeping efforts in Côte d'Ivoire had been previously handed over to the African Union—an event that some summit participants described as a failure on their organization's part. The summit postponed plans to introduce a common currency by July 1, 2005.

In March 2005 ECOWAS launched the Regional Market Systems and Traders' Organizations in West Africa in an effort to improve regional cooperation in trade, with a particular focus on agriculture. The program was seen as the first step toward development of an ECOWAS common agricultural policy. Progress was also subsequently reported in regard to the proposed common external tariff for ECOWAS, a key component of the planned free trade area. Meanwhile, on the political front, ECOWAS was active in early 2005 in helping to resolve the turmoil in Togo; the Community also subsequently assisted in Liberia and Côte d'Ivoire.

At the April 12, 2006, summit, held in Niamey, Niger, the ECOWAS Heads of State approved organizational changes, making its Secretariat into a Commission to increase efficiency and productivity. They approved various efforts to improve the members' economy and infrastructure, including moves toward a common airline and a common standard for mobile telephones. On April 12, 2006, the group's trade ministers met in Abuja to evaluate progress toward the second phase of negotiations with the EU on an Economic Partnership Agreement. This prospective agreement would lead to creation of a free trade area between the two regions.

INDIAN OCEAN COMMISSION (IOC)

Commission de l'Océan Indien

Established: Formation by Madagascar, Mauritius, and Seychelles announced July 17, 1982; General Agreement of Cooperation signed January 10, 1984, in Victoria, Seychelles.

Purpose: To organize and promote regional cooperation in all sectors, with particular emphasis on economic development, to affirm an Indian Ocean identity, and to represent the Indian Ocean islands regionally and internationally.

Headquarters: Quatre Bornes, Mauritius.

Principal Organs: Council of Ministers, Committee of Permanent Liaison Officers, Secretariat.

Secretary General: Monique Andreas Esoquelomandroso.

Membership (5): Comoro Islands, France (representing the French Overseas Department of Réunion), Madagascar, Mauritius, Seychelles.

Origin and development. On July 17, 1982, Aneerood Jugnauth, the newly elected prime minister of Mauritius, announced at the conclusion of a state visit by President France Albert René of the Seychelles that an Indian Ocean Commission (IOC) had been formed by their two countries and Madagascar to examine possible regional cooperation. In December the three members' foreign affairs ministers agreed on an IOC constitution, which was submitted to their national parliaments for approval prior to signing a general agreement of regional cooperation in January 1984 in Victoria, Seychelles.

In January 1985 an IOC ministerial session approved the membership request of the Comoro Islands and endorsed France's proposed accession to represent the island of Réunion. The Comoros and France were formally installed as members at the January 1986 ministerial session. At its 1989 session the IOC elected its first secretary general and settled on Mauritius as the site of its permanent headquarters.

Structure. The Council of Ministers is the highest IOC authority, meeting once per year; its presidency rotates among the membership annually. A Committee of Permanent Liaison Officers convenes three times per year to prepare proposals for council sessions, to carry out council decisions, and to promote cooperation between the council and national administrations. The Secretariat, headed by a secretary general, is responsible for the conduct of the organization's daily activities; the secretary general serves a four-year, nonrenewable term. Technical committees, made up of experts from each of the member countries, identify sectoral projects suited to regional cooperation. After approval of a particular project, the responsible committee assumes a managerial role.

At the second IOC Summit of Heads of State or Government, held in December 1999 in St.-Denis, Réunion, the participants decided that henceforth informal summits would convene every four years.

Activities. IOC activities have greatly depended on external assistance, particularly from the European Community/European Union (EC/EU). Areas addressed by IOC projects and programs have included tuna fishing research and development, exploration of new and renewable energy sources, tourism promotion, environmental conservation, oil spill contingency planning, coral reef monitoring, intraregional trade, investment regulations and capital transfers, regional meteorological cooperation, and technical cooperation.

Partly to try pushing integration beyond the "good intentions" state, the first IOC heads of state or government summit was held March 16, 1991, in Antananarivo, Madagascar. In June 1992 the IOC ministers endorsed a new integration plan and in October agreed to a review of the IOC organizational structure. Subsequently, a degree of discord was reported among IOC members who were apparently excluded from a recent initiative spearheaded by Mauritius to form a larger and more formidable Indian Ocean Rim Association. Officials from Australia, India, Kenya, Oman, Singapore, and South Africa attended preliminary meetings in Mauritius in early 1995 on the proposed organization, with discussions focusing on economic cooperation.

As a consequence, the IOC was shunted to the sidelines. France expressed deep concern for the lack of direction and progress of the IOC in the face of direct competition for resources and attention from the new "Anglo-Saxon" Indian Ocean Rim Association, which was officially inaugurated in March 1997 (see the article on the IOR-ARC). One criticism leveled against the IOC by the French was that the organization collected no dues from its members and instead merely served as a channel for foreign development aid. Furthermore, Paris argued that "most IOC projects must be filed away as disappointing failures" because "results are unpredictable, coordination insufficient, and priorities little apparent."

The second IOC Summit of Heads of State and Government met December 3, 1999, in Réunion, although the government of the Comoro Islands, installed after an April coup, was not represented. (None of the other IOC members recognized its legitimacy.) The session was organized around four broad topics: economic and development issues, including regional cooperation and integration; political matters, including the IOC's relationship with other regional organizations; peacekeeping and security, including civil defense, drug trafficking, and money laundering; and culture, including matters of education and information technology. Earlier in the year, the island of Zanzibar (a component of the United Republic of Tanzania) requested independent membership, without success.

Over the next several years IOC activities were restrained by domestic political difficulties. In February 2002 the Organization of African Unity (OAU) and the IOC dispatched a joint mediation mission to Madagascar to help resolve a postelection crisis. On October 30–31, 2003, an extraordinary meeting of foreign ministers in Moroni, Comoro Islands, discussed preparations for a quadrennial summit, which was scheduled to be held in Moroni, but continuing political instability in the Comoros ultimately resulted in a decision to delay the gathering until 2004. (In late December 2003 the Comoran factions reached an accord, and a follow-up committee with IOC representation was organized under the auspices of the African Union.) The October meeting also focused on the fight against international terrorism and appointed a Committee of Sages to propose organizational reforms and to help define a future direction for the IOC.

In late 2003 the IOC's controversial secretary general, Wilfrid Bertile of Réunion, indicated his intention to resign to seek reelection to the Réunion legislature, the Regional Council. He came under criticism from some quarters for not having resigned his legislative seat after taking over as IOC secretary general in 2001.

The July 22, 2005, summit, held in Antananarivo, was attended by all member heads of state, including Jacques Chirac, the French president, representing Réunion. France appeared to be taking an interest in energizing the group, which was doing better as relations improved between Mauritius and the Seychelles. These countries, together with Réunion, are the richest OC members. The meeting gave permission for Réunion to apply for membership in the Common Market for Eastern and Southern Africa (Comesa) (see separate article on Comesa). During 2005 the IOC also signed an agreement with the EU, which was to provide 30 million euros (US$50 million) to finance its programs.

INDIAN OCEAN RIM ASSOCIATION FOR REGIONAL COOPERATION (IOR-ARC)

Established: By charter signed at a meeting of 14 insular and littoral Indian Ocean countries March 6–7, 1997, in Port Louis, Mauritius.

Purpose: To "increase cooperation in trade, investment, infrastructure, tourism, science, technology, and human resource development."

Headquarters: Vacoas, Mauritius.

Principal Organs: Council of Ministers, Committee of Senior Officials, Indian Ocean Rim Business Forum, Indian Ocean Rim Academic Group, Coordinating Secretariat.

Director of the Coordinating Secretariat: Devdasslall Dusoruth (Mauritius).

Membership (18): Australia, Bangladesh, India, Indonesia, Iran, Kenya, Madagascar, Malaysia, Mauritius, Mozambique, Oman, Singapore, South Africa, Sri Lanka, Tanzania, Thailand, United Arab Emirates, Yemen.
  Observer (1): Indian Ocean Tourism Organization.

Official Language: English.

Origin and development. Responding to a proposal by the government of Mauritius, on March 29–31, 1995, representatives of Australia, India, Kenya, Oman, Singapore, and South Africa met in Mauritius to discuss economic cooperation, trade liberalization, and potential investment opportunities based on "principles of open regionalism and inclusivity." To follow up, a working group of government officials, businessmen, and academics developed a charter for a tripartite regional organization. At a ministerial-level meeting March 6–7, 1997, in Port Louis, Mauritius, representatives of the 14 founding states—Indonesia, Madagascar, Malaysia, Mozambique, Sri Lanka, Tanzania, and Yemen in addition to the seven that met in 1995—signed the charter for the Indian Ocean Rim Association for Regional Cooperation (IOR-ARC).

At the second biennial meeting of the Council of Ministers, held in March 1999 in Maputo, Mozambique, the countries of Bangladesh, Iran, Seychelles, Thailand, and the United Arab Emirates were invited to join the IOR-ARC. They were welcomed into the organization at an extraordinary Council of Ministers session in Muscat, Oman, in January 2000, although Seychelles decided to withdraw in July 2003. "Dialog Partners" are China, Egypt, France, Japan, and the United Kingdom. Turkey also has requested dialog status.

Structure. The Council of Ministers, comprising the foreign ministers of the member states, is the highest authority of the IOR-ARC, setting policy, reviewing progress toward the organization's goals, and creating new organizational bodies. It meets biennially in regular session, but ad hoc meetings also may be called. Convening as needed, a Committee of Senior Officials supervises implementation of council decisions, drafts work programs, and helps seek financing for projects. Working in cooperation with the senior officials are the Indian Ocean Rim Business Forum and the Indian Ocean Rim Academic Group. All organs reach decisions by consensus. The Coordinating Secretariat, headed by a director, is located in Vacoas, Mauritius.

Activities. Apart from providing a regional forum and conducting research in such areas as sectoral tariff levels, the IOR-ARC accomplished little in its first six years. During the March 1999 Council of Ministers session participants agreed to promote trade facilitation and liberalization as well as economic and technical cooperation. Accordingly, they set up a Working Group on Trade and Investment (WGTI), which met for the first time in conjunction with the extraordinary Council of Ministers session in Muscat in January 2000.

Meeting April 7–8, 2001, in Muscat, the Council of Ministers authorized formation of a High Level Task Force (HLTF) with a mandate that included proposing a future direction for the organization, devising a medium-term strategic plan, defining criteria for dialog partners, raising the IOR-ARC's international profile, and examining the functioning and funding of the secretariat. On October 7–13, 2003, the various IOR-ARC organs held meetings in Colombo, Sri Lanka. At the culminating session, the Council of Ministers adopted the HLTF report, which offered recommendations on work programs and provided guidelines for organizing the secretariat.

Long-range organizational goals include eventual elimination of internal tariffs, but some observers have noted that such broad measures will be difficult to achieve. Wide economic disparities persist among the member states, which also participate in other intergovernmental organizations that frequently have competing goals. In addition, there have been reports of major differences between the IOR-ARC members with the largest economies, namely India and Australia.

Recent commentary suggests that the organization has not lived up to its promise. Before July 2005, however, it agreed to allow projects to go ahead with the support of at least six members, rather than by full consensus, and this change in rules might help drive more action. The IOC-ARC has no website, and information about its activities must come from member governments, all of which voice support, and from general news reports.

Ministerial meetings were held August 26–27, 2004, in Colombo and February 21–22, 2006, in Tehran, Iran.

INTER-GOVERNMENTAL AUTHORITY ON DEVELOPMENT (IGAD)

Autorité Intergovernementale pour le Développement

Established: As the Inter-Governmental Authority on Drought and Development (IGADD) by six-nation summit meeting of heads of state and government January 15–16, 1986, in Djibouti; present name adopted March 21, 1996.

Purpose: To coordinate efforts to combat drought and desertification, to develop regional policies on short- and medium-term economic development and, since March 1996, to assist in preventing and resolving conflicts in the region.

Headquarters: Djibouti, Djibouti.

Principal Organs: Assembly of Heads of State and Government, Council of Ministers, Committee of Ambassadors, Secretariat.

Executive Secretary: Attalla Hamad Bashir (Sudan).

Membership (7): Djibouti, Eritrea, Ethiopia, Kenya, Somalia, Sudan, Uganda.

Origin and development. In view of cyclical droughts, which brought widespread famine and death to the region, the leaders of Djibouti, Ethiopia, Kenya, Somalia, Sudan, and Uganda established IGADD during a January 15–16, 1986, conference in Djibouti. Eritrea was admitted in September 1993.

The name of the group was changed to the Inter-Governmental Authority on Development (IGAD) on March 21, 1996, in conjunction with an expansion of the organization's role to include regional conflict prevention and resolution, infrastructural development, and food security and environmental protection.

Structure. The policymaking IGAD body is the Assembly of Heads of State and Government, also called the IGAD annual summit; implementation of its decisions rests with a Council of Ministers, which meets at least twice per year, and a small Secretariat in Djibouti. The March 1996 restructuring increased the size of the Council of Ministers to 14 (2 from each member state) and directed that decisions would henceforth require the vote of two-thirds of the members. The executive secretary, who serves a four-year, once-renewable term, oversees three Secretariat divisions: economic cooperation, agriculture and the environment, and political/humanitarian affairs. Supporting the council and the Secretariat is a Committee of Ambassadors, which comprises the principal representatives of the member states to Djibouti.

Activities. The founders of the IGADD identified the new organization's first priority as the development of a regional "early warning system" to deal with the effects of drought. Other proposed projects emphasized agricultural research, human resources development, and creation of a regional plan for the storage of food and its distribution to needy areas in times of shortage. However, little effective action was achieved by 1990, in large part because of the civil wars in Ethiopia, Somalia, and Sudan and, to a lesser extent, continued sporadic rebel activity in Uganda. Consequently, by 1992 many Western donors had reportedly lost their "enthusiasm" for continued IGADD financing. In May the Council of Ministers announced its intention to restructure the IGADD Secretariat according to the wishes of donors. The council also endorsed France's proposal that IGADD cooperate with the Arab Maghreb Union (AMU) and the Permanent Inter-State Committee on Drought Control in the Sahel (CILSS) in creating an umbrella organization to monitor drought and desertification throughout much of North, East, and West Africa.

Western support for the IGADD was subsequently reported to be regaining strength, particularly as a result of its growing role in the Sudanese peace negotiations. Consequently, the IGADD Council of Ministers in January 1995 decided to establish the "Friends of IGADD," a forum for informal consultation with current and potential development partners such as Canada, Netherlands, Norway, the United States, and the United Kingdom. In addition, in April a special one-day summit in Addis Ababa, Ethiopia, of six IGADD heads of state (the turmoil in Somalia still precluding that nation's participation) appointed a ministerial committee to review proposals for "revitalizing and expanding" the organization. Restructuring of the IGADD was approved at a second extraordinary summit March 21, 1996, in Nairobi, Kenya, at which time the organization became the IGAD.

At the eighth IGAD summit, which met November 23, 2000, in Khartoum, Sudan, the closing declaration reflected a desire to move forward on many other concerns while continuing efforts to find resolutions for the conflicts in Somalia and Sudan. The declaration called for drafting a trade protocol; promoting infrastructural cooperation in transport, communications, and power; establishing a disaster preparedness mechanism; and devising national and regional food security programs. The summit also requested the Secretariat to prepare a draft protocol for a Conflict Early Warning and Response Mechanism (CEWARN). The completed protocol

was then signed at the ninth summit January 10–11, 2002, in Khartoum. At the same time, the IGAD was actively participating in preparations for the African Union's planned African Economic Community, serving as the "northern sector" representative within the Common Market for Eastern and Southern Africa—Comesa (see separate article).

The tenth ordinary summit, which met October 20–25, 2003, in Kampala, Uganda, came in the context of renewed hope for resolution of the Sudanese and Somalian conflicts. In the preceding 15 months, as a consequence of ongoing IGAD-sponsored peace talks, a number of agreements were reached between the Sudanese factions, including the July 2002 Machakos (Kenya) protocol, which included the right of self-determination for southern Sudan; an October 2002 memorandum of understanding on ending hostilities; a February 2003 power-sharing accord; and, most recently, a September 2003 agreement on an interim security arrangement. With regard to Somalia, the latest peace talks were initiated under IGAD auspices October 2002 in Eldoret, Kenya, and then transferred in February 2003 to the Kenyan capital, Nairobi. By October the discussions reached a critical juncture regarding a transitional federal charter, and an agreement was ultimately signed January 29, 2004. The agreement caused a Transitional Federal Government (TFG) for Somalia to be formed, temporarily based in Kenya until conditions in Somalia improved. As a consequence of these peace efforts, the IGAD has received wide international praise and has greatly increased its visibility.

Despite its necessary focus on Sudan and Somalia, in 2002–2003 the IGAD also addressed many other concerns. Recognizing the difficulty of financing development projects in the region, in 2002 the Assembly of Heads of State and Government directed the Secretariat to investigate establishing a Special Fund for that purpose. A Conference on the Prevention and Combating of Terrorism was held in June 2003 in Addis Ababa, while a first-ever Conference on Internal Displacement in the IGAD Subregion concluded in September.

Events in Somalia did not turn out as planned. The TFG moved to Somalia in 2005, but remained deeply split among the various warlords. IGAD offered peacekeeping troops to Somalia as early as January 2005, but by mid-2006 this deployment had not occurred. Elements of the TFG objected to receiving ethnic Somali peacekeepers from neighboring countries, and by June 2006 the whole picture changed when an Islamist militia drove warlord groups out of Mogadishu, the Somali capital.

IGAD's 11th summit, held March 20, 2006, in Nairobi expressed more satisfaction over the outcome of the agreements over Sudan, though it called for all possible international help in returning refugees from the conflict.

INTERNATIONAL ORGANIZATION OF THE FRANCOPHONIE (OIF)

Organisation Internationale de la Francophonie

Established: As *La Francophonie* under a Charter that was adopted on December 18, 1996, in Marrakesh, Morocco, by a Ministerial Conference of francophone states and then endorsed on November 15, 1997, by the Seventh Francophone Summit, held in Hanoi, Vietnam; present name adopted by the Ministerial Conference of the Francophonie on December 4–5, 1998 in Bucharest, Romania.

Purpose: To facilitate the exchange of cultural, educational, scientific, and technological information, particularly but not exclusively among countries with French in common usage; to promote cultural and linguistic diversity, including the teaching of French; to encourage democracy and respect for human rights; to advance the economic development of member states.

Headquarters: Paris, France.

Principal Organs: Conference of Heads of State and Government of Countries Using French as a Common Language (Francophone Summit), Ministerial Conference of the Francophonie, Permanent Council of the Francophonie, General Secretariat, Agency of the Francophonie (Intergovernmental Agency of the Francophonie), Parliamentary Assembly of the Francophonie.

Secretary General: Abdou Diouf (Senegal).

Membership (49): Belgium, French Community of Belgium, Benin, Bulgaria, Burkina Faso, Burundi, Cambodia, Cameroon, Canada, Canada–New Brunswick, Canada–Quebec, Cape Verde, Central African Republic, Chad, Comoro Islands, Democratic Republic of the Congo, Republic of the Congo, Côte d'Ivoire, Djibouti, Dominica, Egypt, Equatorial Guinea, France, Gabon, Guinea, Guinea-Bissau, Haiti, Laos, Lebanon, Luxembourg, Madagascar, Mali, Mauritania, Mauritius, Moldova, Monaco, Morocco, Niger, Romania, Rwanda, St. Lucia, Sao Tome and Principe, Senegal, Seychelles, Switzerland, Togo, Tunisia, Vanuatu, Vietnam.

Associate Members (4): Albania, Andorra, Greece, Macedonia.

Observers (5): Czech Republic, Lithuania, Poland, Slovakia, Slovenia.

Official Language: French.

Origin and development. Efforts to bring together the French-speaking countries of the world date back to the 1960s, some 80 years after the term *"francophonie"* was first used to identify those peoples and states speaking or otherwise using French. International cooperation initially centered on educational policy and institutions, followed in 1967 by creation of the International Association of French Language Parliamentarians (*Association Internationale des Parlementaires de Langue Français*—AIPLF). Near the end of the decade the francophone movement began to assume a somewhat more formal character as the First International Conference of Francophone Countries, meeting on

February 17–20, 1969, in Niamey, Niger, proposed creation of a clearinghouse for members in the areas of culture, education, and technology. Spearheading the efforts were three African heads of state: Habib Bourguiba of Tunisia, Hamani Diori of Niger, and Léopold Sédar Senghor of Senegal. As a result, the Agency for Cultural and Technical Cooperation (*Agence de Coopération Culturelle et Technique*—ACCT) was established by a convention signed March 21, 1970, in Niamey, during the Second International Conference of Francophone Countries. The ACCT subsequently grew to encompass all major French-speaking states except Algeria, as well as a number of countries in which French culture was deemed important, although not dominant.

In the 1980s and 1990s the ACCT was involved in the proposed establishment of a full-fledged francophone "Commonwealth." Although the idea was first suggested to ACCT members in 1980, disputes both within Canada and between Canada and France over the issue of Quebec separatism delayed the convening of a Francophone Summit to work on the proposal until February 17–19, 1986. The summit, held outside Paris, was attended by delegations from 42 countries and regions and adopted a 13-point program of action that called, inter alia, for the formation of a francophone television network, the provision of linguistic data to the francophone world by means of videotext, and the strengthening of cooperation among francophone delegations at the United Nations. Responsibility for a number of the summit's proposals was given to the ACCT, whose ministerial-level General Conference met in an extraordinary session in December to consider structural and financial reforms that would permit it to assume greater francophone authority. Concurrently, Canada, already the ACCT's leading financial contributor, announced it was doubling its level of support.

A second summit, attended by 43 delegations from 37 countries (including all ACCT members except Cameroon and Vanuatu), was held September 2–4, 1987, in Quebec, Canada. African economic issues, particularly the external debt crisis and falling world commodity prices, dominated the meeting, during which Canada announced that it was forgiving about $330 million in debts owed by seven African countries. Discussion also continued on the future role of the ACCT in whatever francophone structure might emerge from the summits.

The Third Francophone Summit, held in May 1989 in Dakar, Senegal, maintained the emphasis on Third World debt and development problems. French President Mitterrand garnered the biggest headlines by announcing he intended to ask the French Parliament to forgive 40 percent (an estimated $2.3 billion) of the debt owed to France by the world's 35 poorest countries. The Fourth Francophone Summit was held November 19–21, 1991, in Chaillot, France, the venue having been changed from Zaire because of objections to Zairean President Mobutu's apparent antipathy toward political reform.

Continued friction between Canada and France over the role of the ACCT was subsequently reported, Paris apparently charging the agency with promoting Canadian interests at the expense of broader francophone concerns. However, an understanding on the matter was reportedly reached at the Fifth Francophone Summit, held October 16–18, 1993, in Port Louis, Mauritius. France acquiesced to a second term for ACCT Secretary General Jean-Louis Roy, a Canadian, apparently in return for the summit's agreement to expand the authority of the Permanent Francophone Council (*Conseil Permanent de la Francophonie*—CPF), which had been established by the 1991 summit. The council was authorized to make "political decisions" on behalf of the francophone countries as well as to coordinate the institutional activities of the francophone community, including the ACCT, between summits. Meanwhile, the summit also approved the renaming of the AIPLF (which in 1989 had changed from *Association* to *Assemblée*) as the Francophone Consultative Assembly (*Assemblée Consultative de la Francophonie*—ACF) and welcomed the grouping under the expanding francophone umbrella.

In anticipation of the next francophone summit, ACCT Secretary General Roy suggested that the group adopt a "more political" approach to enhance its effectiveness, observers taking this to mean, among other things, greater emphasis on such issues as democratization and human rights. However, as expected following the election of rightist Jacques Chirac as the new president of France in May 1995, the sixth summit, held December 2–4, 1995, in Cotonou, Benin, concentrated on economic matters. Among other things, Chirac indicated France would press other leading industrialized nations not to reduce their financial assistance to African nations. He also called for efforts to prevent English from becoming, at the expense of French and other languages, the default language of the Internet and the "information superhighway."

Returning to the issue of a greater political emphasis, the Francophone Ministerial Conference (*Conférence Ministérielle de la Francophonie*— CMF) in 1996 proposed a new francophone "charter," which was approved by the Seventh Francophone Summit, held November 14–16, 1997, in Hanoi, Vietnam. It was agreed that a permanent General Secretariat would be established for *La Francophonie* on January 1, 1998, under the leadership of former UN secretary general Boutros Boutros-Ghali of Egypt, whose selection as secretary general of the new body reportedly caused consternation among some French-speaking African countries. The summit also approved a "plan of action" regarding support for human rights, democratic values, and economic cooperation. In addition, the new charter directed that the ACCT would subsequently be known as the Agency of the Francophonie (*Agence de la Francophonie*); the former ACCT thus became the lead agency of the newly formalized Francophonie, with the summit leaders then selecting Roger Dehaybe of Belgium as the new general administrator of the agency. The summit also confirmed a shift in emphasis, as evidenced by the attendance of several countries with, at best, tangential interest in French language concerns. All, however, had indicated their desire to join forces with other countries attempting to ward off "global domination" by Anglo-Saxon (particularly American) culture and language.

The CMF, meeting in Bucharest, Romania, December 4–5, 1998, endorsed Boutros-Ghali's efforts to heighten the profile of the francophone community, henceforth to be known as the International Francophone Organization (*Organisation Internationale de la Francophonie*— OIF). In addition, the CMF endorsed renaming the ACF as the Parliamentary Assembly of the Francophonie (*Assemblée Parlementaire de la Francophonie*—APF) and asked it to play a wider role in helping to solidify legislative institutions in developing countries.

In 1999 the OIF decided that the Agency of the Francophonie would be commonly, although unofficially, referenced as the Intergovernmental Agency of the Francophonie (*Agence Intergouvernementale de la Francophonie*—AIF) to better reflect its character.

Structure. The Conference of Heads of State and Government of Countries Using French as a Common Language, better known as the Francophone Summit, usually meets every two years to set policy for the OIF. The Ministerial Conference of the Francophonie (CMF), consisting primarily of the members' foreign ministers, is responsible for seeing that summit decisions are carried out. Two additional "Permanent Ministerial Conferences" address matters of education and of youth and sports; sectoral ministerial conferences also may be convened. The Permanent Council of the Francophonie (CPF), comprising the personal representatives of the members' heads of state and government, has among its responsibilities organizing summits and seeing that summit decisions are implemented.

The secretary general, who is elected by the summit for a four-year term, has multiple functions, including heading the General Secretariat, chairing the CPF, carrying out international policy, and serving as the OIF's principal international presence and spokesperson. In addition, he ranks as the senior official of the Agency of the Francophonie (unofficially, the Intergovernmental Agency of the Francophonie—AIF) and proposes that organ's general administrator. As the OIF's principal executing body (*opérateur principal*), the AIF has as its main responsibility carrying out the cultural, scientific, technical, economic, and legal cooperative programs endorsed by the summit. The CMF also sits as the General Conference of the Agency, while the CPF periodically convenes as the agency's Administrative Council.

In January 2004 a new body, the High Council of the Francophonie (*Haut Conseil de la Francophonie*) convened for the first time. Encompassing between 30 and 40 individuals selected by the secretary general for once-renewable terms of four years, the High Council has as its mission reflecting on matters of French language and cultural diversity. The 37 individuals named to the first High Council included politicians, artists, writers, media specialists, teachers, jurists, economists, and entrepreneurs from around the globe.

The OIF sponsors four specialized agencies (*opérateurs directs*): the Agency of Francophone Universities, the French-language TV5 international channel, the Senghor University of Alexandria, and the International Association of Francophone Mayors. Other affiliated bodies and offices include the Francophone Institute for Energy and the Environment in Quebec, Canada, and the Francophone Institute for New Information and Training Technologies in Bordeaux, France. A Parliamentary Assembly serves an advisory role.

Activities. The formal establishment of the OIF solidified efforts by the international francophone community to expand its membership and mission. Recent additions to the membership include Albania, Guinea-Bissau, and Macedonia, none of which has a significant French-speaking population; all, however, have been seeking wider international integration and access to economic and development assistance. In addition to advancing French cultural and linguistic programs, including sponsorship of over 140 rural reading centers in a dozen African countries, the OIF promotes crisis prevention and resolution, strengthening of democratic practices and institutions, ratification of human rights conventions, and adoption of coordinated policies in multilateral trade negotiations. In furtherance of

such goals it has established permanent missions to the United Nations, the European Union, and the African Union and has opened regional AIF offices in Libreville, Gabon; Lomé, Togo; and Hanoi, Vietnam.

The Francophone Summit that convened September 3–5, 1999, in Moncton, New Brunswick, Canada, focused its attention once again on matters of cultural diversity. The meeting's final declaration noted that "cultural goods are in no way reducible to their economic dimension" and that the participating leaders "affirm the right of [their] states and governments to freely define their cultural policies and appropriate tools of intervention." The declaration cited the perceived threat posed by multilateral talks and globalization without, however, explicitly referencing an ongoing U.S.-Canadian dispute over Ottawa's efforts to protect Canadian publications, music, and other media from U.S. domination.

The summit also broadly promoted political equality, security, and democracy. The assembled leaders steered clear of openly disputing various members' human rights records, despite a recent assertion by Amnesty International that 35 of the OIF's members and observers were guilty of human rights violations. In addition, the Moncton session set sustainable economic development as a leading goal. The summit declaration placed particular emphasis on the developing information society, including the need for exchange of knowledge and expertise in science and technology.

Having been postponed from October 2001 following the September 11 terrorist attacks on the United States, the ninth Summit met October 18–20, 2002, in Beirut, Lebanon. The session was largely dominated by the looming crisis over Iraq's alleged weapons of mass destruction. A summit resolution noted the "essential role" of the United Nations in resolving the conflict, and the overall stance of the participants clearly supported French President Chirac's opposition to preemptive military action in the absence of Security Council authorization. The ongoing political crisis in Côte d'Ivoire also drew the attention of the participants, who elected former Senegalese president

Abdou Diouf as the new OIF secretary general. In a noteworthy development, the summit was attended by Algerian President Abdelaziz Bouteflika, who pointedly dismissed questions from the press about whether or not his country would seek admission to the OIF.

The OIF continues to promote French language and the shared traditions of the Francophone community. The secretary general frequently travels beyond the French-speaking world in support of this mission. The OIF has never failed to condemn antidemocratic moves in French-speaking Africa or to praise prodemocratic efforts, such as voters' approval of a new constitution in the Democratic Republic of the Congo in December 2005.

MANO RIVER UNION

Union du Fleuve Mano

Established: By the Mano River Declaration issued by the presidents of Liberia and Sierra Leone on October 3, 1973, and accompanying protocols signed in 1974.

Purpose: To promote the economic development of member states by the elimination of tariff barriers and the creation of new productive capacity, with particular emphasis on the hydroelectric potential of the Mano River; also, in recent years, to further peace, security, and stability in the region.

Headquarters: Freetown, Sierra Leone.

Principal Organs: Ministerial Council, Secretariat.

Secretary General: H. E. Jallow.

Membership (3): Guinea, Liberia, Sierra Leone.

Working Languages: English, French.

Origin and development. The Mano River Union (MRU) was founded in the hope that it might lead to the economic integration of a number of West African states. Guinea joined the group on October 3, 1980, and on May 28, 1981, a customs union was established, with tariff barriers eliminated between the original members and transitional arrangements established for Guinea. However, political conflicts between members, financial problems within the union, and political and economic turmoil within the three member states have precluded the attainment of many of the organization's original objectives.

Meeting May 7–8, 2000, in Conakry, Guinea, the three countries' heads of state approved formation of a Joint Security Committee, a Technical Committee, and Border Security and Confidence-Building Units to resolve security issues and reinvigorate the union.

Structure. General policy, including approval of the union's budget, is normally established by the Ministerial Council, which is to meet yearly. Day-to-day administration is the responsibility of the Secretariat, which maintains offices in Monrovia and Conakry as well as in Freetown, Sierra Leone; in 1980 an Industrial Development Unit was formed within the Secretariat. A more recent emphasis on security matters led to formation of a Joint Security Committee and a supporting Technical Committee in 2000.

Activities. From the mid-1980s the MRU was increasingly beset not only by perennial financial problems but also by adverse political developments. In November 1985 Liberian President Samuel K. Doe accused Sierra Leone of involvement in an attempted coup by an opposition group. Guinea also was charged with complicity and, despite denials by both governments, borders with the two countries were closed. The tension caused virtually all activities to cease and left the organization without an approved budget.

Following mediation by Guinea President Lansana Conté, in July 1986, President Joseph Saidu Momoh of Sierra Leone joined Doe and Conté in the first summit since 1983 in Conakry, Guinea, the three agreeing to end their differences "in the spirit of the Mano River Union." In November 1986 the three heads of state concluded a treaty of nonaggression and security cooperation that prohibited subversive activities by one member against another and called for the creation of a joint committee for settling disagreements within the framework of the Organization of African Unity (OAU). Existing bilateral defense cooperation agreements between Sierra Leone and Guinea and between Liberia and Guinea were incorporated into the agreement.

Ministerial sessions in 1989 and early 1990 authorized feasibility studies on a number of "harmonization" proposals, including the creation of a common currency and development of regional marketing and pricing policies. Also under discussion were road and telecommunications projects and the creation of a regional airline (Mano Air). Subsequently, however, progress was severely compromised by the prolonged civil war in Liberia. Effective regional cooperation was further constrained by the military coup in Sierra Leone in late April 1992, with Guinea sending troops to assist forces remaining loyal to President Momoh before announcing that it would cooperate with the new Freetown government. The presidents of the union members, meeting for the first time in over two years on July 21, 1994, in Conakry, Guinea, again called for the "revitalization" of the grouping. However, political affairs remained tumultuous in all three member states through 1997, yielding a virtual standstill in union activity and the abandonment of the Freetown headquarters by the secretary general.

In the context of continuing turmoil, the MRU's heads of state met U.S. presidential emissary Jesse Jackson in November 1998 in Conakry. The members pledged to abide by the union's nonaggression and security cooperation agreement and called for more international aid to the area. In March 1999 Felix Downes-Thomas, head of the UN office in Liberia, encouraged revival of the union which, he asserted, might help resolve distrust between Sierra Leone and Liberia and provide a multilateral forum for addressing regional problems, including refugees, internally displaced persons, arms, and ex-combatants. Nevertheless, repeated efforts by individual countries, the OAU, and, especially, the Economic Community of West African States (ECOWAS) to mediate the multiple disputes proved unavailing until a foreign ministerial meeting of the three principals on March 18–19, 2000, in Monrovia announced that the union's Secretariat would be revived after a decade of inactivity. On May 7–8 Presidents Conté of Guinea, Charles Taylor of Liberia, and Ahmad Tejan Kabbah of Sierra Leone, joined by ECOWAS Chair Alpha Ouma Konare of Mali, met in Conakry and approved proposals from the March ministerial meeting that included establishing a Joint Security Committee. Through mid-2001, however, mutual hostility continued to characterize interactions between Liberia and its two neighbors, highlighted by ambassadorial expulsions and accusations of support for rebel and opposition groups.

A consultative meeting of foreign ministers held August 13–15, 2001, in Monrovia was followed by an August 22–23 meeting of the new Joint Security Committee, attended by ministers of foreign affairs, security, defense, internal security, and justice. After reviewing the regional security situation the ministers agreed that restoration of peace and stability required measures to "rebuild the confidence of the three member states." Proposed steps included apprehending and returning to the country of origin dissidents, armed groups, and paramilitary forces responsible for destabilization and enforcing compliance with the Non-Aggression and Security Cooperation Treaty, which had been signed in Freetown on November 20, 1996, and with the 15th Protocol to the Declaration of the Mano River Union on Defense, Security, Internal, and Foreign Affairs, signed at the May 2000 Conakry summit. The participants also agreed to deploy Joint Border Security and Confidence-Building Units along their mutual borders, to encourage repatriation of refugees, and to seek international funds for reviving union organs and programs. Additional ministerial and Joint Security meetings were held in September, and another presidential summit was proposed for 2002.

Under the auspices of King Mohamed VI of Morocco, presidents Conté, Kabbah, and Taylor met in a one-day summit in Rabat, Morocco, on February 27, 2002, in what proved to be yet another abortive effort to resolve their countries' differences and reactivate the MRU. In late March the Joint Security

Committee convened in Freetown, while in early April the three members' foreign ministers met in Rabat to discuss the peace process, including securing their borders and repatriating refugees, and to plan for another summit meeting. Thereafter, a renewed rebellion in Liberia halted progress and ultimately led, in 2003, to the forced resignation and exile of President Taylor. In August 2003 Liberia's interim chief executive, Moses Blah, paid visits to Guinea and Sierra Leone, as did the chair of a transitional government, Gyude Bryant, in November, in the expectation that 2004 could prove to be a more fortuitous year for the region. These expectations were aided by a meeting in Conakry on May 20, 2004, between the heads of state of the four member countries at which the Mano River Union was formally reactivateed.

Meanwhile, a number of nongovernmental organizations in the three MRU states also have been attempting to promote peace and stability. In March 2002 a group of civil society organizations proposed a ten-year action plan that included disarming child soldiers, repatriating refugees, organizing general elections, and encouraging socioeconomic development. In December 2003 the United Nations awarded a key human rights prize to the MRU Women's Peace Network. Other recently active groups have included the Mano River Human Rights Network and the MRU Peace Forum. Speaking at the latter's launching in Freetown in February 2004, MRU Secretary General H. E. Jallow identified human rights abuses, the proliferation of small arms, and a lack of press freedom as having contributed to the chaos of the preceding decade.

NONALIGNED MOVEMENT (NAM)

Established: In the course of an increasingly structured series of 11 nonaligned conferences, the first of which met September 1–6, 1961, in Belgrade, Yugoslavia, and the most recent, February 24–25, 2003, in Kuala Lumpur, Malaysia.

Purpose: To promote a "transition from the old world order based on domination to a new order based on freedom, equality, and social justice and the well-being of all"; to pursue "peace, achievement of disarmament, and settlement of disputes by peaceful means"; to search for "effective and acceptable solutions" to world economic problems, particularly the "disparities in the level of global development"; to support self-determination and independence "for all peoples living under colonial or alien domination and foreign occupation"; to seek "sustainable and environmentally sound development"; to promote "fundamental rights and freedom"; to contribute to strengthening "the role and effectiveness of the United Nations" (Final Declaration, Belgrade, 1989).

Headquarters: None.

Principal Organs: Conference of Heads of State, Meeting of Foreign Ministers, Coordinating Bureau (25 members).

Chair: Abdullah Ahmad Badawi (Malaysia). Malaysia is Chair of the group from 2003–2006.

Membership (116): Afghanistan, Algeria, Angola, Antigua and Barbuda, Bahamas, Bahrain, Bangladesh, Barbados, Belarus, Belize, Benin, Bhutan, Bolivia, Botswana, Brunei, Burkina Faso, Burundi, Cambodia, Cameroon, Cape Verde Islands, Central African Republic, Chad, Chile, Colombia, Comoro Islands, Democratic Republic of the Congo, Republic of the Congo, Côte d'Ivoire, Cuba, Cyprus, Djibouti, Dominica Dominican Republic, Ecuador, Egypt, Equatorial Guinea, Eritrea, Ethiopia, Gabon, Gambia, Ghana, Grenada, Guatemala, Guinea, Guinea-Bissau, Guyana, Honduras, India, Indonesia, Iran, Iraq, Jamaica, Jordan, Kenya, Democratic People's Republic of Korea, Kuwait, Laos, Lebanon, Lesotho, Liberia, Libya, Madagascar, Malawi, Malaysia, Maldives, Mali, Malta, Mauritania, Mauritius, Mongolia, Morocco, Mozambique, Myanmar, Namibia, Nepal, Nicaragua, Niger, Nigeria, Oman, Pakistan, Palestine (represented by the Palestinian Authority), Panama, Papua New Guinea, Peru, Philippines, Qatar, Rwanda, St. Lucia, St. Vincent and the Grenadines, Sao Tome and Principe, Saudi Arabia, Senegal, Seychelles, Sierra Leone, Singapore, Somalia, South Africa, Sri Lanka, Sudan, Suriname, Swaziland, Syria, Tanzania, Thailand, Timor-Leste, Togo, Trinidad and Tobago, Tunisia, Turkmenistan, Uganda, United Arab Emirates, Uzbekistan, Vanuatu, Venezuela, Vietnam, Yemen, Zambia, Zimbabwe. The 1979 conference refused to seat either delegation (representing the Khieu Samphan and Heng Samrin regimes) from Cambodia, that country being represented by an "empty seat" at subsequent NAM summits until the 1992 meeting. One of the NAM's founding members, Burma (now Myanmar), withdrew in 1979 but was readmitted in 1992. Venezuela shifted from full member to observer because of a boundary dispute with Guyana and then back to full membership (effective 1989). In September 1991 Argentina's President Carlos Menem announced his nation's withdrawal on the ground that the NAM "no longer had any reason to exist." A June 1994 NAM meeting of foreign ministers refused to seat a delegation from the Federal Republic of Yugoslavia (the Serbian and Montenegrin constituent republics of the dissolved Socialist Federal Republic of Yugoslavia), which was attempting to claim the predecessor state's founding membership in the NAM. Yugoslavia's membership remained suspended thereafter, and in July 2001 the Federal Republic applied for observer status, which was granted and retained upon the country's transformation to the State Union of Serbia and Montenegro. Cyprus and Malta became observer states in 2004 when they joined the EU. In May 2006 Antigua and Barbuda and Dominica, previously observers, became full members.

Observer States (16): Armenia, Azerbaijan, Brazil, China, Costa Rica, Croatia, Cyprus, El Salvador, Kazakhstan, Kyrgyzstan, Malta, Mexico, Paraguay, Serbia as the successor state after the June 2006 split of Serbia and Montenegro, Ukraine, Uruguay. In addition, the following organizations attended the 2003 summit as observers: the African Union, the Afro-Asian People's Solidarity Organization, the Arab League, the Kanaka Socialist National Liberation Front (New Caledonia), the Organization of the Islamic Conference, the New Independentist Movement of Puerto Rico, and the United Nations.

Guests (32): Australia, Austria, Bosnia and Herzegovina, Bulgaria, Canada, Czech Republic, Finland, France, Germany, Greece, Hungary, Ireland, Italy, Japan, Republic of Korea, Macedonia, Netherlands, New Zealand, Norway, Poland, Portugal, Romania, Russia, San Marino, Slovakia, Slovenia, Spain, Sweden, Switzerland, United Kingdom, United States, Vatican. (In addition, many intergovernmental organizations had guest status at the most recent NAM Summit in 2003.)

Origin and development. The first Conference of Nonaligned Heads of State, at which 25 countries were represented, was convened in September 1961 in Belgrade, largely through the initiative of Yugoslavian President Josip Tito, who

had expressed concern that an accelerating arms race might result in war between the Soviet Union and the United States. Subsequent conferences, which attracted more and more Third World countries, were convened in Cairo, Egypt, in 1964; Lusaka, Zambia, in 1970; Algiers, Algeria, in 1973; Colombo, Sri Lanka, in 1976; Havana, Cuba, in 1979; New Delhi, India, in 1983; Harare, Zimbabwe, in 1986; Belgrade in 1989; Jakarta, Indonesia, in 1992; Cartagena, Columbia, in 1995; and Durban, South Africa, in 1998. The most recent summit was held February 24–25, 2003, in Kuala Lumpur, Malaysia.

The 1964 conference in Cairo, with 47 countries represented, featured widespread condemnation of Western colonialism and the retention of foreign military installations. Thereafter, the focus shifted away from essentially political issues, such as independence for dependent territories, to the advocacy of occasionally radical solutions to global economic and other problems. Thus, in 1973 in Algiers there was an appeal for concerted action by the "poor nations against the industrialized world"; this became a basis of debate within the United Nations for a New International Economic Order (NIEO) and led to the convening of an inconclusive Conference on International Economic Cooperation in late 1975 in Paris, France.

At the 1979 Havana meeting, political concerns resurfaced in the context of an intense debate between Cuban President Castro, who was charged with attempting to "bend" the movement in the direction of the "socialist camp," and Yugoslavian President Tito, who urged that it remain true to its genuinely nonaligned origins. In search of a compromise, the Final Declaration of the Havana Conference referred to the movement's "non-bloc nature" and its opposition to both "hegemony" (a euphemism used in reference to presumed Soviet ambitions) and all forms of "imperialism, colonialism, and neocolonialism." In addition, the conference reiterated an earlier identification of "Zionism as a form of racism."

At the 1983 New Delhi conference, delegates focused on the precarious financial condition of Third World countries. The conference's declaration stated, in part, that developed countries should meet with developing countries to discuss debt relief, reduced trade barriers, increased aid for development, and increased cash flow. Its economic proposals, already widely accepted by the world banking community, called for the rescheduling of Third World debt and an increase in Special Drawing Rights by the International Monetary Fund (IMF).

The eighth NAM summit was held in Harare, Zimbabwe, in 1986, the 25th anniversary of the movement. The site was chosen to underscore the group's main concern: the South African government's policy of forced racial segregation. A final declaration called on nonaligned nations to adopt selective, voluntary sanctions against South Africa pending the adoption of comprehensive, mandatory measures by the UN Security Council. The members demanded international pressure to eliminate apartheid, Pretoria's withdrawal from Namibia (South-West Africa), and an end to its aggression against neighboring states.

With Liberia, Singapore, and a number of other members dissenting, the United States was severely criticized for its lack of sanctions against Pretoria, as well as for its policies toward Angola, Libya, and Nicaragua. In implicit criticism of the Soviet Union, the withdrawal of foreign forces from Afghanistan also was urged. The group denounced Israel for its occupation of Arab territory and its activities in Lebanon, while reiterating support for the Palestinians' "just struggle." An appeal was made for the end of interference by unspecified "outsiders" in the Cambodian conflict, and both sides were encouraged to negotiate for peace in the Iran-Iraq war. In addition, an Independent Commission of the South on Development Issues was established to study the causes of underdevelopment and produce common strategies to combat it.

Some of the NAM's most radical members (including Cuba, Iran, and Iraq) stayed away from the 1989 Belgrade summit after preparatory talks revealed that most members favored fewer polemics and a return to the group's original posture of neutrality. Consequently, the meeting's final declaration was markedly less anti-American and anti-Western than previous declarations. Instead,

the summit emphasized the need for the movement to "modernize" and develop "a realistic, farsighted, and creative" approach to international issues in which concordance would be favored over confrontation. The declaration also praised Washington and Moscow for their recent rapprochement, which, by reducing tensions in many areas of the world, had created a "window of opportunity for the international community." At the same time, the Belgrade declaration described the economic situation in the "vast majority of the developing countries" as having "deteriorated dramatically," with many of those nations "suffocating" from the outflow of capital. NAM leaders reaffirmed the NIEO as a "difficult but valid goal," appealing for the developed world to do a better job of addressing the needs of the developing countries.

Structure. By convention, the chief executive of the country hosting the most recent Conference of Heads of State serves as the NAM's chair. Foreign ministers' meetings are generally held annually between conferences, which are usually convened every three years. A Coordinating Bureau, established at the 1973 conference, currently numbers 25 (including the chair, a rapporteur-general and, on an ex officio basis, the immediate past chair) with the following regional distribution: Africa, 10; Asia, 9; Latin America and the Caribbean, 4; Europe, 2. In addition to a Political Committee, an Economic and Social Committee, and a Committee on Palestine, the NAM has created various Working Groups over the years. Those functioning as of 2003 addressed matters of Disarmament, Peacekeeping Operations, Human Rights, Sixth Committee Matters (terrorism), and the Restructuring of the Security Council.

Activities. The NAM emerged somewhat revitalized from its tenth summit, held in 1992 in Jakarta, Indonesia. At the conclusion of the meeting the NAM declared its intention to project itself as a "vibrant, constructive, and genuinely independent component of the mainstream of international relations." With anti-Western rhetoric having been kept to a minimum, the NAM asked developed nations to give "urgent priority" to establishing "a more equitable global economy" and to assist developing nations in resolving the problems of low commodity prices and "crushing debt burdens." The summit agreed to establish a broad-based committee of experts to devise a debt reduction approach. For their part, reflecting the organization's increasingly pragmatic approach, NAM members committed themselves to a measure of "self-reliance" in such areas as population control and food self-sufficiency. The Jakarta Message also called for extended South/South trade and investment cooperation. In addition, the NAM said it would press for a restructuring of the United Nations that would include the diminution or elimination of the veto power of the five permanent members of the Security Council and an expansion of council membership.

The most contentious issue at the summit appeared to be the question of Yugoslavian membership, many Arab countries having called for expulsion of the Federal Republic because of events in Bosnia and Herzegovina. Ultimately, the summit postponed a decision in the matter, opting instead to condemn "ethnic cleansing by Serbs" of Muslim communities, without reference to Yugoslavia.

Yugoslavia remained unrepresented at the NAM Meeting of Foreign Ministers held in May–June 1994 in Cairo, Egypt, while action on politically sensitive membership applications from Macedonia and Russia was deferred indefinitely. However, in what was considered one of the high points of the movement's history (in view of its long-standing anti-apartheid stance), South Africa was welcomed to the NAM ranks following the installation of a multiracial government in Pretoria.

The NAM continued to press for UN restructuring at the 11th summit, held October 18–20, 1995, in Cartagena de Indias, Colombia. It also argued that UN peacekeeping efforts should be cut, so more resources could be used for combating poverty. The summit's communiqué strongly criticized the United States for continuing its heavy economic pressure against Cuba and urged the industrialized nations to adopt a more "just" system of world trade. However, the movement remained plagued by questions of its relevancy in the post–

Cold War era, with NAM supporters arguing that the organization's attention should focus on the long-term global division between the North and the South.

The 12th NAM summit, held September 2–3, 1998, in Durban, South Africa, was expected to concentrate on economic issues, but the ongoing fighting in the Democratic Republic of the Congo diverted attention. With regard to the May 1998 testing of nuclear weapons by India and Pakistan, the NAM called on both members to settle their disputes peacefully and articulated its concern over the development of all weapons of mass destruction. The summit also condemned terrorism, insisting that it be countered in accordance with UN principles, not by unilateral initiatives, and expressed regret that the Middle East peace process remained at a standstill—a situation it attributed to Israeli intransigence.

On the economic front, the summit called for the IMF and the World Bank to expand funding to the developing world and for changes in international financial institutions to prevent the kind of economic crisis that was currently plaguing much of Asia. In more general terms, the NAM criticized the direction of globalization, arguing that economic integration was leading many of the poorest countries toward greater poverty.

The NAM was divided over the Kosovo crisis of 1999, with Muslim member states supporting intervention on behalf of the Kosovars and predominantly backing the US-led NATO air war against Yugoslavia in March–June. The division came in the context of a more fundamental concern that the movement was being eclipsed by the (then) 133-member Group of 77, which had gained increasing recognition as an effective voice for the economic interests of developing countries.

The organization's 13th Ministerial Conference met on April 8–9, 2000, in Cartagena, where the topics under discussion included barring participation by military regimes that had overthrown democratically elected governments. Championed by India, the proposal was generally viewed as an effort to establish democracy as the norm for all members, but observers also noted that New Delhi was clearly targeting Pakistan for exclusion.

The 13th summit was planned for October 2001 in Bangladesh, but the meeting was postponed because of preparations for that country's October 1 national election. In November the newly installed Bangladeshi government announced that it was unable to host the meeting, which had been rescheduled for April 2002, for reasons that included the country's recent economic downturn, inadequate hotel accommodations and other infrastructure and, in the context of the September terrorist attacks on the United States, an inability to guarantee security for the 5,000 or more expected attendees. The venue was subsequently changed to Amman, Jordan, but instability in the Middle East ultimately led the Coordinating Bureau, meeting in April 2002 in Durban, to designate Malaysia as the host. Thus the 13th summit convened on February 24–25, 2003, in Kuala Lumpur.

Attended by some 60 heads of state or government, the first day of the summit included an address by the outspoken, soon-to-retire Malaysian Prime Minister, Mahathir bin Mohamad, who lambasted the West for using undemocratic means to force democracy on other countries, permitting international financial agencies to ignore the debt burden of developing countries, and leaving poorer countries "oppressed and terrorized." Among the specific issues debated at the summit were the threat of war against Iraq and the nuclear crisis in North Korea. In a "Statement Concerning Iraq," the movement warned against the dangers of preemptive action by the United States and its allies, but it also advised the Saddam Hussein regime to comply with UN Security Council resolutions. With regard to North Korea's nuclear program, the summit ultimately supported Pyongyang's contention that a solution would best be found if the U.S. George W.

Bush administration would agree to negotiate directly instead of insisting on multilateral involvement. In addition, as at previous summits, the participants voiced support for the Palestinian people and condemned Israeli actions and alleged human rights abuses in the West Bank and Gaza.

In keeping with its overall theme of "Continuing the Revitalization of the Non-Aligned Movement," the 2003 summit approved the Kuala Lumpur Declaration, which broadly called for multilateral efforts to prevent the marginalization of poorer states but also focused on steps to be taken by the movement's members. Among other things, the declaration urged the wider international community to ensure that globalization leads to the "prospering and empowering of the developing countries, not their continued impoverishment and dependence." In addition, the declaration called upon member states to improve the effectiveness and efficiency of the movement; to enhance unity and cohesion "by focusing on issues that unite rather than divide us"; to meet more frequently with the Group of 77 to improve South-South coordination and cooperation; to bring together states, civil society, and the private sector in a partnership that might bridge the "digital divide"; and to improve North-South understanding through "constructive dialog and interaction" with the Group of Eight and other development partners.

Because the NAM has no central headquarters, it has perhaps suffered in recent years from lack of an official, external face. Malaysia has attempted to address this problem with a very comprehensive website, or "E-Secretariat," which not only documents Malaysia's leadership of the organization, but also thoroughly records all aspects of the movement's work. The fourteenth Conference of Heads of State was scheduled to take place from September 11–16, 2006, in Havana, Cuba.

ORGANIZATION OF ARAB PETROLEUM EXPORTING COUNTRIES (OAPEC)

Established: By agreement concluded on January 9, 1968, in Beirut, Lebanon.

Purpose: To help coordinate members' petroleum policies, to adopt measures for harmonizing their legal systems to the extent needed for the group to fulfill its mission, to assist in the exchange of information and expertise, to provide training and employment opportunities for their citizens, and to utilize members' "resources and common potentialities" in establishing joint projects in the petroleum and petroleum-related industries.

Headquarters: Kuwait City, Kuwait.

Principal Organs: Ministerial Council, Executive Bureau, Judicial Tribunal, General Secretariat.

Secretary General: Abdul Aziz A. Al-Turki (Saudi Arabia).

Membership (10): Algeria, Bahrain, Egypt, Iraq, Kuwait, Libya, Qatar, Saudi Arabia, Syria, United Arab Emirates. (Egyptian membership was suspended 1979–1989.)

Official Language: Arabic.

Origin and development. Established by Kuwait, Libya, and Saudi Arabia in early 1968 in recognition of the need for further cooperation among Arab countries that relied on oil as their principal source of income, OAPEC was expanded in May 1970 by the accession of Algeria, Bahrain, Qatar, Abu Dhabi, and Dubai. In May 1972 the last two combined their membership as part of the United Arab Emirates. In December 1971 the founding agreement was liberalized to permit membership by any Arab country having oil as a significant—but not necessarily the major—source of income, with the result that Syria and Egypt joined in 1972 and 1973, respectively. Also in 1972, Iraq became a member. A Tunisian bid for membership failed at the December 1981 ministerial meeting because of Libyan opposition stemming from a dispute with Tunis over conflicting claims to offshore oil deposits. Tunisia was admitted in 1982 but four years later withdrew from active membership because it had become a net importer of energy and could not make its OAPEC contributions.

OAPEC joint ventures and projects include the Arab Maritime Petroleum Transport Company (AMPTC), founded in 1973 with headquarters in Kuwait; the Arab Shipbuilding and Repair Yard Company (ASRY), established in Bahrain in 1974; the Arab Petroleum Investments Corporation (Apicorp), set up in 1975 in Damman, Saudi Arabia; and the Arab Petroleum Services Company (APSC), founded in 1977 and operating from Tripoli, Libya. The Arab Engineering Company (Arec), established in 1981 in Abu Dhabi, was dissolved in 1989. Shareholders in these ventures are typically either the member governments themselves or state-owned petroleum enterprises.

Subsidiary companies are the Arab Drilling and Workover Company (ADWOC), based in Tripoli since its formation in 1980; the Arab Well Logging Company (AWLCO), established in 1983 in Baghdad; and the Arab Geophysical Exploration

Services Company (AGESCO), formed in 1984 in Tripoli. The APSC is the sole shareholder in AWLCO and the principal shareholder in the other two. The Arab Company for Detergent Chemicals (Aradet), founded in 1981 in Baghdad, is an Apicorp subsidiary.

Structure. The Ministerial Council, OAPEC's supreme authority, is composed of the members' petroleum ministers, who convene at least twice a year to draw up policy guidelines and direct ongoing activities. An Executive Bureau, which meets at least three times a year, assists the council in management of the organization. A Judicial Tribunal, established in 1980, serves as an arbitration council between OAPEC members or between a member and a petroleum company operating in that country, with all decisions final and binding. The Secretariat, headed by a secretary general and no more than three assistant secretaries general, encompasses the secretary's office and four departments: Finance and Administrative Affairs, Information and Library, Economics, and Technical Affairs. The last two comprise the Arab Center for Energy Studies. A largely ceremonial national presidency of the organization rotates annually among the member states.

Activities. Although OAPEC's activities are directly affected by the world oil market, it plays no institutional role in determining either output quotas or prices, deferring in both cases to the more encompassing Organization of Petroleum Exporting Countries (OPEC). Instead, OAPEC focuses on coordinating related policies within the Arab community. Over the years, it has also invested billions of dollars in its associated ventures and affiliates. Apicorp, for example, has helped finance petroleum and petrochemical projects around the world, including gas liquefaction plants, refineries, pipelines and other means of transport, and facilities for making fertilizers and detergents. In addition to its administrative tasks, the OAPEC Secretariat has compiled and continually updates a comprehensive database of information on oil and energy markets, reserves, production, refining, consumption, and downstream industries, such as petrochemicals. OAPEC also conducts related research projects, sponsors seminars, and produces technical papers and studies.

The December 1990 Ministerial Council meeting was held in Cairo, Egypt, that city having been chosen as OAPEC's temporary headquarters following the Iraqi invasion of Kuwait the previous August. In mid-1992 a report co-authored by OAPEC estimated that the Gulf crisis had cost Arab countries as much as $620 billion and had contributed to rising inflation and a decline of 7 percent in the gross national product of 21 Arab nations in 1991. The destruction of oil wells, pipelines, and other infrastructure alone cost Iraq an estimated $190 billion and Kuwait $160 billion, the report said.

Arab oil affairs remained turbulent into 1994 as several OAPEC members continued to quarrel over OPEC production quotas. There was ongoing disagreement over how and when Iraq would resume oil exports, while OAPEC officials described recent wide fluctuations in oil prices as making it difficult for member states to plan development programs effectively. The organization hoped, however, to return to a degree of normal activity following return to its permanent headquarters in Kuwait at midyear.

Low oil prices remained a major OAPEC concern throughout 1998, a December session of the Ministerial Council urging all oil-producing countries to exercise restraint regarding production levels. In 1999 OAPEC officials also suggested that some members might be well served to encourage private investment in their oil sectors as a means of accelerating economic advancement.

Oil output and the condition of world oil markets, which experienced a dramatic increase in prices in 2000, remained a major focus of the four Ministerial Council sessions held in 2000–2001 in Cairo. In mid-2000 an OAPEC report indicated that Arab countries were contributing about 26 percent of world oil production and that, as of 1999, Arab reserves amounted to 63 percent of the world total.

In recent years OAPEC has also been giving increasing attention to environmental concerns, in part to ensure that the economic standing of its members is not adversely affected by international initiatives intended to reduce greenhouse gases and other pollutants. The Eighth Coordinating Meeting of Environmental Experts was held in Cairo on September 29–30, 2001, its principal focus being coordination of member countries' positions regarding, for example, the UN Framework Convention on Climate Change and the associated Kyoto Protocol. At the same time, OAPEC was preparing for the Seventh Arab Energy Conference, held May 11–12, 2002, in Cairo, where again the focus was on "Energy and Arab Cooperation." Other organizations sponsoring the conference were the Arab Fund for Economic and Social Development (AFESD), the Arab League, and the Arab Industrial Development and Mining Organization (AIDMO).

During 2001–2003 oil prices and resultant income remained somewhat volatile despite improving communication between oil suppliers and consuming nations. At the same time, OAPEC reported, Arab petroleum-refining capacity was increasing, as was regional consumption of natural gas. Known Arab reserves of the latter commodity, about one-fourth of the world total, nevertheless continued to increase as new discoveries outpaced consumption. OAPEC also projected that global oil consumption would rise by about 1.6 percent annually, from 76 billion barrels per day in 2000 to nearly 90 billion barrels per day in 2010.

In March–May 2003 the invasion of Iraq by U.S.-led forces had a minimal impact on oil supplies. It was unclear, however, given the dilapidated state of Iraq's petroleum infrastructure, when or if Iraqi oil production would regain the levels that predated the 1991 Gulf War. A representative of the U.S.-sponsored interim Iraqi Governing Council was expected to attend the Ministerial Council session held in Cairo on December 13, 2003, but he withdrew because of an unspecified "emergency." In December 2005 the Ministerial Council canceled 70 percent of the debt owed the organization by Iraq.

A July 2005 report from OAPEC said that member countries planned to increase their share of world oil production from the (then) 32.2 percent to between 38 and 40 percent by 2010. The report noted that the increase would require substantial new investment by all member countries but particularly by Egypt, Algeria, and Libya. In December 2005 OAPEC announced that the organization's presidency would go to Qatar in 2006, not, as in the normal rotation, to Iraq.

ORGANIZATION OF THE ISLAMIC CONFERENCE (OIC)

Established: By agreement of participants at the Conference of the Kings and Heads of State and Government held September 22–25, 1969, in Rabat, Morocco; charter signed at the Third Islamic Conference of Foreign Ministers, held February 29 March 4, 1972, in Jiddah, Saudi Arabia.

Purpose: To promote Islamic solidarity and further cooperation among member states in the economic, social, cultural, scientific, and political fields.

Headquarters: Jiddah, Saudi Arabia.

Principal Organs: Conference of Kings and Heads of State and Government (Summit Conference), Conference of Foreign Ministers, General Secretariat.

Secretary General: Ekmeleddin İhsanoğlu (Turkey).

Membership (57): Afghanistan, Albania, Algeria, Azerbaijan, Bahrain, Bangladesh, Benin, Brunei, Burkina Faso, Cameroon, Chad, Comoro Islands, Côte d'Ivoire, Djibouti, Egypt, Gabon, Gambia, Guinea, Guinea-Bissau, Guyana, Indonesia, Iran, Iraq, Jordan, Kazakhstan, Kuwait, Kyrgyzstan, Lebanon, Libya, Malaysia, Maldives, Mali, Mauritania, Morocco, Mozambique, Niger, Nigeria, Oman, Pakistan, Palestine, Qatar, Saudi Arabia, Senegal, Sierra Leone, Somalia, Sudan, Suriname, Syria, Tajikistan, Togo, Tunisia, Turkey, Turkmenistan, Uganda, United Arab Emirates, Uzbekistan, Yemen. Afghanistan's membership was suspended in January 1980, following the Soviet invasion, but in March 1989 the seat was given to the government-in-exile announced by Afghan guerrillas and subsequently to the Afghan government formed after the guerrilla victory. The advent of the Taliban regime in September 1996 in Kabul yielded competition for OIC recognition between it and the overthrown government, with both being refused formal admittance to the OIC foreign ministers' conference in December in Jakarta, although Afghanistan as such continued to be regarded as a member. Egypt's membership, suspended in May 1979, was restored in April 1984. Nigeria's government approved that nation's admission into the OIC in 1986, but the membership was formally repudiated in 1991 in the wake of intense Christian opposition; the OIC has not recognized the latter decision. Uncertainty also surrounds the status of Zanzibar, whose membership request had been approved in December 1992; eight months later it was announced that Zanzibar's application, which precipitated contentious legislative debate in Tanzania, was withdrawn pending the possible forwarding of a Tanzanian membership request.

Observers (10): Bosnia and Herzegovina, Central African Republic, Economic Cooperation Organization, League of Arab States, Moro National Liberation Front, Nonaligned Movement, Organization of African Unity, Thailand, Turkish Republic of Northern Cyprus, United Nations.

Official Languages: Arabic, English, French.

Origin and development. Although the idea of an organization for coordinating and consolidating the interests of Islamic states originated in 1969 and meetings of the conference were held throughout the 1970s, the Islamic conference only began to achieve worldwide attention in the early 1980s. From a base of 30 members in 1969, the OIC has doubled in size, with the most recent member, Côte d'Ivoire, being admitted in 2001.

Structure. The body's main institution is the Conference of Foreign Ministers, although a summit of members' heads of state and government is held every three years. Sectoral ministerial conferences have also convened in such areas as information, tourism, health, and youth and sports.

Over the years many committees and departments have evolved to provide input for policy decisions and to carry out the OIC's executive and administrative functions. The organization's general secretary, who serves a four-year, once-renewable term, heads the General Secretariat and is aided by four assistant secretaries general—for science and technology; cultural, social, and information affairs; political affairs; and economic affairs—and a director of the cabinet, who helps administer various departments. The secretariat also maintains permanent observer missions to the United Nations (UN) in New York, United States, and Geneva, Switzerland, and an Office for Afghanistan was recently established in Islamabad, Pakistan. Other OIC organs include the Al-Quds (Jerusalem) Committee, the Six-Member Committee on Palestine, the Standing Committee for Information and Cultural Affairs (COMIAC), the Standing Committee for Economic and Trade Cooperation (COMCEC), the Standing Committee for Scientific and Technological Cooperation (COMSTECH), and various additional permanent and specialized committees. Recent ad hoc committees and groups have included an Ad Hoc Committee on Afghanistan and Contact Groups for Jammu and Kashmir, Sierra Leone, and Bosnia and Herzegovina and Kosovo.

To date, the OIC has established four "specialized institutions and organs," including the International Islamic News Agency (IINA, founded in 1972); the Islamic Development Bank (IDB, 1974), the Islamic States Broadcasting Organization (ISBO, 1975), and the Islamic Educational, Scientific, and Cultural Organization (ISESCO,

1982). Of the organization's eight "subsidiary organs," one of the more prominent is the Islamic Solidarity Fund (ISF, 1977). The founding conference of a Parliamentary Union of the OIC Member States was held in June 1999.

Activities. During the 1980s three lengthy conflicts dominated the OIC's agenda: the Soviet occupation of Afghanistan, which began in December 1979 and concluded with the final withdrawal of Soviet troops in February 1989; the Iran-Iraq war, which began in September 1980 and ended with the cease-fire of August 1988; and the ongoing Arab-Israeli conflict. At their August 1990 meeting the foreign ministers described the Palestinian problem as the primary concern for the Islamic world. However, much of the planned agenda was disrupted by emergency private sessions concerning the Iraqi invasion of Kuwait on August 2. Most attending the meeting approved a resolution condemning the incursion and demanding the withdrawal of Iraqi troops. In addition to other ongoing conflicts among conference members (such as the dispute between Mauritania and Senegal), the Gulf crisis contributed to the postponement of the heads of state summit that normally would have been held in 1990.

When the sixth summit was finally held December 9–11, 1991, in Dakar, Senegal, more than half of members' heads of state failed to attend. Substantial lingering rancor concerning the Gulf crisis was reported at the meeting, while black African representatives asserted that Arab nations were giving insufficient attention to the problems of sub-Saharan Muslims. On the whole, the summit was perceived as unproductive, with *Middle East International* going so far as to wonder if the conference would "fade from the international political scene" because of its failure to generate genuine "Islamic solidarity."

In the following three years much of the conference's attention focused on the plight of the Muslim community in Bosnia and Herzegovina. The group's foreign ministers repeatedly called on the UN to use force, if necessary, to stop Serbian attacks against Bosnian Muslims, but the conference stopped well short of approving creation of an

Islamic force to intervene on its own in Bosnia and Herzegovina, as reportedly proposed by Iran and several other members.

The seventh OIC summit, held December 13–15, 1994, in Casablanca, Morocco, reached consensus on a code of conduct regarding terrorism and religious extremism in the hope of improving the "global image" of Islam. Among other things, the OIC nations agreed that their territories would not be used for terrorist activities nor would any of them support, "morally or financially," any Muslim "terrorists" opposed to member governments. However, with states such as Iran and Sudan (both charged with supporting extremist fundamentalists in other nations) signing the OIC statement, some observers described the document as a "face-saving" measure that masked ongoing deep divisions on the issue.

OIC efforts to improve the international image of Islam continued in 1995, notably in conjunction with ceremonies marking the organization's 25th anniversary. U.S. Vice President Gore held talks with OIC Secretary General Hamid Algabid in March in Jiddah, Saudi Arabia, receiving assurances of the OIC's "unwavering" support for international stability and offering in return a U.S. commitment to dialogue with the Islamic world in the interests of peace and mutual understanding. The desire for a greater Islamic role in resolving international disputes, expressed in an anniversary declaration issued in September, was also apparent in enhanced OIC participation in UN and other mediatory frameworks.

The 24th OIC foreign ministers' conference, held December 9–13, 1996, in Jakarta, Indonesia, reiterated familiar positions, including the demand for an independent Palestinian state and Israel's withdrawal from all territory "captured in war." With regard to Afghanistan, neither the new Taliban regime nor the government ousted in September was accorded official status, it being resolved that Afghanistan's OIC seat should remain vacant pro tem "without prejudice to the question of recognition of the government of Afghanistan." A Taliban delegation was also sent to an extraordinary summit of heads of government held March 23, 1997, in

Islamabad to celebrate 50 years of Pakistani independence. While it was again denied official recognition, the delegation was allowed to attend.

The renewed Palestinian *intifada* and the Israeli response to it provided a principal focus for OIC meetings in 2000. These included the June 27–30 Conference of Foreign Ministers in Kuala Lumpur, Malaysia, and the ninth summit November 12–13 in Doha, Qatar, which devoted its first day to discussing "the serious situation prevailing in the Palestinian occupied territories following the savage actions perpetrated by the Israeli forces." Representatives of Iraq, Sudan, and Syria insisted that waging jihad against Israel was required, while others urged political and economic retaliation.

An eighth extraordinary session of the foreign ministers met May 26, 2001, in the context of the continuing hostilities. Meeting June 25–29 in Bamako, Mali, the regular 28th Conference of Foreign Ministers reiterated a call for member countries to halt political contacts with the Israeli government, sever economic relations, and end "all forms of normalization." The concluding declaration of the session also urged resolution of a familiar list of other conflicts involving, among others, Afghanistan, Armenia and Azerbaijan, Cyprus, Jammu and Kashmir, Iraq, Kosovo, and Somalia. In other areas, the conference urged member states to ratify the Statute of the International Islamic Court of Justice, called for formation of an expert group that would begin drafting an Islamic Convention on Human Rights, condemned international terrorism, noted the progress made toward instituting an Islamic Program for the Development of Information and Communication (PIDIC), and cautioned that care must be taken to ensure that the economic benefits of globalization are shared and the adverse effects minimized.

Immediately after the September 11, 2001, terrorist attacks against the United States, the OIC secretary general, Abdelouahed Belkeziz, condemned the terrorist acts, as did an extraordinary Conference of Foreign Ministers session in Doha. The Doha session did not directly oppose the ongoing U.S.-led military campaign against al-Qaida and the Taliban regime in Afghanistan, although it did argue that no state should be targeted under the pretext of attacking terrorism. The foreign ministers session also rejected as counter to Islamic teachings and values any attempt to justify terrorism on religious grounds. Four months later, as part of an effort to foster intercultural dialogue, the OIC foreign ministers met in Istanbul with counterparts from the European Union.

On April 1–3, 2002, a special OIC session on terrorism convened in the Malaysian capital, Kuala Lumpur. In addition to establishing a 13-member committee to implement a plan of action against terrorism, the session issued a declaration that, among other things, condemned efforts to link terrorism and Islam and called for a global conference to define terrorism and establish internationally accepted procedures for combating it. Notably, however, the conference did not voice consensual support for a speech by Malaysian Prime Minister Mahathir bin Mohamad in which he described all attacks on civilians, including those by Palestinians and Sri Lanka's Tamil Tigers, as terrorist acts. The call for a UN-sponsored conference on terrorism was repeated by the Council of Foreign Ministers at their June session in Khartoum.

The impending U.S.-led war against the Saddam Hussein regime in Iraq generated a Second Extraordinary Session of the Islamic Summit Conference on March 5, 2003, in Doha. The meeting included an exchange of personal insults by the Iraqi and Kuwaiti representatives and a warning from the secretary general that a U.S. military campaign would lead to occupation and foreign rule. Concern was also expressed that the Israeli government was taking advantage of the world's preoccupation with the Iraqi crisis to intensify its campaign against Palestinians. The session concluded with a call for the elimination of all weapons of mass destruction (WMDs) from the Middle East.

The tenth OIC Summit Conference, which met October 16–18, 2003, in Putrajaya, Malaysia, featured an address by Prime Minister Mahathir that many Western countries condemned as anti-Semitic because of its stereotypical description of Jewish and Israeli intentions and tactics. The comments came in the context of Mahathir's argument that the Islamic world should focus on winning "hearts and minds" by abjuring violence and adopting new political and economic strategies. The summit concluded with issuance of the Putrajaya Declaration, which noted the "need to restructure and strengthen the Organisation on the basis of an objective review and evaluation of its role, structure, methodology, and decision-making processes, as well as its global partnerships." Included in the closing declaration's plan of action were provisions that called for drafting strategies to strengthen unity, especially at international forums; engaging in further dialogue with the West and international organizations; completing a review of the structure, methods, and needs of the secretariat; promoting the advancement of science and technology (particularly information and communication technology) among member states; and taking steps to encourage the expansion of trade and investment.

In response to subsequent international developments, the secretary general praised improved cooperation between Iran and the International Atomic Energy Agency; condemned the November 2003 terrorist attacks against synagogues in Istanbul as well as those against a housing complex in Riyadh, Saudi Arabia; and welcomed Libya's decision to end the development of WMDs. On February 25, 2004, the OIC argued before the International Court of Justice in The Hague, Netherlands, that the security wall being constructed by Israel on Palestinian land was illegal.

The OIC subsequently continued to condemn acts of terrorism around the world, including the March 2004 bombings in Madrid, Spain; the attacks against London's transit system in July 2005; and the explosions at the Egyptian resorts of Sharm El-Shiekh and Naama Bay later the same month. With regard to developments in Iraq, in August 2005 the OIC urged "prudence and consensus" during deliberations on the draft Iraqi constitution. In particular, the OIC advocated a policy of inclusion, cautioning that the "exclusion of any component of the population" (implicitly, the Sunni minority) would ill serve "the creation of commonly desired conditions of democracy, stability, peace, and welfare in this important member of the OIC."

A third extraordinary session took place December 7–8, 2005, in Jiddah to address the violent worldwide Islamic outrage following publication in a Danish newspaper of cartoons critical of the Prophet Mohammad. The conference condemned violence, saying that Islam was in a crisis, and offered an ambitious ten-year plan to "revamp Islamic mindsets." Symbolic of this decision was the intention to reorganize the OIC itself, and to build it a new headquarters in Saudi Arabia. By mid-2006 a design competition for the new facility was under way. Subsequent statements by the secretary general reinforced a nonviolent message.

The 33rd meeting of OIC foreign ministers, held June 19–22, 2006, in Baku, Azerbaijan, reinforced the message of moderation in the Islamic world. Specifically it warned the two rival factions in Palestine from dragging that territory into civil war.

PERMANENT INTER-STATE COMMITTEE ON DROUGHT CONTROL IN THE SAHEL (CILSS)

COMITÉ INTER-ETATS DE LUTTE CONTRE LA SÉCHERESSE DANS LE SAHEL

Established: Following a March 1973 declaration of a drought-related disaster in the Sahel by Burkina Faso (then Upper Volta), Mali, Mauritania, Niger, and Senegal.

Purpose: To overcome drought, ensure food security, fight desertification, and promote sustainable cooperative development in the Sahel region.

Headquarters: Ouagadougou, Burkina Faso.

Principal Organs: Conference of Heads of State and Government, Council of Ministers, Regional Committee for Programming and Follow-up, Executive Council, Executive Secretariat.

Executive Secretary: Musa Mbenga (Gambia).

Membership (9): Burkina Faso, Cape Verde, Chad, Gambia, Guinea-Bissau, Mali, Mauritania, Niger, Senegal.

Working Languages: French and English. (The introduction of Portuguese and Arabic as working languages was approved in principle.)

Origin and development. The CILSS was formed in 1973 by Burkina Faso (then Upper Volta), Mali, Mauritania, Niger, and Senegal in parallel with efforts by the new UN Special Sahelian Office to marshal aid for countries seriously affected by the 1968–1973 Sahelian drought. Chad soon joined its neighbors in the CILSS, as did Gambia in 1974 and Cape Verde in 1975. By then the Special Sahelian Office was superseded by the UN Sudano-Sahelian office (UNSO), which closely coordinated its activities with the CILSS. (In 1994 the UNSO was reorganized as the UN Development Programme's Office to Combat Desertification and Drought, which was replaced in 2002 by the Drylands Development Centre in Nairobi, Kenya.)

In its first year of existence the CILSS proposed some 300 projects directed toward its principal goals: preparing for future droughts and thereby mitigating their adverse effects, achieving regional security in cereals and other staple foods, and advancing development. The first Sahelian UNSO/CILSS donor conference in July 1975 in Geneva, Switzerland, attracted considerable support for some 50 short-term projects expected to cost $150 million. Also in 1975 the CILSS and various donor countries agreed to establish the Sahel Club, which was inaugurated in March 1976 as an informal forum for coordination and strategy formulation.

In 1984 the CILSS approved the establishment of the Sahel Fund to finance and coordinate national food strategies. The most recent member, Guinea-Bissau, joined in 1986.

Structure. The CILSS was initially a relatively unstructured organization that met in plenary session at least once per year to approve an annual budget and discuss major undertakings. At other times it held joint meetings with such bodies as the UN Food and Agriculture Organization (FAO) to address matters of common concern.

At present, the principal CILSS policymaking organs are the Conference of Heads of State or Government, which meets every three years to provide general direction and define major objectives, and a Council of Ministers, which is charged with realizing the organization's objectives. A Regional Committee for Programming and Follow-up reports to the ministers, while an Executive Council monitors overall operations, including budget preparation. The Executive Secretariat is headed by an executive secretary, who serves a three-year term, and includes four councilors responsible for food security, natural resources management, planning, and communications. Affiliated specialized agencies are the Sahel Institute in Bamako, Mali, and the Agrometeorology and Operational Hydrology Center (Agrhymet) in Niamey, Niger.

Activities. In the 1980s regional programs were created to develop an early warning system for food shortages, improve the quality and distribution of grain seeds, expand water supplies, protect plant life, educate the population on ways to counter the effects of drought and desertification in everyday life, and promote alternative energy sources. In addition, the Conference of the Heads of State addressed several related problems, including the region's economic difficulties and its high population growth rate.

The 1992 CILSS summit endorsed a "renewed mandate" for the organization, which experienced severe financial problems for several years because of arrears in members' payments. With the financial crisis continuing, the 11th summit, held in April 1994 in Praia, Cape Verde, approved a cutback in the CILSS staff from more than 100 employees to approximately 30. The heads of state also agreed to solicit additional external aid for the grouping, based in part on an expanded CILSS emphasis on economic integration, which presumably would make the region more attractive to international investors. As a result of subsequent discussions about assuring adequate funding, the CILSS established the Foundation for Sustainable Development of the Sahel.

At the 12th heads of state and government summit, held in September 1997, in Banjul, Gambia, many outside donors praised the CILSS for its progress. The European Union (EU), for one, called the CILSS one of the continent's most credible institutions and announced it would be one of the three primary organizations in the region to play an important role in the implementation of the Convention for West Africa between the EU and affiliated African, Caribbean, and Pacific (ACP) countries. However, the donors stressed that their continued support was contingent on members meeting their financial obligations to the CILSS. The financial situation of the CILSS was described as "precarious," with the amount members owed to the committee totaling more than $1 million in 1996. To help raise money, the heads of state and government endorsed a Council of Ministers' proposal to set up an endowment.

In late 1998 CILSS ministers, meeting in Banjul, approved a program geared toward assisting women's organizations and improving the management of land and water resources in cooperation with the Islamic Development Bank (IDB) and Organization of the Islamic Conference (OIC). Particularly since a June 1994 CILSS-sponsored Regional Conference on Land Tenure and Decentralization, held in Praia, the CILSS had also placed greater emphasis on land tenure issues, and a Project on Local Development in the Sahel (*Projet d'Appui au Développement Local au Sahel*—PADLOS) was set up to study national land policies.

The 13th CILSS summit convened November 25–26, 2000, in Bamako immediately after sessions of the Regional Committee and the Council of Ministers. Leadership of the Conference of Heads of State and Government passed to Mali's Alpha Oumar Konaré, while Musa Mbenga of Kenya was elected executive secretary for a term that began in February 2001. At the council session ministers reported that, once again, the Sahel was experiencing a "large cereal deficit."

Convening January 25, 2004, in Nouakchott, Mauritania, the 14th conference reappointed Secretary General Mbenga for a second term and passed the leadership reins to the host country's president, Maaouya Ould Sid' Ahmed Taya. Most significantly, the conference resolved to reorient the CILSS toward its original objectives of fighting desertification, addressing regional water needs, and establishing food security. In addition to redefining its focus, the CILSS sought to eliminate duplication of efforts by other regional organizations and to emphasize funding for projects with concrete goals.

This refocusing of attention seems to have helped. Annual crop yields in 2004 and 2005, despite poor rains, were considerably better than forecasted. With better food security, the organization had the opportunity to plan forward. In April 2006 it announced a grant of 79 million euros ($102 million) for a system of 500 solar-powered well pumps throughout its territory. This project was targeted for completion in 2008.

REGIONAL AND SUBREGIONAL DEVELOPMENT BANKS

Regional development banks are intended to accelerate economic and social development of member states by promoting public and private investment. The banks are not meant, however, to be mere financial institutions in the narrow sense of the term. Required by their charters to take an active interest in improving their members' capacities to make profitable use of local and external capital, they engage in such technical assistance activities as feasibility studies, evaluation and design of projects, and preparation of development programs. The banks also seek to coordinate their activities with the work of other national and international agencies engaged in financing international economic development. Subregional banks have historically concentrated more on integration projects than have regional development banks.

African Development Bank (AfDB)

Banque Africaine de Développement (BAD)

The Articles of Agreement of the AfDB were signed August 4, 1963, in Khartoum, Sudan, with formal establishment of the institution occurring in September 1964 after 20 signatories had deposited instruments of ratification. Lending operations commenced in July 1966 at the bank's headquarters in Abidjan, Côte d'Ivoire.

Until 1982 membership in the AfDB was limited to states within the region. At the 1979 Annual Meeting the Board of Governors approved an amendment to the bank's statutes permitting nonregional membership as a means of augmenting the institution's capital resources; however, it was not until the 17th Annual Meeting, held in May 1982 in Lusaka, Zambia, that Nigeria announced withdrawal of its objection to the change. Non-African states became eligible for membership December 20, 1982, and by the end of 1983 more than 20 such states had joined the bank.

The bank's leading policymaking organ is its Board of Governors, encompassing the finance or economic ministers of the member states; the governors elect a bank president, who serves a five-year term and is chair of a Board of Directors. The governors are empowered to name 18 directors, each serving a three-year term, with 12 seats to be held by Africans. The bank's African members are the same as for the Organization of African Unity (OAU), save for the inclusion of Morocco (no longer a member of the OAU) and the exclusion of the Sahrawi Arab Democratic Republic.

While limiting the bank's membership to African countries was initially viewed as a means of avoiding practical difficulties and undesirable political complications, it soon became evident that the major capital-exporting states were unwilling to lend funds without having a continuous voice in their use. In response to this problem, an African Development Fund (ADF) was established in November 1972 as a legally distinct intergovernmental institution in which contributing countries would have a shared managerial role. The ADF Board of Governors encompasses one representative from each state as well as the AfDB governors, ex officio; the 12-member Board of Directors includes six nonregional designees. Nonregional contributing countries—all of whom, except the United Arab Emirates, are now AfDB members— are Argentina, Austria, Belgium, Brazil, Canada, China, Denmark, Finland, France, Germany, India, Italy, Japan, the Republic of Korea, Kuwait, the Netherlands, Norway, Portugal, Saudi Arabia, Spain, Sweden, Switzerland, the United Kingdom, and the United States. In addition, in February 1976 (with effect from April 1976), an agreement was signed by the bank and the government of Nigeria establishing a Nigeria Trust Fund (NTF) with an initial capitalization of 50 million Nigerian naira (about $80 million). Unlike the ADF, the NTF is directly administered by the AfDB. Together, the AfDB, the ADF, and the NTF constitute the African Development Bank Group.

Earlier, in November 1970, the AfDB participated in the founding of the International Financial Society for Investments and Development in Africa (*Société Internationale Financière pour les Investissements et le Développement en Afrique*— SIFIDA). Headquartered in Geneva, Switzerland, with the International Finance Corporation (IFC) and a large number of financial institutions from advanced industrial countries among its shareholders, SIFIDA is authorized to extend loans for the promotion and growth of productive enterprises in Africa. Another related agency, the Association of African Development Finance Institutions (AADFI), inaugurated in March 1975 in Abidjan, was established to aid and coordinate African development projects, while the African Reinsurance Corporation (Africa-Re), formally launched in March 1977 in Lagos, Nigeria, promotes the development of insurance and reinsurance activity throughout the continent. The AfDB holds 10 percent of Africa-Re's authorized capital of $50 million. Shelter-Afrique, established to facilitate lending that would improve Africa's housing situation, began operations in January 1984 in its Nairobi, Kenya, headquarters. The AFDB has also participated in the formation of the African Export-Import Bank (Afreximbank), which began operation in 1993.

At the bank's 1988 annual meeting U.S. officials surprised observers by announcing that Wash-

ington was now willing to support concessional interest rate rescheduling for the "poorest of the poor" African countries. However, African representatives called for additional debt measures, such as extension of maturities and pegging repayment schedules to a country's debt-servicing "history" and "capacity." The bank also called for closer cooperation with the World Bank in structural adjustment lending and pledged to incorporate environmental and women's concerns into project planning. Following up on discussions initiated at the annual meeting on growing arrears in loan repayments and capital subscription payments, the bank announced late in the year that the countries involved faced suspension of existing loan disbursements and would not be eligible for new loans until the arrears were cleared.

During the 1989 annual meeting and 25th anniversary celebration, at which the bank was described as "probably the most successful of the African multinational institutions," the Board of Governors pledged that lending activity would continue to accelerate. On the topic of debt reduction, the bank praised the initiatives launched at the recent Group of Seven summit but called for further measures, including more debt cancellations by individual creditor nations.

A dispute between regional and nonregional members regarding the bank's future continued at the May 1993 AfDB annual meeting as Western nations continued to press for a stricter policy on arrears, better evaluation of project performance, and greater support for private sector activity. In addition, at the insistence of donor countries, an independent task force was established, under the chairmanship of former World Bank vice president David Knox, to review all bank operations. The task force report, released shortly before the AfDB's May 1994 annual meeting, strongly criticized the bank for keeping poor records, maintaining a top-heavy bureaucracy, and emphasizing the quantity of lending at the expense of quality. The report also supported the contention of donor countries that the accumulation of arrears (more than $700 million) had become a threat to the bank's future. The nonregional members subsequently proposed that regular AfDB lending be limited to "solvent" nations, but African members rejected their advice.

Fractious debate continued at the May 1995 annual meeting. Outgoing AfDB President Babacar N'Diaye, blamed by some for the bank's deteriorating reputation, issued the counterclaim that responsibility rested with the Board of Directors, many of whose members, he charged, were concentrating on their own "finances and perquisites" at the expense of bank activity. Further tarnishing the bank's image, the governors were unable to elect a successor to N'Diaye, with regional and nonregional members backing different candidates. However, at a special meeting in Abidjan, in late August the Board of Governors, after nine rounds of balloting, finally chose Omar Kabbaj, one-time official of the International Monetary Fund and a former member of the Moroccan cabinet, as the new AfDB president. Shortly thereafter, Kabbaj announced that an external committee would be established to evaluate the bank's operations, internal structures, and fiscal status. The new president also pledged that the AfDB would immediately begin to give greater emphasis to private sector loans, one issue on which regional and nonregional members appeared in agreement. Meanwhile, talks on the ADF replenishment remained suspended pending Kabbaj's restructuring proposals, expected by the end of the year.

Under the leadership of Kabbaj the AfDB subsequently cut approximately 240 employees (20 percent of the staff) and otherwise restructured the bank's operations, paving the way for an infusion of new capital. At the annual meeting held May 21–22, 1996, the ADF was replenished with $2.6 billion, though this entailed a cut from prior levels. The United States' contribution was significantly lower than in the past, and several other Western nations also reduced their participation. However, led by Japan, 16 nations added another $420 million to the ADF in June. When ADF lending resumed shortly thereafter, the AfDB adopted guidelines recommended by the World Bank under which the number of states eligible for new loans was reduced from 53 to 12.

Although those changes were widely perceived as representing genuine progress, the AfDB "governance report" released in mid-1996 delineated several continuing problems. The report argued that further "stark" measures needed to be taken to prevent the bank from being relegated to the role of a minor player on the continent. Specific issues to be addressed included "incompetence" in some bank operations, low morale among the remaining employees, and a lack of "financial credibility" stemming from arrears of $800 million amassed by 25 out of 53 recipients. (About 75 percent of the late payments were owed by Angola, Cameroon, Congo, Liberia, Somalia, Sudan, and Zaire.)

In July 1996 a special summit was held in Libreville, Gabon, to discuss issues raised in the report and to plot the future of the Bank, particularly in regard to the contentious issue of "control." Led by Nigeria, some African countries opposed giving Western members additional decision-making power, despite the bank's weakened condition. The governance report outlined several alternatives, ranging from a 50–50 split of control between Western and African nations, to no change at all (which might have meant the cessation of Western contributions). Compromise alternatives called for a modest increase in Western decision-making power via a reduction in the total number of seats on the executive board as well a revision of AfDB voting procedures.

The debate over how much control the nonregional members should have continued at the May 1997 annual meeting, with the issue tied directly to discussions on the proposed fifth general increase in capital. Some African members reportedly argued that the capital increase should be refused if it meant turning "veto power" over to the nonregional members. A compromise was reached in March 1998 when it was agreed that a capital increase of about 35 percent ($7.65 billion) would be implemented, with the nonregional share being set at 40 percent. Significantly, while the African members were allowed to retain control of 12 of the 18 seats on the Board of Directors, future discussions would require 70 percent (at least one nonregional vote) endorsement by that board on "crucial" issues.

Under President Kabbaj's leadership, significant structural reforms were implemented during the latter 1990s, contributing to improved international credibility for the bank. Collaterally, a vision statement approved by the Board of Governors in 1999 gave greater emphasis to reducing poverty and increasing productivity, with other concerns including good governance, regional cooperation and development, gender mainstreaming, and environmental sustainability. Operationally, the AfDB was rededicated to meeting client needs through strategic planning and compliance monitoring. An executive restructuring, to take effect in early 2002, included the establishment of two additional vice presidencies, raising the total to five. Areas of vice presidential responsibility were defined as planning, policy, and research; operations in the Central and Western regions; operations in the Northern, Eastern, and Southern regions and the private sector; corporate management; and finance. The reorganization also involved establishing two "operational complexes": sector departments, with responsibility for project management, and country departments, with responsibility for such broader areas as macroeconomic analyses, lending policy, and public sector management.

At the same time, lending by the AfDB group resurged. In 2001 new loan commitments reached 2.4 billion units of account ($3.0 billion, at the year-end exchange rate of $1.26 per UA), the highest level in ten years and 20 percent more than in 2000. The total included $1.7 billion in concessional loan commitments through the ADF and $6.4 million from the Nigeria Trust Fund, for a loan to Mauritius. (In 2000 the trust fund approved loans to Botswana, Gambia, and Guinea, the first new commitments since 1996.) The bank also saw a fivefold increase in private sector activity in 2001, which kept with the 1999 vision statement. Countries that received the most AfDB resources were Tunisia, Morocco, and Algeria, while the comparable ADF leaders were Ethiopia, Mozambique, and Tanzania.

Total bank approvals reached $3.28 billion in 2005, compared to $4.32 billion in 2004, $2.62 billion in 2003, and $2.77 billion in 2002. The decline in 2005 approvals from 2004 was attributed to reduction in HIPC debt relief. As of the end of 2005, cumulative disbursements reached $33.3 billion for more than 3,000 loans and grants. In December 2004 the bank won a new three-year replenishment for the ADF of $5.4 billion, a 43 percent increase over the previous three-year replenishment.

In February 2003 the AfDB temporarily moved its headquarters from Abidjan to Tunis, Tunisia, because of the outbreak of civil war in Côte d'Ivoire. International institutions (led by the Group of Eight) subsequently announced plans for the AfDB to manage a new fund slated to provide as much as $10 billion a year to improve infrastructure in Africa. However, some analysts suggested that the parameters of the new initiative might be reviewed in light of the long and often rancorous battle in mid-2005 to elect a successor to AfDB President Kabbaj, who was retiring after ten years in the position. After numerous ballots that weeded out several candidates, the Board of Governors elected Donald Kaberuka, the finance and economy minister from Rwanda, over Olabisi Ogunjobi, a Nigerian who worked at the bank since 1978. It was widely reported that Kaberuka had enjoyed the support of most of the bank's Western members.

Arab Bank for Economic Development in Africa

Banque Arabe de Développement Economique en Afrique
(BADEA)

The idea of an Arab bank to assist in the economic and social development of all non-Arab African states was first discussed by the Arab heads of state during the Sixth Arab Summit in Algiers, Algeria, in November 1973. The BADEA, with headquarters in Khartoum, Sudan, began operations in March 1975. Its main functions include financing development projects, promoting and stimulating private Arab investment in Africa, and supplying technical assistance. BADEA financing, which cannot exceed $15 million, is limited to 80 percent of projects with total costs up to $12 million and 50 percent of those above that level. Technical assistance is provided in grant form. All member states of the Organization of African Unity, except Arab League participants, are eligible for funding. To date the preponderance of aid has been devoted to infrastructural improvements although the Board of Directors has also accorded additional priority to projects promoting increased food production. The bank has traditionally favored the least-developed countries in its disbursements.

The bank's highest authority is the Board of Governors (one governor for each member), with day-to-day administration assigned to a Board of Directors, one of whose eleven members serves as board chair. The Board of Governors appoints the bank's director general from among the countries not represented on the Board of Directors. The subscribing members of the bank, listed in descending order of contribution, are Saudi Arabia, Libya, Kuwait, Iraq, United Arab Emirates, Qatar, Algeria, Morocco, Oman, Tunisia, Lebanon, Jordan, Bahrain, Sudan, Palestine, Egypt, Mauritania, and Syria. Egypt's membership was suspended from 1979 to 1988.

In a review of its first 25 years of activity, the BADEA reported that infrastructure received more than 50 percent of total commitments, followed by agriculture (30 percent), energy (8 percent), banking (4 percent), and industry (2 percent). In addition to maintaining support for "traditional fields of intervention," beginning with its 1990–1994 five-year plan the bank has placed greater emphasis on projects with a "direct impact on the life of African citizens," such as water supply and food security projects.

In 2000 the BADEA approved $119 million (for 16 projects) in new loans and $5.0 million in technical assistance (for 21 projects), for a total of $124 million. This marked a significant increase over the 1996 total of $90 million. Lending concentrated on potable water supplies, irrigation, and transportation (roads and rail) but also included projects involving fisheries development, a shipyard, an industrial training center, and a hospital.

In 2000 cumulative commitments reached $2.08 billion for 284 development projects, 15 lines of credit, 14 special emergency aid operations, and 239 technical assistance operations. Cumulative disbursements reached $1.17 billion, while cancellations reached $444 million. The BADEA has also administered 37 "soft" loans totaling $214 million that were extended through the Special Arab Fund for Africa (SAAFA) from its commencement of operations in 1974 until 1977, at which time the SAFAA capital was incorporated into that of the BADEA. The bank's subscribed capital is currently $1.5 billion.

The fourth five-year plan (2000–2004) projected $675 million in new commitments—a 35 percent increase over its predecessor—including $125 million in its first year. In general, loans were to carry an interest rate of 1–4 percent over an amortization period of 18–30 years, with a grace period of 4–10 years. The plan included continued financing of Arab exports to African countries, which the bank has handled as a revolving fund.

The BADEA approved $129 million in new loans in 2001, $134 million in 2002, $140 million in 2003, and $139 million (for 21 projects) and $5.7 million in technical assistance (for 24 projects) in 2004. Lending in 2004 centered on infrastructure projects and agriculture. Cumulative disbursements reached $1.6 billion at the end of 2005. In December 2004 the Board of Directors approved the fifth five-year plan, which projected new lending of $900 million in 2005–2009.

Central African States Development Bank

Banque de Développement des Etats de l'Afrique Centrale
(BDEAC)

The Central African States Development Bank was established on December 3, 1975, as a joint venture of Cameroon, the Central African Republic, Chad, (People's) Republic of the Congo, and Gabon, with Equatorial Guinea, previously an observer, joining as a sixth full member in 1986. The bank commenced operations January 2, 1977, as an affiliated organ of the Central African Customs and Economic Union (*Union Douanière et Economique de l'Afrique Centrale*—UDEAC), which was succeeded in 1994 by the Central African Economic and Monetary Community (*Communauté Economique et Monétaire d' Afrique Centrale*—CEMAC; see separate entry). Shareholders include the regional states, the African Development Bank, the Bank of Central African States (*Banque des Etats d'Afrique Central*—BEAC), and the governments of France, Germany, and Kuwait, all of whom are represented on the Board of Directors. The member states hold 51 percent of the bank's capital, some 57.2 billion CFA francs in 2001 ($76.8 million at the year-end exchange rate).

The bank's principal mission is to promote economic and social development through financing multinational and economic integration projects in the borrowing member countries. Particular attention is directed toward productive sectors, including efforts to modernize, convert, and privatize; rural infrastructure and development; and operations that contribute to economic integration and realization of the objectives of the CEMAC.

Throughout the 1990s the bank was under severe pressure as the result of growing arrears in loan repayments, unstable economic conditions in the region, and a series of political crises in various member countries. In fiscal year 1991–1992 only two loans, totaling 3.9 billion CFA ($15 million at the time) were approved, bringing the number of cumulative loans to 85. An external audit in 1992 recommended that the bank's operating costs be reduced, and in early 1993 the bank was temporarily closed and placed under military guard after it was announced that half the 80 staff positions would be eliminated. For the rest of the decade the BDEAC failed to regain its momentum amid efforts to establish appropriate administrative structures and policies in the member states.

On January 9, 2001, Director General Emannuel Dokouna of the Central African Republic was suspended following allegations of mismanagement, which reportedly included spending more than 200 days abroad (most of them in the Central African Republic) during the 1999–2000 fiscal year, using unauthorized funds to rehabilitate his official residence, and consuming most of the bank's investment budget on personal missions. An audit was undertaken by the BEAC, the central facility for the CEMAC states. The post of director general remained vacant until August, when the CEMAC heads of state, meeting in Franceville, Gabon, named former CAR prime minister Anicet Georges Dologuélé to the post. The heads of state had already indicated a desire to revitalize the BDEAC, and the new director general was expected to move rapidly toward addressing the perennial problem of arrears in loan repayments while also seeking renewed support from external partners.

By 2004 it appeared that Dologuélé made progress in restoring the credibility of the BDEAC, with most outstanding repayments collected and the bank having paid off its own debts. It was also reported that technical experts replaced some "political" appointees on the bank's Board of Directors, while greater authority was given to external shareholders such as France and Kuwait. The BDEAC announced plans to focus new lending on small- and medium-sized businesses. At the end of 2005, BDEAC reported 13.9 million CFA francs ($26.7 million) in loans for the year.

East African Development Bank (EADB)

The charter of the East African Development Bank was contained in an annex to the December 1967 treaty establishing the East African Community (EAC), which collapsed in June 1977 because of tensions among its members: Kenya, Tanzania, and Uganda. Because the bank was not supported by EAC general funds, it remained formally in existence, with headquarters in Kampala, Uganda. Subsequently, a mediator responsible for dividing the community's assets among its former members was charged with making recommendations concerning the bank's future, and in late 1979 a new tripartite treaty providing for a revival of EADB activity was drafted. The bank's revised charter, completed during the first half of 1980 and signed by the three members in July, sought to rechannel the thrust of bank lending toward agricultural, infrastructural, and technical assistance efforts.

The bank's principal organ is the Governing Council, which comprises the members' ministers of finance. A Board of Directors includes representatives of the African Development Bank (AfDB), the three member countries, and the private sector. The Danish International Development Agency (Danida) was also represented until it withdrew from the bank in 2000. An Advisory Panel of international financial experts also meets regularly.

In 1990 it was reported that 71 of the EADB's outstanding loans were in arrears, and officials in late 1991 indicated that the bank was experiencing severe operational problems. Much of the difficulty was attributed to currency devaluations arising from members' imposition of structural adjustment policies requested by the International Monetary Fund (IMF) as a condition for further support. (In 1984 the IMF gave the EADB permission to utilize its special drawing rights [SDR] as a unit of account.) Consequently, only two loans totaling SDR 1.53 million ($2.2 million) were approved in 1991, while the bank suffered the first operating loss in its history. The EADB subsequently announced that a "major restructuring" would be implemented.

In 1995 the bank announced it accepted the recommendations of an external panel of experts, who suggested that the EADB become more aggressive in collecting debts, give greater attention to the quality of its loans, and expand its financial advisory services. In addition, the EADB decided to emphasize export-oriented loans as well as those geared to promote tourism in the region. Lending approvals in 1998 totaled $42.1 million, compared to $30 million in 1996 and 1997.

In 1999 the AfDB announced its intention to increase its equity in the bank from SDR 0.35 million to SDR 5.0 million, and loan approvals rose to SDR 34.6 million ($47.3 million, at the year-end exchange rate) before dropping marginally to SDR 34.0 million ($44.3 million) in 2000. Infrastructure (48 percent) and the service sector (28 per-

cent) accounted for most new loans. At the same time, disbursements rose slightly, from SDR 25.2 million ($34.6 million) in 1999 to SDR 27.3 million ($35.5 million). Total assets at the end of 2000 amounted to SDR 133 million ($174 million).

In 2000 the Governing Council approved a long-term strategic plan for 2001–2005 that envisaged an expansion of assets to SDR 300 million ($391 million), partly in anticipation of strengthened international standing occasioned by the revival of the EAC (see separate entry). The final ratification of the new EAC treaty was accomplished July 7, and the three-member community was formally relaunched January 15, 2001. "Total investments" of $51.2 million were reported in 2003, with disbursements registering $23.5 million. In its annual report for 2004 the bank reported loan approvals for the year of $84.4 million, with disbursements of $29.13 million. Approvals were concentrated in the transport and communications and agriculture and fisheries sectors.

The EADB and the China Development Bank signed an agreement in June 2006 to cooperate in mutually agreed development projects in East Africa. At the signing ceremony, the EADB's Director General Godfrey Tumusiime described EADB as "poised to be transformed into the leading agency for facilitation of East African regional integration and development."

West African Development Bank

Banque Ouest-Africaine de Développement
(BOAD)

An agreement to establish a West African Development Bank was initialed at a Paris, France, summit meeting of French-speaking African states on November 13–14, 1973. The bank formally commenced operations January 1, 1976, with headquarters in Lomé, Togo. The BOAD provides regional financing for the eight members (Benin, Burkina Faso, Côte d'Ivoire, Guinea-Bissau, Mali, Niger, Senegal, and Togo) of the West African Economic and Monetary Union (*Union Economique*

Monetaire Ouest-Africaine—UEMOA; see separate entry), its goal being to promote equitable development and achieve economic integration through priority development projects. The other bank members are the African Development Bank, Belgium, the Central Bank of West African States (*Banque Centrale des Etats de l'Afrique de l'Ouest*—BCEAO), the European Investment Bank (EIB), France, and the German Development Company. The unit of account is the CFA franc, valued as of July 1, 2006, at CFA 513.01 per U.S. dollar.

The organs of the bank include the Council of Ministers of the UEMOA and a Board of Directors comprising two directors from each UEMOA member, one director from the other six members, and the BOAD president, who serves as board chair.

A meeting of member ministers in October 1983 in Niamey, Niger, yielded approval of a bank proposal to implement regional integration projects, harmonize national development policies, and facilitate maximum utilization of internal and external resources. Later in the decade the BOAD, having considerably expanded its association with the international banking community, pledged to use the additional resources, in part, to assist member states in making the economic policy reforms requested by major international financial institutions. In 1989 the BOAD also agreed to seek regional projects for funding, more than 80 percent of loans to that point having been for strictly national projects.

After undergoing internal restructuring to promote greater efficiency and better evaluation of loan performances, the BOAD announced in 1994 that upcoming lending would increase support for the private sector and efforts to strengthen the region's financial infrastructure. Much of that activity was expected to take place in conjunction with the new UEMOA, which was established in January 1994 as successor to the West African Economic Community (*Communauté Economique de l'Afrique de l'Ouest*—CEAO). Since then, the BOAD has been considered a "specialized institution" of the UEMOA.

Industry and agro-industry, rural development, transportation, telecommunications, energy, tourism, and other services have been among the sectors receiving support in recent years. In addition, the bank has supported feasibility studies, development of small- and medium-sized enterprises (SMEs), and partnerships with other financial institutions. Regional integration has focused particularly on agricultural processing and on transport infrastructure.

In 2000 the bank approved some 24 projects—including its first to Guinea-Bissau, for a water and energy project—totaling CFA 72.4 billion ($104 million at the year-end exchange rate) in loans, an increase of about 4.7 percent from 1999. About 62 percent of lending went to the public sector, with greater emphasis on integration efforts and projects promoting poverty control. Lending to the private sector concentrated on privatization, industry, and refinancing for SMEs. BOAD cumulative lending reached CFA 555 billion ($796 million) for more than 300 operations, about two-thirds of them public. Leading recipients were Côte d'Ivoire (26 percent) and Benin (19 percent). The BOAD also participated in the multilateral Highly Indebted Poor Countries initiative, and in August 2001 BOAD President Yayi Boni indicated that the bank intended to move forward with a debt reduction program financed primarily by external sources and linked to reforms in individual countries.

In mid 2002 Boni announced BOAD would expand its support to the least-developed countries in the region, calling on national leaders to cooperate in formulating a new regional "vision" for reducing poverty. The bank, which celebrated its 30th anniversary in 2003, agreed to mobilize outside financial support to assist in integrating the region's financial markets and to protect private investors. Apparently in support of that initiative, the World Bank in 2004 approved a new financing package for BOAD totaling $409 million for the next five years. Late in 2004 attention focused on a membership application, eventually successful, from China.

Boni's position as bank president became vacant in April 2006 following his election and inauguration as president of Benin.

SOUTHERN AFRICAN DEVELOPMENT COMMUNITY (SADC)

Established: By the Treaty of Windhoek, signed August 17, 1992, in Windhoek, Namibia, by representatives from the ten members of the former Southern African Development Coordination Conference (SADCC); Agreement Amending the Treaty signed August 14, 2001, in Blantyre, Malawi.

Purpose: To achieve self-sustaining development and economic growth based on collective self-reliance and interdependence; to achieve sustainable use of natural resources while protecting the environment; to promote and defend regional peace and security; to enhance the standard of living through regional integration, including establishing a free trade area.

Headquarters: Gaborone, Botswana.

Principal Organs: Summit Meeting of Heads of State or Government; Council of Ministers; Organ on Politics, Defense, and Security; Executive Secretariat.

Executive Secretary: Tomaz Augusto Salomao (Mozambique).

Membership (14): Angola, Botswana, Democratic Republic of the Congo, Lesotho, Madagascar, Malawi, Mauritius, Mozambique, Namibia, South Africa, Swaziland, Tanzania, Zambia, Zimbabwe.

Working Languages: English, French, Portuguese.

Origin and development. The SADCC originated in a "Southern African Development Coordination Conference" convened in July 1979, in Arusha, Tanzania, by Angola, Botswana, Mozambique, Tanzania, and Zambia (the "Front-Line States" opposed to white rule in southern Africa). A draft declaration entitled "Southern Africa: Towards Economic Liberation" was drawn up proposing a program of action to improve regional transportation, agriculture, industry, energy, and development planning, with a view toward reducing economic dependence on the Republic of South Africa. As a follow-up to the Arusha meeting, the SADCC was formally established during a summit of the heads of state or government of nine countries (the original five plus Lesotho, Malawi, Swaziland, and Zimbabwe) that convened April 1, 1980, in Lusaka, Zambia. Namibia joined the SADCC after achieving independence in 1990.

The SADCC was considered one of the most viable of the continent's regional groupings although its actual accomplishments were modest compared to its members' development needs. During its first six years the SADCC concentrated on the rehabilitation and expansion of transport corridors to permit the movement of goods from the interior of the region to ocean ports without the use of routes through South Africa. In 1986, however, SADCC leaders concluded that such infrastructure development would not reduce dependence on South Africa sufficiently unless accompanied by broad, long-term economic growth in the region. Consequently, the SADCC announced that additional emphasis would be given to programs and projects designed to increase production within the private sector and in enterprises with government involvement, expand intraregional trade, support national economic reform, and encourage international investment. The program of action eventually encompassed some 500 projects including small feasibility studies and large port and railway construction projects.

Throughout the 1980s the conference called for the international community to impose comprehensive, mandatory sanctions against Pretoria to protest apartheid. However, consensus was not attained on regional action, such as the severance of air links with Pretoria, primarily because of objections from Lesotho and Swaziland, the SADCC members whose economies were most directly linked to South Africa.

At their tenth anniversary summit in August 1990 the SADCC leaders discussed proposals to expand the conference's mandate and influence, in part by enhancing the authority of the secretariat. The heads of state, concerned with the region's stagnant export revenue and mounting debt burden, emphasized the need to increase intraregional trade over the next decade. In addition, they endorsed "automatic membership" for South Africa once apartheid was dismantled.

While participants in the 1991 summit urged that sanctions be continued against Pretoria pending further democratic "progress," they endorsed preliminary discussions with representatives of the "liberation movements" in South Africa regarding future coordination of economic policies. In addition to possible resolution of the South African issue, peace initiatives in Angola and Mozambique were subsequently cited by SADCC officials as cause for hope that after three decades of violence the region might be headed for a sustained period of peace. With this in mind, a treaty signed August 17, 1992, in Windhoek, Namibia, transformed the SADCC into the SADC, through which members were to seek development and integration in several areas, leading to a full-fledged common market. Although most details of the new organization were left to subsequent negotiations, the SADC members agreed to concentrate for the short term on

joint infrastructure development, coordination of investment procedures, and establishment of regional production policies. Arrangements for the free movement of goods, capital, and labor among members were to be made at an undetermined date. The most ardent SADC integrationists also suggested the community might eventually pursue political union, perhaps through a regional parliament, and security coordination.

One immediate concern for the SADC was its relationship with the Preferential Trade Area for Eastern and Southern African States (PTA), established in 1981 with many of the same goals as those adopted by the SADC. In late 1992, with eight of the (then) ten SADC members also belonging to the PTA (with Botswana and Namibia as exceptions), the PTA called for a merger of the two organizations. Not surprisingly, the SADC Executive Secretariat opposed the proposal and at a January 1993 meeting the SADC, reportedly concerned over the PTA's history of ineffectiveness, rejected the overture. However, the SADC subsequently indicated it would try to avoid duplicating PTA activities, suggesting that the PTA could assume full responsibility for economic cooperation among the 11 "northern" or non-SADC countries, with the SADC doing the same for its members.

In one of a summer-long series of remarkable international events precipitated by the democratic transition in Pretoria, the SADC accepted South Africa as its 11th member at a summit held in late August 1994, in Gaborone, Botswana. While welcoming South Africa to their ranks, the other SADC members reportedly expressed concern they might be overwhelmed by its economic might. The summit also began to weigh greater security responsibilities, addressing such proposals as the creation of a mechanism for the peaceful resolution of conflicts among members and the establishment of regional peacekeeping and defense forces. Thus, the SADC defense ministers in November endorsed the concept of a "regional deployment force," which would not be a permanent army but one available for quick mobilization from national armies.

Mauritius became the 12th SADC member in August 1995. The Seychelles and Democratic

Republic of the Congo became the 13th and 14th members on September 8 and 9, 1997, respectively, although in 2003 the Seychelles, citing its inability to pay its annual membership fee, announced its intention to withdraw as of mid-2004. At the same time, Madagascar expressed its interest in joining. The 2005 summit welcomed Madagascar as its 14th member.

Structure. Under the terms of the Lusaka Declaration issued in 1980, individual members of the SADCC were assigned coordinating roles over specified economic concerns. Thus, in July 1980 the conference's first operational body, the Southern African Transport and Communications Commission, was formed under Mozambique's leadership. Other states received the following assignments: Angola, energy; Botswana, livestock production, animal disease control, and crop production research; Lesotho, soil and water conservation, land utilization, and tourism; Malawi, fisheries, forestry, and wildlife; Swaziland, manpower development and training; Tanzania, industry and trade; Zambia, development funding and mining; and Zimbabwe, regional food security.

When the SADC was established to replace the SADCC in 1992, it was decided to keep the existing SADCC structure intact for the time being, with additional or reassigned sectoral responsibilities subsequently made: Mauritius, tourism; Mozambique, culture, information, and sports; Namibia, marine fisheries and resources; South Africa, finance and investment; and Zambia, employment and labor. Other changes were made in response to the community's postapartheid regional security concerns, which led in mid-1996 to creation of an Organ on Politics, Defense, and Security. The objectives of the organ included fostering cooperation with regard to issues of law and order, defending against external aggression, and promoting democracy. The organ was also authorized to mediate domestic disputes and conflicts between members.

At an extraordinary summit held March 9, 2001, in Windhoek the SADC approved a report on restructuring that called for phasing out, within two years, the nearly two dozen sector coordinating units and replacing them with four directorates:

trade, finance, industry, and investment; infrastructure and services; food, agriculture, and natural resources; and social and human development and special programs. The structural reform was viewed as essential to advancing regional integration and strategic planning, efficient use of available resources, and equitable distribution of responsibilities.

Under the reorganization, the SADC's chief policymaking organ, the Summit of Heads of State or Government, meets at least once per year, with the position of chair continuing to rotate annually. Between summit meetings, policy responsibility rests on a troika of the SADC chair, his predecessor, and his successor, with other national leaders coopted as needed. The Organ on Politics, Defense, and Security was given a rotating chairmanship, with the organ's internal structure and functions detailed in a Protocol on Politics, Defense, and Security that was signed at the August 2001 summit. The Council of Ministers remains responsible for policy implementation and organizational oversight. A Standing Committee of Senior Officials, comprising a permanent secretary from each member country, serves as a technical advisory body to the council, with an emphasis on planning and finance.

In addition, the restructuring called for creation of an Integrated Committee of Ministers (ICM) to ensure "proper policy guidance, coordination and harmonization of cross-sectoral activities." The ICM, replacing the Sectoral Committee of Ministers, is primarily responsible for overseeing and guiding the work of the new directorates. It answers to the council and includes at least two ministers from each SADC state. To provide policy coordination, particularly with regard to interstate politics and international diplomacy, a new body, the Ministers of Foreign Affairs, Defense, and Security, was subsequently added to the SADC structure.

Duties of the secretariat, which is headed by an executive secretary, include strategic planning, management of the comprehensive SADC program of action, and general administration. Within the secretariat, a new Department of Strategic Planning, Gender, and Development and Policy

Harmonization was established. At the individual state level, representatives of government, the private sector, and civil society meet as SADC national committees to provide input to the central SADC organs and to oversee programs within each jurisdiction.

During the 2000 summit SADC leaders signed a protocol establishing an SADC tribunal, as provided for in the founding treaty. The tribunal will have with responsibility for interpreting the treaty and subsidiary documents and for adjudicating disputes between members.

Activities. The dominant concern for the SADC in 1995 remained the "dual membership" problem regarding the PTA, an issue further complicated by the recent signing of a treaty establishing the Common Market of Eastern and Southern Africa (Comesa). Although most SADC members signed the treaty, several postponed ratification, while South Africa and Botswana indicated their lack of interest in the alignment. Consequently, the SADC summit held August 28 in Johannesburg, South Africa, called for an immediate joint summit between the SADC and PTA/Comesa to resolve the matter. Meanwhile, SADC leaders endorsed the proposed elimination of trade barriers between SADC members and the establishment of a common SADC currency. The summit also signed a protocol for cooperation in water management and launched negotiations on similar protocols in the areas of tourism and energy.

During the summit held August 23–24, 1996, in Maseru, Lesotho, the SADC again declined to merge with Comesa and instead reemphasized its own goal of establishing a Southern Africa Free Trade Area within eight years. (Lesotho and Mozambique subsequently announced they did not intend to ratify the Comesa treaty, while Tanzania eventually dropped out in favor of continued membership in the SADC.) Other protocols were also signed at the SADC summit in the areas of energy, transportation and communications, and illicit narcotics, although an agreement could not be reached on the free movement of people among the SADC countries.

The Organ on Politics, Defense, and Security, launched at the 1996 summit, was at the center of controversy at the September 1997 summit, particularly because of its relative independence from the other SADC institutions. South African President Nelson Mandela, chair of the summit, insisted on bringing the organ under the direct control of the summit, while Zimbabwean President Robert Mugabe, chair of the organ, opposed such a move. Mandela also surprised the summit by proposing the SADC punish members via sanctions if they did not adopt the democratic values central to the organization. His proposal was particularly aimed at Swaziland's King Mswati III and Zambian President Frederick Chiluba, both of whom were unmoved, in Mandela's opinion, by attempts to encourage democracy in their countries.

A March 1998 SADC summit established a high-level committee to address the lingering question of how the community should respond to domestic political and security problems. Particular concern was expressed over renewed turmoil in Angola and the troubled nature of political affairs in Lesotho. In May the SADC sent observers to monitor the legislative elections in the latter country; although the SADC team initially approved the conduct of the election, the community was subsequently drawn into a dispute over opposition charges that massive fraud had occurred.

An SADC summit in late July 1998 in Namibia attempted to refocus the community's attention on economic cooperation. Attendees pledged to eliminate tariffs and other restrictions on 90 percent of intracommunity trade by 2005. However, security matters, particularly the recent outbreak of fighting in the Democratic Republic of the Congo (DRC), returned to the fore at the SADC summit September 13–15 in Mauritius. Several countries urged action in support of the government of DRC President Laurent Kabila; SADC members Angola, Namibia, and Zimbabwe reportedly had already sent troops to the DRC to oppose anti-Kabila rebels. The SADC summit, at Kabila's insistence, refused to meet with the representatives of Rwanda and Uganda (apparent supporters of the

DRC rebels) who traveled to Mauritius to discuss the matter.

The SADC's role in domestic affairs became even more clouded shortly after the summit when South African and then Botswanan troops entered Lesotho to quell unrest generated by anger over the May election, which was followed by a mutiny within the Lesotho Defense Force (LDF). The initiative was described as an SADC intervention based on the community's established principles and procedures, but some SADC members reportedly objected to that classification. By May 1999 an advisory team mandated to help retrain and restructure the LDF replaced the troops.

The 19th summit, held August 18–19, 1999, in Maputo, Mozambique, was dominated by the ongoing instability in the DRC and Angola. Although the summit offered what was described as "moral support" to Angola's government in its campaign against rebel forces, DRC President Laurent Kabila withdrew from the meeting because of what he considered its lack of support for his regime. In economic affairs, the summit confirmed its intention to move forward with establishing a Southern Africa Free Trade Area, as provided for in 1996. Concern was expressed, however, about how small- and medium-sized local businesses should be protected as trade barriers drop.

The August 6–7, 2000, summit in Windhoek drew widespread international criticism for a decision to support the Mugabe government's expropriation of white-owned land in Zimbabwe. The summit's final communiqué also focused on such economic concerns as rising external debt, a regional cereal deficit, the HIV/AIDS crisis, and continuing poverty. The communiqué noted that GDP growth among member states recently rose, but not at the projected 6.8 percent annual rate needed to achieve actual poverty reduction. The crisis in the DRC, which at a January 16 summit generated a call from the SADC for the deployment of UN peacekeepers, also remained an ongoing concern.

The March 9, 2001, summit in Windhoek, in addition to approving the organizational changes called for in a report on restructuring (see Struc-

ture, above), elected Mauritian Prega Ramsamy as successor to Namibian Kaire Mbuende, who was dismissed as executive secretary in 2000. In addition, the summit continued to emphasize matters of defense and security. Considerable tension, particularly between South Africa and Zimbabwe, arose over Robert Mugabe's refusal to step aside as chair of the Organ on Politics, Defense, and Security. Some members clearly felt that Mugabe had misused his position in support of the Kabila regime in the DRC. Subsequently, however, it was agreed that the chairmanship would pass to Mozambique's President Chissano at the August 12–14 annual summit. Held in Blantyre, Malawi, the annual session again focused on regional security issues but also formally approved a package of treaty amendments to accommodate the previously accepted structural reforms. The summit additionally authorized formation by Botswana, Mozambique, and South Africa of a task force to confer with Zimbabwe on domestic economic and political issues. Fearing that the land reform crisis would spill over into neighboring countries, the SADC held an extraordinary summit September 11–12 in Harare, Zimbabwe. For the first time, the Mugabe government was publicly chastised from the chair, by Malawi's Bakili Muluzi, for its methods of land redistribution.

In September 2001 South Africa became the first SADC country to implement the free trade protocol signed in 1996 in Maseru. By then, however, the original free trade target date for the community as a whole was pushed back to 2008, when "substantially all" intra-SADC trade is to become tariff free. Exceptions are to be permitted on a country-by-country temporary basis for "sensitive products." Looking further ahead, the SADC intends to introduce a customs union in 2010 and a full common market in 2012.

A January 14, 2002, extraordinary summit in Blantyre focused on conflicts and security matters in the DRC, Angola, and especially Zimbabwe. The SADC sent a ministerial delegation to Harare in December 2002 that received reassurances from the Mugabe regime about meeting democratic standards for the forthcoming presidential election, but the conduct of the balloting in March 2002 was nevertheless widely condemned internationally. At the October 2–3, 2002, summit in Luanda, Angola, the SADC took no substantive action with regard to Zimbabwe, the main issue under discussion being drought and a resultant food crisis that was severely affecting Lesotho, Malawi, Mozambique, Swaziland, Zambia, and Zimbabwe.

By the August 25–26, 2003, summit in Dar es Salaam, Tanzania, the food crisis had abated, and the SADC turned its focus to economic and social planning, adopting a blueprint called the Regional Indicative Strategic Development Plan (RISDP). The summit also adopted an SADC Charter on Fundamental Social Rights, a Strategic Indicative Plan for the Organ (SIPO), and a mutual defense pact. The defense pact provides for collective action against armed attack and denies support to groups seeking the destabilization of other members, but it continues to uphold the principle of nonintervention in members' internal affairs. Recent security-related measures have also encompassed controlling trafficking in drugs, diamonds, and small arms and light weapons.

A meeting of the Council of Ministers on March 12–13, 2004, in Arusha, Tanzania, officially launched the RISDP, which includes among its economic concerns food security, sustainable growth, trade promotion, regional integration, and development of transport and communications infrastructure. To further emphasize the importance given to combating food shortages and chronic malnutrition, the SADC scheduled an extraordinary summit on agriculture and food security for May 2004.

In the area of social and human development, concerns addressed by the RISDP include gender equality and the AIDS epidemic. In recent years the SADC has given a high priority to advancing gender equality, including the increased participation of women in government and economic development. With regard to HIV/AIDS, however,

the SADC's record is less consistent. In July 2003 a special summit on HIV and AIDS convened in Maseru, but only 4 of the SADC's 14 heads of state or government participated in the effort to draft a comprehensive regional plan for confronting the epidemic. How to deal with HIV/AIDS remains a politically charged issue in several SADC countries, especially South Africa. Meanwhile, regional infection rates are among the world's highest, and AIDS has become a major obstacle to economic development.

In the past several years the relationship with Comesa has become less contentious, and a joint SADC/Comesa task force meets regularly. In addition, both have actively supported the African Union's New Partnership for Africa's Development (Nepad). In the wider international sphere, the SADC and the European Union (EU) continue to hold biennial ministerial meetings. SADC/EU working groups have focused on political, security, and economic matters. Negotiations on an SADC/EU Economic Partnership Agreement opened in 2004 in Windhoek. These discussions took a different direction in March 2006 when the SADC, under South African leadership, asked the EU to negotiate a bilateral agreement with the SADC, as opposed to discussions about joining a larger agreement between the EU and less-developed countries.

At the August 2005 summit in Gabarone, Botswana, Tomaz Augusto Salomao of Mozambique was appointed as the new SADC executive secretary. Other activity included the appointment of the first five members of the SADC tribunal. Also in 2005 the SADC activated the first standby brigade of five planned brigades of SADC peacekeeping forces. The force was planned to be full strength by 2010. In June 2006 South Africa proposed that the standby brigade be augmented by a military inspection and surveillance organization, to be called the African Defense Audit Association.

UNITED NATIONS (UN)

Established: By charter signed June 26, 1945, in San Francisco, United States, effective October 24, 1945.

Purpose: To maintain international peace and security; to develop friendly relations among states based on respect for the principle of equal rights and self-determination of peoples; to achieve international cooperation in solving problems of an economic, social, cultural, or humanitarian character; and to harmonize the actions of states in the attainment of these common ends.

Headquarters: New York, United States.

Principal Organs: General Assembly (all members), Security Council (15 members), Economic and Social Council (54 members), Trusteeship Council (5 members), International Court of Justice (15 judges), Secretariat.

Secretary General: Kofi Annan (Ghana).

Membership: 192.

Official Languages: Arabic, Chinese, English, French, Russian, Spanish. All are also working languages.

Origin and development. The idea of creating a new intergovernmental organization to replace the League of Nations was born early in World War II and first found public expression in an Inter-Allied Declaration signed on June 12, 1941, in London, England, by representatives of five Commonwealth states and eight European governments-in-exile. Formal use of the term United Nations first occurred in the Declaration by United Nations, signed on January 1, 1942, in Washington, D.C., on behalf of 26 states that subscribed to the principles of the Atlantic Charter (August 14,

1941) and pledged their full cooperation for the defeat of the Axis powers. At the Moscow Conference on October 30, 1943, representatives of China, the Union of Soviet Socialist Republics, the United Kingdom, and the United States proclaimed that they "recognized the necessity of establishing at the earliest practicable date a general international organization, based on the principle of the sovereign equality of all peace-loving states, and open to membership by all such states, large and small, for the maintenance of international peace and security." In meetings in Dumbarton Oaks, Washington, D.C., between August 21 and October 7, 1944, the four powers reached agreement on preliminary proposals and determined to prepare more complete suggestions for discussion at a subsequent conference of all the United Nations.

Meeting from April 25 to June 25, 1945, in San Francisco, California, representatives of 50 states participated in drafting the United Nations Charter, which was formally signed June 26. Poland was not represented at the San Francisco Conference but later signed the charter and is counted among the 51 "original" UN members. Following ratification by the five permanent members of the Security Council and most other signatories, the charter entered into force October 24, 1945. The General Assembly, convened in its first regular session January 10, 1946, accepted an invitation to establish the permanent home of the organization in the United States; privileges and immunities of the UN headquarters were defined in a Headquarters Agreement with the U.S. government signed June 26, 1947.

The membership of the UN, which increased from 51 to 60 during the period 1945–1950, remained frozen at that level for the next five years as a result of U.S.-Soviet disagreements over admission. The deadlock was broken in 1955 when the superpowers agreed on a "package" of 16 new members: four Soviet-bloc states, four Western states, and eight "uncommitted" states. Since then, states have normally been admitted with little delay. The exceptions are worth noting. The admission of the two Germanies in 1973 led to proposals for admission of the two Koreas and of the two Vietnams. Neither occurred prior to the formal unification of Vietnam in 1976, while action in regard to the two Koreas was delayed for another 15 years. On November 16, 1976, the United States used its 18th veto in the Security Council to prevent the admission of the Socialist Republic of Vietnam, having earlier in the same session, on June 23, 1976, employed its 15th veto to prevent Angola from joining. Later in the session, however, the United States relented, and Angola gained admission. In July 1977 Washington dropped its objection to Vietnamese membership as well.

With the admission of Brunei, the total membership during the 39th session of the General Assembly in 1984 stood at 159. The figure rose to 160 with the admission of Namibia in April 1990, fell back to 159 after the merger of North and South Yemen in May, advanced again to 160 via the September admission of Liechtenstein, and returned to 159 when East and West Germany merged in October. Seven new members (Estonia, Democratic People's Republic of Korea, Republic of Korea, Latvia, Lithuania, Marshall Islands, and Federated States of Micronesia) were admitted September 17, 1991, at the opening of the 46th General Assembly. Eight of the new states resulting from the collapse of the Soviet Union (Armenia, Azerbaijan, Kazakhstan, Kyrgyzstan, Moldova, Tajikistan, Turkmenistan, and Uzbekistan) were admitted March 2, 1992, along with San Marino. Russia announced the previous December that it was assuming the former USSR seat. Three of the breakaway Yugoslavian republics (Bosnia and Herzegovina, Croatia, and Slovenia) were admitted May 22. Capping an unprecedented period of expansion, Georgia became the 179th member on July 31.

The total dropped back to 178 with the dissolution of Czechoslovakia on January 1, 1993, then moved up to 180 when the Czech Republic and Slovakia joined separately on January 19. On April 8 the General Assembly approved the admission of "The former Yugoslav Republic of Macedonia," the name being carefully fashioned because of the terminological dispute between the new nation and Greece. Monaco and newly independent Eritrea were admitted May 28, followed by Andorra on July 28. Palau, which had finally achieved independence following protracted difficulty in concluding its U.S. trusteeship status, became the 185th member December 15, 1994. Kiribati, Nauru, and Tonga were admitted September 14, 1999, and Tuvalu joined September 5, 2000.

A change of government in October 2000 led to the November 1, 2000, admission of the Federal Republic of Yugoslavia (FRY). On September 22, 1992, the General Assembly, acting on the recommendation of the Security Council, decided the FRY could not automatically assume the UN membership of the former Socialist Federal Republic of Yugoslavia. The assembly informed the FRY that it would have to apply on its own for UN membership, and such an application was submitted the following day. However, no action on the request was taken by the assembly because of concern over the Federal Republic's role in the conflict in Bosnia and Herzegovina and, later, its actions regarding the ethnic Albanian population in the Yugoslavian province of Kosovo. As a consequence, the FRY was excluded from participation in the work of the General Assembly and its subsidiary bodies. Throughout this period, however, the UN membership of the Socialist Federal Republic of Yugoslavia technically remained in effect. A certain ambiguity, apparently deliberate, surrounded the issue, permitting the FRY and others to claim that it was still a member, albeit excluded from active participation, while some nations argued that the membership referred only to the antecedent Yugoslavian state. In any event, the flag of the Socialist Federal Republic of Yugoslavia, which was also the flag of the FRY, continued to fly outside UN headquarters with the flags of all other UN members, and the old nameplate remained positioned in front of an empty chair during assembly proceedings. In October 2000 the Security Council, in a resolution recommending admission of the FRY, acknowledged "that the State formerly known as the Socialist Federal Republic of Yugoslavia has ceased to exist." A representative of the FRY took up the empty seat, and a new FRY flag replaced that of the former Yugoslavia.

On September 10, 2002, the UN admitted Switzerland, which had long maintained a permanent observer mission at UN headquarters and had actively participated as a full member of the various UN specialized and related agencies. The Swiss government, having concluded that UN membership in the post–Cold War era would not jeopardize its long-standing international neutrality, sought admission after winning majority support from Swiss voters at a March 2002 referendum. Timor-Leste became the 191st member on September 27.

In 2003 the FRY became the "state union" of Serbia and Montenegro, which dissolved in June 2006, following a successful independence referendum in Montenegro. Accordingly, on June 28 the world's newest independent state, Montenegro, was admitted as the UN's 192nd member. Serbia, as the successor state to the state union, retained the UN seat held to that point by the FRY.

The Holy See (Vatican City State) has formal observer status in the General Assembly and maintains a permanent observer mission at UN headquarters. In July 2004 the UN granted the Holy See the full range of membership privileges, with the exception of voting.

Structure. The UN system can be viewed as comprising (1) the principal organs, (2) subsidiary organs established to deal with particular aspects of the organization's responsibilities, (3) a number of specialized and related agencies, and (4) a series of ad hoc global conferences to examine particularly pressing issues.

The institutional structure of the principal organs resulted from complex negotiations that attempted to balance both the conflicting claims of national sovereignty and international responsibility, and the rights of large and small states. The principle of sovereign equality of all member states is exemplified in the General Assembly; that of the special responsibility of the major powers, in the composition and procedure of the Security Council. The other principal organs included in the charter are the Economic and Social Council (ECOSOC), the Trusteeship Council (whose activity was suspended in 1994), the International Court of Justice (ICJ), and the Secretariat.

UN-related intergovernmental bodies constitute a network of Specialized Agencies established by intergovernmental agreement as legal and autonomous international entities with their own memberships and organs and which, for the purpose of "coordination," are brought "into relationship" with the UN. While sharing many of their characteristics, the International Atomic Energy Agency (IAEA) remains legally distinct from the Specialized Agencies; the World Trade Organization, which emerged from the UN-sponsored General Agreement on Tariff and Trade (GATT), has no formal association with the UN.

The proliferation of subsidiary organs can be attributed to many complex factors, including new demands and needs as more states attained independence; the effects of the Cold War; a subsequent diminution of East-West bipolarity; a greater concern with promoting economic and social development through technical assistance programs (almost entirely financed by voluntary contributions); and a resistance to any radical change in international trade patterns. For many years, the largest and most politically significant of the subordinate organs were the United Nations Conference on Trade and Development (UNCTAD) and the United Nations Industrial Development Organization (UNIDO), which were initial venues for debates, for conducting studies and presenting reports, for convening conferences and specialized meetings, and for mobilizing the opinions of nongovernmental organizations. They also provided a way for less developed states to formulate positions vis-à-vis the industrialized states. During the 1970s both became intimately involved in activities related to program implementation, and on January 1, 1986, UNIDO became the UN's 16th Specialized Agency.

One of the most important developments in the UN system has been the use of ad hoc conferences to deal with major international problems.

Security Council

Permanent Membership (5): China, France, Russia, United Kingdom, United States. (The other permanent members in late December 1991 accepted Russia's assumption of the seat previously filled by the Union of Soviet Socialist Republics.)

Nonpermanent Membership (10): Terms ending December 31, 2006: Argentina, Denmark, Greece, Japan, Tanzania; terms ending December 31, 2007: Republic of the Congo, Ghana, Qatar, Peru, and Slovakia.

Security Council: Peacekeeping Forces and Missions

In addition to the forces and missions listed below, the United Nations Command in Korea (established on June 25, 1950) remains technically in existence. The only UN member now contributing to the command is the United States, which proposed in June 1975 that it be dissolved. As of mid-2006 no formal action had been taken on the proposal.

United Nations Mission for the Referendum in Western Sahara

Mission des Nations Unies pour le Référendum dans le Sahara Ouest (MINURSO)

Established: By Security Council resolution of April 29, 1991.

Purpose: To enforce a cease-fire in the Western Sahara between Morocco and the Polisario Front, to identify those eligible to vote in the proposed self-determination referendum there, and to supervise the referendum and settlement plan.

Headquarters: Laayoune, Western Sahara.

Force Commander: Maj. Gen. Kurt Mosgaard (Denmark).

Composition: As of July 1, 2006, 192 military observers, 6 civilian police, and 27 troops from Argentina, Austria, Bangladesh, China, Croatia, Denmark, Egypt, El Salvador, France, Ghana, Greece, Guinea, Honduras, Hungary, Ireland, Italy, Kenya, Republic of Korea, Malaysia, Mongolia, Nigeria, Pakistan, Poland, Russia, Sri Lanka, and Uruguay. An additional 2,200 troops and observers had been authorized but not deployed because of the lack of progress in referendum negotiations.

United Nations Mission in Ethiopia and Eritrea (UNMEE)

Established: By Security Council resolution of July 31, 2000.

Purpose: To monitor the cessation of hostilities, the redeployment of Ethiopian and Eritrean forces, and the temporary security zone (TSZ); to chair the Military Coordination Commission formed by the UN and the Organization of African Unity; to coordinate and provide technical assistance for humanitarian mine-action activities in and around the TSZ; and to coordinate mission activities with other humanitarian and human rights activities.

Headquarters: Asmara, Eritrea, and Addis Ababa, Ethiopia.

Force Commander: Maj. Gen. Mohammad Taisar Masadeh (Jordan).

Composition: As of July 1, 2006, 3,373 military personnel, including 221 military observers, from Algeria, Austria, Bangladesh, Bosnia and Herzegovina, Bulgaria, China, Croatia, Czech Republic, Denmark, Finland, France, Gambia, Germany, Ghana, Greece, Guatemala, India, Iran, Jordan,

Kenya, Malaysia, Namibia, Nepal, Nigeria, Norway, Paraguay, Peru, Poland, Romania, Russia, South Africa, Spain, Sweden, Switzerland, Tanzania, Tunisia, Ukraine, United States, Uruguay, and Zambia.

United Nations Mission in Liberia (UNMIL)

Established: By Security Council resolution of September 19, 2003.

Purpose: To support implementation of the recent cease-fire agreement in Liberia; to support humanitarian and human rights activities; and to assist in training national police and the proposed new restructured military.

Headquarters: Monrovia, Liberia.

Force Commander: Maj. Gen. Joseph Owonibi (Nigeria).

Composition: As of July 1, 2006, 14,840 troops, 184 military observers, and 1,051 civilian police from Bangladesh, Benin, Bolivia, Brazil, Bulgaria, China, Croatia, Czech Republic, Denmark, Ecuador, Egypt, El Salvador, Ethiopia, Finland, France, Gambia, Germany, Ghana, Indonesia, Ireland, Jordan, Kenya, Republic of Korea, Kyrgyzstan, Malawi, Malaysia, Mali, Moldova, Mongolia, Namibia, Nepal, Niger, Nigeria, Pakistan, Paraguay, Peru, Philippines, Poland, Portugal, Romania, Russia, Samoa, Senegal, Serbia, South Africa, Sri Lanka, Sweden, Togo, Turkey, Uganda, Ukraine, United Kingdom, United States, Uruguay, Yemen, Zambia, and Zimbabwe.

United Nations Mission in the Sudan (UNMIS)

Established: By Security Council resolution of March 24, 2005.

Purpose: To support implementation of the peace agreement signed by the government of Sudan and the Sudanese People's Liberation Movement in January 2005; to provide humanitarian assistance; and to protect and promote human rights in Sudan.

Headquarters: Khartoum, Sudan.

Force Commander: Lt. Gen. Jasbir Lidder (India).

Composition: As of July 1, 2006, 8,034 troops, 635 military observers, and 596 civilian police from Argentina, Australia, Austria, Bangladesh, Benin, Bosnia and Herzegovina, Brazil, Burkina Fuso, Cambodia, Canada, China, Croatia, Denmark, Egypt, El Salvador, Fiji, Finland, Germany, Ghana, Greece, Guatemala, India, Indonesia, Italy, Jamaica, Jordan, Kenya, Kyrgyzstan, Malawi, Malaysia, Mali, Moldova, Mongolia, Mozambique, Namibia, Nepal, Nigeria, Norway, Pakistan, Paraguay, Peru, Philippines, Poland, Romania, Russia, Rwanda, Samoa, Spain, Sri Lanka, Sweden, Switzerland, Tanzania, Thailand, Turkey, Uganda, United Kingdom, Yemen, Zambia, and Zimbabwe.

United Nations Operation in Burundi

Opération des Nations Unies au Burundi (ONUB)

Established: By Security Council resolution of May 21, 2004.

Purpose: To help implement the Arusha Agreement negotiated by the parties to the conflict in Burundi.

Headquarters: Bujumbura, Burundi.

Force Commander: Maj. Gen. Derrick Mbuyiselo Mgwebi (South Africa).

Composition: As of July 1, 2006, 5,650 troops, 200 military observers, and 120 civilian police from Algeria, Belgium, Benin, Bolivia, Burkina Faso,

Cameroon, Chad, China, Egypt, Ethiopia, Gambia, Ghana, Guatemala, India, Jordan, Kenya, Republic of Korea, Kyrgyzstan, Malawi, Malaysia, Mali, Mozambique, Namibia, Nepal, Niger, Nigeria, Pakistan, Paraguay, Peru, Philippines, Portugal, Romania, Russia, Senegal, Serbia, South Africa, Sri Lanka, Thailand, Togo, Tunisia, Uruguay, Yemen, and Zambia.

United Nations Operation in Côte d'Ivoire

Opération des Nations Unies en Côte d'Ivoire (ONUCI)

Established: By Security Council resolution of February 27, 2004.

Purpose: To facilitate implementation of the peace agreement signed by the parties to the conflict in Côte d'Ivoire. (ONUCI was a successor to the United Nations Mission in Côte d'Ivoire [*Mission des Nations Unies en Côte d'Ivoire*—MINUCI], a political mission that had been established by the Security Council in May 2003.)

Headquarters: Abidjan, Côte d'Ivoire.

Force Commander: Maj. Gen. Gerardo Cristian Chaumont (Argentina).

Composition: As of July 1, 2006, 6,703 troops, 191 military observers, and 707 civilian police from Argentina, Bangladesh, Benin, Bolivia, Brazil, Cameroon, Canada, Central African Republic, Chad, China, Democratic Republic of the Congo, Croatia, Djibouti, Dominican Republic, Ecuador, El Salvador, France, Gambia, Ghana, Guatemala, Guinea, India, Ireland, Jordan, Kenya, Lebanon, Moldova, Morocco, Namibia, Nepal, Niger, Nigeria, Pakistan, Paraguay, Peru, Philippines, Poland, Portugal, Romania, Russia, Senegal, Serbia, Sri Lanka, Togo, Tunisia, Turkey, Uruguay, Yemen, and Zambia.

United Nations Organization Mission in the Democratic Republic of the Congo

Mission de l'Organisation des Nations Unies en République Démocratiquedu Congo
(MONUC)

Established: By Security Council resolution of November 30, 1999, which specified that MONUC would comprise the military liaison personnel authorized by a resolution of August 6, 1999. MONUC's authorized strength was increased in October 2004.

Purpose: In cooperation with the Joint Military Commission (JMC) of the states that signed the July 1999 cease-fire accord, to implement, monitor, and investigate violations of the cease-fire; to assist in the disengagement, redeployment, disarmament, demobilization, resettlement, and reintegration of combatants; to assist in planning and conducting mine-action activities; to assist in the release of prisoners of war, military captives, and remains; to facilitate humanitarian assistance and human rights monitoring, in cooperation with various organizations; and to cooperate with and provide assistance to the Facilitator of the National Dialogue.

Headquarters: Kinshasa, Democratic Republic of the Congo. Liaison offices are maintained in Addis Ababa, Ethiopia; Bujumbura, Burundi; Harare, Zimbabwe; Kampala, Uganda; Kigali, Rwanda; Lusaka, Zambia; and Windhoek, Namibia.

Force Commander: Lt. Gen. Babacar Gaye (Senegal).

Composition: As of July 1, 2006, 15,591 troops, 786 military observers, and 1,103 civilian police, from Algeria, Bangladesh, Belgium, Benin, Bolivia, Bosnia and Herzegovina, Burkina Faso, Cameroon, Canada, Chad, China, Czech Republic, Denmark, Egypt, France, Ghana, Guatemala, Guinea, India, Indonesia, Ireland, Jordan, Kenya, Madagascar, Malawi, Malaysia, Mali, Mongolia,

Morocco, Mozambique, Nepal, Netherlands, Niger, Nigeria, Pakistan, Paraguay, Peru, Poland, Romania, Russia, Senegal, Serbia, South Africa, Spain, Sri Lanka, Sweden, Switzerland, Tunisia, Ukraine, United Kingdom, Uruguay, Vanuatu, and Zambia.

Security Council: International Criminal Tribunals

In the absence of a permanent international court with jurisdiction to prosecute and try cases involving accusations of war crimes, genocide, and crimes against humanity, the Security Council established the International Criminal Tribunal for the former Yugoslavia (ICTY) in 1993 and the International Criminal Tribunal for Rwanda (ICTR) in 1994. Meeting in Rome, Italy, in 1998, a UN conference approved formation of a permanent International Criminal Court (ICC), which by April 2002 had obtained sufficient ratifications for its establishment in July.

As of August 2006 the ICTY had brought public indictments against 161 individuals, including those who had been acquitted and those whose cases had been withdrawn. Twenty-two individuals were serving sentences and 18 had completed their sentences. Fifty-three individuals were detained, nine individuals were on provisional release, and six indicted individuals remained at large.

Biljana Plavšić, former president of the Serb Republic of Bosnia and Herzegovina, was one of the most prominent people to surrender. On November 2, 2002, she pleaded guilty to one count of a crime against humanity for political, racial, and religious persecution, and on February 27, 2003, she was sentenced to 11 years in prison. By far the most prominent figure turned over to the court by national forces was former Yugoslav president Slobodan Milošević, who died on March 11, 2006, during his trial.

As of July 2006 the ICTR had brought public indictments against some 75 individuals and had arrested more than 50 people. Twenty-five cases had reached their conclusion (with 22 convictions),

and 25 trials were in progress. The highest-ranking defendant, former Rwandan prime minister Jean Kambanda, pleaded guilty to genocide in 1998 and was sentenced to life in prison.

In August 2000 the Security Council unanimously indicated its support for forming a third war crimes tribunal, for Sierra Leone, that began its proceedings in 2003, although not as a subsidiary body of the Security Council. A similar joint criminal tribunal in Cambodia to prosecute and try former *Khmers Rouges* is expected to begin its proceedings in 2007.

International Criminal Tribunal for Rwanda (ICTR)

Tribunal Pénal International pour le Rwanda (French)
Urukiko Nshinjabyaha Mpuzamahanga Rwagenewe u Rwanda (Kinyarwanda)

Formal Name: International Criminal Tribunal for the Prosecution of Persons Responsible for Genocide and Other Serious Violations of International Humanitarian Law Committed in the Territory of Rwanda and Rwandan Citizens Responsible for Genocide and Other Such Violations Committed in the Territory of Neighboring States, between 1 January 1994 and 31 December 1994.

Established: By Security Council resolution of November 8, 1994.

Purpose: To prosecute crimes allegedly committed by Rwandans and others in Rwanda, and by Rwandans in neighboring states, between January 1, 1994, and December 31, 1994, the subject offenses being violations of the 1949 Geneva Conventions, genocide, and crimes against humanity.

Headquarters: Arusha, Tanzania. The office of the prosecutor is located in Kigali, Rwanda.

Chief Prosecutor: Hassan Bubacar Jallow (Gambia).

Permanent Judges: Erik Møse (Norway, President), Arlette Ramarosen (Madagascar, Vice President), Charles Michael Dennis Byron (St. Kitts and Nevis), Sergei Alekseevich Egorov (Russia), Mehmet Güney (Turkey), Khalida Rachid Khan (Pakistan), Liu Daqun (China), Theodor Meron (United States), Fausto Pocar (Italy), Jai Ram Reddy (Fiji), Inés Mónica Weinberg de Roca (Argentina), Wolfgang Schomburg (Germany), William Sekule (Tanzania), Mohamed Shahabuddeen (Guyana), Joseph Asoka Nihal De Silva (Sri Lanka), and Andrésia Vaz (Senegal). There are also nine *ad litem* judges.

Registrar: Adama Dieng (Senegal).

Economic and Social Council: Regional Commissions

The primary aim of the five Regional Commissions, which report annually to ECOSOC, is to assist in raising the level of economic activity in their respective regions and to maintain and strengthen the economic relations of the states in each region, both among themselves and with others. The commissions adopt their own procedural rules, including how they select officers. Each commission is headed by an executive secretary, who holds the rank of under secretary of the UN, while their Secretariats are integral parts of the overall United Nations Secretariat.

The commissions are empowered to make recommendations directly to member governments and to Specialized Agencies of the United Nations, but no action can be taken in respect to any state without the agreement of that state.

Economic Commission for Africa (ECA)

Established: April 29, 1958.

Purpose: To "initiate and participate in measures for facilitating concerted action for the economic development of Africa, including its social aspects, with a view to raising the level of economic activity and levels of living in Africa, and for maintaining and strengthening the economic relations of countries and territories of Africa, both among themselves and with other countries of the world."

Headquarters: Addis Ababa, Ethiopia.

Principal Subsidiary Organs: Conference of African Ministers of Finance Planning and Economic Development; Sectoral Ministerial Conferences; Technical Preparatory Committee of the Whole; Follow-up Committee on the Conference of Ministers; seven expert-level committees: Women in Development, Development Information, Sustainable Development, Human Development and Civil Society, Industry and Private Sector Development, Natural Resources and Science and Technology, Regional Cooperation and Integration; Secretariat. The Secretariat includes an Office of Policy Planning and Resource Management and six substantive divisions: African Center for Gender and Development, Development Information Services, Development Policy Management, Economic and Social Policy, Sustainable Development, and Trade and Regional Integration. Subregional Development Centers are located in Tangier, Morocco, for Northern Africa; Kigali, Rwanda, for Eastern Africa; Yaoundé, Cameroon, for Central Africa; Niamey, Niger, for Western Africa; and Lusaka, Zambia, for Southern Africa.

Executive Secretary: Abdoulie Janneh (Gambia).

Membership (53): Algeria, Angola, Benin, Botswana, Burkina Faso, Burundi, Cameroon, Cape Verde Islands, Central African Republic, Chad, Comoro Islands, Democratic Republic of the Congo, Republic of the Congo, Côte d'Ivoire, Djibouti, Egypt, Equatorial Guinea, Eritrea, Ethiopia, Gabon, Gambia, Ghana, Guinea, Guinea-Bissau, Kenya, Lesotho, Liberia, Libya, Madagascar, Malawi, Mali, Mauritania, Mauritius, Morocco, Mozambique, Namibia, Niger, Nigeria, Rwanda, Sao Tome and Principe, Senegal, Seychelles, Sierra Leone, Somalia, South Africa, Sudan, Swaziland,

Tanzania, Togo, Tunisia, Uganda, Zambia, Zimbabwe. (Switzerland also participates in a consultative capacity.)

Recent activities. In early 1993 ECA Executive Director Layashi Yaker, a former Algerian trade minister, joined the heads of the Organization of African Unity (OAU) and the African Development Bank in criticizing the industrialized world's handling of the African debt problem, arguing that many of the continent's countries had made "bold efforts to reform and adjust their economies" but were still facing negative resource flows. At the same time, the trio reproached national leaders in Africa for not having pursued regional economic integration with sufficient vigor. In 1994 Yaker told African finance ministers that the role of government in certain economic areas needed to be strengthened rather than weakened, as external donors had insisted. In particular, "public investment" was required in infrastructure and the development of agricultural technology, Yaker argued, while a "close partnership" was needed between governments and other major institutions in defining national economic strategies. Furthermore, in his end-of-the-year analysis of the continent's economic affairs, Yaker renewed his criticism of Western donors for failing to completely honor their commitments under the UN's New Agenda for Development of Africa in the 1990s.

In 1995 Yaker was succeeded as ECA executive secretary by K. Y. Amoako of Ghana, who stressed the need for national governments to provide "a sound and secure environment for private enterprise" in order to attract additional foreign aid. Amoako, a longtime employee of the World Bank, also launched a wide-ranging evaluation and, ultimately, reorganization of ECA operations to improve efficiency and sharpen the ECA's focus. Subsequently, in the spring of 1996, the ECA was given a number of responsibilities in the new $25 billion UN System-Wide Special Initiative on Africa, launched by the World Bank, a number of other UN-related agencies, and the OAU. Among other things, the initiative was designed to expand basic education and health care on the continent, promote

"better governance," and improve water and food security. The reforms sought to reduce the number of meetings and reports, to provide greater cooperation with other important actors in Africa, to encourage more technical support for members as well as greater interaction with them, to stimulate the formation of "strategic partnerships," and to refocus the ECA from nine subprograms covering 21 areas to "five core programs and two cross-cutting themes." The five core programs were "facilitating economic and social policy analysis, ensuring food security and sustainable development, harnessing information for development, promoting regional cooperation and integration, and strengthening development management." The two themes, permeating all five core programs, were fostering the leadership and empowerment of women and strengthening the ECA's capacities. In 1997 the ECA's five Multinational Programming and Operational Centers (MULPOCs) were reorganized as Subregional Development Centers (SRDCs) with an expanded mission and a planned increase in their share of the organization's personnel and budget. The SRDCs were established to facilitate planning, integration, development, cooperation, and information gathering and dissemination at national and regional levels.

Recent ECA initiatives have included sponsorship of African Development Forums, the first of which convened in Addis Ababa in October 1999. Looking toward the 2001 Third UN Conference on Least Developed Countries (LDCs), in November 2000 Executive Director Amoako proposed a "New Global Compact with Africa" as a contribution to the ongoing debate over how best to effect debt relief and expand aid to the developing world. In return for increased development assistance, debt relief under a reformed international financial system, and improved market access, "Africa should be able to put in place the necessary political and economic reforms to ensure that their economies take off," Amoako said. He has also advocated, with increasing urgency, a coordinated, expanded program to fight the HIV/AIDS epidemic, noting, during a speech to the April 2001 OAU Special Summit on HIV/AIDS and Related Infectious

Diseases, held in Abuja, Nigeria, that health is a prerequisite for development and that "without a healthy population, economic growth is going to remain a mirage."

In 2002 the ECA reported that growth in Africa was falling short of expectations, and the commission endorsed the recently proposed New Partnership for Africa's Development (NEPAD). The ECA proposed a "ground up" approach for that initiative, whereby attention would first focus on development at the national level before progressing to the subregional, regional, and continental levels.

ECA activity in 2003–2005 included criticism of increased U.S. subsidies for U.S. agricultural products. The commission called for revitalization of negotiations in the World Trade Organization that would provide better access to global markets for African commodities. The ECA also noted that the much-publicized debt relief initiative of recent years had to date helped only a handful of African countries. Meanwhile, in mid-2005 the ECA urged its members to deregulate and otherwise reform their communication sectors in order to participate in the "information economy."

WEST AFRICAN ECONOMIC AND MONETARY UNION (UEMOA)

Union Economique et Monétaire Ouest-Africaine

Established: By treaty signed in Dakar, Senegal, on January 10, 1994, by the seven West African countries in the CFA franc monetary zone, with effect from August 1.

Purpose: To coordinate the economic policies of the member states, particularly with regard to human resources, territorial management, agriculture, energy, industry, mines, transportation, infrastructure, and telecommunications; to promote regional monetary and economic integration, coordinated trade policies, and a common external tariff; to create a common market based on the free circulation of people, goods, services, and capital.

Headquarters: Ouagadougou, Burkina Faso.

Principal Organs: Conference of Heads of State and Government, Council of Ministers, Commission, Court of Justice, Court of Accounts, Interparliamentary Committee.

President of the Commission: Soumaila Cissé (Mali).

Membership (8): Benin, Burkina Faso, Côte d'Ivoire, Guinea-Bissau, Mali, Niger, Senegal, Togo.

Official Language: French.

Origin and development. The UEMOA was established in 1994 as successor to the West African Economic Community (*Communauté Economique de l'Afrique de l'Ouest*—CEAO). The CEAO, which traced its origins to an earlier West African Customs and Economic Union (*Union Douanière et Economique de l'Afrique de l'Ouest*—UDEAO), had been established under a treaty adopted June 3, 1972 in Bamako, Mali, and related protocols signed April 16–17, 1973, in Abidjan, Côte d'Ivoire. CEAO signatory states included Benin (then Dahomey), Burkina Faso (then Upper Volta), Côte d'Ivoire, Mali, Mauritania, Niger, and Senegal; the organization came into formal existence on January 1, 1974, although it did not become fully operational until later that year. In addition to advancing cooperation in such sectors as agriculture, animal husbandry, fishing, industry, transport, communications, and tourism, the CEAO was envisaged as a step toward establishing a regional common market.

Constrained by such factors as income disparities among its members, rising trade barriers enacted by national legislatures, and huge payment arrears, by 1993 the union was described as "virtually moribund." It had also been damaged in the 1980s by a financial scandal involving misappropriations from its Solidarity and Intervention Fund (Fosidec), which had been created in 1977 to aid development in poorer member states.

By the early 1990s the larger Economic Community of West African States (ECOWAS), to which all the CEAO members also belonged, was pushing for establishment of a single West African economic community that would absorb other subregional groupings. Chafing at ECOWAS's presumption of regional preeminence, the francophone CEAO instead moved toward creation of an economic and monetary authority that would function more effectively than the CEAO. Accordingly, at a CEAO summit in January 1994 the participating states signed the treaty establishing the West African Economic and Monetary Union (UEMOA), which superseded the CEAO on August 1, following completion of the requisite ratifications. Guinea-Bissau became the eighth UEMOA member on May 2, 1997.

Structure. The UEMOA's principal policymaking organ is the Conference of Heads of State and Government, which meets annually. Supporting organs include a Council of Ministers; a Court of Justice; an administrative Commission, which is headed by a president elected for a four-year term; and an Interparliamentary Committee. The last was officially installed March 1998 in Bamako, Mali, as an interim step toward creation of a community parliament. Also included within the UEMOA structure is the pre-existing West African Monetary Union (*Union Monétaire Ouest-Africaine*—UMOA), which was established by a treaty of November 1973 to oversee financial institutions in the West African CFA franc zone. Affiliated with the UEMOA as specialized autonomous institutions are the Central Bank of West African States (*Banque Centrale des Etats de l'Afrique de l'Ouest*—BCEAO) and the West African Development Bank (*Banque Ouest-Africaine de Développement*—BOAD; see separate entry under Regional Development Banks).

Activities. At its first meeting held May 1996 in Ouagadougou, Burkina Faso, the Conference of Heads of State and Government called for establishment of a customs union, initially with a target date of January 1998. Although that target was subsequently pushed back by two years, the UEMOA moved progressively toward the twin goals of reducing internal tariffs and establishing a common external tariff. In July 1996 the union initiated a transitional preferential tariff scheme that eliminated internal levies on locally produced agricultural goods and crafts while reducing by 30 percent import duties on industrial products originating within the union. The second UEMOA summit held June 1997 in Lomé, Togo, was quickly followed by a further cut of 30 percent on industrial levies. The summit had also agreed to reorganize the Abidjan stock exchange as a regional exchange, the *Bourse Régionale des Valeurs Mobilières* (BRVM).

Meeting at Lomé, the Conference of Heads of State and Government convened twice in 1999, in January and December. In January a principal focus was regional indebtedness, with the session's final communiqué noting that, despite successful national efforts to improve government finances, growth and development continued to be hampered by external debt servicing. In December the attendees adopted a Common Industrial Policy and a Convergence, Stability, Growth, and Solidarity Pact. Shortly thereafter, on January 1, 2000, in perhaps the UEMOA's most significant accomplishment to date, the member states, with the exception of politically troubled Guinea-Bissau, eliminated tariffs on all internally produced goods and instituted a common external tariff (CET) capped at 22 percent. In the following two years it also adopted a code governing transparency of public financing, and common policies with regard to energy and agriculture. At the same time, it moved toward accommodation with ECOWAS, in anticipation of the formation of a second regional monetary union by anglophone non-UEMOA ECOWAS members. Although "macroeconomic and political instability" in the region led ECOWAS to delay introducing the second monetary zone until at least 2005, the ultimate goal remains that of merging the parallel unions into a single West African monetary zone.

A growing convergence of views among the UEMOA members and the other ECOWAS countries has also been evident in other multilateral arenas. For example, following conclusion in June 2000 of the Cotonou Agreement between the European Union (EU) and the associated African, Caribbean, and Pacific (ACP) countries, the members' trade and finance ministers collaborated on preparations for negotiating an Economic Partnership Agreement with the EU. A similar strategy was adopted toward World Trade Organization discussions. Concurrently, the UEMOA reached agreement with the United States on improving trade and investment relations and pursued similar arrangements with several Northern African countries. In addition, the UEMOA actively sought to improve world market conditions for a leading regional commodity, cotton, and took steps to prevent use of the CFA franc, with its direct link to the euro, in money laundering and the financing of terrorism.

At the January 29, 2003, Conference of Heads of State and Government in Dakar, Senegal, discussions were dominated by the political crisis that had erupted in Côte d'Ivoire in 2002. While noting such accomplishments as liberalized intracommunity commerce and progress in harmonizing fiscal legislation, statistics, and macroeconomic policies, the conference also cited a number of deficiencies, including delays in adopting a uniform investment code. The conference called for accelerating structural and institutional reforms as well as measures that would permit freedom of movement, liberalize trade in services as well as goods, and establish community-wide rights of residence and entrepreneurship. In other business, the conference decided to move forward with creation of a Union Parliament.

In the following year, Ivorian instability continued to have a significant impact on the other UEMOA states, not only because Côte d'Ivoire's econ-omy had previously accounted for 40–50 percent of the union's collective GDP, but also because the hostilities had deprived landlocked Burkino Faso, Mali, and Niger of access to their principal seaport, Abidjan. As a consequence, in 2002 the economic growth rate within the union had dropped to 2.7 percent, down from the 3.8 percent of 2001 and well below the 2002 projection of 4.4 percent.

At its January 10, 2004, session in Niamey, the conference reaffirmed regional integration as the cornerstone of development and reiterated its commitment to creation of a customs union and common market. To accelerate growth and promote sustainable development, the attendees adopted a Regional Economic Program (*Programme Economique Régional*—PER) with an emphasis on modernizing infrastructure and reducing cost factors in production. The conference directed the commission, the BCEAO, and the BOAD to seek financing necessary to carry out the PER. Development of agriculture, transportation, and information and communication technology was also given priority.

In its annual report for 2005, UEMOA noted an improved rate of economic growth among its members, 3.6 percent in 2005 as against 3.2 percent in 2004. The report gave credit chiefly to improved agricultural practices. Growth was uneven however, ranging from 7.5 percent for Burkina Faso to 1 percent for Côte d'Ivoire and Togo.

PART FOUR

APPENDIXES

APPENDIX A: CHRONOLOGY OF MAJOR AFRICAN EVENTS, 2006

ALGERIA

March. Security Forces Remain on Offensive. Security forces launch a campaign against "Islamist militants" (officially estimated to be fewer than 800) in remote mountainous regions.

May 24. Prime Minister Resigns. Prime Minister Ahmed Ouyahia (National Democratic Rally) resigns. He is succeeded the same day by Abdelaziz Belkhadem (National Liberation Front), who announces a largely unchanged cabinet on May 25.

July. Paris Club Debt Payments Set. Algeria repays half of its $8 billion debt to the international Paris Club of official creditors and signs bilateral accords with other Paris Club member countries for early repayment.

September. Exiled FIS Leader Returns, Seeks Peace. Rabeh Kebir of the banned Islamic Salvation Front, saying he wants to "bolster peace," returns from self-imposed exiled in Germany and asks militants to disarm.

ANGOLA

January. Elections Postponed. The constitution remains in the hands of the assembly, and it is widely reported that no elections will take place until 2007, after President José Eduardo dos Santos backs away from his initial affirmation that elections would be held in 2006.

August. Thousands Die in Cholera Epidemic. The World Health Organization reports that more than 2,000 have died in the six-month cholera epidemic that has now reached all of the country's 18 provinces.

October. Voter Registration Begins. The official campaign for November voter registration begins, with an election date still unspecified.

BENIN

March 19. New President Elected. President Boni Yayi wins a landslide victory in second-round balloting after leading 26 candidates in first-round balloting on March 5.

BOTSWANA

October. "Diamonds for Development" Campaign Under Way. Government officials take their positive message about the diamond industry, long associated with conflict in Africa, to the UN and other international organizations. President Festus Mogae estimates that diamond revenue to Botswana has enabled every child in the country under the age of 13 to receive free education.

BURKINA FASO

August. Key Opposition Leader Leaves Politics. Joseph Ki-Zerbo, a leading opposition figure and one of the fiercest critics of the Compaoré administration, retires from politics, citing health reasons.

BURUNDI

April. UN Plans to Withdraw Peacekeepers. The UN announces that it will gradually withdraw its peacekeepers during the year.

September. President, Rebels Sign Cease-Fire Agreement. President Pierre Nkurunziza signs a cease-fire agreement with Agathon Rwasa, the leader of the National Forces of Liberation (FNL) rebel holdouts. Negotiations were still pending regarding the final disarmament of the FNL and its conversion into a political party.

October. Rebel Activity Continues. Rebel activity reportedly continues in the north and southwest. Rebels seek release of all political prisoners.

CAMEROON

April. Cameroon Receives Debt Relief. Cameroon reaches its completion point of the Heavily Indebted Poor Countries initiative.

September 22. Cabinet Reshuffled. President Paul Biya reshuffles the cabinet, drawing criticism for not trimming or merging some of the more than 60 ministerial positions.

CAPE VERDE

January 22. Ruling Party Retains Majority. The African Party for the Independence of Cape Verde (PAICV) wins 41 of 72 seats in National People's Assembly balloting.

February 12. President Reelected. Gen. (Ret.) Verona Rodrigues Pires (PAICV) is reelected to another five-year term. Pires receives 50.98 percent of the vote, defeating former prime minister and opposition leader Carlos Alberto Wahnon de Carvalho Veiga, who receives 49.02 percent.

September 14. Private TV Stations Get a Tryout. Cape Verde agrees to a two-month trial period to allow broadcast licenses for privately owned television stations after thousands protest the closing of an independent station a month earlier.

CENTRAL AFRICAN REPUBLIC

January 1. President Bozizé Rules by Decree. Parliament grants the president, Gen. François Bozizé, authority to rule by decree for three months, beginning January 1, to deal with growing violence and economic challenges. Meanwhile, the International Monetary Fund approves $10.2 million in emergency assistance to help stabilize the economy.

February 1. Agreement Allows Repatriation. The CAR signs an agreement with Sudan to provide for the return of 10,000 Sudanese refugees who had lived in the CAR for the past 16 years. The agreement sets the legal framework for voluntary repatriation.

August 18. Rebel Leader Sentenced to Death. Jean-Jacques Larmassoum, who claimed former president Ange-Félix Patassé engaged him to plot to return Patassé to power, is sentenced to death on conspiracy and other charges.

August 30. Former President Convicted in Absentia. Former president Ange-Félix Patassé, who is in exile in Togo, is sentenced to 20 years of hard labor and fined $12,000 after being convicted in absentia of fraud.

September 29. Repatriation Resumes. The CAR allows the UN to resume voluntary repatriation of thousands of refugees to southern Sudan. The effort had been suspended because of extreme violence in the region.

CHAD

March. Soldiers Arrested in Alleged Assassination Plot. More than 100 soldiers are arrested after an alleged attempt to shoot down President Idriss Déby's airplane. In the ensuing unrest, more than 300 are killed in fighting between government troops and rebel insurgents from the Sudanese border.

May 3. President Reelected. President Déby is reelected for another five-year term.

October. UN Cites Urgent Need for Relocations. The United Nations High Commissioner for

Refugees says continued fighting in northeastern Chad and neighboring Darfur, Sudan, will mean moving another 40,000 Sudanese refugees further inside Chad. In response to accusations by the Sudanese government, Chadian officials deny any involvement in fighting between the Sudanese army and rebels.

COMORO ISLANDS

May 14. President Reelected. Ahmed Abdallah Mohamed Sambi is reelected for a four-year term in a unionwide runoff election. The president subsequently reasserts that his country has sovereignty over the disputed French island of Mayotte.

CONGO, DEMOCRATIC REPUBLIC OF THE

February 18. New Constitution Promulgated. President Joseph Kabila signs a new constitution.

June 12. Troops Deployed in Advance of Elections. The EU announces it will send 2,000 troops to safeguard the first democratic elections in the Democratic Republic of the Congo in 40 years. Approximately 17,000 UN peacekeepers are already present.

July 27. Militia Disarms. The three main militia groups in the troubled eastern province of Ituri agree to disarm in exchange for amnesty and army positions.

July 30. Landmark Elections Held. In first-round balloting for the first democratically elected president, incumbent Joseph Kabila wins 44.81 percent of the vote. In second place, with 20.03 percent of the vote, is Vice President Jean-Pierre Bemba of the Movement for the Liberation of the Congo (MLC). In National Assembly balloting on the same day, the People's Party for Reconstruction and Democracy wins 111 of 500 seats, followed by the MLC with 64. The second and final round is set for October 29.

September 20; October 3. Thousands Flee Violence. Armed gangs force approximately 700 peo-

ple to flee the northeast in September, while at least 1,000 flee the area in October following fighting between army forces and tribal warriors.

CONGO, REPUBLIC OF THE

January 25. Congo Leads African Union. The Republic of the Congo is chosen over Sudan to head the African Union as a result of opposition to the situation in Darfur.

March 9. Congo Debt Relief Approved. The World Bank and the International Monetary Fund determine that the Republic of the Congo qualifies for several billion dollars in debt relief under the Heavily Indebted Poor Countries initiative.

CÔTE D'IVOIRE

January. Withdrawal of Assembly Support Prompts Protests. The International Working Group (IWG) established in 2005 by the UN announces it will not endorse the proposed extension of the mandate of the current assembly, a primary source of support for President Laurent Gbagbo. Protests follow, including the occupation of UN headquarters in Abidjan. Gbagbo later extends assembly mandate; the IWG differs but takes no action.

February. Peace Talks Lead to Promise of Elections. Various factions reach a tentative agreement to hold elections in October. The UN bolsters its peacekeeping mission.

April. Debt Relief Approved. Côte D'Ivoire qualifies for International Monetary Fund and World Bank debt relief.

October 6. Talks Under Way to Resolve Political Crisis. West African leaders begin talks in an effort to break the political deadlock. At issue is the status of President Laurent Gbagbo. Elections tentatively set for October do not take place as rebels fail to disarm and the government halts the identification of undocumented Ivorians.

October 18. Transition Period to Be Extended. The African Union (AU), in accordance with the UN, recommends that Côte d'Ivoire's current transition be extended for 12 more months, with President Laurent Gbagbo remaining in office despite rebel and opposition leaders insisting he step down. The AU also recommends that control of the army be transferred to Prime Minister Charles Konan Banny. The recommendations are to be worked into a new resolution by the UN Security Council.

DJIBOUTI

March 10 and 31. Local Elections Boost President's Power. In regional and communal elections, the Popular Rally for Progress wins overwhelming victories, further solidifying the president's power down to the local level.

May. Drought Continues to Plague Djibouti. Drought is a major concern in the Horn of Africa during most of 2006, prompting countries worldwide to donate hundreds of millions of dollars as the UN makes repeated urgent requests for aid.

EGYPT

February 14. Local Elections Delayed Two Years. President Husni Mubarak postpones local council elections scheduled for April, saying this will provide time to enact laws for greater decentralization. The move is also seen as an effort to block the growing influence of the Muslim Brotherhood, an Islamic group (represented in parliament) that was expected to gain more support in local elections.

April 24. Terrorist Explosions Again Hit Sinai. Bomb explosions allegedly executed by the Islamic group Jamaat al-Tawhid wal-Jihad (Monotheism and Holy War) kill at least 24 people and wound more than 60 in Egypt's southern Sinai resort of Dahab. Israel closes its border with Egypt in response. The explosions mark the third attack in two years at resorts on the Sinai Peninsula.

May 19. "Unprecedented" Security at Sinai Conference. Security forces swarm Sharm el-Sheik on the Sinai Peninsula in preparation for World Economic Forum.

August. Egypt Praises Hezbollah. Egyptian leaders praise *Hezbollah* guerrillas for the way they fought the Israelis after *Hezbollah* members crossed the border and kidnapped two Israeli soldiers, igniting a war in July. Egypt also supplies humanitarian aid to war-torn Lebanon.

EQUATORIAL GUINEA

August 10. Prime Minister, Cabinet Resign. After having been criticized for poor performance by President Teodoro Obiang, Prime Minister Miguel Abia Biteo Borico and the entire cabinet resign. The president subsequently appoints Ricardo Mangue Obama Nfube (Democratic Party of Equatorial Guinea) to head a new cabinet (appointed August 16).

ERITREA

May. Peacekeeping Scaled Back. The UN Security Council cuts its peacekeeping mission for Eritrea and Ethiopia by 1,000 soldiers and extends the mission by only four months instead of the normal six months.

October 18. Eritrea Reportedly Breaches Security Zone. The UN condemns Eritrea's reported incursion into the buffer zone between Eritrea and Ethiopia.

ETHIOPIA

May. Hundreds Face Trial on Treason Charges. Trials of approximately 100 detainees begin despite calls for President Meles Zenawi to adopt a more conciliatory stance toward the protesters, who include journalists and opposition leaders. Most are charged with treason and face possible death sentences.

May. Border Talks End in Deadlock. Eritrea's reported refusal to lift restrictions on UN peacekeepers halts talks between Ethiopia and Eritrea on resuming the demarcation of their common border.

August 16. Hundreds Die in Floods. Flooding from 11 days of rain brings devastation. The UN focuses rescue efforts in the south, where more than half of the 600 deaths occurred.

October 20. Border Security Unstable. Tensions increase along the disputed border between Eritrea and Ethiopia after Eritrea moves approximately 1,500 troops to the area, according to UN officials.

GABON

January 20. New Prime Minister Appointed. President El Hadj Omar Bongo Ondimba appoints Jean Eyéghe Ndong (Gabonese Democratic Party) as prime minister.

October. President to Seek Reelection. President Bongo announces he will seek another term in the December election.

GAMBIA

January. Pay Raise for Government Workers Prompts Economic Concerns. President Yahya Jammeh announces an unbudgeted 10 percent salary increase for all government workers in a move that raises concerns about economic stability.

March. Arrest Made in Coup Plot. A former army chief is arrested after an alleged attempted coup d'état.

August. Refugees Pour into Gambia. Thousands of refugees from Senegal's southern Casamance region flee to Gambia to escape fighting between Senegalese forces and Casamance separatists.

September 22. President Reelected. President Jammeh (Alliance for Patriotic Reorientation and Construction) is reelected to another five-year term with 67.3 percent of the vote.

GHANA

February. Gold Project Gets Financing. The World Bank approves a $75 million loan for a gold-producing project that is projected to generate between $300 million and $700 million for the country over the next two decades.

GUINEA

April 5. President Dismisses Prime Minister. President Lansana Conté dismisses Prime Minister Cellou Dalein Diallo for alleged gross misconduct.

May 29. President Reshuffles Cabinet; Prime Minister Post Vacant. President Conté reshuffles the cabinet, creating six new, large ministries but leaving the post of prime minister vacant.

GUINEA-BISSAU

April. Offensive Resumes against Rebels. The army resumes its offensive against Casamance rebels along the border with Senegal, resulting in approximately 12,000 civilians fleeing the border region and prompting calls for a cease-fire by the UN.

May. UN Appeals for Aid for Farmers. The UN appeals for $3.6 million to help those in northern Guinea-Bissau who were cut off from the rest of the country by land mines, leaving farmers unable to get to the cashew fields in time for the harvest.

Oct. 3. UN Chief Says Guinea-Bissau Risks Setback. UN secretary-general Kofi Annan says in a report that, although Guinea-Bissau has made some progress toward political reconciliation, the country's poverty and political tensions continue to make it vulnerable to the risk of a major setback.

KENYA

February. Corruption Scandal Rocks Government. Three cabinet ministers resign in the wake of a report alleging that up to 30 members of the government had participated in a phony contracts scheme.

March 2. Government Orders Raid of Media. The Kenyan government orders a police raid of a newspaper and its sister television station, outlets critical of President Emilio Mwai Kibaki's handling of recent corruption scandals. The shutdown is only temporarily sustainable.

April 10. Lawmakers Die in Military Cargo Plane Crash. Five members of parliament are among those killed in an airplane crash in the country's north. They were on a peace mission regarding ethnic tensions in an area north of Nairobi.

July 24. Elections Disputed. By-elections to replace the five members of parliament who were killed are hotly contested by the National Rainbow Coalition of Kenya, among others, and are also marred by charges of vote buying.

September. Urgent Aid Requested as Drought Continues. International aid agencies issue urgent appeals for aid as drought continues and 3 million people face starvation.

LESOTHO

October. New Flag Unfurled. On the 40th anniversary of its independence from Britain, Lesotho unveils a new flag.

LIBERIA

January 16. New Government Installed. The country's new government replaces transitional government following elections in late 2005.

March 25. Taylor Extradited. Nigeria honors a request to extradite former president Charles Taylor to stand trial before the UN-backed Special Court for Sierra Leone on charges of crimes against humanity.

April 11. Liberia Qualifies for Debt Relief. With international debt of $3.2 billion, Liberia qualifies for debt relief under the Heavily Indebted Poor Countries initiative, the International Monetary Fund announces.

June. Taylor to Be Tried at The Hague. The International Court of Justice at The Hague agrees to host Taylor's war crimes trial. The court in Sierra Leone, fearing renewed tensions in the region, had asked that the trial be moved.

July 24. Electricity Restored. Fulfilling a promise made at her inauguration, President Ellen Johnson-Sirleaf turns on street lights in Monrovia, which had been without electricity for 15 years.

October 20. Sanctions Lifted. The UN Security Council announces it will relax trade sanctions it imposed on Liberia's timber in 2003. Earlier in the year the Security Council had partially lifted an embargo on the importation of arms to Liberia.

LIBYA

March 5. Prime Minister Appointed. Al-Baghdadi Ali al-Mahmudi is appointed as secretary general of the General People's Committee (prime minister) by the General People's Congress. The cabinet is reshuffled, with six new secretaries added.

May 15. United States Restores Full Diplomatic Ties. The United States restores full diplomatic relations with Libya and removes Libya from its list of state sponsors of terror. Diplomatic ties had been severed since 1980.

October. Arms Contracts Near. Reports indicate that Libya and France are close to reaching an agreement on arms sales to Libya.

MADAGASCAR

March. Protests Canceled. Major rallies by opposition groups seeking amnesty for those arrested in the 2001–2002 conflict are canceled after the government deploys riot police in the capital.

May 10. New Presidential Election Set. Madagascar's high court upholds President Marc Ravalomanana's recommendation to hold new presidential balloting on December 3.

September 4. Opposition Blasts "Unconstitutional" Election Plan. The opposition demands that President Ravalomanana resign, claiming he has circumvented the constitution by organizing elections before the end of the constitutional term.

MALAWI

February. High Court Overrules President's Attempt to Dismiss Vice President. The high court rules that President Bingu wa Mutharika lacks the constitutional authority to dismiss Vice President

Cassim Chilumpha on charges related to undermining the government.

April. Chilumpha Arrested. Chilumpha, accused of plotting to assassinate Mutharika, is arrested on treason charges.

April. Aid Program Approved. Citing economic progress, the International Monetary Fund approves a three-year aid program.

July 27. Former President Arrested. The Anti-Corruption Bureau charges former president Bakili Muluzi with 42 counts of corruption, fraud, and theft.

September. Debt Canceled. Malawi qualifies for debt relief under the Heavily Indebted Poor Countries initiative.

MALI

January. Mali, China Agree on Economic Pact. Mali signs a broad economic agreement with China. Mali will export more cotton to China; in exchange, China will expand investment in Mali's agriculture, tourism, and telecommunications sectors.

May. "Taureg Issue" Resurfaces. Taureg fighters launch attacks on several cities and military bases in the north.

July. Rebels Agree to Halt Fighting. Taureg rebels agree to stop their militancy in return for intensified government investment in the northern region.

MAURITANIA

February. EU Aids Transitional Government. The European union offers $7 million to help with the government transition following a bloodless coup in 2005.

June 25. Constitutional Amendments Approved. In a referendum, voters overwhelmingly approve amendments proposed by the transitional government to limit a president to two terms of five years each and set a maximum age limit of 75 for a president.

MAURITIUS

October. Preferential Trade Agreement Readied with India. India and Mauritius are poised to sign a preferential trade agreement, which would go into effect in 2007.

MOROCCO

January. Free Trade Agreement Under Way. Morocco's free trade agreement with the United States, negotiated in 2004, goes into effect.

February. U.S. Praises Counterterrorism Efforts. U.S. secretary of defense Donald Rumsfeld visits Morocco and praises King Mohamed VI for his cooperation with U.S. counterterrorism efforts.

MOZAMBIQUE

April. No Agreement on Electoral Reforms. A bipartisan assembly commission, established in 2005 to propose electoral law reforms, disbands without reaching agreement.

July 1. New Currency Introduced. A "new metical" is introduced, but both old and new meticals will be legal tender through the end of the year.

July 3. Debt Canceled. The World Bank cancels most of Mozambique's debt under a plan agreed on by the Group of Eight (G-8) nations at a 2005 summit.

NAMIBIA

June 17. Government Responds to Polio Outbreak. The government begins widespread immunization campaigns (through August) to eradicate an outbreak of polio.

NIGER

January. Food Crisis Prompts Urgent Appeal for Aid. The International Monetary Fund joins an urgent appeal for donor assistance to alleviate the food crisis in Niger.

NIGERIA

January. Turmoil Disrupts Oil-Rich Niger Delta Region. Two groups claim responsibility for several attacks on pipelines and kidnappings designed to disrupt production and to prompt compensation for environmental damage done by oil companies in the state of Bayelsa.

March 25. Nigeria Extradites Former Liberian President. At the request of Liberian president Ellen Johnson-Sirleaf, Nigeria arrests Charles Taylor, turning him over to a special UN court for trial on charges of crimes against humanity.

April 21. Nigeria Pays Off International Debt. Capitalizing on high oil prices, Nigeria makes its final installment payment to the Paris Club of creditor nations.

May. Senate Rejects Changes to Constitution. The Senate rejects proposed changes to the constitution, which would have allowed President Olusegun Obasanjo to stand for a third term in 2007.

June. Court Orders Oil Company to Pay "Reparations." One of the groups that claimed responsibility for pipeline attacks and kidnappings declares a "cease-fire" after a Nigerian court orders the Shell oil company to pay $1.5 billion in environmental "reparations."

August. Nigeria Turns Over Disputed Land to Cameroon. Nigeria hands over the disputed Bakassi Peninsula to Cameroon under the terms of a 2002 International Court of Justice ruling. The Nigerian government resettles those who were living on the peninsula.

RWANDA

January. Governors Appointed for New Provinces. In accordance with constitutional amendments approved in late 2005, Rwanda's provinces are reduced from 12 to 5, and governors are appointed in each province for the duration of the transition period until elections.

February. Constitutional Change Aids Returning Refugees. The language in the constitution regarding property rights is strengthened to assist returning refugees in recovering their property.

May. U.S. Boosts Bilateral Aid. During a meeting between President Paul Kagame and President George W. Bush in Washington, the United States announces it is increasing bilateral aid to Rwanda.

SAO TOME AND PRINCIPE

March. Prime Minister Appointed. Tomé Soares da Vera Cruz is appointed as prime minister by the president following the legislative elections of March 26. Vera Cruz heads a minority government.

July 30. President Reelected. Fradique de Menezes is reelected (as the candidate of an alliance of the Democratic Movement of Forces for Change and the Party of Democratic Convergence) for a second five-year term.

August 29. Opposition Leader Resigns. Guilherme Posser da Costa, president of the main opposition party, Movement for the Liberation of Sao Tome and Principe–Social Democratic Party, resigns. He cites his role in the party's defeat in the most recent local, legislative, and presidential elections.

SENEGAL

February. Former Prime Minister Released from Prison. A special anticorruption court dismisses embezzlement and subversion charges against former prime minister Idrissa Seck. He is released from prison, enabling him to launch his 2007 presidential campaign.

August–October. Army, Casamance Rebels Clash; Thousands Seek Refuge in Gambia. The army launches an offensive against Casamance separatists, forcing thousands of refugees to flee to Gambia.

SEYCHELLES

May. Assembly Rejects Opposition's Election Proposal. An opposition motion to dissolve the assembly to allow for parliamentary elections at the same time as presidential balloting in 2006—a year ahead of schedule—is rejected by the full body.

July 28–30. Michel Elected President. James Alix Michel (Seychelles People's Progressive Front) is elected to a five-year term in presidential balloting. Joseph Belmont, Michel's running mate, is elected as vice president.

SIERRA LEONE

January. Mano River Peace Talks Held. Representatives from Sierra Leone, Liberia, and Guinea meet to discuss ways to restore peace in the Mano River basin.

May. Government Cited for Poverty Reduction Efforts. The International Monetary Fund, citing the government's "considerable progress" toward economic stability and addressing widespread poverty, approves a new three-year poverty reduction program for Sierra Leone.

July. New Election Boundaries Raise Concerns. The National Electoral Commission draws criticism for creating new election boundaries that reportedly favor the ruling Sierra Leone People's Party.

August 4. Election Set for July 28, 2007. President Ahmad Tejan Kabbah announces that the next presidential election will be held during the rainy season. Opposition groups criticize the date, saying some regions are hard to reach during the rainy season.

SOMALIA

February. Transitional Assembly Meets for First Time. The full Transitional National Assembly meets for the first time. Following riots prompted by the publication in Denmark of cartoons deemed offensive to Muslims, fighting intensifies in Mogadishu between the Islamic Courts Union (ICU) militias and the warlords, who earlier formed the Alliance for the Restoration of Peace and Counter-Terrorism.

April. U.S. to Patrol Coast. Prime Minister Ali Mohammed Ghedi gives the United States permission to patrol off the coast of Somalia to suppress piracy.

June. Islamists Seize Control of Mogadishu. Islamists rout the warlords and take control of Mogadishu and surrounding areas. The ICU subsequently establishes a Council of Islamic Courts to govern the capital.

July 28. Gunman Kills Cabinet Minister. Rioting follows the assassination of the minister for constitutional and federal affairs in Baidao, the temporary seat of government.

July–August. International Airport, Main Seaport Reopen. Mogadishu's airport and seaport are open for the first time in 11 years.

August 7. President Dismisses Cabinet. Following numerous cabinet dismissals and resignations from May to early August, President Abdullahi Yusuf Ahmed announces that the entire cabinet has been dismissed; however, Prime Minister Ghedi remains in office.

August 20. Ethiopian Troops Move into Baidao. In response to tensions between the transitional government and the ICU, Ethiopian troops backed by tanks move into Baidao in support of the government.

August 21. New Cabinet Named. Prime Minister Ghedi announces a new cabinet of 31 ministers.

October. Peace Talks Continue. Ongoing peace talks between the Transitional Federal Government and the ICU take place in Kenya.

October 12. UN Opens More Refugee Camps in Kenya. The United Nations High Commissioner for Refugees announces the establishment of more camps in eastern Kenya to accommodate thousands of refugees from Somalia.

SOMALILAND

Note: Somaliland still lacks international recognition in 2006.

February. African Union Assesses Proposed Recognition of Somaliland. An African Union fact-finding mission concludes that Somaliland's status is "unique" and that recognition of its independence will not open a "Pandora's box" of new secessionist movements across the African continent, as leaders of other countries had feared.

May. House of Elders Extends Its Term. The House of Elders (currently appointed) extends its term of office until October 2010 even though the first elections for the house had been scheduled for October 2006. President Dahir Riyale Kahin supports the extension.

October 24. President Declares Support for Sharia. President Kahin, in response to pressure from Muslim scholars to clarify his position, announces that sharia is the basis of law in Somaliland.

SOUTH AFRICA

March 1. ANC Overwhelming Winner in Local Elections. The African National Congress (ANC) wins handily in municipal polling.

May. Party Official Acquitted of Rape Charge. A judge finds former deputy president of the republic Jacob Zuma not guilty of rape, and he is reinstated as deputy president of the ANC.

June. China Hails Partnership with South Africa. Chinese premier Wen Jiabao visits South Africa and declares the republic is "China's key partner of strategic cooperation in Africa."

September 20. Zuma Bribery Case Dropped. Bribery charges stemming from a 2005 case against Zuma are dismissed, reportedly boosting any potential bid for the presidency.

SUDAN

February 8. Sudan Signs Peace Agreement with Chad. The Tripoli Agreement ends the border conflict in the region that began in December 2005.

April. Sudan Rejects UN Mission. Sudan rejects a proposal from UN secretary-general Kofi Annan to replace the African Union (AU) peacekeeping mission with a more expansive UN-led operation that would have included European and, possibly, U.S. forces.

April 30. African Union Peace Plan Accepted. The Sudanese government accepts a comprehensive peace plan developed by the AU. The plan calls for the disarmament of the *Janjaweed* militias, elections within three years, and the provision

of $500 million for the establishment and operation of an autonomous regional authority. Only one faction of the Sudan Liberation Movement/Army agrees to sign.

May 5. Main Rebel Faction in Darfur Agrees to Cease-Fire. The Sudanese government and the Sudan Liberation Movement/Army sign the AU-backed peace accord.

September. African Union Boosts Troops in Darfur. The AU agrees to increase the number of troops in Darfur and extend the mandate through the end of the year.

October 22. Government Orders UN Envoy to Leave. Jan Pronk, the top UN envoy to Sudan who made comments about low morale in the army, is ordered to leave the country.

SWAZILAND

April. King Says Country Not Ready for Democracy. King Mswati III rejects calls to allow political parties in Swaziland.

July. King Endorses Anticorruption Unit. Tough new anticorruption laws give authority to a ten-year-old entity, among other measures.

TANZANIA

January 6. New Cabinet Installed. The assembly approves a Revolutionary Party of Tanzania cabinet following the party's victory in elections of 2005.

May. Tanzania Gets $11 Million to Fight Corruption. The United States grants Tanzania $11.15 million for an anticorruption campaign.

June. Debt Relief Approved. Tanzania is approved for debt relief through the Heavily Indebted Poor Countries initiative.

TOGO

April. Togo Qualifies for Debt Relief. The World Bank includes Togo among 11 countries approved for debt relief under the Heavily Indebted Poor Countries initiative.

September. New Prime Minister Named; Unity Government Formed. Yawovi Agboyibo, leader of the opposition Action Committee for Renewal, is named prime minister. He assumes the office on September 18, and on September 20 he names a national unity government, including 16 new ministers.

TUNISIA

Sept. 8. Tunisia Draws Criticism for Canceling NGO Summit. The Tunisian government angers Europeans after calling off at the last minute a conference on employment and the right to work. The EU expresses disappointment over what it says is Tunisia's "negative signals" in the area of human rights.

UGANDA

February 23. First Multiparty Elections in Two Decades. Incumbent Yoweri Museveni garners nearly 60 percent of the vote in defeating four challengers and securing another five-year term as president. The ruling National Resistance Movement also retains an overwhelming majority in the legislature.

Early 2006. Rebel Attacks Continue. Rebels in the Lord's Resistance Army (LRA) continue to abduct children and allegedly commit atrocities as the 20-year war with rebels in the north continues. President Museveni pledges after reelection that his government will begin resettling villagers displaced by LRA rebels.

July 16. Uganda's Leaders Begin Talks with LRA. Ugandan officials call on the rebels to cease all hostilities and to disarm during peace talks in Juba, southern Sudan. President Museveni ultimately offers amnesty to LRA leader Joseph Kony if he agrees to quit fighting.

August 25. Uganda, LRA Sign Preliminary Peace Agreement. Under provisions of the agreement, LRA rebels were to leave Uganda and their bases in Sudan and the Democratic Republic of the Congo for areas designated by and protected by the government of southern Sudan.

September. Troops to Deploy to Somalia. Uganda approves sending government troops to war-torn Somalia.

October 15. Uganda, Rebels Violate Truce. Both sides acknowledge they have breached provisions of the agreement, casting further doubt on the success of a final, comprehensive peace accord.

ZAMBIA

April 5. Electoral Reforms Adopted. Zambia's assembly adopts a controversial electoral reform bill establishing the president's authority to set election dates and requiring only a plurality in a single-round election to decide presidential balloting, among other provisions.

July 26. President Sets Election Date. Using the authority granted him under the new electoral reform law, President Levy Patrick Mwanawasa calls for tripartite elections to be held on September 28; opposition groups claim the date, three months earlier than anticipated, does not give them enough time to prepare.

September 28. Mwanawasa, Ruling Party Dominate Elections. President Levy Patrick Mwanawasa (Movement for Multiparty Democracy [MMD]) wins reelection to another five-year term with 42.98 percent of the vote. MMD dissident Michael Sata receives 29.37 percent, and the third-place candidate receives 25.32 percent of the vote. The results are noted by observers in light of Mwanawasa's push for reforms to allow for victory by plurality. In assembly balloting, the MMD wins 72 of 150 directly elected seats.

ZIMBABWE

January–May. Hundreds of Thousands Displaced in Slum-Clearing Program. The government's move to drive out urban dwellers, allegedly those who voted against the ruling party, continues into 2006. Operation Roundup clears an estimated 700,000 people from Harare. President Mugabe pledges to spend hundreds of thousands of dollars over three years to rebuild homes and businesses.

April. Economic Conditions Grow More Dire. Zimbabwe's annual inflation rate hits more than 1,000 percent, among the highest in the world. Millions of people are said to be suffering from food shortages.

April. Zimbabwe Seeks White Farmers. In light of the food crisis following the collapse of the agriculture-based economy after white-owned farms were seized, white farmers are invited to lease back their land from the government. The few white farmers still in Zimbabwe are reported to be largely uninterested in the offer.

July–August. Emergency Reforms Enacted. The government devalues the currency and introduces emergency reforms, issuing new currency in August and seizing cash from citizens and businesses in an effort to curtail trade in the black market.

APPENDIX B: SERIALS LIST

Africa Confidential
Africa Research Bulletin (Economic Series)
Africa Research Bulletin (Political Series)
The Annual Register
The Boston Globe
The Christian Science Monitor
The Economist
Editor & Publisher International
The Europa World Year Book
Facts on File
Financial Times
IMF Article IV Reports
IMF Balance of Payments Statistics
IMF Direction of Trade Statistics
IMF Government Finance Statistics
IMF International Financial Statistics
IMF Survey
IMF World Economic Outlook

Indian Ocean Newsletter
Keesing's Record of World Events
Le Monde (Paris)
The New York Times
People in Power
Permanent Missions to the United Nations
UN Chronicle
UN Handbook
UN Population and Vital Statistics Report
UN Statistical Yearbook
UNESCO Statistician Yearbook
US CIA Heads of State and Cabinet Members
US Department of State, Diplomatic List
The Washington Post
Willings Press Guide
World Bank Atlas
World Bank Country Reports
World Development Report

INDEX

Entries of only a single page number, and the first number in a multiple-page entry, indicate the first or primary reference to that individual. Additional page numbers typically indicate first references in a different section of a profile or in a closely related profile.